An Encyclopedia of
WORLD HISTORY

Collaborators

JAMES B. HEDGES
Professor of History, Brown University

WILLIAM THOMSON
Professor of Arabic, Harvard University

CRANE BRINTON
Professor of History, Harvard University

PENFIELD ROBERTS
Late Professor of History, Massachusetts Institute of Technology

MICHAEL KARPOVICH
Professor of History, Harvard University

ROBERT H. PFEIFFER
*Lecturer in Semitic Languages and Curator of the Semitic Museum
Harvard University*

MASON HAMMOND
Associate Professor of History, and of Greek and Latin, Harvard University

CHARLES S. GARDNER
Formerly Assistant Professor of Chinese, Harvard University

DONALD C. McKAY
Professor of History, Harvard University

LAURISTON WARD
*Lecturer on Anthropology and Curator of Asiatic Archaeology in the Peabody
Museum, Harvard University*

JOHN K. FAIRBANK
Associate Professor of History, Harvard University

PAUL P. CRAM
Formerly Instructor in History, Harvard University

ROBERT O. SCHLAIFER
Formerly Teaching Fellow in History, Harvard University

EDWIN O. REISCHAUER
Associate Professor of Far Eastern Languages, Harvard University

ROBERT S. CHAMBERLAIN
Formerly Assistant in History, Harvard University

New Edition revised with the assistance of
HANS W. GATZKE
Assistant Professor of History, Johns Hopkins University

An Encyclopedia *of*
WORLD HISTORY

Ancient, Medieval, and Modern, Chronologically Arranged

COMPILED AND EDITED BY

WILLIAM L. LANGER

Coolidge Professor of History, Harvard University

REVISED EDITION
Illustrated with Maps

HOUGHTON   MIFFLIN   COMPANY   BOSTON

The Riverside Press Cambridge

LIBRARY OF CONGRESS CATALOGUE CARD NUMBER 52–9589

PRINTED JANUARY, 1962

The Riverside Press
CAMBRIDGE, MASSACHUSETTS
PRINTED IN THE U.S.A.

Preface to the First Edition

THIS *Epitome of History* itself has a long and interesting history. More than seventy years ago Dr. Karl Ploetz, in his time a well-known German teacher, published an *Auszug aus der alten, mittleren und neueren Geschichte*, intended as a factual handbook for the use of students and for the convenience of the general reader. That his compilation filled a real need is attested by the fact that within a few years it went through seven editions, and by the further fact that to date more than twenty editions have appeared in Germany, revised and edited by noted scholars. The book has easily held its own despite competition of numerous similar works.

Ploetz' *Epitome* was translated into English by William H. Tillinghast and published by Houghton Mifflin Company in this country in 1883. The translator, recognizing that the original was designed particularly to meet the needs of the German student and that therefore the history of central Europe was weighted as against the history of France, England, and America, took the opportunity to enlarge a number of sections and to add others. No less a scholar than Edward Channing contributed the new sections on modern England and the United States. Furthermore, Tillinghast first added brief sections on the Middle and Far Eastern countries, which had been completely omitted from the German version. The book appeared under the title *An Epitome of Ancient, Medieval, and Modern History*, and proved so popular that no less than twenty-four printings were necessary before 1905. Occasional revisions were made and in 1915 the title was changed to *A Handbook of Universal History*.

Since historical knowledge and historical conceptions are notoriously fluid, it is not to be wondered at that even so sound and reliable a book as the old Ploetz-Tillinghast *Epitome* should ultimately have fallen behind the times. After the World War the publishers therefore commissioned Dr. Harry Elmer Barnes to overhaul the book and bring it up to date. The new editor, with a number of collaborators, left the kernel of the old work (the Greek and Roman history, the medieval sections, and the early modern parts) as it was, judging quite rightly that in the large it was not so badly out of line as to justify rewriting and resetting. But the sections dealing with the early Near East, of which little was known in Ploetz' day, were completely redone, and a great deal of material on the period from 1883 to 1923 was added. The *Epitome*, thus revised, was published in 1925 as *A Manual of Universal History*. Like the preceding versions it has been widely used by students and laymen alike.

But despite revisions of one kind or another, it became increasingly clear that sooner or later the original book would require drastic changes if it were to keep abreast of modern knowledge and meet contemporary requirements. It stands to reason that in seventy years our command of the facts and our views of even those subjects best treated by Ploetz and Tillinghast have changed substantially. Above all, the past fifty years have witnessed the expansion of western influence over the entire globe and, as a result, there is now a much greater need to know something of the past of non-European countries and cultures, and a much livelier interest in formerly neglected fields. To fill the new requirements no amount of revision of the old book would do, for the original author wrote as a German and treated European history primarily as it touched his own country's development. Tillinghast attempted to give the English translation a somewhat more Anglo-American slant, and Dr. Barnes did what was humanly possible to adapt the old text to a more world-wide approach. But the point had been definitely reached where adaptations and adjustments would no longer suffice. The publishers therefore invited me to undertake a complete rewriting of the entire book, securing the aid of collaborators qualified to treat of special fields where it seemed desirable. It was my great good fortune to be able to interest fifteen of my colleagues to take over particular sections and to secure from them the most whole-hearted co-operation in what, after all, was an enterprise of some magnitude. Their names, with the sections for which they made themselves responsible, are listed at the end of the preface.

When embarking upon this project I still had hope that considerable parts of the old book might yet be salvaged and that a thoroughgoing revision would prove adequate for the ancient, medieval, and early modern sections. But it soon became apparent to all of us engaged in the work that the whole plan and approach required rethinking and that, consequently, there was but little use in trying to adhere to the old text. Here and there a few pages (thoroughly emended) have been retained, but they are relatively so few in number as to be hardly worth mentioning. Almost nothing of the substance of the old book remains; every single section has been gone over in thorough fashion, reduced or expanded and, above all, brought into line with present-day knowledge. Many other sections, naturally, have been newly written, so that I think we can honestly say that the book is no longer a manual of European history with some perfunctory reference to other countries, but genuine world history, in which the geographical divisions are dealt with on their merits.

In the course of rewriting we have, however, stuck by Ploetz' original conception. That is, we have tried to compile a handbook of historical facts, so arranged that the dates stand out while the material itself flows in a reasonably smooth narrative. Individual judgments have been kept in the background and divergent interpretations have been adduced only where they seemed to be indispensable. The great diversity of type which had crept into the old book has been done away with and we have broken the uniformity of the print only by the use of small and capital boldface and very occasional employment of italics. The number of genealogical charts has been much increased: new tables have been added for some of the non-European dynasties and all charts have been brought up to date. Furthermore, a considerable number of maps have been included, not with the idea of supplying a complete historical atlas, but simply for the convenience of the user who, when he is checking one event or another, cannot be expected to have always at hand the necessary map material.

In the preface to the 1925 edition Dr. Barnes referred to the growing interest in non-political aspects of history and to his attempt to expand sections dealing with economic and cultural developments. Though deeply interested in these phases of history, Dr. Barnes felt obliged to recognize that the majority of those who would use the book would come seeking information on political, military, and diplomatic history and that therefore those angles would have to be primarily considered. I subscribe entirely to this view, but I take this opportunity to point out further that cultural history does not lend itself readily to the method of treatment upon which this particular work is based. The backbone of this book is chronology which, in the case of general economic trends, religious and artistic movements and intellectual currents, is both hard to define and of relatively less significance. For methodological reasons, if for no other, we could therefore give but slight emphasis to these aspects of history. In addition we had to consider the further difficulties presented by space limitation: obviously anything like adequate treatment of literature, art, science, and economics would have taken us so far afield that the results could not possibly have been enclosed within two covers. In some sections the reader will find brief summaries of cultural activities, in others not; but in any case we offer them only for what they may be worth, as a matter of convenience, without any thought of sufficiency, much less exhaustiveness. And these remarks apply equally to the special sections at the beginning of the nineteenth century, entitled *Social Thought and Social Movements*, *Scientific Thought and Progress*, and *Mechanical Inventions and Technical Achievements*. The material we adduce in these sections appeared to us indispensable for an understanding of nineteenth-century development. It cannot be suitably included under any one country, for its application is general. We could not aim or hope for completeness; hence our only objective in these sections has been to bring together an irreducible minimum of pertinent information.

Each successive editor of this *Handbook* has come away from his task impressed with the difficulties of attaining accuracy in dealing with so vast a number of dates covering so wide a range of time and territory. I am no exception to the rule and am far from being arrogant enough to suppose that this new book is even more free from error than the old. There is some consolation, however, in the thought that we collaborators have all done what we reasonably could to guard against blunders and that, as a matter of fact, many dates are so uncertain or disputed that they will probably never be satisfactorily fixed.

The success of the *Epitome of History* over a period of more than two generations is ample proof of the need for a manual of this type. In the revised and extended form here presented, it ought to be more valuable than ever. Its use for students of history is obvious enough, but it ought to prove as helpful to many others. Students of the history of literature and of art should find a concise guide to political history a great boon and all readers of historical novels or biographies should welcome a book of reference to events of the past, to genealogical relationships, and so on. My own experience with the old book was that I used it more as I became better acquainted with it. Nothing would please me more than to have the new edition find a secure place on the shelves of all book-lovers.

In presenting the new *Epitome* I cannot refrain from expressing my profound gratitude to all the contributors and also to Professors

Walter Clark and Vincent Scramuzza, to Professor Sterling Dow, Mr. Eugene Boardman, and to Miss Katharine Irwin for the ready help they gave in reading proof. My secretaries, Mrs. Elizabeth Fox and Mrs. Rosamund Chapman, took care of countless loose ends and deserve more than a little credit for whatever merit the book may have.

CONTRIBUTORS

Dr. Lauriston Ward: The Prehistoric Period (Section I).

Professor Robert Pfeiffer: Early Empires of Africa and Asia (exclusive of India and China; Section II, A, 1-9 inc.).

Dr. Robert O. Schlaifer: Ancient Greece (Section II, B; D).

Professor Mason Hammond: Roman History (Section II, C; E; F).

Professor Charles S. Gardner: China throughout and India to c. 1600 (Sections II, A, 10-11; G, 2-3; III, E, 2-3; IV, F, 4; V, J, 5; VI, F, 10).

Professor Edwin O. Reischauer: Japan and Korea throughout (Sections II, G, 4-5; III, E, 4-5; IV, F, 5-6, V, J, 6-7; VI, F, 11).

Mr. Paul Cram: Western Europe in the Middle Ages (Section III, A, 1; B, 1, 3c; C, 1).

Professor William Thomson: The Moslem World in the Middle Ages (Sections II, G, 1; III, A, 3; B, 3, b, e, f, g).

Professor Michael Karpovich: Russia and Poland throughout and Scandinavia since c. 1500 (Sections III, B, 2, a, c, d; C, 2, a, b, c; IV, A, 7-9; B, 8-10; V, D; VI, B, 12-15).

Professor Crane Brinton: Western and Central Europe c. 1500-1815 (Section IV, A, 1-6; B, 1-7; V, B).

Mr. Robert S. Chamberlain: Latin America throughout (Sections III, F; IV, C; V, H; VI, D).

Professor James B. Hedges: North America, exclusive of Mexico, throughout (Sections IV, D; V, G; VI, C).

Professor Donald C. McKay: Western and Central Europe, 1815-1914 (Sections V, A, 1, 2, 3; C).

Professor John Fairbank: India since c. 1600 (Sections J, 3, 4; VI, F, 8, 9).

Professor Penfield Roberts: Western and Central Europe since 1918 (Section VI, B, 1-9).

Mr. Geoffrey Brunn: The Second World War (Section IV, H).

For all other sections the editor is alone responsible.

Foreword to the Revised Edition

THE ORIGINAL EDITION of the *Encyclopedia of World History* carried the chronology of world events down to the outbreak of war in Europe in September, 1939. Since then the Second World War has been fought and hostilities have come to an end. The dropping of the atomic bombs on Hiroshima and Nagasaki prefaced the end of Japanese resistance and at the same time ushered in what has already been recognized as the new, atomic age.

The happenings of six years of total war, the crowded record of military campaigns and of political upheavals certainly call for adequate treatment in a reference work of this kind. This new edition, therefore, takes full account of the developments of the most recent period. At the same time advantage has been taken of the opportunity to make numerous corrections of detail in other parts of the book. The original edition was given a wide and enthusiastic reception and in many instances readers took the trouble to send in comments and suggestions. For the most part these were constructive and proved to be valuable contributions to the improvement of the book.

The additions embodied in this new edition were prepared almost entirely by Dr. Geoffrey Bruun, who has worked tirelessly to put the revised text and tables into the best possible shape. The editor and publisher join in expressing to him their appreciation and gratitude, and also to Mr. H. Robinson Shipherd who prepared the new index.

WILLIAM L. LANGER

Foreword to the Revised Third Edition

FOUR YEARS have passed since the appearance of the second, revised edition of *An Encyclopedia of World History*. The intervening years have been truly a period of world crisis, a crucial span during which the nations of the Western World have banded together and embarked upon a common effort to rearm against Communist subversion, as it was successfully applied in Czechoslovakia, or against open military aggression, as it was tried in Korea.

The *Encyclopedia of World History* has, over the past decade, earned for itself an enviable place among the small number of really indispensable reference books. In stormy times like the present it is more needed than ever as a guide through the bewildering thicket of news which constitutes the record of developments in individual countries and throughout the world at large. It is essential, therefore, that the *Encyclopedia* be brought up to date at fairly frequent intervals.

The present revised edition provides a digest of events since 1945, and in addition embodies a number of changes and corrections based on the criticisms and suggestions submitted by interested readers from all parts of the globe. The additional material has been compiled by Professor Hans Gatzke of Johns Hopkins University, who has spared himself no pains in reviewing the mountainous data of recent history, and who has done a superb job of condensation and organization. The *Encyclopedia* has gained greatly in usefulness through his conscientious and intelligent analysis.

WILLIAM L. LANGER

Contents

I. THE PREHISTORIC PERIOD

A. INTRODUCTION **1**
 1. Definition, Data, and Methods 1
 2. The Origin of Man 1
 3. Cultures and Their Dating 2
  a. Cultures and Periods 2
  b. Relative Dating 2
  c. Absolute Dating 3

B. THE PALAEOLITHIC PERIOD 4
 1. Culture and Industries 4
 2. Europe 4
 3. Africa 5
 4. Asia and Oceania 6
 5. America 7
 6. Interrelationship of Palaeolithic Cultures 7
 7. The Dates of Palaeolithic Cultures 8
 8. Physical Types of Palaeolithic Man 9

C. THE POST-PALAEOLITHIC PERIOD 10
 1. Nature and Sequence of Post-Palaeolithic Cultures . . 10
  a. Mesolithic Period 10
  b. Neolithic Period 10
  c. Chalcolithic Period 11
  d. Bronze Age 11
  e. Iron Age 11
 2. Modern Races of Man 12
 3. Regional Distribution of Post-Palaeolithic Cultures . . 13
  a. Asia 13
  b. Europe 14
   (1) Climatic Changes and Time-Scale. . . . 14
   (2) Cultural Changes and Periods 15
   (3) Movements of Peoples 16
   (4) Regional Distribution of Cultures . . . 16
  c. Africa 18
  d. Oceania 18
  e. America 19

II. ANCIENT HISTORY

A. EARLY EMPIRES OF AFRICA AND ASIA . . .   21
   1. Egypt   21
   2. Mesopotamia   25
      a. Sumer and Akkad   25
      b. Babylonia   26
      c. Assyria   26
   3. Upper Mesopotamia (Mitanni)   28
   4. Palestine   29
      a. Israel and Judah.   30
      b. The Jews   31
   5. Phoenicia   32
      a. Carthage   34
   6. Syria   34
      a. Damascus   35
   7. Asia Minor   36
      a. Hittites   36
      b. Phrygians   36
      c. Lydians   37
      d. Hellenistic Monarchies   37
   8. Armenia   38
      a. The Kingdom of Van (Urartu)   38
      b. Armenia   38
   9. Iran   39
      a. Elamites   39
      b. Medes.   40
      c. Persians   40
  10. India   41
  11. China   44

B. GREECE   46
   1. The Early Period, to C. 500 B.C.   46
      a. Geographical Factors   46
      b. The Aegean Civilization   46
      c. The Invasions   47
      d. Aristocracy and Tyranny; Colonization and Trade .   47
      e. Formation of the Greek States   48
         (1) Asia Minor   48
         (2) The Peloponnese.   48
         (3) Athens   50
         (4) Central and Northern Greece   52
         (5) Sicily and Magna Graecia   52

2. The Persian Wars 53
3. The Fifth Century 54
    a. The Peloponnese, 479–461 54
    b. Athens and the Delian League, 479–461 55
    c. The First Peloponnesian War 55
    d. Athens, 460–431 56
    e. Sicily, 499–409 57
    f. The Great Peloponnesian War. 57
    g. Economic and Social Conditions 61
4. The Rise of Macedon 62
    a. Spartan Hegemony 62
    b. Theban Hegemony 63
    c. Macedon under Philip and Alexander the Great . 64
    d. The West during the Fourth Century 66
    e. Greek Culture in the Fourth Century 67

C. ROME, TO 287 B.C. 68
1. The Early Period 68
    a. Geographical Factors 68
    b. Early Populations of Italy 68
    c. The Roman Monarchy 69
2. The Early Republic 70

D. THE HELLENISTIC WORLD 75
1. Cultural Development 75
2. The Wars of the Diadochi 77
3. Sicily to the Roman Conquest 78
4. Macedon and Greece to the Roman Conquest 79
5. The Seleucid Empire and Pergamum 80
6. Parthia 83
7. Bactria 83
8. Ptolemaic Egypt, to the Roman Conquest 83

E. ROME, THE MIDDLE AND LATER REPUBLIC . 85
1. The Punic and Macedonian Wars 85
2. Domestic Strife and Eastern Conquest 91

F. THE ROMAN EMPIRE 101
1. The Early Empire (31 B.C.–192 A.D.) 101
2. The Third Century (192–284) 113
3. The Later Empire (284–527) 117

G. THE EMPIRES OF ASIA 124
1. The Neo-Persian Empire of the Sassanians (226–651 A.D.) 124
2. India, to 500 A.D. 128
    a. Northern India 128

b. Southern India 132
c. Ceylon 132
3. China, to 618 A.D. 132
4. Korea, to 562 A.D. 137
5. Japan, to 645 A.D. 138

III. THE MIDDLE AGES

A. THE EARLY MIDDLE AGES 141
1. Western Europe 141
    a. The Early Papacy 141
    b. Invaders of the West 142
        (1) The Huns. 143
        (2) The Visigoths 143
        (3) The Vandals 144
        (4) The Burgundians 145
    c. The Ostrogoths in Italy, 489–554 145
    d. The Frankish Kingdom, 481–752 147
       The Carolingians 149
    e. The Lombards and the Popes, 568–774 150
       The Papacy in the Carolingian Period . . . 152
    f. The Empire of Charlemagne and Its Disintegration 153
    g. The West Franks under the Carolingian Kings,
       843–987 158
    h. Germany under the Carolingian and Saxon Em-
       perors, 843–1024 159
    i. Spain 163
        (1) The Visigothic Kingdom, 466–711 . . . 163
        (2) Moslem Spain, 711–1031 163
        (3) Christian Spain 164
    j. The British Isles 164
        (1) England, to 1066 164
        (2) Scotland, to 1034 168
        (3) Ireland, to 1171 168
    k. Scandinavia 170
2. Eastern Europe 170
    a. The Eastern Empire to 1025 170
    b. The First Bulgarian Empire to 1018 181
3. The Moslem World 184
    a. Mohammed and Islam 184
    b. The Omayyad Caliphate, 661–750 186
    c. The Abbasid Caliphate, 750–c. 1100 188

B. THE AGE OF THE CRUSADES 191
  1. Western Europe 191
    a. The British Isles 191
      (1) England, 1066–1307 191
      (2) Scotland, 1034–1304 201
      (3) Ireland, 1171–1307 201
    b. Scandinavia 203
      (1) Denmark, 950–1320 203
      (2) Sweden, 993–1319 203
      (3) Norway, 872–1319 204
    c. Germany under the Salian and Hohenstaufen
      Emperors, 1024–1268 205
      (1) The Teutonic Knights 214
    d. Italy and the Papacy, 888–1314 215
      (1) The Norman Kingdom in South Italy and
        Sicily, 1105–1194 223
      (2) The Development of Italian Towns . . . 223
      (3) The Rise of Venice to 1310 224
    e. France, 987–1314 225
    f. The Iberian Peninsula, 1037–1284 233
      (1) Moslem Spain 233
      (2) Castile 233
      (3) Barcelona and Catalonia 235
      (4) Navarre 237
      (5) Aragon 237
      (6) Portugal, to 1279 238
  2. Eastern Europe 239
    a. The Slavs 239
    b. Bohemia and Moravia, to 1306 239
    c. Poland, to 1305 241
    d. Russia, to 1263 242
    e. Hungary, to 1301 244
    f. Serbia, to 1276 246
    g. The Second Bulgarian Empire 247
  3. The Near East 248
    a. The Eastern Empire, 1025–1204 248
    b. The Seljuk Turks 254
    c. The Crusades 255
    d. Latin and Greek States in the Near East, 1204–1261 . 258
    e. The Mongols 260
    f. Moslem Egypt 262
    g. Moslem Dynasties of North Africa 263

C. THE LATER MIDDLE AGES 264
  1. Western Europe 264
    a. The British Isles 264
      (1) England, 1307–1485 264
      (2) Scotland, 1305–1488 272
      (3) Ireland, 1315–1485 272
    b. France, 1314–1483 273
    c. The Iberian Peninsula 280
      (1) Castile, 1312–1492 280
      (2) Aragon, 1276–1479 282
      (3) Portugal, 1279–1495 284
    d. Italy and the Papacy 286
      (1) The Papacy, 1305–1492 286
      (2) Sicily and Naples, 1268–1494 290
      (3) Florence, to 1492 293
      (4) Milan, to 1500 296
      (5) Venice, 1310–1489 298
    e. The Holy Roman Empire 299
      (1) Bohemia, 1306–1471 304
      (2) The Swiss Confederation, to 1499 . . . 306
      (3) The Hanseatic League 307
      (4) The Teutonic Knights 310
    f. Scandinavia 310
      (1) Denmark, 1320–1387 310
      (2) Sweden, 1319–1387 312
      (3) Norway, 1320–1387 312
      (4) The Union of Kalmar, to 1483 312
  2. Eastern Europe 313
    a. Poland, 1305–1492 313
    b. Lithuania 316
    c. Russia, 1263–1505 316
    d. Hungary, 1301–1490 317
    e. The Serbian States, 1276–1499 318
    f. The Eastern Empire, 1261–1453 320
    g. The Ottoman Empire, 1300–1481 325

D. AFRICA DURING THE MIDDLE AGES 328

E. ASIA DURING THE MIDDLE AGES 330
  1. Persia 330
  2. India 330
    a. Northern India 330
    b. Western India 331

  c. Southern India 335
  d. Ceylon 339
 3. China, 618–1471 339
  a. Burma 347
  b. Siam 347
  c. Malaysia 348
 4. Korea 348
 5. Japan, 645–1543 349

F. PRE-COLUMBIAN AMERICA 360
G. THE GREAT DISCOVERIES 362
 1. Asia 362
 2. Africa 363
 3. America 365
  a. Pre-Columbian Discoveries 365
  b. The Voyages of Columbus 366
  c. Post-Columbian Discoveries 367

IV. THE EARLY MODERN PERIOD

A. EUROPE AND THE NEAR EAST, 1500–1648 . . 369
 1. England, Scotland, and Ireland, 1485–1649 . . . 369
 2. The Netherlands to 1648 379
 3. France, 1483–1641 381
 4. The Iberian Peninsula 387
  a. Spain, 1479–1659 387
  b. Portugal, 1495–1640 390
 5. Italy 392
  a. The Italian Wars, 1494–1559 392
  b. The Papacy 395
  c. Venice 397
  d. Other Italian States 397
 6. Germany 398
  a. Germany, 1493–1618 398
  b. The Thirty Years' War 403
   (1) The Bohemian Period, 1618–1625 . . . 404
   (2) The Danish Period, 1625–1629 404
   (3) The Swedish Period, 1630–1635 405
   (4) The Swedish-French Period, 1635–1648 . . 407
  c. The Swiss Confederation 408
 7. Scandinavia 410
  a. Denmark and Norway, 1513–1645 410
  b. Sweden, 1523–1654 410

  8. Poland-Lithuania, 1492–1648 413
  9. Russia, 1505–1645 415
 10. Bohemia, 1471–1627 418
 11. Hungary, 1490–1648 419
 12. The Ottoman Empire, 1481–1656 420

B. EUROPE AND THE NEAR EAST, 1648–1789 . . 425
  1. England, Scotland, and Ireland 425
  2. The Dutch Republic 437
  3. France 440
  4. The Iberian Peninsula 448
   a. Spain 448
   b. Portugal 452
  5. Italy and the Papacy 454
   a. Italy (general) 454
   b. The Papacy 455
   c. Savoy (Sardinia) 457
   d. Naples 458
   e. Other States 458
  6. The Swiss Confederation 459
  7. Germany 461
  8. Scandinavia 471
   a. Sweden 471
   b. Denmark and Norway 474
  9. Poland 475
 10. Russia 478
 11. The Ottoman Empire 482

C. LATIN AMERICA 486
  1. Nature of the Conquest 486
  2. The West Indies and the Isthmus 486
  3. Venezuela and New Granada 488
  4. Peru and the West Coast 489
  5. The Rio de la Plata 490
  6. New Spain 490
   a. The Conquest of Mexico 490
   b. Expansion to the South 491
   c. Expansion to the North 492
   d. The Gulf Coast, Florida, and the Carolinas . . 493
  7. Foreign Encroachments and Territorial Changes . . 494
  8. The Spanish Colonial System 496
   a. Population 496
   b. Administration 496

c. The Church and the Missions 498
d. Economic Conditions and Policies 499
e. Education, Learning, and Fine Arts 500
9. Portuguese America 500
10. The Portuguese Colonial System 503

D. NORTH AMERICA 505
1. Exploration and Settlement 505
a. The French in North America 505
b. The English in North America 507
(1) Exploration 507
(2) Virginia 508
(3) New England 508
(a) Massachusetts 508
(b) Connecticut and Rhode Island . . 509
(4) Maryland 510
(5) Island Settlements 510
c. Dutch and Swedish Settlements 510
2. Colonial History 511
a. New England 511
b. New York, New Jersey, Pennsylvania 512
c. Virginia, Delaware, and Maryland 513
d. The Southern Colonies . . . . . , . . . 513
3. Wars of England with France and Spain 514
4. The American Revolution 517

E. AFRICA, 1517–1800 524

F. ASIA 526
1. Persia, 1500–1794 526
2. Afghanistan, to 1793 530
3. India 530
4. China 536
a. Burma 541
b. Siam 541
c. Malaysia 541
5. Korea 542
6. Japan, 1542–1793 542

V. THE NINETEENTH CENTURY

A. SCIENCE AND SOCIETY 549
1. Social Thought and Social Movements 549
2. Scientific Thought and Progress 551

3. Mechanical Inventions and Technical Achievements . . 553
4. Arctic Exploration 558
   a. Earliest Explorations 558
   b. The Sixteenth Century 559
   c. The Seventeenth and Eighteenth Centuries . . . 559
   d. The Nineteenth Century 562
   e. The Twentieth Century 566
      (1) Conquest of the Pole 566
      (2) The Canadian Arctic 567
      (3) Greenland 568
      (4) The Spitsbergen Area 569
      (5) The Russian Arctic 570
5. Antarctic Exploration 571

B. THE REVOLUTIONARY AND NAPOLEONIC
  PERIOD 578
  1. Background of the Revolution 578
  2. The National Assembly 579
  3. The Legislative Assembly 580
  4. The National Convention 581
  5. The Directory 584
  6. War of the Second Coalition 586
  7. The Consulate 587
  8. The First Empire 591
  9. The War of the Third Coalition 591
 10. The Peninsula War 593
 11. The War Against Austria 594
 12. Europe, 1810–1812 595
 13. The French Invasion of Russia 596
 14. The Wars of Liberation 598
 15. The Peace Settlements 601
 16. The Hundred Days 602

C. WESTERN AND CENTRAL EUROPE 604
  1. The Congress System, 1815–1822 604
  2. The British Isles 604
    a. The End of the Tory Régime, 1815–1830 . . . 604
    b. An Era of Reform, 1830–1846 606
    c. Palmerston and Russell, 1846–1868 612
    d. Disraeli and Gladstone, 1868–1894 614
    e. A Decade of Unionism, 1895–1905 618
    f. The Liberal Régime, 1905–1914 619

3. The Low Countries 621
   a. The Kingdom of the Netherlands, 1815–1830 (1839) 621
   b. The Kingdom of Belgium, 1831–1914 623
   c. Kingdom of the Netherlands, 1830–1914 . . . 625
4. France 626
   a. The Restoration Monarchy, 1814–1830 626
   b. The July Monarchy, 1830–1848 628
   c. The Second Republic, 1848–1852 630
   d. The Second Empire: the Authoritarian Period,
      1852–1860 632
   e. The Liberal Empire, 1860–1870 633
   f. The Third Republic, 1870–1914 636
5. The Iberian Peninsula 643
   a. Spain 643
   b. Portugal 648
6. Italy 650
   a. The Italian States, 1815–1848 650
   b. The Italian War of Independence, 1848–1849 . . 654
   c. The Unification of Italy, 1849–1870 655
   d. The Kingdom of Italy, 1870–1914 659
7. The Papacy, 1815–1914 663
8. Switzerland 666
9. Central Europe 667
   a. Germany, 1815–1848 667
   b. The Hapsburg Monarchy, 1815–1848 670
      (1) Austria 670
      (2) Hungary 671
   c. The Revolution of 1848–1849 in the Hapsburg
      Dominions 673
   d. The Revolution of 1848–1849 in Germany . . . 675
   e. The Austrian Empire, 1849–1867 678
   f. The Unification of Germany 678
   g. The German Empire, 1871–1914 688
   h. Austria-Hungary, 1867–1914 693
      (1) Austria, 1867–1914 694
      (2) Hungary, 1867–1914 695

D. NORTHERN AND EASTERN EUROPE 697
  1. Scandinavia 697
     a. Denmark 697
     b. Sweden and Norway 699
  2. Russia 701

E. THE BALKANS AND THE NEAR EAST . . . 710
1. The Balkan States 710
   a. Greece 710
   b. Serbia 712
   c. Montenegro 715
   d. Bulgaria 717
   e. Rumania 719
2. The Ottoman Empire 721

F. INTERNATIONAL RELATIONS, 1870–1914 . . . 733

G. NORTH AMERICA 764
1. The United States 764
   a. The United States, 1789–1861 764
   b. The Civil War, 1861–1865 776
   c. The United States, 1865–1917 780
2. British North America, 1783–1914 792
   a. The Dominion of Canada 792
   b. Newfoundland 797
3. Alaska 798

H. LATIN AMERICA 799
1. The Wars of Independence 799
   a. Causes 799
   b. Earlier Insurrections, 1721–1806 799
   c. The Río de la Plata 800
   d. Paraguay 801
   e. The Banda Oriental (Uruguay) 801
   f. Chile 801
   g. Peru and Bolivia 801
   h. Venezuela 802
   i. Great Colombia (New Granada, Venezuela and Quito) 802
   j. New Spain (Mexico) 803
   k. Guatemala and Central America 804
   l. Brazil 805
2. Latin America, 1825–1914 806
   a. Argentina 806
   b. Chile 808
   c. Paraguay 810
   d. Uruguay 810
   e. Bolivia 811
   f. Peru 812
   g. Ecuador 813

h. Colombia (New Granada) 814
i. Venezuela 816
j. Brazil 817
k. Panama and the Panama Canal Zone 818
l. Central America 819
   (1) General 819
   (2) Territorial Adjustments 820
   (3) Nicaragua 820
   (4) Honduras. 821
m. Mexico 821
n. The West Indies 823
   (1) Cuba 823
   (2) Puerto Rico 824
   (3) The Dominican Republic 824
   (4) Haiti 825

I. AFRICA 826
  1. General: Exploration 826
  2. Egypt and the Sudan 828
  3. Ethiopia and the Red Sea Area 834
  4. Northern Africa (Morocco, Algeria, Tunisia, Libya) . . 837
  5. West Africa and the Sudan (French West Africa, Gambia, Sierra Leone, Gold Coast, Togoland, Nigeria, Cameroons, Rio de Oro, Portuguese Guinea) 840
  6. The Congo Region (French Equatorial Africa, Spanish Guinea, Belgian Congo, Angola) 843
  7. East Africa (Kenya, Uganda, Tanganyika, Nyasaland, Mozambique). 846
  8. South Africa (Cape of Good Hope, Orange Free State, Natal, South African Republic, Rhodesia, German South-west Africa). 850
  9. Madagascar 859

J. ASIA 862
  1. Persia 862
  2. Afghanistan 866
  3. India 868
  4. Indo-China 872
    a. Burma 872
    b. Siam 872
    c. French Indo-China 874
    d. British Malaya 875
    e. The Malayan Archipelago 876

5. China 877
6. Korea 885
7. Japan 887

K. THE PACIFIC AREA 894
  1. General: Exploration and Annexation 894
  2. Australia 896
  3. New Zealand 904
  4. The Philippines. 908
  5. Hawaii 910
  6. Samoa 911

VI. TWO WORLD WARS AND THE INTER-WAR PERIOD

A. THE FIRST WORLD WAR 913
  1. The Western Front, 1914 913
  2. The Eastern Front, 1914 914
  3. The War at Sea, 1914 917
  4. The War in the Colonies, 1914–1918 918
  5. The Ottoman Front, 1914–1915 919
  6. The Western Front, 1915 921
  7. The Eastern Front, 1915 921
  8. Naval Operations—Submarine Warfare 922
  9. The Intervention of Italy 923
  10. The Balkan Situation, 1914–1915 925
  11. The Mesopotamian Campaign, 1914–1916 927
  12. Political Changes, 1915–1916 929
      a. England 929
      b. France 929
      c. Italy 930
      d. Russia 930
      e. Austria-Hungary 930
      f. Germany 930
  13. Verdun and the Somme, 1916 930
  14. The War at Sea. Battle of Jutland 931
  15. The Italian Front, 1916 932
  16. The Eastern Front, 1916 932
  17. The Balkan Front, 1916 932
  18. The Intervention of Rumania 934
  19. Peace Negotiations, 1916–1917, and the Intervention of
      the United States 935
  20. Campaigns in Asiatic Turkey, 1916–1917 937
      a. Arabia 937

b. Nejd 937
c. Arab Revolt 937
d. Mesopotamia 938
21. The Western Front, 1917 938
22. The Submarine War, 1917 939
23. The British Offensives, 1917 939
24. The Russian Front, 1917 940
25. The Balkan Situation, 1917 940
26. The Collapse of Italy, 1917 941
27. Political Developments, 1917–1918 941
a. France 941
b. Austria-Hungary 941
c. Germany 942
d. Italy 942
28. The Settlements in the East, 1917–1918 943
29. Operations in the West, 1918 944
30. The Action at Zeebrugge and Ostend 946
31. The War in the Air, 1914–1918 946
32. The Russian Situation, 1918 947
33. The Collapse of Turkey 948
34. The Collapse of Bulgaria 948
35. The End of the Hapsburg Monarchy 949
36. The Allied Victory in the West 950
37. The Peace Settlements 951
a. The Treaty of Versailles 951
b. The Treaty of St. Germain 953
c. The Treaty of Neuilly 953
d. The Treaty of Trianon 953
e. The Treaty of Sèvres 954

B. EUROPE 955
1. International Affairs 955
a. The Period of Settlement 955
b. The Period of Fulfillment 959
c. The Period of Repudiation and Revision. . . . 961
2. The British Isles 967
a. Great Britain 967
b. Ireland 971
3. The Low Countries 974
a. Belgium 974
b. The Kingdom of the Netherlands 975
4. France 976

5. The Iberian Peninsula 980
   a. Spain 980
   b. Portugal 985
6. Italy and the Papacy 986
   a. Italy 986
   b. The Papacy 992
7. Switzerland 994
8. Greater Germany 995
   a. The German Reich 995
   b. The Republic of Austria 1005
9. Czechoslovakia 1009
10. Hungary 1013
11. The Balkan States 1016
   a. Yugoslavia 1016
   b. Albania 1019
   c. Greece 1020
   d. Bulgaria 1022
   e. Rumania 1024
12. Russia (Union of Socialist Soviet Republics) 1027
13. Poland 1037
14. The Baltic States 1041
   a. General 1041
   b. Lithuania 1041
   c. Latvia 1043
   d. Estonia 1044
15. The Scandinavian States 1045
   a. General 1045
   b. Denmark 1045
   c. Norway 1046
   d. Sweden 1047
   e. Finland 1047

C. NORTH AMERICA 1049
  1. The United States 1049
  2. The Dominion of Canada 1057
  3. Newfoundland 1060

D. LATIN AMERICA 1062
  1. General 1062
  2. Argentina 1064
  3. Chile 1064
  4. Paraguay 1065
  5. Uruguay 1066

6. Bolivia 1067
7. Peru . . . . , . . 1068
8. Ecuador 1068
9. Colombia 1069
10. Venezuela 1070
11. Brazil 1070
12. Central America 1071
    a. General 1071
    b. Panama 1072
    c. Costa Rica 1072
    d. Nicaragua 1073
    e. Honduras 1073
    f. Salvador 1074
    g. Guatemala 1074
13. Mexico 1074
14. The West Indies 1077
    a. Cuba 1077
    b. Haiti 1078
    c. The Dominican Republic 1078
    d. Puerto Rico 1079
    e. Virgin Islands 1079

E. AFRICA 1081
1. General 1081
2. Egypt and the Sudan 1081
3. Ethiopia 1085
4. North Africa: Morocco, Algeria, Tunisia, Libya . . . 1086
5. West Africa and the Sudan 1088
6. The Congo Region: French Equatorial Africa, Spanish Guinea, Belgian Congo, Angola 1089
7. East Africa: Kenya, Uganda, Tanganyika, Nyasaland, Mozambique 1090
8. South Africa and Southwest Africa 1091
9. Madagascar 1093

F. ASIA 1094
1. Turkey 1094
2. Syria 1098
3. Palestine and Transjordania 1100
4. Saudi Arabia and Yemen 1104
5. Iraq 1105
6. Iran 1106
7. Afghanistan 1109

8. India 1111
9. Indo-China 1114
    a. Siam 1114
    b. Other States 1116
10. China 1117
11. Japan 1123

G. THE PACIFIC AREA 1128

1. General 1128
2. Australia 1128
3. New Zealand 1131
4. The Philippines 1132
5. Hawaii 1134

H. THE SECOND WORLD WAR 1135

1. Political and International Affairs, 1939–1945 1135
2. The Campaigns in Poland and Finland, 1939–1940 . . 1145
3. The Invasion of Denmark and Norway, 1940 1146
4. The Conquest of the Netherlands and Belgium and the
    Fall of France 1146
5. The Battle of Britain 1148
6. The Balkan Campaigns, 1940–1941 1149
7. The Campaigns in Russia, June, 1941–December, 1944 . 1151
8. Defense of the Western Hemisphere 1154
9. Naval Warfare and Blockade 1156
10. Campaigns in Africa, 1940–1943 1159
11. The Invasion of Italy 1162
12. The Liberation of France and Belgium 1163
13. The Battle of Germany, 1945 1164
14. The War in Asia 1165
15. The War in the Pacific, 1941–1945 1167
16. The Organization of Peace 1170

VII. THE POST–WAR WORLD

A. THE UNITED NATIONS 1172
B. EUROPE 1174
1. International Affairs 1174
2. The British Isles 1175
    a. Great Britain 1175
    b. Ireland 1178

3. The Low Countries 1178
    a. Belgium 1178
    b. The Kingdom of the Netherlands 1179
4. France 1179
5. The Iberian Peninsula 1180
    a. Spain 1180
    b. Portugal 1181
6. Italy and the Papacy 1181
    a. Italy 1181
    b. The Papacy 1182
7. Switzerland 1183
8. Germany 1183
9. Austria 1186
10. Czechoslovakia 1187
11. Hungary 1188
12. The Balkan States 1188
    a. Yugoslavia 1188
    b. Albania 1189
    c. Greece 1189
    d. Bulgaria 1190
    e. Rumania 1191
13. The Soviet Union 1192
14. Poland 1193
15. The Scandinavian States 1194
    a. Denmark 1194
    b. Norway 1194
    c. Sweden 1194
    d. Finland 1195

C. NORTH AMERICA 1196

    1. The United States 1196
    2. The Dominion of Canada 1198

D. LATIN AMERICA 1199

    1. General 1199
    2. South America 1199
        a. Argentina 1199
        b. Chile 1199
        c. Paraguay 1199
        d. Uruguay 1200

e. Bolivia 1200
f. Peru 1200
g. Ecuador 1200
h. Colombia 1200
i. Venezuela 1200
j. Brazil 1201
3. Mexico and Central America 1201
a. Mexico 1201
b. Panama 1201
c. Costa Rica 1201
d. Nicaragua 1201
e. Honduras 1202
f. Salvador 1202
g. Guatemala 1202
4. The West Indies 1202
a. Cuba 1202
b. Haiti 1202
c. The Dominican Republic 1202
d. Puerto Rico 1202

E. AFRICA 1203

1. Egypt and the Sudan 1203
2. Colonial Africa 1203
3. Union of South Africa 1204

F. ASIA 1206

1. The Middle East 1206
a. Turkey 1206
b. Syria 1206
c. Lebanon 1206
d. Palestine (Israel) 1207
e. Transjordan (Jordan) 1207
f. Iraq 1208
g. Iran 1208
h. Afghanistan 1208
2. India 1209
a. British India 1209
b. The Dominion of India 1209
c. Pakistan 1211
d. Ceylon 1211

3. Burma 1211
4. Siam (Thailand) 1212
5. Indo-China 1212
6. The Republic of Indonesia 1214
7. China 1215
8. Japan 1217
9. Korea 1218

G. THE PACIFIC AREA 1221
1. Australia 1221
2. New Zealand 1221
3. The Philippine Republic 1222

LIST OF EVENTS FROM JANUARY 1, 1951, TO APRIL, 30, 1952 1223

APPENDICES

I. Roman Emperors 1231
II. Byzantine Emperors 1232
III. The Caliphs, to 1256 1233
IV. Roman Popes 1234
V. Holy Roman Emperors 1236
VI. British Ministries since Walpole 1237
VII. French Ministries, 1815–1870 1238
VIII. Presidents and Prime Ministers of the Third French Republic 1239
IX. Italian Ministries since 1860 1242
X. List of Presidents of the United States 1243

INDEX, covering events to 1945 i
SUPPLEMENTARY INDEX, covering events from 1946 to April 30, 1952 lxxxiv

Genealogical Tables

The Julian-Claudian House 104
The Merovingian Kings 148
The House of Pepin 149
The Carolingian Dynasty 156
The Saxon Emperors 161
The Macedonian Emperors 178
The Norman and Plantagenet Kings 195
The Scottish Succession 202
The Salian Emperors 205
The Welf and Hohenstaufen Families 209
The Capetian Kings 226
Rulers of Leon and Castile 234
The Houses of Navarre, Aragon, and Barcelona 236
Kings of Portugal, Burgundian House 238
The Comneni and Angeli 251
Lancaster and York 269
The French Succession, 1328 274
The Valois House 275
The House of Castile 281
The House of Aragon 283
Kings of Portugal 285
The House of Anjou 291
The Neapolitan Anjous 292
The Medici Family 295
Rulers of Milan 297
The House of Hapsburg 300
The House of Luxemburg 301
The House of Wittelsbach 303
Rulers of Denmark, Norway, and Sweden, 1263–1533 . . 311
The Palaeologi 321
Succession to the English Crown, 1553–1603 371
The House of Burgundy 380
The French Succession, 1498 382
House of Lorraine and Guise 383
The House of Bourbon, to 1610 385
The Portuguese Succession, 1580 391
The Hapsburg House in the Sixteenth Century 399

Cleve-Jülich Succession, 1609 403
Kings of Denmark, 1448–1670 411
The House of Vasa in Sweden, 1523–1660 412
Kings of Poland, 1445–1668 414
Russian Rulers, 1462–1676 417
Ottoman Sultans, 1451–1649 421
The House of Stuart 433
The Houses of Orange and Nassau, 1559–1843 438
The French Bourbons, 1589–1830 441
The Spanish Succession, 1700 444
The Spanish Bourbons, 1700–1868 449
The House of Braganza, 1640–1826 453
The House of Savoy, 1553–1878 456
The German Hapsburgs, 1556–1835 462
The Hohenzollern House, 1415–1840 464
The House of Vasa, 1523–1818 470
The Danish House of Oldenburg, 1588–1906 473
The House of Romanov, 1613–1801 480
Ottoman Sultans, 1649–1839 483
The Safavid Dynasty 527
The Mogul Emperors 532
The Manchu (Ta ch'ing) Dynasty, 1644–1795 538
The Tokugawa Shōgun, 1603–1867 545
The House of Bonaparte 589
The British Royal House (Hanover, Saxe-Coburg, Windsor). 610
The House of Coburg, 1800–1945 624
The Dutch Royal House, 1815–1939 625
The French Bourbons, 1715–1883 627
The House of Bourbon-Orléans 629
The Spanish Bourbons, 1814–1931 644
The House of Coburg-Braganza 649
The Neapolitan Bourbons 652
The House of Savoy 653
The House of Savoy-Carignan 653
The House of Hapsburg-Lorraine 672
The House of Hohenzollern 679
The Kings of Hanover 682
The Kings of Saxony 683
The Kings of Württemberg 684
The Kings of Bavaria 685
Kings of Denmark since 1746 698
Kings of Sweden since 1751 700

Russian Tsars, 1796–1917 703
Kings of Greece (Danish House) 712
Rulers of Serbia (Yugoslavia) 713
Rulers of Montenegro 716
Rulers of Bulgaria 717
Kings of Rumania 721
Ottoman Sultans, 1703–1922 730
Khedives and Kings of Egypt since 1811 829
The Kajar Dynasty 863
The Barakzai Dynasty 867
The Manchu (Ta Ch'ing) Dynasty, 1795–1912 878
The (Wahabi) Dynasty of Ibn Saud 1103
The Hashimite Dynasty of Iraq 1106
The Pahlavi Dynasty of Iran 1107
Rulers of Afghanistan since 1929 . . . . 111c
Japanese Emperors since the Restoration 1124

List of Maps

Ancient Empires (Egyptian, Assyrian, Babylonian, Persian) . 22
Greek City-States 49
The Kingdoms of Alexander's Successors 76
The Roman Empire Before the Barbarian Invasions . . 101–102
The Frankish Empire 154
England in Alfred's Day 165
The Byzantine Empire Under Justinian 171
The Mohammedan World About 732 185
Dominions of Henry II 192
The Mongol Empire 261
Italy in the Fifteenth Century 287
The Hanseatic League and the Teutonic Knights 308
Poland, Lithuania, and Russia in the Fifteenth Century . . 314
Conquests of the Ottoman Turks, 1418 324
China in the Last Half of the Twelfth Century 338
India to the Mohammedan Conquest 338
Europe in the Sixteenth Century 369–370
Growth of Russia in Europe to 1725 416
Europe in the Seventeenth Century 425–426
The Partitions of Poland 476
Colonial Latin America 487
Early Settlements on the Continent of North America . . 506
The United States During the Revolution 519
Growth of British Power in India 531
The Arctic Regions 560
Antarctic Claims in 1939 572
Napoleon's Empire 597
Europe in 1815 605–606
Unification of Italy 656
Europe in 1900 667–668
Central Europe, 1815–1866 668
The Balkans, 1914 711
The Expansion of the United States 765
The United States During the Confederation Period . . . 767
The Civil War, 1860–1865 777
Canada 794
Latin-American States After the Revolutions 807

The Partition of Africa 827
Asia in 1914 869
Australia and New Zealand 897
The Western Front 912
The Eastern Front 915
The Italian Front 924
The Near Eastern Theater of War 928
The Balkan Front 933
World War Losses 956
South America in 1930 1063
Africa 1082
Western Asia 1099
Japanese Gains in World War II 1115
German Advance in Europe, World War II 1147
Retreat in Russia, World War II 1152
Battle of the Atlantic, World War II 1157
Europe and Africa during German Seizure, World War II . 1161
Japanese Advance into Asia, World War II 1168
Central Europe, 1950 1177
India-Pakistan, 1950 1210
Southeast Asia, 1950 1213
Korea 1219

I. THE PREHISTORIC PERIOD

A. INTRODUCTION

1. DEFINITION, DATA, AND METHODS

HISTORY in its broadest sense should be a record of Man and his accomplishments from the time when he ceased being merely an animal and became a human being. The efforts to reconstruct this record may be classed under two heads: (1) **History** (in the stricter sense), which is based on written documents and covers part of the last five thousand years of Man's activities, and (2) **Prehistory**, which is based largely on archaeological evidence and covers all the long preceding period, which probably amounts to more than one million years.

The prehistoric period is important, not only by reason of its vast length, but also because during this time Man made almost all his major discoveries and adaptations to environment and group-life (except those connected with the recent machine age) and evolved physically into the modern racial types. Hence at least a brief summary of the prehistoric period is a necessary introduction to any account of the recorded history of Man.

The main body of material upon which the work of prehistoric reconstruction is based comprises: first, remains left by early peoples, largely in the form of tools and other artifacts, found by excavation in old habitation sites or burials; secondly, other traces of their activities, such as buildings and rock-carvings or rock-paintings; and lastly, the bones of the people themselves. This material gives good evidence of the physical type of prehistoric peoples and their material culture, very slight evidence of their social, intellectual, and religious life and no evidence of their language. It can be supplemented to some extent—and with great caution—by a comparative study of the physical types, languages, and material culture of modern peoples.

The time when prehistory ends and true history begins varies greatly in different parts of the world. Traditional history often covers the borderline between the two and can sometimes be successfully correlated with the archaeological evidence.

In prehistory, dates are entirely a matter of estimate and cannot be used as fundamental landmarks, as in the case of recorded history.

2. THE ORIGIN OF MAN

MAN'S PLACE AMONG THE ANIMALS. The various living and extinct species of Man are assigned by zoologists to the family *Hominidae*, which belongs to the sub-order *Anthropoidea* (containing monkeys, apes, and baboons), of the order **Primates** (containing also *Tarsius* and the lemurs), of the class **Mammalia**. His nearest living relatives are the four genera of the family *Simiidae* (the so-called Anthropoid Apes): the gorilla and chimpanzee of equatorial Africa and the orang-utan and gibbon of southeastern Asia and the East Indies. Man is distinguished from the higher apes by the greater size of his brain (especially the forebrain), his fully erect position in walking, the better adaptation of his hands for grasping and holding, and his use of language for communication.

MAN'S ANIMAL ANCESTORS. No remains have yet been found of Man's immediate precursor, the primitive and more ape-like animal from which he is supposed to be descended. Neither have we yet found any certain traces of the postulated animal (often popularly termed the *Missing Link*) from which both Man and the anthropoid apes are descended. Several forms of fossil apes have been found, however, which show a kinship to Man in some particulars and help to bridge over this gap: notably, *Propliopithecus*, from the Lower Oligocene of Egypt; *Sivapithecus*, from Miocene India; *Dryopithecus*, from Miocene France; and *Australopithecus* (the "Taungs skull"), from the Pliocene or Pleistocene of South Africa.

DATE OF MAN'S ORIGIN. This has not yet been definitely established. The ancestors of the great apes and the ancestor of Man probably diverged from one another as early as the Miocene period, and Man acquired certain essentially human characteristics probably in the Pliocene period. The earliest known skeletal remains that are accepted as human are believed to date from the early or middle part of the Pleistocene period. For the purposes of the prehistorian, who has to rely largely on archaeological evidence, the record of Man may be said to begin at the moment when he was able to fashion the first stone tools which can be unmistakably recognized to be of human workmanship. This was early in the Pleistocene, or possibly in the very late Pliocene.

PLACE OF MAN'S ORIGIN. This is still entirely a matter of speculation. The old theory of Central Asia as the "Cradle of Mankind" was based on false premises, which have been abandoned. From the distribution of the living and fossil great apes, it is thought that Man's divergence from the general anthropoid stem is likely to have taken place somewhere in the area comprising western Europe, the northern half of Africa, and southern Asia, with the preference perhaps slightly in favor of Africa or Asia, but there is no real evidence at present to warrant a final conclusion.

3. CULTURES AND THEIR DATING

a. CULTURES AND PERIODS

Archaeological investigation of the material remains of prehistoric Man has shown that a wide variety of cultures flourished in different parts of the world and at different times. For convenience these have been grouped into a series of major cultures based primarily on the nature of the principal material used for implements (whether stone or one of the metals), and sometimes on the technique used in fashioning these implements. The oldest culture in the world was characterized by the use of chipped stone for implements and has been named Palaeolithic culture. Neolithic culture, on the other hand, was characterized by the use of polished stone implements; Bronze culture, by the use of bronze implements, and so forth.

In most parts of the world the discovery and use of these different materials and techniques took place in a regular sequence in time. In the absence of fixed dates, it was thus found convenient to use these cultural terms in a chronological sense. Accordingly prehistoric times have usually been divided into the following series of periods or ages (beginning with the oldest): **Palaeolithic** (Old Stone), characterized by chipped stone implements; **Mesolithic** (Intermediate Stone), a transitional period; **Neolithic** (New Stone), with polished stone implements; **Chalcolithic** (Stone and Copper), characterized by the first tentative use of copper implements; **Bronze Age**, with full development of copper and bronze implements; and **Iron Age**, with iron implements.

These names are excellent to identify cultures, but their use to designate periods of time has led to much inaccuracy and confusion, as the dates of the cultures to which they refer differ widely in different parts of the world. It is proper, for example, to speak of the Bronze Age of Hungary or some other limited area, where the beginning and end of the bronze culture can be fairly accurately dated. But it is quite impossible to speak with any meaning of the Bronze Age of the Old World, for this period began some thousand or fifteen hundred years earlier in Mesopotamia, for instance, than it did in western Europe, and it gave way to the Iron Age one or two thousand years earlier in Asia Minor than it did in some parts of Siberia; while in Japan there was no true Bronze Age and in Australia no Bronze Age at all. The names of these periods are, however, too well established to be abandoned and are often useful, if employed with caution.

DATING. As there are no written documents, a variety of other means have been employed to determine the duration and dates of prehistoric cultures.

b. RELATIVE DATING

This is established by the following methods:

(1) **Stratigraphy.** When there is accurate excavation of a site, the undisturbed remains in any given level may fairly safely be assumed to be earlier than the remains in the levels that overlie it.

(2) **Typology.** The age of a given culture may sometimes be determined approximately when most of the objects representing it appear to be identical in type with objects found elsewhere in a culture which has been dated by other means.

(3) **Geology.** The relative age of different remains can often be ascertained by finding the relative age of the geological strata in which the remains occur, as in the case of a series of sedimentary deposits, or river terraces and raised beaches, marking former

shorelines or flood levels in valleys at times when the mutual relation of land and water was different from that of the present.

(4) **Palaeontology.** The presence (with the human remains) of extinct or still existing species of animals (including marine and lacustrine fauna) frequently provides a fairly exact basis for dating the human remains, in terms of geological periods.

(5) **Palaeobotany.** The presence of plant remains furnishes a further basis for assigning associated human remains to certain geological periods.

(6) **Climatic evidence.** When the past record of major climatic sequences in an area is known, human remains can often be dated in terms of glacial advances and retreats or pluvial and dry periods, if the remains are found in deposits characteristic of such periods. The kinds of animals and plants found in association with the human remains frequently show whether the climate of the period in question was wet or dry or warm or cold. Thanks to the great progress which has recently been made in palaeobotany it is now possible to trace climatic fluctuations (as reflected by the immigration of new forest forms) through microscopic examination of pollen grains preserved intact for thousands of years in peat beds and elsewhere. Associated archaeological remains can thus often be referred with great accuracy to a given climatic phase.

There is considerable room for error in the use of each of these methods, unless the greatest care is exercised, but they are all sound in principle and in general they may be relied upon, particularly when one confirms another. The ideal system would make use of all the methods listed above, establishing for any area the sequence of climatic changes, earth movements and deposits, and using this as a chronological framework into which to fit the successive cultures, reconstructed on the basis of the stratigraphy of the archaeological remains. For very few regions has this been done.

c. ABSOLUTE DATING

This is more difficult, but several methods have been used.

(1) **Estimate of the time needed to produce observed changes in culture.** There is no exact basis for such estimates, and this method, though often the only one available, is extremely inaccurate and inadequate.

(2) **Estimate of the time necessary for the performance of certain geological work.** This is used to date geological horizons in which human remains occur. For example, the date of a high river terrace may be given if it is estimated that it must have taken the river at least one hundred thousand years to cut down its bed to the present level. Such estimates are almost equally uncertain and inadequate for the purposes of the prehistorian.

(3) **Extent of the breakdown of radioactive minerals in certain rocks.** This method is based on a process that can be measured with some exactness and has been used to determine the age of the great geological epochs but cannot yet be applied accurately to any period that is much under half a million years.

(4) **Geochronology;** that is, the counting of the annual layers (varves) of sediment deposited by the melt-waters of a retreating ice-sheet. This method, first devised by the Swedish scientist, De Geer, has been applied to the Scandinavian region as the basis of an absolute system of chronology covering the last twelve thousand years. Owing to the scarcity of archaeological remains found *in situ* in dated varves, this system is of value principally in correlating and dating the different stages of the retreat of the last ice-sheet and the major fluctuations in sea-level in the Baltic area. These in turn serve to date many deposits which, by pollen analysis, can be assigned to the various post-glacial climatic cycles. Thus indirectly the archaeological remains found in these deposits can be tentatively dated.

(5) **Dendrochronology.** This method, devised by Douglass and applied first in the southwestern United States, is based on the fact that certain species of trees, especially in arid regions, show by the thickness of their annual rings of growth the alternation of relatively wet or dry years. By matching many specimens from trees of various ages it has been possible to construct a time scale by which to date timbers found in prehistoric ruins.

(6) **Historical evidence.** Late prehistoric cultures in backward areas can sometimes be dated in a general way by the presence of imported objects from a known historical culture in some more advanced area, where written documents already exist.

It is thus seen that dates assigned to prehistoric periods are, for the present at least, almost entirely a matter of estimate. In some cases the estimates of most experts are in more or less general agreement, but often they vary widely, depending upon the person who makes them and the particular methods he relies upon as a basis for his dating.

B. THE PALAEOLITHIC PERIOD

(Probably over one million years in duration, ending about 8000 B.C.*)*

1. CULTURE AND INDUSTRIES

THE word *Palaeolithic* is used to describe a stage of human culture, the earliest of which we have sure evidence. Although this culture persisted longer in some parts of the world than in others, we can use the term with reasonable accuracy to characterize a period of time. This period includes probably 99 per cent of Man's life on earth (at least since he became a tool-using animal), all the other periods down to the present covering the remaining 1 per cent.

Our knowledge of Palaeolithic culture is based principally on implements and animal and human bones found in the gravels of old river terraces, in open camp sites, and in caves. Disregarding the variations of time and place, one may say in general that Palaeolithic men knew the use of fire and lived by hunting and collecting vegetable foods, as the Australian natives and the Bushmen of South Africa do today. They had no agriculture and no domestic animals, excepting possibly the dog. For shelter they probably made wind-breaks and crude huts of branches, occasionally occupying caves. Their clothing was undoubtedly of skins (no textiles). Their tools and utensils were of stone, bone, and undoubtedly also of wood and basketry (no metal and no pottery). We know almost nothing of their social organization, religion, and intellectual life, except that late cave paintings and burials indicate belief in magic (in con-nection with hunting) and in some kind of existence of the individual after death. It is fairly safe to assume, however, that a large part of the fundamental institutions and beliefs of modern primitive peoples and of our own early historical ancestors had their origin and first development in this period.

The **stone tools**, which are such important criteria for this period, were usually made of flint or other hard rock by a process of chipping. They are classified as **core tools**, when the basis of the implement was a piece of rock, improved by chipping, or **flake tools**, when one of the flakes knocked off from a core (which is then termed a nucleus) was used as the basis for the implement. Sometimes the core was made ready for flaking by first creating a flat surface or striking-platform. Chips were removed by striking with another stone (hammer stone) or by pressure (pressure flaking). Sometimes the edges of a flake were improved by secondary chipping or flaking (retouching). The principal types of implements were hand-axes or *coups de poing* (large pear-shaped or almond-shaped cores, chipped on both sides); scrapers of various shapes; points; awls (borers); and, in late times, long blades with roughly parallel edges, and gravers (small tools of many shapes improved for use as chisels or gouges by striking a special blow near the point).

2. EUROPE

The **Pleistocene period**, or Ice Age, in which Palaeolithic culture developed and flourished, was marked, at least in the Alpine regions, by four major glacial advances (Günz, Mindel, Riss, and Würm), separated by three warmer inter-glacial periods. The last glaciation had two maxima (Würm I and II), during which much of northern Europe was covered by a sheet of ice, but between them was a comparatively warm period, the Laufen oscillation.

PRE-PALAEOLITHIC. Assigned to this period, at the end of the Pliocene and early part of the Pleistocene, are certain occasional finds of crude, shapeless stones, called *eoliths*, which are supposed by some archaeologists to show traces of Man's first attempts at chipping, but this is still a matter of dispute. Here also come three so-called industries of Reid Moir: the Iceian industry, characterized by rostrocarinate tools; the Darmsdenian, a pebble industry; and the Harrisonian, an industry of so-called utilized flakes.

LOWER PALAEOLITHIC. This period covers the greater part of the Pleistocene.

Almost our only information about the peoples and movements of this time consists of what may be inferred from the stone implements, which show, according to Breuil, the contemporary but more or less independent development and mutual inter-influence in western Europe of four separate techniques of manufacture (industries): (1) **Hand-axe** industry (French *biface*), developing through Pre-Chellean (Abbevillian) to Acheulean types; (2) **Clactonian** industry, characterized by rough flakes with an unfaceted striking-platform inclined at a high angle to the main flake surface; (3) **Levalloisean** industry, characterized by large flakes struck from a previously prepared core (tortoise core) and retaining a faceted striking-platform; and (4) **Mousterian** industry, consisting of smaller flakes of various forms, usually exhibiting a characteristic technique of retouching the edges (stepped retouch). These industries are found both separate and mixed, and there are additional intermediate forms. Chronologically they have been grouped into four periods: (1) **Pre-Chellean** (Abbevillian) period, characterized by extremely crude hand-axes; (2) **Chellean** period (now usually included with Acheulean), having hand-axes somewhat less crude than the Abbevillian, as well as some Clactonian tools; (3) **Acheulean** period, marked by more highly evolved hand-axes and, particularly in its later stages, by Levallois flakes; and (4) **Mousterian** period (sometimes designated as Middle Palaeolithic), with typical flake tools (points and scrapers) and a continuation in some places of Levallois flakes. The Mousterian industry proper (which has Pre-Mousterian or Proto-Mousterian forerunners in northern and eastern Europe) is found particularly in the caves of central France, associated with bones of mammoth and reindeer and of Neanderthal Man.

UPPER PALAEOLITHIC. This is a relatively short period, coinciding with the last part of the Ice Age and marked by the appearance of new flint industries and men of modern type (*Homo sapiens*). Three principal cultures are noted: (1) **Aurignacian** culture. This was the earliest. Evidence shows that the climate was comparatively warm. The people were nomadic hunters, living in open camps and caves. The stone industry was marked by great use of the blade and included a variety of characteristic scrapers, gravers, points (Châtelperron, Gravette, Font Robert types), and beginning of very small tools (*microliths*); also bone implements and ornaments of shell and bone. Aurignacian remains are found widely through central and western Europe and the Mediterranean region. (2) **Solutrean** culture. This is distributed from eastern and central Europe as far as France, intruding on the Aurignacian. The climate was cold. The Solutreans lived in open camps and rock shelters, were great hunters of horses, and introduced the technique of pressure flaking (willow-leaf and laurel-leaf points). (3) **Magdalenian** culture, the latest to develop, flourished in northern and central Europe and southern France. The climate was somewhat colder and the Magdalenians lived frequently in caves, where they made remarkable rock-carvings and paintings, representing animals and men. Besides stone tools there was a high development of bone carving (spearheads, harpoons, *bâtons de commande*, and representations of animals).

The Palaeolithic period in Europe ended with the great changes in climate, fauna, and flora that marked the termination of the Pleistocene or Ice Age.

3. AFRICA

The Palaeolithic of Africa is characterized by a variety of stone industries, some of which are purely local, while others are similar to or practically identical with certain of the industries of Europe. Geological investigation, which has only recently been undertaken on an adequate basis, indicates that owing to fluctuations in rainfall the Pleistocene period throughout most of Africa can perhaps be divided into a succession of pluvial and interpluvial periods, which it is hoped may eventually be correlated in some way with the glacial and interglacial periods of Europe. The succession of cultures is well established for certain areas, but not yet for the continent as a whole.

NORTHWEST AFRICA. Heavily patinated hand-axes of definitely Chellean and Acheulean types together with an early fauna have been found, usually without stratigraphy, in Tunisia, Algeria, Morocco, and to the south in the Sahara region, which was apparently once less arid than now. A so-called Mousterian industry (accompanied by a later fauna) is also represented, and excavations show an evolution from Levalloisean types, without typical Mousterian, to a special development known as the **Aterian** industry, characterized by small, tanged leaf-shaped points, delicately trimmed all over both faces. This was succeeded by two contemporary cultures, the early **Capsian** and the **Oranian** (Ibero-Maurusian), which were Upper Palaeolithic in date and marked by blades, gravers, and microlithic forms, the earliest phases of which bear a fundamental though distant relationship to the early Aurignacian of Europe.

EGYPT. The presence of Palaeolithic Man is shown by discoveries of the following succession of industries, all *in situ*, in the terraces of the Nile Valley: Chellean, a primitive Acheulean and an Egyptian form of the Clactonian, in the 100-foot terrace (no human implements were found in the 150-foot terrace); developed Acheulean in the 50-foot terrace; Levalloisean (first reported as Early Mousterian) in the 30-foot terrace; and developed Levalloisean (reported as Egyptian Mousterian) in the 15- to 10-foot terrace. These were followed, in deposits of later age, by an Egyptian version of the Aterian and a local industry, the Sebilian.

EAST AFRICA. According to Leakey, who has done the most work in this area, there is an early series of industries in Kenya, Uganda, and Tanganyika, which apparently evolved from simple pebbles, roughly chipped to an edge on one side (**Kafuan** industry), through pebbles chipped to an edge on both sides (**Oldowan** industry) and through other intermediate forms to the true hand-axe types (Chellean and Acheulean industries). In higher geological horizons, and thought to be partly contemporary with one another, are found two series of industries, Aurignacian and a sparsely represented Levalloisean (followed by the Stillbay)—both with many stages. Leakey assigns the Kafuan to the First Pluvial period of East Africa (Lower Pleistocene), the Chellean and Acheulean to the Second or Kamasian Pluvial period (Middle Pleistocene), and the Aurignacian and Levalloisean-Stillbay to the Third or Gamblian Pluvial period (Upper Pleistocene).

SOUTH AFRICA. Here the **Stellenbosch** culture, involving Chellean and Acheulean types (hand-axes and cleavers and Victoria West cores), was followed, stratigraphically, by the **Fauresmith** culture (hand-axes and also flakes with faceted striking-platform, suggesting Levalloisean influence), which together form the so-called Older Stone Age. The Middle Stone Age was marked by a series of more or less contemporary flake industries (Mossel-bay, Glen Grey Falls, Howieson's Poort, Bambata Cave, Stillbay, etc.), suggesting by the shapes and technique of their implements a combination of Levalloisean and Aurignacian influences, together with pressure-flaking in one case (Stillbay).

OTHER AREAS. Occasional finds of implements similar to those of some of the industries already described have been reported from Nigeria, the Sudan, Abyssinia, Somaliland, the Congo region, and northern Rhodesia.

4. ASIA AND OCEANIA

WESTERN ASIA. A remarkably complete sequence of stone industries, paralleling quite closely those of Europe, has been established for the Palestine-Syria region. Surface finds of Chellean implements are supplemented (in three caves in the Wady-el-Mughara, near Mt. Carmel) by the following stratigraphic series: Tayacian, Upper Acheulean, Levalloiseo-Mousterian (with skeletons of Neandertaloid type), Aurignacian, and Natufian (a Mesolithic industry). Occasional sites with implements of one or another of these types have been reported from northern Arabia, Asia Minor, Armenia, Transcaucasia, Mesopotamia, and Persia.

INDIA. Many implements of Chellean type, as well as Acheulean hand-axes and cleavers, have been reported in northern, central, and southern India. In the Punjab, De Terra found Acheulean hand-axes in a deposit contemporary with the second Himalayan glaciation or somewhat later. These were succeeded by a crude pebble industry (Soan industry) in strata contemporary with the third Himalayan glaciation. A few Upper Palaeolithic types, with some suggestions of Aurignacian, have also been found in central and northwestern India, as well as cave sites with rock paintings of uncertain age.

CHINA. Skulls of Peking Man (*Sinanthropus pekinensis*), together with traces of fire and very shapeless stone tools, have been excavated in Middle Pleistocene deposits at Chou-kou-tien, southwest of Peiping. Implements of general Upper Palaeolithic type were found in the Ordos region, accompanied by remains of animals related to those associated with the last glacial advance in Europe. Other finds of a similar nature have been reported from Mongolia and Manchuria, but none to date from Japan.

SIBERIA. Hearth sites, Palaeolithic implements and remains of extinct animals have been found in southwestern and central Siberia, especially in the basin of the Ob River and its tributaries, the valleys of the Upper Yenisei (Minusinsk region) and Angara Rivers and around Lake Baikal. Some of the implements resemble quite closely certain Mousterian, Aurignacian, and Magdalenian forms of western Europe. The deposits in which they occur and the fauna suggest that they belong to the Upper Palaeolithic period.

SOUTHEASTERN ASIA AND OCEANIA. The occurrence of a Palaeolithic culture in parts of this region has been reported, as evidenced by crude chipped stone tools unaccompanied by polished stone or pottery, and (in Tonkin) these actually occur below levels containing polished stone tools and pottery. Many of the familiar types of Palaeolithic tools are lacking, however, and recent investigation has revealed that these industries definitely date from the New Stone Age or at earliest from the Mesolithic. In Burma, however, a new Lower Palaeolithic culture (Anyathian), associated with extinct fauna, has been discovered in the Middle Pleistocene terraces of the Irrawaddy River. In Java an important series of remains of early Man has been found, including *Homo modjokertensis*, in a Lower Pleistocene horizon; the famous *Pithecanthropus erectus*, which is now shown by the associated fauna to be Middle Pleistocene in date; and Solo Man, belonging to the Upper Pleistocene. Surface finds of implements of Lower Palaeolithic type and points and scrapers of general Upper Palaeolithic appearance have also been reported from Java. No Palaeolithic remains have been found in Polynesia.

5. AMERICA

For an account of alleged Palaeolithic cultures in America, see below.

6. INTERRELATIONSHIP OF PALAEOLITHIC CULTURES

It should be clear from the foregoing that at present we know a great deal more about Palaeolithic stone implements than we do about the Palaeolithic people who made them. Our data are still too insufficient to warrant any sure account of the way in which the various elements of Palaeolithic culture were developed by different groups of mankind and spread by them throughout the world. However, three fundamental facts relating to this problem may be regarded as reasonably well established:

First, some of the more highly evolved implements and groups of implements found in widely different areas are so similar in shape and technique that we are forced to infer that the cultures in which they occur bear some time-relationship to one another, i.e. the art of making the typical implements in question (such as the hand-axe, the Levallois flake and the Aurignacian blade, to name three fundamental examples) was not evolved independently at different times and in different places but was spread from some original center, either by actual migrations of people or by cultural diffusion.

Second, the geographical distribution of these various type implements, although very wide, is not haphazard, but each one of the fundamental industries has its own distinct area of major development, with outliers along natural routes of migration. For example, the industry characterized by core implements of hand-axe type is found in one continuous area, comprising southwestern Asia, eastern and northern Africa, and southern and western Europe, with outliers in South Africa and India. A less sharply definable industry, characterized by the use of flake implements in preference to cores and (in its most developed form) by the use of flake implements of Levalloisean type with a faceted striking-platform, has its home in the same area, with addition of a broad belt stretching through central and eastern Europe and northern Asia. Finally the blade industry has a distribution which is practically identical with that last described, though with a less characteristic development in South Africa and India. The southeastern part of Asia, from the North China plain to Indonesia, seems to form a separate culture province, with an almost entirely inde-

pendent development throughout Palaeolithic times.

Third, the three major industries just
referred to had their principal development
at different periods of time, as is shown by
the fact that wherever there is stratigraphic
evidence they occur in the same order of
succession, with the hand-axe industry the
earliest, succeeded in turn by the Levalloisean flake industry and that by the
blade industry, the latest of all. The foregoing outline is, of course, oversimplified
and disregards many problems of local
development and relations, but it is based
on a mass of evidence, it represents the best
opinion of archaeologists today, and it may
be accepted provisionally as a true interpretation of the facts.

7. THE DATES OF PALAEOLITHIC CULTURES

The Palaeolithic period of Man's development is considered to be roughly
contemporary with the Pleistocene period
of the earth's history and has to be dated
in geological terms. The Pleistocene may
be broadly divided, on the basis of faunal
remains, into Lower, Middle, and Upper or
(in Europe at least), on the basis of Alpine
glacial deposits, into four major periods of
glacial advance (Günz, Mindel, Riss, and
Würm) with three corresponding interglacial periods. The dating of Palaeolithic
industries in terms of Alpine glacial and
interglacial periods is still, however, a
highly speculative affair, owing to the fact,
which is not always properly appreciated,
that almost no archaeological remains have
yet been found in actual glacial deposits of
the Alpine region. Attempts have been
made to correlate glaciations in Asia and
Africa with these Alpine glaciations and to
correlate with both the series of implement-
bearing river terraces (especially of the
Thames, Somme, and Nile) and implement-
bearing deposits of so-called Pluvial periods
in non-glaciated regions (notably in East
Africa), but only preliminary work has
yet been done on this large and complicated
problem. Hence statements of experts
regarding the age of the earlier Palaeolithic
cultures differ greatly and should be regarded as opinions or theories only, which
require further evidence before they can be
accepted as established fact.

That tool-making man existed as early
as the Lower Pleistocene period has been
contended by a number of authorities.
Teilhard de Chardin has dated the Sinanthropus finds at Chou-kou-tien as possibly Lower Pleistocene, and Breuil con-
siders that deposits containing his Abbevillian (Pre-Chellean) industry and the earliest
Clactonian industry belong to the First
(Günz-Mindel) Interglacial period. Various
alleged implements of a very primitive
nature (including the so-called *eoliths*)
found in Europe and Africa have been
ascribed to this period and Reid Moir
claims to have found tools of primitive
types in deposits that are presumably of
pre-Günz age. Such early dates are not yet
universally accepted by archaeologists and
geologists.

When we come to the Middle Pleistocene,
however, there is a more general agreement
that the early phases of the hand-axe and
flake industries (Chellean, Clactonian, etc.)
in Europe and Africa probably existed in
the Second (Mindel-Riss) Interglacial
period. De Terra has found similar implements in India in deposits contemporary
with the end of his Second Himalayan
Glacial Advance or the following interglacial period (which may be contemporary
respectively with the Second or Mindel
Glaciation of Europe and the Mindel-Riss
Interglacial).

Furthermore, it is thought very probable
that in Europe the fully developed Acheulean and associated Levalloisean industries
belong to the Third (Riss-Würm) Interglacial period, the typical Mousterian to
the end of this period and the first maximum of the Fourth Glacial period (Würm
I), the Aurignacian to the time of the
Laufen oscillation, the Solutrean to the
second maximum of the Fourth Glacial
(Würm II), and the Magdalenian to the
last stages and retreat of Würm II. African
and Asiatic implements that show relationship to some of the above industries
are probably roughly contemporary with
them.

It is impossible to give an absolute date
to these periods in years. Most recent
geological opinion assigns a duration of one
and one half to two million years for the
Pleistocene. This would mean that the
earliest man whose tools we have found and
certainly identified lived perhaps as much
as a million years ago. It is estimated
(largely on the basis of De Geer's studies
of varves in the Scandinavian area) that
for Europe the Pleistocene period ended
(and with it the Palaeolithic Age) circa
8000 B.C.

8. PHYSICAL TYPES OF PALAEOLITHIC MAN

Very few human skeletal remains have been found which can be assigned with any certainty to the Lower or Middle Pleistocene or which are so primitive in type that they are assumed to belong to these early periods. The principal ones are *Homo modjokertensis*, from the Lower Pleistocene of Java; *Pithecanthropus erectus*, from the Middle Pleistocene of Java; *Sinanthropus pekinensis* (**Peking Man**), from the Middle Pleistocene of China; *Eoanthropus dawsoni* (**Piltdown Man**), found in England and generally thought to belong to the Lower Pleistocene; *Homo heidelbergensis*, from an early interglacial deposit of Germany; and **Rhodesian Man** (Broken Hill skull), from South Africa, of very uncertain age.

For succeeding periods we have more satisfactory data. Belonging to the latter part of the Pleistocene, and mostly to the time of the first maximum of the last ice (Würm I) are many remains of **Neanderthal Man** (*Homo neanderthalensis*), a type which has been found, with many variations, from western Europe to Palestine (usually associated with Mousterian implements). All the primitive types so far mentioned differ greatly in their physical characteristics, and their exact relationship to one another and to modern races of men is still a subject of discussion, but it is questionable whether any one of them was a direct ancestor of *Homo sapiens* (modern or **Neanthropic Man**), the species to which all present races of men belong.

Alleged early occurrences of individuals of this Neanthropic type (e.g. Foxhall, Galley Hill, Olmo, and Castenedolo Man) are not accepted as valid by most anthropologists, but beginning with Upper Palaeolithic times, contemporary with the Laufen oscillation and the Würm II glacial maximum—in other words with the Aurignacian, Solutrean, and Magdalenian periods of Europe—representatives of modern man appear on the scene. Some of these, such as **Cro-Magnon, Combe-Capelle, Chancelade,** and **Grimaldi** in France, are generally long-headed (*dolichocephalic*) and on the whole like present-day long-headed peoples of the White or European group, though some of the Grimaldi skeletons have been claimed to show slight Negroid characteristics. Others, like **Boskop Man,** of South Africa, are more definitely related to present Negroid types. Still others, such as **Wadjak Man** (Java) and **Talgai Man** (Queensland), show relationships to the present Australian natives (Australoid type). Remains of a few round-headed (*brachycephalic*) individuals of the White group, apparently dating near the very close of the Palaeolithic, have been found in Europe—at Solutré, for example. No remains of Palaeolithic men of Mongoloid type have yet been reported.

C. THE POST-PALAEOLITHIC PERIOD

1. NATURE AND SEQUENCE OF POST-PALAEOLITHIC CULTURES

IN THE absence of exact dates, archaeologists have divided the time from the end of the Palaeolithic to the present into the following major periods: Mesolithic period, Neolithic period, Chalcolithic period, Bronze Age, Iron Age, and Modern Age. As has been previously pointed out, this nomenclature has many disadvantages, since the names refer really to cultural stages rather than to periods of time. The words were first employed in the description of cultures as observed in Europe and the order of succession is not always the same for other continents. Furthermore, it is impossible to assign even estimated dates to these so-called periods, for each one began and ended at a different time in different parts of the world. On the whole, however, this chronological division does represent the general progress of culture, in the Old World at least, and although it often leads to confusion, unless applied with the greatest care, still it has the advantage of convenience and almost universal usage. The dividing line between prehistory and history comes at no particular place in this series, but varies in different areas. Following is a brief definition of the different periods, after which the Post-Palaeolithic cultures of the world will be described by geographical areas.

a. MESOLITHIC PERIOD

The disappearance of the last ice-sheet, which marked the end of the Pleistocene period and, with it, the end of the Palaeolithic, led to the rise of a new culture, generally referred to as the Mesolithic, in which the Palaeolithic economy of food-gathering, though basically unchanged, was partly modified in some parts of the world under the influence of new climatic conditions. The big animals of the Pleistocene, on which the Palaeolithic hunters had largely depended for their food, disappeared everywhere except in parts of Africa, and their place was taken by the present-day fauna. Also with the ice retreat new regions were opened to settlement. The stone implements of the Mesolithic cultures were still produced by chipping, but a preference was shown for extremely small forms (*microliths*), often of geometric shapes. Some of these forms had a wide distribution in Asia, Africa, and Europe, showing that there were certain cultural relations and also actual movements of peoples—the latter probably connected to some extent with the drying up of the Sahara and Central Asiatic regions. The Mesolithic period is usually considered to have begun (in northern Europe at least) circa 8000 B.C., and Mesolithic cultures lasted for several thousand years until supplanted (at different dates in different areas) by the food-producing economy of the Neolithic peoples.

b. NEOLITHIC PERIOD

The next stage of development, the Neolithic, is marked by the invention and almost universal adoption of four important new features: **agriculture, domesticated animals, pottery,** and **polished** (instead of chipped) **stone tools.** These changes and the results which flowed from them were revolutionary. Man ceased being a nomad, eternally following his food supply, and became a sedentary being, residing and growing his food in one spot. He now had an assured food supply to carry over lean seasons and this led to a great increase in the population, in most of the formerly inhabited areas, and the opening to settlement of new areas, such as loess lands of Asia and Europe. The altered conditions likewise made possible the accumulation of possessions, the creation and satisfaction of new needs, the leisure for invention and speculation, the growth of large communities and cities, the development of more complex social organization, and in fact all the progress that has taken place since that time.

The four new culture traits which characterize the Neolithic were not necessarily originated at the same time and in the same place, and there is some evidence to indicate that there may have been an early stage, with primitive hoe agriculture and the pig as a domestic animal, before the advent of the Full Neolithic, with oxen, sheep, and plow agriculture. However, there is good reason to believe that Neolithic culture as a whole was developed in one general center and spread from there in successive waves to the ends of Asia, Africa, and Europe, but not, in any significant sense, to the New World. This original center was probably western Asia, for the wild relatives of the cereals and animals that were first domesticated have their home there, and it was the region in which the higher culture or civilization which the Neolithic discoveries made possible was first developed. The earliest remains of Neolithic culture which have yet been found are in Mesopotamia, Syria, Palestine, and Egypt. They represent a fully developed stage of the culture, with wheat and barley in cultivation and cattle, sheep, goats, and pigs as domesticated animals. The date of these remains is considered to be about 4000 B.C.—a period immediately prior to the first use of copper.

Neolithic remains of a much more primitive character have been found in other parts of the Old World, but they are all apparently later than this in date. The first traces of the Neolithic that have been found in Europe are apparently not older than 3000 or 2500 B.C., and Neolithic culture did not begin in many parts of Asia and Africa until much later still.

c. CHALCOLITHIC PERIOD

In a strict sense this is not a true period at all. The word *Chalcolithic* is a term conveniently but loosely used to describe a culture which is still essentially Neolithic in character, but in which the metal copper is just beginning to be used, without, however, replacing stone as the principal material for implements. Chalcolithic cultures are thus transitional. People in many areas of the world did not pass through this intermediate stage, but obtained their first knowledge of copper directly from other peoples who had already fully developed the art of copper metallurgy. The dates of Chalcolithic cultures differ everywhere, depending upon the time which it took for the knowledge of metal-working to spread. The earliest cultures in which copper has been found are in the Near East, and their estimated date is somewhere between 4000 and 3500 B.C. Copper did not appear in Europe much before 2000 B.C.

d. BRONZE AGE

In most regions of the Old World (but not in all of them) there was a period in which copper or bronze came into general use as a material for tools and weapons, but iron was still practically unknown. This period is for convenience termed the **Bronze Age** (although strictly speaking the word *bronze* should refer only to true bronze, a mixed metal composed of copper, alloyed with a certain percentage of tin). The date and duration of the Bronze Age in different parts of the Old World vary greatly. As has already been stated, the earliest known use of copper was in the Near East—in Mesopotamia and Egypt—toward the middle of the 4th millennium B.C. Considerable evidence points to the mountainous ore-bearing regions of Asia Minor, Armenia, and Caucasia as the probable area in which copper metallurgy was first discovered and developed. Copper was in widespread use in the Near East by 3000 B.C. and this may be considered a good rough date for the beginning of the Bronze Age in western Asia, although the general use of true bronze itself did not begin until six or seven centuries later.

The Bronze Age in Europe did not begin until 2000 B.C. or later, and it was more retarded or entirely absent in parts of Asia, most of Africa, and all of Oceania. The first use of iron for implements brought the Bronze Age everywhere to a close.

e. IRON AGE

The **Iron Age** is usually considered by archaeologists to be the period of some centuries immediately following the time when iron began to replace bronze as the principal material for implements and weapons. In one sense, we are still living in the Iron Age, but the term is actually seldom used in connection with any specific culture which is later in date than the beginning of the Christian Era, except in referring to primitive peoples, living in remote regions. Rare examples of early ornaments made of meteoric iron are known, and at least two cases of objects made of iron that was not meteoric (and hence may have been smelted) have been reported in Mesopotamia from levels dating before 2500 B.C. The first certain development of iron metallurgy on any scale, however, began in Asia Minor about the 14th century B.C. and in Europe in the Hallstatt region of Austria in the 11th or 10th century B.C. Iron did not penetrate to large parts of Asia and Africa until many centuries later and did not form part of any culture in the New World until introduced from Europe in the 15th and 16th centuries A.D.

2. MODERN RACES OF MAN

Although the various physical types of modern man began to develop and differentiate in the Palaeolithic period, they assumed their present shape in Post-Palaeolithic times and such tentative conclusions as can be established regarding their major migrations, distribution, and mixture form an essential part of any reconstruction of later prehistoric times.

Unfortunately the task is complicated by two factors: first, that we are still largely in ignorance of the exact ways in which biological processes work to form new physical types, and, second, that all groups of mankind can interbreed and have interbred in varying combinations over an immensely long period of time. Thus such things as pure racial types cannot truthfully be said to exist. Rather one must consider that the population of the world is made up of an almost infinite number of physical types which grade imperceptibly into one another. For this reason attempted classifications of races differ widely and the lack of a standard nomenclature is the cause of much confusion.

In spite of all these difficulties, most anthropologists believe that, on the whole, biological and historical considerations justify a division of modern man into three major groups—the **White** (or European) group, **Negroid** group, and **Mongoloid** group—and the establishment of certain sub-groups or races within each of these larger divisions. Making use provisionally of such a classification, it is possible to trace in a general way the more important movements of peoples in the prehistoric and early historic periods.

THE WHITE GROUP. Representatives of this group have had a primary distribution over the western and northern portions of the Old World. In a series of migrations—some of them clearly known to us and some of them still only guessed at—the blond and slightly long-headed **Nordics** occupied the northern third of Europe; the round-headed **Alpines** took possession of a central zone stretching from Russia to France, and one branch of the dark, long-headed **Mediterraneans**, with their relatives, the Arabs, Berbers, etc., spread through southern Europe, northern Africa, and the Near East, while another, it is believed, thrust down into India and Indonesia and the easternmost islands of the

Pacific. Vaguely identified remnants of archaic White strains have been traced in various points in Siberia and Japan (Ainus) and are thought to be the basis of the Veddoid type (Ceylon and southern India) and the Australoid type (Australia). Other alleged races or sub-races, such as the prominent-nosed Armenoid, in the Near East, the blond but round-headed East Baltic type in northern Europe and the tall, round-headed Dinaric type of the Balkans, were apparently the result of local specialization and had a more limited distribution.

THE NEGROID GROUP without much question developed in the southern half of the Old World and its representatives stretched in an uninterrupted belt across Africa and southern Asia. Today we find two fundamental Negroid types: the short-statured, somewhat round-headed Negrito (Pygmy) in Africa and in Southeastern Asia and Indonesia; and a second type, with normal stature and long head, occupying much the same areas, the True or Forest Negro branch living in central and western Africa and the Oceanic Negroes (Papuans and Melanesians) in the island world to the southeast of Asia.

THE MONGOLOID GROUP quite evidently had its center in eastern central Asia, and from there its various representatives spread northeast to Siberia, east to China and Japan, southeast to Malaysia and Polynesia, and west in a long series of migrations through the Near East and Russia.

Many special races or sub-races developed which may have been the result of crosses between these three major groups. Notable among these are the Australian (Archaic White and Negroid), Bushman-Hottentot (Mongoloid and Negrito), Dravidian (Mediterranean, Australoid, and Melanesian), and Indonesian, Malay, and Polynesian (which seem to be mixtures in varying proportions of Mediterranean and Mongoloid with some Negroid strains).

The **American Indians** do not form a single race, but consist of many types, most of them Mongoloid in their principal characteristics, but many of them, like the long-headed Eskimo and the tall, long-headed type of the eastern Woodlands, suggest the presence of other than Mongoloid strains in their makeup.

3. REGIONAL DISTRIBUTION OF POST-PALAEOLITHIC CULTURES

a. ASIA

MESOPOTAMIA. Excavations at Warka, Ur, Kish, Tello, Fara, and other sites reveal the existence of a Late Neolithic and Chalcolithic culture in southern Mesopotamia during the 4th millennium B.C. It has been divided into four periods:

c. 4000 B.C. The Al Ubaid period began probably shortly before 4000 B.C. and was characterized by a simple agricultural economy and the use of painted pottery with geometric designs. The **Uruk period**, which followed, saw the first development of monumental architecture, copper, seals, and pictographic writing.

c. 3200-3000 B.C. The Jemdet Nasr period marked the culmination of the prehistoric culture and led up to the **Early Dynastic** (Sumerian) **period** and the beginning of recorded history. A similar progress can be traced in northern Mesopotamia, though the lowest levels at Nineveh, Gawra, and Arpachiyah show a somewhat different culture, marked by the brilliant Tell Halaf pottery.

PALESTINE AND SYRIA. A Mesolithic culture, the **Natufian**, followed the end of the Upper Palaeolithic in Palestine and lasted until perhaps 5000 B.C.

c. 5000- It was succeeded later by the **Tahunian** and (at Jericho) by a so-called Neolithic culture, at first without pottery and later with pottery, but without polished stone implements.

c. 3000-2000. With the **Early Bronze Age** recorded history begins in this area, although our information for many centuries comes from Egyptian sources, supplemented by the results of excavations at Beisan, Megiddo, Jericho, etc. An Early Bronze Age culture in Phoenicia has been revealed at Ras Shamra and Byblos, while Late Neolithic or Chalcolithic levels have been unearthed in northern Syria, at Sakje-Geuzi, Carchemish, Tell Judeideh, and Chagar Bazar.

ARABIA. Practically nothing is known of this area before the time of the historical Minaean and Sabaean kingdoms of southern Arabia in the 1st millennium B.C.

ASIA MINOR. A prehistoric culture, of Chalcolithic type, flourished in Asia Minor at the beginning of the 3d millennium B.C., as shown by excavations at the famous site of Troy (Troy I, 3000-2400 B.C.; Troy II, 2400-2000 B.C.) and Alishar Hüyük (Chalcolithic Age, 3000-2800 B.C.; Copper Age, 2800-2300 B.C.; Early Bronze Age, 2300 B.C. on). The historical period begins with the founding of the first Hittite kingdom about 1900 B.C.

ARMENIA AND TRANSCAUCASIA. Almost nothing is known of this region before the 1st millennium B.C. A Chalcolithic culture has been discovered at Shamiramalti, on Lake Van, and there are dubious Neolithic and Bronze Age finds south of the Caucasus. During the Early Iron Age, however, Georgia and Russian Armenia were occupied by a people who buried their dead in megalithic graves and had an advanced metallurgy.

PERSIA AND RUSSIAN TURKESTAN. During the 4th millennium B.C. a highly developed Chalcolithic culture, comparable in some respects to that of Mesopotamia and characterized by fine painted pottery, flourished in many parts of this area, notably at Anau, Tepe Hissar, and Rayy in the north, at Tepe Giyan (Nihavand) in the west, and at Susa, Tepe Mussian, and Persepolis in the southwest. This was followed by the Full Bronze Age in the 3d millennium B.C. In the latter part of the 2d millennium B.C. a new people, who buried their dead in megalithic graves, appeared in the mountain region of western Persia and the ancestors of the Indo-European Medes and Persians probably entered Persia at about the same time.

INDIA. Scattered finds of microlithic implements and polished stone celts attest the probable existence of Mesolithic and Neolithic cultures in India, but practically nothing is known about them. In the middle of the 3d millennium B.C., the remarkable **Indus culture** flourished in the northwest. The excavations of Mohenjo-daro and Harappa reveal a civilization that rivaled that of Egypt and Mesopotamia. This was followed at a slightly later date by the so-called **Jhukar and Jhangar cultures** in the same region, but little that represents a real Bronze Age has been found outside the Indus Valley. History begins for northern India shortly after the invasion of the Indo-Aryans toward the end of the 2d millennium B.C., but no archaeological remains have been found there dating much before 500 B.C. The rest of India is largely a blank to us until a century or two before the Christian Era, although in central and southern India there are a great number of Iron Age cemeteries (with burials in cists, cairns, stone circles, urns, etc.), some of which are prehistoric and others probably date to some time well within the Christian Era.

SIBERIA AND MANCHURIA. This is a marginal area, which apparently retained a Mesolithic and later a Neolithic culture longer than other parts of the continent. The Bronze Age is represented in a few places, particularly the Minusinsk region of the Upper Yenisei Valley and the region from the western slopes of the Altai Mountains to the upper courses of the Ob and Irtish Rivers. Iron was introduced late in most parts of Siberia and in the extreme north and east many of the tribes were living in a Neolithic stage of culture until the Russian explorations and colonization in the 17th century A.D.

CENTRAL ASIA. Mesolithic and Neolithic cultures existed in Mongolia, but archaeologically we know little about them and practically nothing about Chinese Turkestan and Tibet before the opening centuries of the Christian Era. Such information as we have about this area from Chinese records does not run much before the beginning of Han times (3d cent. B.C.).

CHINA. Implements of Neolithic type but of uncertain date have been found in many parts of China. The Yang-shao culture, characterized by the absence of metal and the presence of painted pottery suggesting that of western Asia, existed in Honan and neighboring provinces of northern China at about 2000 B.C. This was succeeded by a culture characterized by black pottery (in lower levels at Cheng-tzu-yai and An-yang), which was followed in turn shortly after 1400 B.C. by the rich Bronze Age culture of the Shang Dynasty and the first written documents (as found at An-yang). In the western province of Kansu interesting but undated archaeological remains, with some suggestion of western influences, have been ascribed to the Neolithic and Bronze Ages.

JAPAN AND KOREA. The Jomonshiki culture (Neolithic) flourished in the northern half of the Main Island of Japan (Earlier period, before 200 B.C.; Middle period, 200 B.C.–200 A.D.; Later period, 200 A.D.–600 A.D.

and even later). In the southern half of the Main Island and Kyushu there was a somewhat different Neolithic culture, represented by scattered finds dating before 200 B.C. This was followed by the Yayoi-shiki culture (200 B.C.–200 A.D.), which was essentially Neolithic and had its nearest relationships with Korea, from which there were occasional imports of bronze implements. Last of all was the Yamato culture (200 A.D.–600 A.D.), of Korean origin, which introduced iron implements and megalithic burials and which spread gradually through the whole of the Main Island.

SOUTHEASTERN ASIA. A series of prehistoric cultures has been reported from Indo-China, especially from the Hoabinhian and Bacsonian areas in Tonkin. The earliest are Mesolithic, with Palaeolithic survivals (Archaic period and Intermediate period of Hoabinhian and Keo-Phay period of Bacsonian), and possibly belong to the 3d millennium B.C. They were followed by certain Proto-Neolithic cultures (Latest period of Hoabinhian and Early and Late Bacsonian). The full Neolithic is represented by the Somrong-Sen culture, which spread through all parts of Indo-China in the 2d millennium B.C. and lasted until the beginning of the Bronze Age, about 500 B.C. Cultures somewhat similar to those of Indo-China have been reported from Burma and the Malay Peninsula.

b. EUROPE

In its broad outlines the prehistory of Europe from the close of the Palaeolithic Age is a record of (1) a series of profound climatic changes, producing modifications of culture and the settlement of new areas; (2) a series of cultural influences coming in from Asia and Africa; (3) a series of invasions of new peoples from Asia and Africa; and (4) the formation of new peoples and the development of new cultures as a result of the interaction of these major factors.

(1) *Climatic Changes and Time-Scale*

By counting and comparing the varves, or annual layers of gravel and clay laid down in post-glacial lakes in many parts of the Baltic area, archaeologists have been able tentatively to tell the year in which each layer was formed over a period covering the past 10,000 years. The thickness of the varves and an analysis of the pollen contained in them and other deposits furnish a record of the progressive climatic changes year by year and date with reasonable accuracy typical archaeological remains found in some clear relation to these deposits. This gives a basic time-scale for northern Europe, which can be applied (in a general way and with modifications) to the rest of Europe, and can be checked, for the later periods, against tentative dates determined archaeologically on the basis of contacts with the historical cultures of Mesopotamia, Egypt, Greece, and Rome. Following is the sequence of climatic periods in the Baltic region:

-8300 B.C.   Sub-Arctic period. Contemporary with the Götiglacial stage of the ice retreat and end of the Palaeolithic period. Very cold and characterized by *Dryas* flora, dwarf birch, willow, and tundra and steppe types of animals.

8300-6800.   Pre-Boreal period. Contemporary with the Finiglacial stage of the ice retreat, the Yoldia Sea and first half of the Ancylus Lake phase of the Baltic and the beginning of the Mesolithic period. Less cold, and characterized by birch, pine, and willow trees and mixed tundra and forest types of animals.

6800-5600.   Boreal period. Post-glacial and contemporary with the last half of the Ancylus Lake phase of the Baltic. Rise in sea-level. Cool, dry "continental" climate, with birch and pine dominant, but alder and oak-mixed forest coming in and animals mostly of forest and lake type.

5600-2500.   Atlantic period. Contemporary with the transgression of the Litorina Sea in the Baltic. Sea-level still high. Warm and moist "oceanic" climate (the so-called *period of climatic optimum*), with alder and oak-mixed forest (oak, elm, and lime) dominant, and forest, lake, and sea types of animals.

2500-700.   Sub-Boreal period. Land relatively stable with relation to the sea and the Baltic Sea largely landlocked as at present. Dry, warm climate.

700-   Sub-Atlantic period. Wet, cold climate.

(2) Cultural Changes and Periods

The principal outside cultural influences which came into Europe at different times followed four main routes: (1) from western Asia through Russia to central and western Europe; (2) from Asia Minor through the Aegean to Greece and also through Thrace to central Europe; (3) from the Near East and the Aegean by sea to the western Mediterranean; and (4) from North Africa to Spain and western Europe. Thus the general direction of cultural movement was from south to north and from east to west; hence at any given moment in time the southern and eastern areas were apt to be enjoying a more advanced form of culture than were the more peripheral regions to the northwest. This is well illustrated by the course which developments took in each of the principal periods.

c. 8000-   In the Mesolithic period, lasting for several thousand years, the **Tardenoisian** culture, which was most closely related to cultures in Africa and Spain and which was characterized by microlithic implements, spread from the south over most of Europe. At the same time, with the amelioration of the climate, there was a northward movement of peoples following the forests that gradually occupied the steppes and tundras of the North European plain and a forest culture was developed, characterized by the use of the chipped stone axe (Maglemosean and Ertebølle cultures).

c. 4000-3000.   The Neolithic period had a similar gradual development. **Neolithic culture** appeared for the first time in Crete in the 4th millennium B.C. By 3000 B.C. some slight Neolithic influences had penetrated as far as western Europe from the east, via Russia, and from the south, via Spain. The earliest full-fledged Neolithic culture in Europe proper appeared in the Danube area of central Europe in the 3d millennium B.C., and spread from there to the Rhine Valley and throughout western Europe. Somewhat later the Megalithic culture, characterized by dolmens, passage graves, cists, and other rough stone monuments, spread along the coastal regions of western Europe from Spain to the Baltic.

c. 3000-   The **Bronze Age culture** began, for Europe, in the Aegean and Greece shortly after 3000 B.C. and copper axes appeared in Hungary a little before 2000 B.C.—in both cases due to Asiatic influence. Other copper influences came into Europe by way of Spain about 2000 B.C. and diffused widely, apparently in association with the Bell Beaker culture. At the same time there were further developments of the Megalithic culture throughout its area. The Bronze Age for Europe as a whole is usually considered to cover the period from about 2000 to 1000 B.C. and is divided into three sub-periods: Early, Middle, and Late Bronze Age (or Bronze I, II, and III).

c. 1000-   The **Iron Age** began not long after 1000 B.C. with the development of iron metallurgy in Austria and its spread through the rest of Europe. The first part of the Iron Age is usually referred to as the **Hallstatt period** (about 1000 B.C. to 500 B.C.), the second part of the **La Tène period** (500 B.C. to 1 A.D.).

(3) Movements of Peoples

It is still uncertain to what extent the spread of all the various cultures was due to trade and borrowing, and to what extent it involved wholesale movements of peoples. The population of Europe in the early part of the Mesolithic period probably consisted largely of the descendants of the food-gathering Upper Palaeolithic peoples and was predominantly of the long-headed, White or European stock, sometimes called Atlanto-Mediterranean. Round-headed peoples began to crowd in early in Mesolithic and Neolithic times, from the east (as shown at the site of Offnet in Bavaria) and possibly from Africa (as shown in certain sites in Portugal and Spain). During the succeeding millennia the three fundamental modern European types became established in their respective areas: the Mediterraneans in southern Europe, the Alpines in central and western Europe, and the Nordics in northern Europe. During the latter part of the Bronze Age and especially in the Iron Age we have further witness to great movements of peoples in the spread of Indo-European languages over the larger part of Europe. Greek-speaking and Illyrian-speaking peoples came down through the Balkans into Greece, and Italic-speaking peoples into Italy; Celtic-speaking peoples moved west through central and northern Europe as far as France and the British Isles, and were followed over much the same route by Teutonic-speaking and, for part of the way, by Slavic-speaking peoples. We know that these groups were of mixed types, but we still have insufficient information about their physical characteristics.

(4) Regional Distribution of Cultures

AEGEAN AREA AND GREECE. In Crete a Neolithic culture, related to that of Asia Minor, flourished for at least several centuries in the 4th millennium B.C. This was followed by a high Bronze Age civilization (with its center at Knossos), which has been divided into three major periods: Early **Minoan,** 3000–2200 B.C.; Middle Minoan, 2200–1600 B.C.; and Late Minoan, 1600–1100 B.C. Similar Bronze Age cultures have been reported from Melos and other islands of the Cyclades, namely: Early Cycladic, 2800–2200 B.C.; Middle Cycladic, 2200–1650 B.C.; and Late Cycladic, 1650–

1300 B.C. On the mainland of Greece a third series of related cultures flourished in central Greece and the Peloponnesus: Neolithic, shortly before 2800 B.C.; Early Helladic, 2800–2100 B.C. Middle Helladic, 2100–1600 B.C.; and Late Helladic, 1600–1100 B.C. In Thessaly were two Neolithic cultures, with northern affinities: Thessalian I, before 2600 B.C., and Thessalian II, 2600–2400 B.C., followed by two of the Bronze Age cultures: Thessalian III, 2400–1800 B.C.; and Thessalian IV, 1800–1200 B.C. In Cyprus the Neolithic began before 3000 B.C., after which developed a series of Bronze Age cultures. During the latter half of the 2d millennium B.C. the so-called **Mycenaean culture** (Late Helladic), with its center in Mycenae in the Peloponnesus, spread throughout Greece and the whole Aegean area, with extensions to western Asia Minor, Cyprus, and Syria. The Iron Age in Greece began about 1000 B.C. with the Geometric period, the close of which marked the beginning of history in this area.

RUSSIA. A Mesolithic culture, related to Tardenoisian, developed in southern Russia before 3000 B.C. and was followed by an Early Neolithic, resembling the Campignian. A rich Late Neolithic and Bronze Age development, related in some details to that of northern Persia, had its center in the Kuban area in the 3d millennium B.C. From 2500 to 1500 B.C. the Late Neolithic and Bronze Age were represented by two distinct series: Tripolye A and B, in the Ukraine, and the Red Ochre Graves, in the steppe region between the Volga and the Dnieper. The most important later culture was that of the Scythians, beginning in the 6th century B.C. In northern and central Russia a version of Mesolithic, with Baltic affinities, survived late and, with influences from the so-called Battle-Axe People, developed in the 2d millennium B.C. into the Fatyanovo culture of central Russia.

CENTRAL EUROPE. In Mesolithic times the principal culture in this region was Tardenoisian, with Azilian influences in the extreme western part. A full-fledged Neolithic, Danubian I, appeared in the Danubian area about 2700 B.C., having come presumably from the east and south. It was succeeded by a second phase, Danubian II (2400–2200 B.C.). Contemporary Neolithic cultures, characterized by painted pottery, have been found at Erösd, Cucuteni, and other places in the Balkans. In the next few centuries there was a further development of the Danubian, with influences from the Corded Ware of Poland and Russia and the Bell Beaker culture.

This extended into the Alpine region (Swiss Lake Dwellings), eastern Germany, and the Rhine Valley. With the Bronze Age (about 2000–1000 B.C. or later) there were distinctive local developments in Hungary, Bohemia, Austria, Switzerland, and other sub-areas and several important cultures with wider distribution, of which the principal ones were the Aunjetitz, Knoviz, Tumulus, Urnfield, and Lausitz. The Iron Age began here shortly after 1000 B.C., with the development of the **Hallstatt culture**, followed by the La Tène, which continued to Roman times.

ITALY. Until late prehistoric times Italy was divided into two rather distinct provinces. In southern Italy and Sicily the Tardenoisian persisted until the introduction of the Neolithic in the 3d millennium B.C. This in turn gave way to Chalcolithic in Sicily (Siculan I, 2000–1500 B.C.), with a similar development on the mainland, and a Bronze Age culture in Sicily (Siculan II, 1500–1000 B.C.), also with connections on the mainland. The relations of these were with the Aegean area and the Balkans. They were followed by Siculan III and the Punic Early Iron Age. In northern Italy there were traces of Tardenoisian, then a Neolithic culture, succeeded by Bell Beaker influences and a Chalcolithic culture (Remedello and Italian Lake Dwellers). The Full Bronze Age in this area began about 1600 B.C., and a century or two later the **Terramare culture** appeared in the Po Valley and spread as far as southern Italy. This was followed in the Iron Age by the **Villanova culture** (1000–600 B.C.) with Hallstatt affinities, and the settlement of the Etruscans (800–400 B.C.) in central Italy.

ISLANDS OF THE WESTERN MEDITERRANEAN. A remarkable Neolithic development, characterized by massive stone temples and underground structures, took place in Malta. In Sardinia there was a distinctive Chalcolithic culture (Anghelu Ruju) shortly after 2000 B.C., followed by various phases of Megalithic (Giants' Tombs, dolmens, and Nuraghis), much of which dates to the early half of the 1st millennium B.C. There was a related Bronze Age culture, with stone constructions (Navetas and Talayots) in the Balearic Islands.

SPAIN. There were several cultures in the Iberian peninsula in the Mesolithic period: Final Capsian in the south and center, Tardenoisian and Azilian in the north and two special developments, the Portuguese Kitchen Middens in the west and the Asturian culture in the northwest. Some of these lasted well into the 3d millennium B.C. and were succeeded by various Neolithic cultures of which the most important developments were in the southeast (Almerian culture) and in Portugal and Galicia (Megalithic). The **Bell Beaker culture** (about 2000 B.C.) ushered in the Bronze Age, which was marked by a continuation of the Megalithic and, in the southeast, by the development of the **El Argar culture** (middle of 2d millennium B.C.) in southeastern Spain. In the early part of the 1st millennium B.C. there was a local Iron Age culture, with Hallstatt affinities, which lasted until the time of the first Punic and Greek colonies (about 500 B.C.).

WESTERN EUROPE. Two cultures, the Tardenoisian and the Azilian, were dominant in western Europe during the Early Mesolithic period, with the Asturian (late Mesolithic) partially represented in southern France and the Maglemosean (Early Mesolithic) in northern France and Belgium. Neolithic influences were late in arriving, but by the middle of the 3d millennium B.C. there was a Neolithic culture, of Mediterranean origin, in the south, and the Campignian and Omalian cultures, of central European origin, in the north. The Bell Beaker culture appeared here shortly after 2000 B.C., while the Megalithic culture spread through the coastal region (especially in Brittany), and influences from central Europe and the Rhine contributed to the development of the Bronze Age in France. Well along in the 1st millennium B.C. this gave way to a western version of the Hallstatt culture, which was followed, as elsewhere in Europe, by the La Tène.

The **British Isles** had a somewhat similar but still more retarded development. In the Mesolithic period a survival of the Upper Palaeolithic Creswellian culture was modified in certain areas by the introduction of Azilian influences into southwestern Scotland, Maglemosean in southern and eastern England, and Tardenoisian more or less generally. About 2500 B.C. or a little later, Neolithic features first appeared, in connection with the Windmill Hill culture and the Long Barrows. Bronze came into England some time after 2000 B.C. (Beaker culture, Long Barrows, and Round Barrows). About 1000 B.C. new bronze-using peoples from the continent invaded England, bringing some iron with them. The true Iron Age began about 400 B.C. with an invasion of continental peoples enjoying a predominantly Hallstatt culture (Iron Age A). They were followed, in the 1st century B.C., by La Tène peoples (Iron Age B), the Belgae (Iron Age C), and the Romans. Modified forms of some of these cultures reached Scotland and Ireland but at considerably later dates.

BALTIC REGION. In the early part of the Mesolithic, which corresponds to the Pre-Boreal period (8300–6800 B.C.), Tanged-point cultures (Remouchamps, Ahrensburg-Lavenstadt, and Swiderian) occupied the North European plain from Belgium to Poland, with outliers in northern and western Norway (Komsa and Fosna cultures), but there were traces of an early Tardenoisian and the beginning of the new forest or axe cultures (Lyngby). In the Boreal period (6800–5600 B.C.), a Mesolithic axe culture, the Maglemosean, with many local variants, spread widely over the whole area from Yorkshire to Estonia. The Komsa and Fosna cultures continued in Norway, and Tardenoisian developed further at various points on the North German plain. In the Atlantic period (5600–2500 B.C.) the Ertebølle culture developed out of the Maglemosean, while the Komsa, Fosna, Tardenoisian, and a late version of Maglemosean survived in marginal areas. The beginning of the Neolithic period is synchronous with the beginning of the Sub-Boreal phase, circa 2500 B.C. At about 2000 B.C. the Early Neolithic elements, of eastern origin, were profoundly modified by the introduction of the Megalithic civilization, which had spread along the Atlantic seaboard. Several distinct but contemporary cultures developed, viz.: Megalithic (in three phases, characterized respectively by dolmens, passage graves, and stone cists), Battle-Axe, Separate Graves, Arctic, and Dwelling-Place cultures. In 1500 B.C. or thereabouts the Scandinavian Bronze Age began, which was followed later by the Iron Age.

c. AFRICA

EGYPT. The Mesolithic period witnessed the final stages of the Sebilian culture. The Neolithic period began early in the Nile Valley (probably before 4000 B.C.) and is represented by the Fayum, Merimdean, Tasian, and Badarian cultures. During the 4th millennium B.C., under combined African and Asiatic influences, the important **Predynastic culture** developed (Amratian, Gerzean, and Semainian phases), and ended about 3000 B.C. with the establishment of the First Dynasty and the beginning of the historical period.

NORTHWESTERN AFRICA. Mesolithic cultures (final stages of Capsian and Oranian) were, at dates as yet undetermined, modified and transformed by the infiltration of Neolithic influences, which spread gradually through Tunisia, Algeria, and Morocco and south across the Sahara. Bronze was late in reaching most parts of this area, and generally stone did not give way to metal until the Punic Iron Age in the 1st millennium B.C.

EAST AFRICA. Following the close of the Upper Palaeolithic period in this area two Microlithic cultures developed (Wilton A and B) and another culture (Elmenteitan), but the dates of all three may be somewhat late as pottery was already present in Elmenteitan. The succeeding cultures (Gumban A and B, Njoroan, Wilton C, and Tumbian) were clearly Early Neolithic in character but not necessarily in date. There was apparently no true Bronze Age in this part of Africa and iron gradually replaced stone during the Christian Era.

SOUTH AFRICA. In what is termed the Later Stone Age of this area, two Mesolithic cultures, Wilton and Smithfield, spread through the greater part of South Africa, beginning at some time after the close of the Pleistocene and continuing with modifications until the Bantu invasions brought iron to the region at a comparatively recent date. South Africa had no true Neolithic period or Bronze Age, although some traces of agriculture and occasional polished stone implements have been found.

CENTRAL AND WEST AFRICA. This also was a marginal region. Mesolithic implements have been found in parts of the Sudan. The Tumbian culture (Mesolithic) was represented in the Congo Basin and persisted after the introduction of polished stone. Various other Neolithic cultures of more fully developed form but uncertain date have been reported from the Sudan and Nigeria. A true Bronze Age is not found here, and iron was late in arriving, but during the Christian Era iron metallurgy received a special development, notably in Benin.

d. OCEANIA

The prehistory of this area is still very obscure, but it is believed that it was peopled by a series of migrations from southeastern Asia. Certain groups of people occupied first the nearer islands (Indonesia), then New Guinea, Australia, and Melanesia and finally the far islands of the Pacific (Micronesia and Polynesia). The Negritos (pygmies), remnants of whom are now found in remote inland districts of New Guinea and the Philippines, were perhaps the first to enter this region. They were either followed or preceded by some of the ancestors of the Australians and the now-extinct Tasmanians. At a later but undetermined date the Papuans pushed out and occupied New Guinea and they were followed by the Melanesians, who settled largely in the islands to the east of New Guinea. Lastly, the Malays and the Polynesians entered the area, the Polynesians apparently for the most part passing by the already occupied regions and pressing east across the Pacific to Micronesia and Polynesia.

It is debatable whether the Polynesians had already assumed their present racial type before the great migrations began or whether the different groups of peoples (Mongoloid, White, Negroid, etc.) which seem to form their ancestry moved east at different times and by different routes and interbred after their arrival in the islands. In any case the date of these movements was comparatively recent. Navigation received its real development in this part of the world in the 1st millennium B.C. The first long voyages into Micronesia and Polynesia probably did not begin until the 4th century A.D., and the farther islands were not settled until some centuries later.

The majority of the peoples who took part in the settlement of Oceania were in a Neolithic stage of culture, although the Australians and Negritos still practiced a Palaeolithic economy of hunting and food-gathering when the European colonization began.

e. AMERICA

North and South America were peopled from Asia, at a relatively recent date. The immigrants apparently came from Siberia, across Bering Strait to Alaska. Many of them probably followed a route which led up the Yukon Valley, over the divide into the Mackenzie River Basin and down the eastern foothills of the Rockies to Central and South America. Theories that some groups of people may have come from a more southern part of Asia or Oceania directly across the Pacific, bringing elements of a high culture with them, are based on very unsatisfactory evidence and are generally considered to be unproved.

There is difference of opinion on the date when the first immigrants reached America. The majority of American archaeologists have held that this was some time after the close of the last glaciation. Suggestions of Palaeolithic types have been found among the stone implements in various regions, but no complete industry that is closely related to any Palaeolithic industry of the Old World has yet been reported, and no skeletal remains have been found which are appreciably outside the range of modern American Indians. However, recent excavations from California to Texas and as far north as Colorado (Mojave Desert, Lake Cochise, Clovis, Silver Lake, and the Lindenmeier site) have brought to light implements (Folsom point, Yuma point, Abilene flints, etc.) found in deposits which were laid down at a time when the climate was considerably colder and wetter than it is today. In some cases the implements were discovered in association with the bones of mammoth, camel, ground sloth, and other extinct animals. Accordingly there is a growing tendency to consider that man may have made his appearance in America soon after the close of the last (Wisconsin) glaciation, if not actually in the Glacial Age itself.

Studies of the physical characteristics of American Indians show these to be predominantly Mongoloid, but also reveal the presence, in mixture, of other types, some of which are European or even Negroid in their suggestions, while there seems to be in both continents a marginal distribution of a long-headed stock which may represent the descendants of a group of very early arrivals.

At the time of the first European contact with America in the 16th and 17th centuries A.D., some Indians were still hunters and food-gatherers, like their Palaeolithic ancestors, but the great majority were in a Neolithic stage of culture. The fact that they had no cereals that were cultivated in the Old World and no Old World domestic animals except the dog has led to the general opinion that agriculture and the domestication of animals were in this case independent developments after arrival in the New World. Certain polished stone tools, however, and even certain types of pottery show relationship to forms found in northeastern Asia. So two of the four main elements of Neolithic culture may show some evidence of a continuation of Asiatic tradition. In a few cases American Indian groups passed beyond the Neolithic stage, as is indicated by the use of metal.

The first advanced culture in the western hemisphere is believed to have had its origin about two thousand years ago in the Andean region of South America and in the highland region of Central America and Mexico. Here grew up a high civilization, parallel in many striking ways to that of the Old World but probably entirely independent of it. The cultivation of Indian corn (*Zea mais*) was the basis of the new economy. Rich textiles, fine pottery, and magnificent ornaments of gold, silver, and copper were produced. Great city centers arose, with canals and gardens and monumental temples on lofty pyramids. A highly complex social organization was developed, with priest-emperors, standing armies, schools, courts, and systematized religions. Intellectual progress was marked by astronomical research, the invention of accurate calendars, and—in Yucatan and Mexico—an elaborate hieroglyphic writing.

In the Peruvian area the early Nasca and Chimu cultures were followed by Tiahuanacan and, in immediately pre-Columbian times, by the Inca civilization. Influences spread from this center across the Andes into the Amazon Basin and down the Andes to the Argentine region. Farther north, the Chibchan and Chorotegan cultures occupied the intervening area between Peru and Yucatan, where the **Maya civilization**, the climax of native American achievement, developed during the 1st millennium B.C. and reached its culmination shortly before the Spanish Conquest. Similarly, in the Valley of Mexico the Archaic and Toltec cultures culminated in the **Aztec civilization**, discovered by the Spaniards. The effect of these powerful centers of influence must have been felt in lessening degree throughout much of North America, especially in the advanced cultures of the Pueblo area of the southwest, the southeast, and the Mound Builder area in the Mississippi drainage. Simpler cultures occupied the Woodlands area of the northeastern United States and Canada and the Central Plains. California was a marginal region, occupied largely by food-gatherers of a low stage of culture, while the Indians of the Northwest coast and the Eskimos of Alaska and northern Canada had, each in their own way, developed highly specialized cultures, which suggest to some extent Asiatic relationships.

II. ANCIENT HISTORY

A. EARLY EMPIRES OF AFRICA AND ASIA

1. EGYPT

GEOGRAPHY. Egypt (in ancient Egyptian: *Kemet, the black [land]*) is the valley of the Nile, from the Delta to the first cataract at Assuan. The valley, extending for about 550 miles, has an average width, south of the Delta, of 12 miles, and comprises only about 13,000 square miles of cultivable ground (less than the area of Switzerland). Before Menes, the Delta (Lower Egypt) and the valley (Upper Egypt) formed two distinct kingdoms. The principal cities of Lower Egypt were: Tanis, Bubastis (i.e. *house of Bast*), Busiris (*house of Osiris*), Saïs, On (Greek: *Heliopolis*), and Memphis (near Cairo). Those of Upper Egypt, south of the Fayum (with Lake Moëris), were: Heracleopolis, Siut, Abydos, Thebes, Jeb (Greek: *Elephantine*), Philae. Egypt was divided into 42 provinces (*nomes*), 20 in Lower Egypt and 22 in Upper Egypt. Egypt was "the gift of the Nile" (Herodotus): its fertility depended on the overflow of the river (June–October) which has deposited, in the course of centuries, 30 to 40 feet of rich black soil in the valley; laborious irrigation was, however, indispensable.

POPULATION. The estimates of the population given by Diodorus (7,000,000) and by Josephus (7,500,000) are slightly exaggerated. Racially the Egyptians are a mixture of several stocks and are ascribed to the Mediterranean race; their anthropological characters have hardly changed to the present day. Ancient Egyptian is related to the Semitic and to the Berber languages; in a lesser degree to the Galla and Somali dialects.

CIVILIZATION. The basic economic, social, and political institutions of ancient Egypt were developed in the pre-dynastic period: agriculture was, and remained, the foundation of the economic life. A calendar with a solar year of 365 days, according to Edw. Meyer and others, was introduced in 4241 (more probably in 2781). The writing went through pictographic, symbolic, syllabic, and alphabetic stages before Dynasty IV, but retained them all to Roman times; it had a monumental (**hieroglyphic**) and a cursive (**hieratic**) form from earliest times; a simpler cursive, called **demotic**, was introduced in the 7th century. During the **Old Kingdom** the Pharaoh (*Per-o*, "Great House") was deified in life and in death, and exercised despotic authority, ruling through an elaborate, carefully trained bureaucracy; architects erected colossal pyramids and magnificent columned palaces and temples; sculptors and painters portrayed gods, humans, and animals with admirable realism and grace; literature began to flourish; some rudimentary sciences were cultivated for practical purposes; industrial crafts reached a high degree of perfection. This culture of the Old Kingdom remained the ideal of later epochs.

RELIGION. In the earliest period each town had its own deity: **Ptah** was worshiped at Memphis, **Atum** at Heliopolis, **Horus** at Edfu, **Amon** at Thebes, **Osiris** at Busiris, etc. Most of the gods were conceived as animals: Ptah and Atum as bulls, the goddess Hathor of Dendera as a cow, the goddess Bast of Bubastis as a cat, Anubis as a jackal, Thoth as an ibis, Amon as a ram, etc. **Horus** was the god of the kings of Lower Egypt, **Set** of those of Upper Egypt, but later Horus became the royal god of both kingdoms. Horus (the hawk) was at first the god of heaven, then of the sun; however, the solar religion that ultimately prevailed in Egypt originated at Heliopolis, where the priests of Atum-Re developed the first theological system of Egypt and made of the worship of **Re** (whose symbols are obelisks) the state religion (Dynasty V): Re was accordingly identified with many local gods, particularly with Amon. In the pyramid texts (Dynasties V and VI) the deceased king sails over the sky in the ship of Re. Another conception of life after death in the same texts is connected with the myth of Osiris, who was killed by his brother Set, but was restored to life by his son Horus or, in later versions, by his wife Isis, and became at first the king of the underworld, and later the judge of the deceased (see the *Book of the Dead*). Corpses were embalmed (mummies) and buried under pyramids or in rock-hewn chambers.

magical and religious texts were inscribed inside the tombs and the departed were provided with food and drink, furniture, statuary, and paintings.

CHRONOLOGY. Manetho, an Egyptian priest (c. 280 B.C.), wrote a history of his country in Greek, of which fragments have been preserved by Josephus, Julius Africanus, and Eusebius. He grouped the kings of Egypt from Menes to Artaxerxes III (343 B.C.) into 30 dynasties. Although his chronology is far from accurate, his dynastic arrangement is still used. The most valuable ancient sources are the **Palermo stone** (a chronicle written in the 5th Dynasty) and the **Turin papyrus** (a list of kings, arranged by dynasties, dating from the 19th Dynasty: it reckons 955 years for the first 8 dynasties and 213 for the 12th). Extant data furnish a fairly accurate chronology, based on "dead reckoning" and astronomical data, for the period after 2000 B.C.; all earlier dates, anywhere, are uncertain.

c. 2900-2700. Dynasties I-II (capital: Thinis). The two kingdoms of Upper and Lower Egypt were united under the rule of **Menes** and his successors.

2700-2200. THE OLD KINGDOM: Dynasties III-VI (capital: Memphis). **Zoser,** the founder of Dynasty III (2700-2650), built the step pyramid of Sakkara. **Snefru** (Dynasty IV, 2650-2500) built the pyramid of Medum and developed navigation; his three successors, **Cheops, Chephren,** and **Mycerinus,** erected the three colossal pyramids at Gizeh. The first pyramid texts appear under Unis, the last king of Dynasty V (2500-2350), and continue under Dynasty VI (2350-2200); Egyptian art reached its culmination during Dynasty V.

2200-2100. Dynasties VII-X. The dissolution of the power of the Pharaohs allowed the nomes to become autonomous.

2100-1788. THE MIDDLE KINGDOM: Dynasties XI (2100-2000), with the capital at Thebes, and XII (2000-1788), with the capital at Lisht (near Memphis) or (with Amenemhet III) in the Fayum. Dynasty XII marks the classical age of Egyptian literature, which was no longer purely religious (fiction begins with the story of Sinuhet); architecture and the plastic arts flourished as well. **Amenemhet I** (2000-1970) curbed the power of the provincial barons and began the wars of conquest continued by Sesostris I (1980-1935), Amenemhet II (1938-1903), Sesostris II (1906-1887), Sesostris III (1887-1849); the

latter conquered Nubia and made a campaign in Palestine. Amenemhet III (1849-1801) reorganized the mining operations in Sinai, carried out hydraulic works in the Fayum (Lake Moëris) and built there the great group of palaces known as the *Labyrinth.*

1788-1580. A period of usurpation (Dynasty XIII; capital: Thebes), of shadowy vassal rulers (Dynasty XIV; capital: Xois), and of foreign domination (Dynasties XV-XVI [Hyksos], 1680-1580; capital: Avaris in the Delta). The **Hyksos** (*Rulers of Countries*) were a mixed horde consisting chiefly of Semites and Hurrians from Palestine, Syria, and farther north; they introduced the horse into Egypt. Objects inscribed with the name of the Hyksos king Chian have been found in Crete, Palestine, and Babylonia. Dynasty XVII (1600-1580) began the war against the Hyksos.

1580-1090. THE EMPIRE (New Kingdom).

1580-1350. Dynasty XVIII (Capital: Thebes). **Amosis** (1580-1557) drove out the Hyksos, reconquered northern Nubia, and put an end to the authority of the local nobles. **Amenophis I** (1557-1536) and Thutmosis I (*Thothmes*) (1536-1520) fought in Palestine and Syria, reaching the Euphrates. The real ruler, from 1520 to her death in 1480, was **Hatshepsut,** the half-sister and the wife first of Thutmosis II, then of Thutmosis III. The great **Thutmosis III** (1501-1447) in 19 years (17 campaigns) conquered Palestine (through the victory at Megiddo in 1479), Phoenicia, and Syria (Kadesh on the Orontes was taken in 1471), to the 36th parallel; although he reached Carchemish, this city and Aleppo remained under the rule of Mitanni. Obelisks of his stand in Istanbul, Rome, London, and New York. **Amenophis III** (1411-1375) preserved the integrity of the Asiatic Empire through diplomacy; the *Tell-el-Amarna letters,* written in Assyrian on cuneiform tablets, preserve much of the international correspondence during his and his son's reign. His rule marks a time of great prosperity and cultural refinement. **Amenophis IV** (Ikhnaton) (1375-1358) envisioned a single god of the whole world, Aton (the sun disk and its life-giving rays), but his religious reformation, owing to the opposition of the priests of Amon-Re at Thebes, did not survive him. Meanwhile, with few exceptions, the cities of Palestine, Phoenicia, and Syria, through internal disaffection and outside pressure (Hittites and Amorites in the north, Habiru-Hebrews in the east), were slipping away from Egyptian control. Ikhnaton built a new capital at Tell-el-Amarna, where a new style in painting and sculpture made its appearance. He was followed on the throne by two sons-in-law: the second was **Tutankhamen,** whose richly furnished unviolated tomb was discovered by Carnarvon and Carter in 1922.

1350-1200. Dynasty XIX (capital: Thebes). **Haremhab** (1350–1315) was a general, but devoted himself chiefly to internal reorganization. **Seti** (Sethos) I (1313–1292) and **Ramses II** (1292–1225) fought against the Hittites for the restoration of Egypt's Asiatic empire. The war ended with a treaty of peace and alliance between Ramses II and Hattushilish (1271); only southern Palestine, however, was incorporated into the Egyptian Empire. During the remaining 46 years of his reign Ramses built prodigiously from the Delta (Pithom and Raamses; Ex. 1 : 11) to Abu Simbel in Nubia. **Merneptah** (1225–1215) (under whom, probably, Moses led the Israelites out of Egypt) quelled a rebellion of Palestine (1223) and repelled the combined attack on Egypt of the Libyans and of the *Peoples of the Sea* (Sardinians, Sicilians, Achaeans, Lycians) (1221). The movement of these Aegean peoples is connected with the Homeric war against Troy and brought about the end of the Hittite Kingdom.

1200-1090. Dynasty XX (capital: Thebes). **Ramses III** (1198–1167) defeated on land and water another wave of the *Peoples of the Sea,* now including also the Danaï, the Philistines, and others (1190); the Philistines (whose culture was Aegean) settled on the Palestinian coast and probably introduced iron there. Ramses' feeble successors (Ramses IV–XII, 1167–1090) were unable to check the growing power of the high priests of Amon. Egyptian authority in Asia became purely nominal (cf. the *Story of Wen-Amon).*

1090-945. Dynasty XXI. The high priests of Amon at Thebes (**Hrihor** and his line) and the nobles of Tanis (**Smendes** and his line) strove for the royal authority.

945-712. Dynasties XXII-XXIV. Shoshenk (later Sheshonk; *Shishak* in 1 Kings 11 : 40; 14 : 25) (945–924), one of the Libyan chiefs who had for some time played a considerable rôle in the Delta, founded a Libyan dynasty (XXII, 945–745) with capital at Bubastis. The highpriestly family of Amon at Thebes founded the independent southern Nubian kingdom with capital at Napata (c. 850); Libyan princes became high priests of Amon at

Thebes. Anarchy and civil war prevailed during Dynasties XXIII (745–718) and XXIV (718–712).

712-663. Dynasty XXV (Ethiopian) founded by Shabaka, King of Napata, who conquered Egypt. After defeating Taharka (*Tirhakah,* 2 Kings 19 : 9) (688–663), Essarhaddon made of Egypt, as far as Thebes, an Assyrian province (671), but Ashurbanipal was forced to undertake two more campaigns into Egypt (668 and 661), during the second of which Thebes was sacked.

663-525. Dynasty XXVI (capital: Saïs). **Psamtik** (Psammetichus) (663–609), son of Necho, the governor of Saïs under Essarhaddon, was appointed governor of Saïs and Memphis by Ashurbanipal (663), but, allying himself with Gyges, King of Lydia, he soon rebelled, and by 652 he was master of Egypt and inaugurated the **Saïtic revival** not only in the applied arts but also in sculpture, painting, architecture, literature, and religion—a renaissance deliberately imitating the masterpieces of the Old and Middle Kingdoms. Greek mercenaries and merchants were encouraged to come to Egypt. **Necho** (609–593), according to Herodotus, failed in his attempt to connect the Nile with the Red Sea by means of a canal, but Africa was successfully circumnavigated in three years by Phoenician sailors at his orders. He attempted to regain Egypt's lost Asiatic empire: he conquered Judea through his victory over Josiah at Megiddo (609), but he was ignominiously driven out of Asia after being completely routed at Carchemish (605) by **Nebuchadrezzar,** the crown prince of Babylon. Necho's successors were likewise unsuccessful in their military campaigns: Psamtik II (593–588) in lower Nubia (Ethiopia), Apries (588–569) against Nebuchadrezzar at the siege of Jerusalem and against the Greeks of Cyrene. Amasis (569–525), while apparently curtailing the privileges of the Greek merchants, allowed them to make of Naukratis a purely Greek city and the most important commercial center of the kingdom.

525-404.   Egypt under Persian rule after Cambyses defeated Psamtik III at Pelusium in 525 (Dynasty XXVII).

404-332.   Dynasties XXVIII–XXX comprised ephemeral native rulers under whom Egypt was in some degree independent from the Persian kings.

332-323.   Egypt under **Alexander the Great.**

323-30.   Egypt under the Ptolemies.
(*Cont. p.* 83.)

2. MESOPOTAMIA

GEOGRAPHY. The Mesopotamian plain (modern Iraq), extending for 600 miles from the southern slopes of the Armenian plateau, from which spring the Euphrates and the Tigris, to the Persian Gulf, which in antiquity reached the vicinity of Ur (60 miles north of the present shore), was divided into **Assyria** in the north and **Babylonia** in the south: the line of demarcation was roughly the 34th parallel. The principal cities of Assyria (so named after its god and its oldest capital) were its four royal cities on or near the Tigris: Ashshur, Calah, Nineveh, and Dur-Sharrukin (*Sargonburg*, now Khorsabad); also Arbela (Sumerian: *Urbillum*, now *Erbil*, the oldest living city in the world). The principal cities of northern Babylonia, or Akkad, were Babylon (*Bab-ili: Gate of God*), Borsippa, Dilbat, Kish, Kuthah, Opis, Sippar, Akkad; those of southern Babylonia, or Sumer (Hebrew: *Shinar*), were Nippur, Adab, Lagash, Umma, Larsa, Erech (Uruk), Ur, Eridu. Most of the cities of Babylonia were on or near the Euphrates.

RACES. Little is known of the race of the earliest inhabitants of Babylonia; the few known skulls are not unlike those of modern Arabs. During the 4th millennium the Sumerians occupied the southern country (Sumer) and "Semitic" Akkadians the northern part. The race and place of origin of the Sumerians are disputed; their language, which is agglutinative, has no close connections with any other linguistic group. Other "Semites," the Amorites from northern Syria, entered Babylonia at the end of the 3d millennium and founded the Hammurabi dynasty. From the northeast, uncultured mountaineers invaded the country about 2270 (the Gutium) and 1600 (the Kassites). Finally the "Semitic" Arameans overran the countryside along the course of the Euphrates (beginning about 1100); one of their tribes, the Chaldeans, produced the dynasty of Nebuchadrezzar. Although Assyrian is a dialect of Akkadian, the Assyrians were not Akkadians, but probably a mixture of Proto-Arameans and Hurrians. It should always be kept in mind that the term "Semites" does not refer to a race but to a group of peoples speaking "Semitic" languages (Akkadian, Hebrew, Phoenician, Aramaic, Arabic, etc.).

a. SUMER AND AKKAD

SUMERIAN CIVILIZATION AND RELIGION. Sumer was divided into city-states ruled by a "tenant farmer" (*ishak*) of the city-god. These cities were in frequent conflict over border lines and water rights and fought for the hegemony of the country, which passed from one to the other. As a result of these wars the Sumerians were superior to the contemporary Egyptians in military equipment (they had a war chariot, drawn by donkeys, 1000 years before the Egyptians) and organization (the phalanx of Alexander is pictured on the *Stela of the Vultures* of Eannatum). Although agriculture was the chief industry, commerce with distant lands flourished: the Sumerians were influential in establishing commercial and banking practices, standard weights and measures, forms of written contracts, etc., in western Asia and were the first to codify civil law in writing; prices and wages were sometimes fixed by law. Their sexagesimal system (soon combined with the decimal) still survives in the divisions of the day (24 hours, 60 minutes, 60 seconds) and of the circle (360 degrees). Out of pictographs they developed a **cuneiform writing** suitable for clay tablets. Sumerian sculpture, even in the time of Gudea, was stiff and crude in comparison with that of the Old Kingdom in Egypt. Sumerian buildings, with monotonous windowless walls of unbaked (or rarely baked) bricks, were ephemeral and purely practical. Originally each city had its own god and goddess; eventually a pantheon was developed with the triad **Anu** (the sky), **Enlil** (the atmosphere and the earth), and **Ea** (the waters) at its head; Enlil, the god of Nippur, became the supreme god. The temples usually had an irregular three-stepped pyramid (*ziggurat*) surmounted by a small shrine. Myths related the creation of the world, the deluge, the fruitless search for eternal life. Life after death was conceived as a shadowy existence in the subterranean *land of no return*, the *Hades* of Homer and the *Sheol* of the Old Testament.

c. 2850-c. 2450. First dynasty of Ur (Mesanni-padda, A-anni-padda); "royal tombs" of Ur. Mesilim, King of Kish. The **First Dynasty of Lagash** was founded by Ur-Nina (*Ur-Nanshe*): Eannatum defeated Umma (*Stela of the Vultures*). Urukagina instituted social reforms, but was defeated by Lugalzaggisi, King of Erech.

c. 2450-c. 2270. The Akkadian Empire. Sargon and Naram-Sin ruled over Akkad, Sumer, Elam, Assyria, and northern Syria. The Sumerian culture was adopted and modified by the Akkadians, who made notable progress in sculpture.

c. 2270-c. 2145. The barbaric Gutium from the eastern hills conquered Babylonia and ruled it for 125 years. Lagash, however, flourished under **Gudea** (c. 2250), whose reign marked the classical period of Sumerian sculpture and literature. Utu-hegal, King of Erech, drove out the Gutium.

c. 2140-c. 2030. The **Empire of Ur,** under the Third Dynasty of Ur (Ur-Nammu [*Ur-Engur*], Dungi [*Shulgi*], Bur-Sin, Gimil-Sin, Ibi-Sin), extended from Ashshur and Arbela to the Persian Gulf, from Susa to the Lebanon. Commerce thrived, as shown by the thousands of business contracts of the time.

c. 2030-c. 1900. The **Sumerians,** under the mutually hostile dynasties of Isin and Larsa, declined and lost their national identity.

b. BABYLONIA

CIVILIZATION AND RELIGION. In all its manifestations, Babylonian culture represents a development of the Sumerian. The foundations for Babylonia's great commercial expansion, for the elaborate government administration, for the admirable code of laws promulgated by Hammurabi, for the architectural and artistic works, for the literature and religion, were laid by the Sumerians, particularly during the time of the 3d Dynasty of Ur. When Babylon became a great metropolis and the capital of an empire, its god **Marduk** acquired a new importance and, by being identified with Enlil and assuming his functions, such as the creation of the world, he became the supreme god of the pantheon and was later called **Bel,** *Lord,* a Semitic designation of Enlil. The most characteristic and influential features of Babylonian religion, aside from its mythology, were the elaborate systems of magical practices (incantations) and the interpretation of omens (divination), particularly the movements and position of the heavenly bodies (astrology), the actions of animals, and the characteristics of the liver of sacrificial victims.

c. 1900-1600. The **First Dynasty of Babylon** (Amoritic). Its sixth king, the great **Hammurabi** (about 1800), defeated Rim-Sin of Larsa, conquered all of Mesopotamia, carried out extensive public works, and introduced an excellent administration and a code of laws unsurpassed before Roman times. After his death a dynasty arose in the Sea Land, on the Persian Gulf (c. 1740-1370).

1600-1150. After a Hittite raid, the Kassites conquered Babylonia and ruled it for 450 years. The horse became common in Egypt and western Asia after 1600. Diplomatic intrigues in 14th century (*Tell-el-Amarna letters*).

1146-1123. **Nebuchadrezzar I** defeated the Elamites but was routed by the Assyrians.

c. 1100-900. Invasion of Aramaic tribes into Babylonia.

900-625. The wars with Assyria were disastrous for Babylonia. In 729 **Tiglath-pileser III** of Assyria became King of Babylon (with the name of *Pul*), and from then to 625, except for occasional periods of open insurrection, Babylon remained a part of the Assyrian Empire.

625-538. THE NEO-BABYLONIAN (CHALDEAN) EMPIRE.

625-605. **Nabopolassar** and his ally Cyaxares, King of Media, destroyed Nineveh (612) and divided between themselves the Assyrian Empire. Through the victory of Nebuchadrezzar over Pharaoh Necho at Carchemish (605), Judea became subject to Babylonia.

605-561. **Nebuchadrezzar** took Jerusalem twice (597, 586), but failed to capture Tyre, which he besieged for 13 years (585-573). The buildings and city walls of Babylon, admired by Greek historians, were erected by Nebuchadrezzar.

555-538. **Nabonidus** (reigning in conjunction with Belshazzar) devoted his time to archaeological excavations and restorations of temples.

538. **Gobryas,** a general of Cyrus, King of Persia, took Babylon.

538-332. Babylonia under **Persian** rule.

332-323. Babylonia under **Alexander the Great.**

312-171. The dynasty of the **Seleucids** ruled Babylonia.

171 B.C.-226 A.D. Babylonia under the **Parthians** (Arsacid Dynasty).

226-641 A.D. The **Sassanian Dynasty.**

c. ASSYRIA

CIVILIZATION AND RELIGION. Assyrian culture was deeply indebted to the Babylonian, to the Hittite, and to the Hurrian. Except for the Assyrian royal annals, which are historical sources of the greatest value and are inspired by Hittite models, for the most part Assyrian literature consisted in new editions of the ancient Babylonian works. **Ashurbanipal** took special pains to collect in his library copies of the ancient writings. In sculpture (particularly in the bas-reliefs depicting realistically religious scenes, hunts, and military operations) and in architecture (influenced by the Hittite styles) the Assyrians surpassed the Babylonians, as also in the fields in which they made their greatest contributions, military equipment and imperial administration. Their fragmentary codes of law (c. 1350) are, however, decidedly inferior to the Code of Hammurabi, although the latter was not unknown among the Assyrians. In religion the Assyrians contributed only the worship of their national god, Ashur, and of Ishtar of Nineveh.

c. 2600-c. 2000. The city Ashshur, at first Sumerian in culture, became part of the Akkadian Empire; rebuilt after a destruction (probably by the Gutium), it was subject to the Third Dynasty of Ur.

c. 1920-c. 1850. Under native rulers Assyrian merchants established a prosperous colony in Cappadocia.

c. 1830-c. 1810. Assyria under Babylonian rule.

c. 1810. Shamshi-Adad made Assyria independent and extended its territory.

c. 1600-1380. Assyria was hard pressed by the Hittites, the Egyptians (Thutmosis III), and the Hurrians of Mitanni.

1380-1341. Ashur-uballit restored the fortunes of Assyria.

1341-1232. Through campaigns in all directions, Assyria consolidated its position.

1232-1116. After a period of weakness due to the fall of the Hittite Kingdom (which seriously affected Assyrian trade) and a revival of Babylonian power, Assyria slowly recovered and began to work iron.

1116-1093. Tiglath-pileser I through successful campaigns gained control of the main trade routes of western Asia.

1093-933. Hard pressed by Aramean nomads, Assyria was barely able to survive.

933-782. THE FIRST PHASE OF THE ASSYRIAN EMPIRE.

883-859. Ashur-nasir-pal II campaigned successfully in the northeast and in the northwest and reached the Mediterranean, where the Phoenician cities paid him tribute. He improved the provincial administration and the military equipment, particularly the battering-rams and the siege engines, adorned his palace at Calah with remarkable bas-reliefs, but was ruthless in war.

859-824. Shalmaneser III fought against the kingdom of Urartu (Van) and against Ben-Hadad of Damascus and his allies, including Ahab of Israel, at Qarqar

(854); he conquered Carchemish (849), defeated Hazael of Damascus without taking his capital (841), received the tribute of Tyre, Sidon, and of Jehu of Israel, and thus gained control of the Mediterranean trade routes.

810-806. Semiramis (*Shammu-ramat*) was the widow of Shamshi-Adad V (824-810) and the mother of Adadnirari III (806-782).

782-745. Assyria, ruled by incompetent rulers, was unable to check the growing power of the kingdom of Urartu (Van).

745-625. THE SECOND PHASE OF THE ASSYRIAN EMPIRE.

745-727. Tiglath-pileser III restrained the expansion of Urartu, conquered Arpad, receiving the tribute of Menahem of Israel and of other Syrian princes; in 734 he forced the submission of Israel, in 732 he took Damascus, in 729 he became King of Babylon (with the name of *Pul*). He consolidated his conquests by deporting entire populations.

727-722. Shalmaneser V besieged Samaria for three years.

722-705. Sargon II (*Sharrukin*) took Samaria (722), took Carchemish, and raided Urartu (717-714). He then reconquered Babylonia (710-709), where Merodach-baladan had become king in 721. He built a new capital (Dur-Sharrukin) near Nineveh.

705-681. Sennacherib (*Sin-ahê-erba*), faced with a general insurrection, fomented by Egypt and Babylonia, in Palestine and Syria, took Sidon and Ashkalon, defeated the Egyptians at Eltekeh, devastated Judah but failed to take Jerusalem (701): all rebellious vassals were forced into submission. In 689 he destroyed Babylon.

681-668. Essarhaddon (*Ashur-ah-iddin*) had difficulty in holding back the hordes of the Cimmerians in the north. He permitted the rebuilding of Babylon, directed a campaign against Tyre and Sidon (676), and conquered Egypt (671).

668-625. Ashurbanipal (*Sardanapalos* in Greek) made two successful campaigns into Egypt (668, 661), but he could not prevent Psamtik from becoming master of that country (652). Palestine and Syria, however, remained submissive. His half-brother Shamash-shumukin, who had been appointed by Essarhaddon viceroy of Babylonia, rebelled: the resulting civil war lasted from 652 to 648 (when Shamash-shumukin committed suicide), but operations were continued against the Chaldeans, the Arabs, and Elam (completely devastated in the course of two campaigns in 646 and 640).

Ashurbanipal was a patron of arts and letters, and assembled a great library of cuneiform tablets at Nineveh.

625-605. Rapid disintegration of the Assyrian Empire. Nineveh was destroyed by Cyaxares, King of Media, and Nabopolassar, King of Babylonia (612). For a few years an Assyrian general, **Ashur-uballit,** attempted to save a remnant of the Assyrian Empire with Harran as its capital, but he failed dismally (605) and the Assyrian nation ceased to exist.

3. UPPER MESOPOTAMIA (MITANNI)

GEOGRAPHY. The homeland of the **Hurrians** was probably in the Nairi lands, as the Assyrians called the region east and north of Lake Van where the original nucleus of the Kingdom of Van was later located. From there, early in the 17th century B.C., the Hurrians moved southward, east and west of Assyria, founding a number of principalities that were eventually joined together under the rule of the kings of Mitanni. The Kingdom of Mitanni extended from Carchemish on the Euphrates to the vicinity of the upper Tigris, comprising the valleys of the Balich, of the Habur, and the province of Nisibis, and, east of the Tigris, it included also the region of Arrapkha (modern Kirkuk), which had previously been a separate Hurrian kingdom. Whether Arbela was also included is not known. The Hurrians overran also parts of Asia Minor, Syria, and Palestine, without, however, organizing permanent kingdoms: their presence is attested about the middle of the 2d millennium at Boghaz Keui (the Hittite capital), at Ras Shamra (northern Phoenicia), at Jerusalem and Taanach, and in the land of Edom (the Horites); the Hyksos probaby included Hurrian contingents.

CIVILIZATION AND RELIGION. The Hurrian language is imperfectly known through the letter of Tushratta, King of Mitanni, to Amenophis III of Egypt, through some tablets in a cuneiform alphabet found at Ras Shamra, through some records from the Hittite archives at Boghaz Keui, and from occasional words in the cuneiform tablets from Nuzi (near Kirkuk). It was probably related to Vannic and Elamitic, but it cannot be classed within any well-known linguistic group. The racial connections of the Hurrians are unknown. The royal dynasty and the nobility of Mitanni were of Indo-Iranian extraction: they took their oaths by the Indo-Iranian deities Indra, Mithra, Varuna, and the Nasatya. The greatest contribution of the Hurrians, or rather of their Indo-Iranian leaders, was the introduction of the two-wheeled horse-drawn war chariot into Egypt and western Asia, where it became common after 1600. A treatise on horse-training written by a Hurrian named Kikkuli, found in the archives of Boghaz Keui, contains many Indian technical terms. The so-called *Hittite* bas-reliefs from northern Syria (Carchemish, Senjirli, Tell Ahmar) and Upper Mesopotamia (Tell Halaf), dating from the middle of the 2d millennium to the 9th century, are probably Hurrian in style if not in origin, as can be verified by comparison with Hurrian seal impressions. The chief deities of the Hurrian pantheon are **Teshub,** the storm-god, and **Hepa** (*Hepat*), a sun-goddess; of several other deities nothing is known but the name.

c. 1690. Beginning of the Hurrian migration.

c. 1600-1500. The Hurrians organized principalities such as the little Kingdom of Arrapkha (including Nuzi) of which we know three kings: Itkhi-Teshub (son of Kibi-Teshub), Itkhiya, and Kirenzi.

c. 1475-1275. THE KINGDOM OF MITANNI (capital: Washshukanni on the upper Habur).

c. 1475. Saushshattar, the son of Parsashatar, conquered Aleppo and held it, with northern Syria, in spite of the victorious campaigns of Thothmes III; Assyria was reduced to vassalage and, to judge from a letter of Saushshattar found at Nuzi, the Hurrian principality of Arrapkha was incorporated into the kingdom.

c. 1440. Artatama preserved the integrity of the kingdom, if he did not extend it. A friendly policy toward Egypt prevailed.

c. 1410. Shutarna was on friendly relations with Pharaoh Amenophis III, to whom he gave his daughter Giluhepa in marriage.

c. 1390. Tuhi, the leader of the anti-Egyptian party, slew the legitimate heir (Artashuwara) and crowned his brother **Tushratta;** the latter executed the rebels, but lost part of his kingdom (Hanigalbat), where the anti-Egyptians made his brother **Artatama II** king. Tushratta was allied with Pharaoh Amenophis III, Artatama with Shubbiluliu, King of the Hittites,

who conquered Tushratta's vassal principalities west of the Euphrates.

c. 1370. Shutarna II was appointed by his
father Artatama II as regent, after
the assassination of Tushratta and
of his supporters; only Mattiwaza,
a young son of Tushratta, was
saved from the slaughter.

c. 1360. Mattiwaza was placed on the
throne by Shubbiluliu, King of the
Hittites, his father-in-law. Assyria under Ashuruballit became

independent of Mitanni and began its wars
against it.

c. 1350-1300. Decadence of Mitanni. Adadnirari I of Assyria conquered
Mitanni as far as the Euphrates,
sacking the capital Washshukanni
(c. 1300).

c. 1275. Shalmaneser I of Assyria defeated
Shattuara, King of Hanigalbat, and
devastated his kingdom. Thus the
Kingdom of Mitanni disappeared
from history.

4. PALESTINE

GEOGRAPHY. Palestine is the southern
part of Syria, extending between the Mediterranean and the Syrian Desert, from Mt.
Hermon to the southern end of the Dead
Sea, or "from Dan to Beersheba." West of
the Jordan its length is about 150 miles; its
width in the north 23 miles, in the south
about 80 miles. The term *Palestine*, derived from the name of the Philistines, was
first used by Herodotus; the Hebrew name
for the land west of the Jordan was *Canaan*.
The country is divided into four zones,
running parallel to the coast: the maritime
plain (Philistia and the plain of Sharon,
south of Mt. Carmel); the western plateau,
divided by the plain of Jezreel (the strategic
key to the conquest of Canaan) into Galilee
in the north and the mountains of Ephraim
and of Judah in the south; the Jordan
Valley, lying below sea-level (the Lake of
Galilee lies 600 feet below sea-level, the
Dead Sea 1300 feet), tropical in climate; the
plateau of Transjordania, cut by numerous
valleys (the three important rivers are the
Jarmuk, the Jabbok, and the Arnon) and
occupied, from north to south, by the Arameans, the Ammonites, and the Moabites
(the occupation of some regions by the
Israelitic tribes of Reuben, Gad, and part
of Manasseh was precarious). The Kingdom of Edom extended from the southern
end of the Dead Sea to the Gulf of Elath
on the Red Sea; the list of the eight Kings
of Edom that ruled about 1200-1000 is
found in Genesis 36 : 31-39.

POPULATION. Nations of Semitic
speech, commonly called *Semites*, occupied
the land in successive waves since the beginning of the Bronze Age (c. 3000 B.C.): the
'amw (= Hebrew '*am*, nation) of the Egyptian records dating from about 2500; the
Amorites from the Lebanon (c. 2000); the
Hebrews (*Habiru* in the *Tell-el-Amarna
letters*) in the early 14th century; the **Israelites** (c. 1200); the **Arabs** (c. 500). The term
Hebrews includes, in the *Old Testament*, the
nations tracing their ancestry to Abraham

(Ishmael and the sons of Isaac, i.e. Israel
and Edom) and his brother Harran (sons
of Lot: Moab and Ammon); the **Arameans**
were said to be the sons of Nahor, brother
of Abraham. The most important non-
Semitic invaders of Palestine were the
Hurrians (presumably the Horites that
occupied the land of Edom before the
Edomites), the Hittites, and the Philistines,
a contingent of the Aegean *Peoples of the
Sea* (c. 1200).

CIVILIZATION   AND   RELIGION
(1600-1200). The language of Canaan
was Hebrew (as known from the Old Testament), a northwestern Semitic dialect akin
to Phoenician, Moabitic, Amoritic, etc. The
civilization was deeply influenced by Babylonia, particularly in commercial terms and
practices, and Egypt, whence amulets and
religious objects were imported. The influence of the Mycenaean culture antedates
the coming of the Philistines. Each locality
worshiped its local **Baal** (master), usually
at an open-air sanctuary on top of a hill
called "high place." **Astarte** was the goddess most commonly worshiped.

c. 3200-2100. Early Bronze Age (I: 3200–
2900; II: 2900–2600; III: 2600–
2300; IV: 2300–2100).

c. 2100-1500. Middle Bronze Age (I: 2100–
1850; II: 1850–1500). Relations
with Egypt (story of Sinuhet; expedition of Sesostris III, c. 1870).
Hyksos period (1680–1580).

c. 1500-1400. Late Bronze Age I. Thutmosis III of Egypt (1501–1447)
conquered Palestine (battle of
Megiddo, 1479).

c. 1400-1200. Late Bronze Age II. Egyptian control of the country began
to relax in the Amarna period, particularly
during the reign of Amenophis IV or Ikhnaton (1375–1358), when the *Habiru* (Hebrews) from the east and the Amorites and
Hittites from the north were intriguing with
vassal princes or attacking them. Palestine
was reconquered through the campaigns of

the Pharaohs of the 19th Dynasty (1350–1200), particularly Haremhab, Sethos I, Ramses II, and Merneptah.

c. 1200-900. Early Iron I. The Israelites occupied the Mountain of Ephraim, the Philistines the coastal plain, where they organized five city kingdoms (Ascalon, Ashdod, Ekron, Gath, and Gaza).

a. ISRAEL AND JUDAH

RELIGION. Through Moses, **Jehovah** (Hebrew: *Yahweh*) became the god of Israel after the deliverance from Egyptian bondage. Jehovah was originally the god of a sacred mountain (Sinai or Horeb). As national god, Jehovah led the Israelites into Canaan and after assuming the functions of the *Baals* and taking over their sanctuaries, he became the god of Canaan as well as of Israel. By declaring that Jehovah was an international god of justice, Amos (c. 750) paved the way to the recognition of Jehovah as the only god in existence, in Isaiah 40–55 (c. 550). The combination of this prophetic theology with the elaborate temple worship proposed by Ezekiel at that time produced a new religion, **Judaism**, a revealed religion of salvation possessing a body of inspired scriptures that grew from the **Law of Moses** in Deuteronomy (published in 621) to the *Old Testament* (without the *Apocrypha*), the canon of which was closed about 90 A.D.

LITERATURE. The **Old Testament** was written and edited in the course of the millennium that elapsed from the *Song of Deborah* in *Judges* 5 (c. 1150) to the *Book of Esther* (c. 130). The **Pentateuch**, published in its final edition about 400, embodies writings dated in the six preceding centuries. The *historical books* (Joshua, Judges, Samuel, and Kings) were edited as religious works about 550 and were canonized about 200, but the admirable biographies of Saul and David in the most ancient parts of the *Books of Samuel* date back to about 950. The great prophets (Amos, Hosea, Isaiah, Micah, Jeremiah, Ezekiel, Isaiah 40–55) were active between 750 and 550; their writings and those of the others of later date were canonized (with the exception of Daniel, dating from 164) about 200, together with the historical books. Some *Psalms*, *Proverbs*, and perhaps the *Book of Job* are earlier than the downfall of the state in 586; the rest of the *Old Testament* belongs to Persian and Hellenistic periods. The **Apocrypha** range in date from about 180 B.C. (*Ecclesiasticus*) to the beginning of our era. The **Apocalypses,** dating from the beginnings of Christianity, were not recognized by official Judaism, but they were influential in oriental Christianity.

The legalistic literature of Judaism was collected in the *Mishna* (about 200 A.D.) and in the *Talmud* (about 500 A.D.).

c. 2000-1225. The patriarchs of the sagas in *Genesis* are legendary heroes, artificially connected with Israel. Some of the Hebrew clans entered Canaan in the Amarna period (14th cent.); others roamed in the wilderness. The Joseph tribes settled at Goshen, in the eastern delta of the Nile.

c. 1225-1200. Moses (whose name is Egyptian and means *son*) led a revolt of the Joseph clans in Egypt, after they had been enslaved by Ramses II, and brought them to the oasis of Kadesh.

c. 1200. The tribe of Reuben settled east of the Jordan, where the tribe of Gad was already living. The tribe of Judah began to move northward from the wilderness south of the Dead Sea. The Joseph tribes, under Joshua, crossed the Jordan and occupied the Mountain of Ephraim. The other tribes of Israel were already in Canaan, where Merneptah attacked them in 1223.

c. 1200-1028. Living among the Canaanites, ten tribes, without central government, worshiped Jehovah and regarded themselves as parts of Israel. Three other tribes (Simeon, Levi, Judah), living in the extreme south of Palestine, became part of Israel later, through David. Six of the ten tribes answered the summons of Deborah and fought victoriously against the Canaanites of the Valley of Jezreel. Victorious tribal leaders (**Judges**) ruled over their tribes, but, with the exception of Gideon, who was followed by seventy sons ruling jointly, and by Abimelech, they founded no dynasty. Ehud killed Eglon, King of Moab; Jephtah, a Gileadite, defeated the Ammonites. The tribe of Benjamin was nearly exterminated in a civil war. Samson of Dan is a figure of legend, symbolizing the beginning of the conflict with the Philistines, as a result of which the tribe of Dan moved to the extreme north of Palestine.

1028-1013. Under the pressure of the Philistine domination (c. 1080–1028), the Israelites made **Saul** their king, after his spectacular deliverance of Jabesh in Gilead. He defeated the Philistines at Michmash, but took his life after their victory at Gilboa.

1013-973. For seven years after the death of Saul, Ishbaal, his son, ruled in Mahanaim, east of the Jordan, while **David,** a Philistine vassal, was King of Judah at Hebron. As King of all Israel, David conquered Jerusalem and made it his capital.

Breaking the power of the Philistines, David fought successfully against the Moabites, the Ammonites, and the Edomites; however, the jealousy between Judah and Israel provoked the rebellions of Absalom and of Sheba.

973-933. In alliance with the Pharaoh of Egypt and with Hiram, King of Tyre, **Solomon** undertook far-reaching trading operations by land and sea. He introduced taxation and forced labor, built the temple, the royal palace, and the city wall at Jerusalem, and public buildings elsewhere. The magnificence of his reign became proverbial.

933. Solomon's son, **Rehoboam,** refused the demand of the northern tribes for relief from taxation and they seceded, making Jeroboam their king.

933-722. KINGDOM OF ISRAEL.

933-887. Jeroboam I chose Shechem as his capital. His son Nadab (912) was slain by Baasha (911), who resided at Tirzah. Elah (888) was killed by Zimri (887).

887-843. Omri (887) overcame Tibni and built a new capital, Samaria: he inaugurated the period of expansion and power of the northern kingdom. He placed northern Moab under tribute, but failed to subdue the Arameans of Damascus. **Ahab** (875) allowed his wife Jezebel, the daughter of Ethbaal, King of Tyre, to spread the worship of Melqarth, her Baal, in Samaria, provoking the reaction of **Elijah** and Elisha, which eventually wiped out Omri's dynasty. Ahab failed against Mesha, King of Moab, but imposed his peace terms on Ben-Hadad II of Damascus and fought with him at Qarqar (854) against Shalmaneser III of Assyria. Ahaziah (853) and Joram (852) were the last kings of Omri's dynasty.

843-744. Jehu (843) exterminated the princes of Israel and Judah within reach and the worshipers of the Tyrian *Baal* in Samaria. He paid tribute to Shalmaneser III. Hazael of Damascus, in revenge, raided his Transjordanian provinces. Under Jehoahaz (816) and Joash (800) Israel was likewise helpless against Damascus, but **Jeroboam II** (785) reconquered the lost provinces while Damascus was attacked by Assyria (773), and ruled over a kingdom at the height of its power and prosperity. However, Amos and Hosea foresaw the impending ruin of Israel. The last king of the dynasty of Jehu, Zechariah (744), was assassinated by Shallum (744).

744-722. **Tiglath-pileser III** of Assyria (745-727) forced Menahem (744) and Pekahiah (738) to pay tribute. Pekah (737) allied himself with Damascus (taken by Tiglath-pileser in 732) and his kingdom was devastated. Hoshea (732) refused to pay tribute to Shalmaneser V (727-722) and was deposed; after a siege of three years (725-722) Samaria was taken by Sargon (722-705), who exiled 27,290 Israelites. The Kingdom of Israel ceased to exist.

933-586. THE KINGDOM OF JUDAH.

933-780. Rehoboam (933), Abijah (917), and Asa (915) fought against the Kings of Israel with small success; Jehoshaphat (875) made an alliance with Ahab. Edom rebelled against Jehoram (851). Ahaziah (844) was killed by Jehu, and his mother Athaliah, a daughter of Jezebel (843), ruled until a palace revolution placed Jehoash (837) on the throne; the latter paid tribute to Hazael of Damascus. Amaziah (798) defeated the Edomites but was taken prisoner by Joash, King of Israel.

780-586. Azariah (Uzziah) (780) enjoyed a prosperous reign owing to Israel's revival under Jeroboam II. Jotham (740) was attacked by Pekah and Rezin (last King of Damascus); Ahaz (735), contrary to the advice of Isaiah, called Tiglath-pileser to his help. Hezekiah (720), however, defied Sennacherib, but after a disastrous war (701) he came to terms. Manasseh (692) remained a faithful vassal of Assyria and encouraged the worship of its gods, as also Amon (639). Josiah (638) reformed the worship, centralizing it in the temple at Jerusalem, and fell at Megiddo (609) fighting against Pharaoh Necho, who deposed Jehoahaz (607) and placed Jehoiakim (607) on the throne. Through Nebuchadrezzar's victory over Necho at Carchemish (605), Judah passed under Babylonian rule. Jehoiakim rebelled in 598, dying soon after; Jehoiachin (598-597) was taken captive to Babylonia, together with the Judean leaders (among them Ezekiel). Zedekiah (597), against the advice of Jeremiah, defied Nebuchadrezzar, who destroyed Jerusalem (586) and brought to an end the Kingdom of Judah.

b. THE JEWS

586-538. The Jews under Babylonian Rule. In Judea the Jews were poor and hard pressed between the Edomites and the Samaritans; in Babylonia they were prosperous and progressive.

538-332. The Jews under Persian Rule. The temple in Jerusalem was rebuilt (520-516), but conditions remained wretched until **Nehemiah** (445 and 433) came to rebuild the walls of Jerusalem and enforce the observance of the Law, thus precipitating the Samaritan schism.

332-198. The Jews under the Rule of Alexander (332–323) and of the Ptolemies of Egypt (323–198).

198-168. The Jews under the Seleucids.

168-63. Led by Judas Maccabeus and his brothers, the Jews rebelled against Antiochus IV (Epiphanes) (175–164), who had declared Judaism illegal (168). Religious freedom was achieved in 164, and, after wars under the leadership of Jonathan (161) and Simon (143), political freedom was attained (142). John Hyrcanus (135), Aristobulus I (104), Alexander Jannaeus (103), and Alexandra (76–67) continued the struggle for conquest until the rivalry between Aristobulus II (67–63) and his brother Hyrcanus II forced Pompey to place the Jews under Roman rule.

63 B.C.-395 A.D. Palestine under Roman Rule. Under Hyrcanus II (63–40) the real ruler was his prime minister Antipater, who appointed his own sons Herod and Phasael as governors. A Parthian expedition placed Antigonus, the son of Aristobulus II, on the throne (40–37). **Herod the Great** (37–4 B.C.) ruled as King of Judea by appointment of the Roman Senate. He began the rebuilding of the temple in Jerusalem, erected a temple of Augustus in Samaria (renamed Sebaste in honor of Augustus), and improved the harbor of Caesarea; he was, however, hated by Sadducees, Pharisees, and Zealots. **Jesus of Nazareth** was born in the latter part of his reign (between 6 and 4 B.C.). Herod's three sons succeeded him: Archelaus as ethnarch of Judea and Samaria (4 B.C.–6 A.D.), Antipas as tetrarch of Galilee and Peraea (4 B.C.–39 A.D.), and Philip as tetrarch of Batanaea, northeast of the Lake of Galilee (4 B.C.–34 A.D.). After their death, except for Herod Agrippa's brief rule over the combined territory (41–44) and his son's (Herod Agrippa II, 50–100) interrupted rule over parts of it, Palestine was placed under the administration of Roman procurators. During the war of the Jews against Rome (66–73), Jerusalem was destroyed by Titus (70). After another war under Trajan (115–117), the Jews, led by Bar Cocheba, rebelled in the time of Hadrian (132–135). After the devastation of Judea, Jerusalem was made into a Roman colony (*Aelia Capitolina*) and was barred to the Jews. Henceforth the centers of Jewish learning were in Galilee (Tiberias) and in Babylonia; the two great editions of the *Talmud* were prepared there at the end of the 5th century.

5. PHOENICIA

GEOGRAPHY. The Phoenician cities lie along the coast of the Mediterranean, west of the Lebanon, and, except for Dor, north of Mt. Carmel. From south to north the most important ones, already mentioned in the *Tell-el-Amarna letters* of the 14th century B.C., are: Acco, Tyre (*Sôr*, "the rock"), Sidon, Beirut, Byblos (*Gebal*), Symira, Arwad, Ugarit (the present Ras Shamra, near Laodicea).

CIVILIZATION. The Phoenicians (called *Sidonians* in Homer and the *Old Testament*) were a branch of the Canaanites, if we may judge from their language, which is one of the western Semitic dialects, closely akin to the Hebrew spoken in Canaan. The greatest contribution of the Phoenicians to civilization was the invention, in the 14th century or earlier, of the **alphabet** (22 consonants, no vowels) from which the principal ancient and modern alphabets are derived. A cuneiform alphabet of 29 letters, whose existence was unknown before 1929 A.D., was used at Ugarit (Ras Shamra), in the extreme north of Phoenicia, in the 14th century or earlier. After the decay of the Minoan and Mycenaean sea-power, the Phoenicians became great sea-traders and after the 12th century established thriving colonies in Cyprus, northern Africa (Utica; Carthage, founded in 814), southern Spain (Tarshish), and, later, in other regions. The main industries, according to the Greeks, were purple dye, weaving, and glass-making. Phoenician art lacks originality: Egyptian and Babylonian motifs prevail.

RELIGION. It is only in the mythological poems of the 14th century, recently found at Ugarit (Ras Shamra), that a real Phoenician pantheon appears: **El**, "the king, father of years," was the supreme god, the creator, the father of **Mot** (the rival of **Aleyan Baal**) and of **Shepesh** (the sungoddess); **Ashera** "of the sea" (probably his consort) was the mother of the gods and had seventy sons; the virgin **Anat** searched for her dead brother Aleyan and presumably restored him to life; other gods are also mentioned. For the rest, each Phoenician city had its local *Baal* (master), who seldom had a personal name (even the name *Melqarth*, the Baal of Tyre, means simply "king of the city," *malk-qart;* the Greeks identified him with Heracles); **Baal Hammon** was the god of Carthage. The chief goddess was **Astarte** (*Aphrodite* for the Greeks), whose great sanctuaries were at Sidon and at Byblos (where she was called *Baalath*, or lady, of Byblos); at Carthage she was usually called *Tanit*. **Adon** ("Lord," *Adonis* in Greek) at Byblos, the Babylonian **Tammuz**, and **Eshmun** (Greek *Asklepios*) at Sidon and Beirut were gods of vegetation, dying and coming back to life (in Egypt Adonis was identified with Osiris).

c. 2900-2000. Egyptian expeditions went to Byblos to obtain cedar of Lebanon logs. Byblos and other cities were occasionally under Egyptian rule. Sumerian and Akkadian raids reached the Mediterranean.

c. 2000-1500. Practically nothing is known of Phoenicia. Byblos was subject to Egypt.

1500-1447. Thutmosis III of Egypt conquered most of Phoenicia.

1411-1358. The **Amarna period** (Pharaohs Amenophis III and IV). The Amorites, under Abd-Ashirta and his son Aziru, in alliance with the Hittites, defeated the Egyptian vassal princes in Phoenicia, particularly Ribaddi of Byblos and Abimelek of Tyre; Zimrida of Sidon joined the ranks of the enemies of Egypt.

1350-1300. Egypt reconquered Phoenicia.

c. 1300-1200. Mycenaean culture at Ugarit. Close contacts with Egypt.

c. 1200-1000. After the Aegean migration, the great cities of Phoenicia, with the exception of Beirut (subject to the Amorites) and Ugarit (permanently destroyed), flourished as independent kingdoms. The oldest inscription in the Phoenician alphabet is on the sarcophagus prepared by King Ittobaal of Byblos for his father Ahiram (c. 1200?). Tiglath-pileser of Assyria (c. 1100) visited Arwad.

c. 1000-774. Hegemony of Tyre. Hiram I, son of Abibaal (969-936), provided Solomon with craftsmen and materials for his building operations and equipped for him a fleet on the Red Sea. He subjected the colony of Utica, which had rebelled. Abd-Ashtart (918-909), his grandson, was assassinated by the four sons of his nurse, three of whom ruled in succession (909-887). Ittobaal (*Ethbaal*) (887-856), priest of Astarte, founded a new dynasty and ruled over Phoenicia as far north as Beirut and part of Cyprus. Under Pygmalion (820-774) Carthage was founded (814).

774-625. Assyrian period. Ashur-nasir-pal II (883-859) and Shalmaneser III (859-824) received tribute from Phoenician cities, without subjecting them. Tiglath-pileser III (745-727) received the tribute of Matanbaal of Arwad, Sibittibaal of Byblos, and Hiram II of Tyre (738); a greater levy was paid to him by Metinna (Mattan) of Tyre in 730; the Valley of the Eleutheros (subject to Hamath) became an Assyrian province. Elulaios (Assyrian *Lule*) of Tyre (c. 725-690) reconquered Cyprus, that had been occupied by Sargon (722-705), and fled there when Sennacherib (705-681) conquered Phoenicia, with the exception of Tyre, in 701; Urumilki was then King of Byblos and Abdiliti of Arwad. Phoenicia and Cyprus were subject to Essarhaddon (681-668) and Ashurbanipal (668-625), who mention Matanbaal and Yakinlu of Arwad and Milkiasaph (followed by Yehawmelek) of Byblos, in addition to three kings of Cyprus. Essarhaddon defeated Abdimilkat of Sidon and destroyed the city (675). Tyre was not conquered, but its king Baal sent his son Yehawmelek with heavy tribute to Ashurbanipal.

625-586. Temporary independence of Phoenicia.

586-538. Chaldean period. Nebuchadrezzar (605-561) subjected Phoenicia (586) but besieged Tyre, under Ittobaal II, for 13 years (585-573) without success; Tyre asserted its independence under Baal II (572-563), under judges (563-556), and under Balatoros (556-555), Marbaal (555-552), **Hiram II** (552-532).

538-332. Persian period. Phoenicia was divided into four vassal kingdoms (Sidon, Tyre, Arwad, Byblos, in the order of their importance) and prospered; it furnished fleets to the Persian kings. A rebellion of Sidon led by Tennes in 350 was crushed with a great loss of life by Artaxerxes III.

332-323. Alexander the Great took Tyre by connecting this island city with the mainland (332) and gained control of the other Phoenician cities by peaceful means.

323-286. Phoenicia was ruled in succession by Laomedon (323), Ptolemy I (320), Antigonus (315), Demetrius (301), and Seleucus (296).

286-197. Phoenicia was under the Ptolemies of Egypt. Sidon's vassal rulers were high priests of Astarte (Eshmunazar I, Tabnit, Eshmunazar II).

197-82. Phoenicia was part of Kingdom of Syria under the Seleucids. Tyre became autonomous in 126, Sidon in 111. Phoenicia was increasingly Hellenized.

82-69. Rule of Tigranes I, King of Armenia, over the Kingdom of the Seleucids.

64. Pompey organized the Roman province of Syria, including Phoenicia.

a. CARTHAGE

814. Carthage ("New City") was founded, according to tradition, by Tyrian colonists in the time of Pygmalion (820–774); according to legend, by Elissa or by Dido (a sister of Pygmalion who became the tutelar deity of the city). The language of Carthage (*Punic*) is a Phoenician dialect. Its two chief magistrates (*suffetes*) were elected annually by the Senate; the popular assembly, in cases of conflict, had the final decision.

600-480. Under the successive commands of Malchus (executed about 535), Mago (who died about 500), and Hasdrubal (who died in Sardinia about 485), the Carthaginians waged wars of conquest in Africa, Sicily, and Sardinia.

480-405. After **Hamilcar** had been defeated and slain at the **battle of Himera** (Sicily) (480) against Gelo of Syracuse, Carthage developed its sea-power and gained control of the western Mediterranean, including the Straits of Gibraltar. The sons of Hamilcar, Himilko and Hanno, explored the Atlantic coasts of Europe (Himilko) and of Africa (Hanno) about 450. As a result of imperial and commercial expansion Carthage flourished greatly. In 409 **Hannibal** avenged his grandfather Hamilkar by storming Selinus and Himera; three years later Hannibal and Himilko

took Agrigentum, and western Sicily became subject to Carthage.

405-367. The Carthaginians fought four wars against **Dionysius I of Syracuse** (405-367). In the first one Himilko besieged Syracuse but was utterly defeated (398-397); in the second Mago was equally unsuccessful and Dionysius gained control of five-sixths of the island (392); the third war was undecisive (383-376); and the fourth (368-367), ending with the death of Dionysius, was inconclusive.

367-268. The wars in Sicily were continued intermittently. Timoleon defeated the Carthaginians at Crimissus (340) and Agathocles invaded Africa (310-307), besieging Carthage. Soon afterward the Carthaginians regained control of most of Sicily and Pyrrhus, King of Epirus, could not drive them out (278-276).

268-146. WARS WITH ROME. After the **First Punic War** (268-241) (see p. 86), Hamilcar conquered Spain to the Ebro (237-228). In the **Second Punic War** (219-202) Hannibal, in a brilliant campaign, marched from Spain to Italy, defeating the Romans at **Cannae** (216); but after his disastrous defeat at **Zama** in Africa (202), Carthage was forced to accept humiliating terms of peace. The **Third Punic War** (149-146) ended with the destruction of Carthage.

122-B.C.-439 A.D. Carthage under Roman rule.

6. SYRIA

GEOGRAPHY. The term *Syria* (used for the first time by Herodotus) in its wider sense indicates the whole region between the Euphrates and the eastern Mediterranean south of the Taurus range (so Strabo: this corresponds to the Roman province of Syria); in a narrower sense it includes only the northeastern part of this territory with the exclusion of Palestine and Phoenicia; since Hadrian divided the province into Palestine, Phoenicia, and Syria, the term is generally employed in its narrower sense. Syria's principal ancient cities, moving southward, were Sam'al, Carchemish, Arpad, Aleppo, Antioch, Kadesh, Hamath, Palmyra, Damascus. Syria has never been an independent political unity; it was merely at one time, in a general way, the land of the Arameans.

The **ARAMEANS** appear as "Semitic" Bedouins out of the Syrian Desert in the 14th century under the names of *Ahlame* and *Suti;* the name *Arameans* is used about 1100 for the first time. The movement of

the Arameans may have been provoked by the expulsion of the Hyksos from Egypt (1580). In the 13th century they threatened to invade the Tigris Valley, but owing to the pressure from the Hittites and the Assyrians they were pushed back into the Syrian Desert, where they remained in the following century after the great Aegean migration of the *Peoples of the Sea.* Important trading centers, like **Palmyra,** were developed in the 11th century. In the 10th century powerful **Aramaic kingdoms** were organized in Syria (Damascus) and uncultured Aramaic tribesmen from the desert were invading Mesopotamia: Assyria withstood the pressure, but in Babylonia Aramaic tribes occupied the valleys of the Euphrates and the Tigris and became the basic population of the countryside after the 9th century: the most important among them were the **Chaldeans.** The Arameans were the international traders on land from the 10th century to the 4th; their language became the *lingua franca* of western Asia during the Persian period and was not displaced as the vernacular until the Moslem conquest; much of the religious literature of the Jews and Christians (Syriac) is in Aramaic.

c. 2450-c. 2350. Sargon of Akkad and Naram-Sin led campaigns into northern Syria; the reference to *Aram* in the latter's inscriptions is puzzling.

c. 2140-c. 2030. Syria under the **Third Dynasty of Ur.**

c. 1800. Syria probably subject to **Hammurabi** of Babylon.

c. 1900. Beginning of the Hurrian invasion.

c. 1600. Aleppo was conquered by Murshilish I, King of the Hittites.

1580-1375. Syria subject to the **Pharaohs** of the 18th Dynasty. Thutmosis III (1501–1447) conquered Syria with the exception of Carchemish and Aleppo, which were subject to the Kings of Mitanni.

1375-1350. During the reign of Amenophis IV (Ikhnaton) the Amorites under Abd-Ashirta and his son Aziru, the Hittites under Shubbiluliu, and local rulers ended Egyptian control in Syria.

1350-1200. Syria remained under Hittite rule in spite of the campaigns of Ramses II.

c. 1200. The great Aegean migrations of the *Peoples of the Sea.*

c. 1200-1000. Some Hittite principalities in Syria continued to preserve their identity after the fall of the Hittite Kingdom in the midst of the flood of Aramaic migrations: **Carchemish**, where Shubbiluliu had appointed his son Biyushshilish as king before 1350, was the most important of these kingdoms and lasted until 717, when it was conquered by Sargon of Assyria. **Aleppo**, where Shubbiluliu had made his son Telipinush king, surrendered in 853 to Shalmaneser III of Assyria. The culture of these kingdoms remained Hurrian-Hittite even after they became Aramean.

c. 1000-700. Aramean kingdoms in Syria and in Upper Mesopotamia. East of the Euphrates: Beth-Eden (Bit-Adini), with Til Barsip as its capital, paid tribute to Ashur-nasir-pal II (883–859) and was devastated by Shalmaneser III (857); Gozan (Tell Halaf); Hadippe (capital: Suru), and other principalities paid tribute to Adad-nirari II in 894. West of the Euphrates:

Gurgum (capital: Marqash, now Mar'ash), Sam'al or Ya'udi (now Senjirli), Hattin (including probably Arpad), Hamath, Damascus, and the Aramean (Syrian) kingdoms named in *II Samuel* 10: 6. The kings of Sam'al were Haian, son of Gabbar (c. 858), Sha'ul (*Saul*), Kalamu (c. 800), Panammu I, Barsur, Azariah (d. 740), Panammu II (740–732), Barrekeb (d. c. 725). The last of the Aramean kingdoms of Syria were conquered by Sargon II of Assyria in 720 and in 709.

a. DAMASCUS

c. 1450-1350. Damascus under Egyptian rule.

c. 1350-1200. Damascus under Hittite rule.

1198-1167. Ramses III conquered Damascus.

c. 1000-732. Aramean Kingdom of Damascus. The dynasty was founded about 970 by Rezon (Hezion?), son of Eliada, a general of Hadadezer, King of Zobah. He was followed by Tabrimmon (c. 916), Ben-Hadad I (c. 900), Ben-Hadad II (Hadadezer), who was defeated by Ahab but led the coalition against Shalmaneser III of Assyria (**battle of Qarqar**, 854), Hazael (842–c. 810), Mari (Ben-Hadad III), who was besieged in his capital by Adad-nirari III in 805 and was prevented by the successful resistance of Zakir (King of Hamath) from extending his power to northern Syria, Tabeel (c. 772), and Rezin, who was executed by Tiglath-pileser III after the fall of Damascus in 732.

732-538. Damascus, which had lost all importance, was subject to the Kings of Assyria (732–625) and Babylonia (625–538).

538-332. Revival of Damascus under the Persian kings.

332-85. Hellenistic period: Antioch took the place of Damascus as the most important city of Syria.

333-323. Syria was conquered and ruled by Alexander the Great.

323-301. Ptolemy I conquered Syria for Egypt in 320, but lost it to Antigonus in 315; through his victory at Gaza against Demetrius, son of Antigonus (312), he took possession of southern Syria; northern Syria remained under Antigonus until his death at the **battle of Ipsus** (301).

301. Northern Syria passed under the rule of Seleucus.   (*Cont. p.* 80.)

7. ASIA MINOR

GEOGRAPHY. Asia Minor or Anatolia is a bridge between Asia and Europe, easily accessible by sea from the west and by land from the east. The great Taurus range in the south and a series of mountains in the north constitute powerful barriers to population movements, except for such strategically important passes as the Cilician Gates. The high central plateau (Cappadocia, Lycaonia, Phrygia) is surrounded by mountains and sinks in its central part around a salt-water lake (Tatta) in the midst of a desert.

RACE. The basic population of Anatolia today as in antiquity has the characteristics of the "Armenoid" type, such as a very prominent nose in line with a receding high forehead. These features are intensified in the representation of Hittites on native bas-reliefs and on Egyptian monuments of the 19th Dynasty. Other racial types (particularly the "Mediterranean") are also represented in Asia Minor.

a. HITTITES

CIVILIZATION. The cuneiform tablets from royal archives at Hattushash (now Boghaz Keui) date for the most part from the 13th century and are generally written in the "Hittite" (*nashili*) language (Indo-European grammar and diction); however, these archives yield information on archaic languages (proto-Hattic and Balaic), on Luvian (a dialect of "Hittite"), and on Hurrian. The decipherment of Hittite hieroglyphics is still in its initial stages. The Hittite kingdom was essentially a feudal aristocracy: the king was crowned by the nobles during the Old Kingdom (1750–1500), but the monarchy became hereditary during the New Kingdom (1350–1200), although the feudal organization persisted to the end. A late fragmentary copy of a code of laws, based on an earlier codification, is characterized by the humaneness of the punishments. Agriculture and shepherding were the chief industries. In literature, impartial historical narratives appear first among the Hittites. The so-called *Hittite* bas-reliefs in Asia Minor and in Syria are apparently Hurrian in style, if not in origin.

RELIGION. The Hittite pantheon included archaic native deities, some of which were worshiped in languages no longer in ordinary use. At the head of the "proto-Hattic" deities was the sun-goddess of Arinna (the supreme deity of the kingdom). There are also "Hittite," Hurrian (Teshub and his consort Hepa or Hepat), and even Babylonian-Assyrian deities.

c. 1750–1500. THE OLD KINGDOM.

c. 1750. Anitta, King of Kushshar (Cappadocia), defeated Bijustis, King of Hatti (capital Hattushash, now Boghaz Keui).

c. 1650. Under Labarnash (or Tabarnash), the founder of the Old Kingdom, and his son Hattushilish I, the capital was Kushshar.

c. 1600. Murshilish I captured Aleppo and raided Babylon. He moved the capital to Hattushash (Boghaz Keui).

c. 1500. Telepinush came to the throne after three usurpers and fixed the royal succession on a hereditary basis.

c. 1500–1430. Obscure period in which the Hurrians probably dominated. Tribute was paid to Thutmosis III of Egypt.

c. 1430–1200. THE NEW KINGDOM.

c. 1430–1390. During the reigns of Tudkhaliash II, Hattushilish II, and Tudkhaliash III, the Hurrian Kingdom of Mitanni grew in power at the cost of the Hittite Kingdom.

c. 1390–1350. SHUBBILULIU, the greatest of the Hittite kings, reconquered Anatolia, subjected northern Syria, and reduced Mitanni to the position of a small vassal kingdom.

c. 1350–1320. Arnuandash I (1350) and Murshilish II preserved the integrity of the empire.

c. 1320–1287. Muwatallish defeated Ramses II at Kadesh on the Orontes.

c. 1287–1281. Urkhiteshub.

c. 1281–1260. Hattushilish III made a treaty of peace and of alliance with Ramses II (1271), in which the Syrian possessions of the Hittites were recognized by the Egyptians.

c. 1260–1230. Tudkhaliash IV was forced to undertake military operations in western Anatolia.

c. 1230–1215. Arnuandash II was confronted with general unrest and insurrections.

c. 1200. The Hittite Kingdom came to an end as a result of the great Aegean migrations (the *Peoples of the Sea* of Egyptian records), of which the Homeric war against Troy was an incident.

b. PHRYGIANS

CIVILIZATION. The Phrygians (as well as the Mysians) came from Thrace with the great Aegean migrations about 1200 B.C.

and occupied central Anatolia, west of the Halys. Their language belonged to the Indo-European group. Their capital was Gordion. Tumuli (sepulchral mounds) are typical of the Phrygians, although graves cut into the rock also occur.

RELIGION. The chief deities of the Phrygians were **Cybele** (*Ma*, the Great Mother riding in a chariot drawn by lions), whose orgiastic cult was introduced into Rome in 191 B.C., and **Attis**, the god who died as a result of castration but came back to life; his priests, Galli, were eunuchs.

c, 1000-700. The Kingdom of Phrygia, the history of which is not known, was organized and grew in power. **Midas** (*Mita* of Mushku in the inscriptions of Sargon II of Assyria) ruled about 715.

696. The **Cimmerian invasion** devastated the kingdom; somehow the Phrygian nation survived until the time of Cyrus (547).

c. LYDIANS

GEOGRAPHY. Lydia, whose capital was Sardis, lies in western Asia Minor, between the Ionian cities on the coast and Phrygia; it borders on Mysia in the north and Caria in the south.

CIVILIZATION AND RELIGION. Whereas Phrygia constituted a barrier between Greece and the Orient, Lydia became the link between east and west, culturally and commercially; if the Etruscans, or at least their nobility, came from Lydia (according to a classical tradition going back to Herodotus which modern scholarship is inclined to accept), the Lydians contributed materially to the civilization of ancient Italy. The Lydians were great merchants and expert craftsmen; they probably invented coinage. They were fond of horsemanship in the early period, and later contributed to the development of music and the dance; according to Greek tradition, Aesop was a Lydian. Little is known about the religion of the Lydians: the gods **Santas** (*Sandon*) and **Baki** (*Bacchus, Dionysos*) were named in their inscriptions.

670-652. Gyges, founder of the dynasty of the Mermnadae, in alliance with Ashurbanipal of Assyria, defeated the Cimmerians and extended the borders of the kingdom. But after sending Carian and Ionian mercenaries to the help of Psamtik, who drove the Assyrians out of Egypt, Gyges fell in battle against the Cimmerians.

652-547. Dynasty of the Mermnadae: Ardys, Sadyattes, Alyattes, Croesus. After overcoming the Cimmerian menace, Ardys and his successors carried out the

conquest of the Greek cities on the coast (begun by Gyges), except Miletus, and of the interior of Asia Minor as far as the Halys, with the exception of Lycia. Lydia reached the zenith of her power under Croesus, who attacked the Persian Empire, but was defeated and taken prisoner by Cyrus in 547.

547-333. Asia Minor under Persian rule.

d. HELLENISTIC MONARCHIES

333-323. Antigonus Cyclops was appointed governor of Greater Phrygia by Alexander the Great.

323-25. After the death of Alexander, Antigonus, who assumed the title of king in 306, extended his dominions to cover most of Asia Minor. He died at the battle of Ipsus in 301. The coastal regions of Asia Minor were soon divided between the Ptolemies and Seleucids (p. 77).

The following kingdoms arose in Asia Minor during this period: **Pergamum:** Philetarus (d. c. 263), a steward of Lysimachus, made Pergamum an independent principality (283); Eumenes I (263–241) withstood Antiochus II; Attalus I (241–197) defeated the Galatians and assumed the title of king; Eumenes II (197–159) extended his kingdom over most of western Asia Minor; Attalus III (138–133) bequeathed his kingdom to Rome. **Bithynia:** an independent principality before Alexander's conquests, it became a kingdom with Ziboetes in 297; Nicomedes I (278–250) and his successors increased the power of the kingdom until Nicomedes III (91–74) bequeathed it to the Romans. **Cappadocia:** Ariarathes I was an independent king in the time of Alexander, but he was crucified in 322 by Perdiccas; after passing successively under the rule of Eumenes, Antigonus, Lysimachus, and Seleucus, it became again a separate kingdom under Ariarathes II (c. 260) and his successors until Tiberius reduced it to the status of a province in 17 A.D. **Pontus** (including Paphlagonia): Mithridates I after the battle of Ipsus (301) founded a dynasty that came to its end with the great Mithridates VI Eupator (120–64), the implacable enemy of the Romans. **Galatia:** 20,000 Celts from among those that had invaded Greece with Brennus (279) crossed over to Asia Minor (278–277) at the invitation of Nicomedes I of Bithynia; in 232, after they had ravaged western Asia Minor for 46 years, Attalus I of Pergamum confined them to the territory called from their name (*Galli*, Gauls) Galatia: the tribal organization was retained until 63, when Pompey made Deiotarus king; after the death of its third king (25 B.C.), Galatia became a Roman province.

8. ARMENIA

a. THE KINGDOM OF VAN (URARTU)

GEOGRAPHY. The borders of Urartu (Ararat) cannot be fixed exactly: in a general way the kingdom was located between the Caucasus and Lake Van.

POPULATION. The basic population seems to have been Hurrian; the Hurrian and Vannic languages seem to be related.

CIVILIZATION AND RELIGION. The Vannic inscriptions, written in Assyrian cuneiform characters but still very obscure, were chiefly annals recording wars and building operations, particularly hydraulic works (the irrigation canal of Menuas is still in use). The Vannic people showed special aptitude in industrial arts, particularly metallurgy. At the head of the pantheon, which included numerous deities, stood a triad: **Haldi,** the national god, **Tesheba** (the Hurrian storm-god Teshub), and **Ardini** (a god or goddess of the sun). The temple of Haldi and his consort Bagbartu at Musasir, pictured on a bas-relief of Sargon II of Assyria at Khorsabad, is surprisingly similar to the Greek temples in the Doric style.

c. 1270-850. The Assyrian name for the Kingdom of Van (*Uruatri*, later *Urartu*) occurs for the first time in the inscriptions of Shalmaneser I (c. 1270). The lands of the Nairi (east and north of Lake Van) were divided into numerous Hurrian principalities and subject to repeated attacks by the Assyrian kings, particularly by Tukulti-Ninurta I (c. 1250), Tiglath-pileser I (c. 1100), Ashurbelkala (c. 1070), Adad-nirari II (c. 900), Tukulti-Ninurta II (c. 890), and Ashur-nasir-pal II (883-859).

c. 860-843. Arame, first known King of Urartu, was defeated by Shalmaneser III (859-824), who captured his capital Arzashkun.

c. 832-820. Sardur I, son of Lutipri, was probably a usurper; he chose Tushpa (Assyrian *Turushpa*, the present Van) as his capital and fortified it. He founded the principal dynasty.

c. 820-800. Ispuini conquered Musasir, appointing his son Sardur II viceroy there, and was attacked by Shamshi-Adad V of Assyria.

c. 800-785. Menua, who was at first co-regent with his father Ispuini, enlarged the kingdom considerably, leaving inscriptions over a vast area.

c. 785-760. Argishtish I annexed the territory along the Araxes and around the Lake of Erivan. Shalmaneser IV of Assyria had no success in his campaigns against Urartu.

c. 760-733. Sardur III preserved the integrity of the kingdom.

c. 733-612. The last kings of Urartu, Rusas I (c. 733-714) (probably the founder of a new dynasty), Argishtish II (c. 714-685), Rusas II (c. 685-650), Sardur IV (c. 650-625), and Rusas III (c. 625-612), ruled over a much restricted territory. The Cimmerian invasion and the raid of Sargon II of Assyria (714) weakened the kingdom, which met its doom after the Scythian invasion, when the Medes conquered the country (612). The Vannic nation ceased to exist.

b. ARMENIA

The Armenians are mentioned for the first time by Darius (519). They were probably a Phrygian tribe and they gradually occupied the territory of Urartu after 612. They adopted the religion of the Persians.

612-549. Armenia under the Kings of Media.

549-331. Under the Persian kings, Armenia was a satrapy administered by a member of the royal family.

331-317. Under Alexander and his immediate successors, Armenia continued to be ruled by Persian satraps.

317-211. Ardvates (317-284), one of these Persian satraps, made the country independent of the Seleucids and founded a dynasty that ruled until 211.

211-190. Antiochus III, after removing Xerxes, the Armenian king, by treachery, divided the country into two satrapies, giving the western one (*Armenia Minor*) to Zadriades and the eastern one (*Armenia Major*) to Artaxias.

190-94. After Antiochus was defeated at Magnesia (190), Zadriades and Artaxias made themselves independent rulers, founding two separate dynasties.

94-56. Tigranes I, a descendant of Artaxias, deposed Artanes, the last king of

Armenia Minor, and united the two countries under his rule. From 83 to 69 he was the most powerful king in Asia, ruling over northern Mesopotamia, Syria, and parts of Asia Minor. Defeated by Lucullus in 69, he was stripped of his conquests, but was allowed by Pompey to rule over Armenia as a vassal of Rome.

9. IRAN

GEOGRAPHY. The Iranian plateau extends from the mountains east of the Tigris to the Indus Valley, and from the Persian Gulf and the Indian Ocean to the Caspian Sea and the Jaxartes River. Media (capitals: Ecbatana and Rhagae), Elam (capital: Susa), and Persia (capital: Persepolis) in the west played a much more important historical rôle than Sogdiana, Bactria, Aria, Drangiana, and Arachosia in the east. In the north-central region, the Parthians became Rome's rivals in the Near East.

POPULATION. In the 4th and possibly the 5th millennium B.C., a population of unknown race living at Susa used copper and made pottery decorated with realistic and conventionalized animals. The mountaineers of the Zagros range (Gutium, Lullubu) and the Elamites predominated in the 3d millennium. The Kassites, who ruled Babylonia from 1550 to 1180, were quite distinct from the Elamites. The Aryans, the Indo-European ancestors of the Indo-Iranians, invaded Iran from the northeast (probably about 1800) and became its basic population.

RELIGION. The religion of the early Iranians was similar to that of Vedic Indians: the worship of **Mithra** and **Varuna**, of the Asuras (Iranian *Ahura*), and of the Devas (degraded to demons by Zarathustra), the myths about the first man Yama (Iranian *Yima*) and about the killing of the dragon, and the conception of *rita* (Iranian *asha* or *urta*) or the inflexible order of the world, and the preparation, offering, and divinization of the sacred drink *soma* (Iranian *haoma*) are common to the Aryans of India and Iran and must date back to the time preceding their separation. **Zoroastrianism** was a reform of this ancient Aryan religion and preserved some of its elements even though it took issue with its naturalistic polytheism. **Zarathustra** (*Zoroaster:* "rich in camels") may have been born in Media about 660 B.C., but seems to have been active in Bactria, where according to tradition he converted King Vishtasp (*Hystaspes*). His teaching is preserved in the *Gathas*, the oldest hymns in the **Avesta.** The *Avesta* is divided into five parts: the *Yasna* (liturgical hymns including the *Gathas*), the *Vispered* (another liturgical book), the *Vendidad* (a code of ritual and ethical laws), the *Yasht* (mythological hymns in praise of the gods), and the *Khorda Avesta* (a prayer book for private devotions). The great doctrines of the finished Zoroastrian system, monotheism, dualism, individual and universal salvation, are present in germ in the *Gathas*. In the cosmic battle between good and evil each person should contribute to his own salvation and to that of the world by obeying the will of the good god **Ahura Mazda** (*Ormuzd:* "Lord Wisdom"). In the later parts of the *Avesta* the god of evil or supreme devil is called *Angro-mainyu* or **Ahriman** (the evil spirit). After death the pious cross the Cinvat bridge to their reward, whereas the wicked fall from it and suffer in the *House of Lies*.

a. ELAMITES

c. 2850-2150. Sumerians and Akkadians frequently defeated and subjected the Elamites, whose civilization was fundamentally Sumerian. **Dynasty of Awan** (c. 2450–2150).

c. 2150. Kudur-nahunte of Elam plundered the temples of Akkad.

c. 1920-1800. Kudur-mabug of Elam placed his son Warad-Sin on the throne of Larsa. The latter's brother and successor, Rim-Sin, was deposed by Hammurabi.

c. 1176. Shutruk-nahunte raided Babylonia taking to Susa the stela of Hammurabi and other monuments.

c. 1130. Nebuchadrezzar I of Babylon defeated the Elamites.

721-640. Merodach-baladan of Babylon and Humbanigash of Elam joined forces against Sargon of Assyria, who was defeated at Der by the Elamites (721). Shutruk-nahunte II allowed Sargon to depose Merodach-baladan (709). Hallushu (699–693) carried into captivity Sennacherib's son, who was ruling Babylonia (694). Umman-menanu (693–689) (who succeeded Kudur-nahunte) fought at Halule against Sennacherib (691). Umman-haldash I (689–681). Umman-haldash II (681–674) raided Sippar during Essarhaddon's Egyptian campaign. Urtaku (674–664) ruled peacefully. Teumman (664–655) was defeated by Ashurbanipal and his kingdom was occupied by the Assyrians. Ummanigash

(655–651) sent his forces to the help of Shamash-shumukin, King of Babylon, who had rebelled against his brother Ashurbanipal. Ummanigash was assassinated by his cousin Tammaritu. Tammaritu (651–649) was deposed by Indabigash and sought refuge in Nineveh. Umman-haldash III (648–646) was defeated by Ashurbanipal, who conquered Susa, and was deposed by Tammaritu II. Tammaritu II was taken prisoner by the Assyrians (646). Umman-haldash III (646–640) returned to the throne, but was taken prisoner by Ashurbanipal, who completely devastated the land of Elam and destroyed Susa. The elimination of the Kingdom of Elam facilitated the task of Cyrus, who a century later founded the Persian Empire, with Susa as one of its capitals.

b. MEDES

835–705. Media, divided into small principalities, was attacked successively by Assyrian kings, from Shalmaneser III (in whose inscriptions the Medes are mentioned for the first time) to Sargon II.

705–625. Media under **Assyrian rule.** The two kings Dejoces (708–655) and Phraortes (655–633) mentioned by Herodotus were probably local chieftains.

625–593. Cyaxares was the founder of the Median Empire and of its dynasty. In alliance with Nabopolassar of Babylon (a daughter of Cyaxares was given in marriage to Nebuchadrezzar), Cyaxares destroyed Nineveh (612) and conquered the Assyrian territory east of the Tigris, as also Urartu (Armenia) and eastern Iran.

593–550. Astyages was deposed by Cyrus and Media became part of the Persian Empire (550).

c. PERSIANS

c. 600–550. Achaemenian kings of Anzan (in Elam): Teispes, Cyrus (I), Cambyses, Cyrus (II) the Great.

550–530. Cyrus the Great deposed his sovereign Astyages of Media (559), conquered Lydia (546) and Babylonia (538), and founded the Persian Empire, which extended from the Indus to the Mediterranean, from the Caucasus to the Indian Ocean.

530–521. **Cambyses,** son of Cyrus, conquered Egypt (525).

521–486. **Darius I,** son of Hystaspes, after pacifying the empire torn by revolts, notably that of Gaumata or Smerdis, and extending its borders beyond the Indus (521–519), divided it into 20 satrapies. His royal residences were Susa, Persepolis, Ecbatana (Hamadan), and Babylon. Darius was a Zoroastrian. Good roads, with stations for royal messengers, made possible regular communications within the empire. A canal was dug from the Nile to the Red Sea. A general revolt of the Ionian Greeks in Asia ended with the fall of Miletus (500–494), but the war against the European Greeks was unsuccessful (**battle of Marathon,** 490).

486–465. After **Xerxes I** (*Ahasuerus*) was defeated by the Greeks on the sea at Salamis (480), and on land at Plataea and Mycale (479), Persia abandoned her plans for conquering Greece.

465–424. Athens took the offensive against **Artaxerxes I Longimanus,** by sending troops to aid a revolt in Egypt (456–454) and by attacking Cyprus (450), but finally signed a peace treaty (446). The Persian Empire began to decline.

424–404. **Xerxes II** was assassinated by his brother Sogdianus (424), who in turn fell at the hands of his brother Ochus or Darius II Nothus (424–404).

404–358. **Artaxerxes II Mnemon** defeated his rebellious brother Cyrus, the satrap of Anatolia, near Babylon at Cunaxa (401); Cyrus lost his life in the battle and his "ten thousand" Greek mercenaries, after great hardships, reached the Black Sea (Xenophon's *Anabasis*) in March of the year 400. Another insurrection broke out in Asia Minor under the leadership of Datames, the governor of Cappadocia, and spread to the western satrapies (366–360). Egypt became more or less independent after 404.

358–338. **Artaxerxes III Ochus** succeeded, through energetic measures, in asserting the royal authority over the satraps. He was followed by Arses (338–336).

336–330. **Darius III Codomannus** was killed after Alexander the Great, through the victories at Granicus (334), Issus (333), and Gaugamela, near Arbela (331), conquered the Persian Empire.

10. INDIA

An early urban civilization in the Indus Valley produced the polished stone, metals, incised seals, and pictographs excavated since 1920 at Harappa and Mohenjo Daro. Not yet known is its relationship to Mesopotamian culture of c. 3000 B.C., and to the much later historic civilization of India. Indian history begins with invasion from the Iranian plateau by **Aryans** of uncertain antecedents, who gradually conquered or pushed back from the rich plains of northern India the earlier black Dravidian and Austro-Asiatic Munda populations. The conquest is variously placed at 2000–1200 B.C.

c. 1200-c. 800 B.C. The Indian Aryans worshiped nature-gods similar to those of Greece and Rome but less personified. The chief were **Indra,** god of the air and of the storm, with **Agni,** the sacrificial fire, and **Soma,** the intoxicant used for libations. Interesting, among many others, was **Varuna,** guardian of cosmic regularity, including individual human acts. The oldest sacrificial hymns, composed in northern India west of the Ganges (perhaps c. 1200–1000), are contained in the *Rigveda,* which dates from c. 1000 B.C., possibly two centuries prior to the related Gathas in the *Avesta* of Iran; and, like the later *Samaveda,* antiphonal selections from the *Rig; the Yajurveda,* hymns and sacrificial prose; and the *Atharvaveda,* a repertory of relatively late magical formulae. The *Rigveda* reveals an Indo-European hieratic literary language remarkable for clarity of structure and wealth of inflection which was, however, probably not written until the 5th century. It depicts a wholesome patriarchal society, engaged in cattle-raising and agriculture, characterized by usual monogamy, adult marriage, and normal widowhood. The Aryan tribes were frequently at war among themselves and with surrounding indigenous tribes. The attitude toward life was vigorous and objective, with none of the pessimism and subjective traits characteristic of later India.

c. 800-c. 550 B.C. A transition period during which the Aryans expanded eastward through Magadha (modern Bihar) is known chiefly from the *Brahmanas,* commentaries upon the *Vedas* (c. 800–600), and the earlier *Upanishads* or confidential teachings (c. 600–300). The Vedic division of Aryan society into three honorable classes: priests (*brahman*), noble warriors (*kshatriya*), and commonalty (*vaisya*), including both farmers and artisans, began

gradually to crystallize into a **caste system,** augmented by a fourth group, the slaves (*sudra*), who were the first to be segregated because of their black color. Progressive evolution of caste may be traced to desire of priest and noble to perpetuate supremacy, to diversification of specialized occupation, and to indigenous rules of endogamy absorbed through the sudras, many of whom improved their servile status. Continual elaboration by the priesthood of an already exaggerated ritual had become devoid of religious significance. The doctrine of continuous rebirth (*samsara*), conditioned by the inescapable results of former acts (*karma*), which may be derived from indigenous animism, was first expressed in the early *Upanishads* (c. 600–550). The *Upanishads,* too, teach that the soul may escape from the suffering inherent in individual existence only by the realization of its identity with an impersonal cosmic soul. Union with the latter is possible through knowledge, but not through Brahman ritual.

c. 550-321. The Aryan area was divided among many petty states. Sixteen are enumerated in an early list. Kosala (King Prasenajit, contemporary of the Buddha) was the largest, extending from Nepal to the Ganges, including modern Oudh. Magadha was its small neighbor on the east, south of the Ganges. The King of Avanti ruled at Ujjain. The capital of the Vamsas (King Udena) was at Kosambi (on the Jumna below Agra). Ten tribal republics are named in the oldest Pali records.

Dissent from Brahmanism, to abolish authority of its scriptures and rites, was undertaken by many schools, among them the **Jains,** followers of the Jina ("Victorious"), Vardhamana Mahavira (?540–468?), who elaborated the doctrines of an earlier prophet **Parsya,** and in Magadha under Kings Bimbisara (?543–491?) and his parricide son Ajatasatru (?491–459?). Parsya had enjoined four vows: to injure no life, to be truthful, not to steal, to possess no property. **Mahavira** added chastity and rigid asceticism as means to free man's immortal soul from bondage to the material world. He set the example by personal attainment of omniscience and freedom through twelve years of austerities.

BUDDHISM was founded in the same period and region by **Siddhartha** (?563–483?) of the clan of Gautama and the hill tribe of Sakya, who attained "illumination" (*bodhi*) at Bodh-Gaya after he had convinced himself that Brahman doctrine and asceticism were alike ineffective. He accepted rebirth to the recurrent suffering of life in accordance with fate (*karma*), which depends on individual effort, and extended reward and punishment to heavens and hells. He taught the means of escape to **Nirvana,** a state of peaceful release from rebirth, through a twofold way of life, withdrawal for meditation and personal religious experience, combined with strict morality and self-sacrificial altruism. Shortly after the Buddha's death 500 disciples met at Rajagriha to rehearse together his doctrine (*dharma*) and his code of discipline (*vinaya*) for the monastic community (*sangha*) which he founded. That community served as the instrument for propagation of his religion, which, like Christianity, offers salvation to all who accept simple doctrine and ethics and seek for personal religious experience. A second council at Vaisali a century after the Buddha's death was concerned with the *vinaya*, but may have begun the schism between conservative **Sthaviravadins** (Pali Theravadins) and liberal **Mahasanghikas.** About this time were formed the four *Nikayas*, earliest extant anthologies from more primitive collections (*Pratimoksa*, etc.).

517-509 B.C.   Darius I of Achaemenid Persia seized Gandhara from the disunited Aryans and sent his Greek admiral Skylax to explore the Indus. *Kharoshthi* script used in northwestern India (5th cent.) is based on Aramaic of the Persian scribes. It was confined to the northwest, doubtless because *Brahmi*, a script which was probably derived from some Semitic alphabet of c. 800 B.C., and ancestor of later Indian writing, was already current in the Jumna basin. The *Sutras* (c. 6th–2d cent. B.C.), "Threads" through the *Brahmanas*, prescribe rules of conduct of various Vedic schools, regions, and periods, for sacrifice and, incidentally, for life. They describe a society in which plural marriage is permitted, child marriage recommended, while numerous taboos mark the beginning of an elaborate theory of caste defilement. **Panini** (? c. 350–300) gives in his *Sutra* the earliest extant Sanskrit grammar, with a wealth of illustration which is augmented by the *Varttikas* or supplementary rules of Katyayana (c. 180) and the rich Mahabhashya (Great Commentary) of Patanjali (c. 150 B.C. or later).

327-325.   Alexander the Great invaded the Punjab, crossed the Indus (Feb. 326), was welcomed to the rich and cultured city of Takshasila (Taxila), won a battle on the banks of the Jhelum, and withdrew on demand of his troops, sending Nearchus with a fleet by sea.

c. 321-c. 184.   THE MAURYA DYNASTY was founded by **Chandragupta** (c. 321–c. 297), who first united northern India from Herat to the Ganges delta, with his capital at Pataliputra (Patna), and who defended it against Seleucus Nicator (c. 305). Megasthenes, a Seleucid envoy, wrote a detailed account of India, now lost. The emperor ruled with aid of a privy council and an elaborate official hierarchy, paid army, and secret service. Administration of public works embraced highways and irrigation.

A Jain high-priest **Bhadrabahu** led a portion of his community south into the Carnatic to escape a 12-year famine in Bengal. On their return (c. 300) the still resident monks in church council at Pataliputra undertook to collect the Jain scriptures, but were unable to record some of the older *purvas*. The canon of the Svetambara sect, the *Siddhanta*, written in its present form at the council of Valabhi (5th or early 6th cent. A.D.), is consequently incomplete. The returning monks maintained a stricter rule, avoided the council, and, as the **Digambara sect,** have steadily maintained that the true canon is lost. The Jain community had then already begun a westward migration to Ujjain and Mathura.

c. 274-c. 236.   ASOKA'S EMPIRE, extended by conquest of Kalinga (Orissa with the Circars, c. 262), embraced two-thirds of the peninsula. As a devout convert he ruled at home and abroad in accordance with Buddhist law. Besides many pious foundations, he engraved on rocks and pillars throughout his empire in true Achaemenid style edicts in vernacular Prakrit exhorting respect for animal life, reverence, and truth, and appointed censors to enforce these injunctions. He sent Buddhist missions to Syria, Egypt, Cyrene, Macedonia, and Epirus, and with much greater success to Burma and Ceylon (c. 251–246; Aryan conquest of Ceylon, traditional date 483 B.C.). The Punjab and Gandhara became a stronghold of the liberal Mahasanghikas, who developed a canonical tradition enriched by legends to bring the life of the Buddha into that region. The canon was then or in the 2d century in Kausambhi, Sanchi, and Malwa expanded and fixed in Pali to form the *Tripitaka* ("Three Baskets"): *sutra* (doctrine), *vinaya* (monastic code), and *abhidharma* (philosophical discussion). The Pali tradition, which was carried to Ceylon and there preserved intact, says a third church council was held at Pataliputra under Asoka, but since his inscriptions ignore it, it probably was restricted to the conservative Theravadin of Magadha and vicinity.

Asoka's pillar at Sarnath near Benares is in form and finish Persian. It is surmounted by four lions facing outward which, with a frieze of animals in low relief, may well have been executed by a Hellenistic sculptor, perhaps from Bactria.

The west remained the chief stronghold of **Brahman doctrine** which now underwent a counter-reformation. Efforts by the priesthood to syncretize popular native gods with the Vedic pantheon, and so retain for themselves religious leadership, led to emergence of cults which constitute a new religion. Rudra, a minor Vedic divinity, was exalted as **Siva**, personification of cosmic forces of destruction and reproduction implicit in all change. **Vishnu**, god of the sacrifice, was recognized as incarnate in **Krishna**, a hero presented by popular legend at Mathura as romantic lover of 1000 herd-girls, and on the west coast as a somber warrior. A second avatar of Vishnu was **Rama**, symbol of conjugal devotion. Siva and Vishnu were linked as one Hari-Hara and were equated with a newly personified god Brahma as elements of a *Trimurti* or trinity.

The *Mahabharata*, an epic poem composed by several generations of bards, seems to have taken form about the 2d century B.C., although probably revised early in our era. The original 9000 verses were swelled to 100,000 by later accretions, largely from the *Puranas* (disordered genealogies of kings compounded with legends, put in present form 4th cent. A.D. and later). It recounts a feud between the wily and aristocratic Kurus and the fierce Pandus, a family who are unknown in early literature. Krishna takes prominent part in the struggle in unscrupulous aid of Arjuna, the Pandu chief. Noteworthy within the epic is the *Bhagavadgita* ("Song of the Lord"), which first urges personal love and devotion (*bhakti*) to Krishna. The *Ramayana*, although traditionally ascribed to Valmiki (?6th cent. B.C.), is in its present form later than the *Mahabharata*. It recounts the trials of Rama in rescuing with an army of apes his wife Sita from a fiend. Both epics are composed in a popular form of Sanskrit.

206. **Antiochus III** of Syria occupied Gandhara, but shortly lost it to the Greek (Yavana) King Demetrius of Bactria, who (c. 185) seized the Punjab also. Eastward expansion of the Yavanas was halted (after c. 162) by civil war between the houses of Euthydemus, represented especially by the warrior-philosopher Menander, and Eucratides.

c. 184-c. 72. THE SUNGA DYNASTY was founded in the Ganges Valley and in Malwa by **Pushyamitra**, who overthrew the Maurya, repulsed the Yavanas under Menander, and by a Brahman reaction may have stimulated Buddhist emigration to Bharhut, Sañchi, and Mathura. The dynasty in its later years was overshadowed if not actually displaced by its line of Brahman advisers, the Kanvas.

A brilliant flowering of **Buddhist sculpture** is chiefly represented by railings and gates about stupas at Bharhut, Bodh-gaya, and Sañchi. The railing at Bharhut (c. 150 B.C.) is almost purely Indian in design and relatively primitive in execution. A Garuda pillar at Besnagar proves by inscription of a Greek envoy from Taxila contact of central India with the northwest, which is evidenced also by technical progress and by the west Asiatic motifs of the rails at Bodhgaya and the opulent gates at Sañchi (1st cent. B.C.). Narrative is surrounded with a festive naturalism which is wholly Indian. Presence of the Buddha in these sculptures is suggested solely by symbols (the elephant of his conception, the lotus of birth, the stupa of consecration, the tree of deliverance, or the wheel of the law). At the same time (c. 100 B.C.-50 A.D.) flourished in Gandhara a school of sculpture which created a Buddha image by adding to the Greek Apollo some of the 32 marks of a Buddha specified in Indian texts. Only a few decadent monuments (mostly 1st cent. A.D.) bear dates (318, 356, 384 with coin of Kadphises, 399) by reference to a Mauryan era (? of 322 B.C.) or more probably the Seleucid era of 312 B.C. Stylistic influence of the art of Gandhara was exerted chiefly in Afghanistan (frescoes of Bamiyan and Dukhtar-i-Nushirwan), where it was fused with Sassanian influences; eastern Turkestan; China of the North Wei dynasty; and Japan. But its iconographic formulae were accepted by the entire Buddhist world. Meanwhile, in western India (near Bombay) were cut in rocky cliffs Buddhist *chaityas* or temple halls, of which the earliest (c. 125–100 B.C.) are at Bhaja, Kondane, Pitalkhora, and Ajanta (cave 10); the largest, finest, and latest (1st cent. A.D.) at Karli. Jain caves in the Udayagiri hills of Orissa are of similar date.

Scythian **Sakas** who, dislodged by the Yüechi from the Jaxartes, had overwhelmed the Greeks in Bactria (c. 135 B.C.), only to be expelled thence also by the Yüeh-chih (shortly after 128), invaded the Punjab from Baluchistan and Sind (Greek Indo-Scythia). (*Cont. p.* 128.)

11. CHINA

Present information indicates that the Chinese parent people, their language, and their civilization are alike native to North China. It seems probable that, at a primitive stage, they diverged from the Miao-tzu, who now find refuge in the southern mountains, the various T'ai peoples (Dioi, Laotians, Siamese) of Kwangsi and Indo-China, and the Tibeto-Burman peoples (Lolo, Mosso, Shan, and Tibetans) of southwestern China. **Peking Man,** who had some Chinese characteristics, lived in the Tertiary Pleistocene epoch. Palaeolithic culture deposits (without skeletal material as yet) are known. Three independent Neolithic cultures are found, characterized by: (1) crude gray pottery with pointed foot; (2) red and black painted pottery similar to that found near Odessa and at Susa; (3) thin black pottery tentatively attributed to a Pacific civilization. The latter is linked with historic China through use of tripod vessels with hollow legs, and bone divination.

Two literary sources contain genealogies of the early dynasties, with chronologies which diverge prior to 841 B.C. Neither earlier chronology has any authority whatever. Nor can historical value be attached to legends which describe a pre-dynastic golden age of fabulous culture-heroes and model rulers. Of the **Hsia Dynasty** we have only the calendar, honorific use of the name, and the putative genealogy of seventeen kings. It was followed by the **Shang** or **Yin Dynasty** of thirty kings, who practiced fraternal succession and who were masters of the Yellow River plain from the mountains of Shansi and the Mongolian plateau to the Shantung massif. Probably the last twelve ruled at An-yang from about the 12th century. The names of twenty-eight kings are found in oracular inscriptions from this site. Advanced pictographic and ideographic script; conventional decoration and perfect casting of bronze vessels; reliance upon ancestral guidance through divination.

c. 1000-950 B.C. THE WESTERN CHOU DYNASTY established its capital at Hao in the Wei Valley. It exercised actual control over its feudatories only until the murder of King Yu in 771. The king was responsible for sacrifices to his ancestors and to gods of the soil, and for the agricultural calendar, as well as for administration. Tenure of land and office was restricted to a pedigreed aristocracy, whose clan names suggest a possible early matriarchate. The peasantry lived a communal life in the summer fields and winter villages, tilled common land for their prince, and practiced exogamic group betrothals and marriages. The Chinese communities were still surrounded and interspersed with "barbarian," i.e. less cultured, tribes.

770-256. THE EASTERN CHOU DYNASTY reigned powerless at Loyang with diminishing moral authority over the frequently warring princes of surrounding (nominally) feudal states.

722-481. **"Annals"** period of loose confederation. The chief states were Ch'i and Lu, which divided modern Shantung; Sung, west of Lu; Yen, on the northeast; Chin, in modern Shansi; Ch'in, in the former Chou lands to the west; and Ch'u, in the middle Long River Valley.

458-424. **Partition of Chin** among three vassal houses: Han, Chao, and Wei.

412. Institution of **ever-normal granary** by Marquis Wen of Wei.

403-221. **Epoch of the Warring States,** opened by royal recognition of the partition of Chin.

391. **Change of dynasty in Ch'i,** which, with Chin, had been a chief bulwark of the "middle kingdoms" against the largely non-Chinese states of Ch'u and Ch'in.

334. Ch'u expanded eastward, annexing the coastal state of Yüeh.

333. **"Vertical"** (i.e. north and south) **alliance of six states,** arranged by Su Ch'in, failed to restrain Ch'in, which conquered Shu (in modern Szechuan) in 316.

307. Prince Wu-ling of Chao gained military advantage for his state by adoption of Tatar dress (Iranian trousers, belt, and boots, which now gradually displaced the loose Chinese costume) and enlistment of cavalry archers, but the continual wars of the eastern states weakened them all, paving the way for

230-221. CONQUEST BY CH'IN OF ALL ITS RIVALS. Golden age of philosophy in China, as in Greece. Four major schools of ethics, which absorbed the practical Chinese to the exclusion of abstract speculation: (1) Coherent teaching embodied in *The Canon of the Way and of Virtue* (5th cent. or later?), attributed to **Lao-tzu,** of whom nothing is known: Man is part of an harmonious universe governed by transcendent law, and finds his best ethical guide in his own nature. **Yang Chu,**

an individualist, sought self-expression in harmless hedonism. **Chuang Chou** (fl. 339–329), the most brilliantly imaginative and subtle of all literary stylists, through parables taught *laissez faire*, mysticism, and relativity of truth. (2) **Mo Ti** (5th–4th cent.?) taught universal love, pacifism, economy, and the duty of the wise to set up standards. New dialectic method borrowed by all later writers. From him stem the schools of pacifists and sophists. (3) **K'ung Ch'iu** or **Confucius** (551–479 or later?) taught that clear thinking and self-discipline lead the superior man to correct action in all his relationships. Through moral influence and education he should lead the common herd with kindliness and justice; paternalism; golden rule. Having failed as minister of justice in Lu (500–496) to secure co-operation of his prince, he edited the *Annals* of that state (722–481) to illustrate his monarchical doctrine of political morality. (A much richer chronicle of the feudal states, composed c. 300, is now appended to these *Annals* as part of the *Tso Commentary*.) His precepts were gathered a century later. **Meng K'o** or **Mencius** (fl. 324–314) urged the now independent princes to win the world, i.e. North China, by exemplary conduct, declaring popular welfare to be the objective and condition of royal authority. A humanitarian, he elaborated the moral code to assure proper development of man's beneficent nature. **Hsün K'uang** or **Hsün-tzu** (c. 300–235) taught that man requires education and formation of correct habit to realize his capacity to order nature. He suggested forced conformity to standards. He synthesized earlier doctrines, and, although a muddy writer, so impressed his students that even mutually opposed thinkers for a century claimed succession from him. (4) **Shang Yang**, minister of Ch'in, 359–338, organized strong centralized government, created an official hierarchy, and encouraged agriculture in that state under a severe legal code. His reforms paved the way for the triumph of Ch'in. **Han-Fei-tzu** (d. 233) and **Li Ssu** (d. 208), disciples of Hsün-tzu, developed further the legalist doctrine of compulsion to justify Ch'in's use of military force to unify the warring states.

Greek influence, probably traceable to Alexander's invasion of Sogdiana (c. 327), is seen in correct statement of the intervals of the Pythagorean musical scale by Lü Pu-wei, prime minister of Ch'in (c. 250), and in diagrammatic illustration of the Pythagorean theorem. (*Cont. p.* 132.)

B. GREECE

1. THE EARLY PERIOD, TO C. 500 B.C.

a. GEOGRAPHICAL FACTORS

Greece proper forms a southward extension of the Balkan Mountains. It lies between two seas, the Aegean, which separates it on the east from Asia Minor, and the Adriatic and Ionian Seas, which separate it on the west from Italy and Sicily. Greece itself is almost split in two by the Gulf of Corinth, which runs in from the west, and the Saronic Gulf on the east. These are separated by the narrow Isthmus of Corinth, which connects the southern part, the Peloponnese, with the northern. Thus Corinth, which portaged the sea-trade from gulf to gulf and which controlled land communications between south and north, played an important rôle in Greek history from an early date.

The Greeks were forced to become sailors by the mountainous character of their country, a factor which also conditioned the eventual rise of hundreds of small, autonomous, self-centered states, scattered throughout most Greek lands. The Greek name for such a state was πόλις (polis), usually translated city-state, but including an area of countryside in addition to the city proper. This area was usually small; Sparta (c. 3000 square miles) and Athens (c. 1000 square miles) were exceptionally large poleis. Since the best harbors lie on the east coast of Greece and since the Aegean is full of islands, which made primitive navigation easy, the earliest expansion of the Greeks was to the Asia Minor coast, similar in aspect but more fertile than Greece proper. Later they penetrated into the Euxine (hospitable) Sea, so-called by an apotropaic euphemism because of its inhospitable character. The closeness of southern Italy to the island of Corcyra also drew them west to the Gulf of Tarentum and Sicily, where again they found a familiar but more smiling landscape.

Some parts of Greece, like Attica and Corinth, were early in the historical period deforested. The resultant soil erosion and rapid off-flow of water made agriculture difficult and unremunerative. The inhabitants, therefore, unable themselves to grow enough grain, imported it from Euboea, Thessaly, the Euxine, or Sicily. They in turn cultivated the olive and vine, to export oil and wine, or developed manufactures, particularly that of pottery. Thus not only geography but economic need encouraged them to become seafarers and individualists.

b. THE AEGEAN CIVILIZATION

The pre-Hellenic inhabitants of Crete early developed an elaborate Bronze Age civilization which spread gradually to the Aegean islands and the surrounding coasts. Its effects were felt throughout the eastern Mediterranean Basin, and it, in turn, was considerably influenced from Egypt. But it made little direct contribution to later Greek civilization, save perhaps in religion and myth (Hera, Athena, Minos, the Idaean Zeus).

c. 4000 B.C. **The Bronze Age** began in Crete with an increased skill in crafts, especially pottery.

c. 2300. A hieroglyphic writing came into use.

c. 2000. The island was unified under one or two dynasties, notably those at Cnossus and Phaestus. There was at Cnossus an elaborate palace, with storehouses for taxes in kind and room for a large administrative staff. The palace seems also to have been the religious center, with a priest-king. The inhabitants lived in cities built closely round the palaces. While the basis of economy was agriculture (cereals, olive, vine), handicrafts and trade (especially with Egypt) flourished.

c. 1600. The palaces at Cnossus and Phaestus were destroyed and rebuilt, perhaps in consequence of a revolution. There followed the height of Cretan prosperity. A linear script replaced the hieroglyphic. The Cretan civilization spread to Greece proper, notably to Mycenae, Tiryns, Argos, Sparta, Orchomenus, and, in a lesser degree, to Athens. The princes of this Mycenaean civilization were native Greek tribal chiefs who adopted the higher Cretan culture. They built strongly fortified cities as places of refuge for their subjects. Their supreme power was limited by the traditional custom of consulting their nobles and of obtaining the approval of a popular assembly in important matters. This civilization is portrayed in the Iliad and the Odyssey.

c. 1400. The palaces of Cnossus and Phaestus were destroyed a second time, by sea-raiders who were either the revolting lords of Mycenae or the Achaeans, who had occupied the mainland cities. Cretan civilization rapidly declined and during the succeeding two centuries its Mycenaean derivative, deprived of its source and subject to increasing pressure from northern barbarians, followed suit. By 1250, if not before, the Achaeans occupied Crete, and by 1100 the Dorians overran it and introduced the Iron Age.

c. THE INVASIONS

Greece was apparently uninhabited in Palaeolithic times, but the remains of Neolithic peoples occur throughout the Aegean area. Their ethnic character remains unknown, though they presumably did not speak an Indo-European tongue and were related among themselves. In later times such isolated tribes as the Leleges in Greece, the Carians in Asia Minor, or the Eteocretans in Crete probably represented their survivors.

c. 3000-2000. THE GREEKS, speaking a language belonging to the western (*centum*) division of the Indo-European family, began to spread southward from the northwestern corner of the Balkans.

c. 1300. The Arcadians had already settled in the central Peloponnese and the **Achaeans,** who had migrated from Thessaly to occupy Mycenae, raided throughout the eastern Mediterranean. With the aid of their Thessalian kin (**Achilles**) they sacked Ilium (**Troy**), traditionally after a ten years' war (c. 1184). Their migration may have been due to pressure from new invaders, since the **Ionians** appear to have occupied Attica and the **Boeotians** central Greece, while a backward group in Epirus were the original **Dorians.** Farther north, two peoples of the eastern (*satem*) division of the Indo-European family had settled, the **Illyrians** along the east coast of the Adriatic and the **Thracians** north of the Aegean.

c. 1100. The Dorian invasion began. One branch, the Phocians, thrust east to the Euripus; another south to the Gulf of Corinth, whence they crossed into the Peloponnese and drove out or subdued and enserfed the previous inhabitants (later known in Lacedaemon as *helots*, in Thessaly as *penestae*). The Dorians finally mastered Megara, the Argolid, and Laconia.

c. 1000. The Greeks, who had learned seamanship from the Cretans, had long been migrating to Asia Minor for a number of reasons: the adventurous spirit, increase of population, and the Dorian pressure. Some reached Cyprus, though they never fully displaced the Phoenicians. The Dorians occupied Crete. On the Asia Minor coast three distinct groups emerged: Aeolians from Thessaly in the north, with a religious center at Gryneium and the cities of Mytilene on Lesbos, Cyme, Magnesia on the Hermus, and Smyrna (which later became Ionian); Ionians from Attica and Euboea in the middle, with a religious center at Mycale and the cities of Phocaea, Colophon, Ephesus, and Miletus and the islands Chios and Samos; and Dorians from the Peloponnese in the south, with a religious center at Cnidus and the cities of Halicarnassus and the islands Cos, Rhodes, and Crete.

d. ARISTOCRACY AND TYRANNY; COLONIZATION AND TRADE

c. 900-600. Monarchies were replaced throughout Greece by **aristocracies,** and the kings vanished or were reduced to a titular office (the *archon basileus* at Athens) save in Sparta, where they retained considerable power, especially in warfare. The nobles became the dominant power in the state through the possession of good iron arms and the acquisition of property at the expense of poorer farmers. It was for such nobles that the *Iliad*, on the Trojan War, and the *Odyssey*, on the wanderings of Odysseus (Ulysses), were composed, probably gradually and orally out of traditional material by a series of bards in Asia Minor, though the final form is possibly due to a single **Homer** (c. 800?). Slightly later came the *Homeric Hymns*, really introductions to epic recitations, and **Hesiod** (c. 700?) of Boeotia, whose *Works and Days*, a farmer's almanac, voiced the distress of the poor and whose *Theogony* canonized Greek mythology. This was the period of the **geometric style** in vase-painting.

c. 800-600. Distress and food shortage, due to monopolization of the land by the nobles, led to **colonization,** encouraged first by the aristocrats to get rid of discontent and then by the tyrants for political and commercial advantages. The traditional dates of the more important colonies in east and west, which were entered almost simultaneously, follow: Miletus colonized Cyzicus (757), and Abydus (756) on the Euxine. But through friendship with Psammetichus I of Egypt, Miletus also founded the important trading post of Naucratis on the Nile (640). Phocaea settled Massalia (Marseilles) in Gaul (600). Rhodes settled Gela (688) and Gela founded

Acragas (580), both in Sicily. Thera colonized Cyrene in North Africa (630). Chalcis and Eretria in Euboea sent colonies to the Chalcidice (northern Aegean) and to Sicily, notably Catana and Leontini (728), Rhegium (730); also Cumae (Bay of Naples, 760). Megara controlled the Hellespont with Chalcedon (660) and Byzantium, as well as settling the Sicilian Megara Hyblaea (728). Corinth occupied the strategic Potidaea (northern Aegean, 609), Corcyra (735), and Syracuse in Sicily (735). In southern Italy (Magna Graecia) Achaea settled Sybaris (721) and Croton (710); while Sparta, occupied with the conquest of Messenia, founded only Taras (Tarentum, 705).

Trade had preceded colonization and in turn colonization encouraged trade, since not only the settlers but the peoples among whom they settled desired luxury products (oil, wine, and manufactures) from Greece, which they repaid with raw materials. Greater skill in technical processes like metallurgy and pottery allowed the Greeks to compete favorably with the Phoenicians and encouraged the growth of an industrial population, as well as a trading one, in the cities. Slavery increased and coined money was introduced from Lydia into Ionia and thence into Greece, traditionally by King Pheidon of Argos (c. 680). The two prominent standards of currency were the Euboean and the Aeginetan.

c. 650-500. Tyrannies arose in Greece, for a variety of causes. The aristocracies refused political equality to the landless traders and manufacturers, the peasants were oppressed by the rich and encouraged to get into debt and then were reduced to slavery or exile; slaves began to compete with free labor. Ambitious individuals capitalized this discontent to overthrow the constituted governments and establish themselves as tyrants in almost all the Greek cities, with the notable exception of Sparta, whose landlocked situation, agricultural character, and entrenched ruling class enabled it to preserve its aristocratic form. The tyrants were on the whole popular and successful; they kept the people happy with festivals and public works, they diminished the power of the nobles, and they abolished class or racial distinctions. They fostered, especially, the artistic and intellectual life. Lyric poetry flourished; Archilochus the father of satire (c. 700); the individual lyric of the Aeolians, Alcaeus and Sappho of Lesbos (c. 600); the choral lyric of the Dorians, Stesichorus (c. 650) and Arion (c. 600). Contact with Lydia led to the replacing of the geometric style in art by the oriental (animal) style. Phi-

losophy began with the Milesian School: Thales (predicted an eclipse in 585), Anaximenes, and Anaximander. Among the important tyrants were: Thrasybulus of Miletus (c. 620); Polycrates of Samos (c. 530), noted for his navy, with which he almost dominated the Aegean, his building, and his alliance with Amasis of Egypt; Cleisthenes of Sicyon (c. 600); Theagenes of Megara (c. 640); Periander of Corinth (c. 600), patron of poetry, who recovered control of Corcyra from the oligarchs; and the Peisistratids in Athens. The tyrannies generally were overthrown in the second generation, since they had served their purpose, and the tyrants' sons, born to power, tended to become oppressive. Moreover, Sparta consistently opposed them.

e. FORMATION OF THE GREEK STATES

(1) *Asia Minor*

c. 705. The Kingdom of Phrygia (traditional kings Midas and Gordius), which had considerably influenced the Asiatic Greeks, was destroyed by the Cimmerians, invaders from southern Russia. Its place was taken by the Kingdom of Lydia, in which Gyges founded the active Mermnad Dynasty (c. 685). He and his successors raided the Greek cities, but were prevented from conquest by further incursions of the Cimmerians, who sacked Sardis and slew Gyges (c. 652).

585, May 28. Alyattes, third King of Lydia, and Cyaxares, King of Media, ended their war by a treaty defining their boundary at the river Halys. Thales is said to have predicted the eclipse which induced them to treat and which, therefore, determines the date. Croesus acceded to the Lydian throne (c. 560) and began to reduce the Ionian cities to a tributary condition, save for Miletus. His mild rule, however, did not check their political growth (tyrannies) but stimulated their economic and intellectual life.

546 (539?). CYRUS, who had united his Persian kingdom with the Median by his defeat of Astyages (550), now defeated Croesus, crossed the Halys, sacked Sardis, and captured Croesus himself. His general, Harpagus, subdued the Ionian cities, save Miletus, which retained its favorable status, and put in pro-Persian tyrants. With the loss of freedom intellectual activity diminished.

(2) *The Peloponnese*

c. 800. Sparta had become mistress of Laconia and had colonized the coast of Messenia. She warred with Tegea, chief city of the backward and disunited

Greek City-States

Athens and Piraeus

Arcadians, who maintained a loose religious union centering about the primitive worship on Mt. Lycaeum. Politically, kingship survived in Arcadia into the 5th century. **Corinth**, under the close oligarchical rule of the Bacchiadae, had become commercially important and, until c. 720, dominated its smaller neighbor **Megara**. **Argos**, though claiming the hegemony of Greece as heir of Mycenae, remained a weak state.

c. 736-716. In the **FIRST MESSENIAN WAR**, Sparta, led by **King Theopompus**, conquered Messenia and divided the rich plain into lots, which the Messenians, as helots, worked for their Spartiate masters. Besides helots and Spartiates, there was a third class of Laconians, the *perioeci* (dwellers-around), who were free but not possessed of citizen rights. Sparta still, however, had an artistic and intellectual life equal to any in Greece, especially in respect to choral poetry.

c. 680. King **Pheidon** made Argos for a brief space powerful. He defeated Sparta allied with Tegea in the **battle of Hysiae** (669), and, in support of revolting Aegina, crushed Epidaurus and her ally Athens. Pheidon is said to have introduced coinage into Greece, perhaps with a mint on Aegina. After his death, the powers of the rulers were curtailed and Argos declined.

c. 650-630. In the **Second Messenian War**, Sparta with difficulty crushed her revolting subjects, who were led by Aristomenes, master of Arcadia, and who took refuge on Mt. Eira.

c. 610. By the so-called *Eunomia*, the Spartans, fearing further revolts, completely reorganized the state to make it more severely military. Youths from the age of 7 were taken for continual military training. Men of military age lived in barracks and ate at common messes (*syssitia, phiditia*). Five local tribes replaced the three Dorian hereditary ones and the army was correspondingly divided, creating the **Dorian phalanx**. In the tribes were enrolled as citizens many non-citizens. The *gerousia*, comprising 28 elders and the two kings, had the initiative in legislation, though the *apella* of all citizens had the final decision. The chief magistrates, *ephors*, were increased to five, with wider powers especially after the ephorate of **Cheilon** (556). Later ages attributed the reforms to the hero **Lycurgus** in the 9th century, perhaps because the new laws were put under his protection.

c. 560. Sparta finally reduced the Tegeates to the status of subject allies, not helots. She then (c. 546, **battle of the 300 Champions**), took the plain of Thyreatis from Argos. The kings Anaxandridas and Ariston extended the policy of alliances to all the Peloponnesian states save Achaea and Argos to form the **Peloponnesian League**, in which the allies had equal votes on foreign policies, contributed two-thirds of their forces in war, and paid no tax except for war. Sparta's policy was hereafter anti-tyrant; she expelled the tyrants of Sicyon, Naxos, and, later, Athens (510), and sought to do so in Samos (c. 524, Polycrates).

c. 520. The young king **Cleomenes I** tried to reassert the royal power against the ephors. When the expulsion of the tyrants from Athens led not to a pro-Spartan oligarchy but to the democratic reforms of Cleisthenes, he led an expedition into Attica, which, however, failed because of the opposition of the other king, **Damaratus**, and the defection of Corinth through jealousy of Sparta's power. Nevertheless, by his defeat of Argos in the **battle of Sepeia** (494) he so increased the power of Sparta and of himself that he was emboldened to depose Damaratus, despite the opposition of the ephors, on a charge of illegitimacy. Public opinion then turned against him and he fled to Arcadia, whence he forced his return by arms. Traditionally, he soon after (c. 489) went mad, was imprisoned, and committed suicide, but this tale may conceal a real arrest and execution by the ephors. He was succeeded by **Leonidas.**

(3) *Athens*

Attica was gradually unified by the device of *synoecism*, through which the numerous small independent cities surrendered their local citizenship for that of Athens. This process had by 700 taken in all Attica except Eleusis, which was soon added. Traditionally the whole process was accomplished by King Theseus.

In the **Ancient Constitution of Athens** the people were divided into four hereditary tribes (*phylai*), each made up of a number of brotherhoods (*phratriai*), which had common religious ceremonies and gave assistance to members in legal strife and blood feuds. The nobles (*eupatridai*) formed smaller associations of clans (*genê*); the *phratriai* contained eventually both members of these clans (*gennetai*) and common people (*orgeones*), although at first perhaps only the former. Each tribe was divided for administrative purposes into 12 *naucrariai*, which handled the revenue and cared for the navy. The people were grouped, chiefly for military purposes, into three classes: *hippeis* (knights), *zeugitai* (those with a yoke of oxen), and *thetes* (laborers).

The nobles gradually restricted the power of the king by giving first his military functions to a *polemarch* and then his civil functions to an *archon*.

683. The hereditary kingship was abolished and made into an annual office (*archon basileus*) like the archon and polemarch. Six *thesmothetai* were created to determine the customary law. These, with the archon basileus, the polemarch, and the *archon eponymous* (civil archon), were known as the **nine archons.** They were chosen from the nobles by the **areopagus,** a council of nobles which was the greatest power in the state. The **ecclesia** (assembly of all the freemen) had either gone out of use or was completely without power.

632. **Cylon,** a noble related to Theagenes, tyrant of Megara, attempted to establish a tyranny, but was foiled. Many of his followers were tricked into surrendering and then slaughtered by Megacles of the Alcmaeonid clan ("Curse of the Alcmaeonids").

621. Publication of the law by **Draco,** the unfairness of the nobles in administering the traditional law having led to a demand for its publication.

c. 600. Athens seized Sigeum from Mytilene; the resulting war was arbitrated (c. 590) in favor of Athens by Periander of Corinth.

594. **SOLON** was made sole archon to remedy the distress caused by the introduction of coined money and high rates of interest (usually 18 per cent); all parties agreed to give this man of the middle class complete powers of reform. By the **Seisachtheia** (shaking-off-of-burdens) all debts on land were cancelled; all debt slaves in Attica were freed; those sold abroad were redeemed at state expense; securing of debts by the person was forbidden. By his **judicial reforms** a new and milder code of laws replaced all of Draco's except the laws on homicide; a court of all the citizens, the *Heliaea*, was created and a right of appeal to it from decisions of the magistrates was granted. By his constitutional reforms election of magistrates was given to the **ecclesia** of all freemen; a council (boulê) of 400 (100 from each tribe) was created as a deliberative body which had the initiative in all legislation: the assembly could only accept or reject its proposals. The areopagus, hereafter composed of ex-archons, continued as guardian of the laws to have large supervisory powers over the magistrates. Four classes of citizens were defined: *pentacosiomedimnoi* (who had revenues of 500 medimni of corn and/or metretai of wine or oil); the *hippeis* (300); the *zeugitai* (200); and the *thetes* (all the

rest). Some time later these classes were redefined in terms of money, and based on property rather than income. Only the first two classes were eligible to the archonship; the first three to the lower offices; the fourth could participate only in the heliaea and the ecclesia. By his economic reforms, Solon devalued the drachma by about a quarter; weights and measures were increased in size; the exportation of all agricultural produce except oil was forbidden; and immigration of artisans was encouraged by ready grants of citizenship.

Solon's reforms were inadequate, chiefly because no provision was made to supply the freed slaves with land or to relieve the *hectemoroi* (share-croppers), who received only one-sixth of the produce of the land for themselves. Besides, the rising class of artisans and traders was deprived of political power by the assessment of the classes on an agricultural basis. Violent party strife continued immediately after Solon's archonship. The rich nobles of the plain (*pediakoi*) were led by **Lycurgus,** the middle class (*paralioi*) by **Megacles** the Alcmaeonid.

c. 565. Peisistratus acquired fame as the successful general in the **conquest of Salamis** from Megara. He organized a new party, the *diakrioi*, of the small artisans, shepherds, and other poor folk.

561-527. **PEISISTRATUS** made himself tyrant, but was almost immediately driven out by Megacles and Lycurgus. In 560-559 he won Megacles over and was restored. About 556 he was again expelled after a break with Megacles. After he had spent some years in gaining wealth from his mines in Thrace, he was restored with aid from Thessaly and Lygdamis of Naxos, whom he had made tyrant (c. 546). Peisistratus' opponents were now exiled and their confiscated lands used to provide for the poor. The *hectemoroi* were made landowners. Peisistratus encouraged industry and trade, and introduced the popular **cult of Dionysius,** in order to break down the power held by the nobles through their hereditary priesthoods. Miltiades and a few Athenians, with Peisistratus' encouragement, set up a tyranny over the Thracians of the Chersonese. Delos was purified. Abroad, Peisistratus pursued a policy of friendship with all near neighbors; at home, he ruled without abolishing existing forms.

527. On the death of Peisistratus his sons **Hippias and Hipparchus** succeeded to the tyranny. Athens protected Plataea against Thebes (519), which was trying to force her into the Boeotian League.

514. An attempt was made by **Harmodius and Aristogeiton** to overthrow the tyranny, but only Hipparchus was killed. Hippias was finally expelled by the exiled Alcmaeonids with Spartan aid (510). Party strife followed between the nobles led by Isagoras and the commons led by the Alcmaeonid **Cleisthenes,** who was finally victorious and inaugurated a

508. Democratic reform of the Constitution. In order to merge the new citizens completely with the old, *demes* (townships) were created to a number of over 150, and citizenship was made dependent on membership in one of these rather than as before in a *phratria*. To break the power of the noble clans, which were connected with the old hereditary tribes, a new system of 10 local tribes (*phylai*) was created: Attica was divided into three sections: Athens and its vicinity, the coast, and the interior. The *demes* in each section were associated in ten *trittyes*, and each tribe was composed of one *trittys* from each section, not always contiguous. A new council (*boulê*) of 500 replaced the Solonian 400; its members were chosen by lot, 50 from each tribe and from each *deme* in proportion to its population. The army was reorganized into ten tribal regiments, each of which in 501 was put under an elective general (*strategos*).

507. At the appeal of Isagoras, **Cleomenes** of Sparta invaded Attica, expelled Cleisthenes, and tried to restore the aristocracy. The Athenians rose, expelled the Spartans, and recalled Cleisthenes.

506. A second expedition of Cleomenes was prevented by King Damaratus and by Corinth. The Athenians crushed the Boeotians and Euboeans and annexed part of Chalcis' territory. They disregarded an ultimatum from Darius of Persia that they restore Hippias, whom Darius had made tyrant of Sigeum.

498. The Athenians sent 20 ships to the aid of the revolting Ionians, but after one campaign withdrew and tried to conciliate Persia by electing Hipparchus, a Peisistratid, to the archonship (496).

493/2. **Themistocles** was elected archon by the anti-Persian party and commenced the fortification of the Piraeus, but his naval policy was opposed by Miltiades, also anti-Persian, who had fled the Chersonese after the failure of the Ionian revolt.

(4) *Central and Northern Greece*

Some time before 700 the cities of Thessaly had been grouped in four *tetrads*, each under a *tetrarch*. Now they were organized into a loose **Thessalian League,** which elected, when common action was necessary, a general (*tagos*). There was a federal assembly which levied taxes and troops on the members. Until the 6th century this league possessed the strongest army in Greece; Thessalian cavalry was always unsurpassed. The looseness of the organization, however, prevented Thessaly from playing a leading rôle in Greece. Thessaly dominated the **Amphictyony of Anthela,** a religious league which by 600 included all the states of central Greece.

c. 590. In the **FIRST SACRED WAR,** under the leadership of Thessaly, and with help from Sicyon and Athens, the Amphictyony of Anthela defeated and demolished Crisa (Cirrha), in whose territory the shrine of Delphi lay. The pretext was the tolls levied by Crisa on pilgrims to Delphi. Delphi was put under the administration of the Amphictyons and their headquarters were transferred thither; Athens and the Dorians of the Peloponnese were admitted to membership.

c. 570. In **Euboea** the two states of importance, Chalcis and Eretria, had been very active in colonization and industry (c. 800–650). The Euboean coinage and weights and measures spread through the Greek world.

c. 570. Chalcis, supported by Corinth, Samos, and Thessaly, now became engaged in the **Lelantine War** with Eretria, aided by Aegina, Miletus, and Megara, over the possession of the rich Lelantine plain. Chalcis was victorious.

c. 600-550. Thebes formed a **Boeotian League** by bringing pressure on the other states of Boeotia. After a long struggle the powerful Orchomenus was reduced.

519-506. Plataea refused to join the league and entered into alliance with Athens. In the ensuing conflict, the Boeotians and Euboeans were defeated by the Athenians.

(5) *Sicily and Magna Graecia*

The original people of Sicily were Sicans; these were displaced by the Sicels from southern Italy. Before 800 the Elymians entered, probably from Spain, and occupied the western corner of Sicily. The Phoenician trading posts in Sicily (p. 32), which had covered the coast, were gradually driven out after 735 (foundation of Naxis) by the Greek colonization, except for Motya, Panormus, and Solus, in the west. Meanwhile **Carthage** (p. 34) had grown into an imperial power by founding colonies of her own and by protecting the older settlements after Tyre and Sidon were weakened by foreign domination after 669.

c. 580. An attempt of the Spartan Pentathlus to colonize western Sicily was defeated by the Elymians.

c. 570-554. Phalaris, tyrant of Acragas, pursued a policy of energetic and ruthless expansion, with extreme cruelty at home.

c. 550. The Carthaginian Malchus campaigned successfully in Sicily.

535. In the naval battle of Alalia, off Corsica, the Carthaginians and Etruscans defeated the Phocaean settlers and forced the abandonment of their colony. Shortly after this Massilia defeated Carthage and imposed a treaty limiting Carthaginian influence in the north and west.

510. Sybaris was destroyed by Croton, which was at this time ruled by the sect of the Pythagoreans. An attempt of the Spartan Dorieus to colonize western Sicily was prevented by the Carthaginians.

The conquest of Ionia by Persia led to a shift of intellectual and artistic effort to Greece proper and, thanks to their wealth, to the western colonies. Tragedy began at Athens with Thespis (539); the poets Pindar, Simonides, and Anacreon flourished c. 500. Attic black-figured vases gave way to red (c. 525). Sculpture became more common, in the archaic style (Athens, Delphi). Heraclitus of Ephesus, last of the Ionian physicists, advocated "change" against the "one" of Parmenides of Elea (*Eleatic School*) in southern Italy. Pythagoras founded his sect of mystic philosophers in Croton.

2. THE PERSIAN WARS

499-494. The Ionians revolted under the leadership of Aristagoras of Miletus, against the Persians and the pro-Persian tyrants. Aristagoras made a trip to Greece to solicit aid; Sparta refused, but Athens responded with 20 ships (498) and Eretria with five. The rebels made a dash on Sardis, burned it, and retired to Ephesus. Greek disunion and the desertion of the Samians and Lesbians led to the defeat of the Greek fleet in a battle off the island of Lade (494). Darius' control of the sea now enabled him to take and sack Miletus. This practically ended the revolt. Darius subdued all the Greek cities, but did not again force tyrants upon them.

492. First Persian expedition under Mardonius, sent to punish Athens and Eretria for their aid to the rebel cities. Mardonius subdued Thrace and accepted the submission of Macedonia, but the Persian fleet was dashed to pieces while rounding the rocky promontory of Mount Athos in a storm. Mardonius thereupon retreated.

490. Second Expedition of the Persians, across the Aegean, under Artaphernes and Datis. Artaphernes besieged Eretria on Euboea while Datis landed at Marathon, the center of Peisistratid strength. When Eretria fell through treachery, Miltiades, one of the ten generals, persuaded the Athenians to attack. The Athenians won a complete victory in the BATTLE OF MARATHON (Sept. 12) and reached Athens in time to prevent its betrayal to Artaphernes by the now pro-Peisistratid Alcmaeonids. The Persians returned to Asia.

Miltiades failed to capture Paros and was condemned to a heavy fine. He died soon.

489. Athens waged an indecisive war with Aegina until c. 483.

488-482. By a reform of the Athenian constitution (488/7), the nine archons were hereafter chosen by lot from 500 candidates elected by the demes; at some later time this was changed to 10 preliminary candidates elected from each tribe, and still later the preliminary candidates also were chosen by lot. This change naturally reduced the power of the polemarch in favor of the 10 elected generals, of whom one might be selected by the people at large as general-in-chief (*strategos autocrator*). To guard against tyranny, the device of ostracism was devised. In a meeting in which not less than 6000 votes were cast (*ostraka* were potsherds used for voting), the man with the greatest number was obliged to leave Athens for ten years; he remained a citizen, however, and his property was not confiscated. Hipparchus was ostracized in 487/6; Megacles the Alcmaeonid in 486/5; Xanthippus of the same party in 484/3. The anti-Persian party, of which the noble faction was led by Aristides and the commons by Themistocles, regained power. Themistocles prevailed upon the people to use a rich new vein of silver found in the state mine at Laurium for the building of 200 triremes, a newly invented type of warship. Aristides was ostracized due to his opposition to this measure, and from now on ostracism was used as a measure of party government. By 480 Themistocles headed the state as *strategos autocrator*.

480. CAMPAIGN OF THERMOPYLAE.

Xerxes, who had succeeded Darius in 486, demanded earth and water (submission) from all the Greek states, most of which refused. Xerxes thereupon led a carefully prepared expedition of about 180,000 men (not the traditional 900,000) into Greece through Thrace and Macedonia. A Greek force sent to hold the pass of Tempe retired when it was found untenable; the Greek army then occupied the **pass of Thermopylae,** and the fleet the Gulf of Artemisium: the plan was for the army to hold the Persians while the fleet won a victory and thus compelled retreat. The naval fighting, however, was indecisive. Under the guidance of the Greek Ephialtes, a Persian company traversed a side path, routed a small Phocian outpost, and turned the Greek position at Thermopylae. Most of the Greeks withdrew, but **Leonidas,** with 300 Spartans and 700 Thespians, refused to retire and they were annihilated. The Boeotians, Phocians, and Locrians immediately "medized"; the Greek army retreated behind a wall built across the Isthmus of Corinth, and the fleet moved to the Saronic Gulf between Athens and Salamis. The Persians occupied Attica and destroyed Athens, whence the citizens had fled to Salamis and the Peloponnese.

BATTLE OF SALAMIS. The Greek fleet was bottled up in the Saronic Gulf by the superior Persian forces. Themistocles craftily warned Xerxes that the Greeks were about to escape by night, and the Persians thereupon rushed into the narrows, became entangled, and were thoroughly defeated. Since it was impossible to force the isthmus merely by assault, this meant the end of the year's campaign. Xerxes returned to Sardis with a third of the army, Artabazus to Thrace with another third, and Mardonius wintered in Boeotia with the rest.

479. BATTLE OF PLATAEA. After unsuccessfully trying to detach the Athenians from the Greek cause, Mardonius again invaded Attica. The Peloponnesians, urged by the Athenians, advanced to Plataea under the Spartan **Pausanias.** Mardonius attacked them as they were confusedly shifting their position, but the day was won by the superiority of the heavy-armed Greek *hoplites* and the discipline and bravery of the Spartans. Mardonius was killed, his camp plundered, and the Persian army routed. The Greeks then took Thebes by siege, and abolished the medizing oligarchy in favor of a democracy. In the meantime, the Spartan **Leotychidas** had sailed with a small fleet to guard the Cyclades against Persia. The Samians and Chians prevailed upon him to attack the Persians, who were at Samos. The Persians, fearing to meet him on the open sea, drew up their ships on land at **Mycale** near Samos. Leotychidas stormed their position, but the Persians succeeded in burning their ships before the Greeks could seize them. The Ionians and several of the island cities (Samos, Lesbos, Chios) now revolted from Persia and joined the Greek fleet, which laid siege to Sestos in the Thracian Chersonese. The Spartans returned home in the fall, but the Athenians and Ionians succeeded during the winter in reducing Sestos (478).

3. THE FIFTH CENTURY

a. THE PELOPONNESE, 479-461

479. Pausanias, in command of the allied fleet, reduced Cyprus and Byzantium. By his domineering he alienated the Ionians and caused the ephors to fear lest his power become excessive; they recalled him and after a first acquittal he was later (c. 471) starved to death in the temple of Athena of the Brazen House. The Ionians refused to recognize his successor Dorcis and went over to Athenian leadership. Thus Sparta's prestige in the Peloponnese fell very low. In 471 Elis united herself under a democratic government by *synoecism* and Tegea deserted Sparta to form an alliance with Argos, probably fostered by Themistocles.

470. After a drawn **battle at Tegea** all of Arcadia except Mantinea joined the anti-Spartan alliance. While Argos was occupied in reducing Tiryns and Mycenae (c. 469), however, Sparta crushed the allies at Dipaea and restored her hegemony.

464. An earthquake in Sparta gave the helots of Messenia a chance to revolt (**Third Messenian War**); after a defeat they retired to Mt. Ithome, where the Spartans besieged them. Unable to take the place, the Spartans called on the aid of their allies, including Athens. Athens sent a force under Cimon which was shortly dismissed (462), probably because many of its members were really hostile to Sparta; this marked the end of the Spartan-Athenian alliance. The fall of Ithome ended the revolt (461), and the Messenians were given safe-conduct to Naupactus, which Athens had just acquired from the Ozolian Locrians.

462. **Megara,** involved in a border war with Corinth, appealed unsuccessfully to Sparta and then made an alliance with Athens.

b. ATHENS AND THE DELIAN LEAGUE, 479-461

479. Athens and the Piraeus were fortified by Themistocles, despite the opposition of Sparta.

478-477. The Ionians, disgusted with Spartan leadership, made an alliance with Athens for the expulsion of the Persians from all Greek territory. Each ally was to contribute either a quota of ships, or money in lieu of this: the smaller states chose the latter. **Aristides** ("The Just") assessed the tribute, using the old Persian tribute as a guide: the total was probably about 200 talents at first. The league had a general assembly (*synedrion*) on Delos, which at first controlled league policy, although it was soon dominated by Athens.

476. **Cimon** made an expedition to Thrace and captured the Persian forts along the coast except Doriscus; the siege of Eion occupied the winter. Some time later Carystus in Euboea was compelled to join the league. These successes enabled Cimon to procure the ostracism of Themistocles (471), probably because the latter wished to follow an anti-Spartan policy. Themistocles went to Argos, where he conspired against Sparta; he was later (467) outlawed by Athens and fled to Persia, where Artaxerxes gave him a refuge (464).

467. When **Naxos** attempted to withdraw from the Delian League, though the treaty of alliance made no provision for withdrawal, Athens forced the city to raze its walls, surrender its fleet, and henceforth pay tribute. Athens after this often interfered in the internal affairs of the tributary states, which were soon considered subjects and not equal allies. Commercial disputes between citizens of two subject states or between those of a subject state and Athens, as well as capital criminal cases, were tried in the Athenian courts. Part of the rebels' lands were often taken, especially during Pericles' supremacy, to establish an Athenian *cleruchy* (colony), serving a military purpose as well as relieving unemployment in Athens. Garrisons were left under military captains (*phrourarchoi*) if necessary; sometimes only civil commissioners (*episkopoi*) were sent. Athenian surveyors (*taktai*) reassessed the tribute, and the Athenian people controlled its use, as well as the use of the contingents of the autonomous allies.

466. Cimon defeated the Persians in a great naval victory at the **Eurymedon River** on the south coast of Asia Minor. He then crushed a revolt of Thasos (465-463). Under the leadership of **Ephialtes,** a man of great probity and ability, a popular party was rising against the domination of Cimon. He was charged with having accepted a bribe from Alexander of Macedon, but was acquitted and prevailed over Ephialtes in having a force sent to Sparta against the helots (462). When the Spartans dismissed Cimon, the strong anti-Spartan feeling in Athens caused him to be ostracized (461). Ephialtes then succeeded in depriving the areopagus of all its powers except the jurisdiction in homicide cases; the other powers were distributed among the ecclesia, the council of 500, and the popular courts, which by this time, owing to the press of imperial business, had been changed from one panel of 6000 to several panels of from 201 up. Ephialtes was murdered shortly afterwards, and **Pericles,** on his mother's side an Alcmaeonid, took his place in the leadership of the popular party.

c. THE FIRST PELOPONNESIAN WAR

460. **Inaros,** who had previously raised a revolt in Egypt and defeated a Persian force, appealed to Athens for aid and was sent a fleet (probably not of 200 sail), which took Memphis. Simultaneously war broke out between the Athenians and the Peloponnesians, caused in part by the Megarian alliance of 462, which the Athenians had followed with alliances with Argos and Thessaly.

459. The Athenians were defeated at Halieis by the Corinthians and Epidaurians, but their fleet won a victory at **Cecryphaleia.** The Aeginetans joined the Peloponnesians (458), but their combined fleet was defeated by the Athenians in a **battle off Aegina** and the island was invested by a force of Athenians under Leosthenes. The Corinthians raided the Megarid to create a diversion but were defeated by the Athenian old men and boys under Myronides.

457. The Aeginetans were forced to surrender, join the Delian League as tributaries, and surrender their fleet.

Sparta then entered the war, sent an army across the Corinthian Gulf, and restored the Boeotian League under the hegemony of Thebes. Athens was defeated at **Tanagra,** but the Spartans returned home, leaving the Athenians to defeat the Boeotians at **Oenophyta** and enroll all the cities except Thebes in her league; Phocis and Opuntian Locris also entered. The Athenians connected the Piraeus with Athens by two long walls.

456. A Persian force under **Megabyzus** defeated the Athenians, who were besieging Leukon Teichos, the citadel of Memphis. The Athenians were in turn besieged on the Nile island Prosopitis.

455. The Athenian **Tolmides** sailed around the Peloponnese, raiding the coast, burning the Spartan shipyard at Gytheum, and gaining Achaea for the Athenian League.

454. Pericles crossed the Isthmus and made an unsuccessful campaign in the Corinthian Gulf. But meanwhile the Athenians in Egypt were defeated and slaughtered, and a relief squadron met the same fate. As a result the treasury of the Delian League was moved to Athens.

451. After three years of inactivity **Cimon** returned from exile and negotiated a five years' truce with Sparta. Thus, being unprotected, Argos had to make a thirty years' peace with Sparta. Cimon then took a large force to Cyprus (450) but a plague (famine?) caused his death and necessitated the return of the force to Athens. As it was departing, the fleet won a great **victory off Salamis,** a town of Cyprus. An understanding was then reached with Persia (the so-called **Peace of Callias**).

449-448. THE SECOND SACRED WAR was begun when Sparta took Delphi from Phocis and made it independent; Athens immediately restored it to the Phocians.

447. **Boeotia** revolted and an inadequate Athenian force under Tolmides was crushed at Coronea. Moderate oligarchies were set up in all the Boeotian cities. The Boeotian League was re-established on a federal principle: a total of 11 Boeotarchs were sent by the cities in proportion to their sizes; for each Boeotarch a city was entitled to 60 seats on the federal council. Both local and federal councils were divided into four sections, of which each in turn served as council, while the four together constituted a plenary assembly. There was a federal treasury and coinage. Troops were levied in proportion to population. Phocis and Locris followed Boeotia in quitting the Athenian League.

446. **Euboea** revolted and Pericles crossed over with an army. Simultaneously the Peloponnesians invaded the Megarid and drove out the Athenian garrison. Pericles returned, but not daring a battle retired to Athens and when the Peloponnesians reached Eleusis came to terms satisfactory to the enemy, who withdrew. Pericles then crushed the revolt in Euboea, and established a cleruchy on the territory of Histiaea. Negotiations with the Spartans continued, and during the winter

446/5. THE THIRTY YEARS' PEACE was concluded: Megara returned to the Peloponnesian League; Troezen and Achaea became independent; Aegina was to be tributary but autonomous; disputes were to be settled by arbitration. Disgust among the Athenian conservatives at the failure of the anti-Spartan policy led to an attempt to ostracize Pericles, but it resulted in the ostracism (445) of their leader Thucydides, son of Melesias (not the historian). Pericles enjoyed undisputed control until 430.

d. ATHENS, 460-431

457. Pericles made the *zeugitae* eligible to the archonship; the *thetes* were never legally eligible, but in fact were soon permitted to hold the office. Athenian imperialism was extended to the far west by an alliance with Segesta and Halicyae in Sicily (453). An extremely important measure for the development of the democracy was the institution (451) of pay for the *dicasts* (jurors) of the popular courts, which made it possible for the poorest citizens to serve. At the same time Pericles carried a bill restricting Athenian citizenship to those both of whose parents were Athenians (repealed 429, re-enacted 403), and when Athens received a gift of free corn from Psammetichus of Egypt in 446/5 the lists were revised and 5000 citizens removed. The western policy was continued with the foundation of Thurii (443) and the alliances made with several Ionic cities of Sicily.

441. Miletus, involved in a war with Samos, appealed to Athens, which replaced the oligarchy in Samos with a democracy.

440. Samos revolted and threw out the democracy, but the Athenians after a long siege took the city (439) which lost its fleet, its walls, and its autonomy, being made tributary. Chios and Lesbos were now the only autonomous allies in the league.

437. A policy of expansion in the north was begun with the foundation of **Amphipolis** in Thrace, controlling the mines of Pangaeus; it also relieved unemployment and served as a garrison against disaffected allies. Perhaps in the same year Pericles made an expedition into the Euxine and established good relations with the princes of Panticapaeum, who exported the grain badly needed by Athens. Athenian settlers were sent to various Pontic cities. In the Corinthian Gulf about this time Phormio made an alliance with some of the Acarnanians.

e. SICILY, 499-409

The first decades of the fifth century witnessed the rise of tyrants in the Sicilian cities, of whom the most important were **Theron of Acragas** (488–472) and **Gelon of Gela,** later of Syracuse (485–478). Gelon made Syracuse the first city of Sicily, largely by transporting thither populations from conquered neighbors. He differed from the usual tyrant in favoring the landed nobles (*gamoroi*) at the expense of the commons.

480. **Terillus,** tyrant of Himera until Theron conquered that city, appealed for Carthaginian help. Carthage, fearing the alliance of Gelon and Theron, responded with a force under Hamilcar, which was utterly defeated at Himera by the allies. Hamilcar was killed and Carthage forced to pay an indemnity.

478-466. **Hieron I,** brother of Gelon, marks the height of the first Syracusan tyranny. He moved the citizens of Catana to Leontini and resettled Catana with his mercenaries under the name Aetna. In alliance with Aristodemus of Cumae he defeated the Etruscans in a naval **battle off Cumae** (474).

472. **Thrasydaeus,** a cruel and hated ruler, succeeded his father Theron at Acragas. He immediately became involved in a war with Hieron and was decisively defeated. The people of Acragas and Himera expelled him and set up a democracy.

466. **Thrasybulus** succeeded his brother Hieron at Syracuse, but was expelled directly; a democracy was established. The attempted tyranny of **Tyndaridas** (Tyndarion) led to the introduction of *petalism,* like Athenian ostracism.

467/6. **Rhegium and Taras** were defeated with heavy losses by the native Italian Iapyges. A democracy was established in Taras and the Pythagoreans were expelled from the Italian cities generally.

463-460. After a series of conflicts the mercenaries of the deposed Sicilian tyrants were left in possession of **Messana** (formerly Zancle).

459/8. The Sicels united under **Ducetius** and founded a capital at Palice.

453. The Elymian towns of Segesta and Halicyae became involved in a war with Selinus and made an alliance with the aid of Athens.

450. Syracuse and Acragas finally succeeded in defeating Ducetius at Noae; he was exiled to Corinth and the Sicel federation fell apart. As a result of this victory Syracuse and Acragas fell out over the division of territory (c. 445). Syracuse was finally victorious and became the recognized leader of Sicily. In fear of her, Rhegium, Leontini, Catana (?), and Naxos (?) made alliances with Athens (443). Athens at the same time refounded the site of Sybaris as Thurii, calling in colonists from all of Greece.

440/39. **Ducetius,** who had returned in 446, restored the Sicel federation, and after founding Cale Acte, died; his federation was completely ended; Syracuse destroyed Palice.

427-424. **A general war** broke out in Sicily. Naxos, Catana, Leontini, Rhegium, Camarina, and most of the Sicels opposed Syracuse, which was supported by Gela, Messana, Himera, Lipara, and Locri. Gorgias of Leontini went to Athens and made an appeal for aid, which was granted. After indecisive fighting the aristocrat Hermocrates of Syracuse persuaded the warring cities, which had assembled in the **Conference of Gela,** to make peace and cease to call in the Athenians.

416. Segesta, at war with Selinus, again obtained Athenian aid under the treaty of 453.

415-413. The **Athenian expedition** against Syracuse, during the Peloponnesian War. The Athenians were finally defeated at the Assinarus. A democratic reform was instituted in Syracuse by Diocles (412): privileges of the lower classes were extended and many offices were made elective by lot. Hermocrates, who had commanded a naval squadron in aid of Sparta, was banished after the **battle of Cyzicus** (410).

f. THE GREAT PELOPONNESIAN WAR

Thucydides considered the war of 431-421 (the **Archidamian War**) and that of 414-404 (the **Decelean** or **Ionian War**) to be in reality one, and together they **are** called the **Peloponnesian War.** Thucydides' incomplete history covers the period to 410. The basic cause of the war was the fact that there existed in Greece two great rival systems of alliances, comprising practically all of continental and Anatolian Greece, each of which was deemed essential by its leader. Thus neither leader could afford to tolerate any action threatening the solidity of its league, nor could it afford to allow the other to attain power appreciably superior to its own. Hence any minor conflict was bound to involve all Greece, and such a conflict was sure to arise.

435. Corcyra, quarreling with Corinth over the latter's interference in their joint colony Epidamnus, defeated the Corinthian fleet in the **battle of Leucimne.** Corinth began preparation of a great expedition, and the Corcyreans in fear appealed (433) to Athens for an alliance, which was granted, since Athens desired a station on the route to the west (to a small degree for commercial reasons), and especially since she feared Corinth's prospective naval power should the latter acquire the Corcyrean fleet. Ten ships were dispatched to Corcyra. The Corinthians attacked at Sybota, but when it was clear they were winning, the Athenians entered the battle, and the arrival of 20 more ships caused the Corinthians to return home. Athens then demanded that her subject Potidaea, a Corinthian colony, cease to receive her annual magistrate from Corinth, and raze her seaward walls.

432. Assured of Peloponnesian aid, the **Potidaeans** revolted in the spring. An Athenian force won a battle before Potidaea in the fall. Pericles passed a bill barring the Megarians from all the harbors of the Athenian Empire, ruining them economically; the Peloponnesians alleged that this was contrary to the Thirty Years' Peace, but the truth is uncertain. The Corinthians, Megarians, and Aeginetans forced the Spartans to take action and, although opposed by King Archidamus, the ephor Sthenelaïdas persuaded the Spartan assembly to declare the peace broken. The **Peloponnesian League** was then assembled and declared war. The winter was taken up by fruitless negotiations.

431. The war began when a band of Thebans by treachery entered Athens' ally Plataea; the Thebans were induced to surrender and were then killed.

The strategy of the Athenians, devised by Pericles, was to refuse a land battle, in which they would almost certainly be defeated, remain within their walls, and let their country be ravaged; they could support themselves through their control of the sea, and hoped to wear down the Peloponnesians by coastal raids and destruction of their commerce. They also ravaged the Megarid twice annually, when the Peloponnesian army was not assembled. The strategy of the Peloponnesians was to ravage the land of Attica annually and, if possible, lure the Athenians into battle; they also gave encouragement and support to revolting allies of Athens.

431. The Athenians expelled the inhabitants of Aegina and replaced them with Athenian cleruchs. Thucydides put in Pericles' mouth the famous *Funeral Oration* for the war dead of this year.

430. A great plague broke out at Athens. When an Athenian expedition against Epidaurus failed, it was sent to Potidaea, but returned after infecting the troops there with the plague. Disgusted, the Athenians deposed Pericles. During the winter Potidaea surrendered.

429. The plague continued. Pericles was re-elected *strategos* in the spring, but died soon after. Instead of invading Attica, the Peloponnesians laid siege to Plataea. The Athenians sent Phormio to block the Corinthian Gulf. Off **Naupactus** he won two battles against superior forces.

428. Cleon succeeded to the leadership of the radical party in Athens, which favored war; the conservatives, opposed to war, were led by **Nicias.** All Lesbos except Methymna revolted on the promise of Spartan aid. To meet this emergency the Athenians levied the first direct property tax (*eisphora*) since 510 and sent out a large fleet under Paches.

427. Mytilene fell before the dilatory Spartan admiral, Alcidas, arrived. The leaders were executed and Athenian cleruchs were sent to the island. Plataea was finally taken by the Spartans; half the garrison had previously escaped; those who remained were executed. The oligarchs in Corcyra, wishing to end the alliance with Athens, opened civil war on the democrats, but the latter, with Athenian help, put down the rebellion; many oligarchs fled to the mainland opposite.

426. The Spartans offered peace to Athens, but it was refused.

425. The Athenian general, **Demosthenes,** in co-operation with the Acarnanians, took Anactorium. He was then sent to reinforce a fleet in Sicily but on the way seized **Pylos,** on the west coast of the Peloponnesus. Demosthenes was left with five ships, to use this station to stir up the Messenian helots against Sparta. But the Spartans besieged this force on Pylos by landing a force on Sphacteria, an island in the bay. The Athenian fleet returned, defeated the Peloponnesians, and blockaded Pylos. Cleon, in Athens, accused Demosthenes of dilatoriness and, on the motion of Nicias, was sent himself to do better. To everyone's surprise, Cleon and Demosthenes captured the 120 Spartiates on Sphacteria. These were held as hostages to prevent another invasion of Attica.

424. Nicias seized **Cythera.** Cleon almost tripled the tribute assessment; pay for the dicasts was raised from 2 to 3 obols a day. Demosthenes and Hippocrates seized Nisaea but were prevented by Brasidas, on his way to Thrace, from taking Megara. **Brasidas,** with 700 helot hoplites and 1000 Argive mercenaries, continued to Thrace, Athens' only vulnerable point, and raised rebellion in several cities. Demosthenes and Hippocrates planned a synchronized invasion of Boeotia from the west and east respectively, to be aided by Boeotian democrats. The Thebans prevented Demosthenes from invading Boeotia from Acarnania and inflicted a heavy defeat on his colleague Hippocrates at Delium. Brasidas took Amphipolis. Thucydides, the historian, commanded a fleet near-by and was exiled at Cleon's instance on a charge of negligence. The fleet in Sicily returned after the **Conference of Gela.**

423. The Athenians made a year's truce with Sparta. Brasidas, however, continued to raise rebellions in the Thracian cities, so the Athenians broke off negotiations.

422. **Cleon** took a force to Thrace, but was routed and killed before **Amphipolis; Brasidas** also killed: thus the leaders of the war parties on both sides were eliminated and negotiations reopened. Sparta's position in the Peloponnese was being shaken by trouble with Mantinea and Elis, the imminent expiration of the peace with Argos, and the Athenian possession of Pylos, Cythera, and the 120 captives. Athens had exhausted her reserves, which had amounted to 6000 talents in 431.

421. THE PEACE OF NICIAS was negotiated, to last for 50 years. The Athenians were to keep Nisaea until the Boeotians restored Plataea; the Chalcidian cities were to be autonomous but tributary; Amphipolis was to be restored; the captives on both sides were to be freed. The Spartans restored the Athenian prisoners, but Brasidas' successor Clearidas refused to give over Amphipolis. The Corinthians, Megarians, Eleans, and Boeotians refused to sign the treaty: the former two because they received no benefits from the whole struggle,

the Eleans because of a private quarrel over Lepreum, and the Boeotians because they did not wish to restore Plataea. To protect herself, Sparta made an alliance with Athens for 50 years. Thereupon, Elis, Mantinea, Corinth, and the Chalcidian cities made an alliance with Argos, whose treaty with Sparta had expired. Megara and Boeotia delayed action.

420. Sparta broke the terms of the Athenian alliance by making a separate treaty with Boeotia, whereby Boeotia was to restore Panactum to Athens. The Boeotians, however, first razed Panactum, and the Athenians continued to hold Pylos. The action of Boeotia caused Corinth to quit the Argive League. Athens formed the **Quadruple Alliance** with Argos, Mantinea, and Elis, for 100 years. The two latter states at this time were already at war with Sparta.

418. The Spartans under **Agis** invaded Argos and, after considerable delay, the Athenians sent troops to Argos' support. Agis decisively defeated the Athenians, Argives, and Mantineans (the Eleans dropped out) in the **battle of Mantinea** and restored Sparta's hegemony in the Peloponnese. The Spartans then sent an ultimatum to Argos, which proceeded to repudiate the quadruple alliance and make a 50 years' alliance with Sparta. In the spring of 417, the Spartans put an oligarchic government into Argos, but it fell immediately and the democrats renewed the treaty with Athens for 50 years. During the next two years various Spartan armies raided Argos; the Athenians each time sent troops which arrived too late to encounter the Spartans.

416. Athens took by siege the island of Melos, which had refused to join the empire. The men were killed, the women and children enslaved; a cleruchy was established.

Selinus attacked Segesta, which appealed to Athens. Athens had by now a reserve of 3000 talents; the industrial and trading elements desired westward expansion. Against Nicias' opposition an expedition to Sicily was voted, to be commanded by Nicias, Alcibiades (the prime mover), and Lamachus.

415-413. **The Sicilian expedition** set out with a fleet of 134 triremes, carrying 4000 hoplites. Nicias refused Lamachus' proposal to attack Syracuse immediately. Alcibiades was recalled on charges of sacrilege, mutilating the *Hermae* and profaning the Eleusinian Mysteries. He fled to Sparta. The Athenians won over Naxos and **Catana,** but accomplished nothing more.

414. Hermocrates was elected to command the defense of Syracuse. The Athenians almost succeeded in enclosing the city by a wall, but were prevented by the arrival of the Spartan Gylippus with a small force; his seizure of the heights called *Epipolae* permanently prevented circumvallation.

413. Reinforcements were sent under Demosthenes. His night attack on Epipolae failed and he advocated immediate return, but was prevented by Nicias' superstitious fear of an eclipse (Aug. 27). When the Athenians finally attempted to leave, the Syracusans, who had strengthened their fleet, defeated them in two naval battles. The Athenians withdrew by land; the rear under Demosthenes lagged behind and was defeated; the van under Nicias was crushed at the Assinarus. The generals were executed; the prisoners were kept for a time in the stone quarries and then sold into slavery.

414. The Athenians sent a fleet against the coasts of Sparta. The Spartans declared the peace broken.

413. The Spartans seized Decelea in Attica. This post was fortified and a garrison kept there continually; the Athenians were thus absolutely prevented from using their own land. The radical party in Athens, led by Peisander and Androcles, fell after the Sicilian defeat and a conservative reform took place. A college of 10 "deliberators" (*probouloi*) received many of the functions of the old council. The imperial tribute was replaced by a 5 per cent import and export levy in all harbors of the empire.

412. A small Spartan squadron stirred up revolts along the coast of Ionia. The Athenians voted to use their last 1000 talents, laid away for extreme emergency, and built rapidly a large fleet, which recovered Lesbos and Clazomenae. The Treaty of Miletus was negotiated by Alcibiades between Sparta and Tissaphernes, satrap of Sardis. Sparta recognized the Persian king's rights to all lands ever belonging to any of his ancestors, while Persia was to furnish the money to maintain the Peloponnesian fleet.

The Athenians laid siege to Miletus, but were forced to withdraw by the arrival of the Peloponnesian fleet. The Athenian fleet at Samos received reinforcements and sent a detachment to blockade Chios. During the winter the Peloponnesian fleet was united at Caunus, but had difficulty in paying its crews, since Tissaphernes' policy, suggested by Alcibiades, was to wear out both sides and let neither win a real victory.

The Peloponnesians took Rhodes, where they obtained supplies and money.

411. Sparta made a new treaty with Persia, signed by both Tissaphernes and Pharnabazus, satrap of Phrygia. The king's claims were limited to Ionia.

Alcibiades claimed that he could win Tissaphernes to the Athenians if the democracy were abolished. The oligarchic clubs in Athens (*hetairai*) by terrorism carried a motion to restrict citizenship to about 5000 of the wealthiest Athenians. Pay for public offices was abolished; all citizens except the 5000 were to be completely without political rights. A provisional committee of 400 was to rule until the 5000 had been chosen. The 400, however, continued to rule without choosing the 5000. The crews at Samos, who refused to recognize the new government and constituted themselves as the Athenian people, elected new generals, notably Thrasybulus and Thrasyllus. They forcibly prevented an attempt by Athenian and Samian oligarchs to restore the oligarchy in Samos which had been put down the year before. Alcibiades was recalled and made commander-in-chief; he demanded the abolition of the 400 in Athens, although he approved of the 5000. When the extremists among the 400 seemed ready to surrender to Sparta after four months of rule, the moderates, led by Theramenes, secured their deposition. Nine thousand citizens were enrolled as councilors, to serve in four sections as in Boeotia (so-called Government of the 5000). Pay for civic offices was not restored. This government fell before the beginning of the civil year 410/9, and the democracy was restored, with pay for the dicasts.

Meanwhile the Spartans raised revolts in many Hellespontine and Thracian cities and especially in Euboea. The Athenians under Alcibiades defeated the Spartans at Cynossema and Abydos.

410. In the battle of Cyzicus, Alcibiades annihilated the Peloponnesian fleet. Sparta offered peace on the *status quo*, but the radical party in Athens, which had risen again under the leadership of Cleophon, rejected the offer. Pharnabazus paid for the building of a new Peloponnesian fleet.

409. An Athenian expedition under Thrasyllus failed to take Ephesus. Sparta recovered Pylos; Megara had already recovered Nisaea.

408. The Athenians made a truce with Pharnabazus and sent ambassadors to the king, but before they arrived the king had received a Spartan embassy and decided to help Sparta energetically. He sent his son **Cyrus** to replace Tissaphernes. Alcibiades recovered Byzantium.

407. Thrasybulus recovered Abdera and Thasos. Alcibiades was elected general and commander-in-chief at Athens and returned to the city in triumph. Cyrus arrived in Asia Minor and formed cordial relations with Lysander, the able Spartan admiral (*nauarchos*).

406. When **Alcibiades** went off to collect money, his guard squadron at Ephesus was **defeated off Notium** by Lysander. Alcibiades lost all influence and fled to the Hellespont. Callicratidas replaced Lysander, but could not get along with Cyrus. The Athenian Conon was defeated at **Mytilene**. The Athenians with a great effort built another fleet.

406. In the **battle of Arginusae**, Conon won a decisive victory over the Spartan fleet. Eight of the Athenian generals, however, were later tried and, despite Socrates' opposition, sentenced to death for not rescuing the shipwrecked sailors; two fled. The Spartans again offered peace on the *status quo*, but Cleophon again had the offer rejected. On Cyrus' demand, Lysander was sent with the Peloponnesian fleet, nominally as secretary, in reality to command.

405. The Athenians followed Lysander to the Hellespont and, through the gross carelessness of the commanders, the fleet was annihilated while drawn up on the shore at **Aegospotami**. Oligarchies of 10 (*decarchiai*) under Spartan harmosts were set up in all the Athenian subject states.

404. Theramenes negotiated peace after Cleophon, who held out against surrender to the last, was finally tried and executed. Athens was to raze her long walls and the fortifications of the Piraeus, surrender her navy, and make an alliance with Sparta.

404. The Athenian oligarchs, supported by Lysander and led by Theramenes, set up **a commission of thirty** which was to make a few immediate reforms and devise a new constitution. Instead of this, the Thirty with Critias at their head seized power and ruled as the **Thirty Tyrants**. They executed Theramenes when he advocated a more moderate course. Finally 3000 of the richest citizens were nominally enfranchised, but never exercised any real power. Many citizens were exiled or fled, and these were supported by Argos and by Thebes, who feared the excessive power of Sparta. In the autumn of 404 Thrasybulus led back some exiles, who occupied Phyle and then the Piraeus. In the beginning of 403, the Athenians deposed the Thirty,

who fled to Eleusis, and elected a **government of Ten**. These, instead of bringing in the democrats from the Piraeus, asked help from Sparta, which sent Lysander. Then the anti-Lysander party in Sparta replaced Lysander with King Pausanias, who brought about a settlement by which the democracy was restored, and a general amnesty with few exceptions decreed. The decarchies in the former Athenian dependencies were soon abolished.

g. ECONOMIC AND SOCIAL CONDITIONS

The decline of Ionia and the growing prosperity of the western Greeks led, after the Persian Wars, to a shift of trade and industry to Greece proper, toward which converged the routes from both west and east, where the Greeks now sought an outlet for manufactures and a source of raw materials. Corinth and Aegina were the leading commercial states in Greece at the beginning of the 5th century, but they were soon outstripped by Athens. This growth of industry caused a rapid rise in the number of slaves, and many **metics** (*metoikoia*, resident aliens) migrated to the commercial states of Greece, where they were well treated: Athens especially was liberal in granting citizenship from Solon's time until 451. The industrial states were all dependent on the **importation of food**. In Greece itself, only Thessaly, Macedonia, and Sicily exported grain; Sparta, Boeotia, and the backward states of the west and north were self-sufficing. Athens exported wine and oil. The economy of almost all Greek states was now on a **money basis** (e.g. at Athens the Solonian classes had been converted into a money assessment of all property). The Athenian coinage became the predominant medium of exchange. **Prices** had risen tremendously since the 6th century. **Wages** were on a bare subsistence level, and the large number of slaves prevented any increase.

Shipping and agriculture remained very primitive. In Sparta and Thessaly great estates existed, but elsewhere ownership of land was much divided, and even in an industrial state like Athens the large majority of the citizens remained landowners. Foreigners were usually prohibited by law from owning land.

Public finance was simple, with no public debt and few surpluses. The chief source of revenue was indirect taxation; Athens profited greatly from her state-owned mines and depended on semi-compulsory contributions by wealthy citizens (*liturgiae*) for such expenses as the equipment of triremes or production of plays. Direct property taxes were used only in case of extreme need. Expenses in most states were correspondingly low; Athens used the revenues from the empire for extensive public works, and also had a large number of citizens on the public pay-roll. The Peloponnesian War, however, not only exhausted the public finances throughout Greece, but also created economic dislocation, and impoverishment among individuals. These losses must, nevertheless, have been made good rapidly, as the 4th century witnessed a high level of prosperity.

During the 5th century art and poetry attained their finest expression in Greece, especially in Athens, whose prosperity favored an artistic life. This was fostered by Pericles, who herein, as in other policies, resembled the 6th-century tyrants. In the choral ode, Pindar of Thebes (518–442) and Bacchylides (c. 480), in the epigram, Simonides (556–468), distinguished the early part of the century. At Athens the three great dramatists, Aeschylus (525–456), Sophocles (495–405), and Euripides (480–406) developed tragedy from a crude choral performance to unsurpassed perfection. Aristophanes (c. 448–385), who overlapped into the 4th century, was the acknowledged master of the Old Comedy. Prose lagged behind verse, but the Ionian Herodotus, writing at Athens (484–428?), made the Persian Wars the motif of a delightfully discursive history. Thucydides (471–c. 400) perfected history in his account of the Peloponnesian War. In philosophy the conflict of unity against multiplicity was solved by the atomic theories advanced by Empedocles in Sicily (c. 444), by Anaxagoras, an Ionian at Athens (500–425? mind or nous), and by Leucippus (c. 450?). But philosophy turned from physics to ethics and the Sophists became the teachers of Greece and advocates of the subjectivity of standards (nomos, convention, against phusis, nature). The leading Sophists were Protagoras, Prodicus, Hippias, and Gorgias, the last of whom came from Leontini in Sicily to Athens in 427.

In architecture, the heavy and luxurious temples of the early part of the century in Sicily, especially at Acragas (Agrigentum), were succeeded by the perfection of Pericles' Doric and Ionic buildings on the Acropolis at Athens, the Parthenon, or temple of Athens (447–432), the Propylaea, or entrance gate (437–432), and the Erechtheum (420–408), or temple of the hero Erectheus. Sculpture reached its height in the works of Myron (c. 450) and Polycleitus (c. 430) of the Argive School and Pheidias (500–431) the Athenian. Attic red-figured vase-painters developed line-drawing in a series of exquisite styles (to 415), and Polygnotus (c. 480) mastered the technique of large-scale painting.

4. THE RISE OF MACEDON

a. SPARTAN HEGEMONY

401-400. Darius II of Persia had been succeeded in 404 by his eldest son, Artaxerxes II. A younger son, Cyrus, collected a Greek mercenary force in Asia Minor and marched against his brothers (the anabasis or "going up") in 401; he was killed in the battle of Cunaxa, and with great difficulty the Greeks, one of whose leaders was the Athenian Xenophon, made their way back to the Euxine by 400.

400-394. When Tissaphernes besieged Cyme in 400, Sparta sent Thibron to hire a mercenary army and to liberate the Ionians from Persia. Dercyllidas took over the command in 399 and ravaged some Persian territory. A truce was maintained (398–397) while Artaxerxes prepared his fleet and put the Athenian Conon in command. In 396/5 King Agesilaus, succeeding Dercyllidas, ravaged Persian territory. In 394 Agesilaus returned to Greece with most of the troops.

395-387. The Corinthian War. In the winter of 396/5 Persia sent Timocrates of Rhodes to bribe the leaders of Athens, Thebes, Corinth, and Argos to attack Sparta. Athens made a defensive alliance with Boeotia which Corinth, Argos, Megara, Euboea, and other states joined. In 394, the Spartans won battles at Nemea and at Coronea, but their fleet, under Peisander, was annihilated by the Persian fleet, under Conon, at Cnidus. Persia granted autonomy to the Asiatic Greek cities and withdrew her garrisons. The Ionians revolted from Sparta and established democracies; the Cyclades followed in 393. Conon returned to Greece, and rebuilt the Athenian long walls. Athens recovered Lemnos, Imbros, Scyrus, and Delos; and made alliances with Chios, Mitylene, Rhodes, Cos, and Cnidus. In 392, an attempt at a general settlement was rejected by the Athenian imperialists, who had just come to power. The Persians deposed Conon, who soon died. In 390, Evagoras of Cyprus revolted from Persia. In 389, the Athenian navy under Thrasybulus recovered Thasos, Samothrace, Tenos, the Chersonese, Byzantium, Chalcedon, *et al.*; garrisons were placed in the more important towns, and 5 per cent harbor tolls levied, which really constituted a revival of the **Athenian naval league**. Thrasybulus was killed in action (388).

387-386. THE KING'S PEACE. In 387, the Spartan Antalcidas negotiated with Persia a general Greek settlement. All Greek cities were to be autonomous except those in Asia, which were to belong to Persia. In 386, the Spartan navy forced Athens to accept by blockading the Hellespont; Thebes was frightened into acceptance. Thus the Boeotian and the new Athenian leagues were dissolved.

385-379. Sparta broke Mantinea up into villages (385), seized the citadel, or Cadmeia, of Thebes (382), and captured Olynthus and dissolved its Chalcidian League (379).

379-378. The Theban democratic exiles led by Pelopidas recovered the Cadmeia by a *coup* and established a democracy in Thebes. The raid of the Spartan Sphodrias on the Piraeus caused an Athenian alliance with Thebes (378). Sparta raided Boeotia in 378 and 377.

377. SECOND ATHENIAN LEAGUE AGAINST SPARTA. Shortly after 386, Athens had renewed her alliances with several naval powers. In 377, these, Thebes, and many others united in the "second" (really third) league against Sparta. All decisions were to be made jointly by a council (*synedrion*) of the allies, excluding Athens, and the Athenian *ecclesia*; funds were to be derived from contributions levied by the *synedrion* and handled by Athens; Athens was to command in war; Athens gave up all claims to its former cleruchies. A fleet was quickly built up. In 376 Chabrias crushed the Spartan fleet off **Naxos**, and gave Athens control of the sea. Meanwhile, Thebes restored the Boeotian League on a democratic basis.

372. Jason, who succeeded his father Lycophron in the tyranny of Pherae, unified Thessaly by having himself made perpetual commander (*tagos*) until his murder in 370.

371. A **general peace settlement** was reached with Sparta in the summer of 371; but when he was not permitted to sign for all Boeotia, the Theban **Epaminondas** withdrew. Sparta immediately sent King Cleombrotus to chastise Thebes, but he was decisively defeated at **Leuctra** by

Epaminondas. This shattered Spartan prestige and ended her chance of hegemony over Greece. Thebes withdrew from the Athenian League, and with her Acarnania, Euboea, and the Chalcidian cities.

b. THEBAN HEGEMONY

370. An **Arcadian League** was formed under Theban protection as counterweight to Sparta. Mantinea was restored as a city. The government of the league comprised a general assembly (the **Ten Thousand**) of all free-born citizens, with sovereignty in matters of war, peace, etc.; a council of *damiurgoi*, which gave proportional representation to the member cities; a college of generals (*strategoi*) as civil and military executive; a standing mercenary army (*eparitoi*). The Theban army, under **Epaminondas**, liberated Messenia from Sparta and the city **Messene** was built. In 369 Athens and Sparta made an alliance on equal terms. The Arcadians founded **Megalopolis** as a federal capital. In the following years, Thebes secured the union of all of Thessaly save Pherae under a single ruler (*archon*). The pro-Spartan party of Callistratus in Athens was replaced in power by the party of Timotheus, and peace was made with Thebes on the basis of the *status quo* (365). Pelopidas was killed in battle against Alexander of Pherae (364), whom Epaminondas then defeated (363).

362. Because of financial difficulties, the federal army of Arcadia was disbanded. The oligarchs, who could serve at their own expense, came into control of many cities, which then made peace with Elis. The radicals appealed to Epaminondas, and the league broke up: Tegea and Megalopolis remained pro-Theban, while the others made an alliance with Elis and Achaea; all these jointly made an alliance with Athens; Mantinea was allied with Sparta. Epaminondas faced this coalition at Mantinea, but was killed in battle. A general peace was made on the basis of the *status quo*, but it was not accepted by Sparta, which refused to recognize the independence of Messenia.

359. PHILIP II became regent and, in 356, by the deposition of his ward, **King of Macedon**. Since he was troubled by his unruly barbarian subjects and Athens was involved in war with the Thracian Odrysae, both were glad in 358 to make a treaty by which Philip gave up his claim to Amphipolis and Athens promised to surrender Pydna. Philip now thoroughly reorganized his army, placing more importance on the **phalanx** of infantry, and with it subdued the rebellious barbarians. By agreement with Athens, he conquered Amphipolis (357) to exchange it for Pydna, since Athens was occupied in recovering Euboea from Thebes and the Chersonese from the Thracians.

357-355. The Athenian allies were angry at Athenian policy, e.g. the sending of cleruchies to Samos (365) and Potidaea (361), the subjection of Ceos and Naxos to Athenian jurisdiction (363/2), and especially the arbitrary financial exactions of Athenian generals; further, the decline of Spartan power had removed the league's *raison d'être.* Under encouragement from **Mausolus** (Mausollos, 377-353), who had succeeded Hecatomnus (395-377) as ruler of Caria, Chios, Rhodes, Cos, and Byzantium joined in revolt, known as the **Social War,** i.e. "War of the Allies." After the defeat and death of Chabrias at Chios, the Athenians, under the incompetent Chares, finally withdrew from Ionia and recognized the independence of many of their allies (355). Mausolus in 353 annexed Rhodes and Cos.

c. MACEDON UNDER PHILIP AND ALEXANDER THE GREAT

355-346. THE THIRD SACRED WAR began when the Phocians refused to pay a fine levied on certain of their people by the Amphictyonic Council at the instigation of Thebes (355). The Phocians seized Delphi and made alliances with Athens and Sparta. When the Amphictyons declared war, the Phocians used the sacred money of Delphi to recruit a very large mercenary army. Though they were defeated by the Boeotians at Neon (354), they seized Thermopylae and Orchomenus (353). When Philip attempted to oppose them in Thessaly, their general Onomarchus twice defeated him, but in 352 Philip defeated and killed Onomarchus. Philip then united Thessaly, which continued loyal to him. His march south was stopped by Athenians, Achaeans, and Spartans, at Thermopylae. The war continued indecisively in Phocis until Athens made the **Peace of Philocrates** with Philip (346). Philip then conquered Phocis, prohibited the carrying of arms, and spread the Amphictyonic fine in installments.

356-346. When Athens refused to surrender Pydna to Philip in return for Amphipolis, he conquered the former, kept the latter, made a treaty against Athens with Olynthus, and took Crenides, renamed **Philippi,** from the Odrysae. After the end of the **War of the Allies** (355), Athens was financially exhausted and the imperialist party of Chares and Aristophon was re-

placed by the pacifists under Eubulus. All financial surpluses were put into a **theoric fund** and used for the entertainment of the citizens. Athens allowed Philip to expand eastward almost unchecked. But in 351 Olynthus, suspicious of Philip, appealed to her for aid. **Demosthenes** appeared as the leader of the anti-Macedonian party, urging action in his three *Olynthiac orations.* An alliance was made with Olynthus (349), but an attempt to divert the surplus from the theoric to the military fund failed. Philip induced Euboea to revolt from Athens and the latter, against Demosthenes' advice, divided its efforts by sending a force there as well as to Olynthus (348). Phocion was successful in Euboea, but his successor, Molossus, lost the country. Philip took Olynthus, which he razed, and enslaved the citizens (348). Athens could secure no help from the Greeks, and even Demosthenes favored peace.

346. PEACE OF PHILOCRATES. On the motion of Philocrates, ten ambassadors, including himself, Aeschines, and Demosthenes, were sent at Philip's invitation to negotiate a peace: the terms restored the Chersonese, except Cardia, to Athens, cancelled Athens' claim to Amphipolis, and left other possessions as they should be when the peace was sworn. Athens could not secure the inclusion of her ally Phocis in the terms. On the return of the ambassadors, the assembly accepted the terms and sent them back to swear the oaths; they delayed on the way and Philip profited by this to conquer more of Thrace. After the conclusion of the peace, Philip conquered the Phocians, took their seat in the Amphictyonic League, and, as its chairman, presided over the Pythian games; Athens refused to send a delegation until Philip's threats forced her to recognize his membership in the league.

344-339. Despite the friendly attitude of Philip, Demosthenes persuaded the Athenians to make alliances against him in Euboea (341) and the Peloponnese (340), and to help Byzantium to repel him (339). Demosthenes, now in control in Athens, urged opposition to Philip in his *Philippic orations.* He reformed the system of paying for the navy by replacing the individual liturgy (*trierarchia*) with more equitable and efficient groups of contributors (*symmoriae*). He devoted surplus income to the war fund instead of to the theoric. Philip tried to get the Amphictyons to fine Athens for insulting Thebes, but Aeschines cleverly diverted them against Amphissa.

339-338. When this caused the **Fourth Sacred War,** the Amphictyons called in Philip. Athens, terrified at this, made an alliance with Thebes on terms very favorable to the latter. The allies won some minor successes. But Philip annihilated their mercenaries near Amphissa.

338. In the **BATTLE OF CHAERONEA,** Philip crushed the allied citizen armies. He garrisoned Thebes, but let Athens go free. Philip called a **congress at Corinth,** and all states, except Sparta, entered a **Hellenic League.** There was proportional representation in the league council, which was presided over by the king in wartime, otherwise by a chairman; autonomy of the members was guaranteed; existing constitutions were not to be altered and no private property confiscated; no tribute was required and no garrisons left, except in a few places; the king had the military command; the Amphictyonic Council served as a supreme court. Philip announced plans for an Asiatic campaign.

337. A second congress at Corinth (337) declared war on Persia, and Philip sent an army under his general, Parmenio, to Asia Minor (336).

336. Philip was assassinated, allegedly at the instigation of his recently divorced wife Olympias.

337-323. ALEXANDER III, THE GREAT (b. 356), succeeded.

On the rumor that Alexander had died, Thebes revolted with Athens, Arcadia, Elis, and Aetolia, but Alexander swiftly took Thebes, destroyed it, and enslaved the inhabitants. The others submitted (335).

334-331. Alexander, leaving Antipater behind as his governor in Greece, crossed the Hellespont in the spring of 334 with an army of 32,000 infantry and 5000 cavalry, supported by a navy of 160 ships, mostly allied. Memnon of Rhodes, commander of Darius' Greek mercenaries, wished to retreat, laying waste the country, but the satraps, hoping to protect their provinces, forced him to take a stand at the river **Granicus,** where he was completely defeated by Alexander (334).

Most of the Greek cities revolted from Persia. Alexander subdued Caria and (spring, 333) Cilicia. Meanwhile, Memnon died and Darius summoned the mercenaries to Syria. Alexander went on to Myriandrus, where he faced Darius, who had raised a large but motley army. Since Alexander feared to come on to the open plain, Darius went behind him to the plain of Issus.

333. BATTLE OF ISSUS. Alexander attacked and completely defeated Darius. Darius offered to give up all Asia west of the Euphrates and pay 10,000 talents, but Alexander demanded unconditional surrender. All Phoenicia, except Tyre, submitted after Issus, and, by a difficult siege of seven months, Tyre was reduced (332).

332-331. Alexander's **expedition to Egypt** was unopposed; while in Egypt, he founded **Alexandria** and visited the oracle of Ammon.

331. Leaving Egypt in the spring, Alexander met and defeated the Persian army at **Gaugamela** (Oct. 1) and went on to Arbela, where he seized much Persian treasure. Babylonia and Susa surrendered, but at Persepolis resistance was offered, so that the place was looted and burned and immense treasure was taken.

331. Sparta under King Agis III, aided by Persian money and in alliance with Elis, Achaea, and part of Arcadia, defeated a Macedonian force and besieged Megalopolis, but was crushed when Antipater arrived with a greatly superior force.

330. In the spring of 330, Alexander pursued Darius through Media, where Darius was murdered by the satrap Bessus. Alexander subdued the Caspian region and marched southward. When Parmenio's son Philotas had been executed for complicity in a plot, Alexander sent messengers who murdered Parmenio in Media: Alexander feared a revolt and Parmenio was too powerful to be discharged.

329. Alexander went on into Bactria and overcame the Iranians under Spitamenes only with a great deal of trouble (328). Alexander now commenced **the adoption of Persian dress** and court etiquette. In a drunken fury, he murdered his friend Cleitus who had reproached him. He had 30,000 natives trained in Macedonian fashion for the army. He married the Persian **Roxana.** He began to foster **a belief in his divinity** as the best means of dealing with the Greeks as an absolute ruler and yet without offending their sentiments of liberty. Though the Greeks had deified living men before this, Alexander's move met so much opposition that he dropped it temporarily.

327-324. Alexander was invited into **India** by Taxiles against Porus. In the **battle of the Hydaspes** (326), he defeated Porus and advanced as far as the Hyphasis. Here the army refused to go farther. Alexander, therefore, returned via the Hydaspes and Indus to the Indian Ocean (325). Thence **Nearchus** went back with the fleet to explore the Indian Ocean and Alexander returned through the desert of Gedrosia.

They met in Caramania and, after a rest, went on to Susa (324).

324-323. In his policy of fusion of the Greek and Asiatic peoples, Alexander had left in office many of the native governors (satraps); most of these, and many of the Macedonian satraps, were now found to have ruled badly; some had enlisted private mercenary armies. These satraps were replaced, usually with Macedonians; the private armies were ordered disbanded. Pursuing the policy of fusion, Alexander, 80 officers, and 10,000 men married native women. Alexander paid all debts of his men. He ordered all exiles recalled by the Greek cities; to give himself a basis for this interference, contrary to the constitution of the Hellenic League, he ordered the Greek states to recognize him as **son of Zeus Ammon.** At Ecbatana Alexander's closest friend, Hephaestion, died.

323, June 13. Alexander died at Babylon.

His exploration had fostered commerce; over 25 cities which he had founded served to Hellenize the east, although his policy of direct fusion failed. The organization of his complex empire he left much as he found it, differing in each area. The officers wished to make the unborn son of Alexander and Roxana king, but the privates preferred a Macedonian, the imbecile **Philip III Arrhidaeus,** son of Philip II. When a son, **Alexander IV,** was born to Roxana, a joint rule was established under the regents Craterus and Perdiccas.

330-322. Athens had recouped her strength under the financier Lycurgus, who, among other reforms, established compulsory military training for all young men (*epheboi*). In 330, Demosthenes had been acquitted in the trial brought by Aeschines on the justness of the award to Demosthenes of a civic crown. In 326 Lycurgus fell from power, and in 324, Demosthenes was exiled for embezzling some of the money which Alexander's treasurer, Harpalus, brought to Athens. On the report of Alexander's death, Athens, led by the radical orator **Hypereides,** organized a new Hellenic League in central Greece and the Peloponnese. The allies under Leosthenes besieged Antipater in Lamia (winter, 323), and eventually forced his retirement to Macedonia. There Craterus joined him from Asia (322).

322. The Athenian fleet was wiped out forever at **Amorgos.** When the allied army was indecisively defeated at **Crannon** the league broke up. Athens received a Macedonian garrison, took back her exiles, and accepted an oligarchic constitution by which only those possessing 2000 drachmas had the franchise, perhaps 9000 out of 31,000 free citizens. Demosthenes, who had been recalled, fled but was caught and committed suicide.

d. THE WEST DURING THE FOURTH CENTURY

413-405. After the defeat of the Athenian expedition, **Syracuse** made democratic reforms. In 410 many oligarchs, including Hermocrates, were banished. Then Segesta, warring with Selinus (409), called in the **Carthaginians,** who, despite Syracusan opposition, sacked Selinus and Himera (408) and, in a second expedition, Acragas (406).

405-367. Dionysius I secured his election as one of the ten generals in Syracuse and then made himself tyrant. He made peace with the Carthaginian forces, who were suffering from a plague. He distributed the confiscated land of the oligarchs to the poor and enfranchised the serfs. He conquered Catana (403), Naxos, and Leontini (400). In a **first war with Carthage** (398–392), he attempted to drive the Carthaginians out, but failed. However, he reduced the Sicels, and then began the conquest of southern Italy (390–379), where he crushed the Italiote League at the **battle of the Elleporus** (389). But he suffered a severe defeat in a **second war with Carthage** (383–381?), which he failed to retrieve in a third (368).

366-344. On the death of Dionysius, his weak son, **Dionysius II,** succeeded under the regency of his uncle **Dion.** Dion brought in Plato to educate Dionysius, but both were forced out (366). Dion regained Syracuse in 357 and ruled tyrannically until his murder in 354. After two more sons of Dionysius I had seized the power and fallen, Dionysius II returned (347), but the Syracusans called in first **Hicetas,** tyrant of Leontini (345), and then **Timoleon** of Corinth.

344-337. Timoleon defeated the Carthaginians at the **Crimissus** (341) and made peace, with the Halycus River as the boundary (339). The tyrants were expelled from the Greek cities, which formed a military league against Carthage. Timoleon established a moderate oligarchy in Syracuse, with the priest (*amphipolos*) of Zeus as chief magistrate and a council of 600 composed of rich citizens. He then retired (337).

338-330. The Greeks in Italy (Italiotes), hard pressed by the natives, called in first **Archidamus of Sparta** (338), who was killed, and then **Alexander of Epirus** (334). The latter defeated the natives and made an alliance with Rome, but was finally assassinated during a battle (330).

e. GREEK CULTURE IN THE FOURTH CENTURY

The death of Alexander the Great marked the end of the great age of Greece in literature, philosophy, and art. Xenophon (431–354), though a writer far inferior to Thucydides, wrote an able continuation of his history from 410 to 362, as well as other historical works. The lesser writers of Middle Comedy were followed by Menander (343–c. 280), the most outstanding of the writers of New Comedy, or comedy of manners. But it was in oratory and philosophy that the 4th century was most distinguished. Of the ten Attic orators the best known were Lysias (445–c. 380), Demosthenes (384–322), and the advocate of pan-Hellenism, Isocrates (436–338). Phi-losophy was dominated by the figure of Socrates (469–399), executed by the Athenians for atheism. His greatest pupil, Plato (427–347), founded the Academy in the grove of the hero Academus, and Aristotle (384–322), the pupil of Plato and tutor of Alexander, founded the Peripatetic (walking about) school or Lyceum, in the grove of the hero Lycus. In sculpture a refined and less vigorous style was preferred by Praxiteles (385–c. 320), Scopas (400–c. 340), and Lysippus (c. 380–c. 318). The center of activity began to shift to Ionia, as seen in the tomb of Mausolus of Caria (the Mausoleum), completed c. 350, and the new temple of Artemis at Ephesus (the old one was burned by Herostratus in 356). (Cont. p. 75.)

C. ROME, TO 287 B.C.

1. THE EARLY PERIOD

a. GEOGRAPHICAL FACTORS

Italy is a long, narrow peninsula of which the central portion comprises the mountains and isolated valleys of the Apennines. At the northern end, the Apennines swing west and enclose between themselves and the Alps a wide and fertile valley, Cisalpine Gaul, traversed by the Po, which flows east into the head of the Adriatic. The eastern (Adriatic) coast of Italy is infertile and lacks good harbors, while the Adriatic itself, because of prevailing northerly winds, hindered the penetration of the Greeks. Moreover, the rugged opposing shore of Illyria was occupied by wild and piratic tribes, whose forays constituted a continuous threat to commerce. The eastern Italian peoples, therefore, remained backward compared to the western. The western part, though mountainous at the northern end, contains fertile plains in its central portion (Etruria, Latium, and Campania), with good harbors, especially around the Bay of Naples. Its rivers, however (the Arno and the Tiber), are too swift to be readily navigable, so that early civilization sprang up along the coast, while the inland peoples remained rude and simple. The western (Tyrrhenian) Sea is enclosed by the islands of Sardinia and Corsica, the former fertile and rich in metals, the latter a wild seat of pirates. Southern Italy, where the mountains begin to fall away, was a land of pastures where later herds moved seasonably from sea to hills under the charge of slave bands of shepherds, whose brigandage formed a constant threat to travelers. Around the Bay of Tarentum, however, the Greek settlers early found a hospitable welcome, and the western toe of Italy afforded ready access, across the narrow Straits of Messana, to the prosperous island of Sicily, whose rich Greek colonies and lavish crops played an important part in Roman history. The western apex of Sicily in turn led towards Africa and the Phoenician colony of Carthage, which became Rome's chief rival for the control of the western Mediterranean.

b. EARLY POPULATIONS OF ITALY

Traces of Palaeolithic, cave-dwelling Man are found throughout Italy, save in Latium, which was still volcanic. Bones from Liguria, the mountainous area around Genoa, suggest that there were at least two races, a Negroid (Africa) and the later, Cro-Magnon (France). Neolithic Man, after the Ice Age (c. 2500–2000), lived in huts and developed more elaborate stone tombs. He practiced agriculture and herding, made pots, and eventually used copper. He belonged to the new race (Mediterranean) which occupied the whole Mediterranean Basin at this time and which survived perhaps in the later Ligurians (northwest) and Piceni (east-central), and in the pre-Greek inhabitants of southern Italy (Iapyges) and Sicily (Sicels). During this period **Illyrians** settled along the east coast, to survive in the **Veneti** (northeast), the **Picentes** of central Italy, and the **Messapians** of Apulia (extreme south).

c. 2000. AN INDO-EUROPEAN PEOPLE of the *centum* branch, closely related to the Greeks, began invading Italy either from Switzerland or from the Danube Valley. They brought with them a type of settlement built on piles, first in the lakes of northern Italy (*palafitte*) and then on dry land (*terramare*), in a regular, rectangular form perpetuated in the Roman camp. They already knew the use of bronze.

c. 1000. THE TERRAMARE PEOPLES had spread their settlements and culture southward through Italy and into Sicily and had come into contact with the maritime peoples of the Aegean world. They probably became the later **Samnite**, **Sabine**, and **Latin** tribes. In the meantime, perhaps, a related people had entered northeastern Italy from the Danube Valley, bringing with them the use of iron and a more advanced culture known, from the site of the chief excavations, as *Villanovan.* Some archaeologists deny, however, that this advance represented an intrusion of new stock and assume only closer cultural relations with the Danube Valley. These peoples possibly became the **Umbrians** and **Oscans**.

c. 900. THE ETRUSCANS first appeared in Italy, probably by sea from Asia Minor (Lydia?) in consequence of the break-up of the Hittite Empire. They established themselves north of the Tiber in Etruria, probably as a conquering minority among enserfed Villanovan (?)

natives. The power was apparently held by an aristocracy of princes (*lucumones*), whose fortified cities (traditionally twelve, though the precise constituents varied from time to time) formed a loose league, and whose elaborate tombs were at first furnished with bronze utensils and armor, then painted and supplied with imported luxuries, notably Greek vases. They extended into the Po Valley and into Latium and Campania until the end of the 6th century, when the pressure of **Celtic invaders** into the Po Valley cut off their northern settlements and the Cumaeans and Hiero of Syracuse broke their control of the sea and Latium revolted. Thereafter they declined until their absorption by Rome during the 4th century. Their culture preserved its identity until the Sullan land distributions in the 1st century so disorganized it that within a century thereafter it had become dead. The Etruscans made no original contribution to Rome save for certain forms (lictors, curule chair, purple-striped toga of office) and a gloomy religion (perhaps the three divinities Latinized as Jupiter, Juno, and Minerva, and certainly the practice of prophesying by consulting the entrails, *haruspicium*), but they first introduced to Rome Greek culture, though in a debased shape, mythology, the heavy Tuscan temple (from the Doric), and perhaps the alphabet.

c. 760.   GREEK COLONIZATION began in the Bay of Naples in southern Italy, and in Sicily. The Greeks were prevented from further expansion to the west and north, save for Marseilles (Massilia), by the Phoenicians and the Etruscans. Despite victories over both peoples by the tyrants of Syracuse in the early 5th century, the Greeks never succeeded in dominating all of Sicily or southern Italy. From the 4th century their fortunes declined until their eventual absorption by Rome during the 3d. Nevertheless they not only impregnated these areas with a Greek culture which lasted throughout the Roman period, but, by their contact with Rome during the formative period of her national culture, first through the Etruscans and then directly, so Hellenized the Romans that when the latter conquered the Mediterranean world they respected and extended the Hellenistic civilization and, by absorbing it, preserved for later ages the Greek heritage.

c. THE ROMAN MONARCHY

753.   FOUNDATION OF ROME, according to Cicero's contemporary, the antiquarian Varro. Traditionally the founder, **Romulus,** was son of a princess of Alba Longa, Rhea Silvia, and the god Mars. The kings of Alba Longa, in turn, were descended from **Aeneas,** a fugitive of the Trojan War and son of the goddess Venus (Aphrodite). This tradition dates, however, from the period when Rome was assimilating Greek culture. Actually during the 8th and following centuries small settlements on the Palatine, Esquiline, Quirinal, and Capitoline Hills united into one, with a common meeting-place in the valley between, the **Forum.** These peoples may have been of different racial stocks, chiefly Latin but partly Sabine, Etruscan, and perhaps pre-Italic. The importance of Rome is less likely to have been economic (trade up the Tiber or across the ford at this point is not attested by archaeology) than military, an outpost of the Latins against the encroaching Etruscans. This would account for the inculcation in the Romans from an early date of habits of obedience, organization, and military drill. The traditions of the four early kings (**Romulus,** 753–715, **Numa Pompilius,** 715–673, **Tullius Hostilius,** 673–641, and **Ancus Marcius,** 641–616) are historically unreliable.

Early government. Rome emerged into history with a king (elective, not hereditary), limited by the existence of a **senate** of 100 elders (*patres*) which was advisory, not compulsory, and by a popular assembly of the clans (*curiae*), the **comitia curiata,** which conferred upon the newly elected king his *imperium* and may have had slight legislative power. There were two classes in the state: **patricians,** who alone could belong to the Senate, and **plebeians.** Most probably the patricians were simply the more prosperous farmers, who for their own advantage organized themselves in *curiae,* set themselves up as a superior class and usurped certain privileges (another theory is that the plebeians were the conquered native people). As a result of the plebeians' lack of power to defend themselves, many attached themselves as clients to patrician patrons, who protected them in return for attendance and service.

The early religion was simple, chiefly the worship of Mars (an agricultural divinity who only later became god of war, and of animistic forces. Religious ceremonies were simple to the point of being magical; by their proper performance the divine power (*numen*) inherent in gods or objects was compelled to act, and failure to get results indicated some fault in the ceremony.

c. 616. **Tarquinius Priscus** (616–578) and his successors, **Servius Tullius** (578–534) and **Tarquinius Superbus** (the

Proud, 534–510), may represent the Etruscan domination in Rome and emerge more clearly than their predecessors. Tarquin the First was a great builder (*Cloaca Maxima*, Temple of Jupiter Capitolinus, *Circus Maximus*). To weaken the patrician influence, he is said to have increased the Senate to 300. He fought successfully against Sabines, Latins, and Etruscans. **Servius Tullius,** traditionally of slave and Latin descent, fought against Veii and brought Rome into the **Latin League.** His chief achievement, traditionally, was to substitute for the hereditary clans a new military division into **classes** and **centuries,** based on wealth and arms (cf. reforms of Solon in Athens). It may be, however,

that this reform should really be dated about 450 and, in any case, the surviving (and conflicting) descriptions of his arrangements probably portray them in the state which they reached after the 3d century B.C. Upon this arrangement depended a new assembly, the **comita centuriata.** Since group voting was taken over from the *comitia curiata,* the wealthy, who though few in numbers constituted the majority of the centuries, controlled this assembly as, presumably, the patricians had the former. The last, **Tarquin the Proud,** was expelled in a revolt which according to tradition was led by L. Junius Brutus and was due to the rape of Lucretia by Sextus Tarquinius, son of the king.

2. THE EARLY REPUBLIC

The early constitution: two annual **consuls,** originally called *praetors* (generals), held equally the undivided *imperium* of the king; either could prevent the other from acting, but could not force him to act. They had absolute command of the army in the field, including power over life and death; in the city they were provided with *coercitio,* a sort of summary police power, but with slight civil and no criminal jurisdiction. They were elected by the *comitia centuriata,* but their *imperium* was conferred by the *comitia curiata* (*lex curiata*), later represented by 30 lictors.

The judicial system: cases of high treason were handled by the *duouiri perduellionis*; all other criminal cases of which the state took cognizance were handled by the *quaestores parricidii* (investigators of murder), later known simply as *quaestors*. From their collecting of fines, the quaestors became the main financial officers of the state, and in this capacity they became attached to the consuls as comptrollers; later they lost their judicial functions. Civil cases were usually handled by arbitration, but gradually the consuls came to take a larger part, until in 367 there was created a special officer (*praetor*).

In time of crisis the Senate could restore unity of command by instructing the consuls to appoint a **dictator** (*magister populi*), who appointed as his assistant a master of the horse (*magister equitum*); the dictator had absolute power in all fields, but had to resign when his task was completed, and in no case could remain in office for more than six months.

The plebs seem already to have had an organization of their own, the *concilium plebis,* with its own officers, *tribunes*

(? originally commanders of the tribal regiments) and *aediles* (custodians of the temple of Ceres on the Aventine, where were kept the plebeian treasury and archives). When the first 17 rustic tribes were organized shortly after the foundation of the republic (the four urban tribes are ascribed by tradition to Servius Tullius, but may be later), the *concilium plebis* was reorganized on the basis of these; some time later a *comitia tributa* of the whole people was organized on the same basis, perhaps to break up the power of the hereditary clans (cf. Cleisthenes, at Athens). It is uncertain how long the *concilium plebis* remained distinct from the *comitia tributa*; in the later republic the difference was merely technical. A resolution of the plebs alone was called a *plebiscitum,* and was originally binding only on the plebeians, as opposed to a *lex* of the entire *populus,* adopted in a *comitia*.

At the beginning of the republican period, Rome was probably the dominant power in the Latin League, but apparently lost this position because of the continued Etruscan pressure; the next two centuries (to c. 280) were characterized externally by Rome's conquest of the primacy in Italy and internally by the struggle of the oppressed plebs, of which the richer members desired social and political equality with the patricians, while the poorer wanted simply protection from unjust treatment at the hands of the patrician magistrates.

509. TRADITIONAL DATE OF THE FOUNDING OF THE REPUBLIC. L. Junius Brutus and **L. Tarquinius Collatinus** (husband of Lucretia) became consuls. Almost all of the history of the first century of the republic, including the names of the first two or three decades of consuls, is unreliable, but it is not yet possible to establish the truth. The dates given here are those of Cicero's contemporary Varro, adopted by Livy. They are subject to errors of up to ten years in the 1st century of the republic, gradually decreasing to become practically certain from c. 300.

A **lex Valeria de prouocatione** is said to have been passed by the *consul suffectus* (filling another's unexpired term), L. Valerius Poplicola, guaranteeing citizens in Rome (not on military service) the right of appeal to the *comitia centuriata* from a consul who proposed to execute or flog them; probably a retrojection of later legislation, but such a right was recognized by the **Twelve Tables**.

508.   A Treaty with the Carthaginians recognized Carthage's exclusive interests in Africa and Rome's in Latium. Doubt has been cast on the genuineness of this treaty, but probably unjustly.

Lars Porsena of the Etruscan Clusium attacked Rome and probably restored the Etruscan domination for a short time, although Roman tradition claimed he had been turned back by the exploits of **Horatius Cocles** (defense of the *pons sublicius*, or wooden Tiber bridge), Cloelia, and Q. Mucius Scaevola.

496.   The dictator A. Postumius, in the **battle of Lake Regillus**, defeated the Latins, who, with the help of Aristodemus of Cumae, had some time before freed themselves from Etruscan rule by the **battle of Aricia**.

494.   **The plebeians**, oppressed by debt, **seceded to the Sacred Mount** (probably the Aventine). The patricians were forced to make some concessions before the plebs would return. The latter further protected themselves by swearing to the *leges sacrae*, by which they bound themselves to avenge any injury done to their officials, the **tribunes**, the aediles, and the *decemuiri stlitibus iudicandis*. These officials were therefore called *sacrosanct*. They were not officials of the state, but officers of a corporate group within the state. But because of the unanimous support of the plebs they had *de facto* great powers, which were never legalized but became gradually respected by custom. The basis of the tribunes' powers was the *ius auxilii*, by which they could intervene to save anyone threatened by the action of a magistrate. This *intercessio* against a specific act of a magistrate developed later (when the tribunes secured admission to the Senate) into the right of interposing a veto against any proposed law or decree. They presided over the *concilium plebis*. The

original number of the tribunes was 2 or 4; it eventually became 10. The aediles handled the fines imposed by the tribunes or the *concilium*, and through the use of this money came to have control of the free distributions of corn to the poor and over the repair of public buildings, etc., which were later extended into a general police power. The *decemuiri stlitibus iudicandis* conducted trials in which the status of persons as slaves or freedmen was in question.

493.   A Treaty of Sp. Cassius with the Latin League provided that booty was to be equally divided; new territory to be colonized in common; the rights of *connubium* and *commercium* (to contract valid marriages between members of different states and to carry on commerce with full legal protection) were restored as they had been before Rome's break with the league (c. 508). The reason for this peace was certainly the increasing pressure of the attacks of the neighboring Volsci and Aequi. The Hernici were later admitted to the alliance on terms of equality with the other two members (486).

491.   Gn. Marcius Coriolanus traditionally tried to bribe the plebeians with free grain into giving up the tribunate; when he failed and was summoned to trial, he fled to the Volsci and led them against Rome, but was finally turned back by the prayers of his mother and wife.

486.   The consul Sp. Cassius attempted to make himself tyrant but was executed. This much may be true, but the story that his method was a proposed division of the public land, which was of insignificant extent for a long time, is probably a retrojection from the Gracchan era.

477.   Battle of the Cremera. War had broken out with the Etruscan Veii (483), which was supported by Fidenae, a town controlling the upper Tiber and thus essential to Rome. A large number of Fabii took up a position on the Cremera to prevent the two cities from joining their forces, but were annihilated by the Veientines. Traditionally, only one of 300 escaped. A peace was made in 474.

458.   L. Quinctius Cincinnatus, called from his field to assume the dictatorship, rescued a Roman army and defeated the Aequi, who had pressed into the valley of the Algidus.

451.   Agitation of the plebs for codification of the law to curb the arbitrariness of the patrician magistrates led to the creation of **ten patrician decemvirs** in place of consuls. According to legend, an embassy had been sent to Athens in 454 to procure the laws of Solon for study. The first decemvirs published ten tables, but since these proved insufficient new decemvirs were created in 450 and drew up two additional tables. Thenceforth the **Twelve Tables** constituted the fundamental law of Rome until the 2d century. Tradition alleges that this decemviral board continued illegally in office in 449 under the extreme patrician **Appius Claudius.** When he attempted to get for himself by false legal process the maiden Virginia, her father Virginius stabbed her and the plebeians seceded to the Aventine and Sacred Mounts. The decemvirs had to abdicate and Appius committed suicide.

448. The moderate patrician consuls Valerius and Horatius passed a series of **Valerio-Horatian laws** weakening the patrician power. Traditionally, these (1) made the *plebiscita* as valid as *leges*; (2) compelled all magistrates, including the dictator, to allow appeals from their decisions; and (3) affirmed the inviolability of the tribunes and also the aediles. All these changes are probably mere retrojections of later reforms. Two more quaestors were added specially for the military treasury, making a total of four. Though patricians, they were elected in the *comitia tributa*, and in 421 the quaestorship was opened to the plebeians. The tribunes acquired the right of taking auspices (necessary before any public business and later convenient as a means of blocking action) and the privilege of sitting on a bench inside the senate, though near the door.

445. A law (plebiscite?) of the tribune Canuleius allowed marriage between patricians and plebeians, the children to inherit the father's rank.

444. As a compromise in the face of agitation that the consulate be opened to plebeians, **6 (?3) military tribunes with consular power.** who might be plebeians, were substituted for the consuls. Two patrician *censors* were also created to hold office for 5 (4?) years, later reduced to 18 months every 5th year. They had no *imperium*, but only a *potestas*, but because usually older and distinguished ex-consuls, they came to outrank even consuls. Their tasks gave them importance, since they made up the citizen lists for tax and military purposes (the *census*), enrolled senators (*lectio senatus*) and knights (*recognitio equitum*), and examined into public morals (*regimen morum*), so that at the end of their term they could perform the ceremony of purification for the state, the *lustrum*, a word which came to be applied to their

five-year cycle. They also made up the state budget, handled its property, and let out contracts for public works.

439. Traditionally, Sp. Maelius was put to death by Servius Ahala, master of the horse for the dictator Cincinnatus, because his free distribution of grain to the people seemed an attempt at a tyranny.

431. The dictator A. Postumius Tubertus decisively defeated the Aequi at the Algidus and drove them out of the valley. The Volsci were then continually driven back and are said to have made peace in 396.

426. Fidenae, which, with Veii, had declared war in 438, was destroyed by the dictator Mamercus Aemilius and the master of the horse A. Cornelius Cossus; thus Veii was forced to make peace for 20 years (425).

405-396. In the siege of Veii, tradition alleged that, because the army had to be kept in the field all winter, pay for the troops was introduced. The dictator M. Furius Camillus finally took the town; it was destroyed, and, since the Latins had not contributed to the siege, the territory was annexed directly to Rome and organized in four new tribes. From this time on Rome really outweighed its ally, the Latin League; the Hernici had long been inferior to the other two.

390. **Rome was sacked by the Gauls** under Brennus, who defeated the defending army at the **Allia** on July 18. According to tradition the Gauls held all of Rome except the Capitol, which was only saved by the geese. Their withdrawal after seven months is attributed to Camillus, but they were probably bought off. The Latins and Hernici took advantage of Rome's plight to break off their alliance.

384. The patrician M. Manlius Capitolinus was, according to tradition, convicted of aspiring to a tyranny by releasing plebeian debtors at his own expense, and was executed by being thrown from the Tarpeian Rock.

367. **Licinio-Sextian Laws.** After ten years of agitation the tribunes C. Licinius and L. Sextius secured the passage of reform measures: (1) some sort of relief was granted to debtors; (2) the amount of public land which one person could hold was limited to 500 iugera (1 iugum = 5/8 acre). This provision is almost certainly a retrojection from the Gracchan era. (3) The practice of giving a consular *imperium* to military tribunes was abolished, and one consulship was opened to the plebs. Tradition incorrectly states that both consul-ships were opened to the plebs, and that one of them had to be filled by a plebeian. At the same time a third *praetor* was cre-ated, to handle the judicial functions of the other two chief magistrates, who thence-forth were usually known as consuls. Two patrician *curule aediles* were created, with functions much like the plebeian aediles. The plebeians were soon admitted to all offices, the last being the religious colleges of *pontifices* and *augures*, by the **lex Ogulnia** of 300. As a result of these changes, a new nobility of office-holding families, both patrician and plebeian, grew up, and the patriciate lost all significance. This no-bility soon became quite exclusive, so that a *novus homo* (a man without office-holding ancestors) had great difficulty in obtaining an office.

367-349. Four wars were waged against the Gauls, who made incursions from Cisalpine Gaul into central Italy. In them are supposed to have been fought the single combats against Gallic champions of T. Manlius Torquatus (361) and M. Valerius Corvus (349). Peace was finally concluded c. 334.

362-345. Wars with the peoples immedi-ately around Rome. The Hernici and the revolting Latin cities were forced to rejoin the Latin League on severer terms; southern Etruria was brought under Roman supremacy; and the Volsci and Aurunci were reduced, thus putting Rome in contact with the Samnites.

348. Second treaty between Rome and Carthage; some sources and some modern authorities call this the first treaty.

343-341. THE FIRST SAMNITE WAR was started by a request for aid from the Samnite tribes in the Campanian plain against the hill tribes. After minor Roman vic-tories the war ended in a draw.

340-338. THE LATIN WAR began with the revolt of the Latin cities from the league and their demand for complete equality. In the course of the war, P. Decius Mus sacrificed himself for the victory of his army. The consul T. Manlius brought the war to a close in the **victory of Trifanum.** The Latin League was dissolved and its members made dependent on Rome without even *commercium* and *connubium* among themselves. In Rome their inhabi-tants received private rights but not the vote (*ciuitas sine suffragio*, later called *latinitas*). Some cities ceded land for settlement of Romans, some were made into Roman colonies, others were made dependent states.

339. Leges Publiliae, passed by the ple-beian dictator Q. Publilius Philo, gave *plebiscita* the force of law provided they obtained the subsequent consent of the senate (*auctoritas patrum*); for regular *leges* it was provided that this consent should now be given in advance, as a pure formality.

326-304. THE SECOND SAMNITE WAR began when Rome made Fregellae a colony and the first pro-consul (an ex-consul whose *imperium* was extended for carrying on a military command), Q. Publilius Philo, captured Naples (327). The Romans had the support of the Apu-lians and Lucanians, and later of certain Sabellian cities. After initial successes the consuls Sp. Postumius and T. Veturius were surrounded in the **Caudine Forks** and forced to surrender with their whole army. The Romans only slowly recovered Campania, but in 312 the censor Ap. Claudius began the great military road, the **Via Appia,** from Rome to Capua to secure Campania. The northern Etruscans joined Rome's enemies but were defeated at **Lake Vadimo** in 310. In 308 the peoples of central Italy, Um-brians, Picentini, Marsians, etc., attacked Rome. The Romans countered by using their first war-fleet in the Adriatic. The Samnites were defeated by M. Fulvius and L. Postumius in 305. In 304 peace was made, slightly to Rome's advantage in that she secured undisputed hegemony of Campania.

313. A law of the consul Poetilius (*lex Poetilia*) secured insolvent debtors against personal imprisonment if they surrendered their property entirely to their creditors.

312. Appius Claudius (later Caecus, "the blind"), as censor, is said to have distributed freedmen not holding land among all the tribes, but in 304 they, and freedmen of small landed property, were confined to the four urban tribes. This may reflect later debates as to the dis-position of freedmen. In 304 a freedman of Appius, Gnaeus Flavius, is said to have made public the rules of legal procedure (*legis actiones*), to which he had access as clerk to the magistrates. This completed the work begun by the decemvirs in pro-tecting the poor from manipulation of the law by the rich.

At about this time (or perhaps earlier, after the Gallic sack), the Roman army was reorganized so that in place of a solid phalanx with the long thrusting spear (*hasta*) the legion consisted of small groups, maniples of 120 men in two centuries (now purely titular), arranged in echelon in three lines (*hastati* and *principes* with the throwing javelin, *pilum*, and only the rearmost *triarii* with the spear) for greater mobility in mountainous areas.

During the ensuing years, Rome secured the Apennines by colonies, Sora, Alba Fucens, Carsioli, and Narnia, and built the *Via Flaminia* north to Narnia and the *Via Valeria* to Alba Fucens.

298-290. THE THIRD SAMNITE WAR was a final effort of the Samnites, aided by the Lucanians, Gauls, and Etruscans, to break the power of Rome. Their capital, Bovianum, was taken in 298, but their army managed to combine with the Gauls, only to be defeated in 295 at **Sentinum**, where a second Decius Mus secured a Roman victory by self-sacrifice, perhaps in fact the only instance. The Gauls scattered, the Etruscans sued for peace in 294, and the Samnites finally made peace as autonomous allies, though the colony of Venusia was planted in the south to watch them, as well as Minturnae, Sinuessa, and Haria farther north. The Sabines, northeast of Rome, were annexed and given Latin rights.

285-282. The Romans, despite defeats, annihilated the Gallic Senones, crushed the Etruscans at Lake Vadimo and Populonia, and occupied the Greek cities in Lucania: Locri, Croton, and Thurii. This advance brought on the war with Tarentum and Pyrrhus.

287. The **lex Hortensia**, passed by the dictator Q. Hortensius, fully equated *plebiscita* with *leges* by requiring the *auctoritas patrum* for the former to be given in advance as well as for the latter; its passage was brought about by another secession of the plebs, this time to the Janiculum. The plebs had thus achieved complete legal equality with the patricians, but the old problem remained in the oppression of the poor by the rich patricio-plebeian nobility, which was in full control of the *concilium plebis* and the *comitia tributa* because, since the voting was by tribes, only the rich members of the more distant tribes could afford to come to the meetings in Rome. Further, in the assemblies all initiative was in the hands of the presiding magistrates, and these were now almost always from the nobility and under the control of the Senate. As the problems of government became more complex with the expansion of Rome the control of the Senate became still more effective.

Rome had now established her supremacy throughout central Italy. Her relations with the other communities may be summarized as follows:

(1) *Municipia* retained their own municipal administration and enjoyed only the private rights (*connubium* and *commercium*) of Roman citizenship, not the franchise or right of holding office (*ciuitas sine suffragio*).

(2) *Coloniae* were settlements established by Rome for military purposes, usually on land taken from the conquered peoples. Smaller ones, Roman, were real garrisons and their settlers retained full citizenship. At first they may have been administered directly from Rome. Larger ones reflected real attempts to relieve surplus population and included both Latins and Romans, the latter accepting only Latin citizenship, or *ciuitas sine suffragio*. They may have had some local government from the beginning. Ultimately colonies came to have administrations closely modeled on the Roman, with two executive magistrates (*duumuiri*) and a senate or *curia* whose members were called *decuriones*.

Whatever the original form of government of the various *municipia* may have been, it tended to approximate the oligarchical model of Rome and the *coloniae*, with a small executive, often four (*quattuoruiri*), and a *curia*. Moreover, recent study suggests that this general pattern of municipality may not be at all early, may, in fact, date only from Caesar's municipal reforms, and that before that both *municipia* and *coloniae* were governed by officials sent out from Rome, as was certainly the case with *municipia* which, by revolt, were deprived of self-government (e.g. Capua later).

(3) *Ciuitates foederatae* were independent allies (*socii*) of Rome, whose obligations were regulated by treaty. They enjoyed freedom from direct interference in their affairs and from taxation (*libertas et immunitas*) and usually provided auxiliary troops or ships rather than legionaries. But their foreign relations were determined by Rome, and, in fact, they suffered considerable control.

(4) There were, in addition, groups or communities which did not have a civic organization and which, consequently, were administered under various names (*fora, conciliabula, uici, pagi*) either directly from Rome, by *praefecti*, or by neighboring cities to which they were attached as *attributi*.

(*Cont. p. 85.*)

D. THE HELLENISTIC WORLD

1. CULTURAL DEVELOPMENT

The Hellenistic Age was characterized politically by the **atrophy of the city-state.** The cities of Greece were dominated increasingly by their richer or better educated members and the mass of the population lost power. In their external relations the cities either passed under the control of the various monarchs or joined together in leagues, whose attempts at representative federal government marked an advance in government which unfortunately bore no further fruit during the Roman period. Athens was a university town, respected for its past grandeur but of little political weight after 262. Sparta, however, played a lone and considerable hand in the Peloponnese. To offset the decay of Greece itself, the Hellenistic Age witnessed the **spread of Greek culture** by the conquests of Alexander and his successors as far as the Indus Valley, the creation of Greek cities throughout Asia, and the development of monarchical governments. In the new Greek cities, municipal administration and public building reached a high level, as at Priene (Asia Minor) or Alexandria (Egypt). **Social experiments** ranged from state control of the grain supply (Athens) or distribution of grain to citizens (Samos) to extreme agrarian reforms at Sparta. Private or royal munificence benefited the cities on a grand scale, and the cities themselves substituted for political rivalry that of the splendor of games, buildings, and honors. The administration of the three chief kingdoms was conditioned by their background. In **Macedon** the army, representing the Macedonian people, retained considerable influence, and the king was never so absolute as his Asiatic *confrères.* The **Seleucids** developed a system of provincial administration and of communications based on the Persian satrapies; but their capital, Antioch, never attained the excellence of Egypt's Alexandria and its Hellenism was strongly affected by Syrian emotionalism. The **Ptolemies** administered Egypt as had the Pharaohs, as a state monopoly. They granted a privileged position, however, to Macedonian settlers and to the city of Alexandria, which was kept apart from the rest of Egypt as a Greek city, though it contained also a large Jewish population, for whom, during the 3d century, a Greek

translation was made of the Hebrew *Bible,* called the *Septuagint* from the 70 elders traditionally responsible for it. Alexandria was distinguished by its excellent administration and its magnificent buildings, among which were a lighthouse (*pharos*) and an academy of scholars (*museum,* temple of the Muses) with a magnificent library.

The economic life of the eastern Mediterranean was much stimulated by unification in Greek hands, by the opening of new areas, and by improved navigation and communications. The cities became very rich. In particular, the opening of the treasures of the Near East vastly increased the amount of gold and silver in circulation. Two countries were, however, adversely affected. Greece, naturally poor, was drained of men by the opportunities offered for trade or mercenary soldiering in Asia, and could no longer compete with the more fertile areas now opened for exploitation. Egypt's resources, though ample for her self-contained economy, were exhausted by the expenditures of the Ptolemies in their attempt to create an Aegean empire. Nevertheless, in general, the period was one of complacent prosperity throughout the eastern Mediterranean.

Under the great librarians of Alexandria, **Zenodotus** (c. 280), **Aristophanes** of Byzantium (257–180), and **Aristarchus** (217–145), philology, textual criticism, and kindred subjects replaced creative writing. But great advances were attained in science by such men as **Euclid** the geometrician (c. 300), **Eratosthenes** the astronomer and geographer (c. 240), and **Archimedes** the physicist (287–212, in Syracuse). **Literature** became imitative, artificial, and overburdened with learning, as in the poetry of **Callimachus** (c. 260), or the epic *Argonautica* of **Apollonius Rhodius** (295–214). Only the pastoral achieved a delicate and spontaneous freshness in the poems of **Theocritus** (c. 270, from Syracuse). The Attalids, notably Eumenes II, tried to make Pergamum into an intellectual rival of Alexandria, but their capital became famous chiefly for its **Pergamene school of art,** whose exaggerated style is best seen in the friezes of the Altar of Pergamum. Another school flourished in the prosperous

THE KINGDOMS OF
ALEXANDER'S SUCCESSORS
(about 200 B.C.)

Kingdom of the Seleucids
Egypt
Macedonia

KINGDOM OF THE BACTRIANS

KINGDOM OF THE ARSACIDS

KINGDOM OF THE SELEUCIDS

KINGDOM

ARABIA

KINGDOM OF THE PTOLEMIES

EGYPT

Jaxartes R.

Oxus R.

Aral Sea

Indus R.

Arachosia

Drangiana

Gedrosia

Carmania

Persis

Persian Gulf

CASPIAN SEA

MEDIA ATROPATENE

ARMENIA

Tigris R.

Euphrates R.

Seleucia

Babylon

ARABIAN SEA

BLACK SEA

PONTUS

CAPPADOCIA

GALATIANS

Pergamum

Antioch

SYRIA

Damascus

Tyre

Cyprus

Crete

Athens

MEDITERRANEAN SEA

Alexandria

Memphis

RED SEA

Nile R.

Danube R.

THRACE

MACEDONIA

Epirus

0   200   400 Miles

island of Rhodes. Much of Hellenistic art dealt with simple subjects of daily life in a realistic fashion, as in the charming pottery figurines from Tanagra, in Greece. In philosophy, the Academy continued the Platonic tradition but with increasing skepticism about the possibility of attaining truth. The Peripatetics devoted themselves almost wholly to scientific and historical studies. Two new schools, however, answered the spiritual needs of the time. Stoicism was founded by Zeno (336–264), a half-Phoenician from Cyprus, who taught in the Painted Porch (*stoa poikile*) at Athens, and Epicureanism by Epicurus (342–270), who withdrew from the world into his garden. Both sought the same end, a mind which would be so self-sufficient through inner discipline and its own resources that it would not be disturbed by external accidents. The Stoics sought this undisturbed state of mind (*ataraxia*) by modifying the Cynic asceticism to a doctrine of neglect of outward honors and wealth and devotion to duty. A belief that the world was ruled by a universal reason in which all shared led them to a humanitarian view of the brotherhood of men which transcended national, racial, or social differences. This internationalism and the doctrine that the ruler should embody divine reason allowed them to support monarchical government. The Epicureans sought the same end by following the Cyrenaics in advocating an inactive life (*apraxia*) and a moderate, not an excessive, self-indulgence. To free the mind from wrong, they attacked religion and superstition and adopted the atomic metaphysics as a mechanical explanation of the universe.

In religion, the Hellenistic Age witnessed a loss of belief in the simple Greek pantheon and a turning to more emotional oriental worships, like those of Cybele, the Great Mother of Asia Minor, the Persian Mithra, or the Egyptian Isis. A fatalistic view of external events led to the personification of Fortune (*tyche*) as a goddess. And a combination of flattery, legalism (since a god could always rule a city without changes in the constitution), skepticism (since many considered that the gods were originally famous men), and real gratitude for the benefits of government introduced the worship of rulers, both dead and living, which the Macedonian monarchs alone refused.

2. THE WARS OF THE DIADOCHI

322-315. When Perdiccas became regent for Philip III Arrhidaeus, the other generals, Antipater, Antigonus, Craterus, and Ptolemy, refused obedience. Perdiccas was murdered when he attempted to dislodge Ptolemy from Egypt, but his general Eumenes defeated and slew Craterus in Asia Minor (321). Antipater and Ptolemy at Triparadeisus in Syria agreed that Antipater should be regent. Antipater sent Antigonus to dislodge Eumenes, who took refuge in the hills (320). When Antipater died (319), he left Polyperchon as regent, but Ptolemy defied him and annexed Syria. Antigonus seized Phrygia and Lydia. Polyperchon gave Eumenes command of the troops in Cilicia. Antipater's son, Cassander, seized the Piraeus, garrisoned it, and left Demetrius of Phalerum as virtual dictator of Athens (317). Cassander took Macedon from Polyperchon (317), executed Olympias and Philip Arrhidaeus, when they attacked him, and imprisoned Roxana with her son Alexander IV, both of whom he put to death in 310. In the meantime, Antigonus, after a drawn battle at Paraetacene (317), had defeated Eumenes in Gabiene (316) and executed him. Ptolemy in Egypt, Cassander, and Lysimachus in Thrace formed a coalition against Antigonus (315).

315-307. Antigonus seized Syria, but his son, Demetrius, was defeated at Gaza (312) by Ptolemy, who had already occupied the Cyclades (314) and the Peloponnese (313). Ptolemy then sent Seleucus to capture Babylon from Antigonus. An attempted settlement in 311 merely allowed Antigonus to continue fighting Seleucus, Cassander to secure the throne of Macedon (above), and Ptolemy to continue his expansion in the Aegean. Antigonus sent Demetrius to Athens, whence he expelled Demetrius of Phalerum and restored the democracy (307).

307. ANTIGONUS I, MONOPHTHALMOS ("one-eyed") or Cyclops, and Demetrius I Poliorcetes ("besieger") took the title of king, whereupon Ptolemy and Seleucus, Cassander, and Lysimachus did the same. The unity of Alexander's empire was thus openly ended.

306. Demetrius crushed Ptolemy in a naval battle off Cyprian Salamis but Ptolemy repelled a land attack by Antigonus. Demetrius failed to reduce Rhodes by a year's siege (305-304), but relieved Athens from the Four Years' War waged by

Cassander (307–304). He then revived the Hellenic League of Philip (302).

301. BATTLE OF IPSUS (in Phrygia). The allies, Cassander, Lysimachus, and Seleucus, but not Ptolemy, finally crushed and slew Antigonus. Demetrius, who had been recalled by Antigonus, escaped to Corinth. By the division of spoils, Seleucus was given Syria, Lysimachus western and central Asia Minor, Cassander kept Macedon, but his brother Pleistarchus received southern Asia Minor. Ptolemy, however, seized Coele-Syria.

299. Pleistarchus was driven out by Demetrius, and Cassander himself died in 298. His eldest son, Philip IV, died also, so that two younger sons, Antipater and Alexander V, divided his realm.

295. Demetrius, after a bitter siege, recovered Athens, where one Lachares had made himself tyrant. He then murdered Alexander V (294) and took Macedon. He mastered northern and central Greece save for Aetolia.

288. A coalition was formed against Demetrius, and Lysimachus and King Pyrrhus of Epirus drove him out of Macedon. He attempted a campaign in Asia Minor, but finally Seleucus captured him in Cilicia (285).

283. Demetrius died in captivity, leaving a son in Greece, Antigonus.

281. Seleucus defeated and slew Lysimachus at the **battle of Corupedium** and became master of Asia Minor. When he tried to seize Macedon, however, he was assassinated by Ptolemy Ceraunus, who acquired control of Macedon. Ptolemy, in turn, was slain in an invasion of Celts (279).

279. The **Celts** ravaged Macedon, defeated the Greeks at Thermopylae, and reached Delphi. A second band ruled Thrace until 210, while a third crossed to central Asia Minor and established the **Kingdom of Galatia.**

276–275. Meanwhile, Antigonus recovered Macedon for himself, founding a dynasty that lasted until 168.

3. SICILY TO THE ROMAN CONQUEST

317–289. AGATHOCLES made himself tyrant of Syracuse in consequence of a civil war (c. 323–317) in which he, as democratic leader, expelled the oligarchs with Carthaginian aid and divided their property among the poor. He successfully defended himself against the neighboring cities and the exiled oligarchs until these appealed to Carthage.

311. The Carthaginian general **Hamilcar** defeated Agathocles at the **Himera River** and besieged Syracuse. In 310, Agathocles slipped across to Africa, where he maintained himself until 307. But his army, under his son, was annihilated during his absence.

305. Agathocles came to terms with Carthage and the oligarchs, and took the title of king. In the meantime the Tarentines had made peace with the Samnites (c. 320) and Rome (304), but were hard pressed by the Lucanians.

302. When a Spartan commander, Cleonymus, failed to relieve them, the Tarentines called in Agathocles. He also failed to accomplish much and died at Syracuse in 289, bequeathing their freedom to the Syracusans, who restored the democracy. Certain of the Campanian mercenaries of Agathocles, calling themselves **Mamertines** ("sons of Mars"), seized Messana.

282–275. The **Tarentines,** angered by Roman occupation of towns in southern Italy, destroyed a Roman fleet which, in violation of the treaty of 304, had passed the Lacinian promontory. They then drove the Romans from Thurii. When Rome declared war, they called in Pyrrhus. Upon his departure in 275, the Greeks of southern Italy remained under Rome, while those of Sicily passed under Carthaginian power, save for Syracuse.

269–216. Hiero II made himself tyrant of Syracuse and defeated the Mamertines at Mylae. He took the title of king (265), and joined the Carthaginians in besieging the Roman force which occupied Messana in 264. But when he was defeated and besieged in Syracuse, he made peace with Rome (263). At the end of the First Punic War all Sicily save Syracuse and a few other pro-Roman cities passed into Rome's possession. Syracuse was reduced in 211 during the Second Punic War.

4. MACEDON AND GREECE TO THE ROMAN CONQUEST

290. Emergence of the **Aetolian League**, a military federation in western Greece. It had a council with proportional representation and a semi-annual assembly. Affairs were handled by a committee of 100 *apokletoi* and a single general (*strategos*) in wartime. The league expanded into Phocis (254) and Boeotia (245) and dominated Greece from sea to sea. It also included Elis and part of Arcadia (245) and made an alliance with Messene, thus separating Sparta from the Achaean League.

280. Formation of the **Achaean League**, consisting of twelve towns in the northern Peloponnese. It had a general (two until 255), a board of ten *demiourgoi*, a federal council with proportional representation of members. There was also an annual assembly of all free citizens. After 251, Aratus of Sicyon dominated its policy and was *strategos* (general) in alternate years. He extended it to include many non-Achaean cities, especially Corinth (243).

276-239. ANTIGONUS II GONATAS ("knock-kneed"?) had to repel an invasion by **Pyrrhus of Epirus** (274–273). Pyrrhus was then called into Greece by the pretender Cleonymus, who sought to oust King Areus (309–265) from Sparta. Pyrrhus was slain at Argos by the Argives and Antigonus (272). Antigonus established tyrants in several cities of the Peloponnese and made peace with the Aetolian League.

266-262. Ptolemy I of Egypt stirred up Athens and Sparta to wage the **Chremonidean War** (from Chremonides, an Athenian leader) against Antigonus. Areus of Sparta was defeated and killed at the Isthmus (265) and, when Ptolemy failed to give energetic aid, Athens was obliged to surrender after a two-year siege (262). Antigonus garrisoned several strong points of Attica and imposed a moderate oligarchy on Athens.

258 (?256). Antigonus defeated Ptolemy in a naval **battle off Cos** and took the Cyclades, though he had to reconquer them later in the **battle of Andros** (245).

c. 252. Antigonus' governor of the Peloponnese, Alexander, revolted and held the peninsula until his death (c. 246).

251. **Aratus of Sicyon** recovered that city from Antigonus' tyrant, and then joined the Achaean League, which he soon dominated.

245-235. Sparta had fallen into a serious economic crisis because of the excessive concentration of land and wealth in the hands of a few. Coined money had been introduced by King Areus. The number of full citizens who could contribute to their mess-tables (*syssitia*) had fallen to 700. When **King Agis IV** (244–240) tried to redistribute the land into 4500 equal lots, the great landowners executed him. **Cleomenes III**, who had married Agis' widow, became king (235).

241. Antigonus sent the Aetolian League to ravage the Isthmus.

239-229. **Demetrius II** succeeded his father, Antigonus. He protected Epirus against Aetolia, so that the latter broke with Macedon and made an alliance with Achaea. Demetrius attacked it in the **War of Demetrius** (238–229), but was recalled by invasions from the north (233). Argos expelled the pro-Macedonian tyrant Aristomachus and joined the Achaean League (229), while Athens asserted her independence.

229-221. **Antigonus III Doson** ("going to give," i.e. always promising) succeeded his cousin Demetrius as guardian of the latter's nine-year-old son, Philip, whom he deposed in 227 to become king himself. He made peace with Aetolia and drove the barbarians out of Macedon.

228-227. Cleomenes defeated the Achaeans under Aratus. He then seized the power in Sparta, redivided the land, and enfranchised 4000 *perioikoi* and abolished the *ephorate*. With an increased citizen army, he reduced Aratus to appeal to Antigonus (225).

222. Antigonus formed a new Hellenic League and crushed Cleomenes at the **battle of Sellasia** (222). Cleomenes fled to Egypt. Antigonus abolished the Spartan kingship, restored the ephors, and forced Sparta into his league.

221-178. Philip V, son of Demetrius II, succeeded Antigonus III. At his instigation the Hellenic League assembled at Corinth to declare

219-217. The War of the Allies, or Social War, against the Aetolians because of the latter's piracy. The Aetolians allied with Elis and Sparta, where an anti-Macedonian faction tried to recall Cleomenes. When he was slain in Egypt, the Spartans nevertheless restored the dual kingship. Philip ravaged Elis (219–218), molested the Aetolian sanctuary of Thermum, and laid waste Laconia.

217. Rhodes and Egypt negotiated the **Peace of Naupactus** between the discouraged Aetolians and Philip, who wanted freedom to act against Rome.

215-205. In the **FIRST MACEDONIAN WAR** Philip V of Macedon attempted to help Hannibal and the Carthaginians against Rome, but a Roman fleet in the Adriatic prevented him from crossing to Italy and the Romans secured the support of the Aetolian League and Pergamum (212), as well as of Elis, Mantinea, and Sparta (210). Sparta in particular, after a period of attempted social reform under King Cheilon (219), had risen to power under Machanidas, regent for the young King Pelops. When the Achaean League under Philopoemen (since the murder of Aratus in 213) slew Machanidas at Mantinea (207), Nabis became regent and soon, by deposing Pelops, king. The Greeks came to terms with Philip in 206 and Rome accepted the settlement by the **Peace of Phoenice** (205).

203-200. Philip, allied with Antiochus III against Egypt (203), began operations in the Aegean, but was defeated by Rhodes and Attalus of Pergamum in the **battle of Chios** (201).

200-196. The **SECOND MACEDONIAN WAR** arose from an appeal by Attalus and Rhodes to Rome (201). When Philip refused to keep the peace, all the Greeks joined Rome (200–198), and Flamininus defeated Philip at **Cynoscephalae** (197), and proclaimed the freedom of Greece at the Isthmian Games (196). Flamininus was forced to check Nabis of Sparta (above), who had carried through agrarian reforms (207–204) and expanded his power in the Peloponnese, especially by acquiring Argos (198). He now lost Argos and much of Laconia, and gave control of his foreign policy to Rome (195). Upon the murder of Nabis (192), Sparta was forced into the Achaean League by Rome, and Messene and Elis soon joined, so that the league controlled all the Peloponnese.

192-189. The Aetolians declared war on Rome and secured the support of Antiochus III with a small force. The Achaeans and Philip supported Rome. The Romans drove Antiochus back to Asia in the **battle of Thermopylae** (191), and the Aetolians were finally made subject allies of Rome by M. Fulvius Nobilior (189).

189-181. Philopoemen humbled Sparta but lost his life in suppressing a revolt in Messenia (183). His successor in the Achaean League, Callicrates, was subservient to Rome and allowed Sparta to revive.

179-167. Perseus became King of Macedon on the death of his father Philip V. He had already persuaded Philip to execute his pro-Roman brother Demetrius, and now Eumenes II of Pergamum laid charges against him at Rome.

171-167. In the **THIRD MACEDONIAN WAR** Perseus was crushed by Aemilius Paullus at **Pydna** (168). He later died in captivity in Italy and the Antigonids came to an end. Rome made Macedon into four unrelated republics, paying a moderate yearly tribute (167). In Aetolia, 500 anti-Romans were slain. One thousand hostages, including the historian Polybius, were taken from Achaea to Italy.

149-148. The **FOURTH MACEDONIAN WAR** was begun by Andriscus, who pretended to be a son of Perseus. On his defeat, Macedon became a Roman province (148).

146. When the Achaean hostages had returned (151) and Callicrates had died (149), the Achaean League attacked Sparta, but was crushed by the Roman general Mummius (146). The Roman Senate ordered Mummius to abolish the leagues, substitute oligarchies for all democracies, sack Corinth, and place Greece under the supervision of the governor of Macedon. This marked the end of Greek and Macedonian independence, though some Greek states retained autonomy for a long time.

5. THE SELEUCID EMPIRE AND PERGAMUM

305-280. SELEUCUS I NICATOR ("conqueror"), after securing his position against Antigonus (310–306) and assuming the royal title (305), ceded India to **Sandracottus** (Chandragupta) for 500 elephants (304–303). Though Ptolemy took Coele-Syria (301), Seleucus secured Cilicia from Demetrius (296–295). Seleucus failed to reduce **Mithridates I of Pontus**, but got control of western Asia Minor on the defeat of Lysimachus (281).

280-261. Antiochus I Soter ("saviour") succeeded upon the murder of Seleucus. He fought and finally defeated the Galatians (279–275) by terrifying them with his elephants. In the **Damascene** (280–279) and **First Syrian** (276–272) Wars he lost, to Ptolemy II, Miletus, Phoenicia, and western Cilicia.

263-241. Eumenes I made himself virtually independent of Antiochus as ruler of Pergamum, where his uncle, Philetarus, had ruled as governor first for Lysimachus and then for the Seleucids.

261-246. Antiochus II Theos ("god"), son of Antiochus I, secured the support of Antigonus II and Rhodes against Egypt in the **Second Syrian War** (260–255). The succeeding peace restored to Antiochus: Ionia (including Miletus), Coele-Syria, and western Cilicia (255).

250-230. Diodotus I declared himself independent King of Bactria. In 248–247, Arsaces I of the nomad Parni established himself in the province of Parthia.

246-226. SELEUCUS II CALLINICUS ("gloriously victorious"), son of Antiochus II by his divorced wife, Laodice I, succeeded. Berenice II, daughter of Ptolemy II, whom Antiochus had married in 252, provoked the

246-241. Third Syrian War ("Laodicean War" or "War of Berenice") in favor of her infant son. Though she and her son were murdered in Antioch, her brother, Ptolemy III, invaded Asia and ultimately forced Seleucus to surrender the coasts of Syria and southern Asia Minor (241).

241-197. Attalus I, Soter ("saviour"), who succeeded his father's cousin, Eumenes I, as ruler of Pergamum, took advantage of Seleucus' difficulties to secure for himself western Asia Minor by crushing the Galatians near **Pergamum** (230), after which he took the title king and received the surname *Soter*.

237. Seleucus attacked **Antiochus Hierax** ("falcon"), a younger son of Laodice, whom Seleucus in 241 had recognized as ruler of Asia Minor. Hierax secured the aid of Mithridates II of Pontus and the Galatians. The Galatians crushed Seleucus at Ancyra (236).

c. 235. Arsaces II (Tiridates), second ruler of the Parni (246–c. 211), also seized the opportunity to conquer Parthia

and Hyrcania and found the **Parthian kingdom** (p. 83). He made peace with Diodotus II of Bactria (c. 230) and an expedition of Seleucus against him was ineffective. Arsaces likewise converted Armenia into an independent kingdom.

229-226. Attalus I of Pergamum drove Hierax out of Asia Minor (229–228), after which Seleucus drove him out of Syria (227) to Thrace, where he died (226).

226-223. Seleucus III Soter or Ceraunus ("thunderbolt"), son of Seleucus II, was murdered during a war with Attalus I (224–221).

223-187. ANTIOCHUS III, THE GREAT, brother of Seleucus III, regained from Attalus most of the territory lost since 241. He recovered the Mesopotamian provinces from the revolting governor, Molon (221). But in the

221-217. Fourth Syrian War, despite initial successes, he finally retained on the Syrian coast only Seleucia, the port of Antioch.

209-204. In a number of campaigns, Antiochus reduced the Parthian Arsaces III Priapatius to vassalship, made an alliance with Euthydemus, who had usurped the Bactrian throne of Diodotus II, and even secured the submission of the Indian rajah Sophagasenus. Thus he restored the Seleucid Kingdom to its former extent.

201-195. The Fifth Syrian War resulted from the treaty which Antiochus III had made with Philip V of Macedon in 203. The war was decided in 200 by Antiochus' victory of Panium. After several campaigns in Anatolia, Antiochus secured from Egypt most of Coele-Syria and southern Asia Minor (save Cyprus). Although Eumenes II Soter of Pergamum (197–159), son of Attalus I, induced Flamininus to order Antiochus out of Asia Minor, Antiochus did not heed, but confirmed his conquests by a peace with Egypt (195).

192-189. WAR WITH ROME. Antiochus' continued disregard of the Senate led to a war in which he was driven from Greece (191) and his fleet was defeated at Myonnesus (190). The Roman army entered Asia Minor and defeated Antiochus himself at Magnesia (190). In the peace (189), Antiochus paid a large indemnity, lost his fleet, and surrendered Asia Minor, which was divided between Rhodes and Pergamum. This defeat led to the complete breaking away of Armenia (under Artaxias) and of Bactria, where a succession of Greek rulers preserved Hellenism until the invasions of the Sacae (c. 150–125). An offshoot of the Bactrian

Kingdom flourished in the Punjab (c. 175–c. 40), and though its rulers adopted Buddhism (c. 150) it introduced Hellenistic art and ideas into India.

187-175. **Seleucus IV Philopater** ("loving his father") succeeded his father Antiochus, and during his reign the empire gradually recovered strength. Meanwhile Eumenes II of Pergamum fought against Prusias I of Bithynia (186) and Pharnaces I of Pontus (183–179).

175-163. **Antiochus IV Epiphanes** ("god manifest") succeeded upon the murder of his brother Seleucus. Though friendly to Rome, he was prevented by the Romans from concluding successfully his war against Egypt (171–168). The Romans also weakened Rhodes by making Delos a free port (167). Insurrection of the Jews under **Judas Maccabeus,** after Judaism had been declared illegal (168). The Jews attained religious freedom in 164 and, after a series of wars, established political independence in 142 (p. 30). Upon his death, Antiochus left as king his young son **Antiochus V Eupater** ("of a noble father"), under the regent Lysias (163–162).

162-150. **Demetrius I Soter** ("saviour"), son of Seleucus IV, returned from Rome to eject Antiochus V, but was slain in 150 by a pretender, **Alexander Balas** (150–145), who claimed to be the son of Antiochus IV and was supported by Attalus II Philadelphus ("loving his brother") of Pergamum (159–138) (who had succeeded his brother Eumenes II), by Ptolemy VI of Egypt, and by Rome. Ptolemy, however, soon invaded Syria in favor of Demetrius II, the son of Demetrius I, who slew Balas in 145.

145-139. **Demetrius II Nicator** ("conqueror") won several victories (140) over Mithridates I of Parthia, who had seized Media (c. 150) and Babylon (c. 141). Mithridates, however, captured Demetrius by treachery in 139. In the meantime, a son of Alexander Balas, Antiochus VI Epiphanes Dionysus ("god manifest"), had held Antioch from 145 to 142, when he was expelled by the mercenary leader Diodotus, who took the title of King Tryphon (142–139). He was expelled by a brother of Demetrius II.

139-127. **Antiochus VII Euergetes Eusebes Soter Sidetes** ("benefactor, pious, saviour") did much to restore the Seleucid power. However, after several victories over Phraates II of Parthia, he was finally defeated and killed at Ecbatana (127).

138-133. **Attalus III Philomater** ("loving his mother") **of Pergamum,** a son of Eumenes II, succeeded his uncle, Attalus II. In his will, he bequeathed his kingdom to Rome, apparently in order to protect his subjects from absorption by their neighbors. Rome had to suppress the pretender Aristonicus before it could make the Kingdom of Pergamum into the Province of Asia (129).

129-125. Demetrius II was sent back to Syria by Phraates II in 129 and was slain in 125 by a pretender with Egyptian support, Alexander Zabinas. Demetrius' son, **Seleucus V,** assumed the diadem but was put to death at once by his mother Cleopatra Thea

125-96. **Antiochus VIII Epiphanes Philomater Callinicus "Grypus"** ("god manifest, loving his mother, gloriously victorious, hook-nosed"), a younger son of Demetrius II, reigned with Cleopatra until her death (c. 120). The pretender, Alexander Zabinas, was killed in 123. In 117 Antiochus was forced into retirement by a half-brother, **Antiochus IX Philopater, "Cyzicenus"** ("loving his father, of Cyzicus"), son of Cleopatra and Antiochus VII. After an indecisive series of battles (113–112), they divided the realm in 111 and both reigned until Antiochus VIII was murdered in 96 by his favorite, Heracleon.

95-64. **Seleucus VI,** son of Antiochus VIII, defeated and killed Antiochus IX (95). The son of the latter, **Antiochus X,** defeated and killed Seleucus VI, but the latter's brother, Demetrius III, seized Damascus. Another son of Antiochus VIII, **Antiochus XI,** was defeated and killed, but his brother Philip I continued the war with Antiochus X. The latter was killed in 93 fighting the Parthians in Commagene. Demetrius III and Philip I engaged in civil war until Demetrius was captured by the Parthians in 88. **Antiochus XII,** another son of Antiochus VIII, seized Damascus, which he held until he was killed on an expedition against the Nabataeans in 84. An insurrection expelled Philip I from Antioch, and Tigranes of Armenia seized Syria and held it until he was defeated by Lucullus in 69. **Antiochus XIII,** son of Antiochus X, was installed at Antioch (68) and soon had to fight with Philip I, son of Philip I. The Arabian prince of Emesa slew Antiochus XIII by treachery in 67; Philip was unable to secure his rule. In 64 Pompey made Syria a Roman province.

6. PARTHIA

331-323. **Rule of Alexander the Great.**

312-282. Seleucus I founded the dynasty of the Seleucids, ruling over Babylonia and Syria; he built the city of Seleucia near Ctesiphon on the Tigris.

249-247. Arsaces I founded the Kingdom of Parthia, including at first only Parthia and Hyrcania, between the Seleucid Kingdom in the west and the Bactrian Kingdom in the east.

247-212. Arsaces II (Tiridates I), though defeated by Seleucus II (238), was able to establish the independence of Parthia.

212-171. Arsaces III withstood the attacks of Antiochus III the Great in 209; he was followed by Arsaces IV (Priapatius) and Arsaces V (Phraates I).

171-138. Mithridates I conquered Babylonia and Media from the Seleucids; later he added to his kingdom Elam, Persia, and parts of Bactria, thus founding the Parthian Empire. Ctesiphon-Seleucia became the capital.

138-124. Phraates II (138–127) defeated Antiochus VII in Media (129), and as a result the Seleucids were permanently excluded from the lands east of the Euphrates; but he died in battle fighting the Tochari (the *Scythians* or *Sacae* of the Greeks), a tribe driven forth from Central Asia by the Yue-chi. The kingdom was devastated and Artabanus I (127–124) fell likewise fighting against the Tochari.

124-88. M I T H R I D A T E S I I , T H E GREAT, defeated the Scythians and also Artavasdes, King of Armenia Major. In 92 he made a treaty with Rome.

88-70. Parthia suffered a collapse and was greatly reduced in territory by Tigranes I of Armenia.

70-57. Phraates III restored order, but was not strong enough to resist the Roman advance, led by Lucullus and Pompey.

57-37. Orodes I defeated Crassus at Carrhae (53) and regained Mesopotamia.

37-32. Phraates IV defeated Antony in 36, but could not prevent him from conquering Armenia in 34. After a period of dynastic disturbances

A.D. 51-77. Vologesus I, after a war with Rome, obtained recognition of his brother Tiridates as King of Armenia (63), thus establishing an Arsacid dynasty in that country. In Parthia itself the utmost confusion prevailed after 77, with two or more kings (all of them little known) ruling at the same time and constantly challenged by other claimants.

(*Cont. p.* 124.)

7. BACTRIA

328-323 B.C. **Bactria under the rule of Alexander.** A mutiny of Greek auxiliaries after Alexander's death was crushed at once by Perdiccas.

323-302. **Bactria under Perdiccas** (d. 321), Antipater (d. 319), Eumenes (d. 316), Antigonus (d. 301). In his wars against Antigonus, Seleucus I conquered the eastern provinces (311–302).

302-c. 250. Bactria under the Seleucids.

c. 250-c. 139. Diodotus, the satrap of Bactria, made himself an independent ruler and conquered Sogdiana.

He founded a dynasty that withstood the attacks of the Seleucids.

After the defeat of Antiochus III at Magnesia (190), Euthydemus and his son Demetrius began the conquest of the Indus Valley. But Eucratides made himself King of Bactria (c. 170) while Demetrius was founding a kingdom in the Punjab. About 150 the Tochari (*Scythians* or *Sacae*) occupied Sogdiana, and about 139 Bactria. The line of Eucratides maintained itself in Kabul until about 40 B.C., but most of the region was ruled by Scythian dynasties.

8. PTOLEMAIC EGYPT, TO THE ROMAN CONQUEST

305-283. PTOLEMY I SOTER ("saviour"), the son of Lagus (hence the "Lagid" house), had been governor of Egypt since 323 and king since 305. He had seized Coele-Syria in 301, and acquired from Demetrius, Pamphylia and Lycia

(296–295), and Caria and the island of Cos (286).

**285-246. PTOLEMY II PHILADEL-
PHUS** ("lover of his sister") adopted a Pharaonic practice by marrying his sister Arsinoe II (276), founder of the Museum at Alexandria. He explored the upper Nile and extended his power along the Red Sea and into northern Arabia (278) for commercial purposes.

280-272. In the **Damascene War** (280–279) and **First Syrian War** (276–272), he suffered initial defeat from Antiochus I and the revolt of his half-brother Magas in Cyrene. But he finally defeated both and secured Miletus, Phoenicia, and western Cilicia. He subsidized Pyrrhus against Antigonus (274), aided Athens and Sparta in the Chremonidean War (266–262), and incited Alexander II of Epirus to attack Macedon (264). He likewise incited Eumenes of Pergamum to revolt from Antiochus (262) and supported the seizure of Ephesus (262–259) by his own son, Ptolemy "the Son." These activities brought Antiochus II, Antigonus II, and Rhodes together to wage

260-255. The **Second Syrian War** (260–255), in which Antigonus defeated Ptolemy in the **battle of Cos** (258 or 256). Though by the resulting peace he lost Cilicia and western Pamphylia (255), he later recovered the Cyclades (250) and also Cyrene (c. 248), which had become independent in 258.

246-221. Ptolemy III Euergetes ("benefactor") supported his sister Berenice II in the **Third Syrian War** (246–241) and acquired the coasts of Syria and southern Asia Minor, as well as some Aegean ports, including Ephesus. But he lost the Cyclades to Antigonus through the **battle of Andros** (245). Height of the Ptolemaic power.

221-203. Ptolemy IV Philopater ("loving his father") was a weak monarch, dominated by his minister, Sosibius. In the **Fourth Syrian War** (221–217) he at first lost much of the Syrian coast to Antiochus III, but the victory of **Raphia** (217) brought the recovery of all save the port of Seleucia.

203-181. Ptolemy V Epiphanes ("god manifest"), a young boy, succeeded his father. While the Egyptian natives revolted in the Delta (201–200) Antiochus III attacked him in

201-195. The **Fifth Syrian War**, as a result of which Ptolemy retained only Cyprus of his Asiatic possessions. When

he came of age (195), he succeeded in suppressing the native revolts.

181-145. Ptolemy VI Philomater ("loving his mother") followed Ptolemy V under the regency of his mother, Cleopatra I. In consequence of Ptolemy's cowardice during the war with Antiochus (171–168), the people of Alexandria forced him to associate his brother, **Ptolemy VII**, in the rule. Rome prevented Antiochus from capturing Alexandria (168). When Ptolemy VI was expelled by his brother (164), the Roman Senate restored him and gave Cyrene and Cyprus to Ptolemy VII, who, however, secured only Cyrene (163). Ptolemy VI expelled Demetrius I from Syria (152–151) and supported Demetrius II against Alexander Balas (147–145), but was slain in the war.

145-116. Ptolemy VII Euergetes II ("benefactor") or Physcon ("fat-bellied") reunited the empire after his brother's death and restored order. At his death, he left Cyrene separately to his son Apion, who willed it to Rome in 96, though it was not actually annexed until 75. Another son, Ptolemy IX, received Cyprus, which was ultimately bequeathed to Rome and annexed in 58.

116-47. Ptolemy VIII Soter II ("saviour") or Lathyrus, son of Ptolemy VII, was eventually expelled by his brother **Ptolemy IX Alexander I** (108–88). The people of Alexandria, however, slew Ptolemy IX and restored Ptolemy VIII (88–80). **Ptolemy X Alexander II**, son of Ptolemy IX, succeeded but was at once slain by the people of Alexandria (80), who set up an illegitimate son of Ptolemy VIII, **Ptolemy XI Auletes** ("flute-player") or **Neos** ("new") **Dionysos**. Though expelled in 58, he bribed the "first triumvirate" (p. 96) to send Gabinus to restore him (55). On his death in 51, he left his throne jointly to his children, **Cleopatra VII** and **Ptolemy XII** (51–47). When Ptolemy expelled his sister, Caesar forced her restoration (48) and, since Ptolemy died during the fighting about Alexandria (48–47), Caesar joined with Cleopatra a younger brother, **Ptolemy XIII** (47–44), whom Cleopatra murdered on Caesar's death (44).

47-30. Cleopatra VII sought to restore the Ptolemaic Empire by winning to her support Caesar and later Antony (41), with whom she sought to establish a Hellenistic monarchy (36). Upon Antony's suicide after Actium (31), she sought to fascinate the young Octavian, but failed and committed suicide rather than adorn his triumph (30). This brought to an end the last of the Hellenistic monarchies.

E. ROME, THE MIDDLE AND LATER REPUBLIC

1. THE PUNIC AND MACEDONIAN WARS

During the 3d and 2d centuries B.C. Rome's internal history was marked by the consolidation of the rule of the patricio-plebeian aristocracy. The extension of Rome's external relations and the consequent complexity of her internal problems raised questions impossible of settlement in the unwieldy and uninformed *comitia*, which came more and more to surrender the initiative in government to the Senate, composed as it was of ex-magistrates, urban, military, and provincial, who had the necessary background and experience. They, in their turn, had come to regard government and office as a prerogative of themselves and their children. This distinction was furthered by the increased opportunities for wealth opened to the ruling group through conquest and provincial government. Since custom, confirmed by a *lex Claudia* of 218, forced senators to invest chiefly in land, they built up large estates, partly by renting public land, which through long tenure they came to regard as their own, and partly by acquiring the holdings of poorer farmers. The poorer farmers, in turn, subjected to the devastations of the Hannibalic Wars, and to the demands of long-term military service abroad, found it difficult to exist, and tended either to emigrate, remain in the army, or congregate as an idle mob in Rome. The political, social, and economic problems thus raised finally caused the ruin of the senatorial republic by the Gracchan troubles.

Rome's position in Italy became increasingly strong during these centuries. In consequence, the senatorial class began to act with increasing arbitrariness toward Rome's Italian allies and to impose on them the burdens of conquest while reserving the rewards for themselves or using them as sops to the Roman citizens. The citizens, who found that citizenship paid in privilege, in some share in the public land, in free entertainment at Rome, eventually in a government-controlled food supply, and probably in the indirect benefits of bribery and corruption, became unwilling to extend the franchise. The discontent of the Italians found ultimate expression in the Social War, which won for them Roman citizenship.

In the Mediterranean, Rome, without really so desiring, was forced to extend her sway, *imperium*, more and more widely. The Senate, like such landed aristocracies as Sparta or the English Tories, was not imperialistic. Nor, on the whole, was the *populus*. But the fear of attack from strong powers led Rome to attack such as might threaten her, and experiments in allowing her rivals a feeble and divided independence (*diuide et impera*, divide and rule) proved unsatisfactory. Either her creations quarreled among themselves and forced her to intervene, or they became the willing or unwilling prey of stronger powers. Hence Rome was forced into annexation. But conquest led ultimately to the corruption of both Senate and people, to the creation of a financial group, the *equites*, interested in imperialism, and to ~pportunities for self-aggrandizement on the part of generals and governors. In consequence, the discontented peoples of Asia supported Mithridates, the equestrian class became a possible rival to the Senate, and the way was opened for the domination of the state by military commanders.

282-272. WAR WITH PYRRHUS arose from an attack by the Tarentines on Thurii and their destruction of a Roman fleet which entered the harbor in violation of a treaty forbidding Roman warships from sailing east of the western promontory of the Gulf of Tarentum. Tarentum called in **Pyrrhus of Epirus** (p. 79). In 280, with an army of 25,000 men and 20 elephants, he won a hard-fought victory over the Romans at **Heraclea.** Though the Bruttians, Lucanians, and Samnites then joined Pyrrhus, the Senate, instigated by Ap. Claudius, the blind ex-censor, rejected the peace offers of Pyrrhus' ambassador Cineas. In 279 Pyrrhus won his second victory at **Ausculum,** but with losses so great that he exclaimed, "Another such victory and we are lost" (a "Pyrrhic victory"). Pyrrhus then crossed to Sicily. Rome rejected peace with Pyrrhus and made one with his enemy, Carthage. Pyrrhus returned to Italy after two years but was defeated at **Beneventum**

in 275 and returned to Greece. His general, Milo, then surrendered Tarentum to the Romans (272), who destroyed its military resources, but left it its own municipal administration. Rome rounded out her subjugation of Italy by the recapture in 270 of Rhegium from the Mamertines and the reduction of the Bruttians, Lucanians, Calabrians, and Samnites.

264-241. THE FIRST PUNIC WAR arose from the fact that certain of the Campanian mercenaries, or Mamertines who were holding Messana against Hiero II of Syracuse (p. 78), appealed to Rome while others appealed to Carthage. The Roman assembly, though the Senate hesitated, sent a fleet and army which found the Carthaginians already in possession. The Romans drove them out and were in turn besieged by the Carthaginians. In 264 the consul Ap. Claudius Pulcher relieved them, but failed to take Syracuse. During the following year two Roman armies invaded Sicily and Hiero shifted to a Roman alliance.

262. The Romans defeated the Carthaginian general Hanno and took Agrigentum (Acragas).

260. After losing the consul Cn. Cornelius Scipio with 17 ships off the Lipara Islands, the Romans under C. Duilius won the **naval victory of Mylae,** west of Messana.

257. The Romans sent 330 ships under the consuls M. Atilius Regulus and L. Manlius Vuiso to carry troops from Sicily and effect a landing in Africa. This fleet defeated the Carthaginians off the south coast of Sicily at Ecnomus (256) and landed just east of Carthage. Regulus, left with half the troops, offered such stringent terms that Carthage continued her resistance under the leadership of the Spartan mercenary Xanthippus.

255. Xanthippus captured Regulus and part of his army. The Romans sent a fleet which took off the remainder, but was lost in a storm, as happened again two years later.

254. Rome seized Panormus and, in 251, defeated the new Carthaginian general, **Hasdrubal,** son of Hanno. On the advice, traditionally, of Regulus, who had been sent to negotiate an exchange of prisoners with the Carthaginians, they refused to do so and Regulus returned to die in Carthage.

249. The consul Claudius Pulcher, after throwing the sacred chickens overboard because they refused to give a good omen by eating grain, lost his fleet at **Drepana.** The Romans were unable to dislodge the Carthaginian **Hamilcar Barcas** ("lightning") from the strong promontory of Eryx, whence his ships harried their coasts.

241. At the Aegates Islands, off Lilybaeum, the Romans annihilated the Carthaginian fleet. Carthage received peace on condition of the surrender of Sicily and the payment of 3200 talents in ten years. Rome left eastern Sicily to Hiero of Syracuse but undertook to govern the remainder herself as her **first province,** regularly constituted in 227.

241-217. Some time during this period the *comitia centuriata* suffered a radical reform, probably because the centuries had lost their military significance. The centuries of *equites* lost the right of first vote, which was hereafter determined by lot among the centuries of the first class. The number of centuries was increased to harmonize in some way with the tribal divisions and divided into seniors and juniors. Perhaps there was one century each of seniors (over 46) and juniors from each of the five classes in each of the 35 tribes, i.e. $2 \times 5 \times 35 = 350$, $+ 18$ of knights and 5 of propertyless persons $= 373$. Though the reform passed for democratic, its basis remained one of property and age, since the first class (wealthy) probably had a proportion of centuries (almost one fifth) in excess of its proportion of population and since the elders, naturally fewer than the younger, had nearly half of the centuries. At the same time (241) the final two tribes were added, making a total of 35. Thereafter new citizens were enrolled in the existing tribes, so that these lost their geographical significance.

238. Rome seized Sardinia, rich in minerals, during a revolt of the mercenaries in Carthage. It later (227) formed a province with Corsica.

235. The first recorded closing of the temple of Janus since its foundation by Numa indicated that Rome was at peace with all nations.

229-228. The first Illyrian War. Rome sent a fleet of 200 vessels to suppress the pirates of Queen Teuta. The grateful Hellenes admitted the Romans to the Isthmian Games and the Eleusinian Mysteries and thus recognized her as a civilized power. In a second war (219), Rome defeated Teuta's successor, Scerdilaidas.

225-222. Large hordes of Celts moved from the Po Valley to Etruria. The Romans surrounded and slew a considerable body at **Telamon** (225) and gradually reduced the Insubres, around Milan. In the **battle of Clastidium** (222) M. Claudius Marcellus slew a Gallic chief in single combat. The Romans founded the fortress colonies of Placentia, Cremona, and Mutina, and extended the *Via Flaminia* from Spoletum to Ariminum.

218. A **lex Claudia** forbade senators to own a ship of more than 300 *amphorae* (225 bushels), only enough to care for their farm produce; they were thus forced to invest in land rather than in industry or commerce.

218-201. THE SECOND PUNIC WAR arose from Rome's jealousy of Carthaginian expansion in Spain, where Hamilcar Barcas (236-228) and, after his death, his son-in-law Hasdrubal (228-221) had established themselves. Rome made Carthage promise not to attack Saguntum or Emporiae, Greek foundations south of the Ebro, or to cross that river. After the assassination of Hasdrubal, his twenty-five-year-old successor **Hannibal** destroyed Saguntum in 219 (perhaps without the full support of his home government), the conservative element in which was jealous of the power and independence of the Barcids. Carthage, however, refused to disown him.

218. Hannibal executed a daring land march through southern France and by an undetermined Alpine pass advanced into the Po Valley. The Roman consul **P. Cornelius Scipio** reached Marseilles with his fleet too late to stop Hannibal. He therefore sent his brother Cnaeus with most of the fleet to Spain and returned himself to meet Hannibal, who had perhaps 26,000 men and a few elephants, at the **Ticinus**, a branch of the Po. He was defeated, as was his colleague soon after at the **battle of the Trebia**, another branch of the Po. As the Romans took refuge in Placentia and Cremona, the Gauls rallied to Hannibal.

217. Hannibal crossed the **Apennines** west of two new Roman armies posted at Ariminum and Arretium. The consul C. Flaminius followed him from the latter place and was led into an ambush and annihilated at **Lake Trasimene.** The Romans, terrified, appointed **Quintus Fabius Maximus** dictator. Hannibal moved east again to the Adriatic and then south, in hopes of a general Italian rising. The cities, however, refused to receive him and Fabius, without joining battle (hence his title *Cunctator*), harried his army. The Romans were dissatisfied with this policy.

216. The consuls L. Aemilius Paullus (conservative) and C. Terentius Varro (popular) led an army of 86,000 Romans and Italians against Hannibal. Consuls, when together, now commanded on alternate days, and Varro, on his day, unwisely attacked Hannibal at **Cannae,** in Apulia. The Romans, including Paullus, were practically annihilated, though Varro escaped. When, during the same year, a legion was destroyed in Cisalpine Gaul, a rift appeared in the allegiance of Italy to Rome. Capua deserted, along with the Samnites, Lucanians, and other peoples of southern Italy. The Romans checked all public grief, refused Hannibal's terms, and sent out an army under M. Claudius Marcellus. Carthage made alliances with Philip V of Macedon, and Hieronymus, grandson of the lately deceased (217) Hiero of Syracuse. Hannibal wintered at Capua.

215. Marcellus, now pro-consul, defeated Hannibal at **Nola** and forced him into Apulia. The government at Carthage gave Hannibal almost no support and he was unable to receive aid from his brother Hasdrubal in Spain.

218-211. Publius Scipio had rejoined his brother Cnaeus in Spain and between them, with varying fortune, they kept Hasdrubal busy and stirred up Syphax, King of western Numidia, against Carthage.

215-205. By using a few troops for the **First Macedonian War** (p. 80), the Romans prevented the irresolute Philip from helping Hannibal. In 211 they organized a Greek alliance, under the lead of the Aetolians (**Treaty of Naupactus**) including even Thracians, Illyrians, and Pergamum, against him. After her Greek allies quit in 206, Rome was forced to make the disadvantageous **Peace of Phoenice.**

214-210. Marcellus carried the war into Sicily, where he defeated a Carthaginian army and sacked Leontini. Though Hieronymus had been murdered, the Syracusans renewed their alliance with Carthage (213), but, despite the ingenious defensive machinery devised by Archimedes, **Marcellus reduced Syracuse in** 211. The rest of Sicily quickly fell again under Roman control.

212. Hannibal seized **Tarentum,** save for the citadel. He compelled the Romans to raise the siege of Capua, defeated two armies, but retired again to Tarentum. Both Scipios were slain in Spain by the Carthaginians, who drove the Romans to the Ebro.

211. Hannibal returned to relieve Capua. The Romans this time refused to abandon the siege, so he marched to within a mile of Rome, but as they did not falter, he again had to retire. Capua surrendered to Rome and was deprived of all self-government. As Hannibal seemed unable to weaken Rome or reduce the citadel of Tarentum, his prestige sank and his Italian allies went back to Rome.

210. P. Cornelius Scipio, son of the late general, was sent to Spain with proconsular powers, though only 25 and a mere exaedile. In Sicily, the Romans reduced Agrigentum.

209. Scipio captured New Carthage in Spain. Marcellus defeated Hannibal and Fabius reduced Tarentum. In the following year, Hasdrubal evaded Scipio and reached the Po Valley.

207. In the battle of the Metaurus River (Sena Gallica), the consul M. Livius Salinator, supported by his colleague C. Claudius Nero, who had made forced marches from the south, where he was holding Hannibal in check, defeated and slew Hasdrubal. Hannibal withdrew to Bruttium.

206. Scipio drove the Carthaginians out of Spain and made a secret treaty with their ally Massinissa, King (in 208) of eastern Numidia. He returned to Italy and was elected consul under age, for 205.

204. Scipio took a force to Africa and, with Massinissa's help, defeated the Carthaginians and Syphax (203). Carthage was forced to recall Hannibal, who attempted in vain to negotiate.

202. In the battle of Zama, Scipio annihilated the Carthaginian army, though Hannibal escaped.

201. Carthage accepted Rome's terms: surrender of Spain and all other Mediterranean islands; transfer of the kingdom of Syphax to Massinissa; payment of 200 talents a year for 50 years; destruction of all except ten warships; promise not to make war without Rome's permission. Scipio, now entitled *Africanus*, celebrated a splendid triumph. The unfaithful Italian allies were in part forced to cede land, in part deprived of independence. Rome founded many colonies in southern Italy.

205-178. Spain was divided into two provinces (197), Hither Spain (*Hispania Citerior*) in the Ebro Valley, and Farther Spain (*Hispania Ulterior*) in the south around Gibraltar and the Guadalquivir River. Constant warfare, however, was necessary to subdue the Lusitanians.

200-191. The resubjugation of the Po Valley required considerable effort. Rome founded colonies and built the *Via Aemilia* as a continuation of the *Via Flaminia* from Ariminum to Placentia.

The newly acquired overseas territories could not be governed either from Rome or as had been just possible in Sicily, by creating new praetors. This last method was tried in Spain, but it became more economical to retain the governors there for two years so that their *imperia* were "prorogued" for another year. The device of extending an *imperium* without renewing the corresponding magistracy was apparently first employed to keep the experienced commander Philo in command against Naples. As the number of provinces grew, this custom was regularly applied to the consuls and praetors, who came to expect a profitable year (for governorships were reduced to this) in a province to recoup themselves for the heavy expenses entailed in securing election (bribery) or incident to the tenure of office (games, etc.). A further effect of the transmarine provinces was that it became necessary to maintain a standing army. In the second and first centuries B.C. the soldier not only could not return to his farm for harvest or the winter — that had long been impossible — but he could not look for a discharge at the end of a year of service, for the government could not afford to send new armies each year across the sea. Though the fiction of annual re-enlistment and the requirement of a property qualification were maintained, the soldiers became in fact professional and served for 20 years or more. They could not then return to farms which would have passed into other hands or fallen into decay, and so they had either to be settled in colonies or allowed to congregate in Rome. As they looked to their commander for rewards in war and protection of their interests at home, they shifted their loyalty, and oath (*sacramentum*), from the state to him. It is therefore extraordinary that for nearly a century the corporate class consciousness of the *nobiles* was sufficient to prevent disloyalty to the senatorial government.

200-197. Rome was drawn into the SECOND MACEDONIAN WAR by an appeal from Pergamum, Rhodes, and Athens, which were harried by Philip and Antiochus III of Syria. The Senate, fearful of Philip's growing power, frightened an unwilling *comitia centuriata* into declaring war by visions of a renewed invasion of Italy. T. Quinctius Flamininus, supported by both the Aetolian and Achaean Leagues, finally (197) defeated Philip at **Cynoscephalae** in Thessaly and forced him to make peace (196) on the following terms: surrender of Greece; payment of 1000 talents in 10 years; reduction of his forces to 5000 men and 5 ships; promise not to declare war without permission of Rome. At the ensuing Isthmian Games, Flamininus proclaimed the independence of the Greek cities. Rome sought to balance the Achaean League by curtailing but not destroying the power of King Nabis of Sparta.

192-189. THE SYRIAN WAR (p. 81). Antiochus III, invited by the Aetolians, invaded Greece, but the consul M. Acilius Glabrio landed in Epirus, moved into Thessaly and, with M. Porcius Cato, repeated the maneuver of Xerxes at Thermopylae to rout Antiochus (191).

190. The Roman fleet, helped by the Rhodians, won two victories. The Roman army, under L. **Cornelius Scipio** (later *Asiaticus*) and his brother Scipio Africanus, crossed the Hellespont and defeated Antiochus in the **battle of Magnesia,** near Smyrna. Antiochus was obliged to make peace on the following terms: surrender of all European and Asiatic possessions as far as the Taurus Mountains; payment of 15,000 talents in 12 years; surrender of Hannibal, who had fled from his enemies at Carthage (195). Though Hannibal escaped, he finally poisoned himself (183) at the court of Prusias I of Bithynia, who was about to betray him. Rome divided the Anatolian territory of Antiochus between Pergamum and Rhodes and aided Eumenes II of Pergamum against the Galatians (189). In Greece, Rome subjected the Aetolians, but left the other cities free. Philip was not rewarded as he had hoped.

171-168. THE THIRD MACEDONIAN WAR was waged against Rome by Perseus, the successor of Philip V. After several unsuccessful campaigns, the Romans sent L. Aemilius Paullus.

168. Battle of Pydna. Paullus utterly defeated Perseus and brought him back in his triumphal procession. So much booty accrued from his victory that Roman citizens were thereafter relieved of direct taxation, the *tributum*. Macedonia was broken up into four wholly distinct confederacies. Illyria was reduced to three

tributary confederacies, and Epirus was devastated. From the Achaean cities 1000 of the chief citizens were taken as hostages and kept in Italy for 16 years. Rome likewise dictated to Eumenes of Pergamum, to Rhodes and to Antiochus IV, who was prevented by the ambassador C. Popilius Laenas from making war on the Ptolemies of Egypt.

153. On account of an uprising in Spain, the consuls entered office on Jan. 1 instead of Mar. 15. Thus Jan. 1 became established as the beginning of the civil year.

151. A law forbidding re-election to the consulship superseded an earlier one of 342 which had imposed a ten-year interval between two tenures. It lasted, with some exceptions, until Sulla revived the older law. Possibly the same law raised the minimum ages for the tenure of all magistracies from those established by a *lex annalis* of the tribune Villius (180) to those of Cicero's time: quaestorship after the thirtieth year, aedileship after the thirty-sixth, praetorship after the thirty-ninth, and consulship after the forty-second.

149. The tribune L. Calpurnius Piso enacted a *lex Calpurnia* which set up a permanent commission to hear the suits of provincials to recover from governors money unjustly collected (*quaestio de rebus repetundis*). This commission differed from previous specially created boards of investigation (*quaestiones*) or panels of special judges (*reciperatores* or *iudices*) in being made always available (*perpetua*) without special legislation. Like its predecessors, the membership for different cases was drawn by lot from a panel of senators and the board met under the presidency of a praetor. The new court soon became an instrument whereby the Senate could discipline governors. Decisions were motivated not by justice but by class selfishness. It is probable that further courts of this type were established before the revision of the system of Sulla.

149-146. THE THIRD PUNIC WAR arose from alarm among conservative Romans over Carthage's revival, typified in the phrase with which Cato expressed his opinion on any question which was discussed in the Senate: *ceterum censeo Carthaginem esse delendam* ("but I declare that Carthage must be destroyed"). The occasion was an attack by Carthage (150) on Rome's ally, the now aged Massinissa. When a Roman army landed in Africa, the Carthaginians offered submission, but refused to vacate the city. With almost no resources they withstood a siege until **Scipio Aemilianus** captured and destroyed Carthage (146). The Romans organized a small area around Carthage as the Province of Africa, but left the rest to the sons of Massinissa (d. 149).

149-148. THE FOURTH MACEDONIAN WAR. A pretended son of Perseus, Andriscus, who called himself Philip, provoked the war, but was defeated by Q. Caecilius Metellus. In 146 Macedonia became a Roman province.

146. When the 300 surviving hostages returned to Achaea, the Achaeans made war on Sparta. Their leaders, Critolaus and Diaeus, were defeated by Metellus and L. Mummius. The latter took Corinth, sent its art treasures to Rome, sold its inhabitants into slavery, and burned the city (at the order of the Roman Senate). The territory of Corinth passed in part to Sicyon, in part became Roman public land. The remaining Greek cities retained a certain measure of autonomy under the governor of Macedonia, though they paid tribute. Not until later (127) did they become organized as the Province of Achaea.

143-133. Continuous unrest in Spain grew into a **war in Lusitania,** led by Viriathus (assassinated 139, thanks to Roman bribery), and in northern Spain, where the city of Numantia took the lead. Numantia fell in 133 and all Spain, except the northwestern part, passed under Roman domination.

135-132. The First Servile War broke out when the ill-treated slaves of the large Sicilian estates revolted under the Syrian Eunus, who called himself King Antiochus. Eunus held Henna and Tauromenium against Roman armies, but was finally captured and his supporters brutally executed.

Rome now possessed **eight provinces:** Sicilia (241), Sardinia (238) with Corsica (c. 230?), Hispania Citerior (205), Hispania Ulterior (205), Gallia Cisalpina (191?), Illyricum (168), Africa (146), Macedonia and Achaea (146). The first four were at first governed by praetors and then, as these became useful at Rome for the new standing courts and as the system of proroguing *imperia* became regular, they were governed by pro-praetors (in the less important or "praetorian" provinces) or proconsuls (in the more important or "consular"). After the middle of the 2d century, consuls and praetors less frequently took command of a province or army while in office, though this was probably never forbidden by law. Wars were conducted either by the governors or by commanders specially endowed with an *imperium* and ranking usually as pro-consuls, even though they had not held the consulship.

Provinces were generally organized by their conqueror with the aid of a commission of ten senators sent out by Rome. The charter of organization was called a *lex data,* as it was authorized in advance by the *comitia* but not brought before it (*rogata*). Usually the Senate rather than the *comitia* confirmed such arrangements. The Romans tended to leave undisturbed existing arrangements where they could; e.g. the charter of Sicily incorporated the usages of Hiero of Syracuse, the *lex Hieronica.* Moreover, organized cities were left to themselves for purposes of local government. The Roman governor was chiefly concerned with warfare and general police duties, with settlement of disputes between cities, of important native trials, of all cases involving Roman citizens, and with the public land and tax-collections. Since, however, Rome had no elaborate administrative organization, the actual management of such lands (when not distributed to Roman citizens) and the collection of taxes were auctioned off at Rome (but not the taxes of Sicily), as were contracts for public works, every fifth year by the censors to companies of private capitalists (*publicani*), whose members came to be called *equites* because they had the census requisite for membership in the centuries of knights. (The actual cavalry, composed usually of sons of senators and distinguished by the grant from the state of a horse, the *equus publicus*, had been abolished by Scipio Aemilianus at the siege of Numantia.) The evils of the publican system lay not so much in extortionate collections, since the rates were laid down in the contract, as in the fact that on the one hand, a bad year might endanger the revenues, except in Sicily, and lead to undue hardship in the collection and that on the other the municipalities, who were responsible to the *publicani* for the payments, might fall into arrears and have to borrow, which they did from the same *publicani* (acting as bankers, *negotiatores*) at very high rates. Once behindhand, they found it hard to get out of debt. The rates on such loans were in time laid down by law, but the governor, who was often a silent partner in the company (a senator could openly invest only in land), would connive at illegal practices, especially since for a time after the Gracchi, and again after 70 he would be likely to be called to account for his own administration before a court imposed of *equites*.

Roman literature began with the production in 241 of a translation of a Greek play by Livius Andronicus, who had been captured at Tarentum in 272. The most important early writers, all strongly under Greek influence, were: for verse, **Naevius** (269-199), who wrote plays and an epic on the First Punic War (*Bellum Punicum*); **Plautus** (254-184), writer of comedies; **Ennius**, who dabbled in many fields and produced in quantitative (Greek) dactylic hexameters (instead of the old, native, accentual "Saturnians") an epic on all Roman history, the *Annales*; **Pacuvius** (220-130), a tragedian; Caecilius (d. 166) and **Terence** (190-159), authors of comedy; and **Lucilius** (180-103), the "inventor" of satire; for prose, a number of historians who wrote in Greek, like **Fabius Pictor** (c. 200), on the Second Punic War, and **Polybius**; **Cato** (234-149), "founder" of Latin prose with his *Origines* (Italian history) and his work on agriculture. Despite the conservative opposition, Greek rhetoric and philosophy were studied by the liberals who gathered about Scipio Aemilianus, whose "Scipionic circle" included Polybius, Terence, Laelius, and the Stoic Panaetius of Rhodes.

2. DOMESTIC STRIFE AND EASTERN CONQUEST

133. Ti. **Sempronius Gracchus,** a noble, was elected tribune on a platform of social reform. Traditionally his motive was to stop the spread of great estates (*latifundia*) at the expense of the small peasants, but since this tendency was restricted to Etruria and Campania, he was more probably motivated by the problem of the proletariat in Rome. He proposed **an agrarian law** (perhaps only a re-enactment of a law of 367) limiting holdings of public land to 500 iugera (312 acres) per person, with an additional 250 for each of two sons. This measure hurt both the great nobles and certain Italian cities. The Senate persuaded a tribune, M. Octavius, to veto the measure, but Gracchus violated custom and had the assembly depose Octavius; the bill was then passed. A commission of three (Tiberius Gracchus, his brother Gaius, and his father-in-law Ap. Claudius) was appointed to recover land held in violation of this law and distribute it in inalienable lots of 30 iugera. To obtain funds for the new settlers Gracchus again violated custom, which left provincial affairs to the Senate, and proposed that the people accept Attalus' legacy of the Kingdom of Pergamum; probably this measure was not passed. Again contrary to custom, Tiberius stood for a second tribunate, on an even more radical program. The *optimates* (reactionary party of the nobles, contrasted with the democratic *populares*), led by **P. Cornelius Scipio Nasica,** murdered him and 300 of his followers during the election, and afterwards the Senate had more of his partisans executed as public enemies without the right of appeal.

133-129. Apparently the commission carried out in part the redistribution of the public land. In 129, Scipio Aemilianus, who had married a sister to Tiberius and, espousing a middle course, perhaps favored some concession to the increasing bitterness of the Italians, was found dead with suspicions of murder.

129. After the defeat of the pretender Aristonicus, Pergamum became the **Province of Asia.**

125. The Senate balked the attempt of the democratic consul **M. Fulvius Flaccus** to extend the franchise to all Italians and sent him to Liguria, where, by helping Marseilles against the Gauls, he began the conquest of southern Gaul. The **revolt of Fregellae,** a town which despaired of peaceful means, was ruthlessly suppressed. In 123 the **Balearic Islands** were conquered and in 121 southern Gaul became the province of **Gallia Narbonensis,** so-called from the newly established colony of Narbo Martius (Narbonne).

123. **Gaius Gracchus,** the more forceful brother of Tiberius, became tribune. To the motive of social reform was added that of revenge, and in this and the following year, when he secured a second tribunate, he put through a far more extreme program than Tiberius had envisaged. The precise order and interrelation of his measures is uncertain, but the most important were the following: by a *lex iudiciaria* (probably the surviving *lex Acilia repetundarum*) he transferred membership in the court on extortion (*quaestio de rebus repetundis*, and any others that existed) from senators to equestrians. He also passed a law reorganizing the Province of Asia, and particularly changing the tax rate into a tithe on produce, as in Sicily. The collection was to be auctioned off to the *publicani*, as heretofore. The two measures were probably intended to relieve the provincials, but they only served to separate the equestrians from the Senate; the former were now able to avenge themselves on a governor who sought to check their rapacity or divert the profits to his own account.

In behalf of the proletariat Gaius passed three measures: (1) a revival of his brother's **land law**; (2) the foundation of **three commercial colonies** (Capua, Tarentum, and Carthage) to take care of veterans and Oriental freedmen, who comprised the majority of the Roman proletariat and who, it was recognized, would not make good farmers; (3) **a law obliging the government to provide grain at a fair price** (probably not below the average market level) to protect the poor against famine and speculation. The transmarine colonies failed because the proletarians preferred the pleasures of Rome to life in remote provinces. The state control of the grain supply became a means whereby demagogues could win popular support (by reducing the price and by increasing the number of eligible beneficiaries). Less important bills mitigated the conditions of military service and reaffirmed the laws against execution without appeal to the people. Finally, Gracchus planned to extend the full franchise to Latin cities and to grant Latin rights to all other Italians. This measure was naturally unpopular with the Roman *populus*, now fully conscious of the advantages of citizenship. The Senate took advantage of Gracchus' absence in Africa to undermine his influence, and he was defeated in the election for his third tribunate. When a riot ensued over the repeal of his colonization bill, the Senate invoked a right based on recent custom and of dubious validity, to declare a state of emergency and to call upon the consuls and other magistrates to see to it, even by use of force, that the state suffered no harm (*senatus consultum ultimum: ut consules . . . opera dent ne quid res publica detrimenti capiat*). This was a substitute for the dictatorship, the last effective use of which had been made in 216. In the ensuing struggles, Gaius Gracchus and many of his supporters were slain.

121-111. A series of measures, ending with the *lex agraria* of 111, recognized the failure of the land distributions by discontinuing them, by relieving the lots of rent and by making them alienable. After various experiments, the courts also were completely restored to the control of the Senate.

111-105. The Jugurthine War resulted from the usurpation of the African Kingdom of Massinissa's descendants by King Micipsa's nephew, **Jugurtha**. The latter murdered one rival, bribed a senatorial commission to support his claim, and captured Cirta (Constantine), capital of the surviving son of the king. The death of some Italians at Cirta led Rome to declare war, but Jugurtha again bought peace. A second murder led to hostilities, waged with varying success by Q. Caecilius Metellus.

107. Gaius Marius, a self-made man and legionary commander (*legatus*) of Metellus, appealed to the Roman people over the head of a hostile Senate and secured the consulship, with command in the war. Since the Senate refused to grant him an army, he called for volunteers and took men without the requisite property qualification. There resulted a thorough **reform of the military system,** carried through by P. Rutilius Rufus in 105: for the manipular system with its three ranks was substituted a division of the legion (6000 men, gradually sinking to about 4500 during the first century) into 10 cohorts, each composed of three maniples; the old military tribunes lost their importance and the command was held by a delegate of the general (*legatus*); the backbone of the legion became the centurions (commanders of the maniples); to each legion was attached an equal number of auxiliary troops, levied from the subject peoples and usually organized in their own fashion; about 300 professional cavalry replaced the old noble *equites*, abolished by Scipio Aemilianus; from the time of Scipio the general had also a special bodyguard (called from his headquarters *praetorium*), the *cohors praetoriana* or praetorian guard.

107-105. Marius' aristocratic quaestor, **L. Cornelius Sulla,** secured the surrender of Jugurtha by the latter's ally and father-in-law, Bocchus, King of Mauretania. Marius triumphed in 105, Jugurtha died in prison, and his kingdom was divided between Bocchus and a grandson of Massinissa.

105. THE CIMBRI, a German (or Celtic) people originally located east of the Rhine, who in 113 had moved into the Alpine regions and across the Rhone, ravaged Gaul and defeated two Roman armies at Arausio, on the Rhone.

Marius was elected consul for the second time, and then continuously for four more annual terms (contrary to the law of 151).

The Cimbri, defeated in Spain and again in northern France by native tribes, joined with the Germanic Teutones and other peoples. Most of the Cimbri then moved on Italy, while the Teutones, some Cimbri, and others advanced into southern Gaul to approach Italy from the west.

104. By a *lex Domitia* the pontiffs and augurs were made elective, but by a minority (17) of the 35 tribes, chosen by lot so that the gods might exercise their influence. This law was repealed by Sulla but revived by Caesar in 63 to secure his election as chief priest (*pontifex maximus*).

103-99. A **Second Servile War** in Sicily, under Tryphon and Athenion, was suppressed with difficulty by the consul, M. Aquillius.

102. Marius, having deflected the invading barbarians from the Little St. Bernhard Pass and having followed them to Aquae Sextae (Aix in Provence), annihilated them there. He then returned to the support of Catulus in northern Italy, which had been invaded by the main body of Cimbri coming over the Brenner Pass.

101. **Marius and Catulus** defeated the Cimbri at **Vercellae** (Campi Raudii). Marius became the national hero.

100. Marius, consul for the sixth time, but despised by the Senate, turned to the demagogues C. Servilius Glaucia (a praetor) and L. Appuleius Saturninus (a tribune) to secure land with which to reward his veterans. A number of extreme bills were passed, including one which defined treason no longer as internal revolt (*perduellio*) but as impairing the "majesty" of the Roman people (*lex Appuleia de maiestate imminuta* — later *laesa*). When Glaucia secured the murder of his rival for the consulship, the Senate passed the *senatus consultum ultimum* and Marius was obliged to besiege and kill his former supporters on the Capitoline. Marius then left for a tour of the east.

91. The tribune, **M. Livius Drusus,** son of an opponent of the Gracchi, brought forward several liberal bills: to compromise the problem of the courts by adding 300 *equites* to the Senate; to distribute land; to cheapen the price of grain; and to extend the citizenship to all Italians. The first three measures were passed as one bill, whereupon the Senate, in virtue of a recent law against such omnibus bills (*lex Caecilia Didia* of 98), declared them void.

91-88. The **Social War** (i.e. War of the Allies). The disappointed Italians, save for Latins, Etruscans, Umbrians, and some southern cities, flared into open revolt. They formed a republic, Italia, with a capital at Corfinium. Though Marius and Gn. Pompeius Strabo succeeded in suppressing it in the north, the consul L. Julius Caesar suffered reverses in the south.

90. The danger of the secession of the Etruscans and Umbrians led to the passage by Caesar of a *lex Iulia* by which citizenship was granted to all Italians who had remained faithful.

89. The war in the north was concluded and L. Cornelius Sulla won successes in the south. The two new consuls moved a *lex Plautia Papiria* which extended citizenship to all Italians who applied for it within 60 days, but enrolled them in only eight designated tribes, to prevent them from dominating the assemblies. Cities in Cisalpine Gaul received Latin rights by a *lex Pompeia*, though the precise status of the region between the Po and the Alps, the Transpadanes, remained a matter of dispute until 49. This concession brought the war to a close in 88 and showed that the Italians preferred to remain with Rome rather than to be independent. It also frankly recognized that citizenship was no longer a right, since personal participation in the assemblies at Rome was impossible for most Italians and no system of representation was devised, but a privilege which ensured to its possessors the special protection of Rome, favored treatment in the provinces, and a share in the profits of conquest.

88-84. FIRST MITHRIDATIC WAR. Contemporaneously with the Social War, **Mithridates IV Eupator,** ambitious King of Pontus since 120, made war on Rome. He had absorbed Colchis at the east end of the Pontus (Euxine, Black Sea), the Kingdom of the Bosporus in Tauric Chersonese (Crimea), Paphlagonia, and Cappadocia. He then came into conflict with Nicomedes of Bithynia, in northwestern Asia Minor, who was supported by the Romans. Mithridates routed both Nicomedes and the Romans, overran the province of Asia, and is said to have commanded the natives to put to death 80,000 "Romans" (Italian traders?) on a single day. Sulla, consul for 88, joined his army at Nola to start for Asia.

88-82. But **civil war** broke out in Rome. The demagogue **P. Sulpicius Rufus** carried several measures by violence, notably one distributing the new Italian citizens among all the tribes, and another conferring the eastern command on Marius. Sulla marched his troops to Rome, stormed the city, and slew Sulpicius and others. Marius fled to Africa. Sulla put through conservative reforms, which did not last, and went as proconsul to Asia in 87.

87-84. The demagogic consul **L. Cornelius Cinna** turned to violence against the optimates under the other consul, Cn. Octavius. He was driven from the city, raised an army, and secured the support of Marius, who returned from Africa. They seized Rome, instituted a reign of terror, a **"proscription"** of the optimates, who were either slain or, if they escaped, lost their property. Cinna and Marius became consuls for 86 (Marius' seventh consulship). Marius soon died and his successor, **L. Valerius Flaccus,** went out to command in the east. Cinna tyrannized at Rome until his death in a mutiny in 84.

87-84. In the meantime, Sulla, in Greece, drove the generals of Mithridates, Archelaus and Aristion, back into the Piraeus and Athens respectively. When, in 86, Athens fell, Archelaus retired from the Piraeus by sea to Boeotia, where he was defeated by Sulla at **Chaeronea** and, in 85, at **Orchomenos.**

84. Sulla, supported by a fleet collected in Asia and Syria by **L. Licinius Lucullus,** moved around the Aegean into Asia, where Mithridates made peace on the following terms: evacuation of all his conquests, surrender of 80 warships, and an indemnity of 3000 talents. Sulla then won over the troops of the democratic general C. Fimbria, who had secured command by murdering Flaccus and now committed suicide. Sulla left these two legions to police Asia and to help Lucullus collect an immense fine of 20,000 talents from the Asiatic cities, while he himself returned to Italy.

83-79. Sulla made a cautious advance from Brundisium against the successors of Cinna, in the course of which the army of the consul Lucius Scipio deserted him after the defeat of the other consul, C. Norbanus. After wintering at Capua, Sulla conducted a brilliant campaign against the various opposing forces which culminated in the **battle of the Colline Gate** (Nov., 82), when he repulsed from Rome a large force of Samnites, who had taken advantage of the civil war to revolt. Sulla punished severely the cities that had sided with his opponents, and then had himself appointed dictator for the purpose of restoring the state (*rei publicae constituendae*).

Sulla's dictatorship was only in name a revival of the old institution. It was not an "emergency" office and was not limited in time, so that actually it was a tyranny. Sulla's objective was to restore the old senatorial system. To this end he sought, by a series of laws (*leges Corneliae*) to subordinate to the Senate all those powers which had been set up against it: magistrates, governors, knights, and people. The size of the Senate was increased from 300 to 600 by the addition of new members, probably equestrians; admission became automatic for those who held the quaestorship, whose numbers had increased to 20. Thus the censors lost the control which they had

hitherto had over admissions to the Senate, though probably Sulla only confirmed what had already become a general practice. But he also deprived the censors of the right to remove unworthy members. The *lex annalis* was revived, with permission for re-election to the consulship after ten years. The number of praetors was increased to eight. Governors were forbidden to take troops outside their province by a law which made such action treason. The number of **standing courts** (*quaestiones perpetuae*) was increased to at least seven: *de rebus repetundis, de maiestate, de ui* (violence), *de peculatu* (embezzlement), *de ambitu* (corrupt electioneering), *de falsis* (fraud) and *inter sicarios* (assassination). Membership was definitely restricted to senators, thus depriving both magistrates and people of judicial power. The **tribunes' veto** was confined to the protection of individuals (*auxilium*) and they were probably forbidden to bring any measure before the people without previous approval of the Senate. Moreover, election to the tribunate disqualified a man for further political office, so that men of ambition would avoid it. The public distribution of grain, an instrument of demagoguery, was perhaps abolished.

Of these reforms, the only one of enduring importance was that of the **judicial system.** Though sentimentally the Laws of the Twelve Tables continued to be regarded as the fountainhead of the Roman Law, in actual fact the *leges Corneliae* laid the foundations of Roman criminal law by defining the types of crime (which had naturally increased as Rome grew) and by providing a more expeditious system of court trial than the hearings before the *populus*. The importance of the praetors, who (except the *urbanus* and *peregrinus*) normally presided over the courts, was thus vastly increased. During this same period, by the *lex Aebutia* (probably c. 150), the civil law was liberated from the restraints of the old, ritualistic, narrow "actions at law" (*legis actiones*) by the recognition of the praetor's *formulae*. The *formulae*, borrowed by the urban praetor from the peregrine (i.e. praetor for foreigners) were general definitions of civil wrongs not covered by specific laws, for which remedies would be granted. Such formulas were published by the praetor either on special occasions (*edicta repentina*) or in the edict with which he assumed office (*edictum perpetuum*). A large body of such material was naturally passed on from praetor to praetor and became "tralatician" (*edictum tralaticium*). Thus the praetors, until the time of Hadrian, could widen the scope of civil law to meet new needs, and the praetor's edict became the chief authority for civil law.

As soon as his reforms were completed, Sulla voluntarily retired from public life (79). He died in the following year.

83-81. THE SECOND MITHRIDATIC WAR, resulted from a Roman invasion of Cappadocia and Pontus. After victory, peace was renewed on the terms of 84.

80-72. Q. Sertorius, the democratic governor of Hither Spain (83) was expelled by Sullan troops. When the Lusitanians invited him back in 80, he established an independent state modeled on Rome. He soon extended his sway over much of Spain and held the Romans at bay until he was murdered in 72 by a jealous subordinate, M. Perperna. Pompey, who had been sent to Spain in 77, quickly defeated and executed Perperna.

78-77. The democratic consul **M. Aemilius Lepidus** sought to undo Sulla's work. When he was blocked, he raised in Etruria an army of the discontented. He was defeated before Rome by his colleague Q. Lutatius Catulus and the remnant of his army was wiped out in northern Italy in 77 by the brilliant young Roman commander **Gnaeus Pompeius** (Pompey), son of a general in the Social War and a protégé of Sulla.

74. Cyrene, which had been tentatively bequeathed to Rome in 154 and again in 96, finally became a province.

73-71. Third Servile War. The Thracian gladiator **Spartacus** and other gladiators started a war by seizing Mt. Vesuvius, to which rallied many fugitive slaves. The praetor **M. Licinius Crassus** (b. 112), a favorite of Sulla who had enriched himself by buying the property of the proscribed, defeated Spartacus twice, and Pompey, returning from Spain, finished off the stragglers. For his achievements during this period, Pompey became known as "the Great" (*Magnus*).

70. Crassus and Pompey openly deserted the optimate cause and used their troops to win for themselves the consulship for 70, though both were under the age set in 151. As consuls, they secured the restoration to the tribunate of the privileges of which Sulla had deprived it. Already, in 75, the disqualification of tribunes for higher office had been abolished and, in 72, the censors had recovered the privilege of removing unworthy senators. Thus Sulla's restoration of the Senate was largely undone. The prosecution of the corrupt propraetor of Sicily, Verres, by Cicero in 70 brought to a head discontent with the senatorial courts and the praetor L. Aurelius Cotta introduced a *lex Aurelia* under which the senators retained only one third membership on the juries and the other two thirds were filled from the *equites* and a group of slightly lower property census, the *tribuni aerarii*, whose origin is uncertain but whose sympathies were equestrian.

68-67. Defeat of the Mediterranean pirates by Q. Caecilius Metellus Pius. There had been a rapid increase of piracy (especially kidnapping for the slave market at Delos) in the eastern Mediterranean after the defeat of Carthage, Rhodes, and Syria and during the civil wars in Italy. The centers were Crete and Cilicia and the situation began to interfere seriously with Rome's grain supply. Efforts to suppress the pirates met with little success until Metellus took Crete (68). It was made a province (67) and later joined to Cyrene.

67. The tribune A. Gabinius secured the passage of the *lex Gabinia*, which conferred upon Pompey for three years the command of the Mediterranean and its coasts for 50 miles inland, equal to that of the governors in each province (*imperium aequum*). Thus enabled to mobilize all available resources, Pompey in three months cleared the sea of pirates and pacified Cilicia.

74-64. THE THIRD MITHRIDATIC WAR. Mithridates, encouraged by Rome's troubles at home, supported his son-in-law, **Tigranes I of Armenia**, in the annexation of Cappadocia and Syria.

74. Nicomedes III of Bithynia bequeathed his kingdom to Rome, presumably to protect it against Mithridates, who nevertheless occupied it. The consul for 74, **L. Licinius Lucullus**, gradually drove Mithridates back and occupied Pontus (73). Mithridates fled to the court of Tigranes.

69. Lucullus defeated Tigranes at Tigranocerta and started to push on into the mountains of Armenia. His troops, many of them brought out twenty years before by Flaccus, mutinied and forced him to retire to Asia (68). This failure and his efforts to relieve Asia by wholesale reduction of the indebtedness of the *publicani*, to say nothing of his optimate sympathies, made him unpopular at Rome.

66. The tribune C. Manilius, moved a bill (*lex Manilia*), which was supported by the rising orator, **M. Tullius Cicero** (b. 106), which gave Pompey a command over all Asia equal to that of the governors and valid until the conclusion of the war (*imperium aequum infinitum*, i.e. without time limit).

Pompey quickly drove Mithridates to the east end of the Black Sea, after which he captured Tigranes at Artaxata and deprived him of all territories save Armenia, besides imposing a fine of 6000 talents.

65. Pompey pursued Mithridates until the latter fled to the Crimea, where he committed suicide on hearing of the revolt of his son (63).

65-62. Reorganization of Asia and Syria by Pompey. He formed four provinces: Bithynia-Pontus (excluding eastern Pontus), which became a client kingdom; Asia, the old province, which was again heavily taxed; Cilicia, including Pamphylia and Isauria; and Syria, the region about Antioch. As client kingdoms he left eastern Pontus, Cappadocia, Galatia (under King Deiotarus), Lycia, and Judaea.

64. Pompey took **Jerusalem**, in order to pacify Judea. He left in charge the Maccabean high-priest Hyrcanus and a civil adviser, Antipater, from the non-Jewish district of Idumaea. Judea was under the supervision of the governor of Syria and was subjected to a light tax.

Pompey's reorganization of Asia had enduring significance. He followed the Roman practice of making cities the responsible agencies of local government and founding new ones wherever advisable. In order to keep the support of the equestrian class, he extended the pernicious publican system throughout the east. The Senate was loath to confirm his arrangements or look after his veterans, but he did not turn against the government. Instead, he dismissed his army at Brundisium (61) and entered Rome as a private citizen.

64-63. Conspiracy of Catiline. The discontented classes at Rome (debtors, veterans, ruined nobles, those proscribed by Sulla, etc.) found a leader in **L. Sergius Catilina.** He may at first have had the support of Crassus and of Crassus' demagogic agent, **C. Julius Caesar** (b. 102 or 101). Caesar belonged to a poor branch of the patrician *gens Iulia*, but his aunt had been the wife of Marius and his (Caesar's) wife was a daughter of Cinna. Catiline tried to run for the consulship on a radical program in 66, but could not get his name presented to the *comitia centuriata*, as he was threatened with prosecution for extortion while pro-praetor in Africa. After a plot to murder the consuls had failed (65), he ran again in 64, but was defeated by Cicero. Catiline turned to even more extreme methods (sedition in Rome and levying a force in Etruria). Then, if not before, Crassus and Caesar abandoned him. The

plot was detected, and Cicero, in virtue of a *senatus consultum ultimum*, arrested the conspirators. With the Senate's approval he had them put to death as *hostes* without appeal, despite the law of Tiberius Gracchus. The forces in Etruria were dispersed. Cicero's famous *Orations against Catiline.*

60. THE FIRST TRIUMVIRATE. Caesar returned from a pro-praetorship in Spain and brought his master Crassus into alliance with Pompey, who had fallen out with the Senate because of the unwillingness of the latter to confirm his eastern arrangements. This informal union became known as the first triumvirate.

59. Caesar, as consul, put through the program of the trio: distribution of the Campanian land to Pompey's veterans; confirmation of Pompey's eastern settlement; grant to himself (*lex Vatinia*) for the unprecedented period of five years of the province of Cisalpine Gaul, with Illyria. To this was added later Gallia Narbonensis, with the possibility of action throughout Transalpine Gaul. The political union was cemented by the marriage of Caesar's daughter Julia to Pompey.

58-51. CONQUEST OF GAUL by Caesar, both to enrich himself and to forge for himself an army and a military reputation to rival Pompey's. He used as an excuse the attempt of the Helvetii to move from Switzerland into Gaul. His plan of campaign was to move down the Rhine, separate the Gauls from the Germans, and then turn back on the Gauls. In 58 he defeated the **Helvetii** at **Bibracte** (Autun) and the German Ariovistus near Vesontio (Besançon). He then reduced the **Belgii** (57), including the stubborn Nervii, in northwestern Gaul. He defeated the **Veneti** on the southern coast of Brittany and the Aquitani in southwestern Gaul (56). After he had repulsed the Germanic Usipetes and Tencteri, Caesar built a wooden bridge over the Rhine near Coblenz to make a two weeks' demonstration in Germany (55). He also tried with little success to invade Britain.

58. To remove opposition at Rome, the triumvirs secured the mission of the irreconcilable **M. Porcius Cato** (the younger) to investigate the affairs of Cyprus, and allowed the violent demagogue and tribune **P. Clodius** to move a bill against Cicero for the execution of Roman citizens without appeal. Cicero voluntarily withdrew to Epirus, the bill was passed and his property was confiscated. Clodius also made the distribution of grain free to a large number of poor, perhaps 300,000.

57. An optimate tribune, T. Annius Milo, secured the recall of Cicero, and organized a following to oppose that of Clodius. The optimates summoned up enough courage to attack Caesar's land bill.

In consequence of the shortage of grain, the Senate conferred on Pompey the supervision of the grain supply (*cura annonae*) and an *imperium aequum* over the areas concerned, but without what he really wanted, viz. military force.

56. Worried by the revival of opposition, Caesar, Pompey, and Crassus met at Luca, on the southern boundary of Caesar's province, and laid plans for the future.

55. In pursuance of these plans, Pompey and Crassus became consuls. By a consular *lex Pompeia Licinia*, Caesar's command in Gaul was prolonged for five years. By a tribunician law (*lex Trebonia*), Crassus was given Syria and Pompey both Spains for the same period. Crassus hurried east, but Pompey, contrary to custom, remained near Rome and governed Spain through his *legati*.

54. INVASION OF BRITAIN. Caesar was more successful than in 55 and defeated King Cassivellaunus somewhere north of the Thames, perhaps at Wheathampstead near Verulamium (St. Albans). Nevertheless, he withdrew to Gaul without any permanent result save to open Britain somewhat to the penetration of trade and Roman influence. In 53 he made a second demonstration across the Rhine.

54-51. Breakup of the Triumvirate. This began with the death of Julia in 54.

53. Crassus was utterly defeated and slain by the Parthians at Carrhae in Mesopotamia.

52. All Gaul flared into revolt under Vercingetorix. Caesar failed to take Gergovia (Clermont in Auvergne) and was himself surrounded while besieging Vercingetorix in Alesia (Alise near Dijon), but finally won a complete victory and captured Vercingetorix. He spent the year 51 ruthlessly suppressing the remaining insurgents.

52. Milo's ruffians killed Clodius in a street fight at Bovillae.

As it had not yet been possible to elect magistrates for this year, the Senate passed a *senatus consultum ultimum* and illegally appointed Pompey sole consul, i.e. in fact dictator. Milo, tried in a special court under Pompey's presidency, was condemned despite Cicero's faltering defense. Pompey then made the optimate Metellus

Scipio, father of his new wife, Crassus' widow, his colleague, thus openly returning to the side of the Senate. Afraid, however, of a decisive break with Caesar, he tried, by a series of indirect moves, to jockey him out of office long enough to leave him open for prosecution in the courts. Since prosecutions could not be brought against one in office, Caesar had so arranged his tenure of Gaul (the details are uncertain) that, by being allowed to canvass in absence during 49, he could proceed direct to the consulship in 48.

49. The Senate finally passed a *senatus consultum ultimum* which declared Caesar a public enemy unless he should disband his army (Jan. 7). The tribunes favorable to him fled to Ravenna, where he was waiting. During the night of Jan. 10-11, Caesar with one legion crossed the Rubicon (*alea iacta est*, "the die is cast"), the brook south of Ravenna on the Adriatic which marked the limit of his province. He thus broke not only Sulla's law on treason, but also an old custom by which a general could bring armed forces into Italy only for a triumph. He justified his action as aimed to protect the sacrosanct tribunes.

49-46. Pompey, fearful of the legions in Gaul, left Italy for Greece, where he might have the resources of the east behind him. Most of the Senate went with him. Caesar, after failing to trap Pompey at Brundisium, turned to Spain, where he defeated the latter's commanders at Ilerda (Lerida) north of the Ebro. Marseilles surrendered to him on his way back to Italy.

48. Caesar landed in Epirus and defeated Pompey at Pharsalus. Pompey fled to Egypt, where he was treacherously slain by order of the minister of the young king, Ptolemy XII.

48-47. When Caesar reached Alexandria in pursuit of Pompey, he was besieged by Ptolemy and the natives during the winter, until he was rescued by an army from Asia. Since Ptolemy perished, Caesar made his sister Cleopatra and a younger brother, Ptolemy XIII, joint rulers of Egypt. Cleopatra soon disposed of her brother and set herself to restore the power of the Ptolemies with Roman aid. She charmed Caesar into remaining three months with her and perhaps siring her son Caesarion.

47. Caesar advanced into Syria to meet a son of the great Mithridates, Pharnaces, who had invaded Pontus. On Aug. 2 Caesar defeated him at Zela (*ueni, uidi, uici*).

46. On his return to Rome Caesar subdued a mutiny of his devoted Tenth Legion. He then crossed to Africa and defeated the Pompeians, led by Pompey the Great's son Sextus, at **Thapsus** (Apr.). Cato committed suicide at Utica (hence called *Uticensis*). A part of Numidia, whose Pompeian king, Juba, had committed suicide, was added to the province of Africa; the rest was left to the king of eastern Mauretania. After four simultaneous triumphs in Rome (July) Caesar went to Spain, where Sex. Pompey had joined his brother Gnaeus.

45. Caesar utterly routed them at **Munda** (Mar.). He then returned to Rome (Sept.).

Caesar's position was that of an absolute monarch. In 49 he had been dictator for 11 days to hold elections. In 48 he was consul for the second time. After Pharsalus he was given the consulship for a five-year term and was given the dictatorship annually; perhaps also some of the tribunician powers (*tribunicia potestas*), since being a patrician he could not be tribune. In 46 he was consul for the third time with Lepidus. After Thapsus he was made dictator for ten years and *praefectus morum* (supervisor of morals). In 45 he was sole consul. After Munda he was made consul for ten years; in 44, dictator and *praefectus morum* for life; his tribunician power was extended to include *sacrosanctitas*. Thus his position was essentially a revival of the Sullan dictatorship. His plans for the future are not definitely known, but while he certainly planned to continue as monarch, it is doubtful that he planned to take the crown or move the capital to Ilium.

The **Senate was increased to 900** by enrolling ex-centurions and provincials, as much to weaken it as to make it representative of the empire. To provide for its maintenance at this size Caesar doubled the number of quaestors and praetors (to 40 and 16 respectively); the quaestors were later reduced. His agrarian and colonization program was like that of all reformers since the Gracchi. The citizenship was considerably extended, beginning in 49 with the confirmation of the Transpadanes' long disputed claim. The *lex Iulia municipalis* may perhaps have been a measure to give to the cities in the west something of the autonomy enjoyed by those in the east. The **calendar was reformed** in the light of Egyptian knowledge on the nearly correct basis of 365¼ days per year; this system continued in use in some countries into the 20th century. The number of those receiving free grain was reduced from 320,000 to 150,000. The publican system was somewhat restricted, since Caesar had considerable concern for the provinces and none for the *equites*.

44. ASSASSINATION OF CAESAR.
Caesar's greatest weakness was an inability to choose trustworthy subordinates. A conspiracy of such people, together with the high-minded patriots and disgruntled optimates, led by M. Junius Brutus, Decimus Brutus, and G. Cassius Longinus, assassinated him in the Senate on the Ides (15th) of March. The famous *Et tu Brute* ("Thou too, Brutus") may have been addressed to Decimus, not Marcus.

The conspirators had no organization ready to take charge. **M. Antonius** (Mark Antony), formerly Caesar's master of horse, got control, in part by appealing to the sympathies of the proletariat by his funeral oration and in part by seizing Caesar's papers and treasure. The conspirators fled, Decimus Brutus to Cisalpine Gaul, Marcus Brutus to Macedonia, and Cassius to Syria, provinces already assigned to them, and over which the Senate now gave them commands superior (not equal) to those of other governors (*imperia maiora*), so that they could raise armies against Antony. Antony secured from the people the transfer of Cisalpine Gaul and Macedonia to himself and Syria to his colleague, P. Cornelius Dolabella. In the meantime, Caesar's eighteen-year-old great-nephew, **Gaius Octavius**, whose mother, Atia, was daughter of Caesar's sister, Julia, and who had been named as heir and adopted in the will of Caesar, came to Rome to claim his inheritance. Antony refused to give him the money and prevented the passing of the *lex curiata* necessary to ratify his adoption. Octavius nevertheless called himself **Gaius Julius Caesar Octavianus.** He borrowed money and, illegally, as a private citizen, levied a force among Caesar's veterans in Campania.

43. Antony marched north to dislodge Decimus Brutus from Mutina (Modena). The Senate sent the new consuls Hirtius and Pansa to relieve Decimus and joined to them Octavian with the command (*imperium*) of a pro-praetor. In two battles, **Forum Gallorum and Mutina,** Antony was forced to retire westward toward Gaul. But the consuls were killed. Octavian, marching to Rome (July), forced the Senate to hold special elections in which he and Pedius were elected to replace the dead consuls. He had his adoption duly confirmed. By a *lex Pedia* vengeance was declared on the conspirators who had assassinated Caesar. In the meantime, **Marcus Lepidus,** governor of Transalpine Gaul, had allied with Antony and Decimus had been slain. Octavian thereupon changed his support from the Senate to Antony in a meeting at Bononia (Bologna).

43, Nov. SECOND TRIUMVIRATE. A tribunician *lex Titia* confirmed their arrangements: Antony, Lepidus, and Octavian were appointed a commission of three to establish the state (*triumuiri rei publicae constituendae*), which amounted to a Sullan dictatorship in commission and differentiated this second triumvirate from the first by recognizing it legally. The triumvirs proceeded with a widespread proscription inspired both by political hatred and by the need for money and lands with which to reward their troops. Octavian acquiesced in the **execution** of Cicero by Antony's agents (Dec. 7).

42. The triumvirs secured the erection of a temple to Caesar in the Forum, where he had been burnt, and his deification. The magistrates were forced to take an oath to support all Caesar's arrangements (*acta*). Antony and Octavian then crossed to Thrace, where they met the combined forces of Cassius and Brutus at **Philippi**. Cassius, defeated by Antony and misled by a false report of Brutus' defeat, committed suicide. Brutus, though actually victorious over Octavian, was finally defeated twenty days later and also killed himself. Antony betook himself to the eastern provinces, where he met Cleopatra at Tarsus in the summer of 41. Either fascinated by her charms or desiring to get control of her resources, he remained with her in Egypt for a year.

41-40. Octavian, who shared the western provinces with Lepidus, had a difficult war against Antony's wife Fulvia and brother Lucius Antonius before finally reducing them at **Perusia** (Perugia) in 40.

40. By a pact made at **Brundisium**, Antony married Octavian's sister Octavia (since Fulvia had recently died). Octavian took Gaul from Lepidus, who was left only Africa.

39. Sextus Pompey, who had conducted a piratical career since Munda, was now a power to be reckoned with, as he controlled Sicily and his fleet could interrupt Rome's grain supply. His possession of Sicily, Sardinia, Corsica, and the Peloponnese was recognized by the triumvirs in the **pact of Misenum.** Octavian divorced his second wife, Scribonia, and married **Livia**, previously wife of Tib. Claudius Nero.

37. Octavia engineered a **second pact at Tarentum.** Octavian gave troops to Antony for his Parthian War and Antony supplied ships for use against Pompey.

The triumvirate was renewed for five years more, though the precise date set for its termination is uncertain.

36. Octavian's fleet, under his general **M. Vipsanius Agrippa**, defeated Pompey, who fled to Miletus, where he died. Lepidus, after landing in Sicily ostensibly to help Octavian, tried to secure the island. When, however, his troops deserted to Octavian, the latter annexed his rival's territory but, because Lepidus himself had become chief pontiff (*pontifex maximus*) on the death of Caesar, kept him in honorable captivity at Circeii until his death in 13. Octavian spent the following years consolidating Roman power in the Alps and Illyria.

36. Antony suffered a severe defeat from the Parthians in 36, but managed to retreat to Armenia. He openly married Cleopatra (though already married to Octavia).

34. At Alexandria he established her as a Hellenistic monarch and distributed Roman provinces to her children as subordinate rulers. How far he intended to be her consort cannot be determined, but Octavian made the most of such a probability.

32. When Antony prepared to attack Octavian, the latter had the support of the west, which was both terrified by fear of an oriental domination under Cleopatra and angry at Antony's highhanded disposition of Roman territory. After the consuls, friends of Antony, fled to him, Octavian had the *imperium* of Antony under the triumvirate annulled by the *comitia.* He published a will purporting to be Antony's in which the Roman possessions in the east were bequeathed to Cleopatra. Italy, and perhaps all the western provinces, took a military oath (*coniuratio Italiae*) to support Octavian. In virtue of this, since he no longer had any legal *imperium* himself if the triumvirate was at an end, he levied troops, outwardly to meet Cleopatra. Antony formally divorced Octavia.

31, Sept. 2. BATTLE OF ACTIUM. The rival fleets met outside the bay. The course of the battle is uncertain, but Cleopatra fled to Egypt, followed by Antony, whose army then surrendered to Octavian. In the following year,

30. Antony, on hearing a false report of Cleopatra's suicide, killed himself. Upon Octavian's arrival at Alexandria, Cleopatra tried to win him as she had his predecessors. When she failed, she committed suicide (the story of the asp is perhaps false) lest she have to grace his triumph. Egypt passed finally into Rome's possession.

29. Octavian celebrated three triumphs and by closing the temple of Janus, something recorded only twice before (by Numa and in 235), signalized the restoration of peace throughout the Roman world.

If the crossing of the Rubicon marked the final fall of the republic, the battle of Actium signalized the final triumph of the empire. The last century of the republic was characterized by the collapse of popular government because of the wide extension of citizenship, the considerable adulteration of the citizen body at Rome by the introduction of un-Romanized Orientals, chiefly through the manumission of slaves, the growth in Rome of an unemployed proletariat, the rise of demagogues, and the complexity of the problems of government. The increasingly corrupt Senate had lost control of the assemblies, the armies, and the generals. The financiers, as well as the governors, saw in the provinces only a field for exploitation. Italy had been exhausted by civil war, proscriptions (which especially reduced the upper classes), recruitment, and land confiscations.

The last century of the republic witnessed a vigorous literary activity at Rome. Hellenism, thoroughly absorbed into Roman education, formed a constituent element in thought rather than something imposed from without. At the same time the native talent of the Romans adapted Hellenism to their own particular needs. **Lyric poetry** found expression in **Catullus** (87–54) from Verona, who, besides his imitations of the Alexandrine poets, produced strongly personal and intense lyrics on his hates and loves. The Epicurean **Lucretius** (99–55) wrote his epic "On the Nature of Things" (*de Rerum Natura*) to expound a materialistic atomism. Caesar's (102–44) *Commentaries* on the Gallic Wars, continued by his officers for the other campaigns, are, despite their apologetic purpose, admirably clear and impartial. Minor writings which have survived are the historical monographs on Catiline and the Jugurthine War by **Sallust** (86–35) and the *Lives* by **Nepos** (100–29). Outstanding among antiquarians was **Varro** (116–27), while the **Scaevolae,** father and son, in the Sullan period, were outstanding students of jurisprudence. But the figure who gave his name to the age was **Cicero** (106–43). In spite of his active public life, he not only published his forensic and judicial speeches but wrote extensively on philosophy, rhetoric, and politics. He passed on to the Middle Ages much of value from Greek thought, especially from Plato, the Stoics, and the New (Skeptic) Academy. But he added thereto a Roman color and much of his own thought and experience. Finally, his correspondence, published after his death, gives a deep insight into both the writer and his times.

Roman art began during this century to emerge with a definite character. Though buildings still preserved the heavy lines and ornament of the Etruscans, they acquired majesty and splendor under direct Greek influence. Portrait sculpture, though executed by Greeks, portrayed the individual to a degree unknown in idealizing Hellenic art.

F. THE ROMAN EMPIRE

1. THE EARLY EMPIRE (31 B.C.-192 A.D.)

31 B.C.-14 A.D. IMPERATOR CAESAR OCTAVIANUS (b. Sept. 23, 63), later called **Augustus**, established his government in 27 (Jan. 23), with some modifications later, especially after a serious illness in 23. He proclaimed that he would "restore the republic," i.e. resign his extraordinary powers and put the Senate and Roman people again at the head of the state. He held the consulship annually until 23, but only twice thereafter for a short part of the year. He also received, and retained after 23, a proconsular command superior to those of other senatorial proconsuls and unlimited in time, though actually renewed at intervals (*imperium proconsulare maius infinitum*). Although he received a special dispensation to retain his *imperium* within the *pomoerium*, it is uncertain to what extent he could actually exercise it over Rome or even Italy, the sphere of the consuls. However, in virtue of the *imperium*, he controlled all the armed forces of the state and appointed as legionary commanders his own senatorial delegates (*legati*). He also divided the provinces between the emperor and the Senate. Augustus himself took charge of all provinces in which the presence of troops was required and appointed to govern them other senatorial delegates, called in this case *legati pro praetore*. The Senate sent proconsuls to the pacified provinces where troops were no longer needed. Thus Augustus hoped to prevent that rivalry of independent commanders which had brought about the downfall of the republic. He also sought to assure better government in the provinces by the payment of salaries to all governors, senatorial and imperial. Two major districts received special treatment. The command of the legions on the Rhine was given to a special legate, independent of the imperial government of the Gallic provinces, and only later did this command develop into two territorial provinces. Egypt was administered by Augustus as a private estate under an equestrian praefect (*praefectus Aegypti*) appointed by himself, who directed the elaborate machinery inherited from the Pharaohs and Ptolemies for the benefit of the new imperial treasury (*fiscus*), which

was distinct from the old senatorial treasury (*aerarium Saturni*). Smaller districts were governed, not by senatorial *legati*, but by equestrian procurators or praefects. Imperial governors of all sorts tended to have longer terms than the senatorial and thus to perform their task better. Since, however, the imperial *legati*, in both provinces and the army, were drawn from the Senate and usually held proconsulships later, no sharp distinction was drawn between the republican and imperial administration in the upper ranks.

A distinct **imperial civil service** did, however, grow up among the equestrians, partly in the provinces where, besides the minor governorships above mentioned, they held financial posts as stewards (*procuratores*) of the emperor or of his treasury (*fiscus*) and partly in various administrative posts in Rome and Italy, of which the chief were those with which Augustus supplemented the inadequate republican administration of the city of Rome. The most important officer was a consular senator, the *praefectus urbi* who had general supervision of the city with three "urban cohorts" of soldiers for police. This office, however, may have become permanent only under Tiberius. The other three major officials were equestrian. A *praefectus annonae* had charge of the grain supply for Rome. A *praefectus uigilum* had seven cohorts of freedmen as firemen, one for every two of the 14 regions into which Augustus divided the city. And a *praefectus praetorio* had charge of the nine cohorts of the imperial or "praetorian" guard (praetor-general), which Augustus kept scattered through Italy, but which Sejanus later concentrated in a camp at Rome. Because of the importance of this post, later emperors frequently divided it between two incumbents.

In 23, Augustus secured the consolidation and extension of certain tribunician privileges which had been granted to him because, as a patrician, he could not be a tribune. The value of this tribunician power (*tribunicia potestas*) was in part its traditionally popular appeal and in part the privileges of sacrosanctity, *auxilium*, veto, direct jurisdiction in Rome, consultation of the Senate, and, most important,

The Roman Empire
before the Barbarian Invasions

the initiation of legislation. Augustus, during his reign, initiated a series of far-reaching laws (*leges Iuliae*) in an attempt to reform the criminal law, regulate social classes, and revive morality and family life. With respect to the social order, he purified the Senate of Caesarian intruders by a series of "selections" (*lectiones*); he restricted severely the freeing of slaves and the attainment of full citizenship by freedmen; and he bestowed the citizenship on provincials very grudgingly. However, he did increase the recipients of free grain from Caesar's 150,000 to 200,000. The final law in his effort to restore morality was the consular *lex Papia Poppaea* of 9 A.D., which supplemented his own *lex Iulia de maritandis ordinibus* of 18 B.C. These laws encouraged marriage in the senatorial and equestrian orders by penalizing the unmarried and offering privileges to the fathers of children, especially of three (*ius trium liberorum*).

Augustus likewise held a number of minor offices or titles. Though he did not become chief priest (*pontifex maximus*) until after the death of Lepidus in 13, he undertook to revivify the old Roman religion in the face of an influx of exotic eastern cults. He also allowed the worship of his genius, allied often with the goddess Roma, in Italy and the provinces. After his death he, like Caesar, was deified and temples were erected to him as *diuus Augustus*; but the official worship of living emperors during the early empire is questionable. Besides revising the rolls of Senate, knights, and people either as censor or with censorial powers, he controlled admission to the Senate by various methods. He alone could grant the wide stripe (*latus clauus*), the sign of a senatorial career, to those who did not inherit it as sons of senators. He appointed to the minor military posts which were a necessary qualification for the republican magistracies. And the privilege of either recommending (*nominatio*) or requiring (*commendatio*) the election of certain candidates for office allowed him to advance those whom he thought most fit. The republican magistracies continued with only minor changes save that the term of the consulship suffered progressive diminution until it averaged two months. When the opening pair of consuls (*consules ordinarii*) left office, there followed a succession of *consules suffecti*. Finally, in virtue either of specific enactments or of his general authority (*auctoritas*), Augustus undertook many improvements throughout the empire: roads, buildings, colonies, etc.

The title by which he is best known, **Augustus**, was bestowed on him by the Senate in 27 (Jan. 16) and expressed a semireligious feeling of gratitude for his achievements. He did not, however, set himself up outwardly as a monarch, and the term which he himself used informally, though not as an official title, to describe himself was **princeps**, chief among equals.

29. The closing of the temple of Janus for the first time since 235 signified the achievement of longed-for peace throughout the empire (cf. year 9, below).

20. By a treaty with **Parthia**, Augustus recovered the standards lost by Crassus and Antony and thereby vindicated Roman honor.

17. A celebration of the *Ludi Saeculares*, religious ceremonies, concluded the fifth era (*saeculum*) since the founding of Rome.

16-15. The defeat of Lollius by the Germans necessitated the presence of Augustus in Gaul and Tiberius in Germany. Rhaetia, Noricum, and Vindelicia were annexed so that the frontier reached the upper Danube.

12-9. Tiberius was summoned to Pannonia by a severe revolt. Drusus fought against the Germans until his death in 9.

9. The altar of Peace (*ara Pacis*), voted by the Senate four years before, was dedicated (cf. year 29, above).

9-7. Tiberius carried on the conquest of Germany, but was sent to Armenia in 6. For some reason now unknown, he retired to Rhodes until the death of the sons of Agrippa and Augustus' daughter, Julia, made him the only possible successor to Augustus. He returned to Rome in 2 A.D., on the death of Lucius Caesar at Marseilles, and was adopted in 4 A.D., after the death of Gaius Caesar in Asia.

4 B.C. THE BIRTH OF JESUS (p. 32) probably occurred not in the traditional year, but shortly before the death of Herod the Great, son of Antipater the Idumaean, who had obtained the Kingdom of Judea from the triumvirs in 40. In 6 A.D. some of his territories were distributed among his sons, but Judea itself was placed in charge of an imperial procurator.

The Christian Era begins with the year 1 A.D., which follows directly on the year 1 B.C., since no year is numbered o. Hereafter dates A.D. (*anno Domini*, "year of our Lord") will appear without designation and dates B.C. (before Christ) will be indicated as such.

4-6. Upon his adoption, Tiberius was sent again to Germany. From there he was recalled to suppress revolts in

Pannonia and Dalmatia until 9. He finally established the frontier on the middle Danube. At the same time (6) the creation of the Province of Moesia and the reduction of Thrace to a client state advanced the frontier to the lower Danube.

6. Augustus set up a special treasury, the *aerarium militare*, to pay bonuses to retiring legionary veterans. Though land grants to veterans occurred thereafter, this bonus system finally solved the problem of caring for veterans. Augustus reduced the number of legions from 70 or more to 27 or 28 at his death. These, with about an equal number of auxiliary troops, gave a total army of some 300,000 men.

9. The legate, **P. Quinctilius Varus,** with three legions, was annihilated by the German Arminius in **the battle of the Teutoberg Forest,** perhaps near Paderborn. This defeat put an end to Augustus' plans for the conquest of Germany to the Elbe and established the Rhine as the future border between Latin and German territory. Augustus discontinued his conquest because of the financial difficulties involved in replacing the lost legions and levying enough additional forces to subdue Germany permanently.

14. AUGUSTUS DIED at Nola on Aug. 19. Legally, his position could not be inherited, since the various powers and offices composing it ceased with his death and could be received by another only from the Senate and Roman people. In fact, however, Augustus had throughout his life sought so to indicate a successor as to insure the perpetuation of the principate. In this attempt he tried to combine inheritance, by either blood, marriage, or adoption, with selection of the best available man, through the bestowal of a secondary proconsular *imperium* and the tribunician power. After several possible successors had predeceased him, he selected **Tiberius,** son of his wife Livia by her first husband. Though, at the death of Augustus, Tiberius held the tribunician power and an unusually extensive *imperium,* he perhaps sincerely laid before the Senate the option of restoring the republic. The Senate, however, realized the impossibility of such a step or, according to ancient authorities, found its freedom of action impeded by the hypocrisy of Tiberius. Revolts of the legions in Pannonia and Germany showed the need of a single strong commander to prevent a recurrence of the civil wars of the later republic. Tiberius already occupied too strong a position for anyone else to be chosen. The Senate therefore conferred on him the powers and titles of Augustus.

14-37. TIBERIUS Claudius Nero (b. 42 B.C.), emperor. He transferred the elections from the assemblies to the Senate. Already the passage of laws in the assemblies had become a formality and though continued until the time of Nerva, the assemblies hereafter had no official share in the government save to confirm the grant of the *imperium* and *tribunicia potestas* to a new emperor. The Roman mob, however, continued by its frequent riots to exert a pressure upon the government out of proportion to its importance.

14-16. **The revolt of the Pannonian legions** was suppressed by Tiberius' son, the younger Drusus. The son of Tiberius' brother Drusus, who is known by his father's title, **Germanicus,** and whom Augustus had forced Tiberius to adopt as a possible successor, suppressed the German mutiny and campaigned in Germany with some successes. He defeated Arminius, whose kingdom then broke up, and recovered the eagles of Varus' legions. He was, however, recalled, probably not because Tiberius begrudged his victories, but because he found them too costly.

17. On the death of their kings, Cappadocia and Commagene became a province.

17-19. Germanicus, sent to install a king in Armenia, conducted himself in a high-handed manner both in Syria and in Egypt. When, however, he died in Syria the enemies of Tiberius rallied about his wife Agrippina, and charged the legate of Syria, Piso, before the Senate with having poisoned him. Piso's consequent suicide gave color to the probably unjust suspicion that Tiberius, or even Livia, had encouraged the supposed poisoning.

19. **Maroboduus,** who had built up a strong kingdom in Bohemia, was forced by internal dissensions to take refuge with the Romans. Thereafter, the Romans were not seriously threatened on the Rhine or upper Danube until the time of Marcus Aurelius.

21. A revolt broke out in Gaul among the Treveri, led by Julius Florus, and the Aedui, led by Julius Sacrovir. Though soon suppressed by the commander in upper Germany, Gaius Silius, it showed that anti-Roman feeling was still strong in Gaul, even among the chiefs who had received Roman citizenship, as these Julii from Caesar or Augustus.

23-31. Tiberius fell increasingly under the influence of the ambitious and treacherous equestrian praefect of the guard, **Sejanus,** who quartered the praetorian cohorts in one camp outside Rome.

The Julian-Claudian House

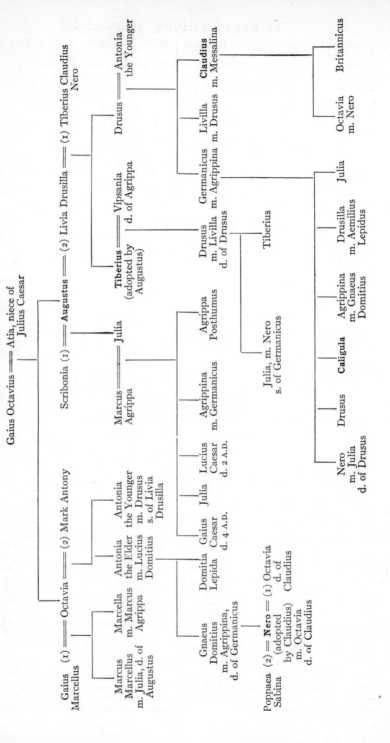

He encouraged the gathering of information against those hostile to Tiberius by unscrupulous informers (*delatores*, many of whom were of the nobility) and the prosecution of the accused under the law of treason (*lex de maiestate imminuta*), since actions against the person of the emperor were regarded as harmful to the majesty of the state. When such trials involved senators or important equestrians, they were heard by the Senate, which came increasingly to act as a court under the presidency of the emperor or the consuls. Ancient writers have, however, much exaggerated the abuse of this law under Tiberius. In 23, Sejanus probably poisoned Tiberius' son Drusus, in order to intrigue for his own succession.

26. Sejanus persuaded Tiberius to retire from the annoyances of an increasingly hostile Rome. Tiberius eventually settled on **Capreae** (Capri), an island in the Bay of Naples, where the popular imagination, probably wrongly, imagined him as giving way to the most abominable vices. Actually, Tiberius was of rigid morality and of the utmost conscientiousness in governing the empire and in carrying out the policies of Augustus.

29. Livia, accused of attempting to dominate the empire after Augustus' death, died. Sejanus secured the exile of **Agrippina**, wife of Germanicus (she died in 33), and the arrest of his two eldest sons, Nero (d. 31) and a third Drusus (d. 33).

(30). PONTIUS PILATE, procurator of Judea (26–36), ordered the crucifixion of **Jesus** of Nazareth, called the Christ (the Greek *Christos* is a translation of Messiah, "anointed" in Aramaic), accused of sedition.

31. The plots of Sejanus finally came to the notice of Tiberius, who engineered his arrest and execution. Tiberius remained in rigid seclusion in Capreae.

36. Artabanus, King of Parthia, made peace with Rome. Rome was saved from a serious Parthian threat throughout this period by dynastic quarrels within Parthia and by disputes over the possession of Armenia.

37. Tiberius, dying at Misenum (Mar. 16), indicated as his successors his young grandson, Tiberius Gemellus, and the surviving son of Germanicus, Gaius Caesar nicknamed *Caligula* ("Little Boot"). Gaius at first favored Tiberius Gemellus, but soon put him to death.

37-41. Caius CALIGULA (b. 12), emperor. If not insane at his accession, Caligula was at least a megalomaniac and soon became unbalanced. Though the follies ascribed to him may be exaggerated, his conduct was extremely irrational. Behind it may have lain the desire for an absolute monarchy after the pattern of his great-grandfather, Antony. He established many client kings, including Julius Agrippa I, wrongly called Herod Agrippa, a grandson of Herod the Great. He had himself worshiped as a god, though his attempt to erect a statue of himself in the temple at Jerusalem was blocked by the legate of Syria, Petronius.

39. Caligula's campaign into Germany was stopped by a conspiracy led by Gaetulicus.

40. A campaign against Britain was also a fiasco.

41, Jan. 24. Caligula was assassinated by conspirators led by Cassius Chaerea.

An attempt by the Senate to revive the republic was frustrated when the praetorian guard found in the palace a scholarly, neglected younger brother of Germanicus, Claudius. Being loyal to the family, the guard imposed him upon the Senate as emperor.

41-54. Tiberius CLAUDIUS Drusus (b. 10 B.C.), emperor.

He was regarded at Rome as a driveling imbecile, subject to the whims of his wives and freedmen. Of the former he had four. The third, Messalina (a great-granddaughter of Antony) used her power to gratify her lusts until her enemies, the freedmen, secured her execution in 48. The last wife was Claudius' niece, Agrippina the Younger. She used her power to insure the succession to Lucius Domitius Ahenobarbus, her son by a former husband. The most prominent of Claudius' freedmen were **Narcissus**, secretary for the imperial correspondence (*ab epistulis*), and **Pallas**, financial secretary (*a rationibus*). Henceforth these secretaryships and others like them, on petitions (*a libellis*), on legal precedents (*a studiis*), etc., which had hitherto been simply posts in the imperial household inherited from the establishments of the republican nobility, became real offices of state, heads of a great bureaucracy. Though they never again conferred such power as they had under Claudius, their administrative importance grew and they were later filled by equestrians. In fact, for all his domestic weaknesses, Claudius took a real and intelligent interest in the administration of the empire. Without departing widely from Augustan precedents, he extended the citizenship and opened the Senate to noble Gauls (48). He incorporated the client provinces of Mauretania Tingitana and Mauretania Caesariensis (42), Lycia with Pamphylia (43), and Thrace (46). Though he made Agrippa king of all Judea in 41, he resumed it as a procuratorial province on Agrippa's death in 44. He restored Macedon and Achaea to the Senate in 44.

43. Aulus Plautius invaded Britain. The precise motives for the Roman conquest are unknown. Claudius himself visited the island to receive the surrender of Camulodunum (Colchester in Essex) in the same year. Thereafter the conquest proceeded slowly north to Lindum (Lincoln) and west to Deva (Chester) and Isca Silurum (Caerlon, i.e. *Castra Legionum*) on the Welsh border. The British leader **Caractacus** was finally captured in 51.

47. Claudius revived the censorship and celebrated secular games (*ludi saeculares*).

48. On the execution of Messalina, Claudius was permitted by a special senatorial enactment to marry his niece Agrippina. In 50, he adopted her son, Lucius Domitius Ahenobarbus who took the name **Nero** and ousted from the succession Claudius' son by Messalina, Britannicus (b. 41 or 42 and inheriting his name from his father's British triumph). In 53, Nero married Claudius' daughter by Messalina, Octavia.

53. Claudius secured a decree of the Senate by which jurisdiction was granted to imperial procurators in financial cases. This marked an important stage in the increase of the importance of imperial officials at the expense of senatorial.

54. Claudius died (Oct. 13), reputedly from poison administered by Agrippina in a dish of mushrooms. When Agrippina secured the recognition of **Claudius Nero Caesar** as successor by the praetorian guard, the Senate had to confer on him the imperial powers.

54-68. Nero (b. 37), emperor. He began his rule well under the guidance of the philosopher **Seneca** and the praefect of the guard **Burrus**. But in spirit he was an actor and wished to play the monarch in the grand manner. He discharged the freedman financial secretary (*a rationibus*) **Pallas** and poisoned Britannicus in 55. He deserted Octavia, first for the freedwoman **Acte** and then for **Poppaea Sabina**, the wife of his friend Otho. Finally he murdered his mother Agrippina in 59. After the death of Burrus in 62, he divorced, exiled, and murdered Octavia, and married Poppaea.

55-63. The general **Corbulo**, who had been successful under Claudius in Germany, was sent to settle the Parthian problem. After spending three years build-

ing up the morale of his troops, Corbulo successfully invaded Armenia and took Artaxata (58) and Tigranocerta (59). In 61, however, Nero replaced him by Paetus, who was thoroughly defeated at Rhandeia (62). In 63, therefore, Corbulo's solution, peace without conquest, was accepted by Nero, whose vanity was satisfied when the Parthian Tiridates came to Rome in 66 to receive his crown.

56. By a decree of the Senate, the tribunes were forbidden to usurp the judicial functions of higher magistrates and the power to fine of the tribunes and aediles was limited. At the same time the senatorial treasury (*aerarium Saturni*) was put under special praetorian praefects chosen by the emperor. The senatorial treasury constantly required subventions from the emperor. In 61, there is evidence that the city praefect (*praefectus urbi*), originally a military or police official, had acquired a jurisdiction which was competing with that of the city praetor (*praetor urbanus*). These instances show how even in Rome the imperial officials were gaining power at the expense of the republican.

60. St. Paul, before his conversion to Christianity a Jew of Tarsus named Saul belonging to the rigid sect of the Pharisees, was brought to trial before the procurator of Judea, Felix, and appealed to the emperor.

61. While Suetonius Paulinus, governor of Britain since 59, was engaged in the subjugation of the Druidical center, Mona (Anglesey, an island off northwest Wales), the queen of the Iceni (Norfolk), **Boudicca** (not *Boadicea*, as usually spelled) led a determined revolt and sacked Camulodunum (Colchester), Verulamium (St. Albans) and Londinium (London). Paulinus succeeded in defeating and killing Boudicca.

64. A great fire destroyed most of Rome. Nero's "fiddling," if genuine, was singing to the lyre a poem on the burning of Troy. When suspected of having set the fire himself, Nero found convenient culprits in the new and despised sect of the Christians, already a considerable group in Rome, with their prophecies of an imminent second advent of Christ and a world-wide conflagration. They were put to death with refined tortures.

65. A widespread conspiracy was organized to put **Gaius Calpurnius Piso** into the principate. Its noble leaders conducted it with such pusillanimity that it was discovered and many senators including Seneca, his nephew Lucan the poet, Faenius Rufus (successor to Burrus as praetorian prefect), and Petronius (the writer and friend of Nero), were executed or forced to commit suicide.

66. Nero's hostility to the opposition culminated in the execution of the irreconcilable Stoics, Thrasea Paetus and Barea Soranus.

66-70. REVOLT IN JUDEA, resulting from misgovernment by a succession of Roman procurators. When the governor of Syria failed to suppress it, **Vespasian** was sent as special legate with three legions (67). He slowly reduced the country, took prisoner the pro-Roman Jewish historian, **Josephus,** and laid siege to Jerusalem (69). After his proclamation as emperor, Vespasian left his son **Titus** to continue the siege against the Zealot leader, John of Giscala, who had removed his rival Eleazar. Jerusalem fell (7 Sept.). Titus celebrated a triumph in 71, which is commemorated on the surviving Arch of Titus at Rome. Some of Judea was given to Marcus Julius ("Herod") Agrippa II, son of Agrippa I, but most of it became imperial domain. The Temple was destroyed, the Sanhedrin (Jewish national council) and high-priesthood abolished, the two-drachma tax paid by Jews to the temple was diverted to a special account in the imperial treasury *fiscus Iudaicus*), and a legion under a senatorial legate superior to the procurator, was quartered in Jerusalem.

67. Nero undertook an artistic tour in Greece, in the course of which he executed Corbulo, and two ex-legates of Germany.

68. On Nero's return to Italy, he heard that **C. Julius Vindex,** legate of Gallia Lugdunensis, had revolted. Though the revolt was put down by the legate of upper Germany, L. Verginius Rufus, who refused to be saluted as emperor (*imperator*) by his troops, the two legions in Hispania Tarraconensis, on the suggestion of Vindex, had already (March) saluted as emperor their elderly legate, Servius Sulpicius **Galba.** When the praetorian guard, under the praefect Nymphidius Sabinus, recognized Galba, the Senate declared Nero a public enemy (*hostis*). He committed suicide in a villa outside Rome ("*what an artist I perish*") and the Julio-Claudian line came to an end.

68-69. Servius Sulpicius GALBA (b. 5 or 3 B.C.), emperor. By the recognition of Galba, the helpless Senate admitted that, in the words of Tacitus, "emperors could be made elsewhere than at Rome." The success of Augustus' compromise depended on the loyalty of the troops to the person to whom the Senate might grant the powers of the principate. It had already been made clear that the

Senate could not resist accepting a candidate of the praetorian guard; now the provincial legions, disabused of their loyalty to the Julio-Claudian house by the unwarlike conduct of Nero, and jealous of the privileges of the praetorians, asserted themselves during this year of the four emperors (Galba, Otho, Vitellius, and Vespasian).

69, Jan. 1. The eight legions on the Rhine refused allegiance to Galba, and on Jan. 3 the four in lower Germany saluted as emperor their legate **Aulus Vitellius** (b. 15). He was also accepted by the legions of upper Germany under Hordeonius Flaccus. Galba, whom Tacitus called "in the judgment of all, capable of ruling if he had not ruled" (*capax imperii nisi imperasset*), had reached Rome, where he adopted as his successor the aristocrat Piso Licinianus.

Thereupon, Marcus Salvius **Otho** (b. 32), the dissolute friend of Nero, who had been made legate of Lusitania so that Nero could marry his wife Poppaea and had returned with Galba, secured the support of the praetorians and had Galba and Piso murdered (Jan. 15). Otho was then recognized by the helpless Senate.

Meanwhile, the troops of Vitellius approached Italy in two divisions under Valens and Caecina. They met in the plain of the Po and defeated the forces of Otho (Apr. 19) in the **first battle of Bedriacum** (near Cremona), whereupon **Otho** committed suicide. The Senate immediately recognized Vitellius, who presently reached Rome himself.

In the meantime (July 1) the praefect of Egypt, Tiberius Julius Alexander, proclaimed as emperor **Vespasian,** legate in Judea. Mucianus, legate of Syria, lent his support. Antonius Primus, commander of the seventh legion in Pannonia, rallied all the Danubian legions to Vespasian and moved rapidly into northern Italy. There he defeated the forces of Vitellius in the **second battle of Bedriacum** and sacked Cremona (late Oct.). When Antonius approached Rome, Vespasian's brother seized the Capitol, which was burnt in the ensuing struggle. The Vitellians fought bitterly in the city streets, but Vitellius was finally slain (Dec. 20). The Senate immediately recognized Vespasian. When Mucianus reached Rome in Jan. (70), he ruled it until Vespasian arrived during the summer.

69-79. Titus Flavius VESPASIANUS (b. 9), emperor and founder of the Flavian dynasty. He was the son of a humble tax collector from the Italian municipality of Reate. Vespasian was confronted with the task, not only of restoring the principate, but of equating himself with his aristocratic Roman predecessors. He himself, with his son Titus, held the opening consulship of every year of his reign save 73 and 78. A surviving law (*lex de imperio Vespasiani*) may be part of an inclusive measure whereby all the powers accumulated by preceding emperors were conferred specifically and together on Vespasian. Such events as the restoration of the Capitol (70, dedicated by Domitian in 82), the triumph of Titus (71), the erection of a temple of Peace (71–75), the closing of the temple of Janus (71), the destruction of Nero's extensive "Golden House" and parks, on the site of which a vast public amphitheater, the Coliseum (or Colosseum, *amphitheatrum Flavianum*), was begun, served to surround the new dynasty with material glamor. To reorganize the Senate, Vespasian felt compelled to revive the censorship with Titus in 73, instead of tacitly assuming the right of enrollment (*adlectio*) exercised by his predecessors. In 74 he granted Latin rights to all of Spain. He reorganized and rigidly controlled the finances.

69–71. The revolt of some Batavian auxiliaries under their native commander, Julius Civilis, won the support of some of the legions of Germany. This inflamed the Gallic Treveri under Julius Classicus and Julius Tutor and the Lingones under Julius Sabinus. Hordeonius Flaccus was slain at Novaesium (Neuss) on the lower Rhine. Petillius Cerialis, with six legions, took advantage of disagreements between Gauls and Batavians to crush the revolt piecemeal. The movement, though ostensibly begun in the interests of Vespasian, had in reality aimed at the establishment of an independent Gallic empire; the last instance of dangerous national separatism during the early empire. Thereafter auxiliaries were not employed in the country of their origin and the corps soon came to be composed of recruits of different nationalities. By this time the praetorian guards were alone recruited in Italy; the legions drew from Roman settlers in the provinces or Romanized provincials, to whom citizenship was often granted to secure their enlistment. Thus the army had become less Italian, more provincial in its sympathies. After the revolt, Vespasian disbanded at least four disloyal legions.

70. By putting Cappadocia in charge of the imperial governor of Galatia, by moving the eastern legions from Syria to forts on the upper Euphrates (Satala, Melitene. and Samosata), and by absorbing a number of small native principalities in Asia and Syria, Vespasian consolidated the eastern frontier against Armenia and Parthia and prepared the way for Trajan's expansion.

71. Titus, though a senator, was made praetorian praefect, a post hitherto equestrian. He also received both the pro-consular command (*imperium*) and the tribunician power (*tribunicia potestas*), whereby Vespasian made it clear that he would follow the hereditary principle of succession.

73-74. Vespasian began the conquest of the territory east of the upper Rhine and south of the Main, the later *agri decumates* (or *decumathes*; the meaning is uncertain). He furthermore reorganized the defenses of the upper and lower Danube.

73. At about this time Vespasian banished and later executed Helvidius Priscus, son-in-law of Thrasea and his successor as leader of the Stoic opposition to the empire. He also banished the professors of philosophy, perhaps because their doctrines encouraged disloyalty.

77-84. Conquest of Britain. Cn. Julius Agricola (40–93) as imperial governor continued the conquest carried on by his predecessors Cerialis (72–74) over the Brigantes around Eboracum (York) and Frontinus (74–77) over the Silures in Wales. In 83 he fought a successful engagement against the Caledonians at **Mt. Graupius** (not *Grampius*), possibly near Aberdeen in Scotland, the farthest point reached by Roman arms. But Domitian recalled him in the following year, due to the fact that troops were needed for the German war. Despite later revolts Romanization progressed rapidly thereafter in Britain.

79-81. TITUS Flavius Vespasianus (b. 39) emperor, succeeding on the death of his father, Vespasian (June 24). Though popular, Titus was more concerned with playing the prince charming than with the economical administration of the empire. Public opinion forced him to put away the Jewish princess Berenice, already thrice married sister of Agrippa II.

79. An eruption of **Mt. Vesuvius**, on the Bay of Naples, buried the cities **Pompeii** and **Herculaneum**. In 80, a severe fire occurred in Rome. During this year, however, Titus dedicated magnificently the Coliseum and some elaborate public baths (*Thermae Titianae*).

81-96. Titus Flavius DOMITIANUS (b. 51) succeeded upon the death of his older brother, Titus (Sept. 13).

Naturally of a suspicious, perhaps cruel, temperament, Domitian had apparently borne with ill grace the favor and preference shown to his brother and came to the throne determined to rule without respect for others, especially the Senate. Nevertheless, despite the hatred which his reign aroused, he appears to have been an able administrator and general. He legislated against immorality and strictly controlled the governors.

83. Domitian crossed the Rhine at Mainz to **campaign against the Chatti.** His victory allowed him to begin the construction of a series of forts connected by a road and later by an earth rampart surmounted by a wooden palisade which served to prevent the infiltration of barbarians into Roman territory and as a base for offensive or defensive operations, though it would not have withstood a full-fledged invasion. This system, which later extended along the central Rhine, then from Mainz outside the *agri decumates* to the upper Danube so as to straighten the dangerous re-entrant angle of the frontier at that point, and along the upper Danube north of Rhaetia, was known as the *limes.*

84. Through his election as consul for ten years and censor for life, Domitian openly subordinated the republican aspect of the state (Senate and magistrates) to the monarchical. By increasing the pay of the troops by one-third (probably in itself a needed reform), he secured their loyalty. And with lavish shows and buildings, he ingratiated himself with the Roman mob. He revived the excessive use of the law of treason with its attendant encouragement of informers. After the abortive **revolt of Saturninus,** legate of upper Germany, in 88, he proceeded bitterly against the opposition; expulsion of the philosophers in 89 was followed in 93 by the execution of Herennius Senecio, Junius Arulenus Rusticus, and Helvidius Priscus. Flavius Clemens, a first cousin of Domitian, was executed in 95 on a charge of atheism (Christianity?), though perhaps the real ground was fear of him as a possible rival. Domitian, besides widening the cult of his deceased father and brother, had himself addressed as "lord and god" (*dominus et deus*), in the tradition of Gaius and perhaps Antony.

85-89. An **invasion of the Dacians** across the Danube into Moesia in 85 was repulsed by Domitian in person. In 89, however, the complete reduction of Dacia was prevented by his defeat at the hands of the Marcomanni and Quadi, who had occupied Bohemia, west of Dacia. Domitian made a somewhat humiliating peace with the Dacian king, **Decebalus,** who re-

tained his independence and **defeated, but** did not crush, the Marcomanni, Quadi, and Iazyges (a Sarmatian people) in 92. Thus the situation on the middle and lower Danube remained dangerous.

88. In consequence of the revolt of Saturninus, Domitian ceased the quartering of more than one legion in one camp to prevent any commander from gaining excessive power. The individual legions became permanently fixed in separate camps and no longer highly mobile, as they had been meant to be by Augustus.

96. Assassination of Domitian (Sept. 18) in a palace plot. The senate decreed the removal of his name from all public inscriptions (*damnatio memoriae*) and cancellation of his arrangements (*rescisio actorum*). Thus ended the Flavian house.

Since the conspirators, wisely, had a candidate ready to receive the Senate's grant of powers, the armies remained quiet and **Nerva,** an elderly and distinguished senator, acceded without difficulty. This marked the last attempt at self-assertion on the part of the old republican element in the principate. Already the old aristocratic families had become exhausted by persecution and race suicide. Their places had been taken by a new nobility of families elevated from the cities of Italy and the provinces through the imperial (equestrian) organization to senatorial rank. Despite a sentimental attachment to the traditions and forms of the Republic, the new generation admitted that the emperor was master, not, as Augustus had pretended, servant of the Senate.

96-98. Marcus Cocceius **NERVA** (b. 35), emperor. He was forced to recognize that the wishes of the army should be consulted by adopting in the autumn of 97 as his successor the successful general **Trajan.** Since Nerva and his three successors had no sons of their own, the principle of adoption, triumphing over heredity, secured a succession of capable rulers known as **the five good emperors** (Nerva, Trajan, Hadrian, Antoninus Pius, Marcus Aurelius). Nerva's two important contributions were to shift from the cities to the imperial treasury the cost of the postal service maintained for government dispatches (*cursus*) and to supplement existing private charity by a system of state aid for orphans (*alimenta*) supported by government grants or, under Trajan, by the interest on permanent loans to small farmers. Both reforms are symptomatic of the gradual breakdown of local economy and the municipal system. The last reference to legislation in the assemblies is to an agrarian law (*lex agraria*) in his reign. Nerva died Jan. 25, 98.

98-117. Marcus Ulpius TRAIANUS (b. 53), emperor. At the time he was in command in lower Germany, but was accepted at Rome without difficulty, though he was the first provincial emperor (born near Seville) and though he did not visit Rome until 99. On one Rhine frontier, Trajan continued the boundary palisade (*limes*) begun under Domitian.

101-107. In two **Dacian Wars** (101-102, 105-107), whose precise chronology is uncertain, Trajan first seriously exceeded the limits set to the Empire by Augustus. Upon the final death of Decebalus, Dacia, north of the Danube, became a Roman province. The war was commemorated by a column, covered with a spiral band of continuous reliefs in the magnificent Forum of Trajan in Rome. Trajan had many fine buildings and arches erected throughout the empire.

111-112 (?). **Pliny the Younger** was sent by Trajan as special legate with pro-consular power to reorganize the senatorial province of Bithynia. The appointment of Pliny is symptomatic of a spreading bankruptcy of municipalities, particularly in the Greek east, which necessitated imperial interference. The emperor not only sent special legates to senatorial provinces but appointed special supervisors for cities (*curatores rei publicae*). Extravagance and increased cost of administration, both municipal and imperial, thus started locally the crisis which disrupted the whole empire during the third century. Further indications of financial stringency appear in the enlargement of the alimentary system and in the burning of records of unpaid taxes in the Forum. During his governorship, Pliny corresponded with Trajan on many problems, including the treatment of Christians, toward whom Trajan instructed him to be lenient.

113-117. Parthian War. When the Parthian monarch **Chosroes** set up his puppet in Armenia, thus violating the compromise reached under Nero, Trajan declared war on Parthia. In 114, on the death of the Parthian puppet, he annexed Armenia. As he advanced, he formed the provinces of Mesopotamia (115) and Assyria (116) and made the Tigris the eastern boundary of the empire. He was, however, recalled from the Persian Gulf by a widespread **revolt of the Jews** and of the newly conquered areas. Both were suppressed with great severity. In 117 Trajan was repulsed from the desert town of Hatra. He died at Selinus in Cilicia (June 22 or July 9) after having adopted on his death-bed (some suspected his wife Plotina of having invented the adoption) his ward and cousin, **Hadrian**, at the time legate of Syria. Trajan's conquests, though spectacular, were of no permanent value and probably hastened the financial collapse by increasing the military expenses.

117-138. Publius Aelius HADRIANUS (b. 75), emperor. He was recognized as emperor by the Senate on Aug. 11. Almost immediately he abandoned the new provinces across the Euphrates. His lack of military ambition may have been responsible for the serious conspiracy, in 118, of four generals of consular rank, whom the Senate put to death. Hadrian then took an oath, which had become a test of constitutionalism, not to execute senators without trial by their peers. Under him the appointment of equestrians rather than freedmen to the important posts in the imperial secretariat became regular. He spent most of his reign (121-126, 129-134) traveling through the provinces, where he erected many buildings. He especially favored the Greek cities, notably Athens. In Britain he built (122-127) the elaborate combination of road, ditches, and stone wall from the Tyne to the Solway which constituted a boundary (*limes*) between the Roman province and the unconquered Caledonians. In Numidia he completed the extensive permanent camp of the Third Augustan Legion at Lambaesis.

In the collection of taxes, the companies of *publicani* had given way to individual collectors (*conductores*) under municipal supervision. Like his predecessors, Hadrian lightened or remitted certain taxes. Yet the economic difficulties continued. He had to deal with the problem of deserted farm lands (*agri deserti*), an indication that peasants were finding agriculture unprofitable, and with complaints from tenants (*coloni*) on the imperial estates in Africa. The replacement of slaves by tenants on large estates had begun when the cessation under Augustus of wars of conquest put an end to large supplies of cheap slaves. The oppression of tenants on both private and imperial estates by rising rents, heavier taxation, and forced labor rendered their lot ever more wretched.

131. The **Praetor's Edict** was definitively codified by the jurist Salvius Julianus under Hadrian's orders. Since no praetor could thereafter alter it, the extension of legal procedure by praetorian *formulae* ended. Senatorial decrees became only a confirmation of the imperial speech (*oratio principis*) which initiated them. The tribunician privilege of introducing business had been extended to the first five motions in any meeting so that the emperor presented all important matters. The only source of law was now the edicts of the emperor. The emperor hereafter summoned to his advisory council (*concilium*) distinguished jurists, who profoundly influenced the development of law.

132-135. The Jews of Judea revolted upon the founding of a Roman colony (Aelia Capitolina) in Jerusalem and the dedication of a temple to Jupiter Capitolinus on the site of their temple. Their leaders were the priest **Eleazar** and the fanatic **Simon Bar-Cocheba.** The suppression of the revolt all but depopulated Judea and thereafter Jews could enter Jerusalem but once a year. This completed the denationalization of the Jews begun by Vespasian. Until 1919 the Jews of the Dispersion (*Diaspora*), scattered among other peoples and, generally despised, possessed only a racial and religious unity.

138. Upon the death (Jan. 1) of his first choice for successor, **Lucius Ceionius Commodus,** Hadrian adopted (Feb. 25) the competent Titus Aurelius Fulvius Boionius Arrius **Antoninus,** who received the imperial powers and took the name Imperator Titus Aelius Antoninus. He, in his turn, had to adopt the young son of Commodus, Aelius Aurelius Commodus (later Lucius Aurelius Verus) and his own nephew, Marcus Annius Verus, henceforth called Marcus Aurelius Antoninus. Hadrian died on July 10.

138-161. Titus Aurelius ANTONINUS PIUS (b. 86) emperor. Warned by Hadrian's unpopularity with the Senate, he spent his reign in Rome. For his filial piety in securing the deification of Hadrian from a hostile Senate, he received the title *Pius.* His uneventful reign marked the culmination of the happy age of the Antonines.

142-143. Quintus Lollius Urbicus, legate of Britain, suppressed a revolt of the Brigantes in Yorkshire and, along the temporary line of forts built by Agricola from the Forth to the Clyde, constructed a turf wall north of Hadrian's. This however, was soon abandoned.

147. Marcus Aurelius, who had married Faustina, daughter of Antoninus, received the imperial powers. Antoninus apparently passed over the younger and incompetent Verus.

155. A brief war with **Vologesus of Parthia** ended in an inconclusive peace.

161-180. MARCUS AURELIUS Antoninus (b. 121) became emperor on the death of Antoninus (Mar. 7). Loyal to the wishes of Hadrian, he shared the imperial powers in full equality with **Lucius Aurelius Verus** (b. 130). This constitutes the first sure instance of complete collegiality in the imperial position, save for the office of chief pontiff (*pontifex maximus*), which remained unshared until Pupienus and Balbinus.

The reign of Marcus represents the triumph of Stoicism. Politically, the emperor was regarded as the human counterpart of the guiding reason of the universe and as obliged to rule for the good of his subjects. In law, the doctrine of the universal brotherhood of man, transcending limits of city or station, emphasized the humanizing trend which had long been operative, especially in legislation on slaves and women. Socially, the municipal and provincial aristocracy, which had appeared in the Senate through the imperial service, had wholly replaced the old Roman nobility and worked in complete loyalty with the emperor. Economically, the empire most nearly approximated unification. Italy had yielded her economic supremacy to the increased prosperity of the provinces and was losing its favored political position. It received from the emperor four special judges (created by Hadrian, abolished by Antoninus, revived by Marcus).

162-165. Verus was sent by Marcus to command in the east against Parthia, adumbrating the later territorial division of the empire. Though Verus dissipated at Antioch, his generals sacked Artaxata, Seleucia, and Ctesiphon, put a Roman puppet on the throne of Armenia, and made part of Mesopotamia a province.

166-167. The troops of Verus brought from the east a terrible plague, which seriously depopulated the empire.

166-175. The upper Danube was crossed by hordes of **Marcomanni** from Bohemia, with kindred tribes. Marcus created his young sons, Lucius Aelius Aurelius Commodus and Marcus Annius Verus, Caesars. He himself, with his colleague Verus, set out at once for the north. Verus died in 169. Just when Marcus had settled with the Marcomanni and had set an extremely important precedent by importing (172?) considerable numbers of them to occupy areas in the empire which had been depopulated by the plague, the **Sarmatians** attacked the lower Danube frontier.

175. Avidius Cassius, a distinguished general and legate of Syria, revolted, perhaps misled by a false report of Marcus' death. Though his revolt was crushed before Marcus could reach the east, it prevented a final settlement of the Sarmatian war.

177. Marcus' eldest son, **Commodus,** became Imperator, then Augustus, coequal with his father. The younger son had died in 169. Marcus is said to have issued a severe **rescript against the Christians.** In any case, they were subjected to increasingly bitter and far-reaching persecution, probably as fomenters of trouble by their prophecies of evil, and as disloyal to the state because they would not swear oaths to the emperor or offer incense to his statues or serve in the army.

178-180. The Marcomanni again opened war so that Marcus and Commodus had to go to the Danube. The wars of Marcus were commemorated on a column in Rome. Marcus died at Vindobona (Vienna) Mar. 17, 180).

180-192. Marcus Aurelius **COMMODUS Antoninus** (b. 161), as Marcus' son was now called, was the first emperor since Domitian to succeed by birth rather than by adoption. He made a peace with the Marcomanni which, though temporarily satisfactory, lost him favor with the troops. He returned to Rome, where he gave himself up to pleasure. The government was at first managed by the capable praetorian praefect **Perennis,** but on his unwarranted execution in 185, at the request of a deputation of mutinous soldiers from Britain, it fell to the mercenary freedman **Cleander,** who, in turn, was sacrificed in 189 to the Roman mob, which blamed him for a grain shortage. Commodus, already hostile to the Senate in consequence of an abortive conspiracy in 182, became extravagantly despotic. He identified himself with Hercules and lavished wealth acquired from the treasury or by confiscation on his favorites, the praetorians, whose pay he increased by a quarter, and on hunts of beasts, in which he participated. On Dec. 31, 192, his concubine Marcia, his chamberlain Eclectus, and the praetorian praefect Laetus had him strangled by a wrestler named Narcissus. Thus ended the Antonine line.

The important trends in the early empire were: politically, the transformation of the *princeps,* agent of the republican Senate and Roman people, into a Stoic king, head of a state in which all good men co-operated for the common weal; administratively, the subordination of the republican magistracies and organs to the will of the emperor and the growth of the imperial secretariat and equestrian civil service; socially, the substitution for the irreconcilable republican nobility of a new aristocracy drawn from the better classes throughout the Empire, which, though sentimentally republican, accepted the Empire if the emperor was good; economically, the financial breakdown of the municipal system, which was accompanied by a loss of local pride, and the increased burdens of the imperial government; and militarily, greater and more constant pressure on both frontiers, north and east, at the same time.

The literature of the early empire falls into two periods; the **Augustan Age,** which, with the preceding Ciceronian Age, forms the **Golden Age;** and (after 14) the **Silver Age** of the Julio-Claudians, Flavians, and Antonines. Under Augustus, the chief figures gathered around his friend, their patron **Maecenas: Publius Vergilius Maro** or Virgil (70–19 B.C.) author of the *Bucolics, Georgics* and the *Aeneid,* and **Quintus Horatius Flaccus** or Horace (65–8 B.C.), author of *Odes, Epodes, Satires,* and *Epistles.* Besides these, **Albius Tibullus** (54–19 B.C.) and **Sextus Propertius** (50–15 B.C) wrote erotic elegies and **Publius Ovidius Naso** or Ovid (43 B.C.–17 A.D.) composed the erotic *Amores, Heroides, Ars Amatoria,* etc., and the longer *Metamorphoses, Fasti, Tristia, Letters from Pontus,* etc. **Titus Livius,** or Livy (59 B.C.–17 A.D.) composed his *History of Rome* (*Libri ab urbe condita*), a prose glorification comparable to the *Aeneid.* The writers of the Silver Age are numerous and less outstanding: **Aulus Persius Flaccus** (34–62 A.D.) and **Decimus Iunius Juvenalis** (55–138) wrote satire, and **Marcus Valerius Martialis** (40–104) composed satirical epigrams. **Lucius Annaeus Seneca** the Philosopher (1–65), son of Seneca the Rhetorician (55 B.C.–40 A.D.), and his nephew, **Marcus Annaeus Lucanus** (39–65), author of the epic *Pharsalis,* belong, like Martial, to the Spanish group of authors prominent in the first century, as does also **Marcus Fabius Quintilianus** (35–100), teacher of rhetoric and author of an *Institutio Oratoria.* **Gaius Petronius Arbiter** (d. 66), the Epicurean friend of Nero, probably composed the *Satyricon,* a picaresque novel. **Publius Cornelius Tacitus** (55–118?), author of the *Dialogue on Oratory,* the life of his father-in-law *Agricola,* the *Germania,* the *Annals,* and the *Histories,* **Gaius Plinius Caecilius Secundus** (61–113?), whose *Letters* are preserved, and nephew of the erudite Gaius Plinius Secundus (23–79), the author of the *Natural History* who died in the eruption of Vesuvius, and the biographer **Gaius Suetonius Tranquillus** (70–121?), whose *Lives of the Twelve Caesars* extend from Caesar through Domitian, belonged to the literary circle which flourished under Trajan. Under

Hadrian began a revival of interest in pre-Ciceronian Latin language and literature, while under the Antonines, a school of African writers introduced a florid and exaggerated style. Its chief exponent was **Lucius Apuleius** (124-?), whose *Metamorphoses* and other writings cast light on the mystery religions and neo-Pythagoreanism. The surviving writings of emperors, apart from administrative edicts, etc., are the succinct account of his life by Augustus, preserved on inscriptions at Ancyra (Ankara, *Monumentum Ancyranum*) and, in fragments, elsewhere; some speeches and letters of Claudius in inscriptions or papyri; and the *Meditations*, in Greek, of Marcus Aurelius.

In **philosophy**, Stoicism remained dominant throughout the period and claimed among its chief exponents the statesman **Seneca** (1-65), the slave **Epictetus** (60-140), and the emperor **Marcus Aurelius**. But it had to compete with mystical tendencies which found expression in astrology, in such **oriental religions** as those of the Egyptian **Isis**, the Persian **Mithras**, and the Jewish **Jesus Christ**, and in a revival of the early Greek mystical philosophy of Pythagoras. **Christianity**, which had begun as a Jewish sect but was universalized and widely spread by the ardent convert, **Paul**, soon developed both an organization and a literature. The organization consisted of independent churches governed by boards of elders (*presbyters*) among whom one frequently secured pre-eminence as bishop (*episcopos*, overseer). Those churches which traced their foundation to the immediate associates of Christ, the **Apostles**, or which arose in big cities, tended to overshadow the less important ones and their bishops, especially, in the west, the Bishop of Rome, became authorities in ecclesiastical quarrels. Heresies appeared from the beginning, like **Gnosticism** and, about **150**, **Montanism**. Christian literature commenced with the *Gospels* and *apostolic* (or pseudo-apostolic) *writings*. The early martyrs, **Ignatius of Antioch** (d. 117?) and **Polycarp of Smyrna** (d. 155?), as well as the Greek bishop, **Irenaeus of Lyons** (c. 130-200), who attacked the heretical transcendentalism of the Gnostics, wrote largely for Christians. But the increasing hostility of the public and government occasioned apologetic writings addressed to non-Christians, like those of **Justin Martyr** (153?) and others.

Augustan art, like Augustan literature, achieved a happy blend of native Roman realism and Greek idealism, as best appears in the sculpture of the *Ara Pacis* or the famous "Prima Porta" statue of Augustus. Julio-Claudian art aped the manner without attaining the excellence of Augustan. Under the Flavians, a certain heaviness and materialism, characteristic of the period, appeared. But two relief techniques were perfected, that of illusionism, the attempt to represent space, as on the panels of the Arch of Titus, and the continuous style, by which a series of events was represented in an unbroken sequence, as on the Column of Trajan. Hadrian's reign witnessed a revived interest in and copying of Greek archaic art. Under the Antonines, a crudeness appears on the Column of Marcus, though not in the reliefs from his arch. Mention should be made of the **wall-paintings** of all periods from the 2d century B.C. to 79 A.D. preserved at Pompeii and of the common red pottery with appliqué reliefs known as **Arretine ware** (modeled on the Greek Samian ware) made first in Italy, at Arretium (Arezzo), and then progressively at various places in Gaul and even in Britain.

In **architecture**, the grandeur of the Augustan Age, as in the porch of the Pantheon or the Maison Carrée at Nîmes, gave way to massiveness, as in the temple of Venus at Rome and the Coliseum. But the Roman engineers produced at all periods substantial and useful structures: aqueducts, theaters, circuses, baths, harbors, roads, etc.

2. THE THIRD CENTURY (192-284)

The third century is characterized by the complete collapse of government and economics throughout the Mediterranean. Upon the death of Commodus, the armies asserted themselves against the Senate as they had in 68. The ultimate victor, **Septimius**, finally and frankly unmasked the military basis of the imperial power. After an attempted revival of "constitutional" government under Alexander, the imperial position became the reward of successful generals of increasingly provincial and uncultured origins. The one ideal which still dominated the armies was the preservation of the frontiers against the Germans and Persians. Even the separatist movements were aimed, not at independence, but at the preservation of the *imperium Romanum*. To secure this end and their own support, the troops made and unmade emperors and drained the scanty resources of the civilians by taxation, depreciation of coinage, and exactions of food, quarters, etc. The military wholly absorbed the civil administration. Intellectual life ceased, inscriptions became rare, and archaeological finds show a rapid decline in skill and taste.

193. Publius Helvius PERTINAX, emperor. He was chosen by the Senate, but his strict and economical rule led to his murder (Mar. 28) by the praetorian guard, which then auctioned off the empire to him who promised them the highest gift of money, **M. Didius Severus Julianus** (b. 133?). The British legions proclaimed as emperor the legate, **D. Clodius Septimius Albinus;** the Pannonian, the legate of Upper Pannonia **L. Septimius Severus** (April or May); and the Syrian, the legate **C. Pescennius Niger Justus.** Septimius at once seized Rome, where the Senate deposed and executed Julianus (June 1).

193-211. L. SEPTIMIUS SEVERUS (b. 146, at Leptis in Africa), emperor. He dissolved the existing praetorian cohorts, composed of recruits from Italy, and enrolled new ones from deserving legionary veterans. He kept Albinus quiet by recognizing him as Caesar (i.e. heir). He then defeated Niger in **battles at Cyzicus** and **Nicaea** and at **Issus** (the Cilician Gates), and put him to death near Antioch (194). Byzantium held out until 196, when it was sacked and reduced to the status of a village. Albinus, who now claimed full equality, was defeated and slain (197, Feb. 19) at Lugdunum (Lyons), which was also sacked and never recovered its prosperity.

Severus created three new legions, one of which was quartered on the Alban Lake in Italy, hitherto free from the presence of legionary troops. He appointed equestrians to command these legions contrary to the Augustan rule and also put the new province of Mesopotamia under an equestrian. He thus initiated the replacement of senators by equestrians in military posts which culminated under Gallienus. Military marriages were recognized, since the immobilization of the legions had made these usual. Auxiliaries were settled on public land in return for military service and the legionary pay was raised. Severus humiliated the Senate, which had supported Albinus, and put equestrian deputies to watch senatorial governors. When he closed down the now almost defunct courts (*quaestiones*), he transferred the jurisdiction over Rome and the area within 100 miles to the praefect of the city and over the rest of Italy to the praetorian praefect, who also exercised jurisdiction on appeal from the provinces.

After the fall of the single and powerful praetorian praefect Palutianus (205), Severus returned to the practice of having two, one of whom was the distinguished jurist Papinian. In the criminal law, a distinction was drawn between the privileged classes (*honestiores*), who were treated favorably, and the ordinary people (*humiliores*). The emperor began the subdivision of provinces into smaller units, which culminated under Diocletian and extended the organization of municipalities as the basis of tax-collecting even to Egypt, which shows how valueless municipal status had become. He created a new treasury in addition to the *fiscus* (the original imperial treasury) and the *patrimonium Caesaris* (originally the ruler's private property, then crown property), namely the *res privata*, his personal funds. He depreciated the silver content of the denarius to 60%. Despite all of these difficulties, his administration was good.

197-198. In a successful **Parthian war** Severus advanced as far as Ctesiphon and reconstituted the Province of Mesopotamia under an equestrian governor with two legions.

205-211. A recurrence of **troubles in Britain**, which had suffered from invasion in 155 and revolt in 180, required the presence of Septimius himself to fight the Caledonians. He definitely withdrew from the wall of Antoninus to that of Hadrian, which he rebuilt. He died at Eboracum (York) on Feb. 4, 211.

211-217. CARACALLA (properly Caracallus), so named from a Gallic cloak which he wore. He was the oldest son of Septimius and had been associated with him as Augustus (198). To strengthen the bond between the Severi and the Antonines he had changed his name from Septimius Bassianus to Marcus Aurelius (Severus) Antoninus (197). Upon his accession, he murdered his colleague (since 209) and younger brother, P. (originally L.) Septimius (Antoninus) Geta (b. 189), along with the jurist Papinian and many others. He increased the pay of the troops to a ruinous degree and called them all *Antoniniani*. To meet the consequent deficit he issued a new coin, the *Antoninianus*, with a face value of 2 *denarii* but a weight of only one and two thirds. He erected at Rome the vast **Baths of Caracalla** (*thermae Antoninianae*).

212. The **EDICT OF CARACALLA** (*constitutio Antoniniana*) extended Roman citizenship to all free inhabitants of the empire save a limited group, perhaps including the Egyptians. His motive has been much disputed; citizenship now meant

so little that this step was a natural culmination of the levelling down of distinctions which had been continuous throughout
the empire. Moreover, he may have hoped
to extend to all inhabitants the inheritance
tax paid by Roman citizens.

213-217. Caracalla successfully defended
the northern frontier against the
Alamanni in southern Germany and the
Goths on the lower Danube (214), and in
the east he annexed Armenia (216). But
as he was preparing an invasion of Parthia,
he was murdered by a group of his officers
(217, Apr. 8).

217-218. **M. Opellius (Severus) MACRI-
NUS** (b. 164?), emperor. He was
a Mauretanian who had risen from the
ranks to be praetorian praefect, and was
the first equestrian emperor. He surrendered Caracalla's eastern gains and sought
to reduce the pay of the troops, who set up
as a rival (218, May 16) at Emesa in Syria
a grandnephew of Julia Domna, the Syrian
wife of Septimius. Macrinus fell on June
8, 218.

218-222. **ELAGABALUS** (Heliogabalus, b.
c. 205), emperor. He derived his
cognomen from the Emesa god, whose priest
he was. To legitimize his rule, he changed
his name from (Varius) Avitus to Marcus
Aurelius Antoninus and claimed to be a
son of Caracalla. While Elagabalus surrendered himself to license and introduced
the worship of his god to Rome, the empire
was really ruled by his forceful mother,
Julia Maesa. She obliged him to adopt
his cousin (Gessius) Bassianus (Alexianus?),
son of her sister, Julia Mamaea. The praetorians murdered Elagabalus (222, Mar.
11).

222-235. **Marcus Aurelius SEVERUS AL-
EXANDER** (b. c. 208), emperor.
He was the adopted son of Elagabalus and
was dominated by his mother, Mamaea.
She established a regency committee of
senators and used the advice of the jurists
Paulus and Ulpian. The new rule was an
attempt to revive the Antonine monarchy.
It was marked, however, by an extension
of governmental control over the trade
guilds (*collegia*) and further depreciation of
the coinage.

227. **The New Persian (Sassanid) Empire**
(p. 124) was founded by **Ardashir**
(Artashatr, Artaxerxes), a Persian who
overthrew the Parthian Arsacids, Artabanus V and Vologaesus V. The strength
of the new empire lay in a revival of Zoroastrianism.

231-233. **Persian attacks** required the
presence of Alexander, who seems
to have won some success before his recall
to the west.

234-235. Alexander was forced to buy
peace from the Alamanni on the
Rhine. The disgruntled troops murdered
him (235, Mar.). With his death the last
attempt to preserve a civil or "constitutional" government came to an end and
military anarchy began.

235-238. **C. Julius Verus MAXIMINUS**
"Thrax" (b. c. 172), a Thracian
peasant of huge size and no culture, was
elevated by the Rhine legions, but was not
recognized by the Senate, which put forward the senators **M. Clodius Pupienus
Maximus** and **D. Caelius Calvinus Balbinus.** In the meantime, the African legions
proclaimed the eighty-year-old pro-consul
Marcus Antonius Gordianus I and his son
Gordianus II. Though the praefect of
Mauretania defeated and slew them, the
populace of Rome forced the Senate to join
the grandson, **Gordianus III,** with Pupienus
and Albinus. Maximin was slain by his
troops while besieging Aquileia (238, June)
and the praetorians murdered Pupienus and
Balbinus (238, June?).

238-244. **Marcus Antonius GORDIANUS
III** (b. 225) was dominated by the
wise praetorian praefect **C. Furius Timesitheus** (Misitheus?), whose daughter he
married (241). Timesitheus drove the son
of Ardashir, Shapur (Sapor), out of Antioch
(241-243) but died himself of disease. The
new praetorian praefect, an Arabian, made
himself co-Augustus, then murdered Gordian (early in 244).

244-249. **M. Julius PHILIPPUS "ARABS"**
bought peace with the Persians
and, at Rome, celebrated the *ludi saeculares*
for Rome's thousandth birthday (248). He
was killed at Verona (249) in battle against
his commander in Dacia, Decius.

249-251. **C. Messius Quintus Traianus
DECIUS** (b. 200?), instituted the
first general **persecution of the Christians,**
and perhaps of all who would not sacrifice
to the emperor. Emperor-worship though
used as early as Pliny as a test against
Christians, seems now to have become a
requirement of all loyal subjects, which indicates a growing belief in the actual divinity of the emperor. Decius was slain
by the Goths in Dacia (251) because
of the disloyalty of the legate of Moesia,
Gallus.

251-253. **C. Vibius Trebonianus GALLUS**
(b. c. 207) put to death his co-
Augustus, **Hostilianus,** son of Decius. In
his reign began a fifteen-year plague. When
he marched against his successor in Moesia,
the Moor M. Aemilius Aemilianus, his own
troops slew him (before Oct., 253).

253-259. **P. Licinius VALERIANUS** (b. c.
193), commander in Germany, be-

came emperor, with his son Gallienus as co-Augustus. He fought unsuccessfully against the Franks, who crossed the Rhine in 256, the Alamanni, who reached Milan, and the Goths. As the frontiers ceased to hold, cities within the empire began to build walls. Valerian recovered Antioch again from Shapur (256–258) but was treacherously seized at a parley (259?) and died a captive at an uncertain date.

259-268. P. Licinius Egnatius GALLI-ENUS (b. 218) continued to reign alone, though pretenders appeared throughout the empire and the period has been called that of the "thirty tyrants." He completed the substitution of equestrians for senators as legionary commanders and as governors.

The Goths, who had broken through to the Black Sea, harried Asia and the Aegean area from ships.

258-267. Odenathus, ruler of Palmyra in the Syrian Desert, kept the Persians out of Asia (260), but his queen and successor **Zenobia,** declared her independence (267).

259-268. Postumus set himself up as emperor in Gaul. **Gallienus** was finally murdered by his own troops before Mediolanum (Milan), where he was besieging the pretender **Aureolus** (before Sept., 268). Aureolus in his turn was slain by Claudius II.

268-270. M. Aurelius CLAUDIUS II "Gothicus" (b.?) was the first of a series of capable Illyrian emperors who prepared the way for Diocletian. He repelled a Gothic invasion of the Balkans (269, whence his title) at **Naissus** (Nisch) and settled numbers of Goths in the vacant lands of the Danubian provinces. Upon his death from plague, the Balkan legions elevated his compatriot and assistant, Aurelian (before July, 270).

270-275. L. Domitius AURELIANUS (b. c. 214?) was rightly entitled "restorer of the world" (*restitutor orbis*). He abandoned trans-Danubian Dacia and settled its Roman inhabitants in a new Dacia carved out of Moesia. He repulsed the Alamanni from Italy (271) and built the existing walls of Rome (271–276) as a protection against future incursions.

271-272. Probus, and then Aurelian himself, defeated and captured Zenobia and, upon a second revolt, sacked Palmyra (273), which remained a ruin.

273 or 274. Aurelian recovered Gaul from the successor of Postumus, Tetricus, in a battle at Châlons. Both Zenobia and Tetricus adorned his magnificent triumph in Rome (274). He was murdered

by some officers while preparing to invade Persia (275).

275-276. M. Claudius TACITUS (b.?), an elderly senator, was appointed emperor against his will by the Senate, to whom the troops left the choice (275, autumn?). Though he defeated the Goths and Alans, who had invaded Asia Minor, the troops slew him and, soon after, his brother M. Annius Florianus.

276-281. M. Aurelius PROBUS (b.?), an Illyrian, was saluted by the eastern armies (276, early summer?). He repelled from Gaul the Franks and Alamanni and other peoples, who had inflicted great devastation. He also strengthened the Danube frontier, quieted Asia Minor, and suppressed pretenders in Gaul. When he tried to use the troops in works of peace, e.g. clearing the canals in Egypt, they murdered him (281, autumn?).

281-283. M. Aurelius CARUS, an Illyrian (?) and praetorian praefect to Aurelian, succeeded and campaigned successfully against the Persian monarch Varahran. He perished (murder, disease, or lightning? in 283, midsummer?) and his son Marcus Aurelius Numerius Numerianus, co-Augustus with him, was murdered (284, autumn). A second son, M. Aurelius Carinus, tried to hold the west against **Diocletian,** an officer whom the eastern army had elected emperor, but he was slain by his own troops during the battle at the river Margus in Moravia (285, summer?).

The troubles of the third century had two main causes: the increased pressure on the frontiers from the new Germanic tribes and from the vigorous Persian Empire, and the economic collapse within, the causes of which cannot be wholly established. In part, at least, the economic crisis was due to the heavy burdens of government and defense and to the oppressive and erratic system of taxation; in part, perhaps, to a "fatigue of spirit." Literature ceased almost entirely. Of art and building notable examples survive, like the Arch of Septimius, the Baths of Caracalla, and the Walls of Aurelian at Rome, but these are imitative and uninspired. **Roman law,** however, reached its heights under the Antonines and Severi. Though the two great schools of jurisprudence, the **Sabinians** and the **Proculians,** originated under Augustus or Tiberius, the great jurists were **Salvius Julianus** under Hadrian, who dealt with the **Praetor's Edict, Gaius** under the Antonines, whose *Institutes* became a standard textbook, and the triumvirate of **Papinian, Paul, and Ulpian** under the Severi, whose various works provided most of the material for Justinian's *Institutes*. In **philosophy,**

neo-Pythagoreanism gave way to neo-Platonism, whose chief exponents were Plotinus (204-270), Porphyrius (233-306), and, later, Iamblichus (d. 333?).

Despite the persecutions under the Antonines, Severus, Maximin, and Decius, the Christian Church grew in numbers and power. Its chief competitor was the cult of the Persian Mithras, a god popular with and widely spread by the troops. The major internal problems of the church in the third century were the heresy called Montanism (an extreme asceticism) and the acute question of the treatment of those who lapsed from their faith during persecutions (*lapsi*) or betrayed the sacred books (*traditores*). Those who had confessed their faith in the face of persecution (*confessores*) opposed the readmission of backsliders to full communion, while the church as a whole, led in the west by the Bishop of Carthage, Cyprian, and the Bishop of Rome, Stephen, advocated a milder policy. The extremists were called Novatians in the third century and Donatists in the fourth, after a certain Donatus, whose riotous bands of schismatics (*circumcelliones*) terrorized the province of Africa. Christian apologetics gave way to homiletic and theological writings in the hands of the African Tertullian (150-225) and Cyprian (200-258) and the Alexandrians Clement (d. 215) and Origen (182-251), the last two of whom combined Platonism with Christianity in the manner of contemporary neo-Platonism.

3. THE LATER EMPIRE (284-527)

284-305. C. Aurelius Valerius DIOCLETIANUS (b. 245, saluted as emperor 284, Nov. 17?), was of humble Illyrian stock. Faced with the task of bringing order out of chaos, he desired to emulate Augustus, to revive the happy days of the early empire, but he succeeded only in creating an oriental despotism.

Since it is difficult to distinguish how far the reorganization of the empire was due to Diocletian and how far to Constantine, a brief outline will be given here. In general, all these reforms were merely a regularization and crystallization of practices developed in the 3d century. Although the Senate continued to meet and the higher republican magistrates survived to varying dates, e.g. the consulship in the east until its abolition by Justinian, and although two provinces, Asia and Africa, still received senatorial pro-consuls, nevertheless the whole administration was organized in a pyramid of interlocking bureaus emanating from the emperor.

According to Diocletian's system, which operated only sporadically, there were to be two coequal emperors (*Augusti*), as in the case of Marcus and Verus. Now, however, the empire was divided for practical administrative purposes into two spheres, eastern and western, the line between which ran from the Danube to the Adriatic south of Dalmatia. Each part was administered by one of the Augusti. But the edicts of the emperors were issued conjointly and they might on occasion command in one another's spheres.

The emperors ruled absolutely, in virtue of selection by the troops and without the consent of the Senate (since 282). Each surrounded himself with the pomp of an oriental court. No longer was he the first citizen among equals (*princeps*), but, since Aurelian, "lord" (*dominus*). All connected with him was "sacred" (the "sacred court," *sacra aula*, appeared under the Severi). Each emperor chose an assistant and successor (*Caesar*).

Under these four rulers, praetorian praefects, now wholly civilian magistrates, administered the four praefectures, Gaul, Italy, Illyrium, and the east. Each praefecture was divided into several dioceses under vicars (*uicarii*) independent of the praefects and directly responsible to the emperor. The dioceses were subdivided into provinces under presidents (*praesides or rectores*). These provinces were subdivisions of those of the early empire and their number increased from 60 to 116.

The military power, which during the third century had absorbed all the functions of government, was now wholly separated from the civilian. Each province had a duke (*dux*) or count (*comes*) in charge of its permanent garrison, which was not, as in the early empire, concentrated in large camps, but scattered in smaller posts along the frontier, often in the guise of soldier-peasants (*limitanei, riparienses*, border or riverbank men). In each praefecture, under masters of the infantry and of the horse (*magistri peditum, equitum*), were mobile forces which could be rushed to strengthen threatened points (*comitatenses*, companions of the emperor). The emperors, moreover, had large bodies of special guards (*protectores or domestici*). The old legions were split into smaller, more mobile but less highly trained units of about 2000 men. Heavy armed cavalry (*cataphractarii*) played a large part in warfare. The auxiliary troops were mostly mercenary bands of barbarians, whose chiefs became extremely influential. The total forces now numbered about 500,000 men, an increase over the Augustan 300,000 which accounts in part for the financial problems of the later empire.

Besides the separate and elaborate administration for each territorial unit, the emperors had an extensive central bureaucracy, the various "offices" (*officia*) under such officials like the quaestor of the sacred palace (*quaestor sacri palatii*, the chief judicial officer), the chancellor (*magister memoriae*, master of records), and the personnel manager (*magister officiorum*, master of the offices, very powerful because he had a finger in every department). These men automatically belonged to the Senate, and other high officials had the titles of honor formerly reserved for equestrians, who vanished as a class. The senators also now formed a class of dominant and very wealthy landowners throughout the empire, who might seldom actually attend the Senate, but who enjoyed privilege and exemption. The rest of the population were crushed by heavy taxes, which were largely collected in kind (*annona*) after the collapse of the currency, and which were reassessed every fifteenth year by an "indiction" (*indictio*). Both labor and property were evaluated in terms of a unit of wheat-producing land (*iugum*). The taxation bore especially heavily on the members of the municipal senates (*curiales, decuriones*), who continued to be held responsible for the collection of taxes and the payment of arrears, and on the small landowners, who had to provide recruits for the army and see that waste lands (*agri deserti*) were kept under cultivation. Thus freemen found it wisest to flee the country, enter monasteries, or become serfs (*coloni*) on large estates. Craftsmen and tradesmen were rigorously confined to their professions. The whole caste system was arranged to insure the maintenance of the administration and the army. Since, therefore, it benefited no one but the great landlords or imperial officials, the vast majority of the population lost interest and either accepted the barbarian invasions supinely or even welcomed relief from oppression. Whether, however, this lethargy, which pervaded not only the political and economic life but also the intellectual, save in the Christian Church, resulted from the system or whether the unwieldy and inflexible

system indicated the poor mental caliber of the rulers, so many of whom were of peasant or barbarian origin, and the effeteness of the hereditary upper class, cannot be determined.

285. Upon the defeat of Carinus, Diocletian chose as his colleague (Caesar in 285, Augustus in 286) the Illyrian **M. Aurelius Valerius Maximianus** (b. c. 240?), who was a harsh, uneducated man but a competent general. They assumed the titles respectively of *Jovius* and *Herculius*. Diocletian took up his residence in the east, at Nicomedia in Bithynia, from which the main road to the upper Euphrates frontier began, while **Maximian**, in the west, lived mostly at Mediolanum (Milan) in northern Italy, which was a better center for the defense of the northern frontier than Rome. Despite its sentimental pre-eminence, Rome thereafter declined in practical importance. But the departure of the imperial court gave the Bishop of Rome increased scope.

293, Mar. 1. Diocletian chose as Caesar **C. Galerius Valerius Maximianus** (b. c. 250), who became his son-in-law and received the government of Illyricum; Maximian chose **Flavius Valerius Constantius** (misnamed Chlorus) (b. ?) who divorced his wife Helena to marry Maximian's daughter Theodora; he received the praefecture of Gaul. He at once drove out the rebel Carausius from Boulogne and subdued the Franks.

294. A revolt was raised in Egypt by Achilleus, whom Diocletian besieged in Alexandria (295) and captured.

296. **Narses,** King of Persia, invaded Roman Mesopotamia and defeated Galerius, but the latter gathered reinforcements in the winter and returned to defeat Narses (297) and recover Mesopotamia; Roman influence was restored in Armenia, whose king became Christian.

297. Constantius crossed to Britain and his lieutenant defeated and killed Allectus, who had murdered and replaced Carausius.

298. Constantius returned to Gaul and defeated the Alamanni.

301. An edict limiting prices of goods and labor was passed by Diocletian in an attempt to end the economic distress caused by the collapse of the currency; no attempt was made to enforce it in the west, and in the east it soon proved impracticable.

303, Feb. 23. Galerius persuaded Diocletian to declare a general persecution of the **Christians,** which, however, Constantius did not enforce in his praefecture. The persecution was stopped in the entire west in 306 but raged in the east until 313.

305, May 1. Diocletian and Maximian abdicated; Galerius and Constantius became Augusti; Diocletian and Galerius selected as Caesars Flavius Valerius Severus under Constantius, receiving the praefecture of Italy, and for Galerius his own nephew **Galerius Valerius Maximinus Daia,** who received Syria and Egypt. The hereditary claims of Maximian's son Maxentius and Constantius' son Constantine were neglected.

306-337. Flavius Valerius CONSTANTINUS I THE GREAT (b. 288? of Constantius and Helena) fled from Galerius to his father in Britain. On the death of the latter (July) Constantine was saluted as emperor by the troops, but made an agreement with Galerius by which he became Caesar and Severus became Augustus. In Rome the praetorians and the people proclaimed **Maxentius Augustus** (Oct. 28); he called his father Maximian to be Augustus and temporarily took the title of Caesar. When the Emperor Severus came with an army, it deserted and he surrendered to Maximian and was later executed by Maxentius. In fear of Galerius, Maximian went to Constantine in Gaul; Constantine recognized him as senior Augustus and married his daughter, Fausta. Galerius attempted an invasion of Italy (307), but disloyalty in his army forced its abandonment. Maxentius took the title of Augustus (308) and Maximian fled to Constantine; for four years Maxentius ruled in Italy very oppressively. Galerius induced Diocletian to preside over a conference at Carnuntum, where it was decided that Maximian should abdicate, **Valerius Licinianus Licinius** was to be Augustus in the west, and Constantine was to return to the rank of Caesar. Constantine refused and Galerius gave him and Daia the rank of *filius Augusti*; both were still unsatisfied, and were finally given the rank of Augustus (310). Maximian made an attempt to revolt, but was killed by Constantine. When Galerius died of disease (311, May), Daia seized Asia Minor, leaving the Balkans to Licinius.

312. Constantine suddenly invaded Italy and after winning a battle over Maxentius' general at Verona defeated and killed Maxentius himself near Rome at the **Milvian Bridge** (Saxa Rubra) (Oct. 28). Before the battle he is said to have seen in the sky a cross and the device *in hoc signo vinces.* Sometime later he became a Christian. He dissolved the praetorian guard. At a meeting with Licinius in Milan (early

313?) equal rights were proclaimed for all religions and the property confiscated from the Christians was restored by the **Edict of Milan.**

313. Daia crossed to Europe, but was defeated by Licinius at **Tzirallum** and fled to Tarsus, where he died soon after. Licinius now held the entire east and Constantine the west.

314. After a brief war, in which Licinius was defeated at **Cibalae** (Oct. 8), a peace was made giving Constantine all of the Balkans except Thrace.

323. Relations between the two were strained by Licinius' anti-Christian policy, and war finally broke out. Licinius was defeated at **Adrianople** (July 3), his fleet was defeated by Constantine's son Crispus, and Licinius was again defeated at Chrysopolis in Anatolia (Sept. 18). He surrendered and was executed in the next year.

324-337. CONSTANTINE REUNITED THE EMPIRE under his sole rule. He had already interfered in the affairs of the Church (at its invitation) when in 316 he tried to settle the Donatist schism.

325. He now summoned the **first oecumenical** (world-wide) **council of the Church,** to meet at **Nicaea** in Asia Minor. It was to settle a controversy which had arisen in Alexandria between the priest **Arius,** who maintained that Christ was of different substance from God (*heter-ousios*), and the Bishop Alexander (succeeded in 328 by **Athanasius,** who continued his doctrine), who supported the doctrine that they were of the same substance (consubstantiality, *homo-ousios*). The council agreed on a creed favorable to Alexander (not the present "Nicene" creed); in addition it adopted certain canons giving privileges to the Bishops (Patriarchs) of Alexandria, Antioch, and Rome. Constantinople later acquired similar rights. The **primacy of Rome,** although in a very restricted sense, had been generally recognized in the west since the **Council of Arles** in 314. The prominent part taken by Constantine in this council laid the basis for the later supremacy of the emperor in the eastern Church. Though Arius died a horrible death in 336, Constantine and his successors swung the Church increasingly toward Arianism, and strife in the Church on this subject was not ended until the reign of Theodosius I. The west remained firmly Athanasian.

330, May 11. Constantine dedicated as his capital **CONSTANTINOPLE,**

which he had spent four years in building on the site of Byzantium, commanding the strategic center of the east, the Bosporous.

337, May 22. Constantine died at Nicomedia. He had been induced (326) by his wife Fausta to execute Crispus, his son by his first wife. His heirs were three sons and two nephews. Of the sons, all Augusti, Constantinus II (b. 317) received the praefectures of Italy and Gaul; Constantius II (b. 317) took the east; and Constans (b. 323?) got Illyricum and part of Africa. The nephews, Dalmatius and Annibalianus, were at once executed by Constantius.

337-361. RULE OF CONSTANTINE'S SONS. While Constantius carried on an indecisive war against Persia, Constantinus attacked Constans, but was slain at Aquileia (340). Constans was killed by the pretender **Magnus Magnentius** (350, Jan.).

351, Sept. 28. Constantius defeated Magnentius at **Mursa**, near the confluence of the Danube and Drave. The latter slew himself at Lugdunum (353) and the empire was once more united.

351, Mar. 15. Constantius chose his cousin Gallus as Caesar, but had him executed in 354.

355, Nov. 6. Constantius chose as Caesar the half-brother of Gallus, **Julian**, who was given command against the Alamanni and Franks.

360. Julian marched against Constantius, who died before Julian reached the east (361).

361-363. JULIANUS, "the Apostate," (b. 332). He is known chiefly for his attempt to substitute paganism for Christianity and to organize a pagan church. After continuing his successes against the Franks, he campaigned against the Persians, but died on his way back from an attack on Ctesiphon (363, Jul. 26). With him ended the line of Constantine.

363-364. JOVIANUS (b. c. 331), was elected by the troops. He surrendered Mesopotamia to the Persians and died soon after (364, Feb. 17).

364-375. FLAVIUS VALENTINIANUS I (b. 321) was the next choice of the troops. He ably defended the west against the barbarians and made his brother **Valens** co-Augustus in the east (364, Mar. 28).

367. Valentinian made his son Gratian co-emperor in the west. Valentinian died on an expedition against the Quadi and Sarmatians (375, Nov. 17).

375-383. GRATIANUS (b. 359), named his half-brother **Valentinian II** (b. 371) co-Augustus in the west.

376. The Visigoths (West Goths) crossed the Danube. Valens fell in battle against them at **Adrianople** (378, Aug. 9). The Goths continued to ravage the Balkan region.

379, Jan. 19. Gratian appointed as co-Augustus for the east, **Theodosius**, son of a successful general in Britain.

382. Gratian, at the request of Bishop Ambrose, removed from the senate-house the pagan altar of victory and gave up the title of *pontifex maximus*.

379-395. FLAVIUS THEODOSIUS "THE GREAT" (b. 346). He supported orthodoxy (i.e. Athanasianism) in the east, and came to terms with the Goths by settling them as military allies (*foederati*) in the Balkans.

383. The British legions proclaimed **Magnus Maximus**, who seized Gaul. Gratian was slain at Lugdunum (Aug. 25). Theodosius recognized Maximus.

387. When Maximus drove Valentinian II from Italy, Theodosius captured and executed him at Aquileia (388, July 28).

390. Theodosius cruelly massacred 7000 people at Thessalonica in revenge for an insurrection. Bishop Ambrose of Milan forced him to do penance for this act and emphasized thereby the independence of the western church from imperial domination.

392, May 15. The Frankish count (*comes*), **Arbogast**, murdered Valentinian II at Vienne and set up as emperor the pagan rhetorician **Eugenius.**

394, Sept. 5. Theodosius defeated and slew Eugenius and Arbogast at the Frigidus, just east of Aquileia. The empire was reunited for a brief space.

395, Jan. 17. Theodosius died at Milan. The empire was divided between his elder son **Arcadius** (made Augustus in the east in 383) and the younger son **Honorius** (made Augustus in the west in 393). The division proved to be permanent, though at the time the unity of the empire was fully accepted in theory and was always envisaged as a practical possibility. One consul regularly held office in Rome (until 472) and one in Constantinople (until 541).

395-408. ARCADIUS (b. 377), emperor of the east. He married Eudoxia, daughter of the Frank, Bauto (395). The praetorian praefect, Rufinus, managed to check the inroads of the Visigoths in the Balkans until his murder by the troops, but thereafter the eunuch Eutropius failed to prevent the invasions of the Visigoths or of the Huns, who overran Asia.

395-423. HONORIUS (b. 384), emperor of the west. He fell wholly under the influence of the Vandal Stilicho who, as master of the troops (*magister militum*), commanded all the forces and married his daughter Maria to Honorius (398).

396-397. Stilicho drove the Visigoths, led by Alaric, out of Greece.

402, Apr. 6. He frustrated their efforts to invade Italy (victory of the Romans at Pollentia).

406, Aug. 23. Stilicho at Florence broke up a miscellaneous force of barbarians which Radagaisus had led into Italy.

At about this time Gaul was overrun by Vandals, Alans, Suevi and Burgundians.

407. EVACUATION OF BRITAIN by the Romans. Constantine, whom the troops in Britain had proclaimed emperor, crossed to Gaul with his forces and it is probable that Roman troops were never sent back. The Romanized natives were left to deal as best they could with the inroads of Caledonians (Picts) from the north and of various German tribes coming by sea. The Saxons seem to have secured a permanent footing at the mouth of the Thames about 441.

408, Aug. 22. Murder of Stilicho, at Honorius' order.

408-450. THEODOSIUS II (b. 401), emperor of the east. He was the son of Arcadius and was a weak ruler dominated by his sister Pulcheria. With Valentinian III, Theodosius issued the earliest collection of existing laws, the Theodosian Code (438). The Huns, under Attila, continued to ravage the empire and extort tribute.

409. Alaric again invaded Italy and set up a usurper, Attalus (praefect of Rome, the last pagan "emperor"). Alaric soon deposed him again.

410, Aug. 14 or 24. ALARIC SACKED ROME. He died soon after in southern Italy. His brother Athaulf led the Visigoths into Gaul (412) and thence began the conquest of Spain from the Vandals (415). There Wallia (416-419), successor of Athaulf, established the first recognized barbarian kingdom (419).

411. Constantine was defeated by Honorius' commander Constantius, near Arles.

423-425. Johannes usurped the purple on the death of Honorius at Ravenna (which he had made the capital in place of Milan).

425. Forces sent from the east by Theodosius II captured Johannes and put him to death.

425-454. VALENTINIAN III (b. 419), emperor of the west. He was the son of Honorius' half-sister Galla Placidia and the general Constantius, who had been made Augustus in 409, but had died almost at once. Valentinian was recognized by Theodosius II and married his daughter Eudoxia (437).

429. The general Bonifatius tried to set himself up as independent in Africa, with the aid of the Vandals, who crossed from Spain under Gaiseric (*Genseric*). But the Vandals seized Africa for themselves after a two-year siege of Hippo Regius (430-431) during which the bishop, St. Augustine, died (430, Aug. 28).

430. Aëtius, master of the troops, disposed of his rivals, Felix and Bonifatius (recalled from Africa in 432). He then devoted himself to clearing Gaul of barbarians, which he did by a resounding victory over the Visigoths (436) and by suppressing an uprising of the peasants and slaves (*Bagaudae*, 437).

435. The Vandal Kingdom in Africa was recognized. The Vandals took Carthage in 439.

450-457. MARCIAN, emperor of the east. Pulcheria, sister of Theodosius II (d. 450), had married Marcian, an able general. He allowed the Ostrogoths (east Goths) to settle as military allies (*foederati*) in Pannonia.

450. Attila, leader of the Huns, decided to bring his people from the east into Gaul.

451, June. Aëtius, aided by the Visigothic king, Theodoric I (*Theoderich, Theoderid*), defeated the Huns in the battle of Châlons (actually the *campi Catalauni* or Mauriac plain, near Troyes).

452. Attila invaded Italy, but turned back, traditionally because warned by Pope Leo I, but probably because well paid. Attila died in 453 and his hordes broke up.

454, Sept. 21. Valentinian rewarded Aëtius by murdering him with his own hand.

455, Mar. 16. Valentinian was murdered by two of Aëtius' guards. End of the house of Theodosius.

455-472. A succession of puppet rulers in the west. In 455 Eudoxia, widow of Valentinian, set up **Petronius Maximus** at Rome. On his murder, in the same year, she called the Vandals from Africa.

455, June 2-16. **Gaiseric and the Vandals sacked Rome.** By the thoroughness of their destruction they attached a permanent stigma to their name.

456. **Avitus** advanced from southern Gaul to Rome, but was deposed by his able general, the Suevian **Ricimer.** Ricimer retained power by securing the consent of the eastern emperors to his nominees, who were **Majorianus** (457-461), **Severus** (461-465), and after a two-year interregnum, **Anthemius** (467-472), and **Olybrius** (472). When in 472 both Ricimer and Olybrius died, the eastern emperor, Leo I, appointed **Glycerius** (473), and **Julius Nepos** (473-475).

457-474. **LEO I** (b. ?), a Thracian (?), succeeded Marcian as emperor of the east. To offset his master of the troops, the Alan Aspar, he married his daughter Ariadne to Zeno, an Isaurian from the mountains of southern Asia Minor (467) and made Zeno's son, Leo, his colleague (473).

474. **Leo II,** who succeeded on the death of Leo I. His father, Zeno, made himself his colleague. Leo died the same year.

474-491. **ZENO** (b. 426), disposed of the pretender Basiliscus, brother-in-law of Leo I (475). He then tried to control the Goths by setting the rival chiefs, Theodoric, son of Strabo, and Theodoric the Amal, against each other.

475. The master of the troops, **Orestes,** removed Nepos in favor of his own son, whose name combined those of the founder of Rome and of the Empire,

475-476. **ROMULUS AUGUSTUS** (nicknamed *Augustulus*).

476, Sept. 4. After defeating and killing Orestes at Pavia, the Herulian **Odovacar** (*Odoacer*) deposed Romulus Augustulus, the last emperor of the west, at Ravenna. Traditional end of the Roman Empire.

The eastern emperor, **Zeno,** apparently recognized Odovacar as "patrician" (*patricius* had become the title of honor for barbarian commanders). Nepos retained titular claim as emperor until his death in 480 and after that date the empire was theoretically reunited under the eastern

emperors, but actually Odovacar ruled as an independent king in Italy.

481. On the death of Theodoric, the son of Strabo, Zeno recognized his rival as patrician and master of the troops. His people were established in Moesia as *foederati*.

488. **Theodoric,** ostensibly as **Zeno's** agent, invaded Italy.

493, Feb. 27. After a three-year siege of Ravenna, Odovacar surrendered. He was soon after murdered by Theodoric. Italy was united under Theodoric the Great (b. c. 455) as the kingdom of the Ostrogoths (p. 145).

491-518. **ANASTASIUS I** (b. 431) emperor of the east. He married Zeno's widow and removed the Isaurians from power, thus causing a serious revolt in Isauria (suppressed only in 497).

The inroads of the Slavic Getae forced him to protect Constantinople by a wall.

502-506. The emperor waged a long war with the Persians (p. 126).

514-518. Conflict with the pretender Vitalian, commander of the Bulgarian *foederati.* Anastasius died in 518 (July 1).

518-527. **JUSTINUS I** (b. 450?), a humble Illyrian who had risen to be commander of the imperial bodyguard. He took as his colleague his able nephew Justinian (527) and died the same year.

527-565. **JUSTINIAN.** (For his reign see Byzantine Empire, p. 170.)

Diocletian and his successors managed to delay, but not to stop the decay which had attacked the empire during the 3d century. The administrative reforms added to the burdens of taxation without stopping the military domination and rivalry for the purple. The army became increasingly barbarized and immobilized by settlement on the land as peasant militia or barbarian *foederati.* The active defense was entrusted to barbarian mercenaries under their powerful chiefs, who came to dominate the state. Thus, the empire in the west did not fall: it petered out; and the establishment of the barbarian kingdoms simply recognized the end of a gradual process. In the east the empire, in Greek garb, maintained itself, at times as a very great and splendid power, until the conquest of Constantinople by the crusaders in 1204 and the definitive fall of the city into the hands of the Turks (1453).

In architecture, the later empire continued the able engineering of earlier days, as in the Baths of Diocletian at Rome, his palace at Spalato, or the Basilica of Maxentius and Constantine at Rome. But art showed a rapid decline, e.g. in the frieze of the Arch of Constantine at Rome.

The second half of the 4th century witnessed a revival of pagan Latin literature in **Symmachus**, the praefect of the city who vainly urged Valentinian II to restore the altar of victory (384), the Gallic poet **Ausonius**, consul in 379, and the Alexandrian **Claudius**, court poet of Honorius and Stilicho. **Boethius**, the last classical philosopher, whether he was pagan or Christian, wrote his *Consolation of Philosophy* in prison before his execution by Theodoric the Ostrogoth (524).

Active intellectual life, however, appeared chiefly in the Church. The great Latin fathers were: **Lactantius** (d. c. 325), **Ambrose** (340–397), Bishop of Milan (374), **Jerome** (340–420), who retired from Rome to Bethlehem, where he translated the Bible into Latin (the *Vulgate*), and **Augustine** (354–430), Bishop of Hippo Regius in Africa (395), who founded Christian theology on Platonism. The important Greek fathers were: **Basil** of Caesarea (330–379), his brother **Gregory** of Nyssa (d. c. 394), and **Gregory** of Nazianzus (329–389), all three Cappadocians, and **John Chrysostom** (329–389), Patriarch of Constantinople (381). **Eusebius** (264–340), orthodox Bishop of Caesarea (315), who should be distinguished from the contemporary Arian, Eusebius of Nicomedia, is noted for his *Ecclesiastical History* and other historical works.

During the 5th and 6th centuries the eastern Church was torn by the **monophysite heresy**, whose doctrine was that Christ had a single nature. The orthodox doctrine, that Christ combined divine and human, had the support of Pope Leo of Rome and was approved at the **Council of Chalcedon** (451), but the eastern emperors on the whole were monophysite. In the west, as imperial authority weakened, and as rival bishoprics passed into barbarian hands, the Bishop of Rome — or **pope** (*papa*) as he came to be known — became supreme, and such great popes as **Damasus** (pope, 366–384) and **Leo I, "the Great"** (pope, 440–461) became temporal as well as spiritual leaders of their people. A claim of territorial sovereignty began to be based on a fictitious **"Donation of Constantine"** to Pope Sylvester of the lands around Rome. A significant missionary effort of the Church was the sending of **Ulfilas to the Goths** (c. 340–348), who converted them to Arianism. But the chief feature of the Church during this period was the introduction of **monasticism**. In the east, the single solitary had long been common and **St. Antony** first gathered some of them together for a common life (*coenobite*) in Egypt in about 285. **Basil of Caesarea** (above) established a monastic rule popular in the east. Monasticism spread to the west under the efforts of **Martin of Tours** (362) and **Jerome** (above). **Cassian of Marseilles** (c. 400) wrote *Institutes* for his monastery, but the rule which became dominant was that of **St. Benedict** (*regula Sancti Benedicti*), who founded his monastery at Monte Cassino, near Naples, in 529. His rule was adopted by Cassiodorus (480–575), secretary to Theodoric the Ostrogoth, who founded a monastery at Beneventum in 540. The closing of the schools at Athens by Justinian, the execution of Boethius, and the founding of Benedict's monastery mark the transition from classical to mediaeval intellectual life.   (*Cont. p.* 141.)

G. THE EMPIRES OF ASIA

1. THE NEO-PERSIAN EMPIRE OF THE SASSANIANS (226-651 A.D.)

226-240 A.D. Ardashir I (*Artaxerxes, Artahshatr*), son of Papak, a vassal-king of the Parthian Empire ruling in Fars (Persia proper), revolted against Artabanus, last king of the Arsacid dynasty of Parthia, and defeated him finally at **Hormuz** (226–27), where Artabanus was slain.

Merv, Balkh, and Khiva conquered by Ardashir; submission of the kings of Kushan, Turan, and Makran received; India invaded and tribute levied on the Punjab.

229-232. War with Rome (p. 115). Rome summoned to evacuate Syria and the rest of Asia. Armenia, the real objective of Ardashir's campaign, subjugated after the murder of its Arsacid king, Chosroes.

Under Ardashir a strongly centralized nation supported by the priesthood created; Zoroastrianism revived and the privileges of the Magi restored; collection of the text of the *Zend Avesta* under Arda-Viraf. He was succeeded by

240-271. Shapur I (*Sapor, Shahpuhri*). Revolts in Armenia and Hatra crushed (240).

241-244. FIRST WAR WITH ROME (p. 115). Shapur invaded Mesopotamia and Syria, took Nisibis and Antioch, but was finally driven back across the Euphrates and defeated at Resaina by the Emperor Gordian. Gordian was murdered and peace was concluded by his successor, Philip. In the east, Balkh apparently independent.

258-260. SECOND WAR WITH ROME (p. 116). Shapur again invaded Mesopotamia and Syria, taking Nisibis, Edessa, and Antioch, and defeating and capturing near Edessa the Emperor Valerian, who remained a captive until his death (265–66). Asia Minor also invaded, Caesarea Mazaca in Cappadocia taken, but no attempt made to consolidate and hold the conquered territory.

260-263. Palmyra. In a brilliant campaign Odenathus, the Arab prince of Palmyra, drove the Persians back across the Euphrates, defeated Shapur and besieged Ctesiphon, seized and occupied Mesopotamia, Syria, and other provinces west of the Euphrates, and was recognized by Gallienus as co-regent for the east.

Shapur's later years were devoted to public works, of which the greatest was the dam at Shuster. He also founded many cities, among them Nishapur. In his reign appeared Mani (215–273), founder of **Manichaeism**, whom Shapur at first favoured, then banished.

271-293. Shapur was succeeded by his son, Hormisdas I (271–272), who was followed by his brother, Varahran I (272–275). Mani executed. Insufficient support given to Zenobia of Palmyra (p. 116), the widow of Odenathus, against Aurelian, whose Persian expedition came to an end with his murder (275). Varahran succeeded by his son, Varahran II (275–293). An eastern campaign, in which the Sakae of Sistan were subdued, was brought to a close by a Roman invasion of Persia under the Emperor Carus, who conquered Mesopotamia and took Ctesiphon (283). The mysterious death of Carus ended the war (284). Armenia seized by Tiridates, the son of the murdered Chosroes, with the help of the Emperor Diocletian (286). Varahran III, son of Varahran II, reigned four months, and was succeeded by his brother,

293-301. Narses, who finally worsted his brother and rival, Hormisdas, and drove Tiridates from Armenia (296).

296-297. WAR WITH ROME (p. 118). The Roman army under Galerius routed near Carrhae (296). The Persian army surprised by Galerius in the following year and almost annihilated. Peace concluded (297). Terms: 1. Cession to Rome of the five provinces west of the Tigris. 2. The Tigris to be the boundary instead of the Euphrates. 3. Cession to Armenia of Median territory up to the fort of Zentha. 4. Iberia (*Georgia*) to be a Roman protectorate.

Abdication of Narses and accession of his son, **Hormisdas II** (301–309), noted for his activity in building and for setting up a court of justice at which the poor were encouraged to make complaint against the oppression of the rich. Upon his death his natural heir, Hormisdas, was set aside by the nobles, who elected his posthumous son, the famous

309-379. SHAPUR II.

309-337. His minority and early campaigns. Persia invaded by the Arabs of Bahrain and Mesopotamia; Ctesiphon sacked. At the age of seventeen Shapur grasped the reins of state, adopted an active policy, invaded Arabia and exacted a terrible revenge upon the Arabs.

337-350. FIRST WAR WITH ROME (p. 120). The Romans were defeated in the field, but Shapur was unable to capture the Roman strongholds. Nisibis invested three times in vain (338, 346, 350). Constantius routed at Singara (348). Persecution of the Persian Christians (from 339 on). Treaty with Armenia (341), but in 351 Armenia went over to Rome. Successful campaigns in the east against the Huns, Euseni, and Gilani (350-357).

359-361. SECOND WAR WITH ROME. Syria invaded, Amida taken after a heroic defense (359). Singara and Bezabde captured (360). Constantius attempted in vain to recapture the latter place, and died in the following year. His successor, Julian, invaded Persia, forced the passage of the Tigris, defeated the Persians north of Ctesiphon, but retreated before investing that city and was mortally wounded in a battle near Samarra (363). His successor, Jovian, concluded peace with Shapur for thirty years. Terms: (1) restoration of the five provinces ceded by Narses; (2) surrender of Nisibis, Singara, and a third fortress in eastern Mesopotamia to Persia; (3) Armenia declared to be outside the Roman sphere of influence. Conquest of Armenia by Shapur and invasion of Iberia.

371-376. THIRD WAR WITH ROME. No decisive results and an obscure peace. Persian power at its zenith at the death of Shapur II. His immediate successors weak and unenterprising. Ardeshir II (379-383) and Shapur III (383-388). Shapur concluded a peace with Rome (384) by the terms of which Armenia was partitioned between Rome and Persia. Varahran IV (388-399). Khusru (Chosroes), the satrap of Persian Armenia, who had revolted, was deposed and succeeded by Varahran's brother. Varahran was killed in a mutiny and succeeded by his son,

399-420. Yezdigird the Wicked. A peaceful reign. A firman issued permitting Christians to worship openly and rebuild their churches (409), a decree as important to the eastern church as the Edict of Milan to the church of the west. The Council of Seleucia adopted the decrees

and the creed of the Council of Nicaea. Yezdigird possibly contemplated baptism and persecuted the Magians, but returning to his old faith he authorized the destruction of the Christian sect. A terrible persecution for four years. Yezdigird succeeded by his son,

420-440. Varahran V. Brought up among the desert Arabs who supported him against his cousin, Khusru, the choice of the nobles, who finally accepted him peacefully. He continued persecution of the Christians and declared war on Rome (420), when the Christians crossed the border seeking Rome's protection. Varahran was defeated and peace concluded (422). Christians to be allowed to take refuge in the Roman Empire, persecution of the Christians to cease. Declaration of the independence of the eastern church at the Council of Dad-Ishu (424). Persian Armenia reduced to a satrapy (428). Campaign of Varahran against the White Huns or Ephthalites (Haytal), of Turkish stock probably, in Transoxania. They invaded Persia, but were surprised and defeated by Varahran, who crossed the Oxus and forced them to sue for peace. Varahran succeeded by his son,

440-457. Yezdigird II. War declared upon Rome and peace concluded the same year (440). Successful campaigns against the Ephthalites of Transoxania (443-451). Armenia forcibly converted to Zoroastrianism (455-456), after the defeat of the Christian party at the hands of the Persians and their Armenian supporters. Persecution of Christians spread to Mesopotamia. Khorsan again invaded by the Ephthalites, who inflicted a severe defeat upon Yezdigird, after he had driven them across the Oxus. At his death his younger son, Hormisdas, seized the throne, but the elder son,

459-483. Firuz (Perozes), defeated and captured Hormisdas with the aid of the Ephthalites. A famine of several years; wise measures adopted by Firuz. Unsuccessful campaigns against the Ephthalites ending in a humiliating peace (464-480?). A further defeat at the hands of the Kushans of the maritime provinces of the Caspian Sea (481) led to the revolt of Iberia and of Armenia under Vahan (481-483). This was still smouldering when Firuz, breaking his troth, attacked the Ephthalites, was defeated and slain. Succeeded by

483-485. Volagases (Balas), his brother. Tribute paid by Persia to Khush-Newaz, the Ephthalite Khan, for about two years. Conciliation of Armenia. **Edict of toleration** granted Christians, after Vahan aided Volagases in a civil war. Thereupon Armenia and Iberia contented provinces of the empire. Nestorian Christological doctrine of the two natures in Christ established by **Bar-Soma** in the Persian Church with royal authority; the college of Edessa driven out by Zeno and set up at Nisibis by Bar-Soma (489). Repudiation by Armenia of the **Council of Chalcedon** (491). Volagases succeeded by his son,

485-498. Kobad (first reign), who had taken refuge with the Ephthalites after an abortive attempt to seize the throne. Successful campaign against the Khazars, dwelling between the Volga and the Don. Many converts gained for his communistic and ascetic doctrines by **Mazdak**, a high priest of Zoroastrianism, among them the king. Unrest in Armenia and Persia owing to the intolerant proselytism of the Mazdakites, leading to a conspiracy of the Chief Mobed, nobles, and army against Kobad, who was deposed and succeeded by his brother **Zamasp**, who reigned from 498 to 501. Kobad escaped to the Ephthalites, who espoused his cause with vigor. Zamasp resigned the crown voluntarily.

501-531. Kobad (second reign). Official support withdrawn from Mazdak.

503-505. FIRST WAR WITH ROME. Cause: non-fulfillment of the Eastern Empire's agreement to pay a share of the expenses of the defense of the pass of Derbend, the usual route taken by nomadic tribes in their invasions of Persia and the Eastern Empire. Roman Armenia invaded; Theodosiopolis taken; sack of Amida in northern Mesopotamia (502). An Ephthalite raid forced Kobad to conclude peace on the basis of the *status quo ante*.

503-523. Successful and final campaign against the Ephthalites (503–513). Massacre of the Mazdakites (523). Rebellion in Iberia.

524-531. SECOND WAR WITH ROME. Cause: Erection of the fortress of Daras within a day's march of Nisibis by the Emperor Anastasius. The first campaign ended in the defeat of the Romans (526), who were again defeated in 528, but were finally victorious in the **battle of Daras** (528) under Belisarius. An indecisive battle near Callinicum brought the war to a close. Kobad was succeeded by

531-579. ANUSHIRWAN THE JUST (*Chosroes*), his son. The most illustrious member of the Sassanian dynasty. Succession disputed. Execution of all his brothers and their male offspring with one exception. Massacre of Mazdak and his followers. Conclusion of the **Endless Peace with Rome** (533). Terms: (1) Rome to pay

11,000 pounds of gold toward the upkeep of the Caucasian defenses. (2) Rome to keep Daras as a fortress, but not as its headquarters in Mesopotamia; (3) restoration on both sides of captured strongholds in Lazica; (4) eternal friendship and alliance. Within seven years, however, Anushirwan, alarmed at Justinian's successes in Africa and Italy (533–539) and prompted by the Ostrogoths and Armenians, began a defensive war.

540-562. WAR WITH ROME. Syria invaded. Antioch sacked. Terms of peace agreed upon and ratification of the treaty received by Anushirwan at Edessa. He nevertheless extracted ransoms from the cities along the route of his return march, whereupon Justinian denounced the treaty.

540-557. Campaigns in Lazica. Lazica (ancient *Colchis*), a Roman protectorate since 527, appealed to Anushirwan for help to throw off the Roman yoke. Petra taken by the Persians (540). Lazica a Persian province. Petra retaken by the Romans (550), and the Persians driven out of the country (555). A truce agreed upon (557). **Definitive peace with Rome** (562). The terms included: (1) cession of Lazica to Rome; (2) payment by Rome of 30,000 pieces of gold annually; (3) free exercise of their religion guaranteed to the Christians of Persia; (4) commercial intercourse restricted to certain roads and marts; (5) Daras to remain a fortified town; (6) arbitration of all disputes and free diplomatic intercourse; (7) inclusion in the treaty of the allies of either party; (8) the defense of the Caspian gate to be undertaken by Persia alone; (9) the peace to hold for fifty years.

554. Subjugation of the Ephthalites with the aid of the Turks and the division of their territory with the Oxus as boundary. Successful campaign against the Khazars.

572. Declaration of war on Persia by Justin. Syria ravaged by Anushirwan and Daras taken (573). Abdication of Justin. A peace purchased by Tiberius.

576?. Arabian campaign. The Abyssinians driven out of southern Arabia, which became a Persian province.

576-578. Alliance of the Turks with the Eastern Empire. Ill-success of their invasion of Persia. Armenian campaigns. An Indian campaign also reported. Under Anushirwan the administration was reorganized. The empire was divided into four great satrapies: the east comprising Khorasan and Kerman; the west including Iraq and Mesopotamia; the north comprehending Armenia and Azerbaijan; and the south containing Fars and Khuzistan. A fixed land tax was also substituted for the former variable tax on produce, and its collection placed under the supervision of the priests. Irrigation and communications were improved, the army reformed, foreigners protected, agriculture encouraged, laws revised, the Christians granted toleration, learning subsidized, Indian tales and chess introduced. Anushirwan was succeeded by his son,

579-589. Hormisdas IV (*Hormazd*). War with Rome continued. The Persians were defeated at Constantia (581) and again at Arzanene near Martyropolis (588). In 589 the Persians took Martyropolis and defeated the Romans, who, however, gained a signal victory near Nisibis soon thereafter.

589. Invasion of Persia by Arabs, Khazars, and Turks. The advance of the Turks constituted a real danger, but they were defeated by the great Persian general, Varahran (*Bahram*). Bahram was then ordered to invade Lazica, but was met and defeated by the Romans on the Araxes. Superseded and insulted by the king, he rebelled. Hormisdas was deposed, and murdered, and succeeded by his son,

589-628. KHUSRU PARVIZ (*Chosroes II*), the last famous king of the Sassanian dynasty. Under him the Neo-Persian Empire reached its greatest extent and suffered also a sudden downfall. Defied by Bahram, Khusru was forced to flee to Constantinople, whereupon Bahram seized the throne and reigned as Bahram (*Varahran*) VI (590-591). Restoration of Khusru with the aid of the Emperor Maurice. Flight of Bahram to the Turks, by whom he was assassinated.

603-610. A victorious war against Phocas, the murderer of Maurice. Capture of Daras, Amida, Harran, Edessa, Hieropolis, Berhoea (Aleppo), etc. Armenia, Cappadocia, Phrygia, Galatia, and Bithynia ravaged.

610. A Persian force defeated by the Arabs at Dhu-Qar, a famous day in the annals of the tribes.

610-620. Accession of Heraclius as Roman emperor. War with Rome continued. Sack of Antioch and Apamea (611) by the Persians. Invasion of Cappadocia (612). Capture of Damascus (614). Sack of Jerusalem and capture of the *True Cross* (615). Capture of Pelusium and Alexandria by Shahr-Baraz. Subjugation of Egypt (616). Chalcedon taken. The Persians within a mile of Constantinople (617). Ancyra and Rhodes captured (620). Khusru had now restored the empire of Darius I,

and the condition of the Roman Empire was desperate. Thrace was overrun by the Avars. Heraclius decided to flee to Carthage, but was prevented by the citizens of Constantinople. He determined as a forlorn hope to make use of his one great advantage, the possession of sea power, and carry the war to enemy territory.

622-627. The famous **campaigns of Heraclius.** Disembarkment at Issus and defeat of Shahr-Baraz (622). Expedition to Lazica and invasion of Armenia (623). Retreat of Khusru and wintering of Heraclius in Albania. The second invasion of Armenia. Surprise and defeat of Shahr-Baraz (624). Invasion of Arzanene and the recovery of Amida and Martyropolis. Campaign in Cilicia. Indecisive **battle of the Sarus.** Retreat of Shahr-Baraz (625).

626. THE SIEGE OF CONSTANTINOPLE. Alliance between Khusru and the Avars. Two Persian armies placed in the field, one against Heraclius in Asia Minor, the other to co-operate with the Avars in the siege of Constantinople. The first under Shahen, the captor of Chalcedon, was defeated by the emperor's brother, Theodore. The second was prevented by the Roman command of the sea from assisting the Avar assault on Constantinople, which failed.

627. Invasion of Assyria and Mesopotamia by Heraclius. Defeat of the Persians near Nineveh. Flight of Khusru. Heraclius marched on Ctesiphon, but did not besiege it. His retreat to Canzaca. Mutiny of the Persian troops in Ctesiphon under Gurdanaspa, their commander. Imprisonment and murder of Khusru, he was succeeded by

628-629. Kobad II (*Siroes*), who made peace with Heraclius on the basis of an exchange of conquests and prisoners and the surrender of the "True Cross." The massacre of his brothers and his death by plague (629). The usurpation of Shahr-Baraz and his murder by his own troops (629). The reign of **Purandukht** and that of **Azarmidukht**, daughters of Khusru Parviz, followed by a period of anarchy, in which pretender after pretender aspired to the throne and perished almost immediately (629-634).

634-642. Yezdigird III, grandson of Khusru Parviz, and last Sassanian king of Persia, whose story is that of the expansion of the Muslim Caliphate eastwards.

633-651. Arab invasion of Iraq under Khalid ibn al-Walid. Hira and Obolla taken. The Arab advance checked temporarily at the **Battle of the Bridge.** The

Persians under Rustam were decisively defeated by the Arabs under Sa'd ibn-abi-Waqqās at Qadisiya (637). Mesopotamia invaded by Sa'd and Ctesiphon (*Madain*) captured. Defeat of the Persians at Jalula (637). Invasion of Susiana and Fars (639). Defeat of the Persians at Ram Hormuz; Shuster taken; conquest of Khuzistan (640).

Final defeat of the Persians under Firuzan at Nehawand (642). Conquest of the Persian provinces and their incorporation into the caliphate. Flight of Yezdigird to Balkh; his appeal for help to the Emperor of China; his murder in a miller's hut near Merv (651).

2. INDIA, TO 500 A.D.

a. NORTHERN INDIA

1st cent. B.C. Dating of the known Saka rulers, the **"Great King Moga"** or Maues, Azes, and Azilises, raises a complex chronological problem affecting the whole epoch from 100 B.C. to 200 A.D. It springs from multiplicity of eras, which are hardly ever explicitly identified. The sequence of rulers has been well established by E. J. Rapson, with the aid of numismatic evidence. Moga appears to date an inscription at Taxila ("78" = c. 72 B.C.) with reference to a Scythian era of c. 150 B.C. Azes seems to have begun a new era, for "136 ayasa" (= AZOY) is identified (although disputed) in the Chir Tope, Taxila. There is no positive evidence that either the "Vikrama" era of 58 B.C. or the Saka era of 78 A.D. originated or was ever used in the Northwest. A Jain text prior to 1428 A.D. purports to explain their origin in Ujjain, but no certain examples of their use are found until 372 A.D. and 578 A.D. respectively. Accession of Azes, however, presumably took place not far from 58 B.C. which may be employed as a working hypothesis.

The Pahlavas (Parthians closely related to the Scythians) under Vonones and his brother Spalirises became independent in eastern Iran with the title of King of Kings sometime (c. 30? B.C.) after the death of Mithradates II (88 B.C., supposed by L. de la Vallée Poussin to begin a Pahlava era; or does such an era begin with appropriation of the imperial title?). Azes II, son of Spalirises, succeeded the Sakas in the Punjab. The period of these events depends on the era intended in the Takht-i-Bahi inscription in the 26th year of his successor Gondopharnes, dated "103." He ruled 19–45 + A.D. if the era is that of Azes-Vikrama; c. 11 B.C.–c. 15 + A.D. if it is that of c. 88 B.C. To him St. Thomas was sent according to a legend current by 250. Pacores was the last to rule as suzerain, although others probably continued as satraps.

The Kushana **Kujula Kadphises** forcibly united the five tribes of Yüeh-chih in Bactria (end 1st cent. B.C.) and seized from the Pahlavas the Kabul Valley and adjacent regions. His son **Vima Kadphises** conquered northwestern India and ruled it by deputy till his death at 80. An inscription near Panjtar speaks of a "Gushana Great King" under date "122" which is 64 or 34 A.D. by the Azes or Pahlava systems. The inscription of "136" similarly belongs to 78 or 48 A.D.

c. 78–176 + A.D. A second Kushana dynasty was founded by

c. 78–96 + A.D. KANISHKA, who extended his rule from Benares and Kabul to the Vindhyas, and established his capital at Peshawar. His inscriptions are dated from "3" to "18," and that of "9" is explicitly dated as of his reign. Whether or not the era which he founded is the "Saka" era of 78 A.D., he probably came to the throne near that date. The Chinese *Later Han History* says:

84. A Yüeh-chih king was allied to Sogdiana by marriage, and by presents to him Pan Ch'ao secured the help of the latter against Kashgar.

88. The king presented precious stones and lions with a request for a Chinese princess, peremptorily refused by Pan Ch'ao.

90. A punitive army of 70,000 sent across the Pamirs under the Yüeh-chih viceroy Hsieh was starved into surrender by Pan, the ablest strategist of his time, who exacted payment of annual tribute. Although the king is not named, only a powerful ruler could have played so strong a hand across the mountains. Some scholars identify Kanishka rather with King Chien of Khotan, who was killed in error by a Chinese envoy in 152 A.D. The Chinese source does not, however, suggest any connection of this king with the Yüeh-chih or with India.

Kanishka appears to have been tolerant in religion, and built a great stupa at Peshawar over relics of the Buddha. A fourth church council, unknown to the Pali sources, was apparently convoked at Jalandhara in the Punjab by the powerful Sarvastivadin, a realist sect of the conservative Sthaviravadin. It probably supervised translation into Sanskrit of the canon which had been fixed in Prakrit in Mathura, the Punjab, and Kashmir in the last centuries B.C. The four Sanskrit *Agamas* agree with the earliest Pali *Nikayas*, but the seven *Abhidharma* books contain catechism, comment, and doctrine peculiar to the school. The *Vibhasha* commentary on one of the *Abhidharmas*, completed by Kashmir professors after the death of Kanishka, cites conflicting doctrines of diverse sects.

The earliest and most vigorous classical Sanskrit is found in Asvaghosha's *Saundarananda* ("Conversion of Nanda") and the *Buddhacharita*, an artistic versified life of the Buddha, together with a work long supposed to be his *Sutralamkara*, which is now identified as the *Kalpanamanditika* of Kumaralata, a junior contemporary.

2d cent. A.D. Kanishka's successors with their inscriptions (dated in terms of his reign) are: his son Vasishka (24, 28, 29); the latter's son Kanishka II (41); his younger brother Huvishka (29 or 33–60); Vasushka, son of Kanishka II (68, 74); and Vasudeva (76–98).

Asoka's inscriptions name three **Tamil states** in the Carnatic: Pandya (extreme south), Chola (southeast), and Chera or Kerala (southwest coast, chief port Muziris). These competed with Maesolia at the mouth of the Kistna and especially with the rich western port of Barygaza (Broach) in thriving trade with the Roman Empire. An embassy to Augustus (c. 22 B.C.) was sent by a king "Pandion" who may have been a Pandya. Strabo (d. 21 A.D.) speaks of fleets of 120 ships from Egypt to India, and Pliny (23–79) values annual imports from India at 50 million sesterces.

THE DECCAN was dominated (from c. 100 B.C. to c. 225 A.D.) by a dynasty of Dravidian or **Munda kings**, called *Andhra* by the late *Puranas* but *Satavahana* or *Satakani* in their own Prakrit inscriptions. Founded by Simuka on the ruins of the Sunga-Kanva power, with capital at Pratishthana (Paithan) on the upper Godaveri, its early conquests to north and northwest were appropriated by the Saka satraps. A Saka satrap **Bhumaka** established Scythian power on the northwest coast (c. 70 A.D.). Nahapana, junior to him, ruled many years over Surashtra (Kathiawar) and the adjacent coast with capital probably at Junnar, east of Bombay. Named Mambanos in the *Periplus* (c. 89), his inscriptions are dated "41–46" (?119–124 A.D.), probably with reference to the Saka era of 78 which he may have founded.

c. 109-132+.   **Gotamiputa Siri Satakani** conquered Surashtra from Naha-

pana, and in an inscription at Nasik (18th year of his reign, c. 126) claimed not only the Deccan from the Vindhyas to Banavasi, but less probably Malwa as well. Very likely by this epoch the Satakani had extended control over the properly Andhra Telugu (Dravidian) lands of the Godaveri and Kistna deltas. The Prakrit poems of the *Sattasai* "Seven Centuries" in part date from this time. Liberal towards all religions, the Satakani especially exalted the Brahmans. Sculptures about the great Buddhist stupa of Amaravati on the lower Kistna reveal union of Hindu traditional style with its crowding and naturalism, already more refined than at Bharhut and Sanchi, with Greco-Buddhist motifs which were borrowed from Gandhara and in turn transmitted to Malaya, Sumatra-Java, Cambodia, and Champa.

c. 120-c. 395. A DYNASTY OF WESTERN SATRAPS of Ujjain was probably founded by Bhumaka's son Chashtana (Tiastanes of Ptolemy, c. 150).

c. 170.   **Rudradaman,** Chashtana's grandson, in a Sanskrit inscription at Girnar in Kathiawar, records repair of a dam which broke in 150 A.D., defeat of northern tribesmen, and repeated rout of the southern Satakani.

Ujjain became a center of Sanskrit learning, and was taken as meridian by Indian astronomers. At Mathura, where sculpture early resembled that of Bharhut and Sanchi, and later clumsily imitated the forms of Gandhara, the heavy drapery of the Hellenistic school was rendered transparent, and schematized in decorative ridges, creating the so-called *Udayana Buddha*, carried to China and Japan.

The Buddhist community was now divided between two means to salvation: the **Hinayana** or *Lesser Vehicle*, which retained much of the primitive simplicity of the "Law" *Dharma*, by which "Buddhism" was then named; and the **Mahayana** or *Great Vehicle*, which emphasized personal devotion to Sakyamuni and to a pantheon strange to him. Although practically deified in the *Lalitavistara* (2d cent.?, Chinese trans. 308) and *Saddharma-pundarika-sutra*, "Lotus of the Good Law" (Ch. trans., 265–316), he is regarded as but the human representative (*manushi-buddha*), for the current epoch, of an infinite series of buddhas. Some of these, identified as *dhyani-buddhas*, dwell permanently in various heavens as spiritual guides to more active colleagues. Amitabha, says the longer *Sukhavativyuha* (Ch. trans. by a Yüeh-chih before 186), is the Buddha of Boundless Light who reigns in a western paradise

(Iranian influence). Maitreya, who is destined to complete human salvation as next manushi-buddha, waits in Tushita heaven as a *bodhisattva*, a being capable of enlightenment (Chinese trans. 265-316). No less popular bodhisattvas are Avalokitesvara (*Lotus Sutra*, ch. 24), Manjusri (*Avatamsaka-sutra*, 2d-3d cent., Chinese trans. 317-420), Samantabhadra, and Kshitigarbha, all of whom have deferred their own illumination to succor struggling mankind. The goal of effort is no longer sainthood or final absorption in nirvana, but direct attainment of buddhahood or rebirth to indefinite residence in a celestial paradise. Nagarjuna (2d cent.), founder of the Madhyamika school, in his *Madhyamika Sutra* teaches that all sensory and mental experience is illusion, and comments on the *Prajñaparamita*, "*Perfect Wisdom*" (Chinese trans. 160) which consists in recognition of the Buddhist law as sole reality.

Already before our era Indian writers recognized and wrote treatises about three phases of human existence: *dharma*, religious and moral duty; *artha*, politics and practical life; and *kama*, love. The *Arthasastra* (compounded from earlier materials c. 300-330) aims to teach a prince the whole science of successful rule according to accepted principles. It assumes autocratic monarchy, justification of all means by the end (personal aggrandisement), and chronic war. It advocates use of spies in all quarters; deception, intimidation, false witness, and confiscation to obtain money; cunning and assassination. Virtuous rule is described because desirable to win affection of a conquered people. The *Kama-sutra* ("Laws of Love") by Vatsyayana Mallanaga (c. 4th cent. or later) imitates the *Artha-sastra* in both form and morals.

320-c. 535. THE GUPTA DYNASTY united northern India after five centuries' division.

320-c. 330. Chandragupta I ruled from Pataliputra (Patna), having strengthened his position by marriage into the ancient Lichchavi tribe. His son

c. 330-c. 375. Samudragupta completed the conquest of the north (Aryavarta) and won glory by traversing Telugu lands to force homage of the Pallava. Claiming to receive tribute from southeastern Bengal, Assam, and Nepal, with presents from the Kushan "son of Heaven and king of kings" (now actually vassal of the Sassanids) in Kabul-Kapisa-Gandhara, the Satrap of Ujjain, and King Meghavanna (352-379) of Ceylon (who founded a monastery at

Gaya for his subjects), he revived the Vedic horse-sacrifice which sanctified claim to the title of "universal monarch." He was a patron of poetry and music.

c. 375-c. 413. Chandragupta II Vikramaditya (on throne in 379) ended the Satrapy of Ujjain by conquest of Malwa, Gujerat, and Surashtra (between 388 and 401). He moved his capital to Ayodhya (in Oudh) and then to Kausambi on the Jumna.

c. 413-455. Kumaragupta I probably founded the monastic community at Nalanda which was the principal Buddhist seminary till it burned c. 988.

455-c. 467. Skandagupta repulsed the White Huns, as heir apparent and as emperor (455).

477-496+. Budhagupta, last emperor of the dynasty, ruled from northern Bengal to eastern Malwa, perhaps to Surashtra. After c. 500 the chief branch of his house ruled as kings of Magadha till the 8th century.

The **Brahman legal writers** defined the social structure in sloka metre. The *Dharma Sastra* of **Manu** (1st cent. B.C.?) was respected and freely utilized by later writers. The *Dharma Sutra* of **Vishnu** (3d cent. A.D.), like the epics, recognized *suttee*, widow-burning, though it is not yet recommended. The days of the week were named from Greek sources. **Yajnavalkya** (4th cent.) admitted documentary evidence, and recommended use of ordeals of ploughshare, scales, and poison in addition to Manu's fire and water. **Narada** (5th cent.) first omitted religious and moral precepts from legal discussion. **Brihaspati** (c. 600 or 700) cited nine ordeals. Punishments: impalement, hanging, burning, mutilation, fines and outcasting, were adjusted to caste. A plaintiff might enforce justice by fasting to death on a debtor's premises. **Fa-hsien**, pioneer Chinese Buddhist pilgrim at the height of Gupta power, stated that fines were usually imposed, and that mutilation was reserved for brigands and rebels. He was enthusiastic about the peace and happiness of northern India (401-409) and Ceylon (410-411).

Six schools of **Hindu philosophy** (or rationalized religion) developed during the first centuries before and after Christ. They enjoy orthodox status in that all recognize the primordial and eternal character of the *Veda*, although in fact they do not derive from it. None is concerned primarily with ethics, but all seek freedom from bondage through deeds to rebirth. Escape for the soul is found in knowledge and cessation of thought. The Purvami-mamsa is a systematization of rules for sacrifice. The *Vaiseshika-sutras* are variously dated from the 2d cent. (Masson-Oursel) or 4th-5th cent. (Stcherbatsky). They elaborate an analysis of matter as composed of atoms combined in molecules under influence of time and direction. Souls are bound through linkage to such matter. The Nyaya is a system of logic calculated to attain that knowledge necessary to freedom. The *Yoga-sutras* (5th cent.?) teach rigid concentration of mind and body, a method open to all and regarded as valuable by many diverse religious groups. The *Samkhya-karika* is attributed to Isvarakrishna (3d or 4th cent.? Ch. trans. c. 560). It sets forth a dualistic system teaching that the eternal soul can be freed by realization that it is not material like the world about it. The *Brahma Sutra* (c. 350–400) gives the first clear expression of the Vedanta *darsana* or "point of view," developed continuously from the older *Upanishads*: God is everything, the soul is God, and it is the task of the high-caste Brahman to realize in contemplation this identity.

Vasubandhu (c. 300–350), leading philosopher of Hinayana Buddhism, in his *Abhidharmakosa sastra* gave a classic summary of the Vibhasha and of the Vaibhashika school based upon it, with illuminating comments on the competing Sautrantika school founded by Kumaralabdha (c. 150–200) and developed by Harivarman. Vasubandhu was converted to the Mahayana by his brother Asanga, founder of the Vijñanavadin (Idealist) or Yogachara (Mystic) school, which explains phenomena as mere reflections of ideas and exalts the bodhisattvas, in particular Maitreya. The active translator to Chinese, Kumarajiva (c. 344–413), and the logician Dignaga (c. 5th cent.) were both adherents of this school, which developed important branches at Valabhi and Nalanda (6th–7th cent.). Fahsien first reported Mahayanist monasteries separate from those of the Hinayana.

Literary studies at Ujjain blossomed under the Guptas into the **golden age of classical Sanskrit.** Arya Sura in the *Jatakamala* (Ch. trans. 428) put into elegant *kavya* verse tales of former births of the Buddha which had been best known through the *Divyavadana* (Ch. trans. in part, 265). Secular fables gathered into the *Panchatantra* passed through Pehlvi (531–570), Syriac (570), and Arabic (750) into the languages of Europe. The *Sakuntala* and *Vikramorvasi* of Kalidasa (c. 400–455) rank first among Indian dramas (Greek influence), his *Meghaduta* equally high as a lyric poem, while his *Kumara-*

sambhava, and *Raghuvamsa* mark the apogee of *Kavya*, scholarly epic poetry. Literary taste survived the Gupta Empire: witness **Sudraka's** drama, *Mrichchakatika* ("Little Clay Cart"), and **Dandin's** romance *Dasakumaracharita* (both 6th cent.) and **Santideva's** brilliant poem of Mahayanist altruism, *Bodhicharyavatara* (late 7th cent.).

As in literature, so in **art** the Gupta period is one of dignity, restraint, and refinement: classicism in a land given to exaggeration. Neither the Dhamekh Stupa at Sarnath nor Buddhist sculpture copies the motifs of Gandhara, yet they have assimilated its spirit to chasten the exuberant naturalism of Sañchi and Amaravati. At Ajanta new caves were cut, both *chaitya* halls (nos. 19 and 26) and monasteries (nos. 1 and 2). Many of these were decorated with troweled fresco paintings (still visible in caves 1, 2, and 17), which are impressive in scale, graphic facility, and sensitive naturalism, but marred by crowding and incoherence. Slightly later frescoes survive in caves at Bagh (s.w. Vindhyas), and at Sigiri, the rock fortress of parricide king Kassapa (526–552) of Ceylon.

Indian medicine largely parallels the Greek, but was limited, and surgery atrophied, by objection to dissection. An ethical code like the Hippocratic oath appears in works of Charaka and Susruta (prior to 4th cent., though present texts date from 8th and 11th cent.). Greek origin is clear for many astronomical ideas in the (4th cent.?) treatises summarized in **Varahamihira's** *Panchasiddhantika* (c. 550). Zodiacal division of the ecliptic replaces the (Babylonian?) Nakshatras; planetary motion is explained by epicycles; parallax and eclipses are calculated, etc. But many Indian inconsistencies suggest that Greek astronomy was known imperfectly, perhaps through rule-of-thumb manuals. **Aryabhata** (499) taught rotation of the earth and the value of π as 3.1416 (epic value 3.5). **Brahmagupta** (b. 598) systematized the rules of astronomy, arithmetic, algebra, and geometry. His integral solution of an indeterminate equation, with another method given by Bhaskara in his *Siddhantasiromani* (1150) is called by Hankel the finest thing in numerical theory before Lagrange (1736–1813). The abacus was described in the *Abhidharmakosa* from first-century sources long before its use in China (1303–1383). More important, the zero (actually a superscribed dot) is attested in Indian literature (600), and the decimal position in a Sanskrit inscription in Cambodia (604) before they passed to the Arabs of Syria (662), and thence to the Europeans.

b. SOUTHERN INDIA

The whole Indian peninsula south of the Vindhyas, save for a part of Maharashtra (Nasik and Pratishthana) easily accessible from Malwa and already Aryanized before our era, was occupied by **Dravidians**: Canarese on the northwest, Telugu on the east, and Tamil in the Carnatic. Jainism, brought to Sravana Belgola in Mysore under Chandragupta (end 4th cent. B.C.), flourished in the Digambara, "naked clergy," form which the north rejected. Buddhism with its stupas and sculpture was brought to Amaravati and Mysore under Asoka. Sanskrit and Hindu culture were carried from the south to Cambodia about the opening of our era. Sanskrit influence is clear in the early (pre-Christian?) Tamil grammar *Tolkappiyam*, and the *Kural* of Tiruvalluvar, lofty songs of a priest of pariahs (2d–3d cent. A.D.). Brahman colonies with Hinduism and the caste system were at various periods imported from the Ganges Valley and endowed by local rulers, as was done also in Bengal.

The south, however, placed its own impress on what it received, and developed linga-worship, *bhakti* devotion to Vishnu and Siva, organization of Saiva monasteries and laymen, occasional violent religious intolerance, and municipal and corporate life with a sacrificial spirit of personal loyalty.

c. 225. Breakup of the Satakani Empire led to establishment in Maharashtra near Nasik, of a
c. 250-c. 500. Traikutaka dynasty, probably founded by chiefs of the pastoral Abhira tribe, which used for dating an era of Aug. 26, 249, possibly based on a usurpation of the throne of Ujjain. Another local dynasty,
c. 300-c. 500. The Vakatakas, extended their power from the fortress of

Gawilgarh in northern Berar to Nagpur, Bundelkhand, and Kuntala, probably limiting Gupta expansion to the south. At Ajanta caves 16 and probably 17 date from the reign of Harisena (c. 475-500).

Farther south the **Chutu branch of the Satakani,** called *Andhrabhrityas* in the Puranas, ruled at Banavasi (c. 200-c. 250) where they were succeeded by
c. 350-c. 500. The **Kadamba dynasty,** founded by a Brahman rebel from the Pallava. His great-grandson **Kakutsthavarman** (c. 435-475) married his daughters to a Gupta, a Vakataka (445), and a Ganga of Mysore.

In the Telugu lands, the Andhras were succeeded by the **Ikshvaku dynasty** (3d cent.), notable for donations to a Buddhist stupa on the Nagarjunikonda (hill), on the Kistna above Amaravati; by the
c. 300-450. Salankayana of Vengi; and by the
c. 400-611. Vishnukundins, a dynasty of at least ten kings at the same place.

c. CEYLON

Ceylon traditionally received Buddhism from Asoka under
?247-?207 B.C. **Devanampiya Tissa,** who founded the Mahavihara or Great Monastery at his capital Anuradhapura. The Pali *Tripitaka,* which reflects Theravadin tradition, was written under
89-40 or 29-?17 A.D. **Vattagamani,** who founded the rival Abhayagiri Monastery. His epoch is supported by the geography (c. 90-200 A.D.) of the *Mahaniddesa,* a commentary admitted late to the Canon. Under
412-434. **Mahanaman,** Buddhaghosha of Magadha, author of the *Visuddhimagga* or "Way of Purity,"[1] recorded in Pali Singhalese traditions. (*Cont. p.* 330.)

3. CHINA, TO 618 A.D.

221-207 B.C. **THE CH'IN DYNASTY** established by the self-styled *First Emperor* (Shih Huang Ti, b. 259; acceded 247; d. 210), advised by Li Ssu. Territorial reorganization into thirty-six *chün*, each under civil, military, and supervisory officials. Disarmament by melting down weapons. Standardization of law, weights and measures, and axle length to facilitate interstate commerce.
214. Earlier ramparts linked by convict labor to form the **Great Wall** against the Turkish Hsiung-nu or Huns.

Strategic roads. Wholesale transportation of families, especially criminals, to strengthen defenses and weaken particularism. Central South China conquered, from T'ai and Miao tribes, as far as the Southern Mountains and Canton, with the help of a new canal at Hsing-an, from present-day Hunan into Kwangsi.
213. Proscription of books which had been employed by enemies of the new order. Exception made for all scientific works and for those in the hands of seventy official scholars. Introduction of roll silk

as writing material led to improvement of hair brush (attributed to Gen. Meng T'ien, d. 209) and to standardization and simplification of script (attributed to Li Ssu). Old complex characters were quickly forgotten.

206. Epic struggle of Hsiang Yü against Liu Pang (posthumous temple name (Han) **Kao Tsu**), who founded

202 B.C.-9 A.D. THE FORMER OR WESTERN HAN DYNASTY, with capital at Ch'ang-an. Classic illustration of the typical Chinese dynastic pattern: foundation by rude warrior and administrator; gradual weakening of ruling line; renaissance under a strong successor whose reign reveals cultural progress; further degeneration of dynasty, weakening of control over officials, oppression, revolts, dissolution. In general the Han continued the Ch'in system of administration, gradually increasing the *chün* from 36 to 108.

200. The emperor was surrounded for seven days by the Hsiung-nu, who had formed the first Turkish Empire in Mongolia during the preceding decade. The gift of an imperial princess as consort (repeated in 173), with other presents, secured peace till 166.

196. Chao T'o was recognized as king of southern Yüeh (the modern Kwang provinces) which he had conquered for the Ch'in in 218–214. An expedition against him in 181 ended in disaster.

191. Withdrawal of proscription of conservative literature permitted private scholars in the cultured East to begin its restoration and (equally vital) to transcribe it into modern characters.

155-130. Liu Teh, Prince of Ho-chien, collected a library of archaic texts. His cousin, Liu An, Prince of Huai-nan (d. 122), directed an inclusive compilation of early (especially Taoist) philosophy.

140-87. The reign of Wu Ti, *The Martial Emperor*, was notable alike for foreign conquests and for the establishment of Confucian scholarship in control of civil administration.

140. Tung Chung-shu advocated Confucian training for a civil service, and urged limitation of private holding of land and slaves to remedy undue concentration of wealth which resulted from commerce and mining on a national scale. As result of his efforts the emperor appointed in

136. Doctors of the Five Classics. These were the *I* or Changes (an early divination manual); the *Shih* or Odes; the *Shu* or History (documents compiled in the 6th century); the *Ch'un Ch'iu* or Annals of Confucius; and the *Shih-li* (now *I-li*) or Rituals. All were studied in terms of moralistic and ritual commentaries. The Han had followed the bad precedent of the Chou by granting fiefs to relatives and assistants, and found that direct efforts to weaken them resulted in revolt of seven princes (154).

127. Chu-fu Yen solved the problem by suggesting that younger sons should share by inheritance one-half of their father's fief. He thus also demonstrated the utility of the scholars.

126. Chang Ch'ien returned empty-handed, but with new knowledge of Central Asia and India, from a mission (138) to secure help against the Hsiung-nu from the Yüeh-chih, an Indo-European people who had been driven by the Hsiung-nu west from the Chinese border into Ili, and had thence invaded Hellenistic Bactria.

124. Creation of a Grand College to train officials for civil service through study of what was now fast becoming Confucian orthodoxy.

121-119. The Hsiung-nu were driven north of the Gobi by **Ho Ch'ü-ping** (d. 117, aged 22). They then split into northern and southern divisions (54).

111-110. Subjugation of eastern Yüeh and southern Yüeh (along the coast from modern Chekiang to Tonkin), and of the southwest. These conquests rounded out the frontiers of modern "China proper," and gave the Chinese all the best lands in their known world. During the next century Chinese officials traveled on the coasting vessels of local southern merchants at least as far as the Indian Ocean, exchanging gold and silk for glass and pearls.

110. Wu Ti inaugurated the sacrifice to Heaven which has since been the primary prerogative and obligation of imperial office.

108. Conquest of Ch'ao Hsien, a border kingdom of Korea.

102. Conquest of the petty states of the Tarim Basin and Ferghana (Ta Yüan) by Li Kuang-li and a large army. Indo-European languages were spoken throughout this region: Tokharian and Kuchean in the northern oases, Eastern Iranian or Shaka in those of the south, while Sogdian served as *lingua franca*.

Imperial finances, drained by war, were

replenished by sale of military titles (123), monopolies of salt and iron (119), forced contributions by the nobility (112), and commutation by fines of judicial sentences (97). They were inflated by debasement of currency (119). The government, guided by Sang Hung-yang, entered the grain business (110), buying cheap and selling dear until exactions of greedy officials led to repeal under Chao Ti (86–73).

The *Shih Chi* or *Historical Memoirs*, first general history of China and a model for later dynastic histories, was compiled by **Ssu-ma Ch'ien** (d. c. 87). **Tai Teh** and **Tai Sheng** compiled standard repertories of early ritual texts, the *Ta Tai Li-chi* and *Li-chi*. **Liu Hsiang** (79–8) prepared a series of reports on the contents of the imperial library. His son **Liu Hsin** (d. 23. A.D.) digested these to form the first classified inventory of extant literature, and rescued from archaic script several important texts, notably the *Tso-chuan* (cf. supra) and the *Chou-li* or Chou Ritual.

1-8. A.D.　Wang Mang served as regent for child-emperors.

6. All candidates for office were required to take **civil-service examinations.** Tribute of a live rhinoceros was presented on request by the distant but unidentified southern state of Huang-chih.

9-23. WANG MANG reigned as emperor of the Hsin Dynasty, and undertook radical reforms: nationalization of land with division of large estates and manumission of slaves had to be repealed (12); a tax on slaveholding was substituted in 17. To monopolies of salt, iron, and coinage was added one on wine, and other mining profits were taxed. Seven regional commissions were directed to establish annual high, low, and mean price levels for staple products; to buy surplus goods at cost; and to peg the market by sales above the seasonal index. To curb usury, loans were offered free up to 90 days for funerals, and at 3 per cent a month or 10 per cent a year for productive purposes. Merchants and capitalists employed as administrators provoked revolts, in one of which Wang was killed.

25-220. LATER OR EASTERN HAN DYNASTY, founded by a collateral imperial scion, (Hou Han) Kuang Wu Ti (25–57), reigned at Loyang. Buddhism was introduced by missionaries from Central Asia, and later from India, probably about the time of Christ. In 65 A.D. the presence of monks and lay believers at his brother's court was favorably mentioned in a decree by Emperor Ming (58–75).

The story of official introduction following a dream of this emperor has been shown by Maspero to be a pious legend, completed in its main outlines by the end of the 2d century.

43. Ma Yüan conquered Tonkin and Annam, much of which remained (except for brief revolts) under Chinese control until 939. A few natives adopted the Chinese classics, Confucianism, and Buddhism; but the masses retained their own language and customs. Commercial relations through the southern seas were gradually extended. "Java" (perhaps then Sumatra) sent tribute early in 132, and traders from the Roman Empire reached Cattigara or Chiao-chih (now Tonkin) in 166 and 226. A newly organized Malay people, the Chams, occupied Quangnam, the region of Tourane, c. 192; but when they came farther north they were repelled (270, 360, and 446).

74-94. Pan Ch'ao, by personal diplomacy and strategy, brought into submission all the petty states of Turkestan, opening the way for extensive silk trade with the Roman Orient (**Ta Ch'in**). His lieutenant Kan Ying penetrated to the Persian Gulf (97). Even the Yüeh-chih, who had recently founded the Kushana Kingdom in the Indian Punjab, sent tribute in 90. The northern Hsiung-nu, as a result of successive defeats by the southern Hsiung-nu (85), by the Mongol Sien-pi (87), and by the Chinese general Tou Hsien (89), in part submitted, in part migrated westward, leaving their lands to the Sien-pi, who in 101 in turn began raiding the frontier. To the west the Ch'iang Tibetans disturbed the peace of modern Kansu for several decades until repulsed by Chao Chung, 141–144.

After only two vigorous reigns the court was dominated by women, by their relatives, and by eunuchs by whom they were surrounded.

82. Empress Tou altered the succession, and, with her family, ruled as dowager (88–97).

105-121. **Empress Teng** ruled as dowager for her infant son and his boy successor till her death, when her most prominent relatives chose suicide.

124. A change in succession made by Empress Yen was violently reversed in the same year.

132. Empress Liang secured honors for her father, and ruled for three youthful emperors from 144 until her death in 150. A younger empress of the same family survived until 159.

CHINA, 159 A.D.–577 A.D. 135

159. Emperor **Huan** finally compassed the death of Liang Chi, brother of the elder empress.

184. **Rebellion of the Yellow Turbans,** provoked by the rapacity of the eunuchs, against whose influence and ruthless murder of scholars opposed to them there had been vigorous protests in 135–136.

189. Massacre of the eunuchs by Yüan Shao.

190-220. Emperor **Hsien,** last of the Later Han dynasty, never really governed, the actual power having passed to competing military dictators.

Insecurity of life and property contributed to the popularity of **religious Taoism,** a cult of mysticism and occultism which promised longevity or even immortality as a reward for support, faith and monastic austerity. Its founders, **Chang Ling** (according to tradition he ascended into heaven in 156 at the age of 123) and his son **Chang Heng,** claimed authority from Laotzu and philosophic Taoism, but followed the practices of alchemy, breath-control, and magic inherited from charlatans who had infested the courts of Ch'in Shih Huang Ti and Han Wu Ti. Their successors slavishly imitated Buddhism by creation of a divine hierarchy, a voluminous textual canon, and a monastic community.

Cultural tradition was maintained by **Pan Ku** (32–92), who compiled the dynastic *History of the Former Han,* his sister **Pan Chao,** whose *Lessons for Women* codified the standard of feminine morality, and **Hsü Shen,** who completed in 100 the first lexicon of archaic script, *Shuo wen chieh tzu.* The rhymed and rhythmic prose-form *fu* was developed at this time. In 105 the eunuch **Ts'ai Lun** presented to court **paper** made of vegetable fibers: bark, hemp, fish nets, and rags. Paper rolls now rapidly supplanted bamboo or wooden slips strung with cords, and the costly roll silk and silk floss paper. **Ma Jung** invented the device of double-column commentary (138–140). Six classics were first engraved on stone (175–183) to perpetuate the academic victory of the conservative school of commentators, who accepted only the earliest renderings into modern script. Figure painting (portraits of 28 generals) and calligraphy (text for stone classics written by Ts'ai Yung) emerged as fine arts. Mortuary chapel of **Wu Liang** decorated with stone flat reliefs (151).

220-264. **Three kingdoms** divided the empire, each claiming imperial status.

220-264. **Wei** dynasty formally founded by Ts'ao P'ei, son of Ts'ao Ts'ao who had dominated the court since 196.

Loyang remained the capital. Eunuchs excluded from government. Families of empresses excluded from future exercise of regency (222). Three classics cut in stone (240–248) to establish versions sponsored by the Archaic Text School, founded by Liu Hsin.

221-264. **Shu** or **Shu-Han** dynasty founded in the west by Liu Pei (d. 223), antagonist of Ts'ao Ts'ao since 194. Capital at Ch'eng-tu. Chu-ko Liang chief minister 221–234. Rapid development of Szechuan.

222-280. **Wu** dynasty founded by Sun Ch'üan in the lower Long River Valley with capital at Chien-K'ang (modern Nanking).

c. 245-250. K'ang T'ai mission to **Fu-nan,** Khmer state in southern Cambodia (first tribute 243), learned details of southern Asia from the envoy of the Indian king.

265-317. Nominal reunion under weak **western Chin dynasty,** established by rebellion of Ssu-ma Yen against the Wei. Institution of the censorate.

317-589. **Southern and Northern dynasties** divided the empire. Six dynasties (counting the eastern Wu) ruled at Chien-K'ang. The later five are considered legitimate:

317-420. **Eastern Chin dynasty,**

420-479. **Former (or Liu) Sung dynasty,** so called from the eight emperors of the Liu family,

479-502. **Southern Ch'i dynasty,**

502-557. **Southern Liang dynasty,**

557-589. **Southern Ch'en dynasty.**

Meantime a series of barbarian dynasties was established in the north by invasion and infiltration of diverse peoples who avidly sought Chinese culture, followed Chinese precedents, and were rapidly absorbed.

304-439. **Sixteen kingdoms** established along the northern marches by three Chinese and leaders of five northern peoples: three Turkish Hsiung-nu, five Mongol Sien-pi, three Ti, one Chieh, and one Tibetan Ch'iang.

386-534. **Northern Wei dynasty,** founded at Ta-t'ung by the Toba Tatars who spoke a Mongol dialect strongly palatalized by contact with the Tungus. In 495 the capital was transferred to Loyang.

534-550. **The Eastern Wei dynasty** ruled at Ye (present Anyang) as did their successors,

550-577. **The Northern Ch'i.** Meanwhile at Ch'ang-an

535-556. The Western Wei were succeeded by
557-581. The Northern Chou, who overthrew the northern Ch'i in 577.

This long epoch of political division retarded cultural progress. Pseudo-reconstruction of texts which had been added to the *Canon of History* by K'ung An-kuo in the 2d cent. B.C., but lost in the 1st cent. A.D., was probably carried out c. 250, and was presented to the throne in 317–322. Thirteen texts, including the *Bamboo Annals*, were recovered (281) from a tomb which was closed in 299 B.C. Gen. Wang Hsi-chih (321–379) provided the classic models (cut in stone) for formal and cursive calligraphy. Ku K'ai-chih (c. 344–c. 406) perfected the technical refinement of episodic figure-painting.

Buddhism flourished in China already by the close of the Han. The splendor of the Buddhist pantheon and ritual, with its novel conceptions which embraced ten heavens, ten hells, re-birth, and salvation of individual souls of common men, proved irresistible. Sutras were translated in terms borrowed from philosophic Taoism chiefly by Indian and Central Asiatic missionaries among whom the most prolific was Kumarajiva (c. 344–413, to China 383), son of an Indian and of a princess of Kucha. Indian sectarian divergencies became reflected especially in versions of the monastic law (*vinaya*). Desire for direct intelligence of authoritative texts led at least 82 Chinese pilgrims to visit India during the period 200–600 (61 in the 5th cent. alone). Fahsien blazed the desert trail across Central Asia and returned by sea (399–414), and Sung-yun followed the land route to and from Udyana and Gandhara (518–522). Most popular text of the 6th century was the *Parinirvanasutra*, which recounts the birth, illumination, first teaching, and death of the Buddha. Unfavorable Confucian appraisal of Indian asceticism, parasitic practices (celibacy, monasticism, mendicancy), and unrestrained imaginative metaphysical literature, together with hostility of the competing Taoist priesthood, led to brief persecution by the Northern Wei (446) and by the Northern Chou (574).

The Northern Wei cut cave temples in the Yün-kang cliffs near Ta-t'ung and decorated them with Buddhist sculpture in imitation of the Caves of a Thousand Buddhas at Tunhuang, then the point of bifurcation of trade routes north and south of the Tarim basin. After 495 new caves were cut at Lung-men near Loyang. The various Buddhas, Bodhisattvas (future Buddhas), Lohan (Skt. Arhat or Saints), and militant guardians of the law reflect

Indian iconography given form by Greek artisans in Gandhara, as well as Iranian influence.

In Central Asia the Juan-juan or Avars founded the first Mongol empire throughout Mongolia (407–553). Revolt by the T'u-chüeh in the Altai (551) led to establishment in imitation of it of a Turkish empire which shortly (572) split into eastern and western divisions. The Western Turks assailed Sassanian Persia from the east, and by weakening it contributed to the triumph of Islam a few decades later.

581-618. The Sui dynasty was founded at Ch'ang-an by Yang Chien (Wen Ti), chief minister (580) of the Chou.

585 and 607-608. Reconstruction of the Great Wall (as in 543 by the Eastern Wei and in 556 by the Northern Ch'i), against the Eastern Turks of the Orkhon.

589. REUNION OF THE EMPIRE by conquest of the southern Ch'en dynasty.

Active patronage of Buddhism, the common religion of north and south, multiplied shrines and images. Chinese Buddhists increasingly neglected the intangible goal of Indian theology, the eventual ending of the perpetual chain of sentient existences by nihilistic absorption into nirvana; and stressed more practical objectives: immediate response to prayer by the protective Bodhisattva Kuan-yin (Avalokitesvara), direct rebirth into the Western Happy Heaven (Sukhavati) of O-mi-t'o (Amitabha), and salvation by the coming Buddha Mi-lo-fo (Maitreya). Early Chinese philosophic divergencies reappeared within Buddhist sectarian doctrine. Taoist thought was reflected in the increasingly influential Ch'an sect which taught that the Buddha-nature is in every man, and that illumination is to be sought solely through meditation, to the exclusion of prayer, asceticism, and good works. Confucian reaction was evident in the emphasis by the T'ien-t'ai school, founded (575) in the mountains of Chekiang by Chih-i (531–597), upon education as necessary to realization of the Buddha-nature. Strongly synthetic, approval was given to ecstasy, ceremonial, discipline, and to a variety of texts which were interpreted as corresponding to stages in the Buddha's teaching. Perfection was reached in the Lotus (*Saddharmapundarika*) Sutra, which thenceforth surpassed all others in popular favor.

602-605. Liu Fang suppressed rebellion in Annam, repelled the Chams, and sacked their capital Indrapura (near Tourane). The Chams now paid tribute for a century and a half. They controlled (until the 10th cent.) the trade in spices for China, and in silk and porcelain for the Abbasids, which was largely in the hands of Persian merchants. Probably before this time the Cambodian kingdom of Chen-la overthrew its suzerain Fu-nan, and now resumed tribute missions to China (616 or 617).

605-618. Yang Ti, a parricide (604), was ruined by extravagance at home and fruitless foreign wars.

605. The Grand Canal was formed by linking existing waterways from the sumptuous new capital at Loyang (604) to the Long River. It was extended to Cho-chün (near modern Peking) by a million laborers in 608, and to Hangchou in 610.

606. The National College was enlarged, and the doctoral *chin-shih* degree first awarded. The first Japanese embassy was received from the Empress Suiko.

607. Appointment of P'ei Chü to command in the west led to defeat (608) of the Mongol T'u-yü-hun, who had entered the Koko-nor region in the early 4th century, and submission of minor kingdoms (609), but provoked the Eastern T'u-chüeh, who invested the emperor in Yen-men (615).

610. The king of the Liu-ch'iu Islands (or Formosa?) was killed by Ch'en Leng.

611-614. Disastrous wars with Kao-li in the Liao Basin and Korea completed exhaustion of the empire and provoked

613-618. Domestic revolts which led to murder of Yang Ti.

618-907. The T'ang dynasty was founded. (*Cont. p.* 339.)

4. KOREA, TO 562 A.D.

Korea is a mountainous peninsula 100 to 150 miles wide and about 400 miles long extending southward from Manchuria towards the western tip of Japan. High mountains and the cold Japan Sea have retarded the development of the east coast, but the milder climate and more suitable terrain of the west coast facing China and the south coast opposite Japan have made these regions the natural centers of Korean history.

The people since prehistoric times seem to have been closely related racially, linguistically and culturally to the ancient peoples of Manchuria and Siberia as well as to the Japanese, but their post-neolithic civilization came largely from China.

c. 300-200 B.C. A semi-Sinicized state called **Choson** (Japanese: Chōsen) developed in the northwest, and other less civilized states appeared in the south and east.

108 B.C. Emperor Wu-ti of the Han dynasty of China conquered Choson and established four prefectures covering central and western Korea and centering around Lo-lang near the modern P'yŏng-yang (Ch. P'ing-jang, J. Heijo), where an extensive Chinese colony grew up.

c. 150 A.D. Koguryŏ, founded over 100 years earlier in Manchuria and northern Korea, and other states in the south and east asserted their independence of the Chinese colony.

c. 210. The Kung-sun family of southern Manchuria obtained control of Lo-lang and established Tai-fang to the south of it.

c. 238. The Wei dynasty of China captured Lo-lang and Tai-fang by sea.

c. 250. Northern invaders established the state of **Paekche** in the southwest.

313. The last remnants of the Chinese colonies were extinguished by native states, and Chinese civilization was diffused throughout the peninsula by the dispersed Chinese colonists. This marked the beginning of

313-668. THE THREE KINGDOMS PERIOD. After the elimination of China, Korea remained for several centuries divided between Koguryŏ in the north, Paekche in the southwest and Silla, established probably in the second or third century, in the southeast.

c. 360-390. Period of greatest Japanese influence and activity in Korea through their foothold on the coast between Silla and Paekche.

372. Koguryŏ received Buddhism from China.

413-490. King Changsu brought Koguryŏ to the height of its power and

moved the capital from the banks of the Yalu River to P'yŏngyang (427).
528. Silla adopted Buddhism. The last of the Korean states to do so and culturally the most backward, Silla at this time began to make rapid progress and to expand at the expense of the Japanese sphere.

554. Silla won an outlet on the East China Sea in central Korea, giving her easy sea communications with China.
562. Silla destroyed Japan's sphere in Korea.   (*Cont. p.* 348.)

5. JAPAN, TO 645 A.D.

GEOGRAPHY: Japan proper consists of a group of islands running eastward from the southern tip of the Korean peninsula for some 700 miles and then turning abruptly northward for about the same distance, approaching the Asiatic mainland once more off the coast of the Maritime Province of Siberia. The cold Japan Sea enclosed by this island arc gives the inner side of the archipelago a cold damp climate, but because of the Japan Current the Pacific coast of southwestern Japan enjoys a warm temperate climate. Consequently, here the main centers of civilization have developed. Four main islands account for most of the land area of Japan. Hondō, the largest, extends for the greater part of the arc. The next largest, Hokkaidō or Ezo, lies to the north of Hondō. Kyūshū at the southwestern extremity and Shikoku east of it, together with the westernmost portion of Hondō, almost surround a long narrow strip of water known as the Inland Sea. Among the many lesser islands Tsushima and Iki are of most significance, for they lie in the straits between Korea and Japan.

The two most important areas of Japan are the group of small plains lying in Hondō at the eastern end of the Inland Sea and the great Kantō Plain around Tōkyō Bay in eastern Hondō. The Inland Sea, as an artery of communications, and northern and western Kyūshū, which face the Asiatic mainland, are also important regions.

The rivers are all short and shallow and are consequently of little significance. Mountains cover almost the entire area and are particularly high in central Hondō. Many of them are volcanic, and eruptions and earthquakes are frequent. The climate is temperate throughout the land, and rain is abundant. Since antiquity rice has been the principal crop.

ETHNOLOGY: The origin of the Japanese people is still in question. Archaeology and physical anthropology indicate a close connection with the Koreans and the Tungusic peoples of northeastern Asia. Linguistic evidence, though more hotly disputed, tends to support this. However, ethnographical evidence and mythology suggest South Chinese, Malaysian or even Polynesian origin. Furthermore, the Ainu (also called Ezo and Emishi), possibly a proto-Caucasian people, originally inhabited the northeastern half of Japan and undoubtedly contributed to the racial composition of the Japanese. One may conclude, therefore, that, though the early Japanese seem to have been primarily a Mongolian people, there was probably some admixture of blood from southeastern Asia and from the Ainu.

RELIGION: The primitive religion of Japan was a simple worship of the manifold manifestations of the powers of nature combined with a system of ritualistic observances, notable among which was an insistence on physical and ritual purity. The deities tended to become anthropomorphic and to merge with memories of past heroes. They were also affected by attempts to explain the origins of man and society in mythological terms. This eventually resulted in an organized mythology centering around the sun-goddess (*Amaterasu*) and her descendants, the imperial family. After the introduction of Buddhism this combination of nature-worship, ritualistic observances and ancestor-honoring mythology was given the name of Shintō to distinguish it from the Indian religion.

CIVILIZATION: Japan's earliest known civilization was a neolithic shell-mound culture, which before the Christian era gave way to a culture featured by sepulchral mounds over dolmens containing pottery and iron and bronze objects which show a predominantly north Asiatic influence. Prehistoric Japanese civilization seems to have come from what is known linguistically as the Altaic region and seems early to have been influenced strongly by the much higher Chinese civilization.

HISTORY: The first authentic historical accounts of Japan occur in Chinese histories of the 3d century A.D., and picture western Japan, if not all of Japan, as divided among a great number of small political units, among which feminine rule was not uncommon. Some of these petty states had direct relations with the Chinese colonies in Korea, and embassies from Japanese states to the Chinese capital are recorded from 57 to 266.

Japanese historical mythology commences with the accession of the first emperor, Jimmu, in 660 B.C., a date arbitrarily chosen, probably over thirteen centuries later. The mythology hints at the migration of the future imperial clan from Kyūshū up the Inland Sea to the plain of Yamato or Nara, and a successful contest for supremacy with another clan in Izumo on the Japan Sea. The Izumo clan seems to have had a rather distinctive culture and to have had close relations with Korea. During the first four centuries of the Christian era the imperial clan in Yamato seems gradually to have established its suzerainty over most of central and western Japan in a long series of wars with neighboring clans and with the Ainu in the east and the Kumaso in the west, a people apparently of alien and quite possibly of southern origin.

c. 230 A.D.　With the accession of the tenth emperor, Sujin, Japanese records begin to contain some material of probable historical accuracy. The victories of the half-legendary Prince Yamatodake over the Kumaso and the Ainu seem to reflect a period of rapid expansion in the early decades of the 4th century.

c. 360.　The story of the conquest of Korea by the Empress Jingō, ruling in the name of her deceased husband and later in the name of her son, probably refers to Japanese campaigns in the peninsula. Korean records mention Japanese inroads during this century, and a Korean inscription of 391 proves that their armies were widely active in the peninsula at that time. From this period probably dates the establishment of a Japanese protectorate over a group of miniature states in southern Korea known as Kara or Imna (J., Mimana), which had for long constituted a Japanese sphere of influence, and at the same time a semi-protectorate over Paekche, a larger state in southwestern Korea. Japan in the 5th century claimed suzerainty over all of Korea, but in reality her power was on the wane even in the south, as Silla, a vigorous kingdom in the southeast, gradually rose to supremacy. The chief significance of the Korean contacts was that Japan through them was able to imbibe deeply of Chinese civilization and was able to open the way

once more for direct relations with China, which was accomplished in 413.

About the end of the 4th century or early in the 5th scribes able to read and write Chinese are said to have come from Korea. This implies the official adoption of Chinese writing, but not the first knowledge of it in Japan. Writing spread slowly, but was early used for historical records, for by the first half of the 6th century the traditional Japanese chronology becomes reasonably accurate.

Japan's social organization as it emerged at that time was that of a large group of clans (uji) under clan chiefs (uji-no-kami). The members of a single clan all claimed descent from a common ancestor, often the clan god (ujigami). The clan chief acted as high priest to the clan god, and his political rule was tinged throughout with a sacerdotal flavor. The chief and his immediate family often had one of several hereditary titles (kabane), which in time came to be grouped hierarchically. Below the clans were hereditary occupational groups (be or tomo), often called guilds or corporations. They were the economic foundation of the clan system. Below them in turn was an inconsiderable number of slaves.

The imperial clan at first was little more than hegemon among the various clans. Its chief was the emperor, and its clan god was made the national deity. Its rule over the country was extremely loose and feeble. The clans with the two most important hereditary titles, Omi and Muraji, were controlled through a chief Omi (Ōomi) and a chief Muraji (Ōmuraji). Tomo-no-miyatsuko were placed over the imperial clan's hereditary occupational groups and Kuni-no-miyatsuko over its rice lands. Chieftains of the Kume, Ōtomo and Mononobe clans served as imperial generals and those of the Nakatomi and Imube clans (also pronounced Imibe and Imbe) clans were in charge of the court religious ceremonies.

The importation of Chinese civilization and an influx of Korean immigrants seriously shook the clan system. In imitation of China there developed a greater centralization of power in the hands of the imperial clan and its ministers, who at times even aspired to the throne themselves. Imperial lands were gradually extended, and imperial authority grew, eventually leading to a complete political and economic reorganization of Japan on the Chinese model.

? 527.　A serious revolt in Kyūshū prevented the crossing of an army to Korea to aid Imna. Dissension among the Japanese and the treason of some of their officers in Korea seriously reduced their prestige in the peninsula and opened the way for the conquest of Imna by Silla.

? 552. The official introduction of **Buddhism** from Paekche, which itself had received it in 384, marked the beginning of a new epoch in Japan. There probably were Buddhist converts in Japan prior to 552, but at this time Buddhism first began to play a significant rôle in Japanese history and to stimulate the influx of Chinese civilization by way of Paekche. Supported by the powerful Soga clan and strengthened by the arrival of clerics from Korea, Buddhism made headway at court, but soon a temporary proscription of it was brought about by the Nakatomi and Mononobe clans, the political rivals of the Soga. It was presently restored, and the Emperor Yōmei (585–587?) embraced the faith shortly before his death.

? 562. Silla drove the Japanese out of Imna, ending their long direct control of a portion of Korea.

? 587. The Soga crushed their rivals in a short civil war, thereby establishing their political supremacy and the right of Buddhism to an unhampered development in Japan.

592. Soga Umako (d. 626) had his nephew, the Emperor Sushun (587–592), murdered.

593-628. Suiko, the first officially recognized empress, ruled over the land at the crucial period when Buddhism was taking root and the importation of Chinese civilization was strongly influencing the basic forms of Japanese government and society. The leading spirit during her reign was the crown prince, **Shōtoku** (d. 621 or 622), who was the real establisher of Buddhism in Japan, the pioneer in laying the foundations for the Sinicized form of government of the next several centuries and the founder of such great monasteries as the Shitennōji (593), the Hōkōji (588–596) and the Hōryūji (607?).

604. Prince Shōtoku issued the so-called Seventeen Article **"Constitution,"** a moral code consisting of somewhat vague injunctions imbued with Confucian ethics and the Chinese political theory of a centralized imperial government. Thus it served as an ideological basis for political centralization. The constitution was also strongly influenced by Buddhism and shows that the prince was aware of its moral and philosophical import and not merely of its supposed magical powers, which chiefly attracted the contemporary Japanese. In this same year, in imitation of China, official grades known as "cap ranks" (*kan'i*), an official calendar and regulations for court etiquette were adopted.

607. Ono Imoko, the first official envoy from the central government, was dispatched to the Sui court in China. This and a second embassy to the Sui in 608 were followed in the course of the next two and a half centuries by twelve embassies to the T'ang. Since Japanese students, scholars and monks accompanied the envoys to China and sometimes remained there for prolonged periods of study, these embassies were a very important factor in the importation of Chinese civilization to Japan.

630. First embassy to the T'ang.

643. Prince Yamashiro no Ōe, the heir of Prince Shōtoku, was forced to commit suicide by Soga Iruka (d. 645), the son of Emishi (d. 645), the kingmaker of the period. The prince had twice been overlooked in the imperial succession by the Soga, whose obvious imperial aspirations brought about

645. THE DOWNFALL OF THE SOGA in a *coup d'état* led by the future Emperor Tenchi (661–672) and by Nakatomi Kamatari (d. 669), the founder of a new clan, the Fujiwara. This incident gave the progressive element at court a chance to begin a series of sweeping reforms along Chinese lines, which mark the beginning of a new era in Japan. (*Cont. p.* 349.)

III. THE MIDDLE AGES

A. THE EARLY MIDDLE AGES

1. WESTERN EUROPE

a. THE EARLY PAPACY

The Church before the emergence of the Bishops of Rome. The center of gravity was in the east. Possession of the Holy Places and the presence of the emperor gave the east political and ecclesiastical supremacy.

Rise of the episcopate. The bishops, originally overseers (*episcopus*), thanks to their consecration, the tradition of apostolic succession, and their control of the sacraments, were distinguished among the clergy. Each church was originally independent, but the evolution of an ecclesiastical counterpart to the centralized civil state gave the bishop a clearly monarchical quality in the 3d century. The lay and ecclesiastical states met in the person of the emperor, and the original loose autonomy of the independent churches began to be lost in a centralized system. The precedence of **metropolitans** (i.e. the bishops of the great sees) was recognized (341), without reducing the accepted superiority of the **patriarchs**. The five patriarchates (ecclesiastical equivalents of exarchates) were (save for Rome) in the east — Jerusalem, Antioch, Alexandria, Constantinople. The west (including Rome) was either poorly represented or not represented at all at the oecumenical councils in the east. Vague precedence in honor was conceded to Rome, but no more.

Oecumenical councils settled general problems of dogma and discipline. These councils were called by the emperor and presided over by him in person or by legate. Local problems were dealt with in synods.

EMERGENCE OF THE BISHOPS OF ROME.[1] *Papa* was a title applied to all bishops until c. 425, and did not take on its present meaning until the 7th century. Bishop Victor of Rome (c. 190) exercised a kind of spiritual sovereignty which was continued in the 3d century. Gradually the recession of the Church of the east, the loss of Africa, and the rise of powerful churches in the east, left Rome isolated in the west. As the sole western apostolic see, the scene of the martyrdom of Peter, and

guardian of the tombs of Peter and Paul, Rome enjoyed a unique spiritual prestige, and until the reign of Diocletian (284–305) it was the administrative center of the empire. After that the capital was at Milan, and this see at times was almost equal to Rome in influence. With the removal of the imperial capital to Constantinople (330), Rome lost prestige, especially in the east. On the other hand, between 330 and 395, since there was no emperor permanently resident in the west, the Bishop of Rome had no political rival.

(1) The emperors supported the Roman campaign against paganism and against heresy (e.g. Arians and Donatists) with civil penalties, and confirmed and deprived bishops.

(2) The Roman See as early as the days of Diocletian was rich, and was further enriched by the emperors until it was the wealthiest in the Church; the Bishop of Rome enjoyed the "presidency in charity" throughout Christendom.

(3) Sporadic intervention (usually on appeal) was made outside his direct jurisdiction by the Bishop of Rome, but until after 1000 the Bishop of Rome "never once on his own special authority pronounced upon any doctrinal point addressed to the Catholic world." Nor did he interfere between a bishop and his flock in ordinary diocesan affairs or collect money except within his own immediate episcopal jurisdiction.

(4) **The Petrine theory,** on the basis of Matthew 16: 18, 19, asserts that Peter was designated by Christ as the founder of the Church, and that Christ conferred the "power of the keys," i.e. "the power to bind and loose," upon Peter, who transmitted it to his successor the Bishop of Rome, through whom it passed to all bishops. This theory was given currency by **Pope Celestine I** (422–432). In effect this abandoned the original concept of the Bishop of Rome as *episcopus inter episcopos* for the more radical monarchical concept of the Roman bishop as *episcopus episcoporum*. Early writers give no indication of such interpretations, and Cyprian (d. 258) in a famous passage avers that the Bishop of

---

[1] A complete list of the popes will be found in Appendix IV.

Rome is no more than a bishop among other bishops.

340. The introduction of **eremitical monasticism** into the west by Athanasius marked the beginning of a strong ascetic reaction against the corruption of western life. Supported by Jerome, Ambrose, and Augustine, this development led to a great growth of monasticism. Bishop Eusebius of Vercelli (d. 371), by insisting that his clergy lead a monastic life, began a practice which led to the general ordination of monks. Martin of Tours founded (c. 362) a cenobitic community of monks near Poitiers.

343. The **Council of Sardika** apparently recognized the right of appeal from a provincial synod to the Bishop of Rome. The oldest extant decretal dates from the episcopacy of **Siricius** (c. 384–398).

THE LATIN FATHERS OF THE CHURCH: Jerome (c. 340–420), a Dalmatian, devoted to pagan learning despite his keen ascetic convictions. The first great western exponent of monasticism. One of the greatest scholars of the Latin Church, his translation of the *Bible* into Latin (the *Vulgate*) is still authoritative in the Roman Church today. This excellent version exerted stylistic and theological influence throughout the Middle Ages. Ambrose (c. 340–397) of Trier, a Roman provincial governor, elected (374) Archbishop of Milan before he was baptized. His *Duties of the Clergy* (based largely on Cicero, *de Officiis*) was for centuries the standard work on ethics, and is probably the chief single source of the Stoic tradition in early western thought. He made Milan almost the equal of Rome in prestige, and forced the Emperor Theodosius to do penance, maintaining that in ecclesiastical matters a bishop was superior to an emperor. Augustine (354–430) of Hippo, greatest of the western fathers. Converted to Christianity after ventures in Neo-Platonism and Manichaeism, he was the founder of western theology, the link between the classical tradition and the mediaeval schoolmen. Through him a great stream of Platonic and Neo-Platonic thought came into the Church. For a thousand years all thought was influenced by Augustine, and theology betrays his influence to this day. He gave wide currency to the doctrines of original sin, predestination, salvation through divine grace, and his influence was felt by Calvin and Luther. His *City of God* presents a dualism of the heavenly city (identified with the Christian Church) and the earthly city (Rome), and is written to prove that the misfortunes of Rome (e.g. the sack of 410) were not due

to Christianity. The *Confessions* set the fashion in spiritual autobiography.

402–417. INNOCENT I asserted that the pope was custodian of apostolic tradition and claimed universal jurisdiction for the Roman Church.

440–461. LEO THE GREAT, the first great pope, a highly cultivated Roman, vigorous foe of the Manichaean heresy. He procured an edict from Emperor Valentinian III (445) declaring that papal decisions have the force of law. Leo was probably the first pope to enunciate the theory of the mystical unity of Peter and his successors, and to attribute all their doings and sayings to Peter. Leo, repudiating the decrees of the Robber Council of Ephesus (449) at the Council of Chalcedon (451), dictated without discussion, and with imperial support, his solution of the greatest doctrinal controversy since 325. His *Tome* promulgated the doctrine of the union of the two natures. He refused to accept the decree of the council that the Patriarch of Constantinople was supreme in the Church. The tradition of his miraculous arrest of Attila's advance and his efforts to stop Gaiseric's attack (455) won the papacy tremendous prestige in later days. (*Cont. pp.* 150, 215).

b. INVADERS OF THE WEST

ORIGINS OF THE INVADERS. The Germanic race was established in Scandinavia (Denmark) and between the Elbe and Oder as early as the 2d millennium B.C. Eastward lay the Balts (Letts) and to the west of the Elbe were the Celts.

EXPANSION. (1) The West Germans (Teutons) displaced (c. 1000 B.C.) the Celts, moving up the Elbe and Rhine (the Main reached c. 200 B.C.). South Germany was occupied (c. 100 B.C.); Gaul threatened (cf. Caesar's *Commentaries*). These invaders were a pastoral, agricultural folk, tending to settle down. By the time of Tacitus' (c. 55–c. 117 A.D.) *Germania* they were wholly agricultural. Later new tribal names and a new kind of federated organization appeared. (2) The East Germans (Scandinavians) crossed the Baltic (c. 600–300 B.C.) and pushed up the Vistula to the Carpathians. (3) The North Germans remained in Scandinavia.

NEW GROUPINGS AMONG THE WEST GERMANS. Alamanni (of Suevian stock) on the upper Rhine; Franks (i.e. "free" of the Romans) and Saxons between the Weser and the Elbe, inland to the Harz; Thuringians, south of the Saxons.

GOVERNMENT. All were tribal democracies, some under kings, others under *grafs*. In each case the head of the state was elected by the assembly of free men, the kings chosen from a royal house, e.g. Amals (Ostrogoths), Balthas (Visigoths). Mervings (Franks), the *grafs* without such restriction.

PROGRESS OF MIGRATIONS. The East Germans (Bastarnae, Burgundians, Gepids, Goths, Heruls, Rugians, Sciri) moved toward the Black Sea where they had arrived by 214 A.D. The division of Visigoth (West Goth) and Ostrogoth (East Goth) probably arose after their arrival at the Black Sea.

(1) *The Huns*

The **Huns,** nomadic Mongols of the Ural-Altaic race group, probably under pressure from the Zhu-Zhu Empire in Asia, swept into Europe in the 4th century and halted for some 50 years in the valley of the Danube and Theiss.

372. They defeated the Alans and Heruls, destroyed the Ostrogothic empire of Hermanric, absorbed the Ostrogoths for a time in their own empire, routed the Visigoths under Athanaric on the Dniester River, and then began a new thrust to the west.

445-453. Height of the Hun power under Attila. Honoria, sister of Valentinian III, to escape an unwelcome marriage, sent her ring to Attila and asked for aid. Attila claimed this to be an offer of marriage. About the same time Gaiseric the Vandal was intriguing to induce Attila to attack the Visigoths. By a clever pretense of friendliness to both sides, Attila kept the Romans and Goths apart, and set out westward with a great force (451) which included Gepids, Ostrogoths, Rugians, Scirians, Heruls, Thuringians, Alans, Burgundians, and Ripuarian Franks. Metz was taken and the Belgic provinces ravaged. To meet Attila the Roman Aëtius mustered a force of Salian Franks, Ripuarians, Burgundians, Celts, and Visigoths under Theodoric I, as well as his own Gallo-Romans. Attila apparently declined battle near Orleans and turned back.

451. Aëtius overtook him at an unknown spot near Troyes, the so-called *Lacus Mauriacus* (**Châlons**), and a drawn battle was fought. Attila continued his withdrawal. Still claiming Honoria, Attila turned into Italy, razed Aquileia, ravaged the countryside (foundation of Venice) and opened the road to Rome. Pope Leo, one of a commission of three sent by the em-peror, appeared before Attila. Attila retreated after plague had broken out in his force, food supply had run low, and reinforcements arrived from the east for the Roman army. Attila's death (453) was followed by a revolt of his German vassals led by the Gepids, and (454) the defeat of the Huns on the Nedao (in Pannonia). The remnant of the Huns settled on the lower Danube, the Gepids set up a kingdom in Dacia, the Ostrogoths settled in Pannonia.

(2) *The Visigoths*

After their defeat by the Huns, the Visigoths (perhaps 80,000 in number) sought refuge in the Roman Empire.

376. The **Emperor Valens** ordered them disarmed and allowed to cross the Danube in order to settle in Lower Moesia. Faced with the unprecedented problem of these refugees, the Roman government bungled the administration, failed really to disarm the Goths and ultimately had to fight a two-year war with them.

378. The Visigoths, under **Fritigern,** defeated and killed **Valens** near Adrianople, thereby making the first decisive break in the Rhine-Danube frontier. This defeat of the Roman infantry by mounted warriors forecast the revolution in the art of war which determined the military, social, and political development of Europe throughout the Middle Ages. Fritigern, hoping to carve a Visigothic empire out of the Roman provinces, ravaged Thrace for two years, but could not take Adrianople. After his death (379), the Emperor **Theodosius** arranged a pacification of the Visigoths as part of a general policy of assimilation. He won over some of the chieftains, including **Alaric** of the royal house of Balthas, who hoped for a career in the Roman service. Alaric, disappointed in his hopes at the death of Theodosius, was elected king by the Visigoths, and ravaged Thrace to the gates of Constantinople. Arcadius, emperor of the east (395–408), was helpless until the arrival of Stilicho, *magister utriusque militiae* (field marshal of both services) in the east.

Stilicho, a Vandal by blood, married to Theodosius' sister, was guardian of Theodosius' sons, Arcadius and Honorius. He faced Alaric in Thessaly and the Peloponnesus, avoiding battle, apparently on orders from Honorius. Alaric was made *magister militum* in Illyricum, and Stilicho, out of favor in Constantinople, was declared a public enemy.

401. Alaric began a thrust into Italy, probably because of the triumph of an anti-German faction in Constantinople, and ravaged Venetia. Simultaneously Radagaisus (an Ostrogoth) began an invasion of Raetia and Italy. Stilicho, firmly against any Germanic invasion of the west, repulsed Radagaisus.

402. Pollentia, a drawn battle between Stilicho and Alaric, was a strategic defeat for Alaric. Alaric's next advance was stopped, probably through an understanding with Stilicho. Halted again (403) at Verona, the Visigoths withdrew to Epirus.

406. The Rhine frontier, denuded of troops for the defense of Italy, was crossed by a great wave of migrants, chiefly East Germans: Vandals, Sueves, and Alans (non-German). The usurper **Constantine** having crossed from Britain to Gaul, Alaric in Noricum was paid a huge sum of gold by the Senate, as a sort of retainer for his services against Constantine. Stilicho, his popularity undermined by these events and by the hostility of Constantinople, was beheaded. There is no evidence of treason by Stilicho. His execution was followed by a general massacre of the families of the barbarian auxiliaries in Italy, and some 30,000 of them went over to Alaric in Noricum.

410. Alaric took Rome after alternate sieges and negotiations. He sacked it for three days, and then moved south toward Africa, the granary of Italy. Turned back by the loss of his fleet, Alaric died and was buried in the bed of the Busento. His brother-in-law Ataulf was elected to succeed him. Ataulf, originally bent on the destruction of the very name of Rome, now bent his energies to the fusion of Visigothic vigor and Roman tradition.

412. Ataulf led the Visigoths north, ravaged Etruria, crossed the Alps, ravaged Gaul and married (against her brother Honorius' will) Galla Placidia (414) after the Roman ritual. He was forced into Spain (415), where he was murdered. **Wallia** (415–c. 418), after the brief reign of Sigeric, succeeded him.

Ulfilas (311–381), a Gothic bishop of Arian convictions, invented the Gothic alphabet for his translation of the *Bible.* This translation, the first literary monument of the German invaders, had enormous influence, and recalls the wide extent of the **Arian heresy,** which won every important Germanic invader except the Franks, a development with the greatest political consequences, since the lands where the Germans settled were peopled by orthodox Roman Catholics.

Spain had already been overrun by a horde of Vandals, Sueves, and Alans (409),

and the Roman blockade made food hard to get. Wallia planned to cross to the African granary, but lost his ships, was forced to make terms with Honorius and restore Galla Placidia to her brother. He agreed to clear Spain of other barbarians. Succeeding in this he received the grant of *Aquitania Secunda* (i.e. the land between the Loire and the Garonne) with Toulouse as a capital. Thus began the

419-507. KINGDOM OF TOULOUSE.
The Visigoths received two-thirds of the land, the remainder being left to the Roman proprietors. A Gothic state was created within the Roman state. Honorius, hoping to counteract alien influences, revived a Roman custom of holding provincial councils, decreeing an annual meeting of the leading officials and the chief landowners for discussion of common problems. The most important rulers of Toulouse were

419-451. Theodoric I, who fell in the battle of Châlons, and

466-484. Euric, whose reign marked the apogee of the kingdom. He continued the pressure of the Visigoths upon Gaul and Spain, and by 481 extended his domain from the Pyrenees to the Loire and eastward to the Rhone, securing Provence from Odovacar (481). Euric first codified Visigothic law, but the *Breviary of Alaric* (506), a codification of Roman law for Visigothic use, had immense influence among the Visigoths and among many other barbarian peoples. Under Visigothic rule the administration in general remained Roman and the language of government continued to be a Latin vernacular. The Gallo-Roman population and clergy were hostile to the Visigoths as Arians, and this hostility opened the way for the **Frankish conquest** (507), which reduced the Visigothic power to its Spanish domains.

507-711. The Visigothic Kingdom of Spain dragged out a miserable existence under more than a score of rulers, some mere phantoms, until the arrival of the Moslems (p. 163).

554. Belisarius' invasion of Spain, part of Justinian's reconstruction of the Roman Empire (p. 172), was a brilliant campaign, but reduced only the southeast corner of Spain, later regained by the Visigoths, who also reduced the Sueves in the north.

(3) *The Vandals*

406. The Vandals (Asding and Siling), allied with the Sciri and Alans, crossed the Rhine near the Main, followed the Moselle and Aisne (sacking Reims,

Amiens, Arras, Tournai), then turned southward into Aquitaine, and crossed the Pyrenees into Spain (409).

429-534. THE VANDAL KINGDOM IN AFRICA. The Vandals and Alani had been established in southern Spain under Gunderic. His brother **Gaiseric** received an appeal from Boniface, the revolted Roman governor of Africa, following which the Vandals (perhaps 80,000 in number) crossed into Africa (429).

430. The first siege of Hippo failed, but Boniface, now reconciled to the regency of Galla Placidia, was annihilated, and the city fell (431). **St. Augustine,** Bishop of Hippo, died during the siege. The creation of a great Vandal power in Africa, supported as it soon was by a powerful navy, distracted the attention of the Roman government from the new barbarian kingdoms of the west and had a decisive effect of a negative kind.

In Africa the Vandals spared nobody and nothing and the treaty made with the Romans was no restraint. After the arrival of a fleet from Constantinople, a second treaty was made. Eudoxia, daughter of Valentinian, was betrothed to Gaiseric's son, Huneric, and the Vandals received most of the Roman territory except the region about Carthage.

439. Gaiseric took Carthage from the Romans, and made it his capital and naval base.

455. Gaiseric attacked Rome, on the invitation (according to tradition) of Valentinian's widow Eudoxia. ⸙ He took it easily, and for two weeks pillaged the city, scientifically and ruthlessly, but without wanton destruction.

In Africa the Vandals were hated as Arians, and they had to deal with serious Berber revolts, but their power was not broken until the

533-548. Vandalic Wars of Justinian. Belisarius quickly defeated the Carthaginian power of the Vandals; the ensuing Berber revolt was not put down until 548.

(4) *The Burgundians*

411-532. The Burgundians, arriving from the Oder-Vistula region, moved along the Main athwart the Rhine, entered Gaul under King Gundicar, and finally settled as federates of the Roman Empire in upper Burgundy (i.e. the lands including Lyons, Vienne, Besançon, Geneva, Autun, Macon). King **Gundibald** (d. 516) codified Burgundian law in the *Lex Gundobada.* The Burgundians were finally conquered by the sons of Clovis (c. 532), but the Burgundian state remained separate under Frankish

control with Merovingian princes until 613. After 613 it was a province of the Frankish Empire.

c. THE OSTROGOTHS IN ITALY, 489-554

On the breakup of the Hunnic Empire (after Nedao, 454), the Ostrogoths settled in Pannonia (their first settlement inside the Roman frontier) as federates of the empire. Under the Huns the emergence of a single ruler had been impossible. Thiudareiks (ruler of the people), corrupted into Theodoric, educated as a hostage at Constantinople, was elected (471) merely a *gau* king, but soon became leader of his people on a march into the Balkan Peninsula where he forced the Emperor Leo to grant them lands in Macedonia. His ambition for imperial appointment was realized (483) when he was made *magister militum praesentalis* and (484) *consul.* He quarreled with the emperor and marched on Constantinople. To get rid of him the emperor commissioned him (informally) to expel Odovacar from Italy. Arriving in Italy (489) the Ostrogoths triumphed over Odovacar, but did not reduce Ravenna until 493. Theodoric killed Odovacar with his own hands and had his troops massacred.

489-526. THEODORIC THE GREAT. In general Theodoric continued Odovacar's policy, substituting Ostrogoths for Odovacar's Germans, and assigning one-third of the Roman estates (as Odovacar had probably done) to his people. Theodoric's rule was officially recognized (497) by Constantinople. Together with the emperors he named the consuls in the west, but never named an Ostrogoth. Theodoric was the only member of his people who was a Roman citizen, constitutionally the others were alien soldiers in the service of the empire. No Roman was in military command, no Ostrogoth in the civil service. Imperial legislation and coinage continued. The so-called *Edictum Theodorici* is a codification of Theodoric's administrative decrees rather than a body of legislation, as none of Theodoric's "laws" were anything more than clarifications of imperial legislation. Theodoric's secretary of state was the learned Italian, **Cassiodorus,** and the dual state was paralleled by a dual religious system. Theodoric was tolerant of the orthodox Catholics and a protector of the Jews. His chief aim was to civilize his people under the Roman environment and to keep peace.

Theodoric's co-operation with the other Germanic peoples was close, and he cemented his associations by marriage alliances (one daughter married Alaric II the Visigoth, another in Burgundy, and he himself married Clovis' sister). He intervened to protect the Alamanni from Clovis and tried to save the Visigoths. Provence was acquired from Burgundy and annexed to Italy. He was regent and protector of his grandson Amalaric after Alaric II's death, and virtually ruled the Visigothic Kingdom until his death (526).

To the Italians Ostrogothic rule was alien and heretical and they resented it. The end of Theodoric's reign was marked by a growing ill-feeling and suspicion which may have been due to this. **Boethius**, the Roman philosopher and commentator on Aristotle, author of the *Consolation of Philosophy*, an official of Theodoric's government, and his father-in-law, the brilliant and polished Roman **Symmachus**, were both executed (c. 524) on a charge of treasonable conspiracy.

535-554. RECONQUEST OF ITALY BY THE EMPEROR. Justinian, as part of his grandiose reconstitution of the Roman Empire, dispatched **Belisarius** and later **Narses** who reduced the stubborn Ostrogoths and drove them over the Alps to an unknown end.

After the expulsion of the Ostrogoths the **Exarchate of Ravenna** was established under the Emperor Maurice (582–602). The exarch had military and civil powers and received full imperial honors. He exercised imperial control over the Church, including the Bishopric of Rome. War and pestilence had completely ruined northern Italy; Rome, in ruins, had sunk from her imperial position to be a provincial town; the way was open for the Lombard invaders.

Ravenna had been the capital of the west (c. 402–476) and was the home of Theodoric's brilliant court. The architecture of the city offers a unique series of examples of Roman and Romano-Byzantine buildings begun under the emperors and continued by Theodoric. The name and glory of Theodoric have survived in German tradition in Dietrich von Bern (i.e. of Verona, where he had a palace).

PROGRESS OF THE PAPACY. Gelasius (492–496) was the first pope to proclaim the independence of the papacy from both emperor and church council in matters of faith. He asserted that two powers rule the world, the *sacerdotium* and the *imperium*. The *sacerdotium*, since it is the instrument of human salvation, is superior to the *imperium*.

As soon as Italy ceased to be a ruling state, there began a long effort to create national unity and to establish national independence. The barbarian invasions had isolated Italy, accentuated the break with the

empire and left the pope as the sole native representative of ancient unity and Italian hegemony. At the same time the Ostrogoths (half romanized as they were) did not destroy Italian culture, but allowed the Church to transmit the Greco-Roman tradition (linguistic, social, cultural, administrative, and religious) in the west.

529. Western monasticism, representing a wide ascetic reaction against current corruption in life and supported by Jerome, Ambrose, and Augustine, had expanded rapidly in the 6th century and reached a chaotic condition ranging from extremes of eremitical asceticism to the laxest kind of cenobitic worldliness. **Benedict** of Nursia, scandalized at conditions, withdrew to Monte Cassino where he founded a colony and gave it (traditionally in 529) the famous *Benedictine Rule*. This rule, which dominated western monasticism for centuries, was a remarkable and characteristic Roman compromise adapted to the average man. It placed the monks under the control of an abbot, made each house autonomous in a loose federation (not strictly an order at all), and provided for careful recruiting and probation. Discipline was efficient but not extreme, and great stress was laid on labor, especially in the open air (*laborare est orare*). The individual was merged in an ascetic, self-contained, self-sufficient corporation. The spread of the Benedictines was rapid, and soon the only important survival of eremitical monasticism was in the Irish monks of St. Columban. The order became the chief instrument for the reform of the Frankish (Gallic) Church, and for the conversion and civilization of England and Germany. In the course of history it gave the Church 24 popes, 200 cardinals, 5000 saints, 15,000 writers and scholars.

Ruined by invasion, its aqueducts cut, Rome was reduced in population from a half million to perhaps 50,000 Its aristocracy had fled, and mediaeval decay had replaced pagan grandeur. The city was not revived until the Renaissance.

554. Justinian's Pragmatic Sanction restored the Italian lands taken by the Ostrogoths and made a *pro forma* restoration of government, but agricultural lands were depopulated and grown into wilderness, the rural proprietors were sinking into serfdom. Town decline was similar. The Roman Senate ceased to function after 603 and the local *curiae* disappeared at about the same time.

Duces were appointed, probably over each *civitas*, as part of the imperial administration, but they gradually became great landowners and their military functions dominated their civil duties. A fusion of the ducal title and landownership ensued and a new class of hereditary military proprietors emerged beside the clergy and the old nobles. The details of this process are, of course, hard to determine, the more so as evidence is scant.

d. THE FRANKISH KINGDOM, 481-752

The Franks first appear as settlers on the lower Rhine in two divisions, the **Salians** (dwellers by the sea, *sal*) and the **Ripuarians** (dwellers by the riverbank, *ripa*). By the end of the 4th century the Salians were established in the area between the Meuse and the Scheldt as federates of the Roman Empire; the Ripuarians in the tract between the Rhine and Meuse. They formed no permanent confederations, and, unlike the other Germanic peoples, did not migrate as a nation, but expanded.

431-751. THE SALIAN FRANKS UNDER THE MEROVINGIANS.

451. Chlodio (son of Merowech) invaded Artois, and was defeated by Aëtius. Salian Franks were in the Roman forces at the **battle of Châlons.** King Childeric (d. 481) fought as a federate of the empire at Orléans when Aëtius defeated the Visigoths, and he later defeated the Saxons on the Loire. His tomb was found (1653) at Tournai, the "capital" of the Salians.

481-511. CLOVIS (Chlodovech), son of Childeric, in the service of Julius Nepos and Zeno. He defeated the Gallo-Roman general Syagrius at Soissons (486), expanding Salian power to the Loire. The story of the **Soissons vase** is significant of the friendly relations between Clovis and Bishop Remigius. Siegebert, the Ripuarian, defeated an Alamannic invasion at Tolbiac (496) with Salian support. Clovis in the same year defeated the Alamanni (Strasburg?) and later, after election as King of the Ripuarians, emerged as master of the Franks on both sides of the Rhine.

496. The traditional date of the conversion of Clovis to Roman Catholicism is 496. He had previously married a Burgundian, Clotilda, who was of the Roman communion. The Burgundians in general were Arians, and Clovis' choice may have been deliberate. In any case his conversion won him powerful papal and episcopal support and opened the way to wide conquests from the heretic (i.e. Arian) German peoples. Burgundy was conquered (after 500), the Visigoths defeated at Vouillé (507), and their whole kingdom north of the Pyrenees (except Septimania and Provence) was soon subjugated. These conquests were warmly supported by the Gallo-Roman

clergy as a religious war. Clovis founded the Church of the Holy Apostles (Ste. Geneviève) at Paris, and shortly moved his "capital" from Soissons to Paris. He was made an honorary consul by the Emperor Anastasius, a proceeding which brought the Franks technically into the empire.

511-628. Divisions of the Frankish lands after the death of Clovis: (1) His four sons established four capitals — Metz, Orléans, Paris, Soissons. Expansion eastward continued along the upper Elbe; Burgundy was added, and the territory of the Ostrogoths north of the Alps. After a period of ruthless conflict, only **Lothair** (Chlothar) survived, and for a brief time (558–561) the Frankish lands were under one head again. (2) Lothair's division of his lands among his four sons led to a great feud from which three kingdoms emerged: Austrasia (capital Metz) lying to the east (Auster) and mostly Teutonic; Neustria (the "new land" as the name implies) (capital Soissons), Gallo-Roman in blood; Burgundy, which had no king of its own but joined Neustria under a common ruler. The Prince of Neustria exterminated the rival house in Austrasia, but the local baronage preserved the kingdom's identity. Under Lothair II all three kingdoms were united again (613) under one ruler.

628-638. Dagobert (Lothair's son), the last strong ruler of the Merovingian House, made wide dynastic alliances and found wise advisers in Bishop **Arnulf** and **Pepin of Landen.** His firm rule led to a revolt. Under the *rois fainéants* following Dagobert the **mayors of the palace** emerged from a menial position to a dominant rôle in the government both in Austrasia and Neustria.

Merovingian government retained the Roman *civitas* as a unit of administration and set a count (*comes* or *graf*) over it. The source of law was not the king, but local custom administered by the *graf* with the aid of local landowners. Military leaders of large districts were the *duces* who were over several counts. Land grants were made in lieu of pay to officials.

Gregory, Bishop of Tours (c. 540–594), a Frank, wrote in Latin the *History of the Franks*, the best single source on the history of the Merovingian period.

Decline of the royal power under the last of the Merovingians, and beginning of feudal decentralization. (1) Concentration of landownership in the hands of a few (i.e. a landed aristocracy of which the mayors of the palace were representative). (2) The breakdown of the old clan and tribal organization without an effective state to replace it, leading to personal and economic de-

The Merovingian Kings

pendence on private individuals rather than on the state (e.g. commendation, *beneficium*, immunity). (3) Military service on horseback became attached to the benefice as early as the 8th century; for example, Martel's cavalry (see *infra*) for service against the Saracens. Since these grants involved church lands to a considerable degree, Martel in effect compelled the Church to help support national defense. (4) The royal domain was exempt from visitation except by the king's personal administrators. This immunity was extended to royal lands granted to others, and then to lands never in the royal domain. The upshot of the system was complete decentralization by the delegation of the royal powers to local officials who tended to become entirely independent.

The Carolingians

Emergence of the Carolingians in Austrasia. The son of Arnulf married the daughter of **Count Pepin I** (of Landen, d. 639), mayor of the palace, founding the line later called Carolingian.

656. Pepin's son Grimoald made a premature effort to usurp the crown, which cost him and his son their lives, and led to a reaction in favor of the Merovingians.

678-681. **Ebroin**, mayor in Neustria, united the mayoralties under one house; he was murdered (681).

687. **Pepin II** (of Heristal), grandson of Pepin I, gained supremacy in Austrasia and Neustria by his victory at Tertry.

The House of Pepin

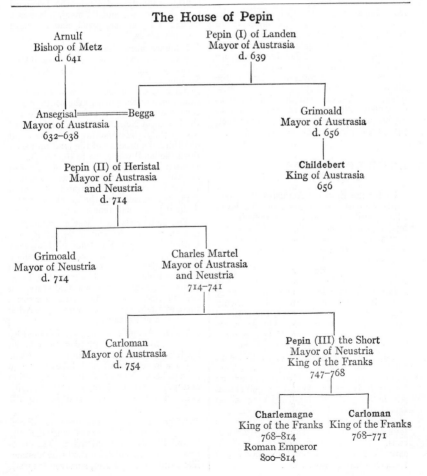

Arnulf
Bishop of Metz
d. 641

Pepin (I) of Landen
Mayor of Austrasia
d. 639

Ansegisal======Begga
Mayor of Austrasia
632–638

Grimoald
Mayor of Austrasia
d. 656

Childebert
King of Austrasia
656

Pepin (II) of Heristal
Mayor of Austrasia
and Neustria
d. 714

Grimoald
Mayor of Neustria
d. 714

Charles Martel
Mayor of Austrasia
and Neustria
714–741

Carloman
Mayor of Austrasia
d. 754

Pepin (III) the Short
Mayor of Neustria
King of the Franks
747–768

Charlemagne
King of the Franks
768–814
Roman Emperor
800–814

Carloman
King of the Franks
768–771

The kingdom was on the verge of dissolution (ducal separatism), and Pepin began an effort to reduce the landed aristocracy from which he himself had sprung.

714-741. Charles Martel (i.e. the Hammer), Pepin's son, an ally of the Lombards, supported Boniface's mission in Germany (Boniface testified that his achievements would have been impossible without Martel's aid).

732. Martel's great victory at **Tours** arrested the advance of the Moslems in the west, and was followed by their final retreat over the Pyrenees (759).

Pepin's conquest of the Frisians was continued, five wars were waged against the Saxons, and powerful decentralizing forces (notably in Burgundy and Alamannia) were broken down.

739. Pope Gregory III, threatened by the Lombards, sent an embassy to Martel, and offered the title of *consul* in return for protection against the Lombards. Charles, an ally of the Lombard king, ignored the appeal. At the end of his life Martel, like a true sovereign, divided the Merovingian lands between his sons, Austrasia and the German duchies going to Carloman, Neustria and Burgundy to Pepin. Carloman and Pepin ruled together, 741-747; Pepin ruled alone, 747-768.

(*Cont. p.* 158.)

e. THE LOMBARDS AND THE POPES, 568-774

Under the Emperor Augustus the Lombards were still established on the lower Elbe (Bardengau) and were defeated (5 A.D.) by the Romans. Their history for the next 400 years is confused and often blank. They were members of the Hunnic Empire and were subdued by the Heruls (505), whom they then destroyed (508). They were probably Arians by this time. Resistance to the Gepids began (c. 546). They were given land by Justinian in Noricum and Pannonia and aided (553) the imperial attacks on the Ostrogoths. The Avars arrived (c. 560) from the Volga, entered Thuringia (562), were defeated by the Franks, and allied themselves (c. 565) with the Lombards against the Gepids, who were annihilated. The Lombards moved on toward Italy and the Avars occupied Dacia. Alboin (d. 573), the Lombard king, killed the Gepid king, Cunimund, with his own hand and married his daughter Rosamund (story of Cunimund's skull as a drinking-cup). The Lombards took part in Belisarius' conquest, and soon the nation began to move south toward Italy.

568. THE LOMBARD CONQUEST OF ITALY. Italy, worn out by the Gothic wars, famine and pestilence, offered little resistance. Constantinople was indifferent, and the conquest was easy. The Lombards, always few in numbers, had associated other peoples (including 20,000 Saxons who soon departed, and some Slavs) in their invasion, but even then they were not numerous enough to occupy the whole peninsula. Rome and Naples were never held, and Ravenna only briefly. The coast was not really mastered. The Lombards (unlike even the Vandals) did not enter into a compact with the empire, and Italian feeling against them was bitter. Pavia became the capital (Italy, until 774, had always two and usually three capitals: Rome, the papal capital; Ravenna, the Byzantine capital; and Pavia the Lombard capital after 573) and the peninsula was a mosaic of Byzantine, papal, and Lombard jurisdictions.

Lombard occupation (virtually military rule at first) covered inland Liguria, inland Tuscany, inland Venetia, the Duchy of Spoleto and the Duchy of Benevento. **Imperial Italy** comprised Venice and the land from north of Ravenna to the south of Ancona, and included the Duchy of Rome and the Duchy of Naples, as well as the toe and heel of Italy. *Hospitalitas* was revived and one-third the produce of the land (not one-third the land) was given to the Lombards. Lombards also took the lands of the dead and the exiled. At first lands were assigned with a full title, but Liutprand introduced (713, 735) leases, and the grant of estates without permanent tenure.

The Lombards took Roman titles and names, and in the end accepted Roman Catholicism. By the time of **Liutprand** (712-744) their speech was clearly Italian, but the natives were loyal to their past, and remained sharply divided from the Lombards. Legally there was a dual system of private law, and in Lombard territories there was a dual episcopal system (i.e. Arian and Roman).

573-584. Alboin's murder was followed by the rule of Cleph (d. 575) and then by ten years of anarchy and private war under a loose federation of dukes (some 36 in number). Roman Catholic opposition and papal negotiations with the Franks alarmed the Lombards, and led to the election of

584-590. Authari, a grandson of Alboin, who was endowed with half the baronial lands as royal domain. The dukedoms were gradually absorbed (the marches like Friuli, Trent, Turin, survived longest).

Authari's widow Theodolinda, a devoted Roman Catholic, bidden to choose a husband who should also be king, selected a Thuringian,

590-615. Duke Agilulf, of Turin, who was friendly to the Roman Church and the true founder of the Lombard state. Gregory the Great blocked an Italian conspiracy against the Lombards. Rothari (636-652) became a Roman Catholic. He collected Lombard customary law in Latin and began the consolidation of Lombard power. Eventually Roman law triumphed and Lombard law survived only in the schools (e.g. Pavia).

The Italian bishops since 476 had been the leaders of the peaceful civilians in the cities, the protectors of the oppressed, and the dispensers of charity. Under the Lombards a system of **episcopal immunities** emerged which made the bishops virtually local temporal sovereigns and enabled them to preserve the local spirit of municipal independence and organization (e.g. consuls, guilds). The urban population was free of feudal bonds, and the town walls (often built by the bishops) were refuges. Milan resumed her greatness and almost equaled Rome. These developments prepared the way for the great assertion of Italian town independence against Roman clerical and German feudal encroachments. **Paul the Deacon** (c. 720–c. 800), the first important mediaeval historian, wrote the *History of the Lombards*.

590-604. GREGORY THE GREAT. Of medium height, good figure, large, bald head, brown eyes, aquiline nose, thick red lips, prominent bearded chin, with exquisite tapering hands. His family was a rich senatorial house and Gregory was prefect of Rome (573). He founded (c. 574) six monasteries in Sicily and one at Rome (St. Andrews) into which he immediately retired as a monk. Embassy to Constantinople (c. 579–586). As Abbot of St. Andrews (586) his rule was severe. Elected pope (590) against his will, he began a vigorous administration. Discipline within his patriarchate was rigorous (stress on celibacy, close watch on elections, insistence on exclusive clerical jurisdiction over clerical offenders). Church revenue was divided into four shares for the bishop, the clergy, the poor, and church buildings. His administration of the wide estates of the Church was honest and brilliant, and the revenue was expanded to meet the tremendous demands on Rome for charity. The pope continued the old imperial corn doles in Rome and elsewhere, aqueducts were repaired, urban administration, especially in Rome, reformed.

Outside his immediate patriarchal jurisdiction Gregory expanded the influence and prestige of the pope, maintaining that the pope was by divine designation head of all churches. Appeals to Rome were heard even against the Patriarch of Constantinople, whose claim to the title of universal bishop was denied. Gregory boldly assumed the rôle of the emperor in the west, and the powers of a temporal prince, counterbalancing the prestige of Constantinople. From his administration date the foundations of later claims to papal absolutism. Gregory was the real leader against the Lombards, appointing governors of cities, directing the generals in war, and receiving from Constantinople pay for the army.

As the first monk to become pope, Gregory made a close alliance between the Benedictines and the papacy (at the expense of the bishops). The monks were given charters and protected from the bishops, the Benedictine Rule was imposed, and a great missionary campaign was begun with monkish aid: (1) The mission to Britain (596) under **Augustine of Canterbury** and the conversion of England provided a base from which the Frankish (Gallic) Church was later reformed and the German people converted; (2) campaigns against paganism in Gaul, Italy, and Sicily, and against heresy in Africa and Sicily.

Gregory was the last of the four great Latin Fathers, and first of the mediaeval prelates, a link between the classical Greco-Roman tradition and the mediaeval Romano-German. Not a great scholar, he was a great popularizer, and spread the doctrines of Augustine of Hippo throughout the west. At the same time he gave wide currency through his *Dialogues* to the popular (often originally pagan) ideas of angels, demons, devils, relic worship, miracles, the doctrine of purgatory, and the use of allegory. Gregory reveals the clerical contempt for classical Latin which profoundly influenced the Latin of the Middle Ages. His *Pastoral* remained for centuries an essential in the education of the clergy. There was a school of music at Rome, but how much Gregory had to do with it, and how much with the introduction of the Gregorian Chant, is doubtful. Gregory introduced the papal style, *Servus Servorum Dei.*

CONTINUED ALIENATION OF ITALY FROM THE EAST. (1) The **Monothelete controversy**: condemnation by the Lateran Synod (649) of Emperor Heraclius' *Ecthesis* (of 638) and Emperor Constans II's *Typos* of 648. Arrest (653) by the exarch of Pope Martin I (649–655), who died in exile in the east. **The Council of Constantinople (680–681)** compromised on the controversy, taking a position in favor of Rome. The Council of Constantinople (692) reasserted the equality of the Patriarchates of Constantinople and Rome. (2) **Emperor Leo the Isaurian's** (717–740) attempt to bring Italy back to obedience: heavy taxation to reduce the great landowners angered Pope Gregory II (the largest landowner in Italy) and Leo's iconoclastic decree (726) aroused all Italy. Gregory III excommunicated all Iconoclasts (731). Gregory's defeat and final humiliation weakened the pope and opened the way for the final Lombard advance.

712-744. DESTRUCTION OF THE LOMBARD KINGDOM. Liutprand, fearing Frankish, Slavic, Hungarian, Byzantine, and papal hostility, began to consolidate his kingdom, reducing the duchies of Benevento and Spoleto. Ravenna was taken temporarily. During the Iconoclastic controversy Liutprand's sincere efforts at rapprochement with the papacy met a brief success.

749-756. Aistulf continued Liutprand's policy of consolidation. The pope, alarmed at Lombard progress, had already (741) made overtures to Charles Martel. Martel, busy with the Moslems, remained faithful to his alliance with the Lombards, but Aistulf's continued advance brought a visit (753) from Pope Stephen II. Stephen had already begun negotiations with Pepin, and the mutual needs of the rising papacy and the upstart Carolingian dynasty drew them into alliance.

754, 756. Pepin in two expeditions forced Aistulf to abandon the Pentapolis and Ravenna (bringing the Lombards virtually to their holdings of 681). Legally the lands involved in the **Donation of Pepin** (756) belonged to the Eastern Empire. The Donation was a tacit recognition of implicit claims of the popes to be the heirs of the empire in Italy. Most important from the papal point of view was the fact that the Church had won a powerful military ally outside Italy. Henceforth the Carolingians maintained a protectorate over the papacy in Italy.

774. Charlemagne, heir to the traditions of Pepin, having repudiated the daughter of the Lombard king, Desiderius, appeared in Italy to protect the pope. After a nine-month siege Pavia was taken, Spoleto and Benevento were conquered, Charles absorbed the Lombard Kingdom into the rising Frankish Empire, and assumed the crown of the Lombards. On a visit (774) to Rome (the first of any Frankish monarch), Charlemagne confirmed the Donation of Pepin, but made it plain that he was sovereign even in the papal lands. At no time did Charlemagne allow the pope any but a primacy in honor (in this respect following the

strict Byzantine tradition). The Donation of Pepin was the foundation of the Papal States and the true beginning of the temporal power of the papacy. Henceforth there was neither the Lombard menace nor the overlordship of the exarch to interfere with the rising papal monarchy. In this sense the fall of the Lombard Kingdom was decisive in papal history. It was equally decisive in Italian history, for the papal victory over the Lombards terminated the last effective effort to establish national unity and a national government until the end of the 19th century. For the Carolingian monarchy the episode was equally significant.

Under the successors of Charlemagne the emperors continued to participate in the papal elections and did what they could to protect Italy against the attacks of the Moslems from Africa.

827-831. The Moslems conquered Sicily.

837. They attacked Naples, pillaged Ancona (839) and captured Bari (840).

846. In the battle of Licosa, Duke Sergius of Naples defeated the Moslems at sea.

847-848. Construction of the **Leonine Wall** by Pope Leo IV (847–855) to defend St. Peter's from the Moslems.

875-877. The Emperor **Charles the Bald** continued to support the papacy against the invader and came to Rome (875) to be crowned, having forced Charles the Fat to retreat and having induced his brother Carloman to sign a truce and withdraw. He was then elected King of Italy by the local magnates.

888. Berengar of Friuli was crowned emperor at Pavia.

891. Guido of Spoleto was consecrated emperor with his son Lambert as co-emperor and co-king.

893. Zwentibold (illegitimate son of Arnulf) was sent to Italy in response to an appeal from Pope Formosus (891–896), but he accomplished nothing. Arnulf then came in person (894) and received an oath of fealty from the Italian magnates, but Guido continued as emperor and was succeeded by

892-899. Lambert. Arnulf embarked upon a second expedition, took Rome and was formally crowned (896).

The Papacy in the Carolingian Period

POPE NICHOLAS I (858–867), one of the few great popes between Gregory I and Gregory VII, was the arbiter of western Christendom. Elected by the favor of Louis II. Three great controversies: (1) **Support of Ignatius,** Patriarch of Constantinople, resulting in the excommunication (863)

of Ignatius' rival, Photius. Photius' futile deposition (867) of Nicholas. This controversy brought the Eastern and Western Churches closer to the final rupture (1054). (2) **Discipline of King Lothair** of Lorraine because of the divorce of his wife Theutberga. Lothair had been allowed (Synod of Aix) by his pliant bishops to remarry, and Nicholas reopened the case at the Synod of Metz (863), which found for Lothair. Nicholas (supported by Charles the Bald) quashed the entire proceeding, disciplined the bishops, and, despite the invasion (864) of the Leonine City by Louis II, compelled Lothair to submit. (3) **Vindication of the right of appeal to Rome** by a bishop against his metropolitan — humiliation of the powerful Archbishop Hincmar of Reims. First papal citation (865) of the *Forged Decretals* (brought to Rome, 864). Emergence of the theory that no bishop may be deposed or elected without papal approval.

867- Decline of the papacy, after the pontificate of Nicholas and the death of Louis II. As the popes had no powerful protectors outside Italy until 961, they fell increasingly under the dominance of the Roman and Italian feudal aristocracy. The lapse of the imperial power left room for the insinuation of a new **doctrine of papal autonomy,** well formulated in the *False Decretals.* Outside Italy the relaxation of papal control and the decline of papal prestige, accompanied by the rise of dominant local feudal lords, accentuated the power of the bishops and made the unity of the western Church a mere shadow until the papacy, having learned to cope with feudalism in the second half of the 11th century, once again made its supremacy felt in the Church.

(*Cont. p. 215.*)

f. THE EMPIRE OF CHARLEMAGNE AND ITS DISINTEGRATION

747-768. PEPIN THE SHORT, who attempted to conciliate the Church by granting and restoring lands to it.

752. Pepin was elected king by the Frankish magnates. Both the house of Pepin and the papacy (in the act of usurping political control from the emperor at Constantinople) needed each other's support. The immediate need of the popes was protection against the expanding Lombard monarchy. **Aistulf,** King of the Lombards, had taken Ravenna (751), the seat of the exarch, besieged Rome, and exacted tribute.

754. Pope Stephen II arrived in Gaul, annointed Pepin, and by conferring

the title *Patricius* (which could legally come only from Constantinople) designated him in a sense *regent and protector of Italy.* The net result was to give some shadow of authority to Pepin's new title as King of the Franks.

754. Pepin marched into Italy, defeated the Lombards, and required them to hand over the exarchate and Pentapolis to the pope. The Lombards failed to do so.

756. Pepin returned and, after defeating the Lombards again, made his famous Donation. The **Donation of Pepin** (which Pepin had no legal right to make) established the Papal States (*Patrimonium Petri*) and began the temporal power of the papacy. It also established the Franks, a distant, non-Italian power, as the allies and defenders of the papacy.

759. Pepin conquered Septimania, disciplined Aquitaine, and so brought effective Frankish rule to the Pyrenees. On his death his lands were given to his sons: Charles receiving Austrasia, Neustria, and northern Aquitaine; Carloman, southern Aquitaine, Burgundy, Provence, Septimania. The brothers ruled together, 768–771; Charles alone, 771–814.

771-814. CHARLES THE GREAT (Charlemagne), a reign of the first magnitude in European history. Charles was a typical German, six feet in height, a superb swimmer, of athletic frame, with large, expressive eyes and merry disposition. He understood Greek, spoke Latin, but could not learn to write. He preferred the Frankish dress. In general he continued the Frankish policy: (1) expansion of Frankish rule to include all the Germans was completed (omitting only Scandinavia and Britain); (2) close understanding with the papacy; (3) support of church reform (which settled the foundations of mediaeval Christian unity).

Italian conquest and reduction of German tribes: Already overlord of the Lombards, Charles married King Desiderius' daughter, soon repudiated her, conquered

773-774. Lombard Italy, and became King of the Lombards, whose kingdom was absorbed into the Frankish Empire. Charlemagne also established his rule in Venetia, Istria, Dalmatia, and Corsica.

787-788. Bavaria was incorporated, its Duke Tassilo first made a vassal and then deposed.

785. Saxony, after a costly and bitter struggle of thirty years, involving eighteen campaigns, was conquered, and Christianity forcibly introduced despite stubborn pagan resistance. Foundation of the Bishopric of Bremen (781).

The Frankish Empire

Original Possessions
Conquests of Charlemagne

Scale of Miles
0 50 100 200 300

795-796. The Avars (on the lower Danube) were reduced.

801. After the Frankish defeat at Roncesvalles (778), the Moslems in northeastern Spain were gradually reduced (Barcelona taken, 801), and the **Spanish March** created.

Establishment of marks (after c. 782) to hold the conquests: Dane Mark, the Altmark (against the Wends), Thuringian Mark, Bohemian Mark, Ostmark (against the Avars), Friulian Mark (on the Italian border), and the Spanish Mark. These marks were also centers of colonization and germanization.

Relation to the Church. Charlemagne held it to be his duty to defend the Church and the pope, and to maintain the faith. He treated the pope like any Frankish bishop, but recognized his unique spiritual prestige. His visit (774) to Rome was the first of a Frankish sovereign: the Donation of Pepin was confirmed, but the terms are not clear. The pope crowned Charles' son, Pepin, King of Italy (781), his son Louis, King of Aquitaine.

REVIVAL OF THE ROMAN EMPIRE IN THE WEST. Pope Leo III, a submissive pontiff, notified Charlemagne of his election to the Holy See, and dated his pontificate by Charlemagne's regnal years. Driven from Rome (799) by a conspiracy and riot, he sought refuge at Charlemagne's court and was restored by Frankish troops.

800. **Charlemagne arrived in Rome,** allowed Leo to clear himself of a series of charges by oath (avoiding the trial of a pope), and was crowned emperor in St. Peter's on Christmas Day. According to Einhard, Charlemagne avowed his regret at the coronation. He cannot have been unaware of the general plan, and his feeling may have been due to modesty or concern at Byzantine reactions or hostility to papal pretensions. Charlemagne disregarded the imperial title in a partition of the empire (806), and arranged to have his son Louis crown himself (813). Theoretically the coronation of 800 marked a return to the dualism of Theodosius I (i.e. two emperors over an undivided empire). In fact the Frankish Empire was more German than Roman in population and institutions. Byzantium regarded Charlemagne as a usurper; Charlemagne seems to have meditated a marriage with the Empress Irene as one solution of the difficulty. The papal coronation, an act of rebellion in Byzantine eyes, marked a definite break between Rome and Constantinople. The Emperor Michael I recognized (812) Charlemagne's

title in the west in return for sovereignty in Venice, Istria, Dalmatia.

GOVERNMENT: (1) **In the Church:** Charlemagne's rule was a theocracy, and he insisted on supremacy over the Frankish Church, legislating on all subjects, settling dogmatic questions, deciding appointments, presiding at synods. (2) **In the Frankish state:** centralization continued; taxation in the Roman sense (which survived only under local and private auspices) was replaced by services in return for land grants (the economic basis of Carolingian society). Such services included forced labor on public works among the lower ranks, the provision of food for the court and public officials on duty, and judicial and military obligations (primarily among the upper ranks). Charlemagne's continuous campaigns reduced the small farmers, accentuating the tendency to serfdom. Charlemagne tried to offset this tendency by allowing groups of poorer farmers to co-operate in sending a single soldier, and by excusing the poorest from ordinary field service. Systematization of the army and of military service was also begun. Commendation and immunity continued, and the basis of later feudal development was firmly established.

Administration: The tribal dukes were largely eliminated and government was carried on by counts, appointed for life, but frequently removed. This system was extended to Italy, Bavaria, and Saxony. To prevent the counts establishing an hereditary tenure, and to limit local abuses, the *missi dominici* (usually a bishop and count) were introduced (802) as officers on circuit in a given district. The *missi* held their own courts, had power to remove a count for cause, and were charged with the supervision of financial, judicial, and clerical administration. They formed an essential link between the local and central government. Under the counts were viscounts and vicars (*centenarii*). Margraves (*Mark grafen*) were set over the marks with extended powers to meet the needs of their position. Local administration of justice was reformed by the introduction of *scabini*, local landowners appointed by the counts to sit as permanent judiciary officers.

The Carolingian revival of learning: Charlemagne, perhaps out of concern for the improvement of ecclesiastical education, set up the Palace School under **Alcuin** from the School of York, later Abbot of Tours. Various clerics were also given liberal grants that they might establish local schools, though no general system of education was introduced in the Frankish Empire. In general, the source of inspiration was Latin

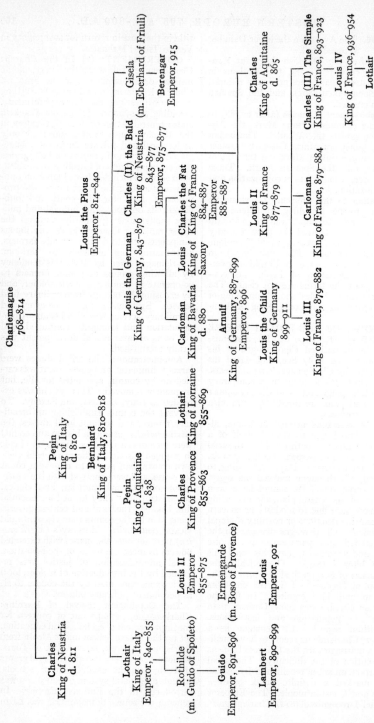

The Carolingian Dynasty

rather than Greek. Einhard, for example, who came to the Palace School from Fulda, wrote his biography of Charlemagne in the manner of Suetonius. At Charlemagne's court were gathered scholars and literary men of almost every nationality, including **Peter of Pisa**, the grammarian, the Visigothic poet **Theodulf**, the Lombard historian, **Paul the Deacon** (*History of the Lombards*). Great care was given to the copying of texts, and the refined Carolingian minuscule was evolved.

814-887. THE DISINTEGRATION OF THE CAROLINGIAN EMPIRE. Such efficiency as the Carolingian government possessed under Charlemagne derived rather from his personality than from permanent institutions. Local administration was carried on by unpaid officials whose compensation was a share of the revenue. Local offices tended to become hereditary. The tentative partitions of the empire in Charlemagne's lifetime followed Frankish tradition, and had no relation to any racial or national elements. One son, Louis the Pious, survived, and the empire was passed on to him (quite by accident) undivided. The decisive stage in the partition of the empire came under Louis and his heirs.

814-840. LOUIS the Pious (emperor), educated at the Palace School, crowned in his father's lifetime. Sincerely religious, a reformer of his court, the Frankish Church, and the monasteries, he allowed himself to be crowned again by the pope (816). Ineffectual as a soldier and ruler. Louis and his heirs concentrated on a long struggle (leading to civil war) over territorial questions, to the neglect of government, foreign policy, and defense, a program which hastened the breakup of the empire.

817-838. A significant series of **partitions** involving Louis' sons: Lothair (d. 855), Louis the German (d. 876), Pepin (d. 838), and their half-brother, Charles the Bald (d. 877).

The division of **817**: Aquitaine and parts of Septimania and Burgundy went to Pepin as sub-king; Bavaria and the marches to the east were assigned to Louis the German as sub-king; Francia, German and Gallic, and most of Burgundy were retained by Louis and his eldest son Lothair. Italy went to a third sub-king.

The division of **838:** Charles the Bald was assigned Neustria and to this was added Aquitaine on the death of Pepin. Charles' holding, which had no name, approximated (accidentally) mediaeval France and was mainly Romance in speech.

840-855. LOTHAIR I (emperor). On the death of Louis the Pious the three heirs continued their struggle, and after the indecisive **battle of Fontenay** (841) Carolingian prestige sank to a new depth. Charles the Bald and Louis the German formed an alliance against Lothair (who was supported by the clergy in the interests of unity) in the bilingual (Teutonic and Romance) **Oaths of Strassburg** (842), sworn by the rulers and their armies, each in their own vernacular. They then forced a family compact upon Lothair at Verdun.

843. THE TREATY OF VERDUN divided the administration and control of the Carolingian Empire as follows: (1) **Lothair** kept the (empty) title of emperor, and was King of Italy and of an amorphous territory (the "middle kingdom") which was bounded roughly by the Scheldt, the upper Meuse, Saône, and Rhone on the west, and by the Rhine and Frisia on the east (i.e. the territory of Provence, Burgundy, and what was later called *Lotharingia*). (2) **Louis the German**, as King of the (East) Franks, ruled a realm essentially Teutonic in blood, speech, and geography, extending from the Rhine (except Frisia) to the eastern frontier of the empire. (3) **Charles the Bald**, as King of the (West) Franks, received a realm (loosely called Karolingia for a time) made up of West Francia and Aquitaine, Gascony, Septimania, etc., mainly Romance in speech, approximating mediaeval France in general outline.

855-875. LOUIS II (emperor). At Lothair I's death his lands were divided as follows among his sons: Louis II received Italy, Charles (d. 863) the newly formed Kingdom of Provence (centered around the city of Arles), and Lothair II the inchoate aggregate (from Frisia to the Alps and from the Rhine to Scheldt) which began to be called *Lotharii regnum* or *Lotharingia* (modern Lorraine).

870. Treaty of Mersen, following the death (869) of Lothair II, King of Lorraine. Louis the German forced Charles the Bald (crowned King of Lorraine, 869) to divide equally and solely on the basis of revenue the lands of Lothair outside of Italy. Thus Louis gained a strip of land which brought his frontier west of the Rhine.

875-877. CHARLES THE BALD, emperor.

877-881. Anarchy and interregnum in the empire.

879. The **Kingdom of Burgundy** (Cisjuran Burgundy) was established by Boso of Provence.

888. The **Kingdom** of **Juran Burgundy** (i.e. Besançon, Basel, Lausanne, Geneva, etc.) was erected by Rudolf I. It passed to the empire by bequest in the time of Conrad II.

c. 787-925. THE NINTH CENTURY INVASIONS:

(1) **In the North.** Bands of Northmen (Scandinavians, p. 170), under pressure of population and resentful at the rise of local kings, pushed outward from Scandinavia. The Swedes penetrated into Russia, the Norwegians and Danes moved into the northern islands (including the British Isles) and south to the Continent. Within a half century of the first raid (c. 787) on England, the British Isles had been flooded. Masters of the sea in the west, the Northmen pushed inland from the mouths of the great rivers (e.g. Rhine, Scheldt, Somme, Seine, Loire), sacking the cities (e.g. Utrecht, Paris, Nantes, Bordeaux, Hamburg, Seville). "Normandy" was invaded (841) and a simultaneous attack made (845) on all three Frankish kingdoms. The Mediterranean was entered (843). In the east Constantinople was attacked by Swedes (*Rus*), who came down from Russia. A great attack on Paris (885) was heroically met by Count Odo (Eudes), son of Robert the Strong. Raids were pushed farther into France and the Mediterranean in the course of the 9th century.

(2) **In the East.** Bulgarian expansion produced a great Bulgar state between the Frankish and Byzantine Empires. The Bulgars were converted to the Greek communion (870). Hungarians (Magyars), closely followed by Petchenegs, crossed the Carpathians and the lower Danube, pushing into Venetia, Lombardy, Bavaria, Thuringia, Saxony, the Rhineland, Lorraine, and Burgundy (925).

(3) **In the Mediterranean.** Moslem domination of Sicily, Corsica, Sardinia, and the Balearic Islands made the Mediterranean virtually a Moslem lake. Raids were almost continuous, Rome was attacked (846) and later Monte Cassino.

852-886. Under the combined influence of the disruption of the Carolingian Empire and the pressure of the 9th-century invasions, the great fiefs of France began to appear as the only effective centers of local resistance to invasion, and feudalism may be said to have struck root.

Feudalism. Its origins may be traced to the German *comitatus* and the proprietary system of the later Roman Empire. Essentially it was an informal system of contracts for the disposal of land and honorable services, and was in no sense a form of government. Inseparable from it was

the agricultural organization (*manorialism*) which rested on servile tenures and contracts for manual labor and services. Antedating feudalism, manorialism was also derived from the Roman proprietary system. The feudal system evolved in each country under local conditions and followed a different development. The feudalism of France is ordinarily regarded as typical.

g. THE WEST FRANKS UNDER THE CAROLINGIAN KINGS, 843-987

843-877. CHARLES THE BALD (emperor, 875-877). His kingdom under the Treaty of Verdun was roughly equivalent to modern France with additions in the north and south and a restricted frontier on the east. Charles was effective master of Laon, but his sway over Neustria was nominal, his control sporadically maintained by war and intrigue. Charles granted three great fiefs as a buffer for his frontiers: The County of Flanders to his son-in-law, Baldwin Iron-Arm (862); Neustria to Robert the Strong as "Duke between Seine and Loire"; the French Duchy of Burgundy to Richard, Count of Autun. Brittany (Amorica) was semi-independent under its own dukes and counts in the 9th century and continued so virtually to the end of the Middle Ages. Aquitaine, joined to Neustria for Charles (838), soon emerged as a duchy and was consistently hostile. The Duchy of Gascony was joined to Aquitaine in 1052. From Neustria were carved the Counties of Anjou (870) and Champagne. Septimania remained refractory.

870. Carloman, Charles' son, emerged from monastic retirement and led a series of intrigues which ended when he was blinded and fled to his uncle, Louis the German. He died in 874. Charles was further weakened by his intrigues in Lorraine and Italy, and by his efforts to win the imperial crown, leaving France open to invasion, anarchy, and brigandage.

The crown, impotent and virtually bankrupt, commanded no respect from magnates or prelates, and the **Capitulary of Mersen** (847) shows clear evidence of the progress of essentially feudal ideas: every free man is to choose a lord; none may quit his lord; each must follow his lord in battle. It must be noted that this was purely a military measure. France was already divided into *comtés* under counts theoretically removable by the king.

875. Expedition of Charles to Italy and imperial coronation.

877. The Capitulary of Kiersy made honors hereditary, but lands were still granted only for life.

877-879. LOUIS II (*the Stammerer*), son of Charles the Bald, maintained himself with difficulty despite the support of the Church. His sons

879-882. LOUIS III and

879-884. CARLOMAN divided their heritage, Louis taking Neustria, Carloman Aquitaine, Septimania, and Burgundy, and reduced their rivals to impotence. Louis' victory over the Northmen (Saucourt, 881) did not stop their raids.

884-887. CHARLES THE FAT, son of Louis the German, already King of the East Franks (879) and emperor (881-887), was chosen King of the West Franks instead of Charles the Simple, the five-year-old brother of Louis and Carloman. Charles the Fat, having failed (886) to aid the gallant Odo (Eudes) against the Northmen, was deposed (887).

888-898. Odo (Eudes), Count of Paris, Marquis of Neustria (son of Count Robert the Strong, whence the name *Robertians* for the line before Hugh Capet) was elected King of the West Franks by one faction of magnates to avoid a minority on the deposition (887) of Charles the Fat. Another faction chose Charles III, the Simple, son of Louis II (Carolingian). Despite five years of civil war

893-923. CHARLES III ruled from Laon, the last Carolingian with any real authority in France. Charles, unable to expel the Northmen from the mouth of the Seine, granted (911) Rollo (Hrolf the Ganger, d. 931), a large part of what was later Normandy, for which Rollo did homage.

Formation of Normandy. Rollo was baptized (912) under the name Robert, acquired middle Normandy (the Bessin, 924) and the western part of the duchy (Cotentin and Avranche, 933). The colony was recruited with fresh settlers from Scandinavia for the best part of a century, and was able to retain a strong local individuality. Yet soon after 1000 the duchy was French in both speech and law. Between this period and the accession of Duke William I (the Conqueror) Norman history is fragmentary.

923-987. The French kingship. Robert, Count of Paris, *Duke between the Seine and Loire*, won the West Frankish crown with the aid of his sons-in-law, Herbert, Count of Vermandois, and Rudolf, Duke of Burgundy, but was killed (923), leaving a son (later Hugh the Great) too young to rule.

929-936. RUDOLF followed Robert as the foe of Charles the Simple, and ruled with no opposition after Charles' death. Hugh the Great, master of Burgundy and Neustria, declined the crown,

preferring to rule through the young Carolingian heir,

936-954. LOUIS IV, a son of Charles the Simple. Hugh's title, *Duke of the French*, seems to have implied governmental functions as much as territorial sovereignty, and he held most of the northern barons under his suzerainty.

954-986. LOTHAIR succeeded his father Louis IV. On the death of Hugh the Great, his son Hugh, known as *Capet*, succeeded him (956).

978. Lothair's effort to gain Lorraine led to an invasion by Emperor Otto II to the walls of Paris. Hugh Capet, in alliance with Emperor Otto III, and aided by Gerbert of Reims, reduced Lothair's rule at Laon to a nullity. Lothair's son

986-987. LOUIS V was the last Carolingian ruler of France.

987. ELECTION OF HUGH CAPET, engineered by Adalbero, Bishop of Reims, and by Gerbert. Hugh was crowned at Noyon with the support of the Duke of Normandy and the Count of Anjou. His title was recognized by the Emperor Otto III in exchange for Hugh's claims to Lorraine. The emergence of the new house of Capet was not the victory of a race, a nationality, or a principle, but the triumph of a family, already distinguished, over a decadent rival.   (*Cont. p. 225.*)

h. GERMANY UNDER THE CAROLINGIAN AND SAXON EMPERORS, 843-1024

843-876. LOUIS THE GERMAN. Increasing Slavic and Norse pressure (general Norse attack, 845, on Carolingian lands). Louis had three sons: Carloman (d. 880), Louis (d. 882), and Charles the Fat. Carloman was assigned Bavaria and the East Mark; Louis, Saxony and Franconia; Charles, Alamannia. Contest with Charles the Bald for Lorraine. By the Treaty of Mersen (870) Louis added a strip of land west of the Rhine.

876-887. CHARLES THE FAT. He blocked Charles the Bald's advance toward the Rhine. Emergence of the Kingdom of Cisjuran Burgundy (i.e. Dauphiné, Provence, part of Languedoc) under Boso (879). Expedition to Italy and coronation by John VIII (881). Negotiations (882) with the Northmen, now permanently established in Flanders. While Charles was in Italy settling a papal election, a great Norse invasion burst on France (Odo's defense of Paris, 886). Deposition of Charles by the Franconian, Saxon, Bavarian, Thuringian, and Swabian magnates at Tribur (887).

887 (896)-899. ARNULF (illegitimate son of Carloman, grandson of Louis the German). A certain supremacy was conceded to Arnulf by the various rulers of Germany and Italy who rendered a kind of homage to him. Victory over the Norse on the Dyle (Löwen, 891); resistance to the Slavic (Moravian) advance (893), with Magyar aid. Magyar raids after 900. Arnulf dared not leave Germany to answer the appeal of Pope Stephen V (885–891) for aid. His illegitimate son Zwentibold was sent on the call of Pope Formosus (891–896), but accomplished nothing (893). Arnulf went to Italy in person (894), was crowned king and received an oath from most of the magnates. On another appeal from Formosus (895) he took Rome and was crowned emperor (896).

900-911. LOUIS THE CHILD (born 893), last of the Carolingians, elected king by the magnates at Forchheim (900). Increasing Norse, Slavic, and Magyar pressure and devastation.

The weakening of the royal power as the East Frankish Kingdom of the Carolingians declined, and the survival of tribal consciousness, left the way open for the emergence of the Stem (German *Stamm*, a tribe) duchies. These duchies preserved the traditions of ancient tribal culture, and their independent development under semi-royal dukes (beginning in the 9th century) ensured the disruption of German unity for a thousand years. These Stem duchies were: Franconia (the Conradiners ultimately drove the Babenbergers into the East Mark, later Austria); Lorraine (not strictly a stem duchy but with a tradition of unity); Swabia (the early ducal history is obscure); Bavaria (under the Arnulfings; repulse of the Magyars, acquisition of the Mark of Carinthia); Saxony (under the Liudolfingers; repulse of the Danes and Wends, addition of Thuringia); the Frisians (no tribal duke appeared).

911. End of the East Frankish line of the Carolingians, with the death of Louis the Child (899–911); the German magnates, to avoid accepting a ruler of the West Frankish (French) line, elected Conrad, Duke of Franconia.

911-918. CONRAD I. Magyar raids and ducal rebellions in Saxony, Bavaria, and Swabia met vigorous but futile resistance from Conrad. Lorraine passed (911) temporarily under the suzerainty of the West Frankish ruler, Charles the Simple. Conrad nominated his strongest foe, Henry, Duke of Saxony, as his successor, and he was elected.

919-1024. THE SAXON (OR OTTO-NIAN) HOUSE.

919-936. KING HENRY I (called *the Fowler,* supposedly because the messengers announcing his election found him hawking). Tolerant of the dukes, he forced recognition of his authority; cool to the Church, he avoided ecclesiastical coronation.

920-921. Reduction of the Duke of Bavaria; alliance with Charles the Simple.

923-925. Lorraine restored to the German Kingdom and unified into the **Duchy of Lorraine,** a center of spiritual and intellectual ferment. Henry's daughter married the Duke of Lorraine (928).

924-933. Truce (and tribute) **with the Magyars,** fortification of the Elbe and Weser Valleys (Saxony and Thuringia), palisading of towns, villas, monasteries, etc., establishment of *Burgwarde,* i.e. garrisons (which later often became towns like Naumburg, Quedlinburg), where one-ninth of the Saxon effectives were on duty and trained as horsemen each year.

928. Saxon expedition across the frozen Havel River **against the Wends:** Branibor (Brandenburg) stormed; the Wends driven up the Elbe; creation of the Marks of Branibor, Meissen, and (later) Lusatia as guardians of the middle Elbe.

933. Henry ended the Magyar truce with his **victory at Riade** on the Unstrut River, the first great defeat of the Magyars. Occupation of the land between the Schlei and the Eider (Charlemagne's Dane Mark), and erection of the Mark of Schleswig, guardian of the Elbe mouth; the Danish king was made tributary and forced to receive Christian missionaries. Henry had prepared the way for his son whose election was a formality, the succession becoming virtually hereditary.

936-973. KING OTTO I (*the Great*). Otto revived the policy of Arnulf, was crowned and anointed at Aachen, Charlemagne's capital; his coronation banquet revived the Carolingian coronation banquet (of Roman origin) at which the Duke of Franconia served ceremonially as steward, the Duke of Swabia as cup-bearer, the Duke of Lorraine as chamberlain, and the Duke of Bavaria as marshal.

Otto's vigorous assertion of royal authority (a three-year war reduced the Dukes of Bavaria, Franconia, Lorraine, and Saxony). He followed the policy of keeping the great duchies (except Saxony) in his own hands or those of his family. Taking Conrad, the boy King of Arles (Provence and Burgundy), under his protection (937), Otto forced the recognition of his overlord-

The Saxon Emperors

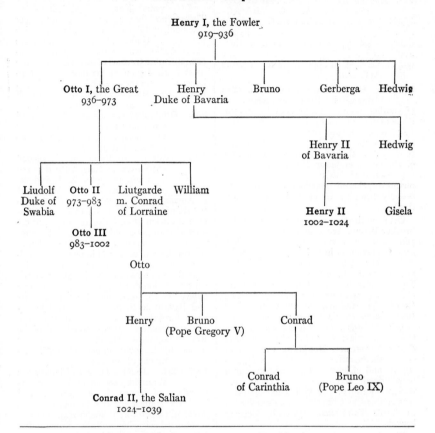

ship (forestalling Hugh of Provence); Conrad's sister, Adelheid, married Lothair, one of the claimants to the crown of Italy, and later Otto himself. The Bavarians defeated Otto (944) at Wels, but Otto conquered (950) Duke Boleslav of Bohemia and put the duchy under the suzerainty of Bavaria.

951-952. Otto's first expedition to Italy to keep the passes through the mountains open. Marriage to Adelheid and assumption of the crown of Italy; the pope refused him imperial coronation; Berengar of Ivrea, forced into vassalage, ceded the Marks of Verona, Friuli, Istria (the keys to the passes), to Otto's brother Henry, Duke of Bavaria.

953. Revolt of Otto's son (Liudolf, Duke of Swabia), his son-in-law Conrad (Duke of Lorraine), and others (suppressed, 955).

955.   BATTLE OF THE LECHFELD. Otto, with an army recruited from all the duchies, ended the Magyar menace by a great victory. Defeat of the Wends on the river Recknitz. Re-establishment and colonization with Bavarians of Charlemagne's East Mark (Austria).

968. The bishoprics established among the Slavs (e.g. Brandenburg, Merseburg, Meissen, Zeitz) were consolidated under the new **Archbishopric of Magdeburg.** German bishoprics were everywhere filled with bishops loyal to the monarchy, marking the alliance of the king and the Church against feudal opposition.

961-964. Otto's second expedition to Italy on the appeal of Pope John XII for protection. Assumption of the crown of Italy at Pavia.

962. IMPERIAL CORONATION BY THE POPE: REVIVAL OF THE ROMAN EMPIRE IN THE WEST. Otto put a temporary end to feudal anarchy in Rome, deposed one pope and nominated another, and compelled the pope to recognize the emperor's right to approve or reject papal elections.

966-972. Otto's third expedition to Italy: deposition of one pope, restoration of another; nomination of a new pope; punishment of the Romans. Imperial coronation (967) of the future Otto II and assertion of suzerainty over Capua and Benevento (967). Betrothal of **Theophano** (daughter of the Greek emperor, Romanus II) to the future Otto II (969); coronation of Theophano (972) and marriage to Otto (supposedly bringing Greek Italy as her portion).

Otto, with the able assistance of his brother Bruno, Archbishop of Cologne, began a cultural revival (the so-called *Ottonian Renaissance*) in the manner of Charlemagne; late in life, he learned to read, but not to speak, Latin; Bruno knew Greek. The cosmopolitan court literary circle included Irish and English monks, and learned Greeks and Italians, notably **Liutprand of Cremona** (*Historia Ottonis*; *Legatio Constantinopolitana*). Great literary activity of the monasteries: **Widukind of Corvey** (*Res Gestae Saxonicae*); **Roswitha**, the nun of Gandersheim, author of the *Carmen de gestis Ottonis* and of learned Latin comedies in a bowdlerized Terentine style, celebrating saintly virginity (9th century), a Christian epic; **Ekkekard of St. Gall's** *Waltherius*, inspired by German legends.

The German rulers and nobles of the 9th century had regarded the monasteries as their personal property and prepared the way for a strong clerical reaction toward reform supported by the regular clergy (e.g. Cluny), opposed by the seculars who were rapidly passing under feudal influences.

973-983. OTTO II. The revolt of Henry the Wrangler, Duke of Bavaria, in alliance with Boleslav of Bohemia, and others, required five years to put down; Henry was banished (978). Repulse of a Danish incursion.

978. Lothair, King of the West Franks, invaded Lorraine and was forced to abandon his claims by Otto's invasion of France (980).

981-982. Otto's campaign in southern Italy,

to expel the Saracens and reduce the Byzantine power, ended in defeat.

983-1002. OTTO III (an infant of three years). Rule of his brilliant mother Theophano (983–991), his grandmother Adelheid, and Archbishop Willigis of Mainz (991–996). Under Theophano's influence his education was in the Byzantine tradition; his tutor **Gerbert of Aurillac**, one of the most learned men of his day, whose brilliance won him the nickname *Stupor Mundi*. Henry the Wrangler proclaimed himself king, but was forced to submit.

996. Otto's first expedition to Italy ended Crescentius II's sway in Rome; Otto designated his cousin Bruno as pope (Gregory V).

998. Returning to Rome on his **second expedition to Italy,** Otto deposed the Crescentine pope, John XVI, and decapitated Crescentius. Otto made Gerbert of Aurillac pope, as Sylvester II. Sylvester shared Otto's devotion to the Carolingian tradition of an intimate union and co-operation of pope and emperor. Otto's romantic antiquarianism led him to a plan of reform through universal imperial overlordship independent of the German crown. He settled down at Rome and began a theatrical restoration of the splendors of the city: palace on the Aventine, Byzantine court and Byzantine titles, futile revival of ancient formulae (seals inscribed *Renovatio imperii romani*, etc.); rapid alienation of the Roman populace. He left no heir and was buried by his own orders beside Charlemagne at Aachen.

1002-1024. HENRY II (son of Henry the Wrangler, cousin of Otto, great-grandson of Henry the Fowler) emerged from the contest for the throne, and was crowned emperor at Rome (1014). Devout (canonized with his wife, St. Kunigunde), but a political realist and firm with the Church, he concentrated his attention on Germany. Against episcopal objections he founded (1007) the great Bishopric of Bamberg, endowed it richly as an outpost of German culture against Slavdom; the cathedral, one of the glories of German architecture, contains his tomb. Vigorous (Gorzian) monastic reform with many confiscations.

1002. Successful **revolt of Ardoin** in Lombardy (reduced temporarily in 1004, and finally in 1014).

1003-1017. A long, unsuccessful struggle with Boleslav Chrobry (992–1025) of Poland, Duke of Bohemia, who had acquired Lusatia and Silesia.

1006-1007. Unrest in Burgundy and revolt of **Baldwin of Flanders** (suppressed, 1007).

In practice Henry had no choice but to allow the great fiefs to become hereditary. He relied heavily on the clergy to supply advisers and administrators, and looked to the Church also for military and financial support, but he dominated the Church in Germany through his control of the episcopal appointments. Extensive secularization and reform of the monasteries of the Church resulted.   (*Cont. p.* 205.)

i. SPAIN

(1) *The Visigothic Kingdom,* 466-711

In the time of **Euric** (466-484) the Visigothic rule extended from the Loire to Gibraltar and from the Bay of Biscay to the Rhone. The capital was Toulouse.

507. Clovis' victory in the **battle of Vouillé** obliged the Visigoths to withdraw over the Pyrenees, retaining only Septimania north of the mountains. The new capital was Toledo.

The Visigoths in Spain were a small minority (about one in five) and were rapidly romanized (e.g. the *Breviary of Alaric*). The conversion of King Reccared (587) from Arianism to Roman orthodoxy brought an end to their religious separateness, accelerated the process of romanization and initiated the domination of the clergy over the monarchy. The **Synod of Toledo** (633) assumed the right to confirm elections to the crown. After 600 the Jews were forced to accept baptism, for which reason they later on welcomed the Moslem invasion. Visigothic speech gradually disappeared and the current vernacular was of Latin origin. Roman organization and tradition survived to a marked degree. **Isidore of Seville** (c. 560-636), a bishop, theologian, historian, man of letters, and scientist, produced in his *Etymologiae* a general reference work which remained a standard manual for 500 years and served as a medium for the transmission of much ancient knowledge to the mediaeval world.

(2) *Moslem Spain,* 711-1031

711-715. THE MOSLEM CONQUEST. In 711 a mixed force of Arabs and Berbers, led by the Berber **Tariq** (whence Gibraltar — *Gebel al-Tariq*) crossed from Africa. Roderick, the last Visigothic king, was completely defeated in the **battle on the Guadalete** (Rio Barbate), whereupon his kingdom collapsed. The Moslems took Cordova and the capital, Toledo. Tariq was followed (712) by his master, **Musa,** who took Medina Sidonia, Seville, Merida, and Saragossa. The Moslems soon reached the Pyrenees (719), having driven the remnants of the Christians into the mountains of the north and west.

732. In the **battle of Tours** the Moslems, having crossed into France, were decisively defeated by Charles Martel and the Franks. By 759 they had been entirely expelled from France.

756-1031. THE OMAYYAD DYNASTY OF CORDOVA.

756-788. Abdurrahman, emir. He was the grandson of the Omayyad Caliph of Damascus, and was the founder of the Moorish state in Spain. Christians were given toleration in return for payment of a poll tax. The Jews were very well treated. But Abdurrahman met with vigorous opposition from the Arab nobility, which was supported from abroad by Pepin and Charlemagne.

777. **Invasion of Spain by Charlemagne,** checked by the heroic defense of Saragossa. Annihilation of his rear-guard by Basques at Roncesvalles (778 — *Song of Roland*). Wars with the Franks continued throughout the rest of the century, Charlemagne ultimately conquering northeastern Spain as far as the Ebro River (capture of Barcelona, 801).

788-796. **Hisham,** son of Abdurrahman, emir, during whose reign Malikite doctrines were introduced in Spain.

796-822. **Hakam,** son of Hisham, emir. Revolts in Cordova (805, 817) and Toledo (814). The Cordovan rebels, expelled from Spain, went to Alexandria and thence to Crete, which they reconquered.

822-852. **Abdurrahman II, son of Hakam.** During his reign Alfonso II of Leon invaded Aragon. He was defeated and his kingdom destroyed. The Franks too were driven back in Catalonia. The Normans first appeared on the coasts. In 837 a revolt of Christians and Jews in Toledo was suppressed, but Christian fanatics continued to be active, especially in Cordova.

852-886. **Mohammed I.** He put down another Christian uprising in Cordova, and carried on extensive operations against the Christian states of Leon, Galicia, and Navarre (Pampeluna taken 861).

886-888. Mundhir.

888-912. Abdullah, brother of Mundhir.

912-961. ABDURRAHMAN III. The ablest and most gifted of the Omayyads of Spain, who assumed the titles of *Caliph* and *Amir al-Mu'minin* in 929, thus asserting supremacy in Islam as against the Abbasid Caliphs of Bagdad. Abdurrahman's reign was marked by the pacification of the country, by completion of governmental organization (centralization), by naval activity, by agricultural advance and by industrial progress. **Cordova** (population c. 500,000) became the greatest intellectual center of Europe, with a huge paper trade, great libraries, and pre-eminent schools (medicine, mathematics, philosophy, poetry, music; much translation from Greek and Latin).

The height of **Moslem learning** was reached by **Averroës** (ibn Rushd, c. 1126–1198), philosopher, physician and commentator on Plato and Aristotle, master of the Christian schoolmen.

The aristocracy, by this time almost extinguished, was replaced by a rich middle class and feudal soldiery. The Christians and Jews continued to enjoy wide toleration.

Abdurrahman continued the wars with Leon and Navarre, which extended over most of his long reign. By the **Peace of 955** with Ordono III of Leon, the independence of Leon and Navarre was recognized and the Moslem frontier withdrawn to the Ebro; on the other hand, Leon and Navarre recognized the suzerainty of the caliph and paid tribute. This peace was soon broken by Ordono's brother Sancho (957) who, after his defeat, was expelled by his subjects but restored by the caliph (959).

961-976. Hakam II. He continued the wars against Castile, Leon, and Navarre and forced their rulers to sue for peace (962–970). At the same time he waged successful war against the Fatimid dynasty in Morocco, which was brought to an end (973) and replaced by the Omayyad power.

976-1009. Hisham II, whose reign marked the decline of the Omayyad dynasty. Power was seized by Mohammed ibn Abi 'Amir, with the title of *Hajib al-Mansur* (European: *Alamansor* = the Victorious Chamberlain), a brilliant reforming minister (army and administration). He carried on successful campaigns against Leon, Navarre, Catalonia, and Mauretania, and temporarily checked the religious and racial separatism which later on brought about the collapse of the Omayyad Caliphate. On his death in 1002 he was succeeded by his son, Abdulmalik al-Muzaffar (the Victorious), who several times defeated the Christians, and was followed by his brother, Abdurrahman, named Sanchol. The latter obliged Hisham to proclaim him his heir, whereupon a revolt took place in Cordova under the leadership of Mohammed, a member of the royal family. Hisham was compelled to abdicate in favor of Mohammed, and Sanchol was executed. In the meanwhile the Berbers nominated Sulayman as caliph. Civil war ensued, reducing Spain to more than a score of petty kingships (*taifas*) and making easier the Christian reconquest.

1027-1031. Hisham III, the last Omayyad caliph.

(3) *Christian Spain*

CASTILE AND LEON, 718-1065

718-737. Pelayo, successor to Roderick the Visigoth, created the **Kingdom of the Asturias,** a theocratic elective monarchy in the Visigothic tradition. Beginning of the reciprocal alliance of kings and clergy under

739-757. Alfonso I, who assigned to the Church a generous share of the lands conquered from the Moslems and used the clergy as a counterweight to the aristocracy.

899. Miraculous discovery of the bones of **St. James the Greater** and erection of the first church of Santiago de Campostella, which became the center of the Spanish national cult and one of the most influential shrines in Europe.

910-914. García, King of Leon, began a rapid expansion of his domain to the east (construction of numerous castles, hence the name *Castile*).

c. 930-970. Count Fernán González, Count of Burgos (later Castile), marked the rise of the Counts of Burgos. By intrigue and alliance with the Moslems he expanded his domains at the expense of Leon, and made the country of Castile autonomous and hereditary. His progress was arrested by Sancho the Fat of Leon (d. 966), who was in alliance with Abdurrahman III.

970-1035. Sancho the Great of Navarre effected a close union of Castile and Navarre and began the conquest of Leon.

1035-1065. Ferdinand I, of Castile, completed the work by conquering Leon (1037) and assuming the title of *King of Leon.*   (*Cont. p. 233.*)

j. THE BRITISH ISLES

(1) *England to* 1066

Prehistoric Britain. The prehistoric inhabitants of Britain (called *Celts* on the basis of language) were apparently a fusion of Mediterranean, Alpine, and Nordic strains which included a dark Iberian and a light-haired stock. Archaeological evidence points to contacts with the Iberian Peninsula (2500 B.C.) and Egypt (1300 B.C.).

1200-600 B.C. The true Celts are represented by two stocks: Goidels (*Gaels*), surviving in northern Ireland and

ENGLAND
IN
ALFRED'S DAY

The Danish
Boroughs *underlined*_ Lincoln
The Chief Districts of
Danish Settlement ------

SCALE OF MILES
0   50   100

IONA
Picts
(Dalriada)
Scots of
Scotland
Edinburgh
LINDISFARNE
English
Northumbria
Jarrow
Wearmouth
Brunanburh
Strath
Irish
Scots
Galloway
Whitby
Solway Firth
de
Cumbria
Danish
Northumbria
ISLE OF
MAN
York
THE
Dublin
RECHIN
ISLAND
Chester
DANELAW
Nottingham
Derby
Lincoln
Offa's Duke
English Mercia
Watling
(DANISH MERCIA)
Lichfield
Stamford
Leicester
East
Anglia
Wexford
Street
South Wales
(Damnonia)
London
SHEPPEY
THANET
Malmesbury
Kingston
Canterbury
Glastonbury
Wilton
The Weald
Athelney
S E
Devon
E   S   S   E   X
Wilton
Winchester
WEST
CORNWALL
W
ISLE OF
WIGHT
Seine

high Scotland, and Cymri and Brythons (*Britons*) still represented in Wales. The Brythons were close kin to the Gauls, particularly the Belgi. Their religion was dominated by a powerful, organized, priestly caste, the Druids of Gaul and Britain, who monopolized religion, education, and justice.

57 B.C.-c. 450 A.D. ROMAN OCCUPATION began with Julius Caesar's conquests in Gaul and Britain (57–50 B.C.); Emperor Claudius' personal expedition and conquest (43 A.D.) were decisive in the romanization of Britain. Reduction of the "empire" (5–40 A.D.) of Cymbeline and suppression (61) of the national revolt of Boudicca (*Boadicea*). Conquest of Wales (48–79). Construction of the great network of Roman roads began (eventually 5 systems, 4 centering on London). Bath emerged as a center of Romano-British fashion.

78-142. Roman conquests in the north began under Agricola; results north of the Clyde-Forth line were not decisive. The Emperor Hadrian completed the conquest of Britain in person: construction of Hadrian's Wall (123) from Solway Firth to Tyne mouth. Firth-Clyde rampart (c. 142).

208. Emperor Septimius Severus arrived (208), invaded Caledonia (Scotland), restored Roman military supremacy in the north, and fixed Hadrian's Wall as the final frontier of Roman conquest.

300-350. Height of villa construction in the plain of Britain. Chief towns: Verulamium (St. Albans), Colchester, Lincoln, Gloucester, York. The skill of the artisans and cloth-workers of Britain was already famous on the Continent in the 4th century. The island south of the Wall was completely romanized.

c. 350. Piratic raids of Irish (*Scoti*) and Picts were common, and the Teutonic conquest of Gaul cut Britain off from Rome in the 5th century, leaving the Romano-British to defend themselves against Saxon attacks on the south and east which soon penetrated the lowlands.

410-442. Withdrawal of the Roman legions and the end of the Roman administration coincided with an intensification of Nordic pressure and the influx of Jutes, Angles, and Saxons, which permanently altered the racial base of the island. By c. 615 the Angles and Jutes had reached the Irish Channel and were masters of what is virtually modern England. A Celtic recrudescence appeared in the highlands of the west and northwest. The history of Britain for two centuries (c. 350–597) is obscure. Christianity had not made much progress under the Romans.

Seven Anglo-Saxon kingdoms, the *Heptarchy*, emerged after the Teutonic conquest: Essex, Wessex, Sussex (probably prevailingly Saxon as the names suggest); Kent (Jutes); East Anglia, Mercia, Northumbria (Angles).

560-616. The supremacy of **Ethelbert of Kent** in the Heptarchy coincided with the

597. Arrival of **Augustine the Monk** and the conversion of Kent to the Roman Church. The hegemony in the Heptarchy passed eventually to **Edwin of Northumbria** (which had also been converted).

633. The defeat and death of Ethelbert's brother-in-law Edwin at the hands of the heathen Mercians ended the Northumbrian primacy and temporarily overwhelmed the Roman Church. A period of anarchy ensued.

633. Oswald of Northumbria called Aidan from Iona, whose mission began the great influence of Celtic Christianity, which for a time threatened to replace the Roman Church.

664. The **Synod of Whitby** turned Britain back into the orbit of the Roman Church and the Continent, and prepared the way for the decisive rôle of

669-690. **Theodore of Tarsus,** Archbishop of Canterbury. Theodore introduced a strictly Roman parochial system and a centralized episcopal system which became the model for the secular state and created a new concept of kingship. National synods brought the rival kingdoms together for the first time, and began the long evolution destined to create English nationality and national institutions, and to spread them through the civilized world.

Theodore's episcopate was marked by the reintroduction of Greco-Roman culture and the permanent establishment of a new cultural tradition which produced **Bede** (673–735), the father of English literature, and culminated in the wide influence of the great School at York, which extended to the Continent (e.g. **Alcuin** at the court of Charlemagne). The Archbishopric of York was founded, 735. Romance ecclesiastical architecture and church music flourished.

757-796. Under **Offa II** the Kingdom of Mercia, supreme south of the Humber, reached its maximum power, after which it broke up.

787. The first recorded raid of the **Danes** in England was followed by the

Danish inundation of Ireland. In the pause before the great wave of Viking advance, Wessex under

802-839. Egbert, who had been in Charlemagne's service, emerged supreme (conquering Mercia), exercised a vague suzerainty over Northumbria, and received the homage of all the English kinglets.

856-875. Full tide of the first Viking assault. Wessex was the spearhead of resistance.

871-899. ALFRED THE GREAT purchased peace until he could organize his forces and build up a navy. Almost overwhelmed by the winter invasion of 878, he finally defeated the Danes and forced the Peace of Wedmore, whereby Guthrun the Dane became a Christian and divided England with Alfred. The *Danelaw*, north of the Thames-Lea line, went to Guthrun; the south, together with London, went to Alfred.

878-900. The Danes were masters of the northeast, and under Danish pressure Scotland began to take on shape and unity.

Alfred proceeded to organize the defense of his kingdom. London was walled and garrisoned with burghers charged with its defense. Earth forts (*burhs*) of the Viking type were thrown up and garrisoned. The *fyrd* and the fleet were reorganized, the army increased, the *thegns* began to be used as a mounted infantry. Henceforth all citizens of the requisite wealth were forced to thegnhood, i.e. to join the military class attached to the royal household. A Danish reaction (892–896) was firmly put down.

Alfred's patronage of **learning**. Foreign scholars and learned refugees were welcomed at court. Alfred translated Bede's *History*, Orosius, and Boethius' *Consolatio* into the vernacular. To provide trained administrators, Alfred established schools for the sons of thegns and nobles. The Anglo-Saxon *Chronicle* was started.

899-924. Edward, Alfred's son, succeeded him, and with his sister, Ethelfreda of Mercia, began the conquest of the Danelaw, which was completed under

924-939. Ethelstan, Edward's son. The sons of Alfred were the first true kings of England; his grandson Edgar (959–975) was recognized as such. Archbishop Dunstan, Edgar's chief counselor, was a great ecclesiastical reformer (simony and morals) of the Church and the people. He followed a policy of fusion and conciliation toward the Danes, and Oda, a full-blooded Dane, became (942) Archbishop of Canterbury. The absorption of the Danelaw by Wessex left the Celtic fringe in Scotland and Wales independent under a vague kind of vassalage to the king.

As the Danelaw was absorbed, the shire system was extended to it with the old Danish boroughs as a nucleus. The administration was often in the hands of men of Danish blood. The Anglo-Saxon farmers had no love for war, and the thegns began to emerge as a professional soldier class. The old tribal and clan organization was superseded by a system of quasi-feudal form whereby each man had a lord who was responsible for him at law. The great earldoms were beginning to emerge.

No common law existed; shire and hundred courts administered local custom with the freeman suitors under the king's representative-ealdorman, shire-reeve, or hundred-reeve. From the days of Edgar, the feudal element tended to encroach on royal authority, especially in the hundred courts. The old monasticism had been destroyed by the invasions, and the Church in England fell into corruption and decadence, only reformed by the influence of Cluny and Fleury and the Norman Conquest.

991. An ebb in Viking raids was followed by a fresh onset during the reign of Ethelred the Redeless (978–1016), led by Sven I (*Forked Beard*), King of Denmark. *Danegeld* had been sporadically collected under Alfred; now it was regularly levied and used as tribute to buy off the invaders. This tax, and the invasions, led to a rapid decline of the freeholders to a servile status. Under Canute, the Danegeld was transformed into a regular tax for defense. Collection of the Danegeld, originally in the hands of the towns, fell increasingly to the lord of the manor, and it was only a step from holding him for the tax to making him lord of the land from which the tax came.

1013-1014. Sven I (d. 1014) was acknowledged by the English, and Ethelred fled to Normandy, the home of his second wife, Emma.

1017-1035. King Canute, one of the two sons of Sven, elected by the Witan. The Witan was a heterogeneous body of prelates, magnates, and officials without any precise constitutional status. Canute was "emperor," on the model of Charlemagne, over a northern empire which included Denmark, Norway, and England, and, but for his early death, might have played a more important rôle. His reign was marked by conciliation and fusion. The Church was under Anglo-Saxon clergy. Canute maintained a good navy, and his standing army included the famous *house-carls*, which soon had an Anglo-Saxon contingent. The four great earldoms, Wessex, East Anglia, Mercia, Northumbria, and seven lesser earldoms can be distinguished in this period. The greatest of the earls was **Godwin of Wessex.** Canute's sons were incompetent, and his line ended, 1042.

Godwin was chiefly responsible for the election of the successor to Canute's line, Edward, son of Emma and Ethelred, who married (1045) Godwin's daughter.

1042-1066.　EDWARD THE CONFESSOR, of the line of Alfred, was under Godwin's domination. Brought up at the Norman court, speaking French, he tried to Normanize the English court. Godwin's influence led to the deposition of the Norman Archbishop of Canterbury and the selection of the Saxon Stigand by the Witan. As Stigand had supported an antipope, Alexander II favored the Normans, as did Hildebrand, the power behind the papal throne. Godwin's son, **Harold,** succeeded (1053) him as Earl of Wessex, and dominated Edward as his father had. Another son of Godwin, Tostig, became Earl of Northumbria. Harold (c. 1064) was driven ashore on the Channel, fell into the hands of William, Duke of Normandy, a cousin of Edward the Confessor, and was forced to take an oath to aid William to attain the crown of England, which William declared Edward had promised him.

1066. Tostig, exiled after the Northumbrian revolt (1065), returned with Harold Hardrada to attack Northumbria. The Confessor died in January (1066) and William at once began vigorous preparations for the conquest of England.

1066. On Edward's death **Harold** was chosen king by the Witan and was guarding the coasts of England against William when Tostig and Hardrada appeared in the north. After a brilliant dash northward, Harold defeated them at Stamford Bridge in September, at the very moment that the Norman invaders arrived in the Channel. Rushing southward after his victory, Harold confronted the Normans, who had already landed, with a reduced, wearied, and shaken force, and was beaten and killed in the

OCT. 14.　Battle of Hastings, or Senlac.

(*Cont. p.* 191.)

(2) *Scotland to* 1034

Racial origins obscure. A wave of Neolithic peoples from the Mediterranean was followed by Celts, Goidels, Brythons, Saxons in the 6th century B.C., and then by Picts. The Romans arrived at the end of the first century, A.D., but made no permanent impression.

450-600.　Four political nuclei: Picts (Pentland Firth to the central plain); **Dalriada** (Argyllshire and the islands of Jura and Islay); **"Welsh" refugees** in Strathclyde; **Ida of Bernicia's realm** (from the Tweed to the Firth of Forth).

c. 565.　COLUMBA arrived from Iona and converted the King of the Picts to the Celtic Church, giving Scotland her first cultural contact with the civilized world.

664.　The Synod of Whitby turned England to the Roman Church and temporarily isolated Scotland. The Picts ultimately went into the Roman communion (c. 700) and Iona itself followed (716).

685. The English power was broken on the southern frontier, and Scotland began her independent evolution. Under **Kenneth I** (d. 858) began the first Scottish union.

794.　Arrival of the Norse. Iona burned (802); a series of devastations followed.

921.　Edward, son of Alfred the Great, was acknowledged lord of Scotland. Ethelstan enforced the bond in arms (934) and a Scottish effort to revolt was crushed (937).

1005-1034. Under **Malcolm II,** Lothian was added to the Scottish crown and Strathclyde completed (**1034**) the union of the four nuclei under

1034-1040. Duncan, but without a homogeneous racial or political basis. The Isles and the north were under Scandinavian dominance, and England aimed to make Scotland her vassal. (*Cont. p.* 201.)

(3) *Ireland to* 1171

Racial origins. The Neolithic inhabitants, followed by Celts and Goidels (c. 600–500 B.C.). The "fifths" (i.e. Ulster, Leinster, Connaught, East and West Munster) may date from the Goidel arrival. Belgic and other Brythonic migrations (300–150 B.C.) probably in the southeast. Supremacy of the Brythonic **Kingdom of Tara** in the 4th century of the Christian Era. The **Picts** pushed into Antrim and Down. There is an enormous body of legend dealing with the early origins.

431. Traditional date for the arrival of **Bishop Palladius** and his mission.

432.　PATRICK, a pupil of Germanus of Auxerre, especially trained for this mission, arrived to continue Palladius' work. He founded churches in Meath, Ulster, Connaught, and probably established the Bishopric of Armagh. Chieftains were converted, but much paganism survived. Patrick began the education of the priesthood. Patrick's ecclesiastical organization was probably close to that of Britain and Gaul, but with the withdrawal of the Roman legions from the latter countries the Roman connection was cut, and there was a recrudescence of paganism. The diocesan organization of Patrick apparently slipped back into the native system.

Chieftains, on their conversion, made donations of land to the Church, and at first the ecclesiastical offices seem to have remained in the hands of the sept, with the *coarb* (inheritor) as bishop or abbot. The cenobitic organization of the 5th century was that of a sept, whose chief was a Christian. Later there was a rigorous form which separated the sexes. As the earlier diocesan organization declined, the number of bishops rose to fantastic figures. There was a great exodus of Irish scholars and monks to Europe during the 8th and 9th centuries.

c. 500-800. The Golden Age of Irish monastic scholarship occurred in the 6th to the 9th centuries. A great school founded by Eudo, Prince of Oriel (c. 450–540), at Aranmore drew scholars from all Europe. Establishment of the monastery of Clonard (c. 520) under Welsh inspiration. Here there were said to be 3000 students living in separate, wattled huts under open-air instruction. From Clonard went forth the so-called *Twelve Apostles of Ireland,* founding schools all over Ireland and later the Continent.

c. 533. True monasticism began with the work of Columba. Columba founded Iona (563), the mother Church of Scotland, whence Aidan, the apostle of England, founded Lindisfarne (635) for the conversion of Northumbria. The *Book of Kells* and the flowering of Gaelic vernacular poetry date from this period.

590. Columban of Leinster, from Bangor, began his mission to Europe, founding Luxeuil and a great series of other foundations (e.g. Gall, Würzburg, Salzburg, Tarantum, Bobbio). The 8th century saw a great wave of missions from the Rhine-Meuse area inland to the Rhone-Alps line. This powerful advance of Celtic Christianity at one time seemed destined to win northern Europe from Rome. The chief formal differences from Rome were in tonsure, the date of Easter, the consecration of bishops. In the 7th century the Irish Church conformed to Roman usage, but the bond with Rome was not close.

723. Boniface (Winfred) the Anglo-Saxon, arrived on the Continent to begin the organization on Roman lines of the Celtic establishments among the Franks, Thuringians, Alamanni, and Bavarians.

Before the coming of the Norse there were no cities, no stone bridges in Ireland, and no foreign trade of importance.

795. The first Norse attack. Dublin (840), Waterford, and Limerick founded as centers of Norse trade with the Continent. Soon a mixed race, the Gallgoidels (whence Galloway) arose, and a Christian decline set in. The Scandinavians remained chiefly in the ports.

1002-1014. Brian of Munster established his supremacy. A period of road- and fort-building. At Clontarf (1014) Brian defeated the Norse, ending the domination of Dublin, though the Norse remained in their cities. Brian fell in the battle and anarchy followed — the struggle of the O'Brians of Munster, the O'Neils of Ulster, the O'Connors of Connaught — which ended in an appeal to King Henry II of England by Dermond (or Dermot) MacMurrough.

1152. The Synod of Kells established the present diocesan system of Ireland, recognized the primacy of Armagh, and the Archbishoprics of Cashel, Tuam, Dublin. Tithes were voted.

1167-1171. The Norman Conquest. Henry II, on his accession, had the idea of conquering Ireland. John of Salisbury records that on his request as Henry's envoy (1155), Pope Adrian IV sent Henry a letter granting him lordship of Ireland, and a ring as the symbol of his investiture. Henry seems never to have availed himself of the papal grant.

1167. On the appeal of Dermond MacMurrough, Henry issued a letter allowing Dermond to raise troops in England for his cause. Dermond came to terms with Richard of Clare, a Norman, Earl of Pembroke, and with other Normans, most of whom were related to one another. A series of expeditions to Ireland brought into the island a group of Norman families (e.g. Fitzmaurices, Carews, Gerards, Davids, Barries, *et al.*), who began to establish a powerful colony, which alarmed Henry.

1171. HENRY II, with papal sanction landed in Ireland to assert his supremacy and to reconcile the natives. The Synod of Cashel, at which Henry was not present, acknowledged his sovereignty.

(Cont. p. 201.)

k. SCANDINAVIA

ORIGINS: References in Pytheas, Pomponius Mela, Pliny the Elder, Tacitus, Ptolemy, Procopius, Jordanes. Archaeological remains indicate Roman connections in the 3d century after Christ, but there is no evidence for close continental relations until the Viking period.

VIKING PERIOD. Scandinavia developed in isolation during the barbarian migrations until the 2d century after Christ. The Viking expansion from Scandinavia itself prolonged the period of migrations in Europe for four hundred years. The traditional participation of Scandinavia in the Viking migration through Europe was as follows: (1) **Norwegians** (outer passage): raids in Scotland, Ireland, France (Hrolf the Ganger, i.e. "Rollo"). (2) **Danes** (the middle passage): British Isles, France, the Low Countries. (3) **Swedes** (eastward passage): across Slavdom to Byzantium (foundation of Novgorod 862, Kiev, c. 900). There never was a mass migration, and probably all stocks shared in the various movements to some degree. Causes: (1) pagan reaction, including renegade Christians; (2) pressure of population; (3) tribal warfare and vassalage of the defeated, especially after 872 (this is the traditional explanation for Rollo's migration, 911); (4) love of gain; (5) fashion and love of adventure.

NORWEGIAN COLONIZATION. (1) **Ireland**: the Norwegian conquest began c. 823 and centers were established at Dublin (the kingdom endured until 1014), Waterford, and Limerick. Exodus of learned monks to Europe (**Scotus Erigena?**). Attacks by the Picts and Danes. The subsequent colonization of the Scottish Islands drew Norwegians from Ireland and accelerated the celtization of the colonists who remained there. (2) **The Islands**: Hebrides, Man, Faroes, Orkneys, Shetlands. (3) **Iceland**: reached by Irish monks c. 790; discovered by the Norsemen in 874 and colonized almost at once; establishment of a *New Norway*, with a high culture. (4)

Greenland: visited by Eric the Red of Iceland (981) and colonized at once; expeditions from Greenland to the North American Continent (p. 365). The Norse settlements in Greenland continued until the 15th century.

CIVILIZATION. Large coin hoards indicate the profits of raids and trade with the British Isles, Mediterranean, Byzantium, and Moslem Asia. Export of furs, arms (to eastern Europe), and mercenary services to rulers (e.g. bodyguards of Ethelred, Canute, Slavic princes, Byzantine emperors). Trade eastward was cut off by the Huns and Avars (5th and 6th century), but resumed after Rurik's expedition (862) reopened Russia.

Runes (from a Scandinavian root, meaning to inscribe) were already ancient in the Viking period, and probably are modified Roman letters. The *Eddas*, dramatic lays (prose and verse) of the Norwegian aristocracy (especially in Iceland) dealing with gods and heroes (many in the German tradition, e.g. Sigurd and the Nibelungs), are the highest literary production of heathen Scandinavia.

Scandinavian society rested on wealth from raids and commerce and consisted of a landed aristocracy with farmer tenants with the right and obligation to attend local courts; there were few slaves. The only general assembly was the *Allthing* of Iceland (established 930), the oldest continuous parliamentary body in existence.

Mythology and religion. The Norwegians had a more complicated mythology than any other Teutonic people: giants, elves, dwarfs, serpents, succeeded by the triumph of **Odin**, his wife **Friga**, and his son **Thor**.

Conversion to Christianity. The first Christians (probably captives) appeared in the 6th century. The first Christian missionary was the Anglo-Saxon, **Willibord** (c. 700), who accomplished but little. A Carolingian mission (c. 820) was welcomed by King Bjorn of Sweden. A few years later (c. 831) the Archbishopric of Hamburg was established and became at once the center for missionary work in the north.

(*Cont. p. 203.*)

2. EASTERN EUROPE

a. THE EASTERN EMPIRE TO 1025

527-565. JUSTINIAN. A Macedonian by birth and the chief adviser of his uncle, Justin, since 518. Justinian was a man of serious and even somber tempera-

ment, but of strong, even autocratic character, sober judgment, grandiose conceptions. He was strongly influenced by his wife **Theodora** (d. 548), a woman of humble origin, probably unduly maligned by the historian Procopius. Theodora was cruel, deceitful, and avid of power, but a woman of iron will and unusual political

THE BYZANTINE EMPIRE
UNDER JUSTINIAN

Scale of Miles

Byzantine Empire at
its greatest extent.

judgment. Justinian's whole policy was directed toward the establishment of the absolute power of the emperor and toward the revival of a universal, Christian Roman Empire. The entire reign was filled with wars in the east and in the west, punctuated by constant incursions of the barbarians from the north.

527-532. The first Persian War of Justinian. His commander, **Belisarius,** won a victory at Dara (530), but was then defeated at **Callinicum.** The conflict ended with the **Perpetual Peace of 532,** designed to free the imperial armies for operations in the west.

532. The Nika Insurrection (so-called from the cry of the popular parties, *Nika = Victory*). This was the last great uprising of the circus parties and led to great violence and incendiarism. Much of Constantinople was destroyed by fire. Justinian was deterred from flight only through the arguments of Theodora. Ultimately Belisarius and the forces put down the insurrection with much cruelty (30,000 slain). Therewith the period of popular domination came to an end and the epoch of absolutism began.

533-543. CONQUEST OF NORTH AFRICA. Belisarius, with a relatively small force, transported by sea, defeated the Vandal usurper, Gelimer, and recovered the whole of North Africa for the empire.

535-554. THE RECONQUEST OF ITALY. Belisarius landed in Sicily, overran the island, conquered southern Italy from the Ostrogoths and took Rome (Dec. 9, 536). The Ostrogoth king, **Witiges,** besieged the city for a whole year (537-538), but failed to take it. In the following year Belisarius advanced to the north, took Ravenna and captured Witiges, but, after the recall of Belisarius, the new Ostrogoth leader, **Totila,** reconquered Italy as far as Naples (541-543). He took Rome (546) and sacked it. Belisarius returned, captured the city, but then abandoned it to the Goths (549). He was later replaced by **Narses,** who invaded Italy by land from the north with a large army composed chiefly of barbarian mercenaries. He defeated the Ostrogoths decisively in the **battle of Tagina** (552) and brought all of Italy under imperial rule.

540. The Huns, Bulgars, and other barbarian tribes crossed the Danube and raided the Balkan area as far south as the Isthmus of Corinth.

540-562. The great Persian War against Khusru I (*Chosroes*). The Persians invaded Syria and took Antioch, after which they attacked Lazistan and Armenia

and raided Mesopotamia. In 544 they besieged Edessa, but in vain. A truce was concluded in 545, but hostilities were soon resumed in the Transcaucasus region. The Persians took Petra (549), but lost it again (551). By the fifty-year **Peace of 562,** Justinian agreed to pay tribute, but Lazistan was retained for the empire.

542-546. Constantinople and the empire were visited by a very severe and disastrous epidemic of the bubonic plague.

554. The **conquest of southeastern Spain** by the imperial armies. Cordova became the capital of the province.

559. The **Huns and Slavs,** having advanced to the very gates of Constantinople, were driven off by Belisarius.

JUSTINIAN AND THE CHURCH. Peace had been made with Rome in 519 and Pope John I had visited Constantinople in 525. Justinian made a great effort to maintain the unity of the western and eastern churches, but this led him into trouble with the **Monophysites** of Syria and Egypt. He attempted to reconcile them also, but with indifferent success. The cleavage between Latin and Greek Christianity became ever more marked. Justinian suppressed all heresies and paganism (closing of the Neo-Platonic Academy at Athens, 529). Extensive missionary work was carried on among the barbarians and in Africa. For the rest the emperor, with a great taste for dogma, set himself up as the master of the Church and arrogated to himself the right to make binding pronouncements in even purely theological matters.

ADMINISTRATION. The emperor insisted on honesty and efficiency. He abolished sale of offices, improved salaries, united the civil and military powers of provincial authorities, etc. In order to hold back the barbarians, he built hundreds of forts along the frontiers and established a regular system of frontier forces (*limitanei*). Financially the empire suffered greatly from the extensive military operations and from the great building activities of the court.

LAW REFORM. In order to clarify the law, Justinian appointed a commission headed by the jurist, **Tribonian.** This commission collected and ordered all the constitutions promulgated since the time of Hadrian and published them as the *Codex Justinianus* (529). There followed the collection of opinions of the jurists, the *Digest* or *Pandects* (533), and a general textbook of the law, the *Institutes*. Justinian's own legislation was collected in the *Novellae* (565). By this great work of codification Justinian assured for the Roman Law an immense prestige and far-reaching influence, but at the same time diminished its chances of further development.

BUILDING ACTIVITY. The period was one of unexampled construction, ranging from whole towns to public baths, palaces, bridges, roads and forts, as well as countless churches and cloisters. It was a period of much free experimentation and originality, resulting in unusual variety of types, all of them, however, marked by grandeur and splendor. The **Church of St.** Sophia (constructed between 532–537 by Anthemios of Tralles and Isidoros of Miletus) is the greatest of the many monuments of Justinian's reign.

LITERATURE. An age of revival. The *Secret History* of **Procopius**; the historians **Agathias** and **John** of Ephesus. Renascence of Greek classical poetry; creation of religious poetry by **Romanos**.

565-578. **JUSTIN II**, nephew of Justinian, who seized the throne with the aid of Tiberius, commander of the guard. Justin was a careful, economical ruler, who continued the policies of his predecessor, but attempted to concentrate attention upon the economic plight of the empire and the growing danger from the barbarians. In 574 he became insane, after which the empire was ruled by Tiberius, in conjunction with the Empress Sophia.

568-571. The **Lombard invasion of Italy** led to the loss of most of the imperial possessions in the north and center, though Ravenna, Rome, and Naples were retained.

572-591. **War with Persia**, growing out of an insurrection in Armenia, which was supported by the emperor. The Persians took Dara (573) and devastated Syria. In 575, Khusru ravaged the country as far as Cappadocia, but was finally driven back by the imperial commander, Maurikios.

578-582. **TIBERIUS**, emperor. His reign was marked by a great inundation of the Slavs, who advanced into Thrace and Greece and settled in large numbers, thus changing profoundly the ethnographic composition of the Balkan populations.

582-602. **MAURICE** (*Maurikios*), emperor. Like his forerunner, Justin, he pursued a policy of retrenchment, which only made him unpopular in the capital. The reign was marked by constant disturbances and by widespread dissatisfaction.

583. The **Avars**, grown to be a formidable power, took the forts along the Danube.

589-591. **Last phase of the Persian War.** Khusru I had died in 579. In 589 a military revolt led to the deposition of

Khusru II, who fled to Constantinople. The emperor, espousing his cause, led a great army to the east (591) and restored him to the throne. In return the emperor received Dara and the larger part of Armenia.

591. The Avars raided to the very gates of Constantinople.

593. The imperial armies, under **Priscus**, proceeded against the Avars. The latter were defeated at **Viminacium** (601) after which Priscus pushed on to the Theiss.

602. **A mutiny of the troops on the Danube,** led by Phocas, resulted in a march to the capital, the outbreak of popular insurrection in the city, and the flight of the emperor.

602-610. **PHOCAS**, emperor. He was an untutored soldier, cruel and utterly incompetent. Maurice was captured and executed with his sons. All his supporters met with a like fate.

606-608. **Resumption of the Persian War.** The Persians again captured Dara and overran Syria and Mesopotamia (608) advancing through Anatolia as far as Chalcedon.

610. **Conspiracy against Phocas,** led by Priscus and supported by the Exarch of Africa. The latter sent an army by land which conquered Egypt, while a fleet from Carthage arrived at Constantinople. The mob thereupon rose, slew Phocas and proclaimed Heraclius, the son of the exarch, as emperor.

610-641. **HERACLIUS I,** founder of a new dynasty, in whose reign the empire became definitely a Greek (*Byzantine*) monarchy. Heraclius found the empire in a parlous state, threatened from the north by the Avars and from the east by the Persians. But he showed himself an able organizer, general and statesman, and found in the Patriarch Sergius a courageous supporter.

611-622. **The Persian advance.** They took Antioch, Apameia, Emesa, and Kaisareia; Damascus (613); Jerusalem (614), which was sacked, the inhabitants and the Holy Cross being transferred to Ctesiphon. In 615 the Persians were at Chalcedon. In 619 they conquered Egypt.

616. The imperial possessions in Spain were lost to the Visigoths.

619. The **Avars appeared at Constantinople,** which was threatened on the Asiatic side by the Persians. Heraclius was deterred from flight to Africa only by the influence of the patriarch.

622-630. DEFEAT OF THE PERSIANS.
Heraclius, with a newly organized army and supported by a tremendous outburst of religious enthusiasm (the *Byzantine Crusade*), took the offensive against the Persians and carried on three brilliant campaigns in the Transcaucasian region, refusing to allow himself to be distracted by the constant attacks of the Avars in the Balkans. In the battle of Nineveh (Dec. 12, 627) he won a decisive victory, which enabled him to advance to Ctesiphon (628). The death of Khusrau (628) and dynastic disorders in Persia made possible the conclusion of a victorious peace. All the Persian conquests were returned and the Holy Cross restored to Jerusalem.

626. The Avars and Slavs attacked Constantinople by land and sea, but were unable to storm the walls. This marked the height of the Avar power.

634-641. The Arab conquests (p. 184).
They took Bostra (634); Damascus (635); by the battle of Yarmuk (636) gained all Syria; forced the surrender of Jerusalem (637); overran Mesopotamia (639) and conquered Egypt (640–642).

635. Alliance between the emperor and Kuvrat, King of the Bulgars, intended to break the power of the Avars.

638. The *Ecthesis*, a formula elaborated by the Patriarch Sergius and other churchmen in the hope of reconciling the Monophysites, who were welcoming rather than opposing the Islamic advance. The formula recognized one will in the two natures of Christ (*monotheletism*), but failed to win acceptance in Syria and Egypt. On the contrary, it called forth much opposition in the strictly orthodox Italian and African possessions.

641. HERACLIUS CONSTANTINUS, son of Heraclius, became emperor, but died in a few months under suspicious circumstances.

641. HERACLEONAS, younger son of Heraclius, emperor, under his mother's tutelage. He was almost at once overthrown by the army.

641-668. CONSTANS II (*Constantinus*), grandson of Heraclius, emperor. He was an energetic and able ruler, who did his utmost to check the Arab advance. With this object in view he reorganized the provincial administration by establishing themes (*themata*) under military governors with wide powers (*strategoi*) and authority over the civil officials. This system greatly strengthened administrative control and was the basis of the imperial organization for centuries.

643. The Arabs took Alexandria, last outpost of the Greeks in Egypt.

647-648. Arab invasion of North Africa.

648. The Arabs, having assembled a fleet, took Cyprus.

649. Pope Martin condemned the teaching of the *Ecthesis*, but was soon arrested by the Exarch of Ravenna (653) and sent to Constantinople.

653. The Arab advance continued. Armenia was conquered (653) and Rhodes plundered (654). In 655 the Arab fleet defeated an imperial armada under the emperor's own command off the Lycian coast. But in 659 a truce was concluded with the Arab commander in Syria.

663-668. Transfer of the court to Italy.
Constans was intent on blocking the Arab conquest of Sicily and Italy and had dreams of restoring Rome as the basis of the imperial power. But he failed to make any conquests in Italy at the expense of the Lombards and in his absence the Arabs annually invaded and devastated Anatolia.

668. Constans was murdered in the course of a mutiny at Syracuse.

668-685. CONSTANTINE IV (*Pogonatus*), the son of Constans, a harsh character, but an able soldier. He had been in charge of affairs and had come to Sicily to put down the revolt that had resulted in his father's death. On his return to Constantinople, the troops obliged him to accept his brothers Heraclius and Tiberius as co-rulers, but after 680 Constantine was sole emperor. His reign witnessed the high point of the Arab attack, accompanied, as usual, by repeated incursions of the Slavs in the Balkans.

673-678. The Arab attacks on Constantinople. After a siege by land and sea (Apr.–Sept. 673), the assailants blockaded the city and attacked it every year for five years. The city was saved by the strength of its walls and by the newly invented Greek fire, which raised havoc with the Arab fleet. In 677 the Greeks destroyed the Arab fleet at Syllaeum and secured a favorable thirty-year peace (678). Never again did the Arab menace become so pressing. The empire had proved itself a formidable bulwark of Europe.

675-681. Repeated assaults of the Slavs on Thessalonica. The city held out, but the settlement of Thrace and Macedonia and northern Greece by Slavic tribes continued uninterruptedly.

679. Appearance of the Bulgar menace. The Bulgars, a people of Turkish race, had pressed westward through southern Russia and settled in Bessarabia. The emperor failed in his efforts to defeat them there. They crossed the Danube, settled in the region between the river and the Balkan Mountains, gradually fused with the Slavs and became largely Slavicized, and founded the first coherent Slavic power in the Balkans.

680-681. The sixth oecumenical council at Constantinople condemned the monothelite heresy and returned to pure orthodoxy. Since the loss of Syria and Egypt, there was no longer any need for favoring the monophysite view. The return to orthodoxy was a victory for the papal stand and was probably intended to strengthen the Byzantine hold on Italy. In actual fact the Patriarchs of Constantinople (now that the Patriarchs of Antioch, Jerusalem, and Alexandria were under Moslem power) became more and more influential in the east and the primacy of the Roman pope was hardly more than nominal.

685-695. JUSTINIAN II, the son of Constantine and the last of the Heraclian dynasty. He ascended the throne when only sixteen and soon showed himself to be harsh and cruel, though energetic and ambitious like most members of his family.

689. The emperor defeated the Slavs in Thrace and transferred a considerable number of them to Anatolia.

692. The Byzantine forces were severely defeated by the Arabs in the battle of Sebastopolis.

695. A revolt against the emperor, led by Leontius and supported by the clergy and people, initiated a period of twenty years of anarchy. Justinian was deposed and exiled to the Crimea (Cherson).

695-698. LEONTIUS, emperor. His reign was marked by the domination of the army.

697-698. The Arabs finally took **Carthage** and brought to an end the Byzantine rule in North Africa.

698-705. TIBERIUS III, made emperor by another revolt in the army. The reign was distinguished by an insurrection against Byzantine rule in Armenia and by constant Arab raids in eastern Anatolia.

705-711. JUSTINIAN II, who returned to the throne with the aid of the Bulgar king. He took an insane revenge on all his enemies and instituted a veritable reign of terror.

711. The emperor failed to suppress a serious **revolt in the Crimea,** supported by the Khazars. The insurgent

troops, under Philippicus, marched on Constantinople and finally defeated and killed Justinian in an engagement in northern Anatolia.

711-713. PHILIPPICUS, emperor. He proved himself quite incompetent and was unable to check the raids of the Bulgars (reached Constantinople in 712) or the ravages of the Arabs in Cilicia (they took Amasia, 712).

713-715. ANASTASIUS II, emperor, the creature of the mutinous Thracian army corps. He attempted to reorganize the army, but this led to new outbreaks.

715-717. THEODOSIUS III, an obscure official put on the throne by the army. He was helpless in the face of the Arabs, who in 716 advanced as far as Pergamon. The invaders were finally repulsed by the *strategos* of the Anatolian *theme*, Leo, who forced the abdication of the emperor and was enthusiastically proclaimed by the clergy and populace of the capital.

717-741. LEO III (*the Isaurian*), founder of the Isaurian dynasty, an eminent general and a great organizer. Leo used drastic measures to suppress revolts in the army and re-established discipline by issuing new regulations. The finances were restored by heavy, systematic taxation, but steps were taken, by an **agrarian code,** to protect freemen and small holders. By the *Ecloga* (739) the empire was given a simplified law code, distinguished by the Christian charity of its provisions. In the administrative sphere Leo completed the **theme organization,** dividing the original units and making seven *themes* in Asia and four in Europe.

717-718. Second great siege of Constantinople by the Arabs. The siege, conducted by land and sea, lasted just a year and ended in failure, due to the energetic conduct of the defense.

726. Beginning of the great iconoclastic controversy. Leo found the empire generally demoralized and a prey to superstition and miracle-mongering. Like many devout persons (especially in the Anatolian regions), he disapproved of the widespread image-worship, which he proceeded to forbid. Behind these measures there undoubtedly lay the desire to check the alarming **spread of monasticism,** which withdrew thousands of men from active economic life and concentrated great wealth in the cloisters, which were free from taxation. The first measures led at once to a revolt in Greece (727), whence a fleet set out for Constantinople with an anti-emperor. This was destroyed by the Greek fire of the imperial fleet. The pope at Rome (Gregory II) likewise declared against the emperor's iconoclasm and the population of the Exarchate of Ravenna rose in revolt and made an alliance with the Lombards. Only with the aid of Venice were a few crucial stations held by the imperial forces. A fleet from the east failed to restore Byzantine authority (731). In revenge the emperor in 733 withdrew Calabria, Sicily, and Illyria from the jurisdiction of the pope and placed them under the Constantinople patriarch.

739. The Byzantine forces won an important victory over the Arab invaders of Anatolia in the **battle of Akroinon.**

741-775. Constantine V (*Kopronymos*), the son of Leo and for years associated with him in the government. Constantine was autocratic, uncompromising, and violent, but withal able and energetic as well as sincere. A revolt of his brother-in-law, Artavasdos, was supported by the idolaters and by part of the army. It took fully two years to suppress it.

745. The emperor, taking the offensive against the Arabs, carried the war into Syria.

746. The Greeks destroyed a great Arab armada and reconquered Cyprus.

746. The empire suffered from the greatest **plague epidemic** since the time of Justinian.

751-752. The emperor led a successful campaign against the Arabs in Armenia. The Arabs were weakened by the fall of the Omayyad Caliphate and the removal of the capital from Damascus to Baghdad (p. 189).

751. The Lombards conquered the Exarchate of Ravenna. The pope thereupon called in the Franks and was given the former Byzantine territory by Pepin (*Donation of Pepin*) (p. 153).

753. The Church Council of Hieria approved of the emperor's iconoclastic policy. Therewith began the violent phase of the controversy. The monks offered vigorous resistance, but the emperor was unbending. The monks were imprisoned, exiled, and some even executed; monasteries were closed and their properties confiscated; images were destroyed or whitewashed.

755-764. Nine successive **campaigns against the Bulgars.** The emperor won important victories at Marcellae (759) and Anchialus (763), and, despite some re-

verses, forced the Bulgars to conclude peace (764).

758. The Slavs were defeated in Thrace and a large number of them settled in Asia.

772. Renewal of the **war with the Bulgars,** marked by further victories of the emperor.

775-780. LEO IV, the son of Constantine. In religious matters he simply continued his predecessor's policy.

778-779. Victory over the Arabs at **Germanikeia** (778) and their expulsion from Anatolia.

780-797. CONSTANTINE VI ascended the throne as a child, wholly under the influence of his ambitious, unscrupulous, and scheming mother, **Irene,** and her favorites. Irene, anxious to secure support for her personal power, devoted herself almost exclusively to the religious question. The Arabs, who again advanced to the Bosporus (782), were bought off with heavy tribute (783). On the other hand, the general, Staurakios, carried on a successful campaign against the Slavs in Macedonia and Greece (783).

787. The Council of Nicaea abandoned iconoclasm and ordered the worship of images. Tremendous victory for the monkish party, which soon advanced far-reaching claims to complete freedom for the Church in religious matters.

790. The army, opposed to the monks, mutinied and put Constantine in power. Irene was forced into retirement. The emperor set out on campaigns against the Arabs and Bulgars, but met with indifferent success.

792. Constantine recalled his mother and made her co-ruler. She took a vile advantage of him and, after his divorce and a remarriage arranged by her (795), put herself at the head of a party of the monks in opposing the step. A rising of the army put her in control and she had her son taken and blinded (797).

797-802. IRENE, the first empress. Though supported by able generals (Staurakios and Aëtios), she preferred to buy peace with the Arabs (798) and devote herself to domestic intrigue.

800. Resurrection of the empire in the west, through the coronation of Charlemagne. The Eastern Empire refused all recognition of the claim.

802-811. NICEPHORUS, who was put on the throne by a group of conspiring officials of the government. Irene, deposed, died in 803. Nicephorus was a firm ruler, who carried through a number of much-needed financial reforms.

803. The emperor made **peace with Charlemagne**, the Eastern Empire retaining southern Italy, Venice, and Dalmatia.

804-806. The Arabs resumed their raids in Anatolia and ravaged Cyprus and Rhodes, ultimately forcing the conclusion of a humiliating peace.

809. Banishment of the monks of Studion, who, under Theodoros of Studion, took the lead in advancing claims of church freedom. They went so far as to appeal to the Roman pope and offer to recognize his primacy.

809-813. War with **Krum**, the powerful king of the Bulgars. The emperor was defeated and killed in a great battle (811).

811. STAURAKIOS, son of Nicephorus, was emperor for a few months.

811-813. MICHAEL I (*Rhangabé*), brother-in-law of Staurakios, emperor. He proved himself quite incompetent, being unable to check the advance of Krum to Constantinople, or the success of the party of monks in domestic affairs.

813-820. LEO V (*the Armenian*), called to the throne by the army. Though personally not much moved by the religious controversy, he could not avoid taking up the challenge of the monks.

815. THE COUNCIL OF ST. SOPHIA marked the return to iconoclasm and the beginning of the second period of active and violent persecution of the monks.

817. The emperor won a great victory over the Bulgars at **Mesembria,** Krum having died (814). The Bulgars were obliged to accept a thirty-year peace.

820-829. MICHAEL II (*Phrygian dynasty*), succeeded to the throne after the murder of Leo by conspirators.

822-824. Insurrection of the general, **Thomas,** in Anatolia. This was supported by the lower classes and encouraged by the Arabs. Thomas attempted twice to take Constantinople, but was ultimately defeated and executed in Thrace.

826. Crete was seized by Moslem freebooters from Spain and until 961 remained the headquarters of pirates who ravaged the eastern Mediterranean.

827-878. Conquest of Sicily by Moslems from North Africa.

829-842. THEOPHILUS, emperor. He was an arrogant, theologizing fanatic who promulgated a new edict against idolaters (832) and pushed the persecution to the limit.

837-838. War against the Arabs. The Byzantine armies, after invading the caliphate, were repulsed. After a long siege, Amorion, one of the key positions on the frontier, was taken by the Moslems (838).

842-867. MICHAEL III, for whom his mother Theodora was regent. Advised by her brother, **Bardas,** she decided to end the religious controversy.

843. Image-worship was restored. This was a great victory for the opposition party, but only in the matter of doctrine. Politically the power of the emperor over the Church remained unimpaired, if not strengthened.

849. Reduction of the Slavic populations of the Peloponnesus, followed by their conversion.

856. Theodora was obliged to retire, but her brother Bardas, an able but unprincipled politician, remained the real ruler of the empire by exploiting to the full the weaknesses of the emperor.

860. First appearance of the Russians (*Varangians*) at Constantinople.

863-885. Missionary activity of **Cyril and Methodius** of Thessalonica among the Slavs of Moravia and Bohemia. They invented the **Glagolitic** (i.e. Slavic) **alphabet** and by the use of Slavic in the church service paved the way for the connection of Slavic Christianity with Constantinople.

865. Tsar Boris of Bulgaria (852–889) allowed himself to be baptized. Although Michael III acted as godfather, the Bulgarian ruler was for a time undecided between the claims of Rome and Constantinople to religious jurisdiction in Bulgaria.

866. Bardas was murdered by Michael's favorite, Basil.

867. Michael himself was deposed and done away with at Basil's order.

867. Schism with Rome. The great patriarch, **Photius,** had replaced Ignatius in 858, whereupon the latter had appealed to the pope for an inquiry. Photius came to represent the Greek national feeling in opposition to Rome. He took a strong stand towards the papal claims and the **Council of Constantinople** (867) anathematized the pope, accused the papacy of doctrinal aberrations, rejected the idea of Rome's primacy, etc.

867-886. BASIL I, founder of the *Macedonian dynasty* (he was really of Armenian extraction, though born in Macedonia). His reign initiated what was probably the most glorious period of Byzantine history. The empire had by this time become a purely Greek monarchy, under an absolute ruler. Settlement of the iconoclastic controversy released the national energies and there followed a period of brilliant military success, material prosperity, and cultural development. An important departure was the recognition of the idea of legitimacy and of an imperial family. This was paralleled by the gradual emergence of a feudal system.

Basil I was himself an intelligent, firm, and orderly ruler, a good administrator and general, whose ambition was to restore the empire both internally and externally. He rebuilt the army and especially the navy, and did much to revise the legal system: the *Procheiros Nomos* (879), a compilation of the most important parts of the Justinian code; the *Epanagoge* (886), a manual of customary law.

869. The eighth oecumenical synod. Photius had been banished (867) and Ignatius recalled. The latter made peace with Rome on papal terms, but conflict and friction continued.

871-879. Campaigns in the east. Border warfare with the Arabs was chronic, but the campaign against the Paulicians (Christian purists hostile to the empire) was a new departure. The imperial armies advanced to the upper Euphrates and took Samosata (873). In 878-879 victorious campaigns were carried through in Cappadocia and Cilicia. By land the

The Macedonian Emperors

Basil I
867–886

Romanus I══Zoë══Leo VI
Lecapenus   886–912
919–944

Alexander
912–913

Constantine VII
Porphyrogenitus
912–959

Romanus II═══════Theophano═══════Nicephorus Phocas
959–963   963–969

Theophano,   Basil II   Constantine VIII
m. Emperor   963–1025   963–1028
Otto II

Zoë   Theodora
m. (1) Romanus III   1054–1056
       1028–1034
    (2) Michael IV
       1034–1041
    (3) Constantine IX
       1042–1054

Byzantine forces were gradually taking the offensive against the Moslems, wracked by internal dissensions.

875. The Byzantine forces seized **Bari** in southern Italy. Some years later (880) they took Tarentum and then (885) Calabria, establishing two new themes in southern Italy, which became a refuge for Greeks driven from Sicily by the completion of the Saracen conquest (Syracuse taken, 878; Taormina taken, 902).

877. Photius was restored as patriarch and the break with Rome was renewed.

880-881. A number of naval **victories over the Moslem pirates** of the eastern Mediterranean marked the beginning of a long campaign against this scourge.

886-912. LEO VI (*the Wise*), a somewhat pedantic philosopher, but nevertheless a determined ruler with a high sense of his office and obligations. He deposed Photius at once and put the Ignatians back in power. The result was a renewal of the union with Rome (900), which, however, could hardly be more than external. The reign of Leo was marked also by further legislative work. The *Basilika* (887–893) provided a series of 60 new law books, consisting largely of a compilation of decrees since the time of Justinian.

889- **War with the Bulgarians,** who now entered the period of greatness under Tsar Symeon (893–927). The emperor encouraged the Hungarians to attack by way of diversion and most of Symeon's reign was taken up with continued campaigns against this enemy. Symeon was educated at Constantinople and was deeply impressed with Greek culture, which he introduced in Bulgaria.

904. The Saracen corsair, **Leo of Tripoli,** stormed Thessalonica, plundered it and carried off some 20,000 of the inhabitants.

907. **The Russians,** under their prince, Oleg, appeared again at Constantinople and secured rights of trade.

912-913. ALEXANDER, the brother of Leo, emperor for less than a year.

913-959. CONSTANTINE VII (*Porphyrogenitus*) ascended the throne as a child, with a regency composed of his mother Zoë, the Patriarch Nikolas, and John Eladas. Constantine was a learned man of artistic tastes. He never really governed, leaving the actual conduct of affairs to strong men who were associated with him.

913-917. **The Bulgarian threat.** Tsar Symeon, who had established a brilliant capital at Preslav (seat also of the Bulgarian patriarchate), styled himself Emperor of the Romans, and undoubtedly hoped to possess himself of the imperial crown. In 913 he appeared at Constantinople; in 914 he took Adrianople, only to lose it again. But in 917 he defeated a Byzantine army at Anchialus. The war continued, indecisively, for years. In 924 Symeon again appeared at Constantinople.

915. A Byzantine victory over the Arabs at Garigliano assured the empire of its possessions in South Italy.

919-944. ROMANUS LECAPENUS, co-emperor with Constantine. He was the emperor's stepfather, an able but ruthless Armenian, whose whole policy was designed to strengthen his own control and establish that of his family.

920-942. Brilliant campaigns of the Byzantine general, **John Kurkuas,** in the east. He took the modern Erzerum (928) and Melitene (934), and extended the imperial power to the Euphrates and Tigris.

920. Official reunion with Rome.

924. The piratical fleets of **Leo of Tripoli** were completely defeated off **Lemnos.** Nevertheless, the Moslem pirates continued to be the scourge of the Mediterranean.

927. The empire suffered from a **great famine,** which probably explains the stringent legislation of the government to prevent the purchase of small holdings by the great landed magnates.

941. A great armada of Russians, under **Prince Igor,** was signally defeated by the Greeks.

944. **The Emperor Romanus** was seized and imprisoned (d. 948) by the very sons whose interests he had attempted to serve. The Emperor Constantine became officially the sole ruler, but governed with the aid of the great general, **Bardas Phocas,** and under the influence of the Empress Helena and her favorite, Basil.

955. Visit to Constantinople and baptism of **Princess Olga** of Russia.

959-963. ROMANUS II, the young and dissipated son of Constantine.

961. Reconquest of Crete from the Saracen pirates. A great armada was sent out under Nicephorus Phocas. Candia was stormed, the Moslems expelled from the island or converted to Christianity.

962. Otto I, Roman emperor in the west, claimed suzerainty over the Lombards in southern Italy, initiating a period of friction with Constantinople, which was only temporarily broken by the marriage of Otto II and the Byzantine princess, Theophano (972).

963-1025. BASIL II, an infant at the death of his father. The principle of legitimacy was carefully respected, but before Basil II really assumed power, the empire was governed by two great generals associated with him.

963-969. NICEPHORUS PHOCAS, who had carried on a successful campaign in the east. He seized control and married the widowed Empress Theophano. Never popular, especially with the clergy, Nicephorus, by his victories in the field, helped to raise the empire to its greatest glory.

964-968. Victorious campaign in the east. Adana was taken (964) and then Tarsus (965). Cyprus was reconquered and in 968 northern Syria was invaded. **Aleppo** and even **Antioch** fell into the hands of the Greeks.

966-969. The Bulgarian campaign, carried through with the aid of Sviatoslav and the Russians. The latter, with their fleets, were so successful on the Danube that the Greeks made peace with the Bulgars.

969. Nicephorus Phocas was overthrown by a conspiracy of officers led by his own nephew

969-976. JOHN ZIMISCES, an Armenian by birth and one of the greatest of Byzantine generals.

969. Sviatoslav, the Russian, crossed the Balkan Mountains and took Philippopolis. John Zimisces marched against him, defeated him near Adrianople, and, with the aid of the Byzantine fleet on the Danube, forced him to evacuate Bulgaria (972). John thereupon annexed eastern Bulgaria as far as the Danube to the empire. The Patriarchate of Preslav was abolished.

971. A great feudal insurrection, led by Bardas Phocas, was put down only with difficulty.

972-976. Continuation of the campaigns in the east. John took Edessa and Nezib (974), Damascus and Beyrut (976), and advanced to the very gates of Jerusalem, where he was halted by the Moslem forces from Egypt.

976. Sudden death of John Zimisces, at the early age of 51.

976-1025. BASIL II (*Bulgaroktonos* = *Slayer of the Bulgarians*) now became sole emperor. He was only 20 years old, but serious and energetic, cynical and cruel. Until 989 he was much influenced by Basil the Eunuch, the illegitimate son of Romanus Lecapenus. The reign of Basil

began with another great feudal upheaval, led by Bardas Skleros, who marched his armies from the east through Anatolia and to Constantinople. Basil appealed to Bardas Phocas, defeated leader of the earlier rising, to save the situation, which he did by defeating Skleros at Pankalia (979).

976-1014. Tsar Samuel of Bulgaria. He built up another great Bulgarian empire, with its capital at Ochrid and extending from the Adriatic to the Black Sea and from the Danube to the Peloponnesus. In 981 he defeated Basil near Sofia.

987. Rising of Bardas Phocas and Bardas Skleros against Basil and the imperial authority. The great feudal barons overran Anatolia. In 988 they threatened Constantinople, but the movement collapsed with the defeat of Phocas at Abydos (989) and his subsequent death. Skleros then submitted.

989. Conversion of Prince Vladimir of Russia, at Cherson. This initiated the general conversion of the Russians to eastern Christianity and the close connection between Kiev and Constantinople.

992. Extensive trade privileges in the empire were granted to **Venice,** by this time quite independent of imperial control, but in close coöperation with Constantinople in the Adriatic.

995. Victorious campaigns of the emperor in the east. Aleppo and Homs were taken and Syria incorporated with the empire.

996. Land legislation of Basil II. Many of the great estates were confiscated and divided among the peasants and provision made to prevent the further development of feudalism.

996-1014. THE GREAT BULGARIAN CAMPAIGNS. In 996 Basil defeated Samuel on the Spercheios River and reconquered Greece. In 1002 he overran Macedonia. Samuel recovered, however, reconquered Macedonia and sacked Adrianople (1003). In 1007 Basil subdued Macedonia again and after years of indecisive conflict annihilated the Bulgarian army at **Balathista** (1014). He sent several thousand blinded soldiers back to Samuel, who died of the shock. The Bulgarians finally submitted (1018), but were left their autonomy and an autocephalous church at Ochrid. Many of the Bulgarian noble families settled in Constantinople and merged with the Greek and Armenian aristocracy.

1018. The Byzantine forces won a great victory over the combined Lombards and Normans at **Cannae,** thus assuring continuance of the Greek domination in southern Italy.

1020. **The King of Armenia,** long in alliance with the Greeks against the Arabs, turned over his kingdom to Basil to escape the new threat from the Seljuk Turks. Thereby the empire became firmly established in Transcaucasia and along the Euphrates.

BYZANTINE CULTURE reached its apogee in the late 10th and early 11th centuries. The empire extended from Italy to Mesopotamia and its influence radiated much farther. Constantinople, indeed, was the economic and artistic center of the Mediterranean world.

Government: The emperor was an absolute ruler, regarded almost as sacred. Under the Macedonian emperors the idea of legitimacy became firmly established. The imperial court reflected the emperor's power and splendor. There was an extensive and elaborate ceremonial (cf. the *Book of Ceremonies* of Constantine Porphyrogenitus); the administration was highly centralized in Constantinople and was unique for its efficiency; the treasury was full and continued to draw a large income from taxes, customs, and monopolies; the army and navy were both at the peak of their development, with excellent organization and leadership; the provinces were governed by the *strategoi*; there were by this time 30 *themes* (18 in Asia and 12 in Europe), but throughout this period there was a steady growth in the number and power of the provincial magnates (*dunatoi*), feudal barons who acquired more and more of the small holdings and exercised an ever greater influence, even challenging the emperor himself. All the legislation of the Macedonian emperors failed to check this development.

The Church was closely connected with the throne, but during this period it too became more and more wealthy and gradually produced a clerical aristocracy. The union with Rome, when it existed, was a purely formal thing. The Greek patriarchate in practice resented the Roman claim to primacy and the popular dislike of the Latins made any real co-operation impossible.

Economic life. This was closely controlled by the state, which derived much of its income from the customs and monopolies. Yet it was a period of great commercial development, Constantinople serving as the *entrepôt* between east and west.

It was also a great center of the industry in luxuries (organization of trades in rigid guilds, etc.).

Learning. The University of Constantinople (opened c. 850) had quickly become a center of philosophical and humanistic study, in which the emperors took a direct interest. In the 11th century there appeared the greatest of the Byzantine scholars, **Psellus,** reviver of the Platonic philosophy and universal genius. In the field of literature there was a conscious return to the great Greek models of the early Byzantine period; historians, **Constantine Porphyrogenitus, Leo the Deacon,** etc. The great popular epic, *Digenis Akritas,* describing the heroic life of the frontier soldiers (*Akritai*), dates from the 10th century.

Art. The period was one of extensive construction, especially in Constantinople; full exploitation of the St. Sophia type in church architecture; mosaics; ikons; gold and silver work. Byzantine influence in this period permeated the entire Mediterranean world, Moslem as well as Christian.
(*Cont. p.* 248.)

b. THE FIRST BULGARIAN EMPIRE TO 1018

The Bulgarians, first mentioned by name in 482 as a people living to the northeast of the Danube, were members of the Finno-Tatar race, probably related to the Huns and at first ruled by princes of Attila's family. They were organized on the clan system, worshiped the sun and moon, practiced human sacrifice, etc.

584-642. KURT, or **KUBRAT,** of the Dulo family, the first authenticated ruler. His dominions lay in the eastern steppes, from the Don to the Caucasus. In 619 he visited Constantinople to secure aid against the Avars, at which time he became converted to Christianity, though this step seems to have had no consequences for his people.

643-701. Isperikh (*Asperuch*), the son or grandson of Kurt. The old Great Bulgaria was disrupted by the attacks of Avars and Khazars, and various tribes of Bulgars moved westward into Pannonia and even into Italy. Those under Isperikh crossed the Danube (650–670) and established a capital at Pliska. In 680 they defeated a Byzantine army and occupied the territory between the Danube and the Balkan Mountains. At the same time they still held Wallachia, Moldavia, and Bessarabia. The amalgamation with the Slavic inhabitants was probably very gradual, the upper, military classes remaining strictly Bulgar for a long time.

701-718. **Tervel,** who established friendly relations with the Emperor Justinian II, who paid a subsidy or tribute to the Bulgars, but only after the imperial forces had been defeated at Anchialus (708) and after Tervel had advanced to the very gates of Constantinople (712).

718-724. Ruler unknown.

724-739. **Sevar,** during whose reign the peace with the empire was maintained. The Dulo dynasty came to an end with Sevar, whose death was followed by an obscure struggle of noble factions.

739-756. **Kormisosh,** of the Ukil family. Until the very end of his reign he maintained peace with the empire, until further domestic disorders gave the signal for Byzantine attacks (755 ff.).

756-761. **Vinekh,** who was killed in the course of an uprising.

761-764. **Telets,** of the Ugain family. He was defeated at Anchialus by the Byzantines (763) and put to death by the Bulgarians.

764. **Sabin,** of the family of Kormisosh. He was deposed and fled to Constantinople.

? 764. **Pagan,** who finally concluded peace with the emperor.

766. **Umor,** who was deposed by

766. **Tokt,** who was captured and killed by the Greeks. This entire period is one of deep obscurity, the years 766–773 being a complete blank.

? 773-777. **Telerig,** whose family is unknown. The Greeks renewed their attacks, which were on the whole successful and resulted in the subjugation of Bulgaria.

777-791. Ruler unknown.

? 791-797. **Kardam,** whose reign marked the turning of the tide. He took advantage of the confusion in the empire to defeat the Greeks at **Marcellae** (792) and to relay the foundations of the state. What happened after his death is unknown.

808-814. **KRUM,** one of the greatest Bulgarian rulers. He appears to have been a Pannonian Bulgar, who rose to power as a result of his victories over the Avars. During his short reign he organized the state and encouraged the Slav elements at the expense of the Bulgar aristocracy. His objective seems to have been the establishment of the absolute power of the khan. For five years (808–813) he carried on war with the Byzantine Empire. The Greeks sacked Pliska (809; 811), but Krum de-

feated and killed the emperor in a battle in the mountains (811). In 812 he took the important fortress of Mesembria and in 813 won another victory at Versinicia. In the same year he appeared at Constantinople. The city was too strong for him, but he retired, devastating Thrace and taking Adrianople.

814-831. **Omortag,** the son of Krum. After a defeat by the Greeks (815), he concluded a thirty-year peace with them (817), returning Mesembria and Adrianople. Construction of the earthwork barrier (the *Great Fence*) on the Thracian frontier. Founding of the new capital, **Great Preslav** (821). During the peace in the east, the Bulgars began systematic raids into Croatia and Pannonia (827–829).

831-852. **Malamir,** the son of Omortag, the period of whose reign is vague, excepting for gradual expansion into upper Macedonia and Serbia (839).

852-889. **BORIS I.** He continued the campaigns in the west, but suffered severe defeats by the Germans (853) and a setback from the Serbs (860). Boris' reign was important chiefly for his

865. **Conversion to Christianity.** The way had undoubtedly been prepared by numerous prisoners of war, but Boris was induced to take the step under pressure from Constantinople, where the government was eager to frustrate a possible German-Roman advance. Boris had all his subjects baptized, which led to a revolt and the execution of a number of noble leaders. For some time Boris was undecided whether to lean toward Rome or toward Constantinople. To counteract the aggressive Greek influence he accepted the primacy of Rome (866), but then turned to Constantinople (870) when the pope refused to appoint an archbishop for Bulgaria. In 885 the Slavonic liturgy was introduced among the Slavs of Bulgaria by the successors of Cyril and Methodius. In 889 Boris voluntarily retired to a monastery.

889-893. **Vladimir,** the son of Boris, who was soon exposed to a violent aristocratic, heathen reaction.

893. Boris re-emerged from retirement, put down the revolt, deposed and blinded his son, completed the organization of the Church and made the Slavonic liturgy general in its application. The capital was definitely moved to Preslav. Boris then returned to his monastery, where he died (907).

893-927. **SYMEON,** another son of Boris, the first Bulgarian ruler to assume the title *Tsar.* Symeon had been educated at Constantinople, as a monk. He was deeply imbued with Greek culture and did much to encourage translations from the Greek. Splendor of Great Preslav and Symeon's court; development of a second cultural center at Ochrid, under St. Clement and St. Nahum.

894-897. Symeon's reign was filled with wars against the Byzantine Empire, which grew originally out of disputes regarding trade rights and ultimately developed into a contest for possession of the imperial throne. The war began in 894, with the defeat of a Greek army. The emperor thereupon induced the Magyars, located on the Pruth River, to attack the Bulgarians in Bessarabia (895). Symeon induced the Greeks by trickery to withdraw and then defeated the Magyars, after which he returned and fell on the Greeks at Bulgarophygon. Peace was made in 897, the emperor paying tribute.

In the meanwhile the **Magyars**, driven westward by the Patzinaks (Pechenegs), advanced into Transylvania and Pannonia, which were lost to the Bulgars.

913. Symeon, taking advantage of the dynastic troubles in the empire, advanced to Constantinople, but withdrew with many presents and the promise that the young emperor, Constantine Porphyrogenitus, should marry one of his daughters. Symeon evidently hoped to attain the crown for himself, but was frustrated by the seizure of power by Zoë. He thereupon made war (914), raiding into Macedonia, Thessaly, and Albania. But the Patzinaks, instigated by the Greeks, invaded and occupied Wallachia (917), while Symeon defeated the Greeks near **Anchialus** (917). In 918 Symeon defeated the Serbs, who had also been aroused by the empress.

919-924. Symeon four times advanced to the Hellespont and Constantinople, but was unable to take the city because of his lack of a fleet. In 924 he had an interview with the Emperor Romanus Lecapenus and finally made peace.

925. Symeon proclaimed himself **Emperor of the Romans and the Bulgars.** The Greek emperor protested, but the pope recognized the title.

926. Symeon set up Leontius of Preslav as a patriarch.

926. Conquest and devastation of Serbia.

927-969. Peter, the son of Symeon, a pious, well-intentioned but weak ruler, who married the granddaughter of Romanus Lecapenus. Peace with Constantinople was maintained, the Greek emperor

recognizing the Bulgar ruler as emperor and acknowledging the Bulgarian patriarchate. Bulgaria was, during this period, occupied by the constant threat from the Magyars (raids, 934, 943, 958, 962) and the Patzinaks (great raid of 944). Internally the period seems to have been one of unrest and religious ferment (founding of monasteries; St. John of Rila; beginning of the **Bogomil heresy**, c. 950, a dualistic creed possibly inspired by the Paulicians settled in the Thracian region by the Byzantine emperors).

967. Invasion of Bulgaria by Sviatoslav and the Russians. Tsar Peter roused the Patzinaks, who attacked Kiev in 968 and forced Sviatoslav to withdraw.

969-972. Boris II. The reign was filled with the second invasion of Sviatoslav, who took Preslav and captured Boris and his family (969). The Greeks, in alarm, sent an army against him and defeated him at **Arcadiopolis** (970). In 972 the Emperor John Zimisces attacked the Russians by land and sea. He took Preslav and destroyed it, besieged Sviatoslav at Dristra on the Danube and finally forced him to evacuate Bulgaria. Boris was obliged to abdicate, the patriarchate was abolished, and Bulgaria came to an end as a separate state.

976-1014. **SAMUEL**, son of a governor of one of the western districts, which had been unaffected by the Russian invasion, set himself up as ruler. He soon expanded his domain to Sofia, and re-established the patriarchate (ultimately fixed at Ochrid, which was the center of the new state).

986-989. **Samuel took Larissa** after several annual raids into Thessaly and c. 989 took also Dyrrhacium on the Adriatic coast. In the east he extended his power to the Black Sea.

996-1014. The campaigns of Basil II (*Bulgaroktonos = Slayer of the Bulgarians*) against Samuel. Basil proceeded to reduce one stronghold after another. Samuel avoided open battle as much as possible, but throughout suffered from defection of his leaders, who were bribed by attractive offers by the emperor. The crowning defeat of the Bulgarians at Balathista (1014) and the sight of his 15,000 blinded warriors brought on Samuel's death.

1014-1016. **Gabriel Radomir** (or *Romanus*), the son of Samuel. He tried to make peace, but was murdered by his cousin

1016-1018. John Vladislav, who continued the war, but was killed in a battle near Dyrrhacium. He left only young sons. The Bulgar leaders thereupon decided to submit. Bulgaria was incorporated into the Byzantine Empire (*themes* of Bulgaria and Paristrium); the patriarchate was abolished, but the Archbishop of Ochrid retained practical autonomy. The Bulgarian aristocracy settled in Constantinople and merged with the leading Greek families.

(*Cont. p.* 247.)

3. THE MOSLEM WORLD

a. MOHAMMED AND ISLAM

Arabia before the time of Mohammed was inhabited by tribes of Semitic race, those in the desert areas (*Bedouins*) of nomadic, pastoral habits, those in the coastal valleys along the Red Sea (Hedjaz, Yemen) much more settled, engaged in agriculture and trade. The towns of Mecca and Medina were centers of considerable commercial and cultural development, in which Greek and Jewish influence was probably quite marked.

570-632. MOHAMMED. He was the posthumous son of Abdullah of the Hashimite sept of Mecca. Having lost his mother when about six, he was brought up by his grandfather, Abdul-Muttalib, and his uncle, Abu Talib. Mohammed became a merchant in the caravan trade, serving Khadija, a widow of means whom he married when he was about 25, thus achieving for himself a modest independence. Given to religious meditation and affected by the Christian and Jewish ideas and practices, he began his prophetic career about 612, preaching the One God, the Last Judgment, Alms, Prayers, and surrender to the will of God (Islam). Gaining a few adherents, but rejected and persecuted by his townsmen, he and his followers fled to Medina, on July 2, 622.

622, July 15. The traditional (though erroneous) date of **Mohammed's flight** (*Hijrah, Hegira*). This date has been adopted as the beginning of the Moslem era.

622-632. In Medina, Mohammed organized the **commonwealth of Islam** by welding together the Meccan fugitives and the Medinan tribes in and around the town (the Aus and the Khazraj), and expelling or devoting the Jewish tribes, into a community based on the will of God as revealed to his prophet, and on the common law of the tribesmen. At the same time he carried on war against the Meccans.

624-630. The Moslems defeated the Meccans at **Badr** (624), but were themselves defeated at Ohod (625). The Meccans thereupon besieged Medina (627) but were repulsed. By the **Treaty of Hudaybiya** (628): Mohammed and his followers were granted permission to make the pilgrimage to Mecca. When the treaty was broken by the allies of the Meccans, the war was resumed and Mohammed took Mecca (630). Many of the Arab tribes were subdued before Mohammed's death (632).

The **six essential articles of the Moslem faith** are: Belief in the One God, **Allah**, in his angels, and in his prophet, **Mohammed**, the last of the prophets; belief in his revealed books, of which the *Koran* is the last and the only one necessary; belief in the Day of Resurrection, and in God's predestination, which determines the fate and the actions of men.

The **six fundamental duties** are: The recitation of the profession of faith; attesting the unity of God and the mission of Mohammed; the five daily prayers; the fast in the month of Ramadhan; the pilgrimage to Mecca; and the Holy War.

632-661. The Orthodox Caliphate, including the first four caliphs.

632-634. Abu Bakr, the first caliph or vicegerent of the Prophet, chosen by acclamation. Defeat of the so-called false prophets, Tulayha and Musaylima; reduction of the rebellious tribes (632).

632-738. EXPANSION BEYOND ARABIA. First incursion into Iraq (Persia) under **Khalid ibn al-Walid** (633). Hira, the ancient Lakhmid capital, and Obolla taken and put to ransom. The main advance, however, was against Syria. Defeat of Theodore, brother of the Emperor Heraclius, at Ajnadayn (*Jannabatayn*) between Gaza and Jerusalem (634). Death of Abu Bakr, who appointed as his successor

634-644. Omar, who first assumed the title of *Amir al-Mu'minin* (*Prince of the Faithful*) and established the primacy of the Arabs over their taxpaying subjects.

Conquest of Syria. Defeat of the Byzantines under Baanes at Marj al-Saffar, near Damascus, by Khalid (635). Damascus and Emessa taken, only to be given up, however, under the pressure of superior forces. Decisive defeat of the Byzantines

The Mohammedan World
about. 732

SCALE OF MILES

100 200 300   600

▨ Territory overrun by Mohammedans

▨ The Byzantine Empire

at **Yarmuk**, south of the Lake of Tiberias (636). Damascus and Emessa retaken. Subjugation of northern Syria, Aleppo and Antioch taken. Capitulation of Jerusalem (638). Caesarea captured (640). The seacoast occupied. Northern boundary of the caliphate the Amanus Mountains. Subjugation of Mesopotamia (639–641). **Conquest of Persia.** After a disastrous defeat at the **Battle of the Bridge**, the Moslems resumed their attack on Persia. Invasion and occupation of Iraq (635–637). Defeat of the Persians under Mihran at Buwayb by Muthanna (635). The Persian chancellor, Rustam, defeated by Sa'd ibn-abi-Waqqās at **Qadisia** (637). Al-Madain (*Ctesiphon*) taken (637). Persians defeated again at Jalula, fifty miles north of Madain (637). Invasion and occupation of central Persia (638–650). Final defeat of the Persians at Nehawand (641). **Conquest of Egypt.** Invasion of Egypt by the Arabs under Amr ibn al-'As (639). Pelusium taken (640). Byzantines defeated at Heliopolis (640). Death of the Emperor Heraclius (641). Capture of Babylon (642). Capitulation of Egypt arranged by Cyrus, Patriarch of Alexandria (642). Terms: security of person and property guaranteed to the inhabitants on payment of a tribute and free exercise of their religion. Omar assassinated (644). His successor was chosen by a body of electors.

644-656. **Othman**, a member of the Omayyad family of Mecca, notorious for his nepotism. The official redaction of the *Koran* made by Zayd ibn Thabit in this reign.

Occupation of Barqa and the Pentapolis (642–643). Revolt of Alexandria, inspired by the appearance of a Byzantine fleet (645). The city retaken by assault (645). Creation of an Arab fleet by Abdullah ibn Sa'd, governor of Egypt. Capture of Cyprus (649) and Aradus (650). Expedition against Constantinople, annihilation of the Byzantine fleet at Dhat al-Sawari on the Lycian coast (655). Disaffection of Arab troops in Iraq and Egypt owing to Othman's nepotism, led to the assassination of Othman in Medina. He was succeeded by

656-661. **Ali**, the prophet's cousin and son-in-law, whose succession was disputed.

First civil war. Revolt of Talha and Zobayr, two old companions of the Prophet, and 'Aisha, the Prophet's favorite wife, in Iraq. They seized Basra, but were defeated by Ali in the **Battle of the Camel**, near that town. **Revolt of Mo'awiya**, Omayyad governor of Syria, who demanded revenge for the

murder of his kinsman, Othman. **Indecisive battle of Siffin** (657). Hostilities suspended by an agreement to arbitrate the dispute. Arbitration of Adhroh (658). Rejection of the decision by Ali, who was deserted and opposed by a party of his followers, the Kharijites, whom he decimated at Nahrawan. Egypt taken for Mo'awiya by its first conqueror, Amr (658). Murder of Ali by a Kharijite.

b. THE OMAYYAD CALIPHATE, 661-750

661-680. Mo'awiya, founder of the Omayyad dynasty.

Hasan, Ali's eldest son, was proclaimed caliph, but abdicated in the face of Mo'awiya's advance on Iraq. Mo'awiya, who had been proclaimed caliph in Jerusalem in 660, moved the seat of government to Damascus. Expedition against Constantinople, Chalcedon taken, Constantinople besieged (669). Ifriqiya (North Africa from the eastern limits of Algeria to the frontiers of Egypt) invaded and the conquest consolidated by the founding of Qairawan by 'Oqba ibn Nafi' (670). In the east under Mo'awiya's brilliant viceregent, Ziyad ibn Abihi, Sind and the lower valley of the Indus were overrun by Mohallib. Eastern Afghanistan invaded. Kabul taken (664). The Oxus was crossed and Bokhara captured (674). Samarcand taken (676). Moslem advance to the Jaxartes.

Blockade of Constantinople by the Moslem fleet (673–678). Failure of the Moslem attack. Peace concluded for thirty years (678). Death of Mo'awiya, who had proclaimed as his successor in 676,

680-682. **Yazid I.**

The second civil war. Husayn, the second son of Ali, was invited by the Kufans in Iraq to assume the caliphate. Advancing from Mecca he was basely deserted by the Kufans, defeated, and slain at the famous **battle of Kerbela** (680), whence the Shi'ite celebration of the martyrdom of Husayn each year in the month of Muharram.

Revolt of Abdullah ibn Zubayr, the candidate for the caliphate supported by the Meccans and Medinans. Defeat of the Medinans on the Harra near the town. Siege of Mecca; the Ka'ba burned. Death of Yazid.

The son and successor of Yazid, **Mo'awiya II**, died some months after his father. **Ibn Zubayr's** caliphate accepted in Arabia, Iraq, Egypt, and by the adherents of the Qais tribe in Syria. The Omayyad party with its adherents of the Kalb tribe chose **Marwan ibn al-Hakam**, a cousin of Mo'-

awiya I. The Qais were defeated with great slaughter at Marj Rahit (684), north of Damascus, which began the disastrous feud between the so-called northern and southern Arabs, which was largely responsible for the fall of the Arab kingdom of the Omayyads.

684-750. THE MARWANIDS.

684-685. Marwan I. Proclaimed caliph in Syria. Egypt was recovered from Ibn Zubayr. Death of Marwan. He was succeeded by his son,

685-705. Abdulmalik, creator of the Arab administration of the empire.

Inroads of the Mardaites of the Amanus, encouraged by the Byzantines, occupied Abdulmalik's first years. His rival, Ibn Zubayr, was occupied by Shi'ite and Kharijite revolts in Kufa and Basra, Arabia and Persia.

The **Shi'ite** sect were supporters of the claims of the "House of the Prophet," the descendants of the Caliph **Ali,** and of the prophet's daughter, Fatima. Later they developed the dogma of the **Imamate,** that the Imam (the leader of the people) was the representative or incarnation of the deity and the only seat of authority both religious and civil.

The **Kharijites** held that any Moslem in good standing could be elected by the community as caliph. They held that *Works* were an essential part of religion and that those who committed mortal sins were unbelievers. Both sects were bitter opponents of both the Omayyad and the Abbasid dynasties.

Mus'ab, Ibn Zubayr's brother and governor in Iraq, was defeated by Abdulmalik on the Tigris (690). Medina was captured by Abdulmalik's general, Hajjaj, later his governor in Iraq (691). Mecca was besieged and captured (692). Ibn Zubayr was killed and Abdulmalik became undisputed master of the empire. The Kharijites (Azraqites) were crushed in Iraq and Persia by Muhallib (693-698). A rebellion in the east under Ibn al-Ash'ath, who was proclaimed caliph, was put down by Hajjaj (699). Kabul retaken.

In Africa Oqba ibn Nafi, now a saint, had raided as far as Tangier, but had met death on his return march (683). Carthage, however, was finally taken (698), and peace concluded with the Berbers, after they had defeated the Arabs under Hassan ibn No'man near Mons Aurasius (703). Thereupon the Berbers became allies of the Arabs. Death of Abdulmalik. He was succeeded by his son,

705-715. Walid I, who built the cathedral mosque at Damascus. Conquest of Transoxania under Qutayba (705-715).

Bokhara taken (709), Samarkand (712), Ferghana (714). It is reported that Qutayba invaded China and reached Kashgar (c. 713). Conquest of Sind and part of the Punjab by Mohammed ibn Qasim (708-715). Invasion of Cilicia (710-711) and of Galatia (714). Preparations for a grand attack on Constantinople by land and sea. Subjugation of the western Berbers and pacification of North Africa by Musa ibn Nusayr (708-711).

711-715. CONQUEST OF SPAIN. Invasion of Spain by a mixed force of Arabs and Berbers under Tariq, a freed slave of Musa (711). The Goths under their king, Roderick, were totally defeated in Wadi Bekka, near Rio Barbate (not at Xeres de la Frontera) (July, 711). Fall of Ecija, Cordova, and the capital, Toledo. Tariq master of half of Spain. The advance of Musa himself (712). Capture of Medina Sidonia, Carmona, Seville (712), Merida (713), and Saragossa. Resistance to Arab arms continued only in the mountains of Asturias. Death of Walid. He was succeeded by his brother,

715-717. Sulayman. Conquest of Jurjan (*Hyrcania*) and Tabaristan by Yazid ibn Mohallib (716). Siege of Constantinople by the caliph's brother, Maslama (717-718), which failed. The crossing of the Pyrenees and invasion of southern France by Hurr, the successor of Musa. Sulayman succeeded by his cousin,

717-720. Omar ibn Abdul-Aziz, who attempted to reorganize the finances of the empire. Members of the subject races, who had become Moslems, were placed on the same footing as the Arabs in respect to taxation. Narbonne in southern France taken by Samh, the successor of Hurr. Omar was succeeded by the third son of Abdulmalik,

720-724. Yazid II. Samh was defeated and killed by the Duke Eudo before Toulouse (721). Revolt of Yazid ibn Muhallib in Iraq. His defeat at Akra on the Euphrates by Maslama. Outbreak of internecine strife between the Yemenites (Kalb) and Modharites (Qais) (the so-called southern and northern Arabs) throughout the empire, especially in Khorasan and Transoxania, where propaganda for the Abbasids (descendants of the prophet's uncle, Abbas) also began. Yazid was succeeded by his brother,

724-743. Hisham. Defeat of the Khazars, conquest of Georgia (727-733).

732. Invasion of southern France by Abdurrahman, governor of Spain; his defeat at Poitiers (Tours) by Charles Martel.

738. Kharijite revolts in Iraq, insurrection of Sogdians and Arabs in Khorasan supported by the Turkomans of Transoxania, was quelled by Chalid ibn Abdallah al-Kasri, governor of Khorasan.

740. Shi'ite revolt in Iraq under Zayd, grandson of the martyred Husayn; his defeat and death. Hisham was succeeded by his nephew.

741-742. The Revolt of the Kharijites and Berbers in North Africa was put down by Hanzala, the viceroy in North Africa.

743-744. Walid II, who was killed in a Yemenite revolt led by his cousin, who succeeded him as Yazid III, only to die a few months later. He was succeeded by the last Omayyad,

744-750. Marwan II, the grandson of Marwan I. Insurrections in Syria at Homs and in Palestine. Kharijite revolt in Mesopotamia (745), and in Arabia (745-746). Mecca and Medina seized by the rebels. Shi'ite insurrection in Iraq and Persia under Abdullah, grandson of Ali's brother, Ja'far, which was joined by Kharijites and Abassids (745-747). The black standard of the Abassids was raised by Abu Muslim in Khorasan (747). Marwan's governor of Khorasan, Nasr, was defeated at Nishapur and Jurjan by Abu Muslim's general, Kahtaba, who routed the Omayyad forces again at Nehawand and Kerbela. Marwan himself was defeated at the battle of the Zab, and was pursued to Busir, Egypt, and killed (750). Slaughter of the Omayyad princes. Few escaped, but among those was Abdurrahman, grandson of Hisham, who later founded the Omayyad Kingdom of Cordova in Spain (755).

c. THE ABBASID CALIPHATE, 750-c.1100

750-1258. THE ABBASID CALIPHATE. Spain never recognized it, nor did Morocco. Abbasid authority was re-established in the Province of Africa as far as Algiers in 761, but only for a short period.

750-754. Abu-l-Abbas al-Saffah, the first Abbasid caliph. Omayyad revolts in Syria and Mesopotamia. Byzantine raids into the northern provinces. Abu al-Saffah was succeeded by his brother,

754-775. AL-MANSUR, the real founder of the dynasty. The revolt of his uncle, Abdullah, governor of Syria, was crushed by Abu Muslim, who was then murdered at Mansur's orders (754). Revolt of Abu Muslim's followers in Khorasan (755). A Byzantine invasion was repulsed with great slaughter. Cappadocia reoccupied; Malitia (*Melitene*), Mopsuestia, and other cities rebuilt and fortified against Byzantine raids (758). Annexation of Tabaristan (759); Shi'ite revolt in Iraq and Medina under the Hasanids, Mohammed and Ibrahim (762). Foundation of Baghdad (762). Khazar invasion of Georgia repelled (762). Insurrection of Ustad Sis in Khorasan and Sistan (767). Rise of the Barmecides to power as viziers of the realm (752-803). Mansur was succeeded by his son,

775-785. AL-MAHDI, noted for his improvement of the communications of the empire, his fortification of important centers, his founding of towns and schools, and his encouragement of the arts.

Persecution of the Manichaeans. Revolt of the veiled prophet, Mokanna, in Khorasan (775-778). Rise of a communistic, nihilistic sect, the Zindiqs, in Khorasan, western Persia, and Iraq. Invasion of the Byzantines, who were routed. Moslem advance against Constantinople; the Empress Irene forced to sue for peace (783-785).

Mahdi was succeeded by his son,

785. Al-Hadi, who reigned only a year and was succeeded by

786-809. HARUN AL-RASHID (of *Arabian Nights'* fame). Kabul and Sanhar were annexed to the empire (787). Khazar invasion of Armenia (799). Fall of the Barmecides (803). Kharijite revolts.

791-809. War with the Byzantines. Defeat of Nicephorus at Heraclea or Dorylaeum (798). The peace, which was concluded, was broken by Nicephorus, and the Moslems invaded Asia Minor led by the caliph in person. Capture of Tyana (806). Advance to Ancyra. Meanwhile Cyprus (805) and Rhodes (807) were ravaged by the Moslem fleet. Iconium and Ephesus in Lydia captured, Sideropolis, Andrasus, and Nicaea reduced. Heraclea Pontica on the Black Sea taken by storm. Nicephorus again invaded Moslem territory in 808, but troubles in Khorasan compelled Harun to march east, where he died. In his reign the Hanafite school of law began to assume a systematic form.

He was succeeded by his son,

809-813. AL-AMIN, against whom his brother Mamun rebelled and was accepted as caliph in Persia. Siege of Baghdad by Mamun's general, Tahir (813). Amin was murdered after surrendering on terms.

813-833. MAMUN THE GREAT.
His reign probably the most glorious epoch in the history of the caliphate. The arts and sciences were liberally endowed. Two observatories were built, one near Damascus, the other near Baghdad. A *House of Knowledge*, provided with a rich library, was erected near the Baghdad Observatory. Literary, scientific, and philosophical works were translated from Greek, Syriac, Persian, and Sanscrit. A liberal religious attitude adopted. Mu'tazilitism became the established faith. The Mu'tazilites maintained, like the Qadarites of the later Omayyad period, man's free will, also that justice and reason must control God's action toward men, both of which doctrines were repudiated by the later orthodox school of the Ash'arites.

Transference of the capital by Mamun from Merv to Baghdad, owing to Omayyad and Shi'ite revolts in Arabia, Iraq, and Mesopotamia. To meet this crisis he had proclaimed as his heir-apparent, Ali al-Ridha, a descendant of the Caliph Ali (817).

Conquest of Crete (from Egypt) by Arabs who had been expelled from Spain by the Omayyads (825); of Sicily by the Aghlabites of North Africa (827). Palermo taken (831). Only Syracuse and Taormine left in Byzantine hands.

Terrorization of the northern provinces by the Magian, **Babek,** leader of the communistic Khurramites, from his stronghold in Azerbaijan (816-833). Byzantine invasions in his support were repulsed by Mamun in person (829-833). Death of Mamun. In his reign the Tahirids of Khorasan became practically independent (820-872). Mamun was succeeded by his brother,

833-842. Al-Mu'tasim. Transference of the capital to Samarra (836). Formation of a standing military corps composed of Turkish slaves and mercenaries, of whom the later caliphs were the mere puppets.

Revolt of the Jats or Gypsies on the lower Tigris (834). Babek was defeated by Afshin and put to death (837-838). War with Byzantium (837-842). Defeat of the Byzantines at Anzen on the Halys, Ancyra destroyed; Amorium, the place of origin of the Byzantine dynasty, captured (838). Preparations for the siege of Constantinople. Arab fleet destroyed by a tempest. Death of Mu'tasim (842) and his succession by his son,

842-847. Wathiq, who continued his father's policy of aggrandizing the Turks at the expense of the Arabs and Persians. Interchange of prisoners between the Byzantines and Moslems. Wathiq's reign marks the beginning of the decline of the caliphate. He was succeeded by his brother,

847-861. Mutawakkil, who sought to reestablish the traditional Moslem faith. Mu'tazilite doctrines were abjured, their professors persecuted. Shi'ites, Jews, and Christians also persecuted. The mausoleum of Husayn, the martyr of Kerbela, was razed to the ground. Damietta in Egypt was taken and Cilicia ravaged by the Byzantines. Mutawakkil was murdered by his Turkish guard and was succeeded by his son,

861. Muntasir, who reigned only six months, when he was deposed by the Turkoman chiefs of his guard, who raised to the throne another grandson of Mu'tasim, **Musta'in** (862-866), who escaped from the Turks to Baghdad, but was forced by them to abdicate and was later murdered by an emissary of his successor, **Mu'tazz** (866-869), in whose reign Egypt became virtually independent under **Ahmad ibn Tulun,** founder of the Tulunid dynasty. Mu'tazz was murdered by his mutinous troops and succeeded by **Muqtadi** (869-870), a son of Wathiq, who was compelled to abdicate by the Turks, who chose as his successor the eldest surviving son of Mutawakkil,

870-892. Mu'tamid, who transferred the court to Baghdad; and for this and the next two reigns the power of the Turkish guard was successfully checked.

The Zenj rebellion in Chaldaea (869-883), which devastated this region for fifteen years, was put down finally by the caliph's brother, Muwaffiq. A Byzantine invasion of Syria was repelled by the Tulunid governor of Tarsus.

In this reign the caliphate lost its eastern provinces. The Saffarid dynasty was founded by Ya'qub ibn Layth, who established himself in Sistan, drove out the Tahirids of Khorasan, and became master of the whole of modern Persia. The dynasty lasted from 870 to 903, when it was extinguished by the Samanids of Transoxania, who had succeeded the Tahirids there (872), and who, after the overthrow of the Saffarids, ruled from the borders of India to Baghdad and from the Great Desert to the Persian Gulf. Their power was finally broken by the Ilak Khans of Turkestan (999), who then ruled over Transoxania, Kashgar, and eastern Tatary from Bokhara (932-1165). Under the Samanids, Bokhara was the intellectual center of Islam.

Mu'tamid was succeeded as caliph by his nephew,

892-902. Mu'tadid, who restored Egypt to the caliphate and reformed the law of inheritance. His successor, Muqtafi (902–908), brought Egypt under his direct control and repulsed the Byzantines, storming Adalia.

891-906. The Carmathian revolt. These communistic rebels overran and devastated Arabia, Syria, and Iraq, took Mecca, and carried away the sacred Black Stone. Muqtafi was succeeded by

908-932. Muqtadir, his brother, during whose reign occurred the conquest of North Africa by the Fatimid, Obaydullah al-Mahdi, who also drove out the last Aghlabite, Ziyadatullah, from Egypt. Establishment of the Ziyarids in Tabaristan, Jurjan, Ispahan, and Hamadhan as independent sovereigns (928–1024). Rise of the Buwayhids (932–1055) under the patronage of the Ziyarids. Conquest and division of Persia and Iraq by the three Buwayhid brothers, Imad al-Dawla, Rukn al-Dawla, and Mu'izz al-Dawla. Mu'izz granted the title of Amir al-Umara (Prince of the Princes) by the Caliph Mustaqfi (945). The caliphs became puppets of the Amir al-Umara. The Buwayhid dominions fell piecemeal to the Ghaznawids, the Kakwayhids of Kurdistan (1007–1057), and the Seljuks, owing to divisions among the Buwayhid rulers.

962-1186. THE GHAZNAWIDS. Founder of the dynasty was Subaktagin, a Turkish slave of Alptagin, himself slave and commander-in-chief of the Samanids in Khorasan and independent prince of the petty fief of Ghazna in the Sulayman mountains. Subaktagin defeated the Rajputs and received Khorasan from the Samanids (994). His successor, **MAHMUD** (*the Idol-Breaker*), one of the greatest figures in the history of Central Asia, became master of Khorasan (1000) and invaded India several times. His court was the resort of famous scholars and poets, such as Beiruni and Firdausi. The Ghaznawids were overthrown by the Seljuks.

929-1096. Meanwhile in Syria and Mesopotamia four Arab dynasties and one Kurdish dynasty held sway.

929-1003. The Hamdanids of Mosul and Aleppo, the most famous of whom, Sayf al-Dawla, took Aleppo from the Ikhshidids of Egypt (944) and warred successfully against the Byzantines. His court was one of the brilliant centers of Islam in the 10th century. The great Arab poet, **Mutannabi**, was its chief ornament. The Hamdanids were descendants of the Arab tribe of Taghlib. Their dominions were absorbed by the Fatimids and the Buwayhids.

1023-1079. The Mirdasids of Aleppo, of the Arab tribe of the Banu Kilab, were engaged in continual warfare with the Fatimids and the Buwayhids, and were finally driven out by the

996-1096. 'Uqaylids of Mosul, a division of the Banu Ka'b tribe, who succeeded the Hamdanids in Mosul, and whose dominions under **Muslim ibn Quraysh** extended from the neighborhood of Baghdad to Aleppo. Their domain was ultimately merged in the Seljuk Empire.

990-1096. The Marwanids of Diyar-Bakr, established by the Kurd, Abu-l Ali ibn Marwan, ruled over Amid, Mayyarfariqun, and Aleppo. They too fell before the Seljuks.

1012-1050. Mazyadids of Hilla, a tribe of the Banu Asad. The fourth ruler of this dynasty, The Sadaqa, was one of the great heroes of Arab history. The state was ultimately absorbed by the Zanjids.

(*Cont. p.* 254.)

B. THE AGE OF THE CRUSADES

1. WESTERN EUROPE

a. THE BRITISH ISLES

(1) *England*, 1066-1307

1066-1087. WILLIAM I (*the Conqueror*), of medium height, corpulent, but majestic in person, choleric, mendacious, greedy, a great soldier, governor, centralizer, legislator, innovator.

1066-1072. Rapid collapse, speedy submission or reduction of the south and east. The Confessor's bequest, acceptance by the Witan, and coronation "legalized" William's title. Reduction of the southwest (1068). Reduction of the rest of England (1067-1070): a series of local risings leniently dealt with; construction by forced native labor of garrison castles (Norman mounds). Great **rising of the north** (Edwin and Morca's second) with Danish aid (1069) put down by William in person. The "harrying of the north" (1069-1070), a devastation (often depopulation) of a strip from York to Durham (the consequences survived to modern times) ended Scandinavian opposition in England. **Reduction of Hereward's last stand** (the "last of the English") in the Isle of Ely (1070-1071); raid into Scotland (1072).

Norman fusion, conciliation, innovation: (1) **Feudalization** on centralized Norman lines (on the ruins of the nascent Saxon feudalism) followed military reduction and confiscation of the rebel lands (1066-1070). Theoretically every bit of land in England belonged to the crown; in practice only the great estates changed hands and were assigned to William's followers on Norman tenures. The king retained about one sixth of the land; less than a half of the land went to Normans on feudal tenures. Except on the border few compact holdings survived; the earldoms, reduced in size, became chiefly honorific. Some 170 great tenants-in-chief, and numerous lesser tenants emerged. A direct oath (the *Oath of Salisbury*) of primary vassalage to the crown was exacted from all vassals, making them directly responsible to the crown (1086). Construction of castles (except on the borders) subject to royal license; coinage a royal monopoly; private war prohibited. (2) **The Anglo-Saxon shires (34)**

and hundreds continued for local administration and for local justice (bishops no longer sat in the shire courts and the earls were reduced) under the sheriffs (usually of baronial rank), retained from Anglo-Saxon days, but subject to removal by the king. The sheriffs were an essential link between the (native) local machinery and the central (Norman) government. Communities were held responsible for local good order; sporadic visitations of royal commissioners. Anglo-Saxon laws little altered. (3) Early grant of a charter to London guaranteeing local customs. (4) **Innovations of the centralizing monarch:** a royal council, the **Great Council** (*curia regis*), meeting infrequently (three stated meetings annually) replaced the Anglo-Saxon Witan and was of almost the same personnel: tenants-in-chief, the chancellor (introduced from Normandy by Edward the Confessor), a new official, the justiciar (in charge of justice and finance, and William's viceroy during his absences), the heads of the royal household staff. This same body, meeting frequently, and including only such tenants-in-chief as happened to be on hand, constituted the **Small Council,** a body which tended to absorb more and more of the actual administration.

The **Church** retained its lands (perhaps a fourth of the land in England). Pope Alexander II had blessed William's conquest, and William introduced the (much-needed) Cluniac reforms. Archbishop Stigand and most of the bishops and great abbots were deprived or died, and were replaced by zealous Norman reformers; **Lanfranc** (an Italian lawyer, a former Prior of Bec), as Archbishop of Canterbury, carried through a wide reform: celibacy enforced, chapters reorganized, new discipline in the schools, numerous new monastic foundations. By royal decree episcopal jurisdiction was separated from lay jurisdiction and the bishops given their own courts, a decisive step in the evolution of the common law as an independent force. William refused an oath of fealty to Pope Gregory VII for his English conquests, and (despite the papal decree of 1075) retained control of the appointment of bishops and important abbots, from whom he drew his chief administrators

DOMINIONS OF HENRY II

Lands held by
Henry as king

Lands held as fiefs
by inheritance

Lands held or claimed through
marriage with Eleanor

Lands which Henry claimed as
fiefs held of him

NORTH
SEA

SCOTLAND

York

Native Irish

Dublin

Wexford

WALES

ENGLAND

London

Dover

ENGLISH CHANNEL

Calais

FLANDERS

Rouen

Paris

CHAMPAGNE

R. Rhine

Caen

NORMANDY

BRITTANY

MAINE

ANJOU

POITOU

BURGUNDY

GUIENNE

R. Rhone

Bordeaux

R. Garonne

TOULOUSE

Bayonne

GASCONY

KINGDOM

OF

CASTILE

KINGDOM

OF

ARAGON

MEDITERRANEAN

SEA

(thereby making the Church, in effect, pay for the administration of the state). No papal bull or brief, no papal legate might be received without royal approval and no tenant-in-chief or royal officer could be excommunicated without royal permission. The king retained a right of veto on all decrees of local synods. The great prelates were required to attend the Great Council, even to do military service.

1086. The great Domesday survey: royal commissions on circuit collected on oath (sworn inquest) from citizens of the counties and vills full information as to size, resources and present and past ownership of every hide of land. The results, arranged by counties in *Domesday Book*, gave a unique record as a basis for taxation and administration.

Royal finance: (1) non-feudal revenues: Danegeld, shire farms, judicial fines; (2) the usual feudal revenues.

Military resources of the crown: (1) (non-feudal) the old Anglo-Saxon *fyrd* (including *ship fyrd*) was retained (i.e. a national non-feudal militia, loyal to the crown, was used, e.g. against the Norman rebellion of 1075); (2) (feudal) about five thousand knights' fees owing service on the usual feudal terms. The prosperity of England under Norman rule was great and an era of extensive building (largely churches, cathedrals and monasteries) began under the Conqueror and continued even through the anarchy of Stephen and Matilda.

1087-1100. WILLIAM II (*Rufus*), a passionate, greedy ruffian, second son of the Conqueror, designated by his father on his death-bed (Robert, the eldest, received Normandy; Henry, cash). A Norman revolt (1088) was put down, largely with English aid, and William firmly settled on the throne. Justice was venal and expensive, the administration cruel and unpopular, taxation heavy, the Church exploited. On Lanfranc's death (1089), William kept the revenues of the See of Canterbury without appointing a successor until he thought himself dying, when he named (1093) Anselm (an Italian, Abbot of Bec, a most learned man, and a devoted churchman), who clashed with William over the recognition of rival popes; Anselm maintained church law to be above civil law and went into voluntary exile (1097). William, deeply hated, was assassinated (?) in the New Forest.

1100-1135. HENRY I (*Beauclerc, Lion of Justice*), an educated, stubborn, prudent ruler, a good judge of men, won the crown by a dash to the royal treasury at Winchester and a quick appeal to the nation by his so-called *Coronation Charter*, a

promise of reform by a return to the good ways of the Conqueror (a promise often broken). Henry married Edith (of the line of Alfred), whose name became Maud out of deference to the Norman's difficulties with Saxon names. Anarchy in Normandy under Robert's slack rule, an invitation from the revolting Norman barons, and the victory of **Tinchebray** (1106), gave Henry Normandy (Robert remained a prisoner until his death), and made a later struggle between the new English kingdom and the rising Capetian power in France inevitable. Anselm, faithful to the reforming program of the revived papacy, on his recall from exile refused homage for the archiepiscopal estates (i.e. he refused to recognize lay investiture) and refused to consecrate the bishops who had rendered such homage. Henry temporized until firmly on the throne, then seized the fiefs and exiled Anselm. Adela, Henry's sister, suggested the **Compromise of 1107** which terminated the struggle by clerical homage for fiefs held of the king, while the king allowed clerical investiture with the spiritual symbols. The crown continued to designate candidates for the great prelacies.

This reign was marked by a notable expansion, specialization, and differentiation of function in the royal administration (e.g. the exchequer, influenced by accounting methods from Lorraine or Laon). Extension of the jurisdiction of royal courts: growing use of royal writs, detailing of members of the Small Council as judges on circuit (hitherto a sporadic, now a regular practice), who not merely did justice but took over increasingly the business formerly done by the sheriffs (e.g. assessment and negotiation of aids and other levies), and brought the *curia regis* into closer contact with shire and hundred courts.

Prosperity was general and trade in London attracted Norman immigrants. The Cistercians arrived (1128) and began an extensive program of swamp reclamation, mill and road building, agricultural improvement, and stock-breeding. Henry began the sale of charters to towns on royal domain.

Influence of the Conquest on English culture: (1) Architecture: wide introduction of the Norman (Romanesque) style (e.g; St. John's Chapel in the Tower of London, end of the 11th century; Durham Cathedral, c. 1096–1133). (2) Literary: Anglo-Saxon, the speech of the conquered, almost ceased to have a literary history, rapidly lost its formality of inflections and terminations, and became flexible and simple if inelegant. Norman French, the tongue of the court, the aristocracy, the schools, the lawyers and judges, drew its inspiration from the Continent until the loss of Normandy (1204). The Normans then began to learn English, and the Anglo-Saxon was enriched with a second vocabulary of Norman words, ideas, and refinements.

Anglo-Norman culture: (1) Historical writing: Geoffrey of Monmouth, *History of the Kings of Britain* (written in Latin, before 1147), created the tale of Arthur for Europe. **Walter Map** (c. 1140–c. 1200), author of Goliardic verse, welded the Grail story into the Arthurian cycle, giving it a moral and religious slant; **Wace** (c. 1124–c. 1174) *Roman de Brut* and *Roman de Rou*; **Marie de France**; all three were at the court of Henry II. **(2) Science: Walcher of Malvern** observed the eclipse of 1092 and attempted to calculate the difference in time between England and Italy. Walcher began to reckon in degrees, minutes, and seconds (1120). **Adelard of Bath**, a student of Arabic science in the service of Henry II, observed and experimented (e.g. the comparative speed of sound and light), translated Al-Khwarizmi's astronomical tables into Latin (1126) and introduced Al-Khwarizmi's trigonometric tables to the west. **Robert of Chester** translated Al-Khwarizmi's algebra into Latin (1145). **(3) Philosophy: John of Salisbury** (d. 1180), pupil of Abélard, the best classical, humanistic scholar of his day, attached to the court of Henry II, and later Bishop of Chartres, wrote the *Policraticus*, etc. **Beginnings of Oxford University** (c. 1167) on the model of Paris, a center of national culture.

1135-1154. STEPHEN. Henry's son drowned on the White Ship (1120), and Henry had had his daughter **Matilda** (widow of the Emperor Henry V) accepted as his heir and married to Geoffrey of Anjou, as protector. Stephen of Blois (son of Henry's sister Adela) asserted and maintained his claim to the throne at the price of a dynastic war (till 1153) with Matilda, the climax of feudal anarchy, and the ruin of English prosperity. Archbishop Theobald finally negotiated a compromise (1153) whereby Matilda's son Henry should succeed to the crown on Stephen's death. The reign was remarkable for a tremendous amount of ecclesiastical building.

1154-1399. THE HOUSE OF PLANTA-GENET (Angevin).

1154-1189. HENRY II. Master of a hybrid "empire" (England, Normandy, Anjou, Maine, Touraine, by inheritance; Poitou, Aquitaine, Gascony, by marriage with Eleanor of Aquitaine (1152); Brittany (acquired, 1169), and Wales, Ireland, and Scotland (on a loose bond) without unity save in the person of the ruler. **Dynastic marriages:** daughter Eleanor to the King of Castile, Joan to the King of Sicily, Matilda to Henry the Lion. King Henry was a man of education, exhaustless energy, experience as an administrator, realistic, violent of temper.

Restoration of England to the good order of Henry I: dismissal of mercenaries, razing of unlicensed castles (1000?), reconquest of Northumberland and Cumberland from the Scots, resumption of crown lands and offices alienated under Stephen. Reconstitution of the exchequer and Great Council. After 1155 Henry felt free to leave England, and spent less than half his reign in the realm.

1155-1172. Struggle to reduce clerical encroachment on the royal courts: Under Stephen anarchy and the theories of Roman law had favored the expansion of clerical courts, extending benefit of clergy to include even homicides. **Thomas Becket** (a deacon and crony of Henry's at the time of his elevation to the chancellorship, 1155) resigned as chancellor when he became Archbishop of Canterbury (1162), and clashed at once with Henry over the criminous clerks. The *Constitutions of Clarendon* (1164), largely a restatement of old customs (including the Conqueror's), provided (*inter alia*) for the indictment of clerics in royal courts, their trial in ecclesiastical courts, and their degradation, followed by their sentence and punishment in royal courts. They also extended royal (at the expense of clerical) jurisdiction, and asserted royal rights of control in episcopal elections. Becket yielded, was dispensed from his oath by the pope, violated the *Constitutions*, and fled to France. Reconciled (1170) with Henry, Becket returned, excommunicated certain bishops friendly to Henry, and was murdered in the Cathedral of Canterbury by four knights of Henry's court, spurred by Henry's outbreak of fury against Becket, but not by Henry's orders. Henry escaped excommunication by promising to abide by the papal judgment, and was reconciled with the papacy (1172) after an oath denying all share in the crime. After this incident Henry had no choice but to tolerate benefit of clergy, which continued to be an increasing scandal in England until the reign of Henry VII. Henry retained the right of presentation and virtual control over episcopal elections. The **Assize of Clarendon** (1166) contains the first civil legislation on heresy since Roman days.

1170. Extensive replacement of the (baronial) sheriffs with men of lower

The Norman and Plantagenet Kings

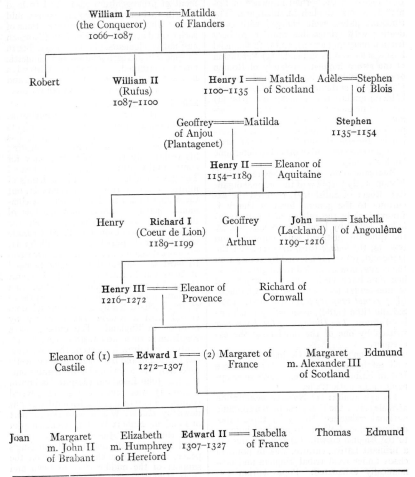

William I══════Matilda
(the Conqueror) | of Flanders
1066-1087

Robert   William II   Henry I ═══ Matilda   Adèle══Stephen
(Rufus)   1100-1135 | of Scotland | of Blois
1087-1100

Geoffrey══════Matilda   Stephen
of Anjou   1135-1154
(Plantagenet)

Henry II ═══ Eleanor of
1154-1189 | Aquitaine

Henry   Richard I   Geoffrey   John ═══ Isabella
(Coeur de Lion) | (Lackland) | of Angoulême
1189-1199   Arthur   1199-1216

Henry III ═══ Eleanor of   Richard of
1216-1272 | Provence   Cornwall

Eleanor of (1) ═══ Edward I ═══ (2) Margaret of   Margaret   Edmund
Castile   1272-1307   France   m. Alexander III
of Scotland

Joan   Margaret   Elizabeth   Edward II ═══ Isabella   Thomas   Edmund
m. John II   m. Humphrey   1307-1327 | of France
of Brabant   of Hereford

rank, trained in the royal service. Henceforth the barons ceased to hold the shrievalty.

1173-1174. **Reduction of the last purely feudal revolt;** Henry's only use of mercenary troops in England.

1181. **The Assize of Arms:** by this reorganization of the old *fyrd* every freeman was made responsible, according to his income, for his proper share in the defense of the realm. The king thus ensured a national militia for the defense against the baronage.

Henry was not a great legislator, but he initiated a remarkable series of innovations in government which fixed the political framework of national unity.

Judicial Reforms: (1) Increasing concentration of judicial business in the Small Council. (2) Designation (1178) of five professional judges from the Small Council as a **permanent central court;** extension of the transfer of judicial business to royal courts by the increase and specialization of royal writs (the fees a valuable source of revenue); formalization and regularization (c. 1166) of the itinerant justices (*justices in eyre*), the great source of the **Common Law** (a law universal in the realm). One of the judges, **Glanvill,** wrote the *Treatise on the*

Laws and Customs of the Kingdom of England, the first serious book on the Common Law revealing the formal influence of Roman Law, but English in substance. The itinerant judges were charged with cases dealing with crimes like murder, robbery (soon forgery and arson), and with financial business as well as judicial. (3) **Expansion of the sworn inquest** (probably of Roman origin, introduced into England by the Conqueror): statements by neighbors (freeholders) under oath in the shire courts: (a) *jury* (12 members) *of presentment in criminal cases* (Assize of Clarendon, 1166), a process which expanded (after 1219), replacing the ordeal; and (b) the *use of juries* (recognitions) instead of ordeal to determine landownership.

Reorganization of the exchequer: Nigel, Bishop of Ely (nephew of the original organizer, Roger of Salisbury), restored the exchequer to the general form of Henry I. **Innovations in the raising of revenue:** (a) *tallage,* levied by local negotiations (i.e. by the itinerant justices) with boroughs and tenants; (b) *hidage (carucage)* replaced the Danegeld; (c) *scutage,* levied by Henry I on the clergy, now extended to knights' fees in lieu of military service (due to Henry's need of non-feudal levies across the Channel); (d) *personal property taxes* (the first, 1166), Saladin tithe (1188), assessed by neighborhood juries. *The Dialogue of the Exchequer* written by one of the officials of the exchequer.

Extension of trade: German merchants well established in London (1157); large Italian business (wool); extensive development of domestic trade.

Foreign affairs: (1) **Norman penetration of Wales** since the Conquest bred a sporadic national resistance; Henry by three expeditions reduced Wales to nominal homage to the English crown. (2) **Ireland,** despite a brilliant native culture, was in political chaos under rival tribal kinglets and economically exhausted. Pope Adrian IV, hoping that Henry would reform the Church in Ireland, "gave" Ireland (1154) to Henry. Richard of Clare's (Strongbow) expedition (1169–1170) established a harsh rule; Henry landed (1171), temporarily reduced the rigors of the baronial administration, and reformed the Irish Church (Synod of Cashel, 1172). **John Lackland** (Henry's son) was appointed Lord of Ireland (1177), arrived (1185) but was soon recalled for incompetence.

Intrigues and revolts (beginning 1173) of Henry's sons, supported by their mother Eleanor, King Louis VII, and later Philip II of France, as well as by disgruntled local barons.

The ruling class continued to speak French during this reign, but the establishment of primogeniture as applied to land inheritance insured that younger sons would mingle with the non-aristocratic sections of society and accelerate the fusion of Norman and native elements. Manor houses began to appear in increasing numbers as domestic peace continued. Numerous Cistercian houses spread new agricultural methods and especially improved wool-raising.

1189-1199. RICHARD I (*Coeur de Lion*).

Neither legislator, administrator, nor statesman, but the greatest of knights errant, an absentee ruler who spent less than a year of his reign in England, visiting his realm only twice, to raise money for continental ventures. Taxation was heavy. The government remained in the hands of ministers largely trained by Henry II, but there appeared a tendency toward a common antipathy of barons and people toward the crown. Richard (having taken the Cross, 1188) went on the Third Crusade with Frederick Barbarossa and Philip II, his most dangerous foe. On his return trip Richard was captured by Duke Leopold of Austria and turned over to the Emperor Henry VI, who held him for a staggering ransom. John and Philip bid for the prisoner, but Richard finally bought his freedom (1194) with a ransom raised partly by taxation in England. The crusade gave Englishmen their first taste of eastern adventure, but drew few except the adventurous portion of the baronage. The domestic reflection was a series of anti-Semitic outbreaks. John Lackland (despite his known character) was given charge of several counties; his plot against Richard was put down by **Hubert Walter** with the support of London. Hubert Walter, Archbishop of Canterbury and Justiciar (1194–1198), ruled England well, maintained the king's peace, and began a clear reliance on the support of the middle class in town and shire. Charters were granted towns (London received the right to elect its mayor)—and the knights of the shire were called on to assume a share of county business as a balance to the sheriffs. Knights (elected by the local gentry) served as coroners and chose the local juries, a departure looking to the day when local election and amateur justices of the peace would be the basis of government. The first known merchant guild, 1193.

1194-1199. Richard's continental struggle against Philip II, in which Richard more than held his own. Château Gaillard, a new departure in castle architecture based on eastern lessons, built by

Richard on the Seine, as an outpost against Philip.

1199-1216. JOHN (*Lackland, Softsword*), cruel, mean, licentious, faithless, weak of will, without counterbalancing virtues. Crowned with the support of the Norman barons against his nephew Arthur's claims (by primogeniture), he became Arthur's guardian.

1202-1204. John's first contest with Philip (to protect his French possessions): struggle over Brittany, Maine, Anjou (temporary acceptance of John's title by Philip, 1200). John's marriage to Isabella of Angoulême (already betrothed to his vassal Hugh of Lusignan), led Hugh to appeal to Philip II as their common overlord. John ignored Philip's summons to judgment (1202); his French fiefs were declared forfeit, and Philip began a war with rapid successes. The death of Arthur (1203), possibly by John's own hand, ruined John's cause, and Philip, already master of Anjou, Brittany, and Maine, took Normandy (1204) and soon Touraine. John's vassals in southern France (preferring an absent Angevin to an encroaching Capetian) resisted Philip's advance south of the Loire. John's loss of the lands north of the Loire reduced the power and prestige of the English crown, cut the Norman baronage in England from their French connections, and turned their interests back to the island, with decisive constitutional and social consequences.

1205-1213. John's struggle with Pope Innocent III: after a double election to the See of Canterbury, Innocent rejected both elections (including John's nominee) and named (1207) **Stephen Langton**, a noted scholar and theologian. John refused to accept Langton, confiscated the estates of the see, expelled the monks of Canterbury; Innocent laid an interdict on England (1208). John confiscated the property of the English clergy who obeyed Innocent's ban without arousing serious public opposition. Innocent excommunicated John (1209), but John, holding as hostages the children of some of the barons, weathered the storm. Innocent deposed John (1213) and authorized Philip II to execute the sentence. John, aware of treason and mounting hostility, promised indemnity to the clergy, did homage to the pope for England and Ireland, agreed to an annual tribute, and was freed of the ban.

1213-1214. Final contest with Philip II (to regain the lands north of the Loire): John's great coalition (including his nephew, Emperor Otto IV, and the Count of Flanders) against Philip; most of the English baronage held aloof. Crushing defeat of the coalition at **Bouvines** (1214) ended all hope of regaining the lands north of the Loire (formal renunciation of English claims, 1259).

1215. MAGNA CARTA. The first politico-constitutional struggle in English history: in origin this struggle resulted from an effort of the feudal barons, supported by Archbishop Langton (notwithstanding papal support of John) and public opinion, to enforce their rights under their feudal contract with the king; it did not aim to destroy the monarchy or the royal administration. Preliminary demands of the barons (1213); John's concessions to the Church and negotiations with Pope Innocent; civil war. London opposed John (despite his liberal charter to the city). John's acceptance of the **Great Charter** at Runnymede. Magna Carta was essentially a feudal document, exacted by feudal barons from their lord but with national implications in its reforms: (1) concessions to the barons: reform in the exaction of scutage, aid, and reliefs, in the administration of wardship and in the demands for feudal service; writs of summons to the Great Council to be sent individually to the great magnates, collectively proclaimed by the sheriffs to the lesser nobles (i.e. knights); (2) concessions to the agricultural and commercial classes: Mesne tenants granted the privileges of tenants-in-chief; uniform weights and measures; affirmation of the ancient liberties of London and other towns; limitation on royal seizure of private property; reform of the forest law; reform of the courts; (3) concessions to the Church (in addition to John's charter of 1214): promise of freedom and free elections.

The **most significant provisions of the Great Charter:** (1) Chapter 12: no scutage or aid (except for the traditional feudal three) to be levied without the consent of the Great Council; (2) Chapter 14: definition of the Great Council and its powers; (3) Chapter 39: "*No freeman shall be arrested and imprisoned, or dispossessed, or outlawed, or banished, or in any way molested; nor will we set forth against him, nor send against him, unless by the lawful judgment of his peers and by the law of the land.*" Even these clauses were feudal and specific in background, but centuries of experience transformed them into a generalized formula of constitutional procedure, making them the basis of the modern English constitution. At the time their chief significance lay in the assertion of the supremacy of law over the king. Careful provisions were made for the enforcement of the charter by the barons, even by force of arms, but in practice such enforcement was impossible. The charter was repeatedly reissued by succeeding rulers. The pope, as John's feudal suzerain, declared the Great Charter void. Civil war followed; a Francophil section of the barons called Louis, son of Philip II, to the throne (1216). John opportunely died; his young son Henry, with the support of the Anglophil barons, succeeded him, and Louis abandoned his pursuit of the crown (1217). ·

1216-1272. HENRY III (a boy of nine). Guardianship (1216–1219) of William Marshal, Earl of Pembroke; an able, patriotic régime: two reissues (1216, 1217) of the (modified) Great Charter; elimination of French influence and interference, opposition to papal encroachments, reduction of feudal castles. William Marshal had designated the pope as Henry's guardian, and the government passed on his death (1219) to the papal legate Pandulph, the justiciar Hubert de Burgh, and Peter des Roches, tutor to Henry. Arrival of **the Dominicans** (1220) and **the Franciscans** (1224). Henry's personal rule (1227–1258) was marked by a major constitutional crisis.

Growth of national consciousness: After a futile but expensive effort (1229) to recover Aquitaine, Henry, always devoted to the papacy, gave free reign to papal exactions. At the same time the increase of papal provisions filled the English Church with alien (usually absentee Italian) appointees, to the exclusion of natives. A bitter anti-papal outbreak (perhaps supported by De Burgh) drove De Burgh from office; Des Roches succeeded him (1232–1234), filling the civil offices with fellow Poitevins. Henry's French marriage increased the alien influx and public opinion grew bitter. The papal collector was driven out (1244), and the Great Council refused (1242) a grant for Henry's effort to recover Poitou, which failed. Henry's acceptance of the crown of Sicily from the pope for his second son Edmund (1254), and his permission to his brother, Richard of Cornwall, to seek election as emperor (1257), both costly ventures, added to public ill-feeling. Finally, in a period of great economic distress, Richard asked the Great Council for one-third of the revenue of England for the pope. This grant was refused and the barons set out to reform the government with public approval (1258). A committee of 24, representing king and barons equally, brought in a proposal,

1258. THE PROVISIONS OF OXFORD, a baronial effort to restore the

charter, with strong clerical and middle-class support: creation of a council of fifteen (containing a baronial majority) with a veto over the king's decisions; the Great Council to be superseded by a committee of twelve, meeting thrice a year with the permanent council of fifteen; the chancellor, justiciar, and treasurer were to be chosen annually by the council. All officials, including the king and his son, took an oath of loyalty to the Provisions.

1260-1264. The knights, alienated by the baronial oligarchy, appealed to Edward (Henry's eldest son). Gradually there emerged a group of progressive reformers (younger barons, many of the clergy and knights, townsmen, notably of London and Oxford); the more conservative barons turned to the king. Henry obtained papal release from his oaths (1261) and replaced the council of fifteen with his own appointees; chaos was followed by civil war (1263). Papal exactions continued. Louis IX (asked to arbitrate the Provisions of Oxford), in the *Mise of Amiens* (1264), decided in favor of the king. This decision was rejected by London and the commercial towns, and civil war soon broke out.

1264. Simon de Montfort (son of Simon of the Albigensian crusade), Henry's brother-in-law, of French blood and education, a friend of Grosseteste, Bishop of Lincoln (a lifelong champion of ecclesiastical and governmental reform), emerged as leader of the reforming group. This group, ahead of its time, manifested strong religious fervor, and even traces of democratic ideas. Simon's victory at **Lewes** (1265), capture of Henry and exaction of the *Mise of Lewes* (a return to the reforms of 1258).
  In the course of this reign the Great Council came to be called *Parliament* (c. 1240) and at various times knights of the shire were summoned to share in its deliberations. Parliament was still as much concerned with administration and justice as with "legislation"; its membership, control of finance, and specific functions were by no means precisely defined. The summoning of the knights in effect merely transformed the negotiation of shire business into a collective negotiation by the same men who managed it locally.

1265. De Montfort's parliament: two knights from each shire, and two burgesses from each borough were summoned, probably the first summons to townsmen in parliamentary history.

1265. Edward, now leader of the baronial, conservative opposition, defeated

De Montfort at **Evesham** (death of De Montfort).

Henry's return to power was formal, as Edward was the real ruler, and Edward and the barons were aware of the need of reform. Edward, on a crusade with Louis IX when Henry died, was proclaimed king while still absent, spent a year in Gascony on the way back, and was not crowned until 1274.

1272-1307. EDWARD I (*Longshanks;* the *English Justinian*), an able ruler and a great legislator, fit to rank with Frederick II, Louis IX, and Alfonso the Wise. He observed his motto, *Pactum serva* (Keep troth), but tempered it with realism. The first truly English king, he surrounded himself with able ministers and lawyers. The reign was marked by a frequent consultation of the knights and townsmen, not always in Parliament. The institutions of the English state began to take shape.

EXTERNAL AFFAIRS:

1276-1284. Reduction of Wales. Wales during the reign of Henry III had gotten out of hand, and a national revival had set in (bardic poetry and tribal union under the Llewelyns around Snowdon in the north). **Llewelyn,** Prince of Wales, joined De Montfort's opposition, refused homage (1276), and, with his brother David, renewed war with the English (1282). Edward marched into Wales, killed Llewelyn and executed David (1283), asserting the full dominion of the English crown. In these wars Edward became aware of the efficiency of the Welsh longbow. Edward's fourth son Edward (later Edward II) was born at Carnarvon (1284), and with him began the customary title, **Prince of Wales,** bestowed on the heir to the English throne. Local government was organized in Wales, and the *Statute of Wales* settled the legal status of the newly disciplined Welsh.

1285-1307. Scotland. William the Lion had purchased freedom from homage to the English king from Richard I in 1189, but his successors continued to do homage for their English lands. The Scottish nobility were largely Normanized. Margaret, the *Maid of Norway* (daughter of Eric of Norway) was granddaughter and heir of King Alexander II of Scotland. After Alexander's death (1286), Edward arranged a marriage for her with the Prince of Wales (1290), but she died on her way to England and Edward's hope of a personal union of the two crowns vanished. There were three collateral claimants to the Scottish crown: **John Baliol, Robert Bruce, John Hastings.** Edward, asked to arbitrate, demanded (1291) homage and acknowledgment of paramountcy from the Scots, which was

given (the commons protested). He awarded the crown to Baliol (1292), who did homage for Scotland. Edward's insistence on appellate jurisdiction alienated the Scots and disposed them toward France, and an alliance began (1295) which endured intermittently for 300 years. Edward invaded Scotland, defeated Baliol at **Dunbar** (1296), declared himself King of Scotland, received the homage of the nobles, took away the coronation stone of Scone. Oppressive administration by Edward's officials led to the rising of **William Wallace** (1297), who was supported by the gentry and commonalty, but got little aid at first from the nobles. Wallace won a victory at Stirling. Edward, using the longbow to open the way for a cavalry charge, defeated Wallace at **Falkirk** (1298), drove him into exile, and completed his second conquest of Scotland (1304). Wallace was taken (1305) and executed, and Scotland incorporated under the English crown. Scottish law was retained, Scottish representatives sat in Parliament, but the nobles had to yield their fortresses, and an English lieutenant was sent to rule Scotland with a council and with power to amend the laws. Scottish nationalism found a leader in **Robert Bruce** (grandson of the claimant to the crown), who was crowned at Scone. Edward died (1307) on an expedition against Bruce.

1293-1303. France. Ill-feeling between sailors from the Cinque Ports (Sandwich, Dover, Romney, Hythe, Hastings, and [later] Rye and Winchelsea) and the French, culminated in a victory for the Anglo-Gascon fleet (1293) and Edward's summons to the court of his French overlord, King Philip IV. Under a *pro forma* compromise (1294), Edward turned over his Gascon fortresses to Philip, who refused to return them, and declared Gascony forfeited. Futile expeditions of Edward (1294, 1296, and 1297, in alliance with the Count of Flanders) against Philip. Philip, busy with his contest against Boniface VIII and other matters, returned Gascony to Edward (1303).

DOMESTIC AFFAIRS:

1290. Expulsion of the Jews: Hitherto the Jews had been protected by the kings, as they were important sources of loans. By this time public opinion was hostile to the Jews, and the Italian houses, like the Bardi and Peruzzi, were ready to finance royal loans. Foreign trade, like banking, was in the hands of foreigners, and there were few native merchants, except for wool export, where Englishmen did about 35 per cent of the business, Italians 24 per cent. The English wool staple was established in Antwerp under Edward.

1296. The clash with Pope Boniface VIII: Winchelsey, Archbishop of Canterbury, in accordance with the bull *Clericis laicos,* led the clergy in refusing a grant to the crown. Edward, with the general support of public opinion, withdrew the protection of the royal courts, and thus promptly brought the clergy to an evasion of the bull through "presents" to the crown; the lands of recalcitrant clergy were confiscated, the pope soon modified his stand, and the victory of Edward was complete.

Institutional and "legislative" developments: (1) The Parliament of 1275 granted (hitherto permission had not been asked) an increase of the export duty on wool and leather to the king, to meet the rising cost of government. (2) **Distraint of knighthood:** Various enactments (beginning in 1278) to insure that all men with a given income (e.g. £20 a year from land) should assume the duties of knighthood. Probably primarily an effort to raise money, the acts also ensured a militia under royal control. (3) *Statute of Gloucester* (1278), providing for *quo warranto* inquests into the right of feudal magnates to hold public (i.e. not manorial) courts. (4) *Statute de religiosis* (Statute of Mortmain, 1279), forbade gifts of land to the clergy without consent of the overlord (a usual policy elsewhere in Europe). Such consent was often given; the statute frequently evaded. (5) *Second Statute of Westminster* (*De donis conditionalibus,* 1285) perpetuated feudal entail (i.e. conditional grants of lands), and led to the later law of trusts. It also reorganized the militia and provided for care of the roads. (6) *Third Statute of Westminster* (*Quia emptores,* 1290) forbade new sub-infeudations of land. Land could be freely transferred, but the new vassal must hold direct of the king or from a tenant-in-chief.

1295. The Model Parliament. The writs of summons included (probably by accident) the famous phrase, *quod omnes tangit ab omnibus approbetur* (let that which toucheth all be approved by all). Bishops, abbots, earls, barons, knights, burgesses, and representatives of the chapters and parishes were summoned. The clergy did not long continue to attend Parliament, preferring their own assembly (*Convocation*) and left only the great prelates, who sat rather as feudal than ecclesiastical persons.

1297. The Confirmation of Charters (*Confirmatio cartarum*), a document almost as important as *Magna Carta,* extorted by a coalition of the barons (angered by taxation and the Gascon expedition) and

the middle classes (irritated by mounting taxes) under the leadership of Archbishop Winchelsey. In effect the Confirmation included *Magna Carta* (and other charters) with the added provision that no non-feudal levy could be laid by the crown without a parliamentary grant. Edward left the actual granting of this concession to his son Edward as regent, and Pope Clement V later dispensed Edward from the promise in exchange for the right to collect (for the first time) annates in England. Edward did not surrender tallage, despite the so-called statute *de tallagio non concedendo.*

1303. The *carta mercatoria* granted the merchants full freedom of trade and safe conduct, in return for a new schedule of customs dues.

1305. The petition from the barons and commonalty of the Parliament of Carlisle to end papal encroachments, notably in provisions and annates. Edward enforced the petition except in the matter of annates.

The reign is remarkable for frequent consultation of the middle class (in Parliament and out), for the encouragement of petition to Parliament (now one of its chief functions), and for frequent meetings of Parliament, which educated the nation not merely in the elements of self-government but in ideas, and kept the crown in close contact with public opinion. The word *statute* as used of this reign means any formal royal regulation intended to be permanent, and does not imply formal parliamentary enactment.

Judicial developments. Under Edward the differentiation of the great common law courts is clear: (1) **Court of King's Bench** (concerned with criminal and crown cases); (2) **Court of Exchequer** (dealing with royal finance); (3) **Court of Common Pleas** (handling cases between subjects). The **King's Council** (Small Council) still remained supreme as a court by virtue of its residual and appellate jurisdiction, and the councillors were expected to take the councillor's oath to the king. Edward began the practice of referring residual cases which did not readily come within the jurisdiction of the common law courts to the chancellor with a committee of assessors from the council. This chancellor's court tended to absorb the judicial business of the council and finally emerged as a court of equity. The **Year Books,** unofficial, verbatim reports in French (the language of the courts) of legal proceedings, a record unique for completeness in the period, began in this reign. Coherence and continuity of tradition among the lawyers was greatly facilitated by the establishment of the **Inns of Court** under the three Edwards. Here the lawyers assembled their libraries, lodged, and studied, transmitting with increasing strength the living force of the Common Law, to the virtual exclusion of Roman Law.

PROGRESS OF ENGLISH CULTURE: Architecture: Early English Gothic (under French influence): Canterbury, begun 1175; Lincoln, 1185-1200; Salisbury, 1220-1258. Decorated Gothic: Choir of Lincoln, 1255-1280; York, west front, 1261-1324.

Painting and minor arts: St. Albans at the opening of the 13th century was the greatest artistic center in Europe (manuscript painting by Matthew Paris). The court of Henry III was a mecca for European craftsmen, especially Frenchmen.

Literature: Orm's *Ormulum* (early 13th century), a translation into English of portions of the Gospels; the *Ancren Rewle*, rules for the ascetic life tinged with the cult of the Virgin (c. 1200); Layamon's *Brut*, an English verse translation of Wace's *Brut*. Political songs and satires of the Barons' War, etc. (e.g. *Song of the Battle of Lewes; the Husbandman's Complaint*). Matthew Paris (c. 1200–1259), a friend of Henry III, monk of St. Albans, in his compilation, the *Historia Maior*, covered the history of the world, but in the portion dealing with the years 1235-1259 produced a work of original research in which he glorified England and things English.

Foundation of **Cambridge University** (1209). Foundation of University College (1249); Balliol (1261); Merton (1264) began the collegiate system of Oxford.

Science and learning: Bartholomew Anglicus (c. 1230), *On the Properties of Things*, a popular encyclopedia influenced by Pliny and Isidore, combining accurate observation (e.g. the domestic cat) with discussion of the fantastic (e.g. the griffin).

The English Franciscans at Oxford: Robert Grosseteste (d. 1253), Bishop of Lincoln: insistence on the study of the sources (the Fathers and the Bible); knew Greek and Hebrew, a precursor of the Christian humanists; student of philosophy, mathematics, astronomy, physics, teacher of Roger Bacon. Roger Bacon (d. 1292), greatest mediaeval exponent of observation and experiment. Foresaw the application of mediaeval power to transport, including flying; "formula" for gunpowder; author of the *Opus Maius* and *Opus Minus*.

Opponents of the Thomist rationalists: Duns Scotus (c. 1270-1308) and William of Occam (c. 1300-1349). (*Cont. p. 264.*)

(2) *Scotland*, 1034-1304

1034-1286. Racial and political turmoil. Duncan I was followed by his murderer, the usurper

1040-1057. Macbeth, and his son and avenger

1059-1093. MALCOLM CANMORE. Malcolm was forced to do some kind of homage by William the Conqueror (1072) and by William Rufus (1091), and Anglo-Norman penetration began. Malcolm's wife, (Saint) Margaret (sister of Edgar Aetheling, grand-niece of Edward the Confessor), was a masterful and remarkable woman whose Anglicizing influence on Scottish culture, on the national life and the native Church was profound. Her three sons, especially

1124-1153. DAVID I, continued the so-called "bloodless Norman conquest," and the new Anglo-Norman aristocracy (e.g. Baliols, Bruces, Lindsays, Fitz Alans, i.e. Stewarts) became the bulwark of the crown.

1153-1286. The next four reigns were notable for the consolidation of Scotland, and for signs of impending collision with the English monarchy. William the Lion, captured in a raid by the English, accepted (1174) the feudal lordship of the English crown and did ceremonial allegiance at York (1175). Richard I weakened England's position, John tried to restore it.

1249-1286. ALEXANDER III did homage (1278) to the English king for his English lands, "reserving" his Scottish fealty. All of Alexander's issue were dead by 1284, leaving only his granddaughter Margaret, the *Maid of Norway*. Margaret's death (1290) made impossible the personal union of England and Scotland (by Margaret's marriage to Edward I's heir). Thirteen claimants to the Scottish crown were narrowed down to the candidacy of Robert Bruce and John Baliol. Edward I of England, called upon to arbitrate, awarded the crown to Baliol (1292), but when Baliol ignored a summons to attend Edward and instead embarked upon an alliance with France (1295), the English invaded the country and, after some years of warfare, reduced it in 1304 (p. 199). (*Cont. p. 272.*)

(3) *Ireland*, 1171-1307

The period following the expedition of Henry II (1171) was marked by a steadily developing conflict between the feudal system of the incoming Normans and the

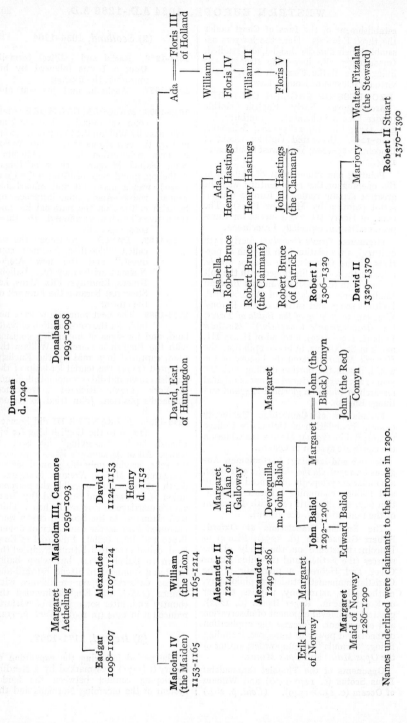

The Scottish Succession

Names underlined were claimants to the throne in 1290.

old tribal organization of the Irish. In its later phases this struggle bred centuries of discord and bloodshed. Henry's authority was precariously maintained by a viceroy who had orders to be fair to the natives, a policy which estranged the Norman elements.

1185. Henry's son, John Lackland, returned to England after a short and inglorious rule as Lord of Ireland, but his authority was maintained by his representative, William Marshal, Earl of Pembroke, who married the daughter of Richard of Clare.

1213. John abandoned Ireland, along with England, to Pope Innocent III.

1216-1272. Under Henry III the power and possessions of the Anglo-Norman colony expanded rapidly: bridges and castles were built, towns prospered and guilds were formed.

1272-1307. Edward I's revolutionary legislation in England was extended to Ireland, which continued to prosper, at least in the Anglo-Norman sections. But the cleavage between the two races had become very marked and the native clans remained restive. (*Cont. p. 272.*)

b. SCANDINAVIA

(1) *Denmark,* 950-1320

c. 950-985. HAROLD BLUETOOTH, whose reign saw a steady advance of Christianity and expansion of Danish power over Schleswig, the Oder mouth, and Norway. But the kingship was of little importance until the reign of

985-1014. SVEN I (*Forked-beard*). He defeated the Norwegians, Swedes, and Wends and conquered England (1013).

1014-1035. KNUT THE GREAT (*Canute*), Sven's son, was King of Denmark, Norway (1028), and England (1016-1035), the first "northern empire." Knut's conversion completed the conversion of his people. He imported priests, architects, and artisans from his English realm, and new influences spread from Denmark to Norway and Sweden. On his death Norway broke away, England passed to Edward the Confessor.

1157-1182. Under **WALDEMAR THE GREAT,** the founder of the Waldemarian dynasty, a great expansion eastward took place at the expense of the Wends; Copenhagen was established as the capital.

1182-1202. KNUT VI made conquests in (Slavonic) Mecklenburg and Pomerania.

1202-1241. WALDEMAR II (*the Conqueror*) led crusading expeditions into Livonia, Estonia (Reval founded), and penetrated the Gulf of Finland, making the southern Baltic a Danish lake (the second "northern empire"). This empire collapsed in 1223, and the advance was in fact more in the nature of a crusade than of permanent imperial expansion. The monarchy was now dominant, the nobles largely feudalized, the clergy (with royal grants) powerful, the bourgeoisie vigorous (fisheries and cattle-raising), the yeoman class strong and independent.

1241-1250. ERIC PLOWPENNY, whose reign was taken up with civil war against his brothers Christopher and

1250-1252. ABEL, who was supported by his brother-in-law, the Count of Holstein, and also by the Swedes and by the city of Lübeck.

1252-1259. CHRISTOPHER. His effort to tax the Church opened a struggle that lasted nearly a century.

1259-1286. ERIC (V) GLIPPING. He was forced by the nobility to sign a charter, the Danish Magna Carta (1282), recognizing the national assembly and initiating the subordination of the king to the law. He continued the contest with the clergy, fought against dynastic rivals, planned expansion in Mecklenburg and Pomerania, and lost Scania and North Halland to Sweden.

1286-1320. ERIC (VI) MENVED, during whose reign the conflict between the crown and the Church came to a head. By a compromise (1303) the rights of the Church were guaranteed, but the king's right to levy military service on church lands was upheld. (*Cont. p. 310.*)

(2) *Sweden,* 993-1319

The origins of the Swedish kingship are obscure, but the kingdom may be dated back to the union of Gothia and Svealand (prior to 836). The conversion of the country to Christianity took place in the 9th century and

993-1024. OLAF SKUTKONUNG was the first Christian ruler. He was the son of Eric the Conqueror, the founder of the Northern Kingdom, and brought to Sweden many Anglo-Saxon workers. His wars with St. Olaf of Norway led to some conquests, which were soon lost. The century following his death was marked by wars between the Goths and the Swedes and by what appear to have been religious conflicts.

1134-1150. SVERKER. Amalgamation of
the Swedes and Goths with alternation of rulers from the two peoples (an
arrangement which continued for a century). The monarchy gradually became
established on a firm basis and the progress
of Christianity was marked by the foundation of many bishoprics (including Uppsala,
1163). The first monasteries also belong to
this period.

1150-1160. ERIC IX (*the Saint*), whose
reign was a short golden age. He
led a crusade into Finland, the
first real expansion of Sweden.
The line of St. Eric came to an end
with

1223-1250. ERIC LAESPE, whose reign
was dominated by his brother-in-
law, Jarl (i.e. Earl) **Birger Magnusson,** the
greatest statesman of mediaeval Sweden.
He controlled the government from 1248–
1266 and had his son elected king in 1250,
thus founding the Folkung line.

1250-1275. WALDEMAR. As regent, Jarl
Birger abolished judicial ordeal by
fire, ended serfdom by choice, encouraged
commerce, favored the settlement of German artisans, checked the power of the
baronage. He attempted to introduce typical European feudalism, setting up his other
sons in quasi-independent duchies.

1279-1290. MAGNUS LADULOS, who
had dethroned and imprisoned his
brother Waldemar. Magnus continued his
father's feudal innovations, extended the
powers of the clergy and set up an hereditary nobility. Town charters became numerous as the burghers became prosperous
through trade and mining.

1290-1319. BIRGER (son of Magnus). His
rule was chaotic, due to civil war
with his brothers, whom Birger ultimately
captured and executed. This led to a popular uprising and the expulsion of Birger,
who was followed by his three-year-old
nephew.   (*Cont. p.* 312.)

(3) Norway, 872-1319

Norway was a region with little natural
unity, which in the earlier mediaeval period
was ruled by numerous petty kings.

872-930. HAROLD HAARFAGER (*Fairhair*) began the unification of the
country by deposing many of the chieftains
(traditionally including Hrolf or Rollo). It
was in this period that the Norsemen supposedly made their conquests in Iceland,
the Faroes, Shetlands, Orkneys, Hebrides,
Scotland, and Ireland.

935-961. HAAKON THE GOOD, who attempted, prematurely, to convert
the country to Christianity.

995-1000. OLAF (I) TRYGVESSON, who,
with the aid of English clergy,
converted Norway, Iceland, and Greenland.
He was defeated by the Kings of Denmark
and Sweden, who supported the Norwegian
nobility. There followed a period of feudal
disruption.

1016-1028. OLAF II (*St. Olaf*) reunited the
country and established Christian-
ity on a firm footing.

1046-1066. HARALD (III) HARDRADA,
who was defeated by King Harold
of England in the **battle of Stamford Bridge**
(p. 168). There followed another period of
confusion, marked by constant wars of
succession, and by a struggle against the
growing power of the clergy. Nevertheless
the expansion of trade brought increasing
prosperity.

1184-1202. SVERRE. He was able to maintain a strong monarchy in the face
of aristocratic and clerical opposition,
thanks to support from the small landowners. Nevertheless Norway continued to
be troubled with dynastic conflict.

1223-1262. HAAKON IV, a strong king,
who temporarily restored order,
conquered Iceland, but was defeated in a war with Scotland.

1262-1299. ERIK THE PRIEST-HATER,
whose reign was marked by a war
with the Hansa towns, in which he suffered
a reverse. As a result he was obliged to
grant the towns full privileges in Norway
and to join the Hanseatic League.

1299-1319. HAAKON V, marking the culmination of decline of the royal
power.

The crown in Scandinavia depended on
its vassals for soldiers and for administration. The introduction of cavalry (first
recorded in Denmark, 1134) accentuated
this feudal tendency, and a new nobility
emerged. This nobility was a professional
military class always ready for war, exempt
from taxes; it quickly became a governing
class receiving local offices and lands as a
reward for military services. From Denmark this new society spread to Norway
and Sweden. Henceforth the nobles added
a further complication to dynastic wars,
causing a series of crises, and restricting the
normal evolution of royal power.

German capital and German merchants
began to penetrate Scandinavia, achieving
by the second half of the 13th century a
dominating position. The growth of the
Hanseatic League delayed the progress of
the native bourgeoisie, but commerce led to
the active growth of towns and town life.
Population was increasing rapidly, lands
were cleared, the arts were advancing
in distinction and perfection under the

patronage of wealthy kings and prosperous prelates.

The heroic age of the Icelandic *skalds* (court poets) in the 10th and 11th centuries brought the art to an involved perfection and a concentration on war that ultimately killed it. Meantime the kings, interested in politics as well as war (notably Sverre of Norway, c. 1185) began to patronize the Norwegian story-tellers, particularly the Icelanders, and the **Sagas** emerged. The greatest master of the new form was an Icelander, **Snorri Sturleson** (1179–1241), an active political figure in both Iceland and Norway. Snorri's *Younger Edda* in prose and verse, containing the rules of versification, the old myths, and a collection of ancient Icelandic poems, is unique. History was written by **Saxo Grammaticus** (died c. 1208), whose *Historia Danica* is the chief source for the Hamlet story. Both Snorri and Saxo were preoccupied with the ideals of national unity, strong royal power, and resistance to baronial particularism.

(*Cont. p.* 312.)

c. GERMANY UNDER THE SALIAN AND HOHENSTAUFEN EMPERORS, 1024-1268

1024-1125. THE FRANCONIAN (or Salian) **HOUSE.** Dawn of the great imperial age.
1024-1039. CONRAD II (the Salian). He continued the general policy of Henry: personally interested only in the churches of Limburg and Speyer, he was firm in his dealings with the Church in general and relied on the lesser nobles to balance the clergy and magnates. The *ministeriales,* laymen of humble or even servile origin, were used to replace the clergy in many administrative posts; regalian rights were retained and exploited. Dukedoms were not regranted as they fell vacant, but were assigned to Conrad's son Henry, who on his accession to the crown held all but the duchies of Lorraine and Saxony. By encouraging the making of fiefs heritable Conrad weakened the dukes and got the support of the lesser nobles, but insured the ultimate feudalization of Germany. Conrad's imperial coronation (1027), one of the most brilliant in mediaeval Rome, was witnessed by two kings, Canute the Great and Rudolf III of Burgundy. Burgundy, willed to Conrad by Rudolf III, guardian of one road to Italy, was reincorporated (1033) in the empire on the death of Rudolf. Failure of an expedition (1030) against Stephen of Hungary; successful disciplinary expedition (1031) against the Poles; recovery of Lusatia; payment of homage by the Poles.

1039-1056. HENRY III (*the Black*). Imperial authority at its height. A period of great town prosperity, due to development of trade. His wife, Agnes of Poitou, was an ardent devotee of Cluny; Henry, an honest reformer, abandoned simony, purified the court along Cluniac lines, but retained a firm hold on the Church. Strongest of the German emperors, he asserted his mastery in Poland, Bohemia, and Hungary; Saxony was the only duchy to keep a trace of its original independence; resumption of the dangerous practice of granting duchies outside the royal house made Germany a feudal vol-

---

The Salian Emperors

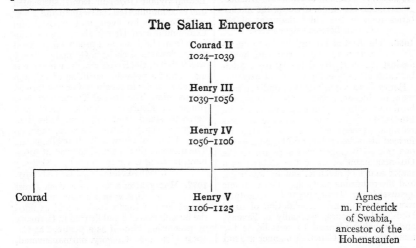

Conrad II
1024–1039

Henry III
1039–1056

Henry IV
1056–1106

Conrad   Henry V
                1106–1125

Agnes
m. Frederick
of Swabia,
ancestor of the
Hohenstaufen

cano; use of the *ministeriales* in administration, but retention of the bishops as principal advisers and administrators. Henry's reforms alienated the bishops, the magnates, and the nobles.

1043. Henry proclaimed the "**Day of Indulgence**," forgiving all his foes and exhorting his subjects to do likewise; Bratislav of Bohemia forced (1041) to do homage; pagan reaction in Hungary put down (1044); final peace in Hungary (1052), which became a fief of the German crown. Homage of Denmark, repudiated soon after.

1046. Synods of Sutri and Rome: deposition at Henry's instigation of three rival popes and election of his nominee, Clement II, the first of a series (Clement, Leo IX, and Nicholas II) of reforming German popes; reaffirmation of the imperial right of nomination to the papacy.

1047. Godfrey the Bearded, Duke of Upper Lorraine, disappointed at Henry's refusal to award him Lower Lorraine, stirred up serious disaffection, and finally joined Baldwin of Flanders in a revolt at first supported by Henry of France (1047); he married (1054) Beatrice, widow of Boniface, Marquis of Tuscany, one of the most powerful Italian supporters of the popes.

1056-1106. HENRY IV. (Aged six at his accession; nine-year regency of his pious, colorless mother Agnes.) During the regency lay and clerical magnates appropriated royal resources and sovereign rights with impunity, and dealt a fatal blow to the German monarchy.

1062. Anno, Archbishop of Cologne, kidnaped the young king and with **Adalbert**, Archbishop of Hamburg-Bremen, governed in his name, dividing the monasteries (one of the chief resources of the crown) between themselves.

1066. The Diet of Tribur, thanks to the reaction of the clergy and nobles against Adalbert, freed Henry from Adalbert and his personal government began.

Henry was a remarkable but undisciplined man, intelligent, resolute, ill-balanced, and headlong, with the odds against him from the start; under papal pressure he was reconciled (1069) with his wife Bertha, reformed his personal life, and began a vigorous rule. His policy was a return to the Ottonian habit of using the Church as a major source of revenue; simony was open, and the reforming party appealed to Rome against Henry. Henry began the recapture, reorganization, and consolidation of royal lands and revenues, especially in Saxony, and probably planned to consolidate the monarchy in the Capetian manner around

a compact core of royal domain in the Harz-Goslar region.

1073. A great conspiracy of the leading princes led to a rising of virtually all Saxony. Henry came to terms with the pope, played one faction off against the other, won the South German baronage, and finally defeated the rebels (1075).

1074. Charter of Worms, the first imperial charter issued direct to citizens without episcopal intervention.

1075-1122. THE STRUGGLE OVER LAY INVESTITURE. The German bishops, alarmed at Hildebrand's reform policy (p. 218), opposed his confirmation as pope, but Henry, in the midst of the Saxon revolt, sanctioned it, and apparently promised reforms in Germany. The sudden abolition of lay investiture would have reduced the emperor's power in Germany and would have made government impossible. With the end of the Saxon revolt Henry's interest in reform vanished.

1075. Pope Gregory, at the Lenten Synod, issued a rigorous reform program and later sent a stern warning to the emperor and the German episcopate. Henry, under pressure from his bishops, called

1076. The Synod of Worms: The bishops repudiated their allegiance to Pope Gregory, addressed a list of (ridiculous) charges to him, and declared him deposed. Henry's letter to the pope associated him with the charges and demanded Gregory's abdication in the most insolent and violent terms. Public opinion was shocked at the letter, but the North Italian bishops at Piacenza supported Henry. Gregory at the Lenten Synod (1076) in Rome, suspended and excommunicated the German and Lombard prelates involved, and deposed and excommunicated Henry, absolving his subjects from allegiance and producing political and ecclesiastical chaos in Germany. Henry was isolated, the Saxon rebellion broke out again, and a powerful coalition of German magnates eager to regain power was formed against him. The Diet of Tribur (October) compelled Henry to humble himself and agree to stand trial and clear himself of Gregory's charges before Feb. 22, 1077, on pain of the withdrawal of their allegiance. The princes called a synod to meet at Augsburg, inviting Gregory to preside; Gregory accepted and started for Germany.

1077. Henry, after a midwinter dash across the Alps with his wife, was welcomed by the North Italians and avoided the humiliation of a public trial in Germany by presenting himself as a penitent at Canossa (Jan. 21). Gregory, outmaneuvered, hesitated three days, and finally, on the appeals of the Countess Matilda and Abbot Hugh of Cluny (Henry's godfather), accepted Henry's promises and solemn oaths of contrition, and absolved him. The penance at Canossa is hardly mentioned by contemporaries, and made much less impression in Germany than the excommunication; the chief source on the episode is Gregory's letter of justification to the disappointed German nobles; Gregory, after some months of waiting for a safe conduct into Germany, turned back.

1077. A faction of the nobles elected an anti-king, **Rudolph of Swabia**, with the approval of Gregory's legates, but without papal confirmation.

1077-1080. Civil war ensued, but Henry, loyally supported by the towns, gained strength steadily; Rudolph of Swabia was defeated and killed (1080); Gregory again excommunicated and deposed Henry, but a synod of German and North Italian prelates then deposed Gregory, naming as his successor Guibert of Ravenna, a reforming bishop and former friend of Gregory (1080).

1083. Henry, at the end of a series of expeditions to Italy (1081-1082), besieged Rome; after futile efforts at reconciliation he gained entrance to the city and Gregory called in his Norman allies. Henry, crowned at Rome by his anti-pope, invaded Apulia; **Robert Guiscard** expelled him from Rome and sacked (1084) the city. The horrors of the Norman sack made it impossible for Gregory to remain in Rome and he departed with his allies, dying as their "guest" in Salerno (1085). The papal position was justified by **Manegold of Lautenbach's** theory that an evil ruler violates a contract with his subjects and may therefore be deposed by the pope, who is responsible for the salvation of mankind. Henry's advocate, **Peter Crassus**, based his denial of this right on historical precedent backed by citations of Justinian (one of the earliest examples of such quotations).

1093-1106. Gregory's successors, unbending champions of reform, supported the revolts of Henry's sons in Germany and Italy: Conrad (1093), and the future **Henry V** (1104). Henry was elected king, but his father retained the loyalty of the towns to the end. Henry V shamefully entrapped and imprisoned his father, who abdicated, escaped, and was regaining ground when he died.

1106-1125. HENRY V (married to Matilda, daughter of Henry I of England in 1114). A brutal, resourceful, treacherous ruler, Henry continued his father's policies.

Skillfully pretending to be dependent on the princes he continued lay investiture, opposed papal interference in Germany, and retained the support of the lay and clerical princes; meantime, relying on the towns and *ministeriales*, he built up the nucleus of a strong power. Wars against Hungary, Poland, and Bohemia (1108-1110).

1110-1111. Imposing expedition to Italy to secure the imperial crown, universally supported in Germany. In Italy the Lombard towns (except Milan) and even the Countess Matilda yielded to Henry. Pope Paschal II (1099-1118) offered to renounce all feudal and secular holdings of the Church (except those of the See of Rome) in return for the concession of free elections and the abandonment of lay investiture, a papal humiliation more than equal to the imperial mortification at Canossa. At Henry's coronation the clergy repudiated Paschal's renunciation, there was a scuffle, Henry took the pope and cardinals prisoners, and forced the pope to acknowledge the imperial powers. The net result was nil, but papal prestige was badly damaged.

1114-1115. A series of revolts (Lorraine, along the lower Rhine, in Westphalia, and soon in East Saxony and Thuringia). Henry was saved by the loyalty of the South Germans.

1115. **Matilda, Countess of Tuscany,** who had made over all her vast holdings to the papacy, retaining them as fiefs with free right of disposition, willed these lands to Henry on her death, and Henry arrived in Italy to claim them (1116-1118).

Both pope and emperor were weary of the investiture controversy, Europe was preoccupied with the Crusades (p. 255), and the time was ripe for compromise. The first important compromise negotiated by the pope was with Henry I of England (1107) and provided that the king should not invest with the spiritual symbols (the ring and the staff), but that he was to be present or represented at all elections. After due homage the king should then invest with the symbols of temporal authority. In France a similar compromise was reached in practice with Philip I (c. 1108). Pope Calixtus II convinced Henry that neither Henry of England nor Philip of France had suffered by their compromise.

1122. At the **Synod of Worms,** under the presidency of a papal legate, the **Concordat of Worms** was drawn up in two documents of three brief sentences each which provided that: (1) elections in Germany were to be in the presence of the emperor or his representative, without simony or violence; in the event of disagreement the emperor was to decide; the emperor was to invest with the temporalities before the spiritual investiture; (2) in Italy and Burgundy consecration was to follow within six months of election; the emperor to invest with the *regalia* after homage. This concordat ended the investiture struggle, but not the bitter rivalry of pope and emperor, for the papacy, now clearly the independent spiritual leader of Europe, could not long tolerate an imperial rival.

1125. Henry left no direct heir, and at the bitterly fought election of 1125 the Archbishops of Mainz and Cologne, foes of the anti-clerical Salian line, cleverly prevented, with papal aid, the election of the nearest heir, Frederick of Swabia, of the House of Hohenstaufen, on the ground that the hereditary principle was dangerous, and Lothair of Supplinburg, Duke of Saxony, was chosen, opening the great struggle of Welf and Waiblinger (Hohenstaufen) in Germany (**Guelf and Ghibelline** in Italy).

1125-1137. LOTHAIR II. Elected by the support of the clergy, he remained loyal to the Church, was the first German king to ask papal approval of his election and did not exercise his rights under the Concordat of Worms for some years. Bitter civil war against the Hohenstaufens (1125-1135); vigorous policy of German expansion among the Wends and Scandinavians; renewal of Wendish conversions (1127).

1133. Influenced by Bernard of Clairvaux, Lothair decided in favor of Pope Innocent II (against Anacletus II) and went to Italy to settle the papal schism; he was crowned; had the Concordat of Worms confirmed, and received the lands of Matilda as fiefs.

1135. The "year of pacification" in Germany — general peace proclaimed. Lothair apparently planned to create a vast dynastic holding for his son-in-law, the Welf Henry the Proud, to include Bavaria, Swabia, Saxony, the allodial lands and fiefs of Matilda of Tuscany, and to secure him the imperial crown. Lothair died suddenly on his return from an expedition against King Roger II of Sicily, and in the election (1138) the clergy, led by Adalbert of Treves, had the Waiblinger, Conrad of Hohenstaufen, chosen. Conrad almost at once put Henry the Proud under the ban, gave Saxony to Albert the Bear, Bavaria to Leopold of Austria, his half-brother, and reopened the civil war.

1138-1268. The **HOUSE OF HOHENSTAUFEN** (from Staufen, their Swabian castle). The first German dynasty to be conscious of the full historical implications of the imperial tradition and the significance of Roman law for imperial pretensions. Their consequent devotion to a policy of centralization and to the aggrandizement of the lay imperial power in the face of the new spiritual supremacy and political aspirations of the Papacy precipitated a second great struggle between the popes and the emperors, centering in Italy but turning upon a sharp conflict between rival spiritual and political concepts.

1138-1152. CONRAD III, a gallant, knightly, attractive, popular hero, but no statesman. The Welf, **Henry the Lion** (son and successor of Henry the Proud), acknowledged Conrad's title, but regained Saxony by force and was granted it by the peace (1142); the struggle of Welf and Waiblinger reduced Germany to chaos and Conrad left on the Second Crusade. On his return Conrad found Germany in worse confusion.

The most significant development of the reign was the renewal of **expansion against the Slavs and Scandinavians** (chiefly on the initiative of Albert the Bear and Henry the Lion): a regularly authorized German crusade against the Slavs (1147); colonization of eastern Holstein; foundation of Lübeck (1143); conversion of Brandenburg and Pomerania; Albert the Bear began to style himself Margrave of Brandenburg; Henry the Lion began the creation of a principality east of the Elbe. Conrad took no share in these developments; was the only king since Henry the Fowler not to attain the imperial title. Alienated from the Church toward the end of his life, Conrad was preparing a more vigorous assertion of the imperial position, and supported the strong imperialist Frederick of Swabia, his nephew, as candidate for the throne. On Conrad's death anarchy was so prevalent in Germany that even the magnates favored a strong ruler, and Conrad's candidate, Frederick, Duke of Swabia, was unanimously elected.

1152-1190. FREDERICK I (*Barbarossa,* i.e. *Red Beard*), a handsome man with flowing golden hair, who could both frighten and charm, the embodiment of the ideal mediaeval German king. A close student of history and surrounded with Roman legists, he regarded himself as heir to the tradition of Constantine, Justinian, and Charlemagne (whom he had canonized by his anti-pope), and aimed at restoring the glories of the Roman Empire. He began the style *Holy Roman Empire.*

The Welf and Hohenstaufen Families

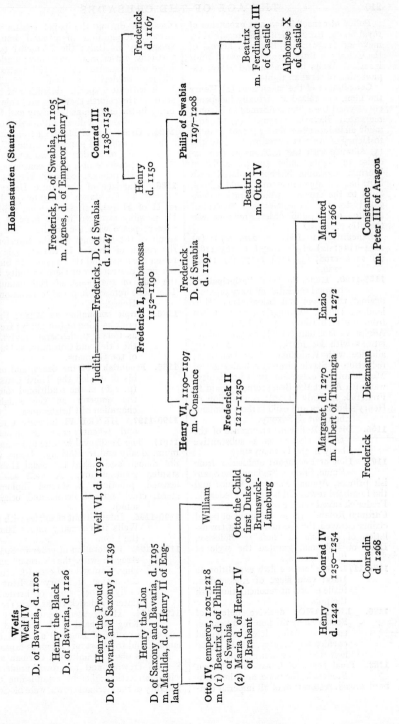

Policy of consolidation and expansion of royal lands: Burgundian lands regained by marriage (1156) with Beatrice, heiress of the County of Burgundy; purchase of lands from the Welfs in Swabia and Italy; exploitation of regalian rights.

Conciliation of the magnates: (1) Henry the Lion, recognized as virtually independent beyond the Elbe; confirmed in Saxony; regranted Bavaria (1156). (2) Austria made an independent duchy (1156), granted to Henry of Austria in return for Bavaria. (3) Alliance with the episcopate: free exercise of rights under the Concordat of Worms; reforming bishops replaced with hard-headed appointees of the old school, loyal to the crown. Administration delegated to the *ministeriales.* Successful maintenance of public order; Frederick won the title *pacificus.*

Expeditions to Italy (*p.* 219, *seq.*): (1) 1154–1155; (2) 1158–1162; (3) 1163–1164; (4) 1166–1168; (5) 1174–1177; (6) 1184–1186.

1156–1180. Henry the Lion's "principality" beyond the Elbe: military progress against the Slavs and colonization (Hollanders, Danes, Flemings); Bremen taken from the archbishop (1156), Lübeck from Adolph of Holstein (1158); commercial relations with Denmark, Sweden, Norway; alliance with Waldemar II of Denmark; reduction of Slavic pirates; colonization of Mecklenburg, extension of Christianity; war with Albert the Bear; refusal of aid to Frederick in Italy (1176); confiscation of Henry's holdings and exile (1180); dismemberment of Saxony.

1156. Diet of Ratisbon: emergence of the *prince electors* as a substantive body in the German state.

1157. Diet of Besançon: emissaries from Rome, France, England, the Spanish princes, Apulia, Tuscany, Venice and the Lombard towns did honor to Frederick. Frederick saved the life of the papal legate, Cardinal Roland, whose statement of papal claims enraged the German nobles (translation of *beneficia* as "fiefs"). Boleslav, Duke of Bohemia, granted the style of "king" (1158).

1174–1177. Frederick's fifth expedition to Italy: vain siege of Alessandria, futile efforts at reconciliation with the pope.

1176. LEGNANO: decisive defeat of Frederick by the Lombard League, the first major defeat of feudal cavalry by infantry, herald of the new rôle of the bourgeoisie.

1183. Final peace of Constance between Frederick, the pope, and the Lombard towns: restoration of all imperial confiscations during the papal schism confirmed, recognition of general imperial suzerainty in Italy; the Lombard towns virtually autonomous city-states under a loose administration by imperial legates and vicars. Frederick retained the Matildan lands without a specific definition of their status. Henceforth there was no shadow of unity in the empire, as Germany and Italy followed a divergent development.

1184. Great Diet of Mainz: a tremendous mediaeval pageant for the knighting of Frederick's two sons in the presence of a great concourse, 70 (?) princes, 70,000 (?) knights.

1186. Marriage of the future Henry VI to Constance (daughter of Roger II of Sicily), heiress of King William II; possibly arranged in the hope of permanent peace with the empire. The net result of the marriage was the transfer of the center of gravity in the struggle between the popes and the emperors to Sicily, the final destruction of German unity and the ruin of the house of Hohenstaufen. The pope refused imperial coronation to Henry.

1186. Triple coronation at Milan: Frederick as King of Burgundy; Henry as *Caesar* (a deliberate revival of the title), and Constance as Queen of the Germans.

1186. Frederick took the Cross, and until his death led the Third Crusade (p. 256) in the traditional rôle of the emperor as the knightly champion of Christendom.

1190–1197. HENRY VI (already Caesar and regent, crowned emperor, 1191). The Mediaeval Empire at its maximum, ideally and territorially. Henry was not robust, and lacked the usual Hohenstaufen good nature. A good soldier, learned, practical, a shrewd diplomat, stern, cruel, but of heroic and original mind.

1190–1195. Intermittent struggles with the Welfs in Germany under Henry the Lion.

1191–1194. Restoration of order in Sicily: struggle with the Norman anti-king, Tancred of Lecce (d. 1194); coronation of Henry as King of Sicily (1194); birth of Frederick (later Frederick II) at Jesi (1194).

1192–1194. Henry used the captivity of King Richard I of England to make the crown of England a fief of the empire, and to extort an enormous ransom. Henry's plans to unite the German and Sicilian crowns, and to crown Frederick without election, thereby establishing the heredity of the German crown, were blocked by powerful German and papal opposition. Frederick was elected King of the Romans (1196). Plans (traditional with the Norman Kings of Sicily) for the foundations of a Mediterranean empire on the ruins of the Byzantine Empire as the basis for a universal dominion; dynastic marriage with the Greek imperial house; active preparations for a crusade; advance in central Italy and conciliation of northern Italy. Sicilian outbreak against the German administration brutally crushed. Henry's sudden death was followed by a bitter anti-imperial reaction in Italy, by fourteen years of civil war in Germany.

1197-1212. Civil war in Germany, chaos in the empire. Rival kings; Henry's brother, the Waiblinger **Philip of Swabia** (supported by King Philip II of France) and the Welf **Otto of Brunswick**, son of Henry the Lion (supported by King Richard I of England). The German nobles played one side off against the other. Chaos in Sicily, where Pope Innocent III acted as guardian of Frederick (after 1198). Otto's title validated by Innocent (1201); assassination of Philip (1208); imperial coronation of Otto (1209); papal break with Otto (1210) and support of Frederick (with Philip II); Frederick's second election (1211) and dash to Germany.

1211-1250. FREDERICK II (*Stupor Mundi*), a valetudinarian of middle height, courteous, amiable, charming, pitiless, arrogant; the most brilliant ruler and one of the most learned men of his day; a legislator of the first order, able soldier, diplomat, skeptic, one of the leading scientific investigators of his time; an astrologer with the mind of a Renaissance rationalist; Sicilian by taste and training, half Norman by blood, with little of the German about him. Crowned: King of the Romans, 1212; King of the Germans, at Aachen, 1215; Emperor, at Rome, 1220.

1212. Alliance with **King Philip II of France.**

1213. The **Golden Bull of Eger:** Frederick, who had already sworn an oath to keep his two crowns separate and to support the pope, abandoned the German Church to Innocent (conceding the free election of bishops, the right of appeal to Rome) and undertook to support the pope against heretics.

1214. The **battle of Bouvines** (p. 230): Frederick and Philip II completed the defeat of Otto and the Welfs. On the death of Innocent III (1216) Frederick's personal rule may be said to have begun.

1216-1227. Frederick on tolerable terms with Pope Honorius III, his old tutor: election (1220) of Frederick's son Henry as King of the Romans (a violation of Frederick's promise); Frederick allowed to retain Sicily during his lifetime; renewal of his crusading oath; grant of generous privileges (1220) to the clergy: exemption of the Church from taxation and of clerics from lay jurisdiction, making clerical princes virtually independent territorial princes; support of the bishops against the towns; promises to suppress heresy. Crusade postponed until 1225.

1222. First appearance of the **Mongols in Europe** (p. 260); capture of Cracow (1241); defeat of the Hungarians and Silesians.

1226. The conversion of **Prussia** undertaken by the Teutonic Order (p. 214).

1226-1232. Renewal of the ancient imperial claims in Lombardy, formation of the Second Lombard League, and appearance of the **First League of the Rhineland;** town leagues in central Italy; Pope Gregory alienated.

1227-1229. Frederick's crusade (p. 257): return of Frederick due to illness; first excommunication (1227); resumption of crusade (1228); violent papal and imperial propaganda and recrimination; the Teutonic Knights under Hermann of Salza remained faithful to Frederick. Aware of the commerical value of Moslem friendship Frederick negotiated a ten-year truce (1229) with El-Kamil, Sultan of Egypt, which restored Jerusalem, Nazareth, and Bethlehem to Christian hands. Frederick crowned himself King of Jerusalem. Papal war (1228–1229) of devastation in Apulia (first known papal mercenaries, the *soldiers of the keys*); Frederick on his return expelled the papal forces and threatened the *Patrimonium Petri* with invasion.

1230. Hollow peace of **San Germano** with Pope Gregory IX: Frederick promised to protect the papal domains, confirmed papal rights over Sicily, and was absolved. In preparation for the next struggle Frederick concentrated on Italy, especially Sicily. Frederick's son Henry on his majority (1228) devoted himself to Germany, and favored the towns. Frederick, like Barbarossa, had leaned heavily on the German episcopate, especially Engelbert of Cologne, and had increased the independence of the lay princes and *ministeriales*; administrative offices tended to become hereditary, and after Engelbert's death (1225) the administration had become less efficient. Settlement of the Teutonic Knights in Prussia: union (1237) with the Livonian Brothers of the Sword and eastward expansion: foundation of

Thorn (1231), Kulm (1232) and Marienwerder (1233).

1231. Privilege of Worms. Hoping for
German support for his Italian
policy, Frederick extended to the lay
princes his generous grants of 1220 to the
clergy; giving them control over local justice, minting rights, roads, and streams, etc.
From this grant dates a clear emergence in
Germany of the territorial sovereignty of
both lay and clerical princes. The **Decree
of Ravenna** (1232) allowed expansion of the
power of the princes at the expense of the
towns. Henry objected, revolted (1234),
and tried to win the German and Italian
towns to his side.

**1231. Completion of the reorganization of
Sicily:** clean sweep of private titles
and royal privileges in the Norman manner;
resumption of royal domain; destruction of
private garrisons and feudal castles; ban on
private war; criminal jurisdiction transferred from feudal to royal courts; towns
deprived of magistrates and put under royal
officers; clergy taxed and excluded from
civil office. Sicily reduced to order (1221-
1225): feudal revolts put down, towns
brought to heel; large Saracen garrison-
colonies (loyal to Frederick and indifferent
to papal threats) established at Lucera and
Nocera. Recognizing in Sicily the true
source of his strength in money and men,
Frederick aimed to unify Sicily and Italy
into a kingdom of the empire. Local risings
(1228-1230 and 1232) in Apulia and Sicily;
unrest (1234) in southern Italy.

1231. The Constitutions of Melfi, the
most conspicuous and constructive
single piece of "legislation" in the Middle
Ages, completed the Sicilian reorganization:
an efficient divine right absolutism (much
of it a return to the policy of Roger II) profoundly influenced by Roman law; centralization under an expert departmentalized
bureaucracy; clerical jurisdiction limited to
ecclesiastical matters; heresy a civil crime;
simony in civil office a capital offense; gift
or sale of Church land forbidden. Feudal,
clerical, and municipal administration replaced by royal officials; supreme court at
Capua; justices on annual circuits; careful
financial organization. The University of
Naples (the first European university on a
royal charter) founded (1224) to train state
officials, and given a monopoly of higher
education; Salerno revived as a school of
medicine.

Advanced economic policy in Sicily based
on Arab practice: abolition of internal
tolls; mercantilistic regulation, state monopolies. Replacement of feudal dues by
fixed payments; direct taxation in crises,

efficient customs collection and internal
prosperity.

**1235-1237. Frederick's last visit to Ger-
many:** deposition, arrest, and imprisonment of Henry, who committed suicide in prison (1242) and was succeeded by
his brother Conrad (1237); conciliation and
peace with the Welfs strengthened Frederick in Germany. Great reform **Diet of
Mainz** (the German Melfi, 1235); issue of
the model *Landfrieden*. Frederick was unable to stem the steady progress of towns
(resting on expanding commerce) in Germany or Italy.

1237. Frederick at Cortenuova smashed
the Second Lombard League and
humiliated Milan.

**1239. Pope Gregory's second excommuni-
cation** of Frederick, followed by a
tremendous battle of pamphlets and preaching: Frederick painted as a heretic, rake,
anti-Christ. He retorted with a demand for
reform of the Church and an appeal to the
princes of Europe, proposing a league of
monarchs against the papacy.

Beginning of the amalgamation of northern and central Italy with the imperial
administration on Sicilian lines: a system
of general vicariates under imperial vicars,
each city with an imperial *podestà* (generally Apulians, and often relatives of
Frederick).

**1241. Gregory's call for a synod at Rome
to depose Frederick:** Frederick
ravaged papal territory, almost took Rome,
and his fleet captured a large delegation of
prelates off Genoa on their way to the
synod; annexation of papal Tuscany to the
empire. Gregory's death (1241). During
the two-year interregnum in the papacy
Frederick intrigued for a friendly pope, and
welcomed

1243. The election of Sinobaldo Fiesco
(*Innocent IV*), who turned out to
be the architect of his ruin.

**1244. Frederick's invasion of the Cam-
pagna** and vain efforts at reconciliation with the pope; Innocent's
flight to Lyons, and call for a
synod.

1245. The Synod of Lyons: appeal to
the Germans to revolt and elect
a new king; deposition of Frederick; Louis
IX's efforts at conciliation and Frederick's
offers rebuffed by the pope: Innocent unleashed the Franciscans and Dominicans in
a war of propaganda and proclaimed a crusade against Frederick. Henry Raspe,
Duke of Thuringia (d. 1247), was set up
(1246) as an anti-king in Germany, followed
by

1247-1256. William of Holland, who was
supported by a newly formed

league of Rhenish towns. Innocent's ruthless but vain campaign against Frederick's episcopal allies in Germany; bitter warfare in northern Italy with extreme cruelty on both sides; Italian conspiracy to assassinate Frederick (probably with Innocent's knowledge) put down in cold blood; Piero della Vigne, Frederick's most trusted official, supposedly implicated. He was arrested, blinded, and died a suicide (1249); capture of Frederick's son Enzio (1249) who died in prison (1272).

1248. The defeat of Frederick after a long siege of Parma did not destroy his hold on northern Italy.

1250. Sudden death of Frederick; burial in the cathedral at Palermo, where his sarcophagus still remains.

1250-1268. Relentless persecution of the Hohenstaufens by the popes:

1250-1254. CONRAD IV, emperor, and King of Sicily by the will of his father, Frederick; Manfred, his illegitimate half-brother, regent of Sicily; Pope Innocent IV's offer (1253) of the Sicilian crown under papal suzerainty to Edmund (son of Henry III of England); renewal of Conrad's excommunication and proclamation of a crusade against him; papal invasion of the kingdom (i.e., southern Italy and Sicily).

1254-1273. THE GREAT INTERREGNUM. An epilogue to the mediaeval struggle of the popes and the emperors, marks the end of the mediaeval Holy Roman Empire and the failure of imperial efforts to establish German unity; it was a prologue to the complete triumph of particularism which dominated German life until well into the 19th century.

1255-1261. Manfred regained southern Italy (1255) and Sicily (1256), was crowned King of Sicily (1258), and after the Sienese (Ghibelline) victory over Florence at Montaperto (1260) almost dominated Italy; Alexander V's peace offers were rejected by Manfred (1261).

1257. Double election in Germany of two foreigners: Richard of Cornwall (brother of Henry III of England, brother-in-law of Frederick II), and Alfonso X of Castile.

1266. Charles of Anjou (brother of Louis IX of France), accepting Urban IV's offer (1262) of the Sicilian crown under papal suzerainty, invaded southern Italy in accordance with papal plans and with his own ambitions to create a Mediterranean empire. He defeated Manfred who fell in the battle (Benevento, 1266), ending any hope of a native ruler for Italy.

1268. Conradin (Conrad IV's son, aged 15), called from Germany by the Italian Ghibellines, was defeated at Tagliacozzo, betrayed to Charles of Anjou, and beheaded at Naples with, at least, the tacit approval of Pope Clement IV. European public opinion was shocked, and Henry III of England and Louis IX of France were aroused. The heir of the house of Hohenstaufen was Constance, daughter of Manfred, whose husband, Pedro III of Aragon, was destined to become the first Aragonese king of Sicily (1282-1285) (p. 282).

The imperial title remained (1268-1802) an appendage of the German monarchy, but as the Germans were little interested in the title the way to the imperial throne was opened to ambitious foreigners. The bitter struggle of the Hohenstaufens and the popes, followed by removal of the papacy to French soil, alienated the German people from the Roman popes and bred a lasting suspicion of the Latin Church that bore fruit in the nationalism of the Reformation.

The princes of Germany, busy consolidating their own power, were not eager to elect a king, and there was no election until Pope Gregory X, alarmed at the progress of Charles of Anjou and the degeneration of Germany, which reduced papal revenue and indirectly strengthened France, and needing an imperial leader for the crusades, threatened to name an emperor.

SIGNIFICANT ELEMENTS IN 13TH-CENTURY GERMANY:

I. **Great tenants-in-chief:** (1) Four ancient princely houses: the **Ascanians** (Brandenburg and eastern Saxony with the ducal title); the **Welfs** (Brunswick); the **Wittelsbachs** (Upper Bavaria, the County Palatine of the Rhine, Lower Bavaria); the **Wettins** (Saxony after the 15th century); (2) **Ottokar**, King of the Slavic Kingdom of Bohemia (1253-1278), with claims to Austria, Styria, Carinthia, Carniola.

II. **Great ecclesiastical tenants-in-chief:** especially in the Rhineland (notably the Archbishops of **Mainz, Trier,** and **Cologne**).

III. **Three minor houses** about to emerge into importance: (1) **Luxemburgs,** (2) **Hapsburgs,** (3) **Hohenzollerns.**

IV. **Lesser tenants-in-chief** (the so-called *Ritterschaft*), who regarded the central power as their defense against the great princes.

V. **Imperial cities** (*Reichstädte*), growing richer and more powerful and disposed to support the crown against the princes.

Tendency of the cities to organize as leagues.

The informal (until the 14th century) constitution of the German monarchy: (1) Election of the king (originally by tribal chieftains) devolved upon the tenants-in-chief, then upon a group of them; election to be followed by ratification by the others. In the 13th century the group election became final election and was confined to a body of seven electors (of varying personnel.) (2) The ancient feudal *Reichstag* (*curia regis*) became (in the 13th century) the German *Diet* (equivalent to Parliament or the Estates-General) divided into two houses: princes and electors. Its functions remained vague and amorphous. Towns were admitted in 1489.

The great ecclesiastical states of the Rhineland and their feudal satellites reached the zenith of their power in the 13th century, and strove to maintain their position in the face of the rising lay states to the east (Saxony, Brandenburg, Austria, and Bohemia) by electing to the monarchy feeble princes who could pay well for election and would remain amenable. The lay states became dynastic principalities primarily concerned with their own fortunes and anti-clerical in policy. (*Cont. p.* 299.)

The Teutonic Knights

1190-1191. Crusading origin. Merchants of Lübeck and Bremen founded a hospital at Acre which soon became attached to the German church of Mary the Virgin in Jerusalem.

1198. The brethren of this hospital were raised to a military order of knighthood (as the *Order of the Knights of the Hospital of St. Mary of the Teutons in Jerusalem*) by the Germans gathered for Henry VI's crusade. Henceforth membership in the order was open only to Germans, and knighthood only to nobles. Pope Innocent III gave them the rule of the Templars. Headquarters were successively at Acre (1191-1291), Venice, and (after 1309) Marienburg, clear evidence of the new orientation of the Knights. Intense rivalry existed between the order and the Templars and Hospitalers in the Holy Land until the failure of the Crusades turned them to other fields of action. The robes of the Teutonic Knights were white with a black cross.

Reconstitution of the order and **transfer to the eastern frontier** of Germany. The eastward advance (*Drang nach Osten*) of the Germans, begun under Charlemagne, had never wholly ceased, and colonization with Netherlandish farmers and German merchants, coupled with Cistercian efforts during the days of Adolf of Holstein, Albert the Bear (self-styled Margrave of Brandenburg), and Henry the Lion of Saxony, established the Germans firmly in Mecklenburg and Brandenburg. Lübeck (founded 1143) early became an important commercial center. The foundation of Riga (1201), as a crusading and missionary center, the establishment of the *Livonian Brothers of the Sword*, and an influx of Westphalian nobles and peasant immigrants insured the continued advance of Germanization and the progress of Christianity (largely under Cistercian auspices) in Livonia. The defeat of the Danes at Bornhöved (1227) by the combined princes of North Germany, cost them Holstein, Lübeck, Mecklenburg, and Pomerania, leaving only Estonia to Denmark. The Poles had already begun the conversion of the Prussians and East Pomeranians.

1210-1239. Under **HERMANN VON SALZA,** the first great grand master, the order, at the invitation of Andrew of Hungary, was established (1211-1224) in Transylvania as a bulwark against the Comans (Cumani) until their progress alarmed the Hungarian monarch.

Hermann was an intimate friend of Emperor Frederick II, and was the real founder of the greatness and prosperity of the (still relatively poor and insignificant) order.

1226. By the **Golden Bull of Rimini,** Frederick laid down the organization of the order (on Sicilian lines) and prepared the Knights for a new career as pioneers of Germanization and as Christian missionaries on the eastern frontier. Frederick repeatedly made them generous gifts, used them for his own crusade, and employed individual knights on important missions. The grand master was given the status of a prince of the empire.

Organization of the order. Districts, each under a commander; a general chapter, acting as advisers to the grand master; five chief officers; the grand master elected for life by the Knights. The order was nominally under the pope and the emperor, but in the days of its might only strong popes exerted any influence.

1229. The call to Prussia. (The name *Prussia* is probably derived from a native word *Prusiaskai* and not from *Bo-Russia*.) An appeal (1225-1226) from Conrad of Masovia, Duke of Poland, for aid, coinciding with Frederick's reorganization, was accepted by Hermann of Salza, and the Knights embarked on a unique crusade comparable only with that in the Iberian Peninsula, as champions of Christianity and Germanism. Conrad gave (1230) them Kulmerland, and promised them whatever they conquered from the Prussians. Frederick confirmed their rights.

1234. The Knights transferred all their holdings to the pope, receiving them back as fiefs of the Church and thus had no other lord than the distant papacy.

1237. **Union with the Livonian Brothers** was followed by notable progress in Livonia and plans for the conversion of the Russians from the Greek Church to the Roman, which led to a serious defeat for the order. Courland was also gained and Memel founded (1252) to hold the conquests. Eventually the southern Baltic coast from the Elbe to Finland was opened by the order to the missions of the Church and the trade and colonies of the Germans.

A great era of town foundations (some 80 in all) opened under the order: Thorn (castle, 1231), Kulm (castle, 1232), Marienwerder (1233), Elbing (castle, 1237), Memel (1252), Königsberg (1254), *et al.*

1242-1253. **A Prussian revolt** was put down, and the conquest of Prussia continued with aid from Ottokar of Bohemia, Rudolf of Hapsburg, Otto of Brandenburg.

1260. **The battle of Durben,** a disastrous defeat of the order by the Lithuanians, was followed by another Prussian revolt which had national aspects and was put down with Polish aid. The suppression was marked by deliberate extermination and the virtually complete Germanization of Prussia ensued. Castle Brandenburg was built (1266) and the reduction of Prussia completed (1285).

The order allowed great freedom to the towns (especially after 1233); no tolls were collected, only customs dues. The large commercial towns joined the Hanseatic League (p. 307). The Knights were also generous (after 1236) in charters to German (and Polish) nobles, the peasants were well treated, and mass migrations into territories of the Knights became common.

1263. The pope granted the order permission to trade, not for profit, a concession later expanded (by devious means) into full commercial freedom. As a result the order, founded as a semi-monastic crusading society, eventually became a military and commercial corporation of great wealth and selfish aims, and a serious competitor of the very towns it had founded. The Knights escaped the fate of the Templars, though temporarily on the defensive.

Great state was kept at the headquarters in Marienburg, and under Grand Master Winrich (1351-1382) the order was the school of northern chivalry, just as later it became a great cultural influence through the foundation of schools everywhere in its domains and the maintenance of its houses as centers of learning.   (*Cont. p.* 310.)

d. ITALY AND THE PAPACY, 888-1314

The papacy was a local and secular institution until 1048; Italy was without effective native rule.

888-924. Berengar I, last of the phantom "emperors" (vacancy in the empire, 924-962), was the grandson of Louis the Pious. Surviving rival "emperors" were Guido of Spoleto, Lambert his son, and Louis of Provence, who was crowned emperor in 915. **Raids of Saracens** (c. 889) and **Magyars** (c. 898) into Lombardy; a Saracen stronghold at Freinet controlled the Alpine passes; Saracen settlements in southern Italy, and the **Moslem conquest** (827) **of Sicily** began the isolation of that area; Italian urban life had become almost extinct; the invasions were checked, not by the shadowy monarchs, but by the rise of feudal defenders.

914-963. **The nadir of the papacy** (the *pornocracy*): the landed aristocracy of Rome, under the leadership of the Senator Theophylact, his wife Theodora, and his daughter Marozia (mistress of Pope Sergius III, and mother of Sergius' son John, later Pope John XI) dominated the Curia.

928. Marozia, having imprisoned Pope John XI, took control of Rome until her son

932-954. Alberic II assumed power; the *Patrimonium Petri* was a plaything of the **Crescentii** (Marozia's family), who maintained an intermittent supremacy in Rome during the 10th century. The papacy was without political power or spiritual prestige and the Western Church for all practical purposes became a loose organism under its bishops, who gave "national churches" such coherence as they had, and acknowledged a vague kind of allegiance to Rome.

924. Rudolf of (Juran) Burgundy elected king, followed by

926-945. Hugh of Provence.

945. Lothair II (d. 950), Hugh's son and co-regent, was declared sole king. Lothair's rival,

950-961. Berengar II, imprisoned his widow Adelheid, who appealed (according to tradition) to Otto the Great.

951-952. Otto the Great's first expedition to Italy.

961-964. Otto's second expedition to Italy, in answer to the appeal of the profligate pope, John XII, for protection against Berengar. Otto's coronation at Pavia as King of Italy and his coronation by the pope as Roman Emperor, marked the

962. REVIVAL OF THE ROMAN EMPIRE. Otto confirmed his predecessors' grants in the *Patrimonium Petri* (probably with additions), but made careful reservation of the imperial right to sanction papal elections, and treated the pope like a German bishop (i.e. subject to the state). Otto also exacted a promise from the Romans not to elect a pope without imperial consent. He established a precedent by calling a synod at Rome which deposed (963) Pope John XII for murder and other crimes, and selected a (lay) successor, Leo VIII (963-964). This synod opened a period of about a hundred years when the papacy was dominated by the German emperors and by the Counts of Tusculum, vassals of the emperors, with the title of *patricius* in Rome. In the same period the bishops in the west lost the position they had won in the 9th century, and became increasingly dependent on the kings and feudal nobility, and increasingly secular in outlook. The homage of Pandolf I for Capua and Benevento (967) and his investiture with the Duchy of Spoleto, mark the beginning of one imperial effort to include southern Italy in the empire.

964. Leo VIII was expelled by the Romans shortly after his election, and **Benedict V** was (964-965) elected by the Romans without imperial consent.

966-972. Otto's third expedition to Italy: Otto held a synod which deposed Benedict. **Pope John XIII** (elected with imperial co-operation) was soon expelled by the Romans, and Otto, after a terrible vengeance on Rome, restored him. Imperial coronation of the future Otto II (967) by John XIII, coronation of Theophano and her marriage to Otto in Rome (972).

980-983. Otto II's expedition to Italy: Otto crushed Crescentius I, Duke of the Romans, restored the pope (981), and was utterly defeated in his effort to expel the Saracens from southern Italy by a Greco-Moslem alliance (982). Otto nominated **Pope John XIV** (983-984).

983. Great Diet of Verona: remarkable unity of the Italian and German magnates; resolve on a holy war against the Moslems; election of the future Otto III as successor to his father. Venice, already profiting by her Moslem trade, refused ships and defied the emperor.

996. Otto III, on his first expedition to Italy deposed the *Patricius*, Crescentius II, and (at the request of the Roman people) nominated as pope his cousin Bruno, **Gregory V** (996-999), the first German pope, an ardent Cluniac. Gregory and Otto compelled Gerbert to yield the Archbishopric of Reims to the German Arnulf, and forced the French episcopate to acquiesce. Gregory censured King Robert of France. As the successor to Pope Gregory, Otto named **Gerbert of Aurillac.**

999-1003. SYLVESTER II (Gerbert of Aurillac), the first French pope, a man of humble origin, one of the most learned men of his day (Arabic, mathematics, and science). An intriguer and diplomat who co-operated with Otto in his mystic renewal of the empire; he was a moderate reformer, asserting that simony was the worst evil of the Church.

1012-1046. The Tusculan popes were either the relatives or the creatures of the Counts of Tusculum: **Benedict VIII** (1012-1024), something of a reformer; **John XIX** (1024-1032), his brother, and **Benedict IX** (1033-1044), a debauchee who sold the papacy for cash (i.e. the Peter's Pence from England) to his godfather, a priest, **Gregory VI** (1044-1046), who bought the See of Peter in order to reform it. The emperors, preoccupied with German affairs, made only rare visits to Italy.

Notable local efforts were made by the Church to reform itself and society:

(1) Local synods decreed clerical celibacy (e.g. Augsburg, 952; Poitiers, 1000; Seligenstadt, 1023; Bourges, 1031), and attacked simony.

(2) Foundation (910) of the **Abbey of Cluny** by William the Pious, Duke of Aquitaine, as a reformed Benedictine house, wholly free of feudal control, directly under the Holy See. Centralization of all daughter and affiliated houses (priories) under a single Abbot of Cluny; rapid spread of Cluniac organization (France, Lorraine, Germany) and ideas of reform into western Europe: celibacy of the clergy; abolition of lay investiture; and of simony.

(3) Gerard, Lord of Brogne, founded (923) a monastery on his own estate which became a center of ecclesiastical reforms among existing foundations in Flanders and Lorraine.

(4) Synods in Aquitaine and Burgundy

(where monarchical opposition to feudal anarchy was weak) pronounced (c. 989) anathema on ravagers of the Church and despoilers of the poor, initiating a long series of clerical efforts throughout Europe to force feudal self-regulation, which go by the name of the **Peace of God**. These decrees, repeatedly renewed and extended, were supplemented (after c. 1040) by the **Truce of God**, an effort to limit fighting to certain days and seasons of the year.

(5) An effort to restore the central authority of the Church by reference to past decrees, of which the most notable were the so-called *Isidorean* (or Forged) *Decretals*, attributed to Isidorus Mercator, and produced (c. 850) by a Frankish cleric. A combination of authentic and forged papal decrees, they aimed to establish the authority and power of the bishops and the position of the pope as supreme lawgiver and judge, and to make him supreme over councils.

(6) Notable increase in new ascetic orders in Italy and monastic schools north and south of the Alps; outstanding individual reformers (e.g. **Peter Damian,** d. 1072; Lanfranc, d. 1089; Anselm, d. 1109).

ITALY AT THE OPENING OF THE 11TH CENTURY: Sicily was in the hands of the Saracens; Apulia and Calabria under the feeble rule of Constantinople; Gaeta, Naples, Amalfi, were city republics; Benevento, Capua, and Salerno the capitals of Lombard principalities. Norman pilgrims arriving (1016) at the shrine of St. Michael on Monte Gargano began the penetration of the south by Norman soldiers of fortune in the service of rival states: the first permanent Norman establishment was at Aversa (c. 1029); the sons of the Norman Tancred of Hauteville (including Robert Guiscard) appeared (after c. 1035), and their steady advance at the expense of the Greeks led Benevento to appeal for papal protection (1051). Feudal anarchy prevailed in the north.

1027. Conrad II, in Italy for his coronation, restored order in the north, reducing the Lombard nobles.

1037. On a second expedition he disciplined Archbishop Aribert of Milan, restored order in the south; his *constitutio de feudis* made Italian fiefs hereditary.

1044-1046. GREGORY VI purchased the papal throne to reform the papacy, but the end of his reign saw three rival popes (Gregory, Sylvester III, and Benedict IX). All three were deposed by the **Synods of Sutri and of Rome** (1046) under pressure from the reforming emperor, Henry III, who made Suidgar, Bishop of Bamberg,

pope as **Clement II** (1046–1047), the first of a series of German pontiffs: Damasus II (1048), Leo IX (1048–1054), Victor II (1055–1057), representing strong Cluniac influences. Henry pacified southern Italy, reaffirmed the imperial right of nomination to the papacy, and left Italy in sound order.

1049-1085. Restoration of the independence of the papacy, resumption of papal leadership in the Church and of spiritual supremacy in the west.

1049-1054. LEO IX (Bruno of Toul, a kinsman of Henry III) began the identification of the papacy with Cluniac reforms, and the restoration of the spiritual primacy of the Holy See. He insisted on his own canonical election to the papal throne, reorganized the chancery on the imperial model, reformed the Church by personal or legatine visitation, giving reform reality in the west. The **Synod of Rome** (1047) had issued stern decrees against simony and clerical marriage.

1052. Henry III granted the Duchy of Benevento to the papacy.

1053. Leo, in his personal effort to enforce papal rights in the south, was utterly defeated by the Normans at Civitate.

1054. The long doctrinal controversy with the **Greek Orthodox Church,** which really hinged on fundamental divergences between east and west, ended with the final schism between the eastern (Orthodox) and western (Roman) Church (p. 249).

1054-1057. VICTOR II. Elected at the urging of Hildebrand (later Gregory VII), who dominated this pontificate and the following one and who made the papacy the leader in reform. Beatrice, mother of Matilda, and widow of Count Boniface of Tuscany, married (1054) Godfrey the Bearded, Duke of Upper Lorraine, Henry's most dangerous foe in Germany, as Boniface had been in Italy. Henry arrested Beatrice and her daughter Matilda, Boniface's heiress; Godfrey fled; Matilda remained all her life a powerful ally of the papacy, and kept middle Italy loyal to the popes.

1057-1058. STEPHEN IX (brother of Godfrey the Bearded), a zealous Cluniac. The **Pataria** (c. 1056), a popular movement (the result of a preaching campaign), gained wide currency in the Milan region for its demands of clerical celibacy, the end of simony and for apostolic simplicity among the clergy. It came into sharp conflict with the bishop and clergy. Peter Damian, sent by the pope, maintained the papal position (1059), and brought the archbishop to terms; there was a later outbreak of the Pataria.

1058-1061. NICHOLAS II.

1059.   The Synod of the Lateran, by its electoral decree, replaced the vague traditional rights of the Roman clergy in papal elections by an electoral college of cardinals: the prerogative voice in the election went to the seven cardinal bishops; the cardinal clergy represented the clergy and people at large; a Roman prelate (if worthy) was to be preferred; the election to be at Rome if possible. Henry's rights were provided for, but the provision seems to have been personal rather than general.

1059.   Under Hildebrand's influence an alliance was made with the Norman, Richard of Aversa, and Nicholas after exacting an oath later invested Robert Guiscard with the Duchy of Apulia and Calabria, and promised him Sicily if he could conquer it, thereby establishing papal suzerainty over southern Italy, the first great expansion of temporal suzerainty by the popes. The Synod of Melfi condemned (1059) the marriage of clergy.

1061-1073. ALEXANDER II. His election without consultation of Henry IV created serious tension; the Synod of Basel declared the election invalid, and chose an anti-pope. Alexander, on friendly terms with William the Conqueror, blessed the Norman conquest of England.

1071.   Robert Guiscard (d. 1085) captured Bari, ending the Greek power in Italy; his capture of Palermo (1072) began the

1072-1091. Norman conquest of Sicily. Roger I (d. 1101) succeeded Guiscard as lord of southern Italy (except Capua, Amalfi, and papal Benevento).

1073-1085. GREGORY VII (*Hildebrand*). Short, corpulent, with glittering eyes, the son of an Italian peasant educated at Rome under strong Cluniac influence. Inspired by Gregory the Great, Gregory VI, and the study of the Decretals, he was neither an original thinker nor a scholar, but was intensely practical and of lofty moral stature. After a brilliant career in the *Curia* he was acclaimed pope by the Romans before his election. German bishops protested the election, and Gregory postponed his consecration, awaiting Henry's decision in a sincere effort to live up to his ideal of perfect co-operation between pope and emperor in the interest of peace, reform, and the universal monarchy of the papacy. His program was summed up by his *Dictatus*, an informal memorandum which asserted: (1) The Roman Church has never

erred, can never err; (2) the pope is supreme judge, may be judged by none, and there is no appeal from him; (3) no synod may be called a general one without his order; (4) he may depose, transfer, reinstate bishops; (5) he alone is entitled to the homage of all princes; (6) he alone may depose an emperor.

1075-1122. THE INVESTITURE STRUG-GLE: vindication of the spiritual supremacy and leadership of the papacy (p. 206).

The Emperor Henry IV after his Saxon victory forgot his promises of reform in Germany. The Synod of Rome (1075) passed severe decrees against simony, clerical marriage, and (for the first time) against lay investiture, providing deposition for clerical offenders, excommunication for laymen. Gregory's letter of remonstrance and rebuke to Henry was ignored, and Henry, on the urging of the German bishops, called a Synod at Worms (1076). This synod deposed Gregory. Henry's first excommunication and the so-called humiliation at Canossa (1077) profited neither party; Henry's second deposition (1080) was without serious effect. After a series of invasions (1081-1084), Henry entered Rome and was crowned by his anti-pope, only to be expelled by Gregory's Norman ally, Robert Guiscard, with a motley army which included Saracens; the atrocity of the Norman sack made it impossible for Gregory to remain and he died a virtual exile, almost a prisoner of his allies at Salerno, leaving Henry and his anti-pope master of Rome for the time.

Gregory was on excellent terms with William the Conqueror and responsible for Alexander's blessing of the Conquest (1066), but William, true to the Norman conception of strong monarchy, ignored Gregory's pressure to make England a fief of the papacy, and forbade the circulation of papal bulls in England without his permission. Gregory asserted papal suzerainty over Hungary, Spain, Sardinia, and Corsica. After a vacancy of a year, a close friend of Gregory was elected pope, Victor III (1086-1087), an aged, unwilling pontiff, soon driven from Rome by Henry's partisans.

1088-1099. URBAN II. A Frenchman of noble blood, long intimate with Gregory; handsome, eloquent, learned, he continued Gregory's policy of maintaining the complete independence of the papacy and vigorous opposition to the emperors. Urban arranged the marriage of Countess Matilda and the son of the (Welf) Duke of Bavaria (1089).

Henry invaded northern Italy successfully, but Matilda held out in the hills; Urban, profiting by the anarchy in Germany, urged Henry's son Conrad to a revolt (1093) which was taken up by half of Lombardy. Urban at the **Synod of Piacenza** (1095) renewed the decrees against simony and clerical marriage, added a ban on clerical homage to laymen, and received the appeal of the Byzantine emperor for help against the Turks at the **Synod of Clermont** (1095) (p. 255). Urban excommunicated King Philip I of France for adultery, and proclaimed the **First Crusade**, directing his appeal to the nobles and peoples rather than the monarchs, most of whom were hostile to the papacy. On a visit to southern Italy, Urban made Roger of Sicily his legate (1098), thus exempting him from the visits of an ordinary legate. At the **Synod of Bari,** Urban was as much interested in keeping the papal leadership in the Crusade as he was in the debates on the procession of the Holy Ghost. The First Crusade was the first great victory for the reformed papacy; the papal dominance of the military effort to defend Christendom is significant of the new prestige of the papacy and the decline of the emperors.

1099-1118. PASCHAL II renewed the excommunication of Henry IV; intrigued with Henry, his son; Anselm waged the investiture battle in England (1103–1107), ending in a compromise (1107), followed almost at once by the lapse of lay investiture in France (formerly one of the worst offenders). Paschal's humiliating renunciation (1111) of papal fiefs and secular revenues, his repudiation by his clergy, and his arrest by Henry V made a much more profound impression in Europe than Canossa. Paschal recalled (1112) his concessions.

1115. The Countess Matilda, having made a donation (1086 and 1102) of her allodial lands (the second great addition to papal holdings) to the papacy (subject to free testamentary disposition), willed them at her death (1115) to Henry V, who came and occupied the Matildine lands (1117), destined to be a bone of contention between the popes and emperors for a century.

1118-1119. GELASIUS II was forced to flee Rome; Henry V appointed his own pope; Gelasius having excommunicated (1118) Henry, was finally driven to France.

1119-1124. CALIXTUS II, a Burgundian, related to half the rulers of Europe and a skilled diplomat, arranged the **Concordat of Worms** (1122) which closed the investiture controversy with a compromise. The **Synod of Reims** (1119) renewed the decrees against simony, clerical marriage, and lay investiture, as well as the excommunication of Henry V.

1130-1138. Papal schism: precipitated by the corrupt election of the (Cluniac) Cardinal Pierleone (son of a rich converted Jewish banker of Rome), as **Anacletus II** (1130-1138), and the hostility of the rival houses of Corsi and Frangipani. The rival pope, **Innocent II** (1130-1143), supported by Bernard of Clairvaux and most of Europe, was given military support by Lothair in return for confirmation of his rights under the Concordat of 1122, imperial coronation, and investiture with the Matildine lands. Anacletus confirmed Roger II's title as king in return for his support.

1139. The Second Lateran Council (the tenth general council in the west) was attended by a thousand bishops. It marked the end of the schism.

1143. The Commune of Rome: established in opposition to the non-Roman pope, it defied three feeble popes (Celestine II; Lucius II; Eugenius III). **Arnold of Brescia,** pupil of Abélard, emerged as the eloquent leader with bitter denunciations of clerical wealth and papal bloodshed and burning appeals for a return to apostolic poverty and simplicity. Temporary restoration of the ancient Roman state, appeal to the emperor's protection. **Bernard of Clairvaux** agreed with Arnold's indictment (cf. *De Consideratione*, addressed to Pope Eugenius), but saw salvation for the Church in purification from within, not in diminution of its great powers, and opposed Arnold as he had Abélard.

1147-1149. The Second Crusade (p. 256).

1154-1159. Adrian IV (Nicholas Breakspear, the only English pope). Son of a poor man, learned, kindly, of high character, he had risen by his own merits; Roman anarchy ended by a stern interdict. Arnold expelled; alliance with **Frederick Barbarossa** against William, King of Sicily; altercation with Frederick over his haughty refusal of ceremonial service to the pope (stirrup episode). The bitter hostility of the Romans to pope and emperor forced a surreptitious coronation and hurried departure from Rome.

1155. Frederick executed Arnold as a heretic, but abandoned Adrian to the Normans and forced him to an independent Italian policy (i.e. alliance with an anti-Norman league of southern barons and with Constantinople) which brought William of Sicily to his knees as the pope's vassal. Adrian accepted the Roman Commune and returned to Rome.

1158-1162. Frederick's second expedition to Italy: the **League of Pavia** (Brescia, Cremona, Parma, Piacenza) supported Frederick; Milan and its league were reduced to submission. The great **Diet of Roncaglia**: Frederick, using Roman law to justify an extreme assertion of imperial rights and a brusque resumption of imperial regalia, substituted an imperial *podestà* for the consuls in the Lombard cities, drove Milan into open revolt (1159-1162) and turned the towns to alliance with the pope. Renewal of the papal alliance with Byzantium; formation of an alliance of Lombard towns under papal auspices.

1159-1181. ALEXANDER III (imperialist anti-popes: Victor IV, Paschal III, Calixtus III). Frederick, citing precedents from Constantine, Charlemagne, and Otto the Great, held a synod at Pavia to adjudicate the claims of Alexander III and Victor IV. Alexander ignored the synod, Victor was recognized. Alexander, after an exile in France, returned and excommunicated Frederick (1165). Renewal of the town leagues (1164); Milan rebuilt, expulsion of imperial *podestàs*.

1167-1168. Frederick's fourth expedition to Italy: Alexander's flight to the Normans; Frederick's capture of Rome; renewal of the Lombard League (1168): promises of mutual aid; organization for federal administration; erection of Alessandria, a great fortress city (named for the pope), to guard the passes (1168); Italy virtually independent.

1174. Frederick's fifth expedition to Italy: vain siege of Alessandria, complete **defeat at Legnano** (1176); preliminary peace of Venice (1177, the centenary of Canossa).

1179. The Third Lateran Council decreed a two-thirds vote of the conclave to be necessary for a valid papal election.

1181-1198. A series of unimportant popes, often exiled from Rome by local anarchy until 1188, when papal recognition of the Commune of Rome made peaceful residence again possible.

1183. Peace of Constance: imperial suzerainty in Italy recognized; resumption by the Lombard towns of all *regalia* they had ever enjoyed, including the right to maintain an army, to fortify, to keep the league or expand it, full judicial jurisdiction, control of their own coinage, abolition of the imperial *podestàs*. The only relic of imperial control was the reservation of the emperor's right to confirm elected consuls, the right of appeal to the imperial court, and the retention of the *fodrum* as a contribution to military needs. The Lombard towns were autonomous for all practical purposes under a very loose system of imperial legates and vicars.

1184. Frederick's sixth expedition to Italy: utilizing the split in the Lombard League (after 1181) and local feuds in Tuscany and Bologna, Frederick created a strong imperial party in middle Italy and by a liberal charter (1185) even won over Milan.

1189-1192. The Third Crusade (p. 256).

1198-1216. INNOCENT III. A tough-minded Italian patrician of German blood (whose family provided the Church with eight popes), chosen by the cardinals to restore the political power of the papacy. Animated by an historical mysticism, he looked on Christendom as a single community in which he aimed to combine moral unity with a world-state under papal guidance. He deduced the papal powers from the Petrine Theory, the *Old Testament*, the *Donation of Constantine*, and from the duty of the pope to insure justice, maintain peace, prevent and punish sin, and aid the unfortunate. With a clear grasp of essentials, he never lost sight of this concept, but his frequent opportunism destroyed his moral grandeur. Insistence, not on moral or theological, but on historical grounds (i.e. the Translation of the Empire) on the right (claimed by Gregory VII) to pass on imperial elections. A brilliant administrator, he first brought the papal chancery into systematic organization (division into four sections under experts, careful systematized treatment of documents) and made a great collection of canons and decretals. This pontificate was the zenith of the mediaeval papacy.

Restoration of the Papal States (Spoleto, Ancona, Romagna regained); many towns succeeded in escaping and keeping their local autonomy. Tuscany: an anti-imperial league under papal auspices; towns like Florence, Lucca, and Siena retained their appropriations of the Matildine lands (a partial foundation of their later power); the rest of the Matildine lands were regained by the Church. Innocent used his position first as protector, then as guardian of Frederick II, in an attempt to alienate Sicily from the Hohenstaufens.

Steady insistence on a crusade: The Fourth Crusade (p. 256) combined opportunity to attack the infidel with a chance to reunite the Roman and Orthodox Churches; Innocent reconciled himself to the sack of Constantinople by the organization of the new Latin Church of Constantinople. The Albigensian Crusade (p. 229), directed against the spreading heresy of southern

France, drenched that region with blood and exterminated one of the most advanced local cultures in Europe, under revolting circumstances of feudal cynicism and clerical intolerance. Simon de Montfort nullified Innocent's efforts to divert the crusaders' ardor to Spain against the Moslems.

Vindication of the political claims of the papacy: (1) Asserting his right to pass on imperial elections, Innocent rejected the Hohenstaufen claimant (Philip of Swabia) to the imperial crown, ignored the undoubted rights of Frederick, crowned and supported Otto (in return for large promises of obedience to papal authority), and then procured (in alliance with King Philip II) the election of Frederick II. (2) By excommunicating Philip II (1198) he forced him to a formal recognition of his wife Ingeborg, but was coldly rebuffed when he intervened in Philip's struggle with the Angevins. (3) Maintaining the rights of his nominee to the See of Canterbury (Langton), Innocent forced King John of England (interdict, 1208) to cede England to the Holy See and receive it back as a fief (1213). (4) Innocent received the homage as papal vassals of the following states: Aragon, Bulgaria, Denmark, Hungary, Poland, Portugal, Serbia, and brought the Roman Church to its closest approximation to an ideal Christian, universal commonwealth.

The struggle against urban heresy: The Church, long organized to deal with a predominantly rural society, was increasingly out of touch with the rising bourgeoisie and urban proletariat as town life revived and expanded; the anti-clericalism of the cities had become a major problem. The Italian, Francis of Assisi, and the Spaniard, Dominic, organized the spontaneous response within the Church to this crisis: Francis (d. 1226), a converted gilded youth, as the joyous "troubadour of religion" began preaching the beauties of humbleness, poverty, simplicity, and devotion, of the brotherhood of man, of man and the animals, of man and nature. His cheerful vernacular hymns won tremendous success in the towns of Italy. Founded as a brotherhood, whence the name Friars Minor (*Minorites, Grey Friars*, also *Cordeliers*), the Franciscans won cautious support from Innocent, but not formal ratification as a corporation until 1223.

The second of the Mendicant Orders, the Dominicans, born of Dominic's campaign against the Albigensian heresy, was sanctioned by Innocent (1215). Organized as a preaching order, the Dominicans (*Friars Preachers, Black Friars*, or *Jacobins* in Paris) patterned their constitution on the Franciscan. These two mendicant orders were not monastic, rural monks, but town-dwellers devoted to preaching and charity. The conduct of the Inquisition was entrusted to them (1233) and their direct influence on education (especially that of the Dominicans) was enormous.

1215. The Fourth Lateran Council was the climax of Innocent's pontificate (attended by 400 bishops, 800 abbots and priors, and the representatives of the monarchs of Christendom) and its decrees were of tremendous significance: (1) The Church was pronounced one and universal; (2) the Sacraments were decreed the channel of grace, and the chief sacrament, the Eucharist; (3) the Dogma of transubstantiation was proclaimed; (4) annual confession, penance, and communion were enjoined; (5) careful rules were made as to episcopal elections and the qualifications of the clergy, and (6) injunctions for the maintenance of education in each cathedral and for theological instruction were formulated; (7) the Albigensian and Catharist heresies were condemned; (8) trial by ordeal and by battle forbidden; (9) relic worship regulated, and (10) rules of monastic life were made more rigorous. Finally, another crusade was proclaimed.

1216-1227. HONORIUS III, a high-minded noble of conciliatory disposition who managed to keep on relatively good terms with Frederick II.

1227-1241. GREGORY IX, a relative of Innocent III, aged and fiery, he never relaxed his relentless pressure on Frederick. **Canonization of Francis of Assisi** (1228) and **Dominic** (1234).

1243-1254. INNOCENT IV, a canon lawyer. Supposedly friendly to Frederick, he continued the uncompromising attack on the emperor, and encompassed the final ruin of the Hohenstaufen.

1271-1276. GREGORY X (*Visconti*), a high-minded pope with three aims: to pacify Italy; to check Charles of Anjou and the rising power of France; and to pacify Germany. At the **Synod of Lyons** (1274) he provided for the seclusion of conclaves to avoid corruption. His successors were occupied with Italian affairs (the war of Naples and Sicily, baronial anarchy in Rome, etc.), and the advancement of their own houses: **Nicholas III** (*Orsini*) (1277–1280), a foe of Charles of Anjou; **Martin IV** (1281–1285), a puppet of Charles of Anjou; **Honorius IV** (*Savelli*) (1285–1287); **Nicholas IV** (*Colonna*) (1288–1292). The rivalries of the great houses was so close that two years were required to elect Nicholas' successor, a hermit dragged unwilling (as a result of Cardinal Malabranca's dream) to the Holy See, **Celestine V** (1294), who never saw Rome, a puppet of Charles of Anjou and Cardinal Caetani. Induced (probably) by Caetani (the midnight voice, a megaphone over the papal couch) he resigned (*The Great Refusal*, Dante, *Inf.* III, 60) and was kept a prisoner by his successor, Boniface VIII (*Caetani*).

1294-1534.   THE SECULARIZED PAPACY: absorption in secular politics to the exclusion of spiritual leadership.

1294-1303.   BONIFACE VIII (*Caetani*). Surpassed all his colleagues in the Sacred College as lawyer, diplomat, and man of affairs. A skeptic in religion, but a believer in amulets and magic, well read in the pagan classics, he was the *last mediaeval pope*, and the last pope to claim the universal authority of the papacy as asserted by Gregory VII and maintained by Innocent III. Addicted to low company, he was not as vicious as contemporary propaganda painted him. Handsome and vain, he substituted on occasion imperial dress and regalia for papal vestments (*I am pope, I am Caesar*). Rude beyond belief, domineering and well-hated, his chief aim was the aggrandizement of the Caetani family. An intelligent patron of architecture and art: Giotto in Rome.

1295.   Bent on regaining Sicily for the papacy, Boniface continued the support of the Angevin claimant, Charles II of Naples, arranged the **Peace of 1295**, by which James of Aragon exchanged Sicily for the investiture of Sardinia and Corsica, and the extinction of French claims in Aragon.

1296.   The Bull *Clericis laicos*, designed to bring the kings of France and England to accept papal intervention, forbade the payment of taxes by the clergy to lay rulers without papal consent (a vain attempt to maintain a mediaeval custom in the face of rising national states). Philip IV of France answered with an embargo on the export of bullion; Edward I of England with outlawry of the clergy; both were supported by public opinion expressed in their national assemblies (pp. 200, 232).

1297.   Angered by the Colonna, their insistence on the validity of Celestine V's election, their appeal to a general council, and their support of the Aragonese in Sicily, the pope began a veritable crusade which exiled the Colonna (Palestrina, the family stronghold, razed).

Recognition of the rights of Robert (second son of Charles II) in Naples (exclusion of Carobert of Hungary). Beginning of the formation of a Caetani *state* as a threat to the barons.

1300.   THE GREAT JUBILEE, zenith of the pontificate, one of the magnificent pageants of the mediaeval papacy, managed with tremendous pomp by Boniface; huge donations (raked over public tables by papal "croupiers"); the proceeds intended by Boniface for the second Caetani state to be formed in Tuscany and for the subjection of Sicily.

1302.   Charles of Valois' failure to dislodge Frederick, the Aragonese claimant in Sicily, forced Boniface to the **Peace of 1302** which ended the War of the Sicilian Vespers, left Frederick king, and provided for the ultimate reunion of Naples and Sicily under the Aragonese.

1302-1303.   Boniface's defeat and humiliation by the national states.

The **Bull** *Unam sanctam* (1302) marked the climax of papal claims to superiority over national states and lay rulers. Philip IV (his appeal for a compromise rejected) dispatched Nogaret to bring the pope to French soil for trial by a general council called by Philip.

1303.   The **"Terrible Day at Anagni":** Nogaret and Sciarra Colonna penetrated to the papal apartment, found Boniface in bed, threatened him with death, tried to force his resignation, took him prisoner. Faced with a public reaction against them as foreigners, Nogaret and Colonna fled, and Boniface died shortly of humiliation. The papacy, so lately triumphant over the empire, found itself defeated by a new force, national feeling supporting national monarchy, and the defeat vindicated the claim of the new states to tax clerics and to maintain criminal jurisdiction over them.

1303-1304.   BENEDICT XI. Exiled to Perugia by the anarchy in Rome, he promulgated a bull condemning the principals in the affair at Anagni, and died almost immediately (reputedly by poison). The cardinals, almost evenly divided for and against Boniface, after a conclave of ten months, chose a compromise candidate, the French Archbishop of Bordeaux, Bertrand de Got (supposed to be a bitter foe of Philip IV), who assumed the name

1305-1314.   CLEMENT V (1305-1314). Clement never entered Italy and became friendly (bribed?) to Philip. The **Synod of Vienne** (1311-1312) exonerated Boniface's memory despite Philip's pressure, but Philip had his way with the Templars (1307) (p. 232). Italy was in anarchy, but Clement was bent on returning there as soon as he had made peace between England and France and launched a crusade. To escape Philip, Clement established the papal court at Avignon. (Avignon was an enclave in the Venaissin which was papal territory). (*Cont. p.* 286.)

(1) The Norman Kingdom in South Italy and Sicily, 1105-1194

1130-1154. The Norman Count **Roger II** of Sicily (1105–1130) succeeded the Norman Duke William of Apulia (1111–1127) and in 1130 assumed the title of King of Sicily, Apulia, and Capua with the approval of anti-Pope Anacletus II. Excommunicated by Pope Innocent II (1139) for his alliance with Anacletus, he defeated Innocent (1140), took him prisoner, and forced recognition of his title. By skillful diplomacy he prevented a joint invasion of Sicily by the Greek and Roman emperors. Planning a Mediterranean commercial empire, Roger established an extensive North African holding (at its maximum, 1153).

1154-1166. **William I,** continuing Roger's policy, defeated (1156) the Byzantine allies of Pope Adrian IV and compelled Adrian to recognize his title in Sicily, Apulia, Naples, Amalfi, and Salerno. He supported Pope Alexander III against Frederick I.

1166-1189. **William II** continued this policy, but as he planned a Mediterranean empire and wished a free hand, he welcomed the marriage (1186) of Constance (Roger II's daughter), his heiress, to the future Emperor Henry VI. He himself married Joan, sister of King Richard I of England, and intended to lead the Third Crusade as part of his imperial plans. On his death,

1190-1194. **Tancred of Lecce** (son of Roger, Duke of Apulia, the brother of Constance) led a vigorous native resistance to the Emperor Henry VI (king, 1194–1197) with the support of the pope and Richard I. Henry reduced Sicily, southern Italy, and part of Tuscany, with the aid of Pisa and Genoa, retained the Matildine lands in central Italy, organized an imperial administration of his holdings, and planned a great empire with Italy as its base. **Purely Norman rule ended with Tancred.**

The Norman kingship in southern Italy and Sicily was theocratic, on Byzantine lines; the administration was an efficient, departmentalized bureaucracy. Tremendous prosperity and efficient taxation made the Sicilian monarchs perhaps the richest in Europe. Dealing with a cosmopolitan kingdom containing Italian, Greek, and Saracen elements, and needing settlers, the Norman rulers practiced a tolerant eclecti-

cism which provided for wide racial divergences in law, religion, and culture.

Roger II's cosmopolitan court and generous patronage of the learned produced a brilliant circle including: the Arab geographer Edrisi, Eugenius the translator of Ptolemy's *Optics*, and Henry Aristippus, translator of Plato's *Phaedo* and Book IV of Aristotle's *Meteorologica*.

(2) The Development of Italian Towns

No continuous tradition of mediaeval and classical town government in Italy can be traced. The post-Carolingian anarchy left defense in local hands and rural refuges and town walls were the work of local co-operation. The bishops in Lombardy, traditional guardians of their flocks, with large episcopal and comital powers delegated from the monarchs, played a decisive rôle in communal organization for defense (e.g. Bergamo, 904). The first cases of true urban autonomy were in Amalfi, Benevento, and Naples (1000–1034), a development cut short by the advent of the Normans.

The great urban evolution took place in the north, and particularly in Lombardy, where sworn municipal leagues and urban associations appeared (probably) in the 10th century. In these cities the nobles (since ancient times town-dwellers for at least part of each year) played an important part, though they were always balanced by the bishops. The emperors, busy in Germany or preoccupied with the popes, made wide grants of regalian rights over local coinage, tolls, customs dues, police powers, and justice (diplomas of Henry I, Lothaire II, and Conrad II); there were also considerable delegations of local episcopal powers. Full-fledged communes appeared in the 11th and 12th centuries (e.g. Asti, 1093; Pavia, 1105; Florence, 1138; and Rome itself, by papal charter, 1188). Expansion in the great maritime and commercial republics was rapid (e.g. Pisa's new walls, 1081; Florence's second wall, 1172–1174; Venetian expansion in the Adriatic after the capture of Bari from the Saracens, 1002).

As a result of revolt and negotiation the towns of Lombardy were largely self-governing communes by the opening of the 12th century, and the consulate or its equivalent was in full activity by the end of the century. Typical town organization: an assembly (legislation, declaration of war and peace, etc.); the consuls, core of the magistracy, usually four to twenty in number, serving a one-year term, and chosen from the leading families; the town council and minor magistrates.

The development of the merchant and craft guilds led to a vigorous class warfare as the rising bourgeoisie asserted itself, and brought in the podestate (the *podestà*), a kind of local dictator, during the last quarter of the 12th century.

In Tuscany the towns treated the counts as the Lombards had treated their bishops. Venice, thanks to her peculiar circumstances, evolved a unique commercial oligarchy.

(3) The Rise of Venice to 1310

Fugitives from the Huns found refuge among the fishing villages of the lagoons; the permanent establishment of Venice seems to date from the Lombard invasion (568). Venetian aid to Belisarius began the formal connection between Venice and Constantinople and a (largely) theoretical connection with the Eastern Roman Empire. The *tribuni maiores* (a central governing committee of the islands) dated from c. 568.

687. Election of the first doge. A salt monopoly and salt-fish trade were the sources of the first prosperity of Venice. Two great parties: (1) pro-Byzantine aristocrats favoring an hereditary doge; (2) democrats friendly to the Roman Church and (later) the Franks. Venice offered asylum to the Exarch of Ravenna fleeing from Liutprand, and gained trading rights with Ravenna. When Charlemagne ordered the pope to expel the Venetians from the Pentapolis and threatened the settlement in the lagoons, Venice turned again to Constantinople, and in a treaty

810. Charlemagne and Nicephorus recognized Venice as Byzantine territory and accepted her mainland trading rights.

1000. After a two-hundred-year expansion in the Adriatic, Venice completely reduced the Dalmatian pirates, and the doge took the title of Duke of Dalmatia. Venice was mistress of the sea road to the Holy Land (commemorated in the wedding of the doge and the sea).

1032. The aristocratic effort to establish an hereditary doge was defeated. Establishment of a council and senate.

1043. The construction of the Church of St. Mark begun; one of the most notable and influential examples of Byzantine architecture in the west.

1063. The first three crusades established Venetian trading rights in a number of Levantine ports (e.g. Sidon, 1102, Tyre, 1123) and founded the power of a wealthy ruling class. A war with the Eastern Empire (financed by the first known government bonds) was unsuccessful, and led to the institution of a deliberative assembly of 480 members (the germ of the Great Council).

1171. Appointment of the doge was transferred to this council, a complete triumph for the commercial aristocracy.

1198. A coronation oath (in varying terms) began to be exacted of the doge.

1204. IN THE FOURTH CRUSADE (p. 256) Venice gained the Cyclades, Sporades, Propontis, the Black Sea coasts, Thessalian littoral, and control of the Morea. She administered this vast empire on a kind of feudal tenure, portioning it out to families charged with defense of the seaways. Venice had also gained a further foothold in Syrian ports.

From this period dates a great epoch of building and increasing oligarchic pressure as the government began to become a closed corporation of leading families.

1253-1299. THE STRUGGLE WITH GENOA for the Black Sea and Levantine trade. The feud of Genoa and Venice was ancient, and trouble began at Acre (1253). The first war with Genoa ended in the complete defeat (1258) of the Genoese.

1261. The Greeks seized Constantinople during the absence of the Venetian fleet; they favored Genoa, turning over Galata to her.

1264. The Venetians destroyed the Genoese fleet at **Trepani**, and soon returned to their old status in Constantinople.

1289-1299. The advance of the Turks (capture of Tripoli, 1289, of Acre, 1291) led Venice to a treaty with the new masters of Asia Minor. Genoa met this by an effort to close the Dardanelles, and won a victory (1294) at Alexandretta; Venice forced the Dardanelles and sacked Galata. The Genoese defeated the Venetians at **Curzola** (1299), but Matteo Visconti negotiated an honorable peace (1299) for them.

1284. The first ducat was coined.

1290-1300. The perfection of the great galleys. Establishment of the Flanders galleys (1317).

1297. The Great Council was restricted in membership to those who had been members within the preceding four years. A commission added other names and then the council was closed to new members (except by heredity). In effect this excluded a large section of the citizens from any share of the government in favor of a narrow, hereditary, commercial oligarchy. Popular reaction led to a revolt (1300), the leaders of which were hanged.

1310. **Tiepolo's rebellion,** the only serious uprising in Venetian history, was crushed. This seems to have been a patrician protest against the extreme oligarchy, and led to the creation of an emergency committee of public safety, the **Council of Ten,** which soon became permanent (1335).

The Venetian government thus consisted of: The Great Council (i.e. the patrician caste); the Senate (a deliberative and legislative body dealing with foreign affairs, peace, war, finances, trade); the Council of Ten, a secret, rapidly acting body concerned with morals, conspiracy, European affairs, finance, the war department, which could override the Senate; the *Collegio* or Cabinet (the administrative branch); the doge and his council, which, sitting with the Ten, made the Council of Seventeen.

(*Cont. p.* 298.)

e. FRANCE, 987-1314

987-1328. **DIRECT LINE OF THE CAPETIAN HOUSE** (the dynasty continued until 1792).

987-996. **HUGH** (called *Capet,* from cloak he wore as abbot of St. Martin de Tours). At Hugh's accession the kingship was at its nadir; such power as Hugh had was feudal; the royal title meant little more than an hegemony over a feudal patchwork, an ill-defined area called France, and the prestige of ancient monarchical tradition sanctified by ecclesiastical consecration. Hugh's own feudal domain consisted of the Île de France (extending from Laon to Orléans, with its center at Paris) and a few scattered holdings. The great barons of the so-called royal fiefs recognized Hugh as their suzerain, but never did homage nor rendered service. Hugh's special interest was to maintain his control over his chief resources, the Archbishopric of Reims and the great bishoprics (Sens, Tours, Bourges) and abbeys of the Île de France, and to wean northeastern France away from the Carolingian and imperial interest. Despite clerical pressure, he avoided submission to imperial suzerainty, a policy which facilitated the demarcation between France and Germany. In defiance of pope and emperor he forced his own candidate into the Archbishopric of Reims. Hugh crowned his son shortly after his own coronation and began a practice (*co-optation*) which the early Capetians continued (until Philip II no longer felt it necessary), thus insuring

the succession, and weakening the principle (dear to the feudality) of elective kingship.

996-1031. **ROBERT II** (*the Pious*), an active, well-educated, polished, amiable ruler, a good soldier, supported by the Duke of Normandy in constant wars against his neighbors, and by the religious houses of Burgundy in attacks on the Dukes of Burgundy. The Duchy of Burgundy escheated to the crown, and was given to Robert, a younger son. Robert the Pious, like his father, supported the Cluniac reformers. Minor territorial additions signify the revival of royal power.

1031-1060. **HENRY I,** an active, brave, indefatigable ruler, whose reign nevertheless marked the lowest ebb of the Capetian fortunes. The rebellion of his brother Robert, supported by Eudes, Count of Chartres and Troyes, was put down with the aid of the Duke of Normandy, and Robert was pacified by the grant of the Duchy of Burgundy (which continued in his family until 1361). Henry supported the Duke of Normandy (1047), but led a coalition against him two years later, and was defeated. He boycotted the pope and his synod at Reims, and, like his son and successor, opposed the reform movement in the Church. The *prévôts* were introduced to administer justice and taxation in the royal lands. The Kingdom of Burgundy passed (1032) to the empire.

1035-1066. **RISE AND EXPANSION OF NORMANDY. William I** became duke (1035) and until 1047 faced a series of baronial revolts. With the aid of his feudal suzerain, King Henry of France, William defeated his revolting barons (1047) and razed their castles. The union of Normandy and Maine was completed (1063) against powerful opposition from the Counts of Anjou. William's alliance with Henry was broken (1053), and Henry ravaged the heart of Normandy (1058). Normandy was now a fully developed feudal state under firm ducal control. Military service, assessed in knights' fees, was attached to specific pieces of land, no castles could be built or maintained without ducal license. Private warfare and blood feud were strictly limited. Coinage was a ducal monopoly. The legal jurisdiction of the duke was wide, local government was under the duke's representatives (the *vicomte*) who commanded the local forces, guarded the castles, did justice, collected the revenue (a large part of which was cash). The Church had been revivified, but here too the duke was supreme, naming bishops, most of the abbots, and sitting in provincial synods.

The Capetian Kings

Hugh Capet
987–996

Robert II the Pious
996–1031

Henry I
1031–1060

Robert, Duke of Burgundy
founder of the Burgundian line

Philip I
1060–1108

Hugh the Great
Count of Vermandois

Louis VI the Fat
1108–1137

Louis VII the Young
1137–1180

Henry   Robert   Peter   Constance

Mary   Alice   Margaret   Alice   **Philip II (Augustus)**
1180–1223   Agnes

Louis VIII
1223–1226   Philip   Mary

Louis IX (Saint Louis)
1226–1270   Robert   Alphonse   Charles
King of Sicily

Robert   Blanche
m. Edmund, Earl of Lancaster

Philip III the Bold
1270–1285   John   Peter   Robert
m. Beatrice
of Burgundy   Isabella   Blanche   Margaret   Agnes

Louis I, Duke of
Bourbon, ancestor
of the Bourbon line

Philip IV the Fair
1285–1314   Charles
Count of Valois   Louis   Margaret
m. Edward I
of England

Philip VI, of Valois,
founder of the Valois line
1328

Louis X
1314–1316   **Philip V**
1316–1322   **Charles IV**
1322–1328   Isabella
m. Edward II
of England

Norman relations with England had grown closer, and this tendency culminated (1002) in the marriage of Duke Robert's sister Emma with King Ethelred. The son of this marriage, Edward the Confessor, educated largely at the Norman court, came to the throne of England (1042), and died without heirs (1066). The Witan at once elected Harold, Earl Godwin's son. William I of Normandy with a volunteer force (perhaps 5000–6000) collected from Normandy and the Continent, defeated Harold in the battle of Hastings (Oct. 14) and was crowned King of England on Christmas Day (p. 168). The *Bayeux Tapestry* forms a unique and probably contemporary record of this expedition.

1060-1108. PHILIP I, enormously fat, but active and vigorous; excommunicated and unpopular with the clergy as the result of an adulterous marriage (1092) and because of his hostility to clerical reform. He defeated (1079) Duke William of Normandy (the *Conqueror*) and steadily supported **Robert Curthose,** William's son, against Anglo-Norman pressure. Systematic expansion of the resources of his house, and regular annexations to its domains in the face of stubborn feudal resistance. The *Chanson de Roland*, the national epic of France, was probably composed during this reign.

The growth of feudalism tended to diminish anarchy and to improve the general security of life, and ultimately led to decisive economic recovery in western Europe, a trend toward urban economy, and the emergence of a bourgeoisie who were beginning to accumulate capital. This development was a determining factor in the economic, social, and monarchical evolution of the 13th century. The **Peace of God** in the 10th century, and the **Truce of God** (first mentioned, 1027), promoted by the Church with Capetian support, were significant rather than effective attempts to reduce warfare.

1108-1328. A period in which the Capetians reduced the great feudatories north of the Loire and began the transformation of the vague ecclesiastical, judicial, and military rights derived from Carolingian tradition into royal powers over the French people as a whole.

1108-1137. LOUIS VI (*the Fat*). A brave soldier, of tremendous physique, intelligent, affable, avaricious, but liked by the peasantry, commercial class and clergy, the first popular Capetian. Consolidation of his Norman frontier (wars with Henry I of England: 1109–1112; 1116–1120), and steady reduction of his lesser vassals as far as the Loire. His charters to colonizers

(*hôtes*) of waste lands, and frequent if inconsistent support of the communes, especially on the lands of the Church and the baronage, began the long alliance of the Capetians with bourgeois interests; Louis' *charter of Lorris*, widely copied in town charters, was a significant sign of the **great urban development** setting in all over Europe in this period. As protector of the Church, Louis gained a foothold in the lands of his vassals. Careers at court were opened to talented clergy and bourgeois: great influence of **Suger** (see below). Louis' compromise with the Church over feudal patronage and investiture initiated the King of France's effective rôle as *eldest son of the Church.* He was the first Capetian to intervene effectively outside his own feudal lands. He defeated the alliance of Henry I of England with the Emperor Henry V, and stopped (1124) a German invasion. The marriage (1137) of his son Louis to Eleanor, heiress of William X of Aquitaine (i.e. Guienne [*Aquitania Secunda*] and Gascony), marked the Capetian effort to balance the Anglo-Norman menace in the north by additions of territory south of the Loire. The Anglo-Norman danger had appeared in aggravated form when in 1129 Geoffrey became Count of Anjou, Maine, and Touraine. He had in 1128 married Matilda (daughter of Henry I of England), and proceeded (1135) to conquer Normandy.

DEVELOPMENT OF ROYAL ADMINISTRATION UNDER THE EARLY CAPETIANS. The court of the king, usually known as the *curia regis*, consisting as it did of magnates, royal vassals, and court officials (mainly chosen from the baronage), was essentially feudal in spirit and tradition. Meeting at royal summons and relatively frequently, its early duties were undifferentiated, its functions judicial, advisory, legislative. The royal administration was in control of the great officers of the crown whose aim was to concentrate power in their own hands, a process which culminated in a virtual monopoly of such power by the **Garlande family** early in the 12th century. Louis VI, after a struggle (1128–1130), terminated their dominance, and thenceforth the Capetians relied increasingly on lesser and more docile nobles, clerics, and bourgeois men of affairs. Such men were career men devoted to the crown rather than to feudal ambitions, and their presence in the *curia regis* began the differentiation of its functions and its subjection to royal rather than feudal influences. Most notable of these careerists was **Suger,** Louis' old tutor, a cleric of humble origin, who became Abbot of St. Denis (1122). An able statesman, his influence was decisive in the reign of Louis and his son Louis VII. Suger began (c. 1136) the new abbey church of St. Denis, the first edifice wholly Gothic in design.

1100-1400. RISE OF TOWNS. The economic revival of western Europe was paralleled by a resumption of town life and development throughout the west, which was most notable in France, where the movement reached its apogee in the 12th century, before the consistent advance of the Capetian monarchy began to retard its progress. Types of town development were by no means uniform, but important general categories can be distinguished: (1) The *commune* proper, a collective person endowed with legal rights and powers (e.g. financial, judicial), able to hold property. As a feudal person the *commune* could have vassals, render and exact homage, establish courts for its tenants, and even declare war and make treaties. Symbols of its independence were the belfry, town hall, and seal. Typical *communes* of northern France and Flanders were the *communes jurées* (e.g. Beauvais, St. Quentin [chartered before 1080], Rouen [chartered 1145], and Amiens [chartered in the 12th century]); in southern France the corresponding *communes* were called *consulates*, which enjoyed even greater rights than in the north, especially in Roussillon, Provence, Languedoc, Gascony, and Guienne. In the south the nobles took an active part in the formation of *consulates* and shared in their government. (2) *Villes de bourgeoisie* (or *communes surveillées*) had elements of communal powers in varying degrees, but lacked full political independence (i.e. they were privileged but unfree). They were found all over France, but especially in the center, and were the prevailing type on the royal domain. Citizens enjoyed specific privileges, but the crown retained judicial and other powers in varying degrees. (3) *Villes neuves* (characteristic of the commercial north) and *bastides* (typical of the south, and usually strongholds) were small rural creations of kings or feudal lords, given a charter from the first, establishing their status. (4) *Peasant associations* and village federations (influential in the north) which sought to define and guarantee the rights of their citizens. Governmentally town development seems to have been hardly the result of conscious effort to introduce a new political dispensation. It was rather an attempt to establish and define the rights of non-feudal groups, and aimed at economic prosperity and personal security. The movement constantly enjoyed royal support, but royal policy toward it was governed by immediate political or financial considerations, and the crown always strove to reduce or control town independence in the interest of its own power. Ultimately monarchy triumphed, but not before the bourgeois groups and the serfs had altered their position to their own advantage.

1137-1180. LOUIS VII (*the Young*), not a strong king, but pious and therefore popular with the clergy. He remained under the influence of Suger until the latter's death in 1151. A papal interdict on the royal lands, resulting from Louis' insistence on his feudal rights, led to intervention by Bernard of Clairvaux.

1147. Louis inspired the **Second Crusade** (p. 256). He induced the Emperor Conrad III and Bernard of Clairvaux to join him and, leaving the kingdom in the hands of Suger, he set out for the east. He returned (1149) beaten, humiliated, and estranged from his wife Eleanor, who had accompanied him. The marriage was annulled (1152), probably due to lack of a male heir. This step cost the Capetians the territories of Poitou, Guienne, and Gascony, for Eleanor at once married Henry, Duke of Normandy, who in 1151 had succeeded his father as Count of Anjou, Maine, and Touraine. The acquisition of Eleanor's domains made Henry master of more than half of France and put him in a position to bring pressure on the holdings of the King of France both from the north and the south. When Henry in 1154 became King of England, the so-called Angevin Empire extended roughly from the Tweed to the Pyrenees.

1173. Louis supported **Thomas Becket** (p. 194) against Henry II of England, and was saved from Henry's wrath only through the mediation of the pope, Alexander III, a refugee in France against whom the Emperor Frederick had raised an antipope. It was Louis' interest to support the anti-imperial party, because of the pressure of the emperor upon Burgundy.

During the reign of Louis VII the appointment of non-feudal experts to the *curia regis* continued, and their influence on the administration began to be decisive. Grant of town charters also continued. The period was, moreover, one of marked

Cultural progress: The guild of masters (germ of the University of Paris) was recognized (c. 1170) and a number of eminent scholars appeared on the scene: **St. Bernard of Clairvaux** (1091-1153), member of the Cistercian Order, a great preacher, fervent reformer, and dominant spiritual figure of the west; **Roscellinus** (died c. 1121), champion of nominalism; **Anselm** (d. 1109), Abbot of Bec, later Archbishop of Canterbury, champion of realism; Peter Abélard (d. 1142), eminent master at Paris (after about 1115), supporter of conceptualism, a middle ground in the great controversy over universals. Abélard's *sic et non* presented without solution the conflicting theological arguments on 158 important problems. John of Salisbury (d. 1180), Bishop of Chartres, favored the humanistic rather than the dialectical approach to knowledge. Peter Lombard, Bishop of Paris (1159), in his *Sententiae* offered a cautious solution of theological and philosophical problems which became a standard text of the Paris schools. In literature the period produced the *chansons de geste* and the troubadour lyrics.

1180-1223. PHILIP II (*Augustus*). He began his rule at fifteen and had no time for education (he knew no Latin). A calculating realist, perhaps the outstanding figure of his time, he was the consolidator of the monarchy and the founder of the organized state. As the "maker of Paris" he paved the streets, walled the city, and began the building of the Louvre.

1180. A six-year alliance with King Henry II of England enabled Philip to defeat Philip of Artois and the Counts of Champagne, to crush a baronial league against him, and to gain recognition for his title to Artois and Vermandois. Philip intrigued with the sons of Henry, welcomed the rebellious Richard (1187), and, joining him, defeated Henry (1189), who died the same year.

1191. Philip, under pressure of public opinion, joined King Richard on the Third Crusade (p. 256); eclipsed by Richard, he quarreled with him, returned to France, and intrigued against him with John during his (Richard's) captivity (1192–1194).

1194-1199. Richard, in a pitiless war of vengeance, built Château Gaillard on the Seine and restored the Angevin power in northern France.

1198. Excommunicated by Pope Innocent III for his divorce of Ingeborg of Denmark, Philip was forced by public opinion to a reconciliation, but sharply refused Innocent's offer of mediation with John, who succeeded Richard (1199).

1202-1204. The final duel with John for, and conquest of, the Angevin lands north of the Loire. On King John's refusal to stand trial as Philip's vassal on charges by Philip's vassal, Hugh of Lusignan, Philip declared John's French fiefs forfeited (1203), and supported John's nephew, Arthur of Brittany. The murder of Arthur (1203) cost John his French support, Châ-

teau Gaillard was lost (1204), Normandy and Poitou followed, and Philip emerged master of the Angevin lands north of the Loire.

New royal officials, the *baillis* (*sénéchaux* in the south), paid professionals (often Roman lawyers), superseded the now feudalized *prévôts* as the chief local administrators (financial, judicial, military) on the Capetian lands (c. 1190). In the course of the 13th century *baillis* began to be assigned to regular districts (*baillages*), but they continued responsible to and removable by the king. As the royal domain expanded, royal administration was extended to it, and the foundation laid for a national, specialized, professional system.

Philip, henceforth master in the north, left the conquest of the south to his successors and devoted himself to statecraft rather than war. He played the barons off against each other, used his position as protector of the Church to weaken them further, and sought the support of the towns and rich bourgeoisie as a balance to the feudality. Part of this process involved the systematization of the royal finance, the regular exaction of feudal aids and obligations due to the crown as well as the systematic collection of customs, tolls, fines, and fees, though as yet there was no such thing as taxation in the modern sense. The levy of the Saladin tithe (1188) was, however, a forerunner of true taxation. Philip's reign also saw the formation of a semi-permanent royal army.

1208-1213. The Albigensian-Waldensian Crusade. The Albigensians (Catharists of Albi) and the Waldensians (followers of Peter Waldo) represented originally a reaction of the lower classes against clerical corruption, but the movement was soon espoused by the nobles, who saw in it a chance to appropriate church lands. Innocent III, after a vain appeal to Philip, proclaimed a crusade against these heretics. Philip took no direct part in the action, but allowed his northern vassals to begin the penetration of the south and thus prepare the way for the advance of the Capetian power. Simon de Montfort (the elder), a baron of the Île de France, emerged as the leader of the crusaders. His victory at Muret (1213) sealed the fate of the brilliant Provençal culture, of the leading southern barons, and of the heretics. After a long chapter of horrors the conquest was finally completed in a campaign by Louis VIII (1226). In the reign of Louis IX the County of Toulouse passed under Capetian administration and the royal domain was extended to the Mediterranean.

1213-1214. The great anti-Capetian Alliance (John of England, Emperor Otto IV, the Courts of Boulogne and Flanders, and most of the feudality of Flanders, Belgium, and Lorraine).

1214, July 27. BATTLE OF BOUVINES. Philip, in alliance with Emperor Frederick II, defeated the coalition near Tournai and thereby established the French monarchy in the first rank of the European powers, at the same time ruining John of England, assuring Frederick II of the imperial crown, and bringing Flanders under French influence. Militarily speaking the battle was a triumph of Philip's professional cavalry and bourgeois militia over the older infantry.

1223-1226. LOUIS VIII, a pallid reflection of his father. The first Capetian king not crowned in his father's lifetime.

1224. Temporary conquest of the lands between the Loire and the Garonne; the English soon regained all but Poitou, the Limousin, and Perigord (1225).

1226. Renewal of the Albigensian Crusade and Louis' conquest of the south. Louis began the dangerous practice of bestowing great fiefs as appanages of the princes of the blood, a practice which later had almost fatal consequences to the monarchy (the case of Burgundy).

1226-1270. LOUIS IX (*St. Louis*, canonized 1297). The most chivalrous man of his age and the ideal mediaeval king. Handsome and lofty in character, Louis' careful education prepared him for a unique reign, in which ethics dominated policy. His justice won him national support and made him the arbiter of Europe. His reign was the golden age of mediaeval France.

1226-1234. Minority of Louis IX and regency of his able and devout mother, Blanche of Castile. With the support of the Church, the royal officials and the people, Blanche was able to suppress a number of feudal rebellions (1226-1231). By the **Treaty of Paris** (1129) Raymond of Toulouse surrendered, and his heiress was betrothed to Louis' brother, Alfonso. Louis himself was married to Margaret of Provence and thus began the severance of that province from the empire.

1233. As part of the campaign against heresy, Pope Gregory IX granted independent authority to investigate heresy to the Dominicans, requiring the bishops to co-operate with them. Louis later supported the Inquisition, despite episcopal objections.

1241. Louis induced the Emperor Frederick II to release the prelates and delegates captured off Genoa while *en route* to a synod at Rome, but, without directly attacking the Church, he associated himself with Frederick's grievances against the pope and refused to intervene against the emperor (1247).

1242. Invasion of France by Henry III of England, in coalition with the rebellious feudal lords of southern France. The whole movement collapsed and was followed by the final submission of Aquitaine and Toulouse (1243).

1244. Louis took the Cross, against his mother's advice, and sailed on his first crusade (1248). His aim was to free Palestine by the capture of Egypt, but the expedition was poorly managed, Louis was captured (1250), and most of his army was put to the sword. Louis himself was ransomed and returned to France.

1258. The Treaty of Corbeil, representing a peaceful adjustment of conflicting claims between France and Aragon, to the advantage of France. Louis' son, Philip, was betrothed to Isabella of Aragon.

1259. Treaty of Paris. Louis, in the interest of amity, yielded Perigord and the Limousin to the King of England, despite protests from both provinces. In return he received the renunciation of English claims to Normandy, Maine, Poitou. Henceforth Guienne became distinct from Aquitaine. This pacific gesture displeased opinion in both countries and weakened the French position in the south as the Hundred Years' War approached.

1265. Louis permitted his brother, Charles of Anjou, to accept the crown of Sicily, a step which later involved France in Italian problems, with decisive consequences.

1270. Louis' second crusade. Probably influenced by Charles of Anjou, who cherished far-reaching Mediterranean ambitions, Louis set out for Tunis. He died of pestilence, without accomplishing anything.

Louis' reign was marked by rigorous insistence on inherent royal rights even at the expense of the Church, and despite episcopal protests. Royal justice was notably efficient and was constantly expanded. The right of appeal from feudal to royal courts was clearly established. The old *curia regis* had already become somewhat differentiated: a *chambre des comptes* and a *parlement* (i.e. high court) were already recognizable. Louis introduced the *enquêteurs*, itinerant investigators, to supervise the *baillis* and *sénéchaux*, but he made few other administrative innovations. Many of his diplomats, *baillis*, and other officials were chosen from the royal household, notably from the so-called *chevaliers du roi*, and from the clergy. Assemblies of royal vassals, irregularly held, gave such "national" sanction as there was to royal policy. Louis was the first king to issue *ordonnances* (i.e. legislation) for the whole realm on his sole authority. By *ordonnance* he outlawed private warfare, the carrying of arms and trial by battle as part of the royal judicial process, and extended the royal coinage to the whole realm. By 1270 the communal movement was already in decline and the crown profited by enforcing a more rigorous control over the towns. Only one new charter (to the port of Aigues Mortes) was granted during the reign. The bourgeois oligarchy of the towns got on increasingly bad terms with the lower orders, often reducing the town finances to chaos. Louis took advantage of this state of affairs to introduce a town audit (1262). The country at large was prosperous in this period, but the financing of the two crusades and of the grandiose schemes of Charles of Anjou led to complaints that royal taxation was leading to bankruptcy and formed a bad precedent for Philip IV.

A brilliant cultural advance accompanied the general material and political progress of the time of Philip II and Louis IX; Perfection of the **French Gothic:** Cathedral of Chartres (c. 1194, Romanesque and Gothic); Amiens (c. 1200); Reims (1210); Louis IX's *Sainte Chapelle*; progress of naturalism in Gothic sculpture. **University of Paris:** Foundation charter (1200); regulations of Innocent III (1215); endowment of Robert de Sorbon (hence Sorbonne) in 1257. Advance of **vernacular literature: Villehardouin's** (died c. 1212) *Conquest of Constantinople* (the first vernacular historical writing); **Chrétien de Troyes** and the Arthurian romances; Goliardic verse (with pagan touch); *fabliaux* (risqué, semirealistic bourgeois tales); *Aucassin and Nicolette* (a *chante fable* marked by irony and realism); **Jean de Meun's** (d. 1305) completion of William of Lorris' *Roman de la Rose* (a satire on the follies of all classes, especially women and clergy); **Jean de Joinville's** *Histoire du roi Saint Louis* (1309), the first vernacular classic of lay biography. **Paris the center of 13th-century philosophy:** harmonization of the Greek philosophy, especally Aristotle (newly recovered during the Renaissance of the 12th century in Latin translations) with Christian orthodoxy: **Vincent of Beauvais'** (d. 1264) *Speculum Maius* (a compendium of contemporary knowledge); **Albertus Magnus** (a German, d. 1280), chief of the

great Dominican teachers in Paris; **Thomas Aquinas** (an Italian, d. 1274), the pupil of Albertus Magnus. Thomas Aquinas' *Summa Theologiae* reconciled reason and religion, completed the integration of the classical learning and the Christian theology and remains to this day the basis of all Catholic theological teaching.

1270-1285. PHILIP III (*the Rash*), a hasty, ill-balanced king, victim of his favorites. The death of Philip's uncle, Alfonso of Poitiers, brought Languedoc under royal sway and established the royal power firmly in southern France (1272). The walls of Carcassonne and Aigues Mortes were built, the latter place giving access to the Mediterranean. Unsuccessful candidacy (1273) of Charles of Anjou for the imperial crown. Crusade (1282) against the King of Aragon, Philip acting as papal champion against the successful rival of the House of Anjou in Sicily.

1281-1285. The pontificate of Martin IV brought to an end an anti-French period of papal policy; papal support of Charles of Anjou's ambitious dreams of Byzantine conquest until the **Sicilian Vespers** (p. 290). There followed another period of papal opposition to French ambitions.

1285-1314. PHILIP IV (*the Fair*). His reign had a distinctly modern flavor and was marked by ruthless expansion of the royal power and notable consolidation of the monarchy: royal finance superseded the feudal; Roman lawyers (trained at Bologna and Montpellier) rather than clerics dominated the government; papal pretensions were reduced and the national Church made virtually autonomous under royal domination.

1286. Edward I of England did homage for Guienne.

1293. Philip treacherously confiscated Gascony, which had been temporarily surrendered by Edward as a pledge, after a Gascon-Norman sea-fight.

1294-1298. War with Edward I over Guienne. Philip announced a war levy on the clergy and followed a protest with a violent anti-papal pamphlet campaign. To finance the war Philip debased the coinage. He first made an alliance with the Scots (1295) and excluded English ships from all ports. In 1297, Edward invaded northern France, in alliance with the Count of Flanders, but the war was brought to a close by a truce negotiated by Pope Boniface VIII.

1296-1303. Philip's conflict with Pope Boniface VIII, who put forward extreme claims to papal supremacy. The bull *Clericis laicos* (1296) forbade secular rulers to levy taxes on the clergy without papal consent. Philip retorted by forbidding the export of precious metals (a serious threat to the papal finances) and by a vigorous propaganda campaign. Boniface, engaged in a feud with the Colonna in Rome and absorbed in Sicilian affairs, gave way and practically annulled the bull (1297). But the great papal jubilee of 1300 was followed by a resumption of the quarrel, culminating in 1302 in the bull *Unam sanctam*, the most extreme assertion of the doctrine of papal theocracy in the Middle Ages. On the **"Terrible Day"** of Anagni (1303, p. 222), Nogaret and Sciarra Colonna attacked the papal palace, demanded the resignation of the pope, and had a violent scene with Boniface. The death of the aged pontiff followed shortly.

1302. The first well-authenticated convocation of the **Estates-General**, including representatives of the towns in their feudal capacity. The meeting was called mainly to insure national support for the king's struggle with the pope.

1302, July 11. **Battle of the Spurs** (at Courtrai), brought about by the troubles in Flanders. Philip had antagonized the Count of Flanders by his efforts to penetrate his territory, and the count had turned to Edward I of England for support. The Flemish nobility betrayed him (1300) and he lost both his liberty and his county. But French rule soon alienated the independent burghers and led to the massacre of the French (*Matin de Bruges*), followed by the **battle of Courtrai,** in which the burghers defeated the flower of the French chivalry.

1305. **Election of Clement V** (a Frenchman) as pope. Clement reluctantly accepted French royal domination, lingered in France after his election, and finally took up his residence at Avignon, thus beginning the **Babylonian** or **Avignonese Captivity** of the papacy (p. 223). During the Captivity (1309-1376) the French monarchy exercised an important influence on the papacy. Clement was obliged to quash the bulls of Boniface, to absolve the assailants of Anagni, and to support Philip's suppression of the Knights Templar (see below). Philip may properly be called the founder of **Gallicanism** (i.e. of the autonomy of the French Church).

1306. The Jews were arrested, despoiled, and expelled from France.

1307. The Order of the Knights Templar, a rich, decadent organization which acted as banker to the popes and which was a creditor of Philip, had become almost a state within the state. Philip now launched an attack upon it. He had its lands occupied by royal officers and its property sequestrated. The country was stirred up against the Order by a vigorous propaganda campaign and by an appeal to the States-General (1308). Clement was obliged to co-operate and the Inquisition was made use of in the trial, the entire affair being conducted with unparalleled ruthlessness and horror (torture freely used to extort confessions).

1312. The Order of the Templars was abolished by the **Synod of Vienne.** Its property was transferred to the Hospitalers (except in Spain, and in France where it passed to the crown). Philip made the Temple treasury a section of the royal finance administration.

New economic and social alignments. The rapid expansion of France and especially the wars of Philip III and Philip IV against England and Flanders, raised an acute financial problem. Philip IV tried every device to raise money (feudal *aides*, war levies to replace military service, tallage of towns, special levies on clergy and nobles, "loans" and "gifts," the *maltôte* or sales tax, debasement of the coinage, attacks upon the Jews and Templars), but without finding an adequate solution. It was this situation primarily that explains the emergence of the

Estates-General. Levies on the nobles and clergy had long been arranged in meetings of representatives of these two orders; by negotiations between the towns and the royal agents the burghers had been brought to contribute. Provincial estates had been called frequently during the 13th century. The convocation of the Estates-General simply meant the substitution of national for provincial or local negotiation, and implied no principle of consent or control over royal taxation. The royal revenue was increased perhaps tenfold between the time of Louis IX and the time of Philip IV, but this meant overtaxation of all classes, harmful effects upon economic life, and estrangement of public opinion. Anti-tax leagues were organized and local assemblies drew up lists of grievances. Philip was obliged to call the Estates-General again in 1314, but as the bourgeoisie and the nobility distrusted each other, no effective measures were taken and no permanent constitutional development took place. Characteristic of the period was

Pierre Dubois' *De Recuperatione Sanctae Terrae* (c. 1306), ostensibly an appeal to Philip to undertake a crusade to recover the Holy Land from the Saracens, in reality an extensive program of reform in the interests of stronger national monarchy. Dubois envisaged the formation of a European league to enforce peace through common military action and economic boycott, disputes between parties to be settled by judicial methods. He called also for a system of universal education and for the secularization of church property.   (*Cont. p. 273.*)

f. THE IBERIAN PENINSULA, 1037-1284

(1) *Moslem Spain*

1037-1086.   THE MULUK AL-TAWA'IF (i.e. *Party Kings*). These were petty dynasties founded on the ruins of the Omayyad Caliphate: the Hammudids of Malaga (from 1016 onward) and of Algeciras (1039–); the Abbadids of Sevilla (1031–); the Zayrids of Granada (1012–); the Jahwarids of Cordova (1031–); the Dhul-Nunids of Toledo (1035–); the Amirids of Valencia (1021–); the Tojibids and Hudids of Saragossa (1019– and 1031–). Most of these dynasties were absorbed by the most distinguished of them, the Abbadids, who summoned the Almoravids from Africa to aid them against Alfonso VI of Castile.

1056-1147.   THE ALMORAVIDS, a Berber dynasty, founded by the Berber prophet **Abdullah ibn Tashfin.** They conquered Morocco and part of Algeria and were called into Spain by the Abbadids to help in the defense against the Christians. They defeated Alfonso of Castile at Zallaka (1086) and proceeded to annex Moorish Spain, with the exception of Toledo and Saragossa.

1130-1269.   THE ALMOHADES, a dynasty founded by the Berber prophet **Mohammed ibn Tumart.** His successor, Abdul-Mu'min, annihilated the Almoravid army (1144), after which Morocco was conquered (1146).

1145-1150.   The Almohades invaded and conquered Moorish Spain, after which they conquered Algeria (1152) and Tunis (1158). They were finally defeated by the Christian kings of Spain in

1212, July 16.   The battle of Las Navas de Tolosa, which was followed by their expulsion from Spain. Thereafter only local Moslem dynasties remained, of which the **Nasrids of Granada** (1232-1492) alone offered much resistance to the Christians until union of the Christian states brought about their defeat.

(2) *Castile*

1072-1109.   ALFONSO VI, OF CASTILE. He captured Toledo from the Moors (1085) and created his son-in-law, Henry of Burgundy, Count of Portugal (1093).

1086.   The Moslems, alarmed by Alfonso's progress, called from Africa the great **Yusuf ibn Tashfin** (d. 1106), leader of the newly dominant sect of Berber fanatics, the Almoravids. Ibn Yusuf landed at Algeciras (1086), and with the support of Seville, began a successful counter-thrust against the Christians (defeat of Alfonso at **Zallaka,** 1086). Yusuf, recalled by the African situation, did not at once exploit his advantage, but on his return to Spain his energetic, puritanic reforms strengthened the Moslems and brought them into an integral relation (c. 1091) with his great African empire which was centered in Morocco. This empire quickly disintegrated on Yusuf's death.

Alfonso resumed the Christian reconquest with the aid of **Rodrigo (Ruy) Diaz** of Bivar, the Cid (*Cid* as applied by the Moslems means *lord* or *master*). Alfonso's style of "emperor" represented personal prestige and a vague hegemony rather than political reality.

The **Cid,** a Castilian originally in the service of Sancho II of Castile, later passed to that of Alfonso VI; was exiled (1081); returned to Castilian service (1087-1088); went over to the Moslem king of Saragossa after his second exile. Eventually he became ruler of Valencia. The Cid served both sides, was cruel, selfish, and proud. Despite these characteristics the legendary figure of the man became the great national lay hero of Spain. On his death (1099) Valencia was soon abandoned to the Almoravids.

In the course of the 11th century French influence began to penetrate the peninsula. The Cluniacs, already (1033) strong in Catalonia, Castile, and Aragon, reinforced French influence, and stimulated clerical reform and the reconquest. A literary reflection of this is to be found in the *Cantar de mio Cid* (c. 1140), which already shows French elements in the cycle of the Cid (a cycle which continued into the 15th century).

1126-1157.   ALFONSO VII, crowned "emperor" (1135) on the basis of military ascendancy and an intense feeling of equality with rival monarchs, especially the Holy Roman emperors. The weakening of the Almoravids by luxury, and the rise

Rulers of Leon and Castile

Constance (2) ══════ Alfonso VI ══════ (3) Jimena Muñoz
King of Leon, 1065–1109
King of Castile, 1072–1109

Raymond ══ Urraca
of Burgundy │ 1109–1126

Teresa ══ Henry of
Burgundy

Berenguela ══ Alfonso VII
of Barcelona │ 1126–1157

Alfonso Henriques
King of Portugal
1114–1185

Blanca ══════ Sancho III
of Navarre │ King of Castile
1157–1158

Ferdinand II ══ Urraca of
King of Leon │ Portugal
1157=1188

Alfonso VIII ══ Eleanor of
King of Castile │ England
1158–1214

Henry I │ Blanca │ Urraca │ Berenguela ══ Alfonso IX
King of Castile │ m. Louis VIII │ m. Alfonso II │ King of Leon
1214–1217 │ of France │ of Portugal │ 1188–1230

Ferdinand III
King of Castile, 1217–1252
King of Leon, 1230–1252

Alfonso X
1252–1284

Sancho IV
1284–1295

of rivals (the Almohades) in Africa (c. 1125), made possible a resumption of the reconquest (1144–1147) with wide raids into Andalusia. The Almohades, summoned from Africa (1146), completed (1172) the second restoration of Moslem unity, and made Moslem Spain a province of their African empire, reducing the Arab influence in Spain to nothing in favor of Berber fanatics. Alfonso's death was followed by a minority and an eight-year dynastic crisis from which his son Alfonso VIII finally emerged as master.

1158–1214. ALFONSO VIII. After a series of successful attacks on the Moslems, Alfonso was overwhelmingly defeated (**Alarcos,** 1195) by the Almohades, then at the zenith of their power. Leon and Navarre promptly invaded Castile, but Alfonso triumphed over them, and, with the aid of Pope Innocent III and the clergy, began the preparation of a unified general assault on the Moslems which led to the greatest victory of the reconquest, **Las Navas de Tolosa** (1212), soon followed by the decline of the Almohade power in Spain and Africa and by Christian dissension.

1179. Portugal's independence and royal title were recognized by Pope Alexander III.

1217–1252. FERDINAND III ended the dynastic war in Castile and attacked the Moors in the Guadalquivir Valley, taking Cordova (1236) and Seville

(1248). On the appeal of the Almohade emperor he sent aid to him, gaining in return a line of African fortresses, and permission to establish a Christian church at Marrakah. His plans for an invasion of Africa were cut short by death. After the capture of Jaen (1246), the emir was allowed to establish himself at Granada, the last Moorish stronghold, as Ferdinand's vassal.

The long history of guerrilla warfare in Castile disorganized tillage, made the people averse to agriculture, led to a concentration of population in the towns, and accounts for the poverty of Castilian agriculture, the tremendous influence of municipalities in mediaeval Castile, the development of a race of soldiers, and the isolation of Spanish thought from general European currents. In general the Moors were not disliked, and intermarriages were not unusual until the 13th century. Then the preaching of crusades as part of the reconquest and papal propaganda prepared the Spanish mind for the burst of intolerance and fanaticism which began in the second half of the 15th century.

The war of Christian reconquest gave birth to three great native military orders, modeled partly on Moorish societies for border defense, partly on the international crusading orders, notably the Templars already established in the Peninsula. Some members took the regular monkish vows, others did not. Two Cistercian monks assumed (1158) the defense of Calatrava (when the Templars gave it up), and the **Order of Calatrava** which grew up was confirmed by the pope (1164). The **Order of Santiago** (established 1171) was the largest and richest, the **Order of Alcántara** (founded c. 1156) an offshoot of Calatrava, was the most clerical in type. By 1493 these orders had grown to stupendous size (the largest, Santiago, having 700,000 members and vassals, and an annual income of close to a million dollars, present value).

In the period following 1252 fear of the infidel was no longer a dominant force in Iberian politics and the nobles turned from assaults on the Moors to attacks upon the monarchy. The struggle between crown and baronage (which found a parallel all through Europe) was notable in Spain for the depth of governmental degradation which it produced. The new elements in the situation were clearly indicated in the reign of

1252-1284. ALFONSO X (*the Learned*), a versatile savant, distinguished as an astronomer (*Alfonsine Tables*), poet, historian, patron of learning, a pre-eminent lawyer and codifier (*las Siete Partidas*), devoted to the Roman ideal of centralized absolute monarchy, but a futile, vacillating monarch. Lavish concessions to the nobles (1271) to avoid civil war established the aristocracy in a position from which it was not dislodged until the reign of Ferdinand and Isabella. Debasement of the coinage to relieve poverty produced economic crises; alternate alliance and war with the vassal King of Granada, and hostilities with Aragon, accomplished nothing. The Kingdom of Murcia was regained (1266) with the aid of James I of Aragon, and was then incorporated with Castile.

In foreign affairs Alfonso abandoned the long peninsularity of Spanish sovereigns, made a series of dynastic alliances, and attempted to give Castile an important European position.

1263-1267. Efforts to rectify the Portuguese boundary with advantage to Castile ultimately produced an actual loss of territory (in Algarve); Alfonso began the long effort to regain Portugal, which finally succeeded under Philip II (1580). Claims to (English) Gascony were revived (1253) and abandoned (1254); desultory wars fought with France. A twenty-year effort to win the crown of the Holy Roman Empire (despite papal opposition and public opinion) met with two defeats (1257 and 1273). The death of Alfonso's eldest son Ferdinand (1275) led at once to a bitter struggle over the succession organized by Alfonso's son Sancho.

(3) Barcelona and Catalonia

The **Spanish Mark** was established as a result of the conquest of Catalonia by Charlemagne (785-811). The County of Barcelona (erected 817) under the Frankish crown became independent, perhaps as early as the 9th century. By the beginning of the 12th century the Counts of Barcelona had large holdings north of the Pyrenees (notably in Provence), to which they added for a brief period (1114-1115) Majorca and Iviza, and permanently Tarragona.

1137. The union of Catalonia and Aragon, begun by Raymond Berenguer IV of Catalonia, was epochal, for it created a powerful state with access to the sea. Catalonian territories included Cerdagne, a large part of Provence, etc., with the later addition of Roussillon (1172), Montpellier (1204, under French suzerainty), Foix, Nîmes, Béziers (1162-1196).

1213. The battle of Muret (see below) definitely turned Catalonia back into the Spanish orbit.

In the 13th century **Barcelona**, utilizing the skill of her native sailors and the local (mostly Jewish) accumulations of capital,

The Houses of Navarre, Aragon, and Barcelona

Sancho the Great === Mayor of
of Navarre   Castile
1000-1032

KINGS OF NAVARRE   KINGS OF ARAGON

Estefania === Garcia   Ramiro I
of Barcelona | King of Navarre   King of Aragon
             | 1035-1054   1035-1063

Sancho V   Ramon   Sancho Ramirez
King of Navarre   King of Aragon, 1063-1094
1054-1076   King of Navarre, 1076-1094
              Ramiro

Garcia Ramirez IV   Pedro I   Alfonso I   Ramiro II
King of Navarre   King of Aragon   King of Aragon   1134-1137
1134-1150   and Navarre and Navarre
                    1094-1104   1104-1134

Sancho VII   Ramon   Petronilla
King of Navarre   Berenguer IV === Queen
1150-1194   Count of Bar-   of Aragon
                    celona, 1131-1162 1137-1162

Theobald === Blanca Sancho VIII   Alfonso II
of Champagne| King of Navarre King of Aragon
            | 1194-1234   1162-1196

Teobaldo I   Pedro II
King of Navarre   King of Aragon
1234-1253   1196-1213

Teobaldo II   Henry I   James I
King of Navarre King of Navarre   King of Aragon
1253-1270   1270-1274   1213-1276

               Juana I   Pedro III
               Queen of Navarre   1276-1285
               1274-1305

and profiting by Italian commercial pioneering, began an extensive slave trade in Moorish prisoners. Aragonese imperial expansion in the Mediterranean (Sicily and the Greek Archipelago, pp. 284, 290) gave Barcelona further commercial advantages and made it one of the most active Mediterranean ports.

Ramon Lull (1232–1315) was the greatest Catalonian intellectual figure of the Middle Ages, a vernacular poet, novelist, missionary, mystic, educator, reformer, logician, scientist, and traveler.

(4) *Navarre*

Navarre gained its independence from Carolingian rule in the 9th century and fell heir to the Carolingian rights in Aragon, which was absorbed by Navarre in the 10th century. Sancho the Great (970–1035) secured the succession of Castile, conquered most of Leon and temporarily united the Iberian kingdoms. By his will Aragon passed to his son Ramiro (d. 1063) and the union came to an end. On the death of **Alfonso the Warrior** (1104–1134), Navarre returned to its old ruling house until it passed under French control (1234) for two centuries.

(5) *Aragon*

Aragon, beginning as a county on the river Arago under Carolingian control, emerged from Carolingian domination in the middle of the 9th century, passed under the control of Navarre, and then became independent under Ramiro (d. 1063). The period from 1063 to 1134 is marked by confusion, intrigue, some progress against the Moors, and the annexation of Navarre (1076).

1104-1134. ALFONSO I (*the Warrior*) advanced to the Ebro, captured Saragossa (1118), and made raids to the Mediterranean. On Alfonso's death, Aragon chose his brother, **Ramiro,** a monk who emerged from retirement long enough to marry and produce a daughter, Petronilla, whom he married off to Raymond Berenguer IV (1131–1162), Count of Catalonia. He then returned (1137) to his monastery, leaving Petronilla under the guardianship of her husband, and the succession settled. The resulting union of Catalonia and Aragon was a decisive event in Spanish history.

After the union the Aragonese kings, preoccupied with Spanish affairs, let Provence drift, and on the death of Alfonso II (1162–1196) it passed to his son Alfonso, nominally under the suzerainty of his brother Peter II (1196–1213), but, in fact, lost for good. Alfonso tried to keep his Provençal holdings clear of the Albigensian heresy, but Raymond, Count of Toulouse, a supporter of the heresy, sought to win Peter II to his views. Peter went to Rome (1204) for a papal coronation, declared himself a vassal of the Holy See, and bore an honorable part at Las Navas de Tolosa, but was forced by the horrors of the Albigensian Crusade and the legitimate appeals of his vassals to oppose Simon de Montfort at Muret, where he fell.

1213. The battle of **Muret** marked the real end of Aragonese interests north of the Pyrenees.

1258. By the Treaty of Corbeil the King of France renounced his claims to Barcelona, Urgel (etc.), Cerdagne, Roussillon (etc.). Aragon ceded: Carcassonne, Foix, Béziers, Nîmes, Narbonne, Toulouse (etc.). All rights in Provence passed to Margaret, wife of Louis IX; a marriage was arranged between Louis' son Philip and Isabella, daughter of James I of Aragon.

1213-1276. JAMES I (*the Conqueror*). After the weakness and anarchy of his minority, James, one of the greatest soldiers of the Middle Ages, conquered Valencia in an intermittent campaign (1233-1245), took the Kingdom of Murcia for Castile (1266), and freed the Aragonese frontier of the Moslem menace. James also attempted to establish his overlordship over Tlemcen and Bugia in North Africa, and to secure a hold in Tunis. Against the will of his Aragonese nobles, but with the support of his Catalonian and French vassals, James conquered the Balearic Islands (1229–1235), thus beginning the creation of an Aragonese Mediterranean empire.

SPANISH CULTURE in the middle ages was very largely conditioned by external influences.

Architecture: (1) **Pre-romanesque** architecture revealed traces of Visigothic, Carolingian, Persian, Byzantine, and Moslem traditions. (2) **Romanesque architecture** showed particularly the influence of Auvergne and Languedoc (e.g. second church of Santiago de Compostella). (3) **The Gothic** was marked by strong elements of the Burgundian style, brought by the Cluniacs. The full tide of the Gothic was probably introduced by the Cistercians (e.g. cathedrals of Toledo, c. 1230; Burgos 1126; Leon, c. 1230). Catalan Gothic shows German influences (cathedrals of Barcelona, 1298; Gerona, 1312). The later Spanish Gothic revealed French, German, and Flemish currents (e.g. cathedral of Seville, begun 1401; west towers of Burgos cathedral, 1442). (4) **Moorish architecture** had a development of its own: the great mosque of Cordova (completed 1118), the Alcazar, Seville (c. 1181), and the Alhambra (mostly 14th century).

Foundation of the first universities: Palencia (1209); Salamanca (1242).

(*Cont. p.* 280.)

(6) *Portugal to* 1279

1055- Reconquest from the Moors of much of present-day Portugal by **Ferdinand the Great** of Leon and Castile. Ferdinand organized the territory as a county, with Coimbra as the capital.

1093-1112. Henry of Burgundy, a descendant of King Robert of France, came to Spain with other knights-adventurers, to fight against the Moors. In return the King of Castile granted him the County of Portugal and gave him the hand of his (illegitimate) daughter, Theresa. Henry himself was a typical crusader, restless and enterprising, whose main hope

appears to have been to establish a dynasty in Castile.

1112-1185. AFONSO HENRIQUES, the founder of the Portuguese monarchy and of the Burgundian dynasty. Afonso was only three years old at the death of his father. His mother Teresa ruled as regent, but soon became involved in a struggle with Galicia and Castile. Being defeated, she agreed to accept Castilian domination, but

1128. Afonso assumed authority, repudiated the agreement, and, after defeating the Spaniards, drove his mother into exile.

1139. **Afonso,** one of the most famous knights of his age, began a long series of struggles against the Moors by defeating them in the **battle of Ourique.**

1143. Afonso was proclaimed king by the Córtes. The pope arranged the **Treaty of Zamora** between Portugal and Castile, the latter recognizing Portuguese independence, while Portugal accepted the suzerainty of the pope.

Kings of Portugal, Burgundian House

1147. The Portuguese took Lisbon and established a frontier on the Tagus.

1169. Further conflicts with Castile led to Afonso's attack on Badajoz. He was defeated and captured, but soon released.

1185-1211. SANCHO I, the son of Afonso Henriques. His reign was noteworthy for the development of towns and for the establishment of military orders of knighthood. Sancho did much to settle colonists on the lands that were won back in the prolonged wars against the Moors.

1211-1223. AFONSO II. Beginning of the king's conflict with the clergy, which led to interference by the pope and to restlessness among the nobility.

1223-1245. SANCHO II. His trouble with the clergy and nobility led ultimately to his deposition by the pope, who offered the crown to

1245-1279. AFONSO III, the brother of Sancho II and Count of Boulogne. His title being weak, Afonso was much dependent on the Córtes, in which the commons were for the first time represented. **War with Castile** was ended by a peace in 1253. (*Cont. p.* 284.)

2. EASTERN EUROPE

a. THE SLAVS

The Slavs, an eastern branch of the Indo-European family, were known to the Roman and Greek writers of the 1st and 2d centuries A.D. under the name of *Venedi* as inhabiting the region beyond the Vistula. The majority of modern scholars agree that the "original home" of the Slavs was the territory to the southeast of the Vistula and to the northeast of the Carpathian Mountains, in the upper basins of the Western Bug, the Pripet, and the Dniester. In the course of the early centuries of our era the Slavs expanded in all directions, and by the 6th century, when they were known to Gothic and Byzantine writers as *Sclaveni*, they were apparently already separated into three main divisions: (1) the western Slavs (the present-day Poles, Czechs, Slovaks, and Moravians); (2) the southern Slavs (the Bulgarians, Serbs, Croats, and Slovenes); (3) the eastern Slavs (the Russians, subsequently subdivided into the Great Russians, the Little Russians or the Ukrainians, and the White Russians).

However, some recent theories insist that the "original" settlements of the Slavs extended much farther south and west than the area indicated above, and thus minimize the importance of the subsequent Slav migrations.

Closely related to the Slavs were the Lithuanians who, together with the Letts and the ancient Prussians, formed the Baltic branch of the Indo-European family. They inhabited the southeastern coast of the Baltic Sea, between the present location of Memel and Estonia.

b. BOHEMIA AND MORAVIA, TO 1306

The earliest recorded attempt at the construction of a Slavic state was that made by

c. 623-658. **Samo,** who appears to have been a Frankish tradesman traveling in central Europe. Probably taking advantage of the defeat of the Avars by the Greeks in 626, he managed to unite the Czechs and some of the Wends, and succeeded in repulsing not only the Avars, but also the Franks under King Dagobert (631). But on the death of Samo the union of the tribes disintegrated.

870-894. **Sviatopluk,** a Moravian prince, succeeded in uniting under his authority Moravia, Bohemia, and present-day Slovakia and managed to maintain his position as against the Germans. During his reign the western Slavs were converted to Christianity by the Greek missionaries, **Cyril and Methodius** (d. 885 in Moravia), but in the last years of the century the German clergy redoubled its efforts and won Bohemia and Moravia for the Latin Church, thus establishing the ecclesiastical dependence of the western Slavs on Rome.

906. **The Kingdom of Moravia** was dissolved as the result of a great defeat by the Hungarians.

929. **Death of St. Wenceslas,** of the house of Premysl, which had emerged in the late 9th century. Wenceslas was murdered by his younger brother, representing the forces of the heathen reaction, who ascended the throne as

929-967. **BOLESLAV I.** He seems to have carried on constant warfare against the encroaching Germans, until forced (950) to accept German suzerainty. To the eastward he made many conquests and included Moravia, part of Slovakia, part of Silesia, and even Cracow in his kingdom. Furthermore, he appears to have established a fairly strong royal power over the old tribal chiefs.

967-999. BOLESLAV II, son of the preceding. He apparently continued the policies of his father and saw to the final victory of the Christian faith (foundation of the Bishopric of Prague, 973). Missionaries from Bohemia took an active part in the conversion of Hungary and Poland.

The entire 11th and 12th centuries were filled with repeated dynastic conflicts between members of the Premysl family and the various claimants appealing to Poland and more particularly to the German emperors for support. The result was an ever-increasing German influence and the gradual integration of Bohemia with the empire.

999-1000. Boleslav the Brave of Poland took advantage of the anarchy in Bohemia to conquer Silesia, Moravia, and Cracow. In 1003 he became Duke of Bohemia, but was driven out in the next year by a German army. There followed another period of disorder, marked only by

1031. The reacquisition of Moravia, which thenceforth remained connected with Bohemia.

1034-1055. BRETISLAV I (*the Restorer*), who overran Silesia, took Cracow (1039) and for a time ruled Poland, which had now entered upon a period of disruption.

1041. Emperor Henry III, alarmed by the expansion of the Bohemian power, invaded the country and advanced to Prague. Bretislav agreed to give up his Polish conquests and pay tribute to the emperor.

1055-1061. Spytihnev, son of Bretislav, whose reign was uneventful.

1061-1092. VRATISLAV II, who, throughout his reign, loyally supported the German emperor, Henry IV, in his struggle with the papacy and took part in the Italian campaigns. He was rewarded by Henry with a crown (1086), but only for his own person.

1092-1110. Bretislav II.

1111-1125. Vladislav I.

1125-1140. Sobeslav I.

1140-1173. VLADISLAV II. Like his predecessors, he supported the German emperors in the main, and was rewarded (1156) by Frederick Barbarossa with an hereditary crown for his aid against the Italian cities.

1173-1197. Another period of dynastic

conflict, during which there were no less than ten rulers.

1197-1230. OTTOKAR I. He took full advantage of the struggles for the succession which now began to wrack the German Empire. Siding now with one party, now with another, he made the Bohemian king (an imperial elector since the early 12th century) one of the decisive powers in German affairs. On the other hand, a long-drawn conflict with the clergy (1214–1221) led to the almost complete independence of the Church.

1212. The Golden Bull of Frederick II recognized the right of the Bohemian nobility to elect its own ruler.

1230-1253. WENCESLAS (VACLAV) I. His reign was marked by large-scale immigration of Germans, encouraged by the ruler, possibly to counteract the growing power of the nobility. Germans had been coming in for a long time (chiefly clergy and nobility), but they now began to open up large forested tracts and to build cities, which were given practical autonomy under German (Magdeburg) law.

1247-1250. Rising of the nobility against the king, possibly in protest against the favor shown the Germans.

1251. The Austrian estates, after the death of the last Babenberg duke, elected Ottokar, son of Wenceslas, as duke.

1253-1278. OTTOKAR II (*the Great*) whose reign marked the widest expansion of Bohemian power and was characterized by great prosperity (opening of the famous silver mines, which made Bohemia one of the wealthiest countries in the later Middle Ages).

1255. Ottokar carried on a successful campaign in support of the Teutonic Knights against the heathen Prussians.

1260. After defeating the Hungarians, Ottokar took from them the province of Styria.

1267. A second northern campaign, against the Lithuanians, achieved little.

1269. Ottokar, taking advantage of the interregnum in the German Empire, extended his power over Carinthia, Carniola, and Istria.

1273. Election of **Rudolph of Hapsburg** as emperor. Ottokar refused to recognize him. The Diet of Regensburg (1274) therefore declared all Ottokar's acquisitions void. The emperor, supported by the Hungarians and by some of the

Bohemian nobility, attacked Ottokar, who agreed to give up all but Bohemia and Moravia, and to recognize Rudolph's suzerainty even over these.

1278. New war between Rudolph and Ottokar. Ottokar was decisively defeated on the **Marchfeld** (Aug. 26) and killed.

1278-1305. Wenceslas II, a boy of seven, for whom Otto of Brandenburg at first acted as regent.

1290. Wenceslas was elected and crowned King of Poland.

1301. His son, Wenceslas, was elected King of Hungary (ruled to 1304).

1305-1306. Wenceslas III. He gave up the claim to Hungary and was murdered while en route to Poland to suppress a revolt of the nobles. **End of the Premyslid line.** (*Cont. p.* 304.)

c. POLAND, TO 1305

The Polish state emerged in the 10th century, the result of the unification of some six tribes under the **Polani**, who were ruled by the members of the semi-mythical family of Piast. From the outset the Poles were obliged to fight against the encroachment of the Germans from the west, the Prussians from the north, the Bohemians from the south, and the Hungarians, also in the south.

c. 960-992. MIESZKO I, of the house of Piast, the first historical ruler. He conquered the territory between the Oder and the Warthe Rivers, but was defeated by Markgraf Gero and obliged to recognize German suzerainty (973).

966. Mieszko was converted to Christianity by Bohemian missionaries, probably for political reasons, to deprive the Germans of any further excuse for aggression. The acceptance of Latin Christianity meant the connection of Poland, like Bohemia and Hungary, with western European culture.

992-1025. BOLESLAV I (*Chrobry = the Brave*). He ascended the throne at 25 and was the real organizer of the Polish state. An energetic, but at times treacherous and cruel ruler, he built up an efficient military machine, laid the basis for an administrative system (*comites = castellani = Burggrafen*, with civil and military powers), organized the Church (establishment of Benedictine monasteries, etc.). Politically his aim appears to have been the union of all western Slavs under his rule. He conquered eastern Pomerania and gained access to the Baltic (992-994), added Silesia, Moravia, and Cracow to his domain (999), and induced Otto III to erect an in-

dependent Archbishopric of Gnesen (1000). On the death of Otto he took advantage of the confusion in Germany to occupy Lusatia and Meissen, and in 1003 made himself Duke of Bohemia. The new emperor, Henry II, carried on long wars against Boleslav to break his power (1004-) and ultimately forced the abandonment of Bohemia and Lusatia (1005). But by the **Treaty of Bautzen** (1018) Boleslav was given Lusatia as an imperial fief, and just before his death Boleslav was able to make himself King of Poland (1025).

1025-1034. MIESZKO II, a much weaker ruler. The Poles, like the other Slavs, divided the domain among the various sons of a deceased king, thus creating endless dynastic conflict and ample opportunity for intervention by neighboring rulers. During Mieszko's reign most of the territorial gains of Boleslav were lost: St. Stephen of Hungary conquered Slovakia (1027); Bretislav of Bohemia took Moravia (1031); Iaroslav of Russia acquired Ruthenia (1031); Canute of Denmark took Pomerania (1031). In 1032 the Emperor Conrad actually divided Poland between Mieszko and two of his relatives.

1034-1040. A period of violent dynastic struggle and general insurrection, including a heathen reaction (burning of monasteries, massacre of the clergy) and a peasant uprising against the landlords. In the meanwhile Bretislav of Bohemia seized Silesia (1038).

1038-1058. CASIMIR I (*the Restorer*), who succeeded, with the aid of the Emperor Henry III, in reconquering his domain, re-establishing Christianity and restoring order. Silesia was recovered (1054). In return Casimir was obliged to give up the royal title (becoming merely a *grand duke*) and to make numerous concessions to the nobility and clergy, thus initiating a baneful practice.

1058-1079. BOLESLAV II (*the Bold*), one of the great mediaeval rulers. In the great struggle between the emperor and the pope he consistently supported the latter, as a counterweight to German influence. At the same time he did his utmost to throw off the pressure of the nobility. In his countless campaigns he reconquered upper Slovakia (1061-1063) and marched as far as Kiev, to put his relative upon the Russian throne (1069). In 1076 he reassumed the royal crown, with the pope's approval. But his entire policy estranged the nobility, which ultimately drove him from his throne.

1079-1102. Vladislav I (*Ladislas*), Hermann, an indolent and unwarlike ruler, brother of Boleslav. He resigned the royal title and attempted to secure peace by supporting the Emperor Henry IV, as well as by courting the nobility and clergy.

1102-1138. BOLESLAV III (*Wry-mouth*), who acquired the throne only after a violent struggle with his brother Zbigniew. He was one of the greatest Polish kings, who defeated the Pomeranians (battle of **Naklo**, 1109) and, by the incorporation of Pomerania (1119–1123), re-established the access to the sea. At the same time he defeated the Emperor Henry V (1109, battle of **Hundsfeld**, near Breslau) and checked the German advance. On the other hand, his campaigns in Hungary (1132–1135) had no definite results.

Boleslav completed the organization of the state, in which the great landlords (*nobiles*=magnates), gentry (*milites*=knights =*szlachta*) had become well-defined social classes, the peasantry having steadily lost in the periods of confusion. The Church was reorganized under the Archbishop of Gnesen, by the papal legate Walo. In order to avoid dispute, Boleslav fixed the succession by seniority. Poland was divided into **five principalities** (Silesia, Great Poland, Masovia, Sandomir, Cracow) for his sons; Cracow was established as the capital, and was to go, with the title of *grand duke*, to the eldest member of the house of Piast. In actual fact this arrangement by no means eliminated the dynastic competition, but introduced a long period of disruption, during which the nobility and clergy waxed ever more powerful and the ducal or royal power became insignificant. Only the weakness of the neighboring states saved Poland from destruction.

1138-1146. Vladislav II (Ladislas).

1146-1173. Boleslav IV, an ineffectual ruler, during whose reign the Germans, under Albert the Bear and Henry the Lion, supported by Waldemar of Denmark, drove back the Poles from the entire territory along the Baltic and west of the Vistula (1147). The Emperor Frederick Barbarossa intervened and forced the humble submission of Boleslav (1157).

1173-1177. Mieszko III, a brutal and despotic prince who antagonized the nobility and was soon driven out by them.

1177-1194. CASIMIR II (*the Just*) was practically elected by the magnates, who extorted privileges from him. In the **Assembly of Lenczyca** (1180) the clergy was also given far-reaching concessions. Casimir attempted to preclude further strife by making Cracow and the primacy hereditary in his own line.

1194-1227. Leszek I (*the White*), whose reign was punctuated by constant wars against Mieszko III, who attempted to regain the throne (d. 1202), and against the latter's son Vladislav Laskonogi (1202–1206). The period was one of complete feudal anarchy, with the nobility and clergy controlling the situation.

1227-1279. Boleslav V, an unhappy reign marked by complete disruption and by constant aggression by neighboring states.

1228. Arrival of the **Teutonic Knights,** called to Prussia by Duke Conrad of Masovia (p. 214). Within the next 50 years they conquered Prussia and erected a most formidable barrier to Polish access to the sea.

1241. Beginning of the great **Mongol invasions** (p. 262), of which there were constant renewals throughout the rest of the century. The Poles managed to stave off Mongol domination, but the country was devastated. One result was the calling in of large numbers of German settlers, some of whom cleared forest land and colonized new areas in Silesia and Posen, others of whom settled in the towns. In all cases large concessions in the direction of autonomy were made (*Magdeburg law*). The German influence meant greater and more efficient exploitation of the soil, development of trade, cultural advance.

1279-1288. Leszek II (*the Black*).

1288-1290. Further dynastic and feudal warfare, with the brief reign of Henry Probus.

1290-1296. Przemyslav II. He was crowned king with the consent of the pope (1295), but was murdered soon afterward.

1300-1305. Wenceslas I, son of the King of Bohemia, elected by the nobility but challenged by claimants of the Piast family. He soon resigned the position and returned home.   (*Cont. p.* 313.)

d. RUSSIA, TO 1263

The **eastern Slavs** settled on the territory of present-day European Russia in the period from the 5th to the 8th century A.D. Little is known of their political history during these centuries, but undoubtedly there were attempts at political organization in the shape of both tribal principalities and city-states formed around important commercial centers. In the 8th century some of the eastern Slavs were under the protectorate of the **Khazars,** a Turkish tribe which established a strong and prosperous state along the lower Volga. After the end of the 8th century the northern part of Russia began to be penetrated by the Scandinavian vikings called in the old Russian chronicles **Varangians** or *Rus* (hence the name of *Russia*). In the course of the 9th century the Varangians constantly moved southward along the main waterway leading from the Baltic to the Black Sea, gradually establishing their political domination over the Slav communities. According to tradition, the Scandinavian chieftain **Riurik** (Rorik?) ruled in Novgorod in the 860's. Later he was recognized as the founder of the Russian princely dynasty.

860. The first recorded appearance of the Russians (*Varangians*) at Constantinople. This was a raid not unlike those of the Norsemen on Britain and France at the same period.

c. 880-912. PRINCE OLEG, who succeeded in uniting under his control both Novgorod and Kiev (on the Dnieper River). Kiev subsequently became the political center of a loose federation of Russian states.

911. The Russians again appeared at Constantinople and extracted trade privileges from the Byzantine emperor. Trade became a leading occupation of the Russian princes, who, with their followers (*druzhina*), protected the merchant ships. Russians also began to take service with the Greek emperors in considerable number and came to play an important rôle in the mercenary corps.

945. Further trade agreements with the Greek Empire testify to the ever closer economic connections and no doubt to an increasing cultural contact.

957. The Russian princess, Olga, visited Constantinople and was converted to the Christian faith. This was, however, a purely personal conversion, and may in fact have been Olga's second.

964-972. SVIATOSLAV, the son of Olga. He was the first of the great conquering princes. In 965 he defeated the Khazars on the lower Volga and proceeded to establish a Russian state in place of the Khazar Empire. Called to the Balkans to aid the Greek emperor against the powerful Bulgars, he carried on a successful campaign (967) and decided to establish himself on the lower Danube. At this time his power extended from Novgorod in the north to the Danube in the southwest and to the lower Volga in the southeast. He was forced to abandon Bulgaria in order to resist the **Patzinaks** *(Pechenegs)*, who had

entered southern Russia from the east and were threatening Kiev. Having repulsed them (968), Sviatoslav returned to Bulgaria, but he was no more welcome to the Greeks than were the Bulgars. In 971 he was defeated and driven out by the Emperor John Zimisces (p. 180). Sviatoslav was defeated and killed by the Patzinaks on his way back to Kiev (972).

972-978. A dynastic struggle between the sons of Sviatoslav ended in the victory of

978-1015. VLADIMIR THE SAINT, in whose reign (c. 990) the Russians were converted in mass to Christianity in the eastern (Byzantine) form. The Russian Church was organized on the Greek pattern and was considered to be under the canonical authority of the Patriarch of Constantinople. From this time on the cultural relation between Constantinople and Kiev was very close.

1015-1019. Further dynastic conflict between the sons of Vladimir.

1019-1054. IAROSLAV (*the Wise*), the greatest ruler of Russia in the Kievan period. He was finally successful in the struggle with his brother Sviatopolk, but was obliged to leave to another brother, Mstislav, that part of the principality east of the Dnieper River until Mstislav's death in 1036. Iaroslav was then supreme ruler of all Russia. Extensive building activity at Kiev (Cathedral of St. Sophia). Religious activity (metropolitan Hilarion and the Monastery of the Caves). Promotion of education. Revision of the *Russian Law* (the earliest known Russian law code), under Byzantine influence. Dynastic alliances with western states (Iaroslav's daughter, Anna, married Henry I of France).

The period following the death of Iaroslav the Great was one of disintegration and decline. Technically the primacy of Kiev continued and the power remained concentrated in the family of Iaroslav. Actually Kiev continued to lose in importance, and authority became divided between members of the princely family on a system of seniority and rotation, leading of necessity to much dynastic rivalry and countless combinations, sometimes with Poles and Hungarians.

At the same time the Kievan state was subjected to ever greater pressure from the nomads (Patzinaks and Cumans) moving into southern Russia from the east. The period witnessed also a shifting of the older trade routes, due to the decline of the Baghdad Caliphate and the conquest of Constantinople (1204) by the Latin crusaders.

Emergence of new political centers: Galicia and Volynia in the southwest, principalities characterized by a strongly aristocratic form of government; Novgorod the Great, in the north, controlling territory to the east to the Urals. In Novgorod the assembly of freemen (*Vieche*) reached its fullest development; Suzdal-Vladimir in central Russia, the precursor of the Grand Duchy of Moscow. In this region the princely power was dominant.

1113-1125. VLADIMIR MONOMAKH, Prince of Kiev. He carried on numerous campaigns against the Cumans of the steppes and his reign marked the last period of brilliance at Kiev, which soon thereafter became a bone of contention between the Princes of Volynia and Suzdal.

1147. First mention of **Moscow in** one of the chronicles.

1157-1174. ANDREI BOGOLIUBSKI, Prince of Suzdal. He repressed the rising power of the nobles (*boyars*), united a large block of territory and established his capital at Vladimir.

1169. Andrei conquered Kiev, which became part of the Vladimir principality. But the new state underwent a marked decline on the death of the ruler.

1199-1205. Zenith of the Galician principality under Prince Roman.

1201. Foundation of Riga, which became the center of German missionary enterprise and commercial expansion.

1202. Foundation of the German Order of Swordbearers by Bishop Albert of Livonia (Latvia).

1219. Conquest of **Estonia** by Waldemar II of Denmark.

1223. BATTLE OF THE KALKA RIVER, near the Sea of Azov. The Mongols (Tatars, see p. 260), under Sabutai, invaded southern Russia from the Transcaucasus region and completely defeated a coalition of Russian princes and Cuman leaders. They retired, however, without pressing their conquests.

1226. The Teutonic Knights (p. 214) were commissioned to conquer and convert Prussia. They united with the Swordbearers in 1237.

1236-1263. ALEXANDER NEVSKI, prince first of Novgorod and after 1252 of Vladimir.

1237-1240. THE MONGOL CONQUEST, under the leadership of Batu. The great armies of the invaders swept over southern and central Russia and into Europe, coming within 60 miles of Nov-

gorod. They took Kiev (1240) and ultimately established themselves (1242) at Sarai on the lower Volga. The **Khanate of the Golden Horde** for two centuries thereafter acted as suzerain of all Russia, levying tribute and taking military contingents, but for the rest leaving the princes in control, respecting the Russian Church and interfering little.

1240. **Alexander Nevski** defeated the Swedes under Birger Jarl on the Neva River and thus broke the force of the Swedish advance.

1242. Alexander defeated the Teutonic Knights in a **battle on Lake Peipus.**

1252. As Prince of Vladimir, Alexander Nevski did his utmost to prevent insurrections against Tatar rule and built up a system of protection based upon submission and conciliation.

1253. **Daniel of Volynia** attempted to organize a crusade against the Tatars. In order to secure papal aid he accepted the union of the Russian Church with Rome, but his efforts came to nothing.

1263. **Death of Alexander Nevski** on his way back from the Golden Horde.

RUSSIAN CULTURE in this period was still primarily religious and largely Byzantine in character. Noteworthy churches were built at Kiev, Novgorod, and Cernigov in the 11th and 12th centuries, decorated with fine frescoes. Church literature was active and there appeared further the first chronicles and epics of fights against the nomads. (*Cont. p.* 316.)

e. HUNGARY, TO 1301

896. The Hungarians, organized in a number of tribes, of which the **Magyars** were the leading one, occupied the valley of the middle Danube and Theiss. Under **Arpad** (d. 907) they had come from southern Russia by way of Moldavia, driven on by the Patzinaks (Pechenegs) and other Asiatic peoples. The Hungarians were themselves nomads of the Finno-Ugrian family. For more than half a century after their occupation of Hungary they continued their raids, both toward the east and toward the west.

906. The Hungarians destroyed the rising Slavic kingdom of Moravia.

955. **Battle of Augsburg,** in which Emperor Otto I decisively defeated the raiding Hungarians. From this time on the Hungarians began to settle down and establish a frontier.

972-997. Geza, Duke of the Magyar tribe, and the organizer of the princely power. He began to reduce the tribal leaders and invited Christian missionaries from Germany (Pilgrin of Passau, 974; St. Adalbert of Prague, 993). Christianization had already begun from the east, and was furthered by large numbers of war prisoners.

997-1038.   ST. STEPHEN (I), greatest ruler of the Arpad dynasty. He suppressed eastern Christianity by force and crusaded against paganism, which was still favored by the tribal chiefs. Stephen took his stand definitely by the west, married a Bavarian princess, called in Roman churchmen and monks (Benedictines) and endowed them with huge tracts of land. With the help of the clergy he broke the power of the tribal chieftains, took over their land as royal domain, administered through counts (*Ispan*), placed over counties (*Comitat*). The counts and high churchmen formed a royal council. Every encouragement was given to agriculture and trade and a methodical system of frontier defense was built up (large belt of swamps and forests, wholly uninhabited and protected by regular frontier guards; as time went on this frontier was gradually extended).

1001.   Stephen was crowned with a crown sent by the pope. He was canonized in 1083.

1002.   Stephen defeated an anti-Christian insurrection in Transylvania.

1030.   Attacks of the Germans under Conrad II, who tried to enforce German suzerainty over Hungary, were repulsed.

1038-1077.   A period of dynastic struggles over the succession, every member of the Arpad family claiming a share of the power, and sometimes calling in the Germans for support.

1038-1046.   Peter Urseolo, son of Stephen's sister and the Doge of Venice, succeeded to the throne. He called in German and Italian favorites, aroused the hostility of the Hungarians and was driven out (1041). For a few years Samuel Aba, the brother-in-law of Stephen, occupied the throne, but he in turn was expelled by Peter, who returned with the Emperor Henry III, to whom he swore fealty.

1046.   Peter was overthrown in the course of a great pagan rising of the tribal chiefs under Vatha, who massacred the Christians and destroyed the churches. This was the last serious revolt of the kind.

1047-1061.   Andrew I, who managed to restore the royal power.

1049-1052.   The three campaigns of Emperor Henry III against the Hungarians. Andrew managed to hold his own, and in 1058 the emperor recognized Hungary's independence of the empire.

1061-1063.   Bela I, brother of Andrew and popular hero of the campaigns against the Germans.

1063-1074.   Solomon, the son of Andrew the candidate of the German party. He was defeated by his cousin

1074-1077.   Geza I.

1077-1095.   ST. LADISLAS I (canonized 1192), the first great king after St. Stephen. He supported the pope in his conflicts with the emperor, and at home restored order and prosperity.

1091.   Ladislas conquered Croatia and Bosnia, but left these regions self-government under a *ban*.

1095-1114.   Coloman (*Kalman*) I. Another strong ruler, who, in

1097-1102.   Conquered Dalmatia from the Venetian Republic.

1114-1131.   Stephen II, in whose reign the dynastic struggles were resumed.

1131-1141.   Bela II. He had been blinded by Coloman, and now took a horrible revenge on his opponents.

1141-1162.   Geza II. The intestine conflicts were greatly complicated by the efforts of the Greek emperor, Manuel, to extend his sway over Hungary. But a number of campaigns carried out to this end (1097-1102) led to no success, though at one time (1156) the Hungarians recognized Byzantine suzerainty.

1150.   Saxon (i.e. Germans from the Moselle region) settlement in the Zips and southern Transylvania regions. They were called in to help defend the frontiers against Poland and against the Greeks, and had much to do with developing agriculture, trade, and town-building. In this period many Pechenegs and Szeklers were also established for frontier protection.

1162-1172.   Stephen III.

1172-1196.   BELA III, who had been educated at Constantinople. He married the sister of Philip Augustus of France and established a close dynastic connection with France. Bela was a strong ruler who successfully defended Dalmatia against Venice.

1196-1204.   Emeric I, whose position was challenged by his brother Andrew.

1204-1205.   Ladislas III, dethroned by Andrew.

1205-1235.   ANDREW II. The most disastrous reign in the Arpad period.

Andrew was renowned for his extravagance and for his generosity to his foreign favorites. A crusade to the Holy Land (1217) cost him much money, which he raised by alienating huge tracts of the royal domain, thus paving the way for the emergence of large landed magnates or oligarchs.

1222. THE GOLDEN BULL, forced upon Andrew by the lesser nobility or gentry, led by Andrew's own son, Bela. This document became the charter of feudal privilege. It exempted the gentry and the clergy from taxation, granted them freedom to dispose of their domains as they saw fit, guaranteed them against arbitrary imprisonment and confiscation and assured them an annual assembly to present grievances. No lands or offices were to be given to foreigners or Jews.

1224. The privileges of the Transylvanian Saxons were set down. They were given practical self-government, directly under the king.

1235-1270. BELA IV. A strong ruler who tried desperately to make good the losses of the preceding reign. The magnates, in reply, attempted to set up a rival ruler, and Bela in turn allowed some 40,000 families of the Cumans, who were driven westward by the Mongol invasions, to settle in the Theiss region in the hope of securing support against the magnates.

1241. THE GREAT MONGOL INVASION, which took the country by surprise in the midst of its dissensions. Bela's army was overwhelmingly defeated at Muhi on the Theiss and he was obliged to flee to the Adriatic. The Mongols followed him, but suddenly gave up their conquests when news arrived of the death of the **Great Khan.** But the Mongol invasion left the country devastated. For defense purposes the nobility was allowed to build castles and these soon became bases for feudal warfare and for campaigns against the king himself.

1246. Bela defeated Frederick of Austria, the last of the Babenbergs, who had taken advantage of the Mongol invasion to appropriate some of the western provinces.

1265-1270. Wars of Bela against Ottokar II of Bohemia.

1270-1272. Stephen V, a weak ruler.

1272-1290. Ladislas IV. His efforts to curb the feudal aristocracy were of little avail, but in alliance with Rudolph of Hapsburg he succeeded in breaking the power of Ottokar in the **battle of Dürnkrut** (1278).

1290-1301. Andrew III, last of the native dynasty. He continued the struggle against the domination of the feudal aristocracy, but with little success.

(Cont. p. 317.)

f. SERBIA, TO 1276

650. Approximate date of the completion of the Slav occupation of the Balkan area. Part of the Slav people extended as far west as Carniola and Carinthia, but these (the Slovenes) were conquered by the Franks in the early 9th century and were thenceforth part of the German Empire.

818. The **Croats,** who had also been conquered by the Franks, revolted, but were again subdued.

924. Tomislav became King of Croatia, accepting his crown from the pope. He ruled over later-day Croatia and over the territory as far south as Montenegro, though the coastal towns were mostly under Byzantine control.

960. Death of Chaslav, who made the first effort to unite the Serbs. The Serbs, inhabiting a mountainous area, were divided into tribes and clans, under headmen or *zupans.* The grand zupan held an honorary pre-eminence. Technically the territory was under Byzantine suzerainty, which, when the Eastern Empire was strong, was effectively exercised. By the end of the 10th century the inhabitants of present-day Serbia and eastern Bosnia had for the most part accepted eastern Christianity, while western Bosnia and Croatia leaned toward Roman Catholicism. But the conflict of the churches drew the southern Slavs this way and that, becoming frequently an important political as well as religious issue.

1077. Mikhail of Serbia was crowned by a papal legate.

1081-1101. Bodin established a Serbian state in Zeta (i.e. Montenegro).

1102. Croatia was joined with Hungary in a dynastic union, after the defeat of the last ruler, Petar, by King Ladislas. This involved the definitive victory of the western orientation in Croatia and the separation from the other southern Slavs.

1168-1196. STEPHEN NEMANYA, founder of the Nemanyid dynasty in the Raska (i.e. *Rascia* or Serbia proper). Though only grand zupan, Stephen appears to have made considerable progress in uniting the various clans. He definitely adopted the Greek Orthodox faith and persecuted the Bogomils, who were forced across the frontier into Bosnia, which at that time was ruled by a strong prince, Kulin (d. 1204). The death of Manuel I Comnenus (1180) and the subsequent decline of the Eastern Empire gave Stephen an opportunity to establish his independence of Constantinople and to conquer extensive territories to the south. In 1196 he retired to a monastery on Mt. Athos which had been founded by his son, St. Sava. Stephen died in 1200.

1196-1223. STEPHEN NEMANYA II, the son of the preceding. The beginning of his reign was marked by a struggle with his elder brother, Vukan, to whom Montenegro had been assigned. The Hungarians, who became an ever greater menace to Serbia, supported Vukan, and Stephen was forced to flee to the Bulgarian court. He returned with an army of Cumans supplied by Kaloyan (see below), who appropriated for himself most of eastern Serbia, including Belgrade and Nish. Stephen's brother, St. Sava, finally mediated between the two contestants and Stephen became ruler of Serbia proper.

1217. Stephen was crowned king by a papal legate (hence *Stephen the First-Crowned*).

1219. St. Sava, fearful of the Roman influence, visited Nicaea and induced the Greek patriarch to recognize him as archbishop of all Serbia and as head of an autocephalous church.

1222. Stephen was recrowned by St. Sava with a crown from Nicaea, thus re-establishing the eastern orientation.

1223-1234. Radoslav, the son of Stephen, a weak ruler, who was deposed by his brother

1234-1242. Vladislav. He married a daughter of Tsar John Asen II of Bulgaria and during this period much of eastern Serbia was under Bulgarian domination.

1242-1276. Urosh I, brother of the preceding two rulers. He married a daughter of the deposed Latin emperor, Baldwin II, and established an alliance with Charles of Anjou, heir of the Latin claims to Constantinople.

1254. The Hungarians, who already held part of northern Serbia, established their suzerainty over Bosnia and Herzegovina. (*Cont. p. 318.*)

g. THE SECOND BULGARIAN EMPIRE

Following the collapse of the First Bulgarian Empire in 1018, Bulgaria was, for 168 years, an integral part of the Byzantine Empire. The more stringent taxation and other grievances led to a serious revolt in 1040, led by **Peter Deljan**, a son of Gabriel Radomir, and confined to the northwest and western parts of the former empire. Delyan had himself proclaimed *tsar*, but the movement suffered from his rivalry with Tikhomir of Durazzo. In 1041 Delyan was defeated and captured by the imperial troops. Another uprising, led by **George Voitech**, in 1072-1073, never assumed the same proportions and was suppressed without much difficulty. During the Byzantine period the country was constantly exposed to marauding raids by the Patzinaks (1048-1054), many of whom settled in northeastern Bulgaria, and by invasions of the Cumans (1064). The **Bogomil heresy** continued to spread, despite persecution by the government (1110 ff.). Under the leadership of the monks it became to a certain extent a reaction to the Greek influence exerted by the higher clergy.

1185. RISING OF JOHN AND PETER ASEN, two Bulgarian lords from the vicinity of Tirnovo. Defeated by the Emperor Isaac Angelus (1186) they fled to the Cumans and returned with an army of the latter. After raiding into Thrace, they accepted a truce which left them in possession of Bulgaria north of the Balkan Mountains.

1189. The Asens attempted to effect an alliance with Frederick Barbarossa and the leaders of the Third Crusade, against the Greeks. This came to nothing, but the Bulgarians resumed their raids into Thrace and Macedonia. An imperial army under Isaac Angelus was completely defeated in a battle near Berrhoe.

1196. Peter Asen succeeded to leadership of the movement after the murder of John by boyar (i.e. noble) conspirators.

1197. Peter himself fell a victim to his boyar rivals.

1197-1207. KALOYAN (*Joannitsa*), the younger brother of John and Peter. He made peace with the Greeks (1201) and then engaged (1202) in campaigns against the Serbs (taking of Nish) and the Hungarians, whom he drove back over the Danube.

1204. The collapse of the Eastern Empire (p. 254) gave Kaloyan an excellent opportunity to reaffirm his dominion. By recognizing the primacy of the pope, he succeeded in securing the appointment of a primate for Bulgaria and in getting himself crowned *king* by the papal legate. At the same time he took over the whole of western Macedonia.

1205. Supported by the Cumans and the local Greeks, Kaloyan completely defeated the Frankish crusaders near Adrianople and captured the Emperor Baldwin I.

1206. Kaloyan put down a revolt of the Greeks and besieged Adrianople and Thessalonica. He was murdered in 1207.

1207-1218. Boril, the nephew of Kaloyan, whose position was not recognized by all other leaders, some of whom attempted to set up independent principalities.

1208. Boril was completely defeated by the Franks under Henry I in the **battle of Philippopolis,** and ultimately (1213) was obliged to make peace.

1217. Ivan (*John*) **Asen,** son of Kaloyan, supported by the Russians, began a revolt in northern Bulgaria. He besieged and took Tirnovo, and captured and blinded Boril (1218).

1218-1241. JOHN ASEN II, whose reign marked the apogee of the Second Bulgarian Empire. John was a mild and generous ruler, much beloved even by the Greek population.

1228-1230. Owing to the youthfulness of the Emperor Baldwin II, a number of Frank nobles at Constantinople projected making John Asen emperor and thereby securing themselves against the aggression of Theodore of Epirus (p. 260). The scheme was opposed by the Latin clergy and ultimately came to nothing.

1230. John Asen defeated Theodore of Epirus at **Klokotnitsa** on the Maritza River and captured him. He then occupied all of western Thrace, Macedonia,

and even northern Albania, leaving Thessalonica and Epirus to Theodore's brother Manuel, who became his vassal.

1232. John broke with Rome and the Bulgarian Church became independent.

1235. Alliance of John with the Greek emperor of Nicaea against the Franks. The Greeks recognized the patriarch of Tirnovo. Together the allies besieged Constantinople, which was relieved by a fleet and forces from Achaia.

1236. The Hungarians, instigated by the pope, began to threaten the Bulgarians and forced John to withdraw from operations against the Latin Empire.

1241-1246. **Kaliman I,** the son of John Asen II. His reign was distinguished chiefly by the great incursion of the Mongols, returning from the expedition into central Europe (1241).

1246-1257. **Michael Asen,** the youngest son of John, and a mere child. The Nicaean emperor, John Vatatzes, took advantage of the situation to conquer southern Thrace and Macedonia, while Michael of Epirus appropriated western Macedonia.

1254. On the death of John Vatatzes, Michael Asen attempted to recover the lost territories, but was badly defeated by Theodore II Lascaris at **Adrianople** and later (1256) in Macedonia.

1257-1258. **Kaliman II,** who, with support of the boyars, drove out Michael Asen, only to be deposed and expelled in his turn. He was the last ruler of the Asen dynasty.

(*Cont. p.* 325.)

3. THE NEAR EAST

a. THE EASTERN EMPIRE, 1025-1204

The period of the later Macedonian emperors (to 1050) and the succeeding thirty years was a period of decline, marked by the rule of women, barbarian invasions in the Balkans, the advance of the Normans in Italy and the expansion of the Seljuk Turks (p. 254) in Anatolia. Within the empire there was a steady development of the clerical and bureaucratic nobility in the capital and of the feudal baronage in the provinces, leading ultimately to sharp conflict between the two interests.

1025-1028. CONSTANTINE VIII, the younger brother of Basil II, a man suspicious of the military commanders, who granted many high offices to court favorites.

1027. The Patzinaks, who had invaded the Balkans, were finally driven back over the Danube by the general, Constantine Diogenes.

1028-1050. ZOË, empress. She was the third daughter of Constantine and, though 48 years old at her accession, married three times, associating her husbands in the imperial office.

1028-1034. ROMANUS III (*Argyropolus*), an official 60 years old, first husband of Zoë. He made great efforts to gain popularity by catering to the populace, the nobility, and especially the Church. The patriarchate was permitted to persecute the Monophysites of Syria, thousands of whom fled to Moslem territory. The hatred engendered by this policy helps to explain the Seljuk advance in subsequent years.

1030. Romanus suffered a severe defeat in a campaign against the Moslem emirs who attacked Syria.

1031. The situation was saved by the victories of **Georgios Maniakes**, greatest imperial general of the period.

1032. A combined Byzantine-Ragusan fleet completely defeated the Saracen pirates in the Adriatic.

1034-1041. MICHAEL IV (*the Paphlagonian*), second husband of Zoë. He was a man of lowly origin, who promptly established his brothers (mostly men of energy and ability) in high office.

1034-1035. The Byzantine fleets, manned by the Norseman Harald Hardrada and Scandinavian mercenaries, repeatedly defeated the Saracen pirates off the Anatolian coast and ravaged the coasts of North Africa.

1038. Maniakes and Hadraade, with Scandinavian and Italian mercenaries and with the support of the Byzantine fleets, stormed Messina and defeated the Sicilian Saracens, first at **Rametta** (1038), then at **Dragina** (1040).

1040. Revolt of the Bulgarians under Peter Deljan, a descendant of Tsar Samuel. The revolt was directed against the harsh fiscal policy of the government. The Bulgars attacked Thessalonica, but the city held out. Ultimately the movement collapsed, as the result of dissension among the leaders. Bulgaria was then incorporated in the empire and the autocephalous church of Ochrid became a prey of the patriarchal hierarchy.

1041-1042. MICHAEL V (*Kalaphates*), one of Zoë's favorites. He attempted to secure sole power by shutting the empress in a cloister, but this led to a rising of the Constantinople nobility and to the incarceration of Michael in a monastery.

1042-1054. CONSTANTINE IX (*Monomachus*), the third husband of Zoë, a scholarly person, wholly out of sympathy with the army and with the military aristocracy. He systematically neglected the frontier defenses and the forces.

1042. Maniakes totally defeated the Normans, who had begun the attack on southern Italy, in the **battle of Monopoli** (near Naples).

1043. Revolt of Maniakes, representing the disaffection of the military classes. Maniakes landed at Durazzo and prepared to march on the capital, but he was accidentally shot and killed on the way.

1046. The Byzantine forces occupied Ani and took over the government of Armenia, which became another field for clerical exploitation.

1047. Another military uprising, led by Leo Tornikios, failed.

1048. The imperial generals defeated the advancing Seljuk armies at **Stragna.**

1050. Death of Zoë. Her husband Constantine continued to reign alone.

1051. Expulsion of the Patzinaks from Bulgaria, after years of ravaging and unsuccessful Byzantine campaigns.

1054-1056. THEODORA, empress. She was the elder sister of Zoë, an intelligent, vigorous, and popular ruler, but already advanced in age.

1054. Final schism between Rome and Constantinople. The long-standing friction between the papacy and the eastern patriarch had come to a head with the conquest of parts of southern Italy by the Normans, who were supported by the papacy. The Patriarch Michael Kerularios disputed the claim of Pope Leo IX to jurisdiction in southern Italy. Negotiations were opened, but each side assumed an uncompromising attitude and the rift became unavoidable. The enmity it left behind was of the utmost importance for the development of the next years.

1056-1057. MICHAEL VI (*Stratioticus*), who was overthrown almost at once by a revolt of the Anatolian feudal barons.

1057-1059. ISAAC COMNENUS, proclaimed by the insurgents. He was an able and energetic army man, who promptly abolished a host of sinecures, undertook the reform of the finances, etc. Isaac, already advanced in years, soon found his work too arduous and abdicated in favor of

1059-1067. CONSTANTINE X (*Dukas*), a high official of the finance department. Constantine introduced a period of domination by the civil officials, Church and scholars, during which the army was viewed with suspicion, neglected, and driven into hostility.

1060. The Normans took Rheggio, completing the conquest of Calabria.

1064. The Seljuks, under Alp Arslan, took Ani and ravaged Armenia.

1065. The Cumans, having crossed the Danube, flooded the Balkan area as far as Thessalonica. They were finally driven back by local forces.

1067-1071. ROMANUS DIOGENES, who, on Constantine's death, married the widowed empress, Eudoxia. Romanus was an ambitious soldier, who did his best to check the advance of the enemy in the east and the west.

1068. The Normans took Otranto, and then Bari (1071), the last Byzantine outpost. This marked the end of the Byzantine rule in Italy.

1068-1069. Romanus succeeded in repulsing the Seljuks, though they repeatedly raided through the whole of eastern Anatolia.

1071. BATTLE OF MANZIKERT (north of Lake Van). Romanus had concentrated huge forces for a decisive battle, and he rejected all offers of a settlement. In the course of a hard-fought battle he was deserted by Andronicus Dukas and other Byzantine magnates. Romanus was defeated and captured, but then released by the Seljuks. He attempted to regain the Byzantine throne, but was defeated by his opponents and blinded. He died very soon afterward.

1071-1078. MICHAEL VII (*Parapinakes*), a son of Constantine X. His elevation meant another victory for the bureaucratic group. Michael made the great scholar, Michael Psellus, his chief adviser and devoted himself to the pursuit of learning. The military system was again allowed to fall into neglect.

1074. The emperor concluded a treaty with the Seljuks in order to secure their aid against his uncle, who had set himself up as a pretender. The Seljuks defeated the pretender, but took advantage of the situation to spread themselves over a large part of Anatolia.

1078. Revolt of Nicephorus Briennius in Albania. Another military revolt broke out in Anatolia, led by Nicephorus Botaniates, who was supported by the Seljuks.

1078-1081. NICEPHORUS III (*Botaniates*), emperor after Michael's abdication. His accession was greeted by a number of insurrections in various parts of the army, but these were suppressed by the able general Alexius Comnenus.

1081. Revolt of Alexius Comnenus himself. He seized Constantinople with a force of mercenaries, who thereupon plundered the capital. The victory of Comnenus meant the final success of the military aristocracy and the beginning of a new period of military success.

1081-1118. ALEXIUS COMNENUS, an able general, vigorous administrator, conscientious ruler and shrewd diplomat. Having to rely upon the great feudal families, he attempted to win their support by lavish grants of honors and ranks. At the same time he tried to use the high clergy to counterbalance the influence of the nobility. He reformed the judicial and financial systems and systematically used his resources in money to buy off the enemies he could not conquer.

1081-1085. The war against the Normans under Robert Guiscard. The latter landed in Epirus with a large force and besieged Durazzo (*Dyracchium*). Alexius bought the support of the Venetians with extensive trade privileges (1082), but Guiscard defeated the emperor in the battle of Pharasalus, after which he took Durazzo. The war was continued by Robert's son, Bohemund, who again defeated Alexius and in 1083 conquered all Macedonia as far as the Vardar. But the advance was broken by the resistance of Larissa, by the guerrilla tactics of the natives (who hated the heretical Latins), and by the Seljuk cavalry employed by the emperor. In 1085 the combined Byzantine and Venetian fleets defeated the Normans near Corfu. The death of Robert Guiscard at the same time led to dissension among his sons and the abandonment of the Balkan project.

1086-1091. Revolt of the Bogomils in Thrace and Bulgaria. The heretics were supported by the Patzinaks and Cumans and were able to defeat Alexius and a large army (battle of Drystra or Dorostolon, 1087). The Cumans then ravaged the entire eastern Balkan region as far as Constantinople until Alexius bought them off, took them into imperial service and used them (1091) to annihilate the Patzinaks (battle of Leburnion).

1092. Death of Malik Shah, ruler of the Seljuk empire of Iconium, which controlled almost all of Anatolia. The death of Malik led to disputes as to the succession and paved the way for the partial reconquest of Anatolia.

1094. Constantine Diogenes, a pretender to the throne, crossed the Danube with an army of Cumans and besieged Adrianople, but was then defeated in the battle of Taurocomon.

1096-1097. THE FIRST CRUSADE (p. 255). The crusaders, of whom

The Comneni and Angeli

Bohemund was one of the leaders, were looked upon with great suspicion in the east, where there was little interest in a movement organized by the heretical Latin pope. But Alexius was unable to stop the crusaders, and therefore devoted himself to managing the movement. He induced them to promise to do homage to the empire for all territory reconquered from the infidel. The crusading **victories at Nicaea**

and **Dorylaeum** (1097) enabled Alexius to recover the entire western coast of Anatolia.

1098-1108. Second war with the Normans. The crusaders, having regained Antioch (lost to the Turks only in 1085), turned it over to Bohemund, who refused to recognize Alexius' suzerainty. War broke out. Bohemund returned to Italy and raised a huge army, with which he appeared in Epirus (1104). He failed in his siege of Durazzo, and Alexius wisely avoided open battle. Ultimately (1108) Bohemund agreed to make peace, recognizing Byzantine suzerainty over Antioch.

1110-1117. War against the Seljuks, who again advanced to the Bosporus. In 1116 Alexius won a resounding victory at **Philomelion**, which induced the Turks to make **peace at Akroinon** (1117): they abandoned the entire coastal area of Anatolia (north, west, and south) and all of Anatolia west of a line from Sinope through Ancyra (Ankara) and Philomelion.

1111. Trade privileges granted to the Pisans. This was part of the emperor's effort to draw the Pisans away from the Normans and at the same time to counterbalance the extensive trade position of the Venetians in the empire.

1118-1143. JOHN COMNENUS, a ruler of high moral integrity, mild, brave, and sincere. He devoted his attention chiefly to the east, with the object of recovering the old frontier of the Euphrates and of subjecting the Latin states of Syria to the empire.

1120-1121. In a successful campaign against the Seljuks, John recovered southwestern Anatolia. He was diverted from further conquests by continued incursions of the Patzinaks in the Balkans.

1122. The Patzinaks were completely defeated and thenceforth were no longer a threat to the empire.

1122-1126. War with Venice, resulting from John's refusal to renew the extensive trading privileges, which the Venetians had been exploiting to the full. The Venetian fleets ravaged the islands of the Aegean, occupied Corfu and Cephalonia, and ultimately (1126) forced John to renew the privileges.

1124. Intervention of the emperor in behalf of Bela II in Hungary, initiating a policy which continued throughout the century. The objective of the Comneni was to prevent the Hungarians from establishing control over the Slavic regions of Dalmatia, Croatia, and Serbia. By the **Peace of 1126** the emperor secured Branicova, a vital bridgehead on the Danube.

1134-1137. Conquest of Cilician (Little) Armenia, which was allied with the Latin Kingdom of Antioch. John forced Raymond of Antioch to do homage for his domain.

1143. John died from a wound incurred while hunting. He was just about to renew his campaigns in Syria.

1143-1180. MANUEL COMNENUS, the son of John, a noble, intelligent, chivalrous idealist, and yet an adroit statesman and ambitious soldier. He was the greatest of the Comneni and the most splendid. In his reign Constantinople came to be accepted as the capital of the world and the center of culture. Its brilliant art was imitated in the east as in the west. Manuel married a Latin princess (Maria of Antioch) and throughout his career cherished the hope of resurrecting a universal empire. Hence his association with and employment of Latin nobles, who intermarried with the Greek aristocracy, his constant toying with the idea of reunion with Rome, his designs on Italian territory and his antagonism to the Hohenstaufen emperors. All this tended to arouse much hostility among the Greeks (accentuated by the high-handed activities of the Italian traders), cost the empire inordinate sums of money and involved repeated conflict with the Normans. The emperor's preoccupation in the west at the same time forced him to neglect the east, where the Seljuk Sultanate of Iconium (Rum) was able to effect a marked recovery.

1147-1158. War with Roger of Sicily. The Norman fleets ravaged Euboea and Attica, took and plundered Thebes and Corinth, carried away large numbers of silk-workers, who were established at Palermo. The emperor, having neglected the Byzantine fleet, was obliged to buy the aid of Venice with extensive trading rights (1148). The Venetians helped to reconquer Corfu (1149) and paved the way for the Byzantine conquest of Ancona (1151). But efforts to extend the Greek power in Italy met with failure (1154) and Manuel in the end had to agree to an inconclusive peace (1158).

1147-1149. THE SECOND CRUSADE (p. 256). The crusaders, having plundered the Balkan region, almost came to blows with the Greeks at Constantinople, but Manuel by diplomacy prevented a clash. The Greeks did nothing to prevent the defeat of the crusaders in Anatolia.

1152-1154. Successful war against the Hungarians, who attempted to make good their claims to Serbia and Bosnia. Peace was made in 1156, the Hungarians recognizing the emperor's suzerainty.

1155. Trade privileges granted to Genoa, the emperor hoping thereby to counteract the domination of the Venetians.

1158-1159. An expedition against Raymond of Antioch forced the latter to renew his homage.

1161. Kilidj Arslan IV, Sultan of Rum, made peace with the empire, recognizing the emperor's primacy.

1165-1168. War with the Hungarians. The imperial forces took Dalmatia and in the final peace (1168) received also part of Croatia. The following years Manuel interfered actively in Hungarian dynastic affairs. Bela III (1173–1196) was practically his vassal.

1170-1777. War with Venice, the natural result of the Byzantine acquisitions in Dalmatia and in Italy. The emperor arrested all Venetian traders in Constantinople and confiscated their goods, but with a neglected fleet he was able to do little. The Venetians conquered Ragusa (1171) and Chios (1171), though they failed in an attack on Ancona (1173). In 1175 the Venetians made an alliance with the Normans against the empire and thereby forced Manuel to yield. By the **Peace of 1176** the trade privileges were renewed and the emperor paid a heavy indemnity.

1176-1177. War against the Seljuks. The Byzantines were defeated at **Myriocephalon** (1176), but in the next year Manuel defeated the enemy in Bithynia, while John Vatatzes drove them out of the Meander Valley.

1180-1183. MANUEL ALEXIUS II, the son of Manuel, who ruled under the regency of his mother, Maria of Antioch. The regent relied almost entirely upon Latins in her service.

1182. Revolt of the populace of Constantinople against the Latins, officials, and traders, who were brutally cut down in a great massacre. The mob forced the proclamation of

1182-1185. ANDRONICUS COMNENUS, an uncle of the boy-emperor, who ruled first as co-emperor, but in 1183 had Alexius strangled and became sole ruler. Andronicus had intrigued innumerable times against Manuel and was renowned for his lack of principle. But he was a man of great personal charm, intelligent, vigorous, unscrupulous, and cruel. Through per-

secution, confiscations, and executions he cleaned the court circle, got rid of the hated Latins, abolished sale of offices, sinecures, etc.; reformed the judiciary, lightened the taxes. All this was a policy directed against the powerful official and landed aristocracy and might, had it been carried through, have led to a thoroughgoing reform of the empire.

1185. The Norman attack. The Normans took Durazzo, sent an army and a navy against Thessalonica, which they stormed, and massacred the Greeks. This attack led to a revolt of the Greek nobility against Andronicus, who was deposed, tortured, and executed.

1185-1195. ISAAC ANGELUS, leader of the insurgents. His accession meant a return of the old negligence and corruption. Within a brief space the entire empire began to go to pieces. In the provinces the powerful feudal families (i.e. Sguros in Greece; Gabras at Trebizond) began to set up as independent potentates.

1185. Victory of the Byzantine general, Alexius Branas, over the Normans at Demetritsa. By 1191 the Normans were driven out of the Balkans and even out of Durazzo and Corfu.

1186-1188. The great insurrection in Bulgaria, led by Peter and John Asen. This was due primarily to the extortion of the imperial fiscal agents. The revolt was supported by the Cumans and resulted in the devastation of much of the Balkan region, with the annihilation of much of the Greek population. Though at times successful, the Greek commanders were unable to suppress the movement, which resulted in the formation of a new Bulgarian state north of the Balkan Mountains (1188).

1187. Fall of Jerusalem. Isaac, in fear of another crusade, allied himself with Saladin.

1189. THE THIRD CRUSADE (p. 256). Frederick Barbarossa was welcomed in Bulgaria by John Asen, who offered him an army for use against the empire. But Frederick avoided friction as well as might be, and Isaac did not oppose the crossing of the crusaders into Anatolia. The death of Saladin (1193) relieved the danger from the east.

1190-1194. Continuation of the war in Bulgaria. The Byzantine forces were defeated at Berrhoe (1190) and at Arcadiopolis (1194).

1195-1203. ALEXIUS III, the brother of Isaac, whom he deposed and blinded.

1196. The western emperor, Henry VI, heir to the Norman domains, demanded Durazzo and Thessalonica. Alexius settled for a huge money payment, and Henry's death (1197) removed the immediate threat from that quarter.

1201. Peace with the Bulgars, who were allowed to retain most of the eastern Balkan area, under the younger brother of the Asens, John (*Joannitsa, Kaloyan,* 1197–1207).

1202-1204. THE FOURTH CRUSADE (p. 256). The leaders were the Venetian doge, **Enrico Dandolo**, and **Boniface of Montferrat.** Alexius, the son of Isaac, appealed for aid against his uncle and promised great concessions. Dandolo succeeded in diverting the expedition against Constantinople. The crusaders took Durazzo (1203) and arrived at Constantinople (June, 1203). The emperor thereupon fled to Adrianople (July). His deposed brother, Isaac, was set upon the throne with his son, the accomplice of the crusaders.

1203-1204. ALEXIUS IV. He was wholly under the control of the crusaders and was forced to pay a heavy tribute. Popular discontent led to

1204, Jan. 25. A revolution and the proclamation of

1204. Alexius V (*Dukas*). Alexius IV was killed. The new ruler refused payments to the crusaders and demanded their withdrawal.

Apr. 12. The crusaders stormed the city, which was given over to a merciless sack. The emperor succeeded in escaping.   (*Cont. p.* 258.)

b. THE SELJUK TURKS

1037. The Seljuks, a sept of the Ghuzz Turks, under the brothers Tughril Beg and Chagar Beg, invaded Khorasan and defeated the Ghaznawid armies. They then conquered Balkh, Jurjan, Tabaristan, and Khwarizm.

1055. Entry of Tughril Beg into Baghdad, where he was proclaimed *sultan,* with the title *King of the East and the West.* Invasion of Byzantine Cappadocia and Phrygia by Tughril Beg.

1063-1073. Alp Arslan, brilliant nephew of Tughril, succeeded the latter. He conquered Georgia and Armenia.

1071. BATTLE OF MANZIKERT (Malaz Kard). Alp Arslan defeated the Byzantine emperor, Diogenes Romanus, and virtually destroyed the Byzantine power in Asia Minor.

1073-1092. Malik Shah, son of Alp Arslan. His vizier, **Nizam al-Mulk**, was one of the ablest administrators ever produced by Asia. At the same time he was a patron of learning, founder of colleges in Baghdad (the Nizamiya) and other principal cities. Under him was undertaken the reform of the calendar by the famous poet, **Omar Khayyam.**

1084. The Seljuks took Antioch.

1090. Rise of the Ismailian fraternity of the **Assassins**, founded by Hasan Sabbah, a schoolfellow of Nizam al-Mulk, and a Fatimid propagandist. He captured the mountain stronghold of Alamut in the Elburz range in Mazendran. The Assassins later became masters of many mountain fortresses in northern Persia, Iraq, and Syria. The crusaders came into contact with the Syrian branch.

1091. Nizam al-Mulk was murdered by one of Hasan's emissaries, after two expeditions against the Assassins had failed.

1092. Barkyaruk (Rukn al-Din), son of Malik Shah, sultan. Civil war broke out between the new ruler and his brother, Mohammed, over Iran and Khorasan, and separate branches of the Seljuk family attained virtual independence in different parts of the empire, although the main line still preserved the nominal sovereignty down to 1157. The Seljuk Empire of the East ultimately fell before the attack of the Khwarizm Shah (1157). The Seljuks of Kirman (1041–1187) were overthrown by the Ghuzz Turcomans; the Seljuks of Syria (1094–1117) by the Burids and Ortuqids; the Seljuks of Iraq and Kurdistan (1117–1194) by the Shahs of Khwarizm. The Seljuks of Rum (Iconium, Koniah), who ruled most of Anatolia, absorbed the Danishmandid princedom in Cappadocia, but were ousted by the Mongols and the Othmanli (Ottoman) Turks (p. 325).

1100-1200. During the 12th century the whole of the Seljuk Empire, excepting Rum, fell into the hands of captains of the Seljuk armies, the so-called *Atabegs* (regents). The **Burid dynasty** of Damascus (1103–1154) was founded by Tughtugin. The **Zangid dynasty** of Mesopotamia and Syria (1127–1250) by Imad al-Din Zangi, whose son, Nur al-Din, was famous as an opponent of the crusaders. The Zangids absorbed the Burids (1154). The **Ortuqid dynasty** of Diyar-Bakr (Diarbekr) was founded by Ortuq ibn Akrab (1101), whose sons, Sukman and Il-Ghazi, both won renown in the wars against the Latin princes of Palestine. The dynasty lasted until 1312. Sukman Qutbi was the first of the

Shahs of Armenia (1100–1207). The Atabeg house of Azerbaijan (1136–1225) was founded by Ildigiz, whose son, Mohammed, was the actual ruler of the Seljuk Kingdom of Iraq. The Salgharids held Fars (1148–1287), the Hazaraspids Luristan (1148–1339); and Anushtigin, a Turkish slave of Balkatigin of Ghazna, was the grandfather of the first independent Shah of Khwarizm, Atsiz. At one time the rule of the Khwarizm Shah was almost co-terminous with the Seljuk Empire.

1095. The crusaders, having invaded the dominions of the Sultan of Rum, took Antioch, with frightful slaughter. They stormed Jerusalem (1099) and founded the Latin Kingdom of Jerusalem. By 1109 Caesarea, Tripoli, Tyre, and Sidon were captured. Constant warfare between the crusaders and the Moslems (Fatimids, Burids, Zangids, Ortuqids, and finally Saladin, the Sultan of Egypt). (*Cont. p.* 325.)

c. THE CRUSADES

PRECURSORS OF THE CRUSADES:
(1) **Penitentiary pilgrimages** probably dating from the days of Helena, mother of Constantine; after the Arab conquest of Jerusalem (638) the Holy City was a joint shrine of Christian and Moslem; protectorate of Charlemagne over the Holy Places (recognized by Harun-al-Rashid, 807); abrogated by the mad Caliph Hakim (1010); (2) **Charlemagne's war** of Christian reconquest in Spain; (3) the **Cluniac revival** and its stress on pilgrimages led to a steady increase of pilgrimages (117 known in the 11th century) without serious opposition from the tolerant Moslems until the advent of the Seljuks; (4) **Wars of Christian reconquest** in the west began European reaction to Moslem pressure; Pisan reconquest of Sardinia (c. 1016) with papal support; alliance of Castile and Aragon in the reconquest of Spain (c. 1050); Norman reconquest of Sicily (1060–1090).

1087. **Genoa and Pisa,** by capture of Mahdiyah in Africa, gained command of the western Mediterranean from the Moslems. Appeal of the Greek emperor after Manzikert (1071) to Pope Gregory VII; preparation of an army (alliance with Roger Guiscard) by Gregory (1074) to aid the Greeks.
Transformation by Pope Urban II of military assistance to Constantinople into a new kind of holy war (a sort of ecclesiastical imperialism) under the auspices of the revived and regenerated papacy.

1095. Appeal from the Greek emperor at the Synod of Piacenza; Urban's call at the **Synod of Clermont** (1095): Urban, a Cluniac and a Frenchman, speaking to Frenchmen, recited the glorious deeds of the French and tales of Moslem atrocities, made open allusions to the chances of profit and advancement, attacked feudal violence at home, and brought the audience to wild enthusiasms; he himself distributed crosses. Urban's propaganda journeys and the preaching of **Peter the Hermit** and others stirred the west, but had the greatest effect in France and Lorraine, the area most under Cluniac influence. The great rulers were all at odds with the papacy or busy at home; the rest of Europe indifferent, and the Crusades began as they continued, largely under French auspices.

1096-1099. THE FIRST CRUSADE. Five popular, aimless mass migrations (1096), emptying whole villages and often accompanied by pillage and anti-Semitic outbreaks, of which two (perhaps 7000 under Peter the Hermit and perhaps 5000 under Walter the Penniless) reached Asia Minor and were annihilated. The Norman-French baronage flocked to the Cross and converged in three divisions on Constantinople: the Lorrainers under **Godfrey of Bouillon** and his brother Baldwin, via Hungary; the Provençals under Count **Raymond of Toulouse** and the papal legate, Adhemar of Puy, via Illyria; the Normans under **Bohemund of Otranto** (the most effective leader) via Durazzo by sea and land. Perhaps they were 30,000 in all.

The Greek emperor, Alexius Comnenus, expecting mercenaries and unprepared for crusaders, provided food and escort and punished the plunderers. He exacted an oath of fealty from the leaders (Raymond refused) in an effort to insure his title to any recovered "lost provinces" of the Greek Empire.

The **Moslem opposition:** the Seljuks had merely garrisoned Syria and were not popular with the native population. Moslem unity in Asia Minor ended with the death of Malik Shah (1092), and Syria was divided politically, racially, and theologically (Sunnite *vs.* Shi'ite; the Fatimite capture of Jerusalem (1098) from the Shi'ites).

1097. **Nicaea,** the Seljuk capital in Asia Minor, taken by the combined Greek and crusading force; defeat of the Moslem field army at Dorylaeum; excursion of Baldwin and Tancred, and rivalry in Cilicia; Bohemund established himself in the Antioch area. Siege and capture (by treachery) of Antioch (1097–1098); counter-siege of the Christians in Antioch by the Emir of Mosul; election of Bohemund as leader. Baldwin's conquest of Edessa (1097); death of Adhemar of Puy (1098);

Christian divisions: rivalry of Norman and Provençal (the *Holy Lance*).

1099. **March to Jerusalem** (Genoese convoy and food supply); siege, capture, and horrors of the sack. The death of the papal legate left the organization of the government of Jerusalem to feudal laymen. **Godfrey of Bouillon**, elected king, assumed the title of *Advocate of the Holy Sepulcher* (for pious reasons). The main body of the crusaders soon streamed back home. The Norman effort to dominate the government through their patriarch Dagobert led to his deposition by the anti-Norman party and Jerusalem became a feudal kingdom rather than theocracy under papal domination. The government (as revealed by the *Assizes of Jerusalem*, the most complete feudal code extant) was narrowly feudal, the king a feudal suzerain, not a sovereign, the tenants-in-chief dominant. Besides the feudal organization there were burgher and ecclesiastical organizations, with their own courts.

Continued divisions among the Moslems and the weakness of the Greeks favored the progress of the Latin states: the **Kingdom of Jerusalem**, in close commercial alliance with the Italian towns (Genoa, Pisa, and later Venice), profited by the commerce through its ports and extended south to tap the Red Sea trade. The other states: the **County of Edessa** (established by Baldwin), the **Principality of Antioch** (established by Bohemund), and the **County of Tripoli** (set up by Raymond of Toulouse), were fiefs of Jerusalem (divided into four great baronies and into lesser fiefs). The departure of the main body of the crusaders left the Franks without enough reinforcement to prevent their orientalization and decline. After the capture of Jerusalem (1187) the Kingdom of Jerusalem ceased to be an organized state.

Moslem unification in Syria was completed by the *Atabegs* (regents) of Mosul and signalized by the capture of Edessa (1144). Mosul soon mastered Egypt; Saladin emerged supreme in Egypt (1171), quickly reduced Damascus and Aleppo, and brought Syria and Egypt under a single efficient rule.

1147-1149. **THE SECOND CRUSADE.** **Bernard of Clairvaux**, persuaded by Pope Eugenius III, somewhat against his will, preached (1145) the Second Crusade. Emperor Conrad III and King Louis VII of France took the Cross. To avoid conflicts the two monarchs went by separate routes; there never was coherent direction or unity of command. The Norman Roger of Sicily profited by the Second Crusade to seize the Greek islands and to attack Athens, Thebes, and Corinth. Nothing of importance was achieved by the Second Crusade and the movement was discredited throughout Europe.

1184. Saladin's steady advance led to a great appeal to the west; King Philip II of France and Henry II of England declined the crown of Jerusalem, but levied a **Saladin tithe** (1188) to finance a crusade. Christian attack on a caravan (said to be escorting Saladin's sister) provoked Saladin's holy war (1187-1189): **capture of Jerusalem** (1187) without a sack (Saladin's humanitarianism) and reduction of the Latin states to the cities of Antioch, Tyre, Tripoli, and a small area about each.

1189-1192. **THE THIRD CRUSADE.** Precipitated by the fall of Jerusalem, a completely lay and royal affair despite the efforts of the papacy to regain control. It was supported partly by the Saladin tithe, and was led by the three greatest monarchs of the day: (1) **Frederick Barbarossa** (a veteran of the Second Crusade) as emperor, the traditional and theoretical military leader of Christendom, headed a well-organized and disciplined German contingent starting from Regensburg (1189), which marched via Hungary, entered Asia Minor, and disintegrated after Frederick was drowned (1190); (2) **King Richard I of England** and (3) **King Philip II of France,** who went by sea. Already political rivals, they quarreled in winter quarters in Sicily (1190-1191); Richard turned aside in the spring and took Cyprus which he sold to Guy de Lusignan. The quarrels of Philip and Richard continued in the Holy Land, and Philip returned to France after the capture of Acre (1191). Richard's negotiations with Saladin (Richard proposed a marriage of his sister Joanna to Saladin's brother, who was to be invested with Jerusalem) resulted (1192) in a three-year truce allowing the Christians a coastal strip between Joppa and Acre and access to Jerusalem. Captivity of Richard (1192-1194) and heavy ransom to the Emperor Henry VI. The Third Crusade ended the golden age of the crusades.

1202-1204. **THE FOURTH CRUSADE.** Emperor Henry VI, King of Sicily (by virtue of his marriage to the Norman Constance) and heir of the traditional Norman plan of creating an empire on the ruins of the Greek Empire, was determined to continue his father Frederick's crusade, and began to encroach on the Greek lands: homage of Cyprus and Lesser Armenia (1195); the marriage of Henry's brother Philip to Irene, daughter of the deposed

Emperor Isaac Angelus, established a Hohenstaufen claim to the Greek throne. Henry died 1197.

Pope Innocent III determined to regain control of the crusading movement, and hoping to unite the Greek and Latin Churches, issued a call to the monarchs; it was ignored (Philip II and King John of England were at odds, Germany in chaos, the Spanish rulers busy with the Moors), and the brunt fell again on the French baronage. Egypt, the objective, could only be reached by water; negotiations with Venice (1201): terms, 85,000 marks and half the booty. **Meeting of Hagenau** (1201) between Philip (brother of Henry VI), Boniface of Montferrat, and (?) Alexius; decision to divert the crusade to Constantinople (a return to the plans of Henry VI); Venice may have shared in the decision. As it was impossible to raise 85,000 marks, Venice agreed to fulfill her bargain if the Christian city of Zara were taken by the crusade. Despite Innocent's furious opposition, Zara was taken and sacked (1202); Innocent excommunicated the crusade. Constantinople was entered (1203); Isaac Angelus and his son Alexius IV were restored; Greek opinion was furious at the new exactions to pay the clamorous crusaders, and Alexius V soon succeeded Isaac. The crusaders stormed and took Constantinople (1204), the first **capture of Constantinople** in history, and sacked it with unparalleled horrors. The Latin Empire of the East (*Romania*) replaced the Greek Empire at Constantinople from 1204 to 1261; the first emperor, Baldwin of Flanders; a Latin patriarch, a Venetian (Morosini), replaced the Greek patriarch, and technically the schism was ended; actually the Greeks refused all union. Venice acquired three-eighths of the city, Adrianople, Gallipoli, Naxos, Andros, Euboea, Crete, and the Ionian islands. Innocent III was horrified and helpless. The government of the Latin Empire was completely feudal under the *Assizes of Romania* (copied from the *Assizes of Jerusalem*). The Greek emperors ruled at Nicaea (1204-1261) until Michael VIII surprised and took Constantinople, 1261. The Fourth Crusade shocked Europe, discredited the papacy and the whole crusading movement, and facilitated the advance of the Turks.

1208. THE ALBIGENSIAN CRUSADE, a European crusade against the Albigensian heretics in southern France, proclaimed by Innocent III (1208) (see p. 229).

1212. The so-called **Children's Crusade,** preached by the lad Stephen of Vendôme and by Nicholas of Cologne in Germany. Stephen's contingent reached Marseilles and was sold into slavery. Nicholas' company was turned back. The whole episode is supposed to have been the origin of the story of the Pied Piper.

1218-1221. THE FIFTH CRUSADE. Innocent III, unwilling to let the crusading idea lapse, preached the Fifth Crusade at the Fourth Lateran Council. Egypt was to be the objective; the date 1217; John of Brienne, King of Jerusalem, was replaced by the papal legate Pelagius as leader (1218). Capture of Damietta (1219); rejection (in the expectation of Frederick II's arrival) of the offers of the sultan (1219) to exchange Jerusalem for Damietta; failure of the march on Cairo; **Treaty of 1221:** eight-year truce, Damietta lost; retreat.

1228-1229. THE SIXTH CRUSADE, of the Emperor Frederick II. Essentially lay, the crusade continued the policy of Frederick's father, Henry VI. Frederick, King of Jerusalem by his marriage (1225) to Yolande of Brienne, sailed (1227) after careful preparation, returned ill with fever, and was excommunicated. He sailed again (1228); the pope proclaimed a crusade against Frederick's Sicilian lands and renewed the excommunication; Hermann of Salza, Master of the Teutonic Order, remained loyal to Frederick. Frederick, the first crusader to understand the Moslems, negotiated a treaty (1229) with Malik-al-Kamil, nephew of Saladin, Sultan of Egypt; peace for ten years, grant of Nazareth, Bethlehem, Jerusalem, etc., and a corridor from Jerusalem to the coast for the Christians. The Patriarch of Jerusalem opposed Frederick at every turn, and Frederick had to crown himself king (1229) in the Church of the Holy Sepulcher. He returned home at once to repel the papal crusade in his lands. The capture of Jerusalem by a rush of Moslem mercenaries (1244) led to the crusades of King Louis IX of France, but Jerusalem was not again in Christian hands until General Allenby captured it (1917).

The **crusades of Theobald of Navarre** (1239) and **Richard of Cornwall** (1240-1241) were forbidden by the pope and were fruitless.

1248-1254. THE SEVENTH CRUSADE, the first of King Louis IX of France. Poorly organized; Damietta taken without a blow; march to Cairo (1249); rout of the army; capture of Louis; massacre of the army; loss of Damietta. Louis, ransomed, spent four years on a pilgrimage to Jerusalem (1251-1254).

1267. Charles of Anjou, aiming at the conquest of Constantinople, became heir (by treaty) to the Latin Empire. He planned to unite Sicily and Jerusalem, but was balked by the Sicilian Vespers (1282).

1269. James the Conqueror, of Aragon, under papal pressure, made a futile crusading expedition to Asia Minor.

1270. THE EIGHTH CRUSADE, the second of King Louis IX and Edward of England (the last of the western crusaders who arrived (1271) and did nothing permanent). Attack on Tunis, possibly at the insistence of Charles of Anjou; death of Louis; the expedition continued by Charles; nothing accomplished.

1274. Preaching of a crusade at Lyons by Pope Gregory X; every ruler took the Cross; Gregory's death ended the project. Acre fell, 1291.

Local and specific crusading expeditions were subsequently undertaken under various circumstances at different times; there was a revival of crusading zeal with the fall of Constantinople (1453) under papal urging, but the true crusades were over.

The crusades gave rise to great orders of knighthood which combined chivalry and monasticism.

THE KNIGHTS OF ST. JOHN or the *Hospitalers* (black mantle with a white cross), originally a Chilian order founded at Jerusalem by Amalfitan merchants (c. 1070) to care for the Hospital of St. John; militarized (c. 1130) on the model of the Knights Templar; transferred to Cyprus (1291); to Rhodes (1310-1522) (the *Knights of Rhodes*) and then to Malta (*Knights of Malta*). Noble blood was a requisite to knighthood in the order.

THE KNIGHTS OF THE TEMPLE (their house in Jerusalem stood near the Temple) or *Templars* (white mantle with a red cross) founded (c. 1120) by Hugh of Pajens to guide and protect pilgrims; confirmed by the Synod of Troyes (1128) and Pope Honorius III. Bernard of Clairvaux drew up their rule, a modification of the Cistercian; they took the threefold monastic vows of poverty, chastity, and obedience, and their rule in general was that of the canons regular. They consisted of knights, men-at-arms, and chaplains. Admission to knighthood in the order was open only to those of noble blood. Organization: by commanderies under a grand master. Transferred to Cyprus (1291), the order was dissolved by the Synod of Vienne (1312) (see p. 232).

The other great orders were associated with national or racial influences, and do not represent the older international aspects of knighthood:

The Knights of the Hospital of St. Mary of the Teutons in Jerusalem (*Teutonic Knights*) (white mantle with a black cross) founded (c. 1190); headquarters at Acre. (For their history in Germany, see p. 214.)

The great Spanish orders: Calatrava (founded, 1164); Avis (Portuguese, founded 1166); St. James of Compostella (founded 1175); Alcantara (founded, 1183).

Famous orders of chivalry of royal foundation: The Order of the Garter (English), founded c. 1344. The Order of the Star (French) founded 1351, replaced by the Order of St. Michael (1469-1830). The Order of the Golden Fleece (Burgundian) founded, 1429, became Hapsburg, 1477.

d. LATIN AND GREEK STATES IN THE NEAR EAST, 1204-1261

Division of the Eastern Empire after the fall of Constantinople: A council, composed equally of crusaders and Venetians, decided to award the imperial crown to Count Baldwin of Flanders, while a Venetian (Pier Morosini) was made Patriarch of Constantinople. Boniface of Montferrat was made King of Thessalonica and the remaining parts of the empire were assigned to various feudal barons as vassals of the emperor. In Anatolia the crusaders were never able to establish themselves excepting in a part of Bithynia near the Bosporus. In Europe they were constantly exposed to the attacks of the Bulgarians. The Kingdom of Thessalonica at first extended over part of Thrace, Macedonia, and Thessaly, but to the westward the Greek, Michael Angelus Comnenus, set himself up as Despot of Epirus and soon began to expand his dominion eastward. Attica and the Peloponnesus were conquered by crusading barons in a short time, and these territories were organized on a feudal basis as the Lordship of Athens (Otto de la Roche, 1205-1225; Guy I, 1125-1263; John I, 1263-1280), and the Principality of Achaia (conquered by Guillaume de Champlitte and Geoffroy de Villehardouin in 1205). Achaia was in turn divided into twelve feudal baronies, a perfect example of the French feudal system. Under the Villehardouin family (Geoffroy I, 1209-1218; Geoffroy II, 1218-1246; Guillaume, 1246-1278) it was well-governed and popular with the Greco-Slavic population, which was considerately treated.

The Venetians took as their share of the empire most of the islands and other important strategic or commercial posts. They kept for themselves part of Constantinople, Gallipoli, Euboea, Crete, the southwestern tip of the Peloponnesus (Coron and Modon), Durazzo, and other posts on the Epiran coast, as well as the islands of the Ionian and Aegean Seas. For the most part these possessions were granted as fiefs to the leading Venetian families (Triarchies of Euboea, Duchy of the Archipelago, etc.).

1204-1205. BALDWIN I, Latin emperor.

1204-1214. MICHAEL ANGELUS COMNENUS, Despot of Epirus.

1204. Theodore Lascaris, with most of the Byzantine leaders, established himself in Bithynia; Theodore Mancaphas set himself up at Philadelphia; Leo Gabalas took over Rhodes; Manuel Maurozomes established himself in the Meander Valley; Alexius and David Comnenus organized a state on the north coast of Anatolia, with David at Sinope and Alexius at Trebizond, thus founding the **Empire of Trebizond,** which lasted until the Ottoman conquest of 1461.

1204. Theodore Lascaris made an alliance with the Sultan of Rum and with Mancaphas of Philadelphia to resist the advance of the crusaders into Anatolia, but was defeated by the latter under Peter of Bracheuil.

1205. The Bulgars, under Kalojan, defeated Emperor Baldwin and Doge Dandolo in battle near Adrianople. Baldwin was captured and died in captivity. The Bulgars then overran much of Thrace and Macedonia, exterminating a large part of the Greek population.

1205-1216. HENRY I, Latin emperor. He was the brother of Baldwin, and the ablest of the Latin emperors.

1206-1222. THEODORE I (*Lascaris*), proclaimed emperor at Nicaea and founder of the Nicaean Empire.

1207. Kalojan and the Bulgarians besieged Thessalonica, but in vain. Kalojan died suddenly, probably murdered.

1207. Theodore Lascaris, allied with the Seljuks of Rum, defeated David Comnenus and drove him back to Sinope. Theodore then concluded a truce with the Emperor Henry, in order to oppose the advance of Alexius of Trebizond, who was now allied with the Seljuks.

1209. Theodore repulsed a second attempt by Peter of Bracheuil and the crusaders to conquer Bithynia.

1210. The **Parliament of Ravennika,** at which the feudal lords of Greece finally recognized the suzerainty of the emperor at Constantinople. In practice this meant little, and the emperor was left to shift for himself, with such support as the Venetians saw fit to give him.

1211. Theodore Lascaris defeated Alexius of Trebizond and the Sultan of Rum, both of whom were captured. As a result a large part of the Anatolian coast was added to the Empire of Nicaea.

1212. Henry I defeated Theodore at Luparcos and began the invasion of Anatolia. Theodore made peace, abandoning to the Latin Empire part of Mysia and Bithynia.

1214-1230. THEODORE DUKAS ANGELUS, nephew of Michael, became Despot of Epirus. He began the work of expansion at the expense of the Latins and Bulgars, taking Durazzo and Corfu from the Venetians (1214).

1216-1217. PETER OF COURTENAY, Latin emperor. He was the brother-in-law of Baldwin and Henry and was in Europe when Henry died. On the way from Durazzo to Thessalonica he was captured by Theodore Dukas of Epirus. He died in 1218.

1217-1219. Regency of Yolanda, the wife of Peter of Courtenay.

1218-1228. ROBERT OF COURTENAY, Latin emperor. His domain was reduced to Constantinople and he spent most of his time soliciting aid in the west.

1222. Theodore Dukas of Epirus captured Thessalonica and extinguished the kingdom. He then had himself proclaimed *Emperor* of the West, and before long had extended his conquests to the vicinity of Philippopolis and Adrianople.

1222-1254. JOHN DUKAS VATATZES, emperor at Nicaea. He proved himself a great ruler as well as an able general. During his reign agriculture was encouraged, trade and industry developed, the finances reformed. The Nicaean Empire enjoyed a period of real prosperity and power.

1224. John Vatatzes defeated the Franks at Poimanenon. In succession he took the islands near the Anatolian coast (Samos, Chios, Lemnos) and subjected Rhodes. An army was even sent across the Straits to capture Adrianople.

1224. Theodore of Epirus defeated an army of the Latin emperor at Serres and then drove the invading Nicaean army away from Adrianople.

1228. On the death of Robert of Courtenay, it was proposed that a regency be established under the Bulgarian ruler, John Asen II (1218-1241), but this suggestion was frustrated by the Latin clergy.

1228-1261. BALDWIN II, Latin emperor. He was the eleven-year-old son of Peter of Courtenay. The reign was a helpless one, during which the emperor was reduced to the point of peddling the Constantinople relics through Europe.

1229-1237. Regency of John of Brienne, former King of Jerusalem, for the boy-emperor. John became co-emperor in 1231.

1230. Theodore of Epirus was defeated and captured by John Asen in the **battle of Klokotnica.** The Bulgarian ruler thereupon appropriated most of the eastern sections of the Empire of the West. Thessalonica and Thessaly passed to

1230-1236. MANUEL, the brother of Theodore.

1235. An expedition sent by **John Vatatzes** against the Venetians in Crete failed to achieve anything.

1236. An attack of the Nicaean Greeks, allied with John Asen of Bulgaria, on Constantinople. The city was saved by the Venetians and by a force sent by the Duke of Achaia.

1236-1244. JOHN, the son of Theodore Dukas of Epirus, became Despot of Thessaly and Emperor of the West.

1236-1271. MICHAEL II, Despot of Epirus.

1242. John Vatatzes, in company with Theodore, who had been liberated by the Bulgarians, set out with an army and besieged Thessalonica. He failed to take the city, owing to his lack of sea-power, but John, the Despot of Thessaly, was obliged to give up the title Emperor of the West and to recognize the suzerainty of the Nicaean emperor.

1244. The **Mongol** invasion of Anatolia, after the defeat of the Seljuks in the **battle of Erzingan.** The Mongols reached Ancyra (Ankara). John Vatatzes established friendly relations with them and succeeded to much of the Seljuk territory in central Anatolia.

1246. Second Expedition of John Vatatzes to the Balkans. He conquered northern Macedonia and finally took Thessalonica, deposing Demetrius Angelus, despot since 1244.

1254. Michael II, of Epirus, recognized Nicaean suzerainty, after a defeat by the forces of John Vatatzes.

1254-1258. THEODORE II (*Lascaris*), Greek emperor at Nicaea.

1255. Theodore defeated the Bulgarian armies of Michael Asen in northern Macedonia.

1257. Revolt of Michael II of Epirus, who managed to defeat the Nicaean forces sent against him.

1258-1261. JOHN IV (*Lascaris*), emperor. He was a mere child and his accession led to a military uprising, led by Michael Paleologus, who became regent.

1259-1282. MICHAEL VIII (*Paleologus*), who was first co-emperor with the boy John, whom in 1261 he had imprisoned and blinded. Michael was an able and energetic general, whose great objective was to re-establish the Greek power at Constantinople.

1259. Michael II of Epirus, allied with the King of Sicily and with the Prince of Achaia, attacked Thessalonica, but was defeated and driven back by the Nicaeans (battle of Pelagonia).

1261. RECONQUEST OF CONSTANTINOPLE. Michael made an alliance with the Bulgarians and concluded the **Treaty of Nymphaion** with Genoa, promising the Genoese all the privileges hitherto enjoyed by the Venetians. On July 25 a Greek army under **Alexius Stragopulos,** taking advantage of the absence of the Venetian fleet, crossed the Bosporus and retook Constantinople without much difficulty. Baldwin II fled (d. 1273). End of the Latin Empire.   (*Cont. p.* 320.)

e. THE MONGOLS

Under the last caliphs, the caliphate had regained its temporal power in Iraq, Mesopotamia, and Fars, and its spiritual authority was greater than at any time since the death of Wathiq (847), but the caliphate was soon threatened by the Mongols, who, in the late 12th century, had advanced from Mongolia.

1206. The Mongol chief, **Temujin** (1162–1227), was proclaimed supreme ruler, *Jenghiz Khan* (Very Mighty King), of all the Mongols. Under his leadership the Mongol armies swept over northern China and over Azerbaijan, Georgia, and northern Persia. Transoxania was invaded and Bokhara taken (1219); Samarcand captured (1220) and Khorasan devastated. Destruction of Merv and Nishapur. Capture of Herat.

1223. Battle of the Kalka River, in southern Russia. The Mongols defeated a strong force of Russians and Cumans, but after their victory returned to Asia.

1237-1240. Mongol armies under **Batu** (actually commanded by Subutai) overran and conquered southern and cen-

The Mongol Empire

Limit of Northern Forest

LAPLAND

HUNGARY

Moscow · Kazan

Kiev

Sarai

BYZANTINE EMP.

Constantinople

GEORGIA

Trebizond

Tabriz

TURKESTAN

MONGOLIA

Karakorum

Shangtu

KATHAY

Peking

Bokhara

Samarkand · Kashgar

Merv

Suchow

Changan

Yellow R.

MAMELUK EMP.

Cairo

Baghdad · Ispahan

Nishapur · Balkh

Kabul

Khotan

Chengtu

Suchu

MANG

Hanoi

Kerman

Herat

IRAN

PERSIA

Ormuz

TIBET

Mecca

Delhi

INDIA

Ganges R.

SIAM

Pagan

Cambay

Myuthia

Pegu · KHMER

Angkor

Chahar

Aden

Ely

Marco Polo 1293

MALAYA

Ceylon

SUMATRA

JAVA

I N D I A N   O C E A N

Mongolian invasions

Raisz

tral Russia and then invaded Poland and Hungary.

1241. The Mongols defeated the Poles and Germans in the **battle of Liegnitz** (Wahlstatt) in Silesia, while another army defeated the Hungarians. But because of political complications arising from the death of the Great Khan, Batu withdrew from western Europe, subjugating, on the way back, Bulgaria, Wallachia, and Moldavia. Subsequently he settled on the lower Volga, where a Mongol (Tatar) state was organized under the name of **Golden Horde,** with Sarai as the capital. The Golden Horde, like other Mongol khanates, recognized the supreme authority of the Great Khan, whose capital was first at Kara-Korum in Mongolia, then at Khanbalyk (present-day Peiping) in China. But after the death of **Kublai Khan** (1294) the unity of the empire was purely nominal.

1245-1253. Continued ravages of the Mongols in Mesopotamia, Azerbaijan, Armenia, and Georgia.

1256-1349. THE IL-KHANS OF PERSIA. Hulagu, the grandson of Jenghiz Khan, was sent by his brother, Mangu, to crush the Assassins and extirpate the caliphate.

1256. Suppression and extinction of the Assassins.

1258. CAPTURE AND SACK OF BAGH-DAD. Hulagu executed the caliph, Musta'sim. He then invaded Syria and took Aleppo.

1260. Great victory of the Mamluks of Egypt, under Baybars, at **Ain Jalut.** This victory checked the Mongol advance and saved Egypt, the last refuge of Moslem culture. Baybars revived the caliphate by inviting to Cairo Ahmad Abu-l-Qasim, a scion of the Abbasid house, who was acknowledged as caliph under the title of *Mustansir l' Illah.*

1344-1349. Reign of **Nushirwan,** last of the Il-Khans of Persia. The dynasty was succeeded by a number of lesser families.

f. MOSLEM EGYPT

868-905. Dynasty of the Tulunids.

935-969. Dynasty of the Ikhshidids. Both these dynasties also ruled Syria.

968-1171. THE FATIMID DYNASTY, under which Egypt became the most brilliant center of Moslem culture. The Fatimids claimed to be descendants of the Caliph Ali, and of Fatima, the daughter of the Prophet. They rose to power as a result of Shi'ite (Ismailian) propaganda among the Berbers, begun about 894 and directed from Yemen. Abu Abdullah, an Ismailian missionary, had won over the powerful Kitama tribe and had overthrown the Aghlabids (909). Obaydullah, son of the Ismailian hidden Imam, then appeared and was proclaimed caliph and mahdi in Qairowan (910). In 922 he reduced the Idrisids, but an attempt to conquer Egypt failed. His son, Al-Qa'im, who succeeded him in 934, was defeated again and again and was besieged in his capital by the Kharijite, Abu Yazid Makhlad. Al-Qa'im's son, Al-Mansur, finally defeated Abu Yazid (947), and brought the whole of North Africa, Sicily, and Calabria under Fatimid rule, though he lost Morocco to the Omayyads of Spain. He was succeeded by his son, Al-Mu'iz, in 952. The latter recovered Morocco and drove the last Byzantine forces out of Sicily (966).

968. Al-Mu'iz took Egypt and transferred the seat of the Fatimid government to Cairo (founded 969).

975-996. Al-Aziz, son of Al-Mu'iz, sultan. He conquered Syria and part of Mesopotamia, and ruled from the Euphrates to the Atlantic.

996-1020. Al-Hakim, son of Al-Aziz, sultan. He was known as the *Mad Caliph,* having affirmed his own divinity. He tried to make Shi'ism the orthodox religion of Egypt. The cult of Hakim as an emanation of deity still survives among the Druses of Syria.

1020-1035. Reign of Al-Zahir, marking the beginning of the decline of the Fatimid power. Most of Syria was lost.

1035-1094. Reign of Al-Mustansir. The holy cities of Mecca and Medina disclaimed their allegiance (1047) and North Africa threw off the Fatimid yoke. On Al-Mustansir's death civil war broke out among his sons, Nizar and Ahmad. Nizar was defeated and killed, and Ahmad reigned as

1094-1101. Al-Musta'li. He lost Jerusalem to the crusaders (1099). The Fatimid power continued to decline.

1167. Shirkuh, general of the Zangid Nur al-Din of Damascus, entered Egypt to assist the last Fatimid Caliph, Al-Adid. Shirkuh was appointed vizier, in which office he was succeeded by his nephew, **Salah al-Din** (*Saladin*), who founded the

1169-1250. Ayyubid dynasty. Saladin ruled at first as viceroy of Nur al-Din, but on the latter's death (1173) asserted his independence and consolidated his power over Egypt, part of Nubia, Hijaz, and Yemen.

1172. Saladin drove the Normans out of Tripoli.

1174. Invasion of Syria and conquest of Damascus. Aleppo taken (1183).

1185-1186. Saladin seized Mosul and reduced Mesopotamia.

1187. Battle of Hittin. Saladin destroyed the crusading Kingdom of Jerusalem.

1190-1193. Saladin defended his conquests against the Third Crusade.

g. MOSLEM DYNASTIES OF NORTH AFRICA

788-985. The **Alid dynasty** of the Idrisids in Morocco, founded by Idris ibn Abdullah, a great-grandson of the Caliph Ali's son Hasan. This dynasty was overthrown by the Miknasa Berbers.

801-909. The **Aghlabid dynasty** in Tunis, founded by Ibrahim ibn Aghlab, the Abbasid governor of Africa. This dynasty conquered Sicily (827-878), took Malta and Sardinia and invaded southern Italy. The dynasty was ultimately destroyed by the Fatimids.

1056-1147. The **Almoravids**, a Berber dynasty founded by Abdullah ibn Tashfin, conquered Morocco and part of Algeria and intervened actively in the affairs of Spain.

1130-1269. THE ALMOHADES, another Berber dynasty founded by the prophet, Mohammed ibn Tumart. His successor, Abdul-Mu'min, annihilated the Almoravid armies (1144). Morocco was conquered (1146) and Spain invaded. Algeria was subjugated in 1152, and the Normans driven out of Tunis (1158). Tripoli too was annexed. But in 1235 the Almohades were defeated and gradually ejected from Spain.

1228-1534. The **Hafsid dynasty**, which succeeded the Almohades in Tunis.

1235-1339. The **Ziyanids**, successors of the Almohades in Algeria. They were ultimately absorbed by the

1296-1470. Marinids of Morocco, a dynasty founded in 1195 which took the Moroccan capital from the Almohades in 1296.

C. THE LATER MIDDLE AGES

1. WESTERN EUROPE

a. THE BRITISH ISLES

(1) *England*, 1307-1485

1307-1327. EDWARD II. Married to Isabella, daughter of Philip IV of France. Ignorant of his task and bored with the business of kingship, Edward was dominated by his favorite, **Piers Gaveston**, a Gascon. The Scottish war was continued in desultory fashion. The baronage, angered by Gaveston, followed the leadership of Edward's nephew, Thomas, Duke of Lancaster, an ambitious, incompetent person. They forced Edward to accept a committee of reform, the twenty-one **Lords Ordainers** (1310), whose reform ordinances, suggestive of the Provisions of Oxford, were confirmed by Parliament (1311). The ordinances required a baronial consent to royal appointments, to a declaration of war and to the departure of the king from the realm, this consent to be given through Parliament. Gaveston was captured and slain (1312).

1313-1314. The Scottish War. By 1313 only the castle of Stirling remained in the hands of the English. Edward set out (1314) to relieve the castle; Lancaster and the baronial party refused to support the expedition. At **Bannockburn** (1314) Edward was overwhelmingly defeated, and Scottish independence won.

In Gascony the French kings began a policy of egging Edward's vassals on to resistance, a process which culminated in the French conquest of Gascony and its retention by the French with the consent (1327) of the regents who ruled after Edward's abdication.

1314-1322. Supremacy of Lancaster. Lancaster offered no opposition to Scottish raids; private wars broke out in England; Edward was under a new favorite, Hugh le Despenser. Parliament exiled Despenser (1321). Edward defeated Lancaster at **Boroughbridge** (1322) and beheaded him. The Parliament of York repealed the Ordinances.

1322-1326. Rule of the Despensers, father and son: Scottish truce (1323); decline of the popularity of the Despensers; alienation of Queen Isabella. Isabella went to France (1325), arranged the marriage of her son, the future Edward III, to Philippa of Hainault, and returned (1326) with Mortimer and foreign troops. Supported by the barons, Isabella gained London, the Despensers were hanged, and the **Parliament of Westminster** (1327), dominated by Isabella and by Edward's enemies, forced an abdication that was tantamount to deposition. Edward was brutally murdered in prison eight months later.

Baronial reform was cynical and selfish in aim, but made no effort to destroy the monarchy. Burgesses and knights sat in the parliaments of 1311, 1322, and 1327, and retained a share in the grant of taxes.

1327-1377. EDWARD III (aged fifteen at his accession). Council of regency and rule (1327-1330) under Mortimer, Isabella's paramour; Bruce's invasion of England forced the acknowledgment of Scottish independence (1328). Edward led the baronial opposition to Mortimer (hanged, 1330) and opened his personal rule (1330).

1337. OUTBREAK OF THE HUNDRED YEARS' WAR. Edward did homage (1329) for his French lands and renewed it (1331). French support of Scottish aggression continued and Edward, profiting by civil war in Scotland, supported Baliol; after a series of expeditions he avenged Bannockburn at **Halidon Hill** (1333). French intrigues to alienate Aquitaine continued; Edward sought allies in the emperor, the German princes, and his wife's relatives in Hainault and Holland, but could not win the Count of Flanders, the vassal of Philip VI. The economic interdependence, due to the wool trade, of England and the Flemish cities, made an English alliance with them inevitable. Philip continued his advance into the English lands south of the Loire (1337) and open hostilities broke out (1338). Edward ravaged northern and eastern France without a decisive battle. Urged on by the Flemings, Edward proclaimed himself King of France (in right of his mother Isabella), and enabled the Flanders towns under Jan van Arteveldt to support him without violating their oaths.

1340. The naval **victory of Sluys** transferred the mastery of the Channel from France to England (until 1372). Intermittent truces (1340–1345) were followed by Edward's invasion of France, and

1346, Aug. 26. Great **VICTORY AT CRÉCY** where English longbowmen, supported by dismounted horsemen, routed the undisciplined chivalry and mercenary crossbowmen of France. This tactical innovation, the result of English experiences in Wales and Scotland, began the joint participation of the yeomanry and the aristocracy in war, and gave the English a unique military power and new social orientation. Artillery may have been used in Crécy.

1346. The invasion of Philip's Scottish allies was halted at **Neville's Cross,** and the King of Scotland captured.

1347. **Calais was taken** after a long siege in which artillery was used. (Philippa's intervention in behalf of the burghers of Calais.) Calais remained an English military and commercial outpost in France until 1558.

1347-1355. A series of truces with France was ended by the expedition of Edward's son, **Edward, the Black Prince,** to Bordeaux, followed by ruthless plundering raids from there as a base, which enriched the English and alienated the populace.

1356, Sept. 19. BATTLE OF POITIERS. The Black Prince, using the tactics of Crécy, defeated King John, capturing him, his son, and the King of Bohemia, as well as the flower of French chivalry.

1359-1360. Edward's last expedition to France penetrated to the walls of Paris; the south had been so devastated that the English could hardly find food.

1360. PEACE OF BRETIGNY, ending the first period of the war. (1) France, utterly exhausted and in chaos, surrendered the full sovereignty of Aquitaine, Calais, Ponthieu; and (2) fixed John's ransom; (3) Edward waived his claims to the crown of France.

THE BLACK PRINCE IN THE SOUTH. The Black Prince, ruling as Duke of Aquitaine, supported Pedro the Cruel of Castile against Henry of Trastamara (allied with Charles V and aided by Du Guesclin). Having defeated Du Guesclin and Henry (**Navarrete,** 1367), the Black Prince, disgusted at Pedro's character, his army dis-

sipated by illness, and seriously ill himself, withdrew. Taxation in Aquitaine to pay for the expedition led the southern baronage to appeal to Charles V, who summoned the Black Prince to answer to him as his feudal lord (alleging a technical defect in the **Peace of Bretigny**). The prince defied Charles, and Parliament advised Edward to resume his claims to the French crown. Du Guesclin avoided open battle, pursuing a warfare of attrition which wore out the Black Prince and alienated the Aquitanians from the English. After the hideous **sack of Limoges** (1370) the Black Prince returned to England (1371) and was replaced (1372–1374) by his brother, **John of Gaunt,** Duke of Lancaster, an incompetent soldier, who lost town after town until only Calais, Cherbourg, Brest, Bayonne, and Bordeaux remained in English hands (1375).

Edward's personal rule and domestic developments in England. Edward, a majestic, affable man, opened his reign with generous concessions to the baronage, and a courteous welcome to the complaints of the middle class. He grew steadily in popularity. He was fond of war and the war was popular; the nation backed him.

Progress of Parliament. The necessities of war finance played into the hands of Parliament, and (after 1325) the knights and burgesses began to establish a privileged position for their common petitions. Without immediate redress when the king broke promises of reform, they were able to apply financial pressure in crises. The king could still legislate outside Parliament by ordinances in council, but Parliament was gaining the initiative: non-feudal levies and changes in levies require parliamentary sanction (1340); a money grant made conditional on redress, and auditors of expenditure appointed (1340–1341); all ministers of the king declared (1341) to be subject to parliamentary approval (soon repealed); demand that a grant be spent as directed (1344); a specific grant voted for defense against the Scots (1348); appointment of parliamentary treasurers and collectors (1377). Parliament continued to sit as a single body, but deliberated in sections: the magnates and prelates sitting in the parliament chamber with the King's Council (thus forming the **Great Council**); the knights and burgesses met separately until 1339–1349, when they began joint sessions (i.e. emergence of the **Commons**) and designated (before 1377) a representative, the speaker, to voice their views in debate. Royal officials ceased to attend the Council-in-Parliament, leaving the council to the prelates and magnates (now sitting virtually by hereditary right). The outline of the **House of Lords** began to appear.

Development of justices of the peace. The conservators of the peace established under Henry III to keep the peace had no judicial powers; the Statute of 1327 allowed them to receive indictments for trial before the itinerant judges. In 1332 their jurisdiction was made to include felonies and trespass. Established as police judges in each county (1360) they were also charged with price and labor regulation. By 1485 they had absorbed most of the functions of the sheriffs. Chosen from the local gentry, under royal commission, they constituted an amateur body of administrators who carried on local government in England until well into the 19th century.

1348-1349. The ravages of the Black Death may have reduced the population one-half; coupled with tremendous war prosperity, this dislocated the wage and price structure, producing a major economic and social crisis. Wages and prices were regulated by a royal ordinance (1349) followed by the **Statute of Laborers** (1351) fixing wages and prices, and attempting to compel able-bodied unemployed to accept work when offered. The labor shortage accelerated the transition (already begun) from servile to free tenures and fluid labor; the statute in practice destroyed English social unity without markedly arresting servile emancipation or diminishing the crisis.

War prosperity affected everybody and led to a general surge of luxury (e.g. the new and generous proportions of contemporary Perpendicular Gothic). Landowners, confronted with a labor shortage, began to enclose for sheep-raising, and the accumulation of capital and landholdings founded great fortunes, which soon altered the political and social position of the baronage. The yeomanry, exhilarated by their joint military achievement with the aristocracy, and their share of war plunder, lost their traditional passivity, and a new ferment began among the lower sections of society.

Growth of national and anti-clerical (antipapal) feeling. Hostility to the Francophil papacy at Avignon: **Statute of Provisors** (1351), an effort to stem the influx of alien clergy under papal provisions (renewed several times); **Statute of Praemunire** (1353), forbidding appeals to courts (i.e. Avignon) outside England (renewed several times); rejection (1366) by Parliament of the papal request that John's tribute (intermitted by Edward, 1333) be renewed, and declaration that no king could make England a papal fief without Parliament's consent; Parliament declared bishops unfit for state offices (1371). **Progress of the vernacular.** English became, by statute (1362), the language of pleading and judgment in the courts (law French retained in documents). English began to be taught in the schools (1375). Parliament was opened (1399) with a speech in English.

c. 1362. Growth of social tension. Langland's *Piers Plowman*, a vernacular indictment of governmental and ecclesiastical corruption, and an appeal (unique in Europe) in behalf of the poor peasant, appeared. Langland, a poor country parson, typical of the section of the Church directly in contact with public opinion, was the voice of the old-fashioned godly England bewildered and angered by a new epoch. Preaching of scriptural equalitarianism by various itinerant preachers (e.g. John Ball); growing bitterness against landlords and lawyers.

c. 1376. John Wiclif, an Oxford don and chaplain of Edward, already employed (1374) by the government in negotiations with the papacy over provisions, published his *Civil Dominion,* asserting in curious feudal terms that, as Christians hold all things of God under a contract to be virtuous, sin violates this contract and destroys title to goods and offices. Wiclif made it plain that his doctrine was a philosophical and theological theory, not a political concept, but extremists ignored this point. A remarkable precursor of the Reformation, Wiclif advocated a property-less Church, emphasizing the purely spiritual function, attacked the Caesarian clergy, and insisted on the direct access of the individual to God (e.g. abolition of auricular confession, reduction of the importance of the sacraments, notably penance) and the right of individual judgment. He also was responsible (with Purvey and Nicholas of Hereford) for the first complete, vernacular **English Bible.** He wrote pamphlets, both in Latin and English, and carried on a wide agitation through his poor priests for his doctrines (**Lollardy**) until it was said every fourth man was a Lollard.

1369-1377. Edward, in his dotage, was under the domination of Alice Perrers; the Black Prince (after his return, 1371) was ill and lethargic; government in church and state was sunk in the depths of corruption, society in an orgy of luxury.

1374. John of Gaunt, returning from France, struck a bargain with Alice Perrers, became the leader of the state, set out to use the strong anti-clerical feeling and social unrest for his own ends, and probably aimed at the succession.

1376. The Black Prince, awakened from his lethargy, led the Good Parliament in a series of reforms: the Commons refused supply until an audit of accounts; two notorious aristocratic war profiteers (Lyons and Latimer) were impeached before the King's Council (i.e. the future Lords), the first impeachment of officials by Parliament in English history.

1377. After the death of the Black Prince (1376) John of Gaunt's packed Parliament undid the reforms and passed a general poll tax (4d.).

1377. Gaunt, aiming at the confiscation of clerical estates, supported Wiclif, but the bishops, unable to touch Gaunt, had Wiclif called to account. A violent scene between Gaunt and Bishop Courtenay ended with public opinion on the bishop's side and Gaunt in flight. Attempts to discipline Wiclif failed because of public opinion, but his denial of transubstantiation (1380) alienated Gaunt and his aristocratic supporters.

ART AND LITERATURE.

Perpendicular Gothic: Gloucester, transepts and choir (1331-1335); cloisters (1351-1412). Minor arts: *Louterell Psalter* (opening of the 14th century), illuminations. English influence on craftsmen of the Rhineland, Paris, Lorraine.

Popular songs: Anti-French songs in celebration of victories at Halidon Hill, Sluys, the capture of Calais, etc., c. 1377 first mention of Robin Hood.

Historical writing: Higden's *Polychronicon* (before 1363), a brilliant universal history in Latin; Walsingham of St. Albans' (end of the 14th century) *Chronicle*, in Latin, rivaling Froissart in brilliance of description. English translation (1377) of the fictional account of the *Travels of Sir John Mandeville* by Jean de Bourgogne.

The Pearl, a mystical poem of lament for a dead daughter, influenced by the *Roman de la Rose,* and suggestive of Dante's mystical visions.

Geoffrey Chaucer (c. 1340-1400), son of a London burgher, a layman, attached to the circle of John of Gaunt, a diplomat, active at court, later member of Parliament, combined observation with learning. Translator of Boethius' *Consolatio,* etc. Representative of the new cosmopolitanism of English society, he was under Italian and French influences; probably knew Petrarch. Creator of English versification; recaster of the English vocabulary by adding continental grace to the ruder Anglo-Saxon word-treasury. The influence of Wiclif, Oxford, Cambridge, the court, and above all, Chaucer, fixed Midland English as the language of the English people. The

Canterbury Tales are a witty, sympathetic, sophisticated, realistic picture of contemporary society (omitting the aristocracy). John Gower (d. 1408), last of the Anglo-Norman poets, wrote in both Latin and French, and later (perhaps due to Chaucer) in English: *Confessio Amantis; Vox Clamantis* (expressing the alarm of a landowner at the Peasants' Revolt).

Foundation of Winchester School (St. Mary's College) by William of Wykeham (1393).

1377-1399. RICHARD II (son of the Black Prince, aged ten at his accession).

1377-1389. Minority. Marriage to Anne of Bohemia (1382); rule by the council under the domination of John of Gaunt; activity of Parliament: insistence by the Commons on the nomination of twelve new councillors. Renewal of war in France (1383): loss of the Flanders trade, complaints at the cost by Parliament. Poll taxes (1370 and 1380); sporadic violence, growing tension in the lower orders of society.

1381. PEASANTS' REVOLT. Efforts by the landlords to revert to the old servile tenures culminated in a peasant rising, the burning of manors, destruction of records of tenures, game parks, etc., assassination of landlords and lawyers, and a march (100,000[?] men) from the south and east of England on London led by Jack Straw, Wat Tyler, and others (release of John Ball from prison). London admitted the marchers; lawyers and officials were murdered, their houses sacked, the Savoy (John of Gaunt's palace) burned. Significant demands: commutation of servile dues, disendowment of the Church, abolition of game laws. The Tower was seized, Archbishop Sudbury (mover, as chancellor, of the poll taxes) was murdered. Richard met the rebels (Mile End), rapidly issued charters of manumission, and started most of them home. After the murder of Wat Tyler, Richard cleverly took command of the remnant (possibly 30,000), deluded them with false promises, and dispersed them. Cruel reaction ensued: Richard and Parliament annulled the charters; terrible repression followed, and a deliberate effort was made to restore villeinage. This proved impossible and serfdom continued to disappear.

1381. Passage of the first Navigation Act, followed by clear signs of growing national monopoly of commerce.

1382. Wiclif, who had alienated his upper-class supporters by a denial of transubstantiation, was discredited by the Peasants' Revolt, and condemned by the Church, and withdrew to Lutterworth

(1382–1384), where he continued to foster Lollardy until he died (1384). His body, by order of the Council of Constance, was dug up and burned (1428).

1382. Archbishop Courtenay purged Oxford of Lollardy, thus separating the movement from the cultured classes and destroying academic freedom, with serious results alike for reform and education in England. Parliament refused to allow persecution of the Lollards. The position of the English Church was not wholly due to its own corruption nor to the paralysis of the Avignonese Captivity, but was partly a result of the fact that secular learning, secular society, and the secular state had overtaken the position of the Church.

1385. Futile expedition of Richard to Scotland; threatened French invasion (1386); general demands for reform in government. Parliament blocked Richard's effort (1385) to set up a personal government, and appointed a commission of reform. The Lords Appellant (led by Richard's uncle, the Duke of Gloucester) secured the impeachment and condemnation (1388) of five of Richard's party (in the *Wonderful,* or *Merciless Parliament*).

1389–1397. Richard's personal and constitutional rule. Truce with France (1389), peace negotiations, marriage to Isabella, infant daughter of Charles VI (1396). Richard was on good terms with Parliament, England prosperous and quiet. Livery and maintenance forbidden by statute (1390); re-enactment of the Statutes of: Provisors (1390); Mortmain (1391); Praemunire (1393).

1397–1399. Richard's attempt at absolutism. Richard, furious at a parliamentary demand for financial accounting, had the mover (Haxey) condemned for treason (not executed). In the next Parliament (Commons, packed for Richard; Lords friendly) three of the Lords Appellant were convicted and executed for treason, Richard was voted an income for life (1398) and the powers of Parliament delegated to a committee friendly to Richard. Heavy taxation, ruthless exactions, and a reign of terror opened the way for the **conspiracy of Henry of Bolingbroke** (exiled son of John of Gaunt).

1399. Bolingbroke landed while Richard was in Ireland, got him into his power on his return, and forced him to abdicate. Richard was thrown into the Tower and later died (murdered?) in prison (1400). Parliament accepted the abdication and, returning to the ancient custom of election, **made Henry king.** Henry's title by he-

redity was faulty; his claim was based on usurpation, legalized by Parliament, and backed by public opinion.

1399–1461. THE HOUSE OF LANCASTER.

1399–1413. HENRY IV. The reign, in view of the nature of Henry's title to the throne, was inevitably a parliamentary one. Henry, an epileptic, was not a great king, but a national monarch was now a necessity to England. To retain the support of the Church, Henry opposed the demand (1404) of the Commons (perhaps a reflection of Lollardy) that church property be confiscated, and applied to poor relief. The request was renewed (1410). The statute, *de Heretico Comburendo* (1401), increased the power of the Church over heresy (primarily, of course, against Lollardy) and was the first law of its kind in England.

1400–1406. Rebellions and invasions: (1) Revolt in behalf of Richard (1400); (2) Scottish invasion (1402) stopped by the Percies, the leading barons of Northumberland, at **Homildon Hill;** (3) Owen Glendower's revolt in Wales (1402–1409) joined by (4) the revolt of the Percies (1403–1404); (5) French landing in Wales (1405); (6) Archbishop (of York) Scrope's rebellion (1405); (7) attack by the Duke of Orléans in Guienne (1406).

1413–1422. HENRY V, a careful king, whose military achievements brought England to the first rank in Europe. Bent on the revival of the Church, he led a strong attack on Lollardy: **Sir John Oldcastle** (Lord Cobham), the leading Lollard, was excommunicated by Archbishop Arundel, but escaped; a Lollard plot against the king's life was discovered; Henry attacked (1414) and captured a Lollard group, most of whom were hanged; anti-Lollard legislation allowing seizure of their books; Oldcastle, the last influential Lollard, executed (1417). Henceforth Lollardy was a lower-class movement driven underground until the Reformation.

1415. Henry, in alliance with Burgundy, reasserted his claims (such as they were) to the throne of France. Relying on the anarchy in France and hoping by military successes to unite the English behind the house of Lancaster, he advanced into France.

1415, Oct. 25. BATTLE OF AGINCOURT. Henry's great victory over vastly superior forces opened the way to

1417–1419. The reconquest of Normandy and an advance to the walls of Paris (1419). The temporary union of the

Lancaster and York

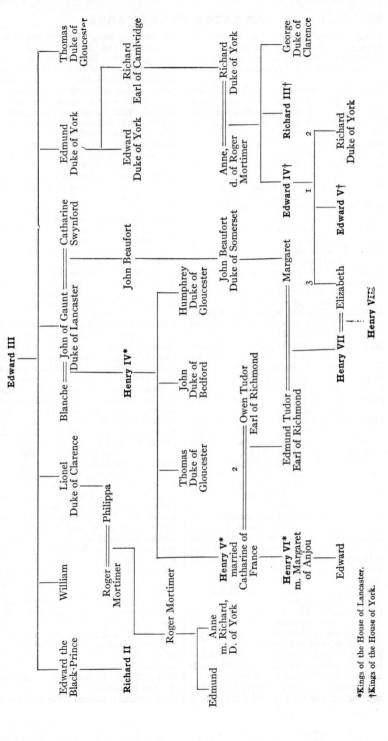

*Kings of the House of Lancaster.

†Kings of the House of York.

Armagnac and Burgundian factions in France was broken by the assassination (1419) of the Duke of Burgundy, followed by the renewal of Anglo-Burgundian alliance and

1420. The Treaty of Troyes. The dauphin (later Charles VII) was disinherited; Henry V was designated regent of France and successor to the mad Charles VI, was given control of northern France, and was married to Charles' daughter Catherine. Henry, busy in the reconquest of France, died suddenly, followed shortly by Charles VI (1422).

1422-1461. Henry VI (aged nine months on his accession), acclaimed King of France; his uncle, the Duke of Gloucester, regent (under the council) in England; another uncle, the Duke of Bedford, regent in France.

1424. Bedford defeated the French at Verneuil, but his ally the Duke of Burgundy was angered by Gloucester's foolish invasion of Hainault. Bitter feud of Gloucester and Beaufort, Bishop of Winchester and chancellor.

1428-1429. English failure at Orléans (Jeanne Darc, p. 278); coronation of Charles VII at Reims (1429).

1431. The English burned Joan of Arc at Rouen and crowned Henry VI King of France in Paris. Steady advance of Charles VII; unpopularity of the war in England; parliamentary resistance to grants; loss of the Burgundian alliance (1435) and of Paris (1436).

1436-1437. Richard, Duke of York (heir to throne), regent in France. He was replaced, after a few successes, by the Earl of Warwick (1437-1439), but later returned to France (1440-1443). Continued rivalry of Beaufort and Gloucester. Beaufort, supported by the king, who liked his peace policy, attended the conference of Calais (1439).

1442. French conquest of Gascony except Bordeaux and Bayonne.

1444. The king's new favorite, the Duke of Suffolk, arranged the marriage of Henry and Margaret of Anjou, concluded a truce of two years, and promised to surrender Maine to Charles VII. Margaret was unpopular in England and Maine was not turned over.

1448. Charles VII, in a vigorous renewal of the war, took Maine, completed the conquest of Normandy (1450), and regained Bordeaux and Bayonne (1451). The English effort to reconquer Gascony failed (1453), leaving only Calais in English hands at the end of the Hundred Years' War.

Domestic disorders. Henry, declared of age (1437), was unfit to rule; the council

continued in power, factions and favorites encouraged the rise of disorder. The nobles, enriched by the war and the new sheep farming and progress of enclosures, maintained increasing numbers of private armed retainers (livery and maintenance) with which they fought one another, terrorized their neighbors, paralyzed the courts, and dominated the government. The government lost prestige; Gloucester, arrested (1447) for treason, died in prison, Suffolk (impeached 1450) was killed as he sailed into exile.

1450. Cade's rebellion: a revolt of perhaps 30,000 men of Kent and Sussex, including many respectable small landowners, who marched on London to demand reform in government and the restoration of the Duke of York to power. Admitted to London, the marchers were finally crushed after they resorted to violence. **Richard of York** returned from Ireland and forced his admission to the council (1450). York was regent during Henry's periods of insanity (1453-1454; 1455-1456), but on his recovery (1454) Somerset returned to power.

1455-1485. THE WARS OF THE ROSES: a dreary civil war between the houses of Lancaster and York (the Yorkists wearing a white rose, the Lancastrians [later] a red rose). The nation as such took little part. **Battle of St. Albans** (1455): Somerset defeated and killed. **Battle of Northampton** (1460): the Yorkists defeated the royal army and took Henry prisoner. York asserted his hereditary claim to the throne, and the Lords decided that he should succeed Henry on his death (excluding Henry's son, Edward).

1460. Queen Catherine raised an army in the north, defeated Richard of York, who fell on the field (Wakefield, 1460). Southern England rallied to Richard's son Edward (aged nineteen) who defeated the Lancastrians at **Mortimer's Cross** (1461), but was defeated at the **second battle of St. Albans** (1461), and lost possession of King Henry. London stood firm against Margaret, admitted Edward to the town, and after his victory at Towton acclaimed him king (1461).

Growth of the powers of Parliament under the Lancastrians: Profiting by the cloud on the royal title and by the pressing needs for war supply, Parliament reached the zenith of its influence: (1) Grant of supply delayed until the end of the session after redress of grievances; agreement by the king not to alter petitions when drafted into statutes. Petitions began to take the form of bills, which when approved by the king became statutes in the modern sense.

(2) Beginnings of the Commons' control over the initiation of financial legislation. (3) Enforcement of reform (1404) in the royal administration; members of the council named in Parliament; appointment of the new council enforced (1405). (4) Parliament forced a reversal of the Haxey judgment (1399), establishing its right to freedom of speech in debate. (5) Opposition to packing began to develop and a statute was padded defining the franchise for elections (1430); this statute was in force until the Great Reform Bill of 1832.

The king could still legislate by ordinances in council. Under Henry VI the autocratic council ruled, and in the end dominated Parliament; finally the chaos of the Wars of the Roses saw the temporary eclipse of Parliament as well as of ordered government.

1461-1485. THE HOUSE OF YORK.

1461-1483. EDWARD IV. Parliament declared the three Lancastrian kings usurpers and Henry VI, his wife, son, and chief adherents, traitors. Edward closed the session with a speech of thanks to the Commons, the first time an English king had addressed that body. The mass of Englishmen now wanted a monarch to keep order in the state, and allow them to attend to trade, industry, and agriculture. Civil war continued intermittently, and Henry VI was finally captured (1465) and put in the Tower. Edward's marriage to the commoner, Elizabeth Woodville, and the beginnings of the creation of a new nobility, angered the older nobles, especially the Earl of Warwick. Edward's sister Margaret was married to Charles the Bold, Duke of Burgundy, and master of the Netherlands (1468). Warwick abandoned the king for his brother, the Duke of Clarence, and began to foment trouble for Edward, now increasingly unpopular (1469–1470). Edward's victory (partly due to artillery) at **Stamford** (1470) was followed by the flight of Warwick and Clarence.

1471. Warwick next turned to the Lancastrians (under the astute guidance of King Louis XI of France), returned to England with Lancastrian support. Edward's victory at Barnet (1471), where Warwick was killed. Edward then turned on Queen Margaret at Tewksbury, and defeated her. Henry VI died (in all probability murdered) in the Tower. The only surviving claimant to the crown was Henry, Earl of Richmond, an exile aged 14, descended from John of Gaunt and his mistress, Catherine Swynford.

Edward's vigorous plans for war against **Louis XI:** Parliamentary grants were too small, so he began a new practice — benevolences (supposedly free, but in fact forced gifts).

1475. Landing in France, Edward got no support from Charles the Bold, and was bought off by Louis XI. Charles the Bold was killed (1477) and Edward was left without an ally.

1483. EDWARD V, aged twelve. Richard, Duke of Gloucester, Edward's uncle, an able man, good soldier, cruel and cynical, skilled at winning popular support, had been appointed guardian by Edward's will. Fearing the Woodvilles (family of Edward's mother), Richard struck at them, taking Earl Rivers and Sir Richard Grey prisoners; the queen mother took sanctuary at Westminster; assassination of Lord Hastings (a supporter of the queen); execution of Grey and Rivers; attacks on the legitimacy of Edward; Parliament declared Gloucester the heir and he was crowned Richard III. Edward was sent to the Tower.

1483-1485. RICHARD III. The Duke of Buckingham, a former supporter of Richard, led (under the skilled direction of Morton, Bishop of Ely) a rebellion in behalf of Henry, Earl of Richmond. The rebellion failed, Buckingham was beheaded, Edward and his brother were murdered in the Tower (1483), and universal indignation was aroused. Richard and the Earl of Richmond were both candidates for the hand of Elizabeth of York, daughter of Edward IV, now heiress to the throne. As she was Richard's niece, even his own followers were shocked.

1485. Henry, Earl of Richmond, landed at Milford Haven, there were open defections from Richard by the nobles, and Henry defeated Richard on **Bosworth Field** (Aug. 22), where Richard fell. The crown of England was found on a bush and passed to the first ruler of the great **house of Tudor,** by virtue of his victory in arms and a later act of Parliament.

Cultural movements. The Italian humanist, Poggio Bracciolini's visit (1418–1423) to England. *The Paston Letters* (1422–1509), a remarkable collection of the correspondence (in the vernacular) of a middle-class English family. *The Libel of English Policie* (c. 1436), a militant nationalistic exposition of the economic value of sea-power. **Eton founded** by Henry VI.

Humphrey, Duke of Gloucester (d. 1447), influential patron of classical learning and Italian humanism, was the donor of 279 classical manuscripts to Oxford, the nucleus of the university library. **Sir John Fortescue** (d. c. 1476), chief justice of the

King's Bench, a Lancastrian exile during the anarchy of the Wars of the Roses, wrote *On the Governance of the Kingdom of England*, and *De Laudibus Legum Angliae*, contrasting the "political" (i.e. constitutional) spirit of the English Common Law with the absolutism of the Roman Law, and comparing the French monarchy unfavorably with the English. Many of his ideas foreshadowed the policies of Henry VII, in form if not in spirit.

Caxton's printing press set up at Westminster (1476) under the patronage of Edward IV. Malory's *Morte Arthure* printed (1484), the first book in poetic prose in the English language.

(*Cont. p.* 369.)

(2) Scotland, 1305-1488

1305. The conquest of Scotland by Edward I of England saved the country from civil war. Edward's plan of union seemed possible for a brief period until the emergence of Bruce's grandson, Robert, who turned against the English and maintained himself until the incompetence of Edward II gave him a chance to extend the opposition to the English.

1311-1313. Bruce began a great advance into England and besieged Stirling (1314).

1314, June 24. BATTLE OF BANNOCK-BURN. Bruce completely defeated the English and established himself on the throne, thus postponing for centuries the union with England. Bruce's daughter, Margaret, married Walter "the Steward" and became the founder of the house of Stuart.

1315-1318. Edward Bruce, brother of the king, led an unsuccessful invasion of Ireland.

1323. A truce of five years with England was followed by the Treaty of Northampton, which recognized Robert Bruce's title and provided for the marriage of his son David to Joanna, daughter of Edward III.

1329-1371. DAVID II, son of Robert, king. His minority was followed by an incompetent rule.

1332. Edward Baliol, with English support, was crowned, and Bruce fled to France. After Baliol's recall to England, Bruce returned and was defeated and captured at

1346. The battle of Neville's Cross, in an effort to aid France by invading England. He was not ransomed until 1357. This futile reign gave the Scottish Parliament its chance; the burghs had sent representatives to the Parliament of 1326, but

the practice was not a regular one until 1424. On at least two occasions the parliamentary majority went home (1367, 1369), leaving the session to commissions, thus establishing the Lords of Articles, who assumed deliberative functions and soon became tools of the crown. Nevertheless, Parliament managed to establish a considerable control over royal acts, and kept its hand on the declaration of war and peace and the coinage. The lower clergy began sending representatives to Parliament (e.g. 1367, 1369, 1370).

1356. Edward Baliol handed over his crown to Edward III.

1363. David Bruce's scheme for a union with England if he died childless was blocked by Parliament's refusal to approve it (1364).

1371. THE STUART LINE was established on the Scottish throne by the accession of

1371-1390. ROBERT II, grandson of Robert Bruce. It maintained itself for three centuries despite a succession of futilities and minorities. The rival house of Douglas was finally extinguished (1488).

1390-1424. ROBERT III, king. The arrival of James I (1424) after a long imprisonment (since 1405) in England began a vigorous, if premature reform, reduction of violence, restoration of the judicial process, and new legislation which ended anarchy and disciplined the Church. The country lairds were given representation in Parliament as a support to the crown (1428). James was assassinated, 1437.

1437-1460. JAMES II.
From James I to Charles I (1625) every sovereign was a minor on his accession. The reduction of the Earls of Douglas (1452), followed by confiscation of their lands, enriched the crown. Rosburgh was taken from the English, leaving only Berwick in alien hands.

1460-1488. JAMES III, a feeble figure, was kidnaped (1466) by Lord Boyd, who ruled as governor (by vote of Parliament). The Orkneys and Shetlands were acquired from Norway (1472). France kept Scotland in contact with the Continent.   (*Cont. p.* 369).

(3) Ireland, 1315-1485

1315. Edward Bruce, brother of Robert Bruce of Scotland, landed in Ireland and, with the aid of native chieftains, had himself crowned (1316). But he was able to maintain himself only until 1318.

The Anglo-Norman colony began to weaken from internal quarrels while Edward III was preoccupied with the Hundred Years' War. The chieftains thereupon seized their opportunity to encroach still further upon the position of the outsiders. From this period dates the gradual ebb of English influence. The Black Death (1348–1349) made matters even worse.

1366. The Statute of Kilkenny (passed during the viceroyalty of Lionel, Duke of Clarence) had two aims: (1) to maintain the allegiance of the English colony and keep it to the English tradition, and (2) to reduce the grounds of racial conflict. Marriages with the Irish were forbidden, though this was not an entirely new measure. English was enjoined as the speech of the colonists, and English law was insisted on. Nevertheless, the viceroys and governors were unable to maintain order.

1398. Expedition of Richard II to reduce Ireland. This was without permanent results. Under Henry V misery in Ireland reached a new peak and perhaps half of the English colony returned home. The danger in this situation is mentioned in the *Libel of English Policy* (c. 1436). Fear that Ireland might pass into other hands was widespread.

1449. Richard of York arrived as viceroy and ingratiated himself equally with colonists and natives. He departed to England in 1450, but on his return made Ireland virtually independent, with the approval of the Irish Parliament. English rule was repudiated and a separate coinage established. Richard continued this policy until his death, but Edward IV resumed a harsh and anarchic policy. Under Richard III the strongest figure in Ireland was Kildare, leader of the Yorkists. (*Cont. p. 369.*)

b. FRANCE, 1314-1483

1314-1316. LOUIS X (*the Quarrelsome*). The real ruler was Louis' uncle, Charles of Valois. A reaction against the monarchy forced concessions from the king. Louis' daughter, Jeanne, was an infant; there was no male heir. A great national council (1316) decreed that there could be no queen regnant in France, and gave the crown to Louis' brother, Philip.

1316-1322. PHILIP V (*the Tall*). There were frequent meetings of assemblies which included burghers. Philip, in an enormous number of royal ordinances, gave definitive form to the Capetian government. He left no male heir.

1322-1328. CHARLES IV (*the Fair*), the last Capetian of the direct line, succeeded his brother Philip, to the exclusion of Edward III of England, grandson of Philip IV. This established the principle, later called the Salic Law, that the throne could pass only through males. On Charles' death, an assembly of barons declared that "no woman nor her son could succeed to the monarchy."

1328-1498. In this period the Capetian house of Valois freed the soil of France from the alien occupation of the English; completed the creation of French national unity and the establishment of a strong national monarchy; prepared France for its brilliant political and cultural rôle in the Renaissance, and began French expansion south of the Alps.

1328-1350. PHILIP VI (nephew of Philip IV, son of Charles of Valois), the nearest male heir. Jeanne, daughter of Louis X, became Queen of Navarre. Edward III did homage for his French fiefs (1329 and 1331). Brittany, Flanders, Guienne, and Burgundy remained outside the royal sway. The papacy was located in France under powerful French influence; rulers of the Capetian house of Anjou were seated on the thrones of Naples, Provence, and Hungary; French interests were firmly established in the Near East; French culture was dominant in England and northern Spain, and was making headway on the fringes of the empire; Dauphiné, the first important imperial fief added to French territory, was purchased (1336). The king had become less accessible; the kingdom, regarded as a possession rather than an obligation, was left to the administration of the royal bureaucracy.

1338-1453. THE HUNDRED YEARS' WAR. English commercial dominance in Flanders precipitated a political crisis. The communes made the Count of Flanders, Louis of Nevers, prisoner (1325-1326); Philip marched to his relief, massacred the burghers on the field of Cassel (1328), and established French administration in Flanders. Edward III retorted with an embargo on wool export from England (1336); the weavers of Ghent, under the wealthy James van Artevelde, became virtual masters of the country and made a commercial treaty with England (1338). On Van Artevelde's insistence, Edward declared himself King of France; the Flemings recognized him as their sovereign, and made a political alliance with him (1340).

1338. Philip declared Edward's French fiefs forfeited and invested Guienne. Edward was made Vicar of the Empire and his title as King of France was recognized by the emperor. Thus began the Hundred

The French Succession, 1328

Philip III 1270-1285

Philip IV 1285-1314 — Charles Count of Valois — Louis

Louis X 1314-1316 — Philip V 1316-1322 — Charles IV 1322-1328 — Isabella

Philip VI 1328-1350

John II 1350-1364

Charles V 1364-1380

Charles VI 1380-1422

Catharine — Henry V King of England and France

Charles VII 1422-1461

Henry VI King of England and France

Philip m. Jeanne of Navarre

Charles the Bad

Edward I of England — Edward II of England — Edward III — John of Gaunt — Henry IV

Jeanne Queen of Navarre

John 1316

Jane — Philip BURGUNDY

Margaret — Louis FLANDERS

Blanche — Philip ORLÉANS

Charles the Bad NAVARRE

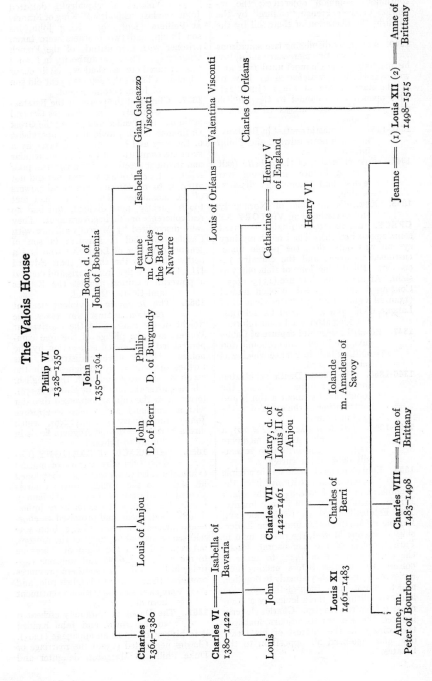

The Valois House

Philip VI
1328–1350

John
1350–1364 == Bona, d. of John of Bohemia

Charles V
1364–1380

Louis of Anjou

John
D. of Berri

Philip
D. of Burgundy

Jeanne
m. Charles the Bad of Navarre

Isabella == Gian Galeazzo Visconti

Charles VI
1380–1422 == Isabella of Bavaria

Louis of Orléans == Valentina Visconti

Louis

John

Charles VII
1422–1461 == Mary, d. of Louis II of Anjou

Catharine == Henry V of England

Louis of Orléans

Charles of Orléans

Henry VI

Charles of Berri

Iolande
m. Amadeus of Savoy

Louis XI
1461–1483

Charles VIII
1483–1498 == Anne of Brittany

Jeanne == (1) Louis XII (2) == Anne of Brittany
1498–1515

Anne, m.
Peter of Bourbon

Years' War, really a series of wars with continuous common objectives: the retention of their French "empire" by the English, the liberation of their soil by the French.

1340. Philip, by dismissing two squadrons of Levantine mercenary ships, lost his mastery of the Channel until 1372 and was overwhelmingly defeated by Edward at the **naval battle of Sluys** (June 24). This opened the Channel to the English and gave them free access to northern France.

1341-1364. A dynastic contest in Brittany, in which both Edward and Philip intervened.

1341. First collection of the *gabelle* (salt tax) in France; increasing war levies and mounting dissatisfaction.

1346. Edward's invasion of Normandy and overwhelming **VICTORY AT CRÉCY,** Aug. 26 (10,000 English defeated some 20,000 French). The French military system was outmoded, the people unaccustomed to arms, and the chivalry inefficient. Blind King John of Bohemia was slain. Artillery came into use (1335–1345). Continued war levies led to open refusal (1346) of a grant by the Estates-General of Langue d'Oil, and a demand for reforms. The king attempted some reforms.

1347. Edward's siege and **capture of Calais** gave the English an economic and military base in France which was held until 1558.

1348-1350. The **Black Death** penetrated northern Europe, reducing the population by about a third, and contributing to the crisis of 1357–1358 in France.

1350-1364. JOHN II (*the Good Fellow*), a "good knight and a mediocre king," a spendthrift who repeatedly debased the currency.

1355. English renewal of the war in a triple advance: into Brittany; from the Channel; and from Bordeaux by the Black Prince. Virtual collapse of French finance. The Estates-General of Languedoc and Langue d'Oil (the latter under the leadership of Etienne Marcel, the richest man in Paris, provost of the merchants), forced the king (ordinance of 1355) to agree to consult the Estates before making new levies of money, a policy already in practice, and to accept supervision of the collection and expenditure of these levies by a commission from the Estates. Charles cleverly induced the Estates to adjourn, debased the coinage in the interest of his treasury, and organized his opposition to the Estates.

1356. The Black Prince (the English "model of chivalry") defeated John, the last "chivalrous" King of France, at Poitiers (Sept. 19). King John, his son Philip, and two brothers were taken prisoner with a multitude of the French aristocracy. The royal authority in France was reduced to a shadow; civil chaos reigned. Charles the eighteen-year-old son of John, became regent.

1357. Climax of the power of the **Estates-General:** The Estates-General again had to be called and passed the **Great Ordinance** which provided for supervision of the levy and expenditure of taxes by a standing committee of the Estates, regular and frequent meetings of the Estates, poor relief, and many other reforms, but did not attempt to reduce the traditional powers of the monarchy. The Estates had met too frequently, were divided, and had no real coherence or skill in government. They were discredited by Marcel's alliance with Charles the Bad of Navarre (a son of Jeanne, daughter of Louis X) who had a better claim to the throne than Edward III. Charles V fled from Paris and created a powerful coalition against the Estates and Charles the Bad.

1358. The *Jacquerie* (a violent peasant reaction against war taxes, the weight of the ransoms of the captives at Poitiers and the pillage of the free companies) led to a merciless reaction by the nobles. Marcel, already distrusted, was further discredited by intrigues with the revolted peasantry and with the English. Charles, after the murder of Marcel (1358), returned to the capital, repressed disorder with a firm hand, and refused to approve John's preliminary peace (1359), which virtually restored the old Angevin lands in France to Edward.

1360. THE PEACE OF BRETIGNY (Calais) (virtually a truce of mutual exhaustion): Edward practically abandoned his claims to the French crown; Charles yielded southwestern France (Guienne), Calais, Ponthieu, and the territory immediately about them, and promised an enormous ransom for John. King John was released on partial payment of the ransom, but returned after the flight of a hostage to die in his luxurious and welcome captivity in England. The southern provinces protested their return to English rule, and there were clear signs of national sentiment born of adversity.

1361. The **Duchy of Burgundy** escheated to the crown, and John handed it to his son Philip as an appanage (1363). Charles negotiated (1369) the marriage of Duke Philip to Margaret, daughter **and**

heiress of Louis de Male, last Count of Flanders, in order to keep Flanders out of English hands. As Mary brought Flanders, the County of Burgundy, Artois, Nevers, and Rethel under control of the Dukes of Burgundy, this marriage added a new danger on the east and north to the Plantagenet threat in the west. Philip further strengthened his house by marriage alliances with the children of the Wittelsbach, Albert of Bavaria, which added holdings in Hainault, Holland, and Zealand.

1364-1380. CHARLES V (*the Wise*), neither strong of body, handsome, nor chivalrous; a pious, refined, realistic statesman of modern cast. He saved France and made it plain to the nation that national well-being depended on the monarchy rather than on the Estates-General.

The reign opened with a bad harvest, plague, and pillage by the free companies (discharged soldiers). The Breton, Bertrand du Guesclin, the first great soldier on the French side in the Hundred Years' War, was sent with some 30,000 of these men to support Henry of Trastamara against Pedro the Cruel of Castile, who had become an ally of the Black Prince.

Charles managed to dominate the new financial machinery set up by the Estates-General, continued the war levies (e.g. hearth-tax, *gabelle*, sales taxes) and utilized the peace for general reform and reconstruction: castles were rebuilt, and royal control of them strengthened; permanent companies of professional cavalry and infantry were established; artillery was organized and supported by pioneers and sappers; a military staff and hierarchy of command established in the army (1374); the navy was reorganized, and French seapower restored. New walls were built around Paris.

The government and finance were reorganized and the general frame of the financial structure fixed until 1789. The grant of the Estates-General of Langue d'Oil (1360) for John's ransom had been for a term of six years; their grant of a hearth-tax (1363) was without a time limit. Following these precedents, Charles was able (1369) to induce the Estates to agree to the general principle that old grants of funds need not be renewed by the Estates unless their terms were to be changed. This freed the king from control by the Estates unless new taxes were needed and meant that the Estates no longer had a vital function. The financial control established by the Estates (1357) was transferred to the royal *chambre de comptés* in Paris.

1369. The appeal of the Count of Armagnac to Charles against the Black Prince and the Black Prince's refusal to appear at Charles' court served as an excuse for the **resumption of the war.** Du Guesclin became (1370) Constable of France (a title usually reserved for great nobles), abandoned chivalrous tactics, and allowed the English to parade through France. Avoiding pitched battle, he harassed the invaders with a picked force. The reconquest of Poitou and Brittany (1370–1372) was followed by the death of the Black Prince (1376); the French fleet, supported by the Castilian, regained control (La Rochelle, 1372) of the Channel, and blocked English transport in the north. By 1380 the English held only Bordeaux, Bayonne, Brest, Calais, Cherbourg, Valais, and their immediately surrounding territory. France was cleared of the enemy, but was in ruins.

1378. With the end of the Avignonese Captivity (1376) the **Great Schism** in the Church began; Charles and his successors supported the French line of popes. On his deathbed Charles forbade the hearth-tax.

1380-1422. CHARLES VI. A minority accompanied by the disruptive rivalry of the king's uncles (the Dukes of Anjou, Berry, and Burgundy, the "Princes of the Lilies"), who exploited France for their own ends. This was followed by the intermittent insanity of the king, and paralysis in the government.

General economic distress, popular unrest, and general revolts, usually against taxes (vigorously repressed): the *Tuchins* (1381) in Languedoc; the *Maillotins* (1382) in Paris, and elsewhere; and the outbreak in Flanders (1382) under Philip (son of James) van Artevelde. The French feudality, under leadership of the Duke of Burgundy, ended this revolt by the victory of **Roosebeke** (1382), following it up with atrocious repression. Flanders on the death of the Count (1384) passed to Burgundy; its pacification was completed in 1385. The hearth-tax was renewed and taxation remained heavy.

1388. The death (1384) of the Duke of Anjou had left the Duke of Burgundy in a position of great power, and Charles, angered at Philip of Burgundy's policies, began his personal rule by replacing the duke by his own brother, Louis, Duke of Orléans, and by restoring (1389) his father's old advisers, men of humble birth (whence their nickname, the *Marmousets*). Louis of Orléans was a refined, talented spendthrift, unpopular in Paris, and Philip of Burgundy (supported by

Queen Isabella) was able to pose as a reformer and lead the opposition, bringing the rivalry of Burgundy and Orléans into the open.

1392.   Charles' first (brief) attack of insanity was soon followed by longer seizures; Philip of Burgundy (as regent) replaced Louis of Orléans in power and the situation returned to what it was before 1389.

1396.   Twenty-year truce with England; annihilation of the French knights on a crusade to free Hungary from the Turk (Nicopolis, p. 326).

1404.   John (*the Fearless*), an able, ambitious man, became **Duke of Burgundy.** After the sudden transfer of Isabella's support to Louis of Orléans, John's orders led to the assassination of Louis, Duke of Orléans (1407). John became the hero of Paris, but caused the emergence of two great factions in France and began the civil war of the **Armagnacs** against the Burgundians. The Armagnacs, named for their head, the Count of Armagnac (father-in-law of Charles, the new Duke of Orléans), were strong among the great nobles, drew their strength from the south and southeast, were a reactionary, anti-English, war party. The Burgundians, supported by the people, the University of Paris, and the Wittelsbachs, were strong in the north and northeast, favored peace, were pro-English, and supported Pope Clement VII and his papal successors.

1413.   The Cabochian revolt (named for the skinner, Simon Caboche) in Paris forced attention to reform, and led to the **Cabochian Ordinance** (1413), inspired by the University of Paris and aimed at efficiency in government rather than democracy. It provided for three councils to conduct public business, and a general detailed program of reform. The Armagnacs returned to control in Paris and led a feudal reaction, which destroyed all hope of reform and opened the way for the English. The Duke of Armagnac (Constable, 1415) repeated the traditional military errors of the feudal class, which understood tournaments but not war.

1415, Oct. 25.   THE BATTLE OF AGINCOURT: Henry V, with 10,000 men, defeated three times that number of French; the Duke of Orléans was taken prisoner; **Normandy was reconquered** (1415–1417) by the English, undoing for the time the work of Philip Augustus; the dauphin (later Charles VII) fled to the south of France (1418); the Burgundians returned to power and there was a massacre of Armagnacs in Paris (1418).

1419.   Rouen fell; the Burgundians, alarmed at the English advance, began negotiating with the Armagnacs; John of Burgundy was assassinated at a conference with the dauphin at the Bridge of Montereau, and the Burgundians returned to the English alliance.

1420. Charles, under Burgundian influence, and supported by his wife Isabella, accepted the **Treaty of Troyes** (which repudiated the dauphin as illegitimate), adopted Henry V of England as his heir and immediate regent (with the approval of the University of Paris and the Estates-General, 1421). Charles' daughter, Catharine, was married to the future Henry V and, also under the treaty, the English were allowed to retain all their conquests as far as the Loire. King Henry V drove the forces of the dauphin across the Loire and began the steady conquest of France which continued uninterrupted until his death (1422). The dauphin remained at Bourges (whence his nickname, *the Roi de Bourges*).

1422–1461.   CHARLES VII (*the Roi de Bourges*, not crowned until 1429). Physically weak, bowed and lethargic from misfortune, the puppet of unscrupulous advisers until the advent of a better group (including Dunois, Richemont, brother-in-law of the Duke of Burgundy, La Hire, *et al.*), after 1433, when he became known as "Charles the Well-Served." **Regency of the Duke of Bedford** (1422–1428) for the infant Henry VI of England, who was recognized as King of France in the north, supported by the Burgundians, and crowned in Paris (1436).

1424. Bedford's decisive victory at Cravant was followed by the defeat of the Armagnacs and the Scots at Verneuil.

1428.   The English began the siege of Orléans. Jeanne Darc (later D'Arc in Charles' patent of nobility), born in 1412 at Domrémy, was of comfortable village family, illiterate, but a good seamstress. A devout mystic, she began to have visions at the age of thirteen.

1429. Jeanne presented herself to the king at Chinon, and was allowed to lead an army (with the empty title of *Chef de Guerre*) to the relief of Orléans. The relief of the city, followed by Charles' coronation (1429) at Reims, was the turning point of the war and marked a decisive change in the spirit of the king and the nation. Jealous ministers (e.g. *La Trémoille*) of Charles soon undermined Jeanne's position, despite the progress of the royal cause.

1430. Jeanne was captured at Compiègne by the Burgundians, ransomed by the English. Without intervention by Charles on her behalf, she was tried for witchcraft. The process was probably a typical ecclesiastical trial. After her confession and its repudiation she was burned (1431) by the English at Rouen ("We have burned a saint"), and Charles returned to his old ways.

1432. Charles favored the **Council of Basel,** which was pro-French and anti-papal.

1435. **Separate Peace of Arras,** reconciliation with Burgundy: Charles agreed to punish the murderers of Duke John of Burgundy and recognized Philip as a sovereign prince for life. Burgundy was to recognize Charles' title; the Somme towns were to pass to Burgundy (subject to redemption). The English refused to make peace on acceptable terms. **Charles recovered Paris** (1436).

1436-1449. Period of military inaction, utilized by Charles for reforms of the army paid for from the *taille*. The Estates-General agreed to permanent taxation for support of the army. Charles entered Paris and was welcomed (1437).

1437-1439. Famine, pestilence, the anarchy of the *écorcheurs*, but steady progress against the English.

1438. **THE PRAGMATIC SANCTION OF BOURGES:** assertion that a church council is superior to a pope; suppression of the annates; provision for decennial councils; maintenance of the autonomy of the French national Church (*Gallicanism*) and its isolation from Rome.

1440. **The Praguerie,** part of a series of coalitions of great nobles against the king, with support from the dauphin (later Louis XI), was put down; the dauphin was ordered to the Dauphiné, where he continued his intrigues.

1445-1446. **Army reforms:** establishment of the first permanent royal army by the creation of 20 companies of élite cavalry (200 *lances* to a company, 6 men to a *lance*) under captains chosen by the king; a paid force, the backbone of the army, assigned to garrison towns; regularization of the auxiliary free archers (*francs-archers*), a spontaneous body dating from the reign of Charles V (opposed by the nobles), under royal inspection (1448) and under territorial captains (1451). Establishment of artillery (the Bureau brothers).

1444. Louis the dauphin made a **treaty of alliance with the Swiss cantons.** The alliance was strengthened (1452) and an alliance made with the towns of Trier,

Cologne, *et al.* (1452), and with Saxony, as part of a developing anti-Burgundian policy. Intermittent support for the house of Anjou in Naples and the house of Orléans in Milan. Under **Jacques Coeur,** the merchant prince of Montpellier, royal finances were reformed, control of the public revenue by the king established, and French commercial penetration of the Near East furthered (c. 1447).

1449-1461. **Expulsion of the English:** Normandy and Guienne regained; Talbot slain (1453).

1456. Retrial and **rehabilitation of Jeanne Darc,** to clear Charles' royal title.

1461-1483. **LOUIS XI** (*the Spider*), of simple, bourgeois habits, superficial piety, and feeble, ungainly body, the architect of French reconstruction and royal absolutism. He was well-educated, a brilliant diplomat, a relentless statesman an endless traveler throughout his kingdom. He perfected the governmental system begun under Charles V (revived by Charles VII), and established the frame of the constitution until 1789. The recognized right of the king to the *taille*, the *aides*, and the *gabelle* made a good revenue available for defense and diplomacy. Louis improved and perfected the standing army with added emphasis on the artillery, but seldom waged war. Feudal anarchy and brigandage were stopped; a wise economic policy restored national prosperity despite grinding taxes.

1461. Louis' first step in the reconstruction of the kingdom was a *rapprochement* with the papacy by the formal **revocation of the Pragmatic Sanction of Bourges.** Little of the royal power was sacrificed, and the national Church remained under the firm control of the crown. Louis steadily reduced urban liberties and began the extinction of local and provincial administrative independence in the interests of royal centralization.

1462. **Acquisition of Cerdagne and Roussillon;** redemption of the Somme towns (1463) revealing the resumption of national expansion.

1465. **League of the Public Weal,** a conspiracy against Louis by the Dukes of Alençon, Burgundy, Berry, Bourbon, Lorraine.

1465. Louis' defeat by the league at Montl'héry. The **Treaty of Conflans** restored the Somme towns to Burgundy, and Normandy to the Duke of Berry. Louis began to evade the treaty at once, and split the league by diplomacy.

Louis' greatest rival was **Duke Philip the Good** of Burgundy. Philip was head of the first union of the **Low Countries** since the days of Charlemagne, a curious approximation of the ancient Lotharingia, which included: the Duchy and County of **Burgundy,** Flanders, Artois, Brabant, Luxemburg, Holland, Zealand, Friesland, Hainault. The dukes lacked only Alsace and Lorraine and the royal title.

1467. The accession of **Charles the Bold** as Duke of Burgundy opened the final duel with Burgundy.

1468. Anglo-Burgundian alliance; marriage of Charles the Bold to Margaret of York.

1468. The affair at Péronne: Charles, assuming Louis' treachery in the revolt of Ghent, arrested him at a conference at Péronne.

1469. The Duke Sigismund ceded Charles' rights in Alsace; Charles occupied Alsace and Lorraine (1473). Louis formed an alliance with the Swiss (1470) and seized the Somme towns (1471).

1474. Louis formed the **Union of Constance** (a coalition of the foes of Burgundy, under French subsidies) which opened the war on Charles.

1475. **Edward IV,** an ally of Charles, invaded France; Louis met him at Piquigny and bought him off.

1476. Charles' conquest of Lorraine and war on the Swiss cantons: defeat of Charles at Granson and Morat.

1477, Jan. 5. DEFEAT AND DEATH OF CHARLES AT NANCY (triumph of the Swiss pikeman over cavalry); end of the Burgundian menace. Louis united the Duchy of Burgundy to the crown and occupied the County of Burgundy (Franche Comté). Flanders stood by the daughter of Charles, Mary of Burgundy, and was lost to France forever. Mary hurriedly married the Hapsburg Prince Maximilian, the "heir" to the empire.

1480. On the **extinction of the house of Anjou,** Anjou, Bar, Maine, and Provence fell to the French crown. Bar completed Louis' mastery on the eastern frontier.

The most significant internal fact of the reign is the development of a clear basis for royal absolutism. Only one meeting of the Estates-General was held (1469), and on that occasion the Estates asked the king to rule without them in future. Legislation was henceforth by royal decree, a situation which facilitated Louis' thoroughgoing reform of the government and administration.

Philippe de Commines, a Fleming who left the service of Charles the Bold for that of Louis, produced in his *Memoirs* the finest piece of critical history since the days of

the great historians of antiquity, and was a precursor of Machiavelli.

François Villon (b. 1431), a lyric poet of the first rank.

Jan (d. 1440) **and Hubert van Eyck,** Flemish painters in the service of the court of Burgundy, perfected oil technique; religious painting; portraiture, raising the painter's art to the highest stage of proficiency and perfection. (*Cont. p.* 381.)

c. THE IBERIAN PENINSULA

(1) *Castile,* 1312-1492

The successors of Alfonso X were not conspicuous for capacity. Frequent minorities and constant dynastic contests still further weakened the authority of the crown. Most outstanding of the Castilian rulers in this period was

1312-1350. ALFONSO XI, who decisively defeated the joint attack of the Spanish and Moroccan Moslems. His victory at Rio Salado (Oct. 30, 1340) ended the African menace forever and was the chief battle in the whole history of the reconquest.

Throughout the **Hundred Years' War** (p. 273) Castile supported France, but attempted to avoid hostility with England as much as possible.

1350-1369. PETER (*Pedro, the Cruel*). His reign was in fact little more than a nineteen-year dynastic conflict with his half-brother, the bastard **Henry of Trastamara.** The French, alienated by Peter's outrageous treatment of his wife, Blanche of Bourbon, supported Henry and sent Du Guesclin to Spain. The English (the Black Prince) supported Peter. Henry was defeated at **Navarrete** (1367), but the English were soon estranged by Peter's vicious character. Ultimately Henry defeated and killed Peter (1369).

1369-1379. HENRY II (Trastamara), who renewed the alliance with France. The Castilian fleet, by its victory over the English in the **battle of La Rochelle** (1372), restored command of the Channel to the French. Peace between Castile on the one side and Portugal and Aragon on the other concluded at **Almazan** (1374).

1375. Rapprochement of Castile and Aragon, through the marriage of Henry's son, John, to Eleanor, daughter of Peter IV of Aragon.

Castilian leadership in the reconquest of Moslem Spain led to a maximum of local and municipal self-government between the middle of the 12th and the middle of the 14th century. The Córtes apparently originated from councils of nobles dating from Visigothic days. The Castilian rulers freely

The House of Castile

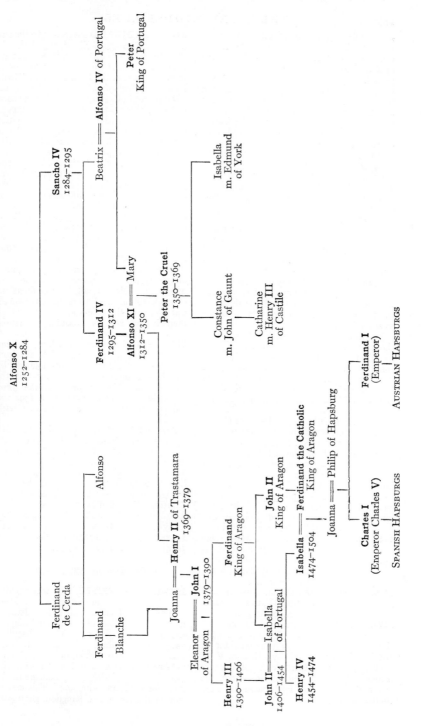

Alfonso X
1252–1284

Ferdinand
de Cerda

Ferdinand
Blanche

Sancho IV
1284–1295

Beatrix ═ Alfonso IV of Portugal

Peter
King of Portugal

Ferdinand IV
1295–1312

Alfonso XI ═ Mary
1312–1350

Peter the Cruel
1350–1369

Constance
m. John of Gaunt

Catharine
m. Henry III
of Castile

Isabella
m. Edmund
of York

Alfonso

Joanna ═ Henry II of Trastamara
1369–1379

Eleanor ═ John I
of Aragon │ 1379–1390

Ferdinand
King of Aragon

John II
King of Aragon

Henry III
1390–1406

John II ═ Isabella
1406–1454   of Portugal

Henry IV
1454–1474

Isabella ═ Ferdinand the Catholic
1474–1504   King of Aragon

Joanna ═ Philip of Hapsburg

Ferdinand I
(Emperor)

AUSTRIAN HAPSBURGS

Charles I
(Emperor Charles V)

SPANISH HAPSBURGS

granted *fueros* (charters of self-government) to towns in the early stages of the reconquest, and definite elements of democracy appeared in municipal government in this period. By calling the burghers to the Córtes, the kings found allies against the baronage, and this process began in Castile and Leon at least as early as 1188 (in Aragon probably not before 1250). The Córtes reached its zenith in the 14th and 15th centuries, but petitions to the crown were received and embodied in legislation as early as the 13th century.

Urban groups, the *hermandades* (brotherhoods), sworn to defend the laws of the realm and the lives and property of their members, were clearly developed in the 13th century (e.g. Sancho's, 1282, directed against his father, Alfonso X) and usually supported the kings in periods of crisis (minorities, succession struggles, baronial assaults). The decline of the *hermandades* is associated with the municipal decline and the appearance of the royal *corregidores* in the towns (14th century), but it is not clear whether the crown hastened the decay of the towns and the brotherhoods or sought to stave it off.

Despite all this support, the battle of the kings with the aristocracy, firmly entrenched during the early stages of the reconquest, was a losing one. The nobles were exempt from taxes and from many laws; in general the same was true of the clergy, and some of the great bishops were virtual sovereigns.

The status of the lower classes of Castile was, however, far from desperate: Jew and Moslem were protected for their economic value, though the tendency toward jealousy and toward the segregation of the Jews was already appearing and the Jewish population was declining. The status of rural workers and serfs tended to improve by the definition and limitation of the landlord's rights. Slavery had probably disappeared by the 15th century.

1454-1474. HENRY IV, during whose reign the feudal anarchy reached its apogee. The monarchical power was saved primarily through the support of the towns.

1469. Marriage of Isabella, stepsister and heiress of Henry IV, to **Ferdinand,** heir of the King of Aragon.

1474. ISABELLA succeeded to the Castilian throne. Isabella's succession was challenged by the daughter of Henry IV, supported by Alfonso V of Portugal. But the Córtes of Segovia (1475) recognized Isabella and Ferdinand and the latter defeated the Portuguese in 1476 **(battle of Toro).**

1479. FERDINAND succeeded to the rule of Aragon, Catalonia, Valencia. A form of dyarchical government was set up for the united Castilian and Aragonese crowns. Rule of the Catholic kings (Ferdinand and Isabella). Restoration of the royal power in Castile: by revising the town charters, the towns were made centers of resistance to feudal aggression; formation of the *Santa Hermandad,* a union of Castilian towns in the interest of royal authority and order. The great feudal magnates were deprived of many of their possessions and rights and a royal administration was gradually established. The *Libro de Montalvo* (1485), the first codification of Spanish law. **Concordat of 1482** with the pope, carefully restricting the power of Rome over the Spanish Church: the king became grand master of the powerful religious orders of knighthood. **The Inquisition** (established in 1478) wholly under royal control, used primarily for the persecution of the Marranos (converted Jews secretly practicing their old faith). Confiscations of property did much to increase the financial power of the rulers and to strengthen them in the work of subduing the feudal opposition.

1492. Fall of Granada, marking the end of the reconquest of Spain from the Moors. This was speedily followed by a spiritual reconquest, the work of the Inquisition. The **expulsion of the Jews** (possibly as many as 200,000) in 1492 was followed by that of the Moors in Castile (1502).

Art and literature. Castilian painting showed the influence of the school of Giotto (after c. 1380), and in the 15th century came under Flemish inspiration (visit of Jan van Eyck, 1428–1429). In general literature and learning followed the same foreign tendencies as architecture and painting: French influence came in early, followed later by Italian and English (notably Dante, Petrarch, Boccaccio, Gower). Introduction of printing at Valencia (c. 1474) and in Castile (c. 1475).

(2) *Aragon, 1276-1479*

1276-1285. PETER III, who was married to Constance, daughter of Manfred and heir of the Hohenstaufen. In 1282 he sailed on a long-planned expedition for the **conquest of Sicily** (which he disguised as an African crusade). He landed at Collo, was called to the throne, defeated Charles at Anjou and became Peter I of Sicily (1282-1285), refusing to do homage to the pope for his island kingdom. This expansion of the Aragonese Kingdom gave Ara-

The House of Aragon

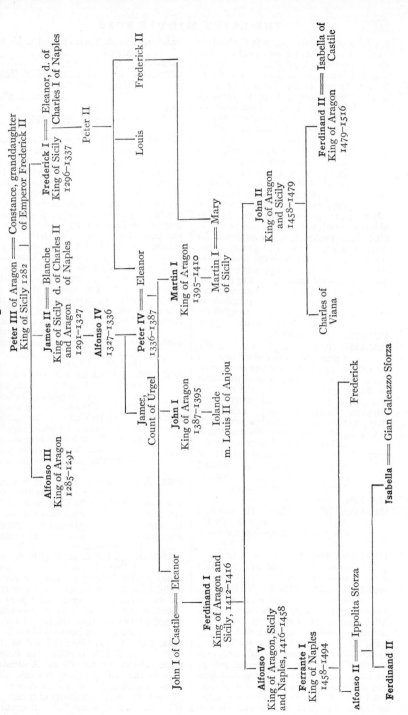

gon for a time predominance in the western Mediterranean. But it estranged the Aragonese aristocracy, as well as the towns. The nobility therefore formed the **Union for Liberty** and, in the Córtes of 1283, extorted from Peter a **General Privilege** which defined the rights and duties of the nobles, affirmed the principle of due process of law, and provided for annual meetings of the Córtes.

1285-1291. ALFONSO III was obliged to make a sweeping regrant of the Privileges of Union (1287), the so-called *Magna Carta of Aragon*.

1291-1327. JAMES II (King of Sicily, 1285-1295). He exchanged the investiture of Sardinia and Corsica for that of Sicily (1295), which thereupon passed to his brother Frederick, who established the separate Sicilian dynasty. James began the expulsion of the Genoese and Pisans from Sardinia (1323-1324), a process not finally completed until 1421. For a period Aragon held the Duchy of Athens (first indirectly through Sicily, 1311-1377, then directly, to 1388), thanks to the activity of the **Grand Catalan Company (p. 322).**

1327-1336. ALFONSO IV.

1336-1387. PETER IV. He was virtually a prisoner of the revived union of the nobility and had to confirm their privileges. But, after a victory over the union (at **Epila**, 1348), he broke up the coalition and gradually restricted the power of the aristocracy in Aragon and Valencia. The clergy and the towns had far less power than in Castile, while the rural workers and serfs suffered a much harder lot.

1377. On the death of **Frederick II** of Sicily, Peter IV, as the husband of Frederick's sister, sent his son Martin as viceroy to Sicily.

1387-1395. John, king.

1395-1410. Martin, king. He reunited Aragon and Sicily (1409). On his death the native dynasty came to an end.

1410-1416. Ferdinand I, of Castile, a grandson of Peter IV, succeeded to the throne.

1416-1458. ALFONSO V (*the Magnanimous*). His attention was engrossed by the desire to conquer Naples. After long diplomatic intrigues and occasional combats, he succeeded (1435), being recognized as king by the pope in 1442. Alfonso, a lover of Italy and passionate *dévoté* of the Renaissance, shifted the center of gravity of the Aragonese Empire and subordinated the interest of Aragon to that of Naples. Aragon was ruled by his brother John, as viceroy. On the

death of Alfonso, Naples passed **to his son** Ferrante (1458-1494).

1458-1479. John II, king.

1479-1516. FERDINAND II, king. **Union of Aragon with Castile.**

(*Cont. p.* 387.)

(3) Portugal, 1279-1495

1279-1325. DINIZ (*the Worker*), the best-known and best-loved king of mediaeval Portugal. An ardent poet, he did much to raise the cultural level of the court. His interest in agriculture and constant effort toward economic development (commercial treaty with England, 1294) resulted in greater prosperity. Beginning of **Portuguese naval activity** (under Venetian and Genoese guidance). Foundation (1290) of the University of Lisbon, which was soon (1308) moved to Coimbra.

1325-1357. AFONSO IV (*the Brave*), whose reign was scarred by dynastic troubles. The murder of **Inez de Castro** (1355), the mistress and later the wife of Afonso's son Peter, at the behest of Afonso. This episode, the subject of much literature, led to a revolt of Peter.

1340. The Portuguese, in alliance with Castile, defeated the Moors in the **battle of Salado.**

1357-1367. PETER I (*the Severe*) a harsh and hasty, though just ruler, who continued his predecessor's efforts in behalf of the general welfare.

1367-1383. FERDINAND I (*the Handsome*), a weak ruler whose love for Leonora Telles led him to repudiate his betrothal to a Castilian princess and so bring on a war with Castile.

1383. Regency of Queen Leonora in behalf of Ferdinand's daughter, Beatrice, who was married to John I of Castile. This arrangement led to strong opposition among the Portuguese, who detested both the regent and her lover and resented all control from outside.

1385-1433. JOHN I, an illegitimate son of Peter I, established the **Avis dynasty** after leading a successful revolt and driving the regent out of the country. He was proclaimed king by the Córtes of Coimbra, but his position was at once challenged by the Castilians, who twice invaded Portugal and besieged Lisbon.

1385, Aug. 14. THE BATTLE OF ALJUBARROTA, in which the Portuguese defeated the Castilians. A decisive date in the history of the country, this battle established the independence of Portugal beyond all possibility of challenge. With the Avis dynasty Portugal entered upon the greatest period of her history. The king himself was an able and enlightened ruler, who enjoyed the aid of five outstanding sons, of whom **Henry the Navigator** (1394–1460) became the greatest figure in the history of the epoch-making discoveries of the 15th century (p. 363).

1386, May 9. The Treaty of Windsor, by which England and Portugal became permanently allied. King John married Philippa, the daughter of John of Gaunt. The dynasty thereby became part English.

1411. Peace was finally concluded with Castile.

1415, Aug. 24. The Portuguese took **Ceuta** from the Moors, thus initiating a policy of expansion on the African mainland.

1433-1438. Edward (Duarte) I, a learned and intelligent prince, eldest son of John. His short reign was marked by a terrific epidemic of the plague and by

1437. The disaster at **Tangier,** where the Portuguese were overwhelmingly defeated. They were obliged to promise to

---

Kings of Portugal

Afonso III === Beatrice, d. of
1248–1279 | Afonso X of
Castile

Diniz === Elizabeth, d. of
1279–1325 | Peter III of Aragon

Afonso IV === Beatrice, d. of
1325–1357 | Sancho IV
of Castile

Constance
m. Ferdinand IV
of Castile

Constance of === Peter I
Castile | 1357–1367
(illegitimate)

Eleanor
m. Peter IV
of Aragon

Maria === Afonso XI
of Castile

Leonora === Ferdinand I
Telles | 1367–1383

Beatrice
m. John I
of Castile

John I of Avis === Philippa, d. of
1385–1433 | John of Gaunt

(illegitimate)

Edward I
1433–1438

Peter

Henry the
Navigator

John

Elizabeth
m. Philip the
Good of Burgundy

Afonso

House of
Braganza

Afonso V
1438–1481

Eleanor
m. Emperor
Frederick III

Joanna
m. Henry IV
of Castile

Ferdinand

John II
1481–1495

Emanuel I
1495–1521

Afonso
d. 1491

return Ceuta, and to leave in Moorish hands the youngest brother of the king, **Ferdinand** (*the Constant Prince*), who died in captivity after five years of suffering. Ceuta was not returned.

1437-1481. AFONSO V (*the African*), an attractive and chivalrous ruler, but lacking the hard-headed realism of his predecessors. The reign began with the regency of the king's mother, Eleonora, a Spanish princess, who again was confronted with Portuguese opposition to a Spanish connection. The nobility revolted, the regent fled, and the king's uncle, Peter, was made regent. His able and enlightened rule came to an end when the king, having reached his majority, allowed himself to be persuaded by favorites to make war on Peter. The latter and his son were defeated and killed in the **battle of Alfarrobeira** (1449).

1446. The Ordenaçoes Affonsinas, the first great law code of the Portuguese, representing an amalgam of Roman, Visigothic, and customary law.

1463. Campaigns against the Kingdom of Fez. The Portuguese captured Casablanca and

1471. Tangiers.

1476. Battle of Toro. Defeat of the Portuguese by the Castilians, after Afonso, who had married a sister of Isabella, attempted to dispute the latter's succession to the throne.

1481-1495. JOHN II, an energetic prince who at once undertook to restrict the property and power of the nobility, which had become very great during the preceding reign. This led to a revolt of the nobles, led by **Ferdinand of Braganza** and supported by the Catholic Kings of Castile and Aragon. The revolt was suppressed in 1483; Braganza and many of his followers were executed. The royal power thenceforth was more firmly established than ever before.   (*Cont. p.* 390.)

d. ITALY AND THE PAPACY
(1) *The Papacy*, 1305-1492

1305-1378. THE AVIGNONESE PAPACY (*Babylonian Captivity*): during seven pontificates the popes, exiled from the spiritual capital of the west, preferred to contend against the pressure of the French crown rather than face the disorder of Rome and Italy.

1310-1313. Expedition of the Emperor Henry VII to Italy (p. 301). Henry asserted his independence of the spiritual power and claimed control of

Italy. Clement V and Philip IV (opposed to him as a rival of the Angevins) combined against him.

1316-1334. JOHN XXII, who supported the Angevins in Naples. His attempt to decide the validity of Emperor Louis IV's title led to a long struggle (1323-1347). Louis was supported by the German people, who resented the Avignonese papacy, and by the Franciscans. John was unable to return to Italy because of the continued anarchy.

1334-1342. Benedict XII, and

1342-1352. CLEMENT VI, whose pontificate was marked by the

1347. REVOLUTION OF COLA DI RIENZI at Rome. With the support of the populace, Cola overthrew the rule of the patricians, set himself up as tribune of the people and summoned an Italian national parliament. Expelled by his opponents (1348), he returned in 1352 and was appointed senator by the pope (1354), but was in the same year slain by his baronial opponents. The lords of the Papal States resumed control and were, to all intents and purposes, independent of papal authority.

1352-1362. INNOCENT VI. He sent the Spanish cardinal, Albornoz, to Italy and the latter succeeded in reducing the powerful barons to obedience, thus making possible an eventual return of the pope.

REFORM OF THE CURIA during the Avignon period. General work of centralization and departmentalization: (1) the *camera apostolica*; (2) the chancery; (3) justice; (4) the penitentiary (punishments and dispensations). Centralization put important clerical appointments throughout Europe under direct papal control through an extraordinary extension of the papal rights of reservation and provision; made a virtual end of local elections, filled ecclesiastical offices with aliens and strangers, and outraged public opinion everywhere. A parallel reorganization and departmentalization of the papal financial administration led to a new efficiency in the levy and collection of papal taxes, fees, etc., which bore hard on the clergy, and drained large sums from the national states, stirring public opinion still further, especially in England. Significant items of the budget of John XXII: war, 63.7%; upkeep and entertainment, 12.7%; alms, 7.16%; 0.4% stables; 0.33% art; library, 0.17%.

Vying with the growing magnificence of the monarchies of Europe, the Avignonese popes and cardinals became proverbial for their pomp and luxury, and these tendencies

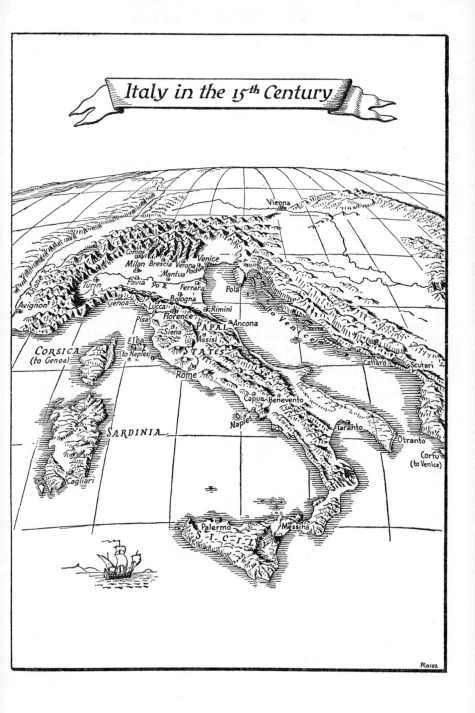

Italy in the 15th Century

spread to the episcopate despite the thunders of the Franciscans and the decrees of local synods. The insubordination of outraged reformers like the **Fraticelli**, the Bohemian preachers, and **Wiclif** soon penetrated to the masses.

Virtually every pope (notably Clement V and John XXII) made serious and honest efforts to combat these alarming developments, but the general anarchy in Europe made success impossible. There was a notable **expansion of missions to the Far East:** China (an archbishop and ten suffragans, 1312; fifty Franciscan houses, 1314; missions to Persia). Rome, the ancient spiritual center of the west, was reduced to an anarchic, poverty-stricken, provincial city, and clamored for the return of the popes. Petrarch's extreme denunciations of the Avignonese popes had little justification.

1362-1370. URBAN V. Return to Rome with the co-operation of Emperor Charles IV; the city a dismal ruin; return to Avignon on the entreaties of the cardinals (a majority of whom were French).

1370-1378. GREGORY XI visited Rome and died before he could leave. The conclave, under threat of personal violence from the Roman mob, yielded to demands for an Italian pope, electing

1378-1389. URBAN VI, a blunt, avaricious man, who alienated the cardinals by announcing that his reform of the Church would begin with the Sacred College.

1378-1417. THE GREAT SCHISM: the papacy divided and dishonored. Thirteen cardinals, meeting at Anagni, elected

1378-1394. CLEMENT VII, thus dividing western Christendom into obediences:

The **Roman Line**	The **Avignonese Line**
Urban VI	**Clement VII**
(1378–1389)	(1378–1394)
Boniface IX	**Benedict XIII**
(1389–1404)	(1394–1423)
Innocent VII	
(1404–1406)	
Gregory XII	
(1406–1415)	

Allegiance to the rivals was determined partly by practical considerations, but often was settled after careful study of the claims of each and consultation with the clergy (e.g. King Charles V of France, John of Castile); England's decision was based largely on hostility to France; Scotland's on its hostility to England; in Naples and Sicily the rulers and their subjects took opposite positions.

EMERGENCE OF THE CONCILIAR MOVEMENT: The basic ideas were inherent in such writers as **Marsiglio of Padua;** specific arguments that a general council is superior to a pope, can be called by a king, and is competent to judge a pope or call a new conclave, were advanced in 1379 (**Henry of Langenstein**) and from then on grew in importance. King Charles VI of France (influenced by the University of Paris) called a **national synod** (1395), which voted overwhelmingly to urge the resignation of both popes. The Avignonese cardinals approved with only one negative; the popes refused to resign. The French clergy voted (1398) to withhold papal taxes and dues, and were endorsed by the king. Benedict's cardinals deserted him in panic and he fled, producing a reaction of public opinion against the King of France. Two Roman popes were elected with the understanding that they would resign if Benedict XIII would do so. The two colleges of cardinals joined in a call for a general council to meet at Pisa, 1409.

1409. THE COUNCIL OF PISA: attended by 500 prelates and delegates from the states of Europe. Two parties: (1) a moderate majority with the sole aim of ending the schism; (2) radical reformers (including d'Ailly and Gerson from Paris), who were compelled to accept postponement of reform to a council supposed to meet in 1412. After hearing specific charges against both popes, the council deposed both. The conclave chose **Alexander V** (d. 1410) and then the ecclesiastical *condottiere*, Cardinal Baldassare Cossa, a man without spiritual qualities. Neither the Roman nor the Avignonese pope resigned, and the schism was a triple one.

1410-1415. JOHN XXIII, expelled from Rome by Ladislas of Naples, was forced by the Emperor Sigismund to issue a call for the **Council of Constance** (1414) in return for protection. This marked the passing of the initiative in reform from the King of France to the Roman Emperor, a return in theory to the days of the Ottos.

1414-1417. THE COUNCIL OF CONSTANCE: one of the greatest assemblies of mediaeval history; three aims: (1) **restoration of unity to the Church;** (2) **reform in head and members;** (3) **extirpation of heresy,** particularly the Hussite heresy (p. 305). Following university practice, voting was by nations and the numbers of the Italian prelates did no good to Pope John. John, seeing a chance to divide the council and the emperor, allowed the imprisonment of Hus (in violation of the imperial safe-conduct).

Hus, heard three times by the whole council (and cleverly induced to expand his doctrine that sin vitiates a clerical office to include civil office as well), lost Sigismund's support, was condemned and executed (1415) as was his companion, Jerome of Prague (1416).

John XXIII, having agreed to resign if his rivals did so, fled the council, was brought back, tried, and deposed (1415); Gregory XII resigned (1415); Sigismund, unable to induce Benedict XIII to resign, won away his supporters, and isolated him. Reform was again postponed, but two decrees are significant: *Sacrosancta* (1415), asserting that a council is superior to a pope; and *Frequens* (1417) providing for stated meetings of general councils.

The conclave elected Cardinal Colonna as Martin V. Christendom ignored the obstinate Benedict, and the schism was over.

1417-1431. MARTIN V (Colonna), a Roman of Romans, declared it impious to appeal to a general council against a pope and dissolved the **Council of Constance.** Evasion of general reform and the threat of general councils supported by powerful monarchs, through the negotiation of concordats with the heads of states (i.e. by dealing with the bishops through lay rulers, a complete negation of the theory of a universal papal absolutism, and a virtual recognition of national churches). **Recovery of the Papal States:** most of the cities were under their own lords who bore *pro forma* titles as papal vicars but were in fact independent. Concentration on Italian political problems at the expense of the universal spiritual interests of Christendom.

1431-1447. EUGENIUS IV, an obstinate Venetian who favored summoning the Council of Basel.

1431-1449. THE COUNCIL OF BASEL, dominated by strong anti-papal feeling. Dissolved by Eugenius because of negotiations with the Hussites, the council ignored the order and decreed (with the support of the princes) that no general council can be dissolved without its consent, continued in session, and summoned Eugenius and the cardinals to attend. Eugenius ignored the summons, but was forced (1433) to accept the council. Temporary compromise with the Hussites registered in the *Compactata*. **Reforms voted:** abolition of commendations, reservations, appeals to Rome, annates, etc.; provision for regular provincial and diocesan synods: confirmation of the right of chapter elections; ap-

peal from a general council to a pope pronounced heresy. Already divided over these reforms, the council split over reunion with the Greek Church. Eugenius and his cardinals ignored a second summons, were pronounced contumacious; Eugenius dissolved the council and called another to meet at Ferrara; the papalists left Basel. The rump council continued to meet, deposed Eugenius (1439), elected Amadeus of Savoy,

1440-1449. FELIX V, because he could pay his own way. Moved to Lausanne, the council continued with dwindling numbers and prestige.

1438-1445. THE COUNCIL OF FERRARA-FLORENCE (under the presidency of Eugenius). After months of futile discussion (over the *filioque* question, unleavened bread at the sacrament, purgatory, and papal supremacy), the Greeks were forced to accept the Roman formula for union (1439) and the schism between east and west, dating from 1054, was technically healed. As the Greeks at home repudiated the union, it was of no effect. Isidore of Kiev and Bessarion remained as cardinals of the Roman Church.

1438. A French national synod and King Charles VII accepted the *Pragmatic Sanction of Bourges* embodying most of the anti-papal decrees of the Council of Basel (basis for the Gallican Liberties). The *Pragmatic* checked the drain of money from France to the papacy.

1439. The Diet of Mainz accepted the *Pragmatic Sanction of Mainz,* abolishing annates, papal reservations, provisions, and providing for diocesan and provincial synods.

Aeneas Sylvius Piccolomini, sent to win Germany back for the papacy, came to an agreement with Emperor Frederick III on such cynical terms that the German princes flocked to Felix V, but a provisional concordat, embodying the *Pragmatic* of 1439 enabled Aeneas Sylvius to detach the princes one by one.

1448. Concordat of Vienna, Eugenius' greatest triumph, accepted the supremacy of a general council, but restored the annates and abandoned most of the restrictions on papal patronage.

1449. Dissolution of the Council of Basel: abdication of Felix V (who became a cardinal). Papal celebration of the triumph over the conciliar movement in the **Jubilee of 1450.** Postponement of moderate reform made the radical Reformation of the 16th century inevitable.

1447-1455. NICHOLAS V, former librarian of Cosimo de' Medici, scholar, humanist, collector of manuscripts, founder of the **Vatican Library.** Rome temporarily a center of humanism: Nicholas' circle included: **Poggio Bracciolini, Alberti,** and **Lorenzo Valla** (a scientific humanist and critic who had just demolished the *Donation of Constantine* as a forgery). Plans for a new St. Peter's.

1453. **The Turkish capture of Constantinople** (p. 327) ended the Greek Empire of the East and removed all serious rivalry by the patriarch to the position of the Roman pope.

1455-1468. **CALIXTUS III** (an Aragonese), an aged invalid, anti-humanist, energetic supporter of war against the Turk, an ardent nepotist (three Borgia nephews, one of them later Pope Alexander VI).

1458-1464. **PIUS II** (Aeneas Sylvius Piccolomini). In his youth a gay dog; in later life austere; most brilliant and versatile of the literary popes, a humanist, lover of nature, eloquent essayist, orator, and Latin stylist. A short, bent man with smiling eyes, a fringe of white hair, seldom free of pain, a tireless worker, always accessible. Advocate of papal supremacy, obstinate foe of conciliar reform. His appeals for a crusade ignored by a preoccupied Europe, he gallantly took the Cross himself to shame the princes of Christendom, and died at Ancona. His family was large and poor and he was a nepotist.

1467-1471. **PAUL II,** a Venetian, rich, kindly, handsome, a collector of jewels and carvings, founder of the Corso horse-races. A strong centralizer, supporter of the Hungarian crusade. The Turkish victory at **Negropotone** (1470) gave the Turks mastery of Levantine waters.

1471-1484. **SIXTUS IV** (della Rovere) aimed to consolidate the Papal States and reduce the power of the cardinals; methodical nepotist (three nephews, the Riarios, one of them later Pope Julius II).

1475. Rapprochement with Ferrante of Naples; alienation of the Medici who were replaced as papal bankers by the Pazzi. The Riarios organized with Sixtus' knowledge, if not approval, the **Pazzi Conspiracy** (assassination of Guiliano de' Medici, 1478). This destroyed the alliance of Florence, Naples, Milan, to maintain the Italian balance of power and led to a war involving most of Italy; the war was terminated by the capture of Otranto (1480) and by the diplomacy of Lorenzo de' Medici. Sixtus' coalition with Venice led to the Ferrarese War (1482-1484). Sixtus and Julius II were the great beautifiers of Rome:

Sistine Chapel (c. 1473), paving and widening of streets and squares; patronage of **Ghirlandaio, Botticelli, Perugino, Pinturicchio,** *et al.*

1484-1492. **INNOCENT VIII,** a kindly, handsome Genoese, a compromise cipher, the first pope to recognize his children and to dine publicly with ladies. A baronial revolt (1485-1487) in Naples (supported by Innocent and, *secretly,* by Venice) led to a revival of the Angevin claims to Naples. Florence and Milan, fearing French intervention in Italy, opposed the war, and peace and amnesty were arranged. Ferrante's cynical violation of the amnesty led the exiles (on Ludovico Sforza's advice) to call in King Charles VIII of France. Sforza struck an alliance with Charles to protect Milan and opened the road into Italy to this alien invader (1494). Italy was not again to know full independence from foreign domination until the end of the 19th century.

Girolamo Savonarola (1452-1498), a Dominican, Prior of San Marco in Florence (1491), eloquent reforming preacher and precursor of the Reformation, was already denouncing the new paganism of the Renaissance, the corruption of the state and the papacy, and foretelling the ruin of Italy.

(*Cont. p. 395.*)

(2) *Sicily and Naples,* 1268-1494

1268-1285. **CHARLES I,** (Angevin) King of Naples and of Sicily (1268-1282). His grandiose scheme for the creation of a Mediterranean empire in succession to the Byzantine (a revival of the Latin Empire under French auspices) was frustrated by the **Sicilian Vespers** (1282) and the war in Sicily which continued until 1302. Sicily maintained its independence and offered the crown to **Peter III of Aragon** (husband of Constance, heiress of the Hohenstaufen), an ally of Constantinople against Charles. Peter accepted the offer (1282), ejected the Angevins and established the house of Aragon on the throne.

1282- **SICILY UNDER ARAGONESE RULE:** Peter (1282-1285); **James** (1285-1295). James exchanged the investiture of Sardinia and Corsica for that of Sicily, and Sicily passed to his brother, **Frederick** (1295-1337). Frederick brought to a close the war with Naples (**Peace of Caltabelotta, 1302**), marrying the daughter of Charles I and accepting the stipulation that the Sicilian crown should pass to the Angevins on his death. This agreement was not fulfilled, with the result that the struggle continued until, in 1373, Joanna of

The House of Anjou

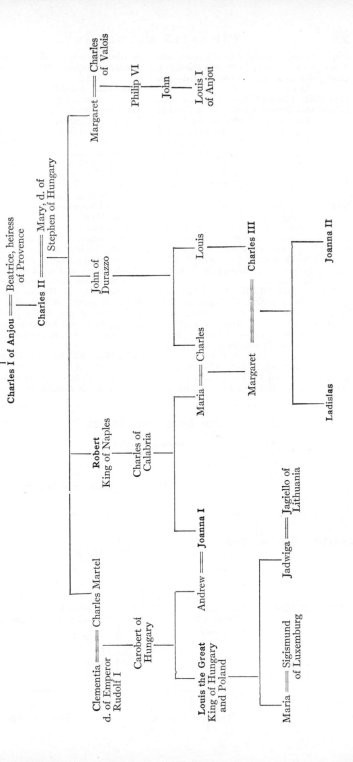

Naples abandoned Sicily to the Aragonese in return for tribute. Sicily was ruled as a viceroyalty until the reunion with Aragon in 1409.

1285-1309. Charles II (Angevin) of Naples.

1309-1343. Robert (Angevin) of Naples. He was the leader of the Italian Guelfs and, having been appointed imperial vicar on the death of Emperor Henry VII, planned to create an Italian kingdom.

1343-1382. Joanna I, Queen of Naples.

1382-1386. Charles III, a grandnephew of Robert.

1386-1414. Ladislas, son of Charles III, finally succeeded in establishing some measure of order in the kingdom and began a vigorous campaign of expansion in central Italy. In 1409 he bought the States of the Church from Pope Gregory XII, but his designs were blocked by Florence and Siena.

1415-1435. JOANNA II, sister of Ladislas. The amazing intrigues of this amorous widow with her favorites, successors designate, and rival claimants to the throne kept Italian diplomacy in a turmoil, and culminated in a struggle between **René,** the Angevin claimant (supported by the pope), and **Alfonso V of Aragon** (supported by Filippo Maria Visconti). This conflict ended in the triumph

of Alfonso, who secured Naples in **1435** and was recognized as king by the pope in 1442.

1435-1458. ALFONSO (*the Magnanimous*) reunited the crowns of Naples and Sicily and made Naples the center of his Aragonese Mediterranean empire (p. 284). He supported Filippo Maria Visconti of Milan, who apparently willed his duchy to him on his death. Alfonso avoided arousing Italy by claiming the duchy, but Ferdinand of Aragon later revived the claim. Alfonso's pressure drove Genoa into the arms of France. Loyal to the pope, Alfonso supported Eugenius IV against Francesco Sforza. He centralized the administration, reformed taxation, and arranged a series of dynastic marriages in Italy. But he failed to subdue his barons entirely. He preferred Italy to Aragon, was a passionate *dévoté* of Italian culture and acted as a Renaissance Macecenas, the patron of Lorenzo Valla. The Academy of Naples was composed mostly of poets. Alfonso divided his domain, Aragon and Sicily passing to his brother, John, and Naples (correctly called the Kingdom of Sicily) going to his illegitimate son

1458-1494. FERRANTE (Ferdinand I), one of the most notoriously unscrupulous Renaissance princes. He triumphed in his struggle for the succession

The Neapolitan Anjous

Louis I of Anjou
(d. 1385)

Louis II === Iolande of Aragon

Louis III   René the Good === Isabella of Lorraine   Charles D. of Maine   Mary === Charles VII of France

John of Calabria   Margaret m. Henry VI of England   Iolande === Frederick of Vaudemont   Louis XI   Charles VIII

René I, D. of Lorraine

Dukes of Lorraine   Dukes of Guise

with the aid of Francesco Sforza and Cosimo de' Medici (who was alarmed at the presence of the French in Genoa). Ferrante generally supported the triple Italian alliance (p. 295) except for the period 1478–1480. Pope Innocent V, angered at Ferrante's suspension of tribute, supported the Angevin pretender, and Ferrante made a hollow peace until he could crush a baronial revolt. Then, supported by the Colonna and Orsini in Rome, he turned on Innocent, who was saved only by Lorenzo de' Medici. Innocent (1492) guaranteed the succession in Naples. Alexander VI stood by the bargain, and opposed Charles VIII's demand for investiture.

THE CLAIMS OF THE VALOIS KINGS TO NAPLES. Based on (1) the marriage of Margaret (daughter of Charles II of Naples) and Charles of Valois, the parents of King Philip VI; and on (2) the claims of the so-called "second" house of Anjou founded by Duke Louis I (d. 1385) of Anjou, Count of Provence. Louis was grandson of Philip VI, and grandfather of (1) Mary, wife of Charles VII of France, mother of Louis XI; and of (2) Duke Louis III (d. 1434) and his brother René of Lorraine (d. 1486).   (*Cont. p.* 398.)

(3) *Florence, to* 1492

EARLY HISTORY. The Margraviate of Tuscany, set up by the Carolingians, extended from the Po to the Roman state under the Margrave Boniface (d. 1052) whose daughter, the great Countess Matilda (1052–1115), was probably the strongest papal supporter in Italy. Associated with her in the government was a council of *boni homines*, whose administration during her frequent absences, and after her death, laid the foundation for the emergence of the commune. Florence, already a great commercial center, opposed the Ghibelline hill barons, who preyed on her commerce. The burghers continued Guelf in sympathy; trade and financial connections with France made them Francophil and friendly to Charles of Anjou. Under Matilda the guild organization emerged, which came to form the basis of the city government. Control of the government was concentrated in the hands of the great guilds (one of which included the bankers). Consuls appeared after 1138. The populace was divided into two great groups, the *grandi* (nobles) and the *arti* (guilds). Consuls were chosen by the *grandi*.

On the breakup of the margraviate following Matilda's death, Florence began her advance, and by 1176 was master of the dioceses of Florence and Fiesole. The in-

stitution of the *podestate* after 1202 was favored by the feudal elements and the lesser guilds. Intermittent rivalry of the noble houses continued. Wars were fought with Pisa, Lucca, Pistoia, Siena. Under the *podestà* the commune developed a strong organization paralleled by the growth of the *popolo* under its *capitano*.

The great struggle of **Guelf and Ghibelline** was reflected in Florentine civil strife. After a Guelf régime, Frederick of Antioch (son of Frederick II) as imperial vicar instituted the first mass expulsion in Florentine history by driving out the Guelfs (1249).

1252. The first gold florin was coined, and soon became the standard gold coin in Europe.

1260. Siena, with the aid of Manfred and the Florentine Ghibellines, inflicted a great defeat on the Florentine Guelfs (**Montaperti**), beginning a Ghibelline dominance which lasted until Manfred's death (1266). This was followed by a reaction, and the expulsion of the Ghibellines. Under the Ghibelline régime the *popolo* lost all share in the government.

In the reaction following the Ghibelline régime, Ghibelline property was confiscated to support persecution of the Ghibellines. Under Charles of Anjou the formulae of the old constitution were restored; the party struggle continued. The Sicilian Vespers (1282) weakened Charles, strengthened the commune, and the Florentine "republic" became in effect a commercial oligarchy in the hands of the greater guilds.

1282. By the **Law of 1282** nobles could participate in the government only by joining a guild. The last traces of serfdom were abolished (1289) and the number of guilds increased to 21 (7 greater, 14 lesser).

1293. The **Ordinance of 1293** excluded from the guilds anyone not actively practicing his profession, and thus in effect removed the nobles from all share in the government.

Two factions arose: the Blacks (*Neri*), extreme Guelfs led by Corso Donati; the Whites (*Bianchi*), moderate Guelfs (and later Ghibellines) under Vieri Cerchi. The Neri favored repeal of the Ordinance of 1293.

Emperor Henry VII was unable to capture Florence, but

1320-1323. Castruccio Castracani, Lord of Lucca, humiliated the city in the field. Growing financial troubles, partly the result of Edward III's repudiation of his debts to the Florentine bankers, culminated in the failures of the Peruzzi (1343) and Bardi (1344), and damaged Florentine banking prestige. The government was discredited and civil war ensued. **Walter of Brienne** (Duke of Athens) was called in, reformed the government, began a usurpation, and was expelled (1343). The restored commune was under the domination of the business men who had three objectives: access to the sea (hence hostility to Pisa), expansion in Tuscany (to dominate the trade roads), and support of the popes (to retain papal banking business). Social conflict continued and grew as the oligarchy gained power and the Guelfs opposed the increasing industrial proletariat. The lesser guilds were pushed into the background, the unguilded were worse off. The first social revolt came in 1345.

1347-1348. Famine followed by the **Black Death** reduced the population seriously, but recovery was rapid.

1351. The commutation of military service for cash marked the decline of citizen militia and the golden age of the *condottieri*. War with Milan resulted (1351) from Giovanni Visconti's attempt to reduce Florence and master Tuscany.

1375-1378. Papal efforts to annex Tuscany led Florence into a temporary alliance with Milan.

1378. Continued pressure by Guelf extremists to exclude the lesser guilds, led to a series of violent explosions. **Salvestro de' Medici,** Gonfalonier, ended the *admonitions* which were the basis of the Guelf terrorism, and a violent **revolt of the** *ciompi* (the poorest workmen) broke out. The *ciompi* made temporary gains, but Salvestro was exiled, and by 1382 the oligarchy was back in the saddle and even *admonitions* were revived.

FLORENTINE CULTURE: Precursors of the Renaissance. (1) **Dante** (1265–1321): *Vita Nuova*, in the Tuscan vernacular; the *Divine Comedy*, a brilliant poetic synthesis of mediaeval ideas and culture which established Tuscan as the literary vernacular of Italy; *De Vulgari Eloquentia*, a defense of the vernacular, written in Latin. **Petrarch** (1304–1374), of Florentine origin, greatest of Italian lyrists, brilliant Latinist, the first great humanist; he never mastered Greek. Interested in every aspect of humanity, a lover of nature, a universal mind. **Boccaccio** (1313–1375), friend of Petrarch, knew both Greek and Latin, the first modern student of Tacitus, collector of classical manuscripts, first lecturer on Dante (1373). His *Decameron*, an epitome of bourgeois sophistication. Founder of Italian prose. **Giotto** (1276–1337), architect (employed on the cathedral), sculptor, painter, revealing Renaissance tendencies.

Villani (d. 1348), *Chronicle* with clear bourgeois elements. **Chrysoloras** (called from Constantinople), the first public lecturer on Greek in the west (1396–1400); he had many famous humanists as pupils.

1382-1432. A half-century of oligarchic domination in Florentine politics, in many ways the zenith of Florentine power. Constitutional reform (1382) broadened popular participation in government, but nothing much was done for the *ciompi*, and sporadic revolts continued as the Guelfs slowly regained power.

1393. Maso degli Albizzi's long control of the government began with the exile or disenfranchisement of the Alberti and their supporters. Capitalism had destroyed the guild organization as a vital political force, and Albizzi ruled for the advantage of his own house and the *Arte della Lana* (wool) with which he was associated. Democratic elements in the state had vanished.

1397-1398. Florence resisted the Visconti advance into Tuscany.

1405. Pisa was bought and reduced to obedience (1406), giving Florence direct access to the sea. Leghorn was purchased (1421) and the *Consuls of the Sea* established. Filippo Maria Visconti's drive into Tuscany led Florence to declare war. The peace party was led by **Giovanni de' Medici,** a wool dealer and international banker, probably Italy's richest man. Several defeats of Florence were accompanied by a decline of Florentine credit and a number of serious bankruptcies. Alliance with Venice and defeat of the Visconti, who accepted peace on onerous terms (1429); Venice monopolized the gains of the war.

1427. Taxation reform, the *catasto*, an income tax intended to be of general and democratic incidence, supported (?) by the Medici.

1433. The fiasco of the war on Lucca (1429–1433) led to Cosimo (son of Giovanni) de' Medici's imprisonment as a scapegoat, and his sentence to ten-year exile. The next election to the Signory favored the Medici, and Cosimo was recalled (1434). Rinaldo degli Albizzi, Rodolfo Peruzzi, *et al.*, were in turn exiled, and the Medici dominance in Florence began, opening three centuries of close identity between the fortunes of the family and those of Florence. Cosimo, without holding office, dominated the government, determining who should hold office.

1434-1494. DOMINATION OF THE MEDICI.

1434-1464. COSIMO (*Pater Patriae*).

The Medici Family

Giovanni de' Medici

Cosimo
1434–1464

Lorenzo

Piero
1464–1469

Grand Dukes
of Tuscany
1569–

Lorenzo
the Magnificent
1478–1492

Giuliano
1469–1478

Giulio
(Pope Clement VII)

Piero
1492–1495

Giovanni
(Pope Leo X)

Lorenzo
1512–1519

Catharine de' Medici
m. Henry II of France

1440. Florence and Venice in alliance defeated Filippo Maria Visconti at Anghiari. The *castato* was replaced by a progressive income tax designed to lighten the burdens of the poor (i.e. the Medici adherents). Cosimo supported Francesco Sforza's contest for the Duchy of Milan and aided him in his war with Venice. For commercial reasons he favored France, but backed Ferrante of Naples against the Angevin claims. He was thus the real creator of the **triple alliance** of Florence, Milan, and Naples in the interest of the Italian equilibrium and security.

1464-1469. Piero the Gouty, son of Cosimo, a semi-invalid who was opposed by Luca Pitti.

1469-1478. Lorenzo and Giuliano de' Medici, and

1478-1492. LORENZO DE' MEDICI (*the Magnificent*) alone. Lorenzo continued the general policy of Cosimo. He enjoyed the power and prestige of a prince, though he had neither the title nor the office. His marriage to Clarice Orsini was the first princely marriage of the Medici.

1471. Lorenzo's effort to conciliate Pope Sixtus IV netted him a confirmation of the Medici banking privileges and the appointment as receiver of the papal revenues.

1474. Pope Sixtus and Ferrante of Naples were asked to join the alliance of Florence, Venice, and Milan (concluded in 1474), but Ferrante, feeling isolated, and Sixtus, angered at Lorenzo's opposition to his nephews, the Riarios, drew together. Italy became divided into two camps. The Pazzi family, rivals of the Medici, were given the lucrative position as receivers of the papal revenues.

1478. The Pazzi Plot. The Riarios (apparently not without Sixtus' knowledge), plotted to have Lorenzo and Giuliano assassinated in the cathedral at Easter mass. Giuliano was killed, Lorenzo wounded. The Medici almost exterminated the Pazzi and hounded the fugitives all over Italy. Sixtus laid an interdict on

Florence, excommunicated Lorenzo; Alfonso of Calabria invaded Tuscany. Venice and Milan stood by Florence, Louis XI sent Commines as his representative. Ferrante engineered a Milanese revolt, the Turks diverted Venice at Scutari, plague broke out. Desperate, Lorenzo visited Ferrante (the cruelest and most cynical despot in Italy), and by his charm and the threat of a revival of Angevin claims, arranged (1480) a peace. Florence suffered considerable losses, but Lorenzo was a popular hero and succeeded in establishing the *Council of Seventy*, a completely Medici organ, the instrument of *de facto* despotism, but a source of real stability in government.

Lorenzo's brilliant foreign policy was costly; he had neglected the family business, and apparently used some of the state money for Medici purposes; he also debased the coinage. Florentine prosperity, under the pressure of rivals, heavy taxation, and business depression, was declining. Nonetheless, Lorenzo, the leading statesman of his day, brought a twelve-year calm before the storm to Italy, resuming the Medici alliance with Naples and Milan to balance the papacy and Venice, and to keep a united front against alien invasion. Florence, on good terms with Charles VIII, regained most of her Tuscan losses. Savonarola, Prior of San Marco (1491), had already begun his denunciations of Florentine corruption and his attacks on Lorenzo (p. 290).

1492. PIERO succeeded Lorenzo on his death. Son of an Orsini mother, married to an Orsini, he supported Naples, angered Florence, and threw Ludovico Sforza into alliance with the Neapolitan exiles who summoned Charles VIII.

1494. Charles' invasion began the age-long subjugation of Italy to alien invaders who dominated the national evolution until 1870. Piero, alarmed at public opinion, fled the city.

Florence, center of the Italian Renaissance. For over a century the Medici were the greatest patrons of the Renaissance, and led the rich bourgeoisie of Florence in fostering the most brilliant development of culture since the days of Pericles. **Cosimo** was an enthusiastic patron of manuscript collectors, copyists, and humanists, established the library of San Marco and the Medici library. The Council of Ferrara-Florence sat in Florence (1439) and brought a number of learned Greeks who stimulated Platonic studies in Florence. Under Cosimo's auspices **Ficino** was trained to make his great translation of Plato (still ranked high) and the **Platonic Academy** was founded. **Lorenzo,** a graceful poet (carnival songs, etc.), ardent champion of the vernacular, and lover of the countryside, a generous patron, drew about him a brilliant circle. He continued the support of Ficino. Florentine leadership in Renaissance: (1) **painting: Massaccio** (1401-1429?), **Botticelli** (1444-1510), **Leonardo da Vinci** (1452-1519) (sculptor and polymath); (2) **architecture: Brunelleschi** (1377-1446); **Alberti** (1405-1471); (3) **sculpture: Donatello** (c. 1386-1466), **Ghiberti** (1378-1455); **Verocchio** (1435-1488); **Michelangelo** (1475-1564) (also painter, poet, architect); (4) **history and political theory: Machiavelli** (1469-1527); **Guicciardini** (1485-1540); (5) **romantic poetry: Pulci** (1432-c. 1487). (*Cont. p.* 398.)

(4) *Milan, to* 1500

EARLY HISTORY. Milan, ancient center of the agriculture of the Lombard Plain, self-sufficient in food, master of important passes (Brenner, Splügen, St. Gothard) of the Alps, was for a long time surpassed in wealth only by Venice.

Establishment of Pavia as the Lombard capital (569). Emergence of Milan as the center of Italian opposition in the Lombard Plain to alien and heretical domination. Rise of the archbishop as defender of native liberty and orthodoxy laid the basis for the evolution of archepiscopal temporal power (military, administrative, judicial) exercised through his viscounts. The end of Lombard domination (774), followed by Carolingian destruction of the great Lombard fiefs, strengthened the episcopal power still further.

The spirit of municipal independence emerged from intense rivalries for the archepiscopal see and the necessities of defense; Milan became an island of safety and justice in the Lombard Plain, a populous, self-sufficient, city-state. Under **Archbishop Heribert** (1018-1045) the *carroccio* (arc of municipal patriotism) was set up; expansion in the Lombard Plain began (reduction of Lodi, Como, Pavia). The moat was dug after Emperor Frederick I's destruction (1162); the city was rebuilt by its allies, Bergamo, Brescia, Mantua, and Verona. (For the Lombard League and the wars with Frederick, see p. 220.) Rapid growth, extension of the walls (after 1183). Chief industry armor manufacturing and the wool trade, later silk manufacture; irrigation made the plain productive.

Government: (1) *Parlamento* (*consiglio grande*) (membership successively reduced

Rulers of Milan

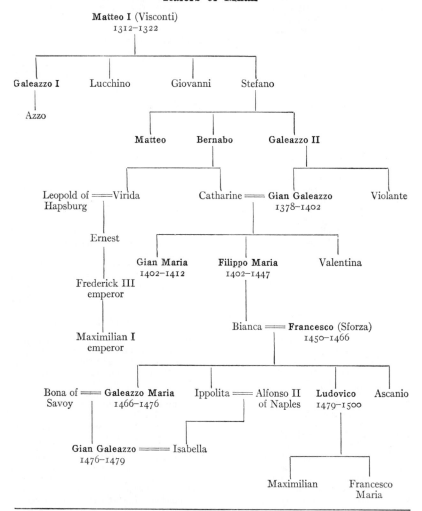

to 2000, 1500, 800). (2) *Credenza*, a committee of twelve for urgent and secret business. (3) *Consuls* (the executive) elected for a year, responsible to the assembly.

Rise of the Della Torre and the Visconti. Bitter warfare between populace and nobles led to the rise of two great families, the Della Torre (lords of the tower, i.e. castle) and the Visconti (i.e. the viscounts).

1237-1277. Rule of the (Guelf) **DELLA TORRE.** Martino established the *catasta*, a tax of democratic and uniform incidence. The title *signore*, i.e. Lord of Milan, established (1259): defeat and capture of the (Ghibelline) Visconti and their adherents. Milan established her power over Bergamo, Lodi, Como, and Vercelli.

1277-1447. Rule of the **VISCONTI.** Established by Archbishop Otto Visconti. Brief restoration of the Della Torre (1302) in a Guelf reaction with outside support. Establishment (1312) of the Visconti supremacy (Matteo designated *imperial vicar*). Ruthless Visconti rule and expansion over northern Italy (including Genoa). Stefano's sons, Bernabo, Galeazzo, Matteo, divided the domains but ruled jointly until Matteo was assassinated (1354) by his brothers. Intolerably harsh joint rule of Bernabo (1354–1385) at Milan and Galeazzo (1354–1378) at Pavia; ostentatious patronage of learning and art.

1378-1402. **GIAN GALEAZZO** succeeded his father Galeazzo and did away with Bernabo (1385), thereafter ruling alone (1385–1402). Gian Galeazzo married Isabella, daughter of King John of France; one of his daughters married Lionel, son of Edward III of England; another, Valentina, married Louis of Orléans (the source of Louis XII's claims to Milan). Gian Galeazzo began the creation of a northern Italian kingdom: mastery of Verona, Vicenza, Padua (1386–1388); Tuscan advance blocked by Florence (1390–1392) and by the rebellion of Padua. Created hereditary duke (1395) by Emperor Wenceslaus, he added Pisa and Siena (1399), Assisi and Perugia (1400) to his domains, and routed (1401) Elector Rupert III (in Florentine pay). The *Certosa* and *Duomo* were begun. Gian Galeazzo's death (1402) saved Florence and opened a period of anarchy in Milan under his sons Gian Maria (1402–1412) and Filippo Maria (1402–1447), which undid much of their father's work.

1402-1447. **FILIPPO MARIA,** after the assassination (1412) of Gian Maria, regained Gian Galeazzo's lands (even Genoa). Venice joined Florence against Filippo and took Bergamo, Brescia (1425). Filippo, last of the Visconti, was followed by

1447-1450. **The Republic** and the supremacy of Francesco Sforza, the condottiere, son-in-law of Filippo, who fought his way to mastery, defeating Venice and conquering the Lombard Plain.

1450. Francesco Sforza was invested with the ducal title by popular acclaim.

1450-1500. Rule of the **SFORZA**. Francesco, eager for peace, came to terms with Cosimo de' Medici and Naples (the so-called triple alliance for the Italian balance of power). Louis XI was on intimate terms with Francesco and made him his political model. Francesco completed the Certosa and the Duomo with Florentine architects under Renaissance influence and began the *Castello*. Patron of the humanist Filelfo, Francesco gave his son Galeazzo and his daughter Ippolita a humanist education; Ippolita was famous for her Latin

style. His court was full of humanists and learned Greeks.

1466-1476. **GALEAZZO MARIA SFORZA** was assassinated after a cruel but able rule. His son

1476-1479. **GIAN GALEAZZO,** husband of Isabella of Naples, under the regency of his mother, supported Florence against Naples after the Pazzi conspiracy (1478). Gian Galeazzo's uncle Ludovico usurped the duchy (1479).

1479-1500. **LUDOVICO** (*il Moro*), alarmed at his isolation after the death (1492) of Lorenzo de' Medici, supported the appeals of Neapolitan refugees to Charles VIII of France, whose expedition (1494) began the destruction of Italian independence. In Charles' train came Louis of Orléans, who, as Louis XII (1498–1515), added claims to Milan to his other Italian claims, took Milan (1499) and captured Ludovico (1500), who ended his days (1508) as prisoner of Louis.

Ludovico's generous patronage marked the **golden age of the Renaissance in Milan.** Ludovico, an artist, man of letters, economist, and experimenter, beautified the city, improved irrigation, bettered agriculture. He was the patron of Bramante and Leonardo.   *(Cont. p. 397.)*

(5) *Venice,* 1310-1489

In the early 14th century Venice already dominated the trade of the Adriatic and possessed many colonies throughout the Near East. Her position in the eastern trade was challenged primarily by Genoa, at that time at the height of her power.

1353-1355. **War between Venice and Genoa.** The Venetians were defeated at **Sapieanza** (1354) and suffered the loss of their fleet. Peace was mediated by Milan.

1378-1381. **THE WAR OF CHIOGGIA** between Venice and Genoa. This grew out of the grant, by John V Palaeologos, of the island of Tenedos, key to the Dardanelles. Luciano Doria, the Genoese admiral, defeated the Venetians at **Pola,** seized Chioggia and blockaded Venice. The Venetians, under **Vittorio Pisano,** blocked the channel and starved out the fleet of Pietro Doria, forcing its surrender. From this blow Genoa never recovered. Henceforth Venice was mistress of the Levantine trade, which made an outlet for her goods over the Alpine passes more urgent than ever. The war with Genoa had demonstrated the importance of a mainland food supply and thereby inaugurated an inland advance which had a decisive influence on Italian politics. Venice had already taken

Padua from the Scaligers of Verona (1339), but by agreement had turned it over to the Carrara family. Treviso and Belluna, however, were retained.

1388. **Treaty of the Venetians with the Ottoman Turks,** the first effort to assure trade privileges despite the rise of the Turkish power.

1405. Venice seized Padua, Bassano, Vicenza, and Verona after the breakup of the Visconti domains (1402) and the defeat of the Carrara family.

1416. **First war of Venice against the Ottoman Turks,** the result of Turkish activity in the Aegean. The **Doge Loredano** won a resounding victory at the Dardanelles and forced the sultan to conclude peace.

1423. The Venetians took over Saloniki as part of a plan of co-operation with the Greek emperor against the Turks.

1425-1430. **Second war against the Turks.** The Turkish fleets ravaged the Aegean stations of the Venetians and took Saloniki (1430). The Venetians were obliged to make peace in view of

1426-1429. **The war with Filippo Maria of Milan,** by which the Venetians established a permanent hold over Verona and Vicenza, and gained in addition Brescia (1426), Bergamo (1428), and Crema (1429).

1453. Participation of the Venetians in the **defense of Constantinople** against Mohammed II (p. 327). After the capture of Constantinople, Mohammed proceeded to the conquest of Greece and Albania, thus isolating and endangering the Venetian stations.

1463-1479. **THE GREAT WAR AGAINST THE TURKS.** Negroponte was lost (1470). The Turks throughout maintained the upper hand and at times raided to the very outskirts of Venice. By the **Treaty of Constantinople** (1479) the Venetians gave up Scutari and other Albanian stations, as well as Negroponte and Lemnos. Thenceforth the Venetians paid an annual tribute for permission to trade in the Black Sea.

1482-1484. **War with Ferrara,** as a result of which Venice acquired Rovigo. This marked the limit of Venetian expansion on the mainland. The frontiers remained substantially unaltered until the days of Napoleon.

1489. **Acquisition of Cyprus** (partly by gift, partly by extortion), from Catharine Cornaro, widow of James of Lusignan.

Venetian culture in the Renaissance. Preoccupied with her commercial empire, her expansion on the mainland, and the advance of the Turk, Venice, despite her wealth, unique domestic security, and the sophistication of wide travel, long stood aside from the main currents of the early Renaissance. Her architecture remained under Gothic and Byzantine influences until the end of the 15th century, and the Palazzo Vendramini (1481) is perhaps the first important example of the new style. The Bellinis (Jacopo, 1395-1470, and his two sons) were the most notable early Venetian painters, and there was little promise of the brilliant if late achievement of the 16th century. The printing press apparently appealed to the practical Venetian nature and the Senate decreed (1469) that the art should be fostered. Much of the finest early printing issued from the Venetian presses of the 15th and 16th centuries. (Cont. p. 397.)

e. THE HOLY ROMAN EMPIRE

1273. The election fell to **Rudolf of Hapsburg** (b. 1218), who ranked as a prince, wished to restore and retain in his family the Duchy of Swabia, and had three daughters to marry off. The Hapsburgs (from *Habichts-Burg,* Hawk-Castle) originally (10th century) of the district of Brugg (junction of the Aar and Reuss) had steadily expanded their lands in the Breisgau, Alsace, and Switzerland, emerging as one of the leading families of Swabia.

1273-1291. **RUDOLF I.** Indifferent to the Roman tradition, he concentrated on the advancement of his own dynasty, and founded the greatness of the Hapsburgs on territorial expansion of the family holdings and dynastic marriages. Edicts for the abolition of private war and support of local peace compacts (*Landfrieden*).

1276-1278. **Struggle with Ottokar,** King of Bohemia, over the usurped imperial fiefs of Austria, Styria, Carinthia, Carniola (p. 240). Rudolf expelled Ottokar from Austria by force (1276), but allowed him to retain Bohemia and Moravia (after homage) as a buffer against Slavdom; dynastic alliance with the Hapsburgs. Ottokar was ultimately defeated and killed (1278, Aug. 26, **battle of the Marchfield**); investiture of Rudolf's sons with the imperial fiefs of Austria, Styria, Carniola (1282) established the Hapsburgs on the Danube until 1918.

Rudolf threw away the last remnants of Frederick II's great imperial fabric: confirmation of papal rights in Italy and Ange-

The House of Hapsburg

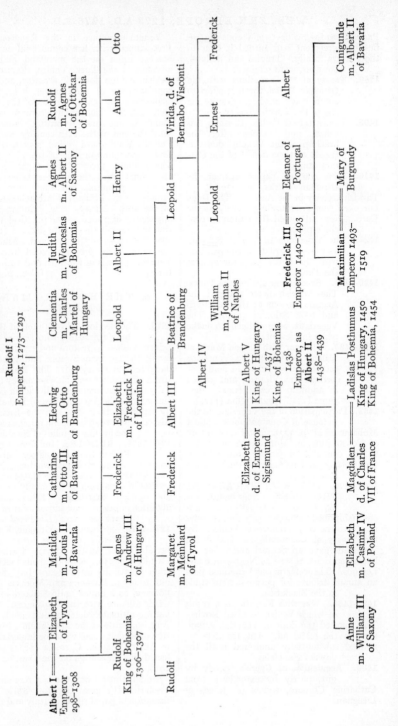

,'in rights in southern Italy (1275); renunciation of all imperial claims to the Papal States and Sicily (1279).

1291. Alarmed at the rapid rise of the Hapsburgs to first rank, the electors passed over Rudolf's son, choosing instead **Adolf of Nassau** in return for substantial considerations.

1291. Revolt of the three Forest Cantons, Uri, Schwyz, and Unterwalden, and formation of a (Swiss) confederacy (p. 306).

1292-1298. ADOLF, a strong imperialist, and able. He supported the towns and lesser nobles and entered into alliance with Edward I of England against Philip IV of France to protect the imperial fiefs of Franche Comté, Savoy, Dauphiné, Lyonnais, and Provence, long under French pressure; the alliance came to nothing, as the German princes were indifferent. The princes, alarmed at Adolf's advance in Meissen and Thuringia, deposed him (1298), electing Rudolf's rejected son Albert.

1298-1308. ALBERT I (Albrecht). Firm reduction of the ecclesiastical electoral princes (aid of the French and the towns); double dynastic marriage with the Capetians; acquisition of the crown of Bohemia (on the extinction of the Premyslids, 1306); Albert supported the Angevin Carobert's acquisition of Hungary; the Rhineland was filled with Francophil clerical appointees of the pope, and the election of 1308 was dominated by French influence. Charles of Valois procured the election of

Henry of Luxemburg, brother of the Archbishop of Trier.

1308-1313. HENRY VII (*Luxemburg*), Francophil, devoted to Italian culture, and bent on restoring the empire. The marriage of his son John to the sister of King Wenceslas of Bohemia brought the throne of Bohemia to the house of Luxemburg (1310–1489).

1310-1313. Expedition to Italy at the urging of Pope Clement V and the Ghibellines; order restored, Milan, Cremona, Rome reduced; imperial coronation (1312); alliance of the pope and King Philip IV of France to save Naples from Henry.

1314-1347. LOUIS IV (*Wittelsbach*). A Hapsburg anti-king, **Frederick the Handsome,** and civil war (until 1325). Bitter papal opposition (1323–1347, refusal of confirmation of Louis' title to the empire); Louis, backed by the German people, against the Avignonese pope. Violent war of propaganda: **Marsiglio of Padua** (*Defensor Pacis,* 1324) and **William of Occam,** defending the imperial position, gave wide currency to pre-Reformation ideas; **Dante's** *De Monarchia;* papal supporters, **Augustino Trionfans** and **Pelagius.**

1327-1330. Louis' futile expedition to Italy and "lay" coronation (1328); his demand for a general council welcomed by the Italian Ghibellines.

Effort to give the German monarchy a formal constitution.

1338. The Day at Rense: formation of a strong electoral union (*Kurverein*);

The House of Luxemburg

Henry VII
1308–1313
|
John of === Elizabeth, d. of
Bohemia | Wenceslas II of Bohemia

Charles IV   Bona   John Henry   Wenceslas
1346–1378   m. John II of   Duke of Luxemburg
        France

Wenceslas   Sigismund === Mary, d. of   John
King of Bohemia   1410–1437 | Louis of Hungary
Emperor
1378–1400

Elizabeth === Albert II (V) of
| Hapsburg

Ladislas Posthumus
King of Hungary and
Bohemia

declaration by the electors that election by a majority of the electors without papal confirmation is valid. The **Diet of Frankfurt**: declaration (the *Licet juris*) that the electors are competent to choose an emperor (i.e. papal intervention is not necessary); in effect the Holy Roman Empire was divorced entirely from the papacy.

1346. Louis was deposed, but fought against his successor, Charles (son of King John of Bohemia, who had been elected after an open alliance with the pope).

1347-1378.   CHARLES IV (*Luxemburg*). Concentration on the advancement of his dynasty (in Silesia, the Palatinate, Lusatia, Brandenburg) and on the progress of Bohemia. Prague became one of the chief cities of the empire (the University founded, 1348). The **Black Death** (1348-1349); the Flagellants; anti-Semitic massacres. Promulgation of the Swabian League and numerous *Landfrieden* reduced private warfare. Dauphiné and Arles continued to drift into the French orbit.

Further elaboration of a formal constitution of the empire.

1356.   THE GOLDEN BULL (in force until 1806) transformed the empire from a monarchy into an aristocratic federation, to avoid the evils of disputed elections. Seven **electors**, each a virtual sovereign: the Archbishops of Mainz, Trier, and Cologne, the Count Palatine of the Rhine, the Duke of Saxony, the Margrave of Brandenburg, the King of Bohemia. Secular electorates to be indivisible and pass by primogeniture. Elections to be by majority vote and without delays; urban leagues forbidden without specific license; other restrictions on the towns. No mention of papal rights or claims. The electors to exercise supervision over the empire, a new function. The crown to remain in the house of Luxemburg.

Charles openly regarded the empire as an anachronism, but valued the emperor's right to nominate to vacant fiefs.

1364.   Treaty of Brünn with the Hapsburgs, whereby either house (Luxemburg or Hapsburg) was to succeed to the lands of the other upon its extinction.

Little improvement in internal anarchy; climax of localism and the *Faustrecht*; the only islands of order and prosperity were the walled towns; the only basis of order were the town leagues (e.g. revival of the **Rhine League** [1354] ; the **Swabian League**); bitter warfare of classes, and princely opposition to the towns. Charles' vain appeal to the princes of Europe to resist France and end the Avignonese Captivity.

Apogee of the **Hanseatic League** (p. 307).

1378-1400.   WENCESLAS (Wenzel, son of Charles IV, King of Bohemia, 1378-1419). Formation of the **Knights' League** (*League of the Lion*) followed by a series of political quarrels between the knights and lords on one side and the towns on the other, ending in the town war (1387-1389) and the defeat of the towns, but not their ruin. Rising Bohemian nationalism: revolts, 1387-1396.

1400.   Deposition of Wenceslas for drunkenness and incompetence. He refused to accept the decision, and the result was that at the end of the confused period (1400-1410) there were **three rival emperors** (Sigismund, Jobst, and Wenceslas) to correspond to the three rival popes.

1410-1437.   SIGISMUND (*Luxemburg;* King of Bohemia, 1419-1437; King of Hungary by marriage). His main concern was to end the Great Schism, and he succeeded the King of France as protagonist of conciliar reform by forcing Pope John XXIII to call the **Council of Constance** (p. 288). Establishment of the **House of Wettin** in Saxony (14.2); the **Hohenzollerns (Frederick)** in Brandenburg (1415). Sigismund's failure at Constance not merely alienated Bohemia, but also ended any hope of German unification.

1410. Utter defeat of the Teutonic Knights by the Polish-Lithuanian army at **Tannenberg**; beginning of the decline of the Teutonic Knights.

1411. Peace of Thorn, halting of the Slavic advance.

1420-1431. Emergence of **BOHEMIAN NATIONALISM** and the **HUSSITE WARS** (p. 305).

1433. Called to the **Council of Basel** (p. 289), the Hussites finally accepted the *Compactata* (which embodied the *Four Articles*), but the Church by its devious dealings alienated them, and they began a final break from the Roman Church. Bohemian nationality asserted itself increasingly in the 15th century, and Bohemia never returned to the German orbit.

Sigismund struggled against the Turkish advance (1426-1427) and was crowned at Rome (1432). In the election of 1438, Frederick of Brandenburg (candidate of the political reformers in Germany) withdrew, making the choice of Albert of Hapsburg (Sigismund's son-in-law) unanimous. Albert also succeeded Sigismund on the thrones of Hungary and Bohemia. Henceforth the imperial crown in practice became hereditary in

The House of Wittelsbach

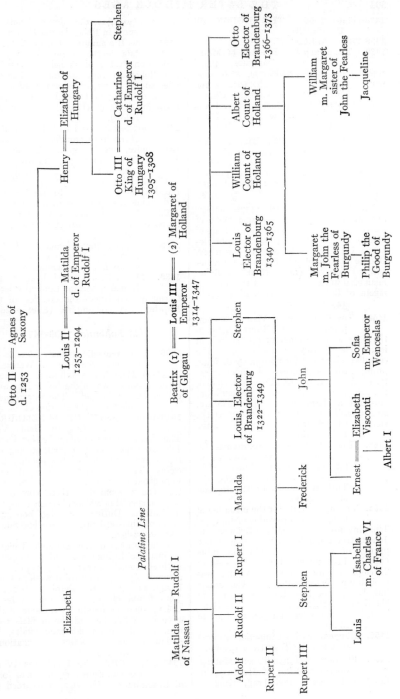

1438-(1740) 1806. THE HOUSE OF HAPSBURG.

1438-1439. ALBERT II.

1439. The Pragmatic Sanction of Mainz (abolition of annates, papal reservations, and provisions), a preliminary agreement between the papacy and the emperor, left the German Church under imperial and princely control and postponed reform till the days of Martin Luther.

1440-1493. FREDERICK III. The last emperor crowned (1452) at Rome by the pope; a handsome, placid *fainéant*, amateur astrologer, botanist, mineralogist, he ignored the existence of diets, debates, and appeals for crusades.

Ladislas Posthumus (d. 1457), nephew and ward of Frederick, became Duke of Austria (1440), was acknowledged King of Hungary (1445) and elected King of Bohemia (1440) with a council of regency. George Podiebrad (champion of the *Compactata*) emerged (1452) from the Bohemian civil war (Catholics vs. Utraquists) as regent of Bohemia, and later king (1458-1471) (p. 305).

1448. The Concordat of Vienna: a compromise on cynical terms between the pope and the emperor on the reform issue: The papacy triumphed over the conciliar movement for reform, by dividing profits with the princes and emperor; external episcopal jurisdiction was excluded, the princes retained rights of presentation, obtained a share in episcopal taxation, and established an authority over the German Church which survived even the Reformation.

1453. The capture of Constantinople (p. 327) and end of the Eastern Empire left the Roman Empire without a rival and brought the Turkish menace to the frontier of Germany.

1454. Traditional date for the invention of printing from movable metal type. This invention is usually attributed to Johann Gutenberg (c. 1398-1468) of Mainz, printer of the so-called Mazarin Bible (1456). Printing had been in process of development for many years and was probably perfected not only by Gutenberg, but by others like Lourens Coster at Haarlem (1440), Albrecht Pfister of Bamberg, Peter Schoeffer and Johann Fust of Mainz.

1456. Hunyadi (without imperial support) repulsed the Turk from Belgrade.

1458. Election of Hunyadi's son Mathias Corvinus, King of Hungary (to 1490) and George Podiebrad, King of Bohemia (to 1471), the climax of national spirit in Bohemia and Hungary.

1462. Pius II's annulment of the Compactata and the excommunication and deposition (1466) of Podiebrad reopened the Bohemian religious wars. Ladislas (elected 1468) succeeded on Podiebrad's death, as King of Bohemia (1471-1516), becoming King of Hungary in 1490 (see below).

1473. Frederick, faced with the threat of (French) Burgundian expansion in the empire, avoided giving Charles the Bold, Duke of Burgundy, the royal title (p. 280), and married his son Maximilian to Charles' daughter Mary (1477), bringing the Hapsburg fortunes to their zenith, and giving reality to his own monogram: A.E.I.O.U. (*Austriae est imperare orbi universo*, or, *Alles Erdreich ist Oesterreich unterthan.*)

1485. Expelled from Vienna by Mathias Corvinus, Frederick became a cheery imperial mendicant.

1486. **Maximilian,** elected King of the Romans, became the real ruler of Germany and began the creation of the Hapsburg dynastic empire. (*Cont. p. 398.*)

(1) *Bohemia,* 1306-1471

1306. The Premyslid dynasty came to an end with the death of Wenceslas (Vaclav) III. There followed an interregnum, during which the Bohemians were driven out of Poland. The interregnum ended with the election of

1310-1346. JOHN OF LUXEMBURG, son of the Emperor Henry VII. The circumstances of his accession forced John to issue a charter guaranteeing the rights and privileges of the nobility and clergy. Thus limitations of the royal power were fixed by written law. At the same time the national diet, theretofore called only on special occasions, became a regular institution. During this reign Bohemian overlordship over Upper Lusatia and Silesia was established.

John supported the Teutonic Knights against the Lithuanians and participated in three campaigns (1328, 1337, 1346). For a time (1331-1333) he ruled western Lombardy, as well as the Tyrol (1336-1341). John found his death in the battle of Crécy, where he fought on the side of the French. While he had shown little concern for Bohemian domestic affairs, he had made Bohemia a power in international politics.

1347-1378. CHARLES I (Charles IV as German Emperor), the son of John of Luxemburg. His reign is regarded as the "golden age" of Bohemian history. A series of charters issued in 1348 established an order of dynastic succession and determined Bohemia's place in the Holy Roman Empire. Moravia, Silesia, and Upper Lusatia were to be indissolubly connected with the Bohemian crown. By the **Golden Bull** (1356, see p. 302) the King of Bohemia was given first place among the empire's secular electors. At the same time Bohemia's internal independence was guaranteed. Acquisition of Lower Lusatia (1370) and Brandenburg (1373). Charles ruled as a constitutional king and spared no effort to promote material well-being and cultural progress. A new code of laws, the *Maiestas Carolina*, was published. Prague was rebuilt and beautified. The **University of Prague** founded (1348), the first university in central Europe.

1378-1419. WENCESLAS (Vaclav) IV, son of Charles. Gradual weakening of the connection with the German Empire. Loss of Brandenburg (1411). Continued conflicts with the barons. This was hastened by the development (since the end of the 14th century) of a national-religious movement which culminated in **Hussitism. John Hus** (1369-1415), a professor at the University of Prague and a popular preacher in the vernacular, was deeply influenced by the teaching of Wiclif and the Lollards in England. He attacked sale of indulgences, demanded reforms in the Church, challenged the primacy of the pope, and emphasized the supreme authority of the Scriptures. He also supported the native element in the university in the struggle which ended in the exodus of the alien Germans (1409), becoming rector of the university. Excommunicated by the pope and eager for vindication, he went to the **Council of Constance** (1415) under a safe-conduct from the emperor. His arrest in violation of this guaranty, his trial and burning (July 6), identified religious reform with Bohemian nationalism and split the empire in the

1420-1433. HUSSITE WARS. Refusal to recognize Sigismund as king. The reformers divided into two groups: (1) The moderate **Calixtines**, with the university as a center, favored separation of religious and political reform and formulated their program in the **Four Articles of Prague** (1420): full liberty of preaching, the cup to the laity (*Utraquism*), exclusion of the clergy from temporal activity and their subjection to civil penalties for crime. (2) The radical **Taborites**, under extreme Waldensian, Catharist, and Wiclifite influences, with a program of democracy and apostolic communism. The papal proclamation of a

Bohemian **Crusade** (not opposed by the Emperor Sigismund) united the nation behind **John Ziska**, a brilliant soldier, who led the Hussites in a series of victories (1420-1422). Ziska's "modernization" of tactics: improved, mobile artillery, use of baggage wagons for mobile cover. Ziska's death (1424) did not affect the movement. Under a priest, **Procop the Great**, the Hussites defeated one crusade after another (1426, 1427, 1431) and carried the war into neighboring regions of Germany, on one occasion (1432) advancing as far as the Baltic. Then civil war broke out between the Calixtines and the Taborites (led by Procop the Great), the latter suffering defeat (1434).

1431-1436. The Council of Basel. The Hussites finally accepted a compromise, the *Compactata* (1436), recognizing them as true sons of the Church and conceding them the cup in the communion.

1436. Sigismund was finally accepted as king by all parties. He attempted a Catholic reaction, which was cut short by his death in the following year. Disputes continued between the Catholics and the Hussites, complicated by factional struggles between Hussite moderates and radicals and by social tension between nobility, townsmen and peasantry.

1437-1439. ALBERT OF AUSTRIA (son-in-law of Sigismund), elected king. An opposition group chose Ladislas, King of Poland. Albert died in the course of a civil war.

1439-1457. LADISLAS POSTHUMUS, the son of Albert. The Emperor Frederick III acted as his guardian, and for many years kept him from Bohemia. In the midst of continued factional conflict, a young nobleman, **George of Podiebrad,** rose to power.

1448. George seized Prague and became head of the Hussites. He was recognized as administrator of the kingdom (1452) and devoted himself to the task of reconciling Catholics and Hussites. The radical wing of the latter was completely suppressed by the **capture of Tabor** (1452). George ultimately succeeded in bringing the young king to Prague, but Ladislas died before he could accomplish much in behalf of the Catholics.

1459-1471. GEORGE PODIEBRAD elected king. Policy of conciliation: vigorous persecution of the Bohemian Brotherhood, a puritanical sect with outspokenly democratic leanings, dating from the teaching of **Peter of Chelchich** (d. 1460), and, like the Taborites, rejecting all subordination to Rome. George, an avowed

Hussite of the moderate school, was technically a heretic and soon found himself in conflict with the pope.

1462. The pope denounced the agreements of Basel, and deposed George (1465). Thereupon the Catholic nobility of Bohemia elected **Mathias of Hungary** as king. George defeated him in a series of engagements, but the issue was undecided when George died. (*Cont. p.* 418.)

(2) The Swiss Confederation, to 1499

Lake Lucerne and the original **Forest Cantons** belonged to the Duchy of Swabia, and the expansion of powerful Swabian families during the Great Interregnum led the Forest Cantons to a determined effort to replace feudal allegiances to various nobles with a single direct allegiance to the emperor. Most powerful of the Swabian families was the rising **house of Hapsburg** (whose original lands expanded in the 13th century into the Aargau, Breisgau, and Alsace). **Rudolf III** (b. 1218) of Hapsburg sought to restore the Duchy of Swabia under his house.

The **Forest Cantons of Uri** (already acknowledged independent of any but a loose imperial allegiance in 1231), **Schwyz**, and **Unterwalden**, emerged as champions of local independence and masters of the St. Gotthard Pass into Italy. Rudolf during the Interregnum expanded his suzerainty, but as emperor was too busy to assert it.

1291. First (known) **League of the Three Forest Cantons**, an undertaking for mutual defense, a kind of constitution, but not an independent federal league, as the cantons did not claim independence. Emperor Adolf confirmed the status of Uri and Schwyz, Henry VII that of Unterwalden, and henceforth the three Forest Cantons were thought of as a unit. The Swiss sent Henry VII three hundred soldiers for his Italian expedition, the first recorded use of Swiss troops outside their own borders.

1315, Nov. 15. Battle of Morgarten. Leopold of Austria, in an effort to crush the Swiss and punish them for support of Louis IV against the Hapsburg Frederick the Handsome, was thoroughly beaten at Morgarten, a battle which began the brilliant career of the Swiss infantry in Europe. Renewal and strengthening of the league and its confirmation by Louis IV.

1332-1353. Additions to the three Forest Cantons: Canton of Lucerne (1332); Canton of Zürich (1351); Canton of Glarus (1352); Canton of Bern (1353),

bringing the number to seven, half of which were peasant cantons, the other half urban.

1386, July 9. BATTLE OF SEMPACH. The confederation, supported by the Swabian League, defeated the Hapsburg Leopold II of Swabia. In 1388 another victory was won at **Näfels.**

1394. Twenty-year truce between the confederation and the Duke of Austria. Austria abandoned claims on Zug and Glarus. The confederation became solely dependent on the empire, which amounted to practical independence.

The confederation was controlled by a **federal diet** (1393), but the cantons retained the widest possible autonomy. Throughout the succeeding period there was but little evidence of union. The various cantons followed their own interests (Lucerne and Schwyz looked to the north; Bern to the west; Uri to the south) and wrangled among themselves. Only the threat from Austria invariably united them against the common enemy. In the meanwhile the 15th century was marked by continual struggles and conflicts with neighbors, as a result of which further territories were brought into the confederation and some approach was made to natural frontiers.

1403. The Canton of Uri began expansion southward, to get control of the passes to the Milanese. In 1410 the whole Val Antigorio was conquered, with Domodossola. The Swiss were driven out by the Duke of Savoy in 1413, but in 1416 regained mastery of the country.

1415. Conquest in the north of the Aargau, from Frederick of Austria, at the behest of his rival, the Emperor Sigismund.

1419. Purchase of Bellinzona, which, however, was seized by the Visconti of Milan (1422).

1436-1450. Civil war between Zürich and some of the neighboring cantons over the succession to the domains of the Count of Toggenburg. Zürich allied itself with Emperor Frederick IV (1442), but was defeated by Schwyz (1443); Zürich besieged (1444). Frederick called in the French, but after a defeat near Basel, the French withdrew. The emperor made **peace at Constance** (June 12, 1446) and in 1450 peace was made within the confederation. The general effect of the war was to strengthen the confederacy.

1460. Conquest of the Thurgau from Austria gave the confederation a frontier on Lake Constance.

1474-1477. The great war against **Charles the Bold** of Burgundy, whose designs on Alsace were regarded as a menace to the confederation. The Swiss allied themselves with the South German cities. This combination was joined by the emperor (perpetual peace, Mar. 30, 1474: Austria again renounced claims to Swiss territory). Louis XI of France also joined, but in 1475 both the emperor and the king withdrew again. Great victories of the Swiss at **Grandson** (Mar. 2, 1476), **Morat** or Murten (June 22, 1476), and at **Nancy** (Jan. 5, 1477) sealed the fate of Charles' plans and established the great military reputation of the Swiss, who were thenceforth sought far and wide as mercenaries.

1478. **War with Milan.** Victory of the Swiss at **Giornico** (Dec. 28). Alliance with the pope, who was allowed to engage Swiss forces.

1481. **Solothurn and Fribourg** were admitted to the Confederation after a long dispute among the members. The **Diet of Stans** drew up a covenant by which federal relations were regulated until 1798. Henceforth the urban cantons were in a majority.

1499. **War with the emperor** over disputed territories in the east. The emperor was supported by the South German cities, while the Swiss enjoyed the support, especially financial, of the French. The Swiss won a series of victories (especially **Dornach,** July 22) and forced the emperor to conclude the **Treaty of Basel** (Sept. 22) which granted the confederation independence of the empire in fact, if not formally (this came only in 1648). By the inclusion of **Basel and Schaffhausen** (1501) and later **Appenzell** (1513), the confederation rounded out its northern frontier.

The Swiss at the end of the 15th century enjoyed immense military prestige, but within the confederation there was much social unrest, especially among the peasants, and a good deal of demoralization in the towns. **Hans Waldmann,** bürgermeister of Zürich (1483–1489), was only the most outstanding of the typical ruthless, mercenary, cynical figures which dominated the scene and which remind one of the contemporaneous Italian despots.

(*Cont. p.* 408.)

(3) The Hanseatic League

Hansa (Old French *Hanse*; Med. Latin *Hansa*), meaning a group, company, or association.

Associations (*Hansas*) and partial unions of North German towns date from the 13th century and were an important aspect of the great town development of Germany in that period.

c. 1000. German traders were established on the island of Gothland and in London.

c. 1150-c. 1250. Revival of the German river trade, notably along the Rhine, centering in the towns of Cologne, Dortmund, Soest, and Münster. At the same time the German expansion toward the Slavic east extended the sphere of German trade along the Baltic coasts. In the later 12th century the German settlement on Gothland (**Wisby**) became autonomous and established an offshoot at **Novgorod** (*St. Peter's Yard*) which became the focus of the important Russian trade.

1226. **Lübeck** (founded 1143) secured an imperial charter from Frederick II. Hamburg followed in 1266–1267.

1237. Wisby secured trading rights in England, and soon afterward in Flanders.

1241. Lübeck and Hamburg formed an alliance to protect the Baltic trade routes.

1256. **The Wendish towns** (Lübeck, Stralsund, Wismar, Rostock, Greifswald, and later Lüneburg) held their first recorded meeting. Lübeck began to emerge as the dominant North German town, a position which it retained throughout the history of the Hanseatic League. Most of the commercial towns followed the *Code of Lübeck*, which was an early source of unity between them. By the end of the century the Wendish towns had taken the leadership from the Gothland merchants.

1282. The Germans in London formed a corporation and established their own guildhall and steelyard. Other German yards were opened at York, Bristol, Yarmouth, Lynn, and Boston. The London trade was dominated by Cologne, but the yards at Lynn and Boston were under the control of Lübeck and Hamburg.

THE HANSEATIC LEAGUE. No date can be fixed for its organization, which was evidently the result of the lack of a powerful German national government able to guarantee security for trade. Its formation was no doubt facilitated by the mediaeval affinity for co-operative action and for monopoly. The term *Hanseatic League* was first used in a document in 1344. The exclusion of Germans abroad (1366) from the privileges of the Hansa indicates a growing sense of unity, but league members spoke of the association merely as a *firma confederatio* for trade, and throughout its history it remained a loose aggregation. This looseness of organization allowed a

The Hanseatic League and
The Teutonic Knights

SCALE OF MILES

0 20 40 60 80 100   200

The cities of the league are marked by dots o

Represents the possessions of the
Teutonic Knights at their greatest extent

Novgorod

ESTHONIA

LIVONIA

Dwina R.

COURLAND

SAMOGITIA

Niemen R.

LITHUANIA

Königsberg

PRUSSIA

Marienburg

Danzig

POMERELLA

Vistula R.

Dobrin

POLAND

Cracow

Breslau

Oder R.

GOTLAND

Wisby

BALTIC SEA

Stockholm

SWEDEN

Kalmar

RÜGEN

Berlin

Magdeburg

Merseburg

Schonen

DENMARK

Copenhagen

Lübeck

Hamburg

Elbe R.

NORWAY

C. Bergen

NORTH SEA

Weser R.

Bremen

Cologne

Rhine R.

Meuse R.

Scheldt

Bruges

ENGLAND

Norwich

Sourbridge Fair

London

York

Longitude   East   12°   from   Greenwich

52°

28°

28°

20°

20°

12°

4°

4°

52°

maximum of independence to its members and was not modified until the league was put on the defensive in the 15th century. The league never had a true treasury or officials in a strict sense; its only common seal was that of Lübeck; it had no common flag. Assemblies of the members (*Hansetage*) were summoned by Lübeck at irregular intervals and were sparsely attended, except in times of crisis. The objectives of the league were mutual security, extortion of trading privileges, and maintenance of trade monopoly wherever possible. The chief weapon against foreigners or recalcitrant members was the economic boycott and (rarely) war. Primarily concerned with the North European trade, the Hansa towns dealt chiefly in raw materials (timber, pitch, tar, turpentine, iron, copper), livestock (horses, hawks, etc.), salt fish (cod and especially herring), leather, hides, wool, grain, beer, amber, drugs, and some textiles. The four chief *kontors* were Wisby, Bergen, London, and Bruges.

1340-1375. WALDEMAR IV of Denmark, who freed his country of the German domination and took up the struggle against the powerful Hansa towns. He threatened the Hanseatic monopoly of the herring trade by his seizure of Scania, and in 1361 cut the Russian-Baltic trade route by his capture of Wisby. In 1362 he defeated the German fleets at **Helsingborg.** By the **Peace of Wordingborg** (1365) the Hansa was deprived of many of its privileges in Denmark.

1367. THE CONFEDERATION OF CO-LOGNE, effected by a meeting of representatives of 77 towns, organized common finance and naval preparations for the struggle. Reconstruction of Scandinavian alliances to meet the threat from Waldemar. After a series of victories, the German towns extorted from the Danish *Reichsrat*

1370. THE PEACE OF STRALSUND, which gave the league four castles in Scania (dominating the Sound), control of two-thirds of the Scanian revenues for 15 years, and the right to veto the succession to the Danish throne unless their monopoly was renewed by the candidate. The treaty marked the apogee of Hanseatic power and virtually established control over the Baltic trade and over Scandinavian politics. The Baltic monopoly was not finally broken until 1441, after a war with the Dutch. Wisby itself never recovered from Waldemar's sack, and was long a nest of pirates (e.g. the famous **Victual Brothers**).

FLANDERS. The Germans in Bruges received a special grant of privileges in 1252, which allowed them their own ordinances and officials. They later (1309) established exemption from the usual brokerage charges levied on foreigners and eventually won an influential voice in the affairs of the city, notably in foreign policy. The revised statutes of the Bruges Kontor (1347) recognized the division of the Hanseatic League into thirds: The Wendish-Saxon; the Prusso-Westphalian; and the Gothland-Livland thirds. Bruges was the most ardent champion of Hanseatic unity, and, with Lübeck, was the chief source of such cohesion as the League attained. A boycott in 1360 brought the town into complete submission to the League.

ENGLAND. The Hansa towns, by maintaining friendly relations to the crown, were able to ignore the growing national hostility to alien traders (directed at first mainly against the Italians) and to avoid granting reciprocal privileges to the English in return for their own exclusive rights (notably those claimed under Edward I's *Carta Mercatoria* of 1303). One source of Hanseatic influence derived from loans to the crown, especially during the Hundred Years' War. The English themselves began to penetrate into the Baltic (c. 1360) and growing public resentment against the league led to increased customs dues, but Richard II in 1377 renewed the privileges of the league, thus firmly establishing the Hanseatic power in England. The Sound was opened to the English in 1451, and the league, profiting by the Wars of the Roses, secured full title to the steelyard in London (1474) and the renewal of rights in Boston and Lynn. Not until the days of Elizabeth were the Hanseatic privileges finally reduced.

DECLINE OF THE LEAGUE. Externally the league was weakened by the disorders of the Hundred Years' War; by the rise of Burgundy and the new orientation thereby given to Dutch trade (e.g. Brill wrested the monopoly of the herring trade from the league); and by the great discoveries and the opening of new trade routes. But above all, the monopolistic policies of the league aroused ever sharper opposition in the countries where the league operated (notably in England, Holland, Scandinavia, and Russia; Ivan III destroyed the Novgorod Kontor in 1494). Internally the league continued to suffer from lack of organization. The inland towns held aloof from the Baltic policy and Cologne sent no representatives to the assembly until 1383. The assembly itself was summoned only at irregular intervals. The delegates were strictly bound by their mandates and their votes were subject to review by their home towns. Decisions were not binding on all members until 1418. In the 15th century the league was further weakened by the struggle within the member towns between the democratic guildsmen and the patrician oligarchy. The league threatened the expulsion of "democratic" towns. The German princes (notably the Hohenzollerns of Brandenburg) gradually reduced the freedom of various powerful members of the league and rivalries broke out within the league itself (Cologne and the Westphalian towns stood together, as did Danzig and the Prussian towns, especially after 1467). The South German towns opened direct trade relations of their own with Flanders, Breslau, Prague, and other centers, and began to establish their own fairs. Leipzig, for example, replaced Lübeck as the center of the fur trade.

1629. The Assembly entrusted the guardianship of the common welfare to Lübeck, Hamburg, and Bremen.

1669. The last assembly (attended by six towns) was held. The league by this time was the merest shadow of its former self, but its Kontors survived in Bergen until 1775, in London until 1852, and in Augsburg until 1863.

(4) *The Teutonic Knights*

The 14th century marked the apogee of the power of the **Teutonic Order** in eastern Europe. The Knights began the penetration of Poland, where Germans settled some 650 districts and where the middle class of the towns became German in speech and law, much to the alarm of the rulers and nobles. At the same period the Knights advanced into Lithuania, a huge region extending from the Baltic to the Black Sea, the last heathen area in Europe. German colonization and town-building first opened and civilized this region.

1326-1333. THE FIRST POLISH WAR, marking a sharp reaction to German penetration and putting the order for the first time on the defensive. With the aid of John of Bohemia, Louis of Hungary, Albert of Austria, Louis of Brandenburg, and others, the order emerged triumphant and the Poles were obliged to conclude a truce.

1343. PEACE OF KALISCH. The Poles, despite papal support of their claims to Pomerelia, were obliged to recognize the Order's possession of the territory, in return for a promise of aid against the Lithuanians. Poland was thus cut off from the Baltic.

1343-1345. The Estonian Revolt, one of the worst *jacqueries* of the Middle Ages. Estonia was taken by the Order from the Danes in 1346.

1385. **Union of Poland and Lithuania** under Jagiello and Jadwiga, thus creating a strong barrier to the further advance of the Germans and indeed, sealing the ultimate fate of the Order.

1410, July 15. Defeat of the Knights in the battle of **Tannenberg** by a huge army of Poles and Lithuanians. Poland, unable to exploit the victory, concluded

1411. THE FIRST PEACE OF THORN, which cost the Knights only Samogitia and an indemnity.

1454. The Prussian Revolt, a great uprising against the oppressive rule of the Order in which the Prussian nobility and towns took part. The movement was supported by the Poles, and Casimir of Poland declared war on the Order.

1466. SECOND PEACE OF THORN. Prussia was divided: (1) West Prussia (including Danzig, Kulm, Marienwerder, Thorn, and Ermeland) went to Poland, thus cutting East Prussia off from the rest of Germany and securing for Poland access to the sea. (2) **East Prussia** was retained by the Order, with Königsberg as capital. East Prussia, Brandenburg, and Memel were all to be held as Polish fiefs. The Order was opened to Polish members. This peace marked the definitive end of the German advance until the partitions of Poland.

The decline of the Order continued (growing commercialization, exclusiveness, lack of new blood, loss of discipline, Slavic pressure) despite efforts at reform by various grand masters.

1525. East Prussia was finally secularized by the grand master, Albrecht (Hohenzollern) of Brandenburg, and became a fief of the Hohenzollerns under the Polish crown.

1561. The Livonian holdings were similarly transformed and became the Duchy of Courland.

The Order itself survived in Germany until 1809 and was later revived in 1840 under Hapsburg auspices with its original functions (e.g. ambulance service in war).

f. SCANDINAVIA
(1) *Denmark*, 1320-1387

The active and on the whole successful reign of **Eric Menved** (1286-1320) was followed in Denmark by a period of weakness

Rulers of Denmark, Norway, and Sweden (1263-1533)

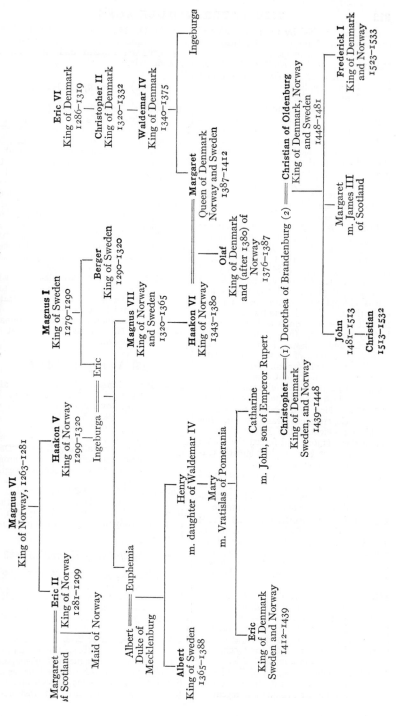

and decline, marked by the ascendancy of the nobility and the constant advance of German influence.

1320-1332. CHRISTOPHER II, elected king after a capitulation, the first in Danish history, limiting the royal power in the interest of the nobility and clergy. The Hansa towns, having acquired a monopoly of trade in Denmark, soon became dominant in Danish politics.

1332-1340. A period of complete anarchy. Christopher was driven from the throne by Gerhard, Count of Holstein, who parceled out the territories of the crown, established German nobles in all the important fortresses, and gave the German traders full rein. Gerhard was murdered in 1340.

1340-1375. WALDEMAR IV, the youngest son of Christopher and one of the greatest Danish kings. At home he did his utmost to break the German influence and to restrict the power of the nobility and the clergy. The Church was subordinated to the royal power and the nobles and towns obliged to perform their military obligations. Abroad Waldemar devoted himself to the reconquest of the territories lost by his father. In wars with Sweden, Holstein, and Schleswig he regained Zeeland (1346), most of Fünen and Jutland (1348), and Scania (1360). His seizure of Gothland (1361) brought him into direct conflict with the powerful Hansa towns, which were supported by Sweden.

1361-1363. First War against the Hansa. Copenhagen was sacked, but Waldemar defeated the Hansa fleets at **Helsingborg** (1362) and forced the Hansa to accept peace (1363) which greatly curtailed their privileges.

1368. A revolt against heavy taxation led to Waldemar's flight. His return (1370) was purchased by tremendous concessions. Meanwhile

1368-1370. THE SECOND WAR WITH THE HANSA had broken out. The German towns were supported by Sweden, Norway, Holstein, Mecklenburg, and even by some of the Danish nobles. Waldemar, badly defeated, was obliged to accept

1370. THE PEACE OF STRALSUND, renewing the privileges of the German Hansa, turning over the larger part of the revenues of four places, and accepting interference in the royal succession. This treaty marked the ascendancy of the Hansa in the Baltic.

1376-1387. Olaf, grandson of Waldemar, who, until his death, ruled with his mother Margaret as regent.

1387-1412. Margaret, mother of Olaf, was queen, ruling at the same time Norway and Sweden and thus uniting Scandinavia.

(2) *Sweden,* 1319-1387

1319-1363. MAGNUS II (*Smek*), aged three at his accession and, until 1333, ruler under the regency of his mother. He was a weak and ineffectual ruler, but through his mother succeeded (1319) to the Norwegian crown and, during the troubled period in Denmark, managed to acquire, temporarily, Scania, Halland, and Bleking (given up again in 1360, to Waldemar IV). His long minority and his reliance on unworthy favorites led to a striking weakening of the royal power and an equally striking rise of the aristocratic party (first *Riksdag*, including burghers 1359). Magnus was ultimately deposed, and was succeeded by

1363-1388. Albert of Mecklenburg, who from the outset was merely a tool of the nobility. The magnates eventually deposed him and defeated him, calling to the throne

1388-1412. MARGARET, the regent of Denmark.

(3) *Norway,* 1320-1387

1319-1343. Magnus II, who was also King of Sweden. In 1343 he turned over Norway to his son

1343-1380. Haakon VI, who was married (1363) to Margaret of Denmark.

1380-1387. Olaf, the son of Haakon and Margaret, already King of Denmark, succeeded to the throne. His death ended the Norwegian line.

1387-1412. MARGARET, mother of Olaf, was elected to the throne, thus introducing into Norway the system of election already in practice in Denmark and Sweden.

(4) *The Union of Kalmar to* 1483

1387-1412. MARGARET OF DENMARK, ruler of all three Scandinavian kingdoms. She had her grand-nephew, Eric of Pomerania, elected king of all three countries in 1389, but retained effective power herself.

1397. Coronation of Eric. Margaret presented a draft for the union of the three kingdoms. Vague and incomplete, the plan provided for a single king, established rules of succession, and set up a system of common defense. It was never ratified by the councils of the three kingdoms, but as long as Margaret lived, it worked relatively well. The union left the internal government of each kingdom much as it was. Margaret, an able despot (the Lübeck delegates called her "the lady king"), repressed the nobles, maintained order, and began the recovery of the Danish royal domain. In general the Danes profited by the union, and Danes and Germans were gradually insinuated into power in Sweden and Norway. Effective government of Scandinavia was centered in Denmark.

1412-1439. ERIC, Margaret's successor, proved himself less able. His efforts to regain control in Schleswig led to a long contest with the Dukes of Holstein, who, in alliance with the Hansa towns, finally conquered Schleswig completely (1432). At the same time much unrest developed among the peasantry (especially in Sweden, where **Engelbrecht Engelbrechtson** emerged as a leader of the lower classes).

1434. Engelbrecht marched through eastern and southern Sweden, seizing castles and driving out bailiffs, until the **Diet of 1435** recognized his demands, electing him regent. This diet included representatives of all four orders and for four hundred years continued to be an important institution. The movement of revolt spread to Norway, where it was taken up and controlled by the nobles. Eric finally took flight and the Danish council called in

1439-1448. CHRISTOPHER of Bavaria, cousin of Eric, who again ruled all three countries (elected in Sweden, 1440; in Norway, 1442). His reign marked the nadir of the monarchy, for Christopher was entirely dependent on the Hansa towns and was obliged to renew all their privileges, despite protests from the Danish burghers.

1448-1481. CHRISTIAN I (of Oldenburg) was elected by the Danish council under a capitulation which left all real power in the hands of that body. He had to accept a similar engagement on assuming the crown of Norway. The Swedish nobility, on the other hand, elected **Knut Knutsson** as king with the title of **Charles VIII** (1449-1457). Charles tried to secure the throne of Norway, but was ousted by Christian.

1457. Charles VII was driven out of Sweden by a revolt inspired by the Church. Christian I was then crowned, but the real power was in the hands of the Stures (Sten, Svanee, and Sten the Younger). Christian kept a great state, but his court, like that of Christopher and Eric, was filled with Germans, and he was financially dependent on the Hansa cities. The **union of Schleswig and Holstein,** each autonomous under the crown of Denmark, was arranged in 1460. Christian founded the **University of Copenhagen** (1479).

Sweden in the later 15th century: The crown was a plaything of the nobles, while the clergy supported the King of Denmark. A rising commerce and industry was, however, creating a burgher class which was soon to assert itself. Sten Sture the Younger, who came into power with the death of Charles VIII, repulsed Christian of Denmark (1471) with the aid of the towns (especially Stockholm) and returned to the reforms of Engelbrecht. The **University of Uppsala** was founded (1477) and **printing** was introduced soon afterward.

(*Cont. p.* 410.)

2. EASTERN EUROPE

a. POLAND, 1305-1492

The history of Poland in this period was concerned chiefly with the efforts of the kings to reunite the various duchies and to establish the royal power. This policy was opposed, with success, by the nobility, which, as elsewhere in Europe, managed to extract countless privileges and to erect a type of oligarchical government. Externally the Poles were involved in a long struggle with the Teutonic Knights, designed to secure an outlet to the Baltic. This conflict alternated with a policy of expansion to the southeast, toward the Black Sea.

1305-1333. VLADISLAV IV (*Lokietek*), under whom Poland regained its independence after a brief period of Bohemian domination. Vladislav was obliged to continue the struggle against Bohemia, and was not crowned until 1320. For protection he concluded dynastic alliances with Hungary (his daughter married Charles Robert of Anjou) and Lithuania (his son Casimir married the daughter of Gedymin). He did much to reunite the various duchies and established a new capital at Cracow. But he failed to secure Pomerania, which in 1309 passed from Brandenburg to the Teutonic Order. A papal decision in 1321 awarded the region to Poland, but the Knights ignored

POLAND, LITHUANIA
AND RUSSIA
IN THE 15TH CENTURY

Scales of Miles

0   200   400   600

the order to turn it over, and continued their raids into Polish territory (1326–1333).

1333-1370. CASIMIR III (*the Great*), an astute and cautious statesman. He introduced an improved administration, reduced the influence of the German town law (a new law code published), developed national defense and promoted trade and industry (extensive privileges to the Jews, 1334). In 1364 he founded a school at Cracow, which became a university in 1400 and the chief intellectual center of eastern Europe.

In foreign affairs Casimir abandoned claims to Silesia and Pomerania, turning his attention toward the southeast, where dynastic problems in the Ukraine called forth dangerous rivalry between Poles, Lithuanians, and Hungarians. By an agreement with Hungary (1339), Casimir, who had no direct heir, promised that on his death the Polish crown should pass to Louis, the son of Charles Robert of Hungary. Louis was to reconquer the lost territories and to respect the privileges of the Polish nobility. This marks the beginning of the disastrous elective system, which gave the magnates an unequaled opportunity for extracting further rights (first real diet — *colloquia* — in 1367). In 1340 Casimir seized Halicz, Lemberg, and Volhynia. War ensued with Lithuania over Volhynia, and ultimately the Poles retained only the western part (1366).

1370-1382. LOUIS (of Anjou). He paid but little attention to Poland, which he governed through regents. To secure the succession to his daughter Maria (married to Sigismund, son of Emperor Charles IV) he granted to the nobility the *Charter of Koszyce* (Kaschau), the basis of far-reaching privileges.

1382-1384. Opposition to Sigismund led to the formation of the **Confederation of Radom** and civil war between the factions of the nobility.

1384-1399. JADWIGA (Hedwig), a daughter of Louis, was elected queen.

1386. Marriage of Jadwiga to **Jagiello,** Grand Duke of Lithuania, who promised to become a Christian and to unite his duchy (three times the size of Poland) with the Polish crown. As a matter of fact, though the marriage prepared the way for union, Jagiello was obliged to recognize his cousin, **Witold,** as Grand Duke of Lithuania, and the connection continued to be tenuous.

1386-1434. JAGIELLO (title **Vladislav V**). He had great difficulty in keeping his fractious nobility in order and in 1433 was obliged to grant the *Charter of*

Cracow, reaffirming and extending their privileges.

1410, July 15. BATTLE OF TANNENBERG (Grünwald), a great victory of the Poles, using Bohemian mercenaries under John Ziska and supported by the Russians and even the Tatars, against the Teutonic Knights. The Poles thereupon devastated Prussia, but Jagiello, unable to keep his vassals in order, concluded the

1411, Feb. 1. FIRST PEACE OF THORN, which left matters much as they were and failed to secure for the Poles an access to the Baltic.

1434-1444. VLADISLAV VI, son of Jagiello, succeeded to the throne. Since he was only ten years old, the country was ruled by a regency. Vladislav's brother, Casimir, was offered the Bohemian throne by the Hussites (1438), and Vladislav himself became King of Hungary (1440). Thenceforth he devoted himself to Hungarian affairs, leaving Poland in the hands of the magnates. Vladislav lost his life in 1444 at the **battle of Varna** (p. 326) against the Turks.

1444-1447. An interregnum, followed by the reign of

1447-1492. CASIMIR IV, brother of Vladislav. He was able to make use of a rift between the great nobles (magnates) and the gentry (*szlachta*). The *Statute of Nieszawa* greatly limited the power of the former and granted substantial rights to the latter (no laws to be passed, no war to be declared without their consent). At the same time the independence of the church was curtailed (bishops to be appointed by the king).

1454-1466. War against the Teutonic Order. The Poles took advantage of the Prussian Union (Prussian nobles and towns in opposition to the Order). The war was carried on in desultory fashion, marked by constant shifting of the feudal forces and of the mercenaries from side to side, but the Poles ultimately gained the upper hand and secured

1466, Oct. 19. THE SECOND PEACE OF THORN, by which Poland finally secured an outlet to the Baltic. Poland acquired Kulm, Michelau, Pomerania, Marienburg, Elbing, and Christburg. The Order became a vassal of the Polish crown, and half its membership became Polish.

1471-1516. Vladislav, the son of Casimir, became King of Bohemia, which involved a long and indecisive war with Hungary (1471–1478). Eventually Vladislav became King of Hungary also (1490).

(*Cont. p.* 413.)

b. LITHUANIA

Of the early history of Lithuania little is known. The numerous heathen tribes were first brought to some degree of unity by the threat of the German Knights (after 1230).

c. 1240-1263. Mindovg, one of the Lithuanian chieftains, in order to deprive the Knights of their crusading purpose, accepted Christianity and was given a crown by Pope Innocent IV. He later broke with the Teutonic Order (1260) and relapsed into paganism. He was killed by one of his competitors. Of the following period almost nothing is known.

1293-1316. Viten re-established a Lithuanian state.

1316-1341. GEDYMIN, the real founder of Lithuania. Blocked by the Germans on the Baltic, he took advantage of the weakness of the Russian principalities to extend his control to the east and south (acquisition of Polotsk, Minsk, and the middle-Dnieper region). Vilno became the capital of the new state.

1341-1377. OLGERD, the son of Gedymin, was the ablest of the dynasty. Defeated by the Knights (1360) he too turned eastward. Siding with Tver in the dynastic conflicts of Russia, he advanced several times to the very outskirts of Moscow. During his reign the domain of Lithuania was extended as far as the Black Sea, where Olgerd defeated the Tatars (1368).

1377-1434. JAGIELLO, the son of Olgerd, married Jadwiga of Poland (1386) and established the **personal union with Poland.** Through him Lithuania became converted to Roman Catholicism and the Polish and Lithuanian nobility gradually became assimilated. In 1387 and 1389 Moldavia and Wallachia, and in 1396 Bessarabia accepted Lithuanian suzerainty.

1398. Jagiello was obliged to recognize his cousin, **Vitovt** (Witold) as Grand Duke of Lithuania. Vitovt hoped to re-establish the independence of the country from Poland, but his failure in a crusade against the Tatars greatly weakened him.

1447. Casimir IV of Poland, having been Grand Duke of Lithuania before his accession, once again united the grand duchy and the Polish kingdom.

(*Cont. p.* 413.)

c. RUSSIA, 1263-1505

The period following the death of **Alexander Nevski** (1263) was marked by the continued and repeated disruption of the Russian lands, due to the complicated and unfortunate system of succession in the princely family. Russia was under the suzerainty of the Tatars, who played off one candidate against another, thus increasing the confusion and perpetuating the weakness of the country. The **rise of Moscow** (first mentioned 1147) to prominence among the Russian principalities was perhaps the most important development looking toward the future. Centrally located, Moscow was in the most favorable position to serve as nucleus for a revived Russian state.

1325-1341. IVAN I KALITA (*Moneybag*), Grand Prince of Moscow. His was the first of a series of noteworthy reigns. Extremely cautious and parsimonious, Ivan bought immunity from Tatar interference and was ultimately entrusted by the Tatars with the collection of tribute from the other princes.

1341-1353. Simeon I continued the policy of his predecessor and was placed, by the Tatar overlord, above all the other princes.

1353-1359. Ivan II Krasnyi (*the Red*).

1359-1389. DMITRI DONSKOI (of the Don), who ascended the princely throne at the age of nine. His reign was filled with a struggle against **Michael of Tver,** his chief rival, who was supported by Olgerd of Lithuania. At the same time he began the conflict with the Tatars, whose power was fading, but who also enjoyed the support of Lithuania.

1380, Sept. 8. THE BATTLE OF KULIKOVO. Dmitri completely defeated the Tatar armies before the Lithuanians arrived. The victory was in no sense decisive, for the Tatars on several occasions thereafter advanced to the very gates of Moscow. But Kulikovo broke the prestige of the Tatar arms and marked the turning point.

1389-1425. Basil I. He annexed Nishni-Novgorod and continued the struggle with the Tatars and the Lithuanians, without forcing a decision.

1425-1462. Basil II, whose reign was distinguished by a relapse into anarchy. A long civil war with his rivals, Yuri and Shemyaka, was followed by Tatar invasion (1451, the Tatars beaten back from Moscow). Nevertheless the Moscow principality managed to maintain itself. In 1439 Basil refused to accept the union of the Eastern and Western Churches, arranged for at the Council of Florence. Thenceforth the Russian metropolitan, who had moved to Moscow in the time of Ivan Kalita, became more and more the head of an independent Russian Church.

1462-1505. IVAN III (*the Great*), who may be regarded as the first national sovereign of Russia. By a cautious but persistent policy he annexed most of the rival principalities and, after a series of wars, subjected Novgorod, where the patrician elements tended to side with Lithuania. In 1471 Novgorod was obliged to renounce the alliance of Lithuania and to pay tribute. After a second war, in 1478, Novgorod's independence was ended and the troublesome upper classes were deported to central Russia. In 1494 Ivan drove out the German merchants and closed the Hanseatic Kontor. Thus he acquired the huge territory of Novgorod, extending eastward to the Urals. Indirectly he greatly reduced the danger of Lithuanian interference. The annexation of Tver (1485) put an end to the most formidable rival of Moscow.

1472. Marriage of Ivan with Zoë (Sophia), niece of the last Greek emperor of Constantinople. This was arranged by the pope in the hope of bringing the Russians into the Roman Church, but all efforts in that direction failed. The marriage was of importance in establishing the claim of Russian rulers to be the successors of the Greek emperors and the protectors of Orthodox Christianity (theory of the Three Romes, of which Moscow was to be the third and last). It also served to introduce into Moscow the Byzantine conception of the autocrat (Ivan took the title of *Tsar*, i.e. Caesar) and the practice of court ceremonial. Rebuilding of the grand ducal palace (Kremlin) with the assistance of Italian architects brought in by Zoë. The court hierarchy (precedence in rank of princes and nobles, etc.).

1480. Ivan threw off the Tatar yoke after a last Tatar advance on Moscow. Ivan avoided open warfare, but took advantage of the disunion among the Tatars. The Khan of the Crimea (Mengli Girai) became his ally against the Lithuanians.

1492. Invasion of Lithuania, made possible by dynastic troubles in Lithuania and Poland. A second invasion (1501) led to the conclusion of peace in 1503, which brought Russia many of the border territories of White Russia and Little Russia. Moscow had by this time become an important factor in European affairs and enjoyed a considerable prestige. Resumption of active diplomatic relations with western countries.   (*Cont. p.* 415.)

d. HUNGARY, 1301-1490

At the beginning of the 14th century Hungary was already an essentially feudal country, in which the great magnates and the bishops, richly endowed with land, ruled as virtually independent potentates ("little kings"), while the lower nobility, organized in the *Comitats* (provincial governments), had, to a large degree, control of the administration. The nobility, freed of taxation, was responsible for defense, but acted only as it saw fit.

1301-1308. The extinction of the Arpad dynasty led to a period of conflict, during which Czech, German, and Italian parties each attempted to put their candidates on the throne. Wenceslas, son of the King of Bohemia, only thirteen years old, was first elevated, but could not maintain himself. The same fate befell Otto of Bavaria.

1308-1342. CHARLES I (Charles Robert of Anjou), a grandson of Mary, the daughter of Stephen V, was elected and founded the brilliant and successful Anjou line. Charles established his capital at Visegrad and introduced Italian chivalry and western influences. After 15 years of effort he succeeded in subduing the "little kings" of whom Mathias of Csak and Ladislas of Transylvania were the most powerful. Recognizing the hopelessness of suppressing the nobility entirely, he regulated its position and obliged it to furnish specified contingents to the army. Regulation of taxation (first direct tax); encouragement of towns and trade. Charles left the royal power well entrenched, but only as part of an avowedly feudal order.

1342-1382. LOUIS (*the Great*), the son of Charles, a patron of learning who established a brilliant court at Buda. He attempted to solidify the position of his house in Naples and embarked on a successful expedition to Italy to avenge the murder of his brother Andrew (1347). In conjunction with Genoa he carried on a long struggle with Venice, which ended in the Peace of 1381: Venice ceded Dalmatia and paid tribute. In the east the Hungarian power made itself felt throughout the Balkans: Serbia, Wallachia, and Moldavia recognized the suzerainty of Louis; foundation of the border districts (*banats*) south of the Danube and the Save, as protection against the Turkish advance. War against the Turks: Hungarian victory in northern Bulgaria (1366).

1370. Louis became King of Poland but paid little attention to his new obligations. In Hungary he continued the work of his father: the *jus aviticum* (1351) restricted the freedom of the great magnates to dispose of their property.

1382-1385. Mary of Anjou, queen. She was married to Sigismund of Luxemburg, who became guardian of the kingdom. His position was challenged by

Charles of Durazzo and Naples, who had many adherents, especially in southern Hungary and Croatia.

1385-1386. Charles II (of Naples). He was assassinated after a very brief reign, which led to a new revolt in Croatia.

1387-1437. SIGISMUND (of Luxemburg), who became German Emperor in 1410 and King of Bohemia in 1436. His reign marked a great decline in the royal power, due in large measure to Sigismund's constant absence from the country and his practice of selling royal domains in order to get money for his far-reaching schemes elsewhere. In general Sigismund relied on the towns and lesser nobility against the great magnates (who imprisoned him for four months in 1401). Hence the grant of ever greater rights to the Comitats.

1396. The disastrous **crusade of Nicopolis** against the Turks (p. 326). Loss of Dalmatia to the Venetians. Hussite invasions of Hungary, resulting from Sigismund's attempts to gain the Bohemian throne.

1437-1439. Albrecht of Hapsburg, son-in-law of Sigismund, also German Emperor and King of Bohemia. He was obliged to sign far-reaching capitulations (nobles not obliged to fight beyond the frontiers).

1437. First victory of **John Hunyadi** over the Turks. Hunyadi was a powerful frontier lord of uncertain origin.

1440-1444. Vladislav I (Vladislav VI of Poland), a weak ruler, whose reign was distinguished chiefly by the continued victories of Hunyadi (1443). Crusade against the Turks.

1444, Nov. 10. Disaster at Varna and death of Vladislav.

1444-1457. Ladislas V, the son of Albert of Hapsburg, also King of Bohemia. He was only four years old at his accession and Hunyadi was therefore appointed governor of the kingdom until 1552.

1456. Crusade against the Turks, preached by John of Capistrano and led by Hunyadi. The Turks were turned back from the siege of Belgrade, but Hunyadi died in the same year.

1458-1490. MATHIAS CORVINUS (*the Just*), the son of John Hunyadi and one of the greatest of the Hungarian kings. He was fifteen at his election, but soon distinguished himself as a soldier, statesman, and patron of art and learning.

Intelligent, firm, crafty, yet just and noble, he re-established the power of the crown and made Hungary the dominant power in central Europe, if only for the brief space of his reign. He once again broke the power of the oligarchs and drew on the support of the lesser nobility. Development of a central administration; regulation and increase of the taxes. Great wealth and luxury of the court. The *Bibliotheca Corvina*, consisting of more than 10,000 manuscripts and books, many beautifully illuminated by Italian artists. Mathias patron of Renaissance learning. Famous law code (1486). Creation of a standing army (*Black Troop*), composed first of Bohemian, Moravian, and Silesian mercenaries. This gave Mathias one of the most effective fighting forces in the Europe of his day. **Mathias' aims:** to secure the Bohemian throne and ultimately the empire and then to direct a united central Europe against the Turks. Long struggles against **George Podiebrad** of Bohemia ended with George's death in 1471, after Mathias had been proclaimed King of Bohemia (1470). Equally prolonged struggle against Emperor Frederick III, who had been elected King of Hungary by a faction of nobles in 1439. Frederick was finally bought off (1462), but trouble continued. Mathias, disposing of much greater funds and forces than Frederick, conquered not only Silesia and Moravia, but also lower Austria. His capital established at Vienna (1485). Mathias died at 47, leaving Hungary the dominant state in central Europe and a decisive factor in European diplomacy.   (*Cont. p.* 419.)

e. THE SERBIAN STATES, 1276-1499

By the end of the 13th century the Serbian states, like others of eastern Europe, had evolved a strong secular and clerical aristocracy which, to a large extent, controlled even the more outstanding rulers. In view of the general unsettlement of the law regarding succession and inheritance, the tendency toward dynastic conflict and territorial disruption was very pronounced. In the western Balkans the situation was further complicated by the rivalry of the western and eastern forms of Christianity, to say nothing of the persistence of the heretical Bogomil teaching, especially in Bosnia.

1276-1281. Dragutin, with the aid of the Hungarians, seized the Serbian throne from his father, **Urosh I.** Having been defeated in battle by the Greeks, he abdicated after a short rule.

1281-1321. Milyutin (*Stephen Urosh II*), the brother of Dragutin. He was a pious and yet dissolute ruler, but above all a political and religious opportunist. Taking full advantage of the growing weakness of the Byzantine Empire, he gradually extended his possessions in Macedonia, along the Adriatic, and, in the north, toward the Danube and the Save.

1321-1331. Stephen Dechanski (*Stephen Urosh III*), the illegitimate son of the preceding. His reign was marked chiefly by the great victory of the Serbs over the Greeks and Bulgarians near **Küstendil** (Velbuzhde) in 1330. The Serbs now held most of the Vardar Valley.

1331-1355. STEPHEN DUSHAN (*Stephen Urosh IV*), the greatest of the Serbian rulers in the Middle Ages. Dushan began his career by deposing his father, who was strangled soon afterward. For most of his reign he attempted to maintain friendly relations with Hungary and Ragusa, in order to have a free hand to exploit the dynastic war in the Byzantine Empire between the Palaeologi and John Cantacuzene. By 1344 he had subjected all of Macedonia, Albania, Thessaly, and Epirus. His daughter was married to the Bulgarian tsar and Bulgaria was under Serbian supremacy.

1346. Dushan set up his capital at Skoplye (Usküb) and proclaimed himself *Emperor of the Serbs, Greeks, Bulgars, and Albanians*. At the same time he set up a Serbian patriarchate at Peč (Ipek), for which he was anathematized by the Greek patriarch. Dushan established a court wholly Byzantine in character, with elaborate titles and ceremonial. In the years 1349-1354 he drew up his famous law code (*Zabonnik*), which gives an invaluable picture of Serbian conditions and culture at the time.

1349. Attack upon Dushan by the ruler of Bosnia. This led to the invasion of Bosnia by the Serbs, who found much support among the Bogomils, resentful of the Catholic proclivities of their rulers. The conquest of Bosnia was not completed because of Dushan's diversion elsewhere.

1353. Dushan defeated Louis of Hungary, who had been instigated by the pope to lead a Catholic crusade. The Serbs now acquired Belgrade.

1355. Dushan died at the age of 46 as he was en route to Constantinople. Thus perished his hope of succeeding to the imperial throne and consolidating the Bal-

kans in the face of the growing power of the Ottoman Turks (p. 325).

1355-1371. Stephen Urosh V, a weak ruler who was faced, from the outset, by the disruptive ambitions of his uncle Simeon and other powerful magnates. He was the last of the Nemanyid house.

1358. Hungary obtained most of Dalmatia, after defeating Venice. Ragusa became a Hungarian protectorate.

1371. Battle of the Maritza River, in which the Turks, having settled in Thrace, defeated a combination of Serbian lords.

1371. Zeta (Montenegro) became a separate principality under the Balsha family (until 1421).

1371-1389. Lazar I, of the Hrebelyanovich family, became *Prince* of Serbia.

1375. The Greek patriarch finally recognized the Patriarchate of Peč.

1376. TVRTKO I, Lord of Bosnia from 1353-1391, proclaimed himself *King of Serbia and Bosnia*, taking over parts of western Serbia and controlling most of the Adriatic coast, excepting Zara and Ragusa. Tvrtko was the greatest of the Bosnian rulers and made his state for a time the strongest Slavic state in the Balkans.

1389, June 20 (traditional June 15). **BATTLE OF KOSSOVO,** a decisive date in all Balkan history. Prince Lazar, at the head of a coalition of Serbs, Bosnians, Albanians, and Wallachians, attempted to stop the advance of the Turks under Murad I. Murad was killed by a Serb who posed as a traitor, but his son Bayazid won a victory. Lazar was captured and killed, due to the reputed desertion of Vuk Brankovich. Henceforth Serbia was a vassal state of the Turks.

1389-1427. STEPHEN LAZAREVICH, the son of Lazar I. He was a literary person, but withal an able statesman. During the early years of his reign he loyally supported the Turks, being present with his forces at the **battles of Nicopolis** (1396) and **Angora** (1402). In return the Turks recognized him as *Despot of Serbia*, and supported him against Hungary and other enemies.

1391. Death of Tvrtko I of Bosnia; gradual disintegration of the Bosnian Kingdom.

1392. Venice acquired Durazzo, beginning the process of establishment on the Dalmatian and Albanian coasts. Scutari was acquired in 1396, and when, in 1420, Venice secured **Cattaro**, she possessed practically all the fortified coast towns.

1393. Hungary recovered Croatia and Dalmatia from the Bosnian Kingdom. Hungarian campaigns against Bosnia itself continued for years, until the native elements in 1416 called in the Turks.

1427-1456. GEORGE BRANKOVICH, the nephew of Stephen Lazarevich, Despot of Serbia. He built himself a new capital at Semendria (Smederovo) on the Danube and attempted, with Hungarian support, to hold his own against the Turks. This policy led to a Turk invasion (1439) and conquest of the country, the Hungarians, however, saving Belgrade. But in 1444 Brankovich, with the aid of **John Hunyadi** (p. 318), recovered his possessions and the Serbian state was recognized in the **Treaty of Szegedin.** Thereafter Brankovich deserted Hunyadi and tried to maintain himself through close relations with the Turks.

1456-1458. Lazar III, the son of George Brankovich. On his death he left his kingdom to

1458-1459. Stephen Tomashevich, the heir to the Bosnian throne. Stephen, as a Roman Catholic, was much disliked by the Serbs, who consequently offered less resistance to the Turks.

1459. The Turks definitively conquered and incorporated Serbia with the empire.

1463. The Turks overran and conquered Bosnia.

1483. Turkish conquest of Herzegovina (Hun).

1499. Conquest of Zeta (Montenegro) by the Turks.

f. THE EASTERN EMPIRE, 1261-1453

After the recapture of Constantinople by the Greeks in 1261, the **Empire of the Palaeologi** was still a relatively small domain, consisting of the former Nicaean Empire, the city of Constantinople and its immediate surroundings, the coastal part of Thrace, southern Macedonia with Thessalonica, the islands of Imbros, Samothrace, Lesbos, and Rhodes. In Anatolia the northeastern part was still held by the Greek Empire of Trebizond, which in the course of the 13th century had managed to hold a balance between the Seljuk Turks and the Mongols and had become the great entrepôt of the eastern trade coming to the Black Sea by way of Persia and Armenia. The city and the court reached its

highest prosperity and brilliance under the Emperor **Alexius II** (1297-1330), whose reign was followed by a period of dynastic and factional struggle, marked by unbelievable degeneracy and cruelty. The reign of **John Alexius III** (1350-1390) marked a second period of splendor, but the 15th century was one of decline. The empire came to an end with the Ottoman conquest in 1461 (last ruler, **David,** 1458-1461).

The European territories of the earlier empire were divided between the Greek Despotate of Epirus and the Greek Duchy of Neopatras (Thessaly, Locris), the Latin Duchy of Athens, the Latin Principality of Achaia, and the Venetian Duchy of the Archipelago.

1261-1282. MICHAEL VIII (*Palaeologus*). He was the ablest of the Paleologi, a man who devoted himself to the restoration of Byzantine authority throughout the Balkan area, persisting despite many setbacks.

1261. Michael established a foothold in the southeastern part of the Peloponnese (Morea), which was widely expanded in the ensuing period. **Mistra** (Misithra) became the capital of a flourishing principality and one of the great centers of late-Byzantine culture.

1262. Michael II of Epirus was forced to recognize the suzerainty of the Constantinople emperor. In a series of campaigns much of the despotate was regained for the empire (Janina taken, 1265).

1264-1265. Constant raids of the Bulgars into Thrace led to a formidable campaign against them and the reconquest of part of Macedonia.

1266. **Charles of Anjou** became King of Sicily. He made an alliance with Baldwin II, the last Latin emperor, and, through the marriage of his son with the heiress of the Villehardouins, extended his authority over Achaia. He soon became the most formidable opponent of the Greeks, for by the **Treaty of Viterbo** (1267) he took over the claims of Baldwin II.

1267. Michael permitted the Genoese to establish themselves at Galata, across from Constantinople. This was part of his policy of encouraging the Genoese at the expense of the Venetians, to whom, however, he had to grant privileges also (1268).

1271. **Death of Michael II of Epirus.** Charles of Anjou had already taken Corfu (1267) and now undertook the conquest of the Epiran coast, the essential base for any advance on Thessalonica and

Constantinople. Durazzo was taken in 1272. John Angelus, driven out of Epirus, set up as Lord of Neopatras (to 1295). Nicephorus I was the titular ruler of a much-reduced Epiran state (to 1296). Charles of Anjou proclaimed himself *King of Albania* and entered into alliance with the Serbs, who had begun the construction of a large state by advancing down the Vardar Valley.

1274. THE COUNCIL OF LYON. Michael, in order to escape from the Angevin danger, accepted the Roman creed and the primacy of the pope, thus effecting the reunion with Rome. This move, purely political in intent, met with vigorous resistance on the part of the Orthodox Greek clergy and in the long run only served to accentuate the antagonism of Greek and Latin.

1274. Campaigns of Michael against the Angevins in Epirus. These campaigns were carried on year after year, with varying success.

1278. The death of William of Villehardouin, Prince of Achaia, gave the Greeks an opportunity to expand their holding in the southeastern part.

1281. Michael VIII won a great victory over the Angevins at Berat. Thereupon Charles made an alliance with the papacy and with Venice, with which the Serbs and Bulgars were associated. Michael in reply effected a rapprochement with Peter of Aragon.

1282. The Sicilian Vespers (p. 290). This blow at the Angevin power in Sicily served to relieve the pressure on the Greek Empire.

1282-1328. ANDRONICUS II, the son of Michael, a learned, pious, but weak ruler, whose first move was to give up the hated union

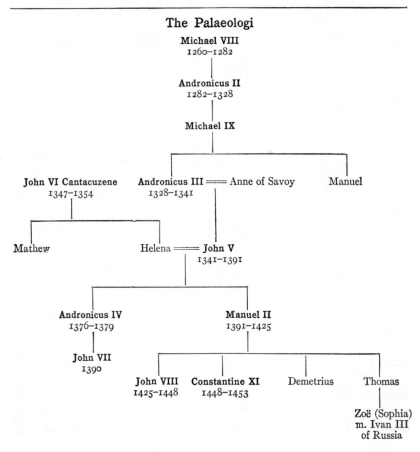

The Palaeologi

Michael VIII
1260–1282

Andronicus II
1282–1328

Michael IX

John VI Cantacuzene
1347–1354

Andronicus III === Anne of Savoy
1328–1341

Manuel

Mathew

Helena === John V
1341–1391

Andronicus IV
1376–1379

Manuel II
1391–1425

John VII
1390

John VIII
1425–1448

Constantine XI
1448–1453

Demetrius

Thomas

Zoë (Sophia)
m. Ivan III
of Russia

with Rome and conciliate the Orthodox clergy.

1285. Venice deserted the Angevin alliance and made a ten-year peace with the Greeks.

1295-1320. MICHAEL IX, son of Andronicus, co-emperor with his father.

1296. The Serbs, continuing their advance, conquered western Macedonia and northern Albania. Andronicus was obliged to recognize these losses (1298).

1302. Peace between the Angevins and the Aragonese. Andronicus, once again exposed to Angevin ambition, engaged Roger de Flor and 6000 Catalan mercenaries (the *Catalan Company*) to fight against the Italians. They raised havoc at Constantinople, where 3000 Italians are said to have been killed in the disorders.

1304. The Catalans repulsed an attack of the Turks on Philadelphia, but they then turned and attacked Constantinople (1305–1307), without being able to take it.

1305. Murder of Roger de Flor. The Catalan Company became a veritable scourge, roaming through Thrace and Macedonia and laying the country waste.

1311. The Catalans, having advanced into Greece, took the Duchy of Athens, where they set up a dynasty of their own.

1321-1328. Civil war between the emperor and his grandson Andronicus. In the course of the struggle much of the empire was devastated.

1325. Andronicus was obliged to accept his grandson as co-emperor.

1326. RISE OF THE OTTOMAN TURKS in northwestern Anatolia. In 1326 they took Brusa from the Greeks, and in 1328 Nicomedia (p. 325).

1328-1341. ANDRONICUS III, the grandson of Andronicus II, who finally forced the emperor's abdication (d. 1332). Andronicus III was a frivolous and irresponsible ruler, wholly unequal to the great problems presented by the rise of the Turkish and Serb powers (Sultan Orkhan, 1326–1359; Tsar Stephen Dushan, 1331–1355).

1329. The Greeks managed to take the important island of Chios from the Genoese.

1330. The Serbs defeated the Bulgars in a decisive battle and put an end to the Bulgar power.

1334-1335. Andronicus conquered Thessaly and part of Epirus from the despot, John II Orsini.

1336. The Greeks reconquered Lesbos.

1340. Stephen Dushan, having conquered the Albanian coastal territory (as far as Valona) from the Angevins, drove the Greeks out of the interior and took Janina.

1341-1376. JOHN V, the son of Andronicus III, ascended the throne as a child, under the regency of his mother, Anna of Savoy.

1341-1347. CIVIL WAR IN THE EMPIRE. John Cantacuzene, supported by the aristocratic elements, set himself up as a rival emperor. John V was supported by the popular elements. In the ensuing war much of Thrace and Macedonia was ravaged. The war proved to be the undoing of the empire, since both sides freely called in Serbs or Turks to support them.

1341-1351. THE HESYCHAST CONTROVERSY in the Greek Church, which added to the confusion. The controversy was really a conflict between the mystic teachings emanating from the monasteries of Mt. Athos (founded 962 ff.) and the rationalism of the clergy. The Hesychasts (*Zealots*) supported Cantacuzene and were victorious with him. In the interval the dispute led to a great popular, almost socialistic rising in Thessalonica, where the extremists set up an almost independent state (1342–1347).

1343. The Venetians, taking advantage of the civil war, seized Smyrna.

1346. Stephen Dushan was crowned Emperor of the Serbs and the Greeks and made preparations to seize Constantinople and replace the Greek dynasty.

1347. Cantacuzene managed to take Constantinople, through treachery.

1347-1354. JOHN VI (*Cantacuzene*), sole emperor. He made his son Manuel despot of the Morea (1348). The Serbs held all of Macedonia.

1351. Stephen Dushan besieged Thessalonica.

1353. The Ottoman Turks, called in by Cantacuzene, defeated the Serbs.

1354. The Turks established themselves in Europe, at Gallipoli, thus beginning their phenomenal career of expansion (p. 325).

1355. John V took Constantinople and forced the abdication of Cantacuzene (d. 1383). At the same time Dushan, having taken Adrianople, was advancing on the capital. His sudden death (1355) led to the disintegration of the Serb Empire and to the removal of a great threat to the Greeks. On the other hand, it left the Christians an easier prey to the advancing Turks.

1365. The Turks, having overrun Thrace, took Adrianople, which became their capital.

1366. John V, who had been captured by Tsar Shishman of Bulgaria, was liberated by his cousin, Amadeo of Savoy.

1369. John V appeared before the pope at Avignon and agreed to union of the churches, in order to secure the aid of the west against the Turks.

1376-1379. ANDRONICUS IV, the son of John V, who dethroned his father with the aid of the Genoese.

1379-1391. John V, supported by the Turks, managed to recover his throne.

1386. The Venetians recovered Corfu, which they held until 1797.

1388. The Venetians purchased Argos and Nauplia.

1389. Battle of Kossovo (p. 319). End of the great Serb Empire.

1390. John VII, a grandson of John V, deposed the latter, but after a few months the old emperor was restored by his second son, Manuel.

1391-1425. MANUEL II, an able ruler in a hopeless position. By this time the empire had been reduced to the city of Constantinople, the city of Thessalonica, and the province of Morea. The Turks held Thrace and Macedonia.

1391-1395. The Turks, under Bayazid I, blockaded Constantinople, and only the Christian crusade that ended in the disastrous battle of Nicopolis (1396) gave the Greeks some respite.

1397. Bayazid attacked Constantinople, which was valiantly defended by Marshal Boucicault. This time the advance of the Tatars under Timur distracted the Turks. The defeat and capture of Bayazid in the battle of Angora (1402), led to a period of confusion and dynastic war among the Turks.

1422. The Turks again attacked Constantinople, because of Manuel's support of the Turkish pretender Mustapha, against Murad II.

1423. The Venetians bought the city of Thessalonica.

1425-1448. JOHN VIII, the son of Manuel, whose position was, from the outset, desperate.

1428. Constantine and Thomas Palaeologus, brothers of the emperor, conquered Frankish Morea, with the exception of the Venetian ports. In these last years the Morea was the most extensive and valuable part of the empire.

1430. The Turks took Thessalonica from the Venetians.

1439. THE COUNCIL OF FLORENCE. John VIII, having traveled to Italy, once again accepted the union with Rome and the papal primacy. As on earlier occasions this step raised a storm of opposition among the Greeks and to some extent facilitated the Turk conquests.

1444. A second crusade from the west ended in disaster when the Turks won a decisive victory at Varna.

1446. The Turks frustrated an attempt of the Greeks to expand from the Morea into central Greece. Corinth fell into Turkish hands.

1448-1453. CONSTANTINE XI, the last Byzantine emperor.

1453. The siege and capture of Constantinople by Mohammed the Conqueror (p. 326). End of Eastern Empire after a thousand years of existence.

1460. Conquest of the Morea by the Turks. End of the rule of the Palaeologi in Greece.

1461. Conquest of the Empire of Trebizond, the last Greek state, by the Turks.

BYZANTINE CULTURE in the time of the Palaeologi. The territorial and political decline of the empire was accompanied by an extraordinary cultural revival, analogous to the Renaissance in Italy. The schools of Constantinople flourished and produced a group of outstanding scholars (philosophy: **Planudes, Plethon, Bessarion**). In theology the dominant current was one of mysticism (**Gregory Palamas** and the *Hesychasts*; **George Scholarius**). Historical writing reached a high plane in the work of **John Cantacuzene, Nicephorus Gregoras**, and, in the last years of the empire, of **Phrantzes, Ducas, and Chalcocondylas**. Art, especially painting, was distinctly humanized and three different schools (Constantinople, Macedonia, and Crete) cast a flood of splendor over the closing years of the empire. **Mistra**, the capital of the Morean province, became in the early 15th century the center of a revived Greek national feeling and a home of scholars and artists.

Conquests of the
Ottoman Turks, 1418

Danube
Vienna
HUNGARY
Szeged
MOLDAVIA
Buda
Belgrade
CROATIA
WALLACHIA
Semendria 1462
CRIMEA
Kaffa
SERBIA 1459
Vidin
DOBRUJA
Ragusa
BOSNIA 1463
Nish
Kosowo 1389
Sofia 1382
BULGARIA
Varna
Cernomen 1371
RUMELIA
BLACK SEA
Sinope
MACEDONIA
Scutari
Kroia
ALBANIA
THRACE
Constantinople 1453
Adrianople
Trapezunt
Durazzo
Salonika
Gallipoli
Nicaea
Nicomedia
ARMENIA
Otranto
EPIRUS 1449
Arta
Negroponte 1470
Brusa 1326
Angora 1402
Erzinjan
Corfu
Athens
Smyrna 1424
ANATOLIA
Malatia
Corinth 1460
MOREA
Mistra
KARAMAN 1466
MESOPOTAMIA
Rhodes
Euphrates R.
CRETE
(to Venice)
CYPRUS
Famagusta
SYRIA
Aleppo
ARABIA
(to Venice)

Wall of 450
Golden Horn
Pera
Galata
Chain 1453
BOSPORUS
Constantinople
Scutari
(Chrysopolis)
Old Serai
New Serai
Sta. Sophia
Chalcedon
1 mile

Raisz

g. THE OTTOMAN EMPIRE; 1300-1481

The presence of the Turks in central Asia can be traced back to at least the 6th century A.D. (**Orchon inscriptions**, dealing with the period 630–680). These Turks, of the Oghuz family, were conquered by the Uighurs in 745 and continued under their rule until 840, when they in turn were conquered by the Kirghiz, coming from the west. In the 9th and 10th centuries the Turks were converted to Islam, and in the 11th century, having pushed their advance into southeastern Russia and Iran, began to attack the Byzantine Empire. The **Seljuks**, a branch of the Turks, took Baghdad in 1055, and in the following two centuries built up an imposing empire in Anatolia and the Middle East (p. 254).

1243. **The Mongols** defeated the Seljuks at **Kösedagh.** Anatolia under Mongol suzerainty; disintegration of the Seljuk Empire in Anatolia; appearance of local dynasties in many places, especially along the Aegean coast.

1289. Traditional date of the **death of Ertogrul,** half-legendary leader of a Turkish tribe serving as frontier guards on the border of the Byzantine Empire.

1290-1326. **OSMAN** (Othman) I, traditional founder of the Ottoman dynasty. He continued the work of his father, but gradually extended his territory at the expense of the Byzantine Empire, which was weakened by the transfer of many of its frontier guards to the Balkans. The Turks were almost certainly more civilized and less nomadic than has generally been supposed. There is evidence to show that Osman had at his command well-organized forces (*Akhi*, a type of semireligious and possibly mercantile as well as military society). But the Turkish advance seems to have taken the form of gradual infiltration more than outright conquest.

1317-1326. Siege of Brusa by the Ottoman Turks. The town was finally starved into submission.

1326-1359. **ORKHAN I,** the first well-authenticated ruler and obviously the organizer of the empire.

1329. The Turks defeated a Byzantine force under Andronicus III at **Maltepe.**

1331. Nicaea taken by the Turks.

1337 or 1338. Nicomedia (Ismid) taken by the Turks.

1345. The Ottomans first crossed into Europe, called in by the Emperor John Cantacuzene, to support his claims against the Empress Anna. Orkhan married Theodora, daughter of Cantacuzene.

1349. The Turks again called in by Cantacuzene, to aid him against the Serbian conqueror, Stephen Dushan.

1354. **First settlement of the Turks in Europe** (Tzympe, on Gallipoli), as a result of a third appeal by Cantacuzene for aid. They spread rapidly through Thrace. On Orkhan's death the state was already well-organized (first Ottoman coins) and the Turkish ruler was able to dictate to the Byzantine emperors.

1359-1389. MURAD I.

1365. Adrianople taken by the Turks, who soon made it their capital (1366), replacing Brusa. Organization of the Janissary corps (date uncertain) composed of captives taken in war, and later of levies of Christian children.

1365. Ragusa made a commercial treaty with the Turks, paying tribute.

1366. **Crusade of Amadeus of Savoy.** He took Gallipoli, but was soon obliged to abandon it. Victory of Louis of Hungary near Vidin.

1369-1372. Conquest of Bulgaria to the Balkan Mountains. Shishman, ruler of Bulgaria, became a vassal of the Turks.

1371. Defeat of the Serbs by the Turks at **Cernomen** on the Maritza River; conquest of Macedonia by the Turks. Raids into Albania and Greece. Continued interference of the Turks in Byzantine affairs.

1385. Capture of Sofia by the Turks.

1386. Capture of Nish. Lazar of Serbia became a Turkish vassal.

1387. Genoa made a treaty with Murad.

1388. Venice made a treaty with the Turks.

1389, June 20 (June 15 traditional). **BATTLE OF KOSSOVO.** Murad defeated a coalition of Serbs, Bulgars, Bosnians, Wallachians, and Albanians. Lazar was killed in battle, Murad assassinated just after it, by a Serb.

1389-1402. BAYAZID I. He began his career by having his brother Yakub strangled. The Serbs were treated leniently and Bayazid turned his attention to Anatolia.

1391. Invasion of Karamania (the leading Anatolian emirate) by Bayazid, who conquered part of it. Several of the other emirates peacefully absorbed. By 1395 the Ottoman Empire extended east to Sivas.

1391-1398. First siege of Constantinople by the Turks. Bayazid made and unmade emperors and extracted a heavy tribute.

1396. CRUSADE OF NICOPOLIS, led by Sigismund of Hungary, supported by Balkan rulers and by French, German, and English knights, as well as by the Roman and Avignon popes. Venice and Genoa negotiated with both sides. The knights assembled with great pomp at Buda and proceeded along the Danube of Nicopolis, pillaging and slaying. On Sept. 25 they met the Turks about four miles south of Nicopolis. The knights ignored all advice and pressed forward; after an initial success they were completely overwhelmed and many captured. Forces were about 20,000 on each side.

1397. Invasion of Greece by the Turks, who advanced as far as Corinth, though they did not take Athens.

1400. Invasion of Anatolia by the Mongols under **Timur** (p. 330). They took Sivas. Provocative attitude of Bayazid.

1402, July 20. BATTLE OF ANGORA (Ankara). Bayazid, deserted by most of his Turkish vassals, was completely defeated and captured. Timur restored many of the Turkish emirs and advanced to Nicaea and Brusa. The Ottoman Empire on the verge of dissolution. Dispute of Bayazid's sons for the succession.

1403. **Mohammed** defeated his brother **Musa** and became sultan of the remaining Asiatic possessions (retirement of Timur from Anatolia, 1403). **Suleiman** became sultan of the European territory.

1405. Suleiman crossed to Anatolia and drove Mohammed into the mountains. Most of the emirs reinstituted by Timur were reduced to obedience.

1406. On Suleiman's return to Europe, Mohammed regained control in Anatolia. He sent his brother Musa to Wallachia to attack Suleiman from the north.

1410. Musa took Adrianople, but was defeated by Suleiman.

1411. Suleiman, having returned to Anatolia, was captured and strangled. His place in Europe was taken by Musa.

1413. Mohammed crossed to Europe, defeated and killed Musa, and reestablished his power over the whole empire.

1413-1421. MOHAMMED I (*the Restorer*). He devoted most of his energy to consolidating his authority

1416. First war with Venice, due chiefly to Turkish activity in the Aegean. The Doge Loredano destroyed a Turkish fleet off Gallipoli, whereupon Mohammed wisely made peace.

1421-1451. MURAD II.

1422. Mustafa, a supposed son of Bayazid, supported by the Greek emperor, **Manuel II**, defeated Murad's troops near Adrianople, but failed to get any support from Anatolia. He was ultimately captured and executed. Murad, in revenge, began to besiege Constantinople, but soon gave up the attempt.

1423. The Venetians took over Saloniki from the Greeks, as part of a plan of co-operation against the Turks.

1425-1430. War between Venice and the Turks. A Turkish fleet ravaged the Aegean stations of Venice, and in 1430 the Turks took Saloniki. They then conquered most of Albania and Epirus. The Venetians, having become involved in war with Milan, were forced to make peace.

1442. The Turks, having invaded Hungary, were defeated by **John Hunyadi**, a frontier lord of uncertain origin, most famous of the fighters against the Turks.

1443. Crusade against the Turks, instigated by the pope and composed of Hungary, Poland, Bosnia, Wallachia, and Serbia. The crusaders, led by Hunyadi, took Nish and advanced to Sofia. Murad thereupon made the ten-year **Truce of Szegedin**, with **Vladislav** of Hungary; by it Serbia was freed and Wallachia abandoned to Hungary.

1444. Murad voluntarily abdicated in favor of his fourteen-year-old son, Mohammed. The Hungarians, encouraged by the pope, thereupon broke the truce and renewed the crusade (Sept.). They advanced through Bulgaria to Varna, where they were to meet the ships of Venice that were to carry them to Constantinople. But the Venetians stayed at Gallipoli and did not even prevent Murad from crossing from Anatolia. Murad resumed the throne and on Nov. 10 completely defeated the crusaders at **Varna** (Vladislav killed).

1448, Oct. 17. Second battle of Kossovo. Murad defeated Hunyadi, who had again invaded Serbia.

1451-1481. MOHAMMED II (*the Conqueror*). He was only 21 when he succeeded his father, but seems to have been unusually well-educated and, like others of the early sultans, a man of pronounced intellectual tastes. From the very outset he devoted his attention to the capture of Constantinople, the center of intrigue against Turkish rule.

1452. Mohammed completed the **Castle of Europe** (*Rumili Hissar*) at the narrowest point of the Bosporus, opposite the older **Castle of Asia** (*Anadoli Hissar*). This assured freedom of passage between Anatolia and Europe and at the same time controlled the supplies of Constantinople. Its erection led to war with the Byzantine emperor, Constantine.

1453, Feb.-May. SIEGE OF CONSTANTINOPLE, at that time largely depopulated and very poor. Constantine had only some 10,000 men at his command and was unpopular because of his efforts to reunite the eastern and western churches. He received some aid from the Venetians and Genoese, but his chief asset was the tremendous wall-system of the city. The Turks concentrated between 100,000 and 150,000 men outside the city. They had a substantial fleet, but this was shut out from the Golden Horn by an iron chain. Most important was the heavy artillery, built by a Hungarian renegade, Urban, for Mohammed. The walls were continually bombarded, but the defenders managed to close the breaches. Finally Mohammed had some 70 light ships dragged overland from the Bosporus to the Golden Horn. These forced the defenders to divide their attention. On May 29 the Turks delivered a great attack on the Romanos Gate and forced an entry. Constantine was killed in the mêlée and many of the defenders escaped on Venetian and Genoese ships. The city was given up to pillage for three days. Mohammed tried at first to populate it with Turks, but had indifferent success. He then repopulated it with Greeks and other Christians, chiefly artisans, and gave the Greek patriarch, **Gennadios,** considerable civil as well as religious authority over the Orthodox inhabitants throughout the empire. Somewhat later similar authority over the Armenian community was given to the Armenian patriarch (millet system). Constantinople (Istambul) soon became the Turkish capital. Churches were transformed into mosques (notably **Santa Sophia**) and palaces built (**Old Serai**, completed 1458; **New Serai**, completed 1467). The seat of government became more firmly fixed and Mohammed evolved a complete administrative system, with an elaborate system of training (palace school; slave household). Much of the court ceremonial was borrowed from the Greeks, though the institutions were fundamentally Turk.

1456. Mohammed besieged Belgrade, after repeated raids by Hunyadi, who relieved the city, but died soon afterward (Aug.). Thereupon Mohammed subdued Serbia (1456–1458) and Bosnia and Herzegovina (1458–1461), where many of the upper classes accepted Islam. In the same years the Turkish fleet took most of the Genoese stations in the Aegean and an army overran the Morea, deposing the last Palaeologi.

1456-1463. The Albanian campaign, against **Scanderbeg** (George Castriota), a *condottiere* educated at the Turkish court, who had escaped in 1443. Scanderbeg was in the pay of Alphonse of Aragon-Naples until 1458 and thereafter in the pay of Venice. He was repeatedly driven back by the Turks, but from his stronghold at Kroia he maintained a vigorous resistance. When he died (1467), Albania was quickly conquered and incorporated in the empire.

1463-1479. FIRST GREAT WAR BETWEEN THE TURKS AND VENICE, resulting from interference with trade and from the Turkish threat to the Venetian stations on the Greek and Albanian coasts. The humanist pope, Aeneas Silvius (Pius II), attempted to organize a crusade and Hungary joined Venice. But only a small and miscellaneous force was collected at Ancona.

1468. The Turks raided Dalmatia and invaded Croatia.

1470, July. The Turks, with a huge fleet and landing force, conquered Negroponte (Euboea) from the Venetians.

1473. The Venetians induced the Persians to attack the Turks, while they raided the Anatolian coasts. The Persians were defeated at Erzingan.

1477-1478. The Turks took Kroia, Alessio, and Drivasto in Albania. Scutari was twice besieged and Turkish raiders reached the very outskirts of Venice.

1479. Peace between **Venice** and the **Turks.** The Venetians gave up Scutari and their Albanian stations, but they kept Dulcigno, Antivari, and Durazzo; they gave up Negroponte and Lemnos and paid an annual tribute of 10,000 ducats for permission to trade in the Black Sea.

1480. A Turkish force occupied **Otranto** in southern Italy.

1480-1481. Siege of **Rhodes**, held by the Knights of St. John, last Christian outpost in the eastern Mediterranean. Mohammed died before the siege could be successfully completed.

(*Cont. p.* 420.)

D. AFRICA DURING THE MIDDLE AGES

AFRICA

(For the history of Mediterranean Africa see pp. 262-263)

The earliest history of Africa is shrouded in obscurity. In the north the original inhabitants appear to have been of some white stock (the ancestors of the Berbers), while south of the Sahara the country was populated by Negrillos, a small race of Negroes of whom the Pygmies, Bushmen, and Hottentots are probably the descendants. The Negrillos were evidently pushed to the northwest and south by a great invasion (possibly c. 30,000 B.C.) of a larger Negro race arriving from the other side of the Indian Ocean and landing on the central part of the eastern coast. From the newcomers the Bantu derive. A second great invasion from overseas followed and pushed the Negrillos even farther to the west, though there seems to have been much intermixture in the region north of the equator, forming the various Sudanese tribes. In all likelihood there was also a good deal of infiltration of Semitic stocks into the northern part of the continent, both west (Carthage) and east (Syria). The earlier inhabitants were chiefly hunters, but the Negro invaders brought pastoral and agricultural pursuits and introduced polished stone and iron. Very few monuments of the earlier ages have survived. The great stone ruins (**Zimbabwe**) of Rhodesia have been variously dated from the 10th century B.C. to the 15th century A.D. They may have been built by the Bantu, though the weight of expert opinion seems to favor the Sabeans from the Yemen (10th century A.D.) or Dravidians from India.

c. 1st to 6th century A.D. The Kingdom of Axum in northern Ethiopia and in southwestern Arabia (obelisks of Axum); direct contact with the Greek world; conversion of the country to Christianity by **Frumentius** (early 4th century). The connection with the Christian east was broken by the Arab conquests (640–).

640-710. CONQUEST OF NORTH AFRICA BY THE ARABS, beginning with Egypt and spreading westward (p. 184 et seq.).

c. 980. Settlement of Arabs from Muscat and Persians from Shiraz and Bushire along the eastern coast, south as far as Cape Corrientes. They founded the towns of Mogdishu, Melinde, Mombasa, Kilwa (Quiloa), and Sofala and traded with the natives of the interior in slaves, ivory, and gold that was shipped to India and Arabia.

10th century. Apogee of the Kingdom of Ghana (capital Kumbi), which had been founded in the 4th century, supposedly by people of Semitic extraction. It extended from near the Atlantic coast almost to Timbuktu and was an essentially Negro state consisting of a group of federated tribes with a surprisingly developed culture (visits of the Arabs Ibn Haukal and Masudi in the late 10th century). There appears to have been an active trade with Morocco by way of the Sahara.

1054. Beginning of the **Islamic conquest** of West Africa by the Almoravids under Abdallah ben Yassin. Several of the native dynasties were converted, though the masses appear to have retained their original beliefs.

1076. The Almoravids pillaged Kumbi, the capital of Ghana, which never entirely recovered. Its decline was evidently hastened by the growing barrenness of the region. The **breakup of the Ghana Empire** led to the formation (11th century) of succession states (Diara, which existed till 1754), Soso, the two Mossi states south of the bend of the Niger, and Manding. The ruler of Manding was converted to Islam, as was also the ruler of Songhoy, a great empire which sprang up (c. 690) on the middle Niger and came to divide West Africa with Manding.

1203. Sumanguru, greatest of the rulers of Soso, plundered Kumbi.

1224. Sumanguru conquered and annexed Manding.

1235. Sun Diata, powerful king of the Mandingos, defeated the ruler of Soso and re-established his independence. In 1240 he destroyed Kumbi.

1307-1332. Apogee of the Mandingo Empire under Gongo Musa, who extended his dominions until they covered most of West Africa, after defeating and subjecting the Songhoy Empire (1325). Brilliant culture of Timbuktu (founded 12th cent.).

1352-1353. The great Arab traveler, **Ibn Batuta,** having crossed the Sahara, visited the Mandingo Empire, of which he wrote a description.

1433. The Tuaregs from the Sahara took and sacked Timbuktu.

1433. The Portuguese explorers first rounded Cape Bojador, beginning a long series of expeditions along the coast (p. 363).

1468. The Songhoy ruler recaptured Timbuktu from the Tuaregs.

1471. The Portuguese founded the post of San Jorge d'el Mina on the Guinea coast.

1487. The Portuguese reached Timbuktu overland from the coast.

1490. The Portuguese ascended the Congo for about 200 miles and converted the King of the Congo Empire (14th cent.-). They established a post at São Salvador and exercised a wide influence in the region until the end of the 16th century.

1493-1529. Greatness of the Songhoy Empire under **Askia Mohammed,** who conquered the larger part of the Mandingo Empire and pushed his conquests to the east beyond the Niger. Visit of Leo Africanus (1507).

1505-1507. The Portuguese took Sofala and Kilwa from the Arabs and founded Mozambique. In 1513 they ascended the Zambezi, establishing posts at Sena and Tete. Missionaries probably penetrated much of the hinterland, but details are not known.

(*Cont. p.* 363.)

E. ASIA DURING THE MIDDLE AGES

1. PERSIA

1349. The end of the troubled reign of **Nushirwan** was also the end of the dynasty of the Il-Khans of Persia. They were succeeded by

1336-1411. The Jalayrs, in Iraq and Azerbaijan;

1313-1393. The Muzaffarids in Fars, Kirman and Kurdistan;

1337-1381. The Sarbadarids in Khorasan. The Muzaffarids and Sarbadarids were overthrown by Timur, and the Jalayrs by

1378-1469. The **Turkomans of the Black Sheep,** who ruled Azerbaijan and Armenia until they were succeeded by

1387-1502. The **Turkomans of the White Sheep.**

1369-1405. TIMUR (*Tamerlane*), the vizier of the Mongol Chagatay Khan Suyurghatmish, usurped the power of his master. Between the years 1380 and 1387 he overran Khorasan, Jurjan, Mazandaran, Sijistan, Afghanistan, Fars, Azerbaijan, and Kurdistan. In 1391 he completely defeated Toqtamish, the Khan of the Golden Horde.

1393. Timur took Baghdad and reduced Mesopotamia. After an invasion of India (1397) he marched against Anatolia and routed the Ottoman Turks at **Angora** (p. 326). The empire of the Timurids (until 1500) was soon restricted to Transoxania and eastern Persia.

1404-1447. SHAH RUKH, fourth son of Timur, whose reign was noted for its splendor. He carried on successful campaigns against Kara Yusuf, head of the Turkoman dynasty of the Black Sheep (1390-1420), who ruled Azerbaijan, Shirvan, and other regions of the northwest. Kara Yusuf was obliged to recognize the suzerainty of the Timurids, though Kara

Yusuf and his successor, Kara Iskender (1420-1438), and Jehan Shah (1435-1467) were effective rulers of all northwestern Persia. Jehan Shah for a brief period (1458) held even Herat.

1452-1469. Abu Said, last of the Timurid dynasty. This period was marked by the great expansion of the Turkoman power under

1453-1478. UZUN HASAN, of the dynasty of the White Sheep. This dynasty had established itself under Hasan's grandfather, Osman Beg Kara Iluk (d. 1435) and ruled the territory about Diabekr. Hasan rapidly extended his authority over Armenia and Kurdistan. His defeat by the Ottoman Turks (1461) turned his attention eastward, and led to five large-scale raids into Georgia.

1467. Uzun Hasan defeated and killed Jehan Shah of the Black Sheep and took over his territories.

1469. Uzun defeated, captured, and killed Abu Said, the Timurid sultan, who had marched against him. Thereupon Hasan became effective ruler of Armenia, Kurdistan, Azerbaijan, and Iran. He entered with Venice into a treaty directed against the Ottoman Turks, but the artillery that was sent him never reached him, and he was defeated by Mohammed II in

1473. The battle of Ersindjan. On his death he was succeeded by his son

1478-1490. JAQUB, who continued his father's policies and gave the country firm and enlightened rule.

1492-1497. RUSTAM SHAH, who succeeded to the throne after a severe dynastic conflict. His death was followed by confusion and by the emergence of the new Safavid dynasty, under Shah Ismail.

(*Cont. p.* 526.)

2. INDIA

a. NORTHERN INDIA

The **White Huns** or Hephthalites, a branch of the Mongol Juan-juan who dominated Central Asia (407-553), had oc-

cupied Bactria (425) and, after defeat by Sassanid Bahram Gor (428), Gandhara. Victory over Sassanid Peroz (484) freed them for raids from the Punjab into Hindustan.

c. 500-502. Toramana ruled as far as Eran (E. Malwa, inscrip. of his 1st year).

502-c. 528. Mikirakula from Sialkot controlled Gwalior (inscrip. of 15th year) and Kashmir. Bhanugupta probably expelled him from Eran (510). Yasodharman of Mandasor (?) boasts (533) of victory over him. Although the Huns in Central Asia were crushed by Turks and Sassanians (553-567), their chiefs kept rank in the Punjab and Rajputana till the 11th century.

606-647. HARSHA, fourth King of Thaneswar north of Delhi (new era Oct. 606), succeeded his brother-in-law as King of Kanauj (royal title 612), and quickly conquered an empire across northern India, to which he left no heir. He received an embassy (643) from the Emperor T'ang T'ai-tsung. A poet and dramatist, he patronized men of letters. He is well known through Bana's poetic romance *Harshacharita*, which is fashionably studded with recondite vocabulary drawn from lexicons of rare words; and by the *Hsi yü chi* (*Record of Western Lands*) of his guest, the pilgrim Hsüan-tsang, whose exact observations in India (630-643) have given priceless guidance to modern archaeology. Hsüan-tsang too, after long study at Nalanda, brought together in his *Vijnaptimatratasiddhi*, the classic anthology of texts and comment of the Yogachara or Dharmalakshana school.

Tantrism meanwhile sought to secure for its adepts in magic arts, through esoteric texts (*tantra*) and charms, rapid attainment of Buddhahood or at least supernatural powers. Partial syncretism with Sivaism led to a cult of Vairochana and various new divinities, largely terrible or erotic. Spells (*dharanis*) appear early (Ch. trans. 4th cent.), but the *Panchakrama* is in part the work of Sakyamitra (c. 850). Tantrism seems to have flourished chiefly along the northern borderland. Buddhism, however, progressively disappeared from India from the 9th century, lingering in Bengal and Bihar until the Moslem conquest (1202). It was largely absorbed by Hinduism or united with it.

647. A second Chinese embassy, under Wang Hsüan-tse, having been attacked by a usurper on a local throne (Tirhut, north of Patna ?), secured 7000 troops from Amsuvarman, King of Nepal, and 1200 from his son-in-law, Srongtsan-sgampo, King of Tibet; captured the malefactor, and haled him to Ch'angan (648).

c. 730-c. 740. YASOVARMAN, King of Kanauj, an author, patronized the Prakrit poet **Vakpatiraja** and **Bhavabhuti,** a Sanskrit dramatist ranked by Indian criticism next to **Kalidasa.**

c. 725-1197. The Pala Buddhist kings ruled Bengal (till c. 1125) and Magadha. Leading rulers: Dharmapala (c. 770-c. 833), and Devapala (c. 883-c. 881), who endowed a monastery founded at Nalanda by Balaputradeva, King of Sumatra.

c. 1125-c. 1225? Senas from the Carnatic gradually advanced from North Orissa into Bengal.

c. 1169-c. 1199. Lakshmanasena patronized Jayadeva, whose *Gitagovinda*, mystic call to love of Krishna, is hailed by Keith as a world masterpiece in union of sound with sense. Tightening of caste restrictions was accompanied by origin of **kulinism:** prohibition of marriage of any girl below her own caste, which led to infanticide; and rise in caste by marriage to man of higher caste, which led to polygamy of high-caste husbands to collect dowries.

b. WESTERN INDIA

Western India, thanks to many impregnable fortresses in Rajputana, was usually divided among local dynasties from the time of the Gupta power to the advent of the Mohammedans.

c. 490-766. A dynasty of **Maitrakas,** foreigners of the Rajput type, usually independent at Valabhi in Surashtra, created a Buddhist scholastic center which rivaled Nalanda. Their gifts reveal that Buddhist images were honored with *puja* of the kind devoted to Hindu gods.

c. 550-861. THE **GURJARA** horde of central Asiatic nomads established a dynasty of twelve kings at Mandor in central Rajputana. Two retired to Jain contemplation, and a third to self-starvation.

712- **Arab raids** from Sind devastated Gujerat and Broach (724-743) and finally shattered the Maitraka dynasty (766).

c. 740-1036. THE **GURJARA-PRATHIHARA DYNASTY,** by uniting much of northern India, excluded the Moslems till the end of the 10th century. Prominent early rulers were Nagabhata I (c. 740-c. 760), who defeated the Arabs; Vatsaraja (c. 775-c. 800); and Nagabhata II (c. 800-836), conqueror of Kanauj.

746-c. 974. The Chapas (or Chapotkatas), a Gurjara clan, founded Anahillapura (or Anandapura, 746), the principal city of western India until the 15th century.

831-1310. A Dravidian dynasty of Chandellas (in present Bundelkhand) built numerous Vaishnava temples, notably at Khajuraho, under Yasovarman (c. 930–954) and Dhanga (954–1002).

c. 840–c. 890. Mihira, or Bhoja, devoted to Vishnu and the Sun, ruled from the Sutlej to the Narmada, but failed to subdue Kashmir.

c. 950–c. 1200. The Paramaras of Dhara, near Indore, were known for two rulers: Munja (974–c. 994) who invaded the Deccan, and Bhoja (c. 1018–1060), author of books on astronomy, poetics, and architecture, and founder of a Sanskrit college.

c. 974–c. 1240. The Chalukya or Solanki Rajput clan, led by Mularaja (known dates 974–995) ruled from Anahillapura over Surashtra and Mt. Abu.

977-1186. The Ghaznavid (Yamini) dynasty ruled at Ghazni and Lahore. It was founded by Subaktagin (977–997), a Turkish slave converted to Islam, who extended his rule from the Oxus to the Indus and broke the power of a Hindu confederacy which included King Jaipal of Bhatinda, the Gurjara-Prathihara King of Kanauj, and the Chandella King Dhanga.

998-1030. MAHMUD OF GHAZNI made 17 plundering raids into the Punjab (defeat of Jaipal, 1001) to Kangra (1009), Mathura and Kanauj (1018–19), Gwalior (1022), and Somnath (1024–26). Vast destruction, pillage of immensely rich Hindu temples, and wholesale massacre resulted only in enrichment of Ghazni and annexation of the Punjab. Ghazni, heir to the rich artistic heritage of the Samanids of northeastern Persia, was now one of the most brilliant capitals of the Islamic world. Alberuni (973–1048) of Khiva, the leading scientist of his time, followed Mahmud to the Punjab, learned Sanskrit, and wrote the invaluable *Tahkik-i Hind* (*Inquiry into India*).

1093-1143. The Chalukya ruler, Jayasimha Siddharaja, a patron of letters, although himself a Saiva, organized disputations on philosophy and religion, and favored a Jain monk, Hemachandra, who converted and dominated

1143-1172. Kumarapala. As a good Jain, he decreed respect for life (*ahimsa*), prohibited alcohol, dice, and animal fights, and rescinded a law for confiscation of property of widows without sons. He also built (c. 1169) a new edifice

about the Saiva temple of Somanatha, which had been reconstructed by Bhimadeva I (1022–1062) after destruction by the Moslems.

1151-1206. The Shansabani Persian Princes of Ghur (Ghor) having burned Ghazni (1151), drove the Yamini to the Punjab and deposed them there (1186).

1172-1176. Ajayapala, a Saiva reactionary, ordered the massacre of Jains and sack of their temples until he was assassinated, when Jain rule was restored under a mayor of the palace whose descendants displaced the dynasty (c. 1240).

Two Jain temples at Mt. Abu are the work of a governor, Vimala Saha (1031), and a minister Tejpala (1230). Built of white marble with a profusion of ornamented colonnades, brackets, and elaborately carved ceilings, they are the most elegant version of the northern or Indo-Aryan architectural style.

Kashmir, already (c. 100 A.D.) an important home of the Sarvastivadin Buddhist sect, remained a center for Buddhist studies (till the 10th cent.; degenerate before the Moslem conquest, 1340) and of Sanskrit literature (until today). Its history from c. 700 is rather fully known through the *Rajatarangini* of Kalhana (c. 1100), the sole early Indian historian who consulted literary sources and inscriptions but accepted even absurd tradition without criticism.

1175-1206. Mohammed of Ghur, Mu'izz-ud-Din, undertook conquest of Hindustan by capture of Multan and Uch. He ruled from Ghazni as governor for his elder brother, Ghiyas-ud-Din Mohammed, whom he succeeded as ruler of Ghur (1203).

1192. A battle at Taraori (14 m. from Thanesar) decisively crushed a new Hindu confederacy led by the Chauhan King of Ajmer and Delhi. Cumbersome traditional tactics, disunited command, and caste restrictions handicapped the Hindu armies in conflict with the mounted archers from the northwest. Victory led to occupation of Delhi (1193), to conquest of Bihar where the organized Buddhist community was extinguished (c. 1197), Bengal (c. 1199), and the Chandella state in Bundelkhand. Mohammed appointed Kutb-ud-din Aibak, a slave from Turkestan, viceroy of his Indian conquests, and left him full discretion (1192, confirmed 1195).

1206-1266. A dynasty of slave kings, the first of six to rule at Delhi (until 1526), was founded by Aibak (killed playing polo, 1210).

The numerically weak early Moslem rulers in India were forced to employ Hindu troops and civilian agents, welcome allegiance of Hindu landholders, and afford their native subjects much the same limited protection (including tacit religious toleration) and justice to which they were accustomed. Rebels, both Hindu and Moslem, were slaughtered with ruthless barbarity.

1211-1236. Shams-ud-din Iltutmish, ablest slave and son-in-law of Aibak, succeeded to his lands in the Ganges Valley only, but recovered the upper Punjab (1217), Bengal (1225), the lower Punjab with Sind (1228), and Gwalior after a long siege (Feb.–Dec. 1232). He advanced to sack Ujjain (1234).

1229. He was invested as Sultan of India by the Abbasid Caliph of Baghdad.

Islamic **architects** brought to India a developed tradition of a spacious, light, and airy prayer chamber covered by arch, vault, and dome, erected with aid of concrete and mortar, and ornamented solely with color and flat linear, usually conventional, decoration. This formula was applied with recognition of local structural styles and of the excellence of Hindu ornamental design. Aibak built at Delhi (1193–96) with the spoils of 27 temples a mosque of Hindu appearance to which he added (1198) an Islamic screen of arches framed with Indian carving. He began (before 1206) a tower for call to prayer, which was finished (1231–32) and named *Kutb Minar* to honor a Moslem saint (d. 1235) by Iltutmish, who also enlarged the mosque in strictly Islamic style.

Upon the death of Iltutmish actual power passed to a group of 40 Turks who divided all offices save that of sultan, and controlled the succession.

1266-1290. A new dynasty at Delhi was founded by **Balban** (d. 1287), a slave purchased by Iltutmish (1233); made chamberlain (1242), father-in-law and lieutenant (1249–52 and 1255–66) of King Mahmud (1246–1266). Balban as king, aided by an effective army and corps of royal news-writers, repressed the 40 nobles, ended highway robbery in south and east, and rebellion in Bengal. His son repelled the Mongols established in Ghazni (since 1221), but was killed by them (1285).

The **tomb of Balban** is the first structure in India built with true arches instead of Hindu corbelling.

1290-1320. The Khalji dynasty of Delhi was founded by **Firuz** of the Khalji tribe of Turks, long resident among the Afghans. Senile mildness led him to release in Bengal 1000 Thugs (murderers in honor of Siva's consort Kali) captured in Delhi.

1296-1316. Ala-ud-din, his nephew and murderer, bought allegiance with booty secured by surprise attack upon Devagiri in Maharashtra (1294–95). He consolidated the empire.

1297. He conquered and despoiled Gujarat with its rich port Cambay. Frequent revolts prompted a program of repression which included espionage; confiscation of wealth (esp. of Hindus), endowments and tax-exempt lands; prohibition of liquor and all social gatherings. Mongol invasions (1299 and 1303) led to

1303. Decrees which by fixing low prices for all products permitted reduction of army pay and increase of strength to nearly 500,000 cavalry. Mongol armies were destroyed (1304 and 1306) and expeditions, usually led by a eunuch, Kafur, entitled Malik Naib, effected

1305-1313. Conquest of Malwa (1305) and the Deccan: Devagiri (1306–1307, annexed 1313), Warangal (1308), the Hoysala capital at Dvarasamudra and that of the Pandyas at Madura (1310–11), and the central Deccan (1313), with enormous treasure.

The *Alai Darwaza* (1311), southern gateway of a proposed vast enlargement of Aibak's mosque, represents the finest ornamental architecture of the early Delhi sultanate, fortunately continued in Gujarat. **Amir Khusrav** (1253–1325), greatest Indian poet to write in Persian, was son of a Turk who had fled before Jenghiz Khan to Patiala. He was prolific as court poet to Ala-ud-din and later in religious retirement. Another excellent Persian poet of Delhi was **Hasan-i-Dihlavi,** who died at Daulatabad (1338).

1320-1413. The Tughluk dynasty was founded by the old but vigorous **Ghiyas-ud-din Tughluk** (d. 1325), a pure Turk who boasted 29 victories over the Mongols. He reduced to provincial status Warangal (1323) and eastern Bengal (1324). He encouraged agriculture, corrected abuses in tax collection, and perfected a postal system by which runners covered 200 miles a day. At Multan he erected a splendid octagonal tomb of Persian character for the saint, Rukn-i-Alam. Increasing austerity marked the architecture of his house.

1325-1351. Mohammed Tughluk hastened to the throne by deliberate parricide. A half-mad military genius, his administrative measures were warped and defeated by his own unwisdom, inordinate pride, inflexibility, and ferocious indiscriminate cruelty. Revolt of a cousin in the Deccan (1326) led to

1327. Transfer of the capital to Devagiri, renamed *Daulatabad*, handsomely rebuilt with European feudal fortifications about an impregnable rock citadel. As a punitive measure

1329. All remaining citizens of Delhi were forced to move thither. He raised taxes so high in the Doab as to force rebellion and then destroyed both fields and cultivators.

1330. Emission of copper fiat money equivalent to the silver *tanga* of 140 grains failed because of easy counterfeiting.

1334. Ibn Batuta, a Moorish traveler, was welcomed with fantastic gifts like other foreigners who might help in world conquest. He left on a mission to China (1342).

1334-1378. Madura revolted under a Moslem dynasty, ended by Vijayanagar.

1337-38. An army of 100,000 horse, sent through Kangra into the Himalaya to conquer Tibet and China, was destroyed by rains, disease, and hill-men; and with it resources needed to avert

1338. Loss of Bengal to the house of Balban, independent until 1539. Moslem architects used at Gaur, its capital, local brick and terra cotta to build, e.g., the bold Dakhil Gateway (1459-74?).

1340. Mohammed sought recognition (received 1344) from the caliph in Egypt. He vainly tried to restore prosperity by redistricting, and appointing undertakers to supervise fixed (unscientific) crop rotation, and to maintain a mounted militia. Increased penal severity culminated when he began

1344-45. Wholesale extermination of his centurions, revenue collectors who usually failed to meet their quotas. Rebellion begun by them in Gujarat led to permanent loss of the whole South.

1346-1589. Shah Mirza (1346-1349) founded a Moslem dynasty in Kashmir. He substituted the usual land tax of one-sixth for the extortionate rates of the Hindu kings.

1347-1527. The Bahmani dynasty, founded by rebels against Mohammed Tughluk, who elected Bahman Shah (1347-1348), at first ruled four provinces: Gul-

barga, Daubatabad, Berar, and Bidar. The capital at Gulbarga and many other fortresses were built or strengthened with European science to serve against Gujerat, Malwa, and Khandesh in the northwest, the Gonds, Orissa, and Telingana in the northeast, and Vijayanagar in the south.

1351-1388. Firuz Tughluk (b. 1305) restored rational administration. He exacted tribute from Orissa (1360), Kangra (1361), and Sind (1363). He refused to disturb the Bahmani Kingdom of the Deccan, its tributary Warangal, or the rebels from it, the Khans of Khandesh between the Tapti and Narbada (independent 1382). He built several towns, notably Jaunpur north of Benares (1359), many mosques, palaces, hospitals, baths, tanks, canals, and bridges; but with cheap materials and little artistic quality. His successors were too weak to prevent further dissolution of the empire.

1358-1375. The Bahmani Mohammed I gave lasting organization to the government of the new dynasty.

1363-1364. Warangal was forced to cede Golconda, with much treasure.

1367. Victory of the Bahmani over immense but ineffectual armies of Vijayanagar. It was the first of several successes and was won with artillery served by Europeans and Ottoman Turks. The subsequent massacre of 400,000 Hindus led to agreement to spare noncombatants. The Great Mosque at Gulbarga was completely roofed with domes.

1392-1531. Malwa (formally independent in 1401) was ruled by the Ghuris and the Khaljis (1436). Hushang Shah (1405-1435) fortified the capital at Mandu above the Narbada, and erected there the durbar hall *Hindola Mahall*, together with a great mosque. These buildings are impressive through structural design rather than surface ornament.

1394-1479. Jaunpur, with Oudh, became independent under the Sharki (eastern) dynasty, founded by the eunuch, Malik Sarvar, and his adopted sons, probably of African Negroid descent. The second ruler, Ibrahim Shah (1402-1436), was a cultured and liberal patron of learning.

1396-1572. Gujerat prospered under a Moslem Rajput dynasty.

1398-1399. INVASION OF TIMUR (*Tamerlane*) of Samarkand, who had already conquered Persia, Mesopotamia, and Afghanistan (p. 330). He desolated the whole Kingdom of Delhi. Crossing the Indus (Sept. 24), he marched 80 miles a day for two days (Nov. 6–7) to overtake fugitives at Bhatnair, massacred 100,000 Hindu prisoners before Delhi (Dec. 12), sacked the city (Dec. 17), stormed Meerut (Jan. 9), and fought his way back along the Himalaya to the Indus (Mar. 19).

1411-1442. Ahmad Shah built Ahmadabad as a capital and beautified it with the *Tin Darwaza* (Triple Gateway) and *Great Mosque*, one of the most imposing structures in the world.

1414-1526. THE KINGDOM OF DELHI, reduced to the Jumna Valley, with tenuous control over the Punjab, was ruled by the Sayyids, who laid nebulous claim to Arab descent from the Prophet, but could collect their revenues only by force. Later the Afghan Buhlul Lodi (1451–1489) founded the Lodi dynasty.

1420-1470. Zain-ul-Abidin, learned and tolerant, recalled the exiles, permitted Brahman rites, employed convicts on public works, and exacted communal responsibility for order.

1422-1436. Ahmad Shah enrolled 3000 foreign mounted archers, who, like the Turks, Arabs, Mongols, and Persians, when employed as ministers, earned by superior qualities and disdain the envy and hostility (massacre 1446) of the native-born Deccanis, Africans, and Muwallads, halfbreed offspring of the latter.

1429. Bidar, rebuilt under Persian decorative influence, became capital.

1458-1511. Mahmud I, called *Begarha* (*Two Forts*) because of his conquest of Girnar (with Kathiawar, 1469–1470) and Champanir (near Baroda, 1483–1484), when 700 Hindu Rajputs preferred ritual death (*jauhar*) to Islam. He built magnificently and in exquisite taste: the Great Mosque at Champanir; the palace at Sarkhej; the step-well at Adalaj; and the pierced stone window-screens of Sidi Sayyid's mosque. The tiny Rani Sipari mosque at Ahmanabad (1514) displays harmonious perfection of the ornamental style.

1463-1482. Mohammed III conquered the Konkan and Teligana to both coasts. He died at 28 of drink, the curse of nearly all his house, and of remorse at having slain (while drunk) his best minister, Mahmud Gavan, the builder of the large quadrangular college at Bidar.

1490. Ahmadnagar (1490–1633), Bijapur (1490–1686), and Berar (1490–1574) became in fact independent of Mahmud (1482–1518), the incompetent prisoner of his minister, Kasim Barid, whose dynasty mounted the throne of Bidar in 1527 (till 1619).

c. SOUTHERN INDIA

100-200. King Karikalan of early Tamil poems is credited with construction of a great irrigation dam on the Kaveri River, east of Trichinopoly.

c. 300-888. The Pallava warrior dynasty of foreign (Pahlava?) origin, using Prakrit and later Sanskrit, held from Kañchi (near Madras) hegemony of the Deccan, which it disputed with the Chalukyas of Vatapi (550–753), the Rashtrakutas of Malkhed (753–973) and the Chalukyas of Vengi (611–1078).

c. 500-753. The first Chalukya dynasty in Maharashtra advanced from Aihole on the upper Kistna to near-by Vatapi (or Badami, c. 550) and to Banavasi (566–597) at the expense of the Kadambas. Construction of the earliest temples at Aihole was followed by that of Mahakutesvara (c. 525) and completion of the cave-temple to Vishnu at Vatapi (578).

c. 575. The Pallava Simhavishnu seized the Chola basin of the Kaveri, which his family held until after 812.

c. 600-625. The Pallava Mahendravarman I, converted from Jainism to Sivaism, destroyed a Jain temple, but dug the first (Saiva) cave-temples in the south (at Trichinopoly, Chingleput, etc.). From his reign date Buddhist monasteries (in part excavated) and *stupas* on the Samkaram Hills (near Vizagapatam).

609-642. The Chalukya Pulakesin II placed his brother on the throne of Vengi, where he ruled as viceroy (611–632), repulsed an attack by Harsha of Kanauj (c. 620), sent an embassy to Khosroes II of Persia (625), and enthroned a son, who headed a branch dynasty in Gujerat and Surat (c. 640–740). Hsüan-tsang (641) describes the prosperity of the country just before the Pallavas pillaged the capital (642), a disaster which was avenged by pillage of the Pallava capital, Kañchi, by Vikramaditya (c. 674).

611-c. 1078. The Eastern Chalukyas of Vengi (independent after 629–632), were continually at war with Kalinga on the north, the Rashtrakutas on the west, and the Pandyas on the south.

c. 625-c. 645. The Pallava Narasimhavarman defeated Chalukya Pulakesin II (c. 642) and took Vatapi. He defeated also his southern neighbors and enthroned Manavalla in Ceylon (?). He improved the port of Mamallapuram, near Kañchi, and cut there the first of five *raths*, monolithic sanctuaries in the form of cars, the earliest monuments of the Dravidian style; also the cliff-relief depicting the descent of the River Ganges from Heaven.

c. 675-c. 705. The Pallava **Narasimhavarman II** built in stone and brick the Shore temple at Mamalla, and the central shrine of the Kailasa temple at Kañchi, completed by his son.

c. 700. Conversion of King Srimaravarman to Sivaism by Tirujnana Sambandhar, the first of 63 *nayanmars* or Tamil saints, led the king to impale 8000 Jains at Madura in a single day, since celebrated by the Saivas. Another saint, Manikka Vasagar (9th cent.) wrote poems of his own religious experience which correspond to our *Psalms*. The Tamil Vaishnavas, too, had their saints, twelve *alvars*, who also expressed emotional religion and whose works were collected c. 1000–1050.

733-746. The Chalukya **Vikramaditya II** thrice took Kañchi, and distributed presents to the temples. He imported Tamil artists and his queen commissioned Gunda, "the best southern architect," to build the temple of Virupaksha. The frescoes of Ajanta caves 1 and 2 are believed to date from this period. So too the Saiva and Vaishnava sculptures of the Das Avatara cave-temple at Ellora.

c. 735-c. 800. **Nandivarman II,** a collateral kinsman twelve years of age, accepted the Pallava throne offered him by the ministers and elders, who defended him against rival claimants.

753-973. The Rashtrakuta dynasty of Canarese kings, already enthroned in North Berar (631) and in Gujerat (c. 700) was elevated to empire by Dantidurga, who soon overthrew the Chalukyas.

758-772. Rashtrakuta **Krishnaraja I** cut from the cliff and decorated with Saiva sculpture the Kailasa(natha) temple at Ellora to rival that of Kañchi. To the same Canarese dynasty if not to the same reign belong the equally classic Saiva sculptures of the cave-temples at Elephanta (an island in Bombay harbor). The successors of Krishnaraja were Govinda II (779) and Dhruva (783), who defeated the Pallava Nandivarman II and the Gurjara Vatsaraja.

774-13th cent. The Eastern Gangas ruled Kalinga, waging constant war with the Chalukyas of Vengi and the Princes of Orissa.

c. 788-c. 850. **Samkara of Malabar** revitalized the Vedanta, creating an unobtrusively new but consistent synthesis of tradition, which he speciously traced to the *Upanishads* and to Badarayana, author of the *Brahma sutra*. His doctrine became accepted as orthodox Brahmanism. He taught a rigorous monism (*advaita*) which admits release for the soul only in union with *brahman* through the higher knowledge that the phenomenal world (and individual personality) do not exist save for those who think objectively. For these latter, however, engrossed in worldly phenomena (*maya*), he recognized that a simpler kind of knowledge was necessary; and for them he was a practical apostle of Sivaism. Although he denounced Buddhism he imitated its moral teaching by opposition to sectarian extravagance, its ecclesiastical strength by organization of an ascetic order for zealous youth (hitherto debarred till later life from religious activity). He founded four scholastic monasteries (*maths*) which still survive at Sringeri (Mysore), Puri (Orissa), Badrinath (the Himalaya), and Dwaraka (western Kathiawar). Ramanuja (c. 1055–1137) of Kañchi (Conjeeveram, near Madras) also interpreted the Vedanta. For him souls are distinct from *brahman*, whose representatives they are, and from the material world with which they are entangled. It is through piety toward Vishnu and his saving grace that they may recover their divine nature.

c. 790. The Chalukya **Vikramaditya II** was defeated by the Rashtrakuta Dhruva (779–794).

794-813. Rashtrakuta **Govinda III** seized Malwa with Chitor from the Gurjaras, and enthroned his brother as head of a second Rashtrakuta dynasty in Gujerat (till c. 900). He took from the Pallava (c. 800) tribute and territory as far as the Tungabhadra.

c. 812-844. Pallava **Nandivarman III** helped Govinda III to crown Sivamara II as Ganga King of Mysore. At the same time

c. 812- Pandya **Varaguna I** imposed suzerainty on the Pallavas.

817-877. Rashtrakuta **Amoghavarsha I** moved the capital from Nasik to Malkhed, the better to carry on war against the Vengi. He abdicated and died in saintly Jain fashion. The last of his line found death in Jain starvation (982).

c. 825-1312. The Yadavas, early suzerains of a score of petty vassal kings, occupied in turn three capitals: (modern) Chandor and Sinnar (1069), both near Nasik, and the fortress of Devagiri (c. 1111) renamed Daulatabad (1327). They fell heir to the northern possessions of the Chalukyas of Kalyani.

843-1249. The Silaharas, another petty dynasty, under Chalukya or Rashtrakuta suzerainty, provided forty-five kings in three different areas along the west coast north of Goa. The Parsis (Parsees), refugees in Kathiawar, had probably already reached Thana near Bombay during the 8th century.

844-888. Gunaga Vijayaditya III fought successfully against western and northern enemies and by the defeat of the Pallava Aparajita and the Pandya Varaguna II helped the rising Chola to supersede both. His association of two brothers as kings-consort led ultimately to succession struggles which placed eight kings on the throne in ten years (918-927).

c. 844-870. Pallava Nripatungavarman recovered Tanjore and obtained the submission of Varaguna II (862-) and of Ganga Prithivipati I.

c. 870-888. Pallava Aparajitavarman, with Ganga Prithivipati, crushed Varaguna II, but was himself defeated and killed by the Chola Aditya I. Numerous Pallava chiefs continued to rule locally. Perungina, in the Tamil South, claimed imperial titles for at least 31 years.

888-1267. The Chola dynasty of Tamil kings from Tanjore, under Aditya I (870-c. 906), with the aid of the Chalukyas of Vengi, replaced the Pallavas at Kanchi. The Chola territory extended along the east coast from Telugu to the Pandya lands.

927-934. A royal inscription is the earliest extant specimen of Telugu literature. It records the erection of a Saiva temple and sectarian hostel.

973-c. 1190. The Chalukyas of Kalyani (near Bombay) were restored to power by Taila II (or Tailapa), who spent his reign fighting the Cholas and Paramaras.

985-1014. Chola Rajaraja I acquired hegemony over the Deccan.

994. Conquest of the Cheras and Pandyas justified the title *Thrice-crowned Chola*, marking the first historical union of the southern peninsula.

999. The conquest of Vengi drove a usurper from the East Chalukyan throne and was extended (1000) to Kalinga.

1001-1004. A successful invasion of Ceylon permitted assignment of Singhalese revenues to the Saiva Great Pagoda of Rajarajesvara, which Rajaraja I built at Tangore, the masterpiece of baroque Dravidian architecture. He also endowed a Buddhist monastery built at Negapatam by a king of Srivijaya (Sumatra).

1014-1042. Rajendra Choladeva, who had helped his father since 1002.

1014-1017. A second invasion of Ceylon secured the regalia and treasure of the Pandya kings, so that a son of the Chola could be consecrated king of Pandya.

1024. An invasion of Bengal enabled the Chola to assume a new title and establish a new capital near Trichinopoly.

c. 1030. By use of sea-power, the Chola exacted tribute from Pegu, Malaiyur (Malay Peninsula), and the empire of Srivijaya.

1040-1068. Rashtrakuta Somesvara I founded Kalyani, the capital until c. 1156. He drowned himself with Jain rites in the Tungabhadra, a sacred river of the south.

1042-1052. Chola Rajadhiraja I, who had aided his father since 1018. He was killed in battle at Koppam against Somesvara I of Kalyani.

1062-1070. Chola Virarajendra defeated the Chalukyas and gave his daughter to Vikramaditya VI. He founded a vedic college and a hospital. His two sons fell into conflict and extinguished their line by assassination (1074).

1073-1327. The Hoysalas, at first a petty dynasty, ruled at Dvarasamudra (Halebid) in Mysore.

1074-1267. The Chalukya-Chola dynasty, founded by Rajendra, son and grandson of Chola princesses, King of Vengi (1070-), who took the vacant throne of Kanchi (1074) and thenceforth ruled Vengi through a viceroy. His authority was recognized by the Ganga King of Kalinga.

1075-1125. Vikramaditya VI of Kalyani began a new era in place of the Saka era, but with small success. One of his many inscriptions is at Nagpur in the northern Deccan, while in the south one of his generals repelled the Hoysalas. His people enjoyed unwonted security. He built temples to Vishnu, but made gifts also to two Buddhist monasteries which must have been among the last in the south to withstand Hindu reaction and absorption. Bilhana of Kashmir, in return for hospitality, a blue parasol, and an elephant, wrote the *Vikramankacharita* in praise of his host.

1076-1147. Anantavarman Codaganga extended his authority from the Ganges to the Godavari, and built at Puri (south of Cuttack) the temple of Jagannath (Vishnu) which, at first open to all Hindu castes, is now barred to fifteen. The great

CHINA

IN THE LAST HALF OF THE
TWELFTH CENTURY

INDIA

TO THE MOHAMMEDAN
CONQUEST

Sun temple, in form of a solar car, known as the *Black Pagoda*, at Konarak, may be earlier than its attribution to Ganga Narasimha (1238–1264).

1111-1141. **Bittideva,** independent, fought successfully against Chola, Pandya, and Chera. As viceroy before accession he was converted from Jainism to Vishnu by Ramanuja, at that time a refugee from Saiva persecution at the Cholas. He began construction at Belur and Halebid of temples in a distinctively ornate Hoysala style, featured especially by a high, richly carved plinth of stellate plan.

c. 1150-1323. The **Kakatiyas** reigned in the east at Kakati or Warangal between the Godavari and the Kistna. They held an important kingdom under **Ganapati** (1197–1259) and his daughter (1259–1288), whom Marco Polo knew.

c. 1156-1183. A revolt against the Rashtrakuta ruler **Taila III** (known dates 1150–1155) led to usurpation by a general who was soon assassinated by Basava, who was in turn compelled to commit suicide. Basava created and organized the Lingayat sect of fanatic, anti-Brahman worshipers of Siva under a phallic emblem. The movement at the outset appeared in the form of a religious and social (equalitarian) war.

1183. Taila's son **Somesvara IV** regained Kalyani, but was unable to resist the Hoysalas (last date 1189).

1292-1342. The Hoysala ruler **Viraballala III** inherited an empire comprising most of southern India.

1327. After sack of Halebid by **Mohammed Tughluk**, Viraballala moved his capital to Tiruvannamalai (South Arcot).

c. 1335-1565. **Vijayanagar** (present Hampi),

founded by two brothers from the region of Warangal, fought steadily against the Moslem sultans north of Kistna and Tungabhadra. It became an important center for Brahman studies and for Dravidian nationalism and art. **Madhava** wrote at Sringeri (c. 1380) the *Sarva darsana samgraha*, which remains the classic summary of the various Brahman philosophical points of view.

1520. Division of the Moslems into five rival sultanates (late 15th cent.) gave Krishnadeva (c. 1509–1529) a chance to win a victory over the Sultan of Bijapur.

1542-1565. Ramaraja sought to profit by further division of the Moslems but provoked a coalition which crushed him and razed Vijayanagar.

d. CEYLON

846. The capital was moved south to Polonnaruva to escape Tamil invasions, which later culminated in

1001-1017. The two great invasions (1001–1004 and 1014–1017) by Chola Rajaraja and his son Rajendra.

1065-1120. Vijayabahu ruled prosperously despite further incursions (1046, 1055).

1164-1197. **Parakramabahu I** repelled the Tamils (1168), invaded Madura and united the two rival monasteries.

1225-1260. **Parakramabahu II** repelled two attacks (c. 1236 and c. 1256) by a King of Tambralinga (Ligor on the Straits of Malacca), with Pandya help.

1284. The king sent a relic of the Buddha to Kublai Khan. (*Cont. p.* 530.)

3. CHINA, 618-1471

618-907. **THE T'ANG DYNASTY,** founded by

618-626. **LI YÜAN** (T'ai Tsu) and his son Li Shih-min. The T'ang used Loyang and Ch'ang-an as eastern and western capitals. Sui institutions were in general retained. The central administrative organization remained essentially unchanged from this time until 1912. The emperor ruled through daily audience with a grand council composed of (1) heads of a secretariat and chancery, which for safety divided transaction of business (a feature later discarded); (2) representatives of the six ministries of civil office, finance, ceremonial, war, justice, and public works; and

(3) specially appointed dignitaries. The censorate and nine independent offices, notably a clan court and a criminal high court, together with three technical services including the national college and flood-prevention bureau, reported to him directly. Although the empire was divided into ten (627), later fifteen (733) districts for supervisory purposes, the prefectures (*chou*) depended directly from the central administration, the prefect being responsible for duties corresponding to those of the six ministries. Each prefecture sent an annual quota of candidates to join graduates of two state universities in civil-service examinations. These led to the eighth or

ninth (bottom) ranks in the official hierarchy. Appointment to a corresponding office depended on a further searching examination before each term until the sixth rank was reached. Promotion was based on performance.

627-649. **The reign of T'AI TSUNG (Li** Shih-min) is illustrious not alone because of the military conquests which established stimulating contacts with Iranian and Indian civilizations, but still more for the liberal, tolerant spirit of the emperor and his patronage of art and letters.

630. The Eastern Turks, who had attacked Ch'ang-an in 624 and 626, were crushed.

631-648. Chinese suzerainty was acknowledged by the petty states of western and eastern Turkestan. The Western Turks were divided and defeated (641).

635. A Nestorian missionary, A-lo-pen, was officially welcomed to Ch'ang-an; and given (638) both freedom of the empire and an imperial church at the capital.

641. A Chinese princess was married to the first King of Tibet, Srong-tsan-sgam-po, and helped convert Tibet to Buddhism, later (after 749) modified by Padmasambhava towards Tantrism.

645. **Hsüan-tsang,** returned from a pilgrimage to India, recorded his precise observations, and headed a commission which translated 75 books in 1335 volumes, creating for the purpose a consistent system for transcription of Sanskrit. He introduced the scholastic doctrine of **Vasubandhu** (which still survives), that the visual universe is only a mental image. The **Pure Land** or **Lotus School** of Buddhism for the next seventy years enjoyed far more popular favor. Based on texts translated in the 2d and 5th centuries, it is called the *Short-Cut School* because it teaches direct salvation by faith in Amitabha and invocation of his name. Religious **Taoism,** fully organized on the Buddhist model, now also received imperial patronage on the ground that Lao-tzu, whose surname legend gives as Li, was the ancestor of the ruling house. A 4th century apocryphal text, *Hua Hu Ching,* which claims Lao-tzu to be a prior avatar of Buddha, was actively debated. It was proscribed (668) but again tolerated (696). Imperial commissions completed or newly compiled eight standard histories to bring the series down to date from the Three Kingdoms. Another prepared the first literary encyclopedia, *I Wen Lei Chü.*

657-659. **Dispersal of the Western Turks** (T'u-chüeh), some of whom eventually migrated across southern Russia to Hungary while others followed Mahmud of Ghazni to India.

671-695. I-ching made the pilgrimage to India by sea, stopping to learn Sanskrit in Srivijaya (southeastern Sumatra), a state which became tributary (670–73), and remained powerful until the close of the 14th century.

684-704. Empress Wu temporarily altered the dynastic title to *Chou* (690–704), and decreed use of capriciously deformed written characters.

712-756. **HSÜAN TSUNG,** popularly known as Ming Huang, ruled over a court of brilliant High Renaissance literary and artistic attainment. He founded the **Academy of Letters** (725) and established schools in every prefecture and district in the empire (738). **Li Po** (705–762) and **Tu Fu** (712–770) created and excelled in lyric verse. In painting, continuous composition was substituted for episodic treatment. **Wu Tao-hsuan** (c. 700–760) ranks foremost among figure-painters. Li Ssu-hsün (651–c. 720) and Wang Wei (698–759) created two of the first and most influential landscape styles. Slackening of genuine religious enthusiasm is conspicuous alike in the tone of Buddhist votive inscriptions and in the monumental realism of the sculpture which becomes increasingly secular, then perfunctory. T'ang potters freely borrowed forms of Iranian flask and ewer, Indian ritual drinking vessel, and Greek amphora. They made these resplendent with new colors in soft lead glaze applied over slip with new technical versatility. From about this time dates probably also the first true porcelain with high-fired felspathic glaze. The Buddhists, too, now enlarged the seal and produced wood blocks for printing on paper (earliest extant printed book dated 868).

732. **Manichaeism** was condemned as perverse doctrine, but was permitted to Persians and Tokharians who had introduced it (694 and 719) and who were favored for their competence in astronomy and astrology.

738. The title *King* was conferred on a T'ai ruler who (730) united six principalities as **Nan Chao** with capital at Ta-li (741). After two disastrous efforts at conquest (750 and 754), the T'ang made peace (789–794), leaving the kings of Nan Chao full autonomy. They still had to be repelled, twice from Ch'eng-tu (829 and 874); once from Hanoi (863).

745. Uighur Turks overthrew the Eastern Turks and set up their own empire on the Orkhon, ruling from Ili to Tibet and the Yellow River. Their *kaghan* was given a title and a Chinese princess (758).

747. Kao Hsien-chih led an army across the Pamirs and Hindukush, but

751. Defeat by the Arabs at Talas lost Turkestan to China.

751-790. Wu-k'ung made the pilgrimage to India through Central Asia on the eve of displacement of Buddhism by Islam.

755. Revolt of An Lu-shan, a Turkish adventurer who had been adopted by the emperor's favorite concubine, Yang Kuei-fei, and had united three military commands, plunged the empire into particularly sanguinary and destructive civil war.

756-757. The emperor fled to I-chou (renamed Ch'eng-tu) which was developed rapidly as a cultural center. He there abdicated in favor of his son. Despite gradual suppression of the rebellion by Kuo Tzu-i and Li Kuang-pi, power remained in hands of territorial military leaders.

762-763. The Uighur kaghan sacked the eastern capital at Loyang, then in rebel hands, but was himself there converted to Manichaeism, which became the Uighur state religion.

763. The Tibetans, by a surprise attack, sacked Ch'ang-an. Through fear of the Uighur, who tried to convert the T'ang, Manichaeans were allowed to build temples in the capitals (768) and seven)ther cities (771 and 807). The kaghans were given rich gifts of silk, and a princess (821).

840-846. Overthrow of the Uighur Empire by the Turkish Kirghiz and Karluk led to migration of many tribes from the Orkhon to the Tarim basin, where they carved out a second Uighur empire in which the Turkish language extinguished the Indo-European dialects.

841-846. The reign of Wu Tsung, under Taoist influence, was filled with persecution of Manichaeans (843), Buddhists, Nestorians, and Mazdeans (845). Buddhism alone was now naturalized and able to survive. The most prominent place in an epoch of increasing anarchy was taken by the Ch'an (Skt. *Dhyana*, Jap. *Zen*) sect which offered refuge in introspective contemplation. Bodhidharma, an aged Persian who had come to Loyang from India

prior to 534, was now hailed as fabulous founder of the school, although in fact he was still obscure as late as 728.

CULTURAL PROGRESS continued despite military alarms. Wei Pao was commanded (744) to prepare an authentic version of the *Canon of History* by collation of variant manuscripts. It was included, together with all three competing rituals and all three commentaries on the *Annals*, among twelve classics which were cut in stone at Ch'ang-an (836–841). Han Yü (768–824) not only wrote excellent poetry, as did Po Chü-i (772–846), but created and set the classic model for the essay style. The first historical encyclopedia, the *T'ung Tien*, was compiled (766–801) by Tu Yu; and the practice of writing monographs on individual prefectures and districts was begun.

907-959. Five dynasties of short duration asserted imperial authority but seldom exercised it outside the Yellow River Basin: Later Liang (907–923), Later T'ang (923–936), Later Tsin (Chin) (936–947), Later Han (947–950), and Later Chou (951–960). Among ten competing secession states the most considerable were southern Han at Canton (904–971), and southern T'ang which from Nanking ruled much of the east and south (937–975).

932-953. Nine classics were first printed from wood blocks, as cheap substitute for stone engraving, at the Later T'ang capital at Loyang by Feng Tao, who had seen the process in Shu (Szechuan). The text was that of the stone inscriptions of 836–841.

907-1123. KHITAN MONGOLS under their dynastic founder Ye-lü A-pao-chi (907–926) conquered all Inner Mongolia, the Kingdom of Po Hai in the Liao Valley, and 16 northern districts of China. His suzerainty was recognized even by the Uighurs. His son Ye-lü Te-kuang (927–947) both helped set up the Later Tsin dynasty at Ta-liang (modern K'ai-feng) and destroyed it. He took Yen-chou (Peking) as his own southern capital (938), and adopted the Chinese dynastic name *Liao* with periodic reign-titles (947–1125).

960-1279. THE SUNG DYNASTY marks the advent of modernity, not only in governmental and social organization, but in thought, belief, literature, and art; not least in the diffusion of learning through print. It was an age of humanism, of scholar statesmen who were at once poets, artists, and philosophers. The first half of the dynasty is often distinguished as the Northern Sung (960–1127) when the capital was at K'ai-feng, then variously called Ta Liang, more properly Pien-liang, or Pien-ching.

960-976. Chao K'uang-yin or (Sung) T'ai Tsu gradually restored unity and order under accustomed forms with the help of a paid army.

965. The Annamese secured independence before South China could be subdued and shortly (c. 982) sacked the Cham capital Indrapura before Chinese pressure forced them to peace. Although the Chams (c. 1000) moved their capital south to Vijaya (Cha-ban, near Binh-dinh), the Annamese resumed the war (1043) and sacked it also.

967. The emperor deliberately refused to invade the territory of the native kings of Nan Chao in Yünnan, a policy observed by his successors. He permitted temporary autonomy to the King of Wu Yüeh (modern Chekiang) who had retained his throne (897–978) by pledging loyalty to each Chinese dynasty.

972 ff. The Buddhist canon was printed in Szechuan by imperial order from 130,000 blocks. It was reprinted with additions in Fukien (1080–1104), and elsewhere thereafter.

976-997. T'ai Tsung completed reunion of the empire (979), but was twice repulsed from Peking by the Liao (979 and 986).

997. Division of the empire into 15 provinces (*lu*) later extended to 18 (1023–31) and 23 (1078–85).

990-1227. The Western Hsia (Hsi Hsia) Kingdom of Tangut on the northwest frontier with capital at Ning-hsia appealed often to arms (996, 1001–1003, 1039–1042) despite grant of the imperial surname *Chao* and office (991, 997, 1006) and royal investiture (1044).

1004. An invasion by the Liao reached the Yellow River near Pien-Liang. They were granted annual tribute. These payments, increased in 1042, and the hire of a large standing army bade fair to bankrupt the treasury.

1006. Granaries for emergency relief were established in every prefecture. In 1069 grain so stored was valued at 15 million strings of cash.

1069-1074. WANG AN-SHIH (1021–1086) carried out a program of radical reform with the full confidence of Shen Tsung (1068–85), and in face of bitter opposition of conservative statesmen.

Through a new financial bureau (1069) he cut the budget 40% and raised salaries to make honesty possible for ordinary officials. To avoid excessive transport costs and to control prices he empowered the chief transport officer to accept taxes in cash or kind, to sell from the granaries, and to buy in the cheapest market, using capital of 5 million strings of cash. Further to protect poor farmers against usurers and monopolists, loans of cash or grain were offered in spring against crop estimates to be repaid in autumn with interest of 2% a month (moderate in China). Ambitious officials forced these loans upon merchants and others who did not want them. Objection to both principle and administration of these measures, which were accompanied by alarming centralization of power and disregard for precedent, led to wholesale resignations and transfers of the best officials whose help alone might have made them successful. **Conscript militia** were organized (1070) and trained for police purposes and national defense. The standing army of over a million inefficient men was gradually cut in half. By 1076 the militia, volunteer guards, and border bowmen numbered over 7 million men. **Cash assessments** graded in proportion to property were substituted (1071) for compulsory public services which had borne too heavily upon thrifty rural families. The exemption of officials, clergy, and small families was reduced by half. Necessary local services were now performed by paid volunteer agents. **State banking and barter offices** were opened (1072) first at the capital and later in every prefecture, with the object of controlling prices for the popular benefit.

1074-1085. The reform program was continued, despite complaints of excessive cash levies and other malpractices, until the emperor's death, for a time (1075–1076) by Wang himself.

1085-1093. Regency of the hostile grand dowager empress (under the reign title Yüan Yu) and recall of Ssu-ma Kuang, Su Shih, and the conservative faction to rescind the whole of the reform scheme (1085–1086). Extreme reaction in turn provoked reaction. On the death of his grandmother,

1093-1100. Che Tsung again favored reform, as did his younger brother

1101-1125. Hui Tsung who permitted Ts'ai Ching to proscribe (1102) 98 of the Yüan-Yu partisans, finally (1104) 309 conservatives, living and dead, headed by Ssu-ma Kuang. Eventually much that was good in the measures of 1070 and 1071 was retained. Hui Tsung, himself an able painter, was an active patron of the arts and letters. He founded the imperial academy of painting, and sponsored catalogues of his collections of painting and of archaic bronzes, some of which were obtained by excavation.

The Northern Sung is the golden age of landscape painting, when compositions of majestic breadth and exquisite detail were rendered in monochrome and color on long rolls or broad panels of silk. Tung Yüan (late 10th cent.) and Kuo Hsi (c. 1020–90) combined mastery of continuous composition and linear technique with that of suggestion of atmosphere through gradations of ink-tone. Li Kung-lin (c. 1040–1106) excelled in vigorous contrasts of light and shade, of broad and delicate line, and in airy architectural renderings in ruled and measured style. Mi Fei (1051–1107) used hardly any lines, building mountains and forests from graded accumulations of blobs of ink.

Scholarship flourished no less. Two great encyclopedias were compiled by imperial order, the T'ai P'ing Yü Lan (977–983) and the Ts'e Fu Yüan Kuei (1005–1013). Ou-yang Hsiu (1007–1072), a prominent statesman, prepared the New History of the T'ang, the first repertory of early inscriptions, and a monograph on the peony. Ssu-ma Kuang's greatest work is an integrated history of China, 403 B.C.–A.D. 959, compiled 1066–1084. Su Shih (1036–1101), better known as Su Tung-p'o, was distinguished as an independent statesman, and one of China's greatest essayists, poets, and calligraphers. Wang An-shih held his own with these as a brilliant writer of state papers and classical expositor.

Use of tea, first mentioned as substitute for wine under the Wu dynasty (222–280), spread through North China.

It is not known when or by whom the principle of magnetic polarity, known to the Chinese at least since the 1st cent. A.D., was applied in the mariner's compass with floating needle. The Malays in the 16th century employed, like the Chinese, a compass rose with 24 points, in contrast to the Arab rose of 32 points; which suggests, but does not prove, that the Malays received both compass and rose from the north. The compass is plainly mentioned by Chinese writers of the early 12th century. The volume of maritime commerce swelled greatly as Arabs in the 9th and 10th centuries entered into competition with Persians at Canton and Ch'üan-chou (Zayton), later at Lin-an. It was trade in cotton goods which brought 70 families of Jews from Persia and India to settle at the capital Pien-liang, where they remained unmolested until gradually absorbed.

1114-1234. Jurchen Tungus tribes overthrew their Khitan rulers in Man-churia (1114–16) and, with short-sighted Chinese aid, seized all the Liao lands in China (1122–23). Ye-lü Ta-shih of the Khitan led the remnant of his people to found a new state, Kara-Khitai, in eastern Turkestan (1130) and Turkestan proper (1141–1211). Meantime

1122. The Jurchen prince declared himself emperor of the Chin (or Kin) dynasty. He attacked the Sung so vigorously that although

1125. Hui Tsung abdicated in favor of his son,

1126. Ch'in Tsung and his father were both captured with the entire court in the capital. Hui Tsung died in captivity (1135).

1127-1279. THE SOUTHERN SUNG. A junior prince fled southeastward across the Long River from city to city, even by sea to Wen-chou; but, when the Chin retired north of the Long River (1130) and set up the puppet buffer state of Ch'i (1130–37), the capital was established (1135) at Lin-an (modern Hang-chou). The gallant general Yüeh Fei won several successes until put to death by Ch'in Kuei who made

1141. A peace dictated by economic exhaustion, accepting as frontier the line of the Huai and upper Han rivers.

1161. Explosives were used by Yü Yünwen in defeating the Chin at Ts'ai-shih (in Anhuei near Nanking). The Chin, like the Liao before them, avidly absorbed and adopted Chinese culture.

Early Chinese philosophers devoted nearly all their effort to the practical study of ethics. Buddhism, however, insistently raised the problems of ontology and epistemology. It is the merit of the Sung philosophers to have achieved a synthesis of ancient ethics with a new rationalized metaphysics. Chou Tun-i (1017–1073) revived a diagram of the ancient diviners to illustrate his conception of causation: emergence of paired forces from primal unity, and differentiation of natural phenomena by their interaction. Ch'eng Hao (1032–1085), the leading member of a commission which initiated the valuable Public Services Act of 1071, was in philosophy a mystic synthesist who found benevolence in all things. His brother Ch'eng I (1033–1107) was an analyst who discovered in the Li Chi the Ta Hsüeh or "Great Learning," a short work on method which stresses knowledge as essential to self-improvement on which all human welfare depends. Ideas of the school were systematized and crystallized by Chu Hsi (1130–1200), who equated as universals

Primary Unity, an impersonal but just and benevolent Heaven, and Righteousness, which correspond to the physical, metaphysical, and ethical spheres. From these proceed as co-ordinates the dual modes of production, the decrees of Heaven, and the processes of self-improvement. The final products are, respectively, the diversity of natural phenomena, conscience, and character. All these activities of parallel evolution are expressions of a universal divine law. Acceptance of knowledge as an element in self-improvement, and consequent emphasis on objective study, pointed the way towards scientific research; but this tendency was promptly combated by **Lu Chiu-yüan** (1139–1192), who stressed the teaching of Mencius that goodness springs from within.

Painters under the Southern Sung reproduced most often the mild misty landscapes of the Hang-chou region rather than the beetling crags found south of Ch'ang-an which had often inspired northern artists. **Ma Yüan** (1190–1224), **Hsia Kuei** (c. 1180–1230), and their school placed special emphasis on economy of line and representation of mists and clouds. Secular painters came increasingly under domination of conventions which grew up in the academy founded by Hui Tsung, and elegance, charm, and impeccable taste tended to replace more virile virtues; but religious painters, both Buddhist and Taoist, continued to produce vigorous work until the close of the dynasty. **Ch'en Jung** (c. 1235–1255) ranks as China's greatest painter of dragons.

Sung ceramists applied to pottery and porcelain in forms of subtle and sophisticated elegance both incised and molded decoration, together with a wide variety of high-fired glazes, some of which have never since been equaled. Although most wares were ostensibly monochrome, the potters learned to control color-transmutation of their pigments. The potters of Tz'u-chou for the first time employed penciled decoration both under and over glaze.

c. 1190-1294. THE MONGOLS. In central Asia Temujin (c. 1155–1227) created a new Mongol empire which was rapidly expanded by strategy and a military machine employing discipline, extreme mobility, espionage, terrorism, and superior siege equipment.

1194. The Yellow River, after repeated alterations of its bed, flowed south of the Shantung massif until 1853.

1206. Temujin was proclaimed *Jenghiz Khan* ("Emperor within the Seas") at Karakorum. He employed as chancellor a Uighur scholar Tatatonga, who applied to Mongol the Uighur script which was derived from Phoenician through Aramaic, Old and New Sogdian. Enforcement of peace and order within the empire promoted both commerce and cultural exchanges.

1211-1222. The Chin were driven south to the Yellow River (from Yen-ching, 1215).

1227. After several campaigns (1205, 1207, 1209) the Hsi Hsia Kingdom was destroyed, with massacre at Ning-hsia. Temujin bequeathed the empire to a grandson and three sons: to Batu, son of his eldest Juchi, Kipchak in Russia; to Chagatai, the former Kara-khitai empire; to Ogedei, Outer Mongolia; and to Tului (regent 1227–1229), eastern Mongolia and North China.

1229-1241. Ogedei was elected khan by plenary kuriltai on the Kerulen.

1231. Ye-lü Ch'u-ts'ai (1190–1244), a sinicized scion of the Khitan royal house and adviser to Temujin since 1215, proved his ability to collect taxes in China by traditional methods, and was appointed chancellor. Korye (Korea) was conquered and placed under 72 Mongol residents.

1233. Pien-liang fell after a flanking campaign by Tului through Hanchung and Szechuan (1231–1232), and a long siege by Sabotai in which the Chin defenders used explosive bombs.

1234. The Chin Empire was annexed. Belated Chinese attack provoked Mongol seizure of Szechuan (1236–1238).

1237. Ye-lü Ch'u-ts'ai secured 4030 scholars, one quarter of whom were freed from slavery, through civil service literary examinations; and restored full civilian administration.

1237-1241. Sabotai subjugated Russia and led an invasion through Hungary to Cattaro which was recalled only by death of Ogedei (p. 244).

1246-1248 or 1249. Guyuk, son of Ogedei and his widow Turakina (regent 1242–1246), was elected khan in presence of Plano Carpini, envoy of Innocent IV.

1251-1259. Mongka, son of Tului, was elected over the son of Guyuk's widow (regent 1249–1251).

1252-1253. Mongka's brother Kublai crushed Nan Chao. The king was named *maharaja* and hereditary administrator under the eyes of a Mongol garrison commander and Chinese resident. More autonomy and an imperial princess were conferred in 1284.

1254. Mongka, the son of a Nestorian woman and employer of a Nestorian chancellor, told William of Rubruck, envoy of Louis IX of France, that religions are like the fingers of one hand. He yet favored Buddhism, and after public disputation (1255) proscribed Taoist books for forgery. Kublai shortly followed this example (1258).

1257. The capital was transferred to Shang-tu, north of present Peking.

1258. The Mongols pillaged Hanoi, while, at the other end of the empire, Hulagu with a Nestorian wife and general destroyed the Abbasid Caliphate of Baghdad.

1260-1368. THE YÜAN DYNASTY (as distinguished from the Mongol Empire) was effectively founded when **Kublai** (1214–1294) had himself elected khan by his own army at Shang-tu (1260), although he adopted the dynastic title only in 1271. He ruled in China according to Chinese precedents. His dynastic name is Shih tsu.

1264. The Mongol Empire was reunited by capture of Kublai's brother Arikboga, who had been proclaimed khan at Karakorum (1260). Twice (1277 and 1287–1288) its unity was defended against Khaidu, head of the house of Ogedei. Kublai's authority was respected by his brother Hulagu and the succeeding Ilkhans of Persia, and in theory by the Golden Horde on the Volga. He transferred (1264) the winter capital to Yen-ching where he constructed Khanbalig, modern Peking (1267). He erected an astronomical observatory on the city wall, wherein were installed bronze instruments cast by Kuo Shou-ching (1279).

1268-1273. A siege of Hsiang-yang and Fan-ch'eng on the Han was ended after 4 years 5 months only by engineers and machines from Mesopotamia. Thereafter the Mongols were free to descend towards the sea.

1276. Capitulation of the empress-regent and boy-emperor at Lin-an (Hang-chou) was followed by capture of Canton (twice, 1277) and destruction of a fleet carrying the last youthful Sung pretender (1279).

1281. Disastrous attack upon Japan. An assault in 1274 having failed, a Mongol army of 45,000 from Korea joined (June) a tardy armada with 120,000 men from the southern Chinese coast in landing

at Hakozaki Bay. The invaders were repulsed by the well-prepared Japanese until (Aug. 15) a typhoon destroyed their fleets, leaving them to death or slavery.

1282-1283. An army sent by sea from Canton to subdue Champa took the capital Vijaya, but was forced by epidemics to withdraw.

1285 and 1287-1288. Abortive expeditions against Annam and Champa by land and sea were massacred and repulsed, but secured admission of vassalage.

1287. The Mongols pillaged Pagan, capital of Burma, received homage (1297), and returned (1300) to pacify competing Shan chiefs.

1292-1293. A naval **expedition to Java,** after temporary success, was forced to re-embark.

1294. Tribute was received from the Siamese kingdoms of Xieng-mai and Sukhotai.

1295-1307. Temur Oljaitu, grandson of Kublai, was the second and last effective ruler of the Yüan dynasty.

1296. A Mongol embassy accompanied by Chou Ta-kuan found Chen-la (Cambodia) much weakened by the attacks of Sukhotai, which had now become a powerful state under its second ruler Rama Kamhing.

ECONOMIC DEVELOPMENTS. Kublai devoted special attention to economic matters: The Grand Canal was restored (1289–1292) from the former Sung capital, Lin-an at Hang-chou (the Kinsay of Marco Polo), now a great and rich city, to the Huai River, and carried north to the outskirts of Peking. Imperial roads were improved, and postal relays of 200,000 horses established. Charitable relief was organized (1260) for aged scholars, orphans, and the sick, for whom hospitals were provided (1271). Imperial inspectors every year examined crops and the food supply with a view to purchase when stocks were ample for storage against famine.

The T'ang first employed paper money orders, to which the Sung and Chin added various bills of exchange. When issue of paper currency was suggested to Ogedei (1236), Ye-lü Ch'ü-ts'ai secured limitation to value of 100,000 oz. of silver. Under Kublai, a Mohammedan financier, Saiyid-i Edjill Chams al-Din Omar (1210–1279), kept annual issues at an average of 511,400 oz. (1260–1269). His successor Ahmed Fenaketi increased emissions (1276–1282) to 10,000,000 oz. annually. After Ahmed's murder, inflation increased until a Uighur,

Sanga, reduced the rate of printing to 5,000,000 oz. (1290–1291). Circuit stabilization treasuries (1264 and 1287) were given reserves inadequate to redeem the flood of bills at $2\frac{1}{2}\%$ discount, the official rate of 1287. The issue of 1260 depreciated until replaced 1 for 5 by that of 1287, which again was replaced 1 for 5 in 1309. All printing was discontinued in 1311; but the credit, financial and moral, of the dynasty was already on the wane. The southern provinces of the empire rapidly fell from its control.

Marco Polo, in the service of the khan (1275–1292), traveled widely in Cathay (from Khitai, hence North China), and Manzi (South China), and to Burma (p. 362). Through his "Division of the World" he first brought detailed and accurate knowledge of eastern Asia to Europe. In his time, and even in that of the Arab, Ibn Battuta (c. 1345), Zayton (Ch'üan-chou) was the busiest deep-sea port in the world, leading Kinsay (Lin-an), Foochow (Fuchou), and Canton in shipping silks and porcelains to Java, Malaya, Ceylon, India, and Persia in exchange for spices, gems and pearls. The itineraries given by Chao Ju-kua (1225) imply in the precision of their bearings the use of a compass needle mounted on a dry pivot.

THE MOSLEM COMMUNITIES of Persian and Arab traders at these ports were small compared to those which now grew up in North China and in Yünnan. Saiyid-i Edjill as governor of Yünnan (1274–1279) built the first two mosques in what became a stronghold of Islam. Most popular religion with all the Mongols was Buddhism. Kublai welcomed a gift of relics of the Buddha from the raja of Ceylon. He conferred the title *Teacher of the State* upon a Tibetan lama Phags-pa, whom he employed to convert the Mongols and to whom he entrusted government of the three provinces of Tibet.

NESTORIAN CHRISTIANS enjoyed full protection. The Patriarch of Baghdad created an archbishopric at Peking (1275); churches were built in Chen-kiang (1281), Yang-chou, and Hang-chou; and a special bureau was created (1289) to care for Christianity. **Mar Yabalaha,** pilgrim from Peking to Jerusalem, was elected patriarch (1281), and his companion Rabban Sauma was sent by him and Argun, Ilkhan of Persia, to Rome and France. He negotiated with Pope Nicholas IV an entente between the Nestorian and Roman churches. **John of Montecorvino** was the first of several Roman missionaries to China (1294–1328). He baptized 5000 converts and was named by the pope (1307) Arch-

bishop of Peking. He received a three-year visit from **Oderic of Pordenone** who reported to Europe the custom of footbinding, which had spread through South China under the Southern Sung, but which was unknown to the Chin and early Yüan.

LITERATURE: the Mongol period introduced the novel and the drama, the latter accompanied by raucous percussion music. Although neither was at once admitted as a form of polite letters, both are now recognized to possess artistic merit.

PAINTING: one group of artists continued traditions of the Southern Sung while another boldly swept away the mists which had shrouded landscape. **Ch'ien Hsüan** (1235–c. 1290) is perhaps the greatest painter of flowers and insects. **Chao Meng-fu** (1254–1322) was particularly adept at depicting the horses and other live-stock which were prominent in Mongol economy. Yüan porcelain reveals in arabesques no less than in the technique of penciling in cobalt blue directly on clear white paste the debt of Chinese potters to Persian models. From these also is derived the Byzantine form of cloisonné enamel.

1368-1644. THE MING DYNASTY was founded by **Chu Yüan-chang** (Ming T'ai Tsu, 1328–1398), a monk turned insurgent amidst anarchy, who seized Chiang-ning (Nanking) in 1356, set up there an orderly government, and proceeded to annex the holdings of surrounding southern war-lords until in 1368 he was strong enough to drive the Mongols from Peking with Shensi, Kansu (1369) and Szechuan (1371). Like all the emperors of this and the following dynasty he ruled under a single reign-title, *Hung-wu* (1368–1398), which is accordingly often used instead of his personal name.

1382. Yünnan was completely conquered, and its prince executed at Nanking. The whole territory of China was now under direct government.

1388. The Mongols were driven from Karakorum and defeated on the Kerulen.

1392-1910. The Li dynasty was founded in Korea upon the ruins of that of Wang, which had reigned since 918 (p. 349).

1403-1424. The Yung Lo reign of Ch'eng Tsu was established by violence against his nephew, who disappeared in a palace fire (1402).

1403-1433. A series of naval expeditions through the southern seas was motivated by desire for commerce and military prestige, but also by uneasiness lest the deposed nephew emerge thence to claim his throne. Secret inquiry by Hu Jung within the empire also was protracted (1407–1416, 1419–1423). A claimant actually appeared in Honan in 1440.

1405-1407. Cheng Ho, the chief eunuch (a Mohammedan whose real surname was Ma), brought back in chains the Prince of Palembang (Sumatra), who had been defeated in battle, as he did

1408-1411. The King of Ceylon and his family, who had attacked the mission. As a result of

1412-1415. A third cruise as far as Hormuz, sixteen southern states sent tribute. Cheng Ho was appointed to lead three more embassies during this reign: 1416–1419 (as far as Aden), 1421–1422, and 1424. Other eunuchs led additional missions.

1410, 1414, 1422-1424. Campaigns into Outer Mongolia were directed at destruction of whatever chieftain or group momentarily possessed sufficient prestige to threaten recreation of the Mongol power.

1421. Transfer of the capital to Peking was mooted in 1409, decreed in 1420. Wisdom of the move is reflected by the fact that the northern frontier was never successfully violated during the five centuries Peking remained capital, save when the Manchus were invited in.

1428-1788. The later Le dynasty in Annam, after a quarter century of fighting, secured recognition of independence (1431) from Hsüan Tsung in the Hsüan Te reign (1426–1435). The royal title was conferred in 1436.

1431-1433. Cheng Ho led a seventh and final embassy to twenty states. As result tribute was sent by Mecca and ten others.

1449. Emperor Ying Tsung (1436–1449 and 1457–1464) was captured in battle by the chief of a new Mongol confederation (Oirat) of four tribes. Although released next year, he recovered his throne from his brother Ching Ti only in 1457.

c. 1470-1543. Dayan, a descendant of Jenghiz, restored unity to Mongolia, but divided it among his own descendants.

1471. Annam finally annexed its southern neighbor, Champa. (*Cont. p.* 536.)

a. BURMA

From early times Burma was under Indian influence. By the 3d century A.D. expanding Hindu peoples had established commercial settlements on the Tenasserim coast and at the principal river mouths which developed into small kingdoms in contact with the Tibeto-Burman tribes of the Irrawaddy Valley. Commercial relations with China were less influential, although an embassy from a Burmese state reached Ch'ang An in 802.

1044. Anawrata seized royal power at Pagan and by his patronage of Hinayana Buddhism and conquests, both north and south, made it the political, religious, and cultural center of Burma; the Burmese written language was developed and Buddhist scriptures translated; architectural monuments followed the inspiration of Ceylon and southern India; able rulers succeeded Anawrata.

1106. A Burmese embassy at the Sung capital in China was received as from a fully sovereign state.

1287. Following the rejection of Mongol demands for tribute (1271 and later), Burmese raids into Yünnan, and the death of Narathihapate (who ruled 1254-1287), Mongol forces looted Pagan and destroyed its power. The invasion of Shan tribes, forced southward by the Mongols, led to the division of Burma into a number of petty states, chief among them being Toungoo (estab. 1280), Pegu in southern Burma, and Ava in the middle and lower Irrawaddy Valley (estab. as capital 1365). (*Cont. p.* 541.)

b. SIAM

During the early centuries of the Christian Era, the Khmer peoples of the Menam Valley came under the influence of Hindu civilization, and about the 6th century there was organized, in the region of Lopburi, the **Kingdom of Dvaravati,** which was Buddhist rather than Brahman in religion, and from which during the 8th century migrants to the upper Menam Valley established the independent and predominantly Buddhist Kingdom of Haripunjaya, with its capital near the present Chiengmai. Early in the 11th century Dvaravati was annexed to Cambodia; but Haripunjaya retained its independence until the 13th century, when it was overrun by a migration of Tai, or Shan, peoples from the north. This migration, accelerated by the Mongol conquest of the Tai state of Nanchao (in modern Yünnan and southern Szechuan) in 1253, led eventually to the suppression of the Khmer kingdoms and the setting up of the Tai Kingdom of Siam with its capital at Ayuthia, founded by Rama Tiboti in 1350. The early Siamese state was from the first under the influence both of Hinayana Buddhism and of Chinese political institutions. Toward the end of the 13th century a form of writing had been invented for the Siamese language.

1350-1460. Siamese **invasions of Cambodia** finally led to the abandonment of Angkor and collapse of the Khmer Empire.

1371. A Siamese embassy at Nanking inaugurated tributary relations with the newly founded Ming dynasty.

1376-1557. Intermittent friction between Siam and the Tai state of Chiengmai in the northern Menam Valley ended only with the destruction of Chiengmai by the Burmese.

During the 14th and 15th centuries strong Siamese influence was exerted over the disunited states of Burma and the northern part of the Malay Peninsula.

(*Cont. p.* 541.)

c. MALAYSIA

Early Indian commercial settlements in Sumatra and Java, at first Brahman in religion and later influenced by Buddhism, became the centers of organized states. Toward the end of the 7th century A.D., **Srivishaya** became the dominant state of Sumatra and built up a commercial empire which at its height (c. 1180) controlled the Straits of Malacca and of Sunda, all of Sumatra and the Malay Peninsula, and the western half of Java; its authority was recognized as far away as Ceylon and Formosa, and in many colonies throughout the East Indies. The **Sailendra dynasty,** rulers of Srivishaya, were ardent patrons of Buddhism, as is shown in the great Borobudur victory monument in central Java. The consolidation of petty Javanese states, begun after the middle of the 9th century, led to the rise of **Singosari** in eastern Java, which under Kartanagara (who ruled 1268–1292) challenged and finally destroyed the power of Srivishaya.

1293. A Mongol expedition, sent to avenge insult offered by Kartanagara, was forced out of Java by a new kingdom, **Madjapahit,** which during the 14th century built up a commercial empire with authority extending over Borneo, Sumatra, and parts of the Philippines and of the Malay peninsula, and profited by an extensive trade with China, Indo-China, and India. After the

1389. Death of Hayam Wuruk, the power of Madjapahit disintegrated.

1405-1407. The first Chinese expedition under Cheng Ho established tributary relations between many Malay states and the Ming Empire; and the authority of Madjapahit rapidly gave way to that of the Mohammedan Arabs. During the 15th century Mohammedan commercial operations, based chiefly on Malacca, were extended to the whole archipelago, and some 20 states accepted Islam as the state religion. (*Cont. p.* 541.)

4. KOREA

612. Emperor Yang-ti of the Sui dynasty of China invaded Koguryŏ, but was repulsed.

645-647. Two T'ang expeditions against Koguryŏ failed.

663. The T'ang destroyed Paekche.

668. The T'ang and Silla together destroyed Koguryŏ.

670. Silla robbed the T'ang of Paekche and southern Koguryŏ, but did not break its allegiance to China.

670-935. SILLA PERIOD.

670-780. Height of Silla power and culture, when Buddhism and art flourished, particularly at the capital near the modern Kyŏngju (J. Keishū).

780-935. Period of political decline, but of closer relations with and increasing imitation of China.

c. 880. Serious rebellions broke out.

918. The state of Koryŏ was founded in west central Korea.

935. Silla peacefully submitted to Koryŏ.

935-1392. KORYŎ PERIOD.

935-1170. Height of Koryŏ power and culture centering around the capital, Kaesong (modern Sŏngdo, J. Kaijō) in west central Korea and P'yŏngyang, the secondary capital.

936. Koryŏ destroyed Later Paekche, thus uniting Korea once more.

996. **The Khitan** (Liao dynasty) forced Koryŏ to recognize them, and not the Sung dynasty of China, as overlords of Korea.

1044. A great wall was completed across northern Korea as a defense against the Manchurian peoples.

1123. **The Juchên** (Chin dynasty) forced Koryŏ to recognize their suzerainty.

1170. Military officers seized the government and proscribed Buddhism.

1196. **The Ch'oe family** established its control over the government with the title of *Kongnyŏng*.

1223. Beginning of over 200 years of attacks on coastal regions by Japanese pirates.

1231. The Mongols invaded Korea, and the Ch'oe removed the government to the island of Kanghwa off the west coast.

1258. The Im (Lim, J. Rin) family supplanted the Ch'oe as *Kongnyŏng.*

1259. Koryŏ submitted to the Mongols, and the Koryŏ kings through intermarriage became merely a branch of the Mongol imperial family and their representatives in Korea. This situation and the rise of Confucianism at this time led gradually to the unquestioning acceptance of Chinese suzerainty and leadership in political and cultural matters.

1356. Koryŏ revolted successfully against the Mongols.

1356-1392. Period of great disorder. The Koryŏ kings, who had depended on Mongol prestige for their authority, were unable to suppress their unruly vassals, and the Japanese pirates were at their worst.

1369. Koryŏ submitted to the Ming dynasty of China.

1392. I (Li, J. Ri) Sŏnggye declared himself king after a series of *coups d'état* and assassinations, thus founding the

1392-1910. I (Li, J. Ri) DYNASTY with its capital at Kyŏngsŏng (modern Sŏul [Seoul], J. Keijō). This new dynasty based its claims to legitimacy on its championing of the Ming cause as opposed to the Mongols, considered by them not to be the legitimate rulers of China. Like their predecessors they remained unswervingly loyal and subservient to China.

1392-1494. Period of greatest prosperity and cultural development.

1419-1451. King Sejong was a patron of learning, and in his time the native phonetic script called *ŏnmun* was introduced. During this reign the Japanese pirates ceased to ravage the Korean coast, and the northeastern corner of present-day Korea was brought under Korean rule.

(*Cont. p.* 542.)

5. JAPAN, 645-1543

645-784. PERIOD OF THE IMITATION OF CHINA. An edict outlining the general principles of national reorganization was promulgated as early as 646 (the *Taika Reform*), but it was only in the course of several decades that the principles were put into practice and even then the reforms often remained on paper. The major features of the new system were: (1) the nationalization of the land, in theory; (2) the adoption of the T'ang system of land distribution and taxation; (3) the reorganization of local government and other measures intended to increase the authority of the central government in the provinces and its income from them, and (4) the reorganization of the central government. The principles and many of the details of the reforms were borrowed directly from China, but in Japan, dominated as it was by an hereditary aristocracy, it was well-nigh impossible to carry them out in full, and from the start they were basically modified in practice. (1) Although the land was nationalized in theory, in actuality the large hereditary estates of the clan chiefs were returned to them as lands held as salary for their official positions and ranks. (2) The land was to be periodically divided among the agriculturalists in accordance with the membership of each family as determined by census, and uniform taxes were to be levied on all alike.

These were (a) the land tax (*so*), paid in rice; (b) the corvée (*yōeki*), often commuted at a fixed rate into a textile tax; and (c) the excise (*chō*) levied on produce other than rice. The system was too closely patterned after the Chinese and functioned badly in Japan from the beginning. Powerful families and institutions, hungry for land, were always ready to deprive the public domain of taxpaying lands, and the peasants, impoverished by taxes, were often anxious to transfer themselves and their lands from the taxpaying public domain to the care of privately owned manors (*shōen*). As a result the history of economic development during the next several centuries is primarily the story of the return of the land into private hands and the emergence of large tax-free estates owned by the court nobility and great religious institutions. (3) The improvement of means of communication helped in the centralization of government and in the collection of taxes, but, although the officials of the provincial governments were to have been appointees of the central government, in practice local leaders retained their supremacy by occupying the lower posts, and it soon became the accepted custom for the high provincial officials to remain at the capital and to delegate their powers to underlings in the provinces. (4) An essential and permanent feature of the reforms was the complete reorganization and great elaboration of the central government. A department of religion (*jingikan*) and a great council of state (*dajōkan*) were established as two parallel organs controlling the spiritual and political aspects of the state. Below the great council were eight ministries, and below them in turn many smaller bureaus. The organization was too ponderous for the Japan of that day. Moreover, with the collapse of the economic supports of the central government through the growth of tax-free estates, this elaborate organism was literally starved to death. Although in theory it continued little changed until the 19th century, actually during most of that period it was merely a skeleton devoid of most of its former powers. In adopting the Chinese form of government the Japanese made one significant change. The official hierarchy of Japan remained a hereditary aristocracy, and with rare exceptions there was little opportunity for the able or learned of low rank to rise far in this hierarchy.

This period was the **classic era of Japanese culture**. Poetry and prose in pure Chinese were composed, and native Japanese poetry reached an early flowering. Japan in the preceding century had already been imitating continental artistic styles, and now the art of T'ang China found fertile soil in Japan and produced there many of the greatest extant examples of Far Eastern art of that day in the fields of architecture, sculpture, painting and the applied arts.

663. The Japanese withdrew from Korea, after the defeat of a Japanese army and fleet, sent to the aid of Paekche, by a combined force from China and Silla (662). Thus ended the first period of Japanese continental expansion. The fall of Paekche in 663 and of Koguryŏ (a North Korean kingdom) in 668 left Silla supreme in the peninsula and resulted in a great immigration of Korean refugees into Japan.

697. The **Empress Jitō** (686–697) abdicated in favor of her grandson, **Mommu** (697–707). This was the first case of the accession of a minor and the second of the abdication of a ruler, but both were soon to become the rule.

702. New civil and penal codes known as the *Taihō Laws* were promulgated. This may have been the first complete codification of the laws embodied in the reforms commenced in 646, although there is mention of an earlier code. These laws, together with a revision of 718 (*Yōrō Laws*, not enforced until 757), have come down to us only through later commenta-

ries, the *Ryō no Gige* of 833 and the *Ryō no Shūge* of 920. A supplementary code, the *Engishiki*, was completed in 928.

710. **Heijō** (or Nara) was laid out on the model of Ch'ang-an, the T'ang capital, as the first permanent capital of Japan. The period during which it was the capital is known as

710-784. THE NARA PERIOD.

712. The *Kojiki*, which records the history of the imperial line since its mythical origins, was written in Chinese characters (used to a large extent phonetically) to represent Japanese words. This is Japan's oldest extant book.

720. The *Nihonshoki* (or *Nihongi*), a more detailed history of Japan written in Chinese, was compiled. It was continued to 887 by five other official histories written in Chinese, which together with it constitute the **Six National Histories** (*Rikkokushi*).

724-749. Shōmu's reign, which included the brilliant Tempyō year period (729–748). This and the period during which Shōmu dominated the court as the retired emperor (749–756) marked the apogee of the Nara Period and its classic semi-Chinese culture.

737. The death of the four grandsons of Kamatari delayed for several decades the complete domination of the imperial court by the Fujiwara clan.

741. Government monasteries and convents (*Kokubunji*) were ordered erected in each province.

752. The dedication of the **Great Buddha** (*Daibutsu*) at Nara marked the completion of the devout Shōmu's most cherished project. The 53-foot bronze figure of the Buddha Rushana (Skt. *Vairocana*) and the huge hall built over it was a tremendous undertaking for the Japanese court and gave witness to the great Buddhist fervor of the time. Many of the objects used in the dedication service together with the personal belongings of Shōmu form the basis of the unique collection of 8th century furniture and art preserved at the imperial treasury in Nara (the *Shōsōin*, commenced in 756).

Shortly before the erection of the Great Buddha the famous monk, Gyōgi (670–749), is said to have propagated the concept that Buddhism and Shintō were two aspects of the same faith. Such beliefs served as a justification for the growing amalgamation of the two religions, which was to lead by the 12th century to the development of Dual Shintō (*Ryōbu Shintō*), in which Shintō gods were considered to be manifestations of Buddhist deities. Faced with a highly developed foreign religion backed by all the prestige of the more advanced Chinese civilization, the simple native cult became for a period of almost 1000 years the handmaiden of Buddhism in an unequal union.

754. The Chinese monk Ganjin (also pronounced Kanshin, etc.; Ch., *Chien-chên*, d. 763), after five unsuccessful attempts to reach Japan, finally arrived at Nara, where he set up the first ordination platform (*kaidan*) and firmly established the **Ritsu** (Skt. *Vinaya*) **Sect**, which stressed discipline rather than doctrine. The Ritsu Sect together with five other sects formed the so-called **Nara Sects**, the oldest sectarian divisions of Japanese Buddhism. These others were the **Sanron** (Skt. *Madhyamika*) **Sect**, said to have been introduced in 625; the **Hosso** (Skt. *Dharmalaksana*) **Sect**, brought from China by Dōshō (d. 700), who had gone there to study in 653; the **Kegon** (Skt. *Avatamsaka*) **Sect**, which was largely responsible for the cult of Rushana, the universal and omnipresent Buddha; the **Kusha** (Skt. *Abhidharmakosa*) **Sect**; and the **Jōjitsu** (Skt. *Satyasiddhi*) **Sect**; which last two may never have existed as independent religious bodies in Japan.

759. The *Man'yōshū*, a collection of over 4000 poems in pure Japanese, composed largely by the court nobility between 687 and 759, was compiled shortly after the latter date. It was followed in later centuries by similar anthologies. In 751 the *Kaifusō*, a small collection of poems in Chinese, had been compiled; it likewise was continued by similar works.

764. A clash for power between **Fujiwara Nakamaro** (also known as Emi Oshikatsu), the leading statesman during Junnin's reign (758–764), and Dōkyō, the monk favorite of the retired nun empress, Kōken (749–758), led to the death of Nakamaro, the exile of Junnin, his subsequent assassination and the reascension to the throne of Kōken as the Empress Shōtoku.

764-770. Dōkyō was all-powerful during Shōtoku's reign and may even have aspired to the throne. Strong opposition and Shōtoku's death led to his ultimate downfall. Perhaps because of the memory of Dōkyō's influence over Shōtoku, for almost nine centuries thereafter no woman occupied the throne.

781-806. The reign of the energetic **Kammu** witnessed the conquest of much of northern Hondō in a prolonged but successful border struggle with the Ainu. After several initial failures the natives of this region, both Ainu and intractable Japanese frontiersmen, were definitely brought under the imperial sway by Sakanoue Ta-

muramaro (d. 811). His campaigns concluded centuries of slow advance into Ainu territory. After a final outbreak in 812 the Ainu menace in the north never again assumed major proportions.

794. Kammu moved the capital from Nagaoka, where it had been since 784, to Heian, the modern Kyōto, where it remained until 1868. The reasons for his abandoning of Nara are not definitely known but were probably: (1) a desire to make a new departure politically and economically; (2) a desire to escape the oppressive influence of the powerful Nara monasteries; (3) the superior location of Nagaoka and Kyōto, which had better water communications with the sea; and (4) the influence of the Hata family (?), which had lands in that region. The reasons for the sudden removal of the capital from Nagaoka to Kyōto, a few miles farther inland, are still more obscure, but may have been connected with Kammu's fear that the first site had incurred the curse of certain spirits. The establishing of the capital at Kyōto marked the beginning of

794-1185. THE HEIAN PERIOD, a long era marked by few violent upheavals but one in which the transition from the period of the imitation of China to the feudal and more strictly Japanese Kamakura period was slowly made. These centuries were characterized by a somewhat effete dilettantist court society, becoming increasingly divorced from political and economic realities; the gradual decline and collapse of the economic and political system borrowed from China; the growth of tax-free manors; the slow emergence of a new military class in the provinces; the full glory and subsequent decline of the Fujiwara family; the appearance and development of the Buddhist sects and cults which dominated much of Japan's religious history; a sounder understanding of the borrowed Chinese civilization and a greater ability to synthesize it with what was natively Japanese, or to modify it to fit the peculiar needs of Japan; a resultant growing cultural independence of China, and the reappearance of more purely Japanese art and literature.

800-816. New offices in the central government, which were to affect profoundly the whole administration, appeared at this time. These were: (1) the *kageushi* (audit office) (c. 800), which in time usurped the prerogatives of the original audit and revenue offices; (2) the *kurōdo-dokoro* (bureau of archivists) (810), which gradually attained control of palace affairs and became the organ for issuing imperial decrees; (3) the *kebiishichō* (police commission) (c. 816), which in time became the primary law enforcement organ of the state and eventually created outside of the official codes its own code of customary law.

804. **Tendai and Shingon, the two** leading sects of the Heian period, were founded by Saichō (Dengyō Daishi 767–822) and Kūkai (Kōbō Daishi 774–835) respectively. Both monks accompanied the eleventh embassy to the T'ang in 804. Saichō returned to Japan the next year to found the Tendai Sect, named after Mt. T'ien-t'ai in China. The syncretistic inclusive nature of the philosophy of the sect appealed to the Japanese, and its central monastery, the Enryakuji, which Saichō founded on Mt. Hiei overlooking Kyōto (788), became the center from which sprang most of the later significant movements in Japanese Buddhism. Kūkai returned from China in 806 bringing with him the Shingon or Tantric Sect, a late esoteric and mystic form of Indian Buddhism. Because of his tremendous personality and the natural appeal of Shingon to the superstitious propensities of the people, the new sect won considerable popular support, and the Kongōbuji monastery on Mt. Kōya, which Kūkai founded (816), became one of the great centers of Buddhism. Tendai and Shingon were more genuinely Japanese in spirit than were the Nara sects, and the Shingon Sect in particular furthered the union of Shintō and Buddhism.

838. The twelfth and last embassy to the T'ang was dispatched. When in 894 Sugawara Michizane (845–903) was appointed to be the next envoy, he persuaded the court to discontinue the practice on the grounds that China was disturbed and no longer able to teach Japan. Although some unofficial intercourse continued between the two countries, this brought to an end the three centuries of the greatest cultural borrowing from China and marked the beginning of a period in which peculiarly Japanese traits asserted themselves increasingly in all phases of Japanese life.

858. The complete domination of the Fujiwara clan over the imperial family was achieved by Yoshifusa (804–872) when he became the *de facto* regent of the child-emperor, Seiwa (858–876). In 866, after Seiwa had attained his majority, Yoshifusa assumed the title of regent (*sesshō*), becoming the first non-imperial regent. Seiwa was the first male adult emperor to have a regent. The typical inner family control which the Fujiwara exercised over the emperors can be seen in the relationship that existed between Seiwa and Yoshifusa, for the latter was both the grandfather and the father-in-law of the young ruler. It was the definite policy of the Fujiwara to have a young imperial grandson of the head of the clan occupy the throne and to have him abdicate early in favor of another child. The period of the domination of the Fujiwara family is often called

866–1160. **THE FUJIWARA PERIOD.**

880. **Fujiwara Mototsune** (836–891) became the first civil dictator (*kampaku*), a post thereafter customarily held by the head of the clan when an adult emperor was on the throne, while the post of regent came to be reserved for the clan head in the time of a minor emperor.

889. The branch of the warrior **Taira clan** which was to rule Japan for part of the 12th century was founded when a great-grandson of Kammu was given this surname. The clan was established in 825 by another imperial prince. In 814 the rival military **clan of Minamoto** was founded by other members of the imperial clan, and in 961 the princely progenitor of the later Minamoto rulers received this surname. The descendants of such imperial princes, reduced to the rank of commoners, often went to the provinces to seek their fortunes, and there some of them merged with the rising class of warriors, who were soon to dominate the land.

891. **The Emperor Uda** (887–897), who was not the son of a Fujiwara mother, made a determined effort to rule independently without Fujiwara influence and refused to appoint a new civil dictator after Mototsune's death. To further this end he used the brilliant scholar, **Sugawara Michizane** (845–903), as his confidential minister, but after Uda's abdication (d. 931), Fujiwara Tokihira (871–909) managed to obtain the removal of Michizane to a provincial post, where he soon died. He was posthumously loaded with honors and deified because it was believed that his vengeful spirit had caused certain calamities. Tokihira throughout his official career strove valiantly but in vain to stem the tide of governmental corruption and disintegration.

905. The *Kokinshū*, an anthology of over 1000 poems in Japanese, was compiled by Imperial order in a revival of interest in Japanese poetry. For over a century almost all literary effort and scholarship had been devoted to prose and poetry in the Chinese language, but Ki Tsurayuki (d. 946) wrote the preface to the *Kokinshū* in Japanese and followed it in 935 by a travel diary (*Tosa Nikki*) also in Japanese. Within the short compass of a century Japanese prose was to rise to great heights of literary achievement. An important contributing factor to the revival of

Japanese literature at this time was the fact that in the preceding century a simple syllabary for writing Japanese phonetically had been evolved from the complicated Chinese characters.

930. The offices of regent and civil dictator were revived after a lapse of four decades when **Fujiwara Tadahira** (880–949) became regent in 930 and civil dictator in 941.

935-941. Civil strife in the provinces broke out on an unprecedented scale, giving witness to the rise of the provincial military class. From 936 until his death in 941 Sumitomo, a member of the Fujiwara clan and a former provincial official, controlled the Inland Sea as a pirate captain, while in eastern Japan an imperial scion, Taira Masakado, after waging war on his relatives and neighbors, declared himself emperor (940), but was presently killed.

949. The **Emperor Murakami** (947–967) did not appoint a successor to Tadahira, but after the former's demise

967-1068. The successive heads of the Fujiwara clan occupied the posts of regent and civil dictator almost uninterruptedly for a full century. This was the heyday of the Fujiwara clan and the core of the so-called Fujiwara period. Court life was ostentatious and extravagant and was characterized by amatorial dilettantism and moral laxity. At the same time petty jealousies and intrigues disrupted the Fujiwara clan, members of the provincial warrior class began to appear on the capital stage as petty military officers and came to be used by the court nobles in their disputes, manors continued to grow apace, further limiting government resources and the general collapse of the central government continued unabated.

985. The *Ōjōyōshū* by the monk **Genshin** (942–1017) gave literate expression to new religious currents which were stirring the nation. A belief had sprung up that the age of *mappō* ("the latter end of the law"), a period of degeneracy to come 2000 years after the Buddha's death, had already commenced. There was a growing belief in the **Pure Land** (*Jōdo*), Paradise of Amida (Skt. *Amitabha*) and salvation through his benign intervention in favor of the believer and not only through one's own efforts, as earlier Buddhism had taught. Emphasis was increasingly placed on *nembutsu*, the repetition of Amida's name or a simple Amidist formula. **Kūya** (903–972), an itinerant preaching monk, was the first articulate voice to express this new religious move-

ment, and Genshin gave it sound literary formulation. It continued to develop, and in the 12th and 13th centuries produced important new Buddhist sects.

995-1028. **FUJIWARA MICHINAGA'S** (966–1028) rule over clan and state saw the zenith of clan power and some of the most brilliant decades of artistic and literary achievement of the epoch. Although he was never officially civil dictator and was regent for only a short period prior to his official retirement in 1017, he was perhaps the most powerful leader the Fujiwara produced. At this time the classic prose literature of Japan reached its height in the *Genji Monogatari* (c. 1008–1020), a long novel by **Murasaki Shikibu**, a court lady, and in the *Makura no Sōshi* (Pillow Book) (c. 1002), a shorter miscellany by another court lady, **Sei Shōnagon**. The refined and somewhat feminine art of the epoch also was at its height. Jōchō (d. 1057), a famous Buddhist sculptor, was already active, and Michinaga's successor, **Yorimichi** (992–1074, regent 1017–1020; civil dictator 1020–1068), built the *Byōdōin*, the outstanding architectural work remaining from the age.

1039. Armed Enryakuji monks invaded Kyōto to force their will upon the government, but were driven off by Taira troops at Yorimichi's command. Such descents upon the capital, known as "forceful appeals" (*gōso*), were common during the 11th and later centuries and sometimes led to actual fighting. The turbulence of the monks, who fought fiercely among themselves as well as with the court, made it necessary for the court to appeal to the Taira and Minamoto for military aid, and the warrior clans consequently became more influential at court.

1051-1062. In the **Earlier Nine Years' War** Minamoto Yoriyoshi, on imperial command, destroyed the **Abe,** a powerful military clan of northern Japan. Thereby he firmly established the prestige of his branch of the Minamoto clan in eastern and northern Japan. Yoriyoshi's ancestors had already started the military renown of the house, and its status at court as "the claws and teeth of the Fujiwara" greatly increased its power.

1068-1073. The **Emperor Sanjō II,** who was not the son of a Fujiwara mother, ruled directly without the interference of the Fujiwara. Although the latter continued to occupy the posts of regent and civil dictator, they never again gained full control of the government. Sanjō II established a records office (*kirokujo*) to examine title deeds of manors in an effort to check their growth, but in this attempt he was blocked by the opposition of the Fujiwara.

1083-1087. In the **Latter Three Years' War** Minamoto Yoshiie (1041–1108) destroyed the Kiyowara family of northern Japan, thereby increasing Minamoto prestige in that region.

1086-1129. The **Emperor Shirakawa** (1073–1086) continued to rule after his abdication as a retired emperor (*jōkō*) and after 1096 as a priestly retired emperor (*hōō*). He built up a complete governmental organization of his own (*insei*, camera government) which was continued during much of the next two and a half centuries by other retired emperors and priestly retired emperors, but after 1156 they lost control of the government to the warrior clans.

1129-1156. The **Emperor Toba** (1107–1123) ruled after Shirakawa's death as a priestly retired emperor.

1156. Civil war (the *Hōgen no Ran*) broke out between the reigning emperor **Shirakawa II** (1155–1158), and the retired emperor, Sutoku (1123–1142). Both were supported by prominent members of the Fujiwara, Minamoto, and Taira clans. Shirakawa II's partisans, among whom were numbered Minamoto Yoshitomo (1123–1160) and Taira Kiyomori (1118–1181), were victorious. Sutoku was exiled, and many of his supporters were executed. This war brought no lasting peace and was soon followed by

1160. A **second civil war** (*Heiji no Ran*), in which Minamoto Yoshitomo and an adventurous young Fujiwara noble, Nobuyori (1133–1160), gained temporary control of the capital by a successful *coup d'état*, but were soon crushed by the Taira. This war left

1160-1181. **Taira Kiyomori** in control of the nation. The two wars of 1156 and 1160 had not been a struggle for power between the court and the military clans, but the result had been to make a single victorious warrior, backed by personal troops, the dominating figure in Japanese politics. Shirakawa II as retired emperor (1158–1192) had some influence in the government, but in 1167 Kiyomori had himself appointed prime minister (*dajōdaijin*), and gave important posts in the central and provincial governments to his clansmen. Kiyomori married his daughters into both the imperial and the Fujiwara families. In 1180 his infant grandson, Antoku, was placed on the throne. Thus he attained the same hold over the imperial family that the Fujiwara had once had.

1175. The **Pure Land** (*Jōdo*) **Sect** was founded by Genkū (Hōnen Shōnin) (1133–1212). It was the first of the Amidist Sects, and this event marked the beginning of a great new sectarian movement.

1179. The **death of Shigemori** (1138–1179), Kiyomori's eldest son and perhaps the wisest of the Taira, removed a stabilizing check on Kiyomori, whose desire for more power was leading him to excesses which were alienating the sympathies of the imperial family, the court nobility, and the Buddhist monasteries. The rapid adoption on the part of Kiyomori and his family of the customs and mentality of the court nobles also estranged many of the provincial supporters of the clan.

1180. An abortive uprising against the Taira led by an imperial prince and by Minamoto Yorimasa (1106–1180), together with certain monasteries, started a general uprising of the remnants of the Minamoto clan under the leadership of Yoshitomo's son, Yoritomo (1147–1199), backed by Taira and other clansmen of eastern Japan.

1183. The Taira were driven out of Kyōto by Yoshinaka (1154–1184), a cousin of Yoritomo. A long campaign in the Inland Sea region followed and culminated in

1185. The **battle of Dan no Ura**, at the western outlet of the Inland Sea, where Yoritomo's younger brother, Yoshitsune (1159–1189), annihilated the Taira. The child-emperor, Antoku, whom the fleeing Taira had taken with them, died in the battle. The elimination of the Taira left Yoritomo, as head of the Minamoto clan, the virtual ruler of the nation and marked the beginning of the first period of feudal rule in Japan known as

1185-1333. THE **KAMAKURA PERIOD.** The outstanding feature of the era was the clear division between the now powerless civil and religious government of the imperial court at Kyōto and the military government (*Bakufu*) of the Minamoto established at Kamakura, near the clan estates in eastern Japan and away from the enervating influence of the court nobility. The transition from civil to feudal military rule had begun with the Taira and was not completed until centuries later, but it was in the Kamakura Period that the most drastic changes occurred and the political and economic institutions of the next several centuries began to take shape.

Feudalism. The usurpation of the powers of the imperial court was largely unconscious and developed naturally out of the economic and political conditions of the late Heian period. Primary factors in this evolution were: (1) The wars of the 11th century had hastened the transfer of the prerogatives of ownership of the great manors of the nobles to the military men who resided on these manors as bailiffs or wardens and who often had feudal ties with the warrior clans. The actual ownership of the estates usually remained unchanged, but ownership was robbed of most of its meaning by a complicated series of feudal rights (*shiki*) which ranged from rights to cultivate the land up through an ascending scale of rights to the income from it. (2) Because of the breakdown of the old centralized government and the need for self-defense feudal military groups had grown up in the provinces with their own "house laws," governing the conduct and the relations of the members of a single group. Moreover, a feudal code of ethics had been developed which emphasized personal loyalty to a feudal chief rather than to a political ideal. (3) Minamoto prestige had for long induced landed warriors to commend themselves and their lands to the Minamoto for the sake of protection. The victory over the Taira greatly increased Minamoto feudal authority both through new additions of this sort and through the confiscation of vast Taira lands. The single Minamoto feudal union consequently had grown so large that it now controlled the nation, and its military government, and not the impotent Kyōto administration, was the real government of the land.

Foreign Relations. For four and a half centuries only a few Japanese monks had gone abroad, and foreign trade had been in the hands of the Koreans and Chinese, but in the Kamakura period the Japanese once more began to take part in foreign commerce. At the same time they began to raid and plunder the coasts of both Korea and China, and in time they became a serious nuisance and occasionally even a national menace to both countries.

Art. Kyōto, though remaining the scene of a colorful court life, was forced to share honors with Kamakura as a center of art and culture. Many Kyōto scholars moved to Kamakura to aid in the civil administration of the military government, and the warrior class brought a new creative energy to art and literature, which were approaching sterility in the late Heian period. Significant artistic trends were: (1) a final great flowering of sculpture before its gradual extinction in following centuries; (2) the introduction from China of two new architectural styles known as the Chinese (*Karayō*) and the Indian (*Tenjukuyō*) styles, which came to blend with the traditional style (*Wayō*); and, (3) the perfection of the narrative picture scroll (*emakimono*). Significant literary trends were: (1) the increasing use of Japanese in preference to Chinese; (2) the revival of native poetry in the *Shin-kokinshū*, an imperial anthology of 1205; and, (3) the popularity of historical military tales written in rhythmical prose.

Religion. The Kamakura period was one of great religious and intellectual ferment. It witnessed the birth and development of new sects growing out of the popular movements of the late Heian period. It saw the introduction of the **Zen Sect** from China and the growth of a military cult glorifying the sword, Spartan endurance and loyalty. From these two elements was born the combination of the aesthetic and mystical penchants of the Zen monk with the qualities of the Kamakura warrior — a combination which remains one of the chief characteristics of the Japanese people.

1185-1199. Yoritomo, as the feudal military dictator, organized the new military government with the aid of Kyōto scholars like Ōe Hiromoto (1148–1225). Already in 1180 he had created a *Saburaidokoro* to perform police duties and to control affairs of the warrior class. In 1184 he had established an administrative board, renamed the *Mandokoro* in 1191. In 1184 the *Monchūjo* had also been established as a final court of appeal. Impartial administration of justice characterized the rule of the Kamakura military government and was one of the chief reasons for its long duration.

In 1185 Yoritomo appointed constables (*shugo*) in some of the provinces and placed stewards (*jitō*) in many of the large manors. A few such appointments had been made in preceding years, but now this system was expanded in order to strengthen his influence in regions over which he had hitherto had no direct control. The constables were special military governors in charge of the direct vassals of the Minamoto. The stewards, who represented Yoritomo on estates not otherwise under his control, levied taxes on the estates for military purposes. Thus the fiscal immunity of the manors was violated, and Kamakura retainers were scattered in key positions all over the country. The constables and stewards gradually grew in importance in the economic and political life of the provinces and in time developed into the feudal lords of later centuries.

1189. Yoshitsune was killed at the orders of Yoritomo, who apparently was jealous of the fame the latter had won as the brilliant general responsible for the greatest victories over the Taira.] Yoritomo similarly disposed of other prominent members of the family, including his cousin Yoshinaka (1184), who as a warrior ranked next only to Yoshitsune, his uncle Yukiie (1186), who was one of the prime movers in the Minamoto uprising, and his brother Noriyori (1193), who also was one of the clan's great generals. His cruel treatment of his own relatives contributed to the early extinction of the family.

1189. Yoritomo crushed the powerful Fujiwara family of northern Japan on the grounds that they had killed Yoshitsune, albeit at his own command. The northern Fujiwara in the course of the previous century had become a great military power and had made their capital, Hiraizumi, a brilliant center of culture. Their elimination removed a serious menace to Minamoto supremacy.

1191. Eisai (1141–1215) propagated the Rinzai branch of the Zen (Skt. *Dhyana*) Sect after his return from a second study trip to China. The Zen Sect enjoyed the official patronage of Kamakura and the special favor of the warrior class in general.

1192. Yoritomo was appointed *Seiidaishōgun* ("barbarian-subduing great general"), or *shōgun* for short. He was not the first to bear this title, but he was the first of the long line of military dictators called *shōgun*.

1199-1219. **Transition period from Minamoto to Hōjō rule.** Yoritomo was succeeded as head of the Minamoto by his eldest son, Yoriie (1182–1204), who was not appointed *shōgun* until 1202, but his mother, Masako (1157–1225), actually ruled with the aid of a council headed by her father, Hōjō **Tokimasa** (1138–1215). The latter, though a member of the Taira clan, from the start had cast his lot with Yoritomo and had exercised great influence in the Kamakura councils before Yoritomo's death. The Hōjō, though loyal to the military government, unscrupulously did away with Yoritomo's descendants and crushed their rivals among the other Minamoto vassals.

1203. Yoriie was exiled and his younger brother, Sanetomo (1192–1219) was made *shōgun* by Tokimasa. The following year Yoriie was murdered.

1205. Tokimasa was eliminated from the government by Masako and his son, Yoshitoki (1163–1224), who then became regent (*shikken*) of the *shōgun*, a post held by successive Hōjō leaders, who were the real rulers.

1219. The Minamoto line came to an end when Sanetomo was assassinated, probably with Hōjō connivance, by his nephew, who in turn was executed.

1219-1333. **THE PERIOD OF HŌJŌ RULE** as regents for weakling *shōgun* of Fujiwara and imperial stock was characterized by administrative efficiency and by justice.

1221. An uprising under the leadership of the retired emperor, **Toba II** (1183–1198), was the gravest menace the Hōjō had to face, but was quickly crushed. Two prominent Hōjō leaders were left in Kyōtō as joint civil and military governors of the capital region (*Rokuhara Tandai*). The estates confiscated from the defeated partisans of Toba II gave Kamakura much needed land with which to reward its followers, and the abortive uprising gave the Hōjō a chance to extend the system of constables, stewards and military taxes to regions hitherto unaffected by it.

1224. Shinran Shōnin (1173–1262), a disciple of Genkū, founded the **True Pure Land** (*Jōdo Shin*) **Sect** as an offshoot from the Pure Land Sect of his master. The True Pure Land Sect introduced innovations such as marriage for the clergy. It was destined to become the most popular of all Japanese Buddhist sects with Zen its only close rival.

1226-1252. Fujiwara nobles as figurehead *shōgun*.

1229. Dōgen (1200–1253) introduced the Sōtō branch of the Zen Sect after his return from study in China.

1232. The *Jōei-shikimoku*, a law code based primarily on custom rather than on earlier sinicized law codes, was adopted for all those directly under the feudal rule of Kamakura. It remained the basis of law codes until modern times.

1252-1333. Imperial princes as figurehead *shōgun*.

1253. Nichiren (1222–1282) **founded the Lotus** (*Hokke*) **Sect,** popularly known as the *Nichiren Sect.* In it the Lotus Sutra was venerated much as the Amidist Sects venerated Amida. A fiery religious and political reformer, Nichiren was an ardent nationalist, and his writings illustrate the gradual emergence of a definite national consciousness at this time. Imbued with the turbulent nature of its founder, the sect had a stormy career.

1274. **FIRST MONGOL INVASION.** The Mongols, already masters of Korea and most of China, repeatedly sent embassies (1268-1273), enjoining the Japanese to submit, but the Kamakura government under the bold leadership of the regent, Hōjō Tokimune (1251–1284), refused. Finally in 1274 the Mongols dispatched an expedition aboard a Korean fleet. The islands of Tsushima and Iki were reduced, a landing was made in Hakata (Hakozaki) Bay in northern Kyūshū, and an inconclusive encounter, in which superior weapons and military organization gave the Mongols the advantage, was fought with the local warriors. But the same night, because of their insecure position and the threat of a storm, the invaders set sail for Korea.

1281. SECOND MONGOL INVASION. Mongol envoys sent to Japan in 1275 and again in 1280 were summarily executed, and the military government hastily prepared defense works in western Japan. In 1281 the Mongols embarked a huge force on two large fleets, one Korean and one Chinese, and again, after capturing Tsushima and Iki, landed in northern Kyūshū. Although the invaders numbered some 150,000, the Japanese checked their advance on land with walls they had prepared for this emergency and worsted them on the sea because of the greater mobility of their smaller craft in close quarters. After almost two months of fighting a terrific storm destroyed a large portion of the invading armada, and the remainder departed with serious losses. The Mongols continued plans for another invasion of Japan until the death of their emperor, Kublai (1294), and the Japanese continued their defense preparations still longer.

The Mongol invasions no doubt spurred on Japan's nascent national consciousness, but it also contributed greatly to the final collapse of the Kamakura government. Military preparations against the Mongols had seriously taxed the nation's resources, and at the end of the two invasions the military government, lacking land confiscated from the enemy, was without the usual means of rewarding its vassals for their valiant efforts. This state of affairs helped undermine the loyalty of the warrior retainers of Kamakura. At the same time the monasteries were becoming increasingly unruly, the court nobility was beginning again to intrigue with disaffected warriors against the Hōjō, and the latter themselves had lost the virtues of frugality and justice which had once characterized the family.

The Hōjō during the final decades of their rule began to resort to **Acts of Grace** (*Tokusei*) cancelling certain indebtedness in an effort to save the lands of their vassals from mortgages, but such obviously unfair measures antagonized certain powerful interests and failed adequately to protect the Kamakura vassals.

1331-1333. THE IMPERIAL RESTORATION of Daigo II and the fall of the Hōjō. The energetic and able emperor, Daigo II (1318–1339), after bringing to an end in 1322 the domination of the court by retired emperors, organized an abortive plot to overthrow the Hōjō as early as 1324. In 1331 open warfare broke out between Daigo II, supported by his able sons, some of the large monasteries in the capital region, and various local nobles and warriors like **Kitabatake Chikafusa** (1292–1354) and **Kusunoki Masashige** (1294–1336), the two outstanding patriot heroes of mediaeval Japan. The following year the emperor was captured and exiled to Oki, but in 1333 he escaped. Most of western Japan declared for the imperial cause. Ashikaga Takauji (1305–1358), one of the two chief generals dispatched by the Hōjō from eastern Japan, deserted to Daigo II's standards, and the sudden capture of Kamakura by another prominent Hōjō vassal, Nitta Yoshisada (1301–1338), brought the military government of Kamakura to an end.

1333-1336. Daigo II in a short period of personal rule, failing to face economic and political realities, attempted to revive the civil imperial rule of the 8th century. However, he did make his able son, Morinaga (1308–1335), *shōgun* and appointed his leading generals military governors of large sections of the land. Because of his dissatisfaction with his share of the spoils in northeastern Japan,

1335. Takauji revolted against the throne. Defeating the Nitta, Kitabatake, and other loyal families,

1336. Takauji drove Daigo II out of Kyōto and set up a new emperor from a branch of the imperial family which had been jealously contending the throne with Daigo II's branch for several decades. He thereby became the virtual dictator of the central government, and, although he was not appointed *shōgun* until 1338, with his capture of Kyōto commenced

1336-1568. THE ASHIKAGA (or Muromachi) PERIOD. The Ashikaga *shōgun* continued the outward forms of the military rule of the Minamoto and Hōjō, but during most of the first and last centuries of the period open warfare disrupted the nation, and at best the Ashikaga exercised only a shadowy control over the great feudatories who made their appearance at this time. The age was characterized by quickly shifting allegiances and by political instability, which at times amounted to anarchy. There was a general redistribution of feudal and economic rights, and the Kyōto nobility, which now lost most of its few remaining lands and provincial sources of income, was reduced to penury. The complicated feudal relations of the Kamakura period broke down into simpler, more compact divisions with practically independent lords, often the former provincial constables, ruling large territories, which were in turn subdivided into smaller units administered by their direct vassals. The collapse of clan unity and an organized feudal system necessitated stronger solidarity within the smaller family and feudal units. The division of patrimonies among heirs was abandoned, and women were reduced to the subordinate status they are still allotted. Lords exercised a closer paternalistic supervision over their vassals, and the latter in turn served their lords with greater personal loyalty.

The overseas trade and pirate enterprises of the Japanese increased in the Ashikaga Period; the central government once more established official relations with China; and another important period of borrowing from abroad commenced. Foreign trade stimulated the growth of towns and provincial ports, such as Sakai (part of the modern Ōsaka), Hyōgo (the modern Kōbe), and Hakata (part of the modern Fukuoka). Despite political disruption and incessant warfare, a phenomenal economic development took place. Nascent industries grew and expanded, and trade guilds (za), usually operating under the patronage of some religious institution, appeared and flourished. However, the unrestricted multiplication of various levies and of customs barriers proved a serious curb to the development of trade.

Kyōto was once more the undisputed political and cultural capital, and there the warrior class and the court nobility tended to fuse. Constant warfare made the period in some respects the intellectual dark ages of Japan, but political disunity helped to diffuse learning throughout the land. Zen monks dominated the intellectual and artistic life of the nation and through their intimate contacts with China, where many had lived and studied, expanded Japan's intellectual and artistic horizons. Although this was a great age of Zen, the other sects, particularly the Amidist sects, flourished and sometimes developed powerful military organizations. It was still a thoroughly Buddhist age, but intellectual life began to free itself from the bonds of Buddhism, Sung Confucian philosophy was introduced from China, and stirrings of new life appeared in Shintō, where for the first time systematic syncretic philosophies were developed.

Despite the violent internecine strife of the early and late Ashikaga period, in the middle decades literature and art, ruled by Zen standards of restraint and refinement, flourished. The *Literature of the Five Monasteries*, as the Zen school at Kyōto was called, revived poetic composition in Chinese, and a great lyric drama called *Nō* appeared. The Sung style of painting, often in monochrome and usually of landscapes, reached its height in Japan with such great masters as Shūbun (c. 1415) and Sesshū (1420–1506), and the two greatest Japanese schools of painting, the Tosa and Kano, flourished. The independent architectural styles of the Kamakura period were blended to form a composite style. Minor arts like landscape gardening and flower arrangement grew up, and the tea ceremony was popular among the upper classes. Under Zen tutelage there developed a refined simplicity of taste and a harmony with nature which has had a lasting influence on Japanese art and psychology.

1336-1392. CIVIL WARS OF THE YO-SHINO PERIOD. When Takauji drove Daigo II out of Kyōto and set up a rival emperor, Daigo II and his partisans, the Kitabatake, Kusunoki and others, withdrew to the mountainous Yoshino region south of Nara, where Daigo II and three imperial successors maintained for almost six decades a rival court, called the *Southern Court* because of its location. During this period, known as the *Yoshino period* or the *Period of the Northern and Southern Dynasties*, civil war convulsed Japan. In support of the legitimacy of the southern court

1339.   Kitabatake Chikafusa wrote the *Jinnōshōtōki*, a history of Japan imbued with extreme nationalistic and patriotic sentiments. It is an important landmark in the growth of a national consciousness and the imperial cult.

1392.   The reunion of the two courts. Although at times the Yoshino warriors even captured Kyōto, the hopes of the southern court gradually waned. Eventually in 1392 peace was made, and Kameyama II (1383–1392) of the southern line abdicated in favor of Komatsu II (1382–1412) of the northern line, with the understanding that the throne should henceforth alternate between members of the two branches of the imperial family, as it had done for several reigns preceding that of Daigo II. However, the northern line never yielded the throne to its rivals despite futile uprisings in their behalf. Official history regards the southern line as the legitimate rulers during the Yoshino period.

1395-1408. Rule of Yoshimitsu as retired *shōgun*. Yoshimitsu, the third Ashikaga *shōgun* (1369–1395), after crushing his principal opponents, uniting the two imperial courts and bringing the Ashikaga power to its apogee, passed on the title of *shōgun* to his son and retired as a monk to his Kitayama estate on the outskirts of Kyōto. The **Golden Pavilion** (*Kinkaku*) he erected there is the outstanding remaining architectural work of the day, and his coterie of artists was the center of the artistic movements of the most creative epoch of the Ashikaga Period. There **Kan-ami** (1333–1384) and his son **Se-ami** (1363–1444) perfected the highly refined *Nō* drama from earlier dramatic and Terpsichorean performances. The luxurious but artistically creative life of the Kitayama estate was continued for several decades after Yoshimitsu's death by his successors.

1449-1490. Rule of Yoshimasa as *shōgun* (1449–1474) and retired *shōgun*. This was the second great creative period of Ashikaga art. In his Higashiyama estate on the edge of Kyōto, Yoshimasa built the **Silver Pavilion** (*Ginkaku*), which as an architectural work ranks second only to the Golden Pavilion of Yoshimitsu, and here he and a brilliant group of artists and aesthetes, presided over by Nō-ami (1397–1476), enjoyed a life of luxury and artistic elegance.

At the same time the complete collapse of what little authority the Ashikaga exercised over the nation became apparent, and there was great social unrest, resulting in numerous popular uprisings. Under the pressure of popular demands, Yoshimasa, like other Ashikaga *shōgun*, repeatedly issued Acts of Grace (*Tokusei*), which, unlike those of the Kamakura period, were sweeping debt cancellations for the benefit of the whole debtor class.

1465. The monks of the Enryakuji destroyed the Honganji, the central

monastery of the True Pure Land Sect in Kyōto. Such affrays between the great monasteries were common at this time. Rennyō (1415–1499), the eighth hereditary head of the sect, fled to the region north of Kyōto, where his teachings met with great success and his numerous followers built up a military organization to defend their interests.

1467-1477. The **Ōnin War**, ostensibly a contest over the succession in the Ashikaga and other great military families, was actually a reshuffling of domains and power among the feudal lords, who divided into two camps under the leadership of two great war lords of western Japan, **Yamana Mochitoyo** (Sōzen) (1404–1473) and his son-in-law, **Hosokawa Katsumoto** (1430 [1425?]–1473), long the chief minister (*kanryō*) of the military government (1453–1464, 1468–1473). Kyōto was soon laid waste, but both leaders died in 1473, and exhaustion eventually brought peace in 1477. However, local struggles went on unabated. In fact, the Ōnin War was merely the prelude to over a century of almost uninterrupted warfare. This period, which is aptly called the *Epoch of a Warring Country*, witnessed a continual shifting of fiefs and power, the elimination of many of the old feudal families, and the emergence of a new group of territorial lords, now known as *daimyō*.

1488. The **True Pure Land Sect** believers north of Kyōto defeated and killed a local lord. This is considered the first of the *Ikkōikki*, or Uprisings of the Ikkō Sect, another name for the True Pure Land Sect. Such uprisings became increasingly common and acted as a medium for popular manifestations of discontent.

1493. **Hosokawa Masamoto** (1466–1507) drove the *shōgun*, Yoshitane (1490–1494, 1508–1521) out of Kyōto and set up a puppet *shōgun* (1494), acts which were repeated by his adopted son, Takakuni (1484–1531), in 1521. Yoshitane's successors suffered similar indignities as the prestige of the Ashikaga dwindled further.

(*Cont. p.* 542.)

F. PRE-COLUMBIAN AMERICA

The aborigines of America, varying among themselves in certain racial characteristics, migrated from Asia to North America in successive waves by way of the Bering Strait. These migrations began at a very early date, and apparently continued until relatively recent times. The migrants, when they arrived, were in a very primitive state. Becoming isolated from other peoples, they slowly expanded throughout both continents and developed autochthonous cultures which ranged from savagery to a relatively high degree of civilization. Many groups at a comparatively early date attained the agricultural stage, and the Inca of Peru achieved the use of bronze. The use of iron and the principle of the wheel were unknown. The dog universally, the turkey, the duck, and, in the Peruvian highlands, the llama, alpaca, and guanaco were the only existing domestic animals, the llama being the sole beast of burden.

At the time of the discovery the peoples of highest culture, most complex society, and greatest political importance were the Aztec, with their center in the Valley of Anáhuac; the Maya of Yucatan and portions of Mexico and Central America; the Chibcha of the Colombian plateau; and the Inca, whose empire centered in the highlands of Peru. Between the higher civilizations of Mexico, Yucatan, and Central America and between those of the Andean region there was extensive interchange of culture over a lengthy period, and it is possible that there was cultural interchange between the peoples of Central America and those of the Andean region. The civilizations of the Aztec and the Inca were built upon preceding cultures of a high order.

THE AZTECS were originally a minor tribe of the great Nahua group. This group evolved the high Toltec civilization which, receiving through cultural transmission mathematical and astronomical knowledge and a calendar from a lowland people, possibly the Maya, reached its height in the 13th century and declined thereafter, being followed by the transitional Chichimec culture. Reaching the shores of Lake Tezcuco in 1325, the Aztecs erected an impregnable capital, **Tenochtitlán**, in the marshes of the lake and, through superior political and military capacity and alliance, extended their control over central and southern Mexico from the Gulf to the Pacific and established colonies in Central America. In 1519 Tenochtitlán was a city of some 60,000 house-holders and the Aztec Empire included perhaps 5,000,000 inhabitants. The government was relatively centralized, with an elective monarch, provincial governors appointed by the central authority, a well-organized judicial system, and a large and efficient army. The Aztecs attained a high degree of development in engineering, architecture, art, mathematics, and astronomy. Principal buildings were of mortar and rubble faced with stucco. There existed a body of tradition, history, philosophy, and poetry which was orally transmitted. Picture writing which was rapidly approaching phonetic was evolved. Music was rudimentarily developed. Agriculture was far advanced and commerce and simple industry flourished. The working of gold and silver and the production of pottery and textiles were highly developed. The religion of the Aztecs was polytheistic, and although it included many lofty concepts the deity of war, Huitzilopochtli, was the principal god and his worship led to the development of one of the most extensive systems of human sacrifice which has ever existed. The priesthood constituted a powerful group, political as well as religious. Certain of the peoples subjected by the Aztecs were restive under their domination and were prepared to rebel at the first opportunity. In the mountains to the east of Lake Tezcuco there existed the powerful republic of Tlaxcala, which, maintaining its independence, regarded the Aztec as hereditary enemies. These conditions created a situation favorable to the Spaniards during the conquest.

THE MAYA before the Christian Era established themselves in the peninsula of Yucatan, Tabasco, Chiapas, northern, central, and eastern Guatemala, and western Honduras. They developed a civilization which, reaching its apogee well before 1000 A.D., was in certain cultural aspects the highest in the New World. The Maya culture in the earlier period extended with considerable uniformity throughout the greater part of their general area, but after about 1000 A.D., tended to center in the northern part of the peninsula of Yucatan. During the period of highest development the Maya did not evolve a unified empire, the area being divided into city states governed by politico-religious rulers or ruling groups. Art, architecture, mathematics, engineering, and astronomy were far advanced, and the Maya had evolved the conception of zero, a vigesimal numerical system, and a calendar more accurate than the Julian. Temples and other major buildings were constructed of stone and mortar and were faced with carved stone. A system of causeways existed. Codices were formed for religious and astronomical purposes, but writing did not exist. A body of traditions, history, and religious prophecies were orally preserved. Religion was polytheistic and relatively humane, and the priestly class, exercising political authority as well as religious, possessed, with the ruling groups, a monopoly of learning. Widespread commerce existed, and weaving and pottery making were well developed. Agriculture was on an exceedingly high level. Civil war occurred during the 13th century and certain Mexican groups conquered the Maya of northern Yucatan. Mexican cultural influences were consequently introduced, especially in art, and religion. In the same century a greater degree of political cohesion appears to have been established in the northern part of the peninsula, and this resulted in a period of peace which endured until the 15th century, when internecine strife led to the destruction of Mayapan in 1451 and the abandonment of the great cities Chichen Itzá and Uxmal. The Maya civilization was decadent culturally and politically when the Spaniards arrived, although certain of the independent provinces were relatively powerful militarily. The Maya of Yucatan numbered perhaps 400,000 to 500,000 on the eve of the Spanish conquest.

THE CHIBCHA. The political organization of the Chibcha, who numbered some 1,000,000, was comparatively cohesive. The Zipa at Bacatá and the Zaque at Tunja were the political rulers, and supreme religious authority was held by the high-priest known as the *Iraca*. The Chibcha possessed a well-developed calendar and numerical system and employed pictographs. Extensive commerce and simple industry existed, ceramics and textiles being highly developed. In gold working the Chibcha were in certain respects unequaled. The Chibcha employed wood and thatch in the construction of buildings.

THE INCA, with their capital at Cuzco, successors to the high coastal and upland cultures of Chimú, Nasca, Pachacamac, and Tiahuanaco, which flourished during the early centuries of the Christian Era, extended their control over the area from Ecuador to central Chile along the coast and inland to the eastern slopes of the Andes including the Bolivian plateau. Expansion was particularly rapid from the 14th century onward and one of the greatest of the conquerors, Huayna Capac, lived until the eve of the Spanish conquest. The empire, with a population of perhaps 6,000,000 to 8,000,000, was a thoroughly organized absolute, paternal, socialistic, and theocratic despotism. All power emanated from the Inca as the ruler and representative of the Sun Deity, whose worship constituted the religion of the Inca. There existed a close-knit and graduated system of provincial and local administration. Each individual had a fixed place in society, and the state benignly provided for the welfare of all. The army was large and well organized, and a system of post and military roads extended to all portions of the empire. In mathematics and astronomy the Inca were not as accomplished as the Maya and Aztec, but in engineering, architecture, and the production of textiles and ceramics they were far advanced. The Inca did not evolve writing, but possessed a device to aid memory in the form of the *quipu*, through which governmental records were kept, tradition was preserved, and messages were sent. In gold working a high degree of skill was attained. Commerce, entailing extensive navigation along the coast, was well developed. A great body of oral tradition and poetry existed, and music was comparatively well developed. Principal buildings were of stone. Politically the Inca were the most advanced of the peoples of the New World. At his death Huayna Capac, contrary to practice, divided the empire between Huáscar, his son by a lawful wife, and Atahualpa, his son by a concubine. A civil war followed, in which Atahualpa, shortly before the arrival of the Spaniards, triumphed and imprisoned his half-brother.

G. THE GREAT DISCOVERIES

1. ASIA

The Crusades left Europe with a greatly expanded horizon, with much more extensive trade interests and connections, and with an accentuated hostility toward Islam. The great conquests of the Mongols in the 13th century (**Jenghiz Khan**, 1206–1227; period of greatness under **Kublai Khan**, 1259–1294), in uniting most of Asia, the Near East, and eastern Europe under one sway opened direct communication between Europe and the Orient and raised the prospect of an alliance against the Moslems.

1160-1173. Rabbi **Benjamin of Tudela** (in Navarre) traveled through Persia, central Asia, and to the very confines of China, but for religious reasons his records had little influence on Christian Europe. The same was true of the researches of the great Arab geographer **Yaqut**, who lived in the late 12th and early 13th centuries and wrote a great geographical dictionary.

1245-1247. Travels of **John of Pian de Carpine,** an Umbrian sent to the court of the Great Khan to propose an alliance against Islam and if possible to convert the Mongols. Traveling by way of southern Russia and the Volga, Carpine crossed central Asia and reached the Mongol court at Karakorum. Though well received his mission proved abortive.

1253-1255. Mission of **William of Rubruck,** a Fleming sent by St. Louis of France to the court of the Great Khan. Rubruck followed much the same route as Carpine and left one of the finest travel accounts of the Middle Ages.

1255-1266. First journey of the Polo brothers, Nicolo and Maffeo, Venetian traders in the Black Sea, who traveled to central Asia, spent three years in Bokhara and proceeded thence to China. They returned to Acre in 1269, bearing letters to the pope from the Mongol ruler.

1271-1295. **Second journey of the Polos,** accompanied this time by Nicolo's seventeen-year-old son, **Marco,** greatest of all mediaeval travelers. They took the route Mosul-Baghdad-Ormuz-Kerman-Khorasan-Pamir-Kashgar and thence across the Gobi Desert to the court of the Great Khan. The Mongol ruler was so favorably impressed that he took them into his service.

During the next fifteen years Marco became acquainted with much of China, Cochin-China, Burma, and India. The Polos returned by sea by way of Sumatra, India, and Persia. Marco's famous *Book of Various Experiences* was dictated, probably in 1297, while he was a prisoner in Genoa. It was almost immediately popular and colored the whole geographic outlook of the succeeding period. Marco died in 1324.

1290-1340. During this period lively trade relations sprang up between Europe and Asia. Specific records are few, but such as they are they indicate the existence of commercial colonies and missionary groups in Persia (Tabriz), in India (Gujerat and Malabar coast), and in China (Peking and other cities). The great trade routes from Central Asia through southeastern Russia and the Black Sea, and from Trebizond through Persia were wide open. Embassies were constantly passing between western rulers and the Ilkhans of Persia, whose emissaries on various occasions came as far as England (1287, 1289, 1290, 1307).

1289. The pope sent out Friar **John of Monte Corvino** to take charge of the newly established Archbishopric of Peking. John remained at his post until his death in 1328 and seems to have built a flourishing Christian community.

1324-1328. Friar **Oderic of Pordenone** traveled to China, leaving one of the best accounts of the country.

1328. The pope established a Bishopric of Quilon and sent out **Jordanus of Severac** to take charge.

1338-1346. **John Marignolli** was sent out to Peking as legate of the pope.

1340. **Francesco Pegolotti,** a Florentine trader at the Genoese station at Kaffa (Black Sea, founded 1266), wrote his *Merchants' Handbook (Della Pratica della Mercatura)*, most valuable business manual of the time, which gives an unrivaled account of the commercial communications with Asia.

1368. Overthrow of the Mongol domination in China. Under the succeeding Ming dynasty foreigners were again excluded. The conquests of Timur the Great, shortly after, served to block the Near-Eastern trade channels once more.

2. AFRICA

During the Middle Ages much of Africa was familiar to the Arabs. **Ibn Batuta,** greatest of Arab travelers, between the years 1325 and 1349 journeyed from his home in Morocco across northern Africa, through Egypt, the Near East, Arabia, eastern Africa, and thence to India. Later he traveled northward to the Crimea and thence through central Asia to India. After spending eight years at Delhi, he went on to Ceylon and China. On his return to Morocco in 1349, he set out across the Sahara and visited Timbuktu and the Niger region. His remarkable journeys serve to record not only the Arab trade from Egypt down the east coast to Africa and to India and beyond, but also the regular caravan trade from southern Morocco across the desert to the **Kingdom of Ghana** (i.e. Guinea) in Nigeria.

1225. Under the tolerant rule of the Almohades and Marinides in Morocco, the Franciscans and Dominicans were allowed to establish their missionary centers in the country. By the end of the 13th century Christian and more particularly Jewish European merchants were engaged in the trans-Saharan trade, dealing chiefly in gold and ivory. In 1447 the Genoese Antonio Malfante penetrated far to the south.

1316. Having heard of a Christian king in East Africa (legend of **Prester John,** widespread in Europe after the spurious letter of 1165), the pope sent eight Dominicans to Ethiopia. Others seem to have been sent in the course of the century.

1402. An **Ethiopian embassy** reached Venice. There were others in 1408 and 1427. In 1452 Ethiopian emissaries arrived at Lisbon and in 1481 at Rome. The object of these embassies, and of those sent in return (especially by the pope in 1453) was to establish a Christian alliance against the Moslem Mamelukes in Egypt and later against the Ottoman Turks. Nothing came of this project, but the exchange of missions served to acquaint Europe with that part of Africa.

1270. Beginning of Portuguese exploration of the west coast of Africa. The Portuguese Malocello visited the Canary Islands (1340–1341). These were assigned by the pope to the crown of Castile (1344).

1291. The two Genoese, Doria and Vivaldo, set out to find a route to India by sea; they never returned and nothing is known of their explorations.

1394-1460. PRINCE HENRY THE NAVIGATOR, the greatest patron of cosmography and discovery. Through his mother a grandson of John of Gaunt. Prince Henry, as general of the *Order of Christ*, was able to turn the crusading enthusiasm as well as the funds of the order into the fields of science and discovery. From 1418 onward the prince sent out, almost annually, expeditions carefully prepared and ably conducted. There can be little doubt that the religious factor dominated the work of the prince, though the scientific and commercial factors were hardly less important. That Prince Henry hoped to open up direct communications with Guinea by sea is clear. That he hoped ultimately to find a sea-route to Ethiopia and thence to India has been questioned by some, but is reasonably certain.

1418-1419. Exploration of the **Madeira Islands,** some of which had been known before. The Azores, some of which appear on the *Medicean Portolano* of 1351, but probably as imaginary islands, were discovered by Diogo de Seville in 1427–1431.

1425. Expedition sent by Prince Henry to conquer the Canaries from Castile. Thereafter the prince tried hard to secure the islands by negotiation and so exclude Castile from any share in the West African trade. Further attacks were made upon them in 1450–1453, but by the **Treaty of Alcaçovas** (1480, Mar. 6) they were definitely assigned to Castile, while West Africa, Guinea, and the islands of the ocean were assigned to Portugal.

1433. After more than ten years of repeated efforts, the Portuguese (under Gil Eannes) succeeded in doubling **Cape Bojador.** The advance then became rapid. Gold and natives were brought back and slave-raiding (later forbidden by Prince Henry) began.

1444. Nuño Tristam reached the Senegal River.

1445. Dinis Dias rounded Cape Verde. By this time the most barren part of the coast was passed and a lively trade with West Africa (c. 25 caravels a year) developed.

1455-1457. Alvise da Cadamosto (Cà da Mosto), a Venetian in the service of Prince Henry, explored the Senegal and Gambia Rivers and discovered the Cape Verde Islands.

1469. After the death of Prince Henry there was a slackening of activity and the King, Afonso V, for financial reasons leased the Guinea trade for five years to Fernão Gomes, with the stipulation that exploration be carried forward at least 100 leagues annually.

1470-1471. Under Gomes' auspices, João de Santarem and Pedro de Escolar reached Mina on the Gold Coast, where the Portuguese established a factory (fort, 1482) and did a rich trade in gold.

1472. Fernando Po discovered the island which bears his name. Lopo Gonçalves crossed the equator and Ruy de Sequeira reached latitude 2° south.

1481. With the accession of John II (1481–1495) the crown once more took in hand the work of exploration, and with greater energy than ever.

1482-1484. Diogo Cão reached the mouth of the Congo River and Cape St. Augustine. In 1485–1486 he advanced to Cape Cross and Cape Negro.

1487. King John organized expeditions by land and by sea in the hope of reaching Ethiopia and India. Pedro de Covilhã and Alfonso de Paiva were sent out by way of Cairo and Aden. Covilhã reached India and on his return followed the east coast of Africa as far south as the mouth of the Zambesi.

1487, Aug.–1488, Dec. VOYAGE OF BARTOLOMEU DIAS. Having followed the African coast, Dias was driven by a great storm (Dec.–Feb.) south of the tip of Africa. He turned east and soon discovered hills running to the northeast, showing him that he had rounded the Cape of Good Hope. He followed the east coast of Africa as far as Mossel Bay and the Great Fish River and then was obliged by his crew to return.

1497, July 8–1499, Aug. 29 or Sept. 9. VOYAGE OF VASCO DA GAMA. This would have been undertaken sooner, excepting for internal troubles in Portugal and disputes with Castile arising from the discoveries of Columbus. Da Gama left with four ships to find the way to India, the feasibility of the route being perfectly clear after the discoveries of Covilhã and Dias. He rounded the Cape in Nov. 1497, reached Quilimane (Jan. 1498), Mozam-

bique (Mar.), and then Mombasa. Despite trouble with the jealous Arab traders, he was finally able to get a pilot from Melindi. He reached Calicut on the Malabar coast (May 22). He started for home in Aug. 1498, touched Melindi (Jan. 1499) and rounded the Cape (Mar.). The exact date of his arrival at Lisbon is disputed.

1500, Mar. 9.–1501, June 23. VOYAGE OF CABRAL, who set out with 13 ships to establish Portuguese trade in the east. After touching Brazil (p. 368) he went on to India, which he reached in Sept. The fleet loaded pepper and other spices and arrived safely in Lisbon. From this time on Portuguese trading fleets went regularly to India, and Lisbon soon became the chief entrepôt in Europe for oriental products.

1501. Vasco da Gama was sent out with 20 ships to punish the Arabs and to close the Red Sea, in order to cut the trade route through Egypt to Alexandria.

1505. Francisco de Almeida sent out as first governor of India. He took Quiloa and Mombasa on the African coast and established forts at Calicut, Cananor, and Cochin on the Malabar coast.

1509, Feb. 2. Almeida destroyed the fleet of the Moslems in the battle of Diu, thus definitely establishing Portuguese control in Indian waters.

1509-1515. Governorship of Afonso de Albuquerque, who in 1507 had conquered Ormuz on the Persian Gulf. Albuquerque made Goa the capital of the Portuguese possessions (1510), and in 1511 took Malacca. He opened communication with Siam, the Moluccas, and China.

1513. Jorge Alvarez first landed near Canton.

1517. Fernão Peres de Andrade appeared with a squadron at Canton.

1542. Antonio da Mota and two companions, driven by a storm, first reached Japan.

1557. The Portuguese established themselves at Macão (near Canton) and initiated regular trade with China.

The opening of the direct route to India at once began the revolution in the conditions of trade between Europe and Asia. The Mamelukes in Egypt had controlled the main routes, from the Persian Gulf to Syrian ports and from the Red Sea to Alexandria, and from these ports the Venetians shipped to western Europe. The Egyptian sultan kept the consignments small (210 tons of pepper per year) and the prices were therefore high. By 1503 the price of pepper in Lisbon was only one-fifth what it was in Venice. When the Portuguese succeeded in blocking the Red Sea route, the Egyptian-Venetian trade was more or less ruined. The conquest of Syria and Egypt by the Turks (1516–1517), though frequently described as a stimulus to the discovery of new routes, had almost nothing to do with the situation. On the contrary the Turkish sultans (notably Suleiman, 1520–1566) did what they could to reopen the Near-Eastern routes.

3. AMERICA

a. PRE-COLUMBIAN DISCOVERIES

790. Irish Monks, searching for religious retreats and for new fields of missionary enterprise, reached Iceland, after discovering the Faroe Islands in the 7th century.

874. The Norsemen (Normans, Vikings) arrived in Iceland and settled.

981. The Norsemen, under Erik the Red, discovered Greenland and settled on the southwest coast (985–986).

1000. LEIF ERICSSON, returning from Norway to Greenland, was driven onto the American coast, which he called *Wineland* (Vinland), from the grapes he found there. Wineland was probably Nova Scotia.

1003-1006. THORFINN KARLSEFNI set out from Greenland with three ships to settle Wineland. He and his party spent three winters on the American continent. There is no general agreement regarding the localities visited by him, which have been placed by different authorities as far apart as Labrador and Florida. One recent writer puts the *Helluland* (Flat-stone Land) of the Greenlandic-Icelandic sagas in northeastern Labrador; *Markland* (Wood Land) in southern Labrador; *Furdustrand* (Wonder Strand) on the north side of the Gulf of St. Lawrence; *Straumfjord* (Stream Fjord), where the first and third winters were spent, on Chaleur Bay (New Brunswick); and *Hop* (Lagoon) on the New England coast, either north or south of Cape Cod. Another recent writer is convinced that Karksefni visited only the Labrador coast and both sides of the northern peninsula of Newfoundland, Straumfjord being, perhaps, in the vicinity of Hare Bay. Wineland was first mentioned in the *Hamburg Church History* of Adam of Bremen (1074 ff.), but most of our knowledge derives from the Norse sagas written down in the 14th century. Supposed Norse remains on the American continent (*Dighton Rock, Old Stone Mill at Newport*) have all been rejected by scholars as spurious, with the exception of the Kensington Stone, found near Kensington, Minnesota, in 1898, under the roots of a tree 70 years old. The stone contains a long runic inscription recording the presence there of a group of Norsemen in 1362. The stone and the inscription are clearly not forgeries, and a majority of geographers as well as many historians are disposed to accept the authenticity of the record. The philologists are less favorable, because of irregularities in the language that are hard to explain. Within recent years a Norse grave, with sword, shield, and two axes, is reported to have been found in Ontario.

How long the Norsemen continued to visit America is obviously an open question. The last definite mention, apart from the Kensington Stone evidence, is for 1189 A.D., but there is some reason to believe that they came at least as far as southern Labrador for ship's timber as late as 1347. After that date the Greenland colonies declined, though the West Colony (in southeast Greenland) continued to exist until at least the mid-15th century and ships appear to have gone there periodically, probably trading in walrus hides and tusks.

1470-1474. Between these years two Germans in the Danish service, Didrick Pining and Hans Pothorst, undertook a voyage to Iceland and the west, supposedly at the request of the King of Portugal. Pining was a great seaman and the terror of the English; from 1478 to 1490 he was governor of Iceland. There is no reason why he should not have been able to reach America, but the evidence does not show that he and Pothorst went beyond Greenland. On a map of 1537 it is stated that a famous pilot, **Johannes Scolvus** (claimed by some to have been a Pole — Jan Szkolny), reached Labrador at this time. It has been held by some scholars that he must have accompanied Pining and Pothorst, but, since Labrador at this time was a name generally used for Greenland, it seems unlikely that Scolvus went beyond the old Norse settlements. From the Portuguese connection with the expedition it has been concluded by some that João Vaz Corte Real went along. There is no satisfactory evidence of this, but in 1474 Corte Real was rewarded with the captaincy of one of the Azores Islands for having made a voyage to the "Land of the Codfish" (?Newfoundland), so that some scholars are well-disposed toward the theory that he may have reached America. But the markings on early maps make it seem likely that he too failed to get beyond Greenland. It is not unlikely, though there is no real evidence, that Breton, Gascon, or Basque fishermen regularly visited the Grand Banks in this period. In any event there is no proof of realization of any pre-Columbian discovery, or of any influence on later attempts.

A great many theories have been advanced in recent years, notably by the Portuguese, but also by others, to show that the Portuguese knew of the existence of America before Columbus sailed. Most of the theories rest upon conjecture and clever deductions. All we can say is that, after the translation of Ptolemy's *Geography* into Latin (1410), the idea of the sphericity of the earth (never entirely lost during the Middle Ages, cf. Roger Bacon's *Opus Majus* of the late 13th century) spread rapidly in scientific circles and revived the idea of reaching Asia by sailing westward. Prince Henry the Navigator, for all his interest in the African route, sent expeditions to the west. In 1427-1431 Diogo de Seville discovered seven of the Azores, which may have been known to the Italians as early as 1351. Flores and Colvo were discovered in 1451-1452. The map of Andrea Bianco (1448) shows land of the proper conformation where Brazil lies. It is clear that after 1450 many Portuguese expeditions set out in search of legendary islands (St. Brandan's, Brazil, Antillia, Island of the Seven Cities, etc.) and, according to some scholars, the Lisbon government enforced a policy of rigorous secrecy with regard to new findings. Nevertheless, no present evidence of Portuguese knowledge of America before 1492 can be regarded as conclusive.

b. THE VOYAGES OF COLUMBUS

1451, bet. Aug. 26 and Oct. 31. CRISTO-FORO COLOMBO (Span. Cristóbal Colón) born near Genoa, the son of Domenico Colombo, a weaver. Almost nothing definite is known of his youth (general unreliability of the biography by his son Fernando). He was probably himself a weaver and probably went to sea only in 1472, when he made a trip to Scio. He seems to have come to Portugal in 1476 and to have made a voyage to England in 1477 (the story of his visit to Iceland is rejected by almost all authorities). In 1478 he appears to have made a voyage to the Madeiras and in 1482 possibly to the Guinea coast. In 1480 he married the daughter of Bartholomew Perestrello, hereditary captain of Porto Santo, near Madeira. By this time Columbus must have learned much about Portuguese discoveries and certainly about the ideas current in Lisbon. His appeal to the great Florentine geographer, **Paolo Toscanelli**, and the latter's reply (1474) urging a voyage to the west, have been called in question by some writers and may be spurious. In any event the idea of seeking India or China in the west was not novel.

1483 or 1484. Columbus appealed to King John II of Portugal to finance a voyage to the west, but whether to seek new islands or a route to Asia is not clear. At this very time the king was authorizing self-financed expeditions to the west of the Azores (1486, Ferman Dulmo) and he might have licensed Columbus had the latter been willing to finance himself. Others maintain that the Portuguese already knew that Asia could not be reached in this way. Apparently Columbus, whose geographical knowledge appears to have been very incomplete, was regarded as a vain boaster. His project was rejected.

1486. Columbus, through the mediation of some Franciscan monks, was able to submit his project to **Ferdinand and Isabella** of Spain. His religious fervor and personal magnetism impressed the queen, but the project was again rejected by experts. In the following years Columbus met the three Pinzón brothers, wealthy traders and expert navigators, from whom he doubtless learned much.

1492. After being recalled to court, Columbus finally induced the queen to finance his expedition. It is not yet clear whether he set out to discover new islands and territories, or whether his object was to find a route to the Indies. He was made admiral and governor of the territories to be discovered, but also carried letters to the Great Khan, which makes it probable that his purpose was twofold.

1492, Aug. 3-1493, Mar. 15. THE FIRST VOYAGE. Columbus left Palos with three ships, of which Martin Pinzón commanded one, and the famous pilot Juan de la Cosa another. He left the Canaries (Sept. 6) and reached land in the Bahamas (probably Watling's Island) (Oct. 12),

naming it *San Salvador*. He then discovered Cuba, which he thought was the
territory of the Great Khan, and Santo
Domingo (Española). A post, Navidad,
was established on Santo Domingo, after
which Columbus returned (1493, Jan. 4),
touching at the Azores (Feb. 15), landing at
Lisbon (Mar. 4) and finally reaching Palos
(Mar. 15). He announced that he had
discovered the Indies, news of which spread
over Europe with great rapidity and caused
much excitement.

1493, May 4. The Line of Demarcation.
At the instance of the Spanish
rulers, who feared counterclaims by Portugal, Pope Alexander VI granted to the
Catholic kings exclusive right to and possession of all lands to the south and west
toward India, not held by a Christian prince
on Christmas Day, 1492, beyond a line
drawn one hundred leagues west of the
Azores and Cape Verde Islands.

**1493, Sept. 25-1496, June 11. SECOND
VOYAGE OF COLUMBUS.** He
left with 17 caravels and 1500 men to
establish Spanish power. On this voyage
he discovered Dominica, Puerto Rico, and
other of the Antilles and Jamaica, explored
the southern coast of Cuba and circumnavigated Española, where he founded the
town of Isabella. He left his brother
Bartholomew in charge, who in 1496 transferred the settlement to the southern coast
(Santo Domingo).

**1494, June 7. TREATY OF TORDESIL-
LAS,** between Portugal and Spain.
The line of demarcation was moved 270
leagues further west, Portugal to have exclusive rights to all lands to the east of it,
and Spain of all lands to the west. The
making of this treaty is not entirely clear,
and it has often been used as an argument
to prove that Portugal already knew of
Brazil, which, by the treaty, was brought
into the Portuguese sphere.

**1498, May 30-1500, Nov. 25. THIRD
VOYAGE OF COLUMBUS.** Dis-
covery of Trinidad Island (1498, July 31)
and South America (Aug. 1) near the mouth
of the Orinoco. He explored the coast
westward as far as Margarita Island. He
then went to Española, where a revolt
broke out against him. He requested the
crown to send out a judge. The government sent out to the Indies **Francisco de
Bobadilla** (1499), who sent Columbus and
his brother to Spain as prisoners. Columbus was released and treated with distinction, but, despite the earlier rights
granted him, was never restored to his
former authority or monopolistic grants.
With Bobadilla direct royal control was
established.

**1502, May 11-1504, Nov. 7. FOURTH
VOYAGE OF COLUMBUS.** He
reached the coast of Honduras and
passed south to Panama, returning after having suffered ship-
wreck at Jamaica.

**1506, May 21. Columbus died in relative
obscurity at Valladolid.** It is
reasonably clear that he believed to the
end of his days that he had discovered outlying parts of Asia, despite the fact that
ever since 1493 the conviction had spread
among experts (e.g. **Peter Martyr**) that a
New World had been discovered.

c. POST-COLUMBIAN
DISCOVERIES

**1497, May 2-Aug. 6. VOYAGE OF
JOHN CABOT.** Cabot was a
wealthy Italian merchant (born in Genoa,
resident in Venice) who had traveled in
the east (Black Sea, Alexandria, Mecca)
and who settled in England about 1490.
For several years he sent out expeditions
from Bristol to seek the island of Brazil,
in the hope of securing the valuable Brazil
wood used in dyeing. Columbus' supposed
discovery of Asia in the west spurred him
on. The expedition reached land (June 24)
evidently on Cape Breton Island, whence
it then cruised along the southern coast of
Newfoundland. Cabot was convinced that
he had discovered the country of the Great
Khan and intended to return, passing south
along the coast to the region of Brazil wood
and spices.

1498, May. John and Sebastian Cabot
sailed with six ships on a second
voyage. They went north, coasted along
the east coast of Greenland, thence passed
to Labrador and went south by Newfoundland, Nova Scotia, and the New England
coast, as far as perhaps Delaware. Thence
they returned to England. The date of
their arrival is not known. Having found
no spices, their efforts evidently no longer
interested the king or country. John Cabot
is not heard of after March, 1499.

1498. King John of Portugal sent out the
famous captain, explorer, and
scientist, **Duarte Pacheco Pereira**, to investigate the lands in the west. Duarte's
account (written in 1505 but published
only in 1892) indicates that he may have
reached the South American coast. He
speaks of a vast continent extending from
70° N.L. to 28° S.L.

1499, May-1500, June. Voyage of **Alonso
de Ojeda** and **Amerigo Vespucci**
in the service of Spain. They landed in
French Guiana, discovered the mouth of
the Amazon and proceeded as far as Cape

St. Roque, after which they returned north and west along the coast as far as the Magdalena River and reached home by way of Española. An earlier voyage (1497–1498) by Vespucci, of which he himself tells in the confused and probably spurious sources, has been generally rejected by scholars. Vespucci (1451–1512) was a Florentine resident in Seville, probably an agent of the Medici banking firm.

1499, Sept.–1500, Dec. Voyage of **Vicente Yañez Pinzón.** Pinzón made a landfall near Cape San Roque (**1500**, Jan.) and thence followed the coast northwestward. At about the same time the Spaniard, **Diego de Lepe,** explored the Brazilian coast from Cape San Roque to about 10° S.L.

1500, Apr. 21. The Portuguese commander, **Pedrálvarez Cabral,** sailing to India with 13 caravels, and accompanied by such distinguished captains as Dias and Duarte Pacheco, landed in Brazil, coming from the Cape Verde Islands. The party stayed only about ten days, but took official possession of the country which Cabral named *Tierra de Vera Cruz.* The idea of Cabral having been the first to discover Brazil, like the idea that his landing there was accidental, has now been given up by some scholars, but the evidence is quite inadequate and the question remains open.

1500. The Portuguese, **Gaspar de Corte Real,** son of João Vaz, voyaged to the east coast of Greenland and to Labrador. In 1501 he set out on a second expedition, exploring Labrador and thence turning south. He himself was lost on this expedition, but his brother Michael carried out yet another voyage in 1502 to the Newfoundland coast. He too was lost at sea.

1501, May–1502, Sept. SECOND VOYAGE OF AMERIGO VESPUCCI, this time in the service of Portugal. The voyage took him south along the Brazilian coast to about 32° S.L. if not farther. It was from the published account of this voyage and from Vespucci's conviction that what had been found was a *New World* that the geographer **Martin Waldseemüller** was led to propose that this New World be called *America* (1507). The name was at first applied only to South America and the use of it spread slowly until its general adoption toward the end of the 16th century.

Further explorations need not be listed in detail. **De Bastidas** traced the coast from Panama to Port Manzanilla (1500–1502); **Vicente Pinzón** followed the mainland from the Bay of Honduras to beyond the easternmost point of Brazil (1508); **Ocampo** circumnavigated Cuba (1508), which was conquered by **Diego Velázquez** (1511); **Juan Ponce de Leon,** the governor of Puerto Rico, discovered Florida (1512).

1513, Sept. 25. **Vasco Nuñez de Balboa** crossed the Isthmus of Panama and discovered the Pacific Ocean.

1515–1516. **Juan Diaz de Solis,** chief pilot of Spain, searching for a strait to the Pacific, explored the coast of South America from near Rio de Janeiro to the Rio de la Plata, where he was slain.

1517. **Francisco Hernández de Córdoba** discovered Yucatan, finding traces of large cities and great wealth.

1518. **Juan de Grijalva** followed the coast north from Yucatan to the Panuco River.

1519. **Alvárez Pineda** completed exploration of the Gulf of Mexico by coasting from Florida to Vera Cruz and back. **Francisco de Gordillo** advanced up the Atlantic coast to South Carolina (1521), and **Pedro de Quexos** as far as 40° N.L. (1525). At the same time (1524–1525) **Esteban Gómez,** sailing from Spain, followed the coast from Nova Scotia in the north to Florida in the south.

1519–1522. CIRCUMNAVIGATION OF THE GLOBE BY FERDINAND MAGELLAN (Fernão de Magalhães, 1480–1521). Magellan was sent out by the Spanish crown to find a strait to the Moluccas. He reached the Brazilian coast near Pernambuco, explored the estuary of the Rio de la Plata and, after wintering at Port St. Julian, passed through the strait which bears his name and entered the South Sea, to which the name *Mare Pacificum* was given. After following the coast to about 50° S.L. he turned northwest and after months of sailing reached the Ladrones and Philippines. In the latter place he was killed in a skirmish with the natives. One of his vessels, under **Sebastian del Cano,** continued westward and reached Spain, thus completing the circumnavigation of the globe.

IV. THE EARLY MODERN PERIOD

A. EUROPE AND THE NEAR EAST, 1500-1648

1. ENGLAND, SCOTLAND, AND IRELAND, 1485-1649

1485-1603. HOUSE OF TUDOR.
1485-1509. HENRY VII. Henry's first act was to imprison the **Earl of Warwick**, son of the Duke of Clarence. His first Parliament (1485) confirmed the crown to him and his heirs. Though the traditional mediaeval checks on the power of the crown were maintained in theory, in practice Henry went a long way toward developing royal absolutism—establishment of the administrative court later called the **Star-Chamber** (1487), suppression of private feudal armies, development of an efficient, if arbitrary, royal financial system (Empson, Dudley, "Morton's Fork").
1487. The pretended Earl of Warwick (Simnel) landed in England, but was defeated at **Stoke** (June 16, 1487), and became one of the king's scullions.
1488-1499. Attempts of **Perkin Warbeck**, a Fleming who personated the Duke of York, to overthrow Henry. Disavowed by Charles VIII in the **Peace of Étaples** (Nov. 9, 1492), which ended the war in which Henry had engaged on account of the annexation of Brittany by Charles VIII (1491), Warbeck found a warm reception in Flanders from the Duchess of Burgundy, sister of Edward IV. Expelled from Flanders, he fled to Scotland, where his claim was recognized. Warbeck and James IV of Scotland invaded England in 1496. In 1497 a formidable insurrection broke out in Cornwall on occasion of an imposition of a tax by Parliament. It was suppressed by the defeat at **Blackheath** (June 22, 1497), and the leaders executed (Flammock). **Peace with Scotland** (Sept. 1497). Warbeck was soon taken and imprisoned in the Tower, whence he escaped, but was recaptured. Plotting another escape with the Earl of Warwick, both Perkin and Warwick were executed (1499).
1494. STATUTE OF DROGHEDA (*Poyning's law*): (1) No Irish Parliament should be held without the consent of the King of England. (2) No bill could be brought forward in an Irish Parliament without his consent. (3) All recent laws enacted in the English Parliament should hold in Ireland.
1496. *Intercursus magnus*, commercial treaty with Netherlands, granted mutual privileges to English and Flemings and provided fixed duties.
1502. Marriage of Henry's eldest daughter, Margaret, with James IV, king of Scotland.
1509-1547. HENRY VIII. He was six times married: (1) **Catharine of Aragon**, widow of his brother Arthur, mother of Mary the Catholic (married June 3, 1509, divorced March 30, 1533). (2) **Anne Boleyn**, mother of Elizabeth (married Jan. 25, 1533, beheaded May 19, 1536). (3) **Jane Seymour** (married May 20, 1536, died after the birth of her son Edward VI, Oct. 24, 1537). (4) Anne of Cleves (married Jan. 6, 1540, divorced June 24, 1540). (5) **Catharine Howard** (married Aug. 8, 1540, beheaded Feb. 12, 1542). (6) **Catharine Parr** (married July 10, 1543, outlived the king). Henry united in his person the claim of both Lancaster and York.
1511. Henry a member of the **Holy League** (pp. 394, 398). Having laid claim to the French crown, he sent troops to Spain, which were unsuccessful (1512). In 1513 the king went to France in person and with Emperor Maximilian won the bloodless victory of
1513, Aug. 17. Guinegate, the *Battle of the Spurs.*
1513, Sept. 9. Battle of Flodden Field. Defeat and death of James IV of Scotland, who was allied with France.
1514, Aug. Peace with France (Tournay ceded to England, afterward [1518] bought by France for 600,000 crowns) and with Scotland.
1515. THOMAS WOLSEY (1475?-1530), the king's favorite, cardinal and chancellor, papal legate.
1520, June 7. Meeting of **Henry VIII and Francis I** of France near **Calais** (*Field of the Cloth of Gold*).

Europe in the 16th century

1521. Execution of the **Duke of Buckingham** on a charge of high treason. Buckingham was descended from Edward III.

1521. Henry wrote the *Assertion of the Seven Sacraments* in reply to Luther, and received the title of *Defender of the Faith* from Pope Leo X.

After the **battle of Pavia (p. 394),** the relations between Henry and the emperor, which had been weakened by the double failure of the emperor to secure the promised election of Wolsey as pope, became so strained that war seemed inevitable, and a forced loan was assessed on the kingdom, which brought in but little. In 1523 an attempt to force a grant from Parliament met with no success. but a rebellion was provoked which was suppressed only by abandoning the demand.

1527. Henry, desiring to divorce his wife in order to marry **Anne Boleyn,** alleged the invalidity of marriage with a deceased brother's wife, and appealed to Rome. The delays of the pope and the scruples of Wolsey enraged the king, who in 1529 deprived the latter of the great seal and gave it to Sir Thomas More (1478–1535; published *Utopia* in Latin, 1516). Sentence and pardon of Wolsey, who, however, died in disgrace (1530). At the suggestion of **Cranmer** (1489–1556) the question was referred to the universities of England and Europe, and a number deciding in the king's favor, Henry married Anne Boleyn. Henry also broke with the Church of Rome. Confiscation of the annates, followed by the resignation of Sir Thomas More (1532).

The pope excommunicated Henry and annulled his divorce from Catharine, which Cranmer, now Archbishop of Canterbury, had pronounced. After the birth of **Elizabeth,** Parliament confirmed the divorce, recognized Elizabeth as heir to the throne (1534), and secured the succession to other children of Anne in case of the death of the princess.

1534. ACT OF SUPREMACY, appointing the king and his successors *Protector and only Supreme Head of the Church and Clergy of England.* This may be taken as the decisive beginning of the **English Reformation.** The break with Rome had political and personal origins; at first there were no real differences in dogma and liturgy. Refusal to take the oath of supremacy was made high treason, under which vote Sir Thomas More was condemned and beheaded (1535).

Thomas Cromwell (1485?–1540), a former servant of Wolsey and his successor in the favor of the king, now vicegerent in matters relating to the Church in England, issued a commission for the inspection of monasteries which resulted in the suppression, first of the smaller (1536). and afterward (1539) of the larger monasteries, and the confiscation of their property. Abbots now ceased to sit in Parliament.

1536. Execution of **Anne Boleyn** on a charge of adultery. Princess Elizabeth proclaimed illegitimate by Parliament. The crown was secured to any subsequent issue of the king, or should that fail, was left to his disposal.

1536. Publication of **Tindale's translation of the Bible,** by Coverdale, under authority from the king.

1536. Suppression of the Catholic rebellion of **Robert Aske,** aided by **Reginald Pole,** son of Margaret, Countess of Salisbury.

1539. STATUTE OF THE SIX ARTICLES, defining heresy; denial of any of these positions constituted heresy: (1) transubstantiation; (2) communion in one kind for laymen; (3) celibacy of the priesthood; (4) inviolability of vows of chastity; (5) necessity of private masses; (6) necessity of auricular confession.

1540. Execution of Cromwell, on a charge of treason. Cromwell had fallen under Henry's displeasure by his advocacy of the king's marriage with **Anne of Cleves,** with whom the king was ill-pleased.

1542. IRELAND MADE A KINGDOM.

1542. War with Scotland. James V defeated at the **battle of Solway Moss (Nov. 25).** James V died shortly afterward. Henry proposed a marriage between his son, **Edward,** and James' infant daughter, **Mary,** but the Scottish court preferred an alliance with France, whereupon Henry concluded an alliance with the emperor.

1544. Parliament recognized **Mary** and **Elizabeth** as heirs to the crown in the event of the death of Edward without issue.

1547. Execution of the **Earl of Surrey,** on charge of high treason.

Henry VIII died Jan. 28, 1547, leaving a will, wherein the crown was left to the heirs of his sister, **Mary, Duchess of Suffolk,** in the event of failure of issue by all of his children.

1547–1553. EDWARD VI, ten years of age; his uncle, Earl of Hertford, was appointed lord protector and **Duke of Somerset,** and assumed the government. Repeal of the Six Articles (1547). Introduction of Protestant doctrines (1549). Execution of Seymour, brother of the Duke of Somerset, who wished to marry the

Succession to the English Crown, 1553-1603

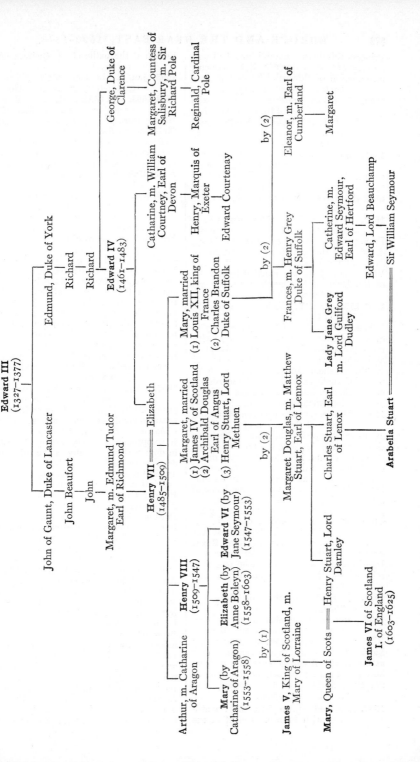

Princess Elizabeth. Establishment of uniformity of service by act of Parliament; introduction of Edward VI's first prayerbook (1549) (second, 1553).

1550. **Fall of the protector, Somerset,** who was superseded by Lord Warwick, afterward **Duke of Northumberland.** Execution of Somerset (1552).

1551. **Forty-two articles** of religion published by Cranmer. These were essentially the basis of Anglican Protestantism, though their form was not final until the thirty-nine articles of Elizabeth's reign.

1553. Edward assigned the crown **to Lady Jane Grey,** daughter of his cousin, Frances Grey, eldest daughter of Mary, daughter of Henry VII, to the exclusion of Mary and Elizabeth, daughters of Henry VIII. Lady Jane was married to the son of the Duke of Northumberland. **Death of Edward VI** (July 6).

1553-1558. **MARY,** who had been brought up a Catholic.

The proclamation of **Lady Jane Grey** as queen by Northumberland meeting with no response, Northumberland, Lady Jane, and others were arrested. **Execution of Northumberland** (Aug. 22, 1553). Restoration of Catholic bishops. **Gardiner,** Bishop of Winchester, author of the Six Articles, lord chancellor.

1553. Marriage treaty between **Mary** and **Philip of Spain,** son of Charles V, afterward Philip II. Philip was to have the title of *King of England,* but no hand in the government, and in case of Mary's death could not succeed her. This transaction being unpopular, an insurrection broke out, headed by Sir Thomas Carew, the Duke of Suffolk, and Sir Thomas Wyatt. The suppression of the rebellion was followed by the **execution of Lady Jane Grey** (Feb. 12, 1554) and her husband. Lady Jane was an accomplished scholar (pupil of Roger Ascham) and had no desire for the crown. Imprisonment of Elizabeth, who was soon released on the intercession of the emperor.

1554. **July 25.** Marriage of **Mary** and **Philip.**

1555. **Return to Catholicism** and persecution of the Protestants (**Bonner,** Bishop of London). Oct. 16, Ridley and Latimer; March 21, 1556, Cranmer burnt at the stake. About 300 are said to have been burnt during this persecution. **Cardinal Pole,** Archbishop of Canterbury and papal legate (1556).

1557. England drawn into the Spanish war with France. Defeat of the French at the **battle of St. Quentin** (Aug. 10, 1557).

1558, Jan. 7. **Loss of Calais,** which was captured by the Duke of Guise.

1558-1603. **ELIZABETH,** brought up a Protestant. Sir William Cecil (Baron Burleigh, 1571), secretary of state. Sir Nicholas Bacon, lord privy seal. Repeal of the Catholic legislation of Mary; re-enactment of the laws of Henry VIII relating to the Church; **Act of Supremacy, Act of Uniformity.** Revision of the prayerbook.

1559, Apr. 2. **Treaty of Cateau-Cambrésis** with France. Calais to be ceded to England in eight years.

On the accession of Francis II, King of France, Mary, his wife, assumed the title of *Queen of England and Scotland.* Conformity exacted in Scotland. **Treaty of Berwick** (Jan. 1560), between Elizabeth and the Scottish reformers. French troops besieged at Leith. **Treaty of Edinburgh** between England, France, and Scotland (1560, July 6). French interference in Scotland withdrawn. **Adoption of a Confession of Faith** by the Scotch Estates. Return of Mary to Scotland (1561) after the death of Francis II, where she was at once involved in conflict with the Calvinists (**John Knox**).

1563. **Adoption of the Thirty-Nine Articles,** in place of the forty-two published by Cranmer. Completion of the **establishment of the Anglican Church** (*Church of England, Episcopal Church*). A compromise Church, largely Protestant in dogma (though many of the thirty-nine articles are ambiguous), but with a hierarchical organization similar to the Catholic, and a liturgy essentially that of the Roman Church translated into English. Numerous **dissenters or nonconformists: Puritans** — even then a broad, inexact term, covering various groups who wished to "purify" the Church; to substitute a simple early-Christian ritual for the existing ritual, to make the Church more "Protestant"; **Separatists,** Puritans who left the Anglican Church entirely to organize their own churches; **Presbyterians,** Puritans who sought to substitute organization by presbyters and synods for organization by bishops within the Anglican Church; **Brownists,** extreme leftist Puritans religiously, the nucleus of the later **Independents or Congregationalists;** Brownists and Catholics, alone of the Elizabethan religious groups could not be brought under the Queen's policy of toleration within the Anglican Church. Elizabeth therefore did not "tolerate"; and did "persecute" Catholics, Brownists, and, of course, Unitarians (who denied the doctrine of the Trinity).

1564. Peace of Troyes with France. English claims to Calais renounced for 222,000 crowns.

In Scotland Mary married her cousin **Darnley**, who caused her favorite Rizzio to be murdered (1566) and was himself murdered (Feb. 10, 1567) by Bothwell. The exact part played by Mary in these intrigues is still debated by historians. Marriage of Mary and **Bothwell** (May 15, 1567). The nobles under Murray, Mary's natural brother, revolted, defeated Mary at **Carbury Hill**, near Edinburgh, and imprisoned her at Lochleven Castle. Abdication of Mary in favor of her son, by Darnley, **James VI** (July 24, 1567). **Murray**, regent. In May, 1568, Mary escaped from captivity; defeated at **Langside**, May 13, she took refuge in England, where, after some delay, she was placed in confinement (1568).

1577. Alliance of Elizabeth and the Netherlands.

1583-1584. Plots against the queen (Arden, Parry); Spanish plot of Throgmorton; execution of the Earl of Arundel for corresponding with Mary. **Bond of Association.**

1585. Troops sent to the aid of the Dutch Republic under the **Earl of Leicester. Victory of Zutphen** (Sept. 22, 1586), death of **Sir Philip Sidney.**

1586. Expedition of **Sir Francis Drake** to the West Indies, sack of St. Domingo and Carthagena; rescue of the Virginia colony.

1586. Conspiracy of **Savage, Ballard, Babington,** etc., discovered by the secretary of state, **Walsingham;** execution of the conspirators. The government involved Mary, Queen of Scots, in the plot. She was tried at Fotheringay Castle (Oct.), and convicted on the presentation of letters which she alleged to be forged. She was convicted Oct. 25 and executed Feb. 8, 1587.

1588. WAR WITH SPAIN. Construction of an English fleet of war. The Spanish fleet, called the *Invincible Armada* (132 vessels, 3165 cannon), was defeated in the Channel by the English fleet (**Howard, Drake, Hawkins),** July 21-29, and destroyed by a storm off the Hebrides.

1597. Rebellion of the Irish under **Hugh O'Neill,** Earl of Tyrone; the failure of the Earl of Essex to cope with the insurrection led to his recall, and his successor Lord Mountjoy quickly subjugated the country (1601). Capture of Tyrone,

flight of the Earl of Desmond. A rebellion of **Essex** in London was followed by his execution (1601).

1600. Charter of the East India Company.

1601. Elizabethan Poor Law, preceded by various measures regulating apprenticeship (1563), vagrancy, etc. This famous law charged the parishes with providing for the needy.

1603-1649 (1714). THE HOUSE OF STUART. Personal Union of England and Scotland.

1603-1625. JAMES I (as King of Scotland James VI), son of Mary Stuart. The Scotch had brought him up in the Protestant faith. He was rather pedantic, and not popular with a people used to the hearty Tudors. Divine right of kingship, divine right of the bishops (*no bishop, no king*). In this century the after-effects of the Reformation made themselves felt in England as on the Continent, and in both places resulted in war. In England, however, owing to the peculiar circumstances of the Reformation, these effects were peculiarly conditioned; the religious questions were confused and overshadowed by political and constitutional questions. Under stress of their quarrel, both the first two Stuarts and the parliamentarians sought to bend the mediaeval English constitution, the Stuarts toward royal absolutism, the parliamentarians toward government by an oligarchy of great nobles and city merchants. Only at the end of the struggle, in the 1640's, did advanced democratic ideas, coupled usually with extreme religious doctrines, appear in minority groups (**Levelers, Fifth Monarchy Men).**

1603, Mar. 24. James I was proclaimed king; he entered London on the 7th of May, and was crowned July 25. Presentation of the **millenary petition** immediately after James' arrival in London, signed by 1000 (800) ministers, asking for the reform of abuses.

The Main and the Bye. The *Main* was a plot to dethrone James in favor of **Arabella Stuart** (see gen. table), concocted by Lords Cobham, Grey, and others. Sir **Walter Raleigh** was also implicated and imprisoned till 1616 (*History of the World* written in prison). The *Bye* or the *surprising treason* was a plot to imprison the king. **Alliance with France,** negotiated by Sully.

1604, Jan. Hampton Court Conference, between the bishops and the Puritans, James presiding. The Puritans failed to secure any relaxation of the rules of the Church. James issued a proclamation enforcing the Act of Uniformity, and another banishing Jesuits and seminary priests. Friction between the king and parliament over a disputed election in Bucks (**Goodwin and Fortescue**).

1604, Mar. 19-1611, Feb. 9. First Parliament of James I. The king's scheme of a real union of England and Scotland unfavorably received. Appointment of a commission to investigate the matter.

Convocation (ecclesiastical court and legislature, at first established [Edward I] as an instrument for ecclesiastical taxation; afterward convened by archbishops for the settlement of church questions; since Henry VIII, convened only by writ from the king, and sitting and enacting [canons] only by permission of the king) adopted some new canons which bore so hardly upon the Puritans that 300 clergymen left their livings rather than conform.

1604. Peace with Spain. James proclaimed *King of Great Britain, France, and Ireland* (Oct. 24). Punishment of many recusants (under the recusancy laws of Elizabeth, whereby refusing to go to church, saying mass or assisting at mass was severely punished).

1605. Nov. 5. GUNPOWDER PLOT, originating in 1604 with **Robert Catesby,** after the edict banishing the priests. Preparations for blowing up the houses of Parliament with thirty-six barrels of gunpowder. Disclosure of the plot through an anonymous letter. Arrest of **Guy Fawkes** in the vaults on Nov. 4, the day before the meeting of Parliament. Trial and execution of the conspirators.

1606. Penal laws against papists. Plague in London. **Episcopacy restored in Scotland.** James urged the union anew, but in vain.

Impositions. The grant of customs duties made at the beginning of every reign (*tonnage* and *poundage*, established by Edward III) proving insufficient to meet James' expenditure, he had recourse to impositions without parliamentary grant, which Mary and Elizabeth had used to a small extent. Trial of Bates for refusing to pay an imposition on currants. The Court of Exchequer decided in favor of the king.

1610. The Great Contract; in return for the surrender of some feudal privileges, the king was to receive a yearly income of £200,000. The agreement was frustrated by a dispute over the impositions. **Dissolution of Parliament** (Feb. 9, 1611).

1611. Plantation of Ulster, which was forfeited to the crown by the rebellion of Tyrone.

1611. Completion of the translation of the Bible, which was authorized by the king and had occupied 47 ministers since 1604.

1613. Robert Carr, the king's favorite (Viscount Rochester in 1611), created Duke of Somerset and lord treasurer, on the death of the Earl of Salisbury (Robert Cecil). Death of Henry, Prince of Wales (Nov. 1612).

1614, Apr. 5-June 7. Second Parliament of James I. Three hundred new members, among whom were **John Pym** (Somersetshire), **Thomas Wentworth** (Yorkshire), **John Eliot** (St. Germains). The whole session was spent in quarreling with the king over the impositions, and Parliament was dissolved without making an enactment, whence it is called the *Addled Parliament.*

1615. Renewal of the negotiation for the marriage of James' son to a Spanish princess (opened in 1611). Imposition of a benevolence, which was resisted by Oliver St. John and condemned by the chief justice, **Sir Edward Coke,** who was afterward dismissed from office. **Rise of George Villiers** in the king's favor; Viscount Villiers, Earl, Marquis, **Duke of Buckingham.**

1617. Sir Walter Raleigh, released from the Tower, allowed to sail for the Orinoco, where he hoped to discover a gold mine. Failing in this he attacked the Spanish towns on the Orinoco. On his return to England in the following year, he was executed under the old sentence, as reparation to Spain.

1621, Jan. 30-1622, Feb. 8. Third Parliament of James I. The Parliament granted a supply for the prosecution of the war in the Palatinate (p. 404), in which James was half-hearted, and then took up the subject of grievances. Impeachment of Mompesson and Mitchell, who had bought monopolies of inn-licensing and the manufacture of gold and silver thread; they were degraded, fined, and banished. Impeachment of **Francis Bacon** (1561-1626), famous essayist and writer on scientific method, lord chancellor since 1618. Bacon admitted that he had received presents from parties in suits, but denied that they had affected his judgment. He was fined £40,000 (which was remitted) and declared incapable of holding office in the future. Petition of the Commons against popery and the Spanish marriage. The angry rebuke of the king for meddling in affairs of state (*"bring stools for these ambassadors"*) drew from the Parliament

1621, Dec. 18. THE GREAT PROTESTA-TION: "That the liberties, franchises, privileges, and jurisdictions of Parliament are the ancient and undoubted birthright and inheritance of the subjects of England, and that the arduous and urgent affairs concerning the king, state, and defense of the realm ... are proper subjects and matter of council and debate in Parliament." The king tore the page containing the protestation from the journal of the Commons, dissolved Parliament (Feb. 8, 1622), and imprisoned **Southampton, Coke, Pym,** and **Selden.**

1623. Charles, Prince of Wales, and the Duke of Buckingham went to Spain and negotiated a marriage treaty, the provisions of which were so favorable to the Catholics as to excite great dissatisfaction in England; finally, being unable to secure any help from Spain in regard to the Palatinate, Charles and Buckingham returned in anger.

1624, Feb. 12-1625, Mar. 27. Fourth Parliament of James I. The Spanish marriage was broken off, but even the anger of Buckingham could not drive the Parliament into a declaration of war with Spain. Supplies voted for defense. Mansfeld raised 1200 men in England who reached Holland, but nearly all perished there from lack of proper provisions. This was, in fact, a breach with Spain. Marriage treaty with France for the marriage of Prince Charles with **Henrietta Maria,** sister of Louis XIII.

1625-1649. CHARLES I.

1625, May 11. Marriage of Charles I and Henrietta Maria. Ships sent to Louis XIII secretly engaged not to fight against the Huguenots.

1625. First Parliament of Charles I. (Assembled June 18; adjourned to Oxford July 11; dissolved Aug. 12). Grant of tonnage and poundage for one year only, and of £140,000 for the war with Spain. Proceedings against Montague. Unsuccessful expedition of Wimbledon against Cadiz.

1626, Feb. 6-June 15. Second Parliament of Charles I. Charles had hoped for a more pliable Parliament, as he had appointed several of the leaders of the first Parliament sheriffs, and so kept them out of the second. But this Parliament, under the lead of Sir John Eliot, was more intractable than the last. Lord Bristol, to whom no writ had been sent by order of the king, received one on the interference of the Lords, but was requested not to appear. He took his seat and brought charges against **Buckingham,** on which that lord was impeached (May). Imprisonment of Sir John Eliot and Sir Dudley Digges, who were set at liberty upon the refusal of Parliament to proceed to business without them.

1626-1630. War against France. Inglorious expedition of Buckingham to the relief of Rochelle (1627).

Exaction of a forced loan to raise money for the French war, and for the subsidy which Charles had agreed to supply to Christian IV of Denmark.

1628, Mar. 17-1629, Mar. 10. Third Parliament of Charles I. (May): Passage of the PETITION OF RIGHT: (1) Prohibition of benevolences, and all forms of taxation without consent of Parliament. (2) Soldiers should not be billeted in private houses. (3) No commission should be given to military officers to execute martial law in time of peace. (4) No one should be imprisoned unless upon a specified charge. Assent of the king (June 7). Grant of five subsidies.

Charles having, after the first year of his reign, continued to levy tonnage and poundage, the Commons drew up a remonstrance against that practice. **Prorogation of Parliament** (June 26). Seizure of goods of merchants who refused to pay tonnage and poundage.

Assassination of Buckingham (Aug. 23), by Felton.

1629, Jan. New session of Parliament. The Commons at once took up the question of tonnage and poundage; claim of privilege in the case of Rolle, one of the merchants, whose goods had been seized, and who was a member of Parliament. Turbulent scene in the House of Commons; the speaker held in the chair while the **resolutions of Eliot** were read: Whoever introduced innovations in religion, or opinions disagreeing with those of the true Church; whoever advised the levy of tonnage and poundage without grant of Parliament; whoever voluntarily paid such duties, was an enemy of the kingdom.

1629. Eliot and eight other members were arrested (Mar. 5); Eliot died in the Tower in Nov. and the others made submission. **Parliament dissolved** (Mar. 10). For eleven years (1629–1640) Charles governed without a Parliament, raising money by hand-to-mouth expedients, reviving old taxes, old feudal privileges of the crown, selling monopolies. These were rarely wholly illegal, but seemed to parliamentarians contrary to recent constitutional developments. **Charles' advisers: William Laud** (1573–1645), Bishop of Lon-··

don, 1628, Archbishop of Canterbury, 1633; **Thomas Wentworth** (1593–1641), Earl of Strafford and Lord Lieutenant of Ireland, 1639. Both were extremists. Strafford's policy of *thorough* further embittered Ireland. **Peace was made with France** (Apr. 1630) **and with Spain** (Nov. 1630). Conformity was enforced, and the communion table inrailed.

1634. The tax which focused hatred on Charles was **ship-money,** by which a writ issued in 1634 extended to the whole country a tax hitherto levied only on seaboard towns. **John Hampden,** a Buckinghamshire country gentleman, defying the tax, was tried in June, 1634, and lost his case in court, but won it with the public.

1637. An attempt to read the English liturgy in Edinburgh, ordered by Charles, produced a **riot at St. Giles'** (June 23). This was followed by the organization of the Scotch Presbyterians to resist episcopacy. On Feb. 28, 1638 was signed the **Solemn League and Covenant** (whence *Covenanters*) for the defense of the reformed religion. In Nov. a general assembly at Glasgow abolished episcopacy, settled liturgy and canons, and gave final form to the **Scottish Kirk.**

1639. The First Bishops' War. The Scots seized Edinburgh Castle and raised an army. Charles marched to meet them near Berwick, but concluded with them, without battle, the **Pacification of Dunse** (June 18). After the armies had been disbanded, the questions were to be referred to a new general assembly and a new (Scotch) Parliament. At the Edinburgh assembly the work of the Glasgow assembly was confirmed, and Parliament proved intractable.

1640. Charles, in trouble in Scotland and financially distressed in England, now called his **fourth Parliament,** the *Short Parliament* at Westminster (Apr. 13–May 5). This Parliament, refusing to vote money until grievances were settled, was immediately dissolved. Riots, attacks on Laud's palace. The Scotch trouble broke out in the **Second Bishops' War,** and the royalists were beaten in a skirmish at **Newburn on the Tyne** (Aug. 28). By the **Treaty of Ripon** (Oct. 26) Charles agreed to pay the Scotch army £850 a day until a permanent settlement could be made. These obligations made the calling of a Parliament inevitable.

1640. THE LONG PARLIAMENT, the fifth Parliament of Charles I (Nov. 3, 1640–Mar. 16, 1660). First session until Sept. 8, 1641.

The fact that the Scotch army was not to be disbanded until paid gave the Commons an unusual hold over Charles. On Nov. 11, **Strafford** was impeached, followed by **Laud,** and both were sent to the Tower. At the trial of Strafford in the following March, the result of impeachment being uncertain, it was dropped, and a bill of attainder introduced, which passed both Commons and Lords in April. Strafford was executed on May 12. Meanwhile, Parliament passed the revolutionary **Triennial Act,** requiring the summoning of Parliament every three years even without the initiative of the crown (May 15, 1641). This was followed in May by a bill to prevent the dissolution or proroguing of the present Parliament without its own consent, which Charles reluctantly signed, along with Strafford's attainder. The culmination of radicalism was the introduction of a bill for the abolition of bishops. This was the **Root and Branch Bill,** on which the moderate Puritans split with the more radical Presbyterians.

1641, July. Abolition of the courts of Star Chamber and High Commission. These courts were a part of the constitution of England, and their abolition shows that Parliament was determined to effect a revolution. In August, a **treaty of pacification** with Scotland was made, and Scotch and English armies were paid with the proceedings of a special poll-tax granted by Parliament. Charles took refuge with the Scotch. On the proroguing of Parliament in Sept., each house appointed a committee to sit in the vacation (**Pym,** chairman of the Commons' committee). Charles attempted to conciliate the moderate parliamentarians by giving office to their leader, Lucius Cary, Lord Falkland.

In Scotland, the **Marquis of Montrose** plotted the seizure of the **Earl of Argyle,** Presbyterian leader. The discovery of the plot seemed to involve Charles himself, who was thus thrown into the hands of Argyle. Charles practically surrendered all control over Scotland to Argyle and the Presbyterians, receiving from the latter only a promise not to interfere in English religious affairs (Oct. 1641).

1641, Oct. 21. Parliament assembled and heard the news of the **massacre of Protestants in Ulster** (30,000 killed). Still unwilling to entrust Charles with an army, it presented him with the **Grand Remonstrance** (Dec. 1) passed in the Commons in Nov. by eleven votes, a summary of all the grievances of his reign. It was ordered printed by Parliament on Dec. 14.

1642, Jan. 3. Charles ordered the impeachment of Lord Kimbolton, and of **Pym, Hampden, Haselrig, Holles, Strode,** of the Commons, for treasonable correspondence with the Scotch in the recent troubles. The Commons refusing to order the arrest, Charles with a few hundred soldiers went to the House and attempted to seize the five members (Jan. 4). Failing to find them, he withdrew. The five members had taken refuge in London, where the Commons followed them, and formed a committee at the Guildhall under the protection of the citizens of London. Charles left London on Jan. 10 and the five members returned. The victorious Commons, emboldened, put before the king bills excluding bishops from the Lords and giving command of the militia to Parliament. From York he refused to sign the latter (March) and there he was joined by 32 peers and 65 members of the Commons. He also had the great seal. The Parliament at Westminster now was obliged to pass ordinances which were not submitted to the king and did not appear under the great seal.

June 2. Parliament made a final approach to Charles, submitting the **nineteen propositions:** that the king should give his assent to the militia bill; that all fortified places should be entrusted to officers appointed by Parliament; that the liturgy and church government should be reformed in accordance with the wishes of Parliament; that Parliament should appoint and dismiss all royal ministers, appoint guardians for the king's children, and have the power of excluding from the upper house at will all peers created after that date. The propositions were rejected.

July. Parliament appointed a **committee of public safety,** and put Essex in charge of an army of 20,000 foot and 4000 cavalry. When on Aug. 22 Charles raised the royal standard at Nottingham, the military phase of the **Great Rebellion** began.

1642-1646. THE CIVIL WAR. Roughly, northern and west-central England stood by the king; East Anglia, London, and the south with Parliament. Socially, the gentry, the Anglican clergy, and the peasantry were royalist; the middle classes, the great merchants, and many great nobles were parliamentarians. But neither *Roundhead* (parliamentarian, Puritan) nor *Cavalier* (royalist) describes completely an economic or social class. Armies were small. Until Cromwell's *Ironsides* the royalist cavalry was superior. The war was relatively free from excesses.

1642. After the drawn **battle of Edgehill** (Oct. 23), where **Prince Rupert** (royalist cavalry leader, son of the Elector Palatine and Elizabeth of England) distinguished himself, the king marched on London, but turned back at Brentford when confronted by Essex (Nov. 12).

The associated counties of Norfolk, Suffolk, Essex, Cambridge, Hertfordshire, and Huntingdonshire raised a force entrusted to **Oliver Cromwell** (1599-1658), which as the *Ironsides* finally became the best troops in the war. Meantime, the war was a series of raids and indecisive battles. **Capture of Reading** by Essex (Apr. 27, 1643); skirmish at **Chalgrove Field** in which Hampden was mortally wounded (June 18). **Capture of Bristol** by Rupert (July 25), counterbalanced by Essex's **relief of Gloucester** (Sept.), gallantly defended by Massey. **First battle of Newbury** (Sept. 20).

1643, July 1. Through all this the **Westminster Assembly,** which sat until 1649, debated religious and theological problems.

Sept. 25. THE SOLEMN LEAGUE AND COVENANT, signed by 25 peers and 288 members of the Commons, agreeing to make the religions of England, Ireland, and Scotland as nearly uniform as possible and to reform religion *"according to the word of God, and the examples of the best reformed churches."* All civil and military officials were required to sign the covenant (nearly 2000 clergymen refused and lost their livings). The Scotch now consented to help the English parliamentarians; a Scotch army crossed the Tweed (Jan. 1644). Charles rashly enlisted Irish Catholic insurgents with whom he concluded peace, thus alienating many Englishmen.

1644, Jan. Charles convened a **royalist Parliament at Oxford.** His opponents established (Feb. 15) a joint committee of the two kingdoms of Scotland and England. At the **battle of Nantwich** (Jan. 25) the royalist Irish were beaten by **Sir Thomas Fairfax,** who, in junction with the Scotch, besieged York while Essex and Waller besieged Oxford.

July 2. BATTLE OF MARSTON MOOR. Prince Rupert, after defeating the Scotch, was decisively beaten by Cromwell and his Ironsides. This was the crucial battle of the war, and gave the north to Parliament. York surrendered (July 16); Newcastle (Oct. 16). In the south Waller was beaten at **Cropredy Bridge** (June 29) and Essex's infantry surrendered to Charles in Cornwall. The indecisive **second battle of Newbury** (Oct.

27), in which Charles was pitted against Essex, Waller, and Manchester, prefaced the so-called **Treaty of Uxbridge,** a truce in Jan. and Feb. 1645, during which Parliament's proposals were rejected by Charles, who had hitherto had the best of the war in south and southwest.

In Scotland, **Montrose,** after slipping into the country in disguise (Aug. 1644), raised highland clans for Charles and gained several victories over the Covenanters (**Tippamuir,** Sept. 1; **Inverlochy,** Feb. 2, 1645; **Auldcarn,** May 1; **Alford,** July 2). At one time he held most of Scotland, but his armies melted away when the Parliament sent General Leslie into Scotland after Naseby, and at **Philiphaugh** (Sept. 13, 1645) the Stuart partisans were decisively beaten. Montrose fled to the Continent.

1645, Jan. **Laud,** tried in March, 1644, was attainted and executed. England was fast moving toward extreme Protestantism. With Cromwell, the **Independents** rose to leadership. **Presbyterianism,** with some reservations for the Independents, became the established Church. The **Self-Denying Ordinance** (April 3) having excluded members of either house from military command, Fairfax superseded Essex as captain-general, and Cromwell, with the Self-Denying Ordinance suspended in his case, became lieutenant-general. The army was re-formed into the *new model* on the lines of the Ironsides.

1645, June 14. **BATTLE OF NASEBY,** decisive defeat of the king, ruin of his cause. Royalist towns and houses surrendered rapidly: Leicester (June 18), Bridgewater (July 23), Bristol (Sept. 11), Carlisle, Winchester, Basing House (Oct.), Latham House (Dec.). At **Stowe-on-the-Wold** (Mar. 26, 1646) Lord Ashley was beaten and captured in the final battle of the war. Charles surrendered himself to the Scotch (May 5).

1646, July. Parliament submitted to the captive Charles **the Newcastle proposals:** that Parliament control the militia for twenty years; that Charles take the Covenant; that he support the Presbyterian establishment. Hoping to profit by the obviously impending breach between the Presbyterians in Parliament and the Independents in the army, Charles rejected the propositions.

1647, Jan. 30. The Scotch surrendered Charles to Parliament in return for their back pay (£400,000). He was brought to Holmby House in Northamptonshire. **Army and Parliament in open conflict.** Parliament reappointed Fairfax commander-in-chief, re-enacted the Self-Denying Ordinance, and voted the disbandment of all soldiers not needed for garrisons or for service in Ireland. This the army refused to accept, claiming full payment for arrears in salary. A detachment headed by Cornet Joyce seized Charles at Holmby House (June 4), and carried him prisoner to the army, thus forestalling an agreement between king and Presbyterians.

June 4. On the same day Cromwell fled from Parliament to the army at **Triptow Heath,** where it had taken an oath not to disband until freedom of conscience was secured, and had erected a council of adjudicators. From St. Albans the army addressed to Parliament a *humble representation* (June 10) and demanded the exclusion of eleven members, among them Holles, obnoxious to it. The two speakers, fourteen lords, and about one hundred of the Commons fled to the army (July). Proposals were presented to the king by the army: that worship be free for all; that Parliament control army and navy for ten years and appoint officers of state; that Parliament serve for three years (**triennial Parliaments**). The king rejected them, and moved to take refuge with the Presbyterian members of Parliament; but the army entered London (Aug. 6) and forced Parliament to take back the members who had fled to the army. Charles removed to Hampton Court, where he rejected a modified form of the previous proposals and fled to the Isle of Wight, where he was detained by the governor of Carisbrooke Castle (Nov. 11).

Dec. 24. "**The four bills**" presented to the king by Parliament: (1) Parliament to command the army for twenty years; (2) all declarations and proclamations against the Parliament to be recalled; (3) all peers created since the great seal was sent to Charles to be incapable of sitting in the house; (4) the two houses should adjourn at pleasure. Charles, who was only playing with the Parliament in the hope of securing aid from Scotland, rejected the four bills (Dec. 28), after he had already signed a secret treaty with the Scots (Dec. 26). Charles agreed to abolish Episcopacy and restore Presbyterianism; the Scots, who looked with horror on the rising tide of toleration in England, agreed to restore him by force of arms.

1648, Jan. 15. Parliament renounced allegiance to the king, and voted to have no more communication with him.

1648. **SECOND CIVIL WAR.** At once a war between Scotland and England, a war between the royalists and the Roundheads, and a war between the Presbyterians and the Independents.

Mar. At a meeting of army officers at Windsor it was decided to bring the king to trial. Parliament having reassembled with 306 members and the Presbyterians again in control, repealed the non-communication resolution and attempted to reopen negotiations with the king (July).

Aug. 17-20. Battle of Preston. Under the Duke of Hamilton, a Scotch army invaded England, but was beaten by Cromwell. This ended the second civil war. The so-called **Treaty of Newport**, between king and Parliament, had no result, as Charles was seized by the army (Dec. 1) and, Parliament having again attempted to treat with the king, **Colonel Pride,** by order of the council of affairs, forcibly excluded 96 Presbyterian

members from the Parliament (*Pride's Purge,* Dec. 6, 7), which is henceforth known as the *Rump Parliament* (some 60 members).

Dec. 13. The **Rump** repealed the vote to continue negotiations with Charles, and voted that Charles be brought to trial. Appointment of a high court of justice of 135 members to try the king was rejected by the Lords (1649, Jan. 2) and the Commons resolved that legislative power resided solely with the Commons (Jan. 4; passed Jan. 6 without concurrence of the Lords).

1649, Jan. 20. The army council drew up a temporary **Instrument of Government.** Charles was tried before the high court (67 members present, Bradshaw presiding) whose jurisdiction he simply denied (Jan. 20–27). **The king was sentenced to death and beheaded at Whitehall** (Jan. 30).

(*Cont. p.* 425.)

2. THE NETHERLANDS TO 1648

The provinces of the **Low Countries,** originally inhabited by Batavians and other Germanic tribes, had formed a part of the empire of Charlemagne and, after the **Treaty of Mersen** (870), belonged in large part to Germany, forming a dependency of the Kingdom of Lotharingia. The decline of the ducal power favored the growth of powerful counties and duchies, such as Brabant, Flanders, Gelders, Holland, Zeeland, Hainault, and the Bishopric of Utrecht. After 1384 the provinces were brought under the control of the Dukes of Burgundy in the following manner: **Philip II** (the Bold), fourth son of John II of France, became Duke of Burgundy in 1363. He married **Margaret,** daughter and heiress of Louis II, Count of Flanders and Artois (d. 1404). Their son was **John the Fearless,** Duke of Burgundy (1404–1419), who was succeeded by his son, **Philip the Good** (1419–1467). Philip acquired Namur by purchase (1425). Brabant and Limburg came to him by bequest (Joanna, daughter of John III, Duke of Brabant, left them to her great-nephew, Antoine, brother of John the Fearless). In 1433 he acquired Holland, Hainault, and Zeeland by cession from Jacqueline, Countess of Holland; and in 1443, Luxemburg, by cession from Elizabeth of Luxemburg. He also added Antwerp and Mechlin. His son, **Charles the Bold** (Duke of Burgundy 1467–1477), acquired Gelderland and Zutphen by bequest from Duke Arnold (1472).

Mary, the daughter and heiress of Charles the Bold, married **Maximilian.** Archduke of

Austria and later emperor (p. 398). Their son, **Philip the Handsome** (Duke of Burgundy), married **Joanna,** the daughter of Ferdinand of Aragon and Isabella of Castile, and thus the Netherland provinces passed ultimately into the hands of Philip's son, **Charles I** (Charles V as emperor).

1548. Charles annexed the seventeen provinces (Brabant, Limburg, Luxemburg, Gelderland, Flanders, Artois, Hainault, Holland, Zeeland, Namur, Zutphen, East Friesland, West Friesland, Mechlin, Utrecht, Overyssel, Groningen) to the Burgundian circle of the empire.

1556. Abdication of Charles. The Netherlands, like Spain, passed to his son,

1556-1598. PHILIP II.

1568-1648. REVOLT OF THE NETHERLANDS. The provinces had long enjoyed ancient and important privileges. The Estates (*staaten, états*) granted taxes and troops. **Calvinism** had taken firm root in the northern provinces (commonly called Holland),ʒbut the southern provinces (now Belgium) remained Catholic. The Spanish garrison, the penal edicts against heretics, the dread of the introduction of the Spanish Inquisition, all these factors led (during the rule [1559–1567] of **Margaret of Parma,** the natural sister of Philip II, and her adviser, **Bishop Granvella**) to the formation of a **league of nobles** (*Compromise of Breda*), headed by Philip Marnix of St. Aldegonde. Presentation of a petition by 300 nobles (*Gueux = Beggars,* **a party**

The House of Burgundy

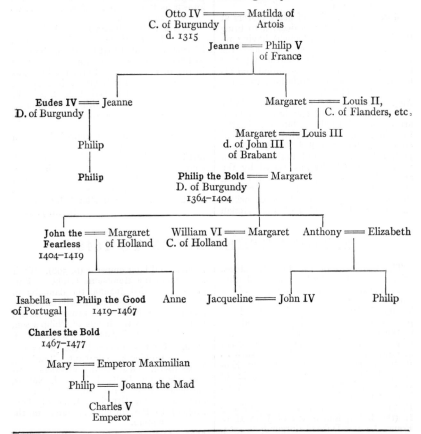

Otto IV ===== Matilda of
C. of Burgundy | Artois
d. 1315

Jeanne ===== Philip V
of France

Eudes IV ===== Jeanne
D. of Burgundy

Margaret ===== Louis II,
C. of Flanders, etc.

Philip

Margaret ===== Louis III
d. of John III
of Brabant

Philip

Philip the Bold ===== Margaret
D. of Burgundy
1364-1404

John the ===== Margaret   William VI ===== Margaret   Anthony ===== Elizabeth
Fearless | of Holland   C. of Holland
1404-1419

Isabella ===== Philip the Good   Anne   Jacqueline ===== John IV   Philip
of Portugal | 1419-1467

Charles the Bold
1467-1477

Mary ===== Emperor Maximilian

Philip ===== Joanna the Mad

Charles V
Emperor

name, originating in the contemptuous remark of the Count of Barlaimont: "Ce n'est qu'un tas de gueux"). Insurrection of the lower classes. Destruction of images and sack of the churches. These disturbances were opposed by **Lamoral, Count of Egmont** (1522–1568) and **William of Nassau,** Prince of Orange (**William the Silent, 1533–1584**), the leaders of the higher nobility, who, however, soon lost control of the movement. Protestant and Catholic parties soon emerged.

1567. Philip sent to the Netherlands the **Duke of Alva** (1508–1582) with an army of 20,000 Spaniards. William of Orange and many thousands of Netherlanders left their native land. Margaret resigned her regency and also departed. Creation of the *Council of Blood.* Ruthless suppression of opposition. **Execution of**

Egmont, Hoorn, and many other prominent figures. The estates of those who failed to appear before the tribunal were confiscated, including those of William of Orange. The latter, with his brother Louis, thereupon invaded the Netherlands, but was repulsed by Alva.

The arbitrary taxes imposed by Alva (the tenth pfenning from the price of every article sold, the hundredth part of every income) produced a new revolt.

1572. Capture of Brill, by the "Water Beggars."[2] The insurrection spread rapidly, especially throughout the north.

1573. Alva was recalled at his own request. His successor, **Luis de Requesens y Zúñiga,** gained a

1574. Victory at Mookerheide, where two brothers of the Prince of Orange fell. But the Spaniards could not suppress the revolt. Requesens died (1576). **Capture and sack of Antwerp, Maestricht, Ghent,** and other towns by the Spaniards led to the

1576. PACIFICATION OF GHENT, a treaty between all the provinces by which they united, without regard to national or religious differences, to drive out the Spaniards. The new governor, **Don John of Austria,** was unable to quiet the country, despite disputes between the various parties. He died in 1578, and was succeeded by

1578-1592. Alexander Farnese (Duke of Parma), a shrewd statesman and an excellent general. Parma ultimately subdued the southern provinces, on the promise that their old political freedom should be restored. The seven northern provinces (Holland, Zeeland, Utrecht, Gelderland, Groningen, Friesland, Overyssel), thereupon concluded

1579. THE UNION OF UTRECHT, followed by a proclamation of **independence from Spain** (1581). The hereditary *statthaltership* was settled on **William of Orange.** After his murder at Delft

(1584, July 10), he was succeeded by his son

1584. Maurice of Nassau, only seventeen years old. Parma continued his victorious campaigns and managed to capture Antwerp. Thereupon the English came to the aid of the insurgents.

1588. Philip II, hoping to put an end to the Anglo-Dutch combination, organized the **Great Armada,** which was defeated by the English and destroyed in a terrible storm (p. 373).

1609. The **Twelve Years' Truce** put an end to sporadic and inconclusive fighting and virtually established the independence of the northern provinces. After its expiration the war was resumed by the Spaniards. The Hollanders, who had grown rich and powerful at sea in the course of the struggle, were well able to hold their own, and finally

1648. THE TREATY OF WESTPHALIA recognized the independence of the Republic of the United Provinces.

(*Cont. p.* 437.)

3. FRANCE, 1483-1641

1483-1498. CHARLES VIII. Death of the Duke of Brittany (1488) called forth a coalition of the empire, Spain, and England to preserve the independence of the duchy, but this proved futile. Charles married Anne, the heiress, in 1491, and concluded the Treaties of Senlis (with the emperor) and **Étaples** (with England). Spain was bought off by the cession of Roussillon and Cerdagne.

1495-1496. Charles' expedition to Italy to claim the inheritance of Naples (through his father from Charles, Duke of Maine and Provence; see geneal. table). Charles marched victoriously through Italy and conquered Naples, but was soon obliged to withdraw in the face of the **Holy League** (Emperor Maximilian, Pope Alexander VI, Spain, Venice, Milan, and ultimately England), formed to protect Italy from foreign domination. Importance of the expedition in furthering the introduction of the Renaissance into France.

1498-1589. HOUSES OF ORLEANS AND ANGOULÊME. Branch lines of the house of Valois (since 1328) whose relation to the main line is shown in geneal. table (p. 382).

1498-1515. LOUIS XII obtained a divorce from Ioanna, daughter of Louis XI and married **Anne of Brittany,** widow of Charles VIII, in order to keep this duchy for the crown; as grandson of Valentina Visconti he laid claim to Milan, drove out Ludovico Moro, who was imprisoned when he ventured to return to Milan (1500).

1501. Louis, in alliance with Ferdinand the Catholic, King of Aragon, conquered the kingdom of Naples. The Spaniards and French soon falling out, the latter were defeated by the Spanish general Gonzalvo de Cordova on the Garigliano (1504). Louis XII gave up his claims to Naples.

1508. Louis a party in the **League of Cambrai** (pp. 393, 398). In 1511 the pope, Ferdinand the Catholic, and Venice renewed the **Holy League,** with the object of driving the French out of Italy. The latter, under the young **Gaston de Foix,** Duke of Nemours, nephew of Louis XII, were at first successful in the war, taking Brescia (1512) by storm (**Bayard,** *sans peur et sans reproche,* 1476-1524), and defeating the united Spanish and papal armies at **Ravenna,** with the aid of 5000 German mercenaries, in the same year; they were, however, compelled by the Swiss to evacuate Milan. In 1513 the French formed a new alliance with Venice,

The French Succession, 1498

Charles V (third king of the house of Valois), 1364-1380

Charles VI
1380-1422

Louis, Duke of Orléans
m. Valentina Visconti

Charles VII
1422-1461

Charles, Duke of Orleans

John, Count of
Angoulême

Louis XI
1461-1483

Louis XII
1498-1515
m. (2) Anne
of Brittany

Charles, Count
of Angoulême
m. Louise
of Savoy

Charles VIII
m. Anne of Brittany,
1483-1498

Claudia ════════════

Francis I
1515-1547

Henry II
1547-1559
m. Catharine de' Medici

Francis II
1559-1560
m.
Mary Stuart

Elizabeth
m.
Philip II
King of
Spain

Charles IX
1560-1574

Henry III
1574-1589
Duke of
Anjou;
King of
Poland

Francis
Duke of
Alençon
and
Anjou

Margaret
m.
Henry IV

but were defeated by the Swiss at **Novara** and withdrew from Italy. **Henry VIII of England,** who had joined the Holy League in 1512, and the **Emperor Maximilian,** who had joined in 1513, invaded France, and defeated the French at

1513, Aug. 17. Guinegate, called the *Battle of the Spurs* from the hasty flight of the French.

France concluded peace with the pope, with Spain (1513), with the emperor, and with Henry VIII (1514). Anne of Brittany having died, Louis took, as his third wife, Mary the sister of Henry VIII. He died soon after the marriage (1515) and was succeeded by his cousin, the Count of Angoulême, who had married Claudia, daughter of Louis XII and Anne, hence heiress of Brittany, which, however, was not actually incorporated with France until later.

1515-1547. FRANCIS I.

1515, Sept. 13-14. Francis reconquered Milan by the brilliant **victory of Marignano** over the Swiss. Peace and alliance between France and Switzerland. Treaty of **Geneva** (Nov. 7, 1515); **Treaty of Fribourg** (Nov. 29, 1516). The latter (*la paix perpétuelle*) endured till the French Revolution.

1516. Increase of the royal power by the **Concordat of Bologna** with the pope, which rescinded the Pragmatic Sanction of 1438 and placed the choice of bishops and abbots in the hands of the king; the pope on the other hand received the annates, or the first year's revenue of every ecclesiastical domain where the king's right of presentation was exercised. Francis also abandoned the principle of the Council of Basel, that the pope was subordinate to an oecumenical council.

1520. Meeting of Francis and Henry VIII of England in the neighborhood

House of Lorraine and Guise

René le Bon, D. of Anjou
and titular King of Naples
and Sicily, m. Isabâla, D.
of Lorraine

Margaret, m.
Henry VI, K.
of England

John II
D. of Lorraine
and Bar

Yolande
D. of Lorraine
m. **Ferri II**, C. of
Vaudemont, Guise, etc.

Nicolas
D. of Lorraine and Bar
no male issue

René II
D. of Lorraine and Bar
C. of Vaudemont, Guise, etc.

Anthony, D. of
Lorraine and
Bar 1508–1544

Claude I, C. of
Aumâle, D. of
Guise (1527)

Francis I
D. of Lorraine
and Bar 1544–1545

Francis, D. of
Guise, murdered
1563

Charles
Card. of
Lorraine

Claude, D.
of Aumâle

Louis
Card. of
Guise

Mary, m.
James V
of Scotland

Mary, Queen
of Scots

Charles II, D. of
Lorraine and Bar
1545–1608

Henry, D. of
Guise, murdered
1588

Charles, D. of
Mayenne

Louis, Cardinal of
Guise, murdered
1588

of Calais (*Field of the Cloth of Gold*). The wars of Francis with **Charles V** (p. 400 ff.) occupied the rest of the reign. Restrictions upon the political rights of the *parlements*. Beginnings of French Protestantism. Reformers of Meaux, **Lefebvre d'Étaples** (1455–1537). King and *parlements* condemned the movement.

1547-1559. HENRY II, son of Francis. Growing power of the house of Guise (**Francis**, Duke of Guise, and **Charles**, Cardinal of Lorraine).

Henry's mistress, **Diana of Poitiers**, Duchess of Valentinois, ruled him almost absolutely. **Montmorency**, constable. Persecution of the Protestants in France; assistance to German Protestants.

1547. Final union of Brittany with the French crown.

1552. War with Charles V (p. 402). Seizure of the three bishoprics (Toul, Metz, and Verdun) by the French.

1556-1559. War with Spain. The French were defeated by the Spaniards, supported by the English, in the **battle of St. Quentin** (1557), and by Egmont at **Gravelines** (1558).

1558. Calais, the last English possession in France, was captured by the Duke of Guise.

1559, Apr. 3. PEACE OF CATEAU-CAMBRÉSIS, which ended the Hapsburg-Valois wars. The French restored all their conquests except Calais and the three bishoprics. Henry II, who died of a wound received in a tournament, was succeeded by his son

1559-1560. FRANCIS II, the first husband of Mary Stuart of Scotland, who was a niece of the Guises. Measures against the Protestants (*chambres ardentes*). The king's mother, Catherine de' Medici (1519-1589), struggled for power and influence against the Bourbon princes: Anthony (King of Navarre); and Louis of Condé, who were descended from Louis IX. The Guises, at first rivals of the queen-mother and then in alliance with her, conducted all the affairs of state and surpassed in influence their opponents, the Catholic constable, Montmorency, and his nephews, the three Châtillon brothers: Gaspard, Admiral de Coligny; François d'Andelot, and Cardinal Châtillon, later leaders of the Huguenots. Conspiracy of Amboise against the Guises. This was defeated (1560). Death of Francis II.

1560-1574. CHARLES IX (ten years old), the brother of Francis. He was wholly under the influence of his mother.

1562-1598. THE RELIGIOUS WARS. Persecution compelled the Huguenots (as the French Protestants were called — derivation uncertain) to take up arms. At the same time they formed a political party. The ensuing struggles, therefore, did not constitute a purely religious war, but also a political, civil war, in which the leaders of both parties endeavored to exploit the weakness of the crown and get control of the government. The Huguenots were recruited primarily from the nobility (between two-fifths and one-half of the French nobility were at one time Protestant) and from the new capitalist-artisan class. Save in the southwest very few peasants became Protestants. Paris and the northeast in general remained Catholic throughout.

The first three wars form properly one war, interrupted by truces called peaces (Amboise, 1563; Longjumeau, 1568; St. Germain, 1570), which bore no fruit. Battles, in which the Huguenots were worsted, were fought at Dreux (1562); Jarnac (1569); and Moncontour (1569). Huguenot cavalry, recruited from the nobility, was excellent; the infantry was generally weak.

The issue of the first period was that the Huguenots, despite defeat, were given conditional freedom of worship, which was guaranteed them by the surrender, for two years, of four strongholds (La Rochelle, Cognac, Montauban, La Charité).

1572, Aug. 23-24. MASSACRE OF ST. BARTHOLOMEW. Murder of Coligny in Paris and general massacre of Protestants in Paris and in the provinces, on the occasion of the marriage of Henry of Bourbon, King of Navarre, with the sister of Charles IX, Margaret of Valois. Henry of Navarre saved his life by a pretended conversion to Catholicism. The massacre led to the

1572-1573. Fourth War. La Rochelle, besieged by Henry, brother of Charles IX, made a brave defense. The election of the Duke of Anjou to the crown of Poland brought about a compromise. Edict of Boulogne (July 8, 1573) ended the war favorably to the Huguenots.

Charles IX died May 30, 1574. His brother, who fled from Poland, became king.

1574-1589. HENRY III.

1574-1576. The Fifth War, during which Henry of Navarre reassumed the Protestant faith, was concluded by conditions more favorable to the Huguenots than those of any previous peace. Peace of Chastenoy (*Paix de Monsieur*, after the Duke of Alençon) May 6, 1576. Hence dissatisfaction among the Catholics. Origin of the Holy League (1576), which, in alliance with Philip II of Spain, purposed the annihilation of the reformed party, and the elevation of the Guises to the throne. The king, out of fear of the league, proclaimed himself its head and forbade the exercise of the Protestant religion throughout France. The Protestants and moderate Catholics had joined forces in 1575 by the Confederation of Milhaud.

1577. Sixth War, wherein the Huguenots were defeated, but obtained favorable terms at the Peace of Bergerac or Poitiers (Sept. 17), as the king was unwilling to let the league become too powerful. In spite of the renewal of the treaty of peace, not one of its articles was executed. This caused the

1580. Seventh War, which was ended in the same year by the Treaty of Fleix (Nov. 26), in which the conditions granted the Huguenots in former treaties were confirmed.

1584. The death of Francis, Duke of Alençon (since the accession of Henry III, Duke of Anjou), the younger brother of the king, rendered the extinction of the house of Valois certain. As it was the intention of the league to exclude from the throne Henry of Navarre, who belonged to the reformed religion, and to give the crown to the latter's uncle, the Cardinal of Bourbon, and as the league meantime had induced the king to revoke the concessions granted to the Huguenots, there broke out the

1585-1589. Eighth War, called the *War of the Three Henrys* (Henry III of Valois, Henry of Navarre, Henry of Guise).

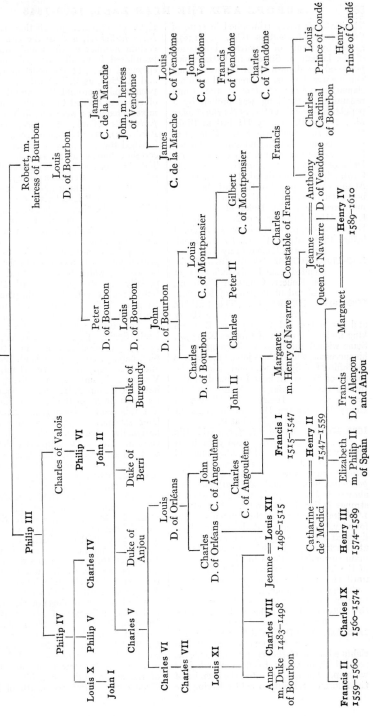

The House of Bourbon (to 1610)

The Catholic party triumphed in spite of the **victory of Coutras** (Oct. 20, 1587), gained by Henry of Navarre. Formation of the **League of Sixteen** at Paris, which purposed the deposition of the weak king. Guise entered Paris, was received with acclamation (*King of Paris*); the timid resistance of the king was broken by a popular insurrection (*Day of the Barricades*, May 12, 1588). Henry III fled to Blois, where he summoned the States-General of the kingdom. Finding no support among them against the league, he caused Henry, Duke of Guise, and his brother, Louis the Cardinal, to be murdered (Dec. 23, 1588). At this news, a revolt of the Catholic party broke out, headed by the brother of the murdered men, the **Duke of Mayenne.** Henry III fled to Henry of Navarre in the Huguenot camp, where he was murdered before Paris, at St. Cloud, by the monk Jacques Clément (July 31).

1589-1792. HOUSE OF BOURBON, descended from Louis IX's younger son Robert, Count of Clermont, husband of Beatrice of Bourbon.

1589-1610. HENRY IV. The Catholic party refused to recognize Henry and made the old Cardinal of Bourbon king under the name of **Charles X** (1590). Some wished the Duke of Mayenne to be his successor, while others joined themselves to Philip II of Spain, who laid claim to the throne of France on behalf of his daughter by his third marriage with Elizabeth of Valois, sister of Henry III. Victory of Henry IV over the Duke of Mayenne at Arques (1589) and at the

1590, Mar. 14. Battle of Ivry, crucial battle of these wars. Henry besieged Paris, which was relieved by Mayenne and the Spanish Duke of Parma. Henry's ultimate success was made possible by the *politiques*, usually moderate Catholics, but above all French patriots who wished a strong national monarchy. **Michel de L'Hôpital** (1505-1573) their precursor and founder. Henry abjured the reformed religion at St. Denis (1593) and was crowned at Chartres (1594). Brissac having thereupon surrendered Paris to him, the power of the league was broken. Not, however, until Henry, after public penance by his ambassadors at Rome, had been freed from the papal ban, was he generally recognized (by Mayenne too). The civil wars of religion were ended by the

1598, Apr. 15. EDICT OF NANTES, which gave the Huguenots equal political rights with the Catholics, but by no means secured them entire freedom of religious worship. The edict granted the exercise of the reformed religion to nobles having the right of criminal jurisdiction (*seigneurs hauts justiciers*), and to the citizens of a certain number of cities and towns, but prohibited it in all episcopal and archiepiscopal cities, at the court of the king, and in Paris, as well as within a circle of twenty miles around the capital. Public offices were opened to the Huguenots and **mixed chambers** were established in four *parlements* (Paris, Toulouse, Grenoble, Bordeaux). The Huguenots obtained some fortified towns, and were recognized, to a certain extent, as an armed political party. The Edict of Nantes was registered by the *parlement* only after a long delay. Though it established nothing like a **"free church in a free state,"** it did give legal status to a kind of toleration not yet formally recognized elsewhere. **Treaty of Vervins** (May 2, 1598) with Spain; restoration of all conquests to France.

Adoption of measures looking to the improvement of the finances and the general prosperity, which had gone to decay, especially by Rosny, afterward **Duke of Sully** (1560-1641). Fantastic plan of the King or Sully to establish a universal Christian republic in Europe, comprising six hereditary monarchies (France, England, Spain, Denmark, Sweden, Lombardy), five elective monarchies (the empire, papacy, Hungary, Poland, Bohemia), and four republics (Switzerland, Italy, Venice, Belgium), which probably would have turned out to be a league against the too great power of the house of Hapsburg. Yet this *great design* was a forerunner of later schemes to organize Europe internationally. Question of Cleves-Jülich succession. Henry IV supported the claims of Brandenburg. In the midst of great preparations for war, **Henry was assassinated** at Paris, 1610 (May 14) by the fanatic **Ravaillac.**

1610-1643. LOUIS XIII, his son, nine years old. Regency of his mother, **Marie de' Medici** (1573-1642). Sully removed from office; the Italian **Concini** was placed in control of affairs. Louis XIII, declared of age in 1614, was in fact all his life under the guidance of others. **Summons of the States-General,** 1614, being the last before the Revolution of 1789. Arrest and murder of Concini; the queen-mother banished to Blois (1617). The king under the influence of his favorite, the Duke of Luynes. By the mediation of **Armand-Jean du Plessis** (1585-1642), **Cardinal-Duke of Richelieu,** a treaty was concluded between Luynes and the queen-mother (1619). **New Civil war.** Contest of the crown with the nobility and the Huguenots. After the death of Luynes

(1621) Marie de' Medici and her favorite, Richelieu, obtained control of affairs. The influence of the latter soon became supreme, and the queen-dowager quarreled with him.

1624-1642. Administration of **Richelieu,** whose influence over the king was henceforward unbroken. Numerous conspiracies against him instigated by Gaston of Orléans, the king's brother.

1625. Revolt of the Huguenots under the Dukes of Rohan and Soubise.

1627-1628. Siege of La Rochelle, under the personal supervision of Richelieu. In spite of the dispatch of three fleets from England to the aid of the Huguenots, the city surrendered Oct. 28, 1628, after an heroic resistance of fourteen months. Defeat of the Duke of Rohan, and complete subjugation of the Huguenots, who thereafter were no longer an armed political party, but only a tolerated sect.

War in Italy with Spain; subjugation of Savoy, Richelieu at the head of the army.

1631. Treaty of **Cherasco.** France renounced all conquests in Italy, but by a secret treaty with Victor Amadeus, Duke of Savoy, Pignerol was surrendered to France (negotiators of these treaties,

Richelieu's confidant, **Father Joseph,** and the pope's agent, **Mazarin).**

A final attempt of Marie de² Medici to overthrow the cardinal failed ignominiously (Nov. 11, 1630, the *Day of Dupes).*

1632, Oct. 30. Defeat of the conspiracy of Gaston and the Duke of Montmorency. Execution of Montmorency.

1631-1648. **FRENCH PARTICIPATION IN THE THIRTY YEARS' WAR** (pp. 405-407).

1635. Foundation of the *Académie Française.*

1641. Conspiracy of Henry d'Effiat, Marquis of Cinq-Mars (*Monsieur le Grand).* His secret treaty with Spain. The plot was discovered by Richelieu.

Richelieu, though not a good financial administrator, helped somewhat to further the power of the royal bureaucracy (*intendants*) at the expense of the nobles, the Huguenots, and the *parlements.* His true greatness, however, lay in the field of foreign affairs. He restored French influence in Italy, in the Netherlands and in Germany, and established it also in Sweden. It was his work that laid the foundation for the power of Louis XIV, and became the traditional basis of French foreign policy.   (*Cont. p.* 440.)

4. THE IBERIAN PENINSULA

a. SPAIN, 1479-1659

1479-1516. **REIGN OF FERDINAND OF ARAGON** and his wife, **ISABELLA,** Queen of Castile (1474-1504). During this period much progress was made, notably in Castile, toward the suppression of the fractious aristocracy and the regulation of the Church. Aragon, on the other hand, retained most of its privileges. The conquest of Granada (1492) ended Moorish power in the Peninsula, while the discovery of America in the same year opened up endless possibilities of overseas empire. In matters of foreign policy, Ferdinand devoted his efforts to the conclusion of profitable marriage alliances and to the furtherance of his designs in Italy, which brought him into conflict with France and other Italian powers.

1493, Jan. 19. Treaty of **Narbonne** with Charles VIII of France. The latter, about to invade Italy, ceded to Ferdinand Roussillon and Cerdagne, in the hope of securing support. Ferdinand, with his usual duplicity, joined the pope, the Emperor Maximilian, Milan and Venice, and helped to frustrate Charles' plans.

1494. Foundation of the *Consulado* for foreign trade at Burgos. This chamber, and the *Casa de Contratación* at Seville (1503) undertook to regulate Spanish trade and had much to do with the commercial expansion of the 16th century.

1500. By the **Treaty of Granada,** France and Spain again engaged to coöperate in Italian affairs, but friction over Naples soon led to hostilities. Victories of the great Spanish commander, **Gonzalvo de Cordova** (especially at **Garigliano,** 1503). Aragon retained Naples. By the **Treaty of Blois** (1505), Louis XII of France ceded his rights to Naples to his niece, Germaine de Foix, whom Ferdinand, a widower since 1504, married.

1504. The death of Isabella made **Joanna** (wife of Philip, Archduke of Austria) legal heiress to Castile. Ferdinand, who had long planned the union of Castile and Aragon, in Joanna's absence secured from the Córtes authority to carry on the government in his daughter's behalf. In

1506 Philip and Joanna came to claim their inheritance. **Treaty of Villafavila** between Philip and Ferdinand, the former securing the regency. Philip's death in the same year and the **insanity of Joanna** (kept in confinement for 49 years, d. 1555) allowed Ferdinand to resume control.

1509-1511. African campaigns, organized, financed, and led by **Cardinal Jiménez de Cisneros** (1436-1517), aided by **Pedro Navarro.** Cisneros was one of the ablest statesmen of his time, who, having reformed the Spanish Church, now devoted himself to the crusade. The Spanish forces took Oran, Bougie, and Tripoli and forced the Moslem rulers to pay tribute.

1511. The Holy League (the pope, Ferdinand, and Venice) against France and the Empire. **Victory of the League at Novara** (1513). (See pp. 394, 398.) At the same time (1512) the Spaniards conquered **Navarre,** which was annexed to the Castilian crown, though it retained its own government (1515).

1516. Death of Ferdinand. Regency of Cardinal Cisneros, who vigorously repressed incipient disturbances by the nobles. The crowns now passed to the son of Philip and Joanna, Charles of Ghent, who became

1516-1556. CHARLES I of Spain, founder of the Hapsburg dynasty. Charles, who had been educated in Flanders, arrived (1517) with a large Flemish following, which regarded the Spaniards with disdain. Dissatisfaction of the Spaniards with Charles' election to the imperial throne (1519) led to widespread opposition to his leaving the country and using Spanish money and men for his imperial purposes.

1520-1521. UPRISING OF THE COMUNEROS. A group of cities (led by Toledo and by the Toledan **Juan de Padilla**) took issue with the government and organized a **Holy League** (*Santa Junta*) at Avila (July, 1520). Though this was originally as much an aristocratic as a bourgeois movement, radical tendencies soon appeared and the upper elements withdrew. After the defeat of the *comuneros* at Villalar (Apr. 23, 1521) the leaders were executed and government authority re-established. But in future Charles avoided as much as possible any infringement of traditional rights.

1521-1529. War between **France and Spain,** the result of French support of the *comuneros* and French designs on Navarre. The French took Pampeluna and Fontarabia, but Charles, supported by the pope, Florence, and Mantua, expelled the French from Milan (1522). In 1524 the Spanish commanders, the **Constable de** Bourbon and the **Marquis Pescara,** invaded Provence and advanced to Marseilles. Francis I was decisively defeated and captured at the **battle of Pavia** (Feb. 24, 1525) and in captivity at Madrid was obliged to sign the **Treaty of Madrid,** by which he abandoned his Italian claims and ceded Burgundy. On his release he violated his promises and the war was resumed. By the **Treaty of Cambrai** (1529), Charles was obliged to renounce Burgundy, while Francis once more abandoned his claims to Naples.

1535. The expedition of Charles to Tunis (p. 422), which was part of a great duel between Spain and the formidable Turkish power.

1535-1538. Another war with France, arising from the succession to Milan (p. 395), led to another invasion of Provence (1536) and to the inconclusive **Treaty of Nice** (1538).

1541. Reverse of the Spaniards at Algiers.

1542-1544. Further hostilities with France.

1551-1559. The last war between Charles and the French kings, ending in the **Treaty of Cateau-Cambrésis** (Apr. 3, 1559). (See below.)

Charles I (Charles V as emperor) gave Spain efficient government, continuing the work of Ferdinand and Isabella. On the other hand, his imperial position resulted in the involvement of Spain in all general European problems and in the expenditure of much blood and money, a drain not so noticeable at the time because of the great influx of gold from the New World. Culturally speaking, the whole 16th and the first half of the 17th century was Spain's golden age, a period of **humanism** (Luis Vives, 1492-1540, for a time professor at Oxford; Luis de León, b. 1528, theologian, poet, and one of those who made Castilian a great literary language) and of religious leadership in the cause of Roman Catholicism. **Arias Montano** (1527-1598) was one of the outstanding scholars at the **Council of Trent** (p. 396); Luis de Granada (1504-1588) was one of the greatest preachers of the century and a religious writer whose books were translated into all leading languages; **Francisco Suarez** (1548-1617), a Jesuit, was a neo-scholastic and an outstanding jurist (*De Legibus ac Deo Legislatore,* 1612); while **Francisco de Vitoria** (1486-1546) wrote extensively on the government of the colonies and became a pioneer of international law (*De Indis et de iure belli relectiones,* 1532). At the same time the Spaniards took the lead in the work of the Catholic Reformation. **Ignatius de Loyola** (1491-1556), after receiving a serious wound in war, made a pilgrimage to Jerusalem (1523–1524) and then studied at Paris (1528–1535). In 1540 he founded the Society of Jesus at Rome, the Jesuit organization from the beginning being placed on a military basis, and engaging in widespread missionary and teaching activity. At the same time Sta. Teresa de Jesús (1515–1582) undertook the reorganization of the Carmelite nunneries and, in her autobiography and her *Castillo interior* made outstanding contributions to mystical literature. St. Jean de la Croix (1542–1591), her disciple, effected similar reforms of the monasteries.

The period was one of equal greatness in the realm of literature and art. Juan de Mariana wrote a popular history of Spain, while Bartolomé de Las Casas (1474–1566), Oviedo, and Gómara distinguished themselves in treatment of the New World. Felix Lope de Vega (1562–1635), who produced over 2000 plays, poems, and stories, was one of the great literary figures of all time and a founder of the modern drama; Pedro Calderón (1600–1681) continued the drama on a high plane; Miguel de Cervantes Saavedra (1547–1616) in his *Don Quijote* (1605) produced an incomparable picture of the Spain of his day and at the same time one of the world's most popular masterpieces.

In the field of art the Italian influence was very strong, though the Escorial (begun in 1563 and built by Juan de Herrera) had a severe style of its own. Prominent sculptors of the age were Gregorio Fernández (d. 1636); Alonso Cano; and Martínez Montañés (d. 1649), but the achievements of painting overshadowed those of the other arts. El Greco (1547–1614; really a Greek from Crete, trained in Italy) came to Spain in 1575 and lived at Toledo until his death in 1614. One of the greatest painters of the Renaissance, he was the first of a number of world-famous artists: José Ribera, called Spagnaletto (1588–1652); Zurbarán (1598–1664); Bartolomé Murillo (1617–1682) and above all the incomparable Diego Rodríguez de Silva y Velásquez (1599–1660). In music Tomas Luis de Vitoria was a worthy contemporary of Palestrina.

On the abdication of Charles I, Spain and the colonies, as well as the Netherlands, Franche-Comté, Naples, and Milan passed to his son

1556–1598. PHILIP II (b. at Valladolid in 1527), the most Spanish of the Hapsburg rulers and a monarch who spent most of his reign (1559–) in Spain. Affable, yet dignified and serious, Philip was a very hard-working bureaucrat as well as an autocrat, and at the same time a hardhearted and vindictive religious fanatic.

His entire policy centered about his determination to defend the faith and to stamp out Protestantism, and further to stand by the Hapsburg interests, outside as well as inside Spain. This involved constant intervention in general European affairs and many costly wars which drained the country. During this period the Spanish infantry (largely volunteer and with a considerable noble element) reached the pinnacle of its prestige.

Philip married four times: (1) **Mary of Portugal,** mother of Don Carlos; (2) **Mary the Catholic,** Queen of England; (3) **Elizabeth of Valois;** (4) **Anne of Austria,** daughter of Maximilian II.

1556–1559. Continuance of the **war with France.** Victories of the Spaniards under the **Duke of Alva,** at **St. Quentin** (Aug. 10, 1557) and at **Gravelines** (July 13, 1558), led to

1559, Apr. 3. The Treaty of **Cateau-Cambrésis,** which reaffirmed the Spanish possession of Franche-Comté and the Italian states. Philip married Elizabeth, the daughter of Henry II.

1560. The capital was definitively established at **Madrid.** In 1563 the construction of the Escorial Palace was begun.

1567. Beginning of the prolonged **struggle for independence in the Netherlands** (p. 379).

1568. **Death of Don Carlos,** the son of the king, whom Philip is sometimes accused of having put away. Don Carlos appears to have been deranged and unmanageable, for which reason he was kept in confinement. There is no evidence of unnatural death.

1569–1571. **Revolt of the Moriscos** (converted Moslems suspected of secretly retaining their original faith). The rising was put down with great severity and ultimately (1609) the Moriscos were expelled from Spain.

1571, Oct. 7. **Battle of Lepanto,** the outstanding event in the long naval duel between the Spaniards and the Turks. **Don John of Austria** (natural brother of Philip), with the aid of a papal and a Venetian fleet, inflicted a tremendous defeat on the Turks (p. 423).

1574. The Spaniards lost Tunis.

1580. Philip succeeded to the **Portuguese throne** (p. 392).

1587. **Sir Francis Drake** destroyed the Spanish fleet at Cadiz. England had for some time been incurring the displeasure of Philip, partly because of the succession of Elizabeth and the progress of Protestantism, partly because of the aid given the Dutch rebels, and partly because of the piratical raids on the Spanish treasure ships. The **execution of Mary Stuart** (1587) brought matters to a crisis, and Philip sent against England

1588. THE GREAT ARMADA, which met with complete disaster (p. 373). The war with England continued in a desultory way until 1603.

1589-1598. War with France, arising from Philip's intervention against **Henry IV.** The Spaniards played an important rôle in this last phase of the Religious Wars in France, but failed to attain their objectives. The war ended with the Treaty of Vervins (p. 386).

1598-1621. PHILIP III, the son of Philip II by his last marriage. A melancholy, retiring, and deeply religious man, the king devoted himself to the interests of the Church (9000 monasteries in this period, and one-third of the population in the church service). Philip left the government to his favorite (*privado*), the **Duke of Lerma,** who initiated the system of court intrigue and corruption. Formation of a court nobility; growth of huge estates; marked decline in agriculture (depopulation through wars and emigration to the colonies). Spain became to a large extent a wool-raising country. Industry and trade, so flourishing in the 16th century, suffered a marked decline. Spain generally entered upon a period of decadence and lethargy.

1609. Expulsion of the Moriscos (see above).

1618. Beginning of the Thirty Years' War (p. 403), into which Spain was drawn by Hapsburg interests and by religious considerations.

1621-1665. PHILIP IV, an amiable prince, not interested in politics and therefore quite content to leave the conduct of affairs to his *privado*, the **Count-Duke Olivares** (1587-1645; Count of Olivares, Duke of Santander), an able and patriotic administrator who, until his fall in 1643, made valiant efforts to modernize the governmental system by means of greater centralization and increase of the royal power.

1622. The occupation of the Valtelline Pass (between Milan and the Austrian lands) by the Spanish led to war with France, which, in a sense, was merely one aspect of the Thirty Years' War. France, under the able leadership of Richelieu, gradually established her ascendancy over Spain (p. 386).

1640-1659. THE GREAT REVOLT IN CATALONIA, a direct result of the policy of Olivares. The king's failure to summon the Catalan Córtes, the imposition of new taxes, the demands for aid for the foreign wars, the quartering of troops in the country and in general the centralizing tendencies of the Count-Duke, precipitated the conflict. The movement was supported by France, which even recognized a **Catalan republic.** After the struggle had gone on for twelve years, Barcelona was finally obliged to submit (1652, Oct.). In the final settlement (1659) the Catalans retained most of their former rights and privileges.

1642. The French occupied Roussillon.

1643, May 19. The battle of Rocroi. Defeat of the Spaniards. This battle is generally taken as marking the end of the supremacy of the Spanish forces.

1647. Revolt of Naples, under **Masaniello** (p. 398).

1648. The Peace of Westphalia (p. 408). This did not apply to the war between France and Spain, which continued for another eleven years.

1658, June 14. Battle of the Dunes; decisive defeat of the Spaniards.

1659, Nov. 7. TREATY OF THE PYRENEES (signed on the Isle of Pheasants, in the Bidassoa River). Spain was obliged to cede to France the frontier fortresses in Flanders and Artois, and also Roussillon and Cerdagne. Louis XIV married Maria-Theresa, daughter of Philip IV. (*Cont. p.* 448.)

b. PORTUGAL, 1495-1640

1495-1521. MANUEL I (*the Great, the Fortunate*), the brother of John II. His reign and that of his successor mark the apogee of Portuguese power and empire, following the great discoveries (**Vasco da Gama's** voyage to India, 1497-1498; **Pedro Alvares Cabral's** discovery of Brazil, 1500; **Magellan's** circumnavigation of the globe, 1520, see p. 363 et seq.). The new empire was at first ruled by men of exceptional ability and courage (**Francisco d' Almeida,** first viceroy of the Indies, 1505; **Afonso de Albuquerque,** viceroy, 1507-1511) and brought in large returns. Lisbon very soon displaced Venice as the entrepôt for Asiatic goods, and became a center of wealth and luxury. Colonial trade was a royal monopoly, and the court became a Mecca for concession-seekers. The old agrarian system became undermined by the introduction of black slavery, while the

The Portuguese Succession (1580)

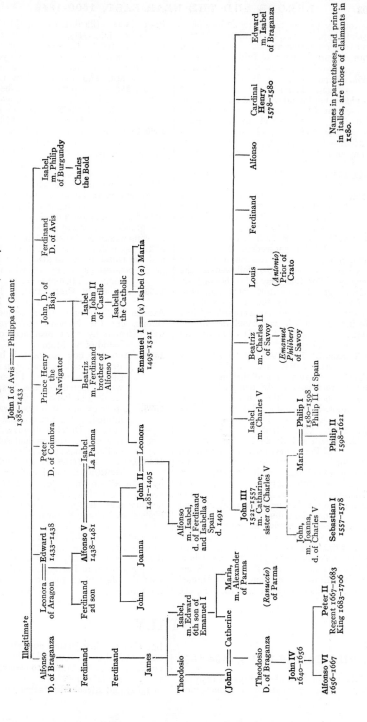

Names in parentheses, and printed in italics, are those of claimants in 1580.

aristocracy to a certain extent abandoned itself to imperial war, to corruption at home and to exploitation abroad. In short, the 16th century, outwardly brilliant, was already the beginning of decadence.

1496. Expulsion of the Jews from Portugal. This step was taken chiefly to please Ferdinand and Isabella of Spain, whose daughter, Isabella, Manuel married (1497; she died in the next year). Persecution and massacre followed the expulsion order, which deprived Portugal of many of its most educated and wealthiest inhabitants.

1521-1557. JOHN III (*the Pious*), during whose reign

1536. The Inquisition was established in Portugal and the **Jesuit Order** invited in. The consequences were much like those in Spain.

1557-1578. SEBASTIAN I, the grandson of John, succeeded. Regency of his mother, Joanna of Austria, a daughter of Charles V, until 1562, followed by the regency of **Cardinal Henry,** brother of John III and grand inquisitor. Sebastian himself was educated by the Jesuits and was consumed with the idea of a crusade against the infidel, which he undertook despite the contrary advice of Philip II of Spain and of the pope.

1578, Aug. 4. THE BATTLE OF AL KASR AL-KABIR (Alcazar-Qivir), in which the Portuguese and their mercenary troops were completely defeated by the Moors. Sebastian, the King of Fez, and the Moorish pretender all lost their lives (*battle of the three kings*).

1578-1580. CARDINAL HENRY, king.

1580. Death of Luis de Camões, greatest of Portuguese poets (*The Lusiads*, published 1572), whose work not only brought to culmination the literary flowering of the 16th century (dramas of Gil Vicente), but served as a profound commentary on Portuguese national life and imperial enterprise.

1580. A regency of five was established to govern the country on the death of Cardinal Henry. There were no less than seven claimants to the throne, of whom the most powerful was **Philip II of Spain** (son of Elizabeth, the daughter of Manuel I) and the most popular was **Antonio,** the

Prior of Crato (illegitimate son of Luis, the brother of John III). Philip's candidacy was supported by the high clergy and by part of the nobility. Antonio enjoyed the support of the townsmen and of the peasants, and was backed by France.

Aug. 25. The Spaniards, under the Duke of Alva, invaded Portugal and defeated their opponents in the **battle of Alcántara,** near Lisbon.

1580-1598. PHILIP I (Philip II of Spain), who was accepted by the Córtes. Philip promised to respect the rights of the country and to rule only through Portuguese. He himself generally observed this obligation, but under his successors it was more and more ignored. First Portugal itself, then the Portuguese Empire, was turned over to Spanish officials. The result was growing discontent in Portugal and increasing weakness abroad. After the defeat of the Spanish armada (1588), the British and the Dutch began to attack the Portuguese possessions, many of which were conquered before 1640.

1583. Antonio of Crato, with a French fleet, established himself in the Azores and prepared to reconquer the throne, but the French-Portuguese fleet was defeated by a Spanish fleet off the island of St. Miguel.

1589. Antonio, now supported by the British, made a landing in Portugal and marched on Lisbon, but was defeated by the Spaniards. He died at Paris in 1595.

1598. Dutch trade with Lisbon was prohibited. This marked the beginning of Dutch enterprise in the east and of the gradual conquest of Portuguese possessions.

1640, Dec. 1. REVOLT OF THE PORTUGUESE, inspired and organized by **João Ribeiro,** a professor at the University of Coimbra, and supported by the nobility and clergy. The insurgents, all disillusioned about Spanish rule, took advantage of the revolt in Catalonia. Like the Catalonians they were supported by France, which was at war with Spain. The Spanish government, unable to devote much attention to Portugal, could not prevent the **election of John of Braganza, to** the throne.   (*Cont. p.* 452.)

5. ITALY

a. THE ITALIAN WARS, 1494-1559

The period from about 1450 to 1550 not only marked the apogee of the Renaissance,

but also the intellectual and artistic primacy of Italy. In the field of history and political science, **Francesco Guicciardini** (1483-1540; *Istoria d' Italia* published only in 1561) and **Niccolo di Machiavelli** (1469-

1527; *Il Principe*, 1513) were outstanding. Pietro Aretino (1492–1552) was a famous publicist of the time, while **Baldassare di Castiglione** (*Il Cortegiano*, 1527) produced a famous handbook of the courtier. **Ludovico Ariosto** (1474–1533; *Orlando Furioso*, 1516) was one of the greatest epic poets of all time. In the field of music **Giovanni da Palestrina** (1525–1594; at St. Peter's after 1551) and **Orlando di Lasso** were men of the first rank. Architects and painters of eminence were too numerous to be listed, and it will suffice to recall names like **Leonardo da Vinci** (1452–1519); **Raffael Santi** (1483–1520; *Sistine Madonna*, 1516); **Michelangelo Buonarroti** (1475–1564; Sistine Chapel paintings, 1508–1512, 1534–1541; dome of St. Peter's, 1547); **Titian** (Tiziano Vecelli, 1477–1576); **Gentile Bellini** (1429–1507); **Tintoretto** (1512–1594); **Paolo Veronese** (1528–1588); **Mantegna, Correggio, Cellini,** etc.

Politically, however, Italy was divided and soon became the "cockpit" of Europe, the victim of the rivalries of the strong monarchies which were arising in the west and all of which coveted the wealth of the Peninsula. There were, at the time, five major states: **Venice,** the strongest of all, deriving her wealth and influence from the extensive eastern trade, from her possessions in the Adriatic, Ionian, and Aegean Seas and from domination of the neighboring mainland; **Milan,** ruled by Ludovico Sforza and commanding the rich valley of the Po; **Florence,** long one of the most progressive of Italian communities, having attained to great splendor under Lorenzo the Magnificent; the **Papal States,** carved from the central part of the Peninsula and in process of expansion under the political popes of the late 15th century; the **Kingdom of Naples,** deeply involved in the Near East, ruled by a branch of the Aragonese house. These states maintained a precarious balance among themselves, but were almost all so imperialistic that they were constantly endeavoring to victimize each other and ultimately reached the point of calling in the foreigner, with the result that Italy became the prey of French, German, and Spanish ambitions.

1492. Formation of a secret alliance between Florence and Naples for the spoliation of Milan. This led to Ludovico Sforza's appealing to Charles VIII of France to make good the Anjou claims on Naples.

1494-1495. THE FRENCH INVASION OF ITALY. Charles arrived in Sept. and met with no real resistance. Florence submitted, but then drove out **Piero de' Medici** (Nov.) and abandoned the French connection. Thereupon Charles attacked and took Florence, which was obliged to give up Pisa and other towns. Charles advanced on Rome (Jan. 1495) and thence into Naples. Alfonso fled to Sicily, leaving Naples to his son Ferrante, who was driven out by a revolt. The French entered Naples (Feb. 22, 1495), but their very success led to the formation of a coalition directed against them: Milan, Venice, Emperor Maximilian, Pope Alexander VI, and Ferdinand of Aragon leagued together against Charles, forcing his retreat to the north. Ferrante and the Spaniards (Gonzalvo de Cordova) soon reconquered Naples. This first French invasion of Italy was poorly planned and carelessly executed, but had much importance in opening up the international side of the Italian problem as well as in disseminating the learning and art of Italy throughout western Europe.

1499, Feb. Venice agreed to support the claims of Louis XII of France to Milan, in return for a promise of Cremona. The French thereupon invaded Italy a second time (Aug.) and forced **Ludovico Sforza** to flee from Milan to Germany. Milan surrendered (Sept. 14). The next year Sforza returned with an army of German mercenaries and obliged the French to evacuate. Before long the German forces began to disintegrate and the French returned to Milan. Ludovico was captured and died (1508) in a French prison. Milan thus became French.

1500, Nov. 11. By the **Treaty of Granada,** Ferdinand of Aragon agreed to support Louis' claim to Naples, which was to be divided between France and Spain. In 1501 (June) the French army, marching south, entered Rome, whereupon the pope declared Federigo of Naples deposed and invested Louis and Ferdinand with the kingdom. The French took Capua (July), while the Spanish fleet seized Taranto (Mar., 1502). So much having been gained, the two allies fell to quarreling over the division of the spoils, and war resulted (July). The Spaniards at first suffered reverses, but in 1503 defeated a French fleet and won a decisive victory at **Cerignola** (Apr. 28). They took Naples (May 13), and, after another victory at **Garigliano** (Dec. 28), forced the French to surrender at **Gaeta** (Jan. 1, 1504). This completed the Spanish conquest of Naples, which, with Sicily, gave them control of southern Italy, as the French had control of Milan in the north.

1508, Dec. 10. THE LEAGUE OF CAMBRAI, organized to despoil Venice of her possessions on the mainland and in

Apulia. Emperor Maximilian promised Louis XII the investiture of Milan in return for support. Ferdinand of Aragon and Pope Julius II joined the coalition. The French attacked and defeated the Venetians at Agnadello (May 14, 1509). Surrender of Verona, Vicenza, and Padua, which were handed over to Maximilian, while the pope occupied Ravenna, Rimini, Faenza, and other Venetian possessions in the Romagna. The Apulian towns, Brindisi, Otranto, etc., fell to Ferdinand. But the Venetians soon rallied and retook Padua (July 17), which was besieged in vain by Maximilian. Vicenza too rose against the emperor and recalled the Venetians. In 1510 the pope, fearful of the power of the Germans, deserted the league and joined Venice, while Ferdinand, having secured his share of the spoils, turned neutral. The papal forces took Modena and Mirandola (Jan. 1511), but the French conquered Bologna (May 13). In Oct. Ferdinand completed a *volte face* and joined Venice and the pope, while Henry VIII of England also adhered. After a French victory at Ravenna (Easter, 1512), even the emperor and the Swiss cantons joined the coalition against the French, who were driven out of Milan (May). In a congress of the league at Mantua (Aug.) the Spaniards forced the Florentines to take back the Medici and join the league. Milan was given to Maximilian Sforza (son of Ludovico). The war continued until the French were badly defeated at Novara (June 6, 1513), after which the pope, Ferdinand, and Henry of England all made peace.

1515. The new French king, Francis I, as deeply interested in Italy as his two predecessors, and quite as adventurous, concluded an alliance with Henry VIII and Venice against the Emperor Maximilian, the pope, Ferdinand, Milan, Florence, and the Swiss. The French won a great victory at Marignano (Sept. 13) by which they recovered Milan. Thereupon the pope came to terms, surrendered Parma and Piacenza, and in return secured the Concordat of Bologna (p. 382). After the death of Ferdinand (Jan. 1516), his successor, Charles I (later Emperor Charles V), confronted with serious problems in Spain and Germany and eager to secure European co-operation against the advance of the Turks, concluded with Francis the Treaty of Noyon (Aug. 13, 1516), by which the French retained Milan, but gave up their claims to Naples. Maximilian returned Brescia and Verona to Venice in consideration of a money payment.

1522-1523. First of the Hapsburg-Valois wars, for many of which Italy became a battlefield. The pope and England supported Charles V against Francis. Having been driven out of Milan, Parma, and Piacenza, the French were defeated at Bicocca (Apr. 27, 1522) and retained only the citadel of Milan. In May they were even driven from Genoa, their all-important sea-base. But in Oct. 1524, the French invaded Italy with a large army. They retook Milan (Oct. 29). The pope changed sides and joined the French.

1525, Feb. 24. THE BATTLE OF PAVIA, the most important engagement of the long Italian wars. The Spanish commanders, Constable de Bourbon (prominent French noble and opponent of Francis), and Marquis de Pescara, completely defeated the French. Francis himself was captured and sent to Madrid. There he concluded the Treaty of Madrid (Jan. 14, 1526), by which he promised to surrender his Italian claims, give up Burgundy, and abandon his suzerainty over Artois and Flanders. These engagements he never meant to observe, and they were repudiated by him as soon as he was liberated.

1526, May 22. THE LEAGUE OF COGNAC, a coalition of Francis I, the pope, Sforza, Venice, and Florence against Charles and the Spaniards. The league was the natural result of the too great success of the Spaniards in Italy and the objective was to restore the *status quo* of 1522. But the Spaniards forced Sforza out of Milan (July 24) and before long attacked Rome (Sept. 21). The pope was helpless and could not prevent

1527, May 6. THE SACK OF ROME by the Spanish and German mercenaries of Charles. The sack was horrible even when judged by the customs of the day, and ended Rome's pre-eminence in the Renaissance. The pope himself was captured.

May 17. Florence rose against the Medici, who were again driven out and replaced by a republic (under Niccolo Capponi). Genoa also revolted, under Andrea Doria (formerly in French service). The French were expelled and a republican constitution established. The French, however, having overrun Lombardy (Oct.) began to march south. Meanwhile the pope, who had fled to Orvieto (Dec.) made his peace with Charles (Treaty of Barcelona, June 29, 1529 — the papal states to be restored and the Medici returned to Florence). The war was ended by

1529, Aug. 3. The Treaty of Cambrai (*Paix des dames*, because negotiated by Charles' aunt, Margaret, and by Francis' mother, Louise of Savoy). Francis once more renounced his Italian claims and the overlordship of Artois and Flanders. Venice was obliged to disgorge her conquests (Apulian towns, Ravenna, etc.). The Duchy of Milan was given to Francesco Maria Sforza, Charles V retaining the citadel. Florence was forced, after an eight months' siege, to take back Alessandro de' Medici as duke. On Feb. 23, 1530, Charles was crowned by the pope as emperor and King of Italy.

1535. The **death of Francesco Sforza** opened the question of the Milanese succession. Charles V claimed it as suzerain, but the French invaded Italy and took Turin (Apr. 1536). After an invasion of Provence by the imperialists, the **Truce of Nice** was concluded for ten years (June 18, 1538). It reaffirmed the Treaty of Cambrai, but the French remained in occupation of two-thirds of Piedmont and the emperor retained the rest.

1542-1544. The war between **Francis I and Charles V**, though fought out in the Netherlands and in Roussillon, had repercussions in Italy. The **Treaty of Crespy** (Sept. 18, 1544) involved abandonment of French claims to Naples, but provided that the Duke of Orléans should marry either Charles' daughter, with the Netherlands and Franche-Comté as a dowry, or else Charles' niece, who would bring Milan. The plan failed through the death of Orléans (1545). Piedmont and Savoy were to be restored to the legitimate ruler.

1556. Alliance of Pope Paul IV and Henry II of France to get Naples. The French, under the **Duke of Guise,** invaded Italy, but were obliged to withdraw after their defeat at **St. Quentin** (1557). This practically ended the French struggle for Italy. The **Treaty of Cateau-Cambrésis** (Apr. 3, 1559) involved the abandonment of French possessions, except Turin, Saluzzo, and Pignerol. Margaret, sister of Henry II, was to marry Emanuel Philibert of Savoy.

b. THE PAPACY

The earlier part of this period marked the nadir of the papacy viewed from the moral standpoint. Most of the popes were typical products of the Renaissance, patronizing the arts, living in splendor and luxury, using their position either to aggrandize their families or to strengthen the temporal position of the Church. Of religious leadership there was almost none, yet politically speaking the period was one of the utmost importance.

1484-1492. **INNOCENT VIII** (Giovanni Cibo), an indolent and altogether corrupt pontiff, who was entirely under the influence of Cardinal Giuliano della Rovere. A long-drawn conflict with Naples ended in marriage alliances of the pope's family with the Aragonese house and with the Medici.

1492-1503. **ALEXANDER VI** (Rodrigo Borgia), a stately, energetic, ruthless, and thoroughly immoral pope, whose life was a scandal even in the Italy of his time. The main objective of his policy was to establish the rule of his family in central Italy. He broke the power of the great Roman families (Orsini, Colonna), and, through his son, **Caesar Borgia** (1475-1507), a former cardinal and the hero of Machiavelli's *Prince*, undertook the conquest of the Romagna. Caesar reduced most of the principalities (1499-1501) and became Duke of the Romagna. In 1501 the Borgias joined France in the attack on Naples, and the French aided Caesar in putting down a revolt of his captains at Sinigaglia (Dec. 1502). But the death of the pope and the hostility of the new pontiff, Julius II, frustrated Caesar's schemes. Forced to disgorge his conquests, he turned to Spain for aid. In 1506 he was arrested at Naples and sent to Spain, where he died (1507).

1503. **PIUS III** (Francesco Piccolomini, a nephew of Pius II), died within 26 days of his election.

1503-1513. **JULIUS II** (Giuliano della Rovere), one of the greatest of the popes and the real founder of the Papal States, a man of great intelligence and boundless energy, more a statesman than a priest. He not only regained the Romagna, but took the lead in the effort to expel the foreigner from Italy. In 1508 he was in the forefront of the **League of Cambrai,** through which he hoped to acquire the Venetian possessions in the Romagna. Having humbled Venice, he turned on the French. In reply Louis XII summoned a church council at Pisa (1511), which obliged the pope to convoke a rival **council at the Lateran** (1512). This remained in session for several years, and first undertook reform of abuses in the Church.

1513-1521. **LEO X** (Giovanni de' Medici, son of Lorenzo the Magnificent), a noteworthy patron of art, but an easygoing churchman, whose pontificate was noted chiefly for the **beginning of the Reformation** in Germany (1517, see p. 399). There is no evidence that the pope realized the gravity of the situation and the only solution he could offer was to ban Luther (1521).

1522-1523. **ADRIAN VI** (of Utrecht), the last non-Italian pope. Adrian was, at the time of his election, regent of Spain for Charles V. An upright and austere man, he attempted to purge the papacy of abuses and tried to reconcile Charles V and Francis I in order to unite Christendom in a crusade against the Turks. His efforts brought him great unpopularity in Italy and conflict, even with Charles V, but he died before accomplishing much.

1523-1534. CLEMENT VII (Giulio de' Medici), a hard-working but undecided pontiff. He failed entirely to cope with the religious revolt in Germany, and failed also to maintain a safe position in the conflict between the French and the Spaniards for domination of Italy. Hence the terrible sack of Rome (May 6, 1527, see above), which may be said to have brought to a close the greatness of Rome in the Renaissance.

1534-1549. PAUL III (Alessandro Farnese), another worldly pope, whose greatest concern was for his family. On the other hand, he recognized clearly the urgency of reform in the Church. By creating cardinals of eminent scholars and serious churchmen he completely changed the character of the college. In 1536 he established a reform commission of nine. The Society of Jesus was founded (Sept. 27, 1540) under his auspices, and the Universal Inquisition was established at Rome (July 21, 1542). Finally the pope yielded to the demand of years, and in 1545 opened the Council of Trent, which undertook the reform of the Church, under Jesuit guidance. The work of the council was several times interrupted and therefore divides into three periods: 1545-1547; 1551-1552; 1562-1564. The first period was perhaps the most important, both for organizational and doctrinal reform.

1550-1555. JULIUS III (Giovanni Maria del Monte), an elegant pope whose reign marked a short return to the papacy of the Renaissance.

1555. MARCELLUS II (Marcello Cervini), whose election marked the victory of the strict reform party. The pope died within 22 days, and was succeeded by

1555-1559. PAUL IV (Gian Pietro Caraffa), a sincere and vigorous reformer and one of the chief inspirers of the Counter-Reformation. The powers and activities of the Inquisition were extended and the first index of forbidden books was drawn up (1559). As a Neapolitan the pope detested the Spanish rule and was soon in conflict with the Hapsburgs. He allied himself with France, but was defeated by the Duke of Alba.

1559-1565. PIUS IV (Giovanni Medici, not related to the famous Florentine family), an amiable pontiff who followed the guidance of his high-minded and able nephew, **Carlo Borromeo**, Archbishop of Milan. He made peace with the Hapsburgs and concluded the Council of Trent (*Professio Fidei Tridentina*, 1564).

1566-1572. ST. PIUS V (Michaele Ghislieri), the last pope to be canonized. Pius was an exceedingly devout and ascetic priest, whose attitude was well reflected in the anathematization of Queen Elizabeth (1570) and in the financing of the naval crusade against the Turks which culminated in the great victory of Lepanto (Oct. 7, 1571, see p. 423). Under Pius' direction the decisions of the Council of Trent were further embodied in the *Catechismus Romanus* (1566), the *Breviarium Romanum* (1568), and the *Missale Romanum* (1570).

1572-1585. GREGORY XIII (Ugo Buoncampagni), who continued the policy of his predecessor and did much to encourage the Jesuit colleges. He is remembered chiefly for his reform of the calendar (1582), which involved the dropping of ten days, and for the future the striking out of leap year at the close of each century, excepting every fourth century. This reform was not accepted by Protestant countries until long afterward (in Russia not until 1918).

1585-1590. SIXTUS V (Felice Peretti), one of the really great popes, who, after suppressing the powerful nobility of the Papal States and purging the territory of bandits, reorganized the government, reestablished the finances on a sound basis, and encouraged industry (silk culture). In the same way he remade the papal curia (college of cardinals fixed at 70; establishment of 15 congregations or commissions of cardinals to deal with particular aspects of church affairs). New edition of the Vulgate Bible. Beautification of Rome, which now took on its characteristic Baroque appearance (construction of the Vatican Palace and Library, the Lateran Palace, the Santa Scala; completion of the dome of St. Peter's according to Michelangelo's plans). There followed the three brief pontificates of

1590. Urban VII, who died in 14 days,
1590-1591. Gregory XIV, and
1591. Innocent IX, who died in two months.
1592-1605. CLEMENT VIII (Ippolito Aldobrandini), a pious, serious pope, who supported the Catholic cause in France and ultimately mediated the peace between France and Spain (1598). His reign was distinguished by the great cardi-

nals, **Robert Bellarmine** (1542–1621), eminent theologian and defender of the papal right to interfere in temporal affairs (*De potestate summi pontificis in rebus temporalibus*, 1610; *De officio principis christiani*, 1619), and **Caesar Baronius** (1538–1607), the great historian of the Catholic Church (*Annales ecclesiastici*, 1588–1607). During this pontificate Ferrara was added to the Papal States by reversion (1597).

1605. Leo IX lived only 25 days, and was succeeded by

1605-1621. PAUL V (Camillo Borghese), whose high idea of the papal power brought him into conflict with Venice and led to a compromise. On the outbreak of the Thirty Years' War the pope gave financial support to the Hapsburgs.

1621-1623. GREGORY XV (Alessandro Ludovisi), a weak old man who was guided by his able nephew, **Ludoviso Ludovisi.** He regulated the papal elections and organized the *Congregatio de propaganda fide* (1622), which united all missionary activity of the Church.

1623-1644. URBAN VIII (Maffeo Barberini). He secured Urbino by reversion (1631), thus completing the dominions of the Papal States. In the Thirty Years' War he attempted to maintain a neutrality which brought him much criticism from the imperialist side. His main concern appears to have been for the States of the Church, which he carefully fortified.
(*Cont. p. 455.*)

c. VENICE

The discovery of the new route to the Indies struck at the old traditional trade through the Levant and at once began to undermine the prosperity of Venice. At the same time the steady advance of the Turks left the Venetians the choice between active opposition or accommodation. In general the latter policy was followed (much to the disgust of other European states), but nevertheless Venice became involved in a number of disastrous conflicts, which cost her most of her outposts in the east (p. 420). The assault upon the possessions of Venice in Italy (**League of Cambrai,** see p. 393) proved less successful than the powers had expected, but thenceforth Venice was obliged to remain on the defensive and to observe, as well as might be, a neutral attitude as between France and Spain and later between France and Austria.

1570. The Turks attacked Cyprus, the largest and most important base of Venetian power in the east. In the course of the ensuing war, the allied Span-

iards and Venetians, supported by the papal fleet, won the great

1571, Oct. 7. Battle of Lepanto, which, however, was not effectively followed up. The Venetians took the earliest opportunity to make peace, and

1573. Venice abandoned Cyprus and agreed to pay a heavy indemnity. Thenceforth only Candia (Crete), Paros, and the Ionian Islands remained in Venetian hands. (*Cont. p. 458.*)

d. OTHER ITALIAN STATES

After the Treaty of Cateau-Cambrésis (1559, see p. 383) all the Italian states, with the possible exception of Venice, were more or less directly under Spanish influence. The Counter-Reformation was soon in full swing, and by the end of the 16th century Italy was already losing the intellectual and cultural primacy which she held during the Renaissance.

MILAN declined rapidly in economic and political importance after 1525. The death of the last Sforza (**Francesco II**) in 1535 brought Milan under direct Spanish rule. In 1556 the Duchy of Milan became an appanage of the Spanish crown, though held as a fief of the empire.

GENOA had been, in the later 15th century, a bone of contention between France and Milan. Torn by internal struggles of rival families (**Adorno** and **Fregoso**), it had lost its great commercial power and was important chiefly as a base of operations for France. In 1528 (Sept. 9), however, the great Genoese admiral, **Andrea Doria,** having left the French service, seized the town and re-established the republic, with a pronouncedly aristocratic constitution. Efforts of the French to recapture it failed. Gian Luigi Fieschi (**Fiesco**) in 1547 staged a spectacular conspiracy that was supported by France. Gianettino Doria, nephew of Andrea, was murdered and Andrea himself forced to flee. The conspirators secured most of the town, but then Fieschi was accidentally drowned and the movement collapsed. **Andrea Doria** returned as doge and the constitution was restored. On Andrea's death (1560) he was succeeded by **Gian Andrea Doria.** The loss of Chios to the Turks (1566) marked the end of Genoese power in the east.

SAVOY was an independent state, the rulers of which governed also Piedmont. Lying astride the Alps and commanding the passes from France into Italy, the state was one of considerable importance, but the feudal organization resulted in such weakness that for long the dukes were unable to pursue an independent policy. In the early 16th century Savoy was decidedly under French influence, and when, in 1536, the duke departed from the traditional policy, his dominions were overrun and for the larger part occupied by the French. **Emanuel Philibert** (1553-1580) was the first really outstanding ruler. By following the Spanish lead he secured his dominions again in 1559, and in the course of his reign he acquired Asti and other territories by negotiation. He made much progress in breaking the power of the nobility and in organizing a central government and an effective army. His successor, **Charles Emanuel I** (1580-1630), squandered much of his father's achievement, waging war and neglecting the economic development of the country. **Victor Amadeus I** (1630-1637) was a wise and just ruler, but his short reign was followed by a civil war, and when finally **Charles Emanuel II** (1638-1675) ascended the throne, his mother **Christina** (daughter of Henry IV of France) dominated the situation as regent.

MANTUA played a fleeting rôle on the international stage in the years 1627-1631, when the death of **Vincenzo II** (Gonzaga) without heirs provoked the **War of the Mantuan Succession.** The best claim was that of **Charles of Nevers,** of the French branch of the Gonzaga line, but the emperor, at Spain's suggestion, sequestered the territory in order to keep the French out. The Spaniards overran the duchy, but the pope and Venice championed Nevers, appealing to France for aid. During 1629 the French fought the Spaniards in the duchy, but both sides were diverted by the larger obligations of the Thirty Years' War. The invasion of Germany by Gustavus Adolphus finally turned the scales in Frances' favor and by the **Treaty of Cherasco** (Apr. 26, 1631), Nevers was invested with the duchy.

FLORENCE, like Milan, sank rapidly in importance during the 16th century. The Medici, restored in 1512, were expelled for a second time in 1527, when the republic was re-established. But in 1530 Charles V appointed **Alessandro de' Medici** hereditary ruler. **Cosimo de' Medici** became duke in 1537 and ruled until 1574. During this period Siena was incorporated with Florence (1555) and Florence became the **Grand Duchy of Tuscany** (1569).

NAPLES, conquered by the Spaniards in 1504, became an appanage of the Spanish crown and was, throughout this period, the headquarters of Spanish power in Italy. Though unpopular, the Spaniards were not threatened in their position excepting by the **revolt of Masaniello** (Tommaso Aniello, a fisherman), in July, 1647. The insurrection, at first completely successful, led to extremism and confusion, in the midst of which Masaniello was murdered.

(*Cont. p.* 454.)

6. GERMANY

a. GERMANY, 1493-1618

1493-1519. MAXIMILIAN I, who first took the title of *Roman Emperor elect.*

1495. The Diet of Worms. Constitutional reform. Attempted "modernization" of the medieval empire. Perpetual public peace. Imperial Chamber (*Reichskammergericht*), first at Frankfurt, then at Speier, and finally at Wetzlar (1689). At the **Diet of Cologne** (1512) the reorganization of the empire was carried further: establishment of ten circles for the better maintenance of public peace (*Landfriedenskreise*): (1) Austria; (2) Bavaria; (3) Swabia; (4) Franconia; (5) Upper Rhine; (6) Lower Rhine; (7) Burgundy (ceded to the Spanish line of the Hapsburgs, 1556); (8) Westphalia; (9) Lower Saxony; (10) Upper Saxony. In all there were 240 states in the empire, exclusive of the imperial knights. Bohemia and the neighboring states (Moravia, Silesia, Lusatia) with Prussia and Switzerland (which was already completely independent in fact) were not included in the circles. Establishment of the **Aulic Council,** a court more under the control of the emperor than the Imperial Chamber, and to which a large part of the work of the latter was gradually diverted.

1508. The League of Cambrai, between Maximilian, Louis XII, Pope Julius II, and Ferdinand the Catholic. The purpose of the league was to break the power of Venice. Maximilian took possession of a part of the republic's territory, but he besieged Padua in vain (1509). The pope withdrew from the league, and concluded with Venice and Ferdinand the

1511. Holy League, directed against France. Maximilian finally (1513) joined in this.

The genealogical table shows the **claim of the Hapsburgs to Spain,** and division of

The Hapsburg House in the Sixteenth Century

Maximilian I ══ Mary, d. of
1493–1519 │ Charles the Bold   Ferdinand ══ Isabella
                                     of Aragon │ of Castile

Margaret   Philip ══ Joanna

Eleanor   Charles V   Ferdinand I   Mary, m.   Catharine
m (1) Emanuel   1519–1556   1556–1564   Louis of Hungary m. John III
of Portugal   m. Isabella of   m. Anne, heiress   of Portugal
(2) Francis I   Portugal   of Bohemia
of France   and Hungary

Philip II   Mary ══ Maximilian II
1556–1598   1564–1576

Don   Isabella   Philip III   Anne   Rudolf II Ernest Elizabeth   Mathias
Carlos m. Albert, 1598–1621 m. Philip II 1576–1602   m. Charles IX 1612–1619
        son of   of Spain   of France
        Maximilian II

---

the house into Spanish and German lines. Through these marriages the central European lands of the Hapsburgs, the Burgundian lands in what are now France and Belgium, and the united lands of the crowns of Castile and Aragon (Spain, Naples, and the Americas) all came by birth to **Charles I of Spain** (eldest son of Philip and Joanna). He acquired the empire and his better known title of **Charles V** by election in 1519.

1517. BEGINNING OF THE REFORMA-TION. Background: Wiclifite (Lollard), Hussite, and other preceding rebellions against the Roman Church; the Babylonian Captivity and the Great Schism, which weakened the prestige of Rome; corruption and worldliness of the Church during the Renaissance; the development of critical scholarship, as represented by **Desiderius Erasmus** of Rotterdam, whose editions of the Church Fathers and whose Greek text of the New Testament (1516) revealed the shortcomings of basic ecclesiastical writings; rise of national feeling and dislike of foreigners, especially in Germany and England; growth of a middle class and a capitalist economy, which felt Roman Catholicism as a restraint (economic interpretation of the Reformation in modern writings of Max Weber and R. H. Tawney); great landed wealth of the Church available for confiscation by ambitious and unscrupulous princes.

Martin Luther (1483–1546), born at Eisleben, the son of a miner; monk in the Augustine monastery at Erfurt; priest (1507); professor at Wittenberg (1508); visit to Rome (1511).

1517, Oct. 31. Luther nailed on the door of the court church at Wittenberg his **95 theses** against the misuse of absolution or indulgences (especially by the Dominican monk **Tetzel**). In the following year another reformatory movement was begun in Switzerland by **Ulrich Zwingli** (1484–1531).

1518. Summoned to Augsburg by Cardinal de Vio of Gaëta (*Cajetanus*), Luther refused to abjure, but appealed to the pope. Mediation of the papal chamberlain, Von Miltitz.

1519. Discussion at Leipzig between **Bodenstein** (called *Carlstadt*) and **Eck.** The latter secured a papal bull against 41 articles in Luther's writings. Luther burned the papal bull and the canon law (1520). Thereupon he was excommunicated.

Basic Lutheran doctrine: justification by faith, which makes priestly offices of the Catholics an unnecessary intermediary between the individual and God.

In the meantime the German electors, despite the claims of Francis I of France, had chosen as emperor the grandson of Maximilian, King Charles I of Spain, who as emperor became

1519-1556. CHARLES V. He came to Germany for the first time in 1520, to preside at a grand diet at Worms (1521). There Luther defended his doctrines, coming under a safe-conduct. The ban of the empire having been pronounced against him, he was taken to the Wartburg by Frederick the Wise of Saxony, and there enjoyed protection. The Edict of Worms prohibited all new doctrines. **Luther's translation of the Bible.**

1521-1526. First war of Charles V against Francis I of France. Charles advanced claims to Milan and the Duchy of Burgundy. Francis claimed Spanish Navarre and Naples. The French, under Lautrec, were driven from Milan, which was turned over to **Francesco Sforza** (1522). The French constable, **Charles of Bourbon,** transferred his allegiance to Charles V. Unfortunate invasion of Italy by the French, under Bonnivert (1523-1524). Imperial forces thereupon invaded southern France. Francis I crossed the Mt. Cenis Pass and recaptured Milan.

1522. Progress of the Reformation. Luther, hearing of Carlstadt's misdoings, returned to Wittenberg and introduced public worship, with the liturgy in German and communion in both kinds in electoral Saxony and in Hesse. The spread of the Reformation was favored by the fact that the emperor was deeply engrossed in the war with France.

1522. The Knights' War. Franz von Sickingen and Ulrich von Hutten advocated the Reformation. Sickingen stood at the head of a league of nobles directed against the spiritual principalities. He laid siege to Trier (1522), but in vain. He was then himself besieged in Landstuhl and fell in battle. Hutten fled the country and died on the island of Ufnau in the Lake of Zurich (1523).

1524-1525. THE PEASANTS' WAR, in Swabia and Franconia. The peasants took the occasion of the disorders attendant on Luther's revolt (inspiration of his passionate attacks on the constituted authorities) to rise against the social and economic inequalities of late German feudalism. They incorporated their demands in the revolutionary **Twelve Articles.** Luther himself repudiated the peasants. They were defeated at **Königshofen** on the Tauber and cruelly punished. Another religious-social revolt was that of the **Anabaptists** in Thuringia, who denied the

efficacy of infant baptism and put forward a program strongly colored with communism. Their leader, **Thomas Münzer,** was captured and executed.

1524. Ferdinand of Austria, younger brother of Charles V, to whom the emperor had entrusted the government of Germany in 1522, at the instigation of the papal legate, **Campeggio,** formed an alliance with the two dukes of Bavaria and the Bishop of southern Germany, in the hope of checking the religious changes.

1525. THE BATTLE OF PAVIA (p. 394). Francis was completely defeated and captured by the imperial forces. In the **Peace of Madrid** (1526) he renounced all claim to Milan, Genoa, and Naples, as well as the overlordship of Flanders and Artois; he also assented to the cession of the Duchy of Burgundy, and gave his sons as hostages.

1526. The League of Torgau formed by the Protestant princes (John of Saxony, Philip of Hesse, Lüneburg, Magdeburg, Prussia, etc.) to oppose Ferdinand and his Bavarian allies. The league procured the enactment of the **Diet of Speier,** favorable to the new doctrine.

1526-1532. War with the Turks (p. 422).

1527-1529. Second war between Charles V and Francis I, who had declared that the conditions of the Peace of Madrid were extorted by force, and hence void. **Alliance at Cognac** between Francis, the pope, **Venice,** and Francesco Sforza against the emperor. The imperial army, unpaid and mutinous, took Rome by storm under the Constable of Bourbon, who fell in the assault; the pope besieged in the Castle of St. Angelo (1527). The French general, **Lautrec,** invaded Naples, but the revolt of Genoa (Doria), whose independence Charles V promised to recognize, and the plague, of which Lautrec himself died, compelled the French to raise the siege of the capital and to retire to France.

1529. Aug. 3. Treaty of Cambrai (*Paix des dames*). So called from the fact that it was negotiated by Margaret of Austria, Charles' aunt, and Louise of Savoy, Duchess of Angoulême, mother of Francis. Francis paid two million crowns and renounced his claims upon Italy, Flanders, and Artois; Charles promised not to press his claims upon Burgundy *for the present,* and released the French princes.

1529. Second Diet at Speier, where, in consequence of the victorious position of the emperor, Ferdinand and the Catholic party took a more decided position. The strict execution of the Decree of Worms was resolved upon. The evangelical states protested against this resolution, whence they were called **Protestants**.

1530. Charles crowned emperor at Bologna by the pope. This was the last coronation of a German emperor by the pope.

1530. Brilliant **Diet at Augsburg**, the emperor presiding in person. Presentation of the **Confession of Augsburg** by **Melanchthon**. The enactment of the Diet commanded the abolition of all innovations.

1531, Feb. 6. **Schmalkaldic League**, agreed upon in 1530, between the majority of Protestant princes and imperial cities.

Charles caused his brother, Ferdinand, to be elected King of Rome, and crowned at Aachen. The Elector of Saxony protested against this proceeding in the name of the evangelicals. In consequence of the new danger which threatened from the Turks, Ferdinand concluded the

1532. Religious Peace of Nürnberg. The Augsburg Edict was revoked, and free exercise of their religion permitted the Protestants until the meeting of a new council to be called within a year.

1534-1535. The Anabaptists in Münster (Johann Bockelsohn of Leyden). Extreme anarchistic (*Antinomian*) consequences of Luther's doctrine of justification by faith.

1534. Philip, Landgrave of Hesse, restored the Lutheran duke, Ulrich of Württemberg, who had been driven out (1519) by the Swabian league of cities. The emperor had invested his brother Ferdinand with the duchy, but the latter was obliged to agree to a compact, whereby he was to renounce Württemberg and in turn be recognized as King of Rome by the Evangelical party.

1534. FOUNDATION OF THE JESUIT ORDER. Ignatius de Loyola (Iñigo Lopez de Recalde, 1491-1556) with five associates founded the *Society of Jesus*, commonly known as the Jesuit Order. It was approved by the Pope Paul III, in 1540. The Jesuits, organized with military strictness, under direct papal control, were the chief agents in spreading the Catholic (or Counter) Reformation.

1535. Charles' successful expedition against Tunis (p. 422).

1536-1538. **Third war** of Charles against Francis I of France. The latter, having renewed his claims to Milan after the death of Francesco Sforza II, without issue, Charles invaded Provence anew, but fruitlessly. Francis made an inroad into Savoy and Piedmont, and besought the

alliance of **Suleiman**, who thereupon pressed his advance on Hungary and sent his fleets to ravage the coasts of Italy. The war was ended by

1538, June 18. The **Truce of Nice**, which was concluded on the basis of possession, and for ten years.

1541. **JOHN CALVIN** (1509-1564) introduced the Reformation into Geneva. Calvin was born at Noyon, France, and published the *Christianae Religionis Institutio* in 1536. He was head of the state in Geneva, save for a short exile to Strassburg (1538-1541), until the time of his death. He systematized Luther's rather emotional revolt, adapting from St. Augustine the rigorous **doctrine of predestination.** Calvinist churches had a strict moral code, and, unlike Lutheran, maintained independence of the Church from the lay authority. In Geneva, in Scotland (**John Knox**, 1505-1572), and briefly in England and even in the New World (at Boston), the Calvinists erected theocratic states. In France and Hungary they became an important minority. In Holland and parts of Germany they were soon the dominant Protestant group.

1541. Charles' unsuccessful expedition against Algiers.

1542. Henry, Duke of Brunswick-Wolfenbüttel, was driven from the duchy by the Schmalkaldic League.

1542-1544. **Fourth war** between Charles and Francis, occasioned by the investiture of Charles' son, Philip, with Milan. The fact that two secret agents whom Francis had sent to Suleiman were captured in Milan, and, when they resisted, were put to death, served Francis as a pretext. Francis in alliance with **Suleiman** and the Duke of Cleve. The allied Turkish and French fleets bombarded and plundered Nice. Charles, in alliance with Henry VIII of England, conquered the Duke of Cleve, and advanced as far as Soissons. Suleiman invaded Hungary and Austria.

1544, Sept. 18. Treaty of Crespy. Francis' second son, the Duke of Orléans, was to marry a princess of the imperial family and receive Milan. He died in 1545, however; Milan continued in the possession of the emperor, who gave it, nominally, to his son Philip, as a fief. Francis gave up his claims to Naples, and the overlordship of Flanders and Artois; Charles renounced his claims to Burgundy.

1545-1563. **COUNCIL OF TRENT** (not attended by the Protestants). The **Tridentine Decrees** effected a genuine internal reform in the Roman Catholic Church, and reaffirmed its essential dogmatic bases (p. 396).

1546-1547. SCHMALKALDIC WAR.
Charles V, since the Treaty of Crespy, unhindered by foreign complications, sought to crush the independence of the states of the Empire in Germany, and to restore the unity of the Church, to which he was urged by the pope, who concluded an alliance with him, and promised money and troops. The leaders of the League of Schmalkalden, John Frederick, Elector of Saxony, and Philip, Landgrave of Hesse, placed under the ban. Duke Maurice of Saxony concluded a secret alliance with the emperor. Irresolute conduct of the war by the allies in upper Germany. The elector and the landgrave could not be induced by General Schärtlin of Augsburg to make a decisive attack, and finally retired, each to his own land. John Frederick of Saxony reconquered his electorate, which Maurice had occupied. Charles V first reduced the members of the league in southern Germany, then went to Saxony, forced the passage of the Elbe, and defeated in the

1547, April 24. Battle of Mühlberg, the Elector of Saxony, captured him, and besieged his capital, Wittenberg. Treaty mediated by Joachim II of Brandenburg. The electoral dignity and lands given to the **Albertine line** (Duke Maurice). The **Ernestine line** retained Weimar, Jena, Eisenach, Gotha, etc. The elector was kept in captivity. Philip of Hesse surrendered, and was detained in captivity. Interim of Augsburg (1548), not generally accepted by the Protestants. The city of Magdeburg, the center of the opposition, placed under the ban. **Maurice of Saxony,** entrusted with the execution of the decree, armed himself in secret against Charles V and

1552. Surprised the emperor, after the conclusion of the **Treaty of Friedewalde** (1551) with Henry II of France, and forced him to liberate his father-in-law, Philip of Hesse, and to conclude the **Convention of Passau:** Free exercise of religion for the adherents of the Confession of Augsburg until the next Diet.

1552-1556. War between **Charles V** and **Henry II,** who, as the ally of Maurice, had seized Metz, Toul, and Verdun. Charles besieged Metz, which was successfully defended by Francis of Guise. The **Truce of Vaucelles** left France, provisionally, in possession of the cities which had been occupied.

1553. Maurice defeated Albert, Margrave of Brandenburg-Culmbach, at **Sieverhausen,** but was mortally wounded.

1555, Sept. 25. RELIGIOUS PEACE OF AUGSBURG. The territorial princes and the free cities, who, at this date, acknowledged the Confession of Augsburg, received freedom of worship, the right to introduce the Reformation within their territories (*jus reformandi*), and equal rights with the Catholic states. No agreement reached as regarded the **ecclesiastical reservation** that bishops and abbots who became Protestant should lose their offices and incomes; but this provision was inserted by imperial decree. This peace secured no privileges for the *reformed* (Calvinist) *religion.*

1556. ABDICATION OF CHARLES V at Brussels (Oct. 25, 1555, and Jan. 15, 1556).
The crown of Spain with the colonies, Naples, Milan, Franche-Comté, and the Netherlands, went to his son **Philip;** the imperial office and the Hapsburg lands to his brother **Ferdinand I.** Charles lived in the monastery of Yuste as a private individual, but not as a monk, and died there in 1558.

1556-1564. FERDINAND I, husband of Anna, sister of Louis II, King of Bohemia and Hungary, after whose death he was elected king of these countries by their estates. Constant warfare over the latter country, which he was obliged to abandon, in great part, to the Turks (p. 423).

1564-1576. MAXIMILIAN II, son of Ferdinand, was of a mild disposition and favorably inclined to the Protestants, whom he left undisturbed in the free exercise of their religion. War with Zapolya, Prince of Transylvania, and the Turks. Sultan **Suleiman I** died in camp before Szigeth, which was defended by the heroic Zrinyi. By the **Truce with Selim II** (1566) each party retained its possessions (p. 423).

REACTION AGAINST PROTESTANTISM: Catholic, or Counter, Reformation.

1576-1612. RUDOLF II, son of the Emperor Maximilian II, a learned man, an astrologer and astronomer, but incapable of governing. New quarrels over the ecclesiastical reservation. The imperial city of Donauwörth, placed under the ban by the emperor because a mob had disturbed a Catholic procession, was, in spite of the prohibition of the emperor, retained by Maximilian of Bavaria, who had executed the ban (1607). These troubles led to the formation of a

1608. Protestant Union (leader, **Frederick IV,** Elector Palatine), which was opposed by the

Cleve-Jülich Succession (1609)

Cleve

Adolph I, d. 1448

John I
1448–1481
m. Elizabeth, heiress of Nevers

Jülich and Berg
William III, d. 1511
m. Sibylla, d. of Albert
Achilles, Margrave of Brandenburg

Counts of Nevers

John II, 1481–1521

Engelbert

Mary ══════ John III, 1521–1539

Charles I

Sibylla, m.
John Frederick I
Elector of Saxony

Anne, m.
Henry VIII
of England

William
1539–1592
m. Mary, d.
of the Emperor
Ferdinand I

Francis, D. of Nevers
d. 1562

(1) Mary Eleanor
m. Albert Frederick
Duke of Prussia

(6) John William
1592–1609

(2) Anna
m. Philip Louis
Count Palatine
of Neuburg

(3) Magdalen
m. John I
Count Palatine
of Zweibrücken

Anna, m.
John Sigismund
Elector of Brandenburg

Magdalen Sibylla
m. John George
Elector of Saxony

Wolfgang
William

1609. Catholic League (leader, Maximilian, Duke of Bavaria). Both princes were of the house of Wittelsbach.

Rudolf, from whom his brother, Matthias, had forced the cession of Hungary, Moravia, and Austria, hoping to conciliate the Bohemians gave them the

1609. Royal Charter (*Majestätsbrief*), which permitted a free exercise of religion to the three estates of lords, knights, and royal cities.

1609. Beginning of the quarrel about the succession of Jülich-Cleve on the death of John William, Duke of Cleve. The Elector of Brandenburg and the Prince of Newburg were the principal claimants.

Rudolf, toward the close of his life, was forced by Matthias to abdicate the government of Bohemia.

1612-1619. MATTHIAS, being childless, and having obtained the renunciation of his brothers, secured for his cousin Ferdinand, Duke of Styria, Carinthia, and Carniola, who had been educated by the Jesuits in strict Catholicism, the succession in Bohemia and Hungary, in spite of the objections of the Protestant states.

b. THE THIRTY YEARS' WAR

1618-1648. The Thirty Years' War is generally divided into four periods, which were properly as many different wars. The first two, the Bohemian and the Danish, had a predominantly religious character; they developed from a revolt in Bohemia into a general conflict of Catholic Europe with Protestant Europe. The two latter, the Swedish and the French-Swedish, were primarily political struggles, wars directed against the power of the Hapsburg house and wars of conquest by Sweden and France, fought upon German soil.

(1) *The Bohemian Period*, 1618-1625

Origin of the war: closing of an Utraquist church in the territory of the Abbot of Braunau, and destruction of another in a city of the Archbishop of Prague. The irritation of the Bohemian Protestants (*Utraquists*) was increased by the transference of the administration to ten governors, seven of whom were Catholics. Meeting of the defensors, and revolt in Prague, headed by **Count Matthias of Thurn.**

1618, May 23. Defenestration of Prague. The governors, Martinitz and Slawata, were thrown from a window in the palace of Prague. They fell seventy feet into a ditch, but escaped with their lives. The rebels then appointed thirty directors. The Protestant Union sent Count Mansfeld to their aid, and from Silesia and Lusatia came troops under Margrave John George of Jägerndorf. The imperial forces were defeated by Mansfeld and Count Thurn.

1619-1637. FERDINAND II. Thurn marched upon Vienna. The Austrian estates, for the most part Protestant, threatened to join the Bohemians, and made rough demands upon Ferdinand, who, by his courage and the arrival of a few troops, was rescued from a dangerous situation. Thurn, who arrived before Vienna shortly afterward, was soon obliged to retire by an unfavorable turn of the war in Bohemia. Ferdinand went to Frankfurt, where he was elected emperor by the other six electors.

Meantime the Bohemians had deposed him from the throne of Bohemia and elected the young **Frederick V** (*The Winter King*) Elector Palatine, the head of the Union and of the German Calvinists, son-in-law of James I, King of England.

Count Thurn, for the second time before Vienna, allied with **Bethlen Gabor** (i.e. Gabriel Bethlen), Prince of Transylvania (Nov. 1619). Cold, want, and an inroad of an imperial partisan in Hungary, caused a retreat.

Ferdinand leagued himself with (1) **Maximilian,** Duke of Bavaria, head of the Catholic League, the friend of his youth,

who helped him subdue the Austrian estates; with (2) Spain (Spinola invaded the County Palatine; **Treaty of Ulm,** July 3, 1620; neutrality of the Protestant Union secured); and (3) with the Lutheran elector of Saxony, who resubjugated Lusatia and Silesia. Maximilian of Bavaria, with the army of the League commanded by **Tilly** (Jan Tserklaes, Baron of Tilly, in Brabant, 1559-1632), marched to Bohemia and joined the imperial general Buquoy. They were victorious in the

1620, Nov. 8. BATTLE OF THE WHITE MOUNTAIN, over the troops of Frederick V, under the command of **Christian of Anhalt.** Frederick was put under the ban, and his lands confiscated; he himself fled to Holland. Christian of Anhalt and John George of Brandenburg-Jägern dorf also put under the ban. Subjugation of the Bohemians, destruction of the royal charter, execution of the leading rebels, extirpation of Protestantism in Bohemia. Afterward, violent counter-reformation in Austria, and, with less violence, in Silesia.

Dissolution of the Protestant Union and transfer of the seat of war to the Palatinate, which was conquered in execution of the imperial ban by Maximilian's general, Tilly, aided by Spanish troops under Spinola.

1622, Apr. Battle of Wiesloch; defeat of Tilly by Mansfeld.

May. Battle of Wimpfen; victory of Tilly over the Margrave of Baden-Durlach.

June. Battle of Höchst; victory of Tilly over Christian of Brunswick brother of the reigning duke and administrator of the Bishopric of Halberstadt.

1623. Maximilian received the electoral vote belonging to Frederick V and the Upper Palatinate; Saxony obtained Lusatia in pledge for the time being.

(2) *The Danish Period*, 1625-1629

Christian IV, King of Denmark and Duke of Holstein, was the head of the Lower Saxon Circle of the empire, and leader of the Protestants.

Albert of Wallenstein (1583-1634), born in Bohemia of an Utraquist family, but educated in the Catholic faith, made Duke of Friedland in 1624, became the commander of an imperial army recruited by himself and provisioned by a system of robbery.

1626. Wallenstein defeated Mansfeld at the **Bridge of Dessau,** and pursued him through Silesia to Hungary, where Mansfeld joined Bethlen Gabor. Death of Mansfeld and of Christian of Brunswick (1626).

Aug. Tilly defeated Christian IV at **Luther am Barenberge,** in Brunswick.

1627. Tilly and Wallenstein conquered Holstein. Wallenstein alone subdued Schleswig and Jutland, drove the Dukes of Mecklenburg from their country and forced the Duke of Pomerania into submission.

1628. Wallenstein besieged **Stralsund.** Heroic defense of the citizens for ten weeks obliged Wallenstein to raise the siege.

1629, Mar. 29. EDICT OF RESTITUTION: (1) Agreeably to the ecclesiastical reservation, all ecclesiastical estates which had been confiscated since the convention of Passau should be restored. This affected two archbishoprics: Magdeburg and Bremen; twelve bishoprics: Minden, Verden, Halberstadt, Lübeck, Ratzeburg, Meissen, Merseburg, Naumburg (the latter three were, however, left in the possession of the Elector of Saxony), Brandenburg, Havelberg, Lebus, and Camin, besides very many (about 120) monasteries and foundations. (2) Only the adherents of the Augsburg Confession were to have free exercise of religion; all other "sects" were to be broken up. Beginning of a merciless execution of the edict by Wallenstein's troops and those of the league.

1629. May 22. TREATY OF LÜBECK, between the emperor and Christian IV. The latter received his lands back, but promised not to interfere in German affairs, and abandoned his allies. The Dukes of Mecklenburg put under the ban. Wallenstein invested with their lands.

1630. Electoral Assembly at Regensburg. The party of Bavaria and the league was hostile to Wallenstein and took up a position of determined opposition to the too powerful general. An excuse was found in the well-grounded complaints of all states of the empire, particularly the Catholics, of the terrible extortion and cruelty practiced by Wallenstein's army. The emperor consented to decree the dismissal of the general and a large part of the army.

(3) *The Swedish Period,* 1630-1635

1630, July. GUSTAVUS II ADOLPHUS (1594-1632), King of Sweden, landed on the coast of Pomerania.

Object and grounds of his interference: **protection** of the oppressed Protestants;

restoration of the Dukes of Mecklenburg, his relatives; the rejection of his mediation at the **Treaty of Lübeck;** anxiety in regard to the maritime plans of the emperor.

Political position of Sweden: Finland, Ingermannland, Estonia, Livonia, belonged to the kingdom of Gustavus; Courland was under Swedish influence; the acquisition of Prussia and Pomerania would have almost made the Baltic a Swedish sea. Gustavus concluded a subsidy treaty with France (**Richelieu**); drove the imperial forces from Pomerania and captured Frankfurt-on-the-Oder. Negotiations with his brother-in-law, George William, Elector of Brandenburg (1619-1640), who was under the influence of Schwarzenberg. Spandau was at last surrendered to him. Negotiations in regard to the surrender of Wittenberg; Saxony, which endeavored to maintain the position of a third, mediatory, party in the empire, a sort of armed neutrality (**Diet of princes of Leipzig,** 1631), was with difficulty brought to form an alliance with an enemy of the empire. Meanwhile

1631, May 20. Capture of Magdeburg by Tilly. The storm was conducted by Pappenheim. Terrible massacre and sack of the city by the unbridled soldiery of Tilly, who did what he could to check the outrages. Fire broke out suddenly in many places far removed from one another, and the whole city with the exception of the cathedral was consumed (*not* by Tilly's command).

Tilly took possession of Halle, Eisleben, Merseburg, and other cities, and burned them. John George, Elector of Saxony, formed an alliance with Gustavus Adolphus, who crossed the Elbe at Wittenberg. Leipzig occupied by Tilly. The imperial army and that of the Swedes and Saxons, each about 40,000 strong, were face to face.

1631, Sept. 17. BATTLE OF LEIPZIG of BREITENFELD. The Saxons were at first put to rout by Tilly, but after a bloody fight Gustavus Adolphus won a brilliant victory.

The Saxons entered Bohemia. Gustavus crossed Thuringia and Franconia to the Rhine, and occupied Mainz.

Meantime Prague was captured by the Saxons under Arnim (Boytzenburg), a former subordinate of Wallenstein. The emperor held fruitless negotiations with the Saxons.

At the urgent request of Ferdinand, Wallenstein collected an army, over which he received uncontrolled command. He recaptured Prague, and drove the Saxons from Bohemia. Their eagerness for **the** war and the Swedish alliance was already chilled.

1632. Gustavus advanced to the Danube by way of Nürnberg to meet Tilly. Conflict at **Rain,** near the confluence of the Lenz and the Danube. Tilly, mortally wounded, died at Ingolstadt.

Gustavus went to Augsburg, vainly besieged Maximilian in Ingolstadt, but forced Munich to surrender. Wallenstein summoned to the assistance of Maximilian.

1632, July-Sept. Fortified camp near Nürnberg. Gustavus and Wallenstein face to face for eleven weeks. Wallenstein declined battle. Reinforced by Bernhard of Saxe-Weimar, the Swedes attacked Wallenstein's entrenchments, but were repulsed with heavy loss. Gustavus advanced to the Danube. Wallenstein turned upon Saxony, now defenseless, Arnim having marched through Lusatia to Silesia with the Saxon and Brandenburg troops. Terrible ravages committed by the bands of Wallenstein. At the call of the Elector of Saxony, Gustavus hastened back by way of Kitzingen and Schweinfurt, joined Bernhard of Saxe-Weimar at Arnstadt, marched upon Naumburg and, hearing that Wallenstein had dispatched Pappenheim from Leipzig to the Rhine, attacked the imperial forces (18,000 against 20,000 Swedes) in the

1632, Nov. 16. BATTLE OF LÜTZEN. Death of Gustavus Adolphus. Pappenheim, recalled in haste, took part in the battle with his cavalry, after three o'clock; he was mortally wounded. The victory of the Swedes was completed by **Bernhard of Saxe-Weimar.**

Bernhard, Gustavus Horn, and Baner took command of the Swedish forces. The conduct of foreign affairs was assumed by the Swedish chancellor, **Axel Oxenstierna** (1583-1654). **League of Heilbronn** between the circles of Swabia, Franconia, Upper and Lower Rhine, on the one part, and Sweden on the other.

1633. Expedition of Bernhard of Saxe-Weimar to Franconia. He took Bamberg and Höchstädt, drove back the Bavarians under Aldringer, and joined Marshal Horn. Bernhard received from the chancellor the investiture, with the Bishoprics of Würzburg and Bamberg, under the name of the Duchy of Franconia, and occupied the upper Palatinate.

Feb. After Wallenstein had tried and punished with death many of his officers in Prague, and had filled their places with new recruits, he marched to Silesia, fought with the Saxon, Brandenburg, and Swedish troops, and negotiated

frequently with Arnim. Negotiations with Oxenstierna.

Nov. Regensburg captured by Bernhard of Saxe-Weimar. Wallenstein found himself unable to go to the assistance of the Elector of Bavaria, as the emperor urged, and went into winter quarters in Bohemia.

Growing estrangement between Wallenstein and the imperial court. The Spanish party and the league wished him removed from his command. Wallenstein conducted secret negotiations with the Saxons, the Swedes, the French. He intended to create, with the help of the army, an independent position for himself, whence he could, with the aid of the two North German electors, liberate the emperor from the control of the Spanish party, and if necessary, *compel* him to make peace and reorganize the internal affairs of the empire. He had resolved upon open revolt if the hostile party continued in power. Whether he harbored a wish for the crown of Bohemia, along with other fantastic plans, it is hard to decide. The court of Vienna succeeded in detaching the principal generals (Piccolomini, Gallas, Aldringer, Marradas, Colloredo) from his cause. Ilow, Trzka, Kinski, remained faithful.

1634, Jan. 24. Imperial proclamation: *"Friedland was concerned in a conspiracy to rob the emperor of his crown."* The chief officers of the army commanded to obey him no longer.

Feb. 18. Second proclamation, formally deposing Wallenstein. On the 24th Wallenstein went to Eger, where he was to be met by Bernhard of Saxe-Weimar, and Arnim. There occurred the

Feb. 25. Assassination of Wallenstein by Captain Devereux, at the instigation of the Irish general, Butler, after his intimate friends had been treacherously massacred. The emperor had not commanded the murder, nor had he definitely desired it; but he had given rein to the party which he knew wished "to bring in Wallenstein, alive or dead," and, after the deed was done, he rewarded the murderers with honor and riches.

1634. Victory of the imperialists under Ferdinand, the emperor's son, and Gallas and the Bavarians (John of Werth), over the Swedes at Nördlingen.

1635, May 30. TREATY OF PRAGUE, between the emperor and the Elector of Saxony. (1) The elector received Lusatia permanently, and the Archbishopric of Magdeburg for his second son, August, for life. (2) Those ecclesiastical lands, not held immediately of the emperor, which had been confiscated before the convention of Passau, should remain to the possessor forever; all others should remain for forty years (from 1627), and in case no further understanding was reached before the expiration of that period, forever, in the condition in which they were on Nov. 12, 1627. (3) Amnesty, except for participants in the disturbances in Bohemia and the Palatinate; common cause to be made against Sweden. The Lutherans alone to be allowed freedom of worship. Brandenburg and the majority of the other Protestant states accepted the peace.

(4) *The Swedish-French Period,* 1635-1648

The policy of Sweden was determined by **Oxenstierna,** that of France by **Richelieu,** and afterward by **Mazarin.** France fought at first in the person of Bernhard of Saxe-Weimar only, with whom subsidy treaties had been concluded, and who was trying to conquer for himself a new state in Alsace, in place of the Duchy of Franconia, which he had lost by the **battle of Nördlingen. Capture of Breisach** (1638). After his death (1639) France took control of his army.

1636. Victory of the Swedes under Baner at **Wittstock** over the imperialists and the Saxons. **Death of Ferdinand II.**

1637-1657. FERDINAND III, his son, was desirous of peace. After the death of Baner (1641) **Torstenson** became commander-in-chief of the Swedes.

1640. Death of George William. Frederick William, Elector of Brandenburg (the **Great Elector,** 1640-1688).

1641. Discussion of the preliminaries of peace in Hamburg. A congress agreed upon.

1642. Second Battle of Leipzig (Breitenfeld). Torstenson defeated the imperialists under Piccolomini. He then threatened the hereditary states of the emperor. These Swedish successes aroused the envy of Christian IV of Denmark. Hence

1643-1645. War between Denmark and Sweden.

1643, Sept. Torstenson hastened by forced marches to the north, conquered Holstein and Schleswig, and invaded Jutland.

Meanwhile the French in South Germany, under Marshal Guébriant, had penetrated to Rottweil. Guébriant fell in battle. Shortly afterward the French, under Rant-

zau, were surprised at **Tuttlingen** by an Austro-Bavarian army under Mercy and Werth, and totally defeated.

1643. Opening of the negotiations for peace in Osnabrück with the Swedes; 1644 in Münster with the French.

Marshal Turenne and the twenty-one-year-old Prince of Bourbon, Duke of Enghien, afterward **Prince of Condé,** appointed commanders-in-chief of the French troops.

1644. The French forced the Bavarians under Mercy to retreat. Condé captured Mannheim, Speier, and Philippsburg. Turenne took Worms, Oppenheim, Mainz, and Landau.

Meanwhile an imperial army, under Gallas, had been sent to the aid of the Danes, who were hard pressed, both by land and by sea by the Swedish admiral, Gustavus Wrangel.

1645, Jan. The imperial force was repulsed by Torstenson and Königsmark, pursued into Germany, and almost annihilated at **Magdeburg.**

March. Brilliant victory of Torstenson over the imperialists at **Jankau** in Bohemia, whereupon, in union with the Prince of Transylvania, Rákóczi, he conquered the whole of Moravia, and advanced hard upon Vienna.

May. Turenne defeated by John of **Werth** at **Mergentheim** in Franconia.

Aug. Turenne, at the head of the French and Hessians, defeated the Bavarians at **Allersheim.**

Peace between Sweden and Denmark at **Brömsebro.**

After a futile siege of Brünn, the plague having broken out in his army, Torstenson returned to Bohemia. He resigned his command on account of illness, and was succeeded by Wrangel.

1646. Wrangel left Bohemia, united to his own force the Swedish troops under Königsmark in Westphalia, and joined Turenne at Giessen. Swedes and French invaded Bavaria and forced the Elector Maximilian to conclude the

1647. Truce of Ulm, and to renounce his alliance with the emperor. After Turenne had been recalled, from envy at the Swedish successes, and Wrangel had gone to Bohemia, Maximilian broke the truce and joined the imperialists again.

1648. **Second invasion of Bavaria** by the French and Swedes; terrible ravages. A flood on the Inn prevented the further advance of the allies, who returned to the Upper Palatinate.

Terrible condition of Germany. Irreparable losses of men and wealth. Destruction of towns and trade. Reduction of population; increase of poverty; retrogradation in all ranks.

1648, Oct. 24. TREATIES OF WESTPHALIA. Negotiations from 1643 to 1648. Imperial ambassadors, Count Trautmannsdorf and Dr. Volmar. French, Count d'Avaux and Count Servien. Swedish, Count Oxenstierna, son of the chancellor, and Baron Salvius. France and Sweden, against the will of the emperor, secured the participation of the states of the empire in the negotiations.

Terms of the Treaties: (A) **Indemnifications:** (1) **Sweden** received as fief of the empire the whole of Hither Pomerania and Rügen, with a part of Farther Pomerania, the city of Wismar (formerly a possession of Mecklenburg) and the Bishoprics of Bremen (not the city) and Verden as secular duchies. Indemnity of five million rix dollars. Sweden became a member of the German Diet with three votes. (2) **France** received absolute sovereignty over the Bishoprics and cities of Metz, Toul, and Verdun (in French hands since 1552); also Pignerol, the city of Breisach, the Landgravate of Upper and Lower Alsace (which belonged to a branch of the Austrian Hapsburgs), and the government of ten imperial cities in Alsace. These cities and the other imperial states of Alsace (particularly Strassburg) retained their membership in the empire. France received also the right to garrison Philippsburg. (3) **Hesse-Cassel** received the Abbey of Hersfeld and part of the County of Schaumburg. (4) **Brandenburg** received, as indemnification for Pomerania (all of which had belonged to Brandenburg by right of inheritance, though only the larger part of Farther Pomerania had been taken over), the Bishoprics of Halberstadt, Minden, and Kammin as secular principalities; the Archbishopric of Magdeburg as a duchy, with the reservation that it should remain in possession of the administrator, August of Saxony, during his life (died 1680). (5) **Mecklenburg** received the Bishoprics of Schwerin and Ratzeburg, as principalities. (6) **Brunswick** was given the alternate presentation to the Bishopric of Osnabrück, where a Catholic and an Evangelical bishop alternated until 1803. (B) **Secular affairs of the empire:** (1) General amnesty and return to the condition of things in 1618. (2) The electoral dignity and the possession of Upper Palatinate were left to the Wilhelmian (Bavarian) line of the house of Wittelsbach, while a new electorate (the eighth) was created for the Rudolfian (Palatinate) line. (3) The territorial superiority (*Landeshoheit*) of all the states

of the empire, as regarded their relation to the emperor, was recognized. This involved the right of concluding alliances with one another and with foreign powers, provided they were not directed against the empire or the emperor. (4) The Republics of the United Netherlands and of Switzerland were recognized as independent of the empire. (C) **Ecclesiastical affairs:** (1) The Convention of Passau and the Peace of Augsburg were approved and extended so as to include the Calvinists. (2) Catholic and Protestant states were to be on complete equality in all affairs of the empire. (3) January 1, 1624, was adopted as the norm (*annus normalis*) by which questions of ownership of ecclesiastical states and the exercise of religion should be determined. As things were on that date, so they were to remain forever, i.e. the ecclesiastical reservation was acknowledged to be binding for the future. The subjugated Protestants of Austria and Bohemia obtained no rights by the treaties, but those Evangelical states which had been won to the Counter-Reformation during the war (i.e. the Lower Palatinate, Württemberg, Baden, etc.) were allowed to resume the exercise of that religion which had been theirs in 1618. The *jus reformandi*, the privilege of deciding by fiat the religion of those subjects to whom the year 1628 did not secure free exercise of religion, was retained for the future by the territorial lords. The right of emigration was, however, reserved to the subjects in such cases. The imperial court (*Reichskammergericht*) was restored and its members were equally divided between Protestants and Catholics.

The Treaty of Westphalia was guaranteed by France and Sweden. (*Cont. p. 461.*)

c. THE SWISS CONFEDERATION

The confederation, at the beginning of the 16th century, was still a loose union of practically independent cantons, each sending two representatives to a federal diet. There were, after 1513, thirteen cantons, of which six (Schwyz, Uri, Zug, Unterwalden, Glarus, and Appenzell) were rural, and seven (Lucerne, Zürich, Bern, Solothurn, Freiburg, Basel, and Schaffhausen) were urban. The Aargau, Thurgau, Ticino, and parts of Vaud were governed by the confederation or one or more of its members. Franche-Comté was under Swiss protectorate. In addition there were a number of states allied with the confederation (St. Gall, Upper Valais, Neuchâtel, Rothweil, Mülhausen, Geneva, etc.).

Swiss military prestige had reached its zenith in the latter part of the 15th century. Swiss mercenaries took an important part in the Italian expedition of Charles VIII and continued to form a crucial part of the French and Italian armies.

1503. The Forest Cantons seized Bellinzona after the French conquest of Milan.

1510. The Swiss joined in the **Holy League** against France. In partnership with the Venetians they restored the Sforza to the Milanese duchy (1512), taking for themselves Locarno, Lugano, and Ossola. Great victory of the Swiss over the French in the **battle of Novara** (June 6, 1513).

1515, Sept. 13-14. In the **battle of Marignano** (p. 382) the French won a decisive victory over the Swiss and Venetians. This led to the conclusion of peace (Nov. 12, 1516): the Swiss retained most of the Alpine passes and received a French subsidy in return for the right for the French to enlist mercenaries.

1519, Jan. 1. Beginning of the **REFORMATION IN SWITZERLAND,** under the leadership of **Ulrich Zwingli** (b. 1484; educated at Basel and Bern; priest at Glarus, 1506; after taking part in the Italian campaigns, became priest at Einsiedeln, 1516; preacher at Zürich, 1518). Zwingli denounced indulgences and other abuses in the Church and made a great impression in Zürich. In 1521 he denounced the hiring of mercenaries, and in 1522 condemned fasts and celibacy (he himself married in 1524). The town, following his teaching, abolished confession (1524) and closed the monasteries. Zwingli acted independently of Luther, from whom he was separated chiefly by difference of opinion on transubstantiation.

1524. Five cantons (Lucerne, Uri, Schwyz, Unterwalden, and Zug) banded together against Zürich and the Reformation movement.

1528. Bern and Basel accepted the Reformation, and were followed by three others. Freiburg and Solothurn remained Catholic and sided with the original five (rural) cantons.

1531. War of the Catholic cantons against Zürich. The Zürichers were defeated in the **battle of Kappel** (Oct. 11) and Zwingli was killed. Thus the division of the confederation was complete; the weakness resulting therefrom made impossible all effective action in the ensuing century.

1536. Geneva (allied with Bern) adopted the Reformation, largely through the efforts of William Farel. In the same year **John Calvin** (1509-1564) arrived in the city. His teaching made a deep impression, but also aroused much opposition. In 1538 he was banished and retired to Strassburg.

1536. Bern subdued Vaud, Chablais, Lausanne, and other territories of the Duke of Savoy, thus laying the basis for a long-drawn duel between the two powers.

1541-1564. **CALVIN,** recalled to Geneva, organized the town as a theocratic state (*City of God*). A consistory of twelve laymen and six clericals controlled the council and the government. Drastic suppression of all godlessness (i.e. everything at variance with Calvinist doctrine).

1553. **Execution of Servetus** for denying the Trinity.

1555. Ruthless suppression of an anti-Calvinist uprising. Geneva a center for Protestant refugees from England and France and a radiating point for Calvinist doctrine. But the Protestant cantons of Switzerland remained predominantly Zwinglian.

1564. Bern was obliged, under pressure from the Spanish power in Italy, to retrocede Gex and Chablais to Savoy. The Savoyards, supported by Spain and also by the Catholic cantons, began a prolonged offensive against Geneva and Bern, which drove the Protestant cantons into the French fold.

1577. Opening of a Jesuit seminary at Lucerne, marking the most active phase of the **Counter-Reformation,** directed chiefly by Cardinal Carlo Borromeo of Milan.

1584. Alliance of Bern, Geneva, and Zürich against Savoy and the Catholic cantons, followed by an alliance of the latter with Spain (1587).

1602. Savoyard attack on Geneva. This was frustrated, but one important result was the renewal of the alliance between the whole confederation and France (the Catholic cantons, however, retained also their alliance with Spain).

1620-1639. Struggle for control of the **Valtelline Pass,** the most important link in the communications between Hapsburg Austria and the Spanish Hapsburg possessions in Italy. The pass was controlled by the **Grisons League,** but in 1620 was seized by the Spaniards, who enjoyed the support of the Catholic faction (under **Rudolf Planta**). Thereupon Bern and Zürich sent aid to the Protestant faction, led by the pastor **George Jenatsch** (1596-1639). The Protestants were at first successful, but in 1621 were expelled by the Austrians, Spain taking over control of the pass. In 1625 it was seized by a Swiss force in French pay. Governorship of the Duke de Rohan. But in 1637 Jenatsch, having turned Catholic in the interest of patriotism, secured Austrian aid and once more drove out the foreigner. By **treaty with Spain** (Sept. 3, 1639) the passes were left open to the use of Spanish troops. The war had been conducted by both sides with the utmost cruelty, typical of the Thirty

Years' War. In that great struggle the Swiss Confederation remained officially neutral, being paralyzed by the division between Catholic and Protestant cantons. Nevertheless, by

1648. The Treaties of Westphalia, the confederation, owing to the efforts and diplomacy of **John Rudolf Wettstein,** burgomaster of Basel, was able to secure a European recognition of its independence of the German Empire. (*Cont. p.* 459.)

7. SCANDINAVIA

a. DENMARK AND NORWAY, 1513-1645

During this period the union of the three Scandinavian kingdoms became dissolved. The attempt of the Danish king,

1513-1523. CHRISTIAN II, to assert Danish supremacy in Sweden by invading the latter and executing the leaders of the national Swedish party (**the massacre of Stockholm,** 1520) led to a

1520. National revolt headed by **Gustavus Ericksson Vasa,** a young Swedish nobleman. The Danes were defeated, and

1523. Gustavus Vasa became first administrator of the kingdom, then king (see below, Sweden).

In his domestic policy Christian II, in alliance with the middle classes, tried to strengthen royal authority at the expense of the nobility and the Church. This caused a rebellion, led by the nobles and the bishops, who invited the Duke of Holstein to rule over Denmark as

1523-1533. FREDERICK I. A civil war followed in which the middle classes sided with Christian II. Christian was defeated and deposed in 1532. After the death of Frederick in 1533, civil war broke out anew (**the Feud of the Counts**). Order was restored with the accession of Frederick's son

1534-1558. CHRISTIAN III. During his reign the **Reformation** finally triumphed in Denmark. Church property was secularized and a national Protestant (Lutheran) Church was established. Simultaneously there was a great strengthening of royal power. Christian III intervened in the religious struggle in Germany siding with the Protestant princes against the emperor.

The continuation of the same policy led to Denmark's participation in the Thirty Years' War (p. 403) under

1588-1648. CHRISTIAN IV. At the same time rivalry with Sweden in the Baltic caused the

1611-1613. War of Kalmar with indecisive results, and

1643-1645. A second war, in which the Swedes were victorious. Denmark lost some territory on both sides of the Sound. Upon the death of Christian IV an aristocratic reaction brought about a temporary weakening of the royal power.

Norway during this period remained under Danish domination: all the important posts in the administration were occupied by the Danes and the Danish language was predominant. However, Norway benefited from the activity of some of the Danish kings. Christian IV improved administration, developed national resources, founded **Christiania.** Under the influence of Denmark, Norway also became Protestant (Lutheran). (*Cont. p.* 474.)

b. SWEDEN, 1523-1654

1523-1654. The **HOUSE OF VASA,** under whom Sweden became the strongest power in the Baltic.

1523-1560. GUSTAVUS I. War with Lübeck, concluded by the **Treaty of 1537,** put an end to the trade monopoly of the Hanseatic League in the Baltic region. In the internal life of Sweden the most important event was the progress of the Reformation. Olaus Petri successfully preached the Lutheran doctrine and translated the New Testament into Swedish (1526).

1527. By the decision of the **Riksdag of Västeras,** bishops were made entirely dependent on the king, payment of the Peter's pence to the pope was discontinued, church estates were partially secularized.

1529. The ordinances of the **Synod of Örebro** modified the church service in the Protestant sense. As

Kings of Denmark (1448-1670)

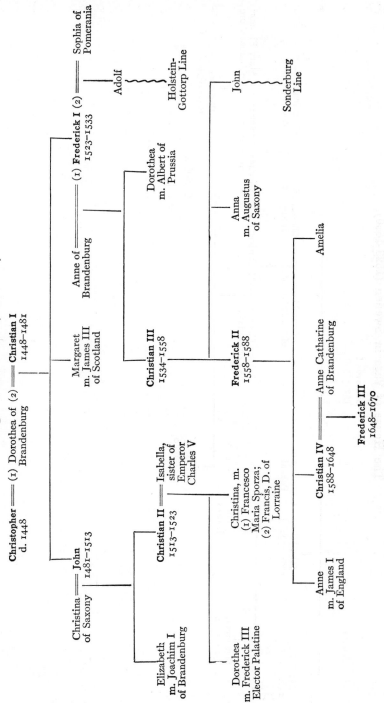

The House of Vasa in Sweden (1523-1660)

the Swedish crown was made hereditary, Gustavus Vasa was succeeded by
his son

1560-1568. ERIC XIV. Under him Baltic
expansion continued and Sweden
came into the possession of Reval (1561)
and the adjoining territory. Toward the
end of his life Eric became insane, and
finally was deposed. Under his brother
John III and John's son **Sigismund** (King
of Poland since 1587), Sweden participated
in the **Livonian War** (p. 417) in which she
acquired all of Estonia with Narva, by the
Treaty of Teusina (1595).

1593. Sigismund's attempt to restore Catholicism was met by the reaffirmation of the Protestant faith, based
on the **Confession of Augsburg,** at the
Convention of Uppsala, while his absolutist
tendencies provoked

1599. A rebellion which ended in his deposition. He was succeeded by
the youngest son of Gustavus
Vasa,

1604-1611. CHARLES IX (in virtual control of the government since
1599) under whom Sweden intervened in Russia during the

Time of Troubles (p. 418). Under his
son and successor,

1611-1632. GUSTAVUS II ADOLPHUS,
war with Russia was ended by
the **Treaty of Stolbovo** (1617): Sweden acquired eastern Carelia and Ingria, cutting
Russia off from the Baltic Sea. This was
followed by

1621-1629. A war with Poland, the result
of dynastic competition, in the
course of which Sweden occupied all of
Livonia. For Swedish participation in the
Thirty Years' War see p. 405.

Gustavus Adolphus' domestic policy was
one of conciliation. A royal charter (1611)
gave the Council and the Estates a voice
in all questions of legislation, and a power
of veto in matters of war and peace. Administration and courts were modernized,
education promoted, commerce and industry sponsored, foreign immigration invited.
The king's chief collaborator was his chancellor, **Axel Oxenstierna** (1583–1654), who
became the actual ruler of Sweden under
Gustavus Adolphus' daughter,

1632-1654. CHRISTINE. For Swedish
acquisitions under the **Treaty of
Westphalia** see p. 408.   (*Cont. p.* 471.)

8. POLAND-LITHUANIA, 1492-1648

The history of Poland in this period was
marked by a constant growth of power on
the part of the lesser nobility, so that Poland became transformed into a republic
of the *szlachta* (*Rzeczpospolita*) with an
elected king as the titular head. All efforts of the kings to strengthen the royal
power, reform the government, and establish a modern standing army met with
failure.

1492-1501. JOHN ALBERT, the son of
Casimir IV, relied upon the gentry
(*szlachta*) to reduce the power of
the great magnates. The result
was the

1496. Statute of Piotrkow (the *Magna
Carta* of Poland) which gave the
gentry extensive privileges at the expense of
the burghers and peasants. The burghers
were restricted from buying land and the
peasants were practically deprived of freedom of movement.

1497-1498. A futile invasion of Moldavia,
which was intended to secure a
throne for the king's brother, resulted in a devastating invasion
by the Turks.

1501-1506. ALEXANDER I, brother of
John Albert and, since 1492,
Grand Duke of Lithuania. His reign was
important only for the war with **Ivan the**

Great of Russia (p. 317), which resulted in
the loss of the left bank of the Dnieper by
Poland (1503), and for

1505. The Constitution of Radom, which
definitely made the national Diet,
elected by the nobles at their provincial
assemblies (the *dietines*), the supreme legislative organ. Henceforth no new laws
were to be passed without the Diet's consent.

1506-1548. SIGISMUND I, brother of
John Albert and Alexander, during
whose reign the Diet (1511) passed
laws finally establishing serfdom
in Poland.

1512-1522. War with Russia over the
White Russian region. The Russians made considerable gains and
in 1514 took Smolensk, the key
city.

1525. Secularization of Prussia and end of
the rule of the Teutonic Knights.
Prussia remained a fief of Poland.

1534-1536. Another war with Russia
brought no success to the Poles.
Smolensk remained in Russian
hands.

1548-1572. SIGISMUND II (*August*). His
reign was distinguished by the
wide spread of the **Protestant Reformation,**
which had taken root in 1518 and had

Kings of Poland (1445-1668)

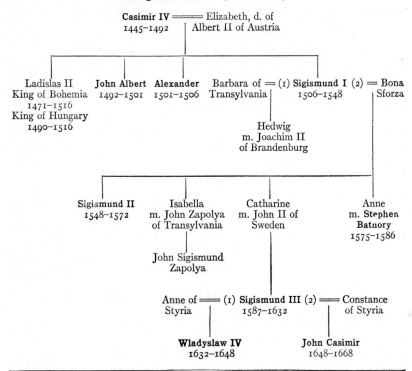

Casimir IV ===== Elizabeth, d. of
1445–1492 | Albert II of Austria

Ladislas II — John Albert — Alexander — Barbara of = (1) Sigismund I (2) = Bona
King of Bohemia — 1492–1501 — 1501–1506 — Transylvania | 1506–1548 | Sforza
1471–1516
King of Hungary
1490–1516 — Hedwig
m. Joachim II
of Brandenburg

Sigismund II — Isabella — Catharine — Anne
1548–1572 — m. John Zapolya — m. John II of — m. Stephen
of Transylvania — Sweden — Batnory
1575–1586

John Sigismund
Zapolya

Anne of === (1) Sigismund III (2) ==== Constance
Styria | 1587–1632 | of Styria

Wladyslaw IV — John Casimir
1632–1648 — 1648–1668

gained ground, especially in the Baltic lands and in the towns, despite many edicts penalizing the adherents, who were known as *Dissidents*. Demands for a national Church, marriage of the clergy, communion in both kinds, Slavonic liturgy, etc. **Calvinism** and **Antitrinitarianism** also established themselves. After the **Council of Trent** (p. 396) the crown, backed by the recently formed Polish-Lithuanian chapter of the Jesuit Order (1565), succeeded in checking the movement and in restoring the supremacy of Roman Catholicism.

1557-1571. The Livonian War, arising from a disputed succession and from the conflicting claims of Poland, Russia, Sweden, and Denmark. The Russians invaded the country (1557) and the Swedes took Estonia, while the Danes acquired part of Courland. In 1561 the Poles took over Livonia, but Ivan the Terrible of Russia conquered part of it in 1563.

1569, July 1. THE UNION OF LUBLIN, which, despite opposition on the part of Lithuania, merged that country with the Polish kingdom. The two nations were to have a common sovereign, and a common diet, though Lithuania was to retain a separate administration and army.

With the death of Sigismund II the **Jagellon dynasty** came to an end and the Polish crown, already elective in theory, became so in fact. The result was a tremendous weakening of the royal power, constant embroilment in the rivalries of other nations, and a growing hopelessness of reform.

1573-1574. HENRY OF VALOIS was elected king on condition of signing the *Pacta Conventa*, formally recognizing the right of the nobility to elect kings and strictly limiting the royal power. The Diet was to meet at least once every two years. Henry paid richly for his election and for the alliance of Poland with France, but, on the death of his brother, Charles IX, he slipped away and returned to France. There followed a period of confusion, during which the Hapsburgs made great efforts to secure the crown. The Poles ultimately elected

1575-1586. STEPHEN BATHORY, husband of Anna, the last Jagellon. Stephen was a strong ruler, but was unable to make much progress against the powerful nobility. His great success was in the field of foreign affairs and war. Plan for a union of eastern Europe under his leadership, preparatory to a united attack upon the Turk. This came to nothing, but Stephen, with a new army of peasant infantry, raised on the royal estates, was able, in the last phase of the Livonian War (1579–1582) to retake Polotsk and to put an end to the steady encroachment of Russia upon the White Russian regions.

1587-1632. SIGISMUND III (*Vasa*), son of King John of Sweden. He had been educated by the Jesuits and threw his entire influence on the side of the Counter-Reformation. For the rest he demonstrated little statesmanship and involved Poland in endless wars with Sweden because of his claims to the Swedish throne.

1595-1596. Attempts to reunite the Greek Orthodox Church in Poland with Rome foundered on the obstinacy of the Jesuits. However, part of the Orthodox formed the so-called **Uniate Church,** retaining Eastern rites but recognizing papal authority. The result was the **Confederation of Vilna** (1599), an alliance between the Orthodox and the Dissidents against the power of the Roman Church.

1609-1618. Polish intervention in Russia during the **Time of Troubles** (p. 418). An attempt to put Sigismund's son, Vladislav, on the Russian throne ended in the expulsion of the Poles from Moscow.

1629. The Treaty of Altmark, a truce in the long conflict with Sweden, signalized the defeat of the Poles and confirmed the loss of Livonia.

1632-1648. WLADYSLAW IV, the son of Sigismund. He was elected without opposition and pursued a policy diametrically opposed to that of his father. But his efforts to restrict the powers of the Jesuits were vain.

1632-1634. War with Russia, which was ended by the **Treaty of Polianov** (1634): Wladyslaw renounced his claims to the Russian throne, but regained the Smolensk region for Poland.   (*Cont. p.* 475.)

9. RUSSIA, 1505-1645

In Russia, as in many other countries, the period was one of conflict between the crown and the powerful landed nobility, accompanied by a decline in the influence of the townsmen and a gradual relapsing of the peasantry into serfdom. In Russia the latter problem was closely connected with defense and territorial expansion. Since 1454 the Grand Dukes of Moscow granted non-hereditary military fiefs (*pomestye*) to secure a supply of fighting men for use in the struggle against the Tatars. The corollary was a steady debasement in the position of the peasants, who consequently tended to run off to newly conquered territories in the southeast. Depopulation in the center resulted in ever more drastic measures to hold the cultivator on the land. At the same time there grew up on the borders the Cossack colonies, wild, free communities which were to play a great rôle in this period.

1505-1533. BASIL III, the son of Ivan the Great and Sophia. The reign was a fairly quiet one, during which the work of consolidation was continued by the reduction of Pskov (1510), Smolensk (1514) and Riazan (1517).

1533-1584. IVAN IV (*the Terrible*), the son of Basil. He ascended the throne at the age of three. The regency was in the hands of his mother, **Helen Glinski** (of Lithuanian family), until 1538, and thereupon fell into the hands of powerful noble (*boyar*) families, notably the **Shuiskys** and **Belskys,** whose oligarchic policy presented the young ruler with an almost insuperable problem.

1547. Ivan assumed power and had himself crowned *tsar*, the first Russian ruler to assume the title formally. At the same time he established a *chosen council*, composed of personally selected advisers, which he hoped to make a counterweight to the power of the **Council of Boyars** (*Duma*). This was followed in 1549 with the convocation of the first national assembly or *Zemski Sobor*, also meant to broaden the support of the crown. In these early years Ivan made considerable progress in breaking down the power of the provincial governors and in establishing a measure of local government.

1552-1556. The conquest of Kazan and Astrakhan from the Tatars gave Russia control of the entire course of the Volga and opened the way for expansion to the east and southeast. Already in the last years of Ivan's reign (1581–1583) Russian traders (the Stroganov family)

Growth of Russia in Europe to 1725

Muscovy in 1480 ◯ *Russia in 1689* ⦂⦂⦂ *acquisitions of Peter the Great*

Russian Rulers (1462-1676)

Ivan III ===== Sophia (Zoë),
1462–1505 | niece of Emperor
Constantine XIII

Basil IV
1505–1533

Roman Yurievich
d. 1543

Ivan IV ==== Anastasia
1533–1584 | Romanova

Nikita
Romanov
d. 1586

Boris
Godunov
1598–1605

Irene = Theodore
1584–1598

Demetrius
d. 1590

Xenia Chestov = Theodore (Philaret)
(Marta the Nun) | Patriarch 1619–1633

Theodore
1605

Eudoxia ==== (2) Michael
Streshnev | 1613–1645

Alexis I
1645–1676

established themselves east of the Urals and Cossack pioneers, under **Yermak,** began the conquest of Siberia.

1553. The British, under Chancellor, reached Moscow by way of the White Sea and Archangel. They were given trade rights in 1555 and formed an important link in Russian communications with the west, which were otherwise cut off by Poland-Lithuania and Sweden.

1557-1582. THE LIVONIAN WAR, arising from the disputed succession to the Baltic territories ruled by the German Knights. Ivan appreciated to the full the importance of an outlet to the Baltic, and seized Narva and Dorpat. In 1563 he conquered part of Livonia, which had been taken over by the Poles.

1564. Conflict of Ivan with the powerful boyars, led by **Prince Kurbsky.** Ivan eventually withdrew from Moscow and issued an appeal to the people, which, through the metropolitan, urged him to return. He took a terrible revenge on his opponents and began a reign of terror marked by incredible excesses and fantastic self-debasement. At the same time Ivan set aside about half of the realm as his personal domain (*oprichnina*), in which he established a new administration and a separate royal army.

1570. Ivan ravaged Novgorod and massacred many of the inhabitants, whom he suspected of sympathy for the Poles.

1571. The Crimean Tatars attacked and sacked Moscow.

1578. Defeat of the Russians by the Swedes at Wenden, in the course of the struggle for the Baltic lands. Polotsk was lost in the following year.

1581. Stephen Bathory, King of Poland, invaded Russia and advanced victoriously to Pskov.

1582. Peace between Russia on the one hand and Poland and Sweden on the other, mediated by the Jesuit Possevino, who had been sent by the pope in the hope of effecting a union of the Orthodox and Roman churches. Ivan was obliged to accept most of his recent losses.

1584-1598. THEODORE I, the son of Ivan, a feeble and utterly weak ruler. The actual government fell again into the hands of the boyars, notably Nikita Romanov (related to Ivan IV's first wife) and Boris Godunov, brother-in-law of Theodore.

1589. Establishment of the Russian patriarchate as separate from that of Constantinople. The Russian Church thus became entirely independent. Theodore dying without issue, a national assembly elected to the throne

1598-1605. BORIS GODUNOV, an intelligent but none too courageous ruler who was faced with the jealousy of other boyar families. Against these he acted by intrigue and persecution.

1604-1613. THE TIME OF TROUBLES, which began with the appearance of a false Dmitri, i.e. a pretender who claimed to be the supposedly murdered son of Ivan IV. Dmitri was an able and forceful person who soon found extensive support among the Poles and the Cossacks. Boris' death at this crucial time initiated a period of utmost confusion during which boyar families struggled for supremacy while their position was challenged by the lower classes (led by the Cossacks), and foreigners (Poles and Swedes) took full advantage of the situation to further their own interests.

1605. Theodore, the son of Boris, succeeded to the throne. He was soon deposed and murdered by the boyars, many of whom accepted Dmitri. The latter advanced to Moscow and established himself on the throne.

1606. Basil Shuisky and a faction of the boyars succeeded in driving out the pretender and murdering him. Shuisky thereupon became tsar. But new pretenders soon appeared, and the situation became desperate when the Cossacks and peasants in the south and east rose in revolt.

1608. The new Dmitri defeated Basil and advanced to Tushino, outside Moscow. In urgent need, Basil ceded Carelia to the Swedes in return for aid.

1609. Sigismund of Poland advanced to Smolensk and made extensive promises to the Russian boyars in the hope of acquiring the crown.

1610. Skopin-Shuisky, nephew of Basil, with a Swedish force under De La Gardie, relieved Moscow, but the Poles continued their advance. The Russians then deposed Basil and a boyar faction offered the throne to Vladislav, son of

Sigismund. The latter, jealous of his son and anxious to secure the throne himself, evaded the offer and advanced to Moscow.

1611. The turn of the tide was marked by the death of the pretender and by a powerful reaction against the Poles, especially in the northern and eastern provinces. A national militia was formed under Pozharsky and this in

1612. Relieved Moscow and drove out the Poles.

1613, Feb. 21. A national assembly (*zemski sobor*) elected to the throne

1613-1645. MICHAEL ROMANOV, grandnephew of Ivan IV and son of the patriotic leader, Philaret. Michael was crowned on July 11 and therewith began the Romanov dynasty, which ruled until 1917. Michael himself was a man of no ability, who was guided by his father and later fell under the influence of favorites. The reign saw the gradual restoration of order, but also the firmer establishment of serfdom and the gradual disappearance of local self-government. The national assembly, which was frequently summoned, failed to establish a regular organization or to develop beyond the status of a consultative body.

1617. Treaty of Stolbovo, with Sweden. The Swedes restored Novgorod, which they had occupied, but Russia was obliged to abandon the few towns which had still been held on the Gulf of Finland.

1634. Treaty of Polianov, with Poland, bringing to a temporary end a long period of conflict. In return for recognition of his title, Michael was obliged to give up many of the frontier towns (including Smolensk) which had been taken by the Poles.

1637. Russian pioneers reached the coast of the Pacific, after a phenomenally rapid advance over the whole of Siberia.

1637. The Cossacks managed to take the important fortress of Azov from the Crimean Tatars. They offered it to Michael, who refused it (1642) in order to avoid conflict with the Turks. The fortress was thereupon returned. (*Cont. p. 478.*)

10. BOHEMIA, 1471-1627

1471-1516. LADISLAS II, son of the King of Poland, first ruler of the Jagiello family, a boy of sixteen at his accession. Ladislas proved himself a gentle but weak and undecided ruler, wholly unsuited to the position. He continued

the persecution of the Bohemian Brotherhood, but made no progress toward unifying the country. As King of Hungary also, he spent most of his time at Pressburg, leaving open the way for the domination of Bohemia by powerful nobles. During the entire later 15th century the aristocracy extended its possessions and power at the expense of the crown and Church. The towns declined in power and the peasantry sank back into serfdom or a status close to it. Great influx of German peasants in the west and north, and also in the towns.

1516-1526. LOUIS, son of Ladislas, who ascended the throne of Bohemia and Hungary at the age of ten. Conditions continued as under Ladislas, further complicated by the spread and persecution of Lutheranism.

1526. Louis was defeated and killed by the Turks at the battle of Mohács. Ferdinand, brother of Emperor Charles V and brother-in-law of Louis, was elected king, opening a long period of Hapsburg rule.

1547. The Bohemian crown was proclaimed hereditary in the house of Hapsburg. Constant growth of the royal prerogative at the expense of the Diet and of town government.

1618. Defenestration of Prague and beginning of the Thirty Years' War (p. 403). Ferdinand II was declared deposed and the Protestant Frederick of the Palatinate was elected king (*the Winter King*).

1620, Nov. 8. BATTLE OF THE WHITE MOUNTAIN; defeat of Frederick and the Bohemians. Bohemia was virtually deprived of independence and a wholesale confiscation of the lands of the native nobility took place.

1627. A new constitution confirmed the hereditary rule of the Hapsburgs and strengthened royal power. The incorporation of Bohemia with the Hapsburg Empire was completed in the 18th century with the extension of the imperial administration under Joseph I (1705-1711) and with the **Pragmatic Sanction of 1720** (p. 463).

11. HUNGARY, 1490-1648

1490-1516. LADISLAS II, King of Bohemia, was elected King of Hungary by the nobles. A weak and ineffectual ruler, he allowed the work of Mathias Corvinus to be undone within a few years. In order to secure recognition from the Hapsburgs, he gave up Mathias' conquests and arranged dynastic marriages with the Hapsburgs (his infant son Louis was married to Mary, granddaughter of Maximilian; his own daughter, Anne, was married to Maximilian's grandson Ferdinand). This policy led to the formation of a national party among the Hungarian nobility, which was led by Stephen Zápolya (Szapolyai), the Vaivode (Prince) of Transylvania. The nobles refused Ladislas all effective financial support, so that he was unable to maintain an army and was soon at the mercy of the feudal elements.

1514. A great revolt of the peasants, led by George Dózsa, was directed against the ruthless exploitation by the aristocrats. It was suppressed in a sea of blood by John Zápolya, leader of the nobility.

1514. The *Tripartitum*, a constitution worked out by Stephen Verböczy, was passed by the Diet. It established the equality of all nobles and at the same time fixed the system of serfdom on the peasantry.

1516-1526. LOUIS II, the son of Ladislas, succeeded his father at the age of ten. A dissolute youngster, devoted to pleasure, he did nothing to stop the disintegration of the royal power. His reign was marked chiefly by the spread of the **Protestant Reformation.** The movement first took root in the German areas and in the towns, and was vigorously opposed by the nobles. In 1523 it was declared punishable by death and confiscation of property, but despite all edicts it took firm hold of the country.

1521. The Turks took Belgrade, beginning their victorious advance into Hungary.

1526, Aug. 29-30. BATTLE OF MOHÁCS. Defeat and death of Louis when the Turks completely overwhelmed his disorganized feudal army of 20,000.

1526-1528. Louis' death was followed by a hot contest over the succession. Part of the nobility, hoping for German aid against the Turks, elected **Ferdinand of Hapsburg,** brother of Emperor Charles V. The national party, on the other hand, elected **John Zápolya** as king. After a civil war lasting two years, Zápolya was defeated. He appealed to the Turks, who supported him vigorously. By the **Peace of Nagyvarad** the two kings recognized each other, each ruling part of the territory. Zápolya became a vassal of the Turks, but Ferdinand continued the war against them which was interrupted only by occasional truces (p. 423).

1540. Death of John Zápolya. The Turks recognized his infant son, **John II** (Sigismund) **Zápolya** (1540-1571). This led to a new clash with Ferdinand, who began the invasion of eastern Hungary. The Turks again invaded and took Buda. They now took over the entire central part of Hungary (the great plain), which was organized in four *pashaliks*. There was no settlement by the Turks, but the territory was granted in military fiefs and subjected to heavy taxation. Religious tolerance of the Turks. Transylvania, under Zápolya, was a vassal state of the Turks, but was left almost entirely free. Under **Cardinal Martinuzzi** it was organized as a state (three nations: Hungarians, Szeklers, and Germans, meeting in a *Landtag*, elected the king and passed laws). The Transylvanians (even the nobility) soon accepted **Calvinism**, so that during the later 16th century the larger part of Hungary was either Lutheran or Calvinist. In 1560 religious toleration was established in Transylvania. The Hapsburgs, on the other hand, held only a narrow strip of western and northern Hungary, and even for this they long paid tribute to the Turk. Warfare was incessant on this frontier (blockhouses and constant raids). The Hapsburgs employed Italian and Spanish mercenaries to defend their possessions, and these ravaged the country as much as the Turkish territory. Ferdinand and his successors governed from Vienna or Prague and with little reference to the traditional rights of the Hungarian nobility. This led to growing friction and later to serious conflict.

1581-1602. Sigismund Bathory, Prince of Transylvania. His efforts to unite with the Hapsburgs for a grand assault on the declining Turk power met with vigorous opposition on the part of the Transylvanian nobility.

1604. Beginning of the Counter-Reformation, under Hapsburg auspices. This resulted in a revolt of the Hungarians, who were supported by the Transylvanians.

1604-1606. STEPHEN BOCSKAY became Prince of Transylvania and, after defeating the Hapsburgs, secured the **Treaty of Vienna,** by which Protestantism was given equal status with Catholicism. Nevertheless, the Counter-Reformation made great strides, especially among the nobility, due to the efforts of Cardinal Pazmany and the Jesuits.

1613-1629. BETHLEN GABOR (Gabriel Bethlen), Prince of Transylvania. He was one of the greatest rulers of the country and made his state the center of Hungarian culture and national feeling. On the outbreak of the **Thirty Years' War,** he openly sided with the enemies of the Hapsburgs and made Transylvania a vital factor in European politics.

1630-1648. GEORGE RÁKÓCZI I, another eminent Prince of Transylvania. He continued the policy of his predecessor and managed to guide the country through the storms of the European crisis. At the same time he took full advantage of the growing weakness of the Turks, making Transylvania virtually an independent state which played a part of some importance in international affairs.

12. THE OTTOMAN EMPIRE, 1481-1656

1481-1512. BAYAZID II, a man of intellectual tastes, but the least significant of the first ten sultans. He was raised to the throne with the support of the Janissaries, but his position was challenged by his younger brother, Jem (**Djem**), who had himself proclaimed sultan at Brusa, and then proposed a division of the empire. Jem was defeated by Bayazid's forces at Yeni-Shehr and fled, first to Egypt, then to Rhodes. The Knights of St. John sent him to France and extracted from Bayazid a treaty of peace. As a valuable hostage many of the European powers tried to get control of him, but he was finally (1489) turned over to the pope, who tried to use him to extract money and support from Bayazid against Charles VIII of France. During the latter's invasion of Italy, Jem

fell into his hands. He died under suspicious circumstances at Naples (1495).

1489. The Venetians acquired Cyprus from the Christian ruler by bequest, and tried to take advantage of Bayazid's weakness to strengthen their position in the Aegean.

1499-1503. War between the Venetians and the Turks. The Turks had a powerful fleet, commanded by Kemal Re'is (possibly a Greek), who defeated the Venetians off Modon. During the war the Turks took Lepanto, Modon, and Koron, while the Turkish cavalry raided Venetian territory as far as Vicenza. In the peace treaty Venice abandoned the stations she had lost, but kept Nauplion and some of the Ionian Islands.

1512-1520. SELIM I (*the Grim*). He

Ottoman Sultans (1451-1649)

Mohamed II
1451–1481

Bayazid II
1481–1512

Jem

Corcud   Ahmed   Selim I
1512–1520

Suleiman I
1520–1566

Mustapha   Bayazid   Selim II
1566–1574

Murad III
1574–1595

Mohamed III
1595–1603

Ahmed I
1603–1617

Mustapha I
1617–1618
1622–1623

Osman II
1618–1622

Murad IV
1623–1640

Ibrahim I
1640–1648

forced his father to abdicate, after a civil war between Bayazid's three sons, Ahmed, Corcud, and Selim.

1513. Selim defeated his brother Ahmed in Anatolia and had him executed.

1514. War against Shah Ismail of Persia, who had supported Ahmed. The struggle was accentuated by religious differences, the Kizilbashes in Anatolia being Shi'ites and wholly in sympathy with the Persians. Selim, a fanatic Sunnite, is said to have slaughtered 40,000 of his own heretic subjects before proceeding against the Persians.

1514, Aug. 23. Selim completely defeated the Persians at Chaldiran, east of the Euphrates. He took and plundered Tabriz, but was obliged to fall back because of the objections of the Janissaries to further advance.

1515. Conquest of eastern Anatolia and Kurdistan by the Turks.

1516. Selim embarked on a second campaign against Persia, but was diverted by the Mameluke Sultan of Egypt, Kansu al-Gauri, who was allied to Persia and appeared at Aleppo with an army.

1516, Aug. 24. BATTLE OF MARJ-DABIK, north of Aleppo. Selim, with the use of artillery, completely defeated Kansu, who was killed. Aleppo and Damascus at once surrendered to the Turks. Selim, anxious to proceed against Persia, offered peace to the new sultan, Tuman Bey, on condition that he accept Turkish suzerainty. This was refused.

1517, Jan. 22. The Turks took Cairo, and sacked it. The **Sherif of Mecca** surrendered voluntarily. The **Caliph Mutawakkil** was sent to Constantinople, but after Selim's death returned to Egypt (legend of his having transferred his authority as caliph to Selim). The important thing was that Selim secured control of the Holy Places in Arabia. Tuman Bey was executed, but Egypt left under the rule of the Mameluke Beys, under a Turkish governor-general. Legend of the Turks cutting the routes of oriental trade: these had really been cut by the Portuguese, operating at the entrance of the Red Sea.

1520-1566. SULEIMAN I (*the Magnificent*), only son of Selim, a highly cultivated but proud and ambitious ruler, generally rated as the greatest of the sultans. In reality he left affairs largely to his famous viziers. **Ibrahim Pasha,** son of a Greek of Parga, practically ruled the empire from 1523 to 1536. In 1524, after an attempt of the Turkish governor of Egypt to set himself up as sultan, Ibrahim completely reorganized the government of the country, with more effective control by the Turks.

1521. Capture of Belgrade, after several assaults. In the succeeding years the Turks raided regularly in Hungary and Austria, creating a panic throughout central Europe.

1522. Capture of Rhodes, which had become the headquarters for Catalan and Maltese pirates who threatened Turkish communications with Egypt. The Knights of St. John put up a valiant defense, but the help expected from the West did not materialize. They thereupon capitulated. In 1530 they were established at Malta by Charles V.

1526, Aug. 29-30. BATTLE OF MOHÁCS. Defeat of King Louis of Hungary and his 20,000 ill-disciplined knights and peasants. Louis was killed and the Turks advanced and took Ofen. Disputed succession in Hungary: John Zápolya elected in Transylvania, Ferdinand of Hapsburg at Pressburg. After two years of civil war Zápolya was defeated. He appealed to Suleiman.

1528. Second campaign in Hungary. **Ofen** retaken by the Turks.

1529, Sept. FIRST SIEGE OF VIENNA. After several assaults the Turks withdrew (Oct. 16), partly because of valiant resistance of the garrison, partly because of wretched weather and inability to bring up the heavy artillery. But Suleiman rejected repeated offers of Ferdinand to pay tribute for Hungary in return for recognition.

1529. Khaireddin Pasha, famous Turkish admiral and corsair (originally a Greek of Mytilene in the service of the Bey of Tunis, 1512; entered Turkish service in 1516) took the Peñon of Algiers.

1531. Turkish campaign in Hungary. The Turks took Güns, after a valiant resistance. Suleiman then retired, because of the threat from Persia.

1533. Peace between **Suleiman** and **Ferdinand.** The latter retained that part of Hungary which he still held; Zápolya remained king of the rest; both paid tribute to the Turks. No peace made with Charles V, so that the naval war in the Mediterranean (Khaireddin and Andrea Doria) continued. Khaireddin evacuated thousands of Moors, expelled from Spain.

1534. Khaireddin drove out the Bey of Tunis and ravaged the coasts of Sicily and southern Italy.

1534. War against Shah Thamasp of Persia, who had been negotiating with Charles V. The Turks marched to Tabriz, and conquered Baghdad and Mesopotamia.

1535, June-July. Great expedition of **Charles V** to Tunis, the fleet commanded by Andrea Doria. The town was taken after Khaireddin had been defeated off the coast. Horrible sack of three days. The Bey, Mulai Hassan, was reinstated.

1536, Mar. Formal alliance between **Suleiman** and **Francis I** of France, against the Hapsburgs. This had been under discussion since 1525 and had led to some measure of co-operation.

1537-1540. War with Venice, forced by the Turkish threat to close the Straits of Otranto. The Sultan and Khaireddin besieged Corfu, with French aid, but were obliged to give up the project.

1538. Holy League against the Turks (Charles V, the pope, and Venice). Abortive efforts of Charles V to buy off Khaireddin. After a defeat at sea (**battle of Prevesa**) the Venetians made peace

(1540), losing Nauplion, their last station in the Morea, and paying a large indemnity.

1538. Turkish naval expedition through the Red Sea to the northwest coast of India. The entire east coast of the Red Sea (Yemen, Aden) was taken over.

1540. Death of John Zápolya, leaving an infant son as his successor, whom Suleiman recognized. Invasion of Hungary by Ferdinand, who tried to make good his claim to the whole country.

1541. Suleiman's campaign in Hungary. He marched to Buda and took over control during the minority of John Sigismund Zápolya. Direct Turkish administrative control established.

1547. Five years' truce between Suleiman and Ferdinand; the Turks retained the larger part of Hungary and Ferdinand paid tribute for the small strip remaining to him.

1548. Second expedition against Persia. Tabriz again occupied.

1551-1562. Renewal of war with Ferdinand. This was carried on in desultory fashion and consisted chiefly of sieges. After Ferdinand's succession to the imperial throne peace was made, Zápolya receiving Transylvania, the Turks retaining Hungary proper, and Ferdinand paying tribute for the western section.

1552. The Persians took the offensive and captured Erzerum.

1553. Suleiman proceeded against the Persians and ravaged the western part of the country. Peace was made in 1555, Suleiman retaining his conquests in Mesopotamia.

1554. Dragut, successor of Khaireddin (d. 1546), took Mehedia, a strong base on the Tunisian coast, from the Spaniards. The conquest of the North African coast was completed in the following two years.

1565. Turkish siege of Malta, the headquarters of the Spanish corsairs. After taking one of the three main forts the Turks were obliged to withdraw.

1566. Renewal of war in Hungary, the result of continued raids ordered by the Emperor Maximilian.

1566, Sept. 5. Death of Suleiman, at the siege of Szigeth. His last years had been embittered by family troubles. His wife, **Roxelana** (probably a Russian captive), and her son-in-law, the Grand Vizier **Rustem Pasha**, so poisoned his mind against his eldest son, Mustafa, that he had

him strangled in 1553. There ensued a conflict between the sons of Roxelana, Selim and Bayazid. The latter took up arms in 1559, but was defeated at Konia. He fled to Persia, where he and his sons were executed in return for a high money payment by Suleiman. But Suleiman left the empire the greatest in Europe and the best organized, an easy match for the European powers, rent by dynastic and religious antagonisms.

1566-1574. SELIM II (*the Sot*), an intelligent but indolent ruler, much given to drink. Divided counsels of **Mohammed Sökölli** (grand vizier, 1560-1579), who favored close relations with Venice and continuance of the war against Spain (peace made with Maximilian in 1568), and the friend of Selim, **Don Joseph Nasi,** most prominent of the thousands of Spanish Jews who settled in Constantinople, Saloniki, Adrianople, and other towns of the empire after the expulsions from Spain and Italy. Nasi had come to Constantinople in 1553 and had financed Selim in the struggle with Bayazid. In return Selim had induced Suleiman to grant Nasi the region about Lake Tiberias, where Nasi undertook to settle Jewish refugees from Italy. In 1566 Selim made him Duke of Naxos and other Aegean islands. Nasi was very hostile to France and Venice, for personal reasons.

1570. Nasi persuaded the Sultan to declare war on Venice, after the latter had refused to cede Cyprus, which Nasi may have intended to make a refuge for Jews. Spain joined Venice in the war, but the two allies were unable to co-operate successfully and their fleets delayed the relief of Cyprus until too late.

1571, May 20. Pope Pius V finally succeeded in organizing a Holy League against the Turks. A great armada, under Don John of Austria, assembled at Messina.

Aug. 3. The Turks took Famagusta, after a siege of eleven months and six assaults.

Oct. 7. BATTLE OF LEPANTO, between the allied fleets (208 galleys, including 6 immense galleasses) and the Turks (230 galleys) under supreme command of Ali Pasha. After a ferocious fight of three hours, 80 Turkish galleys were sunk and 130 captured; 40 escaped from the wing. Greatest naval battle since Actium. Tremendous joy throughout Europe. But the advantages of the victory were lost through continued dissension between the Spaniards and the Venetians, the former insisting on the reconquest of North Africa, the latter desiring to reconquer Cyprus.

The Turks rebuilt their fleet with astounding rapidity, and Don John refused to attack it in the Adriatic in 1572.

1573. Don John took Tunis, which had been captured by the Turks in 1569.

Mar. The Venetians deserted the Spaniards and made peace, abandoning Cyprus and paying an indemnity of 300,000 ducats.

1574. The Turks drove the Spaniards out of Tunis again. Despite the Lepanto disaster, the Turks continued to ravage the coasts of the western Mediterranean during the rest of the century.

1574-1595. MURAD III.

1581. Peace between Spain and the Turks (definitive 1585) based on the *status quo*.

1585. Beginning of the phenomenal **decline of the empire**, due to the degeneracy of the sultans, the abandonment of the government to viziers (mostly favorites), the growth of corruption and harem influence, the emergence of governing cliques (Jews, Greeks, etc.) and the inevitable decline of the military organization, especially the Janissary corps, to which Turks were gradually admitted. As the empire had advanced to the frontier of strong European states, conquests became more difficult and military grants fewer. The soldiers had to be kept quiet with presents and favors. Before long the Janissaries became a veritable praetorian guard, making and unmaking sultans, most of whom were mere puppets in their hands. The period was marked by rising taxation in the empire and general decline in the treasury. On the other hand, the Dutch, English, and French began to develop an extensive trade in the Levant.

1590. Peace between the Turks and Persia, after a long and desultory war which had begun in 1577. The Turks acquired Georgia, Azerbaijan, and Shirwan, thus extending their frontiers to the Caucasus and Caspian.

1593-1606. War between Austria and the Turks, in which **Sigismund Bathory**, Prince of Transylvania, took the side of the emperor.

1596. Turkish victory at Keresztes (near Erlau in northern Hungary). The campaigning, however, remained desultory, due to the preoccupation of the emperor with Transylvania, which he took successively from Bathory and from Michael the Brave of Moldavia. The Turks thereupon supported **Stephen Bocskay** and helped him drive out the Austrians (1605). But the Turks, in turn, were diverted by troubles with Persia.

1602-1618. War with the Persians (**Abbas the Great**), who had completely reorganized their forces (with the help of Sir Anthony and Sir Robert Shirley; mission of Sir Anthony to Europe to secure co-operation).

1603. Abbas retook Tabriz, and then Erivan, Shirwan, and Kars. After a great victory at Lake Urmia, Abbas took Baghdad, Mosul, and Diarbekr. Peace was made in 1612, but the war was renewed in 1616. By the **Treaty of 1618** the Turks abandoned Azerbaijan and Georgia.

1606. Treaty of Zsitva-Torok (first peace treaty signed by the Turks outside Constantinople) between the Turks and Austrians. The Austrians abandoned Transylvania to Bocskay, but were recognized by the Turks as equals and ceased paying tribute for their part of Hungary.

1623-1640. MURAD IV, a boy of fourteen, who found the empire wracked by revolts and at the mercy of insubordinate Janissaries. By savage ruthlessness Murad asserted his authority.

1625. Murad's efforts to retake Baghdad were foiled by new uprisings, which he again suppressed with great ferocity.

1630. Murad took Hamadan from the Persians.

1635. The Turks reconquered Erivan and Tabriz.

1638. Murad retook Baghdad. In the peace the Persians retained Erivan, and the Turks Baghdad.

1638. Murad abolished the tribute in Christian children, reorganized the system of military fiefs, reduced the Janissary corps and began the organization of a new military system. This first effort at reform was ended with his death in 1640.

1645-1664. LONG WAR WITH VENICE, occasioned by Turkish designs on Candia (Crete). The Venetians showed themselves far stronger than the Turks and sent their fleets into the Straits. The Janissaries thereupon revolted, deposed Ibrahim I (1640-1648) and put on the throne

1648-1687. MOHAMMED IV, a boy of ten. There followed another period of anarchy, brought to an end in 1656 by a great Venetian victory off the Dardanelles.

1656. Mohammed Kiuprili, made grand vizier. He was a simple Albanian pasha, noted for his energy and firmness. (*Cont. p.* 482.)

B. EUROPE AND THE NEAR EAST, 1648-1789

1. ENGLAND, SCOTLAND, AND IRELAND

1649-1660. THE COMMONWEALTH, a republican form of government. Power in the army and its leader **Cromwell.** Theoretically legislative power still in the *Rump* (some 50 Independent members of the Long Parliament), executive power in a council of state of 41 (3 judges, 3 officers of the army, 5 peers, 30 members of the Commons). Title and office of king abolished, as was the House of Lords.

1649, Feb. 5. The Scotch proclaimed **Charles II** in Edinburgh and the Irish rose in his favor under Ormond. Cromwell went to Ireland himself and quickly suppressed the rebellion at the **storming of Drogheda** (Sept. 12) and of **Wexford.** Massacres of both garrisons. Cromwell returned to London (May) leaving Ireton to complete his work. By 1652 the Cromwellian settlement had been achieved. Catholic landholders had been dispossessed in favor of Protestants; many Catholics had been killed. The Irish question took on a new bitterness.

1650. **Montrose** came again to Scotland, was beaten at **Corbiesdale** (April 27), captured and executed at Edinburgh (May 21).

June 24. **Charles II** landed in Scotland, took the covenant, and was proclaimed king. At the **battle of Dunbar** (Sept. 3) the Scotch under Leslie were totally defeated by Cromwell. Charles II, however, was crowned at Scone and marched on into England while Cromwell took Perth (Aug. 2, 1651). Cromwell then turned and pursued the king, completely defeated the royal army at the **battle of Worcester** (Sept. 3). Charles in disguise escaped to France, after romantic adventures.

1651, Oct. 9. First Navigation Act passed forbidding the importation of goods into England except in English vessels or in vessels of the country producing the goods. This typical measure of mercantile economy helped the British merchant marine to gain supremacy over the Dutch.

1652, July 8. War with the Dutch broke out because of this act. It was almost wholly naval. English commanders, Blake, Monk; Dutch, Van Tromp, De Ruyter. The English won off the **Downs** (May, before the declaration of war); defeated Van Tromp off **Portland** (Feb. 18, 1653) and off the **North Foreland** (June 2–3). Monk won an important victory of the **Texel** (July 31) where Van Tromp died. **Peace with the Dutch** (April 5, 1654).

Trouble had long been brewing between the *Rump* and the army. Negotiations for the return of confiscated royalist estates led to charges of bribery of members. After an **Act of Indemnity and Oblivion** (Feb. 1652) and an **Act of Settlement for Ireland** (Aug.) had been passed,

1653, Apr. 20. Cromwell turned out the *Rump* and dissolved the council of state. He set up a new council and a nominated parliament of 140 members, called **Barebone's** or the **Little Parliament** (July 4). The Cromwellians in Parliament resigned their powers to Cromwell (Dec. 12) who set up the **Protectorate** (Dec. 16).

1653, Dec. 16–1658, Sept. 3. CROMWELL, LORD PROTECTOR OF THE COMMONWEALTH OF ENGLAND, SCOTLAND, AND IRELAND. The *Instrument of Government,* a written constitution. The executive (lord protector) had a co-operative council of 21; there was a standing army of 30,000; Parliament was to be triennial, and composed of 460 members; once summoned, it could not be dissolved within five months. The protector and council could issue ordinances between sessions, but Parliament alone could grant supplies and levy taxes.

1654, Sept. 3. The new Parliament quarreled with the protector, who ordered an exclusion of members (Sept. 12). After voting that the office of protector should be elective instead of hereditary, the Parliament was dissolved (Jan. 22, 1655).

1655, Mar.-May. The rising of Penruddock at Salisbury was suppressed and Penruddock executed. England was divided into 12 military districts, each with a force supported by a tax of 10% on royalist estates. Anglican clergy were forbidden

Europe in the 17th century

to teach or preach. Catholic priests ordered out of the kingdom. Censorship of the press. Rigid "puritanical" rule in arts and morals.

Oct. Pacification of Pinerolo, with France: the Duke of Savoy stopped the persecution of the Vaudois and Charles II was to be expelled from France.

1656-1659. War with Spain. An English raid under Penn and Venables which had captured Jamaica in the West Indies (May), brought on the war. Capture of Spanish treasure ships off **Cadiz** (Sept. 9, 1656). Victory of Blake off **Santa Cruz** (April 20, 1657).

1656, Sept. 17-1658, Feb. 4. Cromwell's third Parliament witnessed another exclusion of members, and the **Humble Petition and Advice** (March-May, 1657) altering the constitution. Establishment of a second house; reduction of the power of the council of the state; the protector deprived of the power of excluding members; fixed supply for army and navy; toleration for all trinitarian Christians except Episcopalians and Catholics. Cromwell rejected the title of king (May 8).

1658. Dunkirk besieged by the **English and French.** A Spanish relieving force was beaten in the **battle of Dunes** (June 4). Dunkirk surrendered to the English, who retained it at the **Peace of the Pyrenees** (p. 440).

1658, Sept. 3. Death of Oliver Cromwell.

1658, Sept. 3-1659, May 25. Richard Cromwell, Oliver's son, lord protector. A new Parliament met (Jan. 27, 1659) and was soon involved in a dispute with the army, which induced Richard to dissolve Parliament (Apr. 22). The Rump Parliament came together under Lenthall as speaker (May 7) and Richard was induced to resign as lord protector. After the futile insurrection of Booth (Aug.) the army, under Lambert, expelled the Rump and appointed a military committee of safety (Oct.). There was a reaction against military *coups d'état*, and the Rump was restored (Dec. 26).

1660, Feb. 3. General Monk led his army from Scotland to London, assumed control as captain-general, and reestablished the Long Parliament with the still living members excluded by Pride's Purge restored (Feb. 21). Final dissolution (Mar. 16).

1660, Apr. 14. Charles issued his **Declaration of Breda,** proclaiming amnesty to all not especially excepted by Parliament, promising liberty of conscience and the confirmation of confiscated estates in the hands of the actual holders. A Con-vention Parliament, 556 members chosen without restrictions (Apr.), returned a favorable answer to Charles (May 1) and proclaimed him king (May 8); on May 29 he entered London.

1660-1685. CHARLES II. The king's brother, James, Duke of York, appointed lord high admiral and warden of the Cinque Ports; Monk (later Duke of Albemarle), captain-general; Sir Edward Hyde (later Earl of Clarendon), chancellor and prime minister. Abolition of the rights of knight service, worship, and purveyance in consideration of a yearly income for the king of £1,200,000. Restoration of the bishops to their sees and to the House of Lords. Acts of indemnity for all political offenses committed between Jan. 1, 1637, and June 24, 1660 (the regicide judges were excepted from this act). All acts of the Long Parliament to which Charles I had assented were declared in force. This meant that the Restoration was by no means a restoration of "divine right" monarchy, but rather a restoration of the moderate parliamentarian régime aimed at by Pym and Hampden. The army was disbanded (Oct. 2) except some 5000 men. The Cromwellian settlement of Ireland was reaffirmed.

1660, Dec. 29. Dissolution of the Convention Parliament. Rising of Fifth Monarchy men in London put down (Jan. 1661). Bodies of Cromwell, Ireton, Bradshaw disinterred and scattered. Royalist Parliament in Scotland **abolished the Covenant** and repealed all preceding parliamentary enactments for the last twenty-eight years.

1661, May 8-1679, Jan. 24. First Parliament of Charles II. The Cavalier **Parliament,** overwhelmingly royalist. Social reaction against puritanism; revival of games, dancing, the theater. Parliament enacted a series of repressive measures since known as the **Clarendon Code** (Clarendon himself was opposed to many of these measures). They were: (1) The **Corporation Act** (Nov. 20, 1661) by which all magistrates were obliged to take the sacrament according to the Church of England, to abjure the covenant, and take an oath declaring it illegal to bear arms against the king. (2) The **Act of Uniformity** (Aug. 24, 1662) which required clergymen, college fellows, and schoolmasters to accept everything in the Book of Common Prayer (those who refused were the *Nonconformists*). (3) The **Conventicle Act** (May, 1664) which forbade nonconformist (dissenting) religious meetings of more than five persons, except in a private household. (4) The **Five-Mile Act** (Oct. 1665) which required all who had not subscribed to the Act of Uniformity to take an oath of non-resistance, swearing never to attempt any change in Church or State; and which prohibited all who refused to do this from coming within five miles of any incorporated town, or of any place where they had been ministers. The code, and especially this last act, was impossible of strict enforcement.

1662, May 20. Charles married **Catherine of Braganza,** daughter of John IV of Portugal. Dunkirk was sold to France for £400,000.

1665-1667. War with Holland, marked by the defeat of the Dutch by the English fleet off **Lowestoft** (June 3, 1665). France entered the war against England (Jan. 1666). Albemarle beaten by De Ruyter and De Witt off the North Foreland. Defeat of the Dutch in another naval fight (July 25). The Dutch rallied, burnt Sheerness, entered the Medway (June, 1667); low point of English naval power.

1665-1666. Two great domestic disasters: the **great plague** in London (April, 1665); the **great London fire** (Sept. 2-9, 1666) burning 450 acres. St. Paul's cathedral rebuilt by Wren.

1666. The Scotch Covenanters revolted against restrictions laid on them by the triumphant Episcopalians, and were crushed by Dalziel in the **battle of Pentland Hills** (Nov. 28).

1667, July 21. Treaties of Breda between England, Holland, France, Denmark. England received from France Antigua, Montserrat, St. Kitts; France received Acadia; England and Holland adopted the *status quo* of May 21, 1667, England retaining New Amsterdam and Holland Surinam. The Navigation Acts were modified to permit the bringing to England in Dutch vessels of goods brought down the Rhine.

1667. Clarendon, who had had to bear the burden of unpopularity for much of the work of the Cavalier Parliament, was forced to resign, and was impeached and exiled. The chief officers of state now began to be looked on as a distinct (if perhaps unconstitutional) council, the nucleus of the future cabinet system. This was emphasized by the accession to power of the so-called **Cabal** (Clifford, Arlington, Buckingham, Ashley, Lauderdale). There was no cabinet solidarity, and no clear party system. The court and the country factions did, however, foreshadow the later **Tories** and **Whigs.** The court (Tory) party were supporters of the royal prerogative, and in a sense heirs of the Cavaliers; the country (Whig) party, supporters of the power of Parliament and heirs of the majority group

in the Long Parliament, but *not* democrats or radicals. Both *Whig* and *Tory* were originally terms of reproach, the first Scotch, the second Irish in origin.

1668, Jan. 13. The triple alliance between England, Holland, and Sweden negotiated by Sir William Temple and John De Witt as a check on Louis XIV. Charles II went behind Parliament and signed with Louis the **Treaty of Dover** (May, 1670) in secret provisions of which he agreed that he and his brother James would openly join the Church of Rome as soon as expedient, and that he would support Louis in his wars with Spain and Holland. Louis promised Charles £200,000 a year while the war lasted and the assistance of 6000 men in case of an insurrection. James, Duke of York, at once professed his belief in Roman Catholicism.

1672, Mar. Charles issued a **Declaration of Indulgence,** which aimed to free both nonconformist Protestants and Catholics from restrictions. Parliament, insisting that the royal power of dispensing from statutory obligations could be applied only to particular, never to generalized, cases, forced him to withdraw the indulgence (1673).

1672, Mar. 17-1674, Feb. 9. WAR WITH HOLLAND, pursuant to the policy of the treaty of Dover. English naval victory at **Southwold Bay** (May 28, 1672). William of Orange, Dutch stadtholder. Marriage of the Duke of York with the Catholic Maria d'Este of Modena (Nov. 21, 1673). The war was concluded by the **Treaty of Westminster** (Feb. 9, 1674).

1673. The Test Act, an attempt to salvage something from the Clarendon Code, and to attack the Duke of York and his supporters. All persons holding office were compelled to take oaths of allegiance and of supremacy, to adjure transubstantiation, and to take the sacrament of the Church of England. This act was not repealed until 1828, but it was nullified after 1689 by the typically English practice of passing bills of indemnity to legalize the acts of magistrates who had not conformed — i.e. taken communion in the Established Church — while in office. Such officials were commonly dissenters rather than Roman Catholics.

1673. Shift in the ministry; the Duke of York, Shaftesbury, Clifford resigned, being superseded by Prince Rupert, Sir Thomas Osborne (later Earl of Danby). Sir Heneage Finch (later Earl of Nottingham). Buckingham out of office.

1677, Nov. 4. Marriage of Mary, daughter of the Duke of York, with **William of Orange** (later William III).

1678, Sept.   The Popish Plot. Titus Oates
began the scare by alleging that
Don John of Austria and Père la Chaise had
plotted to murder Charles and establish
Roman Catholicism in England. In the ensuing wave of frenzy against the "papists,"
five Catholic lords (Powys, Bellassis, Stafford, Petre, Arundel) were sent to the
Tower. Coleman, confessor of the Duchess
of York, convicted and executed. Passage
of the **Papists' Disabling Act,** excluding
Roman Catholics from Parliament (repealed 1829).

**1679, Jan. 24.   Dissolution of the Cavalier
Parliament.** Danby, who had
been impeached (Dec. 1678) on a charge
of criminal correspondence with France,
was dismissed from the office of lord high
treasurer. The Duke of York left the
kingdom.

**1679, Mar. 6.–1680, May 27.   Third Par-
liament of Charles II.** Danby's
impeachment resumed, but not carried; he
remained in the Tower until 1685. A new
cabinet council composed of Sir William
Temple, Viscount Halifax, the Earl of
Essex, the Earl of Sunderland, and Shaftesbury (afterward in opposition). Introduction of a bill to prevent the Duke of
York, as a Catholic, succeeding to the
throne. Charles fought various exclusion
bills, which were backed by Shaftesbury,
until he had secured his brother's succession.

1679, May.   The Habeas Corpus Act.
Judges were obliged on application
to issue to any prisoner a writ of *habeas
corpus*, directing the jailer to produce the
body of the prisoner, and show cause for
his imprisonment; prisoners should be in-
dicted in the first term of their commitment, and tried not later than the second;
no person once set free by order of the court
could be again imprisoned for the same
offense.

1679.   The Covenanters again rose in
Scotland against the repressive
measures of Lauderdale. Murder of Archbishop Sharpe (May 3). Defeat of Claverhouse by the Covenanters under Balfour
at **Drumclog** (June 1). Defeat of the
Covenanters by the Duke of Monmouth at
Bothwell Brigg (June 22). Covenanters,
Conventiclers, Cameronians — all shades of
Presbyterians repressed, but not successfully. Passage of a **Test Act** against the
Presbyterians (1681) caused some eighty
Episcopalian bishops to resign. Trial and
condemnation of Argyle (Dec. 1681), who
fled the kingdom.

1679, Oct. 7. Charles, without advice of
the cabinet, prorogued his third
Parliament before it had done any business.

Temple, Essex, and Halifax resigned, and
were succeeded by the Earl of Godolphin
and Laurence Hyde, Earl of Rochester.
Another alleged papist conspiracy (**meal-
tub plot**) disclosed by Dangerfield. Petition that Parliament be called; whence
petitioners (country party, Whigs) and
those who expressed their abhorrence at this
interference with the prerogative, **abhorrers**
(court party, Tories).

**1680, Oct. 21–1681, Jan. 18.   Fourth
Parliament of Charles II.** The
exclusion bill passed the Commons, but lost in the Lords (Halifax).

1681, Mar. 21-28.   Fifth Parliament called
at Oxford, and immediately dis-
solved when the exclusion bill was
introduced.

1683, June. Judgment given against the
City of London on a *quo warranto*;
forfeiture of the charter, which was ransomed. The process repeated for other
corporations. Confederacy of leaders of the
country party against the policy of Charles,
which seemed to them a repetition of earlier
Stuart attempts to extend the power of the
crown (Essex, Russell, Grey, Howard, Sidney, Hampden, Monmouth). This was
supplemented by, and at the same time
confused with, the **Rye House plot,** a plan
concerted by quite different persons to
assassinate the king. Both plots were revealed. Essex committed suicide; Russell
and Sidney were executed, becoming republican martyrs for later generations;
Monmouth (natural son of Charles and
Lucy Walters) was pardoned, and retired
to Holland. The Duke of York was reinstated in office (Sept.) and Oates, now
known to be a liar, was fined.

1685, Feb. 6.   Charles died knowing that
his brother would succeed and that
the Whigs were at the moment
worsted.

1685-1688.   JAMES II, a Roman Catholic,
whose tactless attempt to secure
freedom of worship for his co-religionists
united against him Whigs and Tories in
defense of the Anglican Church (*not*, as far
as the Tories were concerned, in defense of
parliamentary supremacy).

**1685, May 19–1687, July 2.   Parliament of
James II.** Halifax, president of
the council; Sunderland, secretary of state;
Godolphin, chamberlain; Clarendon, lord
privy seal; Rochester, treasurer. Trial and
condemnation of Baxter, a dissenting
clergyman. Danby and the five Catholic
lords were liberated. Oates and Dangerfield were tried, condemned, and sentenced
to whipping, from which Dangerfield died
(May, 1685).

1685. Rebellion of Monmouth and Argyle. Argyle landed in Scotland, but could not arouse the Covenanters. He was captured and executed (June 30). Monmouth landed in Dorsetshire and proclaimed himself king, but his motley followers were easily beaten at the **battle of Sedgemoor** (July 6) — the last formal warfare in England until German naval attacks and Zeppelin raids in 1914–1918. **Monmouth was executed,** and Jeffreys sent on a circuit in the west to try the rebels (*the Bloody Assizes*). Jeffreys became lord chancellor; Halifax was dismissed; Sunderland, converted to Catholicism, took his place.

1686. James set out to test the **anti-papal laws.** By dispensation, he appointed a Catholic, Sir Edward Hales, to office. In a test suit, decision was rendered in favor of the king by judges he had appointed. Compton, Bishop of London, refused to remove the rector of St. Giles', who had disobeyed a royal order against violent doctrinal sermons. He was tried before a new court of ecclesiastical commission (July) and suspended. The fellows of Magdalen College, Oxford, having refused to accept Farmer, a Catholic, whom James had appointed their president, were expelled from the college (1687). These and other specific cases were rapidly rousing opinion against the king.

1687. James generalized his action; he issued the first **Declaration of Liberty of Conscience,** granted liberty to all denominations in England and Scotland (Apr.). A second declaration of liberty of conscience (Apr. 1688) was ordered to be read in all churches. Sancroft, Archbishop of Canterbury, and six other bishops were committed to the Tower for having petitioned the king not to insist on their reading what they held to be an illegal order.

June 10. Birth of a son to James, said by Whigs at the time to have been introduced in a warming-pan. The knowledge that James' policies might be continued by a son to be brought up as Catholic turned against him many Tories hitherto loyal.

June 29, 30. Trial of the bishops for seditious libel. The bishops were acquitted. Great popular enthusiasm. An invitation was dispatched to William of Orange to save England from Catholic tyranny: it was signed by the *seven eminent persons* (Devonshire, Shrewsbury, Danby, Compton, Henry Sidney, Lord Lumley, Admiral Russell).

Sept. 30. Declaration of William accepting the invitation. William's real purpose in accepting was to bring England into the struggle against Louis XIV, begun by the **League of Augsburg.** His success reversed the policy of Charles II and James II, which had been broadly pro-French, and re-established English foreign policy along lines which were later considered "traditional" — opposition to any overwhelmingly powerful continental state, especially if that power threatened the Low Countries.

James, frightened by the declaration, dismissed Sunderland and tried to retrace his steps. **William** left Helvoetsluys with 14,000 men (Oct. 19), but was driven back by a gale.

Nov. 5. William succeeded in landing at Torbay. Risings in various sections of England. **Grafton** and **Churchill** (later **Duke of Marlborough**) went over to William (Nov. 22). James issued writs for a new Parliament and endeavored to treat with William. The queen and the baby prince were sent to France (Dec. 10) and James, throwing the great seal into the Thames, fled on Dec. 11. **Interregnum,** rioting in London, seizure of Jeffreys.

Dec. 12. The peers set up a provisional government in London. James, stopped at Sheerness, was brought back to London, but succeeded in escaping to France (Dec. 22), after William had entered London (Dec. 19). Louis XIV set up the exiled Stuarts at the Court of St. Germain.

1689, Jan. 22–1690, Jan. 27. Convention Parliament, summoned by advice of the peers. On Jan. 28 the Commons declared: "That king James II, having endeavored to subvert the constitution of the kingdom by breaking the original contract between king and people, and by the advice of Jesuits and other wicked persons having violated the fundamental laws, and having withdrawn himself out of the kingdom, has abdicated the government, and that the throne is vacant." Also: "That it hath been found by experience to be inconsistent with the safety and welfare of this Protestant kingdom to be governed by a popish prince.²² The Lords objected to the use of the word "abdicated," and to the declaration of the "vacancy" of the throne, but an agreement being reached in a conference of the two houses, the crown was offered to Mary and the regency to William; this being refused, Parliament offered the crown to William and Mary jointly.

1689, Feb. 13. The offer was accompanied by the **Declaration of Rights,** asserting the "true, ancient, and indubitable rights of the people of this realm": (1) **That** the making or suspending law without consent of Parliament is illegal; (2) that the exercise of the dispensing power is illegal; (3) that the ecclesiastical commission court and other such like courts are illegal; (4) that levying money without consent of Parliament is illegal; (5) that it is lawful to petition the sovereign; (6) that the maintenance of a standing army without the consent of Parliament is illegal; (7) that it is lawful to keep arms; (8) that elections of members of Parliament must be free; (9) that there must be freedom of debate in Parliament; (10) that excessive bail should never be demanded; (11) that juries should be empaneled and returned in every trial; (12) that grants of estates as forfeited before conviction of the offender are illegal; (13) that Parliament should be held frequently. William and Mary were declared King and Queen of England for life, the chief administration resting with William; the crown was next settled on William's children by Mary; in default of such issue, on the Princess Anne of Denmark and her children; and in default of these, on the children of William by any other wife. The crown was accepted by William and Mary, who were on the same day proclaimed King and Queen of Great Britain, Ireland, and France.

1689-1702. WILLIAM III AND MARY (until 1694). Privy councillors: Earl of Danby (Marquis of Carmarthen), president; Nottingham, Shrewsbury, secretaries of state; Marquis of Halifax, privy seal; Schomberg (Duke of Schomberg), master-general of ordnance; Bentinck (Earl of Portland), privy purse.

1689, Feb. 22. The Convention Parliament was transformed by its own act into a regular Parliament. Oaths of allegiance and supremacy were taken by the houses, the clergy, etc. Six bishops and about 400 clergymen refused them, and were deprived of their benefices (1691). These non-jurors ordained their own bishops, and maintained their own private Church of England until the 19th century.

Mar. 14. James landed in Ireland with a few followers, was joined by Tyrconnel, and entered Dublin (Mar. 24) amid popular enthusiasm. Irish Parliament (May 7). James besieged the Protestant town of Londonderry (April 20-July 30) which was finally relieved by Kirke.

The first **Mutiny Act**, to punish defection in the army, made necessary by the **Declaration of Rights** (Mar.), passed henceforth annually. The Protestant dissenters who had disdained James' gift of freedom were rewarded by the **Toleration Act** (May 24) which exempted dissenters who had taken the oaths of allegiance and supremacy from penalties for non-attendance at the services of the Church of England.

1689, May 7. WAR BROKE OUT WITH FRANCE. In Scotland Claverhouse (Viscount Dundee) raised his standard for James among the Highlanders, after episcopacy had been abolished by law. At the **battle of Killiecrankie** (July 17) he defeated the Whig general, Mackay, but fell on the field. The revolt gradually petered out.

1689-1690. A series of measures made the constitutional adjustments necessitated by the **Glorious Revolution.** The system of requiring estimate and accounts for supplies, and of specific appropriations — i.e. the nucleus of modern budgetary systems — now became fixed. The **Bill of Rights** (Dec. 16, 1689) was a parliamentary enactment of the **Declaration of Rights,** repeating the provisions of that paper, settling the succession, and enacting that no Roman Catholic could wear the crown. William's **second Parliament** (Mar. 20, 1690-May 3, 1695) by an act of recognition further legalized the already legal acts of the Convention Parliament, settled William's civil list (at a smaller figure than James' or Charles') and by the **Act of Grace** (May 20, 1690) gave indemnity to all supporters of James II except those in treasonable correspondence with him. Shrewsbury and Halifax resigned.

1690. William went to Ireland, and defeated James at the crucial **battle of the Boyne** (July 1). James fled to France. Dublin and Waterford fell quickly. Limerick resisted successfully under Sarsfield (Aug.). In the open field Ginkel defeated Sarsfield and the French St. Ruth at the **battle of Aughrim** (July 12, 1691). Limerick, besieged a second time, surrendered (Oct. 3) under the conditions known as the **pacification of Limerick:** Free transportation to France of all Irish officers and soldiers so desiring. (The Irish Brigade in the French armies had a long and distinguished history.) All Irish Catholics to have the religious liberty they had had under Charles II, carry arms, exercise their professions, and receive full amnesty. The English Parliament confirmed the treaty, but the Irish Parliament, consisting wholly of Protestants, refused to ratify it (1695) and enacted severe anti-Catholic legislation contrary to the pacification terms.

1690, June 30. Defeat of the English fleet by the French at the **battle of Beachy Head.** Lord Torrington, the English admiral, was tried by court-martial and acquitted, but dismissed the service. This defeat was redeemed by the **English naval**

victory under Russell over the French under Tourville at **Cap de la Hogue** (May 19, 1692).

1692, Feb. 13. Massacre of Glencoe. The Highlanders, incompletely pacified after Dundee's rising, had been given until Dec. 31, 1691 to take oath to William. This had been done by all the chieftains save MacIan of the MacDonalds of Glencoe. He took the oath on Jan. 6, 1692, but this fact was suppressed by William's agent, the Master of Stair. A company of soldiers commanded by a Campbell (hereditary foes of the MacDonalds), quartered peacefully at Glencoe, turned suddenly on the Highlanders, killed MacIan and some forty others. The incident was of great political use to William's enemies.

William's land campaigns were unsuccessful; he was defeated by the French at **Steinkirk** (July 24, 1692) and at **Neerwinden** (July 29, 1693) (p. 444). At home he was obliged to turn for support to the **Whig Junto** — Somers, lord keeper; Russel, Shrewsbury, Thos. Wharton, secretaries of state; Montague, chancellor of the exchequer. **Marlborough** had been detected in correspondence with James (Jan. 1692) and disgraced. Sunderland returned to Parliament.

1693, Jan. Beginning of the national debt. £1,000,000 borrowed on annuities at 10%.

1694, July 27. Charter of the Governor and Company of the Bank of England, a company of merchants who, in return for certain privileges, lent the government £1,200,000. Bill for preventing officers of the crown from sitting in the House of Commons (**Place Bill**). Unsuccessful **attack on Brest.** (Treachery of Marlborough?)

1694, Dec. 22. The **Triennial Bill** became law; **Queen Mary died** (Dec. 28); the **Licensing Act** ran out, and was not renewed for the next year, thus abolishing censorship of the press.

1695, Nov. 22-1698, July 5. Third Parliament of William III (first triennial Parliament). Whigs in majority. Recoinage Act. Isaac Newton, master of the mint. Trials for Treason Act (1696); two witnesses required to prove an act of treason. Plot to assassinate William discovered, and conspirators executed; one of them, Fenwick, was the last person to be condemned by a bill of attainder and executed (1696). Formation of a loyal association. Suspension of the *Habeas Corpus Act.*

1697, Sept. 20. TREATY OF RYSWICK (p. 444).

1698, Dec. 6-1700, Apr. 11. Fourth Parliament of William III. London Stock Exchange, the first true stock exchange, formed (1698). **Disbanding Act,** reducing the army to 7000 men (Feb. 1699). Act for the resumption of forfeited estates, aimed at William's Dutch favorites. Further anti-papal measures: Catholic teachers and priests liable to life imprisonment (repealed 1778).

1701, Feb. 6-June 24. Fifth Parliament of William III. Tories in a majority. Harley (later Earl of Oxford) speaker. Portland, Somers, Oxford (Russell). Halifax impeached (Apr.-June).

June 12. **ACT OF SETTLEMENT.** The crown was settled on **Sophia,** Princess of Hanover, granddaughter of James I, and her issue. The sovereigns of Great Britain were to be Protestant and not leave the kingdom without consent of Parliament; the country should not be involved in war for the defense of the foreign possessions of the sovereigns; no foreigner should receive a grant from the crown, or hold office, civil or military; ministers should be responsible for the acts of their sovereigns; judges should hold office for life unless guilty of misconduct.

Sept. 16. **Death of James II.** His son James Edward (the **Old Pretender**) proclaimed King of Great Britain and Ireland by Louis XIV.

1701, Dec. 30-1702, July 2. Sixth Parliament of William III. Attainder of James Edward, "pretended" Prince of Wales. Oath of abjuration reimposed.

1702, Mar. 8. Death of William III.

1702-1714. ANNE, second daughter of James II, wife of Prince George of Denmark. In the first part of her reign Anne was under the influence of her favorite, **Sarah, Duchess of Marlborough,** and her husband, the duke.

1702, May 4. War declared upon France by the Grand Alliance; for this **War of the Spanish Succession,** see p. 445. **Marlborough** was captain-general of the land forces. Godolphin, lord high treasurer; Nottingham, secretary of state. Halifax and Somers not in the privy council.

1702. The campaign: **capture of Venloo** and **Liége** by the allies, loss of the lower Rhine to France. Sir George Rooke failed to take Cadiz, but seized part of the Spanish treasure fleet at Vigo Bay (Oct.).

1702, Oct. 20-1705, Mar. 14. First Parliament of Anne. Harley, speaker.

1703, Nov. Establishment of **Queen Anne's Bounty,** a grant of the first fruits and tithes which Henry VIII had confiscated for the crown, in trust for increasing the incomes of small benefices.

Dec. 27. **Treaty between England and Portugal,** known from its English negotiation as the **Methuen Treaty.** England admitted Portuguese wines at duties one-third less than those paid by French wines, while Portugal agreed to import all her woolens from England.

1703-1706. Progress of the war: Marlborough took Bonn, Huy, Limburg, and Guelders (1703). Sir Geo. Rooke took Gibraltar (July 24, 1704). Marlborough's great victory at Blenheim (Aug. 13, 1704). Capture of Barcelona by Lord Peterborough (Oct. 4, 1705). **Battle of Ramillies** (May 23, 1706) won by Marlborough.

1707, May 1. **UNION OF ENGLAND AND SCOTLAND** under the name of **Great Britain.** This measure, which was made necessary by the omission of Scotland from the Act of Settlement, provided: (1) that Sophia, Princess of Hanover, and her Protestant heirs should succeed to the crown of the united kingdom; (2) there should be one Parliament, to which Scotland should send sixteen elective peers and forty-five members of the Commons. No more peers of Scotland to be created. Scotch law and legal administration to be unchanged; the Episcopal Church in England and Presbyterian in Scotland to be unchanged. Adoption of the Union Jack (Crosses of St. George and St. Andrew) as the national flag of Great Britain.

Oct. 23. **First Parliament of Great Britain.**[1] The influence of Marlborough and his wife had been gradually weakened by Harley and by the influence of the queen's new favorite, Abigail Hill, now Mrs. Masham. Marlborough, however, was still so strong that a hint at resignation secured the dismissal of Harley and St. John from the cabinet, and the substitution of Boyle and Robert Walpole (secretary-at-war). Last royal veto.

1708, Mar. James Edward landed in Scotland; the French fleet sent to help him was beaten by Admiral Byng. The pretender soon returned to France.

1708, Nov. 16–1710, Apr. 5. Third Parliament of Anne (II). Whig ma-

---

[1] Not a new Parliament, but the second Parliament of Anne revived by proclamation. Henceforward Parliaments are numbered without regard to reigns, but here the distinction is retained. The number as a Parliament of Great Britain is indicated by a Roman numeral in parenthesis.

---

jority. Somers, president of the council. Leaders of the Whigs (*Junto*): Somers, Halifax, Wharton, Oxford, Sunderland.

1708-1709. The progress of the war: Marlborough won at **Oudenarde** (July 17, 1708) and again after a bloody battle, at **Malplaquet** (Sept. 11, 1709). Marlborough called by his Tory enemies "the butcher."

1710, Feb.-Mar. **Trial of Dr. Sacheverell** for preaching sermons of an ultra-Tory cast. His conviction further endeared him to the people, and helped the Tory cause.

1710, Nov. 25–1713, July 16. **Fourth Parliament of Anne (III).** Tory majority clear in the Commons. In the Lords it was made certain in 1712 by the creation of twelve Tory peers for the purpose. Complete change in ministry. This election was the first clean-cut peaceful transfer of power under the modern party system in England. Harley (Earl of Oxford in 1711), lord high treasurer. St. John (Viscount Bolingbroke in 1712), secretary of state. Godolphin dismissed. Mrs. Masham, who had gradually supplanted the Duchess of Marlborough in Anne's affections, had a large part in this transfer of power. The Duke of Marlborough was accused of peculation (Nov. 1711), dismissed from his offices, and supplanted as commander-in-chief by the Duke of Ormond. English participation in the war reduced by Tory policy to a negligible point. Complicated peace negotiations begun with France.

1711. **South Sea Company incorporated** by vote of Parliament in a bill dated 1710. Passage of **Occasional Conformity Bill,** directed against dissenters who technically satisfied the Test Act by one communion in an Anglican Church, and then attended a non-conformist "chapel" regularly. **Landed Property Qualification Act,** an attempt by landed proprietors to exclude merchants, financiers, and industrialists from Parliament (repealed 1866). Neither of these Tory measures were long successfully enforced.

1713, Apr. 11. **TREATY OF UTRECHT.** Articles affecting **Great Britain:** renunciation of the pretender by Louis XIV, who recognized the Protestant succession in Great Britain; crowns of France and Spain *not* to be united under one head; fortifications of Dunkirk to be razed and its harbor filled up; cession by France of Hudson's Bay and Acadia, Newfoundland and St. Kitts to Great Britain. **Great Britain and Spain:** cession of Gibraltar and Minorca to England; grant of the Asiento (*el pacto del asiento de negros*), or contract

The House of Stuart

James I (Stuart)
1603–1625

(3) Elizabeth
m. Frederick V
Elector Palatine

(5) **Charles I**
1625–1649
m. Henrietta Maria
d. of Henry IV of France

(12) Sophia
m. Ernest
Augustus, Elector
of Hanover

Charles II
1660–1685

Mary
m. William II
of Orange

James II
1685–1688
d. 1701

by Anne Hyde   by Mary of Este

George I
1714–1727
m. Sophia Dorothea
d. of Duke of
Brunswick and Zell

William III === Mary   Anne
1689–1702 1689–1694 1702–1714

James
Francis
Edward
the Old
Pretender
d. 1766

George II
1727–1760
m. Caroline
of Anspach

Sophia Dorothea
m. Frederick
William, King of
Prussia

Charles Edward
the Young Pretender
d. without issue
1788

Henry
Cardinal
York
d. without issue
1807

Frederick Louis
d. 1751
m. Augusta, d. of
Duke of
Gotha

Frederick II
King of Prussia

George III
1760–1820
m. Charlotte of
Mecklenburg
Strelitz

for supplying slaves to Spanish America, to the subjects of Great Britain for thirty years (Royal African Company). **1714, Feb. 16-Aug. 25. Fifth Parliament of Anne (IV).** Death of Sophia of Hanover (May 28). **Schism Act.** Oxford dismissed (July 27) and succeeded as lord high treasurer by the Earl of Shrewsbury. Many leading Tories, who foresaw that the Hanoverian succession would mean a Whig monopoly of power, attempted negotiations with the pretender.

Aug. 1. Death of Anne.
1714. HOUSE OF HANOVER or BRUNSWICK, changed (1917) to House of Windsor. None of Anne's seventeen children having survived her, the crown, according to the act of succession, descended to the Protestant house of Hanover, the Catholic line of the Stuarts being excluded.
1714–1727. GEORGE I.
1714, Sept. 18. The king landed in England. George I favored the Whigs

in the formation of the first government; Lord Townshend, sec. of state; Shrewsbury resigned, and Halifax was made first lord of the treasury (Shrewsbury was the last lord high treasurer); Sunderland, lord lieutenant of Ireland; Lord Cowper, chancellor; Earl of Nottingham, president of the council; Marlborough, commander-in-chief.

1715, Mar. 17–1722, Mar. 7. **First Parliament of George I (V).** Impeachment of **Bolingbroke, Ormond, Oxford.** Flight of Bolingbroke and Ormond; Oxford in the Tower. Jacobite riots in England.

1715-1716, Sept. "The Fifteen," Jacobite rising in Scotland under the Earl of Mar. Battles of **Sheriffmuir** and **Preston.** Arrival of the pretender ("James III") from France (Dec. 1715). The Duke of Argyle (Campbell, MacCallum More) dispersed the Jacobite troops without a battle, and the pretender fled (Feb. 5, 1716). Impeachment of Jacobite leaders, execution of Derwentwater and Kenmure (Feb. 24).

1716. Partly because of this Jacobite scare, Parliament passed the **Septennial Act,** prolonging its own life to seven years, and making that the full legal term for future Parliaments.

1717, Jan. 4. **Triple alliance** between England, France, and Holland because of the intrigues of the pretender, Charles XII, and Alberoni; the empire joined these in the **quadruple alliance** (Aug. 2, 1718). War between England and Spain (see p. 451).

1718, Jan. Repeal of the Occasional Conformity Act and the Schism Act.

1719. Abortive Spanish expedition to Scotland to help the pretender. **Treaty of Stockholm** (Nov. 20, 1719): Sweden ceded Bremen and Verden to George I (as Elector of Hanover) for 1,000,000 rix dollars.

1720, Jan. Spain joined the quadruple alliance, making peace with England.

1720, Jan. Bursting of the **South Sea Bubble:** disastrous financial panic influenced by the earlier bursting of Law's **Mississippi Bubble** in France (p. 447).

1721-1742. **Administration of Sir Robert Walpole,** first true prime minister. The cabinet system and the party system now took the form they held until 1832. Parallel administration of Fleury in France (1726-1742). Both ministers were cautious and peace-loving, anxious to restore prosperity after the ravages of the "first World War." Period of stability, of common

sense, the **Augustan Age** of European letters, great advances in commerce and industry.

1722, Oct. 9–1727, July 17. **Second Parliament of George I (VI).** **Treaty of Hanover** between England, France, and Prussia (Sept. 3, 1725).

1727-1760. **GEORGE II.** Walpole continued in office. The king was much influenced by his wife, the capable Caroline of Anspach, who remained loyal to Walpole.

1728, Jan. 23–1734, Apr. 16. **First Parliament of George II (VII).**

1729, Nov. 9. Treaty of Seville with Spain: restoration of conquests; England retained Gibraltar; the *asiento* confirmed.

1731, Mar. 16. **Treaty of Vienna** with the empire; dissolution of the Ostend East India Company, which had been formed as rival to the English India Company, by the emperor.

1735, Jan. 14–1741, Apr. 25. **Second Parliament of George II (VIII).**

1736. Porteous riots in Edinburgh.

1736. John Wesley and his brother **Charles** returned from Georgia, set up the little groups of evangelical Christians out of which came the **Wesleyan societies,** and, after the death of John Wesley (1791), the various independent **Methodist churches.** George Whitefield, their great collaborator, was ordained in 1736. The Methodists were emotional and revivalistic, but politically conservative. The movement was probably important in preventing the spread of political radicalism in 18th century England.

1739-1748. **WAR WITH SPAIN** (*War of Jenkins' Ear*). Capture of Porto Bello in Darien by Vernon (Nov. 22, 1739). Futile attack upon Cartagena by Vernon and Wentworth (1740). Voyage of Commodore Anson to Chile and Peru and around the world (Sept. 1740–June, 1744).

1741, Dec. 1–1747, June 17. **Third Parliament of George II (IX).** Fall of Walpole (Feb. 1742). Interim administration of the Earl of Wilmington, followed (1743-1754) by that of **Henry Pelham,** first lord of the treasury. The Whig party tended to disintegrate into rival groups, held together loosely by place and privilege, and by the "interest" of the Duke of Newcastle. *Broad bottom ministry:* Pelham, Pitt, Newcastle, Harrington (later Earl Stanhope), Bedford.

1740-1748. **WAR OF THE AUSTRIAN SUCCESSION.** England took part on the side of Austria. For further details see p. 465.

1745, May 11. Battle of Fontenoy, victory of the French under Saxe over the allies under Cumberland.

1745-1746. SECOND JACOBITE REBELLION (*The Forty-five*). The Young Pretender, **Charles Edward,** landed in Scotland (July 25) and proclaimed his father as James VIII of Scotland and III of England. The Jacobites entered Edinburgh with some 2000 men (Sept. 11), won the **battle of Prestonpans** (Sept. 21), and under Charles Edward himself marched down into England, where they reached Derby, his farthest point, on Dec. 4. Jacobite victories at **Penrith** (Dec. 18) and at **Falkirk Moor** (Jan. 17, 1746). But only in the Highlands was the Jacobite cause strong, and here they were beaten decisively at **Culloden** (Apr. 16). The pretender escaped to France (Sept. 20). This was the last Stuart effort.

1747, Nov. 10-1754, Apr. 6. Fourth Parliament of George II (X).

1748. Treaty of Aix-la-Chapelle, p. 466. England emerged from this war a defeated nation, except in North America. The divisions of the Whigs continued, and their ablest man, **William Pitt** (Earl of Chatham in 1766), was not trusted with power save at the crisis of the **Seven Years' War** (1757).

1752. The Gregorian calendar adopted in England and the colonies. The eleven days between Sept. 2 and 14 were omitted. ("Give us back our eleven days!")

1753. Foundation of the British Museum by government purchase of the collection of Sir Hans Sloane.

1754. On the death of Pelham (Mar.) he was succeeded as prime minister by his brother, the Duke of Newcastle. Henry Fox, secretary of state.

1754, May 31-1761, Mar. 19. Fifth Parliament of George II (XI).

1755-1763. LAND AND NAVAL WAR BETWEEN ENGLAND AND FRANCE. (*Seven Years' War*) originating in boundary disputes in North America, carried on by land in America (and Germany), by sea in all parts of the world. The English had the ultimate advantage of the French almost everywhere. (War in America, p. 516; in India, p. 535.)

1757-1761. Coalition ministry of Newcastle, first lord of the treasury, and the elder Pitt, secretary of state, to centralize war policy and administration. Pitt was the real leader, and helped make possible England's victory in the duel with France.

1759, Sept. 13. Battle of Quebec, death of Wolfe and Montcalm. Naval **battle of Quiberon Bay** (Nov. 20); defeat of the French by Sir Edward Hawke.

1760-1820. GEORGE III.

1761, Aug. 15. Bourbon family compact between France and Spain, with the assumption of the accession of Naples and Parma, for reciprocal guarantee of all possessions and an offensive and defensive alliance.

Oct. 5. Pitt, insisting that war be declared against Spain, resigned. **Lord Bute,** adviser to the king. George attempted to carry out his mother's advice to "be king," but in a way thoroughly consonant with the organization of politics in 18th century England. He built up in Parliament, with Tory aid and by the usual means of patronage and bribery, a party of *king's friends,* and thus brought the Tories into power for the first time since 1714. Newcastle continued prime minister in the new cabinet (Oct. 5, 1761). Egremont and Bute, secretaries of state, George Grenville, leader of the Commons.

1761, Nov. 3-1768, Mar. 10. First Parliament of George III (XII). War declared against Spain (Jan. 1762). Bute became prime minister (May 29, 1762), Grenville, secretary of state.

1763, Feb. 10. TREATY OF PARIS between Great Britain, France, and Spain. (1) France ceded to England: In North America, Canada, and Cape Breton Island; the Mississippi was recognized as the boundary between Louisiana and the British colonies; in the West Indies, Grenada; in Africa, the French possessions on the Senegal. England restored to France Goree in Africa, and Pondichéry and Chandernagor in India. (2) Spain ceded to England Florida, as indemnification for which France had already ceded Louisiana to Spain; Spain received from England all conquests in Cuba including Havana. In consequence of this peace and her acquisitions in India, Great Britain approached the summit of her extent and power; the North American colonies had gradually developed into virtually self-governing states.

1763, Apr. 1-1765, July. Ministry of George Grenville; Halifax and Egremont, secretaries of state; Fox created Lord Holland.

1763-1764. No. 45 of the *North Briton* (Apr. 23, 1763), containing insulting remarks concerning the king by **John Wilkes,** general warrants for the apprehension of the authors, printers, and publishers, were issued. Wilkes was arrested and expelled from the Commons (Jan. 19, 1764). General warrants declared illegal by the chief justice. Wilkes outlawed.

1765, July–1766, July. Ministry of the Marquis of Rockingham; Conway, leader of the Commons. This was succeeded by a ministry headed by **Chatham** (Aug. 1766–Dec. 1767) and then by the ministry of the **Duke of Grafton** (Dec. 1767–Jan. 1770); Townshend, chancellor of the exchequer; Conway, Shelburne, secretaries of state; the Earl of Chatham, lord privy seal. Lord Hillsborough the first colonial secretary.

1768, May 10–1774, June 22. Second Parliament of George III (XIII). Wilkes returned and was elected to the Commons from Middlesex. He was expelled from the House by votes of the "king's friends," but was thrice elected and thrice rejected; at the last election his opponent, Colonel Luttrell, who received a small minority of votes, was declared elected. This was a Pyrrhic victory for George. The affair of the **Middlesex election** stirred up animosities against him, and resulted finally in establishing freedom of election of the House of Commons.

1769-1772. *Letters of Junius,* containing bitter attacks on the Duke of Grafton, Lord Mansfield, and other members of the government, appeared in the *Daily Advertiser.* The author is still unknown, but the weight of evidence favors **Sir Philip Francis.**

1770, Jan.–1782, Mar. Ministry of Lord North, first lord of the treasury and chancellor of the exchequer, and George's favorite. Full Tory government. Under North, third Parliament of George III (Nov. 29, 1774–July 8, 1780) (XIV) and fourth Parliament (Oct. 31, 1780–Mar. 24, 1784) (XV).

Constitutional developments: Establishment of publication of speeches in the Commons, in spite of their protests (1771). Wilkes made lord mayor of London and member for Middlesex. The sixth motion to expunge the resolution rejecting him, as "subversive of the rights of electors," carried (May 3, 1782). Repeal of some of the penal laws against Roman Catholics (1778) helped bring on the **Lord George Gordon** riots in London (June, 1780), originating as a protest against further Catholic emancipation, but degenerating into drunken orgies and brawls. London in the hands of the mob for three days.

The failure of North to subdue the American colonies resulted in a series of motions hostile to him, culminating in that of Sir J. Rous (Mar. 15, 1782) "that the House could no longer repose confidence in the present ministers" (lost by only nine votes). On threat of renewal of the motion, **North resigned,** thus setting a further precedent in parliamentary government.

1775-1783. WAR OF AMERICAN INDEPENDENCE (see p. 520). The war widened in 1778 with the entrance of France against Great Britain, in 1779 with the entrance of Spain against her. Gibraltar, defended by Elliott, besieged by French and Spanish in vain (1779–1782). Holland entered the war against Great Britain (Dec. 30, 1780). In 1781 the English lost Pensacola, Tobago, St. Eustace, Demerara, St. Kitts, Nevis, Monserrat; Cornwallis surrendered at **Yorktown** (Oct. 19, 1781). Minorca lost (1782). A British naval victory near Martinique, Rodney and Hood over De Grasse (Apr. 12, 1782) helped restore the balance. But England was sick of the war, and the new government had, without a formal election, a mandate to make peace.

1782, Mar. 20-July 1. Ministry of Rockingham: Shelburne and **Charles James Fox** (1749–1806), secretaries of state; Thurlow, lord chancellor; **Edmund Burke** (1729–1797), paymaster of the forces; **Richard Brinsley Sheridan** (1751–1816), under-secretary of state. With Chatham, Fox, Burke, Sheridan, the golden age of English oratory. On Rockingham's death (July 1), Lord Shelburne became prime minister in a cabinet (July 1, 1782–Feb. 24, 1783) from which Fox, Burke, and Sheridan were excluded, and **William Pitt** (1759–1806) included as chancellor of the exchequer.

1782, Nov. 30. PRELIMINARY TREATY OF PARIS with the United States (p. 522) followed by the general **Treaty of Paris** (Jan. 20, 1783–Sept. 3) between the United States, Great Britain, France, Spain, and Holland. (1) Recognition of the independence of the thirteen United States. (2) England surrendered Tobago and Senegal to France. (3) Spain retained Minorca and Florida. (4) Holland, badly worsted (separate peace, May 20, 1784), gave Negapatam and the right of free navigation in the Moluccas to England.

1783, Apr. 2-Dec. 13. Coalition ministry of North and Fox, nominally headed by the Duke of Portland; Cavendish, chancellor of the exchequer; North and Fox, secretaries of state; Burke, paymaster. The alliance of two such bitter opponents as North and Fox shocked public opinion and paved the way for the ministry of the younger Pitt.

1783, Dec. 26–1801, Mar. 17. First minis- try of **William Pitt** the Younger, formed after Fox's bill to reform the govern- ment of India was lost in the Lords. Pitt's bill was also rejected, whereupon Parlia- ment was dissolved (1784, Mar. 25) and new elections held.

1784, May 18–1795. Fifth Parliament of George III (XVI).

Aug. 13. Pitt's India bill became law (p. 535).

1788. Temporary insanity of George III. In the course of discussion regard- ing the regency, the king recovered.

1793, Feb. 1. The French Republic declared war on Great Britain (p. 582). The government at once took measures against revolutionary agitation (Traitorous Correspondence Bill; suspension of the *Habeas Corpus* Act, [1794]).

1794, May. Trial of Hardy, Horn Tooke, and Thelwall, on charge of high treason, all of whom were eventu- ally acquitted (Dec.).

Nov. Jay's treaty between the United States and Great Britain (p. 766.)

1796, Sept. 17. The sixth Parliament of George III convened (XVII).

1797, Apr. 15. The mutiny at Spithead. The sailors' demands for better treatment were reasonable and were met by the government (May 17), but imme- diately afterward a more serious outbreak occurred at the **Nore**, which had to be suppressed by force (June 30).

1799. Suppression of the insurrection of the United Irishmen. This or- ganization had been formed in 1791 to se- cure the complete separation of Ireland from England. The French had sent several expeditions to aid them (notably that of Hoche, which was scattered by a storm, Dec. 1796), but the United Irishmen were defeated at **Vinegar Hill** (June 21, 1798) and the insurrection stamped out. As a result

1801, Jan. 1. THE LEGISLATIVE UNION OF GREAT BRITAIN AND IRE- LAND, under the name of the *United*

Kingdom, was brought about. The Act of Union provided that there should be one Parliament, to which Ireland should send four spiritual lords, sitting by rotation of sessions; 28 temporal peers, elected for life by the Irish peerage; and 100 members of the Commons. The churches of the two countries were to be united into one Protes- tant Episcopal Church. Pitt proposed to make some concessions to the Roman Catholics, but the king was persuaded that this would involve a breach of his coro- nation oath. Thereupon

Feb. 3. Pitt resigned.

Mar. 14. His friend **Henry Addington** then headed the cabinet, with Pitt advising, and concluded peace with France, embodied (Mar. 27) in the **Treaty of Amiens.**

The passage of the **Health and Morals of Apprentices Act** in this year marks a step towards government supervision of labor conditions. The Act forbade the hiring out of pauper children for work in the cotton mills until they were nine years of age, restricted their working day to 12 hours, and prohibited their employment at night work.

1803, May 16. The war between Britain and France was renewed. (See p. 590.)

1804, May 10. Pitt returned to office and helped to organize the **Third Coalition** against France. He was stricken by the news of Napoleon's victory at Austerlitz and died on Jan. 23, 1806.

1806. Pitt's place was taken by **Lord William Grenville,** with **Charles James Fox** as foreign secretary until the latter's death, Sept. 13.

1807. Abolition of slavery decreed in the British dominions. The **Duke of Portland** formed his second ministry (March) and held office until May, 1809, when **Spencer Perceval** replaced him, to be followed (June, 1812) by the **Earl of Liverpool,** whose unusually long ministry lasted until April, 1827. (*Cont. p. 604.*)

2. THE DUTCH REPUBLIC

The first half of the 17th century, during which the Dutch provinces were still at war with Spain to secure their independence, was nevertheless the golden age of the Netherlands, a period of unexampled flower- ing in art and literature. This was probably due primarily to the unprecedented ex- pansion of Dutch commerce, which resulted from the closing of Lisbon to Dutch trade after the annexation of Portugal to Spain.

The Dutch were obliged to find their own way to the east and within a remarkably short time they were disputing the com- mand of the Indies with the Portuguese, whom they soon displaced. The **Dutch East India Company** (founded 1602), was given extensive political and military au- thority and became one of the chief organs of Dutch imperialism. In the east, **Batavia** was founded in 1619. The Portuguese

The Houses of Orange and Nassau (1559-1843)

were expelled from Ceylon (1638–1658), and Malacca taken from them (1641). In 1652 the Dutch established themselves at the Cape of Good Hope and in 1667 they took Sumatra. The **Dutch West India Company** (founded 1621) had the same extensive control over the American and African coast trade. In 1623 the Dutch seized Pernambuco and began extensive conquests in Brazil (till 1661). They took the islands of St. Eustace and Curaçao (1634–1635), Saba (1640), and St. Martin (1648). With this far-flung colonial empire, the Dutch provinces became the commercial center of Europe, Amsterdam easily holding the lead as a financial center.

The provinces, however, were politically connected only in the loosest fashion. Despite the stadholdership of the house of Orange, there continued to be (esp. in Holland, the chief province) strong sus-

picion of all centralizing tendencies and an almost fanatical attachment to state rights.

1647-1650.   WILLIAM II, a young man of 23, succeeded his father, Frederick Henry, in the stadholdership. Able, ambitious, and restless, William disapproved of the **Treaty of Münster** (1648), which recognized the independence of the provinces, and would have preferred to continue the war. He soon became involved in conflict with the States-General and, by arresting some of the leaders of Holland and attacking Amsterdam itself (1650), he forced the submission of the state-rights group.

1650, Nov. 6.   William's early death gave the decentralizing party a golden opportunity, for William's son was born posthumously and there was no one to dispute the taking over of control by the

States-General. In 1653 **John de Witt** became grand pensionary of Holland, and through this position exercised control over general policy. An able statesman and adroit diplomat, he easily maintained Dutch prestige and greatness.

1652-1654. THE FIRST ANGLO-DUTCH WAR, the direct outgrowth of the **English Navigation Act** (1651) and the steadily growing competition of English and Dutch, esp. in the east. The English and the Dutch, led by outstanding commanders like Blake, Monk, Tromp, de Ruyter, and de Witt, fought no less than twelve naval engagements, most of them indecisive. By the **Treaty of Westminster** (Apr. 5, 1654) the Dutch agreed to enter a defensive league with England and to pay indemnity. The province of Holland secretly agreed to exclude all members of the house of Orange from the stadholdership (this was due to Cromwell's uneasiness about the relationship of the Stuarts and Oranges — William II having married the daughter of Charles I).

1657-1660. The Dutch interfered successfully in the Swedish-Danish War in order to prevent the entrance of the Baltic from falling into exclusively Swedish control.

1657-1661. War with Portugal, over conflicting interests in Brazil.

1660. On the restoration of the Stuarts in England, the Dutch States-General at once rescinded the exclusion of the house of Orange from the stadholdership.

1662. The Dutch allied themselves to the French to provide against the danger of attack by the British.

1664. The British seized **New Amsterdam** (New York) and appropriated various Dutch stations on the African coast.

1665-1667. SECOND ANGLO-DUTCH WAR. France and Denmark supported the Dutch, who, on the whole, maintained the upper hand at sea (attack on the English fleet in the Medway, etc., see p. 427), but by the **Treaty of Breda** (July 10, 1667) they abandoned claims to New Amsterdam in return for Surinam.

1668, Jan. 13. Triple Alliance of England, Holland, and Sweden to check the aggression of Louis XIV in the Spanish Netherlands. Louis soon managed to buy off the English and the Swedes and thereafter concentrated his hatred upon the Dutch.

1672-1678. WAR WITH FRANCE AND ENGLAND (p. 442). The Dutch were quite unprepared for a land war and

consequently the French were able to overrun much of the country. The result was much agitation against **John de Witt**, who, with his brother Cornelius, was brutally murdered by a mob (Aug. 27, 1672).

1672-1702. WILLIAM III (son of William II), stadholder. With the aid of the emperor and of Brandenburg he was able to hold his own against the French and indeed to force their retirement. The British abandoned the war (1674) and by the **Treaty of Nijmwegen** (Nimwegen, Nimeguen) of 1678, the Dutch came off without losses.

1688, Nov. 5. William III (married in 1677 to **Mary**, the daughter of James II of England) landed in England in response to an appeal from the opponents of James II. In 1689 he was proclaimed king and joint ruler with Mary (p. 429).

1689-1697. WAR OF THE LEAGUE OF AUGSBURG against Louis XIV (p. 443). William was very decidedly the leader in the coalition and threw the whole weight of England as well as of the Netherlands into the struggle. Though rarely successful in the field, William's perseverance and able management saved him from disaster. By the **Treaty of Ryswick** (1697), France and the Netherlands returned to the *status quo ante*.

1702, Mar. 8. The death of William III, without children, brought to an end the direct line of the house of Orange, which, however, was continued by the related house of Nassau. For the time being, however, the States-General resumed control of affairs, which were ably conducted by **Anthony Heinsius**, since 1688 grand pensionary of Holland and close collaborator of William III. Heinsius remained in power until his death in 1720.

1702-1713. THE WAR OF THE SPANISH SUCCESSION (p. 445), in which the Dutch again played their part in conjunction with England. These wars, costly in men and money, reacted most unfavorably on the Dutch position. After 1715 there was a marked and steady economic decline. The republic was soon overshadowed by England and became more and more an adjunct of the English system.

1715, Nov. 15. By the **Barrier Treaty**, the empire ceded to the Dutch a number of strong places on the French frontier in the (since 1713) Austrian Netherlands, as protection against attack by France.

1731. The Dutch signed the **Pragmatic Sanction** of Emperor Charles VI in return for abolition of the Ostend Company, which had been set up as a rival to the Dutch East India Company.

1734. The Prince of Orange-Nassau married Anne, the daughter of George II.

1743. The Dutch Republic joined England in the alliance with Maria Theresa against Prussia and France. The French conquests in the Austrian Netherlands constituted a direct danger to the republic.

1747-1751. WILLIAM IV of Orange-Nassau (grandson of William III's cousin) proclaimed stadholder, a dignity which now became hereditary in the family.

1751. On the death of William IV, his widow, Anne, acted as regent for the three-year-old heir.

1766-1795. WILLIAM V assumed the position of stadholder. He proved himself a weak and ineffectual ruler.

1780-1784. The Dutch went to war with England over the question of the right to search ships at sea. As a result the Dutch lost some of their possessions in both the East and the West Indies.

1785. Beginning of serious conflict between William and the States-General, due to the emergence of the **Patriot Party** (representing the French influence). William ultimately had to call in Prussian troops (1787) to restore his authority.

1793. France declared war on the Dutch Republic as well as on England (friction over the opening of the Scheldt by the French in 1792).

1794-1795. The French general, Pichegru, overran the country, capturing the Dutch fleet while it was frozen in the ice in the Texel. William V fled to England.

1795-1806. THE BATAVIAN REPUBLIC, modeled on France and governed by the Patriots under more or less direct French influence. In the interval the British, still at war with France, seized the Dutch colonies.

1806-1810. LOUIS, the brother of Napoleon, King of Holland. His policy, aimed at the good of his adopted kingdom, brought him into conflict with his brother.

1810. THE KINGDOM OF HOLLAND was incorporated with France as an integral part of the empire.

(*Cont. p.* 621.)

3. FRANCE

1643-1715. LOUIS XIV, who ascended the throne at the age of five. His mother, **Anne of Austria** (daughter of Philip III of Spain) acted as guardian. The government, even after Louis' arrival at majority, was conducted by **Cardinal Mazarin**.

1648-1653. Disturbances of the **Fronde** (**Cardinal Retz; Prince of Condé;** resistance of the *parlement* of Paris), the last attempt of the French nobility to oppose the court by armed resistance. The parlementary, as contrasted with the noble, Fronde, was, however, an attempt to substitute government by law for government by royal or any other irresponsible will. Condé, at first loyal, afterward engaged against the court, fought a battle with the royal troops under Henri de la Tour d'Auvergne, Vicomte de **Turenne**, in the Faubourg Saint Antoine, and took refuge in Spain. The first conspiracy, the old Fronde, ended in 1649, with the second **Treaty of Ruel**; the second conspiracy, the new Fronde, which involved treasonable correspondence with Spain, failed in 1650. A union of the two was crushed in 1653.

(Gaston of Orléans, and his daughter "Mademoiselle.")

1648. Acquisitions of France in the **Treaties of Westphalia**, p. 408.

The war with Spain, which sprang up during the Thirty Years' War (victory of Condé at **Rocroy**, May 18, 1643; alliance with England, 1657; Cromwell sent 8000 men of his army to the assistance of Turenne) was continued till the

1659.   TREATY OF THE PYRENEES: (1) France received a part of Roussillon, Conflans, Cerdagne, and several towns in Artois and Flanders, Hainault and Luxemburg. (2) The Duke of Lorraine, the ally of Spain, was partially reinstated (France received Bar, Clermont, etc., and right of passage for troops); the Prince of Condé entirely reinstated. (3) Marriage between Louis XIV and the infanta **Maria Theresa,** eldest daughter of Philip IV of Spain, who, however, renounced her claims upon her inheritance for herself and her issue by Louis forever, in consideration of the payment of a dowry of 500,000 crowns by Spain.

The French Bourbons (1589–1830)

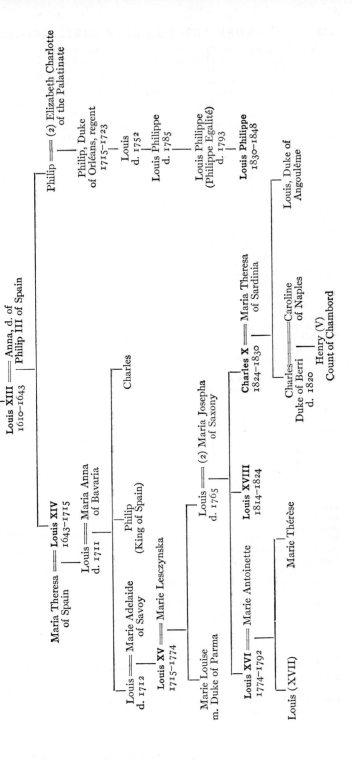

Henry IV ══ (2) Marie de' Medici
1589–1610

Louis XIII ══ Anna, d. of
1610–1643   Philip III of Spain

Maria Theresa ══ Louis XIV ══ Maria Anna
of Spain   1643–1715   of Bavaria

Louis ══ Marie Adelaide   Philip   Charles
d. 1711   of Savoy   (King of Spain)

Louis XV ══ Marie Leszczynska
1715–1774

Marie Louise   Louis ══ (2) Maria Josepha   Louis XVIII
m. Duke of Parma d. 1765   of Saxony   1814–1824

Louis XVI ══ Marie Antoinette   Charles X ══ Maria Theresa
1774–1792   1824–1830   of Sardinia

Louis (XVII)   Marie Thérèse   Charles ══ Caroline   Louis, Duke of
                                     Duke of Berri of Naples   Angoulême
                                     d. 1820

                                     Henry (V)
                                     Count of Chambord

Philip ══ (2) Elizabeth Charlotte
            of the Palatinate

Philip, Duke
of Orléans, regent
1715–1723

Louis
d. 1752

Louis Philippe
d. 1785

Louis Philippe
(Philippe Egalité)
d. 1793

Louis Philippe
1830–1848

1661. Death of Mazarin. Personal government of Louis XIV (1661-1715), absolute, at least in the theory of certain royalist pamphleteers, and perhaps of Louis himself, without Etats-Généraux, without regard to the remonstrances of the parlement of Paris (*L'état, c'est moi*). Louis was in practice, however, limited by his inability to do everything himself. The French bureaucracy was a privileged group, often owning their offices (*vénalité des offices*; *Paulette*, a tax to the crown paid by office owners). Three constitutional limitations on the crown: king must be a Catholic; no woman may occupy the throne (**Salic law**); king may not alienate his lands by *appanage* system. **Colbert,** controller general of the finances from 1662-1683. **Reform of the finances;** mercantile system. Construction of a fleet of war. **Louvois,** minister of war, 1666-1691. Quarrel for precedence in rank with Spain. Negotiations with the pope concerning the privileges of French ambassadors at Rome. The ambition of Louis for fame, and his desire for increase of territory were some of the causes of the following wars, in which these generals took part: Turenne, Condé, Luxembourg, Catinat, Villars, Vendôme, Vauban (inventor of the modern system of military defense).

1667-1668. FIRST WAR (*War of Devolution*) on account of the Spanish Netherlands.

Cause: After the death of his father-in-law, Philip IV of Spain, Louis laid claim to the Spanish possessions in the Belgian provinces (Brabant, Flanders, etc.), on the ground that, being the personal estates of the royal family of Spain, their descent ought to be regulated by the local *droit de dévolution*, a principle in private law, whereby in the event of a dissolution of a marriage by death, the survivor enjoyed the usufruct only of the property, the ownership being vested in the children, whence it followed that daughters of a first marriage inherited before sons of a second marriage. The renunciation of her heritage which his wife had made was, Louis claimed, invalid, since the stipulated dowry had never been paid.

1667. Turenne conquered a part of Flanders and Hainault. By the exertions of John de Witt, pensioner of Holland, and Sir William Temple, England, Holland, and Sweden concluded the **Triple alliance** (1668, Jan. 23) which induced Louis, after Condé had, with great rapidity, occupied the defenseless free country of Burgundy (Franche-Comté) to sign the

1668, May 2. Treaty of Aix-la-Chapelle: Louis restored Franche-Comté (the fortresses having been dismantled) to Spain, in return for which he received twelve fortified towns on the border of the Spanish Netherlands, among others Lille, Tournay, and Oudenarde. The question of the succession was not settled, but deferred.

1672-1678. SECOND WAR (against Holland). The course of Holland in these transactions had inflamed the hatred of Louis against her, a hatred made still stronger by the refuge given by the provinces to political writers who annoyed him with their abusive publications. To gain his purpose, the destruction or the humiliation of Holland, Louis secured the disruption of the Triple Alliance by a private treaty with Charles II of England (the **Treaty of Dover,** 1670, p. 427), and between France and Sweden (1672). Subsidy treaties with Cologne and Münster; 20,000 Germans fought for Louis in the following war.

1672. Passage of the Rhine. Rapid and easy conquest of southern Holland by Turenne, Condé, and the king, at the head of 100,000 men. The brothers De Witt, the leaders of the aristocratic republican party in Holland, were killed during a popular outbreak (Aug. 27), and **William III of Orange** was placed at the head of the state. The opening of the sluices saved the province of Holland, and the city of Amsterdam. Alliance of Holland with Frederick William, Elector of Brandenburg (1640-1688), afterward joined by the emperor and by Spain.

1673. Frederick William concluded the separate **Peace of Vossem,** in which he retained his possessions in Cleves, except Wesel and Rees.

1674. Declaration of war by the empire. Peace between England and Holland. Louis conquered Franche-Comté in person; Condé fought against Orange (drawn **battle at Senef**) in the Netherlands. Brilliant campaign of **Turenne** on the upper Rhine (first ravaging of the Palatinate) against Montecuccoli, the imperial general, and the Elector of Brandenburg. The latter, recalled by the inroad of the Swedish allies of Louis XIV into his lands, defeated the Swedes in the

1675, June 28. Battle of Fehrbellin. In the same year Turenne fell at Sasbach, in Baden (July 27). The French retreated across the Rhine.

1676. Naval successes in the Mediterranean against the Dutch and Spanish. Death of De Ruyter.

1678. Surprise and capture of Ghent and Ypres by the French. Negotiations with each combatant, which had been for some time in progress, resulted in the

1678-1679. TREATIES OF NIMWEGEN (Nijmwegen, Nimeguen). Holland and France (Aug. 10, 1678); Spain and France (Sept. 17, 1678); the emperor, with France and Sweden (Feb. 6, 1679); Holland with Sweden (Oct. 12, 1679). At Fontainebleau, France and Denmark (Sept. 2, 1679). At Lund, Denmark and Sweden (Sept. 26, 1679).

(1) Holland received its whole territory back, upon condition of preserving neutrality. (2) Spain ceded to France: Franche-Comté, and on the northeast frontier, Valenciennes, Cambray, and the Cambrésis, Aire, Poperingen, St. Omer, Ypres, Condé, Bouchain, Maubeuge, and other towns; France ceded to Spain: Charleroi, Binche, Oudenarde, Ath, Courtray, Limburg, Ghent, Waes, etc.; and in Catalonia, Puycerda. (3) The emperor ceded to France: Freiburg in the Breisgau; France gave up the right of garrison in Philippsburg; the Duke of Lorraine was to be restored to his duchy, but on such conditions that he refused to accept them.

Louis XIV forced the Elector of Brandenburg to conclude the

1679, June 29. Peace of St. Germain-en-Laye, whereby he surrendered to Sweden nearly all of his conquests in Pomerania, in return for which he received only the reversion of the principality of East Friesland, which became Prussian in 1744, and a small indemnification.

Louis was now at the height of his power. Stimulated by the weakness of the empire, he established the

1680-1683. Chambers of Reunion at Metz, Breisach, Besançon, and Tournay. These were French courts of claims with power to investigate and decide what dependencies had at any time belonged to the territories and towns which had been ceded to France by the last four treaties of peace. The king executed with his troops the decisions of his tribunals. Saarbrücken, Luxemburg, Zweibrücken, Strassburg (1681), and many other towns were thus annexed to France.

1683. Invasion of the Spanish Netherlands, occupation of Luxemburg, and seizure of Trier (1684). Lorraine permanently occupied by France. To the weakness of the Empire, the wars with the Turks, and the general confusion of European relations since the Peace of Nimwegen, it is to be attributed that these aggressions were met by nothing more than empty protests, and that

1684. A truce for twenty years was concluded at Regensburg between Louis and the emperor and the Empire, whereby he retained everything he had obtained by reunion up to Aug. 1, 1681, including Strassburg.

Louis' mistresses: Louise de la Vallière; Madame de Montespan; Madame de Maintenon, a devout Catholic, whose influence over the king was boundless. Maria Theresa died 1683. Louis privately married to Madame de Maintenon. **War upon heresy.** The dragonnades in Languedoc. Wholesale conversions of Calvinists.

1685, Oct. 18. REVOCATION OF THE EDICT OF NANTES. The exercise of the reformed religion in France was forbidden, children were to be educated in the Catholic faith, emigration was prohibited. In spite of this more than 50,000 families, including military leaders (Schomberg), men of letters, and a large part of the artisans of France, made their way to foreign countries. Their loss was a blow to the industry of the country, which perhaps hastened the approach of the revolution. The exiles found welcome in Holland, England (Spitalfields), Brandenburg, English North America, and South Africa. The Protestants of Alsace retained the freedom of worship which had been secured to them.

1688-1697. THIRD WAR. (War of the League of Augsburg).

Cause: After the extinction of the male line of the Electors Palatine in the person of the **Elector Charles** (d. 1685), whose sister was the wife of Louis XIV's brother, the Duke of Orléans, the king laid claim to the allodial lands of the family, a claim which he soon extended to the greater portion of the country. Another ground for war was found in the quarrel over the election of the Archbishop of Cologne, which Louis was resolved to secure for Von Fürstenberg, Bishop of Strassburg, in place of Prince Clement of Bavaria (1688).

Meantime the unfavorable impression produced throughout Protestant Europe by the revocation of the Edict of Nantes had contributed to the success of the plans of William of Orange, and on July 9, 1686, **The League of Augsburg,** directed against France, was signed by the emperor, the Kings of Sweden and Spain, the Electors of Bavaria, of Saxony, and the Palatinate. In 1688 occurred the revolution in England which placed William of Orange on the throne of that country, and added a powerful kingdom to the new foes of Louis. The exiled James II took refuge with the French monarch (court at St. Germain).

1688, Oct. Invasion and devastation of the Palatinate, by order of Louvois. The military successes of the French on the Rhine were unimportant, especially after 1693, when **Prince Louis of Bavaria** assumed the chief command against them.

1689, May 12. The Grand Alliance, between the powers who had joined the League of Augsburg and England and Holland (Savoy had joined the league in 1687). The principal scene of war was in the Netherlands.

1690, June 30. Battle of Fleurus, defeat of the Prince of Waldeck by Louis' general, Marshal **Luxembourg.** The French expedition to Ireland in aid of James had but a temporary success, and ended in defeat, 1690. French successes in Piedmont; Catinat reduced Savoy; defeat of Victor Amadeus at Staffarda.

1692, May. Defeat of the French fleet under Tourville by the English and Dutch at **Cap La Hogue.** The mastery of the sea passed from the French to the English. Death of Louvois.

July 24. Battle of Steinkirk (Steenkerken). Victory of Luxembourg over William III.

1693, June 30. Battle of Lagos; defeat of the British fleet by the French under Tourville.

July 29. Battle of Neerwinden. Victory of Luxembourg over William III, who in spite of his many defeats still kept the field.

In Italy Marshal Catinat defeated the Duke of Savoy at **Marsaglia. Rise of Prince Eugene of Savoy** (1663-1736).

1695. Death of Luxembourg, who was succeeded by the incapable Villeroy.

1695, Sept. Recapture of **Namur** by William III.

1696, May 30. Separate peace with Savoy at Turin. All conquests were restored to the duke (Pignerol and Casale), and his daughter married Louis' grandson, the Duke of Burgundy. Savoy promised to remain neutral.

1697, Sept. 30. TREATY OF RYSWICK between France, England, Spain, and Holland. (1) Confirmation of the separate peace with Savoy. (2) Restoration of conquests between France and England and Holland; William III acknowledged as King of England, and Anne as his successor, Louis promising not to help his enemies. (3) It was agreed that the chief fortresses in the Spanish Netherlands should be garrisoned with Dutch troops as a barrier between France and Holland. (4) France restored to Spain all places which had been "reunited" since the Treaty of Nimwegen, with the exception of 82 places, and all conquests. (5) Holland restored Pondichéry in India to the French East India Company and received commercial privileges in return.

Oct. 30. Treaty between France and the emperor (and empire). (1) France ceded all the "reunions" except Alsace, which henceforward was lost to the empire.

The Spanish Succession (1700)

Philip III, King of Spain

Anna, m. Louis XIII

Philip IV

Maria Anna m. Ferdinand III

Louis XIV = Maria Theresa

Charles II 1665-1700

Margaret (1) = Leopold I = (2) Claudia = (3) Eleanora Theresa   emperor   of Neuburg

Louis the dauphin

Maria Antoinette, m. Max. Emmanuel of Bavaria

Joseph I emperor 1705-1711

Charles VI emperor 1711-1740 ("Charles III" of Spain)

Philip of Anjou as King of Spain, **Philip V**

Joseph Ferdinand Electoral Prince of Bavaria d. 1699

(2) Strassburg was ceded to France. (3) France ceded Freiburg and Breisach to the emperor, and Phillipsburg to the empire. (4) The Duchy of Zweibrücken was restored to the King of Sweden, as Count Palatine of the Rhine. (5) Lorraine was restored to Duke Leopold (excepting Saarlouis). (6) The claims of Cardinal Fürstenburg to the archbishopric of Cologne were disavowed. (7) The Rhine was made free.

1701-1714. WAR OF THE SPANISH SUCCESSION. The family relations which led to the war will be made clear by the genealogical table.

Leopold I had, besides his daughter **Maria Antoinette,** two sons: by his second marriage, **Joseph I,** emperor from 1705-1711; by his third marriage, **Charles VI,** emperor from 1711-1740.

Charles II, King of Spain, was childless; the extinction of the Spanish house of Hapsburg in the near future was certain; hence the question of the Spanish succession formed the chief occupation of all the European cabinets after the **Treaty of Ryswick.** The question had two aspects: (a) The *legal,* according to which there were three claimants: (1) **Louis XIV,** as son of the elder daughter of Philip III and husband of the elder daughter of Philip IV. The solemn renunciations of both princesses were declared null and void by the *parlement* of Paris. (2) **Leopold I,** the representative of the German line of Hapsburg, as son of the younger daughter of Philip III, and husband of the younger daughter of Philip IV. Both princesses had expressly reserved their right of inheritance. (3) The **Electoral Prince of Bavaria,** as *great-grandson* of Philip IV, and *grandson* of the younger sister of the present possessor, Charles II. (b) The *political* aspect with regard to the balance of power in Europe; in consideration of which the naval powers, England and Holland, would not permit the crown of the great Spanish monarchy to be united with the French, or to be worn by the ruler of the Austrian lands. On this account Leopold I claimed the Spanish inheritance for his second son Charles only, while Louis XIV's claim was urged in the name of his second grandson, Philip of Anjou.

1698, Oct. 11. First Treaty of Partition. Spain, Indies, and the Netherlands to the Electoral Prince of Bavaria; Naples and Sicily, seaports in Tuscany, and the province of Guipuzcoa, to the dauphin; the Duchy of Milan, to Archduke Charles. The negotiations of the powers in regard to the succession, and the conclusion of a treaty of partition without the participa-

tion of Charles II, provoked that monarch. In order to preserve the unity of the monarchy, he made the Prince Elector of Bavaria, then seven years old, sole heir of the whole inheritance; a settlement to which the naval powers agreed.

1699, Feb. 6. Sudden death of the Prince Elector. New intrigues of France (Harcourt ambassador, Cardinal Portocarrero) and Austria at Madrid, while both parties were negotiating a new treaty of partition with the naval powers.

1700, Mar. 13. Second Treaty of Partition. Spain and the Indies to Archduke Charles; Naples and Sicily and the Duchy of Lorraine to the dauphin; Milan to the Duke of Lorraine in exchange. Finally Charles II, although originally more inclined to the Austrian succession, signed a new will, making Louis' grandson, Philip of Anjou, heir. Immediately afterward

1700, Nov. 1. Charles II died. Louis XIV soon decided to follow the will rather than the treaty with England. The Duke of Anjou was proclaimed as **Philip V,** and started for his new kingdom. (*Il n'y a plus de Pyrénées.*)

1701, Sept. 7. Grand Alliance of the naval powers with the Emperor Leopold I, for the purpose, at first, of securing the Spanish possessions in the Netherlands and in Italy for the Austrian house, while France allied herself with the Dukes of Savoy and Mantua, the Electors of Bavaria and Cologne. The other states of the empire, especially Prussia, joined the emperor. Portugal afterward joined the Grand Alliance, and in 1703 Savoy did likewise, deserting France. Three men were at the head of the Grand Alliance against France: **Eugene, Prince of Savoy,** imperial general; **Marlborough,** English general, formerly John Churchill; **A. Heinsius,** after the death of William III, 1702, pensionary of Holland. Spain, the real object of the war, had but little importance in the campaigns, the chief seats of war being Italy, the Netherlands, and Germany. Philip of Anjou was recognized in Spain as **King Philip V.** His strongest support was in Castile.

1701. Commencement of the war by Eugene's **invasion of Italy.** Victory over Catinat at Carpi, over Villeroy at **Chiara;** the latter **was** captured at Cremona (1702).

1702. Eugene and Vendôme fought **a** drawn **battle at Luzzara,** after which the French had the advantage in Italy until 1706.

1703. The Bavarians invaded **Tyrol, but** were repulsed. Eugene went **to** Germany, along the Rhine. Marlborough invaded the Spanish Netherlands. The Archduke Charles landed in Spain, and invaded Catalonia, where he established himself as Charles III. The English captured Gibraltar (1704).

1704, Aug. 13. BATTLE OF HÖCHSTÄDT AND BLENHEIM (BLIND-HEIM), (between Ulm and Donauwörth), Bavarians and French (Tallard) defeated by Eugene and Marlborough.

1706. Charles conquered Madrid but held it for a short time only.

May 23. VICTORY OF MARLBOROUGH AT RAMILLIES over Villeroy. Submission of Brussels, Antwerp, Ghent, Ostend, etc.

Sept. 7. VICTORY OF EUGENE AT TURIN, over Marsin and the Duke of Orléans with the help of the Prussians under Leopold of Dessau. Submission of all Lombardy. Charles III proclaimed at Milan. **The French excluded from Italy.**

1708, July 11. VICTORY OF MARLBOROUGH AND EUGENE AT OUDENARDE over Vendôme and the Duke of Burgundy. Siege and surrender of Lille.

Negotiations for peace. Demands of the allies: surrender of the Spanish monarchy to Charles of Austria, and of the border fortresses of the Netherlands to the Hollanders; restoration of all matters relating to the empire and the emperor to the state prescribed in the peace of Westphalia, i.e. the cession of Strassburg, Breisach, etc. England insisted on the recognition of Anne and the Protestant succession (p. 429) and the banishment of the Pretender. These terms Louis was willing to accept, but when the demand was added that he should drive his grandson from Spain with French weapons, it was too much. The negotiations were broken off, Louis made a successful appeal to the people of France, and the war was continued.

1709, Sept. 11. BATTLE OF MALPLAQUET. The French were again beaten by Eugene and Marlborough, but, by no means broken, retired in good order. The bloodiest battle of the war. The argument of "butchery" helped overthrow the Whigs in England. The allies lost 20,000 men. New approaches on the part of Louis. Capture of Douai, Mons, etc. (1710). In Spain Philip, by the aid of Vendôme, had the advantage of Charles. The Spanish people favored Philip. Renewal of the negotiations at Gertruydenburg. Louis offered to pay subsidized troops against his grandson. The allies demanded that he

should send his armies against Philip. Renewal of the war. Victories of Vendôme over the English (**Brihuega,** 1710) and the imperialists (**Villaviciosa,** in Spain).

1710, Aug. Fall of the Whig ministry in England, and accession of the enemies of Marlborough.

1711. Death of the Emperor Joseph, whereby Charles became heir of all the Austrian possessions, so that the monarchy of Charles V would have been restored had the Spanish inheritance also devolved upon him. These events completely altered all the political relations, in favor of Louis XIV. Marlborough removed from command, the Grand Alliance dissolved, preliminaries of peace between England and France. Death of the dauphin, of Adelaide of Savoy, her husband and their son, the Duke of Brittany.

1712. Victory of the French commander Villars at **Denain** over Lord Albemarle. Recapture of Douai, Le Quesnoy, and Bouchain. Opening of the **Congress at Utrecht.** Each of the allies presented his demands separately. Dissensions between the allies caused the conclusion of separate treaties of peace, which are comprehended under the name of the

1713, Apr. 11. TREATY OF UTRECHT.

(1) **England:** Recognition of the Protestant succession in England; confirmation of the permanent separation of the crowns of France and Spain. France ceded to England Newfoundland, Nova Scotia (Acadia), and Hudson Bay territory, but retained New France (Quebec); Spain ceded to England Gibraltar, the island of Minorca, and the *Asiento,* or contract for supplying the Spanish colonies with African slaves.

(2) **Holland:** Surrender of the Spanish Netherlands to the Republic of Holland, in order that they should be delivered to the Austrians, after the conclusion of a barrier treaty, in regard to the fortresses along the French border from Furnes to Namur, which were to be garrisoned by the Dutch. Lille restored to France. Demolition of the fortifications of Dunkirk.

(3) **Savoy** received the island of Sicily as a kingdom, and an advantageous change of boundary in upper Italy, renounced its claims upon Spain, reserving, however, its right of inheritance in case the house of Bourbon should become extinct.

(4) **Prussia** received recognition of the royal title, and possession of Neuchâtel and the upper quarter of Guelders. Prussia's claim upon the principality of Orange, on the Rhône, was transferred to France.

(5) **Portugal** obtained a correction of boundaries in South America.

Philip V (founder of the Spanish branch of the Bourbons) was recognized as King of Spain and the colonies.

Reservations in the peace: (1) for the emperor, the possession of the appanages of the Spanish monarchy, the Netherlands, Milan, Naples, Sardinia, but *not* Sicily; (2) for the empire the *status quo* of the Treaty of Ryswick, only.

1713. The emperor and the empire continued the war. Unsuccessful campaign of Eugene, who was wretchedly supported. Landau and Freiburg taken by Villars. After these losses the emperor concluded peace with France, in his own name at Rastadt, in that of the empire at Baden (in Switzerland).

1714, Mar.-Sept. TREATY OF RASTATT AND BADEN. Austria took possession of the Spanish Netherlands, after the barrier for Holland had been agreed upon, and retained Naples, Sardinia, and Milan, which she had already occupied. For the empire: ratification of the Treaty of Ryswick; the Electors of Bavaria and Cologne, who had been placed under the ban of the empire, were reinstated in their lands and dignities. Landau was left in the hands of France. No peace between Spain and the emperor, who did not recognize the Bourbons in Spain.

1715-1774. LOUIS XV, five years old, great-grandson of Louis XIV. **Philip, Duke of Orléans,** became regent during the minority of Louis XV (1715-1723), thus setting aside the will of Louis XIV. An attempt was made to use the higher nobility in government by means of councils, but this failed. Under the regent's favorite, **Cardinal Dubois,** a man of low birth who had risen through political skill, the foreign policy of Louis XIV was reversed. Alliance with England and Holland.

1718-1720. War with Spain (p. 450). By the Treaty of The Hague (Feb. 17, 1720) the emperor received Sicily, and Savoy received Sardinia in exchange. In domestic policy, increased religious toleration of Protestants and Jansenists.

1718-1720. Law's Mississippi scheme. In his financial distress the regent grasped at the dazzling plans of the Scotsman **John Law.** Royal bank, Company of the West, grant of Louisiana. Characteristic boom phenomena — rise in value of stock of the Mississippi Company, inflation (made worse by paper). Sudden collapse of the company bringing widespread disaster (1720). Law's boom, like most such speculative manias, left behind it some definite achievements — increased shipping, some colonization in Louisiana, private fortunes for those who had sold out in time. With the contemporary English **South Sea Bubble,** Law's scheme forms an introduction to modern speculative finance.

1723-1726. Administration of the Duke of Bourbon. Louis XV married (1725) the daughter of the deposed King of Poland, **Stanislas Lesczynski,** having broken off a projected marriage with the Infanta of Spain and sent her back, to the great indignation of Philip V. Louis was under the influence of his tutor, **Cardinal Fleury,** who replaced Bourbon and his favorite Prie, and banished them from court.

1726-1743. Administration of Fleury, generally peaceful, and marked by economic growth. Quarrels over the papal bull *Unigenitus,* marked by the government's abandonment of the Jansenists and their defense by the courts (*parlements*). Wave of religious revivalism, similar to Methodism in England (*convulsionnaires,* Archdeacon Pâris). Growth of deism among the literate classes.

1733-1738. France with Spain and Sardinia, took part in the **War of the Polish Succession** (p. 477) and occupied Lorraine (1733).

1740-1748. War of the Austrian Succession (p. 465). France supported the claims of the Bavarian elector and allied with Frederick the Great against Maria Theresa (1741). This involved France in conflict with England, especially in North America and India (pp. 516, 535).

1756-1763. The Seven Years' War (p. 466) in which France played a leading rôle, but this time on the Austrian side, against Prussia. The war overseas (p. 516) led to the loss of most of the French colonial empire.

After the **death of Fleury,** a series of administrations influenced by the royal mistresses, especially the **Marquise de Pompadour** (1745-1764), who helped make possible the Austrian alliance of 1756 (*The Diplomatic Revolution,* p. 467). Heavy expenditures, growth of luxury. The king, once *Louis le bien-aimé,* now hated. **Damiens,** who attempted to assassinate the king (Jan. 5, 1757), was tortured and killed. In spite of general failure in war, France added in this reign Lorraine (1766) and Corsica (1768). In his old age, Louis came under the influence of the politically least able of his mistresses, the plebeian Jeanne Vaubernier, by marriage with a superannuated courtier, **Comtesse du Barry.** Throughout the reign, quarrels with the *parlements*, especially that of Paris, which asserted a claim to something like a power of judicial review over the royal decrees. The *parlements* were abolished in 1771 by the chancellor, Maupéou, and a more simple and efficient system of courts set up, but the reform was very unpopular, and Louis XVI restored the *parlements* as one of the first acts of his reign. The crown was made still more unpopular by the affair of the *pacte de famine*, an attempted corner in the grain trade in which the king himself was implicated. Steady growth of a literature of attack on the government.

1774-1792. LOUIS XVI, grandson of Louis XV. The new king's personal morality and good will were neutralized by a lack of energy and understanding. As dauphin he had (1770) married **Marie Antoinette**, daughter of the Empress Maria Theresa. The queen, always unpopular with the anti-Austrians at court, was a proud and tactless woman, fond of dances, theaters, parties, and was easily made unpopular with the masses by the propaganda of the *philosophes* and their friends. ("Let 'em eat cake.") The scandal of the **diamond necklace** (1785) was especially disastrous to her reputation. She did much, by purely personal choices of favorites, to prevent any consistent or thoroughgoing reforms in French administration.

Yet the early years of the reign were marked by an effort, in keeping with the spirit of "Enlightened Despotism," to achieve reforms. **Turgot**, minister of marine and finance (1774–1776), by the *Six Edicts* made reforms in taxation, dissolved the old trade guilds, and tried to carry out the *laissez-faire* economics of the **physiocrats**, of whom he was one of the leading thinkers. He was dismissed, partly by court intrigue, partly by the opposition of the guilds, and his work largely undone. **Necker**, a Swiss banker, was minister of finances (1777–1781) and effected piecemeal reforms. The greatest achievements of Louis' reforming ministers were those of the **Comte de St. Germain** at the war office. The standing army was improved, especially in the artillery. St. Germain and his aids, **Guibert** and **Gribeauval**, did much to make the victories of the armies of 1792–1794 possible. **Maurepas** was the head of

the ministry, 1774–1781, and on his death was succeeded by the **Comte de Vergennes** (1781).

1778-1783. France intervened in the **War of American Independence** on the side of the colonists (p. 520). Her expenses in this war added disastrously to her financial deficit.

1781. Necker, dismissed from office, published a somewhat disingenuous *compte rendu* of the finances, the effect of which was to bring the deficit dramatically before the public. The next seven years were filled with the desperate expedients of a series of ministers to solve the financial problem. A solution was probably impossible without taxing heavily the *privilégiés* (nobles, state officials, clergy, and even certain commoners). These resisted the efforts of the government, no matter how well intentioned.

1783-1787. Calonne (minister of finances), a facile courtier, contracted an immense debt, but came in the end to the sensible decision to reform the land-tax thoroughly. He encountered resistance, and was forced out in favor of **Loménie de Brienne**. Meanwhile

1787, Feb. 22. An assembly of notables, a purely consultative body, with not very clear constitutional precedents, called to Versailles, was dissolved (May 25) without having achieved any real reform. Loménie de Brienne attempted to issue reform edicts on lines Calonne had worked out, but the *parlements*, headed by the *parlement* of Paris, refused to register them. The *parlement* of Paris was banished to Troyes (Aug. 14). Public opinion was in favor of the *parlement*, and its president, **d'Esprémenil**, became a hero, largely because he had defied the government. The *parlement* was recalled (Sept. 24), but continued its resistance when Brienne proposed new loans. In Jan. 1788, it presented a list of grievances, and was abolished in favor of a *cour plénière* (May 8). Louis and his advisers now decided to give in to many pressures, and summon the old mediaeval legislative body of the realm, the **Estates-General**, which had last met in 1614. In Aug. 1788, **Brienne** resigned and amid popular rejoicing **Necker** was recalled to arrange for the Estates. (*Cont. p.* **578.**)

4. THE IBERIAN PENINSULA

a. SPAIN

The **Peace of the Pyrenees** (1659) marked the end of the Spanish power in Europe, as it established the ascendancy of France. From that time on Spain, far from controlling affairs, came to be looked on more and more as decadent and as suitable spoil for the stronger states.

The Spanish Bourbons (1700-1868)

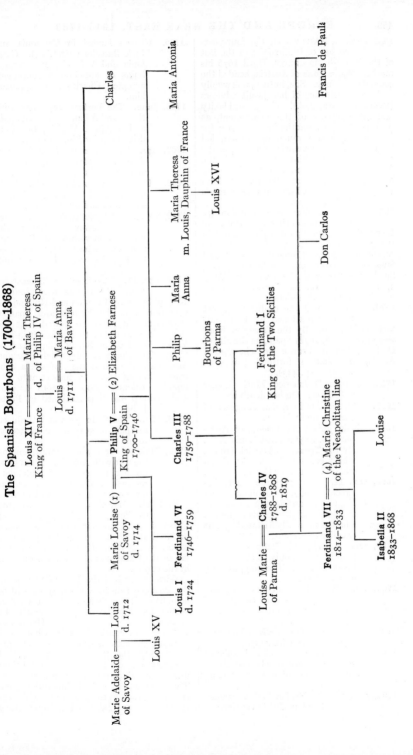

1665-1700. **CHARLES II,** the four-year-old son of Philip IV and the last of the Spanish Hapsburgs. Until 1676 his mother, **Marie Anne of Austria,** headed the council of regency. She, in turn, was wholly under the influence of her Jesuit advisers (**Everard Nitard,** *et al.*). The general laxity and incompetence of the government, as well as the queen-mother's preference for foreigners, aroused much opposition, led by **John Joseph of Austria** and some of the nobles. These ultimately effected the downfall of Nitard and even the departure of the queen-mother. Thereafter John Joseph controlled the king until the former's death in 1679.

1667-1668. **The War of Devolution** (p. 442), representing an attack by Louis XIV on the Spanish possessions in the Netherlands. He was forced, by the combined action of England, Holland, and Sweden, to restore most of his conquests, but by the **Treaty of Aix-la-Chapelle** (May 2, 1668) Louis retained twelve fortified places in Flanders.

1674. Spain joined the coalition against France occasioned by Louis' attack on Holland. By the **Treaty of Nimwegen** (Sept. 17, 1678) Spain, as the ally of Holland, lost to France Franche-Comté, Artois, and sixteen fortified places in Flanders (p. 443).

1680. Charles II married Marie Louise of Orléans. On her death he

1689. Married Marie Anne, daughter of the Elector Palatine.

1690. Spain joined the League of Augsburg (p. 443) against Louis XIV. By the **Treaty of Ryswick** (1697), which concluded the war, Spain was obliged to cede Haiti to France.

1698, Oct. 11. **First partition treaty** between England, Holland, and France, regarding the succession to Spain and the Spanish Empire. Charles, naturally irritated by this cavalier treatment,

1700, Oct. 3. Named **Philip of Anjou,** grandson of Louis XIV, heir to his dominions. The king, long ill, died on Nov. 1.

1700-1746. **PHILIP V,** the first Bourbon king, 17 years old at the time of his accession: a mediocre, irresolute, and pious ruler.

1701-1715. **WAR OF THE SPANISH SUCCESSION** (p. 445).

1703. The powers of the Grand Alliance against France proclaimed Archduke **Charles of Austria** as King of Spain.

1704, Aug. 4. **The British took Gibraltar,** which they have held ever since.

1705. Charles landed in Catalonia and took Barcelona (Oct. 14). Catalonia and Valencia, ever strongholds of anti-French sentiment, accepted Charles and supported him.

1706, June. **The Portuguese,** acting with the Grand Alliance, invaded Spain and occupied Madrid, but were driven out by Philip in Oct.

1707, Apr. The forces of the allies were defeated at **Almanza** by the Duke of Berwick, in Spanish service.

1709. The British seized **Minorca.** Philip was defeated by the Austrians at **Almenara** and **Saragossa,** and

1710, Sept. 28. Charles took **Madrid.** Before long, however, Philip and the French won victories at **Brihuega** and **Villaviciosa** (Dec. 10) and Charles was obliged to abandon Madrid again.

1713, Apr. 11. **The Treaty of Utrecht** (p. 446). Philip was recognized as King of Spain by England and Holland, on condition that the French and Spanish crowns should never be united. At the same time he ceded to his father-in-law, Victor Amadeus of Savoy, the island of Sicily. The English retained Gibraltar and Minorca and secured the *Asiento,* a contract allowing them to import into the Spanish colonies 4000 Negroes a year and to keep one ship stationed at Porto Bello.

1713, May. **The Salic law** was introduced in Spain to govern the succession to the throne.

1714, Mar. 6. **Treaty of Rastatt,** ending the war with Austria. Spain gave up her possessions in Flanders (henceforth the Austrian Netherlands), Luxemburg, and Italy.

Sept. 11. **Barcelona** finally capitulated to Berwick. The privileges of Catalonia and Valencia had already been declared abolished (1707). The provinces were now put under Castilian law and the use of the Catalan language was forbidden in the courts.

With the end of the War of Succession the **Bourbon rule in Spain** may be said to have begun, properly speaking. The rulers of the line soon proved themselves to be no more efficient than the later Hapsburgs and the court continued to be a hotbed of intrigue, dynastic and personal. On the other hand, the Bourbon kings regarded themselves as absolute rulers and did their utmost to reduce the old feudal privileges. They reorganized the administration (central secretariats in the place of the old commissions) and established a bureaucracy (intendants, corregidores). An impressive number of reforming ministers succeeded each other through the century, of whom may be mentioned Patiño, Ensenada, Aranda, Floridablanca, Campomanes, Jovellaños and Godoy. They succeeded in putting the finances on a sounder basis, in rebuilding the army and navy (introduction of conscription — every fifth man), and above all devoted themselves to economic development — road- and bridge-building, encouragement of industry and trade, establishment of technical schools, agricultural improvements, etc.

1714. **Philip married Elizabeth Farnese** of Parma, on the death of his first wife, Marie Louise of Savoy. Elizabeth was a handsome, alert, and very ambitious woman, who soon had the king wholly under her influence. With the aid of her adviser, Abbé (later Cardinal) **Giulio Alberoni**, an Italian of low extraction, she devoted herself to the problem of supplanting the Austrian power in Italy and providing Italian thrones for her children. Philip, on the other hand, appears to have hoped for many years to succeed to the French throne and did his utmost to undermine the position of the French regent, the Duke of Orléans. Thus Spain, though hardly a match for either power, antagonized both France and Austria at the same time.

1717. Philip secretly sent an expeditionary force, which seized Sardinia, and, later (July, 1718), Sicily also.

1718, Aug. 2. Conclusion of the **Quadruple Alliance** (England, France, Holland, and Austria) to counteract the attempts of Philip to overturn the peace settlements. The British fleet landed an Austrian force in Sicily, while the French invaded the Basque country and Catalonia. The war was concluded by

1720, Feb. 17. **The Treaty of the Hague,** by which Philip abandoned his Italian claims in return for an Austrian promise of the succession to Parma, Piacenza, and Tuscany for Charles, the eldest son of Philip and Elizabeth Farnese. At the same time the emperor gave up his claims to Spain. Savoy was given Sardinia in place of Sicily, which was turned over to Austria.

1721, June. Spain joined the alliance of England and France. Louis, son of Philip by his first wife, married Louise Elizabeth of Orléans (1722), while Louis XV of France was betrothed to a daughter of Philip and Elizabeth, who was then only five years old.

1724. **Abdication of Philip,** for reasons not clear. He was succeeded by his son

1724. **LOUIS I,** who, however, died in the same year. Philip then resumed the crown.

1725. The **Duke of Bourbon,** chief minister of Louis XV of France, eager for an heir to the throne, cancelled the engagement of the king to the girl-princess of Spain. In reply Philip allied himself to Austria (work of the adventurer, Baron de Ripperdá) by the **Treaty of Vienna** (Apr. 30, 1725). This alliance, in turn, provoked the **Treaty of Hanover** (Sept. 3) between England, France, Prussia, and Holland.

1727-1729. **War with England and France.** By the **Treaty of Seville** (Nov. 1729), England and France agreed to the Spanish succession in the Italian duchies.

1731. **Charles,** the son of Philip and Elizabeth, on the extinction of the Farnese family, succeeded to the Italian duchies. At the same time Spain recognized the **Pragmatic Sanction** of Charles VI (p. 463).

1733. First *pacte de famille* between France and Spain. Spain thereupon joined France in

1733-1738. **The War of the Polish Succession** (p. 477) against Austria. A Spanish force was sent to invade Lombardy, while another seized Naples and Sicily (1734). By the **Treaty of Vienna** (Nov. 13, 1738) Charles gave up Parma, Piacenza, and Tuscany and instead became King of the Two Sicilies.

1739-1741. **War of Jenkins' Ear,** with England (p. 434).

1740-1748. **War of the Austrian Succession** (p. 465). Spain took part in the war as the ally of France against Austria. By the **Treaty of Aix-la-Chapelle** (1748), Philip, the second son of Philip V and Elizabeth, was given the Duchies of Parma, Piacenza, and Guastalla, while his brother Charles retained Naples and Sicily. Thus the dynastic aspirations of their mother were realized.

1746-1759. **FERDINAND VI,** the second son of Philip V by his first wife. Ferdinand was a good but timid ruler, who did but little to impress his age or his people.

1754. Concordat with the Vatican. Thereby the Spanish Church became practically independent of Rome and was placed under the control of the government.

1756-1763. The Seven Years' War (p. 466). Spain at first remained neutral, though Spanish troops recovered **Minorca** (1756).

1759-1788. CHARLES III, son of Elizabeth Farnese and thitherto King of the Two Sicilies, which he now passed on to his son Ferdinand. Charles has been classified as one of the enlightened despots and he did, in fact, give considerable impetus to administrative and economic reform.

1761, Aug. 15. Second *pacté de famille* with France, against England. In this generally defensive arrangement the Bourbon states of Italy were included.

1762. Spain joined in the war against England. The British seized Cuba and the Philippines. By the **Treaty of Paris** (1763, Feb. 10) Spain recovered these possessions, but lost Minorca and Florida. In return for the loss of Florida, France ceded Louisiana to Spain.

1767, Mar. 1. Without warning or trial the king secretly expelled the Jesuits from Spain. Some 10,000 of them were deported to the Papal States.

1779, June. Spain joined France in the **War of American Independence** against England. The Spaniards seized Florida and Honduras and Minorca (1782), but failed to retake Gibraltar (1779–1783). By the **Treaty of Versailles** (Sept. 3, 1783), Spain retained both Minorca and Florida.

1788-1808. CHARLES IV, the son of Charles III, a well-intentioned but weak and undecided ruler. His ministers, **Floridablanca** and **Aranda**, made great efforts to shut out the teaching and influence of the French Revolution, and the Spanish court did its utmost to save the life of Louis XVI, but the queen effected the overthrow of Aranda and brought into power her favorite, **Manuel Godoy.**

1793, Mar. 7.   FRANCE DECLARED WAR ON SPAIN. Spain made an alliance with England (Mar. 13) and the Spaniards invaded Roussillon and Navarre. But in 1794–1795 the French took the offensive, invading Catalonia and Guipúzcoa. By the **Treaty of Basel** (June 22, 1795), the French returned their conquests and secured in return Santo Domingo. Godoy was given the title *Prince of the Peace.*

1796, Aug. 19. Treaty of San Ildefonso. Spain joined France in the war against England. Defeat of the Franco-Spanish fleet at **Cape St. Vincent** (Feb. 14, 1797). The British seized Trinidad.

1800, Oct. 1. Second Treaty of San Ildefonso. France secured Louisiana in return for a promise to enlarge Parma. By agreement of Jan. 20, 1801, Spain promised to detach Portugal from England, by force if necessary. This latter provision resulted in the **War of Oranges,** between Spain and Portugal (to June 6, 1801).

1802, Mar. Treaty of Amiens, between England, France, and Spain. The Spaniards secured Minorca but abandoned Trinidad.

1805, Jan. 4. Spain entered the **War of the Third Coalition** on the side of France. Defeat of the Franco-Spanish fleet at **Trafalgar** (Oct. 21, 1805). Growing opposition of the Spanish people to the disastrous Francophil policy of Godoy. Ferdinand, the heir to the throne, soon emerged as the leader of the opposition. ,

1807, Oct. 27. Treaty of Fontainebleau, between Napoleon and Spain. Portugal was to be divided between Charles IV and Godoy (who was to become Prince of the Algarves, under Spanish suzerainty). The French were to aid in the conquest, and a French army, under **Junot,** soon arrived in Spain. Invasion of Portugal and capture of Lisbon (Nov. 30, 1807).

1807, Mar. 17. Popular uprising against Godoy at Aranjuez. Charles thereupon abdicated (Mar. 19), but **Murat,** who arrived soon afterward at Madrid, induced the king to retract his abdication and persuaded both Charles and Ferdinand to meet Napoleon.

Apr. 30. The Bayonne Conference. Napoleon told Ferdinand to abdicate the throne he had just assumed. Then Charles was forced to abdicate in Napoleon's favor (May 10). Both princes were given estates in France and handsome pensions.

June 6.   JOSEPH, Napoleon's brother, became King of Spain.
(*Cont. pp.* 593, 643.)

b. PORTUGAL

The story of Portugal in this period parallels that of Spain. The period was one of steady decline economically and socially, accompanied by a growth of the royal power. The last Córtes was called in 1697. The nobility became more and more a court group, dependent on royal favor. The Church, too, was subjected to the state, though within the country the Church possessed great wealth and exercised immense influence.

1640-1656.   JOHN IV, first king of the house of Braganza. He was recog-

The House of Braganza (1640-1826)

John IV ══ Luisa Maria de Gúzman
1640–1656

Charles II ══ Catherine   Alfonso VI   Peter II ══ Maria Sophia
of England   1656–1667 (1683)   (1667) 1683–1706   of Neuburg

Maria Antonia ══ John V
d. of Emp. Leopold I   1706–1750

Ferdinand VI ══ Maria Barbara   Joseph I ══ Maria Anna
of Spain   1750–1777   of Spain

Maria I ══ Peter III
1777–1816   1786

John VI
1816–1826

---

nized almost at once by France and Holland, but Spain fostered a plot of Portuguese nobles against him. This was discovered and the leaders executed. Hostilities with Spain continued in desultory fashion. In 1644 the Portuguese, supported by England and France, took the offensive and invaded Spain (victory of Montijo). This brought a suspension of operations for some years.

1654. The Dutch were finally driven from Brazil, where they had established themselves during the Spanish period.

1656-1667. AFONSO VI, a frivolous, profligate, and vicious young man, during the first period of whose reign his mother, Luisa María de Guzmán, served as regent. In these years hostilities with Spain were reopened. The Spaniards were defeated at Elvas (Jan. 14, 1659), and, when they attempted to invade Portugal (1662) were again overwhelmed (battle of Ameixal, June 8, 1663) in a series of Portuguese victories in 1664-1665.

1661. Charles II of England married Catherine, the daughter of John IV, thus preparing the way for ever closer relations between England and Portugal.

1667. Peter (Pedro), the brother of Afonso, led the opposition to the outrageous conduct of the king. He set himself up as regent and exiled Afonso to the Azores (d. 1683). Peter's rule was more respectable and enjoyed wide popular support.

1668, Feb. 13. Conclusion of peace with Spain, through the mediation of Charles II of England. Spain at last recognized Portuguese independence.

1683-1706. PETER II ruled as king after the death of Afonso. His reign was memorable for the conclusion of

1703, Dec. 27. THE TREATY OF ME-THUEN, with England (concluded by Lord Methuen, the British ambassador). By the agreement English textiles were to be freely admitted into Portugal and England was to admit Portuguese wine at a greatly reduced tariff. The treaty resulted in rapid domination of Portuguese trade by the British.

1704. Invasion of Portugal by the Spanish under Berwick, the consequence of Portugal's participation in the War of the Spanish Succession on the side of England. The British sent a force to Lisbon, the Spaniards were driven out and the Portuguese in turn invaded Spain, taking Madrid (June 28, 1706).

1706-1750. JOHN V, the son of Peter II, a profligate, extravagant, and bigoted ruler, during whose reign the court became another Versailles (construction of the Mafra palace), filled with mistresses and favorites.

1707, Apr. Defeat of the Portuguese by Berwick at Almanza. Thereafter the Portuguese played no important part in the war.

1750-1777. JOSEPH I, during whose entire reign the government of the country was in the hands of the Marquis de Pombal (Sebastião José de Carvalho e

Mello, who became Marquis of Pombal only in 1770), the most remarkable statesman of modern Portuguese history. Pombal was a ruthless and heartless dictator, but at the same time a man affected by the French philosophy of the enlightenment. He devoted himself to breaking the power of the privileged nobility and even more of the Church. On the other hand, he reformed the finances and the army, encouraged industry and trade (establishment of trade companies with monopolistic powers), tried to revive agriculture (silk-raising), and did much to develop primary and technical education.

1755, Nov. 1. THE GREAT EARTHQUAKE AT LISBON, which was accompanied by fire and by flood of the Tagus. Tens of thousands lost their lives in the great disaster. Lisbon was destroyed, with many of its treasures. The city was rebuilt under Pombal's energetic direction.

1758, Sept. Conspiracy of the Tavoras, a plot by a group of nobles against the king and more especially against the all-powerful minister. The leaders, among them members of the highest aristocracy, were tortured and executed.

1759, Sept. 3. Expulsion of the Jesuits, who were deported to the Papal States. This was a direct result of the Tavora conspiracy, in which some Jesuits were involved. Pombal thus set the example for Spain and other states and in fact took a leading part in inducing the pope to abolish the Society of Jesus (1773).

1761. During the Seven Years' War, the Portuguese stood by England. The result was an invasion by Spanish and French forces, but this was repulsed with British aid (Dec. 1762).

1774. Insanity of Joseph I, and regency of his wife, **Maria Anna.** She began gradually to reduce the power of Pombal.

1777-1816. MARIA I, the daughter of Joseph I, queen. She married her uncle, Peter, who assumed the title of king as **Peter III,** but who died in 1786. Under Maria the nobility began to recover its position. Pombal was exiled (d. 1782), but his reform policies were continued at a reduced pace.

1792. Insanity of Maria and regency of her son John. John, ardently supported by the clergy, undertook a drastic repression of all revolutionary agitation and thought.

1801, Feb.-Sept. War of the Oranges, with Spain, resulting from the bargain made between Spain and France. After a Spanish invasion the Portuguese made peace. By the **Treaty of Madrid** (Sept. 29) Portugal paid a heavy indemnity and renounced the treaties with England.

1807, Oct. 27. Treaty of Fontainebleau between France and Spain, envisaging the **partition of Portugal.** The provinces of Entre-Douro and Minho (with Oporto) were to go to Louis, King of Etruria, who was to become King of Northern Lusitania. Alentejo and Algarve were to go to Godoy as Prince of the Algarves; Beira, Tras-ós-Montes, and Estramadura were to be disposed of later.

Nov. 30. Lisbon was taken by a French army under Junot, assisted by the Spanish. The Portuguese royal family thereupon fled to Brazil.

(*Cont. pp.* 593, 648.)

5. ITALY AND THE PAPACY

a. ITALY (GENERAL)

Italy remained, during the late 17th and in the 18th century, a mere geographical expression, politically divided and for the most part under foreign rule. But the cultural decadence of the 17th century gave way in the 18th to a remarkable flowering which again made Italy an important factor in European art and thought and contributed much to the general European enlightenment. In music Italy was outstanding. **Amati** and **Stradivarius** built the finest stringed instruments; the **opera** (dating from 1600) was brought to a high stage of development by **Monteverdi** (1567-1643),

Pergolesi (1710-1736), **Cimarosa,** and **Paisiello.** Two great schools of music at Venice and Naples. **Lorenzo Bernini** (1598-1680), architect and sculptor, was one of the leading artists of the Baroque period, which preceded the Rococo of the 18th century and the classical revival represented by **Canova** (1757-1822). In painting, **Giambattista Tiepolo** (1693-1770) for a time brought Venice a final burst of glory. The **Academy of Arcadia** (1692) started a widespread vogue of the conventional and artificial in literature, which, however, was counterbalanced by the comedies of **Goldoni** (1707-1793) and the serious patriotic drama of **Vittorio Alfieri** (1749-1803). But Italy was pre-eminent also in the fields of social and physical science. Pietro Giannone (1676-1748) created a profound stir with his anti-clerical *Istoria civile del regno di Napoli* (1723); Antonio Genovesi (1712-1769) was an outstanding physiocrat; another distinguished economist was Pietro Verri (1728-1797); Giambattista Vico (1668-1744), with his *Scienza Nuova* (1725), laid the basis of the modern philosophy of history; while Cesare Beccaria (1738-1794) in his *Dei delitti e delle pene* (1764) founded the modern science of penology. In the natural sciences Spallanzani (1729-1799) made fundamental contributions to the study of digestion, while Galvani (1737-1798) and Volta (1745-1827) were in the front rank among the pioneers of electricity.

b. THE PAPACY

Most of the popes of the later 17th and 18th centuries were altogether worthy men, but the currents of the time were against the papacy. By attempting to remain neutral in the great conflicts between the Bourbons and the Hapsburgs, the popes sacrificed the support of both. Furthermore, the Church before long became divided on the question of Jansenism (from Cornelius Jansenius, Bishop of Ypres, who died in 1638, leaving a famous book, *Augustinus*, published in 1640. In this he emphasized inner regeneration rather than external reorganization of the Church, as represented by the Jesuits). Jansenism and Jesuitism soon came into conflict and the papacy was sapped in the process. The enlightenment of the 18th century completed the development and by the time of the French Revolution the papacy appeared as an ineffectual and outworn, as well as superfluous institution.

1644-1655. INNOCENT X (Giambattista Pamphili), a pope who was entirely under the control of his sister-in-law, Olympia Maidalchini, whose machinations brought about almost complete financial collapse. The pope denounced the Treaty of Westphalia because of the abolition of bishoprics, etc., but the protest was of no effect. By the bull *Cum occasione impressionis libri* (May 31, 1653) the pope condemned five propositions in the work of Jansenius, thus initiating the Jansenist controversy.

1655-1667. ALEXANDER VII (Fabio Chigi), an honest and cultured, but apathetic pontiff, who left the conduct of affairs to his nephew, Flavio Chigi. Beginning of friction with Louis XIV over the prerogatives of the Church.

1667-1669. CLEMENT IX (Giulio Rospigliosi), elected by the French influence. He attempted to mediate between Jesuits and Jansenists, but died before much could be achieved.

1670-1676. CLEMENT X (Cardinal Altieri), regarded as pro-Spanish. He disapproved of the French alliance with the Turks and did what he could to support the war of the Hapsburgs against the enemy.

1676-1689. INNOCENT XI (Benedetto Odescalchi), one of the outstanding popes of the period. He undertook a much-needed financial reorganization of the papacy, refused to practice nepotism, enforced regulations to improve the morality of the clergy. At the same time he financed the Austrians in their campaigns against the Turks. The conflict with Louis XIV came to a head when the French ruler called a church assembly at St. Germain (1682) which adopted the four articles: (1) Sovereigns are not subject to the pope in temporal matters; (2) a general council is superior to a pope; (3) the power of the pope is subject to the regulations of a council and a pope cannot decide contrary to the rules of the Gallican Church; (4) decisions of the papacy are not irrevocable. In reply to these articles the pope refused to invest as bishops any French clerics who had taken part in the assembly. Ultimately 35 French bishoprics were vacant. Further friction developed. The pope protested against the suppression and expulsion of the Huguenots and actually approved the expedition of William III to England, as part of an anti-French policy.

1689-1691. Alexander VIII (Pietro Ottoboni).

1691-1700. INNOCENT XII (Antonio Pignatelli), another able pope. By the bull *Romanum decet pontificem* (1692) he definitely limited the number of offices that could be held by relatives of the pope, thus putting an end to nepotism in its worst form. He also checked the sale of offices. In 1697 he made peace with France, winning a substantial victory. Louis XIV abrogated the four articles of 1682, probably in order to win support in the matter of the Spanish Succession.

1700-1721. CLEMENT XI (Giovanni Francesco-Albani), an upright priest, who, though he inclined toward France, attempted to maintain neutrality in the Bourbon-Hapsburg struggle. The Austrians therefore ignored papal claims. In the course of the war they occupied Parma and Piacenza, marched through the Papal States and conquered Naples. In

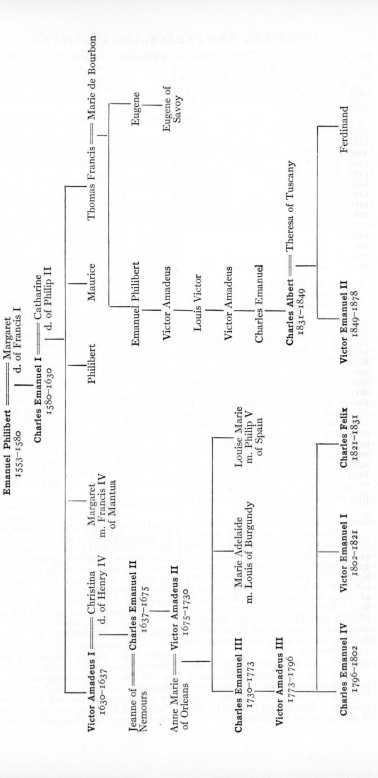

The House of Savoy (1553-1878)

1709 the pope was obliged to recognize Charles as King of Spain. But Clement's pontificate was noteworthy chiefly for the renewed condemnation of Jansenism, which had made extraordinary progress in France. The bull *Unigenitus* (Sept. 8, 1713) was a landmark in the controversy.

1721-1724. Innocent XIII (Michelangelo Conti), a kind but ineffectual pope, who was followed by two other unimportant pontiffs,

1724-1730. Benedict XIII (Cardinal Orsini-Gravosa), and

1730-1740. Clement XII (Lorenzo Corsini).

1740-1758. BENEDICT XIV (Prospero Lambertini), a charming, learned, and serious-minded pope. He was much influenced by the enlightenment in Europe, was a friend of Voltaire and Montesquieu, did much to encourage agriculture and trade. His policy was to seek a compromise with the absolute rulers, whose efforts to establish national churches had so much weakened the papacy. Conclusion of concordats with Naples (1741) and Spain (1753) were important steps in this direction, though they cost the papacy far-reaching concessions.

1758-1769. CLEMENT XIII (Card. della Torre de Rezzonico), a pope elected through the efforts of the Jesuits (*Zelanti*), but who proved too weak and mild to save them. The Jesuits had become unpopular as a result of Jansenist attacks, and because of their interference in politics, their engagement in commercial and industrial enterprise, etc. Their expulsion from Portugal (1759) and France (1762) set the ball rolling, and the next pope,

1769-1774. CLEMENT XIV (Lorenzo Ganganelli), was unable to resist the pressure of the Bourbon governments. By the breve *Dominus ac redemptor noster* (July 21, 1773) the Society of Jesus was ordered dissolved.

1775-1799. PIUS VI, during whose pontificate the papacy felt the full force of the revolutionary doctrine. The pope tried to deter Joseph II from his anti-clerical policy, but was soon confronted with the radical anti-clericalism of the French Revolution. As a result the French armies invaded papal territory (1796) and, after a short truce, intervened in Rome to set up the revolutionary Roman Republic (1798). The pope was taken off to southern France (Valence), where he died in the next year. (*Cont. pp.* 595, 663.)

c. SAVOY (SARDINIA)

The beginning of the period was one of almost complete eclipse for Savoy, where the regency of Duchess Christina for her son, Charles Emanuel II, formed a long interlude of conflict between the French and Spanish factions and brought on a decisive weakening of the ducal power. In the 18th century, however, Savoy re-emerged as a strong military state (the Prussia of Italy).

1638-1675. CHARLES EMANUEL II, who came of age in 1648, submitted to the domination of his mother until her death in 1663. His reign was scarred by the horrible massacres of the Waldenses (1655) which stirred the indignation of Europe.

1675-1730. VICTOR AMADEUS II. His mother, Jeanne de Nemours, acted as regent not only until the young duke attained his majority, but until 1684. She continued the Francophil orientation of Savoyard policy. In 1681 Louis XIV appropriated Casale as part of his reunion plan.

1685. Further persecution of the heretics, at the behest of Louis XIV.

1690. The duke at last made a break in the pro-French policy and joined the League of Augsburg against the French. But in 1696, hoping to make better terms with Louis, he reversed himself and received Pinerolo in return. The French and Savoyard forces obliged the powers of the league to evacuate Italy and agree to its neutralization for the duration of the war.

1701, Apr. War of the Spanish Succession (p. 445). Victor Amadeus stuck by the French connection and allowed the French to occupy Milan and Mantua. But once again the duke changed sides, joining the Grand Alliance in 1703. As a result the French, under Vendôme, overran Savoy in 1704, but the Austrians, under Prince Eugene of Savoy, relieved the situation in 1705. During the following year the French again invaded and besieged Turin until, in Sept., they were again driven out by Prince Eugene. Occupation of Milan by the Austrians and Savoyards (Sept. 24). This practically ended the war in Italy.

1713. By the Treaty of Utrecht, Victor Amadeus was awarded Sicily as his share of the Spanish spoils. At the same time he assumed the royal title.

1717. A Spanish raid on Sicily resulted in war (p. 451) and a new peace settlement, by which

1720. Victor Amadeus gave up Sicily to Austria and received in exchange the island of Sardinia. Henceforth he was *King of Sardinia*.

1730-1773.   CHARLES EMANUEL III,
king. He joined France and
Spain in the War of the Polish Succession,
in the hope of driving the Austrians out
of Italy. By the **Treaty of Vienna** (Oct. 3,
1735), however, his possessions remained
unchanged.

1742-1747. Savoy sided with Austria in
the War of the Austrian Succes-
sion, and by the **Treaty of Aix-la-Chapelle**
(1748) was rewarded with that part of the
Duchy of Milan which lay on the west of
the Ticino.

Savoy-Piedmont had relatively little
share in the intellectual and artistic life
of Italy, being essentially a military state.
The army, however, was not nearly strong
enough to resist the storms of the French
Revolution.

1773-1796.   VICTOR AMADEUS III.
Strongly anti-revolutionary by
temperament and policy, the king in 1792
joined Austria in the war against France,
rejecting French offers of Lombardy. His
territories were soon overrun by the French
and

1796. Napoleon's appearance in Italy
sealed the fate of the kingdom.
The armies of the king were quickly defeated and, by the **armistice of Cherasco**
(Apr. 28) the king was obliged to abandon
the Austrian alliance. Napoleon's defeat
of the Austrians led to a fundamental re-
making of the whole Italian situation (p.
585).   *(Cont. pp.* 585, 650.)

d.   NAPLES

The Spanish rule continued in Naples
until the War of the Spanish Succession
(p. 445). During this conflict

1707. The Austrians occupied Naples, and

1713. By the **Treaty of Utrecht,** Spain
ceded to Austria Sardinia and
Naples, while Sicily passed to Savoy. In
1720 Austria exchanged Sardinia for Sicily,
but, after the War of the Polish Succession

1735. Austria ceded Naples and Sicily to
the Spanish Bourbons, on con-
dition that they should never be
united with Spain as one crown.

1735-1759.   CHARLES IV (son of Philip V
of Spain), King of Naples and
Sicily. His reign was one of reform and
enlightenment, guided by **Bernardo Tanucci.** Restriction of feudal privilege, reform of finance and taxation, reorganization
of prisons, reduction of church wealth and
power (**Concordat of 1741**). Naples the
musical and intellectual center of Italy.
Excavation of Herculaneum (1738) and dis-

covery of the temples at Paestum (1752)
paved the way for neo-classicism in art
(Winckelmann, etc.).

1759-1825.   FERDINAND I, the third son
of Charles, succeeded to the throne
when his father was called to assume the
Spanish crown. Ferdinand was only nine
years old, and continued under the influence of Tanucci until the latter's fall in
1771. By that time his wife, **Maria Carolina** (daughter of Maria Theresa) already
dominated him. She, in turn, followed the
lead of an English adventurer, **Sir John
Acton,** who was busily engaged in rebuilding
the Neapolitan army and navy. The result
of Maria Carolina's policy was to break
down the Spanish influence and to direct
the king toward the Austrian connection.
(Cont. pp. 586, 650.)

e.   OTHER STATES

VENICE continued to fall into ever
deeper decline, the old aristocratic rule becoming ever more unsuited to the demands
of the European world. In international
affairs Venice became entirely devoted to
peace and neutrality, and only in the wars
with the Turks was there some reflection
of earlier glory.

1645-1669.   The Candian War (p. 424),
during the earlier part of which
the Venetians won resounding naval victories at the Dardanelles (under Grimani and
Mocenigo). The war ultimately centered
on the siege of Candia (1658-1669). France
came to the aid of Venice and the Venetians
themselves put up a stout defense, under
Francesco Morosini. Finally, however,
the Venetians were obliged to yield. By
the peace settlement they lost Candia
(Crete).

1684. Venice joined with Austria and Poland in the war against the Turks
(p. 483). In 1685 Morosini began the conquest of the Morea, which was completed
in 1687. The Venetians even captured
Athens (explosion of the ammunition stores
in the Parthenon). By the **Treaty of Karlowitz** (p. 484), the Venetians retained the
Morea.

1718. By the **Treaty of Passarowitz** (p.
484), the Venetians, who had
joined in the Turkish War at the side of
the Austrians, lost the Morea. Thenceforth
Venice retained only the Ionian Islands and
the Dalmatian coast. Politically Venice
stagnated, while artistically it remained
one of the most active centers in Europe.

MILAN remained under Spanish rule
until, by

1713. The Treaty of Utrecht it passed to Austria. Mantua was incorporated with the Duchy of Milan, after the last Gonzaga had, in 1701, sold it to Louis XIV. Parma and Piacenza changed hands several times during the 18th century.

1731. On the extinction of the Farnese family, the duchies were given to Charles, the son of Philip V of Spain and his second wife, Elizabeth Farnese. In 1733 (War of the Polish Succession) Charles conquered Naples and Sicily, and these territories were awarded him in the peace settlement. In return he abandoned Parma and Piacenza to Austria.

1748. As a result of the War of the Austrian Succession, Maria Theresa ceded Parma and Piacenza to Philip, the younger brother of Charles of Naples. Philip ruled until 1765 and was succeeded by his son Ferdinand, who married a daughter of Maria Theresa and generally followed the lead of the Vienna government.

The GENOESE REPUBLIC, like the Venetian, remained independent, though constantly exposed to encroachment by Savoy, France, and Austria.

1730. Revolt of Corsica against Genoese rule. After a long and variable struggle, during which a German adventurer, Baron Neuhof of Westphalia, appeared for a time as King Theodore I (1736), the Genoese called upon the French for assistance. After many engagements (especially against Pasquale Paoli, the Corsican leader), the French subjugated the island, which the Genoese ceded to them (1768).

TUSCANY (Florence) continued under the decadent and unedifying rule of the Medici (Cosimo III, 1670-1723; Gian Gastone, 1723-1737) until the extinction of the line in 1737.

1737-1745. Francis of Lorraine, Grand Duke of Tuscany. He became the husband of Maria Theresa and, after his election as German emperor, turned over Tuscany to his second son

1745-1790. Leopold I, who devoted himself to the thoroughgoing reform of his dominion. The administration was remade, serfdom abolished, trade and industry encouraged. Tuscany became perhaps the best ruled and most progressive region of Italy.   (*Cont. p.* 650.)

6. THE SWISS CONFEDERATION

The century from 1650 to 1750 was one of stagnation and decline in Switzerland. The confederation continued to be the loosest kind of union, the cantons divided against each other by religious issues. Within the cantons patrician oligarchies became dominant and ruled in a reactionary fashion. The main occupation of the Swiss continued to be fighting, and mercenaries were engaged by foreign states (especially France) by the tens of thousands. Only after 1750 was there a renaissance, which brought Switzerland to the threshold of the French Revolution.

1653. A peasant revolt, led by Nicholas Leuenberg, brought the insurgents to the very gates of Bern, but was suppressed with the aid of other cantons.

1655. Proposals for the establishment of a more centralized state, put forward by Zürich, were defeated by the Catholic cantons.

1656. THE FIRST VILLMERGEN WAR, in which Bern and Zürich were pitted against the Catholic cantons. The Protestants were defeated at Villmergen (Jan. 24) and complete control of religious affairs had to be left to the individual members of the confederation.

1663. Renewal of the alliance with France, enabling Louis XIV to draw as many mercenaries as he chose from the cantons. The alliance was opposed by Zürich and some of the Protestant cantons, and in the ensuing period there was much friction between France and Switzerland over the question of service with France against Protestant states, over the reception of Huguenots expelled from France, etc.

1663-1776. During more than a century there was no meeting of the federal Diet, indicating the almost complete collapse of the federal connection.

1678. Franche-Comté, hitherto under federal protection, was annexed to France.

1693. The Protestant cantons, incensed by French use of mercenaries against the Dutch, agreed to supply soldiers to the Dutch, and later to the English. Thereupon the Catholic cantons made an agreement to supply men to the Spaniards. In the War of the Spanish Succession (p.

445) the Swiss fought by the thousands on both sides.

1707. A popular insurrection at Geneva led by Peter Fatio, was suppressed with the aid of the Bern and Zürich oligarchies.

1708. The house of **Hohenzollern** succeeded to the principality of Neuchâtel. Louis XIV was prevented by the war from pressing the claims of the Prince of Conti.

1712. THE SECOND VILLMERGEN WAR, another conflict between Catholics and Protestants. This time the Bernese won a decisive victory, again at Villmergen (July 25), after which the dominance of the Protestant cantons was firmly established.

1723. Revolt of Abraham Davel in the Vaud, against the oppressive rule of Bern. The whole affair was a harebrained undertaking, inspired by noble motives. After taking Lausanne, Davel was easily outmaneuvered, captured, and executed.

1725. Renewal of the treaty with France, but this time with the abstention of the Protestant cantons.

1734, 1737. Further uprisings in Geneva led to some constitutional revision in the popular direction.

With the middle of the century there came a distinct economic improvement in Switzerland, marked by the expansion of industry. This brought with it a falling-off of the mercenary system, but also a rise of the-middle class and an intellectual renaissance: Zürich (with **Johannes J. Bodmer,** 1698-1783, **Albrecht von Haller,** 1708-1777, and **Johannes C. Lavater,** 1741-1801) became an important center of German literature and thought; Geneva (with **Rousseau,** 1712-1778, **Voltaire,** resident in the vicinity after 1755, etc.) became a refuge for advanced thinkers of the French school. The **Helvetic Society** (founded 1762) was an exuberant organization devoted to the new ideas.

1776. The whole confederation once more allied itself with France, but Swiss mercenaries in French service fell to less than 10,000.

1789-1792. In the first years of the French Revolution the Swiss oligarchies were strongly hostile and seriously considered intervention by the side of Austria and Prussia. In the end they determined on neutrality, though pursuing at home a repressive policy (crushing of unrest in the Vaud by the Bern government).

1792, Dec. 5. A revolutionary coup at Geneva put the government in the hands of the popular party. Thenceforth the developments in France were faithfully mirrored in Geneva.

1793. The French Republic annexed the Bishopric (not the town) of Basel.

1797, Oct. Napoleon, following his successes in Italy, annexed the Valtelline and Chiavenna to the Cisalpine Republic.

Dec. Revolutionists seized the town of Basel.

1798, Jan. 23. The French declared the Vaud free from Bernese rule and organized it as the **Lemanic Republic.**

Feb. 9. France decreed the establishment of a **Helvetic Republic.** The move was inspired by the Helvetic Committee in Paris, a revolutionary group headed by **Frédéric-César de La Harpe,** 1754-1838, a Vaudois whose great aim was the liberation of his homeland from the hated Bernese aristocracy, and by **Peter Ochs,** a less high-minded radical. The new republic was to be organized along French lines: excepting for territory annexed to France, all the cantons, together with the subject territories, were to be made into 23 cantons, the whole bound together by a centralized government consisting of an elected chamber of deputies (eight members from each canton) and a senate (four from each canton). At the head was to be a directory of five.

The French move finally convinced the Swiss oligarchies of the danger. Bern declared war and the Bernese defeated the French army under Brune at **Laupen** (Mar. 5). But another Bernese force was vanquished on the same day by Gen. Schauenberg. Bern surrendered and was sacked. Indemnity of 17 million francs.

Apr. Five Forest (Catholic) cantons revolted against the French, under Aloys von Reding. They won some successes, but then made peace, accepting the Helvetic constitution on condition that the French should not interfere or occupy territory of the five cantons.

Apr. 26. Geneva was annexed to France.
(*Cont. pp.* 586, 666.)

7. GERMANY

1658-1705. LEOPOLD I, the son of Ferdinand III. After 1663 a permanent Diet at Regensburg, consisting of representatives of the 8 electors, the 69 secular princes, and the imperial cities; an ineffectual legislature, often degenerating into a squabble for precedence ("a bladeless knife without a handle"). *Corpus Catholicorum* and *Corpus Evangelicorum,* the corporate organizations of the Catholic and Protestant states, the latter being the most important. This organization of the Protestant states had existed, in fact, since the latter half of the 16th century, but it was legally recognized in the Treaty of Westphalia, which decreed that in the Diet matters relating to religion and the Church should not be decided by a majority, but should be settled by conference and agreement between the Catholic and Protestant states, as organized corporations.

1661-1664. War against the Turks (p. 483).

1666. Settlement of the contested **succession in Cleve-Jülich:** Cleve, Mark, and Ravenstein, as well as half of Ravensberg, were given to Brandenburg; afterward the whole of Ravensberg in place of Ravenstein.

1668. The empire joined in the **War of Devolution,** against Louis XIV of France (p. 442), and likewise in

1674. The **Dutch War,** siding with the Dutch against the ambitious aggression of the French king.

1682-1699. THE LIBERATION OF HUNGARY as a result of a prolonged war against the Turks. Hungary had undergone a marked decline in the mid-century. The greatness of Transylvania came to an end with George II Rakoczi (1648-166c) whose ambitious dynastic policy (alliance with Sweden; attempt to secure the Polish crown) had led to trouble with the Turks, who finally drove him from the throne. In that part of Hungary ruled by the Hapsburgs there continued to be persecution of the Protestants and, under Leopold I, extension of the royal power, confiscation of estates of opponents, etc. This led to much unrest (insurrection of Imre Tökölli), but the reconquest of the country entirely transformed the situation. For details of the **war against the Turks** see p. 483. After the siege of Vienna (1683), the imperial generals, Charles of Lorraine and Louis of Baden, advanced into Hungary. Buda was taken (1686) and, after the **victory at Mohacs** (1687) the Turks were driven beyond the Danube. Eugene of

Savoy's great **victory at Zenta** (1697) brought the war to a close. By the **Treaty of Karlowitz** (Jan. 26, 1699) the Hapsburgs secured all Hungary excepting the Banat of Temesvar. In the meanwhile the Hungarian Diet had (1687) fixed the succession to the throne in the male line of the Hapsburgs. In view of the general devastation and depopulation the government began an extensive policy of colonization (1690: Serbs in southern Hungary; 1720-1800: large-scale settlement of Germans). The reconquered territories were awarded in large part to German commanders and soldiers and during the whole century following the reconquest there was a steady increase of royal power and an ever greater concentration of authority in the Vienna government bureaus. The ancient constitution of Hungary subsisted, but it fell more and more into neglect. The higher aristocracy tended to devote itself to the pleasures of the Vienna court, and the opposition of the gentry (concentrated in the local assemblies or comitats) was not sufficient to stem the tide of absolutism.

1688-1697. War of the League of Augsburg, against Louis XIV (p. 443). This war distracted the empire to such an extent that the reconquest of Hungary was delayed for a decade.

During this period several of the German princes were elevated in rank:

1692. Hanover became an electorate (the ninth).

1697. Augustus II, Elector of Saxony, was elected King of Poland on the death of John Sobieski. He thereupon adopted the Catholic faith.

1701, Jan. 18. FREDERICK III, Elector of Brandenburg (1688-1713), with the consent of the emperor, assumed the title of *King of Prussia* (*König in Preussen*) (Frederick I) and crowned himself at Königsberg.

1701-1714. War of the Spanish Succession (p. 445). The emperor, though he and his allies failed to prevent the succession of the Bourbon house in Spain, nevertheless effected the breakup of the Spanish dominions in Europe. By the final settlement Austrian power and influence replaced that of Spain in Italy, and Austria also succeeded to the Spanish Netherlands (henceforth the Austrian Netherlands).

1703-1711. Revolt of the Hungarians under **Francis II Rakoczi.** This was the result of widespread discontent with the policy of the Vienna govern-

The German Hapsburgs (1556-1835)

ment. Ultimately the movement became a real social upheaval. Rakoczi soon controlled most of Hungary and even began to threaten Vienna. But his followers accepted the **Peace of Szatmar** (May 1, 1711), by which the emperor promised respect for the Hungarian constitution and redress of grievances. Rakoczi himself refused these terms and took refuge in Turkey (d. 1735).

1705-1711. JOSEPH I, son of Leopold.
He was succeeded by his brother,

1711-1740. CHARLES VI.

1713-1740. FREDERICK WILLIAM I, son of Frederick I, King of Prussia, by wise economy, military severity, and the establishment of a formidable army, laid the foundation of the future power of Prussia. Maintenance of a standing army of 83,000 men, with a population of two and a half million inhabitants. **Prince Leopold of Anhalt-Dessau** (*der alte Dessauer*).

1714-1718. War of the Turks with Venice, and after 1716 with the emperor (p. 484). The seizure of Sardinia (1717) and Sicily (1718) by Spain, where Elizabeth of Parma, the second wife of Philip V, and her favorite, the minister and Cardinal **Alberoni**, were planning to regain the Spanish appanages lost by the **Treaty of Utrecht,** brought about the

1718, Aug. 2. Quadruple Alliance for the maintenance of the **Treaty of Utrecht,** between France, England, the emperor, and (1719) the Republic of Holland. After a short war and the fall of Alberoni, who went to Rome (d. 1752), the agreements of the Quadruple Alliance were executed in 1720: (1) **Spain** evacuated Sicily and Sardinia, and made a renunciation of the appanages forever, in return for which the emperor recognized the Spanish Bourbons. (2) **Savoy** was obliged to exchange Sicily for Sardinia. After this time the **Dukes of Savoy** called themselves **Kings of Sardinia.**

The Emperor Charles VI was without male offspring. His principal endeavor throughout his whole reign was to secure the various lands which were united under the scepter of Austria against division after his death. Hence he established an order of succession under the name of the **Pragmatic Sanction,** which decreed that: (1) the lands belonging to the Austrian Empire should be indivisible; (2) that in case male heirs should fail, they should devolve upon Charles' daughters, the eldest of whom was **Maria Theresa,** and their heirs according to the law of primogeniture; (3) in case of the extinction of this line the daughters of

Joseph I and their descendants were to inherit.

To secure the assent of the various powers to the Pragmatic Sanction was the object of numerous diplomatic negotiations. The Hungarian Diet accepted it in 1723. A special agreement between Austria and Spain (1725), in regard to this measure, produced the **Alliance of Herrenhausen,** in the same year, between England, France, and Prussia in opposition. Prussia soon withdrew from the alliance and joined Austria by the **Treaty of Wusterhausen.** The alliance between Austria and Spain was also of short duration.

1733-1735. WAR OF THE POLISH SUCCESSION, after the death of Augustus II.

Cause: The majority of the Polish nobles, under the influence of France, elected **Stanislas Lesczynski,** who had become the father-in-law of Louis XV, king, a second time. Russia and Austria induced a minority to choose **Augustus III,** Elector of Saxony (son of Augustus II), and supported the election by the presence of troops in Poland. France, Spain, and Sardinia took up arms for Stanislas.

The seat of war was at first in Italy, where Milan, Naples, and Sicily were conquered, and the Austrians lost everything except Milan; and afterward on the upper Rhine, where the old **Prince Eugene** fought unsuccessfully, and Francis Stephen, Duke of Lorraine, the future husband of **Maria Theresa,** alone upheld the honor of the imperial arms. Lorraine occupied by the French. Kehl captured. Preliminaries of peace (1735), and, after long negotiations,

1738, Nov. 18. TREATY OF VIENNA: (1) **Stanislas Lesczynski** made a renunciation of the Polish throne, receiving as compensation the duchies of Lorraine and Bar, which at his death were to devolve upon France. Stanislas died 1766. (2) The Duke of Lorraine, **Francis Stephen,** received an indemnification in **Tuscany,** whose ducal throne had become vacant by the extinction of the family of Medici, 1737. (3) **Austria** ceded Naples and Sicily, the island of Elba and the Stati degli Presidi to Spain as a *secundogeniture* for Don Carlos, so that these lands could never be united with the crown of Spain, receiving in exchange Parma and Piacenza, which Don Carlos had inherited in 1731 upon the death of the last Farnese, his great-uncle. (4) **France** guaranteed the Pragmatic Sanction.

1736-1739. Unsuccessful war with the **Turks** (p. 484).

The Hohenzollern House (1415-1840)

1740, May. Death of **Frederick William I** of Prussia.

1740-1786. **FREDERICK II, THE GREAT** of Prussia.

1740, Oct. With the death of **Charles VI**, the male line of the Hapsburgs was extinct.

1740-1780. **MARIA THERESA**, Queen of Bohemia and Hungary, Archduchess of Austria, etc., married **Francis Stephen** of the house of Lorraine, Grand Duke of Tuscany (co-regent).

1740-1748. **WAR OF THE AUSTRIAN SUCCESSION:**
Cause: The following claimants for the Austrian inheritance appeared: (1) **Charles Albert**, Elector of Bavaria, who had never recognized the Pragmatic Sanction, a descendant of Anna, the eldest daughter of Ferdinand I. He based his claim upon the marriage contract of Anna, and upon the will of Ferdinand I, whereby the Austrian inheritance was (he claimed) secured to the descendants of Anna, in case the *male* descendants of her brother should become extinct. (The *original* will, however, read, in case the *legitimate* descendants of her brother became extinct.) (2) **Philip V**, King of Spain, relying on a treaty between Charles V and his brother Ferdinand, on occasion of the cession of the German lands, and upon a reservation made by Philip III in his renunciation of the German lands. (3) **Augustus III** of Saxony, the husband of the *eldest* daughter of Joseph I.

The claims advanced by **Frederick II** to a part of Silesia, and his desire to annex the whole of Silesia to his kingdom, the rejection of the offer which he made at Vienna to take the field in favor of Austria if his claims were recognized, brought about, before the commencement of hostilities by the other claimants, the

1740-1742. **FIRST SILESIAN WAR.**
Legal claims of Prussia to a portion of Silesia: (1) The principality of Jägerndorf was purchased in 1523 by a younger branch of the electoral line of Hohenzollern, and the future acquisition of Ratibor and Oppeln secured at the same time, by an hereditary alliance. In 1623 Duke John George was placed under the ban by the Emperor Ferdinand II, as an adherent of Frederick V, the Elector Palatine, and in spite of the Peace of Westphalia, neither he nor his heirs had been reinstated. (2) The Elector Joachim II had made an hereditary alliance in 1537 with the Duke of Liegnitz, Brieg, and Wohlau, which Ferdinand I had forbidden as King of Bohemia and feudal superior of the duke. After the extinction of the ducal house

(1675) Austria took possession of the inheritance. In 1686 Frederick William, the Great Elector, renounced the Silesian duchies, in return for the cession of the circle of Schwiebus. The latter, however, was secured to Austria by a secret agreement with the prince elector, and was restored by him, as Elector Frederick III in 1695.

1740. Occupation of Silesia by Frederick's troops. Capture of Glogau.

1741, Apr. 10. Prussian victory of **Mollwitz.**

May. Secret **alliance of Nymphenburg** against Austria concluded by France, Bavaria, and Spain, afterward joined by Saxony, and lastly by Prussia. The allied French (Belle-Isle) and Bavarian army invaded Austria and Bohemia. Prague taken in alliance with the Saxons. Charles Albert caused himself to be proclaimed archduke in Linz, while Frederick II received homage in Silesia. Charles Albert was elected emperor in Frankfurt as

1742-1745. **CHARLES VII.** Meantime **Maria Theresa** had gone to Hungary. **Diet at Pressburg** (1741); enthusiasm of the Hungarian nobility which was guaranteed immunity from taxation; two armies raised; alliance concluded with England. An Austrian army conquered Bavaria where Maria Theresa received the homage of Munich; a second besieged the French in Prague.

1742, May 17. The victory of Frederick at **Czaslau** and **Chotusitz**, and Maria Theresa's desire to rid herself of a dangerous enemy led to the separate

1742, June and July. Treaty of Breslau and Berlin between Austria and Prussia: (1) **Frederick** withdrew from the alliance against Maria Theresa. (2) **Austria** ceded to Prussia upper and lower Silesia and the county of Glatz, retaining only the principality of Teschen, and the southwestern part of the principalities of Neisse, Troppau, and Jägerndorf, the Oppa forming the boundary. (3) **Prussia** assumed the debt upon Silesia held by English and Dutch creditors, to the amount of 1,700,000 rix dollars.

Austria prosecuted the war against the allies with success, driving them entirely out of Bohemia (1742), and Bavaria (1743); the Pragmatic army (English, Hanoverians, Hessians), under King George II, defeated the French in the

1743, June 27. Battle of **Dettingen.** The Emperor Charles VII was a refugee in Frankfurt.

These Austrian successes and the treaties with Sardinia and Saxony (1743) made the King of Prussia anxious about his new acquisitions. He concluded a *second* alliance with Charles VII and France, and began the

1744-1745. SECOND SILESIAN WAR, by forcing his way through Saxony with 80,000 men and invading Bohemia. He took Prague, but, deserted by the French, was soon driven back into Saxony (1744).

1744. East Friesland, upon the extinction of the reigning house, fell to Prussia.

1745, Jan. Alliance between Austria, Saxony, England, and Holland against Prussia. The French and Bavarians took Munich. Charles VII died (1745, Jan.). His son **Maximilian Joseph** concluded the

Apr. Separate **Treaty of Füssen,** with Austria. (1) **Austria** restored all conquests to Bavaria. (2) The **Elector of Bavaria** surrendered his pretensions to Austria and promised Francis Stephen, the husband of Maria Theresa, his vote at the imperial election.

The French under Marshall **Maurice of Saxony** (*Maréchal de Saxe*, son of Augustus II and the Countess Aurora of Königsmark) defeated the Pragmatic army in the

1745, May 11. BATTLE OF FONTENOY (Irish Brigade), and began the conquest of the Austrian Netherlands.

Frederick the Great defeated the Austrians and Saxons under Charles of Lorraine in the

June 4. Battle of Hohenfriedberg, in Silesia, and the Austrians alone in the

Sept. 30. Battle of Soor, in northeastern Bohemia.

By the election of the husband of Maria Theresa as emperor, the

1745-1806. HOUSE OF LORRAINE-TUSCANY acceded to the imperial throne in the person of the emperor,

1745-1765. FRANCIS I.

After a victory of the Prussian general, Leopold von Dessau, over the Saxons at **Kesseldorf,** Dec. 15, the

1745, Dec. 25. TREATY OF DRESDEN was concluded between Prussia and Austria (Saxony). (1) Ratification of the **Treaty of Breslau and Berlin** in regard to the possession of Silesia. (2) **Frederick II** recognized Francis I as emperor. (3) **Saxony** paid Prussia one million rix dollars.

After the flower of the English army had been recalled to England, where they were needed in the contest with the "young pre-

tender" (p. 435) **Marshal Saxe** obtained at **Raucoux** (1746) a second victory over the allies of Austria and completed the conquest of the Austrian Netherlands.

At the same time, the naval war between France and England, and the war in Italy between Spain, France, and Austria, were carried on with varying fortune. Sardinia had concluded peace with Austria as early as 1743. At last the Empress of Russia, **Elizabeth** (p. 481), joined the combatants as the ally of Austria and sent an army to the Rhine. Congress, and finally,

1748, Oct. TREATY OF AIX-LA-CHA-PELLE. (1) Reciprocal restoration of all conquests. (2) Cessions of Parma, Piacenza, and Guastalla to the Spanish infant, Don Philip, making the second *secundogeniture* of the Spanish Bourbons in Italy. The following guaranties were given: that Silesia should belong to Prussia; that the Pragmatic Sanction should be sustained in Austria; that the house of Hanover should retain the succession in its German states and in Great Britain.

Change in the relations of European states induced by the rise of Prussia to the rank of a great power. Envy between Prussia and Austria; the latter seeing a disgrace in the loss of Silesia to a smaller power, and intriguing for the recovery of the lost province. Thus began the

1756-1763. THIRD SILESIAN, or SEVEN YEARS' WAR.

Cause: Before the Treaty of Aix-la-Chapelle Maria Theresa had concluded a **defensive alliance** with Frederick's personal enemy, Elizabeth, Empress of Russia (May, 1746). Secret articles of this treaty provided for the reunion of Silesia with Austria under certain specified conditions. In Sept. 1750, George II of England, moved by anxiety for his principality of Hanover, signed the main treaty, the secret articles being excepted. Saxony (minister, Count Brühl) signed the treaty unconditionally. **Prince Kaunitz** (until 1753 Austrian ambassador in France, then chancellor of the empire in Vienna) succeeded in promoting a reconciliation between the cabinets of Versailles and Vienna, and securing the Marquise de Pompadour in favor of an Austrian alliance. Formation of a party inimical to the Prussian alliance at the French court.

Maria Theresa and Kaunitz induced England to conclude a new subsidy treaty with Russia in 1755. In June of the same year, however, hostilities broke out between England and France in North America without any declaration of war. Dreading a French attack upon Hanover, George II concluded, in January, 1756, a treaty of neutrality with Frederick at Westminster, which caused a rupture between England and Russia. Kaunitz made skillful use of the indignation at Versailles over the **Treaty of Westminster.** In May, 1756, conclusion of a defensive alliance between France and Austria. In June, 1756, war broke out between France and England, in Europe.

Frederick, well informed concerning the alliances of the powers, and knowing that Russia and France were not in condition to take the offensive against him in 1756, decided to take his enemies by suprise.

1756, Aug. He invaded Saxony with 67,000 men and took Dresden (Sept. 2). On Oct. 1 he defeated the Austrians at **Lobositz,** and on Oct. 15 the Saxons (18,000) surrendered at **Pirna.**

1757, Jan. 10. War was declared on Frederick in the name of the empire. Hanover, Hesse, Brunswick, and Gotha, however, continued in alliance with Prussia. Conclusion of an agreement between Austria and Russia (Jan.) concerning the partition of the Prussian monarchy. Offensive treaty between Austria and France (May 1).

Frederick invaded Bohemia in four columns, and won a

May 6. Victory over the Austrians at **Prague.** Death of Schwerin. Frederick besieged Prague and attacked Daun, who attempted to relieve the city. But Frederick was defeated in the

June 18. Battle of **Kolin,** as a result of which he had to evacuate Bohemia.

July 26. Victory of the French over the British at **Hastenbeck,** which led to the capitulation of the British army (Duke of Cumberland) at **Kloster-Zeven** (Sept. 8). The French occupied Hanover, though the treaty was rejected by the British government.

July 30. Battle of Grossjägerndorf, in which the Russians, under Apraxin, after invading East Prussia with a large force, defeated the Prussians, under Lehwald. Nevertheless the Russians withdrew from East Prussia and did not exploit their success. But the Swedes in the meanwhile began to occupy Pomerania, promised them in return for participation in the war.

Nov. 5. BATTLE OF ROSSBACH, one of the most spectacular victories of Frederick. The French, under Soubise, had joined the imperial army, under Duke Frederick William, for the purpose of liberating Saxony. But Frederick surprised them on the march and completely over-

whelmed them. He then led his victorious army into Silesia, where the Austrians had just won a victory over the Duke of Brunswick-Bevern at Breslau (Nov. 22).

Dec. 5. Battle of Leuthen. Frederick completely defeated the Austrians under Charles of Lorraine and Daun.

1758. Frederick campaigned in Moravia, but failed to take Olmütz. In the west, Ferdinand of Brunswick drove the French back over the Rhine and defeated them in the

June 23. Battle of Crefeld. But the greatest Prussian victory of the year was Frederick's defeat of another invading Russian army in the

Aug. 25. Battle of Zorndorf. But this was counterbalanced by the

Oct. 14. Battle of Hochkirch. The Austrians had invaded Lusatia and Frederick had hurried to the relief of his brother Henry. Daun defeated the Prussians at Hochkirch, but was not able to drive Frederick out of Saxony and Silesia.

1759. The French resumed the offensive in the west, and, under the Duke of Broglie, defeated Ferdinand of Brunswick at Bergen, near Frankfurt (Apr. 13). Later in the year Ferdinand made good this defeat by his victory over the French in the

Aug. 1. Battle of Minden.
The Russians once again advanced into Germany and defeated the Prussian general, Wedell, at **Kay** (July 23). Frederick was unable to prevent their union with the Austrians under Laudon and suffered a major reverse in the

Aug. 12. BATTLE OF KUNERSDORF. The Austrians thereupon captured Dresden. On Nov. 20 Daun surrounded and captured 13,000 Prussians under Fink at **Maxen.**

1760, June 23. The Prussians, under Fouqué, were defeated and captured by the Austrians in the battle of **Landshut,** but

Aug. 15. Frederick's victory over Laudon in the battle of **Liegnitz** (Pfaffendorf) enabled him to prevent the union of the Austrians and Russians. The latter, under Tottleben, nevertheless

Oct. 9-12. Surprised and burned **Berlin,** retreating only as Frederick hurried to the relief.

Nov. 3. Victory of Frederick over Daun at Torgau.

1761. Frederick established a defensive position opposite the united Austrians and Russians near Bunzelwitz. But on Oct. 1 the Austrians took Schweidnitz and the Russians occupied Kolberg before the year was out (Dec. 16). By this time Frederick, deprived of the English subsidies by the accession of George III (1760), was in great distress. His position was saved by

1762, Jan. 5. The death of Elizabeth of Russia. Her successor, **Peter III,** was an admirer of Frederick and very soon concluded the

Mar. 16. Truce of Stargard, which was followed by the

May 5. Treaty of St. Petersburg. Russia restored all conquests and both parties renounced all hostile alliances. The defection of Russia brought with it also the

May 22. Treaty of Hamburg between Sweden and Prussia, which restored the *status quo ante bellum.* The alliance between Prussia and Russia was soon broken off by the deposition of Peter III (July 9). His successor, **Catherine II,** recalled her troops from Frederick's army; nevertheless their inactivity upon the field contributed to the

July 21. Victory of Frederick at Burkersdorf (Reichenbach) over the Austrians (Daun).

After Prince Henry in the

Oct. 29. Battle of Freiburg had defeated the Austrians and the imperial forces, and the preliminaries of the **Treaty of Fontainebleau** between England and France had made it certain that the French armies would be withdrawn from Germany, Austria and Prussia concluded the

1763, Feb. 15. TREATY OF HUBERT(U)SBURG: (1) Ratification of the Treaties of Breslau and Berlin, and that of Dresden, i.e. Prussia retained Silesia. (2) Prussia promised her vote for the Archduke Joseph at the election of the King of Rome. Saxony (restoration to the *status quo*) and the empire were included in the peace.

Frederick's endeavors to heal the wounds inflicted by the war upon his kingdom; distribution of the magazine stores; remission of taxes for several provinces; establishment of district banks, of the Bank (1765) and the Maritime Company (1772) at Berlin. Afterward, however, introduction of an oppressive financial administration; tobacco and coffee were made government monopolies. Drainage of the marshes along the Oder, Werthe, and Netze. Canal of Plauen, Finow, and Bromberg. Reform of the jurisdiction. Codification of the common law by grand chancellor von Carmer, a part of which was published in 1782.

1765-1790. JOSEPH II, emperor, for the Austrian lands co-regent only with his mother, **Maria Theresa,** until 1780, and without much influence.

1778-1779. WAR OF THE BAVARIAN SUCCESSION. Cause: Extinction of the electoral house of Bavaria with Maximilian Joseph (1777). **Charles Theodore,** Elector Palatine, the legal heir of the Bavarian lands, as head of the house of Wittelsbach, and in consequence of various treaties, was persuaded by Joseph II to recognize certain old claims of Austria to Lower Bavaria, and a part of the Upper Palatinate. **Treaty of Vienna** (1778, Jan.): Occupation of Lower Bavaria by Austrian troops. Charles Theodore was childless; his heir presumptive was Charles Augustus Christian, Duke of the Palatinate of Zweibrücken (Deux-ponts). **Frederick II** opened secret negotiations with this wavering and irresolute prince through Count Eustachius von Görz and encouraged him, under promise of assistance, to make a formal declaration of his rights against the Austrian claims. Saxony and Mecklenburg, also incited by Frederick, protested as heirs presumptive of a part of the Bavarian inheritance. As direct negotiations between Austria and Prussia were without result, Joseph and Frederick joined their armies, which were already drawn up face to face on the boundary of Bohemia and Silesia.

Saxony allied with Prussia. No battle in this short war. Frederick and Prince Henry invaded Bohemia (July, 1778). Impossibility of forcing Joseph from his strong position along the upper Elbe, or of getting around it. The armies maintained their positions of observation so long that want began to make itself felt. In the autumn Prince Henry retired to Saxony, Frederick to Silesia. Unimportant skirmishes along the frontier. A personal correspondence between Maria Theresa and Frederick, commenced by the former, led in the following spring, with the help of Russian and French mediation, to a truce and a congress, and soon after to the

1779, May 13. TREATY OF TESCHEN. (1) The Treaty of Vienna with Charles Theodore was abrogated. Austria retained only the district of the Inn, in Bavaria, i.e. the part of Lower Bavaria between the Inn, Salzach, and Danube. (2) Austria agreed to the future union of the margravates of Ansbach and Baireuth with the Prussian monarchy. (3) Saxony obtained some hitherto disputed rights of sovereignty and nine million rix dollars; Mecklenburg the *privilegium de non appellando.*

1780-1790. JOSEPH II. Period of his reign alone and of his attempts at reform. The prudent government of Maria Theresa (d. 1780), with its carefully matured scheme of reform, was succeeded by the essentially revolutionary reign of Joseph II, whereby the ancient forms were shaken to their foundations, and their substance, reluctant and stiff from lack of change, forcibly subjected to experiments made in sympathy with the enlightenment of the century. Joseph II is the best representative of the contradictions of the 18th century, and of its philanthropy and its devotion to right, and again of its severity and lack of consideration, where there was question of executing some favorite theory. Filled with dislike of the clergy and the nobility, and entertaining the ideal of a strong, centralized, united state, Joseph pursued his reforms with the purpose of breaking the power of the privileged classes mentioned above, of destroying all provincial independence, and of establishing unity in the administration (centralization). Despite all his failures, despite the fact that, with few exceptions his reforms did not outlive him, Joseph's reign regenerated the Austrian monarchy, lending it mobility and vitality.

1781, Oct. 13. Edict of tolerance. Within eight years 700 monasteries were closed and 36,000 members of orders released. There still remained, however, 1324 monasteries with 27,000 monks and nuns. For those which remained a new organization was prescribed. The connection of the ecclesiastical order with Rome was weakened, schools were established with the property of the churches, innovations in the form of worship were introduced, nor did the interior organization of the Church escape alteration. Futile journey of Pope **Pius VI** to Vienna (1782), undertaken to prevent these changes. Reform of jurisdiction. The feudal burdens were reduced to fixed norms, and attempts were made to abolish completely personal servitude among the peasants.

1781. Disputes between Joseph and the Dutch; the emperor arbitrarily annulled the **Barrier treaties** (p. 447). He demanded that the Scheldt, which had been closed by the Treaty of Westphalia to the Spanish Netherlands, in favor of the Dutch, should be opened. Finally, after four years of quarreling, French mediation brought about the **Treaty of Versailles** (1785).

Joseph withdrew his demands in consideration of ten million florins.

Joseph attempted to improve the legal system of the empire. His encroachments in the empire. Violent proceedings in the case of the **Bishop of Passau** (1783).

1783. The endeavors of Frederick the Great to conclude a union of German princes (1783), which should resist the encroachments of the emperor, and to strengthen Prussia in her political isolation by a "combination within the empire," were at first but coldly supported by his own ministers and the German princes. Frederick's plan was not taken into favor until news was received of

1785. Joseph II's plan of an exchange of territory, according to which Charles Theodore was to cede the whole of Bavaria to Austria, and accept in exchange the Austrian Netherlands (Belgium), excepting Luxemburg and Namur, as the Kingdom of Burgundy. France maintained an attitude of indifference. Russia supported the project and endeavored by persuasion and threats to induce the heir of Bavaria, the Count Palatine of Zweibrücken, to consent to the scheme. The latter sought help from Frederick the Great, who, a year before his death (d. 1786, Aug. 17), succeeded in forming the

1785, July. League of the German Princes between Prussia, the Electorate of Saxony, and Hanover, which was afterward joined by Brunswick, Mainz, Hesse-Cassel, Baden, Mecklenburg, Anhalt, and the Thuringian lands, directed against Joseph's scheme.

Opposition to Joseph's reforms in the Austrian Netherlands and in Hungary. The removal of the crown of Hungary to Vienna produced so great a disturbance that the emperor yielded and permitted its return. The revocation of the constitution of Brabant caused a revolt in the Belgian provinces (1789). War with the Turks (p. 485). **Death of Joseph II** (1790). His brother became

1790-1792. LEOPOLD II, emperor. He suppressed the Belgian insurrection, but restored the old constitution and the old privileges. A conference at **Reichenbach** prevented a war with Prussia, which (Jan. 31, 1790) had concluded a treaty with the Turks, in order to procure more favorable conditions for the latter from Austria and Russia (p. 485).

(*Cont. pp.* 581, 667.)

The House of Vasa (1523–1818)

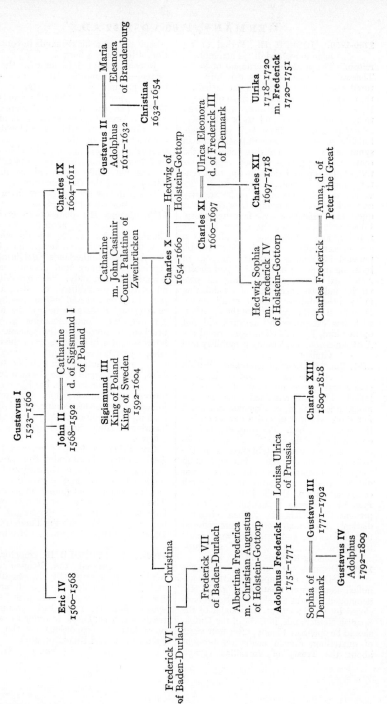

8. SCANDINAVIA

a. SWEDEN

Gustavus Adolphus and his able lieutenants and successors took advantage of the Thirty Years' War to lift Sweden to the rank of a first-class power, with dominance over the whole Baltic area. But the greatness of Sweden was to be short-lived. During the later 17th century the royal power was greatly strengthened, but nevertheless Sweden lacked the resources to compete with the neighboring powers, like Prussia and Russia. The attempts of the Swedish kings to establish control in Poland and the extravagant schemes of Charles XII soon reduced Sweden to the position of a second-class power.

1654. Queen Christine, the daughter of Gustavus Adolphus, abdicated the throne and spent the rest of her life as a converted Catholic, devoted to religion and art. She left the throne to her cousin, Charles Gustavus of Pfalz-Zweibrücken, son of a sister of Gustavus Adolphus, who became

1654-1660. CHARLES X GUSTAVUS. His reign was pre-eminently one of military activity, devoted to

1655-1660. The First Northern War. Charles declared war on Poland on the pretext that John Casimir (of the house of Vasa) refused to acknowledge him. Actually Charles' purpose was to extend the Swedish possessions on the southern Baltic coast.

1656. The Swedes, allied with the Elector of Brandenburg (**Treaties of Königsberg and Marienburg**) invaded Poland and won a great **battle at Warsaw.** Thereupon Russia, Denmark, and the empire declared war on the Swedes, and Brandenburg soon deserted the Swedish cause to join the coalition (Poland recognized the elector's sovereignty over East Prussia).

1657. The Swedes were driven out of Poland, but

1658. Charles twice invaded Denmark. The valiant defense of Copenhagen saved the Danish monarchy from annihilation and the death of Charles facilitated the

1660, May 3. Treaty of Oliva: John Casimir of Poland abandoned his claims to the Swedish throne and ceded Livonia to Sweden. By the **Treaty of Copenhagen** Denmark surrendered to Sweden the southern part of the Scandinavian Peninsula, but retained Bornholm and Trondheim. The **Treaty of Kardis** (1661) between Sweden and Russia re-established the *status quo ante bellum.*

1660-1697. CHARLES XI.

1672-1679. Sweden took part in the Dutch War as an ally of France (p. 442), but the Swedes achieved little. The invasion of Brandenburg resulted in the

1675, June 28. Battle of Fehrbellin, in which the Swedes were defeated by the forces of the Great Elector. A severe blow to Swedish military prestige. The elector then invaded Swedish Pomerania, took Stettin, Stralsund, and Greifswald; but, by the **Treaty of St. Germain-en-Laye** (1679), Sweden, through her French ally, was able to recover all that had been lost.

In the internal history of Sweden this reign was marked by the establishment of an **absolutist government.** The council was reduced to impotence, and the Estates were kept in submission.

1680. Under the pressure of the king the Estates passed a law by the terms of which all earldoms, baronies, and other large fiefs should revert to the crown. This wholesale confiscation of estates dealt a severe blow to Swedish aristocracy.

1697-1718. CHARLES XII. He ascended the throne at the age of 15, but was soon to prove himself one of the military geniuses of modern times. His reign was taken up almost entirely by the

1700-1721. GREAT NORTHERN WAR, which, in a sense, was one aspect of the general war in Europe during the first fifteen years of the century.

The **Northern War** was caused by the common opposition of Russia, Poland, and Denmark to the Swedish supremacy in the Baltic region. **Peter of Russia** was firmly determined to make his country a naval power, and to get possession of the harbors of the Baltic; **Augustus II,** Elector of Saxony and King of Poland, had a scheme for the reunion of Livonia with Poland; the **King of Denmark,** besides desiring general weakening of Sweden, resented Swedish support of the Duke of Holstein-Gottorp in his struggle with Denmark. A secret alliance between the three sovereigns was concluded in the fall of 1699, and next year the war opened with an invasion of Schleswig by the Danes, and of Livonia by

Augustus' Saxon troops. Unexpected landing of Charles XII of Sweden in Zeeland; he threatened Copenhagen and extorted from the Danes the

1700, Aug. 18. Treaty of Travendal: (1) Indemnification of the Duke of Holstein. (2) Denmark promised to abstain from hostilities against Sweden for the future.

Meantime the Saxons were besieging Riga (in Livonia), and the Russians Narva (in Ingermanland).

Nov. 30. Landing of Charles XII with 8000 men and decisive **victory of Narva** over the Russians. Instead of pursuing the Russians, Charles turned west, relieved Riga (1701, June 17) and then invaded Poland.

The following six years were spent by Charles in an effort to defeat Augustus II. After a series of victories over the Poles and Saxons, Charles invaded Saxony and compelled Augustus to sign the

1706, Sept. 24. Treaty of Altranstädt: (1) Augustus abdicated the Polish crown and recognized the previously elected **Stanislas Lesczynski** (the candidate of the pro-Swedish party) as King of Poland. (2) Augustus broke his alliance with the Russian Tsar.

1707, Sept. After this, Charles took the field against Peter, who had employed the interval in making conquests and establishing his power in the Baltic (St. Petersburg founded at the mouth of the Neva in 1703, Narva captured in 1704), and in forming a trained and well-supplied army.

1708. Charles advanced in the general direction of Moscow, and then suddenly turned south into the Ukraine where his secret ally, the Cossack hetman, **Mazeppa,** had promised him a general anti-Russian uprising. The uprising failed to materialize, and the Swedish army found itself in a difficult situation. Meanwhile the Russians had intercepted and defeated an auxiliary Swedish corps, under Loewenhaupt, which was moving south from Livonia with supplies for Charles' army. In an attempt to seize the city of Voronezh, Charles besieged the fortress of Poltava which lay on his way there, and Peter led his main army to the rescue of the stronghold.

1709, July 8. BATTLE OF POLTAVA. The Russian army, superior in numbers and equipment, completely defeated the Swedes, who were exhausted by long marches and lack of food. The Swedish army was broken up, and a large part of

it captured. Charles, accompanied by Mazeppa, found refuge in Turkey. Two years later he induced the Porte to declare war against Peter.

1711. Peter, allied with the rulers of Moldavia and Wallachia, moved to the river Pruth, but was surrounded by a much larger Turkish army and was obliged to conclude the **Treaty of the Pruth:** (1) Azov given back to the Porte. (2) Charles allowed to return to Sweden.

Charles XII, indignant at this treaty, refused to depart, and remained in Turkey for three more years. Meanwhile (1709) Augustus II drove King Stanislas from Poland. Peter occupied all of Livonia, Estonia, Ingermanland, Carelia, Finland. The Danes took Schleswig away from the Duke of Holstein-Gottorp, conquered the Swedish Duchies of Bremen and Verden, which they afterward sold to Hanover upon condition that that state should take part in the war against Sweden, and jointly with the Poles invaded Pomerania. The Prussians occupied Stettin.

1714. Charles XII at last returned to his kingdom through Hungary and Germany. After this the war dragged on for several years with Russia, Saxony, Poland, Denmark, Prussia, Hanover allied against Sweden.

1718, Dec. 11. Charles XII was shot near Friedrichshall, during a military expedition to Norway. He was succeeded by his sister

1718-1720. ULRIKA ELEONORA, who was accepted on condition that the Riksdag should be allowed to draw up a constitution. The **new constitution** provided for joint rule of the monarch and the council when the Riksdag was not in session. While the Riksdag was sitting, the principal decisions were to be made by a secret committee composed of members of the three higher estates (nobility, clergy, and burghers). The peasants were, however, to be heard in matters of taxation. This new system involved the re-establishment of the political power of the nobility and clergy and continued until 1771. But the ruling class was divided in the 18th century, between the party of the *Caps,* who favored a prudent foreign policy, and that of the *Hats,* who were eager to regain Sweden's supremacy in the Baltic.

1720-1751. FREDERICK I (of Hesse-Cassel), the husband of Ulrika Eleonora, to whom she turned over the government. Cautious policy of the minister, **Count Arvid Horn,** a Swedish Fleury, who allowed the dangerous connection with France to lapse, and sought better relations with England and Russia. In 1738 he **was**

by Guldberg, and after his fall (1784) by the

1784-1788. Administration of an able and enlightened statesman, **Count Andreas Peter Bernstorff,** who began by regulating relations between the landlords and their peasant tenants, and then passed a series of measures (1787-1788) virtually abolishing serfdom in Denmark.

In **NORWAY,** which remained under Danish domination, this period saw the vigorous growth of a national cultural movement: literary activity of **Ludwig Holberg** (1684-1754), formation of the **Norwegian Society** among the university students in Copenhagen (1772).

(*Cont. pp.* 595, 697.)

9. POLAND

1648-1668. JOHN II CASIMIR. His reign was marked by grave internal disturbances and unsuccessful foreign wars against the Swedes, the Russians, and the Turks. Frequent uprisings of the serfs and of the Ukrainian Cossacks.

1654. The hetman of the Cossacks, **Bogdan Khmelnitsky,** placed himself under the protection of Russia, thus precipitating a prolonged conflict between Russia and Poland for possession of the Ukraine.

1655-1660. War between Sweden and Poland (p. 471). Invasion of the Swedes. By the **Treaty of Oliva** (May 3, 1660), Poland lost to Sweden her last Baltic territories.

1667, Jan. 20. Treaty of Andrussovo, ending the conflict with Russia. Poland ceded to Russia the eastern Ukraine and Smolensk.

1668. John Casimir abdicated and there followed a period of ardent struggle for the throne. The Poles finally elected a national candidate,

1669-1673. MICHAEL WISNIOWIECKI, during whose short reign the Cossacks again rose in revolt and appealed to the Turks for aid.

1672-1676. War with Turkey. The Turks, having taken Kameniec, secured from the disheartened Polish king the **Treaty of Buczacz** (1772), by which Poland lost Podolia and recognized the western Ukraine as independent under Turkish protectorate. The Polish Diet refused to ratify the treaty and the Poles resumed the struggle under the lead of **John Sobieski,** an able commander who gradually drove the Turks back.

1674-1696. JOHN III SOBIESKI, king after the death of Michael. After a victory over the Turks at Lemberg (1675), he concluded with them the

1676, Oct. Treaty of Zuravna, by which the Turks retained only part of the Ukraine.

1683, Mar. 31. John Sobieski made an alliance with Austria in order to present a united front to the Turkish advance on Vienna. The Poles then played an important rôle in the relief of Vienna from the famous second siege (p. 483). Sobieski continued to participate in the reconquest of Hungary until 1685.

These military successes, however, were not enough to arrest the process of decline which resulted from the basic defects of the Polish political organization, viz. the absence of real unity, the lack of strong central authority, the impotence of the national Diet (repeatedly paralyzed by the use of the *liberum veto* or right of each individual member of the Diet to defeat a resolution by his protest, and thus to break up the session).

1697-1733. AUGUSTUS II (Elector of Saxony), King of Poland. He attempted to strengthen the royal power, but without much success.

1699, Jan. 26. Treaty of Karlowitz, ending the long war against Turkey (p. 484). By this settlement the Poles regained Podolia and the Turkish part of the Ukraine.

1700-1721. The Great Northern War (p. 471), which was fought largely on Polish soil. The Poles had made an agreement with Russia to despoil Charles XII of Sweden. They invaded Livonia (1700), but in 1701-1702 Charles invaded Poland, taking Warsaw and Cracow (1702). The Polish magnates then dethroned Augustus, and elected

1704-1709. STANISLAS LESCZYNSKI as king. By the **Treaty of Altranstädt,** with Sweden (1706), Augustus gave up his claims. The empire, Brandenburg, England, and Holland all recognized Stanislas. But after the defeat of Charles at Poltava (1709), Augustus returned and drove out his rival. Poland suffered tremendously from the Swedish invasion and the civil war, yet gained nothing whatever from the defeat of Charles.

1715-1717. Further disorders, resulting from a rising of the nobles against

THE PARTITIONS
OF POLAND

Partition of 1772
" " 1793
" " 1795

English Miles
0 50 100 150

TO RUSSIA

TO PRUSSIA

TO AUSTRIA

EAST PRUSSIA

SILESIA

HUNGARY

Riga

R.Duna

R.Niemen

Danzig

Warsaw

R.Bug

R.Vistula

Cracow

R.Oder

R.Dnieper

R.Desna

Kieff

R.Dniester

Budapest

Vienna

R.Danube

the absolutist policies of Augustus. This offered an opportunity for Russian intervention and initiated the gradual subordination of Poland to Russia.

1733-1735. WAR OF THE POLISH SUCCESSION. The Poles, supported by France, elected Stanislas Lesczynski, who had become the father-in-law of Louis XV. The Russians and Austrians insisted on the election of Augustus of Saxony, son of Augustus II. A huge Russian army invaded the country and drove out Stanislas, who withdrew to Danzig. France, supported by Spain and Sardinia, declared war on the empire. French expedition to the Baltic to relieve Danzig (besieged by the Russians from Oct. 1733 onward).

1734, June 2. Capitulation of Danzig; Stanislas fled to Prussia. In the meanwhile the main fighting was done in Italy (French and Spanish victories, p. 451) and on the Rhine (indecisive). The war was finally ended by the **Treaty of Vienna** (Oct. 5, 1735, ratified 1738), which wrought profound changes in Italy and assured the victory of the Russian-Austrian policy in Poland.

1734-1763. AUGUSTUS III, king. He spent but little time in Poland and did little to prevent Russian encroachment, especially during the Seven Years' War. Growing agitation for reform in Poland after 1740: two parties, led by the **Potocki** and **Czartoryski** families. The former looked to France for support and aimed at the establishment of an aristocratic constitution; the latter, relying on Russian support, envisaged strengthening of the royal power, abolition of the *liberum veto*, etc.

1764-1795. STANISLAS PONIATOWSKI, king. He was a nephew of Prince Czartoryski and was the favorite of Catharine II of Russia. By agreement of Apr. 11, 1764, Russia and Prussia had arranged for co-operation in Polish affairs. Poniatowski and the reformers attempted to introduce changes, but Russia soon showed herself lukewarm on the subject.

1766-1768. Question of the Dissidents (Greek Orthodox Catholics and Protestants), who were granted equal rights with Roman Catholics, at the insistence of Russia and Prussia. This raised a storm of protest in Poland and led (1768) to the formation of the **Confederation of Bar,** an anti-Russian association which soon enjoyed the active support of France. Civil war of the most violent type broke out in Poland; invasion and campaigns of the Russians against the Confederates. Ulti-

mately the Turks, encouraged by the French, declared war on Russia, in support of Polish "liberties."

1772, Aug. 5. THE FIRST PARTITION OF POLAND. This resulted directly from the Russian victories against the Turks, which so alarmed the Austrians that they came to the point of making war on Russia. Frederick the Great, fearing involvement in a general European conflict, engineered the partition of Poland, by which Russia might make gains unobjectionable to Austria, while Prussia and Austria might participate in the spoils. By the first partition Russia acquired White Russia and all territory to the Dvina and Dniepr, about 1,800,000 inhabitants (mostly Greek Orthodox); Austria took Red Russia, Galicia, and western Podolia, with Lemberg and part of Cracow (2,700,000 inhabitants); Prussia took Polish Prussia, except Danzig and Thorn (416,000 inhabitants). In all Poland lost about one-third of her territory and about one-half of her inhabitants.

1773. The Polish Diet, forced to accept the partition, began to effect reforms (council of state, divided into five ministries, to govern when the Diet was not in session). Intellectual awakening under the influence of French ideas, educational reforms, etc.

1788-1792. The Four Years' Diet, dominated by the progressive patriotic party, supported by Prussia. Austria and Russia being at war with the Turks (p. 485), the Prussian minister **Hertzberg** hoped to secure Danzig and Thorn by agreement with a reformed Poland. Developments in France led to an agreement between Prussia and Austria and to postponement of the scheme.

1791, May 3. The Polish patriots put through a **NEW CONSTITUTION** which (1) converted the elective monarchy into an hereditary monarchy (the Elector of Saxony to succeed Poniatowski and to establish a Saxon dynasty); (2) conferred the executive power upon the king and council of state; (3) vested the legislative power in a diet of two chambers; (4) abolished the *liberum veto*. Prussia and Austria accepted this change, but the Russians organized

1792, May 14. The Confederation of Targowitz, in defense of the old constitution. Russian invasion was followed by similar action on the part of the Prussians, and finally led to a bargain between the two powers in the

1793, Jan. 23. SECOND PARTITION OF POLAND. Russia took most of Lithuania and most of the western

Ukraine, including Podolia (3,000,000 inhabitants); Prussia took Danzig and Thorn, as well as Great Poland (1,100,000 inhabitants). In addition, Russia forced Poland to accept a **Treaty of Alliance**, whereby Russia was given free entry for her troops in Poland and the right to control Poland's relations with other powers.

1794, Mar. 24.   NATIONAL UPRISING in Poland, led by **Thaddeus Kosciuszko** (1746–1817). After an unequal struggle against the forces of Russia and Prussia, the Poles were defeated (capture of Kosciuszko, surrender of Warsaw to

Suvorov), and Austria joined Russia and Prussia in the

1795, Oct. 24.   THIRD PARTITION OF POLAND. Russia took what remained of Lithuania and the Ukraine (1,200,000 inhabitants); Prussia secured Mazovia with Warsaw (1,000,000 inhabitants), while Austria obtained the remainder of the Cracow region (1,000,000 inhabitants). Courland, long under the suzerainty of Poland, but since 1737 practically under Russian influence (Biron, Duke of Courland), was incorporated with Russia.

10. RUSSIA

1645-1676.   ALEXIS, the son of Michael Romanov, who ascended the throne at the age of sixteen. His reign was marked by much internal unrest (serious revolt in Moscow, 1647) and by the adoption by a national assembly (1649) of a new code of law (in force until 1832) designed to improve the administration and to eliminate various abuses. In some of its provisions, however, it involved the final establishment of peasant serfdom in Russia.

1654-1667.   War with Poland for the possession of the Ukraine, after the Cossack hetman, **Bogdan Khmelnitsky,** had placed himself under Russian protection. By the **Treaty of Andrussovo** (Jan. 20, 1667) Russia obtained the Smolensk region and the eastern Ukraine, with Kiev. The outcome of the war was of great importance, since the Russian gains first brought them in contact with the Turks in the Balkans.

1667.   Revision of the Russian church ritual and liturgical books in accordance with Greek practice. This reform, undertaken by the patriarch, **Nikon,** resulted in secession from the Church of the so-called **Old Believers,** who were condemned by a church council as schismatics.

1670-1671. A great **peasant revolt** in the Southeast, led by the Don Cossacks, under **Stephen Razin,** was suppressed with great difficulty.

By the end of the reign of Alexis the government had established more effective control and the crisis of the early 17th century was definitely overcome. The tsar, indeed, felt strong enough to discontinue calling the national assembly. At the same time there was a rapid infiltration of Western influences, which foreshadowed the westernizing reforms of Peter the Great.

1676-1682.   THEODORE III, the son of Alexis, during whose short reign

Russia fought the first of many wars against the Ottoman Turks. By the **Treaty of Radzin** (1681) the Turks abandoned most of the Turkish Ukraine to Russia.

1682-1689.   IVAN V (son of Alexis' first wife), with whom was associated **Peter I** (son of Alexis' second wife) as cotsar. **Sophia,** the daughter of Alexis, acted as regent. In 1689 the partisans of Peter overthrew Sophia and

1689-1725.   PETER I (*the Great*) was effectively the sole ruler, though Ivan V lived until 1696. Peter, an intelligent but ruthless and headstrong ruler (b. 1672), spent the first years of his reign in a process of self-education (chiefly technical and military). He established close relations with members of foreign colonies in Moscow and prepared for his later campaigns through his military and naval "games."

1689.   Conflict with China, resulting from the penetration of Russian pioneers into the Amur region. By the **Treaty of Nerchinsk** (1689) — the first Russian treaty with China — the Russians were obliged to withdraw from the occupied territory.

1695-1696.   Peter's expeditions against **Azov,** the fortress commanding the Sea of Azov and the entrance to the Black Sea. The first expedition, by land, was unsuccessful, but the second, supported by a naval force, resulted in the capture of the stronghold (July 28, 1696).

1697-1698.   Peter's European journey, which he undertook *incognito* as part of a grand embassy sent to secure allies in western Europe for a crusade against the Turks. Peter was the first Russian sovereign to go abroad and his travels in France, England, and Holland strengthened him in the determination to "westernize" Russia. He returned to Moscow to suppress a revolt of the Streltsy (soldiers of the Moscow garrison, among whom there were many Old Believers), and then embarked upon his first reforms. At the same time he prepared for war with Sweden for possession of the Baltic coast, having failed to induce the western powers to continue the Turkish war beyond the year 1699 (Treaty of Karlowitz, p. 484). Peace was concluded with the Turks in 1700, Russia retaining Azov.

1700-1721. THE GREAT NORTHERN WAR (p. 471). Peter was at first no match for Charles XII, who defeated him at Narva (Nov. 30, 1700). But Charles spent the next years campaigning in Poland, thus giving Peter an opportunity to reorganize his army on European lines and to construct a fleet in the Baltic. The capital was moved to the newly founded city of St. Petersburg (modern Petrograd and Leningrad) in 1703.

1709, July 8. THE BATTLE OF POLTAVA, a decisive battle in Russian history. Charles XII, having allied himself with Mazeppa, the Cossack hetman, began to march on Moscow, but then turned off south. At Poltava Peter won a resounding victory which broke the power of Charles and marked the emergence of Russia in place of Sweden as the dominant power in the north.

1710-1711. War with Turkey, due to pressure from Charles XII (a refugee in Turkey) and France. The Russians were surrounded by the Turks on the Pruth River and Peter had to buy himself off. By the Treaty of the Pruth (July 21, 1711), he was obliged to return Azov to the Turks.

1721, Aug. 30. Treaty of Nystadt, between Russia and Sweden, concluding the Northern War. Russia acquired Livonia, Estonia, Ingermanland, part of Carelia and a number of Baltic islands. Thus Peter had achieved his great purpose of acquiring a "window" on the Baltic which would open up connections with the west. Russia now definitely took her place as a European power.

INTERNAL REFORMS OF PETER: centralization of the administration. The old council of the boyars was abolished and was replaced by a governing *senate* (1711), consisting of nine members appointed by the tsar. New government bureaus were set up (1718) under the name of *colleges*. The nobility was made to serve the state (establishment of a hierarchy of offices) and Peter did much to encourage trade, industry, and education (Academy of Science opened the year after Peter's death). In order to subordinate the Church to state

control Peter abolished the patriarchate and in its place established (1721) a synod composed of bishops, but presided over by a layman (procurator of the Holy Synod). Many of Peter's reforms were incomplete and even more of them were hasty and premature, but his drastic innovations no doubt did much to arouse Russia from the stagnation of the preceding period.

Alexis, the son of Peter I, who had become the center of opposition to Peter's policies, died in prison in 1718. In 1722 Peter issued a law which empowered the reigning sovereign to appoint his own successor. He himself died without making use of this right. Upon his death the officers of the palace guard elevated to the throne his second wife,

1725-1727. CATHARINE I, a woman of lowly birth, but intelligent and energetic. During her short reign the most influential member of the government was Prince Menshikov, one of Peter's closest collaborators. Catharine named as her successor

1727-1730. PETER II, the son of Alexis and grandson of Peter I, a boy of 12. There ensued a struggle between the Menshikov and the Dolgoruki families, which ended in the exile of the former. Peter II died young and was succeeded by

1730-1740. ANNA, daughter of Ivan V, who was married to Frederick, the Duke of Courland. Anna was an ineffectual person, dominated by her favorite, Biron (properly Bühren). The government began to fall almost entirely into the hands of Germans, many of them adventurers, but many of them extremely able. Foreign affairs were competently handled by Ostermann, while the army, under Münnich, scored great successes in its campaigns.

1733-1735. War of the Polish Succession (p. 477). As a result of the internal weakness of Poland, the Russians were able to establish on a firm basis their control over Polish affairs and to prepare the way for the final partitions.

1736-1739. War against the Turks (p. 484), in alliance with Austria. The war was the result of Russian action in Poland. The Russians recaptured Azov and, after some reverses in 1737, Münnich advanced victoriously into Moldavia. French mediation deprived Russia of gains she might have made. By the Treaty of Belgrade (Sept. 18, 1739) the Russians retained Azov, but agreed to raze the fortifications and not to build a fleet on the Black Sea.

1740-1741. IVAN VI, the grandson of Anna's sister Catharine. Ivan's

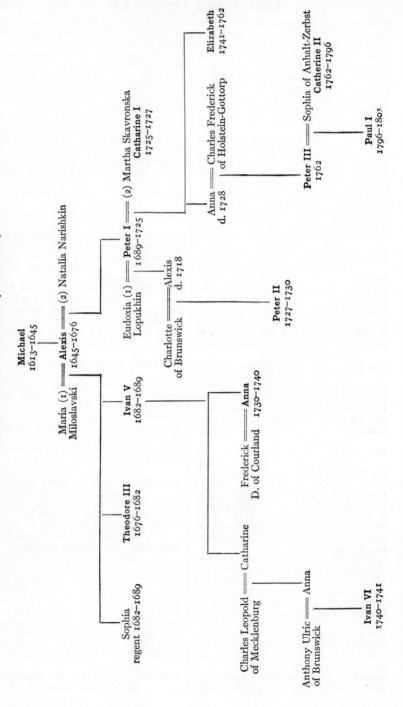

The House of Romanov (1613–1801)

mother, the Duchess of Courland, conducted the government for a short time after the fall of Biron (effected by Münnich), but a military revolt soon placed on the throne

1741-1762. ELIZABETH, the youngest daughter of Peter the Great, a thoroughly Russian character, politically keen, but dissolute and easy-going. Nationalist reaction against German favorites. Elizabeth set up a brilliant if somewhat uncouth court and gave wide rein to the court nobility. Golden age of the aristocracy, which began to emancipate itself from onerous obligations of service to the state, while gradually increasing its privileges. Development of learning and science: **first Russian university** founded at Moscow (1755); activity of the Academy of Sciences (**Michael Lomonosov,** 1711-1765, the first outstanding native scientist).

Foreign policy was, during most of the reign, directed by **Alexis Bestuzhev-Riumin,** and was based on the alliance with Austria and England as against Prussia and France. The great objectives of Russia continued to be expansion at the expense of Sweden, domination of Poland and conquest at the expense of the Turk.

1741-1743. War with Sweden, provoked by the pro-French party in Sweden. After some fighting, the Swedes, by the **Treaty of Abö** (1743, Aug. 7) were obliged to cede to Russia further territory in Finland.

1746, June 2. By treaty with Austria, Russia finally joined in the **War of the Austrian Succession** (p. 465), in which, however, the Russians played an insignificant rôle.

1756-1763. THE SEVEN YEARS' WAR, in which Russia took an active and important part. The "diplomatic revolution" of 1756, which brought Austria and France together, led to the estrangement of Russia and England, and to the downfall of Bestuzhev. Russia fought on the side of Austria and France against Frederick the Great (p. 467ff.), but made no direct gains as a result of the war.

Elizabeth named as her successor **Peter,** Duke of Holstein-Gottorp, her sister's son, who in 1744 married Sophia-Augusta of Anhalt-Zerbst. Sophia took the name Catharine on conversion to the Orthodox faith.

1762. PETER III, a weak and incompetent ruler. As an intense admirer of Frederick the Great, he effected Russia's withdrawal from the war, thereby causing much resentment among the officers and the aristocracy (despite the fact that he proclaimed the freedom of the nobility from

obligatory state service). After a six months' reign, Peter was deposed (July) by a military revolution led by the **Orlov brothers.** A few days later he was killed while in captivity. Peter was succeeded by his wife

1762-1796. CATHARINE II (*the Great*), an exceptionally astute and energetic ruler, who completed the work initiated by Peter the Great. In domestic affairs Catharine was guided by the teachings of the French Enlightenment (especially Voltaire) and tried to establish a benevolent despotism. On the other hand, she was obliged to cultivate the good will of the nobility, to which she owed her power. In order to codify the Russian law and also in order to learn the needs of the country, she convoked at Moscow a legislative commission (1767-1768), consisting of representatives of all classes excepting the serfs. Although no law code was produced, Catharine made good use of the commission's findings in planning her later legislation.

1766-1768. Drastic interference of Catharine in the affairs of Poland, where one of her favorites, Stanislas Poniatowski, had been placed on the throne (p. 477). The Russian advance in Poland led to

1768-1772. WAR WITH THE TURKS (p. 484), in which the Russians won unprecedented victories. The prospective gains of Russia so excited the Austrians (thitherto the partners of the Russians in the advance against the Turks) that the two powers came to the very verge of war. In order to prevent a general conflagration, Frederick the Great engineered the

1772, Aug. 5. FIRST PARTITION OF POLAND (p. 477). The Russian operations against Turkey were hampered further by

1773-1775. Pugachev's revolt, a formidable insurrection of the peasants and Cossacks of southeastern Russia, which was suppressed only with great difficulty.

1774, July 21. The Treaty of Kuchuk Kainarji ended the war against Turkey. Russia acquired Kinburn, Yenikale, and Kertch in the Crimea and secured the right of free navigation for commercial ships in Turkish waters. The Tatars of the Crimea were recognized as "independent" and Russia was given important rights of intervention in Moldavia and Wallachia and in behalf of Christians in the Ottoman Empire (for details see p. 484).

1775. The statute of provincial administration was a direct result of Pugachev's revolt, which convinced Catharine of the need for reform. It completely reorganized local government (small administrative units, better division of functions among the branches of government, some measure of self-government, more particularly for the nobility). Catharine did not dare, however, to touch the evil of serfdom. On the contrary, this institution reached its fullest development in her reign. Catharine's encouragement of education, art, and letters contributed to the growth of a liberal public opinion on the social problem. After the outbreak of the French Revolution, Catharine became decidedly hostile to this movement. **Alexander Radishchev** (1749–1802) was arrested and exiled to Siberia (1790) for having published his *Journey from St. Petersburg to Moscow*, which contained a vigorous protest against serfdom.

1780. Armed neutrality at sea, an idea advanced by Russia during the War of American Independence, as a method of protecting commerce. The idea was supported by Denmark and Sweden (1780) and later by Prussia, Austria (1782) and Portugal (1783); France and Spain recognized the principle, but England prevented Holland from joining the league by declaring war on the Dutch. The demands of the **League of Armed Neutrality** were: (1) free passage of neutral ships from port to port and along the coasts to combatants; (2) freedom of enemy goods in neutral ships (*le pavillon couvre la marchandise*), excepting for contraband; (3) definition of blockade (nominal, "paper" blockade not sufficient; a blockade, to be legal, must be effective).

1780. Visit of the Emperor Joseph II to Catharine and conclusion (1781) of an **Austro-Russian treaty.** Catharine's *Greek Scheme* for the disruption of the Ottoman Empire and division of the Balkans between Russia and Austria (p. 485). In keeping with her Near-Eastern plans, Catharine carried through

1783. The annexation of the Crimea, on the plea of restoring order. The Turks were with difficulty dissuaded by

England and Austria from declaring war on Russia.

1785. Charter to the nobility, recognizing their corporate rights. A similar charter was issued for the towns, but not for the peasantry.

1787-1792. Second war of Catharine against the Turks (p. 485). Austria joined in the war. The Russians advanced to the Danube, but were badly distracted by

1788-1790. War with Sweden, and the Swedish invasion of Finland (p. 474). Under Prussian pressure, the Austrians finally backed out of the Turkish war, and Russia concluded the **Treaty of Jassy** (1792, Jan. 9), by which she secured Oczakov and the boundary of the Dniestr River.

1793, Jan. 23. The second partition of Poland, between Russia and Prussia (p. 477). Catharine, though very hostile to the French Revolution, took care not to become involved. Instead, she furthered her own designs in Poland, and, by

1795, Oct. 24. The third partition of Poland (p. 478) helped to extinguish the kingdom. By her immense gains in Poland, Russia advanced far into central Europe and became an ever more important factor in European affairs. Catharine was succeeded by her son

1796-1801. PAUL I, a tyrannical and mentally unbalanced ruler. Nevertheless, he was the first Russian ruler who tried to put certain limits to the spread of serfdom (1797, manifesto limiting the peasants' work for the landlord to three days a week).

1797. Paul repealed the law of succession of Peter the Great and decreed that succession should be by genealogical seniority.

1799-1801. Russia participated in the **War of the Second Coalition** against France (p. 586).

1801, Mar. 24. Paul was assassinated in the course of a palace revolution, and was succeeded by his son

1801-1825. ALEXANDER I.
(*Cont. pp.* 586, **701.**)

11. THE OTTOMAN EMPIRE

1656-1661. Mohammed Kiuprili, grand vizier. Through unlimited ruthlessness he tamed the restless Janissaries, executed incapable commanders, purged the court, raised the finances (taxes and confiscations). The war with Venice was vigorously pressed and Lemnos and Tenedos retaken

(1657). George II Rakoczy of Transylvania was defeated and deposed.

1661-1678. Ahmed Kiuprili (son of Mohammed), grand vizier. Order having been restored, he ruled with a lenient hand, humoring the sultan and outwitting his enemies. The war with Venice he tried, in vain, to bring to an end by compromise.

1663-1664. War with Austria. After the Treaty of Westphalia, Austria was able to devote attention to the Near East once more.

1664, Aug. 1. Battle of St. Gotthard, a victory of the imperial general, Montecucculi, over the Turks. A 20-year truce concluded at Vasvar, the Turks losing no territory, but recognizing the election of the Prince of Transylvania by the local estates.

1669. Fall of Candia, after a long siege. In the peace with Venice (1670) the latter retained only three fortified posts on the island.

1672-1676. War with Poland, the result of countless border raids (Tatars and Cossacks) and rivalry for control of the Ukraine. The Turks raided as far as Lemberg, but were twice defeated by King John Sobieski. In the **Treaty of Zuravna** (Oct. 16, 1676) the Turks acquired most of Podolia and the Polish Ukraine, thus coming in contact with Russia.

1677-1681. First war with Russia, following Cossack raids. By the **Treaty of Radzin** (1681) the Turks were obliged to give up most of the Ukraine and accord the Cossacks trading rights on the Black Sea.

1678. Kara Mustafa (brother-in-law of Ahmed Kiuprili), grand vizier. He was an incompetent but ambitious man, who at once supported Emeric Tökölli as King of Hungary against the Emperor Leopold I.

1682-1699. War with Austria, which was allied to Poland.

1683, July 17-Sept. 12. SIEGE OF VIENNA by Kara Mustafa. Violent assaults on the walls; extensive mining operations; valiant defense by the garrison under **Rüdiger von Stahremberg.** Successful relief of the city by a united German and Polish army under **Charles of Lorraine and John Sobieski.**

1684. Venice joined Austria and Poland in a **Holy League,** sponsored by the pope. The Poles, however, soon withdrew, influenced thereto by Louis XIV of France. The Austrians advanced rapidly to Budapest (1686), while the Venetians took most of the fortresses in the Morea and the Russians laid siege to Azov (1687, 1689).

1687, Aug. 12. Second battle of Mohacs. Charles of Lorraine defeated the Turks and the Diet of Pressburg conferred hereditary succession to the Hungarian throne upon the male line of Austria. Panic in Constantinople; deposition of Moham-

Ottoman Sultans (1649-1839)

med IV, who was succeeded by Suleiman III (1687–1691).

1688. The Austrians took Belgrade and then (1689) Vidin.

1689. Mustafa Kiuprili (brother of Ahmed), grand vizier.

1690. The Turks drove the Austrians out of Bulgaria, Serbia, and Transylvania and retook Belgrade (flight of the Serbs into southern Hungary).

1691, Aug. 19. The Turks defeated by Louis of Baden in the **battle of Salem Kemen;** Mustafa killed. The war continued, but was not pressed by Austria, which had become involved in war with France (**War of the League of Augsburg,** 1688–1697).

1696, July 28. Peter the Great finally took Azov from the Turks.

1697, Sept. 11. Battle of Zenta, a great victory of **Eugene of Savoy** over the Turks.

1699, Jan. 26. TREATY OF KARLO-WITZ, concluded for 25 years: Austria received all of Hungary (except the Banat of Temesvar), Transylvania, Croatia and Slavonia; Venice received the Morea and most of Dalmatia; Poland obtained Podolia. Russia continued the war until 1702, when the peace treaty recognized the Russian conquest of Azov. Peter was obliged to postpone his far-reaching plans to liberate his coreligionists in the Balkans.

1710-1711. War with Russia, instigated by France and by Charles XII of Sweden, who had fled to Turkey after his defeat by the Russians at Poltava (1709). Peter posed as the champion of the Balkan Christians and made efforts to stir up revolts. But in 1711 he was surrounded on the Pruth River by a vastly superior Turkish army and had to buy himself off. By the **Treaty of the Pruth** (1711, July 21) Russia was obliged to give up Azov again.

1714-1718. War with Venice. Corinth and the Venetian stations in Candia were taken, but Austria entered the war and pressed the campaign in Hungary.

1716, Aug. 5. Eugene of Savoy won a victory at **Peterwardein** and captured Belgrade (1717),

1718, July 21. TREATY OF PASSARO-WITZ: The Turks lost the Banat of Temesvar, northern Serbia, and Little Wallachia, but they retained the Morea.

1725-1727. The Turks, by agreement with Russia, secured the western part of Transcaucasia. This led to war with

Persia (**Nadir Shah**), who drove the Turks out (1730).

1736-1739. War with Austria and Russia, partly the result of Turkish protests against Russian action in Poland, partly of French pressure. The Russians retook Azov and raided the Crimea, but in the campaigns of 1737 the Turks were successful against both Russians and Austrians.

1739. Spectacular advance of the Russian general, Münnich, to Jassy. Austria, alarmed by the successes of Russia, accepted French mediation.

1739, Sept. 18. TREATY OF BELGRADE. Austria gave up northern Serbia and Belgrade. The Russians, deserted by Austria, joined in the peace, agreeing to raze the fortifications of Azov and not to build a fleet on the Black Sea.

1743-1746. An indecisive war with Persia, marking, in a general way, the end of a long duel. The mid-century was, on the whole, a period of peace (European powers involved in the War of the Austrian Succession and the Seven Years' War) and cultural progress (**Raghib Pasha,** grand vizier, 1757-1763). But the unaggressiveness of the central government soon led to the rise of the **Derebeys** (lords of the valley), who established themselves in many parts of Anatolia and set themselves up as semi-independent potentates.

1768-1774. First war of Catharine the Great against the Turks. This arose from the Russian policy in Poland, the rising of the Poles and their subsequent flight into Turkey, whither they were pursued by Russian troops. The Porte, instigated by France, declared war. Catharine, though she did not want the war, threw herself into it energetically. Her generals overran Moldavia and Wallachia and sent agents to Greece to raise a revolt, which was officered by Russians.

1770, July 6. Battle of Chesmé, in which a Russian fleet, officered by British, having come from the Baltic to the Anatolian coast, defeated the Turkish fleet.

1771. The Russians conquered the Crimea. Frederick the Great, alarmed by the Russian successes, offered mediation and arranged the first partition of Poland (p. 477), but the war went on until the Russians were diverted by the great revolt of Pugachev (1773).

1774, July 21. TREATY OF KUCHUK KAINARJI (a village near Silistria on the Danube): Russia received Kinburn, Yenikale, and Kertch in the Crimea and obtained the right of free navigation for trading vessels in Turkish waters; the Tatars of the Crimea were recognized as "independent" on condition that they accept the sultan as caliph (first move of the sultan to exploit his claim to religious leadership of Islam); Moldavia and Wallachia were returned to Turkey on condition that they be leniently ruled (Russia reserved the right to intervene on their behalf); Russia was given the right to build a Greek church in Galata (foreign quarter of Constantinople); the Turks promised protection to the Christian churches and recognized the right of Russia to make representations in behalf of the church to be built in Galata. These provisions were to become the basis of much Russian interference later.

1781. Austro-Russian Treaty, following a famous meeting of Catharine and Joseph II (1780). Catharine's *Greek Scheme* to drive the Turks out of Europe and restore the Greek Empire, with her grandson Constantine (born 1779) as emperor. The Austrians were to receive the whole western half of the Balkans.

1783. The Russians incorporated the Crimea, on the plea of restoring order. England and Austria persuaded the outraged Turks to accept the inevitable.

1787-1792. Second War of Catharine against the Turks, resulting from Turkish intrigues with the Crimean Tatars and from Russian designs on Georgia. Austria joined Russia (1788) under the terms of the alliance treaty of 1781.

1788. The campaign was indecisive, the Russians being unprepared and the Turks having difficulty in getting troop contingents from the Derebeys.

1789-1807. SELIM III, an intelligent ruler, bent on victory and reform of the empire.

1789. The Austrians took Belgrade and the Russians, under Prince Potemkin and Gen. Suvorov, advanced to the Danube.

1791, Aug. 4. The Austrians, under Prussian pressure, made the separate **Treaty of Sistova,** giving back Belgrade in return for a strip of northern Bosnia.

1792, Jan. 9. TREATY OF JASSY, between Turkey and Russia, which, worried by Prussian activity in Poland and deserted by Austria, decided to end the war: Russia obtained Oczakov and a boundary along the Dniestr River, but returned Moldavia and Bessarabia.

(*Cont. pp.* 586, 710, 721.)

C. LATIN AMERICA

1. NATURE OF THE CONQUEST

In the broader sense the conquest and colonization of Spanish America progressed logically outward from the earliest colony in Santo Domingo until by 1600 the territory from New Mexico and Florida on the north to Chile and the Río de la Plata on the south was, with the exception of Brazil, effectively under the rule of the crown of Castile.

The motives which inspired the Castilian sovereigns to create a vast empire in the Americas were the desire to achieve more extensive realms, propagate Christianity, and obtain increased revenues. The early *conquistadores* were impelled by several motives which varied in intensity with regard to individuals, time, and place: desire to gain wealth and position, desire to add to the glory of the Castilian crown, zeal to propagate Christianity, and love of adventure. The most important of the early conquests were achieved at no direct cost to the crown. Individual leaders by their own initiative, in the name of the sovereign or by virtue of royal patents, conquered territory at their own expense, hoping to receive or to be assigned authority and revenues in the lands subjugated. In this manner Cortés conquered Mexico, Alvarado Guatemala, Pizarro Peru, Jiménez de Quesada New Granada, and Montejo Yucatan. The crown of Castile soon established direct and absolute control and evolved complex machinery of government to rule

its vast colonial empire. The Church, over which the crown exercised patronage, achieved complete organization and exercised vast influence. The military triumphs of the Spaniards over incredible numerical odds was the triumph of indomitable representatives of a more highly developed society over those of a lesser. The conquest was accompanied by great cruelty, but it was no greater than that of contemporary conquest elsewhere. Ruthless exploitation of the natives followed colonization, but such was the common lot of subject peoples during the period. The intent of the Castilian crown toward the Indian masses, if not the actual practice, was beneficent. While the production of gold and silver was the chief source of crown revenues in the Indies and became the basis of much private wealth, agriculture, grazing, and commerce were soon highly developed and local industries of various types came into existence. Certain colonies like Chile, Yucatan, and the Río de la Plata were almost exclusively agricultural and pastoral. A relatively large measure of intellectual activity came into being in the larger cities and within the Church. The existence of a large Indian population, many groups of which possessed high cultures of long standing, and the impact of European culture and Christianity on the New World civilizations led to fundamentally important social, cultural, and racial developments.

2. THE WEST INDIES AND THE ISTHMUS

Santo Domingo became the first seat of Spanish government in the Indies. Immigration to Española, although not heavy, increased and mining and agriculture were developed.

1501. Negro slavery was introduced. The Indian population rapidly disappeared as a result of warfare, enslavement, and disease.

1508-1511. Puerto Rico was conquered, San Juan being founded, and Jamaica was settled.

1511-1515. Diego Velásquez, as lieutenant of the viceroy, Diego Columbus,

conquered Cuba and founded Santiago and San Cristóbal de la Habana.

1509-1513. Under royal patents Alonso de Ojeda founded a colony on the coast of South America east of the Isthmus of Panama and Diego de Nicuesa founded Nombré de Dios on the Isthmus. The settlement founded by Ojeda was transferred to the Isthmus at the suggestion of Vasco Núñez de Balboa (1474-1519). There the colonists united with those of Nicuesa.

1513. Balboa became governor of the colony and as such he discovered

COLONIAL LATIN AMERICA

Cibola
TEXAS
Zacatecas
Guadalajara Tlaxcala
Mexico Veracruz Tampeche Havana
Oaxaca R. Guatemala YUCATAN C U B A
Tehuante. Santiago
GUATEMALA HONDURAS ESPAÑOLA PUERTO RICO
NICARAGUA San Juan R. Porto Bello
COSTA RICA Darien Nombre de Dios
Panama 1519 Cartagena
Santa Marta
VR. OF NEW SPAIN

1567
Caracas Cumaná
VENEZUELA Trinidad
Portobelo Bogotá VR. OF NEW
Magdalena Orinoco R.
Guayaquil Quito GRANADA GUIANAS
Tumbez
Cajamarca Amazon R.
Unexplored forest

Lima
Cuzco Belem
Titicaca (Pará) São Luis de Maranhão

VR. OF PERU Charcas 1538 B R A Z I L Natal Parahyba
Valparaiso Recife
Santiago Mendoza MINAS GERAIS Olinda 1536
Córdoba Paraguay R. Salvador 1549
VR. OF CHILE Asunción Paraná R. Bahia Porto Seguro 1537
São Paulo Tijuco Rio de Janeiro
VR. OF LA PLATA BANDA Santos, 1532
ORIENTAL Rio Grande do Sul 1736
Buenos Aires Río de la Plata
1580 Montevideo 1723

Str. of
Magellan

Raisz

the South Sea (Pacific Ocean) and took possession for the crown of Castile.

1513-1514. A jurisdiction independent of Española, **Castilla del Oro** (Darien), was created in the region of the Isthmus and **Pedro Arias de Ávila** (1442–1531) was appointed royal governor, bringing some 1500 colonists from Spain.

1514-1519. Ávila dispatched expeditions by land and sea to adjacent areas, including the Gulf of Nicoya, Zenú, and the Gulf of San Miguel, founded **Panama** as the seat of government, refounded Nombre de Dios, and established a route across the Isthmus. Balboa, as *adelantado* of the South Sea and subordinate to Ávila, continued explorations on the Pacific coast, but as a result of quarrels with the governor, was executed by him (1519).

1522-1523. Under authority independent of Ávila, **Gil González Dávila** and Alonso Niño led a combined land and sea expedition westward from the Isthmus. Dávila conquered the area about the Gulf of Nicoya and Lake Nicaragua and Niño sailed to Fonseca Bay. Ávila then dispatched **Francisco Hernández de Córdoba** to conquer Nicaragua for himself.

1523-1531. Dávila, returning to Española, secured license to continue exploration and conquest, and returned to Central America by way of Honduras. Hernández de Córdoba, after establishing a short-lived colony on the Gulf of Nicoya, entered Nicaragua and founded León and Granada. Forces sent northward by him were defeated by Dávila, who in turn was overcome by Cristóbal de Olid. Hernandez de Córdoba rebelled against Ávila and was executed, after which Ávila became governor of Nicaragua. In this capacity he dispatched an expedition along the San Juan River to the sea, exploration which was continued after his death (1531).

3. VENEZUELA AND NEW GRANADA

Early efforts to colonize the eastern portion of the north coast of South America met with no success.

1521. An attempt made by **Bartolomé de las Casas** (1474–1566) to found a colony at Cumaná in accord with his theories of peaceful reduction failed.

1530. Antonio de Sedeño achieved but little success in an effort to occupy Trinidad Island.

1531-1535. The efforts of **Diego de Ordaz** to explore the region of the Orinoco, led to no result. Ordaz lost his life. In the western areas permanent colonization was established at an early date.

1527. Juan de Ampués, commissioned by the *Audiencia* of Santo Domingo, founded Santa Ana de Coro. This territory was granted by the Emperor Charles V to the **Welsers**, the great Augsburg banking firm to which he was heavily indebted.

1529. The Welsers at once sent out colonists and established an administration. Exploration was carried on through the valley of the Orinoco and into the Andes. The government of the Welsers was marked by ruthless enslavement and maltreatment of the Indians. On that account and because of protests in Spain against grant of lands in the New World to foreigners, their concession was ultimately revoked (1546–1556). The conquest and colonization of Venezuela was then undertaken by the Spaniards. Caracas was founded by Diego de Losada in 1567.

The history of the **conquest of the Chibcha Indian empire** by Quesada has been overshadowed by the fame of Cortés in Mexico and Pizarro in Peru, though it was in some respects no less striking.

1525. **Rodrigo de Bastidas** founded Santa Marta, the first permanent settlement in what was to become New Granada. **Cartagena** was founded in 1533 by Pedro de Heredia, acting directly under royal authority.

1536-1538. Gonzalo Jiménez de Quesada (1495–1576), under commission from the governor of Santa Marta, moved up the Magdalena River, reached the plateau of Bogotá, reduced the Chibchas (p. 361) and founded **Santa Fé de Bogotá.**

1539. **Nikolaus Federmann,** an agent of the Welsers, arrived at Bogotá after three years of wandering in the lowlands. Very soon afterward there appeared from the west coast **Sebastian de Belalcázar,** one of Pizarro's lieutenants. A dispute arose regarding jurisdiction. Finally the three captains went to Spain to lay the controversy before the crown. Federmann died. Belalcázar was confirmed in the governorship of Popayán, but Quesada's claims were rejected in favor of those of the son of the deceased governor of Santa Marta.

1549. The *Audiencia* of **New Granada** was created. It included Santa Marta, Cartagena, Popayán, and Santa Fé (Bogotá), the latter town being the seat of government over this large area.

4. PERU AND THE WEST COAST

1522. Continuing exploration southward from Panama, **Pascual de Andagoya** (c. 1495–1548) reached a point south of the Gulf of San Miguel and advanced into Biru (Peru), where he learned of the rich and powerful **Inca Empire** (p. 361). Andagoya planned the conquest of the lands reported, but was forced to relinquish the project by ill health.

1524-1528. **Francisco Pizarro** (1470–1541), under authority of Ávila, in association with Diego de Almagro (1475–1538) and Hernando de Luque, a priest, determined upon the conquest of Peru. An initial expedition reached the San Juan River and a second the Gulf of Guayaquil and Túmbez, where evidence of the high civilization and great wealth of the Inca was encountered.

1528-1529. Pizarro went to Spain and concluded a capitulation with the crown by which he was granted the right of discovery and conquest in Peru for a distance of 200 leagues south of the Gulf of Guayaquil with the offices of *adelantado*, governor, and captain general. Almagro was assigned command of the fortress of Túmbez, and Luque was named Bishop of Túmbez.

1531. Returning to Panama, accompanied by his brothers, Gonzalo (c. 1505–1548) and Hernando, and a small group of recruits, Pizarro organized an expedition of 180 men, with 27 horses and two pieces of artillery, and sailed for the conquest. Pizarro consolidated his position at Túmbez and founded San Miguel. After having been joined by further recruits, Pizarro moved into the interior with 62 horse and 102 foot, invited by the Inca **Atahualpa,** and reached Cajamarca on the central plateau, near which the Indian monarch was encamped with a large army.

1532, Nov. 16. When Atahualpa visited the Spanish camp, Pizarro seized him. This bold stroke produced great moral effect among the Inca and paralyzed the machinery of government. While a prisoner, Atahualpa caused his rival half-brother Huascar to be murdered.

1533. The Inca paid an enormous ransom in gold and silver, but for political reasons was executed by the Spaniards. Having been joined by Almagro, Pizarro occupied **Cuzco,** the Inca capital, and set up **Manco,** brother of Huascar, as Inca.

1535. Pizarro, having left Cuzco, founded **Lima,** which became the capital of the later viceroyalty of Peru. In Pizarro's absence the natives revolted under Manco and conducted a lengthy but unsuccessful **siege of Cuzco.** This was the only serious attempt of the Incas to expel the Spaniards (1535–1536).

In the following years the area of Spanish dominion was greatly extended. In the south the region about Lake Titicaca was reduced and Chuquisaca founded (1536–1539). The rich silver mines of **Potosí** were opened in 1545. To the north the region of Quito, where lieutenants of Atahualpa had established control after his seizure, was reduced in 1534 by Pizarro's subordinate, Belalcázar (1495–1550). **Pedro de Alvarado,** governor of Guatemala, having heard of rich lands in Peru, led an expedition of some 500 men from Central America and sought to secure control of Quito in 1534–1535. Alvarado was ultimately induced to relinquish his claims in return for monetary compensation. Belalcázar founded Cali and Popayán (1535–1536) and advanced to the Bogotá plateau, where in 1539 he encountered Quesada. In the same year Gonzalo Pizarro, governor of Quito, led an expedition across the Andes and reached the upper Amazon. One of his lieutenants, **Francisco de Orellana,** seeking to gain territory for himself, continued down the Amazon and reached the sea (1541). He went to Spain and secured authority to conquer the Amazonian area, but died on the return to the New World. His followers accomplished nothing.

1537. After a dispute with Pizarro regarding jurisdiction over the city of Cuzco, Almagro occupied the city, thus beginning a series of civil wars between the Spaniards. Almagro was defeated and executed (1538).

1541. Dissension continued. Partisans of Almagro assassinated Pizarro and set up Almagro's son as governor, but the younger Almagro was, in turn, overthrown by the royal governor Vaca de Castro (1542).

In the meanwhile the Spaniards had begun **expansion into Chile.**

1535-1537. Almagro the elder had advanced as far as the Maule River.

1540-1553. **Pedro de Valdivia** (c. 1498–1553) penetrated the fertile valley and founded **Santiago** (1541). A series of wars ensued with the **Araucanian Indians,** most warlike of the tribes.

Valdivia having lost his life in the wars (1553), the conquest was continued by

García Hurtado de Mendoza (1557–1561) whose forces advanced to the Straits of Magellan. The conquest was extended into Cuyo and the town of Mendoza founded.

With the creation of the viceroyalty and *audiencia* of Peru (1542), **Blasco Núñez Vela**, the first viceroy, proclaimed the **New Laws**, with provision for eventual abolition of *encomiendas* (1544). This aroused much opposition, culminating in open revolt under the leadership of **Gonzalo Pizarro**. Vela was deposed and Pizarro assumed the position of governor (1544). The viceroy sought to quell the revolt, but was defeated and killed (1546).

1546-1550. The emperor, fearing a separatist movement, appointed **Pedro de la Gasca**, a churchman with high qualities of statesmanship, his representative and endowed him with virtually unlimited powers. De la Gasca, adopting a conciliatory policy and promising remedy of the causes of complaint, won over many of the opposing party, defeated Pizarro in the **battle of Xaquixaguana** (1548), and restored direct royal authority. Gonzalo Pizarro was executed.

1550-1551. **Antonio de Mendoza** was named viceroy of Peru, but died after a short period in office. The *audiencia* exercised interim authority, crushing a revolt of yet dissatisfied elements led by Francisco Girón, until the arrival of Andrés Hurtado de Mendoza (1557).

1569-1581. **Francisco Alvarez de Toledo,** a proved soldier and diplomat, and one of the greatest of the magistrates of the colonial period, as viceroy of Peru systematized the administration. Codes were promulgated, mining was stimulated and regulated, *corregimientos* on the Castilian model were erected for both Spanish and Indian districts, the tribute of the natives was regularized, the *mita*, or system of enforced labor of the Indians in the mines, on the *haciendas* and for public works was established, the natives were concentrated in towns to facilitate administration and indoctrination, and public works were constructed. **Francis Drake** raided the coast of Peru during the incumbency of Toledo.

5. THE RIO DE LA PLATA

1526-1532. **Sebastian Cabot**, in the service of a group of merchants of Seville, set out with an expedition to reach the Moluccas, but diverted it to the **Río de la Plata** in search for a passage to the east. The expedition passed up the Paraná and Paraguay Rivers and founded a short-lived settlement on the lower Paraná.

1535. Permanent colonization of the La Plata was undertaken by the expedition of **Pedro de Mendoza**, to whom the conquest of the area was assigned.

1536. Mendoza founded **Buenos Aires** (Santa María de Buenos Aires) on the estuary of the La Plata. Expeditions were sent to explore the Paraná and Para-

guay and search for a route to Peru. A fort was established at Asunción (1537) to which the colony at Buenos Aires was soon transferred. Mendoza died (1537) on a voyage to Spain, and Domingo Martínez de Irala was elected governor.

1542-1544. **Alvar Núñez Cabeza de Vaca,** named by the crown to replace Mendoza, reached Asunción with more colonists, having traveled overland from southern Brazil. He was opposed by Irala, who again became governor and was at length confirmed by the crown.

1573. **Juan de Garay**, with colonists from Asunción, founded Santa Fé and a few years later refounded Buenos Aires (1580).

6. NEW SPAIN

a. THE CONQUEST OF MEXICO

1518-1519. To continue the discoveries of Hernández de Córdoba and Grijalva (p. 368), Diego Velásquez and **Hernándo Cortés** (1485–1546) organized an expedition of some 600 men, with 17 horses and 10 cannon. Cortés was put in command. Sailing from Cuba despite Ve-

lásquez' orders, he followed the coast of Yucatan, subjugated Tabasco and reached San Juan de Ulloa. There he renounced the authority of Velásquez and, acting as a direct agent of the crown, founded **Villa Rica de la Vera Cruz**. Cortés was elected chief magistrate by the soldiers and sent representatives to Spain to secure confirmation.

After negotiations with **Moctezuma** (Montezuma), ruler of the Aztecs (p. 360),

and after winning the support of the Totonac, a people subject to the Aztec, Cortés
moved into the interior, overcame Tlaxcala,
and formed an alliance with the republic.
Moving on the Aztec capital, Cortés
thwarted a treacherous attempt to destroy
his force at Cholula and entered **Tenochtitlán** (1519, Nov. 8), where he was amicably
received by Moctezuma. To safeguard his
position, Cortés soon made the native ruler
a prisoner, and the latter and his chiefs swore
fealty to the Castilian sovereign.

1520. Meanwhile Velásquez, named royal
adelantado of the lands discovered
by Hernández de Córdoba and Grijalva,
sent an expedition under **Pánfilo de Narváez** to reduce Cortés to obedience. Cortés,
placing Pedro de Alvarado (1485–1541) in
command at Tenochtitlán, went to the
coast and by combined subterfuge and
vigorous action won over the majority of
the force of Narváez, thereupon returning
to the Aztec capital. Harsh rule by Alvarado aroused the Aztecs to revolt against
the Spaniards and Moctezuma, and Cortés
was forced to evacuate Tenochtitlán with
heavy losses (1520, June 30). Moctezuma,
who had been injured by his own subjects,
died or was killed by the Spaniards at the
time of the evacuation. Cortés retreated
around the northern end of Lake Tezcuco,
overcame an overwhelming Aztec army at
Otumba (1520, July 7), and reached Tlaxcala, which remained loyal. At Tlaxcala
Cortés reorganized his forces. He then
conquered the province of Tepeaca, founding Segura de la Frontera. An expedition
was sent into southern Vera Cruz, and two
outposts were established. Having received
reinforcements, among them the members
of the Garay expedition to Pánuco, Cortés
established his base at Tezcuco and undertook the investment of Tenochtitlán by
land and water.

1521, May 26-Aug. 13. After a prolonged
and desperate siege the Spaniards,
aided by a horde of native allies, captured the Aztec capital, making prisoner
Cuauhtémoc, who had become emperor
and had organized resistance. Spanish
control was firmly established over the
immediate vicinity and the conquest was
rapidly extended. Tenochtitlán was razed
and **Mexico City,** which became the seat
of government of the later viceroyalty of
New Spain, was erected. A bitter suit
between Cortés and Velasquez, carried on
before the crown during the period of the
conquest, terminated in favor of Cortés and
the emperor named him *governor* and
captain-general of New Spain (1522, Oct.
15).

b. EXPANSION TO THE SOUTH

1522-1524. **Cristóbal de Olid** subdued
Colima and part of Jalisco. An-
other settlement was made in Michoacan,
the territory of the independent and civilized Tarascans, whose ruler had given
allegiance to Cortés. Farther south Oaxaca
and Tehuántepec were reduced, the latter
by Alvarado.

1523-1525. Embassies from certain towns
of Guatemala having made sub-
mission, Cortés sent Alvarado to that region.
Alvarado conquered the civilized Quiché
and Cakchiquel and founded the city of
Guatemala. The conquest was then extended into **Salvador,** and Alvarado become
governor of the general district of Guatemala. Chiapas was reduced by expeditions
from New Spain (1523–1528).

1524-1526. Cortés then sent Olid to conquer and settle **Honduras.** Olid
sought to free himself from the authority
of Cortés and overcame Gil González
Dávila, but was defeated and later killed
by a lieutenant of Cortés. Trujillo was
founded during this period (1523–1526).
Cortés led an expedition overland to Honduras by way of Tabasco and Petén, and
established his authority, thereupon returning to Mexico (1524–1526).

1526-1536. Almost complete anarchy continued in Honduras, despite appointment of royal governors. The acting
governor, **Andrés de Cerezeda,** established
the majority of the colonists in the area of
the Río de Ulúa (Higueras), and soon summoned Alvarado to preserve the colony
(1534–1536). Alvarado as governor founded
San Pedro and dispatched an expedition
to found Gracias a Dios, but departed for
Spain without definitely reducing the area
(1536).

1527-1535. The conquest of Yucatan was
assigned to Francisco de Montejo
(c. 1473–1553) as *adelantado.* The first
attempt of Montejo to conquer the Maya
failed after eight years of effort, and he
was diverted to Honduras upon appointment as governor. The final conquest and
colonization of Yucatan was achieved by
the son and nephew of Montejo under his
general direction. Campeche, Mérida, Valladolid, and Salamanca (Bacalar) were
founded (1539–1545).

1537-1539. Francisco de Montejo, as royal
governor, conclusively subjugated
Higueras, founding Comayagua. Alvarado,
upon returning, again became governor, but
after his death (1541) governmental affairs
fell into confusion. Stability was created

with the establishment of the *Audiencia of Confines* (1542–1544).

1546. A serious revolt of the Maya was crushed.

Tabasco, which had been colonized at an early date but was in danger of abandonment, was assigned to the jurisdiction of Montejo and was pacified by him and his son (1529–1540). The area of Petén was not conquered until the close of the seventeenth century.

c. EXPANSION TO THE NORTH

1522-1527. The initial efforts of Garay to colonize Amichel having failed, Cortés subdued the region of the Panuco River and founded a town. Further efforts by Garay were forestalled, and a revolt of the natives was put down by one of Cortés' lieutenants (1523). The Panuco district became a special jurisdiction under the crown, with Nuño de Guzmán as governor (1527).

1531-1550. In the interior Spanish expansion was slower. Querétaro was reduced and the town of that name was founded. The Zacatecas and Guanajuato silver mines were opened, the former proving to be the richest in New Spain. San Luis de Potosí, in which mining was soon developed, was conquered by Francisco de Urdiñola, whose son continued the work of colonization.

1539. Reports brought by Cabeza de Vaca and the legend of the *Seven Cities of Cíbola* caused the viceroy, Mendoza, to send the Franciscan Fray Marcos de Niza northward. Having reached the Zuñi pueblos of New Mexico, the friar returned with exaggerated accounts.

1540-1542. Francisco Vásquez de Coronado, governor of New Galicia, with the authority of the viceroy, led an expedition overland to the new lands, while Hernando de Alarcón proceeded by sea along the west coast. Coronado reached the Zuñis and his lieutenants reached the Moqui pueblos and the Grand Cañon of the Colorado. In search of Gran Quivira, Coronado traversed northern Texas, Oklahoma, and eastern Kansas before his return.

1562-1570. Francisco de Ibarra, governor and captain-general, conquered New Vizcaya and founded Durango.

1598-1608. Under royal patent, Juan de Oñate secured the submission of New Mexico and sent out expeditions which explored the region from Kansas to the Gulf of California. Santa Fé was founded soon after the resignation of Oñate.

In the meanwhile the Spaniards had extended their conquests far up the Pacific Coast.

1529-1531. Nuño de Guzmán, president of the first *audiencia* of New Spain, subjugated a considerable area to the north and west of Mexico City, including Jalisco and Sinaloa. This region was called *New Galicia*, of which Campostela became the capital.

1532-1533. In search of a strait and of new lands, Cortés dispatched expeditions which reached northern Sinaloa and Lower California.

1535. Cortés himself attempted, though without success, to found a colony in Lower California, but Francisco de Ulloa, in command of an expedition organized by Cortés, reached the head of the Gulf of California (1539). Alarcón, co-operating by sea with Coronado's expedition to New Mexico, reached the same district and passed up the Colorado River (1540).

1541. In the absence of Coronado, the natives of New Galicia rose in revolt, but were finally subdued by the viceroy, Antonio de Mendoza.

1542-1543. As part of his project for South Sea discovery, Mendoza sent Juan Rodríguez de Cabrillo to search for a northern strait. Cabrillo, and, after his death, the pilot Bartolomé Ferrelo, explored the Pacific coast as far as Oregon, but failed to discover the Bays of Monterey and San Francisco.

1548. An *audiencia* was created to govern New Galicia, Guadalajara becoming the political and ecclesiastical capital.

1602. The occupation of the Philippines (p. 908), the development of trade, and the need for protection against English, French, and Dutch aroused renewed interest in the California coast and the possibility of a northern strait. The Madrid government having ordered the exploration of the coast, Sebastian Vizcaino proceeded to a point above San Francisco Bay, which, however, he did not discover. Plans to colonize the Monterey Bay region did not materialize.

1680. The Spaniards, driven from New Mexico by a revolt of the natives, reconquered the area somewhat later (1696).

1720-1722. Fearing loss of territory to France, the Spaniards permanently occupied Texas, mainly through the efforts of the Marquis of Aguayo, governor of Coahuila.

1769-1786. Under Gálvez' direction Upper California was occupied. San Diego (1769), Monterey (1770), Los Angeles (1781), and San Francisco (1776), were founded and a system of *presidios* and missions, the latter under the Franciscan order, was established.

1774-1776. Juan Pérez, Bruno de Heçeta, Bodega y Quadra, and other Spanish explorers were sent north along the coast to counter British and Russian activity. They discovered the mouth of the **Columbia River** and advanced as far as 60° N.L.

1776. José de Gálvez, minister of the Indies, erected New Vizcaya, Sinaloa, Sonora, the Californias, Coahuila, New Mexico, and Texas into the *Provincias Internas* under the governorship of a commandant-general responsible directly to the crown.

1789-1795. Attempts were made to colonize the region north of California. Settlements were made on Vancouver Island and at Cape Flattery, but without permanent results.

d. THE GULF COAST, FLORIDA AND THE CAROLINAS

1521. Juan Ponce de León, under royal patent, tried unsuccessfully to colonize Florida.

1526-1528. A colony, **San Miguel de Gualdape**, was established in the Carolinas by **Lucas Vásquez de Ayllón**, but was abandoned on his death.

1528. Pánfilo de Narváez, having secured authority to colonize the territory assigned to Garay on the Gulf coast and to Ponce de León in Florida, landed in Florida with colonists from Spain. After exploration he tried to reach the area of the Pánuco River. The expedition was wrecked on the coast of Texas and most of the colonists died of hunger and disease, or at the hands of the Indians.

1536. Alvar Núñez Cabeza de Vaca and three companions, after six years of captivity, escaped and traversed Texas and northern Mexico, reaching Culiacán.

1539-1543. Hernando de Soto (1499-1542), granted a patent for the colonization of the Gulf coast (Florida), headed an expedition from Spain, landed in Florida, explored the southeastern portion of the United States, discovered the Mississippi River (1541), traversed Arkansas and Oklahoma to the Arkansas River, and followed the latter river to the Mississippi. While moving down the Mississippi, De Soto died (1542) and the expedition, under Luis de Moscoso, continued on to the area of the Pánuco (1543). Luis de Cancer, a Dominican, and certain companions sought to bring the nations of Florida to obedience by peaceful means, in accord with theories of Las Casas, but De Cancer was killed, and the attempt was abandoned (1549).

1559-1561. Under directions from the crown, the viceroy, Velasco, dispatched a large expedition under Tristán de Luna to colonize the region of the Carolinas (Santa Elena). De Luna established a garrison at Pensacola, moved inland, and founded a settlement. The colonists were soon transferred to Pensacola. Villafañe replaced De Luna as governor and sought without success to colonize the Carolinas. The garrison left at Pensacola was soon withdrawn. In view of constant failure, Philip II ordered that no further attempt be made to colonize Florida (1561), but need for protection of the Bahama Channel (the route for the return to Spain of plate and merchant fleets) and French attempts to occupy the region led to a reversal of this policy.

1562. Jean Ribaut failed in an attempt to establish a French Huguenot settlement at Port Royal (in South Carolina), but shortly afterward **Laudonnière** founded Fort Caroline, on the St. John's River (1564). Ribaut arrived with a third expedition, with instructions to establish a fortified place to command the route of the Spanish plate fleets. As a result of these activities Philip II determined upon the expulsion of the French and the permanent colonization of Florida.

1565. As *adelantado* of Florida **Pedro Menéndez de Avilés founded St. Augustine**, captured Fort Caroline, and slew the garrison. Thus danger of French occupation was removed.

1565-1574. Menéndez de Avilés established *presidios* and posts throughout a wide area and explored and sought to colonize the area north of the peninsula. **Jesuits, and later Franciscans**, supported by the *adelantado*, established missions as far north as Virginia. The peninsula of Florida was secured for Spain by Menéndez de Avilés, but the attempts to achieve permanent possession of the territory to the north failed.

7. FOREIGN ENCROACHMENTS AND TERRITORIAL CHANGES

The commercial and territorial monopoly of Spain in the Indies, international war, and religious conflict caused England, France, and the Netherlands to attack Spanish shipping and coastal towns in the colonies and to colonize within areas controlled by Spain.

16th cent. French corsairs early attacked Spanish vessels off the coasts of Europe and at the Azores and Canaries and soon extended their activities into the Caribbean, where they attacked towns as well as commerce. In the latter half of the 16th century English freebooters, with the tacit approval of the crown, became active in the Atlantic, Caribbean, and Pacific. The raiding of the Pacific coast by **Drake** during his voyage around the world (1577–1580) is the most outstanding example of English activity in the Pacific during this period. The activities of British freebooters became official after the outbreak of war between Spain and England. Spanish commerce suffered greatly, and many towns were held for ransom or sacked, among them Nombre de Dios, Cartagena, Santo Domingo, and Valparaiso. **Drake, Hawkins, Oxenham,** and **Cavendish** were the most important of the English mariners, and two of the expeditions commanded by Drake constituted formidable armaments. Coincident with the struggle for independence in the Netherlands, Dutch mariners became active.

17th cent. With the decline of Spanish power, official colonization of the lesser Antilles, neglected by Spain, was undertaken by England, France, and Holland. Settlements were established by these powers in the Guianas. England colonized Bermuda and the Bahamas, the Netherlands unsuccessfully sought to colonize the Pacific coast of South America, and France and Holland sought to gain possession of portions of Brazil. Powerful Dutch armaments were dispatched to American waters, one of which, under Piet Heyn, captured a plate fleet from New Spain (1628). An expedition sent against Spanish possessions by Cromwell captured Jamaica (1655), of which England remained in permanent possession. Western Española, in which French buccaneers had secured a foothold and official colonization had later been undertaken, was ceded to France by the Treaty of Ryswick (1697). The activity of English, French, and Dutch freebooters in the Caribbean reached its height during the 17th century, and played an important part in the decline of Spanish commerce. The Englishman **Henry Morgan** was the most important of these freebooters, and during his career captured numerous cities and towns, including Puerto Bello and Panama (1655-1671).

18th cent. The European wars in which Spain was involved in the 18th century and the early part of the 19th had important consequences in the Americas. Control of the seas by Great Britain and the naval weakness of Spain rendered protection of the colonies increasingly difficult. The Spanish commercial monopoly was, moreover, incapable of enforcement, and extensive illicit commerce participated in by British, French, and Dutch merchants developed.

1701-1713. During the **War of the Spanish Succession** there was considerable fighting between the allied Spaniards and French in the West Indies and Florida. By the **Treaty of Utrecht** (1713) Great Britain was granted the *asiento*, or monopoly of the slave trade with the Spanish possessions and the right to send one ship each year to trade with Atlantic ports of the Spanish colonies.

1718-1720. Incident to war between France and Spain, military operations took place in Florida and Texas, as a result of which Spanish possession of Texas was assured, although the boundary remained disputed.

1739-1748. In the "War of Jenkins' Ear," which merged into the **War of the Austrian Succession,** Spain, as a result of reforms introduced by the Bourbons, maintained a successful defense of her possessions. Inconclusive operations took place in Florida and on the frontier of Georgia, and a powerful British expedition under Admiral Vernon was repulsed at Cartagena, which had been heavily fortified as a principal bulwark of colonial defense (1741). The **Treaty of Aix-la-Chapelle** (1748) provided for no important territorial changes.

1762. When Spain entered the **Seven Years' War** as an ally of France, British expeditions captured Havana and Manila (1762). By the **Treaty of Paris** (1763) Spain ceded Florida to Great Britain and received Havana, Manila being restored later. France ceded Louisiana to Spain, although Spanish authority was not established in the latter without opposition from the French colonists.

With the temporary elimination of France by the Seven Years' War, Great Britain and Spain became the great colonial powers, and **Charles III** (1759–1788), convinced that Great Britain would seek to possess herself of the Spanish colonies, believed a decisive conflict inevitable. Internal and colonial reforms introduced by Charles III raised Spain to the highest position of power and influence enjoyed since the 16th century, and she was comparatively well prepared for an eventual conflict.

1771. A dispute between Spain and Great Britain concerning possession of the **Falkland Islands** brought the two nations to the verge of war, but France refused to afford the support anticipated under the **Family Compact** (p. 452) and Spain was forced to agree to an accommodation.

1775-1783. The **American War of Independence**, becoming a European war after the alliance between France and the colonies, afforded Spain a desired opportunity to check British expansion, and she entered the conflict (1779). Spanish forces captured Mobile and Pensacola, overran the Bahamas, and blocked British attempts to gain control of the Mississippi (1779–1783). By the **Treaty of Versailles** (1783) Spain regained Florida, but relinquished the Bahamas.

1789. Controversy between Great Britain and Spain arose over the seizure of British ships at Nootka. Considering sovereignty involved, Spain invoked the **Family Compact** and prepared for war. The French revolutionary government failed fully to support Spain and she yielded. Great Britain and Spain adjusted the incident by treaty (1790–1794).

1795. By the **Treaty of Basel** Spain relinquished the eastern two-thirds of Española to France. This territory was returned to Spain by the **Treaty of Paris** (1814). Trinidad was ceded to Great Britain (1797). Great Britain during the 18th century gained permanent control of Belize and established a protectorate over the Mosquito Indians of Honduras and Nicaragua.

Controversy arose with the **United States** concerning the navigation of the Mississippi, the mouth of which Spain controlled through the acquisition of Louisiana.

1800. France under the consulate forced Spain to return **Louisiana**, guaranteeing that the territory would not be transferred to any power other than Spain.

1803. France notwithstanding soon **sold Louisiana to the United States.** As a result of increasing pressure from the United States, Spain sold **Florida** to that nation (1819–1821).

The establishment of territorial jurisdiction in South America in accord with the **Line of Demarcation** (p. 367) created much friction between Spain and Portugal. Colonia was established on the left bank of the estuary of the Río de la Plata by the Portuguese (1680–1683) and Montevideo was founded some years later by the Spaniards to prevent Portuguese expansion (1723). Colonia soon became a base for illicit British and Portuguese trade with the province of the Río de la Plata. The **Treaty of Madrid** (1750), an attempted settlement, provided that Colonia should be given to Spain in return for seven Jesuit *reductions* on the east bank of the Uruguay; that Portuguese claims to the basins of the Amazon and Paraná and Spanish claims to the Philippines be recognized, and that boundaries be surveyed. The Guaraní of the seven *reductions*, incited by the Jesuits, rebelled against transfer, and it became necessary for the Portuguese to subdue them by force, the **War of the Seven Reductions** (1752–1756). Portugal, notwithstanding, retained Colonia, and Charles III annulled the Treaty of Madrid (1761). Spanish forces captured Colonia (1762) and invaded Río Grande do Sul (1762), but these territories were returned by the **Treaty of Paris** (1763). Pombal (p. 454) desired to expand Portuguese territory, and, relying on British support, encroached upon Spanish territory. Rivalry between Spain and Portugal continued, and when Great Britain, because of developments in Europe and North America, failed effectively to support Portugal, Charles III dispatched a strong force which captured Colonia and moved against other Portuguese territories (1776–1777). With the dismissal of Pombal (1777) hostilities were suspended and the **Treaty of San Ildefonso** was concluded (1777), by which Colonia and disputed Paraguayan territory were assigned to Spain, and Portuguese claims to the interior were recognized. Meanwhile the **Viceroyalty of La Plata** had been created as a defensive as well as an administrative measure (1776). The Portuguese later occupied the disputed missions territory incidental to European hostilities (1801), but by posterior settlements Spain received Colonia and Uruguay while Portugal secured Río Grande do Sul. Attempts of Great Britain to secure territory in the region of the Río de la Plata failed completely (1806–1807).

8. THE SPANISH COLONIAL SYSTEM

a. POPULATION

Emigration to the Indies was rigidly controlled by the crown and the *Casa de Contratación*. Heretics, Moors, Jews and their descendants were excluded. The vast majority of immigrants were from the realms of the crown of Castile. In the early 16th century the crown adopted active measures to encourage immigration. Negro slavery, introduced at the opening of the century, was extensive only in the West Indies and northern South America. Intermixture between male Spaniards and native women produced a large mixed group (*mestizos*). In 1574 the Spanish population was estimated at some 160,000, and at the close of the colonial period the estimated population was 3,276,000 whites, 5,328,000 *mestizos*, 7,530,000 Indians, and 776,000 Negroes (New Spain 1,230,000 whites, 1,860,000 *mestizos*, 3,700,000 Indians; Guatemala, 280,000 whites, 420,000 *mestizos*, 880,000 Indians; Peru and Chile, 465,000 whites, 853,000 *mestizos*, 1,030,000 Indians; Colombia and Venezuela, 642,000 whites, 1,256,000 *mestizos*, 720,000 Indians; Río de la Plata, 320,000 whites, 742,000 *mestizos*, 1,200,000 Indians; Cuba and Puerto Rico, 339,000 whites, 197,000 mixed, 389,000 Negroes). Negroes in all colonies except Cuba and Puerto Rico numbered 387,000.

Social composition. There existed six relatively distinct groups in the population of the colonies: Spanish colonial officials; upper grade creoles (those of Spanish blood born in the Indies) and socially superior Spanish immigrants; lower grade creoles and Spanish immigrants, high rank *mestizos* and Indian nobility; *mestizos* (mixed white and Indian), mulattoes, *zambos* (mixed Negro and Indian), and certain Indians; Indians, who constituted the largest group numerically; Negro slaves. The two upper classes possessed virtually all the wealth of the colonies.

b. ADMINISTRATION

The discovery of America was accomplished under commission of the sovereign of Castile and the new lands consequently became realms of the Castilian crown, from which all authority emanated. In accord with the theory of royal absolutism the crown abrogated governmental authority granted Columbus and the early conquista-dores and established direct royal control. The machinery of royal government was fully formed by the third quarter of the 16th century.

After appointment to supervise preparations for the second voyage of Columbus (1493) **Juan Rodríguez de Fonseca** became virtual minister of the Indies, and as such laid the foundation for the expansion of the machinery of royal government. With the development of trade the *Casa de Contratación* was established at Seville to control colonial commerce and maritime enterprise (1503). The nucleus of a council to administer the Indies was evolved and this body, under the presidency of Rodríguez de Fonseca, rapidly developed into a formal **Council of the Indies** (*Consejo de Indias*). Upon the death of Rodríguez de Fonseca the *Consejo de Indias* was reorganized (1524) and by the close of the reign of Charles V its organization and functions were fully developed. The *Consejo de Indias* exercised supreme administrative, judicial, and ecclesiastical authority over the Indies and possessed supervisory authority over the *Casa de Contratación*. The legislation for the Indies promulgated by the crown and *Consejo de Indias* was codified in the *Recopilación de Leyes . . . de las Indias*, one of the greatest of colonial codes (1680). At the opening of the 17th century a *Junta de Guerra y Armadas de Indias*, to administer the armed forces and the dispatch of fleets to the Indies, and a *Cámara de Indias*, to control ecclesiastical affairs and appointments, were created as adjuncts to the *Consejo de Indias*. Early in the Bourbon period the office of *Minister of the Indies* was created with the establishment of a *Secretaría de Guerra, Marina e Indias* (1714). This secretariat underwent numerous changes and before the close of the century a separate **secretariat of the Indies** was formed. With the creation of these institutions the *Consejo de Indias* declined in importance.

Direct royal government in the Indies was instituted with the appointment of **Francisco de Bobadilla** as judge and governor of Española and the removal of Columbus (1499–1500). Bobadilla was succeeded by Nicolás de Ovando (1502), and he by Diego Columbus, son of the admiral, named governor at the will of the crown (1509). A tribunal of three royal judges was created in Santo Domingo as a check on the governor (1511), and this body was later established in a fully developed form as the *Audiencia of Santo Domingo* and given governmental authority over the West Indies (1526).

On the mainland government was at first permitted to rest with those who had conquered the several areas under royal patent or with crown recognition and who governed with the titles of *adelantado*, governor, or captain-general. The threat to royal absolutism inherent in government by powerful vassals with privileged positions caused early extension of direct government to the mainland.

The institution of the *adelantado* was of great importance during the period of conquest. By capitulation with the crown the *adelantado* undertook the conquest of a specified area at his own cost and in return was assigned governmental authority and hereditary privileges. The institution was of value in bringing new lands under Spanish dominion, but its character threatened royal authority and the powers granted were revoked after achievement of the royal purpose.

An *audiencia* was created to govern New Spain (1527), but proved weak in its executive aspects and shortly after a *viceroy*, Antonio de Mendoza, was appointed (1529), although he did not take office for some years (1535). The Viceroyalty of Peru was created by the New Laws (1542), which also established an *audiencia* at Lima. The Viceroyalty (or *Reino*) of New Spain, with its capital Mexico City, came to include all Spanish territory north of Panama, the West Indies, Venezuela, and the Philippine Islands. That of Peru, with its capital Lima, included Panama and all Spanish territory in South America except Venezuela.

Audiencias, each with its definite area, were created for Guatemala (1542), New Galicia (1548), New Granada (1549), Charcas, or Upper Peru (1556), Quito (1563), and the Philippine Islands (1583–1593).

The viceroys, as direct representatives of the sovereign, possessed wide civil and military authority, and certain ecclesiastical powers. They were presidents of the *audiencias* of their capitals. The *audiencias*, composed of a president, *oidores*, a *fiscal* (crown prosecutor), and lesser officials, exercised supreme judicial authority within their districts, and the *audiencias* not directly under viceroys exercised governmental authority. The viceregal *audiencia* acted as an advisory council to the viceroy and in this function evolved legislative power. The *audiencias* were co-ordinate in judicial affairs, appeals going directly before the *Consejo de Indias*, and they were empowered to correspond directly with the crown. The *audiencias* varied in status according to the rank of the presiding officer, i.e., viceroy, president and captain-general, or president. The presidents of the *audiencias* of Santo Domingo, Guatemala, and New Granada were early accorded military authority and became presidents and captains-general. As such they became practically independent of the viceroys. Guadalajara, Quito, and Charcas remained presidencies. In the absence of the viceroy or president and captain-general the *audiencia* assumed the government. During the Bourbon period New Granada, Panama, Venezuela, and Quito were erected into the Viceroyalty of New Granada (1717–1739), the Viceroyalty of La Plata was established (1776), the captaincies-general of Venezuela (1773), Cuba (1777), and Chile (1778) were created, and *audiencias* were established in Buenos Aires (1783), Caracas (1786), and Cuzco (1789).

Major administrative areas were divided into *gobiernos*, *corregimientos*, and *alcaldías mayores*, of which the *gobiernos* were, in general, the more important and frequently consisted of more than one province. This organization persisted until the reign of Charles III, when a system of intendants was established throughout the Indies (1769–1790). The intendants possessed administrative, judicial, financial, and military authority, and in fiscal and economic matters were directly responsible to the crown.

In accord with mediaeval Castilian traditions the municipalities at first enjoyed a large measure of self-government under their *cabildos*, composed of *regidores* (councilmen) and *alcades* (mayors), the former elected by the householders and the latter by the *regidores*. Before the close of the 16th century the election of *regidores* gave way to royal appointment, hereditary tenure, and venality of office. *Cabildos abiertos* of all citizens were at times held to discuss important matters. The municipal government exercised executive, legislative, and judicial authority within its district, although frequently under control of royal officials.

Fiscal administration was from the first directly under the crown through the *Casa de Contratación* and *contadores*, *factors*, *tesoreros*, and *veedores* in the New World jurisdictional areas. With the establishment of the intendants those officials assumed administration of fiscal affairs.

The Castilian institutions of the *residencia*, *visita*, and *pesquisa* were early instituted in the New World.

The principal sources of crown revenues were the *quinto*, or one-fifth of the products of the subsoil (gold, silver, precious stones) under the theory of crown ownership of the subsoil; the *almojarifzgo* (customs imposts); the *alcabala* (sales tax); the tributes of the natives; the *media anata* of civil and ecclesiastical offices, and the sale of the *Crusada*. Although revenues from the Americas were great, they at no time during the period of Spanish greatness exceeded 25% of the total income of the crown.

The presence of a great **Indian population** created extraordinary administrative problems. Municipal governments on the Castilian model were established in the Indian towns. Local Spanish officials had jurisdiction over the native towns in their districts. Protectors of the Indians were created for general and local districts to guard their interests. The *repartimiento-encomienda*, which early developed, was an institution of great political, social, and economic importance. In the earlier period this institution involved the assignment of specified towns to *conquistadores* and colonists, the Indians of which gave tribute, labor, and service to the *encomendero*, who was obligated to afford protection, indoctrination in Christianity, and instruction. Abuses caused the crown to regulate the system. Fixed quotas of tribute were established and labor and service were eliminated about the middle of the 16th century. Before the close of the century the *encomienda* was virtually reduced to the right to enjoy the revenues from specified towns. The crown after the publication of the **New Laws** (1542–1543) assumed control of many towns, and grants of *encomiendas* were brought under control of higher authorities. Attempts were made to abolish the system, notably in the New Laws, but it was not until the first part of the 18th century that abolition was definitely decreed. In certain areas the institution persisted almost until the close of the colonial period. Forced labor of the natives in the mines, on the *haciendas*, and for public works, the *mita*, was established late in the 16th century. Indians not within the *encomienda* system were required to pay an annual tribute and after the abolition of the *encomienda* this was required of all.

Extensive **enslavement of Indians** took place during the period of conquest under the law of just war, but this was prohibited by the New Laws. The natives were regarded as wards of the crown and throughout the colonial period legislation was promulgated for their welfare and protection, notable examples of such legislation being the Laws of Burgos (1512), and the New Laws. A section of the Laws of the Indies was devoted to Indian legislation (1680). The beneficent intent of the crown was to a large degree rendered nugatory by the difficulties of administration and the conflict of theory and practice. Many Spaniards acted as advocates of the Indians, the greatest of whom was **Bartolomé de las Casas** (1474–1566).

c. THE CHURCH AND THE MISSIONS

The union of State and Church in the Spanish Americas was exceedingly close. The crown early secured almost complete control of ecclesiastical affairs through the patronage of the Indies (*real patronato de Indias*) granted by Alexander VI in the bulls *Inter caetera* (1493, May 4) which assigned dominion over the Indies and exclusive authority to convert the natives, and *Eximiae devotionis* (1501, Nov. 16), which granted the titles and first fruits of the Church in the Indies, and by Julius II in the bull *Universalis ecclesiae* (1508, July 28), which conceded universal patronage. The extent and nature of the patronage was further defined by bulls issued at intervals throughout the colonial period. The crown exercised ecclesiastical control through the *Consejo de Indias* and later through that body and the *Cámara de Indias*. Papal bulls were not permitted to be placed in effect without the approval of the crown.

The full **organization of the Church** in the Indies followed closely upon the conquest and colonization, and at the close of the colonial period there existed 7 archbishoprics and some 35 dioceses. The Church possessed its own courts, with jurisdiction over all cases touching the clergy and spiritual affairs. The Spanish **Inquisition** was introduced (1569), and tribunals were established in Mexico City and Lima (1570–1571). This institution rapidly achieved great religious and political influence. Indians, considered incapable of rational judgment, were exempt from the Inquisition.

The Church played an important part in the Indies through conversion of the natives, aid in the maintenance of Spanish political authority, transmission of culture, and education. It achieved vast wealth and a privileged position, and at the close of the colonial period is estimated to have controlled half of the productive real estate in the Indies.

The **religious orders**, Franciscan, Dominican, Jesuit, Augustinian, Capuchin, and others, early achieved complete organization and carried on an exceedingly important work in converting the natives and instructing them in the rudiments of European civilization. The task of preserving and extending Spanish control in outlying areas was assigned to the religious orders, especially the Franciscan, Dominican, Capuchin, and Jesuit, as official agencies of the crown. Missionaries, accompanied by small groups of soldiers, and frequently by colonists, established missions and instructed the natives in Christianity. They developed agriculture, grazing, and simple industry. *Presidios* were established to protect the missions. Civilian colonists occupied the territory and secularization followed. Carrying forward on the northern frontier of New Spain, toward the close of the 17th century, Jesuits under the leadership of **Eusebio Kino**, began the establishment of missions in Pimería Alta (Arizona) and under **Juan María Salvatierra** in Lower California, over which the order was granted complete authority. A wide area was eventually brought under Spanish control. Early in the 18th century a system of missions and *presidios* was established in Texas and late in the century in California. Dominicans and Franciscans were active in Guatemala, Capuchins in the area of the lower Orinoco, to check French, English, and Dutch encroachments, and Jesuits in the territory of the Araucanians and Paraguay. The mission system in Paraguay was one of the most important in the New World. Granted complete authority to convert and organize the Guaraní east of Asunción, the Jesuits established missions (*reductions*) along the upper Paraná. The natives were later transferred farther south because of Portuguese slave raids. A complete governmental organization was established, controlled by a father superior at Candelaria, the natives were instructed in Christianity and the rudiments of European civilization, and agriculture and industry were extensively developed. By the **Treaty of Madrid** (1750) seven *reductions* were transferred to Portugal. The Guaraní, incited by the Jesuits, rose in revolt to resist transfer, but were defeated. By later adjustments the territory remained in Spanish possession. With the expulsion of the Jesuits (1767) the Paraguayan *reductions* were given to Franciscans, but failed to prosper.

d. ECONOMIC CONDITIONS AND POLICIES

Mining of gold and silver, fostered by the crown, rapidly became the most important industry in the Spanish colonies.

Rich silver deposits were early discovered throughout central Mexico, especially in the districts of Zacatecas, Guanajuato, Pachuca, Taxco, and San Luis Potosí, and at Potosí in Upper Peru (1530–1600). Gold deposits were worked throughout the Indies. Silver production came to surpass that of gold, and after the third quarter of the 16th century Peru produced about two-thirds of the total output of precious metals.

Agricultural and pastoral pursuits were highly developed. All plants and animals of Spain were introduced into the Indies and native plants, especially maize, potatoes, cotton, tobacco, and cacao were cultivated.

Local textile, iron, pottery, shipbuilding, gold and silver working, and sugar (West Indies) industries developed.

The principal imports into the colonies were manufactured goods, and **exports** consisted almost exclusively of precious metals, raw materials, and agricultural products.

The economic policy of Spain was based upon mercantilist theory. Trade was a monopoly of the metropolis under direct crown control and economic activity in the colonies which competed with that of Spain was prohibited or restricted.

The economic privileges of Columbus were almost immediately rendered inoperative and the crown assumed direct control over all phases of economic activity. In the earliest period Juan Rodríguez de Fonseca as *de facto* minister of the Indies controlled commerce (1493–1503), and trade under license was authorized by the crown (1495–1501). The *Casa de Contratación,* "a board of trade, a commercial court, and a clearing-house for the American traffic," was established at Seville (1503). This body came under the supervisory authority of the *Consejo de Indias.* Seville was accorded a monopoly of the American trade. In the New World Vera Cruz, Cartagena, and Puerto Bello, alone were permitted direct trade with Spain. General intercolonial commerce was early prohibited, and before the close of the 16th century commerce with the Philippines was restricted to Acapulco. Trade between Manila and China was confined to Chinese.

Naval warfare, attacks by corsairs, and the necessity of protection for gold and silver shipments caused the establishment of a system of **convoyed fleets,** one each year for New Spain (the *flota*) and one for Peru, the *galeones* (1543–1561). On the return the fleets united at Havana and sailed for Spain together. Fairs for the exchange of goods were held annually at Puerto Bello and Jalapa (Mexico). Trade between Acapulco and the Philippines

(Manila) was restricted to one vessel a year each way. With the period of Spanish decadence trade declined greatly.

Under the Bourbons many reforms were introduced. By the Treaty of Utrecht (1713) England was conceded the monopoly of the slave trade with the colonies (*asiento*) and the privilege of sending one vessel each year to Puerto Bello to trade. With the establishment of the office of the minister of the Indies early in the 18th century (1714) the *Casa de Contratación* tended to decline in importance. The *Casa de Contratación* and trade monopoly were transferred to Cadiz (1717–1718). To develop trade the monopolistic **chartered companies** of Honduras (1714), Guipúzcoa, or Caracas (1728), Havana (1740), and Santo Domingo (1757) were formed. With the decline in trade the sailings of the fleets had become irregular. Supplies were increasingly carried to the Indies in registered vessels and by the chartered companies and in the middle of the 18th century the fleet system was abolished (1748). Charles III promulgated a series of reform measures authorizing trade between more than twenty Spanish ports besides Seville and Cadiz and a large number of ports throughout the Indies and permitting direct intercolonial trade between New Spain and Peru and Guatemala and New Granada (1764–1782). A great increase in trade resulted. Royal secretaries having increasingly assumed its functions, the *Casa de Contratación* was abolished (1790). During the wars of the French Revolution neutral vessels were permitted to engage in the carrying trade with the colonies (1797).

e. EDUCATION, LEARNING, AND FINE ARTS

Education in Spanish America, with the exception of the rudimentary instruction afforded the Indians by the Church, was largely confined to the upper classes. The earliest universities were those of **Mexico** (1551), **San Marcos de Lima** (1551), and **St. Thomas Aquinas** of Santo Domingo (1558), founded by royal decree. They were modeled after the University of Salamanca. A school of mines was established in Mexico by Charles III (1783).

A vast body of **historical writing**, much of it of high quality, was produced during the colonial period, and important anthropological and linguistic studies were made. In the sciences the most important figures were **Carlos Sigüenza y Góngora** (1645–1700) and **Pedro de Peralta Barnuevo Rocha y Benavides** (1663–1743).

Juan Rúz de Alarcón (d. 1639), a Mexican creole, achieved a high place in the Spanish drama and **Sor Juana Inés de la Cruz** (b. 1651), also a Mexican creole, attained recognition for her poetry.

The first **printing press** was introduced into Mexico by the Viceroy Mendoza (1535). At the close of the colonial period there were a number of presses in operation in the larger cities. Newssheets and scientific and literary publications appeared in Lima and Mexico City toward the close of the 18th century.

Intellectual activity was, in general, seriously hampered by the Inquisition.

In **art and architecture** Spanish models were followed. Local schools of painting developed in Mexico and Quito. Charles III founded the **San Cárlos Academy of Fine Arts** in the former city (1778). An outstanding architectural achievement was the **Cathedral of Mexico**, begun late in the 16th century and completed in the first part of the 19th. (*Cont. p.* 799.)

9. PORTUGUESE AMERICA

1500-1521. Absorbed by interests in the Orient, **Manuel the Fortunate** (1495–1521) made no effective effort to colonize the territory claimed by Portugal in South America, although certain royal expeditions were dispatched and trading posts were established through private enterprise.

1521-1530. French activities having menaced Portuguese possession, **John III** (1521–1557) undertook systematic colonization.

1530-1532. **Martin Affonso de Souza**, as captain-major and leader of a colonizing and exploratory expedition, founded São Vicente and actively furthered colonization, introducing cattle and European grains and fruits and laying the foundations of a sugar industry.

1532-1536. A system of feudal hereditary captaincies under *donatarios* with virtually sovereign authority was established by the crown, but proved unsuccessful and a more centralized administration with a directly responsible governor-general at its head was created.

1549. **Thomé de Souza**, the first governor general, founded **São Salvador** (Bahia), which was made the seat of government. De Souza firmly established the administration and effectively furthered colonization. This task was ably continued by **Mem de Sá** (1558-1572). **São Paulo** was founded shortly after the middle of the century.

1549. Jesuits, headed by Manuel de Nobrega and José de Anchieta, undertook the conversion of the natives and established missions, playing an important part in colonization.

1551. The fundamental relationship between Church and State was established by a bull of Julius III which conceded to the crown complete spiritual jurisdiction over conquests and the right to nominate bishops, collect tithes, dispense church revenues, and receive appeals from ecclesiastical tribunals. The Bishopric of Bahia, suffragan to the Archbishop of Lisbon, was erected (1551).

France, Holland, and England did not permit Portugal to remain in possession of Brazil unchallenged. French efforts to establish an empire in South America passed through two distinct phases.

1555. With the intention of creating an "Antarctic France," a colony was founded on the Bay of Rio de Janeiro under **Nicolas Durand de Villegagnon.**

1565-1567. The Portuguese under leadership of Mem de Sá destroyed the colony and founded the city of **Rio de Janeiro,** ending French attempts in that area. Henry IV projected the establishment of an "Equinoctial France."

1612. After his death, although without direct royal aid, a town was founded on the island of **Maranhão** and exploration was conducted on the mainland with the purpose of occupying the area of the mouths of the Amazon. The State of Maranhão was created (1621), directly subordinate to the home government. The Jesuits established missions along the Amazon and gave Portugal control of the vast river basin. Maranhão was independent of Brazil until 1777.

1615. The Portuguese forced the surrender of the colony, and shortly thereafter founded Belem. These events terminated French efforts to establish an extensive empire in South America.

The personal union of the crowns of Spain and Portugal (p. 392) carried important consequences for Brazil. **English attacks** on coastal towns occurred in the final decades of the 16th century, Santos being sacked.

1624-1625. Dutch activities were far more serious. Shortly after the organization of the **Dutch West India Company** (p. 438), the Dutch captured Bahia (1624),

but were forced to capitulate to a Spanish fleet (1625).

1630. Continuing the effort, a powerful Dutch armament captured Recife and Olinda. The conquest was extended over a wide area.

1637. The West India Company named **Prince Maurice of Nassau-Siegen** governor, and under his able administration Dutch control was established over an area extending from the São Francisco River to Maranhão.

1644. As the West India Company displayed greater interest in profit than in colonization, Prince Maurice returned to Holland.

1645. Immediately thereafter, in a truly popular movement, the Portuguese rebelled and within a decade forced the Dutch to capitulate (1654). These events ended Dutch occupation of Brazilian territory, a situation later recognized by treaty (1661, Aug. 6).

Slave-raiding parties began to penetrate into the interior from São Paulo (1629) and by the middle of the century these Paulistas had explored an extensive area of southern Brazil. They attacked the Spanish Jesuit *reductions* on the upper Paraná, forced their transfer to a more southern area, and made possible Portuguese possession of the region. Simultaneously Portuguese Jesuits established missions in the south, coming into conflict with the Paulistas in their efforts to protect the Indians, in which they received royal support.

1680-1683. Seeking to gain possession of the left bank of the Río de la Plata (*Banda Oriental*), the Portuguese founded **Colonia.** Spain and Portugal immediately came into conflict over this area; **Montevideo** being founded by the Spaniards (1723). The territory changed hands frequently during the remainder of the colonial period.

1693. Decreasing profits from slaving operations and increasingly effective protection afforded the Indians by the Jesuits caused the Paulistas to direct their efforts to a search for gold, and toward the end of the 17th century extensive deposits were discovered in **Minas Geráes.** An influx of gold-seekers ensued, among them many newly arrived Portuguese.

1701-1713. The alliance of Portugal with England during the War of the Spanish Succession led to French attacks on Brazilian ports, **Rio de Janeiro** being sacked and held for ransom by Duguay-Trouin (1711).

1708-1709. Efforts of the Portuguese to displace the Paulistas resulted in open warfare, the **War of the Emboabas,**

in which the former were successful. Through the efforts of the Paulistas Matto Grosso and Goyaz, far to the west of the Line of Demarcation, were gained for Portugal.

1709. With the colonization of the interior the crown created the captaincy of **São Paulo and Minas Geraes,** with a captain-general directly responsible to the sovereign, erected Minas Geraes into a separate jurisdiction (1720), and established the captaincies of Matto Grosso (1744) and Goyaz (1748).

1710-1711. The War of the Mascates. Rivalry between the native Brazilians of Olinda, the political capital of Pernambuco, and the Portuguese of the commercial town of Recife, concerning the elevation of the latter to *villa* status led to armed conflict. Recife, notwithstanding, was accorded municipal privileges and eventually superseded Olinda as the seat of government.

The **Line of Demarcation** never having been surveyed, as Portuguese expansion progressed, efforts were made to establish limits.

1750. In the **Treaty of Madrid,** Spain recognized Portuguese claims to extensive areas in the basins of the Amazon and Paraná, and although this treaty was abrogated, the bases of settlement were reaffirmed by the **Treaty of San Ildefonso** (1777). While the limits were not definitely surveyed, Portuguese claims to territory vastly greater than that assigned under the **Treaty of Tordesillas** (p. 367) were permanently established.

1750-1777. Pombal as minister of Joseph I (p. 453) introduced far-reaching colonial reforms. Administration was unified, the capital being transferred from Bahia to Rio Janeiro and Maranhão being incorporated with Brazil (1777). Commerce between Portugal and Brazil was encouraged, certain restrictions and taxes were removed and trading companies were organized. Native Brazilians were appointed to important governmental posts, racial equality was advocated, and defenses were improved. Pombal strongly pressed Portuguese territorial claims. The Jesuits **were expelled** from Portugal and her possessions during his ministry (1759).

1789. The Conspiracy of Minas. Maladministration, heavy taxes, and reactionary government led to an abortive attempt at revolution in Minas Geraes,

led by **Joaquim José de Silva Xavier** (*Tiradentes*).

1807. The determination of Napoleon to force Portuguese adherence to the Continental System and his plan to partition Portugal exercised a decisive influence on Portuguese and Brazilian history.

1807-1808. Apprised of the designs of the emperor, upon the approach of a French army, **Prince John,** regent after 1792 because of the insanity of María I, created a regency in Portugal, fled to Brazil, and established his government at Rio de Janeiro.

1808-1816. The regent adopted many reforms advantageous to Brazil. Decrees were issued establishing free trade, removing restrictions on industry, promoting agriculture and communications, establishing a royal press, founding the Bank of Brazil, and encouraging the arts and sciences. Brazil was erected into a coordinate member of the **United Kingdom of Portugal, Brazil, and Algarves** (1815, Dec. 16). The regent became **John VI** upon the death of María I (1816, Mar. 1).

1808. Prince John declared war on France and dispatched an expedition which occupied **French Guiana.** This territory was returned by the **Treaty of Paris** (1814). The regent sought also to annex the *Banda Oriental* and supported the designs of his wife, Carlota Joaquina, sister of Ferdinand VII of Spain, to establish her rule over the provinces of the **Río de la Plata.**

1812. The opposition of the viceroy and the revolutionary *junta* of Buenos Aires and British influence caused the regent temporarily to renounce intervention in the area of the Río de la Plata.

1816-1821. After becoming king, John took advantage of the situation arising from the struggle for independence in the *Banda Oriental* and the violation of Brazilian territory by the leader of the movement, **José Artigas** (p. 801). He then intervened again in the *Banda Oriental.* Portuguese troops occupied Montevideo and defeated Artigas, and the territory was incorporated into Brazil as the **Cisplatine Province** (1821). Projects against other provinces of the Río de la Plata were renounced under threat from Ferdinand VII and in face of a potentially united Argentina.

10. THE PORTUGUESE COLONIAL SYSTEM

Population and Race. A complex racial situation developed in Brazil. Intermixture between Portuguese males and Indian women gave rise to a large group of *mestizos*. From the middle of the 16th century onward Negro slaves were introduced in large numbers to meet labor requirements and extensive intermixture of Negro and white blood occurred. There was also intermixture between Negroes and natives. In 1583 the population was estimated at 25,000 whites, 18,000 civilized Indians, and 14,000 Negro slaves. In the mid-17th century, considerable immigration having taken place, at 150,000 to 200,000, three-fourths of whom were Indians, Negroes, and mixed. At the close of the 18th century at 3,000,000, a population already greater than that of Portugal. In 1818 the population was estimated at 843,000 whites, 1,887,500 Negroes, 628,000 mixed, and 259,400 civilized Indians. The bulk of the population was concentrated in São Paulo, Minas Gerães, Pernambuco, and Bahia. Originally the crown permitted any person of Catholic faith to enter Brazil, but after 1591 aliens were excluded.

Portuguese colonial administration was not clearly differentiated from that of the metropolis prior to the union of the crowns of Portugal and Spain. For general purposes there existed an inspector of finances and a *Casa da India*. The *Mesa da Consiencia e Ordems*, with ecclesiastical and financial powers, was created in 1532. Upon the establishment of a more centralized government in Brazil, a commissioner of finances and a chief justice were appointed for the colony (1548). For local administration there were *corregedores*, with judicial and military functions. Municipal organization was patterned on that of Portugal. The fundamental code was the *Ordenanças Manuelinas* (1521).

During the period of the union of the thrones of Spain and Portugal (1580/1581–1640) Spanish administrative forms were introduced. The inspector of finance was replaced by a council, the *Conselho da Fazenda*. A Council of the Indies (*Conselho da India*) was created (1604), a supreme court was established in Bahia (1609), and the title of *viceroy* was introduced (1640). Under Philip III (1598–1621), the *Ordenanças Philippinas*, which permitted greater local autonomy, superseded the *Ordenanças Manuelinas*. The greater portion of these innovations were permanent.

By the close of the 18th century the structure of royal government was fully formed. The **Transmarine Council** (*Conselho do Ultramar*), formerly the Council of the Indies, exercised general religious and military authority over Brazil. Parã, Maranhão, Pernambuco, Bahia, São Paulo, Minas Gerães, Goyaz, Matto Grosso, and Rio de Janeiro were captaincies-general, provinces of the first rank, under captains-general usually appointed by the crown. The viceroy, who was also captain-general of Rio de Janeiro, possessed legal authority over the captains-general in certain matters, but the latter frequently received instructions directly from the crown, with which they could correspond directly. A tendency toward local autonomy existed. There were a number of districts of inferior status, captaincies, subordinate to the captaincies-general. Two superior judicial districts existed, with high tribunals at Bahia and Rio de Janeiro (founded 1757) respectively. Appeals from these courts went directly to Lisbon. The municipalities, with their councils (*senados da camera*), enjoyed a certain degree of self-government.

Portuguese economic policy was founded upon mercantilist theory. Commerce was a monopoly of Portugal until 1808 and trade was restricted to Lisbon and Oporto. In 1649 a monopolistic **Commercial Company of Brazil** was organized and greatly developed commerce. The **Maranhão Company**, also monopolistic, was formed in 1682. Both companies aroused opposition and were abolished in the first part of the 18th century. To foster commerce two chartered companies, one with a monopoly of the trade of Pará and Maranhão and the other with a monopoly of that of Pernambuco and Parahyba, were formed during the period of Pombal, but were abolished after his fall. Between 1548 and the formation of the Commercial Company of Brazil commerce was carried on through convoyed fleets. Discontinued during the existence of the company, the system was re-established upon its abolition and continued until finally abolished by Pombal.

Restrictions were placed upon industry and agriculture which competed with that of Portugal, and a government monopoly, which produced important crown revenues, existed for the exploitation of Brazil wood, mining of diamonds, and other activities. Customs duties were levied, and a royal fifth (*quinto*) of the product of mining activity was required. Agriculture and pastoral pursuits were highly developed. Cotton and sugar cane were the principal agricultural products. The cultivation of coffee was introduced. The mining of gold and diamonds (rich deposits of the latter were discovered in 1721), the gathering of Brazil wood, and the production of sugar and hides were the chief industries. Brazilian sugar production became the greatest in the world and was the basis of the wealth of the colony.

The Church and education. In 1676 Innocent XI created the **Archbishopric of Brazil,** with Bahia as the metropolitan see, at the same time erecting the suffragan bishoprics of Rio de Janeiro and Pernambuco. At the close of the 18th century there were nine bishoprics, two of which were suffragan to the Archbishop of Lisbon. The **Inquisition** was not introduced into Brazil. The **Jesuits** until their expulsion (1759) played an important rôle through conversion of the natives, extension of Portuguese influence, and establishment of schools and colleges, the earliest being that of São Paulo (1554). No institution of university status was created in Brazil during the colonial period, but seminaries and academies were established, among them the seminaries of São Pedro and São José at Rio de Janeiro (founded 1736).

(Cont. p. 805.)

D. NORTH AMERICA

1. EXPLORATION AND SETTLEMENT

a. THE FRENCH IN NORTH AMERICA

Norman and Breton fishermen visited Newfoundland coasts perhaps as early as 1500. There are unconfirmed reports of attempts to explore the Gulf of St. Lawrence in 1506 and 1508, and of an unsuccessful colony on Sable Island in 1518.

1524. Giovanni de Verrazzano, sent out by Francis I, probably explored the coast from Cape Fear to Newfoundland.

1534-1541. Voyages of **Jacques Cartier**. On the first voyage he sighted the Labrador coast, passed through the Straits of Belle Isle and explored the Gulf of St. Lawrence. On the second (1535–1536) he sailed up the St. Lawrence, stopped at the site of Quebec, proceeded to the La Chine Rapids and to the site of Montreal. On the third (1541) he was accompanied by M. Roberval, a Picard nobleman, whom Francis I had made viceroy of Canada, Newfoundland, and Labrador. Unsuccessful attempts were made to establish a settlement at Quebec, and therewith the French efforts to colonize the St. Lawrence Valley came to an end until the 17th century.

In the south the activities of the French necessarily led to conflict with the Spaniards.

1562. Admiral Coligny, as part of his plan to attack Spain, sent **Jean de Ribaut** to establish a colony in Florida. A colony on Port Royal Sound failed, but in 1564 Ribaut and **René de Laudonnière** established **Fort Caroline** on St. John's River. In the very next year the Spaniards, led by Menéndez de Avilés, massacred the French colonists and took the fort. Commanded by the Chevalier de Gourgues, the French (1567) avenged themselves by attacking the Spanish fort on the St. John's and putting the garrison to death.

1598. **Marquis de la Roche** attempted to found a colony on Sable Island. The survivors were rescued five years later.

1600. **Pontgravé, Chauvin, and De Monts,** with a grant of the fur-trade monopoly, made another unsuccessful attempt to colonize, this time at **Tadoussac** on the lower St. Lawrence.

1603. Pontgravé, accompanied by **Samuel de Champlain,** explored the St. Lawrence as far as La Chine Rapids. Champlain also explored the Acadian coast. In the next three years De Monts and Champlain organized a settlement on St. Croix Island, but moved later to **Port Royal.** Champlain followed the New England coast as far as Cape Cod, and returned to France in 1607.

1608, July 3. Champlain, acting as lieutenant for De Monts, founded the settlement of **Quebec.** In the following year, accompanied by a party of Algonquin and Huron Indians, he ascended the Richelieu River to the lake which now bears his name.

1610. Poutrincourt re-established Port Royal.

1613. Champlain explored the Ottawa River to about 100 miles above the present city of Ottawa. In 1615 he went up the river to Lake Nipissing and thence to Georgian Bay, being the first white man to blaze the fur-trader's route into the interior.

1615. Four **Recollet friars** arrived at Quebec, marking the beginning of French missionary activity. In 1625 five **Jesuits** arrived, beginning the work of that order.

1625-1664. **French settlements in the West Indies.** The first was St. Christopher (1625). The **Company of St. Christopher** was formed in 1626, to extend the settlement. This was superseded in 1635 by the **Company of Isles of America.** Guadaloupe, Martinique, and Tortuga were occupied, and between 1648 and 1656 settlements were made on St. Martin, St. Bartholomew, St. Croix, The Saints, Marie Galante, St. Lucia, and Grenada.

1627. Richelieu organized the **Company of the Hundred Associates** to colonize New France. The company was given all lands between Florida and the Arctic Circle, with a monopoly of trade, except in cod and whale fisheries.

1628. Acadia and Quebec captured by the English, but restored in 1632.

1634. Champlain, hearing of a great waterway in the west and believing it might be a passage to China, sent **Nico-**

EARLY SETTLEMENTS ON THE CONTINENT OF NORTH AMERICA

let on an exploring expedition. Nicolet reached Sault Ste. Marie, explored the south shore of the upper peninsula of Michigan, and reached the southern extremity of Green Bay.

1642. De Maisonneuve founded Montreal.

1658-1659. Radisson and Groseillers traded and explored in the country at the western end of Lake Superior.

1665. Father Allouez established the La Pointe Mission near the west end of Lake Superior.

1673. Father MARQUETTE and JOLIET, a trader, followed the Fox and Wisconsin Rivers to the Mississippi, which they descended to the confluence of the Arkansas. In the same year Count Frontenac, governor of New France, founded Fort Frontenac on Lake Ontario.

1679-1683. Explorations of La Salle, along the shores of Lake Michigan and in the Illinois country. He erected Fort Crèvecoeur near present Peoria (1679) and sent Hennepin to explore the upper Mississippi while he himself returned to Fort Frontenac. In 1682 La Salle reached the mouth of the Mississippi and took possession of the whole valley in the name of the King of France.

1683-1689. Attempts of La Salle to establish a French colony at the mouth of the Mississippi, in order to control the fur trade and to provide a base for attack upon Spain in America. He left France with some 400 men in 1684 and reached the West Indies. Continuing his voyage he missed the mouth of the Mississippi and landed at Matagorda Bay, on the coast of Texas. In the meanwhile, Tonty had descended the Mississippi, but had failed to find La Salle (1686). La Salle conducted four expeditions to the northeast in the hope of finding the Mississippi. On the fourth of these (1687) he was murdered by his companions. His colony was completely wiped out by an Indian attack (1689).

1699-1702. To check the Spanish advance, to control the Gulf coast and to forestall possible British occupation of the lower Mississippi, French forces under Iberville established posts at Biloxi and started the French colony in Louisiana (1699). The post was moved to Mobile Bay in 1702 and named St. Louis. Mobile was founded in 1710 and New Orleans in 1718.

1699. A Sulpician mission was set up at Cahokia in the Illinois country. In 1700 Jesuits moved down the Illinois River to Kaskaskia.

1701. Detroit founded by Cadillac, to control the entrance from Lake Erie to Lake Huron and to control the trade with the Illinois country.

1712. Antoine Crozat was granted a monopoly of the trade in the territory from Illinois to the coast. Crozat surrendered his patent (1717) and Louisiana was in the same year taken over by the Compagnie d'Occident, which became the Compagnie des Indes (1719).

b. THE ENGLISH IN NORTH AMERICA

(1) *Exploration*

Following the voyages of the Cabots (see p. 367) the English showed little interest in the New World until the second half of the 16th century.

1562. John Hawkins, having taken a cargo of slaves in Africa, disposed of them in Española. The Spaniards made efforts to stop a second slave-trading voyage (1564-1565), and on his third voyage (1567-1568) Hawkins was driven by a storm into the harbor of Vera Cruz, where his fleet was largely destroyed.

1572-1580. Francis Drake, nephew of Hawkins, carried out reprisals on Spanish commerce. Sailing in 1577 he passed through the Straits of Magellan, up the west coast of South America and north to Drake's Bay, California. He named the region New Albion and took possession for England. He then sailed to the East Indies, across the Indian Ocean, around the Cape of Good Hope, and thence home to England, being the first Englishman to circumnavigate the globe.

1576-1578. After unsuccessful efforts by explorers of the Muscovy Company to find a northeast passage to China, English efforts became concentrated on the search for a northwest passage. Martin Frobisher sailed from England in June, 1576, explored the Labrador coast, crossed Hudson Strait, coasted along Baffin Land, and entered the inlet known as Frobisher's Bay. In 1577-1578 he made a second voyage (p. 559).

1583. Sir Humphrey Gilbert took possession of Newfoundland in the name of Elizabeth, but lost his life on the return voyage.

1585. John Davis explored Davis Strait, but failed to find a northwest passage. A second attempt (1586) was equally unsuccessful (p. 559).

1586-1588. Thomas Cavendish, following Drake's course, plundered Spanish commerce and circumnavigated the globe.

(2) Virginia

1584. **Sir Walter Raleigh**, under patent, sent out Amadas and Barlow to establish a colony. They landed on Roanoke Island and named the country **Virginia.** Supply ships were sent out in 1586, but they found the colony deserted, the colonists having been taken back to England by Drake.

1587. Another party of colonists was sent out, under Governor **John White.** Upon his return in 1591, White found the ruins of the colony.

1602-1606. A number of voyages were made to America, the most important having been that of **George Weymouth** in 1604. Weymouth visited the New England coast and his favorable report did much to stimulate the desire to establish further colonies.

1606, Apr. A group of London men was given a charter to organize the **London Company**, with the object of colonizing the region between 34° and 41° N.L. Another group, composed of Plymouth, Bristol, and Exeter men, was chartered as the **Plymouth Company**, to operate between 38 and 45° N.L. The London Company at once sent out (Dec. 1606) three ships with 120 colonists, under command of Captain **Christopher Newport.**

1607, May. **FOUNDING OF JAMESTOWN COLONY** at the mouth of the James River. The colony was held together largely through the efforts of Captain **John Smith.**

1609. The London Company was enlarged and given a new charter which vested the government in a council, with power to appoint its own officers.

1610, May. Captain **Newport** arrived with 400 more colonists and with **Lord Delaware**, the new governor. Delaware left again in 1611, but remained governor until his death in 1618. **Sir Thomas Dale** was left in command of the colony and ruled with an iron hand.

1612. Beginning of the cultivation of tobacco, which was to play a vital part in the economic and social life of the colony.

1612. Third charter of the London Company. The Bermuda Islands were included in its jurisdiction.

1618. **Sir Edwin Sandys** became the dominant figure in the colony. He carried through a policy of assigning 50 acres of land to every person who would transport one more settler to the colony.

1619. Arrival of the first **Negro slaves** in the colony.

1619. **Sir Thomas Yeardley** arrived as governor, bringing instructions for each plantation to elect two burgesses to a general assembly. The assembly met at Jamestown on July 30 and was the **first representative assembly** in America.

1621. **Sir Francis Wyatt**, the governor, brought over new regulations providing for government through a governor, council of state, and assembly, the latter consisting of two burgesses each elected from every plantation and town.

1624. **Revocation of the charter.** This step was taken as a result of dissension within the company and because of the king's disapproval of popular government and of the raising of tobacco, as well as because of his desire to please the Spanish, who had protested against the founding of the colony. Virginia became a royal colony, with a governor and council appointed by the crown.

(3) New England

(a) Massachusetts

1606. Granting of the charter to the **Plymouth Company.** In this very year two unsuccessful attempts were made to found colonies. In 1607 settlers were landed at the mouth of the **Kennebec River**, but the enterprise was abandoned the next spring.

1614. Captain **John Smith**, of the Virginia settlement, explored the coast of New England and mapped it. He was made *Admiral of New England* by the Plymouth Company (1615) and made an abortive effort to start a colony. Several fishing and trading voyages were made to the New England coast between 1615 and 1620 under the direction of **Sir Ferdinando Gorges**, a member of the Plymouth Company.

1620, Nov. 13. **The Council for New England.** The Plymouth Company having failed to found a colony, Gorges and others secured the incorporation of the council, which was given jurisdiction between 40 and 48° N.L.

1620, Nov. **ARRIVAL OF THE PILGRIMS** at Cape Cod. The Pilgrims were a group of separatists who had migrated from Scrooby to Amsterdam and thence to Leyden in Holland. In 1617 they decided to seek a new home in order to preserve their English identity. They obtained a patent from the London Company and **John Carver** was made their governor. They left England in the *May-flower* and reached Cape Cod, which they found to be outside the jurisdiction of the London Company. They therefore drew up the **Mayflower Compact**, by which they formed themselves into a body politic and agreed to enact laws for the welfare of the colony. The basis of government, then, was the will of the colonists rather than that of the crown. **Plymouth** was selected as the site of the settlement.

1621. William Bradford became governor on the death of Carver.

1623. Settlements at Portsmouth and Dover (New Hampshire) and at Casco Bay and Saco Bay (Maine) were made under the auspices of the Council for New England. A group of Dorchester merchants settled on Cape Ann (1624).

1628, Sept. John Endicott and some 50 colonists arrived at Salem, acting under a patent obtained by Rev. John White of Dorchester from the Council for New England. This patent ran for lands between the parallel three miles north of the source of the Merrimac River and that three miles south of the Charles River.

1629, Mar. ROYAL CHARTER issued confirming the grant to Endicott and his associates, which members of the Gorges family had protested. The new corporation was known as the **Governor and Company of Massachusetts Bay** in New England.

June 27. Five ships, with some 400 settlers, arrived at Salem. John Winthrop and other prominent men meeting at Cambridge (England) agreed to emigrate to Massachusetts Bay, provided the charter and government might be legally transferred to America. The company decided to make the transfer and Winthrop was named governor.

1630. Seventeen ships brought about 1000 persons to the colony. By the end of the year settlements had been made at Dorchester, Boston, Watertown, Roxbury, Mystic and Lynn. The first **general court** of the colony was held at Boston (Oct. 19). From then on no person was to be admitted as a freeman of the corporation unless a member of some church within the colony. In 1634 a representative system was introduced into the general court, because the growth of the colony prevented attendance of all freemen.

1630-1642. The Great Migration to Massachusetts Bay Colony. During these years some 16,000 settlers arrived from England.

1635. The coast of New England was re-apportioned. Gorges received the land in Maine between the Penobscot and

Piscataqua Rivers; **Mason** received New Hampshire and northern Massachusetts as far as Cape Ann; **Edward Gorges** from Cape Ann to Narragansett Bay. In this same year the Council for New England gave up its charter and the king demanded also the charter of the Massachusetts Bay Colony, because of Archbishop Laud's dislike of the Puritan Commonwealth. The king was unsuccessful.

1636. The general court voted £400 toward the founding of a college. In 1638 **John Harvard** bequeathed to the college £780 and 260 books. The institution was named **Harvard College** in 1639.

(b) Connecticut and Rhode Island

1631. The Earl of Warwick, to whom the Council for New England had granted much of the Connecticut River Valley, transferred his rights to **Lord Saye and Sele.**

1633. The Dutch, who had explored the coast, erected a fort on the river near the present Hartford.

1635. Lord Saye, with his associates, sent out settlers under John Winthrop, Jr., who established **Fort Saybrook,** at the mouth of the river. In the same year settlers from Dorchester (Massachusetts), seeking better land, established themselves at Windsor. In 1636 Rev. **Thomas Hooker** led Cambridge settlers to Hartford, while other colonists from Watertown settled at **Wethersfield.**

1638. Rev. **John Davenport** and **Theophilus Eaton** founded a theocratic colony at **New Haven.**

1639. Hartford, Windsor, and Wethersfield drew up **Fundamental Orders,** which provided that the governor and assistants, with four representatives from each town, should constitute the general court. These three settlements were commonly referred to as **Connecticut.**

Meanwhile **Roger Williams** had arrived at Boston, from England (1631). After spending some time at Salem, he repaired to Plymouth, where he concluded that the land rightfully belonged to the Indians and that the king had no right to grant it. He returned to Salem, where he argued that the church and the state should be separated. He denied the right of the magistrate to control the churches, and objected to enforced oaths, since they obliged wicked men to perform a religious act, thereby destroying the freedom of the soul. In Oct. 1635, he was banished from Salem.

1636, June. ROGER WILLIAMS SETTLED AT PROVIDENCE, where he organized a government democratic **in**

character, with separation of church and state.

1638. Mrs. **Anne Hutchinson**, the center of a controversy which shook Massachusetts Bay Colony to its foundations, was banished and took refuge on the island of Aquidneck, later called **Rhode Island**, where she and a small group of associates founded the settlement of **Portsmouth**. The following year another settlement was made at **Newport**.

(4) *Maryland*

George Calvert (later Lord Baltimore) had bought the southeastern peninsula of Newfoundland from **Sir William Vaughan** (1620) and had secured a charter (1623) for a colony, which he called **Avalon**. He visited Newfoundland in 1627 and resolved to abandon the colony because of the unfavorable climate. He then asked for a grant in Virginia, which was made in 1632, despite opposition from the Virginians.

1632, Apr. The charter of the new colony was drawn up in the name of Cecilius Calvert, George Calvert having died. The province was named **Maryland**, and Calvert, as proprietor, was given the right to collect taxes, make grants of land, create manors, appoint ministers and found churches according to the laws of England. As the charter did not forbid the establishment of other churches than the Protestant, Baltimore (Calvert) made use of it to help his co-religionists, the Catholics.

1633, Oct. Baltimore dispatched to Maryland two vessels with some 20 gentlemen, mostly Catholics, and about 200 laborers, chiefly Protestants. Arriving at the mouth of the Potomac (1634, Mar.), they founded the settlement of **St. Mary's**.

(5) *Island Settlements*

1609. A Virginia supply ship, under command of **Sir George Somers**, was wrecked on one of the Bermuda Islands. On his return to England Somers interested a number of persons, mostly members of the Virginia Company, in the islands, with the result that the **Somers Islands Company** was formed (1612) for the colonization of Bermuda. The island had 600 settlers in 1614 and between 2000 and 3000 in 1625. It became an important producer of tobacco.

1625. St. Christopher was settled, and Sir William Courten established the first colony on Barbados. Nevis was occupied by the British in 1628, and settlements were made on Antigua and Montserrat in 1632. By 1640 the island possessions of England had a population of 20,000, devoted chiefly to the cultivation of sugar, which soon supplanted tobacco as the leading crop.

c. DUTCH AND SWEDISH SETTLEMENTS

1602. The United East India Company was chartered by the States-General of Holland.

1609. The company employed **Henry Hudson**, an Englishman, to search for the northwest passage. He sighted land at Newfoundland, explored the New England coast, rounded Cape Cod, proceeded south to Virginia, probably entered Chesapeake Bay, entered Delaware Bay, and explored the Hudson River to Albany. Friendly relations with Iroquois Indians.

1612. Dutch merchants sent **Christianson and Block** to Manhattan Island to engage in fur trade. A post was established in 1613.

1614. Fort Nassau, later Fort Orange, built near present Albany. Exploration by Adrian Block of Long Island Sound, Connecticut coast, Narragansett Bay and Cape Cod. As a result the **New Netherland Company** was formed and given monopoly of trade between the 40th and 45th parallels. Fur trade carried on and the coast explored.

1621. The **Dutch West India Company** was chartered and given a monopoly of trade in Africa and America.

1626. Peter Minuit became director-general of the company. He purchased **Manhattan Island** from the Indians for 24 dollars and founded the settlement of **New Amsterdam**. The company also made settlements in Connecticut, New Jersey, Delaware, and Pennsylvania. Men, known as *patroons*, were given large areas of land on condition that they bring over a stipulated number of settlers. The Dutch, under Governor Kieft of New Netherland, protested in vain against the founding of New Haven.

Meanwhile the attention of Gustavus Adolphus of Sweden was called to the Delaware country by **William Usselincx**, who had withdrawn from the Dutch West India Company. Usselincx received a charter for the **South Company** which came to naught. In 1633 the **New South Company** was organized, but it, too, failed to achieve anything. In 1637 the **New Sweden Company** was organized, chiefly as a result of the encouragement of two Dutchmen, Samuel Blommaert and Peter Minuit.

1638. Two Swedish vessels arrived on the Delaware and **Fort Christina** was

established. This intrusion of the Swedes angered **Peter Stuyvesant** of New Netherland, who urged the West India Company to occupy New Sweden, which was done in 1655.

2. COLONIAL HISTORY

a. NEW ENGLAND

1641. The Body of Liberties, a code of 100 laws, was established by the General Court of the Massachusetts Bay Colony.

1643, May 19. The New England Confederation was formed by Connecticut (Hartford, Windsor, and Wethersfield), New Haven, Plymouth, and Massachusetts Bay for purposes of defense.

1644. Union of Providence and the Rhode Island towns (Newport and Portsmouth) under a charter obtained by Roger Williams. Union of Saybrook and Connecticut under the latter name.

1646. In Massachusetts, **John Eliot** began his missionary work among the Indians. (Translated the Bible into Massachusetts dialect, 1661–1663.)

1649. Incorporation in England of the **Society for Propagating the Gospel in New England.**

1653. Settlements in southern Maine accepted the jurisdiction of Massachusetts.

1662. Charter of Connecticut granted by the king. Assembly composed of the governor, deputy-governor, 12 assistants, and two deputies from each town.

1663. Charter of Rhode Island and Providence Plantations. This was retained throughout the colonial period and was the constitution of the state until 1842.

1664. Union of Connecticut and New Haven, because of the latter's fear of annexation to New York.

1665. Maine was restored to the heirs of Sir Ferdinando Gorges.

Royal commissioners, after an unsuccessful attempt to hear complaints in New England, left the provinces.

1668. Massachusetts reassumed the government of Maine.

1675-1676. KING PHILIP'S WAR in New England. Although primarily due to the advance of the frontier of settlement upon the Indian hunting grounds, there were numerous minor infractions of the law. Christianizing of Cape Cod Indians by John Eliot aroused the suspicions of the Wampanoags, who saw in it an attempt to weaken their power. **Philip,** son of **Massasoit,** chief of the Wampanoags, formed a league comprising most of the Indians from Maine to Connecticut. Border attacks were followed by the white attack upon the stronghold of the Narragansetts near Kingston, Rhode Island, in Dec. 1675, with heavy losses to the Indians. Deerfield was attacked by Indians and most of the houses were burned. During the war 500 white men were captured or killed and nearly 40 towns damaged, 20 being destroyed or abandoned. Chief Canonchet of the Narragansetts was shot (Apr. 1676) and the war came to a close with the death of Philip (Aug. 1676).

1677. The dispute between Massachusetts and the heirs of Sir Ferdinando Gorges regarding Maine having been decided in favor of the latter by the English courts, Massachusetts bought all of the province except that granted to the Duke of York.

1680. **New Hampshire** was separated from Massachusetts by royal charter.

1684. **ANNULMENT OF THE MASSACHUSETTS CHARTER.** The independent course of Massachusetts had long irritated the crown. The heirs of Mason and Gorges charged that Massachusetts had usurped their rights. London merchants claimed the colony evaded the navigation acts by sending tobacco and sugar directly to Europe. Lack of respect for the king's authority and the exercise of powers not warranted by the charter were also charged. In 1679 **Edward Randolph** arrived in Boston as collector of the customs, bearing instructions for the colony to relinquish jurisdiction over New Hampshire and Maine, the latter of which was disregarded. Friction continued, as did Randolph's complaints against the colony, until legal action in 1684 resulted in the annulment of the charter.

1686. DOMINION OF NEW ENGLAND formed through consolidation of the New England colonies. **Sir Edmund Andros** was made governor. *Quo warranto* proceedings were instituted against Connecticut and Carolina. Andros arrived in Boston (Dec. 20) and assumed the government of Plymouth and Rhode Island. In 1687 he assumed the government of Connecticut and demanded the charter which Captain William Wadsworth concealed in a hollow tree, the famous *Charter Oak*.

1689. Upon news of the flight of James II from England, the people of Boston rose in revolt, imprisoned Andros and restored charter government. Similar action was taken in Rhode Island and Connecticut.

1691. New charter for Massachusetts, which included Plymouth, Maine, Nova Scotia, and all land north to the St. Lawrence. A governor, to be appointed by the crown, was vested with the power of calling and dissolving the general court, appointing military and judicial officers, and vetoing acts of legislature. The electoral franchise was extended and religious liberty secured to all except Catholics. **Sir William Phips** was made governor.

1692. Salem witchcraft trials.

1701. Founding of Yale College, New Haven, Connecticut.

1728. William Burnet, governor of Massachusetts, became involved in a quarrel with the legislature over the question of a fixed salary for the governor, which the court refused to grant "because it is the undoubted right of all Englishmen, by Magna Carta, to raise and dispose of money for the public service, of their own accord, without compulsion.":

b. NEW YORK, NEW JERSEY, PENNSYLVANIA

1664. Grant of New Netherland, from the Connecticut to the Delaware, to the King's brother, **James, Duke of York.** The grant included the eastern part of Maine and islands south and west of Cape Cod. The region between the Hudson and the Delaware was granted by the Duke of York to **Lord Berkeley** and **Sir George Carteret.**

1664, Aug. 27. SURRENDER OF NEW AMSTERDAM to the English. Name of the colony changed to **New York.** On Sept. 24 surrender of Fort Orange, whose name was changed to **Albany.**

1673. In the war between England and Holland, the **Dutch captured New York** and established temporary control over Albany and New Jersey. They were restored when peace was made in 1674.

1676. Line of demarcation between East and West New Jersey. Settlement of Quakers in West New Jersey (1677–1681).

1681, Mar. 4. CHARTER OF PENNSYLVANIA signed, granting to William Penn the region between 40° and 43°, extending 5° west from the Delaware River. These limits brought the colony into conflict with New York on the north and Maryland on the south. The dispute with Maryland was finally adjusted when in 1767 two surveyors, **Mason and Dixon,** ran the present boundary between the two states. The form of government of the colony was to be determined by the proprietor. The first body of colonists arrived in 1681 and a frame of government was provided for the government of the colony.

1682-1683. Penn arrived in the colony and **Philadelphia** was laid out (1682). Penn entered into a treaty with the Indians (1683) which had the effect of keeping the colony free from Indian wars.

1683. In response to persistent demands of the people, the Duke of York conceded a legislative assembly to New York. In October, 17 representatives drew up a **Charter of Franchises and Liberties,** which the duke signed, only to reject when he became king.

1688. The Lords of Trade determined to bring New York and New Jersey under the government of Andros. In 1689, New York proclaimed William and Mary.

1702. New Jersey reunited as a royal province.

1715-1750. SETTLEMENT OF THE PIEDMONT, partly by newcomers and old settlers, who crossed the fall line into the areas, partly by Germans, Swiss, and Scotch-Irish entering at the port of Philadelphia and pushing southward through the valleys, especially the Shenandoah. **German immigration,** which began with the founding of Germantown, Pennsylvania (1683), increased greatly in volume after 1710. Occupation of the Piedmont resulted in the formation of a restless, aggressive frontier society which became increasingly important.

1720-1726. William Burnet, governor of New York, began efforts to counteract French attempts to hem in the

English colonies in the west. He prohibited trade between the Iroquois and the French. In 1722, he established a trading post at **Oswego** and carried on negotiations at Albany with the Six Nations. A treaty with the Senecas, Cayugas, and Onondagas (1726) added their lands to those of the Mohawks and Oneidas, which were already under English protection.

1735. Trial in New York of **John Peter Zenger,** printer of a paper, for libel. The court contended that it should decide the libelous nature of the statements made, and that the jury should determine the fact of publication. Zenger's lawyer, Andrew Hamilton, argued that the jury must decide whether or not the publication was libelous. He won his suit, thereby materially safeguarding the freedom of the press.

c. VIRGINIA, DELAWARE, AND MARYLAND

1652. Parliament assumed control of Maryland and suspended the governor.

1659. Virginia proclaimed Charles II King of England, Scotland, and Ireland, and restored the royal governor, **Sir William Berkeley.**

1662. Lord Baltimore was confirmed in the government of Maryland.

1676. **Bacon's Rebellion** in Virginia. Led by Nathaniel Bacon, this revolt was largely the result of the indifference of Governor Berkeley to the problem of frontier defense against the Indians. Jamestown was burned, but the rebellion collapsed with the death of Bacon.

1689. Virginia and Maryland proclaimed William and Mary.

1693. **College of William and Mary** founded in Virginia.

1716. Governor **Spottswood** of Virginia led an expedition to the Blue Ridge, and into the Shenandoah Valley. He recommended the securing of the mountain passes and the establishment of settlements on Lake Erie.

d. THE SOUTHERN COLONIES

1663. **Grant of Carolina** by the king to eight proprietors, including the Earl of Clarendon. The grant included land between 31° and 36° N.L. After Raleigh's unsuccessful effort, the region between Virginia and the Spanish settlements in Florida had received little attention until the grant of the region to Sir Thomas Heath (1629), which also came to naught.

1667. **Grant of the Bahamas** to the Carolina proprietors.

1669. **Adoption of the Fundamental Constitutions,** drawn up for Carolina by John Locke, which provided for an archaic feudal régime totally unsuited to the needs of a frontier colony.

1711. **Tuscarora War** in North Carolina. The Tuscaroras massacred some 200 settlers. Virginia and South Carolina sent aid and the Indians were defeated (1712). Remnants of the Tuscaroras moved to New York and were incorporated in the Iroquois as a sixth nation.

1715. **Defeat of the Yamassees** and allied Indian tribes in Carolina. They were driven across the Spanish border into Florida.

1719-1729. **REORGANIZATION OF THE CAROLINAS.** Economic differences between the northern and southern portions of Carolina had resulted in governmental differentiation. The governor was located at Charleston with a deputy governor in the north. In 1713 the proprietors appointed **Charles Eden** governor of North Carolina and from this time the provinces were virtually separate. Popular discontent with the proprietors because of their indifference to defense against Indians and pirates. The situation was aggravated by refusal of the proprietors to allow the distribution of the Yamassee lands. Meanwhile the proprietors had incurred the ill-will of the British government. Their incompetence in the Yamassee War was the last straw which convinced the Board of Trade that a change was necessary. It upheld the people against the proprietors and in 1729 an act of Parliament established royal governments in both North and South Carolina.

1733. **FOUNDING OF GEORGIA,** the last of the 13 English colonies on the continent. In the triangle between the Carolinas, Florida, and Louisiana, English, French, and Spanish claims conflicted. The international boundaries had never been defined. In 1716 the Carolinians had established a fort on the Savannah River and from 1721 to 1727 had maintained **Fort George** on the Altamaha. In 1730 Sir **Alexander Cuming** was sent on a mission to the Cherokees which resulted in their acknowledgment of English supremacy. The need of a buffer colony on the southern boundary had long been realized by the British. In 1717 Sir **Robert Montgomery** had secured from the Carolina proprietors a grant of the land between the Savannah and Altamaha Rivers, known as the **Margravate of Azilia.** Plans for its settlement proving unsuccessful, **James Oglethorpe** became interested in the settlement of the region. An advocate of a strong policy against the Spanish and a humanitarian interested in improving the condition of imprisoned debtors, he conceived the idea of a barrier colony. In 1732 he secured a charter, granting to him and his associates the region between the Savannah and the Altamaha from sea to sea. Proprietary government was to prevail for 21 years, when the colony was to become a royal province. Religious liberty was guaranteed to all except Catholics. Colonists left England in the autumn of 1732, arriving at Charleston in Jan. 1733. The town of **Savannah** was immediately laid out; and in 1737 a fort was established at **Augusta.**

3. WARS OF ENGLAND WITH FRANCE AND SPAIN

1651-1673. The British Navigation Laws. These applied mercantilist doctrine to colonial trade. The **Act of 1651,** designed to strike a blow at Dutch shipping, required that colonial products be shipped to England in ships of Great Britain or the Plantations. This law was re-enacted in 1660, with the additional provision that certain enumerated articles of colonial production could be shipped only to England. The **Staple Act of 1663** required that articles of European production, destined for the colonies, must be shipped first to England. The **Act of 1673** imposed intercolonial duties on sugar, tobacco, and other products.

1667. Treaty of Breda between England and France. Antigua, Montserrat, and the French port of St. Christopher surrendered to England.

1670. The Hudson's Bay Company incorporated and given a monopoly of the trade in Hudson's Bay Basin.

1689-1697. KING WILLIAM'S WAR, with France. This was the American phase of the general war against Louis XIV known as the **War of the League of Augsburg** (see p. 443). The French were aided by the Indians of Canada and Maine, while the Iroquis supported the English. In 1690 the French and Indians massacred colonists at Schenectady, Salmon Falls, and Casco Bay. An English force under **Sir William Phips** captured Port Royal (1690, May 11), but a Massachusetts expedition against Quebec, led by Phips, resulted in failure. The **Treaty of Ryswick** restored all conquests (1697).

1696-1698. Renewed efforts of the English government to control colonial trade. A **Board of Commissioners for Trade and Plantations** was organized (1696) and a navigation act of the same year was designed to prevent further evasion of earlier regulations. Since the war with France had interrupted the usual trade, the New Englanders had taken up manufacturing. The **Woolens Act** (1698) forbade the colonists to ship wool or woolen products from one colony to another.

1702-1713. QUEEN ANNE'S WAR, the American phase of the **War of the Spanish Succession** (see p. 445). In 1702 the English plundered and burned St. Augustine in Florida, while in 1704 the French and Indians surprised Deerfield in the Connecticut Valley. Their attacks soon spread over much of the frontier and even to the outskirts of Boston. In 1707 the English organized an expedition against **Acadia.** Troops from New England laid siege to Port Royal, but failed to reduce it. The French province was, however, conquered in 1710, when 4000 colonists under **Francis Nicholson,** aided by British ships and a regiment of marines, attacked and captured Port Royal. Acadia then became the British province of **Nova Scotia** and the name of Port Royal was changed to **Annapolis Royal.** For the year 1711 a joint land and sea campaign against Canada was planned. Nicholson's colonials and Iroquois were to attack Montreal, while an expedition was to be led against Quebec by Admiral Sir Hovenden Walker and General Sir John Hill. Seven of Marlborough's best regiments were included. The force gathered at Boston, where it was reinforced by 1500 colonials. In August the fleet entered the St. Lawrence, but the destruction of ten ships compelled the abandonment of the attack. News of this reached Nicholson and induced him to give up the campaign against Montreal. By the **Treaty of Utrecht** (1713) England secured recognition of her claims in the Hudson's Bay country and the possession of Newfoundland and Acadia. The claim of the English to the Iroquois country was also admitted, and St. Christopher was ceded to England.

The French were excluded from fishing on the Acadian coast, but were allowed to retain Cape Breton Island. The **asiento** gave the English the exclusive right for 30 years of bringing Negroes into the Spanish possessions.

1733. The Molasses Act. The increased production of sugar in the French and Dutch West Indies after 1715, the disposition of the English colonists on the mainland (especially the New Englanders) to take advantage of the low prices of sugar, molasses, and rum in the foreign islands, and their desire to avail themselves of the market afforded for their own products in the islands, contributed to bring about a severe depression among the sugar planters of the English island possessions. In response to pleas from the West Indian planters, Parliament enacted the Molasses Act, which placed prohibitive duties on sugar and molasses imported into the colonies from other than British possessions. In 1732 Parliament had stopped the importation of hats from the colonies and had restricted their manufacture. This was in accord with the mercantilist policy of encouraging the production of raw materials (including furs) and of discouraging manufactures that would conflict with those of the mother country.

1739. WAR BETWEEN SPAIN AND ENGLAND (War of Jenkins' Ear, see p. 434). Dissatisfied with the provisions of the Treaty of Utrecht with respect to trade with Spanish possessions, English merchants had resorted to extensive smuggling, which, in turn, had led to the seizure of British ships and the rough treatment of British sailors by the Spanish. The loss of Jenkins' ear was merely one of many similar episodes. In the course of the ensuing war the British captured Puerto Bello and demolished its fortifications (1739). In 1740 they bombarded Cartagena and captured Chagres, while Oglethorpe led an expedition of Georgia, Carolina, and Virginia troops into Florida and made an unsuccessful attack on St. Augustine. The British were likewise unsuccessful in an attack on Santiago (Cuba) in 1741. In the next year they planned, but then abandoned an attack on Panama. The Spanish attacked Georgia (1742), but soon withdrew again to Florida. In 1743 Oglethorpe once more invaded Florida, but failed to take St. Augustine.

1743-1748. KING GEORGE'S WAR, the American phase of the **War of the Austrian Succession** in Europe (see p. 465). The outstanding event in the war in America was the **capture of Louisburg** (1745). The French had made the fortress one of the strongest in the New World. After an invasion of Nova Scotia by the French, Governor Shirley of Massachusetts assembled volunteers from Massachusetts, New Hampshire and Connecticut and placed them under the command of **William Pepperel.** Transports were supplied by the colonies, while warships were provided by the British navy. The expedition appeared before Louisburg on April 30 and the fortress capitulated after a siege (June 16). An attempt of the French to recover Cape Breton and Nova Scotia was made in 1746, but was doomed to failure when a storm destroyed the fleet off the coast. In the interior an abortive attempt of the northern colonies to conquer Canada spurred the French and Indians to attack the frontier as far south as New York (1746–1748). The New York and Pennsylvania frontiers were protected by **William Johnson,** an Indian guide, who kept the Mohawks friendly, and by **Conrad Weiser,** whose support of the Iroquois land claims as against the Delawares kept the Six Nations on the English side. At sea the British twice defeated the French in the West Indies (1745, 1747) and in 1748 the British admiral, Knowles, captured Port Louis on the southern coast of Haiti, bombarded Santiago, and attacked the Spanish fleet off Havana.

1748. The Treaty of Aix-la-Chapelle, based upon European rather than colonial considerations, restored all the conquests of the war. In America the treaty was merely a truce, for Nova Scotia, the Ohio Valley, and the Cherokee country continued to be areas of conflict. In order to strengthen the British hold on Nova Scotia, Lord Halifax sent out 2500 settlers in 1749 and founded the town of **Halifax.** In the Ohio Valley traders from Virginia and Pennsylvania pushed westward as far as the Indian villages on the Mississippi. Virginia frontiersmen made a settlement at **Draper's Meadow** on the Greenbrier River in 1748.

1749. The Ohio Company, organized by a group of Virginians and a number of prominent Englishmen. The company obtained a grant of 500,000 acres on the upper Ohio and sent out **Christopher Gist** (1750) to explore the region as far as the falls of the Ohio. His favorable report led to the erection of a trading house at **Wills' Creek,** the present Cumberland (Maryland), and to the blazing of a trail to the junction of Redstone Creek and the Monongahela River. This activity roused the French to action. In an effort to detach the Iroquois from the English they founded the mission at present-day **Ogdensburg**

(1748). To divert trade from Oswego, they established **Fort Rouillé** on the site of present-day **Toronto** (1749). Another post was located at **Niagara** portage, **Detroit** was strengthened, and in 1749 the governor of Canada sent **Céloron de Bienville** to take possession of the Ohio Valley.

1753. **Marquis Duquesne** sent an expedition of 1500 men to occupy the Ohio country. **Fort Presqu' Isle** was erected and a road was cut to French Creek, where **Fort Le Boeuf** was built. It was planned to establish another fort at the forks of the Ohio. In the same year Governor Dinwiddie of Virginia sent out **George Washington**, a young surveyor, to demand the withdrawal of the French. He proceeded to Fort Le Boeuf, but was told that Dinwiddie's letter would be forwarded to Duquesne. It was quite clear that the French would not leave the valley peacefully.

1754. Virginia troops dispatched to the Ohio, with Washington second in command. The French had, in the meanwhile, built **Fort Duquesne** at the forks of the Ohio. Washington pushed on to Great Meadows where he constructed **Fort Necessity**. He was attacked by the French and forced to surrender.

1754, June 19. The Albany Convention. The advance of the French had shown the need for a common plan of defense. Representatives of New York, Pennsylvania, Maryland, and the New England states met with the Six Nations. Upon the suggestion of **Benjamin Franklin**, the convention drew up a plan of union which was, however, rejected by the colonies. The plan called for union under a president appointed by the crown, with a grand council of delegates elected by the colonial assemblies, this body to have legislative power subject to approval by the president and the crown.

1755-1763. THE FRENCH AND INDIAN WAR, the American phase of the Seven Years' War in Europe (see p. 466). In 1755 the governors of Virginia, North Carolina, Pennsylvania, Maryland, New York, and Massachusetts met in conference at Alexandria (Virginia) with **General Braddock**, the English commander, recently arrived. They planned a fourfold attack on the French: upon Fort Duquesne, Niagara, Crown Point, and Fort Beauséjour. Braddock led the expedition into the Ohio country, but was surrounded and defeated near **Fort Duquesne** (July 9). In the Crown Point campaign the French were defeated in the **battle of Lake George** (Sept. 8), but the English made no attempt to capture Crown Point itself. They built **Fort Wil-**

liam Henry at the southern end of Lake George, while the French fortified **Ticonderoga.** In 1756 war was formally declared between France and England. **Earl Loudoun** was named commander-in-chief of the British forces in America. The French were commanded by **General Montcalm**, who took and destroyed Forts Oswego and George (Aug.) and in 1757 took Fort William Henry (Aug. 9). The garrison, whose retreat to Fort Edward had been guaranteed by Montcalm, was massacred by his Indian allies.

The resistance of the English was weakened by the friction between Lord Loudoun and the Massachusetts general court over quartering of troops, and between the governor and assembly of Virginia over various matters of taxation. In 1758 (July 8) General Abercromby was defeated before Ticonderoga, but Amherst and Wolfe took Louisburg (July 26), Bradstreet took Fort Frontenac (Aug. 27) and Forbes took Fort Duquesne (Nov. 25).

For the year 1759 the English planned four campaigns: against Niagara, against settlements on Lake Erie, against Ticonderoga and Crown Point, and against Quebec. The **battle of the Plains of Abraham** (Quebec) was fought on Sept. 13, both Wolfe and Montcalm losing their lives. Quebec surrendered to the English on Sept. 18. On Sept. 8, 1760 Montreal surrendered and all Canada passed into the hands of the British. In 1762 **Rodney** forced the surrender of Martinique, Grenada, St. Lucia, St. Vincent and the other French West Indies.

1763, Feb. 10. THE TREATY OF PARIS, between Great Britain, France, Spain, and Portugal. France ceded to England all claim to Acadia, Canada, Cape Breton, and all that part of Louisiana situated east of the Mississippi except the Island of Orleans. France retained certain fishing rights on the Newfoundland banks and was given the islands of St. Pierre and Miquelon. England restored to France the islands of Guadeloupe, Martinique, Belle Isle, Maria Galante, and St. Lucia. England restored to Spain, Havana, in return for which Spain ceded Florida to England. France, by a previous treaty (1762, Nov. 3) had ceded to Spain all French territory west of the Mississippi and the Island of Orleans, as compensation for the loss of Florida to England.

1763. The Conspiracy of Pontiac. This was an aftermath to the war. Indian tribes north of the Ohio, fearing eviction by the British, embittered by the arrogance and dishonesty of British traders, and disappointed by the economy of General

Amherst in the matter of presents, were ready to revolt against British occupation of the posts recently held by the French. Pontiac, chief of the Ottawas, organized a rising of the Algonquins and of some of the Iroquois and of tribes on the lower Mississippi. In a simultaneous attack all but three of the northwestern posts fell in May. By 1765, however, the British forces were in possession of the last of the French posts in the west.

1763, Oct. 7. Proclamation of 1763, issued by George III. It created four distinct provinces from the recent conquests: Quebec, East Florida, West Florida, and Grenada. It also closed, temporarily, to white settlement all lands west and north of the streams flowing into the Atlantic Ocean. Fur trade in this Indian reserve was opened to licensed subjects. In 1764 Lord Hillsborough drew up a plan for the management of the Indians and the fur trade. It continued the northern and southern departments for Indian affairs (created in 1755) and provided that in the north all trade must be conducted at regularly established posts and in the south at the Indian towns.

1763-1775. Expansion beyond the mountains. Numerous colonies had been planned by land companies before 1763. With these the Proclamation of 1763 interfered. In 1768, however, a plan for the gradual and controlled establishment of colonies in the west was worked out. In that year treaties with the Creeks, Cherokees, and Iroquois extinguished Indian rights to large areas. A group of Pennsylvanians, including Franklin, organized the **Vandalia Company** for the establishment of a colony in what is now West Virginia. Purchase of land was made in 1769 and by 1775 the proposed colony of Vandalia had been approved by the king and council. The outbreak of the Revolution rendered the plan abortive.

The **Watauga settlement** in eastern Tennessee was made in 1769 and was augmented by the arrival of Virginians and North Carolinians under **James Robertson** and **John Sevier** (1770-1771). Finding themselves beyond the pale of organized law, the settlers, proceeding on the compact theory, formed the **Watauga Association** (1772), organized as Washington County (North Carolina) in 1777.

Richard Henderson, of North Carolina, together with his associates, organized the **Transylvania Company,** purchased land from the Cherokees and established the Transylvania settlement in Kentucky in 1775. **Daniel Boone** was Henderson's agent and cleared the wilderness road to Kentucky. The settlement of Kentucky (1775-1777) was facilitated by the peace forced on the Indians as a result of **Lord Dunmore's War** (1774).

4. THE AMERICAN REVOLUTION

1763-1775. The Preliminaries of the American Revolution. By 1761 the British government was thoroughly aroused by the systematic evasion of the **Molasses Act** of 1733 through colonial smuggling, and by the illicit trade which the colonies had carried on with the enemy during the War of the Austrian Succession and the Seven Years' War. British officials felt that the trade prolonged French resistance. To prevent smuggling, the British resorted to **writs of assistance,** general search warrants, which made possible the search of all premises where smuggled goods might be found. This aroused the opposition of merchants who alleged the writs were illegal. In 1761, when Boston customs officers applied for the writs, the merchants contested their use. **James Otis** argued cogently against their legality before the Massachusetts Supreme Court. Although the court decided they were legal, the argument of Otis did much to shape public opinion.

1763. The Parsons' Cause, argued in Virginia by **Patrick Henry,** still further aroused and molded public opinion against British policy, in this instance the disallowance of a Virginia statute.

1763-1765. George Grenville in power in England. The acquisition of the vast territory from France in America necessitated increased revenues for defense and Indian administration. The ministry decided to enforce the navigation laws, tax the colonies directly and use the revenue to maintain an army in America. Powers of the admiralty courts were enlarged, and colonial governors were instructed to enforce the trade laws.

1764. Enactment of the **Sugar Act,** with the avowed purpose of raising revenue in the colonies and reforming the old colonial system, both economically and administratively.

The **Colonial Currency Act** prevented colonies from paying their debts in England in depreciated currency and forbade issues of unsound money. This act created a shortage of money in the colonies at a time when the Sugar Act injured the West Indian trade of the colonies, which had previously supplied the necessary specie.

1765. Disregarding colonial protests against the two previous acts, Grenville pushed through Parliament the **Stamp Act** providing for stamps on commercial and legal documents, pamphlets, newspapers, almanacs, playing cards, and dice.

The **Quartering Act** was passed, providing that, in the event of insufficiency of barracks in the colonies, British troops might be quartered in public hostelries.

May 29. **Patrick Henry** introduced into the Virginia House of Burgesses a series of resolutions boldly challenging the position of the British government.

June. The Massachusetts General Court sent an invitation to colonial assemblies to send delegates to meet in New York and consider the Stamp Act. Meanwhile the arrival of the stamp officers led to riots in various cities, including Boston, where the house of Lieut.-Gov. Hutchinson was sacked.

Oct. 7. **Stamp Act Congress** at New York. Twenty-eight delegates from nine colonies drew up memorials to the king and Parliament and adopted a **Declaration of rights and liberties** (Oct. 19).

1766. Mar. Repeal of the Stamp Act, followed by the **Declaratory Act** (Mar. 18), declaring that the king, by and with consent of Parliament, had authority to make laws to bind the colonies in all respects.

1767. Suspension of the New York Assembly because of its refusal fully to comply with the Quartering Act.

The **Townshend Acts** imposed duties on glass, lead, painters' colors, tea, and paper imported into the colonies. Out of these revenues fixed salaries were to be paid to royal officials in the colonies. A Boston town-meeting adopted a **non-importation agreement.**

1768. The Massachusetts General Court drew up a petition to the king, sent letters to the ministry, and dispatched a circular letter to the other colonies.

June. The seizure of John Hancock's sloop *Liberty*, because of false entry, led to a riot.

Oct. British troops arrived in Boston and the town refused to provide quarters.

1769. Parliament advised the enforcement of a statute of Henry VIII, allowing the government to bring to England for trial those alleged to have committed treason outside the realm. Resolutions of protest adopted by the Virginia House of Burgesses.

1770. Mar. 5. The Boston Massacre. Popular hatred of the British troops in the city led to a brawl in which several citizens were killed or wounded. Preston, the commanding officer, was acquitted, being defended by John Adams and Josiah Quincy.

An act repealing duties on paper, glass, and painters' colors, but retaining that on tea. This gesture produced a conservative reaction in the colonies, in which the merchants worked for conciliation. This truce was broken by the arbitrary acts of crown officials and by the announcement in

1772. That salaries of governors and judges in Massachusetts were to be paid by the crown, thus rendering them independent of the assembly's control of the purse, and by

June 10. The **Gaspée Affair,** in which a revenue boat, whose commander's conduct had enraged public opinion in Rhode Island, was burned by a mob in Narragansett Bay.

1772, Nov. 2-1773, Jan. Formation of 80 town **committees of correspondence** in Massachusetts under the leadership of **Samuel Adams.**

1773, Mar. 12. The Virginia House of Burgesses appointed a **Provincial Committee of Correspondence** to keep in touch with sister colonies. By Feb. 1774, all the colonies except Pennsylvania had appointed such committees.

To provide relief for the East India Company the government allowed it a drawback of the tea duty in England, but the full duty was to be paid in the colonies. There was a protest to the landing of the tea in Charleston, Philadelphia, and New York, while in Boston there occurred

Dec. 16. The Boston Tea Party in which citizens, disguised as Indians, boarded the ships and dumped the tea into the harbor.

1774. The resistance to the landing of the tea provoked the ministry to a punitive policy. The so-called **Coercive Acts** were passed, including: The **Boston Port Act,** closing the port after June 1; the **Massachusetts Government Act,** depriving the people of most of their chartered rights, and greatly enlarging the governor's powers; the **Administration of**

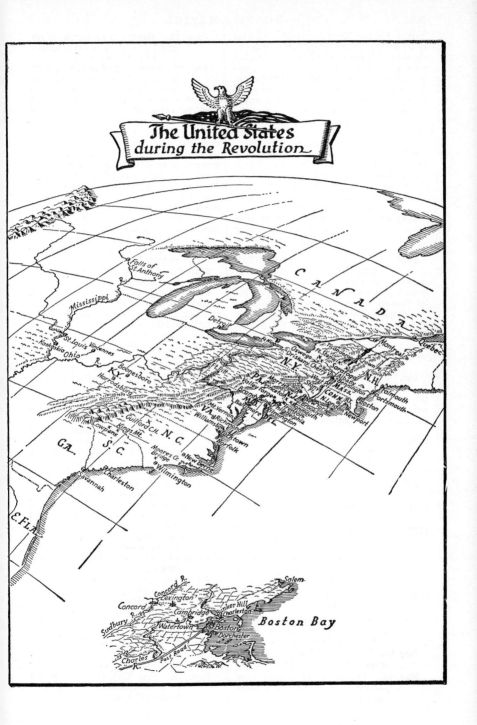

The United States
during the Revolution

CANADA

Falls of
St. Anthony

Mississippi

Detroit

St. Louis Vincennes

Nashville Ohio R.

KY. Boonesboro

Harrodsburg

Oswego Oriskany Cherry
Fort Stanwix

N.Y.

Montreal Quebec

N.H.

Boston

Portsmouth

Valley Forge Monmouth

Mt. Vernon

Williamsburg Yorktown

VIR. Richmond

Guilford C.H. N.C.

Kings Mt.

Cowpens

GA. S.C.

Moore's C. New Berne
Bridge

Charleston

Wilmington

Savannah

E. FLA.

Norfolk

New London Newport

Salem

Concord R.

Concord Lexington

Sudbury Cambridge Bunker Hill
Charlestown

Watertown Boston

Dorchester

Charles R. Post Road

Boston Bay

Justice Act, providing that persons accused of a capital crime in aiding the government should be tried in England or a colony other than that in which the crime was committed; the **Quartering Act**, and the **Quebec Act**, extending the boundary of that province to the Ohio River, cutting athwart the claims of Massachusetts, New York, Connecticut, and Virginia. Although not designed as a punitive measure the Quebec Act was so regarded by the colonies.

County conventions in Massachusetts protested against the acts (Aug.–Sept.). The **Suffolk Convention** resolved that they should be "rejected as the attempts of a wicked administration to enslave America" (**The Suffolk Resolves**).

May 27. The Virginia House of Burgesses adopted resolutions calling for a congress of the colonies. Copies sent to other assemblies.

Sept. 5. The FIRST CONTINENTAL CONGRESS assembled at Philadelphia. All colonies except Georgia represented. Members divided into radicals led by **Samuel Adams** and conservatives led by **Joseph Galloway** of Pennsylvania. The radicals obtained approval of the Suffolk Resolves and defeated Galloway's proposed plan of union, designed to effect an adjustment of difficulties. **Declaration of rights and grievances** drawn up.

Oct. The delegates adopted the *Association* providing for non-importation of English goods after Dec. 1. If redress had not been obtained by Sept. 11, 1775, non-exportation was to go into effect.

1775, Feb. 1. Chatham presented to Parliament a plan of conciliation, based on mutual concessions, but it was rejected.

Feb. 20. Lord North made an unsuccessful effort toward conciliation.

1775–1783. WAR FOR INDEPENDENCE.

1775, Apr. 19. Battles of Lexington and Concord. British troops detailed to destroy stores at Concord became embroiled with provincials at Lexington. Proceeding to Concord, the troops destroyed the stores, but after the fight at the bridge were forced to retreat, first to Lexington, then to Boston.

May 10–12. Ticonderoga captured by **Ethan Allen** and **Crown Point** captured by **Seth Warner**.

May 10. The Second Continental Congress assembled at Philadelphia.

May 31. Troops before Boston were adopted as the **Continental Army** and on

June 15. George Washington (1732–1799) was appointed commander-in-chief of the forces.

June 17. Battle of Bunker Hill, opposite Boston. Americans driven from entrenchments, but only after inflicting great losses on the British.

1775, July–Mar. 17, 1776. Siege of Boston.

1775. A letter by Congress to the people of Canada having failed to enlist their aid, a campaign against them was planned. One force, under **Richard Montgomery**, proceeded by Lake Champlain to Montreal, which was taken on Nov. 12. Another force, under **Benedict Arnold**, advanced by the Kennebec with a view to meeting Montgomery at **Quebec**. Montgomery was killed before Quebec (Dec. 21). Arnold carried on the unsuccessful siege for the remainder of the winter.

1776, Mar. 4. Occupation of **Dorchester Heights** by Washington.

Mar. 17. Evacuation of Boston by the British forces.

Meanwhile the unyielding attitude of the British government, the hiring of German mercenaries, the events on the Canadian frontier, and the burning of Norfolk inflamed public opinion. The appearance of **Thomas Paine's** *Common Sense* crystallized that opinion in favor of independence.

May 15. Congress announced that the authority of the British crown should be suppressed and power of government established under authority of the people of the colonies.

May 15. The Virginia convention, called to form a new government, instructed Virginia delegates in Congress to propose independence.

June 7. Resolution of **Richard Henry Lee** in Congress, "That these United Colonies are and of right ought to be free and independent States." Congress appointed a committee of five to draft a declaration of independence. The committee asked **Thomas Jefferson** to prepare the document.

1776, July 4. DECLARATION OF INDEPENDENCE adopted.

Following the British evacuation of Boston, Washington proceeded to New York. **General Howe** and **Admiral Lord Howe** prepared to attack, but the latter first proffered peace terms which were rejected.

Aug. 27. Battle of Long Island, with defeat of Putnam and retreat to New York.

Sept. 15. New York occupied by the British; Washington retreated to Harlem Heights.

Oct. 11-13. Arnold defeated in two naval engagements on **Lake Champlain.**

Oct. 28. Engagement between Howe and Washington at **White Plains,** followed by retirement of Washington to a line of heights back of his previous position on Oct. 31.

Nov. 16. Surrender of **Fort Washington** to the British, followed by that of **Fort Lee** on Nov. 20.

Nov. 28. Beginning of Washington's retreat across New Jersey into Pennsylvania.

Dec. 26. **Battle of Trenton.** Crossing the Delaware by night, Washington surprised and captured about 1000 Hessians at Trenton. This was followed by the defeat of the British at the

1777, Jan. 3. **Battle of Princeton.** The British plan of campaign for 1777 was to divide the states by the line of the Hudson. Burgoyne was to proceed from Canada by way of Lake Champlain, St. Leger was to co-operate with Burgoyne from Lake Ontario, while Howe was to ascend the Hudson and join Burgoyne.

Aug. 16. **Battle of Bennington,** in which Stark defeated Colonel Baum, sent by Burgoyne to seize stores.

Sept. 19. **First battle of Bemis Heights,** in which Burgoyne held the field, although suffering heavy losses.

Oct. 7. **Second battle of Bemis Heights,** or Saratoga. Burgoyne was defeated and, finding himself surrounded, called a council of war at which it was decided to negotiate terms.

Oct. 17. Burgoyne surrendered his entire force to Gates.

Howe's campaign. Instead of advancing up the Hudson, Howe, on Aug. 25, disclosed his purpose of attacking **Philadelphia.** Washington offered battle, but in the

Sept. 11. Battle of **Brandywine,** the Americans, under Greene, were defeated.

Sept. 27. Howe occupied Philadelphia.

Oct. 4. Attempting to surprise the camp at Germantown, Washington was defeated in the **battle of Germantown.** With the capture of Fort Mifflin and Fort Mercer on Nov. 16 and 20, British control of the Delaware was complete.

1777-1778. Winter suffering of Washington's army at **Valley Forge.** Unsuccessful attempt of the **Conway Cabal** to remove Washington from command.

1777, Nov. 15. **ARTICLES OF CONFEDERATION** and perpetual union agreed upon in Congress. These provided for a confederacy to be known as *The United States of America,* and were sent to the states for ratification.

Burgoyne's defeat and surrender stirred France to action in support of the United States. To re-establish French prestige in Europe, so greatly weakened in the Seven Years' War, was the aim of **Vergennes,** the French minister of foreign affairs. After supplying secret aid in money and supplies to the Americans for two years, France signed,

1778, Feb. 6. **Treaties of Commerce and Alliance** with the United States. **Lafayette** and **De Kalb** had arrived the previous summer to offer their services. **Beaumarchais,** French playwright, had drawn heavily on his personal resources to aid the Americans.

Feb. 17. **Lord North** presented to Parliament his plan for conciliating Americans, which included renunciation of the right of taxation. Commissioners sent to the United States with a peace offer, which was rejected by Congress (June 17). With the French alliance an assured fact, only independence would now satisfy the Americans.

June 18. Evacuation of **Philadelphia** by Sir Henry Clinton, who started to march across New Jersey, where on

June 28. Washington won the **battle of Monmouth.**

July 4. **Wyoming massacre** in Pennsylvania.

July 8. Arrival of **Count d'Estaing's** fleet off Delaware Capes. He and Washington planned a land and sea attack on the British in Newport. After a storm on Aug. 9, which prevented a clash between the French and British fleets, D'Estaing sailed to Boston for repairs, leaving General Sullivan unsupported, who on Aug. 29 gave up the siege of Newport.

Nov. 11. **Massacre of Cherry Valley** in New York.

1779, Feb. **George Rogers Clark,** with a force of Virginians, completed the conquest of the Old Northwest, capturing Hamilton, the British commander, at **Vincennes.**

June. **Spain entered the war** against England, on the promise of France that she would assist Spain to recover Gibraltar and the Floridas.

Sept. 23. Naval victory of **John Paul Jones** of the *Bonhomme Richard* over the *Serapis* and the *Countess of Scarborough.*

Meanwhile the British had decided to try, with the aid of loyalists, to overrun the southern states. In 1778 **Savannah** was captured and in 1780 Sir Henry Clinton laid siege to Charleston.

1780, May. Charleston surrendered.

July. Rochambeau arrived at Newport with 6000 French troops.

Despite brave resistance of Thomas Sumter and Francis Marion, South Carolina was overrun by the British, and in the

Aug. 16. Battle of Camden, Gates was defeated by Cornwallis.

Aug. 18. Sumter's force was defeated by Tarleton, and Marion retreated to North Carolina.

Sept. 23. A plot of **Benedict Arnold** to surrender West Point to Sir Henry Clinton was revealed through capture of the British agent, **Major André.** Arnold escaped, but on

Oct. 2. André was hanged as a spy.

Oct. 7. Battle of King's Mountain, in North Carolina, in which the British, under Major Ferguson, were defeated.

1781, Jan. 17. Battle of the Cowpens, in which the British cavalry under Tarleton was defeated by Morgan.

Mar. 15. Battle of Guilford; British victory.

Sept. 8. Battle of Eutaw; defeat of Greene, followed by retreat of British to Charleston.

Meanwhile British forces under Cornwallis were concentrating in Virginia, where they fortified themselves at **Yorktown.** While Cornwallis remained inactive, Washington, Lafayette, and Rochambeau closed in on him at Williamsburg, and De Grasse, with the French fleet, entered Chesapeake Bay.

Sept. 30–Oct. 19. Siege of Yorktown. Finding himself bottled up,

Oct. 19. CORNWALLIS SURRENDERED with 7000 men.

In the peace negotiations, Vergennes was in the difficult position of trying to please both of his allies, Spain and the United States. This led to delay which aroused the impatience of the American commissioners, who, disregarding their instructions not to negotiate a separate peace with England, proceeded to do so. The British, eager to win American friendship and trade, thereby defeating the aspirations of the French, readily acceded to the American demand for the Mississippi as the western boundary and full rights in the fisheries off the Canadian coast.

1783, Sept. 3. DEFINITIVE TREATY OF PEACE between Great Britain and United States, signed at **Paris.** It recognized the independence of the United States. Provisions of the treaty with respect to the northeastern and northwestern boundaries led to later difficulties with England, while the southern boundary provision led to trouble with Spain.

Full rights in the Newfoundland fisheries were guaranteed to the United States. Creditors of neither country were to encounter legal obstacles to collection of debts, while the Congress would recommend to the states the restoration of the confiscated estates of loyalists.

Navigation of the Mississippi was to be open to both Great Britain and the United States.

1783–1787. THE CRITICAL PERIOD OF AMERICAN HISTORY. The Articles of Confederation had gone into effect in 1781, and with the achievement of independence in 1783 the young nation found itself in a difficult economic situation, not due primarily to the particular forms of government then in operation. Treated as a foreign people by England as well as by other European countries, and denied participation of their ships in the trade of the British West Indies, so important in their economy before the Revolution, far-reaching economic dislocations resulted, producing a deep depression in 1784–1785, from which the country began to recover as early as 1787. While not fundamentally responsible for the unfortunate situation, the Articles of Confederation received the blame and were widely believed to be inadequate. The economic situation was aggravated by paper-money experiments of the states and by the inability of Congress to raise an adequate revenue. The weakness of the central government was dramatized by **Shays' Rebellion** (1786) in Massachusetts, in which the use of state troops was necessary to protect the federal arsenal at Springfield.

1785. The Land Ordinance enacted. The cession by the landed states of their claims to western lands, made necessary by Maryland's refusal to ratify the Articles of Confederation unless such cessions should be made, created the public domain of the United States, for the administration of which a land policy was necessary. This ordinance established the rectangular system of survey, provided for survey in advance of sale, and laid down terms and conditions of sale.

1787. THE NORTHWEST ORDINANCE enacted, providing for the government of the northwest. The region was to be divided into not less than three and not more than five districts, which, after passing through territorial or colonial stage, should be admitted to statehood. This principle of co-ordinancy or ultimate statehood became the basic and distinguishing feature of the American colonial system of the nineteenth century. Slavery and involuntary servitude were prohibited in the area.

1787, May. THE CONSTITUTIONAL CONVENTION assembled at Philadelphia. The inability of Congress to raise revenue, the outbreaks of disorder, and the obstructions to commerce resulted in an increasing desire for a more perfect government. Commissioners from Virginia and Maryland met at **Mount Vernon** in 1785 to consider the possibility of a uniform commercial code. This conference made clear the need of wider co-operation, so Virginia invited all the states to send delegates to a convention at **Annapolis** (1786). This convention was attended by delegates from but five states, who proposed a convention to meet at Philadelphia in May, 1787. Congress officially called such a convention. The convention was to convene on May 5. All states except Rhode Island were represented. After four months of labor,

1787, Sept. 17. The Constitution was signed by the delegates present. The document was sent to the states for ratification, with the provision that it should become operative upon the acceptance of nine states.

1788, June. Ratification by New Hampshire, the ninth state, placed the constitution in operation. In several states the anti-Federalists exacted promises of amendments in return for unconditional ratification. (*Cont. p.* 764.)

E. AFRICA, 1517-1800

1517. Conquest of Egypt by Selim I (p. 422). The country was put under a Turkish governor, but the Mamluk beys were left in effectual control, acting as a landholding oligarchy.

1517. Regular establishment of the **slave trade** through a concession granted by Charles I to a Flemish merchant.

1517. Defeat of the Songhoy ruler by the forces of the **Haussa Confederation,** which became the dominant power east of the Niger, under the leadership of Kebbi.

1520-1526. Mission of **Francisco Alvarez** to Ethiopia. He wrote the first detailed description of the country.

1527. Ethiopia was overrun by the Moslem Somali chief, Ahmed Gran, who used firearms. The negus thereupon called upon the Portuguese for aid.

1534. The Turks, under Khaireddin Barbarossa, took **Tunis** (p. 422).

1535. Spanish conquest of Tunis, completing the conquest of the North African coast begun in 1494 with the acquisition of Melilla.

1541. Abortive expedition of Charles V to Algiers (p. 401).

1541. Portuguese expedition to Ethiopia under **Christopher da Gama,** son of Vasco. The Portuguese succeeded in expelling Ahmed Gran.

1555-1633. THE PORTUGUESE (Jesuit) **MISSIONS IN ETHIOPIA.** Conversion of two successive rulers. Remarkable influence and work of **Pedro Paez.** The conversion led to repeated religious wars against the Portuguese faction. Ultimately the Portuguese were expelled and all Catholic missions prohibited.

1562-1576. John Hawkins initiated the British slave trade, making three voyages from West Africa to the New World with slave cargoes.

1571-1603. Apogee of the **EMPIRE OF KANEM** or **BORNU** (dating from the 13th century) under Idris III. It controlled most of the territory about Lake Chad.

1574. The Spaniards lost Goletta. End of the Spanish rule in Tunis, which became a Turkish regency, with an elected bey.

1574. The Portuguese began the settlement of Angola at **São Paulo de Loanda.**

1578. **Sebastian** of Portugal, called upon to intervene in the dynastic struggles in Morocco and determined to conquer the country for himself, was overwhelmingly defeated at **Kasr al-Kabir. Ahmed al Mansur** established the Sharifian dynasty.

1580. The Spaniards occupied **Ceuta,** which remained technically a possession of Portugal till 1688.

1581. The Moroccans took Tuat, beginning the penetration of the Sahara.

1591. A force of Spanish and Portuguese renegades in the service of Moroccans, crossed the desert and defeated the forces of **Songhoy** by use of firearms. Gao was destroyed and the Moroccans established themselves at Timbuktu. The entire Negro culture was destroyed and the country fell a prey to rival pashas. These made themselves independent of Morocco in 1612 and continued to rule at Timbuktu until 1780.

1595. First establishments of the **Dutch** on the **Guinea coast.**

1598. The Dutch took Mauritius (Isle de France).

1616. The Portuguese, **Gaspar Boccaro,** journeyed from the upper Zambezi to Kilwa on the coast, one of the first recorded explorations of the interior.

1618. Journey of the Frenchman, **Paul Imbert, to Timbuktu.**

1618-1619. G. Thompson ascended the Gambia River for about 400 miles.

1621. The Dutch took **Arguin and Goree** from the Portuguese.

1626. The French established themselves at St. Louis at the mouth of the Senegal.

1626. First French settlements on **Madagascar** (inhabited by various primitive tribes and by the **Hovas,** who had arrived from overseas about 1000 A.D.).

1637. The Dutch took Elmina from the Portuguese and built numerous forts on the Gold Coast.

1637. The French, under de Rochefort, explored the Senegal for about 100 miles and established posts.

1645. Capuchin monks ascended the Congo River, possibly as far as Stanley Falls.

1650. Ali Bey made himself hereditary Bey of Tunis.

1652, Apr. 7. CAPETOWN FOUNDED by the Dutch under **Jan van Riebeeck.**

1660. Rise of the **BAMBARA KING-DOMS** (Segu and Kaarta) on the upper Niger. They defeated and replaced the **Manding Empire** (1670) which thenceforth became a minor state.

1662. Portugal ceded **Tangier** to England.

1662. The British built a fort at James Island at the mouth of the Gambia.

1668. The Dutch advanced their South African settlement as far as Mossel Bay.

1672. Foundation of the **Royal African Company.**

1677. The French conquered the Dutch posts on the Senegal.

1683. The Prussians built the fort of **Grossfriedrichsburg** on the Guinea Coast (abandoned 1720).

1684. The British abandoned Tangier to the Sultan of Morocco.

1684. French expeditions against the piratical deys of **Algiers.** Various coast towns were bombarded and the deys were obliged to surrender Christian slaves.

1686. Louis XIV proclaimed the annexation of **Madagascar.**

1697. The French, under **André de Brue,** completed the conquest of the Senegal region and advanced up the river to Mambuk (1715).

1698. The Portuguese were expelled from their posts on the east coast by Arabs from Oman. Mombasa was abandoned in 1730, but the Portuguese retained Mozambique.

1699. C. **Poncet,** an emissary of Louis XIV, traveled overland from Cairo to Gondar in Ethiopia.

1705. Hussein ibn Ali founded the **Husseinite dynasty** in Tunis and threw off Turkish authority.

1708. The Spaniards were expelled from Oran.

1713. The **Asiento Treaty** (p. 432) gave Britain the right to import African slaves into the Spanish colonies in the New World, thus initiating the most active period of the British slave trade.

1714. Ahmed Bey made himself ruler of Tripoli, founding the Karamanli dynasty which lasted until 1835.

1715. The French took the island of Mauritius.

1723. **Bartholomew Stibbs,** for the African Company, took over the Gambia region as far as the Barrakonda Falls.

1732. The Spaniards retook Oran.

1757-1789. Reign of **Sidi Mohammed** in Morocco. He established law and order and abolished Christian slavery (1777).

1758. The British captured the French possessions on the Senegal.

1760. The Dutch, in South Africa, crossed the Orange River and began the penetration of Great Namaqualand.

1766. **Aki Bey** established himself as ruler of Egypt and proclaimed independence of the Turks. His successor, Mohammed Bey, recognized Turkish suzerainty again (1773).

1768-1773. **James Bruce** explored Ethiopia, traveling from Massawa to Gondar and thence to the Blue Nile. He returned by way of Egypt and reported the Ethiopian Empire in decline, restricted to the area north of the Blue Nile and wracked by rebellion.

1776. Rise of the Tukulor power in West Africa.

1778. The French recovered their possessions on the Senegal.

1778. Explorations of **W. Paterson** in the Kafir country.

1783. By the Treaty of Paris the British secured the Senegal again. They held it until 1790.

1787. The British acquired **Sierra Leone** from the natives. In 1791 it was devoted to the settlement of freed slaves.

1788. Sir Joseph Banks founded the *African Association* for the furtherance of exploration and the development of trade.

1791. The Spanish abandoned Oran, retaining only Melilla and Ceuta and a few minor stations on the North African coast.

1792. **Denmark prohibited the slave trade,** the first country to take this step.

1801. Conquest of the Haussa power by **Usman dan Fodio,** a Tukulor chief, who converted this area to Islam and founded the **Kingdom of Sokoto.**

(*Cont. p.* 826.)

F. ASIA

1. PERSIA, 1500-1794

1500-1524. SHAH ISMAIL, founder of
the **Safavid dynasty,** the first
national dynasty in many centuries. Ismail
traced his descent to **Safi al-Din** of Ardabil
(1252–1334), a supposed descendant of Ali,
the fourth caliph. Safi al-Din founded
among the Turk tribes an order of dervishes,
devoted to mystic teachings and Shi'a
doctrine. His influence and that of his
successors spread over northwestern Persia
and into eastern and southern Anatolia.
Sheikh Joneid, head of the order from 1448–
1460, attempted to extend his temporal
power and ultimately secured the protection
and alliance of **Uzun Hasan,** whose sister
he married. His son, Haidar, married a
daughter of Uzun Hasan and devoted himself to the reorganization of the order, which
became a powerful military instrument
(*Kizil-bashes* = red heads, from their head-
dress). Haidar was defeated and killed by
Jaqub of the White Sheep, but left several
sons, of whom Ismail was one. After years
spent in hiding, Ismail was able to take
advantage of the confusion following the
death of Rostam Shah.

1501. Battle of Shurur, in which Ismail
defeated Alwand of the White
Sheep. He soon took Tabriz and had himself proclaimed shah. With his accession
the Shi'a doctrine became officially established in Persia.

1507-1622. The Portuguese established at
Hormuz.

1510. Ismail defeated the Uzbeks and
drove them out of Khorasan.

1514. BATTLE OF CHALDIRAN, following the invasion of Persia by the
Turks under Selim I (p. 421). Ismail was
defeated and Tabriz taken, though later
evacuated by the Turks. Beginning of a
long duel between Turks and Persians, resulting largely from religious conflict.

1524-1576. SHAH TAHMASP I, the son
of Ismail, who ascended the throne
at ten. The reign was marked by continuous raids and campaigns against the
Uzbeks of Transoxiana and by repeated
incursions of the Turks, who conquered
Mesopotamia and on several occasions took
Tabriz, Sultanich, and Ispahan. **Peace
with the Turks** was finally concluded in
1555.

1561-1563. Anthony Jenkinson, of the
English Muscovy Company,
reached Persia overland through Russia

and opened commercial relations which
continued until 1581.

1576-1577. ISMAIL II, fourth son of
Tahmasp, who succeeded on the
death by poison of his father. He
killed off all his relatives and rivals, but himself died after a year
of office.

**1578-1587. MOHAMMED KHUDA-
BANDA,** the half-blind eldest son
of Tahmasp, who had escaped his
brother's vengeance. Renewal of
the Turkish attack, which was
less decisive than before.

1587-1629. SHAH ABBAS I (*the Great*),
most highly esteemed of the Persian rulers. He was a man of broad outlook
and strong will, though personally suspicious and cruel (he had one son murdered
and two others blinded). In his early years
Abbas was wholly under the domination
of the Kizil-bash chiefs, but he later succeeded in counteracting their influence by
organizing a new tribe of "friends of the
shah," and by building up a new infantry
and artillery force, modeled on the Turkish.
In this he was greatly aided by **Anthony**
and **Robert Shirley,** two brothers who came
with 26 followers in 1598. Robert remained
in Persian service during most of Abbas'
reign.

1590. Abbas made peace with the Turks,
abandoning Tabriz, Shirvan, Georgia, and Luristan. This he did in order to
be free to deal with the Uzbeks, who, under
Abdullah II, had taken Herat, Meshed, and
other towns of Khorasan.

1597. The Persians defeated the Uzbeks,
whose invasions of Khorasan were
stopped for many years.

1602-1627. Further **wars with the Turks**
(mission of Sir Anthony Shirley
to Europe to enlist the co-operation of the
emperor and King of Spain). In 1603
Abbas managed to retake Tabriz, and then
Erivan, Shirvan, and Kars. A great victory
was won over the Turks at **Lake Urmia.**
Thereafter Abbas conquered Baghdad,
Mosul, and Diarbekr. Peace was made in
1612, but war broke out again in 1616.
Efforts of the Turks to retake Baghdad
(1625) failed.

1616. The **British East India Company**
began trading with Persia from
Surat. Their activity was resented by
the Portuguese, who attacked the Eng-

The Safavid Dynasty

Âsh, but were defeated in the **battle of Jask**
(1620).

1622. The English merchants, co-operating with a Persian army, took
Hormuz from the Portuguese, receiving special privileges there.

1629-1642. SHAH SAFI, the grandson
of Abbas. Beginning of harem
rule and rapid decline, as in the Ottoman
Empire fifty years before. Like his contemporary, Murad IV (p. 424), Shah Safi
distinguished himself by wholesale executions.

1630. Murad IV took and sacked Hamadan, the first move in the campaign to retake the conquests of
Abbas the Great.

1635. The Turks took Erivan and Tabriz.

1638. The Turks took Baghdad and forced
the shah to make peace. Erivan
was left to the Persians, while the
Turks retained Baghdad.

1642-1667. SHAH ABBAS II, the son of
Safi. He was only ten when he
reached the throne and at no time
showed any particular ability.

1664. First Russian mission to Ispahan.
Beginning of Cossack raids on the
Caucasus front. In the same year
the French secured permission to
trade in Persia.

1667-1694. SHAH SULEIMAN, the son
of Abbas II, another dissolute
ruler who did nothing to check
the decline.

1694-1722. SHAH HUSAIN, a devout
ruler whose renewed emphasis on
Shi'a doctrine gave his Sunnite
neighbors an excuse for making
trouble.

1709. Rising of the Afghans at Kandahar,
led by Mir Vais, a Ghilzai chieftain and a Sunnite. Mir Vais succeeded in
defeating the Persian armies sent against
him (1711) and established the independence of the Afghan state.

1715-1717. Mir Abdullah, ruler of Kandahar in succession to Mir Vais. He
was overthrown when he attempted to make peace on the
basis of Persian suzerainty over
Kandahar.

1717-1725. Mir Mahmud, ruler of Kandahar. In 1717 the Abdalis of Herat
also revolted and established another Afghan state.

1722. Invasion of Persia by Mir Mahmud
and an army of Afghans. The
Persian court and army were completely
demoralized and offered little real resistance. They were defeated at Gulnabad,
after which Mahmud took Ispahan. Husain abdicated and

1722-1725. Mahmud became shah. Husain's son, Tahmasp, however,
escaped to Mazandaran and tried
to organize national resistance.

1722. Peter the Great, taking advantage
of the confusion, took Derbent on
the plea of supporting Tahmasp. In 1723
he added Resht and Baku, and Tahmasp
agreed to cede all of Shirvan, Daghestan,
Gilan, Mazandaran, and Astrabad in return
for effective aid.

1723. The Turks, hoping for a share of
the spoil, took Tiflis.

1724. Russia and Turkey made an agreement for the dismemberment of
Persia, the Turks reserving for
themselves Tabriz, Hamadan, and
Kermanshah. These places they
occupied in 1724-1725.

1724-1725. Reign of terror in Ispahan,
where Mahmud, gone mad, ordered
the massacre of the Persian nobility and
of all available Safavid princes, to say
nothing of large numbers of soldiers and
inhabitants.

1725-1730. ASHRAF SHAH, in succession
to Mahmud. He was more conciliatory, but from the outset
failed to get much sympathy from
the Persians, or much support
from Kandahar.

1726. Ashraf defeated the Turks, who
were advancing on Ispahan. Peace
was concluded in 1727, Ashraf
securing recognition from the sultan in return for the cession of the
conquered territories.

1726-1728. Tahmasp, supported by Nadir
Kuli, a powerful chief of the Af-
shar tribe of Khorasan, conquered
Meshed and Herat and, after de-
feating an Afghan army, retook
Ispahan.

1730. Final defeat of the Afghans near
Shiraz. Ashraf was murdered on
his way to Kandahar and his
followers fled from Persia as best
they could.

1730-1732. SHAH TAHMASP II was
hardly more than a figurehead,
the real ruler being Nadir Kuli, who married
Tahmasp's sister. Nadir, having defeated
the Afghans, turned against the Turks,
whom he forced to give up Hamadan, Kirmanshah, and Tabriz. He then marched
east to deal with the Abdalis, and Tahmasp,
thinking to complete the victory over the
Turks, met with disaster and lost all that
Nadir had gained. He agreed to the terms
submitted by the Turks, for which Nadir
deposed him.

1732-1736. ABBAS III, the eight-months-old son of Tahmasp, was elevated to the throne as a mere puppet. He was the last of the Safavid dynasty.

1732. By the **Treaty of Resht** the Russians gave up their claims to Mazandaran, Astrabad, and Gilan, which had never been effectively occupied.

1733. Nadir, having been seriously defeated by the Turks in the **battle of Kirkuk,** managed to retrieve his position and blockade Baghdad. But these operations were interrupted by the need for a further campaign in Transcaucasia (1734).

1735. Russia, by treaty, gave up the last Persian acquisitions of Peter the Great, Baku and Derbent, and joined in alliance with Nadir against the common enemy, the Turk. Nadir won a great victory over the Turks at **Baghavand,** and took Tiflis.

1736-1747. NADIR SHAH became ruler on the death of Abbas III. He accepted the throne on condition that the Persians renounce the Shi'a heresy. He himself, being a Turk by race, was also a Sunnite. But he never succeeded in making orthodoxy acceptable to the Persians.

1737. Nadir and his generals reduced Baluchistan and Balkh.

1738. Capture of Kandahar. Nadir thereupon proceeded to invade India. Kabul, Peshawar, and Lahore were taken and in 1739 a huge army of the Mogul emperor was defeated at **Karnal,** near Delhi. Delhi was taken and a tremendous massacre followed. Nadir left the Mogul emperor on the throne, but levied an indemnity of almost half a billion dollars and took all the territory north and west of the Indus.

1740. Nadir subjected **Bokhara and Khwarezm** (Khiva). This marked the greatest extent of his dominion and at the same time marked a turning-point in his career. Nadir was a great soldier, but he lacked real statesmanship and administrative ability. His efforts to stamp out Shi'ism resulted in growing unrest, and the need for suppressing discontent made the shah ever more ruthless and cruel. In the end he ruined the country by his huge contributions and despotic exploitation.

1743-1747. Resumption of **war with the** Turks, the sultan having refused the Persian terms. In 1745 Nadir won a resounding victory near **Kars** and in 1747 was able to secure peace: he gave up his demand for recognition of a fifth (Persian) orthodox sect, but secured recognition for the frontier as it had been in the time of Murad IV.

1747. Nadir Shah was assassinated by one of his own tribesmen.

1747-1750. A period of anarchy, during which the succession was hotly disputed. **Ahmad Kahn Durani** established himself at Kandahar, took Meshed and Herat and annexed Sind, Kashmir, and parts of the Punjab, founding a powerful Afghan state.

1747-1748. Adil Shah, the nephew of Nadir, became shah, but was soon dethroned and executed.

1748-1751. Shah Rukh, grandson of Nadir, was elevated to the throne. He was defeated and blinded by a Shi'a rival, but ultimately established his rule in Khorasan (to 1796). The rest of Persia continued to be hotly disputed between competing chieftains, until

1750-1779. KARIM KHAN, of the **Zand dynasty,** succeeded in maintaining himself against the powerful Kajar leader. Karim Khan, whose strength was in the south (Shiraz the capital), was a just and benevolent ruler, during whose reign the country was enabled to recover.

1763. The English established a factory at Bushire, and somewhat later (1770) at Basra.

1775-1776. Karim Khan sent an expedition against Basra. This important station was taken, but was voluntarily abandoned on the death of Karim.

1779-1782. Another period of anarchy, during which Karim's brothers disputed the succession and the Kajar chief, Aga Mohammed, again took the field.

1782-1785. Ali Murad Shah. He re-established the capital at Ispahan.

1785-1789. Jafar Shah. Continuation of the confusion, marked by cruelty and barbarity.

1789-1794. Lutf Ali Khan, last of the Zand dynasty; a brilliant and chivalrous, but arrogant ruler. Unable to get the better of his rivals, Lutf was finally defeated and killed.

1794. Aga Mohammed founded the Kajar dynasty. (*Cont. p.* 862.)

2. AFGHANISTAN, TO 1793

Prior to the 18th century, Afghanistan was in part ruled by Persia, in part by India and in part by the central Asian khanate of Bokhara. In 1706 **Kandahar** made itself independent and there followed the Afghan conquest of Persia (1722, see p. 528). This remained but an episode, for in 1737 Nadir Shah, having driven the Afghans out of Persia, carried the offensive eastward and subjected all of Afghanistan and western India.

1747-1773. AHMAD SHAH, one of the Afghan generals of Nadir Shah, on the murder of the latter assumed control of the Afghan provinces. He was a member of the Durani (Sauzai) clan of the Abdali tribe and established the **Durani dynasty** and empire. Most of his reign was filled by his nine **expeditions to India,** where he successfully asserted his claim to the Indian provinces of Nadir's empire. The dying Mogul Empire was unable to offer effective resistance. Ahmad took Lahore (1752) and then Delhi, which he plundered (1755). In 1761 he won a resounding victory over the Marathas at **Panipat,** and in 1762 over the Sikhs near Lahore. On his death the Afghan Empire extended from eastern Persia (Meshed) over Afghanistan and Baluchistan and eastward over Kashmir, and the Punjab.

1773-1793. Timur Shah, the son of Ahmad, proved to be a weak and ineffectual ruler. He moved the capital from Kandahar to Kabul, but was unable to prevent the loss of some of the Indian territory or the gradual disintegration of his authority even in Afghanistan.

(*Cont. p.* 866.)

3. INDIA

1498. VASCO DA GAMA, having rounded the Cape of Good Hope, reached Malabar. The Portuguese, after constructing forts at Cochin (1506) and Socotra (1507), soon diverted the spice trade from the Red Sea route.

1504. Yusuf Adil Shah of Bijapur, having annexed Gulbarga, established the Shi'a form of Islam, despite protest from many Sunnites.

1509. The Portuguese, under **Francisco de Almeida,** at Diu destroyed an Egyptian-Indian fleet which had, in the previous year, defeated a Portuguese squadron at Chaul.

1510. The Portuguese acquired Goa as headquarters, in place of Cochin.

1512. Golconda became independent (till 1687).

1526-1537. Bahadur, the last active sultan, with the aid of Khandesh, captured Mandu and annexed Malwa (1531), after which he captured Chitor (1534).

1526-1761 (1857). THE MOGUL EMPIRE in India was founded by **Babar** (1483-1530), descendant of Timur in the 5th generation, who had seized Kabul (1504) and Lahore (1524) as compensation for loss of Ferghana and Samarkand. Decisive victory at **Panipat** over Ibrahim Shah Lodi gave him Delhi and Agra, which he defended in the

1527. Battle of **Khanua** against Rana Sanga of Chitor, chief of a Rajput confederacy.

1529. Victory on the Gogra, where it meets the Ganges, completed conquest of the Kingdom of Delhi to the frontier of Bengal.

Babar's acts, problems, and personality appear in his Turki *Memoirs.*

1530-1540, 1555-1556. Humayun drove Bahadur Shah of Gujarat to flight before Chitor and captured Mandu and Champanir (1535), but lost both through a year of inaction. The same fault and treachery of his brothers lost the empire to the

1539-1555. Sur dynasty of the Afghan **Sher Shah** (1539-1545) who had consolidated power in Bihar and drove Humayun to seek refuge in Persia, whence he returned precariously to Delhi and Agra (1555).

1535. The Portuguese secured by treaty Bassein, and were allowed to fortify Diu, which they defended against an Ottoman fleet and a Gujerati army (1538).

1546. Efforts to expel the Portuguese failed miserably.

1556-1605. AKBAR (b. 1542, personal rule 1562) restored and consolidated the empire throughout northern India.

1556. Guided by **Bairam Khan,** his guardian (till 1560) he crushed the Afghans at Panipat.

1559. Constantine de Braganza seized Daman.

GROWTH OF BRITISH POWER
IN
INDIA

British Territory in 1785
Acquisitions 1785 – 1805
       ,,   1805 – 1819
       ,,   1819 – 1858
       ,,   since 1858
Dependent States – (The
dates are those of the acceptance of British Protection.)

Statute Miles
0   100 200. 300 400

1895
Kashmir 1846
Punjab 1849
British Baluchistan
1815
1801
1803
Rajputana 1818
Oudh 1856
1801
1876
1818
1801
Sind 1843
Behar 1765
Assam 1826
1812
Bengal 1765
1815-18
Malwa 1818
Calcutta 1690
1803-7
Mahratta Lands 1818
Surat 1612
Berar 1853
Bhonsla's Lands 1853
Orissa 1803
Bombay 1661
1817
Nizam's Dominions 1800
Circars 1766
1848
Masulipatam 1620
Kurnool 1839
Kanara 1799
Mysore 1831
Madras 1639
Carnatic
Malabar 1792
Travancore 1788
Ceylon 1795

GEORGE PHILIP AND SON, LTD.

The Mogul Emperors

Babar
1526–1530

Humayun
1530–1556

Akbar
1556–1605

Jahangir
1605–1627

Shah Jahan
1628–1658

Dara   Shuja   Murad   **Aurangzeb**
1659–1707

Azim Shah   **Bahadur**   Mohamed   Kam Bakhsh
1707–1712   Akbar

Azim ash-Shan   Rafi ash-Shan   **Jehandar**   Jehan Shah
1712

Farrukh-Siar   Rafi'ad   Rafi   **Alamgir**   **Mohamed**
1712–1719   Darajat   Addaula   1754–1759   1719–1748

Shah Alam II   **Ahmed**
1759–1806   1748–1754

Akbar II   Bidar Bakht
1806–1837

Bahadur II
1837–1858

Mirza Mughal

Mirza Abu-bekr

1561. Conquest of **Malwa** was effected by the harem party (dominant 1560–1562).

1562. Akbar's marriage to a Rajput princess of Amber (mother of Jahangir) and abolition of the *jizya* tax on non-Moslems (1564) marked a new policy of impartiality and conciliation of subjects.

1564. The Gond Chandels (capital Chauragarh) were conquered. (Construction of the stone fort at Agra was begun.)

1565. A coalition of Ahmadnagar, Bijapur, Bidar and Golconda decisively defeated Vijayanagar at **Talikota,** and led to the execution of the raja. In 1574 Ahmadnagar annexed Berar, which had hindered the allied campaign.

1568. **Chitor** was taken by Akbar and about 30,000 Rajputs massacred.

1571. A new city at Fathpur Sikri, near Agra, was founded and magnificently built, but abandoned on Akbar's death.

1572-1573. Conquest of **Gujarat** gave Akbar access to the sea, new ideas and revenues. To defend his conquest he rode with 3000 horse 450 miles in 11 days.

Re-organization of administration was begun by (1) resumption to the crown of all lands, hitherto held by officials as temporary assignments, but now to be administered and revenue collected directly; (2) establishment of a hierarchy of paid military officials in which civil servants held rank; (3) substitution of a single tax of one-third produce of the land for the traditional levy of one-sixth plus numerous cesses which were now declared abolished; (4) the branding of all horses maintained for government service, to prevent usual fraud.

1576. Bengal was definitely conquered from the Afghans.

1577. Khandesh was induced to submit as first step toward reconquest of the Deccan, actually accomplished only by Aurangzeb (1659–1707).

1578. Public debates on religion, instituted for Moslems only in 1575, were thrown open to Hindus, Jains, Zoroastrians, Sabaeans, and Christians. Akbar showed new respect for animal life (Jain *ahimsa*), Zoroastrian reverence for the sun, and invited to court from Goa the Portuguese Jesuits Antonio Monserrate and Rodolfo Acquaviva (1579; arr. 1580). These, like later missions (1590, 1595), failed despite a friendly reception.

1582. In spite of revolt which followed a claim to infallibility under Moslem law (1579), the emperor decreed a new *Divine Faith* derived largely from non-Islamic ritual. He won for it only limited support, which collapsed at his death.

1589-1591. **Jamal Khan,** minister of Ahmadnagar, an adherent of the Mahdavi heresy which anticipated the advent of the Mahdi (world savior) in A. H. 1000, persecuted both Sunnites and Shiites.

1601-1604. Prince Salim, later Jahangir, rebelled but was restored to favor.

1603. **John Mildenhall,** representative of the English East India Company (London Company, founded Dec. 31, 1600) arrived at Agra, but secured no concession until 1608.

1605-1627. **JAHANGIR** maintained his father's empire in northern India but, himself given to drink, allowed power to pass to his wife Nur Jahan (1611).

1609-1611. **William Hawkins** failed to secure a treaty for James I, as did **Sir Thomas Roe** (1615–1619), but the English won trading rights at Surat after defeating a Portuguese fleet (1612).

1616. Bubonic plague, clearly identified for the first time, became epidemic.

1628-1658. **SHAH JAHAN** (d. 1666) ruled with even less regard for his subjects, but destroyed Ahmadnagar (1632) and defeated Golconda (1635) and Bijapur (1636).

1632-1653. **The Taj Mahal** was built as tomb for his wife, Mumtaz Mahal, for whom he had already built the splendid palace Khass Mahal on the fort at Agra.

1639. The site of **Madras** was granted to an Englishman.

1647. Aurangzeb campaigned unsuccessfully in Badakhshan and Balkh, and

1649-1653. Failed to wrest Kandahar from the Persians.

1653-1658. Again governing the Deccan, he campaigned ambitiously and arrested the revival of Bijapur; but failed to check the Maratha raider Sivaji.

1658. **Aurangzeb rebelled,** following the illness of Shah Jahan and competition for the succession among his four sons. He imprisoned Shah Jahan (d. 1666), and became emperor.

1659-1707. **AURANGZEB** emperor. The Mogul dominion was undermined, in part by Aurangzeb's sacrifice of political stability to religious zeal, and his failure to control his subordinates, of whom he was inordinately suspicious.

1659-1680. Sivaji reduced Bijapur (1659) and sacked Surat (1664 and 1670); the English factory escaped harm. In 1667 he won the title of *raja* from Aurangzeb and began to levy land taxes in Mogul territory (Khandesh, 1670); he successfully organized Maratha government on Hindu principles with the guidance of the poets Ramdas and Tukaram, and was enthroned as an independent ruler (1674).

1666. Chittagong was annexed for Aurangzeb by the Bengal governor.

1669. In the first purely religious persecution since Akbar's accession, the Hindu religion was prohibited and Hindu temples destroyed, with great loss to Indian art, and the *jizya* reimposed on non-Moslems (1679). The period was marked by Jat rebellions (1669, 1681, 1688–1707), Hindu uprisings, and troubles with Afghan tribes and with the now militant and theocratic Sikhs (1675–1678).

1679. Marwar was annexed in war against the Rajputs; hostilities continued nearly thirty years.

1681. Prince Akbar revolted unsuccessfully against his father's misgovernment, and died in exile.

1681-1707. Assuming personal command in the Deccan, Aurangzeb subjugated Bijapur (1686) and Golconda (1687) but failed to check the Marathas.

1685-1688. Aurangzeb seized Surat (1685), intending to expel the English, whose unwise attempt to seize Chittagong lost them all their claims in Bengal (1688); their naval superiority menaced Mogul trade, however, and they were encouraged to return to Bengal (**Calcutta founded, 1690**).

Following the decline of the Portuguese power in India, that of the English had been increased by the acquisition of **Bombay** (1661) and the absorption of Dutch ambitions chiefly in the Spice Islands. Foundation of the French *Compagnie des Indes Orientales* (1664) under strict government control, and numerous settlements (Pondichéry, 1674), now opened the way for acute Anglo-French rivalry.

1689. Capture of Sivaji's successor, **Sambhaji**, failed to crush the Marathas and indecisive warfare continued until 1707.

The intellectual curiosity and luxurious tastes of the Mogul rulers, except Aurangzeb, fostered brilliant cultural progress. Histories, annals, and memoirs, chiefly in Persian, a dictionary supported by Jahangir, and the unsurpassed poems of **Tulsi Das** (1532–1623), formed important literary contributions. Slavish imitation of Persian painting was modified by Hindu and even

European influences; a height of keen observation and delicate rendering was attained under Shah Jahan. Under him also the building of palaces, mausoleums, and mosques in Indo-Persian style attained an exquisite elegance.

1707- Following Aurangzeb's death the empire rapidly disintegrated; various provincial governors became virtually independent (1722 ff.), and wars of succession and foreign invasions culminated in anarchy.

c. 1708. The Sikhs, who had been founded in the 15th century as a strictly religious order, proclaiming Moslem and Hindu fellowship and monotheism, and opposing caste restrictions and priestcraft (except for the secular and religious authority vested in the Guru Hargovind, 1606), became a thoroughly militant order under the last Guru, Govind Singh (1666–1708); they menaced Mogul rights in the Deccan but their strength was broken by Bahadur Shah (1707–1712).

1715. **The English East India Company,** through gifts and medical service, secured exemption from customs duties, and other concessions. The reorganized Maratha government gradually became pre-eminent in India, exacting taxes from the whole Deccan (1720).

1739. A pillaging invasion of Persians under **Nadir Shah** checked the Maratha expansion northward, defeated imperial troops, and withdrew, retaining possession of Afghanistan and the wealth of Delhi (p. 529).

1746-1748. Following the outbreak of the **War of the Austrian Succession in** Europe (p. 465), the French, strengthened by their participation in Indian intrigue under the guidance of **Dupleix,** captured Madras (1746) and defeated the protesting Nawab of the Carnatic. **The Treaty of Aix-la-Chapelle** (1748) restored Madras to England.

1748-1754. **Anglo-French rivalry** continued, each side supporting candidates for the positions of Nizam of the Deccan and Nawab of the Carnatic. French domination, at its height in 1751 when Bussy virtually ruled the Deccan and Dupleix the Carnatic, was checked by **Robert Clive's** (1725–1774) brilliant seizure of Arcot (Sept. 12, 1751). The recall of Dupleix (1754) left English prestige firmly established.

1756. The Nawab (**Suraja Dowla**) of the Bengal region captured Calcutta (June 20) and imprisoned unescaped residents in the *Black Hole.*

1757. The English retook Calcutta and, being again at war with France, seized Chandernagor (destroyed 1759), and under Clive overwhelmed the French and their allies in the **battle of Plassey** (June 22), which practically destroyed French claims in India. From their own candidate as nawab, the English secured rights of landholder over the *zamindari* of Calcutta (c. 882 sq. mi.). A French expedition under Lally arrived too late, and failed to take Madras (besieged Dec. 1758–Feb. 1759).

1758-1760. Maratha occupation of the Punjab (1758) and renewed northern activity (1760) excited allied opposition of Mohammedan rulers, Rohilla Afghans, and Nadir Shah's Afghan successor, Ahmad Shah Durrani, under whose direction the Marathas were crushingly defeated in

1761. The battle of Panipat. Subsequent mutiny caused Ahmad Shah's withdrawal, leaving India in chaotic dissension.

1761. English supremacy in India's foreign relations was assured by their defeat of the Dutch (1759) and capture of **Pondichéry** from the French, who by the **Treaty of Paris** (1763) retained only Pondichéry, Chandernagor, and other scattered stations, with limited numbers of troops. The *Compagnie des Indes* was dissolved in 1769.

1764. The English pensioned the nawab and established uncontested control in Bengal.

1765-1767. Clive administered Bengal affairs for the company: a grant of *diwani* (revenue control) in Bengal, Bihar, and part of Orissa was arranged, the company itself becoming *diwan* in 1771; official perquisites were reduced among the company's servants.

The militarism of the Moguls and the predatory policy of the Marathas led to an emphasis on warfare and piracy as sources of prestige and wealth, and a gradual decline of industry, education, and cultural progress except as maintained by some Vaishnava teachers and Hindu traditions. General economic chaos ensued, with westerners and Indians alike profiting from intrigue and usury. One exception was Indore (1765–1795) under the rule of the pious (**Ahalya Bai**).

During dissension in the Maratha confederacy, **Haidar Ali** (1721–1781) gained power, usurped the throne of Mysore (1761), and

1769. Compelled the British at Madras, who became involved in war against

him (1765), to sign a treaty of mutual assistance.

1772-1774. As governor of Bengal, **Warren Hastings** (1732–1818) initiated reforms, including simplification of the revenue system, reformed coinage, government control of salt and opium manufacture, reduction of dacoity with native co-operation, study of Mohammedan and Hindu law. He became governor-general under the

1774. REGULATING ACT, which provided for government of British India by a governor-general and council; limitation by the crown of the rights of the company's directors, and prohibition of officers' private trade and receipt of presents. Hastings' energetic administration incurred the censure of jealous colleagues, notably **Philip Francis,** and led to his impeachment (after his retirement in 1785), with a trial (1788–1795) resulting in acquittal.

1776. The Amini Commission, appointed by Hastings, brought about the substitution (1781) for the board of revenue (estab. 1772) of a central committee of revenue, which unwisely eliminated all local control.

1778-1782. Hastings sent an expedition across the peninsula from Calcutta to Surat (arr. 1779), which broke the coalition between the Marathas, Haidar Ali, and the Nizam, and by the **Treaty of Salbai** (1782) obtained for Bombay twenty years' peace with the Marathas and the cession of Salsette and Elephanta.

1778. France and England again at war, Hastings took Pondichéry and Mahé. Provoked by this action,

1780-1784. Haidar Ali, with French help, attacked the English in the Carnatic, but was defeated at **Porto Novo** (1781); the **second Mysore war,** continued by his son **Tippoo Sahib,** was terminated when French aid was withdrawn.

1784. PITT'S INDIA ACT, in an endeavor to check territorial expansion, forbade interference in native affairs or declaration of war except in case of aggression; it put the company strictly under crown control, setting up the clumsy "double-government" system which lasted until 1858.

1786-1793. Lord Cornwallis (after a 20-month interregnum of John MacPherson) became governor-general and commander-in-chief, with power to overrule his council (extended clearly over all local authority 1793). Under injunctions to preserve peace, he made administrative reforms (adequate fixed salaries for company officers).

1790-1792. Tippoo attacked Travancore, opening the **third Mysore War;** Cornwallis allied himself with the Peshwa and Nizam, and Tippoo was defeated and ceded half his territory, paying a large indemnity (Mar. 19, 1792).

1793. **Cornwallis' Code** inaugurated substantial reforms. The *Permanent Settlement* stabilized the revenue system by fixing the assessment in Bengal, Bihar, and Orissa (and Benares Province, 1795) with collection through *zamindars*, whose expansive powers allowed corruption to continue nevertheless; it also effected ruthless sale of *zamindar* rights in case of default, led to a "no rent" policy and its faulty remedy, distraint (1799), closed the way to later reliable surveys because of individual interests, and caused great financial loss to company and government. The **judicial** system was reshaped on the British model, but with a paucity of courts and a subordination of Indian officials. *Zamindars* were left only revenue duties, their magisterial and police functions being transferred to European district judges (*zillahs*) and Indian police (*darogas*).

In Madras a careful survey along the lines of local practice led to a system of direct levy from the *ryot* (peasant), more satisfactory than the Bengal system.

Meanwhile the principal Maratha leader, **Mahadaji Sindia** (d. 1794), assumed protection of the emperor, reclaimed Delhi, and extended his power in northern India.

1793-1798. **Sir John Shore,** governor-general.

1798. Ceylon became a crown colony.

(*Cont. p.* 868.)

4. CHINA

1520-1521. The **Portuguese,** who under Albuquerque had seized Malacca (1511), sent Thomé Pires to Peking. Piratical conduct of Simao d'Andrade and others led to their expulsion from China in 1522.

1522-1566. THE **CHIA CHING REIGN** of Shih Tsung was filled with the effort to repel attacks (especially 1542 and 1550) of Altan Khan, Prince of the Ordos; and of Japanese pirates (1523 and 1552), who even besieged Nanking (1555).

1557. A Portuguese settlement was permanently established at **Macao.**

1577. **So-nam gya-tso,** third successor of Tsong-kha-pa (1357-1419), who **reformed Tibetan Buddhism** by foundation of the yellow-capped "Virtuous" church, and himself an incarnation of Avalokitesvara, presided over a Mongol assembly beside Koko-nor. Altan Khan entitled him *Dalai Lama* (Lama of all within the seas), and formally accepted his spiritual authority for his people. The hold of the Tibetan church over Mongolia was cemented by recognition of two new divine incarnations: Manjusri in the Dongkur Hutuktu of the Ordos (1579) and Maitreya in the Jebdzun-damba Hutuktu of Urga (c. 1602).

1573-1620. THE **WAN LI REIGN** of Shen Tsung is famous for cultural attainment.

1592-1593, 1597-1598. Japanese invasions of tributary Korea sent by Hideyoshi were repelled, the first from P'yong-yang (1593), the second from southern Korea.

1615. **Nurhachi** gave military organizations as eight banners to a group of Tungus tribes in eastern Manchuria.

1616. He adopted the title *Chin Khan* and the surname *Aisin Gioro,* "Golden Tribe," to identify his people as heirs of the Chin (1116–1234). They later (1652) called themselves *Manchus* (Man-chou, probably from the Bodhisattva of learning, Manjusri).

1621. He expelled the Ming from the Liao Basin and moved his capital to Liaoyang.

1636. THE **MANCHUS** proclaimed an imperial Ta Ch'ing dynasty at Mukden, and set up a civilian administration copied closely on the Chinese.

1644. The last **Ming emperor** hanged himself when a bandit, Li Tzu-ch'eng, seized Peking.

MING THOUGHT was at first almost wholly dominated by authority of **Chu Hsi** and his school. The *Hsing Li Ta Ch'üan,* a digest of moral philosophy from the works of 120 of these scholars, was published under imperial authority in 1416. Opposition to the positive and authoritarian aspects of such teaching was most vigorously expressed by **Wang Shou-jen** (pen-name *Wang Yang-ming*) (1472–1528 or 1529), who insisted that moral judgments spring from the intuitive faculties within all men. Sages differ from common men in quantity, not quality, of true perceptions. Experience is for him the test of truth. Chu Hsi through emphasis on objective study had opened the door to scientific **re-**

search. Wang, by insistence on subjectivity, did much to prevent it.

The early part of the dynasty saw a vigorous national reaction led by the **Academy of Letters** (Han Lin Yüan) against all things foreign. Buddhism was now almost completely naturalized as Chinese, and Islam was too strongly entrenched in the north and southwest to be eradicated; but both Nestorian and Roman Christianity were suppressed. So too were various secret fraternities with obscure social and political objectives, like the **White Cloud** and the **White Lotus**, which had enjoyed official status under the Mongols.

Matteo Ricci (1552–1610, Macao, 1582) won toleration for the Jesuits and a salary at court (1601) by presenting clocks, etc., to the throne and preparing a huge map of the world. News in Peking (1606) of the arrival in Kansu of **Benedict de Goez**, who had come overland from India (1603–1605), first established for modern Europe identity of **Marco Polo's Cathay** with maritime China (Thinai in the *Periplus*, A.D. 80–89, from Sanskrit Cina). Rapid conversions and private church services at Nanking brought suspicion of secret aims like those of the White Lotus, and consequent deportation (1616) of the missionaries to Macao, whence they gradually returned. **Johan Adam Schall von Bell** (1591–1666, Peking, 1622) was charged (1630) to reform the dynastic calendar (already begun by Jesuits, 1611 and 1629). He cast astronomical instruments; and (1636–1637) twenty 40-lb. cannon, with camel-guns for use against the Manchus.

The **Academy of Letters** supervised an imposing series of official compilations. The *Yung Lo Ta Tien*, an encyclopaedia into which numerous whole works were transcribed, was compiled in 10,000 manuscript volumes of folio size (1403–1409). The precedents of the T'ang, Sung, and Yüan were followed by issue, in numerous editions, of the dynastic legal and administrative codes and a territorial survey of the empire. The practice was begun of gathering many small choice works by various authors into uniform collections. **Mao Chin** published from his private library the *Chi Ku Ko*, fine critical editions of the *Thirteen Classics with Commentaries*, the *Seventeen Standard Histories*, and many other works.

Ming painters, besides much imitation of Sung ink landscape which was now reduced to conventional formulae, revived a coloristic tradition of vivid blues and greens. **Tai Chin** (fl. c. 1446) especially developed a new style of free rapid composition in ink which was better adapted to representation of life and movement than the exquisite but somewhat static Sung technique. The potters of the Hung Wu and Yung Lo reigns achieved bold effects by application of "three-color" glazes (aubergine, turquoise, and yellow) with dark blue to monumental potiches. In the Hsüan Te period they learned to control copper oxide red for decoration of white paste under clear glaze, in addition to the cobalt "Mohammedan blue" of which the purest supply came intermittently from Turkestan. Decoration in overglaze enamels, often in combination with underglaze blue, was used brilliantly on rather bombastic vases in the Chia Ching and Wan Li periods. The imperial kilns at Ching-te-chen in Kiangsi were developed to supply immense quantities of porcelain to the palace.

1644–1912. THE CH'ING DYNASTY entered Peking by surprise when the Manchu regent Dorgun (1643–1650) had helped the Ming general Wu San-kuei to drive off the bandit Li Tzu-ch'eng.

1644–1661. THE SHUN CHIH REIGN of Shih Tsu was filled with military effort to destroy Ming resistance, which centered about Prince Fu at Nanking (1644–1645), Prince T'ang in Fukien (1645–1646), Prince Lu at Shaohsing, Amoy, Chusan (1645–1651), and Prince Kuei from Canton to Yünnan (1646–1659). Conquest was accompanied by imposition of the Manchu shaven head with queue. Footbinding, at first forbidden (1638, 1645, 1662), was at length permitted to Chinese only (1668). Manchus were appointed as colleagues of Chinese in all principal posts of central administration, and garrisons from the eight Manchu banners were distributed among strategic provincial cities; but Chinese were appointed in the provinces both to civil posts and to command of Chinese auxiliary troops. Four Chinese were sent as viceroys to hold the south and southwest.

1645–1683. A pirate dynasty upheld the Ming. Chen Chih-lung (1645–1646, executed at Peking 1661) was succeeded by Cheng Ch'engkung, known to the Portuguese as *Koxinga* (1646–1662). Koxinga seized Amoy (1653), Ch'ung-ming Island (1656), attacked Nanking (1657), and by a long siege of Fort Zelandia (1661–1662) wrested Formosa from the Dutch. So formidable was his naval power that the Manchus decreed (1661) evacuation of the whole coastal population to a depth of ten miles from the sea.

1662–1722. THE K'ANG HSI REIGN of Sheng Tsu (b. 1654, personal rule in form 1667, in fact 1669) opened a period

The Manchu (Ta ch'ing) Dynasty (1644-1795)

Nurachi
T'ien Ming
Ruler of Manchuria
1616–1627
(*T'ai Tsu Kao Huang Ti*)

8   14

16 sons

Huang T'ai Chi
T'ien Ts'ung
Ruler of Manchuria
1627–1635
Ch'ung Te
Emperor of China
1636–1644
(*T'ai Tsung Wen Huang Ti*)

Dorgun
Prince Jui
Regent, d. 1647

9

11 sons

Fu Lin
Shun Chih
1644–1661
(*Shih Tsu Chang Huang Ti*)

3

8 sons

Hsüan Yeh
K'ang Hsi
1662–1722
(*Sheng Tsu Jen Huang Ti*)

4

35 sons

Yün Cheng
Yung Cheng
1723–1735
(*Shih Tsung Hsien Huang Ti*)

4

10 sons

Hung Li
Ch'ien Lung
1736–1795
(*Kao Tsung Shun Huang Ti*)

NOTE: Names in plain type are personal names, taboo after a ruler ascended the throne.
Names in boldface type are reign titles, or year names, adopted for reckoning time, but often applied by Westerners to the emperor himself.
Names in italic type are dynastic titles, or temple names, conferred posthumously to refer to the ruler. *Huang Ti* means simply "emperor."

of cultural achievement which surpassed the greatest of earlier dynasties. The fifteen provinces of the Ming were increased to eighteen by separate recognition of An-huei (1662), Hunan (1664), and Kansu (1705).

The **Dutch** had founded Batavia (1619), their Formosan station (1624–1625), and captured Malacca (1641) from the Portuguese, who lost their commercial empire, but retained Macao. A mission of Pieter van Goyer and Jacob van Keyser (1656) secured nothing better than tributary status, only slightly improved (1667) by the mission of Pieter van Hoorn. Disgruntled by loss of Zelandia,

1663-1664. **Balthasar Bort** with a Dutch fleet helped a Chinese army drive Koxinga's son and successor Cheng Chin (1662–1681) from the Fukien coast to Formosa.

1670. A Portuguese embassy under **Manuel de Saldanha**, like that of Bento Pereyra de Faria (1678–1679), won only confirmation of the status of Macao. The much later missions of A. M. de Souza y Menezas (1726) and F.-X. Assis Pacheco y Sampayo (1742) achieved no more.

1674-1681. Revolt of three viceroys followed imperial orders providing for their withdrawal (1673).

1674. Viceroy Wu San-kuei from Yünnan held Szechuan, Kueichou, Hunan, and Kuangsi for five years (1674–1679). Keng Ching-chung, grandson and heir of the Fukien viceroy, joined him and invaded Kiangsi.

1675. A revolt by Burni in Chahar was quickly suppressed. Cheng Chin's pirates resumed depredations in Chekiang and Fukien.

1676. Shang Chih-hsin forced his aged father, viceroy of Kuangtung, to surrender Canton to the rebels.

1681. Re-entrance of imperial armies to Yünnan City marked complete military triumph, supplemented by

1683. **Surrender of Formosa** by Cheng Chin's son Cheng K'o-shuang (1681–1683). Formosa was for the first time given imperial administration, as appendage of Fukien.

The Russian **Poiarkov** explored the Amur (1643–1646) and Khabarov built a fort at Albazin (1651). A mission under Baikov (1656) proved futile, but Spatar Milescu (1676) performed the kotow (*k'ou t'ou*) with dignity on a reciprocal basis, and mapped Siberia.

1689. By the **Treaty of Nerchinsk** the Russians adopted advice of the Jesuit negotiator Jean-François Gerbillon

to abandon Albazin and military pressure for commercial penetration. L. V. Izmailov (1720–1721) established a trading agent and an Eastern Orthodox church in Peking.

1691. The emperor, at a great assembly of Mongols at Dolon Nor, reorganized the four Khalkha states of central Mongolia which he had just defended (1690) against the provoked attack (1688) of Galdan, chief of the Olöt (West Mongol) Jungars.

1696. Galdan was crushed near Urga and took poison (1697).

1705. Forcible enthronement as Dalai Lama at Lhasa of an imperial candidate aroused Tibetan opposition and appeal to the Olöt (1714).

1712. Domestic peace since 1681 and vigilant administration with frugality not only paid for foreign wars, but led to a permanent settlement of land and poll-taxes on the basis of returns for 1711.

1717. Olöt **seizure of Lhasa** by direction of Galdan's nephew, Tsewang Rabdan (1697–1727), was learned in Peking too late to save a relief column from annihilation (1718). Well-prepared armies from Kansu and Szechuan

1720. Enthroned a popular Dalai Lama and established imperial garrisons in Tibet.

1721. Revolt in Formosa led by Chu I-kuei was suppressed.

The **Jesuits** enjoyed toleration and favor in return for scientific services. **Schall** prepared the dynastic calendar (1645–1664) until imprisoned on representations of jealous Moslem astronomers. **Ferdinand Verbiest** (1623–1688, arr. 1659) was reinstated in control of the almanac (1669), installed a new set of instruments on the observatory (1674), and promulgated a perpetual calendar (1678). **Fontaney** cured the emperor of fever with quinine (1693). **Régis** and eight others prepared the first maps of China to be based on astronomical observation, triangulation, and measurement (1708–1718). Benefits of an edict of toleration (1692) were ruined by a bitter quarrel over Jesuit acceptance of Chinese rites toward Heaven, Confucius, and ancestors. These rites were condemned (1693) by Mgr. Maigrot. Appeal to the emperor (1700) accentuated conflict of imperial and papal authority, which neither of two patriarchs, De Tournon (1705) and Mezzabarba (1720), sent by Clement XI, could reconcile. Dabbling in intrigue for succession among the twenty adult sons of the emperor won only (1722) permanent hostility of the victor, the end of the active mission.

From his accession **Sheng Tsu** labored to win support of the scholar class by daily classical study, honors to Confucius and the Sung Neo-Confucianists (*Ju*), and patronage of scholarship. He founded (1677) the **College of Inscriptions** (*Nan San So*) affiliated to the Academy of Letters. Most important among many books compiled by his order, in addition to the several administrative and archival works prescribed by precedent, were the standard *Ming History* (53 scholars appointed, 1679), *Complete T'ang Poetry* (1707), the *P'ei Wen Chai Shu Hua P'u* repertory of works on painting (1708), the *Yüan Chien Lei Han* encyclopaedia (1710), *P'ei Wen Yün Fu* thesaurus of literary phrases (1711), *K'ang Hsi Dictionary* (1716), and the *T'u Shu Chi Ch'eng* encyclopaedia (5020 vols. 1726). Private scholars were also active: **Huang Tsung-hsi** (1610–1695), the philosopher and critical historian of Sung, Yüan, and Ming philosophy; **Ku Yen-wu** (1613–1681), historical geographer and critic; **Chu I-tsun** (1629–1709) author of the critical bibliography of the classics *Ching I K'ao*; **Hsü Ch'ien-hsüeh** (1631–1694), who brought together 480 vols. of choice classical comment, *T'ung Chih T'ang Ching Chieh*; **Mei Wen-ting** (1633–1721), the mathematician; and many others.

The most brilliant epoch in the history of the imperial kilns at Ching-te-chen followed appointment of **Ts'ang Ying-hsüan** as supervisor (1682). The techniques of enameling on the biscuit, of composite monochrome glazing over colored glaze, of application of underglaze blue in powder form, and of decoration overglaze in transparent *famille verte* enamels were perfected. Progress of the minor arts followed establishment of 28 kinds of artisans within the palace precincts (1680).

1723-1735. THE YUNG CHENG REIGN of Shih Tsung, although peaceful at home, was filled with inconclusive war against Mongols and western tribesmen.

1727. The **Kiakhta Treaty** fixing the Russian frontier was concluded by Sava Vladislavitch after a mission to Peking (1726–1727).

1729. Large-scale operations against the Jungars led to

1732. Establishment of an advisory military council (*Chün Chi Ch'u*) which gradually usurped the executive functions of the grand secretariat (*Nei Ko*).

1736-1795. THE CH'IEN LUNG REIGN of Kao Tsung marks a new advance in population and wealth, which supported imposition of imperial control throughout Central Asia. Cultural activity continued to enjoy imperial patronage and leadership. Corruption of the civil service led by the venal Ho Shen (1750–1799) during the last twenty years of the reign provoked revolts which continued until the end of the dynasty.

1747-1749, 1755-1779. Campaigns of exceptional difficulty were waged to pacify the native tribes of the Tibetan border.

1750. Violence by and against the imperial Residents at Lhasa led to the

1751. INVASION OF TIBET and establishment of control over the succession and the temporal acts of the Dalai Lama.

1755. Amursana, grandson of Tsewang Rabdan, after ten years' succession struggle, was enthroned by imperial troops as Prince of the Jungars, but revolted. Suppression of the revolt, following a smallpox epidemic, depopulated the Ili Valley. The Jungars were annihilated or dispersed.

1757-1842. Restriction of foreign maritime trade to Canton was maintained despite efforts of the British interpreter Flint at Tientsin (1759), Capt. Skottowe at Canton (1761), and the Earl of Macartney at Jehol and Peking (1793).

1758-1759. Kashgaria was conquered by Chao-hui from the Turkish Khoja dynasty.

1765-1769. Invasion of Burma failed to reach Ava, but secured recognition of suzerainty.

1771. The Torgud, who had fled beyond the Volga to escape the Jungars, now dared accept an invitation by T'u-li-ch'en (1712), and migrated back to Ili.

1774. The first Chinese rebellion in nearly a century broke out in Shantung and was traced to the White Lotus Society.

1781, 1784. Revolts in Kansu by Mohammedans, including the Wahabees, were suppressed.

1784. The **United States** entered the profitable Canton trade.

1786-1787. Revolt in Formosa was suppressed.

1792. Invasion of Nepal under Fu-k'ang-an, provoked by attack on Tashilunpo, the seat of the Panchan Lama, resulted in defeat of the Gurkhas and their recognition of imperial suzerainty.

1795-1797. Revolt by the Miao tribes of Hunan and Kueichou was suppressed.

The best critical edition of the 24 *Standard Histories* was issued by imperial authority (1739–1746). Chief among many later imperial literary enterprises was the assemblage (1772–1781) by manuscript transcription, of a select library, *Ssu K'u Ch'üan Shu* or *Complete Work of the Four Treasuries,* embracing 3462 works in 36,300 vols. Seven copies were eventually distributed. The printed critical *General Catalogue* in 92 vols. (1789) contains additional notices of 6734 works not included in the library. The emperor exploited the occasion of compilation to expurgate from Chinese literature all derogatory references to the Manchus and their northern predecessors. More than 2000 works were condemned to total destruction (1774–1782), most of them minor writings of the period 1616–1681. Contrary to precedent, two propagandist histories were compiled fraudulently to identify the Manchus as descendants of the Juchen Chin. The technique of textual criticism was perfected and applied by numerous able scholars, to the classics, especially by **Lu Wen-ch'ao** (1717–1795), **Chiang Sheng** (1721–1799), and **Tuan Yü-ts'ai** (1735–1815). **Wang Ming-sheng** (1722–1797) and **Ch'ien Ta-hsin** (1728–1804) distinguished themselves as commentators on the standard histories. **Pi Yüan** (1730–1797) compiled a supplement to the general history of Ssu-ma Kuang. The practice of gathering choice literature of diverse kinds into uniform collections was spurred by issue from the imperial Wu Ying Tien of a series of 138 works printed from movable wooden type in 800 vols. (1773–1783). **Pao T'ing-po** (1728–1814) published his *Chih Pu Tsu Chai Ts'ung Shu* in 240 vols.

Under direction of **T'ang-Ying** (1736–1749) the imperial kilns at Ching-te-chen developed the elaborate *famille rose* palette of opaque overglaze enamels, which is distinguished by mixed colors and replacement of ferric oxide red by carmine derived from gold.

1795. Kao Tsung abdicated, but continued to direct affairs until death (1798). (*Cont. p.* 877.)

a. BURMA

Following the arrival during the 15th century of a few European travelers (Nicolo di Conti, c. 1435), in

1519. The Portuguese by treaty secured trading privileges at Martaban, and an increasing portion of the foreign trade was conducted by Europeans.

1539. Tabin Shwehti, ruler of Toungoo (1531–1550), captured Pegu, was crowned King of Lower Burma (1542), and after extending his power northward to Pagan (1546) assumed the title of *King of all Burma.* With Portuguese mercenaries he attacked unsuccessfully both Arakan to the west and Siam to the east.

1555. His successor, **Bayin Naung** (ruled 1551–1581), took Ava, destroyed the Tai kingdom of Chiengami (1557) in northern Siam, and subdued Ayuthia (1563) temporarily. Exhausted by these wars, the central power declined; in

1600. Pegu was destroyed and Burma broke up into a number of petty states.

1619. The Dutch and English East India Companies opened factories, but trade did not flourish and they were closed later in the century.

1753. Alaungpaya reunited Burma, with assistance from the English East India Company and in opposition to the French. His second successor destroyed Ayuthia (1767) and subdued Siam for a time, retaining the Tenasserim coast in Burmese possession. (*Cont. p.* 872.)

b. SIAM

Portuguese trading stations were established in the 16th century and about the beginning of the 17th century large numbers of Japanese were active in Siam, in war and trade.

1602. A Dutch trading post was established at Patani, where the British soon followed, until their withdrawal from Siam in 1623.

1664. By a commercial treaty, the Dutch gained a monopoly of Siamese foreign trade, which was, however, thwarted by French intrigue; a French embassy and military expedition (1685) in turn failed to secure the acceptance of Christianity, and French influence, and led to

1688. A popular revolt which began a period of prolonged civil war.

1767. A Burmese invasion destroyed Ayuthia and compelled temporary acceptance of Burmese rule until

1782. Rama I founded a new Siamese dynasty, with its capital at Bangkok, which has ruled to the present day (1939). (*Cont. p.* 872.)

c. MALAYSIA

1511. The Portuguese, under Albuquerque, captured **Malacca,** the center of the East Indian spice trade. They subsequently sent envoys to develop commercial relations with near-by native states, and set up fortified posts from which to dominate the trade.

1594. The Lisbon spice market was closed to Dutch and English traders, thus providing an incentive to direct trade between England and Holland and the Far East. The operations of the English and Dutch East India Companies (formed 1600 and 1602 respectively) led to the destruction of the Portuguese forts.

1605. The Dutch seized Amboyna and in

1619. Established themselves at Batavia.

1623. The English abandoned trade in Siam, Japan, and the East Indies, following a massacre of their people by the Dutch.

1639. The Portuguese were expelled from Japan and finally

1641. The Dutch captured Malacca. For the next century and a half they dominated the East Indies, acquiring a direct overlordship in Java.

1786. The English East India Company secured a grant of Penang (permanent cession 1790), which made a fourth Indian presidency (1805), but proved useless as a naval and commercial base.

(*Cont. p.* 875.)

5. KOREA

1506. A revolt against the cruel ruler, Yonsangun, brought to the throne

1507-1544. Chungjong, whose attempt to curb the great families by means of the Confucian scholars led to the destruction of the latter.

c. 1570. The Confucian scholars gradually established their control over the court, but, although only the orthodox Chu Hsi school of philosophy was tolerated, they broke up into bitterly antagonistic factions. Meanwhile the decline of the Ming brought a similar political and cultural decline in Korea.

1592-1598. Japanese invasions laid waste the land (p. 544).

1623. Injo was put on the throne by the so-called southern faction of Confucianists, which had triumphed over the northern faction. These two groups were originally branches of the eastern faction, which previously had superseded the western faction.

1627. The Manchus overran Korea.

1637. Korea became a vassal state of the Manchus (Ch'ing dynasty) after an invasion led by T'ai-tsung, but the court and people remained loyal to the Ming.

1675-1720. Under Sukchong the western faction of Confucianists returned to power and divided into the old and young factions, which fought bitterly with each other.

1725-1800. A period of great intellectual activity, for the most part limited to moral philosophy and to genealogical research or fabrication.

(*Cont. p.* 885.)

6. JAPAN, 1542-1793

1542 or 1543. Portuguese landed from a Chinese ship on the island of Tanegashima, off the southern coast of Kyūshū. These were the first Europeans to visit Japan. They introduced the musket, which soon modified Japanese warfare. Other Portuguese ships followed and entered into trade relations with the lords of western Japan.

1549-1551. ST. FRANCIS XAVIER (1506-1552), the famous Jesuit missionary, introduced Christianity into Japan, proselytizing in the feudal domains of the west and also at Kyōto, but with no great success. On the whole he was well received and in some cases the feudal lords even encouraged conversions in the hope of attracting Portuguese trade. But the dogmatic intolerance of the missionaries soon earned them the bitter enmity of the usually tolerant Buddhist clergy and led to proscriptions of the new religion in certain fiefs. Xavier left behind two Jesuits and the Japanese converts, who formed the nucleus of the new church.

1568. Oda Nobunaga (1534–1582) seized Kyōto and set up a puppet *shōgun,* Yoshiaki (1568–1573, d. 1597). Lord of the provinces of Owari, Mino and Mikawa east of Kyōto, Nobunaga had acted in response to a secret appeal from the emperor. By this daring blow he became the virtual dictator of central Japan, and with this date commenced

1568-1600. THE PERIOD OF NATIONAL UNIFICATION (usually called the *Azuchi-Momoyama Period*). The process of political disintegration of the nation had already run its course, and in these few decades, through the efforts of three great leaders, the nation was again united as the periphery was gradually subjugated by the military hegemons of the capital region. This was unquestionably one of the most dynamic epochs of Japanese history. The Japanese pirate traders were at their height and were active even in Siamese and Philippine waters. Excess national energy also expressed itself in a great invasion of Korea. Closer contacts with the Asiatic mainland and with Europeans resulted in an influx of new intellectual and artistic currents. Buddhism was in decline, and its monasteries were being deprived of their military power, but militant Christianity was at its height in Japan, and there was a revival of lay learning after the years of warfare. New skills and new products from the Occident profoundly affected the economy of the land, and in these years of relative peace the wealth and productivity of the nation expanded rapidly. The private customs barriers which had hampered trade were abolished, and the old monopolistic guilds (za) for the most part came to an end.

The artistic and intellectual spirit of the period was almost the antithesis of what it had been in Ashikaga times. It was an exuberant, expansive age. Refined simplicity had given way to ostentatious pomp and faddism. Architecture, which perhaps most clearly expressed the spirit of the age, showed a love of gorgeous decoration and majestic size. Castles and palaces rather than monasteries were the typical structures of the day.

1570. Nagasaki was opened to foreign trade by the local lord, Ōmura (sometimes dated 1567 or 1568). A hitherto unimportant fishing village, it soon became Japan's greatest port for foreign commerce.

1571. Nobunaga destroyed the Enryakuji on Mt. Hiei, thus eliminating this the most powerful of all the monasteries, as a military force. In these same years he also waged usually successful wars against other Buddhist groups, especially the militant groups of the True Pure Land sect (Ikkō sect), as in the siege of their central monastery, the Ishiyama-honganji in Ōsaka (1570-1580). Nobunaga's violent opposition to Buddhism as an organized political force finally broke the temporal power of the monasteries.

1576. Nobunaga commenced work on the Azuchi castle on the shores of Lake Biwa. This was the first great castle of Japan and heralded the beginning of several decades of widespread castle-build-

ing. Azuchi was destroyed at the time of Nobunaga's death.

1577-1582. Toyotomi (at this time Hashiba) Hideyoshi (1537-1598), the brilliant but basely born chief general of Nobunaga, conquered much of western Japan from the Mōri family in the name of Nobunaga.

1578. The death of Uesugi Kenshin (1530-1578), together with the earlier demise of his great enemy, Takeda Shingen (1521-1573), removed Nobunaga's two most formidable rivals in eastern Japan.

1578. The conversion of Ōtomo Yoshishige (Sōrin) (1530-1587), one of the greatest lords of Kyūshū, to Christianity gave the foreign religion a greater foothold in the island, where it had already become quite strong since the conversion of some lesser lords of the western littoral, like Ōmura (1562) and Arima (1576). The Christians, who were for the most part confined to the fiefs with Christian lords, were estimated at 150,000 in 1582.

1582. Nobunaga was killed by a discontented general, Akechi Mitsuhide (1526-1582). Hideyoshi returned from his western campaigns and destroyed Mitsuhide. A contest for power with the remaining members of the Oda family, supported by Tokugawa Ieyasu (1543-1616), one of Nobunaga's vassal lords in eastern Japan, brought about the elimination of the Oda and an understanding with Ieyasu, resulting in

1584. The hegemony of Hideyoshi over central Japan. The preceding year he had already commenced the construction of the great Ōsaka castle as his home base.

1585. Hideyoshi was appointed civil dictator (Kampaku), and two years later he became prime minister (Dajodaijin) as well.

1585-1587. A greater stratification of the classes (1, gentlemen-warriors; 2, farmers; 3, artisans; 4, merchants) was brought about by legislation (1585, 1586) and by the disarming of the peasantry (1587).

1587. The subjugation of the Shimazu family of southern Kyūshū completed Hideyoshi's conquest of western Japan.

1587. Hideyoshi issued a decree banishing the Portuguese missionaries from Japan, but failed to enforce it for ten years. His motive for this sudden opposition to Christianity was probably fear of the growing political and military strength of the Christians.

1590. The capture of the stronghold of the Hōjō family at Odawara induced all eastern and northern Japan to accept Hideyoshi's rule and completed the political unification of the land. At this time Hideyoshi's prominent vassal, Tokugawa Ieyasu, moved his administrative and military base to Edo (the modern Tōkyō), a strategic spot for the domination of the great plain of eastern Japan.

1592. THE INVASION OF KOREA. Possibly motivated by the fear of the excess of experienced warriors in Japan, the ambitious Hideyoshi planned the conquest of China. When Korea refused to grant the Japanese transit, he invaded the peninsula. Under the leadership of **Katō Kiyomasa** (1562–1611) and **Konishi Yukinaga** (d. 1600) the expeditionary force of some 200,000 overran almost the whole of Korea, but was forced by a large Chinese army to withdraw to the southern coast in 1593.

1597. The Korean campaign was resumed, but with no great success. After Hideyoshi's death (1598) all the Japanese soldiers returned to Japan. The lasting political results of the Korean venture were negligible, but a rapid development and expansion of the ceramic industry in Japan was brought about by many Korean potters who were taken back to Japan by the retreating captains.

1597. Hideyoshi, irritated by the bickerings between the Portuguese Jesuits and the Spanish Franciscans (who had come to Japan in 1593), and suspecting that Christian proselytizing was merely an opening wedge for the subsequent conquest of Japan by the Europeans, executed 3 Jesuits, 6 Franciscans, and 17 Japanese Christians. The remaining missionaries were ordered to leave, but only a small number did so. Hideyoshi did not press the persecution further, because he did not wish to drive away the Portuguese traders, who were then especially welcome, since direct commercial intercourse with China had been stopped.

1598. Hideyoshi's death was soon followed by a contest for power among his former vassals, culminating in

1600. The battle of Sekigahara, where Ieyasu defeated a coalition of his rivals. This victory made Ieyasu the virtual ruler of the whole land, and, although he was not appointed *shōgun* until 1603, from this time is usually dated

1600-1868. THE TOKUGAWA (or Edo) **PERIOD.** Ieyasu established the military capital at Edo (Tōkyō), which grew phenomenally to become the economic and cultural as well as political capital of the

nation. Because of the fate of the Oda and Toyotomi families, Ieyasu made the perpetuation of the rule in his family his major objective, and this colored the whole spirit as well as the political organization of the epoch, giving them strong conservative and even reactionary tendencies. The feudal lords were divided into the *Fudai* and *Tozama Daimyō.* The former, who were the vassals and allies of Ieyasu before Sekigahara, now occupied the central provinces. The latter, who had only submitted after Sekigahara, were located in more remote regions and were usually excluded from the central government. Both groups were compelled to leave hostages in Edo and to spend alternate periods there and in their fiefs. Important cities were ruled directly by Edo. The building and repairing of castles were strictly limited. The conduct of the warriors was closely regulated, and the emperor and his court, though financially generously treated, were strictly controlled.

The administrative hierarchy, which grew out of the Tokugawa family organization, consisted in order of rank of a *shōgun*; at times, and especially between 1638 and 1684, one or more prime ministers (*tairō*); four or five elders (*toshiyori* or *Rōju*) as a council of state; a group of junior elders (*wakadoshiyori*), who controlled the direct petty vassals of Edo; a class of officials known as *metsuke,* who served as censors or intelligence officers; and a large group of civil administrators called *bugyō.* The laws lacked coherent organization, but were based on certain fundamental moral precepts, primarily that of loyalty. Criminal codes were severe and cruel. There was a stringent stratification of the classes. *Daimyō* were to a large extent autonomous rulers in their own domains, but Edo kept a watchful eye on them, and there was a strong tendency for the feudatories to adopt the laws and organization of Edo.

The peace and prosperity of the early Tokugawa period brought a gradual rise in the standard of living and an increase in population as well as in the national wealth. With the growth of industry and commerce, a powerful merchant class grew up in the larger cities, and a gradual transition from a rice economy to a money economy commenced. This transition, together with the rise in living standards and the increase in population tended to make production inadequate and brought about great economic ills during much of the period.

Political conservatism and isolation from the rest of the world made the Tokugawa period outwardly stagnant, but it was inwardly a time of great intellectual develop-

The Tokugawa Shogun (1603-1867)

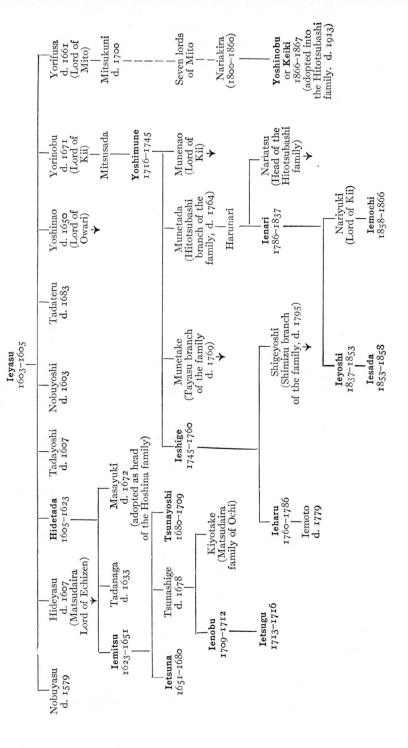

ment. Buddhism was in decline, and Christianity was early stamped out, but there was a great revival of lay learning, the old feudal code of conduct received definite formulation under the name of *Bushidō*, Confucian philosophy enjoyed a protracted period of unparalleled growth and popularity, philosophers and teachers of ethics abounded, there was a revival of interest in Japanese antiquity, Shintō developed new life both as a nationalistic philosophy and as a popular religion, and the newly arisen merchant class contributed greatly to the intellectual and cultural growth of the land.

Literature and art in the Tokugawa period were comparatively free from Chinese influences and were less aristocratic and more popular than in earlier periods because of the influence of the merchant class. A new poetic form, the *haiku*, which consists of only 17 syllables as opposed to the classic form of 31 syllables, was popularized at this time. The novel enjoyed a second great period of flowering. The refined *Nō* drama slowly gave way to more realistic, more exciting, and decidedly less restrained forms, the *Kabuki* and puppet plays, which both developed from long poetic recitations called *Jōruri*. Applied arts reached great heights of technical excellence, but architecture was an uninspired and often debased imitation of 16th-century styles. Painting was largely traditional, but there were able masters of design and an important new school of realism. The most interesting development in painting was the so-called *ukiyo-e* school, a school of popular artists who chose for their subject matter, not Chinese scenes and historical events, but the people, street scenes, and landscapes of contemporaneous Japan. The style was introduced in the 17th century and found its most popular expression in the prints of the great wood-block masters of the 18th and first half of the 19th centuries.

c. 1602. The arrival of Spanish traders in eastern Japan. Ieyasu befriended Spanish missionaries, hoping thereby to persuade Spanish traders to trade directly with eastern Japan, but, although a formal treaty was negotiated with the Spanish acting governor of the Philippines in 1610, few traders ever came.

1605-1623. HIDETADA as *shōgun* (d.1632). This was the formative period of the Edo government, first under the direction of the retired *shōgun*, Ieyasu (d. 1616), and then under that of his uninspired but dependable son, Hidetada.

1608. Hayashi Razan (1583-1657), a Confucian scholar, was appointed attendant scholar (*jidoku*) to Ieyasu. This marked the beginning of a Tokugawa policy of using Confucianism as a stabilizing force in politics and society. Razan, who founded the Edo Confucian temple in 1623, represented the orthodox Sung Confucian school of Chu Hsi (J. *Shushi*), which was the orthodox school in Japan throughout the period. Other schools of Confucian philosophy were those of Wang Yang-ming (J. *Ōyomei*), of Ming China (represented by Nakae Tōju [1608-1648] and Kumazawa Banzan [1619-1691]), and the Ancient School (*Kogakuha*), a reformed school which returned to pre-Sung Confucian commentators (represented by Itō Jinsai [1627-1705] and Ogyū Sorai [1666?-1728]). The Japanese Confucianists made many contributions in various fields of learning and some attacked the pressing economic problems of the time.

1609. The Dutch established a trading post at Hirado in western Japan after an invitation from Ieyasu in 1605. This invitation had been obtained by Will Adams (d. 1620), the English pilot of a Dutch vessel wrecked in Japan in 1600. Adams was forced to remain in Japan by Ieyasu, who made of him an honored adviser.

1612. A definite persecution of Christianity commenced after a series of anti-Christian edicts beginning in 1606. Ieyasu's mounting fears of the political menace from Christianity and his realization that trade with Europe could be maintained without the presence of Catholic missionaries as decoys had made him gradually abandon his at first friendly attitude toward the missionaries.

1613. Cocks established an English factory at Hirado.

1613. Date Masamune (1565-1636), a prominent lord of northern Japan, dispatched an embassy to Spain and to the pope.

1614-1615. The Siege of Ōsaka Castle. Hideyori (1593-1615), the son and heir of Hideyoshi, and the former's mother, Yodogimi (1577-1615), had remained in the Ōsaka Castle after the battle of Sekigahara, constituting a dangerous rallying-point for disaffected elements. Their ultimate destruction was deemed necessary by Ieyasu. In 1614 on a trumped-up charge he laid siege to the castle, and after a short peace captured and destroyed it and its inmates in 1615.

1615. The Bukeshohatto, a collection of general maxims for the warrior class, was issued.

1616. Death of Ieyasu.

1617. Hidetada, aroused by the mutual recriminations of the various European nationalities and religious associations in Japan, intensified the persecution of the Christians (estimated then at 300,000), and for the first time since 1597 European missionaries were executed. Jesuits, Franciscans, and native believers were executed in increasing numbers in the following years (particularly 1622-1624). This marked the height of the Christian persecution. Catholic missionaries still continued to arrive, but eventually all were killed or forced to leave or to apostatize.

1623-1651. IEMITSU as *shōgun.* This was the period of consolidation of Tokugawa rule. As means of achieving this goal the suppression of Christianity was carried to a successful end and the policy of national isolation was adopted.

1623. The English voluntarily left Hirado because their trade with Japan had not proved profitable.

1624. All Spaniards were driven from Japan and all intercourse with the Philippines was stopped.

1636. Japanese were forbidden to go abroad, and those abroad were not allowed to return. Two years later the building of large ships was also proscribed.

1637-1638. The Shimabara uprising. The peasants of the peninsula of Shimabara and the island of Amakusa near Nagasaki, which had been a thoroughly Christianized region for decades, rose in desperation over economic and religious oppression. Some 37,000 of them defended themselves in the dilapidated Hara Castle on the coast of Shimabara for almost three months against vastly superior forces, aided by a Dutch vessel until food and musket ammunition, on which they depended, failed them. They were killed almost to a man in the fall of the castle, and with this slaughter Christianity was virtually stamped out.

1638. The Portuguese traders were expelled because of suspicions as to their complicity in the Shimabara uprising. When they sent an embassy in 1640 to reopen trade, almost the whole party was summarily executed. This left the Dutch at Hirado and some Chinese traders at Nagasaki as Japan's sole means of contact with the outside world.

1641. The Dutch traders were moved from Hirado to the islet of Deshima in Nagasaki Harbor, where they were in virtual imprisonment and were subjected to many inconveniences and indignities.

1651-1680. IETSUNA as *shōgun.*

1651-1652. Two successive abortive *coups d'état* at Edo were the last revolutions the Tokugawa had to face until the 19th century.

1657. Tokugawa Mitsukuni (1628-1701), lord of Mito, commenced the compilation of a *History of Japan (Dainihonshi)* on the model of Chinese dynastic histories. Among the many scholars who aided him were Chinese *émigrés.* The original task was not officially completed until 1720, and supplementary work was continued until 1906. The school of Japanese historians which grew up around this enterprise was one of the important factors in the imperial revival movement.

1657. A great fire destroyed most of Edo and the Edo castle buildings.

1680-1709. TSUNAYOSHI as *shōgun.* Sakai Tadakiyo (1624-1681), prime minister at the time of Ietsuna's death, proposed to have an imperial prince succeed the heirless Ietsuna, but on the insistence of Hotta Masatoshi (1634?-1684) Ietsuna's brother, Tsunayoshi, was made *shōgun,* and presently Masatoshi succeeded Tadakiyo as prime minister. The early years of this period were characterized by vigorous administrative measures until

1684. The assassination of Hotta Masatoshi left Tsunayoshi with inferior counsellors who allowed him to ruin the Edo finances and to bring great hardships on the people by edicts inspired by Buddhism prohibiting the killing of any living creature and extending special protection and privileges to dogs.

1688-1704. The Genroku year period is regarded as the apogee of the vigorous culture of the merchant class of the Tokugawa period. Already by this time the warrior class was becoming mired in debt to the merchants, into whose hands the wealth of the nation was beginning to pass. Consequently, this was a time of ebullient and unsuppressed self-expression on the part of the merchant class. The centers of the gay and extravagant life of the cities were the puppet and *Kabuki* theaters and the licensed quarters, the famous Yoshiwara in the case of Edo. Among the great spirits of the age were **Matsuo Bashō** (1644-1694), who made of the *haiku* a great poetic medium; **Ibara Saikaku** (1642-1693), the author of *risqué* novels about courtesans; **Chikamatsu Monzaemon** (1653-1725), Japan's greatest playwright; and **Hishikawa Moronobu** (1638-1714), an early *ukiyo-e* master. Repressive measures and a gradual amalgamation of the merchant and warrior classes in time tempered the Genroku spirit.

1703. The Chūshingura (called the "Forty-Seven *Rōnin*") **Incident.** Kira Yoshinaka was killed by a group of former retainers of Asano Naganori, Lord of Akō, whose execution in 1701 they felt to be Yoshinaka's fault. The deed thrilled the nation, for, although they had broken the laws of the land, they were but following Confucian ethics in avenging their lord's death. They were eventually ordered to commit suicide.

1703. A great earthquake and fire at Edo was followed in the next five years by several other catastrophes, including the last eruption of Mt. Fuji (1707).

1709-1712. **IENOBU,** as *shōgun*. With the aid of the orthodox Confucian scholar, **Arai Hakuseki** (1657–1725), this able and vigorous ruler carried out a series of much-needed financial reforms.

1713-1716. The infant Ietsugu as *shōgun*.

1715. The quantity of copper allowed exported by the Dutch was greatly reduced. Copper was the mainstay of the Dutch trade, but its export by them and by the Chinese was a drain on the metal resources of the land. This reduction was followed later by even greater reductions and resulted in the limitation of the number of Dutch vessels calling at Japan to two a year.

1716-1745. **YOSHIMUNE** as *shōgun* (d. 1751). Since Hidetada's line had come to an end the new *shōgun* was chosen from the Tokugawa house of Kii, which, with the houses of Owari and Mito, were made by Ieyasu the three Tokugawa cadet branches (*Gosanke*) from which *shōgun* were to be selected when needed. Perhaps next to Ieyasu the ablest and wisest of the Tokugawa rulers, Yoshimune attempted to revive the feudal regimentation and military virtues of Ieyasu's day and to carry through economic reforms. He also encouraged scholarship in all fields, and the Confucian scholar, **Muro Kyūsō** (1658–1734), was one of his chief advisers. Despite this able leadership, economic and social ills began to become acute in Yoshimune's time. The peasants were losing the ownership of their land, and the farm population began to decline because of infanticide and movements to the towns. The military class was badly indebted to the merchants, and to save them from ruin a long series of petty laws in favor of the debtor class was commenced at this time.

These economic conditions led to a mingling of the classes, which began to efface the old rigid class barriers.

1720. Yoshimune removed the ban on the study of Europe and on the importation of European books, exclusive of those on religion. This broadminded move made possible the development of a small but vigorous group of students of Dutch and through this medium of occidental sciences, particularly medicine. A manuscript Dutch-Japanese dictionary was produced in 1745, and in 1774 **Sugita Gempaku** translated a text on anatomy. This early start in the occidental scientific method produced achievements in cartography and military science and proved of great value in Restoration days.

1732-1733. A great famine in western Japan was met with positive measure of relief by Yoshimune.

1742. The criminal law of the land was codified for the benefit of judges and administrators. This codification remained the basis of criminal law during the rest of the Tokugawa period.

1745-1760. **IESHIGE** as *shōgun* (d. 1761). An incompetent sensualist, Ieshige made no attempt to stem the rapid administrative and economic decline which set in after Yoshimune's death in 1751.

1758. **Takenouchi Shikibu** (1714?–1768), a scholar favoring an imperial restoration, and his noble disciples in Kyōto were punished by Edo.

1760-1786. **IEHARU** as *shōgun*. Though an able man, Ieharu was dominated by the tyrannical and avaricious **Tanuma Okitsugu** (often called Mototsugu) (1719–1788), and Tokugawa rule continued its downward course. During this period peasant uprisings became frequent and serious, and they continued to be so until the fall of the Tokugawa.

1783. A great **eruption of Mt. Asama** and a famine in the north came as a double climax to a series of disasters resulting in

1787. Rice riots in Edo.

1787-1793. **Matsudaira Sadanobu** (1759–1829) as head of the government for the child *shōgun*, **Ienari,** carried through a series of reforms. At this same time imperialist opposition to Edo became apparent in Kyōto and the military government became aware of the menace of the rapidly expanding European powers.

(*Cont. p.* 887.)

V. THE NINETEENTH CENTURY

A. SCIENCE AND SOCIETY

1. SOCIAL THOUGHT AND SOCIAL MOVEMENTS

1776. Publication of **Adam Smith's** *Wealth of Nations*, the most influential economic treatise ever written, founding the classical school of political economy and containing the germ of nearly all economic ideas which have since appeared, even in rival systems.

1798. *The Essay on Population* of **Thomas Robert Malthus** (1766–1834), a young clergyman, propounded the stern thesis that population tends to increase more rapidly than food supply and is limited only by such positive checks as war, famine, and malnutritional diseases, or by abstinence from marriage. Hence wages must sink to a subsistence level.

1817. **David Ricardo's** (1772–1823) *On the Principles of Political Economy and Taxation* set forth the famous law of "differential rent", and explained wages as tending to seek the minimum subsistence level. His theories revealed the interests of the different social classes as far from identical and portrayed landholders as innocent but parasitical beneficiaries of the "unearned increment." Ricardian economics enjoyed an immense practical success, culminating in the adoption of free trade in England (1846). Its tenets were enthusiastically adopted by a rising manufacturing class which sought low wages and freedom from governmental interference. These doctrines were rendered more dogmatic in the writings of **James Mill** (1773–1836), **John Ramsay McCulloch** (1789–1864), and **Nassau William Senior** (1790–1864). In France they were systematized by **Jean Baptiste Say** (1767–1832), **Count Pellegrino Rossi** (1787–1848), and **Michel Chevalier** (1806–1879).

1825. *The New Christianity* of **Count Claude Henri de Saint-Simon** (1760–1825), the last work of the first eminent socialist writer of the 19th century. Socialism was a reaction to conditions arising from the industrial revolution and to the teaching of the classical economists. The socialists, instead of stressing the importance and self-sufficiency of the individual, urged state intervention, social planning, changes in the property system, establishment of economic and social equality, etc. Others of this school were **Charles Fourier** (1772–1837), who urged co-operative associations in rural settings (*phalanstères*), the liberation of men's passions, etc.; **Etienne Cabet** (1788–1856), whose *Voyage to Icaria* (1840) proposed an associationist scheme strongly authoritarian in character; **Louis Blanc** (1811–1882), who, in his *Organization of Labor* (1839), urged the elimination of the capitalist through the foundation of producers' associations financed by the state; **Pierre Joseph Proudhon** (1809–1865), who in numerous writings set forth a society in which justice, liberty, and equality should exist and looked forward to anarchy as the ethical ideal. Similar ideas were expounded in England by **Robert Owen** (1771–1858). **Johann Karl Rodbertus** (1805–1875) introduced the French ideas into Germany. The ideas of all these men were strongly influenced by 18th-century thought: perfectibility of man, importance of persuasion and co-operation, value of political action and universal suffrage, essential malleability of social institutions. Their rationalistic outlook and their essentially unhistorical view of society, as well as curious aberrations of some of them, led Marx to dub them *Utopian Socialists*.

1841. **Friedrich List** (1789–1846), in his *National System of Political Economy*, brought the national school to full flower. Following earlier writers like **Jean Simonde de Sismondi** (1773–1842) and **Adam Müller** (1779–1829), he stressed human and particularly national welfare rather than individual wealth and propounded a theory of the relativity of economic policy, contending that each nation passes through definite stages in which different policies should be applied. He declared that the German customs union should adopt a policy of protection in the interest of harmonious development of the productive forces in its existing "agricultural-manufacturing", stage, while awaiting a later development in which free trade would be feasible.

1830-1842. Auguste Comte (1798–1857) became the founder of **Positivism,** a type of social physics describing a society rigidly governed by natural laws, with reason playing a larger rôle in societal evolution. Such evolution was described in three stages: a military-theological stage; a critical-metaphysical; and a scientific-industrial stage. These ideas were further developed by **Herbert Spencer** (1820–1903), who sought to interpret society in terms of principles derived from mechanics. In his *First Principles* he amassed an enormous amount of data, systematically arranged and accompanied by a more or less consistent body of theory. He was properly the founder of sociology and the chief exponent of the philosophy of evolution.

1848. John Stuart Mill's (1806–1873) *Principles of Political Economy,* the most logical and brilliant exposition of the classical economics. But Mill was more sympathetic toward human suffering than his predecessors and favored a mild form of interventionism.

1848. The *Communist Manifesto* of **Karl Marx** (1818–1883) and **Friedrich Engels** (1820–1895) marked the advent of "scientific socialism." Its importance at the time was slight and its basic ideas were later developed at length in Marx's *Capital.*

1862-1864. Activity of **Ferdinand Lassalle** (1825–1864),who borrowed heavily from Louis Blanc and Rodbertus and attempted to start producers' associations with state capital. His importance lay chiefly in arousing and organizing the German workers and in his demonstration of the importance of political action.

1864. Formation of the **First International Workingmen's Association** (*The First International*) by Marx, with headquarters first in London and then in New York. It was devoted to the cause of Marxian socialism and aimed at the organization of workers in the various countries. The fall of the Paris Commune in 1871 (p. 637), which Marx had warmly supported, frightened many of the more moderate elements and generally discredited socialism. **Michael Bakunin** (1814–1876), one of Marx's supporters, was at bottom an anarchist who envisaged the abolition of all governments and the institution of an ultra-individualistic régime. But unlike earlier theorists like **William Godwin** (1756–1836) and Proudhon (see above), Bakunin was ready to hasten the advent of anarchy by every form of "direct action" including the bomb and the revolver. Marx and Bakunin broke with each other (1872) and the First International collapsed (1876). The anar-chist doctrine of Bakunin was developed by **Prince Peter Kropotkin** (1842–1921), who laid more stress on the importance of the collectivist principle, which would harmonize anarchism with social realities (anarcho-communism). From its very nature anarchism could not become an organized mass movement, but during the period 1880–1900 it gained many adherents in France, Italy, Spain, and the United States, where a long series of outrages were committed.

1867-1894. Karl Marx's *Capital,* the basic exposition of his theory. Marx held that the course of history has been determined primarily by economic factors: "The mode of production in material life determines the general character of the social, political, and spiritual processes of life." History has been punctuated by a series of "class struggles" (interpreted in terms of the Hegelian dialectic): The nobility has been overthrown by the bourgeoisie and the bourgeoisie is doomed to destruction by the proletariat, leading finally to a "classless society." The existing struggle of capital and labor was rationalized in terms of the theory of "surplus value": profit-seeking capitalists pay labor subsistence wages and take for themselves the "surplus value" which the workers have added to the product through their labor.

1889. The Second International Workingmen's Association, founded in Paris by representatives of the socialist parties which had been founded in the various countries since 1876. Unlike the First International, it possessed no powerful central authority and was weakened by divergences of interest among the constituent organizations, especially in matters like the attainment of immediate social reform. It was finally discredited by the patriotic participation of the various parties in the First World War.

1908. Georges Sorel's (1847–1922) *Reflections on Violence,* the main work of the leading "syndicalist" thinker. The **syndicalist movement** had succeeded the defunct anarchist movement about 1895, and was widespread in France, Italy, and Spain. The syndicalists accepted the Marxian theory of the class struggle and the need for social revolution, but they insisted that the state must be destroyed (not merely captured) and that this could best be done through the general strike engineered through trade unions. The future society was to be a free and flexible federation of autonomous productive and distributive associations based on collective ownership and functioning in accord with the needs of the community (more concretely each industry should be managed by the workers, organized in *syndicats*). Sorel was interested above all in the capacity of "the myth of the general strike" to moralize the workers and give them an exalted sense of solidarity in the accomplishment of their mission.

1916. The *Treatise of General Sociology* of Vilfredo Pareto (1848–1923), a huge work of psychological analysis aiming to describe an objective social science on the basis of a distinction between the basic motivations of human nature (*residues*) and their superficial appearance or rationalization (*derivations*). The work has had a large influence on political development and on historical writing, as well as on sociology and psychology.

2. SCIENTIFIC THOUGHT AND PROGRESS

1785. The *Theory of the Earth* by **James Hutton** (1726–1797) laid the foundation of modern geology by positing the uniformitarian hypothesis of geologic causation. Impetus was given to the acceptance of the hypothesis by **William Smith** (1769–1839), who assigned relative ages to the rocks and pointed out their fossilized contents, and by **Jean Baptiste de Lamarck** (1744–1829), who classified and compared recent and fossil shells.

1786. **Luigi Galvani** (1737–1798), having noticed the contraction of a frog's leg under influence of an electric discharge, attributed this to animal electricity. **Count Alessandro Volta** (1745–1827) showed that this was not so and invented the primitive primary battery.

1802. Cuneiform writing first deciphered by **Georg Friedrich Grotefend** (1775–1853), opening up a new field of historical research.

1819. Invention of the stethoscope by **René Laënnec** (1781–1826), who introduced auscultation in medical practice.

1821. **Jean François Champollion** (1790–1832) first deciphered hieroglyphics, making possible the modern science of Egyptology.

1824. **Leopold von Ranke** (1795–1886), in his *Zur Kritik neuerer Geschichtschreiber*, completed the earlier critical work of men like **B. G. Niebuhr** (1776–1831) and laid the basis for modern historical criticism.

1825. **James Mill** (1773–1836) published his *Analysis of the Phenomena of the Human Mind*, a basic work of modern psychology.

1830-1833. The *Principles of Geology* of Sir **Charles Lyell** (1797–1875), the basis of modern geology. Lyell assembled all the known facts about fossils and all available evidence of changes in the earth. At about the same time **Adam Sedgwick** (1785–1873) first investigated and named the Cambrian rocks.

1831. **Michael Faraday** (1791–1867) demonstrated the fact of electro-magnetic induction and laid the foundations for three great branches of practical electrical science: electro-chemistry, electro-magnetic induction, and electro-magnetic waves.

1838. **Matthias Jakob Schleiden** (1804–1881) formulated the cell theory in physiology.

1844. An American dentist, **Dr. Horace Wells** of Hartford, demonstrated that nitrous oxide might be used as an anaesthetic.

1846. Another American dentist, **Dr. W. T. G. Morton** of Boston, first used ether as an anaesthetic.

1847. **H. L. F. von Helmholtz** (1821–1894) first set forth the theory of the conservation of energy.

1852. **Paul Broca** (1824–1880) first localized the speech center in the brain.

1852. **Count Joseph Arthur de Gobineau** (1816–1882) in his *Inequality of Human Races* laid the basis for much later writing on race superiority.

1859. *The Origin of Species*, by **Charles Darwin** (1809–1882), the most important work of modern biology. Darwin, inspired by Malthus' population hypothesis, spent twenty years in the collection of data to test his own hypothesis that species evolve through variation and natural selection of those individuals best suited to survive in given environmental conditions. Much the same theory was developed independently by **Alfred R. Wallace** (1823–1913). **Thomas H. Huxley** (1825–1895) was one of the most ardent defenders of the Darwinian theory against opponents drawn chiefly from the religiously orthodox. In Germany much the same mission was assumed by **Ernst Heinrich Haeckel** (1834–1919).

1865. An obscure Austrian monk, **Gregor Mendel** (1822–1884), whose work was rediscovered much later, experimented on the cross-breeding of peas and revealed that in heredity certain characters are indivisible units. Mendel established the mechanics of heredity and introduced a "quantum conception into biology."

1865. **Joseph Lister** (1827–1912) initiated the practice of antiseptic surgery

1869. Sir Francis Galton (1822–1911), a cousin of Darwin, applied the latter's ideas of heredity to man's mental inheritance, his statistical results pointing to the enormous importance of inheritance in relation to individual ability.

1871. *The Descent of Man* and the *Expression of the Emotions in Man and Animals* (1873), works in which Darwin raised the question of the evolution of mental powers and of morality.

1872. The *Principles of Physiological Psychology* of Wilhelm Wundt (1832–1920) created modern experimental psychology and devised a method of analysis.

1873. Walter Bagehot (1826–1877) in *Physics and Politics* made a significant contribution to social psychology, applying the principles of natural selection to the evolution of custom and institutions.

1876. Cesare Lombroso (1836–1909) founded the science of criminal psychology.

1880. Charles Laveran (1845–1922) discovered the malaria germ. Sir Ronald Ross showed (1898) that malaria can be transmitted to birds by mosquitoes, and Giovanni Grassi proved (1900) that the disease is carried by the *Anopheles* mosquito.

1881. Louis Pasteur (1822–1895) applied the principle of immunization through vaccination to rabies. This followed years of experimentation by Pasteur and Robert Koch (1843–1910) on fermentation, which Pasteur showed to be caused by organisms, not by spontaneous generation. Koch, through his studies of anthrax, demonstrated that germs were the cause, not merely the concomitant of disease.

1882. Koch discovered the germ of tuberculosis.

1883. The diphtheria germ was identified by Edwin Klebs (1834–1913). It was isolated by Friedrich Löffler (1852–1915) and a serum developed (1894) by Emil von Behring (1854–1917).

1884. Koch discovered the germ of cholera.

1885. Pasteur developed inoculation against hydrophobia. He also succeeded in bringing under control the costly pebrine epidemic in silkworms and developed the process of "pasteurization" of milk.

1890. Gabriel de Tarde (1843–1904) published his *Laws of Imitation*, a pioneer work in the field of social psychology.

At the same time Pierre Janet (1859–1947) opened a new era in pathological psychology, and soon afterward Gustave Le Bon (1841–1931) published his *Psychology of Crowds* (1895).

1892. The electron theory was formally announced by Hendrik Antoon Lorentz (1853–1928).

1894. The germ of the bubonic plague was discovered by Shibasaburo Kitasato (1856–1931) and Alexander Yersin (1863–1943). Robert Koch (1843–1910) demonstrated in 1897 that the germ is transmitted by fleas from rats.

1895. Sigmund Freud (1856–1939) launched his first work on psychoanalysis, a study of the subconscious. Different aspects of the subject were developed by Carl Jung (1875–) and Alfred Adler (1870–1930). Wilhelm Konrad Roentgen (1845–1923) detected X-rays.

1896. Anti-typhoid inoculation was introduced by Sir Almroth E. Wright (1861–1947), after the germ had been identified (1880) by Karl Eberth (1835–1926). Antoine Henri Becquerel (1852–1908) discovered that Uranium gave off rays similar to those detected (1895) by Roentgen.

1898. Pierre Curie (1859–1906) and Marie Curie (1867–1934) observed the phenomenon of radioactivity and isolated Radium.

1900. Walter Reed (1851–1902) proved that yellow fever was transmitted by the mosquito. Max Planck (1858–1947) propounded the Quantum Theory.

1901. Adrenalin was isolated by Jokichi Takamine (1854–1922).

1902. The disintegration theory to explain radioactivity was suggested by Ernest Rutherford (1871–1937) and Frederick Soddy (1877–).

1905. Albert Einstein (1879–1955) offered his Special Theory of Relativity.

1906. Vitamins were discovered by Sir Frederick G. Hopkins (1861–1947). August von Wasserman (1866–1925) introduced the blood test for syphilis.

1910. The hydrogenation of coal to produce liquid fuels was successfully achieved.

1911. Ernest Rutherford bombarded the atom with particles discharged by radioactive substances.

1912. Frederick Soddy demonstrated the existence of isotopes.

1913. An improved method of measuring the distance of stars through spectroscopic observations was developed by **Harlow Shapley** (1885–   ).

Typhus control was rendered possible by **Charles Nicolle** (1866–1936) who demonstrated that the disease is transmitted by lice.

1920. Ernest Rutherford suggested a method for the artificial disintegration of the atom.

1921. Frederick G. Banting (1891–1941), Charles H. Best (1899–   ), James W. MacLeod (1876–1935) and James B. Collip (1892–   ) perfected a technique for extracting insulin from the pancreas and purifying it for use against diabetes.

1925. Collip obtained an extract of the parathyroid gland for the treatment of tetany.

1926. Liver extract was utilized for the treatment of pernicious anemia.

1927. **Werner Heisenberg** (1901–   ) propounded the principle of uncertainty to explain new phenomena observed in physics.

1930. A ninth planet, Pluto, was located.

1931. "Heavy Hydrogen," an isotope of hydrogen, was detected at the Bureau of Standards at Washington and isolated at Columbia University by **Harold Clayton Urey** (1893–   ) in 1933.

1932. Albert Einstein offered his Unitary Field Theory.

Vitamin D was discovered.

1935. The therapeutic virtue of sulfanilimide was demonstrated by **Gerhard Domagk** (1888–   ).

1940. The possibility of splitting the atom of U 235 was demonstrated.

1943. The United States Army adopted the new formula known as DDT as its standard insecticide.

Penicillin was successfully applied to the treatment of numerous chronic diseases.

1944. The total synthesis of quinine was achieved.

1945. The synthesis of Vitamin A was patented.

The release of atomic energy for explosive purposes was demonstrated by the use of an atomic bomb dropped on the Japanese city of Hiroshima (Aug. 8).

3. MECHANICAL INVENTIONS AND TECHNICAL ACHIEVEMENTS

1766. Discovery of **hydrogen** by **Henry Cavendish** (1731–1810), making possible the development of the balloon.

1769. **JAMES WATT** (1736–1819) invented the modern steam engine and introduced revolutionary developments in the form of a separate condenser for steam economy, as well as the principle of double action. The non-condensing, high-pressure engine was the invention of **Richard Trevithick** (1771–1833) and **Oliver Evans** (1755–1819), an American.

1783. Stephen and Joseph Montgolfier invented the balloon, a paper bag filled with hot air. They made the first ascent. The Robert brothers were responsible for the first hydrogen balloon, constructed later in the same year.

1784. The Robert brothers developed the first **airship**, a melon-shaped hydrogen balloon of silk, having a long car suspended under it with six men using silken oars for propulsion.

1794. The **semaphore telegraph** developed by **Claude Chappe** (1763–1805). The first line was from Lille to Paris

and was so successful that the system rapidly spread to other countries.

1797. **Charles Newbold,** an American, patented the **iron plow.**

1798. The first **printing press with an iron frame,** constructed by the **Earl of Stanhope.**

1802. The tug *Charlotte Dundas,* built by **William Symington** (1763–1831) was the first practical **steamboat,** equipped with stern paddle.

1803. The **Fourdrinier brothers** invented the paper-making machine.

1804. **Trevithick built a locomotive and** was the first to use a steam carriage on a railway.

1805. Robert Fulton built the **first torpedo.**

1807. **ROBERT FULTON** (1765–1815) and **Robert R. Livingston** (1746–1813) steamed from New York to Albany in 32 hours in the *Clermont,* first **successful steamboat.**

1807. **Gas lights** first introduced in London. By 1820 much of the city was lighted.

1809. The **arc lamp,** invented by **Sir Humphry Davy** (1778–1829).

1812. Friedrich König and Andreas Bauer, Saxons, and James Bensley, an Englishman, invented the first cylinder press, which was promptly adopted by the London *Times*.

1814. George Stephenson (1781–1848) completed the adaptation of the steam engine to the railroad.

1816. The celeripede of Nicéphore Niepce (1765–1833), a primitive two-wheeled bicycle propelled by action of the feet on the ground.

1818. Regular transatlantic service was initiated by the *Black Ball Line*, using fast sailing ships between New York and Liverpool.

1818. Introduction of the use of iron in shipbuilding (the lighter *Vulcan*, built near Glasgow).

1819. The steamer *Savannah* crossed to Liverpool, chiefly under steam.

1821-1831. Michael Faraday (1791–1867) developed the electric motor and generator. He was followed by Sir Charles Wheatstone and others.

1822. William Church of Connecticut designed the first type-setting machine.

1824. Henri J. Paixhans (1783–1854), a French artillerist, introduced the shell gun, a revolutionary invention in the history of warfare.

1825, Sept. 27. OPENING OF THE STOCKTON AND DARLINGTON RAILROAD in England, the world's first railway line.

1826. First all-steam crossing of the Atlantic, by the Dutch steamer *Curaçao*.

1827. Nicéphore Niepce (above) secured the first camera image.

1829. The first railroad opened in the United States (Carbondale to Honesdale, Pennsylvania). The first railroad opened in France (Lyon–St.-Etienne Line). Both used English locomotives.

1830. Opening of the Liverpool-Manchester railroad in England, the first to use locomotive power for traction exclusively and the first to be built for passenger traffic as well as freight. Railroads spread rapidly on both sides of the Atlantic, especially in the 1840's.

1832. SAMUEL F. B. MORSE (1791–1872) developed the first practical electrical telegraph, after a large number of experiments in the preceding hundred years.

1834. Cyrus McCormick patented the reaping machine.

1836. The Prussian needle-gun, invented by Johann N. Dreyse (1787–1867), made practical the breech-loading principle.

1836. Introduction of the screw propeller, developed by John Stevens (1749–1838) and later applied by John Ericsson (1803–1889) and Sir Francis Smith (1808–1874).

1836. The *Balloon of Nassau*, the first large-scale balloon, which flew from London to Weilburg, nearly 500 miles.

1836. Invention of the revolver by Samuel Colt, an American.

1837. Introduction of the steel plow in America, an invention of John Deere.

1839. The first real bicycle, an invention of Kirkpatrick MacMillan of Dumfries.

1839. Accidental discovery of the process of vulcanizing rubber, by Charles Goodyear, an American.

1839. Moritz Jacobi's rotary motor (invented 1834) was successfully applied to a boat carrying 14 passengers.

1839. The Peninsula and Oriental Line (*P. and O.*) established regular steamship service from England to Alexandria, to meet the ships of the East India Company coming up the Red Sea.

1840. Samuel Cunard (1787–1865) founded the first important transatlantic steamship line.

1840. The first incandescent electric light, invented by Sir William R. Grove (1811–1896).

1842. W. H. Phillips invented the first helicopter using steam power to leave the ground.

1844. Morse transmitted the first telegraph message over a line between Baltimore and Washington. The telegraph was rapidly developed after this, especially by the railroads. During the 1850's most of the large cities in America and Europe were connected.

1846. Elias Howe, an American, patented the sewing machine.

1851. Introduction of the wet collodion process by Scott Archer. This revolutionized the photographic film.

1851. The first successful submarine telegraph cable was laid between Dover and Calais. This was made possible by the introduction of gutta-percha as an insulator.

1851. Charles Page's electric locomotive drew a train of cars from Washington to Bladensburg, Maryland, at 19 miles an hour. The cost of batteries delayed the further development of the electric railway.

1852. The first practical **dirigible balloon,** driven by steam power, was built by **Henry Giffard.**

1855. Opening of the Soo Canal, between Lakes Superior and Huron, making possible sea transport of iron ore.

1855. The principle of **rifling** was applied to the manufacture of artillery and small arms by **Sir Joseph Whitworth** (1803-1887) and **W. G. Armstrong** (1810-1900). It increased both range and accuracy.

1856. **Henry Bessemer** developed the Bessemer process of making steel "without fuel," by means of an oxidizing blast.

1856-1857. Development of the dry collodion process in photography, making possible the extension of the art to amateurs.

1859. Opening of **Drake's oil well** at Titusville, Pennsylvania, marking the beginning of the commercial exploitation of petroleum.

1859. The first **ironclad frigate** (*La Glorie*) built for Napoleon III by **Stanislas Dupuy de Lôme** (1816-1885).

1860. **Oliver F. Winchester** (1810-1880) introduced the **repeating rifle.**

1862. **Richard J. Gatling** (1818-1903) invented the **machine gun.**

1862. The first **engine** (Beau de Rochas cycle) **using commercial gas.**

1864. **George Pullman** built the first **sleeping car,** for use on railroads.

1865-1866. After two unsuccessful attempts, two **transatlantic cables** were laid, long-distance reception having been made possible by the invention of the mirror galvanometer by **William Thomson,** later **Lord Kelvin** (1824-1907).

1865. **William Bullock** of Philadelphia invented the **web press,** using a web or roll of paper and adding speed (similar to the **Walter press** developed for the London *Times*).

1865. Using the regenerative gas furnace principle of **Sir William Siemens** (1823-1883), **Pierre Martin** (1824-1915) developed the **open hearth** process of making steel.

1865. **Pierre Lallement** developed the **two-wheeled velocipede,** the first crank-driven bicycle (the *boneshaker*).

1866. The first efficient **locomotive torpedo,** invented by **Robert Whitehead** (1823-1905).

1868. The **Sholes typewriter** was first put to commercial use.

1869. The **Westinghouse airbrake** was patented.

1869. Introduction of **refrigeration in railway transportation.**

1869. First **color photography,** done by **Ducos du Haroun.**

1869. Nov. 16. Official **OPENING OF THE SUEZ CANAL,** under construction for 10 years under the direction of **Ferdinand de Lesseps** (1805-1894). This revolutionized communications between Europe and the Orient.

1870-1875. The use of steel gradually replaced the use of iron in **shipbuilding.**

1871. Introduction of the **"dry plate"** process in photography, invented by R. L. Maddox, who discovered the possibilities of an emulsion of isinglass, gelatine, and bromide of silver.

1872. First application of the **moving-picture principle** by **Edward Muybridge,** who recorded the progressive motion of race-horses through the use of a series of co-ordinated cameras, for Senator Leland Stanford of California.

1874. The **triple expansion engine** introduced by **A. C. Kirk.** It became the normal type of marine steam engine.

1875. The **rotary perfecting press** (printing both sides of a sheet at once and delivering the cut and folded newspaper in one operation) was invented by a number of printers, notably **Andrew Campbell** and **Stephen D. Tucker,** both Americans.

1876. The **"safety"** (rear-wheel-driven) **bicycle,** invented by **H. J. Lawson.** This was substantially the model used thereafter.

1876. **ALEXANDER GRAHAM BELL** (1847-1922) invented the **telephone.**

1876. The **Otto Silent Gas Engine** of **Nikolaus Otto** (1832-1891) introduced the principle of the internal combustion engine.

1877. **Hydroelectric power** first developed at Niagara Falls. **Nikola Tesla** (1857-1943) discovered the rotating magnetic field, making possible the long-distance transmission of electric power.

1877. **Thomas A. Edison** (1847-1931) invented the **phonograph.**

1878. Edison developed the **bipolar dynamo.**

1878. **Sidney Gilchrist Thomas** (1850-1885) and his cousin, **Percy Gilchrist** (1851-1935), developed the **Thomas-Gilchrist** or **"basic"** process for removing phosphorus from iron ore, thus making phosphorus ore available for steel manufacture.

1879. First automatic **switching system for telephones.**

1879. Edison perfected the incandescent electric lamp.

1879. Introduction of the electric street car, by Werner von Siemens. The first use in America was in Baltimore (1885).

1882. The Edison system of central station power production gave the first real commercial impetus to electric power production.

1883. John Carbutt of Philadelphia introduced the coated, cut, celluloid film for photography.

1884. The compound steam turbine of Sir Charles Parsons (1854–1931) revolutionized steam engineering.

1884. Boston and New York connected by telephone, the beginning of long-distance transmission.

1885. Invention of the linotype by Ottmar Mergenthaler (1854–1899), a German-American. Invention of the monotype (casting single characters and assembling them in lines) by Tolbert Lanston (1844–1913), also an American.

1885. The first motorcycles introduced in France and Germany.

1885. Heinrich Hertz (1857–1894) verified James Clerk Maxwell's prediction of the existence of radio waves. At the same time he discovered photoelectricity, fundamental to the development of television.

1885 ff. The first naval submarines were built by Thorsten Nordenfeldt (1842–1920), Gustave Zedé (1825–1891), and John P. Holland (1841–1914).

1886. GOTTLIEB DAIMLER (1834–1900) invented the internal combustion engine, using gasoline. He applied it chiefly to boats.

1886. Introduction of smokeless powder and high explosive by the French. They were developed chiefly by Eugène Turpin (1848–1927) and Paul Vieille (1854–1934).

1887. Edison invented a motion-picture machine in which tiny pictures, mounted specially on a cylinder, in the pattern of a phonograph groove, were viewed in motion under a microscope.

1887. DAIMLER'S AUTOMOBILE, the first successful one. The automobile was promptly developed by a host of engineers on both sides of the Atlantic.

1889. Introduction of the pneumatic rubber tire by John Boyd Dunlop. This became basic for the development of the bicycle and automobile.

1889. Panhard and Levassor began to manufacture Daimler engines in France and to develop the automobile.

1889. The straight-line press, invented by Joseph L. Firm, an American. The last fundamental invention in printing.

1889. Edison perfected the motion picture, using the film on nitro-cellulose base manufactured by George Eastman. Edison's new "kinetoscope" was the first successful motion picture. First showings in New York (1894).

1893. Walter Scott designed the first color press for the New York *World*.

1894. Sir Hiram Maxim (1840–1916) carried on extensive experiments with heavier-than-air machines along lines marked out by Sir George Cayley (1773–1853), William S. Henson, and John Stringfellow (1799–1883). Maxim designed a mammoth machine which just failed to leave the ground.

1894. The first gasoline automobile, a Panhard, incorporated many of the essential features of the modern car.

1895. Invention of the Diesel engine by Rudolf Diesel (1858–1913). It supplanted the earlier heavy oil engines of Priestman (1885) and Hornsby-Akroyd (1890). The Diesel engine had spontaneous ignition (no explosion) of the fuel spray under relatively constant pressure. It has been widely used, especially as a marine motor.

1895. GUGLIELMO MARCONI (1874–1937) invented wireless telegraphy, sending messages one mile (1895) and soon across the Atlantic (1901).

1895. The cinématographe of Louis and Auguste Lumière and the vitascope of Thomas Armat, an American. These did much to solve the problem of projection of moving pictures.

1896. Invention of the gyroscope by Ludwig Obry. This was first used to give direction to the torpedo.

1896. Samuel P. Langley (1834–1906) flew a powered airplane model 3200 feet and built a plane powered by an ingenious gasoline engine by Charles M. Manly. This twice failed to fly (1903), but was successfully flown later (1914).

1897. The *Avion* of Clement Ader (1841–1925), though it did not actually fly, was judged "capable of flight."

1897. Introduction of the French 75 mm. gun, designed by Gustave Canet (1846–1908). This was based on the quick-firing principle and revolutionized field artillery.

1898. Alberto **Santos-Dumont's** (1873–1932) **non-rigid airship.** He built about 14 in all, with which he had amazing accidents and adventures. Experimentation with non-rigid types came to a close with the disaster to the Italian ship *Roma* in 1922.

1898. Count **Ferdinand von Zeppelin** introduced the principle of the **rigid airship.** His first ship was 420 feet long, with two motors. The first practical one was completed in 1906. Passenger service was begun in 1910. Zeppelins were much used by the Germans in raiding England during the World War.

1901. Professor **Berson** and **Dr. Süring** made an altitude record of 35,000 feet in a balloon. This was long unexceeded.

1902. Invention of the **arc transmitter** by **Valdemar Poulsen.** This was of great value in the development of wireless telegraphy.

1903, Dec. 17. First really successful **AIRPLANE FLIGHT,** by **Wilbur Wright** (1867–1912) and his brother, **Orville** (1871–1948). They studied gliders and developed a gasoline motor. Their motor-driven plane, carrying a man, made four sustained flights at **Kitty Hawk,** North Carolina, the longest lasting 59 seconds at a speed of 30 miles per hour.

1904. The first **sound moving picture.** The idea was Edison's, who had intended the kinetoscope to be complementary to his phonograph. The cameraphone synchronized projector and phonograph, but its popularity was short-lived.

1906. Launching of the British warship *Dreadnought,* the first all big-gun warship, which revolutionized the construction of capital ships.

1906. G. A. **Smith** and Charles **Urban** developed the first process of **motion-picture color photography** (*kinemacolor*).

1906. Eugene **Luste** invented the production of sound from photographed vibrations on a film, projected upon a selenium cell, an important step in the development of the sound motion picture.

1907. Lee De **Forest** patented the **three-electrode vacuum tube,** later of great importance in the development of radio.

1908. Louis **Bréguet** and Charles **Richet** built a combined helicopter and biplane, which flew 64 feet.

1909. Henry **Ford** announced that his automobile factory would there-

after manufacture only the **model T chassis.** This heralded the advent of the automobile as a universal method of individual transportation and brought it within reach of the average man.

1909, July 25. LOUIS BLÉRIOT (1872–1936) flew a monoplane across the English Channel from Calais to Dover, in 37 minutes.

1915. Anthony H. G. **Fokker** (1890–1939), a Dutchman whose services were declined by the Allies, built for the Germans the first of his famous planes, with synchronization of machine-gun fire through a revolving propeller.

1916. Igor Sikorsky (1889–) developed a **twin-motored plane,** laying the foundation for multi-motored planes, essential for bombing operations and later for the development of commercial transports.

1918. Development of **long-range artillery.** The German gun, *Big Bertha,* bombarded Paris at a distance of 76 miles.

1919, June 15. Capt. JOHN ALCOCK and Lieut. ARTHUR W. BROWN first crossed the Atlantic in an airplane, flying from Newfoundland to Ireland, 1936 miles, in 15 hours and 57 minutes.

1920. Juan de la Cierva designed the **autogiro** (combination monoplane and helicopter). It was first flown in 1923.

1920. First **commercial radio broadcasting,** by the Westinghouse station in East Pittsburgh.

1924. First **circumnavigation of the globe** by four United States Army **airplanes.** Elapsed time, 175 days.

1925. Talking pictures at last successfully introduced.

1927, May 21. CHARLES A. LINDBERGH made the second transatlantic flight and the first continuous flight from New York to Paris, in his monoplane *Spirit of St. Louis* (3605 miles in 33 hours, 39 minutes).

1927, June 29. Lieuts. Albert F. Hegenberger and Lester J. Maitland flew from Oakland, California to Honolulu (2400 miles), the longest over-water flight to that date.

1927, Oct. 15. Capt. Dieudonné Coste and Lieut. Commander Joseph Le Brix made the first east-west flight across the Atlantic, from Senegal to Rio de Janeiro.

1927. First actual **transmission of television signals** (New York to Washington) by the American Telephone and Telegraph Company.

1927. First transatlantic telephone service opened.

1928. The first North Atlantic east-west flight accomplished by two Germans, Baron Gunther von Hühnefeld and Capt. Koehl, and Commandant James Fitzmaurice (Dublin to Greeneley Island, near Newfoundland).

1928. First transpacific flight by Capt. Charles Kingsford-Smith (the overwater leg from Honolulu to Java, 3138 miles, was unprecedented).

1929. The German dirigible, *Graf Zeppelin* (commander, Hugo Eckener), circumnavigated the globe. It was then put into regular passenger service from Europe to South America. Zeppelin passenger service from Europe to the United States was opened in 1935, but was interrupted after the disastrous burning of the *Hindenburg* (1937).

1930, Sept. 2. First non-stop Paris to New York flight, by Capt. Coste and Maurice Bellonte.

1931, May. Prof. Auguste Picard ascended 52,000 feet in a balloon, the first venture into the stratosphere.

June. Wiley Post and Harold Gatty, Americans, circled the globe by airplane in 8 days, 15 hours elapsed time.

1933. Wiley Post alone circled the globe in 7 days, 18 hours.

1933. World distance record for airplanes made by Maurice Rossi and Paul Codos (New York to Syria, 5657 miles, non-stop).

1935. Capt. A. W. Stevens set an altitude record in a stratosphere balloon, rising to 72,395 feet.

1935. Pan American Airways established transpacific service by airplane from California to Manila, with connection to Hongkong. Regular commercial lines had already been established to the East Indies (Royal Dutch Airlines), to Indo-China (Air France lines), to Hongkong and Australia (Imperial Airways), to Brazil (Deutsche Lufthansa), and from the United States to South America (Pan American Airways).

1937, June. V. P. Chkalov, G. P. Baidukov, and A. V. Beliakov, three Russian fliers, flew non-stop from Moscow over the north pole to Vancouver (5288 miles).

1937, July 14. Mikhail Gromov and two companions, all Russians, flew non-stop from Moscow over the pole to Riverside, California (6262 miles in 62 hours, 17 minutes), a non-stop distance record.

1938, July 10-14. Howard Hughes, an American, with four companions flew around the world by way of Europe and Siberia, in 3 days, 19 hours and 17 minutes, averaging between 225 and 250 miles per hour.

1939, May 20. Pan American Airways inaugurated regular commercial flights between the United States and Europe, by way of the Azores.

4. ARCTIC EXPLORATION

a. EARLIEST EXPLORATIONS

The first known civilization within the Arctic regions appears to have been that of the Norsemen, who, before the birth of Christ, seem to have superseded the Finns in Scandinavia. For a thousand years the Norsemen developed a rude form of political democracy and, from their own rocky coasts, ranged the coasts of western Europe.

c. 870. The Norseman, Ottar (Othere), claimed to have sailed around northern Norway, along the Murman Coast, and into the White Sea as far as the Kola Peninsula, in search of the walrus. Thereupon King Harald of Norway declared annexed all territory as far as the White Sea. His successors made various expeditions to that region, both for trade and conquest.

875-900. COLONIZATION OF ICELAND (previously discovered by Irish anchorites, see p. 365).

877. Günnbjorn Ulfsson, driven westward from Iceland, sighted Greenland.

982-985. Eric the Red, outlawed from Iceland, founded a colony in western Greenland (c. 61° N.L.). The Norsemen seem to have carried on sealing and whaling expeditions as far north as Disco Bay (14th-century records indicate stations as far north as 72° 55′). The settlement lasted until the 14th or 15th century.

1000-1006. LEIF ERICSSON and THORFINN KARLSEFNI, from Greenland, explored and tried to settle the North American coast (p. 365).

1194. Iceland annals record the discovery of modern Spitsbergen (*Svalbardi*). In the course of seal, walrus, and whale hunting the Norsemen explored the White, Barents, and Greenland Seas and reached

Novaya Zemlya. But after 1300 Norse enterprise seems to have fallen off (loss of Norwegian independence [1349] and domination of the Hanseatic League).

b. THE SIXTEENTH CENTURY

During this period the initiative in Arctic discoveries was taken by England. Bristol had long carried on trade with Iceland and the Bristolers were therefore well acquainted with the northern routes. After the discovery of the route to India by way of the Cape of Good Hope, the English hoped to find an alternative passage to Cathay either by the northwest, around North America (rediscovered by the Cabots, 1497, see p. 367), or to the northeast, around Siberia. The Cabots, who were intent on finding a **northwest passage**, having failed in their quest, attention became focused on the Siberian route.

1553-1554. Expedition of **SIR HUGH WILLOUGHBY** and **RICHARD CHANCELLOR.** Two of their three ships reached the Russian coast near the mouth of the Pechora River and some new land which may have been Novaya Zemlya or Kolguev Island. They turned back to winter on the Kola Peninsula, where Willoughby and all his men died. The third ship, under Chancellor, reached the site of modern Archangel, whence Chancellor made a trip to Moscow. In 1554 he reached England with a letter from the tsar. One result of the expedition was the

1555. Foundation of the **Association of Merchant Adventurers** (*the Muscovy Company*), to trade with Russia. The company at once took the lead in northern exploration. Chancellor left on a mission to Moscow in 1555, but was lost on the return voyage (1556).

1556. Stephen Burrough, one of Chancellor's men, was sent out by the Muscovy Company to find the rumored Ob River. He discovered Novaya Zemlya and Kara Strait. In 1580 Arthur Pet and Charles Jackman were sent out on a similar mission, but they got no farther than the Kara Sea.

1565. The **Dutch,** under Olivier Brunel and Philip Winterkönig (a Norwegian) became interested in the northeast route and made a trade settlement on the Kola Peninsula, followed by another (1578) near present-day Archangel. Brunel traveled overland as far as the Ob and visited Novaya Zemlya.

1576. Expedition of **SIR MARTIN FRO- BISHER** to find a northwest passage. Frobisher had carried on a long agitation in favor of this course and he had

the support of Queen Elizabeth as well as the London merchants. Frobisher discovered Frobisher Bay in southern **Baffin Land,** which he was sure was the desired passage. Rumors of gold in some earth which he took back led to further expeditions in the succeeding years. On the last of these Frobisher penetrated **Hudson Strait,** but was deterred from "sailing through to China" by orders to bring back loads of "gold ore".

1585-1587. Voyages of **JOHN DAVIS,** sent out by London merchants to follow up the work of Frobisher. Davis landed on the west coast of Greenland at Gilbert's Sound and thence crossed the strait named for him. He cruised along the Baffin coast south to Cumberland Sound, convinced that he had found the passage. Forced to turn back by contrary winds, he resumed operations the following year and followed the coast south of Labrador. In 1587 he explored the Greenland side of Davis Strait as far as 72° 41'. On his return voyage he followed up Cumberland Sound and passed Hudson Strait without realizing its importance.

1594-1597. The three voyages of **WILLEM BARENTS** and **CORNELIS NAY.** Barents and his Dutchmen explored much of the western coast of Novaya Zemlya, while Nay sailed into the Kara Sea and reached the west coast of the **Yalmal Penin- sula.** Finding the sea open beyond, he was convinced that he had found the northeast passage. In 1595 he and Barents returned and tried to get through, but in vain. In 1596 Barents struck north through the sea that bears his name, discovered **Bear Island** and sighted and named Spitsbergen, which he supposed to be part of Greenland. He rounded the north end of Novaya Zemlya and wintered at Ice Haven (the *first expedition to weather an Arctic winter successfully*). Barents died on the return voyage (1597), having laid the foundation for the lucrative Dutch whale and seal fisheries of the 17th and 18th centuries.

c. THE SEVENTEENTH AND EIGHTEENTH CENTURIES

During the 17th century the English and the Dutch continued their efforts to find a passage to China not under Spanish or Portuguese control. The Muscovy Company and individual members of it promoted most of the British expeditions (notably **William Sanderson,** who supported Davis, and **Sir Thomas Smith,** first governor of the East India Company). Richard Hakluyt's *Voyages* (1582) and *Principal Navigations* (1598–1600) as well

THE ARCTIC REGIONS

Scale of Miles
0   200   400   600   800   1000

as the collections of his successor, **Samuel Purchas**, were intended to preserve the records of English achievement and actually provided a great stimulus to exploration and colonization.

1607-1611. Voyages of **HENRY HUDSON**, commissioned by the Muscovy Company. In 1607 he set out in the *Hopewell* for China by way of the north pole. He discovered the East Greenland coast at 73°, passed thence to Spitsbergen (exploring the west coast). On the return he discovered **Jan Mayen** Island. In 1608 he examined the edge of the ice pack between Spitsbergen and Novaya Zemlya in the vain search for a through passage. In 1609 he made yet another attempt, this time in behalf of the Dutch East India Company. Finding his way barred in the Barents Sea, he turned west to North America, where he discovered the Hudson River. In 1610, with English support, he sailed through Hudson Strait and explored the eastern coast of Hudson Bay. The party wintered and on the return voyage the crew mutinied and set out Hudson and the sick and weak to perish in a small boat. Hudson's Spitsbergen explorations had much to do with the development of the Spitsbergen fisheries. In 1609 **Jonas Poole** was sent out from England. Having seen the whales for himself, he promptly made three more fishing expeditions. In 1612 the Muscovy Company was given a monopoly over fishing in those waters. In 1613 it fitted out a large fleet under Benjamin Joseph. But the English were never able to exclude the Dutch and the Danes, who finally secured the best fishing grounds on the northern shore of Spitsbergen.

1610-1648. The Russian Cossacks, in the course of the conquest of Siberia, reached the Siberian north coast at the mouths of the great rivers (Yenisei, 1610; Lena and Yana, 1636; Kolyma, 1644). There is strong evidence that in 1648 a Cossack named **Simon Dezhnev** led an expedition from the Kolyma through Bering Strait into the Gulf of Anadyr.

1612-1613. Sir **Thomas Button** reached the western coast of Hudson Bay and spent the winter at the mouth of the Nelson River. In the following summer he explored the shore of Southampton Island.

1615-1616. Robert **Bylot** (a former member of Hudson's crew) and **William Baffin** explored the coasts of Hudson Strait. On their second voyage they penetrated Baffin Bay and explored the coast far beyond the point reached by Davis. Baffin's fine scientific observations enabled Prof.

Hansteen of Christiania to draw up his *first magnetic chart*.

1631. The Englishmen, **Luke Fox** and **Thomas James**, on separate expeditions, continued the exploration of Hudson Bay (extreme north and extreme southern parts).

1664. **Willem de Vlamingh**, in search of new whaling grounds, rounded the northern end of Novaya Zemlya and sailed east as far as 82° 10′. In the meanwhile Spitsbergen was becoming better known scientifically. In 1671 Frederick Martens, a German surgeon, visited the region and wrote the best historical and geographical account prior to Scoresby's work. In the years 1700–1728 the **Van Keulens**, father and son, made a famous chart embodying Dutch knowledge of the Spitsbergen region.

1670. **Royal charter granted to Hudson's Bay Company**, under the auspices of Prince Rupert, for the purpose of trading with the Indians. The company sent out a reconnoitering expedition under Zachariah Gillan (Gillam), who wintered on Rupert's River and established a station at Fort Charles. Trading stations multiplied rapidly, but exploration was badly neglected for nearly a century, the only fruitful expeditions being those sent out by the admiralty to look for a northwest passage: in 1742 **Christopher Middleton** discovered Repulse Bay and Frozen Strait; in 1746 **William Moor(e)** explored Wager Inlet.

1721. **Hans Egede**, a Norwegian pastor, touched by the story of the lost Norse colony in Greenland, enlisted the support of Frederick IV in an effort to find it. He failed, but on the other hand began the modern colonization of Greenland. With a party of 40 he founded a settlement at Gotthaab and began to convert the Eskimos. Other colonists, including missionaries, followed, and, despite great hardships, multiplied the settlements and spread along the west coast. Trade (skins of seal, reindeer, fox, and bear, eiderdown, whalebone, walrus tusks, and dried cod) was organized as a monopoly in private hands from 1750 to 1774, and, after it became less profitable, passed into government hands.

1725. **Vitus Bering**, a Dane in Russian service, was dispatched by Peter the Great to explore the waters off northeastern Siberia. In a series of voyages (1728–1741) he discovered **Bering Strait**, explored the Aleutian Islands, and discovered and named Mt. St. Elias on the American side.

1732-1743. Great survey of the whole Siberian coast, sponsored by the Russian government. Two Russian officers in 1738 made the voyage from Archangel to the mouths of the Ob and the Yenesei. In an effort to effect a passage from the Yenesei to the Lena, a journey was made (1738–1739) eastward past Taimyr Bay to Cape Sterlegov, and repeated attempts were made to round the northernmost point of Siberia by boat. These efforts were blocked by the ice. But in 1743 S. Chelyuskin succeeded in making the trip by sledge. Dmitri Laptiev in a series of voyages (1737, 1742) completed the delineation of the coast east from the mouth of the Lena to Cape Baranov.

1750-1820. Height of the English whaling industry in the Spitsbergen and Greenland Seas. From 1733 the introduction of bounties had infused new life into the fisheries. In 1776 £5000 was offered to the first ship to pass 89° N.L. and £20,000 for making the northwest passage. Outstanding among the whaling captains for exploration and scientific work were the William Scoresbys, father and son.

1760-1768. Russian merchants of Archangel, hoping to find silver in Novaya Zemlya, sent several expeditions to the islands. The first circumnavigation was by the pilot Loshkin (1760).

1770-1773. Liakhov, a Russian fur merchant, discovered three of the New Siberia Islands. In 1771 he obtained from Catherine the Great monopoly of the mammoth fossil ivory of Liakhov Islands, of which he and his successors made a profitable trade.

1773-1778. Exploration of the Canadian Arctic. In 1773 Capt. C. J. Phipps was sent out to search for an opening to the north of Spitsbergen. He reached 80° 48′ N.L. before he was stopped by the ice. In

1778. Capt. James Cook, sent by the admiralty to Bering Strait to find a passage northeast or northwest from the Pacific to the Atlantic, sailed north from Kamchatka in the *Resolution* and the *Discovery*. He rounded Cape Prince of Wales, cleared Bering Strait and penetrated eastward to Icy Cape before turning west again to discover and name Cape North on the Asiatic side.

d. THE NINETEENTH CENTURY

1806. William Scoresby reached a record north in the Spitsbergen region (81° 30′). In 1820 William Scoresby, Jr.,

published his *Account of the Arctic Regions*, which at once became the standard work.

1818. The British government, at the instigation of Sir William Barrow, renewed the offer of £20,000 for making the northwest passage and £5000 for reaching 89° N.L.

1818. Capt. John Ross and Lieut. Edward Parry set out on a twin expedition to Baffin Bay. It confirmed Baffin's work and pointed the way to the subsequent lucrative whale fishery in that region. Ross named Melville Bay and Cape York.

1819-1820. Parry returned to northern Baffin Bay, penetrated Lancaster Sound and Barrow Strait, discovered Wellington Channel, Prince Regent Inlet, and the island of North Somerset, and finally advanced westward to Melville Sound and Melville Island, where the expedition wintered. On the return voyage (1820) he surveyed the western coast of Baffin Bay to 68° 15′. The expedition was noteworthy for the scientific care with which it was conducted.

1819-1826. Exploration by land, carried on by the Hudson's Bay Company to fill in the "missing" coastline of northern Canada. The work was entrusted to Lieut. (later Sir) John Franklin. In 1820–1821, with Dr. John Richardson, George Back and Robert Hood, he made a trip from Great Slave Lake to the Coppermine River and down the river to the polar sea. They explored 550 miles of coast east to Cape Turnagain.

1821. Lieut. P. F. Anjou, in Russian service, was sent out to survey the Arctic coast of Siberia. At the same time Baron Wrangel explored the coast from Cape Chelagskoi to the mouth of the Kolyma (1820–1823).

1821-1823. Parry's second expedition, in quest of a passage at a lower latitude. He spent the first winter in Hudson Bay (Winter Island) and the second among the Eskimos at Igloolik. During the summer of 1821 he verified the dead end of Repulse Bay. In 1822 he turned north to Fox Channel and discovered the ice-choked Fury and Hecla Strait.

1822. William Scoresby, Jr., in the specially constructed *Baffin*, forced his way through the ice and reached the east coast of Greenland, which he surveyed for 400 miles (75° to 69°).

1823. Capt. Douglas Clavering continued Scoresby's work and charted the East Greenland coast from 72° to 76°, while his associate, Capt. Edward Sabine, established for the admiralty a magnetic observatory on Pendulum Island.

1824. **Parry's third expedition,** on which he hoped to follow the Fury and Hecla Strait west to Prince Regent Inlet. He had to abandon the attempt when one of his ships was badly damaged.

1825-1826. **Franklin's second expedition** by land. He descended the Mackenzie River to the sea and advanced westward to Cape Beechey. A party under Dr. Richardson reached the shore between the Mackenzie and Coppermine Rivers, discovered and named Union and Dolphin Strait and Wollaston Land.

1826. Capt. **F. W. Beechey** led an expedition to the Arctic by way of Bering Strait, to connect with Franklin's explorations. He traced the coastline as far west as Point Barrow, and narrowly missed connection with Franklin's party.

1827. **Parry tried to reach the North Pole** from northern Spitsbergen, using sledge-boats, but the southward drift of the floe was too fast and the party did not get beyond 82° 45′ N.L. This remained the record north for fifty years.

1829-1830. Capt. **W. A. Graah** (Danish navy) led an expedition around Cape Farewell and explored the East Greenland coast from the extreme south as far north as 65° 18′.

1829-1833. Capt. **John Ross** and his nephew, **James Clark Ross,** embarked on a private quest for the northwest passage through Prince Regent Inlet. They found their way into the Gulf of Boothia, where they wintered. In 1830 James Ross crossed the Isthmus of Boothia by sledge, discovering to the west King William Land. In

1831, June 1. **JAMES ROSS** located and planted the British flag on the **north magnetic pole.** The expedition remained in the Arctic until 1833 and was rescued in Lancaster Sound by a whaler.

1833. Sir **George Back** and Dr. **Richard King** made an effort to reach the Rosses overland from Great Slave Lake and Great Fish River, which they descended to the mouth. Failure of supplies forced them to turn back.

1837. **Thomas Simpson** and **P. W. Dease,** of the Hudson's Bay Company, descended the Mackenzie and explored the remainder of the coast westward from Cape Beechey (Franklin's farthest west) to Point Barrow. In 1839 Simpson explored east from the mouth of the Coppermine to Simpson Strait and the mouth of the Great Fish River. From there he went on to

Montreal Island and as far as Castor and Pollux River. On the return trip he explored the southern coasts of King William Land and of Victoria Land.

1845-1848. **THE EXPEDITION OF SIR JOHN FRANKLIN,** in the *Erebus* and *Terror,* to seek a northwest passage by way of Lancaster Sound. Franklin first tried to get through Wellington Channel, but was blocked by ice. He wintered at Beechey Island, where the deterioration of a large part of the stores was discovered, restricting the expedition to two winters in the Arctic. In 1846 he sailed south down Peel Sound and Franklin Strait and in the winter 1846–1847 was beset by heavy polar ice drifting on the northwest coast of King William Land. In the spring a party went south as far as Cape Herschel, thus completing the **discovery of the northwest passage,** although unable to navigate its full length. Sir John died in June, as did twenty-three others in the course of the following winter. The rest abandoned ship (Apr. 22, 1848) and started for Great Fish River. According to later reports by Eskimos "they fell down and died as they walked." Not one member of the expedition survived.

1847. Dr. **John Rae** closed the gap remaining in the Canadian coastline between Boothia and Fury and Hecla Strait. He and his men of the Hudson's Bay Company explored 655 miles of new coast, on foot, and established the fact that Boothia is the northernmost extremity of the American continent.

1848-1859. **THE FRANKLIN RELIEF EXPEDITIONS:**

1848-1849. Sir **James Ross** followed Franklin's route by way of Lancaster Sound and explored the northern and western coasts of North Somerset, never realizing, when he turned back, how near he had come to solution of the Franklin mystery.

1848-1851. Dr. **Rae** and Sir **John Richardson** searched the American coast between the mouth of the Mackenzie and the mouth of the Coppermine.

1850-1851. A great relief expedition was organized in various sections and dispatched by the admiralty: Capt. **Horatio Austin** led a renewal of the search from Barrow Strait. He found Franklin's Beechey Island camp and in 1851 sent out sledge parties on a systematic quest. Though they found no further trace of Franklin, these parties made an immense addition to geographical knowledge, for members of the expedition covered 7025 miles, of which 1225 were new land.

1851-1852. Capt. **William Kennedy** and Lieut. **J. R. Bellot** (French Navy) were sent out by Lady Franklin to search Prince Regent Inlet. They discovered Bellot Strait and turned back just before reaching Franklin's course.

1850-1854. Capt. **Richard Collinson** and Capt. **Robert M'Clure** were sent out by the admiralty to attack the problem from Bering Strait. M'Clure wintered in Prince of Wales Strait, whence he could see Banks Strait, blocked by ice. Once again the northwest passage was found, but could not be navigated. Collinson traced the shore of Prince Albert Land and reached Melville Island, thus connecting with previous explorations from the east. He investigated also the south shore of Victoria Land, coming within a few miles of Franklin's location.

1852. Capt. **Edward A. Inglefield** advanced north in Baffin Bay to Smith Sound, which he correctly surmised to be a channel to the Arctic Ocean. He named Ellesmere Land and explored 600 miles of new coast.

1852-1854. Sir **Edward Belcher** was sent out by the admiralty on a last effort to solve the Franklin mystery from the east. He and Sherard Osborn went north through Wellington Channel, discovered Belcher Channel and explored the northern coasts of Bathurst Island. A subdivision of Belcher's command, under Capt. H. Kellett, spent the winter of 1852–1853 at Melville Island, whence sledge expeditions were sent out. They completed the exploration of Melville Island and Prince Patrick Island.

1853-1855. An American relief expedition under Dr. **E. K. Kane** advanced up Smith Channel, wintered at Van Rensselaer Harbor, and in 1854 discovered the great Humboldt Glacier. In 1855 Kane abandoned ship and retreated to the Danish settlement of Upernivik. In 1860 the American Dr. **I. I. Hayes** followed the course of Kane and traveled for a week in Ellesmere Land.

1854. Dr. **Rae**, exploring in the region of King William's Land, secured from the Eskimo the first information and relics of the Franklin expedition, thus winning the £10,000 admiralty award.

1857. Lady Franklin sent out Capt. **Leopold M'Clintock**, famous organizer of sledge operations on earlier expeditions, to complete the search. His party went over the Boothia and King William Land regions, and at Point Victory and Point Felix found the records and many relics of Franklin's party. In the last analysis the Franklin catastrophe resulted in the exploration of more than 7000 miles of coastline.

1858-1872. **Swedish exploration of Spitsbergen.** Seven expeditions were sent to Spitsbergen and two to Greenland.

1860-1871. Expeditions of **Charles Hall**, an American. He explored Countess of Warwick Land and came across the ruins of a house built by Frobisher in 1578. The years 1864–1869 he spent looking for relics of Franklin along the south shore of King William Land. In 1871 he went north through Smith Channel, Kane Basin, and Kennedy Channel to Robeson Channel (82° 16′ N.L.).

1863. Capt. **E. Carlsen** first circumnavigated **Spitsbergen.** In 1864 Capt. Tobiesen circumnavigated Northeast Land.

1868. Prof. **A. E. Nordenskiöld** penetrated the pack ice north of Spitsbergen to 81° 42′.

1869-1870. The Germans, inspired by Dr. A. Petermann, organized a great Greenland expedition under Capt. **Karl Koldewey**. He and his lieutenant, **Julius Payer** (an Austrian), explored the east coast of Greenland by sledge to Cape Bismarck in Germania Land. One of the ships, the *Hansa*, was crushed by the ice and for nearly a year her crew drifted 1100 miles south on a floe, eventually landing near Cape Farewell.

1870. Nordenskiöld and Dr. Berggren explored the interior of Greenland, advancing 35 miles from Auleitsivikfjord on the west coast and reaching an altitude of 2200 feet.

1871-1874. **DISCOVERY OF FRANZ JOSEPH LAND,** by the Austrians, Julius Payer and Carl Weyprecht. In 1872 they sought a northeast passage around Novaya Zemlya, were caught in the ice and drifted northwest for nearly a year. This brought them to Franz Joseph Land, where they wintered. In 1874 they did some exploration by sledge, but ultimately had to abandon ship and return to the open sea, where they were rescued by a Russian schooner.

1875-1876. The British, under Sir **George S. Nares,** resumed the effort to penetrate the northwest passage. From Smith Sound they entered Lady Franklin Bay, where one ship wintered. The other wintered in Robeson Channel. In 1876 **Albert H. Markham,** of the expedition, reached a new record north (83° 20′ on May 11). Another member, Lieut. Aldrich, explored the north coast of Ellesmere Land to Cape Columbia, while Lieut. Beaumont followed the north coast of Greenland to Cape Britannia.

1876. Foundation of the Danish committee for the geographical and geological investigation of Greenland. This committee stimulated popular interest and sent out many expeditions.

1878. The Dutch, under **Koolemans Beynen,** began sending out annual expeditions in the specially constructed *Willem Barents* to make scientific observations in the Spitsbergen area.

1878-1879. NORDENSKIÖLD for the first time made the **northeast passage** in the *Vega*. Rounding the northernmost point of Siberia (Cape Chelyuskin) on Aug. 19, 1878, he was frozen in and obliged to winter on shore. The voyage was completed in the next year, Bering Strait being reached on July 20, 1879.

1879-1881. The American expedition of **Lieut. G. W. de Long** in the *Jeannette*, financed by Gordon Bennett. The purpose was to explore the northern coast of Siberia from Bering Strait. The ship was crushed in the ice and sank (June 13, 1881). De Long and most of the party perished, but a few reached the coast by way of the New Siberian Islands, two northern outliers of which group, Jeannette and Henrietta Islands, were discovered by this expedition.

1880. Leigh Smith, an Englishman, reached Franz Joseph Land from Spitsbergen and explored the southern coast, naming it Alexandra Land. In 1881 his ship sank and the party, after wintering, made its way to Novaya Zemlya in small boats.

1881. Lieut. Berry, sent out to search for De Long, landed on Wrangel Island (sighted and named by Kellett in 1849) and explored it.

1882. Establishment of **international polar stations,** an idea put forward in 1875 by Weyprecht and promoted at the polar conferences of 1879-1880. Norwegians, Swedes, Danes, Russians, Dutch, British, Germans, Austrians, and Americans agreed to co-operate. The Dutch were unsuccessful in establishing a station at the mouth of the Yenesei, but the other expeditions carried out their assignments. An American mission, under **Lieut. A. W. Greely,** carried on observations in Lady Franklin Bay for two years (1881-1883). Greely explored the north coast of Greenland and reached a new record north (83° 24') at Lockwood Island. In 1882 Greely penetrated Grinnell Land, discovered Hazen Lake and sighted a fjord to the southwest.

In 1883 Lieut. **James Lockwood** crossed Grinnell Land to Greely Fjord. Relief ships having failed to arrive, the party had to winter in Smith Sound. All but six of the party of 24 were dead of starvation when the relief ships arrived in June, 1884.

1883. Nordenskiöld penetrated 84 miles into the interior of Greenland, reaching an altitude of 5000 feet.

1886. Lieut. Robert E. Peary advanced 50 miles inland from Disco Bay and reached an altitude of 7500 feet.

1888. FIRST CROSSING OF GREENLAND, by Dr. Fridtjof Nansen, Otto Sverdrup, and five others. From near Kjoge Bay on the east coast they covered 260 miles of glacier on skis, reaching an altitude of nearly 9000 feet and striking the west coast near Gotthaab.

1892. Peary made a 1200-mile dog-sledge journey from Inglefield Gulf in northwest Greenland, north and east over the inland ice to Independence Fjord and back again.

1893-1896. EXPEDITION OF NANSEN in the *Fram*. Surmising that there was a drift across the polar basin, Nansen decided to be frozen in and travel with it. With Sverdrup he entered the pack off the New Siberian Islands in Sept. 1893, drifted northwest until Nov. 15, 1895. Thence the ship moved southward until it broke free off northern Spitsbergen (Aug. 1896). The ship reached 85° 55' N.L. in the summer of 1895, but Nansen and Hjalmar Johansen in March left the ship and traveled north with skis and dog-sledges, reaching a record north of 86° 14' on Apr. 7. Realizing the hopelessness of reaching the drifting ship, they made for Spitsbergen, wintered at Frederick Jackson Island (one of the newly discovered Whiteland Islands). In the spring of 1896 they were picked up by the relief ship *Windward*.

1894-1897. The Jackson-Harmsworth expedition to Franz Joseph Land reached 81° 19' N.L. and surveyed a number of islands. Jackson covered about 600 miles of new coastline and demonstrated the complexity of the archipelago. A number of other expeditions continued the investigations (E. Baldwin, 1898; W. Wellman, 1898, 1900, discovered Graham Bell Island; W. Ziegler, 1901, 1903-1905, reached 82° 4' N.L.).

1897. S. A. Andrée, a Swedish flyer, undertook a balloon flight northeastward from Spitsbergen. His decapitated body was found on White Island in Barents Sea in 1930, with a diary which revealed that the balloon had come down on the ice pack after 65 hours and that the party had reached White Island, where all had perished.

1897-1898. **Sir Martin Conway** carried on extensive exploration in the interior of Spitsbergen, as did also Dr. A. G. Nathorst.

1898-1902. Capt. **Otto Sverdrup** in the *Fram*, blocked by ice in his effort to circumnavigate Greenland, made several journeys over Ellesmere Land, discovering its western coast. In 1899–1902 he explored and mapped that part of the Arctic Archipelago which had not been reached by Franklin and his successors. He discovered Axel Heiberg Islands. Altogether this expedition charted 1750 miles of coast line.

1899. The Russian admiral, Makarov, arranged a trial trip into the ice off Spitsbergen, using the great ice-breaker *Yermak*. Though unsuccessful he paved the way for later development of the ice-breaker.

1899-1900. Expedition of the **DUKE OF THE ABRUZZI** to Franz Joseph Land. From Rudolf Land his lieutenant, Capt. Umberto Cagni, led a dog-sledge party on a 753-mile trip and reached a new northern record of 86° 34′ N.L. (200 miles from the pole).

1900. **G. C. Amdrup** made a survey of the East Greenland coast from Scoresby Sound south to Angmagssalik, thus completing the discovery and mapping of this coast from Cape Farewell north to Cape Bismarck.

1900. **Peary**, from his base in Lady Franklin Bay, made a journey along the northern coast of Greenland, rounding the northernmost point and reaching Cape Wyckoff, where he built a cairn (82° 57′ N.L.). He made an effort to advance over the frozen sea to the north, but found the ice too rough.

e. THE TWENTIETH CENTURY

(1) Conquest of the Pole

1901. **Peary**, discouraged with Greenland as a taking-off place for the pole, tried a route from Ellesmere Land, but was again blocked by rough ice.

1905-1906. Peary, with **Capt. Robert Bartlett**, went by ship to northern Grant Land and thence westward by sledge to Cape Hecla. From there he claimed to have reached 87° 6′ early in 1906. The claim is questioned by some geographers, since Peary was the only white man in the final party and because the record is unsatisfactory in certain respects.

1907-1908. **Expedition of Dr. F. A. Cook.** He followed a route discovered by Sverdrup (from Cape Sabine across Ellesmere Land and north along the coast to the northern tip of Axel Heiberg Island).

1908, Apr. 20. **Cook** claimed that he reached the pole on this date. Experts regard the claim as improbable, though not impossible. His observations were fuller than Peary's, but not very good. His chronological table of distances was entirely reasonable. The claim has not yet been accepted by authoritative opinion.

1909. Apr. 6. **Peary** claimed to have reached the pole on this date, from Cape Columbia, the northernmost extremity of Grant Land. Though generally accepted, the claim is questioned by some experts because of the inadequacy of the observations and the incredible time-table submitted. Possibly neither Cook nor Peary actually reached the pole.

No further progress in polar exploration was made until the aeroplane began to open up new possibilities.

1925, May. **Roald Amundsen** (Lieut. Riiser-Larsen as pilot) and **Lincoln Ellsworth**, in two flying-boats, flew from King Bay, West Spitsbergen, to 87° 43′ N.L., where they landed. With great exertion and delay they finally got one of their craft into the air again and managed to return.

1926, May. **COMM. RICHARD BYRD** and **FLOYD BENNETT** flew from King Bay and reached the pole (May 9). Using the Fokker monoplane *Josephine Ford*, they covered the 750 miles and return in 15 hours.

1926, May. **ROALD AMUNDSEN, GEN. UMBERTO NOBILE,** and **LINCOLN ELLSWORTH,** forestalled by Byrd in their effort to reach the pole first, took off in the dirigible *Norge* to fly from King Bay across the pole to Alaska. They landed safely near Nome, having sighted no land in the Beaufort Sea area.

1928, May. **Nobile,** in the dirigible *Italia*, made a number of flights from King Bay, one of which (from Cape North around the northern end of Franz Joseph Archipelago, southeast toward Severnaya Zemlya and back over the northern end of Novaya Zemlya and Northeast Land) covered almost 20,000 square miles of unexplored regions. No new land was seen. The last flight was made (May 24) over northeastern Greenland to the pole. On the return flight the ship encountered a storm and crashed on the ice. Among many relief expeditions, Amundsen's ended disastrously in Barents Sea. Amundsen was lost. The

Italia survivors were rescued by other planes and by the Russian icebreaker *Krassin*.

1937. May 26-1938, February 19. A SO-VIET POLAR STATION organized by Prof. Schmidt, and consisting of four members, was transported by plane to a floe near the pole (89° 26' N.). Oceanographical and meteorological observations were taken over a period of nine months. After seven months the drift became strong and ultimately carried the party to the east coast of Greenland.

1937, June. Three Russian aviators (V. P. Chkalov, G. P. Baidukov, and A. V. Beliakov) flew non-stop from Moscow over the North Pole to Vancouver.

1937, July 14. Mikhail Gromov and two companions, all Russians, flew non-stop over the pole from Moscow to Riverside, California (6262 miles in 62 hours 17 minutes, a non-stop distance record).

(2) The Canadian Arctic

1903-1906. Capt. Roald Amundsen navigated the northwest passage by way of the east coast of King William Land, spending two winters at Petersen Bay and charting the coast of Victoria Land. Proceeding westward in 1905, he was frozen in and spent the winter at King Point, but in Aug. 1906, he finally reached Bering Strait. This was the first time a ship passed from sea to sea.

1906-1908. The Anglo-American Polar Expedition, led by Einar Mikkelsen and Ernest Leffingwell, with V. Stefansson, took soundings in Beaufort Sea, but discovered no land.

1908-1910. THE CANADIAN GOVERNMENT took formal possession of all islands to the north of the continent. Capt. J. E. Bernier, sent out by the government, formally annexed Banks and Victoria Islands. In 1910 he failed to make the northwest passage by way of Melville Island, but surveyed the west coast of Baffin Land.

1908-1912. Stefansson and Dr. R. M. Anderson made an extensive study of the Eskimos in the Mackenzie Delta region.

1913-1917. Donald B. MacMillan led the Borup Memorial Expedition to Ellesmere Land. From a base at Etah observations were made over a period of four years and a permanent meteorological station was established. In 1914 MacMillan traveled 1200 miles across Ellesmere

Land and Axel Heiberg in search of Peary's Crocker Land, which was found not to exist. In 1915 W. E. Ekblaw made an equally extensive trip to explore northwestern Grant Land, where he found numerous ruins of Eskimo houses. MacMillan in 1916 attempted to explore King Christian Island, but was frustrated by a blizzard.

1913-1918. Stefansson led the Canadian Arctic Expedition, one section of which made observations for three years in the Coronation Gulf district, while the other, in command of Stefansson, was beset off northern Alaska. One of the ships, the *Karluk*, was driven westward in a gale and was wrecked near Wrangel Island. Capt. Bartlett made his way to the mainland and eastward 700 miles to Alaska. Stefansson himself remained in the field for four years and continued his investigations in a series of remarkable sledge journeys in the vicinity of Banks Island and Melville Island. Many smaller islands were discovered.

1921-1924. Knud Rasmussen, with two companions, carried out a 20,000-mile expedition across Arctic America by way of Fox Channel, Hudson Bay, King William Land, Coronation Gulf, and the Mackenzie Delta to Alaska. The results of this expedition, primarily ethnological, are laid down in Rasmussen's study of the Eskimos, *Across Arctic America* (1927).

1922- The Canadian government established an annual police patrol of the islands and opened a large number of government stations designed for observation, exploration, and the development of the Eskimos. The discovery of a navigable steamship lane through the Mackenzie Delta has led to the development of this waterway as an outlet for the products of the interior. Aerial surveys have become a regular part of government activities.

1934- J. M. Wordie led two Cambridge University expeditions to West Greenland, Baffin Land, and outlying islands.

1934-1935. The Oxford University Ellesmere Land Expedition organized by Edward Shackleton, son of the famous antarctic explorer, and led by Noel Humphreys, made a sledge journey from Etah to northern Grant Land where the British Empire Mountains were discovered. The expedition explored Grinnell Land, the eastern coast of Ellesmere Land, and Scoresby Bay.

1936- The British-Canadian Arctic Expedition, under T. H. Manning, carried out scientific surveys around Southampton Island, Repulse Bay, and Melville Peninsula.

(3) Greenland

1905. The Duke of Orleans in the *Belgica* traced the northeastern coast from Cape Bismarck to a new northern point (78° 30′, Duc d'Orléans Land).

1906-1908. L. Mylius-Erichsen led a Danish expedition from near Cape Bismarck to Northeast Foreland. It was discovered that Greenland extended much farther east than appeared in Peary's chart. A party under Lieutenant J. P. Koch advanced to the northwest and connected with Peary's earlier explorations, thus completing the discovery of the entire Greenland coast. Mylius-Erichsen and another party were lost on a return trip from Peary's Navy Cliff. His body and part of the records were discovered the next spring by Koch.

1909-1912. Einar Mikkelsen led an American expedition to search for records of Mylius-Erichsen and to settle the question whether Peary Channel was really a channel or a fjord. In 1910 he made a 1400-mile sledge journey from Shannon Island to Danmark Fjord, where he found Mylius-Erichsen's statement that Peary's Channel does not exist. On return to Shannon Island, he found that his ship had been crushed and the rest of the expedition taken home in another boat. He and his party spent two more winters alone before being rescued.

1912. Knud Rasmussen made two crossings of interior Greenland, the first eastward from Inglefield Gulf to Danmark Fjord, whence he explored Peary Land and Independence Fjord. Finding that Peary Channel did not exist, he was obliged to make a second crossing from Navy Cliff to Inglefield Gulf.

1912. Dr. de Quervain, a Swiss scientist, crossed Greenland from Disco Bay to Angmagssalik, discovering the lofty mountain chain which contains Mt. Forel.

1912-1913. J. P. Koch and Dr. Alfred Wegener, a German, after spending a winter on the inland ice at an altitude of 4000 feet, led a party on the long 700-mile crossing over the unknown middle part of Greenland. They reached an altitude of 9500 feet.

1917. Rasmussen, with two Scandinavian scientists, explored a number of fjords in northern Greenland in an attempt to find the northwest outlet of Peary's Channel.

1917. Denmark strengthened her claim on Greenland by treaty with the United States, ceding the Virgin Islands in settlement of American claims to areas discovered by Peary.

1919. Foundation of the **Danish East Greenland Company.** This led to the establishment of trapping stations at Danmark Harbor and Germania Harbor and later at other places.

1920-1923. Lauge Koch led a Danish expedition to northern Greenland to complete the survey of Peary Land. Extensive investigations were carried on over a period of years.

1921. Denmark **proclaimed sole sovereignty** over the whole country and closed the coasts to foreigners. The Norwegians, however, continued to press a long-standing claim based on original discovery and settlement by the Norsemen.

1924. **Greenland Agreement** between Denmark and Norway, providing that, until 1944, Norwegian hunters and landing parties should suffer no restrictions on the east coast between 60° 27′ and 81°, except at Angmagssalik and the new Eskimo colonies around Scoresby Sound. Similar concessions made to the British. **Greenland became a crown colony of Denmark,** which exercises a trade monopoly and has undertaken a paternalistic program to preserve Eskimo culture.

1925. Richard Byrd and Floyd Bennett made several trial flights from Etah northwest over Ellesmere Land and over East Greenland, surveying more than 30,000 square miles.

1926, 1929. J. M. Wordie led two Cambridge University expeditions to East Greenland, mapping in detail a large area of mountains and glaciers around Clavering Island. On the second expedition Petermann Peak (9600 feet) was ascended.

1926-1927, and 1931-1934. Lauge Koch continued the Danish government surveys from Scoresby Sound northward. Four winter stations were established with radios, and various air surveys were carried out. A large group of scientists carried out an ambitious program of research.

1930. Capt. **Ahrenberg** made an airplane flight from Sweden to Angmagssalik. In August of the same year **Wolfgang von Gronau** flew over the southern end of Greenland and landed at Ivigtut on his way from Iceland to the United States.

1930-1931. The German Inland Ice expedition under Dr. Alfred Wegener established parties at Scoresby Sound and at Kamarujuk Bay (West Greenland) and set up meteorological stations for winter observation. The expedition made some use of propeller-driven sledges and echo-sounding apparatus for measuring the thickness of the icecap.

1930-1932. The British Arctic Air-Route Expedition, led by twenty-three-year-old H. G. Watkins, established a base west of Angmagssalik and set up a weather station at an altitude of 8000 feet. Much of the coast was photographed from the air, and the lofty Watkins Mountains were discovered. In 1931 a party climbed Mt. Forel (11,100 feet). Another party crossed the icecap to Ivigtut, while yet another section crossed by a more northern route to Holsteinsborg. Watkins, with two companions, made a boat trip around the southern coast of Greenland carrying out careful surveys. In 1932 Watkins returned to East Greenland and disappeared in the region around Lake Fjord, probably drowned.

1931, Aug. Von Gronau made a second and much longer flight over the Greenland icecap from Scoresby Sound to Sukkertoppen.

1931, July 10. Norway formally annexed the coastal region north of Scoresby Sound, calling it *Erik the Red's Land*. After protests by Denmark the matter was referred to the Hague Court which decided in favor of Danish sovereignty (Apr. 5, 1933).

1932-1933. The Danish Scoresby Sound Committee undertook large-scale aerial photography. Mikkelsen and Rasmussen worked out a technique for rapid mapping of large areas which was applied by the Danish Air Survey in 1933 both in East and West Greenland.

1934. Martin Lindsay led the **British Trans-Greenland Expedition** from Disco Bay to the west slope of the Watkins Mountains, following the range southward for 350 miles. The expedition traversed one of the largest "blank spots" and reached an icecap altitude of 10,400 feet.

1935-1936. The Oxford University Greenland Expedition, under H. Hayward, continued extensive investigations in West Greenland. In 1936 a second expedition under Peter Mott extended the survey.

1935. A. Courtauld, a former companion of Watkins, scaled the highest known peak in the Arctic (about 12,200 feet) in the Watkins Range.

(4) The Spitsbergen Area

1907-1920. Dr. W. S. Bruce in a series of six expeditions made a complete cartographical, geological, and zoological survey of Prince Charles Foreland. In addition he staked a mining claim on which the Scotch Spitsbergen Syndicate was founded (1909), and took an active part in developing the mineral resources of the country.

1911. Count Zeppelin in the *Mainz* set up a German meteorological station at Ice Fjord. At the outbreak of the World War it was turned over to the Norwegian government, which moved it to Quade Hook.

1912. Lt. Schroeder-Stranz led an expedition to the north coast of Spitsbergen on which he and about half the participants lost their lives.

1921-1924. A series of three **Oxford University** expeditions, largely promoted by George Binney, initiated the University School of Explorers, composed largely of undergraduates and professional scientists. In Spitsbergen these expeditions carried out extensive scientific investigations, as they did in Greenland. Great attention was devoted to little known Northeast Land. In 1924 Binney introduced a seaplane for geographical exploration and succeeded in making many aerial photographs.

1923. Lt. Mittelholzer, a Swiss aviator, made a successful 500-mile flight over Spitsbergen and Northeast Land.

1925. Norway acquired sovereignty over the Spitsbergen Archipelago and Bear Island, the whole area becoming officially known by the old Norse name *Svalbard*. Since 1906 the government has supported annual surveying cruises, mostly under the leadership of Prof. Adolf Hoel. Since 1911 meteorological and other stations have been established and in 1936 aerial mapping was begun. Svalbard has a great deal of high-grade coal which is being exploited by Swedish and Russian companies whose pre-existing claims were accepted by Norway as a condition of her sovereignty.

1925. A **British Arctic expedition**, under Grettir Algarsson and Comm. F. A. Worsley, carried out soundings and other investigations between Spitsbergen and Franz Joseph Land.

1925. Beginning of the polar flights of Amundsen, Byrd, Nobile, etc., which all started from King Bay (p. 566).

1931. The Norwegian-Swedish expedition to Northeast Land, under Prof. H. Ahlmann, carried out a sledge tour over the inland ice and made many valuable scientific contributions.

1933-1936. Two Oxford University expeditions, led by A. R. Glen, concentrated on the little known New Friesland icecap in West Spitsbergen, explored and mapped the greater part of the interior, and carried on extensive biological researches. The second expedition (1935-1936) went to Northeast Land and carried out the most comprehensive scientific program of any British Arctic expedition. Two observation stations were maintained on the inland ice throughout the winter.

(5) *The Russian Arctic*

The development of Siberia and the need for better communications with the Far East served as an important stimulus to Arctic work.

1910. The government inaugurated annual hydrographic cruises along the Siberian coast by the ice-breakers *Taimyr* and *Vaigach*, and between 1912 and 1914 established five meteorological stations in the Arctic.

1912. Three Russian expeditions to Franz Joseph Archipelago and Novaya Zemlya all met with disastrous ends. Lieut. Sedow spent two winters off northern Novaya Zemlya and perished in the effort to reach the pole in 1914.

1913. Capt. B. Vilkitski, in an attempt to navigate the northeast passage from east to west, discovered several new islands of the New Siberia group and, above all, the new and extensive Severnaya Zemlya (North Land), about 50 miles north of Cape Chelyuskin.

1914-1915. Capt. Otto Sverdrup first used radio successfully in the Arctic, communicating with the ice-breakers off Cape Chelyuskin.

1915. Vilkitski arrived at Archangel, having completed the east-west passage.

1916. The Russian government annexed Franz Joseph Land (claimed by Austria after the discovery in 1873). At the same time the government claimed Wrangel Island, Henrietta Island, and Herald Island, all discovered by Americans in the late 19th century.

1918-1925. Capt. Roald Amundsen, with Dr. H. Sverdrup, in the specially built *Maud*, navigated the northeast passage and spent two winters (1918-1920) in

the ice preparatory to his projected drift over the pole. The drift was carried out in 1922-1925, nearly duplicating that of the *Fram*, but without important geographical results.

1921. Stefansson attempted to plant a British colony on Wrangel Island, which he regarded as a possible future air base. Most of the colonists died before they could be relieved in 1923.

1921. Prof. R. Samoilovich, of the new *Institute for the Exploration of the North* (founded 1921), initiated the annual exploration cruises into the Barents Sea, Kara Sea, and Russian Arctic.

1923-1929. Prof. Meschachev led a series of cruises to the Franz Joseph Archipelago for the *Moscow Scientific Maritime Institute.*

1924. The Soviet government founded a colony on Wrangel Island, which has been maintained ever since.

1924. The government created the *Islands Administration of the U.S.S.R.* and placed Novaya Zemlya, Kolguev, and Vaigach under its jurisdiction.

1925-1928. Prof. S. V. Obruchev explored the practically unknown territory between the Kolima and Indigirka Rivers, discovering some very high mountain ranges.

1926. The Soviet government hoisted the flag over Herald Island, and, after Amundsen's flight in the *Norge*, claimed all lands and islands that might be discovered north of Russia and Siberia by flight across the Arctic.

1927. The Soviet established a permanent station on the New Siberia Islands. First Russian hydroplane flight from Cape North to Wrangel Island.

1929-1931. Samoilovich and Prof. Otto Schmidt carried on extensive exploration in the Franz Joseph Archipelago and about Severnaya Zemlya.

1931. The German dirigible, *Graf Zeppelin*, commanded by Dr. Hugo Eckener, cruised over the Franz Joseph Archipelago, Severnaya Zemlya, the Taimyr Peninsula, and unexplored parts of northern Novaya Zemlya.

1932. The Soviet government claimed Victoria Island, though this is generally regarded as part of the Spitsbergen group.

1932. Prof. Schmidt, in the ice-breaker *Sibiriakov*, made a record passage by the northeast route from Archangel

(July 28) to Yokohama (Nov. 5), that is, 3000 miles in 9 weeks. It was the first time the passage had been made in one season. Since then at least one ship has gotten through each year. In 1936 fourteen ships made the passage.

1932. The government established a **polar radio station** on Prince Rudolf Land, in the Franz Joseph group.

1932. Prof. N. N. Zubow first circumnavigated the Franz Joseph Archipelago.

1935. Foundation of the **CENTRAL ADMINISTRATION OF THE NORTHERN SEA ROUTE** by the Soviet government. This was a chartered company entrusted with the exploration and development of all Soviet territory north of 62°. Under Prof. Schmidt it employed about 40,000 people. The extensive new program included: navigation of the great Siberian rivers and building of ports at their mouths (to be kept open by ice-breakers); establishment on the coast of permanent stations (there were 57 in 1936) with radio

and other scientific equipment; maintenance of planes for reconnaissance of ice conditions, etc.; charting of coasts and currents (warm currents discovered along the edge of the continental shelf in 1935); construction of a railway from the Yenesei to the Dudinka and Norilsk mining regions (coal, nickel, platinum, and copper); agricultural stations to develop a food supply for colonists (work on rapidly maturing wheat, etc.); education and development of the natives, and protection of reindeer herds, etc.

1937, May-1938, Feb. **ESTABLISHMENT OF THE SOVIET POLAR STATION** near the North Pole (p. 567).

1938. The Administration of the Northern Sea Route, like many other branches of the Soviet government, was subjected to a drastic "purge." Prof. Schmidt and many other leading officials were removed and imprisoned, but some of them were later reinstated. Russian activity in the Arctic continued.

5. ANTARCTIC EXPLORATION

A legend dating from Greek antiquity and supported by Ptolemy related to the existence of an enormous continent in the southern hemisphere. This land-mass is shown by mediaeval cartographers, and even on maps as late as the end of the 16th century, on many of which it is extended to tropical latitudes in each of the three oceans. A series of voyages in southern latitudes during the 15th, 16th, and 17th centuries (Da Gama, 1497; Magellan, 1520; Drake, 1579; Tasman, 1642; and others, who were blown southward from their courses) progressively reduced the possible area of this legendary continent by pushing its limits farther and farther southward.

1738-1739. **Pierre Bouvet**, a French naval officer, deliberately set out to prove or disprove the existence of the southern continent, and 1400 miles south of Capetown he sighted land (Bouvet Island, 54° S.L.).

1756. The Spanish ship *Leon* discovered South Georgia (54°-55° S.) in the Atlantic.

1768. Capt. **James Cook**, on his first voyage, circumnavigated New Zealand, hitherto supposedly part of the Antarctic continent.

1771-1772. Capt. **Yves Kerguelen**, sent out by France to look for "a very large continent." He discovered Kergue-

len Island in the Indian Ocean (50° S.), which he named *New France.*

1772-1775. **SECOND VOYAGE OF CAPT. COOK.** He was the first to cross the Antarctic Circle (Jan. 17, 1773). He circumnavigated Antarctica, and made extensive exploratory cruises in the surrounding waters, pushing to 71° 10′ S. on Jan. 30, 1774 (1130 miles from the pole and the record south for the 18th century). He discovered the South Sandwich Islands, annexed South Georgia, and reported the presence there of enormous herds of seals.

1778-1839. **Explorations by the sealers.** Suspension of exploration as such. The discoveries made in this period were in the main incidental to the operations of British and American whalers and sealers drawn south by Cook's reports.

1778. British sealers began operations at South Georgia.

1819. Capt. **William Smith**, of the British brig *Williams*, discovered and took possession of the South Shetland Islands for the British.

1820. **Edward Bransfield**, in the *Williams*, charted 500 miles of the southern coast of the South Shetlands, discovered his strait, and sighted Graham Land.

1820-1821. Capt. **Fabian Gottlieb von Bellingshausen**, sent out by Alex-

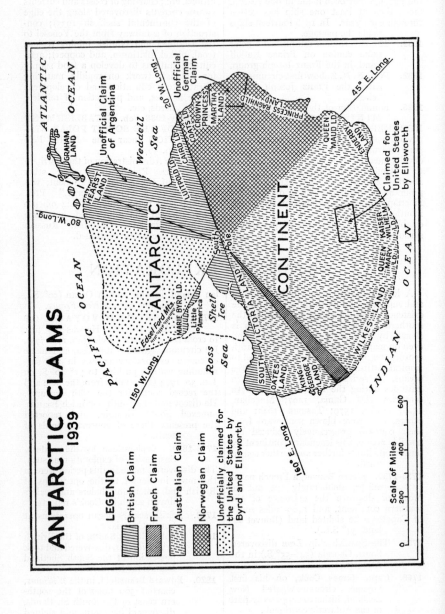

ander I of Russia, circumnavigated Antarctica, and discovered Alexander I Land and Peter Island (68° S.), the first land sighted within the Antarctic Circle.

1821. George Powell, a British sealer, and Nathaniel B. Palmer, an American sealer, discovered the South Orkney Islands, and Powell surveyed and annexed them for the British. Palmer and other American sealers further explored Palmer Archipelago, which skirts Graham Land.

1823. Capt. James Weddell, an Englishman, discovered and penetrated Weddell Sea, establishing on Feb. 20, 1823, the record south of his day (74° 15′, 945 miles from the pole).

1831-1832. John Biscoe, an English sealer, circumnavigated Antarctica, named and annexed Graham Land, discovered the Biscoe Islands, Queen Adelaide Island, and sighted Enderby Land. In 1839, John Balleny, another English captain, discovered the volcanic Balleny Islands, just on the Antarctic Circle, off the coast of Oates Land.

1837-1840. Capt. J. S. C. Dumont D'Urville of the French navy, in the *Astrolabe* and *Zelée*, sighted Joinville Island, Louis Philippe Land (in Graham Land), and Adélie Land on the mainland due south of Tasmania.

1839-1840. Capt. Charles Wilkes of the U.S. Navy was antedated in his discovery of Adélie Land by D'Urville, but he cruised westward along the coast of Antarctica from 148° E. to 108° E., where he found his way blocked by Termination Barrier (Shackleton Ice Shelf).

1841-1843. CAPT. JAMES CLARK ROSS (sent out by the British admiralty) in the *Erebus* and the *Terror* crossed the Antarctic Circle (Jan. 1, 1841), aiming to plant the Union Jack on the south magnetic pole and reach as high a latitude as possible. He got through the ice pack, but, finding his way barred by the lofty Admiralty Range behind Cape Adare, cruised southward for 430 miles into Ross Sea, along the scarped eastern coast of South Victoria Land. There he sighted and named, besides the Admiralty Range, the Prince Albert Range and the volcanic mountains Erebus and Terror on Ross Island. Finding further passage southward barred at the latter point by the Great (Ross) Ice Barrier, he cruised eastward along it for 350 miles, before returning to Hobart, Tasmania (Apr. 1, 1841). The following summer he returned to the head of Ross Sea near King Edward VII Land and made a record south (78° 9′, 710 miles from the pole) which held for 60 years. In 1842 he cruised off Graham Land, but made no important discoveries. Altogether Ross charted about 1000 miles of coastline. He also took possession for Great Britain of all the continental land and islands which he discovered in 1841.

After the voyages of Ross there was a lull of 30 years in systematic exploration of the Antarctic, attention having shifted to the North Pole.

1872-1874. H.M.S. *Challenger* (Capt. George S. Nares), the first steampropelled vessel to cross the Antarctic Circle, renewed the study of oceanography in the Antarctic and helped to redirect public attention to the south.

1873-1875. Capt. Eduard Dallmann (German) in the steamship *Grönland* established the fact that Palmer Land was an archipelago by sailing behind it, and, beyond, discovered Bismarck Strait and the Kaiser Wilhelm Archipelago to the south off Graham Land.

1893. Capt. C. A. Larsen (Norwegian) in the *Jason* explored Weddell seacoast, discovering and naming Foyn Coast in Graham Land, King Oscar Land, Mt. Jason, and Robertson Island.

1894-1895. Capt. Leonard Kristensen (Norwegian) in the *Antarctic* discovered Ridley Beach at Cape Adare, where the first landing on the continent was made in January by Carsten Borchgrevink. He found the first vegetation in the Antarctic — a lichen at Possession Island.

1895. The Sixth International Geographical Congress in London called attention to Antarctic exploration, which it described as the most pressing geographical requirement of the time, and did much to stimulate interest in the problem, both on the part of governments and of private individuals.

1897-1899. Lieut. Adrien de Gerlache (Belgian) in the *Belgica*, with Roald Amundsen as mate, coasted Graham Land, discovered and made several landings in Belgica Strait (subsequently Gerlache Channel), discovered and named Danco Land to the east, and passed south of Peter Island. Here on Mar. 3, 1898, they were beset and remained, the first prisoners through an Antarctic night, drifting with the pack ice until Feb. 14, 1899.

1898-1900. Carsten Borchgrevink, in the whaler *Southern Cross*, led the first party (British and Scandinavian) to winter on the continent, at Cape Adare, where meteorological observations were taken, penguin life studied, and geological collections made. Picked up by their ship in Jan. 1900, they made several landings on the eastern shore of Victoria Land, discovered the Emperor Penguin rookery at Cape Crozier, and cruised along the Ross Barrier. Feb. 19, they made a sledge journey on its surface to 78° 45', a new record south.

1901-1903. The German National Expedition, led by Prof. Erich von Drygalski in the *Gauss*, discovered and named the Gaussberg and Kaiser Wilhelm II Land, where they sent out the first sledge parties on the Antarctic ice coast. This expedition founded a magnetic station on Kerguelen Island.

1901-1903. The Swedish Expedition, led by **Dr. Otto Nordenskiöld** and Capt. Larsen in the *Antarctic*, made exploratory cruises around Graham Land and in Weddell Sea, where they discovered another great ice barrier stretching from Robertson Island to Mt. Jason, surveyed the east coast of Graham Land and outlying islands from Erebus and Terror Gulf to 66° S., and discovered and charted the Crown Prince Gustav Channel and James Ross Island as well as the northern archipelago lying around it. The *Antarctic* was crushed and sunk by the pack ice and the expedition was obliged to spend two winters at Snow Hill Island, where it was finally rescued by an Argentine ship.

1902-1904. CAPT. R. F. SCOTT (British), commanding a large expedition, including **Lieut. Shackleton** and **Dr. E. A. Wilson,** in the *Discovery* reached Cape Adare, Jan. 1902. Cruising southward along Ross's course in 1842, he discovered and named the Drygalski and Nordenskiöld ice tongues, Granite Harbor, and the Royal Society Mountains. He succeeded in surpassing his predecessor's record, reached the eastern end of Ross Barrier, sighted and named King Edward VII Land on the eastern shore of Ross Sea, and charted 150 miles of its coast. Upon the return to winter at Ross Island in McMurdo Sound, Mt. Erebus was found to be an active volcano.

1903, Nov.-1904, Feb. Scott, Wilson, and Shackleton made a southern trip of 930 miles over the Ross Barrier in an effort to ascertain its limits. They discovered that its western boundary was formed by 350 miles of scarped coastline, backed by the lofty Britannia and Queen Alexandra Ranges, the latter containing 15,000-foot Mt. Markham. Their record south was 82° 17' (500 miles from the pole), near Shackleton Inlet, an enormous ice strait, where they were obliged to turn back. At the same time a reconnaissance party under Lieut. **Albert Armitage** made a western trip on to the continental ice-sheet of South Victoria Land's 9000-foot inland plateau, discovering and naming the Ferrar, Taylor, and Blue Glaciers. The following season (1903-1904) a party under Scott pushed 200 miles farther over the plateau and on the return trip discovered and explored Dry Valley.

1903-1905. The Scottish National Expedition, led by **Dr. W. S. Bruce** in the *Scotia*, carried on oceanographical explorations in Weddell Sea, and wintered on Laurie Island. In March, 1904, again exploring southward in Weddell Sea, they discovered Coats Land.

1903-1905. Jean B. Charcot (French) in the *Français* operated off the west coast of Graham Land, charted the western side of Palmer Archipelago, sighted Alexander I Land, and discovered Loubet Land.

1907-1909. SIR ERNEST SHACKLETON (British), privately financed in the *Nimrod*, led an expedition including Douglas Mawson and Prof. T. W. E. David to the Ross Sea sector. First ascent of Mt. Erebus and discovery of the live crater (Mar. 5-10, 1908). From a base at Cape Royds on Ross Island, he and three others started on a journey to the pole (Oct. 29, 1908). Surpassing Scott's record, they discovered and passed the southern end of Ross Barrier, formed by the Commonwealth Range, and struggled (Dec. 7-27) more than a hundred miles up to the head of Beardmore Glacier, where they discovered a seam of low-grade coal. At its head (9820 feet) they emerged upon the South Polar Plateau, across which they traveled to 88° 23' S., on Jan. 9, 1909, where a desperate food shortage obliged them to turn back, only 97 miles short of their goal.

1908, Oct. 5-1909, Feb. 4. David, Mawson, and Mackay on a 1260-mile sledge trip, explored and surveyed 200 miles northward along the coast of Victoria Land, crossed Drygalski Glacier, and turning inland climbed up the 7000-foot Northern Plateau to reach and plant the British flag on the **south magnetic pole** (1200 miles from the true South Pole) on Jan. 16, 1909. The land was claimed for King Edward. Altogether Shackleton's expedition discovered about 1000 miles, and explored 300 miles more of territory previously discovered. All the new land explored was formally declared to be British.

1908. Great Britain issued letters patent constituting the *Falkland Dependency* (South Georgia, the South Shetlands, the Sandwich Group, and Graham Land) under the jurisdiction of the governor of the Falkland Islands. The Dependency established a sector between 80° and 20° W. Long. running from 50° S. Lat. to the pole.

1908-1910. Second expedition of Jean Charcot. He charted 200 miles of the west coast of Graham Land, extending his previous survey 100 miles beyond Loubet Coast. The new land was called Fallières Coast. Then advancing southward Charcot first reached Alexander I Land, but could not determine whether it was an island or mainland. In 1910 he discovered Charcot Land, farther to the southwest, and verified Bellingshausen's discovery of Peter Island.

1910-1912. DISCOVERY OF THE SOUTH POLE BY CAPT. ROALD AMUNDSEN. Beaten by Peary at the North Pole, Amundsen hoped to anticipate Scott at the South Pole. He chose a base on the Bay of Whales and with four others made the trip with dog-sledges (1911, Oct. 19-Dec. 14). The Norwegian flag was hoisted at the pole on Dec. 16, 1911. On the trip Amundsen discovered the 15,000-foot Queen Maude Range which bounds Ross Barrier. He ascended this range to the Polar Plateau by way of Axel Heiberg Glacier, and discovered the Devil's Glacier beyond.

1910-1913. SCOTT'S LAST EXPEDITION. He aimed for the pole, but was interested mainly in scientific research. From a base at Cape Evans in McMurdo Sound, he and four others started (Nov. 3, 1911) and followed Shackleton's route up Beardmore Glacier. Failure of transport and deficient food resulted in ever slower progress. **The pole was reached Jan. 16, 1912,** but the party was so exhausted that before getting back it was overtaken by bad weather. Halfway across Ross Barrier they all died in a blizzard (about Mar. 29). The bodies were found by a relief party in Nov. 1912.

1910-1912. Lieut. Shirase (Japanese), after an unsuccessful attempt to reach Ross Sea (1911), effected a landing on the Bay of Whales. Learning that Amundsen had already reached the pole, he contented himself with a short sledge journey across the Barrier.

1911-1912. Dr. Wilhelm Filchner (German), in an attempt to find out whether Ross and Weddell Seas are connected by a strait, discovered Leopold Land, delimited the southern boundary of Weddell Sea and discovered the Wilhelm Ice Barrier, which fills its head.

1911-1913. Dr. Douglas Mawson (British) led a large-scale, well-equipped expedition to explore the 2000 miles of practically unknown coast between Cape Adare and the Gaussberg. He was the first Antarctic explorer to use wireless. The larger section of the expedition broke through the pack ice and discovered Mertz Glacier, stretching 60 miles out to sea, and beyond it D'Urville Sea. Here the party made its base on Commonwealth Bay and (Nov. 1911-Jan. 1912) Mawson, Mertz, and Ninnis sledged 280 miles over the great ice plateau into King George V Land, crossing the Mertz and the still larger Ninnis Glacier, but Mawson was the only one who got through alive. Another party explored the coast to the east for 275 miles, and a third contingent was taken 1200 miles westward in the *Aurora* past the great ice barrier which they named Shackleton's Ice Shelf, discovered Davis Sea, and named the land on its shores Queen Mary Land. The party camped on Shackleton Ice Shelf, on which Denman and Scott Glaciers were discovered. From here also a party made a 215-mile trip to Gaussberg in Kaiser Wilhelm Land and back.

Mawson discovered that the greater part of Antarctica is bordered by ice coasts. Altogether his expedition discovered and explored 1320 miles of land, mapped 800 miles of coastline, and made more geographical and scientific discoveries than any previous expedition, although it worked under far worse weather conditions in the most desolate, blizzard-ridden part of the continent.

1914-1917. SIR ERNEST SHACKLETON, in the *Endurance*, proposed to cross Antarctica from Weddell to Ross Sea *via* the pole (1800 miles, half over unknown territory) to meet the complementary party under **Mackintosh** in the *Aurora.* This aim was defeated, Shackleton's way south to the destined landing-place being barred by heavy pack ice in Weddell Sea, but he confirmed Bruce's discovery of Coats Land, between which and Leopold Land to the southwest, he discovered Caird Coast, which contains the Dawson Lampton Glacier — probably the world's largest. Feb. 22, 1915, the *Endurance* was fast beset and drifted 570 miles northwest with the pack until Nov. 21, 1915, when she was crushed and sunk by the pressure ice. The party drifted on the disintegrating floe until Apr. 9, 1916, when they took to small boats. On Apr. 14 they reached Elephant Island, where they were obliged to winter. Shackleton and five others made the 800-mile trip to South Georgia for help in a 20-foot open boat in 16 days, arriving May 10, 1916. A fourth relief expedition to Elephant Island was finally successful in removing the marooned party on Aug. 30, 1916.

The Ross Sea party in the *Aurora* was left stranded with insufficient equipment at its base at Cape Evans when the ship was carried away by the pack in May, 1915.

Scantily-clad, half-starved, and suffering from scurvy, the land party nevertheless fulfilled its part of the plan, laying depots all the way to Beardmore Glacier for Shackleton to use on the last lap of his polar journey. This party was rescued by the *Aurora* in Jan. 1917.

1921-1922. J. L. Cope and **G. H.** (now Sir Hubert) **Wilkins** (British), landed by Norwegian whalers on the west coast of Graham Land, were foiled in their plan to cross it to Weddell Sea, because the country was too rugged for sledging.

1923, July 30. A British order in council constituted the Ross Sea sector a British dependency, known as the *Ross Dependency*, under the governor-general of New Zealand, and fixed as its boundaries the meridians of 150° W., 160° E., and the 60th parallel S., a delimitation which included a large part of Amundsen's discoveries and excluded part of Scott's route to the pole across King Edward Plateau, part of Oates Land, and all of the extensive lands discovered by Mawson, including the south magnetic pole area, which had been claimed for the British by David in 1908.

1924. The French government put Adélie Land (between 136° 20′ and 142° 20′ E. Long.) under the governor of Madagascar.

1928-1930. F I R S T A N T A R C T I C FLIGHTS, BY SIR HUBERT WILKINS. The expedition was sponsored by the American Geographical Society and largely financed by W. R. Hearst. From Deception Bay, Wilkins, piloted by C. B. Eielson, made a 1200-mile flight (Dec. 20, 1928) southwest over Graham Land, discovering Crane Channel, the Lockheed Mts. and Stefansson Strait which separates Graham Land from the mainland (named Hearst Land). On Dec. 31, 1929, Wilkins, piloted by A. Cheesman, flew over Charcot Land, discovered that it was an island and dropped a flag claiming it for Britain. Altogether Wilkins mapped about 80,000 sq. miles, discovered a new portion of the continent and determined the insularity of Graham Land.

1928-1930. COMM. RICHARD BYRD (American) led a large, scientifically equipped expedition with three aeroplanes. In Jan. 1929, they built the base *Little America* on Ross Barrier. A flight on Jan. 27 revealed the new Rockefeller Mts. and neighboring Scott Land. Another on Nov. 18 discovered the Charles V Bob Mt. Range east of the Queen Maude Range.

1929, Nov. 28-29. Byrd, Balchen, June, and McKinley, in the plane *Floyd Bennett*, flew to the pole and back (1700

miles) by way of the 10,000-foot pass over Liv's Glacier. In a further flight on Dec. 5 Byrd went beyond the Rockefeller Mts., crossed the British boundary, and discovered the huge Edsel Ford Range in a new territory which he named *Marie Byrd Land* and claimed for the U.S. (between 150° and 120° W.).

1929-1931. SIR DOUGLAS MAWSON led the co-operative British, Australian, and New Zealand Antarctic Research Expedition, in the *Discovery* (Capt. Davis), to explore the 2500-mile uncharted coastline between King Wilhelm II Land and Coats Land, including Kemp and Enderby Lands. Planes were carried along, to be used in cases where pack ice prevented approach to the mainland coasts. Dec. 29, 1929: Discovery of MacRobertson Land near Kemp Land by flight from the *Discovery*. Jan. 13, 1930: Landing in Enderby Land, of which formal possession was taken for the crown. A large range of mountains discovered there was named after Scott. Jan. 14, 1930: The *Discovery* met the *Norvegia* (Capt. Riiser-Larsen), which was also exploring. It was decided that the British should keep to the east and the Norwegians to the west of 40° E. (later changed to 45° E. by the two governments). The following (1930-1931) season a landing was made at Mawson's old base on Commonwealth Bay and all land from there eastward to Oates Land was claimed for the British crown under the name *King George V Land*. The coast west of Cape Denison was explored by plane and additional surveys of Adélie Land were made. Further discoveries were: Banzare Land (west of 127° E.), Sabrina Land (between 115° and 116° E.), Princess Elizabeth Land (between the Gaussberg and MacRobertson Land), and Mackenzie Sea, a huge bay in MacRobertson Land. These two cruises resulted in the discovery of new coasts covering 29° of longitude, about 1000 miles of which was charted. Mawson's major achievement on his two expeditions (1911-1914 and 1929-1931) was the demonstration that the coastline is continuous from Cape Freshfield in King George V Land to Enderby Land — more than 2500 miles.

1933. The British government accepted the **Australian claim** to the huge sector between 45° and 160° E. Long., exclusive of French Adélie Land.

1929-1931. Capt. Hj. Riiser-Larsen (Norwegian) led an expedition in the *Norvegia* to look for new whaling grounds and new land. He carried two planes and on Dec. 22, 1929, he flew to the coast of Enderby Land. Jan. 15, 1930, he discovered Queen Maude Land (southwest of Enderby Land) and (Feb. 18) Crown Princess Martha Land (by flight), to which 150 miles of coastline was added by a flight on Feb. 20. The following (1930–1931) season he extended his explorations of Queen Maude Land 200 miles farther to the west, the new land (between 24° and 30° E.) being called *Princess Ragnhild Land*.

1934-1935. THE SECOND EXPEDITION OF COMMANDER BYRD. The equipment included four planes, four tractors, and an autogyro, and from Jan. 17, 1934, to Feb. 6, 1935, a comprehensive set of observations was taken in the fields of meteorology, biology, geophysics, botany, and cosmic rays. Byrd himself undertook to man single-handed a weather observation station 100 miles inland through the Antarctic winter, but fell ill and injured himself after three months, so that a relief expedition had to be sent after him in one of the tractors. Dr. Poulter's investigations of Ross Barrier bore out the Japanese contention that much of it was aground. One tractor party explored a new plateau discovered to the southeast of Little America, and another, aiming south, pushed up the glaciers bordering the Barrier, explored mountains only two hundred miles from the pole, where they found plant-fossils, coal, fossilized wood, and other indications that the climate had once been subtropical, and discovered a huge plateau to the east of Thorne Glacier.

Explorations were also carried on by flight, the main achievement being the demonstration that no strait connects Ross and Weddell Seas and that Antarctica is thus one continent. A new range called the *Horlick Mountains* was discovered east of Thorne Glacier.

1934-1937. The British Graham Land Expedition, under John Rymill (Australian). In 1935–1936 it operated from a base at the Argentine Islands, exploring the Graham Land coast to Cape Evensen and discovering that it consists of an 8000-foot plateau, rising abruptly from the sea. In July, 1936, two parties surveyed the coastline north from a base at Barry Island (Fallières Coast). On Aug. 15 a flight was made westward along the shore of Alexander I Land, which was photographed. A flight on Sept. 15 revealed to the south a long, ice-covered strait (King George VI Channel), which the expedition attempted to penetrate with sledges. At

72° S.L. the channel appeared to open into a large bay, which proved that Alexander I Land is larger and extends farther south than previously supposed. Meanwhile another sledge party penetrated the interior of Graham Land, discovered and scaled a 7500-foot pass and reached a point overlooking the east coast, which was mapped for 140 miles, south to 70° 40'. The expedition revealed that what looked like straits to Wilkins were in reality glaciers several thousand feet high and that Stefansson Strait, Casey Channel, and probably Crane Channel are fjords. Graham Land may, after all, be part of the Antarctic continent.

1935-1936. LINCOLN ELLSWORTH (American) in the *Wyatt Earp*, commanded by Sir Hubert Wilkins, succeeded in his third attempt at a transcontinental Antarctic flight. On Nov. 23, 1935, with Herbert Hollick-Kenyon (Canadian) he took off in the *Polar Star* from Dundee Island in the northern part of the Antarctic Archipelago for the Bay of Whales, 2300 miles away. The trip was made in six stages, the last one by sledge after the exhaustion of their fuel. They reached Little America Dec. 15, and were picked up Jan. 15, 1936, by the *Discovery II*, an Antarctic research ship. The new territory between Hearst Land and Marie Byrd Land (80° to 120° W.) was named *James W. Ellsworth Land* and claimed for the U.S., and a high mid-continental plateau was named after Hollick-Kenyon. Ellsworth also discovered the 12,000-foot Eternity Range in Hearst Land and the Sentinel Range in James W. Ellsworth Land.

1936. Australia proclaimed her control over all Antarctic territory south of the 60th parallel between 160° and 45° E. Long. (except Adélie Land), this being the territory explored by Mawson on his two expeditions. It constitutes an area almost as large as that of Australia.

1938-1939. Ellsworth, on another expedition, surveyed a large part of eastern Antarctica by air, claiming some 430,000 square miles for the United States. The Australian government at once protested against this claim.

1939, Jan. 14. The Norwegian government laid claim to Queen Maude Land, Princess Ragnhild Land, and Crown Princess Martha Land, about 1,000,000 square miles covering roughly one-fifth of the Antarctic continent.

B. THE REVOLUTIONARY AND NAPOLEONIC PERIOD

The period of the revolution and empire may be divided into the following sub-periods, distinguished by changes in the form of government:

(1) **Estates-General** and **Constituent Assembly** (*Constituante*) from May 5 (June 17), 1789, to Sept. 30, 1791. Government a limited, constitutional monarchy. Dominance of the upper middle classes.

(2) The **Legislative Assembly** (*Législatif*), from Oct. 1, 1791, to Sept. 21, 1792. The monarchy continued as before, until suspended. Rising power of the lower classes.

(3) The **National Convention** (*Convention Nationale*), from Sept. 21, 1792, to Oct. 25, 1795. Height of the revolution. The convention, called to frame a new constitution, first abolished the monarchy and condemned the king to death; it supported the Reign of Terror, and then overthrew it. It led the resistance to foreign foes.

[N.B. In modern party terms the *Left* of the Constituent was the *Right* of the Legislative (though the actual *personnel* was by law different), and the Left of the Legislative was (at first) the Right of the Convention.]

(4) The **Directory** (*Directoire*), from Oct. 26, 1795, to Nov. 9, 1799 (18 Brumaire, An. VIII). The middle classes recovered their influence. Party divisions. The army. General Bonaparte's *coup d'état*. Form republican.

(5) The **Consulate** (*Consulat*), at first provisional, then definitive, from Dec. 25, 1799, to May 20, 1804; civil and military rule, virtually of one man; progress of French arms. Form still nominally republican.

(6) The (first) **Empire;** from May 20, 1804, to (April, 1814) June 22, 1815. **Napoleon I** made France the controlling power on the Continent, but was finally overthrown.

1. BACKGROUND OF THE REVOLUTION

The spirit of the 18th century — a spirit devoted to the destruction or reformation of existing institutions. Attacks of French writers upon Church and State.

Agrarian conditions. The peasantry was almost wholly free (300,000 out of some 20,000,000 still subject to certain servile restriction), and in many regions owned land. Often its holdings were too small for adequate support. It was subject to certain surviving feudal dues, not in the aggregate large, but annoying, and in 1789 no longer paid for protection. There is evidence that in the last half of the eighteenth century nobles and other owners of these dues were attempting to collect them to the full, and revive those that had lapsed (the so-called *feudal reaction*). Taxation bore heavily on the peasantry, especially the *taille*, a land-tax from which nobles and clergy were exempt. Yet as a whole French peasants were certainly better off than most European peasants, and they took part in the revolution, *not* because they were hopelessly downtrodden, but because they were well enough off to wish to better themselves.

The rise of a middle class, generally excluded from politics, and particularly local politics (access to the royal bureaucracy was open to able and ambitious bourgeois), but which had been growing richer with the expansion of French trade, and which read and listened to the *philosophes*.

An unwieldy and inefficient machinery of government, not so much tyrannical as irresponsible and unsuited to the needs of a large commercial and agricultural state. Taxation was inequitable, neither clergy nor nobility paying their full share (the clergy did pay a not inconsiderable *don gratuit*, and nobles paid the *vingtième* and *capitation*). Moreover, the indirect taxes were farmed out, and the *fermiers généraux* most unpopular. The *gabelle*, or salt-tax, was particularly irregular in its incidence. There was no true representative assembly, though the *parlements*, and especially the *parlement* of Paris, sometimes took upon themselves in the eighteenth century the rôle of such an assembly. Justice was by no means arbitrary, and the judges (*noblesse de robe*), though they owned their offices, were generally competent and conscientious. The famous *lettres de cachet*, royal orders imprisoning without benefit of *habeas corpus* or similar proceedings, were less important in fact than in anti-governmental propaganda. Sometimes used against political offenders, their chief use was to back up the family discipline of the upper classes by providing a means of shutting up wayward sons and otherwise keeping the power of the *pater familias* intact.

An ever-growing deficit, which proved impossible of reduction. The Estates-General were called to remedy practical bankruptcy. Once called, they took upon themselves the wholesale reform of the state. France in 1789 was a fairly prosperous society with a bankrupt government.

2. THE NATIONAL ASSEMBLY

1789, May 5. MEETING OF THE ES-TATES-GENERAL at Versailles, with a double representation of the middle classes, the third estate (*tiers état*), nobles 300, clergy 300, commons 600. Dispute about the manner of debating and voting (whether votes should be cast by the orders as such, or by each member individually) which broke out during the verification of the powers of the members. The nobles and the clergy demanded a separate verification, the commons wished that it should take place in common. The true question was whether the legislative body should consist of a lower house of commons, and an upper house (or two houses) of nobles and clergy which would check the lower, or of one house in which the commons equaled in number the nobles and clergy together. Upon the motion of the **Abbé Siéyès** (author of the remarkable pamphlet asking, *What is the Third Estate?*) the representatives of the third estate assumed the title of the
1789, June 17-1791. NATIONAL ASSEM-BLY (*Constituante*) and invited the other orders to join them.
June 20. Suspension of the meetings for three days; the hall closed to the members, who at last resorted to a neighboring **tennis court** (*jeu de paume*) and took an oath not to separate until they had given the realm a constitution. President Bailly. Many of the clergy and some nobles joined the Assembly.
June 23. Fruitless royal sitting; the king ordered the Assembly to meet in three houses. Principal orator of the Assembly: **Mirabeau** (1749–1791), a Provençal nobleman elected by the third estate. The representatives of the clergy and the nobility joined the third estate by request of the king. Concentration of troops near Paris. Rumors of the king's intention to dissolve the National Assembly, and the **dismissal of Necker** (July 11) caused the
July 14. STORM AND DESTRUC-TION OF THE BASTILLE in Paris (murder of its governor, De Launay).

Paris in the hands of the mob scarcely controlled by the electors who had chosen the deputies from Paris and who now sat at the Hôtel de Ville as a provisional government. **Necker recalled. Lafayette** commander of the newly established **National Guard.** Bailly mayor of Paris. Adoption of the tricolor: blue, red (colors of Paris), white (color of France).

Beginning of the emigration of the nobles, headed by the **Count of Artois,** second brother of the king, **Prince of Condé, Polignac.**

Rising of the peasants against the feudal lords in Dauphiné, Provence, Burgundy, and throughout France. This *Grande Peur* was *not* systematically spread from Paris but occurred sporadically as a series of mass movements with numerous centers. Riots, provisional governments, guards in the provincial cities.

Aug. 4. Voluntary surrender by the representatives of the nobles (Vicomte de Noailles) of all feudal rights and privileges, but only gradually over a period of years, and with compensation to the owners (this compensation was in most cases never paid; under the Convention these provisions were repealed); abolition of titles, prohibition of the sale of offices, dissolution of the guilds, etc.

Aug. 27. Declaration of the rights of man, a bill of rights compounded from English and American precedents and from the political theories current with the *philosophes.* Discussion of the veto power.

Oct. 5, 6. Outbreak of the mob of Paris, caused by hunger and rumors of an intended reaction. March of a band, consisting principally of women, to Versailles. The royal family, rescued by Lafayette, was obliged to go to Paris, whither the National Assembly followed them. 200 members resigned.

Liberal monarchical constitution: one chamber with legislative power and the sole right of initiation. The royal veto was suspensive only, delaying the adoption of a measure for two legislative terms. The king could not declare war and conclude peace without the consent of the Chamber, ratification by which was necessary for the validity of all foreign treaties.

In order to relieve the financial distress the ecclesiastical estates were declared public property. *Assignats*, notes of the government, having for security the public lands, the value of which was not to be exceeded by the issue of notes (a check which was inoperative). The state assumed the support of the clergy.

1790, July 14. National federation in Paris; the constitution accepted by the king. Abolition of the old provinces and governments; France divided into 83 *departments*, named after rivers and mountains; these departments being subdivided into 374 *districts* and *cantons*. The *communes* were left unchanged (44,000); tax qualifications for the exercise of *active* suffrage in the primary assemblies, which chose electors, who then elected the representatives (745) for a legislature with a term of two years. The administrative officers of the departments and districts were selected from the electors; the municipal officers and the judges were taken from the great body of voters, the *active* citizens. Active citizens, who voted, paid direct taxes equal to three days' wages of common labor in their locality: *passive* citizens, who did not vote, paid no direct taxes, or less than the above minimum. Each department and each district had a local assembly. Abolition of the *parlements* and the old judicial constitution. Juries. Abolition of hereditary nobility, titles, and coats-of-arms. Dissolution of all ecclesiastical orders, excepting those having education and the care of the sick for their objects. Civil organization of the clergy; the priests to be chosen by the voters of the districts, the bishops by the voters of the departments. Somewhat

less than half of the clerics submitted to the new constitution by taking the required oath, creating a distinction between the *prêtres assermentés* and the *prêtres réfractaires*.

Growing power of the clubs, which had existed since 1789. The *Jacobins* (meeting in a monastery formerly occupied by Dominicans in the Rue St. Jacques), under the leadership of **Robespierre** soon became the greatest power in the state, making use of a network of daughter societies in the provinces. The *Cordeliers*, who met in a Franciscan monastery (leaders **Danton, Marat, Desmoulins, Hébert**). The *Feuillants*, moderate monarchists who had separated from the Jacobins (**Lafayette, Bailly** belonged to this group).

Reorganization of the municipality (*commune*) **of Paris:** 48 sections, with 84,000 voters in a population of 800,000; general council; executive board (44). Each section had a primary assembly.

Sept. Fall of Necker. Alliance between the court and Mirabeau, who endeavored to stem the revolution and prevent the overthrow of the throne.

1791, Apr. 2. Death of Mirabeau.

June 20-25. FLIGHT OF THE KING and his family to the northeast frontier, where loyal troops were to protect them. The party was recognized and stopped at Varennes, then brought back to Paris. At first suspended, then reinstated by the moderate party (Sept.) **Louis accepted the constitution** (Sept. 14) as revised and completed.

Sept. Annexation of Avignon and Venaissin to France.

Sept. 30. Dissolution of the Assembly, after it had voted that none of its members should be eligible for election to the next assembly.

3. THE LEGISLATIVE ASSEMBLY

1791, Oct. 1-1792, Sept. THE LEGISLATIVE ASSEMBLY, composed of 745 members, elected by the active citizens, still represented primarily the middle class. Parties: The *Right* (constitutionalists, royalists, Feuillants, etc.) became weaker almost day by day. The *Left*, comprising the majority, was divided into (1) the *Plain*, an unorganized group of moderate republicans or timid monarchists, swayed in turn by the next two groups; (2) the *Girondists*, so called because the leading members came from Bordeaux (de-

partment of the Gironde), had in **Guadet, Vergniaud,** and **Brissot** a group of brilliant orators, advocating the establishing of a form of federal republic; (3) the *Mountain* (la Montagne, Montagnards), so called from their seats, which were the highest on the left side of the hall, was composed of the radicals, champions of a united, indivisible republic. The Mountain drew its strength from the Jacobin and Cordelier Clubs. The division between Girondists and the Mountain did not attain its clearest form until the meeting of the Convention (below), but

its beginnings were evident in the Legislative Assembly. **Pétion,** the mayor of
Paris, was a Girondist.

Aug. 27. Meeting at Pillnitz of **Frederick
William II** of Prussia (1786–1797)
and **Leopold II** (1790–1792), the emperor.
The two sovereigns and their ministers
reached a preliminary understanding regarding Near-Eastern affairs (p. 485) and
above all regarding the French situation.
The **Declaration of Pillnitz** was a carefully
worded statement that the two rulers would
intervene in French affairs only with the
unanimous consent of the powers, including
England. But the French interpreted it as
a bald threat of interference.

1792, Feb. 7. **Alliance of Austria and
Prussia** against France.

1792-1806 (1835). **FRANCIS II,** emperor
in succession to Leopold.

1792-1797. **WAR OF THE FIRST COA-
LITION** against France. A Girondist ministry (Roland, Dumouriez) took
the place of the constitutionalist ministry,
whose fall was caused by the Pillnitz Declaration. The Girondists actually sought the
war, while on the Austrian side Francis fell
completely under the influence of the war
party. The French *émigrés* had long been
trying to provoke intervention, while certain
German princes with feudal rights in Alsace
(*princes possessionés*) were demanding compensation for losses under the decrees of
Aug. 4, 1789. Many Prussian and Austrian
leaders thought that France, weakened by
the revolutionary dissension, would be
easily beaten. Exact responsibility for the
war is hard to allocate. In Apr. 1792 both
sides wanted it.

Apr. 20. The French **declared war
against Austria** and put three
armies in the field: Rochambeau (48,000)
between Dunkirk and Philippeville; Lafayette (52,000) between Philippeville and
Lauterburg; Luckner (42,000) between
Lauterburg and Basel. The French suffered
reverses, which increased the revolutionary
excitement in Paris.

June 13. **Fall of the Roland ministry.**

June 20. **Attack of the mob on the
Tuileries;** calm behavior of the
king.

July 11. The Assembly pronounced the
country in danger. Formation of
a voluntary army throughout the country.
Threatening **manifesto of the Duke of
Brunswick,** Prussian commander-in-chief.
The Paris council was broken up and its place
usurped by commissioners from the sections
(new commune of 288 members).

Aug. 10 **STORMING OF THE
TUILERIES** by the mob, in consequence of a command of the king ordering
the Swiss guard to cease firing. Massacre
of the Swiss guards. The king took refuge
in the hall of the Assembly, was suspended
from his functions and confined in the
Temple (old house of the Knights Templar).
Arrests of suspected persons. **Provisional
government:** Danton (1759–1794), minister
of justice; Lebrun, Roland, Servan, Monge,
Clavière. The Assembly virtually abdicated its powers, which passed to the Paris
Commune and the Jacobin clubs. Convocation of a national convention, to be
elected by manhood suffrage, to draw up a
new constitution.

Aug. 20. **Lafayette,** having been impeached and proscribed, fled from
his army, was captured by the
Austrians and imprisoned at Olmütz (till 1796). Verdun taken
by the Prussians.

Sept. 2-7. **THE SEPTEMBER MASSA-
CRES** at Paris. Suspects were
taken from the prisons and, after hasty
trials by improvised tribunals, were summarily done away with by the mob. Blame
seems to lie chiefly with Sergent, Panis, and
other Paris ward politicians. **Danton,** if he
cannot be proved to have instigated the
massacres, certainly allowed them to run
their course. Similar scenes were enacted
at Versailles, Lyons, Rheims, Meaux, and
Orléans.

Sept. 20. **BATTLE OF VALMY.** The
French, under **Dumouriez** and
Kellermann, defeated the Prussians in an
artillery duel fought in a heavy fog. The
engagement, far from important in the
military sense, was yet a crucial test. It
gave heart to the revolutionary armies and
was to prove a turning-point.

4. THE NATIONAL CONVENTION

1792, Sept. 21-1795, Oct. **THE NATIONAL
CONVENTION,** longest-lived of
the revolutionary assemblies. It was
elected by manhood suffrage and was composed entirely of republicans (749 members,
of whom 486 were new men). **Parties: The**

Girondists now formed the Right, while the
Mountain, under Robespierre, the Duke of
Orléans (Philippe Egalité), Danton, Collot
d'Herbois, etc., formed the Left. The **Plain**
(scornfully called the *Marsh* and the *Belly*)
appeared as in the preceding assembly.

Numerically it had the majority, but it was dominated first by the Girondists, then by the Mountain.

1792, Sept. 21. ABOLITION OF THE MONARCHY. France declared a Republic.

Sept. 22 was the first day of the year one of the French republic. *Citoyen et citoyenne*; decree of perpetual banishment against emigrants; *tu et toi.* Inglorious retreat of the Prussians through Champagne to Luxembourg and across the Rhine. The French general, **Custine,** took Speier, Mainz, and Frankfurt on the Main. Occupation of Nice and Savoy (Sept.).

Nov. 6. Victory of the French general **Dumouriez at Jemappes.** He took Brussels and conquered the Austrian Netherlands. The Prussians retook Frankfurt.

Nov. 19. Proclamation of the convention offering French assistance to all peoples who wished to throw off their government.

Nov. 27. Savoy and Nice annexed; the Scheldt opened to commerce.

1792, Dec.-1793, Jan. Trial of Louis XVI before the Convention. Barrère prosecutor; Malesherbes, Desèze, Tronchet, for the defense. Proposed appeal to the nation rejected. Jan. 15, 683 votes out of 721 declared the king guilty. Jan. 16, 361 votes, exactly a majority (among them that of the Duke of Orléans) were cast unconditionally for death, 360 being cast for imprisonment, banishment, or death with respite.

1793, Jan. 21. EXECUTION OF LOUIS XVI.

Feb. 1. War declared against Great Britain, Holland, Spain. England, Holland, Spain, and the empire joined the alliance against France, Sardinia having been at war with the latter power since July, 1792. **Annexation of Belgium.** The *émigrés*, under the Prince of Condé, proclaimed as King **Louis XVII,** who was a prisoner in the Temple.

Mar. Royalist revolt in the **Vendée,** upon occasion of a levy of recruits. (Charette, Stofflet, Cathelineau, La Rochejaquelein).

Mar. 18. The Austrians under the Duke of Coburg defeated Dumouriez at **Neerwinden,** and recaptured Brussels. Dumouriez went over to the Austrians with the Duke of Chartres, **Louis Philippe,** son of Egalité.

At Paris, in the Convention, struggle for life and death, between the **Girondists** and the **Mountain.** After the failure of the plan of the Orléanists, belonging to the Mountain, to make the Duke of Orléans

protector, all power centered in the **Committee of General Security** and the

Apr. 6. Committee of Public Safety (*Comité du salut public*). Composed of 9 (afterwards 12) members, who exercised dictatorial power. Leaders: **Danton** (from the very start); **Robespierre** (1758-1794), **St. Just, Couthon** (these three in July); **Carnot,** who concerned himself exclusively with military matters; **Collot d'Herbois** (Sept.). The third power in the state was the **commune of Paris,** now reorganized on the basis of manhood suffrage and acting through its committee (reduced to 20) at the Hôtel de Ville. Leaders: **Chaumette** and **Hébert** (editor of *Le Père Duchesne*).

Financial difficulties: New issues of *assignats*, based on the lands of the emigrant nobles, the sale of which was ordered. Attempts to check depreciation of the *assignats* by severe penalties.

June 2. Arrest of 31 Girondist deputies, forced on the Convention by an uprising engineered by the Commune and the Jacobin "machine," with the National Guard, commanded by Henriot. Brissot, Vergniaud, Pétion were among the victims. Complete domination of the Mountain, itself the organ of the Paris Commune.

June 22. The Constitution of 1793, an out-and-out democratic system, was sent to the primary assemblies for ratification, but was never actually put into effect.

July 13. Assassination of **Marat** by **Charlotte Corday,** an ardently patriotic girl from the provinces.

1793-1794. THE REIGN OF TERROR. Robespierre gradually came to dominate the whole government. He was never "dictator" in the modern sense, being checked by his colleagues in the Committee of Public Safety, by the opposing Hébertist faction in the Commune and Convention, and by the commissioners of the Convention sent into the provinces (*représentants en mission*). These commissioners, sent out to suppress counter-revolutionary movements, were often responsible for extreme terrorism in their districts. They collaborated with the local Jacobin Clubs and revolutionary committees (*comités de surveillance, comités révolutionnaires*). Horrors perpetrated by Tallien at Bordeaux, Lebon at Arras, Carrier at Nantes, Couthon, Fouché, Collot d'Herbois at Lyons. Some commissioners, however, were fairly clement and spared their regions (the younger Robespierre in the east and south, Lakanal in the southwest).

1793, July. Mainz recovered by the Prussians after a three months' siege.

The Allies also took Condé and Valenciennes. Custine executed by the French for negligence. **British siege of Toulon.** The troops of the republic were driven back on almost all fronts, with the result that revolts multiplied in the interior, frequently inspired by Girondists who had escaped the purge and had fled Paris. Energetic counter-measures of the Committee of Public Safety.

Aug. 23. Levy of the entire male population capable of bearing arms. Fourteen armies hastily organized and put in the field. Caen, Bordeaux, Marseilles conquered by the republicans.

Sept. 17. Establishment of the maximum price for a large number of commodities; fixation of wages. The system was never fully worked out and the *maximum* was frequently violated. It did, however, prevent a catastrophic fall of the *assignats* and insured the provisioning of the armies. The whole experiment was less a socialistic measure than a method of rationing goods during an emergency.

Oct. Lyons captured after a two months' siege. The city was partially destroyed and large numbers of the inhabitants were massacred.

Oct. 16. Execution of Marie Antoinette.

Oct. 20. Defeat of the Vendéans at Chollet, and at **Le Mans** (Dec. 12). Revolutionary tribunal at Nantes (15,000 put to death in three months by Carrier: *noyades, fusillades, mariages républicains*).

Oct. 31. Execution of the Girondists (21). Reign of the revolutionary tribunals and the guillotine (Place de la Révolution, now Place de la Concorde). Fouquier-Tinville, public prosecutor. Neglect of legal forms; sixty executions a month (including Bailly, Philippe Egalité, Madame Roland, etc.).

Nov. 10. Abolition of the worship of God. Cult of Reason (Hébert, Chaumette, Cloots). Profanation of the royal sepulchre at St. Denis.

Revolutionary calendar, dating from the year one of the revolution (Sept. 22, 1792). The months: Vendémiaire, Brumaire, Frimaire; Nivose, Pluviose, Ventose; Germinal, Floréal, Prairial; Messidor, Thermidor, Fructidor. Each month had 30 days, leaving five intercalary days (*sans culottides*) in the year. Every tenth day a holiday.

Creation of the new army, really an amalgamation of recruits with loyal elements of the old army. Successes of the new forces throughout the autumn, under Jourdan, Hoche, and Pichegru.

Dec. Retreat of the Allies across the Rhine. The French captured Worms and Speier, and took Toulon from the British (first appearance of **Napoleon Bonaparte,** a young artillery officer, closely connected with Robespierre and Jacobins).

1704. Robespierre (representing the Committee of Public Safety) finally succeeded in crushing the rival powers represented by Hébert and Danton. Playing off Danton against the Hébertists, he encompassed

Mar. 24. The execution of the leaders (Hébert, Chaumette, Cloots, etc.). Thereupon he turned on the Dantonists, whose past gave ample opening for accusation.

Apr. 6. Execution of Danton, Desmoulins, Hérault de Sechelles, etc.

Apr. 19. Treaty of the Hague between England and Prussia, England paying subsidies for 60,000 men.

May 18. Victory of Pichegru's army at Turcoing.

June 8. Festival of the Supreme Being, a cult of which Robespierre was the high-priest, having abolished the cult of reason.

June 10. Law of 22 Prairial, bestowing great power on the revolutionary tribunal: juries to convict without hearing evidence or argument. Tremendous increase of executions (up to 354 a month).

June 25. Capture of Charleroi by the French.

June 26. BATTLE OF FLEURUS, a French victory which obliged the Duke of Coburg to evacuate Belgium.

July. Conspiracy against Robespierre, by members of the Mountain and by the more moderate elements (Tallien, Fréron, Fouché, Collot d'Herbois, Billaud-Varennes). This was due to jealousy of Robespierre within the Committee of Public Safety, and to rivalry between the two "great committees."

July 27 (9 Thermidor). **FALL OF ROBESPIERRE.** He and his brother, as well as Couthon and St. Just, were arrested. Being released by friends, they were outlawed, surprised at the Hôtel de Ville, and executed, with 18 others. On the following days over 80 of the party met the same fate. The Paris Commune was nearly extinct. This *coup d'état* was carried through by disparate elements, personal enemies of Robespierre, who were opposed to his effort to make France a "republic of virtue." The objective was to remove Robespierre, not to end the Terror. Public opinion, however, forced them to adopt more moderate policies.

1794-1795. End of the Terror. The convention dominated by the moderates (*Thermidoreans*), who gradually broke the power not only of the Commune, but of the Jacobin Clubs (the Paris Club closed Nov. 12).

Dec. 8. The Girondists who had escaped with their lives were readmitted to the Convention.

Dec. 24. Repeal of the maximum. New issues of *assignats*; increased depreciation.

1795, Apr. 1 (Germinal 12). **Bread riots in Paris;** attack on the Convention suppressed; transportation of Billaud, Collot, Barrère, Vadier, and other radicals. Growing reaction in the capital and throughout the country. *Jeunesse dorée*; revival of monarchist agitation; return of some of the *émigré* nobility; the **White Terror.**

May 20 (Prairial 1). Further riots and outbreaks. Fierce attack on the Convention. Firmness of the president, Boissy d'Anglas. The movement was finally gotten in hand and resulted only in the extermination of the remnants of the Mountain.

Meanwhile the armies had been uniformly successful. Having overrun Belgium, Pichegru invaded Holland in the winter of 1794–1795, the Prince of Orange-Nassau fleeing to England (p. 440).

1795-1806. THE BATAVIAN REPUBLIC founded by the French. Flanders was surrendered to France.

1795, Mar. 5. TREATY OF BASEL between France and Prussia. Prussia, financially exhausted and at odds with Austria, withdrew from the war. Saxony, Hanover, and Hesse-Cassel followed suit. France was to retain the left bank of the Rhine until peace should be concluded with the empire, but was to evacuate the right bank. Northern Germany was to be neutralized. Secret articles: Prussia consented to the absolute cession of the left bank to France and was given assurance of compensation through secularization of ecclesiastical territory on the right bank. On June 22 Spain and France concluded peace at Basel, Spain ceding St. Domingo but recovering other lost territories.

June 8. Death of the dauphin (Louis XVII, ten years old) in the Temple. Later numerous pretending dauphins appeared, even in the United States. The death of the dauphin is, however, as certain as such matters can ever be.

June 27. Landing of the British and *émigrés* at Quiberon (Brittany) to aid the royalists of the region (*Chouans*).

July 16-21. Victories of Hoche over the invaders. Over 700 *émigrés* executed. Retaliatory massacre of 1000 republican prisoners by Charette.

Aug. 22. The Constitution of 1795 (third of the revolution): the executive power vested in a directory of five; legislature of two chambers (*Council of Elders*, or Ancients, 250; *Council of Five Hundred*); for the first term, two-thirds of the members of both houses were to be taken from the rolls of the Convention. This self-protective proviso led to opposition in Paris and the provinces. The Paris royalists instigated an outbreak of the sections. On the motion of Barras, the Convention placed Gen. Bonaparte in charge of its troops.

Oct. 5. (Vendemiaire 13). **The Day of the Sections.** Bonaparte's "whiff of grape-shot." Cannonade from the church of St. Roch. Complete victory of the Convention.

Oct. 26. The Convention dissolved, after voting that relatives of *émigrés* should not be permitted to hold office.

5. THE DIRECTORY

1795-1799. THE DIRECTORY. The new government, much maligned by historians and frequently accused of dishonesty and corruption, was faced by an acute financial crisis, the *assignats* having fallen to a fraction of one per cent of their face value. Substitution of *mandats territoriaux*, convertible into a specified amount of land, for the *assignats*. The *mandats* in turn depreciated almost at once.

1796, Mar. 5. Final suppression of the insurrection in the Vendée and in Brittany, by Hoche.

In the **war against the empire**, the Directory, on advice of Carnot, arranged for a triple attack: (1) The Army of the Sambre and Meuse, under **Jourdan**, was to advance from the lower Rhine to Franconia; (2) The Army of the Rhine and the Moselle, under **Moreau**, was to penetrate from the upper Rhine into Swabia and Bavaria; (3) the Army of Italy, under **Bonaparte**, was to drive the Austrians out of Italy and unite with the other armies by way of the Tyrol.

1796. The campaign in Germany. Jourdan and Moreau invaded South Germany, and Baden, Württemberg, and Bavaria were obliged to conclude truces (Aug.), but suddenly the **Archduke Charles** (brother of Emperor Francis II) took the offensive against Jourdan and defeated him at **Amberg** (Aug.) and **Würzburg** (Sept. 3). Jourdan resigned his command. The archduke then turned on Moreau, who retreated through the Black Forest to the upper Rhine.

1796, Mar. 9. Marriage of Bonaparte with Josephine de Beauharnais, former friend of Barras and one of the lights of Paris society.

1796-1797.   BONAPARTE'S   ITALIAN CAMPAIGN. Following the coast from Nice, he defeated the Austrians at **Millesimo** (Apr. 13) and the Piedmontese at **Mondovi** (Apr. 22), compelling Victor Amadeus to conclude a separate peace with France: Savoy and Nice ceded to the French Republic, and the French given the right to garrison Piedmontese fortresses. Napoleon then pursued the Austrians, whom he defeated in

1796, May 10.   The battle of Lodi (storming of the bridge over the Adda).

May 15.   Napoleon entered Milan, and then conquered all Lombardy as far as Mantua. The Dukes of Parma and Modena, the pope and the King of Naples purchased truces at the price of large payments in money and art treasures.

May 16.   Napoleon set up the Lombard Republic.

July-1797, Feb.   Siege of Mantua by the French. Four attempts by the Austrians to relieve the fortress. They were defeated in the **battles of Castiglione** (Aug. 15), Roveredo, Bassano, and in

Nov. 15-19.   The battle of Arcola, and 1797, Jan. 14.   The battle of Rivoli.

Feb. 2.   Mantua surrendered, and Napoleon started on an advance to Rome. The pope thereupon hastily concluded with him

Feb. 19.   The Treaty of Tolentino, ceding the Romagna, Bologna, and Ferrara.

Mar.-Apr.   Bonaparte crossed the Alps to meet the Archduke Charles, advancing from Germany. The inhabitants of Venetia rose against the French, and in the Tyrol too the population was called to arms. In danger of being cut off, Bonaparte opened negotiations which led to

Apr. 18.   THE PRELIMINARY PEACE OF LEOBEN: Austria ceded the Belgian provinces to France; a congress was to arrange peace between France and the empire on the basis of the integrity of imperial territory; Austria ceded the region beyond the Oglio, receiving in return the Venetian territory between the Oglio, Po, and Adriatic (which she was to conquer for herself), Venetian Dalmatia and Istria, and the fortresses of Mantua, Peschiera, and Palma Nova. **Venice** was to be indemnified with the Romagna, Bologna, and Ferrara. Austria recognized the **Cisalpine Republic** which was to be formed in northern Italy.

May. The French declared **war upon Venice,** under pretext of an outbreak at Verona. Abolition of the aristocracy and establishment of popular government. Occupation of the republic by French troops; also of the Venetian islands of Greece (Ionian).

July 9. Proclamation of the **Cisalpine Republic** (Milan, Modena, Ferrara, Bologna, Romagna). Transformation of the Republic of Genoa into the **Ligurian Republic** under French control.

Sept. 4 (18th Fructidor).   **COUP D'ÉTAT AT PARIS.** Victory of the republican party over the party of reaction, which was represented in the Council of Five Hundred, in the Council of Ancients, and in the Directory. The three republican directors, Barras, Rewbel, and La Révellière defeated their colleagues, Barthélemy and Carnot. The latter escaped by flight; Barthélemy and many of his adherents, including Pichegru, were transported to Cayenne.

Oct. 17.   TREATY OF CAMPO FORMIO. (1) Austria ceded the Belgian provinces to France. (2) A congress was convened at **Rastadt** to discuss peace with the empire. (3) Austria received the territory of Venice as far as the Adige, with the city of Venice, Istria, and Dalmatia. (4) France retained the **Ionian Islands.** (5) Austria recognized the Cisalpine Republic and indemnified the Duke of Modena with the Breisgau. Secret articles: (1) Austria agreed to the cession of the **left bank of the Rhine** from Basel to Andernach, including Mainz, to France; the navigation of the Rhine was left open to France and Germany in common; those princes who lost by the cession were to receive indemnification in Germany. (2) France was to use her influence to secure to Austria, **Salzburg,** and that portion of Bavaria which lay between Salzburg, the Tyrol, the Inn, and the Salza. (3) Reciprocal guaranty that Prussia should not receive any new acquisition of territory in return for her cession on the left bank of the Rhine.

1796-1801. PAUL I, Emperor of Russia, succeeded his mother Catharine II (p. 482).

1797-1840. FREDERICK WILLIAM III, King of Prussia.

1797, Dec.-1799, Apr. Congress of Rastadt. No agreement.

1798, Feb. The French occupied Rome. Proclamation of the **Roman Republic.** Captivity of the pope, **Pius VI** (p. 457).

Apr. French invasion of Switzerland. Organization of the **Helvetian Republic** (p. 460). Geneva annexed to France.

1798-1799. BONAPARTE'S EGYPTIAN EXPEDITION, prepared under the mask of an invasion of England (*Army of England* concentrated at Boulogne). Napoleon, having convinced himself of the impracticability of crossing the Channel, persuaded the Directory to deliver a blow at England's Indian empire, by way of Egypt, a country which had long attracted the interest of French political writers. Napoleon sailed from Toulon with 35,000 men and a corps of scientists (May 19, 1798), surprised and took **Malta** (June 12), and landed in Egypt (July 1). **Capture of Alexandria** (July 2).

July 21. BATTLE OF THE PYRAMIDS, outside Cairo. The French easily defeated the mediaeval Mamluk cavalry, and took Cairo (July 22).

Aug. 1. BATTLE OF THE NILE. The British admiral, **Horatio Nelson,** having sought the French in vain throughout the eastern Mediterranean, finally located the French fleet in the harbor of **Abukir,** east of Alexandria. Without much difficulty he managed to destroy the fleet, which, being crowded in the anchorage, was unable to maneuver. Thus Nelson cut Napoleon and his force off from France.

1799, Feb. The Syrian campaign. The Ottoman government having declared war on France, Napoleon invaded Syria, stormed **Jaffa** (massacre of 1200 prisoners), but was frustrated in his efforts to take **Acre.** Outbreak of plague in the French army; hasty retreat to Egypt.

July 25. Battle of Abukir. The Turks, supported by the British, had landed at Abukir, but they were completely defeated by Napoleon and Murat.

Napoleon left Egypt (Aug. 24) to return to France. **Kléber** in command. After long negotiations, he concluded with the Turks the **Convention of El Arish** (Jan. 24, 1800), providing for evacuation of the French forces. This was opposed by the English. Kléber was assassinated (June) and succeeded by Menou, whom the English defeated at Alexandria (Mar. 21, 1801). The French force was repatriated and, by the **Treaty of Amiens** (p. 590), Egypt was restored to the sultan.

6. WAR OF THE SECOND COALITION

1798, Dec. 24. Alliance between Russia and Great Britain, to which Austria, Naples, Portugal, and the Ottoman Empire adhered. This **Second Coalition** against France was the work primarily of Paul I of Russia, whom the Knights of Malta had elected as grand master.

Plan of campaign: An Anglo-Russian army under the Duke of York was to drive the French from the Netherlands; an Austrian army under Archduke Charles was to expel them from Germany and Switzerland; a Russo-Austrian army was to force the French out of Italy.

A Neapolitan army, commanded by the Austrian general, Mack, had attacked the Roman Republic and occupied the city of Rome (Nov. 29), thus beginning hostilities. The French, under Championnet, recaptured the city (Dec. 15) and then overran the entire Kingdom of Naples; Ferdinand was obliged to flee to Sicily, while the French proclaimed

1799, Jan. 23. The Parthenopean Republic, a client state of France. Even before this (Nov.–Dec. 1798) Gen. Joubert had conquered Piedmont and forced the king to flee to Sardinia (Dec. 9). On Mar. 25, 1799 the Grand Duke of Tuscany was driven from his dominions and the French occupied Florence.

Mar. 25. The Archduke Charles defeated Jourdan and the army of the upper Rhine, at **Stockach.** Jourdan retreated across the Rhine and laid down his command. His army and that of the middle Rhine (Bernadotte) were united under command of **Masséna.**

Apr. 5. Battle of Magnano, in which the French army of Italy, under Schérer, was defeated by the Austrians under Kray. **Moreau** succeeded to the command, but was in turn defeated in the

Apr. 27. Battle of Cassano, by the Austrian general Melas and the Russian army under Suvorov. The Allies entered Milan and extinguished the Cisalpine Republic. In the meanwhile,

Apr. 8. The congress of Rastadt had been dissolved. Mysterious murder of the French delegates, Roberjot, and Bonnier, on their way home, by Austrian hussars (Apr. 28).

May 27. Suvorov occupied Turin, and shut up remnants of Moreau's Army in Genoa.

June 4-7. BATTLE OF ZURICH. The Archduke Charles defeated Masséna.

June 17-19. BATTLE OF THE TREBBIA. Suvorov defeated the French army under MacDonald, which had hurried north from Naples. In the interval the King of Naples returned from Sicily and overthrew the Parthenopean Republic (ruthless vengeance, with massacres). The Roman Republic met with the same fate. The Directory now sent to Italy Gen. Joubert with a new army.

Aug. 15. BATTLE OF NOVI. Suvorov and Melas completely defeated Joubert as he attempted to advance from Genoa. Joubert himself was killed.

Suvorov then crossed the Alps by the St. Gothard Pass in order to unite with the second Russian army under Korsakov, who had taken the place of the Archduke Charles in Switzerland.

Sept. 26. Korsakov was defeated and driven out of Zürich by Masséna. Suvorov was unable to recover the position in Switzerland and was obliged to fall back to the Grisons with an army decimated by starvation and want. Masséna took Constance and threatened the flank of the Archduke Charles, who was preparing the invasion of France from the Rhine.

Oct. 18. Convention of Alkmar, by which the British surrendered all prisoners taken in Holland, in return for unobstructed evacuation. The campaign in Holland had been an unqualified failure. The British and Russians had not cooperated effectively and the French, under Brune, had more than held their own in the fighting around Bergen (Sept. 19).

Oct. 22. The Russians withdrew from the coalition, disgusted with the conduct of their allies, especially the Austrians. In the interval (May, 1799) a Russian-Turkish fleet had wrested the Ionian Isles from French control. The islands were organized as a republic (**Septinsular Republic**) under Turkish protection and under Russian guaranty. The Russians occupied them until 1807.

Nov. 9 (18 Brumaire). **THE COUP D'ÉTAT OF BRUMAIRE.** Napoleon had landed at Fréjus unannounced from Egypt (Oct. 8) and had effected an alliance with the directors Siéyès and Roger-Ducos. With the aid of his brother Lucien (president of the Council of Five Hundred), he overthrew the Directory and broke up the council on the following day.

7. THE CONSULATE

1799-1804. THE CONSULATE, representing a new system worked out by Siéyès in conjunction with Napoleon. Napoleon was first consul (term ten years) and was assisted by two other consuls appointed by him (Cambacérès and Lebrun), who had only consultative powers.

1799, Dec. 24. Constitution of the Year VIII, which was submitted to popular vote (3,011,107 in favor; 1567 opposed). It preserved the appearance of the republic, but in reality established the **dictatorship of Napoleon.** Below the consuls were the following institutions: the *Senate* (80), appointed for life from lists of names sent in by the departments, legislative bodies, higher officials; the *Tribunate* (100), which discussed measures submitted by the government, but without voting on them; the *Legislative Chamber* (300), which

accepted or rejected these measures, but without debate; the *Council of State,* appointed by the first consul and his chief support in the work of legislation.

The people voted for notables of the communes, who then elected one-tenth of their own number as notables of the departments, of whom one-tenth again became notables of France. From this final sifting were chosen, by the Senate, the members of the legislative bodies.

Establishment of prefectures (administration of the departments) and **subprefectures** (for the districts or *arrondissements*). The administration was gradually centralized. **New system of tax-collection:** a *receveur-général* for each department, and a *receveur particulier* for each *arrondissement.*

The new system, which proved to be highly efficient and which has, to a large extent, been retained to the present day, owed much to experiments and experience of the revolutionary assemblies and the Directory. The civil service was recruited largely from former Jacobins. In his policy Napoleon, as first consul, followed closely the course marked out by his predecessors. **Napoleon's offers of peace.** These were rejected by the Allies, though Russia had left the coalition. Defensive alliance between Russia and Sweden (1799); drawing together of Russia and Prussia. Friction between Russia and England over Malta. Renewal of the **armed neutrality** of 1780. Northern Convention (1800).

1800. RENEWAL OF THE CAMPAIGN AGAINST AUSTRIA. In Italy the Austrians, having defeated Masséna at **Voltri**, advanced to Nice (Apr.). Obstinate **defense of Genoa** by Masséna and Soult. Capitulation of the city (June 4) after a horrible famine.

May. Napoleon crossed the St. Bernard Pass with 40,000 men, to attack the flank of the Austrians.

June 2. The French took Milan and restored the Cisalpine Republic.

June 14. BATTLE OF MARENGO, a great victory won by Napoleon, but by an extremely narrow margin. Truce between Napoleon and Melas: all fortresses west of the Mincio and south of the Po were surrendered to the French.

In Germany, Moreau was in command. He had crossed the Rhine in April and had advanced into southern Germany.

July. Moreau took Munich, after which operations were suspended for some months, causing dissatisfaction on both sides.

Dec. 3. BATTLE OF HOHENLINDEN. Moreau completely defeated the Archduke John, who had been appointed to take the place of his brother Charles. The French then advanced to Linz. Another army, under MacDonald, advanced into Tyrol, and in Jan. 1801 Brune, with the Army of Italy, crossed the Adige and began the invasion of Austria from the south. This decided the emperor to make peace.

1801, Feb. 9. TREATY OF LUNEVILLE, which practically involved the destruction of the Holy Roman Empire. **Conditions:** (1) Ratification of the cessions made by Austria and to her in the Treaty of Campo Formio (p. 595). (2) Cession of the Grand Duchy of Tuscany (Austrian *secundogeniture*) to Parma, to be indemnified in Germany. (3) The emperor and empire consented to the cession of the left bank of the Rhine to France, the valley of the Rhine (i.e. the middle of the river), the

boundary. The princes who lost by this operation received indemnification in Germany. (4) Recognition of the Batavian, Helvetian, Cisalpine, and Ligurian Republics. Germany lost by this peace, taking the Belgic territory into account, 25,180 square miles with almost 3,500,000 inhabitants. The German princes received an increase of territory. The negotiations over the indemnifications lasted more than two years (p. 590), during which time the ambassadors of German princes haunted the antechambers of the first consul to beg for better terms, and bribed French ambassadors, secretaries, and their mistresses.

Tuscany was transformed into the **Kingdom of Etruria,** for the satisfaction of Parma. Besides losing Parma (a Spanish *secundogeniture*), Spain ceded **Louisiana** to France, which afterward sold it to the United States (1803). The Treaty of Lunéville was succeeded, after conclusion of a truce, by the

Mar. 18. Treaty of Florence with Naples. **Conditions:** (1) Closure of the harbors to British and Turkish vessels. (2) Cession of the Neapolitan possessions in central Italy and the island of Elba. (3) Reception of French garrisons in several Italian towns.

Prussia joined the Northern Convention against England. **Occupation of Hanover.**

1801–1825. ALEXANDER I, Tsar of Russia. Reconciliation between Russia and England (in 1801 England had attacked Denmark, the ally of Russia, and forced her to withdraw from the Northern Convention). The Northern Convention was now dissolved.

1801. CONCORDAT BETWEEN FRANCE AND THE PAPACY, concluded after long and trying negotiations. This was part of Napoleon's policy of pacification. The concordat provided that French archbishops and bishops should be appointed by the government, but confirmed by the pope. Clergy paid by the government. The pope agreed to accept as valid the titles of those who had bought former church property confiscated by the revolutionary government. **Pius VII** (elected 1800) was given possession of the Papal States, but without Ferrara, Bologna, and the Romagna. The liberties of the Gallican Church were strongly asserted. By the new organization of the **Université,** an incorporated body of teachers who had passed a state examination, the entire system of higher education was made dependent upon the government. The **Institut National** was reorganized and divided

The House of Bonaparte

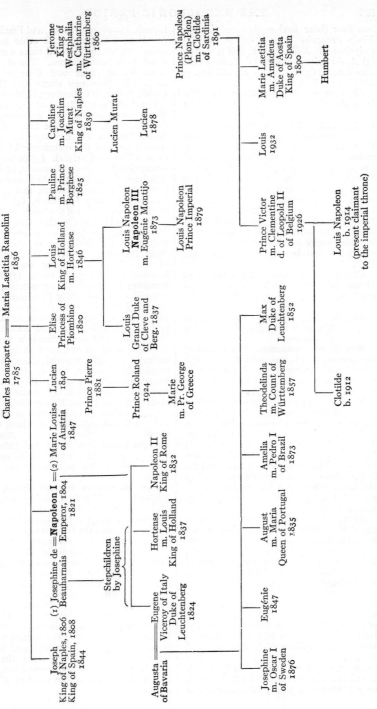

Dates, unless otherwise indicated, are death dates.

into four (later five) academies: (1) *Académie Française* (1635); (2) *A. des Inscriptions et Belles-Lettres* (1663, 1701); (3) *A. des Sciences* (1666); (4) *A. des Beaux Arts* (1648); (5) *A. des Sciences Morales et Politiques* (1832).

After the withdrawal of the younger Pitt from the English cabinet, and after long negotiations, the

1802, Mar. 27. TREATY OF AMIENS was concluded between England and France, thus achieving a complete pacification of Europe. (1) Surrender of all conquests made by England to France and her allies, excepting Trinidad, which was ceded by Spain, and Ceylon, which was ceded by the Batavian Republic. (2) France recognized the Republic of the Seven Ionian Islands. Malta must be restored to the Order of the Knights of Malta. In consequence of this treaty, peace was concluded also between France and the Porte.

Creation of the **Order of the Legion of Honor** (May 19, 1802). Assumption of regal state and authority. By a popular vote (*plébiscite*, 3½ millions),

Aug. 2. Napoleon became consul for life, with the right of appointing his successor.

New (fifth) constitution. The powers of the Senate, which was ruled by the first consul, were enlarged; the importance of the legislative bodies and the Tribunate was very decidedly reduced.

Napoleon had already become president of the **Italian Republic,** as the Cisalpine Republic was henceforward called. Elba and Piedmont were annexed to France. Military interference of the French in Switzerland, which was torn with civil dissensions. The **act of mediation** restored the independence of the separate cantons, but the country remained still so far a single state that it was represented by a landamman and a diet.

As regards the internal relations of Germany, the Treaty of Lunéville was executed according to a plan of indemnification established by France and Russia by the

1803, Feb. Enactment of the delegates of the empire (*Reichsdeputationshauptschluss*): Of the ecclesiastical estates there were left only: (1) The former Elector of Mainz, now Electoral Archchancellor, with a territory formed out of the remains of the Archbishopric of Mainz on the right bank of the Rhine, the Bishopric of Regensburg, and the cities of Regensburg, and Wezlar. (2) The masters of the Order of St. John, and the Teutonic Order. (3) Of the 48 free imperial cities which still existed, only 6 were left, (the 3 Hanseatic cities:

Lübeck, Hamburg, Bremen, and Frankfurt, Augsburg, Nürnberg). All other ecclesiastical estates and imperial cities were devoted to indemnifications. The electoral bishoprics of Trier and Cologne were abolished. Four new electorates: Hesse-Cassel, Baden, Württemberg, Salzburg.

Principal Indemnifications: (1) To the **Grand Duke of Tuscany:** Salzburg, and Berchtesgaden. (2) To the **Duke of Modena:** Breisgau (in exchange for which Austria received the ecclesiastical foundations of Trent and Brixen). (3) To **Bavaria:** Bishoprics of Würzburg, Bamberg, Freising, Augsburg, the majority of the prelacies and imperial cities in Franconia and eastern Swabia, in return for which, (4) **Baden** received that portion of the Palatinate lying on the right bank of the Rhine (Heidelberg, Mannheim). Baden also received: the portion of the Bishoprics of Constance, Basel, Strassburg, Speier, on the left bank of the Rhine, and many ecclesiastical foundations and imperial cities. (5) **Württemberg:** many abbeys, monasteries, and imperial cities, especially Reutlingen, Esslingen, Heilbronn, etc. (6) **Prussia:** the Bishoprics of Paderborn, Hildesheim, the part of Thuringia which had belonged to Mainz (Eichfeld and Erfurt), a part of Münster, many abbeys, particularly Quedlinburg, and the imperial cities, Mühlhausen, Nordhausen, Goslar. (7) **Oldenburg:** Bishopric of Lübeck. (8) **Hanover:** Bishopric of Osnabrück. (9) **Hesse** (Darmstadt and Cassel) and **Nassau** divided the portions of the Archbishoprics of Mainz, Trier, and Cologne, which remained, upon the right bank of the Rhine. (10) **Nassau-Orange:** Bishopric of Fulda, and Abbey of Corvey. As a rule the indemnified princes gained considerably in territory and subjects.

New dissensions between France and England, caused by the refusal to surrender Malta and the quarrels of the journalists. The French occupied Hanover, where they nearly exhausted the resources of the state. The encampment at **Boulogne** threatened England with an invasion.

1804, Feb. Conspiracy against the life of the first consul discovered. Pichegru met a mysterious death in prison, **Georges Cadoudal** was executed. **Moreau** fled to America. The **Duke of Enghien,** a Bourbon prince of the branch line of Condé, was taken by violence from the territory of Baden, condemned by a commission acting in accordance with the wishes and under the order of Napoleon, without the observation of the ordinary forms of law, and shot at Vincennes on the night of March 20–21.

8. THE FIRST EMPIRE

1804-1814 (1815). **NAPOLEON I,** Emperor of the French. He was proclaimed by the Senate and Tribunate on May 18, and consecrated at Paris by Pope Pius VII on Dec. 2. Napoleon placed the crown on his own head (in imitation of Pepin and Charlemagne). His elevation was ratified by a plebiscite (3,572,329 in favor, 2569 opposed). The imperial office was made hereditary, succession to be in the male line and the emperor having the right to adopt the children of his brothers; in default of such children, the crown was to pass to Napoleon's brothers, Joseph and Louis.

Napoleon at once established a brilliant court: grand dignitaries of the Empire; the eighteen marshals of France; development of a new nobility, with many of the privileges of the old, but based on achievement rather than on birth. Napoleon really revived the absolute monarchy, but on a more modern and efficient basis.

1805. Napoleon made himself King of Italy. His stepson, Eugène Beauharnais, became viceroy of Italy. The **Ligurian Republic** was incorporated with France.

9. THE WAR OF THE THIRD COALITION

1805. Formation of the Third Coalition against France. England had been at war with France since May 16, 1803, and was now joined by Austria, Russia, and Sweden. Spain was allied with France.

Napoleon hastily broke up the camp of Boulogne and shelved his plans (genuine or pretended) for an invasion of England. The French armies, under Davout, Soult, Lannes, and Ney, marched quickly to the Rhine to meet the Austrian armies under Archduke Ferdinand and Gen. Mack. In Italy, Masséna commanded the French against the main Austrian army under Archduke Charles. Napoleon then took over the chief command in Germany, crossed the Rhine and marched toward Bavaria, which had been invaded by the Austrians. Bavaria, Würtemberg, Baden, Hesse, and Nassau supported the French.

Oct. 17. Mack was obliged to surrender at **Ulm,** with an army of 30,000 men, whom the French had surrounded.

Oct. 21. BATTLE OF TRAFALGAR, a great victory of **Nelson** (who died of wounds) over the combined French and Spanish fleets. This victory broke the naval power of France and established Britain as the mistress of the seas throughout the 19th century.

The French, after Ulm, marched down the course of the Danube and took **Vienna** without meeting much resistance. In Italy the Archduke Charles was driven back by Masséna, and returned to Germany. In the meanwhile, however, a Russian army under Kutusov, and a second under **Tsar Alexander I** came to the aid of the Austrians in Moravia.

Dec. 2. BATTLE OF AUSTERLITZ (*battle of the three emperors*), one of the greatest victories of Napoleon. The combined Austrian and Russian armies were defeated, the Austrians hastily agreed to a truce, and the Russians retreated.

Dec. 15. Treaty between **Prussia and France.** The Prussians had been on the point of joining the coalition, but after Austerlitz agreed to cede to France the remaining part of Cleve on the left bank of the Rhine, and also Ansbach and Neuchâtel, in return for Hanover.

Dec. 26. TREATY OF PRESSBURG, between France and Austria. (1) **France** received Piedmont, Parma, and Piacenza. (2) **Austria** ceded to the Kingdom of Italy all that she had received of Venetian territory by the Treaty of Campo Formio, as well as Venetian Istria and Dalmatia; Austria also recognized Napoleon as King of Italy. (3) **Austria** ceded to Bavaria the Tyrol, Vorarlberg, the Bishoprics of Brixen and Trent, Burgau, Eichstädt, Passau, Lindau; **Bavaria** also received the free city of Augsburg. (4) **Austria** ceded to Württemberg and Baden what remained of the western lands of the Hapsburgs. (5) **Württemberg** and Baden were recognized as kingdoms. (6) **Austria** was indemnified by being given Salzburg, Berchtesgaden, and the estates of the Teutonic Order, which were secularized. The Elector of

Salzburg received from Bavaria Würzburg as compensation.

Dec. The **Bourbons** in Naples were dethroned by a proclamation of Napoleon from Schönbrunn (*La dynastie de Naples a cessé de régner*).

1806. **Joseph Bonaparte,** elder brother of Napoleon, became King of Naples. The Bourbons withdrew to Sicily, where they enjoyed the protection of the British fleet.

Joachim Murat, brother-in-law of Napoleon, was created Grand Duke of Berg; Marshal Berthier became Prince of Neuchâtel; **Louis,** third brother of Napoleon, became King of Holland (the former Batavian Republic).

July 12. **THE CONFEDERATION OF THE RHINE,** organized under French auspices. Napoleon was protector. **Members:** the Prince Primate, formerly electoral arch-chancellor; the Kings of Bavaria and Württemberg; the Grand Dukes of Baden, Hesse, Darmstadt, Berg; the Duke of Nassau, etc. Afterward all German princes joined the confederation except Austria, Prussia, Brunswick, and the Elector of Hesse. Thus a large part of Germany came under French domination. Territorial changes were constantly made: many princes who held immediately of the empire were mediatized; Bavaria was given the free city of Nürnberg; Frankfurt passed to the Prince Primate (Grand Duke of Frankfurt).

Aug. 6. **END OF THE OLD HOLY ROMAN EMPIRE.** The Austrian emperor, Francis II, had already assumed the title of *Francis I, Emperor of Austria* (1804). He now laid down the old imperial crown.

1806-1807. **WAR AGAINST PRUSSIA AND RUSSIA.** Reasons for Prussia's entry into the war: Establishment of the Confederation of the Rhine; annexation of Wesel; seizure of Verden and Essen; garrisoning of French troops throughout half of Germany; Napoleon's offer to England to take Hanover away from Prussia (on whom he had forced it a short time before). The Prussians were also embittered by the high-handed execution of Palm, a book-seller of Nürnberg, who had published some strictures on Napoleon.

Dangerous position of Prussia at the outbreak of the conflict: the complete separation of the military and civil administration had resulted in the safety of the state resting on a half-trained army composed in part of foreigners, on a superannuated general, and on subordinate commanders who, overconfident in the

military fame of Prussia since the time of Frederick II, regarded the French with contempt. Prussia had no allies, excepting Saxony and far-off Russia. Relations with England were filled with dissension.

The Prussian army was commanded by the Duke of Brunswick, and was concentrated in Thuringia. As it advanced, it was defeated by the French at **Saalfeld** (Oct. 10) and then in the

Oct. 14. **BATTLES OF JENA AND AUERSTÄDT.** The main Prussian armies were completely routed and quickly fell to pieces. A reserve force under the Prince of Württemberg was defeated and scattered at **Halle** (Oct. 17).

Oct. 27. **Napoleon occupied Berlin.** The Prince of Hohenlohe and 12,000 men were forced to surrender at **Prenzlau** (Oct. 28). Blücher, after a valiant defense of Lübeck, was also obliged to surrender at Ratkau (Nov. 7). Hasty surrender of the fortresses of Erfurt, Spandau, Stettin, Küstrin, Magdeburg, Hameln; only Kolberg (Gneisenau, Schill, Nettelbeck) and Graudenz (Courbière) defended themselves resolutely.

Nov. 21. **BERLIN DECREE:** Napoleon proclaimed a (paper) **blockade of Great Britain** and closure of the Continent to British trade, thus inaugurating the *Continental System.*

The French, supported by the Bavarians and Württembergers, invaded Silesia and called on the Poles to revolt.

Dec. 11. **Separate peace between France and Saxony.** The elector became *king,* allied himself with France and joined the Confederation of the Rhine.

The war also became extended to the Near East. The French emissary, **Gen. Sebastiani,** induced the Turks to abandon the alliance with England and Russia. Deposition of the Russophil governors (*hospodars*) of Moldavia and Wallachia (Aug. 1806) resulted in

1806-1812. **WAR BETWEEN RUSSIA AND TURKEY.**

1807. **The French** captured most of the Hanseatic towns and took Breslau and most other fortresses of Silesia. In the meanwhile the Russians advanced to the aid of the Prussians. The combined armies fought against the French in the

Feb. 7-8. **Battle of Eylau,** a bloody but indecisive engagement. The armies then went into winter quarters. King Frederick William withdrew to Memel.

Feb. 17. A British squadron, under Admiral Duckworth, forced the **passage of the Dardanelles** and appeared before Constantinople. Duckworth was, however, obliged to retire with a loss of two ships (Mar. 3), because of the threatening preparations of the Turks, inspired by Sebastiani.

Mar. 18. The British occupied Alexandria, but, meeting with vigorous opposition from the Turkish forces, evacuated again on Sept. 25.

May 26. The French captured Danzig and, advancing eastward, fought

June 14. THE BATTLE OF FRIEDLAND against the Russians. The French were victorious and the Russians fell back. Napoleon then occupied Königsberg and all the country as far as the Niemen River. After the conclusion of a truce, Napoleon met Alexander I and Frederick William III on a raft in the Niemen and concluded

July 7-9. THE TREATIES OF TILSIT, between (A) France and Russia, and (B) France and Prussia.

A. (1) **Russia** recognized the Grand Duchy of Warsaw, which was formed from Polish territory acquired by Prussia through the partitions, under the King of Saxony. (2) Danzig restored to the condition of a free city. (3) A part of New East Prussia (Bialystock) ceded to Russia. (4) Russia recognized Joseph Bonaparte as King of Naples, Louis Bonaparte as King of Holland, Jerome Bonaparte as King of Westphalia, a new kingdom yet to be created; Russia, moreover, recognized the Confederation of the Rhine, and accepted the mediation of Napoleon in concluding peace with the Turks, while Napoleon accepted the like good offices from Alexander in regard to England. In a *secret article*, Alexander agreed to an alliance with France against England, in case the latter refused to accept the proffered peace.

B. (1) **Prussia** ceded: (a) to Napoleon for free disposal, all lands between the Rhine and Elbe; (b) to Saxony, the circle of Cottbus; (c) all lands taken from Poland since 1772 for the creation of a Duchy of Warsaw, also the city and territory of Danzig. (2) Prussia recognized the sovereignty of the three brothers of Napoleon. (3) All Prussian harbors and lands were closed to British ships and British trade until the conclusion of a peace with England. (4)

Prussia was to maintain a standing army of not more than 42,000 men. In regard to the restoration and evacuation of the Prussian provinces and fortresses, it was settled by the **Treaty of Königsberg** (July 12), that Prussia should first pay all arrears of war indemnities.

These indemnifications, fixed at 19 million francs by the Prussian calculations, were set at 120 millions by the French, which sum was raised to 140 millions in 1808. After 120 millions had been paid the fortresses were evacuated, excepting Stettin, Küstrin, and Glogau. Until this occurred the Prussian state, reduced as it was from 89,120 to 46,032 square miles, was obliged to support 150,000 French troops.

Aug. Foundation of the **Kingdom of Westphalia** (capital, Cassel) by a decree of Napoleon, who reserved for himself half of the domains.

Sept. High-handed proceeding of the English against Denmark, which had been summoned to join the Continental system. An English fleet bombarded Copenhagen, and carried off the Danish fleet. Alliance of Denmark with France. Russia declared war upon England. Stralsund and Rügen occupied by the French.

Nov. Portugal, which refused to join the Continental system, occupied by a French army under **Junot** (Duke of Abrantès). The royal family fled to Brazil.

Dec. 17. Milan Decree, reiterating the blockade against British trade. On paper, Napoleon had closed the entire European coastline to the British.

1808, Mar. Spain invaded by 100,000 Frenchmen under the pretext of guarding the coasts against the English. Charles IV (p. 452) abdicated in favor of his son Ferdinand, in consequence of an outbreak which had occurred against his favorite, Godoy. Father and son, with Godoy, were enticed by Napoleon to Bayonne and compelled to renounce the throne (May). Napoleon's brother Joseph became King of Spain, Murat taking the throne of Naples instead of Joseph. General uprising of the Spaniards.

10. THE PENINSULAR WAR

1808-1814. War of the British against the French in Portugal and Spain. The British landed in Portugal, under command of **Sir Arthur Wellesley** (later the Duke of Wellington) and defeated the

French under Junot at **Vimeiro** (Aug. 21, 1808). Nevertheless, Wellesley's successor, Gen. Dalrymple, instead of continuing the campaign, agreed to

Aug. 30. The Convention of Cintra, by

which Junot agreed to evacuate Portugal.
The **popular insurrection in Spain** (May, 1808) led to retirement of the French, under Murat, behind the Ebro. But on July 20 the French managed to recover Madrid. On the same day another French force, advancing toward Cadiz, was defeated by the insurgents and forced to capitulate at **Baylen.**

Sept. The **Congress of Erfurt**, a conference between Napoleon and Alexander I of Russia, attended also by four kings and thirty-four princes, mostly obsequious German satellites. Ostensible reinforcement of the Franco-Russian alliance. Napoleon at the height of his power and splendor. But in secret the French statesman, **Talleyrand**, was negotiating with Alexander behind Napoleon's back, to frustrate further measures against Austria. Immediately after the Erfurt meeting Napoleon proceeded to Spain in person, with an army of 150,000. He advanced at once upon Madrid (which the French had again abandoned), while his marshals defeated the Spaniards at **Burgos** (Nov. 10) and **Espinosa** (Nov. 11).

Dec. 13. **Madrid capitulated** to Napoleon. To distract the French from invasion of the south, the British, under Sir John Moore, invaded northwestern Spain from Portugal. Napoleon turned against him, forcing his retreat.

1809, Jan. 16. Battle of Corunna. Marshal **Soult**, succeeding Napoleon in the command, defeated and killed Moore. The British were forced to evacuate Spain. But in Spain guerrilla warfare continued: heroic **defense of Saragossa** (Palafox), which, however, was obliged to capitulate (Feb. 21). The French, meanwhile, invaded Portugal and took **Oporto**. To protect Lisbon, the British sent out Wellesley with reinforcements. Soult was driven out of Oporto, and the British again invaded northwestern Spain.

July 28. Battle of Talavera, an indecisive engagement, which, however, protected Portugal against further invasion. In the meanwhile the French pushed on with the conquest of the south.

Nov. 12. Battle of Ocana, in which the Spaniards were defeated. The French thereupon overran all Andalusia, excepting Cadiz.

11. THE WAR AGAINST AUSTRIA

After the disasters of 1805–1806, both Prussia and Austria undertook far-reaching political and social reforms, designed to modernize the state and develop greater strength for the further contest with Napoleon. In Prussia the greatest reformer was **Karl, Freiherr vom Stein** (1757–1831), assisted by **Hardenberg**. Reorganization of town government, liberation of industry from burdensome restrictions, abolition of hereditary serfdom, reform of taxation and the whole financial system. Reorganization of the army, on the basis of universal military service, by **Gneisenau, Grolmann, Boyen, Clausewitz, Scharnhorst.** Foundation of the **University of Berlin** (1810), by **Humboldt, Altenstein, Niebuhr,** and **Schleiermacher.** Fichte's famous *Addresses to the German Nation* (1807–1808), a tremendous stimulus to national feeling; foundation of the *Tugendbund*, a patriotic organization; development of gymnastics by **Jahn;** patriotic poems of **E. M. Arndt,** etc.

Similar, though less extensive, reforms were introduced in Austria, where **Count Stadion** became the leading figure. Reorganization of the army by **Archduke Charles.** The Austrians, impressed by the difficulties Napoleon was meeting with in Spain, and encouraged by the British, who promised subsidies, decided to take advantage of the situation.

1809, Apr. The **Archduke Charles** appealed to the whole German people to embark on a war of liberation, and with an army of 170,000 began the invasion of Bavaria. Only Tyrol heeded the appeal, and rose in revolt, under **Andreas Hofer.** Napoleon, having hurried back from Spain, engaged the Austrians in Bavaria (using German troops), drove the archduke across the Danube into Bohemia (battles of Abensberg, Landshut, Eckmühl, Regensburg, Apr. 19–23) and

May 13. The French took Vienna. Napoleon then crossed the island of Lobau, in the Danube, and fought the

May 21–22. BATTLE OF ASPERN AND ESSLING. Napoleon was defeated and forced to recross the Danube, where he united his forces with those of the Italian viceroy, **Eugene**, who had driven the Austrians, under Archduke John, from Italy into Hungary. With the combined forces Napoleon recrossed the river and defeated Archduke Charles in the

July 5-6. BATTLE OF WAGRAM. The Austrians, completely exhausted, agreed to the

Oct. 14. TREATY OF SCHÖNBRUNN: Austria lost 32,000 square miles of territory, with 3,500,000 inhabitants, as follows: (1) to **Bavaria:** Salzburg and Berchtesgaden, the Innviertel and half of the Hausrückviertel; (2) to the **Grand Duchy of Warsaw:** West Galicia; (3) to **Russia:** the Tarnopol section of East Galicia; (4) to **France:** all the lands beyond the Save River (circle of Villach, Istria, Hungarian Dalmatia, and Ragusa). These territories were, together with the Ionian Islands (ceded to France by Russia in 1807), organized by Napoleon as a new state, the **Illyrian Provinces,** under **Marmont** as Duke of Ragusa. Austria further joined the Continental system and agreed to break off all connections with England.

The **Tyrolese,** left to themselves, continued the war against the Bavarians and French with heroic courage, but in the end they were subdued. In Nov. 1809, **Hofer was captured and shot** by the French at Mantua. Southern Tyrol was annexed to the Kingdom of Italy.

Similar **outbreaks in Germany** ended likewise in disaster: The bold attempt of Major Schill, a Prussian, to precipitate a war of liberation in Apr. 1809, was frustrated by news of Napoleon's victories on the Danube. Schill fell while fighting at Stralsund (May 31). Eleven of his officers were court-martialed and shot at Wesel, while the captured soldiers were condemned by Napoleon to hard labor; after serving for six months in the French galleys, they were enrolled in the coast-guard. Another effort was made in 1809 by the Duke of Brunswick, who, with a force of volunteers from Bohemia and Silesia, made his way across Germany to Brunswick (July 31). Forced by superior numbers to withdraw, he managed to reach Bremen and transported his men to England.

12. EUROPE, 1810-1812

1810, Apr. MARRIAGE OF NAPOLEON WITH ARCHDUCHESS MARIE LOUISE, daughter of Emperor Francis I of Austria. Napoleon had divorced Josephine and was eager for an heir to his great empire. The marriage was arranged by **Metternich,** the Austrian foreign minister after 1809, whose policy was that of alliance with France as the only protection for Austria during the period of recuperation. Birth of an heir to the throne, the King of Rome (Mar. 1811).

July 1. Abdication and flight of **Louis, King of Holland,** who had refused to ruin his country by joining the Continental system. Thereupon **Holland was annexed to France** (July 9), followed by the annexation also of the canton of Wallis, of Oldenburg, of a large part of the Kingdom of Westphalia, of the Grand Duchy of Berg, of East Friesland, and of the Hanseatic cities. The French Empire thenceforth comprised 130 departments and extended along the entire Channel and North Sea coast. These annexations were provoked chiefly by the desire to stop smuggling of British goods, but as such they proved rather ineffectual.

THE REVOLUTION IN SWEDEN. By the **Treaty of Tilsit,** Alexander of Russia had been given a free hand to conquer Finland, which he did in 1808, meeting with but feeble opposition from the Swedes. In the course of the war the Russians, under Gen. Barclay de Tolly, crossed the Gulf of Bothnia on the ice, captured the Aland Islands, and threatened Stockholm. This situation, complicated by an unfortunate war between Sweden and Denmark, resulted in a military overturn. On Mar. 13, 1809, **King Gustavus IV** was arrested by Generals Klingspor and Adlerkreuz, and forced to abdicate (Mar. 29). His uncle became king as **Charles XIII** (1808–1818) and a new constitution was promulgated, restoring the power of the aristocracy. The new king concluded with Russia the **Treaty of Friedrichsham** (Sept. 17) by which the Swedes abandoned Finland as far as the Tornea River, and also the Aland Islands. Through the mediation of Russia, the Swedes secured also the **Treaty of Paris,** with France. By this Sweden joined the Continental system, and received in return Swedish Pomerania. In Jan. 1810, the Swedish Estates elected as heir to the throne Prince Christian of Holstein-Augustenburg, and on his sudden death (May) they chose **Marshal Bernadotte** (Prince of Ponte Corvo) as crown prince. Napoleon was unable to resist this compliment and Bernadotte accepted the position (Nov. 5). Thenceforth he controlled the Swedish army and foreign affairs.

ROME AND THE PAPACY. Growing friction between Napoleon and Pius VII after 1805, when the pope returned to Rome. Difficulties about the working of the Concordat of 1801, high-handed action of Napoleon in depriving the pope of some of his territories. Pius steadfastly refused to join in the Continental system, as directed, so that on Feb. 2, 1808, the French, under Gen. Miollis, occupied Rome. On May 17, 1809, the **Papal States were declared incorporated with France.** To this act Pius replied by excommunicating Napoleon (June 10), whereupon the emperor had him arrested (July 6) and taken to Savona, near Genoa, where he was held prisoner. Pius continued his attitude of opposition and in 1812 was removed to Fontainebleau.

PORTUGAL AND SPAIN. The English force in Portugal, under Wellesley, was in 1810 threatened by a twofold attack by the French, under Masséna in the north, and under Soult in the south. The French took **Ciudad Rodrigo** (July 10) and the British fell back towards Lisbon, where they held the lines of **Torres Vedras** (Oct.). All through the winter the two armies confronted each other, until finally Masséna fell back into Spain. The English pursued and besieged **Almeida** and **Badajoz.** In the **battle of Fuentes de Onoro** (May 5) Masséna was defeated, while another British force, under Gen. Beresford, defeated Soult in the south (**battle of Albuera,** May 16). In 1812 (Jan. 19) the British took **Ciudad Rodrigo,** and somewhat later (Apr. 6)

captured **Badajoz.** On July 22 **Wellesley** (Wellington) completely defeated the French under Marshal Marmont, at **Salamanca.** Joseph Bonaparte had to abandon Madrid (Aug. 12) and fall back to the Ebro River. In the meanwhile, a national assembly (*Côrtes*) elected in 1810 in the only part of the country then free, viz. Cadiz and vicinity, promulgated a famous **constitution** (May 8, 1812) of an advanced, democratic type (one-chamber parliament, universal suffrage, popular sovereignty, etc.).

THE OTTOMAN EMPIRE. War against England and Russia (1806–1812). This was conducted in desultory fashion by both sides. 1807: **Revolutions in Constantinople** (p. 722). 1809, Jan. 5: The English concluded the **Treaty of the Dardanelles** with the Turks and withdrew from the war. In the same year the Russians won a victory at **Silistria,** which was followed, in 1810, by the occupation of **Bessarabia, Moldavia,** and **Wallachia.** In 1811 the Russians crossed the Danube and began the advance through Bulgaria. These operations had to be broken off in view of the impending invasion of Russia by Napoleon. Despite French efforts to induce them to continue the war, the Turks were glad to accept the **Treaty of Bucharest** (May 28, 1812), by which they gave up to Russia the province of Bessarabia.

13. THE FRENCH INVASION OF RUSSIA

Causes: Latent rivalry between Napoleon and Alexander, both eager for leadership in Europe. Dissatisfaction of Alexander, aroused by Napoleon's marriage and alliance with Austria. Unwillingness of the Russians to carry through fully the Continental system. Irritation of the tsar over Napoleon's unwillingness to grant him free hand in the matter of Constantinople. Addition of West Galicia to the Grand Duchy of Warsaw (by the **Treaty of Schönbrunn,** 1809) aroused Alexander's fear that Napoleon was planning the restoration of Poland. Deposition of the Duke of Oldenburg and annexation of his territory to France offended Alexander, who was a near relative of the duke.

Preparations: Alliance of Napoleon with Austria (which agreed to furnish 30,000 men) and **Prussia** (20,000). **Denmark,** however, maintained neutrality throughout the war. **Sweden,** which had been forced by Napoleon to declare war on England (1810), now, under Bernadotte's guidance, shook off the French yoke and secured

compensation for the loss of Finland. The French having reoccupied Swedish Pomerania and Rügen (Jan. 1812), the Swedes concluded with Russia

1812, Apr. The Treaty of St. Petersburg: Russia promised Sweden the annexation of Norway, which belonged to Denmark, the latter to be indemnified elsewhere; Sweden agreed to make a diversion against the French in northern Germany.

May 28. Russia made peace with the Turks at Bucharest (above).

June. England made peace with Russia and Sweden.

Military preparations: The Grand Army of Napoleon, originally about 420,000 men, ultimately, with reinforcements, about 600,000, probably the greatest army ever assembled up to that time. It was only in part French, for there were large contingents of Italians, Poles, Swiss, Dutch, and German (from the Confederation of the Rhine members, as well as Austria and Prussia). The **Austrians,** under Schwarzen-

Napoleon's Empire

berg, formed a separate army on the right wing, the **Prussians,** under York, held the left wing.

1812, June. Passage of the Niemen River and **occupation of Vilna.** The Russians, under Barclay de Tolly, retreated, allowing the French main army to reach Smolensk without offering battle. The Prussians meanwhile besieged **Riga** and the Austrians penetrated into **Volhynia.**

Aug. 17-18. Destruction of Smolensk by the French. Barclay de Tolly, criticized for his failure to resist the invasion, was replaced by **Gen. Kutusov,** who fought the French in the bloody

Sept. 7. BATTLE OF BORODINO, on the Moskova River (terrific losses on both sides). The Russians were obliged to retreat farther, and abandoned Moscow.

Sept. 14. The French occupied Moscow, which had been deserted by most of the inhabitants. Napoleon established himself in the Kremlin.

Sept. 15-19. BURNING OF MOSCOW, evidently a disaster planned and executed by the Russians (**Rostopchin**) to make the place untenable. Napoleon of-

fered Alexander a truce, which Alexander rejected. After waiting for five weeks in Moscow, Napoleon, frustrated in his hope of bringing the Russians to terms and unable to maintain himself so far from his bases, began the

Oct. 19. RETREAT FROM MOSCOW toward Smolensk. Attacks on the invaders by Kutusov's army and by swarms of Cossacks and irregulars. Separate corps of the Grand Army fought at **Jaroslavetz** (Oct. 24) and at **Viazma** (Nov. 3). By the beginning of Nov. very severe weather began to set in. Suffering of the troops from hunger and frost, combined with constant attacks by the enemy (e.g. at **Krasnoi** and **Borissov**).

Nov. 26-28. CROSSING OF THE BERESINA, one of the most horrible episodes in the retreat. Ney and Oudinot, with 8500 men, forced the passage against 25,000 Russians. From this point on, the remaining fragments of the army became completely disorganized and the retreat became a wild flight. Napoleon left the army and hastened to Paris, where he arrived on Dec. 18. At about the same time the remnants of the army (not more than 100,000 men) straggled across the Niemen.

14. THE WARS OF LIBERATION

Soon after the catastrophic invasion of Russia, the Prussians deserted the French and joined the tsar in a campaign in Germany. On Dec. 30 Gen. York, in command of the Prussian contingent of the Grand Army, concluded the **Convention of Taurog-gen** (an agreement of neutrality) with the Russian general, Diebitsch. Great pressure was brought to bear upon Frederick William III by his generals and advisers.

1813, Feb. 3. Appeal of Frederick William III, issued from Breslau and calling upon his people to form volunteer corps. Enthusiastic response, especially among the younger men and students.

Feb. 28. Treaty of Kalisch, between Prussia and Russia. (1) Offensive and defensive alliance, enumeration of auxiliary armies to be furnished by either side. (2) In the event of victory Prussia to be given as much territory as she possessed in 1806. (3) Invitation extended to Austria and England to join the alliance.

Mar. 3. Treaty between England and Sweden: England paid one million rix dollars in subsidies and promised not to oppose the union of Norway with Sweden.

Sweden furnished the allies an army of 30,000 men under command of **Crown Prince Bernadotte.**

Mar. 17. Appeal of Frederick William III "To my people," and "to my army." Establishment of the **Landwehr** and the **Landsturm.** Iron Cross.

Mar. 18. Outbreak in Hamburg. Tettenborn and a force of Russians occupied the city. The Dukes of Mecklenburg withdrew from the Confederation of the Rhine.

Great preparations on both sides. The Elbe was the boundary between the combatants; Danzig, Stettin, Küstrin, Glogau, Modlin, and Zamosc, being, however, in the hands of the French.

Mar. 27. Occupation of Dresden by Russians and Prussians under Wittgenstein and Blücher, after the withdrawal of Marshal Davout. Flight of the King of Saxony.

The French army and the contingents of the Confederation of the Rhine concentrated in Franconia, Thuringia, and on the Elbe. Napoleon, after the end of April, was at the head of 180,000 men in

Germany. He was unexpectedly attacked by the armies of the allies, numbering 85,000 men.

May 2. Battle of Gross-Görschen or Lützen. Victory remained with the French, in spite of their losses. The allies withdrew through Dresden to Lusatia. Scharnhorst, severely wounded, died in Prague. Napoleon in Dresden, in close alliance with the King of Saxony, who had returned from Prague.

May 20 and 21. Battles of Bautzen and Wurschen. Napoleon attacked the allies at Bautzen, forced them to retreat across the Spree, and completed the victory at Wurschen, with great loss to himself. Duroc killed. The Allies retreated to Silesia.

May 30. Hamburg occupied by Davout, after the withdrawal of the Russians. The combatants, exhausted, waited for reinforcements and strove to secure the alliance of Austria.

June 4-July 26. Armistice of Poischwitz, afterward prolonged until Aug. 10 (16).

June 15. England concluded a subsidy treaty with Prussia and Russia at Reichenbach.

July 5 (28)-Aug. 11. Congress at Prague. Austria played the part of mediator. After futile negotiations (Metternich, Caulaincourt, William von Humboldt), the congress was dissolved.

Aug. 12. AUSTRIA DECLARED WAR ON FRANCE.

The Allies, all supported by English subsidies, put three armies into the field: (1) **The Bohemian army,** under **Schwarzenberg** (with Kleist and Wittgenstein), was accompanied by the three monarchs; (2) **the Silesian army,** under **Blücher** (with York, Sacken, and Langeron); (3) **the Northern army,** under **Bernadotte** (with Bülow, Tauenzien, and Winzingerode).

Napoleon began operations by attacking Blücher, who retired behind the Katzbach. Meanwhile Schwarzenberg advanced from Bohemia upon Dresden. Napoleon left MacDonald to oppose Blücher and hurried to Saxony. Oudinot and Reynier were to march on Berlin, with the support of Davout, coming from Hamburg.

Aug. 23. Battle of Grossbeeren. Oudinot and Reynier were defeated by Bülow, the Crown Prince of Saxony having looked on inactive. Berlin was saved by this victory.

Aug. 26. Battle of the Katzbach. MacDonald's army was defeated by Blücher, who was made Prince of Wahlstatt.

Aug. 26-27. BATTLE OF DRESDEN. Napoleon defeated the allied army from Bohemia. It was his last major victory on German soil.

Aug. 30. Battle of Kulm and Nollendorf. Vandamme, with a French force that attempted to intercept the retreat of the Bohemian army, was defeated by Ostermann and Kleist.

Sept. 6. Battle of Dennewitz, in which Marshal Ney, attempting to take Berlin, was defeated by Bülow and Tauenzien.

Sept. 9. TREATY OF TEPLITZ, between Russia, Prussia, and Austria: (1) Firm union and mutual guaranty for their respective territories. (2) Each party to assist the others with at least 60,000 men. (3) No separate peace or armistice to be concluded with France. Secret articles provided for the restoration of the Austrian and Prussian monarchies to their territorial status of 1805.

Oct. 3. Battle of Wartenburg. York forced a passage across the Elbe for the army of Silesia. The northern army also crossed the Elbe.

Oct. 8. Treaty of Ried, between Austria and Bavaria. Bavaria withdrew from the Confederation of the Rhine and joined the alliance against Napoleon. In return, the king was guaranteed his possessions as of the time of the treaty.

Oct. 16-19. BATTLE OF LEIPZIG (*Battle of the Nations*). Napoleon had left Dresden in order to avoid being cut off from France by the three allied armies, which were attempting to unite in his rear. The decisive battle was fought around Leipzig. **Oct. 16:** Inconclusive engagement between Napoleon and the army of Bohemia at **Wachau** (south of Leipzig): victory of Blücher over Marmont at **Möckern,** north of Leipzig. **Oct. 17:** The main armies were not engaged; Napoleon sent peace offers to the emperor, who rejected them as too extravagant; toward evening the Allies united, being reinforced with a Russian reserve under Bennigsen (100,000); formed in a huge semicircle, they greatly outnumbered the forces of Napoleon. **Oct. 18:** General attack of the Allies, ending in complete victory after nine hours. The French army was driven back to the gates of Leipzig. The Saxon and Württemberg corps went over to the Allies. **Oct. 19:** Storming of Leipzig by the Allies; capture of the King of Saxony. The army of Napoleon, having lost 30,000 men, began the retreat, harried by the allied forces (**battle of the Unstrut,** and of **Hanau**).

As a result of the French defeat at Leipzig, King Jerome fled from Cassel and the

Kingdom of Westphalia came to an end. The same was true of the Grand Duchies of Frankfurt and of Berg. The old rulers were restored in Cassel, Brunswick, Hanover, and Oldenburg. The central administrative bureau, which had been created under Freiherr vom Stein at the beginning of the war to govern recovered territories, had only Saxony to concern itself with.

THE CAMPAIGN IN SPAIN. The English, unable to take Burgos, had been obliged to fall back again, and King Joseph was able to recover Madrid. But in Feb. 1813, Soult and a large part of the French army had to be recalled to Germany. Once more Wellington advanced to the northeast, to cut off the communications of King Joseph with France.

June 21. **Battle of Vittoria.** Wellington completely defeated Marshal Jourdan. Joseph fled to France and the French abandoned most of the country. The British stormed San Sebastian (Aug. 21) and besieged Pampeluna. In the east, Marshal Suchet was driven out of Valencia into Barcelona. Pampeluna fell to the British and Spaniards (Oct. 31). Wellington crossed the French frontier, defeated Soult (Nov. 10) and invested Bayonne (Dec.).

Nov. **Napoleon crossed the Rhine** at Mainz. Württemberg, Hesse-Darmstadt, Baden, and the remaining members of the Confederation of the Rhine joined the alliance. One city after another surrendered to the allied forces: Dresden (Nov. 11), Stettin (Nov. 21), Lübeck (Dec. 5), Zamosc, Modlin, Torgau (Dec. 26), Danzig (Dec. 30), Wittenberg (Jan. 12, 1814), Küstrin (Mar. 7). But Hamburg (Davout), Glogau, Magdeburg, Erfurt, Würzburg, Wesel, and Mainz remained in French hands until the conclusion of peace.

Nov. 8. **The allies offered Napoleon peace,** leaving France the boundaries of the Alps and the Rhine. When Napoleon failed to accept, the allies (Dec. 1) adopted a resolution to prosecute the war vigorously and to pass the Rhine and invade France.

Nov. 15. **Revolt of the Dutch,** who expelled the French officials. The allied army of Bülow entered Holland, while Bernadotte, with the northern army, invaded Holstein, and in a short winter campaign forced Denmark to accept the

1814, Jan. 14. TREATY OF KIEL: (1) Denmark ceded Norway to Sweden, with a guaranty to the Norwegians of the maintenance of their rights. (2) Sweden ceded to Denmark Western Pomerania and Rügen. At the same time peace

was made between **England and Denmark,** England restoring all conquests except Heligoland.

Meanwhile **the allied armies had crossed the Rhine** (Dec. 21–25). The army of Schwarzenberg crossed through Switzerland, whose treaty of neutrality was disregarded. On Jan. 1, 1814, Blücher crossed the river at Mannheim and Coblenz. Altogether about 200,000 men invaded France. The main army proceeded through Burgundy, while Blücher advanced through Lorraine. Napoleon attempted to prevent their junction by attacking Blücher at Brienne and driving him back (Jan. 29). But Blücher united with part of the main army and defeated the emperor in the

Feb. 1. **Battle of La Rothière.** Napoleon retired behind the Aube River. Difficulties of supply forced the allied forces to divide again. The main army was to advance on Paris by the Seine River, while Blücher was to follow the course of the Marne. Hearing of the division, Napoleon suddenly hurled himself on the various corps of Blücher's army and defeated them in four battles: Champaubert, Montmirail, Chateâu-Thierry, Vauchamps (Feb. 10–15). Then, turning on the main army, he defeated it in engagements at Nangis and Montereau (Feb. 17–18). Blücher was obliged to fall back to Etoges, and Schwarzenberg to Troyes. Meanwhile the Allies met with Napoleon's envoy, Caulaincourt, in the

Feb. 5–Mar. 19. **Congress of Châtillon** (sur-Seine). Napoleon was offered the French frontier of 1792, but, elated by his recent successes, he overplayed his hand and the negotiations failed.

Feb. 27. **Battle of Bar-sur-Aube.** Schwarzenberg defeated Oudinot and MacDonald. Blücher, forced to retire across the Marne and Oise, joined the army of the north under Bülow and Winzingerode.

Mar. 9. **TREATIES OF CHAUMONT,** between the Allies. These were arranged by **Lord Castlereagh,** the British foreign minister, who had hurried to the Continent to forestall any breakup of the coalition. The treaties provided for continuance of the struggle and guarded against a separate peace. The alliance to continue for twenty years.

Mar. 9-10. **Battle of Laon.** The allied armies, combined, defeated Napoleon.

Mar. 12. The British, under Wellington, captured **Bordeaux.** The campaign in the south came to an end with

Soult's final defeat in the **battle of Tou-louse** (Apr. 10).

Mar. 20-21. Battle of Arcis-sur-Aube. Napoleon suffered another reverse. He then formed the desperate plan of throwing himself on the rear of the Allies in Lorraine, summoning the garrisons of the fortresses to his aid, and calling the population to arms. The Allies, with equal boldness, advanced on Paris, and, in

Mar. 25. The battle of **La Fère-Champenoise** defeated Marshals Marmont and Mortier. The French generals threw themselves upon the capital, which was valiantly defended, but which, after

Mar. 30. The storming of the **Montmartre** by the Allies, was obliged to capitulate.

Mar. 31. VICTORIOUS ENTRY OF THE ALLIES INTO PARIS. The

Senate, under Talleyrand's influence, declared that Napoleon and his family had forfeited the throne. The emperor, hastening to the defense of the capital, arrived a few hours too late. His marshals refused to join him in a foolhardy assault on the city, so in the end he was obliged to abdicate in favor of his son (Fontainebleau, Apr. 6). The Allies rejected this solution, and on

Apr. 11. Napoleon abdicated unconditionally. The allies granted him the **island of Elba** as a sovereign principality, with an annual income of 2,000,000 francs, to be paid by France. His wife, **Marie Louise,** received the Duchies of Parma, Piacenza, and Guastalla, with sovereign power. Both Napoleon and Marie Louise retained the imperial title. On May 4 the emperor arrived at Elba.

15. THE PEACE SETTLEMENTS

1814-1824. LOUIS XVIII, King of France. He was the elder of the two surviving brothers of Louis XVI. His restoration to the throne was due in part to the failure of other candidacies (notably that of Bernadotte), in part to the clever managing and maneuvering of Talleyrand. The British were sympathetic and Alexander I of Russia was easily persuaded. Louis was induced by Talleyrand and his other advisers to issue a **constitution,** modeled on that of the English, but with many limitations. This was the charter (*Charte constitutionnelle*), for which see p. 626.

May 30. THE FIRST TREATY OF **PARIS.** Leniency of the Allies, due to their desire to strengthen the Bourbon régime: (1) **France** retained the boundaries of 1792, which included Avignon, Venaissin, parts of Savoy and parts of the German Empire and Belgium, all of which had not belonged to France in 1789. (2) **France** recognized the independence of the Netherlands, of the German states, the Italian states, and of Switzerland. (3) **England** restored the French colonies, excepting Tobago, Ste. Lucia and Mauritius (Isle de France). England also retained Malta. (4) The Allies abandoned all claims for indemnity, etc. (5) **France** promised to abolish the slave trade.

Discussion of the general settlement of the reconquered territories among the Allies at Paris, and during the visit of Alexander I and Frederick William to England (June). In view of the complexity of the problem, it was decided to hold a congress at Vienna.

1814, Sept.—1815, June. THE CONGRESS OF VIENNA, one of the most brilliant international assemblies of modern times. Lavish entertainment offered by Emperor Francis. Most of the rulers of Europe attended the congress, to say nothing of the host of lesser potentates, ministers, claimants, etc. The chief negotiators were: for Austria, **Prince Metternich:** for Prussia, **Hardenberg** and **William von Humboldt;** for Great Britain, **Castlereagh** and **Wellington;** for Russia, the tsar himself and his many advisers (**Czartoryski, Stein, Razumovsky, Capodistrias, Nesselrode**); for France, **Talleyrand;** for the papacy, **Card. Consalvi.**

The main decisions were made by the chief representatives of the four major allied powers, the other members of the grand alliance (Spain, Portugal, Sweden) being allowed to participate only in the treatment of fairly obvious or unobjectionable subjects. The full congress never met officially. Talleyrand, in order to gain admission to the inner councils, tried to raise the **principle of legitimacy** to support his claim, but he was taken into the inner group only when the dispute between the Allies as to the fate of Poland and Saxony led them (Jan. 1815) to the verge of war and the deadlock between the two opposing groups (Russia and Prussia against Austria and England) had to be broken by enlisting the support of France on the anti-Russian side.

The work of the Congress of Vienna was interrupted by the **return of Napoleon from Elba** and the reopening of the war (p. 602), but the various settlements were brought together and signed as

1815, June 8. THE ACT OF THE CONGRESS OF VIENNA. Chief provisions:

(1) **Restoration of the Austrian and Prussian monarchies:** (*a*) **Austria** received, besides her former domain, the Italian provinces of Lombardy and Venetia (to be called the *Lombardo-Venetian Kingdom*); the Illyrian provinces (French Kingdoms of Illyria and Dalmatia); Salzburg and the Tyrol (from Bavaria); Galicia. (*b*) **Prussia** received part of the Grand Duchy of Warsaw (Posen) and Danzig; Swedish Pomerania and Rügen, in return for which Denmark was given Lauenburg; the former Prussian possessions in Westphalia, somewhat enlarged, as well as Neuchâtel; the greater part of Saxony, as compensation for the loss of former possessions, like Ansbach and Baireuth (ceded to Bavaria), East Friesland (to Hanover) and part of the Polish territory (to Russia).

(2) **Formation of the Kingdom of the Netherlands,** comprising the former Republic of Holland and the Austrian Netherlands (Belgium), under the former hereditary statthalter as King William I. England returned the former Dutch colonies, but not Ceylon or the Cape of Good Hope.

(3) **Creation of the Germanic Confederation,** to take the place of the old Holy Roman Empire. Schemes for a unified German state, as advanced by the so-called "patriots," were put aside, and the federal bond was hardly more than a mutual defensive alliance. The confederation comprised 39 states, including four free cities. All other princes remained mediatized. The **Act of Confederation** was signed on June 8, 1815 and was later supplemented by the **Final Act of Vienna** (May 15, 1820).

(4) **The Kingdom of Poland:** Most of the former Grand Duchy of Warsaw was handed over to Russia, and became a Polish kingdom, with the Russian tsar as king. Poland received from Alexander a liberal constitution; Polish was the official language and Poland had her own institutions, including a separate army. Cracow became a free state under the protection of Russia, Austria, and Prussia.

(5) **England** retained Malta, Heligoland, some of the French and Dutch colonies (see above), and assumed a protectorate over the Ionian Islands (**Treaty of Nov. 5, 1815**).

(6) **Sweden** retained Norway, which had been acquired by the Treaty of Kiel (p. 600). **Norway** was given a separate constitution. **Denmark** was indemnified with Lauenburg.

(7) **Switzerland** was re-established as an independent confederation of 22 cantons. Geneva, Wallis, and Neuchâtel (a principality belonging to the King of Prussia) were now included in the federation.

(8) **Restoration of the legitimate dynasties** in Spain, Sardinia (which received Genoa), Tuscany, Modena and the Papal States. The Bourbons were not reinstated in Naples until 1815, since Murat had secured possession of Naples for the time being through his desertion of Napoleon.

16. THE HUNDRED DAYS

News of the discontent in France with the government of the Bourbons, and knowledge of the discord at the Congress of Vienna, to say nothing of the encouragement of his adherents, induced Napoleon to make another effort to recover his throne.

1815, Mar. 1. Landing of Napoleon at Cannes, with 1500 men. He marched at once upon Paris. Troops sent to oppose him (even Ney's corps), espoused his cause.

Mar. 13. Ban against **Napoleon,** issued by the allied monarchs from Vienna. **Flight of Louis XVIII** to Ghent.

Mar. 20. Napoleon entered **Paris** and began the short rule generally called the *Hundred Days* (Mar. 20–June 29).

Mar. 25. Austria, England, Prussia, and **Russia** concluded a new alliance against Napoleon; each engaged to supply 180,000 men. All European nations were invited to join the coalition, and most of them did, but not Sweden, which was engaged in the conquest of Norway. The sum of the contingents furnished against Napoleon amounted to over a million men. The **Duke of Wellington** in command.

May 3. Murat, who had now declared for Napoleon again, was defeated by an Austrian force at Tolentino. Naples was captured (May 22); Murat fled to France. The Bourbon king, **Ferdinand,** restored to the Neapolitan throne

June 14. Napoleon, forced to fight, crossed the frontier into Belgium. Engagement at **Charleroi; the advanced**

guard of the Prussians, under Ziethen, forced back.

June 16. Battle of Ligny. Napoleon obliged Blücher to fall back. The Prussians marched to Wavre. On the same day the Prince of Orange retreated before Marshal Ney in battle of **QUATRE BRAS.** Meanwhile the army of Wellington had been concentrating. This consisted of English, Hanoverians, Dutch, and Germans from Brunswick and Nassau.

June 18. BATTLE OF WATERLOO (*Belle Alliance*). Napoleon hurled himself upon Wellington's army, believing that he had insured against the junction of Blücher and Wellington by ordering **Grouchy** to engage the Prussians. But Grouchy had allowed Blücher to get away. At Waterloo Wellington's army held its lines all day under terrific assaults from the French. The arrival of Blücher toward evening probably saved the day. The French were completely defeated, and the army, pursued by Gneisenau, was soon scattered.

June 22. SECOND ABDICATION OF NAPOLEON. The emperor was soon obliged to flee before the victorious Allies. He reached Rochefort where, after futile attempts to escape to America, he surrendered himself to the British admiral, **Hotham.** He was conveyed to England on the warship *Bellerophon*. By unanimous resolution of the Allies, he was taken, as a prisoner of war, to the island of **St. Helena,** in the South Atlantic Ocean. There he arrived in October. The remainder of his life he spent under close supervision. He died May 5, 1821.

July 7. Second capture of Paris by the Allies. Return of Louis XVIII ("in the baggage of the allies"). Arrival of the allied monarchs.

1815, Sept. 26. THE HOLY ALLIANCE, a document drawn up by the Tsar Alexander I, signed by the Emperor Francis I and by Frederick William III and ultimately by all European rulers, excepting the King of England, the pope, and the Sultan of Turkey. It was an innocuous declaration of Christian principles, which were to guide the rulers in their relations with their subjects and with each other. These vague and unexceptionable principles were probably meant by the tsar merely as a preface to some form of international organization, along the lines recommended by the Abbé de St. Pierre a century earlier. The importance of the document lay not in its terms, but in its later confusion in the public mind with the **Quadruple Alliance** and more particularly with the reactionary policy of the three eastern powers, which were regarded as bound by a pact directed against the liberties of the people, camouflaged by religion.

Oct. 13. Murat, who had made a reckless attempt to recover his kingdom by landing in Calabria, was captured, court-martialed, and shot.

Nov. 20. SECOND PEACE OF PARIS. **Terms:** (1) France was obliged to give up the fortresses of Philippeville and Marienburg to the Netherlands, and Saarlouis and Saarbrücken to Prussia; Landau became a fortress of the Germanic Confederation; the surrounding region, as far as the Lauter River, was ceded to Bavaria. To Sardinia, France was obliged to cede that part of Savoy which she had retained in the First Treaty of Paris. In general she was restricted to the boundary of 1790. (2) Seventeen fortresses on the north and east frontiers were to be garrisoned for not more than five years by troops of the Allies (at French expense). (3) France was to pay 700,000,000 francs for the expense of the war. In addition, art treasures which the French had taken from all over Europe, were now to be returned to their original owners.

Nov. 20. RENEWAL OF THE QUADRUPLE ALLIANCE, between England, Austria, Prussia, and Russia. The members promised to supply each 60,000 men in the event that a violation of the Treaty of Paris should be attempted. They agreed to hold future meetings to facilitate the execution of the treaty. This latter provision laid the basis for the ensuing international congresses and the emergence of a system of "government by conference" (*Confederation of Europe*).

C. WESTERN AND CENTRAL EUROPE

1. THE CONGRESS SYSTEM, 1815-1822

During the **Congress of Vienna** there was general agreement between the powers that some measures should be taken to maintain the peace settlements and to guard against the recurrence of war. But efforts to establish a guaranty of the peace terms came to nothing.

1815, Sept. 26.   THE SIGNING OF THE HOLY ALLIANCE. *See* p. 603.

Nov. 20.   THE QUADRUPLE ALLIANCE, signed by the four victorious powers after the battle of Waterloo and the **Second Treaty of Paris** (p. 603). It developed the principles laid down in the **Treaties of Chaumont** (p. 600) and was concluded for 20 years. It aimed at preventing the return of Napoleon or his dynasty; at preservation of the territorial settlement with France; at the protection of Europe against French aggression through co-operative action by the signatories. It was further provided, at the urgent request of Lord Castlereagh, that representatives of the signatory powers should meet periodically to discuss common interests and problems (**government by conference**).

1818, Sept.   Congress of Aix-la-Chapelle, the first of the meetings. This settled the question of the French indemnity payments and arranged the withdrawal of allied troops from France. France was admitted to the newly constituted **Quintuple Alliance** (the old Quadruple Alliance

being retained, however). Questions of the slave trade, the status of Jews, etc., were also raised and there was indication that the congress system would develop into an effective international machine.

1820-1821.   Congresses of Troppau and Laibach, called to consider the revolutions in Spain and Italy. Metternich induced the three eastern powers to accept the **Troppau Protocol,** directed against revolutions which might disturb the peace. Castlereagh was prevented by English liberal opinion and by British tradition from accepting a policy of interference in the affairs of other states (cf. British state paper of May 5, 1820). This difference of view marked the first serious weakening of the congress system.

1822, Oct.   Congress of Verona, last of the congresses, summoned to consider the Spanish and Greek situations. Castlereagh had committed suicide on the eve of the meeting. His successor, **George Canning** (1770–1827), was unsympathetic to the "European Areopagus," tended to stress the divergence between the "liberal" and the "conservative" powers, and was, above all, determined to prevent intervention in Spain for fear that the effort might be made to extend it to Spanish colonies in the New World. He refused to co-operate with the other powers and, though unable to prevent intervention in Spain, succeeded in destroying the congress system.

2. THE BRITISH ISLES

a.   THE END OF THE TORY RÉGIME, 1815-1830

1815-1820.   The cessation of the Napoleonic wars brought, not the anticipated prosperity, but widespread distress. A long and severe **economic depression** followed. Continental markets failed to absorb the overstocked supplies of English manufacturers; governmental demands for military supplies ceased; prices fell; thousands were thrown out of work. The ranks of the unemployed were swelled by more than 400,000 demobilized men. A

complete dislocation of the country's war-time economic organization took place.

Remedial legislation took the form of: (1) further protection for agriculture (primarily in the interest of the landlords) by the **Corn Law of 1815,** which virtually excluded foreign grain from England until home-grown corn should reach the "famine price" of 80 shillings per quarter, after which it was to be admitted duty free (this measure was in part a blow at the working classes in the form of higher prices for bread); (2) **abolition of the 10 per cent income tax** (1816, Mar.), but with the concomitant enactment of duties on many articles (raising prices); (3) **deflation of the**

currency (1821, May) by the resumption of specie payments by the Bank of England. But the meager and unsatisfactory character of these "remedies" gave rise to widespread dissatisfaction.

Radical agitation turned particularly to demands for parliamentary reform, viewed as a panacea for social and economic ills by such leaders as the journalist, William Cobbett (1763–1835). Clubs were formed, petitions presented to Parliament. As distress became more general the radical movement revealed more extreme elements, violence was resorted to, middle-class moderates were driven more and more into the arms of the reactionary Tory ministry.

1816, Dec. 2. Acts of violence by a crowd gathered in Spa Fields, London, to hear an address on parliamentary reform precipitated the

1817, Mar. Coercion Acts: (1) temporarily suspending *habeas corpus* for the first time in English history; (2) extending the act of 1798 against seditious meetings; (3) renewing the act for the prevention and punishment of attempts to seduce soldiers and sailors from their allegiance; (4) extending to the prince regent all the safeguards against treasonable attempts which secured the king himself. The government's repressive policy stimulated the activity of extremists in the radical movement, which reached a climax in the

1819, Aug. 16. Peterloo Massacre: a crowd gathered at St. Peter's Fields, Manchester, to hear a speech on parliamentary reform and the repeal of the Corn Laws, was charged by soldiers ordered to arrest the speaker; several were killed and hundreds injured. The result was the passage of the repressive code known as the

1819, Dec. Six Acts: (1) provided for the speedy trial of "cases of misdemeanor"; (2) increased the penalties for seditious libel; (3) imposed the newspaper stamp duty on all periodical publications containing news (a blow at the radical journalists); (4) once more greatly curtailed public meetings; (5) forbade the training of persons in the use of arms; (6) empowered magistrates to search for and seize arms dangerous to the public peace. The Six Acts rendered the cabinet unpopular, but its prestige was again momentarily revived when a band of twenty extremists plotted the assassination of the whole cabinet (they were to be destroyed by dynamite as they dined together), and the seizure of enough cannon to overawe the populace, occupy the Bank of England, and establish a provisional government. This was the famous

1820, Feb. 23. Cato Street conspiracy. The plot was discovered in time; the conspirators were arrested at their rendezvous. This conspiracy stimulated anew fears of radicalism, and the cause of moderate reform was dealt a serious blow.

1820, Jan. 29. George III, declared insane and represented by the Prince of Wales as regent since 1811, died. The regent became king as

1820-1830. GEORGE IV, promptly had his cabinet institute divorce proceedings against the queen, Caroline of Brunswick, whom he had married (Apr. 8, 1795) in accordance with an arrangement of his father, but from whom he had separated shortly after the marriage. With the accession of George IV she returned from the Continent to claim her position as queen, was received with tumultuous demonstrations by the public, which viewed her as wronged by a prince whom it had learned to know as debauched and treacherous. The king induced his ministers to institute divorce proceedings, and they brought in

July 5. A Bill of Pains and Penalties, depriving the queen of her royal title and dissolving the marriage. The bill passed the House of Lords by a margin of nine votes, but was dropped by the government (Nov. 10) in face of certain defeat in the Commons. The result of the fiasco was a serious decline in the cabinet's prestige.

1822-1830. Following the death of Castlereagh (1822, Aug. 12), the cabinet received a series of liberal accessions: George Canning as foreign minister; Robert Peel (1788-1850) as secretary for home affairs — son of a self-made factory owner, Oxford-trained, independent, with a mind open to arguments for reform; William Huskisson (1770-1830), liberal financier of wide talent, as president of the board of trade. Between 1822 and 1830 the liberal wing of the Tory cabinet was responsible for a number of moderate but important reforms: (1) Peel secured passage of legislation revising the antiquated criminal code by which more than 200 offenses had become punishable by death. The reforms reduced the number of offenses so punishable by about 100, thus making conviction for many misdemeanors more certain, making the punishment more nearly approximate the offense (reflecting the growing humanitarian sentiment of the nineteenth century). (2) The first breach in the protectionist mercantile system was made by Huskisson in the budgets of 1823–1825, which reduced duties on certain imports (silk, wool, iron, wines, coffee,

Europe in 1815

sugar, cottons, woolens, etc.), and lifted the secular prohibition on the exportation of wool. Huskisson's reform was a foretaste of the sweeping movement toward free trade which began in the mid-forties. (3) **The repeal of the Combination Acts** was largely the work of **Francis Place** (1777–1854), master tailor who had retained his interest in the workers' cause from less fortunate days. Place collected a mass of evidence on the hardships occasioned for labor by the Combination Acts, and interested **Joseph Hume** (1777–1855), radical member of Parliament, in the cause. Hume secured appointment of a select committee to investigate conditions, and the evidence produced convinced Peel and Huskisson. The acts were repealed (1824, June 21). Phenomenal, though short-lived, **development of trade-unionism.** Many strikes followed, accompanied by violence. **A new law** (1825, July 6) allowed workers to combine to secure regulation of wages and hours of employment, but, in effect, forbade them to strike by prohibiting the use of violence or threats, and introducing summary methods of conviction.

The sharp divergences in the cabinet between liberal and right-wing Tories had been smoothed over by the conciliatory **Lord Liverpool,** continuously prime minister from 1812 till 1827, when a stroke of apoplexy obliged him to resign.

1827, Apr. 30. Canning succeeded as prime minister with a cabinet of liberal Tories and moderate Whigs, but died soon after (Aug. 8).

1827, Aug.—1828, Jan. Cabinet of the conciliatory but incapable **Lord Goderich** (1782–1859).

1828, Jan.—1830, Nov. Cabinet of the **Duke of Wellington,** from whose great distinction and wide popularity much was hoped. But Wellington was sympathetic with the reactionary group in his cabinet and alienated the liberal Tories, who resigned. The complete failure of Wellington's policy in the Near-Eastern crisis (p. 723) seriously discredited the cabinet.

1828, July 15. The Corn Law. The patent hardships (for consumers) of the Corn Law of 1815 obliged Wellington to introduce a measure permitting grain to be imported at any time and fixing duties on a sliding scale (high when the price of English corn was low and reducing the duty as the English price advanced). The act alienated the landlords, yet won Wellington no credit with the liberals, who remembered that the duke had earlier defeated the law when it was introduced by Canning.

1829. The Wellington cabinet again alienated its own supporters by its **Catholic emancipation policy.** When Daniel O'Connell (1775–1847), leader of the Catholic emancipation movement, was elected to Parliament in 1828 from the County of Clare in Ireland, the Wellington cabinet was faced by a crisis. Under the provisions of the **Test Act** (p. 427), no Catholic (or Protestant Nonconformist) could hold public office. Wellington and Peel were bitterly opposed to emancipation, but feared that the failure to relieve the Catholics of their disabilities would precipitate civil war in Ireland (the Catholic movement had been gathering strength steadily since the turn of the century).

1828, May 9. The **Test Act was repealed,** and

1829, Mar.-Apr. The **Catholic Emancipation** Bill was driven through Parliament by Wellington in the face of vigorous opposition from the reactionary Tories. It granted the Catholics the right of suffrage and the right to sit in Parliament, and declared their eligibility for any public office, save those of lord chancellor of England and lord lieutenant of Ireland — all this in return for an oath denying the pope any power to interfere in the domestic affairs of the realm, recognizing the Protestant succession, and repudiating every intention to upset the Established Church.

The radical and violent **agitation for parliamentary reform** which followed the Napoleonic wars yielded in the twenties to more moderate demands advocated by individual Whigs, notably **Lord John Russell** (1792–1878). The **July Revolution** in France, a triumph for the middle class (p. 628), stimulated the movement.

1830, June 26. George IV died, and was succeeded by his brother

1830-1837. WILLIAM IV (1765–1837). The accession necessitated a general election (a requirement abolished by the Reform Bill of 1867), and the reform of the House of Commons became a campaign issue. There was a turnover of some 50 seats, almost all of them going to proponents of reform. In caucus the Whigs adopted reform as their program. Wellington maintained an intransigent attitude, but was forced to resign (Nov. 16), ending a continuous Tory rule (with one brief interval) of nearly half a century.

b. AN ERA OF REFORM, 1830-1846

1830-1834. The Tory cabinet of Wellington was succeeded by the **Whig**

cabinet of **Earl Grey** (1764–1845), including a membership of distinguished talents, widely representative of liberal opinion and determined on **parliamentary reform.** The existing system of representation reflected gross inequalities, the result of ancient provisions whose effect was greatly exaggerated by the growth and migration of population under the impact of the industrial revolution. In *pocket boroughs* the patron enjoyed the absolute right of returning candidates. In *rotten boroughs* the elections were controlled by bribery and influence. On the eve of the reform not more than one-third of the House of Commons was freely chosen. Electoral inequalities constituted a second serious abuse: in various boroughs the right to vote rested on the possession of a forty-shilling freehold or some other financial basis, certain residence qualifications, membership in the governing body of the municipality (*close boroughs*). Even in boroughs of democratic electoral qualification the number of electors was usually small enough to be effectively bribed. Electoral conditions in the counties were better, but abuses were many. Grey's ministry undertook to reform this situation by redistributing parliamentary seats and extending the franchise.

1831, Mar. 22. **The First Reform Bill,** the work of Lord Durham and Lord John Russell, was passed on second reading by a majority of one, but defeated by amendment in the committee stage.

Apr. 19. Grey secured a **dissolution of Parliament,** followed by a bitterly fought election, with public opinion warmly supporting "The Bill, the whole Bill, and nothing but the Bill." The election was a Whig triumph.

Sept. 21. **The Second Reform Bill** passed the new House of Commons with a majority of 109, but the House of Lords threw the measure out on second reading (Oct. 8). The ministry prorogued Parliament and prepared a new bill. Extra-parliamentary agitation now became violent, riots broke out, the mob held Bristol for two days.

1832. **THE THIRD REFORM BILL** was passed by the Commons with a larger majority (Mar. 23). But the Lords in committee demanded amendments unacceptable to the ministry. They were greeted by a new blast of popular agitation. With the country on the verge of civil war, Grey advised the king to create enough new peers to pass the measure. The king refused, the cabinet resigned, Wellington was unable to form a ministry. The king recalled Grey, promised to appoint the new

peers, but instead induced the recalcitrant Tories to withdraw during the final vote in the Lords (June 4).

The act disfranchised 56 *pocket* and *rotten* boroughs (returning 111 members); 32 small boroughs were deprived of one member each. The available 143 seats were redistributed: 22 large towns received 2 each, 21 towns a single member each; county membership was increased from 94 to 159; 13 remaining members went to Scotland and Ireland. Extension of the franchise took the form of eliminating antiquated forms in the boroughs and giving the vote to all householders paying £10 annual rental. In the counties the area of enfranchisement was enlarged by retaining the 40-shilling freehold qualification for those owning their own land; other cases were covered by a £10 qualification for freeholders, copyholders, leaseholders for 60 years; and a qualification of £50 was fixed for leaseholders of shorter terms and tenants-at-will.

July-Aug. **Scotland and Ireland** were subjects of separate bills, in which the franchise was remodeled upon lines similar to those adopted in England.

The Reform Bill shifted the balance of power to the industrial and commercial class, revealed that the House of Lords could not defy the popular will, opened an era of reform. It failed to concede the secret ballot and left the bulk of the population still disfranchised.

1831. **Tithe War in Ireland.** The Irish, overwhelmingly Catholic, resented the enforced payment of **tithes** to support the Established Episcopal Church and resorted to violence.

1833, Apr. A **Coercion Bill** gave the lord lieutenant unlimited powers of suppressing public meetings, of subjecting disturbed districts to martial law.

Aug. 2. **The Irish Church Temporalities Bill** introduced by the government as a counterpoise to coercion. The bill established a graduated tax on clerical incomes to relieve ratepayers from the burden of parish expenses, and provided for the reduction of the Irish episcopate. The bill failed to provide for the application to secular purposes of the savings effected, and so outraged O'Connell and his following.

Aug. 23. **Abolition of slavery in the colonies.** Edward Stanley, Irish secretary, had incurred such unpopularity that he was transferred to the colonial secretaryship where he carried the bill emancipating the slaves in the British colonies. The law was the crowning act in the long campaign of the abolitionists, led by **William Wilberforce** (1759–1833), agitation dating particularly from the abolition of the slave trade (p. 826). The act provided for the immediate emancipation of children under six, a period of apprenticeship for those over six (eliminated four years later), and compensation of £20,000,000 to slaveowners.

Aug. 29. Factory Act. Investigations had revealed the frightful working conditions to which children were often subjected and against which the factory acts of 1802 and 1816 gave quite inadequate protection. The result was the Factory Act of 1833, carried in the face of opposition from the Tories and many Whigs (imbued with *laisser-faire* doctrine). It forbade employment of children under 9 years, restricted labor of those between 9 and 13 to 48 hours a week or 9 in a single day, and of those from 13 to 18 years to 69 hours a week or 12 in a day. Children under 13 were to have 2 hours' schooling per day. A system of paid inspectors was set up. The law applied only to factories in the textile industries and was in itself inadequate, but it was the forerunner of further remedial legislation.

1834. Growth of trade-unionism. The movement had taken a phenomenal but short-lived spurt after the repeal of the Combination Laws in 1825, and was given momentum by the general dissatisfaction of the workers with the Reform Act of 1832. The pioneer was **John Doherty** (1797–1854), at whose instigation the **National Association for the Protection of Labor** (a federation of about 150 unions) had been formed in 1830. As the movement spread after 1832, Doherty and **Robert Owen** (1771–1858) decided to attempt to form a general union of skilled and unskilled laborers.

Jan. The Grand National Consolidated Trades Union was organized. Within a few weeks it had over 500,000 members. The avowed policy was to promote a **general strike** for an eight-hour day. But the organization suffered from the confusion of trade-union aims with the co-operative and socialist aspirations of Owen and his disciple, **William Thompson** (1783–1833). The Grand National made one or two small and futile experiments in co-operative production, but spent most of its energies in a series of aggressive and unsuccessful strikes. The government became seriously alarmed and resorted to drastic measures.

Mar. Six Dorchester Laborers, who had formed a lodge of the Grand National, were sentenced to seven years'

imprisonment. The Grand National dissolved in Oct., Owen quit the field, and a period of general apathy followed in the labor movement.

Apr. 22. Quadruple Alliance with France, Spain, and Portugal (p. 645).

July 9. Grey resigned.

July-Nov. First cabinet of **Lord Melbourne** (1779–1848) a right wing Liberal (the terms *Liberal* and *Conservative* were beginning to replace the older *Whigs* and *Tories*). The king had hoped for a coalition government (with Peel), was disappointed at the reconstitution of the Whig ministry and welcomed an early opportunity to accept the **resignation of Melbourne** (Nov. 15), who felt the strength of his party shaken by the loss of the leader in the House of Commons, **Lord John Althorp,** who became Earl Spencer on the death of his father.

Aug. 14. The New Poor Law. Earlier relief legislation was fundamentally altered and given coherent form by the new law, which limited payment of charitable doles to sick and aged paupers and established workhouses where able-bodied paupers were put to work. The law ended the vicious system of giving the dole to laborers as a supplement to low wages. It supplanted the great Poor Law of 1601 and its amendments of 1722, 1782, and 1795.

Nov.-1835, Apr. The short-lived first **Peel ministry.** In the general election of Jan. 1835 Peel set forth his conceptions of a new **liberal Conservatism** (*Tamworth Manifesto*): acceptance of the Reform Act of 1832, readiness to proceed further with "judicious reforms." He won wide support from the moderates of both parties, actively undertook the cause of reform, but was defeated shortly thereafter on the Irish question.

1835-1839. Second Melbourne cabinet. Melbourne promptly undertook the reform of the internal organization and administration of municipal government — untouched by the Reform Act, generally in the hands of self-elected, irresponsible, and corrupt councils.

1835, Sept. 9. The Municipal Corporations Bill provided a uniform plan of government for all boroughs and cities (London and 67 small towns excepted): a town council was to consist of mayor, aldermen, and councilors, the last-named elected for three years by the ratepayers, together with the freemen who had survived the Reform Act (the freemen were a limited number of privileged persons who had formerly chosen the corporations.) The mayor was to be chosen annually, the aldermen every six years by the councilors from among their own number.

Further reforms followed in 1836, notably legislation permitting civil marriages, some equalizations of episcopal and clerical incomes, permission to prisoners charged with felony to have full benefit of counsel, etc.

William IV died (1837, June 20) and was succeeded by his youthful niece,

1837-1901. VICTORIA (1819-1901), then eighteen. Victoria was the daughter of the Duke of Kent (d. 1820) and the duchess, a princess of Saxe-Coburg (for the Hanoverian dynasty see p. 610), who had brought up Victoria in England, but surrounded her by German influences, notably that of her brother Leopold (King of the Belgians, 1831, p. 623). Victoria's education had been solid and sensible, and she brought to her heavy duties graciousness and poise rarely associated with one of her age. She was self-willed on occasion, "rebuked" her ministers, but made no serious attempt to invade their rights under the parliamentary system despite the influence of her German adviser, **Baron von Stockmar** (1787-1863), who urged her to take a stand of greater independence.

The Melbourne government favored a conciliatory Irish policy (opposed by the Conservatives); it was faced by three Irish problems — poor relief, municipal reform, and the settlement of tithes.

1838, July 31. The **Poor Law Bill** extended provisions similar to those in the **New Poor Law** to Ireland. It was opposed by the Irish members of the House of Commons on the ground that the poor were too numerous to be provided for in workhouses. A second bill **converted the tithes** into a fixed rent charge, 75% of their nominal value and payable by the landlord. The municipal corporations in Ireland were controlled by self-appointed Protestant councils. **A new municipal act** (1840) conferred the right to vote on all persons paying £10 rent a year.

Weakened by attack on its policy in England, Ireland, and Canada (p. 793) the Melbourne government was in no position to survive the disaffection occasioned by the settlement of the

1839, Apr. 9. Jamaica problem. Following emancipation of the slaves, economic conditions had grown rapidly worse for the planters, who were guilty of great brutality toward their former slaves. The upshot was the suspension for five years of the **Jamaica Constitution**, a drastic measure carried by only five votes in the Commons. Melbourne felt his position seriously shaken, resigned soon after (May 7).

May. Cabinet crisis. The queen turned regretfully to Wellington, then to Peel. The latter refused to form a ministry unless certain of the queen's lady attendants (all members of Whig families) were changed (the **Bedchamber Question**). The queen was indignant and turned again to Melbourne, who formed

1839, May—1841, Aug. The third Melbourne ministry.

1839. CHARTIST AGITATION. The Chartist movement was a direct outcome of dissatisfaction with the reforms of the Whigs among the laboring classes and of the failure of the trade-union movement. It had its origin when (1836) a **Workingmen's Association** in London set forth its program in a petition or **charter** to Parliament. This demanded: (1) manhood suffrage; (2) vote by ballot; (3) abolition of property qualification for members of Parliament; (4) payment of members; (5) equal electoral districts; (6) annual Parliaments. The working public was rapidly converted to this program by missionaries who toured the country, held huge meetings and organized torchlight processions. Gradually more radical elements emerged, notably **Feargus O'Connor** (1794-1855) who headed a **party of physical force** opposed by **William Lovett's party of moral force**, both within the larger movement.

Feb. The first **National Convention of Chartists** met in London.

May 13. The **charter was presented to Parliament**, which rejected it. The convention adjourned to Birmingham, issued a radical manifesto appealing to members to defend liberty by use of arms.

July. Serious **riots** in Birmingham and elsewhere.

Nov. 4. In a **riot at Newport** (Wales) the crowd was fired on by the constables and 20 were killed. John **Frost**, the leader, and others were sentenced to death, but ultimately transported to the penal colonies. The movement then turned back to more moderate channels.

Nov. 3. Outbreak of the Opium War with China (p. 878).

1840, Jan. 10. A pamphlet by **Rowland Hill** (1795-1879) on postal reform led to the institution of **uniform penny postage** (for letters under half an ounce to any point in the United Kingdom), a substitute for the previous exorbitant rates and the cumbersome system of charges varying with size, weight, and shape of letters — a revolution in communication.

Feb. 10. The queen married her first cousin, **Albert of Saxe-Coburg-Gotha,** a sober and sensible prince, to whom

The British Royal House (Hanover; Saxe-Coburg; Windsor)

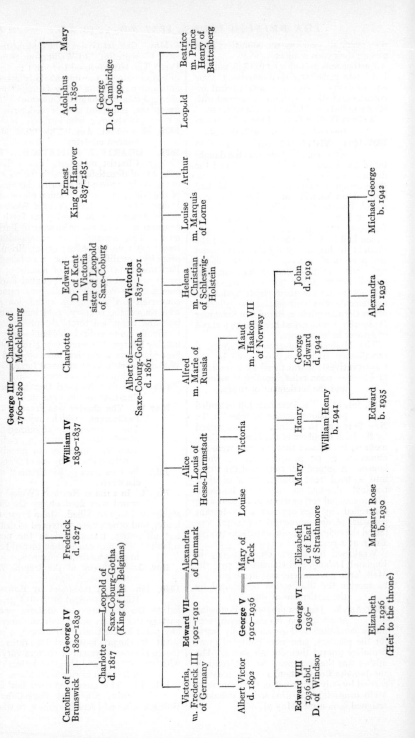

she became profoundly devoted. The marriage was generally condemned by Conservative leaders, and Albert suffered from rumors that he was a "papist" (although all his family were Lutheran), from the demands of the queen that he be named *King Consort* (he was made *Prince Consort* by royal letters patent only in 1857), and that he be voted a civil list of £50,000 (reduced to £30,000), etc. Albert succeeded Melbourne as royal private secretary, and in time became, with the queen, joint ruler of the nation, in fact if not in name.

In the spring of 1841 Melbourne's government was twice defeated on a tariff measure in the Commons, appealed to the country, and was again defeated by the Conservatives.

1841, Aug. 28. Melbourne finally resigned following a vote of censure, and was succeeded by

1841, Sept.—1846, June. The second Peel cabinet, which included a number of men of distinction and young men of promise, notably **William Ewart Gladstone** (1809-1898) as vice-president of the board of trade. Peel turned first to the deficit, the most pressing problem. He **modified the sliding scale of 1828 on corn imports** (1842, Apr. 29) to encourage importation; **removed prohibitory duties** and drastically reduced duties on a vast number of imports, especially raw materials and prime foodstuffs; **revived the income tax** to provide against possible losses from lower tariffs; **abolished import and export duties on wool.** Peel, a protectionist, was already moving in the direction of free trade.

1842, Apr. 12-May 12. Second National Convention of Chartists in London. A second petition to Parliament was again rejected (May 3) and a "turn-out" followed in August. In Lancashire the strike spread rapidly and the moderates were again outmaneuvered by the radicals. Nevertheless the movement gradually collapsed. It remained in eclipse until 1848, when a last national convention was held, a huge demonstration arranged, and the charter once more presented to Parliament.

Aug. 9. Webster-Ashburton Treaty with the United States (p. 773).

1844. The Bank Charter Act, designed to meet the problem presented by the rapid growth of joint-stock banks. These issued great quantities of paper money at a time when British gold reserves were being depleted by shipments abroad, largely to the United States. The Bank Charter Act separated the banking department from the note-issuing department of the Bank of England; required that note issues of the Bank should be covered by coin or bullion, except for £14,000,000 covered by government securities; prohibited new banks from issuing notes and limited old banks to the existing amount. The tendency of the act was to eliminate by degrees all notes except those of the Bank of England.

1845. Peel's **second free-trade budget** eliminated export duties entirely, and also duties on cotton, glass, etc.

1845. Formation of the **National Association of the United Traders for the Protection of Labor,** marking the revival of the trade-union movement. The new organization undertook to deal with disputes between master and men, look after the interests of labor in Parliament. The program showed that the movement had discarded the aggressive policy and ambitious aims of the years 1830-1834. Strikes were deprecated and the idea of the general strike abandoned in favor of conciliation and arbitration.

1845-1846. Anti-Corn Law agitation. This gradually absorbed much of the interest of the working classes. It centered in Manchester and was fostered by the political leaders of the **Manchester School,** notably **Richard Cobden** (1804-1865) and **John Bright** (1811-1889), both manufacturers of middle-class origin. Their interests extended not only to free corn (i.e. grain import), but to **free trade** in general, in which they saw a boon both for the workers (cheap food and higher wages) and factory owners (cheap raw materials and the expansion of markets). The **Manchester Anti-Corn Law Association** (1838) was launched in the midst of the economic depression which began in 1837. Similar organizations rapidly appeared elsewhere, and all joined to form the **Anti-Corn Law League** (1839). The widespread propaganda of the league was met by the bitter opposition of Conservative landlords, but was carried to the farmers as well as the workers. The farmers were attracted by the argument that free trade meant low prices for means of subsistence, and cheap food meant low wages, by which England would be able to compete successfully with foreign competition. The argument that appealed to the workers was as follows: the abolition of the corn duties would reduce the price of food, which would enable the people to spend more on manufactured goods and so increase the demand for them. This in turn would lead to more employment and higher wages in industry.

Peel's support for Corn Law reform finally came as a result of the ruin of the

Irish potato crop and the consequent threat of famine in the island unless prompt relief measures were taken.

1845, Nov. 22. The Whig leader, **Lord John Russell,** announced his conversion to free trade. Unable to forestall a Whig success by the enactment of a repeal measure, **Peel resigned** (Dec. 5), but returned to office (Dec. 20) when Russell was unable to form a government.

1846, Jan. ff. New free-trade proposals met with stiff resistance from a block of Conservatives led by **Benjamin Disraeli** (1804–1881), who denounced Peel for betraying the protectionist principles of his party. A struggle of two months was followed by the

1846, June 6. REPEAL OF THE CORN LAWS. After passage of both the Corn and Customs bills by the Commons (May 15), Wellington again induced the Lords to yield. The **Corn Law** provided for the immediate repeal of earlier legislation and fixed the duty on corn at a shilling a quarter from 1849, preserving a small protective duty in the intervening years. The **Customs Law** abolished the duties on all live animals and nearly every kind of meat, and reduced the duties on cheese, butter, and other foods. Many duties on manufactured goods were abolished and others greatly reduced.

June 15. Oregon Boundary Treaty with the United States (p. 773).

June 29. Peel's government was overthrown by a revolt led by **Benjamin Disraeli,** who objected to a new coercion bill for Ireland.

c. PALMERSTON AND RUSSELL, 1846-1868]

1846, July—1852, Feb. Cabinet of Lord John Russell.

1847-1848. Young Ireland. The Irish famine of the forties resulted in the growth of a revolutionary movement in the island. Even before the **death of Daniel O'Connell** (1847), the leadership of the Irish nationalists had passed to the **Young Ireland Party** (founded 1840), under **William Smith O'Brien** (1803–1864). This radical group rejected O'Connell's peaceful methods to secure repeal of the union. A series of agrarian crimes in the autumn of 1847 was followed by the suspension of the *Habeas Corpus Act* for Ireland. This measure, together with news of the revolutions on the Continent, precipitated an **insurrection in Tipperary** (1848, July 29), O'Brien hoping that the peasantry would support it. The rising proved abortive, as

the rebels fled before a squad of constabulary.

1850. The **Don Pacifico affair.** Don Pacifico was a Moorish Jew, but a British subject. He held large claims against the Greek government which he pressed with vigor until an anti-Semitic mob burned his house in Athens (1849, Dec.). Palmerston ordered a British squadron to the Piraeus to force a settlement of this and other claims on the Greek government. The Greeks proving obstinate, the British laid an **embargo on all Greek vessels** in the Piraeus and finally seized them (1850, Jan.). After abortive mediation by the French, the Greeks were eventually forced to comply (Apr. 26). Palmerston defended his action in his greatest parliamentary speech (June 29), in which he appealed to British pride and nationalism (*civis Romanus sum*).

1850-1851. Formation of the **Amalgamated Society of Engineers,** a new type of labor organization based on high contributions and provision of benefits as well as direct action and collective bargaining. A number of further "amalgamated societies" were organized and their leaders gradually assumed control of the trade-union movement.

The **Oxford Movement** centered at Oxford, and had as its chief **J. H.** (later Cardinal) **Newman** (1801–1890). It endeavored to prove that the doctrines of the Anglican Church were identical with those of the Roman Catholic Church, therefore that every Catholic doctrine might be held by Anglicans. In 1845 Newman and many of his associates seceded to the Church of Rome, whereupon the English people, thoroughly Protestant, became alarmed, fearing that the real object of the *Tractarians* (so-called from the tracts they published) was to reconcile England with Rome. Popular apprehension of "papal aggression" was stirred by a papal bull (1850, Sept. 30) setting up a hierarchy of bishops in England who were to derive their titles from English sees created by the bull. The sympathies of the Whig ministry, and especially of Lord John Russell, the prime minister, were with the people.

1851, Feb. The **Ecclesiastical Titles Bill,** which forbade the assumption by priests and bishops of the Roman Catholic Church of titles taken from any territory or place within the United Kingdom, and declared null and void all acts of possessors of such titles. The law remained a dead letter and was repealed in 1871.

May 1-Oct. 15. The **Great Exhibition of 1851** in Hyde Park, for which Prince Albert was largely responsible, included exhibits from all nations, and was the first of its kind. *Prosperity* was the note it sounded, and it was confidently expected that the exhibition would inaugurate an era of international peace.

Dec. Conflict between the queen and Lord Palmerston. Victoria had long been dissatisfied by the foreign minister's indiscretions and boisterous nationalistic policy, to say nothing of his tendency to ignore royal suggestions and advice. After the Don Pacifico incident, the queen, assisted by Prince Albert and Baron Stockmar, drew up a famous memorandum demanding that the queen be kept informed and that, once she had approved a measure, it should not be arbitrarily altered. Palmerston promised to mend his ways, but in the following months a new crisis occurred. Palmerston at once approved of the *coup d'état* of Louis Napoleon in France (Dec. 2), but the cabinet, adopting the queen's attitude, on Dec. 5 instructed the ambassador at Paris to carry on as though nothing had occurred, passing no judgment. The resulting embarrassment enabled the queen to force **Palmerston's dismissal** (Dec. 19).

1852, Feb. 20. Lord John Russell's cabinet was defeated on a militia bill.

Feb. 27-Dec. 17. Cabinet of Lord Derby (Conservative).

1852, Dec. 28—1855, Jan. 20. Lord Aberdeen's ministry, with a coalition of Whigs and Peelites.

1854, Mar. 28. Outbreak of the Crimean War (p. 727).

1855, Feb. 5—1858, Feb. 22. First Palmerston cabinet, resulting from popular dissatisfaction with Aberdeen's policy in the war.

1857. The Indian Mutiny (p. 870).

1857-1858. War with China (p. 879).

1858, Feb. 25—1859, June 11. Second Derby ministry, after Palmerston's government was defeated on a bill to increase the penalty for conspiracy to murder (following French representations after the Orsini bomb affair, p. 643).

1858, June. An act brought to an end the property qualifications for members of Parliament.

July 23. Removal of disabilities on Jews.

Aug. 2. India Bill, by which the British East India Company's political powers were brought to an end and the government of India was assumed by the crown (p. 870).

1859, June 18—1865, Nov. 6. Second Palmerston ministry, after the defeat of Lord Derby's reform bill.

1860, Jan. 23. The famous **commercial treaty** signed with France (*Cobden-*

Chevalier Treaty) marking a great advance toward free trade on the part of France.

1861, Nov.-Dec. The Trent affair. Crisis in Anglo-American relations resulting from the Civil War (p. 776).

Dec. 14. Death of the Prince Consort. For a period of many years Queen Victoria withdrew more and more from all public functions and thereby suffered a period of marked unpopularity.

1864, Apr. 28. Great Britain abandoned the protectorate over the **Ionian Islands** (assumed in 1815) and made over the islands to Greece, in order to stabilize the new Danish dynasty (p. 710).

1865, Oct. 18. Death of Lord Palmerston.

1865, Nov. 6—1866, June. Second ministry of Lord John Russell. On the death of Palmerston, Russell succeeded as prime minister. He was faced by urgent demands for further electoral reform, which he had previously sponsored in a perfunctory way. Only one man in six possessed the vote, and workers were virtually excluded. Repeated measures for franchise extension had been defeated in the Commons, while industrial growth had exaggerated electoral anomalies left by the Act of 1832.

1866, Mar. Russell introduced an anodyne measure which was defeated as the result of the defection of a section of the Liberals. Russell resigned in June.

1866, July 6—1868, Feb. 25. The third Derby ministry, in which the dominant figure was to be **Disraeli,** once more leader of the House of Commons. Workers' demands for suffrage reform spread rapidly, and Disraeli was literally obliged to adopt the Liberal program of electoral reform, which in the end he had to extend radically, despite the opposition of many Conservatives.

1867, Aug. 15. THE SECOND REFORM BILL extended the suffrage: in *boroughs* to all householders paying the poor rates and all lodgers of one year's residence paying an annual rent of £10; in the *counties,* to owners of land of £5 annual value, to occupying tenants paying £12 annual rental. All boroughs of fewer than 10,000 population lost the right of sending two members to the Commons; Manchester, Birmingham, Liverpool, Leeds were given each a third member; two other large towns, Salford and Merthyr, received a second member; nine *new boroughs* were created; 25 additional members were allotted to the counties. The **Scotch Reform Bill** of 1868

(July 13) founded generally upon the same principles as the English bill, gave Scotland seven new seats. The **Irish Reform Bill** of 1868 (July 13) reduced the borough franchise requirement, left the county franchise unaltered, and left the Irish representation unchanged. A radically democratic step had been taken: the electorate was increased from roughly 1,000,000 to 2,000,000. Disraeli had "dished the Whigs," but had violated his party pledges and had taken a step bitterly opposed by many Conservatives and described even by Derby as a "leap in the dark."

1867-1868. Abyssinian expedition (p. 834).

d. DISRAELI AND GLADSTONE 1868-1894

1868, Feb. 29—Dec. 2. First Disraeli ministry, which came to an end after the sweeping Liberal victory in the elections of Nov. 1868.

1868, Dec. 9—1874, Feb. 17. First Gladstone ministry. Gladstone (1809–1898) was the son of a Liverpool merchant, a product of the aristocratic influences of Eton and Christ Church, Oxford. He was widely learned, profoundly devout, possessed of typical Scotch industry. He had entered politics as a Tory, seceded with the Peelites, ended as a Liberal. He possessed a vast knowledge of internal problems, especially of financial questions. In the field of foreign relations he was hampered in an age of imperialist expansion by humanitarian principles and sympathies with minorities abroad.

1868-1869. The Irish Question. Prior to taking office Gladstone had declared: "My mission is to pacify Ireland." The **Fenian Brotherhood,** formed in 1858 in New York, collected funds among the American Irish, aimed to overthrow British rule in Ireland. **O'Donovan Rossa** and **James Stephens** were arrested (Sept. Nov. 1865) and supplies of arms were taken. A Fenian invasion of Canada (1866) failed (p. 796). A general rising in Ireland miscarried (1867, Mar.). Further "outrages" followed, notably the attempt to deliver two prisoners from Clerkenwell, London (Dec. 13), when a blast in the wall caused the death of 12, the injury of 120 more. Gladstone attacked what he considered the causes of the discontent — disestablishment and land tenure (neither of which had figured among Fenian aims).

1869, July 26. The Disestablishment Act provided that the Irish (Episcopal) Church should cease to exist as of Jan. 1, 1871. The Church's endowments were to be taken away with compensation for interests affected; church buildings, etc., were to be reserved to a new voluntary organization; the tithe rent-charge on estates, the Church's chief source of revenue, was to be purchased by the landlords for some £8,212,500; provision was made for the care of Episcopal clergymen during their lifetime. Irish Catholics were no longer to be obliged to support a state church of which they were not communicants. Despite the opposition of the Episcopal clergy, the Conservatives in general and the House of Lords in particular (again threatened with the creation of new peers), the bill passed.

1870, Aug. 1. Irish Land Act. The sufferings of the Irish were in considerable measure due to the prevalent system of **land tenure.** There was a vast difference between the rural landlord in England and his Irish counterpart — the former putting money into the land and making improvements for the tenants; the latter merely drawing rack-rent which he often spent in England, leaving the tenants to do everything for themselves, and often evicting them wholesale without compensation for improvements. In 1850 a **Tenant-Right League** was founded to obtain for the tenant the "three F's" — a **fair rent, fixity of tenure,** and **free sale.** The movement spread rapidly. In 1870 Gladstone introduced an Irish Land Bill. It contained no recognition of the "three F's," but it gave the tenant the right to compensation for disturbance (that is, eviction) and for improvements (if, without fault on his side, he was evicted, but not where the ejection was for non-payment of rent). The **Bright clauses** of the bill facilitated the creation of a peasant proprietorship by allowing government loans to be granted to tenants who wished to buy their holdings from their landlords. The act did not extinguish the evils with which it was designed to deal. It interfered with the landlord's right of disposing of his land on the absolute basis of free contract, but it did not protect the tenant against increased rent, nor did it give him security of tenure. The Act of 1870 was important chiefly as the first of a great series of Irish agrarian laws. It did not allay Irish agitation. Even while the bill was in progress, in the spring of 1870, agrarian outrages occurred in County Mayo. By the **Peace Preservation Act** (Apr. 4), the government increased its powers of repression.

1870, Aug. 9. An important **Education Bill** aimed to remedy the existing chaotic situation: nearly half of the 4,000-000 children of school age were unprovided for; about 1,000,000 attended schools attached to the Church of England, government inspected and supported by voluntary subscriptions supplemented by government grants; another million attended schools unsupported by the government and uninspected. On the whole English education was far inferior to that in Prussia, Switzerland, the United States. The Education Bill, brought in by **W. E. Forster** (1818–1886), provided for two types of schools: (1) those voluntary schools doing good work were to be retained, government grants were to be increased, but they were to receive no aid from local rates; (2) elsewhere *board schools* (under the control of locally elected boards) were to be set up and maintained by government grants, parents' fees, local rates (the question of compulsory attendance was to be passed on by each local board). The question of religious education was crucial: the voluntary schools were permitted to continue religious instruction; all denominational religious instruction was prohibited in the board schools — a compromise satisfying neither of the extreme groups.

1870, June 4. **Order in council reforming the civil service,** by providing that candidates for ordinary posts should, in the discretion of department heads, be given competitive examinations. The new order was speedily adopted by almost all the chief departments, the foreign office remaining a notable exception.

1871, June. **The University Tests Act** conferred on Cambridge and Oxford students the right to obtain university degrees and to hold lay offices in colleges and universities without subscribing to any religious tests.

The **Army Regulation Bill** virtually reorganized the British army, a reform associated with the name of **Edward Cardwell** (1813–1886), the secretary of war. The system of purchasing commissions was abolished; short service was introduced, which made possible a well-trained reserve (six years with the colors and six in the reserves, instead of twelve years' service); etc.

1872. **The Ballot Act** made voting secret for the first time.

Sept. 14. **Settlement of the Alabama Claims** (p. 781).

The prestige of the Gladstone ministry rapidly declined: the Education Act alienated nonconformists and high churchmen alike; reduction in the number of dockyard workers caused dissatisfaction; the elimination of the purchase of army commissions irritated the upper classes. When Gladstone introduced a bill to unite Irish

colleges in a single university open to Catholics and Protestants alike, he was defeated and resigned (1873, Feb.). Disraeli was reluctant to take office as yet, Gladstone returned, sponsored a notable reform of the law courts in

1873. **The Judicature Act,** which, along with supplementary acts, consolidated the three common law courts, chancery, and various other tribunals into one **supreme court of judicature,** to consist of two principal divisions: (1) The *high court of justice* — (a) queen's bench, (b) chancery, (c) probate, divorce, and admiralty; (2) the *court of appeal,* from which appellate jurisdiction lay to the House of Lords, strengthened in 1876 by the addition of three (later four) law lords of life tenure.

1874, Feb. Gladstone appealed to the country in a general election, was overwhelmed by the Conservatives, who succeeded to power with Disraeli as prime minister.

1874, Feb. 21—1880, Apr. 22. **The second Disraeli ministry** came to power with the expressed purpose of "giving the country a rest" at home and pursuing a foreign policy more in accord with the demands of British prestige and interests. Certain measures of a domestic character were passed, notably a

1875. **Public Health Act,** a codification of earlier legislation which remains even today the backbone of English sanitary law; an

1875. **Artisans' Dwelling Act,** the first serious attempt by the government to grapple with the problem of the housing of the poor.

1876. **The Merchant Shipping Act,** aimed to prevent overloading ships or permitting use of unseaworthy vessels (the act a result of persistent efforts of **Samuel Plimsoll** [1824–1898], the "sailors' friend").

But the country's attention was riveted on foreign and colonial affairs.

1875, Nov. 25. **Purchase of the Suez Canal shares.** The completion of the Suez Canal under the direction of a Frenchman, Ferdinand de Lesseps (1805–1894), and under the auspices of an international company, greatly shortened the distance to India and the east and heightened English interest in Egypt. **Khedive Ismail** of Egypt, who held 44% of the shares, was in perennial financial difficulties, and finally considered mortgaging his shares in Paris. This information came to Disraeli's attention; he sprang a *coup* by negotiating purchase of the shares on his own responsibility. A grateful Parliament subsequently ratified the act. This marked the beginning of British penetration and presently occupation of Egypt (p. 832).

1876, Apr. The **Royal Titles Bill** declared the queen *Empress of India*, deeply flattered Her Majesty, was the occasion of great enthusiasm in India, caused considerable opposition among educated Englishmen — the title was "un-English" and in disrepute through the fall of Emperor Napoleon III and the tragedy of Emperor Maximilian of Mexico (the opposition was allayed by the promise that she would not use it in England).

Aug. Disraeli was elevated to the peerage as the **Earl of Beaconsfield.** During the remainder of its term of office the government was absorbed by the crisis of 1875–1876 in the Near East, culminating in the **Russo-Turkish War** and the **Congress of Berlin** (p. 735), by the **Afghan War** of 1878–1879 (p. 867), and by the war with the **Zulus** in South Africa (p. 853). Beaconsfield's popularity had reached its zenith when he returned from the Congress of Berlin.

1879. A severe **agricultural depression** with the worst harvest of the century accompanied by a decline in trade, strikes, the unpopular Afghan and Zulu wars, obstruction by the new **Irish Home Rule Party** in the House of Commons.

Nov. **Gladstone** roundly denounced the government, alike for its imperialism and its domestic policy, in a series of speeches to his **Midlothian** constituents.

1880, Mar. 8. Beaconsfield appealed to the country in a general election, his party was defeated, and he resigned (Apr. 18), to be succeeded by Gladstone.

1880, Apr. 28-1885, June 8. Second Gladstone ministry. Much of the session of 1880 was occupied by the famous case of **Charles Bradlaugh**, newly elected to the Commons, who as an atheist refused to take the oath (including the words "So help me God") and insisted on an affirmation instead. An **Affirmation Bill** was twice defeated (1881, 1883); Bradlaugh changed his mind, offered to take the oath, was refused the right (as a freethinker). Subsequently he was involved in eight lawsuits, was unseated and re-elected repeatedly, was finally permitted to take the oath (1886, Jan.). Bradlaugh secured passage of a bill (1888) legalizing affirmation both in the Commons and the courts, removing the last religious disability for membership in the House.

1880, Sept. 13. First Employers' Liability Act, granting compensation to workers for injuries not their own fault.

1881-1882. The Irish Question. Foundation (1871) of the parliamentary **Home Rule for Ireland Party** by Isaac Butt, who aimed at securing by peaceful means a separate legislature for Ireland. The dominant figure soon became **Charles Stewart Parnell** (1846–1891), descendant of English Protestant settlers in Ireland, but consumed by hatred for England; brilliant orator, elected to Parliament in 1875. Parnell hoped to unite all elements of Irish opposition and to force the grant of Home Rule by the use of obstruction in Parliament. The Peace Preservation Act of 1875 expired in 1880 and the government, unable to maintain order under ordinary law, was obliged to resort to new **coercive measures.**

1881, Aug. Gladstone then passed the **Land Act,** which aimed to correct the defects in his Act of 1870 and to meet the Irish demand for the three "F's." The act recognized a dual ownership of land and provided for the creation of a court to mediate between landlord and tenant and fix a "fair" rent for a period of 15 years; it gave increased fixity of tenure to tenants who paid those rents, with the right to sell their interest in the holdings to the highest bidder. While it established a land court, with authority to cut down excessive rents, the act made no provision for dealing with accumulated arrears. It pleased neither landlords nor tenants.

Oct. 13. Parnell and others were sent to Kilmainham Prison for inciting Irishmen to intimidate tenants taking advantage of the act. They were released (1882, May 2) when they agreed in the "Kilmainham Treaty" to cease "boycotting" and co-operate with the Liberal Party.

1882, May 6. Lord Frederick Cavendish, new chief secretary for Ireland, and **Thomas Burke,** permanent undersecretary, were murdered in broad daylight by Fenians in **Phoenix Park,** Dublin. Parnell repudiated all connection with the crime and offered to resign his leadership of the Home Rule Party.

July. The government put through the draconian **Prevention of Crimes Bill** (limited to three years) suspending trial by jury and giving the police unlimited power to search and arrest on suspicion. Irish extremists, with whom Parnell denied all connection, resorted to a **campaign of terrorism,** punctuated by dynamiting of public buildings in England.

1883, Aug. The Corrupt and Illegal Practices Act in effect limited the total amounts which might be spent (all parties) in a general election to £800,000 (£2,500, ooo had been spent in the general election of 1880); no candidate might spend more than a fixed sum for election purposes; penalties for corrupt practices were greatly increased.

1884. Gladstone's Franchise Bill aimed to extend the rights enjoyed by the borough voters to the rural classes and to unify substantially the franchise throughout the United Kingdom. The measure virtually provided manhood suffrage — only domestic servants, bachelors living with their families, and those of no fixed abode being excluded. Some 2,000,000 voters were to be added, nearly four times the number added in 1832, nearly twice that added in 1867. The bill passed the Commons, was rejected by the Lords, the Conservatives insisting on the importance of a concomitant redistribution of seats. Negotiations followed; Gladstone yielded in the matter of redistribution; the Franchise Bill itself passed easily (Dec.).

1885, June. A **Redistribution Bill** followed — London received 37 additional members, Liverpool 6, Birmingham 4, Glasgow 4, Yorkshire 16, Lancashire 15; single-member constituencies became the rule, except in the City of London and in cities and boroughs with a population between 50,000 and 165,000; boroughs of fewer than 15,000 population were merged with their counties. By this legislation the historic counties and boroughs ceased to be, as such, the basis of the House of Commons. The individual for the first time became the unit, and numerical equality ("one vote, one value") the master principle.

Despite his resistance to the imperialist policy of Disraeli, his withdrawal from Afghanistan (p. 868), his concessions to the Boers in South Africa (p. 853), Gladstone was fated to play an active rôle in the field of colonial expansion.

1882. Britain was obliged to intervene in Egypt (p. 832), and the prestige of the cabinet was seriously damaged when it failed to rescue General Gordon, isolated in the Sudan (p. 832).

1884-1885. Russian encroachments in Afghanistan nearly led to war, and the pacific policy of the foreign minister, Lord Granville, led to Conservative accusations of truckling to the Russians (pp. 739, 868).

1885, June 9. A hostile amendment to his budget led to **Gladstone's resignation.**

1885, June 24—1886, Jan. 27. First Salisbury ministry. Salisbury had become head of the Conservative Party on the death of Beaconsfield (1881, Apr. 19).

1885, Aug. Ashbourne Act. The Conservatives had previously been the party of Irish coercion, but Salisbury reached an understanding with Parnell that this policy should be reversed in return for Irish Nationalist support. A fund of £5,000,000 was provided by the Ashbourne Act for loans with which Irish tenants could purchase their holdings on an easy-interest, long-term basis (extending a feature of the Liberal Land Act of 1881). **Further Land Purchase Acts** were adopted in 1887, 1891, 1896, and 1903 (the last named providing an eventual sum of £100,000,000).

1886, Feb. 12—July 20. Third Gladstone ministry. Gladstone's support for Home Rule had been secured (1885, Dec.), and during his third ministry he introduced his

1886, Apr. 8. First Home Rule Bill, providing for a separate Irish legislature of two orders (one of 28 representative peers, with 75 other members elected by and from the propertied classes, the other of 204 elected members). The Irish legislature was to have important powers, but legislation relating to the crown, the army and navy, trade and navigation, etc., were still to be dealt with by the British Parliament in which Irish members were no longer to sit. The measure was bitterly attacked by the Conservatives, caused a secession from the Liberal Party of the **"Liberal Unionists"** (Hartington, Joseph Chamberlain), and was finally defeated (July). A general election was called and produced a new defeat for the Liberals.

1886, July 26—1892, Aug. 13. Second Salisbury ministry. Arthur Balfour (1848-1930), the prime minister's nephew, was made chief secretary for Ireland and carried a new **Crimes Bill** (1887) whose passage was facilitated by the publication of a notorious series of articles by the *Times* on "Parnellism and Crime," including an alleged letter of Parnell's declaring he had condemned the Phoenix Park murders only as a matter of policy. Parnell denied authorship of this and other letters, was cleared (1890) by a governmental commission (the author was Richard Piggott, broken-down Irish journalist and subsequent suicide). Soon thereafter Parnell's position was ruined when he was named co-respondent in a divorce suit brought by Captain O'Shea, one of his followers. Gladstone dropped him, a schism followed among the Nationalists, **Justin McCarthy** became leader of the majority. When Parnell died (1891, Oct. 6), **John Redmond** (1856-1918) succeeded him as leader of the minority.

1889, May 31. Naval Defense Act, designed to meet growing sea-power of France and Russia. It provided that the British fleet should always be as strong as the fleets of the two next strongest powers combined (**two-power standard**).

1889, Aug. 15—Sept. 16. Great London dock strike, in which almost all riverside workers joined. This great strike and the formation of the **Miners' Federation of Great Britain** (1888) marked the extension of trade-unionism from the skilled classes (represented in the Amalgamated Societies) to the less skilled.

1892. In the **general election** Gladstone made Home Rule the principal issue of the campaign, advocating also a series of additional reforms (**Newcastle Program**): disestablishment of the Church of England in Wales, and of the Church of Scotland; local veto on liquor sales; abolition of plural voting; extension of the Employers' Liability Act; restriction of hours of labor. The election gave Gladstone sufficient votes, with the aid of 81 Irish Nationalists, to carry his Home Rule plank.

1892, Aug. 18—1894, Mar. 3. Fourth Gladstone cabinet.

1893, Feb. 13. Second Home Rule Bill. Its principal difference from the first bill was the provision that 80 Irish representatives should sit at Westminster. It passed the Commons (Sept. 1), but was overwhelmed by the Lords (Sept. 8). A period of comparative peace followed in Ireland and Home Rule sank in importance, to be revived only two decades later. **John Morley** (1838–1923), Irish secretary (1892–1895), ruled with sympathy and wisdom. The Conservative régime (1895–1905) continued its traditional tactics of killing Home Rule by kindness (new Land Purchase Acts, 1896, 1903).

1893, Jan. Foundation of the Independent Labor Party, a frankly socialist party. Socialism, which had declined in the forties, had revived in the eighties under the influence of the American Henry George's *Progress and Poverty* (1879). In 1884 **H.M. Hyndman** (1842–1921) founded the **Social Democratic Federation,** a Marxist organization. In 1883 was founded the **Fabian Society,** which became prominent with the publication (1889) of the *Fabian Essays.* Prominent among the Fabians were **Sidney** and **Beatrice Webb** (1859–1947, 1858–1943) and **George Bernard Shaw** (1856–1950). They preached practical possibilities — municipal socialism and state control of the conditions of labor — and expected socialism to come as a sequel to the full application of universal suffrage

and representative government. In 1892 the first two avowed socialists were elected to Parliament. One of them, **James Keir Hardie** (1856–1915), was mainly responsible for the foundation of the Labor Party.

1894, Mar. Gladstone had lost his fight for Home Rule, had shattered the Liberal Party. He resigned the premiership and was succeeded by the Liberal imperialist Lord Rosebery (1847–1929).

1894, Mar. 5—1895, June 21. Cabinet of Lord Rosebery. Sir William Harcourt (1827–1904), now leader of the House of Commons, brought in a bill adding £4,000,000 to the budget by equalizing death duties on real and personal property and providing a graduated tax of 1 to 8% — an attempt further to shift the burden of taxation to the wealthy. The cabinet was defeated on a matter of minor importance, and resigned.

e. A DECADE OF UNIONISM, 1895-1905

1895, June 25—1902, July 11. Third Salisbury ministry, with Salisbury himself as foreign minister, Balfour as first lord of the treasury and leader of the Commons. The cabinet included some of the principal Liberal Unionists, notably Hartington (Duke of Devonshire since 1891) and **Joseph Chamberlain.** The latter's political beginnings had been as a radical; as colonial secretary, he now devoted his great energy and ability to the cause of enhancing British imperial prestige. The new government's attention was almost entirely absorbed by events abroad — the **Venezuela Boundary** dispute with the United States (p. 786), the **Armenian Massacres** and the **Greco-Turkish War** (pp. 744, 746), the struggle for power in the **Far East** (pp. 744–746), the **Hague Conference of 1899** (p. 748), the **South African problem** which culminated in the **Boer War** (p. 857).

1900, Feb. Formation of the Labor Representation Committee, with J. **Ramsay MacDonald** (1866–1937) as secretary. The committee represented the Independent Labor Party, Trade-Union Congress, and various socialist organizations. Its aim was to establish a distinct Labor group in Parliament, but it had a hard struggle for existence. Only about 5% of the unions affiliated themselves with it, the Social Democratic Federation soon withdrew, the attitude of the Fabians was cool, and the miners were hostile. At the general election of 1900 the committee ran 15 candidates, of whom only two were returned. But the decision of the Lords in the **Taff Vale case** (1902, July), which declared unions legal entities capable of being sued, consolidated the ranks of labor and created the **Labor Party**, which returned 29 members in the election of 1906.

1901. Jan. 22. Death of Queen Victoria after one of the longest reigns in European history. She was widely mourned, reflecting the respect for her courage, strength of character, and the tact with which she had recognized the constitutional limitations of the crown and yielded to the steadily enlarging powers of her ministries. In the last decades Victoria had come to be regarded above all as the symbol of imperial unity, an aspect of the monarchy upon which attention had been brilliantly and effectively focused by the **Jubilee of 1887** (celebrating the fiftieth anniversary of the queen's accession) and by the **Diamond Jubilee of 1897.** The reign had witnessed a period of incredible industrial expansion and increasing material prosperity. The population of the United Kingdom had increased from 16,261,183 in 1831 to 37,518,052 in 1901.

1901-1910. EDWARD VII (b. 1841). Edward was nearly sixty, and Victoria had deprived him until recently of serious participation in matters political. He was possessed of great social charm and tact, read little, cared nothing for routine, gathered information largely from personal contact. He was gay and fond of pleasure, a yachting enthusiast, patron of the turf, supporter of philanthropic causes, widely popular with all classes before his accession.

1902, July 11—1905, Dec. 4. Cabinet of Arthur Balfour, following the retirement of Lord Salisbury.

1902, Dec. The Education Act was the most important legislative achievement of the Balfour government. For some time it had been felt that the school boards of the Education Act of 1870, although they had worked well in the towns, were on the whole too parochial in personnel and policy. The Act of 1902 abolished the boards, placed elementary and secondary education in the hands of statutory committees of the borough and county councils. The denominational schools, hitherto belonging to and maintained by the Anglicans and Catholics, were brought into the reorganization *pari passu* with the undenominational board schools. For the first time in England the provision of secondary education was recognized as the duty of the state and was brought under public control. Educational progress under the act was rapid; in five years the number of secondary schools doubled.

1903, May. Joseph Chamberlain and the **Tariff Reform League** advocated a sweeping tariff reform, with moderate duties on corn, flour, meats, dairy produce, and foreign manufactures. The new system was to give Britain a basis for bargaining with the colonies, of preventing foreign dumping in Britain, of increasing the revenue. Balfour was unwilling to go so far, and Chamberlain resigned (Sept. 18).

1904. Committee of Imperial Defense. The South African War had revealed serious defects in the army. The report of the commission of inquiry was an "unsparing condemnation of war office methods." The upshot was the organization of the Defense Committee with the prime minister as its head; the commander-in-chief was replaced by an army council which included the war secretary, four military members, one civil and one finance member; a board of selection (Duke of Connaught, president) was to control appointments.

Foreign relations bulked large in a period when Britain settled her differences with France in the **Entente cordiale** of 1904 (p. 752), European peace was threatened in the **Moroccan Crisis of 1905** (p. 753), and the naval rivalry of England and Germany became increasingly embittered (p. 747 ff.).

Balfour's cabinet steadily lost prestige because of its dilatory tactics regarding the tariff question; opposition to its Education Act of 1902, which roused the ire of Nonconformists because it left in existence state-supported denominational schools largely controlled by Anglicans; etc. Balfour resigned, expecting to be recalled, but was succeeded by

f. THE LIBERAL RÉGIME, 1905-1914

1905, Dec. 5—1908, Apr. 5. Cabinet of Sir Henry Campbell-Bannerman, leader of the Liberals. It included **Herbert Asquith** (1852-1928), chancellor of the exchequer, and **Sir Edward Grey** (1862-1933), foreign minister. The **Liberal program of 1906** included: exclusion of Chinese labor from the Transvaal; change of the Education Act of 1902 in favor of the Nonconformists; reduction in the number of liquor licenses and national control of the liquor trade; sweeping measures aimed at social amelioration.

1906, Jan. The Liberals won an over-whelming victory in the elections.

Dec. A **Trade Disputes Bill** met the demands of the trade-unionists by providing that a union could not be made liable for damages on account of illegal acts committed by its members; legalized peaceful picketing, etc.

At the same time a **Workingman's Compensation Act** developed the principle of employers' liability laid down in acts going back to 1880; the employer was now made liable for compensation for accidents to practically all employees receiving less than £250 annually except in case of "serious and willful misconduct."

1908, Apr. 5—1916, May 15. Cabinet of Herbert Asquith, following the resignation of Campbell-Bannerman on account of ill-health (d. Apr. 22).

1909, Jan. The **Old-Age Pension Law,** outcome of thirty years of agitation, provided a pension for every British subject over 70 with an income of less than £31 10s.

1909. The **People's Budget,** brought in by **David Lloyd George** (1863–1945), chancellor of the exchequer, leading spirit of liberal reform. Facing a large deficit (chiefly the result of naval expenditure and social legislation) Lloyd George devised a budget aiming to shift the tax burden from producers to possessors of wealth, in the form of income and inheritance taxes, levies on unearned income, heavy rates on monopolies (such as liquor licenses) and on unearned increments of land. The budget passed the Commons after a hot fight (Nov. 5), but was rejected by the Lords (Nov. 30) until the judgment of the country should have been expressed. The House of Lords was the stronghold of opposition to the program of the Liberal majority in the Commons, and had twice thrown out an education bill (1906, 1908) and a licensing bill (1908).

Dec. 2. Asquith denounced the action of the Lords as a breach of the constitution.

1910, Jan. General election, fought out on the issues of the budget, the veto power of the Lords, and Home Rule for Ireland (the Irish Nationalists having offered their support on condition that the power of the House of Lords should be so far reduced that it could no longer defeat Home Rule). The Liberals lost considerable strength in the election, but determined to go on with their program.

May 6. Death of Edward VII.

1910-1936. GEORGE V (b. 1865), a sound but unimaginative ruler, filled with a sense of responsibility and rigid respect for the constitution.

1910, May 10. Three resolutions passed in the House of Commons: (1) that the Lords should have no right to veto a money bill; (2) that any other measure should become law after being passed in three successive sessions of the Commons, even if vetoed by the Lords, providing that two years had elapsed since its first introduction; (3) that the maximum life of Parliament should be five instead of seven years. In the Lords, Lord Lansdowne offered an alternative measure for the reconstruction of that body.

Nov. 28. Parliament was dissolved and a second general election held (Dec.). The Liberals gained only two seats.

1911, May 15. The Parliament Bill was again passed in the Commons and ultimately passed the Lords (July 20) with amendments unacceptable to Asquith, who threatened to have enough peers created to carry the bill. Thereupon the Lords capitulated (Aug. 10).

Aug. 10. The Commons for the first time voted salaries for their members (£400 per year).

1911, Dec. The **National Insurance Act** provided: (1) insurance for the whole working population against loss of health and for the prevention and cure of sickness; (2) insurance against unemployment. Wage-earners 16 to 65 years old having less than £26 annual income from property were obliged to take health insurance. The second part of the act applied only to 2,250,000 workers engaged in trades specially liable to fluctuations — large building and engineering trades — and gave a maximum benefit of 15 weeks. Both health and unemployment insurance were supported by contributions from employers, employees, and the state.

1911-1912. **Epidemic of strikes,** of which the transport workers' and railwaymen's strikes (1911) and the miners' strike (1912) were outstanding. The strikes were the reflection of stationary wages and rising prices, and showed the influence of syndicalist ideas imported from the United States and the Continent. The **coal strike** (1912), involving 1,500,000 men, brought government action and

1912, Mar. 29. A **Minimum Wage Law,** which, however, did little to relieve unrest.

Apr. 11. The government introduced a bill for **Home Rule in Ireland.** It provided for a bicameral Parliament for Ireland, but with continued representation in the House of Commons. The bill was attacked for its injustice to Protestant Ulster, which would be submerged in a united Catholic Ireland. Opposition brilliantly led by **Sir Edward Carson** (1854-1935).

1913. The **Home Rule Bill** was twice passed by the Commons (Jan. 16, July 7) and twice rejected by the Lords (Jan. 30, July 15). Meanwhile Ulster opposition grew steadily hotter. A **covenant** was signed at Belfast (1912, Sept. 28) pledging resistance to Home Rule and refusal to accept it if it were voted.

July 12. A resolution was adopted by a meeting of 150,000 Ulstermen at Craigavon to resist Home Rule by force of arms if necessary. By Dec. 100,000 **Ulster volunteers** had been raised. Civil war appeared imminent if the government persisted in its Home Rule program, which it had pledged to the Irish Nationalists.

1914, Feb. 10. When Parliament met, Unionist opposition had reached its peak. Asquith offered a compromise (Mar. 9): electors in each of the nine Ulster counties might determine whether their county should be excluded from the new arrangement for six years. The Home Rule Bill was passed for a third time by the Commons (May 26). Under the Parliament Act of 1911 no further action by the Lords was necessary: Ireland had now been given a unitary parliamentary system, with no separate position for Ulster.

June 23. Asquith introduced his compromise of Mar. 9 on Ulster into the House of Lords, which changed the bill to exclude the whole of Ulster without time limit. A three-cornered struggle of Lords, Commons, and Irish Nationalist leaders was overtaken by the World War.

Sept. 18. The **Home Rule Bill** received the royal assent and became law; but by a simultaneous act it was not to come into force until after the war, and the government pledged that, before it was put into force, an amending bill dealing with the question of Ulster would be introduced. The third Home Rule Bill, which never came into operation, was subsequently replaced by the Home Rule Bill of Dec. 1920 (p. 972).

1914, Sept. 18. Welsh disestablishment.
The parliamentary course of the Welsh Disestablishment Bill was almost exactly parallel with that of the Home Rule Bill. A bill for the disestablishment of the Anglican Church in Wales had failed in 1894–1895, again in 1909. Introduced in 1912 (Apr. 12), it passed the Commons twice, but was rejected by the Lords (1913, Feb. 13, July 22). The bill was finally passed by the Commons in 1914 (May 19) and received the royal assent (Sept. 18); but along with it was passed a **Suspensory Bill**, postponing its action until the end of the war. The bill provided that the four Welsh dioceses should no longer form part of the province of Canterbury, that the Welsh bishop should no longer sit in the House of Lords, that all ecclesiastical jurisdiction should be abolished, and that the Welsh Anglicans should be free to set up their own church government.

(*Cont. pp.* 912 *ff.*, 967.)

3. THE LOW COUNTRIES

a. THE KINGDOM OF THE NETHERLANDS, 1815-1830 (1839)

1814, June 21. Protocol of the Eight Articles, concluded between the Prince of Orange and the representatives of the allied powers after the defeat of Napoleon. In order to create a bulwark against France, it was agreed to unite Belgium (the Austrian Netherlands) and Holland to form the **Kingdom of the Netherlands**. This arrangement was confirmed by the Congress of Vienna (1815, June 9).

1815-1844. WILLIAM I, the former Prince of Orange, a well-meaning but rather arbitrary and obstinate ruler. He granted a moderately **liberal constitution** (1815, Aug. 24), but failed to make the union of Belgium and Holland work. Traditions, customs, religion, and interests were different and the Belgians felt throughout that they were put in an inferior position. The seat of the government was in Holland, the king a Dutchman and a Calvinist; despite her larger population, Belgium had only equal representation in the lower chamber of the States-General or assembly; the majority of officers and officials were Dutch; the public establishments (banks, schools) were predominantly Dutch; Dutch was made the official language in all except the Walloon districts of Belgium; the public debt was equally divided, though in 1814 that of Holland was many times greater than that of Belgium; the Catholic Church in Belgium resented the equality of religious denominations; the Belgians disliked the Dutch tariff system, which, being liberal, gave inadequate protection to Belgian industry.

1828, July. The two Belgian parties (Clericals and Liberals) united after the king had estranged the Clericals by concluding a concordat with the Pope (1827) giving him the right to veto the election of bishops, and the Liberals by a harsh press law. The program of the two parties called for freedom of press, instruction, and worship, and for ministerial responsibility. Increased agitation for the redress of grievances, accompanied by much economic distress.

1830, Aug. 25. THE BELGIAN REVOLUTION, stimulated by the July Revolution in Paris and by unrest among the lower classes. The moderate liberal elements asked only an autonomous administration and were willing to accept the king's son as viceroy.

Sept. 23-26. Violent fighting in Brussels between the workers and the troops, who were obliged to evacuate the city. A provisional government was set up with Charles Rogier as leader.

Oct. 4. Proclamation of independence. A national congress was summoned to draw up a constitution.

Oct. 27. Bombardment of Antwerp by the Dutch made the Belgians irreconcilable.

Nov. 4. At the suggestion of England, a conference of the powers met at London and ordered an armistice.

Nov. 10. The Belgian national congress declared the House of Orange deposed, but voted for constitutional hereditary monarchy.

Nov. 15. Advent of Lord Palmerston to the British foreign office, following the downfall of the Wellington ministry. Palmerston was not unsympathetic to the Belgian claims, but was above all eager to check the spread of French influence in Belgium and to prevent war. Louis Philippe, confronted with a serious domestic situation in France, followed the British lead and the two powers induced Russia (paralyzed by the Polish insurrection, p. 701), Austria, and Prussia to abandon the principle of legitimacy.

Dec. 20. The conference practically recognized the independence of Belgium by declaring the dissolution of the Kingdom of the Netherlands.

1831, Jan. 20, Jan. 27. Two protocols set forth the bases of separation. The Dutch accepted the terms, but the Belgians refused.

Feb. 3. The Belgian national congress elected as king the Duke of Nemours, second son of Louis Philippe. Energetic warnings and threats of Palmerston induced Louis Philippe to reject the election.

Feb. 7. The Belgians set up a regency under Surlet de Chokier, and the congress drew up a constitution on the English pattern, one of the most liberal in Europe.

June 4. The Belgians elected as king Prince Leopold of Saxe-Coburg (1790–1865), widower of Princess Charlotte of England and uncle of the future Queen Victoria, a cultured and shrewd prince.

June 26. The London conference, having approved of Leopold, drew up the Eighteen Articles, regulating the separation and more favorable to the Belgians. It was accepted by the Belgians, but rejected by King William of Holland.

Aug. 2. Breaking off the armistice, William sent a large army over the frontier, which quickly defeated an improvised Belgian force. A French army thereupon invaded the country and forced the Dutch to retire.

Oct. 14. The Twenty-Four Articles, drawn up by the London conference and more favorable to Holland. Still King William refused to agree or to evacuate Antwerp.

1832, Nov.-Dec. A French army and a Franco-British fleet expelled the Dutch from Belgium.

1833, May 21. The Dutch were obliged by the English and French to conclude an armistice of indefinite length on the basis of the *status quo*.

1839, Apr. 19. King William finally accepted a settlement much like that of the Twenty-Four Articles. He recognized Belgium and accepted substantially the frontier of 1790, except for Luxemburg and Limburg. The Belgians had claimed the whole of Luxemburg, but only the western part was given them; the rest, including the capital, remained a grand duchy with the King of Holland as grand duke. Limburg was also divided, the Belgians receiving about one half. The Scheldt was declared open to the commerce of both countries and the national debt was divided. Article VII recognized Belgium as an "independent and perpetually neutral state" under the collective guaranty of the powers.

b. THE KINGDOM OF BELGIUM, 1831-1914

1831-1865. LEOPOLD I. During the early part of his reign the Clerical-Liberal coalition continued to rule the country, devoting itself to the consolidation of the kingdom, ably guided by the king.

1847. The coalition gave way to a party system and ministerial responsibility. Until 1884 the Liberals were generally in control of the government, first under the leadership of **Charles Rogier**, then of **Walther Frère-Orban** (1812-1896).

1848. A new electoral law lowered the franchise and doubled the number of voters. The success of the régime was attested by the fact that Belgium was almost alone among the Continental powers in escaping revolution.

1850. The national bank was founded as part of a general policy devoted to economic development.

1861-1862. Commercial treaties with France and England ushered in a period of free-trade policy.

1863. The navigation of the Scheldt was made free.

1865-1909. LEOPOLD II, like his father an able, energetic, strong-willed ruler and a man of vision.

1867-1870. A period of international uncertainty, arising from the designs of **Napoleon III** upon Belgium (p. 635) and culminating in the effort (1869) to secure control of the Belgian railways.

1870, Aug. 9, 11. Under British auspices, treaties were concluded between England, Prussia, and France guaranteeing **Belgian neutrality** during the Franco-Prussian War.

1879, July 1. Education Act secularizing primary education. The public or "neutral" schools were to be supported by the communes with subventions from the government; no public support was to be given to the "free" or Catholic schools. This measure, passed by the Liberals, estranged the Clericals.

1880, June. The Clericals won a majority in the elections. They now replaced the Liberals and remained in power until the time of the World War.

1884, Sept. 10. A new **Education Law** reversed that of 1879 and gave public support for church schools in Catholic districts.

1885, May 2. Establishment of the Congo Free State, with Leopold II as ruler. This great African empire had been built up by Leopold as a personal enterprise. Its recognition by the powers was a most unusual achievement (pp. 739, 843).

1886-1894. Labor unrest, with a series of major strikes. Economic development had been very rapid, with the result that social problems emerged in an acute form. With extensive coal mines, Belgium was able to industrialize to the point where it was the fourth manufacturing power in Europe. Under the circumstances socialism made great strides. The **Labor Party** was founded in 1885 and soon took the place of the declining Liberal Party as the chief organ of opposition to the Clericals. The Socialists demanded universal manhood suffrage and organized strikes as a method of bringing pressure.

1893, Apr. A general strike was proclaimed.

Apr. 27. The government introduced **universal suffrage,** but with a system of **plural voting** which gave two or three votes to about two-fifths of the voters who fulfilled certain requirements as to age, income, education, and family.

1895, Aug. 30. Instruction in the Catholic religion made compulsory in all public schools.

1899, Dec. 24. Adoption of **proportional representation** for the protection of political minorities. An alliance was formed between the Liberals and Socialists to demand "one man, one vote."

1901-1905. Another period of **strike activity,** punctuated by anarchist outrages, especially dynamitings.

1903-1904. The Congo scandal, arising from the revelation in England of labor conditions under Leopold's rule. A commission of inquiry was sent out in 1905. The Congo was ceded by the king to the Belgian nation in 1908 and became the Belgian Congo.

1909-1934. ALBERT I (b. 1875) succeeded his uncle, Leopold II.

1913, Apr. 14-24. A political general strike ended on the assurance of the government that the electoral system would be revised. The reform was delayed by the World War, but was finally accomplished on May 6, 1919, when universal suffrage without plural voting was established and certain women were given the vote.

Aug. 30. Army Law enacted, with the introduction of universal military service in place of the earlier system by which one son was taken from each family.

House of Coburg (1800-1945)

The Dutch Royal House (1815–1939)

William V (Stadholder) ══ Wilhelmina, sister of
1751–1795 │ Frederick William II
of Prussia

Wilhelmina ══ William I
of Prussia │ 1813–1840

Anna, ══ William II
d. of Paul I │ 1840–1849
of Russia

Marianne,
m. Albert of
Prussia

Frederick ══ Louisa, d. of
│ Fred. Will. III
of Prussia

Sophia (1) ══ William III ══ (2) Emma of
of Württemberg │ 1849–1890 │ Waldeck

Henry   Sophia

Louisa,
m. Charles XV
of Sweden

Marie,
m. William
of Wied

William
d. 1879

Alexander
d. 1884

Wilhelmina ══ Henry of Mecklenburg
1890–1948 │

Juliana ══ Bernard of
1948– │ Lippe-Biesterfeld

Beatrix Wilhelmina   Irene   Margriet Francisca
b. 1938   b. 1939   b. 1943

1914, Aug. 2. German ultimatum to Belgium demanding free passage for German armies. Belgium rejected the ultimatum and appealed to England and France.

Aug. 4. Beginning of the **invasion of Belgium** and German declaration of war (p. 912).

(*Cont. pp.* 912 *ff.*, 974.)

c. KINGDOM OF THE NETHERLANDS, 1830-1914

1840, Oct. 7. Abdication of William I, who had become very unpopular because of his obstinate opposition to reform. He died in 1843.

1840-1849. WILLIAM II (b. 1792).

1848, Oct. The king, moved by the European revolutions of 1848 and pressed by the Liberals, under the distinguished jurist and statesman **Johan Thorbecke** (1798–1872) conceded a revision of the constitution: the power of the king was reduced and that of Parliament greatly increased. Ministerial responsibility was provided and the upper house (thus far appointed by the king) was to be elected by the provincial assemblies. The lower house was still elected by a restricted suffrage.

1849-1890. WILLIAM III (b. 1817), an enlightened and benevolent ruler. His reign was marked by great **commercial expansion** and much internal development (canals, etc.). The political life of the country centered on the struggle of parties over the questions of religious education and the extension of the suffrage. The Liberals, largely representative of the trading classes and the towns, demanded a system of free secular schools. They were opposed by the Protestant Conservatives, the Calvinist peasantry and the Catholics, all of whom favored religious control of the public schools.

1862. Slavery abolished in the Dutch West Indies.

1867, Mar. The king made a treaty with France for the **sale of Luxemburg.** This gave rise to an international crisis and the dropping of the project (p. 686).

1887, June 17. Introduction of **suffrage reform,** after a long period of agitation. The electorate was about doubled. The first Socialist was elected to Parliament.

1889, Dec. 6. A Calvinist-Catholic coa-
lition, following on a period of Liberal rule (1871–1888), passed a law providing financial assistance for all private denominational schools. Non-sectarian public schools continued to be state-supported.

1890- . WILHELMINA (b. 1880). Until 1898 the queen-mother, **Emma,** acted as regent.

1894. A serious revolt broke out in the **Dutch East Indies.** Another rising, in 1896, was put down only with considerable difficulty.

1896, June 29. A new electoral law, carried by a Liberal cabinet, again doubled the electorate (from 300,000 to 700,000), but the system was still far removed from universal suffrage and drew fire from the working classes.

1897-1901. The **Borgesius ministry** (Liberal), which passed much **social legislation,** such as accident in-surance, improvement of housing, compulsory education for children, etc.

1901, Feb. 7. The queen married Duke Henry of Mecklenburg-Schwerin.

1901-1905. Dr. Kuyper ministry (Clerical).

1903, Apr. Great railway and dock strikes, which the government broke up by the use of the military, thus arousing the forces of trade-unionism and socialism.

1905. The elections restored the Liberals to power, but the party, never very disciplined, continued to disintegrate.

1913, Aug. 25. An extra-parliamentary cabinet was formed by Cort van der Linden (Moderate Liberal) and set out to settle the suffrage and education questions. In 1917 (Nov.) **universal suffrage** and proportional representation were introduced. At the same time the Clericals were satisfied by the concession in full of the principle of absolute equality with regard to financial support for public non-denominational schools and private sectarian instruction. (*Cont. p.* 975.)

4. FRANCE

a. THE RESTORATION MONARCHY, 1814-1830

1814-1824. LOUIS XVIII (b. 1755), brother of Louis XVI, easy-going, disillusioned, reasonable. He was permitted by the allies to return after the defeat of Napoleon, mainly through the influence of Tsar Alexander of Russia.

1814, June 14. The king granted the *charte constitutionnelle,* or **constitution,** a reflection of the tsar's liberalism and of Louis' desire to meet the demands of the middle classes. It created a system akin to that of the British, with an hereditary monarch, a chamber of peers nominated by the king, a chamber of deputies elected by a limited suffrage, and various guaranties of civil and religious liberty.

1815, Mar. 20. The sudden **return of Napoleon** from Elba obliged Louis to flee from Paris and remain in exile during the Hundred Days (p. 602). After Waterloo he made an undignified return to the capital "in the baggage of the allies" (July 8), whereupon the **second restoration** was accomplished. The king's influence was much reduced and he was unable to prevent a so-called **White Terror,** carried on by fanatical royalists, especially in the south, against revolutionaries and Bonapartists.

Aug. 22. The first parliamentary elections yielded a large majority for the **Ultra-royalist** group (*chambre introuvable*), whose reactionary policy was opposed by the ministry headed by the Duke of Richelieu (1766–1822). The reaction went to such extremes that the king, under pressure from the allied representatives,

1816, Sept. Dissolved the Chamber and called new elections. In the new Chamber a majority of moderates supported the policy of Richelieu and that of his immediate successors, Dessolles (1818–1819), Decazes (1819–1820).

1816-1820. Moderate measures characterized the period of these ministries, among others laws freeing the press (1819, May 1).

1818. The **payment of the French indemnity** and the consequent evacuation of French soil by allied troops, the most notable achievement of Richelieu.

1820, Feb. 13. The murder of the Duke of Berri, presumed to be the last of the Bourbon line, by an obscure fanatic, Louvel, was providential for the Ultras. The ministry of Decazes, favorite of the king, was overthrown and succeeded by a second Richelieu ministry (1820–1821).

The French Bourbons (1715-1883)

Louis XV

Louis, dauphin

Marie Antoinette === Louis XVI   Louis XVIII   Charles X==== Maria Theresa   Elizabeth
of Austria   1774-1792   1814-1824   1824-1830 | of Sardinia

Louis (XVII)   Marie Thérèse === Louis   Charles === Caroline of
                                 D. of   D. of Berri | Naples
                                 Angoulême   d. 1820
                                 d. 1844

                                                Henry (V)
                                                D. of Bordeaux
                                                C. of Chambord
                                                d. 1883

1820. To preserve the country from the increasing danger from the Left, **a new electoral law** was passed (the *Law of the Double Vote*), which established a complicated system of election of two degrees, increased the electoral weight of voters in the upper tax brackets, and aimed to increase the influence of landed proprietors (source of Ultra support) at the expense of the middle class. This law, together with legislation on the press, personal liberty, etc., marked the beginning of the "reaction," which was to end only in the Revolution of 1830.

1823, Apr. Invasion of Spain by French troops, in behalf of Ferdinand VII (p. 644).

1824-1830. CHARLES X (1757-1836).

1821-1827. Under the **Villèle ministry,** a resolute attempt was made to restore, in as large a measure as possible, the position which the monarchy had occupied under the old régime.

1825, Apr. A Law of Indemnity compensated the nobles for the losses of their lands during the revolution, at the expense of the holders of government bonds, largely the upper *bourgeoisie.* The Church was favored in various ways, notably by the adoption of the notorious

1826. Law of Sacrilege, imposing a death sentence for certain offenses of a "sacrilegious" character. The *bourgeoisie* was further alienated by the king's

1827, Apr. 30. Dissolution of the national guard, a preserve of the middle

class. Secret societies sprang up, notably the Liberal electoral society, *Aide-toi, le ciel t'aidera.* Confident of his position, Charles X called a general election to strengthen his majority in the Chamber.

1827, Nov. 17, 24. The election returned a Liberal majority, and the king was obliged to part with his Ultra minister, Villèle, and supplant him with

1828, Jan. 3. Martignac, a moderate who, the king hoped, would please neither the Liberals nor the Ultras.

1829, Aug. 6. The dismissal of Martignac was followed by a revolutionary step, when the king appointed

Aug. 8. A ministry dominated by **Prince** of Polignac, "Ultra of the Ultras" which for the first time since 1816 did not possess the confidence of the Chamber, a departure from the principle of ministerial responsibility, not stated in the Constitution of 1814, but now generally accepted.

1830, Mar. 18. The king's act was censured in the answer to the address from the throne, signed by 221 Liberal deputies. Charles X dissolved the Chamber.

May 16. New elections returned a majority unfavorable to the king, who, relying on the effect of the conquest of Algiers (June-July, p. 837), replied with the

July 26. FIVE "JULY" ORDINANCES, establishing a rigid governmental control of the press, dissolving the Chamber, changing the electoral system in an attempt to insure an Ultra majority.

July 26.   Adolphe Thiers (1797–1877), journalist and Liberal, drew up a protest against the ordinances on behalf of the Parisian journalists. The Liberal majority of the Chamber also prepared a protest. But the dynamo of the **Revolution of 1830** was radical Paris, in whose ranks a republican movement had been for some years forming.

July 28.   The insurgents raised barricades, took the Hotel de Ville, and were masters of Paris (July 29). The **Marquis de Lafayette**, patriarch of the republican cause, headed the radical movement, which aimed to make him president of a French republic. The Liberal deputies hastily turned to **Louis Philippe**, Duke of Orléans and representative of the younger Bourbon line, as the savior of the cause of constitutional monarchy.

July 30.   Orléans was offered the lieutenant-generalship of the realm, was accepted by Lafayette on behalf of radical Paris, and was proclaimed *King of the French* by the Liberals sitting as a rump Chamber (Aug. 7) under the Charter of 1814, revised to insure the perpetuation of the new constitutional régime.

b. THE JULY MONARCHY, 1830-1848

1830-1848.   REIGN OF LOUIS PHILIPPE (1773–1850).

1830-1836.   Agitation of Republicans and other radicals, who had accepted Louis Philippe as a revolutionary monarch only to discover their mistake too late. The radicals were disillusioned by the cautious policy of the

1830, Nov. 2—1831, Mar. 13.   Laffitte ministry with respect to the revolutions in Italy and Poland and by the government's opposition to the demands of the workers.

1831, Mar. 13—1832, May 16.   Ministry of Casimir-Périer, a strong man who managed to restore order, but died in the great cholera epidemic of 1831–1832. Radical agitation and violence continued.

1831, Nov.   A large-scale **insurrection of workers at Lyons** was put down with difficulty. Rapid spread of secret societies. Under a régime of press freedom the king was unsparingly attacked in the radical newspapers and mercilessly caricatured (notably by **Honoré Daumier,** 1808–1879).

1832, Oct. 11—1834, July 15.   Ministry of Marshal Soult (1769–1851), which included the Duke of Broglie, Thiers,

and Guizot, and represented the more conservative wing of liberalism.

1833, June 28.   The Primary Education Law, brought in by Guizot. In the interests of safe doctrine it gave the Church (formerly attacked by the Liberals) effective control of the primary schools.

1834, Apr.   Climax of the radical movement in the **great revolts in Paris and Lyons,** repressed with great severity.

1835, Mar.—1836, Feb.   Ministries of the Duke of Broglie.

1835, July 28.   Sanguinary attempt on the life of Louis Philippe by the Corsican radical, **Fieschi.**

1835, Sept.   The September Laws, including a severe press law and other acts to accelerate the trials of insurgents and assure their conviction. These repressive laws brought the radical movement under control.

1836, Feb.-Sept.   First Ministry of Adolphe Thiers.

1836-1839.   Ministries of Count Molé (1781–1855), the king's personal friend. Louis Philippe managed to establish something like personal rule by playing off the strong men in the Liberal movement and by appointing weak men to office. But the two groups of the opposition (Right Center: *party of resistance,* led by Guizot; Left Center: *party of movement,* led by Thiers) united and overthrew Molé, who was followed by a short-lived Soult ministry 1839, May–1840, Feb.).

1840, Mar.-Oct.   Ministry of Thiers, who led France to the brink of war during the acute Near-Eastern crisis (p. 725).

1840-1847.   Ministry of Soult, in which François Guizot (1787–1874) was the commanding figure. Guizot became premier in 1847 and remained in power until Feb. 1848. He dominated the political scene through political and electoral manipulation and followed the direction of the king in a conservative policy.

1840-1848.   Revival of radicalism and emergence of "utopian" socialism. The period was one of rapid industrial development (600 steam engines in France in 1830, 4853 in 1847; consumption of coal increased fivefold) and extension of communications (**Railway Act** of 1842: provided for government construction of roadbeds, bridges, tunnels, etc.). All this tended to raise a social question, which was treated by such eminent writers as **St.-Simon, Fourier, Cabet, Louis Blanc** (p. 549). The radical movement had been driven under-

House of Bourbon-Orléans

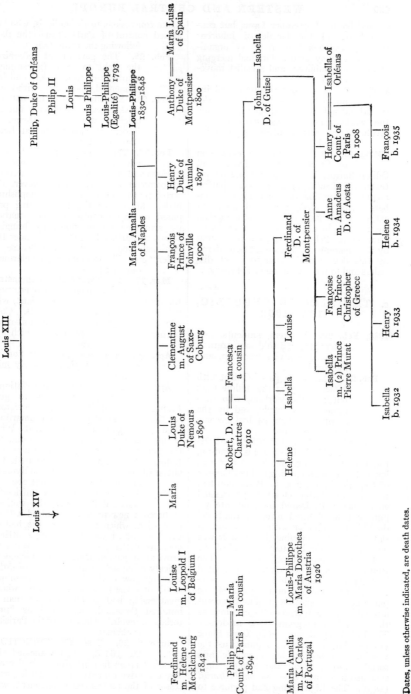

Dates, unless otherwise indicated, are death dates.

ground by the **September Laws,** but continued behind the façade of innocent **friendly societies** and in secret organizations of many kinds. Gradual merging of radical, republican, and socialist movements.

1846-1847. A severe **agricultural and industrial depression** caused widespread unemployment and suffering among the workers and predisposed them to revolutionary action when opportunity offered.

1847-1848. The **parliamentary opposition** to Guizot, led by Thiers and Odilon Barrot, demanding electoral reform (extension of suffrage) and an end of parliamentary corruption (office-holding by members, bribery, etc.), embarked upon an extra-parliamentary **campaign of banquets,** culminating in a great banquet in Paris, arranged for Feb. 22, 1848, but prohibited by the government. The unrest engendered by this demonstration led to street disorders and to the revolution of February.

c. THE SECOND REPUBLIC, 1848-1852

1848, Feb. 22. Workers, students, and others gathered to demonstrate in Paris. Barricades went up, and fighting began.

Feb. 23. The king replaced Guizot with Molé, satisfying the middle class but not the workers, who continued the struggle, and by the morning of Feb. 24 had become masters of Paris.

Feb. 24. LOUIS PHILIPPE ABDICATED in favor of his grandson, the Count of Paris, but the latter was ignored by a rump meeting of the Chamber of Deputies into which the Paris mob had filtered; the latter chose a provisional government, dominated by moderate republicans, which fused in turn at the Hôtel de Ville that evening with a more radical slate. The same evening the **republic was proclaimed** at the insistent demand of the mob (for the second time in France). The Right Wing of the government, dominated by the poet, **Alphonse de Lamartine** (1790–1869), was composed of members of the parliamentary opposition, willing to accept a republic and universal suffrage so long as the republic's program were moderate. The Left Wing, dominated by **Louis Blanc** (1811–1882), viewed the republic as the vestibule to far-reaching economic and social reforms, along the general lines sketched in Blanc's *Organisation du travail* (1839). The Right Wing had perforce to

make concessions to the radicals, who had armed control of Paris during the days following the revolution.

Feb. 25. The government recognized the right to work (government guaranty of work relief) and implemented this promise with the

Feb. 26. Establishment of the national workshops, a large-scale but inefficient work-relief scheme in Paris. It also permitted Louis Blanc to set up

Feb. 28. The Commission of the Luxembourg, a kind of parliament of workers and employers to discuss questions of common interest, soon, however, deserted by the employers and accomplishing little. Meanwhile the Right Wing prepared to regain control of the situation by arranging for elections, by bringing troops to Paris, taking steps to render the National Guard loyal to the "cause of order," etc. The workers became alarmed, organized

Mar. 17. A monster radical demonstration which might have overturned the government but for Louis Blanc, who guided it into moderate channels. Conservatives everywhere now became alarmed by the "specter of communism," which was raising its head.

Apr. 16. A second demonstration of workers in Paris completely miscarried.

Apr. 23. The elections to the National Assembly, which was to give France a new constitution, were a victory for the moderate Republicans (**Lamartine**) with some 500 seats; the Left Wing (**Louis Blanc**) had fewer than a hundred; the Legitimists (seeking the return of the Bourbon line) had about a hundred; the Orléanists (supporters of the fallen dynasty of Louis Philippe), about 200.

May 15. In the face of the unfriendly National Assembly, the workers prepared a new protest, organized a huge procession, which marched to the hall of the Assembly, invaded it during a sitting, overturned the government, set up a new provisional government. The movement quickly collapsed. But the forces of order were by now terrified. They determined to dissolve the national workshops, whose membership had grown to more than a hundred thousand, denounced as "pretorians of revolt." The reply of the Parisian workers was

June 23-26. THE INSURRECTION OF JUNE, which witnessed the bloodiest street-fighting Europe had seen. The executive commission, vacillating successor of the provisional government, was

swept away; **General Louis Cavaignac**
(1802–1857) was made dictator *pro tempore*
and suppressed the movement.

July–Aug. A reaction followed, punctuated by severe press legislation
(aiming to eliminate radical newspapers),
the suppression of secret societies, and laws
for the rigid control of clubs and political
associations.

Nov. 4. The Assembly completed the
new constitution, providing for a
single chamber and a strong president (with
a separation of powers and direct election
under universal suffrage). The moderate
Republicans' candidate, General Cavaignac,
was opposed by **Prince Louis Napoleon**
(1808–1873), nephew of Napoleon I and
pretender to the Napoleonic succession.
Louis Napoleon had profited by the flowering of the "Napoleonic legend"; by the
publicity attending two personal attempts
at a *coup d'état* in France (Strasbourg, 1836;
Boulogne, 1840); and by the demand after
the June Days for a "strong man" to govern
France.

Dec. 10. The presidential elections gave
Louis Napoleon 5,327,345 votes;
his opponents, 1,879,298. He became president, Dec. 20.

1848, Dec. 20. PRINCE LOUIS NAPO-
LEON BONAPARTE took the
oath as **President of the French Republic,**
and promptly gave evidence of his "republicanism" by appointing a ministry
dominated by Orléanists, headed by **Odilon
Barrot,** despite the fact that the majority
of the National Assembly were Republicans.
The president had the support of five
million electors, the Constituent Assembly
was already obsolete.

1849, Jan. 29. Under the menace of troops
quartered in Paris for that pur-
pose, the Assembly was obliged to vote its
own dissolution, after the budget and
certain measures completing the constitution should have been passed.

The conservative forces in society —
such diverse elements as Legitimists, Orléanists, Bonapartists, some moderate
Republicans — were united by means of
a central committee (*Union électorale*) to
win the elections to the new Chamber
on a program of "saving society" ("threatened" by the radical elements of 1848)
through revival of the influence of the
Catholic Church.

1849, Apr.–June. The French intervention
against the **Roman Republic** (p.
655) was part of this program, connived at
by the president. After **General Oudinot's**
first defeat (Apr. 30), "the honor of the
country and of the army" was turned to
account as a slogan by the Conservatives,

who won a large majority of the seats in the
election. Actually the Radical Republicans
fared much better in the elections than
they had anticipated. **Ledru-Rollin** was
returned in five departments by two million
votes.

June 13. He engineered an **abortive
revolt in Paris,** which played into
the hands of the Conservatives: severe
measures were taken against the Radical
Republicans — arrests were made in Paris
and the provinces, banquets forbidden,
mutual benefit societies dissolved. The
severity of these measures overshot the
mark, stimulated Republican propaganda
in turn. The history of the new Legislative
Assembly (*Corps législatif*) now became
that of the struggle between the Catholic
majority and the Liberal and popular opposition groups. Louis Napoleon was determined to be captured by neither, to use the
struggle for his own ends.

Oct. 31. Although French troops had
restored Rome to Pius IX, Louis
Napoleon opposed reintroduction of an
absolutist régime. In this he was supported
neither by his Catholic majority nor by his
own ministry. He accordingly dismissed
Odilon Barrot and summoned **General
d'Hautpoul** as premier, with a cabinet
"devoted to his own person," in which the
dominating figure was **Eugène Rouher**
(1814–1884), minister of justice. With a
ministry of his own men, the president had
in fact established a thinly veiled dictatorship.

1850, Jan. 9. The president extended his
control through a government bill,
placing school teachers under the
control of prefects.

Mar. 15. A second education bill, the
so-called *Falloux Law* (prepared
by the Catholic Legitimist, Vicomte de
Falloux) was grudgingly acquiesced in by
the government, a concession to the Catholic majority. Its effect was to extend
greatly Catholic influence in education,
providing lower standards for Catholic than
for state teachers, giving the clergy wide
powers of school inspection, permitting the
substitution of Catholic for lay schools by
communes and departments (seeking to
avoid the expense of maintaining state
schools).

May 31. A further attack on radicalism
was made in an **electoral law** requiring three years' residence in
one place for all voters (affecting
above all industrial workers, at
once migratory and radical.)

June 9. Another act **forbade clubs and
public meetings,** even for election
purposes. Republican propaganda was

paralyzed by various other means: newspapers overwhelmed with lawsuits and fines, houses of Republicans searched, Republican civil servants dismissed on the slightest suspicion, etc.

By now, the empire was on the horizon. Was it to be accomplished legitimately or by force? Louis Napoleon turned first to legal methods, the revision of Article 45 of the constitution, which forbade two consecutive four-year terms for a president. The president had a clear majority in the Assembly, but a vote of three-quarters was essential to revision.

1851, July 15. The proposal to revise was defeated by nearly 100 votes more than were needed. Not without considerable vacillation the president now decided to resort to force to accomplish his objects.

Dec. 2. THE COUP D'ÉTAT. Plans were laid in great secrecy late in Nov. During the night of Dec. 1–2 (Dec. 2 was the anniversary of the victory of Napoleon I at Austerlitz) **Count Morny,** the president's half-brother, had a proclamation printed, informing the people of the dissolution of the Assembly, the restoration of universal suffrage (Louis Napoleon was here posing as the friend of the people tricked by an unfriendly legislature), convening the electors for a plebiscite concerning fundamental revision of the constitution. The people of Paris found themselves confronted by the army which occupied the Palais Bourbon, seat of the Assembly. Leading deputies, Republican and Royalist (notably generals), prominent journalists *et al.* were arrested in their beds. Two hundred deputies who met and proclaimed the fall of Louis Napoleon were arrested.

Dec. 3. A group of Republican deputies organized a popular rising (Faubourg St. Antoine); barricades went up.

Dec. 4. Troops were hurled against the workers by General **Jacques de Saint-Arnaud,** minister of war; the movement promptly collapsed, but not before many insurgents had been killed and unarmed crowds of pedestrians had been fired upon (*Massacre of the Boulevards*). Large numbers of arrests followed in Paris and the provinces, where numerous risings were summarily repressed.

Dec. 21. The plebiscite, feverishly "prepared" by Morny (now minister of the interior), gave to the president (7,500,000 votes to 640,000) the right to draw up a constitution: the great majority of Frenchmen were obviously weary of parliamentary struggles, alarmed by popular risings, and ready to seek security beneath the authority of a second Napoleonic dictatorship. Repressive measures continued: nearly 20,000 persons were sentenced — 10,000 of them to transportation to Algeria.

1852, Jan. 14. The new constitution declared the chief of the state "responsible to the nation," but gave him "free and unfettered authority"; he commanded the forces on land and sea, could make war and peace, alone could initiate laws, promulgated laws and issued decrees and regulations necessary to carry them into effect, etc. The constitution set up a Council of State, chosen by the president, to formulate laws in secret sessions; a Senate, with members appointed by the president, sitting in secret, empowered to reject laws judged unconstitutional, and to modify the constitution through its *consulta,* subject to the consent of the president; a Legislative Assembly (*Corps législatif*), which could accept or reject legislation, but which had no power to introduce or amend bills. Hence effective power rested in the hands of the president, who appointed the members of the Council of State and the Senate, and who exercised wide influence over the election of members of the Legislative Assembly through presentation of "official candidates," openly supported by the prefects. The constitution expressly stated: "The emperor governs *by means of* the ministers, the Council of State, the Senate, and the Legislative Assembly."

1852, Sept. The president made a provincial tour. Under the influence of handpicked prefects, there were frequent cries of Vive l'Empire! The empire was the logical and obvious next step.

Nov. 2. The *senatus consultum* ratified by plebiscite (Nov. 21) and promulgated by decree (Dec. 2), declared the empire re-established.

d. THE SECOND EMPIRE: THE AUTHORITARIAN PERIOD, 1852-1860

1852-1870. NAPOLEON III, emperor.
1852, Feb. 17. Repressive measures. The press was kept under strict supervision by the police; newspapers could be established only with government permission and were obliged to deposit a large sum (50,000 francs in Paris) as guaranty of good behavior. The minister of the interior discharged and appointed editors, on nomination of the owners; he had power to suspend publication at any time.

Feb. 28. **Promotion of material prosperity.** The government authorized formation of joint-stock banks issuing long-term credit. The government-subsidized *Crédit foncier* (1852) was obliged to make loans at 5% and later (1854) became a state institution. The *Crédit mobilier* (founded 1852 by the Pereire Brothers) was a joint-stock bank whose function it was to initiate and support large companies, participate in public loans, etc. It played a large rôle in the development of railroads, shipping companies, public utilities. Napoleon embarked also upon an active **social policy:** improvement of worker's dwellings, donations to charitable institutions, formation of friendly societies. A huge program of **public works** was initiated, especially the rebuilding of Paris by **Baron Georges Haussmann** (1809–1891), made prefect of the Seine. Streets were widened and new boulevards opened. Paris soon became a new city, enlarged from 12 to 20 arrondissements by the annexation of the suburbs (1860). Its population grew from 1,297,064 in 1851 to 1,825,274 in 1866.

Dec. 25. The **powers of the emperor** were further extended by a *senatus consultum.* He was given authority to conclude treaties of commerce; the budget of every ministry was voted by the Legislative Assembly, but the subdivision of sums granted was to be settled by imperial decree.

1853, Jan. 30. **Marriage of the emperor to Eugénie de Montijo,** Countess of Téba (1826–1920), daughter of a Spanish grandee. Beautiful and charming, the empress was simple and dignified in manner, but she was impulsive and ignorant, incapable of grasping affairs of state. Her rigorous religious training made her an enemy of liberalism and a leader of the Clerical Party at the palace.

Napoleon III continued the policy of **concessions to the Church** initiated by the Falloux Law: Catholic missions were developed, government grants were made to churches and religious bodies of a charitable or educational character, Catholic schools were favored and offered increased competition to state schools. Catholics as a whole welcomed and supported the empire as a "heaven-sent blessing," although the Liberal Catholic wing, notably **Montalembert,** urged the importance of a liberal political régime as the only type under which Catholicism could flourish.

1854, Mar. 28. **FRANCE DECLARED WAR ON RUSSIA** (*Crimean War*, p. 727). The war grew out of a dispute between France and Russia regarding the custody of holy places in Palestine (1850–1853). In part to please the Clericals, in part to assert French claims and maintain French prestige, Napoleon III, mindful of the poor impression made by Louis Philippe's cautious foreign policy, took a strong line and carried England with him.

1855, May-Nov. The **Paris International Exposition** bore witness to the technological and economic progress of France. Wages were rising rapidly, though costs of living rose even more. General prosperity. Height of Napoleon's popularity.

1856, Feb.-Apr. **Peace congress at Paris** (p. 728). France once again the leading power in Europe, enjoying great military prestige.

Mar. 16. **Birth of the Prince Imperial,** assuring the succession to the throne.

1857. A **Railway Law** encouraged railway companies through an elaborate system of state guaranties of bonded interest. Railways developed rapidly from 3627 kilometers in 1851 to 16,207 in 1858.

1858, Jan. 14. **Attempt of Felice Orsini to assassinate Napoleon and the empress.** Two persons were killed and a hundred wounded. This unfortunate episode initiated Napoleon's active participation in the problem of Italy, resting on his interest in oppressed nationalities and national self-determination, as well as the desire to acquire for France her "natural frontiers."

1859, May 12-July 12. **WAR OF FRANCE AND PIEDMONT** against Austria (p. 657). The war, which took a turn not intended by Napoleon, estranged the Clerical elements in France, but brought France

1860, Mar. 24. The **annexation** of the Piedmontese provinces of **Savoy** and **Nice.**

1860, Jan. 23. **Commercial treaty with England,** marking the initiation of a free-trade policy.

e. THE LIBERAL EMPIRE, 1860–1870

1860, Nov. 24. **Extension of the powers of the legislature.** Napoleon, his popularity shaken by the Italian war and the commercial treaty with England, decided to revive parliamentary life, create parties and exercise his power more indirectly by acting as mediator. The decrees of 1860 empowered the Senate and Legislative Assembly to move and discuss freely a reply to the address from the throne; parliamentary debates were to be fully reported (thus saving governmental prestige in cases of failure by emphasizing the approval of a measure by a parliamentary majority). Both parties seized upon these concessions as an opening wedge to demand wider powers, the eventual revival of parliamentary institutions.

1861, Nov. 4. The Financial powers of the legislature were next extended. A grandiose program of public works, an extravagant foreign policy had entailed rapidly mounting expenses. The annual deficit was about 100 million francs; by the end of 1861 the floating debt had reached nearly a billion francs. Financial policy was unsettled by the emperor's power to redistribute the estimates for the various departments after the budget had been voted *en bloc* and by his power to authorize supplementary loans on his own responsibility. To restore the confidence of the business world and to oblige the legislature to share imperial responsibility, Napoleon renounced the right to borrow money while the legislature was not in session and agreed that the budget should be voted by sections. But the emperor retained the right to alter the estimates, section by section. This defeated parliamentary control, gave rise to constant demands for an enlargement of the Chamber's financial powers.

An opposition coalition rapidly grew up in the country, composed of such diverse elements as Catholics (outraged by the papal policy of Napoleon), Legitimists, Orléanists, Protectionists, and even Republicans — republican opposition had been reborn in the legislature when "the Five" (Emile Ollivier, Darimon, Hénon, Picard, Jules Favre) were returned in the elections of 1857 and by-elections of 1858.

Napoleon's position was rapidly undermined during the sixties by a series of failures in foreign policy.

1861-1867. THE MEXICAN EXPEDITION (p. 822). Owing to the refusal of the revolutionary Juarez government to meet its obligations, France, England, and Spain decided (**Convention of London**, Oct. 13, 1861) to force fulfillment of these obligations. They all landed troops at Vera Cruz (Dec. 1861), but the English and Spanish soon withdrew when they recognized Napoleon's more far-reaching plans, viz. to establish a Catholic Latin empire in Mexico while the United States was engaged in the Civil War. French troops took Mexico City (June, 1863) and proclaimed Archduke Maximilian (brother of Francis Joseph I of Austria) as emperor. Maximilian was unable to maintain himself without French support. By 1866 the United States was vigorously demanding the withdrawal of the French and Napoleon was in dire need of his troops because of European complications. He therefore deserted Maximilian, who refused to abdicate (1866, Dec.). He was captured and executed by the Mexicans (June 19, 1867).

1862, Sept. 25. An attempt to conciliate the papacy by warning the Italian government against a march on Rome, succeeded only in estranging the Italian government.

1863. Napoleon's efforts to intervene against Russia in the **Polish Insurrection** (p. 704) broke down through the lukewarm attitude of the English and Austrians and through Prussia's support of Russia. The effect of the policy was to estrange Russia, with which power France had been on close terms of friendship since 1857.

1864. The September Convention. Reversing his attitude on the Roman question, Napoleon agreed to withdraw his troops from Rome within two years in return for a promise from the Italian government not to attack papal territory. This move outraged French Catholic opinion. The pope issued the encyclical *Quanta cura* and the *Syllabus of Errors* (p. 664) which were in part an attack on the French government (e.g. condemnation of the supremacy of the nation and of universal suffrage). Napoleon at once forbade publication of the *Syllabus* in France, and thereby further aroused the ire of the clergy.

These failures led to a more outspoken attitude on the part of the parliamentary opposition, which, in the elections of 1863, had polled a vote of almost two million and had returned 35 deputies to the Chamber, of whom 17 were Republicans. Thiers denounced the extravagance in Mexico (Jan. 11, 1864) and demanded "the indispensable liberties" which became the slogan of his group.

1866, Mar. More than 40 members of the government majority in the Chamber broke away and formed a *Third Party* which asked the emperor "to further the natural development of the great Act of 1860."

1866, July 3. Prussian victory over Austria at Sadowa (p. 686). The French, who had expected a long war ending with French mediation and compensation, regarded the victory as a national humiliation. But the army was not ready and Napoleon's will was crippled by physical suffering occasioned by bladder stones. He failed to mobilize and acquiesced in the formation of the North German Confederation. His belated attempts to secure compensation from Prussia in the Rhineland, Luxemburg, or Belgium (1866–1867) failed completely and left him badly discredited.

1867, Jan. 19. The **right of interpellation** was granted the Chamber, but every interpellation required the previous approval of four committees, so that the majority could prevent undesired questions.

Mar. 12. The Senate demanded and was accorded the **right to examine the projected laws in detail** (instead of merely passing on their constitutionality) and to return them to the Legislative Assembly for further action. Thus the Senate became a collaborator in legislation, though a reactionary one.

Nov. 3. Napoleon again alienated the Liberals and Republicans by sending troops to crush the Garibaldians before they could attack Rome (Mentana, p. 659).

1867-1870. ALLIANCE NEGOTIATIONS WITH AUSTRIA AND ITALY. These were part of the preparation for ultimate conflict with Prussia (regarded as inevitable after the Luxemburg affair of 1867, p. 686). **Napoleon met Francis Joseph at Salzburg** (1867, Aug. 18–21) and Francis Joseph paid a visit to Paris (Oct.). After the reorganization of the French army had been begun (**Army Law of Jan. 1868** adding 100,000 men and providing for complete rearmament), negotiations were initiated first with Austria, then with Italy, leading in 1869 to a draft treaty and to an exchange of letters between the sovereigns. The main obstacles to a firm agreement were the unwillingness of the Austrians to commit themselves to immediate action in a dispute between France and Prussia on a purely German issue, and the insistence of the Italians on the evacuation of Rome by the French. Nevertheless the French government mistakenly proceeded on the supposition that in case of war with Prussia, Austria and Italy could be relied upon to participate.

By 1868 there had been a marked **revival of republicanism** and **radicalism**. Strikes had been permitted by an Act of May 1864 and trade unions, though still illegal, were connived at after an Act of Mar. 25, 1868. The result was a growing epidemic of strikes and a wide spread of trade-unionism, with a corresponding strengthening of the republican sentiment. By 1868 the enemies of the imperial régime could be silenced only by candid concessions.

1868, May 11. A **liberal press law** made possible establishment of a newspaper by simple declaration; eliminated administrative interference in the form of warning, suspension, and suppression.

June 11. **Limited right of public meeting** was granted, each meeting to be held, however, in a closed building subject to supervision by a police officer empowered to dissolve it. Republican newspapers promptly multiplied; workers met to discuss economic problems, to end in attacking the political régime.

1869, May 23, 24. **Parliamentary elections** gave the government 4,438,000 votes to 3,355,000 for the opposition; the new Chamber included 30 Republicans.

June 28. The Third Party interpellated the government, demanded the creation of a responsible ministry. With the co-operation of 40 deputies of the Left, the "116" of the Third Party had a majority. The emperor had to yield or embark on a struggle with at least one-half of his subjects.

July 12. He adopted the program of the 116. By decree of the Senate (Sept. 6), the **new régime** was initiated: the Legislative Assembly was given the right to propose laws, criticize and vote the budget, choose its own officers; the Senate became a deliberative body with public sessions, had the right to discuss laws voted by the Assembly and send them back for consideration; ministers were declared responsible but were to "depend on the emperor alone." — an equivocal position casting doubt on how far the new régime could be considered "parliamentary."

Dec. 28. The Third Party pressed Napoleon for clarification of this situation, and he entrusted their chief, **Emile Ollivier,** with the formation of a "homogeneous cabinet, representative of the majority of the Legislative Assembly." Ollivier was faced by divisions within his own party, by growing revolutionary agitation in the country. **Leon Gambetta's** (1838–1882) Republican **Program of Belleville** demanded universal suffrage, freedom of the press, right of meeting, of combination, of trial by jury for all political offenses, separation of Church and State, suppression of the standing army. Labor was rapidly organizing in trade unions, on one hand, and its more radical elements in the Marxist **First International.** This was twice dissolved in France by official action (Mar. 1868; June 1870). France was swept by an epidemic of strikes.

1870, Jan. 10. When the Republican journalist, **Victor Noir,** was shot by Prince Pierre Bonaparte, cousin of the emperor, his funeral was the occasion for a demonstration against the empire of some hundred thousand people. Ollivier's problem was no longer that of converting a liberal into a constitutional monarchy, but of saving the empire by concessions. Sweeping constitutional reforms followed:

Apr. 20. The Senate was made an **upper house,** sharing legislative power with the Assembly; constituent authority was taken from the Senate and given to the people (no constitutional change was to be made without a plebiscite). The Bonapartists then sought a plebiscite (to strengthen the hand of the emperor): the nation was asked "whether it approved the liberal reforms effected in the constitution since 1860 . . . whether it ratified the *senatus consultum* of April 20, 1870." Battle was joined between empire and republic (Right Republicans, however, as the *Gauche ouverte*, supporting the government).

May 8. The **plebiscite** gave 7,358,786 "ayes," 1,571,939 "noes"; the Napoleonic Empire seemed to have won new strength by this sweeping triumph. Within four months it was to be swept away by the War of 1870 (p. 688).

f. THE THIRD REPUBLIC, 1870-1914

1870, Sept. 2. The **capitulation of Napoleon III at Sedan** (p. 688) was a blow the empire was unable to survive.

Sept. 4. When the news became general in Paris, the mob invaded the Palais Bourbon and obliged the reluctant members of the rump of the Legislative Assembly to join in proclaiming the fall of the empire. In accordance with accepted revolutionary ritual, the **republic was proclaimed** at the Hôtel de Ville after a provisional government of **national defense** had been set up, of which **Gambetta** was the outstanding member, **General Trochu** (who had recently sworn to die defending the Napoleonic dynasty) the president. The new government seemed faced by a hopeless task — winning a war already lost.

Sept. 19. After Sedan two German armies swept on and invested Paris. The government devoted itself to a desperate defense of the country, sent a delegation to Tours to organize resistance in the provinces, presently joined by Gambetta, who escaped from besieged Paris in a balloon and virtually governed France (beyond Paris) in the succeeding months.

The populace of Paris was disgusted by the inactivity of Trochu, possessed of a force superior to Moltke's in size; was further outraged by the "treasonable"

Oct. 27. Surrender of General Bazaine at Metz, with 173,000 men.

Oct. 31. The discontent crystallized in a Paris *putsch* of socialists and radicals, aiming to establish a commune in the tradition of 1792 and carry on the war to the finish. The movement collapsed. By Jan. the Parisian populace was reduced to a miserable state. With only eight days' supply of food remaining,

Jan. 28. Paris capitulated. The armistice agreement yielded the forts to the Germans and an indemnity of 200,000,000 francs, and disarmed the troops of the line in the city. By the armistice Bismarck also agreed to permit election of a representative assembly to determine whether the war should be continued or on what terms peace should be made.

1871, Feb. 8. Elections were held.

Feb. 13. The National Assembly met at Bordeaux. From Tours Gambetta had organized armed resistance in the provinces, with the aid of a young mining engineer, **Charles de Freycinet** (1828–1923); the obstinate fighting of these hastily improvised forces amazed the German command. But by mid-January this resistance had been substantially crushed, the country was exhausted, the majority of Frenchmen wanted peace. Under these conditions only the **Radical Republicans and Socialists** wanted to continue the war "to the last ditch." Hence the country elected an assembly two-thirds of whom were conservatives.

Feb. 16. The Assembly elected **Adolphe Thiers,** who had won a reputation as the Cassandra of imperial collapse, **chief of the executive power.**

Feb. 28. Thiers introduced the **terms of a peace treaty** negotiated with Bismarck by **Jules Favre** and himself providing for the **cession of Alsace and a part of Lorraine,** an indemnity of five billion francs, an army of occupation to remain until the indemnity should have been paid. The terms were hotly opposed by the representatives of Alsace and Lorraine, by Louis Blanc, Gambetta, Clemenceau, and others; but accepted, 546 to 107 (Mar. 1).

May 10. The definitive **treaty of peace was signed at Frankfurt,** embodying the terms accepted Mar. 1, but with certain territorial rectifications, etc. Thiers proclaimed his own neutrality in the face of party division within the Assembly and urged the necessity of the co-operation of all in the task of national recovery (**Pact of Bordeaux**, Feb. 19). The Assembly adjourned (Mar. 11) to meet again at Versailles (Mar. 20).

1871. Mar.-May. THE PARIS COMMUNE. Mar. 1-3. Radical Paris, which had undergone the fruitless suffering of four months' siege, felt itself further humiliated by the entry of German troops into the capital and by the peace terms accepted by the National Assembly; it was alarmed by the composition of the Assembly, whose majority was obviously unfriendly to the republic. Discontent spread rapidly. The National Guard, which the Germans had failed to disarm by the armistice of Jan. 28, appointed a central committee, seized cannon belonging to the regular army, prepared for the eventualities of conflict.

Mar. 18. Thiers sent troops of the line to seize the cannon; they fraternized with the crowd, refused to fire; the mob seized and executed Gens. **Lecomte** and **Thomas**; the troops retired, leaving Paris in the hands of the radicals. Election of a municipal council (the **Commune of 1871**) was called by the central committee of the National Guard for Mar. 26. The **Commune** included Moderate Republicans, Radical Republicans (of the 1793 Jacobin tradition), followers of Proudhon, followers of Blanqui, members of the **First International**. A body of such diverse tendencies had no clear-cut program, "socialist" or otherwise. It sought to decentralize France by enlarging the powers of municipalities; to substitute the National Guard for the standing army; to separate Church and State (law of **Apr. 2**). But opportunity for carrying through a legislative program was cut short by the armed struggle with the government of the National Assembly at Versailles.

Apr. 2. The Versailles troops took the offensive, defeated the troops of the Commune repeatedly, entered Paris, reduced the city in the face of desperate but unorganized resistance behind barricades in the **Bloody Week** (May 21-28). Hostages taken by the Communards, including **Archbishop Darboy** of Paris, had been executed. The victors replied by visiting summary and sanguinary punishment through courts-martial on a large but indeterminate number of prisoners; others in large numbers were deported or imprisoned.

1871-1873. THE MONARCHIST OFFENSIVE. The Monarchist majority of the National Assembly, summoned to answer the question of war or peace, were determined to settle the question of a new régime for France before separating. The Monarchists were divided: of those originally elected, some 200 were **Legitimists** (supporters of the "legitimate" Bourbon line and of its pretender, the **Count of Chambord**), the same number **Orléanists** (supporters of the **Count of Paris**, grandson of Louis Philippe), some thirty **Bonapartists**. Legitimists and Orléanists would hear nothing of a restoration of the "parvenu" Napoleonic dynasty.

1871, July 6. The **Count of Chambord** alienated both the Orléanists and the country by declaring categorically that he must rule under the white flag of the Bourbons. Meanwhile Republicans gained ground in by-elections to the National Assembly.

Aug. 31. Thiers' title became *President of the Republic* by the **Law Rivet-Vitet**, which, however, also declared that the Assembly possessed constituent powers. Thiers, originally a staunch Orléanist, was rallying to the *conservative republic* as a *pis aller* ("the government which divides us least"). The Monarchist majority permitted him to accomplish the patriotic task of paying the German indemnity (through two government loans, June 21, 1871, July 15, 1872), bringing with it **evacuation of French territory** (the last German soldier crossed the frontier, Sept. 16, 1873). They then condemned the government of Thiers as insufficiently "conservative" (vote of 360 to 344).

1873, May 24. Thiers promptly resigned, and **Marshal MacMahon** (1808-1893) was elected president at the same session. MacMahon, soldier by profession, monarchist by predilection, neophyte in politics, was to prepare the way for the restoration.

Aug. 5. The Count of Chambord and the Count of Paris became reconciled, and it was agreed that the latter should succeed the former, who was childless.

Oct. 27. The plan foundered when the Count of Chambord insisted once again on the white flag.

Nov. 20. To give themselves time to re-form their forces, the Monarchist majority conferred the powers of president on MacMahon for seven years (**Law of the Septennate**).

1875. THE CONSTITUTION OF 1875. After prolonged discussion of various constitutional projects, a **Law on the Organization of the Public Powers** was introduced.

Jan. 21. Henri Wallon proposed an amendment: "The president of the republic is elected by an absolute majority of the votes of the Senate and the Chamber of Deputies sitting together as the National Assembly. He is chosen for seven years. He is eligible for re-election." The term *republic* was crucial: acceptance of the amendment meant acceptance of the republic. The *impasse* caused by the failure of the Monarchists had resulted in some disintegration in their ranks.

Jan. 30. The Wallon amendment was adopted by one vote — 353 to 352. The **Law on the Organization of the Public Powers** was accepted as a whole (Feb. 25); the **Law on the Organization of the Senate** had been accepted (Feb. 24). A **Law on the Relation of the Public Powers** (passed July 16) completed the so-called **Constitution of 1875.** The executive was a president (who was not to be a member of the legislative body) elected according to the Wallon amendment, possessed of the usual executive powers (command of the army and navy, right to choose civil officials and military officers, etc.), but requiring a counter-signature for each of his acts by the relevant minister. The ministers were declared responsible, each for his own acts, together for the general policy of the government. The Senate was to have 300 members, 225 chosen for nine years, on the basis of a complicated and indirect system of election, 75 named by the National Assembly (later by the Senate) for life (senators for life were discontinued in 1884). The Senate shared the right to initiate legislation (except finance laws) with the Chamber of Deputies, whose members were elected by universal, direct, manhood suffrage. The Chamber was subject to dissolution only by the president, with the consent of the Senate. The seat of the government was fixed at Versailles, reflecting fear of Republican Paris.

Apr.-May. The famous **war scare** during which the Duc Decazes, French foreign minister, secured the intervention of England and Russia at Berlin (p. 733).

1877, May 16. CRISIS OF *SEIZE MAI.* The National Assembly came to an end and the new Senate and Chamber met for the first time (1876, Mar. 8). The Senate had a Conservative majority, the Chamber was overwhelmingly Republican. In the next quarter-century the new republican institutions were to be repeatedly attacked by their enemies of the Right. The first test came in the affair of the *Seize Mai* when MacMahon, irritated by what he considered inadequate opposition of the

premier, **Jules Simon,** to the anti-clerical attitude of the Left, forced Simon to resign. Had the power of dismissal of ministries been conceded to the president, the Chamber's control of ministries would have disappeared, and the president would have been given the powers held by Louis Napoleon, 1848–1851 (p. 632).

June 19. A new cabinet, headed by the Orléanist **Duke of Broglie,** was given a vote of "no confidence" by the Chamber, 363 to 158; MacMahon dissolved the Chamber with the consent of the Senate (the only dissolution in the history of the Third Republic).

Oct. 14, 28. In the elections, despite vigorous governmental pressure, the Republicans lost only 36 seats.

Nov. 19. The De Broglie ministry was forced to retire by an adverse majority (312 to 205); its successor, the presidential **Rochebouët ministry** (Nov. 24) fared the same.

Dec. 13. MacMahon was forced to beat a retreat, named **Jules Dufaure** to head a ministry enjoying the confidence of the Chamber. The principle of ministerial responsibility had triumphed over that of the personal power of the president.

1879, Jan. 5. In the senatorial election the Republicans gained 58 seats; faced by a hostile majority in the Senate and Chamber,

Jan. 30. MacMahon resigned (although his term of office had more than a year to run), and was succeeded by a Conservative Republican, Jules Grévy.

1879-1887. PRESIDENCY OF JULES GRÉVY (1813–1891). The Conservative Republicans (**Opportunists**), in power from 1879 to 1885, proceeded to a series of **anti-clerical laws:**

1880, Mar. 29, 30. Two decrees (1) enjoining all non-authorized **religious associations** to regularize their position within three months; (2) ordering dissolution and **dispersion of the Jesuits** within three months and dissolution of all religious teaching associations within **six** months (giving effect to the decree of 1762 and later legislation).

July 11. A law providing virtually **full amnesty to the Communards of** 1871.

1881, Mar.-May. French occupation of Tunis (Treaty of Bardo, May 12), largely the work of Jules Ferry (1832–1893); important as marking the emergence of French imperialism and the expansion of the second French Empire (pp. 737, 838).

1882, Mar. 29. Primary education law, making education from 6 to 13 free, obligatory, and "neutral" (i.e. public schools were to give no religious education).

1884, July 27. Law re-establishing divorce substantially as it had been permitted under the civil code (divorce had been abolished by the law of May 8, 1816).
Further important legislation included

1884, Mar. 21. The Trade-Union Act legalizing unions forbidden by the *Loi Chapelier* (of 1791) and subsequent legislation, but tolerated since 1868. By this time the labor movement, temporarily in eclipse after the Commune, had begun to revive and to veer in a Marxian direction. In 1876 Jules Guesde (1845-1922) had returned from exile and had begun to propagate Marxian ideas. At the third congress of French workers (Marseilles) in Oct. 1879 the Guesdists had won the day over the more idealistic co-operative socialists and steps were taken to organize a socialist political party, the *Fédération du Parti des Travailleurs Socialistes de France*. In the party the more moderate group (Possibilists) were at first dominant. In 1882 the Guesdists withdrew and formed the *Parti Ouvrier Français*, while the Possibilists reorganized the majority as the *Parti Ouvrier Socialiste Révolutionnaire Français*.

1884-1885. French advance in Tonkin, resulting in war with China (p. 874) and downfall of the second Ferry ministry (1883-1885).

1886-1889. THE BOULANGER CRISIS. This arose from widespread discontent with the Conservative Republican régime. The Radical Republicans wished to democratize further the constitution and to separate the Church and State; the workers were suffering from depression and demanding state action in their behalf; the Monarchists continued to hope for an eventual restoration; The elections of **1885** were a victory for the Right (202 seats as against 80 in 1881), although the various Republican groups still had 372 seats.

1886, Jan. 4. General Georges Boulanger (1837-1891) became minister of war in the Freycinet cabinet. He was the friend and protégé of Georges Clemenceau (1841-1929), dominant figure among the Radical Republicans, who had imposed Boulanger on Freycinet. Boulanger won popularity in the army through various reforms (improvement of soldiers' food and living conditions, etc.); among the people

by frequent and impressive appearances in public, notably on July 14, 1886. He was celebrated in poem and song, became a national figure with the Schnaebelé incident (p. 740) and the attacks of the German press, and was greeted as the incarnation of the *révanche*.

1887, May 18. When Boulanger left office (fall of the Goblet cabinet), his popularity only increased. The government became alarmed, exiled Boulanger to Clermont-Ferrand as commandant of the 13th Army Corps. The Wilson Scandal shook the prestige of the republic and offered Boulanger an opportunity to widen his contacts. Daniel Wilson, son-in-law of President Grévy, was discovered to have been trafficking in medals of the Legion of Honor: Grévy, although not guilty of complicity, was forced to resign the presidency (Dec. 2). He was succeeded by **Marie François Sadi-Carnot**.

1887-1894. Presidency of **Sadi-Carnot** (1837-1894), an honest but undistinguished politician, grandson of Lazare Carnot, "organizer of victory" in 1793.
During the Wilson crisis, Boulanger maintained relations with the Radical Republicans and made contact with the Orléanist leaders (*Nuits historiques*, Nov. 28-30, 1887) — apparently ready to satisfy his ambitions by whatever path offered. Boulanger, although ineligible for the Chamber, permitted his candidacy to be posed repeatedly as a test of his popularity.

1888, Mar. 27. The government, alarmed, put him on the retired list; he was now eligible for the Chamber, to which he was promptly elected (Apr. 15). He initiated a vigorous **campaign for revision of the constitution** (in what sense was not specified); demanded dissolution of the Chamber as an essential preliminary; resigned from the Chamber (July 12) and was returned in three constituencies simultaneously (Aug. 19).

1889, Jan. 27. Boulanger won a striking victory in Paris. It was believed he would march on the Elysée Palace that night and make himself master of France. But he failed to seize the opportunity to make himself dictator and his popularity rapidly declined. The government prepared to have him tried for treason by the Senate; and he fled into exile (Apr. 8), where he eventually committed suicide on his mistress's grave in Brussels (1891, Sept. 30).

July 17. Meanwhile a law was adopted, forbidding **multiple candidacies.** The general elections of 1889 were a triumph for the Republicans, a crushing defeat for the Boulangists.

1890 ff. The Ralliement. The Boulangist fiasco was a blow to the monarchists and their ally, the Church. **Pope Leo XIII,** discouraged by the failures of the monarchists, turned to a policy of conciliation of the republic.

1890, Nov. 12. Charles Cardinal Lavigerie, Primate of Africa, in a famous toast at a banquet to French naval officers at Algiers (**Algiers Toast**), declared it the duty of all citizens to "rally" to the support of the existing form of government, once that form of government had been accepted by the people. This so-called *ralliement* to the republic was vigorously combated by Monarchists and Clericals on the one hand, and by Radical Republicans and Socialists on the other. But the pope was influenced, notably by the international situation (p. 742), to espouse Lavigerie's policy.

1891, May 15. The encyclical *Rerum novarum* (on the condition of the workers) attempted to win the support of both Radical and Conservative Republicans through a more liberal (though by no means radical) statement of papal views on the social question; more specific support to the movement came in the encyclical *Inter innumeras* (Feb. 16, 1892), which declared that a government once established was legitimate. Despite opposition, the *ralliement* introduced a new spirit into the relations of Church and State in France: the period of the **Méline ministry** (1896–1898) has been termed "the Golden Age of Clericalism." Eventually the *ralliement* foundered in the struggle over Dreyfus (p. 641).

1891, July. Visit of a French squadron to Cronstadt. Beginning of the **Franco-Russian Alliance** negotiations (p. 742).

1892–1893. THE PANAMA SCANDAL. Attracted by the name of **Ferdinand de Lesseps** (1805–1894), builder of the Suez Canal, and president of the Panama Company (*Compagnie du Canal Interocéanique*), French investors, from peasant to capitalist, had contributed to the Panama Canal project to the extent of 1,500,000,000 francs. The company collapsed (1889, Feb.) as a result of corruption and mismanagement, but despite the uproar, it was nearly four years before legal action was taken against de Lesseps and his associates (1892, Nov. 19). In the course of a parliamentary investigation and two trials, it was revealed that the company had made lavish distributions to the press and to a certain number of deputies and senators (in the interest of securing their support for parliamentary authorization of a stock lottery). The company's intermediary was **Baron Jacques Reinach,** Jewish banker of German origin, who was found dead the day after he was summoned for trial. The revelations caused widespread consternation, increased by knowledge that the government had attempted to silence the whole affair.

1893, Feb. 9. Ferdinand de Lesseps and some of his associates were condemned by the court of appeal to pay large fines and serve prison sentences, but the decree of the court was set aside by the *cour de cassation* (June 15) on the grounds that the three years under the criminal statute of limitations had expired. Of the numerous senators, deputies, and others tried before the court of assizes, only three were found guilty, one (Baïhaut) on his own confession that he had received 375,000 francs.

Further development of **socialism** and the **labor movement.** In 1890 a further split in the ranks of the Possibilists had taken place, precipitated by **Jean Allemane,** who criticized the majority for accepting public office and co-operating with the *bourgeoisie.* The new faction took the name *Parti Ouvrier Socialiste Révolutionnaire.* With the progress of the industrial revolution and the consequent growth of the proletariat, the social question became ever more acute. Collisions between workers and the forces of "order" became more and more frequent. In the **Massacre of Fourmies** (1891, May 1) the troops fired on a crowd of demonstrating workers and killed women and children, causing a great sensation. The government of the conservative republicans continued lukewarm in the matter of social reform, with the result that extremist elements in the labor movement became more and more active. The anarchists (disciples of **Michael Bakunin** and **Prince Peter Kropotkin**) began a long series of outrages (dynamiting and assassination). In Mar. 1892, a number of bombings were carried out by **Ravachol,** an anarchist.

1893, Oct. Visit of a Russian squadron to Toulon, followed by the conclusion (1893, Dec.–1894, Jan.) of the **Franco-Russian Alliance** (p. 742).

1893, Dec. 9. Auguste Vaillant, another anarchist, exploded a bomb in the Chamber of Deputies.

1894, June 24. President Carnot was stabbed at Lyons by an Italian anarchist, **Santo Caserio.**

Meanwhile, the various socialist parties had begun to concert action. In 1893 they had elected some 50 deputies. The trade unions, which had developed rapidly after the law of 1884, organized nationally in the *Fédération des Syndicats* (by trades) and in the *Fédération des Bourses du Travail* (each representing the different trades in one locality). Under the influence of anarchism

1894. The Trade-Union Congress at Nantes adopted the principle of the general strike.

1894, June 27—1895, Jan. 17. Presidency of Jean Casimir-Perier (1847–1907), who resigned in disgust.

1895. The Trade-Union Congress at Limoges organized the *Confédération Générale du Travail* (C.G.T.) with a program of direct action, seeking to destroy the capitalist régime and the state by means of the general strike and to prepare for this eventual catastrophe through local strikes, boycotts, and sabotage (a theory later given classic formulation by Georges Sorel in his *Reflections on Violence*, 1908). By the end of the century the workers' organizations — radical revolutionaries harking back to Auguste Blanqui; socialists of various stamps; anarchists; syndicalists — constituted a real power in the country, which was, however, dissipated by divergences of view and mutual antagonism.

1895-1899. Presidency of Félix Faure (1841-1890), prosperous and conservatively minded business man and politician. During his presidency the ministry of Méline (1896-1898) marked the last flowering of conservative, protectionist, clerical republicanism.

1894-1906. THE DREYFUS AFFAIR. Captain Alfred Dreyfus, probationer (*stagiaire*) of the general staff of the army, was arrested (1894, Oct. 15) charged with treason. He was tried by a court-martial *in camera*, condemned (Dec. 22), degraded, sent to Devil's Island in French Guiana. The evidence was a list of military documents (the *bordereau*), apparently submitted by a treasonable member of the general staff to the German military attaché, later purloined from the latter's mail by a French spy and submitted to the French intelligence service. The latter's handwriting experts disagreed as to whether the writing was that of Dreyfus; further "secret" evidence, subsequently shown to be irrelevant or forged, was also introduced and was said to have been considered conclusive. The presence of treason in the general staff had been aired in the press and had excited public opinion; the honor of the army seemed to be engaged; a victim was needed, and Dreyfus was the only one to whom the evidence pointed at all. Moreover, the real culprit was a friend of a member of the general staff, Major Henry, who sought to protect him. Dreyfus was a Jew, intensely disliked by most of his conservative colleagues of the general staff, who were Catholic, royalist, anti-Semitic. Dreyfus, wealthy and ambitious, son of an Alsatian patriot who had opted for France after the cession of 1871, apparently had no motive for treason.

1896, Mar. Colonel Georges Picquart, new chief of the intelligence service, had delivered to him a second document (the *petit bleu*), a card of the type used in the Paris pneumatic postal service. The card was addressed to a former member of the general staff, Major Count Walsin-Esterhazy, then stationed at Rouen, French by birth, former officer in the Austrian army, in the papal zouaves, in the foreign legion; *débauché*, gambler, *arriviste*. Picquart compared a specimen of Esterhazy's writing with that of the *bordereau*, concluded they were identical, submitted his evidence to Gen. Gonse (second in command of the general staff), was told to say nothing of the matter — that the affair could not be reopened. Picquart was transferred to a frontier post in Tunis.

1897, Nov. 15. Mathieu Dreyfus, brother of Alfred, discovered independently that the *bordereau* was in Esterhazy's writing, and demanded the latter's trial.

1898, Jan. 11. Esterhazy was tried by a military tribunal, and triumphantly acquitted.

Jan. 13. The novelist, Émile Zola (1840–1902), promptly published an open letter (*J'accuse*) to the president of the republic, denouncing by name the members of the general staff associated with the condemnation of Dreyfus.

Feb. 23. Zola was tried and condemned to one year imprisonment.

It was presently discovered that a decisive document in the secret Dreyfus *dossier* had been forged by Col. (formerly Major) Henry, now chief of the intelligence service.

Aug. 30. When Henry admitted the forgery (only the first of a series to be discovered), Gen. de Boisdeffre, chief of the general staff, resigned. Henry was imprisoned and committed suicide the next day. A rehearing for Dreyfus was promptly sought by his wife (Sept. 3).

1898, Sept.-Nov. The Fashoda crisis (p. 748) brought France and England to the brink of war.

By this time France was divided into two camps, and the *Affair* had taken on a profound political complexion: **Dreyfusards** (those interested in preserving the republic) ranged themselves against **anti-Dreyfusards** (the army and a large body of Royalists and Catholics—forces interested in a restoration of the monarchy). A violent campaign in the press, both Nationalist and Republican, followed. Street clashes were frequent. The various socialist parties, who had at first considered the *Affair a* mere *"bourgeois* quarrel,"² now saw the republic threatened.

Oct. 16. In a mass meeting in Paris the socialists concerted forces to defend the republic against its "attackers."²

1899, Feb. 16. The sudden **death of President Faure,** opponent of a retrial for Dreyfus, was followed by the election of the colorless **Emile Loubet,** considered a friend of revision.

1899-1906. Presidency of Emile Loubet (1838-1929).

1899, June 3. The *cour de cassation* (highest court of appeal) set aside the condemnation of Dreyfus, and summoned a court-martial at Rennes.

Sept. 9. **Dreyfus was again found guilty,** this time with "extenuating circumstances"; he was condemned to ten years' imprisonment.

Sept. 19. By presidential decree, he was pardoned — first act of pacification of the **ministry of René Waldeck-Rousseau** (1846-1904), formed June 22, 1899, to bring internal peace to the country. The Dreyfusards painfully accumulated new evidence, and Dreyfus finally asked a rehearing. On July 12, 1906 the *cour de cassation* set aside the judgment of the court-martial at Rennes, declaring it "wrongful" and "erroneous." The government decorated Dreyfus (July 13) and raised him to the rank of major.

1901-1905. SEPARATION OF CHURCH AND STATE. The outcome of the Dreyfus Affair was a victory for the republic, a defeat for its enemies (monarchists, the clergy, the army). In matters affecting the Church, Waldeck-Rousseau wished to remain faithful to the Napoleonic Concordat (p. 588), but was a proponent of stringent regulation (not suppression) of religious associations, many of whose members had intervened on the side of the anti-Dreyfusards.

1901, July 1. The result was the **Associations Law,** whose terms relative to religious "congregations" were most important: (1) no congregation could be formed without a law defining its scope and activity; (2) all congregations lacking authorization, or which parliament failed

subsequently to authorize, were to be dissolved. Since the treatment of congregations was to depend on the will of the legislature, the general elections were all-important. The elections were a victory for the Radical Republicans and Socialists.

The **Republican bloc** (formed in 1900 to defend the republic against its anti-Dreyfusard opponents) was determined to proceed with vigor against the Church, viewing the Associations Laws as a *pis aller.*

1902, June 2. Waldeck-Rousseau, unsympathetic with extreme measures, resigned, an unprecedented act for a premier who possessed the confidence of the majority of the Chamber. His successor was **Emile Combes** (1835-1921), known for his probity and anti-clerical convictions. His ministry proceeded to enforce the Associations Law with vigor: closing some 3000 unauthorized schools until they should apply for, and receive, authorization; preparing 54 bills refusing the applications for authorization of as many male congregations (all 54 bills were passed by parliament, 1903, Mar.); etc.

1904, July 7. All teaching by congregations was forbidden by a further law, such congregations to be suppressed within ten years.

Relations of the French government with the papacy were rapidly embittered.

1904, Mar. President Loubet's visit to the King of Italy, the pope's enemy, irritated the papal government, which sent to the Catholic powers an official protest against this offense to papal dignity.

May 21. The French ambassador to the Vatican was recalled.

Nov. Combes, who thus far had wished to preserve the Concordat of 1801, introduced a **bill for the separation of Church and State.** It was not Combes' bill (his ministry came to an end, Jan. 19, 1905), but that ably defended by **Aristide Briand** (1862-1932, reporter of the Chamber's Committee on the Separation of Church and State, that was carried, the law being promulgated Dec. 9, 1905: (1) it guaranteed complete liberty of conscience; (2) it suppressed all connection of the Church with the state — henceforth the state would have no connection with the appointment of Catholic ecclesiastics or with the payment of their salaries; (3) the property of the Church was to be taken over by private corporations formed for that specific purpose. Thus ended the relationship of the state to the Catholic Church as established by the Concordat of 1801, as well as the separate régimes establishing the relation of the state to the Protestant and the Jewish faiths (the Protestant Church had been state-supported and controlled since 1802, under the Organic Articles of Apr. 8; the Jews had been under state control since 1808 and had been given state support in 1831).

Apr. 8. Conclusion of the Entente Cordiale with England (p. 752).

1905. An acute crisis in Franco-German relations, arising from the Moroccan question (p. 753). Dramatic downfall of Théophile Delcassé (June 6), foreign minister since June, 1898.

1906-1913. Presidency of Clément Armand Fallières.

1906-1911. Striking revival of French nationalism and royalism. This was an outcome of the conflict over Dreyfus and particularly of the international tension resulting from the Moroccan crisis. The new "integral nationalism" assumed a sophisticated form in the writing of Charles Maurras (1868–   ) and Léon Daudet (1867–1942) in the newspaper *Action Française* (founded 1899). They sought the restoration of the monarchy, the aggressive development of French power at home and of French prestige abroad. Maurice Barrès (1862–1923), the eminent novelist, though unsympathetic to the restoration of the monarchy, also sought the promotion of national unity in terms of French "traditional development," with decentralization and harmonizing of the forces of nationalism and socialism, an ideology in some respects foreshadowing National Socialism.

1906-1911. Epidemic of strikes and labor troubles. Decline in wine prices caused a crisis in that industry and the organization of vineyard workers in the *Confédération Générale des Vignerons* (1907). There were manifestations on a grand scale in the south, and considerable violence.

1909, Apr.-May. Strike of the Paris postal workers. Civil servants had demanded the right to unionize and affiliate with the *Confédération Générale du Travail.*

The former demand had been granted, the latter refused. The government of **Georges Clemenceau** (1906–1909) met the strikers with severe measures: more than 200 employees were discharged and the right of civil servants to strike was denied. Labor agitation was accompanied by violent passages between radicals and socialists notably between Clemenceau and **Jean Jaurès** (1859–1914), the outstanding figure of French socialism.

1909-1910. The first ministry of **Aristide Briand.**

1910, Oct. 10. A strike of railway workers on the Northeastern Railway was answered by Briand (long a socialist) by calling out the troops. The National Union of Railway Workers and Employees thereupon called a **general strike,** but when it became clear that the movement was collapsing, the strike committee ordered the resumption of work (Oct. 18). Briand defended the use of force to maintain the functioning of the railroads as essential to the life of the nation and its defense.

1911. New strikes of vineyard workers in Champagne, similar to those in the south in 1907.

1911, June-Nov. The second Moroccan (Agadir) crisis (p. 757). The ministries of **Joseph Caillaux** (1911, June 27–1912, Jan. 10) and **Raymond Poincaré** (1912, Jan. 14–1913, Jan. 18) were taken up largely with the Moroccan problem and other questions of international import, notably those arising from the Tripolitan War (p. 758) and from the Balkan Wars (p. 759).

1913, July-Aug. The government of **Louis Barthou** (1862–1934) carried a law increasing the military service from two to three years. This measure was vigorously opposed by the Radical Socialists and Socialists and its revocation was hotly debated until the very eve of the World War.

1913-1920. Presidency of Raymond Poincaré, ardent patriot, one of the most eminent of French statesmen in modern times.

(*Cont. pp.* 912 *ff.*, **976.**)

5. THE IBERIAN PENINSULA

a. SPAIN

1814-1833. FERDINAND VII, restored to the throne (1814, Mar.) after the conquest of Spain by Wellington in the

Peninsula War (p. 600). The king had promised to maintain the liberal Constitution of 1812 (p. 596), but refused to keep his promise, knowing the absolutist temper of the country and relying on the support of the Church and the army. Ferocious

The Spanish Bourbons (1814–1931)

Ferdinand VII = (4) Cristina
1814–1833   of Naples

Francisco = Isabella II
D. of Cadiz   1833–1868

Louisa = Anthony
D. of Montpensier

Isabella

Maria de la Paz
m. Louis Ferdinand
of Bavaria

Eulalia
m. Anthony
of Orléans

Alfonso XII = Maria Cristina
1875–1885   of Austria

Maria de las Mercedes
m. Charles of Bourbon

Maria Theresa
m. Ferdinand
of Bavaria

Alfonso XIII = Victoria
1886–1931   of Battenberg
(d. 1941)

Alfonso
b. 1907

Jaime
b. 1908

Beatrice

Maria
Cristina

John = Maria
b. 1913   Mercedes
(heir   of Bourbon
presumptive)

Maria del Pilar
b. 1936

---

persecution of the liberals and the king's capricious and incapable rule caused widespread dissatisfaction, notably in the army. The loss of the colonies in America (p. 799) deprived the government of one of the chief sources of income and determined Ferdinand (who was encouraged by Russia and France) to undertake their reconquest. Forces were concentrated at Cadiz, one of the chief centers of disaffection, where the troops became demoralized.

1820, Jan. Mutiny of the troops under Colonel Rafael Riego. They began to march to Madrid. Other revolutionary movements broke out in the north and ultimately the garrison in Madrid mutinied. Ferdinand yielded and restored the constitution. The revolutionaries held him practically a prisoner until 1823.

1822. The Congress of Verona (p. 604), after much previous debate among the powers, gave France a mandate to suppress the movement. England, under Canning, did its utmost to prevent intervention, but in vain. A French army

crossed the Pyrenees in the spring of 1823, marched to Madrid to the cheers of the unenlightened peasantry, and drove the revolutionaries south to Cadiz, taking the king with them.

1823, Aug. 31. The battle of the Trocadero brought the revolution to an end. Ferdinand was restored. He ignored the advice of the French to introduce a moderate constitutional régime and delivered the country over to an orgy of repression which lasted until his death.

1823, Dec. 2. Monroe's message to Congress (Monroe Doctrine, p. 770). This warned European countries against intervention in South America, and was the outcome of Canning's approaches to the American minister, Richard Rush, for joint action to oppose reconquest of the colonies. The danger of such action was almost nil on account of the attitude and sea-power of England.

1833, June 30. To assure the succession of his infant daughter **Isabella**, Ferdinand, under the influence of his energetic queen, **Cristina**, set aside the Salic Law, thus depriving his brother, **Don Carlos**, of the throne. The King died Sept. 29.

1833-1868. ISABELLA II (1830–1904). She was represented by her mother, Maria Cristina, as regent. Realizing that she must depend on the Liberals for support, the latter granted

1834. The **Estatuto Real** (royal constitution): Spain was divided into 49 administrative provinces, on the model of the French *départements*; a bicameral legislature (*Côrtes*) was given financial powers, but the government retained the right of dissolution and control of the ministry. The constitution was less advanced than that of 1812, and led to a split in the ranks of the Liberals: the *Moderados* accepted the statute; the *Progresistas* demanded restoration of the Constitution of 1812.

1834-1839. THE CARLIST WAR. Don Carlos, claiming the throne, was supported by the conservative elements, the Church, and much of the north of the country (Basques, Navarre, Aragon, Catalonia) where regional and autonomous feeling revolted against the centralizing tendencies of the Liberals.

1834, Apr. 22. Quadruple Alliance between England, France, Spain, and Portugal, aimed at the support of the constitutionalists against the pretenders. The British government went so far as to suspend the Foreign Enlistment Act and allow the formation of a foreign legion, under **Sir De Lacy Evans**. In 1836–1837 the Carlists were defeated, and the war was concluded by the **Convention of Vergara** (1839, Aug. 31). Don Carlos left the country for France.

1836, Aug. 10. Progressist insurrection in Andalusia, Aragon, Catalonia, and Madrid. Cristina, who had become very unpopular through her secret marriage with **Ferdinand Muñoz** (1833), was obliged to restore the Constitution of 1812 and summon a Progressist ministry, which had the Côrtes adopt the **Constitution of 1837,** a compromise between the Constitution of 1812 and the Statute of 1834.

1840, Oct. Revolt of General Espartero, "Duke of the Victory," who had embraced the Progressist cause. Cristina was forced to leave the country and Espartero became practically dictator, acting as regent.

1841, Oct. Espartero defeated a Cristina insurrection at Pampeluna.

1842, Nov. Rising in Barcelona, accompanied with much bloodshed. A republic was proclaimed, but was suppressed by Espartero (Dec.).

1843, June. A coalition of *Moderados, Progresistas,* and republicans declared against Espartero. **General Narvaez took Madrid** (July 15) and Espartero fled the country (Aug.). Isabella, though only 13 years old, was declared of age, with Narvaez as lieutenant-general of the kingdom. Cristina returned (1844, Mar.), but Narvaez remained practically dictator until 1851.

1845. A new constitution virtually reestablished the Statute of 1834.

1846, Oct. 10. Isabella married her cousin, Francis, Duke of Cadiz, while her sister, **Luisa Fernanda,** married the Duke of Montpensier, youngest son of Louis Philippe of France. The **affair of the Spanish marriages** caused the breakdown of the *entente* between England and France which originated in their collaboration in the Belgian question (1830–1831) and in the Quadruple Alliance of 1834. In 1843 and 1845 Aberdeen and Guizot had made **agreements at Eu,** according to which the choice of Isabella's husband should be confined to the Spanish and Neapolitan branches of the Bourbon house (i.e. the descendants of Philip V). This eliminated the two most desirable candidates, the Duke of Montpensier and Prince Leopold of Saxe-Coburg. It was further provided that the Infanta Luisa should not be married to a French prince unless her sister, the queen, should have first been married and borne children. Ignoring the Eu pacts, Palmerston sent a dispatch to Sir Henry Bulwer, the British ambassador at Madrid (July 19, 1846), mentioning three candidates for Isabella's hand, and Prince Leopold first. The second part of the dispatch discussed the Spanish domestic situation and condemned the French-supported *Moderados* for their violence and arbitrary methods. The French and Spanish governments, united in distrust of Palmerston and fearing British support of the *Progresistas,* precipitated the engagement of Isabella to the Duke of Cadiz and of Luisa to Montpensier. When the double marriage had taken place Palmerston was furious and invoked the Treaty of Utrecht with its precautions against the union of France and Spain. This was of no effect, but Franco-British relations were seriously compromised.

1851, Mar. 16. Concordat with the papacy. It recognized the Catholic religion as the sole authorized faith, gave the Church sweeping control of education and censorship; in return the papacy recognized abolition of ecclesiastical jurisdictions and the sale of confiscated church lands.

1852, Dec. A constitutional reform virtually eliminated the powers of the Córtes and established the dictatorship in law. A camarilla had complete power in its hands.

1854, July. A revolution led by General O'Donnell (a Moderate) and Espartero (Progressive) overthrew the government and forced Cristina to leave the country. O'Donnell then formed a new party, the Liberal Union, espousing a program between that of the moderates and progressives. When the Córtes adopted a law confiscating church lands, Isabella threatened to abdicate.

1856, July 15. Espartero resigned in favor of O'Donnell, who re-established the Constitution of 1845 with an amendment guaranteeing annual assembly of the Córtes and presentation of the budget at the beginning of each session.

1856, Oct. O'Donnell was dismissed and two years of reaction followed, punctuated by numerous insurrections.

1858-1863. O'Donnell back in power, governing with the support of the Liberal Union and avoiding thorny questions of domestic policy.

1859-1860. Successful campaign against the Moors in Morocco.

1861. Annexation of Santo-Domingo (p. 824) followed by insurrection in the island. Relinquishment of the island (1865).

Spain also joined France and England in intervention in Mexico.

1864, Sept. Narvaez made premier, supported by the *Moderados* and many of the absolutists. Reversion to a Catholic and reactionary policy. The Liberal parties united in opposition to the régime, the *Progresistas* boycotting the elections.

1864-1865. Dispute with Peru over the Chincha Islands (p. 813).

1865-1866. War with Chile (p. 809).

1865. A severe press law was accompanied by the dissolution of political clubs.

1866, Jan.-June. An insurrection organized by General Prim failed, but was followed by many executions.

1868, Apr. 23. Death of Narvaez, who had been preceded by O'Donnell (d. 1867, Nov. 5). Gonzalez Bravo attempted to continue the absolutist régime, but the army escaped from his control. The Liberal parties united on a revolutionary program. Scandals which gathered about the queen's name were ruthlessly exposed in the newspapers and undermined her

position. Her latest favorite, **Carlos Marfori**, a cook's son and an actor by profession, was made minister of state.

Sept. 18. Admiral Topete issued a revolutionary proclamation at Cadiz, followed by a manifesto by the Liberal generals. By the end of Sept. the movement had spread to all Spain.

Sept. 28. Royal forces defeated at **Alcolea** by Marshal Serrano. The queen fled to France (Sept. 29) and was declared deposed.

Oct. 5. A provisional government was formed, with **Serrano** at the lead and with **Prim** as the moving spirit. Reactionary laws were annulled, the Jesuit and other religious orders abolished. The government established universal suffrage and a free press.

1869, Feb. A constituent Córtes met.

May 21. The Córtes voted for the continuance of monarchical government.

June 6. The new constitution promulgated.

June 15. Marshal Serrano made regent. Prim head of the ministry. The new régime was bothered by Carlist and republican uprisings and other disturbances, but its chief anxiety was to find a ruler. The Duke of Montpensier was passed over out of consideration for Napoleon III; the Duke of Aosta; Prince Ferdinand of Saxe-Coburg; the Duke of Genoa; General Espartero, all these declined the throne when offered. Finally the offer was made to **Prince Leopold of Hohenzollern-Sigmaringen**, who accepted, but then withdrew. This candidacy became the occasion for the **war between Germany and France** (p. 688).

1870, Dec. 30. The Duke of Aosta, son of Victor Emmanuel II of Piedmont, was prevailed upon to accept. Death of Prim, victim of an assassin.

1871-1873. AMADEO I (b. 1845). Amadeo ruled for two years — isolated, opposed on every side, greeted as a "foreigner" — and then abdicated (1873, Feb. 12).

1873-1874. THE FIRST SPANISH REPUBLIC, proclaimed (Feb. 12) by the radical majority in the Córtes elected in Aug. 1872 (the Carlists having abstained).

1873, May 10. A constituent Córtes, now elected, was divided among partisans of different types of federal republic.

Sept. 8. In the midst of Carlist risings, **Emilio Castelar**, partisan of a centralized republic, was made head of the government, with the mission of restoring order.

1874, Jan. 2. Castelar retired. A military *coup* promptly followed, with Marshal Serrano as head of a provisional government. The Carlist war continued, marked by exceptional brutality.

Nov. 24. Alfonso, son of Isabella, came of age and declared for a constitutional monarchy. A party of Liberal Unionists and Moderates supported him.

Dec. 29-31. A group of generals, disgusted with the republic, **rallied to Alfonso,** who was proclaimed king.

1875-1885. ALFONSO XII. Continuation of the Carlist War, until Feb. 1876, when Don Carlos again fled. The pope, who had recognized Carlos as **Carlos VII,** King of Spain, was won over to recognition of the new régime by a governmental increase of the ecclesiastical budget, closing of Protestant schools and churches, abolition of civil marriages, and other concessions.

1876, July. A new constitution, accepted by the Córtes elected in Jan., was a compromise between the constitutions of 1845 and 1869 and established a system midway between Carlist "absolutism" and republican "anarchy." It provided for a bicameral legislature and a responsible ministry, but with a limited suffrage — a parliamentary régime in appearance only. The Córtes, as before the revolution, was "ministerial" (i.e. elected under government auspices and obedient to the ministry). The ministry, in turn, was selected by the king, who thus remained the effective ruler of the state. Constitutional forms were, however, observed, and during the succeeding decades there was neither *camarilla* nor insurrection. The ministerial power alternated between two parties, both supporting the régime: the **Conservatives** (led by **Canovas del Castillo**) and the **Liberals** (under **Sagasta**). The country prospered, but the king, though courageous and humane, was indulgent and lost much popularity through scandals at court. In foreign policy he followed the lead of the central powers. From 1887 to 1895 Spain was associated with England, Italy, and Austria in the **Mediterranean Agreements** (p. 740).

1885-1902. Regency of Maria Cristina, widow of Alfonso, who ruled for her son, born 1886, May 17, after the death of his father. The Con-

servatives and Liberals continued to alternate in power.

1890. Universal suffrage was again introduced. The economic development of the country led to increasing labor unrest, especially in centers like Barcelona. Anarchist outrages became frequent and resulted in many executions and in much repressive legislation.

1895. The Cuban Revolution (p. 823). It continued for three years and ended in the loss of both Cuba and the Philippines.

1898. THE SPANISH-AMERICAN WAR (p. 787). It left Spain weak and discredited, and resulted in further disintegration of the parliamentary régime. The Conservatives divided into an authoritarian wing (led by **La Cierva,** allied to the clergy), and the **Liberal Conservatives** (followers of **Silvela**). The Liberals (Progressives) were led by **Moret** after the death of Sagasta. A small **Carlist Party** continued to exist in the mountains of the north. A **Republican Party** had its headquarters in Madrid, Andalusia, and Catalonia. A **Socialist Party** was rapidly winning recruits among the laborers of Catalonia and the miners of the Basque region. Anarchists continued their activities and even made attempts upon the king's life. The centralized character of the government system gave rise to a **regionalist movement** in Catalonia, where the **United Catalans** (*Soldiarios*) demanded an autonomous administration and a separate budget. In its literary and linguistic aspects this movement took the form of a cultural revival.

1902-1931. ALFONSO XIII. Though declared of age, he at first allowed his mother to continue the government.

1904. Agreement between Spain and France regarding Morocco (p. 752). This marked the veering of Spanish policy to the side of France and England.

1906, May 31. Marriage of Alfonso to Princess Eugenia of Battenberg, granddaughter of Queen Victoria of England. The succeeding period was one of internal conflict. Army influence secured the passage of a law (1906) to try press offenses "against the fatherland and the army" by court-martial.

1909. When troops were embarked for Morocco, protests of extremists followed, directed against the inequality of the military service régime, under which obligatory service fell on the poorer classes. A general strike was proclaimed at Barcelona and extended to other Catalonian cities under the direction of a revolutionary committee.

July. At Barcelona the insurgents burned convents and massacred priests and monks. Vigorous repression followed, and Señor Ferrer, propagandist of the anti-clerical opposition, was executed (Oct. 13), with resulting criticism throughout Europe and many repercussions in Spain.

Oct. 21. The king called a Liberal ministry. In the succeeding years he even consulted with the Republican leader, **Azcarate**, and declared himself accessible to all parties, even those of anti-dynastic complexion.

1910-1913. The Liberals were in power, supported by the king.

1912, Nov. 12. Assassination of the ad- vanced Liberal premier, **José Canalejas**, pledged to an anti-clerical program. He had passed (1910, Dec. 23) the **Padlock Law**, forbidding the establishment of more religious houses without the consent of the government. The industrial enterprises of the religious orders were taxed, and public worship of non-Catholic bodies was expressly permitted.

Nov. 27. Treaty with France, defining their respective spheres in Morocco (p. 839).

1913, Oct. 27. The **Conservatives returned to power** after the king's unsuccessful attempts to reconcile the Liberals, who had split up after Canalejas' death.

1914, Aug. 7. Spain declared neutrality in the World War, the king having given France assurances that she might denude her Pyrenees frontier of troops.

(Cont. p. 980.)

b. PORTUGAL

1820, Aug. 29. Revolution at Oporto, stimulated by the revolution in Spain. The insurgents drove out the regency, established in Nov. 1807 under British auspices to rule the country during the sojourn of **King John VI** (ruled 1792–1826) in Brazil.

1822. A constitution was adopted similar to the democratic Spanish constitution. Brazil declared independence. King John accepted the invitation to return as constitutional monarch and left the government of Brazil to his eldest son, **Dom Pedro.**

1823, June 5. John revised the constitution in the interest of absolutism. His second son, **Dom Miguel**, in the meanwhile started a civil war (1823–1824) supported by the reactionaries.

1826, Mar. 10. Death of King John. He left the throne to Dom Pedro of Brazil, who became **Peter IV.** Peter drew up a charter providing for moderate parliamentary government of the English type. But he refused to leave Brazil and eventually handed over the Portuguese throne to his infant daughter, **Maria da Gloria,** with Dom Miguel as regent.

1826-1853. MARIA II. Miguel united the reactionaries and clericals in a movement against constitutional government.

1827, Jan.—1828, Apr. 28. A British force landed at Lisbon to support the constitutionalists. They withdrew when Miguel promised to respect the constitution.

1828, May. *Coup d'état* by Miguel, who abolished the constitution and had himself proclaimed king (July 4). Maria da Gloria fled to England.

1828-1834. The Miguelite Wars.

1831, Apr. 7. Dom Pedro abdicated the Brazilian throne and returned to Europe (England), to fight for the restoration of Maria.

1832, July 8. Pedro, with the connivance of England and France, organized an expedition and took Oporto. The Miguelists were defeated and

1833, Sept. Maria was restored.

1834, Apr. 22. Quadruple Alliance between England, France, Spain, and Portugal, aimed at the expulsion of Miguel.

May 26. Final defeat of Miguel, who left the country.

1834-1853. A period of ministerial instability and chronic insurrection, reflecting the conflict between those championing the radical constitution of 1822 and those supporting the Charter of 1826.

1836, Apr. 9. The queen married Duke Ferdinand of Saxe-Coburg.

1853-1861. PETER V.

1861-1889. LOUIS I. Under these two reigns Portugal had some respite from civil strife, and the country was ruled by two opposing factions of professional politicians, the **Regenerators** (or Conservatives) and the **Progressives** (or Liberals) who adopted the system of *rotavism*: skillful manipulation of the electorate, enabling the two parties to hold office in rotation. This sterile, pseudo-parliamentary system resulted in the formation of a **Republican Party** (1881).

The House of Coburg-Braganza

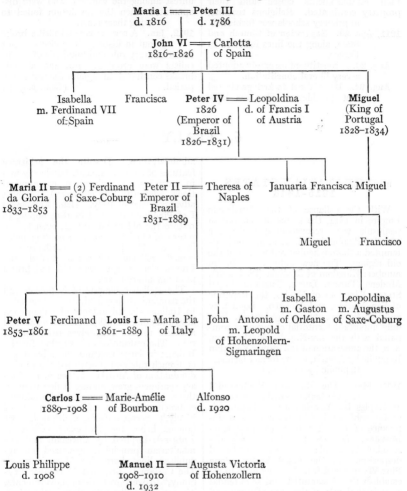

Maria I === Peter III
d. 1816 | d. 1786

John VI === Carlotta
1816–1826 | of Spain

Isabella   Francisca   Peter IV === Leopoldina   Miguel
m. Ferdinand VII   1826   d. of Francis I   (King of
of Spain   (Emperor of   of Austria   Portugal
                            Brazil   1828–1834)
                        1826–1831)

Maria II === (2) Ferdinand   Peter II === Theresa of   Januaria Francisca Miguel
da Gloria | of Saxe-Coburg   Emperor of | Naples
1833–1853   Brazil
                            1831–1889

                                                        Miguel   Francisco

                                            Isabella   Leopoldina
                                            m. Gaston   m. Augustus
Peter V   Ferdinand   Louis I === Maria Pia   John   Antonia   of Orléans   of Saxe-Coburg
1853–1861   1861–1889 | of Italy   m. Leopold
                                                of Hohenzollern-
                                                Sigmaringen

Carlos I === Marie-Amélie   Alfonso
1889–1908 | of Bourbon   d. 1920

Louis Philippe   Manuel II === Augusta Victoria
d. 1908   1908–1910 | of Hohenzollern
                d. 1932

1889-1908. CARLOS I, who gained notoriety by his extravagance and licentiousness. Discontent grew, especially in the cities, and there were sporadic revolts, strikes, and conspiracies.

1906, May 19. The king appointed **João Franco** as prime minister, with dictatorial powers. Parliamentary government was suppressed, the press gagged, and all opposition to the government sternly punished.

1908, Feb. 1. Assassination of King Carlos and the crown prince in the streets of Lisbon.

1908-1910. MANUEL II. He put an end to Franco's régime and restored constitutional government, but, like his father, was scandalously extravagant.

1910, Oct. 3-5. Insurrection in Lisbon. The king was forced to flee to England.

1910, Oct. 5. PROCLAMATION OF THE PORTUGUESE REPUBLIC. A provisional government was organized under Dr. **Theophilo Braga.** It proceeded to a frontal attack upon the Catholic Church, which was regarded as the backbone of royalism. Religious orders were expelled, their establishments closed and their property confiscated. Religious teaching in primary schools was forbidden.

1911, Apr. 20. Separation of Church and State, along the lines followed in France.

Aug. 20. A constituent assembly adopted a very **liberal constitution**.

Aug. 24. Dr. Manoel de Arriaga elected first president. He was con-

fronted with royalist plots and with growing unrest among the workers, who were disappointed when the revolution failed to bring them relief.

1912, Jan. A serious **general strike** broke out in Lisbon. The city was put under military rule and hundreds of syndicalists were arrested. But radical outbreaks continued throughout the rest of the period. (*Cont. p.* 985.)

6. ITALY

a. THE ITALIAN STATES, 1815-1848

With the collapse of the Napoleonic Empire in 1814, the states of the Italian peninsula were reconstituted under the effective domination of Austria, which attempted a thoroughgoing restoration of the old régime. The new states were nine in number: Kingdom of Sardinia (Piedmont), Modena, Parma, Lucca, Tuscany, Papal States, Kingdom of Naples, the Republic of San Marino, and Monaco. Lombardy and Venetia were annexed by Austria. The only important territorial changes, as compared with the pre-Napoleonic situation, were the annexation of the former Venetian Republic by Austria, of the former Genoese Republic by Piedmont.

1815, May. The Bourbon **Ferdinand I** (1751–1825), restored to the throne of Naples by Austrian arms, despite his promises of political liberty and the maintenance of French reforms (**decrees from Messina**, May 20–24, 1815), quickly descended to a rule of almost unrelieved despotism. In the **Papal States, Pope Pius VII** returned from his long exile to reestablish the obscurantist and semi-feudal ecclesiastical rule of the 18th century and to restore the Company of Jesus (suppressed in 1773). In **Modena, Duke Francis IV** entered upon a policy of candid reaction, rigorously concentrating power in his own hands, turning the universities over to the Jesuits. In **Parma and Lucca** the return to the old régime was rapid but less violent than in Modena and the south. **Maria Louisa of Parma** (former Empress of the French) and the Infanta **Maria Louisa of Bourbon-Parma**, Duchess of Lucca, owed their thrones to Austria and heeded the wishes of Metternich. In **Lombardy and Venetia**, with separate governments, Metternich organized a thoroughly Austrian

administration. Despite the arbitrary features of the government, Lombardy was in most respects (education, communications, administrative efficiency) the most advanced part of Italy. **Victor Emmanuel I of Piedmont** returned in 1814 hoping to restore the old régime intact, even to the return of officials who were holding office in 1798. The Jesuits were cordially welcomed, religious toleration denied, the French Code swept away, old and brutal punishments restored.

The Italian conquests of Napoleon and the reorganization of Italy (1) had revealed to Italians the advantages of enlightened laws and administration; (2) had awakened a desire to free themselves from foreign rule. The restorations of 1815 lost for the Italians in large measure the advantages of French rule and substituted the foreign domination of Austria. Hence revolutionary sentiment grew, aiming at first to overthrow existing governments and gradually embracing the idea of unity for all of "Italy."[2] Secret societies multiplied, most famous being the **Carbonari** (*Charcoal-Burners*), inspired by Christian and humanitarian principles, organized on republican lines, borrowing Masonic ritual. The Carbonari prepared to combat "tyranny," to overthrow existing governments. They grew rapidly in numbers in the Kingdom of Naples, and spread to other Italian States.

1820, July 2. The Neapolitan Revolution. Encouraged by news of the success of the revolution in Spain (p. 644), the Carbonari in the army, led by **General Pepe**, precipitated a revolt.

July 13. Ferdinand I granted a constitution similar to that introduced in Sicily under British auspices in 1812. The representatives of the powers, meeting in Congress at Troppau and Laibach to consider the Spanish situation, were persuaded by Metternich (England dissenting because of British public opinion, but not opposing) to adopt the principle of intervention (**Troppau Protocol**) against revolutions which might endanger the European peace. Austria was given a mandate to restore order in Italy. An army was marched to Naples, overthrew the revolutionary government (1821, Mar.) with little difficulty, and restored Ferdinand I to his former position.

1821, Mar. 10. Rising in Piedmont, engineered by the Carbonari, who hoped that **Charles Albert,** Prince of Carignan, would place himself at the head of a constitutional government.

Mar. 12. Victor Emmanuel I abdicated in favor of his brother, Charles Felix, then absent from Turin. Charles Albert was made regent and granted a constitution like that of Spain.

Mar. 22. Charles Felix arrived, ordered Charles Albert to flee, which he did.

Apr. 8. The **Piedmontese revolution** collapsed with the defeat of the constitutionalists near **Novara** by a combined force of royalists and Austrians.

1831, Feb. Risings in Modena and Parma inspired by the July Revolution in Paris (p. 628) and connected with a general movement aiming to free all northern Italy; they were accompanied by widespread revolts in the Papal States.

Mar. With the aid of Austrian troops the insurrections were put down.

May 21. The ambassadors of the powers demanded certain reforms in the Papal States, but the pope contented himself with an amnesty and a few concessions in the administration and the judiciary. Fresh revolts broke out in the Papal States at the end of 1831. Order was again restored by Austria (Jan. 1832), which led to the **occupation of Ancona** by the French (Mar. 1832). It was not until 1838 that the foreign troops were withdrawn.

The failure of insurrections indicated the ineffectiveness of secret societies, notably of the Carbonari, and of small-scale, sporadic risings which they promoted. The importance of unified effort by Italians everywhere and of careful preparation through propaganda and organization was recognized by **Giuseppe Mazzini** (1805–1872), former Carbonaro, who launched a

Mar. New revolutionary society (*Young Italy*). From early youth Mazzini had dreamt of freeing Italy from her present rulers and giving her a republican consti-

tution — as a prelude to a free confederation of all Europe dominated by a spirit of Christian brotherhood. Through the widely ramifying channels of Young Italy, Mazzini launched his propaganda from exile in Marseilles. Before a general rising in Italy (planned for June, 1832) could take place,

1832, Mar. Piedmontese authorities discovered existence of the plans; arrests followed, the rising collapsed.

1834, Feb. Another Mazzinian **attack on Savoy** ended in ludicrous failure. Mazzini now extended the scope of his activity by organizing the **Young Europe movement,** composed of Young Italy, Young Germany, Young Poland, and kindred organizations. From London he carried on his work of direction and propaganda. Abortive risings followed with almost monotonous regularity, but accomplished nothing but the creation of martyrs to the cause.

1843. Publication of **Vincenzo Gioberti's** *On the Moral and Civil Primacy of the Italians,* and of **Count Cesare Balbo's** *The Hopes of Italy.* These two books represented the views of the Italian moderate Liberals, especially in northern Italy. They found Mazzini's republicanism offensive and his methods dangerous and impractical. The moderates distrusted universal suffrage and advocated constitutional reform and some type of unification for the peninsula. Some favored a federation of states under the presidency of the pope. These were the **Neo-Guelphs,** led by Gioberti. Balbo and his followers were intent chiefly on the extrusion of Austria (by peaceful means if possible) and the organization of Italy under Piedmontese leadership.

1846, June 15. THE ELECTION OF PIUS IX (Cardinal Mastai-Ferretti) as pope led to an outburst of liberal enthusiasm and to boundless hopes. In contrast to his predecessor, Gregory XVI, Pius was democratic in his attitude. He proclaimed an amnesty for political prisoners and refugees, relaxed the censorship laws, organized an advisory council composed of laymen, replaced the mercenary army by a civil guard, and established a municipal council for Rome. These reforms were opposed by the reactionaries (Gregorians) at every step, but the pope's popularity grew throughout Italy.

1847, July 17. Occupation of Ferrara by Austrian troops (actually exercising a right conferred by the Treaty of Vienna). This step called forth a storm of indignation among Liberals in all Italy and did much to fan the anti-Austrian sentiment.

The Neapolitan Bourbons

The House of Savoy

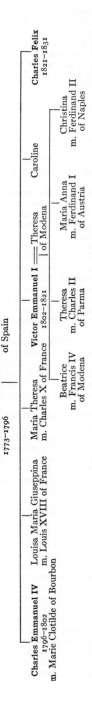

The House of Savoy-Carignan

Oct.   Charles Albert of Piedmont (succeeded Charles Felix in 1831), though conservatively inclined, dismissed his reactionary minister, **Solaro della Margarita,** and began to yield to the liberal agitation (*King Wobble, Re Tentenna*). He consented to the revision of the criminal code, mitigation of the censorship, amendment of the law on public meeting.

1848, Jan. 12.   A revolutionary movement broke out in **Sicily** and stimulated the Neapolitan liberals to action.

Feb. 10.   Ferdinand II (*Bomba,* 1830–1859), unable to secure Austrian aid in the face of the pope's opposition to the crossing of his territory, promulgated a liberal constitution modeled on the French charter of 1830.

Feb. 17.   Grand Duke Leopold of Tuscany was obliged to grant a constitution.

Mar. 4.   Charles Albert promulgated a constitution for Piedmont (the *Statuto*, the basis for the later constitution of the Kingdom of Italy).

Mar. 14.   The pope followed suit, introducing a constitution establishing an elective council of deputies, but nevertheless reserving a veto power to the pope and college of cardinals.

b. THE ITALIAN WAR OF INDEPENDENCE, 1848-1849

1848, Mar. 18-22.   THE FIVE DAYS OF MILAN, marking the culmination of dissatisfaction with Austrian rule and the influence of the news of the revolution in Vienna (Mar. 13). Barricades were thrown up in the narrow streets. The Austrian general, **Radetzky,** held the entire circle of fortifications, preventing the insurgents from communicating with the outside world. The rebels, fighting without plan or organization, but greatly outnumbering the Austrian forces, gradually reduced the garrisons inside the town and, after repeated assaults, took **Porta Tosa** (Mar. 22). Radetzky was obliged to order a general retreat to the famous **Quadrilateral** (four fortresses: Mantua, Peschiera, Legnano, Verona, between Lombardy and Venetia).

Mar. 22.   Proclamation of the Venetian Republic, following agitation and some violence after the arrival of the news from Vienna. A provisional government was established, with **Daniele Manin** (1804–1857) as president.

Mar. 22.   PIEDMONT DECLARED WAR ON AUSTRIA, in response to an appeal from the Milanese. Charles

Albert was very hesitant about allying with the revolution and very suspicious of possible action by the radical French Republic, but finally yielded for fear of radicalism in his own territory.

Apr. 25.   Papal forces under **General Durando** joined the Piedmontese. Contingents also arrived from Naples and other parts of Italy. Wild enthusiasm, but little discipline.

Apr. 29.   A papal encyclical, the result of Austrian protests, disclaimed all intention of making war on the Catholic Austrians. This paralyzed all action by the papal troops.

May 15.   Collapse of the revolution in Naples, after a counter-offensive by the king's Swiss mercenaries. Neapolitan troops withdrawn from the north.

May 30.   The Piedmontese won the **battle of Goito,** but failed to follow up their advantage. Acute danger of intervention by the French Republic, which concentrated 30,000 troops on the Alps. Austrian efforts to secure British support (**Hummelauer mission**). Palmerston urged the abandonment of both Lombardy and Venetia.

June 15.   The Austrian government ordered Radetzky to seek an armistice to permit an offer of independence to Lombardy. Radetzky sent **Prince Felix Schwarzenberg** (p. 674) to Vienna and induced the government to continue the war.

July 24.   BATTLE OF CUSTOZZA. Radetzky overwhelmingly defeated the Piedmontese and (Aug. 4) drove them out of Lombardy. Charles Albert finally appealed to the French for mediation, but after the **June Days** (p. 630) the French government was too deeply engrossed in domestic affairs to be willing to embroil itself with Austria and England.

Aug. 9.   Armistice of Salasco (the general who negotiated it). The Piedmontese gave up Lombardy. Charles Albert accepted joint Anglo-French mediation, on the understanding that he would get Lombardy later. The Austrians accepted mediation after much resistance (Sept. 3), but nothing came of it, especially after the formation of the Schwarzenberg ministry (Nov. 21), which refused to entertain the suggestion of territorial cessions.

Sept. 16.   The pope appointed **Count Pelligrino Rossi** prime minister, after several ephemeral cabinets and a steady growth of radicalism at Rome. Rossi was a disciple of Guizot, a moderate, clear-headed administrator, whose aim was to restore order. His efforts at reform earned him the hatred of all factions.

Nov. 15. Rossi was murdered by a fanatical democrat.

Nov. 16. Popular insurrection in Rome. The pope was forced to appoint a democratic ministry under Monsignor **Carlo Muzzarelli.**

Nov. 25. Pius, alarmed by radical agitation (clubs), fled from Rome to Gaeta where he enjoyed Neapolitan protection. He attempted unsuccessfully to maintain his power in Rome through a commission of regency.

1849, Feb. 9. Proclamation of the Roman Republic, after the meeting of a constituent assembly (Feb. 5).

Mar. 12. Piedmont denounced the armistice with Austria, the king yielding to radical pressure.

Mar. 23. BATTLE OF NOVARA. Radetzky again decisively defeated the Piedmontese. Charles Albert abdicated in favor of his son, **Victor Emmanuel II.** Peace negotiations dragged on through the spring and summer, the size of the indemnity being the chief point in dispute. Peace was finally signed Aug. 9, Piedmont agreeing to an indemnity of 65,000,000 francs.

Mar. 29. On news of the Piedmontese defeat at Novara, the leaders at **Rome set up a triumvirate** (Mazzini, Saffi, Armellini) which introduced a moderate, conciliatory régime and restored order. But since Jan. there had been discussion of intervention by France or Austria, or both, to restore the pope.

Apr. 14. The French Assembly voted funds for an expedition, being led by the government to suppose that the purpose was to forestall the Austrians. In reality the aim of Napoleon was to win the approval of the Catholics.

Apr. 24. The French expedition, under General Oudinot, landed at Cività Vecchia.

Apr. 29-30. Oudinot, supposing that Mazzini's followers were a minority in Rome, attacked the city, but was repulsed by improvised forces led by **Giuseppe Garibaldi** (1807–1882), republican patriot and guerrilla leader.

May 29. Ferdinand de Lesseps (1805–1894), later builder of the Suez Canal, having been sent by the French government to negotiate, signed a treaty with the Roman Republic by which the city gates were to be opened to the French in return for a promise to respect the rights of the republic and to guarantee it against foreign aggression.

June 1. De Lesseps was abruptly recalled and later disavowed. Oudinot was reinforced and ordered to take the city.

June 3. He attacked without warning, but Garibaldi and his men fought so valiantly that the French had to settle down to a siege.

June 30. Garibaldi, regarding the situation as hopeless, made terms with the French.

July 2. After reviewing his troops, Garibaldi marched forth with some 5000 men on his famous retreat. All were presently killed, captured, or dispersed, Garibaldi himself escaping after dramatic adventures.

July 20-Aug. 28. Austrian siege and bombardment of Venice. The city surrendered, ravaged by cholera and faced with starvation.

By this time the revolutionary movement had been everywhere suppressed. Neapolitan troops had reconquered Sicily and entered Palermo (May 15) and the Austrians had entered Florence to support the restored Grand Duke Leopold (May 25).

c. THE UNIFICATION OF ITALY, 1849-1870

The abysmal failure of the revolutionary movements of 1848–1849 revealed the military weakness of the Italian states (hence the need of foreign aid for the extrusion of Austria); demonstrated the unreliability of the pope as a leader of the unity movement; undermined the prestige of the Mazzinians and republicanism in general; pointed to the steadfastness of Piedmont, only state to retain its liberal constitution. Piedmont was henceforth recognized as the hope of liberal Italy. In the parliamentary life of Piedmont there rapidly came to the fore a new man,

1851-1861. Count Camillo Benso di Cavour (1810–1861), a liberal who had drawn his ideas from French and especially English sources; believer in the *juste milieu*, profound admirer of British parliamentarism, convinced of the importance of reforms (commercial, industrial, agricultural, political) if Piedmont were to take its place as the leader of the movement for Italian independence. Scientific farming on western lines he introduced on his father's estates, and then made it the subject of wider propaganda through the medium of the **Agrarian Society** (founded 1842). He was active in the promotion of banking, railroads; welcomed the repeal of the Corn Laws in England (p. 612). He

Unification of Italy

entered actively into the necessarily veiled political activity of the forties; founded the first **Whist Club** at Turin, innocuous façade for political discussions. When Charles Albert reformed the censorship (1847), Cavour promptly founded, with Cesare Balbo, *Il Risorgimento*, a newspaper urging the independence of Italy, a league of Italian princes, and moderate reforms. Cavour assumed a leading rôle in the demand for a constitution during Jan. 1848. The king yielded (Feb. 8); published the new constitution (Mar. 4) providing for a system modeled principally after that of Great Britain, with a Senate, whose life-members were to be appointed by the king; a Chamber of Deputies, with members elected on the basis of a limited suffrage (leaving electoral influence in the hands of the nobility and middle class); a ministry responsible to parliament. Parliament met for the first time, May 8, 1848. Despite vigorous opposition of democratic elements, suspicious of Cavour as an aristocrat, he played an increasingly important rôle in the period following the disasters of 1848-1849.

1850, Mar. On the advice of Cavour, Giuseppe Siccardi was made keeper of the seals by Premier Massimo D'Azeglio. Siccardi brought in a bill (of which Cavour was the author) seriously curbing the powers of the Catholic Church — abolishing ecclesiastical courts, and all their special jurisdictions; eliminating the right of asylum; limiting the number of holidays; restricting the right of religious bodies to acquire real property. Elsewhere these questions had been settled by concordat with the pope; in Piedmont they were settled by unilateral action (Oct. 10).

1850-1851. Cavour entered D'Azeglio's government as minister of agriculture and commerce, the portfolio of the navy being shortly added, and later that of finance.

1852, Nov. 4. After a short period out of office, **Cavour became premier**, a post he was to hold for seven years uninterruptedly. Cavour by now had deserted the Right and governed with the aid of a coalition of the Liberals of the Right Center and Left Center (the *connubio*). His government reorganized finances; negotiated commercial treaties and revised tariffs (first approach to free trade); fostered legislation on co-operative societies, agrarian credit, banks; accelerated railroad construction; reorganized the army.

1855, Jan. 26. Cavour managed to insinuate his country into the **Crimean War** on the side of France and England. The Piedmontese troops took part in the victory of the **Chernaia** (Aug. 16) and thereby regained morale and prestige. Though Piedmont received no reward as a result of her participation (unwillingness of England to estrange Austria), Cavour was given an opportunity at the **Congress of Paris** (p. 728) to expound the grievances of Italy. His moderation made a most favorable impression on the English and French.

1856. Foundation of the National Society by Giuseppe Farina, Daniele Manin, and Giorgio Pallavicino. The organization, aiming at the unification of Italy under the King of Piedmont, enjoyed the secret encouragement of Cavour, and at the same time was backed by many Mazzinian republicans, like Garibaldi.

1858, Jan. 14. The attempt of Felice Orsini to assassinate Napoleon III and the empress (p. 633). From prison Orsini appealed to Napoleon to help free Italy. The effect of the episode was to prick Napoleon (himself originally an Italian conspirator) into action.

July 20. SECRET MEETING OF NAPOLEON III AND CAVOUR AT PLOMBIÈRES. Agreement: Napoleon to join Piedmont in war on Austria provided it could be provoked in a manner to justify it in the eyes of French and European opinion; after expulsion of the Austrians, Italy to be organized as a federation of four states, under presidency of the pope — (*a*) An **Upper Italian Kingdom** of Piedmont, Lombardy, Venetia, Parma, Modena, and the Papal Legations; (*b*) A **Kingdom of Central Italy**, Tuscany with Umbria and the Marches; (*c*) **Rome** and the surrounding territory, to which the temporal power of the pope was to be restricted; (*d*) the **Kingdom of Naples;** France was to be compensated by Savoy and Nice; Princess Clotilde, 15-year-old daughter of Victor Emmanuel, was to marry Prince Jerome Bonaparte, cousin of the emperor.

Dec. 10. The formal treaty signed by France and Piedmont, after Napoleon had assured himself of the good-will of Russia (mission of Prince Jerome to Warsaw, Sept.).

1859, Jan. 1. Napoleon's warning remarks to the Austrian ambassador let the secret out. Strong protests of Napoleon's ministers and of some sections of French opinion. Desperate efforts (Jan.-Apr.) of the English to prevent a clash. These proved abortive, since there was no will to peace on the French and Italian side.

Mar. 9. Piedmontese reserves called to the colors including volunteers, chiefly fugitives eluding conscription.

in Lombardy (a direct provocation to Austria).

Apr. 7.   Austria mobilized.

Apr. 23.   Austrian ultimatum to Piedmont, directing her to demobilize in three days. This was a terrible blunder, since it supplied Cavour with the provocation he needed. The ultimatum was rejected.

Apr. 29.   The Austrians, under General Gyulai, **invaded Piedmont,** but Gyulai delayed action so long that the French had ample opportunity to arrive on the scene.

May.   Peaceful revolutions in Tuscany, Modena, and Parma, engineered by the National Society. The rulers fled the country.

May 30.   Piedmontese victory at Palestro. The allies crossed the Ticino into Lombardy.

June 4.   BATTLE OF MAGENTA, a disorganized fight ending in the retirement of the Austrians.

June 13-15.   Insurrection in the Papal Legations (Ravenna, Ferrara, Bologna).

June 24.   BATTLE OF SOLFERINO and San Martino, sanguinary but indecisive. The Austrians began to withdraw to the Quadrilateral.

Napoleon III had been depressed by the sight of bloodshed on the fields of Magenta and Solferino; was alarmed by the risings in Tuscany and the Papal States with the threat of rapid spread of the unification movement; was faced by the possibility of a Prussian attack on the Rhine and the reality of a prolonged siege of the Quadrilateral fortresses, into which the Austrian army had retired. Without preliminary understanding with Victor Emmanuel, Napoleon proposed an armistice to Emperor Francis Joseph, concluded July 8, followed by the

July 11. Meeting of the two emperors at **Villafranca,** with agreement that Lombardy (except Mantua and Peschiera) should be ceded to France and might then be ceded by France to Piedmont; Venetia was to remain Austrian; Italian princes should be restored to their thrones subject to amnesty of their revolting subjects. These terms were accepted as preliminaries of peace by Victor Emmanuel, who reserved his liberty, however, respecting the risings in central Italy. **Cavour resigned** in a rage. The final **Treaty of Zürich** (Nov. 10) embodied substantially the provisions of the preliminaries of Villafranca.

Aug.-Sept. In Parma, Modena, Tuscany and Romagna, representative assemblies decreed the downfall of their late rulers and union with constitutional Piedmont. The Piedmontese government dared not accept without the consent of Napoleon.

1860, Jan. 20.   Cavour returned to power as premier, negotiated the annexations with Napoleon, whose price was the cession of Nice and Savoy.

Mar. 13-15.   Plebiscites in Parma, Modena, Romagna, and Tuscany resulted in vote for annexation to Piedmont.

Mar. 24.   Treaty of Turin, by which Piedmont ceded Savoy and Nice to France, after plebiscite.

Apr. 4.   Abortive rising in Sicily against the Bourbons.

May 5.   Garibaldi and his Thousand Redshirts sailed from Genoa for Sicily. They had been preparing an expedition to Nice, Garibaldi's natal city, which he meant to hold against the French. He was diverted to Sicily by Cavour, who secretly supported this filibustering expedition.

May 11.   Garibaldi and his force landed at Marsala, in western Sicily. He marched inland, gathering recruits as he went.

May 15. He defeated the Neapolitans at **Calatafimi** and marched on Palermo.

May 27.   Garibaldi took Palermo and set up a provisional government.

July 20. He defeated the Neapolitans at **Milazzo,** whereupon they evacuated Sicily, except Messina.

Aug. 22.   Garibaldi crossed the straits, with the connivance of the British government (Lord Palmerston).

Sept. 7. He took **Naples** after a triumphal march, during which the Neapolitan army faded before him. **Francis II** (succeeded Ferdinand II in May 1859) fled to Gaeta. He had made desperate attempts to ward off the danger by forming a Liberal ministry (June 28) and re-establishing the Constitution of 1848 (July 2), but was faced by defection on all sides.

Garibaldi's plan was to defeat the remnants of the Neapolitan army, march on Rome, and then proceed to the conquest of Venetia. Despite Garibaldi's loyalty to Victor Emmanuel, Cavour became alarmed, fearing French intervention on behalf of the pope and possible action by the Austrians. He therefore decided to take a hand and march Piedmontese troops to the scene, a course favored by the British to thwart supposed French schemes for a Muratist restoration in Naples.

Sept. 8.   An uprising in the Papal States gave Cavour an excuse to intervene. He called upon **Cardinal Antonelli**, papal secretary of state, to disband his "adventurers" (the *Zouaves*, an international force of ardent Catholics). The demand was rejected.

Sept. 10. The Piedmontese crossed the papal frontier.

Sept. 18. They virtually annihilated the papal forces at **Castelfidaro** and advanced into Neapolitan territory, joining forces with Garibaldi.

Oct. 21-22. **Naples and Sicily** voted by plebiscite for union with the north. Similar votes were taken in the **Marches** (Nov. 4) and in **Umbria** (Nov. 5).

Oct. 26. Garibaldi defeated the Neapolitans on the **Volturno.**

Nov. 3—1861, Feb. 13. **Siege of Gaeta.** The operations were much hampered by the French fleet, which made attack by sea impossible until it was withdrawn (Jan. 19).

1861, Mar. 17. **THE KINGDOM OF ITALY** proclaimed by the first Italian parliament, with Victor Emmanuel as first king and a government based on the Piedmontese Constitution of 1848.

June 6. Cavour died at the age of 51.

1861-1862. Ministry of Baron Ricasoli, ardent Tuscan patriot, who embarked upon a vast national **agitation for the annexation of Rome,** still garrisoned by French troops. Garibaldi left his place of retirement, the island of Caprera, and organized the

1862, Mar. 9. **Society for the Emancipation of Italy.** He organized an abortive conspiracy against Austria, then made a triumphant visit to the scenes of his victories in Sicily. Defying the government, he raised the cry *Rome or Death*, crossed to the mainland (Aug. 24) and advanced north.

Aug. 29. **Battle of Aspromonte,** a skirmish in which Garibaldi and his volunteers were defeated. Garibaldi wounded and captured. He and his men were amnestied soon after (Oct. 5).

1864, Sept. 15. The **September Convention,** by which Napoleon finally agreed to evacuate Rome within two years (beginning Feb. 5, 1865), in return for an Italian promise to move the capital from Turin to Florence. Napoleon regarded this as the renunciation of Rome. The agreement raised a storm of protest in Piedmont and was denounced by Garibaldi, but was approved by the parliament.

1866, May 12. **Alliance of Italy and Prussia,** encouraged by Napoleon (p. 681).

June 20. **Italy declared war on Austria.**

June 24. Italians defeated at second battle of Custozza, by Archduke Albert.

July 3. **VENETIA CEDED TO ITALY** after its cession to France by Austria.

July 20. Resounding **defeat of the Italian** fleet by the Austrians under Admiral Tegethoff, **near Lissa.**

Oct. 12. **Treaty of Vienna,** bringing the war to a close.

Dec. **Last French troops withdrawn from Rome.** Garibaldi again placed himself at the head of volunteers and began the invasion of the papal territory, despite disavowals of the government. He was twice captured, but escaped (1867, Sept.).

1867, Oct. 27. A plan for an insurrection in Rome failed, but Garibaldi defeated a papal force.

Oct. 28. A French force landed at Cività Vecchia and marched to Rome.

Nov. 3. **BATTLE OF MENTANA.** Garibaldi defeated by papal troops supported by French, who mowed down the enemy with the new breech-loading *chassepots.* Garibaldi was captured and sent to Caprera. Napoleon tried at first to summon an international congress to discuss the Roman question, but accomplished nothing. The Roman question continued to be an open sore in Franco-Italian relations, and did much to prevent the formation of an alliance (p. 635).

1870, Aug. 19. Final withdrawal of French troops from Rome, in view of the **Franco-German War** (p. 688).

Sept. 20. After a short bombardment **the Italians,** capitalizing the defeat of France at Sedan, **entered Rome** after making a breach at the Porta Pia.

Oct. 2. After a plebiscite, **Rome was annexed** to Italy and became the capital.

d. THE KINGDOM OF ITALY, 1870-1914

1871, May 13. **THE LAW OF GUARANTIES,** defining the relations between the government and the papacy: the person of the pope was to be inviolable; he was granted royal honors and prerogatives and full liberty in the exercise of his religious functions (free intercourse with Catholics throughout the world, liberty to hold conclaves, control of papal seminaries, etc.); representatives of foreign powers at the Vatican were conceded diplomatic rights and immunities; the pope was to have an annual income of 3,250,000 lire from the Italian treasury (the equivalent of his previous income from his territories); he was left in full enjoyment of the Vatican and other palaces, with rights of extra-territoriality. This law was not accepted by the pope, who henceforth posed as *the prisoner of the Vatican.* Relations between the papacy and the Italian government were not regularized until the **Lateran Treaty of 1929** (p. 993).

1873-1876, Ministry of Marco Minghetti (1818–1886) following that of Giovanni Lanza (1869–1873). The outstanding statesman was **Quintino Sella,** minister of finance, whose great aim was to balance the budget and organize the economic life of the new kingdom. He exercised "economy to the bone" (cutting down the civil list, salaries of ministers, etc.) and passed taxes on cereals, incomes, land, etc. The government **reorganized the army** (350,000 men in peacetime) and re-created the navy (Italy the third sea-power by 1885). **Railroads** were pushed to the south (mileage 1758 kilometers in 1860; 7438 in 1876) and the **merchant marine** developed (10,000 tons in 1862; 1,000,000 in 1877, next to England and France).

1876, Mar. 18. FALL OF THE MIN-GHETTI CABINET and of the Party of the Right (the party of enlightened conservatism following the teaching of Cavour, which had ruled the country since 1849).

Mar. 28. First ministry of the Left, under **Agostino Depretis** (1813–1887). Depretis was an early disciple of Mazzini, but had been converted to monarchism. Cold, cynical, disillusioned, he relied for maintenance of his power upon adroit parliamentary tactics, upon corruption and upon political alliances (*trasformismo*). By generous use of government pressure the Right was overwhelmingly defeated in the elections and returned to parliament a mere rump. Depretis remained premier, with two short interruptions, until his death in 1887. The unpopular taxes, against which the Left had protested, were restored and free rein was given to agitation against Austria (*irredentism*), aiming to acquire the **Trentino** and **Trieste** (*Italia Irredenta*), Italian-speaking districts still under Austrian rule. Italian stock in international affairs reached the low point.

1878, Jan. 9. Death of King Victor Emmanuel.

1878-1900. HUMBERT I, king.

1878, Feb. 7. Death of Pius IX.

1878-1903. LEO XIII (Cardinal Pecci, 1810–1903), pope. Various attempts were made to reach an agreement on the Roman question (notably in 1886) but

they all foundered on the pope's demand for at least some part of Rome.

1881. Extension of the franchise, by reduction of the age limit from 25 to 21 and lowering the tax-paying requirement from 40 to 19 lire. The result was an increase of the electorate from about 600,000 to about 2,000,000.

1882, May 20. Triple Alliance of Italy, Austria, and Germany (p. 738).

1885. An act of parliament **farmed out the state railways** to three private companies for 60 years, with possible termination at the end of 20 or 40 years.

Another act introduced **employers' liability for accidents,** but was so poorly administered as to be ineffective, like the act (1877) making elementary education compulsory for children from six to nine years.

1885. Italian occupation of Assab and Massowa on the Red Sea, after the French (1881) had frustrated Italian hopes for Tunis (pp. 737, 838).

1887, July 29. Death of Depretis.

1887-1891. First ministry of Francesco Crispi, minister of interior under Depretis, former republican and member of Garibaldi's "Thousand," a proud, self-centered, vigorous individual. After abortive negotiations with the papacy he turned to a violently **anti-clerical policy:** abolition of ecclesiastical tithes and of compulsory religious instruction in elementary schools. The erection of the **statue of Giordano Bruno** confronting the Vatican (1889) brought relations to such a pitch of tension that the pope seriously considered leaving Rome.

In **foreign policy** Crispi took his stand unwaveringly by the alliance with Austria and Germany (p. 740). He suppressed radical and irredentist organizations. Relations with France became so strained that they almost resulted in a rupture.

1887-1889. The Ethiopian venture. Crispi was a convinced imperialist and was determined to expand the Italian footing on the Red Sea. This led to war with Ethiopia and to a serious setback at **Dogali** (Jan. 25, 1887). Nevertheless the Italians were able to strengthen their position by backing **Menelek,** King of Shoa, against the Ethiopian king of kings, John.

1889, May 2. The Treaty of Ucciali by which, according to the Italian version, Menelek accepted an Italian **protectorate over Ethiopia.** Menelek became king of kings (Nov.) on the death of John.

1891, Jan. 31. Fall of Crispi, after a gratuitous outburst against the Right.

1891-1892. Ministry of Marquis di Rudini, member of the Right, who governed with a coalition cabinet and support from the Left. He attempted to balance the budget, notably by reducing the expenditures for army and navy.

1892-1893. First ministry of Giovanni Giolitti (1842-1928). In the midst of a banking crisis, Giolitti made the managing director of the *Banca Romana*, Signor Tanlongo, a senator. The Senate refused to confirm the appointment; an interpellation resulted in the arrest of Tanlongo and other prominent persons. A parliamentary investigation revealed that he had issued large sums in duplicate bank notes, that two preceding cabinets had been aware of his irregularities, that loans had been made by him to deputies, etc. Giolitti was overthrown and left the country for a time.

1893, Dec. 10—1896, Mar. 5. Second Crispi ministry. The cabinet was faced with serious peasant troubles in Sicily (*fasci*), which were ruthlessly put down by the use of the military. In similar manner Crispi dealt with anarchist outrages. Laws of July 11 and Oct. 22, 1894, suppressed anarchist and socialist organizations.

The desperate financial situation was attacked by **Baron Sidney Sonnino** (1847-1922), the minister of finance. The *Bank of Italy* had been established by a law of Aug. 10, 1893, to liquidate the insolvent *Banca Romana*. The law forbade state banks to make loans on real estate, limited their powers of discount, and reduced the paper money maximum. Other measures sought increased economy and larger income. By 1896 Sonnino had practically balanced the budget despite the added expenses of the war in Africa.

1895-1896. THE ETHIOPIAN WAR. Menelek had rejected the Italian interpretation of the **Treaty of Ucciali** (1891) and all efforts at compromise had failed. By 1895, after Menelek had secured the necessary munitions, he was ready to take up the Italian challenge.

1895, Dec. 7. The Italians, having advanced into northern Ethiopia, were badly defeated at **Amba Alagi** by Ras Makonen, who then besieged the key fortress of Makallé, which fell Jan. 20, 1896. Crispi now felt that Italian honor and his own position were at stake. He insisted that **General Baratieri** make an advance and secure a victory. The general, against his better judgment, obeyed orders.

1896, Mar. 1. BATTLE OF ADUA. The Italians (25,000) were completely defeated by some 100,000 Ethiopians under Menelek. Those who were not killed were for the most part captured and held for ransom. One of the worst colonial disasters

in modern history. The Italians were obliged to sue for peace and signed the **Treaty of Addis Ababa** (Oct. 26), in which they recognized the independence of Ethiopia and restricted themselves to the colony of Eritrea.

Mar. 5. Downfall of Crispi, resulting from a storm of public indignation and unrest.

1896-1898. Second Rudini ministry, based on an understanding with **Felice Cavalotti,** the radical leader. There followed a period of acute unrest.

1896, Sept. 30. Agreement between France and Italy with respect to Tunis. The Italians gave up many of their claims. First step in the policy of assuaging French hostility.

1898, May 3-8. THE "FATTI DI MAGGIO." Serious bread riots in various parts of the country culminated in open conflict with the troops in Milan. Martial law was proclaimed, but order was restored only after considerable loss of life. Heavy sentences by courts-martial, especially against socialists, ensued. Rudini was obliged to resign.

1898, June 28—1900, June 18. Ministry of General Luigi Pelloux. He presented to parliament a drastic **Public Safety Law,** which was violently opposed by all radical groups. An attempt was made to change the Chamber's standing orders, but this was again opposed. Pelloux appealed to the country (1900), but the elections only strengthened the radical elements. Having already granted an amnesty (Dec. 30, 1899), Pelloux was forced to resign.

1898, Nov. 21. A commercial treaty signed with France, bringing to an end the tariff war that had been raging since 1886, much to the detriment of Italy.

1900, July 29. King Humbert assassinated by an anarchist at Monza.

1900- VICTOR EMMANUEL III, king. He was regarded as more liberal than his father and the government's policy gradually turned more and more to the Left for support.

1900, Dec. 14. Franco-Italian agreement exchanging a free hand in Morocco (for France) for a free hand in Tripoli (for Italy). An important stage in the Franco-Italian rapprochement (p. 750).

1901. Development of a **large-scale strike** epidemic, reflecting the growth of socialism, the organization of labor, and the more active spread of radicalism.

1902, Jan.-Feb. Strike of the employees of the Mediterranean Railway, demanding, among other things, recognition of their union. In Feb. there was real danger of a general strike, following a strike of gas employees in Turin. The government met the situation by calling up all railway workers who were reservists. By mediation a settlement was finally reached in June.

1903, Oct.—1905, Mar. 4. Giolitti prime minister. Strikes and disorders continued unabated.

1904, Sept. General strike proclaimed. Much violence in Milan and other large cities.

Oct. In the general elections the socialists and radicals lost considerably, evidently a popular protest against the excesses of the labor organizations, but probably influenced also by the attitude of the pope (Pius X since 1903), who gave permission to Catholics to take part in political struggles involving the safety of the social order.

1906, May 30—1909, Dec. 2. Ministry of Giolitti, following the short-lived cabinets of Fortis and Sonnino.

1908. Giolitti continued his policy of concession to the Church by sponsoring a measure to facilitate religious education, such education to be optional with the communal councils, which were, however, obliged to supply such education if parents desired it.

Dec. 28. An earthquake of appalling severity shook southern Calabria and eastern Sicily, completely destroyed Reggio and Messina and many villages, with loss of life estimated at 150,000. At Messina a "tidal wave" added to the destruction.

1909, Dec. 2. Giolitti's government was overturned and was followed by the cabinets of Sonnino (1909, Dec.–1910, Mar.) and Luzzatti (1910, Mar.–1911, Mar.).

1911, Mar. 29—1914, Mar. 10. Giolitti prime minister again.

1911, Sept. 29—1912, Oct. 15. THE TRIPOLITAN WAR, with Turkey. By various agreements (with Germany and Austria, 1887; with England, 1890; with France, 1900; with Russia, 1909) Italy had secured approval for eventual action to acquire Tripoli. The second Moroccan crisis (p. 757) and the prospects of a French protectorate in Morocco induced the Italian government to act before it was too late. Its decision was influenced in large measure by the pressure exerted by the revived nationalist movement (writings of Gabriele d'Annunzio, Enrico Corradini, *et al.*) after

1908. The pretext used was Turkish obstruction of Italian peaceful penetration. An ultimatum was sent (Sept. 28), but was rejected by the Turks.

1911, Oct. 5. The Italians landed a force at Tripoli and occupied the town. The other coastal towns were taken in rapid succession.

Nov. 5. The Italian government proclaimed the **annexation of Tripoli,** though the country was far from being conquered (valiant opposition of a small Turkish force under **Enver Bey,** supported by the Arabs).

1912, Jan.-Feb. Naval operations in the Red Sea and on the Syrian coast. The Italians bombarded several coastal cities, but the general operations were much hampered by Austrian refusal to permit war on the Balkan or Aegean coasts (forbidden by the Triple Alliance and other agreements). All efforts at mediation by the powers were frustrated by the refusal of the Turks to abandon Tripoli.

Apr. 16-19. Italian naval demonstration at the Dardanelles. The Turks closed the Straits (till May 4) causing much loss to Russian commerce.

May 4-16. The Italians occupied Rhodes and the other Dodecanese Islands. Peace negotiations were finally opened in July, but neither side was ready to yield an iota of its claims and only the threatening Balkan War finally induced the Turks to give in. The preliminary **Treaty of Ouchy** (definitive **Treaty of Lausanne,** Oct. 18) ended the war: the Turks abandoned sovereignty of Tripoli, but the Italians were to recognize a representative of the sultan as caliph (i.e. Turkish religious authority); the Italians were to restore the Dodecanese Islands as soon as the Turks evacuated Tripoli.

June 29. Extension of the franchise, increasing the number of voters from about three to about eight and a half million. This amounted to practically universal suffrage. The same bill provided for salaries for members of parliament.

1913, Oct. The general election gave the Liberals a majority, but showed a marked increase of various socialist groups (78 seats together in place of the previous 41) and the Catholics (35 instead of 14).

1914, Mar. 9. General strike proclaimed at Rome, largely the outcome of popular resistance to taxation made necessary by the war.

Mar. 10. Cabinet of Antonio Salandra, following the resignation of Giolitti. The revolutionary railway union demanded an increase in wages, but the question was finally compromised.

June 7. On the national holiday of the *Statuto*, **riots broke out in Ancona,** where an anti-militarist demonstration had been prohibited. A general strike followed in the town and spread to other parts of the Marches, Romagna, etc. The leader

was Enrico Malatesta. **Benito Mussolini** (p. 986), then editor of the socialist newspaper *Avanti*, took a prominent part. Mobs held a number of towns for a week until nationalists and troops restored order.

Aug. 3. Italy proclaimed **neutrality in the World War.**

(*Cont. pp. 923 ff.*, 986.)

7. THE PAPACY, 1815-1914

In the period of the restoration the papacy recaptured much of the ground lost during the chaos of the revolutionary era. Throughout Europe there was a revival of Catholicism, and even in Protestant states sympathy had grown for the Catholic Church as the mainstay of the throne and the most effective force for holding the revolutionary spirit in check. The governing classes regarded as axiomatic this "union of throne and altar" against the disruptive tendencies of liberalism and nationalism. The papacy was also assisted by the Romantic movement, with its idealization of the past, and by the influential writings of men like **René Chateaubriand, Robert de Lamennais,** and **Joseph de Maistre** (*Du Pape,* 1819), which glorified the Catholic Church and the authority of the pope.

1814, May 24. Ultramontanism reigned in Rome upon the return of the gentle and courageous **Pius VII** (1740–1823). The **Jesuit Order** and the **Inquisition** were re-established in Rome (Aug. 7), and the **Index** was reconstituted.

1815. Through the efforts of his able secretary of state, **Cardinal Consalvi** (1757–1824), the pope obtained from the Congress of Vienna the **restitution of the States of the Church.** The temporal administration was reorganized, a bureaucracy established on the French model. Considerable opposition developed against this highly centralized administration, which excluded laymen from all high offices. Discontent against the "rule of the priests" centered in the **Carbonari,** a Liberal secret society (p. 650).

1821, Sept. 13. After the **rising in Naples** (p. 650), Consalvi had their leaders prosecuted, and the pope condemned their principles.

The chief activity of the papacy in the reign of Pius VII was concerned with efforts to recover its international influence in Europe. Toward the accomplishment of this program, Consalvi negotiated a series of valuable **concordats** with all the Roman Catholic powers save Austria.

1823-1829. **LEO XII** (Annibale della Genga, 1760–1829) continued the policy of Pius VII and secured further advantageous concordats, extending the policy to the South American republics. His **extreme reactionary policy** in domestic affairs strengthened the underlying current of liberalism. He persecuted the Jews, harshly supervised morals, condemned the Protestant Bible societies and all dissenters (1824, 1826), and made vigorous efforts to root out the Carbonari. **On the constructive side,** Leo promoted missions, encouraged scholars, improved the educational system in Rome, reduced taxes, made justice less costly, and found money for public improvements. Of noble character, Leo lacked insight into, and sympathy with, the temporal developments of his period.

1829-1830. **PIUS VIII** (Francesco Castiglione, 1761–1830) — a short, reactionary reign noteworthy for the **Catholic Emancipation Act in England** (p. 606).

1831-1846. **GREGORY XVI** (Mauro Capellari, 1765–1846). Apogee of the reaction. The new pope was greeted by revolts which had broken out under his predecessor and which were promptly suppressed (p. 651).

1832, Aug. 15. The encyclical *Mirari vos* condemned complete and unrestrained liberty of conscience, liberty of the press, and revolt for any reason against an established government. Though Gregory did much to promote **public welfare** (establishment of a decimal coinage and a bureau of statistics, and of a steamship service at Ostia; foundation of public baths, hospitals, and orphanages; lightening of various imposts), he would not concede the demand for separation of the ecclesiastical and the civil administration. The secretary of state, **Cardinal Lambruschini** (1776–1854), suppressed all aspirations for political liberty with extreme severity. The last three years were again occupied with rebellions in the Papal States. The embarrassing financial condition in which Gregory left his dominions was due to his lavish expenditure on architectural and engineering works, and to his liberal patronage of learning.

1846-1878. PIUS IX (Giovanni Mastai-Ferretti, 1792–1878), widely greeted in Italy as the "pope of progress" (p. 651).

1848, Apr. 29. Placing the universal significance of the papacy above national aspirations, Pius proclaimed his neutrality in the national war against Austria. For this he was denounced as a traitor, and forced to flee (for details on Pius IX and the Revolution of 1848, see p. 655).

1850, Apr. 12. Pius returned to Rome, embittered, and henceforth stubbornly hostile to liberalism in all its forms. The Constitution of 1848 was not restored, though half-hearted efforts were made to modernize the state through the grant of self-government, with participation of laymen. In the reactionary policy which prevailed, **Cardinal Antonelli** (1806–1876), secretary of state, with mediaeval views and Machiavellian temperament, exerted a paramount influence. In the achievement of Italian unity (1859–1860) the Papal States were lost, to be followed by the taking of Rome in 1870 (p. 659). Pius and his successors persistently refused the offer of the Italian government to accord the pope the rights and honors of a sovereign, and an annual endowment (p. 660). Faced by the loss of his temporal sovereignty, Pius sought compensation by strengthening the machinery of the Church and the spiritual influence of the papacy. The political reaction following the stormy years 1848–1849 offered promising soil for the pope's efforts to conclude advantageous concordats, and in several countries, notably Spain (1851) and Austria (1855), he was able to regulate Church-State relations to the advantage of the Curia. Pius also reestablished Roman Catholic hierarchies in England (1850) and Holland (1853). Seeking popularity, the pope, unaided by an oecumenical council, promulgated a new dogma, the first since the Council of Trent.

1854, Dec. 8. Dogma of the Immaculate Conception of the Virgin, which made a belief long widely held in the Church an article of faith. The "infallibility" of the pope implied in this act was openly acknowledged in 1870 by the Vatican Council.

1864, Dec. 8. When the temporal power of the papacy was tottering to its fall, Pius flung down the gauntlet of defiance to the new social and political order in the encyclical *Quanta cura*, with the appended *Syllabus errorum*. The pope censured the "errors" of pantheism, naturalism, nationalism, indifferentism, socialism, communism, freemasonry, and various other 19th-century views. He claimed for the Church the control of all culture and science, and of the whole educational system; rejected the liberty of conscience and worship enjoyed by other creeds, and the idea of tolerance; claimed the complete independence of the Church from state control; upheld the necessity of a continuance of the temporal power of the Roman See, and declared that "It is an error to believe that the Roman Pontiff can and ought to reconcile himself to, and agree with, progress, liberalism, and contemporary civilization." The Ultramontane party was loud in its praise of the *Syllabus*, but the Liberals were amazed, and treated it as a declaration of war by the Church on modern civilization. It was also a blow aimed at the **Liberal Catholics,** who were reconciled to religious liberty and democratic government.

1869, Dec. 8—1870, Oct. 20. THE VATICAN COUNCIL. The zenith of Pius' pontificate was attained when the Vatican Council (the first general council since that of Trent, three centuries earlier) proclaimed (1870, July 18) the **dogma of papal infallibility** — the dogma that the pope, when speaking *ex cathedra*, possesses infallibility in decisions regarding faith or morals, in virtue of his supreme apostolic power. The new dogma was attended by important results. It marked the final triumph of the papacy over the episcopal and conciliar tendencies of the Church. It attempted to exalt the papacy above all secular states and to extend "faith and morals" to the political domain.

1870, July 30. Austria immediately annulled the **Concordat of 1855.** In Prussia the *Kulturkampf* broke out (p. 688), and in France the council so accentuated the power of ultramontanism that the state took steps to curb it. At his death in 1878, Pius left the Church shaken to its foundations and in feud with almost every secular government.

1878-1903. LEO XIII (Joachim Pecci, 1810–1903), a gifted diplomat, marked a change. Leo possessed a more liberal and tolerant spirit than his predecessor. He narrowed the intellectual gulf between the Church and modern society: by encouraging a renewed study of Thomas Aquinas in all Catholic seminaries (the result of which was to spread the doctrine that between true science and true religion there was no conflict); by fostering the study of Church history (on the theory that it would augment the prestige of the Church by showing its contributions to the progress of civilization); by supporting experimental science among eminent Catholics.

1885. Leo was appointed arbitrator in a dispute between **Germany and Spain** over the possession of the Caroline Islands. He also acted as arbitrator in a number of other cases. As his reign wore on, Leo perceived that democracy might prove fully as useful as monarchy for preserving and strengthening Catholic principles. He therefore encouraged Catholic political parties, with distinctly liberal tendencies, in Germany and Belgium, and adopted a friendly attitude toward the government of the French Republic. Instructions were given to French Catholics to break with monarchical principles, and to support the republic.

1890. However, the policy of the *Ralliement* in France (p. 640) was also motivated by the pope's desire to secure French aid for the **solution of the Roman question**, the mainspring of his whole policy. Relations with the Italian government had grown steadily worse, and in an encyclical addressed to the Italian clergy (1898, Aug. 5) Leo insisted on the duty of Italian Catholics to abstain from political life while the pope remained in his "intolerable position."

1891, May 15. The encyclical on labor questions, *Rerum novarum*, aimed to apply Christian principles to the relations between capital and labor, and won for Leo the title of "the workingman's pope." It pointed out that the possessing classes, including the employers, have important moral duties to fulfill; that it is one of the first duties of society (State and Church collaborating) to improve the position of the workers.

Of the political principles of Pius IX, Leo altered little. He expressed in his encyclicals the same condemnation of many phases of liberalism and nationalism, and reiterated the view that the Church should superintend and direct every form of secular life. But, unlike his predecessor, Leo never appeared as a violent partisan of any particular form of government. It was his object to bring about harmonious collaboration between Church and State. In the *Kulturkampf* he adopted a moderate and conciliatory attitude, and succeeded in obtaining the repeal of the legislation against the Church.

1903-1914. **PIUS X** (Giuseppe Sarto, 1835–1914), known as the "pope of the poor and the humble," applied himself with determination to the task of fortifying the inner life of the Church. He carried out (1908) an extensive reorganization of the Curia in order to modernize its machinery. Another important reform, the codification of canon law (1904), was undertaken (completed under Benedict XV, promulgated June 28, 1917).

Encouraged by the liberal tendencies in Leo's reign, a group of Catholics known as **Modernists** (notably **Father George Tyrrell**, in England, the **Abbé Loisy** in France, and **Antonio Fogazzaro** in Italy) had begun to agitate for a revision of the dogmas and policies of the Church to bring them in line with the findings of scientific scholarship and the modern spirit. Pius had only bitter scorn for the Modernists.

1907, Sept. 8. The encyclical *Pascendi gregis* expounded and condemned the Modernist system, and set up a new and effective censorship to combat it.

Pius was not greatly interested in political affairs. Relations with the Italian government improved, and the pope qualified the absolute prohibition imposed by his predecessors against the participation of Catholics in political elections (p. 662). But the pope experienced great bitterness in his relations with France, which adopted legislation for the separation of Church and State (p. 642).

1914, Aug. 2. Pius' last circular was an appeal for peace addressed to the Catholics of the world on the eve of the World War.

1914-1922. **BENEDICT XV** (Giacomo della Chiesa), whose reign was taken up by efforts to maintain an even balance between the warring nations, many of them essentially Catholic. The pope twice (1915, July 30; 1917, Aug. 1) appealed to the belligerents to make peace, but these appeals earned him nothing but a reputation for pro-Germanism.

With the victory of the Allies and Italy, the pope began to give up opposition to the Italian government. He definitely revoked (1919) the decree forbidding Catholics to participate in politics, and authorized (1920) Catholic sovereigns to visit the king in Rome. Negotiations were opened which led ultimately to the Lateran Treaty of 1929 (p. 993). (*Cont. p.* 992.)

8. SWITZERLAND

1815, Mar. 20, 29. Two acts of the Congress of **Vienna** regulated the Swiss problem. They laid down the principle of the **perpetual neutrality** of Switzerland, restored the old frontiers, with two exceptions, and smoothed over the internal difficulties of the country. A constitutional convention drew up a new **federal pact** which restored the old institutions, and gave very wide autonomy to the 22 cantons. The Diet had very restricted powers, being little more than a congress of ambassadors representing the cantons. Racial and religious differences, and differences in political ideals still existed among the cantons, which made for division and disunion.

1815-1828. The early part of the restoration period was characterized by a serious economic crisis, due to the war. Swiss industry, no longer protected by the Continental blockade, found itself unable to compete with English industry, especially in the textile trade. The cantons were unable to agree upon a common customs policy. In the political sphere most of the cantons followed reactionary policies. Under the pressure of the Holy Alliance, Switzerland was obliged to persecute the liberal refugees from neighboring countries, and in 1823 was compelled to restrict the freedom of the press.

1828-1848. The so-called "**Era of Regeneration**," in which revision of the constitutions of several cantons was undertaken.

1828-1829. The cantonal governments were wise enough to grant the concessions demanded, such as universal suffrage, freedom of the press, and equality before the law. The movement was strengthened by the July Revolution in Paris. Between 1830 and 1833 some ten cantons liberalized their constitutions.

1832, Mar. 17. The **Siebener Concordat.** The liberal cantons joined together to guarantee their new liberal constitutions.

July 17. The question of revising the federal pact in the direction of a stronger central government was brought before the Diet by a large majority of the cantons, whereupon the conservative cantons concluded an alliance (**League of Sarnen**) to maintain the Pact of 1815.

1834, Jan. 20. The struggle for the revision of the constitution was transformed into a **religious quarrel** when the liberal cantons adopted the *Articles of Baden*, which contained a program of ec-

clesiastical reform. The Liberal party stood for freedom of worship, secular education, a lay state, and was especially irritated by the paramount position in the Catholic cantons of the **Jesuits**, who had returned after 1814. By increasing the power of the central government, the Liberals hoped to be able to impose their views upon the whole confederation. Religious and political passions gradually rose to fever pitch.

1845, Dec. 11. THE *SONDERBUND*. The seven Catholic cantons — Lucerne, Uri, Schwyz, Unterwalden, Zug, Freiburg, and Valois — replied to the organized armed bands of the Liberal cantons by concluding a league (the *Sonderbund*) for the purpose of protecting their interests.

1847, July 20. The Liberals were able to get a vote through the Diet ordering the **dissolution of the *Sonderbund*** as being contrary to the constitution. The seven cantons refused, and war resulted.

Nov. 10-29. The federal general **G. H. Dufour** quickly defeated the forces of the *Sonderbund*. Lord Palmerston's policy of masterly inactivity and Dufour's rapid victory averted an intervention being planned by Metternich and Guizot. The *Sonderbund* was dissolved, the Jesuits were expelled, and the victors proceeded to strengthen the federal government.

1848, Sept. 12. THE NEW CONSTITUTION, replacing the **Pact of 1815**. It organized Switzerland as a federal union closely modeled on that of the United States. While preserving the historic local government of the cantons, it established a strong central government. Legislative authority resided in two chambers: The **Council of State** (*Ständerat*) consisting of two members from each canton; the **National Council** (*Nationalrat*), members of which were elected by universal suffrage in numbers proportional to the population of each canton. The executive was a **Federal Council** (*Bundesrat*) of seven members, elected by the two chambers. Its annual chairman was given the title *President of the Confederation*, but he enjoyed no wider powers than his colleagues.

1848-1857. The **Neufchâtel problem.** The canton of Neufchâtel (part of the confederation, but under the sovereignty of the King of Prussia) had proclaimed a republic (Mar. 1848), the constitution of which was guaranteed by the Federal Diet. In 1856 a conservative revolution aimed at the restoration of the king. War with Prussia was narrowly averted by the mediation of Napoleon III. In May 1857 the king renounced his rights, in return for a money payment, which he later renounced. He kept his title, but this was discontinued by William I.

Swiss internal history in the ensuing period was dominated by economic problems and by a general trend toward **government centralization.** The public services (telegraph and postal systems, customs, currency, weights and measures) had been brought under federal control, and were reorganized.

1874, Apr. 19. A revision of the constitution further enlarged the powers of the federal government, especially in military affairs. Free elementary schools under federal supervision were authorized and the principle of referendum was introduced for national legislation. Thereafter, by means of the initiative and referendum, federal authority was extended to many fields.

1874, Oct. The International Postal Congress met at Berne. Switzerland became a favorite meeting-place for international conventions and headquarters for many international organizations.

1882, May 20. Opening of the St. Gothard Railway; first of the great railroad tunnels through the Alps.

1887, May. The federal government was given a **monopoly of sale of spirits.**

1889. Acute tension in relations with Ger-

many, resulting from the expulsion of a police officer on the trail of political offenders. Switzerland had long been a haven for political refugees and for radicals and conspirators of all hues. The asylum extended to them caused constant friction with neighboring powers.

1890, June. The federal government was empowered to enact measures of **social insurance.**

1898, Feb. The federal government was authorized to **purchase privately owned railways.**

Nov. The federal government was empowered to unify and enforce the civil and penal codes.

1907, Apr. 12. A new army bill reorganized the forces. Although Swiss neutrality was guaranteed by the powers in 1815, growing international tension necessitated precautions. A unique military system was built up (1847, revised 1907): the army was a type of standing militia, with short periods of required training biennially.

Switzerland made steady progress in the economic sphere, but despite growing prosperity and the expansion of federal power, democracy remained. In six of the smallest cantons the people continued to exercise their local powers through mass meetings (*Landesgemeinden*) without the intervention of any assembly. In the larger cantons representative systems were used, but they were based on universal suffrage and in most of them the initiative and referendum were employed. (*Cont. p.* 994.)

9. CENTRAL EUROPE

a. GERMANY, 1815-1848

1815. THE "METTERNICH SYSTEM."
After the Napoleonic wars central Europe (the German states and the Austrian Empire) was subjected to the "Metternich System." Through rigid censorship, elaborate espionage, supervision of the universities, etc., Metternich opposed constitutional and nationalist aspirations awakened during the Napoleonic wars. In the German states he made his will felt through the **Germanic Confederation** (called into being by the Congress of Vienna). It was composed of 38 sovereign powers; its object was to guarantee external and internal peace of Germany, and the independence of the member states (Austria brought only its German states into the confederation); its organ was a diet sitting

at Frankfurt-on-the-Main, organized on a complicated basis into two "assemblies," over both of which the Austrian representative presided. The diet was a diplomatic congress, not a parliament: its members were instructed delegates of the various governments. In Metternich's view, it was a loose confederation (*Staatenbund*) to protect German monarchs against their foreign foes (Russia and France) and their domestic enemy (liberalism).

In 1815 **Prussia** had been the great hope of the Liberals, but with the decay of the influence of the king's principal minister, Hardenberg, reactionary influences came to the fore, capitalizing the growing fear of radical activity and the fact of fundamental disunity (territorial and moral) in Prussia. The constitutional movement was a disappointment elsewhere, except in Bavaria, Baden, and Saxe-Weimar.

Europe in 1900

Central Europe, 1815-1866

Raisz

1815-1819. The Burschenschaften. Universities became the centers of the liberal movement; students were organized in Liberal societies (*Burschenschaften*). The center of the agitation was the University of Jena, where an extremist group followed the lead of **Karl Follen.**

1817, Oct. 18. The Wartburg Festival (organized by Jena students as a joint celebration of the Reformation and the battle of Leipzig), at which emblems of reaction were burned.

1819, Mar. 23. August von Kotzebue, poetaster, reactionary journalist, formerly in the tsar's service, was murdered at Mannheim by a Jena student, **Karl Sand,** as an enemy of liberalism. Metternich was alarmed by this Liberal activity, won King Frederick William of Prussia over to repressive measures, embodied in the

1819, July. CARLSBAD DECREES, sanctioned by the Diet of the Germanic Confederation (Sept. 20), binding sovereigns to control of universities through commissioners, providing a strict censorship of all publications, establishing at Mainz an inquisition into secret societies — an act held to have "fettered opinion and postponed constitutional liberty in Germany for a generation."

1819-1844. THE GERMAN *ZOLL-VEREIN*. A more serious threat to Austrian hegemony in Germany now had its unostentatious beginnings in the movement for a *Zollverein* (customs union). The multiple tariff systems existing in Germany imposed irksome and hampering restrictions on a steadily growing commerce. Prussia took the lead in ending this situation by establishing a uniform tariff for all her territories and signing an initial tariff treaty with Schwarzburg-Sondershausen (1819, Oct.). Prussia was feared for her power and hated for her reaction by the smaller states, which combated her leadership and attempted to set up rival customs unions.

1829, May. Prussia won over the League of Bavaria and Württemberg and gradually added other states. By 1844 the *Zollverein* included practically the whole of Germany, except German Austria, Hanover, Oldenburg, Mecklenburg, and the three Hanse cities. By forming a close economic union of the great majority of the states in the Germanic Confederation, Prussia had won a political victory over Austria.

1830. The July Revolution in Paris (p. 628) not unnaturally had repercussions in Germany, where the revolutionary movement had revived in the hands of the reorganized university movement (1827), in secret clubs, etc. The rulers were forced to abdicate in Brunswick, Saxony, and Hesse-Cassel (Sept.); in these states and in Hanover (1833) new constitutions were introduced. Prussia escaped revolution, due to respect for the king, and especially to administrative reforms which had removed the worst evils of misgovernment.

Metternich saw in the revolutions the working of international radicalism, seeking to undermine the bases of existing society.

1832, May. The new movement was typified for Metternich in the **Hambach Festival,** where a gathering of 25,000 drank to Lafayette, demanded a republic and German unity, resolved to adopt not only peaceful methods of press and platform, but of armed revolt.

June 28. Metternich's answer was the adoption by the Germanic Confederation of **six articles:** imposing on every German sovereign the duty of rejecting petitions of his estates impairing his sovereignty; repudiating the right of estates to refuse supplies or to use this method to secure constitutional changes; providing against legislation by the states prejudicial to the Germanic Confederation, etc.

July. Additional repressive measures included prohibition of all public meetings; surveillance of suspicious political characters; renewal of edicts against universities. The reply of the revolutionists was a crazy plot engineered by international conspirators (probably connected with Mazzinian secret societies), aiming to seize Frankfurt, dissolve the Diet, unify the German states on liberal principles.

1833, Apr. 3. The attempt on Frankfurt was made and promptly collapsed. The Diet's reply (June) was to appoint, at Metternich's instance, a central commission to co-ordinate preventive measures and supervise prosecutions in the various states.

1837. The Metternichian reactionist policy was next extended to **Hanover,** where, on the death of William IV of England, the kingdom passed (in accordance with the Salic Law) to **Ernest Augustus, Duke of Cumberland,** eldest surviving son of George III. The latter set aside the Liberal constitution granted by William IV (1833). (Dismissal of seven eminent professors for refusal to take the oath.) A new constitution, cloak for the king's absolutism, was vigorously opposed in Hanover; the opposition was supported in the diet by

Bavaria and other states; but Metternich secured the support of Prussia for the principles of monarchical absolutism, and the Diet decided that the Constitution of 1833 was invalid, the king justified in overthrowing it.

1840, Aug. Ernest Augustus then imposed a constitution of his own, reducing the legislature to a nullity and recognizing the state domains as the king's private property. Constitutionalists in Germany were outraged by this act, even Conservatives were stirred; Liberals declared the Germanic Confederation a national disgrace.

The long reign of Frederick William III of Prussia came to an end, June 7, 1840, and he was succeeded by his son,

1840-1861. FREDERICK WILLIAM IV (b. 1795), a romanticist, deeply imbued with poetic and mystical conceptions, his ideas often far removed from reality. Like the Liberals, he aimed at greater political freedom and stronger national unity. But he sought to attain these ends, not through constitutionalism, but through the rule of the estates, reviving the position of the nobles and corporations, reflecting the "mystic glories of a divinely consecrated and patriarchial monarchy." In place of the Germanic Confederation, he dreamt of reviving the Holy Roman Empire, in which Prussia would play a glorious rôle, but secondary to that of the Hapsburgs.

1841-1842. The reign began auspiciously. The censorship was made much less stringent, but abuses of the new system resulted in its prompt withdrawal, causing mutual recrimination between government and public opinion.

1841. Provincial diets, established in 1823, were given the right to elect committees to meet in Berlin and discuss legislation for all Prussia.

1842. At the first meeting of the committees, the king explained that they were not to regard themselves as a popular assembly, an irritating and ambiguous statement. They separated after accomplishing but little. The king was impelled to move forward also by financial difficulties which he hoped to ease by some sort of popular representation.

1847. The eventual result was the order summoning the United *Landtag* (combined provincial diets). The king, who affected to despise the formalism of "Liberal constitutions," now presented to the *Landtag* an incredibly complicated and unreal scheme which gave the *Landtag* no effective power over legislation or the budget, made no provision for regular meetings. Opposition developed at once,

demanding above all periodicity of meetings. Two government bills were introduced at this session (dealing with financial matters); both were rejected. The session came to an end amid great discontent of the Liberals.

Having failed in the *Landtag*, the king sought to recover his prestige through a scheme for reform of the Germanic Confederation, giving the Diet new powers and transforming the system in the direction of a federal state. The plan was presented at Vienna (end 1847) by **Joseph Maria von Radowitz**, but no decision had been reached when the scheme was overtaken by the stormy events of 1848.

b. THE HAPSBURG MONARCHY 1815-1848

(1) *Austria*

The Austrian Empire was an anomalous congeries of territories and peoples, united by common obedience to the house of Hapsburg-Lorraine, as provided by the Pragmatic Sanction (p. 463) and by such common institutions as the capital (Vienna), the Austrian court, the army, the bureaucracy, diplomacy, the Austrian Church. Held together by the centripetal forces of these institutions, Austria was a monarchical machine. She was increasingly weakened by the centrifugal forces of nationalism and the discords of inharmonious peoples gathered within her heterogeneous territories. The empire embraced (1) the hereditary lands (principally Austria proper and the territories inhabited by the Slovenes to the south); (2) the lands of the Bohemian crown; (3) the province of Galicia, acquired in the partitions of Poland; (4) the Kingdom of Italy, Venetia, and Lombardy; (5) the lands of the crown of St. Stephen — Hungary, Transylvania, Croatia.

Among these peoples **nationalist movements** took root and flourished, e.g.: (1) the **Illyrian renaissance**, beginning as a literary movement among the Croats and their neighbors and eventuating in resistance to the rule of the Magyars, dominant racial group in the lands of the crown of St. Stephen; (2) the **Czech renaissance**, beginning also as a literary movement and turning in the forties to demands for the restitution of constitutional rights for Bohemia; (3) most important of all, the rise of a nationalist movement **among the Magyars** (p. 671).

1806-1835. FRANCIS I (b. 1768). He was, until the dissolution of the

Holy Roman Empire (1806), Holy Roman Emperor as Francis II. Until 1805 he had been assisted by a cabinet minister (in effect a prime minister) who was in direct control of the various elements in the government. Thereafter Francis acted as his own minister, permitting **Metternich** wide powers in foreign affairs, but holding the threads of domestic government in his own hands. The governmental machine was extremely complicated, the emperor alone representing any synthesis of the various administrative departments. "Austria was administered, but not ruled," remarked Metternich. The infrequent meetings of the various provincial estates were mere form. The police were supreme; spies were everywhere; letters were opened; censorship was extremely severe; instruction was made to conform with conservative principles. The emperor's alarm at popular movements increased.

1832. He combated Metternich's suggestion of a new constitution to reconcile the "opposition between the monarchist principle and the democratic." His will warned his successor to "displace none of the foundations of the edifice of state. Rule, and change nothing."

1835-1848. FERDINAND I (1793-1875), the weak-minded and incapable son of Francis I. He followed his father's advice in leaving Metternich in control of foreign affairs. But he permitted court circles to induce him to create, as supreme governmental organ,

1836. The **State Conference** (*Staatskonferenz*), composed of Archdukes Ludwig and Francis Charles, **Count Kolowrat**, Metternich. In fact the State Conference met less and less often, and the dominant influence in the state was exercised by individual ministers over their several departments, notably by Metternich over foreign affairs, Kolowrat over finance.

Publications within Austria were still subjected to a strict censorship, but Liberal pamphlets, newspapers, etc., were freely introduced from abroad. University professors were (in fact) allowed considerable latitude. Western European Liberal ideas rapidly took root among the educated classes of Austria. In Austria proper these ideas found expression in agitation for constitutional changes. This agitation was least important in the Alpine districts, most significant in Lower Austria and especially Vienna. The assembly of estates in Lower Austria had during the past century lost its political significance, but now began to press for legislative and tax reforms, more effective parliamentary

representation for the cities, etc. The movement for constitutional reform was stimulated by the industrial progress of Austria, giving Vienna and other cities an increasingly large middle class, cultivated, eager to take its place in the political life of the country. Industry also brought a city proletariat with more radical views and destined to play an important rôle in the Revolution of 1848. The masses were goaded by severe economic depression; riots of workers became more frequent. This was the setting for the events of March, 1848.

(2) Hungary

1813-1825. In Hungary, whose constitution remained unchanged, the reactionary Emperor Francis I (p. 670) attempted to rule without summoning the Diet, demanding troops and subsidies directly from the counties. When the latter refused compliance, he was obliged once again to summon the Diet (1825), promise triennial meetings and the exclusive right to grant taxes and recruits. The Hungarian Diet represented exclusively the still semi-feudal nobility. The upper house (*Table of Magnates*) had as members the great nobles (some 130 in number) and certain ecclesiastical dignitaries and high officeholders. The lower house (*Table of Deputies*) was recruited from members of the gentry (about 700,000), with representatives elected by the county assemblies (two each); it included also two members representing all the cities, and delegates from the Diet of the Kingdom of Croatia.

A movement, at once liberal and national, made rapid progress in Hungary, in the thirties and forties. Its moderate wing, inspired by **Count Stephen Széchenyi** (1791-1860), aimed primarily at a cultural renaissance and the economic development of the country along western European lines. The radicals, led by **Louis Kossuth** (1802-1894), sought independence from Austria and parliamentary government for Hungary. Between these two groups, but much nearer Széchenyi, **Francis Deák** (1803-1876) urged a middle course to assure Hungary at once her rightful position of autonomy within the Empire and a modern parliamentary régime. All groups were interested in extending the use of the Magyar language; all favored maintenance of the dominant position of Magyars over other peoples within Hungary.

1836-1844. The Diet won its first victory when Magyar was substituted for Latin as the official language in Hungary. Agitation for reform gathered vigor in the

The House of Hapsburg-Lorraine

All single dates, except where otherwise indicated, are death-dates.

forties. As editor of a newly founded (1841) organ of the radicals, the *Pesti Hirlap* (*Pest Journal*), Kossuth extended the influence of his revolutionary propaganda, attacking Austria violently, fostering Magyar chauvinism by denying the rights of Slavic minorities in Hungary.

1847. The elections of 1847 returned a large majority of Liberals to the Table of Deputies. Deák now united the various Liberal groups on a compromise program of reform, the so-called **Ten Points,** afterward known as the *March Laws*: responsible government; popular representation; larger liberty for the press; incorporation of Transylvania; right of public assembly; complete religious liberty; universal equality before the law; universal taxation; abolition of serfdom with compensation to the landlords; abolition of the *aviticitas*, the rigid system of entail dating from 1351. Deák's program was accepted by the Table of Deputies, but was combated by the conservative Table of Magnates. The deputies negotiated with the imperial government and had reached a deadlock when news of the February Revolution in Paris reached Budapest and precipitated the revolutionary movement there.

c. THE REVOLUTION OF 1848-1849 IN THE HAPSBURG DOMINIONS

1848, Mar. 3. The news of the February Revolution in Paris (p. 630) aroused much excitement in Vienna and Budapest. In a daring speech **Kossuth** denounced the Vienna System and demanded responsible government for Hungary.

Mar. 12. Stimulated by the boldness of the Hungarians, the Viennese began to demonstrate and draw up petitions to the emperor. Through mismanagement the popular commotion led (Mar. 13) to clashes between the troops and the demonstrators (largely students).

Mar. 13. METTERNICH RESIGNED and left the country.

Mar. 15. An imperial manifesto abolished the censorship and promised the convocation of a constitutional assembly. On the same day the Hungarian Table of Deputies adopted the entire Ten Points of Deák, which thus became the **March Laws,** equivalent to a constitution. The Table of Magnates opposed the program vigorously, but the king-emperor accepted it (Mar. 31) as well as further demands (Apr.) which made **Hungary** all but independent, joined to the rest of the Hapsburg posses-

sions only through a personal union. On the same day also the **Croats** organized a national committee which sought autonomous government, i.e. separation from Hungary.

Mar. 18-23. The **glorious Five Days in Milan,** initiating the revolution in Lombardy (p. 654).

Apr. 8. The **Czechs** obliged the Vienna government to promise a constituent assembly for the Kingdom of Bohemia. Other revolutionary movements took place in Moravia, Galicia, Dalmatia, and Transylvania.

Apr. 25. The emperor promulgated a **constitution for Austria** instead of awaiting the work of the assembly promised in March. The constitution set up a constitutional régime with a responsible ministry.

May 15. Dissatisfaction with the constitution and the dissolution of a committee of students and national guard led to a popular demonstration. The government was forced to reconstitute the committee and to promise revision of the constitution in a democratic sense.

May 17. The emperor and his family fled from radical Vienna to Innsbruck.

May 26. An attempt to dissolve the Academic Legion resulted in another demonstration, the raising of barricades and the creation of a **committee of safety,** which controlled Vienna during the following months.

June. The first **Pan-Slav Congress** (composed, however, almost entirely of Czech delegates) met at Prague under the presidency of **Francis Palácky** (1798-1876), the eminent Bohemian historian and national leader. It proclaimed the solidarity of the Slavic peoples (as against the Germans), but stressed also the equality of all peoples, and proposed a European congress to deal with outstanding international problems.

June 12. The Princess Windischgrätz, wife of the commander of the forces at Prague, was accidentally shot and killed during a demonstration. **Prince Windischgrätz,** throughout an advocate of strong repressive measures, seized this opportunity to bring up reinforcements.

June 17. He bombarded **Prague,** crushed the Czech revolutionary movement and established a military dictatorship in Bohemia. First step in the recovery of the governmental power.

July 22. The general diet or constituent assembly (*Reichstag*) met in Vienna. It discarded the constitution previously promulgated by the government and drew up a new document, pronouncedly democratic. Its only act of lasting importance was the **emancipation of the peasants** from feudal burdens (law of Sept. 7).

July 24. General **Radetzky** overwhelmingly defeated the Piedmontese-Italian army in the **battle of Custozza** and re-established control of Lombardy (p. 654).

Sept. 17. Baron **Jellachich**, governor (ban) of Croatia, began an invasion of Hungary. He had been appointed on Mar. 23, in reply to the demand of the Croatians for autonomy. Under his leadership the Croatian-Slavonic Diet had rejected the authority of Hungary (June 5), an action which led to the suspension of Jellachich by the emperor. After Custozza the court party urged the emperor to take vigorous action against the Hungarians, who made no secret of their sympathy with the revolutionary movement in Germany and Italy, which aimed at the breakup of the Hapsburg Empire. The emperor therefore reinstated Jellachich (Sept. 4) and countenanced his attack on Hungary.

Oct. 3. Jellachich was made commander-in-chief of the forces operating against Hungary. He was driven back by the Hungarians, who invaded Austria and came within sight of Vienna.

Oct. 6. Barricades went up in Vienna when it was learned that the court was moving to suppress the Hungarian revolutionary movement. **Count Latour**, the minister of war, was murdered and a radical rump of the constituent assembly declared itself in permanent session.

Oct. 31. Windischgrätz, aided by Jellachich, bombarded **Vienna** into submission. The radical leaders (including **Robert Blum**, delegate from the Frankfurt Parliament, p. 675) were ruthlessly executed. The assembly had already (Oct. 22) been adjourned to the little Moravian town of **Kremsier**, where it attracted less attention.

Dec. 2. Abdication of the Emperor Ferdinand. This was engineered by **Prince Felix Schwarzenberg** (1800–1852), diplomatic adjunct of Radetzky, iron-willed adherent of the restoration and even extension of the imperial power. He induced the heir to the throne, Archduke Francis Charles, to forego his rights in favor of his eighteen-year-old son,

1848-1916. FRANCIS JOSEPH I (b. 1830), who ascended the throne, according to Schwarzenberg, unbound by any of the promises of his predecessor to the Hungarians and others. The efforts of the government were now concentrated on the campaign against Hungary.

1849, Jan. 5. Windischgrätz, in command of the invading armies, won an initial success by occupying **Budapest**, which surrendered without offering resistance.

Feb. 26-27. He defeated General Dembinski at **Kapolna**, but was then obliged by General Görgei to evacuate nearly all of Hungary (Apr.).

Mar. 1. The Austrian *Reichstag* completed its constitutional work. The **Kremsier Constitution** provided for a decentralized, federal form of government and is regarded by many as having offered the last chance for a healthy reorganization of the monarchy.

Mar. 4. Having dissolved the *Reichstag*, **Schwarzenberg** promulgated a constitution of his own, designed to apply to all the Hapsburg possessions, including Hungary. It provided for a highly centralized system, with a representative diet and a responsible ministry. "Provisionally" the emperor governed autocratically.

Apr. 13. Goaded into resistance by the new constitution and rapidly drifting into more radical channels, the Hungarian Diet, meeting temporarily at Debreczen, proclaimed **the Hungarian Republic.**

Apr. 14. Kossuth was elected *"responsible governor-president"* by the Hungarian Diet.

June. Francis Joseph accepted the offer of Tsar Nicholas of Russia to aid in the suppression of the Hungarian revolution.

June 17-18. The Russian general **Paskievich** invaded Hungary from the north while the Austrian general **Haynau** led the invasion from the west. At the same time the Hungarians were faced with serious revolutionary movements among the Serbs in the south and the Rumanians in Transylvania. **Görgei** put up a vigorous resistance, but the Hungarians were unable to face such odds for long.

Aug. 9. The Hungarians were decisively defeated in the **battle of Temesvar.**

Aug. 11. Kossuth abandoned his position in favor of Görgei and fled (with many other leaders) across the frontier into Turkey.

Aug. 13. GÖRGEI SURRENDERED to the Russian commander at Vilagos. Despite promises of clemency, General Haynau visited sanguine vengeance on the

Hungarians at the bloody assizes of **Arad.**
Nine generals were hanged and four shot.

d. THE REVOLUTION OF 1848-1849 IN GERMANY

The **February Revolution in Paris** (p.
630) acted as a catalytic agent to precipitate
widespread discontent in Germany. First
in the south and west, then in the central
states and Prussia, there were popular
demonstrations and demands for constitutional changes and reform. As in the
Hapsburg Monarchy, the movement was
both national and liberal. But whereas in
Austria the revolution aimed at the wrecking or dismemberment of one sovereign
state, in Germany its objective was the
unification of numerous sovereign states
into one new empire. In the excitement of
the first days, the German rulers, taken off
their guard, yielded everywhere. Ministries
were refashioned along liberal lines and pro-
fuse promises of reform were made. Revolutionary changes were effected rapidly and
almost without bloodshed.

1848, Mar. 15. Beginning of the **March
Days** in Berlin. The raising of
barricades led to efforts of the soldiers to
clear the streets, and to some bloodshed
(Mar. 16). King Frederick William, convinced that the whole trouble was due to
the machinations of foreign agitators and
unwilling to slaughter his beloved subjects,
determined to make concessions.

Mar. 18. The censorship was abolished
and a patent was issued summon-
ing the **United** *Landtag.* The king announced his readiness to collaborate in
giving Germany as a whole a constitution.
The crowd, milling about the palace, was
greeted by accidental shots from the troops.
No one was hurt, but barricades went up
again and the insurrection became general
in Berlin.

Mar. 19. The king, extremely agitated,
issued a proclamation "to his
beloved Berliners" urging them to quit
the barricades and promising them that
the troops would then be withdrawn. Before the evacuation of the barricades was
at all complete, the king ordered the
withdrawal of the military. The palace
was unprotected, the king was obliged to
grant the popular demand for arms, and
had to face the humiliation of saluting the
corpses of insurgents as the mob carried
them by.

Mar. 21. The king issued a second proclamation "to my people and the
German nation," promising that he would
assume the leadership of the German people

and that Prussia would henceforth be
"merged in Germany." On the same day
the king suffered a second humiliation when
he paraded through the streets wearing the
tricolor of black, red, and gold (recently
adopted by the Diet as the flag of the new
Germany) and making liberal addresses to
the students.

Mar. 31. The Frankfurt *Vorparlament*
met. On Mar. 5 a self-constituted
committee of 53 Liberals from various
states had met at Heidelberg and had decided to arrange for a constituent body for
all Germany. The *Vorparlament* (preliminary parliament) ordered the holding of elections by direct, manhood suffrage.

May 18. THE FRANKFURT NA-
TIONAL ASSEMBLY (*National-
versammlung*) or parliament met for the
first time in the Church of St. Paul at
Frankfurt-on-the-Main. Its membership
was about 830. Many of the conservatives
who had been elected refused to take their
seats in a revolutionary assembly, but the
parliament nevertheless was weighted
heavily in favor of rank, office, property,
and education. It was preponderantly a
middle-class body, composed of some 200
lawyers, about 100 professors, many phy-
sicians, judges, officials, plus about 140
businessmen. "The most distinguished
constituent body in history." Its debates,
though often of exasperating length and
technicality, were of a surprisingly high
order.

May 19. The parliament chose **Heinrich von Gagern** as president and
devoted itself to the work of
organization.

**May 22. Meeting of the Prussian con-
stituent assembly.** It continued
its debates throughout the summer, becoming gradually more and
more radical.

June 28. The **Frankfurt Parliament,**
having suspended the Diet of the
Germanic Confederation, appointed **Archduke John of Austria** (uncle of Emperor
Ferdinand) imperial regent (*Reichsverweser*)
as head of a provisional executive power.
He was recognized by the various state
governments and appointed a ministry in
which Anton Schmerling (an Austrian) was
minister for foreign affairs and the interior
and Peucker (a Prussian) and Heckscher
(from Hamburg) ministers of war and
justice respectively. The provisional government, lacking all material power (army),
never established its authority firmly, and
the attention of the Parliament itself was
riveted during the summer of 1848 on the
Schleswig-Holstein question, a test case of
the solidarity of German national feeling

and of the power of the Parliament over the state governments.

The two provinces of **Schleswig** and **Holstein** (the former half German, the latter almost wholly so) were possessions of the **King of Denmark.** Holstein was a member state of the Germanic Confederation. In Jan. 1848 Frederick VII succeeded to the Danish throne. He was wholly under the influence of the Danish nationalists (**Eider Danes**) whose object was to integrate Schleswig with the rest of the monarchy. The duchies refused to recognize descent in the female line and supported the claim of the Duke of Augustenburg to succession in the duchies. When Danish troops began to occupy Schleswig, the **duchies rose in revolt** and established a provisional government at Kiel (Mar. 24). The Frankfurt Parliament thereupon decided to intervene and commissioned Prussia to send federal troops, which the Prussians did, despite warnings from both England and Russia, which powers were interested in keeping Prussia from the North Sea coast, and in maintaining Denmark at the entrance to the Baltic. Various British efforts at mediation (June, July) failed, but Frederick William, whose heart had never been in the intervention,

Aug. 28. Concluded the **Armistice of Malmö** for seven months: Danes and Prussians both to evacuate the duchies, which were to be provisionally administered by a joint commission of Danes and representatives of the Germanic Confederation. This arrangement, so favorable to Denmark, raised a storm of protest in the duchies and in the Frankfurt Parliament. The Parliament rejected the armistice at first, but, after a change of ministry,

Sept. 16. The Frankfurt Parliament yielded. Ultimately it accepted a proposal of Palmerston (Feb. 3, 1849) for a separate constitution for Schleswig, but soon afterward (Feb. 26) the Danes denounced the armistice. The war was resumed Mar. 31, the Germans invading Jutland. On July 10 a new armistice was concluded and long-drawn negotiations were initiated. They finally led to the conclusion of **peace between Prussia and Denmark** (July 2, 1850), in which both sides reserved their rights. The **London Protocol** (May 8, 1852), between England, Russia, France, Austria, Prussia, Sweden, and Denmark (not signed by the duchies or by the Germanic Confederation) fixed the succession, the Duke of Augustenburg's claims being settled by a money payment.

By the time the Parliament was ready to devote itself to the constitutional problem, loose parties had emerged from the ranks of deputies. The **Right** (Radowitz, Vincke, Prince Lichnowsky) held to the idea of an imperial constitution in harmony with the separate state governments; the **Left** (Vogt, Ruge, Blum) proclaimed the sovereignty of the people and endeavored to establish a republican, strongly centralized, federal government; the **Right Center** (Gagern, Dahlmann, Gervinus, Arndt, Bassermann, J. Grimm) hoped to persuade the governments to recognize a constitutional monarchy for all Germany; the **Left Center** (Römer, Fallmerayer) insisted on the subordination of the states to the central monarchy. As the various groups debated, the chief governments recovered their authority.

Oct. 31. Windischgrätz took Vienna (p. 674).

Nov. 9. King Frederick William of Prussia, encouraged by the success of the Austrian court and prodded by his generals, exiled the Prussian constituent assembly to Brandenburg-on-the-Havel, as a reply to its action in striking the phrase "by the grace of God" from the royal title, and other radical measures.

Dec. 5. The Prussian constituent assembly was dissolved and the government promulgated a constitution (based upon the work of the assembly, but maintaining the ultimate authority of the king). As elaborated in the succeeding years, the constitution came to provide for an upper house (*Herrenhaus*), bulwark of the privileged orders, and a lower house (*Landtag*), chosen by universal suffrage but under a three-class system of voting based on taxpaying ability, so that 83% of the electorate controlled only one-third of the seats. Though the *Landtag* was given power to vote *new* laws and taxes, there was no ministerial responsibility, and when parliament was not in session, ordinances, with the force of law, could be issued by royal fiat. This constitution remained in force from 1850 to 1918.

The conservatives and the radicals in the Frankfurt Parliament had become seriously divided on the question of what territory should be included in the projected German national state. The radicals were in favor of bringing in the German provinces of Austria (in which they included Bohemia), though this would have involved the disruption of the Hapsburg Monarchy. This group was known as the Big-German (*Grossdeutsch*) party, while the Little-German (*Kleindeutsch*) group thought it wiser to leave Austrian territory out of account. The question became more and more academic as the Austrian government recovered its position and made known its hostility to any infringement of its unity. The whole matter was finally compromised (Oct.) by a decision to include all German territory, but with the proviso that no part of the new state should be connected with non-German territory. In effect this meant the victory of the *Kleindeutsch* group, which looked to Prussia and Frederick William for aid in the constitution of a German national state.

1849, Mar. 27. THE FRANKFURT CONSTITUTION. This followed upon the Austrian Constitution of Mar. 4 which reasserted the unity of the Hapsburg dominions and ended all talk of including part of Austria. The Frankfurt Constitution created a federal state under an hereditary "Emperor of the Germans," who was to have a suspensive veto over legislation passed by a national parliament. Ministers were to be responsible to the parliament, which was to consist of two houses: an upper house (*Staatenhaus*) the members of which were to be chosen, one-half by the state governments, one-half by the lower houses of the state legislatures. The members of the lower house (*Volkshaus*) were to be elected on the basis of universal, direct, secret, equal ballot, with single-member constituencies. Over the courts of the various states was set a supreme court for the *Reich*, with final jurisdiction. The federal government was to have complete control of foreign policy, the army, regulation of economic questions. The constitution was never put in force, but exercised important influence on the later constitution of the North German Confederation (p. 686) and the constitution of the German Republic (p. 996).

Mar. 28. The Frankfurt Parliament elected **Frederick William of Prussia as Emperor.**

Apr. 3. The king told the Parliament's deputation that he could agree only after the princes and free cities had accepted the constitution.

Apr. 21. When the small states had already accepted, the king torpedoed the movement through a declaration that Prussia could not accept the constitution as it stood — a King by "divine right" could not receive a crown at the hands of a popularly elected assembly. The majority of the governments now withdrew their representatives from Frankfurt.

June 18. A "rump parliament" removed to **Stuttgart,** where government troops finally dispersed its members. The attempt to unite Germany under a parliamentary system had failed.

1849-1850. The Prussian Union Scheme.

Though unwilling to accept the crown from an elected assembly, Frederick William still hoped to achieve German unity in accordance with his own ideas and with the consent of his fellow princes. His friend, **Von Radowitz,** produced a plan for a larger confederation to include the German states and the whole of the Austrian dominions, German and non-German, thus creating a great **Middle European bloc** with a population of 60,000,000, with immense economic possibilities. This great empire was to be divided for administration into two parts: (1) an **inner confederation** comprising roughly present-day Germany, under the leadership of Prussia; (2) the **Hapsburg Monarchy,** which would thus remain intact.

1849, May 26. A draft constitution for the inner confederation (**Prussian Union**) not substantially different from that of the later North German Confederation was accepted by Prussia, Saxony, and Hanover. Saxony and Hanover, however, reserving the right to withdraw if it were not accepted by the other German governments, apart from Austria. Nearly all the petty governments, fearing Prussia, promptly joined the new union.

Oct. 19. A national assembly was summoned to meet at **Erfurt.** Saxony and Hanover now withdrew, leaving the union substantially a combination of Prussia and the smaller states (Württemberg and Bavaria refusing to join).

1850, Mar. 20. The **Erfurt Parliament** met, the constitution as proposed by Prussia was accepted, and the Parliament was soon afterward prorogued.

Apr. 29. Frederick William told the princes that he left them free to adhere to the union, but gave them the impression that it was in fact suspended until more auspicious times. With the Hungarian Revolution crushed, Schwarzenberg was now prepared for an active policy in Germany.

May 16. At his invitation, representatives of a number of the petty states and Austria met at Frankfurt and reconstituted the old **Diet of the Germanic Confederation.** If Prussia insisted on the perpetuation of the Erfurt Union, war with Austria appeared inevitable. When a dispute arose from an appeal of the Elector of Hesse to the Frankfurt Diet for support against his parliament, the Austrians sent federal troops into the district, while the Prussians, arguing a right to intervene in view of the fact that Hesse was a member of the Prussian Union, did likewise. Both powers mobilized and war seemed imminent. Tsar Nicholas of Russia, irritated by the pseudo-liberalism of the Prussian ruler, sided with Austria, and Frederick William, who had been averse from war from the very outset, decided to beat a retreat. He sent his new minister, **Otto von Manteuffel**, to negotiate with Schwarzenberg at Olmütz.

Nov. 29. ..THE PUNCTATION OF OL-MÜTZ. The Prussians abandoned the Prussian Union and recognized the re-established Germanic Diet at Frankfurt. It was decided that the future constitution of Germany should be discussed in "open conferences" of all the German states. This was merely a screen to conceal the Prussian retreat, and the whole affair is generally spoken of by Prussian historians as the *Humiliation of Olmütz*.

1850, Dec.-1851, Mar. Conference of the German states at Dresden. This proved fruitless and the old Germanic Confederation was re-established in the original form.

e. THE AUSTRIAN EMPIRE, 1849-1867

1849-1860. The Bach system. The constitution of Mar. 4, 1849, having been suspended (1851), the empire was ruled from Vienna by bureaucratic methods and a concerted effort was made to undermine the national movements by a policy of vigorous **Germanization**. This policy was associated especially with the name of **Alexander Bach**, minister of the interior. Hungary lost its historic identity and was divided into five administrative "governments," ruled by German officials and by gendarmerie directed from Vienna. Croatia, Transylvania, and southern Hungary became separate provinces, and the Slavs and Rumanians in these territories (who had been loyal in 1848) suffered the same fate as the Hungarians.

1855. A concordat with the Catholic Church gave the Church extensive power, especially in matters of education, thus breaking with the tradition of Joseph II, in the interests of counteracting the revolutionary spirit.

1856-1859. The Austrian government felt acutely the results of the Crimean War (p. 727), which undermined Austria's international position and ruined the finances through prolonged mobilization.

1859. WAR WITH FRANCE AND PIED-MONT (p. 658), brought to an abrupt end in part because of financial stringency, in part because of the danger of revolt in Hungary. The government felt impelled to scrap the Bach system and come to an agreement with the national groups.

1860, Oct. 20. The October Diploma, issued by the emperor, set up a federal constitution which recognized wide autonomy for the various "Lands," with an imperial diet of limited powers, to be elected by the provincial *Landtage*. The Hungarians opposed this settlement and demanded the restoration of their own constitution.

1861, Feb. The February Patent, "interpreting" the October Diploma, but really a new constitution which set up a bicameral parliament with an electoral system designed to give the German *bourgeoisie* (the mainstay of the empire) an influence wholly disproportionate to their numbers. Negotiations with the Hungarians failed; Hungary was again ruled administratively and autocratically. The emperor resumed negotiations with the Hungarians in 1865. They were facilitated by the overwhelming defeat of Austrian arms at Königgrätz (p. 686) and by the loyal participation of the Hungarians in the war against the Germans. The result was the

1867, Oct. COMPROMISE OF 1867 (largely the work of **Francis Deák**, seconded by **Julius Andrássy**), which established a political organism *sui generis*: In Hungary (the ancient *lands of the crown of St. Stephen*) the Magyars were permitted to dominate the subject peoples through the constitutional system of 1848. In Austria (the remaining seventeen provinces of the empire) the Germans were to dominate the other peoples through a constitution, based on the February Patent, extended and made perpetual. The two states were joined in personal union in the monarch; in common ministries of foreign affairs, war, and finance (merely an administrator of the common treasury which received the funds contributed by both states for common purposes); in the annual *delegations*, composed of sixty members of each of the two parliaments, empowered to decide matters of common interest; in a decennial treaty regulating tariffs, currency, the military system, etc. The "autocrat of the fifties" now ruled through responsible ministries in both parts of the empire.

f. THE UNIFICATION OF GERMANY

1850-1853. Despite the extent of the humiliation of Prussia by Austria at Olmütz (above), she was able to thwart

The House of Hohenzollern

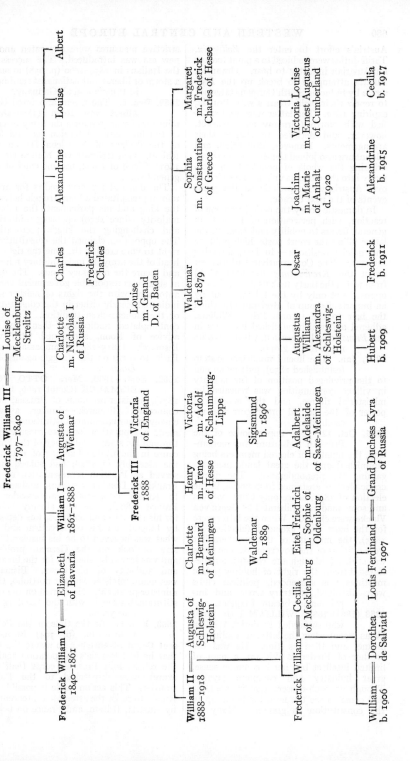

Frederick William III 1797–1840 ═ Louise of Mecklenburg-Strelitz

Children: Frederick William IV 1840–1861 ═ Elizabeth of Bavaria; William I 1861–1888 ═ Augusta of Weimar; Charlotte m. Nicholas I of Russia; Charles; Alexandrine; Louise; Albert

Frederick Charles (son of Charles)

William I ═ Augusta of Weimar — children: Frederick III 1888 ═ Victoria of England; Louise m. Grand D. of Baden

Frederick III ═ Victoria of England — children: William II 1888–1918 ═ Augusta of Schleswig-Holstein; Charlotte m. Bernard of Meiningen; Henry m. Irene of Hesse; Sigismund b. 1896; Victoria m. Adolf of Schaumburg-Lippe; Waldemar d. 1879; Sophia m. Constantine of Greece; Margaret m. Frederick Charles of Hesse

Waldemar b. 1889 (son of Henry)

William II ═ Augusta of Schleswig-Holstein — children: Frederick William ═ Cecilia of Mecklenburg; Eitel Friedrich m. Sophie of Oldenburg; Adalbert m. Adelaide of Saxe-Meiningen; Augustus William m. Alexandra of Schleswig-Holstein; Oscar; Joachim m. Marie of Anhalt d. 1920; Victoria Louise m. Ernest Augustus of Cumberland

Frederick William ═ Cecilia of Mecklenburg — children: William b. 1906 ═ Dorothea de Salviati; Louis Ferdinand b. 1907 ═ Grand Duchess Kyra of Russia; Hubert b. 1909; Frederick b. 1911; Alexandrine b. 1915; Cecilia b. 1917

Austria's effort to enter the *Zollverein*. Tariff duties were reduced to a point too low for Austrian industry to bear. Thwarted, Austria attempted to break up the *Zollverein* by inducing South German states not to renew their tariff treaties with Prussia, expiring 1852. The latter were well satisfied with North Germany as a market, however, and declined to change their arrangements. **Hanover, Brunswick, and Oldenburg** also joined the *Zollverein* (1853), bringing the whole of non-Austrian Germany into the customs union. This victory over Austria was a prelude to the great events of the next decade.

In domestic policy the period was one of reaction, with persecution of Liberals in general, favors to nobility and *Junkers*, the latter filling the court posts, high military and official positions — in fact, directing the state. The Conservatives had as their organ the *Kreuzzeitung* (founded 1848) from which the party took its name. It was opposed not only by the Liberals, but by an important group of Moderates to which the heir to the throne, Prince William, adhered and which published its views in the *Preussische Wochenblatt*, which gave its name to the group.

1852, Jan. The liberal municipal system (established 1850), putting an end to the privileged position of the nobility in village communities, was repealed by ministerial decree, and the magisterial power of the landed proprietors was re-established.

1854, Oct. 12. The upper house of the Prussian legislature was reorganized, the number of elected members being diminished and the great landowners regaining the preponderance. The democratic electors abstained from voting in the election of 1852, hence only Conservatives and some moderate Liberals like **Georg von Vincke** were elected. When the latter were for the most part excluded (elections of 1855), the majority of the members left were officials of the government. The press was stifled (although the constitution declared it free), the right of holding public meetings was suspended, political clubs were dissolved, arbitrary arrest and imprisonment became frequent.

1858 (1861)-1888. WILLIAM I (b. 1796) who succeeded Frederick William IV as regent when the latter was adjudged insane, and then as king. He was the brother of Frederick William, a man of limited intellect but much common sense, great industry and complete loyalty. Though an arch-conservative in 1848, he had come to see the need for living up to the constitution as granted. Many re-

strictive measures were abrogated and a new era was introduced. The success of the Italians in 1859–1860 (p. 658) aroused a storm of liberal and nationalist sentiment in Prussia and all Germany.

1859, Dec. 5. The regent appointed Gen. **Albert von Roon** (1803–1879) minister of war to reform the army in view of the international tension (general fear of the designs of Napoleon III on the Rhine). Gen. Helmuth von Moltke (1800–1891), friend of Roon, became chief of the general staff.

The demand for new credits for army reform precipitated a long struggle between the king and his parliament, the Liberal majority (since 1859) opposing militarism and challenging the king's prerogative. The opposition claimed the constitutional right to vote credits; the king the right, as head of the army, to make military reforms and secure the necessary funds. The issue at stake was responsible government versus autocracy, with the rights of neither side indicated clearly either in the constitution or the Hohenzollern tradition. The king contemplated abdication; then, on the advice of Roon, summoned Otto von Bismarck (1815–1898), ambassador to Paris, to carry on the struggle against the *Landtag*.

1862, Sept.—1890, Mar. OTTO VON BISMARCK (Count 1866, Prince 1871), minister-president of Prussia, later chancellor. Bismarck — Junker, avowed enemy of parliamentary institutions — had made a reputation for ultra-conservatism through his staunch advocacy of the king's cause in the United Landtag of 1847 and the assembly of 1848; had subsequently served as Prussian representative to the Frankfurt Diet (1851–1859), ambassador to Russia (1859–1862), ambassador to France (1862). He was already known for his strength and boldness, was detested by Liberals for his conservatism and for what was believed to be his insular Prussian outlook on the German problem, and was feared by the king for the breadth and audacity of his views. Bismarck was made minister without portfolio, then minister-president. He carried on the constitutional struggle with the Landtag for four years.

1863, Feb. 8. At the time of the Polish insurrection (p. 704) Bismarck sent **Count Alvensleben** to assure the tsar that he had Prussia's co-operation against the rebels; four Prussian corps (half the army) were dispatched to the Polish frontier. This action made it possible for Russia to resist the attempted intervention by Austria, Britain, and France on behalf of the Poles; it won the tsar's trust and friendship during the three wars necessary to German unification.

Agitation for the unification of "Germany" had revived rapidly after 1859. Austria and the South German states favored reform of the Germanic Confederation. German Liberals generally favored a parliamentary *Kleindeutschland* after the Frankfurt tradition of 1848. Bismarck had learned at the Frankfurt Diet to distrust Austria, was convinced she must be extruded from Germany, preliminary to German union under the leadership and domination of Prussia.

1863, Aug. A congress of princes, summoned by Emperor Francis Joseph to reform the Germanic Confederation, but really meant as a bait to German Liberalism, miscarried when Bismarck induced King William to refuse to attend. Bismarck's next opportunity came in connection with the highly complicated **Schleswig-Holstein question.** A royal proclamation of King Frederick VII of Denmark (1863, Mar. 30) in substance announced the annexation to Denmark of the Duchy of Schleswig. This act was a breach of the **London Protocol** (1852) by which the powers had guaranteed at once the inseparability of the duchies and their personal union with Denmark under the king, and also of an engagement given by Denmark to Austria and Prussia (Dec. 1851) not to incorporate Schleswig or treat it separately. Frederick's act also thrust a new charter on the Duchy of Holstein (which retained its independence), without consulting its representatives. This was to fly in the face of the Germanic Confederation, of which Holstein was a member. Expectation of English and Swedish support was an important factor in shaping Danish policy during 1863 and early 1864.

July. The Diet of the Germanic Confederation demanded that the two duchies should be taken forcibly from Denmark and submitted to the rule of the German Duke of Augustenburg (son of one of the claimants to the succession).

Oct. 1. The Diet voted federal execution (i.e. action against Denmark) and instructed Hanover and Saxony to furnish troops.

Nov. 15. Frederick VII died, and was succeeded by

Nov. 18. Christian IX, who promptly signed a newly drafted constitution (of Nov. 13), not formally incorporating Schleswig, but clearly tending to that end.

Dec. 24. Federal troops entered Holstein. The Diet was still supporting the Duke of Augustenburg, whose claims had been discarded by the London Protocol. Hence Bismarck could now separate Prussia from the action of the Diet and declare Prussia the upholder of the Protocol.

1864, Jan. 16. Austria joined Prussia in an alliance, and the two powers agreed to send an ultimatum to Denmark demanding repeal of the constitution (otherwise they would invade), to settle the future course of the duchies only "by mutual agreement."

Feb. 1. Austrian and Prussian troops invaded Schleswig, the new Prussian army of Roon and Moltke receiving its baptism of fire.

Feb. 5. The Danes quickly abandoned the defense of the *Dannewirke*; all Schleswig except Düppel and the island of Alsen were in the enemy's hands. The Düppel forts were not taken until April 18; the Germans were now invading Denmark.

Apr. 25-June. The **London Conference,** engineered by the British to save the Danes, miscarried, due to the cleverness of Bismarck and the stubbornness of the Danes.

June 26. The war was renewed, resulted in a crushing defeat for the Danes, the **surrender of the Duchies of Schleswig, Holstein, and Lauenburg** to Austria and Prussia (definitive **Peace of Vienna,** Oct. 30).

What was to become of the duchies, now the joint possession of Austria and Prussia? After prolonged negotiations, Bismarck maneuvered Austria, seriously embarrassed at home by political demands of the Magyars (p. 678), into

1865, Aug. 14. The **Convention of Gastein:** joint sovereignty was to be maintained, but Austria was to administer Holstein, Prussia to administer Schleswig (Lauenburg going to Prussia in return for a money payment to Austria). An impossible situation was created: Austrian Holstein became a virtual enclave in unfriendly Prussia. Under the skillful hand of Bismarck, Austro-Prussian relations rapidly worsened. Prussian relations with Russia were excellent.

Oct. At Biarritz **Bismarck met Napoleon III,** and appears to have dropped vague hints of compensation for France in the Rhineland, in return for which he won a promise of French neutrality from the emperor, convinced that Austria would be victor in the coming war.

1866, Apr. 8. Bismarck, aided by Napoleon, concluded an offensive and defensive **alliance with Italy:** Italy to join

Kings of Hanover

George III ═══════ Charlotte of
King of England │ Mecklenburg-Strelitz
King of Hanover
1814–1820

George IV   William IV   Ernest Augustus ═══ (3) Frederica
1820–1830   1830–1837   1837–1851 │ of Mecklenburg-
                                                 Strelitz

Marie ═══════ George V
of Altenburg │ 1851–1866

Ernest Augustus ═══ Thyra of   Frederica
D. of Cumberland │ Denmark
d. 1923

Marie Louise   George William   Alexandra   Olga   Victoria ═══ Ernest Augustus
m. Max of Baden   m. Frederick   Louise of │ D. of Brunswick
                            of Mecklenburg-   Prussia │ 1913–1918
                              Schwerin

Ernest Augustus   George William   Frederica   Christian   Henry
b. 1914   b. 1915   b. 1917   b. 1919   b. 1923

Prussia if war broke out between Austria and Prussia within three months, with Venetia as a reward.

Apr. 9. Bismarck introduced a motion for **federal reform** into the Frankfurt Diet, evidently with the idea that Austria would reject it and precipitate a conflict. Both parties began to mobilize. Last-minute efforts to compromise (**Gablenz mission**) proved fruitless.

June 6. The Austrian governor of Holstein summoned the Holstein Diet in order to discuss the future of the duchy. Bismarck denounced this as a violation of the Gastein Convention and ordered Prussian troops into the duchy.

June 12. Austria, realizing that conflict was inevitable, signed a **secret treaty with Napoleon III.** In return for French neutrality, Austria promised to cede Venetia to Napoleon (who was to retrocede it to Italy), whether Austria won or lost the war. In the event of Austrian victory, Austria was to be free to make what changes she wished in Germany, but if these changes disturbed the European balance of power (as they were bound to do), Austria was to

consult with Napoleon before making them. Verbally the Austrians agreed in this case not to oppose the erection of a **neutral buffer state** (client of France) along the Rhine.

June 14. On Austria's motion, the Frankfurt Diet voted **federal execution against Prussia** for violating federal (Holstein) territory. Most of the German states, including the larger ones like Bavaria, Saxony, and Hanover, sided with Austria against Prussia. The Prussian government declared the federal constitution violated and the **confederation at an end.** The war began.

1866, June-Aug. The **SEVEN WEEKS' WAR.** The war was fought in three theaters:

(1) Italy: the Italians were defeated on both land and sea (p. 659).

(2) Germany:

June 27-29. General Vogel von Falkenstein, with an army of some 50,000 men, defeated the Hanoverians at **Langensalza,** and forced them to capitulate. He turned to the South German allies of

Kings of Saxony

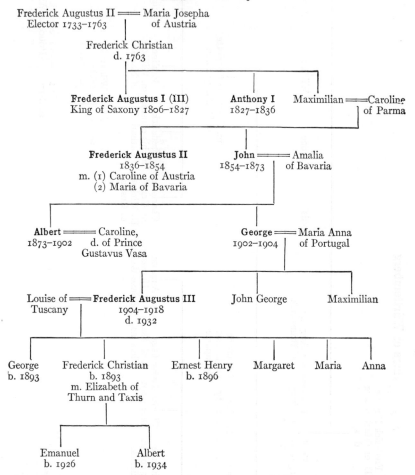

Austria, but before he could reach them the die had been cast in

(3) **Bohemia:** Moltke had learned golden lessons from the American Civil War on the uses of the telegraph and railroad. To accelerate concentration of his forces near Gitschin (Bohemia), he formed three armies, advanced them separately in order to make greatest use of existing railways, co-ordinating their movements from headquarters in Berlin by telegraph.

June 22-23. The First Army (**Prince Frederick Charles**) and the Army of the Elbe (**General Herwarth von Bittenfeld**) entered Bohemia through passes in the Erzgebirge and Riesengebirge. The

Second Army (**Crown Prince Frederick**) moved south through Silesia. The experience of the Austrian commander in chief, **Field Marshal Benedek,** had been limited to Italy, and he had never been called upon to command large numbers of troops. He was summoned to Bohemia so that an Austrian archduke, Albert, might be assured a victory in Italy. Benedek was, as it turned out, a sacrifice to the prestige of the house of Hapsburg.

July 2. Benedek's army was discovered to be within striking distance of the Prussian First Army and Army of the Elbe. At this critical moment the telegraph broke down. Late at night Moltke took

Kings of Württemberg

Kings of Bavaria

Christian III
D. of Zweibrücken
1733–1735

Frederick Michael === Maria Dorothea of Sulzbach

Wilhelmine (1) of Darmstadt === **Maximilian I Joseph** Elector of Bavaria 1799–1805, King of Bavaria 1805–1825 === (2) Caroline of Baden

Children of Maximilian I Joseph:
- **Louis I Augustus** 1825–1848 === Theresa of Hildburghausen
- Auguste m. Eugene Beauharnais
- Caroline m. (1) William I of Württemberg, (2) Francis I of Austria
- Charles
- Elizabeth m. Fred. William IV of Prussia
- Amalia m. King John of Saxony
- Sophie m. Archduke Francis Charles of Austria
- Maria m. Fred. Augustus II of Saxony
- Ludovica m. D. Maximilian Joseph of Bavaria → Ducal Line → Maximilian

Children of Louis I Augustus:
- **Maximilian II** 1848–1864 === Maria of Prussia
- Mathilda m. Louis III of Hesse
- **Luitpold** Regent 1886–1912 m. Auguste of Tuscany
- Adelgunde
- Hildegarde
- Adalbert

Children of Maximilian II:
- **Louis II** 1864–1886
- **Otto** 1886–1913

Children of Luitpold:
- **Louis III** 1913–1918 m. Maria Theresa of Este
- Leopold
- Arnulf
- Louis
- Charles Theodore m. Maria Josepha of Portugal
- Helen
- Elizabeth m. Francis Joseph I of Austria
- Maria m. Francis II of Naples

Children of Louis III:
- Crown Prince Ruprecht === Maria Gabriele of Bavaria
- 10 other children

Child of Ruprecht:
- Albrecht b. 1905

the fateful decision: instructed the First Army and Army of the Elbe to attack at dawn while he sent a courier twenty miles to fetch the crown prince's Second Army.

July 3. Battle of Königgrätz (Sadowa). The Austrians had the better of the battle until early afternoon, when the crown prince came up on the left and decided the issue in favor of the Prussians, who were much advantaged by the breech-loading "needle-gun," enabling the infantry to fire from prone positions at the standing Austrians (using muzzle-loaders).

The sudden and complete victory of the Prussians at Königgrätz was a stunning defeat for the policy of Napoleon, who had expected a long war, exhausting both belligerents.

July 5. Napoleon offered mediation, which Bismarck accepted only on condition that the terms of peace should be determined before an armistice was concluded. Napoleon — ill, his will crippled, unwilling to envisage the use of force — yielded; accepted Prussian terms imposed in the

July 26. Preliminary Peace at Nikolsburg: Hanover, Electoral Hesse, Nassau, Frankfurt were to be incorporated in Prussia; Austria was to be excluded from Germany (the Germanic Confederation came to an end); German states north of the Main River were to form a North German Confederation under Prussian leadership; the South German states were to remain independent and to be permitted to form a separate confederation. King William insisted on taking Austrian Silesia, territory from the South German states and Saxony. Bismarck had seen the importance of not provoking Napoleon for the moment, of not alienating Prussia's potential allies for the future. He resisted and won his point.

Aug. 5. Napoleon advanced his **claims for compensation:** the frontiers of 1814 (Saarbrücken, Landau) and possibly the Bavarian Palatinate or Rhenish Hesse (with Mainz), or Luxemburg. Bismarck brusquely rejected these claims as an offense to German national feeling.

Aug. 16. Napoleon instructed his ambassador, Count Vincent Benedetti, to ask for Luxemburg and for Prussian support for the **acquisition of Belgium** by France. Benedetti was induced by Bismarck to put these demands in writing, along with the French offer to sanction the union of North and South Germany in return (the **Benedetti Treaty**). Bismarck then took advantage of illness (Sept.–Dec.) to evade a definite reply. The

draft treaty was communicated to the English in 1870 and influenced British opinion in favor of Prussia during the war with France.

Aug. 9–22. Bismarck took advantage of the French demands to push his peace negotiations with the **South German states** (Baden, Württemberg, Bavaria). They were let off on very generous terms, but were induced, in return, to conclude with Prussia **military alliances** for the event of French attack.

Aug. 23. The Definitive Treaty of Prague brought the war to a close.

Sept. 8. Bill of Indemnity, by which Bismarck concluded the struggle with the Prussian parliament. An election during the war had strengthened the Conservatives at the expense of the Liberals. Many of the latter had come over to Bismarck in view of the fact that he was accomplishing their program of national unification. The bill of indemnity gave retroactive assent to previous expenditures of the government without the consent of the *Landtag.* It caused an important split in the ranks of liberalism, the majority of the Liberals rallying to Bismarck as the new **National Liberal Party** (leader, **Rudolf von Bennigsen**).

1867. THE NORTH GERMAN CONFEDERATION, formed through treaties between Prussia and the other states north of the river Main. The constitution was primarily the work of Bismarck himself. The new confederation was one in which the component states retained their own governments, but in which the military forces were controlled by the federal government (the King of Prussia, commander in chief). The **presidency** (*praesidium*) was held by the King of Prussia, represented by a **chancellor** (Bismarck), responsible to him alone. The **federal council** (*Bundesrat*) was composed of instructed delegates of the various states, among whom 43 votes were divided, Prussia having 17 and unofficially controlling the votes of several small North German states. The *Bundesrat* had constituent powers, but a two-thirds vote was required for constitutional changes. The **lower house** (*Reichstag*) shared equally with the *Bundesrat* in legislation. It was composed of deputies elected from single-member constituencies on the basis of universal suffrage. Bismarck had thus achieved two objects: the predominancy of Prussia in the new state, and the maintenance of the royal power against Liberal demands for responsible government.

1867, Apr. The Luxemburg crisis. This grew out of Napoleon's efforts (winter 1866–1867) to acquire the Duchy of Luxemburg from the King of the Netherlands, who was suzerain. Bismarck had promised not to oppose the deal, provided it were so engineered that German national feeling should not be aroused. The French mismanaged the affair, the news leaked out, Bismarck was interpellated in the new North German *Reichstag*, and the King of the Netherlands drew back from the arrangements he had made. There followed a period of acute crisis, which was closed by a compromise.

May 7-11. An International conference at London, which finally signed the Treaty of London (Sept. 9): Prussia abandoned her previous right to garrison the fortress of the town of Luxemburg. The duchy ceased to be a member of the Germanic Confederation. Its neutrality and independence were guaranteed by the powers. This settlement was a profound humiliation for Napoleon, who henceforth looked upon a final reckoning with Prussia as inevitable, reorganized his army and initiated negotiations for an alliance with Austria and Italy (p. 635).

July 8. Bismarck brought the four South German states into the *Zollverein* and established a *Zollparlament* (customs parliament) consisting of the North German Reichstag plus representatives of the South German states. This was effectively a parliament for all Germany, though still empowered to deal only with customs questions. In South Germany there was still much opposition to union with Prussia, due to cultural and religious differences and general suspicion, as well as attachment to states' rights. It became increasingly evident to Bismarck that only war with France and the specter of French domination in the Rhineland would drive the South German states into the union. War he regarded as inevitable, convinced as he was that France would not peaceably permit the inclusion of the South German states in the Confederation. The sudden appearance of the greatly strengthened neighbor alarmed the French and led to the demand of revenge for Sadowa and to much loose talk about the need of chastising overbearing Prussia.

1868-1870. The Hohenzollern candidacy for the Spanish throne. After the Spanish revolution (Sept. 1868) and the expulsion of Queen Isabella (p. 646), the provisional government of Marshal Serrano and General Prim made several attempts to secure one of the Portuguese Coburgs or one of the Italian princes as king. From the outset there had been talk of offering the throne to Prince Leopold of Hohen-

zollern-Sigmaringen, distant relative of both King William of Prussia and of Napoleon III. The part played by both French and Prussian diplomacy in the various candidacies is still quite obscure, but the Hohenzollern candidacy was taken up by Bismarck at least as early as Mar. 15, 1870 (mission of Salazar with letters from Prim, Hohenzollern "family" council). Prince Leopold refused to accept unless ordered by the king, but William, averse to the whole business, refused to take an active part. Bismarck, possibly seeking a reply to the French alliance project with Austria and Italy and desiring a connection with Spain which would oblige French troops to guard the frontier of Spain in the event of a Franco-Prussian war, sent special emissaries to Spain who returned (May) with glowing accounts.

1870, June 19. Leopold was induced to change his decision and accept the offer. King William gave a grudging consent, on condition that Leopold should be elected by a substantial vote of the Spanish Córtes.

July 2. Through misunderstanding, the Spanish Córtes was adjourned before a vote was taken. The secret leaked out and created a wave of consternation in France, fanned by the French foreign minister, Duke of Gramont.

July 6. Gramont made a famous speech in the French Chamber indicating war unless the Prussian government withdrew the candidacy. The Prussian government, however, disclaimed all knowledge of the affair, which it insisted on describing as a family matter.

July 9, 11. The French ambassador, Count Benedetti, having followed King William to Ems, where he was taking a cure, asked that he order Leopold to withdraw. The king refused, but sent a secret emissary to advise Leopold to that effect.

July 12. Prince Charles Anthony, father of Leopold, withdrew the candidacy in behalf of his son, who was absent in the Alps. Not content with this diplomatic victory, Gramont and the French government now proceeded to demand satisfaction and guaranties from King William (he was to write Napoleon a letter of apology, officially disavow the candidacy, and promise that it would never be renewed).

July 13. At a famous interview at Ems, the king rejected Benedetti's demands and repulsed all efforts of the ambassador to continue the discussion. On the same day Bismarck met with Roon and

Moltke in Berlin. On receiving a report of the happening at Ems, he revised it for publication, giving it a brusque quality and conveying the impression that the negotiations at Ems had ended in what was tantamount to the rupture of relations. The importance of the **Ems telegram** has probably been exaggerated, for it is now clear that the French court (with the possible exception of Napoleon himself) was determined on a humiliation of Prussia, even at the cost of war.

July 15. The French took the decision for war, relying on the preparedness of the army and on the support of Austria and Italy.

July 19. France declared war on Prussia.

1870-1871. THE FRANCO-GERMAN WAR. Bismarck had at once the armed support of the South German states and the benevolent neutrality of Russia. The war party in Vienna was a threat which would become serious in case of Prussian defeats. In England Gladstone was interested only in the preservation of **Belgian neutrality,** reassured in new treaties with France and Prussia (Aug. 9).

Three German armies invaded France. **General Steinmetz** from the Moselle, **Prince Frederick Charles** from the Palatinate on Metz, **Crown Prince Frederick** from the upper Rhine on Strasbourg. A French army advanced into the Saar, won a minor victory at Saarbrücken. Then the German avalanche began.

Aug. 4, 6. The crown prince won victories over Marshal MacMahon at **Wörth** and **Weissenburg,** forced him to evacuate Alsace, invested Strasbourg, advanced on Nancy. **Marshal Bazaine** was soon shut up in Metz by the other two German armies.

Aug. 16, 18. In bloody battles at **Mars-la-Tour** and **Gravelotte** Bazaine's attempts to break through the Prussian lines were repulsed. Metz was besieged, the advance on Châlons begun. When MacMahon attempted to relieve Bazaine at Metz, he found the road closed, and was decisively defeated in the

Sept. 1. Battle of Sedan. The army, with the Emperor Napoleon himself, capitulated the following day. (For the siege of Paris and remaining events of the war, see p. 636.)

1871, Jan. 18. FOUNDATION OF THE GERMAN EMPIRE. During the war German public opinion demanded the union of North and South Germany. Bismarck negotiated separately with each state, making essential concessions. By the end of November treaties had been signed with all. On Dec. 2, King Ludwig

II of Bavaria addressed a letter to King William (drafted by Bismarck at Ludwig's invitation) inviting him to assume the imperial title. The king was averse to having the Prussian title subordinated to that of the empire, but yielded to the general wish.

1871, Jan. 18. William I was proclaimed German Emperor in the Hall of Mirrors at Versailles. The constitution of the North German Confederation was then remodeled in terms of the agreements reached with the various states and was adopted (Apr. 14) by a freshly elected *Reichstag,* representative of the new empire. The new *Reich* included 25 states — four kingdoms (Prussia, Bavaria, Saxony, Württemberg); five grand duchies; 13 duchies and principalities; three free cities (Hamburg, Bremen, Lübeck). **Alsace-Lorraine** (annexed as a result of the war) was designated *Reichsland,* given an imperial governor (*Statthalter*), and made the common property of all the German states.

g. THE GERMAN EMPIRE, 1871-1914

1871-1883. The *Kulturkampf.* As chancellor of the new German Empire, Bismarck's first struggle was with the Catholic Church in the so-called *Kulturkampf,* from the words used by Rudolf Virchow in the Prussian Diet (1873, Jan. 17): "The contest has taken on the character of a great cultural struggle (*Kulturkampf*)." The conflict grew out of the coincident expansion of papal pretensions and German power: the promulgation of the **dogma of papal infallibility** (p. 664), implying the extension of papal pretensions to defend the Church against encroachments of the state, came just at the time of the creation of the German Empire, determined to subordinate all groups within the state to its sovereign power.

German bishops and the vast majority of lay Catholics promptly accepted the dogma of papal infallibility, despite the resistance of the liberal group (*Old Catholics*).

1871, Mar. Heterogeneous Catholic elements organized the **Center Party** during the first elections to the imperial *Reichstag* to defend Catholic interests — leader, **Ludwig Windthorst** (1812–1891). In general, the Center Party represented particularist Catholic interests in opposition to the pretensions of Protestant Prussia, hence it was anti-imperial. When, of all parties in the *Reichstag,* only the National Liberals supported the new state, the anti-imperial attitude of the Center irritated and alarmed Bismarck. Hence the Prussian government supported Catholic teachers in state schools who refused to accept the dogma of papal infallibility, and

July 8. Abolished the Roman Catholic department for spiritual affairs (recognized by the constitution of 1850). "Have no fear — to Canossa we shall not go, either in body or spirit," declared Bismarck to the *Reichstag* (1872, May 14).

1872, June 25. An imperial law permitted the **expulsion of the Jesuits**; the Jesuit organization was dissolved, the Jesuits expelled from Germany.

1873, May. **The May Laws or Falk Laws.** Dr. Adalbert Falk, Prussian minister of public worship, was responsible for four drastic measures: (1) making it a punishable offense for servants of the Church to impose penalties in matters not of a religious character; (2) placing education of the clergy under state supervision and giving the Government a right of veto on all clerical appointments; (3) facilitating secession from the Church for those who wished to leave it; (4) subjecting ecclesiastical discipline of the Catholic clergy to state control. The struggle rapidly became embittered.

1875, Feb. 6. **Civil marriage was made obligatory** for the empire. A papal letter to Prussian bishops at the same time declared null and void all Prussian laws which denied and sought to undermine the divine sanction and authority of the Church. Publication of this letter was forbidden by the Prussian government.

Apr. 6. The Prussian Diet passed the **Breadbasket Bill,** suspending all grants to the Church in sees whose clergy refused obedience to Prussian laws.

May 8. Religious orders and congregations, with the exception of those engaged in nursing the sick, were dissolved.

May. The war scare, an acute crisis in the relations of Germany and France (p. 733).

May. **SOCIALIST CONGRESS AT GOTHA.** Adoption of the Gotha program and formation of the **Socialist Workingmen's Party.** The growth of socialism was the result of the rapid industrial development of Germany and the conversion of the working classes to political action. **Ferdinand Lassalle** (1825–1864), son of a prosperous merchant, was the founder of German social democracy. In lectures on the "Workers' Program" (1862) he insisted on the importance of universal suffrage as a means of obtaining state help

for producers' co-operative societies. He opposed all violence. In May 1863 he organized the **Universal German Workingmen's Association,** of which he became president, with almost dictatorial power. It numbered fewer than 5000 members at the time of Lassalle's death in a duel (Aug. 31, 1864). Leadership soon passed to the **Marxian Socialists.** After the organization of the International Workingmen's Association (the **First International**) at London in 1864, Karl Marx (p. 550) sent **Wilhelm Liebknecht** (1826–1900) to Germany to organize labor along Marxian lines. Expelled from Prussia, Liebknecht took refuge in Saxony, where he met **August Bebel** (1840–1913), a woodturner of Catholic family and originally of monarchist sympathies. Liebknecht won Bebel to the cause and he became the outstanding parliamentary leader of the movement. At the **Eisenach Congress** of representatives of workingmen's associations (Aug. 1869) the Marxians had a majority and formed the **Social Democratic Workingmen's Party,** devoted to political action. Liebknecht and Bebel, the only two Socialist members of the North German *Reichstag*, withheld their votes when war credits were granted in July 1870 and joined the Lassalleans in voting (Sept. 1870) against the continuation of a war which they regarded as no longer defensive. Bismarck's attacks upon both groups drove them into union. At the **Gotha Congress** (1875) they united on an essentially Lassallean program, which Marx bitterly criticized.

1876, Jan. **Opening of the Imperial Bank** (*Reichsbank*), an institution which was to play a major part in the economic development of the country.

1878, May 11. Attempt on the life of the emperor by **Emil Hödel,** a deranged radical. Bismarck's proposal for repressive legislation rejected by the *Reichstag* (May 24).

June 27. Another attempt on the emperor's life by **Dr. Karl Nobiling,** an educated radical. The emperor was badly wounded.

June 13-July 13. **The Congress of Berlin** (p. 736).

July 30. In the elections for the *Reichstag* the Conservatives made substantial gains at the expense of the National Liberals.

Oct. 19. **PASSAGE OF THE ANTI-SOCIALIST LAW,** renewed at intervals until 1890. The electoral campaign was waged largely on the question of repressing socialism, though neither of the would-be assassins of the emperor was a socialist. The law prohibited meetings, publications, and collections of money which by "means of social democratic, socialistic or communistic designs, aim at the overthrow of the existing order of state or society." Rigorous measures were provided for its execution, though the Reichstag steadfastly refused (Mar. 7, 1879) to gag debate in parliament or to interfere with the Socialist deputies. In the next 12 years socialism was driven underground.

1878-1879. Negotiations with the papacy for the cessation of the *Kulturkampf*. By this time half the bishops in Germany had been displaced and many of them had fled abroad. Hundreds of clerics had been removed and many imprisoned, yet the fight continued as obstinately as ever. In 1878 Pius IX died and was succeeded by Leo XIII, a much more diplomatic pope, who at once opened negotiations with the German government. He demanded the abrogation of the May Laws, but Bismarck would agree to nothing more than administrative dilution of the laws, and only with the proviso that the pope would guarantee pre-notification of clerical appointments to the government (carrying the right of the government to object). This proposal was rejected by Rome.

1879, June 30. Resignation of Falk, the minister officially connected with the policy. Bismarck, satisfied by this time that he had overrated the danger from organized Catholicism and requiring the support of the Center Party for his new tariff program, began to introduce ameliorative measures on his own initiative. Repressive laws were abrogated or neglected over a period of years until by 1883 the *Kulturkampf* may be said to have come to an end.

July 12. The new (protective) **TARIFF LAW.** Thus far Germany had been following a policy of free trade, which was supported by the National Liberals, though opposed by the landholding Conservative groups. But German industry was hard hit by the **financial crisis of 1873** and the ensuing depression, as well as by the **crisis in agriculture** produced by foreign competition. Both the industrialists and the landowners began to inveigh against free trade. The government itself was influenced to return to protection because, depending upon customs and excise duties for its income, it found itself in perennial need of funds. The new tariff gave protection to both industry and agriculture. It was supported by the Conservatives, who gave up their earlier opposition to the empire and became supporters of the government, by the Catholic Center and by part of the National Liberals, representing industry. The Liberal Party split for a second time, the dissidents going over to the Progressive Party.

In the decades following the introduction of protection, German industry underwent a phenomenal development comparable to that of the United States. Possessed of vast supplies of coal and very extensive iron deposits, German industry was able to meet competitors. Between 1860 and 1913 pig-iron production grew from 529,000 metric tons to 19,309,000: Germany passed France and England as producers and was second only to the United States on the eve of the war. She occupied the same position as a producer of steel. Railway mileage grew from 18,887 kilometers (1870) to 61,749 (1914); the merchant marine from 980,000 tons (1870) to 5,450,000 (1914), placing the Germans third after Great Britain and the United States. Foreign trade grew with similar rapidity, doubled between 1902 and 1913; at the latter date Germany was close on the heels of England for first place. With the development of industry, the German social scene rapidly changed: from 1882 to 1907 the number of persons employed in and dependent upon industry rose from 16,058,080 to 26,386,537, while the total number dependent on agriculture decreased more than a million and a half. Urbanization was equally striking: 8,600,000 persons lived in cities of 20,000 or more (1885), representing 18.4% of the population; by 1910 this number had increased to 22,400,000, 34.5% of the population.

1879, Oct. 7. Signature of the alliance between **Germany and Austria,** the foundation of the **Bismarckian alliance system** (p. 736).

1881, June 18. Conclusion of the **Three Emperors' League** (Germany, Austria, and Russia, p. 737). Renewed, 1884, for three years.

1882, May 20. Conclusion of the Triple Alliance (Germany, Austria, Italy, p. 738).

1883, May. Sickness Insurance Law, the first of Bismarck's great measures of "state socialism" by which he hoped to wean the workers from socialism. The law insured workers during sickness; the costs to be paid two-thirds by the workers, one-third by employers. This measure was followed by the **Accident Insurance Law** (June 1884), paid for entirely by the employers and extended to practically all wage-earning groups; the **Old-Age and Invalidity Insurance Law** (May 1889), of which the costs were divided between the employers and workers, with state contributions to pensions.

1883-1885. Foundation of the German colonial empire. Friction with England (p. 738).

1886, Dec.—1887, Mar. Parliamentary conflict over an **army bill,** the Liberal parties making an effort to secure control over appropriations. After elections the government, through the intervention of the pope, secured the support of the Center Party and won its point.

1887, Apr. The **Schnaebele affair,** marking the height of tension in Franco-German relations and in European affairs generally. Renewal of the Triple Alliance, conclusion of the **Reinsurance Treaty** with Russia, formation of the **Mediterranean Coalition** (p. 740).

1888, Mar. 9-June 15. FREDERICK III (b. 1831) who succeeded on the death of William I.

1888-1918. WILLIAM II (1859-1941), who followed on the death of his father, Frederick III, of cancer of the throat. The young emperor, intelligent, charming, idealistic, but impulsive and headstrong, soon evinced the desire to rule the state himself. He showed sympathy for the workers and was called the *Labor Emperor.*

1890, Jan. After two readings of a bill to prolong the anti-socialist law it was rumored that the emperor had changed his mind and favored a policy of mildness. The bill was lost, but it opened a rift between the chancellor and the emperor, which was widened when the latter proposed (Feb.) an international conference on labor questions, opposed by Bismarck as a further weak concession to the Socialists. The emperor wished to set aside the right of the chancellor to be present at interviews of the emperor and ministers. On Russo-German policy the two differed basically (p. 741). The fundamental question was who should rule the empire — the emperor or Bismarck? After further irritating incidents, Bismarck was ordered to "ask permission to resign," but refused.

Mar. 18. RESIGNATION OF BISMARCK, on imperial command. He was made Duke of Lauenburg, but unceremoniously "ejected" from the chancery palace.

1890-1894. Chancellorship of General Georg Leo von Caprivi (1831-1899), able soldier, sober and capable administrator, but without political experience, chosen to carry out the emperor's wishes. The emperor hoped through social legislation to win the workers from socialism.

July 29. Industrial courts were set up to adjust wage disputes. Weekday employment of women and children was restricted, Sunday rest made obligatory for all workers.

1891, June 1. Factory inspection was made more efficient. Workers were given the right to form committees to negotiate with employers on conditions of employment.

1892, Mar. 26. A **labor department** was formed in the imperial statistical office, to bring the whole province of labor under more complete survey. But the emperor's hopes of winning the workers from socialism were disappointed. Socialism spread rapidly after the repeal of the anti-socialist legislation and attracted much non-socialist, liberal support. In the elections of 1890 the Socialists returned 35 deputies to the *Reichstag.* At the **Erfurt Congress** (1891) the party adopted a more strictly Marxian program.

1892-1894. The Caprivi commercial treaties, with Austria, Italy, Switzerland, Spain, Serbia, Rumania, Belgium, and ultimately Russia (1894). They substantially reduced agricultural duties, thereby relieving the prices on foods (seriously high in 1891-1892) and laying the basis for the expansion of German trade in industrial products in the treaty countries. These treaties recognized the preponderance of German industry over agriculture and drew upon Caprivi's head the wrath of the landowners, who organized (1894) the **Agrarian League** (*Bund der Landwirte*), with which the older German **Peasants' League** (*Deutscher Bauernbund*) amalgamated. The Agrarian League wrung numerous concessions from the government and came more and more to serve as a spearhead for conservatism in the political sense.

1894, Oct. 26. Resignation of Caprivi, who had estranged not only the agrarians, but the Center (through his failure to carry the **Prussian School Bill** in 1890), the colonialists (through the **East Africa Agreement** with England, 1890, p. 741), and the militarists (through the **reduction of the term of service in the infantry** from three to two years, 1893). Caprivi was also harassed by the independence and unexpected initiatives of the emperor, with whom he found it increasingly difficult to work.

1894-1900. Chancellorship of Prince Chlodwig zu Hohenlohe-Schillingsfürst (1819-1901), former Bavarian statesman, diplomat, governor of Alsace-Lorraine, *grand seigneur,* now in his old age and little inclined to oppose openly the will and vagaries of the emperor.

1895, June. Opening of the **Kiel Canal** from the North Sea to the Baltic.

1896, Jan. 3. The **Kruger telegram** episode, marking the first violent outbreak of popular hostility between Germany and England (p. 744).

July 1. The **Civil Code** (in process of elaboration since 1871) was enacted, to come into effect Jan. 1, 1900.

1897, Nov. German occupation of **Kiao-Chow**, on the Chinese coast (pp. 746, 882).

1898, Mar. 28. Passage of the first German **Navy Law**, through the efforts of Admiral **Alfred von Tirpitz**, minister of marine since 1897. It marked the beginning of German naval expansion and the gradual emergence of friction with England on this score.

Nov. 27. Preliminary concession for the **Baghdad Railway** secured by the *Deutsche Bank*, marking active German expansion in the Near East and the development of friction with England and Russia (p. 749).

1899, Dec. 7. A law permitting the **federation of societies** of all kinds. This was Hohenlohe's reply to Liberal and Socialist agitation for broadening of the association laws.

1900, Oct. 16. Hohenlohe resigned.

1900–1909. Chancellorship of Count (later Prince) **Bernhard von Bülow**, diplomat, who had been foreign minister and intimate adviser of the emperor since June 1897. Bülow was a man of brilliant parts, an accomplished *causeur* and orator and a finished manipulator of men, but he lacked Bismarck's seriousness of purpose, strength of character and breadth of view. His tenure of office was marked primarily by major issues in foreign and colonial policy (p. 746). In domestic policy the chief developments were the extension of social insurance.

1900. Accident insurance was extended to new occupations. The **Old-Age and Invalidity Law** had already been amended (June 1899) to increase old age and invalid pensions and extend compulsory insurance to various new groups.

June 11. Prussia enacted a law empowering local authorities to remove children from their homes if they were in danger of demoralization and place them in institutions — a law much criticized as invading parental rights.

June 12. The second German Naval Law, providing for a 17-year building program and the construction of a high-

seas fleet which would be second only to that of England. Tirpitz' idea of risk — Germany to have a navy so strong that even the strongest naval power would hesitate before attacking it.

1902, Dec. 14. The new **Tariff Law**, enacted on the expiration of the Caprivi treaties. It restored the higher duty of agricultural products and was the reflection of the power of the Agrarian League. The Conservatives supported the naval policy (advocated especially by big business interests) in return for adequate protection in their own lines.

1903, Apr. 30. The Sickness Insurance Law amended to give longer and more generous help to workers in ill health (26 weeks instead of 13).

1905–1906. The first Moroccan crisis (p. 753).

1906, Dec. Parliamentary crisis. The Center Party, which had held the balance since 1890 and had extracted many favors from the government, turned against the administration, defeated a bill for the reorganization of the colonial office and refused funds for military operations against the Hereros in Southwest Africa (in revolt since 1904). The Reichstag was dissolved and Bülow called on the Conservatives, National Liberals, and Progressives to subordinate party to national interests, to combat the Center and the Socialists. In the elections the Socialists suffered heavily and the government was able to form a coalition of parties in its support.

1906–1910. Dr. **Bernhard Dernburg**, minister for the colonies. He studied British methods of administration, revolutionized the German system and made sweeping changes in favor of the natives.

1908, Dec. 9. A law restricted hours of factory work by young people and women (no children under 13 to be employed, 6-hour day for children 13–14, 10-hour day for those 14–16, etc.).

Nov. *The Daily Telegraph* episode, resulting from the publication in an English paper of an interview with the emperor on Anglo-German relations. The emperor pictured the German people as hostile to England, while he was friendly. The affair created a furor in the *Reichstag* and a widespread demand for some check on the emperor's power. Bülow, who was responsible, directly or indirectly, for the publication of the interview, defended the emperor but weakly.

1909, July 14. Bülow resigned.

1909–1917. Chancellorship of Dr. **Theobald von Bethmann-Hollweg.** Beth-

mann had won a high reputation as minister for the interior. He was a typical bureaucrat of the best type, sound, industrious, honest, well-intentioned, but lacking in imagination and brilliance.

1910. Religious affairs. A violent controversy had developed from the papal encyclical *De pascendi dominici gregis* (1907, Sept. 18), directed against "modernist" heresies and requiring priests and teachers of the Church to take an oath against modernism. This seemed to threaten again an invasion of the state province of education. But the pope promised (in a letter to the German prelacy, 1910, Feb. 1) that the oath would be restricted to priest-professors and would not be required of professors engaged in purely lay functions. Protestant sentiment had also been aroused by the encyclical *Editio saepe* (1910, May 26) which referred in scathing terms to the Reformation and association of certain German princes with it. In reply to a tactful remonstrance from the Prussian government, the pope denied (June 11) any intention of wounding Protestant susceptibilities and decided that the encyclical should not be circulated in Germany.

1910, Nov.—1911, Aug. The **Potsdam Agreement** between Germany and Russia concerning their interests in the Near East (p. 757).

1911, May 26. A law was passed organizing **Alsace and Lorraine as a state**, with a two-chamber legislature and a large measure of autonomy.

May 30. The **Imperial Insurance Code** consolidated all previous workers' insurance laws and amended and extended their provisions. Certain groups of white-collar workers were insured against sickness, old age, and death, by a separate and simultaneous law.

July 1. Mission of the gunboat *Panther* to Agadir, thereby precipitating the **second Moroccan crisis** (p. 757).

1912, Jan. **Elections to the Reichstag.** The Socialists polled 4,250,000 votes and, with 110 deputies, became the strongest party in the Reichstag. By this time the movement had become much modified through the "revisionist" tendency introduced by **Eduard Bernstein** (1850–1932). The revisionists sought to divert interest from the "ultimate goal" of socialism and to fasten attention on the importance of gradual advancement, through parliamentary reforms, toward a new social world. This theory was denounced as a heresy at the **Lübeck Congress** (1901, especially by **Karl Kautsky** and **Rosa**

Luxemburg), but it nevertheless colored the outlook of the party, which was further influenced by the rapid progress of the trade-union movement, dominated by moderate views. After the serious setback of the Socialists in the election of 1907, revisionism became more and more generally accepted. The party began to take an active part in work for social reform and collaborated with the Progressives in organizing the *Reichstag* in 1912. In 1914 the Social Democrats voted for the war credits, defending their action as necessary for the defense of the fatherland against autocratic Russia.

Feb. **Visit of Lord Haldane to Berlin.** Abortive attempt to effect a naval agreement between England and Germany (p. 758).

1913, June 30. The **Army and Finance Bills.** In the midst of the tension which preceded the outbreak of the World War, the government had little difficulty in securing the passage of its army bills. But all previous bills were eclipsed by the bill of 1913, providing for the addition of 4000 officers, 15,000 non-commissioned officers, 117,000 men, as part of a program to increase the peacetime strength of the army from 544,000 to 870,000 men. The Socialists, Poles, and Alsatians voted against it, but all other parties supported the government, and the bill passed. The cost of the measure was estimated at one billion marks, of which 435,000,000 was to fall due in 1913. In the **Finance Law** there was provision for a special national defense tax (*Wehrsteuer*), to be levied only once on real and personal property and income. The incidence was to be on the well-to-do classes, as a concession to the Socialists and other radicals: the Socialists therefore voted the funds, though they had voted against the military measures for which the funds were intended.

1913, Dec. The **Zabern affair**, resulting from the action of a German officer in striking and wounding a lame cobbler with his sword and insulting Alsatian recruits. The incident created much excitement and embittered Franco-German relations. (*Cont. pp.* 912 *ff.*, 995.)

h. AUSTRIA-HUNGARY, 1867-1914

The task of the Emperor Francis Joseph was to make the dualist system work. In law he ruled through responsible ministries in both Austria and Hungary, but in fact little could be done in either state without affecting "common concerns" and in these the emperor-king was able to make his will felt. In foreign affairs and military questions he enjoyed far-reaching powers. The foreign minister was offically responsible to the delegations, but in practice it was almost impossible not to endorse his policy so long as he enjoyed the confidence of the emperor.

(1) *Austria,* 1867-1914

1867, Dec. 21. Four fundamental laws of a liberal character reformed the February Patent (p. 678) and became the Constitution of 1867. This was a concession aimed to win the approval of the German Liberals for the compromise with Hungary.

1867, Dec.—1870, Jan. Ministry of Count Auersperg, representing the German Liberals, who were a minority of all the Germans (these in turn constituting hardly more than a third of the total population). The Liberals were determined to maintain administrative centralization and oppose the federalist pretensions of the Slavs. Once in power they passed a number of anti-clerical measures:

1868, May 25. Civil marriage was restored.

1870, July 30. The concordat with the papacy (of 1855) was suspended as a reply to the promulgation of the dogma of papal infallibility.

1871, Feb.-Oct. 25. Ministry of Count Hohenwart, representing the federalist groups. The Czechs and other Slavs had protested vigorously against the compromise, had boycotted the parliament and had demanded local autonomy. When hopes of recovery of the Austrian position in Germany had disappeared, the emperor, who distrusted the anti-clericalism of the German Liberals, turned to these opposition groups. Hohenwart prepared a scheme to meet the demands of the Czechs, to whom far-reaching promises were made.

Sept. 12. The Bohemian Diet went further, and demanded a position in Austria similar to that of Hungary in the Dual Monarchy. This was opposed by the Hungarians as endangering the "unity" of the empire, and was rejected by the emperor. Hohenwart was obliged to resign.

1871, Nov.—1878. Second ministry of Count Auersperg and the German Liberals. The position of the ministry was unstable after the financial crisis of 1873, when a number of leading Liberals and even ministers were discredited by speculation. The Liberal group rapidly dissolved into conflicting factions.

1875-1878. Acute Near-Eastern crisis, arising from the insurrection in Bosnia-Herzegovina and the war of Russia against Turkey (p. 734).

1878, June-July. The Austrian government, by European mandate, was given the right to occupy Bosnia and Herzegovina, which were put under the administration of the ministry of common finance. The step aroused much opposition among both Germans and Magyars, who disliked the annexation of more Slavs. In the provinces a serious revolt broke out (1882), which was not suppressed until Oct.

1879, Aug.—1893, Oct. 29. Ministry of Count Taaffe, a boyhood friend of the emperor. Faced by the opposition of the German Liberals, Taaffe was obliged to rule with a coalition of Czechs, Poles, and German Conservatives and Clericals (the *Iron Ring*), which in turn extracted from him numerous concessions (language rights, etc.).

In the face of a rising labor movement, Taaffe adopted a policy much like that of Bismarck. Socialism was repressed with great severity, but the government passed legislation providing protection for workers, shortening of the working day, measures of insurance, etc.

1879, Oct. 7. Signature of the Austrian Alliance with Germany (p. 736).

1881, June 18. Austria-Hungary joined Germany and Russia in the Three Emperors' Alliance (p. 737).

1882, May 20. Austria joined Germany and Italy in the Triple Alliance (p. 738).

1885-1888. Acute tension between Austria and Russia resulting from the development of the Bulgarian problem. Non-renewal of the Three Emperors' Alliance (1887), renewal of the Triple Alliance (1887), and conclusion of the Mediterranean Agreements with England and Italy (Feb., Dec. 1887, see p. 740).

1889, Jan. 30. Suicide of Archduke Rudolf, only son of Francis Joseph and heir to the throne, at Mayerling. The Archduke Francis Ferdinand (1863-1914), nephew of the emperor, became heir.

1893, Oct. 29. Resignation of Count Taaffe, due to the breakdown of his governing coalition. The opposition of the Germans, who had formed a nationalist group, and the rise of the Young Czechs (more radical than their predecessors) had rendered his policy of muddling along impossible. Taaffe had tried to solve the problem by introducing a bill providing for universal manhood suffrage (1893, Oct. 10), hoping thereby to counteract the nationalist agitation with the weight of socialism. The bill was rejected by Conservatives and Liberals of all stamps.

1895, Sept.—1897, Nov. Ministry of Count Casimir Badeni, a Polish landlord. He attempted to solve the nationality problem by conciliating the Czechs.

1897, Apr. 5. The Badeni Language Ordinances, establishing parity between German and the local language in a given district.

1897, Apr. Austro-Russian Agreement to maintain the *status quo* in the Balkans (p. 728).

Nov. 28. Badeni was forced to resign as a result of violent German agitation against his language ordinances and hot debate on the decennial renewal of the economic arrangements with Hungary. There followed a period of acute constitutional crisis, which brought the monarchy to the verge of dissolution and made parliamentary government utterly impossible.

1898, Mar. New laws divided Bohemia into a Czech, a German, and a mixed linguistic district, but this effort at compromise satisfied no one. On Oct. 14, 1899, the original arrangements were restored, despite objection and obstruction from the Czechs, who engaged in widespread disorders.

1898, Sept. 10. Assassination of the Empress Elizabeth at Geneva, by the Italian anarchist, Luigi Luccheni.

1900, Jan.—1904, Dec. Ministry of Ernst von Körber, an able bureaucrat, who governed with a ministry of officials, chiefly by decree. His efforts to effect a compromise on the language question proved as fruitless as those of his predecessors.

1907, Jan. 26. Law introducing universal, equal, and direct suffrage for parliamentary elections. This subject had been hotly debated for years and was vigorously demanded by the Socialists. The effect of it was to stress social stratification and interests, though the nationality problem remained an open sore.

The ministries from 1907 to 1914 were for the most part non-parliamentary (i.e. lacked a parliamentary majority), ruling by decree and making concessions to particular groups to secure support for particular measures.

1908, Oct. 6. Annexation of Bosnia and Herzegovina by decree. This ushered in the acute **Bosnian annexation crisis** and a period of tension in Austro-

Russian relations that lasted until the World War (p. 756).

1912-1913. The Balkan wars (p. 759 *f.*). The victories of Serbia and Austrian efforts to block Serbian expansion led to a marked growth of Yugoslav agitation and to a revival of Slavic activity within the monarchy.

1914, June 28. Assassination of the Archduke Francis Ferdinand at Sarajevo. He was known to be hostile to Magyar pretensions and favorably disposed toward a reorganization of the monarchy along "trialistic" lines, i.e. giving the Slavic elements a position on a par with that of Germans and Magyars.

(*Cont. pp.* 914 *ff.*, 1005.)

(2) *Hungary*, 1867-1914

1867, Feb. 17. The Constitution of 1848 was restored in Hungary. A ministry was formed under **Count Julius Andrássy**, remaining in power until Nov., 1871.

June 8. Francis Joseph crowned King of Hungary at Budapest.

1868, May 4. In face of opposition from the Independence party, Andrássy's government agreed to the establishment of a common army for the Dual Monarchy, with German the language of command.

Sept. The king agreed to the **reunion of Croatia** with Hungary (separated since 1848). Despite opposition from military circles, the king also permitted **abolition of the military frontier province** (*Militärgrenze*), adjacent to the southern boundary of Hungary, which had been administered for two centuries by the Austrian war office as a safety zone against the Turks. It was now incorporated with Croatia.

1875, Feb. Formation of the Liberal Party by Kálmán Tisza (1830–1902). It was composed of the larger part of the Independence Party, which had fought the Compromise of 1867, and the larger part of the Deák Party, which had disintegrated.

Aug. The elections gave the new party a great majority.

1875, Oct. 20—1890, Mar. 7. Ministry of Kálmán Tisza. Accepting the compromise, Tisza devoted his energies to strengthening the Magyar position in Hungary, notably by various school and language regulations designed to Magyarize the new generation among the subject nationalities.

1876, Jan. 28. Death of Francis Deák.

1894, Mar. 20.   Death of Louis Kossuth, at Turin. In the previous decade there had been a marked revival of the Independence Party, the leadership of which was assumed by Kossuth's son, Francis. This party kept stressing the weaknesses of the compromise and demanding fuller independence for Hungary. Economic differences between industrial Austria and agrarian Hungary served to sharpen the tension, as demonstrated in the heated arguments over the renewal of the economic compromise in 1897.

1903. The dispute reached the acute phase in the struggle over the army, the Magyars resenting the unified system. An increase in the number of recruits was vigorously opposed by the Independence Party, which insisted on the use of Magyar insignia in the Hungarian regiments and the substitution of Magyar for German as the language of command. This the king flatly refused to consider.

Sept. 16. In a proclamation to the army, Francis Joseph declared that he would "never yield the rights and duties guaranteed to its supreme commander," and that he would maintain the army, common and unified, at all costs. This declaration raised a storm in Hungary.

Oct. 26—1905, Feb. 1.   Ministry of Count Stephen Tisza (1861–1918), son of Kálmán Tisza.

1904. Mar. 11. Tisza secured the passage of the recruits bill after he had threatened drastic measures (*guillotine bill*) to deal with parliamentary obstruction.

1905, Jan. In the elections Tisza and the Liberal Party, having refused to make use of the customary corruption, were completely defeated. The Independents had 163 seats as against the Liberals' 152. Kossuth formed a coalition with several of the smaller parties and renewed the demand for the Magyar language of command, refusing to recognize the non-parliamentary government set up by Baron Géza Fejérváry. The crisis, which continued despite innumerable efforts to reach a compromise, dragged on until broken by the king's threat to introduce universal suffrage. This was designed to break the preponderance of the Magyars and was hotly resisted by all parties.

1906, July.   The Universal Suffrage Bill was actually brought before the Hungarian parliament. This brought the Independence Party to its senses. The military demands were abandoned.

1906-1910.   Parliamentary government of Dr. Alexander Wekerlé, governing with the support of the coalition parties.

1910-1913.   Ministry of Count Khuen-Héderváry, in which Tisza was the dominating figure. Tisza was convinced of the importance of ending the internecine struggles in Hungary and of strengthening the common army in face of European danger of war. By expending large sums of money he reorganized the old Liberal Party as the National Party of Work, and won an overwhelming victory in the elections of 1910. Nevertheless the Independents, again in opposition, continued obstructive tactics.

1912.   Tisza, as president of the lower house, succeeded in modifying parliamentary procedure and forced through the army bill, after ejecting the opposition by force.

1913, June 15—1917, May 23.   Tisza prime minister, exercising far-reaching authority not only in Hungary, but in the councils of the Dual Monarchy.

In Hungary, as in Austria, though to a less extent, the disintegrating forces of nationalism made themselves felt. There was constant friction with the Croatians (especially in 1903) which the government tried to meet by encouraging the Serb elements against the Croats. In Transylvania the Rumanian irredentist agitation developed rapidly. The government suppressed it to the best of its ability, but thereby created much ill-feeling in Rumania proper. Tisza was eager for an understanding, especially with the Rumanians, but like all Magyar statesmen, he rejected the idea of universal suffrage, which would have given the subject nationalities a voice in political affairs (they were 52% of the total population) and would at the same time have enabled the lower classes (both agrarian and industrial proletarians) to challenge the domination of the upper classes. In 1914 Hungary was still essentially a feudal state, ruled by a Magyar aristocracy.   (*Cont. pp.* 914.*ff.*, 1013.)

D. NORTHERN AND EASTERN EUROPE

1. SCANDINAVIA

a. DENMARK

During the Napoleonic period Denmark sided with France, thereby becoming involved in war with England and Sweden (p. 593). By the **Treaties of Vienna** (1815) Denmark abandoned **Norway** to Sweden and **Pomerania** to Prussia, receiving as compensation the little Duchy of **Lauenburg.**

1806-1839. FREDERICK VI, king. The reign was devoted primarily to the work of reconstruction and recovery, especially in finance. Marked growth of liberal and nationalist feeling, stimulated by the Paris Revolution of 1830.

1831-1834. Institution of representative government: four provincial diets established for (1) the islands; (2) Jutland; (3) Schleswig; (4) Holstein. But these bodies had only deliberative and advisory powers.

1839-1848. CHRISTIAN VIII (nephew of Frederick VI). Continuation of reform; improvement of the finances; development of communal self-government; prison reform; constitution granted to Iceland.

1848-1863. FREDERICK VII. His reign began with a war with the German states resulting from the efforts of the Danish nationalists to incorporate Schleswig and Holstein with the monarchy (p. 676).

1849, June 5. Promulgation of a new constitution: Denmark proper became a limited monarchy in which the king shared legislative power with a bicameral national assembly; civil liberties guaranteed. Schleswig and Holstein continued to be governed in the old fashion, since an effort made in 1855 to include Schleswig in the Danish constitutional system resulted in further friction with the German powers.

1857. Abolition of the historic Sound dues, in return for compensation.

1863-1906. CHRISTIAN IX, of a collateral branch of the family.

1864. WAR AGAINST PRUSSIA AND AUSTRIA, over the two disputed duchies. The Danes had tried, by the Constitution of Nov. 13, 1863, to settle the Schleswig problem by violating promises given to Prussia and Austria in 1851. When these two powers demanded the abolition of the objectionable constitution, the Danes, relying on the support of England, Sweden, and possibly France, accepted the challenge. No aid from others having been offered, the Danes were bound to lose in so unequal a struggle. By the peace settlement they had to **cede Schleswig, Holstein, and Lauenburg** to the victors, thus losing some 200,000 Danes resident in northern Schleswig.

1866, July 28. Revision of the Constitution of 1849. The upper chamber (*Landsthing*) was to consist in part of members named by the king, in part of members chosen by indirect vote. The upper chamber was given more extensive power at the expense of the lower (*Folkething*): ministers could govern with support of the upper chamber even in defiance of the lower. This arrangement led to an acute struggle between the Liberal Party, aiming at parliamentary government, and the **Conservative Party,** defending the existing political order. After 1875 the Conservatives were in control for nearly two decades, under the leadership of **Jacob Estrup** (1825-1913).

The last decades of the 19th century were marked by unusual **economic and cultural development** in Denmark. *Society for the Cultivation of Heaths* (1866); improvement of agriculture; expansion of dairy-farming (English market); growth of co-operative enterprise; development of industry and commerce.

1891-1892. Social legislation: the **Old-Age Pension Law** and the **Health Insurance Law** passed. At the same time the peasants were aided in transforming their leasehold tenancies into freeholds (by 1905 about 94% of the farms were freeholds). Continued vigorous growth of co-operatives, which greatly increased the economic well-being of the rural population.

Liberal agitation for a democratic constitution was supported (after 1880) by the new Social Democratic Party.

1901. Formation of a Liberal government, without, however, any constitutional change.

1906-1912. FREDERICK VIII, king.

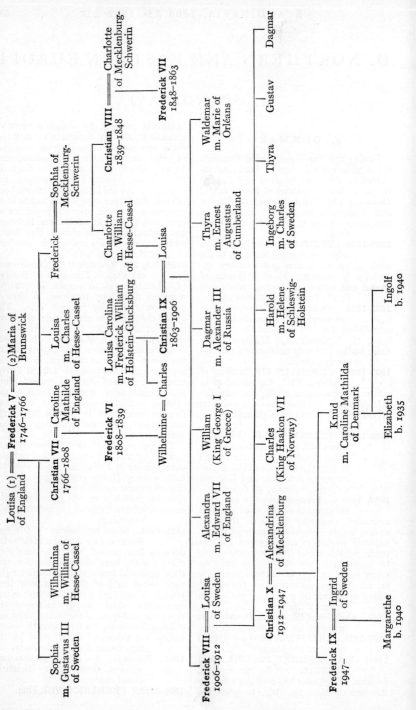

Kings of Denmark since 1746

Louisa (1) of England ══ **Frederick V** 1746–1766 ══ (2) Maria of Brunswick

Sophia m. Gustavus III of Sweden

Wilhelmina m. William of Hesse-Cassel

Christian VII 1766–1808 ══ Caroline Mathilde of England

Frederick ══ Sophia of Mecklenburg-Schwerin

Louisa m. Charles of Hesse-Cassel

Frederick VI 1808–1839

Louisa Carolina m. Frederick William of Holstein-Glucksburg

Charlotte m. William of Hesse-Cassel

Christian VIII 1839–1848 ══ Charlotte of Mecklenburg-Schwerin

Frederick VII 1848–1863

Wilhelmine ══ Charles

Christian IX 1863–1906 ══ Louisa

Frederick VIII 1906–1912 ══ Louisa of Sweden

Alexandra m. Edward VII of England

William (King George I of Greece)

Dagmar m. Alexander III of Russia

Thyra m. Ernest Augustus of Cumberland

Waldemar m. Marie of Orléans

Thyra

Gustav

Dagmar

Christian X 1912–1947 ══ Alexandrina of Mecklenburg

Charles (King Haakon VII of Norway)

Harold m. Helene of Schleswig-Holstein

Ingeborg m. Charles of Sweden

Frederick IX 1947– ══ Ingrid of Sweden

Knud m. Caroline Mathilda of Denmark

Margarethe b. 1940

Elizabeth b. 1935

Ingolf b. 1940

1912-   .   **CHRISTIAN X,** king.

1914-1915. Constitutional amendments passed. The suffrage was extended to all men and most women, and the age limit reduced from 30 to 25 years. The appointive seats in the upper house were abolished, and its former predominance broken. Establishment of regular parliamentary government. (*Cont. p.* 1045.)

b. SWEDEN AND NORWAY

Sweden, by participating in the **War of the Third Coalition** against France (p. 591), for a time lost Pomerania, which, however, was restored in 1810. Finland was lost in the war with Russia (p. 595). Following the deposition of Gustavus IV in 1809,

1809-1818. CHARLES XIII ascended the throne and was obliged to accept **a new constitution.** In 1810 the French marshal, Bernadotte, was elected crown prince under the name of Charles John. Under his lead

1812. Sweden joined Russia in the coalition against France, as a result of which

1814. Sweden acquired Norway from Denmark in return for Pomerania. Under pressure from the Norwegians, the Danes had, in 1807, granted Norway a national administration and a national university. On taking over the country, the Swedes had to agree to

May 17. A new constitution for Norway, providing for a single-chamber national assembly (*Storting*) and denying the king an absolute veto or the right of dissolving parliament. The Norwegians attempted to elect as their king the Danish prince, **Christian Frederick,** but after an invasion of the country by Bernadotte, they were obliged to accept him.

Nov. 4. At a meeting at Christiania, the Norway assembly declared **Norway a free, independent, and indivisible kingdom, united with Sweden** under one king.

1815. A special act of union was ratified by both Sweden and Norway.

1818-1844. CHARLES XIV (Bernadotte), king and founder of a new dynasty. He was a firm defender of the royal prerogative and tended to lean toward a reactionary policy. This led to a chronic **conflict between the king and the estates,** which tried to check royal absolutism.

1832. Opening of the **Göta Canal,** connecting the North Sea with the Baltic.

1842. An elementary-school statute provided for the maintenance of at least one school in every parish.

1844-1859. OSCAR I. Continued growth of Liberal opposition.

1845. The government was obliged to grant some liberal concessions (right to abrogate periodical publications abolished).

1859. Complete religious freedom established.

1859-1872. CHARLES XV. Insistence of the Liberals on electoral reform finally led to

1864, Dec. 8. THE ESTABLISHMENT OF A NEW CONSTITUTION, framed by **Louis de Geer** (1818-1896), the Liberal prime minister. The traditional division of the *Riksdag* into four estates was given up and a modern **bicameral parliament** was established: members of the upper chamber to be elected by provincial assemblies and for a nine-year term; the lower chamber to be elected by direct popular vote, for a three-year term. The franchise was still subject to property qualifications, but was wide enough to include a large part of the peasantry.

GROWTH OF NORWEGIAN NATIONALISM in this period: formation of the **Young Norway Party** by Henrik Wergeland (1808-1845); cultural and intellectual activity: **Magnus Landstad** (1802-1880) published his *Norwegian Folksongs* (1853), while **Peter Andreas Munch** (1810-1863) brought out his *History of the Norwegian Nation* (1852-1863). **Ivar Aasen** (1813-1896) wrote a Norwegian grammar and a dictionary of the folk language (1848, 1850). The great figures of the Norwegian literary revival: Henrik Ibsen (1828-1906), Björnstjerne Björnson (1832-1910), Jonas Lie (1833-1908), Alexander Kielland (1849-1906).

1872-1907. OSCAR II (brother of Charles XV). During his long reign Sweden underwent an **economic and social transformation.** The first twenty years of the new constitutional régime were a period of agrarian domination in politics, but after 1880 the commercial and industrial classes began to come to the fore. The conflict between free-traders and protectionists ended in

1888. The introduction of a protective tariff.

1889. Passage of the first factory laws (extended in 1900). In the meanwhile the industrial workers organized the **Social Democratic Party** (under **Hjalmar Branting,** 1860-1925). Development of trade-unionism and the co-operative movement. Extensive **emigration to America** (between 1870 and 1914 Sweden lost about 1,500,000 inhabitants).

Kings of Sweden since 1751

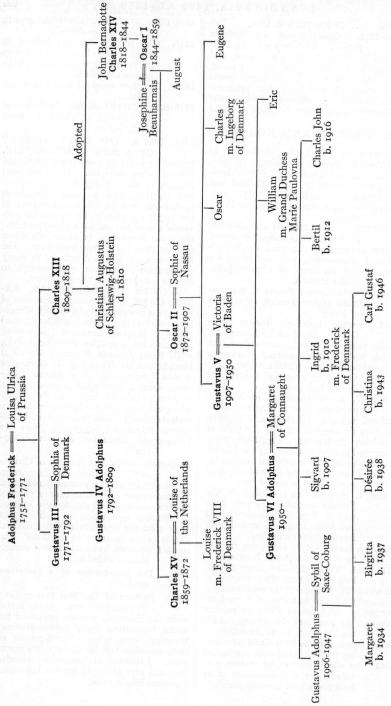

1898. Universal manhood suffrage was introduced in Norway, where the democratic elements, led by **Johan Sverdrup** (1816–1892), dominated the *Storting* after 1884. Rapid growth of the movement for complete independence in Norway. This led to a conflict with Sweden about Norway's foreign representation. The Norwegians, a great trading people, demanded a national flag and a consular service of their own. These concessions the Swedish king refused to make.

1905, June 7. THE NORWEGIAN *STORTING* DECLARED THE UNION WITH SWEDEN DISSOLVED. The decision was ratified by a popular plebiscite (Aug. 13). Finally

Sept. 24. The Swedish *Riksdag* acquiesced, and

Oct. 26. The treaty of separation was signed. Oscar II laid down the Norwegian crown and the Norwegians elected as their king Prince Charles of Denmark, who ascended the throne as

1905- HAAKON VII, King of Norway. His reign was marked by further democratic reforms: suffrage extended to women (1907); royal veto (suspensive) abolished.

1907. Parliamentary government and almost universal suffrage were introduced in **Sweden.**

1907- GUSTAVUS V, King of Sweden. Further constitutional amendments based the elections to the lower house upon real universal suffrage, combined with proportional representation. Property qualifications for election to the upper house were considerably reduced. Conflict between the government and parliament over expenses for national defense led to the growth of radical opposition. In the elections of 1914 the Socialists won about one-third of the seats in the lower Chamber. (*Cont. p.* 1046.)

2. RUSSIA

1801-1825. ALEXANDER I. He had been educated by the Swiss rationalist **Laharpe,** and began his reign by granting an amnesty to political prisoners and exiles, abolishing torture, repealing the prohibition of foreign books, etc. With a group of intimate friends (the *Informal Committee*: **Czartoryski, Kochubei, Novosiltsov, Stroganov**) Alexander discussed various reforms and the project of a constitution for Russia. Though the constitution was not introduced, the central government was reorganized, modern ministries replacing the old "colleges."

1803. A law was passed regulating the **liberation of the peasant serfs** of owners who desired to make the change. This was important chiefly as the first move of the government toward abolition of serfdom. Further reforms were postponed because of the many wars in which Alexander became involved.

1804-1813. War with Persia, resulting from Russian annexation of the **Kingdom of Georgia.** The Russians were victorious and Persia recognized the annexation, besides ceding to Russia **Daghestan** and **Shemakha.**

1805-1812. Russian expansion in North America. Forts were built in Alaska (occupied by Russian pioneers in the late 18th century) and even in northern California.

1805-1807. WAR OF THE THIRD COALITION against France (p. 591). This ended in Russia's defeat and the conclusion of the **Treaty of Tilsit,** by which Alexander and Napoleon became allies.

1806-1812. War against Turkey (p. 592). This was hurriedly concluded in 1812 by the **Treaty of Bucharest,** which gave Russia not only **Bessarabia,** but rather extensive rights in the Danubian principalities.

1808-1809. War with Sweden, through which Russia acquired **Finland.** Finland was organized as an autonomous grand duchy, with the Russian tsar as grand duke. Constitutional government was guaranteed the Finns by a special act.

After these wars, Alexander resumed his reform schemes, with **Michael Speransky** (1772–1839) as his chief counselor.

1810. A council of state was established to draft new laws and watch over the legality of administration. The ministries were also reorganized and a regular system of state budgets introduced. Speransky presented a **plan for a constitution,** but it too remained unrealized. Opposition of the conservatives and personal disagreement with the tsar led to Speransky's downfall and temporary exile (1812).

1812. INVASION OF RUSSIA by Napoleon (p. 596). Formation of the

Grand Alliance and the campaigns in Germany and France led Alexander to devote himself almost entirely to foreign affairs. For his participation in the Congress of Vienna and his project of a Holy Alliance, see pp. 601, 603.

1815. By the Treaty of Vienna, Russia acquired most of the Grand Duchy of Warsaw, which Alexander organized as an autonomous Kingdom of Poland, in permanent union with the Russian Empire. The constitution of Poland provided for a diet, a separate administration and army, official use of the Polish language, etc. Gen. Zaionczek was made viceroy, and the Grand Duke Constantine became commander of the Polish army. After 1820 relations of Alexander with the Poles became ever more strained, partly because of Alexander's unwillingness to abide by the constitution (failure to summon the diet), partly because the Polish nationalists advanced claims to White Russia, Lithuania, and the western Ukraine.

In domestic affairs, Alexander continued to discuss constitutional projects, but in practice he became more and more reactionary, as was shown by his selection of Gen. Alexis Arakcheiev (1769–1834) as his chief adviser. This new departure led to the growth of opposition, more particularly among the younger army officers who had imbibed liberalism in the west. After 1817 secret societies were formed in the army. These finally took the shape of a Northern Society at St. Petersburg (favored constitutional monarchy, abolition of serfdom, etc.), and a Southern Society at Kiev (republican, advocating division of land among the peasants, etc.) under the leadership of Paul Pestel (1793–1826).

1825, Dec. 13. Death of Alexander I in the Crimea. As he had no children the succession would normally have passed to his brother Constantine, but the latter had, in 1822, renounced his claims in favor of the younger brother, Nicholas. This arrangement, however, had been kept secret and Nicholas refused to believe in it until he had secured a further renunciation from Constantine (at Warsaw). The interregnum and the general uncertainty gave an opportunity for

Dec. 26. THE DECEMBRIST RISING, a military revolt started by the Northern Society. The whole affair was ill-planned and half-hearted. Nicholas suppressed it the same day. Of the leaders several were executed and the rest sent into exile. An attempted uprising in the south was also frustrated.

1825–1855. NICHOLAS I, a firm believer in autocracy and a determined

enemy of liberalism both at home and abroad. In foreign policy he combined defense of legitimism with an attempt to secure Russia's commercial interests, especially in the east.

1826–1828. War with Persia, resulting from a Persian attack on Russian possessions in Transcaucasia. The war ended in a Russian victory and in the Treaty of Turkmanchai: Russia secured part of Armenia with Erivan; Persia recognized Russia's exclusive right to have a navy on the Caspian Sea, and granted Russia important commercial concessions.

1828–1829. War against Turkey, growing out of the Greek Revolution and conflict between Russia and Turkey over the terms of the Treaty of Bucharest. For the campaigns see p. 723. By the Treaty of Adrianople (1829) Russia secured the mouth of the Danube and the eastern coast of the Black Sea.

1830–1831. THE POLISH REVOLUTION, long prepared by the Polish nationalists, but provoked by the Paris Revolution and the tsar's proposal to use the Polish army to suppress the new government in Belgium and France. The Russian garrison was expelled from Poland, a revolutionary government proclaimed, the Romanov dynasty declared deposed and the union with Lithuania celebrated. The Russian army, commanded first by Gen. Dibich (Diebitsch) and then by Paskievich, defeated the Poles (divided by internal dissensions between moderates and radicals) at Ostrolenka (May 26, 1831) and finally took Warsaw (Sept. 8). The revolution collapsed and most of the Polish leaders escaped to the west, where they formed a powerful revolutionary faction, especially in Paris. The Polish constitution was abrogated and replaced by an organic statute: Poland lost its political rights and retained only a small measure of administrative autonomy. Beginning of the policy of Russification in Poland.

DOMESTIC POLICY. Nicholas, while recognizing the need for reform, was sternly opposed to all independent public activity. Growth of bureaucracy and of the tsar's personal government. Publication of a new code of law (1832), edited by Speransky. This, with some modification, remained in force until the Revolution of 1917. Partial measures to alleviate the condition of the serfs and to limit the power of the landlords. Progress of technical education. First Russian railroad (St. Petersburg to Tsarskoe Selo, 1838). At the same time drastic repression of all liberal manifestations and tendencies; activity of the secret police (third section of "His

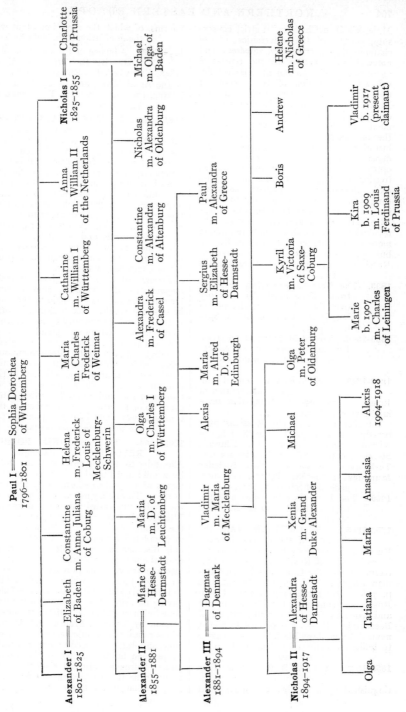

Russian Tsars (1796-1917).

Majesty's Own Chancery"); strict censorship; control of the universities; official championship of **orthodoxy, autocracy, and nationalism.** Despite all the repressive measures, public opinion nevertheless developed. Formation of two schools of thought: the *Westerners*, who held that Russia must follow the lead of western countries in political and social development; and the *Slavophils*, who insisted on the peculiarities of Russian culture and historical evolution, and on the need for independent development. But both groups opposed bureaucratic rule and demanded freedom of thought, abolition of serfdom, etc. Beginnings of **Russian socialism** (under the influence of the Utopian socialists in France): **Alexander Herzen** (1812–1870), **Michael Bakunin** (1814–1876). The revolutions of 1848–1849 simply resulted in more thoroughgoing repression in Russia, but opposition broke through as soon as Russia began to meet with defeats in the Crimean War.

1833. The **Near-Eastern crisis,** resulting from Mohammed Ali's victory over the sultan. Interference of Russia and **Treaty of Unkiar Skelessi** (p. 714).

1839-1840. Second **Mohammed Ali crisis.** Russian co-operation with England. **Straits Convention,** etc. (p. 725).

1848-1849. Revolutions in central and western Europe. Intervention of Russia to suppress the Hungarian revolutionary movement (p. 674).

Advance in Asia. The Russians were pressing on steadily. During the reign of Nicholas they conquered the Khirghiz Steppe and prepared for the **advance into Turkestan.** In the Far East **Nicholas Muraviev** (1809–1881) became governor-general of Siberia in 1847.

1850. The Russians established a settlement at the mouth of the Amur River.

1853-1856. THE CRIMEAN WAR, the outcome of the dispute between Russia and France over the holy places in Palestine and of Russian claims to a protectorate over the Christians in the Ottoman Empire. For details of the war see p. 726 *f.* By the **Treaty of Paris** (1856) Russia lost control of the Danube mouth and ceded to Turkey the southern part of **Bessarabia.** Russia was obliged to accept **neutralization of the Black Sea** and to agree to build no fortifications and to keep no navy in that sea.

1855-1881. ALEXANDER II (the *Tsar Liberator*), whose reign was distinguished by a number of fundamental reforms, of which the most important was the liquidation of the serf problem.

1858-1860. Advance of Russia in the Far East. By the **Treaty of Aigun** (1858) China ceded to Russia the left bank of the Amur River, and by the **Treaty of Peking,** the Ussuri region. **Foundation of Vladivostok** (1860).

1861, Mar. 3. THE EMANCIPATION EDICT, liberating the serfs. The subject had been discussed for years by a special committee, which collected huge masses of material from provincial bodies. Temporary freedom of discussion in the press had also produced much information and difference of viewpoint. The landowners were, on the whole, ready to give the serfs freedom, but not ready to give up much of their land. At the other extreme were the radicals and socialists, who insisted that the land belonged to those who worked it. The final solution was a compromise imposed by the tsar.

Terms: All serfs were given **personal freedom,** together with **allotments of land** for which the owners were paid by the state in treasury bonds. The peasants in turn were to refund the treasury by installments (**redemption payments**) spread over a period of 49 years. The land was not given to individuals, but to the **village communes** (*mir*), which distributed it among the village members according to the size of the peasant family. To assure equality of treatment the land was to be redistributed every 10 or 12 years. The members of the commune were held jointly responsible for the redemption payments.

1863-1864. THE SECOND POLISH REVOLUTION. Attempts of Alexander to win the support of the Poles by a mild and liberal policy: the arrangements of 1815–1830 substantially restored in 1862. This policy met with support from the Polish moderates (**Marquis Alexander Wielopolski**), but was not enough to satisfy the extreme nationalists (*reds*), who aimed at complete independence. After considerable disorder the government decided to draft the malcontents (especially students) into the army. This provoked the insurrection of Jan. 1863, which spread rapidly to Lithuania and White Russia. The Poles having no army, most of the fighting was done by guerrilla bands. **Diplomatic intervention by England, France, and Austria** (similar but not identic protests of Apr., June, and Aug.) produced a strong **nationalist reaction in Russia,** led by the former radical journalist, **Michael Katkov** (1818–1887). The Russian government was able to ignore the protests of the western powers because of the support and co-operation of the Prussian government (**Alvensleben Convention,** Feb. 8, 1863). But the insurrection was not finally suppressed until May, 1864, and then with great severity. Polish autonomy was again abolished and Russian administration re-established; Russian language made obligatory in Polish schools; proceedings of the government against the Roman Catholic clergy; rupture of relations with the Vatican.

1864. ZEMSTVO LAW, one of the most important features of the great reforms. By the law a system of local self-government was organized: local boards (*zemstvos*), on which the nobility, the townsmen, and the peasants were represented (no one class to have a majority of the seats), were empowered to levy taxes for local economic and cultural requirements (roads, bridges, schools, hospitals, etc.).

1864. Reform of the judiciary: the old system of class courts was abolished and a new hierarchy of courts, on the French model, was set up, with thoroughly modernized procedure and jury trial for criminal offenses. **Justices of the peace** were provided to deal with minor civil suits, and the old **peasant courts** were retained for those who wished to use them.

1867. Cession of Alaska to the United States (p. 798). The Russian settlements in California had been abandoned in 1844 and the Russian government now sold Alaska itself to the American government.

1865-1876. Russian advance in central Asia. Conquest of the khanates of **Kokand, Bokhara, and Khiva,** followed by the annexation of the entire Transcaspian region in 1881. This forward policy created much friction between Russia and England, which was fearful for India.

1870. Reform of municipal government, the last of the great reform measures. The old patrician system was abolished and the towns were given self-government, under councils elected by the propertied classes.

1871, Mar. 13. Abrogation of the Black Sea clauses of the Treaty of Paris. The Russian government had taken advantage of the Franco-German War (p. 688) to denounce its obligations. British protests led to the convocation of a **conference at London,** which accepted the fact, but reaffirmed the principle that international obligations cannot be abrogated without consent of all signatory powers.

1874. Army reform, introducing the principle of **universal military liability** in place of the former system of taking recruits only from among the lower classes.

1875. Cession of the Kurile Islands to Japan, in exchange for the southern part of the island of **Sakhalin.**

1875-1878. T H E N E A R E A S T E R N CRISIS, the Russian-Turkish War, and the **Treaties of San Stefano** and **Berlin** (p. 735 *f.*). As a result of the war the Russians received **Bessarabia** (which had been lost in 1856), **Kars** and **Batum.**

Growth of opposition to the tsarist régime, due to the incompleteness of the government reforms. The liberal elements demanded a constitution, while the radicals and socialists aimed at the complete overturn of the social order and a resettlement of the land question. The radicals soon became avowedly revolutionary. Under the leadership of **Herzen, Bakunin, Peter Lavrov** (1823-1900), and **Nicholas Chernyshevsky** (1828-1889) they organized

1876. A secret society under the name *Land and Liberty*. This became the spearhead of the so-called **Populist movement** (the *Going among the People*). The movement met with a qualified reception from the suspicious peasants and was soon persecuted by the police.

In the meanwhile the unsatisfactory outcome of the war with Turkey broadened the base of popular discontent. The liberals were further estranged by the grant of a constitution to the Bulgarians, while the adherents of the new **Panslav movement** (foundation of the *Slavonic Welfare Society* at Moscow, 1857; Panslav congress at Moscow, 1867) became extremely critical of the government for failure to complete the work of liberating the Balkan Slavs. After 1878, therefore, the revolutionary movement secured more popular support.

1879. Organization of the society *Will of the People*, composed of the most radical wing of the older Populist group. The new society was out-and-out terrorist and carefully planned attempts on the lives of prominent officials, finally of the tsar himself.

1880. Appointment of Gen. Loris-Melikov as minister of the interior. After two abortive attempts to assassinate him, the tsar had decided on a policy of concessions, accompanied, however, with ever more stringent police measures against the terrorists. Loris-Melikov propounded a scheme for summoning representatives of the zemstvos to co-operate with the council of state in the discussion of new laws. This compromise plan was approved by Alexander on

1881, Mar. 13. But on the very same day he fell a victim to the bombs of the terrorists.

1881-1894. ALEXANDER III. He was determined to suppress the revolutionary movement and throughout his reign followed the advice of his former teacher and close friend, **Constantine Pobiedonostsev** (1827-1907), who was made procurator of the Holy Synod. After some debate, Loris-Melikov's plan was dropped and the **autocratic system** reaffirmed. Drastic repression of revolutionary activity and silencing of all liberal opposition. Curtailment of the reforms of the preceding reign and restoration of the pre-eminence of the nobility. **Persecution of religious dissenters,** Roman Catholics, Protestants, and especially Jews (beginning of the pogroms in the Ukraine). **Discrimination against national minorities** and attempts at Russification in the border provinces.

1881, June 18. Conclusion of the **Alliance of the Three Emperors** between Germany, Russia, and Austria (p. 737). This was renewed in 1884, but in 1887 was replaced by a separate pact between Russia and Germany (the **Reinsurance Treaty,** p. 741). For the rest, Russian policy was concerned primarily with Balkan affairs, and more particularly with the abortive effort to maintain a predominant position in Bulgarian affairs (p. 739).

1884-1887. Continued advance in central Asia (conquest of Merv, 1884) brought the Russians to the frontier of Afghanistan, where a clash of Russian and Afghan troops in 1885 brought Russia to the very verge of war with England (pp. 739, 868). The matter was finally disposed of by agreement on a Russian-Afghan frontier.

BEGINNING OF THE INDUSTRIALIZATION OF RUSSIA. The government inaugurated a high protective tariff and began to give extensive support to native industry. The rapid expansion of railroads and the opening of the coal and iron fields of southern Russia served as an important stimulus. The guiding spirit in the whole process was **Sergei Witte** (1849-1915), first minister of communications and later minister of finance. Heavy borrowing abroad, especially in France, in the hope that the increased productive power of Russia would make repayment easy. But the growth of industry involved also the emergence of an **industrial proletariat,** living in misery and most inadequately protected by the first factory laws (1882-1886). Unrest in the cities was accompanied by growing disorder in the country, where the plight of the peasants was such (**great famine** of 1891-1892) that the government was obliged to abolish the poll-tax and reduce the redemption payments.

1891-1894. Conclusion of the **Franco-Russian Alliance,** which was to become one of the main features of pre-war international relations (p. 742).

1894-1917. NICHOLAS II, an intelligent but weak-willed ruler, deeply devoted to the memory and to the system of his father. During the first decade of his reign the reaction continued unabated and at the same time the policy of economic development was maintained (**introduction of the gold standard** by Witte in 1897). Liberal tendencies of the zemstvos were vigorously combated and the policy of Russification was extended to Finland, thitherto practically autonomous. But as time went on it became more and more difficult for the government to uphold the policy of Alexander III. Opposition revived in various forms:

1898. Formation of the **Social Democratic Party** among the industrial workers. Marxism had been introduced into Russia by **George Plekhanov** (1857-1918), whose fairly moderate program was, however, soon to be challenged by the more radical wing under the leadership of **Nikolai Lenin** (Vladimir Ulianov, 1870-1924). Lenin was the son of a school inspector and the brother of a prominent terrorist who was executed in 1887 for plotting against the life of the tsar. Lenin himself spent several years in exile in Siberia, but after his escape became one of the most energetic and uncompromising champions of the worker. The socialists were obliged to operate from abroad (especially from Switzerland). **Split in the Social Democratic Party** (1903) at the party congress in London: *Mensheviks* (moderates) and *Bolsheviks* (extremists).

1901. Organization of the Social Revolutionary Party, which took its inspiration from the earlier Populist movement. This party, to which many of the students adhered, was concerned chiefly with the peasant problem and advocated the nationalization of the land. Its methods were those of **terrorism** and the years following its birth were marked by an increasing number of assassinations.

1903. Formation of the Union of Liberation, the third of the opposition parties and at the time the most important. This group consisted largely of intellectuals, members of the liberal professions, and zemstvo workers. Its program called for a liberal constitution.

The development of popular opposition to the government was greatly facilitated by the outbreak and course of the

1904-1905. RUSSIAN-JAPANESE WAR.
This was the direct result of the Russian forward policy in the Far East: construction of the **Trans-Siberian Railway** (1891–1903); intervention after the Sino-Japanese War (1895); **treaty with China** (1896) and penetration of northern **Manchuria**; interference in **Korea**; lease of **Port Arthur** (1898); occupation of **Manchuria** after the Boxer Insurrection (1900–1903); activity of Russian interests in **northern Korea**, etc. (see pp. 744 f., 882). Repeated efforts of the Japanese to reach an agreement were treated with disdain by the Russians, so that long-drawn negotiations ended in the outbreak of hostilities (Feb. 8, 1904). The Russians were consistently defeated (**battles of Liao-Yang**, Aug.; **Sha-ho,** Oct.; **fall of Port Arthur**, Jan. 1905; **battle of Mukden,** Feb. 23–Mar. 10; **naval disaster at Tsushima,** May 27). The government was wholly discredited and popular pressure became ever greater.

1904, July 28. Assassination of Viacheslav Plehve, the ruthless but able minister of the interior. This event induced the government to attempt a policy of conciliation, represented by **Prince Sviatopolk-Mirsky,** but it proved to be too late for halfway measures and the relaxation of repression only gave the opposition better opportunities for organization and expression.

Nov. A great **zemstvo congress** met at St. Petersburg and demanded the convocation of a representative assembly and the granting of civil liberties. Similar demands were advanced by numerous other groups and by the professional classes.

1905, Jan. 22. Bloody Sunday, marked by the first bloodshed and by the emergence of the workers as a factor in the movement. A procession of workers, led by **Father Gapon,** while proceeding to the palace to lay its demands before the tsar, was fired on by the troops: 70 killed and 240 wounded. Growing indignation and unrest; epidemic of strikes.

Mar. 3. The tsar announced his intention to convoke a "consultative" assembly. Further concessions: edict of religious toleration, permission to use the Polish language in Polish schools, relief for the Jews, cancellation of part of the redemption payments.

May 8. Organization of the **Union of Unions,** under the chairmanship of **Prof. Paul Miliukov.** This brought together all the liberal groups in a renewed demand for parliamentary government and the institution of universal suffrage.

June-Aug. Increasing unrest and disorder throughout the country: strikes, agrarian outbreaks, national movements in the border provinces, mutinies in the army and navy (Potemkin episode).
Yielding to the popular pressure,
Aug. 19. The tsar published a **manifesto creating the Imperial Duma,** or assembly, to be elected by a limited franchise and with deliberative powers only. This concession was far too modest to meet the popular demand and the revolutionary movement became ever more widely spread until it culminated in

Oct. 20-30. THE GREAT GENERAL STRIKE, a spontaneous movement in which the whole country joined.

Oct. 26. The St. Petersburg workers formed **the first soviet** (council) to direct the strike. This was essentially a moderate socialist organization and had relatively little influence on the course of events. The strike soon paralyzed the government and forced the tsar to yield. Pobiedonostsev and other reactionary ministers were obliged to resign, and Nicholas, advised by Witte (who had been disgraced in 1903, but had been restored to favor after the conclusion of the **Treaty of Portsmouth** with Japan), issued the

Oct. 30. OCTOBER MANIFESTO, granting Russia a constitution: the projected duma was to have real legislative power, the franchise was to be greatly extended, civil liberties were guaranteed, etc. **Witte was appointed prime minister.** The manifesto satisfied all the more moderate liberal groups, but appeared inadequate to those who had called for a constituent assembly. The immediate effect of the government's capitulation was, therefore, to split the liberal group; the moderates became known as the **Octobrist Party,** while the progressives took the name **Constitutional Democratic Party** (abbreviated to K.D. = *Cadet*). The Social Democrats rejected the whole program of the government and the St. Petersburg soviet (with branches opened in many cities) attempted several times to organize another strike. The sole effect of this policy was to drive more of the liberals into the government ranks. At the same time Witte made every effort to bring back the troops from the Far East. When he felt sufficiently strong,

Dec. 16. The members of the St. Petersburg soviet (about 190) were arrested. This move led to

Dec. 22.-Jan. 1. INSURRECTION OF THE WORKERS IN MOSCOW. Severe street fighting, and much bloodshed.

But the troops remained loyal to the government and the uprising was finally suppressed. Vigorous action by the army during the winter to restore order in the provinces (**Black Hundreds** — punitive raids, etc.). Meanwhile Witte arranged to float a huge loan ($400,000,000) in France and England, so that, when the Duma met, the government might not be dependent on the representatives of the people for funds.

1906, May 2. Dismissal of Witte, who was never popular with Nicholas and who was no longer needed. In his place the tsar appointed **Goremykin,** a conservative bureaucrat of the old school.

May 6. Promulgation of the Fundamental Laws, issued on the very eve of the meeting of the Duma. These extensive regulations decided in advance many of the questions left open by the October Manifesto. The tsar was proclaimed autocrat, and retained complete control over the executive, the armed forces, and foreign policy. Changes in the fundamental laws could be made only with his consent. The legislative power was to be divided between the Duma and an upper chamber, the Imperial Council, half the members of which were to be appointed by the tsar, the other half to be elected by various privileged bodies throughout the country. The government reserved the right to legislate by decree when the Duma was not in session. The budgetary powers of the Duma were closely restricted.

May 10. MEETING OF THE FIRST DUMA, elected by what amounted to universal suffrage. But the radical parties had, for the most part, boycotted the elections and the Cadets formed the largest party. Profoundly disappointed by the fundamental laws, the Cadets criticized the government violently and this first representative assembly ended in a deadlock.

July 21. Dissolution of the first Duma. The Cadet leaders adjourned to Viborg and issued thence the **Viborg Manifesto,** calling upon the country to refuse taxes. The manifesto found but little response in the country, where the revolution was already a thing of the past.

Nov. Agrarian Reform Act of Peter Stolypin (1862–1911), who had become prime minister in June. Though a conservative, Stolypin was far from being a reactionary. He was eager to maintain the constitutional system, and hoped gradually to wean the country from revolutionary sentiment by well-planned reforms. The Agrarian Law put an end to the communal (mir) system of landholding and enabled each peasant to withdraw from the commune at will, receiving his own share of the land in private ownership. Any commune was able to end the old system by majority vote. This law was later approved by the third Duma.

1907, Mar. 5-June 16. THE SECOND DUMA, more radical than the first because of the active part taken in the elections by the revolutionary parties. The Cadets were now anxious to co-operate with the government to save the constitutional system (though they refused Stolypin's invitation to some of the leaders to join the ministry). But these efforts were frustrated by the radicals. The reactionary groups at court, constantly pressing for a return to the simple autocratic system, finally forced the dissolution of the Duma and

June 16. The promulgation of a **new electoral law,** which greatly increased the representation of the propertied classes to the detriment of peasants and workers. At the same time it reduced the representation of the national minorities.

1907-1912. THE THIRD DUMA, elected on the new basis, returned a conservative majority. Stern suppression of all revolutionary outbreaks and disorders (*Union of True Russian Men; League of the Russian Nobility;* drumhead courts-martial, etc.). At the same time Stolypin, with co-operation of the Duma, continued his **reform activities:** social insurance, zemstvo reform, education, police reorganization, land banks, encouragement of emigration to Siberia, etc. With the restoration of order came the resumption of economic expansion, industrialization, etc.

1907, Aug. 30. Conclusion of the Anglo-Russian Entente (p. 752), an important milestone in Russian foreign policy, which definitely aligned Russia with England and France against the Central Powers.

1908-1909. Tension between Russia and Austria over the annexation of Bosnia and Herzegovina (p. 756). Marked **revival of Pan-Slav or Neo-Slav agitation.**

1911, Sept. 14. Stolypin was assassinated by a revolutionary, at Kiev. He was succeeded by **Kokovtsev,** an able financier and a statesman of moderate type, lacking, however, the prestige and will-power of his predecessor.

1912-1916. THE FOURTH DUMA, similar to the third in character and purpose. This period was taken up largely with major questions of foreign policy, notably by the crisis of the **1912-1913. Balkan Wars** (p. 759 *f.*), in which Russia played a very prominent rôle.

In the meanwhile the reforms inaugurated by the government proved insufficient to quiet the political and social unrest. The national minorities, too, were antagonized by the policy of the government (especially in Poland and Finland). On the eve of the World War there was growing dissatisfaction, which spread even into more moderate circles. The latter were irritated particularly by the state of affairs at court, where the tsarina, a deeply religious person, had become the center of a group of mystics and magic healers, originally called in to cure the only son of the imperial couple of an incurable disease. Of this group **Rasputin** was the most remarkable and powerful, and he was to play a most important rôle in the history of Russia during the war.

1914, Aug. 1.   GERMANY DECLARED WAR ON RUSSIA. For the details of the July crisis and Russia's policy in international affairs see p. 762.

(*Cont. pp.* 914 *f.*, **1027**.)

E. THE BALKANS AND THE NEAR EAST

1. THE BALKAN STATES

a. GREECE

1821-1831. Greek War of Independence (p. 722).

1832-1862. OTTO I, king. Otto was a Bavarian prince, 17 years of age. During the first three years the country was governed by a regency of three Bavarian advisers, which attempted to establish a centralized, bureaucratic system, wholly unsuited to the conditions of the country. The entire reign was marked by unpopularity, internal dissension, continued brigandage, and economic want.

1843, Sept. 14. Popular rising in favor of a constitution. Otto yielded and agreed to a fundamental law establishing a bicameral parliamentary régime. This, however, worked but little better than the preceding system.

1850, Jan.-Mar. British blockade arising out of friction over the unsatisfied claims of British subjects (**Don Pacifico affair**, p. 612).

1854, Jan.-Feb. Greek bands invaded Thessaly and Epirus, to take advantage of the war of Russia against Turkey (p. 726). Relations between Greece and Turkey were severed (Mar. 28), but the Greeks were prevented from making war by the **occupation of the Piraeus** by the British and French (this lasted until Feb. 1857).

1862, Feb. 13. A military revolt was successful. Otto deposed (Oct. 23); he left the country (Oct. 27).

1863, Feb. 3. The Greek Assembly proclaimed Prince Alfred of England king, after a plebiscite. The election was rejected by the British government.

1863-1913. GEORGE I, a Danish prince (17 years old), who was finally chosen with the consent of the powers.

1863, June 5. England turned over to Greece the **Ionian Islands** (under British protectorate since 1815).

Nov. 28. A new democratic constitution was introduced, providing for manhood suffrage and a single-chamber parliament (*Boulé*).

1866-1868. Cretan revolt; excitement in Greece; rupture of relations with Turkey (Dec. 1868; resumed Feb. 1869).

1878, Jan. 28. Rising in Thessaly, part of the general upheaval in the Balkans resulting from the war of Russia against Turkey (p. 734). The Greek government declared war on Turkey (Feb. 2), but was constrained by the powers from larger hostilities.

1881, July 2. By a convention with Turkey the **Greeks finally acquired Thessaly** and part of Epirus, promised them at the Congress of Berlin (p. 736).

1886, Apr. 26. Ultimatum of the powers to Greece, to prevent Greek action in harmony with the revolution in Eastern Roumelia (p. 739). The Greeks refused to disarm, whereupon **the powers blockaded Greece** (May 8-June 7) forcing compliance.

1893, Aug. 6. Opening of the **Canal of Corinth.**

1896, Apr. Revival of the **Olympic Games.**

1896-1897. Cretan Insurrection. Intervention of Greece (Feb. 1896) and resultant **war with Turkey** (Apr. 17, 1897). The Greeks were utterly defeated, but were saved by the powers from the fruits of their folly (p. 745).

1898, Feb. International **commission** set up to control Greek finance, after the Greek government had defaulted on its obligations.

Nov. Forced evacuation of **Crete** by Turkish troops, after attacks on British forces. Contingents of England, France, Russia, and Italy remained in occupation of the island.

Nov. 26. Prince George of Greece named high commissioner for Crete.

1905, Mar. 30. Insurrection in Crete, after the powers had repeatedly rejected appeals for union with Greece. The Assembly (leadership of **Venizelos**) decreed union, but the powers, despite attacks upon their troops, remained adamant.

1906, Sept. 25. Prince George resigned as high commissioner for Crete, and was succeeded by **M. Zaimis.**

1908, Oct. 7. The Cretans proclaimed union with Greece, following the annexation of Bosnia and Herzegovina and the declaration of Bulgarian independence (p. 756).

1909, July. England, France, Russia, and Italy withdrew their forces from Crete.

THE BALKANS, 1914

Raisz

Kings of Greece (Danish House)

Christian IX
of Denmark

George I ═══ Olga of
King of Greece │ Russia
1863–1913

Constantine I ═══ Sophia of | George | Nicholas | Marie | Andrew | Christopher
1913–1917 │ Prussia | m. Marie | m. Helena | m. George | m. Alice of
1920–1922 │ | Bonaparte | of Russia | of Russia | Battenberg

George II ═══ Elizabeth | **Alexander** | Helen | **Pauí I** | Irene | Catharine
1922–1923 of Rumania | 1917–1920 | m. Carol II | 1947– |
1935–1947 | | of Rumania | |

1910, Jan. The **Military League**, an association of officers, forced the Greek Assembly to agree to revision of the constitution. Thereupon the league voluntarily dissolved itself (Mar.).

Oct. 18. Venizelos became prime minister. He at once undertook the work of military and financial reform.

1911, June 11. Completion of the revision of the constitution.

1912, May 29. Treaty of Alliance with Bulgaria (p. 759).

Oct. 14. Cretan representatives were finally admitted to the Greek Assembly.

Oct. 17. THE FIRST BALKAN WAR (p. 759).

1913, Mar. 18. Assassination of King George.

1913–1917. CONSTANTINE I, king.

June. SECOND BALKAN WAR (p. 760).

Dec. 10. Crete officially taken over by Greece.

1914. Crisis arising from Greek claims in **southern Albania** and from the question of the **Aegean Islands** (p. 761).

July-Aug. Outbreak of the World War. Constantine rejected appeals from Germany to join in the conflict.

Sept. 7. Resignation of Venizelos (p. 931), marking the beginning of the crisis of Greek neutrality in the World War. (*Cont. pp.* 920 *f.*, 1020.)

b. SERBIA

1804–1813. First Serbian Insurrection, under **Kara George** (p. 721).

1815–1817. Second Serbian Insurrection, under **Milosh Obrenovich** (p. 722).

1817. Milosh recognized by the sultan as **Prince of Serbia** (the Pashalik of Belgrade), which was given a measure of self-government. Cautious policy of Milosh, who, through bribery, gradually secured larger powers from the Porte. During the Greek War, he managed to play a canny game between Russia and Turkey.

1829. The Treaty of Adrianople guaranteed the **autonomy of Serbia,** religious liberty, etc.

1830. The sultan recognized **Milosh** as **hereditary prince,** added some territory to his jurisdiction, obliged the Turkish landlords to sell their holdings, and confined the Turkish troops to a few garrison towns.

1835. Opposition of the notables to Milosh's autocratic and oppressive rule (use of bastinado on his opponents, appropriation of forests, control of the pork business, etc.) forced Milosh to grant a **constitution** providing for a senate of elders with legislative, executive, and judicial powers, and a popular assembly (*Skupshtina*) with control of the budget.

1838. The sultan, supported by Russia, forced **the abrogation of the constitution** and the appointment of a senate of notables with almost complete power.

Rulers of Serbia (Yugoslavia)

(1) Obrenovich

Milosh
Prince, 1817–1839
1858–1860

Ephraim
d. 1856

Milosh

Milan
Prince, 1839

Michael
Prince, 1839–1842
1860–1868

Milan I ═══ Nathalia Keshko
Prince, 1868–1882
King, 1882–1889

Alexander I ═══ Draga Mashin
King, 1889–1903

(2) Karageorgevich

George Petrovich (Kara George)
Lord of Serbia, 1804–1813

Alexander (Karageorgevich)
Prince, 1842–1858

Peter I ═══ Zorka of
King, 1903–1921   Montenegro

Arsène

Paul ═══ Olga of
(Regent   Greece
1934–)

Helen
m. Ivan
of Russia

George
(renounced
throne, 1909)

Alexander II ═══ Marie of
Regent, 1914–1921   Rumania
King, of Yugoslavia
1921–1934

Alexander
b. 1924

Nicholas
b. 1928

Elizabeth
b. 1936

Peter II
b. 1923
King, 1934–1945
Yugoslavia a republic 1945–

Tomislav
b. 1928

Andrew
b. 1929

1839, June 13. Milosh abdicated, in protest against the oligarchic system.

1839. Milan, son of Milosh. He died after a rule of only a few weeks.

1839-1842. MICHAEL, another son of Milosh, only 17 years old. His short rule was marked by constant intriguing on the part of the Karageorgevich faction (*Defenders of the Constitution*) who demanded the convocation of the *Skupshtina*. Michael was finally forced to flee.

1842-1858. ALEXANDER KARAGEORGEVICH, elected by the *Skupshtina*. Loud protests of Russia, which forced the banishment of the popular leaders. Alexander's reign was the quietest in Serbian history, marked by a cautious foreign policy, spread of western influence, growth of trade (especially with Austria), and development of education (Academy of Sciences, 1841; University of Belgrade, 1844). Politically it was a period of factional trouble and corruption, the Senate being in complete control.

1856. By the Treaty of Paris (p. 728), Serbia was placed under the collective guaranty of the powers.

1858, Dec. 23. Alexander forced to abdicate by an opposition faction, supported by the Obrenovichs and by Turkey and Russia.

1858-1860. Restoration of Milosh Obrenovich, now 79 years old. He died after wreaking vengeance on his enemies.

1860-1868. MICHAEL, son of Milosh, reascended the throne. He was a well-educated and intelligent prince, whose great aim was to unite the Balkans in a crusade against the Turks. Introduction of compulsory service in the army and gradual development of an efficient administration.

1862, June 15. Bombardment of Belgrade by Turkish troops, after clashes between the garrison and the populace. Michael appealed to the powers and the sultan was induced to concentrate his forces in three or four places.

1866. Michael appealed again for the withdrawal of Turkish troops. The powers induced the sultan to yield, and the last troops left Serbian territory in Apr. 1867.

1866, Sept. 23. Secret offensive and defensive alliance between Serbia and Montenegro.

1867, May 26. Secret Serbian-Rumanian treaty, with the object of securing independence.

1867, Aug. 26. Secret treaty between Serbia and Greece (Treaty of Voeslau): Serbia was to get Bosnia and Herzegovina,

Greece Thessaly and Epirus. Action was to be taken against Turkey in 1868. A Balkan confederation was envisaged as the ultimate goal. Michael organized a far-reaching propaganda in Bosnia and Macedonia, and established close contact with the Bulgarian revolutionary leaders. Widespread nationalist agitation (United Serbian Youth or *Omladina*, founded 1867).

1868, June 10. Michael assassinated by conspirators aiming at the restoration of Alexander Karageorgevich. But Michael's chief adviser, Garashanin, anticipated them, roused the garrison and had the assassins arrested.

1868-1889. MILAN, grand-nephew of Michael, appointed prince, with a regency, which undertook the revision of the constitution (1869) in a liberal sense, to meet the growing demands of the nationalist organizations.

1876, July. Declaration of war on Turkey, following the insurrection in Bosnia and Herzegovina. Rampant nationalism of the government (Ristich) and of the country. Complete defeat of the Serbs (p. 734).

1877, Dec. 14. Serbia re-entered the war against Turkey, on Russia's side.

1878, July 13. THE TREATY OF BERLIN made Serbia completely independent, but Serbia received but slight increase of territory and the coveted provinces of Bosnia and Herzegovina were occupied by Austria (p. 736).

1881, June 28. Secret treaty with Austria, giving the latter practically a protectorate over Serbia (p. 737).

1882, Mar. 6. MILAN proclaimed himself king, with Austrian support.

1883, Nov. Serious revolt against the government by the newly formed Radical party (Nicholas Pashich, leader), a violently nationalist group.

1885, Nov. 13. War with Bulgaria, after the union of Eastern Roumelia. The Serbs completely defeated at Slivnitza (Nov. 17), but saved from invasion by the intervention of Austria (p. 718).

1888. Aug. Milan divorced his Russian wife, Nathalia, who left the country. Growing split between the Austrian party and the pro-Russian, nationalist factions.

Dec. 16. The Radicals won a victory in the elections.

1889, Jan. 3. Despite warnings from Milan, the Assembly passed a revision of the constitution in a liberal sense.

1889, Mar. 6. Abdication of Milan.

1889-1903. ALEXANDER I, son of Milan, 13 years old at the time of his accession. A regency under Ristich was established.

1893, Apr. 14. *Coup d'état* of Alexander, who abolished the regency.

1894, May 21. Restoration of the constitution of 1869.

1899, Aug. 5. Alexander married Draga Mashin, a lady of questionable position. This and his ruthless persecution of the Radicals led to increased opposition to him.

1901, Feb. 11. Death of Milan, who had spent the last ten years of his life intriguing behind the throne and further discrediting the rule of his house.

1903, June 10. Alexander, Draga, and some 20 members of the court, murdered by a group of conspirators, mostly military men.

June 15. The Assembly elected Peter Karageorgevich to the throne, and restored the Constitution of 1889.

1903-1921. PETER I, a well-intentioned ruler who was, however, wholly at the mercy of the conspirators.

1904, Dec. 10—1905, May 22. First ministry of Nicholas Pashich. Serbian policy became outspokenly nationalist and anti-Austrian.

1905-1907. "Pig War" with Austria, a tariff conflict which did much to embitter relations.

1906, May 1—1908, July 6. Second ministry of Pashich.

1908-1909. Bosnian annexation crisis (p. 756). Acute danger of war between Serbia and Austria. Serbia was obliged to back down, but the crisis left a legacy of hate. Foundation of propagandist societies (*Narodna Odbrana*, 1908; *Union or Death* [Black Hand], 1911).

1912, Mar. 13. Treaty of Alliance with Bulgaria (p. 758).

Sept. 12. Pashich again premier.

Oct. 17. Outbreak of the First Balkan War (p. 759).

1913, June 1. Offensive and defensive treaty of alliance with Greece, concluded for ten years (p. 760).

June 29. Outbreak of the Second Balkan War (p. 760).

1914, June 24. Prince Alexander, heir to the throne, proclaimed regent for the deranged king.

June 28. Assassination of the Archduke Francis Ferdinand at Sarajevo.

July 28. Declaration of war on Serbia by Austria-Hungary (p. 762).

(*Cont. pp.* 916 *f.*, 1016.)

c. MONTENEGRO

1782-1830. PETER I, vladika (i.e. *prince-bishop*). He was a regular ally of Russia in the wars against the Turks.

1799. Selim III recognized the complete independence of Montenegro.

1830-1851. PETER II, a national poet of the southern Slavs.

1851-1860. DANILO I. He abolished the office of prince-bishop and established himself as a secular ruler. His efforts to reform and modernize the state led to opposition which ended in Danilo's murder (Aug. 12, 1860).

1852-1853. One of the numerous clashes between the Montenegrins and the Turks threatened to lead to disaster for the former when Omar Pasha invaded the little state. The Turks were obliged to withdraw (Feb. 1853) under threats from Austria (Leiningen mission).

1860-1918. NICHOLAS I, who, during his long reign, effected many military, administrative, and educational reforms and modernized the state. Montenegro definitely assumed a position among the lesser European powers.

1861. Following a revolt in Herzegovina, supported by the Montenegrins, the country was again invaded by Omar Pasha, who forced the recognition of Turkish supremacy.

1876, July 2. War against Turkey, resulting from the great insurrection in Bosnia and Herzegovina. Successes of the Montenegrins (p. 734).

1878, July 13. TREATY OF BERLIN, recognizing the complete independence of Montenegro, which received some increase of territory.

1905, Dec. 1?. Nicholas finally granted a constitution, with an assembly elected by universal suffrage. Since the advent of the Karageorgevich dynasty in Serbia (1903) there was growing rivalry for leadership of the Southern Slavs, resulting in conspiracy against the life of Nicholas.

1910, Aug. 28. NICHOLAS proclaimed himself king.

1912, Oct. 8. First Balkan War. Montenegro, though not bound to the other states by formal alliance, was the first power to declare war (p. 759).

1913, Apr. 10. Blockade of the Montenegrin coast by the powers, to raise the siege of Scutari. Nicholas took Scutari (Apr. 22), but was forced by Austrian threats to evacuate it (May 5).

1914, Aug. 5. Montenegro declared war on Austria. (*Cont. pp.* 926, 1016.)

Rulers of Montenegro
(Petrovich-Njegosh Dynasty)

Stephen Herakovich Njegosh

Danilo Petrovich Njegosh
Vladika, 1711–1737

Radul

Sava

Nicholas

Sava Petrovich
Vladika, 1737–1782

Vassili Petrovich
Coadjutor of Sava
1744–1766. d. 1766

Nicholas

Ivan

Ivan

Sava

Peter I
Vladika, 1782–1830

Stanko

Peter II
Vladika 1830–1851

Peter
Regent 1851–1854

George

Massan

Mirko ══ Anastasia
Martinovich

Danilo I ══ Darinka Kvekich
Vladika 1851
Prince 1852–1860

Nicholas I ══ Milena Vukotich
Prince, 1860–1910
King, 1910–1918
d. 1921

Olga

'Militza
m. Grand
Duke
Peter of
Russia

Danilo
m. Jutta of
Mecklen-
burg. Re-
nounced
claims
1921

Helena
m. Victor Em-
manuel III
of Italy

Anna
m. Francis
of Batten-
berg

Mirko
m. Nathalia
Constan-
tinovich

Anastasia
m. (1) Duke
of Leuch-
tenberg
(2) Grand
Duke Nicholas
of Russia

Peter
d. 1932

Mirko
b. 1908
(present
claimant)

Rulers of Bulgaria

Augustus ===== Clementine
Prince of Coburg | d. of
Louis Philippe
of France

Marie Louise (1) ==== Ferdinand ============ (2) Eleonora
of Parma | of Saxe-Coburg | of Reuss
Prince of Bulgaria, 1887–1908
Tsar of Bulgaria, 1908–1918

Boris III ==== Giovanna   Cyril   Eudoxia   Nadejda
1918–1943 | of Italy   m. Albert Eugene
of Württemberg

Marie Louise   Simeon II
b. 1933   1943–1946

d. BULGARIA

1762. The monk **Paisi** wrote his *History of the Bulgarian People*, generally taken to mark the beginning of the Bulgarian national renaissance.

1840. Translation of the Bible into Bulgarian by the monk **Neophytos**, aided by the American missionary, **Elias Riggs**.

1858. Opening of the **first American mission** (1861, **Samokov Seminary** founded by **J. F. Clarke**). Rapid growth of Bulgarian national movement, with revolutionary committees at Bucharest and Odessa. Connection of the revolutionaries (**Rakovski** and **Botev**) with Prince Michael of Serbia.

1870. Establishment of the **Bulgarian Exarchate**, a national branch of the Greek Orthodox Church. The exarch was given jurisdiction over large parts of Macedonia and Thrace, as well as Bulgaria.

1875, Sept. Abortive rising of the Bulgarians against Turkish rule.

1876, Apr.-Aug. Great insurrection in Bulgaria, put down by Turkish irregulars (*Bulgarian Horrors*).

1878, Mar. 3. T R E A T Y O F S A N STEFANO, with provision for a large Bulgarian state to include most of Macedonia (p. 735).

July 13. TREATY OF BERLIN (p. 736) establishing a small Bulgarian principality north of the Balkan Mountains and an Eastern Roumelia, south of the mountains. Macedonia left under Turkish rule, with promises (Art. XXIII) of reform.

1879, Feb. 22. A constitution granted the new Bulgarian state, under Russian auspices.

Apr. 29. Alexander of Battenberg elected prince. He was a favorite nephew of the tsar and was intended to serve as a satrap. He soon became involved in conflict with the national assembly (*Sobranye*), of which the Liberal members opposed dictation by Russia.

1879-1886. ALEXANDER I, prince.

1881, July 13. With Russian consent **the prince changed the constitution to give himself greater power.** He appointed a ministry headed by Russian officers.

1883, Sept. 30. Alexander, hounded by Russian concession-hunters (demands for a Rustchuk-Küstendil railway) and confronted with the hostility of the liberal, nationalist elements, **restored the Constitution of 1879,** thereby winning the enmity of the Russians.

1883-1884. Alexander's projected marriage with Princess Victoria, granddaughter of the German Emperor. This was vigorously opposed by Bismarck, fearful of estranging Russia, but ardently championed by Queen Victoria of England.

1885, Sept. 18. R E V O L U T I O N A T PHILIPPOPOLIS, in favor of union of Eastern Roumelia with Bulgaria. Alexander, under nationalist pressure, was obliged to assume leadership of the movement, despite violent protests of Russia.

Nov. 13. DECLARATION OF WAR BY SERBIA, demanding compensation. Defeat of the Serbs at Slivnitza (Nov. 17-19). The Bulgarians invaded Serbia and took **Pirot** (Nov. 27), but were forced to withdraw as a result of intervention by Austria. Peace made Mar. 3, 1886, on the basis of the *status quo.*

1886, Apr. 5. The sultan agreed to appoint **Alexander governor of Eastern Roumelia** for five years, to which the powers consented.

Aug. 21. Kidnaping of Alexander by a band of officers, inspired by the Russians. Provisional government of **Stephen Stambulov,** energetic nationalist leader, who arrested the conspirators and recalled Alexander.

Aug. 29. Return of Alexander. His appeal to the tsar, who replied coldly.

Sept. 4. Abdication of Prince Alexander. Regency, led by Stambulov.

Sept. 25. Mission of the Russian general, **Kaulbars,** who tried to win over the country to the Russian side, but failed. Acute danger of Russian military intervention, frustrated by opposition of the powers (especially Austria and England).

Nov. 10. Prince Waldemar of Denmark elected prince, but refused the offer.

Nov. 20. Departure of the Kaulbars mission.

1887, July 4. The Bulgarian Assembly elected **Prince Ferdinand** of Saxe-Coburg, who accepted and arrived Aug. 14. Protests of Russia. Ferdinand was not recognized by any of the powers, but, with the aid of Stambulov and the nationalists, managed to maintain himself, though the first ten years of his reign were punctuated by plots against him, assassinations of ministers, etc.

1887-1918. FERDINAND I.

1890, July. The Turkish government appointed three Bulgarian bishops to Macedonian dioceses.

1892, Aug. Visit of Stambulov to Constantinople. His policy throughout was one of friendship with Turkey and the extraction of concessions in regard to Macedonia. Suggestions by Tricoupis, the Greek statesman, for formation of a **Balkan League,** were rejected (1891).

1893. Formation of the **Internal Macedonian Revolutionary Organization** (*I.M.R.O.*) to work for an autonomous Macedonia.

1894, June 12. Dismissal of Stambulov, due in part to Prince Ferdinand's desire to pave the way for reconciliation with Russia, partly to pressure of Macedonian elements, dissatisfied with Stambulov's cautious policy.

1895. Formation of the **External Macedonian Revolutionary Organization,** with headquarters in Sofia.

June. Beginning of **raids into Macedonia,** from Bulgaria (**Boris Sarafov,** leader).

July 15. Brutal murder of Stambulov by Macedonian revolutionaries.

1896, Feb. Reconciliation of Russia and Bulgaria, on the occasion of the conversion of the crown prince, **Boris,** to the Orthodox faith.

Feb. 19. Prince Ferdinand recognized by Russia and the other powers.

1901. Arrest of Macedonian leaders, after the assassination of certain Rumanians and acute tension between Bulgaria and Rumania. They were tried, but acquitted.

1902-1903. Great insurrection in Macedonia, accompanied by raids from Bulgaria. Danger of war between Bulgaria and Turkey. Bulgarian government helpless in the face of the Macedonian agitation and revolutionary bands. The situation was cleared by the introduction of the **Mürzsteg reform program** by the powers (p. 752).

1908, Oct. 5. DECLARATION OF INDEPENDENCE by Ferdinand, who assumed the title of *tsar.* Beginning of the Bosnian annexation crisis, which overshadowed the action of Bulgaria (p. 756).

1909, Feb. 21. Visit of Ferdinand to St. Petersburg, where he was received with royal honors.

Apr. 19. Convention with Turkey, which recognized Bulgarian independence. Agreement with Russia, which assumed responsibility for the financial settlement.

Nov. Draft treaty of alliance between **Russia and Bulgaria.** Ferdinand avoided committing himself, preferring to balance between Russia and Austria. Efforts of the Serbs to effect an alliance were evaded, because of Ferdinand's unwillingness to abandon claim to all of Macedonia.

1911, Mar. 22. Gueshov cabinet. Beginning of negotiations with Serbia (Oct.) as a result of the Tripolitan War (p. 662).

1912, Mar. 13. CONCLUSION OF THE ALLIANCE WITH SERBIA (p. 758).

Mar. 29. TREATY OF ALLIANCE WITH GREECE (p. 759).

Oct. 17. OUTBREAK OF THE FIRST BALKAN WAR. Bulgarian victories (p. 759).

1913, May 7. Bulgaria agreed to cede Silistria to Rumania, in compensation for Bulgarian gains elsewhere.

June 14. Danev cabinet. Effort to arbitrate the conflict with Serbia regarding division of the spoils (p. 760).

June 29. OUTBREAK OF THE SECOND BALKAN WAR, following the attack of Gen. Savov and the Bulgarians on the Serbian and Greek positions (p. 760).

July 15. Formation of the Radoslavov cabinet.

Aug. 10. Disastrous Treaty of Bucharest, following Bulgaria's defeat (p. 760).

Sept. 29. Treaty of Constantinople, concluding peace between Turkey and Bulgaria.

1914, July 29. Bulgaria declared neutrality in First World War.

1915, Oct. 14. BULGARIA ENTERED FIRST WORLD WAR.

(*Cont. pp.* 925 *f.*, 1022.)

e. RUMANIA

1774. By the Treaty of Kuchuk Kainarji (p. 484) Russia was given certain rights of intervention in behalf of the Danubian principalities (Moldavia and Wallachia), which were still ruled by *hospodars* (usually phanariot Greeks) appointed by the sultan.

1802. Russia forced the sultan to promise to appoint the hospodars for seven years and not to remove them without Russian consent.

1812. By the Treaty of Bucharest (p. 596), Bessarabia was detached from Moldavia and ceded to Russia.

1829, Sept. By the Treaty of Adrianople Russia strengthened her protectorate and secured for the principalities complete autonomy (p. 724).

1829-1834. Continued Russian occupation. Enlightened rule of the Russian governor, Count Kisselev, who took precautions against the plague, organized a militia, reformed the finances and abolished trade restrictions.

1832. THE ORGANIC STATUTE, worked out by a group of *boyars* (landed gentry) under Russian auspices: an assembly of boyars was to elect the prince from among their own numbers. He was to be elected for life and irremovable without Russia's consent. The result was an

oligarchic system, which continued until 1856.

1832-1856. Period of great economic expansion (demands of western Europe for Rumanian grain; development of steamboat traffic on the Danube) and the rapid spread of French influence (many Rumanian students in France; influence of the Polish emigration). Progressive rule of Prince Michael Sturdza in Moldavia, but both principalities continued under strong Russian influence.

1848, June. REVOLUTION IN WALLACHIA, demanding a liberal régime (leaders Constantine Rossetti, Ion and Dmitri Bratianu). The hospodar accepted a liberal constitution and then fled.

Sept. By agreement with Turkey, Russia invaded the principalities and put down the revolution.

1849, May 1. Convention of Balta Liman between Russia and Turkey: the hospodars were to be appointed for only seven years; assemblies of boyars abolished and replaced by *divans*, appointed by the hospodars. Russia and Turkey were to occupy the country jointly. The Russians stayed until 1851.

1853, July 2. Occupation of the principalities by Russia, following the dispute with Turkey which led to the Crimean War (p. 726).

1854, Aug. 8. Evacuation of the country by the Russians and occupation by the Austrians (till Mar. 1857) in agreement with Turkey (p. 727).

1856, Feb.-Mar. CONGRESS OF PARIS (p. 728). Napoleon III favored union of the principalities (influence of Mme. Cornu and of Ion Bratianu). This was opposed by Turkey and Austria, gradually supported by England. Russia sided with France. It was finally decided that the sultan should summon popularly elected divans to ascertain the wishes of the population. At the same time an international commission was to investigate and suggest an organization.

1857, Mar. Evacuation by Austria. In the elections every kind of pressure and corruption was employed to debar the unionists, who were consequently defeated. France at once demanded annulment, which the sultan refused.

Aug. France, Russia, Prussia, and Sardinia broke off relations with Turkey. Acute danger of war between France and England, the latter supporting Turkey.

Aug. 9. Visit of Napoleon III to Osborne and Osborne Pact between France and England: England agreed to annulment of the elections and approved of a system of common institutions under separate princes (*broad administrative union*).

Sept. New elections; a great victory for the unionists.

1858, Aug. 19. A conference of the powers at Paris decided to establish the **United Principalities of Moldavia and Wallachia,** with separate but identical administrations; delegates from each of the two assemblies to form a central commission for legislation.

1859, Jan. 17. Col. Alexander Cuza, a relatively unknown officer, elected prince in Moldavia.

Feb. 5. The Wallachians also elected Cuza. Napoleon recognized him at once and the other powers followed more or less grudgingly.

1862, Feb. 5. The sultan allowed the **fusion of the two legislatures** and the union of the principalities was recognized, with the new name of *Rumania*.

June 20. Assassination of Catargiu, the Conservative leader and prime minister. Thereafter Cuza, whose sympathy was with the peasant class, appointed a Liberal ministry under **Kogalniceanu** and proceeded to a policy of Liberal reform: **expropriation of the monasteries,** etc.

1864, Mar. 28. *Coup d'état* of Cuza, designed to break the Conservative opposition. A plebiscite approved his proposal to strengthen the prince's power by establishing an appointed senate, etc.

Aug. Cuza introduced a great **land reform** by decree: abolition of serfdom and feudal dues, with compensation to the landlords; the peasants were given a small share of the land.

1866, Feb. 23. Cuza kidnaped and forced to abdicate by a conspiracy of Conservatives and Liberals who desired a foreign prince. The Assembly at once offered the position to the **Count of Flanders,** son of Leopold II of Belgium, who declined.

Apr. 14. The provisional government (with the secret approval of Napoleon III and Bismarck) proclaimed Prince **Charles of Hohenzollern-Sigmaringen.** A plebiscite approved of the action.

May 22. Charles arrived at Bucharest, having crossed Austria in disguise.

July. Introduction of a new constitution, based upon the Belgian Charter of 1831 (liberal, but not democratic).

Oct. 24. The sultan recognized Charles and the powers followed suit.

1866-1914. CHARLES I (Carol). His reign was characterized by rapid economic development (especially petroleum).

1877, Apr. 24. Invasion of Rumania by the Russians during the war with Turkey, after a convention had been forced upon the government.

May 21. Rumania entered the war on Russia's side and **proclaimed independence.** The Russians rejected active help until they were hard pressed at the **siege of Plevna** (p. 735).

1878, July 13. THE TREATY OF BERLIN recognized the **full independence of Rumania,** but the Rumanians were obliged to cede **Bessarabia** to Russia in return for the much less desirable **Dobrudja** (p. 736). By Art. XLIV of the Berlin Treaty the Rumanian government was obliged to promise **protection to the Jews,** of whom there were many in Moldavia. Actually nothing was done and anti-Semitism became rampant in the country; protests of the powers achieved but little.

1881, May 23. PRINCE CHARLES proclaimed king.

1883, Oct. 30. ALLIANCE BETWEEN RUMANIA AND AUSTRIA, acceded to by Germany and Italy. This continued in effect until 1914, but was kept a strict secret by the king, so that only a few chosen ministers were ever initiated. The alliance was the result of Rumanian fear of Russia, but it failed to overcome the basic antagonism between Rumania and Hungary over Transylvania.

1888, Apr. Serious agrarian insurrection, due to the failure of the government to face the vital land question.

1893, Jan. 10. Marriage of Prince **Ferdinand** and Princess **Marie of Edinburgh.**

1900-1901. Tension in relations with **Bulgaria,** arising from conflicting aspirations in Macedonia and the murder of several Rumanians by Macedonian revolutionaries.

1905-1911. Rupture of relations with Greece as the result of friction over the treatment of Kutzo-Vlachs in Macedonia by Greek comitadjis. Large numbers of Greeks were expelled from Rumania.

1907, Mar.-Apr. Great insurrection of peasants in Moldavia, which had to be put down by military forces. Martial law proclaimed throughout the country.

Kings of Rumania

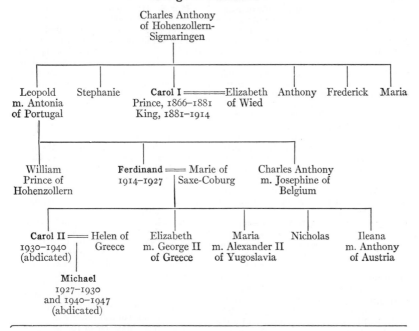

Charles Anthony
of Hohenzollern-
Sigmaringen

Leopold   Stephanie   Carol I ═══════Elizabeth   Anthony   Frederick   Maria
m. Antonia   Prince, 1866–1881   of Wied
of Portugal   King, 1881–1914

William   Ferdinand ═══ Marie of   Charles Anthony
Prince of   1914–1927   Saxe-Coburg   m. Josephine of
Hohenzollern   Belgium

Carol II ═══ Helen of   Elizabeth   Maria   Nicholas   Ileana
1930–1940   Greece   m. George II   m. Alexander II   m. Anthony
(abdicated)   of Greece   of Yugoslavia   of Austria

Michael
1927–1930
and 1940–1947
(abdicated)

1913, May 7. Agreement with Bulgaria by which the latter was to cede Silistria as compensation for gains made in the Balkan Wars. The Rumanian government demanded more.

July 10. DECLARATION OF WAR ON BULGARIA, Rumania joining with Serbia and Greece in the Second Balkan War (p. 760).

1914, June 14. Visit of Tsar Nicholas of Russia and Sazonov to **Constantza,** taken as evidence of Rumania's veering to the side of the Entente powers (p. 761).

Aug. 4. Rumania proclaimed neutrality in the First World War.

Oct. 10. Death of King Charles, heartbroken over the failure of the government to honor the treaty of alliance with Austria.

1914–1927. FERDINAND I, nephew of Charles.

1916, Aug. 27. RUMANIA DECLARED WAR ON AUSTRIA.
(*Cont. pp.* 934, 1024.)

2. THE OTTOMAN EMPIRE

1793. The New Regulations, providing for the complete reorganization of the military system and the establishment of a corps modeled on European lines, revision of commercial arrangements (to get rid of the abuse of *berats* or licenses by foreign representatives), revision of the tax system, etc. These **reforms of Selim III** met with vigorous opposition from the Janissaries and from the religious leaders. Nothing much came of them, though Selim built up a small and effective military force of a few thousand men, trained on European lines.

1798. Napoleon's Egyptian Expedition (p. 586).

1804, Feb. RISING OF THE SERBS, under George Petrovich (**Kara George**), a well-to-do trader in pork. The Serbs had been aroused to national self-consciousness by the writings of **Rajich** and **Obradovich,** but the movement was directed less against Turkish rule than against the oppression of the Janissary garrison at Belgrade. The Janissaries were driven out in Dec. 1806 and in 1808 the supreme command was made hereditary in the family of Karageorge. Encouraged by Russia the movement took on a much larger aspect.

1806-1812. War with Russia (p. 592).

1807, July. Selim III dethroned as a result of a rising of the Janissaries, who put **Mustapha IV** on the throne. **Bairakdar**, the pasha of Rustchuk, led a strong force to Constantinople in the hope of seizing control. He took the city (1808), but his opponents had Selim strangled before he could be restored. Bairakdar thereupon put upon the throne **Mahmud II**, the nephew and pupil of Selim. Having made the mistake of sending most of his troops to the Danube, Bairakdar was soon faced with a new revolt, in which he lost his life. Mahmud was left on the throne only because he was the last of the Ottoman house.

1808-1839. **MAHMUD II,** a proud and obstinate ruler, whose great object was to put down the rebellious pashas in the provinces and to re-establish the absolute power of the sultan. In the first ten years of his reign he succeeded in displacing most of the Derebeys in Anatolia.

1815-1817. **Second rising of the Serbs,** under **Milosh Obrenovich.** The Serbs had been shamefully deserted by the Russians in the Treaty of Bucharest and the first insurrection had been suppressed (1813). Kara George returned from exile in Austria in 1817, but was murdered by his Obrenovich opponents. Beginning of the blood feud between the Obrenovich and Karageorgevich families. Milosh was recognized by the Turks in 1817 as hereditary Prince of Serbia, which at that time was only a very small part of present-day Serbia.

1821-1830. **GREEK WAR OF INDEPENDENCE.** This was the result of growing prosperity of the Greeks in the later 18th century (Black Sea grain trade), the cultural renaissance (Korais, Rhigas), the encouragement of Russia (Catherine's *Greek Scheme*; revolt of 1769-1776, and the influence of the French Revolution and the intrigues of Napoleon. A secret revolutionary society, the *Hetairia Philiké*, was founded at Odessa in 1814 and was in close touch with the Russian government (**Count Capo d'Istria,** close friend of Tsar Alexander I). At the head of the movement was **Alexander Hypsilanti,** member of a powerful Greek Phanariot family from Moldavia and an officer in the Russian army.

1821, Feb. Outbreak of an **insurrection in Wallachia** against Turkish-

Greek rule. This precipitated action by the Greeks.

Mar. 6. **Hypsilanti proclaimed the revolt in Moldavia** and appealed to the tsar for aid. Tsar Alexander, under Metternich's influence, disavowed him and refused to countenance a revolutionary movement. Hypsilanti lost courage, and was defeated by a Turkish force at **Dragashan** (June 26). He fled, but was captured and imprisoned by the Austrians.

At the same time a more imposing insurrection took place in the **Morea,** which was joined by some of the more prosperous islands. The Turks, a small minority, were ruthlessly slaughtered and the movement spread rapidly to the rest of Greece. The Turks retaliated by hanging the Greek patriarch and massacring Greeks in Constantinople. This, in turn, led to protests from Russia and acute danger of war.

July 27. **Russian ultimatum to Turkey,** demanding restoration of Christian churches, protection of the Christian religion, etc. The Turks rejected this and relations were severed. War was prevented only through the efforts of Metternich and Castlereagh, who reminded the tsar of the dangers of supporting revolution.

Oct. 5. **The Greeks took Tripolitsa,** the main Turkish fortress in the Morea. Massacre of 10,000 Turks.

1822, Jan. 13. A Greek assembly at Epidauros declared **Greek independence** and drew up an organic statute (constitution) providing for a liberal parliamentary system and an executive directory of five.

Feb. 5. **A Turkish army finally took Janina** and brought to an end the career of **Ali of Janina,** one of the most powerful of the pashas. The Turks were now free to press the campaign against the Greeks.

Apr. **A Turkish fleet,** under Kara Ali, **took the island of Chios** and either massacred or sold into slavery most of the population.

June 19. The Turkish fleet was destroyed by the Greeks under Kanaris.

July. Invasion of Greece by an army of 30,000, which overran the whole peninsula north of the Gulf of Corinth. The Greek government fled to the islands.

1823, Jan. The Turks were obliged to fall back, having been unable to take the key fortress of Missolonghi, at the entrance to the Gulf of Corinth. The Greeks failed to take advantage of this respite, but devoted themselves to personal rivalries (**Kolokotronis** against **Kondouriot-tis**; conflict between the executive power and the legislature).

1824. First civil war. Kolokotronis was defeated. The government was established at Nauplia. Meanwhile the sultan had appealed for help to his powerful vassal, **Mohammed** (Mehemet) **Ali,** of Egypt, who possessed a strong army and navy. The Egyptians had already conquered Crete (1822–1824).

1825, Feb. Ibrahim, the son of Mohammed, effected a landing in the Morea and quickly subdued the whole peninsula. At the same time the Turks, under Reshid Pasha, invaded from the north and renewed the **siege of Missolonghi** (finally taken by the Turks, Apr. 23, 1826).

The Turkish-Egyptian successes aroused sentiment in Europe, where the Greeks were regarded as descendants of the heroes of old, renewing the struggle against the barbarians. Rapid spread of **Philhellenism** in Germany, Switzerland, France, and England. The governments were obliged to do something and an ambassadorial **conference at St. Petersburg** (1824–1825) discussed projects of establishing Greece as a group of three self-governing but tributary states, but Austria and England were unwilling to follow Russia in action against the Turks.

July 26. The Greeks put themselves under British protection and after the fall of Missolonghi appealed for British mediation.

1826, Apr. 4. St. Petersburg Protocol, signed by England (**Wellington mission** to St. Petersburg) and Russia. The two powers agreed to mediate between the Turks and Greeks on the basis of complete autonomy for Greece under Turkish suzerainty. Canning, who was chiefly concerned with preventing separate action by Russia, tried hard to associate other powers.

Apr. 5. Russian ultimatum to Turkey: demanded return to the *status quo* in the Danubian principalities and dispatch of a special envoy to discuss outstanding questions between Russia and Turkey. The Turks yielded, on the advice of Austria and France.

June 15-16. DESTRUCTION OF THE JANISSARIES. This had been planned by Mahmud ever since his accession. The hopeless inefficiency of the troops gave him an opening and he succeeded in winning over the religious leaders. In May he decreed the formation of a new corps, admission being opened to the Janissaries. But the latter rose in revolt. The small loyal corps of the sultan bombarded the barracks and the mob did the rest. From 6000 to 10,000 Janissaries are said to have been massacred.

1827, Apr. 11. The Greek factions, whose rivalries paralyzed all plans of action, united to elect **Count Capo d'Istria** president for 7 years.

May 17. Constitution of Trozene, which practically deprived the executive of all power and vested it in a single chamber, the Senate. Despite the efforts of the Englishmen, **Cochrane** and **Church,** united action proved illusory.

June 5. The Acropolis capitulated to the Turks.

July 6. TREATY OF LONDON. France joined Russia and England, and it was provided that if the Turks refused an armistice the three powers would threaten to support the Greeks and use their naval forces. In the interval the British made desperate efforts to induce Mohammed Ali to withdraw from the conflict (**Cradock mission**).

Aug. 16. Note of the three powers to the Porte, demanding an armistice. The Turks refused, whereupon the admirals were instructed to stop all reinforcements and supplies from reaching the forces in Greece.

Sept. 8. A large Egyptian fleet with transports landed at **Navarino,** but Ibrahim was induced, by Admiral **Codrington,** to await instructions from Alexandria before continuing operations. When Ibrahim learned that the Greeks were continuing the fighting at Patras, he disregarded the engagement.

Oct. 20. BATTLE OF NAVARINO. The British, French, and Russian squadrons entered the harbor, where the Egyptian fleet was crowded together. The battle was an artillery fight at short range and resulted in the sinking or blowing up of most of the Egyptian fleet. Wild enthusiasm in Europe; indignation of the Turks, who demanded reparation.

Dec. 28. The allied ambassadors left Constantinople.

1828, Apr. 26. Russia declared war on Turkey. The British disapproved (Wellington ministry, Jan. 1828), but the French were friendly to Russia and Austria did not dare raise too many objections.

June 8. The Russians crossed the Danube, but were held up by the garrisons of the fortresses on the south bank (Shumla, Silistria, Varna).

Aug. 9. Anglo-French convention with Mohammed Ali, providing for the evacuation of the Egyptian forces from

Greece. This was carried out by a **French expeditionary force** under Gen. Maison (winter 1828–1829).

Oct. 12. The Russians took **Varna**, but were too exhausted to continue the campaign that winter.

1829, Mar. 22. LONDON PROTOCOL, drawn up by an ambassadorial conference: Greece, south of a line from the Gulf of Volo to the Gulf of Arta, with Negroponte (Euboea) and the Cyclades (but without Crete) to be an autonomous, tributary state, under a prince (*not* to be chosen from the ruling families of England, France, or Russia).

June 11. Battle of Kulevcha. The Russians, under Gen. Diebitsch, opened the road to the Balkan Mountains.

July 15. Diebitsch crossed the mountains (first time a Russian army advanced so far).

Aug. 20. The Russians took Adrianople. In the meanwhile Gen. Paskievich took **Kars** and **Erzerum** on the Asiatic front. The Turkish Empire on the verge of collapse (scheme of Prince **Polignac**, the French prime minister, for the partition of the empire and a complete revamping of the map of Europe).

Sept. 14. TREATY OF ADRIANOPLE, concluded through the mediation of the Prussian officer, Major von Müffling. The Russians, decimated by disease, were hardly in a position to take Constantinople and decided not to try (fear of foreign intervention). The terms were lenient: Russia abandoned her conquests in Europe, but the frontier on the Pruth was extended from the northern to the southern mouth of the Danube; Russia was to occupy the Danubian principalities pending the payment of an indemnity of 15,000,000 ducats in 10 years; the hospodars of Moldavia and Wallachia were to be appointed for life and the Turks were to withdraw all Moslems and raze all fortresses in the two provinces; with regard to Greece the Turks agreed to accept the London Protocol.

Nov. 30. The London Conference decided that Greece should be given complete independence, but the frontier was moved back to the line Aspropotamo–Gulf of Lamia, i.e. almost to the Gulf of Corinth. This decision was embodied in a **new London Protocol** (Feb. 3, 1830), which the Greeks rejected as inadequate. The powers chose **Leopold of Saxe-Coburg** as prince, but he declined the offer on the grounds that the frontiers of the new state were too restricted. For the time being Capo d'Istria ruled the state in dictatorial fashion.

1831, Oct. Assassination of Capo d'Istria. Civil war between his brother, Agostino, and Kolettis.

1832, Mar. The powers chose for the throne the Bavarian prince, **Otto,** and extended the frontiers of the state to the Volo–Arta line.

1832-1833. CONFLICT BETWEEN THE SULTAN AND MOHAMMED ALI of Egypt, who demanded all Syria as a reward for his aid in Greece. When the sultan refused to yield, Mohammed picked a quarrel with the Pasha of Acre and sent Ibrahim with an army to occupy the country. **Ibrahim took Acre** (May 27, 1832), **Damascus** (June 15), and **Aleppo** (July 16). He defeated a Turkish army near **Alexandretta** (July 29) and began the invasion of Anatolia. The sultan appealed to England for aid, but Palmerston was preoccupied with the Belgian situation and did not as yet recognize the threat involved in Mohammed Ali's designs.

1832, Dec. 21. BATTLE OF KONIAH. Ibrahim completely defeated the grand vizier and the main Turkish army. With no further opposition, he pressed the advance to near Brusa and was on the point of overthrowing the Ottoman house. The Russians, however, intervened, offered the sultan aid and warned Mohammed Ali (**Muraviev mission** to Constantinople and Alexandria, Dec.–Feb.).

1833, Feb. 20. A Russian squadron arrived at Constantinople. Alarm of England and France, which began to mediate.

Apr. 8. Convention of Kutahia. France induced the sultan to grant Mohammed Ali all of **Syria** and **Adana.** But the sultan tried to hold out on Adana and the Russians began to land troops on the Asiatic side of the Bosporus. Great tension: British and French fleets at Smyrna. The sultan finally yielded (May 4).

July 8. TREATY OF UNKIAR SKELESSI, between Russia and Turkey, concluded for 8 years: each party to come to the other's aid in case of attack; a secret article relieved the Turks of this obligation in return for an engagement to keep the Dardanelles closed to all foreign warships. The Russians then withdrew from Constantinople (July 10). Vigorous protests of France and England, which took the treaty to mean that the Bosporus was to remain open to Russian warships and that Turkey was to be henceforth at the mercy of Russia.

Sept. 18. Münchengrätz Agreement, between Russia and Austria. The tsar declared for the maintenance of the Ottoman Empire and agreed that if partition became inevitable he would act only in agreement with Austria. But the meeting was taken in England merely as a re-affirmation of the Holy Alliance.

1835. Exploration, by Capt. Francis Ches-ney, of a possible line of com-munication from the Syrian coast down the Euphrates to the Persian Gulf. This re-flected growing British interest in the routes to the east. Growing tension in relations with Mohammed Ali, who obstructed the British schemes and rejected a proposal for a railway from Cairo to the Red Sea. Mo-hammed, on the contrary, pushed his conquests in Arabia as far as the Persian Gulf (1838) and the Indian Ocean, while the British occupied Aden (Jan. 1839). Palmerston became more and more con-vinced of the necessity of defending the Ottoman Empire against both Egypt and Russia (violent anti-Russian propaganda of **David Urquhart**), aided the sultan in the construction of a fleet and concluded an advantageous tariff treaty (1838). The French, on the other hand, became increas-ingly favorable to the Egyptian pasha and encouraged him in plans for a vast Arabo-Egyptian Empire.

1838, Dec.—1839, Apr. Mission of Reshid Pasha to London. In view of Mohammed Ali's threat to declare himself independent, the sultan proposed to the British an offensive and defensive alliance. Palmerston flatly refused anything beyond a defensive pact.

1839, Apr. A Turkish army began the invasion of Syria from the Eu-phrates.

June 24. BATTLE OF NESIB. Ibrahim completely defeated the Turkish forces.

July 1. The Turkish fleet, having gone to Alexandria, **voluntarily sur-rendered** to Mohammed Ali, either through treachery or through fear of the admiral that the grand vizier, Chosrew Pasha, was plan-ning to abandon it to the Russians.

July 1. Death of Mahmud II. The new sultan, **Abdul Mejid** (1839–1861), a mere boy, was ready to yield and make Mohammed Ali hereditary pasha of Egypt and Ibrahim pasha of Syria.

July 27. Collective note of the five great powers to Constantinople: they reserved the right to settle with Mohammed Ali. Palmerston from the outset insisted that Mohammed must give up Syria, while the French were sympathetic to him and refused to consider pressure.

Sept., Dec. Missions of Baron Brunnow to London. In order to effect a break between England and France, the tsar agreed to pressure on Mohammed Ali to force him to abandon Syria, and promised that Russia would not enter the Bosporus without similar action by the British at the Dardanelles.

Nov. 3. HATT-I-SHERIF OF GUL-HANÉ, a reform decree issued by the sultan under the influence of **Reshid Pasha**, who favored reform on western lines and hoped to increase the popularity of the Turks in England. The Hatt was chiefly a declaration of principles, guaranteeing the life, liberty, and property of all subjects and promising military and taxational reform. It was followed, in the next decade, by numerous specific measures resulting in the establishment of a modern, centralized administration, an assembly of notables, provincial councils, mixed tribunals, techni-cal schools, etc.

1840, Feb.-Oct. Ministry of Thiers in France. He resolutely rejected all proposals to coerce Mohammed and at-tempted to mediate between the Turks and Egyptians without intervention by the other powers. This disloyal policy enabled Palmerston to carry a reluctant cabinet for a policy of action with Russia and without France.

July 15. TREATY OF LONDON: Eng-land, Austria, Prussia, and Russia agreed to force a settlement on Mohammed Ali and to support the sultan if necessary. Mohammed was to be offered Egypt as an hereditary possession and southern Syria for life, but was to give up Crete, northern Syria, Mecca, and Medina, and return the Turkish fleet. Failure to accept these terms in 10 days was to mean the withdrawal of the offer of southern Syria; failure to accept the revised offer in 10 days would mean the withdrawal of the whole offer and freedom for the sultan to make other arrangements. Mohammed rejected these terms, relying on France. The British induced the sultan to depose him. Panic in Paris when the treaty became known. Violent bellicosity of Thiers and of the press, **danger of war on the Rhine.**

Sept. 9. The British admiral, **Stopford,** bombarded Beyrut, and Gen. **Napier** landed troops. Revolt against the Egyptians in Syria. Capture of Beyrut (Oct. 10); bombardment and capture of Acre (Nov. 3); Ibrahim forced to evacuate all Syria.

Oct. 20. Resignation of Thiers, reflecting Louis Philippe's decision against war.

Nov. 27. Convention of Alexandria, con-cluded by Napier: Mohammed Ali agreed to return the Turkish fleet and to abandon claims to Syria, in return for he-

'reditary rule of Egypt. The sultan was finally induced to accept (firman of Feb. 13, 1841).

1841, July 13. STRAITS CONVENTION, signed by the five great powers and marking France's return to the European concert: the Straits (Bosporus and Dardanelles) were to be closed to all foreign warships in time of peace.

1844. Visit of Tsar Nicholas to London. Discussions with **Lord Aberdeen** about the precarious condition of the Ottoman Empire. The tsar proposed that, in case of Turkish collapse, Russia and England should consult as to what should be done. **Gentlemen's agreement** to this effect.

1848, Sept. Rising in the Danubian principalities, directed chiefly against the Russian influence. In agreement with the Turks, the Russians invaded the provinces and occupied them until 1851.

1849, Oct. International crisis, resulting from the Russian and Austrian demand on Turkey that the **Hungarian refugees** be extradited. The Turks appealed to England for aid, and Palmerston promised it. France supported England and both powers made a naval demonstration at Besika Bay. On Nov. 1 the British squadron actually entered the Straits, to escape bad weather. It was withdrawn after Russian protests.

1851. Dispute between France and Turkey regarding the privileges of the Roman Catholic monks at the **Holy Places** in Palestine. These had fallen under the control of the Greek Orthodox monks, supported by Russia. Pressure of clerical circles in France induced Napoleon to press the claims of France, traditional protector of the Roman Catholics. In Feb. 1852 the sultan yielded and granted certain privileges to the Latins; these were extended in Dec. Indignation of the tsar, enhanced by his dislike of the upstart French emperor.

1853, Jan.-Feb. Nicholas' talks with Lord Seymour, the British ambassador. The tsar envisaged the demise of the "sick man" and made a bid for an agreement with England concerning the ultimate disposition of the heritage: Russia did not desire Constantinople, but would not allow any other power to take it; Serbia and Bulgaria might be made independent states; England might take Crete and Egypt, etc. Aberdeen, apprehensive of French plans toward England, was not unfavorably disposed toward the Russian advances.

Feb.-May. Mission of Prince Menshikov to Constantinople, to secure

concessions in the matter of the Holy Places and, in return for a promise of support against a western power (France), to secure a treaty recognizing a **Russian protectorate** over Orthodox churches in Constantinople "and elsewhere." These demands Menshikov tried to obtain by intrigue, cajolery, and threats.

Apr. 5. Arrival of Lord Stratford de Redcliffe (British ambassador to Turkey, 1842–1858 — the *great Elchi*) at Constantinople, with instructions to arrange a settlement of the question of the Holy Places in Russia's interest. This he did, only to learn (May 5) of the wider demands of Menshikov. He advised rejection of these and the Turkish grand council voted them down (May 17). Menshikov left (May 21) after many unfulfilled threats.

May 31. The tsar decided to occupy the Danubian principalities as a method of pressure on the sultan; on the same day the British and French governments decided to send their squadrons to Besika Bay. Stratford was empowered to call the fleet to Constantinople, if necessary. Division of the British cabinet: **Aberdeen** pro-Russian; **Palmerston** for strong action; **Clarendon,** the foreign minister, attempting to mediate. Strong public feeling in England against autocratic Russia.

June 13. The British and French fleets at Besika Bay.

July 2. Occupation of the principalities by Russian forces. The powers protested, but restrained the Turks in their desire to declare war.

July 28. THE VIENNA NOTE, drawn up by the French ambassador and submitted to Russia by Austria. This was a formula vaguely worded and designed to give the Russians satisfaction in principle without offending the Turks. The tsar accepted it (Aug. 5), but the Turks insisted (Aug. 19) on an amendment making it clear that the protection of the Christians should depend on the sultan, not on the "active solicitude" of the tsar. The Russians rejected this (Sept. 7), and in a circular revealed the fact that they had intended to derive a virtual protectorate from the original vague phraseology. After a **meeting of Nicholas and Francis Joseph at Olmütz,** the Austrians continued to work for acceptance of the note, but the British and French refused to follow suit.

Sept. 23. After demonstrations and disorders at Constantinople, the **British fleet was ordered to Constantinople.**

Oct. 4. The Turks enthusiastically declared war on Russia.

Oct. 23. The Turks, under **Omar Pasha, crossed the Danube** and in an engagement at **Oltenitza** (Nov. 4) held their own against the Russians.

Nov. 30. A Turkish squadron and transports on the way to the Asiatic front, was caught and destroyed by the Russians off **Sinope.** Great indignation in England.

1854, Jan. 3. At Napoleon's suggestion the **British and French fleets entered the Black Sea,** to protect the Turkish coasts and transports.

Feb. 6. Russia broke off relations with England and France.

Feb. 27. Anglo-French ultimatum to Russia, demanding evacuation of the principalities by April 30. The tsar did not even reply to this.

Mar. 12. Alliance of England and France with Turkey.

Mar. 20. The Russians crossed the Danube.

Mar. 28. England and France declared war on Russia and concluded an alliance with each other (Apr. 10).

Apr. 20. Defensive alliance between Austria and Prussia, each guaranteeing the other's territory for the duration of the war, and agreeing to oppose Russia if the latter made an effort to incorporate the principalities or attempt an advance beyond the Balkan Mountains. Austria began to mass troops in Galicia and Transylvania.

June 3. Austrian ultimatum to Russia: Russia must not carry the war across the Balkans and must state a date for evacuation of the principalities.

June 14. Austrian treaty with Turkey: Austria to occupy the principalities until the end of the war and to intervene in Bosnia, Albania, or Montenegro in case disturbances broke out there.

Aug. 8. The Russians evacuated the principalities, which were occupied by the Austrians (Aug. 22). Beginning of the sharp antagonism between Russia and Austria, which outlasted the century.

Aug. 8. THE VIENNA FOUR POINTS, agreed to by England and France: conditions of peace to be: (1) collective guaranty of the position of the principalities and Serbia; (2) free passage of the mouths of the Danube; (3) revision of the Straits Convention in the interests of the European balance of power; (4) abandonment of the Russian claim to a protectorate over the sultan's subjects and agreement by the five great powers to secure privileges for the Christians without impairing the independence of Turkey. The Russians indignantly rejected these terms.

Sept. 14. Landing of the allied troops at Eupatoria in the Crimea, the campaign in the Balkans (from Varna) having been cut short by the Russian evacuation of the principalities. The English were commanded by Lord **Raglan,** the French by Gen. **St. Arnaud.** The objective was the strong Russian fortress of **Sebastopol.**

Sept. 20. BATTLE OF THE ALMA RIVER, in which the allies, marching south, defeated an inferior Russian force. St. Arnaud died of cholera and was succeeded by Gen. Canrobert.

Oct. 17-19. First bombardment of Sebastopol. The allies, lacking heavy artillery, were unable to make much impression and had to settle down to a siege.

Oct. 25. BATTLE OF BALACLAVA, another allied victory (*charge of the Light Brigade*).

Nov. 5. BATTLE OF INKERMAN, in which the Russians again failed to break through the enveloping forces. In the interval Sebastopol was strengthened through the efforts of Col. **Todleben,** famous military engineer. Horrible sufferings of the allied forces during the winter (lack of fuel, clothing, and supplies); relief work and nursing organized by **Florence Nightingale.**

Dec. 2. Offensive and defensive alliance of Austria with England and France; the latter powers guaranteed Austria's possessions in Italy for the duration of the war and promised support against an attack by Russia; Austria promised to defend the principalities and give the allies free hand there. Austria mobilized all her forces, but still abstained from hostilities.

1855, Jan. 26. Sardinia (Piedmont) **entered the war** on the allied side and sent a force of 10,000 men under Gen. La Marmora, to the Crimea.

Mar. 2. Death of Nicholas I. His successor, **Alexander II,** was more disposed to make peace and engaged in abortive negotiations at Vienna (Mar.–June).

Apr., June. Violent attacks on Sebastopol failed to break the resistance of the Russians.

Sept. 8. The French forces finally succeeded in taking the **Malakov** tower, a key position; the British took the **Redan,** but were driven out again.

Sept. 11. The Russians abandoned Sebastopol, sinking their ships and blowing up the forts.

Nov. 21. Sweden concluded a treaty with the allies: Sweden to make no cessions or exchanges of territory with Russia and the allies to support Sweden against such demands.

Nov. 28. On the Asiatic front **the Russians captured Kars.**

Dec. 28. Austrian ultimatum to Russia, threatening war if Russia refused to accept the Vienna Four Points, plus the neutralization of the Black Sea and the cession of Bessarabia. Russia finally yielded and agreed to preliminary peace conditions at Vienna (Feb. 1, 1856).

1856, Feb. 18. THE HATT-I HUMAYUN, the most important Turkish reform edict of the 19th century, guaranteeing Christian subjects security of life, honor, and property and abolishing the civil power of the heads of the Christian churches. These churches in future were to be governed by a synod of the clergy and a national council of laymen. Full liberty of conscience was guaranteed and all civil offices thrown open to all subjects of the sultan. Christians were technically eligible for military service, but were allowed to buy themselves off. Torture was abolished and prisons reformed. Acquisition of property by foreigners allowed under certain circumstances, etc. These arrangements were opposed by the Turks as too far-reaching, and met with opposition from the Christian communities, but the whole program was worked out by the British, French, and Austrian ambassadors and forced on the Turkish government in order to effect a settlement before Russia could intervene.

Feb. 25-Mar. 30. CONGRESS OF PARIS (**Walewski**, French foreign minister, president; for England, **Clarendon** and **Cowley**; for Austria, **Buol** and **Hübner**; for Russia, **Orlov** and **Brunnow**; for Turkey, **Ali Pasha** and **Mehmed Jemel**; for Sardinia, **Cavour**). Napoleon had high hopes of using the occasion to effect a general revision of the treaties of 1815, with special reference to Italy and Poland. These schemes were frustrated by England, which drew closer to Austria in a policy of preserving the *status quo*; France thereupon began to court Russia. By the **Treaty of Paris** (Mar. 30) the powers admitted **Turkey** to the European concert and promised to respect the independence and integrity of the empire; **Russia** ceded the mouths of the Danube and a small part of Bessarabia; in Asia Russia returned Kars; Russia gave up claims to a protectorate over the Chris-

tians in Turkey and the powers "recognized the high value" of the Hatt-i Humayun; the **Danubian principalities** were placed under the joint guaranty of the powers and the status of the provinces was to be determined later; no change was made in the Straits Convention, but Russia agreed to the **neutralization of the Black Sea;** an **international commission** was established to assure safe navigation of the Danube. Adoption of **four rules of international law:** (1) Privateering remained abolished; (2) the **neutral flag covers enemy goods,** except contraband; (3) neutral goods, except contraband, were **not liable to capture** under an enemy flag; (4) **blockade,** to be binding, must be effective.

Apr. 15. Anglo-French-Austrian Treaty: the three powers agreed to regard any infringement of Turkish independence and integrity as a *casus belli* and to concert measures to meet it.

1856-1858. Settlement of the problem of the principalities (p. 719).

1858. Definitive abolition of feudal holdings in the Ottoman Empire.

1860. Founding of Robert College, crowning achievement of American missionaries in Turkey (since 1820; **Bebek Seminary** founded by **Cyrus Hamlin,** 1840; **Home School for Girls,** later **Constantinople Women's College,** 1871).

1860-1861. Insurrection in Syria and conflict between the Moslem **Druses** and Christian **Maronites,** many of whom were massacred. The powers gave France a mandate to intervene (1860, Aug. 2) and a French expeditionary force restored order. Evacuation of the French (June, 1861); special constitution for the Lebanon region.

1861-1876. ABDUL AZIZ. His reign was distinguished by a rapid **spread of western influence,** resulting from the association with England and France during the Crimean War (first loans to Turkey; construction of railroads from the Black Sea to the Danube, etc.), and by striking **development of liberalism (literary revival,** throwing off of the old Persian manner; **Namik Kemal,** radical dramatist and political writer; his history of the Ottomans and translations of Rousseau, Montesquieu, etc.; phenomenal growth of Turkish journalism). The leading statesmen of the period were **Ali** and **Fuad,** both followers of Reshid Pasha and committed to liberal reform. Encouragement of education: **Lycée of Galata Serai** (1868); **University of Constantinople** (1869); **School of Law** (1870).

1863. Foundation of the Banque Impériale Ottomane.

1864. Vilayet Law, establishing larger provinces under governors-general and subdivision into sanjaks, each with mixed councils and tribunals.

1865. Establishment of the Ottoman National Debt Administration.

1866-1868. Cretan insurrection. The islanders proclaimed their independence and union with Greece (1866, Sept. 2), but after years of fighting the revolt was put down. The sultan then proclaimed the Organic Statute, providing for Christian assessors to assist Turkish officials and for an elective assembly.

1867. Abdul Aziz attended the great exposition at Paris, the first sultan to travel abroad, visiting also London and Vienna.

1868. Concession granted for a railroad to connect Constantinople with the Hungarian lines (work begun 1872).

1868-1876. Elaboration of the Code Civil Ottoman.

1869. OPENING OF THE SUEZ CANAL (p. 830), the effect of which was to put the Ottoman Empire once more on the main trade route to the Far East.

1869. New law of citizenship.

1870. Establishment of the Bulgarian Exarchate, a separate branch of the Greek Orthodox Church; an important stage in the development of the Bulgarian national movement (p. 717).

Oct. 31. Repudiation of the Black Sea clauses of the Treaty of Paris by Russia, taking advantage of the Franco-German War. England and Austria protested, but Germany supported Russia. A conference at London finally (Mar. 13, 1871) accepted the Russian action while declaring against unilateral breaches of international agreements.

1872. A scheme, put forward by Ali Pasha, for the complete reorganization of the empire. The Balkan nationalities were to be given a self-governing status like that of Bavaria in the German Empire. This plan was ruined by the opposition of the nationalities and the protests of Russia.

1874. Financial collapse of the empire, due to heavy borrowing abroad and poor management. Half the interest on the debt was repudiated.

1875, July. INSURRECTION IN HERZEGOVINA AND BOSNIA, then in Bulgaria; war with Serbia and Montenegro; Russo-Turkish War of 1877-1878; Congress and Treaty of Berlin (p. 736).

1876, May 10. Midhat Pasha, dominant figure of a new ministry. Midhat (1822-1884) was the successor of Reshid, Ali, and Fuad, and an ardent reformer. His brilliant administration of Bulgaria (1861-1869) and of Baghdad (1869-1873). His plans for the establishment of a national state, including the Christians in the new Ottoman nationality.

May 30. Midhat and his associates deposed Abdul Aziz and proclaimed his nephew, Murad V, as sultan. Abdul Aziz died soon after, either by suicide or murder.

June 15. Assassination of several members of the government by a Circassian officer. Midhat supreme leader of the victorious reforming party.

Aug. 31. Deposition of Murad V on the plea of insanity.

1876-1909. ABDUL HAMID II.

1876, Dec. 23. PROCLAMATION OF THE CONSTITUTION by Midhat Pasha: it declared the indivisibility of the Ottoman Empire, liberty of the individual, freedom of conscience, the press, and education; equality of taxation; irremovability of judges; parliamentary government based on general representation.

1877, Feb. 5. Dismissal of Midhat Pasha, who was banished.

Mar. 19. Opening of the first Turkish parliament. It made a serious effort to fulfill its mission, but was soon prorogued by the sultan, who allowed the constitution to lapse and devoted himself to the re-establishment of his absolute power. Midhat and others were tried for the murder of Abdul Aziz in 1881 and convicted. Only intervention by the British government saved them from execution.

1878. Insurrection in Crete. After its suppression the sultan granted (Oct.) the Pact of Halepa, giving the Christians a majority in the general assembly and allowing the island practical self-government.

1881. French occupation of Tunis (pp. 737, 740).

1882. British occupation of Egypt (pp. 738, 832).

1885-1888. INSURRECTION IN EASTERN ROUMELIA and resultant eastern crisis (pp. 717, 739).

1888, Aug. 12. Opening of the railroad from Hungary to Constantinople.

Oct. 6. Concession to German interests for a railroad to Angora (Ankara), the first stage in the Baghdad Railway project (p. 749).

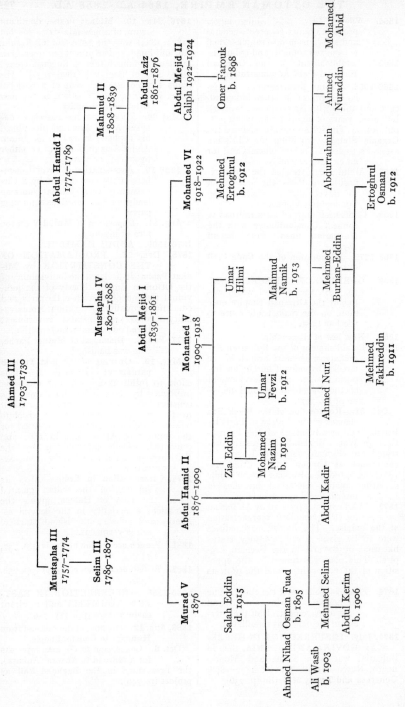

Ottoman Sultans (1703-1922)

Ahmed III
1703-1730

Mustapha III
1757-1774

Selim III
1789-1807

Abdul Hamid I
1774-1789

Mustapha IV
1807-1808

Mahmud II
1808-1839

Abdul Aziz
1861-1876

Abdul Mejid I
1839-1861

Abdul Mejid II
Caliph 1922-1924

Omer Farouk
b. 1898

Mohamed VI
1918-1922

Mehmed
Ertoghrul
b. 1912

Abdul Hamid II
1876-1909

Mohamed V
1909-1918

Umar
Hilmi

Mahmud
Namik
b. 1913

Mohamed
Burhan-Eddin

Ertoghrul
Osman
b. 1912

Abdurrahmin

Ahmed
Nuraddin

Mohamed
Abid

Mehmed
Fakhreddin
b. 1911

Ahmed Nuri

Abdul Kadir

Umar
Fevzi
b. 1912

Zia Eddin

Mohamed
Nazim
b. 1910

Murad V
1876

Salah Eddin
d. 1915

Osman Fuad
b. 1895

Mehmed Selim

Abdul Kerim
b. 1906

Ahmed Nihad

Ali Wasib
b. 1903

1889. Insurrection in Crete, encouraged by Greece. The powers showed little interest and the rising was put down. The sultan thereupon curtailed the Pact of Halepa, reducing the power of the assembly and increasing that of the governor.

1890-1897. ARMENIAN REVOLUTIONARY MOVEMENT and subsequent Armenian massacres, resulting from the growth of a national movement since 1840 and the failure of the powers (1879–1883) to secure reforms for the Anatolian provinces (p. 743 *f.*).

1895. Raids of Bulgar revolutionaries into Macedonia and beginning of the systematic activity of Bulgarian, Greek, and Serbian *komitadjis* (members of revolutionary committees) in that region (p. 718).

1896-1897. CRETAN INSURRECTION, fomented and supported by Greeks and resulting in the Turco-Greek War of 1897 (p. 745).

1896-1908. REVIVAL AND DEVELOPMENT OF THE YOUNG TURK MOVEMENT, harking back to the Constitution of 1876. The Young Turks (mostly exiles in France, Switzerland, and England) hoped to capitalize the discredit of the sultan; their chief aim was to prevent the disruption of the empire and to reconstitute it on a liberal, national basis. To some extent they arranged co-operation with the Armenian, Macedonian, and other revolutionary organizations (1903), but the movement throughout was hampered by dissensions between factions and by the drastic repressive measures of Abdul Hamid, which made all activity within Turkey impossible.

1900-1908. Construction of the Hejaz Railway to the Holy Places in Arabia. The line was built by popular subscription and was intended as a Pan-Islamic project.

1902-1903. Insurrection in Macedonia. Intervention of the powers. **Mürzsteg program** of reforms (p. 752).

1905, Nov., Dec. After prolonged argument between the Turkish government and the powers regarding the number of officers to be employed in the Macedonian gendarmerie, the terms of international control of Macedonian finance, etc., the powers made a naval demonstration and occupied Lemnos, forcing the sultan to yield.

1906, May. Dispute with England regarding the frontier between Palestine and Egypt (**Tabah, Akaba**). The sultan yielded to a British ultimatum.

1907, Dec. Meeting of various **Young Turk** and revolutionary groups at Paris. They concerted plans for action in common, and established contact with groups of discontented army officers (**Committee of Liberty,** founded 1905–1906) and **Masonic** lodges at Saloniki and in other towns of the empire.

1908, June 9. Reval meeting between King Edward and Tsar Nicholas. The Russians agreed to a much more extensive British plan of Macedonian reform. Fear that the three Macedonian provinces would be lost to the empire precipitated action by the Young Turk organization, the **Committee of Union and Progress.**

July 5. Niazi Bey, chief organizer of the revolutionary movement in Turkey, raised the standard of revolt at **Resna,** in Macedonia. When the sultan had a number of officers arrested at Saloniki, others, notably Enver Bey, joined Niazi (July 8). The Committee of Union and Progress adopted the insurrection (July 13), which was supported also by the Albanians. Government troops sent against the rebels deserted to the movement.

July 24. RESTORATION OF THE CONSTITUTION OF 1876 by Abdul Hamid, after several days of debate in the council of ministers. The sultan now posed as a good father who had been misled by his ministers. The revolutionaries gave up all thought of deposing him. Several weeks of frantic joy and fraternization throughout the empire, all nationalities joining with the Turks in the common celebration.

Oct. 5, 6. Proclamation of Bulgarian independence and annexation of Bosnia and Herzegovina by Austria (p. 756).

Dec. 17. First meeting of Parliament, which had a large Young Turk majority. Growing rift between the representatives of the subject nationalities (**Liberal Union**) and the Turkish nationalists, who dominated the Committee of Union and Progress: main issue that of decentralization in favor of the nationalities, and introduction of Turkish as the only official language.

1909, Feb. 13. Fall of Kiamil Pasha, the grand vizier. He was a liberal, sympathetic to reform and to the program of the moderates. The committee forced his resignation and had one of its sympathizers, **Hilmi Pasha,** appointed grand vizier.

Apr. 13. REVOLT OF THE FIRST ARMY CORPS, chiefly Albanian, at Constantinople, after violent attacks upon committee rule by the **Mohammedan**

Union and other conservative forces. The insurgents took the parliament house and telegraph offices and forced Hilmi Pasha to resign. The committee thereupon appealed to the troops in Macedonia.

Apr. 24. Mahmud Shevket Pasha, with an **Army of Liberation** numbering some 25,000, reached Constantinople and after five hours of fighting took the city. The leaders of the mutiny were executed and the control of the committee re-established.

Apr. 26. ABDUL HAMID DEPOSED by unanimous vote of the parliament, because of his approval of the counter-revolution. He was sent into exile at Saloniki (d. Feb. 10, 1918).

1909-1915. MOHAMMED V, brother of Abdul Hamid, a weak and helpless ruler.

1909, Apr. Massacre of Armenians at Adana and other places of Little Armenia. These were provoked by Armenian demonstrations which aroused the Moslems.

Aug. Revision of the constitution: the sultan was henceforth to name only the grand vizier, who was to appoint the other ministers; the sultan was deprived of the power to dissolve parliament; the cabinet was made responsible to parliament, which was given equal right to initiate legislation.

1910, Apr.-June. Insurrection in Albania, the result of Albanian demands for autonomy and the repressive policy of the Turkish nationalists. The revolt was put down with much bloodshed by a large Turkish army. In Arabia, too, there was constant disorder.

1911, Sept. 29. Outbreak of the **WAR WITH ITALY** (pp. 662, 758).

1912, Jan. 18. The sultan dissolved the **first parliament,** after a phenomenal growth of criticism of government by the committee.

Apr. The elections turned out a great victory for the committee, which appears to have used every form of pressure on the electorate.

June 25. Discontented officers at Monastir **(Saviors of the Nation)** joined the Albanians in a new insurrection against the government.

July 21. Cabinet of Ghazi Ahmed Muktar Pasha, a non-committee government representing the victory of the moderate groups over the extreme nationalists. The new government dissolved parliament by force (Aug. 5) and proclaimed martial law.

Oct. 8, 17. OUTBREAK OF THE BALKAN WAR (p. 759).

Nov. 28. Proclamation of Albanian independence, by an assembly at Valona which rejected the grant of autonomy made by the Turkish government on Aug. 20.

1913, Jan. 23. COUP D'ÉTAT OF THE YOUNG TURKS (especially **Enver Bey**) against the government, which was prepared to cede Adrianople to the victorious Balkan states. **Mahmud Shevket Pasha** became grand vizier.

May 30. Treaty of London, closing the First Balkan War (p. 760).

June 11. Assassination of Mahmud Shevket Pasha. This led to a period of Young Turk terrorism, which lasted until the World War. The country was, to all intents and purposes, ruled by **Enver, Talaat,** and **Jemal,** a triumvirate which ruthlessly suppressed all opposition.

July 20. The Turks took Adrianople, in the course of the Second Balkan War (p. 760). This was retained by the **Treaty of Constantinople** (Sept. 29).

Dec. The **Liman von Sanders** crisis (p. 761).

1914, Feb. 8. The Turkish government accepted a program of **reform for the Armenian provinces,** worked out by the powers under the leadership of Russia.

Aug. 2. Secret treaty of alliance with Germany (p. 919).

Oct. 30. RUSSIA DECLARED WAR ON TURKEY (p. 919).

(Cont. pp. 919 f., 1094.)

F. INTERNATIONAL RELATIONS, 1870-1914

The period was characterized at first by the power of Germany, the weakness of France, and the indifference of England. In the first decade Bismarck, whose figure dominated the scene, attempted to follow a policy of the free hand, but the constant friction between Austria and Russia with regard to the Near East made it necessary for him to make a choice between them. Thereby he embarked upon the policy of alliances, which ultimately involved most of the European powers in one group or another. The effect of technical and industrial advance on warfare resulted in growing anxiety for security on all sides, and consequently to alignments for the event of war which, in fact, tended to make war more likely. At the same time the expansion of European powers in Africa and Asia greatly extended the field of possible friction.

1871, Aug., Sept. Meeting of Emperor William and Francis Joseph, with their foreign ministers, at Ischl, Gastein, and Salzburg. The Austrians, their hopes of revenge for 1866 blasted by the defeat of France, were ready for better relations with the powerful German Empire. This policy was represented especially by the Magyars (**Count Julius Andrássy,** foreign minister, Nov. 13, 1871).

1872, Sept. 6-12. Meeting of the three emperors in Berlin (William, Francis Joseph, Alexander II of Russia). Alexander invited himself, for fear lest Austria and Germany should become too intimate. No political agreements were made at the meeting, but Andrássy and Gorchakov, the Russian chancellor, discussed the Near-Eastern situation and agreed to work for the *status quo.*

1873, May 6. Military convention between Germany and Russia, concluded during the visit of the Emperor William, Bismarck, and Moltke to St. Petersburg. If either party were attacked by another European power, the other was to come to its assistance with 200,000 men.

June 6. Agreement between Russia and Austria (Schönbrunn Convention) providing for consultation and eventual co-operation in case of attack on either. These agreements were not concluded for a definite period, and were loose in nature. Together they formed the **Three Emperors' League,** the main aim of which was to emphasize monarchical solidarity against subversive movements and to secure for Germany support in the event of trouble with France (May, 1873, overthrow of Thiers by the French monarchists).

Sept. Visit of King Victor Emmanuel II to Vienna and Berlin. Italy loosely associated with the Three Emperors' League, in order to obtain assurance against action by France in behalf of the pope.

Sept. Completion of the evacuation of French territory by German troops. Activity of the French royalists and clericals. Efforts at alliance with Russia. Friction with Italy and Germany over the question of the papacy and the *Kulturkampf* (p. 688).

1875, Feb. Mission of Von Radowitz to St. Petersburg, reflecting Bismarck's anxiety to hold Russia, in view of tension in relations with France.

Apr. 8. The article "Is War in Sight?" published in the Berlin *Post.* This referred to the new French army law and concluded that war was in sight. Panic in France, where the article was regarded as an inspired one. The **Duc Decazes,** French foreign minister, appealed to England and Russia for support, with the aim of discrediting Bismarck.

May 10. Visit of Tsar Alexander and Gorchakov to Berlin. Warnings of Gorchakov, supported by similar action by the British ambassador, Lord Odo Russell. Acrimonious discussion between Bismarck and Gorchakov. The latter's telegram: "Peace is now assured." Results: Bismarck realized the weakness of the Three Emperors' League and the suspicious jealousy of the other powers. France strengthened by the "moral coalition" that had been formed against Germany and by the knowledge that neither England nor Russia would stand idly by if France were attacked by Germany in a preventive war.

July. Outbreak of the insurrection against Turkish rule in Herzegovina and then Bosnia (p. 729). This initiated three years of acute Near-Eastern tension, which profoundly modified the relations of the powers to each other. The Serbs at once supported the insurgents, in the hope of acquiring the two provinces for themselves. **Russia** was extremely sympathetic (religious affinity, racial relationship to the southern Slavs, Pan-Slav movement and ambitions, secular aims for the destruction of Turkey, opening of the Straits to Russian warships, etc.).

Nov. 25. Purchase of the Khedive of Egypt's shares in the Suez Canal, a master-stroke of British policy (**Benjamin Disraeli**) which indicated England's growing interest in the Near East.

Dec. 12. Efforts at mediation by the powers having led to nothing, the sultan, in order to forestall more energetic action, promulgated reforms for the whole Ottoman Empire which were to meet the demands made by the insurgents.

Dec. 30. The **Andrássy Note,** communicated to all powers signatory of the Treaty of Paris of 1856. It called for complete religious freedom in Bosnia and Herzegovina, abolition of tax-farming, use of local revenue for local needs, and establishment of a mixed Christian-Moslem commission to supervise these reforms. This program was adopted by the powers and by the sultan (Jan. 31, 1876), but failed of its purpose because it was rejected by the insurgents.

1876, Jan.-Feb. **Bismarck's advances to England,** in the hope of meeting a possible Austrian-Russian rupture. This move was ruined by the suspicion of **Lord Derby,** the English foreign minister.

May 13. The **Berlin Memorandum,** drawn up by Andrássy, Gorchakov, and Bismarck after a conference at Berlin. It reflected Andrássy's aversion to any policy of annexations (suggested by Bismarck and Gorchakov) and was an expansion of the Andrássy Note. It called for a two months' armistice, resettlement of the insurgents, concentration of the Turkish troops in a few localities, retention of arms by the insurgents, supervision of reforms by the consuls of the powers. The memorandum was accepted by France and Italy, but was rejected by England, partly for technical reasons, but chiefly because of Disraeli's resentment of the failure to consult England in the drafting of the program.

May-Sept. **Insurrection in Bulgaria,** suppressed with great severity by Turkish irregular troops (*Bulgarian horrors*); thousands slaughtered.

June 30. **Serbia declared war on Turkey,** trusting in Russian support and hoping for the eventual acquisition of the insurgent provinces.

July 2. **Montenegro joined Serbia in the war.**

July-Aug. The **Serbs,** commanded by the Russian general, Chernaiev, defeated in a series of engagements. Serbia invaded.

July 8. Meeting at Reichstadt of Andrássy and Gorchakov. **Reichstadt Agreement:** the two powers to insist on the *status quo ante bellum* in the event of the defeat of Serbia and Montenegro, and on the reforms for Bosnia and Herzegovina laid down in the Berlin Memorandum. In the event of Serbian-Montenegrin victory, these two powers to be given parts of Bosnia and Herzegovina, but the larger part of these provinces to be awarded to Austria. Russia to obtain Bessarabia (lost in 1856). In the event of Turkey's collapse, Bulgaria and Roumelia to be autonomous states or independent principalities; Greece to acquire some territory; Constantinople to be a free city.

Sept. 1. **Complete defeat of the Serbs at Alexinatz.** They appealed to the powers for mediation. The Turks rejected proposals for an armistice, except on very hard terms. Great excitement in Russia and demand for war. Efforts of the Russians to secure assurance of German support in the event of war developing between Russia and Austria. Bismarck's reply: Germany would intervene only to prevent either Russia or Austria being mortally wounded or seriously weakened by the other.

Sept. 6. **Gladstone's pamphlet:** *The Bulgarian Horrors and the Question of the East.* Tremendous agitation in England against Turkish misrule. This greatly hampered the government in a policy of supporting Turkey against Russia.

Oct. 31. Turkey agreed to a six-week armistice, as a result of a **Russian ultimatum** to check the continued successes of the Turks.

Nov. **Russian preparations for war** against Turkey. Bellicose attitude of Disraeli, determined to frustrate the Russian designs.

Dec. 12. First meeting of the **Constantinople Conference,** convoked at the instance of England. Negotiations between **Lord Salisbury,** the British plenipotentiary, and **Count Ignatiev,** the Russian ambassador. *Agreement:* Serbia to lose no territory; Montenegro to secure parts of Herzegovina and Albania conquered from the Turks; Bulgaria (i.e. the regions under the Bulgarian Exarchate, extending over most of Macedonia) to be divided into an eastern and a western province; Bosnia and Herzegovina to be united as a province, and this, as well as the two Bulgarias, to have a governor-general appointed by the powers with approval of the Turkish government, and a provincial assembly; reforms to be supervised by the powers.

Dec. 23. **Midhat Pasha,** the grand vizier and leader of the Turkish liberals and nationalists, published the famous **constitution,** introducing a liberal régime for the whole empire and making reforms in special provinces ostensibly unnecessary.

1877, Jan. 18. An assembly of notables in Constantinople rejected all demands of the powers. Failure of the Constantinople Conference, which closed Jan. 20.

Jan. 15. January Convention (Budapest Convention) between Russia and Austria, to settle disputes as to the terms of the Reichstadt Convention: Austria to remain neutral in an eventual Russian-Turkish war; Austria to occupy Bosnia and Herzegovina when she saw fit; Serbia, Montenegro, and Herzegovina to form a neutral zone. An additional convention, signed Mar. 18 but antedated to Jan. 15, reaffirmed the terms of the Reichstadt Convention with regard to the disposition of Turkish territory; no large state, Slavic or otherwise, to be erected in the Balkans.

Feb.-Mar. Ignatiev mission to western capitals. Efforts of the English to arrange disarmament of both Russia and Turkey.

Apr. 24. RUSSIA DECLARED WAR ON TURKEY, the government yielding to the pressure of the Pan-Slav circles.

May 6. British note to Russia, warning against an attempted blockade of the Suez Canal or occupation of Egypt and reaffirming England's traditional stand with regard to Constantinople and the Straits. Bismarck's suggestions to the British to take Egypt and other parts of the Ottoman Empire rather than provoke war. Evasive reply of the Russians to the British note (June 8).

July 26, Aug. 14. Loose and negative agreement between England and Austria, listing seven points to which they would not agree in the event of a Russian victory. The British cabinet had decided (July 21) to declare war on Russia if the latter occupied Constantinople and did not make arrangements for immediate retirement. The reverses of the Russians at Plevna (July 20 ff.) eased the situation.

Dec. 10. Fall of Plevna, resumption of the Russian advance.

Dec. 12. The Turks appealed to the powers for mediation. This was rejected by Bismarck. Disraeli anxious to act, but his schemes were frustrated by members of his own cabinet (especially Derby). Andrássy contented himself with warning the Russians that Austria and the powers would demand a voice in the peace settlement.

1878, Jan. 9. The Turks appealed to the Russians for an armistice.

Jan. 23. The British cabinet decided to send the fleet to Constantinople, at the sultan's request. Resignation of Lord Derby. The fleet was recalled after reassuring reports had arrived from Constantinople. Derby rejoined the cabinet.

Jan. 28. Andrássy proposed the convocation of a European conference.

Jan. 31. Armistice concluded, the Russians to occupy the lines just outside Constantinople. War fever in England (*"We don't want to fight, but by jingo, if we do, we've got the men, we've got the ships, we've got the money too."*).

Feb. 8. Second British decision to send up the fleet. Other powers invited to join. The fleet started to enter the Straits, but returned when the sultan, under pressure from the Russians, failed to give permission.

Feb. 15. The British fleet finally arrived at Constantinople, having been ordered to proceed even without permission.

Mar. 3. THE TREATY OF SAN STEFANO between Russia and Turkey (ratified Mar. 23): Montenegro to be enlarged and given the port of Antivari; both **Montenegro and Serbia to be independent,** the latter also receiving some territory; **Rumania to be independent,** Russia reserving the right to give Rumania the Dobrudja in return for Bessarabia; **Bosnia and Herzegovina** to be granted reforms; **Bulgaria to** be an autonomous state under an elected prince and to be occupied for two years by Russian troops; it was to include most of Macedonia and to have a seaboard on the Aegean; **Russia** to receive Ardahan, Kars, Batum, and Bayazid on the Asiatic front; Turkey to pay a huge indemnity.

Mar. 6. Andrássy issued invitations to a congress of the powers to meet at Berlin. Long disputes between England and Russia as to what subjects might be discussed at the congress.

Mar. 25. Mission of Ignatiev to Vienna; he failed to reconcile the Austrians to the Russian peace settlement.

Mar. 27. The British cabinet agreed to call out the reserves and to bring troops from India to occupy one or two stations in the eastern Mediterranean. Second resignation of Lord Derby. Lord Salisbury became foreign minister.

Apr. 1. Salisbury's circular, restating the British position in strong and effective fashion. British efforts to establish common action with Austria. These were met by evasion.

May 8. Mission of Count Peter Shuvalov, Russian ambassador to London, to St. Petersburg. He there imposed a policy of agreement with England. He returned May 23 with the offer to push

Bulgaria back from the Aegean, pare it down in the west, and divide it into a north and south part.

May 30.   Secret Anglo-Russian agreement, as arranged by Shuvalov.

June 4.   Secret Anglo-Turkish agreement, reluctantly accepted by the sultan. To meet the Russian advance in Asia Minor, the British promised to defend Turkey against any further attack on the sultan's Asiatic possessions. In return they were to be allowed to occupy **Cyprus.** The sultan promised to introduce reforms in his Asiatic territories.

June 6.   Anglo-Austrian Agreement, following the failure of the Ignatiev mission. The agreement dealt with the future organization of Bulgaria and the length of Russian occupation.

June 13-July 13.   THE BERLIN CONGRESS: Bismarck, the "honest broker"; Gorchakov and **Shuvalov** for Russia; Andrássy for Austria; Disraeli and **Salisbury** for England; **Waddington** for France; **Count Corti** for Italy; **Caratheodory** (a Greek) for Turkey. The main decisions had been made in the preceding secret agreements, but there was much trouble and friction about details, especially after the Anglo-Russian agreement leaked out. **Bulgaria was divided** into three parts: (1) Bulgaria proper, north of the Balkan Mountains, to be tributary and autonomous; (2) Eastern Roumelia, south of the mountains, to have a special organization under the Turkish government; (3) Macedonia, which was to have certain reforms. **Austria** was given a mandate (June 28) to occupy Bosnia and Herzegovina and to garrison the Sanjak of Novi Bazar, a strip lying between Serbia and Montenegro. The territory given to Serbia and Montenegro was reduced. The **Greeks** were put off with promises for the future. **Rumania** was given the Dobrudja, but had to hand over southern Bessarabia to Russia. **Serbia, Rumania,** and **Montenegro** became independent states. **Russia** received Batum, Kars, and Ardahan. Reforms were promised for the sultan's Asiatic provinces. The British occupied Cyprus under the **Cyprus Convention** (above). Objections of the **French** were met by promising them permission to occupy **Tunis.** The **Italians** were put off with suggestions of expansion in Albania. The upshot of the treaty was that it left Russian nationalists and Pan-Slavs profoundly dissatisfied and left the aspirations of Serbia, Bulgaria, and Greece unfulfilled. The Ottoman Empire, wholly at the mercy of the powers, was left with a few fragments of territory in Europe which

were a constant bait for covetous neighbors. The promise of reforms in Macedonia and Asia Minor led to far-reaching agitation and trouble on the part of the Macedonians and Armenians.

Oct. 11.   Agreement between Germany and Austria abrogating the provision of the Treaty of Prague (1866) requiring a plebiscite in North Schleswig. This agreement had really been reached on Feb. 13, 1878, but was post-dated. Its publication (Feb. 4, 1879) was taken to reflect a German rapprochement with Austria.

Nov. 20.   Outbreak of war between England and Afghanistan, the result of the Russian advance in central Asia and the determination of the British to secure their frontier in India (p. 867). The British drove out the Amir, **Sher Ali,** and put **Yakub Khan** on the throne. In Sept. 1879 the British agent, **Maj. Cavagnari,** was murdered and the war flared up anew. **Abdurrahman** entered Afghanistan with Russian support, but made an agreement with the British (July 20, 1880): the British recognized him and gave him a pension.

1879, Sept. 4. Establishment of the **Dual Control** (England and France) in Egypt (p. 831). This grew out of the heavy investments of Europeans in Egypt and the financial difficulties resulting from the construction of the Suez Canal and many other public works by the **Khedive Ismaïl.** The Dual Control was first established in Nov. 1876, but had been suspended in Dec. 1878 when the khedive initiated ministerial government and gave the British and French controllers of finance seats in the cabinet. This plan had not worked, because of the policy of the khedive of retaining power. England and France thereupon forced the **abdication of Ismaïl** (1879, June 26) and the succession of **Tewfik,** who restored the Dual Control.

Oct. 7.   ALLIANCE TREATY BETWEEN GERMANY AND AUSTRIA, concluded for five years, but regularly renewed; it remained in force until 1918 and was the foundation stone of Bismarck's alliance system. *Provisions:* If either party were attacked by Russia, the other should come to its assistance with all forces; if either should be attacked by some other power, the other should preserve at least neutrality; if some other power should be supported by Russia, then each ally was obliged to aid the other. The alliance was the result of a period of tension between Germany and Russia following the Berlin Congress, the Russian nationalists blaming Bismarck for Russia's diplomatic defeat. There had been months of newspaper recrimination culminating in a threatening letter of Tsar Alexander II to William I. Bismarck, always fearful of a coalition built up by Russia against Germany and suspecting that Andrássy would soon be displaced by the pro-Russian party in Vienna, decided on the alliance, which Andrássy welcomed. The negotiations were held up by the obstinate resistance of Emperor William, who yielded only when Bismarck threatened to resign. There was some thought of bringing **England** into the combination; Disraeli was friendly, but the German ambassador, Count Münster, misrepresented the projected alliance as one directed chiefly against France and Bismarck allowed the matter to drop. The immediate result of the negotiation was the **mission of Saburov** to Berlin, in the effort to effect a Russian-German alliance or the revival of the Three Emperors' League (Sept.–Oct. 1879). At the moment Bismarck evaded these advances.

1880, June-Nov.   Montenegrin troubles.
The Albanian League, a union of tribes supported by the sultan, vigorously and successfully resisted the efforts of the Montenegrins to take over the Albanian territory assigned them by the Treaty of Berlin. A conference of the powers at Berlin (June) decided that Montenegro should receive Dulcigno in lieu of some of the disputed territory. The Turks resisted. A naval demonstration of the powers at **Dulcigno** (Sept. 28) had no effect. The British government (under Gladstone since Apr.) took a strong line and threatened to occupy the customs house at Smyrna. The Turks finally yielded (Nov. 25).

1881, May 12.   Treaty of Bardo, establishing a **French protectorate over Tunis.** This went back to the assurances of Salisbury and Bismarck during the Congress of Berlin, but the French government had not acted because of the indifference of French public opinion in matters of colonial expansion and because of distrust of Bismarck's motives. The question was precipitated by the activity of the Italians, determined to make good their failure to secure gains at the Berlin Congress at Austria's expense. The French prime minister, **Jules Ferry,** an ardent imperialist, took advantage of raids by Krumir tribes into Algeria (Mar. 1881) to secure credits from the Chamber. After the invasion of Tunis the bey gave in without much resistance. The affair initiated a long period of **Franco-Italian tension** and modified the Mediterranean situation to England's disadvantage. Gladstone protested, but the British government was committed by Salisbury's assurances.

May 24.   The Turks were obliged to cede to Greece a considerable part of **Thessaly** and part of **Epirus.** These territories had been promised Greece at the Berlin Congress, but the Turks had temporized. In the autumn of 1880 there was acute danger of war. In the end the Greeks had to content themselves with much less than had originally been envisaged.

June 18.   THE ALLIANCE OF THE THREE EMPERORS: Term three years, renewed in 1884 for three more years. *Provisions:* If one of the contracting powers found itself at war with a fourth power (except Turkey), the other two were to maintain friendly neutrality. Modifications of the territorial *status quo* in Turkey should take place only after agreement between the three powers; if any one of them should feel compelled to go to war with Turkey, it should consult its allies in advance as to the eventual results; the principle of the closure of the Straits was recognized; if this principle were infringed by Turkey, the three powers should warn Turkey that they would regard her as having put herself in a state of war with the aggrieved power; Austria reserved the right to annex Bosnia and Herzegovina when she saw fit; the three powers agreed not to oppose the eventual union of Bulgaria and Eastern Roumelia. This treaty, kept rigorously secret, was the outcome of long negotiations between Bismarck and Saburov, the Russians being anxious for an alliance with Germany as protection against Austrian policy in the Balkans, and equally anxious for recognition of the closure of the Straits against possible English action. Bismarck refused an agreement that would not include Austria and the Austrians were hostile to the idea until after the advent of the Gladstone government in England, which was unfriendly to Austria. The final conclusion of the agreement was delayed by the assassination of the tsar (Mar. 13, 1881).

June 28.   Secret treaty between Austria and Serbia, the result of Prince Milan's resentment at being deserted by Russia in 1878 and of his chronic need for Austrian financial support. Term ten years. Serbia promised not to tolerate intrigues against Austria. Austria promised to recognize Milan as king. By Art. IV Serbia engaged not to conclude any political agreement with another power without consulting Austria. In case of war with other powers, each promised the other neutrality. Austria promised that in favorable circumstances she would support Serbia in making acquisitions toward the south. The treaty established more or less of a protectorate over Serbia and roused protests from the Serbian ministers. But Milan assumed personal responsibility.

1882, May 20. TRIPLE ALLIANCE, between Germany, Austria, and Italy, concluded for five years and renewed at intervals until 1915. *Terms:* If Italy were attacked by France without provocation, Germany and Austria were to come to Italy's aid; Italy to come to Germany's aid if the latter were attacked by France; if one or two of the contracting parties were attacked or involved in war with two or more great powers, the non-attacked member or members of the alliance should come to the aid of the other or others; if one of the allies should be forced to make war on some other great power, the others were to preserve benevolent neutrality. The treaty was the result of Italy's isolation after the French occupation of Tunis and also a reflection of popular demand for security against radicalism and the prospect of intervention by other powers in behalf of the pope. The Italians wanted above all a treaty of guaranty, assuring them of the possession of Rome. This neither Austria nor Germany was willing to consider, though Austria was anxious for an agreement that would put an end to **irredentist agitation** (very active since 1876), and Germany was uneasy about the renewed Pan-Slav agitation (speech of Gen. **Skobelev** in Paris, Feb. 1882) and the possibility of a Franco-Russian alliance. The Italians secured no specific guaranty of Rome, but received assurances against attack by France.

July 11. Bombardment of Alexandria by the British fleet.

Sept. 13. Defeat of the Egyptians by the British in the **battle of Tel-el-Kebir. British occupation of Egypt** (p. 832). This was the outcome of a long development and the reflection of Britain's paramount interest in Egypt and the Suez Canal. The re-establishment of the Anglo-French condominium and the reorganization of the government in the interests of foreign bondholders had resulted in the growth of a nationalist, anti-foreign movement, inspired by the Pan-Islamic leader, **Jamal ud-Din,** and led by army officers like **Arabi Pasha.** An Anglo-French note, inspired by Gambetta (Jan. 8, 1882), was designed to strengthen the khedive, but was not followed up by action and only discredited the ruler as a puppet in foreign hands. The British proposal to have the Sultan of Turkey intervene was wrecked by the opposition of the French. On June 12 anti-foreign riots broke out at Alexandria and fortifications were constructed. The French refused at the last moment to take part in the action, as did the Italians. The

British bombarded Alexandria and then landed forces to protect the Suez Canal. After the battle of Tel-el-Kebir, Cairo was occupied. Arabi was sent into exile and the nationalist movement collapsed. During the entire crisis the English had enjoyed the support and encouragement of Bismarck, who thenceforth used the Egyptian question as a lever to bring pressure on Britain in other matters. The affair led to the estrangement between England and France which lasted until 1904 and was therefore a development of prime importance in European diplomacy.

1883, Feb.-Apr. Establishment of the Germans, under Lüderitz, at Angra Pequeña (Southwest Africa), marking the **beginning of German colonialism** (growing agitation from 1875 onward — *German Colonial Society,* 1882) and Bismarck's conversion to imperialism. The German establishment was opposed by the British, more through confusion than through interest, but the German government took the settlement under its protection (Apr. 24). There followed two years of growing **tension between England and Germany,** the dispute extending to East African territory, the Cameroons, etc. Bismarck managed to establish a loose **entente with the French** (Jules Ferry), especially in the question of Egypt (financial conference at London, June–Aug. 1884), and thereby to oblige the British to accept Germany as a colonial power.

Oct. 30. Alliance of Rumania and Austria, to which Germany adhered. This was due to Rumanian dissatisfaction with the settlement of 1878 and fear of violation of Rumanian territory in the event of another advance of the Russians into the Balkans. The Rumanians, by the alliance, shelved their irredentist aspirations in Transylvania, but the agreement was kept exceedingly secret and had little effect on public opinion. *Terms:* Austria to come to the assistance of Rumania in case the latter were attacked without provocation; Rumania to come to Austria's aid if the latter were attacked in a portion of its states bordering on Rumania (i.e. by Russia). The treaty was concluded for five years, but was periodically renewed and remained in force until 1916.

Nov. Battle of El Obeid. Gen. **Hicks** and an Egyptian force defeated by the **Mahdi,** religious leader of a movement directed against Egyptian rule in the Sudan. The British thereupon obliged the very reluctant Egyptian government to decide on the **evacuation of the Sudan.** Gen. **Charles Gordon** was sent out (Jan. 1884) to evacuate the garrisons. Gordon, more or less following ideas of his own, was surrounded and besieged in **Khartum**. The British government belatedly sent out a relief expedition under Gen. **Wolseley** (Aug.), but it was unable to save Gordon. Khartum was taken and Gordon killed (Jan. 26, 1885).

1884, Feb. 26. **British agreement with Portugal**, recognizing the latter's rights to territory at the mouth of the Congo. This was intended to frustrate the designs of King Leopold of Belgium (head of the Congo Association) and of France. France and Germany together protested so vigorously that the British abandoned the treaty (June 26).

1884, Nov. 15—1885, Feb. 26. **The Berlin Conference on African Affairs,** arranged by Bismarck and Ferry. Fourteen nations, including the United States, agreed to work for the suppression of slavery and the slave trade and declared complete liberty of commerce in the basin of the Congo and its affluents and on the adjacent coasts. Freedom of navigation on the Congo and Niger and their affluents was also declared. The Congo Basin was declared neutral. The principle of effective occupation to establish a claim on the coasts was set up. At the same time the various powers recognized the **Congo Free State,** which had developed under Leopold of Belgium from the **International Association for the Exploration and Civilization of Central Africa** (1876), and later the **International Association of the Congo** (1878), financed by Leopold and exploiting the discoveries of **Henry M. Stanley.**

1885, Mar. 31. **Fall of Jules Ferry** from power, after a minor French reverse at Langson in the course of the **war with China** (p. 880) over Annam and Tonquin (July 12, 1884–June 9, 1885). **End of the Franco-German entente;** gradual reconciliation of the English and Germans, with recognition of the German acquisitions in Africa and the Pacific.

Apr. **Acute Anglo-Russian crisis,** resulting from an attack by Russian troops on the Afghan forces at **Penjdeh** (Mar. 30). The Russians had gradually absorbed the central Asian khanates (**occupation of Merv,** Feb. 1884) and reached the territory supposedly under the Amir of Afghanistan. Efforts to delimit the frontier had been unsuccessful, due largely to the temporizing of the Russians. News of the Penjdeh clash brought the two countries to the verge of war. The British occupied **Port Hamilton**, on the Korean coast (Apr. 26), in view of probable operations against Vladivostok. But the British government ultimately drew back, apparently after abortive efforts to secure the consent of the powers for the passage of British war-

ships through the Straits into the Black Sea. The question was adjusted by compromise (Sept. 10, 1885).

Sept. 18. **Revolution in Eastern Roumelia,** initiating another period of tension in the Near East. The movement was directed at union with Bulgaria. Prince Alexander of Battenberg (elected Prince of Bulgaria in Apr. 1879) was obliged to assume leadership or else abandon his position. The Russian tsar at once (Sept. 23) recalled all Russian officers from the Bulgarian army, an expression of the dislike and even hatred for Prince Alexander that had been developing during the preceding years. Bulgaria was saved through the unwillingness of the sultan to send troops, and through the warm sympathy of England, which reversed its attitude on the question of union in order to meet the change in Russian policy. Austria was sympathetic to the union, but embarrassed by the clamor of the Serbs, who, like the Greeks, feared the movement might spread to Macedonia, where they too had claims.

Nov. 13. **Serbia declared war on Bulgaria,** after it had become clear that an ambassadorial conference at Constantinople would not rescind the union of Bulgaria and Eastern Roumelia.

Nov. 19. **Complete defeat of the Serbians in the battle of Slivnitza.**

Nov. 27. Serb defeat at Pirot. Bulgarian invasion. This was stopped only through Austrian intervention to save Serbia (**Khevenhüller mission**).

1886, Jan. 4. Greek note to Turkey demanding the territorial promises of 1878 by way of compensation for Bulgarian claims.

Jan. 24. Note of the powers to Greece warning against attack on Turkey. The Greeks ignored these warnings and prepared for war.

Feb. 1. **Agreement between Bulgaria and Turkey.** Prince Alexander appointed governor-general of Eastern Roumelia for five years. Russia insisted that Alexander should not be specifically named. The powers accepted this compromise and the agreement was signed on Apr. 5.

Mar. 3. **Treaty of Bucharest:** "Peace is restored between Bulgaria and Serbia."

May 10-June 7. **Pacific blockade of the Greek coast** by an international naval force. The Greeks were obliged to disarm.

Aug. 20. Kidnaping and **abdication of Alexander of Battenberg** by a group of officers, supported by Russia. A counter-movement in Eastern Roumelia, led by **Stephen Stambulov**, overthrew the Russian faction and recalled Alexander.

Aug. 28. Arrival of Alexander. He appealed to the tsar for mercy, but received a cold reply.

Sept. 7. Definitive abdication of Alexander of Battenberg. Indignation in Europe generally, but especially in England.

Oct. 27. Bulgarian national assembly at Tirnovo. Despite pressure from Russia (Kaulbars mission) the Bulgarians elected as prince **Waldemar of Denmark**, who declined the offer. Kaulbars and other Russian agents left the country (Nov. 17). Danger of Russian occupation of Bulgaria.

Nov. 13. Speech of Count Kalnóky, the Austrian foreign minister, warning against Russian action. Growing Austro-Russian tension, much deplored by Bismarck, who was constantly urging an agreement based on the division of the Balkans into an Austrian (western) and a Russian (eastern) sphere of influence. Bismarck reminded the Austrians that the alliance of 1879 did not oblige Germany to support a forward policy of Austria in the Balkans, but the Austrians enjoyed the sympathetic support of England.

1886-1887. Rapid development of **nationalist and revenge agitation in France**, the reaction to Ferry's policy of understanding with Germany in colonial expansion. Activity of **Paul Déroulède** and his *League of Patriots* (founded 1882) in behalf of an alliance with Russia. Appointment of Gen. **Georges Boulanger** as minister of war (Jan. 1886). He quickly became the darling of the country and the symbol of revenge on Germany (Longchamps review, July 14, 1886). Corresponding anti-German, pro-French agitation of the Russian nationalists (**Michael Katkov** and the *Moscow Gazette*).

1887, Jan. 11. Great speech of Bismarck, reviewing the international situation, warning the nations against war, redefining the German attitude, and advocating a large increase in the German army.

Feb. 12. FIRST MEDITERRANEAN AGREEMENT, between England and Italy, adhered to by Austria (Mar. 24) and Spain (May 4). The agreement took the form of an exchange of notes (Anglo-Italian; Anglo-Austrian; Italian-Spanish, acceded to by Germany and Austria, May 21). Bismarck had encouraged the combination, exploiting the acute Anglo-French tension (over Egypt) and the Italian-French tension (tariff war, etc.). The notes provided for the maintenance of the *status quo* in the Mediterranean, including the Adriatic, Aegean, and Black Seas. If the *status quo* could not be maintained, the contracting parties were to agree beforehand as to changes. Italy was to support the British policy in Egypt and England the Italian policy in North Africa. The Anglo-Austrian note stressed rather the community of interest of the two powers in the Near East. Spain promised not to make an agreement with France regarding North Africa which should be aimed at Italy, Austria, or Germany. England refused to bind herself to any specific action, but the effect of the agreements was to provide a basis for common action in the event of disturbance in the Mediterranean by France or Russia.

Feb. 20. RENEWAL OF THE TRIPLE ALLIANCE for five years. Negotiations had been carried on since Nov. 1886, the Italians demanding more far-reaching support of their interests in North Africa. This Bismarck was willing to concede, in order to be assured of Italy's friendship in case of a clash with France. But Austria objected, her attention being focused on the Balkans. In the end the old alliance was renewed and additional German-Italian and Austro-Italian agreements made. Germany promised that in the event of French efforts to expand in North Africa, if Italy were obliged to take action or even make war on France, Germany would come to the aid of Italy. If France were defeated, Germany would not object to Italy's taking "territorial guaranties for the security of the frontiers and of her maritime position." The Austro-Italian agreement provided for the maintenance of the *status quo* in the Orient. If this became impossible, neither party should occupy territory except in agreement with the other on the principle of reciprocal compensation. This was not to apply to the eventual annexation of Bosnia and Herzegovina by Austria.

Apr. 20. Arrest of Schnaebelé, a French frontier official who had been condemned by a German court for espionage. It was never determined whether he was arrested by the German police on the German or French side of the border. He was released a week later, when it was shown that he had been invited to a conference by his German colleagues. The affair roused great popular excitement, but was of much less significance than previously supposed.

May 16. Fall of the French cabinet in which Boulanger was minister of war. He was excluded from the new cabinet of Rouvier. Beginning of the reaction against him in French government circles.

May 22.   The Drummond-Wolff Convention, by which England agreed to evacuate Egypt within three years, but reserved the right to reoccupy in case of disorder. This convention was wrecked by the opposition of France and Russia — the first striking case of Franco-Russian collaboration against England.

June 18. Signature of a secret **RUSSIAN-GERMAN TREATY** (the *Reinsurance Treaty*) to replace the expiring Alliance of the Three Emperors, which Russia refused to renew. The two powers promised each other neutrality in the event of either becoming involved in war with a third power, but this was not to apply in case of aggressive war of Germany against France, or of Russia against Austria. They were to work for the maintenance of the *status quo* in the Balkans and Germany was to recognize Russia's preponderant influence in Bulgaria. The principle of the closure of the Straits was once more reaffirmed. An additional and very secret protocol promised German assistance in re-establishing a regular government in Bulgaria and in opposing the restoration of Battenberg. It also promised moral and diplomatic support "to the measures which His Majesty [the tsar] may deem it necessary to take to control the key of his empire" (i.e. the entrance to the Black Sea). This famous treaty represented Bismarck's effort to keep Russia from France and to buy her friendship by signing away things that he knew Russia could never get on account of English and Austrian opposition. On the Russian side the treaty reflected the victory of the foreign minister, Giers, over the extreme nationalist groups.

July 7.   The Bulgarian Assembly elected Prince Ferdinand of Saxe-Coburg-Kohary as prince, despite the opposition of the Russians. He was not recognized by the powers. Continuance of the Bulgarian crisis and of the danger of Russian intervention.

Dec. 12.   S E C O N D   M E D I T E R-RANEAN AGREEMENT (better *Near-Eastern Entente*) between England, Austria, and Italy (Bismarck having refused to participate — Bismarck-Salisbury correspondence, Nov.). It restated the principle of the *status quo* in the Near East and the importance of keeping Turkey free of all foreign domination. Turkey must not cede her rights in Bulgaria to any other power or allow occupation of Bulgaria by any other power. Neither must she give up any rights in the Straits or in Asia Minor. If she resists efforts at encroachment, the three contracting powers will agree as to measures to support her. If she fails to resist, the three powers will consider themselves justified, jointly or separately, in the provisional occupation of such Turkish territory as may be deemed necessary to secure respect for the treaties.

1888, Jan. 28.   Military agreement between Germany and Italy, providing for the use of Italian troops against France in the event of a Franco-German war.

Feb. 3.   Publication of the German-Austrian Alliance of 1879. This was intended as a warning to Russia, where nationalist agitation against Germany and Austria continued. Bismarck vetoed plans of German and Austrian military circles for a "prophylactic" war against Russia.

Feb. 6.   Bismarck's great Reichstag speech, dealing largely with the Russian situation and ending, "We Germans fear God, and nothing else in the world." The main terms of the Triple Alliance and of the Mediterranean Agreements were allowed to leak out at the same time. Taken together they served as a cold *douche* on the hopes and aspirations of both France and Russia.

Feb.   Acute crisis in Franco-Italian relations, Crispi fearing a sudden attack by the French fleet on Spezzia.

May 15. Italy adhered to the alliance of Germany and Austria with Rumania (p. 738).

1889, Mar.   Naval Defense Act, setting up the two-power standard for the British fleet and establishing an extensive building program.

July. Crisis in the relations of Italy and the papacy. The pope was on the verge of leaving Rome. The Italians again feared an attack by France, and induced the Germans and British to issue warnings.

1890, Mar. 18.   DISMISSAL OF BISMARCK (p. 691), resulting at least in part from the dissatisfaction of the young Emperor William II with Bismarck's policy toward Russia and his desire for closer relations with Austria and England.

Mar. 23. A German ministerial conference decided, on the advice of Baron Fritz von Holstein (long a collaborator of Bismarck, who had recently drifted from him), not to renew the Reinsurance Treaty with Russia. It lapsed on June 18, despite numerous Russian attempts to reopen the question of renewal.

July 1.   Anglo-German Colonial Agreement (*Heligoland Treaty*), by which Germany gave up large claims in East Africa and received in return the island of Heligoland, which England had obtained from Denmark in 1815. Since the island at that time was regarded as practically useless, the whole treaty was looked upon as a striking demonstration of German readiness to purchase the friendship of England.

Aug. 17-22. **Visit of the Emperor William to the Tsar at Narva.** Last efforts of the Russians to secure some agreement with Germany, evaded by the Germans.

1891, Feb. 18-27. **Visit of the Empress Frederick,** mother of William II, to Paris. Anti-German demonstrations and Franco-German tension. Russia supported France, but avoided any definite commitment.

May 6. **Premature renewal of the Triple Alliance,** the three documents being merged in one and Germany assuming somewhat larger obligations to support the Italian claims in North Africa. The renewal of the treaty was due to German fears lest France might force Italy into her orbit. The contracting parties were to do their utmost to associate England in support of Italian aspirations.

July 4. Great state visit of Emperor William to London. Much talk of England's association with the Triple Alliance.

July 24. Visit of a French squadron under **Admiral Gervais, to Cronstadt.** Frantic demonstrations of Franco-Russian friendship. The tsar listened to the *Marseillaise* played on one of the French warships. The **Franco-Russian Agreement,** which had been prepared by French loans, etc., began to loom on the horizon, the result primarily of German rejection of the Reinsurance Treaty, the hasty renewal of the Triple Alliance, and the demonstrations of Anglo-German solidarity.

Aug. 21, 27. **THE AUGUST CONVENTION** between France and Russia, first fruit of the negotiations. The French desired a hard-and-fast agreement, but this was watered down by the Russians until it was hardly more than an agreement to consult as to what measures should be taken by the two powers in case the maintenance of peace were threatened or one of the parties menaced by aggression. All efforts of the French to arrange for mobilization, etc. (especially during Giers' visit to Paris, Nov.), proved abortive.

1892, Aug. 1. **Mission of General Boisdeffre to St. Petersburg,** with a draft military convention. He found the Russian military men hesitant, and the draft was subjected to many changes. It was finally accepted "in principle," but as such had no force. Further development of the Franco-Russian alliance was delayed by the outbreak of the **Panama Scandal** (p. 640), which upset the French political scene for a year, and by the great **famine in Russia,** which paralyzed the government for an even longer period.

1893, July 13. **French ultimatum to Siam,** resulting in a short but severe crisis in Anglo-French relations. The French took a strong stand and generally won their point, thereby making a good impression on Russia. The Germans, who were half prepared to back the English, were disgusted by the backdown.

July 15. **Passage of the German military bill,** reducing service in the infantry to two years and increasing the forces. This created much uneasiness in both France and Russia and reminded the Russians of the value of the connection with France.

Oct. 13. Visit of a Russian squadron under **Admiral Avellan to Toulon.** Wild demonstrations of affection for Russia throughout France. Alarm of the British for their position in the Mediterranean.

1893, Dec. 27, 1894, Jan. 4. Exchange of notes between the **Russian and French governments,** formally accepting the military convention worked out 18 months before. The agreement was really political as much as military, but was classed as a military convention in order to circumvent the French constitution, which required submission of treaties to the Chamber of Deputies. The convention was to remain in force as long as the Triple Alliance. It provided: (1) that if France were attacked by Germany, or by Italy supported by Germany, Russia would employ all available forces against Germany; if Russia were attacked by Germany, or by Austria supported by Germany, France would employ all available forces against Germany. (2) In case the forces of the Triple Alliance, or of any one power a member of it, mobilized, France and Russia should mobilize without delay. Other articles provided for the number of troops to be employed, for specific plans of the general staffs, for secrecy, etc.

1894, Mar. **Resignation of Gladstone** and succession of **Lord Rosebery** as British prime minister. Passage of the **Spencer naval program,** providing for a great increase of forces in the next five years. This was the culmination of a severe naval scare and widespread agitation during the winter, the reflection of English anxiety about the Franco-Russian combination as it affected the Mediterranean situation.

Mar. 16. Conclusion of the Russian-German tariff treaty, after years of tariff war and negotiations. This agreement demonstrated the Russian desire not to be drawn into hostilities with Germany.

June. Breakdown of efforts by Rosebery and Kalnóky to revitalize the connection between England and the Triple Alliance. Negotiations had extended over six months and finally failed because of Germany's unwillingness to assume responsibility for any English interest. Beginning of the Anglo-German estrangement.

May 12. Treaty between the British government and the Congo Free State by which the British leased to King Leopold for the duration of his life a large tract on the left bank of the Upper Nile, and to Leopold and his successors a much larger tract lying to the west of the first. In return Leopold leased to the British a corridor 25 kilometers in width between Lakes Tanganyika and Albert Edward, which was to serve as a connecting link for the **Cape-to-Cairo telegraph and railway system,** under discussion since 1888. The treaty was a modified version of an earlier one (**MacKinnon Treaty** of May 24, 1890), which the British government had later disavowed. The British, having become aware of the importance of the Sudan for the assurance of Egypt's water supply, were confronted by encroachments of other powers. The penetration of the Germans into Uganda was checked by the Heligoland Treaty of July 1, 1890 (p. 741) and Uganda was ultimately taken over from the *Imperial British East Africa Company* (Apr. 12, 1894). But Leopold was constantly sending expeditions into the Nile country from the Congo, and the French, who disputed the Congo claims, were also penetrating into the Sudan (**Monteil mission,** May 1893). Efforts of the British to block the French by assigning the crucial area to Germany (agreement of Nov. 1893) were frustrated when the Germans in turn signed away the region to France (agreement of Mar. 15, 1894). The British therefore thought best to lease the territory along the Nile to Leopold, as the least dangerous competitor. The French at once protested, on the basis of their treaties with the Congo. The Germans joined in the protest on account of the corridor, which ran along the frontier of German East Africa. In order to conciliate the Germans, the British abandoned the corridor (June 1894), but in the end they were obliged to allow the whole treaty to lapse. Under pressure from Paris, Leopold (Aug. 14, 1894) was forced to shelve his claims. The whole episode was of vital importance in the British struggle to control the Nile. From the European angle it demonstrated once more the rift between England and Germany and the renewed tendency of Germany and France to collaborate in colonial affairs against England.

Aug. 1. Outbreak of war between China and Japan, over Korea (below, and p. 881).

Aug.-Sept. Armenian massacres. These were the result of the failure of the powers (1878–1882) to secure for the Asiatic provinces of Turkey the reforms envisaged by the Treaty of Berlin. Armenian nationalists, inspired by the example of Russian Pan-Slavs and terrorists, had organized secret revolutionary groups (leader **Avetis Nazarbek**), which, operating from Geneva, Tiflis, Paris, and other places, followed a policy of provoking troubles in Armenia in the hope of calling forth reprisals by the Turks and so bringing about European intervention. From 1890 on there were constant disturbances, culminating in the Armenian rising of Aug. 1894 in the vicinity of **Sassun.** This was put down with ferocity by the Kurdish irregular cavalry (Hamidié regiments). The result was a great outcry in Europe, particularly in England, where ill-informed humanitarians called on the Liberal government to intervene. Ultimately the sultan appointed a **commission of investigation,** which was joined by British, French, and Russian delegates. Lord Rosebery hoped to develop further this **Near-Eastern Triplice,** but Russia, threatened in her own territory by the prospect of an Armenian state, was adverse to any action. The commission produced a fairly innocuous program of reform (Apr. 1895). The sultan, as usual, temporized. Suggestions of the British for the use of pressure were flatly rejected by Russia and nothing was done.

Oct. 6. The British government invited Germany, France, Russia, and the United States to join in **intervention in the Far East,** the Chinese having been regularly defeated in battle with the Japanese. The projected intervention failed because of the unwillingness of the United States and Germany to take part.

1895, Apr. 17. Treaty of Shimonoseki between China and Japan: China and Japan recognized the full independence of **Korea;** China ceded to Japan **Formosa,** the **Pescadores Islands,** and the whole of the **Liaotung Peninsula,** with Port Arthur; China was to pay a huge indemnity; China was to conclude a treaty of commerce, opening seven new ports. *Reaction of the powers:* England reasonably well satisfied, especially with the commercial clauses, and ready to abandon defeated China for the rising power of Japan; **Russia** most directly affected since the beginning of Russian activity in the Far East (*Trans-Siberian Railway* begun 1891) and the development of interest in Manchuria and Korea (important because of its excellent open harbors). The Russians were long undecided whether to oppose the Japanese or to seek an agreement with them. The Tokyo government was quite prepared for a territorial deal, but ultimately the Russians rejected these advances in view of the readiness of the **Germans** to join in action to check Japan (growing German commercial interests in the Far East; above all German anxiety to re-establish close relations with Russia and to divert Russia to the Far East, thus emasculating the Franco-Russian Alliance). **France,** though she had extensive interests and aspirations in southwestern China, followed the Russian lead rather reluctantly, simply in order not to be left out of the picture.

Apr. 23. INTERVENTION OF RUSSIA, GERMANY, AND FRANCE at Tokyo. England refused at the last moment to join in the action. The Japanese were "advised" to retrocede the Liaotung Peninsula in return for an increased indemnity. After some hesitation the Japanese government yielded. Beginning of the acute antagonism between Russia and Japan in the Far East. Formation of the **Far-Eastern Triplice** (Russia, Germany, and France) which, in the following years, exploited the weakness of China.

June 25. Formation of the **Salisbury cabinet** in England, with **Joseph Chamberlain** at the colonial office. Beginning of the most active phase of British imperialism. In view of Britain's isolation and the situation in the Near East, Africa, and the Far East, Salisbury tried at first to throw off the danger of French and Russian advance by reconstituting close relations with Germany and the Triple Alliance.

Aug. 5. FAMOUS INTERVIEW BETWEEN WILLIAM II AND SALISBURY AT THE COWES YACHT RACES. Salisbury hinted broadly at the advisability of partitioning the Ottoman Empire as the best solution of the chronic Near-Eastern troubles. His idea was clearly that the Russians should be allowed to take Constantinople, but the Germans misunderstood the premier's design and interpreted it as a move to embroil the Continental powers in the Near East and smash the reviving friendship between Germany and Russia. The emperor therefore rejected all suggestions. When he discovered his mistake, he tried to arrange a further interview with Salisbury, but this came to naught through further misunderstanding. The result was profound distrust between Salisbury and the emperor (encouraged by Baron von Holstein), which only served to aggravate relations between the two countries.

Oct. 1. First Armenian massacres in Constantinople following a great and provocative Armenian demonstration.

Oct. 17. Under pressure from the powers, the sultan finally accepted the **program of reforms for Armenia.** Nevertheless, the massacres continued, taking place in various cities all over Anatolia. A British squadron was assembled outside the Dardanelles and British action was deferred solely because of apprehension as to what France and Russia might do. The Italians supported the English and **Count Goluchowski** (Austrian foreign minister since June) actually ignored German advice and took the lead in recommending international naval action at Constantinople. During the crisis (Nov.) the Russians planned to send an expeditionary force to the Bosporus **(Nelidov scheme)** and to seize the Turkish capital before the British and their allies could get there. The execution of the scheme was deferred in part because of inadequate preparation, in part because of the unwillingness of the French to become embroiled in war.

1896, Jan. 3. THE KRUGER TELEGRAM, sent by Emperor William to **President Kruger** of the South African Republic **(Transvaal)** congratulating him on the defeat of the raiders led by Dr. Jameson. The raid was the culmination of a long development and of acute tension in the relations between England and the Transvaal (p. 856). The Kruger telegram reflected German policy in this whole question. German interests in the Transvaal were considerable, but not decisive. The Germans made themselves the advocates of the Transvaal because they hoped (this was Holstein's plan) to demonstrate the value of German friendship to England by annoying the British into better relations. When news of the Jameson raid reached Berlin, the emperor, assuming that the British government was privy to the scheme, demanded strong measures and even military intervention on behalf of Kruger. His advisers did their utmost to cool his ardor, but in the end agreed to the telegram of congratulations to Kruger.

This created a storm of indignation and recrimination in England, especially when it became known that the real purpose of the German government was to beat the British into friendship. The governments indeed remained calm, but public opinion on both sides was so stirred up that for the future a policy of friendship became almost impossible. Loud demands for an agreement with France and Russia were met by the British government by an agreement with France (Jan. 15) in which the British abandoned many of their claims in Siam, and by approaches to Russia which, however, led to nothing.

Feb. Reconciliation between Russia and Bulgaria, the new tsar, Nicholas II (1894–1917), desiring to bring the feud to an end, and Prince Ferdinand having expressed his readiness to baptize the Crown Prince Boris in the Orthodox faith. Russia took the initiative in securing the recognition of Ferdinand by the powers, but refused to encourage the Bulgarian agitation in Macedonia, which had become very active since the dismissal of Stambulov (May 1894). Stambulov was murdered by Macedonian revolutionaries (July 17, 1895) and the revolutionary committees (founded Apr. 1895) were attempting to start an insurrection in the province, in order to exploit the Armenian crisis. Russia was anxious to keep the Near East quiet while following her designs in the Far East.

Feb. Outbreak of the insurrection in Crete, fomented by Greeks who were intent on the annexation of the island. Under pressure from the powers the sultan eventually agreed (July 3) to the restoration of the **Pact of Halepa** (1878), which had introduced a large measure of self-government in the island and which had been curtailed after the suppression of a rising in 1889. Greek support of the insurgents continued. The Austrian government proposed a blockade of Crete (July 25). This was rejected (July 29) by England, where anti-Turkish feeling ran high. The sultan accepted a **new reform scheme** (Aug. 25) drawn up by the ambassadors of the powers (Crete to have a Christian governor, named by the sultan with the approval of the powers; the Cretan Christians to have two-thirds of all offices and the Cretan assembly to have wide powers; a European commission was to reorganize the gendarmerie, courts, and finances). This program was accepted by the insurgents (Sept. 12).

Mar. 1. Battle of Adua. Disastrous defeat of the Italians by the Ethiopians. By the **Treaty of Uccialli** (May 2, 1889) the Italians had hoped to establish a protectorate over Ethiopia. This was recognized by the British (agreements of Mar. 24 and Apr. 15, 1891) on condition that the frontier remain 100 miles from the Nile and that the Italians promise not to interfere in any way with the Nile water. Thus the British hoped to use the Italians as a bulwark to protect the Nile. This plan was frustrated by the French (established on the Red Sea at Obock, 1862), who were anxious to get to the Nile and connect their western and eastern African holdings in a great belt. Menelek, Emperor of Ethiopia, denounced the Treaty of Uccialli (1891) and encouraged the French (**Jibuti-Addis Ababa Railway** concession, 1893), who in turn supplied him with munitions. War broke out between Italy and Ethiopia in the autumn of 1895 and led to a series of reverses of the Italians. Pressed by demands from Crispi, Gen. Baratieri decided on a march to Auda. In the mountains his forces became divided, after which they were overwhelmed by much greater numbers of Ethiopians.

Mar. 12. British decision to begin the **reconquest of the Sudan** by an advance on Dongola. This decision was taken less because of the frantic appeals of Italy and Germany for aid, or because of the reports of dervish misrule, than because of the fact that the Italian collapse in Ethiopia meant the collapse of the British system of protecting the Nile on the east. Danger of French advance in that region, as well as from the west (second **Monteil mission,** July 1895; **Marchand mission,** Feb. 1896), despite the famous **Grey declaration** (Mar. 28, 1895) stating that England would regard such action as "unfriendly," obliged the government to re-establish control of the Sudan itself. The French and Russian governments refused their consent to the use of Egyptian funds, but the British circumvented this difficulty by making Egypt a loan.

June 3. Treaty of alliance between Russia and China, signed by **Li Hung Chang** during his attendance at the coronation of the tsar at Moscow. The treaty was the outcome of long negotiations through which the Russians strove to secure a reward for the intervention against Japan in 1895. Its term was 15 years. During this period each party was to aid the other in the event of aggression by Japan against Russian territory in the Far East, China, or Korea. Russia was given permission to run the Trans-Siberian Railway across northern Manchuria to Vladivostok, thus cutting off a large detour to the north and making possible the economic penetration of Manchuria.

June 9. **Lobanov-Yamagata Agreement** between Russia and Japan, regarding Korea. Russian influence had been predominant there since Feb., when the king, in dire dread of the Japanese, who had engineered the murder of the queen, fled to the Russian legation. The Russians rejected a Japanese offer to divide the country into a northern (Russian) and a southern (Japanese) sphere. By the agreement of June 9 both parties promised to withdraw their forces and co-operate in the work of reform. In case of disorder they were to consult before sending troops. The agreement established what amounted to a condominium.

Aug. 26. **Attack on the Ottoman Bank** by Armenian revolutionaries. They seized the building and threatened to blow it up unless their demands were met. Eventually they were induced to withdraw, but other outbreaks occurred in the capital. This led to the greatest of the **Armenian massacres**, lasting three days and resulting in the slaughter of thousands of humble Armenians. The horror was stopped by the vigorous intervention of the ambassadors. Repetition of the crisis of 1895 as regards the European powers. England was anxious to intervene and an effort was made to persuade the tsar (who visited the queen at Balmoral in Sept.) to join in the action, but Nicholas was held back by his advisers (**death of Lobanov,** Aug. 30; ascendancy of Nelidov, ambassador at Constantinople). The Russian government adopted **Nelidov's scheme** for the seizure of Constantinople and the Straits in the event of action by the British (Nov.). But, as in the preceding year, nothing came of the plan, not so much because of the opposition of Witte, the powerful finance minister, as because of inadequate preparation and the lukewarmness of France. With respect to Armenia the powers were unable to agree on any course of action. The disorders continued more or less until June 1897, after which the revolutionary movement, having attained nothing but the massacre of thousands of Armenians, gradually collapsed.

1897, Feb. 2. **Cretan insurrection** resumed, supported by the Greek *Cretan Committee* and the *Ethniké Hetairia*, an organization designed for the realization of Greek aspirations in Macedonia. The Greek government was forced by public opinion to send ships and troops to Crete (Feb. 10, following the proclamation of union with Greece, Feb. 6). The powers, in dread of a rising in Macedonia, were eager to check the movement, despite popular sympathy with the Greeks. At the suggestion of **Muraviev,** the new Russian foreign minister, the powers (Feb. 15) landed troops in Crete, to hold the island in "deposit" for the time being. But England (Feb. 17) rejected a Russian-Austrian proposal that the Piraeus be blockaded. The powers handed in notes to Greece and Turkey (Mar. 2) promising **autonomy for Crete** and demanding withdrawal of the troops on pain of "measures of constraint." The Greek government rejected the note and on Mar. 18 the **blockade of Crete** was proclaimed. The war in Crete went on.

Apr. 17. **WAR BETWEEN GREECE AND TURKEY,** the result of the massing of Greek troops on the Macedonian frontier and attacks by the bands of the *Ethniké Hetairia*. The British had refused to take part in a blockade of Volo, which would have made these preparations impossible. Serbia and Bulgaria were eager to join in the assault on Turkey, but were deterred by strong warnings from Russia.

Apr. 30. **Russian-Austrian Agreement,** concluded during a visit of Francis Joseph and Goluchowski to St. Petersburg. The two powers agreed to maintain the *status quo* in the Balkans, and, if partition became inevitable, to work for the division of the area among the Balkan states, to which was to be added an Albanian state. The joint action of the two powers prevented Serbia and Bulgaria from associating themselves with Greece.

May 10. **The Greeks appealed to the powers,** after a series of decisive defeats by the Turks. They had first been obliged to recall their troops from Crete and to accept in advance the decisions of the powers. An armistice was arranged (May 19) and a peace settlement reached (Sept. 18). Turkey was allowed only a small rectification of the frontier in her favor, and an indemnity. The Cretan question remained open until Nov. 1898, when the powers finally agreed to name **Prince George of Greece** as governor of the island, and withdrew their forces.

Nov. 14. **Landing of German forces at Kiao-chow Bay,** and occupation of Tsingtao, following the murder of two German missionaries (Nov. 1). Ever since 1895 the Germans were determined to secure a port on the Chinese coast as reward for their intervention against Japan. But they had been unable, until 1897, to decide which port was most desirable. Kiao-chow had finally been settled on. Despite the fact that the tsar had given his approval (visit of William II to St. Petersburg, Aug. 1897), the Russian foreign minister raised objections and claimed prior rights. There was a period of acute uncertainty, but the Russians gave up their opposition. The Chinese refused the German demands until Mar. 6, 1898, when an agreement was signed giving Germany a lease of the bay for 99 years and permission to construct two railways in Shantung Province and to operate mines.

Dec. 14. The Russian fleet ordered to proceed to Port Arthur. This was the first step in the acquisition of the port, as recommended by Muraviev and approved by the tsar, though opposed by Witte and all the other ministers (council of Nov. 25).

Dec.—1898, Mar. Conflict between Russia and England over a loan required by China. Both sides put forward extremely hard conditions. Russia demanded a monopoly of railroad-building in Manchuria and the right to build a railroad from the Trans-Siberian south to the Yellow Sea, where she was to be permitted to construct a port; England demanded a concession for a railroad from the Burmese frontier to the Yangtze Basin and a promise not to alienate territory in the Yangtze Valley, as well as other commercial concessions.

1898, Jan. 25. Salisbury's note to Russia, aiming at a compromise. The British premier in effect proposed that all Asia should be divided by a line from Alexandretta to Peking into a northern (Russian) sphere and a southern (British) sphere. The Russians evaded these advances, feeling no need for abandoning half of Asia (the better half) to England. Instead, the Russians pressed on the Chinese a demand for the lease of **Talienwan and Port Arthur** (Mar. 3). This brought the Anglo-Russian crisis to a head.

Mar. 8. Britain sounded the United States government regarding possible collaboration in the Far East, but received no encouragement.

Mar. 17. Chamberlain's advances to the Japanese, which were also abortive, as the Japanese did not yet feel ready to act against Russia and were negotiating with Russia an agreement regarding Korea.

Mar. 27. The Chinese yielded to Russian pressure and leased to Russia Port Arthur and Talienwan for 25 years. The British government had decided (Mar. 25) that the question was not worth a war with Russia and that the best course would be to lease Weihaiwei as a counterweight. The Chinese agreed to this on Mar. 27.

Apr. 10. The French extorted from China an agreement not to alienate the three provinces of Yunnan, Kuangtung, and Kuangsi, and to permit the construction of a railroad to Yunnan-fu. France was given a **lease of Kuangchowwan** for 99 years. Numerous other concessions were extorted from the Chinese government in the following months, initiating the partition of China.

Apr. 25. The Nishi-Rosen Agreement between Russia and Japan. This had been under negotiation since Feb. and was meant by the Russians to circumvent Japanese opposition to the advance in Manchuria. The Russians rejected a Japanese offer of a free hand in Manchuria in return for a free hand in Korea, but recognized Japan's preponderant economic interests in Korea and promised not to obstruct them.

Mar. 28. Passage of the first naval law by the German Reichstag. This was the work of Adm. **Alfred von Tirpitz,** minister of marine, and laid the basis for the naval expansion of Germany. The arguments for a larger fleet were the need for protecting colonies and commerce and the necessity for a fleet if Germany was to make her weight felt in international affairs (especially against England). It was therefore decided to build a battle fleet (influence of the teaching of Mahan) so strong that even the strongest naval power would hesitate before attacking. Tirpitz also hoped that the possession of a fleet would heighten Germany's alliance value in the eyes of Russia and France.

Mar. 29. Beginning of the discussions between **Joseph Chamberlain and the German ambassador,** the object of which was to enlist German support against further Russian encroachments in the Far East. Bülow (German foreign minister since June, 1897) treated the matter evasively, being unwilling to antagonize Russia. In England there was little official or public sentiment for Chamberlain's project. The discussions were complicated by the over-eagerness of **Baron von Eckardstein,** who misled his own government as well as the English. Lord Salisbury, on his return from a vacation, showed little enthusiasm and took the Far Eastern situation less seriously than Chamberlain.

May 13. Chamberlain's great speech at Birmingham, extremely anti-Russian and a bid for the friendship of the United States and Germany. This made an unfavorable impression both in England and in the world at large. Neither the

United States nor Germany did anything to encourage the colonial secretary.

Aug. 30. Anglo-German Agreement regarding the future of the **Portuguese colonies.** The Portuguese government was bankrupt and in urgent need of a loan. This the British government was ready to grant, in return for the cession or lease of **Delagoa Bay,** long coveted as the key to the Transvaal and now of prime importance because of the growing tension in relations between England and the Transvaal. The Germans demanded a hand in the matter and the English reluctantly agreed, for fear of German collaboration with France (advances of June 1898). The two powers agreed to share in a loan to Portugal, with the colonies as security. The northern half of **Mozambique** and all but a central strip of **Angola** was assigned to Germany as the area of which the revenues should serve for the German share of the loan; the southern half of Mozambique and the rest of Angola were assigned to Britain. In the event of default of the Portuguese government these territories were to pass to the contracting powers. The Germans expected the agreement to bear early fruit. The British did all they could to prevent its coming into effect, and regarded the whole agreement as a piece of blackmail.

Sept. 18. Beginning of the **Fashoda crises,** between England and France. Since Mar. 1896 the Egyptian forces, under Gen. **Kitchener,** had been advancing up the Nile. The dervishes were decisively defeated on the **Atbara River** (Apr. 8, 1898) and at **Omdurman** (Sept. 2). During the same period British expeditions were trying to reach the Nile from Uganda, all with the object of heading off the French, with whom the Congo government cooperated. The **Marchand mission,** sent out in Feb. 1896, succeeded, after countless delays and hardships, in reaching the Nile at Fashoda (now Kodok) on July 10, 1898, and establishing itself there. Just before that, in June, a force of Ethiopians, accompanied by a few Frenchmen, had pushed down the Sobat River and reached the Nile just above Fashoda, this being part of a plan to push Ethiopian claims to the right bank of the Nile, while the French established themselves on the left bank. After the battle of Omdurman, Kitchener at once proceeded up the Nile, where he found Marchand. The latter refused to evacuate without orders of his government. There ensued the most acute crisis in Anglo-French relations during the whole pre-war period. The British refused to discuss the *pros* and *cons* of the French claims until

Marchand had evacuated territory which the British claimed for Egypt by right of conquest. The French government, harried by the Dreyfus affair (p. 641), finding itself unprepared for war at sea and securing no support from Russia (visit of Muraviev to Paris, Oct.), yielded to a poorly veiled threat of war. On Nov. 3 the **evacuation of Fashoda** was ordered. The French claims were not settled until Mar. 21, 1899, when they were obliged to renounce all territory along the Nile, in return for worthless districts in the Sahara. The episode left a legacy of hatred for England in France and made more difficult the pursuit of a policy of friendship with England, as advocated by **Théophile Delcassé,** French foreign minister from June, 1898, to June, 1905.

Nov. 21. Commercial treaty between France and Italy, bringing to an end a long and disastrous tariff war. The treaty marked the beginning of the reconciliation of France and Italy and the gradual **defection of Italy from the Triple Alliance** (tacitly renewed for six years in 1896). This policy was necessitated by the collapse of the Italian colonial policy and the instability of the domestic situation (p. 661).

1899, May 18-July 29. FIRST HAGUE PEACE CONFERENCE, which met at the invitation of the Russian tsar (Aug. 24, 1898). It is now known that the Russian proposal was due chiefly to financial stringency and inability to keep up with the armaments of Austria and other powers. The suggestion was regarded with distrust and dislike by most of the powers, not least by France. Twenty-six states were represented, but little more was achieved than the signature of conventions for the pacific settlement of international disputes and the definition of the laws of war (prohibition for 5 years of the use of projectiles thrown from balloons, prohibition of gas warfare and dumdum bullets, provision for better treatment of war prisoners and wounded, etc.). Nothing was done about disarmament or limitation of armament; compulsory arbitration was rejected, but a **permanent court of arbitration** was provided for.

Aug. 9. Extension of the Franco-Russian Alliance, during Delcassé's visit to St. Petersburg. In view of the Austrian constitutional crisis (p. 694) and the possibility of the dissolution of the Hapsburg monarchy, the alliance was extended to provide for the maintenance of the balance of power as well as the maintenance of peace, and the term of the military convention was made indefinite.

Sept. 6. Open Door Note of the American secretary of state, **John Hay.** In view of the division of China into spheres of influence, it proposed that England, Germany, and Russia should not interfere with treaty ports and should not levy higher harbor or railroad dues on foreign goods than on their own within their spheres. This was agreed to by all powers interested, but by Russia only with vague reservations. The note had little immediate importance, but set up an ideal policy often referred to later.

Oct. 9. Outbreak of the **Boer War** (p. 857). Almost from the beginning there were rumors of the possibility of **Franco-Russian-German intervention** against England, and Count Muraviev appears to have made some efforts in that direction, but neither the French nor the Germans showed much desire to become embroiled.

Oct. 14. The so-called Windsor Treaty between England and Portugal. The secret agreement renewed older treaties of 1642 and 1661, involving a guaranty of Portuguese territory, and included a promise by Portugal not to let munitions pass through **Delagoa Bay** to the Transvaal, or to declare neutrality. The agreement was a negation of the spirit of the German-British Agreement of Aug. 1898.

Nov. 1. Agreement between England and Germany regarding the **Samoan Islands.** The disorders in Samoa (p. 911) and the desire of the Germans to acquire the British share of the group had embittered relations between the two countries for almost a year. In view of the war in South Africa the British government finally gave in, though with poor grace. Germany got the islands of **Upolu** and **Savaii,** the British taking in return the **Tonga Islands, Savage Islands,** and lesser islands of the Solomon group, as well as a disputed strip of **Togoland.**

Nov. 25. Baghdad Railway concession granted to a German syndicate. This was the fruit of a decade of German economic activity in the Near East. There had been innumerable schemes for railways in Anatolia, especially from the Syrian coast to Baghdad and the Persian Gulf. The sultan, anxious to increase the income from the more remote provinces and to bind the empire together strategically, had (Oct. 4, 1888) given a German company a concession to build a railroad from opposite **Constantinople to Angora** (Ankara) with the idea of going on through northern Anatolia to Baghdad. This line was completed in 1892, after which there was a scramble for a new concession. The British

were obliged to withdraw when the Germans threatened to discontinue support of their policy in Egypt. On Feb. 15, 1893, the German company received a concession to continue the line from **Angora to Kaisarieh** (this was not built) and for another line, through the more promising southern districts, from **Eskishehr to Konia.** This was finished in 1896 and therewith the question of continuing to Baghdad became an immediate one. Countless projects and applications (British, French, Russian) were put forward, but the Germans remained in the ascendant, especially after the **visit of Emperor William II to Constantinople and the Holy Land** (Oct. 1898) and his proclamation of friendship for the 300,000,000 Moslems in the world. The French ultimately gave up their opposition and agreed to co-operate with German interests. The British were taken up with other affairs and had protected their interests in the Persian Gulf by an agreement with the **Sheikh of Kuwait** (he promised to cede no territory without British consent) on Jan. 23, 1899. The Russians remained vigorously hostile to the German project, but the Germans obtained a preliminary concession for a line from Konia to Baghdad on Nov. 25, 1899. Though primarily an economic enterprise, the Baghdad Railway project quickly became a vital factor in the relations of Germany with Russia and England.

Nov. 20-28. Visit of William II and Bülow to England (the first since 1895). Conversations between Bülow, Chamberlain, and Balfour. Discussion of a possible Anglo-German-American agreement. Bülow suggested that Chamberlain say something publicly of the common interests which bound the two countries. In his **Leicester speech** (Nov. 30) Chamberlain went much further and thereby raised a storm of ill-will in both England and Germany, where pro-Boer sentiments were very pronounced. Bülow, in a Reichstag speech (Dec. 11), rejected the advances and even stressed the need of Germany for a stronger fleet. Marked cooling in Anglo-German relations.

1900, Jan. Acute tension in Anglo-German relations resulting from the stopping of the German ship *Bundesrath* on very inadequate suspicion that she was carrying contraband. The British government eventually gave in (Jan. 16).

Feb. 28, Mar. 3. Muraviev suggested to the French and German governments the possibility of joint "amicable" pressure on England to bring about peace in South Africa. The Germans rejected the suggestion unless action were preceded by a mutual guaranty of territory between the three powers. There was no serious effort made to intervene against England, though the Russians took advantage of England's plight to advance their interests in **Persia**, **Afghanistan**, and **Tibet**, and the French in **Morocco**.

Mar. Russian squadron at Chemulpo. Efforts made to secure a naval base on the southern coast of Korea (**Masampo**). These attempts were frustrated by the vigorous opposition of Japan.

June 12. Passage of the **second German naval law**, providing for a fleet of 38 battleships, to be built in 20 years. This was the basic building program, carried through the Reichstag on a wave of ill-feeling toward England, which the government exploited through the Navy League and other organized propaganda.

June 13-Aug. 14. Boxer rising and siege of the Peking Legations. The rising was the direct outcome of the encroachments of the European powers in China and the division of the empire into spheres of influence. The Boxers were volunteer militiamen, organized and encouraged by the government to block the designs of the foreigners. The legations were finally relieved by an international expeditionary force. The Chinese government was obliged (Sept. 1901) to agree to punish the officials most directly responsible and to pay a huge indemnity. But the whole episode had given the Russian military men (opposed by Witte and the new foreign minister, **Count Lamsdorff**) an opportunity to occupy Manchuria with 100,000 troops. The question of evacuation soon became the key to the whole Far-Eastern problem.

Oct. 16. Anglo-German Yangtze Agreement, the result of British anxiety because of Russian designs. It provided for the maintenance of the "Open Door" in "all Chinese territory as far as they [the contracting powers] can exercise influence," and disclaimed all territorial designs. Other powers acceded to it.

Nov. 9. The Alexeiev-Tseng Agreement, between Russia and the Chinese governor of Manchuria. The Chinese civil administration was to be restored and Russian troops concentrated at Mukden and other points along the railroad. This was disavowed by both the Russian and Chinese authorities.

Dec. 14. Franco-Italian Agreement, by which Italy gave France a free hand in **Morocco** in return for a free hand in **Tripoli**. This marked the full development of the Franco-Italian entente.

1901, Feb. 8. Russian proposals to China for the evacuation of Manchuria. In return for evacuation, the Chinese government was to agree not to keep more than a police force in Manchuria and to give Russia a monopoly of concessions in Manchuria, Mongolia, and Chinese Central Asia, as well as a concession for a railroad running toward Peking. Appeals of China to the powers. Strong stand of Japan, backed by England and, more cautiously, by Germany.

Mar. 15. Bülow's speech in the *Reichstag*, declaring that the Yangtze Agreement did not apply to Manchuria. This brought to an end the first discussions in London on the possibility of an Anglo-German-Japanese bloc directed against Russia. The Germans were unwilling to go beyond a promise of neutrality in a Russian-Japanese or Anglo-Russian war.

Apr. 6. Following new and stronger protests from Japan and England, the Russian government dropped the draft convention with China and denied that it had been authentic.

May 29. Lord Salisbury's memorandum on British policy, a confidential document defending a policy of isolation. This rang the death-knell of the Anglo-German alliance discussions, carried on since March by **Baron von Eckardstein**, secretary of the German embassy in London. Eckardstein reported the British much more anxious for alliance than they were, which induced the German government to insist on an alliance with the whole Triple Alliance. To this the British would not agree, being lukewarm about the whole matter in general.

June. Moroccan missions to Paris, London, and Berlin. Discussion of an Anglo-German pact on Morocco. This the Germans rejected except as part of a larger alliance.

July-Aug. Beginning of the negotiations for an **Anglo-Japanese Alliance.**

Oct.-Nov. Renewed discussions between Russia and China regarding the conditions for the evacuation of Manchuria.

Oct. 16. Resumption of **Anglo-Japanese** discussions by **Baron Hayashi**, the minister in London. Hayashi made it clear that for Japan Korea was the crux and that Japan was interested in Manchuria only as the approach to Korea. The negotiations hinged on the definition of Japan's interests in Korea and on the question whether the alliance should be extended to include Siam and India.

Nov. 25-Dec. 4. Visit of Prince Ito to St. Petersburg. Contrary to expectation he found Witte and Lamsdorff eager for an agreement and willing to make far-reaching concessions to Japan in Korea. Ito was thereby induced to exceed his instructions and draft an agreement with Russia.

Dec. 7. The Japanese government, feeling committed to England, decided to drop the negotiations with Russia and conclude the alliance with England.

1902, Jan. 30. THE ANGLO-JAPANESE ALLIANCE, marking the end of Britain's "splendid isolation." It had been decided, in the later negotiations, to drop the idea of inviting Germany to join. The alliance was concluded for five years and provided for the independence of China and Korea and the recognition of Japan's special interests in Korea; if either party became involved in war with a third party, its ally was bound to maintain neutrality, but if another power or powers should join in the war, the allied power was bound to join in the conflict; neither party was to enter into separate agreements with another power (Russia) without consulting its ally. The treaty was published on Feb. 11.

Mar. 20. Franco-Russian declaration in favor of the principles enunciated in the Anglo-Japanese Alliance and reserving the right to take counsel to safeguard their interests. This was generally taken as a counterblast to the new combination and an extension of the Franco-Russian Alliance to the Far East, but this was probably an exaggeration.

Apr. 8. Russian-Chinese Agreement, providing for the evacuation of Manchuria within 18 months.

May 31. Treaty of Vereeniging (p. 857) bringing to an end the South African War and restoring to England greater liberty of action.

June 28. Renewal of the Triple Alliance for six years. The demands of the Italians for greater concessions were evaded, but they were given assurances with regard to Tripoli.

Nov. 1. Italian note to France assuring her that in the event of her being attacked, Italy would remain neutral; "the same shall hold good in case France, as the result of a direct provocation, should find herself compelled, in defense of her honor or of her security, to take the initiative of a declaration of war." Italy also gave assurance that she was not a party and would not be a party to any military agreement in conflict with this declaration. Com-

pletion of the Italian-French Entente, the work largely of M. Camille Barrère, the French ambassador. **Nadir of the Triple Alliance,** the relations between Italy and Austria being badly strained by irredentist agitation.

Nov. 8. Failure of the **French agreement with Spain** on Morocco. The French had offered the Spaniards a substantial part of northern Morocco as a sphere, but the Spanish government drew back for fear of antagonizing England.

1903, Feb. Russian-Austrian program of reform for **Macedonia.** The country had for years been the prey of rival Bulgarian, Serbian, and Greek bands and had broken out in insurrection in 1902 Mild reforms introduced by the sultan (Nov. 1902) had failed to pacify the region. The Russian-Austrian program called for a gendarmerie composed of Moslems and Christians according to population, appointment of foreign officers, and reorganization of the financial system. It was accepted by the other powers.

Apr. Baghdad Railway crisis. The German company had obtained a definitive concession for the road from Konia to Basra (Jan. 17, 1902) and had done its utmost to secure the co-operation of the British and French governments in arranging the financing of the scheme. The British government was favorably disposed, but the bankers were finally scared off by an organized press campaign against participation. Thereupon the British and French governments refused to become associated. The Russian government, as before, was irreconcilably opposed to the whole project.

May 1-4. Visit of King Edward VII to Paris. This first move toward reconciliation ended as a great success.

May 15. Lord Lansdowne's declaration of British interests in the Persian Gulf: England "would regard the establishment of a naval base or a fortified port in the Persian Gulf as a very grave menace to British interests, and would certainly resist it by all means at her disposal." This was intended primarily as a warning against Russian plans for a railroad across Persia to Bunder Abbas.

July 6-9. Visit of President Loubet and Delcassé to London. Beginning of the conversations that were to lead to the Anglo-French Entente.

Aug. 12. First Japanese note to Russia, following the failure of the Russians to carry through the evacuation of Manchuria. Earlier conversations had failed through the unwillingness of the Russians to abandon their claims in northern Korea (**Yalu concession**, in which even Tsar Nicholas was interested financially).

Aug. 29. Dismissal of Count Witte, the Russian finance minister. This was tantamount to the victory of the group favoring Russian expansion in Manchuria and Korea (notably **Bezobrazov**). The Viceroyalty of the Far East was established to deal with Asiatic affairs independently of the foreign office. The Russians refused to take the Japanese policy seriously. They did not believe that Japan would go the limit and were confident that if she did, Russia would easily defeat her. The notes from Tokyo were treated with disdain and delay.

Oct. 2. The Mürzsteg Program of reform for Macedonia, worked out by Russia and Austria and approved by the powers. This program was to replace the February program, which had been proved inadequate. Austrian and Russian inspectors were to be attached to the inspector-general and a foreign general was to command the gendarmerie. Further administrative and judicial reforms were provided for.

Nov. Anglo-Russian conversations looking toward an understanding. These broke down because of Russia's unwillingness to agree to a partition of Persia into spheres of influence.

1904, Feb. 4. OUTBREAK OF THE RUSSIAN-JAPANESE WAR, following the failure of the Russians to give the Japanese any satisfaction (p. 892).

Apr. 8. THE ANGLO-FRENCH ENTENTE concluded. This had been under negotiation since July and especially since Oct. The outbreak of the Russian-Japanese War undoubtedly served to hasten the conclusion. The agreement represented a complete settlement of colonial differences, particularly with regard to Egypt and Morocco: France recognized the British **occupation of Egypt**, but was given guaranties regarding the Egyptian debt; England was to make effective the Treaty of 1888 providing for the free navigation of the **Suez Canal;** England recognized French interests in **Morocco** and promised diplomatic support in realizing them; secret articles envisaged the eventual breakdown of Moroccan independence and the partition of the country between France and Spain; France surrendered ancient rights on the shores of **Newfoundland**, but retained the right to fish; in return France was given territory near **French Gambia**

and east of the **Niger;** British and French spheres of influence were delimited on the frontiers of **Siam** and disputes regarding **Madagascar** and the **New Hebrides** were adjusted.

Apr. 24-29. Visit of President Loubet and Delcassé to Rome. Acute crisis in the relations of France and the papacy (p. 642) and much ill-feeling between Germany and Austria and Italy, because of the failure of Victor Emmanuel III to make mention of the Triple Alliance in the toasts and speeches.

Sept. 7. British treaty with Tibet, signed by Col. **F. E. Younghusband** after an expedition to Lhasa. The Tibetan Lama agreed not to cede or lease territory to any foreign power or to allow foreign intervention. Thus Britain took advantage of the Russian-Japanese War to destroy the Russian advance in Tibet.

Oct. 3. Franco-Spanish Treaty regarding Morocco. The public clauses reaffirmed the independence and integrity of Morocco, but a secret convention provided for eventual partition. Spain was to have the Mediterranean coast of Morocco (but less of the hinterland than was offered her in 1902). Spain was to take no action without the consent of France, and was not to erect any fortifications.

Oct. 21. The Dogger Bank episode. The Russian fleet, under Admiral Rodjestvensky, passing through the North Sea on its way to the Far East, fired upon British trawlers, supposed to be Japanese destroyers. One trawler was sunk and several lives lost. The Russian fleet continued on its way and the Russian government evaded giving satisfaction. Acute crisis in Anglo-Russian relations. The British fleet was ordered to stop the Russian fleet off Gibraltar, even by force. The situation was finally saved through the efforts of Delcassé, and the matter was adjusted by an international commission (Feb. 25, 1905).

Oct. 27-Nov. 23. German-Russian negotiations for an alliance. These arose from the tension between Russia and England and from British protests against the coaling of the Russian fleet by German companies. The tsar accepted a German draft treaty (Oct. 30) providing for mutual aid in case of attack by another European power. The plan broke down because of Russia's unwillingness to sign before consulting France, which was expected to be drawn in. Ultimately the two powers agreed merely (Dec. 12) to aid each other in the event of complications arising from the coaling of the fleet.

Dec.—1905, Feb. Mission of St. René Taillandier to Fez. He carried to the sultan a program of reforms (police, state bank, communications) which would have given France practically a protectorate over Morocco.

1905, Feb. 3. Speech of Mr. Lee, first lord of the British admiralty, directed against German naval armaments. This reflected the growing anxiety of the British regarding the German naval plans.

Mar. 31. VISIT OF THE GERMAN EMPEROR TO TANGIER, initiating the first Moroccan crisis. Delcassé had wantonly excluded the Germans from the Moroccan negotiations and had not officially communicated the agreement with England. The Germans were uncertain about the Anglo-French Entente, but had declared their disinterestedness in Morocco except for the Open Door, regarding which Delcassé had given assurances. The French had thereupon proceeded to capitalize the free hand secured in the agreements with Italy, England, and Spain. After the failure of the German-Russian negotiations, Bülow and Holstein decided to make the Moroccan affair a test of the strength of the Anglo-French Entente and carried the unwilling emperor along on this course. At Tangier he proclaimed Germany's adherence to the principles of independence and integrity and declared in favor of the policy of equal opportunity for all. His visit at once created a panic in Paris and led to a loud outcry against Delcassé's policy. Delcassé at once offered to make good his mistake and to buy off the German opposition, but the Germans turned a deaf ear.

Apr. 6. The Germans accepted the invitation of the Sultan of Morocco to an international conference.

May 1-5. Efforts of **Rouvier**, the French prime minister, to reach an adjustment with the Germans. He was even ready to concede them a port on the coast of Morocco, but the Germans insisted on a conference.

May 17, 25. British correspondence with France. The British, apprehensive about German designs on the Moroccan coast, proposed "full and confidential discussion . . . in anticipation of any complications." Delcassé took this as the first step toward an alliance and tried to develop the British advance, but Rouvier objected.

June 6. FALL OF DELCASSÉ, who urged the French cabinet to accept the British offers. He argued that the Germans were only bluffing and that a Franco-British front would be invincible. The cabinet voted unanimously against him, fearing that France was poorly prepared for war, that an agreement with England would precipitate war at a time when Russia was rendered helpless by her defeat in the Far East, and that France would bear the burden of German hostility. Rouvier took over the foreign office and renewed his efforts to strike a bargain. The Germans stood by their previous attitude.

July 8. The French government, assured of American support against unreasonable demands, accepted the idea of a conference.

July 24. BJÖRKÖ TREATY, signed by the Emperor William and the tsar during a visit to each other's yachts. The treaty was essentially a return to the draft of Oct. 1904, excepting that it was to be confined to Europe and was to take effect only after the conclusion of peace between Russia and Japan. Bülow objected to its restriction to Europe and threatened to resign, but was persuaded to remain after a pathetic appeal from the emperor. The treaty was warmly opposed by the Russian foreign office and was ultimately wrecked by the refusal of the French government, estranged by the Moroccan crisis, even to consider joining in such a pact (Oct.).

Aug. 12. Renewal of the Anglo-Japanese Alliance for 10 years. The treaty was modified to provide for mutual support in the event of attack by *one* other power, and was extended to include India.

Sept. 5. Treaty of Portsmouth, ending the Russian-Japanese War (p. 892). This was effected through the mediation of President Theodore Roosevelt. Russia ceded to Japan the northern part of Saghalin, but paid no indemnity; Russia recognized Japan's predominant interests in Korea and agreed not to oppose any steps Japan might take in Korea; Russia's lease of the Liaotung Peninsula was transferred to Japan.

Sept. 28. France and Germany finally reached an agreement on the agenda for the Moroccan Conference, which was to meet in Jan. 1906. Most of the French demands were met, in the hope that France would be disposed to accede to the Björkö Treaty.

Oct. Beginning of Anglo-Russian discussions regarding an eventual entente.

1906, Jan. 10. Beginning of Anglo-French military and naval conversations, which had been unofficially initiated in Dec.

The new Liberal government (Sir Edward Grey, foreign secretary since Dec. 1905) refused to promise support to France in the event of German attack, but agreed to non-binding discussions of the modalities of co-operation in case such co-operation should be decided on. Creation of the "moral obligation" of England to France. The cabinet as a whole was not informed of these conversations until 1911.

Jan. 16-Apr. 7. Algeciras Conference on Morocco. France was supported throughout by all the powers except Austria, which sided with Germany. There were countless disputes regarding details, and some danger of war, which was apparently favored by Baron von Holstein until his dismissal on Apr. 5. The Act of Algeciras reaffirmed the independence and integrity of Morocco and "economic liberty without inequality." The French were entrusted with the police on the Moroccan-Algerian frontier. In the rest of the country the police was to be under French and Spanish control. A state bank was to be organized, on which France was to have a larger measure of control than the other powers.

Feb. 10. Launching of the *Dreadnought*, the first all-big-gun battleship (ten 12-inch guns), which revolutionized the world naval situation.

May. The German government decided to increase the tonnage of battleships in the naval program, to add six cruisers to the program, and to widen the Kiel Canal to allow the passage of projected ships of the *Dreadnought* type.

Aug. 15. Visit of King Edward to Emperor William at Cronberg; futile discussion of the naval situation.

Dec. 13. Agreement between Great Britain, France, and Italy regarding Ethiopia. It provided for the independence and integrity of Ethiopia and respect for earlier agreements, but divided the country into spheres of influence for the event of Ethiopia's collapse.

1907, May 16. Pact of Cartagena between Great Britain, France, and Spain. It provided for the maintenance of the *status quo* in the Mediterranean and that part of the Atlantic which washes the shores of Europe and Africa. The agreement was directed chiefly at supposed German designs on the Balearic Islands and the Canaries.

June 10. Franco-Japanese Agreement, providing for the independence and integrity of China and equality of treatment there.

June 15-Oct. 18. SECOND HAGUE PEACE CONFERENCE, called at the suggestion of President Theodore Roosevelt (Oct. 21, 1904), but postponed because of the war in the Far East. All efforts of the British to secure some limitation of armaments were wrecked by the opposition of other powers, for which Germany, fearing a British attempt to check the growth of the German fleet, acted as spokesman. Germany also rejected all proposals for compulsory arbitration. But the conference enlarged the machinery for voluntary arbitration and concluded conventions regulating action to collect debts, rules of war, rights and obligations of neutrals, etc.

July 30. Russian-Japanese Agreement, similar to the Franco-Japanese Agreement (above).

July. Renewal of the Triple Alliance for 6 years, despite the complete lack of faith on the part of Germany and Austria in Italy's loyalty.

Aug. 3-5. Meeting of Emperor William and Tsar Nicholas and their foreign ministers at Swinemünde. Discussion of the Baghdad Railway; assurances of the Russians that any agreement they made with England would not be directed against Germany.

Aug. 31. THE ANGLO-RUSSIAN ENTENTE. This had been discussed at various times since the conclusion of the Russian-Japanese War, and was encouraged by the French. Negotiations had lagged because of opposition in Russian court circles, because of the confusion created by the Russian revolutionary movement (p. 707), and because of the fears of Alexander Izvolski (Russian foreign minister since May, 1906) lest Germany take offense. The agreement was much less extensive than that between France and England: Persia, the root of the Russian-English antagonism, was divided into three spheres of influence: a large Russian sphere in the north, covering the most valuable part of the country; a neutral sphere in the center; and a smaller British sphere in the southeast. Russia agreed that Afghanistan should be outside her sphere of influence and that she would deal with the Amir only through England; England promised not to change the status of the country or to interfere with its domestic affairs. Both governments recognized the suzerainty of China over Tibet and promised to respect its territorial integrity. In a separate note (Apr. 1907) the British government had expressed itself as well disposed toward a change in the Straits Agreements favorable to Russia. In another separate note (Aug. 29) the Russian government recognized Britain's preponderant position in the **Persian Gulf.**

Sept. 5. **Meeting of King Edward and Izvolski at Marienbad,** followed by a meeting of Izvolski and **Count Alois Aehrenthal** (Austrian foreign minister since Oct. 24, 1906). Izvolski gave the most explicit assurances regarding the entente with England and sounded out Austria with regard to an eventual revision of the Straits Convention.

1908, Jan. 27. Count Aehrenthal announced the intention of the Austrian government to build a **railway through the Sanjak of Novi Bazar** toward Saloniki. The purpose of this was to drive a wedge between Serbia and Montenegro, where anti-Austrian agitation had grown rapidly since the advent of the Karageorgevich dynasty (1903; **Serbian-Austrian tariff war,** 1906–1911). The Austrian move was much resented by Izvolski, who claimed it was a violation of the spirit of the Austro-Russian Entente of 1897. He brought forward a rival scheme for a railroad from the Danube to the Adriatic. The British were also much wrought up by the Austrian step, which they regarded as a bribe by Turkey to Austria to induce the latter to oppose further reforms in Macedonia.

Mar. Sir Edward Grey put forward a scheme of **reform for Macedonia** which would have given the three provinces practical autonomy.

Apr. 23. **The Baltic and North Sea Conventions,** the first between Germany, Sweden, Denmark, and Russia, the second between Great Britain, Germany, Denmark, France, the Netherlands, and Sweden. They provided for the maintenance of the *status quo* on the shores of the two seas and for consultation between the signatories in case the *status quo* was threatened.

June 9. Reval meeting, between King Edward and Sir Charles Hardinge on the one hand and Tsar Nicholas and Izvolski on the other. The British secured **Russian approval for the Macedonian reform scheme** and discussed the problems presented by German armaments.

June 23. **Counter-revolution in Persia,** where the shah, **Mohammed Ali,** overthrew the constitution which had been granted (Dec. 30, 1906) as a result of the liberal-nationalist movement of that year. The Russians supported the shah, and the British, bound by the agreement with Russia, were obliged to desert the liberal cause.

July. **Mulay Hafid,** having defeated his brother, **Abdul Aziz,** Sultan of Morocco, in a long civil war, took Fez. The Germans supported Mulay Hafid and the Moroccan question drifted toward another crisis.

July 24. **Victory of the Young Turk Revolution** (began July 6 in Macedonia). The sultan was obliged to restore the Constitution of 1876 (p. 731). The whole movement was a reflection of Turkish excitement about the Reval interview (above) and resulted in the collapse of German influence in Turkey and a period of frantic Anglophilism.

Aug. 11. **Meeting of King Edward and Sir Charles Hardinge with Emperor William at Friedrichshof.** Acrimonious discussion of the naval situation. The emperor flatly refused all suggestions of reduction of the German program, which had been indirectly enlarged by the reduction of the service-term of warships and by the acceleration of German building operations.

Aug. 13. **King Edward and Francis Joseph met at Ischl.** Reputed efforts of the English to enlist Austrian pressure on Germany.

Aug. 27. Austrian reply to a note of Izvolski proposing an agreement regarding Bosnia and Herzegovina on the one hand and the Straits question on the other.

Sept. 16. **BUCHLAU CONFERENCE** between Aehrenthal and Izvolski. After long discussion an informal agreement was reached: Russia was not to oppose the annexation of Bosnia and Herzegovina by Austria and Austria was not to oppose the opening of the Straits to Russian warships, under certain conditions. An international conference was to put the stamp upon these arrangements and other minor modifications of the Berlin Treaty.

Sept. 23. **Visit of Prince Ferdinand of Bulgaria to Budapest.** Aehrenthal evidently gave his approval to eventual declaration of Bulgarian independence. Both Austria and Bulgaria felt threatened by the determination of the Young Turk régime to summon delegates from Bosnia and Herzegovina and from Bulgaria to the new parliament.

Sept. 25. **Casablanca affair.** Three German deserters from the French foreign legion were taken by force from a German consular official. Acute tension in Franco-German relations.

Sept. 26. **Meeting of Izvolski and Baron Schön** (German foreign minister) at Berchtesgaden. Schön agreed to the Russian Straits program on the understanding that Germany should receive compensation (probably in the Baghdad Railway question).

Sept. 28. Meeting of Izvolski and Tommaso Tittoni (Italian foreign minister) at Desio. The Italian minister evidently accepted the Russian program in return for promises of support in Tripoli and Albania.

Oct. 4. Arrival of Izvolski at Paris, where he received a letter from Aehrenthal announcing the coming annexation decree.

Oct. 5. Proclamation of Bulgarian independence.

Oct. 6. PROCLAMATION OF THE ANNEXATION OF BOSNIA AND HERZEGOVINA BY AUSTRIA, who gave up the right to occupy the Sanjak militarily. Excitement in Turkey, where a boycott against Austrian goods was instituted. Frenzy and rage in **Serbia** and **Montenegro,** where the two annexed provinces had long since been looked upon as a future legacy. Military preparations were at once begun and negotiations were initiated looking toward a Turkish-Serbian-Montenegrin-Greek alliance against Austria. In **Russia** the event caused hardly less consternation in nationalist circles, where nothing was known of Izvolski's bargain with Aehrenthal. The prime minister, Stolypin, at once wrote Izvolski instructing him to oppose the Austrian action and it was this primarily that obliged Izvolski to repudiate his agreement, declare that he had been duped, and take the lead in championing the Serbian claims. **The Germans,** though rather outraged by Austria's failure to give advance notice, supported Austria loyally in order to uphold the alliance. **The French and British,** though they resented Izvolski's underhanded negotiation with Austria, supported Russia and demanded the convocation of an **international conference** to consider the Austrian action.

Oct. 7. Crete proclaimed union with Greece, thereby adding to the crisis.

Oct. 9-14. Izvolski's visit to London, to secure support for his Straits program. The British, unwilling to sacrifice the newly found friendship of the Turks and having sounded and found them ill-disposed to any concession to Russia, made their consent to the opening of the Straits conditional on previous Turkish consent. Russian efforts to secure that consent naturally failed. Complete collapse of Izvolski's scheme. He now became virulent in his denunciation of Aehrenthal and his demand for a conference. Aehrenthal, on his part, would agree only to a conference to register (not discuss) the Austrian action. Negotiations on this question continued through the autumn.

Oct. 27. Izvolski in Berlin. The Germans, recognizing his difficulties, made no objection to his Straits program, provided they were given compensation.

Oct. 28. The Daily Telegraph affair (p. 692). The publication of the indiscreet utterances of Emperor William to an English nobleman served to create a crisis in Germany and at the same time to accentuate the Anglo-German antagonism.

Nov. 10. Germany and France agreed to submit the **Casablanca affair** to an arbitral board, which rendered a report on May 22, 1909.

Dec. 4. LONDON NAVAL CONFERENCE, attended by 10 naval powers. The conference agreed on certain regulations of naval warfare (blockade, contraband, prizes, convoy, etc.), but the convention was never ratified.

Dec. 25. Izvolski's Christmas speech advocating a league of the Balkan states and Turkey to resist further encroachments. This program was also supported by England, but came to nothing because of the difficulty of adjusting the Serbian and Bulgarian claims in Macedonia, and because of Turkey's insistence on an offensive as well as defensive alliance.

1909, Jan. 12. Austro-Turkish Agreement (final form Feb. 26), by which Turkey recognized the annexation and was paid compensation. This agreement greatly strengthened Aehrenthal's position, since Turkey was the power chiefly concerned.

Feb. 8. German-French Agreement on Morocco. It reaffirmed the independence and integrity of the country, but Germany recognized France's "special political interests" in return for recognition of Germany's economic interests and a promise to associate German nationals in future concessions.

Mar. 2. The powers intervened to prevent a war between Serbia and Austria. The Serbs had continued to arm and were becoming less and less ready to surrender their claims. The Austrians had also armed and the military party in Vienna (**Conrad von Hötzendorff,** chief of staff) was urging a war in order to clear the situation. The powers advised the Serbs to yield, but the Serbian note to Vienna (Mar. 10) avoided any recognition of the annexation and was generally regarded as unsatisfactory.

Mar. 12. **New British naval appropriations,** the result of a panic called forth by dubious statements by the first lord of the admiralty regarding German strength.

Mar. 18. **Russian-Bulgarian Agreement,** by which Russian financial claims on Turkey (unpaid since 1878) were cancelled to meet the compensation demanded by Turkey from Bulgaria.

Mar. 21. **German note to Russia,** calling upon her to abandon support of the Serbs and to recognize the annexation. The Germans asked for a definite reply, failing which they would allow matters to take their course. Izvolski seems to have been glad for a chance to get out of a hopeless *impasse* (Russia being quite unprepared for war). He yielded, but thereafter set afloat the legend of a German "ultimatum" to Russia. The British were indignant at Russia's "climb-down," which left them in a most embarrassing position.

Mar. 31. **Serbian note to Austria,** recognizing the annexation, declaring that it did not infringe on Serbian interests and promising to check anti-Austrian propaganda and maintain good neighborly relations in the future.

Apr. 9. **Turkey recognized the independence of Bulgaria.**

Apr. 13. **Turkish counter-revolution.** This was put down and Abdul Hamid was deposed (Apr. 27). Gradual revival of German influence.

May. **Mission of Baron Stumm** to London. He was instructed to offer an agreement on naval affairs in return for a defensive alliance, a neutrality agreement or at least a general settlement of colonial questions. These suggestions were coolly received in London, where there was no desire to estrange France and Russia or to weaken the entente. The British view was that the naval agreement must come first.

July 14. **Resignation of Prince Bülow** (German chancellor since 1900). Bülow had come more and more to disapprove of the uncompromising naval policy of the emperor and Tirpitz and his position had been hopelessly weakened by the *Daily Telegraph* episode. His successor, **Theobald von Bethmann-Hollweg,** was, if anything, more conciliatory and eager for an agreement with England.

Oct. 24. **Racconigi Agreement** between Russia and Italy. Both powers promised to work for the *status quo* in the Balkans. Italy agreed to support Russian aspirations in the **Straits,** while Russia agreed not to oppose the Italian designs in **Tripoli.**

Nov.-Dec. **Anglo-German negotiations** (Gwinner and Cassel) looking toward a general settlement, but dealing chiefly with the **Baghdad Railway.** The Germans were prepared to give up all claims to control the railway from Baghdad to the Persian Gulf, but the British demanded full control (not international) of that section, and were unwilling to act without Russia and France.

1910, Feb. **Official Russian-Austrian reconciliation** based on agreement to maintain the *status quo* in the Balkans, the Russians being in constant dread of a further move by the Austrians.

Nov. 4-5. **Visit of Tsar Nicholas** and the new foreign minister, **Sergei Sazonov,** to Emperor William at Potsdam. Tentative agreement on the Near East. The Germans gave the Russians a free hand in **northern Persia,** while the Russians promised no longer to oppose the **Baghdad Railway** and to arrange for the connection of this line with the Persian railways. Disappointment of the British, who had always refused to negotiate without Russia and who were now deprived of their chief support in the Baghdad Railway matter.

1911, Apr.-May. **French advance in Morocco,** following anti-foreign disturbances. The French entered Fez on May 21, despite warnings from the Germans that they were violating the Algeciras Act.

June-Nov. **SECOND MOROCCAN CRISIS,** resulting from the forward movement of the French and the general dissatisfaction of the Germans with the working of the 1909 agreement. The French government was not unwilling to make compensation to the Germans, and M. **Jules Cambon,** the ambassador at Berlin, engaged in conversations with the German foreign secretary, **Kiderlen-Wächter,** at Kissingen (June 20-21). But the Germans refused to advance demands and took the stand that the French should make an offer. Kiderlen was genuinely anxious to liquidate the Moroccan affair and pave the way to better relations with France and England. Negotiations on the French side were hampered by a cabinet change the result of which was the formation of a **ministry under Joseph Caillaux** (June 28).

July 1. **The German gunboat *Panther* arrived at Agadir** on the coast of Morocco, ostensibly to protect German interests, but in reality to frighten the

French into action. The French foreign minister, **M. de. Selves,** appealed to England to join in sending ships. This action was disavowed by Caillaux and rejected by the English (July 4).

July 15. After much fencing, the Germans admitted to the French that they would require the whole of the **French Congo** as compensation for the abandonment of their rights and interests in Morocco. This was regarded by the French as out of the question, but discussions continued, carried on to a large extent irregularly by Caillaux.

July 21. **Mansion House speech of Lloyd George,** in which he declaimed against England's being ignored in the matter and used threatening language. Since Lloyd George had been regarded as pacifically minded, the speech caused a great stir and led to much recrimination between the German ambassador and Grey. The crisis now came to a head and elaborate preparations were made on the British side for eventual war. Nevertheless negotiations continued between the Germans and French and by October substantial agreement was reached. By the **Convention of Nov. 4,** Germany agreed to leave France a free hand in Morocco and not to object even to the erection of a protectorate; in return France ceded part of the French Congo, with two strips of territory connecting the German Cameroons with the Congo and Ubangi Rivers.

Sept. 28. OUTBREAK OF THE TRIPOLITAN WAR between Italy and Turkey (p. 662). This was due in large measure to the desire of the Italians to realize on the agreements with France and to counterbalance the French gains in Morocco. In one way or another all the great powers were bound not to oppose the Italian action, though they all disapproved of it. The Austrians, however, objected from the outset to all operations which would disturb the *status quo* in the Balkans and thereby prevented attacks upon the Adriatic or Aegean coast. Numerous attempts at mediation by the powers broke down through the hasty **annexation of Tripoli** by the Italians, which the Turks stoutly refused to recognize.

Oct. 14-Dec. 6. The Charykov Kite. Charykov, the Russian ambassador at Constantinople and the chief proponent of a Balkan League which would include Turkey and would serve as a bulwark against the dreaded advance of Austria in the Balkans, took matters more or less into his own hands and offered the Turks a guaranty of their territory in Europe in return for accession to such a league and opening of the Straits to Russian warships. The Turks treated the matter in dilatory fashion and, when pressed, appealed to the other powers. Charykov's action was disavowed by Sazonov after a visit to Paris (Dec. 6).

Nov. 11. Russian ultimatum to Persia, followed by an invasion of northern Persia and Russian control of the Russian sphere. The Persian Liberals were trying hard to reform the country (appointment of **Morgan Shuster,** an American, as treasurer-general, with wide powers, Feb. 1911) and the Russians determined to frustrate these efforts. With their connivance the reactionary shah returned to the country (July 18) and began a civil war. He was defeated, but the Russians invaded the country and suppressed the Liberal movement. Despite English protests the Russians forced the dismissal of Shuster and other foreign advisers and made themselves at home in northern Persia. British action was hampered by fear of rupturing the entente with Russia at a time when the Moroccan crisis and the Tripolitan War raised the specter of a general conflagration.

1912, Feb. 8. Haldane mission to Berlin. On the English side this was the outgrowth of dissatisfaction with Grey's policy in the Agadir crisis and discontent with the policy of Russia in Persia, reflected in a demand of the Radicals for better relations with Germany. On the German side Tirpitz and the emperor were determined to increase the fleet beyond the previous program, but Bethmann and Kiderlen were anxious for an agreement with England that would weaken the entente. At Berlin Haldane suggested that England would be willing to support German colonial aspirations in Africa in return for abstention from increase of the fleet. The Germans were unwilling to make naval concessions without a political agreement. Bethmann demanded a promise of neutrality under certain conditions, while Grey refused more than an assurance not to attack or take part in a hostile combination against Germany.

Mar. 8. Publication of the **new German naval bill,** providing for an increase in the number of ships, an increase in personnel, and the establishment of a third squadron in commission. With this the Anglo-German discussions came to an end, though conversations regarding the Baghdad Railway and colonial affairs continued and an effort was made on both sides to put relations on a better footing.

Mar. 13. Treaty of alliance between Bulgaria and Serbia. This had been under discussion since 1908 and had been warmly supported by the Russians (especially Hartwig, the minister at Belgrade). Serious negotiations were initiated in Oct. 1911, in view of the Tripolitan War, but were delayed by the insistence of the Bulgarians that the alliance be directed against Turkey rather than Austria and that Macedonia should receive autonomy. The secret *annexe* of the treaty provided for a possible war against Turkey. In the event of victory Serbia was to receive the Sanjak of Novi Bazar and the territory north of the Shar Mountains; the territory south and east of the Rhodope Mountains was to go to Bulgaria; the rest of Macedonia was to be autonomous, but if partition was decided on later, most of it was to fall to Bulgaria, a disputed area being left to the arbitration of the Tsar of Russia. The treaty was supplemented by a **military convention** (May 12). Its general tenor became known to most of the powers at an early date, but it was not taken very seriously. The Russians, who had sponsored it, regarded it chiefly as a defensive bulwark against Austria and relied on their ability to hold back the Balkan states from aggression against Turkey.

Apr. 18.   **The Italians bombarded the Dardanelles,** which were thereupon closed by the Turks. After vigorous protests from Russia and other powers, they were reopened on May 4.

May 4-16.   **The Italians conquered Rhodes** and other islands of the Dodecanese, thereby establishing a footing in the eastern Mediterranean and causing much uneasiness in England and France.

May 29.   **Treaty of alliance between Bulgaria and Greece.** This had been proposed by Venizelos a year before, but had been evaded by the Bulgarians for fear of becoming involved in a war concerning Crete. Such a war was not provided for in the treaty, and the definition of claims in Macedonia was postponed. A **military convention** was concluded on Oct. 5.

July 16.   **Naval convention between France and Russia,** to supplement the military convention of 1893. This was part of Poincaré's (French premier since Jan. 14, 1912) policy of strengthening the alliance with Russia.

July 22.   **Decision of the British admiralty to withdraw battleships** from the Mediterranean and concentrate them in the North Sea, in view of the growing naval strength of Germany. The French soon afterward reversed the process and withdrew their battleships from Brest to the Mediterranean, chiefly to face the growing power of Italy and Austria.

Aug.   **Visit of Poincaré to St. Petersburg,** where he was first shown the text of the Serbian-Bulgarian Alliance. He saw the import of it and warned Sazonov, but at the same time discussed the need for the strengthening of Russian military preparations in Poland.

Aug. 14.   **Bulgarian note to Turkey,** demanding establishment of autonomy for Macedonia, where outbreaks had become more frequent.

Aug. 14.   **Note of Berchtold** (Austrian foreign minister since Feb. 1912) to the powers suggesting pressure on the Balkan states to keep the peace and pressure on the Turks to institute far-reaching reforms in Macedonia. This was accepted by the powers, which commissioned Austria and Russia to act for them.

Sept. 18.   **Bulgaria and Serbia decided for war** against Turkey, using the demand for reform merely as a blind. The two powers were anxious to take advantage of the Tripolitan War, which was coming to a close.

Sept. 25.   The Turks announced maneuvers, to be held at Adrianople.

Sept. 30.   **Mobilization of the Balkan states.** Russia announced a trial mobilization in Poland.

Oct. 8.   **Austrian-Russian note to the Balkan states,** demanding respect for the *status quo* and promising reforms for Macedonia.

Oct. 8.   **Montenegro declared war on Turkey.**

Oct. 18.   **OUTBREAK OF THE FIRST BALKAN WAR,** between Bulgaria, Serbia, and Greece on the one hand, and Turkey on the other.

Oct. 18.   **Treaty of Lausanne,** between Turkey and Italy. This had been under discussion since July and had been forced by an Italian ultimatum (Oct. 12): Turkey promised to withdraw her forces from Tripoli and the Italians promised to withdraw from the Aegean Islands as soon as the Turkish withdrawal from Tripoli was complete; the Turks were allowed to keep in Tripoli a representative of the sultan as caliph.

Oct. 22.   **Bulgarian victory at Kirk Kilissé,** in Thrace, where the Turks had rashly taken the offensive.

Oct. 24-26.   **Serbian victory at Kumanovo.**

Oct. 28-Nov. 3.   **Great Bulgarian victory at Lulé Burgas.** Advance of the Bulgarians to the Chatalja lines, last line of defense before Constantinople.

Nov. 3-5. Russian warnings to the Bulgarians against the occupation of Constantinople, which the Russians would resist by the use of their fleet.

Nov. 10. The Serbs reached the Adriatic, after overrunning northern Albania.

Nov. 15-18. Serb victory at Monastir.

Nov. 17-18. Bulgarian attack on the Chatalja lines, which failed.

Nov. 21-22. Grey-Cambon correspondence, in which England and France agreed to consult in the event of either one being threatened by attack.

Nov. 24. The Austrians announced their unalterable opposition to territorial access to the Adriatic for Serbia and came out for an independent Albania. Acute international crisis. The Serbs remained steadfast and were at first supported by Russia, which was given assurances by France of support in the event of war with Germany. Austria was supported by Italy, which also opposed the appearance of the Serbs on the Adriatic. The Germans, after some hesitation, promised Austria support if she were attacked while defending her interests. England was sympathetic to the Austrian position and tried to work with Germany for an adjustment without jeopardizing relations to France and Russia. The crisis was most acute in late November and early December, when both Austria and Russia began to mobilize. It was overcome when the Russians, unprepared for war, abandoned the Serb territorial claims.

Dec. 3. Armistice between Turkey, Bulgaria, and Serbia. Greece did not join in it. Operations were to continue around **Scutari** (besieged by the Montenegrins), **Janina** (invested by the Greeks), and **Adrianople**.

Dec. 5. Last renewal of the Triple Alliance, for 6 years from July, 1914. This reflected the closer relations between Italy and Austria and the friction between Italy and England and France growing out of the occupation of the Dodecanese.

Dec. 17. Opening of the London Peace Conference. At the same time an ambassadorial conference at London discussed the status and boundaries of Albania, the fate of the Aegean Islands, etc.

1913, Jan. 6. Breakdown of the London Conference, because of the refusal of the Turks to give up Adrianople, the Aegean Islands, and Crete.

Jan. 22. The powers finally induced the Turks to abandon Adrianople.

Jan. 23. *Coup d'état* at Constantinople; downfall of Kiamil Pasha and victory of the extreme nationalists led by Enver Bey.

Feb. 3. Resumption of the war.

Mar. 5. The Greeks took Janina.

Mar. 26. The Bulgarians took Adrianople.

Apr. 16. The Bulgarians and Turks concluded an armistice, which was accepted by other belligerents.

Apr. 22. The Montenegrins took Scutari, despite protests of the powers, who had assigned it to Albania.

May 3. Under threat of war from Austria, the **Montenegrins gave up Scutari** and the **Serbs evacuated Durazzo** (May 5).

May 7. An ambassadorial conference at St. Petersburg awarded to **Rumania the town of Silistria**, without the fortifications, as compensation for the gains of Bulgaria.

May 20. Reopening of the London Peace Conference. The victorious allies were obliged by an ultimatum from Sir Edward Grey to accept the settlement agreed to by the great powers.

May 30. **TREATY OF LONDON,** ending the First Balkan War. Turkey ceded all territory west of a line between Enos and Midia and abandoned all claim to **Crete**; the status of **Albania** and of the **Aegean Islands** was left to the decision of the powers.

June 1. Treaty of alliance between Serbia and Greece against Bulgaria. This was the result of Serbia's failure to make good her claims on the Adriatic and the unwillingness of Bulgaria to grant Serbia more of Macedonia than had been envisaged in the Treaty of Mar. 13, 1912. The Bulgarians were willing to leave the matter to the arbitration of the tsar, which the Serbs tried to evade.

June 29-July 30. **SECOND BALKAN WAR.** The Bulgarian commander, Gen. Savov, ordered an attack on the Serbian-Greek positions without informing the prime minister, Daney, who was just leaving for St. Petersburg. The government disavowed the action, but the Serbs and Greeks took advantage of the situation to carry out the attack they had long planned. Rumania and Turkey entered the war against Bulgaria, which was rapidly defeated.

Aug. 10. **TREATY OF BUCHAREST.** The Rumanians were given the northern **Dobrudja**, from Turtukaia on the

Danube to Ekrene on the Black Sea; the Serbs and Greeks retained those parts of **Macedonia** which they had occupied. Bulgaria retained only a small part of Macedonia, having lost **Monastir** and **Ochrid** to Serbia and **Saloniki** and **Kavalla** to Greece. On the Aegean seaboard the Bulgarians kept only the stretch between the Mesta and Maritza rivers, with the second-rate port of **Dedeagatch.**

Sept. 23. Invasion of Albania by the Serbs, following Albanian raids into areas assigned to Serbia by the Treaty of London.

Sept. 29. TREATY OF CONSTANTI-NOPLE between Bulgaria and Turkey; the Turks recovered **Adrianople** and the line of the Maritza River.

Oct. 18. Austrian **ultimatum to Serbia,** demanding the evacuation of Albania within eight days. The Serbs yielded.

Oct. 30. Austro-Italian note to Greece, demanding the evacuation of southern Albania by Dec. 31.

Nov.-Dec. THE LIMAN VON SAND-ERS CRISIS. Liman had been appointed by the Turkish government to reorganize the army. He was to have command of the First Army Corps, at Constantinople, and other far-reaching powers. The Russians, who had at first raised no objection, protested when they learned how extensive the authority of the German mission was to be. They demanded that Liman be given a command elsewhere than at Constantinople. The French vigorously supported the Russian stand, but the English were lukewarm. Ultimately a note was sent to the Turkish government (Dec. 13) warning it against too great concessions. The affair was closed (Jan. 1914) when the Germans agreed that Liman should give up the Constantinople command and become inspector-general of the army. The incident left the Russians suspicious of German designs on the Turkish capital and led to much recrimination.

Dec. 13. Grey proposed to the powers the division of disputed southern Albania between Greece and Albania, with compensation to Greece in the Aegean Islands. This was finally accepted, but the Greeks did not evacuate until Apr. 27, 1914, after which the dispute continued with regard to the Aegean Islands. By June 1914 there was an acute danger of war between Greece and Turkey.

1914, Feb. 21. A famous **Russian crown council** discussed the question of the Straits and concluded that Russian aims there could be attained only in case of a European war.

Apr. 22-24. Visit of King George and Grey to Paris. The French, at the request of the Russians, urged the conclusion of an **Anglo-Russian naval convention** (the English refusing to consider an alliance). Discussions were carried on throughout the remaining months of the pre-war period.

June 14. Visit of Tsar Nicholas and Sazonov to Constantza and **Bucharest.** The Russians and Rumanians agreed to co-operate in the event of the closure of the Straits in a Turkish-Greek war, but the Rumanians refused to commit themselves to intervene in the event of an Austrian attack upon Serbia.

June 15. An Anglo-German Agreement initialed. This settled the **Baghdad Railway** problem, the Germans promising not to construct the line south of Basra and recognizing England's preponderant interests in the shipping on the Euphrates. The agreement reflected a real desire on both sides to remove many outstanding colonial difficulties.

June 24. Austrian memorandum for Germany, discussing the Balkan situation as it emerged after the Treaty of Bucharest. The Vienna government favored an alliance with Bulgaria and Turkey to make impossible a reconstitution of the Balkan League under Russian and French auspices. The Germans had, on the other hand, been urging on Vienna a reconciliation with Serbia and Rumania and Greece. On this basic question the two allies had drifted far apart.

June 28. ASSASSINATION OF THE ARCHDUKE FRANCIS FERDINAND at Sarajevo. The assassin was **Gavrilo Princip.** He and other young Bosnian revolutionaries acted as agents of the Serbian society **Union or Death** (*The Black Hand*), a terrorist organization founded in 1911 for agitation against Austria in behalf of Serbian aspirations. The Serbian government was cognizant of the plot, but did little to prevent its consummation or to warn the Austrian government. The Vienna government, though convinced of the complicity of Serbia, was intent on making out a tight case and sent a legal expert to Sarajevo to collect evidence. The world generally was outraged by the assassination and sympathetic toward Austrian claims for satisfaction.

July 5. Mission of Count Hoyos to Berlin. He took the memorandum of June 24 on the Balkan situation, to which had been added some remarks on the need for settling, once and for all, the intolerable activity of the Serbs. Both the emperor and Bethmann recognized the justice of the Austrian stand, promised support (the *Blank Check*) and urged that steps be taken while world opinion was favorable. The Germans evidently regarded a localized settlement as possible, and believed the Russians too unprepared to take an extreme stand.

July 7. Austrian crown council. Most of the members favored war against Serbia, but this course was opposed by the Hungarian premier, **Count Tisza,** who insisted on diplomatic action to avoid larger European complications.

July 13. Baron von Wiesner, sent to collect evidence, reported that he had been unable to find conclusive evidence of Serbian complicity, though the part played by members of the Black Hand Society was clear.

July 14. Austrian crown council. Tisza was won over to a policy of warlike action, on condition that no Serbian territory should be annexed by Austria.

July 20-23. Visit of President Poincaré and Premier Viviani of France to St. Petersburg. Agreement to invite England to join with France and Russia in pressure on Vienna, though the Austrian demands on Serbia were not yet known, except in a vague way. The French apparently disregarded the merits of the case and took the whole matter as a test of the solidarity of the entente in face of action by the Triple Alliance.

July 23. Austrian ultimatum to Belgrade (48 hours). This had been ready on July 20, but had been held back until Poincaré should have left St. Petersburg. It demanded suppression of publications hostile to Austria; dissolution of patriotic organizations engaged in anti-Austrian propaganda; cessation of propaganda in the schools; dismissal of officials accused by Austria of collaboration of Austrian with Serbian officials in the inquiry regarding responsibility for the assassination; judicial proceedings against those accessory to the plot; arrest of two Serbian officials known to be involved; explanations and apologies.

July 24. First formulation of **Russian policy:** Serbia must not be attacked and devoured by Austria.

July 25. Austrian assurances to Russia that no Serbian territory would be annexed. A Russian crown council decided on first military measures against Austria, to be followed by war if Serbia were attacked. **French assurances of support** given to Russia.

The **Serbian reply** to the Austrian ultimatum, generally favorable at first sight, was actually evasive. The crucial point VI was rejected. The Serbian reply may have been due to reports from St. Petersburg of Russia's decision to support Serbia. On reception of the Serb reply the Austrian minister at once left Belgrade. Serbia had ordered mobilization against Austria even before making the reply. Austria at once mobilized against Serbia.

July 26. Sir Edward Grey proposed a conference to deal with the Austro-Serb issue. France accepted; Austria refused to submit a question of national honor to the decision of others; Germany also refused an international discussion of the Austrian claims, though ready for a conference to deal with the Austro-Russian tension; Russia accepted the Grey proposal in principle, though preferring direct conversations with Vienna, which had been initiated.

July 27. First French preparatory measures. The British fleet ordered not to disband after maneuvers. Grey promised Russia diplomatic support and did nothing to hold Russia back from further steps.

July 28. AUSTRIA DECLARED WAR ON SERBIA. Belgrade was bombarded the next day, though Austria was not ready for real operations until about Aug. 12. The declaration of war was meant to create a *fait accompli.* Rupture of the Austro-Russian pourparlers. Germany urged the **occupation of Belgrade** as a pawn, to be followed by negotiations with Russia regarding the Serbian reply. This course was also favored by Grey, but was ignored by Berchtold. France renewed assurances of support to Russia.

July 29. Bethmann, resisting pressure from Gen. von Moltke, chief of staff, urged the resumption of Austro-Russian negotiations and began to bring **pressure on Vienna.** At the same time he made a bid for **British neutrality:** Germany ready to promise not to take French territory in Europe, or Belgian territory, if England promised neutrality. This was rejected.

The Russian tsar yielded to pressure from Sazonov and the military men and agreed to **general mobilization.** The order was recalled and mobilization against Austria alone decided on when the tsar received a telegram from Berlin telling of the Emperor William's efforts to bring the Austrians into line.

July 30. Austro-Russian conversations resumed. Due to technical difficulties the Russian government reversed its action of July 29 and decided for **general mobilization,** despite numerous German warnings.

July 31. Germany proclaimed **"state of threatening danger of war"** and sent a **12-hour ultimatum to Russia** demanding cessation of preparations on the German frontier.

German inquiry in Paris as to what attitude France would take in a Russian-German conflict.

Germany refused a British request that the neutrality of Belgium be respected.

5.00 p.m. Austria decreed general mobilization.

Aug. 1. French reply to Germany: France would be guided by her own interests.

3.55 p.m. French mobilization.

4.00 p.m. German mobilization. Germany offered England a promise not to attack France if England would guarantee French neutrality.

7.00 p.m. GERMAN DECLARATION OF WAR ON RUSSIA, no reply having been received to the German ultimatum.

Aug. 2. The British cabinet, after many meetings and much disagreement regarding support of France, **voted to give France assurances** to protect the coast against German attack (the "moral obligation" arising from previous naval arrangements).

The Germans began the invasion of Luxemburg and submitted to Belgium a demand for permission to cross Belgian territory, in return for a promise to uphold Belgian integrity. This was rejected.

Aug. 3. GERMANY DECLARED WAR ON FRANCE, on the flimsy pretext of frontier violations. In reality the German action was due to military considerations and to the conviction that France would come to Russia's support in any case.

Beginning of the invasion of Belgium.

Aug. 4. ENGLAND DECLARED WAR ON GERMANY, the invasion of Belgium giving Sir Edward Grey a welcome argument in the cabinet and in Parliament.

Aug. 6. AUSTRIA DECLARED WAR ON RUSSIA.

Declarations of War

1914

July	28	Austria on Serbia
Aug.	1	Germany on Russia
Aug.	3	Germany on France
Aug.	4	Germany on Belgium
		England on Germany
Aug.	5	Montenegro on Austria
Aug.	6	Austria on Russia
		Serbia on Germany
Aug.	8	Montenegro on Germany
Aug.	12	France on Austria
		England on Austria
Aug.	23	Japan on Germany
Aug.	25	Japan on Austria
Aug.	28	Austria on Belgium
Nov.	2	Russia on Turkey
		Serbia on Turkey
Nov.	5	England on Turkey
		France on Turkey

1915

May	23	Italy on Austria
June	3	San Marino on Austria
Aug.	21	Italy on Turkey
Oct.	14	Bulgaria on Serbia
Oct.	15	England on Bulgaria
		Montenegro on Bulgaria
Oct.	16	France on Bulgaria
Oct.	19	Russia on Bulgaria
		Italy on Bulgaria

1916

Mar.	9	Germany on Portugal
Mar.	15	Austria on Portugal
Aug.	27	Rumania on Austria
Aug.	28	Italy on Germany
		Germany on Rumania
Aug.	30	Turkey on Rumania
Sept.	1	Bulgaria on Rumania

1917

Apr.	6	United States on Germany
Apr.	7	Panama on Germany
		Cuba on Germany
Apr.	13	Bolivia severs relations with Germany
Apr.	23	Turkey severs relations with United States
June	27	Greece on Austria, Bulgaria, Germany, and Turkey
July	22	Siam on Germany and Austria
Aug.	4	Liberia on Germany
Aug.	14	China on Germany and Austria
Oct.	6	Peru severs relations with Germany
Oct.	7	Uruguay severs relations with Germany
Oct.	26	Brazil on Germany
Dec.	7	United States on Austria
Dec.	8	Ecuador severs relations with Germany
Dec.	10	Panama on Austria
Dec.	16	Cuba on Austria

1918

Apr.	23	Guatemala on Germany
May	8	Nicaragua on Germany **and** Austria
May	23	Costa Rica on Germany
July	12	Haiti on Germany
July	19	Honduras on Germany

G. NORTH AMERICA

1. THE UNITED STATES

a. THE UNITED STATES, 1789-1861

1789, Mar. 4. First Congress met at New York.

Apr. 30. WASHINGTON INAUGU-RATED AS PRESIDENT. Creation by Congress of three executive departments: state, war, and treasury. The **Judiciary Act** of 1789 provided for a system of federal district and circuit courts. The first ten amendments to the constitution, the so-called *Bill of Rights*, were adopted by Congress and sent to the states.

1790, Jan.—1791, Dec. Formulation of **Alexander Hamilton's** fiscal policies. These included the **Funding Bill**, authorizing the treasury to accept old securities at par in payment for new bonds, bearing interest; the **Assumption Bill**, providing for federal assumption of the debts of the states; the **Bank of the United States**; and an excise tax. In his *Report on Manufactures* Hamilton argued cogently for tariff protection, but the tariff, first imposed in 1789, remained primarily a revenue measure.

1791-1814. Economic developments. In 1791 **Samuel Slater** and **Moses Brown** successfully applied power-driven machinery to the spinning of cotton yarn at Pawtucket, R.I. This is commonly taken to date the introduction of the factory system and the beginning of the industrial revolution in the United States. In 1793 **Eli Whitney** introduced the **cotton gin**, which, by rendering profitable the cultivation of short staple cotton in the uplands of the south, had a revolutionizing influence on the south and on the slavery problem. In 1797 **Charles Newbold** took out a patent for an **iron plow**. In 1798 Eli Whitney announced his plan for manufacturing guns on a "new principle," that of standardized, interchangeable parts. In 1814 **Francis Cabot Lowell** and his associates at Waltham (Mass.) combined in one establishment all the processes of cotton manufacture.

1792. Political parties made their appearance, largely because of differences of opinion with respect to Hamilton's policies. **Jefferson,** who became the leader of the **Republican** (later the Democratic) Party, felt that Hamilton's policies were designed in the interest of financial and commercial groups and were inimical to the agrarian elements. **Hamilton and John Adams** became the leaders of the **Federalist** Party.

1793. Washington and Adams re-elected.

With the outbreak of war in Europe between England and France, the latter sent **Genet** as minister to the United States. His efforts to commit the United States to the support of France, even to the point of appealing from the president to the people, forced Washington to ask for his recall. Determined to maintain neutrality in spite of the efforts of Hamilton and Jefferson to influence him in favor of England and France respectively, Washington issued his proclamation of neutrality (Apr. 22). The following year (1794) the **Neutrality Act** was passed.

1794. Whiskey insurrection in western Pennsylvania, resulting from opposition to the excise tax on domestic spirits; put down by militia of Pennsylvania and other states.

The **eleventh amendment** proposed by Congress as a result of the decision of the supreme court in *Chisholm v. Georgia.* The amendment closed the federal courts to suits instituted against a state by citizens of another state or citizens or subjects of a foreign state.

Since the Treaty of 1783 relations between England and the United States had been far from satisfactory. England refused to enter into a commercial treaty and refused to evacuate the posts on the Great Lakes (ostensibly because of failure of the United States to observe the treaty provision with respect to collection of debts owed to British creditors, really in order to obtain control of fur trade and build up an Indian buffer state in the northwest). England was charged with inciting the Indians to hostility, with imprisonment of American seamen, and with capture of American merchant ships. To adjust these differences **John Jay** was sent to England and

THE EXPANSION OF THE UNITED STATES

ATLANTIC OCEAN

CANADA

BAHAMA ISLANDS (British)

CUBA

GULF OF MEXICO

Limit of British Claim

St. Lawrence

L. Ontario
L. Erie
L. Huron
L. Michigan
L. Superior

THE UNITED STATES

1783

ORIGINAL THIRTEEN STATES

FLORIDA

St. Marys R.

Claimed by Spain to 1795

1810 1813

Perdido R.

Purchased from Spain 1819

Mississippi R.

LOUISIANA PURCHASE

Purchased from France 1803

Missouri R.

REPUBLIC OF TEXAS

Annexed 1845

Rio Grande

Ceded by Mexico 1848

ROCK MOUNTAINS

OREGON COUNTRY

Columbia R.

U.S. Claim recognized by Great Britain, by Treaty of 1846

Ceded by Mexico 1848

Colorado R.

Gila R.

Gadsden Purchase 1853

MEXICO

PACIFIC OCEAN

Present State Boundaries

Scale of Miles

0   100   300   500

Nov. 19. Jay's Treaty was concluded. It provided for the evacuation of the border posts in 1796, permitted trade with the British East Indies, placed trade between the United States and Great Britain on a basis of "reciprocal and perfect liberty," and admitted American boats of not more than 70 tons burden to the West Indies. Joint commissions were provided for settling the questions of the debt and the northeast boundary. Claims on behalf of loyalists were dropped, balanced by claims for slaves carried away by the British armies. Claims arising from alleged illegal seizures of ships were referred to commissions. The Senate grudgingly ratified, after striking out the clause with respect to the West Indies.

1795, Oct. 27. Treaty of San Lorenzo or Pinckney's Treaty. Since 1783 there had been constant friction with Spain over the southern boundary of the United States (England having retroceded Florida to Spain), over the navigation of the Mississippi, over Spain's machinations with the Indians of the southwest, and over her intrigues with the frontiersmen. In 1786 negotiations between Jay and Gardoqui came to naught. Finally in 1795 Thomas Pinckney succeeded in negotiating a treaty establishing the southern boundary at the 31st parallel, giving to Americans the right to navigate the Mississippi to its mouth, and granting to them the *right of deposit* at New Orleans for three years.

1796, Sept. 18. Washington's Farewell Address.

1797, Mar. 4. JOHN ADAMS, president, with Jefferson as vice-president. The conclusion of Jay's Treaty with England involved the United States in difficulties with France, who regarded the treaty as evidence of a pro-British policy by the United States. The difficulty culminated in the attempt of the French Directory to extort money from the three American commissioners, Pinckney, Marshall, and Gerry. This is the so-called **X.Y.Z. Affair.** Fighting on the sea occurred, a navy department was created, Washington was named commander of the army, and until Sept. 30, 1800, a naval war was carried on. By the **Treaty of 1800** the treaty of alliance of 1778 with France was abrogated.

1798. Stung by the criticisms of its opponents (many of them French citizens), the Adams administration enacted a series of repressive measures against them: the **Naturalization Act** extending the required time of residence to fourteen years; the **Alien Act;** the **Alien Enemies Act,** and the **Sedition Act.** The last act especially represented an attempt to make a crime of political opposition. These acts led to

1798-1799. The **Kentucky** and **Virginian Resolutions,** penned by Jefferson and Madison respectively, which, in effect, asserted that a state might nullify the force of an act of Congress within its confines, if it regarded such act as contrary to the constitution.

1800. In the election, commonly referred to as the **Revolution of 1800.** Adams was defeated, but, because Jefferson and Burr had the same number of votes, the election was decided by the House of Representatives in favor of Jefferson. The tie led to the movement culminating in the **twelfth amendment** (1804), which altered the method of electing the president and vice-president by requiring that separate ballots be cast for each.

1801. John Marshall, chief justice of the supreme court.

Mar. 4. THOMAS JEFFERSON, the first president to be inaugurated in Washington, the new capital.

1801-1802. Repeal of the internal revenue taxes and of the Judiciary Act of the Adams administration.

1803. Ohio admitted as the 17th state, and the first state to be carved out of the Old Northwest. It had been preceded into the union by Vermont (1791), Kentucky (1792), and Tennessee (1796). The first authorized settlement of Americans north of the Ohio was made by the **Ohio Company** at Marietta (1788). A short time later the **Symmes Company** established a settlement in southwestern Ohio, while in 1796 Connecticut settlers established **Cleveland** in the Connecticut Western Reserve. The planting of these settlements aroused the Indians to opposition. In 1791 Gen. Arthur St. Clair was decisively beaten by them, but in 1794 at **Fallen Timbers** Gen. Anthony Wayne defeated them. By the **Treaty of Greenville** (1795), the Indians ceded all but the northwest quarter of Ohio, thereby paving the way for the increased settlement leading to the admission to statehood.

1803. Marbury v. Madison, the case in which John Marshall established the principle of judicial review of acts of Congress by declaring a section of the Judiciary Act of 1789 unconstitutional.

Apr. 30. THE LOUISIANA PURCHASE. In 1800 Spain had retroceded Louisiana to France. Napoleon was then interested in Louisiana because of his ambition to re-establish a French colonial empire in America. This alarmed

THE UNITED STATES DURING THE CONFEDERATION PERIOD

Jefferson, who feared a strong power at the mouth of the Mississippi. To reassure the west, alarmed at the possible closing of the river to its trade, Jefferson instructed **Livingston**, the American minister to France, to open negotiation for the purchase of a sufficient area at the mouth of the river to guarantee freedom of navigation and transshipment of goods. Monroe was sent to assist Livingston. Meanwhile the failure of Napoleon's army to reconquer Santo Domingo, combined with the ominous turn of events in Europe, caused Napoleon to lose interest in a colonial empire. He therefore sold Louisiana to the United States for 80,000,000 francs, thereby doubling the size of the country. Louisiana included the area between the Mississippi and the Rocky Mountains, plus the island on which New Orleans stands. Uncertainty as to the southern boundary of Louisiana led to prolonged controversy with Spain as to whether it included Texas and West Florida, which was not finally settled until the Treaty of 1819.

1803-1804. New England Federalists, believing the accession of Louisiana would so strengthen the agrarian states as to lead to a decline in New England influence, planned the formation of a **northeastern confederacy**, composed of New England and New York. To carry New York with them they approached **Aaron Burr**, vice-president, who was disgruntled with Jefferson, and proposed that he run for the governorship, with Federalist support. The opposition of Hamilton to this plan was followed by the duel between Burr and Hamilton (July, 1804), in which Hamilton was killed.

1804-1806. Lewis and Clark Expedition. Meriwether Lewis and William Clark were selected by Jefferson to explore the trans-Mississippi country. Leaving St. Louis, they ascended the Missouri to its source, crossed to the head-waters of the Snake River, thence down the Columbia River to the Pacific. The mouth of the Columbia had first been entered in 1793 by Capt. Robert Gray of Boston. Explorations of Lewis and Clark gave the United States another claim to the "Oregon country."

1805. The **Tripolitan War**, which had begun in 1801, brought to a close by a treaty.

    Mar. 4. Thomas Jefferson began his **second term** as president, with George Clinton as vice-president.

    Decision in the *Essex* case, reversing the decision in the case of the *Polly* (1800), and declaring the American re-export trade a violation of the Rule of 1756.

1806, May 16. Fox's order declared the coast of Europe from Brest to the Elbe River to be in a state of blockade, except between Ostend and the mouth of the Seine, where neutral vessels were admitted if not coming from or bound to an enemy port. Napoleon retaliated (Nov. 21) with his **Berlin Decree** declaring a paper blockade of the British Isles. A British order in council of Jan. 7, 1807, closed to neutrals the coasting trade between French ports. On Nov. 11, 1807, an order in council blockaded the coast from Copenhagen to Trieste against neutrals unless they had first entered or cleared from a British port and paid duties there. In Dec. Napoleon replied with his **Milan Decree** which declared that ships lost their neutral character if they obeyed the British order in council of Nov. 11, or if they submitted to search on the high seas by British officers.

1807, June. The *Chesapeake-Leopard* affair. The American ship *Chesapeake* was fired on by the British ship *Leopard* and four deserters taken from her. Although Federalists and Republicans forgot their differences in the face of this national insult, Jefferson, opposed to war, merely ordered British ships of war to leave American waters, and demanded reparation and the abandonment of impressment.

    Aug. 17. Robert Fulton's steamboat, the *Clermont*, steamed up the Hudson from New York to Albany in 32 hours.

    Dec. 22. The Embargo Act. Jefferson, still averse to war, resolved on commercial coercion as a means of forcing France and England to withdraw their restrictions on American trade. The act forbade the departure of ships for foreign ports, except foreign vessels in port at time the act was passed. Coasting vessels were required to give bond to land their cargoes at American ports.

    Aaron Burr tried for treason and acquitted. The trial was the outgrowth of Burr's activities in the west after his duel with Hamilton. He planned the creation of an independent state, either at the expense of the United States or Spain, more probably the latter.

1808. African slave trade prohibited after Jan. 1.

1809, Mar. 4—1817, Mar. 4. JAMES MADISON the fourth president.

    Mar. 15. The repeal of the Embargo Act became effective. It had not brought England and France to terms, but had fallen with great weight upon American shipping. New England opposition to the policy was reflected in Federalist gains in the election of 1808.

May 20. The **Non-Intercourse Law** permitted commerce with all countries except France and England.

1810, Mar. 23. Napoleon's **Rambouillet Decree** ordered the sale of all American ships which had been seized for violation of French decrees.

May 1. **Macon's Bill No. 2** repealed all restrictions on trade with the warring powers and provided that if either should remove its restrictions on American trade, the president should renew nonintercourse with the other. Napoleon announced revocation of the Berlin and Milan Decrees, effective Nov. 1, whereupon Madison, on Nov. 2, proclaimed the renewal of non-intercourse with England within 90 days. Napoleon continued to seize American ships.

1810-1811. **Rise of the war party.** The election of 1810 resulted in the defeat of many of the old members of pacific views and the choice of younger men, especially from the west, who were impatient with the peace policy. These men, commonly known as the *War Hawks*, were especially aroused by the opposition of the Indians, led by **Tecumseh,** to the advance of white settlement in the northwest. In Nov. 1811 occurred the **battle of Tippecanoe,** which made **William Henry Harrison** a hero in the eyes of the frontiersmen. More and more the west became convinced that British aid and encouragement from Canada stiffened the Indian opposition. The result was a growing demand for war with England and the conquest of Canada. Reading the lesson of the election of 1810 aright, Madison adopted a firmer tone toward England.

1812, Apr. **Ninety-Day Embargo** to insure that American ships would be safely in port when war with England began. By this time England, fighting the Peninsular War in Spain, needed American supplies. She therefore would have gladly revoked the orders in council if she could have been certain that Napoleon would absolutely withdraw his decrees against American shipping. A new order in council announced that whenever the Berlin and Milan Decrees were unconditionally revoked, the British decrees would automatically cease. The French foreign minister thereupon produced a decree, dated a year earlier, which declared that the decrees were non-existent, so far as the United States was concerned, after Nov. 1, 1810. The document was drawn up in 1812 and antedated, but the British accepted it and

revoked the orders in council, June 23. Meanwhile,

June 18. **War was declared on England,** on the ground of impressment, violation of the three-mile limit, paper blockade, and orders in council.

1812-1814. **WAR OF 1812.** (See also p. 793.) In the naval warfare of the first year the Americans were surprisingly successful, the *Essex* capturing the *Alert;* the *Constitution,* the *Guerrière* and the *Java;* the *Wasp,* the *Frolic;* the *United States,* the *Macedonian.* Later in the war, however, the American ships were one by one captured or bottled up. Except for the effect on the morale of the people, the victories on the high seas were without influence on the course of the war. On land the campaign of 1812 called for a triple invasion of Canada, which came to naught when **Hull surrendered Detroit** (Aug. 16). In 1813 **Oliver Hazard Perry** won the **naval battle of Lake Erie.** In 1814 the Americans were successful at the engagements of **Chippewa** and **Lundy's Lane** in Canada, which decided nothing, while Capt. **Thomas Macdonough** won the **naval battle of Plattsburg** on Lake Champlain. In the same year the British captured and **burned Washington,** but were repulsed at Baltimore (Sept. 13), whereupon they launched attacks on the Maine coast and on New Orleans. In the southwest **Andrew Jackson** broke the military power of the Creek Indians and dismembered their territory (Aug. 9, 1814), whereupon he proceeded to New Orleans to defend it against the British attack. On Jan. 8, 1815, he won the **battle of New Orleans.**

1814, Dec. 24. The **Treaty of Ghent** brought the war to a close. The treaty was silent on the questions which had been the chief cause of controversy before the war. It restored the *status quo ante,* and provided for joint commissions to determine disputed boundary questions between the two countries.

Dec. **The Hartford Convention.** The New England states, disgruntled since the time of the embargo, had refused the call for militia during the war and had talked freely in terms of state rights. When the federal government stationed no troops in the section and the British invaded the Maine coast in 1814, Massachusetts asked her sister states to join her in a convention to be held at Hartford. The fact that moderates obtained control prevented any possibility of secession, for which the bulk of the New England people were not prepared. The convention contented itself, therefore, with drawing up some proposed amendments to the constitution, designed to safeguard more adequately New England interests. With the conclusion of peace at Ghent the New England states soon forgot their grievances.

1816. The Second **Bank of the United States** chartered. The **Tariff of 1816** provided increased protection. The conclusion of the War of 1812 was marked by an outburst of national feeling hitherto unknown within the country. While the Madison administration had been unwilling to recharter the First Bank in 1811, it now regarded such an institution as necessary to a uniform circulating medium. The Second Bank, chartered for 20 years, was to have a capital of $35,000,000, one-fifth to be subscribed by the government, which should name a like proportion of the directors. The Tariff of 1816 was enacted in response to the demand of young manufactures to be protected from the dumping of English goods, long held back by embargo and war.

1817, Mar. 4—1825, Mar. 4. JAMES MONROE, the fifth president. An era of good feeling, in which party strife seemed about to disappear, as indicated by the re-election of Monroe in 1820 with but one dissenting electoral vote.

1817, Apr. 28. The **Rush-Bagot Agreement** between Great Britain and the United States, limiting naval forces on the Great Lakes.

1818, Oct. 20. A convention between Great Britain and the United States established the 49th parallel as the boundary from the Lake of the Woods to the Rocky Mountains. Being unable to agree on a division of the Oregon country, north of the 42d parallel and west of the mountains, the convention provided for joint occupation for a period of 10 years. This was renewed in 1827.

1819. The *Savannah* crossed the ocean from Savannah to Liverpool, mostly under steam.

Feb. 22. Treaty with Spain. Since 1803 Florida had been a source of difficulty between the United States and Spain. In 1810 Madison took advantage of an insurrection in West Florida to annex that province. After 1815 Amelia Island was a base for smugglers and freebooters. Fugitive slaves escaped to Florida, and raids against settlements in Georgia and Alabama led to trouble. In 1817–1818, in the so-called **Seminole War,** Jackson invaded Florida and executed two British subjects. **John Quincy Adams,** secretary of state, demanded that Spain maintain order in Florida or cede it to the United States. Spain chose the latter because of inability

to comply with the former demand. The United States agreed to pay an indemnity of $5,000,000 to its citizens for their claims against Spain. The treaty also delimited the western boundary of the Louisiana Purchase, and provided for Spain's relinquishment of all claims to territory on the Pacific north of the 42d parallel.

1819-1824. The nationalism of the postwar period was emphasized by a series of notable supreme court decisions by John Marshall. In **McCulloch v. Maryland** (1819), **Cohens v. Virginia** (1821), and **Gibbons v. Ogden** (1824) he gave judicial sanction to the doctrine of centralization of power at the expense of the states. In **Dartmouth College v. Woodward** (1819), as in the earlier case of **Fletcher v. Peck** (1810), the court provided judicial barriers against democratic attacks upon property rights.

1820, Mar. 3. The Missouri Compromise. The admission to statehood of **Louisiana** (1812), **Indiana** (1816), **Mississippi** (1817), **Illinois** (1818), and **Alabama** (1819) had not raised the question of slavery. After the Revolution many southerners had agreed with northerners as to the desirability of the abolition of slavery. Southerners had been prominent in the organization of the **American Colonization Society** (1816) for the purpose of colonizing free blacks in Liberia. With the spread of cotton culture into the interior of the south, following the invention of the cotton gin by Eli Whitney (1792), southern sentiment gradually changed. Meanwhile increasing feeling in the north against the spread of slavery resulted in strong opposition to the admission of **Missouri** as a slave state. The attempt to balance the admission of Missouri as a slave state by admitting **Maine** as a free state having failed, a compromise was arranged whereby Missouri was to be admitted without restriction as to slavery, while in all the remaining portions of the Louisiana Purchase north of 36° 30' slavery was to be forever prohibited. **Maine** was admitted (1820) and **Missouri,** after careful scrutiny of its constitution by Congress, was finally admitted as a slave state (Aug. 10, 1821).

Apr. 24. A **Land Law** was passed abolishing the credit system, established by the Law of 1800, which had encouraged overpurchase of land with resulting distress, especially in the period of declining prices following the close of the war in 1815. The Act of 1820 established the minimum price of public lands at $1.25 per acre.

1823, Dec. 2. THE **MONROE DOCTRINE** enunciated by the president in his annual message to Congress. The background of the doctrine is to be found in the threat of intervention by the **Holy Alliance** to restore Spain's revolting American colonies and in the aggressive attitude of Russia on the northwest coast of America. It was, at the same time, an expression of American national sentiment and of distrust of England, whose foreign minister, George Canning, had proposed a joint declaration. The message stated that *"the American continents, by the free and independent condition which they have assumed and maintained, are henceforth not to be considered as subjects for future colonization by any European powers,"* and that European intervention in this hemisphere could not be viewed *"in any other light than as the manifestation of an unfriendly disposition toward the United States."* It also disclaimed any intention of the United States to take any part *"in the wars of the European powers"* or *"in matters relating to themselves,"* i.e. the European powers.

1824. Robert Owen founded *New Harmony* in Indiana, the first of a large number of communistic experiments in the United States.

Presidential election, in which none of the four candidates, J. Q. Adams, Jackson, Clay, and W. H. Crawford, obtained an electoral majority, although Jackson received a plurality. In the House of Representatives Adams was elected president.

1825, Mar. 4—1829, Mar. 4. **J O H N QUINCY ADAMS**, sixth president.

1825. COMPLETION OF THE ERIE CANAL.

1826. The abortive **Panama Congress** planned by Bolívar and others to present a united American front against Spain and Europe. The Senate reluctantly approved the appointment of an American mission to the congress. One delegate died *en route* while the other arrived after the congress had adjourned.

1828, May 19. The Tariff of Abominations, framed by Jackson men for defeat, to discredit J. Q. Adams and bring about the election of Jackson. To their surprise it passed Congress, was signed by Adams, and promptly aroused strong opposition, especially in South Carolina, where Calhoun penned his *South Carolina Exposition* (1828), which gave the classic statement of the nullification doctrine.

The **American Peace Society** founded in New York by **William Ladd. Elihu Burritt** became the chief leader of the American peace movement.

July 4. The **Baltimore and Ohio Railroad begun,** the first public railroad in the United States.

1829, Mar 4—1837, Mar. 4. **ANDREW JACKSON,** who defeated Adams in the election of 1828, seventh president. The election of Jackson was a triumph of the frontier democracy of the west.

The **spoils system,** the practice of basing appointments on party service, was nationalized by Jackson. The system was already well-established in certain states of the north and west.

1829-1850. Rise of the common man and era of reform. By 1829 the principle of **white manhood suffrage** was established in most states. Between 1810 and 1826 Maryland, South Carolina, and New York had adopted it. Massachusetts reduced her former suffrage requirement to mere tax payment. The Virginia convention of 1830 removed the chief restrictions on the suffrage. Opposition to reform was strongest in Rhode Island.

1829. The **Workingmen's Party** organized in New York, following the example set in Philadelphia the preceding year. The movement spread to other seaboard states in the north. The program of the movement included social reform, free public schools, banking legislation, abolition of imprisonment for debt, etc.

1830. Organization of the **Mormon Church** at Fayette, N.Y., by **Joseph Smith.** *Book of Mormon* first printed.

Great debate between Webster and Hayne on the nature of the union. The debate was really begun by Benton, who protested against New England attempts to limit the sale of western lands.

Jackson's veto of the **Maysville Road Bill.**

1831. William Lloyd Garrison established the *Liberator* at Boston to advocate unconditional emancipation of the slaves. This marks the beginning of the abolitionist movement. The **New England Anti-Slavery Society** (1832) and the **American Anti-Slavery Society** (1833). **Oberlin College** opened its doors to Negroes as well as to women (1833).

1830-1834. Controversy between Georgia and the Cherokee Indians and development of Jackson's **Indian policy.** An act of March 10, 1830, authorized the president to locate on lands west of the Mississippi all Indians who surrendered their holdings east of the river. This act was prompted largely by the controversy between the state of Georgia and the Cherokee Indians. It led to the creation of an area west of Arkansas as the final home for the southern Indians. A commissioner of Indian affairs was created.

1831, July 4. Treaty by which France agreed to pay $5,000,000 in satisfaction of spoliation claims.

1832, July. Tariff Act of 1832, an improvement over the *Tariff of Abominations*, but retaining the protective principle which was unsatisfactory to South Carolina and led to

1832-1833. The nullification episode in that state, in which a state convention declared the tariff laws of 1828 and 1832 unconstitutional and void within the state. On Dec. 10 Jackson issued his proclamation against the nullifiers, and on Jan. 16, 1833, he asked Congress for additional legislation to enable him to enforce the tariff law. On Mar. 1, Congress enacted the Force Bill. Meanwhile Henry Clay brought forward (Feb. 12) his compromise tariff, providing for gradual reduction of the tariff until July 1, 1842, when it should reach the 20% level.

1832. The Bank controversy. The Second Bank of the United States, although capably managed after 1819, had committed certain political indiscretions which, in combination with Jackson's prejudice against the alleged monopolistic tendencies of the bank, aroused his opposition. When Clay and Webster urged the bank to apply for a renewal of the charter in order to embarrass Jackson in the campaign of 1832, Jackson was aroused to the point where he vetoed the measure. Jackson construed his election over Clay as popular approval of his veto of the Bank Bill, and he resolved to crush the institution. In 1833 there began the removal of the deposits, or the transfer of government funds to certain state banks known as the *pet banks.*

1833. The General Trades' Union linked all the trade societies of New York in one organization. Trade unionism began to supersede the workingmen's parties as the characteristic form of labor activity, until the collapse of the movement in the panic of 1837.

1833-1837. The Whig Party. Southern particularists who were angered by Jackson's handling of the nullification episode, those who feared the leveling tendencies of Jacksonian Democracy, the supporters of the bank, and the industrial and financial groups generally formed the Whig Party, largely lacking in constructive principles, but held together by a common hatred for and distrust of Jackson.

1834-1839. Inventions. Cyrus McCormick took out a patent on a reaping machine. **Obed Hussy** had invented a reaper, but lacked the means to make it a commercial success like McCormick's. In 1836 **Samuel Colt** patented his revolving pistol, commonly known as the *six-shooter.* This new weapon was of great importance in the conquest of the Mounted Plains Indians. In 1837 the **John Deere** steel plow was introduced, which, by virtue of its scouring quality, greatly facilitated the conquest of the prairies. In 1839 **Charles Goodyear** accidentally discovered the process for the vulcanization of rubber. He took out his first patent in 1844.

1836. Texan independence. The American colonization of Texas had begun in 1821 when **Stephen Austin** obtained a grant of land on condition that he settle a certain number of families thereon. This was followed by similar grants to other *empresarios* who introduced a substantial number of American settlers. This movement, largely of southerners, was part of the normal westward movement of the American people. Beginning about 1830 difficulties developed. In 1836 the **Republic of Texas** was established. The decisive battle was that of **San Jacinto** (Apr. 21, 1836).

1836. Act for distribution of surplus revenue among the states, theoretically as a loan.

1837, Mar. 4—1841, Mar. 4. MARTIN VAN BUREN, eighth president.

1837. Panic of 1837. Fundamentally this crash was due to the wave of speculation and reckless expansion which swept the country in the years of 1833–1837. The situation was complicated by the failure of certain great business houses in England which had invested heavily in American securities, by poor crops in the west in 1835 and 1837, and by Jackson's **Special Circular** (July 11, 1836) which required that public lands be paid for in "hard" money.

1837-1840. Struggle between Van Buren and the Whigs over the **independent treasury** proposed by Van Buren for the deposit of government funds. The Whig leaders favored the establishment of a third United States Bank. Independent treasury plan adopted (1840).

1837. Mt. Holyoke Seminary, first women's institution of college rank, opened by **Mary Lyon.**

1837-1842. Difficulties between the United States and Canada. The *Caroline* affair (Dec. 1837) in which an American steamer in the service of Canadian rebels was seized by Canadian militia on the American side of Niagara River, and in which an American citizen was killed. One **Alexander McLeod,** a Canadian, boasting that he had killed the American, was arrested and tried in New York courts. His acquittal averted the possibility of serious difficulties between the United States and Great Britain.

Difficulty over the northeastern boundary led to the **Aroostook County War** (1838-1839). The boundary was finally adjusted in the **Webster-Ashburton Treaty** (Aug. 9, 1842).

1838. The **Underground Railroad** organized.

1838-1839. Congress adopted **gag resolutions** against anti-slavery petitions.

1841. The **Pre-emption-Distribution Act.** Benton had long advocated the pre-emption policy with respect to public lands, while Clay had advocated the distribution of the proceeds of the sale of public lands among the states. By a compromise the two measures were now combined, with a proviso, insisted upon by the south, which required that distribution should cease if the tariff should rise above the 20% level.

1841, Mar. 4—1845, Mar. 4.   WILLIAM HENRY HARRISON and **JOHN TYLER**, the ninth and tenth presidents. Harrison died Apr. 4, 1841.

1842. The **Dorr Rebellion** in Rhode Island, occasioned by refusal of conservatives to liberalize the suffrage and to reform representation. It swept away the Charter of 1663, which had served as the constitution of the state of Rhode Island, 1776-1842.

The **Whig Tariff** restored protective features on the expiration of the Compromise Tariff of 1833.

1844, Apr. 12. **Calhoun's treaty** for annexation of Texas signed. Defeated in the Senate June 8, 1844.

Dr. Horace Wills, a dentist of Hartford, demonstrated that nitrous oxide might be used as an **anaesthetic**. In 1846 **Dr. W. T. G. Morton**, a Boston dentist, applied **ether** as an anaesthetic.

S. F. B. Morse transmitted the **first telegraph message** over a line from Baltimore to Washington.

Presidential campaign. The Democrats nominated **James K. Polk** on the platform declaring for reannexation of Texas and the reoccupation of Oregon. The Whigs nominated **Henry Clay**. The Liberty Party nominated **James G. Birney** and took enough popular votes from Clay to enable Polk to carry New York and win the election.

1845, Mar. 1. Tyler brought about **annexation of Texas** by joint resolution of Congress.

1845, Mar. 4—1849, Mar. 4.   JAMES K. POLK, eleventh president.

1846, June 15. **Oregon Treaty** with Great Britain. The two countries had long claimed the Oregon country, between 42° and 54° 40', although the region really in dispute was that between the Columbia River and the 49th parallel. **The Treaty of Joint Occupation** of 1818 was renewed in 1827, with provision that it might be terminated by either party upon a year's notice. British interest in the Oregon country centered in the fur trade, dominated, after 1821, by the **Hudson's Bay Company.** American traders had visited the Oregon coast at an early day. Capt. Gray had discovered the mouth of the Columbia River (1793), Lewis and Clark had explored the region, and John Jacob Astor had established the post of **Astoria** (1811). A Methodist mission was established in the Willamette Valley (1834) and was followed by others. By the early forties a substantial migration of American farmers to the Willamette Valley was under way, so the Anglo-American rivalry became one of fur trader versus settler. The treaty established the 49th parallel as the boundary on the mainland, and then the middle of the channel to the ocean.

Elias Howe patented his **sewing machine.**

The **Walker Tariff** enlarged the free list and established a rate of 26.5% on dutiable imports.

Re-enactment of the **Independent Treasury Act** which the Whigs had repealed in 1841.

1846-1848.   WAR WITH MEXICO. The United States had many grievances against Mexico, while Mexico could not forgive the United States for the annexation of Texas. Polk was determined to have New Mexico, preferably by peaceful means, but when **Slidell's mission** to Mexico for the purpose of purchasing that territory failed (Nov. 1845–Mar. 1846), Polk was prepared for war. By sending American troops into the disputed area between the Nueces and Rio Grande Rivers, he brought about a skirmish which enabled him to say that Mexico had "shed American blood on American soil." An army under Zachary Taylor invaded Mexico and won the **battles of Palo Alto** and **Resaca de la Palma** (May 8 and 9), took **Monterey** (May 24), and won a victory at **Buena Vista** (Feb. 22 and 23, 1847). Col. S. W. Kearny occupied **Santa Fé** (Aug. 18, 1846). Marching inland from Vera Cruz, **Winfield Scott** fought the battles of **Cerro Gordo** (Apr. 17 and 18, 1847), **Churubusco** (Aug. 20), **Chapultepec** (Sept. 12 and 13), and captured **Mexico City** (Sept. 14). On the Pacific an American squadron seized the California ports.

1846, Aug. 8. The **Wilmot Proviso** introduced into the House of Representatives, when Polk asked for an appropriation to enable him to treat with Mexico for territorial cessions. It provided that in any territory acquired from Mexico, slavery should be excluded. Although it never passed the Senate, it raised the slavery issue and aroused the fears of the south.

1848, Jan. 24. Discovery of gold at Coloma, 60 miles east of Sutter's Fort, California. Beginning of the great gold rush.

Feb. 2. The **Treaty of Guadalupe Hidalgo** closed the war with Mexico. Mexico gave up claims to Texas, recognized the Rio Grande as the boundary, and ceded New Mexico and California to the United States in return for $15,000,000 and the assumption of American claims against Mexico.

July 19. First **Women's Rights Convention,** the first in world history, held at Seneca Falls, New York. The movement had started with the visit of **Frances Wright** to America in 1827. Her example aroused to action **Sarah** and **Angelina Grimke, Lucretia Mott,** and **Elizabeth Cady Stanton.**

Presidential campaign, in which the Whig candidate was **Zachary Taylor,** hero of the recent war. The Democrats nominated **Lewis Cass,** who had recently proposed squatter sovereignty as a solution of the problem of slavery in the territories, raised by the Wilmot Proviso. The **Free Soil Party,** favoring homestead and the exclusion of slavery from the territories, nominated **Van Buren,** who, by splitting the Democratic vote in New York, enabled Taylor to carry the state and win the election.

1849, Mar. 4—1853, Mar. 4. ZACHARY TAYLOR and **MILLARD FILLMORE,** twelfth and thirteenth presidents. Taylor died July 9, 1850.

1850. The **COMPROMISE OF 1850.** On Jan. 29, 1850, Clay introduced his compromise resolutions providing that California should be admitted as a free state; that territorial governments should be established in the remainder of the Mexican cession without any action by Congress with respect to slavery; Texas should yield her claims in the boundary dispute with New Mexico, in return for which the United States would assume the Texan debt; the slave trade should be abolished in the District of Columbia; and Congress should enact a more drastic fugitive slave law. Great debate in which Calhoun spoke (Mar. 4) against the compromise; Webster (Mar. 7) for the compromise; Douglas for, Jefferson Davis, Seward, and Chase against. On Apr. 18 the resolutions were referred to a Senate committee of 13, with Clay as chairman. Between Sept. 9 and 20 the separate measures, known collectively as the **Compromise of 1850,** were passed: California to be admitted as a free state; the remainder of the Mexican cession to be divided at the 37th parallel into the territories of New Mexico and Utah, to be admitted to the union ultimately as states, with or without slavery as their constitutions might provide at the time of admission; the claims of Texas to a portion of New Mexico to be satisfied by payment of $10,000,000; the slave trade in the District of Columbia to be abolished and a more effective fugitive slave law enacted.

Land grants to railways adopted by Congress. A grant was made to the state of Illinois to help the **Illinois Central Railroad** and another to Mississippi and Alabama in support of the **Mobile and Ohio** line.

Apr. 19. The **Clayton-Bulwer Treaty** between the United States and Great Britain with respect to British encroachments in Central America and a future interoceanic canal.

June 3. Nashville Convention of nine southern states. Dominated by moderates, it demanded merely the extension of the 36° 30' line.

1851. Maine prohibition law, sponsored by Neal Dow. It became the model for all similar legislation of the period.

June 2. The **Erie Railroad** reached Dunkirk, on Lake Erie, being the first railway to make connections with the Lakes.

1852. The Democratic Party, committed to finality of the Compromise of 1850 as a solution of the problem of slavery in the territories, elected

1853, Mar. 4—1857, Mar. 4. FRANKLIN PIERCE, fourteenth president.

1853. Rail connection established between New York and Chicago. By 1860 the region north of the Ohio River and east of the Mississippi had been firmly attached commercially to the North Atlantic seaboard. The movement of internal trade, originally north and south along the Mississippi, now became predominantly a west-east movement, the shift proving of great economic and political significance.

Dec. 30. The **Gadsden Purchase** rounded out our possessions in the Far West.

1854, May 30. THE KANSAS-NEBRASKA ACT, which repealed the

Missouri Compromise of 1820, opened the Nebraska country to settlement on the basis of popular sovereignty, and provided for the organization of two territories, Kansas and Nebraska. Douglas was the author of the measure, and he was largely motivated by his desire to pave the way for a Pacific railway. The act undid the sectional truce of 1850 and proved the death-blow to the Whig Party.

Mar. 31. Commodore Perry negotiated a treaty with Japan, opening the country to commercial intercourse with the United States.

Oct. 18. The Ostend Manifesto. The American ministers to England, France, and Spain, instructed to confer on the best means of acquiring Cuba, met at Ostend and drew up the manifesto saying that, if Spain refused to sell Cuba, the United States would be justified in taking it by force. This caused great excitement in free states.

The Know Nothing and Republican Parties appeared, the former as a protest against the Kansas-Nebraska Act.

1855. Opening of Soo Canal bet. Lakes Superior and Huron provided cheap transportation of iron ore and laid the basis for rapid development of the steel industry.

1854-1858. War for "Bleeding Kansas." The opening of Kansas to settlement under the Douglas doctrine of popular sovereignty precipitated a mad scramble for control between pro-slavery and free-soil elements. In Apr. 1854 the New England Emigrant Aid Society was formed to colonize free-soilers in Kansas. This aroused the pro-slavery people. Border Ruffians from Missouri interfered in elections in Kansas. A pro-slavery element attacked the town of Lawrence, and in return John Brown staged the massacre at Pottawatomie Creek (May 24, 1856). The Lecompton Constitution was formed by pro-slavery forces, but was denounced by Douglas as a fraud upon the people of Kansas and a violation of the popular sovereignty doctrine. This led to a break between Douglas and Buchanan. The Senate accepted the Lecompton Constitution, but the House rejected it. The deadlock was broken by the English Bill, enacted May 4, 1858, providing for resubmission of the constitution to popular vote in Kansas. If accepted, the state would receive a grant of land; if rejected, statehood must await further growth of population. It was rejected, and Kansas did not become a state until Jan. 1861.

1857, Mar. 4—1861, Mar. 4. JAMES BUCHANAN, fifteenth president.

Mar. 7. The Dred Scott decision, declaring that the Missouri Compromise was unconstitutional because Congress had no right to enact a law which deprived persons of their property in the territories of the United States. Dred Scott, therefore, had not acquired his freedom by being taken into a territory where slavery had been prohibited by the compromise. The decision caused bitter criticism of the court in the north.

Tariff of 1857; reduced duties.

Panic of 1857, following a period of overexpansion and speculation.

1858, Aug. 5. The transatlantic cable completed. It operated only for a short time.

Aug. Lincoln-Douglas debates, seven in number, in the campaign for election to the Senate. Douglas was elected, but Lincoln, by asking Douglas to reconcile his doctrine of popular sovereignty with the Dred Scott decision, forced him to enunciate his Freeport heresy, which was deeply distasteful to the southern wing of the party.

Abandonment of the government ship subsidy policy (introduced 1845), because of opposition of the southern states.

1859, Oct. 19. John Brown's raid on Harper's Ferry still further aroused sectional passions.

Drake's petroleum well, near Titusville, Penn., marked the beginning of the modern oil industry.

1860. The Davis Resolutions, introduced by Jefferson Davis, demanded a Federal slave code for the protection of property in slaves in the territories.

Presidential campaign. The Republicans nominated Abraham Lincoln on a platform opposing further extension of slavery in the territories and supporting homestead and tariff. The Democrats split at Charleston on the question of slavery in the territories. Two platforms were drawn up, one demanding a federal slave code, the other endorsing the Freeport doctrine of Douglas. Subsequently the northern Democrats nominated Douglas, while the southern Democrats named John C. Breckinridge. The Union party nominated John Bell. Lincoln was elected, in a purely sectional contest. He received no electoral support in the slave states.

Dec. 20. South Carolina adopted the Ordinance of Secession, as a protest against the election of Lincoln.

1860, Dec.—1861, Feb. 4. Futile efforts to save the union. The Crittenden Compromise Resolutions, proposing the extension of the Missouri Compromise line to the Pacific; conference of governors of northern states; the **Peace Convention** at Washington, Feb. 4, 1861.

1861, Jan.-May. Mississippi, Florida, Alabama, Georgia, Louisiana, Texas, Virginia, Tennessee, Arkansas, and North Carolina seceded from the union.

Jan. 9. The ship *Star of the West* was fired upon by a battery at Charleston.

Feb. 4. Delegates of the seven seceding states met at Montgomery, Ala., and formed a provisional government, taking the name **Confederate States of America.**

Feb. 8. **Jefferson Davis** elected president and **Alexander H. Stephens** vice-president of the Confederacy.

1861, Mar. 4—1865, Apr. 15. **Abraham Lincoln**, sixteenth president.

b. THE CIVIL WAR, 1861-1865

MILITARY EVENTS. The Confederates, having seized Federal funds and property in the south, proceeded (Apr. 10) to demand the evacuation of the Federal **Fort Sumter** in Charleston Harbor. Major Anderson, in command, having refused unconditional surrender, Gen. Beauregard bombarded it Apr. 12-13, just as a relief expedition of the Unionists approached.

Apr. 15. Lincoln called for 75,000 volunteers to serve three months, and summoned Congress to meet July 4. May 3 he appealed for 42,000 men to serve three years or for the duration of the war. General expectancy of a short conflict. Immense advantages of the north; 23 states with almost 23,000,000 population against 11 states with 5,000,000 white population; financial strength of the north; manufacturing facilities; more extensive railway communications, etc. South largely dependent on cotton-growing and badly hampered by the blockade of the Confederate ports (proclaimed Apr. 19); from the beginning the south was on the defensive.

May 13. Great Britain recognized the Confederate States as belligerents.

July 21. **FIRST BATTLE OF BULL RUN.** By July there were some 30,000 raw troops in and around Washington, under command of Gen. **Winfield Scott.** Across the Potomac lay 25,000 Confederates under **Beauregard** near the Manassas railway junction. Another force, under Gen. **Joseph E. Johnston**, lay in the Shenandoah Valley, near Harper's Ferry. Congress, meeting July 4, demanded action. Gen. **Patterson** was sent to contain this latter force, while Gen. **Irvin MacDowell** reluctantly advanced on Beauregard. But

part of Johnston's army, under Col. **T. J.** (**Stonewall**) **Jackson**, got away and joined Beauregard. At Bull Run the Federal army was routed. It streamed back to Washington in a state of dissolution. The effect of the battle was to open the eyes of the Unionists and to introduce a period of more extensive and systematic preparation.

Nov. 1. Gen. **George B. McClellan** appointed to succeed Scott in command of the Federal forces. McClellan's policy one of cautious, careful preparation and reliance on numbers. He spent the winter training some 200,000 men (Army of the Potomac) for a march on the Confederate capital, Richmond.

Nov. 8. **Mason and Slidell**, commissioners of the Confederate States to Great Britain and France, were taken off the British steamer *Trent* by the Federal steamer *San Jacinto.* Sharp protests of Great Britain and danger of war. War averted by the prudence and skill of **William H. Seward**, secretary of state. The commissioners were given up, in accordance with a principle of international law for which the United States had invariably contended.

1861-1862. **NAVAL OPERATIONS.** To make the blockade of the southern coasts effective and to prevent privateering, a joint naval and military expedition was sent out in Aug. 1861 'o take key positions on the coast.

1861, Aug. 28-29. Attack and capture of Forts Clark and Hatteras on the North Carolina coast.

1862, Feb. 8. Capture of **Roanoke Island** and **Elizabeth City** (Feb. 10).

Mar. 3-4. **Amelia Island,** on the Florida coast, taken.

Mar. 8. The Confederate frigate *Merrimac*, made over as an ironclad, appeared in Hampton Roads and sank the *Cumberland.*

Mar. 9. The Federal ironclad *Monitor* (revolving gun-turret) engaged the *Merrimac* and finally obliged her to withdraw. Epoch-making development in naval warfare.

Mar. 12. **Jacksonville,** Florida, occupied by Federal forces.

Mar. 14. Capture of **New Berne,** North Carolina. This gave the Federal forces a base from which to threaten Richmond, and obliged the Confederates to keep an army near the capital.

Apr. 24-25. A Federal force (27 ships and 15,000 troops), under command of Flag-officer (later Admiral) **D. G. Farragut** and Gen. **Benjamin F. Butler**, ran the forts

THE CIVIL WAR 1860-1865

CANADA

NEBRASKA
TERR.

MINN.
St Paul

WISCONSIN

Madison

MICH.

Detroit

IOWA

Iowa City

ILL.

Chicago

IND.

OHIO

Columbus

Cleveland

Buffalo

N.Y.

Omaha

Ft.Leavenworth

Independence

KANSAS TERR.

Jefferson
City

St.Louis

Springfield

Indiana-
polis

Cincinnati

Marietta

PA.

Pittsburgh

Harrisburg

Boston

MISSOURI

Wilson Creek

Island No.10

Evansville

New Madrid

Paducah

Cairo

KY.

Louisville

Perryville

W. VA.

Harper's Fy.

Staunton

Richmond

Philadelphia

New York

N.J.

Baltimore

Washington

Bull Run

VA.

ARKANSAS

Little Rock

Memphis

Ft.Henry

Ft.Donelson

TENN.

Nashville

Mill Spring

Murfreesboro

Knoxville

Danville

Appomattox

Williamsburg

Ft.Monroe

Hampton Roads

Norfolk

Ft.Pillow

Shilohꞏ Ptsbg.ldg.

Corinth

Iuca

Chattanooga

Chickamauga

Kenesaw Mt.

N.C.

Raleigh

Goldsboro

MISS.

Champion Hill

Jackson

Raymond

Pt. Gibson

ALA.

Atlanta

GA.

Andersonville

Columbia

S.C.

Augusta

Charleston

Ft. Sumter

Ft. Pulaski

Savannah

Wilmington

Bentonville

Vicksburg

Natchez

Port Hudson

Baton Rouge

Mobile

Montgomery

New Orleans

Morgan
Guns

Tallahassee

Jacksonville

FLA.

Key West

50 miles

Gettysburg

PA.
MD.

Antietam

Martinsburg

Frederick

Harper's Ferry

Baltimore

Winchester

Leesburg

Kernstown

Cedar Creek

Front Royal

Manassas

Washington

Bull Run

Culpeper

Bristow

Cedar Mt.

Chancellorsville

Wilderness

Mine Run

Fredericksburg

Spotsylvania

Raisz

below New Orleans and bombarded the city. After the landing of troops, the city was taken (May 1).

1862.   THE PENINSULA CAMPAIGN.
After endless delay, McClellan decided to advance on Richmond, not over-land through territory cut by many rivers, but by water to the mouth of the James River, whence he could proceed up the peninsula between the James and the York. The advance began in April. The Confeder-ates, under Johnston and **Robert E. Lee** (b. 1807, d. 1870; Confederate commander in chief after June 1, 1862), were greatly outnumbered and fell back. They were saved in part by McClellan's vacillation and by the operations of Jackson, who managed to draw a considerable Federal force into the Shenandoah Valley and ulti-mately succeeded in joining Lee with sub-stantial reinforcements. Heavy fighting around Richmond: **battle of Fair Oaks** (May 31); **Seven Days' battle** (June 25–July 1: **Mechanicsville, Gaines' Mill, White Oak Swamp, Malvern Hill**), resulting in the withdrawal of the Federal forces from the peninsula.

Campaign in Maryland. In the autumn of 1862 Lee began to push on toward Wash-ington. Confederate forces under Jackson defeated the Union forces under Banks at **Cedar Mountain** (Aug. 9), while the Union army under Gen. Pope was defeated by Jackson in the **Second Battle of Bull Run** (Aug. 30). The Confederates crossed the Potomac (Sept. 4) and invaded Mary-land.

Sept. 17.   BATTLE OF ANTIETAM, indecisive, but Lee began to fall back into Virginia. McClellan, as usual un-able to take advantage of his opportunities, did little to pursue him and did not cross the Potomac until Oct. 26.

Nov. 7. Gen. **Ambrose E. Burnside** was appointed to succeed McClellan. He pushed the advance in Virginia, but was badly defeated by Lee in the **battle of Fredericksburg** (Dec. 13). Jan. 25, 1863, he was succeeded by Gen. **Joseph Hooker.**

CAMPAIGNS IN THE WEST. In western Kentucky and Tennessee there was active campaigning throughout the year 1862. Brig.-Gen. **Ulysses S. Grant** (b. 1822, d. 1885), serving under Gen. **H. W. Halleck,** in command of the Union troops, on Feb. 6 forced the **surrender of Fort Henry** on the Tennessee River, and on Feb. 16 he secured the **surrender of Fort Donel-son** on the Cumberland. The Confederates abandoned **Nashville** and fell back on the line Memphis–Chattanooga.

Apr. 6-7.   Battle of Shiloh. The Con-federates, under Gen. **Albert S.**

Johnston, attacked Grant's lines at **Pitts-burg Landing.** After an initial success the Confederates (Johnston killed, Beauregard in command) were driven back. They evacuated **Corinth** (May 30) and surren-dered **Memphis** (June 6). The Federal forces commanded the Mississippi as far south as Vicksburg.

Oct. 8.   Battle of Perryville, Ky. A Con-federate force under Gen. **Bragg** had advanced into Kentucky in the hope of compelling the withdrawal of the Union forces to the north. Bragg threatened Cin-cinnati, but the Kentuckians failed to sup-port him. He was retreating southward when he met the Federal army of Gen. **Rosecrans** in the battle of **Murfreesboro** on **Stone River** (Dec. 31, 1862–Jan. 3, 1863).

1863.   EASTERN CAMPAIGNS. After several months spent in reorgani-zation, Hooker on May 1 ordered an advance from Chancellorsville, Va.

May 1-4.   BATTLE OF CHANCEL-LORSVILLE. The Federal forces were defeated by the Confederates (death of Stonewall Jackson). Gen. **George G. Meade** relieved Hooker as commander of the Army of the Potomac (June 28). Mean-while Lee had begun the invasion of the north by way of the Shenandoah Valley, establishing himself in southern Pennsyl-vania. Meade took up his position at Gettysburg.

July 1-3.   BATTLE OF GETTYSBURG.
In three days of heavy fighting Lee was unable to dislodge the Federal forces and was obliged to fall back to the Potomac. Decisive battle of the war. Henceforth the Confederates were obliged to remain on the defensive and the war be-came a test of endurance.

WESTERN CAMPAIGNS. The oper-ations in the west centered first on the taking of **Vicksburg,** key to the control of the Mississippi. On Apr. 30 **Grant** crossed the river below the fortress, marched east and took Jackson and then doubled back, hemming in the fortress.

July 4.   VICKSBURG SURREN-DERED, starved out after a short siege. July 8 **Port Hudson,** farther down the river, surrendered, giving the Unionists command of the entire river and cutting off Texas, Arkansas, and Louisiana from the rest of the Confederacy.

Sept. 9. The Federal troops, under Rose-crans, took **Chattanooga** and pur-sued the Confederates, under Bragg, into Georgia. Defeated in the **battle of Chicka-mauga** (Sept. 19–20), Rosecrans was obliged to fall back to Chattanooga, where he was hard pressed by the Confederates. Reinforced by troops from Vicksburg under Gen. William T. Sherman and from the Potomac under Hooker, Grant, in command of the armies of the west, fought the

Nov. 23-25. BATTLE OF CHATTANOOGA (Lookout Mountain, Nov. 24; Missionary Ridge, Nov. 25), driving the Confederates out of Tennessee and opening the road into Georgia.

1864, Mar. 9. Grant made lieutenant-general and commander in chief of all the armies; Sherman given command in the west. Grant's plan was to defeat Lee's army. He crossed the Rapidan (May 3) and began the advance from near Chancellorsville through the Wilderness.

May 5-6. BATTLE OF THE WILDERNESS. Grant, attacked by Lee, was unable to defeat him, but maintained his ground and continued the advance towards Spotsylvania Court House.

May 8-18. Battles around Spotsylvania Court House, on the North Anna River (May 21-31), and at Cold Harbor (June 1-3). Grant was unable to defeat Lee, but crossed the James River and assaulted Petersburg (June 15-18), 20 miles below Richmond, which he then besieged. In order to create a diversion, Lee sent Gen. Early to threaten Washington. Early carried through raids into Maryland and Pennsylvania, but was defeated by Gen. Philip H. Sheridan in the battles of Winchester (Opequan Creek) and Fisher's Hill (Sept. 19, 21), after which the Confederates were obliged to withdraw from the Shenandoah Valley (battle of Cedar Creek, Oct. 19). Sheridan laid the whole region waste and then rejoined Grant at Petersburg.

SHERMAN'S CAMPAIGN. Sherman started from Chattanooga (May 5) with about 100,000 men to march through Georgia to Atlanta. He was opposed by one of the ablest Confederate commanders, Gen. Joseph E. Johnston, with 65,000 men. Johnston did what he could to impede Sherman's advance, but wisely refused a general battle. Sherman, however, crossed the Chattahoochee River (July 17), as a result of which Johnston was removed from his command. His successor, Gen. John B. Hood, offered battle, but was defeated (battle of Atlanta, July 22).

Sept. 2. Evacuation of Atlanta by the Confederates. Sherman destroyed the factories and stores and urged upon Grant his plan of a march to the sea. Part of the army, under Thomas, was sent north to watch Hood, who was defeated before Nashville (Dec. 15-16). Sherman himself, with 60,000 men, started for the southeast (Nov. 16), ravaging the country as he proceeded. He reached the sea (Dec. 12) and the Confederates abandoned Savannah (Dec. 20). Sherman then turned north into South Carolina. Columbia was taken (Feb. 17, 1865) and the advance continued into North Carolina. A Federal fleet took Charleston (Feb. 18) and Sherman took Goldsboro (Mar. 19).

1865. LAST CAMPAIGNS. The Confederate armies, caught between Grant in the north and Sherman in the south and deprived of food supply, were no longer able to withstand the pressure. Sheridan won the battle of Five Forks (Apr. 1) and thus forced the evacuation of Petersburg (Apr. 2) and the surrender of Richmond (Apr. 3). Grant with all his forces then pursued and surrounded Lee.

Apr. 9. LEE'S CAPITULATION AT APPOMATTOX COURT HOUSE. Johnston, with the southern army, surrendered to Sherman (Apr. 26), and the last Confederate army, under Gen. Kirby Smith, surrendered at Shreveport, La., on May 26. Jefferson Davis, president of the Confederacy, fled to Georgia, but was captured (May 10) and imprisoned.

POLITICAL AND SOCIAL ASPECTS OF THE WAR PERIOD:

1861, Mar. The Morrill Tariff, marking the beginning of successive tariff increases which by 1864 reached duties of 47%.

Aug. Income Tax of 3% on all income in excess of $800.

1862, Feb. First of the Legal Tender Acts, followed by similar acts in 1862 and 1863.

July. The first comprehensive internal revenue act, born of the war.

Sept. 22. The president issued a preliminary proclamation declaring that all slaves in states or parts of states which should still be in rebellion on Jan. 1, 1863, should be free from the latter date on. The formal Emancipation Proclamation was issued on Jan. 1, 1863.

1863, Feb. 25. National Banking Act passed to create a market for United States bonds, to drive out of circulation the notes of banks chartered by the states, to create a powerful financial support for the government, and to provide for the country a uniform circulating medium. Stockholders obtaining a charter could buy government bonds, deposit them with the treasurer of the United States, and then issue national bank notes up to 90% of the current market value of the bonds. The banks having proved slow to take out charters, state bank notes were driven out of existence by a tax of 10% (1865).

June 20. **West Virginia** (the loyal part of Virginia) admitted to the union as the thirty-fifth state.

1864, Nov. 8. **Re-election of Lincoln.** Andrew Johnson, vice-president.

1865, Feb. 1. Resolution in Congress to submit to the states the **thirteenth amendment** to the constitution, prohibiting slavery within the United States. The amendment was ratified by two-thirds of the states by Dec. 18.

1865-1873. Serious and recurring **epidemics** of smallpox, typhus, typhoid, cholera, scarlet fever, and yellow fever in Philadelphia, New York, Boston, Baltimore, Washington, Memphis, and New Orleans led to the realization of the need for improved sanitation. In 1866 a municipal **board of health** was created in New York and in 1869 a state board of health was established in Massachusetts.

1861-1868. **New territories.** In the years just before the war the discovery of precious metals in the Pike's Peak country and in the Washoe Mountains led to mining rushes to those regions, with the result that the territories of **Colorado** and **Nevada** were organized in 1861. Mining rushes elsewhere in the years of the war resulted in the organization of the territories of **Arizona** (1863), Idaho (1863), and **Montana** (1864). **Wyoming** was made a territory in 1868.

1862-1886. **Taming of the Plains Indians.** The constant pressure of white population, combined with broken promises, led to continued outbreaks of the Indians. The **Homestead Act** (1862) played a prominent part in the settlement of the west. The **Morrill Act** (1862), providing for grants of land to states in order to aid the establishment of agricultural colleges, opened up more areas. In 1862 the **Union and Central Pacific Railways** were chartered by Congress and given a large grant of land. They formed the first transcontinental railway (completed May 10, 1869).

In 1862 the **Sioux Indians** of Minnesota were defeated by Gen. Sibley at **Wood Lake.** In 1864 the **Cheyenne** went on the warpath, with the aid of the Arapahoe, Apache, Comanche, and Kiowa tribes. Troops under Col. Chivington staged a massacre of Indians at **Sand Creek,** Colo. (Nov. 1864). Efforts of troops to build an emigrant road from Fort Laramie along the Powder River to the mines of Montana and Idaho led to war with the **Plains Sioux** (1866). A commission authorized by Congress persuaded the Apache, Comanche, and Kiowa tribes to locate in **Indian Territory,** and secured the removal of other tribes from the Plains to more remote regions. In 1869 Congress created the **Board of Indian Commissioners** to supervise all government expenditures for the Indians. Meanwhile the advance of white settlers, slaughter of the buffalo, and the gold rush to the Black Hills caused an outbreak of the Plains Sioux (1876) under **Sitting Bull,** which resulted in the **massacre of Custer** and his men at the **Little Big Horn** (June 25). **Nez Percé Indians** under **Chief Joseph** were defeated (Oct. 1877) and removed to Indian Territory. The last important Indian uprising came in the years 1882-1886, when the **Apaches** in Arizona and New Mexico, under **Victorio** and **Geronimo,** resisted efforts to confine them to reservations. By 1886 the Indians had all been removed to Indian Territory or to reservations.

c. THE UNITED STATES, 1865-1917

1865, Apr. 14. **ASSASSINATION OF LINCOLN;** death Apr. 15. Andrew Johnson, vice-president, succeeded.

Cost of the war. National debt in 1860, $64,842,287; in 1866, $2,773,236,173, which great increase was in addition to the debts incurred by the states and municipalities.

May 29. President Johnson issued a **proclamation of amnesty,** granting pardon to all ordinary persons who had participated in the rebellion on taking an oath of allegiance.

Dec. **Joint Committee of Fifteen on Reconstruction** appointed by Congress.

Dec. 18. **Ratification of the thirteenth amendment,** abolishing slavery.

1866, Feb. Johnson vetoed a measure extending the life of the **Freedmen's Bureau,** thereby increasing tension between himself and Congress.

April. Congress passed over Johnson's veto the **Civil Rights Bill,** declaring all persons born in the United States to be citizens of the United States and entitled to equality of treatment before the law. This was designed to guarantee equal treatment to Negroes in southern states.

June 13. **FOURTEENTH AMENDMENT** sent to states for ratification. Declared ratified July 28, 1868. It incorporated in the constitution the principle of the Civil Rights Act; gave the southern states the choice of Negro enfranchisement or reduced representation in the lower House of Congress; barred from office-holding ex-Confederates who had been federal or state officials before the war, until they should be pardoned by a two-thirds vote of Congress; provided that the war debt of the south should never be paid or that of the union repudiated; and that former masters should never be compensated for their slaves. In the light of subsequent events, the most significant provision of the amendment was the clause, **"nor shall any state deprive any person of life, liberty, or property, without due process of law."** It was generally assumed at the time that this clause was designed solely to safeguard the freedmen in the possession of their civil rights and it was so interpreted by the supreme court in the **Slaughter House Cases** (1873). In 1886, however, in the case of **Santa Clara County v. Southern Pacific Railroad**, the supreme court declared that a corporation was a "person" within the meaning of the amendment and thus entitled to its protection. From this time the **due process clause** of the amendment came to have a new significance. More and more it was applied by the courts to shield business and corporations against hostile legislative action by the states, and by reading into the clause the doctrine of **liberty of contract** the court made it a formidable barrier against the enactment of much-needed social legislation by the states.

July 27. **The Atlantic cable** brought to Newfoundland by **Cyrus W. Field**, thus establishing telegraphic communication with Great Britain.

1867, Mar. 2. **THE BASIC RECONSTRUCTION ACT.** Johnson having advised the southern states to reject the fourteenth amendment, all except Tennessee promptly did so, the quarrel over Reconstruction thereby becoming the major issue in the congressional election of 1866, in which Johnson was repudiated. This act, as supplemented by regulations of March 23 and July 19, 1867, and March 11, 1868, divided the southern states into five military districts. To be restored to the union, the states must hold state conventions, whose delegates must be elected with the aid of Negro suffrage; these conventions must frame constitutions, approved by Congress and ratified by the people of the states; and the legislatures elected under the constitution must ratify the fourteenth amendment.

Mar. 2. **Tenure-of-Office Act.** Mar. 4 it was passed over Johnson's veto.

Mar. 30. **Purchase of Alaska** for $7,200,-000.

1868, Feb. 24-May 26. **Impeachment and trial of Andrew Johnson.** Johnson and Congress had disagreed over the Reconstruction policy. The immediate occasion for the impeachment proceedings was Johnson's alleged violation of the Tenure-of-Office Act. He was acquitted by a vote of 35 to 19, one short of the necessary two-thirds of the Senate.

The Sholes typewriter first put to commercial use.

1869, Feb. 26. **The fifteenth amendment** adopted by Congress. The radicals, fearing that southern whites might obtain power in their states and repeal the provisions of their state constitutions granting the suffrage to the Negro, sponsored this amendment, providing that the right to vote shall not be abridged because of "race, color, or previous condition of servitude." It was declared ratified, Mar. 30, 1870. Virginia, Texas, Mississippi, and Georgia were forced to ratify this amendment as a condition of restoration to the union.

The Westinghouse airbrake patented. In this same year **James Oliver** invented the **plow with chilled steel moldboard**, and **refrigeration** was introduced in railway transportation. In 1875 two carloads of refrigerated meats were shipped from Kansas City to New York and another to Boston.

Sept. **The National Prohibition Party** was organized by a convention in Chicago.

Nov. **The National Woman's Suffrage Convention** met at Cleveland (**Rev. Henry Ward Beecher**, president) and organized the **American Woman Suffrage Association**, indicating increased activity of women in regard to the ballot.

1869, Mar. 4—1877, Mar. 4. **ULYSSES S. GRANT**, eighteenth president.

1871, May 8. **TREATY OF WASHINGTON** with Great Britain, providing (1) for the reference to the German Emperor of the dispute as to the northwest boundary (decided in favor of the United States, Oct. 21, 1872); (2) for a partial settlement of the fishery dispute (**Halifax award**, 1877, which gave Great Britain $5,500,000) — this part of the treaty was abrogated by the United States, 1883; (3) and for the settlement of the **Alabama claims** by an international commission to sit at Geneva.

1872, Aug. 25. **The Geneva Award** of $15,-500,000 to the United States as compensation for direct damages resulting from the depredations of the *Alabama* and other Confederate cruisers.

Nov. Re-election of Grant, the Republican candidate, over **Horace Gree-**

ley, the Liberal Republican candidate, who was endorsed by the Democratic Party, which abstained from placing a candidate in the field. Increasing dissatisfaction of many Republicans with the Grant administration had led to the organization of the **Liberal Republican Party**. Grant received 286 electoral votes to 62 for Greeley.

1873. Crédit Mobilier scandal, resulting from the revelation by congressional investigating committees that **Schuyler Colfax**, the outgoing vice-president, and a number of members of Congress, including James A. Garfield, held stock, for which they had not paid, in the Crédit Mobilier, the construction company which built the Union Pacific Railway. This was merely one of the numerous instances of corruption in the Grant régime. In 1874 **W. A. Richardson**, secretary of the treasury, hastily resigned to escape a vote of censure by Congress. Grant's private secretary, **O. E. Babcock**, was implicated in the **Whiskey Ring**, while **W. W. Belknap**, secretary of war, resigned in 1876 to escape impeachment for bribe-taking. **James G. Blaine**, speaker of the House, was compromised through the **Mulligan letters**.

1873, Sept. Panic precipitated by the failure of **Jay Cooke and Company**. Fundamentally the panic was due to inflated currency, unlimited credit, reckless speculation, and over-expansion. As much of the business expansion had been financed from abroad, a panic in Vienna (May 1873), which spread to other European money centers, caused the withdrawal of much of the foreign capital from the United States.

The Great Bonanza. Important discovery of silver in Nevada.

1874. Washburn and **Pillsbury** introduced the process of reducing wheat to flour by use of chilled steel rollers.

1875, Jan. 14. The Resumption Act passed by Congress, providing for the resumption of specie payment (suspended in 1861) Jan. 1, 1879.

1876. Johns Hopkins University opened in Baltimore. As the first real graduate school in America, it gave great impetus to advanced study.

Feb. 15. Patent for manufacture of **barbed wire**. This was of the utmost significance in the conquest of the Great Plains.

Mar. 10. First intelligible sentence transmitted by **telephone** by Alexander Graham Bell. The invention was patented Mar. 17.

The Granger decisions. These decisions of the supreme court came as a climax to the first important farmers' movement in American history. In 1867 there had been formed the **Patrons of Husbandry**, commonly called the *Grange*, a non-political organization of farmers. At this time the farmers in the middle western states were incensed because of the unfair practices of railways and grain elevators. Organizing farmers' parties, they proceeded (1870-1875) to enact legislation in Illinois, Iowa, Wisconsin, Minnesota, and other states, bringing railways and grain elevators under state control. The Granger decisions established the following principles: (1) A state under its police power has authority to regulate a business which is clothed with a public interest. (2) Until Congress acts in the premises, the states may establish rates for interstate shipments. (3) The determination of the reasonableness of rates is a legislative rather than a judicial function. The second of these principles was set aside in 1886 in the case of the *Wabash, St. Louis and Pacific Railroad v. Illinois*, while the third was undermined and set aside by a series of decisions between 1889 and 1898, the last being the case of *Smyth v. Ames*.

Nov. The disputed election. In the election, **Tilden**, the Democratic candidate, was assured of 184 electoral votes; **Rutherford B. Hayes**, Republican, had 165 electoral votes, with 20 votes in the states of Oregon, Florida, South Carolina, and Louisiana in dispute, with two sets of returns. For election 185 electoral votes were necessary. Since the constitution made no provision for such an eventuality, Congress created on

1877, Jan. 29. The Electoral Commission, composed of five senators, five representatives, and five justices of the supreme court, the fifth justice to be chosen by the four named in the statute. The commission was composed of 8 Republicans and 7 Democrats, and, deciding all questions by a strict party vote, awarded the 20 electoral votes to Hayes, giving him the 185 necessary for election.

Mar. 3. The Desert Land Act, designed to encourage development of irrigation in arid areas by private effort.

July 31. The phonograph patented by **Thomas A. Edison**.

1877, Mar. 4—1881, Mar. 4. RUTHERFORD B. HAYES, nineteenth president.

1878, Feb. The Bland-Allison Act. In 1873 Congress had omitted the standard silver dollar from the list of authorized domestic coins to be minted in the future. This action synchronized with the demonetization of silver by various European countries, and with a marked increase in silver production, especially in the Comstock Lode in Nevada. As a result the commercial price of silver declined sharply, giving rise to a demand by the silver interests for the coinage of silver, which was precluded by the legislation of 1873, commonly referred to as the *Crime of* 1873. The silver producers were supported by the farmers, who believed the free coinage of silver would bring an upturn in the price of farm products. In 1877, therefore, **R. P. Bland** of Missouri introduced into the House of Representatives a bill providing for the free coinage of silver. Although it passed the House by a sectional vote, it was amended in the Senate, and as the **Bland-Allison Act** it was passed over the veto of Hayes. It authorized the secretary of the treasury to purchase from two to four million dollars' worth of silver bullion monthly for coinage.

> The **arc light** introduced by **C. F. Brush.**

1879, Jan. 1. Resumption of specie payment. The success of the policy was greatly aided by the unusual demand abroad for American agricultural products, which brought gold into the country in large quantity.

> **Oct. 21. Thomas Edison** invented the **incandescent electric light,** maintaining incandescence for over 40 hours.

1881, Mar. 4. JAMES A. GARFIELD, twentieth president. Shot July 2 and died Sept. 19, 1881, being succeeded by **Chester A. Arthur,** vice-president.

> **May 21.** The **American Red Cross Society** organized, with **Clara Barton** as president.

1882, May 6. The Chinese Exclusion Act. The increasing immigration of Chinese, especially in California, led to a race riot as early as 1871. The formation of a workingmen's party in that state in 1877 brought the matter into prominence and to the attention of Congress. The Act of 1882 barred Chinese laborers from entrance into the United States for a period of ten years. In 1902 the exclusion was made perpetual and the same act prohibited the immigration of Chinese to the United States from Hawaii and the Philippines. In 1885 an act of Congress prohibited the entrance of all laborers under contract.

1883, Jan. 16. The Pendleton Act. After more or less continual discussion since 1865, Congress provided in this act for a bipartisan commission to set up and administer a system of **competitive examinations** as a test of fitness for appointment to federal office. It also prohibited the levying of **campaign contributions** upon federal office-holders. Although the plan applied immediately only to the executive departments in Washington, to the custom-houses, and to the larger post-offices, the president was authorized, at his discretion, to extend the "classified list."

Tariff Act. Despite a redundant revenue and the recommendation of tariff reductions by a tariff commission, the protective principle, so securely established by the Civil War tariffs, remained intact. Although substantial reductions were made in internal revenue duties, the reductions in import duties averaged less than 5%.

> **Sept. 8.** The **Northern Pacific Railroad** completed (chartered and endowed with an enormous grant of land in 1864). This was the second transcontinental line. The **Southern Pacific** was the third, and by 1893 no less than five were completed. Other lines threaded their way across the prairies and plains to the mountains, letting in the tide of population which brought the frontier to an end.

1883-1890. The problem of the treasury surplus. Cleveland would deal with the surplus by reducing the tariff duties, which he urged in his message to Congress in 1887 and which he made the leading issue in the campaign of 1888. Republicans attempted to remove the surplus by retirement of Civil War bonds, the building of a new navy, and reckless pension legislation.

1884. Presidential campaign between James G. Blaine (Republican) and Grover Cleveland (Democrat). The **Mugwumps,** the reforming wing of the party, deserted Blaine in favor of Cleveland. Cleveland was elected, 219 electoral votes to 182.

1885, Mar. 4—1889, Mar. 4. GROVER CLEVELAND, twenty-second president.

1885. The **linotype** invented by **Ottmar Mergenthaler.**

1886. The **Presidential Succession Law,** providing that in the event of the death of both president and vice-president, members of the cabinet should succeed to the presidency in definite order.

> **Dec.** The **American Federation of Labor** organized. The Civil War years witnessed the formation of a number of national trade unions, which **W. H. Sylvis** attempted to federate into a single nation-wide association known as the **National Labor Union** (1866). In 1869 **Uriah Stephens** formed the **Knights of Labor,** which represented an attempt to combine all labor, skilled and

unskilled. organized and unorganized, into one body. Between 1879 and 1885 they grew rapidly. In 1885–1886 they became involved in a series of strikes on the Gould railway system, in the last of which they were routed and discredited. In 1886 there occurred a widespread movement in favor of the 8-hour day. May 4, 1886, the **Haymarket Square riot** in Chicago still further discredited the Knights of Labor, who now gave way to the American Federation of Labor as the first permanent national labor movement in American history. The germ of the organization dated from 1881, when disgruntled members of the Knights of Labor, led by **Samuel Gompers**, formed the **Federation of Organized Trades and Labor Unions.**

1887, Feb. 4. INTERSTATE COMMERCE ACT. As early as 1874 the **McCrary Bill,** looking to federal regulation of the railways, passed the House of Representatives, but failed in the Senate. In 1878 the **Reagan Bill** passed the House, but was defeated in the Senate. The growing realization of the shocking practices of the railways led to the appointment by the Senate in 1885 of the **Cullom Committee,** which conducted hearings in the principal cities of the country. This was followed by the passage of the **Act of 1887**. It declared that charges of the railways must be reasonable and just, made pooling illegal, contained a long-and-short-haul clause, declared rebates illegal, and created an **Interstate Commerce Commission** with power to inquire into the management of the carriers, summon witnesses, compel the production of papers, and invoke the aid of the federal courts. Up to 1903 the commission was largely frustrated by the courts. In 1897, in the *Maximum Freight Rate Case,* the supreme court denied the commission's authority to prescribe a maximum rate. The long-and-short-haul clause was rendered ineffective and the commission was left with the duty of collecting railway statistics and requiring the publication of rates by the companies.

Feb. 8. The Dawes Act, authorizing the president, at his discretion, to terminate tribal government and communal ownership of land among the Indians and to divide the land at the rate of a quarter section for each head of a family, full ownership to be withheld for 25 years. In 1906 the **Burke Act** authorized the secretary of the interior to bestow full property title whenever convinced of the Indians' fitness.

1888. Presidential campaign. Cleveland (Democrat) against Harrison (Republican). The tariff was the dominant issue. Although Cleveland had a popular plurality, he lost the election, receiving 168 electoral votes to 233 for Harrison. Treachery of Tammany in New York cost Cleveland the election.

1889, Mar. 4—1893, Mar. 4. BENJAMIN HARRISON, twenty-third president.

1889, Apr. 22. Oklahoma opened to settlement. The Territory of Oklahoma was organized in 1890. The movement into the trans-Mississippi country led to the admission of the last states to the union: **Nevada** (1864); **Nebraska** (1867); **Colorado** (1876); **North Dakota, South Dakota, Washington,** and **Montana** (1889); **Wyoming** and **Idaho** (1890); **Utah** (1896); **Oklahoma** (1907); **New Mexico** and **Arizona** (1912).

June 14. Samoan Treaty signed. In 1872 the American consul in Samoa obtained harbor privileges for American ships. In 1878 the United States secured the exclusive right to use the harbor of Pago-Pago. When in 1886 the American consul proclaimed an American protectorate over Samoa, the state department disavowed the act. By the **Treaty of 1889** the United States, Germany, and Great Britain recognized the independence of Samoa, but placed authority in the hands of a chief justice and the Apian municipal council, the members of which were to be chosen by the three countries. By a treaty of Dec. 4, 1899, Germany and the United States partitioned the Samoan Islands, the American share being Tutuila, with the harbor of Pago-Pago.

Oct. 2. First Pan-American Conference convened at Washington. The idea of closer relations among the nations of the western hemisphere, with the United States playing the rôle of an elder sister, had long been in the mind of James G. Blaine, who as Garfield's secretary of state had planned such a congress in 1881. His successor, Frelinghuysen, cancelled the arrangements. As secretary of state in Harrison's cabinet, Blaine carried the idea to fruition. All Latin-American nations except San Domingo were represented. The conference rejected Blaine's plan of reciprocity and refused to adopt a convention calling for the promotion of peace by arbitration, but established the **Pan-American Union,** a bureau of information.

1890, June 19. The Force Bill, providing for federal control of federal elections, reported in the House of Representatives. It aimed to protect Negro voters in southern states against attempts to disfranchise them. It passed the House, but was not adopted by the Senate.

June 27. Disability Pension Act, in reality a service pension act, since it provided pensions for all veterans of 90 days' service who could claim physical or mental disability, regardless of origin, which precluded the gaining of a livelihood by manual labor. Pensions were to be granted to widows of soldiers without regard to the cause of the husband's death if the marriage had occurred prior to 1890.

July 2. THE SHERMAN ANTI-TRUST LAW enacted. After the formation of the Standard Oil Trust in 1879 (revised in 1882), numerous large business combinations made their appearance, thereby raising the specter of monopoly, which led to the demand for legislation by Congress. The **Sherman Act** declared illegal *"every contract, combination in the form of trust or otherwise, or conspiracy in restraint of trade or commerce among the several states or with foreign nations."* The act was loosely drawn and left several important questions unanswered: Did it apply to combinations of labor, did it apply to combinations of the railways, and was the word "every" to be construed literally or reasonably? In the case of *Debs* (1895) the supreme court gave an affirmative answer to the first question, while in the *Trans-Missouri Freight Association Case* (1897) it answered the other two in an affirmative manner.

July 14. The Sherman Silver Purchase Act. The continued decline in the commercial price of silver, plus the strengthening of the silver forces in the Senate by the appearance of senators from the newly admitted states of the northwest, led to a demand for further legislation with respect to silver. As the price of their support of new tariff legislation desired by the conservative wing of the Republican Party, the silver group obtained the desired legislation. The act authorized the treasury to purchase 4,500,000 ounces of silver monthly for coinage into dollars. It provided for the issuance of treasury certificates, to be redeemed in either gold or silver at the discretion of the treasury.

Oct. 1. The McKinley Tariff Act. The purpose of the law was such an increase in protective duties as would diminish the revenue from customs duties, thereby relieving the treasury of the surplus. By placing sugar on the free list and providing a bounty on domestic sugar, a substantial decline in revenue was certain. The law made provision for limited reciprocity treaties.

1892, Feb. 29. Treaty with Great Britain regarding the **Bering Sea seal fisheries.** Blaine, as secretary of state, had carried on a long controversy with Great Britain on this question, basing his arguments on faulty law, history, and ethics. The treaty submitted the controversy to an arbitral court, which in 1893 denied the right of the United States to prohibit fishing beyond the three-mile limit. In 1911 an international convention prohibited pelagic sealing for 15 years.

1892-1895. Labor troubles. A strike of workers in the Homestead Plant of the Carnegie Steel Company was called by the Amalgamated Association of Iron and Steel Workers (June 30, 1892) as a result of disagreement over a wage scale. The use of Pinkerton detectives by the Carnegie Company led to violence, which was followed by the use of state troops to protect the Carnegie properties. Sympathy of the public, at first with the workers, was alienated later. In the end the Amalgamated Association was destroyed. May 11, 1894, a strike occurred in the plant of the Pullman Company, in which the American Railway Union, formed the previous year by **Eugene V. Debs,** participated, with resulting obstruction of the mails and destruction of property. Without consulting Gov. Altgeld, Cleveland sent federal troops to Chicago, and on the advice of Olney, the attorney-general, an injunction was issued ordering the officials of the union to desist from obstruction of the mails or from injuring the property of the railroads. Upon disregarding the injunction, Debs was arrested for contempt of court and sent to jail. The United States circuit court approved the use of the injunction, sentenced Debs to prison for six months, and approved the use of the Sherman Anti-Trust Act against labor unions where they were engaged in a "conspiracy to hinder and obstruct interstate commerce." The next year the supreme court sustained the judgment of the lower court. The use of the injunction gave capital a formidable weapon against labor.

1892, Feb. 22. The People's Party organized at St. Louis. For a decade there had been a gathering discontent of the farmers, resulting from the depressed condition of agriculture. Organizations of farmers, known as the *Southern Alliance* and the *Northwestern Alliance*, had appeared, and held meetings at St. Louis (Dec. 1889), Ocala, Fla. (Dec. 1890), and Cincinnati (May, 1891). They now formed the **People's** or **Populist Party.** In July, 1892, at their Omaha convention, they nominated **James B. Weaver,** a veteran inflationist, as their candidate for the presidency and drew up a platform declaring for a national currency without the use of banking corporations, free and unlimited coinage of silver, a graduated income tax, postal savings banks, and government ownership of railways and telephone and telegraph lines.

Harrison defeated for re-election by **Cleveland,** who denounced the McKinley Tariff and the Force Bill. Cleveland received 277 electoral votes; Harrison, 145; and Weaver, the Populist candidate, 22.

1893-1898. Hawaii became of increasing concern to the United States. Jan. 17, 1893, a provisional government, established with the connivance of the American minister, supplanted the Hawaiian monarchy. Feb. 14 there was signed a treaty annexing Hawaii to the United States. When the Senate failed to ratify before Cleveland came into office, he promptly withdrew the treaty and sent a commissioner to the islands to investigate. Failing in his efforts to bring about a restoration of the monarchy, Cleveland recognized the republic which had in the meantime been established. In June, 1897, McKinley arranged a new treaty of annexation, which was defeated in the Senate. July 7, 1898, Hawaii was annexed by joint resolution of the two houses of Congress.

1893, Mar. 4—1897, Mar. 4. GROVER CLEVELAND president for the second time.

1893. Panic of 1893. Depression had begun to spread over the western world in 1890 when the banking house of Baring collapsed as a result of unfortunate investments in the Argentine. British investors in American securities began to sell, which was largely responsible for the movement of gold from the country. Overexpansion in rails, due to the import of British capital, had created a boom which collapsed when the railways were unable to meet their charges. The situation was complicated by the dissipation of the treasury surplus through reckless pension legislation and the Tariff of 1890, which sharply reduced revenue. To Cleveland there was just one cause of the panic: the world-wide fear of our inability to maintain a gold standard was draining off the supply of the precious metal. For this fear, he alleged, the Sherman Silver Purchase Act was responsible. He therefore asked the special session of Congress to repeal the act. After bitter debate, on

Oct. 30. The Sherman Silver Purchase Act was repealed.

The Anti-Saloon League founded, a milestone in the development of the prohibition movement. It inaugurated a nation-wide campaign in 1895.

1894-1896. Sale of government bonds in an effort to maintain the gold reserve. Finding that repeal of the Silver Purchase Act did not stop the outflow of gold, the treasury, to obtain gold, arranged for sale of bonds by banks in Jan. and Nov. 1894. In Feb. 1895 the Morgan-Belmont syndicate sold $60,000,000 bonds at a profit of $7,000,000, causing much criticism. In Jan. 1896 bonds were offered at public subscription.

1894, Aug. 18. The Carey Act, granting 1,000,000 acres of land to each of the states of Colorado, Idaho, Montana, Nevada, Oregon, Utah, Washington, and Wyoming to encourage irrigation by state action. In 1908 they each received another million acres.

Aug. 27. The Wilson-Gorman Tariff Act, a violation of the Democratic platform, became a law without Cleveland's signature. As a result of Senate amendments to the original bill, the act retained the protective principle, although duties were lowered to about 40%. It contained a provision for a 2% tax on incomes above $4000. On

1895, May 20. The income tax was declared unconstitutional in the case of *Pollock v. Farmers Loan and Trust Co.*, causing much criticism. An income tax declared a direct tax which, in accordance with the constitution, must be apportioned among the states in proportion to population.

The Venezuela boundary dispute. Upon the refusal of Great Britain to submit to arbitration the disputed boundary between Venezuela and British Guiana, Secretary of State Olney, on July 20, 1895, sent a note to Great Britain, asserting that a forcible rectification of the boundary by Great Britain would violate the Monroe Doctrine, and declaring that the one way to settle the dispute was by arbitration. He then stated that *"today the United States is practically sovereign on this continent, and its fiat is law upon the subjects to which it confines its interposition."* **Lord Salisbury** replied (Nov. 26), rejecting arbitration and denying the applicability of the Monroe Doctrine to this dispute. Dec. 17, Cleveland asked Congress to authorize a commission to ascertain the facts in the dispute, and asserted the duty of the United States to support the findings. The commission was authorized and appointed, Jan. 4, 1896. Feb. 2, 1897, Great Britain and Venezuela signed a treaty, submitting the dispute to arbitration. The awards made in 1899 largely supported the British position.

1896. Election of William McKinley, running on a single gold standard platform, over **William Jennings Bryan,** Democratic candidate, supporting free silver. Because of the Democratic espousal of free silver, the Populists supported Bryan. Silver Republicans supported Bryan. McKinley elected, 271 electoral votes to 176 for Bryan.

1897, Mar. 4—1901, Sept. 14. WILLIAM McKINLEY, twenty-fifth president.

1897-1901. Return of prosperity, to which the increased gold production of the world and the unusual demand abroad for American agricultural products were important contributing factors. Great increase in the gold reserve. A period of great activity in the formation of large combinations in the field of business, despite the Sherman Anti-Trust Act. This movement culminated in the organization of the **United States Steel Corporation** (1901), the first billion-dollar corporation. Great concentration of control by banking interests in the business world.

1897, July 24. The Dingley Tariff Act, which, despite McKinley's purpose, was primarily designed to increase protection rather than revenue. It greatly increased the duties and provided for reciprocity treaties with a view to the extension of foreign trade.

1898. THE SPANISH-AMERICAN WAR. The insurrection in Cuba, which broke out in 1895 and toward which Cleveland had maintained an entirely correct attitude, was increasingly attended by inhuman treatment of the rebels which aroused the sympathy of various elements in the United States and afforded an opportunity for the new "yellow press" of the United States to influence American sentiment against Spain. Feb. 15, 1898, the *U.S.S. Maine* was mysteriously blown up in Havana Harbor, producing strong feeling against Spain in the United States. In the face of the belligerent attitude of the press and various groups in the country, McKinley finally yielded to the war clamor, despite the fact that Spain had agreed to every condition laid down by his ultimatum with respect to Cuba. On

Apr. 11. McKinley sent his war message to Congress asking authority for forcible intervention. On

Apr. 20. Congress adopted a resolution authorizing intervention, but disclaiming any intention of annexing Cuba.

Apr. 24, 25. War formally declared. The war consisted of five operations: (1) Defeat of the Spanish fleet at Manila by **Dewey** (May 1); (2) the blockade of Cuba; (3) the search for the main Spanish fleet;

(4) the land and sea battles (**battles of El Caney** and **San Juan Hill,** July; and the **naval battle of Santiago,** July 3); and (5) the invasion of Puerto Rico (July 25). Aug. 12 the **Peace Protocol** was signed and Aug. 13 Manila was captured.

1898, Dec. 10. TREATY OF PEACE SIGNED AT PARIS. Spain withdrew from **Cuba** and ceded to the United States **Puerto Rico, Guam,** and the **Philippines** (for the loss of the latter she was paid $20,000,000). The larger effect of the war was to establish the United States as a world power and to extend the sphere of her political interests and contacts.

1899-1902. Philippine insurrection. Although the Filipinos under **Aguinaldo** aided the Americans against the Spaniards, and had conquered the island of Luzon, they were deeply disappointed when the conditions of the peace treaty were made known. Hostilities broke out in Feb. 1899. For the next three years an American army of 60,000 was engaged in the islands. Guerrilla warfare, with all its attendant horrors, developed. Although Aguinaldo was captured (Mar. 1901) it was not until Apr. 1902 that the insurrection was finally brought to an end.

1899, Sept. 6. John Hay, secretary of state, sent his **Open Door** note to London, Paris, Berlin, and St. Petersburg, asking that the powers claiming spheres of interest in China should pledge themselves to keep the treaty ports open and not interfere with any "vested interest" already in their spheres; that the powers allow the application of the Chinese treaty tariff to the ports under their control without discrimination against nationals of other countries; and that they should not levy higher harbor charges on other nationals calling at their ports.

1900, Mar. 14. Currency Act, declaring other forms of money redeemable in gold on demand, and providing for a gold reserve of $150,000,000. This extended the issue of national bank notes from 90% to full face value of the bonds upon which they were issued and reduced capital requirements of banks in small communities.

Boxer uprising in China. In June the United States participated in the relief expedition against Peking. Hay made this the occasion for reaffirming the Open-Door policy. July 3 he sent a circular note to the powers asking them to preserve the territorial and administrative integrity of China and to safeguard the principle of equal and impartial trade.

Nov. 6. Bryan, running on a platform of free silver and anti-imperialism, defeated by McKinley, who received 292 electoral votes, to 155 for Bryan.

1901, Mar. 2. The Platt amendment respecting Cuba, added to the Army Appropriation Bill for 1901–1902. The Cuban constitutional convention incorporated the amendment in the Cuban constitution (June 12) as a condition of American withdrawal from the island. Cuba agreed not to impair her independence by treaty with foreign powers; not to assume public debt beyond the ability of her ordinary revenues to liquidate; to permit American intervention for the protection of Cuban independence; to sell or lease to the United States land necessary for naval or coaling stations.

The Insular Cases decided. The supreme court held that territory might be subject to the jurisdiction of the United States without being incorporated into the country. The constitution was not applicable, in every particular, to all lands over which the country exercised sovereignty. This enabled the United States to develop a distinctive colonial policy and to enact legislation for the government of backward peoples, where a degree of paternalism was necessary.

Sept. 14. McKinley died from an assassin's bullet.

1901, Sept. 14—1909, Mar. 4. THEO-DORE ROOSEVELT, twenty-sixth president.

1901-1903. Isthmian Canal diplomacy. The **Clayton-Bulwer Treaty of 1850** had provided that any Isthmian canal which might be constructed should be jointly controlled, should not be fortified and should be neutralized for the service of all nations. In later years of the century the United States sought the abrogation of this treaty. In Feb. 1900 the **First Hay-Pauncefote Treaty** was negotiated, only to be rejected by Great Britain. Dec. 16, 1901, the Senate ratified the **Second Hay-Pauncefote Treaty,** which abrogated the Clayton-Bulwer Treaty, provided for American construction and control of a canal, its neutrality to be maintained under the supervision of the United States. After much debate as to the route of the canal, Congress, June 28, 1902, authorized the president to construct a canal across Panama, provided he could obtain the New Panama Canal Company's rights for $40,-000,000 and the acquisition from Colombia of perpetual control over a canal zone. Should he fail in this, he was to construct the canal by the Nicaragua route, provided for in the earlier Spooner Bill. Jan. 22, 1903, the **Hay-Herran Convention** was signed with Colombia, providing for a canal

zone. Although ratified by the United States Senate, the Colombian Senate adjourned (Oct. 31) without ratifying. Nov. 3 Panama revolted and declared her independence of Colombia. United States ships prevented the landing of Colombian troops in Panama and Nov. 6 the United States recognized the independence of Panama. Nov. 18 the **Hay-Bunau-Varilla Treaty** between the United States and Panama granted to the United States the use of a canal zone ten miles wide, transferred to the United States the properties of the New Panama Canal Company and the Panama Railroad Company; provided for the payment of $10,000,000 in gold to Panama and an annuity of $250,000. The United States guaranteed the neutrality of the canal and in return was accorded the right to fortify it.

1902, May 12-Oct. 13. Strike of anthracite coal miners, demanding union recognition, a 9-hour day, and wage increase. In the face of a threatened coal famine, Roosevelt intervened and threatened to work the mines with federal troops, whereupon the owners accepted his suggestion of a commission to investigate. The miners returned to work, but when the commission made its award, union recognition was withheld. Not until 1916 did the miners receive union recognition, with an 8-hour day.

June 17. The Newlands Act providing for the irrigation of the arid lands of the west.

Maryland enacted the first **state workmen's compensation law.** By 1920 all but five states had enacted such laws.

Oregon adopted the thoroughgoing use of the **initiative and referendum.**

1902-1908. Roosevelt and foreign affairs. In 1902, because of the refusal of Venezuela to meet her debt obligations, Great Britain, Germany, and Italy blockaded five of her ports. Dec. 19, upon the urging of the state department and the expressed willingness of **Castro,** the Venezuelan dictator, to submit the European claims to a mediator, the European powers agreed to arbitrate. In Feb. 1903 the blockade was lifted and a mixed commission was set up by the Hague Tribunal to pass upon the claims.

Dec. 2, 1904, Roosevelt enunciated the **Roosevelt corollary of the Monroe Doctrine.** This was occasioned by the debt situation of the Dominican Republic and the pressure of European countries to compel payment. He said that chronic wrongdoing by powers in the western hemisphere might compel the United States under the Monroe Doctrine to the exercise of an international police power as the only means of forestalling European intervention. Under this doctrine the **United States intervened in Santo Domingo** and unofficially collected the customs. July 31, 1907, the American administration left Santo Domingo.

In the summer of 1905 Roosevelt offered his services as **mediator between Russia and Japan** and Aug. 9 the peace conference at **Portsmouth** (N.H.), opened.

In Europe, Roosevelt was instrumental in bringing about the **Algeciras Conference,** Jan. 16, 1906.

In Oct. 1906 the **segregation of Japanese school-children** in San Francisco schools led to strained relations with Japan, which were adjusted by the intervention of Roosevelt. This school controversy, however, proved to be merely one aspect of the general opposition on the Pacific coast to Japanese immigration. Japan declared it was not her practice to issue passports to laborers to come to the United States, though passports were issued for Hawaii, Canada, and Mexico, the holders of which in most cases came to the United States. Japan expressed her intention of continuing this policy, and, relying on this **gentlemen's agreement,** Congress inserted in the Immigration Act of 1907 a clause authorizing the president to exclude from the continental territory of the United States holders of passports issued by any foreign government to its citizens to go to any country other than the United States. By the **Root-Takahira Agreement** of Nov. 1908 Japan confirmed *"the principle of equal opportunity for commerce and industry in China"* and agreed to support the *"independence and integrity"* of that empire.

1903, Jan. 24. Alaskan boundary question referred to a commission of three Americans, two Canadians, and one British. When **Lord Alverstone,** the British member, voted against the Canadians, the dispute was decided in favor of the American contention.

Dec. 17. Wilbur and Orville Wright demonstrated the first motor-driven aeroplane at **Kitty Hawk** (N.C.). Their machine, carrying a man, made four sustained free flights, the longest 59 seconds at 30 miles per hour.

Beginning of effective **state legislation limiting hours of labor of children** and establishing state departments of labor or industrial boards. By 1930, 37 states had established the 48-hour week for children in factories.

Wisconsin enacted the first direct primary law.

1903-1913. Railroad legislation. In 1903 the **Elkins Act** was passed to strengthen the Interstate Commerce Act of 1887, which had proved so ineffective. The Elkins Act forbade railroads to deviate from published schedules of rates and made railway officers as well as the companies liable in cases of rebating. The **Hepburn Act** of 1906 extended the control of the commission to express companies, sleeping-car companies, pipeline, ferries, and terminal facilities. The commission was given power to reduce a rate found to be unreasonable. Passes were abolished and a commodity clause included. The **Mann-Elkins Act** (1910) extended the commission's jurisdiction to telephone and telegraph lines, cable and wireless companies. The long-and-short-haul clause was made effective. Mar. 1, 1913, Taft signed the **Physical Valuation Act,** requiring the commission to evaluate the properties of the railways as the basis for the fixing of rates which would enable the companies to earn a fair return on their investments.

1904, Mar. 14. The Northern Securities Case decided. The efforts of Harriman to gain control, first of the Burlington system and then of the Northern Pacific, had led to the struggle between Harriman and Hill, in which Northern Pacific stock was bid up to fabulous prices, producing the so-called *Northern Pacific Panic* (1901). This was followed by an agreement between the rival groups for the merging of the Northern Pacific, Great Northern, and Burlington systems through the Northern Securities Company. This the supreme court declared to be a violation of the Anti-Trust Act and its dissolution was ordered.

Nov. 8. Roosevelt elected president over **Alton B. Parker,** the Democratic candidate, 335 electoral votes to 133.

1906, June 30. The Pure Food and Drug Act, prohibiting the misbranding and adulteration of foods.

Lee De Forest invented the **oscillating audion,** of great importance in the development of radio.

1908. Oregon adopted the principle of the **recall** of all elective officials.

The supreme court in the case of *Muller v. Oregon,* upheld the Oregon 10-hour law for women in industry. By 1930 all but five states had laws limiting hours of work of women.

Nov. 3. William H. Taft (Republican) elected president over **William Jennings Bryan,** by 321 electoral votes to 162.

1909, Mar. 4—1913, Mar. 4. WILLIAM HOWARD TAFT, twenty-seventh president.

1909–1912. Foreign relations of the United States. In 1909 Taft and Philander C. Knox, his secretary of state, interceded with China to secure the participation of New York bankers with British, French, and German capitalists in the loan for the construction of the Hukuang Railways in China. This gave rise to the charge of **dollar diplomacy.** In May 1910 the American bankers were admitted into the consortium. When in 1912 American bankers were invited to participate in the currency loan to China, Taft gave his approval, but when Wilson in 1913 refused the formal encouragement of the American government, the bankers withdrew.

Sept. 7, 1910, the **Newfoundland fisheries question** was settled by the international court of arbitration at The Hague. American privileges were affirmed and extended.

The unsettled condition of affairs in **Nicaragua** and **Honduras** in 1911 caused Knox to attempt to emulate the example of Roosevelt in Santo Domingo. He negotiated conventions with the two countries providing for loans from American bankers, with an American receiver of customs and with the customs pledged as security for the loans. When the Senate withheld ratification, **American marines** were landed **in Nicaragua** (Aug. 1912), fiscal affairs were turned over to an American collector, the Nicaraguan Bank was controlled by New York bankers, and the Nicaraguan government placed on a monthly allowance. Knox negotiated a **treaty with Nicaragua** giving the United States the right of way for an interoceanic canal, a naval base on the Gulf of Fonseca, and long-term leases over the Great and Little Corn Islands. The Senate refused to ratify, but in 1916 the Wilson administration secured the ratification of a similar treaty. During 1912 troops were concentrated on the Mexican border and the revolutionary Madero government of Mexico was warned that it would be held accountable for loss of life and property.

In 1911 the proposed **reciprocity agreement with Canada** came to naught as a result of the Dominion election.

1909, Aug. 5. Payne-Aldrich Tariff, which disregarded party pledges and maintained protection unimpaired. Strongly opposed by the insurgent Republicans from the west. The first step in the downfall of Taft's administration.

The announcement by **Henry Ford** that thereafter his company would manufacture only the **Model T** chassis heralded the advent of the automobile as a universal method of individual transportation by bringing it within the reach of the average man.

1910, Jan. Taft removed **Gifford Pinchot** from the forestry service as a result of the **Ballinger-Pinchot controversy.**

Mar. 19. Insurgent Republicans in the House moved to shear the speaker of his power by supporting a resolution providing for the election of the rules committee and the exclusion of the speaker from its membership. In 1911 the speaker was deprived of the right of appointing other standing committees of the House.

Aug. 31. Theodore Roosevelt's speech at **Ossawatomie,** Kan., in which he enunciated his doctrine of the **New Nationalism.** This augured ill for Taft.

1911, Jan. 21. National Progressive Republican League organized. Another step in the break in the Republican party. La Follette the leader of the league.

May 1. The supreme court, under the Sherman Anti-Trust Act, ordered the **dissolution of the Standard Oil Company** and the **American Tobacco Company.** In the Standard Oil case the court enunciated the *rule-of-reason doctrine,* indicating its belief that the government should not attempt to outlaw "every" combination in restraint of trade, but should confine action to those contracts which resulted in an "unreasonable" restraint of trade. The enunciation of this doctrine marked a turning-point in the court's attitude toward the so-called "trusts."

Illinois adopted the first state-wide law for **assistance to mothers with dependent children.** In 1912 Colorado took action, while in 1913 18 other states enacted similar laws.

1912. Massachusetts set up a commission to establish **minimum-wage schedules** for women and children. By 1923 14 other states and the District of Columbia had taken similar action, setting up either a statutory minimum or giving commissions mandatory powers. All such laws were dealt a severe blow by the supreme court decision of 1923, in the **Adkins case,** in which the court declared unconstitutional the District of Columbia law because it deprived the individual of liberty of contract.

Feb. 24. Theodore Roosevelt announced he would accept the Republican nomination for president. He carried the preferential primaries over Taft in six states, and was successful in four state conventions. In spite of this the Republican machine brought about

June 22. Taft's renomination. Rooseveft delegates withdrew and Aug. 7 nominated Roosevelt as the candidate of ,the Progressive Party.

July 2. Woodrow Wilson nominated by the Democratic convention on the 46th ballot.

Nov. 5. Wilson elected with 435 electoral votes, with 88 for Roosevelt and 8 for Taft.

1913, Feb. 25. Sixteenth amendment to the constitution, empowering Congress to levy income taxes without apportionment among the states and without regard to any census or enumeration, declared in effect.

Mar. 4. Department of Labor created with a seat in the cabinet.

1913, Mar. 4—1921, Mar. 4. WOODROW WILSON, twenty-eighth president.

1913, May 31. The seventeenth amendment to the constitution, providing for direct election of senators by the people, declared in effect.

Oct. 3. The Underwood Tariff Act reduced the average rate of duty to 26.67%. Based on *ad valorem* rather than specific duties. Reductions covered largely those commodities on which protection had served its purpose or where American goods controlled the markets. Graduated surtax on incomes above $20,000.

Dec. 23. THE FEDERAL RESERVE BANK ACT. The panic of 1907 had emphasized the weakness of the national banking system. The Aldrich-Vreeland Act was passed in 1908 as an emergency measure, and provided for the appointment of a national monetary commission to study the problem. Report of the commission submitted (1912). Wilson asked for legislation which would provide an elastic currency, based on commercial assets rather than bonded indebtedness, mobilization of bank reserves, public control of the banking system, and decentralization rather than centralization. These features were embodied in the **Act of 1913.** The country was divided into 12 districts, each with a federal reserve bank.

1914, Apr. 21—1921. Relations with Mexico. Wilson's refusal to recognize the Huerta régime in Mexico led to the seizure of the port of **Vera Cruz** by American marines (Apr. 21, 1914). Wilson then accepted the mediation of the A.B.C. **powers,** and at the **Niagara Conference** a protocol was signed (June 24), which availed little because Huerta fled the country. In Oct. 1915 an inter-American conference decided to recognize **Carranza,** which prompted Villa to raid Columbus, N.M. ,(Mar. 1916). Punitive **expedition against** Villa under command of **Pershing,** 1916 (see p. 822).

Article 27 of the **Mexican Constitution of 1917** led to the demand by American business interests for intervention which Wilson successfully resisted.

1914, June 15. Panama Tolls Bill signed, repealing the Act of 1912, exempting American coastwise vessels from the canal tolls.

Aug. 15. Panama Canal formally opened.

Sept. 26. Federal Trade Commission Act, abolishing the Bureau of Corporations (1903) and establishing a bipartisan commission of five members, with investigative and regulatory powers in regard to business and corporate practices.

Oct. 15. Clayton Anti-Trust Act, an amendment of the Sherman Act (1890), prohibiting price discrimination, exclusive selling or leasing contracts, intercorporate stockholdings and interlocking directorates in large corporations. It sought to restrict the use of the injunction in labor difficulties, and exempted labor, agricultural, and horticultural organizations from the operation of the anti-trust laws.

Arizona adopted an **old-age pension** system which was declared unconstitutional by the state supreme court. In the 1920's, however, under the intelligent propaganda of the **American Association for Old-Age Security,** many states took up the principle of public responsibility for the aged, and began enactment of old-age pension laws.

1915, Feb. 15—1916, Dec. 18. American neutrality. Feb. 15, the American government protested against the German war-zone proclamation. May 7, the sinking of the *Lusitania,* with loss of American life, led to Wilson's warning to Germany of May 13. He dispatched a second note June 9 and a third July 21. Feb. 1916 the McLemore Resolution to warn Americans to refrain from traveling on armed merchant ships defeated. Apr. 1916 Wilson delivered an ultimatum to Germany as a result of the sinking of the *Sussex* Mar. 24. German concession May 4, with respect to submarine warfare. Dec. 18, 1916, Wilson called upon the belligerent powers to state their war aims. (See p. 935.)

1915-1917. Wilson's policies in the Caribbean. Local disorders in **Haiti** led to the landing of American marines (July 1915) and proclaiming of martial law. In Sept. a treaty was signed by which the Haitian administration was put in American hands. The treaty, proclaimed May 3, 1916, was to run for ten years. Marines continued in occupation. Dec. 29, 1916, an

American naval administration was set up in Santo Domingo. Local parliament suspended. Military occupation continued.

In Nicaragua the **Bryan-Chamorro Treaty of 1916** gave to the United States the right-of-way for a canal, a lease of the Corn Islands, and a naval base on the Gulf of Fonseca.

Jan. 17, 1917, the purchase of the **Virgin Islands** from Denmark was ratified.

1916, July 17. Federal Farm Loan Bank Act passed to improve the agricultural credit situation; established a federal land bank to conduct the lending business, provided for farm loan associations of borrowing farmers, and a federal farm loan board for administrative purposes.

Aug. 29. The Jones Act granting to the Philippines what was practically a territorial status. Declared purpose of the United States to grant independence "as soon as a stable government can be established therein."

Sept. 3. The Adamson Act establishing the 8-hour day on interstate railways.

Sept. 7. The United States Shipping Board formed to acquire merchant vessels for sale or charter to United States citizens. A corporation formed with capital up to $50,000,000 to purchase, lease, or operate the vessels.

1917, Jan. 18. Wilson before the Senate made a plea for termination of the war and outlined the principles necessary thereto.

Jan. 31. Unrestricted submarine warfare renewed by Germany, in violation of the agreement of May 4, 1916.

Feb. 3. Diplomatic relations with Germany severed.

Mar. 1. State department released the **Zimmerman note** showing German efforts to enlist Mexico in support of Germany.

Mar. 12. Presidential order authorizing the arming of merchantmen.

Mar. 16 and 17. Three American ships, homeward bound, attacked without warning and sunk by German submarines.

Mar. 21. Wilson called Congress to meet in special session, Apr. 2.

Apr. 2. Wilson asked Congress to recognize the existence of a state of war between the United States and Germany.

Apr. 6. WAR DECLARED ON GERMANY. (*Cont. p.* 935 *f.,* 1049.)

2. BRITISH NORTH AMERICA, 1783-1914

a. THE DOMINION OF CANADA

1783-1787. Settlement of the loyalists from the United States. Thousands of these established themselves in New Brunswick (separated from Nova Scotia, Aug. 16, 1784) and in Upper Canada. The British government assigned lands to them (100 acres to each head of a family and 50 acres to each member) and spent some $30,000,-000 in equipping them. Effect of the immigration to give Canada a more English composition, and to arouse sentiment of the English settlers against the Quebec Act.

1791, June 10. PASSAGE OF THE CANADA ACT through the British Parliament. It went into effect Dec. 26. Canada divided at the Ottawa River into Upper Canada (chiefly English) and Lower Canada (predominantly French). Each part had a governor, a legislative council appointed by him, and an elected assembly. Colonial laws could be disallowed by the home government within two years of passage. One-seventh of all land granted to be reserved for the maintenance of the Protestant clergy. All rights of the Catholic Church reaffirmed.

1783— EXPLORATION OF THE WEST. In 1783 the **Northwest Company** was organized in competition with the **Hudson's Bay Company.** In 1788 **Captain John Meares** sailed along the Pacific coast and established a fur post at Nootka. In 1789 a Spanish expedition from Mexico took possession of the northwest coast on the basis of discovery in 1775. Several British ships were seized, but in 1790 Spain made reparation for them and abandoned claims to the region (**Treaty of Oct. 28**). In 1792 **Captain George Vancouver** explored the Pacific coast and circumnavigated Vancouver Island. In 1793 **Alexander Mackenzie** reached the coast after the first overland journey from the east. In the meanwhile (1785-1795) **David Thompson** had traversed much of the territory along the coast of Hudson Bay north to Fort Churchill, as well as the regions about Lake

Winnipeg and along the Saskatchewan and Athabasca Rivers. **Jay's Treaty** between the United States and Great Britain (Nov. 19, 1794) provided for a boundary commission to determine the frontier west of the Lake of the Woods. In 1797 Thompson, in the service of the Northwest Company, pushed west along the 49th parallel and to the upper Missouri; in 1798 he explored the region about the headwaters of the Mississippi. During the following years he continued his travels in what are now Manitoba, Saskatchewan, and Alberta, and in 1807 founded **Fort Kootenay**, the first post on the Columbia River. At the same time (1805-1807) **Simon Fraser** and **James Stuart** explored the Fraser River region to the ocean. Thompson continued his work on the Columbia. By 1810 much of the southern half of present-day Canada had been gone over by various explorers and traders. In 1811 **Lord Selkirk** bought from the Hudson's Bay Company 116,000 square miles for settlement in Manitoba, Minnesota, and North Dakota. Scotch settlers arrived there on the Red River in 1812. In 1815 an attack was launched on the colony by agents of the rival Northwest Company; colonists were driven out in 1815 and 1816. An investigation in 1817 upheld the claims of Lord Selkirk and the colony was re-established.

1812, June 18. UNITED STATES DECLARED WAR ON GREAT BRITAIN. Among the causes of conflict was the continued trouble with the Indians, supposedly instigated and equipped by the British in Canada, and the American desire to conquer Canada, which was regarded as easy. A triple attack was planned: on Montreal, on the region opposite Niagara, and on the region opposite Detroit. On the Montreal front and at Niagara the offensive failed to materialize. At Detroit a short advance was made, followed by retreat. The British, under Gen. Isaac Brock, secured the **surrender of Detroit** (Aug. 16, 1812). Brock then turned to Niagara and fought the successful engagement of **Queenston Heights** (Oct. 13), in which he was killed.

1813. The Americans captured **York** (Toronto) Apr. 27, but abandoned it soon afterward (May 2). In Ohio the Americans were vigorously attacked by the British, supported by the Indians (**Tecumseh**). Sept. 10 Lieutenant **Oliver Hazard Perry** with an improvised fleet won the naval **battle of Lake Erie** and forced the British to abandon Detroit. The Americans, under Gen. **William Henry Harrison**, crossed into Ontario and fought the successful engagement on the **Thames River** (Oct.

5), but were unable to follow up the advantage. The campaign against Montreal was begun Oct. 17, but the Americans were defeated by a greatly inferior force (**battle of Crysler's Farm**, Nov. 11) and the advance abandoned. Dec. 10 an American force burned **Newark**, in retaliation for which the British and Canadians, after taking **Fort Niagara** (Dec. 18), burned **Buffalo** (Dec. 29-31).

1814, July 5. The Americans, advancing from Niagara, took **Fort Erie** and won the engagement at **Chippewa Plains**. They advanced to Queenston, but then fell back again.

July 25. Battle of Lundy's Lane, which was indecisive, but the Americans blew up Fort Erie and recrossed the river (Nov. 5).

In the meanwhile 16,000 British troops had been sent to Canada and an invasion was begun by way of Lake Champlain.

Sept. 11. An American naval force under Lieutenant (later Captain) **Thomas Macdonough** won the **battle of Plattsburg** and forced the retirement of the British.

Sept. 21. The British, having invaded Maine, declared all territory east of the Penobscot annexed to New Brunswick.

Dec. 24. The Treaty of Ghent brought the war to a close. All captured territory was returned and a commission to delimit the northeastern frontier provided for.

1817, Apr. 28. Exchange of notes between the United States and Great Britain, by which they agreed to **restrict naval forces on the Lakes** to one each on Lake Champlain and Lake Ontario and two on the upper lakes.

1818, Oct. 20. Treaty between the United States and Great Britain giving Americans the right to fish on the coasts of Newfoundland and Labrador and dry fish in unsettled bays. Boundary between the United States and Canada west of the Lake of the Woods fixed on the 49th parallel to the Rockies. Territory west of the Rockies to be jointly occupied for 10 years.

1821, Mar. 26. The Northwest Company merged with the Hudson's Bay Company under the latter's name. Rights of exclusive trade to the company in the territory allotted to it renewed for 21 years.

1836, July 21. First Canadian railroad opened, from Laprairie on the St. Lawrence to St. Johns on the Richelieu.

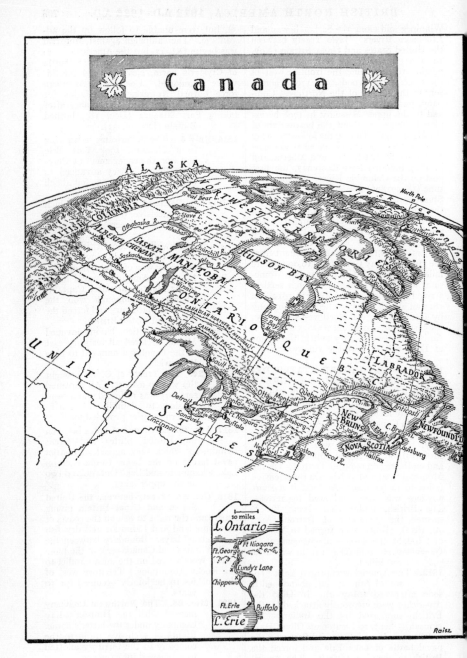

Canada

1837. REBELLION IN UPPER AND LOWER CANADA. This had been brewing ever since 1815 and was the result of constitutional conflict between the governors and the appointed legislative councils, representing bureaucratic and vested interests (*family compact* in Upper Canada, *château clique* in Lower Canada) on the one hand and the popularly elected assemblies on the other. Popular leaders in Upper Canada, **Robert Gourlay** (expelled 1818), **William Lyon Mackenzie, Egerton Ryerson;** in Lower Canada, **Louis Joseph Papineau.** *Grievances:* control of judiciary, control of revenue, supply bills, clergy reserves, established churches, executive council. The situation was worst in Lower Canada, where the British minority, represented by the governor and the council, was opposed by the French majority in the Assembly. In 1822 it had been proposed to reunite Upper and Lower Canada, but the project roused a storm of protest in Lower Canada. A British parliamentary investigation was made in 1828 and led to various administrative reform proposals, but nothing came of them. In 1834 the Assembly of Lower Canada adopted the 92 resolutions, a declaration of rights. By 1837 affairs had reached a deadlock and the popular leaders decided to resort to force.

In Lower Canada the rebellion was confined to an area around Montreal. There were a number of riots and some fighting at **St. Denis** and **St. Charles.** Most of the population remained passive, the rebels were easily defeated, and the leaders fled to the United States. In Upper Canada the rebels, under Mackenzie, attacked **Toronto** (Dec. 5), but were driven off. Mackenzie fled across the border and Dec. 13 seized **Navy Island** in the Niagara River, where he proclaimed a provisional government.

Dec. 29. A Canadian government force crossed the river and burned the American steamer *Caroline*, which had been supplying the rebels; a famous case in international law.

1838, Jan. 13. Mackenzie abandoned Navy Island and was arrested in the United States.

During the year 1838 the rebels, supported by American sympathizers (*Hunters' Lodges*), staged several invasions from the United States, but none of these assumed large proportions.

May 29. Lord Durham arrived at Quebec as governor-in-chief of all the British North American provinces. His lenient treatment of the rebels led to disavowal by the home government. Oct. 9 he resigned.

1839, Feb. 11. Durham's famous *Report on the Affairs of British North America.* He proposed the union of Upper and Lower Canada and the grant of responsible government. The imperial government was to retain control only of foreign relations, regulation of trade, disposal of public lands, and determination of the colonial constitution.

June 20. Lord John Russell introduced in the British Parliament a resolution based on the *Durham Report.*

Oct. 19. Poulett Thomson (Lord Sydenham) arrived at Quebec as governor-in-chief, to prepare the provinces for union.

1840, July 23. THE BRITISH PARLIAMENT PASSED THE UNION ACT. This united Upper and Lower Canada into one government, with one governor, one appointed legislative council, and one popularly elected assembly, in which the former two provinces had equal representation. Various administrative reforms were carried through. The issue of responsible government was evaded, and the principle was not firmly established in practice until the time of **Lord Elgin's** governorship (1847–1854), in the course of the crisis arising from the **Rebellion Losses Bill** (1849).

1842, Aug. 9. Ashburton Treaty between the United States and Great Britain. Great Britain abandoned more than half of the territory claimed on the northeast frontier.

1846, June 15. Oregon Boundary Treaty between the United States and Great Britain, following a period of acute tension.

Aug. 28. British Possessions Act gave Canada the right to fix tariffs.

1849, June 26. Abolition of the British **Navigation Acts,** removing restrictions on foreign shipping. This, following on the abolition of the Corn Laws in 1846, led to an acute economic depression in Canada and to a short-lived agitation for annexation to the United States (**Annexation Manifesto,** Oct. 10, 1849).

1854, June 5. Elgin Treaty, establishing reciprocity between Canada and the United States. This was abrogated by the United States in 1866.

Sept.-Dec. Law converting **clergy reserves** into a special fund to be distributed to counties and cities for secular purposes. Another law abolished **seignorial tenure,** feudal dues being converted into cash rents.

1856, June 24. The legislative council, hitherto appointive, was made elective.

1858, Aug. 2. British Columbia, having been withdrawn from the jurisdiction of the Hudson's Bay Company, was given separate administration.

1866. Beginning of the **Fenian** (Irish-American) **raids,** designed to bring pressure on the British government in favor of Ireland. Fenians from Buffalo seized **Fort Erie** (June 1), but were driven out. Other raids took place from Vermont and Fenian troubles continued to some extent until 1871.

1867, Mar. 29. B R I T I S H   N O R T H   AMERICA ACT united Ontario, Quebec, New Brunswick, and Nova Scotia in the **Dominion of Canada** (effective July 1). The movement for confederation was the result of growing difficulty in the government of United Canada (religious and racial differences, problems of representation), as well as of economic (especially railway) considerations and military (defense) problems in the Civil War period. The movement began in the Maritime Provinces (**Charlottetown Conference,** Sept. 1864), but expanded almost at once (**Quebec Convention,** Oct. 10–28, 1864, in which all provinces were represented). The 72 **Quebec Resolutions** became the basis for the Act of Confederation. They provided for a federal government and provincial governments, a federal parliament of two houses (Senate consisting of 24 members each from Ontario, Quebec, and a third division comprising Nova Scotia and New Brunswick, and an elected lower House). Representatives of the provinces conferred with imperial authorities in London (Dec. 1866) and drew up the **London Resolutions,** which were transformed into the final act.

1867–1868. Lord Monck, first governor-general. (Sir) **John A. Macdonald** first premier of the Dominion.

1868, Dec. 29. Sir John Young (Lord Lisgar) appointed governor-general (1868–1872).

1869, Nov. 19. PURCHASE OF NORTH-WEST TERRITORIES from the old Hudson's Bay Company for $1,500,000, the company retaining one-twentieth of the land. Taken over, 1870.

1869–1870. RED RIVER REBELLION. Half-breeds, led by Louis Riel about Fort Garry (Winnipeg), irritated chiefly by the belief that surveys being made were to rob them of their land, set up a provisional government (Nov. 1869) with Riel president; expedition from Portage Laprairie defeated and captured (Feb. 1870); **Thomas Scott** (Orangeman) executed

(Mar.) and great indignation aroused in Ontario. The rebels dispersed without a blow before the advance of an expedition under Col. Garnet (later Lord) **Wolseley.**

1870, July 15. Manitoba constituted a province of the Dominion.

1871, July 1. British Columbia joined the Dominion; a transcontinental railroad to be commenced within 2 and completed within 10 years.

1871. Sir John Macdonald a member of the British commission to Washington to settle outstanding difficulties with the United States.

1872, May 22. Earl Dufferin appointed governor-general (1872–1878).

1872. General elections; government victory.

1873, June 1. Death of Joseph Howe; Howe had opposed Nova Scotia's entrance to union, but later accepted it rather than agree to radical proposals of annexation to the United States.

July 1. Prince Edward Island joined the Dominion; the Dominion to assume railway debt.

Nov. 7. Resignation of Sir John Macdonald owing to pressure of public opinion following **transcontinental railway** scandal and charges of corruption in last elections. Alexander Mackenzie formed a Liberal cabinet; overwhelming victory at general elections.

1874. Introduction of **ballot voting;** elections on a single day.

1876. Opening of the **Intercolonial Railway** connecting Ontario with the Maritime Provinces; government-owned and operated.

1878, Oct. 5. Marquess of Lorne, governor-general (1878–1883).

Oct. General elections on **tariff issue.** Conservatives victorious in support of protection; Sir John Macdonald premier (Oct. 17), and protective tariff instituted.

1881. Charter given to newly formed **CANADIAN PACIFIC RAILWAY COMPANY** for construction of a transcontinental railroad following financial difficulties of old companies. Government grant of $25,000,000 with 25,000,000 acres of land and 670 miles of track already laid; loan of $20,000,000 in 1884 (repaid 1887). Last spike driven, Nov. 7, 1885, and formally opened May, 1887, with 2905 miles of rail joining coast to coast. Marked results in Canadian development; steamship lines established; flow of immigrants to the west accelerated.

1883, Aug. 18. Marquess of Lansdowne, governor-general (1883–1888).

1885, Mar. 26. Outbreak of the North-west Rebellion; quickly suppressed by the Dominion government with troops from all the provinces transported over the new Canadian Pacific Railway. Riel surrendered (May 15); executed (Nov. 16).

1886. Canadian and Bering Sea fisheries dispute with the United States.

1888, May 1. Lord Stanley (Earl of Derby), governor-general (1888–1893).

1890. Liberals urged policy of "unrestricted reciprocity" to remedy the depression following the United States McKinley Tariff. Continental Union Association formed. The Imperial Federation League (formed 1885) urged preferential trade with the mother country.

1891, June 6. Death of Sir John A. Macdonald; succeeded by Sir John J. C. Abbott (June 16).

1892, Nov. Resignation of Sir John Abbott; succeeded by Sir John S. D. Thompson (Dec. 5).

1892-1893. Bering Sea Arbitration (p. 785).

1893, May 22. Earl of Aberdeen appointed governor-general (1893–1898).

1894, June 23-July 10. Second Colonial Conference held at Ottawa.

Dec. 12. Death of Sir John Thompson. Mr. (later Sir) Mackenzie Bowell succeeded (Dec. 21).

1896. The offer of Newfoundland to enter the Dominion was refused through financial disagreement.

Apr. 27. Resignation of Sir Mackenzie Bowell; Sir Chas. Tupper, premier (Jan. 15, 1895).

July 11. Mr. (later Sir) Wilfrid Laurier became premier (1896–1911) as a result of a Liberal victory in the general elections (June).

1897. British preferential tariff instituted. In 1898 the preference was increased to 25% and in 1900 to 33⅓%. Germany retaliated (July 7, 1899) by depriving Canada of most-favored-nation treatment.

1898. Canadian Northern Railway chartered.

July 30. Lord Minto appointed governor-general (1898–1904).

1899, Oct. 29. The first Canadian contingent sent to South Africa. A second contingent sent in 1900; but the official contingents were withdrawn before the end of the war owing to dissatisfaction in Quebec.

1902, Oct. 31. Cable from Vancouver to Brisbane completed.

1903. Alaskan Boundary Arbitration with the United States (p. 789). High dissatisfaction with the award.

1904, Sept. 26. Earl Grey appointed governor-general (1904–1911).

1905, Sept. 1. Formation of the provinces of Alberta and Saskatchewan.

1908. Civil Service Commission appointed for the selection of civil officials.

1910. Formation of a small Canadian navy.

1911, Jan. 26. Publication of a Reciprocity Agreement with the United States; ratified by the United States Senate (July 22). But in the general elections (Sept. 21) the Liberals were defeated on the issue and reciprocity was dropped. Mr. (later Sir) Robert L. Borden formed a Conservative ministry (Oct. 10).

Mar. 21. Duke of Connaught appointed governor-general (1911–1916).

1913, May 30. Defeat in the Senate of a navy bill providing for the contribution of three dreadnoughts to the imperial navy.

1914, Apr. 7. Completion of the Grand Trunk Pacific Railway.

May 21. *S.S. Komagatu Maru* in Vancouver Harbor; 300 Hindus refused entrance to British Columbia and sent back to India.

May 29. *S.S. Empress of Ireland* sunk in collision in the Gulf of St. Lawrence; 1023 lives lost.

Aug. 4. Entrance of Great Britain into World War. (*Cont. p.* 1057.)

b. NEWFOUNDLAND

1855. Responsible government granted; bicameral legislature, legislative council (15), appointed by the governor-in-council, House of Assembly (36), elective, and a responsible cabinet.

1864. Copper discovered in the north and mining operations begun.

1873. Direct steam communication with England and America established.

1880. Government loan of £1,000,000 to a railway from St. John's to Hall's Bay; completed to Harbor Grace (1884); after financial difficulties, construction was taken over by Mr. R. G. Reid (1893) and built to Port-aux-Basques.

1888. Bait Act took effect, after considerable controversy and protests of the French government, prohibiting capture in Newfoundland waters, for exportation or sale, of bait fish except under special license. French retaliations followed until a *modus vivendi* was enacted (1890). Finally settled in the Anglo-French Convention of 1904.

1894-1895. Bank failures and insolvency; Canadian banks replaced former government institutions; followed by renewed prosperity.

1895-1896. Severe financial depression. Delegation to Ottawa regarding union with Canada. Canada objected to assuming all of the $16,000,000 debt and negotiations were broken off.

1900. Resignation of Sir James Winter; succeeded by Mr. (later Sir) Robert Bond.

1906, Oct. *Modus vivendi* with the United States following difficulties with fishing rights under the Treaty of 1818. Referred to the Hague Tribunal and award (Sept. 1910) allowed Great Britain (Newfoundland) the right to make regulations subject to the Treaty of 1818, and defining the "three-mile limit" in bays as from a line across the bay at a point where distance of 10 miles is not exceeded.

1909. Resignation of premier Sir Robert Bond; succeeded by Sir Edward P. Morris. (*Cont. p.* 1060.)

3. ALASKA

1728. Vitus Bering, a Dane, sailed through the straits now bearing his name.

1741. Bering explored the Alaskan coast. From this time on the Russians were active in the region, establishing sealing and fishing stations.

1776. Captain James Cook made the first English explorations on the coast. He was followed by Vancouver.

1793. Alexander Mackenzie crossed the continent from the east to the Pacific coast, and returned.

1799. The Russian-American Fur Company organized by the Russian government and given a trade monopoly for 20 years (later renewed). A most active period of Russian enterprise under the governorship of Alexander Baranov (1790–1819).

1804. Baranov founded Sitka.

1821. Russian decree claiming the coast south to lat. 51 and forbidding all foreign ships approaching within 100 miles of the coast. Protests of the United States and Great Britain. The matter was settled by treaties between Russia and the United States (Apr. 17, 1824) and between Russia and Great Britain (Feb. 28, 1825), by which Russia was given the territory north of 54° 40' and west of 141°.

1867, Mar. 30. The United States purchased Alaska from Russia for $7,200,000. The formal transfer was made Oct. 18.

1884, May 17. The Organic Act applied the laws of Oregon to Alaska, after a period of government by the war department.

1903. Passage of a homestead law for Alaska.

Oct. 20. Settlement of the boundary dispute between the United States and Canada by a board of three American, two Canadian, and one English jurist. The Canadian case was lost and Canada was debarred from the ocean inlets.

1906. Alaska permitted to elect a delegate to Congress.

1912. Alaska given territorial status. A bicameral legislature was established under a governor appointed by the President of the United States. The legislature was not permitted to pass laws dealing with excise, game, or fur, and the American Congress reserved the right to veto Alaskan legislation.

The population of Alaska increased from 30,000 in 1867 to 55,000 in 1920. The population is engaged chiefly in fishing (halibut, cod, herring) and in the fur trade. A treaty between the United States, England, Russia, and Japan in 1911 prohibited pelagic killing of seals, and the killing on the Pribilov Islands is done only by United States government agents. The value of the furs taken between 1867 and 1925 was over $100,000,000. Mining (especially gold — Klondike gold rush, Aug. 1896) is also an important industry, the value of the product between 1880 and 1927 having been almost $600,000,000.

H. LATIN AMERICA

1. THE WARS OF INDEPENDENCE

a. CAUSES

Political, economic, and social factors inherent in the Spanish colonial system were the fundamental causes which led to the separation of the American colonies from the mother country. The creoles (Spaniards born in America) and *mestizos* (mixed Spanish and Indian) increasingly desired participation in government. The virtual exclusion from more important civil and ecclesiastical offices, the economic policy of Spain, and the exploitation of the colonies, fully revealed by the reforms of Charles III (p. 450), and certain aspects of religious policy created discontent. The freedom enjoyed during the long periods when Spain was at war, and the successful revolution of the North American colonies of Great Britain (p. 517), engendered a desire for independence. The doctrines of the French philosophers and the French Revolution created a demand for reform among intellectuals. Geographical influences, lack of communications, the administrative division of the colonies, and traditional Spanish separation and individualism aided in creating sentiment for independence.

In **South America** the movement for separation was fundamentally liberal. From the first it was led by creoles and originated in the *cabildos*, later expanding to national proportions. In **Mexico** the earliest and unsuccessful phases, led by certain creoles, developed into a servile revolt as well as a movement for independence. Separation was finally achieved by a reactionary movement after the Revolution of 1820 in Spain (p. 644).

The **Wars of Liberation** were also civil conflicts within New World administrative districts. The royal government and the Church, until the Spanish Revolution of 1820, constituted the basis of Spanish resistance. The ignorant masses frequently became a source of manpower for the Spanish régime as well as for the creole movement. In the region of the Rio de la Plata and New Granada provincial separatist tendencies led to internecine strife among proponents of independence from Spain.

The **immediate cause** of the movement which led to the independence of the South American colonies was the domination of Spain by **Napoleon Bonaparte** and his establishment of his brother **Joseph** on the throne (p. 593). The American colonies opposed French control and refused to recognize Joseph, proclaiming allegiance to the deposed **Ferdinand VII.** Certain areas declared their independence when it appeared that Napoleon had established complete control over Spain. The restoration of the absolute rule of Ferdinand in 1814 and his determination to restore the old system (despite the liberal policies which had been adopted by the Spanish agencies representing his authority during the Napoleonic period) turned the movements into a definitely separatist channel. Internal strife and disturbed political conditions in Spain after 1814 contributed to the success of the colonists.

The **Wars of Independence** passed through two phases, that between 1809 and 1816, during which movements for separation failed everywhere except in the area of the Rio de la Plata, and that between 1816 and 1825, during which independence was achieved.

b. EARLIER INSURRECTIONS, 1721 - 1806

The first serious insurrectionary movements occurred in the eighteenth century, the gravest taking place in **Paraguay** (1721–1735), **Peru** (1780–1782), and **Colombia** (1781).

1721-1735. The Comuneros of Paraguay.
   José de Antequera, appointed by the *audiencia* of Charcas to resolve a controversy between the *cabildo* of Asunción and the governor of Paraguay, supported the *cabildo* and was chosen governor (1721). An autonomous commune was created, and Antequera, speaking of the sovereignty of the people, refused to relinquish office on demand of the higher Spanish authorities. Open warfare between the forces of the commune and royal forces ensued. After maintaining their cause for a considerable period, Antequera and the Paraguayans were overcome (1731). Antequera was

executed, but a follower, **Fernando Mompó de Zayas**, revived the organization and continued the struggle, which was finally completely suppressed (1735).

1780-1782. The revolt of Tupac Amarú. Abuses in connection with forced labor under the *mita* and *repartimiento* and with administration caused the natives of the Peruvian highlands to revolt under leadership of **Tupac Amarú**, descendant of the Inca rulers, who proclaimed himself liberator of his people. Two attacks were made on Cuzco by Tupac Amarú at the head of a horde of ill-armed Indians, but the Spaniards crushed the native forces and executed the leader. The revolt was continued and La Paz was twice subjected to siege before the movement was definitely crushed.

1781. The comuneros of New Granada. Attempts to increase royal revenues in New Granada led to a widespread revolt under the leadership of two creoles, **Berbeo** and **José Antonio Galán.** Moving on Bogotá, the insurrectory forces compelled the authorities to consent to their conditions, whereupon they dispersed. The viceroy, receiving reinforcements, suppressed the movement, although later (1784) representatives of New Granada, declaring themselves allies of Tupac Amarú, fruitlessly sought England and French aid for the liberation of South America.

1790-1806. The early efforts of Francisco de Miranda. The greatest of the early leaders who planned the independence of the Spanish colonies was **Francisco de Miranda** (1756–1816). A Venezuelan creole, Miranda served in the Spanish army and became a general in the French revolutionary forces. He early formulated plans for liberation and long but fruitlessly sought the aid of the English, French, and United States governments. Organizing a filibustering expedition in the United States, Miranda captured **Coro**, but Venezuela was not prepared for revolt and the movement failed (1806). Support of the English government was at length secured and an expedition for the liberation of northern South America was being organized under command of Wellington when developments in the Iberian Peninsula caused abandonment of the project.

c. THE RÍO DE LA PLATA

The period of independence in the region of the Río de la Plata was introduced by a British attempt to gain possession of at least a portion of the area.

1806. On his return from the occupation of Cape Colony (p. 851), **Sir Home Popham**, acquainted with the projects of Miranda, on his own initiative occupied **Buenos Aires.** The viceroy fled and **Jacques de Liniers**, at the head of the colonial militia, forced the British to capitulate. Upon his return the viceroy was deposed by a *cabildo abierto* and Liniers was elected to the office, an act of sovereignty which the crown approved.

1806-1807. Although the action of Popham had not been authorized, the British government dispatched an expedition of 10,000 men under **Gen. John Whitelocke.** This force occupied **Montevideo** and moved against Buenos Aires, the defenders of which, under Liniers, forced Whitelocke to capitulate and withdraw from the area of the Río de la Plata. These events stimulated national feeling in the region.

1809-1810. Liniers was replaced by a viceroy appointed by the central *junta* of Spain, but in view of the apparent success of Napoleon he was removed by the *cabildo* of Buenos Aires and a provisional *junta* of the **provinces of the Río de la Plata** was established in the name of Ferdinand VII (1810, May 25). Direct Spanish authority was never restored.

1810-1811. The provisional *junta*, dominated by **Mariano Moreno** (1778–1811), soon rejected the authority of the provisional government of Spain representing Ferdinand VII and sought to extend control over the **Banda Oriental** (Uruguay) and **Paraguay.** An army was dispatched to liberate upper Peru (Bolivia), but was disastrously defeated. Paraguay refused to adhere to the provinces of the Río de la Plata. Forces were sent against the province by Buenos Aires, but were defeated by the royal governor, supported by the majority of Paraguayans (1811). Moreno was forced from office and a triumvirate replaced the provisional *junta*.

1812-1813. **Manuel Belgrano**, placed in command of the northern forces, defeated the royalists near **Tucumán** and at **Salta**, and prevented the invasion of the southern portion of the region of the Río de la Plata. A second attempt to invade upper Peru failed.

1813. Authority was vested in a *director*, the former viceroyalty was divided into provinces, and a congress was convened at Tucumán (1816).

1816, July 9. JUAN MARTIN DE PUEYRREDON was named *supreme director* and **the congress declared the independence of the United Provinces.** Meanwhile **José de San Martín** (1778–1850), one of the two great figures of the period of independence, who was born in the Misiones territory while his father was governor of the province and who had served in the Spanish army in Africa, Portugal, and Spain, was given command of the army of the north (1814).

1814-1817. Comprehending the geographical difficulties of a campaign in upper Peru, San Martín formulated a plan to organize an army in western Argentina, liberate Chile, and move by sea to attack Peru, the center of Spanish authority. San Martín established himself at Mendoza and prepared to carry his plans into effect.

d. PARAGUAY

1811. After the defeat of the forces of Buenos Aires, the **Paraguayans** overthrew the royal governor, and a revolutionary *junta* was established at Asunción.

1811, Aug. 14. PARAGUAY PROCLAIMED INDEPENDENCE FROM SPAIN, and later from Buenos Aires (1813). A republican government with two consuls at its head was created (1813).

1814. The *First Consul* José Rodríguez de Francia (1756–1840) was declared *Dictator*, and was soon made *Perpetual Dictator* (1816).

e. THE BANDA ORIENTAL (URUGUAY)

1811-1814. Spanish control in the Banda Oriental, territory claimed by the Portuguese crown and the provinces of the Río de la Plata, was brought to an end by forces of Buenos Aires and by Uruguayan revolutionaries led by José Artigas (1746–1826). Artigas, who favored a federal system of government, at first maintained allegiance to Buenos Aires, but controversy concerning federal and unitary forms led to conflict and he advocated independence.

1816-1820. After establishing control over an extensive area, Artigas was driven from Uruguay by Brazilian troops, who occupied the province (1816–1820).

1821. The Banda Oriental was incorporated into Brazil.

f. CHILE

1810. Upon the apparent triumph of Napoleon in Spain the captaingeneral of Chile was deposed and a *junta* assumed authority in the name of Ferdinand VII. A general congress convened at Santiago, from which, after controversy concerning reforms and separation from Spain, the radical elements withdrew. The remaining groups constituted themselves into an *executive power*.

1811-1812. José Miguel Carrera overthrew the government and sanctioned a republican organization, at the same time acknowledging the sovereignty of the king. A constitution was framed which assigned supreme authority to a *junta* of three under the control of Carrera, whose rule aroused strong opposition headed by Bernardo O'Higgins (1778–1842).

1814. This dissension enabled the viceroy of Peru to crush the Chilean armies, despite the ultimate co-operation of O'Higgins and Carrera. Santiago was taken and royal government was re-established.

1817. San Martín, having completed his preparations at Mendoza (above), crossed the Andes with some 5200 men, defeated a Spanish army at Chacabuco (Feb. 12) and occupied Santiago. O'Higgins was made *supreme director* after San Martín had refused the post.

1818, Feb. 12. THE INDEPENDENCE OF CHILE WAS PROCLAIMED. A royal army from Peru was defeated by San Martín at Maipú (Apr. 5). With these events the independence of Chile was definitely achieved.

1818-1820. San Martín prepared for the liberation of Peru, receiving support from Buenos Aires and aid from O'Higgins. A navy was organized under Admiral Thomas Lord Cochrane (1775–1860), an able British naval officer, and an army of 4000 men was formed.

g. PERU AND BOLIVIA

1809. The inhabitants of Chuquisaca deposed the president and established a *junta*, while those of La Paz deposed the intendant and also created a *junta*, declaring loyalty to Ferdinand VII. Royal troops soon crushed the movements. Another unsuccessful revolutionary movement occurred at Cuzco (1813). Peru long remained a bulwark of royal authority.

1820. After completing preparations in Chile, San Martín transported his forces to Peru by sea, where he resorted to propaganda rather than immediate military action on a large scale, and opened negotiations with the viceroy. Negotiations failed, but efforts to influence opinion met with success. The viceroy abandoned Lima, and San Martín, invited by the people, entered the capital.

1821, July 28. He proclaimed the INDE-PENDENCE OF PERU, and assumed supreme authority as *protector*.

1823. A factional quarrel among the proponents of independence in Lima led to the establishment of a new government, which invited **Bolívar** to Peru. A force under **Andrés Santa Cruz** was dispatched into Charcas (Bolivia), but was defeated by the royalists. **Sucre** moved to Lima with Colombian troops and Bolívar followed, being proclaimed *dictator*.

1824. Carrying the war to the royalists, under the viceroy, **José de la Serna**, and **José Canterac**, Bolívar and Sucre moved into the highlands and defeated the Spaniards at **Junín** (Aug. 24). Bolívar returned to Lima to assume the government. Sucre continued the campaign, and with some 5800 men defeated la Serna and Canterac, with 9300 men, in the decisive **battle of Ayacucho** (Dec. 9). The Spanish leaders were forced to sign a capitulation which included the withdrawal of the 23,000 royal troops which remained in Peru. With these events the independence of Peru was achieved. Invading Charcas, Sucre liberated the presidency and convened a **congress at Chuquisaca.**

1825, Aug. 6. CONGRESS PROCLAIMED INDEPENDENCE and designated the new state the **Republic of Bolívar** (Bolivia).

h. VENEZUELA

1808. Upon the intervention of Napoleon in Spain the *cabildo* of **Caracas**, proclaiming Ferdinand VII King of Spain and the Indies, proposed the establishment of a *junta*. Two years later an extraordinary *cabildo* deposed the captain-general and created a *junta* in the name of the sovereign (1810).

1811. The *junta* soon disavowed the Spanish regency and claimed for Venezuela a place among free states, inviting other colonies to take similar action. A commission, which included **Simón Bolívar** (cf. below), was sent to England to secure aid. **Miranda** returned to Venezuela to assume leadership.

July 7. A general congress proclaimed VENEZUELAN INDEPENDENCE and a constitution was adopted. Miranda was given command of the revolutionary forces and Bolívar became one of his lieutenants. **Simón Bolívar** (1783-1830), born in Caracas of distinguished creole parents, educated in his native city and widely traveled in Europe, deeply read in the French philosophers and strongly influenced by his republican tutor, Simón Rodríquez, had dedicated himself to the liberation of the Spanish colonies, and became one of the two greatest figures of the independence movement.

1811-1812. Spanish forces under **Juan Domingo Monteverde** achieved marked success in a campaign of reconquest, and internal strife developed.

1812, Mar. 26. An earthquake wrought great destruction and created demoralization in the area controlled by the revolutionists, but spared that held by the royalists. The clergy proclaimed the catastrophe to be divine retribution for disloyalty, with detrimental effect upon the revolutionary cause.

July 25. **Miranda was made dictator** to organize further resistance, but the royal forces made rapid progress and he was forced to capitulate by the **Treaty of San Mateo**, which provided clemency for the revolutionists. Monteverde, notwithstanding, dealt with Venezuela as a conquered province. Bolívar and other leaders, indignant at the capitulation, permitted Miranda to fall into Spanish hands, and he was sent a prisoner to Cadiz, where he died (1816).

i. GREAT COLOMBIA (NEW GRANADA, VENEZUELA, AND QUITO)

1808. Ferdinand VII was proclaimed king at Bogotá upon the invasion of Spain by Napoleon, and in the following year the president of Quito was driven from office. A *junta*, in the name of Ferdinand VII, and a senate, vested with the powers of the *audiencia*, as well as secretaries for war and foreign affairs were created. The viceroy of New Granada was compelled to call an advisory *junta* to consider action with respect to the movement in Quito. This body displayed dissatisfaction with Spanish rule and with its authority a memorial of grievances was drawn up, to be sent to the *central junta* of Spain. An extraordinary *cabildo* at Bogotá, in the name of the king, established a *junta* for the viceroyalty and named the viceroy its president. The *junta* soon expelled the viceroy and broke with the Spanish regency, but again proclaimed loyalty to Ferdinand VII. Principal towns of New Granada, while affirming loyalty to the sovereign, also overthrew the Spanish officials and created provincial *juntas*, certain of which drew up constitutions. Meanwhile the movement in Quito was crushed by the Spanish authorities (1809).

1811, Nov. 11. Cartagena later declared its independence, and was followed by Cundinamarca (1813). A congress drew up an *Act of Federation of the United Provinces of New Granada*, but the provinces displayed marked separatist tendencies and conflict between them weakened the revolutionary cause. Bolívar took service with Cartagena and drove the Spanish forces from the lower Magdalena Valley.

1813. Commissioned by the congress of New Granada to carry the war into Venezuela, Bolívar regained Caracas and **became virtual dictator** under authority of the *cabildo* of the capital.

1814. A savage *war to the death* ensued in which the royalists, under **José Tomás Boves**, triumphed and re-established Spanish control throughout Venezuela.

Returning to New Granada, Bolívar under authority of the congress of New Granada undertook to conquer the separatist provinces of Cundinamarca, Cartagena, and Santa Marta. He brought Cundinamarca under control of the central government, which then established itself in Bogotá, and besieged Cartagena, preparatory to a campaign against Santa Marta.

1815. While the siege of Cartagéna was progressing, an army of 10,000 Spanish veterans under **Pablo Morillo** landed in Venezuela, the close of the Napoleonic wars having made the dispatch of troops possible. Morillo, leaving a portion of his forces in Venezuela, moved into New Granada and everywhere defeated the revolutionary armies. Bolívar, recognizing the hopelessness of the situation, departed for Jamaica. Acting ruthlessly, Morillo restored royal authority virtually throughout New Granada.

1816. After dispatching a commissioner to England to secure support, **Bolívar returned** to the area of Orinoco.

1818-1819. With the aid of **José Páez** (1790–1873), Bolívar secured control over the lower basin of the Orinoco and established headquarters at Angostura. A congress convened at Angostura elected **Bolívar president** and he presented a constitution to that body.

1819. Leaving Páez to contain Morillo, Bolívar, his army augmented by British volunteers, moved up the valley of the Orinoco, crossed the Andes, defeated a superior royalist army at the **Boyacá River** (Aug. 7), and **occupied Bogotá** (Aug. 10). **New Granada was definitely liberated by this campaign.**

Dec. 17. The **Congress of Angostura,** including representatives of New Granada, proclaimed **Great Colombia,** to be constituted of New Granada, Venezuela, and Quito. A constitution was adopted and Bolívar was made president and military dictator.

1820. The **Spanish Revolution of 1820** caused Ferdinand VII to adopt a conciliatory policy and Morillo was instructed to conclude peace on condition that the revolutionists accept the *Constitution* of 1812, which accorded the colonies representation in the Córtes. A six months' truce was concluded (Nov. 25) and Bolívar dispatched emissaries to Spain under instructions to uphold the independence of Colombia. As the crown refused to acknowledge Colombian independence, war was soon resumed. Morillo meanwhile departed, placing **Miguel de la Torre in command.**

1821. Bolívar dispatched his able lieutenant, **Antonio José de Sucre** (1793–1830), to liberate Quito, moved into Venezuela, uniting with Páez, defeated the royalist army at **Carabobo** (June 24), and occupied Caracas (June 29). The battle of Carabobo assured Venezuelan independence.

Aug. 30. A congress at Cucutá framed a republican constitution and named **Bolívar president.** Bolívar placed Páez in command of the army in Venezuela.

1821-1822. Moving by sea to Guayaquil, **Sucre**, aided by forces sent by San Martín, achieved the liberation of Quito through the decisive **battle of Pichincha** (1822, May 24). Bolívar meanwhile, placing authority in the hands of the vice-president, **Francisco de Paula Santander,** moved to aid Sucre. He persuaded the provinces of Quito to unite with Great Colombia (May 29).

1822, July 26-27. San Martín, who had been advancing on Quito, **and Bolívar met at Guayaquil** to consider prosecution of plans for liberation. Comprehending the ambitions of Bolívar, realizing the impossibility of co-operation, and fearing detriment to the cause of independence, San Martín withdrew in favor of Bolívar.

j. NEW SPAIN (MEXICO)

1808. Events in Spain following the intervention of Napoleon caused creole elements to desire a greater share in government. With support from the viceroy, **José de Iturrigaray**, who hoped to advance his own interests, a general *junta* was convened, despite opposition of the *audiencia*, which, composed of Spaniards, mistrusted the creole elements. Within a short time a group of Spaniards, instigated by the *audiencia*, expelled the viceroy. Four viceroys followed in rapid succession (1808–1813).

The first direct action against Spanish rule was led by **Miguel Hidalgo y Costilla** (1753–1811), a creole priest steeped in French philosophy and interested in the welfare of the native masses.

1810. **Hidalgo**, his object being separation and social reform, initiated a revolt in the province of **Guanajuato** with the support of certain creoles (Sept. 16). Joined by Indians, *mestizos*, and an increasing number of creoles, Hidalgo captured Guanajuato, Guadalajara, and Valladolid and reached the vicinity of the capital, from which his ill-armed horde of 80,000 was forced to retreat by a small Spanish force under **Felix Calleja** (Nov. 6). The movement headed by Hidalgo rapidly assumed the character of a servile revolt, with resultant alienation of the upper classes of the creoles.

1811. Assuming the offensive, **Calleja**, with 6000 men, crushed the revolutionary forces at the **Bridge of Calderón**, near Guadalajara (Jan. 17). Hidalgo and a small remnant fled northward, but the leader fell into Spanish hands, was tried and executed (July 31).

The revolt was continued by **José María Morelos** (1765–1815), a *mestizo* priest, who, as a lieutenant of Hidalgo, had been operating west of Mexico City.

1812. Moving southeast, Morelos secured control of a wide area and captured **Oaxaca** (Nov. 25). Turning westward, he took **Acapulco** (1813, Apr. 12).

1813. A congress was convened at Chilpancingo (Sept. 14), Morelos was made head of the government, **independence was declared** (Nov. 6), and administrative, social, and fiscal reforms were adopted.

1814, Oct. 22. The **Constitution of Apatzingan** was promulgated.

Morelos failed in an attempt to take Valladolid and was forced to retreat by **Agustín de Iturbide** (1783–1824), a creole in Spanish service. The revolutionary cause became increasingly hopeless, reinforcements reached the royalists from Spain, and the government was forced to move frequently.

1815. Morelos, having relinquished executive authority though retaining military command, was captured while escorting the government to Tehuacán and was shortly thereafter executed (Dec.

22). The revolutionary congress was dissolved.

1816–1821. The viceroy, **Juan Ruíz de Apodaca**, instituted a conciliatory policy and secured the surrender of the majority of the revolutionary leaders. Spanish authority was again firmly established, and only certain guerrilla leaders among them **Vicente Guerrero** (1782–1831), continued resistance.

1817. An expedition raised in England and the United States under **Francisco Xavier Mina** landed on the Gulf Coast and penetrated to Guanajuato, but was defeated. Xavier Mina was executed (Nov. 11).

1821. The **Revolution of 1820 in Spain** and the restoration of the Constitution of 1812 menaced the position of the clergy and the upper classes, and reactionary and conservative elements determined upon separation. These groups found an instrument in Iturbide, who concluded with Guerrero the *Plan of Iguala*.

Feb. 24. This **PROCLAIMED THE INDEPENDENCE OF MEXICO,** declared that the government should be a constitutional monarchy under Ferdinand VII or another European prince, guaranteed maintenance of the Roman Catholic religion and the preservation of the position and property of the Church, and urged the union of all classes to support the instrument. The royalists, higher clergy, and prominent creoles supported the movement, an army was formed, and the viceroy Apodaca was deposed.

Aug. 24. The newly arrived viceroy, **Juan O'Donojú**, accepted the Plan of Iguala by the **Convention of Córdoba**. The revolutionary army occupied Mexico City (Sept. 27). A **regency under** Iturbide was formed pending choice of a sovereign. A constituent congress was convened.

1822. The Spanish government refused to accept the Convention of Córdoba.

May 19. **ITURBIDE** induced a section of the congress to elect him emperor. He was crowned **Augustín I** (July 25).

k. GUATEMALA AND CENTRAL AMERICA

1811–1814. Several revolutionary movements occurred in the **captaincy-general of Guatemala** (Guatemala, San Salvador, Honduras, Nicaragua, Costa Rica, and Chiapas), but were speedily suppressed.

1821, Sept. 15. Influenced by events in Mexico a *junta* convened by the captain-general in Guatemala City declared for the independence of the provinces with the royal executive as administrative head. **Iturbide** invited the new state to become a part of Mexico.

1822, Jan. 5. **Guatemala accepted,** but the other provinces, tending toward republicanism, opposed union.

1822. After coronation Iturbide demanded that he be proclaimed emperor in the former captaincy-general and dispatched troops under **Vicente Filísola** to force acceptance of his authority. In **San Salvador,** where opposition to union was especially strong, a congress proposed incorporation into the United States of America (1822, Dec. 2). The other states accepted **inclusion in the Mexican Empire** and coercive action was taken against San Salvador.

1823. Upon the abdication of Augustín I (p. 821), Filísola convened a general constituent assembly in Guatemala City (Feb. 21) in which all provinces except Chiapas, which remained incorporated with Mexico, were represented.

July 1. This body declared the provinces of Guatemala, San Salvador, Nicaragua, Honduras, and Costa Rica sovereign as the confederated **United Provinces of Central America.** Mexico recognized the independence of the United Provinces (Aug. 20).

1. BRAZIL

1820-1822. The immediate causes of **Brazilian independence** arose from a complex combination of circumstances in Portugal and Brazil. The administrative system of the court, the position accorded the Portuguese, and the spread of republican theories, evidenced by a revolt in Pernambuco (1817), created discontent among Brazilians, while in Portugal there was growing dissatisfaction with the British-dominated regency (p. 648), the transfer of government to Brazil, and the opening of Brazil to free trade.

1820. Following the example of Spain, the **Portuguese overthrew the regency** and provisionally adopted the Spanish constitution of 1812. The Córtes, convened for the first time in more than a century, summoned the king to return and invited Brazil to send representatives to a constituent assembly.

1821, Feb.-Apr. Vacillating and fundamentally an absolutist, **John VI** was forced by a military rising to accept the **Portuguese constitution** yet to be promulgated, and to appoint a liberal ministry. Upon the demand of the assembly, convened to select representatives to the Portuguese constituent convention, he later

adhered to the provisional Spanish constitution. After excesses on the part of the Brazilian assembly, the king dispersed it by military action and reversed his position.

Apr. 22-26. Convinced of the ultimate necessity of returning to Portugal, John VI designated his son **Pedro** as prince-regent and departed, thoroughly discredited.

1821-1822. Eventual separation of Brazil from Portugal was hastened by the determination of the Córtes to reduce Brazil once again to the status of a dependency. That body, over the protest of Brazilian representatives, created in Brazil directly responsible provisional administrative councils, ordered the regent to visit Europe to study constitutional forms, subordinated the tribunal of Rio de Janeiro to the supreme court of Portugal, and finally, in effect, re-established the commercial monopoly of Portugal.

1822. Meanwhile **Brazilian national sentiment** crystallized about the regent, who, upon petition of his subjects, declared his determination to remain in Brazil (Jan. 9). A design of the Portuguese commander in Rio de Janeiro to carry the regent to Portugal failed and the garrison was later forced to withdraw. Dom Pedro formed a new ministry (Jan. 16) and decreed that no law of the Córtes be put in effect without his assent (Feb. 21). A Portuguese squadron which arrived to convey the regent to Portugal was forced to withdraw.

1822. Having gained the support of Minas Geráes (Mar.), **Dom Pedro** was declared **Perpetual Defender of Brazil** (May 13). He soon convoked a Brazilian constituent assembly (June 3). A visit to São Paulo secured that province.

Sept. 7. **The Grito de Ypiranga** (Cry of Ypiranga). While *en route* to the city of São Paulo, the regent received dispatches from Portugal which offered concessions but made clear the determination of the Córtes to subordinate Brazil. He therefore **proclaimed Brazilian independence.**

Oct. 12. The regent, upon initiative of the Senate, was proclaimed at Rio de Janeiro **constitutional Emperor of Brazil.** Dom Pedro pledged acceptance of the constitution to be formulated by the already summoned convention. His coronation as **Pedro I** followed (Dec. 1). Armed resistance by Portuguese garrisons and Brazilian elements opposed to separation in certain northern provinces and the Cisplatine Province was overcome by the close of 1823, due in large part to the Brazilian navy, organized by **Lord Cochrane.**

2. LATIN AMERICA, 1825-1914

The movement for independence in the Spanish colonies produced ephemeral cooperation between the states of South America and between Mexico and Central America, and there existed the ideal of union, which was one of the objectives of Bolívar. The individualism of the Spaniard, separatist traditions inherited from Spain, the influence of administrative division during the colonial period (which created rudimentary nationalism and in certain instances cultural entity within the upper classes), geographical and climatic factors, lack of communications, and the personal ambition of individual leaders prevented the achievement of union and cooperation between states.

Orderly progress within nations was rendered difficult by these same factors, by ethnic differences, and by class distinctions and vested interests, which independence from Spain did not eliminate. The Church was determined to maintain its vast influence, interests, and privileged position, and wealth and political power remained the possessions of a small minority. Of the peoples of Spanish America some 19% were whites, 31% *mestizos*, 45% Indians, and 4% Negroes. The vast bulk of the population was abjectly ignorant, and large native groups had scarcely been touched by European culture in other than its religious aspects. The educated upper classes had no experience in government other than that afforded by the municipal *cabildos* and the governmental agencies created during the period of liberation. Military influence, resulting from the long period of wars, was strong.

As there existed no community of interest, political, economic, social, and religious dissension and division into bitterly opposed conservative and liberal reforming groups were inevitable. Conditions after independence demanded firm government and capable administrators. San Martín favored monarchical forms and Bolívar, a man of theoretical democratic and republican beliefs, comprehending the problems involved, advocated compromise between monarchy and republicanism. The majority of the intellectual leaders of the independence movement were impractical, idealistic, and doctrinaire republicans. As a result republican forms, for which the peoples were least prepared, were adopted. Republican leaders were divided among themselves on the question of the unitary as opposed to the federal system.

The conflict of forces within the newly formed states made inevitable a long period of instability and adjustment.

a. ARGENTINA

At the achievement of independence, there existed little feeling of unity in Argentina and a fundamental issue at once arose concerning the adoption of a unitary or federal form of government. Buenos Aires favored a unitary system, while the provinces, controlled by local leaders (*caudillos*) and fearing the preponderance of the capital, favored a federal system. The Argentine provinces wished to include Paraguay and Uruguay within the nation, and this laid the basis for foreign complications.

1825. Hoping to achieve the incorporation of Uruguay, **Argentina** aided in a revolt of that state against **Brazil** and made war on the empire.

1827. Argentine and Uruguayan forces defeated the Brazilians, gaining the decisive **battle of Ituzaingó** (Feb. 20).

1828. Through the **mediation of Great Britain** Uruguay was made an independent buffer state.

1829. Almost constant rebellion in the provinces reduced Argentina to anarchy until **Juan Manuel de Rosas** (1793–1877), a provincial leader and a federalist, became governor of Buenos Aires (Dec. 8) after a victory over its forces in the field (Apr.).

1835. Rosas assumed complete authority in Buenos Aires and twelve provinces recognized him as chief executive. The **Argentine Confederation** thus became a reality. Rosas governed with absolute authority. He sought to raise Argentine prestige abroad. and desired to bring Uruguay and Paraguay into the confederation.

1831-1841. Controversies arose with the United States and Great Britain concerning the **Falkland Islands,** which England claimed, and with France concerning treatment of French subjects. This led to a blockade of the Argentine coast (1838).

1845-1850. Further disputes arose with France and Great Britain concerning **intervention in Uruguay** and the closing

San Francisco

M E X I C O

Rio Grande

Mississippi R.

Gulf of Mexico

Mexico

A T L A N T I C

O C E A N

Cuba

BELIZE

Haiti

Puerto Rico

CENTRAL AMERICA

Caribbean Sea

Panama

Caracas

Venezuela

New Granada

Bogotá

C O L O M B I A

GUIANA

Quito

Quito

Amazon R.

B R A Z I L

P A C I F I C

P E R U

Lima

B O L I V I A

O C E A N

Sucre

PARAGUAY

Rio de Janeiro

Asunción

CISPLATINE PROVINCE

Paraná R.

C H I L E

UNITED PROVINCES OF LA PLATA

Santiago

Montevideo

Buenos Aires

LATIN
AMERICAN
STATES
AFTER THE
REVOLUTIONS

A T L A N T I C

O C E A N

Scale of Miles

0   500   1000   1500

of the Paraná to foreign commerce, and resulted in a **blockade of the Río de la Plata** by English and French naval forces. From these controversies Argentina emerged with credit, although the position of Rosas was weakened thereby.

1851. The tyrannical rule of Rosas caused internal opposition, led by **Justo José de Urquiza** (1800-1870), and his intervention in Uruguay aroused the enmity of Brazil.

1852. In alliance with Uruguay and Brazil, Urquiza overthrew Rosas in the **battle of Caseros** (Feb. 3). Despite its drawbacks, the arbitrary régime of Rosas constituted a necessary period of transition between anarchy and constitutional organization. Argentine designs on Uruguay were henceforth relinquished.

1853. **Urquiza** became chief executive and a **federal constitution,** to which Buenos Aires refused to adhere, was promulgated (May 1). A president with a six-year term, a bicameral congress, and an independent judiciary were provided by the instrument.

1854. Buenos Aires drew up a separate constitution (Apr. 12). Both Buenos Aires and the provinces of the federation progressed materially, but fundamental antagonism led to war between the federation and Buenos Aires (1859).

1859. The latter was speedily defeated (Oct. 22) and agreed to union with the federation under constitutional amendments (Nov. 10).

1862. Efforts to adjust differences failed and **Bartolomé Mitre** (1821-1906), governor of Buenos Aires, upon the withdrawal of Urquiza from politics after the indecisive engagement of **Pavón** (1861, Sept. 17), became head of the national government (1862, Aug. 27).

These events gave Buenos Aires ascendancy over the remainder of the nation, and the city was made the national capital for a period of five years. Under Mitre administrative reforms were carried out, material progress continued, and education was promoted. Insurrections in several provinces were suppressed.

1865, May 1. Argentina concluded an alliance with Uruguay and Brazil.

1865-1870. **WAR WITH PARAGUAY.** Dictator López declared war after Argentina refused to permit passage of Paraguayan troops across national territory (p. 810). Mitre commanded the allied forces during the first two years of the war.

1868-1880. During the administrations of Domingo Sarmiento (1868-1874) and Nicolás Avellaneda (1874-1880) edu-

cation, commerce, and immigration were encouraged and the southern frontiers were advanced through subjugation of Indian groups. The first census indicated a population of over 1,700,000 (1869).

1880. The ascendancy of Buenos Aires, the province including 30% of the population, created dissatisfaction in the provinces and they formed the **League of Córdoba,** supporting **Julio Roca** for the presidency. Buenos Aires resorted to civil war to maintain its position, but was defeated (July 20-21). The city of Buenos Aires was erected into a federal district and made the national capital, and the province was made co-ordinate with the remainder. Roca became president (Sept. 21). Thus the problem of the relation of the city and province of Buenos Aires to the remainder of the nation was solved.

1880-1886. Under Roca economic progress continued, and the Indian frontiers were pushed forward.

1886-1890. Excessive speculation and corruption, for which President **Miguel Juárez Celman** was largely responsible, aroused demands for reform. A new party, the *Unión Cívica,* was formed (1890) to achieve this and secure a wider franchise.

1890. An unsuccessful revolt occurred (July 26-27), but **Celman resigned** (Aug. 5) and the vice-president, **Cárlos Pellegrini,** assumed office.

1890-1904. Pellegrini (1890-1892), Luis Sáenz Peña (1892-1895), José Uriburu (1895-1898), and Julio Roca (1898-1904) carried on the task of economic rehabilitation. **Boundary disputes** with Brazil (1895) and Chile (1899, 1902), the latter leading the two nations to the verge of war, were adjusted by arbitration.

1904-1910. The administrations of **Manuel Quintana** (1904-1906) and **José Figueroa Alcorta** (1906-1910) were characterized by labor difficulties and a demand on the part of Radicals for increased suffrage.

1910-1913. **Roque Sáenz Peña,** president. Secret voting and universal suffrage were instituted (1912).

(*Cont. p.* 1064.)

b. CHILE

1818-1823. Supreme Director **Bernardo O'Higgins** (p. 801) laid the foundations of the Chilean state and established a highly centralized government.

1823-1827. Opposition developed and Ramón Freire became chief executive. A federalist form of government was adopted (1826).

1827. In face of discontent Freire resigned in favor of Vice-President Francisco Antonio Pinto. A second federalistic constitution was promulgated (1828). A Liberal Party, advocating democracy and local autonomy, and a Conservative, supported by the upper classes and clergy, advocating a centralized system with a strong executive authority, developed.

1829-1830. Civil war ensued. The Conservatives, under leadership of Diego José Victor Portáles (1793–1837), were victorious (1830, Apr. 17), and entered into a long period of power (to 1861).

1833. A highly centralized constitution, which accorded great powers to the president, was adopted. Roman Catholicism remained the state religion.

1836. Chile opposed the formation of the preponderant Peruvian-Bolivian Confederation by Santa Cruz, and declared war (Nov. 11).

1839. Chilean troops under Manuel Búlnes (1799–1866) overthrew the confederation through the decisive battle of Yungay (Jan. 20).

1841-1851. During the two administrations of Búlnes great internal development took place and steps were taken to extend Chilean sovereignty over the area of the Straits of Magellan. A new Liberal Party, opposed to Conservative oligarchical control and advocating curtailment of presidential powers, developed.

1851-1861. Manuel Montt (1809–1880) succeeded Búlnes and served two terms. Material progress continued, education was promoted, and certain liberal reforms, which alienated reactionaries, were adopted. Two Liberal revolts were suppressed.

1861-1871. With the support of Montt, José Joaquín Pérez, acceptable to the Liberals, was elected. This marked a movement toward greater democracy and a shift of power in favor of the commercial and intellectual elements. Pérez held office for two terms, during which internal development increased and Chilean capital was invested in Peru and Bolivia for exploitation of guano and nitrate. The lands of the Araucanian Indians were made part of the national domain following their final subjugation.

1865. Chile united with Peru in war against Spain (p. 813), and Valparaiso was bombarded (1866).

1871-1876. During the administration of the Liberal Federico Errázuriz education was promoted, anti-clerical reforms were adopted, administrative reforms tending toward increased democratization were introduced, and material progress continued.

1876-1881. Financial problems and war with Peru and Bolivia (pp. 812, 813) developed during the term of Aníbal Pinto (1876–1881), who was followed by Domingo Santa María (1881–1886).

1879-1883. Chile was completely victorious in the War of the Pacific because of superior governmental efficiency and military and naval supremacy, and emerged unquestionably the dominant power of western South America.

1883, Oct. 20. By the Treaty of Ancón, Peru ceded the province of Tarapacá, and Chile was to occupy Tacna and Arica for ten years, after which a plebiscite was to be held.

1884, Apr. 4. By the Treaty of Valparaiso Chile retained possession of the Bolivian littoral. Chile thus gained rich nitrate territories of vast importance to the national economic structure. After termination of the war religious and administrative reforms were adopted, but efforts to separate Church and State failed. The reforms of Santa María aroused much Conservative opposition, and the Liberal Party became divided.

1886. José Manuel Balmaceda followed in the presidency. Parliamentary principles had been evolved (although not envisaged in the constitution) by which a ministry might not remain in office without the support of a majority in Congress. Balmaceda maintained full presidential prerogatives.

1891. Civil war ensued (Jan.) in which the Congressional forces were victorious and the parliamentary principle was established. Balmaceda, driven from office, committed suicide (Sept. 19). Congressional elements were incensed by supposed sympathy of the United States for Balmaceda and when an attack on members of the crew of the *U.S.S. Baltimore* occurred (Oct. 16) at Valparaiso an acrimonious controversy arose. This was adjusted upon agreement by Chile to pay an indemnity.

1891-1896. Jorge Montt, head of the Congressional Party, was made president, and financial and administrative reforms, including the establishment of a large degree of local autonomy, were adopted.

1896-1901. Federico Errázuriz, son of the former president, succeeded Montt. Efforts to solve the territorial question arising out of the War of the Pacific failed. Boundary disputes with Argentina were submitted to arbitration, although war was but narrowly averted.

1901. The Liberal Party, which had lost prestige as a result of the civil war of 1891, regained strength and secured the election of Germán Riesco. The Conservative Party declined thereafter.

1906-1920. During the administrations of Pedro Montt (1906-1911), Ramón Barros Lucca (1911-1915), and Juan Luis Sanfuentes (1915-1920) internal progress took place. The population reached 3,000,000 by 1907.   *(Cont. p. 1064.)*

c. PARAGUAY

1816-1840. José Rodríguez de Francia, Perpetual Dictator of Paraguay (1816) (p. 801), assumed absolute governmental authority and made himself head of the Paraguayan Church. Fearing Argentina, he isolated the country, developed a strong army, and created an intense national feeling. The power of the Church and the influence of the upper classes were broken, and Francia readily established his unlimited control over the docile Guaraní, who constituted the vast bulk of the population. Agriculture (into which state socialism was introduced) and industry were encouraged.

1844-1862. After the death of Francia the government was reorganized and commercial relations were established with other nations. Paraguayan independence was reaffirmed (1842). Cárlos López (1790-1862) became president (1844) and remained in office with dictatorial powers for the remainder of his life. He asserted Paraguayan territorial claims against Argentina and Brazil and peacefully adjusted disputes with the United States, France, and Great Britain. After the fall of Rosas (1852) the danger of incorporation into Argentina disappeared. Commerce, agriculture, and industry were encouraged, and a system of primary schools was established. The first railway was constructed. The population increased to over 1,000,-000.

1862-1870. Francisco Solano López (1827-1870), son of Cárlos López, was made president (1862) and immediately established absolute control. López desired

territory and perhaps envisaged a **Greater Paraguay** which would include Uruguay and the Argentine provinces of **Corrientes** and **Entre Ríos.** He also feared Argentina and Brazil. The army was made the largest and most efficient in South America, and a system of defenses was erected.

1865-1870. The ambitions of López, Brazilian intervention in Uruguay in support of the *Colorados* while López supported the *Blancos* (p. 811), and unsettled territorial claims led to overt acts by the Paraguayan dictator which brought about **war with Brazil, Argentina, and Uruguay** under the *Colorado* government of Flores (Mar. 18). Brazil, Argentina, and Uruguay concluded an alliance, and a large army, of which the greatest part was Brazilian, supported by a Brazilian fleet, invaded Paraguay. After five years of large-scale operations, the Paraguayan nation, despite its valiant resistance, was virtually annihilated and the war terminated when López was killed (1870, Mar. 1). The population was reduced to some 28,000 men and slightly over 200,000 women. After the **occupation of Asunción** by the allies (1868, Dec. 31), a provisional government was established, a treaty of peace was concluded (1870, June 20), and a centralized constitution was adopted (Nov. 25). Paraguay lost some 55,000 square miles of claimed territory, and was saved from greater losses only by Brazilian support against Argentine claims (1872-1876).

1878. Argentina and Paraguay submitted certain territorial claims to arbitration of President Hayes of the United States, who decided in favor of the latter. Heavy indemnities imposed on Paraguay by the treaty of peace were never paid, and the allies did not press for action.

1879. Attempts of Bolivia and Paraguay to adjust territorial claims failed.

1872-1912. The close of the Paraguayan War was followed by a long period of political instability. The *Colorado* or Radical Party, without clearly defined principles, was in control throughout the greater part of this period.

(Cont. p. 1065.)

d. URUGUAY

1828, Aug. 27. Uruguay became a sovereign nation under the treaty which terminated the war between Brazil and Argentina over the status of the **Banda Oriental.** A constitution was framed for the Banda Oriental del Uruguay, and in accord with the treaty this instrument was approved by Brazil and Argentina (1830, May 26).

1836-1843. Factional strife developed and two parties, *Blancos* and *Colorados*, evolved, headed respectively by **Manuel Oribe** and **Fructuoso Rivera.** Rosas, dictator of Argentina, with his expansionist policy (p. 806), supported Oribe, and Rivera was aided by French forces.

1843-1851. Upon withdrawal of the latter, following agreement between the French consul and Rosas, Oribe began an eight years' **siege of Montevideo.** During the period of the blockade of the Río de la Plata, French and British troops occupied Uruguayan territory as a check to Rosas (1845-1849). Efforts to resolve the situation in the Banda Oriental by negotiation were fruitless.

1851. After the conclusion of an alliance between Urquiza, the *Colorado* government, and Brazil (**May** 29), Urquiza forced Oribe to abandon the siege of Montevideo and concluded a treaty which terminated the war and permitted the *Colorado* government to remain in power (Oct. 8). The overthrow of Rosas (1852) removed a serious menace to Uruguayan independence.

1851. Seeking to expand its influence, **Brazil** secured a portion of the **Misiones** territory from Uruguay and intervened to maintain order at the request of the *Colorado* president, **Venancio Flores** (1854).

1863. Internal disorders continued and evolved into a prolonged civil war between the *Blanco* president, **Anastasio Aguirre,** and **Flores.** Brazil pressed claims for injuries to her nationals and when Aguirre proved intransigent an agreement was reached with Flores. Brazilian forces occupied certain Uruguayan frontier towns (1864-1865).

1865. Flores occupied Montevideo and assumed the government (Feb. 22). As **Francisco Solano López,** dictator of Paraguay, had an understanding with Aguirre, these events did much to bring on the **Paraguayan War** (pp. 810, 817), in which Uruguay under a *Colorado* government was allied with Brazil and Argentina (1865-1870).

1870-1872. A protracted civil conflict between *Blancos* and *Colorados*, in which the latter were victorious, followed the war.

1872-1907. Political instability, with many changes of executive, continued through the first decade of the twentieth century. During this entire period the *Colorados* remained in power. Despite political instability, great material progress took place: agriculture became highly developed, commerce expanded, and an extensive railway system was built. The foundations of a system of public education were laid. The population, estimated at 70,000 in 1830, increased to 224,000 by 1860, and almost 1,000,000 by 1900.

(*Cont. p.* 1066.)

e. BOLIVIA

1825-1826. **Bolívar** and **Sucre** organized the government of Bolivia and launched the nation on its career as a sovereign state. Peru recognized the independence of Bolivia (1826) and Bolivian claims to territory on the coast from Cape Sama to the Loa River (1828).

1828. **Antonio José Sucre,** president after the departure of Bolívar for Colombia, was forced to withdraw as a result of discontent in Bolivia and an invasion of Peruvian troops.

1829. **Andrés Santa Cruz** became president, and, with the collaboration of Orbegosa of Peru, **united Bolivia and Peru** (divided into North and South Peru) into a confederation (1835-1836).

1839. **Argentina and Chile** opposed the creation of a preponderant confederation, and Chilean troops under Búlnes defeated the forces of Santa Cruz at **Yungay** (Jan. 20) and brought the union to an end.

1841. An attempt of **President Gamarra** of Peru to annex Bolivian territory during the presidency of José **Ballivián** was thwarted when his invading army was defeated at **Ingavi** and he himself was killed (Nov. 20).

1841-1847. Ballivián sought to promote economic development. He was forced from office by **Manuel Belzu,** who was succeeded by Jorge Córdova (1855).

1857. José María Linares drove Córdova from the presidency and took office. Linares introduced many governmental reforms. He was forced to relinquish office and was succeeded by **José de Achá** (1861), who was unable to preserve order and gave way to **Mariano Melgarejo** (1864).

1866. A treaty was concluded with Chile by which Bolivia ceded the territory between the Salado River and parallel 24° from the Andes to the Pacific and accorded economic privileges. Bolivia also recognized Brazilian claims to a large area on the Madeira and Paraguay Rivers (1867).

1870. Melgarejo was forced from office. **Agustín Morales** became president, but was killed, and **Adolfo Ballivián**

took office (1872). Ballivián sought to reform finances and concluded an alliance with Peru (1873, Feb. 6).

1874-1876. During the administration of **Tomás Frías** the **boundary between Bolivia and Chile** was fixed at parallel 24° (1874). Bolivia agreed that Chileans might engage in mining industry for 25 years without additional taxation.

1876-1880. Hilarión **Daza** became president after a *coup d'état* (1876). An additional tax was placed on nitrate exported from the Bolivian littoral (1878) and the **Chilean Nitrate Company** of Antofagasta appealed to the Chilean government. Despite negotiations Bolivia decided temporarily to rescind the contract of the nitrate company.

1879, Feb. 14. Chilean troops occupied Antofagasta and Bolivia proclaimed a state of war. Peru refused to guarantee neutrality and Chile declared war on the allies (Apr. 5).

1879-1884. WAR OF THE PACIFIC. Chilean troops, everywhere successful, occupied the entire Bolivian littoral, Tarapacá, Tacna, and Arica (1879). **Daza** was overthrown (1880) and **Narciso Campero** took office. Hostilities between Bolivia and Chile were terminated by the **Treaty of Valparaiso** (1884, Apr. 4), which provided for an indefinite truce, Chilean control of Atacama for the life of the agreement, and tariff concessions by Bolivia. Bolivia thus ceded territory rich in nitrate and lost access to the sea.

1888-1892. During the period of office of **Aniceto Arce** a railway was opened between Antofagasta and Oruro, affording Bolivia access to the coast by rail.

1892-1896. Mariano **Baptista** succeeded Arce. Two agreements with Chile envisaging the granting to Bolivia of access to the sea were ratified (1895, May 18, Dec. 9), but not put in effect.

1898. Following an attempt of Conservatives to erect Sucre into a permanent capital, a **revolt headed by José Pando** occurred in La Paz (Nov. 6) which had shared the status of the seat of government with Sucre and other cities. Pando became president (1899).

1899. Brazilians who had entered the rubber-producing **Arce** district proclaimed a separate state (July).

1903. By the **Treaty of Petropolis** (Nov. 17) Bolivia ceded the territory to Brazil and the latter undertook to provide Bolivia with rail and water outlet eastward through construction of a railway around the cataracts of the Madeira.

1904-1909. During the presidency of **Ismael Montes** education and railway construction were encouraged and finances were improved. Public worship of religions other than Roman Catholicism was permitted.

1904, Oct. 20. A treaty between Bolivia and Chile formally terminated the **War of the Pacific**, recognized Chilean possession of the littoral, and provided for the construction by Chile of a railway to connect Arica and La Paz, the Bolivian portion to be turned over to Bolivia 15 years after completion. In a supplementary protocol (Nov. 15), **Bolivia recognized Chilean sovereignty** over the territory between parallels 23° and 24°.

1909-1913. Eleodoro **Villazón** promoted economic development. In the administration of Montes, again president (1913–1917), material progress continued.

1913. The boundary between Bolivia and Argentina was adjusted, and efforts were made to determine the limits with Paraguay.

(*Cont. p.* 1067.)

f. PERU

1825-1826. Bolívar as head of the state aided in the governmental organization of Peru and upon completion of his task departed for Colombia.

1827. José de Lamar as president adopted an expansionist policy, intervened in the affairs of Bolivia, despite recognition of Bolivian independence, and sought to annex southern Colombian provinces. Invading Peruvian troops aided in forcing Sucre to withdraw from Bolivia (1828). A Peruvian fleet took **Guayaquil** (1829, Jan. 21), but the Peruvian army of invasion was defeated by Sucre at **Tarqui** (Feb. 27) and Guayaquil was soon retaken (Feb. 28). The plans of Lamar for northern expansion were thus thwarted.

1835-1839. During civil strife, while **Luis Orbegosa** was president, **Santa Cruz** with the collaboration of Orbegosa established the Peruvian-Bolivian Confederation which was brought to an end by the **battle of Yungay** (p. 811).

1841. Expansionist aims caused President **Agustín Gamarra** to invade Bolivia, but he was defeated and killed at **Ingavi** (Nov. 20).

1842-1845. Civil War followed, from which **Ramón Castilla** (1797–1867) emerged as head of the state, remaining virtual dictator for 15 years.

1845-1862. Castilla established order, sought to stabilize finances, promoted internal development, including exploitation of guano and nitrate, and adopted administrative, religious, and social reforms.

1863-1865. During the administration of Juan Antonio Pezet a long-standing controversy with Spain, which had not acknowledged Peruvian independence, came to the fore. After unsuccessful negotiations a Spanish fleet seized the Chincha Islands (1864, Apr. 14). Pezet concluded a treaty (1865, Jan. 27) by which Spain virtually recognized the independence of Peru, but which contained provisions which aroused the resentment of his countrymen. He was consequently driven from office.

1865. Mariano Prado became president and declared war on Spain (1866, Jan. 14). Alliances were concluded with Chile, Bolivia, and Ecuador. After blockading allied ports and attacking Valparaiso and Callao, the Spanish fleet abandoned hostilities (May 9). An armistice was later arranged through mediation of the United States (1871), and separate treaties of peace were signed.

1868, Jan. 7. While the war with Spain was in progress Prado was overthrown and Pedro Diáz Campero became president. He was followed by José Balta (1868-1872), who undertook an extensive program of internal developments, but created a serious financial situation through heavy expenditures and the contracting of large foreign loans.

1872. Balta was driven from office and murdered (July 26) and was succeeded by Manuel Pardo (1872-1876). Education was promoted and governmental reforms were adopted. The financial situation created by Balta led to governmental bankruptcy.

1873, Feb. 6. Peru and Bolivia concluded a secret treaty of alliance, and when the conflict over Atacama arose between Chile and Bolivia (pp. 809, 812), Peru, under the presidency of Mariano Prado, unsuccessfully sought to mediate. After Peru refused to proclaim neutrality, Chile declared war.

1879-1884. WAR OF THE PACIFIC. Chile was completely victorious: Tarapacá, Tacna, and Arica were occupied, the navy gained undisputed control of the sea, and Lima was taken by an army landed on the coast (1879-1881). The United States sought in vain to mediate between the belligerents.

1883, Oct. 20. Chile concluded the Treaty of Ancón with the government of Miguel Iglesias. By this treaty Peru ceded the nitrate province of Tarapacá and Chile was to remain in possession of Tacna and Arica for 10 years, after which a plebiscite was to be held to determine final disposition. The war brought Peru to the verge of national collapse and a long period of attempted readjustment followed.

1885-1890. Under the administration of Andrés Cáceres the foreign debt was funded and assumed by the Peruvian Corporation, a society of bondholders, in return for the cession of railways and guano deposits for a period of 66 years. Attempts to adjust the question of Tacna and Arica failed, and the 10-year period elapsed without a plebiscite.

1895-1899. Nicolás de Piérola became president after a period of instability, and during his administration monetary reforms were initiated and unsuccessful attempts were made to determine the question of Tacna and Arica.

1899-1903. Under his successor, Eduardo de Romaña, boundary disputes with Ecuador and Brazil developed, and American interests began development of the copper deposits of Cerro de Pasco. A vigorous stand was taken against possible loss of Tacna and Arica, and this was continued by succeeding presidents.

1908-1912. During the administration of Augusto Leguía (1863-1932), Chile having adopted an intransigent attitude, diplomatic relations between Peru and Chile were severed (1910, Mar. 21). While Leguía was in office Peru acknowledged Brazilian sovereignty over a portion of the Arce region and concluded a boundary treaty with Bolivia (1911), which established the basis of a permanent adjustment.

(*Cont. p.* 1068.)

g. ECUADOR

1822-1830. After the liberation of Quito (p. 803), the territory, in accord with the plans of Bolívar, was incorporated into Great Colombia. A movement for independence developed before the death of Bolívar.

1830, May 13. The Republic of Ecuador was created, with Juan Flores (1801-1864) as president (1830-1835). Opposition to separation in Guayaquil was overcome, and by treaty Cauca, which had adhered to Ecuador, was restored to New Granada and the Carchi River was declared the boundary (1832, Dec. 8). Flores became the leader of the Conservative element and Vincente Rocafuerte (1783-1847) of the Liberal.

1834, July. After civil war a compromise political arrangement was reached by the two leaders.

1835-1843. During the administrations of Rocafuerte (1835-1839) and Flores (1839-1843) administrative and social reforms were adopted and material progress was fostered. Upon the re-election of Flores under a new constitution (1843, Apr. 1), Rocafuerte went into exile.

1845, Mar. 6. Flores was overthrown by a Liberal revolt. A period of political instability and foreign complications ensued (1845-1860).

1856, July 9. During this period a portion of the boundary between Ecuador and New Granada was fixed, and Peruvian naval forces blockaded Guayaquil (1860).

1860. After the revolutionist leader Franco had been driven from Guayaquil (Sept. 24), Gabriel García Moreno (1821-1875), an extreme conservative, who was convinced of the supremacy of the Roman Church over all earthly powers, became president (1861).

1861-1875. He dominated Ecuador until his assassination. A new constitution according wide powers to the president was promulgated (1861, Apr. 10). Moreno governed with absolute authority. Order was restored and insurrections were ruthlessly suppressed, internal improvements were carried out, and financial, military, and administrative reforms were introduced.

1862, Sept. 26. A concordat was concluded with the papacy by which the Church was granted great authority, influence, and wide privileges.

1863. President Mosquera of New Granada (p. 815) invited Ecuadorians to overthrow Moreno, and Flores led an army into New Granada, but was defeated (Dec. 6). A treaty restored the *status quo.*

1865-1866. Ecuador united with Peru and Chile against Spain (pp. 809, 813).

1869. A new constitution granting extensive powers to the executive and assuring the position of the Church was adopted (June 9). Toward the close of his career Moreno became increasingly proclerical and Ecuador became virtually a theocracy.

1875-1895. A period of political instability, characterized by strife between Liberals, who sought to restrict the influence of the Church, and Conservatives followed the death of Moreno.

1895-1916. During the administrations of the Liberals Eloy Alfaro (1895-

1901; 1907-1911) and Leonidas Plaza Gutiérrez (1901-1905; 1912-1916) relatively liberal constitutions were adopted (1897, 1906) and the authority, privileges, and influence of the Church were greatly restricted.

1904, May 6. Ecuador recognized Brazilian claims over territory between the Caquetá and Amazón, but efforts to adjust the boundary with Peru were but partially successful.

1908. A railway between Guayaquil and Quito was completed.

1916-1924. Comparative tranquillity existed during the second term of Plaza Gutiérrez and the administration of Alfredo Baquerizo Moreno (1916-1920).

(*Cont. p.* 1068.)

h. COLOMBIA (NEW GRANADA)

Great Colombia as established by Bolívar comprised the viceroyalty of New Granada, the captaincy-general of Venezuela, and the presidency of Quito.

1829-1830. Separatist movements in Venezuela (1829-1830) and Quito (1830) brought the confederation to an end despite the efforts of Bolívar, who, the center of controversy, retired to Santa Marta and soon died (1830, Dec. 17).

1831, Nov. 17. New Granada was declared a separate state, and a centralized constitution was adopted (1832, Feb. 29). Political dissension in New Granada had developed with independence.

1832. Colonial traditions caused reactionary tendencies, the Church was powerful, and sectional rivalry and geography made difficult the attainment of unity. Two parties, almost equal in strength, arose, the Conservative, favoring a centralized administration, the Church, and class privilege, and the Liberal, advocating federalism, secularization, disestablishment, religious toleration, and extended suffrage.

1832-1837. Francisco de Paula Santander (1792-1840), a Conservative, executive while Bolívar was engaged in the liberation of Quito, Peru, and Bolivia, and president of New Granada after the disruption of Great Colombia, was confronted by forces of disunity which he was unable to control.

1837-1842. During the administration of his successor, José de Márquez, a period of civil wars began. Order was temporarily restored by Pedro Herrán, who followed Márquez, and a new centralized constitution was adopted (1842).

1845-1849. During the administration of Tomás Mosquera (1798-1876), a Conservative, a commercial treaty was concluded with the United States by which that government was granted right of transit across the Isthmus of Panama and guaranteed the neutrality of, and New Granadan sovereignty over, that area (1846, Dec. 12).

1849-1853. José López, a Liberal, succeeded Mosquera. Slavery was abolished with compensation for the owners (1851-1852) and Colombian rivers were opened to foreign commerce (1852). A liberal and federalistic constitution was adopted (1853, May 28) during the term of José María Obando (1853-1854), a Liberal, and laws were enacted to separate Church and State (June).

1854, Apr. As the result of a conservative movement Obando was removed and the vice-president, Manuel Mallarino, assumed office. A railway across Panama was completed (1855).

1855, Feb. 27. Panama was given a federal status by a constitutional amendment, which also provided that other provinces might establish that form.

1858. Certain provinces assumed a federal organization and, during the presidency of Mariano Ospina (1857-1861), a federal constitution, which failed to define the powers of the central government, was adopted (Apr. 1), the republic being designated the Granadan Confederation.

1860. Opposing legislation which assigned the central government certain powers in local affairs, Mosquera, who had become a Liberal and governor of Cauca, declared that state independent. Other states took similar action.

1861. Civil war ensued, and Mosquera occupied Bogotá and assumed the presidency (July 18).

1861-1863. Religious reforms were adopted, a congress proclaimed the union of seven sovereign states as the United States of Colombia, and a new federal constitution was promulgated (1863, May 8).

1867. Mosquera quarreled with the Liberal Party and his policies became dictatorial. He was exiled.

1867-1880. The ensuing administrations were characterized by civil war, impotence on the part of the central government, disorganized finances, and increasing opposition of the Conservatives, who became a clerical and traditionalist party.

1878, May 18. A concession for 99 years was granted a French company to construct a canal across Panama.

1880-1898. With Liberal support Rafael Núnez (1825-1894) became president (1880-1882) and introduced economic reforms. After the administration of F. J. Zaldúa (1882-1884) Núnez again became president (1884). He advocated complete reorganization of the nation and became the head of a new group, the Nationalists, composed of Conservatives and Independents. A Liberal revolt (1885, Jan.-Aug.) was suppressed. These events marked a triumph for conservatism, centralized government, and clericalism.

1886, Aug. 4. A centralized constitution was adopted and a concordat was concluded with the papacy (1887, Dec. 31) which accorded the Church a privileged position. Núnez was re-elected (1892), but the vice-president, Miguel Caro, actually exercised authority. Upon the death of Núnez (1894), Caro became president.

1898-1900. During the presidency of Miguel Sanclemente, a Liberal revolt occurred (1899-1900). Vice-President José Marroquín, a Conservative, forced Sanclemente from office (1900, July 31) and assumed authority.

1900-1903. A prolonged civil war ended with a victory of the Conservatives.

1902. The French company, headed by Ferdinand de Lesseps, had begun work on the canal across Panama (1881), but had become bankrupt (1891) and a new company sought to sell the assets (1902).

1903, Jan. 22. Freed from the Clayton-Bulwer Treaty (p. 818), the United States and Colombia negotiated the Hay-Herrán Treaty according to the former canal rights and lease of territory. Colombia delayed ratification.

Nov. 3. The Panamanian elements, fearing choice by the United States of the alternate Nicaraguan route and assured of American support, proclaimed an independent republic. American warships prevented Colombian forces from landing to quell the movement, and the United States recognized the independence of Panama (Nov. 6). These events aroused Colombia, which was unsuccessful in an attempt to secure redress. Colombia refused to recognize the independence of Panama.

1904-1909. Rafael Reyes succeeded Marroquín and governed dictatorially. Efforts were made to reorganize the finances.

1907, Apr. 24. Colombia relinquished to Brazil disputed territory about the mouth of the **Caquetá River** and the headwaters of the **Río Negro.**

1909, Jan. 9. The conclusion of a **convention with the United States** which involved recognition of Panama and abrogation of the Treaty of 1846 aroused resentment, and **Reyes was forced to resign** (July 8).

1910-1914. During the administration of **Carlos Restrepo** educational and governmental reforms, including minority representation in congress and the cabinet (provided for by a law of 1906), were placed in effect and efforts were made to rehabilitate the finances.

1914-1918. José **Concha** succeeded Restrepo.

1914, Apr. 6. The **Thomson-Urrutia Treaty,** by which the United States expressed regret for the differences which had arisen with Colombia, accorded transportation privileges on the Isthmus, and agreed to pay Colombia $25,000,000, and by which Colombia recognized the independence of Panama, was ratified by Colombia, but not by the United States Senate. *(Cont. p.* 1069.)

i. VENEZUELA

1830, Sept. 22. Separatist sentiment increased rapidly in Venezuela after the creation of Great Colombia, and under the leadership of **José Páez** the state was made sovereign.

1830-1846. As president, Páez maintained order, stimulated internal development and commerce, and promulgated religious and administrative reforms. The oligarchic group which controlled Venezuela during the early period became known as the Conservative Party and about 1840 a Liberal opposition made its appearance. The Conservatives advocated a centralized system of government and the Liberals a federal.

1846-1850. José **Tadeo Monagas,** a Conservative elected with support of Páez, appointed a Liberal ministry and became involved in difficulties with congress, whereupon Páez led an unsuccessful revolt and was driven into exile (1850).

1851-1855. Under the presidency of **José Gregorio Monagas,** who succeeded his brother José Tadeo, slavery was abolished with recompense to owners (1854).

1855-1858. José **Tadeo Monagas** again became president. The issue of centralized government as opposed to federal led to civil strife.

1861, Mar. Páez, invited to return, became dictator.

1863-1864. The Federalists gained the ascendancy and an agreement was reached under which Páez relinquished office, a Federalist constitution was promulgated, and the leader of the Federalists, **Juan Falcón,** became president.

1870-1888. After a further period of civil war **Antonio Guzmán Blanco,** a Liberal, assumed authority and controlled Venezuela, directly or through delegates, for 18 years. During this period he was upon several occasions absent in Europe. Internal development was encouraged, administrative and religious reforms were adopted, and two constitutions were promulgated (1874, 1881), the second of which provided for a president elected for two years by a federal council constituted of state representatives.

1889. Reaction against his rule while he was in Europe led to the elimination of Guzmán Blanco from Venezuelan affairs (Oct.).

1892. The attempt of president **Raimundo Anduza Palacio** (1890–1892) to prolong his term beyond the constitutional period led to his overthrow by **Joaquín Crespo** (June 17), who became president under a new constitution (1894).

1895-1896. A serious **boundary dispute with Great Britain** concerning the limits of British Guiana caused the United States to protest vigorously to London under the Monroe Doctrine, and, after a serious crisis had arisen, the dispute was submitted to arbitration (p. 786). The award was largely favorable to Great Britain, but Venezuelan sovereignty over territory at mouth of the Orinoco was confirmed (1899, Oct. 3).

1899. After a successful revolt (May 23–Oct.) against the successor of Crespo, **Cipriano Castro** assumed authority (Oct. 23).

1902, Dec. Claims of nationals because of injuries during revolutionary disturbances caused **Great Britain, Germany, and Italy to institute a naval blockade** of Venezuelan ports. Pressure upon the European powers by the United States led to submission of the claims to arbitration (1903, Feb. 13).

1908. Refusal of Castro to give compensation for injuries to American citizens caused the **United States to suspend diplomatic relations** (June 23). Charges that political refugees were being harbored on the island of Curaçao caused Castro to dismiss the Dutch minister (July 22). The **Netherlands thereupon blockaded** Venezuelan ports (Nov. 7).

1909. While Castro was absent in Europe the vice-president, **Juan Vicente Gómez**, made himself president (Dec. 19). (*Cont. p.* 1070.)

j. BRAZIL

1822-1831. THE REIGN OF PEDRO I. Dissension and opposition arose in the constituent assembly convoked before the declaration of independence.

1823. Dom Pedro dissolved the assembly and promulgated a constitution (1824, Mar. 25).

1824, July 2. Discontent with the acts of the emperor caused the formation of the **Confederation of the Equator** by certain northern provinces, with republican intent, but this movement was suppressed (Sept. 17).

1825. Opposition to Brazilian rule had never disappeared from the **Cisplatine Province** (Banda Oriental), and Argentina desired its incorporation.

1825-1828. War between Brazil and Argentina resulted from an independence movement in the Banda Oriental (1825) and the desire of Argentina to annex that territory. Brazil was decisively defeated in the battle of Ituzaingo (1827, Feb. 20). Through the mediation of Great Britain the Banda Oriental, or **Uruguay**, became independent (1828, Aug. 27).

Opposition to Pedro I arose from his autocratic tendencies, his preference for Portuguese advisers, and, most important, his attempts to secure his daughter **María da Gloria** on the Portuguese throne and his consequent interest in the affairs of Portugal. The loss of the Cisplatine Province increased his unpopularity.

1831, Apr. 7. In face of this opposition he was forced to abdicate in favor of his five-year-old son, **Pedro de Alcantara, Pedro II** (1825-1891).

1831-1840. The regency. During this period anarchy reigned because of factional quarrels and provincial revolts, the most serious of which was a separatist movement in **Rio Grande do Sul** (1835-1845). To re-establish direct monarchical government Pedro II was proclaimed of age (1840).

1840-1889. THE REIGN OF PEDRO II. The provincial revolts were brought to a close and a period of order and progress was initiated, control alternating constitutionally between the Liberal and Conservative Parties.

Great **material progress** took place after 1850. Agriculture, commerce, and industry expanded, railway construction, encouraged by the government, was carried on (about 650 miles in 1870 and over 6000 miles in 1889). Coffee production greatly increased, stock-raising remained important in the south, and sugar production in the north. Rubber production in the Amazon Basin became important after 1880. In 1850 the estimated population was 8,000,000, including 2,500,000 slaves; in 1872 over 10,000,000, including 1,500,000 slaves; and in 1889 over 14,000,000.

In **foreign affairs**, Brazil sought to extend her influence to the west and southwest. She intervened in the affairs of Uruguay, opposed the expansionist policies of Rosas, dictator of Argentina, and aided in his overthrow (1851-1852) (p. 808), and, allied with Argentina and Uruguay, conducted a major **war against Paraguay** (1865-1870) (p. 810). During this period Brazilian prestige increased greatly.

1870-1888. A movement for emancipation of Negro slaves developed rapidly after 1850. After the enactment of a law stipulating that children of slaves should be free (the **Rio Branco Law**, 1871), after the freeing of slaves by the provinces of Ceará and Amazonas, and the freeing of all slaves of over sixty years (1885), a Liberal ministry provided for **complete emancipation** with no recompense for owners (1888, May 13).

1870. Republicanism, originally a movement of intellectuals, at first spread gradually. A republican party was formed (1870). The movement grew rapidly. The monarchy was gradually undermined by a number of forces: the dissatisfaction of the army with the peaceful policies of Pedro II after 1870, friction with the clergy, the rapid growth of republicanism, the alienation of the landed aristocracy through the emancipation of the slaves, the virtual extinction of provincial autonomy, and the unpopularity of the French husband of Princess Isabella, Gaston d'Orléans, Comte d'Eu.

1889, Nov. 15. The army, headed by General **Manoel Deodoro da Fonseca**, revolted and **deposed the emperor.** A republic was immediately proclaimed and a provisional government was established.

1889- THE REPUBLIC. During this period trade, cattle-raising, mining, agriculture, and forestry were greatly expanded and there was some development of manufacturing (cotton textiles). Railway mileage increased greatly. Coffee production came by 1925 to comprise four-fifths of the world supply. Overproduction of coffee led São Paulo, Rio de Janeiro, and

Minas Geraes in 1906–1907 and the central government somewhat later to establish a valorization system. Rubber production reached its height in 1910, after which it declined, because of the introduction of plantation systems in the East Indies. The problems of coffee and rubber production played an important part in creating economic difficulties.

The **population** in 1920 reached a total of over 30,000,000, and in 1935 of over 47,500,-000. During this period there was extensive **immigration**, especially of Spaniards and Italians.

The proper functioning of the national government under the republic was, from the very beginning, rendered difficult by the existence of **illiteracy** (estimated at 80% in 1910 and at 75% in 1920), by **political inexperience** and intolerance, by the absence of real political parties, and by the prevalent tendency toward **military rule.** The southern states, especially São Paulo and Minas Geraes, sought to control the country. Presidential candidates were chosen by caucuses representing controlling political groups of the more important states.

1891, Feb. 24. A constitution which provided for a federal republic, the **United States of Brazil,** a president elected for four years, a bicameral legislature, and the separation of Church and State was promulgated, and **Deodoro da Fonseca** was elected president.

Nov. 23. The dictatorial policies of the president caused a naval revolt and he was forced from office. Vice-President **Floriano Peixoto** assumed authority and governed arbitrarily.

1893–1895. A rebellion occurred in **Rio Grande do Sul,** and the navy revolted under **Admiral de Mello,** but the movements were suppressed after serious fighting.

1894–1910. Presidents **Moraes Barros** (1894–1898), **Manoel de Campos Salles** (1898–1902), **Rodriquez Alves** (1902–1906), **Affonso Penna** (1906–1909), and **Nilo Peçanha** (1909–1910) sought to stabilize finances, secured loans, and adopted fiscal reforms. **Boundary controversies** with Argentina (1895), France (1900), Bolivia (1903), England (1904), and Holland (1906) were adjusted by arbitration or direct negotiations.

1910–1920. The political campaign of 1910 was of unusual significance because it involved the question of militarism in politics. **Hermes da Fonseca,** the candidate of the conservative and army elements, was elected and governed arbitrarily. A

financial crisis resulting from a drop in the prices of rubber and coffee and the resultant need of unity caused the withdrawal of the anti-militarist candidate in the campaign of 1914, and **Wenceslau Braz** was elected.

(*Cont. p.* 1070.)

k. PANAMA AND THE PANAMA CANAL ZONE

Prior to the revolution of 1903, Panama was part of Colombia. The district had long been of interest because of the numerous **projects for an interoceanic canal** which were put forward from time to time from the 16th century onward. Schemes of this kind, involving complicated engineering problems, became practicable only in the later 19th century.

1850, Apr. 19. CLAYTON-BULWER TREATY, between Great Britain and the United States, by which both powers agreed not to obtain or maintain any exclusive control of a proposed canal, and guaranteed its neutrality.

1878, May 18. The Colombian government granted a French company under **Ferdinand de Lesseps** exclusive rights to construct a canal. The French **Panama Canal Company** was organized Aug. 17, 1879, and began construction of a sea-level canal (Jan. 1, 1880). The company failed in 1889 and a second company organized in 1894. Work continued until 1899.

1899, June 10. The United States Congress appointed a **canal commission** to report on possible routes through Panama.

1900, Feb. 5. The First Hay-Pauncefote Treaty, between Great Britain and the United States. This treaty, by which England renounced the right to joint construction and ownership, was rejected by Great Britain.

1901, Nov. 18. SECOND HAY-PAUNCEFOTE TREATY, giving the United States sole right of construction, maintenance, and control.

1903, Jan. 22. Hay-Herrán Treaty, between the United States and Colombia, providing for the acquisition by the United States of a canal zone. The Senate of Colombia failed to ratify this treaty.

Nov. 3. REVOLUTION IN PANAMA; independence from Colombia (p. 815).

Nov. 18. HAY-BUNAU-VARILLA TREATY between the United States and the new Panaman government: Panama granted the United States in perpetuity the use of a zone five miles wide on either side of the future canal, with full jurisdiction. The United States paid $10,000,000 and still pays $250,000 annually. The treaty was ratified Feb. 26, 1904.

1904, Feb. 13. **Adoption of the Panama constitution;** president, unicameral legislature, etc. The constitution also stipulated that if by treaty the United States guaranteed the independence and sovereignty of Panama, that power should also have the right to intervene to maintain order.

1904-1908. **Manuel Amador Guerrero,** first president of the republic.

1904, Apr. 23. The United States acquired the property of the French canal company for $40,000,000. At this time American engineering opinion still favored a sea-level canal.

1906, Feb. 5. The Isthmian Canal Commission reported in favor of a **lock canal.** On June 29 the United States Congress passed an act providing for such a canal.

1907, Apr. 1. Lieut.-Col. George W. Goethals appointed chief engineer.

1914, Aug. 15. **THE PANAMA CANAL WAS OPENED.** Its use during the first years was limited, because of constant landslides. The official and formal opening was postponed until July 12, 1920.

Sept. 2. The boundaries of the Canal Zone were **defined** and further rights of protection were conceded to the United States by treaty. (*Cont. p.* 1072.)

1. CENTRAL AMERICA

(1) *General*

1824, Nov. 22. After separation from Mexico (p. 805) the assembly of the **United Provinces of Central America** promulgated a federal constitution and **Manuel José Arce** was elected president. Guatemala City was made the capital. A Conservative Party (Servile), favoring centralized government and the Church, and a Liberal, advocating the existing federalism and reform, developed.

1826. Discontent with the preponderance of Guatemala, dissension concerning religious questions, and political discord soon developed, and **civil war** ensued. Arce supported the Conservatives and **Francisco Morazán** (1799-1842) became the Liberal leader.

1829. Morazán was victorious, occupied Guatemala City (Apr. 12), and became dictator, later assuming the presidency (1830).

1829-1835. Anti-clerical reforms were adopted, control of the Church was assumed, religious freedom was established, measures were taken against Spaniards and members of religious orders, and the capital was transferred to Salvador.

1837-1838. Political and religious tension led to **civil strife,** and **Rafael Carrera** (1814-1865), of mixed blood, placed himself at the head of the revolt, gaining clerical support.

1839-1840. **The Liberals were defeated** and Morazán was forced into exile. Congress meanwhile had adjourned, and with the defeat of Morazán the confederation dissolved into its component states: **El Salvador, Honduras, Nicaragua, and Costa Rica.**

1840-1865. **Carrera** became dictator of **Guatemala,** in which he established an extremely conservative régime, and dominated a large part of Central America.

1842-1852. **Honduras, Nicaragua, and El Salvador** formed a short-lived union (1842-1844), El Salvador and Guatemala sought to establish co-operation (1845), Honduras, El Salvador, and Nicaragua attempted to form a union (1847), and Honduras, Nicaragua, and El Salvador formed a confederation which was to include Costa Rica and Guatemala (1849-1852), but no permanent results were achieved because of friction or open hostilities.

1855-1862. An attempt by **William Walker,** an American, to establish control over Nicaragua (which he achieved for a short period) and perhaps extend his authority over a wider area, produced political and military co-operation between the Central American states. As a result of this and the antagonism of **Cornelius Vanderbilt,** who desired control of the transit route across Nicaragua, which became important after acquisition of California by the United States, **Walker was defeated** (1855-1860).

1862. **Nicaragua,** supported by Honduras and Salvador, sought to form a Central American union, but with no results.

1876-1885. **Justo Rufino Barrios** (c. 1834-1885), President of Guatemala, attempted without success to form a union (1876). Later he sought to establish a confederation by force. Honduras alone supported Rufino Barrios, while Costa Rica, Nicaragua, and El Salvador placed forces in the field to oppose him. **Barrios invaded Salvador,** but was defeated and killed at Chalchuapa (1885, Apr. 2).

1886-1887. Upon the initiative of Guatemala the Central American states framed a constitution and concluded a **treaty of peace and amity.**

1888-1889. Under this organization congresses met at **San José, Costa Rica,** and **San Salvador.** Definite union was decided upon by the latter congress, but controversy between Guatemala and Salvador prevented consummation.

1895-1898. Representatives of Nicaragua, El Salvador, and Honduras at **Amapala** concluded a **treaty of union** which created a governing commission (1895, June 20). A constitution for a confederation, the **Greater Republic of Central America,** was framed and an executive council met, but opposition in El Salvador brought the union to an end (1898, Nov. 25).

1893-1909. President **José Santos Zelaya** of Nicaragua appears to have projected the establishment of a confederation by force.

1907. In a war with Honduras he placed a president of his choice in power in that country and openly aided a **revolution in El Salvador.** Zelaya prepared to invade El Salvador, which was supported by Guatemala, and a general war threatened. In this situation, through the mediation of the United States and Mexico, a **conference of Central American states** to promote peace, unity, and eventual federation was held in Washington (Nov. 13–Dec. 20). Treaties were concluded providing for unification of currency, communications, tariffs, and similar matters, non-interference in internal affairs, neutralization of Honduras, and the creation of a Central American Court of Justice to determine all disputes. Honduras proposed confederation, but without result. The court of justice was established at Cartago (1908). When Nicaragua ignored its adverse decisions concerning the conclusion of the Bryan-Chamorro canal treaty between that country and the United States, the court lost influence and provision for its continuance was not made.

(2) *Territorial Adjustments*

1823- Great Britain maintained a protectorate over the **Mosquito Indians** of Nicaragua and Honduras, acquired during the colonial period, and the British from **Belize** expanded southward. Desiring a weak Central America, Great Britain was opposed to reunion after dissolution of the confederation.

1841. The **Bay Islands,** occupied by British, were placed under jurisdiction of the superintendent of Belize, and claim was laid to the mouth of the San Juan River.

1848. After acquisition of California by the United States, and with the prospect of canal construction, Great Britain took possession of the mouth of the **San Juan River** in the name of the ruler of the Mosquito Indians.

1850, Apr. 19. Opposition of the United States to British domination of a canal route across the Isthmus led to the conclusion of the **Clayton-Bulwer Treaty,** by which the United States and Great Britain agreed to neutralization of the proposed canal and pledged not to occupy or exercise sovereignty over any part of Central America. Great Britain at first refused to withdraw from the Bay Islands and the Mosquito Coast under this treaty, but eventually agreed to do so upon vigorous American representations.

1859, Nov. 28. A treaty between **Great Britain and Honduras** gave the latter control of the appropriate portion of the Mosquito Coast and recognized the sovereignty of Honduras over the Bay Islands.

1860, Jan. 28. Great Britain recognized **Nicaraguan sovereignty** over the Mosquito territory within its boundaries by a similar treaty, although Nicaragua did not gain full control until the presidency of Zelaya (1894).

1859, Apr. 30. A treaty between **Guatemala and Great Britain** fixed the southern limits of Belize.

(3) *Nicaragua*

1909. The **United States opposed President José Santos Zelaya** of Nicaragua because of his bellicose policies and interference in other states (p. 790), and American pressure together with a Conservative revolt forced him from office (1909, Dec. 16).

1911, June 6. As Nicaraguan finances were unsatisfactory, a treaty was concluded between the **United States and Nicaragua** providing for a loan to be secured by customs, these customs to be collected by a collector-general approved by the United States. **President Taft** appointed a commissioner-general and created a claims commission, and loans were extended. The United States Senate refused to ratify the treaty, and loans were thereupon restricted.

1912. Upon the outbreak of **civil war** (July) the United States intervened to protect the Conservative government. An election was held under supervision of

American forces and **Adolfo Díaz**, a Conservative, was elected (Nov.). A legation guard of American marines was established at Managua. (*Cont. p.* 1073.)

(4) *Honduras*

1907, Feb.-Dec. War between Honduras and Nicaragua. The Hondurans were defeated and the capital occupied by President Zelaya of Nicaragua. **President Bonilla** of Honduras captured. He was replaced by Gen. **Miguel Dávila.**

1909, Dec. Outbreak of a revolt against Davila, led by former President Bonilla. The ensuing civil war lasted until 1911.

1911, Feb. 8. Armistice: both factions agreed to abide by the forthcoming elections.

Oct. 29. Bonilla elected president.

1912, Jan. 9. American marines landed in Honduras to protect American property.

1913, Mar. 21. Death of Bonilla. He was succeeded by the vice-president, **Francisco Bertrand.**
(*Cont. p.* 1073.)

m. MEXICO

1823, Mar. 19. AGUSTIN I (p. 805), confronted by financial difficulty and political discontent, was forced from the throne by a revolt of which one of the leaders was **Antonio López de Santa Anna** (1797–1876).

1824, Oct. 4. A federal republic was established and **Guadalupe Victoria** was made president. Controversy arose between Liberal and Conservative elements, and upon the conclusion of the term of Guadalupe Victoria (1828) a period of disorder was initiated.

1829. During this period, while **Vicente Guerrero** was in office, a Spanish expedition from Cuba took **Tampico** (Aug. 18), but was forced to capitulate (Sept. 11).

1833, Apr. 1. Santa Anna was elected president by the Liberals and for over twenty years dominated Mexican affairs directly or indirectly. Santa Anna alternated in office with Vice-President **Valentín Gómez Farías** (1833–1834), who undertook political and religious reforms. Gómez Farías was driven from office by Santa Anna (1834, Apr. 24).

1835, Dec. 15. A highly **centralized government** was established.

1836, Mar. 2. Americans who had colonized **Texas** opposed direct Mexican control, **proclaimed a republic,** and maintained their independence, defeating and capturing Santa Anna at **San Jacinto** (Apr. 21).

1838, Apr. 16. In enforcement of claims a French expedition occupied **Vera Cruz** and withdrew when Mexico agreed to indemnities (1839, Mar. 9).

1841, Oct. 10. After further civil strife Santa Anna again assumed **dictatorial power** and promulgated a highly centralized constitution (1843, June 12).

1844. A revolt forced him into temporary exile (1845).

1846-1848. THE EXPANSIONIST POLICY OF THE UNITED STATES, boundary disputes, the question of Texas, and unsettled claims had created strained relations between the United States and Mexico, and the annexation of Texas by the United States (1845, Mar. 1) led to **war between the two nations** (p. 773). Mexico was totally defeated, and its capital occupied (1847, Sept. 14).

1848, Feb. 2. By the **Treaty of Guadalupe Hidalgo,** Mexico ceded **Upper California, New Mexico,** and the northern portions of **Sonora, Coahuila,** and **Tamaulipas,** the United States paying $15,000,000 and assuming payment of claims against the Mexican government.

1848-1853. Following the war Presidents **José Joaquín de Herrera** and **Mariano Arista** sought unsuccessfully to rehabilitate finances and restore order.

1853. Santa Anna again became president and established a dictatorship which tended toward monarchy. A Liberal revolt drove him from office and ended his control of Mexican affairs (1855, Aug. 9).

1855. A program of **religious and political reform** was undertaken by the Liberal government, including an attempt to release from mortmain the great holdings of the Church (Ley Juarez, Nov. 23), and a federal constitution was adopted (1857, Feb. 5).

1857-1860. These reforms led to civil war between Conservatives and Liberals, the **War of the Reform.**

1858. The Liberal government, with **Benito Juárez** (1806–1872) as president, established its capital at **Vera Cruz** (May 4), being recognized by the United States (1859, Apr. 6). The Conservative capital was Mexico City. Laws providing for separation of Church and State, confiscation of ecclesiastical property except churches, and suppression of religious orders were promulgated by the Liberal government.

1860, Dec. 22. The Liberal forces triumphed in the field and Juárez placed the reform laws in effect throughout Mexico. The war disorganized Mexican finances and created friction with other powers.

1861. Upon suspension of payment on foreign debts by the Mexican government (May 29, July 17), **France, Great Britain, and Spain,** by the **Treaty of London** (Oct. 31) undertook joint intervention to protect their interests. Napoleon III desired to create in Mexico a Catholic empire under French hegemony, which would provide markets and raw materials and check the expansion of the United States. French designs, supported by Mexican reactionaries, became clear after **allied occupation of Vera Cruz** (Dec. 17), and Spain and Great Britain withdrew (1862, Apr. 8).

1863. French troops occupied Mexico City (June 7), and the **Archduke Maximilian of Austria** (1832–1867) was made **emperor** (1864, Apr. 10). The Mexican Liberal government continued resistance and the liberal policies of Maximilian alienated certain conservative elements.

1865-1867. After the close of the Civil War the United States (which refused to recognize Maximilian and supported Juárez) insistently demanded withdrawal of French troops, as the Monroe Doctrine was definitely involved. In view of the attitude of the United States and the delicate European situation, **Napoleon III withdrew** support from Maximilian (1867, Mar. 12).

1867, May 14. The emperor was forced to capitulate at Querétaro, and was executed (June 19). Juárez restored order, and was re-elected to the presidency (Dec. 19).

1872. Upon the death of Juárez **Sebastián Lerdo de Tejada** became president. Constitutional amendments were enacted to safeguard the liberal reforms earlier adopted (1873, May 29).

1876. **Porfirio Díaz** (1830–1915) overthrew Lerdo de Tejada (Nov. 20) and became president (1877, May 2).

1876-1911. **DÍAZ CONTROLLED MEXICO** with absolute authority until 1911, remaining in office constantly with the exception of the period 1880–1884. Under Díaz order was established, Mexican prestige was raised, finances were stabilized, and vast material progress was achieved. Railways were built, public works were

promoted, industry was developed, and commerce increased. Much foreign capital, especially American, was invested. A mining code was promulgated which, contrary to Spanish law, provided that title to land carried ownership of subsoil products (1884, Nov. 22). A census of 1895 indicated a population of 12,500,000, and that of 1910 a population of 15,150,000 (1,150,000 white; 8,000,000 *mestizos*; 6,000,000 Indians). The government of Díaz favored the upper classes. Lands of the Indians and *mestizos* and communal lands (*ejidos*) were permitted to come into possession of large landowners. Concessions to foreigners acted to the detriment of the Mexican middle class, exploitation of the working classes was general, and peonage developed. Education was neglected and Mexicans, with the exception of a small group, were denied participation in government. By 1910 all elements of political and social revolt had developed.

1911, May 25. **Díaz was overthrown** by a movement begun in 1910 and headed by **Francisco Madero,** who became president (Nov. 6), and an era of revolution was initiated. Madero, whose objectives were largely political, had an imperfect understanding of the fundamental issues involved and the forces he unleashed soon passed beyond his control.

1913, Feb. 18. **Madero was overthrown** by **Victoriano Huerta** and shot (Feb. 22). Venustiano Carranza (1859–1920) headed a movement against Huerta, whom the United States refused to recognize.

1914, Apr. 21. As a result of overt acts, **United States forces occupied Vera Cruz,** and war was narrowly averted.

July 15. Huerta was forced from office by Carranza. Civil war soon broke out between the latter and his lieutenant, **Francisco Villa,** and complete disorder followed.

1915, Oct. 19. The United States and eight other American nations recognized Carranza as *de facto* president.

1915-1916. Injury to life and property of foreigners created a delicate international situation and a demand for intervention arose in the United States.

1916, Mar. 9. A raid by Villa on Columbus, New Mexico, caused the United States to dispatch **punitive expeditions** into Mexico under Gen. **John J. Pershing** (Mar. 15). Carranza opposed this action.

1917, Feb. 5. American troops were withdrawn after having failed in their objective. These developments greatly stimulated Mexican anti-interventionist sentiment. The Carranza government was sympathetic to Germany during the World War. (*Cont. p.* 1074.)

'n. THE WEST INDIES

(1) *Cuba*

During the Wars of Liberation **Cuba** and **Puerto Rico** remained loyal to Spain and served as bases of operations for Spanish forces. Many royalists from revolutionary areas established themselves in Cuba. Arbitrary government and an economic policy which reacted detrimentally upon the expanding Cuban sugar industry over a long period created discontent among Cubans.

1868-1878. THE TEN YEARS' WAR ensued when reforms were not adopted by the Spanish government after the overthrow of Isabella (p. 646). This revolt, in which the Cubans had the sympathy of the United States (which had earlier sought to purchase Cuba for strategic reasons), was terminated by the **Convention of El Zanjón** (1878, Feb. 10), by which Spain promised administrative reforms. The spirit of the Convention of El Zanjón was not observed by Spain, although slavery was eventually abolished (1880, 1886).

1895-1898. Political and economic unrest and a desire for independence led to a new **revolutionary movement.** The Cubans were supported by American opinion, which was further aroused by the ruthless measures adopted by the Spanish authorities.

1897, Nov. 25. The Liberal Spanish premier, **Sagasta,** offered the Cubans a large measure of self-government, but they were determined upon complete independence.

1898. THE SPANISH-AMERICAN WAR. The Cuban situation rapidly became a direct issue between the United States and Spain, which, after the **destruction of the U.S.S.** *Maine* in Havana Harbor (Feb. 15), led to war (Apr. 25). Spain was decisively defeated (p. 787). By the **Treaty of Paris** (Dec. 10), which terminated the war, Spain relinquished sovereignty over **Cuba** and ceded **Puerto Rico** to the United States, and the United States undertook to maintain order in Cuba during the period of occupation. The loss of Cuba and Puerto Rico ended Spanish dominion in the Americas.

1899-1900. Upon termination of the Spanish-American War Gen. **John**

R. Brooke as military governor promulgated administrative reforms. Gen. **Leonard Wood** succeeded Brooke (Dec. 13) and under his direction the civil government was organized, steps were taken to establish a Cuban administration, sanitation and public health measures were initiated (notable among them efforts which led to eradication of yellow fever), legal reforms were instituted, schools were standardized, municipal elections were held, and elections for a constituent assembly were called.

1901, Feb. 21. The constituent assembly adopted a **constitution,** providing for a president and bicameral congress, into which, at the insistence of the United States, was inserted the **Platt Amendment** (June 12) to the American army appropriation bill. This provided that Cuba might not enter into any treaty with a foreign power which impaired her sovereignty, that excessive foreign debts might not be contracted, that the United States might intervene to maintain Cuban independence and a government capable of preserving life, property, and personal liberty, and that lands be leased to the United States as coaling stations.

1902-1906. Tomás Estrada Palma was chosen president and continued the policies initiated by Wood. American forces were withdrawn. A Liberal Party formed in opposition to Estrada Palma, who became leader of conservative elements.

1906. A **Liberal revolt** (Feb. 24-25) followed the re-election of Estrada Palma and upon his appeal President Theodore Roosevelt dispatched **William H. Taft** and **Robert Bacon** to adjust the situation. They were unable to do so and Estrada Palma resigned (Sept. 25). As Congress was unable to agree upon a successor, Taft established a provisional government and American forces occupied the island. **Charles E. Magoon** succeeded Taft (Oct. 3). Order was re-established, electoral reforms were adopted, and further public improvements were carried out (1906-1908).

1908, Nov. 14. Elections were held and **José Miguel Gómez,** a Liberal, became president (1909-1913), whereupon Magoon and the occupationary forces were withdrawn (1909, Feb. 1). But the Liberal Party divided into factions and disorders occurred which brought threat of American intervention. Increasing opposition to the Platt Amendment developed.

1913-1917. During the presidency of the Conservative **Mario García Menocal,** a projected revolt was prevented by American pressure and American forces were landed when a Negro rebellion occurred.

1916-1917. The elections of 1916, in which Menocal was opposed by the Liberal **Alfredo Zayas,** were disputed, and the Liberals, led by ex-President Gómez, revolted (1917, Feb. 9). The United States proclaimed that a government established by force would not be recognized and American forces were landed at Santiago (Mar. 8). **Gómez** was defeated and **Menocal** took office (May 20). (*Cont. p.* 1077.)

(2) *Puerto Rico*

Puerto Rico was discovered by Columbus on his second voyage (1493) and colonization was begun in 1506. During the period of Spanish rule it was several times attacked (by the English under Lord George Clifford, 1598; by the Dutch, 1625; by the English under Abercromby, 1797). Slavery was abolished in 1873, after which a number of reforms were promulgated. In 1897 the Spanish government introduced an autonomous régime.

1898, May 12. During the Spanish-American War, Admiral **Sampson** appeared off San Juan and landed troops (July 25). Fighting continued until Aug. 13.

Oct. 18. Gen. **John R. Brooke** took possession for the United States. A military government was established.

Dec. 10. By the **treaty of peace** Spain ceded the island to the United States. Under the leadership of **Eugenio M. de Hostos,** agitation for "self-determination" began at once.

1899, Jan. An insular police force replaced the Spanish civil guard. This "state constabulary" constituted the sole police force after 1902: some 800 men preserved order for a population of 1,000,000.

Mar. 24. A Puerto Rican regiment was organized to serve as garrison. It was composed entirely of white inhabitants. In 1918 it served as part of the garrison of Panama. In 1920 it became the 65th Infantry, U.S. Army.

Aug. 8. **San Ciriaco hurricane,** the most destructive in the history of the island; 3369 persons killed; coffee plantations destroyed.

1900, Apr. 12. **Foraker Act,** by which Congress established civil government for the island and introduced free trade with the United States.

1901, May 27, Dec. 2. The United States

supreme court decided (*De Lima* v. *Bidwell*) that Puerto Ricans were not, *ipso facto*, United States citizens.

Features and results of civil government: Manhood suffrage was established and proved a stimulant to popular education. Duties collected in Puerto Rico on foreign products were devoted to island affairs. The foreign trade increased between 1900 and 1924 from $16,602,004 to $177,650,164. A corresponding increase of population took place, from 952,243 in 1898 to 1,299,809 in 1920, of which 948,709 were whites. During the American period there has been a rapid extension of the school system, and a reduction of illiteracy from 90% to less than 50%. There has also been much progress in sanitation, the death rate falling from 41 per 1000 in 1898 to 18.6 in 1922. Less commendable was the gradual concentration of wealth in fewer hands. Small holdings decreased by more than 30%.

1909. Two half-mile tunnels were opened through the mountains, providing irrigation for the south side of the island, which is a trade-wind desert.

Growing agitation, under the leadership of **Luis Muñoz Rivera,** for the extension of American citizenship to Puerto Ricans.
(*Cont. p.* 1079.)

(3) *The Dominican Republic*

1808-1809. A revolt in Santo Domingo, aided by English naval forces, established freedom from Haiti and France.

1814. Santo Domingo was again assigned to Spain by the Treaty of Paris.

1821, Dec. 1. Santo Domingo proclaimed independence following the action of other Spanish colonies, and unsuccessfully sought incorporation with Colombia.

1822. **Haiti** under President Boyer conquered **Santo Domingo,** which remained incorporated until independence was established by a revolution (1844, Feb. 27).

1861, Mar. 18. Because of internal disorder and fear of conquest by Haiti, Santo Domingo at its own request was annexed to Spain.

1865, May 1. A nationalist revolution caused Spain to relinquish sovereignty.

1868-1870. An effort to secure annexation to the United States failed when the United States Senate refused approval.

1882-1899. During the presidency of **Ulises**

Heureaux comparative tranquillity and prosperity existed, although heavy debts were contracted abroad.

1899-1904. After a period of turbulence, the government was bankrupt. Heavy loans had been contracted abroad and the possibility of intervention by European powers existed.

1905. Concerned as to the Monroe Doctrine, President Theodore Roosevelt, after rejection by the Senate of a treaty providing for supervision of Dominican finances, arranged by a *modus vivendi* for administration of Dominican customs and appointed a customs receiver (Mar. 31).

1907, Feb. 8. A treaty was later concluded by which the United States was accorded control of customs for fifty years. Under American control Dominican finances were rehabilitated. Loans were floated in New York to aid stabilization.

1916, May. Despite supervision of elections by the United States, disorder developed and **American naval forces were landed** to preserve order. As the result of the refusal of the provisional president, **Francisco Henríquez y Carvajal,** to sign a new treaty providing American financial control, the United States withheld customs revenues. (*Cont. p.* 1078.)

(4) *Haiti*

1697. In the 17th century the French gained control of the western extremity of **Española,** Saint-Domingue, or Haiti, and by the **Treaty of Ryswick** Spain ceded the western part of the island to France. **Saint-Domingue** became a prosperous plantation colony.

1795. In the **Treaty of Basel** Spain ceded the eastern part of Española to France. At this time the population of Saint-Domingue consisted of some 40,000 whites, 28,000 freedmen, and 500,000 Negro slaves.

1794, May 6. The mulattoes and Negroes, desiring equal rights and independence, during the French Revolution revolted, and under leadership of **Toussaint L'Ouverture, Jean-Jacques Dessalines,**

and **Henri Christophe** achieved independence after forcing capitulation of a large French army dispatched by Napoleon (1804, Jan. 1). All slaves were freed. The whites were either killed or forced to flee during the revolution.

1804, Oct. 8. **Dessalines made himself emperor, Jacques I,** and after his assassination (1806, Oct. 17), **Christophe** as **Henri I** and **Alexandre Pétion** established their control in the north and south respectively.

1818, Mar. 20. Jean Pierre Boyer became president after the death of Pétion and the suicide of Christophe (1820, Oct. 8).

1822. Santo Domingo, which had again come under control of Spain (1814), was conquered by Boyer and the island was united as the **Republic of Haiti,** to which France accorded recognition (1838, Feb. 12).

1843, Mar. 13. Boyer was forced from office.

1844, Feb. 27. **Santo Domingo established its independence** through a revolution.

1847. Faustin Soulouque became president and soon proclaimed himself **Faustin I** (1849).

1859, Jan. 15. After oppressive rule he was overthrown and **Fabre Geffrard** assumed power. Fabre Geffrard governed for eight years before being forced from office (1867).

1867-   . An era of instability followed. Haitian finances became disorganized and obligations were contracted abroad.

1914, June 14. France and Germany demanded control of Haitian customs to secure payment, and the United States, with interests in Haiti, also desired control.

1915, July 3. After a series of disorders **the United States landed forces to** restore order. Under American supervision **Philippe Dartiguenave** was named president (Aug. 12). A treaty was concluded by which the United States established a political and financial protectorate for 10 years (Sept. 16). This was later renewed for a second 10-year period to end in 1936. (*Cont. p.* 1078.)

I. AFRICA

1. GENERAL: EXPLORATION

1795-1796. **MUNGO PARK** explored the Gambia and reached the **Niger** at Segu, finally establishing the fact that the great river flowed east.

1798-1799. The Portuguese **Francisco de Lacerda** traveled from Tete on the Zambezi northward to **Lake Mweru.**

1801. The Englishmen, **Sir John Truter** and **William Somerville,** explored Bechuanaland and penetrated the interior almost as far as **Lake Ngami.**

1802-1811. The Portuguese, **Pedro Baptista** and **A. José,** crossed the continent from Angola to Tete on the Zambezi.

1805. **MUNGO PARK EXPLORED THE NIGER** as far as the **Bussa Rapids,** where he was drowned.

1807, 1811. The **British government abolished the slave trade.**

1812-1814. A Swiss, **J. L. Burckhardt,** advanced up the **Nile** and crossed to the Red Sea.

1815. France abolished the slave trade. Other countries (notably Spain and Portugal) followed suit, under British pressure.

1818. **G. Mollien** discovered the sources of the **Gambia and Senegal.**

1820-1822. Egyptian campaigns on the upper Nile. **Khartum** founded (1823).

1822-1825. **Walter Oudney, Dixon Denham,** and **Hugh Clapperton** journeyed from Tripoli across the desert to **Lake Chad** and thence westward to the **Niger,** proving that the river had no connection with the lake.

1825. **Alexander G. Laing** crossed the desert from Tripoli to **Tuat** and thence to **Timbuktu,** the first modern to visit the latter city.

1827. **René Caillé** reached **Timbuktu** from French Guinea and proceeded thence to Fez.

1827. **Linant de Bellefonds** ascended the **Nile** to lat. $13° 6'$ north.

1830-1834. **Richard Lander** explored the **lower Niger** from Bussa to the sea.

1831-1833. **Edouard Rüppell** explored northern **Ethiopia.**

1837-1848. Extensive researches of **A. T. d'Abbadie** in **Ethiopia.**

1839. An Egyptian force, accompanied by **G. Thibaud,** ascended the **Nile** to lat. $6° 30'$ north.

1840-1843. **C. T. Beke** mapped much of Ethiopia.

1848-1863. **J. Petherick** carried on extensive investigations in the **Niam-Niam** country.

1849. **DAVID LIVINGSTONE** crossed the Kalahari Desert and advanced to **Lake Ngami,** returning (1850) to the upper Zambezi.

1849-1853. **Heinrich Barth** and **A. Overweg** crossed from Tripoli to the Niger and Lake Chad, thoroughly studying the country for the first time.

1853-1856. **LIVINGSTONE CROSSED THE CONTINENT** from the Zambezi to Loanda and return, discovering the **Victoria Falls.**

1853. The Portuguese, **Silva Porto, crossed the continent** from Benguella to the mouth of the Rovuma River.

1858-1859. **Richard Burton** and **John Speke** discovered **Lake Tanganyika** and **Victoria Nyanza,** Speke concluding that Victoria Nyanza was the source of the White Nile.

1858-1861. **THIRD EXPEDITION OF LIVINGSTONE,** who traveled from the Zambezi to the interior and discovered **Lake Nyasa** (1859).

1860-1863. **SPEKE AND GRANT** passed through Uganda, **reached the Nile** and descended it to **Gondokoro,** where they met **Sir Samuel Baker** (1863) who had ascended the river to that point.

1864. **Baker,** continuing up the Nile, **discovered Albert Nyanza,** whence he returned to Gondokoro.

1865. Extensive exploration of the **Benuë-Niger** region by **Gustav Rohlfs.**

1866-1871. **LIVINGSTONE** traveled from the mouth of the Rovuma inland to Lake Nyasa and thence to Lake Tanganyika and Bangweolu, whence he returned to Tanganyika.

Span. Sphere 1906
Madeira (Port. 1420)
Morocco Fr. Sphere 1906
Algeria 1830
Tunis 1881
Canary Is. (Sp. 1478)
R. de Oro. Spanish
Tripoli 1912
Egypt Br. Occupation 1882
Gambia 1618
French West Africa
Eritrea 1896
Assab 1881
Br. Somaliland 1884
Port. Guinea
Freetown 1792
Sierra Leone
Nigeria Chartered Co 1885 Col. 1914
Anglo-Egyptian Sudan 1899
French 1862-84
Liberia 1820
GoldCoast
C. Coast Cas. 1667
Togo 1884
Lagos 1861
Fern. Po (Sp. 1778)
Princes I. (Port. 1484)
St. Thomas
1841
Kamerun 84-1911
Abyssinia
Br. East Africa Chartered Co 1885 Col. 1903
French Congo
Congo State 1885 Belgian Congo 1909
German E. Africa 1885
Pemba Zanzibar Br. 1890
Angola 1575-1848
Rhodesia Chartered Co 1889
Mozambique
1886
Madagascar Fr. Col. 1896
Walfish B Br. 1878
Germ. S.W. Africa 1884-1890
1885
1902
Natal 1843
C. of Good Hope 1806
Union of S. Africa 1910
1902

REFERENCE

Up to 1884,	Acquisitions 1885-1914	
		British
		French
		Portuguese
		Spanish
		Italian
		German

THE
PARTITION OF AFRICA
Statute Miles

0   500   1000

GEORGE PHILIP AND SON, LTD

1868. St. Vincent Erskine explored the region of the **Limpopo River.**

1868-1871. G. SCHWEINFURTH went from Khartum to the Niam-Niam country and discovered the **Welle River,** flowing west.

1870. Gustav Nachtigal explored the **Chad region** and crossed from there to Egypt.

1871. HENRY M. STANLEY, searching for Livingstone, found him on Lake Tanganyika. Death of Livingstone (May 1, 1873).

1874. V. L. Cameron crossed the continent from Lake Tanganyika to Benguella, mapping large territories.

1874-1877. STANLEY CIRCUMNAVIGATED VICTORIA NYANZA, proceeded thence to Lake Tanganyika, crossed to the **Lualaba,** which he **descended to the Congo,** ultimately reaching the Atlantic coast.

1874. Charles Chaillé-Long traced the course of the **Somerset Nile** and discovered **Lake Kioga.**

1875. Savorgnan de Brazza explored the region of the Ogowe and **lower Congo.**

1876. Foundation of the International Association for the Exploration and Civilization of Africa, under the auspices of **Leopold II** of Belgium.

1877. The Portuguese, **Serpa Pinto,** crossed from Benguella to Natal.

1879-1886. **Wilhelm Junker** demonstrated

that the Welle River was part of the Congo system and carried on extensive researches about Lake Albert.

1879-1884. Stanley, in the service of Leopold, ascended the Congo and established posts in the Basin.

1878-1881. Joseph Thomson explored the region between Lakes Nyasa and Tanganyika.

1880-1886. HERMANN VON WISSMANN explored the **Congo Basin** and twice crossed the continent.

1882. The Italians, **Matteucci** and **Massari,** crossed the continent from **Suakin** on the Red Sea to the **Niger River.**

1882. **Wilhelm Junker** explored the **Ubanghi River** system.

1887-1890. STANLEY'S EXPEDITION TO RELIEVE EMIN PASHA (Eduard Schnitzer, Egyptian governor of Equatoria, 1877-1888). Stanley ascended the Congo, crossed to the great lakes, traced the **Semliki River** to **Lake Edward,** which he discovered. He found Emin on the upper Nile and induced him to leave for the east coast.

1888. Count **Samuel Teleki,** a Hungarian scientist, discovered **Lakes Rudolf** and **Stephanie.**

1892-1895. V. Bottego explored the **Juba River.** Later explorations have been chiefly of a scientific nature with the object of filling out the map and supplementing the work of earlier travelers.

2. EGYPT AND THE SUDAN

1805. **Mohammed Ali** appointed **governor of Egypt** by the sultan. Mohammed (b. 1769) was a tobacco merchant from Kavalla, who had come to Egypt in 1799 in command of an Albanian contingent. By intervening freely in the intrigues of the Turkish officials and the Mamluks and supporting the latter, he succeeded in driving out the Turkish governor and establishing his own power, which the sultan recognized only with reluctance.

1807. British invasion and occupation of Alexandria. The British failed to make further progress and withdrew (p. 593).

1811, Mar. 1. Massacre of the Mamluks in the citadel of Cairo. They had obviously been intriguing against Mohammed and were probably supported by the sultan. Mohammed invited them to a banquet and had them treacherously slaughtered. Only a few escaped to upper Egypt. Thereafter **Mohammed was su-**

preme. Though illiterate, he was a firm believer in western technique and reorganized the country administratively on the French model. In time he built up a powerful army (organized by Col. **Sèves, or Soliman Pasha)** and a substantial fleet. In order to secure the necessary funds, he gradually took over most of the land, organized **state monopolies** of trade, introduced the **culture of cotton and hemp,** and developed the **irrigation system** (Delta Barrage).

1815. **Revolt of the Albanian regiments,** which resented Mohammed's efforts at Europeanization. Mohammed was forced to flood Cairo, but the revolt was ultimately repressed and the mutinous troops sent to upper Egypt.

1818. Conclusion of seven **years of war against the Wahabis** in Arabia, who had occupied Mecca and Medina and threatened Syria. The campaign was undertaken at the behest of the sultan. The result

Khedives and Kings of Egypt since 1811

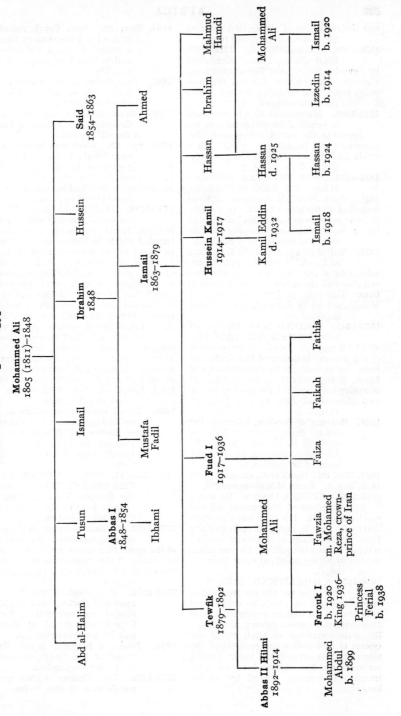

Mohammed Ali
1805 (1811)–1848

Abd al-Halim — Tusun — Ismail — Ibrahim 1848 — Hussein — Said 1854–1863

Abbas I 1848–1854

Ibhami

Mustafa Fadil — Ismail 1863–1879 — Ahmed

Tewfik 1879–1892

Fuad I 1917–1936

Hussein Kamil 1914–1917 — Hassan — Mahmud Hamdi — Ibrahim

Abbas II Hilmi 1892–1914

Mohammed Ali

Faiza — Faikah — Faikah — Fathia

Mohammed Abdul b. 1899

Farouk I b. 1920 King 1936–

Fawzia m. Mohamed Reza, crown-prince of Iran

Princess Ferial b. 1938

Kamil Eddin d. 1932 — Hassan d. 1925 — Mohammed Ali

Ismail b. 1918 — Hassan b. 1924 — Izzedin b. 1914 — Ismail b. 1920 was the subjection of the eastern coast of the Red Sea to Egyptian rule.

1820-1822. CONQUEST OF THE SUDAN (Nubia, Senaar, Kordofan) by Egyptian forces under Mohammed's son Hussein. The primary object of the campaign was to find gold supplies and slaves. Khartum founded (1823).

1823-1828. Mohammed Ali's intervention in behalf of the sultan against the insurgents in Greece. Campaigns of Mohammed's son Ibrahim (b. 1789). As a result Mohammed acquired the governorship of Crete (p. 723).

1832-1833. WAR BETWEEN MOHAMMED AND THE SULTAN (p. 724). As a result Mohammed acquired control of all Syria and Adana. In the subsequent years he expanded his influence as far as the Persian Gulf, arousing the distrust and opposition of England.

1833. Arrival of a group of St. Simonians in Egypt. Their aim was the development of the country on western lines and above all the construction of a canal at Suez. This latter project was opposed by Mohammed Ali for fear of its international implications.

1839-1841. SECOND WAR BETWEEN MOHAMMED ALI AND THE SULTAN (p. 725). Due to the intervention of the powers, Mohammed lost Crete and Syria, but secured the hereditary tenure of Egypt, paying tribute to the sultan and accepting a reduction of the army to 18,000 men (firmans of Feb. 13 and June 10, 1841).

1847. Regency of Ibrahim, following the mental derangement of Mohammed Ali in his later years. In July, 1848, Ibrahim was formally invested as khedive.

1848, Nov. 10. Death of Ibrahim.

1849, Aug. 2. Death of Mohammed Ali.

1848-1854. ABBAS I, khedive. He was a grandson of Mohammed Ali and was born in 1816. His reign was characterized by hostility to European and especially French influence and by a more subservient attitude toward the sultan. He was assassinated by his opponents at court (July 13, 1854).

1854-1863. MOHAMMED SAID, khedive. He was the youngest son of Mohammed Ali (b. 1822), an enlightened ruler friendly to western penetration. He took steps to suppress slavery, abandoned the state ownership of land, ended the system of monopolies, and reorganized the administration along liberal lines. During his reign the first foreign loan was contracted (£3,000,000, floated by British bankers).

1854, Nov. 30. Suez Canal concession granted to Ferdinand de Lesseps, a French diplomat and promoter and a friend of Said's of long standing.

1857. Completion of the railroad from Alexandria to Cairo. This was later extended to Suez.

1858. Organization of the Suez Canal Company, which raised a loan of 200 million francs.

1859, Apr. 29. Work was begun on the Suez Canal. The project had been vigorously opposed by the British (Lord Palmerston) at every step, because of its French connections and because of the supposed threat to India.

1863-1879. ISMAIL, khedive. He was the son of Ibrahim and was born in 1830. Partly educated in France, he had traveled widely in Europe and set himself to complete the modernization of Egypt. In his first years the Civil War in America created a great demand for Egyptian cotton and resulted in widespread prosperity. Ismail took advantage of this and of the readiness of European interests to lend huge sums of money (at usurious rates of interest) to carry through immense public works — Suez Canal, irrigation canals, railroads, telegraphs, harbor works, bridges, etc. Most notable was the development of primary schools, which increased from 185 to 4685 during his reign. On the other hand, Egypt was confronted with a tremendous public debt.

1865. Ismail induced the sultan to put under Egyptian control the ports of Suakin and Massawa on the Red Sea, the beginning of a systematic expansion in that direction.

1869, Nov. 17. OFFICIAL OPENING OF THE SUEZ CANAL; presence of the Empress Eugénie, Emperor Francis Joseph, and many other European celebrities.

1870-1873. Sir Samuel Baker, in Egyptian service, completed the conquest of the upper Nile region, as far as Unyoro, and initiated the suppression of the slave trade, which had seriously depopulated the country.

1872-1875. Occupation of the Red Sea coast and Harrar. The Egyptian control was extended as far as Cape Guardafui and cut off Ethiopia from access to the sea.

1874. Zobeir, a powerful former slave-trader of the Sudan, conquered Darfur for the khedive.

1874-1879. Gen. Charles Gordon governor-general of the Sudan. He completed the work of Baker, established posts on the upper Nile and dealt the slave-traders a mortal blow.

1875, Nov. The khedive, in financial stringency, sold his **176,000 shares in the Suez Canal Company to the British government** for 100,000,000 francs. The British government thereupon became the largest single shareholder.

1875-1879. War with Ethiopia. The Egyptians were at first defeated, but won a crushing victory in Feb. 1876.

1876, Apr. 4. Publication of the **report of Mr. Stephen Cave** on the finances of Egypt. The khedive was accused of unwise borrowing and spending and some measure of European supervision was declared indispensable.

May 2. Establishment of the **Caisse de la Dette** to manage the service of the debt.

Nov. 18. Appointment of a **British and a French controller,** following reduction of the debt and of interest. Anglo-French condominium.

1878, Aug. 15. Appointment of a **ministry under Nubar Pasha,** with an Englishman (**Sir Rivers Wilson**) as minister of finance, and a Frenchman (**M. de Blignières**) as minister of public works. A vigorous effort was made to meet the demands of the European creditors, with resulting hardship on the country and much discontent and hatred of foreigners.

1879, Feb. 18. Fall of the Nubar ministry after a demonstration of army officers, possibly encouraged by Ismail, who resented the curtailment of his own power.

June 25. Deposition of Ismail by the sultan, under pressure from the European powers. He left Egypt and died in exile at Constantinople (1895).

1879-1892. TEWFIK, khedive.

1879, Sept. 4. The **European controllers were reappointed** and henceforth were to be irremovable without the consent of England and France.

1880, July 17. The **Law of Liquidation,** promulgated after another international investigation. It rearranged the finances and provided that all surplus should go to the service of the debt.

1881, Feb. 1. Rising of Egyptian officers, following the dismissal of one of their number. The officers forced the resignation of the Circassian war minister and the appointment of **Mahmud Sami,** a

nationalist, in his place. The movement was led by **Ahmed Arabi** and was the first definite expression of the new **nationalist movement,** inspired by **Jamal ud-Din el-Afghani,** famous Moslem teacher (at Cairo after 1871) who preached resistance to the west and adoption of western political methods for purposes of defense. The national movement in Egypt was primarily directed against foreign control and against the Turkish influence, but also centered on a demand for constitutional government.

Sept. 9. A second rising, led by Arabi, forced the khedive to revoke the dismissal of Mahmud Sami.

1882, Jan. 8. The **Gambetta Note,** handed to the Egyptian government by France and England. It pronounced in favor of the khedive and was intended to strengthen him against nationalist pressure. Its effect was merely to discredit him, since the British refused to follow up the note by any concrete action.

Feb. 5. The khedive was obliged to appoint **a nationalist ministry** under Mahmud Sami, in which Arabi became war minister. The ministry began discussion of a constitution.

Apr. 12. A conspiracy of Circassian officers against the government was discovered and many were arrested.

May 2. Forty of the conspirators were condemned to exile in the Sudan. The khedive thereupon appealed to the powers for support and the ministry summoned the Chamber, evidently with the idea of deposing Tewfik.

May 20. British and French squadrons appeared at **Alexandria** as a demonstration in behalf of the khedive.

May 25. An **ultimatum from England and France** forced the resignation of the nationalist government, under protest.

May 28. The khedive, unable to find another government, was obliged to recall Arabi and the nationalists.

June 12. Outbreak of riots at Alexandria, in which some 50 Europeans were killed. These riots have been attributed by some to the khedive, as part of a scheme to force intervention in his behalf.

June 23. Opening of an ambassadorial conference at Constantinople, to discuss the modalities of Turkish intervention under the supervision of the powers.

**July 11. BOMBARDMENT OF ALEX-
ANDRIA** by the British under
Adm. **Sir Beauchamp Seymour.** The ostensible object was to destroy the earth-
works which the nationalists were throwing
up. The French government refused to
take part in the action, fearing international complications. The British thereupon began to land troops and to send a
force to protect the Suez Canal. The
French and also the Italians refused invitations to participate.

Sept. 13. The British under **Sir Garnett
Wolseley, defeated the Egyptian
forces** of Arabi **at Tel el-Kebir.**

**Sept. 15. THE BRITISH OCCUPIED
CAIRO.** Arabi surrendered; he
was later tried and banished to
Ceylon.

Nov. 9. The dual control of Britain and
France **was abolished.**

1883, Jan. 3. Granville Circular to the
powers, declaring England's desire
to withdraw her forces from Egypt "*as
soon as the state of the country and the organization of proper means for the maintenance of the khedivial authority will admit
of it.*"

Feb. 6. Dufferin Report, proposing the
reorganization of the Egyptian
government.

May 1. THE ORGANIC LAW, embodying the Dufferin proposals, went
into effect: in addition to the cabinet there
was to be a **legislative council** composed of
nominees of the khedive and members
elected by the provincial assemblies; a
general assembly was to include the ministers and legislative council and additional
members chosen by the provincial and
town governments. Neither the council
nor the assembly had more than advisory
power, the real authority resting with the
khedive and through him with the British
representative.

1883-1907. SIR EVELYN BARING (1892
— Lord **Cromer**) **resident** and
consul-general. Cromer's rule was that of
a strong man, who ordered the finances,
developed the economic power of the
country, revised taxation, abolished the
corvée, etc., though doing little for popular
education or for the development of self-
government. British advisers were appointed for all important native officials
and exercised an ill-defined but effective
control.

1883, Nov. 5. Battle of El Obeid. Gen.
Hicks, with an Egyptian force,
was completely defeated and his army wiped
out by the forces of the **Mahdi Mohammed
Ahmed** of Dongola, who set himself up as
a prophet and organized a great movement

throughout the Sudan directed against the
baneful Egyptian rule. Throughout 1882–
1883 he had fought with varying success
against the Egyptians until his victory at
El Obeid gave him control over Kordofan.
Slatin Bey and **Lupton Bey,** governors of
Darfur and Bahr-el-Ghazal respectively,
were soon obliged to surrender, only **Emin
Pasha** retaining his position in Equatoria.
Osman Digna, ablest of the lieutenants of
the Mahdi, carried on a vigorous offensive
against the Red Sea ports.

1884, Jan. 6. The British obliged the reluctant Egyptian government to
decide on the **evacuation and
abandonment of the Sudan.**

Jan. 18. Gen. Charles Gordon was sent
out to effect the evacuation of
Egyptian garrisons. He reached Khartum
on Feb. 18 and offered remission of taxes,
non-interference with the slave trade, and
recognition of the Mahdi as sultan of
Kordofan, his idea being to re-establish
the local chiefs in their positions under
Egyptian suzerainty. These offers were
rejected by the Mahdi, who continued his
conquests.

**June 28-Aug. 2. International confer-
ence** on Egyptian finance at
London. The British proposed the reduction of interest on the debt and the use of
the surplus revenue to meet the heavy
charges of the Sudan campaigns. The
powers rejected these suggestions, Bismarck
working closely with Jules Ferry to frustrate the British (p. 738).

**Sept. 18. The British suspended the
sinking-fund payments,** but were
obliged by protests of the powers
and a decision of the mixed tribunals to give up this course of
action.

**1885, Jan. 26. THE MAHDI TOOK
KHARTUM,** massacring Gordon
and the garrison. A relief force,
sent out from Wadi Halfa (Aug.
1884), reached the city just too
late.

Mar. 27. An international conference
at Paris accepted the French proposals regarding the financial problem —
reduction of interest and a loan under international guaranty. Thus **international control** was in some measure retained, giving
France in particular ample opportunity to
impede the British policy.

June 21. Death of the Mahdi, who was
succeeded by the **Khalifa Abdullah
el Taashi.** On July 30 the dervishes (followers of the Mahdi) took the key position
of **Kassala,** completing their control of the
whole Sudan except for the Red Sea fortresses. In that region and along the new

Egyptian frontier at Wadi Halfa, fighting continued throughout the next ten years.

1887, May 22. Drummond-Wolff Convention between Turkey and Great Britain. The British promised to evacuate Egypt within three years provided conditions were favorable, but retained the right to reoccupy the country if it were menaced by invasion or internal disorder. Under pressure from France and Russia the sultan refused to ratify this convention and the British became more and more convinced that they must remain in the country for some time.

1888, Oct. 29. SUEZ CANAL CONVENTION (Treaty of Constantinople) signed by Great Britain, France, Germany, Italy, Austria, Spain, the Netherlands, Russia, and Turkey, after an international conference at Paris in 1885 had failed to establish a régime for the canal. The **Convention of 1888** declared the canal free and open to merchant and war vessels of all powers in time of war as in time of peace; the canal was not to be blockaded and no acts of hostility were to be committed within its confines, but the sultan and khedive were to be free to take such measures as they *"might find necessary for securing by their own forces the defense of Egypt and the maintenance of public order."* The British government **reserved the application of the convention** in so far as *"they might fetter the liberty of their government during the occupation of Egypt by their forces."* The treaty therefore did not actually go into effect.

1892-1914. ABBAS HILMI II, son of Tewfik, khedive. He was a young and headstrong man who resented the tutelage of the British and, relying on French support, attempted to shake off the domination of Lord Cromer. This led to much friction and an acute **crisis in Jan. 1893,** in which Cromer asserted British authority to the full and increased the forces of occupation.

1896-1898. RECONQUEST OF THE SUDAN by Gen. **Lord Kitchener** (of Khartum). This was due less to indignation at the conditions under dervish rule than to a growing realization of the importance of the Sudan to assure and increase the Egyptian water-supply, and further to the constant advance upon the Sudan of forces of the Belgian Congo and of France. For the international aspects of the Nile problem see p. 748.

1896, Sept. 21. Kitchener took Dongola. He proceeded with the greatest caution, building a railroad as he advanced.

1897, Aug. 7. The Egyptians took Abu Hamed.

1898, Apr. 8. Kitchener's victory at the Atbara River.

Sept. 2. BATTLE OF OMDURMAN, decisive defeat of the Khalifa, who fled. The Egyptian forces took Khartum.

Sept. 19. Kitchener reached Fashoda and found the French under Maj. Marchand in occupation. For the Fashoda crisis see p. 748.

1899, Jan. 19. An Anglo-Egyptian Convention established a condominium in what became known as the Anglo-Egyptian Sudan.

Mar. 21. Convention between Britain and France ending the Fashoda crisis. The French were definitely excluded from the Bahr-el-Ghazal and from all contact with the Nile.

Nov. 24. Defeat and death of the Khalifa, who had been pursued into Kordofan by Sir Reginald Wingate.

1902, May 15. Treaty between Britain and Ethiopia, by which the latter accepted a frontier with the Sudan well removed from the Nile.

Dec. Opening of the Aswan Dam, first of the great storage reservoirs on the upper Nile.

1904, Apr. 8. The Anglo-French entente cordiale finally brought to an end the French obstruction of British policy in Egypt. Great Britain recognized the Suez Canal Convention as in full force.

1906, May 3. A British ultimatum to Turkey obliged the latter to renounce claims to the **Sinai Peninsula,** which became Egyptian territory.

May 9. Agreement between Britain and King Leopold as sovereign of the Congo. After years of friction, Leopold gave up his claims to the Bahr-el-Ghazal (under the Treaty of 1894), but was given the **Lado Enclave** on the upper Nile for the duration of his life.

June 13. The Denshawi affair. Several British officers, on a pigeon-shooting expedition, were attacked by natives and one was killed. The episode revealed popular hatred of foreign rule, and the punishment of the culprits, which was made a demonstration, served to arouse Egyptian national feeling.

1907-1911. SIR ELDON GORST, resident and British consul-general, on the retirement of Lord Cromer (d. 1917). Gorst attempted a more lenient policy, established friendlier relations with the khedive and encouraged popular education.

1907, Dec. 7. First Nationalist Congress and organization of a Nationalist party under leadership of **Mustapha Kamel.** The program was a liberal, pacific, and cultural one.

1908, Feb. 10. Death of Mustapha Kamel, aged only 34, a great loss to the reviving nationalist movement.

Nov. 12. The khedive, possibly to counteract the nationalist movement, appointed as premier a Christian Copt, **Butros Ghali.** This led to violent Islamic agitation.

1909, Mar. 25. The government instituted a system of **press censorship** and supervision to check the extravagances of the Nationalists.

July 4. A law of police supervision enabled the government to exile undesirable agitators.

1910, Feb. 20. Assassination of Butros Ghali by a Nationalist fanatic. The trial and execution of the assassin brought the unrest to a new pitch.

June 16. On the death of Leopold II, the **Lado Enclave reverted to the Sudan.**

1911-1914. **LORD KITCHENER,** resident and consul-general on the death of Sir Eldon Gorst. He proceeded vigorously against disorderly agitation, but at the same time attempted to satisfy Egyptian opinion by liberal concessions.

1913, July 21 The government introduced a **new electoral law and a new constitutional system:** the old general assembly was abolished and all popular authority vested in a new legislative assembly, largely elective, which was given the power to initiate legislation and wide powers of supervising the budget, etc.

1914, Jan. 22-June 17. Meeting of the **first assembly,** which was then suspended during the World War.

Nov 6. Proclamation of a **state of war** with Turkey.

Dec. 18. Declaration of a British **protectorate** over Egypt.

Dec. 19. Deposition of Abbas II, who was accused of intrigue with the Sultan of Turkey and of anti-British designs.

1914-1917. **HUSSEIN KAMIL** (uncle of Abbas II), proclaimed *sultan.*

(*Cont. pp.* 919 *f.,* 1081.)

3. ETHIOPIA AND THE RED SEA AREA

1855. **Ras Kassa** succeeded in deposing **Ras Ali of Gondar** and thereupon conquered the rulers of Tigré, Gojjam, and Shoa, making himself king of kings, under the throne name of *Theodore.*

1855-1868. **THEODORE,** emperor. He was supported by the Englishmen **Walter Plowden** and John Bell in suppressing his rebellious subordinates.

1862, Mar. The French acquired the port of Obock from the Sultan of Tajura.

Oct. After Plowden's death Theodore, through the new British consul, **C. D. Cameron,** proposed an alliance with England against the Turks. Through an oversight no reply was made to this proposal, and Theodore, deeply offended, threw Cameron and other European traders and missionaries into prison at Magdala (Jan. 1864).

1866, Jan. Theodore received Hormuzd Rassam, a British envoy, but threw him also into prison. Several ultimata from the British government failed to reach him.

1868. **EXPEDITION OF SIR ROBERT NAPIER** and an Anglo-Indian force to Ethiopia. Napier proceeded with great caution, but found much support from local chiefs, estranged by Theodore's boundless vindictiveness and cruelty.

Apr. 10. Battle of Arogee. Theodore was defeated and committed suicide.

Apr. 13. The British stormed Magdala and released the prisoners, after which Napier withdrew from the country, which relapsed into anarchy.

1869. The Italian **Rubattino Company** bought the port of **Assab** on the Red Sea, to be used as a station on the new Suez-Red Sea route.

1872-1889. **JOHANNES IV** (ruler of Tigré), king of kings.

1872-1874. **Egyptian occupation of the Red Sea coast,** as far as Cape Guardafui.

1875-1879. **War between Ethiopia and Egypt,** in which the Egyptians were successful, cutting off Ethiopia from the sea.

1882. Johannes, having defeated **Menelek,** King of Shoa, made a pact with him and designated him as his successor.

1882. The Italian government took over Assab, which became the kernel of the colony of **Eritrea**.

1884. Following the Egyptian withdrawal from the Sudan and the Red Sea coast, **England established a protectorate** over part of the **Somali coast**, with **Zeila** as the chief port. The French at the same time expanded their station at Obock into a **French Somali protectorate**.

1885, Feb. 6. The Italians, encouraged by the British, established themselves at **Massawa**, whence they at once began a policy of expansion into the highlands of the interior.

1887-1889. War of Johannes against the Italians. The Ethiopians attacked Massawa and on Jan. 26 annihilated an Italian force in the **battle of Dogali**. The Italians were saved by the attacks of the Mahdist forces in northern Ethiopia, which diverted Johannes.

1887. The French transferred the seat of their protectorate from Obock to **Jibuti**, commanding the chief caravan route to Ethiopia.

1888, Feb. The British and French made an agreement regarding their spheres in Somaliland and engaged not to expand into **Harrar**.

Dec. Revolt of **Menelek** of Shoa against Johannes. He was supported by the Italians, to whom he promised parts of northern Ethiopia in return for munitions.

1889, Mar. 12. Death of Johannes, killed in the **battle of Metemma** against the Mahdists. Menelek's succession was disputed by **Ras Mangasha**, son of Johannes. The Italians supported Menelek and took over Keren and Asmara by way of reward.

1889-1911. MENELEK, emperor.

May 2. TREATY OF UCCIALLI between Italy and Menelek, from which the Italians derived a claim to a protectorate over all Ethiopia. A supplementary agreement (Oct. 1) gave Menelek a loan on the security of the Harrar customs, Harrar to revert to the Italians in default of interest payments.

Aug. 3. The Italians secured from the Sultan of Zanzibar **the entire Benadir coast** from Kismayu to Cape Guardafui.

1890. The Italian Red Sea possessions were organized as the **colony of Eritrea**.

1891, Feb. 9. Menelek, having subdued Ras Mangasha, **denounced the Italian claims** to a protectorate, which were unjustified according to the Amharic text of the Treaty of Uccialli.

Mar. 24, Apr. 15. Two **Anglo-Italian agreements** defined the frontiers of their Red Sea colonies. England recognized the Italian protectorate over the whole of Ethiopia to within 100 miles of the Nile and Italy agreed not to interfere with the water-supply of the Atbara River.

Apr. 10. Menelek's circular to the powers, claiming all territory to the Nile and to Lake Victoria.

1893, May 15. The Italian government leased Italian Somaliland to the **Filonardi Company** for exploitation.

Dec. The Italians defeated and threw back the **Mahdists** who had attacked Eritrea.

1894, Mar. 9. Menelek granted to his Swiss adviser, **Alfred Ilg**, a concession for a **railway from Jibuti** to the new capital, **Addis Ababa**, and thence westward to the Nile.

May 5. Another Anglo-Italian agreement abandoned **Harrar** to Italy (despite the Anglo-French agreement of 1888), but gave Britain the freedom to act there until Italy should take it over.

July 17. The Italians took **Kassala** from the dervishes.

1895, Mar. 25. The Italians began their advance into Ethiopia and took **Adigrat**.

Sept. Menelek declared war against the Italians.

Dec. 8. Defeat of the Italians at **Amba Alagi**.

1896, Mar. 1. BATTLE OF ADUA. An Italian force of some 20,000 was annihilated by some 80,000 Ethiopians under Menelek (p. 745).

Mar. 18. The Italians repulsed a vigorous attack of the dervishes on Kassala.

Oct. 26. Treaty of Addis Ababa between Ethiopia and Italy, the Italians recognizing the independence of Ethiopia and restricting themselves to their coastal possessions.

1897, Mar. 20. Treaty between Ethiopia and France, defining the Somali frontier. The French influence at Addis Ababa was at its height at this time and the French hoped to use Ethiopia as a base for the advance on the Nile.

May 14. Treaty of Ethiopia with Great Britain (**Rodd Mission**); the British abandoned much of the territory claimed in Somaliland, but failed to get Menelek to surrender his claims toward the Nile.

Dec. 25. **The Italians,** hard pressed by the dervishes, **ceded Kassala** to the Egyptians.

1898, June 22. **An Ethiopian force,** accompanied by a French mission, **reached the Nile,** but was unable to effect contact with Marchand coming from the west. Other Ethiopian armies pushed to the north and south and brought all the highland territory under Menelek's control, thus founding the **modern Ethiopian Empire.**

1899, Sept. Rise of the "Mad Mullah," Mohammed ben Abdullah, a Somali chief who proclaimed himself Mahdi and began systematic raids on the British and Italian possessions.

1900, July 10. An **Ethiopian-Italian agreement** defined the frontier of their respective territories.

1901, Dec. 7. **Anglo-Italian agreement** defining the frontier of the Sudan and the Italian possessions. There were many supplementary agreements.

1902, Feb. 6. The French government agreed to subsidize the **Jibuti-Addis Ababa railroad** enterprise. This led to strong protests from Britain and Italy, which demanded the internationalization of the line.

Mar. 18. Agreement between England and Ethiopia regarding the **Nile water-supply,** and an eventual dam at Lake Tana.

May 15. Anglo-Ethiopian agreement regarding the **Sudan frontier;** Menelek gave up all claim to territory bordering the Nile.

1905, Mar. 5. After years of campaigning by England, Italy, and Ethiopia against the Mad Mullah, an agreement was reached with him allowing him territory in Italian Somaliland.

Mar. 16. **The Italian government took over Somaliland** from the Filonardi Company.

1906, July 4. **TRIPARTITE PACT** between Great Britain, France, and Italy: they declared for the independence and integrity of Ethiopia and engaged not to interfere, but for the event of the situation becoming untenable they defined **spheres of influence** (Lake Tana region to England; the railway zone to France; a crescent-shaped belt of territory connecting

Eritrea with Italian Somaliland to the west of Addis Ababa to Italy). Britain and Italy were given seats on the board of the railway company. Menelek protested against the implications of the treaty and reserved his sovereign rights (Dec. 10).

1907, Oct. 26. Menelek, stricken by partial paralysis, organized a cabinet to assist him.

Dec. 6. An agreement between England and Ethiopia defined the frontier with **Uganda** and **East Africa.**

1908, June. Menelek named his grandson, **Lij Yasu** (12 years old), as his heir, with **Ras Tessama** as regent. As Menelek became more and more helpless, a three-cornered struggle for influence developed between the supporters of Lij Yasu and those of the Empress Taitu and those of Ras Tessama. For several years the empress was supreme. **Growing influence of the Germans** during this period.

1908. Resumption of the raids of the Mad Mullah. The British withdrew to the coast, but sporadic fighting continued until 1920, when the Mullah died (Nov. 23).

1911, May 15. **LIJ YASU PROCLAIMED EMPEROR,** on the death of Ras Tessama.

July 15. An Anglo-Italian agreement defined the boundary of **Italian Somaliland** and **British East Africa** at the mouth of the Juba River.

Dec. 12. Death of Menelek.

1916, Apr. **Lij Yasu announced his conversion to Islam.** This aroused a storm of opposition among the local chiefs, who were supported by the British, French, and Italian representatives, who regarded Lij Yasu as a tool of the Germans and his conversion as a step in the direction of an alliance with Turkey and Germany.

Sept. 27. **Lij Yasu was deposed** by the head of the Ethiopian Church and fled to the Danakil country.

1916–1926. The **EMPRESS ZAUDITU** (Judith), a daughter of Menelek, was proclaimed queen of kings, with Ras Tafari as heir. The intestinal struggles in Ethiopia continued for several years.

1918, May 21. Completion of the railroad from Jibuti to Addis Ababa (begun in 1897). *(Cont. p. 1085.)*

4. NORTHERN AFRICA

Morocco, Algeria, Tunisia, Libya

At the beginning of the 19th century these territories were all (except Morocco) more or less under the suzerainty of the Ottoman Porte, but the local rulers were to all intents and purposes independent. They engaged freely in **piratical enterprises** against European commerce in the Mediterranean and made the coast towns veritable slave emporia. Their territories were organized on a tribal basis and their authority did not run far from the coast. Disorder, poverty, and general backwardness were characteristic of the entire area.

1816. Commissioned by the Congress of Vienna, the **British bombarded Algiers** and obliged the dey to put an end to **Christian slavery.**

1827. The French consul at Algiers was slapped in the face with a fly-whisk by the dey, who ignored repeated French demands for satisfaction.

1830, July 5. A FRENCH EXPEDITIONARY FORCE, after a short campaign, **took Algiers** and deposed the dey. A few other coast towns were occupied, but the French seem to have been uncertain of their own further plans.

1832-1834. Attacks upon the French by **Abd el-Kader** of Mascara, proclaimed *dey* by the native chiefs. After suffering several setbacks, the French recognized him as **Dey of Mascara.**

1835. A **Turkish force landed at Tripoli,** put an end to the independence of the country, and replaced the last Karamanli ruler by a Turkish governor.

1835-1837. **Second war** of the French with Abd el-Kader. The French were repeatedly defeated.

1837, May 30. By the **Treaty of Tafna,** the French abandoned most of the hinterland of Algeria to Abd el-Kader.

1840, Dec. Outbreak of the **third war** with Abd el-Kader. The French sent a large expeditionary force under **Marshal Bugeaud,** who began the systematic subjugation of the interior.

1841. Abd el-Kader was driven across the frontier into Morocco, where he secured the aid of the sultan.

1844, Aug. 6. The French, under the Duke of Joinville, began hostilities against **Morocco,** bombarding **Tangier and** occupying **Mogador.**

Aug. 14. Battle of Isly. Bugeaud completely defeated Abd el-Kader and the Moroccans.

Sept. 10. **Treaty of Tangier,** concluding the war of the French against Morocco. The French withdrew.

1845, Mar. 18. Convention of Lalla Maghnia, fixing the boundary between Algeria and Morocco on the Mediterranean coast.

1847, Dec. 23. Abd el-Kader surrendered to Gen. Lamoricière. Contrary to promise, he was sent a prisoner to France. He was released in 1852 by Napoleon III and died at Damascus in 1883.

1848. Algeria was organized as three departments, represented in the French parliament. This system was revoked by Napoleon III, who restored military rule. Continued insurrections in the interior obliged the French to continue operations. By 1870 they had subjugated the central part of present-day Algeria.

1863. An important land law recognized private ownership in Algeria and did much to break up the tribal organization. The French made staunch attempts to settle the country with military colonists, but with indifferent success.

1869. The Bey of Tunis, having borrowed heavily in Europe and having failed to meet his obligations, was obliged to accept an **international financial control** of England, France, and Italy.

1878, July 8. At the **Congress of Berlin** Lord Salisbury offered the French a free hand in Tunis as compensation for the acquisition of Cyprus by Britain.

1879. Algeria was definitively put under civil government.

1879-1881. Acute rivalry between **the French and the Italians in Tunis,** both sides struggling and intriguing for key concessions (railroad, telegraph, land grants, etc.).

1881. Early French projects for a **Trans-Saharan Railway** were brought to an end with the murder of the Flatters mission of investigation.

1880, July 3. MADRID CONVENTION, signed by the leading European powers and the United States, by which the status and privileges of foreigners in Morocco were regulated.

1881, Mar. Raids of Krumir tribes from Tunisia across the frontier into Algeria. Though there was nothing very unusual about these raids, they gave the French a convenient excuse for settling the score with the bey and concluding the competition with Italy.

Apr. 30. A French naval force seized **Bizerta,** while a land force invaded Tunis from Algeria.

May 12. TREATY OF BARDO (Kasr es-Said), by which the Bey of Tunis accepted a **French protectorate.** Loud protests from the Turkish government, from Italy and from England led to nothing, since Bismarck gave the French steady support.

June 30. Outbreak of a serious **insurrection against the French** under **Ali ben Khalifa.** The French were obliged to subdue southern Tunisia in a regular campaign.

July. At the same time a major **uprising against the French in Algeria** was led by **Bou Amama.** This was not suppressed until 1883.

1883, June 8. The Convention of Marsa, between the French and the Bey of Tunis, gave the French effective control (through a resident-general) of Tunisian affairs.

1893. Attacks of the Riff tribes of Morocco upon the Spanish possessions on the coast. The Spaniards had great difficulty in maintaining themselves.

1894. ABDUL AZIZ (a boy of 13) became Sultan of Morocco. He was intelligent and well-intentioned, but was unable to control his powerful ministers or to keep within bounds the growing forces of European penetration. By 1900 the country had fallen into complete anarchy.

1896, Sept. 28. A Franco-Italian agreement brought an end to the long-drawn dispute about the **status of Italian residents in Tunis.** Their nationality and that of their descendants was to be regulated by Italian law.

1898. Reorganization of the government of Algeria; decentralization of the administration; establishment of an assembly with elected members.

1899, Mar. 21. Anglo-French convention defining the hinterland of Tripoli, after the Fashoda crisis. The Italians protested loudly against the large concessions to France in the Sahara.

1900-1903. French occupation of the oases (Igli, Gourara, Timmimun, Tidikelt, Tuat) to the southwest of Algeria. These had belonged to Morocco, though the effective control of the sultan had broken down.

1900, Dec. 14. Secret Franco-Italian agreement, by which France was given a free hand in Morocco in return for a free hand for Italy in Tripoli.

1901, July 20. French agreement with Morocco giving France considerable control of the police on the frontier.

1902-1903. Growing disorder in Morocco: **rising of the pretender Omar Zarhuni.**

1904, Apr. 8. THE ENTENTE CORDIALE between England and France (p. 752). This gave France a free hand in Morocco and assured her of the diplomatic support of England.

May 18. Kidnaping of Mr. Perdicaris, an American citizen, by the Moroccan chieftain **Raisuli.** He was released for a ransom on June 24, but Raisuli continued for years to terrorize the country behind Tangier.

Oct. 3. Franco-Spanish agreement on Morocco: the northern, Mediterranean belt was reserved to Spain as a zone of influence.

1905, Jan.-Mar. Mission of St. René Taillandier to Fez, to induce the sultan to accept a far-reaching scheme of reform under French guidance.

Mar. 31. Spectacular **visit of the Emperor William II** to Tangier. Beginning of the **first Moroccan crisis** between France and Germany (p. 753).

June 3. The Sultan of Morocco invited the powers to a conference to arrange for reform.

1906, Jan. 16-Apr. 7. THE ALGECIRAS CONFERENCE and the **Act of Algeciras** (p. 754), giving France and Spain substantial control of Moroccan reform, but reaffirming the independence and integrity of Morocco and equality of economic opportunity. This was accepted by the sultan on June 18.

1907, July 30. The French occupied Ujda (northwest Morocco) following continued disorders and the **murder of Dr. Mauchamp.**

Aug. 4. The French bombarded Casablanca and then occupied the whole Shawia region on the Atlantic coast, following serious antiforeign outbreaks.

Nov. 24. Mulai Hafid (brother of Abdul Aziz), who had been proclaimed sultan at Marakesh (May 5) was defeated by the sultan's troops.

1908, Jan. 4. Mulai Hafid was proclaimed sultan at Fez.

Aug. 23. Abdul Aziz was defeated at Marakesh.

Sept. 3. The German government notified its intention of recognizing Mulai Hafid. The other powers reluctantly followed suit (Dec. 17) after Mulai Hafid had agreed to respect the Act of Algeciras and other international obligations.

Sept. 25. The Casablanca affair, arising from the seizure of German deserters from the French foreign legion. The matter was adjusted by the Hague Court in May, 1909 (p. 756).

1909, Feb. 9. FRANCO-GERMAN AGREEMENT on Morocco. Germany recognized France's special political position, in return for economic concessions (p. 756).

July-Oct. Attacks of the Riff tribesmen upon the Spaniards at Melilla. Despite heavy losses the Spaniards began to spread in the zone reserved to them.

Oct. 24. Russian-Italian agreement at Racconigi (p. 757). The Russians gave the Italians a free hand in Tripoli.

1910, Mar. 4. Agreement between France and Morocco. The French evacuated Udja and the sultan accepted the program of reform.

1911, Apr. 2. Attack of Berber tribesmen on Fez.

Apr. 26. A French force occupied Fez on the plea of protecting foreigners.

July 1. Arrival of the **German gunboat *Panther* at Agadir.** Beginning of the **second Moroccan crisis** between France and Germany (p. 757).

Sept. 29. Outbreak of **war between Italy and Turkey,** following a short-term ultimatum demanding guaranties for the protection of Italians and Italian enterprises in Tripoli. The war reflected Italy's determination to secure compensation for the French advance in Morocco (p. 758).

Nov. 4. Franco-German agreement regarding Morocco. In return for compensation in the French Congo, the Germans gave the French a free hand in Morocco (p. 758).

Nov. 5. The Italians proclaimed the **annexation of Tripoli and Cyrenaica,** though only a few coastal towns had been taken.

1912, Mar. 30. TREATY OF FEZ. The sultan was obliged to accept a **French protectorate.**

May 24. Gen. Lyautey appointed resident-general in Morocco. By his judicious policy rapid strides were made in the restoration of order and the recognition of French authority.

Aug. 11. Mulai Hafid abdicated rather than rule as the client of France. He was succeeded by **Mulai Yusuf.**

Oct. 18. The Treaty of Lausanne brought the Tripolitan War to a close. The Turkish sultan abandoned Tripoli, but retained religious authority (p. 759).

Nov. 27. Franco-Spanish agreement, defining the position of the Spanish zone in Morocco in relation to the French protectorate and establishing a **special status for Tangier.**

1913. Italian subjugation of the interior of Tripoli (Libya).

1914, Sept. Outbreak of a formidable **insurrection among the Arabs** (Senussi) of Libya. On the entry of Italy into the World War (May, 1915) the movement assumed ever larger dimensions. The Italians were obliged to withdraw from the interior and during the war held only the towns of **Tripoli** and **Homs** on the coast. **Misurata** and other ports were used as German submarine bases. (*Cont. p.* 1086.)

5. WEST AFRICA AND THE SUDAN

French West Africa, Gambia, Sierra Leone, Gold Coast, Togoland, Nigeria, Cameroons, Rio de Oro, Portuguese Guinea

At the beginning of the 19th century the Portuguese, Spanish, French, British, Dutch, Danes, and Swedes all had forts or posts on the coasts of West Africa, engaged in the slave trade and in trade in gold, ivory, and oil. With the abolition of the slave trade many of these stations languished and were abandoned. The interior of the country had to a large extent been conquered by **Tukulor chiefs** with the aid of the pastoral Fulani tribes. Various Tukulor sultans (Moslem) ruled from the Senegal to Lake Chad, the populations of these regions remaining to a large extent pagan. South of the Niger lay a number of strong Negro kingdoms, **Mandingo, Ashanti, Dahomey.** Farther to the east were the empires of **Bagirmi** (dating from the 16th century), which was subjected by Wadai in 1808; and **Waidai** (dating from the 17th century), which was almost chronically at war with the Sultans of Darfur. In the eastern Sudan there arose (1805) the power of the **Senussi,** a puritanical sect of Islam (later centered at Kufra) which made a special point of keeping the infidel Christians from Moslem territory.

1799. Foundation of the **British Church Missionary Society,** which carried on extensive work in West Africa.

1799, July 5. Sierra Leone (acquired 1787 and used for the settlement of freed slaves) was made a separate British colony.

1807. The British settlement on the **Gambia** was put under the government of Sierra Leone, which became a crown colony (1808).

1809. The British captured the French settlements on the Senegal.

1817. The British returned Senegal to the French.

1821. Sierra Leone, the **Gold Coast,** and the Gambia were joined as the **British West African Settlements.**

1822. Foundation of Liberia as a colony for freed American slaves (first colonists had arrived in 1820).

1824-1827. First war of the British on the Gold Coast with the powerful rulers of the **Ashanti.**

1828. The Basel Mission (Swiss) began active missionary work on the Gold Coast.

1829. The **British Slave Trade Commissioners** took over the administration of the island of **Fernando Po,** with Spanish consent.

1842-1843. The French made the first treaties with the native chiefs of the **Ivory Coast.**

1843. **Fernando Po was returned to** Spanish rule.

1843. Gambia was separated from Sierra Leone and made a separate crown colony.

1845. **Edward Saker** and the Baptist Mission established themselves at **Ambas Bay,** on the coast of the Cameroons.

1846. The British Presbyterian Mission began its activities on the Nigerian coast. By this time numerous other missionary societies (British, Swiss, German) had begun to operate. Their success among the Moslem inhabitants of West Africa was rather limited.

1847, July 26. Establishment of the **FREE AND INDEPENDENT REPUBLIC OF LIBERIA.** It was recognized first by Great Britain, and then by other countries.

1849, Apr. 5. The French proclaimed a **protectorate over French Guinea.**

1850, Jan. 24. The Gold Coast was made a separate British colony.

Aug. 17. Denmark sold her four posts on the Gold Coast to Great Britain.

1854-1865. GOVERNORSHIP OF GEN. FAIDHERBE in Senegal. He carried on successful campaigns against **El Hajj Omar,** the powerful Tukulor chieftain, who was ultimately defeated and driven eastward to the upper Niger. He died in 1864, but his sons succeeded to his kingdom, which was rent by dynastic wars until its conquest by the French in 1890. Faidherbe extended and consolidated the Senegal colony.

1860. **German traders** (Woermann and Company) opened a factory **on the Cameroons coast.**

1861, Aug. 6. The British secured possession of the **Lagos coast** through treaties with the chiefs.

1862, June 3. The United States recognized the Republic of Liberia

1863, Feb. 25. The French established a protectorate at **Porto Novo** on the Dahomey coast.

1866, Feb. 19. The British colonies in West Africa were once more united under the jurisdiction of the Sierra Leone government.

1871, Feb. 21. The Dutch sold **El Mina** and other posts on the Gold Coast to Great Britain.

1873-1874. SECOND ASHANTI WAR; campaigns of Sir Garnet Wolseley, who entered the Ashanti capital, **Coomassie,** Feb. 4, 1874.

1878. The Mission of the White Fathers (under **Cardinal Lavigerie**) was given charge by the pope of the Catholic missions in Africa.

1874, July 24. The British West African colonies were once again separated.

1879. Foundation of the **United African Company** (National African Company after 1881) by **Sir George Goldie.** This brought together a number of small British firms trading on the Nigerian coast since 1832 and made possible British expansion in this area.

1882, June 28. An Anglo-French agreement delimited the boundary between Sierra Leone and French Guinea.

1883. Re-establishment of the French on the coast of **Dahomey** and beginning of expansion into the interior.

1883-1888. French conquest of the upper Niger region, from Senegal. A key fort was built at **Bamaku.**

1884, July 5. Gustav Nachtigal proclaimed a German protectorate over the coast of **Togoland.**

July 12. Gustav Nachtigal proclaimed a German protectorate over the **Cameroons coast,** five days before the arrival of the British representative dispatched for the same purpose. The British resigned their rights and recognized the German protectorate May 7, 1885.

1885, Jan. 9. The Spanish proclaimed a protectorate over **Río de Oro** and Spanish Guinea.

June 5. The British proclaimed a protectorate over the **Niger River** region.

Nov. 11. The boundary between **Sierra Leone and Liberia** was defined by agreement.

1885-1886. Campaigns of the French against the powerful Mandingo ruler, **Samori,** in the Ivory Coast hinterland.

1886, Jan. 13. Lagos, on the west coast of Nigeria, was set up as a separate British colony.

May 12. A French-Portuguese agreement defined the frontier between French and Portuguese Guinea.

July 10. THE ROYAL NIGER COMPANY was chartered and given full control of the British sphere in Nigeria. This company succeeded the National African Company.

July 14. An Anglo-German agreement delimited the frontier between the Gold Coast and Togoland.

July 27. An Anglo-German agreement began the delimitation of the Nigeria-Cameroons frontier.

1889, Jan. 10. France established a formal protectorate over the Ivory Coast.

Aug. 10. An Anglo-French agreement defined their respective spheres on the Gold and Ivory coasts and on the Senegal and Gambia.

1890. French war with the **King of Dahomey,** who was defeated and forced to recognize the French protectorate. Beginning of French expansion into the interior.

Aug. 5. An important **Anglo-French** agreement defined their possessions in northern Nigeria by a line running from **Say to Lake Chad.**

1892. Second Dahomey War. The French deposed the king, but were confronted with further risings of the warlike natives in 1893-1894.

1892. Further conquests of the French on the upper Niger. Col. Archinard took Segu and broke the powers of the Fulani.

Dec. 8. A French agreement with Liberia defined the boundary between the Liberian Republic and the Ivory Coast.

1893. Further advance of the French on the Niger. They took Jenné and Timbuktu, defeating the Tuaregs (Dec. 16).

Mar. 10. The colonies of French Guinea (hitherto Rivières du Sud) and the Ivory Coast formally established.

Nov. 15. An Anglo-German agreement defined the Nigerian-Cameroons boundary, leaving the region east of Lake Chad to Germany to within 100 miles of the Nile.

1893-1894. THIRD ASHANTI WAR. The natives were defeated and a British protectorate set up.

1894-1895. Abortive campaign of the French under Maj. Monteil against the forces of **Samori.**

1894, Mar. 15. Franco-German agreement on the boundary between the Cameroons and the French Congo. The French were given the basin of the Shari River and the Bagirmi region, and therewith an open road to the eastern Sudan and the Nile.

June 22. Dahomey was made a French colony.

1895, Jan. 1. The Royal Niger Company proclaimed a **protectorate over Busa** on the middle Niger and **Nikki** in the hinterland of Dahomey.

June. The French possessions in West Africa were united under a governor-general.

1895-1896. FOURTH ASHANTI WAR. Sir Francis Scott took **Coomassie** (Jan. 18, 1896), made the king a prisoner, and proclaimed a British protectorate (Aug. 16).

1897, July 23. A Franco-German agreement defined the boundary between Dahomey and Togoland.

1897-1898. Acute tension in Anglo-French relations arising from competition for the possession of western Nigeria. The French, eager to connect their territories on the Niger with those in Dahomey, dispatched numerous expeditions into the disputed area, which took **Busa** (Feb. 13, 1897) and **Nikki** (Nov. 30). The British protested vigorously and by the spring of 1898 the two countries were on the verge of war.

1898, June 14. THE ANGLO-FRENCH CRISIS was ended by an agreement defining the frontier from the coast (between Dahomey and Lagos) to the Niger. The French retained Nikki, while the British were awarded Busa.

1898, Sept. 29. The French finally defeated and captured **Samori**, thus breaking the Mandingo power. Samori was exiled to Gabun and died in 1900.

1898-1899. The French, under Émile Gentil, organized the entire region along the Shari and Lake Chad. This expedition united near Lake Chad with other missions from the Senegal and Niger and from Algeria, thus establishing the **connection of all the French possessions.**

1899, Mar. 21. Following the **Fashoda crisis** (p. 748), an **Anglo-French agreement** excluded the French from Bahr-el-Ghazal and Darfur, but left them a free hand in Wadai, Borku, and Tibesti in the eastern Sudan.

Aug. 9. The British government took over **Nigeria** from the Royal Niger Company and made it a British protectorate (Jan. 1, 1900).

Nov. 14. An **Anglo-German agreement** settled the Togoland-Gold Coast frontier and abolished the neutral zone previously established on the upper Volta River.

1900, Mar.-Nov. Rising of the Ashantis, who besieged Coomassie. The rebellion was ultimately suppressed and the capital relieved.

Apr. 22. In the **battle of Lakhta** or **Kusseri** the French defeated and killed **Rabah Zobeir**, foster brother of the famous Sudanese slave-trader Zobeir, who since 1878 had been ravaging Wadai, Bagirmi and Bornu.

May. The French conquest of **Tidikelt, Tuat, Insalah,** and other oases south of Morocco and Algeria, gave them control of the northern Sahara.

June 27. A Franco-Spanish agreement defined the frontier of Río de Oro and of Spanish Guinea.

1900-1903. British conquest of northern Nigeria: Kano and Sokoto taken (Feb. 3, Mar. 15, 1903) and subdued.

1901, Sept. 26. The kingdom of Ashanti was definitely **annexed** and joined to the British Gold Coast colony.

1904. Reorganization of the French possessions (Mauretania, Senegal, French Guinea, Ivory Coast, Dahomey, Upper Senegal, and Niger) as **French West Africa,** with capital at Dakar.

1904. Insurrection of the **Ekumekus,** a fanatical sect, in southern Nigeria.

1904-1905. Serious insurrection in the Cameroons.

1906. Native rising in Sokoto.

Feb. 18. The British colony **Lagos** was incorporated with southern Nigeria.

1908-1909. French conquest of **Mauretania** by Gen. Gouraud.

1909. An American commission investigated the finances of **Liberia,** which was bankrupt. The United States supported the government against native insurrections and gave financial aid until an international loan was arranged for (June, 1912).

1909-1911. French conquest of **Wadai.**

1911, Nov. 4. By the **Franco-German agreement** settling the second Moroccan crisis (p. 757) about 100,000 sq. miles of the French

Congo were added to the German Cameroons colony.

1914. The French occupied Tibesti, but owing to the exigencies of the World War, were obliged to abandon the eastern Sudan in 1916. The region was reoccupied in 1920.

Jan. 1. Southern and northern Nigeria were joined under one administration.

1914, Aug. CONQUEST OF THE GERMAN COLONIES, Togoland, and Cameroons, by French and British forces from the neighboring colonies (p. 918).

(*Cont. p.* 1088.)

6. THE CONGO REGION

(French Equatorial Africa, Spanish Guinea, Belgian Congo, Angola)

This area is inhabited by the **Bantu,** who, because of the thick tropical jungles and the consequent difficulty of communication, never built large empires comparable to those of West Africa. In the 19th century the chief "kingdoms" were those of the **Congo** (on the lower reaches of the great river), the **Ansika** (on the Congo plateau, above Brazzaville), **Lounda** (on the border between the present-day Congo State and Angola), **Manyema** (to the west of Lake Tanganyika), and **Balouba** (to the south of Manyema).

1839-1845. The **French** acquired land by treaty on both sides of the **Gabun River.**

1840. The **Portuguese** extended their possessions in Angola south to **Mossamedes.**

1849. The **French founded Libreville,** using freed slaves as settlers.

1857-1859, 1863-1865. Explorations of **Paul du Chaillu** (a Franco-American) in the region of the Gabun and Ogowe Rivers.

1875-1878. Explorations of **Savorgnan de Brazza** in the region north of the Congo.

1876, Sept. 12. King Leopold of Belgium, an ardent imperialist, summoned to Brussels an international congress of geographers, explorers, and scientists and founded the **International Association for the Exploration and Civilization of Central Africa,** one of the chief purposes of which was to suppress the slave trade. Each national group was to establish a national committee to carry on the work in special areas. The Belgian committee was most active, and in the years 1877–1879 began to found posts on Lake Tanganyika.

1878, Nov. 25. The Belgian committee was transformed into the **Comité d'Études du Haut-Congo. H. M. Stanley,** recently returned from his crossing of Africa by the Congo route, was engaged to establish stations in the Congo area. This he did in the years 1879–1884.

1880. The French, alarmed by Stanley's activity, sent out **De Brazza,** who made treaties with the chiefs on the north side of the Congo, founded **Brazzaville** and organized a protectorate.

1882. The Comité d'Études du Haut-Congo was transformed into the **International Association of the Congo,** with trade as a main objective. A number of companies were organized to exploit the Congo region.

1884, Feb. 26. AN ANGLO-PORTUGUESE TREATY gave Portugal both sides of the lower Congo from $5° 12'$ to $8°$ S. Lat. and inland to Noki. Portugal agreed to freedom of navigation on the Congo and promised a low tariff. The treaty was intended primarily to check the French advance. Owing to vigorous parliamentary opposition and to protests from France and Germany, it had to be abandoned (June 26).

Apr. 22. The United States recognized the International Association as a territorial power.

Apr. 23. By treaty France secured the **right of pre-emption** in the event of the International Association alienating its territory.

Nov. 8. Germany recognized the International Association.

Nov. 15-1885, Feb. 26. BERLIN CONFERENCE on Congo affairs, arranged by Germany and France. It provided for freedom of navigation on the Congo and Niger, free trade in the Congo Basin, abolition of slavery and the slave trade, effective occupation of territory claimed, etc.

Dec. 16. England recognized the International Association. France and Russia followed on Feb. 5, 1885, and the

Association took the name **Independent State of the Congo.**

1885, Feb. 5. An agreement, concluded between **France and the Congo State** in connection with the recognition of the latter, defined the frontier between the Congo State and the French Congo at the Congo River and the Ubangi, a northern confluent.

Feb. 14. An agreement between the Congo State and Portugal gave the latter the Kabinda Enclave to the north of the river, and the south bank as far up as Noki.

Apr. King Leopold assumed sovereignty of the Congo State, which became his personal possession. The character of the state became less and less international and the king's objective became more and more the exploitation of the country. Concessionaires were granted large areas, but much of the country (the central portion) was set aside as state land (*domain de la couronne*) and as the king's private domain (*domain privé*).

Aug. 1. Leopold proclaimed the **neutrality of the Congo State** and announced its territorial claims.

Nov. 22. A treaty between France and the Congo State defined the boundary in the Manyanga region.

Dec. 24. An agreement between France and Germany defined the frontier between the French Congo and the Cameroons in the southern part.

1886, Apr. 27. De Brazza was made **commissioner-general** of the French Congo.

May 12. A Franco-Portuguese agreement fixed the boundary of the Kabinda enclave.

Dec. 30. A German-Portuguese agreement fixed the frontier between Angola and German Southwest Africa.

1887, Apr. 29. A new Franco-Congolese treaty defined the frontier as the Ubangi River and the 4th parallel N. Lat.

1888. The French explorer, **Paul Crampel,** opened up the region from the French Congo to Lake Chad. He was followed by others (**Dybowski, Maistre**).

Dec. 11. The French colony of **Gabun was united with the French Congo.**

1888-1889. "RESCUE" OF EMIN PASHA, the governor of Equatoria, by H. M. Stanley. The relief expedition had been largely financed by King Leopold and his friend Sir William MacKinnon, chairman of the Imperial British East Africa Company. Its real purpose was to secure Equatoria and thereby an outlet to the upper Nile for the Congo State.

Aug. 2. Leopold designated the **Belgian State as the heir of the Congo.**

1890, May 24. The MacKinnon Treaty, concluded between Leopold and the Imperial British East Africa Company. In return for a strip of territory between Lake Albert Edward and Lake Tanganyika (important for the project of an all-British Cape-to-Cairo route), the company recognized as Leopold's sphere the western bank of the upper Nile as far as Lado. This agreement, while not officially recognized by the British government, was not disavowed by it.

July 2. THE BRUSSELS ACT, concluding an international conference at Brussels. It arranged for the systematic extirpation of the slave trade, prohibition of the sale of firearms, etc.

July 3. Leopold gave the Belgian State the right to annex the Congo State after 10 years.

July 11. In return the Belgian State granted the Congo a loan without interest and a subsidy for 10 years.

Nov. 14. An agreement between England and Portugal defined the frontier of Angola and South Africa.

1891, Apr. 15. The Katanga Company formed under Leopold's auspices to exploit the rich copper deposits of Katanga, after the defeat of the native king, **Msidi.**

May 25. By treaty the Congo State and Portugal divided Lounda between them.

June 11. A further Anglo-Portuguese agreement assigned Barotseland to England. Later disagreements were arbitrated by the King of Italy (May 30, 1905).

1892, May 8. The natives of the Congo were forbidden to collect ivory and rubber excepting for the state.

May 15. Beginning of a great **rising of the Arab slaveholders** and traders on the upper Congo and in the Tanganyika region. The Belgians proceeded against them. The Arabs were defeated by Baron Dhanis (Nov. 22) and then by Col. Chaltin, who took their chief centers, **Nyangwe** (Mar. 4, 1893) and **Kasongo** (Apr. 22).

Dec. 5. Forced labor of the Congo natives was introduced in the guise of taxes in kind and labor.

Oct. A Belgian force, under **Van Kerckhoven, reached the Nile** at Wadelai and proceeded to take over the region assigned the Congo by the MacKinnon Treaty.

1893, June. The French, alarmed by the advance of the Belgians, sent out Monteil and Decazes to occupy the country from the M'Bomu River to the Nile, after futile attempts to reach an agreement with Leopold.

1894, Mar. 15. A Franco-German agreement regarding the Cameroons frontier left the French free to advance through the Sudan to the Nile.

May 12. THE CONGO TREATY, between England and the Congo State. In order to frustrate the French advance, the British leased to Leopold for the duration of his life the entire region west of the upper Nile from Lake Albert to Fashoda and west to 30° E. Long. The region west of this (to 25° E. Long.) and north of the Congo-Nile watershed, was leased to Leopold and his successors. In return England was to have a lease of a corridor 25 kilometers wide from Lake Tanganyika to Lake Albert Edward. Violent protests of the Germans forced the abandonment of the lease of the strip (June 22) while the threatening attitude of the French obliged Leopold to make an agreement with them.

Aug. 14. FRANCO-CONGOLESE AGREEMENT, fixing the frontier on the M'Bomu River and the Nile-Congo watershed along the parallel 5° 30′ N. Lat. Leopold was thus obliged to give up his claim to the northern part of the lease, but retained the region known as the Lado Enclave.

Sept. Liotard was made French commissioner of the upper Ubangi and was sent out to establish posts in the Bahr-el-Ghazal region. The French had visions of occupying the southern part of the former Egyptian Sudan and thereby forcing the British to evacuate Egypt by a threat of interference with the Nile water-supply. Some even dreamed of extending the French belt from West Africa across the Nile and Ethiopia to French Somaliland.

1895-1897. The Gentil mission opened up the Bagirmi country, the hinterland of the French Congo.

1895, Mar. 28. Statement of Sir Edward Grey in the British Parliament, that any French expedition to the upper Nile would be regarded as an "*unfriendly act.*"

Sept. Visit of King Leopold to Paris. He made an agreement with the French to co-operate on the upper Nile, and during visits to England (Oct., Jan.) attempted to bring about an adjustment of rival claims. His aim was to secure the agreement of England to a lease of the upper Nile region to the Congo State.

1896, Mar. 13. Beginning of the Egyptian reconquest of the Sudan, under Gen. Kitchener. The main object of the reconquest was to prevent the Sudan falling into the hands of France.

June. The Marchand Expedition left France, with instructions to advance to Fashoda and claim the country for France.

1897, Feb. The Belgians, under Chaltin, reached the Nile at Rejaf, and, after defeating the Sudan dervishes, occupied Lado and Wadelai.

Aug. Marchand reached the Bahr-el-Ghazal region, but was unable to proceed because of the low water of the rivers.

Sept. Great mutiny and rising of the Batetelas on the upper Congo. Baron Dhanis proceeded against them in force, but the insurrection was not finally suppressed until Oct. 1900.

1898, July 10. Marchand reached the Nile at Fashoda and established a force.

Aug. 30. Secret Anglo-German agreement for the eventual partition of the Portuguese colonies. Germany was to get the larger part of Angola (p. 748).

Sept. 19. Arrival of Kitchener at Fashoda. Acute crisis in the relations of France and England (p. 748).

Nov. 4. The French government ordered the evacuation of Fashoda.

1899. Granting of concessions in the French Congo to a number of rubber companies. Through rubber taxes and forced labor a form of slavery was introduced not much different from that of the Congo State.

1900, June 27. An agreement between France and Spain defined the boundary of Spanish Guinea.

1902. Great native uprising in Angola, suppressed with difficulty.

July 5. The French possessions on the Congo were divided into two colonies: Lower Congo-Gabun, Chad.

1903, May. Beginning of a large-scale agitation, first in England, then in the United States, Germany, and other countries, directed against the conditions in the Congo. The writings of E. D. Morel and the reports of the British consul, Sir Roger Casement, aroused great indignation.

In July 1904 Leopold sent out a commission of three to investigate. Its report (Nov. 1905) was very unfavorable. The agitation continued until the annexation of the Congo by Belgium.

Dec. 29. The French Congo was divided into four colonies: Gabun, Middle Congo, Ubangi-Shari, Chad.

1905. A serious insurrection broke out in the French Congo. An investigating commission under De Brazza was sent out.

1906, May 9. After years of friction the British finally obliged Leopold to accept a compromise settlement of his claims on the upper Nile. He was given the Lado Enclave, but only for the duration of his life.

1907. Another insurrection in Angola, connected with the Herrero rising in German Southwest Africa.

1908, Oct. 18. By act of the Belgian parliament, the Congo State was annexed to Belgium. Thenceforth the parliament exercised effective control and began the removal of abuses.

Dec. 23. A Franco-Belgian agreement definitively fixed the boundaries of the French and Belgian Congos.

1910, Jan. 15. The French Congo was renamed French Equatorial Africa, and was redivided into three colonies: Gabun, Middle Congo, Ubangi-Shari.

May 2. The labor tax was abolished in the Belgian Congo.

May 14. An Anglo-Belgian agreement gave the Belgian Congo the west shore of Lake Albert.

June 16. The Lado Enclave reverted to the Anglo-Egyptian Sudan on the death of Leopold.

July 1. An extensive program of reform was introduced in the Belgian Congo. At much the same time the French government thoroughly revised the concessions to the companies operating in the French Congo.

Aug. 11. A German-Belgian agreement fixed the frontier between the Belgian Congo and German East Africa.

1911, May 4. An Anglo-Belgian agreement defined the boundary between the Belgian Congo and Uganda.

Nov. 4. THE FRANCO-GERMAN AGREEMENT ending the second Moroccan crisis (p. 758) involved the cession by France to Germany of about 100,000 square miles of the French Congo, on the coast south beyond Spanish Guinea and in the interior two strips, one along the Sangha River to the Congo, and another to the Ubangi River.

1912, July 1. Freedom of trade in the entire Belgian Congo was declared.

1913, Jan. 31. The liquor trade was forbidden in the Belgian Congo.

1914, Feb. 3. An Anglo-Belgian agreement fixed the boundary between the Belgian Congo and British East Africa.

July. The Belgian Congo was divided into four provinces and a general program of administrative decentralization was introduced.

Aug. 15. Angola was given autonomy.
(*Cont. p.* 1089.)

7. EAST AFRICA

(Kenya, Uganda, Tanganyika, Nyasaland, Mozambique)

East Africa is inhabited almost exclusively by Negroes of the **Bantu race.** At the beginning of the 19th century the only European settlements were those of the **Portuguese,** and of these only the more southerly ones remained after the **conquests of the Arabs of Muscat** (Oman) in the late 17th century. From Cape Delgado northward to what is now Italian Somaliland the coast was under the rule of the Sultan of Muscat, who was represented by a viceroy (*Sayyid*) residing first at Mombasa, later at Zanzibar. The Arabs carried on a lively trade in slaves, and in the course of time the slave-raiders penetrated farther and farther into the interior, reaching the region of the great lakes. When the European powers, intent on the suppression of the slave trade and on the expansion of their commerce, began to interest themselves in this region, they were confronted first with the claims of the Arab ruler and then with the pretensions of Portugal.

1823. **Adm. Owen,** commanding a British squadron, raised the British flag on the south shore of **Delagoa Bay,** but this was removed after his departure, by the Portuguese.

1824-1828. Owen occupied Mombasa on the East African coast, the region being in dispute between the Sultan of Muscat and his local representative.

1840. Sayyid Said, representative of the Sultan of Muscat on the East African coast, established his capital at Zanzibar.

1841. The first British consul-general was appointed to Zanzibar. From this time on, British trade interests in East Africa developed rapidly.

1860-1865. Explorations of the German discoverer, von der Decken, in East Africa. He first outlined schemes for a German dominion in this region.

1861. Under pressure from the British, the dominions of the Sultan of Muscat were divided, Zanzibar becoming the seat of the Sultan Majid, who claimed control over some thousand miles of the coast.

1862, Mar. 10. The British and the French recognized the independence of the Sultan of Zanzibar.

1866-1887. Sir John Kirk, British consul-general at Zanzibar. Under his influence the sultan was induced to take measures against the slave trade. British interests became predominant and Kirk to a large extent determined the policy of the sultan.

1870-1888. Barghash Sayyid, Sultan of Zanzibar.

1873, June 5. Under British pressure, the sultan prohibited the export of slaves from his dominions and closed the public slave markets of Zanzibar.

1875. Following the explorations of Livingstone (p. 826), the first British missionaries appeared on the Shiré River and about Lake Nyasa. Blantyre was founded in 1876.

July 24. An arbitral award of President MacMahon of France assigned the south shore of Delagoa Bay to Portugal, rejecting the British claims.

1876. The Sultan of Zanzibar offered his continental possessions to Sir William MacKinnon, chairman of the British India Steam Navigation Company. MacKinnon appealed to the British government for support, and, failing this, declined the offer.

1877. The first Protestant missions arrived in Uganda, following an appeal from King Mtesa (1857–1884), transmitted through Stanley.

1878. The German African Society, as a branch of the International African Association, established a number of posts in the region between Bagamoyo and Lake Tanganyika.

British missionary and trading interests organized the African Lakes Trading Company on Lake Nyasa.

1879. Catholic French missionaries of the White Fathers arrived in Uganda.

1883, Dec. 14. The Portuguese government granted a concession for a railway from Delagoa Bay to the Transvaal to the American promoter, MacMurdo.

1884, Feb. 26. By the abortive Congo Treaty (p. 843) Portugal recognized British claims in the Nyasa area.

Oct. 10. Death of King Mtesa of Uganda. He was succeeded by his young and headstrong son, Mwanga, who soon became involved in struggles with the various religious factions (Moslem-Arab; Protestant-British; Catholic-French).

Nov. 19. Karl Peters, moving spirit of the German colonial movement, signed the first of a long series of treaties with the native chiefs of the regions behind Bagamoyo.

1885, Feb. 12. The German East Africa Company was chartered, to take over the claims established by Peters.

Feb. 17. The German government established a protectorate over East Africa from the Umba River in the south to the Rovuma in the north.

Apr. 8. The Denhardt brothers, Germans, secured the Witu region from the local sultan, for the newly formed Witu Company.

May 27. The German government established a protectorate over Witu.

Aug. 14. The Sultan of Zanzibar was obliged to recognize the German protectorate over Witu, following a naval demonstration and an ultimatum.

Oct. Murder of Bishop Hannington at the command of Mwanga of Uganda. Beginning of a period of persecution of the Christians and general chaos in that region.

1885-1896. Prolonged wars of the British in Nyasaland against the Arab slave-traders and their allies.

1886, May 12. France recognized the Portuguese claims to all territory between Angola in West Africa and Mozambique in East Africa, without prejudice to the claims of others. On Dec. 30 the

German government likewise recognized the Portuguese pretensions.

Oct. 29, Nov. 1. After an investigation of claims by a British-German-French commission (report June 9), the British and German governments concluded an agreement defining the possessions of the Sultan of Zanzibar: the islands of Zanzibar, Pemba, and Lamu; the northern towns of Kismayu, Brava, Merka, Magdoshu, and Warsheikh; and the coastal strip (10 miles wide). The **German and British spheres of interest** were defined by a line from the mouth of the Umba River northwest around the northern base of Mt. Kilimanjaro and thence northwest to the point where the first parallel S. Lat. strikes the east coast of Lake Victoria. In the north the British sphere extended to the Tana River, leaving Witu to the Germans.

1887, May 24. The **British East Africa Company** (Sir William MacKinnon, chairman) secured from the Sultan of Zanzibar a 50-year lease of his coastal strip between the Umba and the Tana Rivers.

1888, Mar. 26. Death of Barghash; **Sayyid Khalifa**, Sultan of Zanzibar.

Apr. 28. The Germans secured from the sultan a 50-year lease of that part of the coast between the Rovuma and the Umba Rivers.

Sept. 3. The **British East Africa Company** was given a charter to develop the territory in the British sphere.

Sept. Victory of the Moslem-Arab faction in Uganda; deposition and flight of Mwanga.

1888-1890. Great **insurrection of the coast Arabs** in the German sphere, under Bushiri. In Dec. 1888 the British joined the Germans in a blockade of the coast. The rising was ultimately mastered by the German explorer and administrator, **Hermann von Wissmann.**

1888-1890. Portuguese expeditions into the regions west of Lake Nyasa and into the Manica district, with the object of establishing Portuguese claims to the whole of the interior, which had been assigned by the British government to the newly founded South Africa Company (p. 855).

1889, Sept. 21. The British proclaimed a protectorate over the Shiré River region.

Oct. 4. Mwanga, supported by the Christians, defeated the Moslems in Uganda. Ascendancy of the Catholic faction.

Dec. Emin Pasha, the governor of Equatoria, having been "rescued" by Stanley (p. 844), arrived at Bagamoyo. He soon took service with the Germans and set out for the region west of Lake Victoria, where he was killed (1892) by Arab slave-traders.

1890, Jan. 10. The British sent to the Portuguese government a stiff **ultimatum** protesting against the expeditions into the interior.

Mar. 4. The British East Africa Company secured from the Sultan of Zanzibar the concession of the **Benadir coast.**

Mar. **Karl Peters,** having entered Uganda by way of the Tana River country, induced Mwanga to sign a treaty, by which it was hoped that the German position in Uganda might be established.

Apr. 14. A mission of the British East Africa Company, under **Frederick Jackson,** arrived in Uganda. Peters withdrew to the south side of Lake Victoria and Jackson succeeded in getting Mwanga to recognize the protection of the company.

May 24. The so-called **MacKinnon Treaty,** concluded between the British East Africa Company and King Leopold as ruler of the Congo. The company recognized Leopold's rights on the west bank of the upper Nile, in return for the cession of a strip of territory between the south tip of Lake Albert Edward and the north tip of Lake Tanganyika. This agreement was not officially sanctioned by the British government.

June 14. The British established a protectorate over Zanzibar. This was recognized by Germany in the agreement of July 1 and by France (in return for recognition of the protectorate over Madagascar) on Aug. 4.

July 1. AN ANGLO-GERMAN AGREEMENT disposed of conflicting claims and aims in East Africa: in return for the cession of Heligoland (p. 741) the Germans gave up all claims to Uganda and abandoned their position in Witu. The frontier between British and German East Africa was extended on the west side of Lake Victoria as far as the frontier of the Congo State.

Oct. 28. Following the suppression of the Arab rising, the **German East Africa Company ceded all its territorial rights to the German government.**

Nov. 19. The British proclaimed a protectorate over Witu and the coastal area as far as the Juba River.

Dec. 18. Arrival of Sir Frederick Lugard with a British force in Uganda.

He induced the king to sign a new treaty (Dec. 26) and attempted to restore peace between the religious factions. In 1891 he moved to the western areas, establishing posts and enlisting remnants of the Sudanese forces which had been in the service of Emin Pasha.

1891, Mar. 24. An Anglo-Italian agreement fixed the Juba River as the boundary between British East Africa and Italian Somaliland.

June 11. AN ANGLO-PORTUGUESE AGREEMENT brought to an end the long-standing dispute about claims in East Africa: Portugal was to have both banks of the Zambezi to a point 10 miles west of Zumbo; the Rovuma River was to be the northern boundary; British claims in Nyasaland were recognized, as also in Manicaland.

July 30. The Portuguese government chartered the **Mozambique Company,** which was financed to a large extent by British capital, to develop the region behind Beira.

1891-1893. The Wahehe War in German East Africa.

1892, Jan. Outbreak of new religious conflicts in Uganda. Lugard intervened energetically and secured the victory of the Protestant faction.

1892-1898. Pacification of Nyasaland through the suppression of Angoni and Arab risings, chiefly by Sir Harry H. Johnston.

1893, Mar. Arrival of Sir Gerald Portal in Uganda. The British East Africa Company had announced its intention of withdrawing and had been induced to stay on only through the intervention and financial support of the missionary interests. The government of Lord Rosebery was eager to take over the country in order to protect the approach to the headwaters of the Nile, but the anti-imperialist element in the cabinet objected. Portal raised the British flag and recommended retention of control by Britain.

Feb. 22. The name of Nyasaland was changed to **British Central African Protectorate.**

1894, Feb. 4. Major Owen, sent out to counteract Belgian expeditions along the Nile, reached the river from Uganda and raised the British flag at Wadelai.

May 12. The Congo Treaty between King Leopold and Great Britain, along the lines of the MacKinnon Treaty (p. 845). The protests of the German government led to the cancellation of the lease, by the Congo State, of a narrow strip of territory adjacent to the German East African frontier, thus frustrating the hope of a Cape to Cairo connection through Africa.

June 18. The British government formally announced a **protectorate over Uganda.**

Sept. 1. A German-Portuguese agreement defined the boundaries between German East Africa and Mozambique.

1895-1899. Native risings in Mozambique greatly hindered the development of the colony.

1895, July 1. Following the dissolution of the British East Africa Company, the British government organized its sphere as the East Africa Protectorate.

1896, June 30. The kingdom of Unyoro was added to the Uganda Protectorate.

Aug. A disputed succession in Zanzibar led to a dangerous Arab movement against British rule and to a **bombardment of Zanzibar** by a British squadron.

1897, Apr. 6. Slavery was abolished in Zanzibar, by decree of the sultan.

July-Aug. New troubles in Uganda, provoked by King Mwanga. He was forced to flee and surrendered to the Germans.

Sept. Outbreak of a great mutiny of the Sudanese troops in Uganda, which was not suppressed until 1898, after a regular campaign by Maj. James MacDonald.

Nov. Daudi Chwa was made King of Uganda. Being a small child, the country was ruled, under the British, by a regency (until 1914).

1898, Sept. Maj. C. G. Martyr took Wadelai and Rejaf on the Nile, as part of the reconquest of the Sudan.

1899, June. Capture of Mwanga and his ally, Kabarega of Unyoro. These two troublesome opponents of British rule were exiled to the Seychelles.

Sept. 13. First ascent of Mt. Kenya, by H. J. Mackinder.

1900, Mar. 10. A definitive treaty between Uganda and Great Britain regulated the form of government: the country is ruled by the king (*kabaka*) with the advice and assistance of the British commissioner.

1901, Feb. 23. An Anglo-German agreement regulated the boundary between German East Africa and Nyasaland.

Dec. 26. The first railroad train reached Lake Victoria by the **Uganda Railway,** from Mombasa (surveyed 1891–1892; constructed 1896–1901, and since then the most important single factor in the opening up of the country).

1902, Apr. 1. The eastern province of Uganda was joined to British East Africa.

1902. A land grant of 500 sq. miles in British East Africa to the **East African Syndicate** initiated white settlement in the upland region (regulated by the **First Crown Lands Ordinance,** Sept. 27).

1905. A serious **rising of Moslems and pagans** in the southern part of **German East Africa** led to the practical extermination of the Angonis, a powerful native tribe.

1906, Oct. 22. Executive and legislative councils were established in British East Africa, the latter composed exclusively of nominated members.

1907, May 23. The government of **Mozambique was organized,** with the establishment of a legislative council on which the European elements were represented.

July 6. The name of British Central Africa was changed back to **Nyasaland Protectorate.**

Sept. 4. Nominated executive and legislative councils were established in Nyasaland.

1908. Mar. 31. Opening of the **Shiré Highlands Railway** to Blantyre.

1912, Feb. 26. Opening of the **railroad from Dar es-Salaam to Tabora,** the main line in German East Africa.

1914, Feb. 1. The Dar es-Salaam Railroad reached the shore of Lake Tanganyika.   (*Cont.* p. 1090.)

8. SOUTH AFRICA

(Cape of Good Hope, Orange Free State, Natal, South African Republic, Rhodesia, German Southwest Africa)

At the end of the 18th century the Dutch were still in possession of Cape Colony, where they had established themselves in 1652. The settlement was originally designed exclusively as a refreshment station for the ships of the **Dutch East India Company** *en route* to the Spice Islands, but the need for supplies had led to the establishment of **free burghers** (1657) who were to grow grain and make wine. To provide the necessary farm labor, **slaves** were introduced from West Africa and from Asia (1657). The neighboring native tribes (**Bushmen** and **Hottentots**) were economically in a very backward state, but early efforts to prevent contact and conflict could not be maintained. The need for fresh meat resulted in trade with the Hottentot cattlemen and to a gradual expansion of the burghers beyond the immediate vicinity of Capetown. The population was increased (1688–1694) by the arrival of several hundred **French Huguenot settlers** who had taken refuge in Holland after the revocation of the Edict of Nantes and whose passage to the Cape was financed by the Dutch East India Company. By 1700 there were about 1000 free burghers at the Cape. Progress during the 18th century continued to be very modest. The stiff regulations of the

company served as a deterrent and European immigration was almost insignificant. Nevertheless, the tendency toward expansion remained potent. Cattle farmers continued to push the frontier of settlement eastward along the coast and northward into the veld. The Orange River was reached in 1760 and the Great Fish River in 1776. Graaff Reinet was founded in 1786. In the last years of Dutch rule there developed also a demand for burgher representation and a more liberal régime. By 1795 this movement had reached the point where local magistrates were driven out and projects for a national assembly brought forward.

1795, Sept. 16. By the **capitulation of Rustenburg,** the Dutch garrison at the Cape surrendered to Adm. Elphinstone and a British fleet. The British acted under mandate from the exiled Prince of Orange, but the chief purpose of the seizure was to prevent the Cape, like Holland, from falling into the hands of the French.

1803, Feb. 21. Under the terms of the **Treaty of Amiens** (p. 590) the **British returned the Cape** to the Dutch (Batavian Republic).

1806, Jan. 10. By the capitulation of **Papendorp** the Dutch garrisons once more surrendered to a powerful British fleet.

1807. **Abolition of the slave trade** throughout the British Empire. This created a serious labor problem in South Africa and brought to the fore the question of drafting the Hottentots.

1809. Legal restrictions on the free movement of the Hottentots were introduced, with the object of forcing them into service.

1814, May 30. By the **TREATY OF PARIS** (p. 601) the British secured definitive possession of the Cape. By an agreement of Aug. 13 the Dutch were paid £6,000,000 funds, ostensibly by way of compensation. Until 1825 the new possession was ruled autocratically by the British governor.

1816. Great influx of **British missionaries** (Moravian missions, 1792; London Missionary Society, 1794; Wesleyans, 1816). The missionaries undertook to convert the natives in the eastern areas and to improve their lot. Through their exertions (esp. Dr. **John Philip**) the problem of native protection was brought to the fore. Philip proposed segregation of the Hottentots and their settlement on the land. All proposals of this type roused strong opposition among the farmers.

1820. About 4000 **British colonists** (*Albany Settlers*) settled in the eastern coastal region by the British government, giving the colony for the first time a noticeable English tinge.

1822. A proclamation provided for the gradual establishment of English in place of Dutch as the official language.

1824, Aug. 27. **Francis G. Farewell** and a group of merchants from the Cape declared **Natal** British, but this step was not recognized by the government. The settlement was renamed **Durban** in 1835.

1825. After an investigation, the British government established an **advisory council** at the Cape (3 official members; 3 nominated) to assist the governor. Two years later provision was made for an **independent judiciary**.

1826. The Cape colony was extended northward to the Orange River.

1828. Through the efforts of Philip an ordinance (the **Fiftieth Ordinance**) was passed, allowing Hottentots to buy and hold land, and abolishing earlier restrictions on free movement.

The old Dutch magistracy (*landdrosts, heemraden*) was replaced by the **English judiciary system.**

1833. In Cape Colony the advisory council was replaced by a **legislative council**, similarly constituted, but with extended powers.

1834. **Abolition of slavery** throughout the British Empire, with compensation to the owners. In South Africa, where 35,000 slaves were freed, there was much complaint about the inadequacy of the compensation.

Great invasion of the eastern regions **by the Bantu** (Kaffirs), irritated by the constant encroachment of the Dutch cattlemen and farmers. The natives were driven back with some difficulty.

1835. British territory was extended eastward to the Kei River (**Province of Queen Adelaide**), but the region between the Keiskamma and the Kei (Kaffraria) was left to friendly natives under supervision as well as to white settlers. The British government, under pressure from philanthropic and missionary interests, disavowed the extension of Cape authority and the province had to be abandoned, much to the disgust of the settlers.

1835-1837. **THE GREAT TREK** of the Dutch (Boer) cattlemen and farmers to the north and the east of the Orange River. Irritated by the restrictions on slavery and by the sympathetic native policy of the government, they sought new lands and freedom from interference. About 10,000 moved northward, seriously depopulating the eastern parts of the Cape Colony. Under **A. H. Potgieter** they passed beyond the Vaal River and settled in what became the Transvaal. Those under **Piet Retief** crossed the Drakensberg and began to occupy Zululand and Natal, regions largely depopulated by the ravages of **Chaka**, the great military leader of the Zulus.

1838, Feb. **Retief** and 60 followers were treacherously **slain by Dingaan,** the powerful king of the Zulus, who massacred the immigrants and thereupon destroyed Durban.

Dec. 16. In the **battle of Blood River** Dingaan was defeated by the Boers, now led by **Andreas Pretorius.** The Boers thereupon settled in Natal (**Republic of Natal**), founding **Pietermaritzburg** (1839).

1840. **Dingaan was defeated** by his rival, Umpanda, who became king of the Zulus and accepted the rule of the Boers. Immigration of the Zulus from Zululand into Natal continued unchecked.

1842. War between the Boers and the British in Natal. The Boers were repulsed and British authority established.

1843, Aug. 8. Natal was made a British colony, with the object of protecting the natives against exploitation. Thereupon many of the Boers departed, moving northward over the Vaal River.

Dec. 13. By treaty with **Moshesh,** powerful leader of the Basutos, **Basutoland** became a native state under British protection. A similar treaty was made with **Adam Kok,** the Griqua chief. Thus many Voortrekkers were put under native jurisdiction.

1844, May 31. Natal was combined with Cape Colony for administrative purposes.

1846-1847. War of the Axe, between the British and the Kaffirs. The latter were defeated and **British Kaffraria** (between the Keiskamma and the Kei Rivers) was set up as a native preserve (1847).

1846. In Natal the first **Location Commission** set up preserves for the immigrant Zulus, under a revived tribal system. Beginning of the policy of **native segregation.**

1848, Feb. 3. Sir Harry Smith, the British governor of the Cape, proclaimed as British territory all the region between the Orange and Vaal Rivers and the Drakensberg. The Boers were disunited, but some, under Pretorius, opposed the British. They were defeated by Smith in the **battle of Boomplaats** (Aug. 29) and the **Orange River Sovereignty** became a reality.

1850-1853. Great Kaffir War on the eastern frontier of Cape Colony.

1852, Jan. 17. By the **SAND RIVER CONVENTION** the British government recognized the **independence of the Transvaal.**

1853, July 1. A **new constitution** was introduced in the Cape Colony, after years of agitation. It provided for an elected legislative council of 15 members and an elected house of assembly with 46 members. The parliament was to be summoned annually by the governor, but the executive was not made responsible to it. The franchise was extended to all British subjects (white and black alike) on fulfillment of certain conditions as to employment, etc., property or salary.

1854, Feb. 17. By the **Convention of Bloemfontein** the British government withdrew from the territory north of the Orange River, despite the protests of some of the settlers. This was the final step in the policy of withdrawal initiated by the Sand River Convention. The settlers thereupon organized the **Orange Free State,** with a president and a volksraad.

1854-1861. SIR GEORGE GREY, governor of the Cape Colony. His administration was distinguished by an active policy of native protection, under white magistrates, the ultimate object being the civilization of the blacks.

1856, July 12. Natal was made a separate colony with an elected assembly.

Dec. 16. Organization of the South African Republic (*Transvaal*), after years of confusion. **Marthinius Pretorius** became president, and Pretoria (founded 1855) the capital. Dissenting groups stood aloof and continued their separate state organizations in **Zoutpansberg, Lydenburg,** and **Utrecht.**

Self-destruction of the Kaffirs, who slaughtered their cattle in the hope, encouraged by their prophets, that the heroes of old would return and drive out the white man. The population, deprived of food, died of starvation and in the end was reduced to about one-third of the original number. This tragedy did much to end the long-standing Kaffir problem.

1857, June 1. The South African Republic and the Orange Free State recognized each other's independence.

1858. Zoutpansberg joined the South African Republic, while Lydenburg and Utrecht united as one state.

1858. Sir George Grey recommended the **federation of the colonies,** including the Orange Free State, but not the South African Republic. The idea was at once repudiated by the home government.

1860. The **first laborers were imported from India** to work (under three-year indenture) on the sugar plantations of Natal. Large numbers were imported in the course of the next generation, many of whom remained in the country after expiration of the indenture. "Free" Indians also immigrated and soon became an important factor in trade and small industry.

Opening of the **first railway in Cape Colony.** In 1864 it reached Wellington.

Lydenburg joined the South African Republic.

1860-1864. Pretorius was at the same time president of the South African Republic and of the Orange Free State, thus establishing a close bond between the two Boer states.

1861. The British occupied islands in **Delagoa Bay,** in order to keep this strategic harbor from falling into the hands of the Transvaal.

1864-1888. Jan Brand, president of the Orange Free State.

1865-1866. War of the Boers of the Orange Free State against Moshesh, the chieftain of the Basutos. Moshesh, defeated, was obliged to cede large tracts of his territory and open them to white settlement.

1866. Kaffraria was joined to Cape Colony.

1867. DISCOVERY OF DIAMONDS NEAR HOPETOWN, on the Orange River. By 1870 a considerable diamond industry grew up in the region between the Vaal and Orange Rivers.

1867-1868. The Orange Free State defeated the Basutos, who had risen in protest against the cession of territory in 1866.

1868, Mar. 12. The British annexed Basutoland, following a petition by Moshesh. His lands were returned to him, despite the protests of the Orange Free State.

Forces from the Transvaal attempted to occupy Delagoa Bay, but withdrew under protest from the British. The question was ultimately arbitrated by President MacMahon of France, who awarded it to Portugal (1875).

1869, July 29. An agreement between the Transvaal and Portugal fixed the boundary in southeast Africa.

1871. The town of Kimberley was founded and soon became the center of the great diamond industry. By 1890 some six tons of diamonds were mined, valued at £39,000,000. The opening-up of this great wealth completely changed the economic set-up in South Africa.

Oct. 27. The British government annexed the diamond region (*Griqualand West*), which had been under the rule of the Griqua (half-breed) chief, Nikolaas Waterboer, under the authority of the Orange Free State since 1854. The Orange Free State vigorously protested against this action, which had much to do with stimulating Boer distrust of the British.

1871-1872. The efforts of the British colonial secretary, Lord Carnarvon, and his special agent, the historian James Froude, to bring about federation of the South African colonies, were frustrated by the opposition of the Cape government (under John Molteno).

1871. The government of Basutoland was taken over by the Cape Colony.

1872. Thomas Burgers, a learned Dutch minister from Cape Colony, became president of the South African Republic.

1872. Responsible government was established in Cape Colony.

1875. Lord Carnarvon, continuing his efforts toward federation, arranged for an informal conference at London (Aug.). As a result the claims of the Orange Free State to the diamond country were settled by a money payment of £90,000.

1876. The Cape government extended its influence up the west coast of Africa, concluding treaties with native chiefs as far as the frontier of Angola, but this policy was disavowed by the home government.

1877-1880. Sir Bartle Frere, governor of Cape Colony. His purpose was to push forward the work toward federation.

1877, Apr. 12. ANNEXATION OF THE SOUTH AFRICAN REPUBLIC by the British under Sir Theophilus Shepstone. This was intended as a step toward federation, but was a flagrant violation of the Sand River Convention. The Boers, under the leadership of Paul Kruger (1825–1904), protested vigorously, but without avail.

1877-1878. Kaffir War. As a result the British annexed all of Kaffraria, and in the following years (1879–1886) extended their authority to the northeast as far as Pondoland.

1877, Mar. 12. The British annexed Walfish (Walvis) Bay on the coast of Southwest Africa. German missionaries had been active on that coast since 1842 (Bethany Mission), and had, in 1868, appealed to the British government for annexation. This appeal had been rejected.

1879. THE ZULU WAR, against Cetywayo (king since 1872). Cetywayo had built up again the military power of the Zulus. Jan. 22 he defeated the British in a battle at Isandhlwana. Reinforcements were rushed to the front, and July 4 Sir Garnet Wolseley won a decisive victory at Ulundi. Cetywayo was captured Aug. 28 and peace was made with the Zulu chiefs Sept. 1.

1879. Foundation of the Afrikander Bond, a Dutch group designed to work for recognition of the Dutch language. Under the influence of Jan Hofmeyr it soon rallied most of the Dutch elements in the Cape Colony, but with a much larger program of South Africa for the South Africans, with gradual elimination of interference from the British government.

1880-1881. REVOLT OF THE TRANSVAAL BOERS against the British. Dec. 30 a Boer republic was proclaimed by Kruger, Joubert, and Pretorius. Jan. 28, 1881, the Boers repulsed a British force under Sir George Colley at **Laing's Nek**, and Feb. 27 they again defeated and killed Colley at **Majuba Hill**. The British government, under Gladstone, was unwilling to contest the desire of the Boers for freedom, and Apr. 5 concluded the **Treaty of Pretoria**, by which the South African Republic was given independence, but under the suzerainty of Great Britain.

1880. Organization of the diamond industry. Two great corporations were founded: the **Barnato Diamond Mining Company** (by Barney Barnato, an English Jew), and the **De Beers Mining Corporation** (by Cecil Rhodes and Alfred Beit).

1880-1881. The **"Gun War"** in Basutoland, resulting from the refusal of the natives to surrender their arms. As a result of this war, the British government in 1883 resumed the government of Basutoland as a crown colony.

1882. Cetywayo was restored as king of the Zulus, but was opposed by the native chiefs. The troubles were ended by Cetywayo's death in 1884.

1882. Establishment of **Stellaland and Goshen**, two Boer states in Bechuanaland. This was part of the Boer expansion to the westward as far as the Kalahari Desert.

1883, Apr. 16. **Kruger became president** of the South African Republic.

Aug. F. A. E. Lüderitz, a German merchant, purchased from the natives a large tract of territory north of the Orange River. A short time before (Feb.) the German government had inquired in London whether the British government exercised any authority in this region. The reply was evasive, but when Lüderitz hoisted the German flag at **Angra Pequena** there was much excitement in London as well as at Capetown. The British government now announced that it regarded any claim to sovereignty in the region between Cape Colony and Angola as an infringement of Britain's legitimate rights. There followed a rather acrimonious discussion between London and Berlin. The Cape government, in the interval, urged the home government to annex all territory north as far as Walfish Bay. But the attempt was frustrated by the **proclamation of German protection** over the region (Apr. 24, 1884), which was extended over all Namaqualand and Damaraland (Oct. 15, 1884). Sovereignty was vested in the Deutsche Kolonial Gesellschaft until it was assumed by the German government (1892).

1884, Feb. 27. The **Convention of London** further defined the relations of the South African Republic to Great Britain.

The Transvaal was deprived of Stellaland and Goshen, but the British government agreed to the omission of definite reference to suzerainty, though the Transvaal government was precluded from making treaties without submitting them for approval to the British government.

May. Fearful of German expansion eastward as far as the Transvaal and the cutting of the route to the north, the British, under the influence of **Cecil Rhodes** (1853–1902), concluded treaties of protection with the native chiefs of **Bechuanaland**.

Aug. The Boers, under Joubert, attempted to establish a republic in **Zululand** and thus secure themselves access to the sea on the east.

Dec. 18. In order to frustrate this move, **the British government annexed St. Lucia Bay** to Natal.

1885, Sept. 30. The **Bechuana territory was organized** as British Bechuanaland (the region between the Orange and the Molopo Rivers) and as the Bechuanaland Protectorate (north of the Molopo).

Nov. 28. The **railroad from the Cape** was opened as far as Kimberley.

1886, Dec. 30. An agreement between Germany and Portugal fixed the frontier between German Southwest Africa and Angola.

1886. **DISCOVERY OF GOLD** on the Witwatersrand in the southern Transvaal. Gold had been found in various parts of the Transvaal before this, but the rich reefs were opened up only at this time. There was a wild rush to the Rand from all parts of the world. **Johannesburg** was laid out (Sept. 1886) and before long had a population of 100,000, of whom half were native workers. By 1890 there were 450 mining companies on the Rand (capitalized at £11,-000,000). The output was almost 500,000 ounces in 1890, and 1,210,865 ounces in 1892. Rhodes and his associates took an active part in the financing and organization of the industry, and his company (**Consolidated Goldfields**) soon controlled a large share of the business.

1887, June 21. The British annexed **Zululand**, in order to block the effort of the Transvaal government to establish territorial communication with the sea.

1888. Amalgamation of the **De Beers and Barnato diamond interests**, giving the De Beers corporation, under Rhodes, practically a monopoly of the industry.

Feb. The **project of a customs union** between the Cape, Natal, and the

Orange Free State was much discussed, but the Transvaal, under Kruger, remained unalterably opposed to all schemes of federation.

Feb. 11. J. S. Moffat, a missionary and agent of Rhodes, concluded a **treaty with Lobengula**, king of the Matabele, by which the latter accepted British protection and promised to cede none of his extensive territories without the consent of the governor of the Cape.

Oct. 30. In a further treaty Lobengula gave the Rhodes interests **exclusive mining rights** in Matabeleland and Mashonaland.

1889. The Cape Colony and Orange Free State concluded a customs union. At the same time the Free State and the Transvaal (South African Republic) concluded a defensive alliance.

Oct. 29. The British government granted a charter to the **British South Africa Company**, headed by Rhodes. It was given almost unlimited rights and powers of government in the huge area north of the Transvaal and west of Mozambique, without northern limit. The effect was to hedge in the Transvaal on the north, Rhodes cherishing the hope that gradually the Boer Republic would be forced into closer economic and political relations with the other states.

1890, July 17. Cecil **Rhodes became prime minister** of the Cape Colony. He enjoyed the support of the Afrikander Bond, under Homeyr, the British and Dutch elements co-operating in a policy of South Africa for the South Africans.

Sept. 12. The town of **Salisbury was founded** in Mashonaland, part of the dominion of the British South Africa Company.

Dec. The railroad from Capetown through the Orange Free State reached the Vaal River.

1891, June 10. Dr. L. Starr Jameson, a close friend of Rhodes', was made administrator of the South Africa Company's territories.

Dec. By an **agreement between the Cape government and the Transvaal**, the Cape advanced money to finance the building of the railway from Pretoria to the Portguese frontier, there to join the line (completed in 1889) to Delagoa Bay. In return the Transvaal government agreed to construct a short line from Johannesburg to the Vaal River and to bridge the river to connect with the line to Capetown. The Cape government was to have the right to fix rates on this short line until Dec. 31, 1894.

1892, Sept. The first trains from the Cape arrived at Johannesburg. An immense traffic developed and the income from the railways came to be a vital factor in the finance of Cape Colony.

In Johannesburg **Charles Leonard** organized the foreign (*Uitlander*) element in the **National Union**, to agitate for better educational advantages, better police, easier franchise requirements, etc.

1893, Apr. 22. Kruger was elected president of the South African Republic for another term of five years.

May 12. Responsible government was introduced in **Natal**.

July. **War of Lobengula** against the Mashonas. The South Africa Company interfered, defeated the Matabeles and took Bulawayo (Nov. 4). The chiefs submitted (Jan. 1894) and the danger passed with the death of Lobengula (Jan. 23).

Nov. 13. By the **Pretoria Convention** Great Britain agreed that the Transvaal should have **Swaziland**, which, however, did not give the Boers access to the sea.

1894, Sept. 25. The **British annexed Pondoland**, thus connecting the Cape Colony with Natal.

Aug. Passage of the **Glen Grey Act** by the Cape Parliament. This provided for a new native policy in the region east of the Kei River: the natives were to be given self-government under native councils, together with a general council, under the British magistrate. Individual landholding was made possible. At the same time the property qualification for black voters in Cape Colony was raised and an educational test introduced.

Nov. Rhodes paid a visit to Kruger and renewed his efforts to induce the Transvaal government to join the other states in a customs union. Having failed once more, Rhodes began to support the Uitlander agitation in Johannesburg and ultimately financed a **revolutionary movement against Kruger's government**.

1895, May 3. The territory of the South Africa Company south of the Zambezi was named **Rhodesia**, in honor of Rhodes.

June 11. The **British annexed Tongoland** in order to block the last possible access of the Transvaal to the sea (through Swaziland and Tongoland).

July 8. **Opening of the Delagoa Bay Railway** from Johannesburg and Pretoria to the sea. This gave the Transvaal at least an economic outlet free of all British influence. The Delagoa Bay route being much shorter than that to the Cape, traffic began to be diverted. This process was hastened by the imposition of prohibitive rates on the short line from Johannesburg to the Vaal River. In order to circumvent this move, the shippers began to use ox-wagons, crossing the fords (*drifts*) of the Vaal and proceeding thence to the Rand. Kruger then ordered the drifts closed, but the British government interfered vigorously and Kruger yielded to an ultimatum (Nov. 8).

Nov. 11. **British Bechuanaland was attached to the Cape Colony.** Northern Bechuanaland became the Bechuanaland Protectorate, but a narrow strip of it, along the Transvaal frontier, was turned over to the South Africa Company on Rhodes' plea that it was needed for the extension of the railway from Mafeking north into Rhodesia. In reality the strip was desired so that the company could station a force at Mafeking, the nearest point on the frontier to Johannesburg. When the revolution, planned for Dec., should have broken out on the Rand, Dr. Jameson was to ride in and take control of the situation. Actually the conspirators in Johannesburg decided to postpone action and Rhodes warned Jameson not to proceed. But the latter, convinced that all that was needed was a little encouragement, disregarded orders and set out on his famous raid.

1895, Dec. 29—1896, Jan. 2. THE JAMESON RAID. With 660 men Jameson tried to cover the 140 miles to Johannesburg, but the Boers, who had learned of the plans, closed in on him, defeated him at **Krugersdorp** (Jan. 1) and forced his surrender at **Doorn Kop** (Jan. 2). At the demand of the British government Jameson was handed over for trial in England. He was condemned, but given a light sentence. The Johannesburg leaders were arrested and several condemned to death by the Transvaal courts. They were ultimately released in return for a large money payment.

1896, Jan. 3. **The Kruger Telegram**, in which the German emperor congratulated Kruger on his success in suppressing the movement. This step created an acute crisis in the relations of Britain and Germany (p. 744).

Jan. 6. Because of his part in the Jameson raid episode, **Rhodes was obliged to resign** as prime minister of the Cape Colony. He did not re-enter politics until 1898.

Mar. In Rhodesia there was another **rising of the Matabele** and (June) Mashona tribes. This was not suppressed until Oct.

Mar. 17. The Transvaal and the Orange Free State concluded an offensive and defensive treaty, a direct reaction to the Jameson raid.

Sept. 26. Aliens Expulsion Act passed in the Transvaal. This, and

Nov. 26. The **Aliens Immigration Restriction Act** and various restrictions on the press and on public meeting, resulted in continuous friction between Great Britain and the Transvaal, culminating in a **dispute about British suzerainty** over the republic.

1897, Aug. Sir Alfred Milner became high commissioner in South Africa.

Nov. 4. The railroad from the Cape reached Bulawayo, in southern Rhodesia. This line was intended by Rhodes ultimately to connect the Cape with Cairo.

Dec. 1. Zululand was annexed to Natal. In Natal the growing feeling of opposition to immigration of Indians led to the prohibition of entry of "free" (i.e. unindentured) Indians and the closing of many occupations to those already in the country.

1898, Feb. 10. **Kruger was re-elected president** of the South African Republic for five years. This meant a defeat for the more progressive element among the Transvaal Boers, which favored a more generous policy toward the immigrant foreigners and an agreement with the other South African states. The result was a marked revival of the **Uitlander agitation,** which met with the fullest sympathy from Milner. By the end of the year Milner was already convinced that the only solution of the problem would be through war, and that the war would amount to little more than a slap in the face. This forward policy, however, had little response in England. The cabinet, confronted with several serious international problems, was eager to avoid an unpopular war if possible, and so resisted Milner's prodding.

1899, Mar. 24. The Uitlanders sent a petition with 20,000 names to Queen Victoria, recounting their numerous grievances.

May 31—June 5. The **Bloemfontein conference** between Milner and Kruger, arranged through the efforts of President Steyn of the Orange Free State. Milner insisted on the immediate grant of the franchise to foreigners who had been 5 years resident in the Transvaal. This Kruger refused and the conference broke down. But July 11 the Transvaal government passed a law granting the franchise on completion of 7 years' residence. The British government thereupon proposed a joint inquiry as to the working of this law, but Kruger countered with the suggestion of reducing the term to 5 years in return for an abrogation of suzerainty. When Britain rejected this, Kruger took back his offer. By this time (Sept.) both sides had begun to make military preparations. Kruger, ever since the Jameson raid, had been convinced that the British were intent on the acquisition of the rich Transvaal, while the British had gradually come to believe that Kruger was actively furthering a plan to drive the British out of South Africa and set up a confederation of Boer republics. Feeling that further negotiation was futile, and wishing to take advantage of the small forces which the British yet had in South Africa, Kruger sent an ultimatum (Oct. 9), which the British rejected. The Orange Free State joined the Transvaal (Oct. 11) and war broke out Oct. 12.

1899, Oct. 12—1902, May 31. THE SOUTH AFRICAN (BOER) WAR. At the outset the British had only about 25,000 men available, the Boers having a distinct advantage in numbers. In addition the Boer forces were admirably equipped with small arms and with Krupp and Creusot artillery. The commander-in-chief, Gen. Joubert, hoped to push through Natal and capture Durban, thus gaining access to the sea. He brushed aside Sir George White at **Laing's Nek** (Oct. 12), suffered a temporary reverse at Elandslaagte (Oct. 21), but won a battle at Nicholson's Nek (Oct. 30) and invested **Ladysmith** (Nov. 2). In the west the Boers invested **Mafeking** (Oct. 13; valiant defense by Colonel Baden-Powell) and besieged **Kimberley** (Oct. 15). The British, under Methuen, drove back Cronje and the Boers on the **Modder River** (Nov. 28), but there soon followed the **Black Week** (Dec. 10–15), when Cronje's victory at **Magersfontein** (Dec. 10–11) frustrated Methuen's efforts to relieve Kimberley and when Buller, commanding in Natal, failed (**battle of Colenso,** Dec. 15) to effect the crossing of the Tugela River in the advance on Ladysmith.

Buller was thereupon relieved of the supreme command, and his place was taken by Gen. Lord Roberts, with Gen. **Kitchener** as his chief-of-staff. They arrived in South Africa on Jan. 10, 1900. In the meanwhile the fighting about Ladysmith had continued indecisive. Jan. 18 Buller finally managed to cross the Tugela and capture **Spion Kop** (Jan. 25), but was again forced back. A third attempt to establish himself beyond the river also met with failure (Feb. 6–7). But French began a vigorous advance to relieve **Kimberley,** which was successful (Feb. 15). Cronje was defeated at

Paardeberg (Feb. 18) and obliged to surrender (Feb. 27). At the same time Buller, having finally crossed the Tugela (Feb. 18), **relieved Ladysmith** (Feb. 28).

The British, now heavily reinforced, were henceforth able to maintain the offensive. Roberts took **Bloemfontein** (Mar. 13), and, advancing up the railroad, arrived at **Kroonstad** (May 12), while in Natal Buller drove the Boers back from Glencoe and Dundee (May 15). The **Orange Free State** having been overrun, it was annexed to the British possessions as the **Orange River Colony** (May 24). **Mafeking was relieved** (May 17–18) and the invasion of the Transvaal begun. **Johannesburg was taken** (May 31) and **Pretoria occupied** (June 5). Buller then forced the passes of the Drakensberg and began the invasion from Natal (June 10). On July 4 the forces of Roberts and Buller effected a junction at Vlakfontein. On Sept. 3, the **Transvaal was annexed** as the Transvaal Colony. Kruger fled to Delagoa Bay and went thence to Europe. All efforts to interest other powers and provoke intervention failed. But the Boer leaders, defeated in regular warfare, now adopted **guerrilla tactics,** thereby prolonging the war by another eighteen months. Small forces repeatedly raided into the Cape Colony, harassed the lines of communication, attacked the railway lines, etc. Ultimately Kitchener (commander-in-chief since Nov. 1900) was obliged to erect a line of **blockhouses** and to organize **concentration camps,** into which some 120,000 Boer women and children were brought (about 20,000 of this number died of disease and neglect). The Boer farms were ruthlessly destroyed and the *guerrilleros* finally harried into submission. At the end of the war Britain had 300,000 troops in South Africa to deal with the 60,000 to 75,000 Boers. By the **Treaty of Vereeniging** (May 31, 1902) the Boers accepted British sovereignty, but were promised representative institutions as soon as circumstances should permit; the British government promised a grant of £3,000,000 to enable them to rebuild their farms.

1903, Feb. Visit of Joseph Chamberlain, secretary for the colonies, to South Africa. He convinced himself of the hopelessness of the policy initiated by Milner of establishing English supremacy throughout the conquered areas. Gradually the government swung back to a policy of conciliation and Anglo-Dutch equality.

Dec. The Transvaal government, under pressure from the mining interests, agreed to the **importation of Chinese coolies.** In a short time over 50,000 of them were brought in, but their disorderliness, marked by several outbreaks and much terrorism, soon brought about vigorous agitation for their repatriation.

1904, Jan.—1908. The great **HERRERO INSURRECTION in German Southwest Africa,** which was suppressed only after many systematic campaigns, by a force of some 20,000 men.

1905, Jan. Gen. **Botha** formed the organization called *Het Volk*, to agitate for the introduction of responsible government in the Transvaal. A similar organization, *Orangia Unie*, sprang up in the Orange River Colony.

Mar. 1. The **Earl of Selborne** succeeded Milner as high commissioner in South Africa.

Apr. 25. The **Transvaal was granted a constitution,** with an elected assembly. This arrangement was condemned by Botha as inadequate.

1906, Dec. 6. By a new constitutional instrument, the **Transvaal was granted responsible government.**

1907, Feb. 26. In the first Transvaal elections, Botha's party, *Het Volk*, won 37 seats, as against 21 for the Progressive Party. Botha thereupon became premier (Mar. 4) and control passed to the conquered Boer element.

Mar. 22. The Transvaal government passed an **Asiatic registration bill** and provided for the restriction of immigration of Indians. The Indian population, led by an Indian lawyer, **Mohandas Ghandi** (1869–1948), later to become leader of the nationalist movement in India, began a long campaign of passive resistance.

June 14. The Transvaal government decided to repatriate the Chinese coolies imported a few years previously.

July 1. A new constitution, with responsible government, was established in the **Orange River Colony.**

1908, Oct. 12—1909, Feb. 3. MEETING OF A CONSTITUTIONAL CONVENTION, first at Durban, then at Capetown. The purpose of the meeting was to discuss the relationship of the Cape Colony, Natal, Orange River Colony, and Transvaal to each other. The older ideas of federation were now brushed aside and the sentiment spread rapidly in favor of union. The convention agreed on a scheme for a Union of South Africa, at the head of which was to be the king, represented by the governor-general. There was to be a two-chamber parliament: the **Senate,** composed of eight

members from each state (province), elected by the representatives of that province in the House of Assembly, sitting with the provincial council of the province; the governor-general was to appoint eight additional members of the Senate (in recent years a number of these appointed members have been men versed in native affairs and fitted to speak for the native population); the term of the Senate was fixed at 10 years; the **House of Assembly** was to be composed of about 150 members, popularly elected, roughly on the basis of population, but in each province under the electoral arrangements in existence there; the term of the House was to be 5 years; it was to have complete budgetary control and the ministry was to be responsible to it. The English and Dutch languages were both established as official languages. The provinces were to be governed by an **administrator** appointed by the Union government; he was to be assisted by an **executive committee,** consisting of himself and four members elected by the provincial council; the **provincial council** was to be popularly elected, have a term of 3 years, and be indissoluble before the completion of the term. The powers of the provincial governments were distinctly limited, and they were clearly subordinated to the Union government. The **seat of the legislature** was established at Capetown, but the **seat of government** at Pretoria; Bloemfontein became the seat of the court of appeal.

1909, Sept. 20. The draft constitution was approved by the British Parliament as the **South Africa Act.** It went into effect on May 31, 1910.

1910, Apr. 27. Botha and Hertzog founded the **South African Party** as the successor to the old *Afrikander Bond* in the Cape Colony, *Het Volk* in the Transvaal, and *Orangia Unie* in the Orange Free State (this name was restored at the time of union). The party was a moderate nationalist party, aiming at equality of English and Boer and at independent status for South Africa within the British Empire.

May 24. Dr. Jameson founded the **Unionist Party,** an English-imperialist group.

Sept. 15. In the first **Union elections,** the South African Party won a decided victory (67 seats as against 37 for the Unionists). **Botha became prime minister** of the Union.

1911, Aug. 17. Northeastern and northwestern Rhodesia were united as **Northern Rhodesia,** under the administration of the South Africa Company.

1913, June 14. An Immigration Act restricted the entry and free movement of Asiatics. This measure was followed by extensive agitation and rioting on the part of the Indians, led by Gandhi.

June 16. The Natives Land Act restricted the purchase or lease of land by natives and set aside further areas as reserves, thus extending the policy of segregation.

1914, June 30. The Smuts-Gandhi letters, in which Smuts, as colonial secretary in the Botha cabinet, promised Gandhi that the law regarding Asiatics would be enforced in a just manner and with due regard to vested interests. So much having been gained, Gandhi departed for India (July 20).

Jan. Gen. Hertzog founded the **Nationalist Party** in opposition to Botha's South African Party. It drew its strength almost exclusively from the rural, Boer areas and became the organ of Boer separatism.

Sept. Botha, despite Hertzog's opposition, secured approval for a policy of supporting Great Britain in the World War and for sending an expedition against German Southwest Africa.

Oct. 13—1915, Feb. Outbreak of **rebellion in South Africa.** The Boer extremists, led by Gens. De Wet, Beyers, etc., had to be suppressed by force. De Wet was captured (Dec. 1) and Beyers was drowned (Dec. 8). The movement then began to collapse.

Dec. 25. The South African forces captured **Walfish Bay**, which had been taken by the Germans.

1915, May 12. Botha took the town of **Windhoek**, the capital of German Southwest Africa.

July 9. The Germans surrendered at Grootfontein. The colony was made a protectorate of the Union and placed under martial law.

(*Cont. pp.* 918, 1091.)

9. MADAGASCAR

Little is known of the original inhabitants of Madagascar, but the island was subjected to several waves of invasion from outside. Arabs came in before the 9th century and settled on the northwest and southeast coasts, where remnants are to be found today. There was evidently also an influx of Africans, probably slaves of the Arabs. But the bulk of the population, speaking one language of many dialects, is of Malayo-Polynesian and Melanesian stock. The most advanced group, which probably arrived from overseas in the 8th to 10th centuries, is the Hova, light in color and of distinct Mongoloid features. They moved from the east coast onto the central plateau, but not until the early 19th century were they able to establish predominance over other tribes.

Madagascar was first discovered by the Portuguese Diego Diaz in 1500. The first Frenchmen landed in 1527, without settling. Portuguese missionaries attempted, though unsuccessfully, to convert the natives (1600–1619). During the 17th and 18th centuries both the Dutch and the French attempted to establish posts along the coasts. The French took Diego Suarez on the northern tip of the island in 1638 and settled on the Bay of Antongil in 1642. They founded Fort Dauphin (extreme southeast coast) in 1643. In 1664 the French posts were turned over to the Société des Indes Orientales and the island

was successively called *La France Orientale* and *Ile Dauphine.* But in 1672 the natives drove the French out of Fort Dauphin, which was destroyed. In the following century the French once again established a foothold, this time on the island of Ste. Marie, off the east coast (1750–1761). In 1774 a Polish adventurer, Benyowski, who had escaped from Siberia, was given a commission for a French settlement. He founded Louisbourg on the Gulf of Antongil and set himself up as ruler of the whole northeast coast. Having returned to France in 1776 to ask for formal protection, he was repudiated. Ultimately he received a subsidy from the United States government, returned to Madagascar and proclaimed himself an independent ruler. He was attacked and slain by a French expedition in 1786.

1787-1810. A N D R I A N A M P O I N M E-RINA, King of the Hovas. He reunited the territory and extended the Hova authority over much of the island.

1803. Under orders from Napoleon, Sylvain Roux and a French force established itself at Tamatave.

1810-1811. The British, under Sir Robert Farquhar, seized Mauritius, Réunion, and the French stations in Madagascar. Réunion was returned by the Treaty of Paris (1814), but Farquhar's efforts to maintain the British position in

Madagascar were not encouraged by the home government.

1810-1828. RADAMA I, King of the Hovas. He was a vigorous ruler, intent on modernizing his kingdom. From the British at Mauritius he secured firearms and military trainers. In other ways, too, he encouraged the spread of British influence.

1818. The London Missionary Society established its first posts in the country, meeting with unusual success. By the end of the century almost half a million of the natives were converted to Christianity.

1818-1819. The French began to occupy posts, notably Fort Dauphin. But in 1825 Radama, supposedly instigated by the British, ejected them.

1828-1861. RANAVALONA I, Queen of the Hovas. From the very outset she showed herself hostile to European influence (British as well as French) and also to missionary enterprise.

1829, Oct. A French squadron bombarded **Tamatave** in protest against the hostile policy of the government, but without real effect.

1830. The new French government of Louis Philippe ordered the withdrawal from all French stations except Ste. Marie.

1835. The Hova government forbade the practice of the Christian religion and forced the English missionaries to leave.

1840-1841. By treaties with the local chiefs, the French acquired a number of the islands off the northwest coast.

1845, May 13. By order of the Hova government, all foreigners were made subject to native law, including trial by ordeal. By way of protest the **French and British together bombarded Tamatave** in 1846, but again without making any impression upon the government. European influence was reduced to almost nothing.

1859. A number of chiefs on the west coast accepted the French protectorate.

1861-1863. RADAMA II, son of Ranavalona. The new king was a Christian, and at once reopened the country to the Europeans.

1862. The Hova government concluded **treaties with both France and Great Britain.**

1863, May 13. The Hova aristocracy (*Andriana*) revolted against the policy of the king, who was taken and strangled.

1863-1868. RASOHERINA, Queen of the Hovas.

1865-1870. Exploration of Madagascar by the French scientist, **Alfred Grandidier,** whose exhaustive researches are still authoritative.

1865, June 27. By treaty with Great Britain, Christians were again tolerated and missions protected.

1868-1883. RANAVALONA II, queen. During her reign and that of her successor (i.e. till 1896) the real ruler of the country was the first minister, **Rainilaiarivony,** who was married to the last three queens in succession. Rainilaiarivony was a Christian, but distinctly suspicious of French designs. His policy, therefore, was to rely upon the British to resist French encroachment.

1868, Aug. 8. TREATY OF FRIENDSHIP AND COMMERCE WITH FRANCE. The French recognized Hova supremacy over the entire island, but in return were given consular jurisdiction over French nationals.

1869. Protestantism was proclaimed the state religion.

1877, Oct. Treaty of commerce with the British, who induced the Hova government to proclaim the **liberation of slaves.**

1879. Beginning of friction with France, growing directly from a dispute as to the inheritance of extensive lands which had been granted to the French consul, **Jean Laborde.**

1882. The French government claimed a protectorate over the entire northwestern part of the island, on the basis of the Treaties of 1840. The Hova government took its stand on the Treaty of 1868.

1883, June 1—1885, Dec. 17. WAR WITH FRANCE. The French government submitted a stiff ultimatum, which was rejected. French squadrons thereupon bombarded **Majunga** and **Tamatave,** which was taken June 13. The war dragged on inconclusively until 1885, when the downfall of the colonialists (Jules Ferry) in France led to the conclusion of

1885, Dec. 17. The treaty with France which gave France control of Madagascar's foreign affairs; **Diego Suarez,** at the northern tip of the island, was ceded to France outright; a heavy indemnity was to be paid, and **Tamatave** occupied until the obligation had been met; France was permitted to send a resident to the court of Tananarive, but with the understanding that there should be no interference with domestic affairs.

1886. The French occupied the Comoros Islands (Mayotte had been taken in 1841).

1890. Great Britain (Aug. 5) and Germany (Nov. 17) recognized the **French protectorate over Madagascar,** as part of the larger general colonial settlements made at that time.

1893. Further friction between the French and the Hova government, which resented the French claims to a protectorate.

1894, Nov. 10—1896, Jan. 16. THE FRENCH CONQUEST. The Hova government rejected a French ultimatum embodying extensive claims. The French thereupon occupied **Tamatave** (Dec. 12) and sent an expeditionary force of about 15,000 men under Gen. **Duchesne** to conquer the country. Duchesne landed at Majunga (Feb. 1895), but was delayed for months by fever and transportation difficulties. Finally a small column was organized to push on to the capital, **Tananarive.** The place was bombarded (Sept. 30) and surrendered at once. The queen agreed to accept the French protectorate on condition that she retain sovereignty, but a treaty along these lines (Oct. 1) was rejected by the French government.

1896, Jan. 16. The French proclaimed possession of the island, after forcing the queen to accept. The immediate result of this step was the outbreak of a widespread anti-foreign and anti-Christian insurrection.

Aug. 6. MADAGASCAR WAS PROCLAIMED A FRENCH COLONY. Gen. **Gallieni** was sent out to pacify the island and organize the government. He remained as governor-general until 1905, by which time order had been restored, administration set up, roads built, native tribunals organized, and some schools opened.

1897, Feb. 28. Gallieni deposed the queen and put an end to the Hova dynasty. Ranavalona was exiled first to Réunion, then to Algeria (d. 1917). The French thenceforth ignored the primacy of the Hovas and dealt with all tribes on an equal basis.

1904, Apr. 8. By the general settlement between Great Britain and France (p. 752) all British claims in Madagascar were disposed of.   *(Cont. p. 1093.)*

J. ASIA

1. PERSIA

1794-1925. THE KAJAR DYNASTY, founded by **1794-1797. AGA MOHAMMED** (crowned 1796), a brutal, avaricious, and ambitious chieftain. He managed to suppress a revolt in Georgia and also to reduce Khorasan, but his successful military operations were cut short by his assassination.

1797-1835. FATH ALI SHAH, the nephew of Aga Mohammed, a ruler fond of wealth and splendor, but no general. His reign was marked by the involvement of Persia in the conflicts of Europe, by the rapid infiltration of foreign influence, and by the beginning of Russia's successful advance in Central Asia.

1798. The British, fearful for India, induced the Persians to attack Afghanistan, thus initiating a long struggle by the Persians to recover their eastern provinces.

1800. Russia annexed Georgia, the last king of which, George XII, appealed for Russian support against Persia.

1800. The first Malcolm mission to Persia. Sir John Malcolm, representing the East India Company, concluded a political and commercial treaty; the shah was to make no peace with the Afghans unless the latter renounced their designs on India. The British were to supply arms and money in the event of an attack on Persia by Afghanistan or France.

1804. War with Russia. The Russians advanced on Erivan, but were forced to retire. Indecisive fighting continued in Gilan.

1806. Arrival of a French mission under Jaubert. Napoleon offered to support the Persians in the reconquest of Georgia and in an attack on India.

1807, May. Treaty of Finkenstein, between France and Persia. The French government sent out Gen. Gardanne with 70 officers to reorganize the Persian army, but after the conclusion of the Treaty of Tilsit (p. 593) the French lost interest.

1808. Mission of Sir Harford Jones. He induced the Persians to dismiss Gardanne, in return for a subsidy and the aid of British officers.

1810. Another mission under Malcolm succeeded in definitely establishing the British influence.

1812. Russian victory over the Persians in the battle of Aslanduz.

1813, Oct. 12. Treaty of Gulistan, between Russia and Persia. The latter ceded Derbent, Baku, Shirvan, Shaki, Karabagh, and part of Talish, and also gave up claims to Georgia, Daghestan, Mingrelia, Imeritia, and Abkhasia.

1814, Nov. 25. Definitive treaty with England. Persia was to cancel all treaties with European powers hostile to England and to exclude all European armies hostile to England. Mutual aid was to be given in case of attack, and England was to pay a subsidy of £150,000.

1821-1823. The last war with Turkey brought Persia some successes, but ended in the Treaty of Erzerum, which involved no territorial changes.

1825-1828. War with Russia resulting from the Russian seizure of Gokcha, disputed territory. The Persians were defeated by Paskievich in the battle of Ganja (1826), after which the Russians took Erivan and Tabriz (1827).

1828, Feb. 22. TREATY OF TURKMAN-CHAI: Persia ceded to Russia the provinces of Erivan and Nakhchivan, and paid a huge indemnity.

1835-1848. MOHAMMED SHAH, who ascended the throne with the support of both England and Russia. His general policy, however, was less friendly to England, and a military mission (1834-1838), which attempted to modernize the army, was ultimately obliged to withdraw.

1837-1838. The Persians besieged Herat, which was valiantly defended (Eldred Pottinger). Finally the shah yielded to British pressure and gave up the operation.

1847. Confirmation of the Treaty of Erzerum (1823), providing for delimitation of the Turkish-Persian frontier. This was not actually completed until Oct. 1914, England and Russia acting as arbitrators.

1848-1896. NASIR UD-DIN, the son of Mohammed, and on the whole the ablest ruler of the Kajar dynasty. In his

The Kajar Dynasty

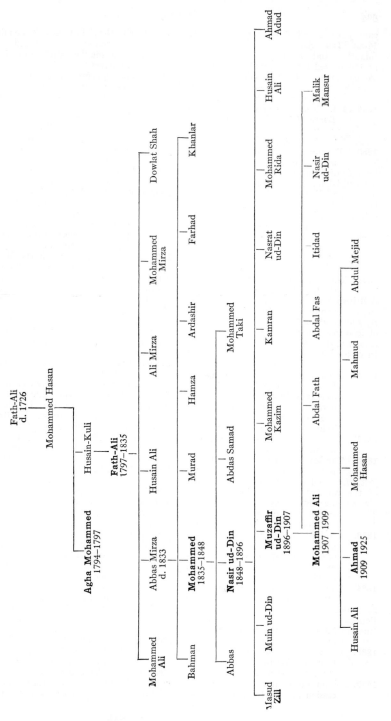

early years (till 1852) his energetic minister, **Mirza Taki Khan,** undertook extensive financial and military reforms, which promised well for the country, but which came to an end with Taki's downfall. The shah himself on three occasions visited Europe (1873, 1878, 1889).

1849-1854. **Russian conquest of the Syr Darya Valley,** beginning the advance of Russia to the Persian frontier in Central Asia.

1850. **Execution of Sayyid Ali Mohammed,** the *Bab* (Gateway), and founder of **Babism,** a new mystical movement in Islam. In the succeeding years the numerous followers of the Bab were ruthlessly persecuted and finally (1864) expelled, most of them finding refuge in Turkey. The Bab's successor, **Baha Ulla** (*Splendor of God*), gave the movement a new turn and founded **Bahaism,** a less strictly Islamic version of the new doctrine.

1856. **The Persians took Herat,** whereupon **the British declared war** on Persia. A British force took Kharak Island and occupied Bushire and (1857) Mohammerah. By the **Treaty of Paris** (1857) the shah was obliged to evacuate Afghan territory and to recognize the independence of the country. In case of dispute he was to make use of British good offices.

1864. Opening of the **first telegraph** in Persia (Baghdad-Tehran-Bushire) constructed by British interests as part of the line to India. The line from Europe (Odessa–Tiflis–Tehran) was opened in 1870.

1872. **The boundary between Persia and Afghanistan was defined.**

1872. **The Reuter concession,** granted to Baron de Reuter, a British subject, envisaged the economic development of the country in many directions and pledged the customs by way of payment. The concession proved impracticable and was cancelled by the government.

1878. Establishment of **the Cossack Brigade,** a force trained by Russian officers and an important instrument for the spread of Russian influence.

1884. **The Russian conquest of Merv** completed the subjection of Turkmenistan and brought Russia to the frontier of Persia. From this time the growth of **Russian influence** in northern Persia was rapid and almost irresistible.

1888. Opening of the **lower Karun River** to navigation by British interests (Lynch Brothers).

1889. Baron de Reuter secured a concession for the **Imperial Bank of** Persia, with the right to exploit the mineral wealth of Persia (except gold and silver). The bank became the focal point of British interests.

1890. The government granted a concession for the production, sale, and export of tobacco, but aroused thereby so much popular and religious opposition that the concession was cancelled.

1892. The British government granted Persia a loan, with the customs of the Persian Gulf coast as security.

1896. **Assassination of the shah,** who was succeeded by his son

1896-1907. **MUZAFFAR UD-DIN,** an incompetent and weak ruler, constantly in need of money for his own purposes. His reign marked the **acute phase of the rivalry of Russia and Britain.**

1900, Jan. Russia, through the Banque d'Escompte de Perse (practically a branch of the Russian finance ministry) granted Persia a loan of $22\frac{1}{2}$ million rubles, with the customs of all Persia, excepting the Gulf coast, as security. Persia was to liquidate the earlier British loan and to accept no other offers for ten years. In Mar. 1902 the Russian government added another loan, receiving in return the **concession for a road from Julfa to Tabriz and Tehran.**

1900. **Russian ships appeared at Bunder Abbas** and plans were being considered for the construction of a railroad across Persia to the Gulf coast. The British government made no secret of its opposition, and finally, in 1903, Lord Curzon made a grand tour of the Persian Gulf to refresh the British ascendancy there.

1901. Mr. W. K. d'Arcy, a New Zealander, secured a 60-year **concession to exploit for oil** through most of the country. The government was to receive £20,000 and the same amount in paid-up shares, and was to have 16% of the annual profits. The concessionaire spent much time and money in futile operations, until, in 1908, the field at Masjid Sulaiman was discovered.

1902, Dec. 13. Russia induced Persia to promulgate a **new tariff,** very favorable to Russian goods and equally unfavorable to the British.

1903. The Persian customs were put under the administration of **M. Naus,** a Belgian national.

1905, Dec. BEGINNING OF THE PERSIAN REVOLUTION. Opposition to the incompetent rule of the shahs went back at least until 1890, and was centered in the commercial classes and the religious leaders. Inspiration of **Jamal**

ud-Din el Afghani, the eminent teacher of Pan-Islamic ideas, who was a Persian by birth (b. near Hamadan, 1838) and was at times closely associated with Shah Nasir ud-Din. In 1905 the movement was directed at the spread of foreign interests and control and at **Ayn ud-Dola,** the powerful and corrupt minister (1903-1906), who was held chiefly responsible.

1906, July. The Great *Bast* at the British legation. Several thousand revolutionaries took refuge on the legation grounds. The shah was obliged to yield to the popular demand. He dismissed Ayn ud-Dola and (Aug. 5) agreed to the convocation of a national assembly (*majlis*).

Oct. 7. The first majlis met at Tehran and drew up a constitution of the accepted liberal type. The shah died just after signing it (Dec. 30) and was succeeded by his son

1907-1909. **MOHAMMED ALI SHAH,** who from the outset was hostile to the new movement and attempted to circumvent the majlis. The result was

1907, Aug. The assassination of his reactionary minister, **Atabeg i-Azam,** and the establishment of a liberal ministry under Nasir ul-Mulk.

1907, Aug. 31. **CONCLUSION OF THE ANGLO-RUSSIAN ENTENTE** (p. 754), by which these two powers, both uneasy about German policy in the Near East, compromised their interests in Persia. Russia recognized Britain's preponderant interest in the Persian Gulf. The southeastern part of the country was reserved as a British sphere, while the entire northern half of the country became a Russian sphere. A central belt was to be left open to concessions for either party. The Persians were in no way consulted, but were not misled by the reaffirmation, in the agreement, of the principle of the independence and integrity of Persia.

1907, Dec. 15. The shah attempted a *coup d'état* and imprisoned the liberal prime minister. This led to a popular uprising in various parts of the country, and the shah was obliged to yield.

1908, June 23. Successful *coup d'état* of the shah. With the secret support of the Russian legation and the aid of the Cossack Brigade, the shah shut down the assembly and had many of the liberal leaders killed. Martial law was established in Tehran, but at Tabriz **the populace revolted** and seized control. The shah sent an army against the city, but a deadlock ensued.

1909. Formation of the **Anglo-Persian Oil Company** to exploit the d'Arcy concession. A pipe line was constructed from the oil fields of southwestern Persia to Abadan Island in the mouth of the Shatt el-Arab and Persia soon became a leading producer of oil.

Mar. 26. A Russian force invaded northern Persia and raised the siege of Tabriz. Brutal action of the Russians in occupying the city for the shah.

June. Ali Kuli Khan, a leader of the Bakhtiari tribe, began the march on Tehran to defend the constitutional régime.

July 12. He took the city and deposed the shah (July 16).

1909-1925. **SULTAN AHMAD SHAH,** the twelve-year-old son of Mohammed Ali. He was wholly under the control of the more radical elements, who set up a regent to govern the country.

1911, May 12. **Arrival of W. Morgan Shuster,** an American, who had been invited to order the finances of Persia. Shuster was given almost dictatorial power by the majlis, and began to organize a treasury gendarmerie. The Russians, already suspicious, frustrated his attempt to secure the services of **Maj. Stokes,** a British officer, and in other ways opposed the constructive efforts of the reformer.

July 18. The ex-shah, evidently with the connivance of the Russians, left his retreat in Russia and landed at Astrabad. His force was defeated by the government (Sept. 5).

Nov. 5, 29. Two Russian ultimata, aiming at the dismissal of Shuster, were rejected by the majlis. Thereupon the Russians began to invade northern Persia. Acute tension in Anglo-Russian relations.

Dec. 24. The majlis was suddenly closed and locked by the action of a group of politicians, who then formed a **directory.** From this time until the outbreak of the World War, Persia was pretty much under the domination of Russia.

(*Cont. pp.* 919 *f.,* 1106.)

2. AFGHANISTAN

1793-1799. ZAMAN SHAH, the son of Timur. His reign marked the beginning of a prolonged period of dynastic conflict and tribal strife, during which the **Punjab was definitively lost to the Sikhs.** Zaman at first defeated his brothers, but finally fell into the hands of his brother Mahmud, who blinded him.

1799-1803. MAHMUD SHAH, who was supported by Persia.

1803-1810. SHAH SHUJA, a brother of Mahmud, who seized control. His reign is memorable chiefly for the **beginning of relations with the British East India Company.**

1809, June 17. First agreement with the British. The latter, fearful of a Persian or French attack on India, induced the Afghans to oppose such a move and promised to support them if necessary.

1810-1818. MAHMUD SHAH, having escaped from captivity and having defeated Shah Shuja, resumed the throne. His main support was the vizier **Fath Ali Khan** of the Barakzai tribe, an able and energetic soldier and statesman.

1816. The Persians captured Herat, but were soon driven out by the Afghans.

1818. Revolt of the tribes after Fath Ali's dismissal by the shah. Mahmud was unable to stay the tide and was driven out of all his territory excepting Herat, where he ruled until 1829. The rest of the country fell to the various brothers of Fath Ali, who established practically **independent khanates** such as Kabul, Kandahar, Ghazni, etc.

1819. Conquest of **Kashmir** by Ranjit Singh, who took advantage of the confusion in Afghanistan.

1826. Dost Mohammed, brother of Fath Ali, member of the Barakzai tribe and ruler of Ghazni, **captured Kabul** and began gradually to extend his influence over much of the country.

1834. Dost Mohammed took over **Kandahar** after defeating the local ruler. In the same year **Ranjit Singh conquered Peshawar.**

1835-1839. DOST MOHAMMED became ruler of all Afghanistan and took the title of *Amir*, founding the **Barakzai dynasty.**

1837. The Persians, supported by the Russians, launched an **attack on Herat.** This offensive led to the conclusion of

1838, July 25. The **Tripartite Treaty** between the East India Company, Ranjit Singh and Shah Shuja, the object of which was to restore the latter to the Afghan throne and block the advance of the Persians and the Russians.

1839-1842. THE FIRST AFGHAN WAR of the British against Dost Mohammed. A British force advanced to Kandahar and thence to Ghazni and Kabul. Dost Mohammed was captured, deposed, and sent to India.

1839-1842. SHAH SHUJA ascended the throne again. Great discontent in the country and agitation against British influence.

1841. Rising against the British. **Murder** of **Sir Alexander Burnes** and **Sir William Macnaghten**, the British envoys.

1842, Jan. The British were obliged to fall back from Kabul. In the course of the retreat they were attacked by the Afghans under **Akbar Khan** (son of Dost Mohammed). With few exceptions the entire force of over 3000 men was massacred. Shah Shuja was murdered.

Sept. 14. Gen. Pollock and a punitive force from India **reoccupied Kabul** and punished the guilty, but the British government insisted on withdrawal from so exposed a position (Oct.).

1842-1863. DOST MOHAMMED again ascended the throne and reestablished his power, though he secured Kandahar only in 1855.

1855, Mar. 30. Treaty of Peshawar, between Dost Mohammed and the British. The treaty was directed against Persian designs on Herat.

1856. The Persians seized Herat on the death of the local ruler. This move led to the declaration of war by England (p. 864) and

1857, Mar. 4. The Treaty of Paris, between England and Persia. The latter power gave up its claim to Herat and recognized the independence of Afghanistan.

1863. Dost Mohammed finally took Herat after a ten months' siege from the khan who had been set up after the Persian evacuation.

1863-1870. Civil war following the death of Dost Mohammed. His third son, Shir Ali, who was recognized by the British, had a hard time asserting his claim against his brothers, who for years held the upper hand.

The Barakzai Dynasty

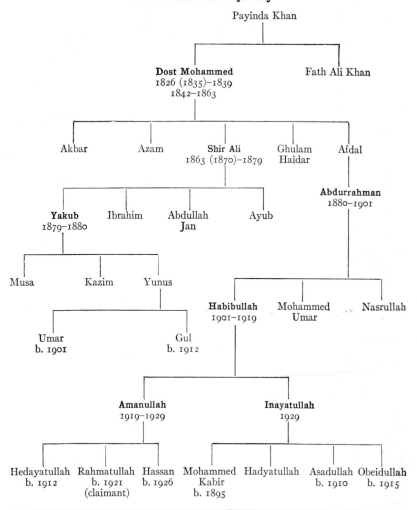

Payinda Khan

Dost Mohammed
1826 (1835)–1839
1842–1863

Fath Ali Khan

Akbar   Azam   **Shir Ali**
1863 (1870)–1879

Ghulam
Haidar

Afdal

Abdurrahman
1880–1901

Yakub
1879–1880

Ibrahim

Abdullah
Jan

Ayub

Musa   Kazim   Yunus

Habibullah
1901–1919

Mohammed
Umar

Nasrullah

Umar
b. 1901

Gul
b. 1912

Amanullah
1919–1929

Inayatullah
1929

Hedayatullah
b. 1912

Rahmatullah
b. 1921
(claimant)

Hassan
b. 1926

Mohammed
Kabir
b. 1895

Hadyatullah

Asadullah
b. 1910

Obeidullah
b. 1915

1870-1879. SHIR ALI, amir. His general policy was to lean on Russia as a counterweight to the British. The result was growing tension in relations with India.

1878, June.   Arrival of a Russian mission under Gen. Stolietov at Kabul and conclusion of a treaty of mutual support (Aug.). The Indian government thereupon insisted upon the reception of a British mission, which Shir Ali refused. The result was

1878-1879.   THE SECOND AFGHAN WAR, in the course of which Shir Ali died (Feb. 1879).

1879.   YAKUB, the son of Shir Ali, became amir. The British having overrun much of the country, he was forced to accept

May 16.   The Treaty of Gandamak, by which the British were to occupy the Khyber Pass, but to pay the amir an annual subsidy of £60,000. The amir was to conduct his foreign relations only through the Indian government. British trade was to have full freedom.

Sept. 3. Native outbreak against the British. Murder of Sir Louis Cavagnari and his escort. The British thereupon advanced and took Kabul once more (Oct. 12).

Oct. 19. Yakub abdicated and surrendered to the British.

1880-1901. ABDURRAHMAN, nephew and opponent of Shir Ali, who had been in retirement in Russia, then became amir. In a general way he accepted the Treaty of Gandamak, but throughout his reign he succeeded in playing off the British and the Russians and thereby protecting his country. At the same time he subdued many of the tribes and established his authority as ruler. The reign was noteworthy also for the gradual fixing of the Afghan frontiers.

1885, Apr. The Penjdeh incident, a clash between Russian and Afghan troops on the disputed border. A severe Anglo-Russian crisis ensued (p. 739), but the matter was finally settled by negotiations (June 18, 1886).

1893, Nov. 12. The Durand agreement, with England, fixed the frontier with India from Chitral to Baluchistan.

1895, Mar. 11. Settlement of the Pamir boundary, after years of friction with Russia. Afghanistan retained a narrow strip which separated the Russian and British possessions.

1901-1919. HABIBULLAH KHAN, son of Abdurrahman, amir. He was a much less effective ruler and fell more and more under harem and religious influences. Gradual penetration of European ideas.

1905, Mar. 21. A new agreement with England reaffirmed earlier engagements. This was a reply to renewed Russian activity since about 1900 (mission of commercial agents, etc.).

1907, Aug. 31. The Anglo-Russian Entente, which involved compromise of Russian and British interests in Persia, included recognition by Russia of Britain's predominant position in Afghanistan. Russia agreed once more to abstain from interference in Afghan affairs. (*Cont. p.* 1109.)

3. INDIA

1798-1805. LORD MORNINGTON (later Marquis of Wellesley) governor-general. He reversed earlier policy by seeking stability through subsidiary alliances by which England supplied troops and protection in exchange for territory or monetary grants, was allowed control of the state's foreign affairs, but pledged non-intervention in internal government, and secured exclusion of every other foreign power from the state's service. The fourth Mysore war (d. Tipu 1799) led to a protectorate over Mysore; various annexations extended British control over nearly all southern India. Costly warfare with Maratha leaders following the Treaty of Bassein with the Peshwa (1802) led to alarm at home, Wellesley's recall, and subsequent reversal of his policy.

1805. Lord Cornwallis again governor-general (d. Oct)., succeeded by Sir G. Barlow.

1807-1813. LORD MINTO, governor-general.

1809. Sutlej fixed as southern boundary, checking the advance of a Sikh confederacy under Ranjit Singh.

1808-1810. To curb French expansion in the east, Minto made treaties with Sind, Persia, and Afghanistan, and captured the French islands in the Indian Ocean and Java, which was under French control (Bourbon was later restored to France and Java to the Dutch).

1813-1823. LORD MOIRA (later Marquis of Hastings) governor-general.

1813. Company's charter renewed for another 20 years, but its monopoly of trade with India abolished.

1814-1816. Gurkhas invaded from Nepal, provoking war and British acquisition of the present Kumaun Division and permanent peace with Nepal.

1816-1818. The Pindari tribes, after raiding British territory, were suppressed and broken up by Hastings; hostile Maratha leaders were also defeated, leaving no native state in India proper altogether independent.

1819. Occupation of Singapore by Raffles (p. 875).

1824-1826. Following Burmese aggression the first Burmese war (see Burma) led to English acquisition of Assam, Arakan, and Tenasserim.

ASIA
1914

Scale of Miles

0   200   400   600

⬚ British Territory

1827. Pretense of subordination to the Delhi emperor abandoned; his name removed from the coinage (1835).

1833. Company's charter renewed for 20 years, but its monopoly of trade with China abolished; European settlement in India allowed; law revision and codification undertaken (Macaulay).

1828-1835. LORD WM. BENTINCK, governor-general. Relative peace favored reform measures: *Suttee* was made a criminal offense (1829), bands of thugs were largely suppressed; more responsibility was given to Indians, and the vernacular was used in court.

In competition with the work of Christian missionaries, who printed many vernacular texts and had begun the first vernacular newspaper (1818), Ram Mohun Roy organized the *Brahmo Samaj* (1828), a reform association supporting western education, which printed Hindu works in vernacular.

1835-1836. SIR C. METCALFE, governor-general, followed by

1836-1842. LORD AUCKLAND.

1839-1842. THE FIRST AFGHAN WAR (p. 866).

1842-1844. EARL OF ELLENBOROUGH, governor-general. Two armies sent into Afghanistan, resulting in recapture of Kabul and replacement of Dost Mohammed (p. 866).

1843. Sind was annexed, following British provocation of hostilities.

1844-1848. SIR H. HARDINGE, governor-general.

1845-1849. First and second wars with the Sikhs, arising from disorders after Ranjit Singh's death (1839), led to acquisition of territory including Kashmir, and annexation of the Punjab, reform of its government, and permanent loyalty of the Sikhs.

1848-1856. EARL OF DALHOUSIE, governor-general, accelerated public works, introducing a uniform postal rate and telegraph service and developing roads, irrigation canals, and railways (first line opened 1853). Regular steamship service to England via Suez overland route had been established in 1843.

Dalhousie adhered consistently, even when an adopted son might rule, to the doctrine of lapse (disavowed 1859), whereby states with no heirs in the ruling line fell to the paramount power; he annexed seven principalities.

1852. Second Burmese war (p. 872) led to annexation of Pegu (lower Burma) and British dominion over entire east coast of Bay of Bengal.

1856. Annexation of Oudh, which aroused increasing resentment.

1856-1862. EARL CANNING, governor-general.

1857-1858. THE GREAT MUTINY. Fear of forcible conversion inflamed undisciplined and discontented sepoys (four-fifths of the army was native), who mutinied at Meerut (May 10, 1857). The rising spread through northern and central India (massacre at Cawnpore June 27) and was suppressed with difficulty (first relief of Lucknow by Havelock Sept. 25, final relief by Campbell Nov. 16). Siege and capture of Delhi (June–Sept.) led to banishment of Bahadur Shah (d. 1862) and end of the Mogul Empire.

1858, Sept. 1. The East India Company came to an end, the crown taking over its duties and treaty obligations. Renunciation of the annexation policy was guaranteed by two *sanads* (Hindu and Moslem 1862), but Britain controlled successions and assumed responsibility for "protected" states, frequently interfering in them (from 1875 Baroda was governed by British regents). Paper currency, license taxes, and an income tax were introduced to meet the heavy debt left in 1859. Regulation of civil service appointments (competitive since 1853), court reform to include Indian magistrates, and legislative and executive councils (1861) including Indian representatives, all strengthened the administration, which also promoted forest conservation, agricultural experiment, famine prevention measures, and sanitation (boards in each presidency 1864).

1862-1863. Lord Elgin, viceroy, succeeded by Lord Lawrence (1864–1869), Lord Mayo (1869–1872), Lord Northbrook (1872–1876), and Lord Lytton (1876–1880).

1865. A small war with Bhutan led to cession of some territory for annual payment. Opening of telegraph service to Europe.

1866. Collapse of a cotton boom which had arisen from increased production during the American Civil War.

1870-1921. Financial stability was enhanced by Mayo's decentralized policy, with fixed annual grants to provincial departments augmented by local taxes.

1876. Occupation of Quetta as a safeguard against Russian encroachment in Afghanistan.

1877, Jan. 1. THE QUEEN WAS PROCLAIMED *EMPRESS OF INDIA.*

1878-1881. THE SECOND AFGHAN WAR (p. 867).

1880-1884. MARQUIS OF RIPON, viceroy (resigned 1884).

1884-1888. LORD DUFFERIN, viceroy, succeeded by **LORD LANSDOWNE** (to 1894).
Imperial Service troops (native forces with British officers) were put under command of the individual states, subject to the commander-in-chief only when on active service.

1885. Third Burmese War (p. 872), provoked by defiance of King Thibaw and his negotiations with France; upper Burma was annexed (Jan. 1886) and united to lower Burma in 1897.

1886. The first National Congress was convened and, although largely lacking Moslem support, came to represent the Indian voice. The Nationalist movement, led by Surendranath Banerji, Gokhale, and Bal Gangadhar Tilak, worked particularly through gymnastic societies and the press.

1892. Legislative councils were enlarged and allowed, within limits, to pass on the budget.

1894-1898. LORD ELGIN, viceroy.

1895. Disputed succession in Chitral led to brief war and permanent peace.

1897. Serious rising of Afridi clans in Tirah.

1898-1905. GEORGE N. (later Lord) **CURZON** appointed viceroy (took office Jan. 6, 1899).

1903-1904. Expedition to Tibet under Sir Francis Younghusband.

1904. Co-operative credit system set up to reduce hoarding and usury (amplified with purchase and marketing societies in 1912; 52,182 co-operatives by 1922).

1905. PARTITION OF BENGAL, which seemed to favor Moslems, aroused Nationalist opposition (boycott on foreign goods, general violence) and led to control of meetings and the press.

1905-1910. EARL MINTO, viceroy, following resignation of Lord Curzon (Aug. 12) in consequence of decision of the home government in favor of Lord Kitchener's proposals regarding Indian military administration.

1907. A meeting of the National Congress led to **rift between extremists** under Tilak, demanding complete independence, and **moderates** advocating parliamentary government.

1909, May 25. INDIAN COUNCILS ACT passed (operative Nov. 15). Powers of legislative councils increased, and a majority of the members made directly elective; separate electorate for Mohammedans. An Indian to be appointed to the viceroy's executive council and two Indians to the secretary's council in England (increased to three in 1919).

1910. LORD HARDINGE appointed viceroy. Wounded by anarchist bomb in Delhi (Dec. 23, 1912). **Growth of Nationalist movement** influenced by: (1) the Asiatic successes in the Russo-Japanese war; (2) the dissatisfaction with the Universities Act (1904, providing greater government control in order to improve standards) and the partition of Bengal; (3) Mohammedan resentment at British acquiescence in the spoliation of European Turkey (1912); (4) the genuine desire of educated Indians for self-government. Agitation for **full self-government** in the National Congress and in the press. The movement was violent in its first years, many outrages being attempted and perpetrated; later development of a non-co-operative movement (1919 *et seq.*).

1911, May 8. Agreement made with China gradually to cut off the supply of opium to China.

Dec. 12. Coronation **Durbar at Delhi:** king-emperor well received. Transfer of the Indian capital from Calcutta to the ancient capital Delhi. **Reversal of the partition of Bengal.**

1914, May 21. Komagatu Maru incident. Gurdit Singh and 400 Indians arrived at Vancouver to test the immigration laws, but were not admitted; resentment in India and some rioting near Calcutta on return of vessel (Oct. 2); 16 killed.

Aug. 4. British **declaration of war** on Germany. India responded loyally with contributions of **money and men.** In all, about 1,400,000 men volunteered for service and took active part in the campaigns in the Near East and Africa (p. 918 *f.*). (*Cont. p.* 1111.)

4. INDO-CHINA

a. BURMA

The modern Burmese state was built upon the conquests of **Alaungpaya** (1752–1860), whose successors managed to repulse **invasions by the Chinese** (1766–1769), but were unable to maintain themselves in Siam (1771).

1781-1819. Bodawpaya, king. Conquest of Arakan (1784) and further encroachments on Indian territory. **Peace with Siam** (1793). Acquisition of the Tenasserim coast (1793).

1819-1837. Bagyidaw, king. He continued the advance toward India, seizing Manipur and Assam (1822) and invading Kachar (1824). This policy of expansion soon brought him into conflict with the British East India Company.

1824-1826.   FIRST BURMESE WAR. Despite vigorous resistance by the Burmese, they were unable to withstand the force of a modern army. The British, under Sir **Archibald Campbell**, took Rangoon, and then Syriam, Tavoy, Mergui, Martaban, and Pegu. An attempt by the Burmese to recapture Rangoon failed (1825). The British advanced up the Irrawaddy and at the same time overran Arakan. Feb. 24, 1826: by the **Treaty of Yandabu** (near Ava) the British secured Assam, Arakan, and the Tenasserim coast, as well as an indemnity and the right to send a resident to Ava (discontinued 1837).

1837-1846. Tharawaddi Min, king.

1846-1852. Pagan Min. Under these reigns the friction with the British continued. The Burmese rulers continued to treat the British with contempt and to hamper the development of British trade.

1852-1853.   SECOND BURMESE WAR. Rangoon was again taken, by Gen. Godwin. Pegu was also occupied and annexed (Jan. 20, 1853). A revolution in the capital led to the deposition of the king and the elevation of

1853-1878. Mindon Min, described as the best king of Burma in modern times. He accepted the British gains without concluding a formal treaty, and attempted, throughout his reign, to maintain friendly relations with his neighbor.

1857.   Mandalay, built by the king, became the capital of the country.

1862.   Conclusion of a commercial treaty with Great Britain. The customs duty was fixed at 5% and the British were given the right to trade throughout the country.

1875.   A British expedition to explore the route from Bhamo into Yunnan was checked by the murder of the British interpreter.

1878-1885. THIBAW, king. He proved himself an apathetic and unwise ruler. From the beginning of his reign he caused trouble by his interference with British trade. At the same time he established contact with French interests and negotiated with them for the organization of a royal bank and for the construction of a railroad from Mandalay to the Indian frontier. This anti-British attitude resulted in

1885.   THE THIRD BURMESE WAR. The British (Oct. 22) sent an ultimatum demanding that Thibaw receive a British envoy and that his interference with trade be stopped; furthermore, that in future the foreign relations of Burma be conducted in accordance with the advice of the Indian government. On the rejection of this ultimatum, a British steamer expedition, commanded by Gen. **Sir Harry Prendergast**, occupied Mandalay (November 28). Thibaw surrendered and was sent to India.

1886, Jan. 1.   UPPER BURMA WAS ANNEXED by the British, but desultory guerrilla warfare continued for years. The **Shan States** were not reduced until 1887 and the **Chin Hills** not until 1891.

July 24.   An Anglo-Chinese convention recognized the British position in Burma. Chinese prestige was saved by a continuation of Burmese decennial tribute missions.

1893.   The boundary with Siam was fixed by convention.

1895.   Agreement with France on the boundary with Cochin-China.

1900.   Agreement with China finally fixed the Burmese frontier on that side.

b. SIAM

1765.   Destruction of Ayuthia by the Burmese marked the end of the old Siamese kingdom. After long years of war the Burmese were driven out of the country and a new dynasty (the **Chakri**) was founded.

1782-1809.   RAMA I (Phra Buddha Yod Fa Chulalok), first of the new line. He finally brought to an end the long conflict with Burma (1793), re-established control over the local potentates throughout the country, and secured part of Cambodia through division of that state with Annam.

1809-1824.   RAMA II (Phra Buddha Loes Fa Nobhalai).

1824-1851.   RAMA III (Phra Nang Klao), whose reign was distinguished by the reopening of contact with the western nations.

1826, June 20. Conclusion of a **treaty of commerce with Great Britain.** This was followed (Mar. 20, 1833) by a similar treaty with the United States. Both agreements left much to be desired, as they did not even provide for the establishment of consuls.

1844. Cambodia passed under the protection of Siam.

1851-1868.   RAMA IV (Phra Chom Klao Mongkut), who, as a monk, had made a study of western governments and who began the work of modernizing Siam.

1855, Apr. 18.   A NEW TREATY WITH GREAT BRITAIN, modeled on the Anglo-Chinese treaty. Opening of **Siam:** consuls to be established; extraterritorial system introduced; right to trade throughout the kingdom. Similar treaties were concluded with the United States (1856, May 29) and with France (1856, Aug. 15), and thereafter with many other powers.

1863. The French established a protectorate over Cambodia. After long negotiations, the Siamese gave up their claims (1867).

1868-1910.   RAMA V (Phra Maha Chulalonkorn), the real founder of modern Siam. After attaining his majority (1873) he devoted himself almost entirely to the reform of his government and the improvement of his country: feudal system abolished; slavery reduced and stamped out; administrative reform (central bureaucracy); taxation and finance reform; postal service; modernization of the army; introduction of the telegraph (1883); opening of the first railway (1893).

1885. Failure of a French **proposal to neutralize Siam** resulted in ever-increasing friction and continuous border disputes, culminating in

1893, May-Aug.   THE SIAMESE CRISIS. The French had been trying for years to extend their dominions westward to the Mekong River, a policy which met with opposition not only from Siam but

from England, which desired to preserve Siam as buffer between Burma and the French possessions. Border clashes in May 1893 led to the mission of two gunboats to Bangkok in July. The Siamese fired upon them, whereupon the French submitted a stiff ultimatum (July 13). This was rejected and the French then instituted a blockade (July 31), which led to a short but acute **Anglo-French crisis** (p. 742). The Siamese were obliged to yield and ultimately accepted the

Oct. 3.   Franco-Siamese treaty, by which the Siamese abandoned all claim to territory east of the Mekong and paid an indemnity of three million francs. The French remained in occupation of Chantabun until 1905.

1896, Jan. 15.   An Anglo-French agreement ended the long friction between the two countries on the Siamese question. The British recognized the gains made by France in 1893 and abandoned their demand for a buffer between Burma and the French colonies. Both sides guaranteed the independence of Siam.

1897. The King of Siam paid an extended visit to the European capitals.

1904, Feb. 13. A further treaty with France replaced the agreement of 1893. France returned Chantabun, while Siam ceded Bassac, Melupré, and that part of Luang Prabang which lay on the right (west) bank of the Mekong; also Krat on the coast.

1907, Mar. 23. By agreement **France retroceded to Siam Battambong, Siemrap, and Sisophon** on the Cambodian frontier, and received in return the region of **Krat and Dansai.** France agreed to **modification of the extra-territorial system,** giving Siam jurisdiction over French Asiatics.

Apr. 8. An **Anglo-French convention** confirmed the independence of Siam, but established **spheres of influence;** territory west of the Menam River to be the British sphere, that to the east the French sphere.

1909, Mar. 10.   Great Britain gave up the system of extra-territoriality, in return for the cession of Kedah, Kelantan, Trengganu, and Perlis to the Malay States.

1910-1925.   RAMA VI (Vajiravudh). Educated in England, he continued the policy of modernization and westernization: irrigation projects, education, calendar reform, reduction of compulsory labor, etc.

1917, July 22.   Siam declared war on Germany and Austria.

(*Cont. p.* 1114.)

c. FRENCH INDO-CHINA

At the beginning of the 19th century most of present-day French Indo-China was ruled by the **Emperor of Annam.** The region was predominantly Chinese in culture and the empire acknowledged the suzerainty of the Chinese emperor. After a long period of **dynastic struggle and civil war** (1772–1802) the imperial domain had been reunited by

1802-1820. GIA LONG (Nguyen Anh), emperor, who had been supported in his struggles by the French missionary, **Pigneau de Béhaine.** Catholic missions had been active in the country since 1615 and had worked with considerable success. The emperor, who was a great organizer as well as a soldier, gave the French Catholics free rein.

1820-1840. MINH-MANG, emperor. A strict Confucian and a great admirer of all things Chinese, Minh-Mang was decidedly hostile to Christians, whom he suspected of supporting the rebellious provincial lords. He therefore ordered them expelled (1824 and on many later occasions).

1840-1847. THIEU-TRI, emperor. He continued the persecution of the Christians and refused flatly to receive foreign missions. During his reign the French naval commanders intervened several times to save the lives of the Christians.

1847-1883. TU DUC, emperor. He was a learned, simple, and pious ruler, who, like his predecessors, attempted to keep his country closed to outsiders. Persecution of Christians continued.

1858. A joint French and Spanish expedition under Adm. **Rigault de Genouilly,** in order to put a stop to the exclusive and unfriendly attitude of the Annamite court, bombarded Tourane on the coast. Unable to proceed to the capital, Hué, the expedition turned south and occupied Saigon in Cochin China. The operations were interrupted by the war of the French against China, but they led ultimately to the

1862, June 5. Treaty of Saigon, by which the emperor abandoned to the French the three eastern provinces of Cochin China and agreed to pay an indemnity of 20,000,000 francs in ten years. Free exercise of the Catholic religion was to be allowed and three ports (Tourane, Balat, and Kuang-An) were to be opened to French trade.

1863-1868. Adm. de La Grandière, governor of Cochin China. He organized the system of government through admirals, so-called, which continued until 1879. Actual administration was left largely in the hands of native mandarins.

1863, Aug. 11. King Norodom (1860–1904) of Cambodia, a Hindu state dependent on both Annam and Siam and constantly threatened by these neighbors, **accepted a French protectorate.**

1867. France occupied the three western provinces of Cochin China, after an insurrection.

1868. French exploration of the **Mekong River,** as far as Yünnan. It was hoped that this would prove a useful route to penetration into southwestern China, but the river was shown to be unnavigable in the upper reaches and the French therefore began to turn their attention to the Red River of Tonkin.

1873. Exploration of the **Red River** by **Jean Dupuis,** a French merchant active in China. The Annamites objected to French activity in Tonkin, but

1873-1874. FRANCIS GARNIER, with a handful of men, attacked and **took Hanoi** and conquered most of the Red River delta.

1874, Mar. 15. BY A TREATY SIGNED AT SAIGON, the emperor was obliged to promise to conform his foreign policy to that of France and to recognize the French possession of Cochin China. Freedom of the Christian religion was once again promised. In return France promised protection and offered to supply gunboats and officers to help suppress piracy. The French returned Hanoi, but the treaty was systematically evaded by the emperor, who now began to appeal to the Chinese for aid against the French.

1882. Insurrection in Tonkin. Death of Henri Rivière and a small force (1883).

1883, Aug. 25. TREATY OF HUÊ. Tu Duc was forced once more to recognize the French protectorate, which was now extended to Tonkin and Annam itself. But the French still had to deal with the pirates and guerrilla Black Flags in Tonkin, who were supported by the Chinese. The result was **war with China** (p. 880), in the course of which the French suffered a setback at **Langson** (Mar. 28, 1885) which in turn led to the overthrow of Jules Ferry, the prime mover for expansion in France. But by the **Treaty of Tien-tsin** (June 9, 1885) China was obliged to recognize the French protectorate over Tonkin.

The year 1883 was marked by severe **internal strife**, following the death of Emperor Tu Duc. The regents elevated and deposed several emperors in succession, and after the French control was established the native ruler was subject to French orders.

1884, June 6. THE TREATY OF HUÊ gave France the right to occupy militarily any place in Annam. Thereby effective French control was established.

June 17. A new treaty with Cambodia gave the protecting power much more extensive control than theretofore.

1885-1895. Pacification of Tonkin and Indo-China generally. There were many revolts in the interior, those in Tonkin being led by the formidable insurgent **De Tham.**

1887. Cochin China, Cambodia, Annam, and Tonkin were administratively united as the *Union Indo-Chinoise.*

1893. FRANCE ACQUIRED A PROTECTORATE OVER LAOS, the interior region along the Mekong which had long been in dispute between Annam and Siam.

1897-1902. Paul Doumer, governor-general. He first inaugurated the far-reaching reforms and administrative arrangements which modernized the region.

(*Cont. p.* 1114.)

d. BRITISH MALAYA

The Malays settled the peninsula from Sumatra in the 14th century, but apparently never established any single control. Of the various sultanates that of Malacca was as important as any.

1511. Conquest of Malacca by the Portuguese, who thenceforth controlled the trade in tin and spices until superseded by the Dutch.

1602. The Dutch East India Company set up a **factory at Patani** and thenceforth rapidly extended its power at the expense of the Portuguese.

1641. THE DUTCH TOOK MALACCA from the Portuguese. For more than a century the Dutch power was dominant in the Malay Peninsula.

1718- Bugis from Celebes attacked and conquered many of the Malay states, establishing dynasties in most of them.

1786. The British East India Company set up a station at Penang, under Francis Light. The island was ceded to the British by the Sultan of Kedah in return for a subsidy (1790).

1795. The British took Malacca to hold for the Dutch, who were under French domination at the time.

1800. The British secured Province Wellesley from the Sultan of Kedah.

1802. Malacca was restored to the Dutch under terms of the **Treaty of Amiens.**

1811. The British retook Malacca, which was used as a base for the expedition against Java.

1818. The Dutch recovered Malacca, under terms of the **Treaty of Vienna.**

1819. FOUNDING OF SINGAPORE by **Sir Stamford Raffles.** The place had been practically abandoned for centuries, but was soon to become the strategic and commercial center of the region, completely overshadowing Malacca.

1824, Mar. 17. The Dutch ceded Malacca to Britain, in return for Bengkulen in Sumatra.

1826. British treaty with Siam (p. 873). Under terms of this agreement the sultanates of Perak and Selangor were recognized as independent, while Siamese control of Kedah was acknowledged. At the same time Perak ceded to Britain **Pangkor Island** and the **Sembilan Islands** for use as bases in the fight against piracy.

1850- Steady influx of Chinese laborers into the peninsula. These were employed chiefly in the tin mines, though many also turned to piracy on the coast. Their presence created much disturbance in many of the states and ultimately provoked British interference.

1867, Apr. 1. End of the rule of the British East India Company. The Straits Settlements thenceforth had the status of a crown colony.

1873, June 20. TREATY OF PANGKOR. After serious Chinese disorders in Perak and a prolonged dynastic conflict, the British obliged the Perak chiefs to accept a British resident and to take his advice on all matters excepting religion and custom. The introduction of this system soon outraged the native chiefs, who in

1875. Rose in revolt. Murder of the British resident, **J. W. W. Birch.** The insurrection was suppressed by a British force and in the ensuing years further treaties were concluded with the other Malay states.

1885, Dec. 11. British treaty with Johore, regulating relations.

1889. Nine of the smaller states were federated and became **Negri Sembilan.**

1892-1894. Two serious risings of the chiefs in Pahang were vigorously suppressed.

1896, July 1. TREATY OF FEDERATION of Perak, Selangor, Negri Sembilan, and Pahang. Together they were to have one British resident-general (the governor of the Straits Settlements), while retaining their separate residents.

1909, Mar. 10. By treaty with Siam, Britain secured suzerainty and protection over **Kelantan, Trengganu, Kedah,** and **Perlis.** Protection was proclaimed July 14, 1909, and treaties concluded with these states in 1910. Together with Johore they comprised the Unfederated Malay States.

1914, May 12. The Sultan of Johore accepted a general adviser and a further measure of British supervision and control.

British Malaya was entirely under British rule or control. The different states were organized as follows:

Straits Settlements (crown colony) comprised Singapore, Penang, Province Wellesley, the Dindings, Malacca;

The Federated Malay States: Perak, Selangor, Negri Sembilan, Pahang.

Unfederated Malay States: Johore, Kedah, Perlis, Kelantan, Trengganu.

(*Cont. p.* 1114.)

e. THE MALAYAN ARCHIPELAGO

Java and neighboring islands were conquered by **Hindu** princes from India during the 1st century A.D. Thereafter a number of Hindu empires divided the region. **Islam** appears to have been introduced from India in the 10th century, but was not important until the 15th century, when Moslem leaders conquered the Hindus and drove them to Bali and other islands. There followed the **Moslem empires of Demak** and later **Mataram.**

In the period from 1510-1525 the **Portuguese** discovered most of the islands and established factories on many of them (Java, Ternate, Borneo). They were succeeded at the very end of the 16th century by the Dutch and British.

1596. The Dutch set up a **factory** at **Palembang** (Sumatra).

1602. The British established themselves at **Bantam** (northwest Java).

1613. The Dutch settled in **western Timor.**

1619. **BATAVIA built by the Dutch.** It became the headquarters of the Dutch East India Company, which monopolized the trade. Not much effort was made to acquire territory, but the trade was worked to the limit.

1623. **Massacre of Amboina:** the Dutch cut down the British settlement and forced its abandonment.

1666. The Dutch took the island of **Celebes** from the Portuguese.

1683. Acquisition of Amboina and Ternate by the Dutch.

1685. The British set up a **factory at Bengkulen** (Sumatra).

During the 18th century the Dutch continued to hold the upper hand. Growing ruthlessness and corruption of the company. At the same time, in order to control the trade, the company was forced to exercise ever wider control over northern Java.

1769. The British East India Company opened stations in northern Borneo, but the settlements (especially **Balambangan,** 1773) had to be given up under pressure from the natives (1775).

1781. The British **conquered** all the Dutch settlements on the west coast of **Sumatra,** Holland having joined the armed neutrality against England.

1783. By the **Treaty of Paris** the British returned the Dutch colonies, but secured the right to trade throughout the Dutch island possessions.

1795. The British again captured Sumatra, and in 1796 Ternate.

1798. End of the Dutch East India Company.

1808. The Dutch subdued Bantam in western Java. Mission of **Marshal Daendels,** who reorganized the Dutch possessions and began the systematic curtailment of the powers of the princes and feudal lords.

1811. A British expedition captured **Batavia** and took over **Java.** Under the administration of **Stamford Raffles** (1811-1816) much of the old system was swept away: extension of European control while retaining native administration; land leases to natives, etc.

1814, 1816. Sumatra and then Java were restored to the Dutch, in accordance with the peace treaties.

1824, Mar. 17. The British ceded **Bengkulen** (Sumatra) to the Dutch in return for Malacca: end of British hold in the island.

1825-1830. REVOLT OF THE JAVANESE against the Dutch, led by

Dipo Negora. The rising was suppressed only with great difficulty. The ultimate effect was to oblige the Dutch to conquer the interior and to extend their control. Later revolts (1849, 1888) had the same effect.

1830. Introduction of the **forced culture system** by the Dutch. This involved government contracts with the natives, crop control, and fixed prices — a system very lucrative to the Dutch interests.

1839. Native chiefs of **Bali acknowledged Dutch control,** but disorders continued until 1849.

1841. The Sultan of Brunei, in northern Borneo, **ceded to Sir James Brooke** the region of **Sarawak,** in return for aid against enemies. Brooke became rajah of the region and ruled until 1868, when he was succeeded by his son (to 1917) and grandson (1917–   ). He induced the British government to take an active part in the work of suppressing piracy in the China Sea.

1847. The British secured from the Sultan of Brunei **the island of Labuan,** off the northwest coast of Borneo, which it was expected would become an important naval base.

1859, Apr. 20. The **Dutch and Portuguese** by agreement **divided Timor** and the neighboring islands between them.

1865. The American government concluded a treaty with the Sultan of Brunei and the **American Trading Company of Borneo** acquired title to lands, but the effort to exploit the region proved abortive.

1870. The Dutch introduced a **new sugar law and a new agrarian law in Java,** which involved a relaxation of the culture system and the gradual extension of private agriculture.

1881. The British government issued a **charter to the North Borneo Company,** organized by Austrian and English interests. This company took over the assets of the American company and secured new concessions from the Sultans of Brunei and Sulu. Protests of the Dutch and Spaniards were of no avail (Spanish claims renounced in 1885).

1888, Mar. 17. **Great Britain established a protectorate over Sarawak.**

May 12. **British protectorate over North Borneo,** which, however, continued to be held and administered by the North Borneo Company.

1891. June 20. The British and Dutch by treaty defined their respective domains in Borneo, the Dutch retaining by far the larger part.

1907, Dec. The Dutch, after many years of warfare, finally **subdued the Achinese** in northern Sumatra (Atjeh), thus completing the pacification of Sumatra.

1908. **Direct Dutch rule** was established in **Bali,** after a series of native insurrections.   (*Cont. p.* 1116.)

5. CHINA

1796-1820. THE CHIA CH'ING REIGN OF JEN TSUNG was filled with revolts which had been postponed only by the prestige of his father.

1796-1804. Suppression of **revolt of the White Lotus Society** impoverished the three provinces of Hupei, Szechuan, and Shensi.

1805. Christian literature was proscribed, and a Catholic priest strangled for presence in China without permission (1815).

1813. An attempt by the **Heavenly Reason Society** to seize Peking failed.

  Scholarship profited by labors of three brilliant critical editors: **Sun Hsing-yen** (1753–1818), **Yen K'o-chün** (1762–1843), and **Juan Yüan** (1764–1849). The last prepared the best edition of the *Thirteen Classics with Commentary* and gathered in 360 vols. the best *Classical Comment of the*

Reigning Ch'ing Dynasty. Robert Morrison (1782–1834), the first Protestant missionary, translator of the Bible and author of the first Chinese-English dictionary, arrived in Canton (1807).

1816. British ambassador, **Lord Amherst,** sent away from Peking without being received.

1821-1850. THE TAO KUANG REIGN OF HSÜAN TSUNG.

1821. The illicit **trade in Indian opium,** 5000 chests annually despite imperial prohibition (1800), was transferred to Lintin Island off the Canton River. The conditions of trade at Canton became intolerable through local official arbitrariness and venality, recurrent conflict of principles of individual as against collective responsibility under criminal law, restrictions on personal freedom, and denial of appeal to the central government.

The Manchu (Ta Ch'ing) Dynasty (1795-1912)

Hung Li
Ch'ien Lung
1736–1795
(*Kao Tsung Shun Huang Ti*)

15

17 sons

Yung Yen
Chia Ch'ing
1796–1820
(*Jen Tsung Jui Huang Ti*)

3   4   5

Min Ning
Tao Kuang
1821–1850
(*Hsüan Tsung Ch'eng Huang Ti*)

Mien K'ai
Prince Tun
d. 1839?

Mien Hsin
Prince Jui
d. 1828

Mien Yü
Prince Hui
d. 1864

1   4   5   6   7

I Wei
Prince Yin Chih
d. 1831

I Chu
Hsien Feng
1851–1861
(*Wen Tsung Hsien Huang Ti*)

I Tsung
d. 1889

I Hsin
Prince Kung
d. 1898

I Huan
Prince Ch'un
d. 1890

I Ho
d. 1868

I Hui
d. 1877

Tsai Shun
T'ung Chih
1862–1874
(*Mu Tsung I Huang Ti*)

Tsai T'ien
Kuang Hsü
1875–1908
(*Te Tsung Ching Huang Ti*)

Tsai Feng
Prince Ch'un
Regent 1908–1911

P'u I (born 1906)
Hsüan T'ung
1909–1912

Note: Names in plain type are personal names, taboo after a ruler ascended the throne.

Names in boldface type are reign titles, or year names, adopted for reckoning time, but often applied by westerners to the emperor himself.

Names in italic type are dynastic titles, or temple names, conferred posthumously to refer to the ruler.

Huang Ti means simply "emperor."

1825-1831. **Kashgaria** was with difficulty defended against Jehangir of the Khoja family and Mohammed Ali of Khokand.

1830-1834. American missionary, medical, and sinological work begun in southern China.

1834. The end of the East India Company's monopoly of British trade with China removed an important element in the Canton system of commercial regulation. The assertion of diplomatic equality by the first superintendent of British trade in China, **Lord Napier,** was followed by the temporary stoppage of trade; Napier d. Oct. 11; his successors followed a "quiescent policy."

1836. Chinese proposals to legalize the importation of opium, and concern over the "drain of silver" to pay for it, led to heated discussions at Peking. Chinese policy remained weak (1837–1838) and lawlessness grew until

1839. Imperial Commissioner Lin Tsehsü arrived at Canton (Mar. 10), forced surrender of opium (annual import 30,000 chests, 1835–1839), and burned it. Hostilities followed (Nov.).

1840. British occupation of Chusan and Canton River forts led to an agreement (**Ch'uanpi Convention**) between Capt. Chas. Elliot and Ch'i-shan (Jan. 1841), which was repudiated by both governments.

1841-1842. THE FIRST BRITISH WAR, with seizure of several coastal ports and Chinkiang on the Grand Canal, ended in dictation by **Sir Henry Pottinger** of the

1842, Aug. 29. TREATY OF NANKING which ended the tributary status and Canton monopolistic system of maritime trade. China ceded **Hongkong** (occupied Jan. 1841) to Britain; opened **Canton, Amoy, Foochow** (Fuchou), **Ningpo,** and **Shanghai** to trade under consular supervision; established **uniform import tariff** of about 5% *ad valorem*; paid £21,000,000 indemnity.

1843, Oct. 8. Supplementary Treaty, also negotiated by Pottinger and Imperial Commissioner Ch'i-ying, conceded "most-favored-nation" status (later extended to other powers) and amplified the details of the new commercial system. Opium traffic continued. The

1844, July 3. Treaty of Wanghsia signed by Ch'i-ying and by **Caleb Cushing** for the United States placed American (ultimately all foreign) residents under extra-territorial criminal and civil jurisdiction of consular and mixed courts. The study of Chinese became legal for foreigners. The French **Treaty of Whampoa** (Oct. 24) secured **toleration of Roman Catholicism,** extended (1845) to **Protestantism.**

1846-1849. Popular opposition to foreign entrance into the city of Canton increased Anglo-Chinese friction.

1851-1861. THE HSIEN FENG REIGN revealed approaching dissolution of the dynasty. Agrarian unrest due to official exactions, to natural calamities, and to absentee landlordism which centered especially in Kiangsi, found expression in the

1850-1864. T'AI P'ING REBELLION. The *Heavenly Kingdom of Great Peace* was founded in Kwangsi by a mystic, **Hung Hsiu-ch'üan,** who borrowed certain forms of Protestant doctrine. With help of an able strategist, **Yang Hsiu-ch'ing,** he led disciplined forces through Hunan to Wuch'ang (1852) and down the river past Nanking, his capital (1853-1864), to the Grand Canal. An advance toward Peking was deflected through Shansi by floods of the Yellow River, which shifted its bed north of Shantung (1853). The rebels were repelled (1855). Neglect of the rebels to provide conquered territory with either protection or constructive administration foredoomed their régime to failure.

1853-1868. **Nien Fei,** organized bandits of Anhuei, N. Kiangsu, and Shantung, later also Shansi, profited by preoccupation of imperial troops with the T'ai P'ing and foreign invaders to plunder. They were suppressed (1865-1868) by the same men who put down the T'ai P'ing Rebellion.

1854, July 12. Capture of Shanghai city by rebels (Sept. 7, 1853) led to inauguration of **foreign inspectorate of customs.**

1855-1873. **Mohammedans** (Panthays) in **Yünnan** revolted and set up an independent state at Tali, the ancient capital of Nan Chao.

1855-1881. **Miao** tribesmen in Kweichow seized the opportunity to revolt.

1856, Oct. 8. Lorcha *Arrow* incident at Canton precipitated Anglo-Chinese hostilities.

1857-1858. **Anglo-French seizure of Canton** and military threat in the north forced the

1858, June 26-29. TREATIES OF TIENTSIN between China and Great Britain (Lord Elgin), France, the United States, and Russia. China opened eleven more ports, permitted legations at Peking and trade and Christian missions in the interior; subsequent tariff and rules of trade (Nov.) established a maritime customs service with foreign inspector-general (H. N. Lay) and staff, and legalized the importation of opium. The **Treaty of Aigun** signed by I-shan and Nicholas Muraviev gave the north bank of the Amur to Russia. Khabarovsk founded.

1859. Refusal of British demands for admission of foreign diplomats to Peking and repulse of attack on the Taku forts (June 25) before Tientsin led to

1860, Oct. 12. Occupation of **Peking** by 17,000 British and French troops. **Burning of the Summer Palace** to punish the court for seizure of envoys (Harry Parkes) under a flag of truce suggested unfortunate parallels with conduct of earlier barbarian invaders. **Peking conventions** (Oct. 24 with England, Oct. 25 with France) increased indemnities, and the French secured right of Catholic missions to hold land. The Russian envoy, **Gen. Ignatiev,** secured cession (Nov. 14) of the **Maritime Province.** Vladivostok was founded. Eruption of the T'ai P'ing rebels from Nanking desolated Kiangsu and Chekiang.

1861. The **Tsungli Yamen was created to** handle foreign affairs.

1861-1864. Tseng Kuo-fan with able help, including Tseng Kuo-ch'üan, Li Hung-chang, Tso Tsung-t'ang, and the Ever-Victorious Army (1862–1863) of **F. T. Ward** and **C. G.** Gordon near Shanghai, suppressed the immensely destructive T'ai P'ing Rebellion by recapture of Anking (1861), Soochow (1863), and Nanking (1864).

1862-1874. THE T'UNG CHIH REIGN OF MU TSUNG. The Dowager Empress Tzu Hsi ruled as co-regent for her son until 1873. Under leadership of **Tseng Kuo-fan** and his protégés reform and study of the west was begun.

1862-1873. Mohammedan rebellions were suppressed by Tso Tsung-t'ang in Shensi (1868–1870) and Kansu (capture of Suchou, 1873).

1863-1908. (Sir) Robert Hart built up the Maritime Customs Service as mainstay of government revenue and credit, with collateral services to train men, light the coast, improve rivers and harbors, and organize a postal service (1896, independent 1911).

1864-1889. Protestant missionaries in China increased from under 200 to nearly 1300, and introduced western medicine and ideas. Communicants numbered 55,000 in 1893.

1868-1870. Anson Burlingame, with two Chinese associates, was sent on a good-will mission to western states.

1870, June 21. The Tientsin massacre, by a mob, of a French consul and missionaries led to a mission of apology to France by Ch'ung-hou (1871–1872).

1871. Cables were laid from Vladivostok via Nagasaki to Shanghai, Hong-kong, and Singapore. A land line was built, Shanghai-Tientsin, in 1881.

1872-1881. 120 Chinese students were brought to the United States by Yung Wing (Yale 1854), and 30 sent to England and France for technical training (1876).

1874. A Japanese expedition to occupy Formosa to punish murder by natives of Liu Ch'iu islanders and Japanese (1871) was withdrawn in return for indemnity; but by revelation of Chinese military weakness served to strengthen demands (since 1867) by Tseng Kuo-fan, Li Hung-chang, and a small group of liberal Chinese statesmen that China undertake reform and establish representatives abroad.

1875-1908. THE KUANG HSÜ REIGN OF TE TSUNG. As the late emperor was childless, an infant cousin (born 1871), a nephew of the Dowager Empress

Tzu Hsi, was adopted as second son of Wen Tsung to carry on dynastic sacrifices, and his prospective offspring was destined to be adopted son of the late emperor. An uncle, **Prince Kung,** was named regent under supervision of the two dowager empresses. Personal rule 1889.

1875-1878. Tso Tsung-t'ang suppressed (1875–1876), the Tungans of the northern T'ien Shan, in revolt since 1862, and reconquered Kashgaria (1877–1878), which had become independent under **Yakub Beg** in 1866. Both areas were organized as one province, the **New Territory,** Sinkiang (Hsin chiang), with capital at Urumtsi (Tihwa).

1876. The Chefoo (or Yentai) **Convention** forced by Britain on occasion of the murder of interpreter Margary on the Burmese border (1875) opened ten additional ports, and improved the status of foreigners in China. Ratified by Great Britain in 1885 with additional article relating to opium, importation of which reached an annual average (1875–1885) of 82,000 chests, an amount greatly exceeded, however, by production in China.

1877-1878. Diplomatic missions, determined in 1875, established legations in London and Berlin (1877), Paris, Washington, and Tokyo (1878), Madrid and St. Petersburg (1879), and Lima (1880).

1879, Sept. 15. The unratified Treaty of Livadia gave Russia much of Ili (occupied by her 1871), strategic passes, and indemnity; but after Chinese threat of war

1881, Feb. 24. The Treaty of St. Petersburg negotiated by Tseng Chi-tse, returned to China most of the Ili Valley and the passes in return for more money.

A French bishop, **Pigneau de Béhaine,** had helped **Nguyen Anh** set up in Annam a new dynasty (1802) upon that of the interloping Tây-so'n (1788). Both alike were accorded imperial investiture in return for biennial tribute. Execution of a missionary bishop (1857) served as pretext for extraction by the French expedition to China of the **Treaty of Saigon** (1862) ceding three provinces of Cochin-China, augmented by three more (1867). Seizure of Hanoi (1873) by Francis Garnier, shortly killed by Black Flag remnants of T'ai P'ing armies, led to a second Treaty of Saigon (1874) which opened the Red River. Second seizure of Hanoi (1882) by Henri Rivière, likewise killed by Black Flags, preceded the forced

1883, Aug. 25. Treaty of Hué, by which Annam accepted a French protectorate with administration of Tonkin by

French residents in disregard of Chinese suzerainty and protests (1881-1882).

1884. Prince Kung and the grand council were **dismissed by the Dowager Empress** Tzu Hsi for failure to repel the French. A preliminary convention signed by Li Hung-chang with Capt. Fournier (May 11) resulted in misunderstanding, and a French defeat at Baclé (June 23) led to **undeclared war.** French naval destruction of the new Foochow arsenal (Aug. 23) and attacks on Formosa were balanced in part by reverses on the Tonkin border (**Langson** Mar. 28, 1885).

1885, June 9. The Treaty of Tientsin, facilitated by negotiations of Robert Hart, recognized the French protectorate in Annam in return for a reciprocal promise to respect the southern frontier of China. Tso Tsung-t'ang in a dying memorial urged modernization and foreign study.

In Korea, a tributary to the Manchus since 1637, China evaded responsibility for persecution of Christians and for the French punitive expedition which was repulsed from Seoul (1866). China did not protest a **Japanese** treaty (1876) recognizing Korean independence, nor a Korean embassy to Japan. Li Hung-chang, however (1882), sent as resident to Seoul **Yüan Shih-k'ai** who was thereafter active in intrigue against Japan, uninterrupted by the

1885, April 18. Li-Ito Convention for withdrawal of troops of both powers from Korea (p. 886).

1886, July 24. British protectorate in Burma was recognized in return for continuance of decennial tribute.

1887, Dec. 1. Portugal secured cession of Macao on promise not to alienate it.

1888. The first imperial railway (Tangshan-Tientsin, 80 miles) was opened and extended to Shanhaikuan (1894) and to Fengt'ai outside Peking (1896). Chang Chih-tung (1837-1909), governor-general of Hupei, opened coal mines, the great Ta-yeh iron mines, and the Hanyang steel works, as necessary preliminaries to interior railway construction.

1890. Abolition of the board of admiralty and subsequent neglect of the new and promising navy, as a result of the resignation of Capt. Lang (British) and the death of Prince Ch'un and Marquis Tseng Chi-tse.

1894. Sun Yat-sen (Sun Wen, 1866-1925) organized at Canton the first of several secret revolutionary societies with which he tried ten times before 1911 to overthrow the Manchu dynasty. After his first failure (1895), he organized the Chinese in Honolulu and America, and was kidnaped and held for ten days by the Chinese legation in London (1896).

1894-1895.   THE   SINO-JAPANESE WAR, the outcome of ten years' rivalry and intrigue in Korea. **Rising of the Tonghak** (*Eastern Learning*) **Society** in southern Korea led to seizure by the Japanese of the Korean queen and appointment of a regent. The British ship *Kowshing* (July 25, 1894), carrying Chinese troops to Korea, sunk by the Japanese; the Korean regent declared war on China (July 27); China and Japan declared war on each other (Aug. 1). Vain efforts of the European powers and the United States to mediate. Easy victories of the Japanese at **Ping-yang** (Sept. 16), off the **Yalu River,** at Port Arthur (Nov. 21), **and at Wei-hai-wei** (Feb. 12) destroyed the Chinese army and navy and forced the Chinese to accept

1895, Apr. 17. THE TREATY OF SHIMO-NOSEKI. *Terms:* China recognized the independence of Korea and ceded to Japan the island of Formosa, the Pescadores Islands, the Liaotung Peninsula; China was to pay an indemnity of 200,-000,000 taels, and to open four more ports to foreign commerce.

China's helplessness in the face of a despised Asiatic neighbor equipped with modern instruments of war was clearly revealed to all. It awakened the majority of the educated Chinese, much as the bombardments of 1863-1864 had roused the Japanese. Chinese demands for reform were further stimulated by the rush of the European powers for political and economic concessions and by their efforts to set up exclusive spheres of influence. Dilemma of the Chinese government: native capital not available for military, railway and industrial development; foreign capital could be secured only at the expense of further extension of foreign control within the empire. Revenue from the customs was limited by interlocking agreements to about 5% in 1858, and to an effective 2-3% in the later 19th century.

Apr. 23. Russia, Germany, and France intervened and obliged Japan to return the **Liaotung Peninsula** to China in consideration of a further indemnity of 30,000,000 taels. For reasons for the intervention see p. 744. All three intervening powers expected to be well repaid by the Chinese.

June 20. France secured extensive territorial and commercial concessions in the southern provinces.

July 6. Franco-Russian loan to China (400 million francs at 4%, to run for 36 years, with the Chinese customs as security).

1896, May 23. An Anglo-German loan (£16,000,000 for 36 years at 5%, secured by the customs revenues, the administration of which was meanwhile to continue as then constituted).

June 3. RUSSIAN-CHINESE TREATY, secretly concluded at the coronation of Nicholas II at Moscow by Li Hung-chang. In return for a defensive alliance for 15 years, China granted Russia the right to build and operate the Chinese Eastern Railway across northern Manchuria, as a link in the Russian Trans-Siberian line to Vladivostok.

July 21. A commercial treaty with Japan, imposed as part of the peace settlement, gave Japan most-favored-nation status and granted all the treaty powers the right to operate industrial enterprises in treaty ports.

1897, Feb. 4. Great Britain was permitted by treaty to extend the Burmese railways into Yünnan (later proved impracticable), and gained further rights in southwest China to offset the French penetration.

Nov. 14. THE GERMANS OCCUPIED KIAOCHOW (Chiao-chou) Bay with Tsingtao, on the pretext of murder of two missionaries in Shantung. The move had been long under consideration and was looked upon by the Germans as the logical sequence to the intervention in favor of China in 1895. But it precipitated the

1898. SCRAMBLE FOR CONCESSIONS, in which most of the great European powers took part.

Feb. Britain secured agreements to open inland waters to foreign steamers, not to alienate any part of the Yangtse River Valley to any other power, and to employ a British inspector-general of customs so long as British trade remained preponderant.

Mar. 6. Germany extracted a convention giving her a 99-year lease on Kiaochow Bay, with exclusive right to build railways and develop mines in Shantung (the Tsingtao-Tsinan Railway opened in 1904). A second Anglo-German loan of £16,000,000 for 45 years at 4½% was secured by certain likin and salt revenues, as well as the customs.

Mar. 27, May 7. Russia extorted from China a 25-year lease of the southern part of the Liaotung Peninsula, including Talien-wan (Dairen, Dalny) and Port Arthur, with the right to construct a railroad from Harbin in the north to the newly leased ports.

Apr. 10. France received a 99-year lease of Kwangchow (Kuang-chou) Bay and the vicinity, with the right to extend a railway to Yunnanfu (completed 1910) and a promise not to alienate to any other power any part of the provinces bordering Tonkin.

Apr. 26. Japan secured a promise from China not to alienate any part of Fukien.

June 9. Britain secured a 99-year lease of Kowloon (Chiu-lung) opposite Hongkong, and (July 1) a lease of Wei-hai-wei to run as long as the Russian occupation of Port Arthur.

June 11-Sept. 16. THE HUNDRED DAYS OF REFORM, embarked upon by the emperor under the guidance of the radical reformer K'ang Yu-wei (1858-1927) and a Cantonese faction of students of foreign education, and of Chang Chih-tung, who wrote Learn, a classic appeal for reform (a million copies sold). The reformers aimed at hastening the construction of the Peking-Hankow Railway (1898-1905), to give western arms to the Manchu Banners, to prepare for naval training, to establish schools and a University of Peking. These measures met with general approval, but the decrees of Aug. 30-Sept. 16 struck boldly at vital interests of the civil and military officials by abolishing sinecures and the Green Banner provincial armies, and by introducing a budget system. To prevent seizure of her own person,

Sept. 22. The empress dowager Tzu-hsi, supported by Jung-lu, seized the emperor and imprisoned him. Reforms contrary to interests of the Manchus and official classes were revoked. Reactionary officials were placed in control of the central government.

1899, Feb. Italian demand for a port and concession in Chekiang was rejected with a show of force and vigorous efforts to strengthen imperial defense.

In response to notes of Sept. and Nov. John Hay, American secretary of state, secured assurances from the great powers that the open door to equal commercial opportunity would be maintained in spheres of special interest in China (p. 749).

Boxers, militia forces organized in Shantung and southern Chihli in response to imperial decrees, showed hostility to aggressive foreign powers by persecution of their visible representatives, Christian missionaries and converts, with encouragement of Yü-hsien, Manchu governor of Shantung until he was replaced by Yüan Shih-k'ai (Dec. 6).

1900. THE BOXERS, driven from Shantung into Chihli, were encouraged by an anti-foreign Manchu clique at court, which hoped to use them as auxiliaries to expel all foreigners from China. Identic notes of foreign diplomats at Peking (Jan.–May) by demanding suppression increased resentment. A **mob attack on Fengt'ai railway station** (May 28) was followed by admission of legation guards to Peking (total 458), but repulse to Tientsin of a joint naval column of 2066 men (June 10–26). **Foreign seizure of the Taku forts** (June 17) was cited in an imperial declaration of war (June 20), disregarded as a forced document both by foreign powers and by Chinese officials outside Chihli and Shansi. Murder of the German minister, **Baron von Ketteler** (June 20), opened a **siege of the legations** which would have succeeded but for Jung-lu's protection. An **international expedition** took Tientsin (July 14) and relieved the legations (Aug. 14). Elsewhere, especially in Shansi, where Yü-hsien was now governor, at least 231 foreign civilians, chiefly missionaries, were killed by imperial order (June 24–July 24). **The court fled** (Aug. 15) to Sian, whence a rescript (Dec. 26) promptly accepted a joint note embodying the allied demands. Russians at Blagovestchensk, in retaliation for Chinese bombardments across the Amur (July 14–15) and in fear of attack by the local Chinese, drove thousands of civilians to death in the river. Russia quickly seized possession of southern Manchuria (Sept. 4–Oct. 10), without being able to secure ratification of a secret convention extorted at Port Arthur (Nov. 11). German troops, which had arrived late at Peking, carried out alone 35 of 46 punitive missions (Dec. 12–Apr. 30, 1901). After eight months' haggling between the allies, the

1901, Sept. 7. Boxer Protocol, signed by twelve powers, provided for expressions of regret, punishment of 96 officials, payment over 40 years of 450,-000,000 taels with interest (or a total value of gold $738,820,707, which became more burdensome as silver depreciated), revision of the tariff to an effective 5%, fortification of an enlarged legation quarter, the razing of all forts and establishment of foreign garrisons along the railway to Shanhai-kuan. The indemnity was to be met from maritime customs surplus, native customs, and salt monopoly, the maritime customs under Hart being given charge of the native customs within 50 *li* of all treaty ports.

1902, Jan. The dowager empress with the emperor returned to Peking by rail. Educational, economic, and military reform immediately undertaken. Death of Li Hung-chang (1901), Liu K'un-i, and Jung-lu (1903) left Chang Chih-tung and Yüan Shih-k'ai her ablest advisers. Intermarriage of Manchus with Chinese was for the first time sanctioned. The most distinguished Chinese jurist, **Shen Chia-pen,** was ordered to revise the legal code. A new code was promulgated (1910).

Sept. 5. Anglo-Chinese commercial treaty, with American and Japanese treaties of Oct. 8, provided for changes in the treaty system and internal reform (largely ineffective).

1904-1905. Defeat of Russia by Japan (p. 892) again revealed to the Chinese the advantages of learning the lessons of the west. The Treaty of Portsmouth returned Manchuria from Russian to Chinese administration (1907). Japan retained only the leasehold in southern Liaotung which had already been definitively conceded to Russia, together with the South Manchurian Railway. Hitherto a Manchu preserve under military government, the three eastern provinces were now (1907) reorganized on a civilian basis and thrown open to Chinese settlement.

1905. Boycott of American goods as a protest against further exclusion of Chinese from the United States reflected growing national consciousness.

On Chang Chih-tung's recommendation of Japanese education, a **ministry of education** was created and Chinese students swarmed to Japan (15,000 there at one time).

Sun Yat-sen organized in Japan the *T'ung Meng Hui,* a union of societies which constantly strove to eject the Manchus from China.

1906. Preparation for constitutional government proclaimed, following the report of a mission sent in 1905 to study foreign states. But **reorganization of the ministries** (Nov. 6) was followed by the appointment of Manchu princes to direct them (1907–1909).

Provision for progressive 10-year **suppression of opium cultivation and consumption** was supplemented by an agreement with Britain which cut imports from 48,530 chests (1907) to 4136 chests in 1915. At the suggestion of the United States (1909) a series of conferences began at Shanghai and later (1912) at the Hague to establish international control over the world drug traffic.

1908, Jan. 13. Foreign loans for a railway

from **Tientsin** to **P'u-k'ou** (opposite Nanking) were contracted on the basis of construction, control, and operation exclusively by the Chinese government. The line was completed and opened in Jan. 1912.

May 13. Remission by the United States of half her share in the Boxer indemnity made possible the establishment of Tsing Hua College (1911) and the sending of about 1100 graduates to America for advanced study (1911–1927).

Nov. 14-15. Death of the emperor and of the dowager empress. Power passed to the reactionary Prince Ch'un, regent for the

1908-1911. HSÜAN T'UNG REIGN OF THE EMPEROR P'U-I (born 1906).

1908, Dec. 3. A draft constitution was published, providing for election of a parliament after nine years. This signified little, for

1909, Jan. 2. The dismissal of Yüan Shih-k'ai and the death of Chang Chih-tung (Oct. 4) placed the whole administration in Manchu hands. Consequently, when provincial assemblies and a national assembly met (1910), they insisted on early convocation of parliament, which was finally promised for 1913.

Scholarship of a high order continued without break through the last reign of the dynasty. The state papers of **Tseng Kuo-fan** and of **Chang Chih-tung** are regarded as models of the classical style. **Wang Hsien-ch'ien** (1842–1918) compiled a supplement in 320 vols. (1886–1888) to the *Classical Comment of the Reigning Dynasty*, the best critical edition of the two Han histories with collected modern comment, and the *Tung Hua Lu*, a judicious selection from the official archives of the dynasty through 1874 (284 vols., 1879–1887). Baron Iwasaki Koyata purchased and took to Tokyo (1907) the library of **Lu Hsin-yüan** (1834–1894), an active critic, archaeologist, and editor of the *Shih Wan Chuan Lou Ts'ung Shu*. **Miao Ch'üan-sun** (1844–1919), bibliographer and archaeologist, thereupon persuaded Governor-General Tuan Fang (1861–1911) to buy the library of the Ting family for Nanking as the **first public library in China**. **K'o Shao-min** (1850–1931) prepared a new standard *History of the Yüan Dynasty*. **K'ang Yu'wei's** *Study of the Classics Forged in the Hsin Era* (1891) and *Study of Confucius as a Reformer* (1897) together served to focus upon early texts historical criticism of a type which had fallen in abeyance since the time of Ts'ui Shu (1740–1816). Chinese envoys to Japan, **Yang Shou-ching** (1835–

1915) and **Li Shu-ch'ang** (1837–1897), found there many early editions which they reproduced in the *Ku I Ts'ung Shu* (1884). A profusion of other early documents, both Chinese and Central Asiatic, was recovered in 1907–1908 by **Aurel Stein** and **Paul Pelliot** from a temple library immured (c. 1000 A.D.) at Tun-huang, the point of bifurcation of mediaeval caravan routes north and south of the T'ien Shan Mts. Discovery in 1899 of a deposit of oracular inscriptions on bone and tortoise-shell from the Shang dynasty was followed quickly by their decipherment by paleographers already trained in the archaic script of ritual bronzes.

1911, Oct. OUTBREAK OF THE CHINESE REVOLUTION, precipitated by discovery of the headquarters of the revolutionary organization at Hankow. The movement, fed by provincial distrust of the central railway administration of Sheng Hsüan-huai, spread rapidly through the west and south, without causing much bloodshed.

Nov. 8. Yüan Shih-k'ai, who had been recalled to military command (Oct. 14) was elected premier by the national assembly.

Dec. 4. Yüan signed a truce with the rebel general Li Yüan-hung, and sent T'ang Shao-i to represent him in negotiations at Shanghai.

Dec. 30. Sun Yat-sen, recently returned from Europe, was **elected President of the United Provinces of China** by a revolutionary provisional assembly at Nanking.

1912, Feb. 12. Abdication of the boy emperor.

Feb. 15. Yüan Shih-k'ai elected provisional president of the Chinese Republic by the national assembly. Sun Yat-sen resigned in order to unite the country.

Mar. 10. The Nanking provisional constitution, which aimed at making the bicameral assembly supreme. Yüan Shih-k'ai soon came into conflict with the assembly through his efforts to strengthen his own power. Formation of opposition parties: the *Harmony or Progress Party* of **Liang Ch'i-ch'ao**, advocating a strong executive; the *Kuo Min Tang or Nationalist Party* of Sun Yat-sen championing the system of parliamentary government.

1913, April 8. Convocation of the elected parliament.

Apr. 21. Yüan secured from Great Britain, France, Russia, and Japan **a loan for £25,000,000**, secured by the salt tax. Fearing that this would strengthen him even more, his opponents started the

July 10. **"Second Revolution"** in the southern provinces. This movement was soon suppressed (Nanking taken, September 1).

Oct. 6. Yüan Shih-k'ai was elected president, and Li Yüan-hung vice-president of the republic. In order to prevent adoption of the constitution, Yüan

Nov. 4. Purged the parliament of its Kuo Ming Tang members, and soon afterward dissolved it (Jan. 10, 1914).

Nov. 5. The Chinese government recognized the autonomy of Outer Mongolia, which had been secured by treaty between Outer Mongolia and Russia a year before (Nov. 7, 1912).

1914, May 1. A "constitutional compact" promulgated by Yüan Shih-k'ai gave him a ten-year term of office, with ample powers. (*Cont. p.* 1117.)

6. KOREA

After the Japanese invasions under Hideyoshi (1592–1598, see p. 544) and the defeat of the Koreans by the Manchus (1637), the kingdom of Korea was shut off entirely from the outside world. It recognized Chinese suzerainty, though the Japanese did not entirely abandon their claims to overlordship. The ensuing two centuries were a period of reasonably efficient and progressive government, and apparently of considerable prosperity. From time to time Europeans were wrecked on the treacherous coast, but for the most part these were kept as captives in the country.

1777. Introduction of Christianity, evidently by Chinese converted by the Jesuits at Peking. The new religion made considerable progress, and by the mid-19th century there were some 10,000 converts in the kingdom. Despite all prohibitions, Catholic missionaries, mostly French, stole into the country in the early 19th century.

1797. Exploration of the east coast of Korea by Capt. W. R. Broughton.

1800-1834. Sunjo, king.

1835-1849. Hŏn-jong, king.

1850-1863. Ch'ŏlchong, king.

1864-1907. Kojong (usually known as I T'ae-wang [the reign title was changed in 1896 and again in 1897]), the 12-year-old grandson of King Sunjo, succeeded. His father, Hŭngsŏn, generally known as Tai Wen Kun (or Tae-wŏngun), became regent, ruled directly until 1873, and was the dominant political figure until his death in 1898. From the outset he was extremely hostile to all foreign influence and especially to Christianity.

1865-1870. Systematic persecution of the Christians. A number of French missionaries were executed.

1866. A French expedition under Adm. Roze, occupied and burned Kanghwa at the mouth of the Han River, but was unable to proceed to the capital, Seoul; after some reverses at the hands of the natives, it was obliged to withdraw.

1867, Oct. Expedition of the German Jew, Ernst Oppert, assisted by an American, Jenkins, with the object of rifling the royal tombs (supposedly of pure gold). The landing force reached the tombs, but was unable to open them. Attacks by the natives forced withdrawal.

1871, May 16. An American naval force, under Capt. Shufeldt and the minister to Peking, Mr. Low, tried to open Korea to foreign trade. Marines were landed at the mouth of the Han, but hostilities ensued and the project had to be given up.

1876, Feb. 26. OPENING OF KOREA, through a treaty with Japan. Japan recognized Korean independence without eliciting a protest from China. Three ports were opened to Japanese trade and Japan was permitted to have a resident at Seoul.

1882, May 22. TREATY WITH THE UNITED STATES, negotiated by Shufeldt and by Viceroy Li Hung-chang (in charge of Chinese-Korean relations): no mention of Korean independence, but the United States secured extra-territorial rights and permission to trade. Similar treaties were concluded with England (Nov. 26, 1883), Russia (July 7, 1884), and other powers.

July 23. An attack by the Koreans on the Japanese legation in Seoul led to intervention by the Chinese. The Japanese were given compensation and the right to keep a legation guard. Yüan Shih-k'ai became Chinese resident at Seoul and during the ensuing decade devoted himself to strengthening the Chinese influence as against Japan. In Korea the regent returned to power and there soon developed between him and the energetic Queen

Min a struggle for control of the government.

1884, Dec. 5-7. The reform party, supported by the Japanese, hatched a conspiracy, assassinated a number of ministers and secured control of the king. The Chinese thereupon dispatched troops to Seoul, recaptured the king and the palace, but provoked further intervention by Japan. The two powers were on the very verge of war, but finally concluded the

1885, Apr. 18. CONVENTION OF TIEN-TSIN (*Li-Itō Convention*): both agreed to withdraw their troops and to notify each other if it became necessary in future to intervene again.

May 12. The British occupied Port Hamilton in the course of the Anglo-Russian crisis, for fear lest Russia might seize a port on the Korean coast. (Despite Chinese protests the British remained until Feb. 27, 1887).

1894-1895. THE SINO-JAPANESE WAR, which was the direct outcome of the rivalry of the two powers for control of Korea. Following an insurrection in southern Korea in the spring of 1894, the king called upon the Chinese for aid (June 10). Several thousand men were dispatched and Japan notified. Thereupon the Japanese sent twice as many men and occupied Seoul (June 25). On the suggestion of the Chinese that both forces be withdrawn, the Japanese insisted first on the introduction of extensive reforms. Hostilities soon broke out and war was declared Aug. 1 (for the course of the war see p. 881). Korea was obliged to conclude an alliance with Japan (Aug. 26) and the Japanese soon took over control of the government.

1895, Apr. 17. Treaty of Shimonoseki, ending the Sino-Japanese War. By this treaty the independence of Korea was recognized by China. The Japanese, still in substantial control, pushed through far-reaching and for the most part unpopular reforms. Opposition of the queen and the court led to the

Oct. 8. Murder of the queen, with the connivance of the Japanese resident, Miura. The commanding position of Japan was, however, at once challenged by popular outbreaks and anti-reform riots. The country became divided into a conservative, anti-Japanese, and a progressive, pro-Japanese party (the latter represented by the *Independence Club*, founded 1896).

1896, Feb. 10. The king fled to the Russian legation in the course of another insurrection. He remained under Russian protection for a year and during this period

the Russians quickly supplanted the Japanese as the dominant influence. Mission of Russian advisers and instructors; foundation of the Russian-Korean Bank; timber and mining concessions to Russia, etc. The situation became so dark for the Japanese that they were glad to conclude with Russia

June 9. THE LOBANOV-YAMAGATA AGREEMENT, which established a type of condominium: Russia and Japan to co-operate in the reform of army and finances. In practice the agreement proved almost worthless and the Russian penetration continued unabated.

1897, Feb. 20. The king left the Russian legation and moved into the new palace. **The king took the imperial title** (Oct. 17).

Dec. An Anglo-Russian crisis, arising from efforts of the Russians to replace the financial adviser, **M'Leavy Brown** (since 1895), by a Russian. A British naval demonstration at Chemulpo made the Russians draw back.

1898, Apr. 25. THE ROSEN-NISHI AGREEMENT between Russia and Japan. Russia, involved in the international crisis following the occupation of Kiao-chow and Port Arthur (p. 747), was eager to avoid friction with Japan and withdrew many of the advisers and officers. By the new convention both sides engaged not to interfere with the internal affairs of Korea, but Japan was given a free hand in economic matters.

Nov. Dissolution of the Independence Club and arrest of many of the leaders resulted in widespread riots and disorders. The conservative (pro-Russian) and progressive (pro-Japanese) groups were now almost at open war with each other.

1900, Mar. 18. The Russians attempted to secure a concession at Masampo for a naval station, but were foiled by the stiff opposition of Japan. Despite all previous agreements, the two powers were gradually moving toward a crisis. The Japanese, determined to exclude Russia from Korea, concluded with England

1902, Jan. 30. The Anglo-Japanese alliance, which again affirmed the independence of Korea. The Japanese then entered upon negotiations with Russia, which was trying to exploit a great timber concession on the Yalu River in northern Korea (first secured in 1896). The negotiations bringing no results, the Japanese embarked on

1904, Feb. 8. THE RUSSIAN-JAPANESE WAR (p. 892). The Japanese at once occupied Seoul, and Korea was obliged to annul all concessions made to the Russians. Once again Korea fell entirely under Japanese control, and was forced to accept Japanese diplomatic and financial advisers (Aug. 22).

1905, Sept. 5. The Treaty of Portsmouth, between Russia and Japan, provided for Russian recognition of the preponderant interest, political, military and economic, of Japan in Korea and provided further that Russia should not oppose any measures for the government of Korea or its protection and control, which the Japanese government might deem necessary to take in conjunction with the Korean government.

1906-1908. Prince Itō, Japanese resident-general. He regulated the relations between Japan and Korea and set the Korean government on the road to reform and modernization.

1907, July 19. Abdication of the emperor under Japanese pressure. His successor was a mere figurehead.

July 25. The administration was placed almost entirely under **Japanese control** and the Korean army was ordered disbanded. This at once led to **widespread insurrection and a war of independence,** which was suppressed only with great difficulty after years of fighting.

1910, Aug. 22. KOREA WAS FORMALLY ANNEXED TO JAPAN, and renamed *Chōsen*.

7. JAPAN

1793. Laxman, a Russian lieutenant, arrived at Hakodate in Hokkaidō with Japanese castaways, but failed to establish friendly relations.

1793-1837. THE PERSONAL RULE OF IENARI as *shōgun* (d. 1841) was characterized by increasing extravagance and inefficiency and by signs of the breakdown of isolation and the collapse of military rule. During this period lived **Ninomiya Sontoku** (1787–1856), a famous peasant-philosopher and economic reformer; **Kyokutei** (or Takizawa) **Bakin** (1767–1848), an author of adventure novels; and **Katsushika Hokusai** (1760–1849) and **Andō** (or Utagawa) **Hiroshige** (1797–1858), two of the best known ukiyo-e woodblock artists.

1795. Broughton, a British explorer, visited Hokkaidō, charting parts of the coast.

1797-1809. American ships traded with Japan nearly every year, on behalf of the Dutch.

1798. The *Kojikiden*, a commentary to the *Kojiki*, was completed after 35 years' labor by **Motoori Norinaga** (1730–1801), the greatest of the Shintō scholars. This achievement was an important event in the revival of Shintō and of the imperial cause. Influential in these movements were also **Kamo Mabuchi** (1697–1769) and **Hirata Atsutane** (1776–1843).

1804. A Russian ambassador, **Rezanov,** representing the Russian-American Company, reached Nagasaki, but after six months failed to obtain a treaty. In 1806–1807 his subordinates raided Sakhalin.

1814. Kurozumi Munetada (1780–1850) founded the **Kurozumi sect,** the first of the modern popular Shintō sects which on the whole stress patriotism and sometimes faith-healing. This and 12 similar sects founded in the course of the next century now have over 17,000,000 believers.

1837. The *Morrison*, an American ship with merchants and missionaries from Macao, visited Napa in the Ryūkyū (Ch. *Liu-ch'iu*) Islands, was bombarded at Edo and Kagoshima and failed to open relations. This was but one of some half a hundred efforts to establish more extensive intercourse with Japan before 1854. One reason for these efforts was that since about 1820 the northern Pacific whaling industry had developed greatly, and more humane treatment of crews of whalers wrecked in Japanese waters was desired, particularly by the United States.

1837-1853. IEYOSHI as *shōgun*. This was a time when the question of opening the nation to foreign trade in compliance with the demands of the occidental nations became pressing. The sentiment in favor of an imperial restoration was growing, and economic ills of the nation were acute, resulting in the impoverishment of many warriors who became *rōnin*, masterless warriors.

1838. Nakayama Miki (1798–1887), a woman, founded the faith-healing **Tenri sect,** the most popular of the modern Shintō sects.

1839-1840. Conservative scholars in an effort to check the rapid growth of occidental learning had restrictive measures instituted and imprisoned two leading scholars of the occidental school (*Rangaku*, "Dutch Learning"), who favored opening of Japan, **Watanabe Kazan** (1793–1841) and **Takano Chōei** (1804–1850).

1841-1843. Mizuno Tadakuni (1794–1851) carried through misguided and ineffectual reforms.

1844. William II of Holland warned the *shōgun* by letter of the futility of the exclusion policy.

1846. American **Commodore Biddle visited Edo Bay**, but trade was refused.

1849. Commodore Glynn succeeded in getting American castaways at Nagasaki.

1851. American **Commodore J. H. Aulick** was commissioned to open relations with Japan, but was removed from his command (Nov.); **Commodore M. C. Perry** appointed as his successor (Mar. 1852); Holland warned Japan of the project. The Perry expedition was sent to improve treatment in Japan of American castaways from whalers, to open one or two ports for trade and supplies, especially coal for California–Shanghai steamship service; instructions pacific in nature.

1853, July 8. PERRY with four ships anchored off **Uraga** in Edo Bay and remained ten days, delivering the president's letter, which was referred to the emperor and to the *daimyō*, an unprecedented course which aroused the whole nation and elicited a largely anti-foreign response.

1853-1858. IESADA as *shōgun*. The feudatories increasingly criticized the action of Edo, and the public became divided into two camps — (1) those in favor of the expulsion of the foreigners (*jōi*), led by emperor-honoring **Tokugawa Nariakira** (1800–1860), ex-Lord of Mito, and (2) the realists who saw that concessions to the foreigners were necessary, led by **Ii Naosuke** (Kamon-no-kami) (1815–1860). The two groups also divided over proposed heirs for the childless Iesada. Naosuke favored **Tokugawa Iemochi**, Lord of Kii. Nariakira favored his own son, **Hitotsubashi Yoshinobu** (Keiki), and resorted to the unprecedented stratagem of seeking imperial backing for his candidate.

1854, Feb. 13. Perry returned to Edo Bay with more ships, hastened by fear of Russian and French efforts to get treaties, and secured the **Treaty of Kanagawa** (Mar. 31), which opened two ports, permitted trade under regulations, provided better treatment of American castaways, and included most-favored-nation clause, but omitted extra-territoriality. This was followed by treaties with England (Oct.

1854), Russia (Feb. 1855), and Holland (Nov. 1855, Jan. 1856), which gave further privileges. Japan was not yet really open to trade. All these treaties were signed by the *shōgun* (called by foreigners *tycoon* [*tai-kun*], and wrongly regarded by them as the "secular emperor").

1854-1855. The Dutch aided the Japanese in laying the foundations for a future navy.

1856, Aug. American Consul-General **Townsend Harris** arrived at Shimoda with instructions to procure a commercial treaty.

1858, Mar.-May. Growing imperial prestige was seen in an extraordinary Edo appeal to the emperor for approval of further foreign intercourse, which was refused. The strong anti-foreign spirit in Kyōto became linked with a pro-emperor movement (*sonnō*).

June. Ii Naosuke appointed *tairō* and soon all-powerful at Edo. He secured the appointment of Iemochi as the *shōgun's* heir and the signature (July 29) without imperial approval of the important commercial treaty previously arranged with Harris, which provided for unsupervised trade and permanent residence at five ports, residence at Edo and Ōsaka, an envoy at Edo, extra-territoriality, a conventional tariff, the prohibition of the import of opium, revision in 1872 or later. Treaties followed with Holland (Aug. 18), Russia (Aug. 19), England (Aug. 26), France (Oct. 7), all on the model of the Harris treaty.

1858-1866. IEMOCHI as *shōgun*. The anti-foreign sentiment continued unabated, and desire for the restoration of the emperor's direct rule increased rapidly.

1859, Feb. Kyōto informed Edo that foreigners were to be expelled as soon as possible.

1859. Foreign merchants settled at Yokohama. A series of attacks upon foreigners followed and resulted in foreign pressure upon Edo for redress. Silver-gold exchange rate of 5 to 1 led to outflow of gold.

Nov. Yoshida Shōin (1830–1859), a leading anti-foreign, pro-imperial spirit of Chōshū (W. Hondō), was executed for anti-Edo activities, but his teachings continued to influence the Chōshū warriors.

1860, Mar. 24. Ii Naosuke was assassinated by former Mito men.

May 17. First Japanese embassy to the United States exchanged treaty ratifications in Washington.

Sept. 17. Nariakira died, and leadership of anti-foreign, pro-imperial movement passed to **Satsuma** (S. *Kyūshū*), **Chōshū**, and **Tosa** (*Shikoku*) fiefs.

1861, Mar.-Sept. Russian occupation of **Tsushima.**

1862, Jan. Mission to European governments. Agreement signed in London (June) postponing until 1868 opening of Niigata and Hyōgo and residence in Edo and Ōsaka.

Sept. 14. An Englishman, **Richardson**, murdered by Satsuma men near Yokohama. This was but one of many murderous attacks on foreigners or their employees by antiforeign warriors.

Oct. The forced residence of *daimyō* in Edo was greatly curtailed and the western *daimyō* began to congregate around the court in Kyōto.

1863, Apr. Iemochi went to Kyōto in response to a summons from the emperor. This unprecedented step signified that the political center of the empire had already shifted back to Kyōto. On June 5 a date (June 25) was chosen for expulsion of foreigners.

June 24. Edo paid indemnity to the English for Richardson and others and announced negotiations would be undertaken for closing of ports.

June 25. Chōshū forts at Shimonoseki fired on an American vessel and later on French and Dutch vessels; direct reprisals by American and French warships.

Aug. 15-16. A British squadron bombarded Kagoshima, thereby convincing Satsuma that expulsion of foreigners was impracticable.

Sept. *Coup d'état* at Kyōto; extremist Chōshū forces expelled.

1864. Internecine strife in Mito robbed it of all leadership in national affairs.

Aug. Chōshū men defeated in pitched battle at Kyōto in effort to regain influence at court.

Sept. 5-8. Allied expedition (British, Dutch, French, American) silenced Chōshū forts at Shimonoseki, thereby breaking back of antiforeign movement. Edo agreed to pay indemnity for Chōshū (Oct.).

1865, Nov. Allied naval demonstration at Ōsaka secured imperial ratification of treaties.

1866, June 25. Tariff convention signed with United States, England, France, and Holland. 5% duty on almost all imports and exports (in force until 1899).

July-Oct. Edo engaged in unsuccessful expedition to punish Chōshū for its extremist activities.

Sept. Iemochi died and was succeeded by

1867. KEIKI (Hitotsubashi Yoshinobu) as *shōgun*. Young leaders, like Saigō (1827-1877) and Ōkubo (1832-1878) of Satsuma, plotted to undermine Edo rule; a vigorous young ruler, **Mutsuhito** (Meiji emperor), came to the throne (Feb.); Keiki, who as a Mito scion was predisposed to surrender to Kyōto, resigned (Nov.), bringing almost 700 years of feudal military government to an end.

1868, Jan. 1. Hyōgo (Kobe) and Ōsaka opened to foreign trade.

Jan. 3. THE EMPEROR assumed direct control of the nation; western clans seized power at Kyōto; remaining Tokugawa forces defeated in civil war (July 4, battle of Ueno in Edo).

Mar. The emperor received French, Dutch, and British representatives.

Apr. 6. Charter oath by the emperor promised a deliberative assembly, decision of public affairs by public opinion.

Nov. Capital moved to Edo, renamed Tōkyō (*Eastern capital*). Meanwhile the year period was changed to Meiji marking the beginning of

1868-1912. THE MEIJI PERIOD. The anti-foreign policy of the imperial party was dropped as soon as it came to power, and Japan entered upon a period of great borrowing from the Occident comparable only to the period of the imitation of China. The remnants of military rule and feudalism were abolished, a strong centralized bureaucratic government fashioned along occidental lines was built up under the able leadership of the Meiji emperor, and Japan became a modern world power. **Rapid industrialization** on western models took place, and, as a consequence, the wealth and population of the land multiplied. In the fields of science, education, philosophy, and even art and literature great transformations were wrought by the impact of occidental civilization, and for a few decades many of the native traits and institutions were somewhat discredited if not completely superseded.

1869, Mar. The *daimyō* of Satsuma, Chōshū, Tosa, and Hizen offered their lands to the emperor as a step toward the abolition of feudalism; others followed this example.

July. *Daimyō* were appointed governors of their former estates with one-tenth their former revenue. Representatives of the 276 fiefs, appointed by their lords, met in an assembly (*kogishō*); this body lacked legislative power, was prorogued in 1870 and abolished in 1873.

1871, Aug. 29. Imperial decree abolished the fiefs and substituted prefectures (*ken*, at first 71, now 44, with 3 prefectural cities [*fu*]). First regular government postal service established (Tōkyō to Ōsaka). Ministry of education reorganized to promote universal education. First daily newspaper.

Sept. 3. Treaty of Tientsin with China signed as between equals. Japan did not gain extra-territorial and commercial rights equal to those of the West, nor a most-favored-nation clause.

Oct. The Iwakura mission (including Ōkubo and Itō) departed to seek treaty revision from the West and to prepare for reforms necessary to that end. It failed to secure revision and returned Sept. 1873.

1872. Universal military service introduced; the army was modeled at first on the French, later on the German. First railway opened (Tōkyō-Yokohama, 18 mi.). National bank regulations issued on American model.

1873, Jan. 1. Solar Gregorian calendar adopted in place of lunar calendar. British officers employed to reorganize the navy. Policy of religious toleration permitted the propagation of Christianity once more.

Oct. A peaceful policy toward Korea was chosen rather than a warlike policy.

1874, April. Expedition sent via Amoy to Formosa to redress murder by natives of Ryūkyū sailors in Dec. 1871; Japan having claimed suzerainty over Ryūkyū and China having avoided responsibility. In Oct. Japan agreed to recall the expedition, China to pay indemnity.

1875. Assembly of prefectural governors convened (not a representative nor a legislative body). A senate (*Genrōin*), convened in 1876, likewise had advisory duties only (abolished 1890). Agitation for representative institutions continued, led by Itagaki of Tosa.

1876, Feb. 26. Japanese naval demonstration secured treaty with Korea, recognizing the latter as independent of China and granting extra-territorial and commercial privileges to Japan.

Aug. Compulsory commutation of the pensions which had been granted the warrior class, and which were a heavy financial burden, and the prohibition of the wearing of two swords signified the end of the warrior class as a separate group. Natural resentment over this led to several disturbances including

1877, Jan.-Sept. THE SATSUMA REBELLION led by Saigō, a leader in the restoration movement. It was crushed by the modern trained army of commoners. A large issue of inconvertible paper money was used to defray expenses.

1878, May. Ōkubo was assassinated.

1879. Prefectural assemblies, elected by males over 25 who paid a land tax of 5 yen or more, were convened with powers to determine local budgets.

1880, July. Promulgation of revised penal code and code of criminal procedure, based largely on French models, in order to remove necessity for extra-territoriality.

1881. Imperial decree promised to convene a national assembly in 1890; fostered organization of political parties (*Jiyūtō* or Liberal Party by Itagaki; *Kaishintō* or Progressive Party by Ōkuma) in opposition to Satsuma-Chōshū bureaucracy.

1882, Jan.-July. In treaty revision conference at Tōkyō foreign minister Inoue failed to secure revision.

Mar. Itō was appointed to draft a constitution and visited the Occident, being particularly impressed by the German political system (returned Sept. 1883).

May 22. Korea opened to western trade by treaty with United States signed by Commodore Shufeldt and Li Hung-chang at Tientsin, which recognized Korea as a sovereign state and thus weakened the Chinese position there; this was followed by similar treaties with the European powers (1883–1886).

July. A Korean mob attacked the royal palace and Japanese legation in Seoul; Japan obtained indemnity (Sept.).

Oct. Bank of Japan established as central bank of European type.

1883, Apr. 16. Revision of the press law with drastic libel regulations.

1884. Creation of a newly organized peerage of 500 members to provide a basis for an upper house.

Dec. *Coup d'état* by pro-Japanese liberal party in Seoul; the Japanese envoy and troops were forced out by Chinese; this led to

1885, Apr. 18. CONVENTION BE-TWEEN ITŌ AND LI HUNG-CHANG: both powers to withdraw their troops and to inform each other of any intention to send them back to Korea; really a victory for Japan. An attempt by Russia to gain a protectorate over Korea prevented. Great Britain occupied Port Hamilton (Apr.), but withdrew (Feb. 27, 1887).

Reorganization of the cabinet on German lines with a premier (Count Itō) and nine departmental ministers responsible to him.

1886, May 1—1887, July 29. Treaty revision conference in Tōkyō, conducted by Inoue as foreign minister, failed to obtain the abolition of extra-territoriality; individual negotiations were then carried on by Inoue's successor, Ōkuma.

Period of rapid commercial expansion with government paper-making and cotton-spinning plants (200 steam factories in Japan by 1890); extension of railroads (959 miles of government lines by 1901 and 2905 of private); increase in steamship tonnage (15,000 by 1893, 1,522,000 by 1905); and unification of telegraph and postal systems (1886).

1888, Apr. Privy council created as an advisory body to the emperor. Kuroda succeeded Itō as premier.

1889, Feb. 11. NEW CONSTITUTION PROMULGATED. The emperor's powers were carefully guarded, including the right to declare war and make peace, and power to issue ordinances having the force of laws. Bicameral Diet; upper house of peers and representatives of merit and wealth (363 members); lower house elected through limited suffrage (463 members); the Diet had restricted control of finances.

Dec. Count Yamagata became premier.

1890. The emperor formally approved the new civil, commercial, and criminal codes of law based on western models, in order to eliminate necessity for extraterritoriality. Mexico had already in 1888 granted Japan judicial autonomy over Mexicans in Japan. The civil code was put in force, 1892 and 1898, and the commercial code, 1899.

July. First general election, by males aged 25 who paid direct national taxes of 15 yen or more (460,000 qualified voters out of 42,000,000).

1891, May. Resignation of Premier Yamagata, Count Matsukata succeeding.

1892, June. Resignation of the cabinet following defeats in the Diet; Count Itō became premier.

1894, Mar. Rising of the anti-foreign Tonghak Society in southern Korea led China and Japan to send troops to Korea.

July 16. Aoki-Kimberley Treaty, signed in London, revised British Treaty of 1858, abolished extra-territoriality in 1899, prepared the way for similar treaties with other powers. By Aug. 4, 1899, all Occidentals were subject to Japanese courts; a new international status for Japan.

1894-1895. SINO-JAPANESE WAR — primarily a struggle for control of Korea (p. 881).

July 23. Japanese forces seized the royal palace in Seoul, leading to the outbreak of hostilities; Japanese victories at P'yŏngyang (Sept. 16), in the naval battle of the Yalu (Sept. 17), invasion of Manchuria, and capture of Port Arthur (Nov. 21) led to abortive Chinese peace overtures (Nov.).

1895, Feb. 12. Japanese capture of Weihai-wei.

Apr. 17. TREATY OF SHIMONOSEKI signed by Count Itō, Count Mutsu, minister of foreign affairs, and Li Hung-chang, Chinese ambassador extraordinary. China recognized the full independence of Korea, ceded to Japan the Pescadores, Formosa, and the Liao-tung Peninsula, paid an indemnity of Tls. 200,-000,000, opened four more treaty ports, and negotiated a new commercial treaty (signed July 21, 1896).

Nov. Japan yielded to tripartite intervention of Russia, France, and Germany and gave up the Liaotung Peninsula, receiving instead from China Tls. 30,000,000 additional indemnity.

1896. Japanese domination and reorganization of the Korean government, following the murder of Queen Min (Oct. 8, 1895) and the recall of the Japanese minister implicated in it (Miura), was checked by the flight of the king to the Russian legation (Feb. 11), where he remained until 1897. Henceforth, Russia became Japan's rival for control of Korea.

June 9. Lobanov-Yamagata Protocol, signed in St. Petersburg, recognized Russia's position in Korea (pp. 746, 886).

Sept. Matsukata again premier.

1897, Mar. 29. Japan adopted the gold standard; ratio, 32½ to 1.

1898, Jan. Itō again premier.

Mar. 15. Russian agent to control Korean finances dismissed after a British and Japanese show of naval force.

Apr. 25. **Nishi-Rosen Protocol** signed, by which Russia agreed to Japanese economic penetration of Korea; both powers were to refrain from interference with internal affairs. Japan increased her military and naval preparations.

Apr. 26. Japan assured by the Tsung-li Yamen at Peking respecting the **non-alienation of Fukien province** to any other power.

June. **Ōkuma-Itagaki ministry** of Kenseitō party formed.

Nov. **Yamagata ministry** formed.

1899, July 17. **Revised treaties with foreign nations took effect.** France and Austria retained consular jurisdiction until Aug. 4.

1900, June 6. **Boxer uprising in China.** Japan joined the international relief expedition.

Oct. Itō formed a **Kenseitō ministry.**

1901, June 2. Viscount Katsura formed a ministry.

Aug. Plans of naval and military reorganization adopted; cabinet ministers for these departments might be civilians, but direct responsibility to the emperor was retained.

1902, Jan. 30. **ANGLO-JAPANESE ALLIANCE** signed (negotiated by Hayashi in London), recognizing the independence of China and Korea and Japanese special interests in Korea; each power was to remain neutral if the other became involved in war with one power, but to make war and peace in common with its ally if another power entered the war; to remain in force five years.

1904. **Continued Russian penetration of northern Korea** and failure to withdraw from Manchuria, together with breakdown of Russo-Japanese negotiations, led to Japanese severance of diplomatic relations (Feb. 6) and

1904-1905. **THE RUSSO-JAPANESE WAR.**

Feb. 8. Japan attacked Port Arthur (*Ryojun*), bottling up Russian fleet.

Feb. 10. **War declared.**

Feb. 23. Treaty between Japan and Korea by which the latter virtually became a protectorate of Japan in return for guaranties of integrity.

May 1. Russians defeated at the **Yalu River** by Kuroki.

May 30. Japanese occupied **Dalny** (Dairen). Nogi began **siege of Port Arthur,** Ōyama advanced northward, and

Aug. 25-Sept. 4. Defeated Russians at Liaoyang. The latter withdrew to Mukden.

1905, Jan. 2. **Port Arthur surrendered.**

Feb. 20-Mar. 9. Russians defeated at Mukden by five combined Japanese armies under Ōyama.

Apr. 5. Japanese representations in the United States, England, France, Germany, and Austria elevated to the rank of embassies.

May 27-29. In naval battle of Tsushima Straits the Russian fleet of 32 vessels, come from European waters, was annihilated by Japanese under Tōgō.

Aug. 12. **Anglo-Japanese alliance renewed** for ten years; *casus belli* redefined as attack by a single power on either party.

Sept. 5. **TREATY OF PEACE** signed at Portsmouth, after a conference which began Aug. 5 through Pres. Roosevelt's mediation. Russia acknowledged Japan's paramount interest in Korea, transferred to Japan the lease of the Liao-tung Peninsula and the railroad to Ch'ang-ch'un, and ceded the southern half of Sakhalin. Manchuria to be evacuated by both powers and restored to China. Because of failure to obtain an indemnity the treaty was unpopular in Japan and riots occurred in Tōkyō.

Nov. 17. Japan secured by treaty control of the foreign relations of Korea. In 1906 Marquis (later Prince) Itō was appointed resident-general. A large immigration of Japanese commenced.

Dec. 22. Confirmation by China of the Russo-Japanese treaty.

1906, Jan. **Resignation of Premier Katsura** because of popular dissatisfaction with Portsmouth treaty. **Kenseitō ministry formed by Marquis Saionji.**

Mar. 16. Bill passed lower house for **nationalization of all railways** at estimated cost of $250,000,000. By 1921 there were 6481 miles of state railways and 1993 of private.

1907, June 10. **Franco-Japanese treaty** guaranteeing the "open door" and integrity of China, *status quo* in the Far East, and a most-favored-nation agreement; mutual promise regarding security of Chinese territory in which each had special interests (for Japan, Fukien and parts of Manchuria and Mongolia).

July 20. **Abdication of the Emperor of Korea** in favor of his son.

July 25. Japan obtained a protectorate over Korea by treaty, with complete control by Japanese resident-general.

July 30. Russo-Japanese treaty similar to the Franco-Japanese treaty (1907), with an agreement about the Chinese Eastern and Southern Manchurian railroads and spheres in Manchuria.

1908, Feb. 18. Plans handed to American minister at Tōkyō for Japanese **restriction of labor emigration to the United States** (*Gentlemen's agreement*) to settle existing difficulties between the two countries.

July. Katsura succeeded Saionji as premier.

Nov. 30. Exchange of notes with the United States (*Root-Takahira Agreement*) on the common policy of the *status quo* in the Pacific and "open door" and integrity of China.

1909, June. Prince Itō resigned after confessed failure to reform Korean administration.

Oct. 26. Itō assassinated by a Korean fanatic.

1910, July 4. Russo-Japanese agreement demarcated spheres in Manchuria, in joint opposition to American proposals (Knox scheme of Nov. 1909) and for common action in defense of their interests.

Aug. 22. KOREA ANNEXED by treaty, and a program of development and attempted assimilation begun. Korea named *Chōsen*, and Terauchi appointed first governor-general.

1911, Feb. 24. New treaty with the United States, continued restriction of emigration of Japanese laborers.

July 13. Anglo-Japanese alliance renewed for ten years without reference to Korea. Neither party to be drawn into war with a nation with which it had a general arbitration treaty.

Aug. Saionji succeeded Katsura as premier.

1912, Feb. 3. Heavy naval program submitted to the Diet, involving eight super-dreadnoughts and eight armored cruisers to be commenced in 1913.

July 8. Secret Russo-Japanese treaty further delimitated spheres in northeastern Asia.

July 30. The Meiji emperor died and was succeeded by his son, Yoshi-hito. The year period was changed to Taishō, marking the beginning of

1912-1926. THE TAISHŌ PERIOD. The movements begun in the Meiji Period continued with no startling new developments. The personal weakness of the Taishō emperor almost eliminated the direct control of the throne over practical politics. The World War and natural economic advance made Japan one of the great world powers.

1912, Dec. 20. Prince Katsura became premier without a majority when Saionji resigned because of opposition to his retrenchment policy in Korea.

1913, Feb. 12. Adm. Yamamoto succeeded Katsura as premier.

May 9. Formal protest sent the United States against proposed anti-alien land legislation in California. The bill nevertheless was signed (May 19), and Japan assured that treaty rights were not infringed.

1914, Apr. Count Ōkuma formed a ministry after Yamamoto resigned because of defeat of a heavy naval budget.

Aug. 15. Japanese ultimatum to Germany demanding withdrawal of German fleet from Far East and the surrender of Kiao-chow within a week. Since no reply was received

Aug. 23. WAR DECLARED ON GERMANY. (*Cont. pp.* 918, *ff.*, 1123.)

K. THE PACIFIC AREA

1. GENERAL: EXPLORATION AND ANNEXATION

1513, Sept. 25. **Vasco Nuñez Balboa** (1475–1517) first sighted the Pacific from the coast of Panama.

1520, Nov. 28. **MAGELLAN** (Fernão de Magelhaes, ?1480–1521) with three ships passed from the Straits of Magellan into the Pacific, which he crossed to the Ladrone and Philippine Islands in the course of 110 days. Only a couple of deserted islands were sighted. Magellan was killed on the island of Cebu, but one of his ships, under **El Cano**, returned to Europe by the Cape of Good Hope, discovering **New Amsterdam Island** on the way (1522).

1527. Portuguese traders to the Spice Islands seem to have touched on the northwest coast of Australia.

1542. The Spaniard, **Lopez de Villalobos**, crossed from Mexico to the Philippines, discovering some of the **Caroline** and **Palau Islands** on the way.

1545. The Spaniard **Ortiz de Retes** touched on the north coast of **New Guinea**, which he named. The island seems to have been sighted by the Portuguese **Antonio de Abrea** in 1511.

1565. The Spaniard **Andres de Urdaneta** discovered the **northern seaway** from the Philippines to New Spain, thus making the return voyage relatively easy. For the **Spanish settlement of the Philippines** and the connection with Latin America see p. 908.

1567. **Alvaro de Mendaña** (Span.) discovered the **Solomon, Marshall,** and **Ellice Islands.**

1578. **Sir Francis Drake crossed the Pacific,** east to west, the first Englishman to make the voyage.

1595. Mendaña, on a second voyage, discovered the **Marquesas** and **Santa Cruz Islands.**

1606. **Pedro Ferñandez de Quiros** (1565–1614), one of Mendaña's captains, continuing the search for new lands and a southern continent (*Terra Australis*), discovered **Tahiti** and the **New Hebrides**. One of his captains, **Luis Vaez de Torres,** sailed through **Torres Straits**, between Australia and New Guinea. In the same year the Dutchman, **Willem Janszoon,** entered Torres Straits from the west side and

coasted along the west coast of York Peninsula.

1616, Oct. 25. The Dutchman, **DIRK HARTOG,** landed on the island named for him on the coast of **West Australia.** During the next ten years Dutch mariners explored the west coast and part of the north coast, and in 1627 part of the south coast.

1616. The Dutchmen, **Willem Cornelisz van Schouten** (1580–1625) and **Jacob Lemaire,** seeking a route to the Indies not under control of the East India Company, first rounded Cape Horn and crossed the Pacific, discovering the **Bismarck Archipelago** and exploring the north coast of New Guinea.

1642-1644. **ABEL JANSZOON TASMAN** (1603–1659), in the service of the East India Company, sailed east from Mauritius, discovered the west and south side of **Tasmania** (Van Diemen's Land), touched on the west coast of **New Zealand,** and on the way back to Batavia discovered **Tonga** and **Fiji.** He proved that Australia was not part of a great Antarctic continent, though in circumnavigating Australia he did not even sight it.

1699. **William Dampier,** an Englishman, coasted along the northwest and west coasts of Australia.

1721. **Jacob Roggeveen** (Dutch), sailing from east to west across the Pacific, discovered **Easter Island** and **Samoa.**

1766-1767. **Samuel Wallis** and **Philip Carteret** rediscovered **Tahiti** and explored the Solomon Islands and the New Guinea coasts.

1767-1769. **Louis Antoine de Bougainville** (1729–1811), a French nobleman seeking new lands for France, explored Tahiti, Samoa, and the New Hebrides.

1768-1771. **FIRST VOYAGE OF JAMES COOK** (1728–1779), the greatest explorer of the Pacific. Cook's party set out to observe the transit of Venus, from Tahiti. Having achieved this end, Cook sailed around New Zealand, proving its insularity, and thence discovered the east coast of Australia. He passed thence to Java and home by the Cape of Good Hope.

1772-1775. SECOND VOYAGE OF JAMES COOK, this time west to east. He attempted to find the Terra Australis (see p. 571) and explored the New Hebrides, New Caledonia, and Norfolk Island.

1772. The Frenchman **Kerguelen-Trémarec** discovered **Kerguelen Island.**

1776-1779. THIRD VOYAGE OF JAMES COOK, in search of a passage from Hudson Bay to the Pacific. Cook discovered **Christmas Island** and (1778) **Hawaii** (Sandwich Islands), after which he passed through Bering Strait and explored the Arctic coasts of America and Asia (p. 562).

1785-1788. Jean François de La Pérouse (1741–1788), one of the greatest explorers of the period, made extensive discoveries in the northwest part of the Pacific, about Japan and Siberia.

1788, Jan. 18. The first shipload of British convicts was landed at BOTANY BAY, Australia, and **England** claimed Australia east of 135° E. Long. For the further development of Australia see p. 896.

1790. Mutineers from the British ship *Bounty* settled on little **Pitcairn Island,** the first British settlers on a Pacific island. Their descendants, by native women, still occupy the island, which was annexed by England in 1838.

1797. The first British mission was established on Tahiti, and soon afterward on the Marquesas and Friendly Islands. The English Protestants were soon followed by **French Catholics,** and, although at first the missions were rather unsuccessful, in the course of the 19th century the islands were for the most part converted.

1798. Fanning Island and Gilbert Island were discovered.

1798. George Bass and Matthew Flinders discovered **Bass Strait,** separating Australia and Tasmania.

1802-1803. Flinders completed the exploration of the south coast of Australia and (1803) circumnavigated the continent.

During the 19th century the **development of European trade** ran parallel with the expansion of missionary activity. Sandalwood, trepang, and coconut oil the chief products. Ruthless treatment of the natives (**Kanaka traffic** to Australia, i.e. kidnaping and selling into slavery). Phenomenal decline of the native populations, due in part, no doubt, to practice of infanticide

and to the **ravages of disease** brought in by the Europeans. The traders, and especially the whalers, completed the exploration of the ocean, while European expeditions extended scientific study.

1818-1819. The Frenchman **Freycinet** explored the coasts of New Guinea, the Mariannes, and Hawaii.

1823-1824. Another Frenchman, **Duperry,** visited and studied the Gilbert, Marshall, and New Britain Islands.

1826-1829. Dumont d'Urville, next to Cook the greatest explorer of the Pacific, investigated New Zealand, New Guinea, New Hebrides, Fiji, and the Mariannes.

1828. The Dutch annexed western New Guinea.

1833-1835. Captain Fitzroy, with **Charles Darwin,** made a famous scientific voyage in the *Beagle* to Tahiti and New Zealand.

1837-1840. Dumont d'Urville, in a second voyage, explored the Louisiades, Fiji, the Solomons, Marquesas, and Tuamotus. He established the division of the island world into *Melanesia, Micronesia,* and *Polynesia.*

1842. The French initiated a policy of annexation by taking the **Marquesas** and establishing a **protectorate over Tahiti and the Society Islands.** In 1844 they took over **Gambier Island** in the Tuamotus, claiming a protectorate over the entire group, which was formally annexed in 1881. In 1853 the French annexed **New Caledonia.**

1857-1859. The Austrian *Novara* expedition, one of the most fruitful scientific voyages.

1864. The French annexed the Loyalty Islands.

1874-1875. The British *Challenger* expedition, under Sir George Nares.

1874, Oct. 10. The British government annexed Fiji, inaugurating an extensive annexationist policy which had been previously rejected by the government, but now appeared necessary in view of French and German activity and because of clamor from Australia and New Zealand.

1880. Tahiti was made a French colony.

1884. England annexed the southeast part of New Guinea, while the Germans appropriated the northeast as well as the islands of the Bismarck Archipelago.

1885. Germany annexed the Marshall Islands and the Solomons.

1887. England and France established

a condominium over the New Hebrides.

1888. The British established a protectorate over the Cook Islands.

1889. England, Germany, and the United States arranged for joint supervision of the affairs of Samoa (p. 911).

1892. The British proclaimed a protectorate over the Gilbert and Ellice Islands (annexed 1915).

1898, Aug. 12. The United States annexed Hawaii (p. 910). By the war with Spain the United States secured the Philippines (p. 909) and Guam.

1899. By purchase, the Germans secured

from Spain the Marianne (Ladrone) Islands and the Palau Islands.

1899. Settlement of the Samoan dispute (p. 911). The United States retained Tutuila and the rest of the islands went to Germany. As compensation the British secured a number of the Solomon Islands from Germany.

1900. British protectorate over the Friendly Islands (Tonga) and Savage Island.

1901. The Cook Islands were turned over to New Zealand for administration.

1906. British New Guinea was turned over to Australia.

2. AUSTRALIA

The Dutch, who discovered and explored the western and parts of the northern and southern coasts of Australia (1613–1627) called the land **New Holland**. James Cook, who discovered and explored the east coast during his first voyage (1768–1771), called that part **New South Wales**. His favorable reports led the British government, after 1783, to consider it for possible settlement by the loyalists from America, but ultimately, after failure of convict settlements in West Africa, it was decided to use New South Wales for the establishment of criminals and offenders who crowded the British prisons after it became impossible to send them to America. The plan was merely to set up a **convict colony** that would support itself.

1788, Jan. 26. Capt. Arthur Philip arrived at Port Jackson (Sydney) **with the FIRST CONVICT TRANSPORTS** and convoy, 11 ships with 717 convicts, of whom about 520 were men. In the following month 15 convicts and escort were sent to organize another settlement on **Norfolk Island** (till 1803). Philip remained governor until 1792, during the most critical period of the colony: scarcity of food; uncertainty of supplies; laziness, incompetence, and quarrelsomeness of the convicts; prevalence of vice of every kind. The colony was protected by the **New South Wales Corps**, raised in England and itself an unimpressive and insubordinate body. The governor enjoyed absolute power and alone formulated policy. The convicts were supplied from government stores, but on expiration of their terms they were given 30 to 50 acres of land. Discharged soldiers were given grants of 80 to 100 acres. The officers were more richly endowed, and some

of them, like **John Macarthur**, soon became wealthy and influential.

1792-1795. Francis Grose and then **William Paterson** acted as vice-governors. As members of the New South Wales Corps, they provided richly for their comrades. The officers were given the service of convicts and were allowed to establish a monopoly of cargoes brought to the settlement. **Importation of rum** was permitted and rum soon became currency, much to the detriment of the settlement.

1793. Arrival of the first free settlers (11 in all), who received free passage, tools, convict service, and land grants.

1794. John Macarthur first began **sheep-raising and breeding**, which soon became a most profitable venture for himself and for the colony.

1795-1800. John Hunter, governor. A mild, well-intentioned administrator, he was soon at loggerheads with the officers of the Corps, through whose influence at home he was ultimately recalled.

1796. George Bass, in a small boat, **discovered Bass Strait** between Australia and Tasmania. Together with **Matthew Flinders** he circumnavigated Tasmania in 1798. Flinders alone in 1802–1803 **circumnavigated Australia**, proving that no strait divided New South Wales from New Holland. He suggested the name *Australia* for the continent, and it gradually came into general use.

1800-1806. Philip King, governor. His main ambition was to break the power of the officers, wherefore he forbade their trading and prohibited the importa-

AUSTRALIA
AND
NEW ZEALAND

Dates indicate formation of separate government
Stuart's transcontinental journey of 1862 ....
Overland telegraph of 1872 ---------------
Principal cable lines --------------

BRITISH ISLES
Comparative Size

tion of spirits. Neither policy proved much of a success, and so King, like his predecessor, was in constant conflict with the officers, of whom Macarthur was the chief leader.

1803-1804. Settlement of Tasmania, carried through by the governor for fear that the French might seize it. Settlements were established near present-day Hobart and near Launceston. In 1808 the convicts on Norfolk Island were transferred to Tasmania. From the very outset the settlers had much trouble with aborigines and bushrangers, i.e. escaped convicts turned bandits and freebooters.

1804. Insurrection of the Irish convicts, who had been sent in large numbers after the suppression of the revolution in Ireland in 1798. The rising was put down with ruthless vigor.

1806-1809. William Bligh, governor. He was appointed in the hope that, as a well-known disciplinarian, he would be able to end the domination of the officer clique and to stop the disastrous liquor traffic. But his drastic methods and fiery temperament resulted merely in the

1808, Jan. 26. Rum Rebellion. The officers, outraged by the arrest of Macarthur, induced the commander, Maj. George Johnston, to arrest Bligh as unfit for office and to hold him captive until the arrival of a new governor (1809). Though the home government condemned this action, it accepted it and removed Bligh.

1809-1821. COL. LACHLAN MAC-QUARIE, governor. His appointment marked the **end of rule by the naval commanders.** Macquarie took his Highland regiment to Australia and obliged the members of the New South Wales Corps to enlist in the regular force or return home, which about one-half of them did. For the rest the new governor devoted himself to the systematic building-up of Sydney, to road construction, establishment of orphanages, and to unrelenting war on the vice prevalent throughout the colony. **Civil courts** were established (1814) and a bank opened (1817). In 1816 the home government removed all restrictions on free emigration to Australia, thus preparing the way for a change in the character of the colony. But by 1810 there were already 3000 free settlers, endowed with large blocks of land. These freemen objected violently to **Macquarie's efforts to secure social equality for the emancipists** (i.e. pardoned convicts or those who had served their time) and to discourage free immigration. As a result, Macquarie, like earlier governors, was en-

gaged in constant struggle, though on a different basis.

1813. Gregory Blaxland with two companions (Lawson and William Charles Wentworth) first succeeded in penetrating the confused mass of mountains along the coast, thus paving the way for the advance to the plateau of the interior.

1815. Bathurst, the first town in the interior, was founded and a road built to it from Sydney.

1817-1818. John Oxley began the exploration of the interior, following the Lachlan and Macquarie Rivers. He found the country more or less flooded, but the discovery of great grassy regions stimulated settlement. The government granted land freely to immigrants and to emancipists, in addition to whom large numbers of squatters began to occupy grazing lands. Brutal and rapid **extermination of the natives,** who had become aggressive after many outrages by the whites (kidnaping of women and children, etc.). Rapid **development of bushranging** (lawlessness of escaped convicts and other bandits, who terrorized the more remote areas).

1819-1821. Inquiry of John T. Bigge, a London barrister sent out to investigate the government and the general condition of the colony. Bigge, having collected much material, recommended liberal land grants to settlers and extensive use of convict labor to open up the country.

1821-1825. SIR THOMAS BRISBANE, the eminent astronomer, served as governor after the recall of Macquarie. The period of his rule was marked by an acceleration of development. Land was granted generously on condition that the grantee take over one convict for every 100 acres. **Sale of crown lands,** but not more than 4000 acres to any one person. Systematic clearing of lands by convict gangs, at fixed prices. Organization of large syndicates: the *Australian Agricultural Company* received a grant of 1,000,000 acres and a monopoly of the coal mining near Newcastle. The *Van Diemen's Land Company* was given a grant of 400,000 acres in Tasmania. Brisbane's administration was distinguished also by the

1823. Establishment of a legislative council, the first step in the development of representative government. The council consisted of 5-7 nominated members, who could act on measures submitted by the governor. In 1828 the council was enlarged by the addition of seven non-official members. Beginning of the **agitation for representative government,** inspired by **William C. Wentworth,** editor of the *Australian* (1824).

1824. Opening of new convict settlements, to take care of the most dangerous elements. One was established at **Moreton Bay** and the town of Brisbane was founded. This colony was maintained until 1842. At the same time **Norfolk Island** was reopened and the worst felons were transported thither. Brutal treatment led to several serious uprisings and in 1855 the penal colony on Norfolk was given up.

1824 - 1825. Explorations of Hamilton Hume and **William Hovell** in the region west of the mountains. They crossed the upper Murray River and ultimately reached the coast near Geelong. The rich country discovered by them was soon penetrated by settlers.

1825. Tasmania (Van Diemen's Land) **was separated from New South Wales** and was thenceforth administered by a lieutenant-governor and a legislative council. Horrible conditions in the island with its large convict population. The bushrangers, under leaders like **Matthew Brady,** were well organized in bands and attacked settlers and natives. The natives, driven to desperation by the treatment of the whites, embarked upon the **Black War,** which cost many lives. The governor, Col. **George Arthur,** finally managed to track down the bushrangers, many of whom were hanged, but his efforts to corral the natives (the *Black Line*) met with failure. Finally **George Robinson,** a Methodist settler, offered to serve as conciliator. He succeeded in getting the remnants of the native tribes to submit and in 1835 the 200–300 who remained were established on Flinders Island, where efforts were made to civilize them. The experiment failed. By 1844 there were only 44 natives left, and these were moved back to Tasmania. The last man died in 1869 and the last woman in 1876.

1825-1831. RALPH DARLING, governor of New South Wales. He was much more vigorous and autocratic than his predecessor and much less favorable to the emancipists. Conflict with Wentworth over freedom of the press; drastic suppression of disorder; **Bushranging Act** (1830) — suspects to be arrested without warrant and held until proved innocent. On the other hand, Darling's rule was distinguished by the extension of the council (see above) and by the introduction of **trial by jury** for criminal cases. Emancipists were permitted to serve on juries, excepting in special cases. Darling continued the policy of **generous land grants** and by the end of his period some 4,000,000 acres had been

assigned in New South Wales, much of it in large blocks.

1825-1827. The government, alarmed by the explorations of the Frenchman, Dumont d'Urville, along the coasts, established posts at **Westernport,** at **Albany** on the southwest coast, **and at Melville Island** on the north coast, but none of these thrived. In 1829 the British government, however, laid claim to the whole of the continent.

1827-1830. Progress of exploration. Allan Cunningham in 1827 discovered the rich Darling Downs, in the hinterland of Brisbane. In 1828 **Charles Sturt,** seeking for the great inland sea which he was convinced existed, discovered the Darling River. On a second journey (1829–1830) he descended the Murray River to its mouth and, with great hardship, made the return trip overland to Sydney.

1829. FOUNDATION OF PERTH, in West Australia. This was the work of **Thomas Peel, James Stirling,** and their associates. A huge tract of land was granted by the government and was divided among the settlers, but dispersal of the population, lack of sufficient labor, etc., led to collapse of the founders' hopes and investments. West Australia led a most precarious existence for many years.

1831-1838. Sir Richard Bourke, governor. The British government fixed the minimum price of land at 5 shillings per acre, thus bringing to an end the unrestricted granting of land. Half of the proceeds from land sales was to be devoted to financing of immigration, the other half to public works. In 1832 the New South Wales government began the encouragement and financing of free immigration.

1834-1836. FOUNDING OF SOUTH AUSTRALIA. Whalers and sealers from Tasmania and America had for some time maintained stations on the coast, but the establishment of the colony was due to the efforts of **Edward Gibbon Wakefield** (1796–1862), the famous colonial theorist. Wakefield argued that land must be sold at a "sufficient price," which meant a price sufficient to oblige the laborer to work for several years before being able to acquire land for himself. In the interval the proceeds from land sales could be devoted to the importation of further labor, and thus a perpetual turnover of capital, land, and labor could be effected. On Aug. 2, 1834, Wakefield's followers, supported by men like the Duke of Wellington, George Grote, and others, secured for their *South Australia Association* a charter to found a colony. The first settlers were landed at Kangaroo Island in 1836, but were soon

moved to the mainland, where **Adelaide was
founded.** Wakefield's theory was not
closely adhered to, but the land sales resulted in widespread speculation, which
ruined the beginnings of the enterprise.
Sir George Grey (lieut.-governor (1841–
1845) finally succeeded in clearing up
the financial muddle and re-established the
colony on the basis of cultivation and
grazing.

**1834-1837.   SETTLEMENT OF VIC-
TORIA.** This was begun by colonists from other parts of Australia and
Tasmania. In 1834 **Edward Henty** and
his brothers from West Australia began
farming and ranching at Portland Bay and
in the following year **John Batman** and his
associates from Tasmania (the *Port Philip
Association*) concluded a fantastic treaty
with the natives at Port Philip and began
to open the country. A rival group from
Tasmania, led by **John Fawkner**, established itself close by. The Sydney government, ill disposed to extension of its responsibilities, warned the squatters off, but
in the end could do nothing more than
dissolve the association and add the region
to New South Wales (1837). Batman
and his friends were the **founders of Melbourne.**

1837. A British parliamentary committee
investigated the whole question of
transportation of convicts and
reached conclusions unfavorable
to the system. Beginning of the
movement to abolish it.

1838. **The minimum price of land** was
raised to 12 shillings per acre (in
1840 to £1 per acre). The government,
however, issued **grazing licenses** for a small
fee, thereby facilitating the occupation of
large tracts in the interior. Between 1840
and 1850 the Darling Downs were opened
up and New South Wales entered upon
the golden age of the grazing and wool-
raising industry.

**1840, Nov. 18.   THE LAST CONVICTS
WERE LANDED IN NEW
SOUTH WALES.** Since 1788 between
60,000 and 75,000 had been brought in, but
in 1840 there were perhaps less than 25,000
under sentence. The free population already greatly outnumbered the convicts
and emancipists.

1840-1841. **Edward J. Eyre** explored the
barren region north of Spencer
Bay as far as Lake Torrens. Thence he
made his way, alone with one native,
across the huge deserts to Albany (West
Australia).

1842. **Reconstruction of the legislative
council,** which henceforth was
to consist of 36 members, of whom 24
were to be elected by the propertied classes.
Emancipists were given the vote provided
they could meet the property qualifications.

1844-1845.   Charles Sturt, starting from
Adelaide, pushed his way north
into the great **Stony Desert** as far as the
Diamantina. At the same time (1845) the
German scientist **Ludwig Leichhardt** ex-
plored the region from Darling Downs to
the Gulf of Carpentaria and as far as Port
Essington (post founded 1831).

1847. By order in council the great pastoralists who had occupied land on
grazing licenses were transformed into **leaseholders,** thus securing fixity of tenure. The
measure reacted favorably on the sheep industry, but accentuated the conflict of
pastoralists and small farmers.

1848. **The British government resumed
transportation of convicts** on the
new Pentonville (conditional pardon) system. Convicts who had proved their good
behavior for a couple of years in England
were transported to Australia and set free
on condition that they should not return
to England until their sentence was completed. The new plan roused a howl of
protest in New South Wales.

**1850-1855.   Construction of the first rail-
way** (Sydney to Goulburn).

1850. Convicts were for the first time sent
to **West Australia,** in response to a
request from the settlers, who were
desperately in need of laborers.

**1850, Aug.   THE AUSTRALIAN COLO-
NIES GOVERNMENT ACT**
passed by the British Parliament. The
colonies were given the right to constitute
their own legislatures, fix the franchise,
alter their constitutions, determine their
own tariffs, all subject to royal confirmation. Thus the Australian states, in conformity with the new colonial policy of the
British government after 1837, were given
self-government. A committee headed by
William Wentworth worked out a **constitution** for New South Wales which was
adopted in Nov. 1855. It provided for **a**
legislative council appointed for life and a
legislative assembly elected on a restricted
franchise, together with cabinet government on the English model. At the same
time the other states (excepting West Australia) adopted similar constitutions, though
for the most part they provided for an
elective upper house.

1851. The legislative council of New South
Wales unequivocally forbade the
landing of further convicts on any
system, and the British government yielded.

1851, July 1.   VICTORIA was separated

from **New South Wales** and became a distinct colony.

1851, Aug. 9. DISCOVERY OF GOLD in large nuggets at Ballarat (Victoria), then at Bendigo and other places. Isolated finds had been made ever since 1839, but the government had discouraged the search for fear of the diversion of labor from grazing. From the Victoria fields about £80,000,000 worth of gold was taken in the first decade. Tremendous **influx of workers and adventurers** from all over the world. The population of Victoria rose from 77,000 in 1851 to 333,000 in 1855. Recrudescence of bushranging. Efforts of the government to secure some part of the new wealth, in the form of mining licenses. Growing discontent on the gold fields culminated in Nov.-Dec. 1854 in **open rebellion**, led by German and Irish revolutionaries who proclaimed the **Republic of Victoria**. The insurrection was put down by government troops without much trouble.

1852. **Foundation of the University of Sydney,** followed in 1853 by that of Melbourne and later other state capitals.

1852. **Arrival of the first steamship** at Sydney. In 1856 the Peninsula and Oriental Steamship Company opened regular service, at first in competition with the fast clipper ships which had greatly reduced the time of passage from England.

1853. **Discontinuance of transportation to Tasmania.** Since 1803 about 67,000 convicts had been landed in the island (about 4000 a year after 1841). The name *Tasmania* now definitively replaced that of *Van Diemen's Land,* and a constitution not unlike that of New South Wales was adopted.

1855. **The convict colony on Norfolk Island was abandoned,** after several serious and bloody insurrections.

1855. The Victoria government passed an **act to restrict Chinese immigration** (33,000 had come to the gold fields since 1851). The new law provided for a poll-tax of £10 on every Chinese immigrant. In 1859 a residence tax of £4 per annum was added. Similar measures were adopted by South Australia (1857) and New South Wales (1861) despite pressure from the British government. The effect was to check Chinese immigration almost completely.

1855. **New South Wales,** having first adopted a railway gauge of 5 ft. 3 in., changed to the 4 ft. 8½ in. gauge, leaving Victoria with the broader gauge. South Australia and West Australia and Queensland, for reasons of economy, adopted the 3 ft. 6 in. gauge, thus producing complete **confusion in the continental railway systems.** In all the colonies the railways soon came under the control of the state.

1859. **QUEENSLAND was established as a separate colony,** following agitation against government from Sydney. **Brisbane** became the capital.

1861. In New South Wales the **Land Occupation** Act limited the tenure of leases and permitted **selection of small holdings** for purchase. The measure was intended to help the small farmer (*selector*), but gave rise to much abuse (selecting of the best part of a large sheep run, e.g., and "dummying" or purchase by selectors who were mere agents of the large holders). Greater and greater efforts were made in most colonies to restrict and break up the large holdings (resumption of crown lands on expiration of leases, compulsory resale, etc.) culminating (1910) in a heavy tax on unimproved estates of over £5000 value. But none of these measures proved entirely successful.

1861. **Robert O. Burke** and **W. J. Wills** headed a lavishly financed and well-equipped expedition across the desert from Melbourne, using camels for the first time. The expedition first **succeeded in crossing Australia** from south to north (Gregory River on the Gulf of Carpentaria), but the leaders lost their lives on the return journey.

1862. **M'Duall Stuart,** on his third attempt to cross the continent from Adelaide to Port Darwin, succeeded. This expedition was of far greater scientific importance than that of Burke and Wills.

1863. **Administration of the Northern Territory** (i.e. central as well as northern Australia), which, since the separation of Queensland, was no longer contiguous to New South Wales, was **assigned to South Australia,** where there was high hope of fertile territory.

1864. Beginning of the **importation of native (Kanaka) laborers** into Queensland from the Solomon and other islands. The system was intended to meet the labor shortage on the sugar plantations Though officially a system of contract labor, it soon degenerated into something closely akin to slave-raiding, until regulated, to some extent, by the government.

1866. The Victoria Parliament, influenced by the writing of **David Syme,** an influential Melbourne editor, gave up free trade and **introduced protection.** The measure led to a great constitutional conflict between the assembly and the council, which was dominated by the squatter oligarchy. Similar struggles continued until finally the farmer and industrial labor groups secured control of the political situation. The other colonies followed the example of Victoria in adopting protection, with the sole exception of New South Wales, which contented itself with a tariff for revenue only.

1867. The **Public Schools Act** in New South Wales laid the basis for the modern system of compulsory education for the young.

1867. The **last convicts were landed in West Australia,** which, since 1853, had received about 10,000. Thus ended the transportation system to any part of the continent.

1870. The **British government withdrew imperial forces** from Australia, after which the different colonies established militia systems of their own.

1872. **Opening of the telegraph line across the continent** from Adelaide to Port Darwin, which was soon afterward connected with Java and so with the lines to India and Europe.

1873. **Introduction of compulsory, secular schooling in Victoria.** At the same time the Victoria government passed the **first factory act,** aimed at protection of children and women and at the maintenance of sanitary and safe working conditions. This pioneer move was improved upon in 1884 and was imitated by the other colonies.

1873. The **New Guinea problem.** Already in 1867 the New South Wales government had appealed to London for action in the non-Dutch part of New Guinea, but the government had turned a deaf ear. In 1873 Capt. **Moresby** raised the British flag on the south coast, but the home government was still cool and refused to act unless the colonies agreed to assume responsibility for the administration of the territory. This some of the colonies were unwilling to do, so that Moresby's action was disavowed.

1874. Crossing of the western half of the continent by **John Forrest,** who made his way from the Murchison River across the desert to the newly constructed south-north telegraph line and thence to Adelaide.

1878. The **Queensland government annexed the islands in Torrens Straits.**

1879. Organization of the **first trade-union congress.** Unions had existed for some years previously and had embarked upon a widespread **agitation for the eighthour day** (one of many points borrowed from the Chartists who had come to Australia after 1848). The unions became powerful factors in New South Wales, Victoria, and South Australia.

1880. Meeting of the **first federal conference at Sydney,** to consider the possibility of federation of the colonies. The idea had been put forward long before by W. C. Wentworth and was ardently championed by **Sir Henry Parkes,** the eminent statesman of New South Wales. Homogeneity of race, common tradition, the needs of defense, etc., favored some sort of union, but the colonies were jealous of their independence and in many respects downright hostile to each other.

1883-1884. THE NEW GUINEA CRISIS. The Queensland government, uneasy about German designs, offered to assume the administration of the island if the home government would annex it. Apr. 4, 1884, the Queensland government, exasperated by delay in London, proclaimed possession, but was disavowed by London. Other colonies joined in the agitation for action. Ultimately, when the home government decided to act, the Germans had already laid claim to the northeastern part, leaving to the British (annexation Nov. 6, 1884) only the southeastern part. This danger at the door appears to have had much to do with furthering the sentiment for federation in Australia.

1883. **Opening of the Sydney-Melbourne railway line.**

1885. The British Parliament authorized the **establishment of a federal council** to meet every two years for the discussion of inter-colonial problems. The first meeting was held at Hobart (1886), after which New Zealand no longer attended. Since the council had merely consultative power it was regarded as inadequate by Parkes and other federalists, who renewed their demands for real union.

1885. **Victoria established wages boards,** empowered to fix wages in sweated industries. These boards, composed of employers and employees, with a neutral chairman, were given extensive powers to regulate entire industries. A daring experiment in labor relations, the system was gradually adopted by other colonies (1908-) under pressure of the labor parties.

1888. The British privy council upheld the **exclusion of the Chinese** as practiced in Victoria. Thereafter the policy was enforced by all the colonies and the idea of a "White Australia" met with general acceptance. As a matter of fact, there was growing hostility to any immigration, especially on the part of labor, and the influx of new settlers rapidly declined to a mere trickle.

1890. The Australian colonies and New Zealand agreed to support financially a British naval squadron, to be maintained in Australasian waters.

1890. **Responsible government** was at last established in West Australia.

1890. A great shipping, mining, and shearing strike resulted in failure, but thereby came to mark an important turning-point in the **development of the labor movement.** In several colonies the trade unions embarked upon political activity and soon became crucial factors in the political situation.

1891, Mar.-July. **THE FIRST AUSTRALASIAN FEDERAL CONVENTION** met at Sydney, under the presidency of **Sir Henry Parkes.** The members were chosen from the colonial parliaments and included most of the outstanding political figures of Australia and New Zealand. The convention worked out a draft constitution, which later served as a basis for the federal system, but the scheme had to be dropped because of the **opposition of New South Wales.** The result was renewed agitation for federation, especially by popular societies and leagues (1893-). The great financial crisis of 1893, the growth of the White Australia sentiment, and the emergence of Australian nationalism contributed further to the desire for union.

1894. South Australia introduced **woman suffrage,** which was later adopted by the other states (West Australia, 1899; New South Wales, 1902; Tasmania, 1903; Queensland, 1905; Victoria, 1909). At the same time South Australia established **compulsory arbitration of industrial disputes,** another experiment in the settlement of labor problems.

1897-1900. **THE ACHIEVEMENT OF UNION.** A federal convention met at Hobart in Jan. 1897 (10 members from each colony except Queensland). This assembly reconsidered the draft constitution of 1891 and finally evolved the arrangement which was later accepted. The federation was modeled in large measure upon the United States system, though with the responsible government characteristic of England. The united states were to be called the *Commonwealth of Australia,* and the new federal government was to be established in a new capital city to be deter-

mined later. The federal government was to have control of foreign affairs, defense, trade, tariffs, posts and telegraphs, currency, naturalization, marriage and divorce, pensions, etc. At the head was to be a governor-general, appointed by the crown. The **executive council, or cabinet,** was to be composed of members of Parliament and responsible to Parliament. Parliament was to be bicameral: the upper house (**Senate**) was to consist of six members from each state, elected directly for a six-year term, one-half renewable every three years; the **House of Representatives** was to be directly elected on the basis of populational districts. A high or **supreme court** was provided for as guardian of the constitution.

The draft constitution was submitted to the colonies for popular vote. Victoria, South Australia, and Tasmania were overwhelmingly in favor, but in New South Wales the proposal was lost by a fairly small vote. In 1898 a conference of prime ministers, in which Queensland joined, arranged for amendments (chiefly financial) to meet the objections of New South Wales. In a new election in New South Wales (1899) the amended draft was adopted. After some discussion of the limitation of appeals to the British privy council, the British government and Parliament accepted the project, which was given royal assent on July 9, 1900. West Australia then decided to join the federation (July 31) and on

1901, Jan. 1. **THE COMMONWEALTH OF AUSTRALIA came into being.** The first cabinet was led by **Edmund Barton,** ardent federationist and protectionist. The opposition, led by G. H. Reid, favored a tariff for revenue only. The **Labor Party** formed the third group. Led by J. C. Watson and better disciplined than the other parties, it was able, from the outset, to control the balance, and thus to carry into the commonwealth field the program of state socialism already introduced in the states. In 1901 New South Wales introduced conciliation and arbitration courts and adopted a scheme for old-age pensions. The Labor Party was particularly determined in the matter of immigration restriction, to which all parties, indeed, were committed.

1902. **The Immigration Restriction Act** (federal) provided that an immigrant, on demand, must demonstrate ability to pass a test in a European language (changed in 1905 to "a prescribed language" to spare Japanese susceptibilities). In this way Orientals and, if desired, Europeans could be excluded at will. The federal government at the same time put a stop to the importation of Kanakas into Queensland (they were repatriated in 1906). A high tariff on sugar protected the sugar-growers from competition from outside.

The **federal tariff** established in 1902 placed the whole continent on the protectionist system.

Woman suffrage was established (1902) for all federal elections.

1902-1904. Alfred Deakin, leader of the opposition, became premier, dependent on support of the Labor Party. When the latter abandoned him

1904. **Watson** formed the first Labor cabinet, which, however, was able to maintain itself for only a few months. Watson was succeeded by

1904-1905. **Reid,** who governed with support of the non-Labor representatives. The combination did not work very smoothly and the Reid cabinet was followed by a

1905-1908. **Deakin** ministry, which enjoyed the support of the Labor Party, now led by **Andrew Fisher.**

1905. British New Guinea became an Australian federal possession, and was renamed *Papua* (the Portuguese name). The territory had been but little developed (white population c. 600), but was regarded as vital for defense, especially in view of the rise of Japan and her victory over Russia.

1908-1909. Second Labor cabinet (Fisher). The government was much preoccupied by foreign affairs and defense. The new tariff (1908) gave British goods a 5% preference, and other efforts were made to draw closer the bonds to Great Britain, chiefly in view of the rising naval power of Germany and the gradual withdrawal of British naval forces from the Pacific. The Australian colonies had all taken part with the mother country in the South African War, and contributions had been made since 1890 to the maintenance of a naval squadron in the South Pacific. In 1908 the Australian government decided on the **construction of a naval force** of its own and began work on a 22-year program.

1909. **The commonwealth capital was finally fixed at Canberra** (New South Wales), the state government ceding the necessary territory, with a strip of land to the sea.

1909-1910. **Another Deakin government,** based on fusion with the following of Reid and his successor, **Joseph Cook.**

1909. **Federal old-age pensions** were established for those over 65 years of age and resident in Australia at least 25 (later 20) years.

1909-1910. **Defense Acts.** After a visit and recommendations by **Lord Kitchener,** the Australian government introduced a system of **compulsory military training** and began to organize a regular military force.

1910. **The Northern Territory,** administered by South Australia, **became a federal possession.**

Apr. In the general election the **Labor Party** for the first time **won a clear majority** of seats in the House of Representatives, thus ending the system of three minority parties working in combination. Fisher formed his second government, which lasted until 1913. **Continuation of the social program** (heavy tax on large and absentee properties, etc.). In order to make the White Australia more secure, the government resumed the **system of assistance to desirable white immigrants,** especially with the view of settling the Northern Territory.

1913. In the general election the **Fusion Party** (Joseph Cook) **secured a majority** of one. Cook formed a ministry, but legislation was effectively blocked by the Labor Party, which still had a majority in the upper house. To break the deadlock the governor-general dissolved both houses, and in the

1914. General election the **Labor Party recovered its majority.** Fisher formed his third government, which in 1915 was taken over by his successor, **William M. Hughes.** (*Cont. p.* 1128.)

3. NEW ZEALAND

New Zealand was discovered by the Dutch captain, **Tasman,** in 1642. But he did not land and the islands were not rediscovered until Capt. **Cook,** on his first voyage, landed (Oct. 7, 1769) and circumnavigated the group. The inhabitants, numbering perhaps 100,000, were located chiefly in the warmer, north island. They were **Maoris,** a people of the Polynesian family, who had probably occupied the country between 900-1400 A.D. Their culture was Neolithic and the practice of cannibalism was general. Tasman and Cook both had occasion to note their fighting qualities.

Though several other explorers touched

New Zealand in the last quarter of the 18th century, it was only after 1792 that **whalers, sealers, and traders** began to arrive more frequently. Merchants from Sydney were interested in the fine **timber** and in the native **flax**, which was bought from the Maoris in exchange for firearms. After securing muskets, native chiefs near the coast began to attack and exterminate tribes of the interior. There followed, especially after 1821, the **depredations of Hongi**, of **Te Rauparaha** (*Satan*), who carried his wars into the South Island, and of **Tu Hawaiki** (*Bloody Jack*), who dominated Otago. By this time the bay whalers were establishing **permanent shore settlements** on the coast of the South Island and in Cook Strait. Escaped convicts from New South Wales and beachcombers of all descriptions made these early settlements by-words for lawlessness and depravity. In the meanwhile

1814. **SAMUEL MARSDEN**, chaplain of the New South Wales penal colony, who had become acquainted with Maoris serving on whaling ships, established the **first Church of England mission** at the Bay of Islands. He himself did not remain in the islands, but opened a seminary for Maori chieftains in his New South Wales home. In New Zealand three lay missionaries and their families were maintained, but little progress was made during the first decade. In 1822 a **Wesleyan mission** was opened, and in 1823 the first Anglican clergyman, **Henry Williams**, arrived and initiated a period of greater activity and success. **William Colenso** translated the Bible into Maori (1827–) and in 1842 **George Selwyn** was named first Anglican Bishop of New Zealand. The missionaries did much to teach the natives and their influence spread far and wide in a relatively short period. In general the missionaries were opposed to settlement by Europeans, desiring to keep the islands for the Maoris. The **first Catholic mission** was opened at Kokianga in 1838.

1826. The **first New Zealand Company** was founded in England. It enjoyed powerful support and at once dispatched colonists. These, arriving at the height of the native wars, were too unfavorably impressed and insisted on going on to Australia.

1833. In order to combat the spread of lawlessness, the British government appointed **James Busby as resident** in the islands. Since the British government did not claim sovereignty, Busby had no real standing and was unable to achieve much.

1837. **Baron de Thierry,** a Belgian-British adventurer, arrived on the northwest coast and attempted to set up a kingdom of New Zealand on land he claimed to have bought from the natives. His venture was only one of many in these years. Missionaries, traders, speculators in Australia and England began to buy land in large blocks and under frequently suspicious circumstances, so that by 1840 land claims amounted to 56,000,000 acres.

1837. Foundation of the **NEW ZEALAND ASSOCIATION** by **Edward Gibbon Wakefield,** who had been chiefly instrumental in the colonization of South Australia (p. 899). The association agitated for annexation and settlement, but met with no favorable response from the colonial office which, like the missionaries, opposed further settlement. Thereupon Wakefield and his followers organized the **New Zealand Company** (May, 1839), bought out the rights of the earlier company, and began to sell land at £1 per acre to prospective colonists and investors. The government still opposing the company, fearful of action by a rival French enterprise (Capt. Langlois and the Nanto-Bordelaise Company), sent out colonists without securing permission of the government.

1840, Jan. 22. THE **FIRST BRITISH COLONISTS** landed at **Port Nicholson** in Cook Strait. A huge tract of land was acquired from the Maori chiefs and the town of **Wellington was founded.** In the interval the British government, also exercised by French designs, proclaimed

Jan. 30. British sovereignty. Capt. **William Hobson** had been sent out as governor, and, with aid of the missionaries, concluded with the native chiefs

Feb. 6. THE TREATY OF WAITANGI, which was subscribed to by some 500 chiefs in the course of the next six months. By the treaty the native leaders ceded their sovereignty to Britain, and in return were guaranteed their lands and other possessions. On May 21 Hobson proclaimed British sovereignty and established the **capital at Auckland.** On Aug. 10 a British force landed at Akaroa (Banks Peninsula), only a day before the arrival of the French colonials. The latter settled for a time, but all danger of French possession was obviously past.

1840-1842. Capt. **William Hobson**, governor. He made desperate efforts to regulate the confused land claims, and by ordinance of June 9, 1841, voided all claims until investigated and approved by the government. This brought him into conflict with the **New Zealand Company**, which had claims to some 20 million acres and which was sending out colonists in large numbers. While the government tried to sell lands at £1 per acre, the company sold at 5s. Ultimately the company's rights to about 283,000 acres were recognized, but in London as in New Zealand the conflict between government and company continued for years.

1840. The company established **settlers at New Plymouth**, renamed *Taranaki* in 1859.

1841. The company settled the south side of Cook Strait, founding the **town of Nelson**.

1843-1845. Capt. **Robert Fitzroy**, governor. In his eagerness to bring in settlers, he permitted purchase of land direct from the natives on payment of 10s. (soon reduced to 1d.) per acre to the government. This measure was disallowed by the home government and Fitzroy was recalled. By that time

1843-1848. THE FIRST MAORI WAR had broken out. It originated from a dispute about land in the Nelson district, where the settlers took the offensive and were cut down (**massacre of Wairau**). There followed anti-foreign outbreaks in the north. Many of the tribes remained loyal and the movement at all times lacked cohesion. To meet the emergency the home government sent

1845-1854. Capt. (later Sir) **GEORGE GREY** from South Australia as governor. With his usual vigor he suppressed the traffic in arms and while putting down disorders asserted his personal authority and gained the confidence of many Maori leaders. He cancelled his predecessor's land ordinances and forbade direct purchase on penalty of heavy fine (1846).

1846, Dec. 23. The British government conferred a constitution on New Zealand (named *New Munster* and *New Ulster*). Each province was to have its own governor, appointed council, and elected assembly. This system, obviously premature, was rescinded in 1848. Meanwhile the Maori wars in the North Island had deterred settlers from colonizing the disaffected regions, but

1846. The advent of the Russell ministry in England introduced an element friendly to the company. The government granted loans and allowed a very liberal land settlement. Under the auspices of the company other organizations took up colonization.

1848. A **Scottish Free Church association** settled **Otago** (capital Dunedin), and in

1850. An organization of **Church of England members** settled **Canterbury** (Christchurch). In the open regions of the South Island, where there were few natives, **sheep-raising** soon established itself (the industry was inaugurated in 1843-1844 and operated on grazing licenses issued by the government).

1851. The government began to issue **grazing leases** for 14 years, thus facilitating the **organization of large holdings**. Wool-raising became the most important industry. By 1871 there were in New Zealand 10 million sheep and wool was exported to the value of £2,700,000.

1851. The **New Zealand Company was dissolved.** By the terms of the settlement the members received £268,000, which became a charge on the New Zealand government.

1852. A NEW CONSTITUTION WAS PROMULGATED. It provided for six provinces, each under a superintendent and each with a provincial (district) council elected on the basis of a property franchise. For the colony as a whole there was to be a governor assisted by a nominated legislative council and a house of representatives elected on the provincial franchise. The regulation of native affairs was reserved to the home government (colonial office). Since the district councils were organized and functioned before the colonial assembly met, the provincial governments secured control over most affairs and until 1875 New Zealand was essentially disunited (**period of provincialism**).

1853. Grey reduced the price of crown lands to 10s. per acre, making possible the establishment of the small farmer.

1856. Responsible government was established in New Zealand. At the same time the provincial councils were authorized to dispose of the crown lands within their districts.

1858. The new province of **Hawke's Bay** was established. There followed the provinces of **Marlborough** (1859), **Southland** (1861-1870), and **Westland** (1873).

1860-1870. THE SECOND MAORI WAR. Like the first, this was a series of outbreaks, confined almost entirely to the North Island. The main cause was the rapid acquisition of native land by the government and the growing feeling of the natives that they were doomed. Development of the **king movement**, which aimed at union of the Maori tribes under a king. This was never more than partially successful. There followed (1865-) the **Hau-Hau movement**, a religious movement compounded of native mythology and Judaeo-Christian lore, the basic idea being opposition to Christianity as well as to European domination. Like the first war, the second, concentrated particularly in the Taranaki and Waikato country, was a matter of guerrilla warfare, and therefore difficult to deal with. Australian troops were sent to aid the government, but the **campaigns of Generals Pratt and Cameron** were indecisive.

1861-1867. SIR GEORGE GREY, governor for the second time. He did what he could to restore order and introduced the system of **confiscating the lands of rebels**. At the same time he made concessions to the Maoris (four chiefs being admitted to the legislative assembly in 1867). By 1870 the native disorders had been for the most part suppressed. During the remainder of the century the Maoris declined rapidly in numbers.

1861. Discovery of gold in Otago and (1865) in **Westland**. The result, as in similar cases elsewhere, was a great inrush of miners, so that the population rose from 100,000 in 1861 to 250,000 in 1870. The South Island became by far the most populous and rich and so it remained throughout the rest of the century.

1862. The government abandoned its right to pre-emption of native lands and established free trade in such lands. In 1865 a **native land court** was established to investigate titles before sale. Under this system the Maoris were quickly separated from their lands, so that by 1892 most of the good land was in the hands of the settlers.

1863. Opening of the first railroad (Christchurch to Ferrymead). The railways were from the start state-owned and operated.

1865. The capital was transferred from Auckland to Wellington, removing a longstanding grievance.

1870. The British government withdrew its troops from New Zealand, following the conclusion of the Maori War.

1870-1890. The "continuous ministry" of Sir Harry Atkinson, representing primarily the large pastoral, landed interests, was in power during most of twenty years. The period was one of deep depression, following the gold rush boom. To meet the situation the government, inspired by **Sir Julius Vogel,** embarked upon a policy of heavy borrowing, extensive railroad building and public works construction generally. In 1873 the **ownership of native land was individualized,** which made purchase from the natives easier. Extensive program of **assisted immigration** for settlers carefully selected in England by an agent of the New Zealand government. The population rose from 256,000 whites in 1871 to about 772,000 in 1901.

1870. Steamship connection was established with San Francisco. The **New Zealand Shipping Company** (1873) also contributed to improvement of communications.

1875. The district councils were abolished (effective Nov. 1, 1876), thus ending the period of provincialism. New Zealand was thenceforth under one government.

1876. Opening of the transoceanic cable to Australia.

1881. Chinese Immigrants Act, similar to the regulations introduced in Australia to restrict the influx of Orientals.

1882. Successful introduction of meat refrigeration on transoceanic steamers. For New Zealand this invention was epoch-making. Sheep thenceforth were raised not merely for wool, but for food. Furthermore, refrigeration made possible the **development of a great dairy industry** to provide the English market.

1887. Annexation of the Kermadec Islands to New Zealand. Already in 1871 the New Zealand government had appealed to England to annex Samoa, but these appeals proved fruitless. The New Zealanders throughout took a frankly imperialist view of southern Pacific affairs.

1888. Adoption of a protective tariff, under pressure from Labor groups. One effect of this change was that the Atkinson party began to divide and disintegrate.

1889. Introduction of manhood suffrage, another concession to popular agitation.

1890. In the general election the **Liberal-Labor Party,** led by John Ballance, defeated the Conservatives. For more than 20 years the progressive elements controlled policy. Under Richard Seddon (prime minister 1893-1906) an energetic social program was realized, which gave New Zealand a world reputation for state socialistic experiment. In the land question the government acted to restrict and break up large holdings through taxes on unimproved values and absentee estates. Every effort was made to establish small farmers on the land. Stringent **factory laws** (1894, 1901) and **progressive income tax.** The Labor Department, under **W. Pember Reeves** (1891–   ) instituted many other measures, some of which are listed below.

1893. **Adoption of woman suffrage.**

1894. Establishment of **industrial conciliation and arbitration boards,** with obligatory clauses. In practice the result was rapid **growth of trade-unionism** and regulation of all industrial conditions by the arbitration courts (wages, hours, factory conditions, etc.). This was the key measure in the New Zealand social program.

1897. **The eight-hour day** established by law.

1898. Introduction of **old-age pensions.**

1899. **Further restriction of oriental immigration:** an educational test was introduced, as in Australia.

1900. **The Cook Islands,** as well as **Savage Island** and **Suvorov Island,** were **annexed to New Zealand.**

1903. New tariff arrangements provided for **preferential treatment of British goods.** New Zealand was extremely loyal to the empire and, like Australia, contributed to the upkeep of the British Pacific squadron. New Zealand sent a contingent to participate in the South African War.

1906-1911. **Joseph Ward** became **prime minister** on the death of Seddon.

During these years New Zealand enjoyed great prosperity, but politically the governing Liberal-Labor Party began to disintegrate and in 1909 the **Labor Party** organized separately. Rapid spread of a strike movement, inspired by the **Federation of Labor** (founded 1907).

1907, Sept. 26. **NEW ZEALAND WAS GIVEN THE STATUS OF A DOMINION** within the British Empire.

1909. The government decided to pay for a battleship to be added to the British navy.

1911. A system of universal military training for those between 14 and 41 was established to meet the growing tension in international affairs.

Oct. **Defeat of the Liberals** in the election. After an interim cabinet

1912. **W. F. Massey,** leader of the Reform (Conservative) Party, became prime minister. The **Reform Party** drew its support from the small farmers and dairymen, chiefly in the North Island, which, since 1906, had again passed the South Island in population and which became ever more influential. One of the first acts of the new government was to transform the crown leaseholders into freeholders.

1913. **Foundation of the United Federation of Labor and of the Social Democratic Party,** designed to protect the interests of the industrial workers.

(*Cont. p.* 1131.)

4. THE PHILIPPINES

1521, Mar. 15. The islands were discovered by **Magellan,** who was killed there (Apr. 25) in a fight with the natives.

1525-1527. In order to strengthen Castilian claims against Portugal, Charles V sent out an expedition under **García Jofre de Loyasa,** who died en route. The expedition visited Mindanao, but Portuguese opposition was encountered and no results were obtained.

1527. Under orders from home, **Cortés** (in Mexico) sent out **Alvaro Saavedra Ceron,** whose fleet was dispersed without accomplishing anything.

1529. Lack of success in these efforts induced Charles V to conclude with Portugal the **Treaty of Saragossa,** by which the line of demarcation in the Far East was fixed 297.5 leagues east of the Moluccas, which remained Portuguese. The Philippines, though within Portuguese

jurisdiction, were not occupied by Portugal.

1532. Charles V granted **Pedro de Alvarado** authority to conduct discovery and colonization in the Pacific. Alvarado abandoned the project in order to attempt the conquest of Quito.

1541. The viceroy of New Spain, **Antonio de Mendoza,** was given authority for the same purpose but was to share the results with Alvarado.

1542-1543. Mendoza sent out **Ruy Lopez de Villalobos,** who landed and named the islands, though he was then driven by the natives and later captured by the Portuguese.

1565-1571. Under instructions from Philip II, the viceroy **Velasco** sent out an expedition under **Miguel Lopez de Legazpi,** who made the first settlement (San Miguel), subjugated the natives and founded **Manila** (May 19, 1571). An *audiencia* was established at Manila (1583) and the islands were subordinated to the government of New Spain.

1762, Sept. 22. An English fleet bombarded Manila and took the city (Oct. 5).

1764, Mar. 31. The British evacuated Manila on the conclusion of peace.

1892. Organization of native secret societies directed against Spanish rule.

1896, Aug. 26. Beginning of the native insurrection, led by **Emilio Aguinaldo.** Execution (Dec. 30) of Dr. José Rizal, one of the most prominent native leaders.

1897, Dec. 14. Pact of Biac-na-bato between the governor-general, Primo de Rivera, and Aguinaldo, bringing the insurrection to an end. Reforms to be introduced within 3 years; Aguinaldo and other leaders left the islands in return for a money payment.

1898, Apr. 21. Outbreak of the **Spanish-American War.**

May 1. Commodore **Dewey's victory** over Spanish fleet in Manila Bay.

May 19. Arrival of **Aguinaldo,** who proceeded to organize a native army under American auspices.

June 12. Aguinaldo proclaimed **independence** and organized a provisional government, with himself as president.

Aug. 13. Manila captured by American forces, assisted by Aguinaldo.

Dec. 10. By the **Treaty of Paris** Spain ceded the islands to the United States for $20,000,000. Government of the islands put in the hands of Gen. **Elwell S. Otis.**

1899, Jan. 5. Aguinaldo protested against American sovereignty and called on the Filipinos to declare independence.

Jan. 20. The Malolos Constitution proclaimed. Aguinaldo named president of the rebel government. The insurrection against American rule began Feb. 4.

Mar. 4. Arrival of the **first Philippine Commission,** under J. G. Schurman. Apr. 4 it promised "the amplest liberty of self-government," but the revolt went on.

1900, Feb. 6. Second **Philippine Commission,** headed by Judge **William H. Taft.** It reached Manila (June 3) and began to take over the administration and to organize a government.

Dec. 23. Formation of the Filipino **Federal Party,** aiming at peace under the sovereignty of the United States.

1901, Mar. 2. The **Spooner amendment** to the army appropriation bill authorized the president of the United States to establish civil government in the Philippines.

Mar. 23. Capture of Aguinaldo by Gen. Frederick Funston as a result of a stratagem. Aguinaldo took the oath of allegiance to the United States (Apr. 2) and issued a proclamation advising submission. Guerrilla warfare continued to some extent until Apr. 1902.

July 4. Judge Taft inaugurated first civil governor of the islands.

Sept. 1. Three Filipinos were added to the Philippine Commission.

1902, Jan. 21. Bureau of Education established.

June 12. Judicial system established: supreme court of seven justices, and sixteen courts of first instance.

July 1. Philippine Bill passed by Congress, the first organic law for the government of the islands: bicameral legislature, consisting of appointive upper house and elected assembly, with veto power reserved to United States Congress.

1903, Mar. 2. Coinage established (silver peso—50¢).

Dec. 22. "Friars' Lands" (c. 400,000 acres) purchased from the Catholic Church for $7,237,000.

1904, Feb. 1. Gen. Luke E. Wright inaugurated as governor.

1906, Apr. 2. Henry Clay Ide inaugurated as governor.

Sept. 20. James F. Smith, governor.

1907, Jan. 9. Election law, providing for 80 delegates to the Assembly.

Mar. 12. Formation of the **Partido Union Nacionalista,** advocating independence.

July 30. Election for the first Assembly. 105,000 voters elected 32 Nationalists, 20 Independents, and 16 Progressives. The Assembly met Oct. 16 and became the lower house of the legislature, of which the Philippine Commission formed the upper house.

1908, May 12. The number of members of the commission was increased to nine, of whom four were to be Filipinos.

1909, Oct. 6. The **Payne-Aldrich Tariff,** allowing free importation into the United States of limited quantities of

Philippine products (sugar and tobacco) and of unlimited quantities of hemp.

Nov. 11. **W. Cameron Forbes** appointed governor-general.

1913, June 1. English became the official language, but the use of Spanish was to be permitted until 1920.

Aug. 21. **Francis B. Harrison,** governor-general.

Oct. 3. The **Underwood Tariff** removed restrictions on the free import of Philippine sugar and tobacco into the United States.

(*Cont. p.* 1132.)

5. HAWAII

1778, Jan. 18. The islands were discovered by Capt. **James Cook** and were named the *Sandwich Islands.* Cook was killed there by the natives (Feb. 14, 1779).

1810. **Kamehameha I** (1795–1819) conquered most of the islands and established his dynasty.

1820. Arrival of the **first American missionaries.**

1826. Treaty of friendship and commerce with the United States. Treaties were signed with Great Britain (1836) and with France (1839).

1842, Dec. 19. The United States recognized the independence of the islands.

1843, Nov. 28. In a convention, England and France recognized the independence of the islands and promised not to annex them. A representative form of government had been introduced in 1840 and the king appointed a number of Americans to administrative and judicial office.

1851. In reply to French demands on the island government, the American government warned France and took the stand that annexation by a European power would not be permitted.

1875, Jan. 30. **Reciprocity Treaty** with the United States. Hawaiian sugar admitted to the United States free of duty. The United States was given the use of Pearl Harbor for a coaling and naval station in 1887 when the treaty was extended.

1891, Jan. 20. **Lydia Liliuokalani** became queen. Growing constitutional unrest.

1893, Jan. 14. *Coup d'état* and new constitution promulgated by the queen. American residents organized a **committee of safety.** American marines landed (Jan. 16) to protect life and property.

Jan. 17. **Provisional government** organized. Monarchy declared abolished.

Feb. 1. The American minister proclaimed a protectorate.

Feb. 14. **Treaty of annexation** by the United States signed. This was withdrawn by President Cleveland (Mar. 9), and a special commissioner sent out. The commissioner, **James H. Blount,** reported the revolution engineered by Americans supported by the American minister. Efforts of American government to restore the queen were wrecked by the opposition of the provisional government.

1894, July 4. **Republic of Hawaii** proclaimed (**Sanford B. Dole,** president). This was recognized by the United States (Aug. 7).

Dec. 8. A royalist revolt broke out, but was soon suppressed.

1897, June 16. **Treaty of annexation** signed with the United States. This was ratified by the Hawaiian Senate (Sept. 9) and by the United States Congress July 7, 1898 (**Newlands' Joint Resolution**).

1898, Aug. 12. **Formal transfer of the islands to the United States.**

1900, April 30. The islands organized as a territory of the United States. Unlike Puerto Rico, Hawaii pays its tariff duties, internal revenue collections, and income tax to the federal treasury.

An acute labor shortage existed on the islands, resulting in considerable **immigration of Japanese.** The government encouraged immigration of Spanish, Portuguese, and Filipino laborers and excluded Japanese, Chinese, and Koreans. In 1910 the total population was 192,000, of whom only 26,000 were Hawaiians and 12,500 part-Hawaiians; on the other hand there were 80,000 Japanese and 21,500 Chinese.

1919. **Pearl Harbor** fortifications and dry-dock completed.

In recent years the population has increased rapidly (426,654 in 1940) and the sugar and pineapple industry has been further expanded. The islands have also become a center of tourist traffic and an important station on the Trans-Pacific air route. (*Cont. p.* 1134.)

6. SAMOA

1722. The Samoan Islands were discovered by the Dutchman, **Jacob Roggeveen.** American and European activity dates from about 1790.

1872, Apr. 9. A number of chiefs petitioned for annexation by the United States.

1878, Jan. 16. Treaty of friendship and commerce with the United States, which secured the harbor of **Pago Pago** as a coaling and naval station.

1879, Jan. 24. Similar treaty with Germany, which secured the harbor of **Apia.**

1880, Mar. 24. Agreement between United States, England, and Germany, recognizing **Malietoa Talavou** as king and providing for an executive council consisting of one American, one German, and one Englishman.

Nov. 8. Death of the king. Civil war between rival factions. The three powers recognized (July 12, 1881) **Malietoa Laupepa** as king.

1887, June 25-July 26. Conference on the affairs of Samoa at Washington, the United States, England, and Germany taking part.

July 24. Demanding satisfaction of claims, the Germans landed troops and proclaimed **Tamasese** king. Malietoa surrendered and was exiled.

1888, Sept. 4. Native revolt under **Mataafa** directed against the Germans.

1889, Mar. 15-16. Terrific hurricane in Apia Harbor. Three American and three German warships driven ashore.

Apr. 29-June 14. **New Samoan Conference** of the three powers at Berlin.

June 14. **The Samoa Act.** The three powers recognized **Malietoa** as king and made provision for joint supervision of the administration.

1898, Aug. 22. **Death of Malietoa.** Mataafa and other chiefs landed by a German warship. Mataafa was elected king (Nov. 12), but was rejected by the American and British consuls. Civil war broke out between Mataafa and **Malietoa Tana,** son of the dead king. Mataafa was successful (Jan. 1899) and a provisional government was set up.

1899, Mar. 15. British and American warships bombarded Apia as a protest against Mataafa and his German supporters.

May 14. Arrival of a joint American-British-German commission. This declared the monarchy abolished.

Nov. 14. **Anglo-German Treaty,** by which England relinquished rights to Savaii and Upolu in favor of Germany, and rights to Tutuila and other islands in favor of the United States. The three powers signed this treaty Dec. 2 and it was ratified Feb. 16, 1900.

The American islands, of which **Tutuila** was the most important, were put under the control of the navy department. Pago Pago became a naval base.

WESTERN FRONT

Scale of Miles

0 10 20 30 40 50

Farthest German Advance Sept. 8, 1914
Line of July 1, 1916
German Offensive March to July 1918
Line of Nov. 11, 1918

VI. Two World Wars and the Inter-War Period

A. THE FIRST WORLD WAR

1. THE WESTERN FRONT, 1914

German strategy was based on the **Schlieffen Plan** (drafted in 1905), which provided for the concentration of the main German forces on the French front, the passage through Belgium, and a huge wheeling movement to encircle Paris. This plan required a massing of forces on the German right flank, but even before the outbreak of war the German chief of the general staff, **Gen. Helmuth von Moltke** (1906–Sept. 14, 1914; d. June 18, 1916; nephew of the great Moltke of Bismarckian times), had transferred some divisions from the right to the left (Lorraine) wing, in order to block an invasion of South Germany. The German forces on the eastern (Russian) frontier were relatively few in number and were intended merely to delay the invaders until a decisive victory could be won in the west.

The **French plan of campaign** (Plan 17) had been drawn up in 1913 by **Gen. Joseph Joffre** (chief of the general staff, July 28, 1911–Dec. 12, 1916), under the influence of the teaching of **Gen. Ferdinand Foch**. The plan ignored the danger of a great German advance through Belgium and depended entirely on a vigorous French offensive on the right wing and center. The French reckoned on a Russian advance in the east with about 800,000 men on the 18th day of mobilization. England was expected to contribute about 150,000.

The Germans concentrated about 1,500,-000 men, organized in seven armies as follows: 1st (**Von Kluck**) and 2d (**Von Bülow**) on the Belgian front; 3d (**Von Hausen**) opposite Liège; 4th (**Prince Albrecht of Württemberg**); 5th (**Crown Prince Wilhelm**) at Luxemburg; 6th (**Prince Rupprecht of Bavaria**) at Metz; 7th (**Von Heeringen**) at Strassburg.

Aug. 4. In the night the **Germans crossed the frontier** of Belgium. Armies I and II were obliged to pass through a narrow strip between Holland and the Ardennes, heavily guarded by the fortifications of Liège. Aug. 5–6 the Germans (**Gen. von Emmich**) by a night attack got past the forts, which were then reduced by

heavy artillery (Aug. 6–17). The Belgians fell back on Brussels and then Antwerp, destroying the bridges of the Meuse.

Aug. 20. **Von Kluck entered Brussels,** after driving the Belgians back in the **battle of Tirlement** (Aug. 18–19).

In the meanwhile the **French offensive** (five armies) had been developing in the region between Mézières and Belfort, Joffre hoping for a break-through on either side of Metz.

Aug. 14-25. Battle of the Frontiers (Lorraine). The French invasion was checked almost at once and the French armies driven out of Lorraine with heavy losses. The 3d and 4th armies were also driven back from Luxemburg, the western wing (**Gen. Lanrezac**) being defeated in the **battle of Charleroi** (Aug. 21–24) and forced to fall back for 12 days. **Namur** taken by the Germans (Aug. 25); **Longwy** (Aug. 27); **Montmédy** (Aug. 30); **Soissons** (Sept. 1); **Laon** (Sept. 2); **Rheims** (Sept. 3); **Maubeuge** (Sept. 7).

The **British expeditionary force** (four infantry and one cavalry divisions, about 90,000 men), under the command of **Sir John French** (till Dec. 1915), had begun to land at Le Havre (Aug. 7–17) and to concentrate on the left of the French 5th army, at **Le Cateau** and **Maubeuge**.

Aug. 23. Battle of Mons. First contact between Germans and English. The latter were obliged to fall back with the French 5th army. Further delaying action fought by the British (**Gen. Smith-Dorrien**) at Le Cateau (Aug. 26).

Spectacular German advance, as the French and British fell back to the **Marne River.** The French government moved to Bordeaux (Sept. 3–Dec. 1914). Joffre hastily formed a 6th army (**Gen. Maunoury**) on his left, to outflank the German 5th army. In the meanwhile Moltke, believing a decision had already been reached by Aug. 25, detailed six corps from the 2d and 3d armies to serve on the Russian front. Two of these were actually dispatched, later being sadly needed on the German flank, and arriving too late in the east to be of much use.

Aug. 30. Von Kluck gave up his advance to the west of Paris, in order to keep contact with Von Bülow's 2d army. By Sept. 4 Von Kluck realized the danger threatening him from Maunoury's 6th French army before Paris. On the same day Moltke ordered Kluck and Bülow to turn southwest to meet this danger. In the course of the operation a gap was allowed to open between the 1st and 2d German armies.

Sept. 5-12. BATTLE OF THE MARNE. Maunoury and Kluck tried to outflank each other (**battle of the Ourcq**). Strongly urged by **Gen. Gallieni** (military governor of Paris), Joffre decided to order a general counter-offensive (Sept. 5) in the hope of breaking in on the right and rear of Bülow's 2d army. Sept. 6–9, no decision. Kluck's efforts to outflank Maunoury increased the gap between the German 1st and 2d armies, but the British and French failed to take full advantage of this. Sept. 9, Von Kluck and Von Bülow began to fall back (oral instructions of **Col. Hentsch**, from German headquarters in Luxemburg). The whole German line began to withdraw west of Verdun. Cautious advance of the British and French.

Sept. 13. The Germans stood, north of the Aisne River. All efforts of the Allies to dislodge them ended in failure (**battles of the Aisne**, Sept. 15–18; of **Picardy**, Sept. 22–26; and of **Artois**, Sept. 27–Oct. 10).

Sept. 22-25. Repeated German assaults at Verdun. **St. Mihiel**, on the left bank of the Meuse, taken.

Oct. 1-9. Operations at Antwerp. Germans (**Von Beseler**) brought up siege guns and finally obliged the Belgian army, with small British supporting force, to evacuate.

Oct. 10-Nov. 10. THE RACE FOR THE SEA. Germans took **Ghent** (Oct. 11); **Bruges** (Oct. 14) and **Ostend** (Oct. 15). From this time until Dec. 22 there was almost uninterrupted fighting in Artois. The Germans failed to push through to the Channel ports, the Belgians having flooded the district of the Yser (**battle of the Yser**, Oct. 18-Nov. 30). Farther south the Germans took Lille (Oct. 12) and massed great numbers of troops for an attack southeast of Ypres. But they did not succeed either in taking the town or wiping out the salient at that point (**first battle of Ypres**, Oct. 30–Nov. 24).

Dec. 14-24. The Allies launched a general attack along the whole front from Nieuport to Verdun, but failed to make any substantial gains. Heavy fighting continued throughout the winter in Champagne (**first battle of Champagne**, Dec. 20, 1914–Mar. 17, 1915).

By the end of 1914 the line on the western front had become fairly well fixed and the war had become a war of position, confined largely to trench warfare. All but a tip of Belgium was in the hands of the Germans. The Belgian government was established at Le Havre, while the occupied area was governed successively by **Gen. von der Goltz** (to Nov. 1914), **Gen. von Bissing** (to Apr. 1917), and **Gen. von Falkenhausen** (to the end of the war). The Germans also retained about one-tenth of the territory of France (21,000 sq. kilometers), including many of the most valuable coal and iron mines and several important industrial areas. The line, which in the course of the next three years did not vary by more than 10 miles, left to the Allies **Verdun, Rheims**, and **Soissons** in Champagne and thence turned northward between **Noyon** (Ger.), **Montdidier** (Fr.), **Peronne** (Ger.), **Albert** (Fr.), **Bapaume** (Ger.), **Arras** (Fr.), **Lens, La Bassée** (Ger.), **Armentières, Ypres** (Brit.), **Passchendaele, Dixmude** (Ger.), **Nieuport** (Brit.), **Ostend** (Ger.).

2. THE EASTERN FRONT, 1914

The Russian plan of campaign (**Grand Duke Nicholas Nicolaievich** commander in chief, Aug. 3, 1914–Sept. 5, 1915) was concerned primarily with the war with Austria; large forces were therefore concentrated on the Galician frontier. The Austrians (**Archduke Frederick** commander in chief, **Gen. Conrad von Hötzendorff**, chief of staff, 1912–1917, commander in chief, 1917–July 16, 1918) on their part had drawn plans which depended on German support through an advance on the **Narev River**. Pressure elsewhere prevented the Germans from keeping this engagement, but the Austrians, unable to abandon eastern Galicia, with its valuable oil-wells, decided to attempt an advance from Lemberg toward Lublin and Cholm, to cut the railways to Warsaw.

Aug. 26-Sept. 2. The Austrians, under **Gen. von Auffenberg**, won a great victory over the Russians (**battle of Zamosc-Komarov**), but at once the Russians (**Gen. Brusilov**) with much larger forces began to drive back the Austrian right wing.

THE EASTERN FRONT

☆ Forts
——— January 1918
- - - Farthest advance of the Russians

Sept. 3. The Russians took Lemberg.
The Austrian left wing was forced
to fall back. The **battle of Lemberg** (Sept.
8–12) obliged the Austrians to abandon
eastern Galicia. The Russians took **Czernowitz** in the Bukovina (Sept. 15) and **Jaroslav** (Sept. 21). At the same time the
Russians invested the key fortress of
Przemysl (Sept. 16) and launched an attack
upon the passes of the Carpathians leading
into northern Hungary (Sept. 24).

On the **Serbian front** the Austrians were
able to concentrate fewer forces than
originally intended. They bombarded **Belgrade** (July 29), and crossed the **Drina
River** (Aug. 13) to begin the first invasion
of Serbia. The Serbs, however, repulsed
them (**battle of the Tser and the Jadar,**
Aug. 17–21) and obliged the Austrians to
withdraw from Serbian territory. In Sept.
the Serbs crossed the Save River and invaded **Syrmia,** while the Austrians again
crossed the Drina (Sept. 8). The Serbs took
Zemlin (Zemun) Sept. 10, but were unable
to continue the advance into Austrian territory. The two opponents fought the long-
drawn **battle of the Drina** (Sept. 8–17),
which was followed by a long series of desultory engagements on the heights along
the river. The Serbs were ultimately forced
to retreat, and the Austrians were able to
take Belgrade (Dec. 2).

The decisive battles on the eastern front
in 1914, however, were fought and won not
by the Austrians, but by the Germans.
In response to French appeals for action
against the Germans, the Russians formed
two armies to invade **East Prussia** from the
east and from the south. The 1st army
(Gen. **Rennenkampf**) began the advance
from between Kovno and Grodno Aug. 17
and defeated the German 8th army (Gen.
von Prittwitz) in the **battle of Gumbinnen**
(Aug. 19–20). The German commander,
having completely lost his nerve, decided
on a retreat to the Vistula, despite the objections of his chief of staff, Colonel (later
General) **Max Hoffmann,** one of the few
geniuses of the war. On learning of Prittwitz' decision, the German high command
at once dismissed him and decided to
send to the eastern front General **Erich
von Ludendorff,** who had distinguished
himself in the taking of Liège and who
was recognized as an outstanding staff
officer. Ludendorff, a junior officer, was to
serve as chief of staff to Gen. (later Field-
Marshal) **Paul von Beneckendorff und von
Hindenburg,** a retired officer of no great
distinction, who was intended to shield
Ludendorff with his seniority.

Aug. 23. Hindenburg and Ludendorff
arrived at Marienburg, only to find that their arrangements had been
anticipated by Hoffmann. The essence of
this joint plan was to withdraw the German
army from in front of Rennenkampf and to
concentrate it against the second Russian
army (Gen. **Samsonov**), which was beginning the invasion of East Prussia from the
southeast. Throughout these and later
operations the Germans were aided greatly
by the interception of unciphered Russian
messages, and by the unreadiness of Rennenkampf to do much to relieve Samsonov,
apparently because of a long-standing personal feud between the two men.

**Aug. 26-30. BATTLE OF TANNEN-
BERG.** The Germans completely
defeated Samsonov's army on both wings.
Brilliant work of **Gen. von François,** who
managed to surround the Russian forces
from the west. The Germans took over
100,000 prisoners. Samsonov, in desperation, shot himself on the field.

The Germans then turned on Rennenkampf's army, which was obliged to fall back
when attacked on the left flank.

**Sept. 6-15. BATTLE OF THE MA-
SURIAN LAKES.** The Germans
(Gen., later Field Marshal, **von Mackensen**)
drove the enemy into the difficult lake
country and succeeded in capturing 125,000
men. Completely demoralized, the Russians began to fall back, and the Germans
advanced to the lower Niemen River and
occupied the *gouvernement* of Suvalki. Early
in Oct. most of the German troops on this
front had to be withdrawn for operations
farther south, so that the Russians were
able to invade **East Prussia** for the second
time.

In the meanwhile it was necessary for the
Germans to do something to relieve the
Austrians. Hindenburg, who now enjoyed
an immense if somewhat fictitious prestige,
was made **commander in chief of the German armies in the East** (Sept. 18). The
plan, as worked out by the German and
Austrian staffs, was for a great combined
attack on Poland. The Austrians took the
offensive in Galicia (Oct. 4), relieved
Przemysl and forced the Russians to withdraw from the Carpathians. In the meantime the Germans (**von Mackensen**), advancing on the Austrian left, pushed on
toward the Vistula.

**Oct. 9-20. BATTLES OF WARSAW
AND IVANGOROD.** Macken-
sen advanced as far as **Warsaw** (Oct. 12),
but was obliged to fall back when the
Russians counter-attacked against the
Austrians farther east. The Austrians retreated to **Cracow,** while the Russians commenced the second investment of **Przemysl**
(Nov. 10) and renewed the invasion of

northern Hungary (Nov. 15). Farther west, heavy fighting about Cracow (**battle of Cracow,** Nov. 16–Dec. 2).

In order to relieve the pressure in the south, Hindenburg and Ludendorff planned a great offensive, which, it was hoped, would knock the Russians out before the onset of winter. They appealed to the high command for the transfer of large forces from the west, but the demand was rejected by Gen. **Erich von Falkenhayn** (minister for war, 1906–Jan. 21, 1915; chief of the general staff, Sept. 14, 1914–Aug. 29, 1916), whose attention at this time was concentrated on the drive for the Channel ports. Hindenburg was therefore obliged to get along with the forces at his disposal. He sent Von Mackensen and the 9th army to the north toward Thorn, whence a German advance was begun to the southeast (Nov. 11).

Nov. 16-25. THE BATTLES OF LODZ AND LOWICZ. A confused and bloody conflict in mud and snow. For a time the Russians, having brought up reinforcements, threatened to surround the Germans, but in early Dec. the Germans were themselves strengthened by the arrival of new divisions from the west front. **Lodz** fell to the Germans (Dec. 6).

On the **Galician front** the Austrians attempted an offensive to coincide with the German advance.

Dec. 5-17. BATTLE OF LIMANOVA. The Austrians were successful, but failed to break the Russian position before Cracow. Throughout the winter the Russians were within 30 miles of the city.

In **Serbia** the Austrians met with even less success. Having taken Belgrade (Dec. 2), they were soon confronted with a formidable Serbian force on the **Morava River.**

Dec. 3-6. Battle of Kolubara. The Austrians were defeated and forced to recross the frontier. **Belgrade** retaken by the Serbs (Dec. 15). End of the second invasion of Serbia.

3. THE WAR AT SEA, 1914

The **British Grand Fleet** (Adm. **Sir John Jellicoe,** commander, Aug. 4, 1914–Nov. 29, 1916) consisted of 20 dreadnoughts and a corresponding number of battle cruisers, cruisers, destroyers, and other craft. The fleet was based on **Scapa Flow, Cromarty,** and **Rosyth,** with **Harwich** as the base for destroyers and submarines. A second fleet, consisting largely of pre-dreadnought types, guarded the Channel. The **Germans** had a **High Seas Fleet** of 13 dreadnoughts, based on the North Sea ports. On both sides an early engagement was looked for, but the Germans remained in port, despite the efforts of Adm. **von Tirpitz** to bring about a more active policy. Nothing was done by the Germans to prevent the landing of the British expeditionary force in France.

1914, Aug. 28. British cruisers, supported by battle cruisers (Adm. **Sir David Beatty**) raided **Heligoland Bight.** The German cruisers came out and drove the English off, but Beatty, coming up with the battle cruisers, was able to sink three ships of the enemy.

The Germans now devoted their attention to mine-laying and **submarine work.** The *U.*9 sank the three old cruisers *Hogue, Cressy,* and *Aboukir* (Sept. 22); the *Hawke* sunk by submarine (Oct. 15). After an attempted German submarine raid on **Scapa Flow** (Oct. 18) the Grand Fleet was withdrawn from that base and concentrated, for a time, on the west coast of Scotland.

Oct. 27 a German mine sank the superdreadnought *Audacious* off the north coast of Ireland.

Apart from these and other occasional sinkings, the war in the North Sea was restricted to raids, chiefly by German battle cruisers (Adm. **von Hipper**), on the English coast (Nov. 3 — **raid on Yarmouth;** Dec. 16 — **bombardment of Scarborough and Hartlepool**).

1915, Jan. 24. Naval action off the **Dogger Bank** between the British and German battle-cruiser squadrons. Hipper, though outnumbered, did much damage to the British flagship and ultimately got away, losing only his poorest ship, the *Blücher.*

When the war broke out, there were eight German cruisers on foreign stations, mostly on the China station. When **Japan** declared war (see p. 893), the commander, Adm. **Count von Spee,** left for the South American coast with the cruisers *Scharnhorst, Gneisenau,* and *Nürnberg.* He bombarded **Papeete** (Sept. 22) and destroyed the British cable station at **Fanning Island.** At **Easter Island** (Oct. 12–18) Von Spee was joined by the cruisers *Dresden* (from the West Indies) and *Leipzig* (from the California coast). Together they proceeded to the Chilian coast.

In the meanwhile Adm. **Cradock,** with three old ships, had been ordered to hunt down Spee.

1914, Nov. 1. NAVAL ACTION OFF CORONEL. Von Spee destroyed two of Cradock's ships (the *Monmouth* and the *Good Hope;* the *Glasgow* escaped).

To meet the danger from the German squadron, all available Allied ships were assembled off the southeast coast of South America. Three battle cruisers were hastily dispatched from the Grand Fleet to the South Atlantic.

Dec. 8. BATTLE OF THE FALKLAND ISLANDS. Von Spee made the fatal decision to stop to attack the **Falklands** on his way homeward. The British squadron (**Adm. Sturdee**), with the battle cruisers and some lighter cruisers, came down upon the Germans unexpectedly and sank four of five of their ships (*Scharnhorst,*

Gneisenau, Leipzig, and *Nürnberg*). **Only** the *Dresden* escaped. Heroic death of Adm. von Spee, his two sons, and 1800 men.

Several of the German cruisers still abroad caused great damage to Allied shipping. The *Emden* (Capt. **von Müller**) left the China station for the Indian Ocean. Between Sept. 10 and Nov. 9 she bombarded **Madras** (Sept. 22) and captured several ships before she was sunk at Cocos Island. The German cruiser *Königsberg* was also very destructive until located and shut into the mouth of the Rufigi River. The *Dresden,* having escaped from the Falklands, engaged in commerce-destroying until cornered at Juan Fernandez, where she was blown up by her own crew (Mar. 14, 1915).

4. THE WAR IN THE COLONIES, 1914-1918

Most of the German colonies were seized by the British and French during the first months of the war.

1914, Aug. 26. Togoland defense force capitulated to an Anglo-French force. The colony was divided between the English and the French in agreements of Aug. 26, 1914, and Dec. 27, 1916.

1914, Aug. 30. A New Zealand expeditionary force occupied **Samoa.**

1914, Sept. 11. An Australian force landed on the **Bismarck Archipelago.** German forces in **New Guinea** surrendered to Australians (Sept. 21).

1914, Sept. 7. A British force from Nigeria invaded the **Cameroons** and took **Duala** (Sept. 27). The French also invaded the colony from the south and east. The Germans were obliged to fall back, and ultimately crossed into Spanish territory (Feb. 9, 1916).

1914, Sept. 19. An English force landed at **Lüderitz Bay**, German Southwest Africa. The Union of South Africa decided to prosecute the war in the German colony, and **Gen. Botha** crossed the Orange River, taking **Swakopmund** (Jan. 14, 1915). He defeated the German forces at **Riet** and **Treckkopje** (Apr. 26, 1915), took **Windhoek** (May 12, 1915) and finally forced the 3500 German and colonial troops to capitulate at Otawi (July 9, 1915).

1914, Aug. 8. The British opened hostilities in German East Africa by bombarding the coast towns of **Bagamoyo** and **Dar-es-Salaam.** Indian forces were then brought to East Africa for the campaign. But the German commander (Gen. von

Lettow-Vorbeck) defeated a greatly superior landing force in the **battle of Tanga** (Nov. 2–5, 1914). There was a certain amount of skirmishing throughout the winter of 1914–1915, but the campaign remained desultory until in Nov. 1915 the British secured naval control of **Lake Tanganyika,** and landing forces took **Tanga** (July 7, 1916) and **Bagamoyo** (Aug. 15, 1916). **Gen. Smuts,** with a force of Afrikanders and Portuguese, now began to push the operations. **Dar-es-Salaam** fell (Sept. 4); **Lindi** (Sept. 16) and **Tabora** (Sept. 19). Lettow-Vorbeck and his troops were obliged to fall back to the southeast corner of the colony. The campaign was resumed in 1917, when the Germans defeated their enemies at **Mahiwa** (Oct. 15–18, 1917) and began the invasion of Portuguese East Africa. Lettow-Vorbeck advanced almost to the mouth of the Zambezi, but then fell back to **Lake Nyasa.** Nov. 2, 1918, he began the invasion of **Rhodesia.** The armistice went into effect Nov. 14, 1918, at which time the Germans were still in the field.

1914, Aug. 23. Japan declared war on Germany and began to land forces in Shantung for an attack on the German position at **Tsingtao.** The Japanese were joined by a British detachment. The bombardment of **Tsingtao** was begun in Oct., and was accompanied by an attack from the land side. An assault on Oct. 31 failed, but Nov. 7 the fortress was obliged to capitulate. During this same period the Japanese naval forces occupied a number of the German islands (**Marshall Islands, Mariannes, Palaw, Carolines**).

5. THE OTTOMAN FRONT, 1914-1915

At the outbreak of the war, the policy of **Turkey** was determined primarily by **Enver Pasha**, the minister of war, whose pro-German inclinations were well known. At the height of the July crisis (July 27) the Turks themselves proposed to the Germans the conclusion of an alliance directed against Russia. The Germans accepted, and the treaty, which was known only to a few of the Turkish ministers, was concluded Aug. 1. The Turks were to enter the war as soon as hostilities were opened by Russia against Germany or Austria (which adhered to the pact). Actually the Turkish government, with the assent of its allies, remained neutral for some time, in order to complete the necessary military preparations.

1914, Aug. 11. The powerful German cruisers *Goeben* and *Breslau* arrived at the Dardanelles, and were allowed to pass through. These two cruisers, stationed in the Mediterranean, had bombarded **Bona** and **Philippeville** in French Africa (Aug. 3) and had then gone on to Messina. The British Adm. **Milne** watched for them at the northern end of the Straits of Messina, but the German Adm. **Souchon** left by the southern end (Aug. 6). A small British squadron (Adm. **Troubridge**) followed the German ships, but did not dare attack. Milne acted too leisurely to prevent the ships from reaching the Dardanelles. Their presence at Constantinople not only served to reveal the trend of Turkish policy, but also helped the Germans to establish a firm influence over that policy. The ships were officially bought by the Turkish government to take the place of two battleships that were building in England and had been taken over by the British government.

Aug.-Oct. Many efforts were made by the English government to secure the neutrality of Turkey, by offering a guaranty of independence and integrity and by promising concessions in the matter of the capitulations. The Turkish government, in the interval, declared the **capitulations abolished** (Sept. 7), but probably never seriously considered either neutrality or alliance with the western powers. Longdrawn negotiations for an alliance with Russia were probably meant only as a blind.

Oct. 29. Turkish warships, including the two German cruisers, suddenly bombarded **Odessa**, **Sevastopol**, and **Theodosia** on the Russian Black Sea coast. England and her allies at once severed relations and sent an ultimatum. **Russia** declared war (Nov. 2) and **England and France** followed (Nov. 5), England on the same day proclaiming the **annexation of the island of Cyprus** (occupied since 1878, see p. 736).

Nov. 14. The sultan, as khalif, proclaimed a **Holy War** (*Jihad*) against all those making war on Turkey or her allies. In the sequel this move proved to be of slight importance.

Dec. 18. The British proclaimed a **protectorate over Egypt** (occupied since 1882, see p. 832), and hastily began to concentrate troops for the defense of this strategic area. (Dec. 1 — first units of the Australian and New Zealand expeditionary force [**Anzac**] arrived in Egypt.)

Gen. Liman von Sanders, head of the German military mission in Constantinople, urged the Turks to attempt the invasion of the Ukraine from Odessa, evidently in the hope of bringing Rumania in on the side of the central powers. But **Enver Pasha** from the outset insisted on a campaign against the Russians in the **Caucasus region**.

Dec. 17. The Turks began their offensive against **Kars**.

Dec. 29-1915, Jan. 2. Battle of Sarikamish. The Turks advanced and took **Tabriz** (Jan. 8), but this important town was retaken by the Russians (Jan. 30) and the whole Turkish offensive gradually ran out. The Caucasus front remained quiet until Apr. (1915) when the Turks began the deportation and **massacre of the Armenians**, whom they accused of aiding the Russian invader. The Armenians rose in revolt at **Van** (Apr. 20) and held the fortress until relieved by a Russian force (May 19). After months of desultory fighting the Russians were finally obliged to abandon Van (Aug. 3, 1915), which was then reoccupied by the Turks (Aug. 5).

In the interval the Turks had initiated **operations against Egypt** also. A force, after making its way across the Sinai Desert, attacked the **Suez Canal** (Feb. 3-4, 1915), but was easily repulsed. Nevertheless, the constant threat of another such attack obliged the British to keep large numbers of troops in Egypt throughout the war.

The entry of Turkey into the conflict had extended tremendously the area of possible operations. In view of the deadlock that had been reached on the west front before the end of 1914, the idea was soon advanced in England (notably by **Winston Churchill**, supported by Lloyd George and by **Lord Kitchener**) that it would be wiser to allow the French armies to hold the western front, while England should devote her newly raised armies to an attempt to attack the enemy in some more vulnerable spot, preferably in the Near East, where a resounding success might serve to bring in the Balkan states on the side of the Entente. This idea was entertained sympathetically by a few French generals (**Gallieni, Franchet-d'Esperey),** but on the whole met with the most vigorous opposition from **Sir John French, Joffre** and the other commanders in France, who stuck to the idea that a decision could be reached only in the main theater of war, and that all available forces must be massed there for another attempt at a breakthrough.

The exponents of an eastern campaign (**Easterners**) continued to raise the issue and advanced three different courses of action: (1) It was proposed to land a force in the **Gulf of Alexandretta,** which might cut the railway between Syria and Anatolia, prevent a Turkish campaign against Egypt, and encourage the Arabs to break with the Constantinople government. (2) It was proposed to send a force to **Saloniki,** a force strong enough to bring Greece and Bulgaria into the war on the Allied side; this force to march either up the Vardar to relieve the Serbs, or else to Constantinople and thence by way of the Danube against Austria. (3) It was proposed to make an attack on the **Dardanelles,** land a force and thus capture the Turkish capital. All these schemes, however, had to be shelved because of the insistence of the generals that the newly raised forces be sent to France.

1915, Jan. 2. The Russians appealed to England for a diversion to relieve the pressure of the Turks in the Caucasus. The War Council, after much debate, finally (Jan. 13) decided on a naval action against the Dardanelles, with Constantinople as the objective. Later (Feb. 16) it was decided to send one division of troops, which was to be reinforced from Egypt.

The Greek government (**Eleutherios Venizelos,** prime minister since 1910) offered to aid the Allied operations with a number of divisions (Mar. 5), but this policy was rejected by **King Constantine,** whereupon **Venizelos resigned** (Mar. 6). It appears that the Russian government was also opposed to the participation of Greece, because of suspicion of Greek designs on Constantinople.

Mar. 4. The Russian foreign minister, **Sazonov,** handed to the French and British representatives a note claiming for Russia, in the event of success, **Constantinople** and a strip along the northern side of the Bosporus, Sea of Marmora, and

Dardanelles, as well as **Thrace** to the Enos-Midia line, and the Asiatic side of the Bosporus to the **river Sakaria.** To this England and France agreed, the latter reluctantly, on condition that Constantinople be made a free port and that merchant ships should be free to pass through the Straits. Further English and French claims in Asiatic Turkey were to be defined later (Mar. 12).

Feb. 19. The British began the naval action against the Dardanelles, and occupied the island of **Lemnos** as a base (Feb. 23). The forts were soon silenced and several companies of marines were landed without great difficulty, suggesting that more extensive military operations at this time would have been relatively easy.

Mar. 18. Adm. de Robeck and 18 warships tried to force the Narrows. Four ships struck mines, whereupon Robeck gave up the attempt, probably somewhat prematurely.

The interval of more than a month that followed was used by the Turks (Gen. **Liman von Sanders** put in command) to strengthen the defenses and to concentrate about 100,000 men. The British sent out about 75,000 men, under the command of **Sir Ian Hamilton.**

Apr. 25. LANDING OF THE BRITISH at several places at the tip of the peninsula, while Australian troops made a feint farther north and a French force landed on the Asiatic side. Poor coordination between the different parties; heroic resistance of the Turks, who managed to keep the various landing parties off the heights and prevented their coalescence (distinguished work of **Mustafa Kemal,** later leader of the Turk national revival, see p. 1094).

Several months of futile fighting ensued, during which the troops suffered from heat, lack of water, flies, etc.

May 12. Hostile submarines began to appear off the Straits. British warships *Goliath, Triumph,* and *Majestic* sunk. Allied submarines ultimately penetrated to Constantinople on a raid (Aug. 1), but for the most part the British squadron was withdrawn to **Mudros** excepting when needed for attack.

Aug. 6. LANDING AT SUVLA, after many additional divisions had been sent out from England. The plan was to cut behind the Turkish position and so reach the Narrows. Four days of heavy fighting (**battle of Sari Bair,** Aug. 6–10). Timid and confused leadership on the British side; staunch resistance of the Turks, who succeeded in retaining the heights.

This second failure turned opinion in England against the whole project. Hamilton was replaced by **Sir Charles Munro** and preparations were made for evacuation (Oct. 16).
Dec. 19-20—1916, Jan. 8-9. The British forces were withdrawn from **Galli-** poli without loss, much to the astonishment of the British command. With the failure of the effort at the Dardanelles, the Straits remained closed and Russia was pretty effectively cut off from supplies which her allies might have furnished her.

6. THE WESTERN FRONT, 1915

The operations in France during this year were devoid of broader interest. The commanders on both sides persisted in the belief that a decision was to be won in this area, and consequently devoted as many men and guns as possible to renewed efforts to break through the opponents' line. None of these "offensives" had a notable permanent effect. All were characterized by appalling loss of life.

1915, Jan. 8-Feb. 5. In heavy fighting along the **La Bassée Canal** and in the **Soissons** region the Germans made some slight gains.

Feb. 16-Mar. 30. After terrific bombardments of the German positions in eastern **Champagne,** the French attacked, with but insignificant results.

Mar. 10-13. The British launched a vigorous attack in the vicinity of **Neuve Chapelle** and succeeded in breaking through the German line for a short distance. Inadequate preparation and management deprived them of any permanent gain.

Mar. 30-Apr. 15. Heavy French attacks on the German salient at **St. Mihiel** left the situation much as it was before.

Apr. 22-May 25. SECOND BATTLE OF YPRES. The original Allied plans for a major offensive were more or less frustrated by the **use of gas** (chlorine) by the Germans (Apr. 22). Though the French had advance information of what was coming, they had made no preparation for it. The troops fled, leaving Ypres exposed. The Germans gained some ground at first, but were apparently themselves skeptical of the effect of the new weapon and unprepared to take full advantage of the situation. In the end the chief significance of the German offensive lay in the fact that it prevented the full participation of the British in the offensive planned by Joffre for May.

May 9-June 18. SECOND BATTLE OF ARTOIS. After an unprecedented bombardment, the French (**Gen. Pétain**) succeeded in breaking through on a six-mile front north of Arras and facing Douai. The advance was about three miles in depth, but was secured at a loss of about 400,000 men.

The western front was unusually quiet during most of the summer, the Allies utilizing this period for preparation of a "great offensive" for the autumn.

Sept. 22-Nov. 6. SECOND BATTLE OF CHAMPAGNE. This was the key operation in Joffre's great offensive. The French attacked on a front between Rheims and the Argonne, making use of an immense concentration of artillery as well as man-power. The Germans, however, held their own on the heights between Rheims and Ste. Menehould, so that after many weeks of desperate fighting Joffre had little to show.

Sept. 25-Oct. 15. THIRD BATTLE OF ARTOIS. This was merely the British contribution to the great offensive in Champagne. The British here first used gas. Greatly outnumbering the Germans, they succeeded in driving the enemy back toward Lens and Loos (**battle of Loos,** Sept. 25-Oct. 8), but then failed to realize on this advantage by hesitation in the use of the reserve. In this way the operation remained without great importance.

The failure of the great offensive of French and British, which Joffre had hoped would work like a pair of pincers to force the German withdrawal from northern France, left the situation in the west substantially what it was a year previous.

7. THE EASTERN FRONT, 1915

During the winter months the fighting on the Russian front was inconclusive.
1915, Feb. 4-22. Winter battle in Masuria. The Germans advanced and took **Memel** (Feb. 17). Further German offensive in East Prussia (**battle of Augustovo Forest,** Mar. 9-10). But in this area the Russians offered stout resistance. They

won a victory between Kovno and Grodno (**battle of Przasnysz**, Feb. 22–27) and retook Memel (Mar. 18), though the Germans succeeded in driving them out of this valuable seaport a few days later (Mar. 21).

The idea of Hindenburg and Ludendorff was to concentrate more and more troops in the east, in the hope of enveloping the Russians by an advance from East Prussia to the southeast. But Falkenhayn insisted on the attempt to reach a decision in the west. This difference of view led to acute tension and a threat by Hindenburg to resign. Ultimately the emperor decided that the newly formed 10th army should be sent to the east, but Falkenhayn managed to have it sent to the Galician front, partly in order to relieve the Austrians, partly to act as the southern shear in a movement to force the further withdrawal of the Russians from Poland.

Mar. 22. The Russians had at last taken **Przemysl** and were in a position to break through the Carpathian passes into northern Hungary.

Apr. 2–25. Austrians, with the aid of a **German South Army** (Gen. von Linsingen) succeeded in driving the Russians back from the Carpathians. An 11th army, under Gen. **von Mackensen**, was then formed to co-operate with the Austrian forces, from the region southeast of Cracow, in the direction of Przemysl.

May 2. Beginning of the great **Austro-German offensive in Galicia.** The Russians, already suffering severely from lack of rifles, artillery, ammunition, and clothing, gave way at once (**battle of Gorlice-Tarnow**). The Austro-German armies crossed the Dunajec (May 3–5) and took Jaroslav (May 14). By May 15 they had reached the San and forced a crossing (**battle of the San**, May 15–23). Przemysl was retaken (June 3) and gradually the whole Russian south front collapsed. **Lemberg** fell (June 22) and farther east **Zuravno** (June 5) and **Stanislav** (June 8). The Dniester River was crossed June 23–27. By the end of June the Austro-German forces had advanced almost 100 miles, had liberated **Galicia** and **Bukovina,** and had taken huge numbers of prisoners. The Russian armies on this front were completely demoralized.

The failure of the British to achieve a success at the Dardanelles enabled the Germans to postpone a projected campaign in Serbia designed to make direct contact with the Turks, and to exploit further their great successes against Russia. The offensive in Galicia had been accompanied by a smaller **advance in Courland** (Apr. 26–) and had resulted in the taking of **Libau** (May 7). It was now planned to organize a much greater movement in northern Poland as part of a pincers movement to trap the Russians.

July 1. Beginning of the **second great offensive.** The Austrians (Archduke Joseph Ferdinand) took **Lublin** and **Cholm** (July 31) and stormed **Ivangorod** (Aug. 4). In Courland the **Germans** took **Windau** (July 18) and **Mitau** (Aug. 1), while in northern Poland the Germans (Gen. von Gallwitz with the 12th army) advanced to the Narev and took **Warsaw** (Aug. 4–7). The Germans took **Kovno** (Aug. 18) and stormed the key fortress of **Novo-Georgievsk** (Aug. 20). Brest-Litovsk fell into their hands (Aug. 25) and Grodno (Sept. 2). In the south the Austrians managed to take **Lutsk** (Aug. 31) and **Dubno** (Sept. 8). The capture of **Vilna** (Sept. 19) may be taken as marking the end of the great offensive.

Sept. 6–16. The Russians offered some resistance to the Austrians (**battle of Tarnopol**) and to the Germans (**battle of Dvinsk**, Sept. 9–Nov. 1), and in Courland **Riga** was held, but when the German advance came to a stop in Sept. the Russians had lost all of Poland, Lithuania, and Courland, to say nothing of the larger part of a million men. Their only success lay in escaping complete envelopment and capture. The line in Sept. ran from west of Riga and Dvinsk almost due south to Baranovici(German) and Pinsk (Russian) and thence farther south to Dubno (Austrian), Tarnopol (Russian), and Czernowitz (Austrian).

Sept. 5. The **Grand Duke Nicholas Nicolaievich** was relieved of the supreme command and sent as viceroy to the Caucasus. The supreme command was taken over by the tsar in person.

8. NAVAL OPERATIONS — SUBMARINE WARFARE

From the very beginning of the war the question of neutral shipping had arisen in aggravated form. Both the British and French governments issued new and more rigorous **interpretations of contraband** (Aug. 20, 25, 1914), adding greatly to the list of contraband goods. To this the United States government replied (Oct. 22) stating that it would insist on the observance of the existing rules of international law. Nevertheless the British continued to revise the list of contraband and to modify the Declaration of London of 1909. Nov. 2 they declared the North Sea a military zone, and Jan. 30, 1915, the British admiralty warned British merchant ships to fly neutral ensigns or none in the vicinity of the British Isles.

1915, Feb. 4. The German government announced that a submarine **blockade of Great Britain** would begin Feb. 18. To this the London government replied with an order in council (Mar. 11) wiping out distinctions in contraband and ordering the seizure of all goods presumably destined for the enemy. Cotton was declared contraband Mar. 18.

Mar. 28. First passenger ship sunk by German submarine (*S. S. Falaba*).

May 1. First American ship (*Gulflight*) sunk without warning.

May 7. *LUSITANIA* SUNK OFF THE COAST OF IRELAND, with a loss of 1198 lives, including 139 Americans. Before the ship left New York a warning against sailing on her had been inserted in the newspapers by the German embassy, but it is not true that a submarine was sent out specially to sink her. The captain failed to observe instructions to zigzag his course, and so came within range of the submarine. The *Lusitania* carried a part-cargo of small arms and munitions.

The sinking of the *Lusitania* brought the United States and Germany to the verge of war, and created a much greater tension than had developed between the American and Allied governments over questions of contraband and blockade. In a speech of May 9 **President Wilson** struck a strong note and defined American policy, though the note of protest to Berlin (May 13) was somewhat milder in tone, demanding reparation and abstinence from such practices in the future.

June 8. **William J. Bryan** resigned as American secretary of state, because of unwillingness to follow the president in his policy. Bryan was succeeded by **Robert Lansing.**

On the very next day a much stronger note was dispatched to Berlin, without eliciting a disavowal or assurance for the future. A third note was sent on July 21.

Aug. 19. **Sinking of the *Arabic*,** with the loss of two American lives. This new offense resulted in a second period of acute tension, but the German ambassador at Washington, **Count Bernstorff,** finally persuaded his government of the real danger of war.

Sept. 1. The German government gave assurances that no liners would be sunk in future without warning and without some provision for the safety of non-combatants, provided the ship made no effort to offer resistance or to escape. These assurances were reasonably well observed during the remainder of the year, and so the first phase of the submarine warfare came to an end.

9. THE INTERVENTION OF ITALY

On the plea that the Austrian action against Serbia was an offensive action and therefore incompatible with the terms of the **Triple Alliance,** the Italian government in July, 1914, refused to join the Central Powers, and declared neutrality instead (Aug. 3). But almost from the outset the Italian government maintained that, under Art. VII of the Triple Alliance, Italy was entitled to some compensation to counterbalance the Austrian gains in the Balkans. These claims were advanced the more persistently when the foreign ministry was given to **Baron Sonnino** (Nov. 3), following the sudden demise of **Marquis di San Giuliano** (Oct. 16).

The necessity for making some concession to Italy in order to keep her neutral was fully recognized in Berlin, but the Austrian foreign minister (**Count Berchtold**) refused to entertain all suggestions of territorial cessions.

1914, Dec. 20. Prince Bülow, former German chancellor, arrived in Rome on special mission. He admitted the Italian claim to the Trentino and the German government made every effort to persuade the Austrians to give in (Mission of Count von Wedel to Vienna, Jan. 16, 1915).

1915, Jan. 13. **Count Burian** appointed Austro-Hungarian foreign minister to replace Berchtold. Burian finally agreed to the cession of territory (Mar. 9), but was willing to offer only the **Trentino,** to be transferred only after the conclusion of peace. This was not enough to satisfy the Italians, who were already veering toward the side of intervention and were already negotiating with the Entente powers. Sonnino demanded of Austria the immediate cession of the **South Tyrol,** the district of **Gorizia** and **Gradisca,** the establishment of **Trieste** and its neighborhood as

a free state, the cession to Italy of the **Curzolari Islands** off the Dalmatian coast, full sovereignty over the island of **Saseno** and over **Valona** on the Albanian coast (Italian occupation of Saseno, Oct. 30, 1914; "provisional" occupation of Valona, Dec. 26, 1914). These demands were entirely too exorbitant, from the Austrian point of view, but the Germans finally (May 10) induced their allies to agree to substantially all the Italians held out for. As it turned out, the Austrians yielded too late.

Apr. 26. England, France, Russia, and Italy concluded the secret treaty **of London.** Salandra, the Italian prime minister, had envisaged Italian intervention on the Entente side almost since the beginning of war, but the non-interventionists, led by **Giolitti**, were too strong to make that at first a practicable policy. During the winter, however, the interventionist movement gathered strength (**Mussolini** broke with the Socialist Party and became an active proponent of intervention). The western powers, meeting with failure on the western front, were ready to offer much. Negotiations were embarked upon in Feb. 1915, but were delayed by the opposition of Sazonov to the assignment of the Dalmatian coast to Italy, in view of the Serbian aspirations in that region. Under the terms of the treaty as finally concluded, a military convention was to be drawn up to protect Italy against the full force of Austrian attack. The political clauses promised Italy the **South Tyrol** and **Trentino, Gorizia, Gradisca, Trieste, Istria,** the most important **Dalmatian islands,** and the southern part of the province of **Dalmatia; Saseno** and **Valona,** full sovereignty over the **Dodecanese Islands** (occupied since 1912); in the event of the partition of Turkey, Italy was to have the province of **Adalia;** in the event of England and France enlarging their empires by the addition of German colonies, Italy was to receive extensions of her territory in **Libya, Eritrea,** and **Somaliland.** Italy was further to receive a loan, and ultimately part of the war indemnity. The Entente powers were to

support Italy in preventing the Holy See from taking diplomatic steps for the conclusion of peace. Italy was to commence hostilities within a month of the signature of the treaty.

May 3. The Italian government denounced the Triple Alliance.

May 10. Conclusion of a **naval convention** between England, France, and Italy.

May 23. Italy mobilized and declared war on Austria-Hungary. Germany at once severed diplomatic relations (May 24), but for various financial reasons Italy did not declare war on Germany until Aug. 28, 1916.

May 29. The Italian government "formally" occupied **Valona. Albania** being in a state of anarchy (flight of Prince William von Wied, Sept. 3, 1914; provisional government of Essad Pasha at Durazzo, Oct. 4, 1914), this little state, the independence of which had been guaranteed by the powers (Dec. 20, 1912), now became a prey to its neighbors.

June 26. The **Montenegrins** occupied **San Giovanni di Medua.**

July 4. The **Serbians** occupied **Durazzo,** which they evacuated again July 17, under pressure from the Italian government.

Aug. 31. Durazzo reoccupied by the **Serbs.**

Dec. 20. Durazzo occupied by the **Italians.**

1915. FIRST BATTLES OF THE ISONZO. The first two years of Italy's participation in the war were taken up with the fighting of 11 successive battles on the Isonzo, along a front of only about 60 miles. The Austrians (commander **Archduke Eugene**) held the two important bridgeheads at Gorizia and Tolmino. The Italians (**Gen. Luigi Cadorna,** commander in chief, May 23, 1915–Nov. 7, 1917) tried to force the passage, but their total advance never exceeded 10 or 12 miles. The Isonzo battles of 1915 were the first (June 29–July 7); second (July 18–Aug. 10); third (Oct. 18–Nov. 3); and fourth (Nov. 10–Dec. 10).

10. THE BALKAN SITUATION, 1914-1915

The three Balkan states, Greece, Bulgaria, and Rumania, all more or less exhausted by the Balkan Wars of 1912–1913, proclaimed neutrality at the beginning of the European conflict. In the early months of the war the Russians entertained high hopes of securing the aid of **Rumania,** which would have been an important factor in the Galician campaign. On various occasions

(July 30, Sept. 16) they attempted to bait the Bucharest government with promises of Transylvania, but so long as **King Carol** lived (d. Oct. 10, 1914) there was no hope of Rumanian intervention, since the king strongly regretted Rumania's failure to side with her Austrian and German allies of prewar days. **King Ferdinand** felt morally less bound, but the prime minister, **Ion Bratianu** (premier and foreign minister Jan. 14, 1914–Feb. 6, 1918), was determined to drive a hard bargain.

1914, Dec. 6. Bratianu rejected allied suggestions that Rumania guarantee Greece against Bulgarian attack or that Rumania make concessions in the Dobrudja to secure Bulgarian support.

1915, Jan. 25. He refused to join Greece in support of Serbia. On the contrary he set an ever higher price on Rumanian support.

May 3. The Rumanians asked not only for **Transylvania**, but also for part of **Bukovina** and the **Banat**.

July. The Russians were prepared to concede most of these demands, but Bratianu was then unwilling to act unless the Allies had 500,000 men in the Balkans and the Russians 200,000 in Bessarabia (Nov. 1915).

THE POSITION OF BULGARIA became crucial after the entry of Turkey into the war in Nov.

1914, Nov. 9. In order to secure Bulgarian help the Allies at once offered Bulgaria the **Enos-Midia line** in eastern Thrace and, after the war, the (1912) **uncontested zone of Macedonia** as far as the Vardar River, this territory being in the possession of Serbia.

It was clear almost from the outset, however, that such an offer would not prove attractive, since the Bulgarians aspired not only to part of **Thrace**, but to most of **Macedonia**, the **Kavalla-Drama-Seres** region of western Thrace, and also that part of **Dobrudja** lost to Rumania in 1913.

1915, Jan. As the Dardanelles campaign was being decided on, the Allies offered to **Greece** the Turkish city of **Smyrna** and its hinterland, on condition that the Greeks cede the **Kavalla** region to Bulgaria and join a Balkan bloc in support of Serbia. **Venizelos** favored this policy strongly, but **King Constantine** preferred the sparrow in the hand to the pigeon on the roof (Jan. 24, 29).

Mar. 6. Venizelos fell from power when the king refused to adopt his policy of aiding the Allies at the Dardanelles (see p. 920). His successor, M. Gounaris (Mar. 9–Aug. 22) was less favorable toward the Entente.

Apr. 12. He rejected a second offer of the Smyrna region, on the plea that the Allies would not guarantee Greek territory (i.e. against Bulgaria).

May 7. The Allies, more eager than ever to secure the aid of Bulgaria in view of the failure at the Dardanelles, gave **Serbia** a conditional guaranty of the eventual acquisition of Bosnia and Herzegovina and "a wide access to the Adriatic," as compensation for the part of Macedonia that was required to bring in Bulgaria.

May 29. A definite offer along these lines was made to **Bulgaria**. But the Sofia government treated these advances dilatorily, and was already leaning to the Central Powers, which were prepared to promise whatever Bulgaria wanted, and were not embarrassed by the fact that Bulgarian aspirations were directed chiefly to Serbian and Greek territory.

July 22. The Germans persuaded the Turks to cede to Bulgaria a strip of territory along the **Maritza River** (definitive agreement Sept. 22). Aug. 8 the Bulgarian government secured from Germany and Austria a loan of 400 million francs.

Sept. 6. **Bulgaria concluded an alliance** and military convention with Germany and Austria, providing for mutual aid against attack by a neighboring state, for a German-Austrian campaign against Serbia within 30 days, and for Bulgarian participation five days later. Bulgaria was to receive **Macedonia**, and, if Rumania joined in the war, **Dobrudja** also; if Greece proved hostile, Bulgaria was to receive the **Kavalla** region as well.

Sept. 21. The Bulgarians **began to mobilize**. The Serbs, being directly threatened, appealed to Greece for aid, under the terms of the Treaty of May, 1913. Venizelos, who had won in the elections of June, 1915, and had returned to power Aug. 22, was as eager as ever to intervene, but made it a condition that the Allies furnish the 150,000 troops which Serbia was required to supply under the treaty terms.

Sept. 24. The English and French governments gave a promise to this effect. Venizelos then secured the secret consent of the king to the landing of the Allied forces at **Saloniki**, but publicly the request of the Allies to land was rejected (Sept. 28).

Oct. 3-5. One **British** and one **French** division were **landed at Saloniki**, followed by two more French divisions at the end of the month. King Constantine now refused to support Venizelos to the extent of joining in the war; the prime minister resigned (Oct. 5, 1915) and was succeeded by **M. Zaimis** (Oct. 6–Nov. 5, 1915).

Oct. 6. Beginning of the great Austro-German campaign in Serbia (Gen. von Mackensen). Belgrade fell (Oct. 9) and Semendria (Oct. 11).

Oct. 11. The Bulgarians crossed the Serbian frontier.

Oct. 14. Bulgaria and Serbia declared war on each other. England and France declared war on Bulgaria (Oct. 15, 16), and so did Russia and Italy (Oct. 19). The Allies made great efforts to induce Greece to join, the English offering them the island of Cyprus (Oct. 16), but this offer too was rejected (Oct. 20).

Nov. 5. Zaimis resigned and was succeeded by M. Skouloudis (Nov. 6, 1915-June 21, 1916). The Greek government then declared its benevolent neutrality (Nov. 8) and agreed not to interfere with the Allied forces at Saloniki, in return for a guaranty of the eventual restoration of Greek territory (Nov. 24).

Oct. 22. The Bulgarians (Gen. Jekov) took Üskub (Skoplje), and then (Oct. 28) Pirot. Nish fell (Nov. 5). An attempt of the British and French from Saloniki to block the Bulgar advance on the Strumitsa (Nov. 3-5) and on the Cerna (Nov. 12) was brushed aside. The Allies were again repulsed on the lower Vardar (Dec. 4-10) and forced to retreat to Greek territory. The British were, by this time, prepared to give up the whole Saloniki adventure, but the French, under Gen. Sarrail, persisted in staying. The result was that even greater forces were tied up at Saloniki, without being able to accomplish much.

Nov. 16. The Bulgarians took Prilep, then Pristina (Nov. 23), Prizrend (Nov. 29), and Monastir (i.e. Bitolje, Dec. 2). The Serbs were now in full flight into Albania, the Bulgars pursuing them and taking Dibra and Okhrid (Dec. 8) and ultimately Elbasan (Feb. 2, 1916).

Dec. 2. The Austrians took Plevlje, and then Ipek (Dec. 6). Mt. Lovchen, guarding Montenegro, was stormed (Jan. 10, 1916) and Cettinje taken (Jan. 13). King Nicholas laid down his arms and retired to Italy.

1916, Jan. 11. The French occupied Corfu as a refuge for the Serbian troops. The Greek government refused its consent, but the Serbs were landed nevertheless (Jan. 15).

Jan. 23. The Austrians took Scutari, then San Giovanni di Medua (Jan. 25) and Berat (Feb. 17). The Albanian provisional government, under Italian protection at Durazzo, left for Naples (Feb. 24), and the town was taken by the Austrians from the Italians (Feb. 27). Mountain warfare between the Austrians and the Italians in Albania continued until the end of the war.

11. THE MESOPOTAMIAN CAMPAIGN, 1914-1916

This campaign, which grew later to large dimensions and absorbed thousands of men, began very modestly when a British force from India occupied Basra (Nov. 22, 1914) in order to protect the oil pipeline from Persia. Then, for the sake of greater security, the British began to extend the sphere of their occupation.

1914, Dec. 4-8. Fighting about Qurna, which was taken by the Anglo-Indian forces (Dec. 9).

1915, Apr. 11-13. Sir John Nixon repulsed Turkish attacks on Basra.

June 3. Gen. Townshend took the town of Amara on the Tigris, and then Nasiriya on the Euphrates (July 25). Beginning of a general advance toward Baghdad.

Sept. 28. BATTLE OF KUT-EL-AMARA. Townshend defeated the Turks and drove them as far as Aziziya.

Nov. 11. Beginning of the advance on Baghdad.

Nov. 22-24. BATTLE OF CTESIPHON. The engagement was indecisive, but both armies began to fall back, Townshend retreating as far as Kut, which was reached Dec. 3.

Dec. 7-Apr. 29, 1916. SIEGE OF KUT-EL-AMARA. Three attempts were made by the British to relieve the garrison (Jan. 18-21, Mar. 8, Apr. 1-9), but the armies were hampered by floods and mud and the operations failed. Efforts were made to buy off the Turks, but these too led to no result.

1916, Apr. 29. CAPITULATION OF KUT-EL-AMARA, with 10,000 men.

In the effort to divert the Turkish forces and to establish contact with the British, the Russians in Nov., 1915, had begun an advance into western Persia, which was followed by an offensive in Armenia. They took Kasvin (Nov. 2), Hamadan (Dec. 14), Kirmanshah (Feb. 26, 1916), Karind (Mar. 12), and, turning westward toward the flank of the Turkish force in Mesopotamia, they took Khanikin (May 15) and Rowanduz (May 15), a detachment actually joining hands with the British on the Tigris.

THE
NEAR EASTERN
THEATER OF WAR
1914–1918

Scale of Miles
0   100   200   300   400   500

The British had occupied Bushire (Aug. 8, 1915).

1916, Jan. 11. Beginning of the Russian offensive in Armenia. The Russians took Koprikoi (Jan. 18), and, after a battle of three days, Erzerum (Feb. 16) and Mush (Feb. 18). Bitlis fell (Mar. 2), and then Trebizond (Apr. 17) and Erzingan (July 25).

June 5. The Turks began a counter-offensive in western Persia. They drove the Russians out of Khanikin (June 5), and retook Kirmanshah (July 1) and Hamadan (Aug. 10).

Aug. 15. In Armenia the Turks also took the offensive, taking Bitlis and Mush (Aug. 15), but losing them again to the Russians (Aug. 24).

IN EGYPT during this period large numbers of troops were kept concentrated to meet the double threat of trouble from the Senussi tribes in the west and from the Turks advancing on the Suez Canal.

1915, Nov. 14. Rising of the Senussi, who drove the Egyptian forces out of a number of posts along the Mediterranean (actions at Wadi Senab, Dec. 11, and Wadi Majid, Dec. 25). They were defeated at Agagia (Feb. 26, 1916) and the town of Sollum was reoccupied (Mar. 14). The British were also obliged to carry on a campaign against the Sultan of Darfur (Mar. 1–Dec. 31, 1916).

1916, Apr. 23. A small Turkish force under the command of Col. Kress von Kressenstein, surprised an Anglo-Egyptian force at Qatia and temporarily seized several posts commanding the approach to the Suez Canal.

July 19. Second Turk attack on the Canal, this time with larger forces. The Turks were almost surrounded in the action near Rumani (Aug. 4), and were obliged to retreat.

12. POLITICAL CHANGES, 1915-1916

During the first years of the war the Allied powers gradually evolved arrangements for heightening the productive efficiency of their countries, and made some effort to establish closer co-ordination of action between themselves.

a. ENGLAND

1915, May 25. The Asquith ministry (since 1908) was reorganized as a coalition. Churchill resigned as first lord of the admiralty (May 27) and was succeeded by Arthur Balfour. An inner group of the cabinet, first called the War Committee and then (June 7) the Dardanelles Committee, took over the conduct of operations. A ministry of munitions was set up (July 2).

June 3. An Allied conference met in Paris to establish concerted action in economic matters. This was followed (Nov. 25) by arrangements for inter-Allied munitions control, and by numerous measures designed to restrict trade with Germany, even by the method of rationing the supply of raw materials, etc., to neutrals (Dec. 23, introduction of the Black List; Jan. 27, 1916, establishment of the Shipping Control Commission; Feb. 23, 1916, organization of a ministry of blockade in England).

1916, Jan. 6. The British Parliament passed the compulsory military service bill, despite the opposition of Labor groups. Thus far the British had at-

tempted to raise more forces by volunteer enlistment. At first this method had been quite successful, and by the beginning of 1916 the British had a million men in France. But by that time other methods had become urgently necessary.

Apr. 20. Sir Roger Casement, the Irish leader, landed on the Irish coast from a German submarine, to start a rebellion.

Apr. 24. Beginning of the great Easter Rebellion in Dublin and other sections of Ireland. After a week of fighting and much bloodshed the insurrection was suppressed (May 1). Several of the leaders, including Casement, were tried and executed (Aug. 3).

June 5. Field-Marshal Lord Kitchener, on secret mission to Russia, was lost when *H.M.S. Hampshire*, on which his party was traveling, was torpedoed off the Orkney Islands.

July 7. David Lloyd George became secretary of state for war to succeed Kitchener.

Dec. 4. The Asquith cabinet resigned. Lloyd George formed a war cabinet (Dec. 7-10), in which Balfour took the place of Sir Edward Grey at the foreign office.

b. FRANCE

1915, Oct. 13. M. Delcassé resigned as French foreign minister and was succeeded by the prime minister, M. Viviani.

Oct. 29.   The Viviani cabinet resigned, and a new ministry was organized by M. Briand, in which the premier himself took the portfolio for foreign affairs.

1916, Dec. 12.   The Briand cabinet was reorganized, and an inner committee of five ministers formed a kind of war cabinet.

c. ITALY

1916, June 11.   The Salandra Cabinet resigned, and was succeeded by the Boselli cabinet (to Oct. 25, 1917).

d. RUSSIA

1915, June 26.   The Russian war minister, Gen. Sukhomlinov, was removed and later tried for malfeasance.

1916, Feb. 1.   The Russian minister-president Goremykin resigned, and was succeeded by M. Stürmer.

July 22.   The Russian foreign minister, M. Sazonov, resigned and the functions of the foreign ministry were taken over by M. Stürmer.

Nov. 24.   M. Stürmer resigned and was followed by M. Trepov.

e. AUSTRIA-HUNGARY

1916, Oct. 21.   The Austrian prime minister, Count Stürgkh, was assassinated. His place was taken (Oct. 28) by Dr. von Körber.

Nov. 21.   The old emperor, Francis Joseph, died, and was succeeded by his grandnephew, Charles.

Dec. 14.   The Körber ministry in Austria resigned, and was followed by a cabinet under Count Clam-Martinitz. Count Czernin took the place of Count Burian as Austro-Hungarian foreign minister.

f. GERMANY

1916, Nov. 20.   The German foreign minister, von Jagow, resigned. His place was taken by Dr. A. Zimmermann.

13. VERDUN AND THE SOMME, 1916

Both Joffre and Falkenhayn were still convinced, at the end of 1915, that a military decision could be reached only on the French front. Joffre planned for a great Anglo-French offensive to begin in the summer, to be supported by simultaneous Russian and Italian offensives. Sir Douglas Haig (who succeeded Sir John French as commander in chief of the British forces Dec. 19, 1915) would have preferred to arrange for an offensive in Flanders, but Joffre insisted on operations in the Somme area, where the British and French could collaborate more easily. Continued argument and friction between Joffre and Haig as to the extent of front which the British should take over.

In the meanwhile Falkenhayn, having disposed of the threat from the east, was able to bring almost half a million men to the west front and to carry out his long-cherished plan for a crushing blow. The plan was not so much for a break-through as for mere attrition. The French were to be bled white at Verdun, a salient with poor communications and hard to hold and yet a place which for sentimental reasons if for no other would have to be fought for to the end. The French, having lost faith in forts, had taken away most of the guns about Verdun, and Joffre, intent on preparations for the Somme offensive, ignored warnings of danger in that area.

1916, Feb. 21.   BEGINNING OF THE BATTLE OF VERDUN. The Germans (Crown Prince Wilhelm in command) concentrated 1400 guns on a short front of 8 miles on the right bank of the Meuse. After a devastating bombardment they took Fort Douaumont (Feb. 25). French reinforcements (Gen. Pétain) were rushed to this sector, but the defense was hampered by the bottle-mouth of the salient.

Mar. 6-Apr. 10.   Renewal of the attack, this time on both sides of the salient. Terrific loss of life on both sides. Gen. Nivelle replaced Gen. Pétain and the French began a series of vigorous counterattacks (May).

June 2.   The Germans finally took Fort Vaux, and before the end of the month the works of Thiaumont (June 23). Heavy attacks continued until July 11, when the Germans went over to the defensive. The French losses have been estimated at about 350,000, the German at somewhat less. But Verdun did not bring a decision much nearer.

The immediate effect of the assault on Verdun was felt in the preparation for the Somme offensive. The French were obliged to reduce their contribution from 40 divisions to 16 and their front of attack from 25 miles to 10, so that the operation was in the main a British one.

July 1. OPENING OF THE BATTLE OF THE SOMME. After a long and intensive bombardment the British advanced on a front of 15 miles toward Bapaume, while the French objective was Péronne. Though the Germans were outnumbered at least six to one at first, the British had but little success. The heavily laden infantry was unable to move fast enough to keep up with an extraordinarily rigid time schedule. British losses on one day were 60,000, heavier than in this or any other war.

July-Aug. The battle continued, both sides fighting desperately and the Allies gradually pushing forward.

Sept. 15. First use of tanks by the British. These had been suggested long before, but the military authorities had been hostile to the idea, and even when they were finally used there were far too few (only 18 on the field) to gain the fullest advantage.

Nov. 18. End of the battle of the Somme, which gradually ran out in rain and mud. The Allies had conquered about 125 sq. miles of territory, but nothing of prime strategic importance. The maximum advance was about 7 miles. British losses were over 400,000 and French almost 200,000. The German losses were between 400,000 and 500,000.

Oct. 24-Dec. 18. The French (Gen. Mangin) **counter-attacked at Verdun,** retaking Forts Douaumont and Vaux (Nov. 2) and making a total advance of about two miles. These operations left the situation at Verdun much as it was early in the year. Both sides were seriously exhausted after the arduous and costly, but wholly inconclusive, operations of 1916.

14. THE WAR AT SEA. BATTLE OF JUTLAND

The second half of 1915 and the first half of 1916 were not marked by any striking events of naval warfare. The Germans continued their efforts to reduce British preponderance by submarine and mine destruction, and at the same time extended their operations against merchant shipping.

1916, Feb. 21. The German government notified the United States government that thenceforth armed merchantmen would be treated as cruisers. **The "extended" submarine campaign** began Mar. 1.

Mar. 24. The *Sussex* sunk by torpedo in the Channel with the loss of American lives. There followed another acrimonious dispute between Washington and Berlin, the Germans showing themselves unwilling to make any concession until what amounted to an American ultimatum induced them to give up unrestricted submarine warfare for the time being (May 10).

In the meanwhile (Jan. 1916) **Adm. Scheer** had succeeded Adm. Pohl in the command of the German High Seas Fleet. The famous minister of Marine, **Adm. von Tirpitz, resigned** (Mar. 14) as a protest against the emperor's unwillingness to make full use of German sea-power. He was succeeded by **Adm. von Capelle.**

Apr. 24-25. A German squadron raided and bombarded **Yarmouth** and **Lowestoft.** Submarines appeared off the Scottish naval bases.

May 31-June 1. BATTLE OF JUTLAND (SKAGERRAK). May 30

Adm. Hipper with the German battlecruiser squadron had been sent to show himself off the Norwegian coast. May 31 he came into contact with **Adm. Beatty** and the British battle cruisers, running southeast before the Grand Fleet. Though decidedly outnumbered Hipper and the Germans, through superior marksmanship, sank two of Beatty's ships. Beatty, sighting the German High Seas Fleet (Adm. Scheer) coming up in battle array, turned to the north to meet Jellicoe and the Grand Fleet, which was hastening to his assistance. The German fleet, having been sucked in, met the Grand Fleet just before 6 P.M. Jellicoe tried to deploy across Scheer's line of retreat, but Scheer turned about suddenly and made away to the south and then to the east, coming up on the flank of the British, in pursuit. Scheer turned again, launching a torpedo attack, which obliged Jellicoe to fall back. Scheer then sent Hipper and the battle cruisers to attack while the High Seas Fleet effected its escape. Night fell, leaving the two fleets steaming southwest about 6 miles apart. But at 9 P.M. Scheer turned east and made for Horns Reef, forcing his way through the tail end of Jellicoe's forces, still steaming south. The German fleet reached Horns Reef in safety at 3.30 in the night. Each fleet lost six ships in the Jutland engagement, but the British ships lost totaled almost twice the tonnage of the Germans. Scheer had to yield to the superiority of the British in capital ships, but in battlecruiser warfare the Germans were completely victorious. They showed themselves

brilliant in maneuvering and in marksmanship.

**Aug. 19, Oct. 26-27. German raids on
the English coast.** At the same
time German light cruisers slipped through
the blockade and ravaged commerce in the
Atlantic, later returning through the lines
to home ports (*Moewe*, Dec. 26, 1915–Mar.
14, 1916; Nov. 26, 1916–Mar. 22, 1917;
Seeadler, Nov. 22, 1916–Aug. 2, 1917;
Wolff, Dec. 1, 1916–Feb. 24, 1918). The
German commercial submarine *Deutschland*
made a trip to America and back (July 10,
1916, at Norfolk, Va.).

15. THE ITALIAN FRONT, 1916

**1916, Feb. 15-Mar. 17. The fifth battle of
the Isonzo**, which, like the previous engagements, led to no substantial
change.

The Austrian chief of staff, Gen. **Conrad**,
had for some time been urging upon the
German high command the desirability of
massing troops in the Trentino for an attack upon the Italian rear and flank, but
Falkenhayn had flatly refused to contribute
forces which he needed for the operations
at Verdun. The result was that the Austrians decided to make the try alone. As
many troops as possible were withdrawn
from the Russian front and prepared for an
advance on the Asiago plateau.

**May 15-June 3. The Austrian offensive
in the Trentino.** The Italians
were taken by surprise and the Austrians
took **Asiago** and **Arsiero** (May 31). But it
soon became evident that the Austrians
lacked sufficient forces to break through,
the more so as the Italians hastily brought
up reserves from the Isonzo front. The
Italian lines held and by June 17 a counter-
offensive was launched. When this came
to a close (July 7) most of the territory had
been recovered, but the Italian losses were
about 150,000 men.

Aug. 6-17. Sixth battle of the Isonzo.
The Italians finally took **Gorizia**
(Aug. 9).

**Sept. 14-18. Seventh battle of the
Isonzo.**

Oct. 9-12. Eighth battle of the Isonzo.

**Oct. 31-Nov. 4. Ninth battle of the
Isonzo.**

16. THE EASTERN FRONT, 1916

**1916, Mar. 19-Apr. 30. Battle of Lake
Naroch.** This inconclusive Russian offensive was intended solely
to relieve the pressure of the
Germans at Verdun.

**June 4. BEGINNING OF THE GREAT
BRUSILOV OFFENSIVE**, initiated somewhat prematurely in order to
meet the Italian appeals for action to distract the Austrians in the Trentino. Brusilov (appointed to the command of the
Russian southern front, Apr. 4) had planned
the offensive for June 15, to coincide with
Joffre's great offensive on the Somme. But
the Brusilov offensive was meant to be
followed by an even larger operation farther
north. The objective in the south was
Kovel, an important railway center, but
the advance extended over a front of 300
miles. The Austrians, taken by surprise,
fell back at once, leaving many prisoners in
Russian hands. The **Russians took Lutsk**
(June 8) and Czernowitz (June 18). Heavy
fighting continued about Kovel, Tarnopol,
and Baranovici (**battles of the Strypa**, June
11–30; **Baranovici**, July 2–9; **Kovel**, July
28–Aug. 17) until Sept. The Russians advanced from 25 to 125 kilometers in the
region from Pinsk south to Czernowitz and
they took half a million prisoners, but they
had difficulties in moving their own troops
from north to south, and ultimately the
offensive was stopped by the arrival of 15
divisions of Germans from the west front.
The Russians had failed to take either
Kovel or Lemberg. Their losses were about
a million men, and the whole operation left
the army demoralized and discontented.

17. THE BALKAN FRONT, 1916

Throughout the summer and autumn of
1916 the Greek situation continued to be
most unsatisfactory from the Entente viewpoint.

1916, May 26. A Bulgarian-German force
occupied **Fort Rupel** in Greek Macedonia,
this action enhancing the suspicion that
King Constantine was secretly bound to
the Central Powers.

June 6-22. The "pacific blockade" of

THE
BALKAN FRONT

Battlefronts at the
end of 1916

Scale of Miles
0   100   200   300

Greece by the Entente Powers. France and England sent Greece an ultimatum (June 21) demanding demobilization of the Greek army and the institution of responsible government. The Greek government yielded. The Skouloudis ministry resigned and a Zaimis cabinet was organized. The army was put on a peace footing (June 27) and new elections were arranged for.

July 25. The reconstituted Serbian army, which had been shipped from Corfu to Saloniki, came into action on that front. Russian troops from France and an Italian contingent also arrived (July 30, Aug. 11).

Aug. 2-21. Battle of Doiran. The Allies began the advance against the Bulgarians on the Saloniki front.

Aug. 17-19. Battle of Florina. The Bulgars and Germans counterattacked and pushed back the Saloniki forces. They took **Seres** (Aug. 19), **Drama,** and **Kavalla** (Sept. 18), where the fourth Greek army corps voluntarily surrendered.

Aug. 30. A Venizelist, pro-Ally movement, fostered by Gen. Sarrail, took place at Saloniki.

Sept. 29. Venizelos and Adm. Condouriotis established a provisional government in Crete. Venizelos then (Oct. 9) went to Saloniki, where the provisional government declared war on Germany and Bulgaria (Nov. 23).

Oct. 10. The **Entente Powers,** incensed by the surrender of the Greek forces at Kavalla, submitted an ultimatum to Athens demanding the surrender of the Greek fleet. The Athens government (Lambros ministry, Oct. 10–May 3, 1917) yielded (Oct. 11), whereupon the Entente Powers demanded (Nov. 19) the dismissal of the representatives of the Central Powers at Athens and the surrender of war material. These demands were rejected (Nov. 30) and in consequence **French and British** landing parties debarked at Piraeus. They withdrew again Dec. 1 after conflicts with the Greeks. Dec. 6 there were clashes between the Greek government supporters and the Venizelists.

Dec. 8. Blockade of Greece. The Allies demanded (Dec. 14) the complete withdrawal of Greek forces from Thessaly. The Athens government once more gave in (Dec. 15), but Dec. 19 the British government decided to recognize the provisional government of Venizelos.

Oct. 5-Dec. 11. The Allied forces under Sarrail began a great offensive in Macedonia (**battle of the Cerna and Monastir, or first battle of Monastir**). Monastir (Bitolje) was taken (Nov. 19) and the Allies finally pushed forward as far as Lake Okhrid. On the Bulgarian frontier no advance was made.

18. THE INTERVENTION OF RUMANIA

Since the spring of 1916 the Russian government had been redoubling its efforts to bring Rumania into the war. The success of the Brusilov offensive and the readiness of the Russian government and its allies to recognize the Rumanian claims to the Bukovina and Banat as well as to Transylvania resulted in the conclusion of a political and military agreement (Aug. 18).

1916, Aug. 27. RUMANIA DECLARED WAR ON AUSTRIA-HUNGARY. Germany declared war on Rumania, and Italy finally declared war on Germany (Aug. 28). Turkey and Bulgaria declared war on Rumania a few days later (Aug. 30, Sept. 1 respectively).

The Rumanians should probably have entered the war in June, when the Russian offensive began, but they had wanted to wait for the harvest and were, in fact, very inadequately prepared even then.

Aug. 28. The Rumanians began the invasion of Transylvania and took Kronstadt (Brasov) and **Hermannstadt** (Sibiu).

Sept. 27-29. The Austro-German forces, hastily assembled in Transylvania and commanded by the former chief of staff, Gen. von Falkenhayn (replaced by Hindenburg, Aug. 29), counter-attacked and surrounded the Rumanians at Hermannstadt (**battle of Sibiu**).

Sept. 26-Nov. 23. Operations of a Bulgarian-German force under Gen. von Mackensen, in the **Dobrudja.** Silistria was taken (Sept. 10), then **Constantza** (Oct. 22) and **Cernavoda** (Oct. 25).

Oct. 7-9. Battle of Kronstadt (Brasov). The Austro-German forces retook the city and advanced to the Carpathian passes.

Nov. 10-14. Falkenhayn forced the **Vulcan Pass** into Rumania and began the invasion of Wallachia.

Nov. 23. Mackensen's troops crossed the

Danube at Sistova and Simnitza and advanced toward Bucharest, as did Falkenhayn coming from Craiova.

Dec. 1-5. The Rumanians tried to counter-attack on the Arges River, but were completely defeated (**battle of Argesul**). The Rumanian government was hastily moved to Jassy, and the capital, **Bucharest, fell into the hands of the enemy** (Dec. 6).

1917, Jan. The Austro-German forces continued the advance both in the Dobrudja and in Moldavia. **Braila** was taken (Jan. 5) and **Focsani** (Jan. 8). By the middle of Jan. the Rumanians had reached the Sereth River, where the campaign came to a stop. Most of Rumania, with important wheat-and-oil-producing areas, was in the hands of the Central Powers.

19. PEACE NEGOTIATIONS, 1916-1917, AND THE INTERVENTION OF THE UNITED STATES

From the very outbreak of the war, **President Wilson** appears to have felt that ultimately the opportunity would present itself for the United States government to step in as mediator. The president himself regarded the work of peacemaking as his great mission, and was prepared to act at once when the moment was opportune.

1916, Jan.-Feb. The president's close friend and intimate adviser, **Col. Edward M. House,** visited Europe and consulted with the leading statesmen. His conferences with Sir Edward Grey resulted in the so-called **House Memorandum** of Feb. 22, which stated that the president was ready, whenever England and France thought the time opportune, to propose a peace conference. If the proposal were accepted by the Allies but rejected by Germany, the United States would probably enter the war on the Allied side. The terms on which the United States would mediate would include the restoration of Belgium and Serbia, the retrocession of Alsace-Lorraine to France, the acquisition of Constantinople by Russia, and the transfer of the Italian-speaking parts of Austria to Italy. Poland was to be independent. Germany would retain some colonies and perhaps be given more. At that time the Allied soldiers and statesmen were still hoping for victory in the 1916 offensive, but the offer illuminates the sympathies of Wilson, House, Page, and other American statesmen.

Public opinion in the United States was still distinctly divided, but sentiment for peace was prevalent, excepting in the eastern states where, almost from the outset, there was some feeling for intervention on the Allied side (influence of English propaganda, etc.). The president was re-elected (Nov. 7, 1916) very largely on a platform of peace, but he applied himself almost at once to the resumption of his mediatory efforts.

Dec. 12. The German government appealed to the United States to inform the Entente governments that the Central Powers were **prepared to negotiate peace.** This offer appears to have been designed to anticipate any move by Wilson and may have been intended to divide the Allies or to prepare the way for the introduction of unrestricted submarine warfare. In any event, the military situation, after the wiping-out of Rumania, could hardly have been more favorable, a fact which was not overlooked in the drafting of the German note. Failure of the Germans to mention any specific terms, and the fact that all the advantages were on their side, made it relatively easy for the Allied governments (new energy of the Lloyd George and Briand cabinets) to reject the German advances (Dec. 30).

Dec. 18. President Wilson transmitted his own proposals to the warring powers. He suggested that the belligerents state their terms for peace and for arrangements to guarantee the world against renewal of conflict. The German, Austrian, and Turkish governments replied (Dec. 26) in an appreciative way, but reiterated their opinion that the best method would be to call a meeting for exchange of views. No definite terms were mentioned. The Allied Powers in their reply (Jan. 10, 1917) named specific terms. These included the restoration of Belgium, Serbia, and Montenegro; the evacuation of French, Russian, and Rumanian territory, with just reparation; the reorganization of Europe on the basis of nationalities; the restoration of territory previously taken from the Allies; the liberation of Italians, Slavs, Rumanians, and Czechoslovaks from foreign rule; the freeing of subject nationalities under Turkish rule and the expulsion of the Turks from Europe.

The far-reaching nature of the Allied terms, at a moment when the military situation was by no means in their favor, estranged even Wilson, who still stuck by the idea of "peace without victory" (speech to the Senate, Jan. 22). The first step, however, was to elicit from the Germans a concrete statement of aims. These were confidentially communicated to the president on Jan. 29: restitution of the part of Alsace occupied by the German forces; acquisition of a strategical and economic zone between Germany and Poland on the one hand and Russia on the other; return of colonies and the granting to Germany of colonial territory in accord with her population and economic needs; restoration of occupied France; renunciation of normal obstacles to normal commerce; compensation for German enterprises and civilians damaged by the war; freedom of the seas, etc.

Though this program was anything but hopeful, the president and the German ambassador, **Count Bernstorff**, continued to negotiate. It was felt that the Allies were rapidly coming to the point where they would be unable to continue the war without American aid and that, when that time came, they would have to accept American mediation and a compromise peace without victory. But these discussions were cut short by the decision of the Germans to begin unrestricted submarine warfare.

1917, Jan. 8. A meeting of the highest military and civil officials of Germany, **at Pless,** finally concluded that the unrestricted use of the submarine was the only method by which England could be brought to her knees and the war won. It was calculated that shipping could be sunk at the rate of 600,000 tons a month and that in six months England would have to yield. It was understood that the decision would probably mean war with the United States, but it was felt that the conflict would be over before the full weight of America could be thrown in. The chancellor, Bethmann-Hollweg, and men like Helfferich were not convinced of the soundness of the policy, but offered no other solution. To counterbalance the hostility of the United States, the foreign minister, Herr von Zimmermann, sent instructions to the German minister in Mexico to work for an **alliance with Mexico and Japan** directed against the United States (Jan. 19).

Jan. 31. The United States was notified that **unrestricted submarine war** would begin on Feb. 1.

Feb. 3. **The United States government severed relations** with the German government. In response to an appeal from

the president, Brazil, Bolivia, Peru, and other Latin-American states followed suit. China did likewise (Mar. 14).

The president had decided not to declare war until the Germans had committed an overt act. Several American ships were in fact sunk during Feb. and Mar. At the same time the British secret service intercepted and deciphered the **Zimmermann note,** revealing German plans against the United States.

Apr. 6. THE UNITED STATES DECLARED WAR ON GERMANY, following the president's war message to the Senate (April 2). War was not declared on Austria-Hungary until Dec. 7, 1917.

1917, Feb.-June. Secret negotiations between the **Emperor Charles** of Austria and his foreign minister, Count Czernin, **and the French and British governments.** The emperor seems to have been determined, from the time of his accession (Nov. 1916), to make peace, even without Germany. The negotiations were carried on through his brother-in-law, **Prince Sixtus of Bourbon,** who was serving in the Belgian army. After several secret meetings in Switzerland, Prince Sixtus went to Vienna, with the full knowledge and approval of the French foreign office, and had a conference with the emperor and Czernin. He returned to Paris with a letter from Charles (dated Mar. 24) in which the writer promised to use his influence with his allies to support "the just French claims relative to **Alsace-Lorraine."** Belgium was to be restored, with compensation for her losses; so also Serbia, which was to have access to the Adriatic. The emperor was also not opposed to Russia's acquisition of Constantinople.

This offer was well received by **Poincaré** and **Briand** and also by **Lloyd George.** The one flaw was the failure to offer adequate gains to Italy. In the ensuing negotiations, which continued till June (second visit of Prince Sixtus to Vienna, May 6-8), it became clear that the Austrians were willing to turn over the **Trentino** to Italy, but not **Trieste,** and that the Italians (statement of Sonnino at the **St. Jean de Maurienne conference,** Apr. 19-21) were unwilling to accept anything short of the full terms of the Treaty of London (see p. 925). Efforts continued to be made by Poincaré and Lloyd George, but the French prime minister, **M. Ribot** (succeeded Briand, Mar. 20), took a hopeless attitude and indeed the Italians made no move in the direction of concessions.

20. CAMPAIGNS IN ASIATIC TURKEY, 1916-1917

1916, Apr. 26. **Anglo-Russian-French agreement** with regard to the future partition of Asiatic Turkey. This agreement had been maturing ever since Mar. 1915, when France and England promised Russia Constantinople and the Straits. It provided that in the independent Arab state that was to be formed, **England** should have as a sphere of influence Mesopotamia and in Syria the ports of Haifa and Acre. The **French sphere** was to include the coastal strip of Syria, the Adana vilayet, Cilicia and southern Kurdistan, with Kharput. **Palestine** was to be under an international administration. **Russia** was to receive Armenia and part of Kurdistan and northern Anatolia westward from Trebizond to a point to be determined later.

May 9. **THE SYKES-PICOT AGREEMENT** between England and France. This made the French and British claims more specific. The territories mentioned in the above agreement were to be the French and British administrative zones, while the rest of Arabia was to be divided into French and British spheres of influence, though organized as an Arab state or federation of states.

1917, Apr. 19-21. **The St. Jean de Maurienne Agreement.** In return for recognition of the Sykes-Picot Agreement, Italy was given further concessions in the regions of Adalia and Smyrna.

Through the Sykes-Picot Agreement the British were involving themselves in serious difficulties for the future, because these agreements were not entirely compatible with other agreements made with Arab chieftains, agreements which, indeed, were not compatible with each other.

a. ARABIA

1914, Oct. 31. **Lord Kitchener** had offered **Hussein**, the Grand Sherif of Mecca, a conditional guaranty of independence. Negotiations between the sherif and the British government were definitely embarked upon in July, 1915.

1915, July 14. **Hussein submitted his terms** for entering upon a campaign against the Turks. Britain was to recognize the independence of the Arab countries south of 37° N. L.

Oct. 24. **The British reply** took exception to the Arab claims to the Mersina-Alexandretta region and to Syria west of Damascus, Hama, Homs, and Aleppo. For the rest the boundaries of the future Arab state were accepted with respect to "those portions of the territories therein in which Great Britain is free to act without detriment to her ally, France."

Nov. 5. **Hussein accepted the British** proposals with regard to Mersina and Alexandretta, but held out for Beirut and Aleppo, as well as Baghdad and Basra, though he was willing to recognize the British right to temporary occupation of the latter places.

Dec. 21. **The French government accepted** the idea of Arab administration of western Syria, but only under French influence.

1916, Jan. 30. **The British accepted Hussein's terms,** leaving the exact status of Baghdad and Basra, and of the sphere of French influence in Syria, undetermined.

b. NEJD

1915, Dec. 25. **The government of India,** after long negotiations with **Ibn Sa'ud,** King of Nejd, concluded an agreement with him (ratified July 18, 1916) by which it recognized Nejd, Qatif, Jubail, and territories along the Persian Gulf coast of Arabia as the independent possessions of Ibn Sa'ud, despite the obvious contradiction between these concessions and those offered to Hussein.

c. ARAB REVOLT

1916, June 5. Beginning of the **Arab revolt in the Hijaz.** Attack on the Turkish garrison at Medina.

June 7. Hussein proclaimed the **independence of the Hijaz.** The garrison of Mecca surrendered (June 10).

Oct. 29. **Hussein proclaimed King of the Arabs.** He summoned all Arabs to make war on the Turks.

Dec. 15. The British government recognized Hussein as King of the Hijaz.

It was largely in order to strengthen the Arab insurrection that **Sir Archibald Mur-**

ray (commander in Egypt, since Mar. 19, 1916) decided on a cautious offensive in Sinai and Palestine.

1916, Nov. 15. Beginning of the advance.

Dec. 21. The British took El Arish, after building a railway and pipeline across the desert. They then took the fortified posts of **Magdhaba** (Dec. 23) and **Rafah** (Jan. 9, 1917).

1917, Mar. 26-27. First battle of Gaza. The cavalry had surrounded the town, but through a misunderstanding was recalled.

Apr. 17-19. Second battle of Gaza. The Turks, in the interval, had strengthened their position and had been reinforced by German troops (*Asienkorps*, under von Falkenhayn). The British were forced back with heavy losses.

June 28. Murray was replaced by **Sir Edmund Allenby.**

July 6. Emergence of the spectacular war hero, **Col. T. E. Lawrence,** who galvanized the Arab movement and took Aqaba, thus beginning the brilliant thrusts against the Turkish garrisons and especially against the guards of the Hijaz railway, the most important link in the Turkish communications.

d. MESOPOTAMIA

Operations on the Mesopotamian front

were also resumed in the autumn of 1916, with **Sir Stanley Maude** in command. After troops and supplies had been collected in large numbers and careful preparations had been made

1916, Dec. 13. The advance was begun toward Kut-el-Amara.

1917, Jan. 9-Feb. 24. Battle of Kut. The city was taken Feb. 23. The victorious British then pursued the Turks toward Baghdad.

Mar. 11. BAGHDAD OCCUPIED BY THE BRITISH. The British campaign in Mesopotamia was accompanied by a new **Russian advance in western Persia.**

1917, Mar. 2. The Russians took Hamadan, then **Kirmanshah** (Mar. 12), **Karind** (Mar. 17), and **Khanikin** (Apr. 4).

Apr. 23. The British reached Samarra, 80 miles north of Baghdad.

July 8. The Russians began to retreat from western Persia: one of the effects of the Russian Revolution.

Sept. 29. The British captured Ramadi on the Euphrates, and then (Nov. 6) **Tikrit** on the Tigris, these points marking the farthest extent of the advance in Mesopotamia in 1917.

21. THE WESTERN FRONT, 1917

The operations of 1917 were prefaced by important changes in the German and French high commands.

1916, Aug. 29. Hindenburg succeeded von Falkenhayn as chief of staff of the German field armies, with **Gen. von Ludendorff** as quartermaster-general. Despite their constant advocacy of a concentration of forces on the eastern front, both Hindenburg and Ludendorff now came to share the opinion of Falkenhayn, that a decision could be reached only on the French front.

Dec. 12. Gen. Nivelle succeeded Joffre as commander in chief of the French armies. Nivelle had distinguished himself in the fighting at Verdun. His energy and dash made a profound impression, and his appointment, it was hoped, would lead to a more fruitful campaign.

Nivelle, like his predecessor, hoped to effect a break-through and planned a great French offensive in the direction of Laon, this to be introduced by a preliminary

Franco-English advance on both sides of the Somme. The execution of this plan was delayed by **disagreement between Nivelle and Haig,** who himself would have preferred an offensive in Flanders and who resented being put more or less under Nivelle. The friction that ensued required a number of conferences between French and English statesmen (Jan.–Mar. 1917).

In the interval Ludendorff had decided that the western front could be made stronger and more defensible if some of the bulges could be eliminated. A strong new position was therefore constructed, which became known as the *Hindenburg Line.* After completely destroying the area between, and after mining the roads

1917, Feb. 23. The Germans effected a preliminary withdrawal between Arras and Soissons.

Mar. 4-Apr. 5. The main withdrawal was carried through. The Germans abandoned **Bapaume, Péronne, Roye, Noyon, and Chauny.**

Though this move on the part of the Germans dislocated the French plans, Nivelle was still optimistic. His own generals warned him and the members of the new **cabinet of Ribot** (succeeded Briand, Mar. 20) and Painlevé (minister of war) brought pressure upon him to give up the plan. This opposition was overcome by Nivelle's threat to resign, which the government yielded to from consideration of public opinion.

Apr. 9-May 4. BATTLE OF ARRAS. The British 3d army (Gen. **Allenby**) began the advance after a thorough bombardment and heavy gas attack (use of the gas projector). **Canadian troops took Vimy Ridge** and the British made a total advance of about 4 miles, without, however, effecting a break-through. On the Somme they advanced to near St. Quentin.

Apr. 16-20. SECOND BATTLE OF

THE AISNE and **THIRD BATTLE OF CHAMPAGNE.** Nivelle's plans had been so well advertised that the Germans had been able to concentrate large forces in the area of attack. The whole operation failed; in the fighting till May 21 the French took only the **Chemin des Dames,** and this with very heavy losses. Discontent and mutiny became widespread in the weary army, till 16 corps were affected (May–June).

May 15. Nivelle was dismissed and his place taken by **Gen. Pétain,** who did what he could to redress the grievances of the troops and wisely decided to stand on the defensive until the American reinforcements could make themselves felt. At the same time the government proceeded with the greatest rigor against socialist and pacifist agitators. Twenty-three leaders were executed.

22. THE SUBMARINE WAR, 1917

The German high command reckoned confidently on winning the war through the destruction of the English food-supply. The prospects were, indeed, excellent. Already in the last months of 1916 German submarines had destroyed 300,000 tons of shipping a month. By the beginning of 1917 the Germans had about 120 submarines, the number being increased to 134 by Oct. 1917.

1917, Apr. Submarine warfare reached the high point. In this month alone 875,000 tons of shipping were destroyed, more than half of it British. This figure exceeded the German estimates (600,000) and brought the British admiralty to the point of despair. Finally, owing largely to

the insistence of Lloyd George, the admiralty agreed to try **convoying** merchant ships (first convoy, May 10). The system proved to be an unqualified success. At the same time the British increased the numbers of their destroyers and submarine chasers, developed the depth bomb and the system of scouting with hydroplanes. Shipbuilding was pushed to the very limit.

By Oct. 1917 the Germans had destroyed about 8,000,000 tons of shipping, but they had lost 50 submarines and their campaign was becoming less and less effective. By the beginning of 1918 the Allies were building more new tonnage than was being destroyed. The German gamble on the submarine had failed.

23. THE BRITISH OFFENSIVES, 1917

The collapse of the Nivelle offensive gave **Haig** greater freedom to act than he had enjoyed before. In view of the great destructiveness of the submarines, based on the Belgian coast, Haig was more determined than ever to start an **offensive in Flanders** and to try to roll up the German right flank. The French command was not enthusiastic about the plan, and pointed out that it could co-operate only to the extent of launching lesser attacks on the Verdun and Champagne fronts.

1917, June 7. Battle of Messines (till June 14). The British 2d army (Gen. **Plumer**) launched a surprise attack on **Messines Ridge.** and was

entirely successful in straightening the Ypres salient.

July 31-Nov. 10. THIRD BATTLE OF YPRES. Despite the opposition of Lloyd George and the skepticism of some of his subordinates, Haig proceeded hopefully to the main offensive. The third battle of Ypres (or **Passchendaele**) was a series of 8 heavy attacks, carried through in driving rain and fought over ground waterlogged and muddy. No break-through was effected and the total gain was about 5 miles of territory, which made the Ypres salient more inconvenient than ever and cost the British about 400,000 men. The British forces were almost as demoralized by this operation as the French by the Nivelle offensive.

Aug. 20-Dec. 15. Second battle of Verdun. Intended to serve as relief for the British in Flanders. The French, after careful preparations, gained several key positions, even on the east bank of the Meuse.

Oct. 23-Nov. 1. Battle of Malmaison. The French, attacking along the Chemin des Dames, managed to cut off a German salient northeast of Soissons. The Germans fell back to the Oise-Aisne Canal.

Nov. 20-Dec. 3. Battle of Cambrai. First great tank raid. Without preliminary bombardment the British launched a surprise attack with 380 tanks. Without much trouble they penetrated the three German lines and were on the point of breaking through into open country, but the exhausted troops were unable to take advantage of the situation. The operation had been planned as a limited one and inadequate reserves were on hand. The British advanced 5 miles in the direction toward **Cambrai** on a 6-mile front, but Nov. 30 the Germans suddenly counter-attacked on both flanks of the salient and forced the British to give up much of the ground they had conquered.

24. THE RUSSIAN FRONT, 1917

The situation in the east was dominated, in 1917, by the developments of the **Russian Revolution** (see p. 1028). But the provisional government (**Paul Miliukov,** foreign minister, Mar. 15–May 16, 1917) was strongly in favor of prosecution of the war in the hope of realizing the national aspirations. The same was true of **Alexander Kerensky** (minister of war, May 16; prime minister, July 16), who hoped to combat disruptive tendencies and galvanize the country by a new military effort.

1917, July 1. Brusilov began a **great offensive on the Galician front** (battles of Brzezany, Koniuchy, and Zloczow). The Russians advanced until the Germans counterattacked.

July 18-28. Battle of East Galicia. The Germans and Austrians drove the Russians back and retook **Halicz, Tarnopol, Stanislav** (July 24–26), and Czernowitz (Aug. 3).

Aug. 1. Brusilov was succeeded by Gen. Kornilov.

Sept. 3-5. Battle of Riga. The Germans attacked Kornilov, surrounded and took Riga (Sept. 3).

Sept. 8-14. Kornilov marched on Petrograd as leader of a counter-revolutionary movement, which failed.

Oct. 11-20. The Germans, having overrun much of Latvia, **conquered the Baltic Islands** (Oesel taken, Oct. 16; Moon Island and Dago, Oct. 17–18).

Nov. 7 (Oct. 25 O.S.). Bolshevik *coup d'état* in Russia.

Nov. 28. The new Bolshevik régime offered the Germans an armistice and peace.

Dec. 15. Armistice concluded on the eastern front.

25. THE BALKAN SITUATION, 1917

The Macedonian front was quiet during the winter of 1916–1917, but operations were resumed in March.

1917, Mar. 11-19. Second battle of Monastir and battle of Lake Presba.

May 5-19. Battle of the Vardar (or Doiran). These engagements were inconclusive, but they served to convince the Allied powers that success on this front would be impossible so long as the Greek government was unreliable.

June 11-12. The newly arrived French envoy (**M. Jonnart**) presented an Allied ultimatum, demanding the abdication of King Constantine and the renunciation of the claims of the Greek crown prince. At the same time Allied troops invaded Thessaly and a French force occupied the Isthmus of Corinth.

June 12. Constantine abdicated in favor of his second son, Alexander.

June 26. Venizelos became premier, replacing M. Zaimis, who had succeeded Lambros on May 3.

June 27. The Greek government severed relations with the Central Powers and definitely **entered the war on the Allied side.**

26. THE COLLAPSE OF ITALY, 1917

During the first part of 1917 the Italian effort continued to center on the Isonzo.

1917, May 12-June 8.   Tenth battle of the Isonzo.

Aug. 17-Sept. 12.   Eleventh and last battle of the Isonzo. As a result of two years of operations the Italians had advanced only about 10 miles, or halfway to Trieste.

In part the Italian failure was due to inadequate artillery and ammunition. Gen. Cadorna had already tried to persuade England and France to send supplies and men in large numbers, so that a knock-out blow might be delivered against war-weary Austria. Gen. Foch and Lloyd George were distinctly favorable to this plan, but Haig had his way and proceeded to the offensive in Flanders.

In the meanwhile **Ludendorff** decided to follow the annihilation of Serbia and Rumania with a similar assault on Italy, which would relieve the pressure on Austria. Six divisions of German troops were sent to reinforce the nine Austrian divisions on the Isonzo front. It was decided to attack on the Upper Isonzo, near Caporetto, in the hope of breaking through and advancing as far as the Tagliamento River.

Oct. 24-Dec. 26.   THE CAPORETTO CAMPAIGN (sometimes called the twelfth battle of the Isonzo). The German-Austrian forces attacked after a short bombardment, but in heavy fog. The Italian forces, worn down by long and inconclusive fighting under trying conditions, broke at once. The Austro-German advance on the first day was fully 10 miles. In three days they were through the hills and almost prevented the completely demoralized enemy from crossing the Tagliamento. **The Italians fell back to the Piave.** French and British troops were hurried to Italy to help hold the front (Nov. 3, 4). The Austro-German forces, outrunning their supply system, were obliged to slow down. The line became fixed on the Piave River, after the Italians had lost almost 300,000 men taken prisoner and even more than that in deserters.

Nov. 7.   Gen. Cadorna was replaced by Gen. Diaz, who devoted himself to establishing a defensive position and above all to restoring the morale of the troops.

27. POLITICAL DEVELOPMENTS, 1917-1918

In the summer of 1917 peace no longer appeared to be far in the future. The inability of both sides to win a decision on the battlefield and the victory of the revolution in Russia led to a wide spread of defeatism, pacifism, and socialism.

a. FRANCE

1917, Mar. 17.   The Briand cabinet was obliged to resign, and was succeeded by a ministry in which **Alexandre Ribot** was premier and **M. Painlevé** foreign minister. It was this cabinet, led by a tired septuagenarian, that had to bear the full brunt of the discontent arising from Nivelle's ill-starred offensive. Deserted by the Socialists, who were outraged by the government's refusal of passports to delegates to the Socialist conference at Stockholm, Ribot resigned (Sept. 9).

Sept. 12.   M. Painlevé formed a cabinet, in which Ribot became foreign minister. This proved to be merely a transition government, unable to stem the tide of war-weariness.

Oct. 23.   M. Barthou succeeded M. Ribot as foreign minister.

Nov. 16.   The Painlevé cabinet fell. Formation of the great **ministry of Georges Clemenceau,** in which the prime minister was also minister of war, while **M. Pichon** was given the foreign office. Clemenceau's policy was one of victory *sans phrase.* He set out at once to hunt down the preachers of disaffection (**Malvy, Humbert, Bolo Pasha, Caillaux**) and to organize the country for victory.

b. AUSTRIA-HUNGARY

In **Austria-Hungary** the continuance of the war and the failure of the emperor's peace efforts resulted in much instability.

1917, May 23.   The Hungarian ministry of Count Tisza resigned.

June 15-Aug. 9.   Count Esterhazy's ministry in Hungary.

Aug. 21-1918, Oct. 24.   Count Wekerle's ministry in Hungary.

1917, June 18. The cabinet of Count Clam-Martinitz in Austria resigned, being succeeded by a new government under **Dr. von Seidler**, which continued in office until June 21, 1918.

1918, Apr. 15. Count Czernin, the Austrian foreign minister, was **replaced by Baron Burian**, who continued in office until Oct. 25, 1918.

c. GERMANY

In Germany the growing unrest led to certain important promises by the government.

1917, Apr. 7. The Emperor William, as King of Prussia, in an **Easter Message** announced the end of the famous three-class system of voting in Prussia. The introduction of a system of equal, direct, and secret suffrage was announced somewhat later (July 11).

July 14. The Chancellor, Theobald von Bethmann-Hollweg, having lost the support of the Conservatives, National Liberals, and Center and having long since become objectionable to the military men, **was allowed to retire.**

July 14–Oct. 30. Chancellorship of Dr. George Michaelis, an almost unknown official who was the appointee of the high command and served chiefly as a cloak for the **power of Ludendorff**, who henceforth directed political as well as military affairs.

July 19. Under the leadership of **Matthias Erzberger** and his Catholic Center Party, the **Reichstag passed a resolution** in favor of a peace of understanding, without annexations (212 Centrists, majority Socialists and National Liberals against 126 Conservatives, National Liberals and Independent Socialists). The new chancellor declared that his aims were attainable within the limits of the resolution as "he understood it." But the German government, like the Austrian, allowed Socialist delegates to attend the conference at Stockholm.

Aug. 5. Richard von Kühlmann succeeded Zimmermann as German secretary for foreign affairs.

Oct. 30. Count Hertling replaced Michaelis as chancellor.

d. ITALY

In Italy the Boselli cabinet resigned at the height of the Caporetto disaster (Oct. 25).

Oct. 29. A new Italian cabinet was formed by Orlando.

The peace offers of Austria, as transmitted through Prince Sixtus (see p. 936), had failed, but they were followed almost at once by new efforts by **Pope Benedict.** After informal soundings in Berlin and in the Allied capitals

Aug. 1. The pope put forward outline proposals to serve as a basis for peace. These included disarmament, arbitration, freedom of the seas, renunciation of indemnities, evacuation and restoration of occupied territory, and conciliatory examination of conflicting claims as in Alsace-Lorraine, the Trentino, the Balkans, Poland, etc. To these suggestions the Central Powers replied accepting the general principles, but evading a commitment with regard to territorial claims. The Allied powers and the United States from the first took an unfriendly stand, insisting that the rulers of Germany were not to be trusted and that it would be impossible to negotiate until Germany had made a definite statement with regard to Belgium and Alsace-Lorraine. The pope made repeated efforts to secure from Berlin a clear statement on these points. The German government, however, though ready to restore Belgium, was unready to make any concessions on Alsace-Lorraine and furthermore refused to publish any terms. It is reasonably clear that at this time, when pacifist sentiment ran fairly high in all countries and extended even into governing circles, **the Alsace-Lorraine question** had become the great obstacle to negotiation. Even the efforts of the Socialists, whose program was not so very different from that advanced by the pope, were unable to make any headway. **The Socialist Congress** which met at **Stockholm** (May 10–) and was enthusiastically supported by the Russian, German, Austrian, and Scandinavian groups, was frustrated by the absence of English, French, and American representatives, whose governments had refused them passports.

28. THE SETTLEMENTS IN THE EAST, 1917-1918

While discussion of peace between the western powers led to an *impasse*, the winter of 1917–1918 produced a settlement in the east.

1916, Nov. 5. **The Germans,** being in occupation of Poland, announced the formation of an independent **Polish state.** The object of this move, inspired by the military men, was to win over the Poles and induce them to enlist on the German side. This hope was sadly disappointed.

1917, Mar. 30. The Russian provisional government recognized the independence of Poland.

Apr. 5. The British government adhered to the principle of an independent and united Poland.

Sept. 12. The Central powers granted a constitution to what was formerly Russian Poland, and appointed a regency council (Oct. 15).

Nov. 7. **The Bolshevik Revolution in Russia** (see p. 1029). Lenin and his followers, who regarded the war as a capitalist and imperialist venture, were in favor of a peace without annexations or indemnities, and were determined to make peace, which the Russian people yearned for. The old Russian Empire, indeed, was already dissolving.

Nov. 20. The Ukrainians proclaimed the **Ukrainian People's Republic.**

Nov. 21. The Bolshevik government, having invited all belligerents (Nov. 8) to make peace on the basis of no annexations and no indemnities, and having elicited no reply, opened separate discussions with the Central powers.

Nov. 28. The local diet proclaimed the **independence of Estonia.**

Dec. 3. **Opening of peace conference at Brest-Litovsk.** Germany (Von Kühlmann), Austria (Czernin), and their allies negotiated an armistice with Russia (represented by Trotsky).

Dec. 6. **Finland proclaimed its independence.**

Dec. 23. **Proclamation of the Moldavian** (i.e. Bessarabian) **Republic.**

Dec. 25. The Central Powers accepted the principle of no annexations and no indemnities on condition that the Allied Powers accept it within 10 days. Trotsky's appeals brought no response and there was nothing to moderate the German demands (these were laid down by the Ger-

man general staff, and were regarded as too extreme by Von Kühlmann).

1918, Jan. 4. Beginning of the peace discussions at Brest, after a suspension of ten days. Trotsky refused to recognize the new Baltic states without a plebiscite, and much acrimonious discussion ensued.

Jan. 12. **Latvia declared its independence.**

Feb. 1. **The Central Powers recognized the independence of the Ukraine.**

Feb. 9. **TREATY OF PEACE between the Central Powers and the Ukraine** signed at Brest-Litovsk.

Feb. 10. Trotsky declared the war ended, without peace having been made.

Feb. 18. The Germans at once resumed hostilities. They took **Dvinsk** (Feb. 18), **Dorpat** (Feb. 24), **Reval** (Feb. 25), **Pskov** (Feb. 25), and **Narva** (Mar. 4), advancing to within 100 miles of Petrograd.

Feb. 28. The Russians, at the insistence of Lenin, renewed negotiations at Brest.

Mar. 2. At the request of the Finnish government the **Germans occupied the Aaland Islands.**

Mar. 3. The Russians signed the **TREATY OF BREST-LITOVSK,** abandoning Poland, Lithuania, the Ukraine, the Baltic provinces, Finland, and Transcaucasia.

Mar. 3. In order to clear the Bolsheviks out of the Ukraine the Germans and Austrians sent an expeditionary force. They occupied **Kiev** (Mar. 3), **Odessa** (Mar. 13), **Nicolaiev** (Mar. 17), **Kharkov** (Apr. 8), and then invaded the Crimea, taking **Sevastopol** (May 1). The Ukraine henceforth became an important granary for the Central Powers, though the returns were never as great as anticipated. Under German direction Gen. **Skoropadski was proclaimed Hetman of the Ukraine** (Apr. 29).

Apr. 3. **German forces landed in Finland** itself. They took **Helsingfors** (Apr. 13) and **Viborg** (Apr. 30). After a five-day battle between Lahti and Tavastehus **the Whites,** supported by the Germans, **defeated the Reds** and the Finnish civil war came to an end (May 7).

June 4. The Lithuanian Assembly elected Duke William of Württemberg king.

Oct. 8. The Finnish Assembly proclaimed Prince Frederick Charles of Hesse king. German troops remained in Finland until Dec. 16, 1918.

RUMANIA was likewise obliged to make peace in the winter of 1918.

1917, Aug. 6–Sept. 3. Battle of Putna. After the failure of the Brusilov offensive (see p. 940) the Germans and Austrians began the invasion of northern Moldavia. Though it had been reorganized by the French general Berthelot, the Rumanian army was forced to fall back.

Dec. 6. Truce of Focsani. Hostilities between the Central Powers and Rumania ceased.

1918, Feb. 6. A German ultimatum demanded the opening of peace negotiations at once. Bratianu resigned and was succeeded by Averescu as premier and foreign minister.

Mar. 5. Preliminary peace between the Central Powers and Rumania.

May 7. DEFINITIVE TREATY OF BUCHAREST. Rumania was obliged to cede Dobrudja to Bulgaria and to turn over the Carpathian passes to Austria-Hungary. The Germans took a 90-year lease of the Rumanian oil-wells.

Apr. 9. The Moldavian Republic (Bessarabia) proclaimed its union with Rumania. The Russian government protested against this (Apr. 23), but the union was recognized by the Central Powers in the Treaty of Bucharest.

29. OPERATIONS IN THE WEST, 1918

The tremendous gains made by the Germans in the east did not serve to improve the situation with respect to the western powers. On the contrary, it was generally felt that the terms imposed on Russia and Rumania were irrefutable proof of Germany's expansionist aims. In the west the demands for peace died away and the governments were able to take a stronger line than ever.

1918, Jan. 5. Lloyd George, in an address to the Trades Unions Congress, formulated the British war aims. These included the restoration of Belgium, Serbia, Montenegro, and the occupied parts of France, Italy, and Rumania. In addition, a "reconsideration" of the great wrong done to France in 1871; the establishment of an independent Poland "comprising all those genuinely Polish elements who desire to form part of it"; genuine self-government of the nationalities in the Austro-Hungarian Monarchy; satisfaction of the Italian national claims, and of Rumanian aspirations; "recognition of the separate national conditions" of Arabia, Armenia, Mesopotamia, Syria, and Palestine. Lloyd George envisaged further some future organization to limit armaments and prevent war.

Jan. 8. in an address to Congress President Wilson outlined a peace program consisting of Fourteen Points, as follows: (1) Open covenants openly arrived at. (2) Absolute freedom of navigation alike in peace and war, except as the seas might be closed by international action to enforce international covenants. (3) The removal, so far as possible, of all economic

barriers. (4) Adequate guaranties that armaments would be reduced to the lowest point consistent with domestic safety. (5) An impartial adjustment of all colonial claims on the principle that the interests of the population must have equal weight with the claims of the government. (6) The evacuation of Russian territory and the free determination of her own political and national policy. (7) Evacuation and restoration of Belgium. (8) Evacuation and restoration of French territory and righting of the wrong done to France in the matter of Alsace-Lorraine. (9) Readjustment of the frontiers of Italy along clearly recognizable lines of nationality. (10) Opportunity for autonomous development for the peoples of Austria-Hungary. (11) Evacuation and restoration of Rumanian, Serbian, and Montenegrin territory, together with access to the sea for Serbia. (12) The Turkish parts of the Ottoman Empire to be given a secure sovereignty, but the other nationalities to be given an opportunity for autonomous development, and the Dardanelles to be permanently opened to the ships of all nations under international guaranties. (13) An independent Poland, to include territories indisputably Polish, with free and secure access to the sea. (14) A general association of nations to be formed to afford mutual guaranties of political independence and territorial integrity to great and small states alike.

The Allied war aims could be realized only through military victory, and prospects of this were not very good at a time when the Germans were able to transfer troops from the east to the west and when the American forces were not yet numerous enough to make much difference. Some efforts had been made, however, to establish greater co-ordination of effort among the Allies, and after the Italian disaster at Caporetto

1917, Nov. 27. The Supreme War Council had been established, consisting of the leading statesmen, with their military advisers (first Sir Henry Wilson, Foch, Cadorna, and Bliss). Even this new board was unable to establish harmony. The British and French were continually dickering about the extent of their respective fronts, the use of the reserves, etc.

The Germans, now disillusioned about the submarine campaign, fully cognizant of the war-weariness of their allies, and feeling acutely the pinch of the blockade, decided to stake everything on a decision in the west, which it was hoped could be reached before the Americans arrived in great force. Ludendorff planned a series of crushing blows to be delivered against the English on a 60-mile front south of Arras, by which he hoped to break through, roll up the opposing forces, and drive them westward to the sea.

The British expected an attack, but not along the southern part of their front, so that the 5th army (Gen. Gough) was left holding an extensive front with relatively few forces.

1918, Mar. 21-Apr. 5. THE GREAT MARCH OFFENSIVE. After cleverly concealed preparations, the Germans began with a bombardment of 6000 guns and a heavy gas attack. They advanced from St. Quentin in a heavy fog, which recurred for several days. The British line broke and in a few days the Germans drove in the British line to a depth of about 40 miles, taking **Péronne, Ham, Bapaume, Chauny, Noyon,** and even **Montdidier.** The hasty and generous supply of reserves by the French helped to check the advance.

Mar. 26. In the midst of the crisis a conference at **Doullens** named Gen. **Foch** to co-ordinate operations on the west front.

Apr. 14. Foch named commander in chief of the Allied armies in France. In practice the national com-

manders (Haig, King Albert, Pershing) retained extensive control.

Apr. 9-29. Battles of the Lys. The second great German blow, delivered south of Ypres on a short front. The Germans stormed **Messines Ridge** and took **Armentières,** opening up a wide breach in the British front. Lack of reserves made it impossible for them to take full advantage of the situation.

May 27-June 6. (THIRD) BATTLE OF THE AISNE. Ludendorff, in order to draw the French reserves from Flanders preparatory to the main offensive there, arranged an attack upon the French between Soissons and Rheims, along the strong and therefore weakly held **Chemin des Dames.** The French were taken by surprise and driven back 13 miles on the first day. The Germans took **Soissons** (May 29) and May 30 reached the Marne River, only 37 miles from Paris. The new salient was 40 miles deep.

June 9-14. Battle of the Matz. Ludendorff, astounded at his own success in Champagne, gave up the idea of an offensive in Flanders and undertook to join up the Soissons and Noyon salients by an attack toward Compiègne. The Germans advanced about six miles, but the move had been hastily prepared and the French were able to meet it.

June 4. The American forces at Château-Thierry. The 2d division, collaborating with the French, managed to break the German advance. In this engagement the Americans first played a substantial rôle.

July 15-Aug. 7. (SECOND) BATTLE OF THE MARNE. Ludendorff threw his weary troops into yet another attack west and east of Rheims. East of Rheims no progress was made, and west of the city, though the **Germans crossed the Marne,** they made but little progress against strong French and American forces. **July 18 Foch ordered a counter-attack,** in which nine American divisions took part. The Germans were forced back over the Marne to the Vesle River, while the French retook **Soissons** (Aug. 2). The Allied counter-offensive was of importance chiefly because it frustrated Ludendorff's plan for a great attack in Flanders, and because it enabled Foch to take the initiative in the months to come.

30. THE ACTION AT ZEEBRUGGE AND OSTEND

Naval operations during the years 1917–1918 were confined largely to submarine and destroyer activities. **The Germans repeatedly raided the English coast** (Apr. 20, 26, 1917; Jan. 14, Feb. 15, 1918) and **attacked British convoys in the North Sea** (Oct. 17, Dec. 12, 1917). But there were no larger engagements, excepting for a British **light cruiser attack off Heligoland,** which was beaten back (Nov. 17, 1917).

In order to meet the constant menace from the submarine, Adm. Keyes of the Dover Patrol had long urged an operation against the submarine bases, Zeebrugge and Ostend, on the Belgian coast.

1918, Apr. 23. After months of careful preparation an **attack was made on the mole at Zeebrugge** while three old cruisers were run in and sunk in the canal entrance. A similar operation at Ostend was unsuccessful, and even at Zeebrugge the blocking was not complete.

Oct. 17-20. The British, in their advance, took Zeebrugge, Ostend, and the other Channel ports.

Nov. 21. Following the armistice **the German High Seas Fleet surrendered to the British at Rosyth.**

1919, June 21. The German fleet (10 battleships, 9 armored cruisers, 8 smaller cruisers, 50 torpedo boats, 102 submarines, totaling about 500,000 tons) **was scuttled** by the crews under command of Adm. Reuter, **at Scapa Flow,** where the fleet had been interned.

31. THE WAR IN THE AIR, 1914-1918

Although only France had done much before the war to develop the military use of the airplane, throughout the war the British and the Germans were the main antagonists.

1914, Aug. 30. **The first German airplane raid on Paris.**

Sept. 22, Oct. 8, Nov. 21. British airplanes raided the German flying-fields at **Düsseldorf, Cologne,** and **Friedrichshafen.**

Dec. 21. **The first German air raid on England** (Dover).

On the western front, and on other fronts to a less extent, the airplane was used for reconnaissance, but almost immediately (Sept. 1914) experiments were made by the British in wireless communication between airplanes and artillery, in aerial photography, and in bomb-dropping. There was not much aerial combat until the middle of 1915.

1915, Oct. The Germans began the use of the **Fokker** plane, equipped with a device allowing the pilot to shoot through the propeller. This plane was so superior that, for the better part of a year, **it gave the Germans mastery of the air,** though the British, with a greater number of planes, kept carrying the fight over the German lines. Great German fighters of this period were **Oswald Boelcke** (d. Oct. 28, 1916) and **Max Immelmann** (d. June 1916).

1916, April. **Battle of Verdun,** including heavy air fighting between Germans and French. The French, with the **Nieuport 3** and the **Spad 3,** succeeded in securing mastery of the air. Great French fighters were **René Fonck** and **Georges Guynemer** (d. Sept. 1917).

July. **Battle of the Somme.** The British, with the new **De Havilland** and **Farman Experimental** planes, definitely put an end to German **Fokker** supremacy. Great British fighters: **Albert Ball** (d. May 7, 1917), **J. T. B. McCudden** (d. July, 1918), **W. A. Bishop,** and **Edward Mannock** (d. July, 1918).

Sept. The Germans introduced the **Albatross and Halberstadt planes** and developed formation flying. This re-established something like a balance on the British front, though the British had a distinct superiority in numbers and continued to take the offensive.

1917. The British began to use the **Scouting Experimental** and **Bristol Fighter.** This period was marked by the spectacular achievements of **Manfred von Richthofen** (d. Apr. 21, 1918) and by the development of ever larger formations and more intricate tactics.

1918. The Allied superiority became more marked, and American air squadrons began to take part (Apr.). The British did much in the development of large-scale bombardment, especially of munitions centers. At sea much use was made of the airplane for scouting and for submarine-chasing.

During these years the Germans continued their raids on England, first with **Zeppelins**, then with airplanes, with the object of drawing back British air forces from France, of interrupting industry, and of demoralizing the civil population.

1915, Jan. 19. First German airship raid on England.

Oct. 13. The worst of the **Zeppelin raids** on eastern England and London. There were 19 such raids in 1915 and 41 air raids in 1916. On Sept. 2, 1916, London was raided by 14 Zeppelins at once. But by the end of 1916 the British had elaborated a fairly good defense against airships (fighting plane, anti-aircraft guns, searchlights, sirens, etc.). The Germans used 80 Zeppelins in the course of the war, of which only 7 remained at the time of the armistice.

1916, Nov. 28. First German airplane raid on London. There were a great many of these in the course of 1917–1918, first by daylight, then by night. There was a considerable loss of life and property, but the raids do not appear to have achieved any marked results.

32. THE RUSSIAN SITUATION, 1918

The **Treaty of Brest-Litovsk** put the Russian régime at the mercy of the Germans and plans were at once evolved by the Allies for reconstituting the eastern front in order to prevent the transfer of German forces to the west.

1918, May 24. General Poole arrived at Murmansk to arrange for an expeditionary force, which landed June 23. The British were joined later by American contingents (Sept. 4) and other Allied forces. They seized part of the railway from Murmansk (opened for service Dec. 8, 1916), and, after a pro-Entente revolution at **Archangel**, took over that port (Aug. 1–2). As a result a practical state of war existed between the Allied governments and the Russian Bolshevik government.

May 26. About 100,000 **Czech troops**, many of whom had deserted from the Austrian armies to the Russians, began hostilities against the Bolsheviks, while being transported across Siberia to Vladivostok. They seized **Samara, Simbirsk**, and **Kazan** on the Volga, and in eastern Siberia they took **Omsk, Irkutsk**, and other points on the Trans-Siberian Railway. Aug. 13 they declared war on Germany and were recognized as a nation by the British (Aug. 13) and the Americans (Sept. 3).

July 26. The Japanese government accepted an American proposal for **joint action in Siberia** in support of the Czechs.

Aug. 3. A British force was landed at Vladivostok, followed by a Japanese force (Aug. 11) and later by Americans and French.

Sept. 5. Japanese forces took **Khabarovsk**.

Oct. 14. British forces reached **Irkutsk**. Contact established with the Czechs, who controlled the railway in western Siberia.

Nov. 18. A counter-revolutionary coup led by Adm. **Kolchak** overthrew the All-Russian (anti-Bolshevik, but liberal) government at Omsk. **Kolchak became Dictator of All Russia**, controlling much of Siberia and part of eastern Russia.

In the **TRANSCAUCASIAN REGION** there ensued a similar conflict between the Russians, Germans, and Turks on the one hand and the British on the other.

1917, Sept. 20. Proclamation of the Transcaucasian Republic.

1918, Jan. 27. Gen. Dunsterville with a British force set out from Baghdad for the Caspian to assure the British position in the oil regions of western Persia. He reached **Enzeli** (Feb. 17). The British took **Kirmanshah** (Feb. 25).

Feb. 24. The Turks began an advance into Armenia. They took Trebizond (Feb. 24) and Erzerum (Mar. 12), then Van (Apr. 5), Batum (Apr. 15), and Kars (Apr. 27).

May 26. Georgia, Azerbaijan, and Armenia declared their independence.

June 8. Georgia and Armenia concluded a peace with Germany and Turkey.

June 12. A German force having been landed at Poti, the Germans advanced and **took Tiflis** (June 12). The Turks meanwhile advanced and took Tabriz (June 14).

July 26. The Bolshevik government at Baku was overthrown, after which a British force occupied the city (Aug. 4).

Aug. 26–Sept. 14. The British defended Baku against vigorous Turkish attacks, but were finally obliged to abandon the city to the Turks.

Nov. 17. After the armistice, the **British reoccupied Baku** and then the whole of Georgia, including Batum (Dec. 27). After the surrender of the Turkish army the **British also occupied Mosul** (Nov. 4).

33. THE COLLAPSE OF TURKEY

On the Palestine front the new British commander, Gen. **Allenby**, had begun his advance in Oct. 1917.

1917, Oct. 31. After a month of heavy fighting between Gaza and Beersheba, the British took the latter town and began rolling up the enemy line, thus forcing the **evacuation of Gaza** (Nov. 7) and Jaffa (Nov. 16).

Dec. 9. ALLENBY TOOK JERUSALEM. The British advance was delayed by the fact that Allenby was obliged to send large contingents to France to meet the crisis of Mar. 1918. The operations of the spring of 1918 were confined to Trans-Jordania. In the interval the Turks devoted themselves more and more to the Transcaucasian situation, neglecting the Palestine front.

1918, Sept. 18. Beginning of the great British offensive in Palestine. **Battles of Megiddo.** The British broke the Turkish lines near the Mediterranean and began to roll up the enemy forces, which were surrounded by cavalry. The German corps managed to escape into Trans-Jordania, and thence to Damascus and Aleppo. The British, assisted materially by the Arabs under Lawrence, were now able to push northward.

Oct. 1-2. British and Arabs took Damascus, then Beirut (taken by French naval forces, Oct. 7), Homs (Oct. 15), Aleppo (Oct. 26).

Oct. 13. The new Turkish sultan, **Mohammed VI** (succeeded Mohammed V July 3, 1918), **dismissed his Young Turk ministers** (Talaat and Enver) and appointed Izzet Pasha as grand vizier. The Turks then (Oct. 14) appealed to President Wilson to arrange an armistice. Having received no reply, they liberated **Gen. Townshend** and sent him to the British naval commander in the Aegean, **Adm. Calthorpe.**

Oct. 30. ARMISTICE CONCLUDED AT MUDROS to take effect the next day. The Turks were obliged to open the Straits, repatriate Allied prisoners, demobilize their armies, sever relations with the Central Powers, and place Turkish territory at the disposal of the Allies for military operations.

Nov. 12. The Allied fleet passed the Dardanelles and arrived at Constantinople (Nov. 13).

34. THE COLLAPSE OF BULGARIA

The Bulgarian front was really the first to break down. Under **Gen. Guillaumat** (succeeded Sarrail Dec. 22, 1917) the forces at Saloniki had been reorganized and greatly strengthened. Guillaumat, having been recalled to France in June 1918, did much to convince the English and French authorities of the desirability of a great attack in the Balkans. There were then 29 divisions (over 700,000 men) available at Saloniki, with **Gen. Franchet d'Esperey** in command.

1918, Sept. 15-24. Battles of Dobropolje or **Monastir-Doiran.** The Allies (Italians on the left, Serbs in the center, French, English, and Greeks on the right) began a great offensive all the way from Albania to the Struma River. The Serbs advanced almost 40 miles in a week and threatened to drive a wedge into the German-Bulgarian forces. On the right the British were less successful, but the Bulgarians, who had been taking soundings for peace since June (June 18, Germanophil Radoslavov cabinet succeeded by **Malinov government**), were unable to hold out longer. They appealed for an armistice.

Sept. 30. ARMISTICE CONCLUDED WITH BULGARIA AT SALONIKI: The Bulgarian army was to be demobilized at once and its equipment put into Allied custody; Greek and Serb territory still occupied was to be evacuated; all means of transport to be put at the disposal of the Allies; Bulgarian territory to be available for Allied operations.

Gen. Franchey d'Esperey's plan was to take advantage of the situation not only to break the communication between Germany-Austria and Turkey, but to attack the Turks in Thrace and force the opening of the Straits. A force was indeed sent into Thrace, and reached the **Maritza River** (Oct. 30). Other forces took over strategic positions in Bulgaria, crossed the whole country, and effected the **passage of the Danube** at Rustchuk (Nov. 10).

Oct. 4. Tsar Ferdinand of Bulgaria abdicated and was succeeded by his son Boris.

Nov. 10. The Allies having entered Rumania, that government now re-entered the war on the Allied side (Nov. 8, resignation of the **Marghiloman ministry**

and formation of a new government under Gen. **Coanda**).

In the center **the Serbs** continued their advance after the armistice. They took **Vranje** (Oct. 5), **Nish** (Oct. 11), and finally **Belgrade** (Nov. 1). Having crossed the Danube they continued the advance into the **Banat of Temesvar**, which was occupied by the end of November.

On the extreme left the **Italians** carried through the **conquest of Albania**, over which they had proclaimed a protectorate as early as June 3, 1917. They took **Elbasan** (Oct. 7), **Durazzo, Ipek**, and **Novi Bazar** (Oct. 14), **San Giovanni** (Oct. 29), **Scutari** (Oct. 31), and **Antivari** (Nov. 4).

35. THE END OF THE HAPSBURG MONARCHY

By the summer of 1918 the **Hapsburg Monarchy** was already in full process of dissolution. Disorders were common in the larger centers, parliamentary government had had to be given up, and desertions from the army had reached a large scale. In Russia, in France, and in Italy there had been formed Czech, Polish, and Yugoslav legions which were fighting for the Allies, while national councils of these subject nationalities were springing up not only in the provincial capitals, but in Paris and London.

1918, Apr. 10. Meeting of the Congress of Oppressed Austrian Nationalities in Rome. Here the Czech, Yugoslav, Polish, and Rumanian representatives proclaimed the right of self-determination, denounced the Hapsburg government as an obstacle to free development of the nations, and recognized the need for fighting against it.

Apr. 21. The Italian government recognized the Czechoslovak National Council as a *de facto* government.

May 29. Secretary **Lansing** declared the sympathy of the United States for the Czechoslovaks and Yugoslavs.

June 3. Allied declarations were made supporting the national aspirations of Poles, Czechoslovaks, and Yugoslavs.

June 30. Italy and France officially recognized the **independence of Czechoslovakia.** Britain followed suit Aug. 13, and the United States Sept. 3.

In view of the rapid disintegration of the monarchy the Austrians made a last bid for military victory.

June 15-24. Battle of the Piave. The Austrians crossed the river, but were unable to maintain their position. They withdrew again after losing some 100,-000 men. From this time on there was steady demoralization of the army.

Sept. 15. The Austrian government appealed to President Wilson to call an informal conference to discuss peace. This plea was rejected by Wilson.

Oct. 4. The Austrians joined the Germans in appealing for an armistice (see p. 951).

Oct. 16. The **Emperor Charles proclaimed** the reorganization of the non-Hungarian part of **the monarchy as a federal state,** with complete self-government for the subject nationalities. This move was patently belated.

Oct. 21. THE CZECHOSLOVAKS DECLARED THEIR INDEPENDENCE.

Oct. 24-Nov. 4. BATTLE OF VITTORIO VENETO. Gen. **Diaz,** after much prodding from the Allies, attacked the Austrian front all the way from the Trentino to the Adriatic. The Austrians held out for a week on the Monte Grappa, the key position in the center, but on the lower Piave they collapsed completely. The Italians advanced to **Vittorio Veneto** (Oct. 30), by which time the Austrian armies were in a state of dissolution, several hundred thousand being captured and the remainder streaming back toward home. The **Italians took Trieste** (Nov. 3) and **Fiume** (November 5).

Oct. 27. Count Julius Andrassy (succeeded Burian as Austrian foreign minister, Oct. 25) notified Wilson that Austria was willing to recognize the rights of the subject nationalities and to make a separate peace.

Oct. 29. THE YUGOSLAV NATIONAL COUNCIL at Agram (Zagreb) **proclaimed the independence of the Yugoslavs.**

Oct. 29. The Austrians offered to surrender unconditionally to the Italians.

Meanwhile disorders in both Vienna and Budapest had resulted in revolutionary changes.

Oct. 30. Formation of a **German National Council in Vienna, for** the German provinces.

Nov. 1. Establishment of an independent Hungarian government, under Count Michael Karolyi.

Nov. 3. CONCLUSION OF AN ARMISTICE between the Allied Powers and Austria-Hungary: complete demobilization of the armies and withdrawal of troops fighting with the Germans; surrender of half the equipment; evacuation of territories still occupied and of territory in dispute between Austrians, Italians, and Slavs; Allied occupation of strategic points; surrender of the fleet, etc.

Nov. 7. A Yugoslav conference at Geneva decided for the union of Croatia and Slovenia with Serbia and Montenegro.

Nov. 12. Abdication of the Emperor Charles.

Nov. 13. PROCLAMATION OF THE AUSTRIAN REPUBLIC.

Nov. 16. PROCLAMATION OF THE HUNGARIAN REPUBLIC.

Nov. 24. PROCLAMATION OF THE UNITED KINGDOM OF THE SERBS, CROATS, AND SLOVENES at Zagreb. King Peter of Serbia became king, with Prince Alexander as regent.

Dec. 1. King Nicholas of Montenegro having opposed union was declared deposed by the parliament, which then voted for union with the new kingdom.

Dec. 1. A national assembly of the Rumanians of Transylvania and the Banat at Alba Julia voted for union of these regions with Rumania.

36. THE ALLIED VICTORY IN THE WEST

After the second battle of the Marne the Allied forces, together with the Americans, gradually went over to a sustained offensive, consisting at first of a series of local attacks, but later merging into a general movement.

1918, Aug. 8-11. Battle of Amiens. The British, after careful and well-concealed preparation, attacked with 450 tanks. They advanced about eight miles the first day, after which the German lines tightened.

Aug. 21-Sept. 3. Second battles of the Somme and of Arras. The British and French gradually extended their attacks. They took Roye (Aug. 27), Bapaume (Aug. 28), Noyon (Aug. 28), and Péronne (Aug. 31), and obliged the Germans to fall back to the Hindenburg Line.

Sept. 12-13. The American forces, attacking on both sides of the St. Mihiel salient, pinched out that area, capturing some 15,000 of the enemy.

Sept. 26-Oct. 15. BATTLES OF THE ARGONNE AND OF YPRES (Sept. 28-Oct. 2). Foch's plan was to execute a pincer movement with an American thrust north through the Argonne and a British thrust eastward toward Cambrai and farther north toward Lille. If successful this would have cut the main lateral German railway and forced a general withdrawal. But at both ends the advance was much slower than expected. By mid-October the Americans had got through part of the Argonne, while the British had taken St. Quentin, Lens, and Armentières (Oct. 1-2).

These blows, together with the news of the surrender of Bulgaria, shook the nerve of Gen. Ludendorff, who, in something of a panic, demanded (Sept. 29) that the government initiate armistice and peace negotiations while the army could still hold out.

Sept. 30. Hertling and his fellow ministers resigned.

Oct. 4. Prince Max of Baden, a Liberal, named chancellor and foreign minister, with support of the Center, Progressive, and Socialist Parties. On the same day the German and Austrian governments appealed to President Wilson for an armistice, accepting the Fourteen Points (see p. 944) as a basis for peace. There followed an exchange of notes between Berlin and Washington that extended over several weeks, Wilson demanding evacuation of occupied territories, insisting that the Allies could negotiate only with a democratic government, etc. In the interval Ludendorff regained some of his composure and began to talk of resistance, renewal of the war in the spring, etc. The home situation, however, was bad and the democratic tide strong. The government (Oct. 27) accepted Ludendorff's resignation. He was succeeded as quartermaster-general by Gen. von Gröner.

During Oct. the British continued to advance in the north. They took Ostend, Zeebrugge, Roubaix, Lille, and Douai (Oct. 18), Bruges (Oct. 19) and Valenciennes (Nov. 1). By that time the American troops also resumed the advance. The Germans began to withdraw rapidly, and by Nov. 10 the Americans were at Sedan. Foch was then planning still another thrust east of Metz, and arranging for the mission of a force through Austria to attack Bavaria.

Nov. 3. Mutiny broke out **in the German fleet** at Kiel, the crews refusing to put to sea on a series of cruiser raids planned by Adm. Scheer. The mutiny spread rapidly to Hamburg, Bremen, and Lübeck and thence to the whole of northwestern Germany.

Nov. 7-8. **Revolution broke out in Munich.** The king abdicated. In Berlin, too, the pressure was great and the ministry convinced itself that the abdication of William II was imperative if the monarchy was to be preserved. The emperor, who was at Spa, resisted the suggestion, but Prince Max, feeling that he was unable to wait,

Nov. 9. **ANNOUNCED THE ABDICATION IN BERLIN.** Scheidemann, the Socialist leader, then **proclaimed the German Republic.**

Nov. 10. **William II,** having been told by Hindenburg and Gröner that they were unable to guarantee the loyalty of the army, took their advice and **fled to Holland.** Meanwhile

Nov. 8. The German armistice commission, headed by **Mathias Erzberger,** the leader of the Center Party, was received by Foch in his railway coach near Compiègne. The terms submitted by the Allies were designed to make Germany helpless and to make certain the acceptance of the peace terms to be worked out. The armistice provided for the immediate evacuation of occupied territory on the west front and of all territory west of the Rhine, which was to be occupied by Allied forces. The **treaties of Brest-Litovsk** and **Bucharest** were to be renounced and German troops were to be withdrawn from Rumania, Austria-Hungary, Turkey, and eventually Russia. Germany was to surrender 5000 locomotives, 5000 motor lorries, and 150,-000 freight cars. She was to turn over 160 submarines and a large number of other warships. The armistice, harsh though the terms were, had to be accepted. It was concluded for a period of 30 days, but was periodically renewed until peace was signed.

Nov. 11.   AT 11 A.M. HOSTILITIES CEASED ON THE WEST FRONT. The Allies at once began to take over the occupied and western German territories. The last German troops crossed the frontier of France Nov. 18 and the frontier of Belgium Nov. 26. French troops occupied Strassburg Nov. 25, while British and American troops began the occupation of Germany Dec. 1.

WORLD WAR LOSSES

The number of known dead has been placed at about 10,000,000 men, the wounded at about 20,000,000, distributed among the chief combatants as follows (round numbers):

	Dead	Wounded	Prisoner
Great Britain....	947,000	2,122,000	192,000
France..........	1,385,000	3,044,000	446,000
Russia..........	1,700,000	4,950,000	2,500,000
Italy...........	460,000	947,000	530,000
United States...	115,000	206,000	4,500
Germany........	1,808,000	4,247,000	618,000
Austria-Hungary.	1,200,000	3,620,000	2,200,000
Turkey.........	325,000	400,000	

The total direct cost of the war has been figured at $180,500,000,000, and the indirect cost at $151,612,500,000.

37. THE PEACE SETTLEMENTS

a. THE TREATY OF VERSAILLES

1919, Jan. 18.   The Peace Conference was formally opened at Paris, with 70 delegates representing 27 of the victorious powers. The Germans were excluded until the terms were ready for submission. The German request for a peace on the basis of Wilson's **Fourteen Points** had been granted by the Allied Note of Nov. 5, 1918, with two reservations, but the Fourteen Points receded into the background as the conflict of views and interests developed at the conference. **President Wilson,** received with the wildest enthusiasm when he arrived in Europe in mid-December, represented the new idealism in international relations and was intent primarily on securing the adoption of a plan for a **League of Nations,** to be included in the peace treaty. **Lloyd George,** the chief representative of Great Britain and the empire, was more or less disposed to make a moderate peace, but was deeply committed by promises made in the general election recently held, to the effect that the war criminals would be brought to justice and that Germany would be made to pay for the war. **Clemenceau,** in turn, was frankly the exponent of the old diplomacy, being intent on revenge, on the interests of France, and on provisions for the security of France. Both England and France were bound further by their agreements with Italy, by commitments in the

Near East, etc. The Italian prime minister, Orlando, played a secondary rôle, but the foreign minister, Sonnino, stood forth as an unbending champion of Italian claims against Austria and against the new Yugoslav state.

The plenary sessions of the conference were of little significance, for the decisions rested from the start with the Supreme Council, the Big Ten, composed of President Wilson and the prime ministers and foreign ministers of the five chief powers (Wilson, Lansing, Lloyd George, Balfour, Clemenceau, Pichon, Orlando, Sonnino, Saionji, Makino). Russia was not represented, though the Russian situation was of vital import. The wars of the counter-revolution were in full swing and the fate of the new states on Russia's western frontiers depended on the outcome. Clemenceau having refused to invite delegates of the warring parties to Paris, a conference was arranged for at the Prinkipo Islands. The Bolshevik government was apparently anxious for some kind of adjustment, but Kolchak and Denikin, the two leading figures of the counter-revolution, refused to enter upon discussion and the whole project fell flat. Public opinion in both France and England was violently anti-Bolshevik and it seems hardly likely that an agreement could have been reached.

Jan. 25. The conference unanimously adopted a resolution for the creation of a League of Nations. A committee was appointed to draft a constitution, and other committees were organized to deal with reparations and various territorial questions.

Feb. In the middle of the month President Wilson returned for a time to America and Lloyd George to London.

Mar. 25. After the return of Wilson and Lloyd George, the statesmen devoted themselves to the working out of the German treaty. The Council of Ten was replaced by the Council of Four, for the expedition of business.

Apr. 28. The Covenant of the League of Nations (worked out by a committee consisting of Wilson, House, Cecil, Smuts, Bourgeois, and Venizelos) was presented in final form. The League was to consist of the signatory states and others admitted by two-thirds vote. The members were to afford each other mutual protection against aggression, to submit disputes to arbitration or inquiry, to abstain from war until three months after an award. All treaties between members which were incompatible with these obligations were declared abrogated; all subsequent treaties were to be registered with the League. The League was to devote itself to problems of disarmament, labor legislation, health problems, international administration, etc. A permanent secretariat was provided for, to be located at Geneva (Sir Eric Drummond, first secretary-general). All member states were to be represented by one vote in a General Assembly, while a Council, consisting of representatives of the five great powers and four others chosen by the Assembly, was to fill the position of executive (Belgium, Brazil, Greece, and Spain were first chosen for the Council). The League, the covenant of which was an integral part of the peace treaty, came into effect in Jan. 1920.

The drafting of the peace terms was marked by violent conflict between the members of the Council of Four. Clemenceau insisted on the separation of the left bank of the Rhine from Germany, and desired also the annexation of the Saar Basin to France. These demands were opposed by Wilson and Lloyd George, and French security was finally arranged for otherwise, Wilson having ordered preparations for his return home (Apr. 7). Other serious disputes arose from the demands of England and France that Germany should be required to meet the costs of the war, a proposition to which Wilson objected. The Polish claims, supported by France, also caused friction, as did the Japanese pretensions in Shantung and the Italian claims in Dalmatia, neither of which Wilson was prepared to recognize. All these questions were finally settled by compromise in order to keep the conference together (the Italian delegates left the conference Apr. 23 and did not return until May 6).

May 7. The treaty was submitted to the German delegation, which had arrived Apr. 29. The Germans (Count Brockdorff-Rantzau, chief of the delegation) protested vigorously that the terms were not in keeping with the conditions on which Germany had laid down her arms and that many of the clauses were impossible of fulfillment. Nevertheless the victorious powers made only slight modifications in the draft and the Germans, after an acute domestic crisis, decided that they would be unable to resist and that their only possible course was to sign.

June 28. SIGNATURE OF THE TREATY OF VERSAILLES in the Hall of Mirrors at Versailles. The treaty provided for the League of Nations and for the following territorial cessions by Germany: Alsace-Lorraine to France; Moresnet, Eupen, and Malmédy to Belgium, with a plebiscite in Malmédy after cession; the

Saar area to be under international administration for 15 years, after which a plebiscite was to be held, France exploiting the coal mines in the meanwhile; northern and central **Schleswig** were to decide their allegiance by plebiscite; in the east, Germany was to cede the larger part of **Posen** and **West Prussia** to Poland; a plebiscite was to be held in **Upper Silesia**; **Danzig** was to be a free state within the Polish customs union; plebiscites were to be held in parts of **East Prussia** to decide whether they should go to Poland or remain with Germany; **Memel** was ceded to the Allies; the **German colonies** were also ceded to the Allies, to be organized as mandates under supervision of the League. Germany, in **Art. 231**, accepted sole responsibility for causing the war. She was henceforth to keep an **army of not more than 100,000 men**, was to have no large guns and only a limited number of smaller ones. The navy was limited to six warships and a corresponding number of other craft; Germany was to have **no submarines or military aircraft**; the fortifications of **Heligoland** were to be dismantled; the Allies were to occupy the **Rhineland** for 15 years, and longer if necessary, and a belt 30 miles wide on the **right bank of the Rhine** was to be demilitarized. The **Kiel Canal** was opened to the warships and merchant shipping of all nations, and the **German rivers** were internationalized. The former **emperor** and other offenders were to be tried. The Germans were required to pay for all **civilian damage** caused during the war, the final bill to be presented by May 1, 1921; in the interval Germany was to pay five billion dollars, the rest to be paid in 30 years. Germany was to hand over all **merchant ships** of more than 1600 tons, half of those between 800 and 1600 tons and a quarter of her **fishing fleet**. She was to build 200,000 tons of shipping for the victors annually for five years. Large quantities of **coal** were to be delivered to France, Belgium, and Italy for ten years. Germany was to bear the **cost of the armies of occupation**. She bound herself further to agree to the sale of German property in Allied countries.

July 7. The German government ratified the treaty, as did France (Oct. 13), Great Britain (Oct. 15), Italy (Oct. 15), and Japan (Oct. 30). The United States government never ratified it, the Senate having first proposed amendments, which failed of the necessary votes. The United States government also refused to ratify the **treaty of alliance signed with England and France** (June 28) providing for assistance in case of attack by Germany. This treaty thus also failed of effect.

b. THE TREATY OF ST. GERMAIN

1919, Sept. 10. Austria signed the treaty which had been submitted July 20. This treaty merely registered the break-up of the Hapsburg Monarchy, at the same time penalizing the new Austrian Republic as the representative of the old régime. Austria recognized the **independence of Czechoslovakia, Yugoslavia, Poland, and Hungary**, these states being obliged to give guaranties of protection of minorities. **Eastern Galicia**, the **Trentino, South Tyrol, Trieste**, and **Istria** were ceded by Austria. The army was limited to 30,000 men and Austria, like Germany, was to pay **reparations** for 30 years. **The union of Austria with Germany** was forbidden, except with consent of the Council of the League.

c. THE TREATY OF NEUILLY

1919, Nov. 27. The Bulgarians signed the treaty of peace, which deprived them of a seaboard on the Aegean and gave them only an economic outlet. Bulgaria recognized the **independence of Yugoslavia**. She agreed to pay **reparations** of $445,000,000. Her **army** was reduced to 20,000 men, and she was obliged to surrender most of her war materials.

d. THE TREATY OF TRIANON

1919, Mar. 22. The republican government headed by **Count Karolyi** was overthrown by a **Bolshevik coup**, headed by Alexander Garbai and **Bela Kun**. This government became involved in war with most of Hungary's neighbors when it became known that territory was to be assigned to them. Ultimately the **Rumanians invaded and took Budapest** (Aug. 4) just after the Bolsheviks had been overthrown (Aug. 1). The monarchists then regained control and appointed **Adm. Horthy as regent** (Feb. 1920). The Rumanians were finally induced to withdraw (Dec. 10, 1919), under pressure from the Allies, but only after they had carried away most of what was movable.

1920, June 4. The Hungarians signed the Treaty of Trianon, by which the old Hungary was shorn of almost three-quarters of its territory and two-thirds of its inhabitants. Czechoslovakia was given **Slovakia**, Austria received **western Hungary**, Yugoslavia took **Croatia-Slavonia** and part of the **Banat of Temesvar**, and Rumania received the rest of the **Banat,**

Transylvania, and part of the **Hungarian plain.** Hungary agreed to pay **reparations,** to keep an **army** of only 35,000 men, to assume part of the old Austro-Hungarian debt, to hand over war criminals, etc.

e. THE TREATY OF SÈVRES

In the settlement of the Turkish question the Allies were much hampered by the downfall of the tsarist régime in Russia, the withdrawal of Russian claims to Constantinople, and the publication by the Bolsheviks of the secret treaties revealing the Allied plan of partition. President Wilson in particular opposed the former program, while American opinion showed little interest in assuming responsibility for either the Straits area or Armenia. The question dragged on through 1919, while in Turkey a nationalist movement under **Mustapha Kemal** (see p. 1094) was building up a strong opposition to the Allied plans.

1919, May 15. The Greeks, with the support of the Allies, **landed troops at Smyrna,** acting as agents for Allied interests. The Italians also landed troops in southwestern Anatolia.

1920, Apr. 18. At a **conference** of the Allied prime ministers **at San Remo** the main lines of the Turkish treaty were agreed upon.

Aug. 20. The feeble and helpless government of the sultan, protected by an international force of occupation at Constantinople, signed the **Treaty of Sèvres.** By this treaty the sultan's government renounced all claims to non-Turkish territory. **The Kingdom of the Hijaz was recognized as independent.** Syria became a mandate of France, and **Mesopotamia** (with Mosul), as well as **Palestine,** became British mandates. Smyrna and its hinterland were to be administered by Greece for five years, after which a plebiscite was to be held. The **Dodecanese** and **Rhodes** went to Italy, while **Thrace** and the remainder of the **Turkish islands** in the Aegean were assigned to Greece. **Armenia** was recognized as independent. The **Straits** were to be internationalized and the adjoining territory demilitarized. **Constantinople** and the strip of territory to the Chatalja lines remained Turkish, as did the remainder of **Anatolia.** This treaty was not recognized by the Turkish nationalists who, under Mustapha Kemal's leadership, continued to build up a military force in Anatolia and to organize a government in defiance of the sultan and the victorious allied powers. As a result of nationalist successes the Treaty of Sèvres was ultimately replaced by the Treaty of Lausanne (p. 1095).

B. EUROPE

1. INTERNATIONAL AFFAIRS

International affairs since the First World War have involved the following **major problems**: (1) The attempt to establish collective security by means of new international bodies, the League of Nations, and the World Court, without creating any form of superstate; (2) the unwillingness of the non-European powers, the United States, Japan, and the British Dominions in particular, to assume responsibility for anything outside their respective spheres of interest; (3) the efforts of Japan to dominate the Far East by force and of the United States to dominate the Americas by a "good neighbor policy"; (4) the struggle between French efforts to maintain the position of leadership on the continent of Europe established by the peace settlements and German endeavors to evade or revise the terms imposed in 1919; (5) the problem of restoring world trade and general prosperity in a war-impoverished world; (6) the attempts to attain security and prosperity by neomercantilist ideas imposed dictatorially as emergency measures.

The era between the wars may be divided chronologically into three phases: (1) The period of settlement (from the peace treaties to the Dawes Plan, 1924); (2) the period of fulfillment (1924 to the evacuation of the Rhineland, 1930); (3) the period of repudiation and revision (1930-1939).

a. THE PERIOD OF SETTLEMENT

1919, June 28. Conclusion of **defensive treaties between France, England, and the United States.** England and the United States were to come to France's assistance in case of aggression by Germany. The United States Senate refused to ratify this agreement and also rejected the Versailles Treaty (Nov. 19), thus knocking out one of the keystones in the international peace structure established at Paris.

1919-1922. The Vilna dispute, between Poland and Lithuania. Gen. **Pilsudski** took the town from the Bolsheviks (Apr. 19, 1919). The **Curzon line** (Dec. 8) established a boundary depriving Poland of the city, which was retaken by the Bolsheviks (June 15, 1920). The Lithuanians took it when the Russians evacuated (Aug.

24), but were driven out by Polish freebooters under Gen. **Zeligowski** (Oct. 9). By decision of the League a plebiscite was to be held to decide the fate of the city, but this was later abandoned (Mar. 3, 1921). A plebiscite (Jan. 8, 1922) held by Zeligowski decided for Poland and the Vilna Diet voted for union. Apr. 8 it was incorporated with Poland, though Lithuania refused to recognize this disposition of the question.

1919-1920. The Teschen conflict between Poland and Czechoslovakia. The Czechs had occupied the disputed area (Jan. 1919) and serious clashes took place (May). The supreme council decided for a plebiscite (Sept. 27), but disorders continued (Mar., May, 1920) until the conference of ambassadors divided the territory (July 28).

1919-1920. The Polish-Russian War, resulting from the effort made by the Poles to push their frontier east to the frontier of 1772. After an initial advance they were repulsed (p. 1033).

1919-1921. The Burgenland dispute between Austria and Hungary. The strip of territory had been assigned to Austria by the peace treaties, it being only 15 miles from Vienna. The population, too, was predominantly German. But Hungarian irregulars were in occupation and refused to evacuate (Aug. 1921). Through Italian mediation a plebiscite was arranged for. This was held (Dec. 1921) and gave Austria most of the area, though Ödenburg went to Hungary.

1919-1922. The Greek invasion of Anatolia (see p. 1094).

1919-1924. The Fiume question. President Wilson had rejected the Italian claim to the town and the coast south of it (Apr. 14, 1919), whereupon the Italians had withdrawn from the peace conference. A compromise, suggested by M. Tardieu, which would have created a buffer state of Fiume (May 30), was rejected by Yugoslavia. **D'Annunzio** led a filibustering expedition which occupied the town and set up a visionary government (Sept. 12). The matter was finally left to Italy and Yugoslavia to settle (Mar. 6, 1920). The **Treaty of Rapallo** (Nov. 12) made Fiume an independent city and gave Italy Zara

WORLD WAR LOSSES
By Germany
By Austria-Hungary
By Bulgaria
By Russia

and a number of Dalmatian islands. But a Fascist coup (Mar. 3, 1922) overthrew the local government, and government troops took control (Mar. 17). By a treaty of Jan. 27, 1924, Yugoslavia abandoned claims to Fiume, but received **Porto Barros** in return.

1919-1922. The Upper Silesian question. The peace treaties had provided for a plebiscite in this valuable area. It was held Mar. 20, 1921 (see p. 997) and returned 717,122 votes for Germany as against 483,154 for Poland. But an armed rising under the Polish commissioner **Korfanty** (May 3, 1922) was acquiesced in by the French commander acting for the League. Aug. 1922, the Council of Ambassadors referred the matter to the League and the League Council accepted a **scheme of partition** by which a majority of the population and more than half of the territory were awarded to Germany, while Poland was given the principal mining and industrial districts.

1920, Jan. 10. Official **birth of the League of Nations.** The Assembly met for the first time Nov. 15. In the first years the League was entrusted with many of the territorial questions and with a host of other problems.

Jan. 23. The Dutch government refused to surrender the **former Emperor William,** though it later agreed to intern him.

Feb.-Mar. The plebiscites in **North Schleswig** gave the northernmost zone to Denmark and the remainder to Germany.

Apr. 19-26. The **San Remo Conference** of the Allied powers, to discuss various territorial problems and to dispose of the Class A mandates.

June 19-22. Conferences of **Hythe and Boulogne,** to discuss the Near-Eastern situation and the reparations problem.

July 5-16. The **Spa Conference,** where the Germans submitted a scheme of reparations payments and signed a disarmament engagement. The Allies decided to apportion reparations money as follows: France, 52%; British Empire, 22%; Italy, 10%; Belgium, 8%; the smaller powers to receive the rest.

Aug. 14. Treaty between **Czechoslovakia and Yugoslavia,** which became the foundation of the **Little Entente.** Its purpose was to enforce observance of the peace treaty by Hungary and to forestall a possible restoration of the Hapsburgs.

1921, Jan. 24-30. Paris Conference, to discuss reparations.

Feb. 19. Treaty between **Poland and** France, providing for mutual assistance in case of attack.

Feb. 21-Mar. 14. London Conference, dealing with reparations. Schedules of payment were worked out for the Germans and the latter made counterproposals. The application of sanctions was agreed upon in case Germany refused to accept the Paris proposals.

Mar. 3. Offensive and defensive treaty between **Poland and Rumania.**

Mar. 8. The French occupied Düsseldorf, Duisberg, and Ruhrort, after an ultimatum to Germany had been evaded.

Mar. 24. The reparation commission declared **Germany in default,** though the Germans, reaching other figures on payments already made, denied the default.

Apr. 23. Rumania joined Czechoslovakia in the Little Entente.

Apr. 27. The reparation commission announced that Germany should pay a **total of 132,000,000,000 gold marks.**

Apr. 29-May 5. London Conference on reparations. It sent an ultimatum to Germany demanding one milliard gold marks by the end of the month on penalty of occupation of the Ruhr. The Germans raised the money by borrowing in London, and accepted the payment schedules.

June 7. Treaty between Yugoslavia and Rumania, completing the Little Entente.

Aug. 24, 25. By separate treaties the United States made peace with Austria and Germany.

Oct. 6. The **Loucheur-Rathenau Agreement,** arranging for payments in kind.

Oct. 20. The **Aaland Islands Convention** signed at Geneva. It provided for the neutralization and non-fortification of the group.

Oct. 20. The former **Emperor Karl** arrived in the **Burgenland** by airplane and began a march on Budapest. Czechoslovakia and Yugoslavia mobilized and the Hungarians, unable to face another war, did not dare restore their Hapsburg king. **Karl was exiled** (Nov. 7) to Madeira, where he died (Apr. 1, 1922) leaving a widow, the former **Empress Zita,** and a number of children, the eldest of whom is Otto, claimant to the Hapsburg thrones.

Nov. 12-1922, Feb. 6. THE WASHINGTON CONFERENCE, which met at the invitation of the United States government to consider naval armaments and Far-Eastern questions. Great Britain,

France, Italy, Belgium, the Netherlands, China, Japan, and Portugal were represented. Russia, not yet recognized by the United States, was not invited, despite her great interests in the Far East. The conference resulted: (1) in the **Four-Power Pacific Treaty**, Dec. 13 (United States, Great Britain, France, and Japan), by which the signatories guaranteed each other's rights in insular possessions in the Pacific and promised to consult if their rights should be threatened. The Anglo-Japanese Alliance came to an end; (2) the **Shantung Treaty** (Feb. 4) by which Japan returned Kiao-chow to China; (3) two **Nine-Power Treaties** (Feb. 6) guaranteeing the territorial integrity and administrative independence of China and reiterating the principle of the "Open Door"; (4) The **naval armaments treaty** (Feb. 6) providing for a 10-year naval holiday during which no new capital ships (defined as ships over 10,000 tons with guns larger than 8-inch) were to be built, and establishing a ratio for capital ships of 5–5–3–1.67–1.67. This meant that Great Britain and the United States were each allowed 525,000 tons, Japan 315,000, and France and Italy each 175,000. Total tonnage of aircraft-carriers was restricted and a maximum size fixed for capital ships, aircraft-carriers and cruisers.

1922, Feb. 15. The **Permanent Court of International Justice** was opened at The Hague.

Mar. 13-17. Conference at Warsaw of the Baltic states and Poland, provided for arbitration and a defensive league in the event of attack by another power.

Apr. 10-May 19. GENOA CONFERENCE, including Germany and Russia, called to consider the Russian problem and the general economic questions of the world. The conference broke down on the insistence of France on the recognition by Russia of the pre-war debt.

Apr. 16. **Rapallo Treaty** of alliance between Germany and Russia, in which both renounced reparations, etc.

May 31. The reparation commission, despite protests from France, granted Germany a moratorium for the remainder of the year, it having become clear that payments were resulting in the collapse of the mark and creating an impossible transfer problem.

June 30. The new **Danube Statute** went into effect.

Aug. 1. Lord **Balfour**, the British foreign secretary, sent a note to the Allied Powers indebted to Great Britain offering to abandon all further claims for payment and all claims to reparations, provided a general settlement could be made which would end "the economic injury inflicted on the world by the present state of things." If the United States, which had not demanded a share of reparations payments, should refuse to cancel the debts owed by European governments, then Great Britain would have to insist on receiving enough from her debtors to pay her own obligations to the United States. The American attitude was that reparations and inter-Allied debts were not connected problems, so that German default on reparations would not excuse default on Allied payments to the United States.

Aug. 7-14. **London Conference.** Poincaré demanded, as conditions for a moratorium, a series of "productive guaranties," among them appropriation of 60% of the capital of the German dyestuff factories on the left bank of the Rhine, and exploitation and contingent expropriation of the state mines in the Ruhr. British and French policy now diverged sharply, as the former refused Poincaré's scheme and Poincaré refused to grant a moratorium.

Nov. 20-1923, Feb. 4. **First Lausanne Conference,** to conclude peace between Turkey and Greece (p. 1095).

Dec. 9-11. **Second London Conference.** Bonar Law offered to cancel Allied debts to Great Britain even if Great Britain had to continue to pay the United States. Poincaré remained adamant, since the reparations expected from Germany were theoretically much greater than the French debt to Great Britain.

Dec. 26. The reparation commission again declared **Germany in default** on the motion of M. Barthou, the French representative. The point at issue was a minor delay in deliveries of timber.

1923, Jan. 2-4. Paris Conference. British and Italian schemes for bond issues, etc., were rejected by the French.

Jan. 9. **Germany declared in default on coal deliveries.**

Jan. 11. FRENCH AND BELGIAN TROOPS BEGAN THE INVASION AND OCCUPATION OF THE RUHR DISTRICT. The British government refused to take any part in it and in a note of Aug. 11 declared that the "Franco-Belgian action . . . was not a sanction authorized by the treaty." The Italian government, though technically associated, took no active part. The activities of the

M.I.C.U.M. (*mission interalliée de contrôle des usines et des mines*), sent into the heart of Germany to supervise business enterprises under military protection, were not, according to the Franco-Belgian note (Jan. 10), to disturb the normal life of the civilian population. But the German government urged **passive resistance** on the people of the Ruhr and recklessly inflated the currency to defray the expense of supporting idle workers and compensating their employers. The French fomented a **separatist movement** in the Rhineland, which failed, after some bloodshed, to establish an independent buffer state.

Apr. 23-July 24. Second Lausanne Conference, on the Near East (p. 1095).

Sept. 26. End of passive resistance in the Ruhr. German paper marks had sunk to the point of being worth less than the paper they were printed on. The effect of the financial collapse could not be confined to Germany. The French franc fell about 25% and by Nov. the French were willing to make an agreement directly with the Ruhr mine operators to secure deliveries. **Stanley Baldwin**, British prime minister, secured a promise of American co-operation to avert the complete economic and financial collapse of the world.

Nov. 30. Two committees were organized to investigate the German economic problem as it touched reparations.

1924, Apr. 9. THE DAWES PLAN. The committee under the chairmanship of the American, **Charles G. Dawes**, presented its report. Based on the slogan, "Business, not politics," this Dawes plan provided for a reorganization of the German *Reichsbank* under Allied supervision. Reparation payments of one milliard gold marks were to be made annually, increasing by the end of five years to two milliard, five hundred thousand. Germany was to receive a foreign loan of 800,000,000 gold marks.

Apr. 16. The Germans accepted the Dawes Plan.

July 16-Aug. 16. A conference at London adopted the Dawes Plan. The *Reichstag* promptly passed the necessary legislation. Of the loan, $110,000,000 was taken up in the United States, the rest in Europe.

b. THE PERIOD OF FULFILLMENT

1924, Oct. 2. The Geneva Protocol (protocol for the pacific settlement of international disputes). This was the product of continued efforts to strengthen the international machinery and to overcome the weakness in the League structure resulting from the absence of Russia, Germany, and the United States. A **draft treaty of mutual assistance**, based on proposals made by Lord Robert Cecil and Colonel Réquin, had attempted a definition of the aggressor and had submitted an ingenious scheme for combining the advantages of a general guaranty and a local system of alliances. The objection of Great Britain and the Dominions to the regional and continental character of the plan had led to its rejection by the League Assembly (Sept. 1923).

The Geneva Protocol, brought forward by **Ramsay MacDonald**, British prime minister, and drafted by Beněs and Politis, was unanimously recommended to the governments members of the League. It provided for compulsory arbitration of all disputes and defined the aggressor as the nation unwilling to submit its case to arbitration. The decisive factor in the rejection of the scheme was the **opposition of the British Dominions**, which regarded the risks in this mutual insurance scheme as too unequal: "We live in a fireproof house, far from inflammable materials" (M. Dandurand for Canada). The newly elected Conservative government in England therefore rejected the Protocol (Mar. 1925).

1925, Feb. 9. The German government proposed a **Rhineland mutual guaranty pact.** The idea was taken up by the British, who were seeking some European arrangement to replace the Geneva Protocol. **Aristide Briand**, who became French foreign minister in Apr. 1925, accepted the suggestion on condition that Germany join the League.

Feb. 11, 19. International Opium Conventions providing more effective control of production and trade in opium.

June 17. Arms Traffic Convention, dealing with international trade in arms and munitions. A protocol was also signed, prohibiting use of poison gas.

Aug. 25. The French **evacuated Düsseldorf, Duisburg**, and **Ruhrort.**

Sept. 1-4. A committee of jurists met in London to draft a security pact.

Oct. 5-16. LOCARNO CONFERENCE AND TREATIES (signed Dec. 1). The treaties included: (1) a **treaty of mutual guaranty** of the Franco-German and Belgo-German frontiers (signed by Germany, France, Belgium, and by Great Britain and Italy as guarantors); (2) **arbitration treaties** between Germany and Poland and Germany and Czechoslovakia; (3) **arbitration treaties** between Germany and Belgium and Germany and France; (4) a **Franco-Polish** and a **Franco-Czechoslovakian treaty for mutual assistance** in case of attack by Germany. The effect of the treaties was very far-reaching. For some years the "spirit of Locarno" gave the European powers a sense of security, though Britain had guaranteed only the western frontiers of Germany and Germany had not specifically bound herself to refrain from aggression to the east and south. Realizing this, France secured herself by alliances with Poland and the states of the Little Entente and proceeded with a program of fortifying the German frontier (Maginot line) and reorganization of the army.

1926, Mar. 17. **The admission of Germany to the League** was postponed because of complications raised by Spain and Brazil regarding seats on the council.

May 18-26. **First meeting of the preparatory commission for a disarmament conference.** This had been appointed by the League in 1925 to tackle the problem of disarmament, foreshadowed in the Treaty of Versailles. The United States was represented, but not Russia (until 1927). The commission held many sessions during the next years.

June 10. **Spain announced withdrawal from the League,** but later rescinded this decision.

Sept. 8. **Germany admitted to the League** and given a permanent seat on the council.

1927, Jan. 31. **End of the Inter-Allied Commission of Military Control** in Germany. Problems of German armament were henceforth put under jurisdiction of the League.

May 4-23. **International Economic Conference at Geneva,** some fifty countries being represented.

June 20-Aug. 4. Great Britain, the United States, and Japan met in a **three-power naval conference at Geneva** in an effort to reach an agreement on cruisers, destroyers, and submarines. The conference failed to reach agreement.

Nov. 30-Dec. 3. At a meeting of the preparatory commission on disarmament, **Maxim Litvinov,** for Russia (now admitted to the meetings), **proposed complete and immediate disarmament,** but this was rejected as a communist trick.

1928, Apr. 13. **Mr. Kellogg,** American secretary of state, submitted to the Locarno powers a **plan for the renunciation of war,** the suggestion flowing out of American-French negotiations.

Apr. 21. **M. Briand,** for France, put forward his draft for a treaty outlawing war.

June 23. **Explanatory note** on the **Kellogg-Briand Pact** sent to England, Germany, Italy, and Japan and to the allies of France and to the British Dominions. There was almost immediate and universal adherence, since the pact only involved renunciation of aggressive war and made no provision for sanctions.

Aug. 27. **THE KELLOGG-BRIAND PACT** signed at Paris (*Pact of Paris*).

Sept. 3-26. The ninth assembly of the League implemented the Kellogg-Briand Pact by a general act providing for conciliation and arbitration and an **optional clause** like that of the World Court, acceptance of which involved compulsory arbitration. This was accepted by 23 nations, in some cases with reservations.

1929, Jan. 5. **General Act of Inter-American arbitration,** analogous to the above, signed at the Pan-American Conference in Washington.

Jan. 19. **Appointment of the Young Committee** to re-examine the reparations problem and make final disposition of it.

Feb. 9. **Litvinov Protocol,** an eastern pact for renunciation of war, signed at Moscow by Russia, Poland, Rumania, Estonia, and Latvia.

Apr. 12. **Report of the Young Committee,** to which the Germans made some counter-proposals.

June 7. **THE YOUNG PLAN.** Responsibility of transferring payments from German marks into foreign currency was to be undertaken by Germany and was to be made under a new institution, the **Bank for International Settlements** at Basel. On the directorate of this bank all the principal central banks were to be represented. Germany was to pay annuities ending in 1988 and increasing gradually for the first 36 years. But only Rm. 660,-000,000 were unconditionally payable annually. The transfer of the rest of the annuity might be postponed for two years. These safeguards were meant to cover any possible crisis in transfer. The unconditional annuity was secured by a mortgage on German state railways. The total annuity of Rm. 1,707,000,000 was less than Germany had been paying with apparent ease under the Dawes Plan, so that experts and diplomats had no doubt that the Young Plan was a permanent settlement.

Aug. 6-31. Hague Conference on the Young Plan. The Germans accepted it and were rewarded by evacuation of the Rhineland, before June, 1930.

Sept. 5-9. M. Briand proposed a European federal union. The plan was discussed by the League, but nothing came of it.

1930, Jan. 21-Apr. 22. LONDON NAVAL CONFERENCE. It led to a treaty, signed by Great Britain, the United States, France, Italy, and Japan, regulating submarine warfare and limiting the tonnage and gun-caliber of submarines. The limitation of aircraft-carriers, provided for by the Washington Treaty, was extended. Great Britain, the United States, and Japan also agreed to scrap certain warships by 1933 and allocated tonnage in other categories. An "escalator clause," permitting an increase over specified tonnages if national needs of any one signatory demanded it, was included. The agreements were to run until 1936.

Oct. 5-12. First Balkan Conference at Athens. These met annually for several years and were the basis for the **Balkan Entente.**

Nov. 6-Dec. 9. Final meeting of the preparatory commission on disarmament. It adopted by majority vote a draft convention to be discussed at a disarmament conference called by the League Council for Feb. 1932. This draft was not approved by the German and Russian representatives, and was much criticized by the Swedish and American delegates. The most obnoxious clauses preserved rights and obligations secured by previous treaties, which France interpreted as including strict maintenance of the military clauses of the Treaty of Versailles, thus barring the way to German equality in armament and to revision in general.

c. THE PERIOD OF REPUDIATION AND REVISION

The years following 1930 were dominated by the great international **economic depression,** which almost ruined world trade and brought many nations to the verge of bankruptcy. The tension in domestic affairs led to a marked turn toward dictatorial forms of government and to widespread repudiation of financial and moral obligations in the effort to solve domestic problems. A number of less favored nations embarked frankly upon a policy of territorial expansion.

1931, May 11. The failure of the Austrian Credit-Anstalt, caused largely by the artificial and impracticable restrictions on commerce and finance imposed by the Succession States of the old monarchy, precipitated an alarming financial and diplomatic crisis in central Europe which threatened to involve the whole continent. A guaranty of the Credit-Anstalt's foreign debts by the Austrian government, backed by a foreign exchange credit from ten of the largest central banks (arranged through the Bank for International Settlements), failed to check the panic. Foreign funds were rapidly withdrawn from Germany. The Bank of France, actuated by the purely political motive of forcing the abandonment of a proposed customs union between Austria and Germany, refused financial support for the Austrian bank.

June 16. The Bank of England, despite difficulties at home, advanced 150,000,000 schillings to the Austrian National Bank. Everywhere, from Austria to Australia, governments, banks, and corporations were exposed to immediate bankruptcy and were in terror of fascist or communist uprisings.

June 20. President Hoover, persuaded by expert opinion that one factor in the crisis was the always difficult problem of transferring sums due as reparation and war-debt payments from one currency to another, **proposed a moratorium** of one year on all intergovernmental debts. French opposition, chiefly political, caused disastrous delay.

July 6. Hoover announced **acceptance of the moratorium** by all important creditor governments. The moratorium showed that there was, in fact, a close connection between inter-Allied debts and reparations, though Hoover reiterated that there was no such connection. European governments regarded the moratorium as an American acknowledgment that inter-Allied debts and reparations would stand or fall together.

Aug. 19. Layton-Wiggin Report, from an international committee of bankers which had met at Basel. It called for a six months' extension of all foreign credits to Germany, expressed in terms of foreign currencies, so that these were "frozen." Germany never after became fully solvent in international transactions, i.e. she remained unable to pay promptly and in full principal and interest on long- and short-term foreign obligations.

Sept. 21. The Bank of England was forced off the gold standard, in spite of credits of £25,000,000 each from the Federal Reserve Bank of New York and the Bank of France, and the formation

(Aug. 24) of a National Coalition ministry which was to balance the budget. Since then Great Britain has experimented with a managed paper currency, and the fluctuations of sterling exchange have been followed by the numerous currencies, such as the Scandinavian, which have been tied to sterling. The depreciation of these currencies in terms of those of countries which remained on the gold standard and did not devalue, amounted to an export subsidy which temporarily stimulated trade and eventually forced devaluation by almost all other countries. But trade was greatly contracted in the absence of any fixed medium of exchange. Capital showed a tendency to flee from one country to another and back again, in a vain attempt to escape the shrinkage of assets involved in devaluation.

Sept. 18. Japanese army leaders, acting apparently without orders from Tokyo, took advantage of the hopeless world situation and of recurrent disorders in China to **occupy Mukden, Ch'ang-ch'un,** and **Kirin,** important Manchurian towns. The result was the opening of an unofficial war between China and Japan that completely changed the complexion of affairs in the Far East (p. 1119).

1932, Jan. 4. Occupation of Shanhaikwan by Japanese troops completed Japanese military control of South Manchuria.

Jan. 29. Naval and military **intervention by Japanese at Shanghai.**

Feb. 2-July. MEETING OF THE DISARMAMENT CONFERENCE at Geneva, 60 nations represented, including the United States and Russia. The session led to nothing chiefly because of the divergence of view between France and the other powers. The French proposed a system of international police and insisted that security must precede disarmament. The Germans demanded equality. In June President Hoover suggested the division of national forces into "police components" and "defense components," the latter to be reduced by one-third. This plan also failed because of many objections.

Mar. 3. The Chinese driven back from Shanghai.

May. Following mediation by the League, the **Japanese withdrew from Shanghai.**

June 16-July 9. LAUSANNE CONFERENCE. Representatives of Germany, France, Belgium, Great Britain, Italy, and Japan reached an agreement which set aside the German reparation debt and substituted for it 5% bonds for Rm. 3,000,000,000, to be deposited with the Bank for International Settlements and issued when and if it became possible to market them at a price of 90% or better, within the ensuing 15 years. Ratification of this agreement was made conditional on a satisfactory agreement between the associated powers and their creditors (i.e. United States). This agreement became impossible when the American Congress (Dec.) passed a resolution that "it is against the policy of Congress that any of the indebtedness of foreign powers to the United States should in any manner be cancelled or reduced." Technically, then, the failure of the Lausanne Agreement meant a return to the Young Plan. Actually Germany made no payments and the National Socialist government repudiated the international form of "interest slavery." England and several other European debtors made small "token payments" to the United States until Congress ruled against such payments. Since then only Finland has paid her installments in full. (The total sum borrowed from the United States was $10,338,000,000, of which $3,261,000,000 was borrowed after Nov. 11, 1918. Between 1923 and 1930 separate agreements were negotiated by a **World War Foreign Debt Commission,** created by Congress, which decided each debtor's capacity to pay and arranged principal and interest payments for a period of 62 years. The original 5% interest was reduced for every debtor, thus cancelling a varying portion of the debt. Payments actually came chiefly from Great Britain — almost $2,000,000,000 — and France — almost $500,000,000. The total actually paid by all debtors remained under $3,000,000,000).

Oct. 4. Lytton Report, drawn by a commission appointed by the League on motion of the Japanese member (Dec. 10, 1931) to investigate the situation in Manchuria. China had appealed to the League under Arts. XI, X, and XV of the Covenant. The commission's findings were mostly adverse to Japan, but instead of ordering Japan out of Manchuria, it proposed a settlement recognizing Japan's special interest there and making **Manchuria an autonomous state** under Chinese sovereignty but under Japanese control.

1933, Feb. 25. The **Lytton Report** was adopted almost *in toto* by the League, despite its rejection by Japan. Japan gave notice of withdrawal from the League (Mar. 27). The whole episode proved to be the **first serious blow at the League structure** and Japan's example proved a stimulus to aggression elsewhere.

Feb. 2-Oct. 14. Meeting of the Disarmament Conference, after the United States government had engineered (Dec. 11, 1932) a **No Force Declaration,** by which Germany, France, Great Britain, and Italy had promised "not in any circumstances to attempt to resolve any present or future differences between them by resort to force." The conference discussed a plan put forward by **M. Herriot** along familiar French lines, but this was nullified by German opposition (advent of Hitler, Jan. 30). **Ramsay MacDonald** put forward (Mar. 16) a scheme by which European armies would be reduced by almost half a million men, and France and Germany would be given equality. Despite strong American support, this proposal also failed because of German insistence that Storm Troops should not be counted as effectives. The conference adjourned in June, to meet again in Oct. In the interval desperate attempts were made to reach an agreement. Great Britain, France, Italy, and the United States were ready not to increase armaments for four years and at the end of that time to allow Germany all such armaments as the other powers had. The Germans insisted on having at least "defensive" weapons at once.

Feb. In view of the danger from the new nationalist Germany, the **Little Entente was reorganized** and given a permanent council.

Mar. Mussolini proposed a **four-power pact** between England, France, Germany, and Italy.

June 12-July 27. INTERNATIONAL ECONOMIC CONFERENCE at London. It disregarded war debts and reparations and tried to secure an agreement on currency stabilization. This was blocked by President Roosevelt's repudiation of it in his message to the conference (July 3). The conference failed.

July 15. Conclusion of the **Four-Power Pact,** proposed by Mussolini, but in a much diluted form. It merely reiterated the adherence of the signatories to the Covenant of the League, the Locarno Treaties, and the Kellogg-Briand Pact.

Oct. 14. Germany announced her withdrawal from the Disarmament Conference and from the League of Nations (Oct. 23).

1934, Feb. 9. Conclusion of the **Balkan Pact** between Turkey, Greece, Rumania, and Yugoslavia. It was the counterpart of the Little Entente and was designed to protect the Balkans from encroachment by other powers. The great weakness of the pact was the absence of Bulgaria.

May 29-June 11. The **Disarmament Conference** met for a brief session, but last-minute efforts to reach an accommodation were wrecked by the stiff French attitude.

Sept. 19. Russia joined the **League of Nations,** another reflection of fear of the new Germany.

Dec. 19. Japan denounced the naval agreements of 1922 and 1930.

1935, Jan. 7. Franco-Italian Agreement, dealing with conflicting interests in Africa, but meant to pave the way to Franco-Italian co-operation in the event of action by Germany.

Mar. 16. GERMANY FORMALLY DENOUNCED THE CLAUSES OF THE TREATY OF VERSAILLES CONCERNING HER DISARMAMENT, reintroduced conscription, and announced that her army would be increased to 36 divisions. This step was based on the failure of the other powers to disarm as provided in the peace treaties and on the steady growth of French and Russian military establishments.

Apr. 11. Stresa Conference between England, France, and Italy establishing a common front in view of the German action.

Apr. 17. The League formally condemned Germany's unilateral repudiation of the Versailles Treaty.

May 2. Franco-Russian Alliance concluded for five years. Each promised the other aid in case of unprovoked aggression.

June 18. Anglo-German Naval Agreement. Germany to have a naval force (including submarines) of not more than 35% that of Great Britain. This separate agreement estranged France.

Sept. BEGINNING OF THE ETHIOPIAN CRISIS (p. 1085).

Oct. 3. The League Council declared that Italy had "resorted to war in disregard of her obligations under Art. XII," though neither Italy nor Ethiopia had declared war.

Oct. 11. Representatives of 51 nations voted in the League Assembly to impose sanctions on Italy, under Art. XVI.

Nov. 18. These sanctions went into effect. They included embargoes on arms, credit and raw materials (not oil), and a prohibition of imports from Italy. Several countries made reservations, leaving loopholes in the scheme. Italy proceeded despite the almost complete unanimity of the nations. Acute tension developed between Italy and England, the leader in the international action. In the course of the winter England concluded with France, Spain, Yugoslavia, Greece, and Turkey agreements providing for mutual support in the event of war arising from action taken under the League. England concentrated an immense naval force in the Mediterranean, but was obliged to withdraw it to Alexandria, in view of the exposure of Malta to air attack.

1936, Mar. 7. GERMAN REOCCUPATION OF THE RHINELAND, violating the Treaty of Versailles and the Locarno Treaties. The Germans took advantage of the Ethiopian crisis and pleaded the danger from the Franco-Russian combination.

Mar. 12. Great Britain, France, Belgium, and Italy denounced the German violation of the Locarno Treaties. The League also recognized this violation, but, despite acute danger of war between Germany and France, the crisis blew over, due largely to England's unwillingness to invoke sanctions. Hitler's vague proposals for a new agreement came to naught through his refusal to consider the extension of the agreement to eastern Europe.

May 5. The Italian army occupied Addis Ababa, bringing to an end the Ethiopian war (p. 1086). Complete collapse of the League as a political machine. Ethiopia, though a member of the League, was abandoned to her fate and Italian aggression, like the Japanese in Manchuria, had proved successful in the face of world opinion and even the application (though incomplete) of sanctions.

July 18. BEGINNING OF THE CIVIL WAR IN SPAIN. From the beginning the insurgents were supported by Italy and Germany, while the Russians assisted the government. The League was helpless, but Great Britain and France arranged an international agreement against intervention, which was generally ignored by the powers interested. The Spanish War divided Europe into fascist and nonfascist groups.

Oct. 25. A German-Italian Pact established the Berlin-Rome Axis, marking the division of Europe into contending groups.

Nov. 14. Germany denounced international control of her waterways. Only France, Czechoslovakia, and Yugoslavia protested.

Nov. 25. A German-Japanese agreement, followed by an Italian-Japanese agreement, directed against communism and the Third International (*The Anti-Comintern Pact*).

1937, Jan. 2. An agreement between Great Britain and Italy for mutual respect of interests and rights in the Mediterranean and the maintenance of the independence and integrity of Spain. This failed to affect the situation materially.

Mar. 25. Conclusion of a non-aggression and neutrality pact for five years between Italy and Yugoslavia. The latter agreed to recognize Italian possession of Ethiopia, while Italy made extensive trade concessions. The agreement brought to an end the long-standing feud between the two powers and reflected Premier Stoyadinovich's anxiety to establish a middle position between the French and the Italians.

Sept. 10-14. The Nyon Conference and Agreement, to deal with piracy in the Mediterranean in connection with the Spanish civil war. Nine powers adopted a system of patrol zones, though England and France assumed the chief burden. Italy, unable to frustrate this action, belatedly joined in the scheme.

Nov. 17. Visit of Lord Halifax, member of the British cabinet, to Hitler, with the aim of discovering the German objectives and, if possible, striking some peaceful settlement. The evidence would indicate that Halifax returned deeply impressed with the magnitude of the German program, especially in central and eastern Europe.

Dec. 1-17. The French foreign minister, M. Delbos, paid an extended visit to France's allies (Poland, Rumania, Yugoslavia, and Czechoslovakia) in the hope of reanimating the French alliance system and preparing for any German moves in central and eastern Europe. Apparently he found but little readiness to take a strong stand against so formidable an opponent as Germany had become. Poland and Yugoslavia, at least, hoped to maintain a free hand policy.

1938, Mar. THE AUSTRO-GERMAN CRISIS and the annexation of Austria by Germany (p. 1009) created remarkably little tension in international relations. Italy, which might have been expected to offer stiff opposition, was so bound up with Spanish and Mediterranean affairs that Mussolini had to accept the inevitable as graciously as possible. France, at the moment, was in the midst of a cabinet crisis. The British appear to have been reconciled to the German move from the outset. Beyond a few half-hearted attempts to revive the Stresa front of 1935, the powers acquiesced and accepted the *fait accompli*.

Mar. 16-19. The Polish-Lithuanian crisis, following on the heels of the German action. Since Lithuania capitulated at once to the Polish ultimatum (p. 1040), the affair had no broader effects.

Apr. 16. CONCLUSION OF THE ANGLO-ITALIAN PACT, which had been under negotiation for some time. The British being eager to free themselves of Italian hostility in the Mediterranean and Near East and Mussolini apparently desiring some counter-weight to the oppressive friendship of Hitler, the two parties succeeded in liquidating their differences. Great Britain was to recognize Italian sovereignty over Ethiopia and use her influence to induce other states to do likewise. Italy was to respect Spanish territory and withdraw her "volunteers" at the end of the war (at that time regarded as very near). Italy was to desist from hostile propaganda in the Near East, and both powers were to collaborate in maintaining the *status quo* in the Red Sea. The provisions of the agreement were to come into force as soon as the Spanish affair had been settled.

May 3-9. Visit of Hitler to Rome, a great and impressive state function evidently designed to demonstrate the solidarity of the Rome-Berlin Axis.

July 19-21. State visit of King George VI and Queen Elizabeth to Paris, clearly meant as a counter-demonstration of Anglo-French solidarity.

Aug. 21-23. Meeting of the Little Entente statesmen at Bled (Yugoslavia). The three powers **recognized Hungary's right to rearm** and arranged for the conclusion of non-aggression pacts.

Sept. THE GERMAN-CZECH CRISIS and the dismemberment of Czechoslovakia as a result of the **Munich agreements** (p. 1012). The German action against Czechoslovakia brought the European world closer to another World War than any issue of the preceding 20 years. Czechoslovakia was abandoned not only by her allies of the Little Entente, but by France, despite numerous assurances by the French government that treaty obligations would be respected. The Russian government appeared ready to support Czechoslovakia, but in the last analysis neither France nor Britain was willing to go the limit. The nature of the German national claim and the relative weakness of France and England (especially in air forces) brought the decision for peace and the capitulation of the western powers at Mu-

nich. As a result of Hitler's immense victory the **Little Entente disappeared as an important factor** in international relations. What remained of Czechoslovakia fell entirely under German influence. Much the same was true of Hungary and the other Danubian countries. The Czech alliances with Russia and France became all but valueless, and the Franco-Russian alliance of 1935 lost most of its significance. Germany now emerged as the strongest power on the Continent.

Nov. 16. The Anglo-Italian Agreement of Apr. 16 was put into force, despite the fact that the conditions of enforcement had been only very imperfectly fulfilled. The British were obviously eager to prevent any recrudescence of the Mediterranean tension.

Nov. 26. Poland and Russia suddenly renewed their non-aggression pact. Poland, directly exposed to the German advance eastward, now required closer relations with Russia and, indeed, made efforts to build up a barrier of Baltic and Balkan states to join with Poland in the interest of the *status quo.*

Nov. 30. Astounding **anti-French demonstrations in the Italian Chamber of Deputies** (demands for Corsica and Tunisia, which were then taken up by the government-controlled press) ushered in a period of acute **tension between France and Italy,** which became even more accentuated with the fascist victories in Spain.

Dec. 6. France and Germany concluded a pact by which they guaranteed the inviolability of the existing frontier and provided for consultation with the aim of settling any disputes pacifically.

Dec. 17. An Italian note to France declared the agreement of 1935 invalid because ratifications had not been exchanged. France rejected this argument.

Dec. 24. The declaration of Lima was adopted by 21 American republics. It reaffirmed their solidarity and decision to oppose any foreign intervention or activity threatening their sovereignty (p. 1062).

1939, Mar. THE SLOVAK CRISIS and the **ANNIHILATION OF THE CZECHOSLOVAK STATE** (p. 1012 *f.*). None of the great powers made a move to check the German annexation of the rump Czech state or the Hungarian conquest of Ruthenia (Carpatho-Ukraine). Yet Hitler's action served to disillusion those who held that his aims were restricted to German territories.

Mar. 23. German annexation of Memel after pressure upon Lithuania which extracted a peaceful settlement. At the same time Hitler submitted stiff demands regarding **Danzig** and **Pomorze** (the "Polish Corridor") to Warsaw. Faced by the project of limitless German expansion on the continent,

Mar. 31. The British government pledged **Anglo-French aid to the Poles** in case of action threatening Polish independence. This was later (Apr. 6) expanded into a pact of mutual assistance.

Apr. 7. Italian invasion and conquest of Albania (p. 1020). Despite the violation of the Anglo-Italian pact, Britain made no move.

Apr. 7. The victorious nationalist government in **Spain** joined Germany, Italy and Japan **in the Anti-Comintern Pact.**

Apr. 13. The Franco-British pledge was extended **to Rumania and Greece.**

Apr. 15. President Roosevelt, in a letter to Hitler and Mussolini, asked assurances against attack on 31 nations of Europe and the Near East. In response Hitler publicly restated German grievances and claims and denied aggressive intentions.

May 12. Announcement of an **Anglo-Turkish mutual assistance pact,** to be followed by a French-Turkish agreement purchased at the expense of the Sanjak of Alexandretta.

May 17. Sweden, Norway and Finland rejected a German offer of a bilateral non-aggression pact, preferring to maintain a rigid neutrality. Denmark, Estonia and Latvia, however, accepted the German proposal. In the interval the British made every effort to draw Russia into the anti-aggression front. The Russians, profoundly suspicious, insisted not only on complete reciprocity in defense, but on guarantee of the independence of the Baltic States which, incidentally, objected to such guarantees.

May 22. Conclusion of a political and **military alliance between Germany and Italy** marking the full development of the Rome-Berlin Axis.

June 23. Treaty between France and Turkey by which the Republic of Hatay was abandoned to Turkey in return for a promise of mutual aid in case of aggression.

Aug. 20-Sept. 1. THE DANZIG-POLISH CRISIS. After months of agitation and recrimination punctuated by incidents on the Danzig-Polish frontier, the long-anticipated crisis broke when Albert Forster, Nazi leader in Danzig, announced publicly that the hour of deliverance was near. At the same time the world was startled by the conclusion of a trade treaty between Germany and Soviet Russia, followed by

Aug. 21. The announcement that Germany and Russia were about to conclude a non-aggression pact. Coming after months of negotiation between England, France and Russia and the mission of a military delegation to Moscow, this move was regarded as a demonstration of Bolshevik perfidy. The *volte-face* of the Russians was evidently due in large measure to Poland's refusal to admit Russian forces in the event of war. Discussion of Russia's inclusion in a peace front was at once dropped. In England and France as well as in Germany military preparations were initiated, the Germans concentrating forces in Slovakia as well as along the Corridor.

Aug. 22. The British government reiterated its pledges to Poland, but at the same time appealed to Germany for a truce in eastern Europe and negotiation of German claims.

Aug. 23. The German-Russian pact was signed at Moscow by the German foreign minister, artisan of the Anti-Comintern Pact of 1936. It provided not only for abstention of either party from attack on the other, but for neutrality of either party if the other were attacked by a third power. Each signatory promised not to join any group of powers "which is directly or indirectly aimed at the other party." As a result of this amazing agreement the Anti-Comintern Pact at once collapsed, Japan resuming freedom of action.

Aug. 24. President Roosevelt appealed to King Victor Immanuel, to Hitler and to President Moscicki of Poland suggesting direct negotiations between Germany and Poland, arbitration or conciliation. Poland agreed to conciliation by a third party.

The British parliament met in special session and voted the government practically dictatorial powers, at the same time **England and Poland signed a pact of mutual assistance.** Poland began to call up reserves.

Forster was proclaimed "supreme head" of the Danzig Free State.

Aug. 25. In discussion with the British ambassador, Hitler renewed his demand for a free hand against Poland. Roosevelt again appealed to Hitler to seek a peaceful solution.

Aug. 26. Premier Daladier of France appealed to Hitler, receiving in reply (Aug. 27) a plea for German-French peace but also a reiteration of the German demands on Poland.

Aug. 28. The British government replied to Hitler, again urging a truce and repeating former warnings of British action in case of German aggression. British shipping was recalled from the Baltic and Mediterranean. In Germany emergency rationing was introduced. On all sides military preparations were accelerated.

Aug. 29. Hitler reiterated to Britain his extreme demands on Poland and refused to negotiate until these demands were met. He called for arrival of a Polish plenipotentiary in Berlin within 24 hours.

Aug. 30. The Poles decreed partial mobilization, while in Germany a six-man "cabinet council for defense of the Reich" was set up under the presidency of Goering.

Aug. 31. The German government published a 16-point proposal to Poland. This was of rather moderate tenor, but before it could be transmitted to Warsaw, communications were cut off. On this same day the Russian Supreme Soviet ratified the pact with Germany and Hitler, claiming his proposals to Poland had been rejected, gave the order to march.

Sept. 1. GERMAN ATTACK ON POLAND on land and in the air. Forster proclaimed the reunion of Danzig and Germany. England and France mobilized but expressed readiness to negotiate if German forces were withdrawn from Poland. Italy declared the intention of remaining neutral.

Sept. 2. Italy proposed a five-power conference to discuss the situation, but England refused negotiation so long as the Germans remained on Polish soil. Hitler having failed to reply to the Anglo-French notes, these two powers sent an ultimatum, to which Hitler replied by a note blaming England for encouraging the Poles in a policy of persecution and provocation. The German government having rejected the Anglo-French demands for withdrawal from Poland,

Sept. 3. ENGLAND AND FRANCE DECLARED WAR ON GERMANY, thus initiating the Second European War of the twentieth century.

2. THE BRITISH ISLES

a. GREAT BRITAIN

Great Britain's losses in the First World War were 750,000 killed and about 1,500-000 wounded. Her total expense exceeded £8,000,000,000 and her burden of domestic and foreign debt was ten times what it had been in 1914. She was faced with the problem of returning soldiers to industry and introducing social reforms loudly demanded by the laboring classes and was confronted at the same time with increased competition in foreign trade in a world generally disorganized and impoverished. In Ireland, India, Egypt, and Palestine she was confronted with urgent and almost insoluble problems. Even the self-governing Dominions demonstrated an enhanced national feeling and a reluctance to be committed to any share in future European wars.

1918, Dec. 14. The Khaki Election, with an electorate increased by the granting of suffrage to all men of 21 and over and to women over 30. The coalition government won a huge majority on a platform promising punishment of the German "war criminals," full payment by the defeated powers of the costs of war, and the prevention of dumping of foreign goods in Great Britain. These promises greatly hampered Lloyd George's freedom of action at the Paris Peace Conference (p. 951).

1919-1922. COALITION GOVERNMENT OF DAVID LLOYD GEORGE.

1919, Mar. 24-29. Strike of coal miners, ending with recognition by the workers of the recommendations of a royal commission (Sankey Commission).

Oct. 18. Another great strike of miners, who won a favorable compromise settlement.

Dec. 9. Milner report on the government of Egypt (p. 1081).

Dec. 23. GOVERNMENT OF IRELAND ACT passed, providing for the division of Ireland (p. 972).

1921, Mar. 3. The Emergency Unemployment Act increased unemployment payments to 20s. a week for men and 18s. for women. There were at this time almost 1,000,000 unemployed.

Mar. 31. Great coal strike begun as government control of the mines ended and proposals for nationalization had been rejected. The strike ended July 1 when the miners accepted a government offer of subsidy and increase of wages.

Dec. 6. TREATY WITH IRELAND (p. 972).

1922, Feb. 28. End of the British protectorate over Egypt (p. 1083).

Sept. 15. Appeal of Lloyd George to the Dominions for support in the Near-Eastern crisis (p. 1095). This was rejected.

Oct. 19. The Unionists decided to withdraw their support from the Lloyd George government, which thereupon resigned.

Oct. 23-1923, May 20. CABINET OF A. BONAR LAW.

Nov. 15. General election. The Conservatives (Unionists) received a majority of the seats. The Liberals split between the followers of Asquith and Lloyd George. The Labor Party (142 seats) became for the first time His Majesty's Opposition.

1923, May 22—1924, Jan. 22. CABINET OF STANLEY BALDWIN, following Bonar Law's retirement owing to illness.

Oct. 1-Nov. 8. Imperial Conference. This recognized the right of the Dominions to make treaties with foreign powers.

Dec. 6. A general election to pass upon Baldwin's scheme for a protective tariff to relieve unemployment resulted in heavy loss for the Conservatives and a decided gain for Labor.

1924, Jan. 22-Nov. 4. FIRST LABOR CABINET, under Ramsay MacDonald; Philip Snowden, formerly a clerk, became chancellor of the exchequer, and **Arthur Henderson,** formerly an iron worker, became home secretary.

Feb. 1. *De jure* recognition of Soviet Russia.

Aug. 8. Commercial treaty with Russia, giving British goods most-favored-nation treatment and promising Russia a British loan if and when the debt of the former tsarist government should have been settled. These treaties were opposed by the Liberals and Conservatives.

Oct. 29. The general election turned out a great victory for the Conservatives, owing largely to the so-called Zinoviev letter (Oct. 25), in which the Third International supposedly instructed British subjects to provoke revolution.

1924, Nov. 7-1929, June 4. SECOND BALDWIN MINISTRY.

Nov. 21. The new government denounced the treaties with Russia.

1925, Mar. 12. Rejection of the Geneva Protocol by Great Britain (p. 959).

May 1. Cyprus (annexed in 1914) made a crown colony.

Dec. 3. Signature of the Irish boundary agreement, fixing the frontier between Northern Ireland and the Irish Free State.

1926, May 1. Strike of coal miners, after a commission report adverse to continuation of government subsidy.

May 3-12. GENERAL STRIKE, in sympathy with coal miners. It involved about 2,500,000 of the 6,000,000 trade-union members in Great Britain. Volunteers, largely from the upper classes, maintained essential transport and other services. The Trade-Union Council called off the strike May 12 with an understanding that negotiations on wages and hours would be resumed. But the miners' union continued to strike until Nov. 19, when it surrendered unconditionally.

Oct. 19-Nov. 18. Imperial Conference. Its report declared that Great Britain and the Dominions "are autonomous communities within the British Empire, equal in status, in no way subordinate one to another in any aspect of their domestic or external affairs, though united by a common allegiance to the crown and freely associated as members of the British Commonwealth of Nations."

1927, May 26. Trade agreement with Russia abrogated, following much friction as to communist agitation in England.

June 28. Trade-Union Law, declaring certain strikes and lockouts illegal.

1928, July 2. An act of Parliament extended the franchise to women on the same terms as men.

Dec. 20. Treaty with China, recognizing the Nanking government and Chinese tariff autonomy, China to abolish coast and interior duties.

1929, May 30. In the general election the Labor Party was victorious, securing 288 seats against 260 for the Conservatives.

June 5-1931, Aug. 24. SECOND MacDONALD CABINET.

Sept. 28-Nov. 1. Visit of Prime Minister MacDonald to the United States and Canada.

Oct. 1. Diplomatic relations with Russia resumed.

1930, Jan. 21. Opening of the London Naval Conference (p. 961).

June 10. Publication of the **Simon Report** on the government of India (p. 1113).

Oct. 1-Nov. 14. Imperial Conference. MacDonald rejected a Canadian proposal for preferential tariff to help Dominion wheat because of Labor policy of free trade and cheap bread.

1931, July. Report of the **May Committee** of financial experts. They claimed the deficit for the fiscal year would be over £100,000 sterling and suggested drastic economies, including a cut in the dole to the unemployed. This report caused a **split in the cabinet,** the majority rejecting the proposals as too burdensome to the workers. There were, at this time, over 2,000,000 unemployed.

Aug. 24. Resignation of the **MacDonald cabinet,** the result of the financial crisis and disagreement as to remedies.

Aug. 25-Oct. 27. A NATIONAL COALITION GOVERNMENT formed to include Conservatives, Liberals, and Labor members, with MacDonald as prime minister. The Labor Party opposed this coalition and expelled those of its leaders who favored it. MacDonald, Snowden, Thomas, and others formed a new **National Labor** group. Henderson became leader of the old Labor Party.

Sept. 10. Passage of a bill embodying most of the economies urged by the May Committee caused rioting in London, Liverpool, Glasgow, and other large cities.

Sept. 15. Mutiny of sailors in the navy, at Invergordon.

Sept. 21. England forced to abandon the gold standard. The pound sterling fell from par ($4.86) to $3.49.

Oct. 27. A general election gave the coalition government a majority of almost 500 seats over the combined opposition. The government was reformed under MacDonald.

1931, Oct. 27—June 7, 1935. NATIONAL COALITION CABINET under MacDonald.

Dec. THE STATUTE OF WESTMINSTER passed by Parliament, giving force of law to the changes in empire relations worked out by the Imperial Conference in 1926.

1932, Feb. 29. Protective Tariff Acts, including a new "corn law" which guaranteed British farmers about $1 a bushel for a specified quantity of home-grown wheat. Abandonment of free trade.

July 21-Aug. 20. Ottawa Imperial Economic Conference. A series of rather grudging agreements for a carefully limited amount of imperial preference led to the resignation (Sept. 28) of the free-trade Liberal members of the cabinet, who went into opposition under the lead of **Sir Herbert Samuel.** The Liberals who remained in the government were led by **Sir John Simon.**

1933, June 12-July 27. World Economic Conference at London (p. 963). The failure of this conference led the British government to extend its neo-mercantilist policy of economic nationalism. Campaign to "buy British." Managed paper currency; control of foreign exchanges through an exchange equalization fund; free trade and *laisser-faire* definitely abandoned. Gradual but slow recovery took place. The budget was kept in balance.

1935, Feb. 1-3. Anglo-French Conference at London regarding action to be taken with reference to Germany's announcement of rearmament. England and France joined in an invitation to Germany to help re-establish confidence and security by concluding pacts of mutual assistance in eastern Europe, guaranteeing Austrian independence, collaborating in disarmament, rejoining the League, etc. Germany expressed willingness to conclude an air pact, but refused to consider an eastern pact, which England and France thought should come first.

Mar. 4. The British government announced that the international situation was such that **England would have to put her defenses in shape.** Most of the new expenditure was devoted to the fleet.

May 6-9. Silver jubilee of George V, an impressive demonstration of loyalty and solidarity.

June 7. Reconstruction of the cabinet, following a general election which continued the majority of the coalition government. **Stanley Baldwin became prime minister** and Sir Samuel Hoare foreign secretary.

June 18. Conclusion of the **Anglo-German naval agreement** (p. 963): Germany to have not more than 35% of the British tonnage. This agreement made a most unfavorable impression in France and resulted in cooling of the Anglo-French relationship.

Aug. 2. The Government of India Act passed by Parliament (p. 1113).

Sept. The Ethiopian crisis (p. 991). The British government, especially after the failure of the Hoare-Laval plan to victimize Ethiopia, gave way to **a**

strong current of British opinion. Under the lead of **Anthony Eden,** who now became foreign secretary, Britain assumed the guidance of the League of Nations in the **imposition of sanctions,** etc. The result was acute danger of war in the Mediterranean. France, Turkey, Greece, and Yugoslavia all agreed to support England in case of conflict, but in the end the London government shrank from extreme measures (oil sanction, e.g.) and the League action failed. Uncertainty regarding the possible attitude or action of Germany no doubt influenced the British cabinet, as did also the military unpreparedness of the country at that time.

**1936, Jan. 20.	Death of George V.**

**1936, Jan. 20-Dec. 10.	EDWARD VIII.**

**Mar. 25.	The London Naval Agreement,** signed by England, France, and the United States after Japan and Italy had abandoned the conference. No quantitative limitation was reached, but limitation of tonnage and size of guns in each ship category was agreed to.

Apr. 30. The government announced plans for the construction of 38 warships, the largest building program since 1921.

Aug. 27. Conclusion of the **Anglo-Egyptian Treaty** on terms very favorable to the Egyptian Nationalists (p. 1084).

**Dec. 10.	Abdication of Edward VIII,** the first voluntary abdication in English history. The Baldwin ministry and the Dominion governments had refused to consent to a morganatic marriage between the king and **Mrs. Wallis Warfield Simpson,** an American-born lady whose second divorce had not yet become final. Edward, apparently at odds with his ministers on other matters also (social policy, etc.), insisted on his right to shape his own life and abdicated rather than abandon his plan. He became **Duke of Windsor** and in June 1937 married Mrs. Simpson in France.

**1936- .	GEORGE VI,** brother of Edward VIII, became king.

1937, Jan. 2. Signature of the **Anglo-Italian Mediterranean Agreement,** which, it was hoped, would bring to an end the dangerous antagonism in that sea. But the general statements of principle of which the agreement consisted proved of very little value in the sequel. On the contrary, the Mediterranean situation became ever more serious with the development of the **Spanish civil war** (p. 983) and the open flouting of the **non-intervention agreements** by the Italian government. From the outset the British government had worked

for non-intervention, in order to prevent the generalization of the conflict. By this policy the government stood despite flagrant violations of the principle by other powers.

**May 28.	Neville Chamberlain became prime minister** on the retirement of Stanley Baldwin. Chamberlain had been chancellor of the exchequer. He was confronted at the outset with a most difficult and dangerous European situation, which overshadowed all issues of purely domestic character. Abandoning the rather aimless, opportunist policy of Baldwin, Chamberlain held that in order to secure peace, it must be definitely worked for. He therefore sought to reach agreements with powers like Germany and Italy, even at the expense of considerable concessions. This became known as the *policy of appeasement.*

**July 8.	Publication of the Peel Report** recommending the ending of the **Palestine mandate** and the division of the country into Arab and Jewish states, England to retain a mandate only over Jerusalem, Bethlehem, and a corridor to the sea. Parliament refused to commit itself to this scheme and the opposition to it on the part of both Jews and Arabs resulted in its reconsideration (p. 1101).

**July.	Outbreak of hostilities in China.** Though British interests were deeply involved and suffered enormous damage, the government avoided challenging Japan in any way, even when the British ambassador was badly injured in an attack of Japanese planes upon the ambassadorial party. The British government co-operated with the United States and France in protests against Japanese bombing and injury of European interests, but for the rest the British were too deeply involved in Europe and too weak navally in the Far East to do more than protest.

**Nov. 17.	Visit of Lord Halifax to Chancellor Hitler** at Berchtesgaden. This was the first concrete step in the policy of appeasement and was obviously intended to elicit a statement of German claims.

**1938, Feb. 20.	Resignation of Anthony Eden,** British foreign secretary and outstanding champion of the system of collective security and action. He resigned in protest against the prime minister's determination to seek an agreement with Italy without waiting for a settlement of the Spanish problem. Lord Halifax became foreign secretary in his place.

Mar. In the **Austrian annexation crisis** (p. 1019) the British government played but a small part, having apparently reconciled itself to this development after Halifax's visit to Hitler.

Apr. 16. Conclusion of the **Anglo-Italian Agreement**, for which Chamberlain had been working for some time. (For terms see p. 965.) The agreement was to come into force as soon as the Italian "volunteers" were withdrawn from Spain.

Apr. 25. Conclusion of a three-year agreement with Ireland, bringing to an end a feud which had continued for years (p. 973).

Sept. THE GERMAN-CZECH CRISIS AND THE MUNICH AGREEMENTS (p. 1012). During the entire development of the Czech problem in the summer, the British government had played a leading rôle, sending **Lord Runciman** as mediator and working generally for a compromise. As the crisis reached the peak, Chamberlain twice flew to Germany to confer with Hitler and ultimately went to Munich to sign the instrument of German victory. By way of compensation he brought back a **peace pact with Germany** which apparently he rated highly, but which other people viewed with considerable skepticism. The desire to appease the national claims of the Germans and the feeling of inferiority in the matter of preparedness appear to have been at the root of Chamberlain's yielding.

Nov. 2. Ratification of the **Anglo-Italian Pact** of Apr. 16, which went into force Nov. 16. The conditions originally laid down had not been fulfilled, but Chamberlain was evidently eager to do what was possible to satisfy Mussolini and prevent too close co-operation between Rome and Berlin.

Nov. 17. Conclusion of **trade agreements between Great Britain, Canada, and the United States.** These had been under negotiation for a long time and involved substantial sacrifices on all sides. They were taken as an indication of growing co-operation between the English-speaking nations.

Dec. 1. Opening of a "national register" for war service. This was entirely voluntary, but was looked upon as an important item of preparedness. After the crisis of 1938 the British government pushed its preparations to the utmost, going so far as to buy large numbers of planes in the United States.

1939, Jan. Visit of Chamberlain and Lord Halifax to Rome. The visit was said to be purely exploratory and indeed appeared to have no very significant consequences.

Mar. 31. British-French pledge to Poland (p. 966), marking the end of the policy of appeasement. The British government, disagreeably surprised by German annexation of Czechoslovakia and Memel, and alarmed by the German threat to Poland, made an epochal departure in foreign policy and devoted itself to building up an anti-aggression pact. After the Italian conquest of Albania (p. 1020) guarantees were given to Greece and Rumania, a mutual assistance pact was concluded with Turkey, and the British government finally embarked on the arduous task of bringing Russia into the *"peace front."* At the same time

Apr. 27. The British government introduced conscription for men of 20–21 years, in order to increase the forces by 300,000 men. Expenditure for armament was fixed at three billion dollars for one year.

Apr. 28. Hitler, in a great *Reichstag* speech, denounced the Anglo-German naval agreement of 1935.

May 17. The British published a new plan for Palestine (p. 1102), after abortive negotiations with both Arabs and Jews. The new scheme met with a storm of opposition from both parties to the dispute.

King George and Queen Elizabeth arrived in Canada for an extended visit, followed (June 8–11) by a visit to the United States obviously intended to strengthen Anglo-Saxon ties in the face of threatening war in Europe.

Aug. 20-Sept. 1. The Danzig-Polish crisis (p. 966) and the

Sept. 3. OUTBREAK OF WAR BETWEEN ENGLAND AND GERMANY.

b. IRELAND

1916, Apr. 24-29. THE EASTER REBELLION, led by P. H. Pearse and the Irish Republican Brotherhood, despite failure of German aid. Suppression by British (p. 929).

1917, June 15. Amnesty granted the rebels of 1916.

July 11. Release of Eamon de Valera, Sinn Fein leader, who was re-elected to Parliament.

Oct. 25-27. A Sinn Fein convention at Dublin adopted a constitution for the Irish Republic and elected De Valera president.

1918, Mar. 6. Death of John Redmond, leader of the Irish Nationalist group in the British Parliament.

Apr. 17. Adoption of **conscription for Ireland.** The Irish Nationalists thereupon deserted the British Parliament and organized opposition to the measure, which was never very successful.

May 18. **De Valera** and other Sinn Fein leaders again arrested.

June 25. Conscription was given up.

Dec. 14. Great victory of the **Sinn Fein** candidates in the elections for the British Parliament.

1919, Jan. 21. The **Sinn Fein members** of Parliament, having decided not to attend, **organized a parliament** of their own for Ireland (the *Dail Eireann*) and declared Irish independence.

Feb. 3. Escape of **De Valera** from prison; he took refuge in the United States.

Sept. 12. The Dail was suppressed and the headquarters of the Sinn Fein party raided.

Nov. 26. Suppression of the **Sinn Fein movement; beginning of war** between the Sinn Fein and the British forces: attacks on the constabulary, arson, etc.

1920, May 15. Arrival of British reinforcements (*Black and Tans*) and initiation of a **policy of reprisal.** There followed several months of ferocious conflict.

Dec. 23. **PASSAGE OF THE GOVERNMENT OF IRELAND ACT** by the British Parliament: **Northern Ireland** and **Southern Ireland** each to have its own parliament, and each to retain representatives in the British Parliament. A **Council for Ireland,** representing the two parts, was to attempt to effect common action in common affairs.

1921, May 13. Elections: in the North the Government of Ireland Act was generally accepted and the new system went into effect. In Southern Ireland the **Sinn Fein** won **124 out of 128 seats.**

June 28. The Parliament for Southern Ireland was opened, but only the four delegates not members of the Sinn Fein attended. The Sinn Feiners declared themselves the Dail Eireann and rejected the settlement proposed.

July 14-21. Conferences of **De Valera** and Sir James Craig (representing Northern Ireland) with Lloyd George and other British representatives. De Valera rejected offers of Dominion status for Ireland.

Oct. 11.-Dec. 6. Second conference with the British leaders; De Valera did not attend and the negotiations for the Sinn Fein were conducted by **Arthur Griffith** and **Michael Collins.**

Dec. 6. **THE IRISH REPRESENTATIVES SIGNED A TREATY** with the British government which granted Ireland **Dominion status** as the **Irish Free State** (Northern Ireland retaining the right of keeping the existing arrangement).

Dec. 8. **De Valera** denounced the settlement made by Griffith.

1922, Jan. 7. The **Dail Eireann accepted** the settlement, 64–57.

Jan. 9. Resignation of **De Valera.** Griffith became president of the executive council and Collins prime minister. The Dail ratified the treaty (Jan. 14).

Mar. 15. **De Valera** organized a new **Republican Society** and began an insurrection against his former colleagues; irregular forces resumed the methods of assassination and arson formerly used against the British.

June 16. The Government forces won a great victory in the elections.

Aug. 12. Death of Arthur Griffith.

Aug. 22. Assassination of **Michael Collins** by the Republicans.

Sept. 9. **WILLIAM T. COSGRAVE BECAME PRESIDENT** of the executive council and, with the aid of **Kevin O'Higgins,** began a policy of rigorous repression of De Valera's movement.

Oct. 25. **THE DAIL ADOPTED A CONSTITUTION,** providing for a two-chamber parliament (a senate, with 12-year term, one-fourth renewable annually, with suspensive veto; a chamber of deputies, popularly elected and with exclusive power in financial affairs; the lower chamber to elect the president).

Dec. 6. The constitution went into effect and the Irish Free State was officially proclaimed.

1923, Aug. 14. **De Valera was captured** by government forces, and imprisoned.

Sept. 10. Ireland was admitted to the League of Nations.

1924, July 16. **De Valera was liberated.** He and his Republicans continued to refuse to take their seats in the Dail, rejecting the necessary oath of loyalty to the king.

1925, Dec. 3. Boundary with the State of Northern Ireland fixed after long negotiations. Compromise proposals having failed, the boundary envisaged in 1920 was retained, but Southern Ireland was relieved of the obligation to assume part of the British national debt.

1926, Mar. 11. De Valera resigned as head of the Sinn Fein.

1927, July 10. Assassination of Kevin O'Higgins, dominant figure of the government. Popular condemnation of the tactics of the Republicans. A drastic public-safety law enacted. Candidates for the Dail henceforth required to promise acceptance of the oath in advance.

Aug. 12. De Valera and other Republican leaders agreed to take the oath and assume their seats in the Dail.

Sept. 15. Elections. The government party had 61 seats against 57 for the Republicans, but failed to secure a clear majority and had to rely on support of the Independents.

1930, Mar. 27. Resignation of Cosgrave, who was soon re-elected (Apr. 2: 80 votes against 65 for De Valera).

1931, Oct. Passage of a new public-safety law to meet the revival of Republican agitation and activity, stimulated by economic stress. The Republican army was declared illegal and military tribunals set up to deal with sedition, illegal drilling, etc.

1932, Feb. Elections. The Republicans won 72 seats against 65 for the government. The Labor deputies supported the Republicans, thus giving them a majority.

Mar. DE VALERA ELECTED PRESIDENT, with a program of abolishing the oath to the king; suspension of land annuity payments; establishment of a high protective tariff, etc.

May 19. The Dail passed a law abolishing the oath, but this was held up by the Senate, with an opposition majority.

July. Outbreak of tariff war with Great Britain, following long abortive negotiations concerning the land annuities which the Irish government suspended.

1933, Jan. 2. De Valera dissolved the Dail and in the ensuing elections (Jan. 24) secured for his party a clear majority of one.

May 3. The Dail abolished the oath of loyalty and soon afterward voted that the approval of the governor-general should no longer be necessary to put legislation into effect; appeals to the British Privy Council were made illegal.

July 23. Formation of the National Guard (*Blue Shirts*) in opposition to De Valera's Republican army.

Sept. 3. Union of the National Guard and the Center (Cosgrave Party) to form the *United Ireland Party*, under Gen. Owen O'Duffy. There followed a period of disorder and conflict between the two groups.

Sept. 22. Resignation of O'Duffy, a reflection of disapproval of his methods by the more moderate opposition elements. Cosgrave became leader of the United Ireland Party.

1934-1935. Continuation of the tariff war with Great Britain. Ireland suffered tremendously from the loss of her export markets, and much discontent developed. The government tried to meet the situation by encouraging the diversification of crops and the establishment of industrial self-sufficiency, but these measures had only qualified success.

1935, Jan. Conclusion of a coal and cattle agreement with Great Britain which enabled the Irish to get rid of at least some of their meat.

July. Anti-Catholic riots in Belfast, leading to expulsion of Catholic families, and reprisals by the Free State government.

1936, Feb. 17. Conclusion of an Anglo-Irish trade pact, bringing to an end the disastrous tariff war. The Irish government agreed to pay the land annuities.

June. Abolition of the Senate. De Valera proposed a new constitution involving the abolition of the governor-generalship.

Nov. 3. THE NEW CONSTITUTION reintroduced the Senate, but as a functional body. The relationship to Great Britain was ignored.

1937, June 14. Parliament approved the draft constitution, which was to be submitted to popular vote.

July 16. The elections resulted in a stalemate, the De Valera party winning exactly one-half of the seats.

1938, Jan. 17. Opening of conversations between the Irish and British governments in the hope of a broader settlement.

Feb. 9. The elections in Northern Ireland resulted in an overwhelming victory for the Unionists, thus blasting any hope there might have been of merger of the Free State and Northern Ireland.

Apr. 25. CONCLUSION OF AN AGREEMENT WITH GREAT BRITAIN for three years. The Ulster (Northern Ireland) problem had to be shelved, but other outstanding questions were adjusted. Ireland was to pay £10,-

000,000 in satisfaction of land-annuity claims. All recent tariff barriers were thrown down. Great Britain turned over to the Free State (*Eire* or *Ireland* in the new constitution) the coast defenses of Cobh, Bere Haven, and Lough Swilly. This agreement, restoring close friendly relations between Ireland and England, was approved by the Irish opposition, which also joined the government party in electing

May 4. DR. DOUGLAS HYDE FIRST PRESIDENT under the new con-

stitution. Hyde was one of the leaders of the Gaelic cultural revival, and a Protestant. His election was taken as a persuasive gesture toward Northern Ireland.

June 17. The elections resulted in a great **victory for De Valera,** who became prime minister under the new system. The growing danger of war in Europe led to ever closer relations between Ireland and England, though negotiations for union of North and South Ireland were actively pressed by De Valera.

3. THE LOW COUNTRIES

a. BELGIUM

Of all the countries involved in the First World War, **Belgium,** an unwilling participant, suffered most. The total damage was estimated at over $7,000,000,000, but the country showed extraordinary recuperative power and soon returned to a peace basis. Politically the country was ruled by the Catholic and Socialist parties. One of the major questions at issue was the demand of the Flemish for recognition of their language.

1919, May 9. A new **electoral law** introduced **universal suffrage** and gave the franchise to certain classes of women.

May 30. By agreement with Great Britain, Belgium was given the **mandate over part of German East Africa** (Ruanda and Urundi). This was later confirmed by the League of Nations.

June 28. By the Treaty of Versailles, Belgium acquired the German districts of **Eupen, Malmédy, and Moresnet.**

Nov. 16. In the elections the Catholic Party lost its majority, though it was still the largest party (73 seats as against 70 for the Socialists).

1920, Sept. 7. Military convention with France. In the following years Belgium acted closely with France in most questions of international import.

1921, Nov. 28. The elections restored the majority of the Catholic Party.

1922, Jan. 1. A law went into effect putting Flemish on a par with French as an official language.

1923, Jan. 11. Invasion of the Ruhr, by French and Belgian troops (p. 958).

July 27. The use of Flemish was introduced in the University of Ghent.

1925, Apr. 3. A treaty with the Netherlands settled a long-standing dispute regarding the **navigation of the Scheldt.**

Apr. 5. The Socialists secured a majority in the elections.

Oct. 16. Belgium was a party to the **Locarno Treaties** (p. 959).

1926, May 22. A treaty with England and France formally abrogated the Treaty of 1839.

July. Financial crisis. The king was given dictatorial powers for six months to solve the problem. Devaluation and stabilization of the Belgian franc. A new currency unit, the *Belga,* equal to five Belgian francs, was introduced.

1929, May 26. In the elections the Catholics regained their preponderance.

1932, July 18. Enactment of **new language regulations.** Henceforth French was to be the administrative language only of the Walloon provinces, while in Flanders the Flemish language was to be official. In Brussels and Brabant there were to be two sets of higher officials. In the secondary schools instruction was to be given in the language prevailing in the district.

July 19. Conclusion of the **Ouchy Convention** between Belgium, Luxemburg, and Holland. The three parties agreed to gradual reduction of economic barriers between them.

Sept. 14. The government was granted **extraordinary power** to deal with the alarming budget deficits. The worldwide depression struck Belgium very hard in view of the cessation of German reparations payments. The government stuck to the gold standard and tried to meet the situation by reduction of salaries, flotation of loans, and steady increase of taxation.

1933, Mar. 16. The victory of the National Socialists in Germany obliged the government to take precautionary measures. 150,000,000 francs were devoted to fortifications along the Meuse and Belgium thenceforth constantly increased appropriations for defense. In Dec. 1936 the term of service for the infantry was extended from seven to eighteen months.

1934, Feb. 17. Death of King Albert I, the result of a mountaineering accident. He was succeeded by his son

1934-1944. LEOPOLD III.

July 12. The government prohibited the formation of military units and the wearing of uniforms by political organizations. This law was directed at the growing fascist movement, and also at the **Labor Defense Militia.** Both organizations were dissolved.

1935, Mar. 25. Paul Van Zeeland, eminent financier, formed a **Government of National Unity,** which was given decree powers for a year to cope with the desperate financial situation. Van Zeeland devalued the belga by 28%, undertook the conversion of the public debt, concluded trade agreements, and, in fact, managed to balance the budget. Nevertheless, strikes and unrest continued, and in the

1936, May 24. Parliamentary elections the fascists, led by Léon Degrelle, and generally called *Rexists*, won 21 seats. Van Zeeland, after reforming his government, introduced an extensive

June 24. Social improvement program, roughly the equivalent of the Popular Front program in France: minimum wage, 40-hour week in certain industries, free holidays, increase of unemployment allowance, etc.

Oct. 14. BELGIUM DENOUNCED THE MILITARY ALLIANCE WITH FRANCE AND RESUMED LIBERTY OF ACTION. This step resulted from the German reoccupation of the Rhineland and was generally taken as a reflection of Belgium's determination not to become embroiled with Germany through connection with the Franco-Russian alliance.

Oct. 22. Martial law was proclaimed to check the **excesses of the Rexists.** Degrelle himself was arrested.

1937, Oct. 13. THE GERMAN GOVERNMENT, in a note to Brussels, guaranteed the inviolability and integrity of Belgium so long as the latter abstained from military action against Germany. This assurance was regarded as a valuable gain for the policy of neutrality.

Oct. 24. Resignation of Van Zeeland, following charges of corruption in connection with the National Bank. After a prolonged cabinet crisis, **Paul Janson**

(Liberal) formed a new coalition government, which

1938, May 13. Gave way to a coalition headed by **Paul Spaak** (Moderate Socialist).

Oct. 16. The municipal elections showed a distinct falling-off of support for the extremist groups on both Right and Left (Rexists only 5% of the total), but the coalition of Catholics, Liberals, and Socialists became harder and harder to work and the political situation therefore remained uncertain.

1939, Feb.-Mar. A prolonged **cabinet crisis** resulted from failure to construct a parliamentary majority. On advice of the Pierlot ministry the king dissolved parliament and called new elections. In a letter to Pierlot he denounced political squabbling in time of national danger.

Apr. 2. The **elections** brought no great change, though the Rexist deputies dropped from 21 to only 4.

Apr. 18. Pierlot formed a **Catholic-Liberal government.**

Aug. 23. King Leopold issued an **appeal for peace** in behalf of Belgium, Holland and the Scandinavian states. This proved of no avail. Belgium mobilized but proclaimed neutrality in the European War that broke out on Sept. 3 (p. 967).

b. THE KINGDOM OF THE NETHERLANDS

Though the Netherlands took no part in the World War, the nation suffered considerably through interference with trade. Toward the end of the war the government was obliged to submit to stringent regulations by the Allies and to permit the requisitioning of Dutch shipping.

1919, Aug. 9. A new electoral law provided for direct election of deputies by all men and women 23 years of age or older.

1920, Jan. 23. The Dutch government refused the Allied demand for the surrender of the **former German Emperor William.** He lived in retirement, first at Amerongen, then at Doorn.

1926, Nov.—1927, July. A great communist revolt in Java and the East Indies was suppressed only with difficulty.

1928, Apr. 4. Palmas Island, near the Philippines, in dispute between Holland and the United States, assigned to Holland by arbitration.

1930, Dec. 22. Conclusion of the **Oslo Agreements** between the three

Scandinavian countries, Holland, Belgium, and Luxemburg. The contracting parties promised not to raise tariffs without notification and consultation. July 19, 1932, Holland, Belgium, and Luxemburg concluded the **Ouchy Convention** arranging for more specific reduction of tariffs. The Oslo Agreements were renewed in 1937, but on July 1, 1938, the trade agreement had to be dropped.

1931, Dec. 22. **The Dutch government,** despite free-trade traditions, **began to increase the tariff** and to set up import quotas, in order to help the agricultural and dairying interests, hard hit by the world depression.

1933, Feb. 7. **Mutiny** on the training ship *Zeven Provincien* in East Indian waters. This resulted from reduction of pay. Mutiny and disorders were finally put down with some loss of life.

Apr. 26. Following the elections, **Dr. Colijn constructed a crisis cabinet** which attempted to deal with the serious financial situation and to check the growth of extremist movements on both Right and Left.

1934, May. The government was granted **emergency powers to regulate trade and industry.** Restriction of agricultural production; program of public works to relieve unemployment. **Drastic measures against extremists:** National Socialists, Revolutionary Socialists, and Socialists debarred from holding office. Despite these measures, the National Socialists continued to increase their numbers and influence throughout 1935.

1936. In view of developments in Germany, the government felt obliged to strengthen its defenses. In 1937–1938 the advance of Japan in China exposed the Dutch East Indies to possible Japanese aggression and led to a strengthening of naval forces in the Far East.

1937, Jan. 7. **Marriage of Princess Juliana** (heiress to the throne) to **Prince Bernhard of Lippe-Biesterfeld.**

May 26. The elections proved to be a setback for the **National Socialist movement.** The Liberal Democratic Party showed a marked gain.

1939, June 30. Resignation of the Colijn government, which was reformed amidst much party dissension.

4. FRANCE

The acquisition of Alsace-Lorraine and of mandates in Africa and Syria (pp. 1088, 1098) did not compensate victorious France for her losses in the war, which had been fought largely on French soil. The 1,385,000 French soldiers known to be dead; 700,000 seriously wounded; 2,344,000 other wounded; 446,000 prisoners or missing meant a loss of man-power proportionately greater than that suffered by any other belligerent. Of Frenchmen who in 1914 were aged between 20 and 32, more than half were killed. Property damage in the war zone in the north and east of France included 300,000 houses destroyed, and as many more damaged; 6,000 public buildings and 20,000 workshops and factories destroyed or badly damaged; 1,360,000 head of livestock killed or confiscated; thousands of acres of farm land and forest ravaged by shell fire. These figures explain the intensity of the postwar demand for security and reparation. Since most Frenchmen believed Germany solely responsible for the war, these losses, which brought suffering to almost every French household, stood in the way of any compromise or co-operation between France and post-war Germany.

1919, July 12. **A new Electoral Law** introduced the *scrutin de liste* and a measure of proportional representation. The effect of this was to make it more difficult than ever for any one party to secure a majority.

Nov. 16. Elections. The coalition which had governed under Clemenceau split into a Right *Bloc National* (Clemenceau, Millerand, Poincaré, Briand) and a *Cartel des Gauches*, led by Herriot. The Royalists, Socialists, and Communists were not included in either group. The elections gave a majority to the *Bloc National*, which was also victorious in the senatorial elections of Jan. 1920.

1920, Jan. 17. Presidential election. Clemenceau was defeated by Paul Deschanel, a reflection of political and public opinion which held the Treaty of Versailles too lenient.

Jan. 18. Resignation of Clemenceau.

Jan. 19–Sept. 24. Cabinet of Alexandre Millerand.

1920, Feb. 18–Sept. 15. PRESIDENCY OF PAUL DESCHANEL.

Apr. 23. Joseph Caillaux, former prime minister, sentenced to three years' imprisonment and other penalties after conviction of dealings with the enemy.

Sept. 15. Resignation of President Deschanel on account of ill health.

1920, Sept. 23—1924, June 11. PRESIDENCY OF ALEXANDRE MILLERAND, who, like Poincaré before him, tried to make the office an effective one.

Dec. 30. The Socialist Party, at the Tours Congress, voted to unite with the Third International.

1921, Jan. 13. The General Confederation of Labor dissolved by court order. This organization (C.G.T.) was the center of the syndicalist movement, which had been joined by many unions.

Jan. 16-1922, Jan. 12. Cabinet of Aristide Briand.

Feb. 19. Defensive Treaty with Poland.

Mar. 9. Peace Treaty with Turkey ending hostilities in Cilicia.

May 28. Diplomatic relations with the Vatican resumed (ruptured in 1904).

June 28. By agreements with the railroad companies the government granted concession till 1950 or 1960 and guaranteed expenses and interest and principal payments.

1922, Jan. 15-1924, June 1. Cabinet of Raymond Poincaré, with a program of forcing reparations payments from Germany, chiefly to meet the expense of restoration of the devastated regions, on which 20 milliard francs had already been spent.

Dec. 15. The Workingmen's Compensation Act of 1898 was extended to agricultural laborers.

1923, Jan. Invasion of the Ruhr (p. 958).

Apr. 1. Compulsory military service reduced to one and one-half years.

1924, Jan. 6. The Catholic Church was given the right to reoccupy its former property under a system of *"diocesan associations."*

Jan. 25. Treaty with Czechoslovakia, providing for mutual aid in the event of unprovoked attack by a third power.

May 11. The elections gave the *Cartel des Gauches* a majority in the Chamber, as a result of the failure of Poincaré's policy of coercing Germany. Poincaré resigned.

June 11. Resignation of President Millerand. This was forced by Herriot, leader of the Radical Socialist Party, the strongest group in the Chamber, who refused to form a government while Millerand was president, on the plea that the president had abandoned the traditional

neutrality and had openly sided with the Right.

1924, June 13—1931, June. PRESIDENCY OF GASTON DOUMERGUE.

June 14—1925, Apr. 10. Édouard Herriot, prime minister.

Oct. 28. *De jure* recognition of Soviet Russia.

1925, Feb. 2. Embassy at the Vatican again suppressed, but a special arrangement made for representation of Alsace and Lorraine. The anti-clerical policy of the government caused a storm of protest from all factions of the Right, and it was finally decided (May, 1925) to retain an embassy at the Vatican.

Apr. Beginning of the insurrection in Morocco (p. 1087).

July. Rising of the Druses in the Lebanon against French rule (p. 1098).

July 26. Agreement with Spain for common action in Morocco.

Oct. 16. The Locarno Treaties (p. 959).

Nov. 27—1926, July 15. Three ministries of Aristide Briand.

1926, June 10. Treaty with Rumania.

July 15. Fall of the Briand ministry as a result of the financial crisis. The franc had declined to the value of 2¢ and the budget could not be balanced, despite the imposition of new taxes and increases of income and other taxes. Bond issues could not be floated, since the old obligations could not be met. War debt, post-war extravagance, and the failure of reparations payments made a partial repudiation of the debt inevitable.

1926, July 28—1929, July 26. National Union ministries of Poincaré. Briand remained as minister for foreign affairs. Six former premiers sat in the cabinet. The new government voted new taxes and drastic economies which balanced the budget. The franc rose to about 4¢.

Aug. 10. The two chambers, sitting as a national assembly, incorporated a sinking-fund measure in the constitution. Income from the tobacco monopoly and from inheritance taxes was to be used to redeem part of the national debt.

1927, July 13. The system of *scrutin d'arrondissement* restored for the elections.

Nov. 11. Treaty with Yugoslavia.

1928, Mar. 28. Military service reduced to one year.

Apr. 22-29. Elections gave the National Union government a majority.

May 24. Conviction of four Alsatian autonomists, who for some time had been agitating for separate status through the *Heimatsbund.*

June 24. The franc was devalued from 19.3¢ to 3.92¢, this being a disguised repudiation of about four-fifths of the national debt. The measure hit the *rentier* class hardest and explains later opposition to further devaluation.

Aug. 27. The Kellogg-Briand Pact (p. 960).

1929, July 27. Resignation of Poincaré, on account of ill health. There followed a series of short-lived cabinets, based on shifting parliamentary blocs rather than on genuine party groupings.

1930, Feb. 3. Treaty with Turkey.

Apr. 30. A National Workmen's Insurance Law passed after years of discussion. It insured 9,000,000 workers against sickness, old age, and death. Workers contributed 3% of wages, employers an equal amount. The state contributed in some cases.

June 30. End of the evacuation of the Rhineland (p. 999).

1931, June—1932, May. PRESIDENCY OF PAUL DOUMER. Briand was passed over, since his efforts at international conciliation had estranged the Right. Death of Briand (Mar. 7, 1932).

1932, May 6. President Doumer assassinated by a Russian *émigré* named Gourgoulov, apparently insane.

1932, May- PRESIDENCY OF ALBERT LEBRUN.

May. The elections gave the Left parties a majority.

June-Dec. Second ministry of Édouard Herriot. He resigned because the government proposal to pay the scheduled debt installment to the United States was voted down by the Chamber. There followed five short-lived ministries in the next 13 months. All were concerned with keeping France on the gold standard and with balancing the budget without resorting to inflation.

1933, Dec. The Stavisky case. Stavisky, a Russian promoter, involved in the floating of a fraudulent bond issue by the municipal pawnshop of Bayonne, fled to escape arrest and when cornered was alleged to have committed suicide. Royalists and fascists stirred up an agitation against the republic which recalled the Dreyfus case. It was believed that important officials and politicians were involved and that their guilt was being concealed. The full facts were never made known.

1934, Feb. 6-7. Serious riots in Paris and other cities, resulting from the Stavisky case.

Feb. 8. Coalition cabinet under ex-President **Doumergue,** including leaders of all parties except Royalists, Socialists, and Communists, formed to avert civil war (general strike Feb. 12–13).

Oct. 9. Assassination, at Marseilles, of King **Alexander of Yugoslavia** and Foreign Secretary Barthou, who had been busily engaged (Apr.–June) in a grand tour of European capitals in the hope of building up a strong alliance system against the new Nazi Germany.

Nov. Fall of the Doumergue ministry, Doumergue having proposed a constitutional reform by which change of ministry should, as in England, necessitate a new election. The coalition was reorganized under **Flandin.**

1935, Jan. 7. Agreement between France and Italy with regard to Africa. In this accord France made a number of concessions to Italy (status of Italians in Tunisia, frontier rectifications, part ownership in the Ethiopian Railway, etc.), all in the hope of establishing a strong front against the growing German menace.

May. The Flandin cabinet was overthrown when it demanded quasi-dictatorial powers to save the franc. A **Laval ministry** followed.

May 2. Conclusion of the alliance treaty with Soviet Russia. For some time the French government had labored not only to resuscitate its alliance with the Little Entente powers and Poland, but to bring Germany and Poland and Russia into an eastern pact which would serve to maintain the *status quo.* Both Germany and Poland evaded this suggestion and, after the announcement of German rearmament (p. 963), the French government hurried into the alliance with Russia, an arrangement by no means popular with the more conservative elements in France.

July 27. The government was granted emergency financial powers and embarked upon a policy of retrenchment. Reduction of state salaries led to much disorder.

Nov. 3. Merger of various Socialist groups to form a *Socialist and Republican Union.* This group soon established close relations with the Communists and with the Radical Socialists, to form a **Popular Front,** the main objective of which was to counteract the agitation of the reactionary groups (**Col. de La Roque** and his *Croix de Feu,* etc.). To meet this new pressure from the Left,

Dec. 28. The government ordered political leagues dissolved. Most of them promptly re-emerged as political "parties."

1936, Jan. 22. Downfall of the Laval government, which was thoroughly discredited by its half-and-half attitude toward Italy during the Ethiopian crisis (p. 991) and which was further suspected of supporting the reactionary currents. There followed a cabinet under Albert Sarraut which was nothing more than a stop-gap.

May 3. The parliamentary elections gave the Popular Front a majority in the Chamber of Deputies and led to the formation of the

June 5. FIRST POPULAR FRONT MINISTRY, under Léon Blum, leader of the Socialist Party. The cabinet was composed of Radical Socialists and Socialists, and enjoyed the support of the Communists. A great wave of sit-down strikes (300,000 workers out) accompanied this important change and led at once to the introduction of a far-reaching program of social reform: establishment of the 40-hour week (June 12); reorganization and ultimately nationalization of the Bank of France; suppression of fascist groups (June 30); nationalization of the munitions industry (July 17); compulsory arbitration of labor disputes, vacations with pay, etc. These measures, hailed by the workers as marking the dawn of a new era, at once aroused the hostility of the capitalist and employing classes. Rapidly rising costs of production brought with them rising prices. The franc began to sink steadily and capital started to flee the country in large amounts. To the increasing financial difficulties was added the enhanced tension in international affairs following the German reoccupation of the Rhineland, the Italian victory in Ethiopia, the collapse of the League system (on which France had depended so much), and the outbreak of civil war in Spain. The government was obliged to expend huge sums on further rearmament and, after Belgium's resumption of neutrality, to undertake the fortification of the Belgian frontier. In the Spanish affair Premier Blum felt impelled to follow the British lead and adopt a policy of non-intervention. Anglo-French relations had grown so cool as a result of Laval's Italian policy that Blum looked upon revival of close relations as worth any cost.

Oct. 2. A bill devaluing the franc, but not definitely fixing its gold content, was finally passed. Co-operation of Great Britain and the United States averted violent fluctuations in the foreign exchanges.

1937, Mar. Premier Blum was obliged to announce a "breathing spell" in the work of social reform, in order to reassure capitalist groups and make possible the flotation of huge defense loans.

June 19. The Senate refused Blum's demands for emergency fiscal powers, whereupon the cabinet resigned. The government was reformed with Camille Chautemps (Radical Socialist) as premier and Blum as vice-premier. The new government secured the necessary powers and devoted itself to the Herculean task of financial reconstruction. At the same time the foreign minister, M. Delbos, embarked upon an extended visit to France's eastern allies (Dec.), without apparently finding much prospect of active collaboration against Germany.

Nov. 18. Discovery of a royalist plot against the republic. The *Cagoulards* (Hooded Ones) appear to have been a terrorist group within a larger revolutionary (fascist) movement. Secret plans, fortified dugouts, caches of weapons and munitions were discovered.

1938, Jan. 14. The Socialists deserted the cabinet, which was reorganized by Chautemps as a Radical Socialist ministry. This the Socialists at first tolerated, but

Mar. 10. Chautemps' government fell when the Socialists rejected a demand for full powers.

Mar. 13-Apr. 10. Léon Blum, after trying in vain to organize a national coalition cabinet to face the acute international situation, formed a new Popular Front government. Like its predecessor it was frustrated by the Senate, which refused Blum all confidence. Forced out of office, Blum made way for

Apr. 10. The cabinet of Édouard Daladier (Radical Socialist) who had served as minister of defense and who stood farther to the Right. Daladier was given decree powers until July 31, and then proceeded to devalue the franc and end a new strike movement. Blum and the Socialists supported him.

July 19-21. State visit of George VI of Great Britain to Paris; a striking demonstration of Anglo-French solidarity in the face of the Berlin-Rome Axis.

Sept. THE GERMAN-CZECHOSLOVAK CRISIS (p. 1011). Despite numerous unequivocal public assurances that France would abide by her treaty obligations to Czechoslovakia, Daladier and the foreign minister, Bonnet, followed the British lead and brought extreme pressure to bear at Prague to oblige the Czechs to give in. During the crisis the French army and navy were partially mobilized and everything was in readiness for war. But the country was strongly in favor of a peaceful settlement and Daladier, like Chamberlain, received a warm reception on his return from Munich. In the larger sense, however, the crisis meant the discrediting of France as an ally. The Little Entente lost all value and the bonds connecting France with Poland and Russia became extremely threadbare. France faced further developments in the certainty of British support, but with little more. On the Continent the French preponderance had been definitely replaced by German hegemony.

Oct. 4. The Daladier government broke definitely with the Socialists and Communists when the former abstained from the vote of confidence on the Munich agreements and the Communists voted in opposition. End of the Popular Front. The government now turned farther and farther to the Right in its search for support.

Nov. 12. The government promulgated a large number of decrees aimed at improvement of the desperate financial situation. Among other things the 40-hour week, retained in principle, was to be much modified in practice. This departure created much ill-feeling, especially in the ranks of the C.G.T. (*Confederation of Labor*) with its 5,000,000 members. A new strike epidemic was launched by the workers and this culminated in

Nov. 30. A general strike of protest, called for 24 hours. The government had prepared to meet the threat, had put railway workers under military orders, and had otherwise requisitioned services. Under threats of punishment the whole movement collapsed, relatively few workers going on strike. Many of the strikers and leaders were arrested and the episode

was made an excuse for sterner action against organized labor. The needs of national defense served as a further argument for measures designed to increase production.

Dec. 6. Conclusion of the Franco-German Pact guaranteeing the existing frontier (p. 965). This made but a slight impression in France, the more so as it coincided with a new

Dec.-1939. Franco-Italian crisis, arising from Italian demands for French colonies and other concessions. The government took an uncompromising attitude toward any cessions of territory and

1939, Jan. Daladier paid a demonstrative visit to Corsica and Tunisia. On the other hand the conquest of Catalonia by the Spanish fascists, supported by the Italians, brought France face to face with a new dictatorship on her frontiers.

Mar. The continued expansion of Germany to the east (p. 1004) produced ever greater tension. Daladier asked for and received from parliament power to govern by decree without express limitations, a situation unprecedented under the Third Republic. The premier used his power to speed up rearmament, to effect partial mobilization, etc. France assumed an attitude of quiet determination, but at the same time joined with Britain in guarantees to Poland, Rumania and Greece, and used all her influence to draw Russia into the non-aggression system.

June 23. Conclusion of a treaty with Turkey providing for cession of Alexandretta to Turkey and conclusion of a mutual assistance pact.

Aug. 20-Sept. 1. The Danzig-Polish crisis (p. 966). The French government throughout stood shoulder to shoulder with England and

Sept. 3. Declared WAR ON GERMANY (p. 967).

5. THE IBERIAN PENINSULA

a. SPAIN

Though Spain was spared the horrors of the World War, the effects of the conflict made themselves felt. The demands of the combatants for iron and for munitions and other goods led to a striking **development of Spanish industry**, centering in Catalonia. The growth of industry in turn resulted in

increased tension between the semi-feudal upper classes, supported by the Church and the army, and the new forces of socialism and anarchism. The movement for autonomy for Catalonia, which had survived the centralizing policies of the 19th century, flared up anew, and the government was throughout confronted with the additional problem of Morocco, where constant native risings required a great military effort and the expenditure of much money. Politically the pre-war system extended through the World War and immediate post-war periods, with a constant change of ministry and the rotation of Liberals and Conservatives in power.

1917, July 5. The Catalan deputies and senators in the Córtes demanded the convocation of a constituent assembly to consider home rule for Catalonia.

1919, Jan. 24. A Catalonian Union met at Barcelona and drafted a program for home rule. The government appointed a commission to consider the question, but its carefully circumscribed project was rejected by the Catalonians as inadequate.

1921, July 21. DISASTER AT ANUAL, Morocco, culmination of the troubles there. Gen. Silvestre and 20,000 Spaniards were defeated by the Riffians under Abdel Krim and some 12,000 killed. Silvestre committed suicide. The disaster precipitated a political crisis and a widespread demand for an investigation of responsibility. A parliamentary commission was established, but its report, when submitted to the cabinet in 1922, was at once suppressed.

1923, Sept. 12. Mutiny of the garrison at Barcelona and outbreak of a separatist movement.

Sept. 13. MILITARY COUP OF GEN. MIGUEL PRIMO DE RIVERA, who acted with the approval of the king, who had gone to France. He took Barcelona, formed a military directorate, proclaimed martial law throughout the country, dissolved the Córtes, suspended jury trial, and instituted a rigid press censorship. Liberal opponents were imprisoned or harried out of the land (Miguel de Unamuno, Blasco Ibañez).

1924, Feb. 7. The Tangier Convention (England, France, Spain) providing for permanent neutralization of the Tangier zone and government by an international commission.

June 30. Outbreak of another rising of the Riffians in Morocco.

Nov. 19-28. Visit of Alfonso XIII and Primo de Rivera to Rome, in return for a visit of the King and Queen of Italy (June). This exchange of visits marked the dictator's efforts to establish a close understanding with Fascist Italy, culminating in the treaty of friendship of Aug. 7, 1926.

1925, July 26. Agreement with France for co-operation in the war against the Riffs.

Dec. 3. End of the dictatorship, because of widespread and increasing popular discontent. But Primo de Rivera was at once named prime minister, with a predominantly military cabinet.

1926, Sept. 11. Spain resigned from the League of Nations, but the resignation was later withdrawn (Mar. 22, 1928).

Nov. 2. Attempted coup in Catalonia by conspirators operating from France.

1927, Feb. 9. International conference at Paris to consider the Spanish demand that Tangier be included in the Spanish zone.

May 31. A consultative assembly was convoked to draft a new constitution.

July. End of the Franco-Spanish campaign in Morocco.

1928, Mar. 3. France agreed to give Spain somewhat larger share in the government of Tangier.

1929, Jan. 29. Military revolt at Ciudad Real, indicating spread of dissatisfaction to the military factions.

Mar. 17. The University of Madrid and soon after other universities were closed in order to put an end to the opposition agitation of the students and intellectuals.

1930, Jan. 28. RESIGNATION OF PRIMO DE RIVERA, discouraged and in ill health (death Mar. 16).

Jan. 30. Government of Gen. Damaso Berenguer, who attempted a policy of conciliation. An amnesty was granted, Primo de Rivera's assembly was dissolved, local government organs restored, juridical rights recognized. The government promised early elections for a national parliament. But the students continued their agitation and Republican leaders openly denounced the monarchy as responsible for national disasters and dictatorship (speech of Alcalá Zamora, Apr. 13; of Miguel de Unamuno, May 4; of Marcellino Domingo, June 24). After the removal of the censorship (Sept.) criticism and demonstrations became the order of the day.

Dec. 12-13. Mutiny of the garrison at Jaca, demanding a republic. This was suppressed only with difficulty.

Dec. 15. Martial law proclaimed again throughout the country, but soon rescinded excepting in Madrid.

1931, Feb. 8. The king announced the restoration of the constitution and fixed parliamentary elections for March.

Popular demand for a constituent assembly. **Berenguer resigned.**

Mar. The government called for municipal and provincial elections and promised a constituent assembly.

Apr. 12. **The municipal elections** resulted in an overwhelming victory for the Republicans. Alcalá Zamora, the Republican leader, called for the king's abdication.

Apr. 14. **KING ALFONSO LEFT SPAIN** without abdicating, stating that he would await the expression of popular sentiment. Alcalá Zamora at once set up a provisional government, with himself as president.

June 28. **Elections** for the constituent assembly gave the Republican-Socialist coalition a huge majority.

Nov. 12. A committee of the assembly declared **Alfonso XIII guilty of high treason** and forbade his return to Spain. The royal property was confiscated.

Dec. 9. **The new constitution** was adopted. It provided for universal suffrage and a single-chamber parliament (Córtes), to be elected for four years. The president of the republic was to be chosen by an electoral college consisting of parliament plus an equal number of electors chosen by popular vote. His term was to be six years. No army officer or member of the clergy was to be eligible. The ministry was to be responsible to parliament. The constitution proclaimed complete religious freedom and separated Church and State; education secularized; church property nationalized; Jesuit Order dissolved (1932, Jan.) and its property taken over. Catalonia was given a measure of local autonomy. The government was granted power to expropriate private property, to socialize large estates, and to nationalize public utilities.

Dec. 10. **Alcalá Zamora elected first president.** He had resigned in Oct. in protest against extremist anticlerical legislation, and had been succeeded by **Manuel Azaña,** who became first prime minister under the constitution. The national assembly continued to function as the first regular parliament.

1932, Aug. 10. **Revolt of Gen. José Sanjurjo,** who seized Seville. The movement was quickly suppressed by loyal troops, but was indicative of conservative opposition to the radical legislation of the new régime. The property of the rebels was confiscated and divided up among the peasants.

Sept. 25. **CATALAN CHARTER OF AUTONOMY.** The home rule leaders had drawn up the charter soon after the revolution and had secured Catalan approval by a plebiscite (Aug. 1931). After much agitation and disorder in the province, the Republican government was obliged to consider and accept it. Catalonia was given its own president, parliament, and government, with extensive taxing and other powers. The Catalans were to have their own flag and Catalan was made the official language. The Catalan Parliament met for the first time in Dec. Success of the movement led to similar demands by the Basques and other regionalists.

1933, Jan. 8. **Great radical rising** (anarchists and syndicalists) in Barcelona, which spread to many other large cities. It was successfully suppressed by government troops, but indicated the impatience of the lower classes at the social reform movement.

Apr. 23. **Municipal elections** reflected a distinct veering of opinion to the Right.

May 17. **An Associations Law** required that heads of all religious orders be Spaniards; members of religious orders were forbidden to engage in industry or trade; church schools were abolished and all secular education by religious orders prohibited; church property nationalized, though left in the custody of the clergy. Vigorous protests of the pope (encyclical *Delectissimi nobis*).

Sept. 8. **Elections for the Tribunal of Constitutional Guaranties** (a body to test the constitutionality of legislation and protect civil liberties) showed a further trend toward the Right.

Nov. 19. **The first regular elections for** the Córtes gave the Right parties 44% of the seats, the Left parties only 21%. There followed a series of coalition ministries, all of them more or less helpless and unpopular.

Dec. 9. **Syndicalist-anarchist rising** in Barcelona, put down only after ten days of fighting.

1934, Jan. 14. **Catalan elections,** resulting in a victory for the moderate Left groups; a protest against the swing to conservatism in Spain generally. **Luis Companys president** of Catalonia.

Apr. **A great strike in Barcelona,** led by Socialists, created further tension with Madrid and was suppressed only with difficulty.

Oct. 4. Cabinet of Alejandro Lerroux, in which the Catholic *Popular Action Party* of Gil Robles was represented. This party was allied with the monarchists, was outspokenly clerical and fascist.

Oct. 5. The Left parties called a general strike in protest against the rising reaction against the democratic, social republic.

Oct. 6. President Luis Companys of Catalonia proclaimed the independence of Catalonia. This rising was suppressed by government troops, as was also an insurrection of the miners in the Asturias where a communist régime had been proclaimed. The revolution in the Asturias was put down with great brutality. As a result of the rising in Catalonia, the Catalan statute was suspended preparatory to revision (Dec. 15).

1935, Sept. The Lerroux cabinet fell, and was succeeded by several ephemeral ministries, all more or less at the mercy of the Right.

1936, Jan. 6. The Córtes was dissolved.

Feb. 16. Elections. The Left parties (Republicans, Socialists, Syndicalists, Communists) combined in a *Popular Front* and won a decisive victory over Conservative Republicans, Clericals, and Monarchists. Manuel Azaña formed a new cabinet (Feb. 19), which at once proclaimed an amnesty and undertook the restoration of Catalan autonomy. The social reform program (distribution of land, development of schools, etc.) was resumed, as was the anti-clerical policy.

Apr. 10. The Córtes voted to remove President Zamora for exceeding his powers.

May 10. Manuel Azaña was regularly elected president.

July 18. OUTBREAK OF THE GREAT SPANISH CIVIL WAR. The conflict began with a revolt of the army chiefs at Melilla in Spanish Morocco. It spread rapidly to the garrison towns of Spain (Cadiz, Seville, Saragossa, Burgos, etc.). In Madrid and Barcelona the government held its own, thus making early success of the Insurgents impossible. All the parties of the Left united in resistance and the government declared the confiscation of all religious property (July 28). The Insurgent leaders, Gen. Francisco Franco and Gen. Emilio Mola (Gen. Sanjurjo was killed at the very outset in an airplane accident) were supported by the bulk of the army and of the air force, and had at their disposal large Moorish contingents. July 30 they set up a Junta of National Defense at Burgos. At an early stage in the war foreign powers began to intervene and Spain became the battleground of rival ideologies. Italian and German "volunteers" joined the Insurgents, while Russia supplied the government with equipment and advisers.

Aug. 15. The rebels captured Badajoz and began a great advance eastward up the Tagus Valley through Talavera and Toledo (relieved Sept. 28 after a ten-weeks' siege of the famous Alcazar fortress by the Loyalists).

Sept. 4. The rebels captured Irun in the north. On the same day a Popular Front government was formed in Madrid under Largo Caballero, with Catalan and Basque Nationalists represented. In Nov. Anarchist-Syndicalists were included. On Sept. 12 the Insurgents took San Sebastian.

Oct. 1. GEN. FRANCISCO FRANCO was appointed by the Insurgents as *Chief of the Spanish State.*

Oct. 8. The government adopted home rule for the Basque provinces, which established the first autonomous Basque government under President Aguirre.

Nov. 6. Beginning of the siege of Madrid by the Insurgents. The government moved to Valencia. Despite heavy fighting in the suburbs of the city and despite appalling air bombardments, the Loyalist troops held the capital and the Insurgent assault ended in deadlock.

Nov. 18. Germany and Italy recognized the government of Gen. Franco. Great Britain and France continued their ban on supplies to the legitimate government and attempted to unite the powers on a policy of non-intervention, for fear lest the war expand into a general conflict. Twenty-seven nations, including Germany and Italy, agreed to participate in a non-intervention committee, sitting at London. A scheme for supervision was introduced, but this, like other methods adopted, failed to prevent participation by those powers which cared to intervene. The Italian government came out more and more openly in support of Franco, and ultimately had from 50,000 to 75,000 troops in Spain.

1937, Feb. 8. The rebels captured Malaga with Italian aid, but failed to cut the road from Madrid to Valencia.

Mar. 18. Loyalist forces defeated Italian troops at Brihuega, capturing large stores. The Insurgents, frustrated in the effort to cut off Madrid, turned to the north and concentrated on Bilbao.

May 17. **A new government, under Juan Negrin**, replaced that of Largo Caballero. Negrin represented the Socialists, but took in members of other Left parties (except the Anarcho-Syndicalists). The new cabinet took the view that the war must be won before the social revolution could be carried further. All defense ministries were unified under **Indalecio Prieto.**

May 31. **Four German warships bombarded Almeria** by way of reprisal for an air attack by the Loyalists upon the *Deutschland.*

June 18. **Bilbao fell to the Insurgents** after weeks of heavy fighting and after countless heavy air bombardments. The Basque resistance soon collapsed and the rebels pushed on to Santander.

June 23. **Germany and Italy quitted the neutrality patrol** off the Spanish coast in protest against the unwillingness of the other powers to secure satisfaction for the attack on the *Deutschland.* At the same time they refused to accept patrol by England and France. Acute international tension, the French being held back from opening the frontier to supplies for the Loyalists only by pressure from England. In the meanwhile "piracy" became rife in the western Mediterranean, mysterious submarines attacking British ships and even warships. Thereupon the British government convoked the **Nyon Conference,** and, with French support, organized a new and drastic anti-piracy patrol (p. 964).

Oct. 21. **Franco's troops finally captured Gijon,** breaking the resistance in the Asturias and **completing the conquest of the northwest.**

Oct. 28. **The Spanish government moved from Valencia to Barcelona,** having taken over control of the Catalan government (Aug. 12).

Nov. 28. Franco announced a **naval blockade** of the entire Spanish coast, using the island of Majorca as a base.

Dec. 5. Beginning of a great Loyalist **counter-offensive around Teruel,** which was taken Dec. 19. This move served to divert the Insurgents from operations to the northeastward. But the government forces, much less adequately supplied and equipped than their opponents, were unable to sustain the offensive.

1938, Feb. 15. **Franco's forces recaptured Teruel** and made a spectacular drive toward the sea.

Apr. 15. **The Insurgents took Vinaroz,** on the seacoast, thus severing Loyalist territory in Castile from Barcelona and Catalonia. A tremendous battle developed along the Ebro River, where the contestants were deadlocked during most of the summer. In accordance with the **Anglo-Italian Agreement** (p. 965), Mussolini withdrew some troops from Spain, but there still remained a substantial force estimated at 40,000.

Dec. 23. Beginning of the great **Insurgent drive in Catalonia.** Despite valiant resistance, the Loyalist forces were gradually driven back toward Barcelona.

1939, Jan. 26. **BARCELONA WAS TAKEN BY FRANCO'S TROOPS,** with Italian aid. The Loyalist resistance now collapsed completely in this sector and within a couple of weeks the Insurgents had overrun all of Catalonia, some 200,000 Loyalist troops crossing the French frontier, where they were disarmed.

Feb. 27. **England and France finally recognized the government of Gen. Franco,** without conditions. Thereupon

Feb. 28. **President Azaña,** who had taken refuge in Paris, **resigned** his position. Efforts of England and France to bring the civil war to an end met with the opposition of Premier Negrin, who enjoyed the support of the more radical elements in Republican Spain, but

Mar. 6. **A military coup in Madrid,** led by Gen. Segismundo Casado, resulted in the removal of Negrin and his colleagues. They fled to France by air, while at Madrid a new *National Defense Council* was organized, with **Gen. José Miaja** (defender of Madrid in 1936–1937) at the head. The Republican fleet escaped from Cartagena and took refuge in the Tunisian port of Bizerta, where it surrendered and was interned by the French authorities. The new Madrid régime was committed to a policy of "peace with honor," but this policy at once led to **conflict with the Communists** in the capital, producing a civil war within the larger civil war. The Communists were finally defeated and Miaja then devoted himself to the task of reaching a compromise with Franco. Failing to secure assurances of leniency, the National Defense Council was finally obliged to accept unconditional surrender.

Mar. 28. **END OF THE CIVIL WAR** came with the **SURRENDER OF MADRID** and Valencia. Members of the Defense Council fled. The war had cost about 700,000 lives in battle, 30,000 executed or assassinated, 15,000 killed in air raids. Franco and his government at once set up special tribunals which convicted hundreds of loyalist leaders, despite efforts of England and France to ensure moderation. The United States recognized the new régime (Apr. 1) and on

Apr. 7. Spain announced **adhesion to the German-Italian-Japanese anti-Communist Pact.** The democratic powers derived some consolation, however, from

May 20-June. The **withdrawal of Italian and German forces** from Spain after an imposing victory parade in battered Madrid. As it turned out, the Germans had some 10,000 men in Spain, mostly in the aviation and tank services. Together with the Italian "volunteers" they had aided Franco greatly in transporting troops from Morocco in the early days of the war, and had played a major rôle in many later engagements.

Sept. 3. Spain indicated her intention of remaining neutral in the great European conflict over Danzig and Poland (p. 967).

b. PORTUGAL

1914, Nov. 23. The **Portuguese National Assembly** voted to join Great Britain and France in the war against Germany, but action in accord with this vote was delayed by

1915, Jan. 28-May 14. The insurrection and dictatorship of Gen. **Pimenta de Castro,** representing a pro-German faction in the army. He in turn was overthrown by a democratic revolt May 14.

1915-1917. Bernardino Machado became president on the resignation of President Arriaga.

1916, Mar. 9. GERMANY DECLARED WAR ON PORTUGAL after the seizure of German ships in the harbor of Lisbon. The Portuguese organized an expeditionary force, which arrived in France Feb. 3, 1917, and took over a small sector of the front.

1917, Dec. 5. Gen. **Sidonio Pães** led another pro-German uprising, arrested and deported the president, and **made himself president-dictator.**

1918, Dec. 14. Pães was **assassinated** by a radical, whereupon the democratic régime was re-established. The situation in the country continued to be utterly confused. In a land which was still

65% illiterate the democratic system could hardly be expected to function well. One cabinet relieved another, the average duration of governments being about four months. Insurrections and coups were hardly less numerous. The financial condition of the country, long parlous, went from bad to worse. Multiplication of offices, widespread political corruption, appalling inefficiency characterized the decade from 1918 to 1928.

1919, Jan. 19-Feb. 14. A royalist uprising in the north assumed substantial proportions, but was ultimately suppressed.

May 6. The Allied Supreme Council assigned to Portugal the **mandate for part of German East Africa,** known as the *Kionga Triangle.*

Aug. 5. Antonio José de Almeida became president.

1920, Apr. 8. Portugal joined the **League of Nations.**

1923, Aug. 6. Teixeira Gomes succeeded as president.

1925, Apr. 18-19. An attempted **military coup** directed against the corruption of the democratic régime led to some shooting and bloodshed in Lisbon, but then collapsed from want of leadership.

Dec. 16. Bernardino Machado was again elected president.

1926, May 28. OVERTHROW OF THE EXISTING RÉGIME by an army movement inspired by **Mendes Cabeçadas** and led by Gen. **Gomes da Costa.** The revolt broke out in the north and was supported by most of the army. Gomes da Costa, an audacious, vain, and politically innocent leader, became a national hero. Machado and the cabinet of Antonio Mara da Silva were overthrown, parliament was dissolved and parties broken up.

July 9. Gen. **Antonio de Fragoso Carmona** deposed the utterly incompetent Gomes da Costa, who was honorably exiled to the Azores.

1927, Feb. 3-13. Insurrection against the military dictatorship broke out at Oporto and then (Feb. 7) at Lisbon. This was described as "communist," but was really inspired by a group of intellectual reformers (group about the *Seara Nova*). After some severe fighting the movement was defeated.

1928, Mar. 25. Gen. **Carmona was elected president.** The new régime, which appears to have had no very specific program, proved itself not much different from its predecessors, excepting for the fact that the spoils were in the hands of the military clique rather than in those of the parliament.

Apr. 27. Antonio de Oliveira Salazar became minister of finance, with extraordinary powers. Born 1889, he had been educated for the priesthood, had then turned to law, and had finally become a professor of economics. In a remarkably short time he solved the long-standing financial muddle (using old-fashioned methods of economy and strict accountancy). Before long he became the dominant figure in Portugal, a retiring, studious, unambitious and unselfish statesman, proponent of a national renaissance.

1930, July 30. Foundation of the National Union, a political-social party of a fascist type. This was the only party permitted by the government and was designed to prepare the way for the *Estado Novo*.

1932, July 5. OLIVEIRA SALAZAR BECAME PREMIER and to all intents and purposes dictator. He ruled with a strong hand, but opposition to fascism and dictatorship continued to smolder, as shown by occasional uprisings and attempts on the life of the dictator.

1933, Feb. 22. The government promulgated a **NEW CONSTITUTION,** which was approved by plebiscite Mar. 19. *Provisions:* a **president** elected for seven years; a **cabinet** appointed by the president and responsible to him alone; a **national assembly** elected by heads of families possessing a certain degree of education; a **corporative chamber** representing occupations (on the Italian model), but with only advisory power.

1934, Jan. 18. A revolutionary movement led by the General Confederation of Labor and by the Communists was suppressed with vigor and the leaders were imprisoned.

Dec. 16. In the elections the voters were allowed to choose among candidates put forward by the National Union; no others were permitted. The first national assembly of the new régime met Jan. 10, 1935.

1935, Feb. 17. President Carmona was elected for another term.

1936, July- . With the **outbreak of the civil war in Spain** (p. 983) the Portuguese dictatorship at once sided with the Insurgents against the republican government. Portugal became one of the main routes by which supplies reached Franco from Germany and elsewhere. This continued until in Apr. 1937 the British government persuaded the Portuguese to permit a British border control. By that time Franco was able to get his supplies through the North Spanish coast towns. The British were obliged to strain themselves to the utmost to uphold the traditional alliance with Portugal, the latter country having become of immense strategic importance because of its location athwart the routes from Africa to Britain and France.

1939, Mar. 18. Portugal concluded a non-aggression pact with Fascist Spain, but at the same time

May 22, 26. Portugal and England reaffirmed their traditional alliance, Portugal thereby demonstrating the desire to stand well with both Fascist and democratic powers.

6. ITALY AND THE PAPACY

a. ITALY

Italy had entered the war primarily to gain territory and to wrest control of the Adriatic from Austria-Hungary. Her military achievement had fallen far below Allied expectations and as a result Italy was given but little say at the peace conference. President Wilson took a very hostile stand toward the provisions of the **Treaty of London** (p. 925) and Italy, in return for 600,000 lives lost, received only 9000 square miles of territory with a population of 1,600,000. None of the former German colonies were assigned to her as mandates. The war, then, left Italy loaded with debt, suffering from high costs of living, and generally restless and discon-

tented. The governments enjoyed no prestige and the political situation was complicated by a rapid spread of communism and by the emergence of an organized clerical party. Efforts of the government to meet the situation by social legislation had little success.

1919, Jan. 19. Formation of the *Partito Popolare*, a Catholic party.

Mar. 23. Formation of the first *Fascio di Combattimento* by **Benito Mussolini** (b. 1883), former radical socialist and editor of *Avanti*, who had turned violently interventionist and nationalist.

Mar. 29. Italian troops landed at Adalia to make good Italian claims to a share in the Turkish spoils.

Apr. 24. The Italian delegation left the

Paris peace conference after the public appeal of President Wilson against the Italian territorial claims on the Adriatic. The Italian delegation returned May 5.

June 19. The Orlando cabinet resigned. A new ministry was formed by **Francesco Nitti**, with **Tittoni** at the foreign office.

July 29. Treaty signed with Greece: Italy to support Greek claims in Thrace and Epirus, Greece to support an Italian protectorate over Albania, Italian claims in Anatolia. Italy was to keep Rhodes for 15 years and the Dodecanese Islands were to be ceded to Greece.

Sept. 2. A new electoral law introduced universal suffrage and the French system of *scrutin de liste* (election by departmental lists) and proportional representation.

Sept. 12. Gabriele d'Annunzio, eminent writer, ardent nationalist, and World War hero, seized Fiume with a band of volunteers. His action was disavowed by the Italian government.

Oct. 5-8. The Socialist Congress at Bologna voted for adherence to the Third International.

Nov. 11. The pope definitely lifted the prohibition against participation by Catholics in Italian political life.

Nov. 16. Elections for parliament. The Socialists secured 160 seats; Catholics 103; Liberals 93; Radicals 58. At the opening of parliament the Socialists refused to hail the king and shouted "Long live Socialism," a striking demonstration of disloyalty.

1920, Apr. 26. The San Remo Conference decided to leave the Fiume question to settlement by Italy and Yugoslavia.

June 9. Fall of the Nitti cabinet, after it had been twice reconstructed. A new government was formed by the veteran, **Giovanni Giolitti**, with **Count Carlo Sforza** at the foreign office.

Aug. 2. Agreement with Albania to evacuate the country, with the exception of the island of Saseno. The Albanians had attacked the Italian forces and made their position untenable.

Aug. 10. Treaty with Greece, confirming cession of the Dodecanese; Rhodes to be given to Greece after 15 years if England ceded Cyprus to Greece, and a plebiscite in Rhodes resulted in favor of Greece.

Aug. 31. A general lockout in the metallurgical factories led to the occupation of the factories by the workers, the beginning of a far-reaching movement. The Socialist Party voted for syndicalization of the factories.

Nov. 12. Treaty of Rapallo with Yugoslavia; Fiume to be an independent state, as envisaged by the peace treaties; Italy renounced claims to Dalmatia, except Zara; Istria divided; Yugoslavia to have Susak.

Dec. 1. D'Annunzio declared war on the Italian government.

Dec. 27. Italian troops bombarded Fiume and forced D'Annunzio to evacuate. Disorders continued in the city between the autonomists and the nationalists.

1921, Jan. 13-22. Congress of the Socialist Party at Livorno. The party split into a moderate and a radical wing, the latter frankly communist.

Feb. 27. Communist and Fascist riots at Florence, inaugurating a period of constant clashes which ultimately approximated civil war between the two factions.

May 15. Elections, the first held under a system of universal suffrage. The Liberals and Democrats won a resounding victory and secured 275 seats, as against 122 for the Socialists and 107 for the Popular (Catholic) Party. The Communists had only 16, the Fascists 22.

June 26. Fall of the Giolitti cabinet, the result of dissatisfaction with its foreign policy. A new ministry was organized (July 5) by **I. Bonomi**.

1922, Feb. 9. The Bonomi cabinet resigned. The new government (Feb. 25) was led by **Luigi Facta,** supported by Liberals and Democrats.

Mar. 3. A Fascist coup overthrew the Fiume government. The town was then occupied by Italian troops (Mar. 17).

May. Fascists drove out the communist city government of Bologna. The conflict between the factions was extended to all the larger cities.

Aug. 3-4. Fascists seized control of the Milan city government. The government seemed quite unable to cope with the aggressive action of the bands.

Oct. 8. Italy denounced the agreement with Greece on the Dodecanese Islands, despite protests from England.

Oct. 16. Formation of a **quadrum virate** under Mussolini (Michele Bianchi, Italo Balbo, Gen. De Bono, Dino Grandi).

Oct. 23. **Treaty of Santa Margherita** with Yugoslavia, reaffirming the Treaty of Rapallo (independence of Fiume).

Oct. 24. **Fascist Congress at Naples.** Mussolini, having refused a seat in the cabinet, demanded the resignation of Facta and formation of a Fascist cabinet. Facta refused, apparently underestimating the power of the Fascist movement which was, to be sure, a minority movement, but one led aggressively and supported by nationalist elements and by business interests which feared communism.

Oct. 28. **THE "MARCH ON ROME"** by the Fascists. The king refused Facta's demand for the proclamation of martial law, whereupon Facta resigned. The Fascists occupied Rome.

Oct. 31. **Mussolini,** summoned by the king from Milan, **formed a cabinet** of Fascists and Nationalists.

Nov. 25. Mussolini was granted by the king and the parliament **dictatorial powers** until Dec. 31, 1923, to restore order and introduce reforms. He then appointed prefects and sub-prefects of Fascist sympathies and, with the support of the army, gradually established control of the government machinery. He still professed the intention of governing constitutionally and the constitution remained technically in force.

1923, Jan. 14. A voluntary **Fascist militia** authorized by the king.

Mar. 24. Reform of the judicial system.

May 16. The Popular (Catholic) Party voted to support the Fascist régime, but the leader, **Don Luigi Sturzo,** resigned. Fascists continued their attacks on the Catholics.

July. Initiation of a rigid policy of **Italianization in Southern Tyrol** (Upper Adige).

Aug.-Sept. **THE CORFU INCIDENT.** Gen. **Tellini** and four members of his staff were assassinated (Aug. 27) while engaged with the commission delimiting the Greek-Albanian frontier. The Italian government sent a stiff ultimatum to Greece (Aug. 29) and Aug. 31 bombarded and occupied Corfu. Greece appealed to the League of Nations and agreed to accept the decision of the council of Ambassadors. The latter sent a note to Greece embodying most of the Italian demands. Under considerable pressure from England and other

powers the Italians evacuated Corfu (Sept. 27), the first Fascist reassertion of power in international affairs having resulted in something of a *débâcle*.

Nov. 14. **A new electoral law.** Before the expiration of his dictatorial powers, Mussolini forced through Parliament a law providing that any party securing the largest number of votes in an election (provided it had at least one-fourth of the total) should receive two-thirds of the seats. The remaining seats were to be divided according to proportional representation. This arrangement would avoid the difficulty of coalitions and blocs in a parliament where no party had a majority.

1924, Jan. 27. **Treaty with Yugoslavia** regarding Fiume. The town was ceded to Italy, Yugoslavia receiving Porto Barros and special facilities at Fiume.

Apr. 6. In the **elections** the Fascists, through government control of the machinery and through liberal use of "squad" methods, polled 65% of the votes and were given 375 seats in the Chamber (as against the 35 they had previously had).

June 10. **MURDER OF THE SOCIALIST DEPUTY GIACOMO MATTEOTTI,** who had written a book, *The Fascisti Exposed*, containing detailed case histories of hundreds of acts of violence illegally carried out by Fascists. The murderers were Fascists, some of them prominent in the party. When tried in 1926 they were either acquitted or given light sentences.

June 15. Most of the non-Fascist third of the new Chamber seceded (*Aventine Secession*) and vowed not to return until the Matteotti affair had been cleared up and the complicity of the government disproved. The opposition demanded the disbandment of the Fascist militia and the cessation of violence. Mussolini, faced by a major crisis (the most serious during his rule), disavowed all connection with the affair and dismissed all those implicated. A rigid press censorship was introduced (July 1) and meetings of the opposition group were forbidden (Aug. 3). The support of part of the Liberal group, under Salandra, helped to break the force of the opposition, which never returned to parliament. In 1926 the seats of the secessionists were declared vacant.

1925. **Continuation of the crisis,** marked by revival of Liberal and Communist demonstrations in various parts of the country. Mussolini twice reorganized the cabinet (Jan. 5; Aug. 30) and extended the work of repression through the *Legge Fascistissime*, which tightened control of the press (all journalists to be registered and every newspaper to have a director appointed by the government), forbade Freemasonry and similar secret organizations (May 19), and established government control of local government through the appointed *podestàs*. Many political opponents of the régime arrested and transported to the Lipari Islands.

1926, Jan. 31. The prime minister authorized to govern by decree when necessity required.

Feb. Acute tension in relations with Germany, arising from the ruthless policy of Germanization in the Southern Tyrol.

Apr. 3. Recognition of a number of labor syndicates and establishment of compulsory arbitration in industrial disputes. Lockouts and strikes made illegal.

Apr. 3. Organization of the *Ballilla*, a Fascist youth association to train the rising generation.

Apr. 7. Mussolini wounded in the nose by Violet Gibson, a deranged Irish noblewoman. Two other attempts were made to assassinate the *Duce* (Sept. 11, Oct. 31) and led to a law providing penalty of death for anyone engaging in actions against the king, queen, or head of the state (Nov. 25).

June 29. By decree the working day was increased to 9 hours. Provincial and municipal elections were suspended indefinitely. All cities except Rome and Naples were put under *podestàs*.

Aug. 7. Treaty of friendship with Spain.

Sept. 25. Beginning of the campaign against the *Mafia*, a loose criminal organization which had dominated Sicilian politics and life for 50 years.

Nov. 27. Treaty with Albania, establishing what amounted to an Italian protectorate.

1927, Apr. 5. Treaty of friendship with Hungary, beginning of the Fascist policy of rallying the "revisionist" states against the Little Entente and its supporter, France.

Nov. 22. Second treaty with Albania.

1928, Feb. 21. The Fascist militia was incorporated with the regular army.

May 12. A new electoral law. Universal suffrage abolished and franchise restricted to men of 21 and over who paid syndicate rates or taxes of 100 lire. Electorate reduced from almost 10,000,000 to about 3,000,000. 400 candidates for elec-tion to be submitted to voters by the Fascist Grand Council, to be voted for or rejected *in toto* by the electorate.

Aug. 2. Treaty of friendship with Ethiopia.

Sept. 23. Treaty of friendship with Greece.

Nov. 15. The Fascist Grand Council made an official organ of the state and charged with the duty of naming candidates for the Chamber and/or co-ordinating all government activities.

1929, Feb. 11. THE LATERAN TREATIES with the papacy (ratified June 7): creation of the state of Vatican City (area 108.7 acres) and its recognition as independent; concordat between the Italian government and the papacy regulating activities of the Catholic Church; payment of an indemnity of 750,000,000 lire and one milliard lire in state bonds to the pope.

Mar. 24. Elections. The 400 official candidates received 8,510,559 votes, with only 135,761 adverse votes.

Apr. 21. National Council of Corporations established to adjust disputes between various groups in the interest of national production. The council was composed of representatives from the syndicates and from the government. Despite much official oratory about the *Corporate State* it does not appear that much actual power was entrusted to the syndicates or corporations. The actual administration appears to have remained in the hands of a highly centralized bureaucracy.

1930, Feb. 6. Treaty of friendship with Austria. Mussolini began to come out more openly as the champion of revision of the peace treaties (speeches of May 24 at Milan and Oct. 27 at Venice).

Apr. 30. Great naval program, the result of failure to secure recognition of Italian parity from France. During the following years Italian naval and air forces were built up to imposing dimensions.

Oct. 25. Marriage of Princess Giovanna to King Boris of Bulgaria. Bulgaria brought more and more within the orbit of Italian influence.

1930-1935. The economic depression, aggravated for Italy because of her lack of basic raw materials and constant adverse trade balance. Great efforts were made to increase the production of food (*battle of wheat*) and to reclaim swamp areas for agricultural exploitation (*Pontine marshes*, etc.), as well as to develop hydro-electric power. Industrial production was increased and cost of production reduced by cuts in wages and other devices. Italy, like many other countries, tried to stave off the worst effect of the depression by the conclusion of **trade pacts**, rigid control of foreign exchange, conversion of the public debt, etc. The result was almost complete government control of finance and industry.

1933, Jan. The advent of the National Socialist government in Germany at once raised the **prospect of Italo-German co-operation**, which would have involved an immeasurable strengthening of Italy's position with respect to Great Britain and France. Göring and von Papen visited Rome at an early date (Apr. 11–19), but the sole result of the *rapprochement* appears to have been the agreement of Germany to join in the

July 15. Signature of the Four-Power Pact between England, France, Italy, and Germany. This represented a favorite idea of Mussolini, who aimed at replacing the influence of the small states in the League of Nations by a bloc of major powers. In actual practice the Four-Power Pact proved of almost no significance.

1934, Jan. 20. The Italian Chamber passed a law completing the organization of the "corporative state."

Mar. 17. Conclusion of the Rome Protocols between Italy, Austria, and Hungary. Dollfuss and Gömbös had come to Rome for conferences, at which the agreements were worked out. They provided for closer trade relations, consultation and common policy, and in general represented the organization, under Fascist auspices, of a Danubian bloc to counterbalance the Little Entente and the French influence.

June 14-15. First visit of Chancellor Hitler to Italy. Though nothing much is known of what occurred, it seems that the two men made a poor impression on each other and that they made no progress toward establishing a common policy. Quite the contrary, considerable tension developed between Germany and Italy, especially with regard to Austria.

July. The abortive Nazi coup in Vienna, which resulted in the death of Dollfuss, was solved in favor of Austria largely through the energetic action of Mussolini, who mobilized a huge army on the Brenner Pass and made clear his determination to intervene in order to frustrate the German designs.

Nov. 10. Establishment of the Central Corporative Committee, a type of economic parliament intended to complete the structure of the corporative state.

Dec. 5. CLASH OF ITALIAN AND ETHIOPIAN TROOPS AT UALUAL, on the disputed Ethiopian-Somaliland frontier. This was seized upon by the Italian government as the point of departure for the conquest of Ethiopia. After the great disaster at Adua in 1896 (p. 661), the Italian designs on Ethiopia had been more or less dormant. **By agreement with England and France in 1906,** Italy had been obliged to accept a relatively unpromising slice of Ethiopia as her sphere of interest. In the post-war period there had been negotiations with England, but these had no concrete results. The Italian government had, indeed, adopted a policy of friendship with Ethiopia and had supported the admission of Ethiopia to the League of Nations. Now, however, this policy was reversed and the old policy of imperialist expansion was resumed.

1935, Jan. 3. The Italians having refused to arbitrate the Ualual affair, **the Ethiopian government appealed to the League** under Art XI of the Covenant, but the League postponed action.

Jan. 7. AGREEMENT BETWEEN FRANCE AND ITALY, negotiated by M. Laval during a visit to Rome. In the hope of winning Italian support against Germany, Laval made large concessions to Italian claims in Africa (p. 963), including more or less of a free hand in Ethiopia. Mussolini at once took advantage of the situation and sent to Eritrea Generals **Di Bono** and **Graziani** with large forces (Feb. 23).

Apr. 11-14. The Stresa Conference, called by France to consider action against the German rearmament and to provide further guaranties for Austrian independence. Italy joined in the declarations and protests, but these were of no avail because of the complications that soon arose from the Ethiopian affair.

May. Italy finally agreed to arbitrate differences, but apparently this was meant merely as a blind to stave off League action.

June 23-24. The British minister for League affairs, **Anthony Eden,** visited Rome and offered Mussolini concessions which the latter, however, rejected as inadequate.

June 25-July 9. Italian-Ethiopian arbitration negotiations at The Hague produced no semblance of agreement. Thereupon

July 25. The League Council set Sept. 4 as the date when it would itself begin to investigate the situation. By that time the Italian preparations were complete and Mussolini no longer concealed the fact that only the annexation of Ethiopia would satisfy him. While the League made belated efforts at adjustment,

Oct. 3. THE ITALIAN FORCES BEGAN THE INVASION OF ETHIOPIA. They took **Adua** on Oct. 6.

Oct. 7. THE LEAGUE COUNCIL DECLARED ITALY THE AGGRESSOR in the Ethiopian affair and began to arrange for sanctions to be applied.

Nov. 8. After a rather slow advance the Italians finally took the fortress of **Makallé.** The command was then taken over by Marshal **Pietro Badoglio**, who carefully reorganized the forces and prepared for the difficult advance through the mountainous country.

Nov. 18. The League of Nations voted the **application of sanctions** against Italy (prohibition of import of Italian goods; arms embargo, financial embargo, etc.). Italy thereupon ended all economic relations with the sanctionist powers and adopted a system of rigid control of food and raw materials to meet the emergency. Britain and France continued their efforts to effect a compromise settlement, but the famous **Hoare-Laval proposals** (very favorable to Italy) were wrecked by public indignation over the suggested reward to a nation branded as the aggressor.

By the end of 1935 the **international tension** had reached a high pitch and England and Italy were coming close to a collision in the Mediterranean. Britain concentrated a huge naval force at Alexandria and secured promises of support from France, Yugoslavia, Greece, and Turkey. But the British forces were poorly prepared, especially with respect to air power, and therefore avoided all provocative action. Italy weathered the sanctionist storm, the more so as the nations could not agree to apply the oil **sanction** (Feb. 1936), which might have proved decisive, but which might also have involved armed conflict. The reoccupation of the Rhineland by Germany (Mar. 1936) diverted the attention of England and France and made all prospects of further action against Italy illusory.

1936, May 5. The Italian forces finally occupied **Addis Ababa** and the resistance of the Ethiopians collapsed (p. 1086).

May 9. THE ITALIAN GOVERNMENT FORMALLY PROCLAIMED THE ANNEXATION OF ALL ETHIOPIA, the King of Italy assuming the title *Emperor of Ethiopia.* Gradual pacification of the country (p. 1086).

July 4. The League Council voted to discontinue sanctions. Complete *débâcle* of League action; a milestone in the history of collective action in behalf of peace (p. 964).

July. OUTBREAK OF THE CIVIL WAR IN SPAIN (p. 983). From the very outset Mussolini took an active part in supporting the Insurgents with men and equipment, on the theory that Italy could not permit the establishment of a "communist" government in the Mediterranean. The expense of sending 50,000 to 75,000 "volunteers" to Spain, added to the cost of the Ethiopian campaigns and the demands for ever greater armaments, necessitated the **devaluation of the lire** (Oct. 5) and the introduction of various forms of levy on capital. At the same time the Italian action in Spain aroused the apprehensions of Great Britain and France and served to increase the tension in the Mediterranean. Mussolini, under these circumstances, was obliged to draw closer to Germany and to conclude

Oct. 26. The Italian-German Agreement regarding Austria (p. 1008), which served as a foundation for Italo-German co-operation, and may be taken as the beginning of the **Rome-Berlin Axis.** Germany recognized the conquest of Ethiopia by Italy (Oct. 25).

Nov. 9-12. Vienna conference between the representatives of the Rome Protocol states (Italy, Austria, and Hungary), marking the gradual consolidation of the Italian position in the Danube Basin.

1937, Jan. 2. Conclusion of a "gentlemen's agreement" between Italy and Great Britain. This affirmed the independence and integrity of Spain, freedom of passage through the Mediterranean, etc. But in the long run it did not dispel the suspicion aroused by Italian activity in the Mediterranean and Near East.

Mar. 16. Imposing visit of Mussolini to Libya (p. 1088), in the course of which he declared his interest and friendship for Moslems everywhere and permitted himself to be hailed as their protector. This was taken as a move directed against British and French dominance over Arab countries, and the Italians were accused of subversive propaganda throughout North Africa, Egypt, Palestine, and Syria.

Mar. 25. Conclusion of an Italian-Yugoslav treaty, guaranteeing the existing frontiers and the maintenance of the *status quo* in the Adriatic. This brought to an end the long period of tension between the two powers and was a serious blow at the Little Entente structure and at French influence.

Nov. 6. Italy adhered to the anti-communist pact between Germany and Japan, thus completing the triangle of states engaged in upsetting the peace treaties and the *status quo*. In keeping with this policy, the Italian government, long critical of the League of Nations, announced

Dec. 11. The withdrawal of Italy from the League.

1938, Jan. 7. The Italian government announced a huge naval construction program, to supplement the great rearmament plan introduced a year previous.

Mar. The German annexation of Austria (p. 1008). The world was astounded at Mussolini's calm acceptance of a situation which involved the breakdown of the Rome Protocol system and brought the powerful German Nazi state to the Brenner Pass. Evidently the Italian commitments in Ethiopia, Libya, and Spain made any other course impossible. In any event, Mussolini thenceforth became more than ever dependent on Germany.

Aug. 3. The Italian government, despite past policy and assurances, introduced a "racial" program directed against the Jews, who were few in Italy. Various regulations barred foreign Jews from Italian schools, ordered all Jews who had taken up residence in Italy since 1919 to leave within six months, discharged Jewish teachers and students from schools and universities, prohibited marriage between Italians and Non-Aryans, etc.

Sept. In the Czechoslovak crisis (p. 1012) Mussolini remained in the background until the tension reached the breaking point. Then he delivered himself of a series of threatening speeches. But in the last instance he appears to have done his utmost to bring about the Munich meeting and the accord which sacrificed a large part of Czechoslovakia to Germany.

Oct. 8. The Fascist Grand Council abolished the Chamber of Deputies, last vestige of the old constitution, and replaced it with a Chamber of Fasces and Corporations.

Nov. 16. Ratification of the Anglo-Italian Pact (concluded Apr. 16). Thereby Great Britain recognized the conquest of Ethiopia and Italy promised to withdraw all troops from Spain on the conclusion of the civil war. In addition the agreement dealt with other outstanding Mediterranean questions. France also recognized the Italian conquest, but only to be confronted with

Nov. 30. A great demonstration in the Italian Chamber, with loud demands for the cession of Corsica and Tunisia. The agitation spread throughout the country, being tolerated by the government. Although no official demand for territory was made of France, the relations between the two powers became extremely strained, a situation made even worse by the Insurgent victories in Catalonia (p. 984).

1939, Jan. 20-23. Count Ciano, the Italian foreign minister, paid a visit to Belgrade and arranged for closer political, economic, and cultural relations between Italy and Yugoslavia. One objective of the Italian government was to bring about a reconciliation between Yugoslavia and Hungary.

Apr. 7. Italian invasion and conquest of Albania, which voted personal union with Italy (p. 1020).

May 22. Conclusion of a political and military alliance with Germany. The closest co-operation was now established, with much coming and going of military men and technical experts. Nevertheless Mussolini, more directly exposed to French and British power, appears to have used his influence to obviate critical developments. At the end of May and early in June the Italian troops were finally withdrawn from Spain.

Aug. Conferences of Count Ciano with the German leaders were kept extremely secret, but were taken to presage the international crisis which broke on Aug. 20 (p. 966). Throughout Germany's dispute with Poland the Italian press strongly supported the German position, though it appears that Mussolini used his influence to effect a pacific solution. When the storm broke on Sept. 1-3, Italy surprised the world by maintaining neutrality, evidently in the thought of serving Germany as a channel for necessary supplies.

b. THE PAPACY

1914, Sept. 3. BENEDICT XV (Giacomo della Chiesa) was elected pope on the death of Pius X (Aug. 20). The new pontiff was confronted with the world conflagration, which he did his utmost to terminate. After various appeals to the warring governments,

1917, Aug. 1. The pope put forward his most comprehensive **proposal for peace,** suggesting a type of "peace without victory" and arrangements to settle future international disputes by arbitration. These efforts bore no fruit (p. 942).

1922, Feb. 6. PIUS XI (Achille Ratti) was elected pope on the demise of Benedict XV (Jan. 22). The reign of Pius XI proved to be one of the most critical in the whole modern history of the papacy. Although the long-standing quarrel with the French government was gradually adjusted by compromise (May 13, 1923, Jan. 18, 1924), in Russia the Bolshevik campaign against religion appalled all Christendom. From the very outset the pope took a strong **stand against communism,** which he condemned publicly on many occasions (most recently in the encyclical of Mar. 19, 1937). In the same way the

1926. Anti-clerical policy of the Mexican government (p. 1075) called from the pope the strongest protests, which were frequently renewed. With the **Fascist government in Italy** there was constant friction, marked by much bitterness, especially in view of the suppression of the Popular (Catholic) Party, which had been formed after the revocation of the papal prohibition of participation in Italian politics (Nov. 11, 1919). Ultimately, however, the two parties to the dispute managed to reach agreement, and the conflict which dated back to 1870 was disposed of by

1929, Feb. 11. THE LATERAN TREATIES, which were ratified June 7. Of these agreements the **Lateran Treaty** proper restored the temporal power of the pope, who was to rule over the **Vatican City,** a small section of Rome (108.7 acres) about St. Peter's and the Vatican, in full sovereignty. A **concordat with the Italian government** defined the position of the Church in the Fascist state, while a **financial agreement** involved the payment by the Italian government of an indemnity of 750,000,000 lire in cash and 1,000,000,000 lire in government bonds. Under the new conditions, the pope gave up his status of voluntary prisoner, and July 25 for the first time left the Vatican. Unfortunately the agreements by no means ended friction between the Church and the government. Much dispute arose regarding the activities of the Catholic youth organization, the *Azione Cattolica.* This particular matter was disposed of by a supplementary agreement of Sept. 2, 1931, by which it was provided that the *Azione Cattolica* should

desist from all political activity and should restrict itself to the religious instruction of youth.

1931. The revolution in Spain (p. 982) ushered in a policy of anti-clericalism on the part of the republican government and so added yet another problem to those already weighing on the papacy. Here again the pope issued protests and, in order to make clear the sympathy of the Church with the needs and aspirations of the lower classes, published

    May 15. An important **encyclical,** *Quadragesimo anno,* to supplement the famous encyclical *Rerum novarum* of Leo XIII (1891). The pope called for social and economic reform, condemned the maldistribution of wealth, and strongly urged fundamental changes to give the worker a fairer share in the product of his labor. At the same time he once more condemned communism and socialism.

1933, July 20. Conclusion of the **concordat with the National Socialist government of Germany.** Although the position of the Church was carefully defined, the anti-clericalism, not to say the atheism and neo-paganism of the new régime in Germany was so strong that conflict was almost inevitable. The Nazi threat to the Church was seen to be no less serious than that from communism. The Church fought for its position as well as it could, but there was no real amelioration of the situation, and the German annexation of Austria, a purely Catholic state, in Mar. 1938, made conditions if anything even worse.

1936, July. The outbreak of the **civil war in Spain** appeared to promise a reaction against the anti-clericalism of the republican régime. The pope therefore supported Gen. Franco and recognized the Insurgent régime (Aug. 27, 1937). But when Pius XI died (Feb. 10, 1939) the Spanish situation was as yet undecided and the world was rent by the conflict of fascism and democracy and communism. In the midst of this confusion the position of the Church had become extremely precarious, but the pontiff had earned world-wide respect for the firmness of his stand against any régime threatening religion or the fundamental rights of the individual (i.e. his **condemnation of the racial policies of Germany and Italy**).

1939, Mar. 2. PIUS XII (Eugenio Pacelli) was elected pope. He had served for years as papal secretary of state and chief adviser to Pius XI and was generally recognized as a man of strong will, combined with great astuteness and diplomatic skill. He devoted himself at once to efforts for the pacification of Europe, but for the rest introduced no basic change of policy.

7. SWITZERLAND

1914, Aug. 1. The Swiss Confederation **mobilized** its forces in view of the international crisis and remained on a war footing throughout the conflict. Aug. 4 the government announced its **neutrality**, and its readiness to defend it no doubt had something to do with respect for Swiss territory on both sides. Naturally the great conflict led to a certain degree of **tension between the French and the German-speaking cantons.** For the rest the war resulted in ever-increasing authority of the federal as against the cantonal governments (the Federal Council was given exceptional powers Aug. 3, 1914). Switzerland suffered much from food shortage and was obliged to establish highly **centralized control of economic activity.** The demands of the combatants and the need for food resulted in a striking **development of Swiss industry,** with a corresponding growth of industrial labor and a spread of socialist and radical thought. By the end of the war the social tension had reached the point where

1918, Nov. 12. A **general strike** was attempted. This, however, ended in grievous failure. Bourgeois and democratic elements were more than ever on their guard, and

Dec. 8. **Switzerland broke off relations with Soviet Russia,** which was suspected of subversive propaganda. To date the Swiss government has refused recognition of the new régime in Russia.

1919, Apr. 11. **Geneva was chosen as the seat of the League of Nations.** The Swiss, though long interested in international collaboration, were nevertheless primarily concerned with maintenance of their neutrality, and were anxious to avoid dangerous commitments. When,

Apr. 11. The people of **Vorarlberg voted** by a large majority for union with **Switzerland,** the federal government ignored the opportunity to extend the confederation. By the

June 28. Treaty of Versailles the powers recognized the **perpetual neutrality** of Switzerland, while the Swiss gave up their treaty right to occupy northern Savoy in the event of war (this right or obligation had not been exercised). The intricate **problem of the free zones** of Upper Savoy and Gex, so important for the defense of Geneva, was left to direct Franco-Swiss negotiations.

Nov. 19. The Swiss parliament voted to join the League of Nations, but the federal government first secured from the League Council

1920, Feb. 13. **The Declaration of London,** by which the League Council agreed that Switzerland should not be obliged to take part in military sanctions under the terms of the Covenant. Thereupon

Mar. 8. **Switzerland formally joined the League.** Nevertheless, a plebiscite arranged to decide the issue, on

May 16. Showed a vote of only 416,000 in favor as against 323,000 opposed.

1921, Aug. 7. **Agreement with France** with respect to the free zones. Switzerland agreed to give up former treaty rights, but this arrangement was repudiated by a Swiss plebiscite (Feb. 18, 1923). Thereupon the French government took unilateral action, moving its customs stations forward to the political frontier (Nov. 10. 1923). The Swiss government protested and it was finally decided to investigate the legal aspects of the problem and to arbitrate the dispute (Oct. 30, 1924, Mar. 18, 1925).

1923, Mar. 29. Conclusion of a **customs union between Switzerland and** the little principality of **Liechtenstein,** which before the war had been closely associated with Austria-Hungary. The Swiss government was henceforth to operate the postal and telegraph services, and to protect the foreign interests of Liechtenstein.

May 10. **V. V. Vorovsky,** Russian delegate to the Lausanne Conference (p. 1095), **was assassinated by Maurice Conradi,** a Swiss who had suffered under the Soviet régime in Russia. Conradi was acquitted by the courts (Nov. 16) and the whole incident brought Switzerland and Russia to a state of extreme tension. The questions arising from the Vorovsky affair were settled only in 1927 (Apr. 15), but even that did not signify a great improvement in relations.

1930, Apr. 13. The Swiss and French governments having failed to reach agreement on the **free zones,** the Permanent Court of International Justice was appealed to and arranged for new discussions (Apr. 13, 1931). These too having broken down (July), the court took matters into its own hands and

1932, June 7. Decided the question in favor of Switzerland. The French government was directed to withdraw its customs stations by Jan. 1, 1934.

Nov. 9. Serious labor disturbances at Geneva resulted from the growing pressure of the world crisis. The police fired upon a crowd of demonstrating socialists, killing twelve persons. The radical leader, Deputy Nicolle, was arrested, and an attempt to proclaim a general strike (Nov. 12) came to nothing. The government now proceeded with ever-greater vigor against all extremists.

1933, May 12. The wearing of party uniforms was forbidden.

Oct. 14. The Federal Council was again given authority to legislate by decree in economic matters.

1934. The Swiss government bitterly opposed the admission of Russia to the League of Nations, and voted against it in the League Council.

1935, Feb. 24. By plebiscite the people voted to extend the period of military training. In view of the rapidly growing international tension, the Swiss began to feel extremely uneasy, and therefore embarked upon an extensive armament program (June 5, 1936) which involved thorough modernization of frontier defenses, mechanization of army units, development of air defense, etc.

1936, Feb. 4. Assassination of the National Socialist leader Gustloff by a Jew, at Davos. The government at once forbade continuation of a national organization of National Socialists. Protests of the German government and rapid development of ill-feeling between the two countries. In the eyes of the Germans the one redeeming feature was the valiant struggle which the Swiss government continued to wage against communism (new measures of suppression, Nov. 3). In some cantons the Communist Party was entirely forbidden.

Sept. 26. The government decided to devalue the Swiss franc, in keeping with the policy of France. This step led to a marked economic revival.

1937, June 15. The government, though it had taken part in economic sanctions against Italy during the Ethiopian crisis (p. 964), decided to recognize the Italian conquest. The ill-concealed aspirations of the Fascists to the Italian-speaking cantons of Switzerland, the conclusion of the Berlin-Rome Axis, and the collapse of the system of collective security made it essential for the Swiss government to avoid pressing matters to the limit.

Dec. 7. Romansch was recognized as a fourth national (though not official) language. This was a step designed to win renewed support from the cantons most directly exposed to Italian designs.

1938, Apr. 30. The government appealed to the Council of the League of Nations to recognize Switzerland's unconditional neutrality, pointing out the great change that had come over Europe since 1919 and stressing the particularly exposed position of Switzerland between the League powers and those of the Rome-Berlin Axis. The League Council accepted the Swiss view (May 14), thus freeing Switzerland from all obligation to take part even in economic sanctions against a future aggressor. The federal government at once brought this new situation to the attention of the German and Italian governments, which, by exchange of notes of June 21, expressed their appreciation and undertook to "acknowledge and respect" the complete neutrality of the confederation.

8. GREATER GERMANY

a. THE GERMAN REICH

1918, Oct. 28. Mutiny of sailors at Kiel, caused by orders from the admiralty to go to sea and fight the British. "Further than Heligoland we will not go."

Oct. 29. Emperor William II, alarmed at demands in the Reichstag for his abdication, left Berlin for army headquarters at Spa.

Nov. 4 and 5. The revolt at Kiel spread to other seaports. Councils of workers and soldiers formed.

Nov. 7. Revolt at Munich, led by Kurt Eisner, an independent socialist, led to the proclamation of a republic in Bavaria (Nov. 8). Similar outbreaks in other cities throughout Germany.

Nov. 8. The emperor refused a demand of the Majority Socialists that he abdicate, and rejected advice from the cabinet of Prince Max of Baden that he do so to save the nation from civil war.

Nov. 9. ABDICATION OF THE EMPEROR announced in Berlin by Prince Max. REPUBLIC PROCLAIMED by Scheidemann. Government turned over to Majority Socialists, led by Friedrich Ebert and Philip Scheidemann. The emperor fled to Holland in his special train. Allowed to cross the frontier by order of

Queen Wilhelmina after some hours of delay. His abdication was not signed until Nov. 28, by which time all other German rulers had abdicated. This revolution in Germany made it impossible to resist armistice terms offered by the Allies, and accepted Nov. 11.

Nov. 10. A joint ministry of Independent and Majority Socialists took control in Berlin. Struggle between the extreme Left, or Spartacist, group, led by Karl Liebknecht and Rosa Luxemburg, who favored a communist régime, and the Social Democrats (Majority Socialists), who wanted a gradual and not a violent abandonment of capitalism.

Nov. 25. A conference of representatives of the new state governments met at Berlin and agreed that a National Constituent Assembly should be elected.

Dec. 16. A congress of workmen's and soldiers' councils at Berlin refused to invite Liebknecht and Luxemburg to take part, showing that the masses favored the moderate policy of the Majority Socialists. The Spartacists opposed the plan of a National Assembly.

1919, Jan. 5-15. Spartacist revolt in Berlin, crushed by the provisional government with the aid of the regular army. The Independent Socialists sided with the Spartacists, now avowed communists. Rosa Luxemburg and Karl Liebknecht were killed while under arrest (Jan. 15).

Jan. 19. Election of members of a national assembly, to draw up a constitution. The Communists refused to take part, but all the other groups both Right and Left were represented. Majority Socialists won 163 seats, Center 88, Democrats 75, Nationalists 42, Independent Socialists 22, others 31.

Feb. 6- National Assembly met at Weimar. It was controlled by a coalition of Majority Socialists, Center Party, and Democrats, led by Scheidemann.

Feb. 11. Friedrich Ebert chosen as first President of the German Republic, by the National Assembly.

Feb.-Mar. Further communist uprisings in Berlin, Munich, etc., suppressed by Gustav Noske, acting for the government.

Feb. 21. Assassination of Kurt Eisner, by a conspiracy to re-establish the monarchy.

Apr. 4-May 1. Soviet Republic established in Bavaria. This was overthrown by armed forces of the federal government.

June 1. Proclamation of a Rhineland Republic, instigated and supported by France. After some months the movement collapsed because of the hostility of the inhabitants.

June 20. The Scheidemann ministry resigned rather than sign the peace treaty dictated by the Allies.

June 21. The German fleet was scuttled at Scapa Flow, by its crews.

June 23. The new cabinet, under Gustav Bauer (Matthias Erzberger, vice-chancellor; Count von Brockdorff-Rantzau, foreign minister), accepted the peace treaty unconditionally after the Weimar Assembly had voted 237 to 138 for conditional acceptance, in order to avoid invasion of the country. In this way the Majority Socialists and Liberals who controlled the Assembly assumed the odium for the hated treaty.

July 12. The Allied blockade was finally lifted, after a large part of the population had been reduced to the verge of starvation.

July 31. ADOPTION OF THE WEIMAR CONSTITUTION. The president, elected for a 7-year term, was to appoint a chancellor who in turn chose a cabinet which could command a majority in the *Reichstag*. By Arts. 25 and 48 the president was empowered to suspend constitutional guaranties and dissolve the *Reichstag* in periods of national emergency. The *Reichsrat*, composed of delegates from 18 states (no one of which was to have more than two-fifths of the seats), could delay but not prevent legislation. The members of the *Reichstag* were elected, not as individuals or as representatives of districts, but by party lists for all Germany. A system of proportional representation insured the representation of minority parties, but also necessitated coalition governments.

Sept. 22. The government was obliged by the Allies to strike out provision for the representation of Austria and to promise to respect Austrian independence.

Oct. 6. The government ordered the evacuation of Latvia by Gen. von der Goltz and his corps, at the command of the Allies.

1920, Feb. 10. Plebiscite in the northern zone of Schleswig resulted in a vote for Denmark. The plebiscite in the southern zone (Mar. 14) was in favor of Germany.

Feb. 12. French troops and the Allied commission of control took charge in Upper Silesia.

Mar. 13-17. KAPP PUTSCH, a monarchical coup, led to seizure of government buildings in Berlin. The government fled to Stuttgart, but the movement collapsed as result of a general strike of the trade unions.

Mar. 19. A great Spartacist rising took place in the Ruhr mining districts.

Mar. 26. Resignation of the Bauer cabinet. A new ministry was formed by Hermann Müller.

Apr. 3. Government troops, having entered the Ruhr, put down the revolt with great severity.

Apr. 6-May 17. French troops occupied Frankfurt and some of the Ruhr towns as a reply to invasion of the Ruhr by German government troops.

Apr. 30. Union of eight central German states to form the new state of Thuringia.

June 6. General elections, to replace the National Assembly by a regular *Reichstag*. The Weimar coalition lost its majority and a new coalition was formed of the People's Party (Liberal), Center, and Democrats. The Müller cabinet resigned (June 8) and a new government was formed by Konstantin Fehrenbach, leader of the Center Party (June 25). The Socialists were excluded.

July 5-16. Spa Conference (p. 957). The Germans signed a protocol of disarmament and arranged for coal deliveries.

July 11. A plebiscite in Allenstein and Marienwerder resulted in a large majority for Germany.

Sept. 20. By decision of the League, Eupen and Malmedy were turned over to Belgium. Five-sixths of the 600,000 inhabitants were German-speaking. The peace treaty did not provide for a plebiscite, but only gave the inhabitants six months to register their preference publicly.

Nov. 9. Danzig proclaimed a free city, as provided for in the peace treaty. It was placed under protection of the League.

1921, Mar. 8. Allied occupation of Düsseldorf, Duisburg, and Ruhrort, because of alleged German default in reparations payments.

Mar. 20. Plebiscite in Upper Silesia, in favor of Germany.

May 2. Korfanty and the Poles started a rising in Upper Silesia.

May 4. Resignation of Fehrenbach. A new ministry was formed by Julius Wirth (May 10).

May 11. Germany accepted the Allied reparations terms (p. 957).

July 16. Trial of war criminals at Leipzig.

Aug. 29. Assassination of Matthias Erzberger by reactionary conspirators, who escaped.

Oct. 12. Award of the League of Nations in the Upper Silesian question (p. 957).

1922, Apr. 16. Treaty of Rapallo with Russia (p. 958).

June 24. Assassination of Walther Rathenau, Jewish industrialist and cabinet minister, by reactionary nationalists. The assassins committed suicide and their accomplices were mildly dealt with by the government.

June 30. Membership in monarchist organizations made a criminal offense.

Aug. Beginning of the collapse of the mark, due to heavy reparations payments.

Nov. 14. Resignation of the Wirth cabinet. A new government was formed by Wilhelm Cuno, an influential industrialist.

1923, Jan. 11. OCCUPATION OF THE RUHR, after Germany had been declared in default (p. 958). The government suspended all deliveries to the Allies, but the Franco-Belgian Commission arrested the recalcitrant mine-owners and took over mines and railroads. The government supported the population in a policy of passive resistance.

Aug. 12. Resignation of Cuno. A new cabinet was formed by Gustav Stresemann, leader of the People's Party. He was supported by the Socialists, Center, and Democratic Parties.

Sept. 26. The government ended passive resistance.

Oct. 21. A Rhineland Republic was proclaimed at Aix-la-Chapelle, with Belgian and French support. The government was faced also with communist troubles in Saxony and with monarchical plots in Bavaria.

Nov. 8-11. "BEER HALL PUTSCH" in Munich, occasioned by the general crisis resulting from the Ruhr occupation and the financial collapse. General Erich Ludendorff and Adolf Hitler, leader of a growing National Socialist Party, attempted to overthrow the Bavarian government. The rising was poorly organized and was easily put down. Hitler was arrested and sentenced to five years in prison. While serving his term he wrote *Mein Kampf*, a book outlining his career, his theories, and his program. He was released after serving less than a year, and at once resumed his propaganda and organizing activity.

Nov. 15. Opening of the _Rentenbank._ Hjalmar Schacht, appointed special currency commissioner, undertook the difficult task of substituting a new monetary unit for the worthless paper currency. The new _Rentenmark_, theoretically secured by a blanket mortgage on all land and industry to the amount of 3,200,000,000 gold marks, was exchangeable for one trillion of the old marks. **Hans Luther,** as minister of finance, tried by drastic economies, including the dismissal of more than 700,000 government employees, to balance the budget. But the Dawes Plan and the foreign loan that went with it were what really made it possible for Germany to emerge from bankruptcy. In the process most of the internal debt, public and private, was wiped out. Most of the capital of the _rentier_ class and the savings of all classes, vanished. But many fortunes were made by clever speculators, some of them Jewish, who incurred general hatred. The drastic deflation, like the signature of the Versailles Treaty, discredited the Liberal groups, who were gradually deserted by the impoverished middle classes. The aristocracy remained monarchist at heart, while the workers tended to become more radical. The business men, who tended to dominate the various coalition governments, were, however, convinced that Germany, in need of raw materials, markets, and new capital, must remain on good terms with England, the United States, and possibly France. Hence the policy of fulfillment represented by **Gustav Stresemann,** who remained in every cabinet until his death in 1929. The policy made possible the flotation of large bond issues, largely in the United States, which helped pay reparations and brought on a fictitious prosperity.

Nov. 23. Fall of the Stresemann ministry. It was succeeded by a government under **Wilhelm Marx** (Center), in which Stresemann became minister for foreign affairs.

1924, Jan. 31. Collapse of the separatist movement in the Rhineland, after the assassination (Jan. 9) of **Heinz,** the president of the autonomous Palatinate government.

Apr. 9. The Dawes Plan (p. 959). It was accepted by the German _Reichstag_ Aug. 28.

May 4. _Reichstag_ elections. Gain of Nationalists and Communists at the expense of the moderate parties.

Nov. 18. Completion of the evacuation of the Ruhr.

Dec. 7. _Reichstag_ elections, in which the Socialists regained some of their losses.

1925, Jan. 15. Cabinet formed by Hans Luther. A Nationalist for the first time was included.

Feb. 28. Death of President Ebert.

Mar. 29. Presidential election. None of the seven candidates received the needed majority, but the Nationalist candidate, **Karl Jarrès,** was in the lead, with 10,416,655 votes against 7,802,496 for **Otto Braun** (Socialist). The constitution provided for a second election, in which the candidate receiving the largest number of votes should be elected. The Socialists and Democrats supported **Wilhelm Marx,** leader of the Center, while the Right parties abandoned Jarrès in favor of Field Marshal **Paul von Hindenburg,** in retirement since 1919. The Communists put forward **Ernst Thälmann.**

Apr. 26. HINDENBURG ELECTED PRESIDENT, with 14,655,766 votes against Marx's 13,751,615. Thälmann polled almost 2,000,000 votes, which, if they had gone to Marx, would have been sufficient to defeat Hindenburg.

Oct. 16. Locarno Treaties (p. 959). The _Reichstag_ voted for ratification Nov. 27.

Nov. 29. The Prussian government settled the **Hohenzollern claims,** leaving the former emperor large tracts of land and many estates, in addition to a money payment of some $7,000,000.

Dec. 5. Resignation of the Luther cabinet. This caused a deadlock which was broken only by Hindenburg's threat to invoke Art. 48. Luther ultimately reformed his cabinet.

1926, Feb. 10. Germany applied for admission to the League, in accord with the Locarno Treaties. Her admission was postponed because of a dispute regarding seats on the council (p. 960).

Apr. 24. Treaty of friendship and neutrality with Russia, extending the Rapallo Treaty of 1922.

May 6. The _Reichstag_ rejected a proposal to confiscate the property of former ruling families.

May 12. Resignation of the Luther cabinet, following its instructions that the old imperial colors should be used in the diplomatic service.

May 17. Second cabinet of Wilhelm Marx.

June 30. Referendum on the confiscation of royal property. The vote was heavily in favor of confiscation, but the total fell short of the number required by law.

Sept. 8. Germany admitted to the League, with a permanent seat on the council.

1927, Sept. 18. President von Hindenburg, in a memorial speech dedicating the Tannenburg monument, repudiated German responsibility for the war (Art. 231 of the Versailles Treaty).

1928, Jan. 29. Treaties with Lithuania, regarding the frontiers and the status of **Memel**, and providing for arbitration.

May 20. **Reichstag** elections. The Socialists so strengthened their number of seats that they had to be included in the government. The Nationalists lost heavily.

June 13. Resignation of the Marx ministry. Hermann Müller (Socialist) formed a new government.

1929, Feb. 6. Germany accepted the Kellogg-Briand Pact (p. 960).

Sept.-1930, June. Evacuation of the Rhineland.

Oct. 3. Death of Gustav Stresemann.

Dec. 22. A referendum upheld the decision to adopt the **Young Plan.** This marked a defeat for the Nationalists, led by **Hugenberg.**

1930, Mar. 27. Resignation of the Müller cabinet. A new coalition was formed by **Heinrich Brüning** (Center), in which parties of the Right replaced the Socialists.

July 16. The *Reichstag* having rejected a **budget bill,** President Hindenburg authorized it by decree. This act was condemned by the *Reichstag*, which was thereupon dissolved, the budget being put into effect by decree.

Sept. 14. *Reichstag* elections. Emergence of Hitler's National Socialists as a major party (107 seats as against their previous 12). The Communists returned 77 candidates. The Socialists retained 143 seats, but all the moderate parties lost heavily. This was probably a reflection of the world economic situation and the cessation of loans by the United States. The German obligations under the Young Plan were heavy and caused much Nationalist feeling. Hitler's program was opposed to all provisions of the Versailles Treaty, and especially to reparations. The election ushered in a period of disorder, with numerous clashes between National Socialist (*Nazi*) and Communist bands.

Dec. 12. Completion of the evacuation of the Saar by Allied troops.

1931, Mar. 21. Publication of a **project for a German-Austrian customs union.** This met at once with vigorous protest from the French government and its satellites, the protest resting on the claim that a customs union involved infringement of Austrian sovereignty, and was therefore contrary to earlier obligations assumed by the Austrian government. The matter was ultimately referred to the World Court, which handed down a decision against the project.

May 11. The failure of the Austrian **Credit-Anstalt** marked the beginning of the financial collapse of central Europe, including Germany. With the financial collapse came a great economic crisis and depression. By the beginning of 1932 the number of unemployed was already more than 6,000,000. Economic hardship brought greater social tension: rapid growth of communism and of its opponent, national socialism.

1932, Mar. 13. Presidential election. Hindenburg secured 18,651,497 votes as against 11,300,000 for Hitler and 4,983,341 for Thälmann (Communist). Hindenburg fell just short of the required majority. In the second election (April 10) he secured a plurality of only 6,000,000 out of a total vote of 36,000,000.

May 30. Brüning, who had been obliged to govern largely by emergency decrees issued by the president, resigned when the president refused to sanction a decree which would have divided bankrupt East Prussian estates into allotments for small farmers. Hindenburg, himself of the Junker class, seems to have felt that the Brüning régime was no longer popular with the public or with the army.

May 31. Franz von Papen was asked by the president to form a ministry responsible to the executive alone. This *ministry of barons* included **Constantin von Neurath** (foreign minister) and Gen. **Kurt von Schleicher** (minister of defense). Brüning had refused the foreign office. National Socialists were excluded.

June 16. The government lifted a ban on Nazi Storm Troops, which had been imposed by Brüning (Apr. 13). The National Socialist movement now gained great momentum. Disorders and clashes of rival groups became the order of the day.

July 20. *Coup d'état* in Prussia. Von Papen removed the Socialist prime minister and other officials. Berlin and Brandenburg were put under martial law, because the activities of the Nazi Storm

Troops had made it difficult for civil authorities to maintain order.

July 31. Reichstag elections, following a dissolution (June 4). The National Socialists returned 230 candidates; Socialists 133; Center 97; Communists 89. Since neither the Nazis nor the Communists would enter a coalition, no majority was possible.

Aug. 13. Hitler refused Hindenburg's request that he serve as vicechancellor under Von Papen. He demanded "all or nothing."

Sept. 12. The Reichstag dissolved. After a presidential decree had been read, a vote was taken, contrary to rules, on a Communist motion of "no confidence." This was passed by 512 votes to 42, indicating the impossibility of securing popular support for the Papen ministry.

Nov. 6. An election failed to break the Reichstag deadlock. The National Socialists lost some seats, while the Communists gained.

Nov. 17. Resignation of Von Papen.

Nov. 24. Hitler rejected the proffer of the chancellorship on certain conditions. His demand for full powers was refused by Hindenburg.

Dec. 2. Gen. Kurt von Schleicher formed a new presidential cabinet.

1933, Jan. 28. Schleicher forced to resign after his efforts to conciliate the Center and Left had failed and Hindenburg had rejected a demand for another dissolution.

Jan. 30. ADOLF HITLER, CHANCELLOR. Von Papen, vicechancellor; Hermann Goering (Nazi), without portfolio; Wilhelm Frick (Nazi), interior; Gen. Werner von Blomberg, defense; Constantin von Neurath, foreign affairs. Von Hugenberg and Seldte, Nationalists, were included. The ministry, regarded as a coalition of National Socialists and Nationalists, with important posts assigned to non-party men of the old governing class, lacked a majority so long as the Center stood aloof. But Hitler refused to compromise with Mgr. Kaas, the Centrist leader, and the Reichstag was dissolved. The new elections were set for Mar. 5.

The **National Socialist German Workers' Party** appealed to prejudices widely held in Germany against Jews, intellectuals, pacifists, communists, socialists, and liberals. Hitler exacted unquestioning obedience from his followers, but promised in return to make Germany strong, self-sufficient, respected — an Aryan nation purified of Jewish elements, able to revive the traditions of early Teutonic heroism. His denunciations of the Versailles Treaty had brought him much support. The middle classes, ruined by inflation and by the economic depression, were offered the elimination of Jewish competition in business and the professions. Thousands of unemployed and hopeless young men were put into uniform as Storm Troops, with the support of which the lieutenants of Hitler, like Goebbels, were able to organize an unusually effective propaganda and imposing demonstrations. To what extent the movement was financed by well-to-do classes and big business interests cannot be definitely ascertained, but by many such people the movement was regarded as the last bulwark against communism. On the other hand, many radical workingmen believed Hitler's rather vague denunciations of "interest slavery" and of the evils of bourgeois capitalism in general. Hitler's fanatical patriotism and extreme nationalism, combined with asceticism, and his extraordinary powers as a popular orator, secured him the backing of many who were moved by a dark discontent with things as they were. At this stage the movement was still pretty much all things to all men.

Feb. 27. A violent **election campaign** culminated in a **fire** set by the Nazis which partly destroyed the **Reichstag building.** Hitler denounced this as a Communist plot and President von Hindenburg issued emergency decrees suspending the constitutional guaranties of free speech and free press, as well as other liberties. The Nazi Storm Troops were able to intimidate and bully their opponents with impunity.

Mar. 5. The **Reichstag elections** gave the Nazis only 44% of the votes, and their Nationalist allies (party of big business and of the old aristocracy) only 8%. The Center Party elected 74, the Socialists 120, the Communists 81, and other non-Nazi parties 23 members. There were 288 Nazis and 52 Nationalists. The vote cast exceeded all preceding ones.

Mar. 23. Passage of the Enabling Act by the **Reichstag** and **Reichsrat.** The National Socialists and the Nationalists found support among deputies of the Catholic Center. The Communist Party had already been outlawed after the Reichstag fire. Only 94 votes (all Social Democratic) were cast against the crucial **Enabling Bill,** which gave the government dictatorial powers until Apr. 1, 1937. Thereby the **Nazi dictatorship** was firmly established.

The **Nazi Revolution** proved to be one of

the greatest overturns in German and in fact in European history. It affected almost every phase of life. The policies and achievements of the first years may be briefly summarized as follows:

(1) *CONSTITUTIONAL CHANGES.* The German states were allowed to continue, but the state governments were gradually shorn of all effective power. *Statthalter* were appointed for all the states (Apr. 7, 1933), and the *Reichsrat*, representing the states, was abolished (Jan. 30, 1934). Thereby the sovereignty of the states came to an end and **Germany became a national rather than a federal state.** Relations between the state governments and the local party organizations (*Gaue*) were not clearly defined, but the tendency was to identify them more and more.

(2) *ADMINISTRATIVE.* By the **Civil Service Law** of Apr. 7, 1933, all non-Aryan (i.e. Jewish) officials of national, state, and municipal governments could be retired, as also notaries, teachers, and other semi-public servants. Thenceforth no opponent of the Nazi régime could hope to retain his position.

(3) *JUDICIAL.* The entire legal system was overhauled, all traditional concepts of law being discarded and the welfare of the state and the Nazi régime became the sole deciding considerations. The **People's Court** (May 3, 1934) was set up to try cases of treason (which was given an extremely wide definition); the proceedings were made secret and there was no appeal except to the *Führer.* Summary execution of sentences became the usual thing. **Concentration camps,** in which thousands of opponents were retained without trial, became standing institutions.

(4) *POLITICAL.* All opposing parties were liquidated under government pressure. Socialist parties were prohibited on May 10, 1933; the Nationalist Party dissolved itself (June 27, 1933); the Catholic parties were obliged to dissolve (July 5, 1933); all monarchist organizations were forbidden (Feb. 2, 1934). In the same way such non-political organizations as the *Stahlhelm* were incorporated with the Nazi party (June 21, 1933) and ultimately disbanded (Nov. 11, 1935). The **National Socialist Party was declared the only political party** July 14, 1933.

(5) *RACIAL.* From the very outset the new régime aroused indignation throughout the world by the ruthless **persecution of the Jews.** A national boycott of all Jewish businesses and professions (Apr. 1, 1933) introduced a long series of outrages. As quickly as possible Jewish businesses were

liquidated and lawyers and doctors barred from practice. By the famous **Nürnberg Laws** (Sept. 15, 1935) the Jews (including all those of one-quarter Jewish extraction) were deprived of rights of citizenship and all intermarriage with Jews was strictly forbidden. Many Jews left the country, though they were required to sacrifice almost all of their property in so doing. After the annexation of Austria the same measures were extended to the new state, and, June 16, 1938, the Jews were required to register all their property, at home and abroad, within a couple of weeks. Early in Nov. 1938 the persecution came to a head when, following the assassination of a German diplomat by a Jew in Paris, well-organized attacks upon synagogues and Jewish property took place throughout the *Reich.* The government levied a fine of one billion marks upon the Jewish community, which amounted to a capital levy of 20% on property above 5000 marks. No secret was made of the determination of the government to drive all Jews (originally some 500,000) out of the country. In view of this desperate situation an **international refugee committee** was organized to arrange ways and means of effecting the emigration of so large a number as soon as possible. One great obstacle to a satisfactory arrangement was the unwillingness of the German government to allow the emigrants to take money or property with them.

(6) *RELIGIOUS.* Though both Catholics and Protestants gave the Nazis considerable support at the outset, it soon became evident that the new régime was bent on co-ordinating all religious organizations with the state machinery. **Neopagan movements,** which were many, were countenanced and even encouraged by the government, while the Christian churches were exposed to great pressure. The Protestant state churches amalgamated to form a new **Evangelical Church** (July 11, 1933), but when the government appointed as national bishop **Ludwig Mueller,** many pastors who objected to him broke away and formed the **German Confessional Church,** which soon found itself in conflict with the authorities. Sept. 28, 1935, the Protestant Church was placed under state control and **Hans Kerrl** was made minister of Church affairs with decree powers. The opposition was led by Pastor **Martin Niemoeller,** who was finally arrested (July 1, 1937). Though acquitted after trial (Mar. 1938), he was at once rearrested by the secret police and returned to a concentration camp. How many other recalcitrant pastors suffered the same fate can only be guessed at. The **Catholic Church** had an equally hard time. July 20, 1933,

the government signed a new **concordat** with the Vatican, replacing the older agreements with separate German states. The Catholic clergy was forbidden to take part in politics and future diocesan appointments were to be made by the Holy See only after consultation with the German government. On the other hand Catholic schools and societies were to be permitted so long as they did not meddle in public affairs. Despite this agreement the government brought pressure to bear to prevent parents from sending children to confessional schools (Catholic or Protestant), and furthermore brought children into the **Youth Movement**, where doctrines wholly objectionable to many Christian parents were freely taught. The policy of the government led to many protests by Catholic leaders (notably Card. **Faulhaber** of Munich). But these proved futile. On the contrary, the government took the offensive (1937), brought many monks to trial on charges of immorality, etc., and in general did its utmost to discredit and break the influence of the Catholic Church.

(7) *ECONOMIC.* The workers' parties, after dissolution, were replaced by the **Nazi Labor Front**, which was given a new constitution (Oct. 24, 1934). Strikes and lockouts had already been forbidden (May 17, 1933), and under the new constitution the employers (as leaders in their respective factories and industries) were given extensive control. On the other hand the new régime succeeded, within a remarkably short time, in **eliminating all unemployment** (chiefly through opening of labor camps for young men and even women, by public works and rearmament, etc.). Many of the workers were won over to the Nazi party by the establishment of the organization *Kraft durch Freude* (**Strength through Joy**) which provided for cheap entertainment, vacations, etc. In the larger sphere the government brought to an end the reparations problem and embarked upon a **policy of self-sufficiency** (autarchy) which would make the country independent (especially in raw materials) in the event of war. This underlay the famous **Four-Year Plan** of Oct. 19, 1936. Germany suffered greatly from the parlous condition of world trade, and considerably also from the boycott of German goods resulting from the anti-Jewish policies. The great costs of government and rearmament were met by internal loans, more forced than voluntary. Industry was more and more brought under government control, just as the peasants were more and more attached to their land.

(8) *MILITARY.* The government restored **universal compulsory military service**

Mar. 16, 1935, and from that time on made rapid progress in rearmament. By 1938 Germany not only had an impressive land army, equipped with the latest weapons, but an air fleet far superior to that of any other country. In the course of 1938 the western frontier was heavily fortified, giving the country further assurance against attack from France.

1933, May 28. The elections in the Free City of Danzig proved to be a victory for the National Socialists (led by **Albert Forster**), who captured 39 out of 72 seats in the Senate. June 20 the Nazis took over the government and thenceforth exerted themselves in the work of conforming with developments in Nazi Germany. The Polish government for a time served as a check, as did also the commissioner of the League of Nations. But after the **German-Polish Agreement** of Jan. 1934 the Polish government concerned itself more exclusively with protection of Poles in Danzig. In the elections of Apr. 7, 1935, the Danzig Nazis secured 43 seats. There soon developed a conflict with the League representative, whom the government boldly defied (July, 1936). The League, discredited by the Ethiopian *débâcle*, was unable to assert its authority, so that during 1937 the Nazis, by one device or another, gradually got rid of their opponents in the Senate. May 14, 1937, the Nationalist Party dissolved itself and a number of its representatives joined the Nazis. The Socialist Party was prohibited Oct. 14, 1937. By 1938 the Nazis had 70 seats in the Senate, the other two going to Poles. The government then began to introduce legislation against the Jews and indeed to follow step by step the lead of Berlin. To all intents and purposes, Danzig was part of the German *Reich*.

Oct. 14. WITHDRAWAL OF GERMANY FROM THE DISARMAMENT CONFERENCE AND FROM THE LEAGUE OF NATIONS. This marked the beginning of an independent policy in foreign affairs.

Nov. 12. Election of a new *Reichstag*. 93% of the voters approved the government's action in withdrawing from the League. 92% voted for the Nazi list of candidates. There were no opposition candidates, but opponents of the régime, despite intimidation, cast about three million invalid ballots, the only way of registering disapproval. The *Reichstag* itself, under the new system, lost all importance and became little more than an assembly of Nazi leaders occasionally convoked to hear addresses by the *Führer*.

1934, Jan. 26. Conclusion of the German treaty with Poland. This followed a period of extreme tension, and provided for non-aggression and respect for existing territorial rights for 10 years. It was the first breach in the French alliance system in eastern Europe. Poland became the first friend of the new régime in Germany.

June 14. Hitler and his chief associates paid a visit to Mussolini at Venice. This move was evidently designed to pave the way for closer relations between the two Fascist states, but instead it proved to be only a prelude to a clash of interests in the Danube Valley.

June 30. THE GREAT BLOOD PURGE, in which, according to Hitler's own admission in the *Reichstag* (July 13), 77 persons, many of them leaders high in the party, were summarily executed because of an alleged plot against Hitler and the régime. In reality this dramatic move appears to have been directed against representatives of the more radical, social revolutionary wing of the party, which aimed at incorporation of the Storm Troops (i.e. party forces) in the army, and at far-reaching property changes. Outstanding among the victims were Gen. von Schleicher and his wife (later said to have been shot by mistake); Ernst Roehm, one of the best organizers in the whole movement; Gregor Strasser, one of the earliest and most energetic, but also one of the most radical of the Nazis; Erich Klausener, prominent Catholic leader.

July 25. Nazi Putsch in Vienna, in the course of which Chancellor Dollfus was assassinated. The coup was the culmination of Nazi propaganda and pressure on the Austrian government (p. 1007). It would probably have succeeded or at least led to German intervention excepting for the fact that Mussolini mobilized his forces on the Brenner Pass and so frustrated any further Nazi action.

Aug. 1. Law concerning the head of the state, combining the Presidency and Chancellorship.

Aug. 2. Death of President von Hindenburg (aged 87), followed by

Aug. 19. A plebiscite which approved **Hitler's assumption of the presidency** and of sole executive power (88% of the votes affirmative). Hitler, however, preferred to retain the title *Der Führer*.

1935, Jan. 13. PLEBISCITE IN THE SAAR BASIN, conducted by the League of Nations and in accordance with the Treaty of Versailles. 90% of the electors voted for reunion of the territory with Germany as against union with France or continuation of League administration. The Nazis had unfolded a tremendous

agitation in the Saar, but there is no reason to suppose that the vote did not accurately represent popular sentiment at the time. The return of the Saar to the *Reich* (Mar. 1) marked the beginning of German expansion under the Hitler régime. With this crucial matter out of the way, the *Führer* was less dependent on the good will of France and England, and on

Mar. 16. Hitler startled the world by denouncing the clauses of the Versailles Treaty providing for German disarmament. Under French lead, England and Italy joined in a strong protest against the German action (Stresa Conference, Apr.) and attempted to secure from Germany some *quid pro quo* in the form of non-aggression pacts, or air-limitation agreements. Nothing came of the discussions excepting the conclusion of an

June 18. Anglo-German naval agreement, by which Germany promised not to extend her navy beyond 35% of that of the British. By this pact Hitler did much to reassure the British and to drive a wedge into the Anglo-French Entente.

1936, Mar. 7. THE GERMAN GOVERNMENT DENOUNCED THE LOCARNO PACTS of 1925 **and reoccupied the Rhineland.** Acute danger of war with France blew over, since all of the powers were deeply involved in the crisis of the Ethiopian War and not even France was prepared to force the issue at that time.

July 11. German-Austrian Agreement, ending a period of great bitterness between the two German states. Hitler promised to respect the sovereignty of Austria and to abstain from interference in Austrian affairs, while Austria engaged to follow a policy that befitted a German state. The agreement seems to have been intended from the German side primarily to pave the way for the

Oct. 27. Formation of the Berlin-Rome Axis, which resulted from a visit of the Italian foreign minister, Count Ciano (Oct. 25-27). This agreement strengthened the position of both Germany and Italy with respect to France and Great Britain, setting up a league of "have-nots" (i.e. revisionist powers) against a league of the "haves."

Nov. 14. Hitler denounced the clauses of the Versailles Treaty providing for international control of German rivers. This created hardly a ripple of protest, though it involved another breach in the treaty system.

Nov. 17. Conclusion of the German-Japanese Pact, ostensibly directed against communism, but in reality an extension of the Berlin-Rome combination and an effective counterweight to the Franco-Russian Alliance (p. 963).

Nov. 18. **The German government recognized the Insurgent government of Gen. Franco in Spain.** From the beginning of the civil war in Spain, the Germans had openly sided with the rebels, supplying Franco with armaments and technical experts, as well as with some troops (few in number compared to the Italian "volunteers"). In this way Hitler not only supported his Italian ally, but created further difficulties for England and France, thus securing for himself a free hand elsewhere.

1937, Sept. 25-28. **Visit of Mussolini to Berlin;** reaffirmation of the Berlin-Rome Axis.

Nov. 24. **Walther Funk replaced Dr. Hjalmar Schacht as minister of economics,** Schacht remaining president of the *Reichsbank.* Schacht had been regarded as the financial wizard who kept the régime going, and he had, in fact, done much to develop German trade through bartering agreements with the Balkan and Near-Eastern countries. But his methods, however clever, were not in accord with the more extreme theories of Nazi circles. In Oct. 1936 the **Four-Year Plan** had been introduced and Gen. Goering had been made economic dictator. Funk's advent marked a further advance of the more extreme Nazi elements.

1938, Feb. 4. **Reorganization of the military and diplomatic command.** Werner von Blomberg (minister of war) and Werner von Fritsch (commander-in-chief of the army) were removed. Hitler assumed the ministry of war, while Gen. Keitel became his representative at the Supreme Command and Gen. Brauschitsch became commander-in-chief of the army. In the foreign office the place of **Constantin von Neurath** was taken by **Joachim von Ribbentrop.** In the broader sense this involved the definitive subordination of both the army and the foreign service to the Nazi Party. The men who were relieved were looked upon as moderates, while the new men were known to be exponents of a bolder, forward policy. The events of the year 1938 seemed to bear out this interpretation.

Feb. 12. **Visit of Chancellor Schuschnigg** of Austria to Chancellor Hitler **at Berchtesgaden.** Harshly taken to task for his policy of opposition to National Socialism in Austria, Schuschnigg was obliged to promise amnesty to imprisoned Nazis, greater scope for their activity, and inclusion of Nazis in the cabinet. This

ushered in the Austrian and indirectly the Czechoslovakian crisis (pp. 1008, 1010).

Mar. 12-13. **GERMAN INVASION AND ANNEXATION OF AUSTRIA** (p. 1008). Thereby over 6,000,000 Germans were added to the *Reich* and the way was paved for future expansion of influence in the Danube Valley.

May 7. **Visit of Hitler to Rome,** a state affair of great magnificence. Politically it demonstrated that the Berlin-Rome Axis continued to function despite the Austrian affair.

May 19-20. **The first Czech crisis** (p. 1010). The strong stand taken by France and England led to the hurried fortification of the western frontier of Germany, carried out by half a million men working day and night.

July 1. By decree all members of the German state were made liable to short-term labor service in emergencies.

Sept. 12-29. **THE GREAT CZECHO-SLOVAK CRISIS** (p. 1011), as a result of which Hitler annexed to Germany over 3,000,000 Germans of the Sudeten region. Politically the German success reduced the Little Entente to ruins, broke down the French alliance system in eastern Europe, and made Germany easily the dominant power on the Continent.

1939, Jan. 20. **Dismissal of Dr. Schacht,** whose place as president of the *Reichsbank* was taken by Walther Funk. Schacht had supposedly warned that the huge armament program must be curtailed if catastrophic inflation was to be averted. Germany's adverse trade balance in 1938 was 432,000,000 marks, and by standards of bourgeois capitalism the country had been bankrupt since 1931. But the more radical elements still proceeded by dictatorial methods and desperate expedients to the most ruthless mobilization of national resources.

Mar. 15. **German occupation of rump Bohemia and Moravia,** and extinction of the Czechoslovak state (p. 1013). Bohemia-Moravia became a German protectorate, Slovakia remained nominally independent.

Mar. 21. **German annexation of Memel.** At the same time extensive demands were made on Poland with regard to Danzig and Pomorze. The firmness of the Poles and the alarm of Britain and France, which guaranteed Poland against attack (p. 966) induced the German government to hold back.

Mar. 24. **A new financial program,** of inflationary character, was announced. The government was to pay its debts to industry 60% in cash and 40% in "tax certificates" of two classes: (1) not discountable, for circulation only in industry; (2) small discountable denominations. These certificates, receivable in payment of taxes, were to be issued in amounts up to 10,000,000,000 marks per year.

Apr. 28. Hitler's *Reichstag* **speech,** in reply to President Roosevelt's appeal (p. 966). He denounced the Anglo-German naval convention of 1935 and the German-Polish agreement of 1934 because of the new policy of "encirclement", supposedly followed by Britain and Poland. At the same time he renewed his demands on Poland and offered any state assurance against aggression. Specific offers of **bilateral non-aggression pacts** were made to the Scandinavian and Baltic states, but only Denmark, Latvia and Estonia accepted.

May 22. Conclusion of a political and **military alliance with Italy,** an obvious reply to the British "peace front" and British efforts to reach an agreement with Russia. With European alignments gradually reverting to the pre-war situation, Germany's position was somewhat weakened, though she was clearly dominant on the continent and more or less mistress of Central Europe.

During the summer the **dispute with Poland** over Danzig and Pomorze rapidly came to a head. Despite repeated warnings from England and France, the Germans reiterated their demands and their determination to secure satisfaction at any cost. At the end of June German "volunteers" began to arrive in Danzig and a "free corps" was organized. Border incidents became frequent and finally, on

Aug. 20, 21. The crisis broke when the German government had succeeded in arranging a pact with **Russia** that marked a complete reversal of the anticommunist policy which had underlain National Socialist theory. Throughout two weeks of tension (p. 966) the Berlin government refused to negotiate directly with Poland and on

Sept. 1. **War between Germany and Poland** began, without formal declaration. This brought in its train almost at once the

Sept. 3. **DECLARATION OF WAR BY ENGLAND AND FRANCE.**

b. THE REPUBLIC OF AUSTRIA

German Austria, with a population almost entirely German, was the most unfortunate creation of the peace conference. Of less than 8,000,000 population, 2,000,000 lived in Vienna, a great industrial center, which was cut off from the former territories of the monarchy and shut in by the high tariff walls of the new neighbors. The economic viability of the country was in question from the very outset. Despite the principle of self-determination, Austria was forbidden to unite with Germany for political reasons. The history of the country since the peace treaty centered upon the conflict between the countryside (conservative and clerical) and the metropolis, controlled by the Socialists; upon the question of union with Germany (*Anschluss*); and upon the question of subsistence.

1918, Nov. 11. **Abdication of the Emperor Charles.**

Nov. 12. A provisional government was established.

1919. The larger part of the year was one of confusion, marked particularly by **communist disorders** aiming at the overthrow of the more moderate elements.

Feb. 16. **Election of a constituent assembly.** The Socialists secured 72 seats, the Christian Socialists (agrarian, clerical) 69, the German Nationalists 26.

Mar. 12. The assembly adopted a **constitution** and voted Austria an integral part of the German *Reich*. Dr. **Karl Renner** (Socialist) became the first chancellor.

Sept. 10. Austria signed the **Treaty of St. Germain,** in which union with Germany was expressly forbidden. The name of the state had to be changed from German Austria to *Republic of Austria*.

1920, June 11. **The Renner cabinet resigned** and was followed by a ministry of all parties under **Michael Mayr.**

Oct. 1. **A new constitution** created a federal state on the Swiss model with eight provinces (Vienna a separate province) and a two-chamber legislature.

Oct. 10. A dispute with Yugoslavia over the **Klagenfurt** area was decided by plebiscite in favor of Austria.

Dec. 9. **Michael Hainisch** elected first president of the republic.

1921. Acute food shortage, leading to much suffering and unrest.

Apr. 24. Plebiscite in the Tyrol, which voted for union with Germany.

May 29. Salzburg voted for union with Germany. The movement of separation was stopped by Allied threats.

June 21. New cabinet of **Johann Schober,** supported by Christian Socialists and German Nationalists.

July-Dec. The Burgenland dispute with Hungary (p. 955).

1922, May 31. CABINET OF IGNAZ SEIPEL (Christian Socialist).

Oct. 4. The League of Nations took over the problem of Austrian reconstruction, following the earnest appeal of the chancellor. An international loan, under guaranty of the League, was accorded and a League commissioner appointed to supervise Austrian finance.

1923, Oct. 20. In the elections the Christian Socialists won a victory over the Socialists.

1924, Nov. 17. Resignation of Seipel because of ill health. His place was taken by his follower, **Rudolf Ramek.**

1925, Sept. 10. The League voted to discontinue control of Austrian finance in July, 1926, the reconstruction scheme having successfully put Austria on her feet.

1926, Oct. 15. The Ramek cabinet gave way to a new **Seipel ministry.** During this period there was a marked recrudescence of agitation in favor of union with Germany, and a growing antagonism between the Christian Socialist government and the Socialist government of Vienna, which carried on a policy of "soaking the rich" in order to carry through elaborate socialist experiments in housing, relief, etc.

1927, July 15. The acquittal of three Nationalists of the murder of two Socialists led to riots and a **general strike in Vienna.** The mob burned the beautiful palace of justice, destroying many valuable records. The disorders were put down with some bloodshed. In the succeeding years clashes between the factions became more and more frequent in various parts of the country, each organizing private armies (the Christian Socialists the *Heimwehr*, the Socialists the *Schutzbund*).

1928, Dec. 5. Wilhelm Miklas elected second president.

1929, Feb., May. Great parades of rival factions in Vienna.

Apr. 30. Ernst Streeruwitz succeeded Seipel as chancellor.

Sept. 26. Second Schober cabinet, supported by Christian Socialists and Nationalists, with a program of restoring order.

1930, Feb. 6. Treaty of friendship with Italy. Beginning of the systematic support of the fascist elements by Italy.

June 17. A law forbade the possession of arms by private organizations. This was aimed at the rival factional armies.

Sept. 30. Cabinet of Karl Vaugoin.

Nov. 9. The elections gave the Socialists 72 seats as against 66 for the Christian Socialists.

Dec. 3. Cabinet of Otto Ender (Christian Socialist), including Schober and Vaugoin.

1931, Mar. 20. The *Anschluss* problem culminated in a projected **customs union with Germany.** This led to loud protests from France, Italy, Czechoslovakia, and other states, where it was held contrary to the maintenance of treaty obligations. The matter dragged on through the summer. Sept. 3 Germany and Austria voluntarily renounced the scheme. Sept. 5 the World Court, by a vote of 8–7 (generally regarded as political) held the project contrary to the Austrian engagement of 1922.

May 11. Collapse of the Austrian Credit-Anstalt, due in part to the withdrawal of short credits by France by way of pressure to force the abandonment of the customs union with Germany. The Austrian government attempted to save the bank, but was ultimately obliged to appeal for aid abroad. France refused support excepting on the most burdensome terms, but at the last moment (June 16) the British government offered a necessary loan. On the same day the **Ender cabinet resigned** and

June 21. Dr. Buresch (Christian Socialist) **formed a new government,** which was concerned primarily with the effort to save the desperate financial situation.

Sept. 13. The Fascist *Heimwehr* attempted **a coup in Styria** and proclaimed **Dr. Pfrimer** "dictator." The movement failed for lack of active support from the police and troops, but it was a significant warning of things to come.

Oct. 3. The national assembly passed **a drastic economy program** in the hope of balancing the budget and then securing a loan from the League of Nations.

Oct. 9. **President Miklas was re-elected.**

1932, Apr. 16. The International Chamber of Commerce met at Innsbruck with unofficial delegates from the Danubian states to consider a **plan for co-operation in the Danube area.** Such a scheme had been advanced by the French premier, André Tardieu, but the French plan was objectionable to many of the powers. The Innsbruck Conference failed likewise because of the opposition of Austria, Germany, and Italy to any plan advanced by France or the Little Entente.

May 20. **A CABINET UNDER ENGELBERT DOLLFUSS** (Christian-Socialist) replaced that of Dr. Buresch. Like its predecessor, the new government represented a coalition of Christian-Socialists and Agrarians.

July 15. The League of Nations finally **agreed to a loan** of 300,000,000 schillings, Austria engaging not to enter into political or economic union with Germany before 1952. This condition roused a storm of protest in Austria, but the agreement was ratified by the assembly Aug. 17.

1933, Mar. Growing anti-governmental **agitation in Austria,** following the victory of the National Socialists in Germany. To meet the situation, Dollfuss **suspended parliamentary government** (Mar. 4) and prohibited parades and assemblies; freedom of the press was also curtailed (Mar. 8). Nevertheless the Austrian Nazis staged a great demonstration and riot in Vienna Mar. 29, and the Styrian branch of the *Heimwehr* became frankly Nazi. In reply the government May 4 forbade the wearing of uniforms by all political parties. Nazi agitators were harried out of the land and relations with Germany became extremely tense. June 1 Hitler instituted a charge of 1000 marks on Germans desiring to visit Austria, thereby completely ruining the Austrian tourist business.

June 14. The Austrian government expelled Herr Habicht, Hitler's "inspector for Austria." The Germans retaliated and in Austria there broke out a series of **terrorist outrages.**

June 19. The Nazi Party in Austria was dissolved. Agitation and terrorism continued, encouraged by a virulent Nazi radio campaign. Oct. 3 an attempt was made to assassinate Dollfuss.

1934, Feb. 11-15. **DESTRUCTION OF THE AUSTRIAN SOCIALISTS.** This followed a decree dissolving all political parties except Dollfuss's *Fatherland Front.* Raids by government forces and *Heimwehr* on Socialist headquarters led to an uprising and the bombardment of the Karl Marx Hof, an elaborate Socialist housing unit, where the leaders had concentrated. These leaders were either captured or forced to flee. By this drastic action Dollfuss and the Christian Socialists permanently antagonized the working classes of Vienna and deprived themselves of what might have been the most effective support against the Nazi threat.

Mar. 17. **Signature of the Rome Protocols,** effecting close relations between Austria, Hungary, and Italy. Dollfuss was obliged to rely more and more upon Italian support against a hostile Germany.

Apr. 1. Promulgation of a **new constitution for Vienna,** which deprived the capital of most of its powers of self-government.

Apr. 30. An extremely complicated **constitution for Austria** was accepted by the national assembly. It set up a **dictatorship under Dollfuss,** who (July 10) reconstructed his cabinet along more Fascist lines.

May 1. **A concordat with the Vatican** gave the Church in Austria wide control of education.

July 25. **NAZI COUP.** A band of Nazis seized the radio station in Vienna and forced the staff to broadcast Dollfuss's resignation. They then entered the chancellery and (probably unintentionally) **shot and killed Dollfuss.** The whole affair was badly mismanaged and the conspirators were routed by *Heimwehr* troops. Action by Germany in behalf of the Nazis was made impossible by the strong stand of Italy and Yugoslavia, which concentrated large forces on the frontier. Thereupon the German government disavowed all connection with the affair and recalled its ambassador to Vienna.

July 30. **Dr. Kurt Schuschnigg,** close collaborator of Dollfuss, **formed a new cabinet** committed to the same policies. Twice in the course of the autumn he visited Mussolini in Italy. Economic agreements with Italy and Hungary led to some improvement of the situation, and political agitation also died down somewhat.

1935, July 4. Repeal of the anti-Hapsburg laws and restoration of part of the imperial property. This move was symptomatic of increased **sentiment for return of the Hapsburgs,** advocated by Prince Stahremberg and supposedly encouraged by Mussolini. The opposition of

the Little Entente and of France served,
however, as an effective damper.

1936, Apr. 1. Reintroduction of conscrip-
tion, in violation of the provisions
of the Treaty of St. Germain. The Austrian
step followed similar action by Germany
(p. 1002) and was intended to give the
Austrian dictatorship an armed force more
reliable than the *Heimwehr.* May 14
Schuschnigg forced **Prince Stahremberg,**
commander of the *Heimwehr,* out of the
offices of vice-chancellor and leader of the
Fatherland Front, thus removing his only
serious rival.

July 11. German-Austrian Agreement,
ending the feud between the two
countries at least temporarily. Germany
engaged to respect the independence of
Austria and Schuschnigg promised to pursue a policy befitting a German state. The
agreement was evidently inspired by Mussolini during a visit by Schuschnigg to
Rome (June 1), Mussolini being anxious,
on the eve of the Ethiopian campaign, to
secure the good-will of Germany.

Oct. 10. Schuschnigg disbanded the
Heimwehr and had the members
absorbed into the *Fatherland Front* militia.
He dropped the remaining *Heimwehr* members from his cabinet, and Oct. 18 had himself proclaimed *Front Führer.*

1937, Feb. 14. Schuschnigg publicly
claimed the right to decide on the
question of Hapsburg restoration. All indications were that he was veering more
and more in that direction. This was highly
objectionable to Hitler and to the entire
Nazi party, and probably accounts for the
recrudescence of Nazi demonstrations and
mutual recrimination (Feb.). Schuschnigg's position was further weakened by the
conclusion of the Rome-Berlin Axis (p. 964)
and by Mussolini's preoccupation with the
Spanish civil war.

Apr. 22. Schuschnigg visited Mussolini
at Venice, where he was warned
that Italy could not be counted on to give
armed support against Germany. Mussolini seems further to have opposed the projected restoration of the Hapsburgs and to
have objected to a suggested alliance
between Austria and Czechoslovakia for
common defense. His advice was that
Schuschnigg make his peace with Hitler
and admit Nazis to the government.
Schuschnigg rejected this advice, but continued throughout the year to further negotiations with Czechoslovakia and the
Little Entente. Indications were that,
deserted by Italy, he was seeking and finding a measure of support from France and
France's allies. This policy, on the other

hand, led to much dissatisfaction in Germany and to ever more outspoken demands
on the part of the Austrian Nazis and Pan-
Germans.

1938, Feb. 12. Schuschingg paid a visit to
Hitler at Berchtesgaden, and
under pressure was obliged to promise an
amnesty to Austrian Nazis who had been
imprisoned, and furthermore to agree to
take certain Nazis into the cabinet. Feb. 16
Arthur Seyss-Inquart (Nazi) became minister of the interior. **Full amnesty** was
granted and (Feb. 19) the *Fatherland Front*
was opened to Nazis.

Feb. 24. Schuschnigg, replying to a
speech of Hitler (Feb. 20) promising protection to 10,000,000 Germans outside the *Reich,* **reaffirmed the independence**
of Austria and appealed for support against
further demands for concessions. This
speech called forth a good deal of enthusiasm in Austria, but the Nazis, confident of
success, assumed the offensive. Mar. 1
serious **disorders broke out at Graz** and
soon all Styria, as well as other places, was
in a state of revolution. The government
was unable to cope with the situation without offending Nazi Germany. Last-minute
efforts of Schuschnigg to arrange a reconciliation with the Socialist working classes
came to nothing. As a last resort, Schuschnigg suddenly announced (Mar. 9) that a
plebiscite would be held on the following
Sunday on the question of Austrian independence; only *Yes* ballots were to be
distributed (those who desired to vote *No*
would have to supply their own ballots, of
specified form). This announcement drove
the Nazis to extremes and plunged the
country into chaos. Hitler seized the opportunity offered him, and

Mar. 11. Germany submitted an ulti-
matum demanding postponement
of the plebiscite and the resignation of
Schuschnigg. German troops began to
concentrate on the frontier. Unable to
resist, **Schuschnigg resigned and Seyss-**
Inquart became chancellor.

Mar. 12. The German army began the
invasion of Austria. No resistance
was offered. **President Miklas**
resigned and

Mar. 13. SEYSS-INQUART PRO-
CLAIMED THE UNION WITH
GERMANY. Hitler arrived in Vienna
Mar. 14 and took formal possession. He
had already decreed a plebiscite to be held
Apr. 10. In the meanwhile the most ruthless revenge was taken on all opponents of
the Nazis, many of whom committed suicide
and most of whom, unable to get away, were
thrown into concentration camps. Schusch-

nigg allowed himself to be arrested and was kept in confinement without trial. The Jews suffered assault and humiliation of all kinds.

Apr. 10. The plebiscite in Austria revealed a vote of 99.75% in favor of the union with Germany. Austria was incorporated with the *Reich* as a new state, and was divided into seven districts (*Gaue*). The union was carried through with such speed and energy on the part of the Ger-

mans that no international complications ensued. England and France protested, but these powers were too deeply involved in Mediterranean and Far-Eastern problems to be able to take further action, the more so as Italy refused to join in protest. Mussolini, though his ally's success brought a powerful state to the Brenner Pass, could do nothing but accept the new situation with as good grace as possible.

9. CZECHOSLOVAKIA

The new state, with a population of about 15,000,000, inherited the most valuable part of the old Austro-Hungarian Monarchy, with most of the industrial areas. Its political life since the war was dominated by the racial problem and the consequent multiplication of political parties.

1918, Oct. 14. The Czechoslovak National Council in Paris organized a **provisional government, with Thomas Garrigue Masaryk** (1850–1937) as president, and **Eduard Beneš** (b. 1884) as foreign minister.

Oct. 28. DECLARATION OF INDEPENDENCE, by the National Council.

Oct. 30. The Slovak National Council voted for union with the Czechs.

Nov. 14. A national assembly at Prague confirmed the republic and the presidency of Masaryk.

1919, Jan. The dispute with Poland regarding the Teschen area (p. 955).

Apr. 16. The Land Reform Bill. This involved the confiscation, with compensation, of the large estates and their division among the peasants in lots of about 25 acres, with state aid.

1920, Feb. 29. Adoption of the constitution, which was closely modeled on that of France.

Apr. 18. The first regular elections. There were numerous parties, representing racial groups and social strata. The country had to be ruled by various coalitions, representing chiefly the bourgeois, democratic elements.

Aug. 14. Treaty with Yugoslavia, the basis of the **Little Entente,** which was directed against Hungarian revisionism and the restoration of the Hapsburgs.

1921, Apr. 23. Treaty with Rumania, completing the Little Entente. It was **renewed** from time to time and in 1934 the

Little Entente was given a permanent organization.

1924, Jan. 25. Treaty of alliance with France.

1925, July 6. Rupture of relations with the papacy, as a result of the celebration of the anniversary of John Hus as a national holiday and a long-standing dispute regarding the delimitation of dioceses and the appointment of bishops. The matter was settled by a compromise (Dec. 17, 1927).

1927, May 27. President Masaryk re-elected. Eduard Beneš remained foreign minister in all cabinets and took an active part in the work of the League of Nations.

July 1. An administrative reform gave a greater measure of self-government to the provinces. This was designed to meet the constant complaints of the Slovaks and Ruthenians that their districts were ruled from Prague by Czechs. In both areas there was an active movement demanding autonomy.

1928, Dec. The arrest and **conviction of Voitech Tuka,** a Slovak deputy accused of irredentist agitation in favor of Hungary, caused great ill-feeling in Slovakia.

1931, Mar. The government, in association with France, offered the most strenuous **opposition to the projected German-Austrian customs union.** When this matter was finally disposed of, the Czech government, beginning to suffer severely from the economic crisis which spread over central Europe after the financial crash in Vienna in May (p. 961), lent all possible support to the French scheme for regional agreements between the Danubian states.

1932, Apr. 6-8. A conference, attended by representatives of Great Britain, France, Germany, and Italy, met at London to discuss the **Danube problem.** The French (Tardieu) plan, which would have excluded Germany and Italy from the projected regional understandings, was wrecked by the opposition of those two countries.

1933, Feb. 14-16. The powers of the Little Entente, meeting at Geneva, concluded a Pact of Organization, providing for a standing council and a permanent secretariat, as well as for co-ordination of policies and for economic collaboration. This step toward greater solidarity was provoked partly by revival of irredentist agitation in Hungary, in part by the advent of Hitler's National Socialist government in Germany. In the course of the year Nazi agitation spread rapidly among the more than three million Germans living along the frontiers of the republic. These areas, being largely industrial, were particularly hard hit by the depression, so that economic grievances were added to the earlier cultural and political ones.

Oct. 4. The Sudete National Socialist Party dissolved itself, on the eve of a government order prohibiting it. Led by Konrad Henlein, the party soon emerged again as the *Sudetendeutsche Partei*, Nazi in its program but officially not directed at the disruption of the state.

1934, Apr. 26. Visit of the French foreign minister, M. Barthou, to Prague. His purpose was to discuss the Danubian situation as it appeared after the conclusion of the Rome Protocols (p. 990) and generally to revivify the Franco-Czech Alliance.

May 24. President Masaryk was once again re-elected.

1935, May 16. Conclusion of a pact of mutual assistance with Russia, together with an air convention. By the terms of this agreement, Russia was obliged to come to the aid of Czechoslovakia in case of attack, provided that France did so. The agreement followed the breakdown of French efforts to engineer an eastern pact, and the conclusion of the Franco-Russian Alliance (p. 963). While giving Czechoslovakia added support in case of conflict with Germany, it also aroused much opposition in Germany and exposed the republic to German wrath.

May 19. In the general elections the government coalition secured 149 out of 300 seats in the Chamber. The Sudete Party won a sweeping victory in the German areas and, with 44 seats, became the strongest single party with the exception of the Czech Agrarians.

June 4. The government of M. Malypetr was reorganized as a coalition of Agrarians, Social Democrats (Czech), National Socialists, Clericals, and Small Traders. Despite all efforts of the premier,

the Slovak Clericals stood aloof. The Sudete Germans were not included.

Nov. 5. Dr. Milan Hodža, a Slovak and the leader of the Agrarian Party, formed a new cabinet along the lines of his predecessor's.

Dec. 13. Resignation of President Masaryk, who had reached the age of 85. He was succeeded by his close friend, the foreign minister,

1935-1938. EDUARD BENEŠ, president. He continued to guide the republic's foreign policy, though Feb. 29, 1936 Dr. Kamil Krofta, well-known Czech historian, became foreign minister.

1936, Mar. 9-10. Premier Hodža visited Vienna. Apr. 2 a trade treaty was concluded between Czechoslovakia and Austria. This *rapprochement*, pursued with ever-greater assiduity, reflected the Austrian desire for support in the face of German hostility and Italian uncertainty, as well as the hope of the Czechs, backed by France, to bring Austria, and perhaps Hungary, into association with the Little Entente to form a stronger bulwark against Germany. The Czech government had already embarked upon an extensive program of armament and had undertaken the construction of a very strong line of fortifications along the German frontier.

Sept. 10. Dr. Goebbels, the German minister of propaganda, publicly accused Czechoslovakia of harboring Soviet army planes and permitting Soviet airdromes on Czech soil. Despite Czech protests, these accusations were repeated with ever-greater frequency and there developed a campaign of denunciation and recrimination reminiscent of the Nazi campaign against Austria.

1937, Sept. 14. Death of President Masaryk.

Oct. 16. The Czech police suppressed a meeting of the Sudete German Party at Teplitz. Some violence having occurred, Henlein protested against the government's brutal methods and demanded complete autonomy for the 3,500,000 Germans in the republic. In view of the general excitement and tension, the government postponed the elections scheduled for Nov. 14. All political meetings were forbidden.

Nov. 29. The Sudete German deputies left parliament, declaring that they had been beaten by the police.

1938, Mar.-May. The first German-Czech crisis. Hitler's speech of Feb. 20 promising protection to German minorities outside the *Reich* presaged an active policy by the Nazis and was answered by Premier Hodžo (Mar. 4) by a firm declaration that Czechoslovakia would defend itself against outside interference. But the **German annexation of Austria** (Mar. 13) completely changed the position of the Czechslovak Republic, which was surrounded on three sides by the new German Empire. The German government gave Prague assurances of its desire to improve German-Czech relations (Mar. 14) and both the French and Russian governments categorically declared their intention to honor their treaty obligations. Nevertheless the situation rapidly grew worse. **The German Activists** (i.e. German parties which had joined the cabinet) **all withdrew** (Mar. 22–25), and Hodža's announcement of a forthcoming **Nationality Statute** made but little impression on the German elements. Apr. 24 the Sudete leader, Henlein, put forward his demands (the **Karlsbad program**: *eight points*: full equality of status for Germans and Czechs; delimitation of the German areas; full autonomy; removal of all injustices and reparation for damages suffered by the Germans since 1918; full liberty for the Germans to proclaim their Germanism and their adhesion to "the ideology of Germans"; furthermore, Henlein demanded complete revision of Czech foreign policy). These demands were rejected by the Prague government, despite strong urging by France and England that the utmost concessions be made. Henlein then paid visits to London and Berlin. On his return disorders began to break out in the German districts. This situation and rumors of German troop concentration on the frontier led the Czech government to mobilize 400,000 men. France and Britain took a strong stand and the crisis (details of which are unknown) blew over. Shortly afterward Henlein began negotiations with the Czech government with regard to the Nationality Statute, but Hitler, with feverish haste, began the fortification of the German-French frontier and ordered a huge increase in the German air forces.

The summer was filled with **negotiations between the government and the Sudete leaders,** but little progress was made. July 26 the government finally published a draft Nationality Statute, based on the principle of proportionality, but falling short of Henlein's Karlsbad program. At the same time it was announced that a British mediator, **Lord Runciman,** would come to Prague. He arrived Aug. 3 and held many conferences with Sudete leaders. In the meanwhile (Aug. 12) the German government announced huge maneuvers which involved calling 750,000 men to the colors,

and Aug. 28 Hitler began a demonstrative tour of the new fortifications in the west. At the same time (Aug. 26) the British government announced the concentration of most of the fleet for early Sept. British statesmen on various occasions warned publicly that British abstention in a crisis should not be counted on. By the beginning of Sept. the situation was clearly critical; various Czech proposals for cantonal organizations, etc., were flatly rejected by Henlein after visits to Hitler. The Karlsbad program was insisted on as a minimum. The French government (Sept. 7) began to call up reservists, so that about 1,000,000 men were under arms.

Sept. 7-29. HEIGHT OF THE GERMAN-CZECH CRISIS. The Sudete leaders broke off negotiations with the government (Sept. 7) after an affray at Moravska Ostrava. Discussions were resumed (Sept. 10), but disorders, provoked by extremists, became more and more frequent. Sept. 12 Hitler, in a speech at Nürnberg, first demanded in no uncertain terms that the Sudete Germans be given **the right of self-determination.** This address was the signal for a widespread series of disorders and the proclamation of martial law by the government (Sept. 13). Henlein and other leaders fled across the frontier (Sept. 15). To meet this dangerous situation, Prime Minister Chamberlain, in agreement with the French government, proposed a personal conference to Hitler.

Sept. 15. CHAMBERLAIN-HITLER CONFERENCE AT BERCHTESGADEN. The German chancellor baldly stated his demand for annexation of the German areas on the basis of self-determination, and did not conceal his readiness to risk a war to attain his end. Chamberlain returned to London, as did Runciman from Prague. Sept. 18 Premier Daladier and M. Bonnet (French foreign minister) arrived in London. Decision reached to advise and urge the Czech government to accept Hitler's terms, promising an international guaranty of the rump state. After long deliberations the Czech government (Sept. 20) **suggested arbitration** on the basis of the German-Czech Locarno Treaty of 1925. This proposal was at once rejected by England and France as inadequate. After further pressure and threats of desertion by France and England, the **Prague government finally yielded** (Sept. 21), despite the fact that Poland and Hungary had both put in additional claims for territory. The **Hodza cabinet resigned** (Sept. 22) and a new government was formed by Gen. **Jan Sirovy,** popular military leader.

Sept. 22-23. CHAMBERLAIN'S SECOND VISIT TO HITLER AT GODESBERG. Further demands of the German chancellor: surrender of the predominantly German territories at once, without removal or destruction of military or economic establishments; plebiscites to be held in areas with large German minority by Nov. 25, under German-Czech or international supervision. These terms were regarded by Chamberlain as quite inacceptable, and as an unwarranted extension of the original German demands.

Sept. 24-29. ACUTE INTERNATIONAL CRISIS, the most serious since 1918. The Czech government ordered full mobilization and the great powers took precautions of every kind. Britain and France began to confer with **Russia,** which had urged a strong stand in behalf of Czechoslovakia from the outset. **Rumania** also was reported favorable. On the other hand, **Italy** came out more and more definitely on the German side. Daladier and Bonnet again came to London (Sept. 26) and the decision was evidently reached to support Czechoslovakia in resisting the extended German demands. Chamberlain appealed to Hitler for a conference, so that the cession of Sudete territory, already agreed on by all, might be effected by discussion, not by force. President Roosevelt also appealed to Hitler and urged a conference (Sept. 27). Finally (Sept. 28) Hitler, apparently persuaded by Mussolini (to whom both Chamberlain and Roosevelt had appealed), agreed to a conference.

Sept. 29. THE MUNICH CONFERENCE AND AGREEMENT. Hitler, Ribbentrop, Mussolini, Ciano, Chamberlain, and Daladier conferred during the afternoon and evening, Czechoslovakia being unrepresented. The agreement (dated Sept. 29) was actually signed just after midnight. Hitler secured about all that he had demanded: evacuation to take place between Oct. 1 and Oct. 10, under conditions arranged by an international commission, which should also determine the plebiscite areas. England and France undertook to guarantee the new frontiers of Czechoslovakia against unprovoked aggression. When the Polish and Hungarian minorities questions should have been solved, Germany and Italy would give a like guaranty. The Czech government felt impelled to acquiesce in this settlement Sept. 30.

The statesmen, returning from Munich, received warm ovations from their peoples and there could be no doubt that the will to peace was strong, not only in England and France, but also in Italy and Germany.

The crisis, however, soon led to much dispute and recrimination. Many felt that the democratic powers had not only deserted the one democratic outpost in central Europe, but that they had suffered a tremendous defeat, which might have been avoided if the strong stand taken just before the Munich conference had been maintained. Others believed that the German case in Czechoslovakia was too strong to justify war against Germany, and that Hitler, far from bluffing, was determined to march. In any event, the final outcome established **German hegemony in central Europe** and opened the way to domination of the entire Danubian area.

THE SETTLEMENTS:

(1) *GERMAN.* The occupation was carried through as scheduled at Munich, taking over all the vital Czech frontier fortresses. The predominantly German regions were determined by the Austrian census of 1910. The international commission caused Germany no trouble, and in the end there were no plebiscites. Germany acquired about 10,000 square miles of Czech territory, with about 3,500,000 inhabitants, of whom about 700,000 were Czechs. By agreement with the Czechoslovak government (Nov. 20, 1938) Germany was given **rights to a highway across Moravia to Vienna, and to a canal connecting the Oder and the Danube Rivers.** The truncated Czechoslovak state, without defensible frontiers, became of necessity a satellite of the *Reich.*

(2) *POLISH.* During the crisis the Polish government had renewed its longstanding **claims to the Teschen region.** Sept. 29 a virtual ultimatum was submitted to Prague, to which the Czech government yielded. Oct. 2 Polish forces occupied the Teschen area and Czechoslovakia lost about 400 square miles of territory with some 240,000 inhabitants (less than 100,000 Poles).

(3) *HUNGARIAN.* The Hungarian **claims to Slovakia** were to be settled by negotiation, and delegates of the two countries met Oct. 9. Agreement proved impossible and serious clashes took place on the frontier. Ultimately the matter was adjusted by joint decision of Germany and Italy. Hungary received a broad strip of southern Slovakia and Ruthenia, almost 5000 square miles, with 1,000,000 population. The Hungarian claim, supported by Poland, for a common frontier with Poland, was denied.

CZECH LOSSES THROUGH THE DISMEMBERMENT: In all the republic lost 5,000,000 inhabitants (retaining 10,-000,000), distributed as follows: Germans,

2,850,000; Hungarians, 591,000; Poles, 77,000; Jews, 60,000; Ruthenians, 37,000; Czechs and Slovaks, 1,161,000. In territory Czechoslovakia lost 16,000 square miles (retaining 38,500).

Oct. 5. **Resignation of President Beneš,** who had been the target of German attack throughout the crisis. He left the country almost at once, going ultimately to the United States. His departure was the signal for a violent campaign directed against him and Masaryk and the policies that had led to Munich.

Oct. 6. **Slovakia was given the full autonomy** which Slovak leaders had demanded for a long time. Mgr. Joseph **Tiso** became premier of Slovakia.

Oct. 8. **Ruthenia was given full autonomy** and was renamed *Carpatho-Ukraine*. This remote region of Europe at once assumed a crucial importance as the base for Ukrainian agitation, supposedly inspired from Berlin. The Polish government made every effort to arrange for its partition between Poland, Hungary, and Rumania, but all such plans were frustrated by German opposition.

Oct. 20. **The Communist Party was outlawed** in Czecho-Slovakia (so spelled after the federal reorganization). This was merely one move in the direction of the new policy planned in conformity with Germany. **Persecution of Jews,** etc., soon followed.

Nov. 30. EMIL HACHA, judge of the high court, **was elected president.**

Rudolf **Beran** (Agrarian), an opponent of Beneš and his orientation towards the west, became prime minister.

1939, Mar. 10-16. **THE ANNIHILATION OF THE CZECHOSLOVAK STATE.** The crisis began when the Prague government deposed Mgr. Tiso, premier of Slovakia, for allegedly working in the direction of separation, with support of the Fascist *Hlinka Guards*. Tiso appealed to Hitler and during a visit to Berlin was given assurances of support. Hitler summoned President Hacha and foreign minister Chvalkovsky to Berlin and induced them to "place the fate of the Czech people . . . trustingly in the hands of the *Führer*," who guaranteed "an autonomous development of its national life corresponding to its peculiarities." Slovakia and Carpatho-Ukraine declared independence. Mar. 15 Bohemia and Moravia became a German protectorate, which was promptly occupied by German forces, the Czechs offering no resistance. On Mar. 16 Tiso put Slovakia also under German protection. **Constantin von Neurath,** former German foreign minister, became **protector of Bohemia and Moravia,** Hacha continuing as "head of the state." The disappearance of Czechoslovakia was momentous, inasmuch as it demonstrated Hitler's readiness to extend his claims beyond German racial areas and to base them on German needs for "living area" (*Lebensraum*). The small states were thrown into a panic, and Britain and France promptly adopted a policy of guarantees to prevent further German expansion (p. 966).

10. HUNGARY

Hungary, left a country of some 8,000,-000 population by the peace settlements, was predominantly agricultural, socially still organized on a semi-feudal basis. Much of the political history after 1918 had to do with the successful efforts of the landholding classes to secure and retain control and with the agitation for revision of the peace treaties and the restoration of the monarchy. The antiquated political arrangements effectively kept the lower classes from exerting much influence.

1918, Oct. 17. The Hungarian parliament, in reply to the Emperor Charles' declaration of reorganization of the monarchy, declared complete independence from Austria, except for the personal union.

Oct. 31. **REVOLUTION IN HUNGARY.** Count Michael Károlyi,

grand seigneur of extremely liberal, republican, and pacifist views, made prime minister in the hope of securing satisfactory peace terms and maintaining the unity of the monarchy.

Nov. 16. The National Council proclaimed **Hungary a republic.**

1919, Jan. 11. Károlyi appointed president **of the republic.** The government at once proceeded to the work of dividing the large estates among the peasants.

Mar. 21. Károlyi resigned in protest to the Allied decision to assign Transylvania to Rumania.

Mar. 21. Formation of a **Socialist-Communist government** under Alexander Garbai (president) and **Béla Kun** (foreign affairs). The Socialists were soon crowded out and a communist dictatorship established under Béla Kun, henchman **of**

Lenin, who had come from Russia in Nov. 1918 but had been imprisoned for communist agitation.

Mar. 28. Hungary declared war on Czechoslovakia and proceeded to the reconquest of Slovakia.

Apr. 10. Rumanian troops began to invade Hungary to forestall reconquest of Transylvania. A provisional government was set up by Count Julius Károlyi (brother of Michael), Count Stephen Bethlen, Admiral Horthy, and Archduke Joseph at Szeged (under French occupation). **Beginning of the counter-revolution.**

June 24. Soviet constitution.

Aug. 1. Béla Kun fled to Vienna in the face of the Rumanian advance.

Aug. 4. The Rumanians occupied Budapest (until Nov. 14).

Aug. 6. Archduke Joseph took control as state governor, but was forced by Allied protests to resign.

1920, Feb. 25. Final evacuation of the country by the Rumanians, who took with them all that was movable.

Mar. 1. Admiral Nicolas Horthy, commander in chief of the forces, appointed **regent and head of the state.**

Mar. 23. He proclaimed **Hungary a monarchy,** with the throne vacant.

June 4. SIGNATURE OF THE TREATY OF TRIANON, consecrating the immense losses of territory and population involved in the establishment of Czechoslovakia, Rumania, and Yugoslavia.

1921, Mar. 27. King Charles returned to Hungary and called on Horthy to give up his powers. Owing to the threatening attitude of the neighboring states, the national assembly voted against restoration and Charles was obliged to return to Switzerland.

Apr. 14. CABINET OF COUNT STEPHEN BETHLEN, who remained in power until 1931.

Aug.-Dec. The Burgenland dispute with Austria (p. 955).

Oct. 21. Second arrival of King Charles, at Ödenburg. With an improvised force he marched on Budapest. Czechoslovakia and Yugoslavia began to mobilize and a government force was obliged to turn back and capture the king, who was exiled to Madeira (d. Apr. 1, 1922).

Nov. 4. A Dethronement Act abrogated the rights of Charles.

1922, June 2. Elections, held under a system of carefully restricted suffrage and open voting, gave the government a strong majority. Bethlen proceeded on a conservative policy designed to maintain the *status quo.* Radical disorders were put down, Jews persecuted. Efforts of the extreme royalists and Fascists (**Awakening Magyars,** etc.) to overthrow the government were summarily dealt with.

Sept. 18. Hungary was admitted to the League of Nations.

1923, Dec. 20. The League of Nations adopted a **scheme for economic reconstruction** of Hungary, not unlike the one successfully applied in Austria. This continued until June, 1926.

1926, Jan. 4. Arrest of a number of high officials, who were convicted (Mar.) of counterfeiting French francs to finance the monarchist movement.

Nov. 11. Re-establishment of an upper house, representing the landed aristocracy.

1927, Apr. 5. Treaty of friendship with Italy, initiating a period of close relations. This was reflected in the growing **agitation for treaty-revision,** which was ardently supported in England by the Rothermere press.

1928, Jan. Austrian customs officials discovered five freight cars loaded with machine-gun parts, shipped from Italy and destined for Hungary. The Little Entente powers protested to the League, which held an investigation.

1930, Nov. 20. Archduke Otto, pretender to the throne, **reached his majority.**

1931, Aug. 15. France granted a loan to Hungary, evidently on condition that revisionist agitation should cease. Hungary suffered severely from the general world depression.

Aug. 19. Resignation of Count Bethlen, officially because of ill health, actually because of inability to cope with the financial situation. His friend, **Count Julius Károlyi,** took his place, but

1932, Oct. 4. Julius Gömbös, former extreme reactionary and anti-Semite, took his place. Gömbös was not averse to a measure of agrarian and electoral reform, but was above all an ardent nationalist and revisionist. He opposed the restoration of the Hapsburgs, but sought to further realization of Hungary's territorial claims by **close co-operation with Fascist Italy.**

1933, Jan. Discovery of another shipment of arms from Italy to Hungary threw some light on the subterranean aspects of European politics. Once again the Little Entente countries took a strong stand.

The advent of Hitler and the National Socialists in Germany led to the rapid **spread of Nazi agitation** to Hungary, where there were large-scale demonstrations already in April.

June. Gömbös visited Berlin, and in July he journeyed to Rome. His great hope was that Germany and Italy could both be brought to support the Hungarian claims. It was only natural, then, that he should reject the Franco-Czech plans for a Danube Federation (Dec.).

1934, Mar. 17. SIGNATURE OF THE ROME PROTOCOLS, establishing close political and economic ties between Italy, Austria, and Hungary and forming a bloc in opposition to the Francophil Little Entente.

Oct. 9. Assassination of King Alexander of Yugoslavia. It turned out that the assassins had operated from Hungary. Acute danger of conflict developed, but the matter was finally adjusted by the League of Nations which, in a masterpiece of diplomatic circumlocution, mildly rebuked the Hungarian government (Dec. 10).

1935, Apr. 11. In the parliamentary elections the opposition groups polled 1,041,000 votes as against 908,000 for the government, but the intricate electoral system enabled the government to retain 166 seats in the Chamber as against 25 for the Agrarians, 14 for the Christian Socialists, and 12 for the Social Democrats.

June 1. Count Bethlen and his followers joined the most important opposition group, the Agrarian Party of Tibor Eckardt. This party resented the dictatorial methods of Gömbös and suspected him of designs against the constitution. At the same time it advocated land reform in behalf of the 3,000,000 landless peasants, and electoral reform as a stage on the road toward real democracy. Only by timely reform along national lines could the threat of Nazism and Fascism be removed.

Oct. 6. Death of Premier Gömbös, who was succeeded by Koloman Darányi. Darányi represented no change in policy, but tried to follow a somewhat more conciliatory course. As a matter of fact, Hungary's position became steadily worse through international developments. The German government showed but little interest in Hungarian revisionism and was downright hostile to all proposals of a Hapsburg restoration. The attention of Italy, too, was diverted by the Ethiopian crisis and the Mediterranean situation. The formation of the **Rome-Berlin Axis** (Oct. 1936) involved the sacrifice of Austria by Musso-

lini. In the same way the **Italo-Yugoslav Agreement** of Mar. 1937 was tantamount to desertion of Hungary in favor of its neighbor. Under the circumstances Darányi during 1937 drew closer to Austria and both Austria and Hungary began to seek contact with the nations of the Little Entente. This policy of necessity estranged Germany (Hungary's most important customer) and produced vigorous opposition on the part of the Hungarian Nazis.

1937, Mar. 5. The existence of a widespread **Nazi plot** was revealed. The Nazi leader, **Ferenc Szálasi,** and other conspirators were arrested, but were treated rather mildly. The Nazi elements had a most effective weapon to use against the government, viz. the promise of land reform and relief for the agrarian proletariat. The government resorted to evermore strenuous methods to repress agitation, but without avail.

Oct. 11. Eckardt and his Agrarian Party joined with the Legitimists. Even the Social Democrats became friendly to the idea of Hapsburg restoration as the most effective way to block the Fascist elements.

Oct. 16. Various Fascist groups united to form the **Hungarian National Socialist Party,** under the leadership of Szálasi. Efforts were made to glorify the regent, Admiral Horthy, and to further his candidacy for the throne. Horthy himself discountenanced these efforts.

1938, Feb. Szálasi was again arrested, with 72 associates. He was sentenced to prison and drastic steps were taken to stamp out the Fascist-Nazi movement. But

Mar. 13. The annexation of Austria by Germany brought the powerful *Reich* to the Hungarian border. The idea of a bloc consisting of Austria, Hungary, and the Little Entente states was exploded and the scheme of a Hapsburg restoration likewise. The large German element in Hungary (c. 500,000) became more and more restless and the Nazi danger became ever more urgent.

May 13. A new cabinet was formed by Béla Imredy, eminent financier, who was regarded by the ruling classes as the strong man needed to manage the situation. Imredy did, indeed, rule with a strong hand. At the same time, however, he initiated certain political and economic reforms (a part of all large estates to be distributed to the peasantry, etc.) and undertook the limitation of Jewish activity in business and the professions. In this way he hoped to steal the thunder of the Nazi agitators. For the rest he tried to maintain good relations with Germany. In Aug. Admiral Horthy paid a visit to Germany, where he was received with great ceremony and splendor.

Nov. 2. ACQUISITION OF SOUTH-ERN SLOVAKIA, as a result of the dismemberment of Czechoslovakia (p. 1012). The Hungarian claims were valiantly championed by both Germany and Italy, two powers which served as arbitrators after the Czech and Hungarian governments had failed to agree. Hungary was given 5000 square miles of territory, with 1,000,000 inhabitants. This was less than the Hungarians claimed as theirs, but Germany vetoed any further reduction of Slovakia and particularly any idea of joining Hungary and Poland (as desired by Poland and also by Italy). Sporadic fighting continued along the new frontier throughout the winter of 1938–1939.

1939, Jan. 20-23. The Italian foreign minister, Ciano, on a visit to Belgrade, devoted himself to the **adjustment of Hungarian-Yugoslav relations,** with what success was not clear. Yugoslavia's unwillingness to consider any cessions of territory to Hungary made any reconciliation difficult.

Feb. 15. Resignation of Premier Imredy. The Nazis, whom he had tried to outdo in his anti-Semitic policy, had taunted him with his own Jewish ancestry. He was finally obliged to admit that he had one Jewish great-grandfather and this admission, he felt, made his retention of the premiership impossible.

Feb. 24. The new government of Count Paul Teleki suddenly suppressed the leading Fascist organization, yet at the same time, to placate Germany, **joined the anti-communist pact** of Germany, Japan, and Italy.

Mar. 15. HUNGARY OCCUPIED CAR-PATHO-UKRAINE and annexed it after heavy fighting with the inhabitants, who had driven out the Czechs and, under Augustin Volosin, had enjoyed independence for one day. Thus Hungary was able to exploit the German absorption of Bohemia and Moravia (p. 1013), securing at last a common frontier with Poland. A small slice of eastern Slovakia was also conquered, with German consent, but the remainder was guaranteed by Germany as to independence and integrity.

Apr. 11. Hungary withdrew from the League of Nations, revealing further influence of German pressure.

May 3. Introduction of drastic **anti-Jewish laws** providing for rigorous limitation of Jews in professions and business, expulsion from government service and eventual emigration within five years.

May 28. In the elections the government secured 180 seats out of 260, but the Nazis increased their representation from 6 to 53, while the Agrarian had 14 seats as against a previous 23.

11. THE BALKAN STATES

a. YUGOSLAVIA

The history of the new state, composed of Serbia, Montenegro, Croatia, Slovenia, and Dalmatia, was marked chiefly by the efforts of the Serbs to establish a centralized Serb state and by the vigorous resistance of the Croats and Slovenes (Roman Catholic and much more westernized than Serbia) to secure some type of autonomy.

1917, July 20. THE PACT OF CORFU, signed by Serbian, Croatian, Slovenian, and Montenegrin representatives, declared that the Serbs, Croats, and Slovenes formed a single nation, to be organized under the Serbian dynasty.

1918, Apr. 8-10. Congress of Oppressed Nationalities (chiefly under Hapsburg rule) at Rome. Italy recognized the unity and independence of the Yugoslav nation.

Oct. 19. The National Council at Zagreb proclaimed itself the authoritative body for the Yugoslavs and declared for union.

Nov. 26. A national assembly in Montenegro proclaimed union with Serbia and declared **King Nicholas,** who had resisted previous efforts at union, deposed (d. Mar. 1, 1921, in exile).

Dec. 1. Prince Alexander of Serbia accepted the regency of the new state.

Dec. 4. THE KINGDOM OF THE SERBS, CROATS AND SLOVENES FORMALLY PROCLAIMED.

1919, Feb. Dispute with Italy regarding the allocation of Fiume and territory on the Dalmatian coast (p. 955).

June 13. The Peace Conference decided that the **Banat of Temesvar,** in dispute between Yugoslavia and Rumania, should be divided between them.

1920, Aug. 14. TREATY OF ALLIANCE WITH CZECHOSLOVAKIA (renewed Aug. 31, 1922, and later), laying the foundation for the **Little Entente** (p. 957).

Oct. 10. Plebiscite in the Klagenfurt area, in dispute between Yugoslavia and Austria (p. 1005).

Nov. 12. Treaty of Rapallo with Italy, settling the Fiume question.

Nov. 28. Elections for a constituent assembly. No party had a majority, but the Croats (leader **Stephen Radich**) refused to take their seats, demanding recognition of the federal principle. This left the field free for the Serbian Centralists (leader **Nicholas Pasich**).

1921, Jan. 1. The new constitution provided for a centralized form of government. Pasich became premier of a coalition of Serbian Radicals and Democrats. The Croats continued in opposition.

June 7. TREATY WITH RUMANIA, second link in the Little Entente.

Aug. 16. Death of King Peter.

1921-1934. ALEXANDER I. He was a hardworking, intelligent ruler, whose aim, however, was to consolidate the kingdom despite opposition from Croats and other groups.

1923, Mar. 18. The elections failed to effect any substantial change. The Croats remained in opposition and boycotted the parliament.

1924, Jan. 27. Treaty of friendship with Italy for five years, following settlement of the Fiume problem. This was not renewed in 1929.

July 18. The Pasich government resigned after Radich had changed his tactics and had upset the parliamentary balance by instructing his followers to take their seats. The Pasich ministry was reconstructed, but efforts to effect a compromise with Radich failed.

Dec. 24. The Croat Peasant Party was **outlawed** and Radich imprisoned.

1925, July 18. Radich having at last **recognized the constitution**, he was liberated and some of his followers were given seats in the cabinet. Radich himself became minister of education (Nov. 18).

1926, Apr. 1. Resignation of Radich and other Croatians from the cabinet.

Aug. 17. Treaty with Greece, settling the question of the Yugoslav **free zone at Saloniki** (p. 1020).

Sept. 18. Treaty of friendship with Poland.

Dec. 10. Death of Pasich, veteran leader of the Radical Party.

1927, June. Rupture of relations with Albania, following repeated frontier incidents (p. 1020).

Nov. 11. Treaty of friendship with France, intended as a reply to the Italian advance in the Balkans.

1928, June 20. Radich and his associates were **fired upon** in parliament by a Radical deputy. **Radich died** Aug. 8. The Croat deputies once again withdrew from parliament.

Aug. 1. The Croats once more demanded the institution of a federal régime as the price of their co-operation. They then set up a separatist "parliament" at Zagreb and refused to have anything more to do with the Belgrade government (Oct.). All efforts of the king to effect a compromise ended in failure.

1929, Jan. 5. KING ALEXANDER PROCLAIMED A DICTATORSHIP. Gen. Zhivkovich premier; the constitution was suspended and parliament dissolved; a rigorous censorship was introduced and local government curtailed. Alexander then set to work to end corruption and purge the administration and army.

Jan. 21. The Croat and all other parties were dissolved.

Feb. 17. A legislative council, with only advisory powers, was set up to replace parliament.

Mar. 27. Treaty of friendship with Greece.

May 22. Arrest of Dr. Vladko Machek, the new leader of the Croats.

June. Beginning of border raids by Macedonian revolutionaries from Bulgaria. Acute tension in Yugoslav-Bulgarian relations; the frontier hermetically closed. This situation continued throughout the following years.

Oct. 3. The name of the kingdom was officially changed to *Yugoslavia*, another indication of the king's effort to wipe out the old historic divisions. The traditional provinces were divided into nine new *banats*, with purely geographical names.

1930, June 14. Machek was acquitted.

1931, Sept. 3. The king announced the end of the dictatorship and introduced a new constitution (two-chamber parliament). The electoral law left no place for purely local parties; two-thirds of the seats were to go to the party receiving the largest number of votes; voting to be open.

Nov. 9. Farcical elections. The government named most of the candidates and therefore won a great victory; most of the opposition groups had abstained.

1932, Nov. 14. The Croat Peasant Party denounced the régime of personal rule and again demanded autonomy, following the imprisonment of the Croat leader, Dr. Machek (Oct. 17).

1933, Jan. Slovene and Croat leaders were arrested.

Feb. 15. Reorganization of the Little Entente, the treaties becoming indefinite in duration and a permanent secretariat being set up (p. 963).

Apr. 29. Machek, Croat leader, was imprisoned for three years for treasonable activity.

Oct.-Nov. Alexander visited Sofia and Istanbul as part of a series of visits exchanged by Balkan rulers in the effort to bring about a Balkan Pact (fear of Nazi Germany).

Dec. 10-13. King Boris of Bulgaria visited Belgrade: initiation of the Bulgarian-Yugoslav reconciliation.

1934, Feb. 9. CONCLUSION OF THE BALKAN PACT between Yugoslavia, Greece, Rumania, and Turkey. Bulgaria refused to recognize the territorial settlement and therefore could not join.

June 1. Conclusion of a trade agreement with Germany; fears that Yugoslavia might veer to the German side, especially in view of the Italian-Austrian-Hungarian *rapprochement*.

June 25. Visit of M. Barthou, the French foreign minister, to Belgrade; he evidently persuaded the government to stick by the French connection.

Sept. 23. Visit of Alexander to Sofia, apparently in the hope of bringing Bulgaria into the Balkan Pact.

Oct. 9. ASSASSINATION OF KING ALEXANDER and M. Barthou at Marseilles. The assassin was a Macedonian revolutionary, working with Croat revolutionists having headquarters in Hungary. The assassination led to acute danger of war between Yugoslavia and Hungary (deportations on both sides), which was finally adjusted (Dec. 10) through the good offices of the League of Nations.

1934- PETER II (b. 1923). Prince Paul (cousin of Alexander) chief regent.

Nov. 15. The Croats offered to coöperate with the government, hoping for concessions from the conciliatory regent.

Dec. 19. Machek pardoned, but the government made no move in the direction of concessions.

1935, May 5. In the elections government pressure was exerted to the full, but the coalition of the Croats and a new party of Serbian peasants polled two-fifths of the votes.

June 3. The Croats resumed boycott of parliament.

June 20. A new cabinet, under M. Stoyadinovich, announced the coming liquidation of the dictatorial régime and a new electoral law. Relaxation of repressive measures and methods, but only for a time.

July 25. A Concordat with the Vatican, granting Roman Catholics wider privileges. The concordat was signed, but Orthodox groups created so much disorder that the government was obliged to drop the project. The total effect was to estrange the Orthodox Church without really winning any support from the Croats.

Aug. 19. Stoyadinovich formed a new Radical Union of Serbian Radicals, Slovene Clericals, and Bosnian Moslems, which reaffirmed the principle of unity and blasted hopes of a federal solution.

1936, May. Conclusion of a barter agreement with Germany. This was made necessary by the falling-off of trade with Italy subsequent to Yugoslavia's imposition of sanctions during the Ethiopian crisis. Ever closer trade relations with Germany brought in their train a political *rapprochement* which appears to have been decidedly unpopular in the country.

1937, Jan. 24. Signature of the BULGARIAN-YUGOSLAV TREATY OF FRIENDSHIP AND PERPETUAL PEACE, bringing to an end the long antagonism between the two states. This was followed by an even more astounding departure in foreign affairs, the

Mar. 25. CONCLUSION OF A NON-AGGRESSION AND ARBITRATION PACT WITH ITALY for five years. Both parties guaranteed each other's frontiers; the Yugoslav minority in Italy was to be given language and school concessions; economic collaboration was envisaged. This new agreement associated Yugoslavia more closely than ever with the Berlin-Rome Axis, and was therefore warmly denounced by the opposition groups in Yugoslavia itself. The government, in the hope of frustrating the opposition by winning over the Croat clerical elements, brought before the Chamber for ratification

Oct. 6. The opposition groups closed ranks and formed the **Agrarian-Democratic Party,** composed of Croats and Serbian democrats. The program called for abolition of the dictatorship and restoration of democratic government. The increasing strength of the opposition obliged Stoyadinovich to renew his efforts to satisfy the Croats, but prolonged negotiations during 1938 led to nothing.

1938, Dec. 11. In the **parliamentary elections** Stoyadinovich managed to secure victory for his party (by corruption, so it was claimed by the opposition), but in Croatia the Peasant Party of Vladko Machek received an overwhelming vote. As a result

1939, Feb. 4. Stoyadinovich was obliged to resign. The new cabinet of **Dragesha Cvetkovich** rested upon the same coalition (Radical Union) as had Stoyadinovich, but it was committed to making larger efforts to conciliate the Croats.

Apr. 27. Substantial agreement was reported reached with Machek, envisaging the reorganization of Yugoslavia as a federal state. In the meanwhile Yugoslavia was courted by both alliance groups in Europe. Count Ciano visited Belgrade and Prince Paul (June 1) visited Berlin, where Hitler in a toast once more assured him of the inviolability of the Yugoslav frontier.

The settlement of the Croat problem hung fire throughout most of the summer until the German-Polish crisis (p. 966) finally precipitated a decision.

Aug. 26. **DEMOCRATIC GOVERNMENT WAS REËSTABLISHED** in Yugoslavia and new elections by secret ballot were arranged for. The state was to be reorganized on a federal basis, the Croats receiving complete autonomy in all cultural and economic matters. Machek became vice-premier and five other Croats joined the cabinet.

b. ALBANIA

1912, Nov. 28. Proclamation of independence by a national assembly at Valona; provisional government under Ismail Kemal.

1913, May 30. The Treaty of London (p. 760) recognized the independence of Albania and set up a commission to determine the boundaries.

1914, Jan. 15. The government of Ismail Kemal gave way to one under **Essad Pasha.**

Feb. 21. Prince William of Wied, a German officer and close relative of Queen Elizabeth of Rumania, was offered the crown by Essad and accepted.

Mar. 2. Northern Epirus (southern Albania) proclaimed independent by Greeks led by **Zographos.** This matter was adjusted by the powers and the area was given autonomy.

Mar. 7. Arrival of Prince William. From the outset friction developed between him and Essad, the real ruler of the country.

Sept. 4. William left the country, after the outbreak of the World War.

Sept. 13. The Italians landed at Valona. During the war the Italians gradually occupied most of southern Albania and the Serbs and Montenegrins the northern part. Both were driven out by the Austrians. The government of Essad fled to Italy (Feb. 24, 1916).

1918, Dec. 25. A national assembly elected **Turkhan Pasha president.** The government had to deal with the incursions of the Yugoslavs in the north and the Italians on the coast. The latter were finally driven out in 1920.

1920, Aug. 2. Italy agreed to evacuate **Valona,** while retaining the island of **Saseno.** The Italians left Sept. 2.

Dec. 17. Albania was admitted to the League of Nations.

1921, June. Erection of the **Mirdite Republic** at Prizrend, under Yugoslav auspices.

Nov. 9. The conference of ambassadors decided on the frontiers of 1913 for Albania, with some slight concessions to Yugoslavia.

1922, Dec. 3. Ahmed Bey Zogu became premier, representing the Yugoslav party.

1924, June 10. A revolution, led by **Bishop Fan Noli** and supported by Italy, led to the **flight of Ahmed Zogu.**

Dec. 12. A **counter-revolution,** organized in Yugoslavia, overthrew **Fan Noli,** who fled to Italy (Dec. 27).

1925, Jan. 6. Ahmed Zogu became premier again.

Jan. 21. **THE NATIONAL ASSEMBLY PROCLAIMED ALBANIA A REPUBLIC,** with Ahmed Zogu as first president.

Mar. 2. A constitution was promulgated, providing for parliamentary government, but granting the president almost dictatorial powers.

Sept. 2. A national bank was organized, under Italian auspices and supported by an Italian loan.

1926, July 30. A final act fixing the frontiers was signed by Great Britain, France, Italy, Greece, and Yugoslavia.

Nov. 20-26. An insurrection in the north, supposedly supported by Yugoslavia, was put down with difficulty.

Nov. 27. TREATY OF TIRANA, between Italy and Albania. The two powers promised each other support in maintaining the territorial *status quo*, and Italy promised not to interfere in Albania except by request.

1927, May-July. A rupture of Albanian-Yugoslav relations was finally patched up by the powers.

Nov. 22. SECOND TREATY OF TIRANA, taken as a reply to the French treaty with Yugoslavia (Nov. 11): the treaty established a defensive alliance for 20 years and provided for military co-operation. It marked the beginning of what became practically an Italian protectorate. The Italians granted Albania substantial loans (especially in 1931) and in return secured valuable concessions (notably oil), supervision of military affairs, construction of roads, educational privileges, etc.

1928, Sept. 1. Ahmed Bey Zogu was proclaimed king as

1928-1939. ZOG I. Throughout he acted as the champion of the modernization of the country (building of Tirana as a modern capital, language reform, educational development, religious independence, etc.).

Nov. 22. The assembly adopted a new monarchical constitution.

1931, June. An Italian loan, spread over 10 years and subject to Italian supervision, established Italian economic control of the country.

1932. King Zog rejected a proposal for a customs union with Italy; beginning of Albanian opposition to too great extension of Italian influence. In Sept. some 200 persons were arrested and seven sentenced to death for allegedly plotting the establishment of a republic.

1933, June. Further friction with Italy, resulting from the closing of Italian schools.

1934, June 23. After further disputes an Italian fleet suddenly appeared at Durazzo and frightened the government into submission. The Italian control of the army was strengthened, Italians were given the right to colonize certain areas, etc.

1936, Mar. 19. Further agreements between Italy and Albania marked another stage in the extension of Italian control, providing as they did for even closer financial and trade relations.

1937, May 15-19. Insurrection of the Moslems in the southern sections. The immediate cause was the government's decree forbidding the veiling of women, but in the larger sense it was another expression of discontent with King Zog's dictatorial rule.

1939, Apr. 7. END OF ALBANIAN INDEPENDENCE. The Italians, long irritated by Albanian resistance to their direction (prohibition of a Fascist party, etc.) took advantage of the confusion produced by German absorption of Czechoslovakia. They bombarded the coast towns and landed an army which, after some resistance by the natives, overran the whole country. King Zog and his queen fled to Greece and then Turkey. On Apr. 12 an Albanian constituent assembly voted personal union with Italy and King Victor Emmanuel graciously accepted the crown. On June 3 Albania was given a constitution providing for a Superior Fascist Corporative Council over which the king, however, retained extensive control.

c. GREECE

1917-1920. ALEXANDER I, king.

1919, April 29. The Dodecanese, in a plebiscite, voted for union with Greece.

May 14. Landing of the Greeks at Smyrna (p. 954).

July 29. Venizelos-Tittoni Agreement: the Dodecanese to be ceded to Greece when the Treaty of Sèvres went into effect.

1920, May 14. Agreement with Italy providing for the immediate cession of the Dodecanese, except Rhodes, which was to have a plebiscite at the end of 15 years.

June 22. Beginning of the Greek offensive in Anatolia (p. 1094).

Aug. 10. THE TREATY OF SÈVRES: Greece obtained Smyrna, the Dodecanese (except Rhodes), eastern Thrace, Imbros, and Tenedos.

Oct. 25. Death of King Alexander. Regency of Queen Olga.

Nov. 14. Defeat of the Venizelists in the election, due to dissatisfaction with the Anatolian adventure. Venizelos resigned.

Dec. 5. A plebiscite, held despite Allied warnings, showed an almost unanimous vote for King Constantine. The Allies thereupon withdrew all support from Greece.

1920-1922. CONSTANTINE I, restored. He announced continuation of the war with Turkey.

1921, Aug. Battle of the Sakkaria. The Greeks failed to reach Angora (p. 1095).

1922, Aug. 18. Turkish counter-offensive. Taking of Smyrna, Sept. 9 (p. 1095).

Sept. 21. Revolt of Gens. Gonatas and Plastiras in Chios.

Sept. 26. The Venizelists took Saloniki and demanded the abdication of the king.

Sept. 27. Abdication of Constantine (d. Jan. 11, 1923).

1922-1923. GEORGE II, who was a mere puppet in the hands of the military men.

Oct. 8. Italy denounced the agreement regarding the Dodecanese on the plea of the collapse of the Sèvres Treaty.

Nov. 13. Trial for treason of the ministers and commanders of Constantine. Gounaris and five others convicted and shot.

1923, May 10. Yugoslavia granted a small free zone at Saloniki for 50 years beginning 1925.

July 24. TREATY OF LAUSANNE (p. 1095). Exchange of populations: In the period till 1930 some 1,250,000 Greeks repatriated, with the help of the League and of the Near-East Relief Commission; great financial and other problems connected with this great transfer, but Greece enriched by influx of artisans and farmers.

Aug. 27. Murder of the Italian officer, Gen. Tellini, and his staff, on the Albanian front. Italian bombardment and occupation of Corfu (Aug. 29). Settlement of the incident by the League of Nations in Dec. (p. 988).

Dec. 16. Great victory of the Venizelists in the elections.

Dec. 18. George II left Greece, under pressure from the military junta.

1924, Jan. 11. Venizelos premier. He opposed the deposition of the king, but, failing to convince the military men, resigned (Feb. 3) and retired from Greece.

Apr. 13. A plebiscite resulted in an overwhelming vote for a republic.

May 1. GREECE PROCLAIMED A REPUBLIC. Adm. Paul Kondouriottis made provisional president.

1925, June 25. *Coup d'état* of Gen. Theodore Pangalos.

Oct. 22-23. Clash of Greek and Bulgarian forces on the frontier, followed by the invasion of Bulgaria. The matter was settled by the League of Nations (Dec. 14), which fined Greece.

1926, Jan. 3. Pangalos made himself dictator, voiding the republican constitution of Sept. 30, 1925.

Mar. 19. President Kondouriottis resigned.

Apr. 11. Pangalos, president.

Aug. 22. Pangalos overthrown by Gen. George Kondylis, who recalled Kondouriottis.

Sept. 24. The new constitution promulgated.

Nov. 7. The Republicans won a bare majority in the elections. A coalition government formed by Alexander Zaimis.

1928, May 31. Return of Venizelos, who formed a cabinet (July 4).

Sept. 23. Pact of friendship with Italy, first step in Venizelos's policy of restoring Greece's international position.

1929, Mar. 17. Settlement of the free zone controversy with Yugoslavia, which was given more extensive privileges at Saloniki than in the agreement of 1923.

Mar. 27. Pact of friendship with Yugoslavia.

May 16. Venizelos restored the Senate (abolished 1862) in the hope of adding stability to the republican régime.

Dec. 10. Retirement of President Kondouriottis. Zaimis provisional president.

1930, Oct. 5-12. First Balkan Conference at Athens, called by Venizelos in the hope of establishing better relations between the Balkan states and improving the economic situation.

Oct. 30. TREATY OF ANKARA with Turkey, following Venizelos's visit to Ankara (p. 1096).

1932, Sept. 25. The Venizelists failed to secure a majority of seats in the election. Growing power of the royalists, strengthened by general economic stringency.

Oct. 31. Venizelos resigned and was followed (Nov. 4) by a moderate royalist cabinet under Panyoti Tsaldaris, who declared his loyalty to the republic and was therefore tolerated by the Venizelists.

1933, Jan. 13. Fall of the Tsaldaris cabinet, defeated on its financial policy.

Jan. 16. Venizelos became premier again, but, after dissolving parliament, suffered

Mar. 5. Defeat in the elections. Plastiras, an ardent republican general, attempted a *coup d'état*, which failed.

Mar. 10. Tsaldaris premier again, despite Venizelist opposition.

Sept. 15. Ten-year non-aggression pact with Turkey. The two countries agreed to close co-operation in foreign policy.

1934, Feb. 9. CONCLUSION OF THE BALKAN PACT between Greece, Turkey, Yugoslavia, and Rumania (p. 963).

Oct. 19. Zaimis elected president for five years.

1935, Mar. 1. Rising of the Venizelists in Athens, Macedonia, and Crete, as a protest against royalism. The movement was put down, after some fighting, by Gen. George Kondylis. Venizelos fled to France.

June 9. In the elections the followers of Tsaldaris and Kondylis secured most of the seats, the republicans having abstained from voting.

Oct. 10. By a coup, Kondylis ousted Tsaldaris and induced parliament to vote for the recall of the king.

Nov. 3. A farcical plebiscite resulted in an almost unanimous call for restoration of the monarchy.

Nov. 24. Return of George II, from exile in England. The king was supported by England (Ethiopian crisis), but was at the mercy of Kondylis.

1935– GEORGE II, RESTORED. He insisted on a general amnesty (Dec. 1).

1936, Jan. 26. The elections were a victory for the Venizelists, who, however, failed to secure a majority of the seats.

Jan. 31. Sudden death of Kondylis.

Mar. 18. Death of Venizelos, in exile at Paris.

Apr. 13. Gen. John Metaxas, premier.

Aug. 4. *COUP D'ÉTAT* OF METAXAS, who made himself dictator, proclaimed martial law and dissolved the parliament. Institution of a régime of rigid repression (parties abolished; censorship; persecution of opponents). The Metaxas régime rested squarely on the army, but real efforts were made to conciliate the population by wage increases, social security legislation, artificially low bread prices, etc., as well as by cancellation of agricultural debts. A huge public works program (esp. rearmament) necessitated a substantial increase of taxation and domination of business by government. In foreign affairs Metaxas drew closer to Germany (barter agreements), but at the same time attempted to retain the good-will of England and France. Relations with Turkey continued to be close.

1938, July 29. A revolt broke out in Crete, but was quickly suppressed. Despite widespread dissatisfaction with the dictatorship, the régime became more and more firmly entrenched, and

July 30. Metaxas became premier for life.

1939, Apr. 13. Britain and France guaranteed Greek independence and integrity following the Italian conquest of Albania and the sudden danger of aggression against Greece.

d. BULGARIA

Defeated in the First World War, Bulgaria not only failed to recover any of the territory lost in the second Balkan war, but was also deprived of some further areas on the Serbian frontier and of all access to the Aegean. The country was flooded with thousands of refugees from Thrace and Macedonia, whom the government, loaded with debt and with heavy reparations payments, was unable to settle. They formed a huge mobile element, easy converts to the revolutionary program of the Macedonian committees or to Bolshevik agitators. The drastic policy of nationalization pursued by the Yugoslav and Greek governments in Macedonia stimulated the unrest in Bulgaria which the government was unable to control. Raids of revolutionary bands across the frontiers became the order of the day, creating a state of chronic tension between Bulgaria and her neighbors.

1918, Oct. 4. Abdication of Tsar Ferdinand.

1918– BORIS III, son of Ferdinand, tsar.

1919, Aug. 17. In the elections the Peasant Party won a great victory.

Oct. 6. Alexander Stamboliski, leader of the Peasant Party, became premier. He had opposed Bulgaria's entry into the war on the side of Germany and had been imprisoned as a result. He now took revenge on his opponents. All members of the Radoslavov cabinet (except the premier, who had escaped) were tried and convicted; they were heavily fined and imprisoned. Stamboliski, moved by hatred of the bourgeoisie and intellectuals, there-

upon embarked on a policy of disappropriation: a drastic land law broke up all crown
lands and estates of over 75 acres; a heavy
income tax was levied on all but the peasants; the university was shut down; freedom of the press was abolished, and all
opponents of the régime were ruthlessly
dealt with. In foreign affairs Stamboliski
followed a policy of fulfillment of the peace
treaties and reconciliation with Yugoslavia.
The Macedonian Revolutionary Organization (IMRO) was broken up.

Nov. 27. Bulgaria signed the Treaty of
Neuilly (terms, p. 953).

1920, Dec. 16. Bulgaria became a member
of the League of Nations.

1922, Dec. 4. Attempted rising of the
Macedonians, under Todor Alexandrov. They took and held the
town of Küstendil for a time.

1923, Mar. 21. Agreement with the Allies
with regard to reparations.

**June 9. STAMBOLISKI WAS OVER-
THROWN** by a conspiracy of
officers, Macedonians, and others
affected by his class policies.

June 10. A cabinet was formed by Alexander Zankov.

June 14. Stamboliski was shot and
killed, allegedly in an effort to
escape. Zankov and the new government
proceeded with great vigor in a policy of
revenge. The condemned members of
the Radoslavov government were released.

Sept. 26-28. An abortive communist
insurrection led to much bloodshed and to violent repression.

1924, Aug. 31. Assassination of Alexandrov, the Macedonian leader, by
members of a rival faction. The IMRO
then broke into two groups, one led by
Protoguerov and the other by Ivan Mihailov. These were mutually hostile and
fought each other as bitterly as they fought
the enemy.

1925, Apr. 16. Bomb outrage in Sofia
Cathedral. The bomb, which
killed 123 persons, was set off by
communists; it only served to
heighten the terrorist policy of the
government.

May 4. Communists were outlawed in
Bulgaria.

Oct. 21. Greek invasion of Bulgaria,
following serious frontier incidents. The matter was settled by
the League (p. 1021).

1926, Jan. 4. A cabinet of Andrew Liapchev followed that of Zankov and
attempted a more conciliatory
policy.

Feb. 4. All political prisoners except
communists were amnestied.

June 10. Liapchev secured from the
League of Nations a huge loan, to
facilitate the settlement of refugees.

July 28. Great raid of the Macedonians
over the Yugoslav frontier.

Aug. 11. Stiff note of Yugoslavia,
Greece, and Rumania demanding
cessation of raids. The government was apparently helpless.

1927, June 19. Further raids on Yugoslav
territory.

Oct. 10. The government proclaimed
martial law along the frontier and
attempted to suppress the Macedonian activity.

1928, July 7. Assassination of Protoguerov
by the Mihailov faction. Open
war followed between the two
groups.

1929, Mar. 6. Treaty of friendship with
Turkey.

Sept. 26. Agreement with Yugoslavia
for the establishment of a frontier
régime.

1930, Jan. 20. The Hague Agreement
greatly reduced the Bulgarian
reparations payments.

Aug. 11. Action by the government
against the IMRO; Mihailov was
arrested.

Oct. 5-12. First Balkan Conference at
Athens. Bulgaria sent delegates,
but from the outset made further
co-operation dependent on a settlement of the minorities question.

Oct. 25. Marriage of Tsar Boris and
Princess Giovanna, daughter of
Victor Emmanuel III of Italy.
Gradual *rapprochement* between
Italy and Bulgaria.

1931, Jan.-Feb. Further frontier incidents
with Greece led to a tense situation
and mediation by the powers.

June 21. In the elections the Peasant
Party won a victory over the Democratic Entente, which had supported Zankov
and Liapchev. A new cabinet was formed
(June 29) by Alexander Malinov, Democrat, in alliance with the peasants.

Oct. 12. Cabinet of Nicholas Mushanov,
also a Democrat supported by the
Peasant Party.

1932, Feb. 8. Bulgaria denounced further
reparations payments.

Sept. 25. Striking success of the Communists in the Sofia municipal
elections. But in the communal
elections (Nov.) the Democrats
and Agrarians won an overwhelming victory.

1933, June 24. The government arrested over a thousand Communists and Macedonians.

Oct. 3. King Alexander visited Sofia, first step in the reconciliation of Yugoslavia and Bulgaria.

Dec. 10-13. Tsar Boris visited Belgrade and was given a tumultuous reception.

1934, Jan. 27. Boris visited King Charles of Rumania.

Feb. 8. Conclusion of the Balkan Pact, without Bulgaria, the government having refused, even by indirection, to recognize the *status quo* established by the peace treaties.

May 19. *Coup d'état* of army officers under Gen. Kimon Gueorguiev, who set up a dictatorship for one year. The policy of reconciliation with Yugoslavia was continued.

June 12. All political parties were declared abolished. Vigorous action taken against the Macedonians, chief opponents of the government's Yugoslav policy.

Sept. 12. Mihailov, the Macedonian leader, fled to Turkey.

1935, Jan. 22. Gueorguiev was forced out and his place taken by Gen. Petko Zlatev, supported by the tsar.

Apr. 18. A purely civilian cabinet was formed by Andrew Tochev, the officers' group having been weakened by factional dissension, and by a disastrous financial policy.

Oct. 2. A plot against the tsar resulted in the arrest of Gueorguiev and other officers, who were, however, soon released.

Nov. 23. A new cabinet was formed by George Kiosseivanov.

1936, Feb. Trial and conviction of a number of military men, including Damyon Veltchev, supposed to be the leader of the military party.

1936, Mar. The Military League was dissolved. To all intents and purposes Tsar Boris was master of the situation. He announced his intention of restoring the constitutional régime, but proceeded very cautiously in that direction. Political parties continued to be forbidden, and steps were taken to keep in check the Zankov group, which had National Socialist leanings.

1937, Jan. 24. CONCLUSION OF THE PACT OF FRIENDSHIP WITH YUGOSLAVIA, bringing to an end the long period of hostility and opening the way for closer relations between Bulgaria and the other Balkan powers.

Mar. The local elections resulted in a striking diminution of the government majorities and revealed the growing dislike for the tsar's personal system.

Oct. 13. More than forty political leaders petitioned the tsar for free elections and a return to constitutionalism. Thereupon the tsar promulgated a new electoral law providing for free voting by men and married women, but forbidding candidates to run as representatives of the old parties.

1938, Mar. The elections were held on four successive Sundays, and resulted in victory for a number of opponents of the government.

May 22. Parliament met for the first time since the military coup of 1935. Its powers were merely consultative.

July 31. AGREEMENT WITH GREECE (acting for the Balkan Entente) recognized Bulgaria's right to rearm. By this time Bulgarian rearmament (in contravention of the treaties) had already made considerable headway, Germany supplying much of the material. This did not, however, imply acceptance of National Socialism by the Bulgarian government. On the contrary, the National Socialist organization was disbanded (Apr. 30) and the government readily accepted an Anglo-French loan of $10,000,000 to support the rearmament program (Aug.). In the growing international tension of 1938-1939 Bulgaria, like most of the lesser states, was pulled this way and that. Great efforts were made to bring her into the Balkan Entente, but this courting merely enabled the government to demand more insistently a revision of the treaties. Claims to the Dobrudja created rather tense relations between Rumania and Bulgaria in the spring of 1939.

e. RUMANIA

1914-1927. FERDINAND I.

1917, July 14. An agrarian law (extended later, 1918-1921, to the new territories) broke up the crown lands and large estates, compensated the owners in state bonds, and distributed the land among the peasants. This policy, long overdue, practically ruined the Conservative Party.

1918, Nov. 10. Rumania re-entered the First World War and occupied Transylvania.

Nov. 27. The National Council of Bessarabia voted for unconditional union with Rumania. This act was not recognized by Russia and the Bessarabian question kept the two countries on tenter-hooks for many years.

Nov. 28. The Bukovina National Council voted for union with Rumania.

Dec. 1. Transylvania and the Banat voted for union.

Dec. 2. A government, headed by Julius Maniu, Transylvanian peasant leader, was soon (Dec. 14) obliged to give way to a cabinet under Ion Bratianu, leader of the Liberal Party, representing the industrial, commercial, and professional classes of the old kingdom.

1919, Apr. Beginning of the Rumanian advance into Hungary. The Rumanians ultimately occupied Budapest (Aug. 4) and did not evacuate until Nov. 14 (p. 1014).

May 18. Russia declared a state of war.

May 28. The Jews were emancipated and given full citizen rights, but anti-Semitism continued to be rampant, especially in the universities, which had to be closed repeatedly because of anti-Semitic riots.

Oct. Various peasant groups won a victory in the elections, but were unable to effect a change in the established régime.

1920, Mar. 2. Armistice with Russia.

Sept. 14. Rumania joined the League of Nations.

Oct. 28. England, France, Italy, and Japan recognized the Rumanian possession of Bessarabia. This treaty was not ratified by England and France until 1924, by Italy until 1927.

1921, Mar. 3. Defensive treaty with Poland and Hungary, directed against Russia.

Apr. 23. ALLIANCE WITH CZECHO-SLOVAKIA, part of the Little Entente treaties (p. 957).

June 7. ALLIANCE WITH YUGO-SLAVIA, completing the Little Entente.

1923-1930. Long dispute with Hungary regarding the disappropriation of Transylvanian landholders who had opted for Hungarian citizenship, and whose property rights were laid down in the treaties. All efforts by the League to effect a compromise failed.

1923, Mar. 27. The new constitution abolished the three-class system of voting and introduced the direct, secret ballot.

1924, Apr. Conference with Russia on the Bessarabian question broke down when Rumania refused to hold a plebiscite in the area.

Oct. 1. Introduction of the Gregorian calendar.

1925, Dec. 28. Prince Charles (Carol) renounced his right of succession to the throne and preferred to live in exile with his mistress, Mme. Lupescu. Bratianu and the Liberals were actively hostile to the prince.

1926, Mar. 25. A new electoral law provided that the party polling 40% of the votes should have one-half of the seats in parliament. This move was designed to prevent due representation to the various peasant parties, which were clamoring louder and louder against the existing régime.

Mar. 26. Treaty of alliance with Poland.

June 10. Treaty of friendship with France.

Sept. 16. Treaty of friendship with Italy, which made a large loan in return for oil and other concessions.

Oct. Fusion of the peasant parties to form the new National Peasants' Party, under Maniu's leadership.

1927, July 20. Death of King Ferdinand.

1927-1930. MICHAEL I (b. 1921). Principal regent Prince Nicholas, brother of Prince Charles, the father of Michael.

Nov. 24. Death of Ion Bratianu, energetic leader of the Liberal Party.

1928, Mar. 18. The peasants loudly demanded the dismissal of the cabinet.

May 6. Congress of the National Peasants' Party at Alba Julia, demanding representative government, decentralization, and reform.

Nov. 9. JULIUS MANIU became premier. He set out to purge the administration, make easier the influx of foreign capital, improve the lots of the peasants, etc.

Dec. 12. In the elections, at last free of pressure and corruption, the Peasants' Party scored a great victory.

1930, June 6. Prince Charles arrived by airplane and was accepted by Maniu. The parliament (June 8) revoked the law excluding him from the throne. Michael was put aside in favor of his father.

1930- CAROL (CHARLES) II. He very soon fell out with Maniu, brought back Mme. Lupescu, and attempted to establish his personal rule.

Oct. 6. Resignation of Maniu, because of ill health. He was succeeded by his lieutenant, George Mironescu.

Dec. 23. Ion Duca became leader of the Liberal Party on the death of Vintila Bratianu, brother of Ion.

1930. The optants' dispute with Hungary settled by the **Brocchi Plan** (worked out by Italy and England): Hungary was to assume the claims of the optants and was to receive contributions for this purpose from Czechoslovakia and other countries.

1931, Apr. 18. The king appointed a coalition (**National Union**) cabinet under Prof. **Nicholas Iorga**, his former tutor. This was regarded as a prelude to a royal dictatorship.

May. A new electoral law assigned 60% of the seats in parliament to professional groups.

June 1. In the elections, manipulated as of old, **the Peasants' Party was completely defeated.**

1932, Jan.-May. Negotiations with Russia, held under Polish auspices at Warsaw, failed to effect a settlement of the Bessarabian question.

May 31. Iorga resigned, after failure to secure a loan from France.

June 6. A new cabinet was formed by **Alexander Vaida-Voevod**, Peasant leader.

July 17. The Peasants won a great victory in the elections. But their position was weakened by the inability of Maniu to get along with the king and by rivalry between Maniu and Vaida-Voevod. **Oct. 20** Maniu took over the premiership (until Jan. 5, 1933).

1933, Jan. A system of **League supervision of Rumanian finances** was introduced for four years.

July. A PACT OF NON-AGGRESSION was finally concluded with Russia; this involved tacit recognition of Rumania's possession of Bessarabia, and was the direct result of the victory of Hitler in Germany and of Russia's preoccupation with the Far-Eastern situation.

Nov. 14. A cabinet was formed by Ion Duca, Liberal leader, the Liberals returning to power as a result of the disintegration of the Peasants' Party.

Dec. 20. In the elections the government groups won a great victory, as usual.

Dec. 29. Duca was assassinated by members of the **Iron Guard**, a fascist, strongly anti-Semitic organization, led by Corneliu Codreanu. Martial law was proclaimed at once and leaders of the Iron Guard arrested. **George Tartarescu** took over the premiership.

1934, Feb. 8. CONCLUSION OF THE BALKAN PACT between Rumania, Yugoslavia, Greece, and Turkey. The consummation of the plan was largely the work of **Nicholas Titulescu**, the Rumanian foreign minister.

May. The peasants supported the Liberal Party in frustrating an effort by the king to establish a dictatorship, following a plot against his life.

June 9. Agreement between Rumania, Poland, and Russia, guaranteeing each other's frontiers.

Sept. Reconciliation of **Maniu** and **Vaida-Voevod.** Renewed attacks of the Peasants' Party upon Mme. Lupescu and the royal camarilla. These were of little effect and the old feud between the peasant groups and the court soon was overshadowed by the rapid **spread of fascism and anti-Semitism.** Early in

1936, Feb. The anti-Semitic **Christian League**, headed by Prof. A. C. Cuza, and the **National Christian Party**, led by the poet Octavian Goga, united with one wing of the Peasants' Party, under Vaida-Voevod, thus forming a strong reactionary bloc not much different from the fascist Iron Guard.

Aug. 29. Foreign minister **Titulescu,** representing close connections with France, Russia, and the Little Entente against Germany, **was forced out** by the groups of the Right, which were favorable to Germany and Nazi ideals. Nevertheless the king and his ministers attempted to maintain friendly relations with France and Czechoslovakia, buying armaments from Prague with money lent by France.

1937, Dec. 21. The elections, to the surprise of the whole world, resulted in **a defeat for the government.** Thereupon the Tartarescu government resigned (Dec. 26) and King Carol, once more astounding the world, appointed

Dec. 28. OCTAVIAN GOGA prime minister, despite the fact that his National Christian Party had gained only 10% of the votes in the election. Goga at once embarked upon an orgy of **anti-Semitic legislation,** forbidding Jews to own land, depriving those naturalized after 1920 of their citizenship, barring Jews from the professions, etc. At the same time Goga aimed at the establishment of a dictatorship by sending his party troops into all localities.

1938, Jan. 18. King Carol dissolved the Parliament, which had not yet met. New elections were arranged for March. This unconstitutional procedure led to protests from the non-fascist parties, while the anti-Semitic policy quickly brought the country to the verge of business collapse. Remonstrances from England and France appear also to have undermined Goga's position. Thereupon

Feb. 10. The king dismissed Goga, using as a pretext the fact that the courts had invalidated several of the anti-Semitic laws. Goga and the fascists had thoroughly discredited themselves and thereby had really strengthened the position of the king, who now assumed complete control of the situation. A new "concentration" cabinet, containing seven former premiers, was established under the leadership of the patriarch, **Miron Cristea. The constitution was suspended and all political parties were suppressed.** Rigid censorship was instituted. These moves were violently opposed both by the fascist Iron Guard and by the Peasants' Party of Maniu, but

Feb. 24. A plebiscite, properly managed by the government, approved **Carol's action** by an overwhelming vote (only 5300 opposed). The king thereupon decreed that in future the Senate should be one-half appointive, that only the crown might initiate legislation, and that the ruler might govern by decree. A new electoral law restricted the franchise to those of 30 years of age and provided for elections on an occupational basis.

Apr. 19. Codreanu was condemned to 6 months' imprisonment for libel, and then (May 27) to 10 years at hard labor for treason. The government's attack upon the fascists now assumed major proportions, hundreds of Iron Guardists being arrested and imprisoned after discovery of an alleged plot against the king.

Aug. 4. A new nationalities statute gave minorities equal rights with Rumanians in language, religion, and race. This was evidently a move designed to secure the government wider support. By a new **administrative arrangement** (Aug. 13) the old racial divisions were wiped out and a new system of 10 provinces was inaugurated.

Nov. 30. DEATH OF CODREANU. He and 13 other Iron Guardists were reported shot by their guards while being moved from one prison to another. The explanation did not satisfy everyone, least of all the German Nazis, who described the episode as cold murder. But the Rumanian government persisted in the chosen course and stopped at nothing to stamp out the fascist movement.

1939, Mar. 6. Armand Calinescu became **premier** on the death of Patriarch Cristea.

Apr. 13. Great Britain and France guaranteed Rumanian independence and integrity following the German annihilation of Czechoslovakia and rumors of a German ultimatum to Rumania. But the Bucharest government nevertheless concluded a **commercial agreement with Germany** giving the latter broad scope for expansion and control of Rumanian industry. In short, the government attempted to straddle the two groups of powers in Europe.

May 10. In the elections under the new system (only official candidates, elected by professional organizations) the government secured a docile body. Both the chamber of deputies and the Senate was reduced in number by one-third.

---

12. RUSSIA
(UNION OF SOCIALIST SOVIET REPUBLICS)

On Germany's declaration of war (Aug. 1, 1914), the opposition parties in Russia declared their readiness to put aside domestic quarrels and support the government in the work of national defense. Since the government failed to respond, political discontent developed rapidly. Public opinion was deeply stirred by

1915, May. The great **Russian defeat in Galicia** (p. 922), and openly accused the government of inefficiency and criminal negligence in failing to supply the armies.

June 25. The tsar was obliged to dismiss Gen. Sukhomlinov, the minister of war (tried and convicted by the

provisional government in 1917), and to admit representatives of the Duma and other public bodies (the Union of Zemstvos and Municipalities, the War Industry Committee, etc.) to direct participation in the work of army supply and the mobilization of industry. Nicholas refused, however, to comply with the demand of the progressive bloc in the Duma for an entirely new ministry enjoying the confidence of the country and committed to a more liberal policy. The situation was aggravated when

Sept. 5. The tsar decided to dismiss the popular commander in chief, **Grand Duke Nicholas,** and to assume the command himself. The tsar's absence from the capital opened the way for **domination of the Empress Alexandra,** known to be bitterly hostile to the Duma and to be under the influence of the notorious adventurer, **Gregory Rasputin.** The government was completely discredited in the eyes of the public when

1916, Feb. 3. Boris Stürmer, arch-conservative and allegedly pro-German, replaced Goremykin as **chief of the cabinet.** July 23 Stürmer took charge of the foreign office. Rumors of treason in high places undermined the morale of the army and of the population generally. To all this was added a **grave economic problem:** shortage of labor, due to repeated mobilizations; disorganization of railroad transport, failure of food and fuel supplies in the cities.

Nov. 18. Meeting of the Duma. In a turbulent session the leaders denounced the "dark forces" in the government and warned the country of impending disaster unless there was an immediate change of policy.

Nov. 24. Alexander Trepov replaced Stürmer as president of the council of ministers and the government embarked upon a policy of repression of dissatisfaction. But opposition continued, and

Dec. 30. Rasputin was assassinated by Prince Felix Yussupov and other aristocrats. Even these drastic measures were barren of results, and in some political and military circles there was discussion of a palace revolution. Before any plans could materialize

1917, Mar. 8. Strikes and riots broke out in St. Petersburg (named *Petrograd* at the beginning of the war). These were followed by

Mar. 10. A general mutiny of the troops in the capital, which sealed the fate of the old régime.

Mar. 11. The Duma refused to obey an imperial decree ordering its dissolution, and established

Mar. 12. A PROVISIONAL GOVERNMENT, headed by **Prince George Lvov** (chairman of the Union of Zemstvos and Municipalities). The new government included Prof. **Paul Miliukov,** leader of the Constitutional Democrats (as minister for foreign affairs); **Alexander Guchkov,** leader of the Octobrists (minister of war); and **Alexander Kerensky,** the only Socialist (minister of justice).

Mar. 15. Nicholas II abdicated for himself and his son in favor of his brother Michael, who in turn (Mar. 16) abdicated in favor of the provisional government pending election by a constituent assembly.

Mar.-Nov. THE RULE OF THE PROVISIONAL GOVERNMENT. At the very outset the new régime proclaimed the **civic liberties** and recognized legal equality of all citizens without social, religious, or racial discrimination. **Finland** was recognized as independent within a Russian federation (Mar. 21); **Poland's** complete independence was accepted (Mar. 30); **Estonia** was granted autonomy (Apr. 12). At the same time the government announced a program of far-reaching **social reforms,** including distribution of land among the peasants (confiscation of imperial and monastery lands, Mar. 30). But the decision on these and other matters was reserved for the **constituent assembly,** which was being arranged for. From the very outset the provisional government, essentially liberal and bourgeois, found itself in

Conflict with the Petrograd Soviet (*Council of Workers' and Soldiers' Deputies*), which had been organized by the Socialists Mar. 12. The government pledged itself (Mar. 18, May 1) to the continuation of the war against the Central Powers, in common with the Allies, until the attainment of a "victorious end." It attempted to maintain and increase the efficiency of the army and proceeded but cautiously toward its democratization. The Soviet leaders, on the other hand, insisted on a radical revision of war aims, renunciation of secret diplomatic agreements concluded by the tsarist government (and promising Russia Constantinople), and the speedy conclusion of a "general democratic peace," without annexations or indemnities. Suspecting the generals of counter-revolutionary tendencies, the Soviet issued (Mar. 14) the famous *Order No. 1,* which deprived the officers of all authority excepting for strategic operations, and entrusted the administration of the army to committees elected by both officers and men. The counter-order of the provisional government was virtually ignored and the committee system was subsequently introduced in all army detachments. The antagonism of the Soviet against the government became more outspoken when

Apr. 16. Vladimir **Lenin,** Zinoviev, Radek, Lunacharski, and other Bolshevik leaders **arrived at Petrograd** from Switzerland, having been transported through Germany in a sealed carriage, the German high command having calculated that these extremists would soon undermine the pro-Allied provisional government. **Lenin's program** was: (1) Transfer of power from the "bourgeois" provisional government to the Soviets; (2) immediate cessation of the war, if necessary by the acceptance of a separate peace with the Central Powers; (3) immediate seizure of land by the peasants, without awaiting the decision of the constituent assembly; (4) control of industry by committees of workers. Lenin was ably supported by **Leon Trotsky** (Bronstein), who returned from the United States and England early in May, but his program was not accepted by the more moderate (Menshevik) wing of the Socialist Party, nor by the Social Revolutionaries. Consequently much difference of opinion and considerable friction was generated within the Soviet.

May 14, 16. Guchkov and Miliukov were obliged to resign from the provisional government as a result of agitation over war aims and army organization. The government was remade, and now accepted a policy of no annexations and no indemnities, though still declaring against a separate peace. Several Socialists were included in the cabinet, and **Kerensky became minister of war.** He undertook to revive the war spirit and the fighting power of the army on the basis of the new "revolutionary discipline." After a spectacular visit to the front and a stirring appeal to the soldiers, he ordered the

June 29-July 7. Russian offensive against the Austro-German forces. After a brief initial success the offensive collapsed and the disorganized Russian troops were completely defeated (p. 940). The radicals now took the initiative.

July 16-18. The Bolsheviks attempted to seize power in Petrograd, but the effort was clearly premature. The movement was suppressed by the government and many of the leaders (including Trotsky) were arrested. Lenin managed to escape and went into hiding in Finland. This coup, as well as disagreement between ministers regarding the burning question of land reform and the status of national minorities (assumption of power in the Ukraine by the local Rada, June 26; establishment of Gen. Kaledin as hetman of the Don Cossacks, June 30; Finnish declaration of complete independence, July 20), resulted in

July 20. The resignation of Prince Lvov, whose place was taken by Kerensky. The position of the government, however, remained very precarious, in view of the growing restlessness of the masses, who suffered from war-weariness and material privations, and were all too ready to listen to Bolshevik propaganda. On the other hand, the conservative elements opposed the government because of its alleged weakness in dealing with the Bolsheviks. The advocates of a strong line found a champion

in Gen. **Lavr Kornilov,** recently appointed commander in chief. A rift between Kerensky and Kornilov finally led to

Sept. 9-14. The Kornilov attack upon the government. Kerensky had dismissed Kornilov, who refused to obey and ordered his troops to advance on Petrograd, his avowed aim being to destroy the Soviet and liberate the provisional government from Socialist domination. The movement broke down because of defection on the part of many soldiers and because of mobilization of the radical elements in the capital, to whom Kerensky appealed for support against the "counter-revolution" (Trotsky and some other Bolshevik leaders were released from prison). **Kornilov was defeated,** but Kerensky now found himself under the domination of his Bolshevik allies. The masses had come to suspect of counter-revolutionary designs not only the army command, but the provisional government also. Bolshevik influence made rapid headway among the factory workers and among the soldiers of the Petrograd garrison. In Oct. the Bolsheviks secured a majority in the Soviet, Trotsky becoming its chairman. Thereupon Lenin decided to attempt a coup.

Nov. 6. (O.S. Oct. 24). **THE BOL-SHEVIK REVOLUTION.** The Bolsheviks, led by the military revolutionary committee, the soldiers of the Petrograd garrison, the sailors from Kronstadt, and the workers' Red Guards, captured most of the government offices, took the Winter Palace by storm, and arrested the members of the provisional government. **Kerensky managed to escape,** and, after a futile attempt to organize resistance, went into hiding and subsequently into exile abroad.

Nov. 7. The Second All-Russian Congress of Soviets, from which the moderate Socialists bolted, approved the coup and handed over power to the Bolsheviks.

The history of Russia (*Union of Soviet Socialist Republics*) after Nov. 1917 may be conveniently divided into **three periods:** (1) The **Period of Militant Communism** (1917-1921); (2) the **Period of the New Economic Policy** (1921-1927); (3) the **Period of the New Socialist Offensive** (1928-).

The new government (organized Nov. 7) assumed the name *Council of People's Commissars.* It was headed by **Lenin,** and included **Trotsky** (commissar for foreign affairs), **Joseph Stalin** (commissar for national minorities). To protect itself and to crush opposition, the council organized (Dec. 20) the *Extraordinary Commission to*

Combat Counter-Revolution (the *Cheka*, later known as the *G.P.U.*).

Nov. 25. **The elections to the constituent assembly** returned 420 Social Revolutionaries as against only 225 Bolsheviks. When the assembly met in Petrograd (Jan. 18, 1918) it was dispersed at once by the Red Troops. Therewith one of the most influential elements of the opposition was disposed of. Some of the Social Revolutionaries joined in the anti-Bolshevik movements which soon began to take form.

1917-1921. **SOCIAL AND ECONOMIC POLICY.** The victorious Bolsheviks at once undertook the reorganization of society along collectivist lines. A **Land Decree** (Nov. 7) ordered immediate partition of the large estates and distribution to the peasants. But Feb. 19, 1918, the **nationalization of the land** was proclaimed (all land to be the property of the state, and only those willing to cultivate it themselves to be permitted to use it). No further efforts were made in the direction of collectivization, but when the civil war brought the cities and the armies into danger of starvation, the peasants were ordered (Dec. 14, 1920) to turn over to the government their entire surplus (the **food levy**). As they were reluctant to do so, and saw no prospect of any return in industrial goods, the government was driven to adopt **forcible requisitioning**, which created widespread discontent.

On their advent to power the Bolsheviks at once declared all **banks nationalized**, confiscating private accounts. The **national debt was repudiated** (Jan. 28, 1918). The workmen were given **control over the factories** (Nov. 28, 1917), and by the summer of 1918 all the larger plants (and subsequently the smaller ones also) were nationalized (law of June 28, 1918). The workers were instructed to join **government-controlled trade unions**, and were denied the right to strike. In emergencies the government resorted to a system of **compulsory labor**. Private trade was gradually suppressed and the government undertook the distribution of food and other commodities among the urban populations, using a **rationing system** as the basis and making use also of the co-operatives. All **Church property was confiscated** (Dec. 17, 1917) and all religious instruction in the schools was abolished. Only civil marriages were thenceforth to be recognized. The Gregorian calendar was introduced on Jan. 31, 1918.

1917-1918. **CONCLUSION OF PEACE WITH THE CENTRAL POWERS.** In accordance with its avowed policy, the new government at once (Nov. 7) published a **Decree of Peace**, that is, an appeal to all belligerent states to start immediate peace parleys. The Russian commander, Gen. Dukhonin, was dismissed (Nov. 21) for refusing to offer an armistice. His place was taken by the Bolshevik, Krylenko.

Nov. 22. Trotsky again proposed to the Allies the conclusion of an armistice. The Allies, unwilling to accept a peace on the basis of no annexations and no indemnities, evaded, but the Germans expressed their readiness to negotiate (Nov. 28). Thereupon the Bolshevik government, in order to expose the designs of the capitalist governments, published (Dec. 5 *et seq.*) the **secret treaties** concluded between Russia and her allies. At the same time

Dec. 5. **An armistice was concluded between Russia and the Central Powers.** Negotiations were opened at Brest-Litovsk Dec. 3, but broke down Dec. 28 when it was revealed that the Germans demanded the cession of Poland and the western Russian territories, supposedly on the basis of self-determination. The Germans therefore arranged for

1918, Jan. 28. **The independence of the Ukraine,** with which they concluded a separate peace (Feb. 9). By way of protest the Bolsheviks

Feb. 10. **Ended the war by proclamation,** but this failed to satisfy the Germans, who resumed the offensive (Feb. 18), advanced on Petrograd and thereby obliged the Bolsheviks to conclude the

Mar. 3. **TREATY OF BREST-LITOVSK,** by which Russia lost Poland, the Ukraine, and all of the borderlands occupied by non-Russian nationalities.

Mar. 9. **The government moved** the capital from Petrograd (renamed Leningrad, Jan. 26, 1924) **to Moscow.** This was partly due to the exposed position of Petrograd with relation to the Germans and their satellites, and partly to the threat of counter-revolution emanating from the borderlands. Monarchists and members of the propertied classes, who favored political and economic restoration, as well as Liberals and Moderate Socialists who were opposed to the Communistic dictatorship were all more or less united in their refusal to accept the disastrous Brest-Litovsk Treaty. The British and French, who regarded the Bolsheviks as the tools of the German general staff and who were eager to keep supplies and munitions from falling into the hands of the Germans, encouraged and supported movements among the opponents of the Bolsheviks. **Independent governments** were established all along the Russian frontiers (**Lithuania**, Dec. 11, 1917; **Moldavia**, Dec. 15; **Republic of the Don**, Jan. 10, 1918; **Ukraine**, Jan. 28; **Transcaucasia**, Apr. 22, etc.). The revolt of the Don Cossacks, led by Gens. **Kornilov** and **Kaledin**, Dec. 9, 1917, may be said to mark the beginning of the

1918-1920. GREAT CIVIL WAR. The Bolshevik government was at first faced with the prospect of war without anything like an adequate trained force. During the first period of the war it suffered one reverse after another, but gradually a new **Red Army** of volunteers was organized. Under the leadership of Trotsky (who had become commissar for war) it developed into a regular army based on conscription and subject to strict discipline. The Bolsheviks had the advantage of fighting on the inside lines and they derived a certain measure of support from the fact that they were defending Russian territory. At the same time the lack of cohesion among the counter-revolutionary movements and the fitful attitude of the Allied Powers constantly hampered the operations of the Whites.

(1) **The War with the Cossacks.** Operations began with the new year. Gen. **Kaledin** committed suicide after a defeat (Feb. 13) and Gen. **Kornilov** was killed in battle soon afterward (Apr. 13). The command in the south was taken over by Gen. **Denikin**, supported by Gen. **Krasnov** (hetman of the Don Cossacks, May 11).

(2) **The Struggle for the Ukraine.** The Ukraine had declared its independence of Russia (Jan. 28, 1918) and the Moderate Socialist government at Kiev had concluded a separate peace with the Germans and Austrians (Feb. 9). Thereupon the Bolsheviks attacked and took **Kiev** (Feb. 18), but they were soon ejected by the Germans (Mar. 2), who then took also Odessa (Mar. 13) and overran the whole Ukraine, from which they tried, rather unsuccessfully, to secure much-needed food supplies. With German aid a more conservative government, under Gen. **Skoropadsky**, was set up, but after the end of the World War, Skoropadsky was overthrown (Nov. 15) by the Ukrainian Socialists, under Gen. **Simon Petliura**. The French occupied **Odessa** (Dec. 18), but the Bolsheviks, having assumed the offensive, took Kiev (Feb. 3, 1919) and expelled the Allied forces from Odessa (Apr. 8). **The Ukraine became a Soviet Republic**, which was conquered by the White armies of Gen. Denikin (Aug.– Dec. 1919) only to be retaken by the Bolsheviks (Dec. 17) and then invaded by the

Poles (May 7, 1920). The Bolsheviks managed to drive the Poles back and Dec. 28 concluded a treaty with the Ukrainian Soviet government, recognizing the latter's independence. Dec. 30 the Ukraine joined with the other Soviet Republics to form the Union of Socialist Soviet Republics.

(3) **The War in White Russia and the Baltic region.** Most of this area continued to be occupied or dominated by the Germans down to and beyond the conclusion of the World War armistice. In the autumn of 1919 a White army under Gen. **Yudenitch** advanced on Petrograd (Oct. 19), but was forced back by the Bolsheviks. The Soviet government recognized the **independence of Estonia** (Feb. 2, 1920), **of Lithuania** (July 12), **of Latvia** (Aug. 11), **and of Finland** (Oct. 14). White Russia continued to be a Soviet Republic until its union with the other Soviet Republics in 1922.

(4) **Allied intervention in northern Russia.** The British landed a force at Murmansk June 23, 1918, primarily with the object of holding German forces in the east and of protecting Allied stores from falling into hostile hands. Aug. 2 the **British and French took Archangel** and began to support a puppet **government of northern Russia**. The Americans also sent a force, and during the spring of 1919 there was considerable fighting between the Allies and the Bolsheviks. The French were the most ardent advocates of more extensive intervention against the Bolsheviks, but neither the British nor the Americans were willing, after the armistice, to go beyond financial and other support for the anti-Bolshevik movements. Sept. 30, 1919, the Allies abandoned Archangel and then (Oct. 12) Murmansk. These territories were quickly taken over by the Bolsheviks.

(5) **Campaigns of Denikin and Wrangel in the Caucasus and southern Russia.** The Caucasian states (**Georgia**, **Armenia**, and **Azerbaijan**) declared their independence Apr. 22 and May 26, 1918. After the withdrawal of the Germans and Austrians from southern Russia, the Bolsheviks made an effort to reconquer this territory, so valuable for its oil, but Gen. **Denikin** defeated them (Jan. 1919). After a rather spectacular advance northward, Denikin was himself driven back to the Black Sea coast (Apr.), where he maintained himself until the autumn. In another swift offensive he then captured Odessa (Aug. 18) and took Kiev (Sept. 2), only to be forced to retreat again (Dec.). By Mar. 27, 1920, his last base fell to the Bolsheviks and Denikin turned over the command to Gen. **Wrangel.** The Bolsheviks meanwhile advanced into the Caucasus and took Baku (Apr. 28), but

Wrangel, starting from the region north of the Sea of Azov, began to overrun much of southern Russia (June–Nov.). Finally, however, the Bolshevik forces, freed by the conclusion of the war with Poland (see below), were able to concentrate against Wrangel, who was forced back to the Crimea (Nov. 1) and then obliged to evacuate his army to Constantinople (Nov. 14). Early in 1921 **Soviet governments were set up in Georgia** (Feb. 25) **and in Armenia** (Apr. 2). By the treaty with Turkey (Oct. 13) **Batum was restored to Russia.** Mar. 12, 1922, the Soviet governments of Georgia, Armenia, and Azerbaijan were combined to form the **Transcaucasian Socialist Soviet Republic,** which Dec. 30 became part of the larger Union of Socialist Soviet Republics.

(6) **The war in Siberia and eastern Russia.** Japanese forces were landed at **Vladivostok** Dec. 30, 1917, at a time when the **Czech legions** (organized before the revolution out of large numbers of Austrian war prisoners) had already started their march toward Vladivostok with the purpose of ultimately joining the Allied forces in Europe. Disagreement between them and the Soviet government led to armed conflict (June 1918), in the course of which the **Czechs seized control of the Trans-Siberian Railway** and formed an alliance with local anti-Bolshevik forces. An autonomous Siberian government had already been formed at Omsk. This government later merged with the directory organized in Ufa by former members of the constituent assembly (mostly Moderate Socialists). Meanwhile the Czechs extended their operations to the Volga region, taking Ekaterinburg (July 26) and other places. At Omsk the military and conservative elements executed a coup (Nov. 18) by which the Socialists were forced out of the government and **Adm. Alexander Kolchak was proclaimed** *Supreme Ruler of Russia.* His Siberian White army then staged an **advance into eastern Russia,** capturing Perm (Dec. 24) and Ufa. But the Bolsheviks initiated a vigorous counter-offensive, taking Orenburg and Ekaterinburg (Jan. 25, 27, 1919) and gradually forcing Kolchak back into Siberia. They recaptured Omsk (Nov. 14) and forced the White army to fall back on Irkutsk. Kolchak gave way to Gen. Semenov (Dec. 17) and was subsequently captured and executed by the Bolsheviks (Feb. 7). The Bolsheviks attempted to take Vladivostok by a coup (Jan. 30), but were obliged to yield to the greater power of the Japanese. In order to avoid conflict, the Soviet government of Russia set up a buffer state in eastern Siberia (Apr. 6). This was known as the **Far Eastern Republic,** with capital at Chita. When the Japanese finally evacuated Vladivostok (Oct. 25, 1922), the city was occupied by troops of the Far Eastern Republic, which was itself annexed to Soviet Russia Nov. 19, 1922.

Other important developments of this confused and crucial period were:

1918, July 6. The assassination of the German ambassador, **Count von Mirbach,** by a social revolutionary. This resulted in increased demands by the Germans on Russia, which in turn ruined all hope of cordial relations between Germany and the Soviet government.

July 10. PROMULGATION OF THE SOVIET CONSTITUTION, which was adopted by the Fifth All-Russian Congress of Soviets. The main lines of the soviet system were these: (1) **Local soviets** elected representatives to the **provincial congresses of soviets,** which in turn sent delegates to the **All-Russian** (subsequently **All-Union**) **Congress of Soviets;** (2) the latter elected the **executive committee,** a permanent body which acted in the intervals between sessions of the congress; the congress also elected the **council of people's commissars;** (3) elections were held on an occupational, and not on a territorial basis: the factory workers were more generously represented than the peasants, while the "non-toiling" bourgeois classes (including the clergy) were disenfranchised; (4) All elections were open, with no provision for secret ballot. In practice this system of "soviet democracy" was dominated by a **dictatorship of** (or for) **the proletariat,** and this in turn was exercised by the Bolshevik Party (renamed the **Communist Party** in Mar. 1918). No other parties were permitted, and the press and other channels of expression were put under sweeping government control. The Communist Party was governed by a **central committee,** within which there was a smaller group called the **political bureau.** This latter was the real governing body of the country. Lenin's authority remained supreme in both party and government until his death.

July 16. Murder of Nicholas II, Tsarina Alexandra, and their children in a cellar at Ekaterinburg, where they had been kept in captivity. On the outbreak of the revolution the imperial family had been confined first in the palace of Tsarskoe Selo. Thence it had been moved to Tobolsk and finally (Apr. 1918) to Ekaterinburg. The murder was perpetrated by local Bolsheviks who feared the imminent capture of the city by the advancing Czechs and Whites.

Aug. 30. An attempt was made by a social revolutionary to assassinate Lenin. Coming at the time of severe crisis, this move created a panic and inaugurated a systematic reign of terror by the Bolsheviks, in the course of which huge numbers of intellectuals and bourgeois of all types were wiped out.

1919, Mar. 2. Foundation of the Third International (Communist), an organization for the propagation of communist doctrine abroad with the purpose of bringing about the world revolution, on which Lenin and his associates reckoned with confidence in the stormy period following the end of the war.

1920, Apr. 25-Oct. 12. WAR WITH POLAND which, in agreement with Petliura, attempted to wrest the Ukraine from the Bolsheviks. The Poles quickly overran the country, taking Kiev (May 7), but the Bolsheviks launched a vigorous counter-attack, and drove the Poles out of Kiev (June 11) and Vilna (July 15). By Aug. 14 the Russians were on the outskirts of Warsaw. But the Poles, vigorously aided by the French (Gen. **Weygand**) made a stand and were soon able to turn the tables. The Bolsheviks were forced to fall back and abandon their Polish conquests. The preliminary treaty of Riga (Oct. 12) was followed by the definitive **Treaty of Riga** (Mar. 18, 1921), which defined the frontier between the two countries.

The effects of the Allied blockade and of the devastating civil war, together with the revolutionary economic policy of the government, led to an almost complete **collapse of the Russian economy** by 1921. There was a sharp decline in production in both industry and agriculture, widespread disorganization of transport, acute shortage of food and fuel, especially in the cities. Popular discontent found expression in numerous **peasant uprisings** during 1920 and in rioting of the factory workers in Petrograd, culminating finally in

1921, Feb. 23-Mar. 17. The mutiny and uprising of the sailors at Kronstadt, which was put down only with difficulty and after much bloodshed. This situation finally forced the Communist Party to adopt

Mar. 17 *et seq.* **THE NEW ECONOMIC POLICY** (often spoken of as the *NEP*), sponsored by Lenin himself. To placate the peasants, the **food levy was abolished,** and in its place there was introduced a limited **grain tax,** thus leaving the peasants at least part of the surplus. To enable them to dispose of this surplus, **freedom of trade** within the country was **partially restored.** Subsequently (1922) a

new **land statute** was passed which made possible reconstruction of small individual farms and even permitted, under certain conditions, limited use of hired labor and lease of land. In industry some of the small plants were returned to former owners and licenses were given to private persons to start new enterprises. **Private commercial establishments** were also permitted in the cities. In course of time the **financial system** was recast on a semi-capitalistic basis: the state bank was given the right to issue bills backed either by goods or by foreign bonds; attempts were made to stabilize the currency (the devaluated paper money was replaced by the new *chervonets* bills). Large industry and transport, however, remained nationalized, and foreign trade continued to be a government monopoly.

The *NEP* was declared to be a "temporary retreat" from communism, necessary for purposes of economic reconstruction. After the **great famine** of 1921–1922 (caused by drought, but aggravated by the economic collapse that preceded it), the national economy recovered at a rapid pace. Production in industry and agriculture reached the pre-war level and there was marked improvement in living standards both in the cities and in the countryside. Along with this recovery went an **abatement of the Red terror** and a slight relaxation of governmental censorship and repression. With the end of the civil war, more attention could be given to cultural work, and the government introduced an ambitious **educational program** aiming at a speedy elimination of illiteracy.

1922, Apr. 10-May 19. Russia took part in the economic conference at **Genoa** (p. 958), thus for the first time indicating a readiness to collaborate with non-Bolshevik countries for common ends. The conference ended in failure, though it resulted in

Apr. 16. THE TREATY OF RAPALLO between Germany and Soviet Russia. The agreement provided for economic co-operation and established close political connections. Despite the indignation of the other powers, Russia and Germany, as outcast powers, held steadfastly to the pact, which was supplemented by a commercial treaty (Oct. 12, 1925), periodically renewed, even after Hitler's advent to power in Germany.

Dec. 30. The Union of Socialist Soviet Republics was organized, bringing together Russia, the Ukraine, White Russia, and Transcaucasia in one federation. The member states retained a large measure of cultural autonomy, but political control was exercised from Moscow through the All-Union Communist Party organization.

1924, Jan. 21. THE DEATH OF LENIN. This important event marked the beginning of a struggle for power within the inner councils of the party and the government. The chief contestants were **Trotsky** and **Stalin.** The latter at first allied himself with **Leo Kamenev** (Rosenfeld) and **Gregory Zinoviev** (Radomyslsky), but these two soon quarreled with Stalin and adhered to the opposition bloc of Trotsky. Open conflict of the factions broke out in 1926.

Feb. 1. Great Britain recognized the Bolshevik régime, and was soon followed by most of the other European and some extra-European powers (Italy, Feb. 7; France, Oct. 28).

1925, Jan. 21. Japan recognized the Soviet government and agreed to withdraw from northern Sakhalin (evacuation Apr. 4).

May 12. Revision of the federal constitution. A number of new republics were added to the federation (**Uzbekistan, Turkmenistan, Kazakistan,** etc.).

1926, July-Oct. Victory of Stalin over the Leftist opposition bloc led by Trotsky. This group insisted on discontinuation of the *NEP* policy, the speeding-up of "socialist construction," and the active resumption of work for the world revolution. Trotsky held that a communist régime in one country was an anomaly and that the proletarian revolution could be safe only when the whole world had been directed into the same channel. Trotsky, Zinoviev, Radek, and other leaders were now expelled from the political bureau of the party.

1927, May 26. Great Britain severed relations with Soviet Russia because of continued Bolshevik propaganda in contravention of treaty agreements.

Dec. 27. Definitive victory of the Stalin faction over the Trotsky group, when the 15th All-Union Congress of the Communist Party condemned all "deviation from the general party line" as interpreted by Stalin. Trotsky and his followers were banished to the provinces after expulsion from the party. In Jan. 1929 **Trotsky was expelled from the Union** and was obliged to take refuge in Constantinople. Later he moved to Norway and ultimately to Mexico. The same party congress made several decisions which signified the end of the *NEP* and the inauguration of a

1928- NEW SOCIALIST OFFENSIVE. A program of speedy industrialization was introduced in the form of several successive **Five-Year Plans** (beginning Oct. 1, 1928). In the realization of this program considerable success was achieved in the **development of heavy industries** (primarily for purposes of national defense). But production of manufactured products still lagged far behind the needs of the population and the government was constantly faced with inefficiency, to say nothing of ill-will (1930– : a series of **trials of technicians** for mismanagement and sabotage). In the field of agriculture the government now returned to a policy of socialization by pooling individual peasant farms in large concerns, such as the **collective farms** (*kolkhoz*) and the **state farms** (*sovkhoz*). The collectivization campaign in the villages was carried out by means of both propaganda and coercion (drastic measures against the recalcitrant peasants and especially against the well-to-do farmers or *kulaks*, who were completely wiped out). The objectives of the government were substantially achieved, and within a few years the great majority of the peasants were collectivized, the government controlling the output of the new farms.

1929, Nov. 17. Expulsion of Bukharin and other members of the Rightist opposition. This group had advocated further concession to the peasants along the lines of the *NEP*. Stalin was now undisputed master of the situation and dictator of Russia.

Dec. 22. An agreement with China brought to an end a prolonged dispute and a period of acute tension over the conflicting claims to the **Chinese Eastern Railway.** In the period from 1924 to 1926 the Soviet government had actively supported the nationalist movement in China, but after a quarrel the Russian agents had been expelled and relations had rapidly degenerated.

1932-1933. Another severe famine swept over Russia, due in part, at least, to the excesses of the government's agrarian policy. The famine centered in the Ukraine and the northern Caucasus and the government did its utmost to conceal it from the world. The desperate situation resulted in a reduction of the amount of foodstuffs taken by the state and in permission to the collective farms to sell at least part of their surplus produce.

1932, July 25. Conclusion of non-aggression pacts with Poland, Estonia, Latvia, and Finland, followed by a similar agreement with France (Nov. 29). These pacts reflected the government's uneasiness about developments in the Far East, notably the establishment of the Manchukuoan state under Japanese auspices. Relations between Russia and Japan degenerated rapidly and considerable tension developed with regard to the **Chinese Eastern Railway**. This particular issue was settled by the sale of the Russians' interest for 140,000,000 yen (Mar. 23, 1935), but Japanese activity on the border of **Outer Mongolia** (allied to Russia and really under Russian protection) gave rise to a series of "incidents" of a dangerous nature. As a result of Japanese expansion in eastern Asia and the growing threat to the Russian position, the Moscow government not only attempted to stabilize relations with its European neighbors, but began to take an active part in the **Disarmament Conference** (p. 962) and in general international co-operation. This new departure was signalized by a notable lull in the activities of the Third International.

1933. Purge of the Communist Party. About one-third of the members (1,000,000) were expelled for one reason or another. In Apr. a number of British engineers were put on trial for sabotage. The British government protested and put an embargo on Russian goods. Though convicted, the engineers were permitted to leave the country, but Anglo-Russian relations continued to be distant.

Nov. 17. Recognition of the Soviet government by the United States brought to an end a long period of estrangement. Trade relations were opened and the Russian government promised to abstain from propaganda in the United States.

1934, Apr. 4. The non-aggression pacts with Poland and the Baltic states were extended into 10-year agreements. In view of the National Socialist victory in Germany (p. 1000) and the openly expressed hostility of the new German régime to communism, the Soviet Union felt more than ever endangered. Trade relations with Germany continued and even developed for a few years, but the Moscow government at once embarked upon an extensive **program of armament** on land, sea, and air. Within a few years the Russians had a formidable air fleet and had made considerable progress toward the construction of a powerful navy (esp. submarines). In accord with the effort to secure support in Europe, Russia made

June 9. Agreements with Czechoslovakia and Rumania, at long last recognizing the loss of Bessarabia. Above all the government

Sept. 18. JOINED THE LEAGUE OF NATIONS, which before had been roundly denounced. Russia now took an active part in all work for the furtherance of collective security and supported France in the scheme for an eastern European pact along the lines of the Locarno agreements.

Dec. 1. The assassination of Serge Kirov, a close collaborator of Stalin, revealed the existence of a strong and desperate opposition to the régime within the ranks of the Communist Party itself. The incident was followed by another **outbreak** of terror and by repeated "purges" of the party and the administration. In several spectacular trials many of the most prominent of the older communist leaders were condemned.

1935, Jan. 15-17. Zinoviev, Kamenev, and several other leaders were **tried for treason** and conspiracy. They were convicted and imprisoned for terms of 5 to 10 years.

May 2. CONCLUSION OF THE FRANCO-RUSSIAN ALLIANCE. This was carefully fitted into the framework of the League of Nations, but in Germany was regarded as a pact directed against the Nazi régime.

May 16. An alliance between Russia and Czechoslovakia obliged the Russians to come to the assistance of Czechoslovakia in the event of attack, provided France decided to act. This agreement enraged the Germans all the more, and they repeatedly accused the Czechs of having made their country a base for Russian air operations against Germany.

July 25-Aug. 20. At a meeting of the Third International it was decided that Soviet Russia, in view of the growing tension between the democratic and fascist states, should throw its weight on the side of the democracies against the common enemy. Henceforth communists in other countries were to give up their opposition to military appropriations and to support the governments, even though these were bourgeois.

1936, Aug. 19-23. Zinoviev, Kamenev, and a group of their followers were put on trial again, this time as Trotskyists, accused of plotting with enemy powers against the existing régime in Russia. They openly confessed to most of the charges brought against them, much to the astonishment of the world. On conviction, sixteen of them were at once executed.

July. On the outbreak of the civil war in Spain (p. 983) the Russian government at once took the side of the Madrid government. While Italy and Germany supported Franco, Soviet Russia sent airplanes and other supplies to the Loyalists. This only served to enhance the division of Europe. In his Nürnberg speech (Sept.) Hitler denounced Bolshevism in the most violent fashion and made but little secret of German hopes of securing Russian territory. The position of Russia became extremely exposed when Nov. 25 **Germany and Japan concluded a pact directed against communism.** All these events drove Russia farther and farther in the direction of the democratic states, a policy which was reflected in

Dec. 5. ADOPTION OF A NEW "DEMOCRATIC" CONSTITUTION for Russia. The Soviet Federation was recast and the Union thenceforth was composed as follows: (1) **Russia;** (2) **Ukraine;** (3) **White Russia;** (4) **Azerbaijan;** (5) **Georgia;** (6) **Armenia;** (7) **Turkmenia;** (8) **Uzbekistan;** (9) **Tadzhikstan;** (10) **Kazakhstan;** (11) **Kirghistan.** Russia and subsequently all other states of the Union adopted an **electoral system** from which no elements in the country were any longer debarred: all votes were to be equal; elections to the higher assemblies were made direct; votes were to be cast on a territorial, not on an occupational basis; the secret ballot was introduced. The place of the congresses of soviets was taken by a two-chamber parliament (the **Supreme Soviet**), consisting of a **Council of Nationalities** (i.e. a federal chamber) and a **Union Council.** This parliament was to appoint a **Presidium** to act while the Council itself was not in session. All civic rights were guaranteed, but the Communist Party continued to be the only political group permitted in the country.

1937, Jan. 23-30. Piatakov, Radek, and other leaders were put on trial and convicted, thirteen of them suffering the death penalty. The various "purges" continued throughout the year and extended through the entire administration, ultimately reaching also the army and the diplomatic service. Political commissioners were appointed to watch over the army commands. May 31 **Marshal Gamarnik** was reported to have committed suicide, and

June 12. Marshal Tukhachevski and seven other generals of the highest rank were executed after a secret court-martial. They were accused of conspiracy with the Germans and the Japanese. There followed further purging, in the course of which all "Trotskyists" and others objectionable to Stalin were "liquidated." These executions and drastic persecutions made a miserable impression throughout the world and did much to discredit Russia as a reliable factor in international relations.

Dec. 12. The first elections under the new constitution were held. Most of the candidates elected were those of the Communist slate, so that no significant change resulted from the new system. The Supreme Soviet met for the first time Jan. 12, 1938, and appointed to the key positions those who were already dominant in the government.

1938, Mar. 2-15. Bukharin, Rykov, Yagoda, and other prominent Bolsheviks were put on trial, accused of wanting to restore bourgeois capitalism and of joining with Trotsky in treasonable conspiracy. They were **convicted and executed.** More and more Stalin trusted to the younger generation, which had never known anything but the Bolshevik régime and which was therefore less apt to criticize.

July 11-Aug. 10. Open warfare broke out between the Russians and the Japanese on the frontier of eastern Siberia and Manchukuo. The Russians held their own and the matter was finally compromised, but Russian-Japanese tension remained near the breaking point. During the Japanese invasion of China (p. 1121) the Russians gave firm support to the Chinese in every practicable way. Meanwhile there was no relaxation of the tension in Europe. During the

Sept. Great Czech crisis the Russian government favored resistance to the German demands and publicly announced its readiness to come to the assistance of the Czechs if France did so. But neither England nor France appeared to relish the idea of communist support and followed a policy of yielding. As a result the Franco-Russian Alliance lost most of its significance and Russia was almost completely isolated in Europe. Indeed, the supposed **German designs on the Ukraine** seemed to presage a conflict between Germany and Russia in the not too distant future.

1939, Mar.-June. The **extinction of Czechoslovakia** and the German annexation of Memel threw Europe into consternation and produced a revolution in British policy (p. 971). The London government extended guarantees to Poland, Rumania and Greece and suddenly opened negotiations to bring Russia into a "peace front" directed against attack upon Poland or Rumania. The Russians, however, proved recalcitrant. They insisted not only on a complete offensive alliance, but upon guarantees for the Baltic States. After weeks of proposals and counter-proposals

May 3. Maxim Litvinov was suddenly dismissed from the post of commissar for foreign affairs, after 18 years of service. Premier Vyacheslav Molotov took his place and publicly uttered sharp criticism of the British suggestions. As a result it was feared on some sides that Russia was preparing to revive close relations with Germany. In any event, Russia had suddenly emerged as a key power in international alignments.

Negotiations with England and France dragged on through the summer, the Russians rejecting one draft after another and making no secret of their distrust of the western powers. They insisted on guarantees to the Baltic States against internal revolution and also on the right to send troops into Poland in the event of aggres-sion by Germany. The vigorous opposition of the parties concerned made it impossible for England and France to concede these points, though they sent military missions to Moscow to demonstrate their sincerity. Finally the real Russian policy was revealed when on

Aug. 20, 21. **A trade pact was concluded with Germany** and announcement was made of a forthcoming **non-aggression pact** (concluded Aug. 23). The seemingly impossible had happened, and the Nazi and Communist régimes, supposedly implacable enemies, joined hands in a **diplomatic revolution** that shook the world. When Germany made war on Poland (p. 967) Bolshevik Russia stood by as a benevolent neutral.

13. POLAND

During the First World War Poland was a pawn in the conflict between Russia and the Central Powers. On the one hand the Russian government, to hold the loyalty of the Poles,

1914, Aug. 14. Promised that Poland should be **restored as an autonomous kingdom.** This policy secured the support of an important faction of Polish nationalists, led by **Roman Dmowski**, who Nov. 25 formed the *Polish National Committee* at Warsaw, which looked to Russia for solution of the Polish problem. On the other hand,

Aug. 16. Gen. **Joseph Pilsudski** (1867–1935, a Russian Pole by birth and several times convicted and imprisoned in Russia for radical, revolutionary activity) founded the *Supreme National Committee* at Cracow, under Austrian protection. The Austrian government permitted the formation of Polish legions to fight against Russia. In the course of 1915 most of Poland was conquered by the Germans and Austrians, who for a time divided the administration of the territory between them. Ultimately, however, the German high command took almost complete control of the country.

1916, July 25. Pilsudski resigned from his command in protest against the failure of the Central Powers to establish a Polish kingdom. The Polish legions were incorporated with the Austro-Hungarian army.

Nov. 5. The German and Austrian governments joined in the proclamation of an "**independent**" **Polish kingdom** and set up a *Council of State*, which adopted a constitution (Jan. 30, 1917). On this council Pilsudski accepted a seat.

1917, Mar. 30. The Russian provisional government declared in favor of an independent Poland, to include all lands in which the Poles comprised a majority of the population.

July 2. Pilsudski resigned from the Council of State in protest against the continued German control and domination of the government. He was thereupon arrested and imprisoned at Magdeburg (until Nov. 2, 1918).

Aug. 15. Dmowski established the Polish National Committee at Paris, the French government having given permission (June 4) for the formation of a Polish army in France.

Oct. 15. The Germans set up a *Regency Council* in Poland which exercised effective control under German supervision. On the collapse of the Central Powers in

1918, Oct. 12. The Regency Council took charge of affairs. But the Ukrainians had already begun the invasion of Galicia and before long

Nov. 1. Poland made war on the Ukraine, reconquering Galicia for the new Polish state.

Nov. 3. THE POLISH REPUBLIC WAS PROCLAIMED at Warsaw. This soon fell under the control of Pilsudski, who returned from his German captivity Nov. 10 and was granted full military power by the Regency Council, which thereupon resigned (Nov. 14). Under Pilsudski's direction the Poles continued their advance in Galicia, taking Lemberg (Nov. 23). At the same time they attempted to realize their aspirations in the west, and

Dec. 27-28. Occupied Posen (*Poznania*) with their troops. Pilsudski succeeded in reaching agreements with other provisional governments (that of **Daszynski** at Cracow and above all that of **Dmowski** and **Ignace Jan Paderewski** at Paris), so that

1919, Jan. 17. Paderewski could form a coalition cabinet, Pilsudski acting as provisional president. A constituent assembly was elected (Jan. 26) and worked out a temporary constitutional system. In the meanwhile the entire effort of the government was devoted to the conquest of the territories belonging to Poland at the time of the first partition of 1772. This brought the Poles into conflict with the Bolsheviks in White Russia and Lithuania. Jan. 5 the Bolsheviks took Vilna. In the west there was desultory fighting with the new Czechoslovak state over the **Duchy of Teschen** and other disputed territories. Having concluded an armistice with the Czechs (Feb. 5), Pilsudski was able to devote himself to the southern and eastern fronts.

Apr. 19. The Poles recaptured Vilna from the Bolsheviks and advanced into White Russia. At the same time they held their own against the Ukrainians and against the Czechs. In the meanwhile the

June 28. TREATY OF VERSAILLES established the Polish frontier in the west, Poland receiving a corridor along the Vistula to the sea (the **city of Danzig** to be a free city under supervision of the League of Nations, but economically connected with Poland), and large parts of **West Prussia** and **Posen.** A plebiscite was to determine the frontier in Upper Silesia. Poland was obliged to accept a **minority treaty** guaranteeing full rights and numerous religious, educational, linguistic, and other privileges to the minority peoples.

Aug. 18. A Polish rising was engineered in the **Upper Silesian region**, as a result of which the Poles secured control of much of the disputed area. In view of continued clashes in Teschen also,

Sept. 27. The Supreme Council arranged for a plebiscite in Teschen.

Dec. 7. Paderewski resigned as premier. Pilsudski, now Marshal of Poland, remained as chief of the state.

Dec. 8. The Supreme Council laid down the so-called **"Curzon Line"** for Poland's eastern frontier. This line deprived Poland of Vilna and was thoroughly unsatisfactory to the Poles for this reason.

1920, Mar. 27. The Poles demanded of the Russians **the boundaries of 1772** with a plebiscite in the region west of that boundary. This the Bolsheviks would

not accept, though they made many efforts to effect a compromise. Breakdown of negotiations led to

Apr. 25-Oct. 12. THE RUSSIAN-POLISH WAR (p. 1033), as a result of which the Poles, with French support, secured not all, but a substantial part of their claims in the east (**Treaty of Riga,** Mar. 18, 1921).

July 11. The plebiscites held in Allenstein and Marienwerder showed an overwhelming vote in favor of Germany, so that these districts were lost to Poland.

Aug. 24. The Lithuanians seized Vilna after its evacuation by the Bolsheviks, but

Oct. 9. Gen. Lucien Zeligowski, with a body of Polish freebooters, **captured the city** and held it for Poland, with the secret approval of Pilsudski. The Polish government agreed, however, to the holding of a plebiscite.

1921, Feb. 19. Conclusion of the **Polish Alliance with France,** followed shortly by a similar

Mar. 3. Alliance with Rumania. For many years Polish foreign policy was based on these agreements (supplemented with less extensive pacts with Czechoslovakia and Yugoslavia as well as with the Baltic states). Poland had a hostile Germany and a hostile Russia on its frontiers and for that reason was bound to France and the French system. The French supplied large sums of money for armaments and for reconstruction of the country.

Mar. 17. ADOPTION OF THE CONSTITUTION, which provided for a president, elected for seven years by a two-chamber parliament (**Senate** and **Sejm**) chosen by popular vote. The whole system was molded closely on that of France.

Mar. 20. The plebiscite in Upper Silesia resulted in a victory for the Germans, but

May 4. The Poles under **Adalbert Korfanty** occupied some of the disputed areas. The matter was referred to the League of Nations, which finally decided, on the plea of economic necessity, to partition the region (Oct. 12).

1922, Jan. 8. The Vilna plebiscite showed a majority in favor of Poland, and the city and district were incorporated Apr. 18. The result was a bitter feud with Lithuania. Nevertheless the Conference of Ambassadors (Mar. 15, 1923) determined the Polish-Lithuanian frontier in such a way as to leave Vilna to Poland. State of war between the two states continued until Dec. 10, 1927.

Mar. 17. Poland concluded **treaties with Latvia, Estonia, and Finland** which provided for maintenance of the treaty settlements and neutrality in case one of these powers should be attacked.

Nov. 5. The elections resulted in a victory of the Rightist parties. Pilsudski resigned as chief of state and became chief of the army staff. The parliament elected

Dec. 9. Gabriel Narutowicz president, but he was assassinated Dec. 18 and

Dec. 20. STANISLAS WOJCIECHOW-SKI became president. The next few years were devoted to the ·work of reconstruction. The finances were ·n bad condition, the parliamentary system ·was distinguished by bitter party strife between the more conservative and nationalist parties and the socialists and peasants. At the same time there was much friction with the minorities (especially the Ukrainians and the Germans). Cabinets changed with the greatest suddenness and rapidity until

1923, Dec. 19. L. Grabski formed a nonparliamentary ministry of experts, which managed to stabilize the currency, made some concessions to meet the demands of the minorities (including Jews), and regulated Polish relations with some of the neighboring states. On Grabski's downfall (Nov. 13, 1925) there followed another period of political confusion, during which

1925, Dec. 28. An important **land law** was passed, providing for the distribution of about 500,000 acres of land to the peasants annually for 10 years.

1926, May 10. Vincent Witos, the leader of the Peasant Party, formed a government, but

May 12-14. PILSUDSKI LED A MILITARY REVOLT against the government and the existing political system. After two days of fighting Pilsudski took the capital, forcing Witos to resign. President Wojciechowski also resigned (May 15), whereupon Pilsudski was elected to take his place. Pilsudski declined the honor, but his friend

June 1. IGNACE MOSCICKI became president. Pilsudski was the real ruler of the country, though he acted through the president, who, by

Aug. 5. A revision of the constitution, was given much greater power.

Oct. 2. Pilsudski assumed the premiership, which he retained until June 27, 1928. His coup and practical dictatorship had aroused great resentment and opposition among the parties of the Left, and no one less than Pilsudski could succeed in breaking the power of the opposition in the *Sejm.* Under Pilsudski the government resorted to the most **drastic methods of repression.** The *Sejm* was dissolved and 54 opposition deputies arrested (Nov. 28, 1927), but new elections indicated the continuance of strong objection to the rule of the military **(rule of the "colonels").**

1930, Aug. 25. Pilsudski again took over the premiership (until Nov. 28) in order to break down the Leftist opposition. Many of the radical leaders were tried and imprisoned (including Witos), and finally

Nov. 16. The elections returned a majority of deputies supporting the government bloc. Pilsudski's control was complete, but the country began to suffer severely from the world depression, and the unrest attending general want produced an ever greater tendency on the part of the ruling group to turn to more conservative policies.

1932, Mar. Parliament granted the president **decree powers for a period** of 3 years, and these were later extended.

1933, May 8. Moscicki was re-elected for a second term of 7 years.

Aug. 5. An **agreement with the city** government of Danzig (which had recently fallen under National Socialist control) assured the Poles in Danzig fair treatment, while guaranteeing to Danzig a certain percentage of Poland's seaborne trade. By this time the new Polish **port of Gdynia** (constructed after 1920 because of the constant friction between Poland and Danzig) had already outstripped its older German neighbor as a trade center.

1934, Jan. 26. Conclusion of a 10-year **NON-AGGRESSION PACT WITH GERMANY,** which gave Poland at least some assurance against a Nazi attempt to recover the Polish corridor by force of arms. The agreement reflected the changed situation resulting from the Nazi victory in Germany. The Poles, guided by the foreign minister, Col. **Joseph Beck,** now began to balance between the alliance with France and friendship with Germany, the great objective being to avoid involvement in the quarrels of others. In keeping with this policy

May 5. The Poles extended to 10 years a non-aggression pact with Russia which had been first concluded July 25, 1932.

1935, Apr. 23. A NEW CONSTITUTION was adopted after years of planning and discussion. The new régime, railroaded through the *Sejm* while the opposition stayed away, brought to an end the democratic, parliamentary system. The Senate henceforth was to be one-third appointed by the president and two-thirds elected by persons of special distinction. The *Sejm* was reduced in numbers by more than one-half. In future it was to be composed of deputies nominated by local councils and corporate bodies. Its powers were greatly curtailed, all real authority going to the president, who was even empowered to nominate his successor. The system was not fully Fascist or National Socialist, but represented a form of authoritarianism often spoken of as **"conducted democracy."**

May 12. Death of Marshal Pilsudski. He was succeeded as head of the army by Gen. (later Marshal Edward Smigly-Rydz, the new power behind the presidential system.

Sept. 8. The elections, in which only 45% of the electorate took part, produced a *Sejm* dominated by the deputies of the government bloc. But even with complete control of the political machinery the army and its supporters were constantly challenged by their opponents. The Socialists and Peasant Party persisted in demanding a return to genuine democracy. The Ukrainians became bolder and bolder in their claims for autonomy or independence.

1937, Mar. 1. Col. Adam Koc organized the *Camp of National Unity*, intended to be an all-inclusive union of those supporting the government. Its program called for maintenance of the constitution of 1935, popular support for the army as the shield of national existence, anti-communism, distribution of land to the peasants, Polonization of minorities, etc. In reply to this move the workers and peasants in the same month joined in a *Workers', Peasants', and Intellectuals' Group*, opposed to Koc and his camp. Peasant strikes became widespread and led to some bloodshed.

1938, Jan. 11. Col. Koc resigned leadership of the camp to Gen. **Stanislas Skwarczynski**, who represented a somewhat more moderate and conciliatory wing of the government group. Apr. 21 the camp broke definitely with the *Union of Young Poland*, an out-and-out fascist and violently anti-Semitic organization founded by Koc.

Nevertheless the extremists on the Right, authors of anti-Semitic excesses, were as much an active danger to the government as were the radical and minority leaders on the Left.

Mar. 16-19. The Polish government, taking advantage of the international situation created by the German annexation of Austria, sent an **ultimatum to Lithuania** demanding an end to hostility and an early regulation of relations between the two countries. Despite years of negotiations no progress had been made toward settlement of the old feud. Now the Lithuanian government, faced by the threat of war, capitulated at once and accepted all Polish demands.

Sept. 29. A POLISH NOTE was sent to Czechoslovakia demanding the cession of the Teschen area (seized by the Czechs during the Polish-Russian War of 1920). The Czechs, face to face with the threat of German invasion and deserted by their friends, were obliged to yield. Oct. 2 Polish forces occupied Teschen. Thus Poland acquired some 400 square miles of territory. In the discussions following the **Munich Agreement** (p. 1012) the Poles ardently championed the Hungarian claims in Slovakia and Ruthenia and tried hard to secure a common frontier with Hungary, but these schemes were frustrated by the opposition of Germany. In the same way the efforts of Col. Beck to induce the Rumanians to participate in a division of Ruthenia (Carpatho-Ukraine) between Poland, Hungary, and Rumania ended in failure. The Poles felt directly menaced by the supposed **German designs on the Ukraine.** They, therefore, began to revive their relations with Russia and with the Baltic states. When the Italian foreign minister, Count Ciano, visited Poland at the end of Feb. 1939 he was given an enthusiastic reception, in the course of which there was much popular demonstration against the Germans. Poland, suffering like Italy from pressure of population, had begun to put forward claims to some share in the reparation of the world's colonies to which the "have-not" powers had devoted themselves.

1939, Mar.-Apr. A Polish-German crisis ensued after the German action in Czechoslovakia and the annexation of Memel (p. 966). At the end of March the German government submitted extensive demands to Warsaw, including the cession of Danzig to Germany and the right to construct an extra-territorial railway and automobile highway across Pomorze (the "corridor"), in return for a guarantee of Polish frontiers and a non-aggression pact.

The demands were rejected, but resulted directly in the

Mar. 31. Anglo-French guarantee of aid to Poland in the event of aggression (expanded Apr. 6 into a mutual pact of assistance "in the event of any threat, direct or indirect, to the independence of either"). In reply

Apr. 28. Hitler denounced the agreement of 1934 with Poland. Relations continued to be tense, with much friction in Danzig. In view of this situation the Poles gave up opposition to a proposed guaranty by Russia and approved the British efforts to bring the Soviet government into the new "peace front."

The Danzig problem developed rapidly during the summer and frontier incidents became frequent. The Germans began to send troops into Danzig and the Poles began to take counter measures, while reiterating their determination to oppose by force any effort to change the *status quo* by force. Finally the crisis broke on Aug. 20 (p. 966). The British and French stood by Poland while the Germans refused to engage in direct negotiations. Two weeks of tension ended with

Sept. 1. THE GERMAN ATTACK ON POLAND, followed by the European War (p. 967).

14. THE BALTIC STATES

a. GENERAL

The development of the three Baltic states after the First World War was more or less along a common line. All of these states were originally part of Russia; they were, during the war, occupied by the Germans, who ruled the three countries through puppet régimes; after Germany's collapse, efforts were made by the Bolsheviks to recover these territories, which gave access to the Baltic. Through German and Allied aid, and by their own efforts, the Baltic forces drove out the Bolsheviks and established independent governments. In all three states there was a German minority of landed wealth and influence, against which **agrarian legislation**, aiming at the breakup of large estates, was directed. The democratic systems set up after the war gave rise to considerable confusion, with much party wrangling between Social Democrats, Agrarians, etc. **Communism** was an ever-present danger, against which all the governments took vigorous measures. But after the victory of National Socialism in Germany the Baltic states hastened to improve their relations with Soviet Russia in order to present a firm front against German intervention in behalf of the German minorities, or German lust of conquest. An entente between the various states had often been discussed, but had been frustrated by Lithuania's demand for recognition of her claims to Vilna. Finally

1934, Sept. 12. THE TREATIES OF THE BALTIC ENTENTE were signed between the three states, the Vilna problem being passed over. **The Baltic Pact** provided for common action in defense of independence and for common action in

foreign affairs, with semi-annual meetings of foreign ministers.

By 1939 all three of the Baltic states had gone over to some form of **dictatorship,** not from deference to the German system, but rather to forge a stronger régime for ultimate resistance to Germany.

b. LITHUANIA

After the victory of the revolution in Russia,

1917, Sept. 23. A Lithuanian conference at Vilna led to the **establishment of a national council** and a demand for independence from Russia. The movement was encouraged by the Germans and resulted in

1918, Feb. 16. A FORMAL DECLARATION OF INDEPENDENCE. The new state was at once invaded by the Bolsheviks, but by

Mar. 3. The Treaty of Brest-Litovsk Russia was obliged to recognize Lithuanian independence. The Germans also recognized the new state (Mar. 23), which entered into alliance with Germany (May 14). Under these circumstances the Lithuanian government was obliged to elect

June 4. Duke William of Urach as king. But when German power collapsed in Nov. this election was rescinded and

Nov. 11. Augustine Voldemaras formed a national government, the first of many short-lived cabinets. The Germans were obliged to withdraw, whereupon the Bolsheviks again invaded the country and

1919, Jan. 5. Took Vilna, which they lost soon afterward to the Poles (Apr. 4).

Dec. 8. The Allied Powers defined the Polish-Lithuanian boundary by the *Curzon Line*, which left **Vilna** to Lithuania.

1920, July 12. The Treaty of Moscow brought to an end the Russian-Lithuanian hostilities. The Bolsheviks, at war with Poland, hastened to recognize Lithuania and the latter's possession of Vilna, which was taken over by the Lithuanians on the evacuation by the Bolsheviks (Aug. 24).

Oct. 9. Gen. Zeligowski and his Polish freebooters seized Vilna by surprise. The Lithuanians refused to give up their claims and the League of Nations arranged for a plebiscite. Meanwhile the Lithuanian capital was fixed at **Kaunas** (Kovno).

1921, Sept. 22. Lithuania joined the League of Nations.

1922, Jan. 8. The Vilna plebiscite, supervised by Zeligowski and his Poles, resulted in a majority vote for union with Poland. The Lithuanians refused to accept this as a valid vote and all intercourse between Lithuania and Poland was cut off. The frontier was closed and a state of war continued until Dec. 1927. All efforts by the League to bring about a settlement were bound to fail, as neither side would yield on the Vilna issue.

Feb. 15. An important **land law** began the process of expropriating the large landowners and distributing the land to the peasants.

Aug. 1. Adoption of the constitution which had been worked out by a constituent assembly convoked in May, 1920. Lithuania became a democratic republic, which was recognized by the United States July 27, and by England, France, and Italy Dec. 20.

Dec. 21. Antanas Stulgenskis became president of the republic.

1923, Jan. 11. INSURRECTION IN MEMEL, engineered by Lithuanians. The city, which was predominantly German, had been under inter-Allied control since 1918. Lithuanian troops now occupied it, obliging a French garrison to withdraw. An inter-Allied commission was sent out to investigate, and thereupon

Feb. 16. The council of ambassadors decided to grant Lithuania sovereignty but to constitute **Memel an autonomous** region in the Lithuanian state. Lithuania accepted (Mar. 16) and the *Memel Statute* was signed by England, France, Italy, and Japan on May 8, 1924.

Nov. 16-17. A military coup led by Gen. Glavatsky resulted in the overthrow of the ministry and the establishment of the conservative elements in power. This coup paved the way for another

1926, Dec. 17. *COUP D'ÉTAT* **OF ANTANAS SMETONA**, who arrested the president and cabinet and had himself made president, with Augustine Voldemaras as premier. The constitution was suspended and the Diet dissolved, Smetona becoming virtual dictator with the support of the Nationalist Union.

1929, Sept. 19. Voldemaras was forced to resign. He was later (May, 1930) tried for high treason, exiled to a village and ultimately convicted and imprisoned for a term of 12 years (June, 1934).

1931, May 6. A treaty of friendship with Russia (first concluded in 1926) was renewed for another 5-year term. By this agreement Russia recognized the Lithuanian claims to Vilna.

Dec. 11. Smetona was re-elected for another 7-year term.

1932, Feb. 6. The arrest of Herr Boettcher, head of the Memel directorate, for alleged treasonable correspondence with Germany, ushered in a period of continued German protests and recrimination. England, France, and Italy periodically made efforts to hold Lithuania to respect for the spirit as well as the letter of the Memel Statute, but with little success. After the advent of Hitler to power in Germany, relations between Germany and Lithuania were strained to the breaking point.

Dec. 16. The Nationalist Union, supporting Smetona, frankly adopted a fascist (of course not German fascist) program.

1934, June 6-7. Followers of Voldemaras attempted a coup, which failed.

Sept. 12. CONCLUSION OF THE BALTIC PACT (see above).

1935, Mar. 25. Conviction of almost 100 Memellanders on a charge of plotting the return of Memel to Germany. Those condemned to death had the sentences commuted and ultimately many were pardoned, but this episode brought the German-Lithuanian conflict to a head. Despite a change in the Memel electoral law, the elections of Sept. 29 returned 24 German members to the directorate as against 5 Lithuanians.

1936, Feb. 6. The government suppressed all political parties excepting the Nationalist Union.

June 9-10. Elections were held for a new parliament along fascist lines. Only Nationalist candidates were presented, and these were elected by local authorities. The parliament met Sept. 1.

1938, Mar. 16. The Polish government sent a stiff ultimatum to Lithuania demanding reopening of the frontier and regulation of relations. After a short crisis the Lithuanian government yielded (Mar. 17) and in the subsequent month most of the questions outstanding since the end of the World War were disposed of.

Dec. 11. The elections in **Memel** brought a vote of more than 90% for the National Socialists. In view of the resurgent power of Germany, the Lithuanian government was obliged to leave the Nazis practically a free hand in Memel.

1939, Mar. 23. The Germans took Memel after extorting an agreement from Lithuania. In return the Germans gave a guaranty of Lithuanian independence and integrity and concluded a commercial treaty establishing close economic relations.

Mar. 28. Gen. Jonas Cernius, the chief of the general staff, formed a new **National Coalition cabinet** in which the forbidden opposition parties were represented. On Apr. 8 Cernius resigned so that the government might not have a military character. Lithuania, practically at Germany's mercy, made efforts to draw closer to Poland, the old enemy.

c. LATVIA

1917, Oct. 29. Formation of the **Latvian National Council,** following the Soviet seizure of power in Russia. Since German forces remained in the country, the National Council was unable to assert its authority or build up an effective national army. For more than a year German efforts to organize a **Baltic Duchy** continued, especially since by

1918, Mar. 3. The **Treaty of Brest-Litovsk** the Bolsheviks were obliged to accept loss of the Baltic States. After the defeat of Germany by the Allied Powers (Nov. 11), the Latvians set up

Nov. 17. A **People's Council,** with **Karlis Ulmanis** as Prime Minister. The Council on

Nov. 18. Proclaimed the independence of the **State of Latvia.** Almost immediately, however,

1919, Jan. 3. A Bolshevik army invaded the country and took **Riga** (Jan. 4). A Soviet government was set up, but

German-Latvian forces, with the approval of the Allies, drove the Soviet troops back (March).

Gen. **von der Goltz** attempted a *coup* (Apr. 16) and eventually retook Riga (May 22). After much confused fighting, a truce was concluded, under pressure of the Allies.

June 28. The **Treaty of Versailles** required the Germans to withdraw from the Baltic States. Von der Goltz was recalled (Aug. 16) at Allied insistence, but fighting between Germans and Latvians continued (German attack on Riga, Oct. 8) until about Nov. 20, when the country was finally cleared of German forces. By

1920, Jan. The last of the Bolshevik troops had also been expelled.

Feb. 1. An **armistice** was concluded between the Latvian and Soviet governments.

May 1. The Latvian **Constituent Assembly** met and drafted a constitution. By the

Aug. 11. Treaty of Riga the Soviet Government recognized Latvian sovereignty and renounced all rights to the territory.

1921, Jan. 26. The Allied Powers recognized the new state and on **Sept. 22** Latvia joined the **League of Nations.**

1922, May 1. The new constitution went into effect. It provided for a single-chamber parliament (Saiema) and ministerial responsibility.

Oct. 8. The elections resulted in a victory for the **Social Democrats.**

Nov. 14. Jan Chakote became President.

1927, Apr. 8. Gustav Zemgalis, president.

1928, Jan. 14. The conservative parties for the first time formed a government.

1930, Apr. 9. Albert Kviesis, president.

1932, Feb. 5. Conclusion of a **non-aggression pact with Soviet Russia.**

1934, May 15. *COUP D'ÉTAT* OF KARLIS ULMANIS, the prime minister, assisted by Gen. **Balodis.** Ulmanis claimed to have anticipated a *coup* by the Marxists. His success represented a victory for the growing conservative elements. Martial law was proclaimed and many of the Socialist leaders were arrested. The constitution was suspended and Ulmanis became virtual dictator.

Sept. 12. **Latvia joined the Baltic Pact** with Lithuania and Estonia (see p. 1041).

1936, Apr. 11. Ulmanis succeeded Kviesis as president.

1939, May. Latvia, directly exposed to the victorious German advance to the east, became an object of great concern to Russia. In the negotiations for an Anglo-Russian pact (p. 966) the Moscow government insisted on a guaranty of the independence of all the Baltic States, but the Latvian government, as ever suspicious of the Soviets, meanwhile accepted the German offer of a mutual non-aggression pact (June 7).

d. ESTONIA

1917, Nov. 28. **The Estonians**, taking advantage of the Bolshevik revolution in Russia, **proclaimed their independence**, but the Soviet government at once undertook the reconquest of this strategically important area. To block the Russian advance, the Germans occupied the country (Dec.) and

1918, Feb. 24. The independence of Estonia was again proclaimed, under German protection. A provisional government was formed by **Konstantin Paets**, who was to play a prominent rôle throughout the entire post-war period.

Mar. 3. By the Treaty of Brest-Litovsk Russia was obliged to recognize Estonian independence.

Nov. 11. The Germans began the withdrawal from the country, following the end of the First World War. They ceded complete power to Paets. But the departure of the Germans simply gave the Bolsheviks another opportunity to recover their position.

Nov. 22. The Russians began a second invasion of the country. The Estonians put up a valiant resistance and were supported by a British fleet.

1919, Jan. The Bolsheviks were finally driven out and the Estonian government was able to establish its control throughout most of the land.

June 15. Adoption of a constitution drafted by a national assembly. Estonia, like Latvia, became a democratic republic, with Reval as the capital. One of the first acts of the government was to pass an

Oct. 10. Agrarian law which inaugurated the policy of breaking up the large estates of the (German) Baltic barons and distributing the land among the peasants.

1920, Feb. 2. **The Treaty of Tartu** (Dorpat) with Russia brought Estonia definitive recognition as an independent state.

1921, Sept. 22. **Estonia joined the League of Nations.**

1923, Nov. 1, 2. Conclusion of **defensive treaties with Latvia and Lithuania** which paved the way for close relations and the ultimate construction of a Baltic bloc (1934).

1924, Nov. 27. **Trial of 150 communists,** most of whom were convicted and imprisoned. Estonia continued to be particularly exposed to communist agitation, which finally culminated in

Dec. 1. A communist uprising, which, however, was suppressed. Fear of communism continued to be a dominant factor in Estonian politics and resulted in a steady growth of conservative, not to say fascist sentiment. The conservative elements organized in a *League of Liberators* (i.e. veterans of the campaigns against Soviet Russia), which succeeded in forcing

1933, Oct. 14-16. A plebiscite in favor of constitutional revision, providing for the election of a president (thus far the premier had acted as head of the state), to whom wide powers were to be assigned.

1934, Jan. 24. The new constitution went into effect. The Liberators at once attempted a *coup* in order to secure control of the government, but this was suppressed and

Mar. 12. **KONSTANTIN PAETS,** aided by Gen. **John Laidoner, set up a virtual dictatorship.** Parliament was prorogued, political parties were abolished, 400 leaders of the Liberators were arrested, and civil liberties were drastically curtailed. But Paets acted in behalf of the conservative and middle-class elements, and from the outset averred his intention of ultimately re-establishing constitutional government.

Sept. 12. Estonia joined in the Baltic Pact (p. 1041).

1936, Feb. 23-25. In a plebiscite, the nation voted 3 to 1 in favor of abolishing the Constitution of 1934 and returning to the democratic system. In Dec. a national assembly was convoked to work out a new constitution.

May 6. About 150 leaders of the Liberators were put on trial for attempting another *coup* in Dec. 1935. Only seven of them were acquitted. Paets continued to be irreconcilably opposed to fascism and national socialism, as he was to communism.

1937, July 29. The new constitution, providing for a president and a two-chamber parliament, was adopted. Restoration of civil liberties was provided for, as were democratic elections. But under the new system the president (to be elected for six years) was to enjoy great authority, with power to appoint and dismiss the cabinet, dissolve both houses of parliament, and rule by decree in national emergencies.

1938, Feb. 24. The election resulted in a chamber containing 63 deputies of Paets' National Front and 17 of opposition groups.

Apr. 24. Paets was elected president.

1939, May. Estonia concluded a mutual non-aggression pact with Germany, acting together with Latvia (see above).

15. THE SCANDINAVIAN STATES

a. GENERAL

The Scandinavian states were all able to preserve neutrality during the First World War, though they were obliged to subject themselves to various regulations and restrictions made necessary by the Allied blockade of Germany. After 1918 they all took an active part in the development of collective security, in which obviously they have a great interest. For the rest they all became thoroughly democratic states, outstanding in the whole world for their progressiveness and enlightenment. In the matter of politics the situation in most cases was rather unstable, due to the relative strength of conservative, liberal, agrarian, and social democratic parties and the difficulty of establishing majority government. In the field of foreign policy efforts were made consistently to develop a program of close co-operation and solidarity, which became all the more necessary after the resurgence of Germany as a powerful military state. Efforts at collaboration go back to the

1914, Dec. 18-19. Meeting of the kings of the three Scandinavian states at Malmö. They discussed various problems of the war, neutrality, etc. Similar meetings took place periodically during the war and post-war periods, and they were supplemented by gatherings of the foreign ministers, which became increasingly frequent.

1926, Jan. 14, 15, 30. Agreements were made between Denmark, Sweden, Norway, and Finland providing for the pacific settlement of all disputes. Ultimately, when these countries began to suffer severely from the world economic crisis,

1931, Sept. 6. Prime ministers of the Scandinavian states met for discussion of economic problems, and there was finally drawn up the

1932, Feb. 7. Oslo Convention, by which the Scandinavian states joined with Holland and Belgium in a scheme of economic co-operation, albeit on a modest scale. More recently Scandinavian solidarity was celebrated by the institution of

1936, Oct. 27. Scandinavia's Day. In view of the collapse of the League system for security and the imposing rearmament of Germany and Russia,

1938, Apr. 5-6. The four Scandinavian foreign ministers met for a discussion of the defense problem. In view of the unwillingness of Denmark to challenge Germany, the specific question of armament and defense had to be left to the individual governments.

July 1. The Oslo mutual trade agreements came to an end. Nevertheless, relations between the so-called Oslo powers continued to be cordial and even close.

1939, June 17. Sweden, Norway and Finland declined the German offer of a mutual non-aggression pact, an offer provoked by President Roosevelt's suggestion, in his letter to Hitler, that Germany's neighbors felt threatened by aggression. The problem was discussed at length by the Scandinavian foreign ministers, most of whom agreed to hold aloof from all commitments to rival power groups. Denmark alone accepted the German offer, being unwilling to give reason for complaint.

b. DENMARK

1912-1947. CHRISTIAN X, king.

1914, Aug. 4. Sale of the Danish West Indies to the United States. The transaction was approved by a Danish plebiscite Dec. 14.

1918, Apr. 21. The system of complete universal suffrage (male and female) went into effect. In the

Apr. 22. Elections under the new system the Conservatives secured 23 seats, the Left (Liberals) 45, the Radicals 33, and the Socialists 39. The government was formed by a coalition of Radicals and Socialists.

Nov. 30. By the Act of Union, **Iceland was recognized as a sovereign state,** united with Denmark only in the person of the ruler. But until 1944 certain affairs were to be handled jointly by the governments.

1920, Feb. 10, Mar. 14. By the plebiscites provided for in the Treaty of Versailles, **a northern zone of Schleswig went to Denmark by** popular vote. It was officially incorporated July 9.

Mar. 8. **Denmark joined the League of Nations.**

1924, Apr. 11. In the elections the Socialists increased their representation from 39 to 55. Thereupon **Theodor Stauning** (Socialist) formed a government.

1926, Mar. 12. The Danish Parliament voted for almost complete disarmament, which was subsequently carried through.

Dec. 2. A Liberal government was formed by **T. Madsen-Mygdal** after a severe setback to the Socialists in the elections.

1929, Apr. 24. Stauning organized another government after Socialist successes at the polls. His party acted in coalition with the Radical Left.

1931, July. A serious dispute with **Norway** developed over the problem of sovereignty over East Greenland (see below).

1933. **Agitation of the Germans in North Schleswig** followed on the victory of the National Socialists in Germany. No serious trouble ensued, however, and Germany and Denmark, closely connected by economic ties, maintained friendly relations, despite the continuance in power in Denmark of the Stauning Socialist-Radical ministry. National Socialism itself made but little progress in Denmark, although Denmark, practically disarmed, remained more or less at the mercy of her powerful neighbor.

c. NORWAY

1905- **HAAKON VII,** king. Norway, much more dependent on trade and fishing than either Denmark or Sweden, has alone among the Scandinavian powers revealed a tendency toward expansion overseas.

1919, Sept. 25. The Allied Supreme Council awarded Norway the sovereignty over **Spitsbergen,** which was thereupon annexed (Feb. 9, 1920). Other acquisitions are mentioned below.

1920, Mar. 5. **Norway joined the League of Nations.**

1924, Oct. 20. In the elections the Conservatives emerged victorious, with 54 seats as against 34 for the Radicals, 22 for the Agrarians, 24 for the Labor Party, and 8 for the Socialists. But in the next

1927, Oct. 17. Elections the Labor Party for the first time became the strongest group (59 seats as against 31 for the Conservatives and 31 for the Liberals). The **first labor government** was organized by **Christopher Hornsrud,** but was soon forced out by its opponents (Feb. 10, 1928). Thereupon **J. L. Mowinckel** (Liberal) formed a cabinet.

1928, Jan. 18. **Annexation of Bouvet Island** and of

1929, Feb. 2. **Peter Island,** both in the South Atlantic and both important as stations for whalers.

May 8. **Annexation of Jan Mayen Island** in the Arctic.

1929-1930. **Explorations of Commander Riiser-Larsen** in the Antarctic Continent (p. 576).

1931, May 8. **P. Kolstad** (Farmers' Party) formed a government.

July 10. **Annexation of the East Greenland coast** between 71° 30′ and 75° 40′ N.L. Norwegian fishermen had settled along the coast and there was some fear that Denmark, which claimed sovereignty, would attempt to make her control effective. Denmark at once protested against the Norwegian action and both parties agreed to refer the matter to the Permanent Court of International Justice. While the case was pending the Norwegian government (July 12, 1932) proclaimed annexation also of part of the more southern coast (60° 30′ to 63° 40′ N.L.), but finally (Apr. 5, 1933) the Permanent Court decided against the Norwegian claims. The Oslo government accepted the decision without demur.

1932, Mar. 5. On the death of Premier Kolstad, his place was taken by **J. Hundseid,** but

1933, Jan. 25. Mowinckel organized another Liberal cabinet, which continued in power even after the elections of Oct. 16 gave the Labor Party 69 seats (Right 30; Left 24; Farmers 23).

1935, Mar. 20. A second Labor government was formed by **Johan Ny-gaarsvold**, with **Halvdan Koht**, an eminent historian, at the foreign office. This government was very successful in overcoming the economic crisis, and became noteworthy for its extension of social security legislation (1937, Jan.: **Workers' Security Law** and **Seamen's Security Law**).

1939, Jan. 14. Norway laid claim to 1,000,000 square miles of **Antarctic territory** extending from 20° W. Long. to 45° E. Long. (Coats Land to Enderby Land, about one-fifth of the entire Antarctic coast, see p. 577).

d. SWEDEN

1907-1950. GUSTAVUS V, king.

1917, Dec. 29. The **Aaland Islands**, following the Bolshevik Revolution in Russia, **voted to join with Sweden**, but later (June 25, 1921) the League of Nations Council assigned them to Finland, with the proviso that they should be demilitarized.

1919, May 26. The introduction of **woman suffrage** completed the democratization of the franchise.

1920, Mar. 4. Sweden joined the League of Nations.

Mar. 10. Hjalmar Branting formed the first purely Socialist cabinet, but he was forced to resign after the defeat of his party in the elections of Oct. 22.

1921, Oct. 13. Branting formed a second government, which remained in office until Apr. 6, 1923, and was followed in

1924, Oct. 18, by the **third Branting government.** The prime minister died Feb. 24, 1925, but his place was taken by **Rickard Sandler**, the cabinet continuing in power until June 1, 1926. These Socialist cabinets enacted a large body of **social reform legislation** for both workers and peasants, and greatly reduced the military establishment. After the downfall of the Socialist government in June, 1926, there followed a number of Liberal and Conservative governments:

1926, June 7. Carl Ekman (Liberal), premier.

1928, Oct. 2. Arvid Lindman (Conservative), premier.

1930, June 1. Ekman again assumed power, but the elections of Sept. 1932 revealed substantial gains by the Social Democrats and Farmers and

1932, Sept. 24. Per A. Hansson became premier of a Socialist government, with **Rickard Sandler** as foreign minister.

This government did much to combat the evils of the depression by introducing large-scale public works, drastically economizing in administration, and passing a long-term unemployment insurance act (May, 1934). The government also undertook a **program of rearming** which appeared essential after the rise of Hitler in Germany and the rapid deterioration of German-Russian relations.

1936, June 13. Axel Pehrsson (Agrarian) formed a cabinet, but after the elections of Sept. 20 (Socialists 112 seats; Conservatives 44; Agrarians 36; Liberals 27),

Sept. 28. Hansson again assumed the premiership, his government representing a coalition of Socialists and Agrarians.

e. FINLAND

1917, Mar. 21. The Russian provisional government recognized Finland as an **independent state** within the proposed Russian federation, but the

July 20. FINNS PROCLAIMED THEIR COMPLETE INDEPENDENCE of Russia, and this was recognized by the Russian Soviet government (Jan. 2, 1918) as well as by Sweden (Jan. 4), France, and Germany (Jan. 6). In Finland itself there ensued a period of

1918, Jan. 28. CIVIL WAR. Finnish communists (*Reds*), supported by the Russian Bolsheviks, seized Helsingfors (Helsinki) and overran much of southern Finland, but in

Apr. The *Whites* (i.e. opponents of Bolshevism), led by **Baron Karl Gustav Mannerheim** and supported by a German force under Gen. **von der Goltz,** retook the capital (Apr. 13) and drove the Reds out of the country (**battle of Viborg,** Apr. 29). For a time Finland remained under strong German influence, and

Oct. 8. The Finnish Diet elected Prince Frederick Charles of Hesse as king. After the defeat of the Central Powers, Frederick Charles himself renounced the crown (Dec. 31). In the interval

Dec. 11. Gen. Baron Mannerheim had become **head of the state,** and the last German forces had departed (Dec. 17).

1919, June 6. War with Russia broke out again, over conflicting claims to Carelia. After much desultory fighting, hostilities were concluded by the **Treaty of Dorpat (Tartu)** of Oct. 14, 1920, by the terms of which Finland was given a narrow strip of territory between Murmansk and the eastern frontier of Norway, with the ice-free port of **Pechenga**. The fate of the Finnish population in Carelia remained a source of friction between the two countries.

July 17. A democratic constitution was adopted and

July 25. KARL J. STAHLBERG was elected president for six years.

1920, Dec. 16. Finland joined the League of Nations, and

1921, June 24. The League Council assigned to Finland sovereignty over the Aaland Islands, on condition that the islands be given an autonomous régime. Oct. 20 the powers concluded a convention neutralizing the islands.

1922, Oct. 14. Passage of an agrarian law which inaugurated the breakup of the large estates and the distribution of the land to the peasants.

1925, Feb. 16. LAURI RELANDER succeeded Stahlberg as president.

1930, Oct. 14. Attempted *coup* of Gen. Kurt Wallenius and his fascist *Lapua* organization. The president of the republic was abducted, but in the end the *coup* failed. The whole movement was directed chiefly against communism, which, with Soviet Russia near by, was a constant factor in the Finnish situation. As a result of pressure from the Lapua group,

Nov. 11. The government enacted drastic measures against communism.

1931, Feb. 16. PEHR SVINHUFVUD became president. During his term of office he threw his entire influence in the direction of conservatism, which encouraged the fascist elements to attempt

1932, Feb. 27-Mar. 7. Another Lapua uprising. Once again the movement failed. Gen. Wallenius was arrested and Nov. 21 more than 50 leaders were convicted. The organization was disbanded, but in 1933 there emerged the *Patriotic*

National Movement, similar to the Lapuan· To meet this continued threat,

1933, May 4. The government forbade the military organization of political parties and groups, and

1934, Apr. The wearing of uniforms and political emblems was prohibited.

1935, Aug. 28. The Finnish foreign minister for the first time joined in the meeting of ministers of the other Scandinavian states. Thereafter Finland regularly participated in these meetings. In view of the changed conditions in the Baltic after Hitler's rise to power, Finland attempted to form a bloc of Scandinavian and Baltic states to hold a balance between Germany and Russia. In close collaboration with these states Finland proceeded to refortification of the Aaland Islands, despite the opposition of the inhabitants.

1937, Feb. 15. KYOSTI KALLIO, premier and leader of the Agrarian Party, was elected president, with support of the Social Democrats. A coalition government of Agrarians, Socialists, and National Progressives was formed, which was outspokenly hostile to reactionary and fascist movements and which was determined to further the close relationship with the other democratic Scandinavian states. In keeping with this policy

1938, Nov. 22. The government dissolved the Patriotic National Movement, which was the spearhead of fascism.

1939, May 17. Finland, together with Norway and Sweden, declined the German offer of a mutual non-aggression pact, but at the same time made known its opposition to the Russian suggestion of a joint Russian-British-French guarantee of the independence of all the Baltic States. Relations with Russia continued cool, the more so as the Soviet delegate blocked League approval of the refortification of the Aaland Islands.

C. NORTH AMERICA

1. THE UNITED STATES

1917, Apr. 6. WAR DECLARED ON GERMANY. Diplomatic relations with Austria-Hungary were terminated Apr. 8, but war was declared only Dec. 7. Diplomatic relations with Turkey were severed Apr. 20, but war was never formally declared on either Turkey or Bulgaria.

May 18. Selective Service Act passed, providing for the registration of those between 21 and 31 years inclusive. June 5 local draft boards registered 9,586,508 men. June 5, 1918, another million (those who had come of age during the year) were added. Sept. 12, 1918, a third registration, of those between 18 and 48 years, added another 13,228,762 men.

June 13. First division embarked for France.

June 15-1918, May 6. The **Espionage Act**, the **Trading-with-the-Enemy Act** (Oct. 6, 1917) and the **Sedition Act** (May 6, 1918).

July. War Industries Board created and placed in complete charge of all war purchases.

Aug. 10. The **Lever Act**, establishing control over food and fuel. **Herbert Hoover**, food administrator.

Sept. 1. Grain Corporation inaugurated, which fixed price of grain and financed the 1917, 1918, and 1919 crops.

Oct. 3. War Revenue Act, greatly increasing income tax and imposing an excess profits tax on business earnings of corporations and individuals.

Nov. 2. Lansing-Ishii Agreement, reaffirming the assurances of the Root-Takahira Agreement (1908), with the admission by the United States that "territorial propinquity" gave Japan special interests in China.

Dec. William G. McAdoo, secretary of the treasury, made director-general of the railroad administration.

Dec. 18. Under stress of war conditions and the need of food conservation Congress had in Aug. 1917 prohibited the use of food products in the making of distilled beverages. Ownership of large numbers of breweries and distilleries by persons of German origin accentuated popular resentment against liquor traffic. As a result, Congress adopted the **18th amendment** and sent it to the states for ratification. It became part of the constitution Jan. 16, 1919.

1918, Jan. 8. Fourteen Points set forth by President Wilson in an address to Congress defining war aims of the United States (p. 944).

Apr. 5. War Finance Commission created with fund of $500,000,000 for financing essential industries.

Apr. 10. Webb-Pomerene Act exempting export associations from the restraints of the anti-trust laws, with a view to encouraging export trade.

July 18-Nov. 11. American troops participated in six prolonged assaults upon German positions. Two of these were conducted wholly by American forces: **battle of Saint Mihiel** (Sept. 12–16) and that of the **Meuse-Argonne** (Sept. 26–Nov. 11), in which 1,200,000 men were thrown into the encounter (pp. 945, 950).

Nov. 11. Armistice signed (see First World War).

Dec. 13. Arrival of President Wilson in France, for the Peace Conference. Accompanied by Col. House, Robert Lansing, secretary of state, Gen. Tasker H. Bliss, and Henry White.

1919, Mar. 2. Senate Round-Robin, declaring the opinion of 39 senators that only after the establishment of peace should the League of Nations concern the negotiators.

June 28. Treaty of Versailles signed.

July 10-1920, Mar. 19. Treaty of Versailles before the Senate. When presented to the Senate July 10, strong objection developed to the treaty. Wilson refused to accept amendments or reservations. Nov. 19, the Senate defeated the treaty with and without reservations. Finally, Mar. 19 the treaty with reservations was rejected by a vote of 49 to 35. Wilson then vetoed a joint resolution of Congress declaring war with Germany at an end. A similar resolution was passed July, 1921, and signed by Harding.

Sept. 22-1920, Jan. 8. Steel strike. Although the public sympathized with the steel workers and regretted the 12-hour day, the strikers were defeated.

Oct. 28. The National Prohibition Act, commonly known as the **Volstead Act**, passed over President Wilson's veto in pursuance of the 18th amendment. It defined as intoxicating all beverages containing more than one-half of 1% of alcohol; provided several regulations for the manufacture and sale of alcohol for industrial, medicinal, and sacramental purposes. Strengthened by amendments of 1921 and 1929.

1920, Feb. 28. Transportation Act signed by President Wilson, giving the interstate commerce commission power to establish and maintain rates which would yield a "fair return upon the aggregate value of the railway property of the country," and power to prescribe minimum rates. Prosperous roads were to share profits with the less prosperous. The commission was empowered to draw up a plan for the consolidation of the railway lines into a limited number of systems, such combinations to be exempt from operation of the anti-trust laws.

Mar. 1. The railroads were returned to their owners.

1920, June 5—1928. Merchant Marine Acts. Under the Act of 1920 the shipping board was to dispose of the war-time merchant fleet to private parties, and to operate those ships which it could not sell; to establish new shipping routes and to keep ships in these services until private capital could be attracted to them. These measures failing to interest private capital, the Merchant Marine Act of 1928 established a revolving fund from which construction loans up to three-fourths of the costs of building were to be made to private operators, and private owners were to be given, as an inducement to shipbuilding and operation, long-term mail-carrying contracts. In effect the Act of 1928 provided for subsidies to the merchant marine.

1920, June 20. Water-Power Act passed, creating a federal power commission composed of the secretaries of war, interior, and agriculture and subordinate appointive officers. Its authority extended to all waterways on public lands, to all navigable streams, including falls and rapids. It might license power companies to utilize appropriate dam sites for periods not exceeding 50 years. The power commission applied the act so generously as to make it largely ineffectual.

Aug. 28. Nineteenth amendment, providing for woman suffrage.

Sept. 8-11. Transcontinental air mail service established between New York and San Francisco, 16,000 letters being carried.

Nov. 2. The Westinghouse Electrical Company arranged the **first general radio broadcast** for the national election. Nov. 31 the same company broadcast the first regular evening program.

Nov. 2. Warren G. Harding (Republican) elected president over **James M. Cox** (Democrat), 404 electoral votes to 137.

1921, Mar. 4—1923, Aug. 2. WARREN G. HARDING, twenty-ninth president.

Apr. 20. Colombian Treaty ratified by the Senate; the United States was to pay Colombia $25,000,000 for the loss of Panama and to grant free access to the Panama Canal. A similar treaty, negotiated by the Wilson administration in 1914, had been rejected by the Senate, largely because of the influence of Theodore Roosevelt, who denounced it as blackmail.

May 19. Immigration Act signed, limiting the immigrants from a given country to 3% of the number of foreign-born persons of such nationality resident in the United States according to the U.S. Census of 1910.

May 27. Emergency Tariff Act, raising duties on agricultural products, wool, and sugar. It placed an embargo on German dyestuffs; those products that could not be made in the United States were put on a licensing basis.

Aug. 24. Treaty of peace signed with Austria.

Nov. 12—1922, Feb. 6. WASHINGTON CONFERENCE. Aug. 11 President Harding issued a call to Great Britain, France, Italy, and Japan to meet for discussion of naval limitation, and to the same powers plus Belgium, Netherlands, Portugal, and China for discussion of questions affecting the Pacific and the Far East. For the agreements concluded see p. 957.

1922, Feb. 11. By the Yap Treaty (Feb. 11) the United States secured equality with Japan and other nations in the use of cable and wireless facilities in Yap and other Japanese mandates.

Mar. 24. Four-Power Treaty ratified by the Senate.

Mar. 29. Five-Power Naval Treaty ratified.

Apr. 1-Sept. 4. Strike of coal miners in protest against wage reductions and in support of the check-off system by which the unions require employers to deduct union fees from wages. **Herrin riots**

in Illinois. Agreement reached with bituminous miners Aug. 15 and with anthracite miners Sept. 4.

July 1-Sept. 13. Railway shopmen's strike in protest against wage reductions set by railway labor board.

Sept. 19. Fordney-McCumber Tariff Act passed. Contained highest rates in American tariff history. *Ad-valorem* duties were to be assessed on the foreign value of the goods. The act explicitly stated that the principle underlying American protection was to be that of equalizing the cost of American and foreign production.

Nov. 20. An American observer sent to the Lausanne Conference. This break with the administration's policy of non-interference in European affairs was largely due to the concern of American oil interests over the oil situation in the Near Eastern fields where a British monopoly was feared.

1923-1930. Refunding of debts owed the United States by Allied Powers. During and immediately following the war the United States lent to foreign powers a total of $10,350,000,000. The first refunding agreement was with Great Britain, which was to pay over a period of 62 years, with interest at 3.3%. The settlement with Italy came in Nov. 1925, with interest rate fixed at 0.4%. That with France was in Apr. 1926, with interest at 1.6%, over a period of 62 years. By May 1930 17 nations had come to terms with the United States.

Aug. 2. CALVIN COOLIDGE became thirtieth president upon death of Warren G. Harding.

1924, Jan. 14. Gen. Charles G. Dawes chosen chairman of reparation commission expert committee. Conference of London (July 16–Aug. 16) used the report as a basis of agreement (p. 959).

Feb.-Mar. Teapot Dome oil scandal. Apr. 7, 1922, **Albert Fall**, secretary of the interior, leased the Teapot Dome Oil Reserve to Harry F. Sinclair, and by agreements of Apr. 25 and Dec. 11, 1922, he leased the Elk Hills Reserve to E. L. Doheny. Secrecy attending the leases, combined with the sudden opulence of Fall, led to Senate investigation under direction of Senator Thomas J. Walsh. It was shown that Sinclair had personally befriended Fall, while Doheny had "loaned" $100,000 to Fall without security or interest. As a result, Denby, secretary of the navy, resigned (Fall had previously resigned), and

in 1927 the supreme court ordered the reserves returned to the government.

May 19. Soldiers' Bonus Bill for veterans of the First World War passed over the president's veto.

May 26. Immigration Bill signed, limiting annual immigration from a given country to 2% of the nationals of the country in the United States in 1890. A further provision of the law stipulated that from July 1, 1927 (later deferred to 1929) the annual immigration should be limited to 150,000, to be apportioned among the different countries in proportion to the relative strength of the various foreign elements represented in the American population in 1920. The bill provided for the total exclusion of the Japanese, thereby abrogating the gentlemen's agreement. Protest from Japan and resulting ill feeling.

May 27. Rogers Bill signed consolidating the diplomatic and consular services.

Nov. 4. Calvin Coolidge elected president over John W. Davis (Democrat) and R. M. La Follette (Progressive) by 382 electoral votes to 136 for Davis and 13 for La Follette.

1925 Mar. 4—1929, Mar. 4. CALVIN COOLIDGE president.

1925-1929. Agricultural legislation. In Feb. 1922 the **Capper-Volstead Act** granted to agricultural associations and co-operatives the right to process, prepare, handle, and market their goods in interstate commerce. In Mar. 1923 the **Federal Intermediate Credit Act** provided for the creation of a system of federal intermediate credit banks for the purpose of handling agricultural paper exclusively. Agriculture continuing in a depressed state, legislation was shortly introduced into Congress with a view to its rehabilitation. The **McNary-Haugen Bill**, a measure designed to make the tariff on agricultural products effective, was defeated in the House in June 1924 and again in May 1926. In June 1926 it was defeated in the Senate, but in Feb. 1927 it passed both houses, only to be vetoed by Coolidge. In Apr. and May 1928 it again passed both houses but was again vetoed by the president. This measure, as well as the export debenture plan, was opposed largely because of price-fixing and subsidy features. In June 1929 the **Agricultural Marketing Act** of the Hoover administration was enacted with its plan for the redemption of agriculture through voluntary co-operation and self-discipline under governmental auspices. Producers were to be encouraged to form effective marketing corporations, owned and controlled by themselves. A federal farm board was created with a revolving fund of $500,-000,000 for loans to co-operatives and with power to create stabilization corporations. Grain and cotton stabilization corporations bought extensively with a view to sustaining prices of farm products, but to little avail.

1925, June. Secretary Kellogg charged the Calles government in Mexico with failure to protect American lives and property rights, creating a tension between the two countries which was increased by the enactment of the Mexican Petroleum Law and the Alien Land Law in Dec. 1925. See p. 1075.

May 20-21. Charles A. Lindbergh made the first non-stop New York to Paris flight, alone in the monoplane *Spirit of St. Louis*. His time was 33 hrs. 39 min.

1927, Oct. Dwight W. Morrow appointed ambassador to Mexico. By his tact and understanding he gained the confidence of Mexico, which was expressed by concessions on controverted points.

Dec. The amendment of the **Mexican Petroleum Law** paved the way for a marked improvement in the relations between the two countries. Morrow also played the rôle of conciliator in the controversy between the government and the Catholic Church in Mexico.

1928, Aug. 27. The Pact of Paris signed. Art. I outlawed war as an instrument of national policy, while Art. II committed the contracting parties to settle all disputes by pacific means (p. 960).

Nov. Herbert Hoover (Republican) elected president over Alfred E. Smith (Democrat) by 444 electoral votes to 87.

1929, Jan. 15. Pact of Paris ratified by the Senate, with the declaration that it did not curtail the country's right of self-defense; that the treaty was not inconsistent with the Monroe Doctrine; and that it did not commit the United States to engage in punitive expeditions against aggressor states.

1929, Mar. 4—1933, Mar. 4. HERBERT HOOVER, thirty-first president.

1929, Oct. STOCK MARKET CRASH, the culmination of the boom market and unrestrained speculation of the Coolidge-Hoover era. Ushered in prolonged depression which gradually settled upon the country with increasing unemployment, bank failures, and business disasters.

1930, Jan. 21-Apr. 22. London Naval Conference, resulting in a three-power treaty by the United States, Great Britain, and Japan. It established a permanent parity between Great Britain and the United States; continued capital ship construction holiday to the end of 1936. It set up an American-Japanese ratio of capital ships which was unsatisfactory to Japan, and fixed limits to building of auxiliary craft within a system of ratios.

Mar. CLARK MEMORANDUM ON THE MONROE DOCTRINE made public by the state department. Written by J. Reuben Clark, undersecretary of state two years before, the Memorandum declared: 1. The Monroe Doctrine is unilateral. 2. *"The Doctrine does not concern itself with purely inter-American relations."* 3. *"The Doctrine states a case of the United States versus Europe, not of the United States versus Latin America."* 4. The United States has always used the Doctrine to protect Latin-American nations from the aggressions of European powers. 5. The Roosevelt corollary is not properly a part of the Doctrine itself, nor does it grow out of the Doctrine.

June 17. Smoot-Hawley Tariff Act signed by Hoover in spite of protest of more than 1000 trained economists. Duties higher than ever. In many instances the duties on raw material were 50 to 100% greater than in 1922 schedules. This led to widespread reprisals and retaliation by other countries. By the end of 1931 some 25 countries had taken steps to retaliate.

July 21. London Naval Treaty ratified by the Senate.

1931, June. Debt and reparations moratorium. In 1929 a committee of experts under the chairmanship of Owen D. Young had submitted the Young Plan to Germany, in which debts and reparations were joined together, despite the refusal of the American state and treasury departments to admit the fact. By June 1931 it was evident that the German financial situation would preclude payments for the year, whereupon Hoover, accepting the inevitable, arranged a year's moratorium on debts and reparations.

June. Wiley Post and Harold Gatty circumnavigated the globe by air in 8 days, 15 hrs. 51 min.

1932, Jan. 7. Stimson Doctrine enunciated by the secretary of state. Stimson, in notes to Japan and China, in which he stated that the United States would not *"recognize any situation, treaty, or agreement which may be brought about by means con-*

trary to the covenants and obligations of the Pact of Paris." This was in protest against Japanese occupation of Manchuria.

Feb. 2. Reconstruction Finance Corporation created with a fund of $500,000,000 and the right to borrow more money, for the purpose of making available government credits to release the frozen assets of financial institutions and to provide aid for the railways.

Feb. Norris Anti-Injunction Act, declaring "yellow-dog" contracts unenforcible before the federal courts and providing that certain types of activity in labor conflicts should be immune from injunctions. It provided that *"no person participating in, or affected by, such disputes shall be enjoined from striking, or from striving for the success of the strike by customary labor-union effort, short of fraud or violence."* The immunity extended to all persons *"in the same industry, trade, or occupation"* rather than merely to employers and their own employees.

Nov. Franklin D. Roosevelt (Democrat) elected president over Herbert Hoover (Republican) by 472 electoral votes to 59.

Dec. 15. Default of various European governments in payment of war debts owed to the United States.

1933, Feb. 6. **Twentieth amendment** to the constitution proclaimed. It provided that after Oct. 15, 1933, senators and representatives should take office Jan. 3 following the election and that Congress should convene annually on that date. The president and vice-president were to take office Jan. 20, after election.

Feb. 14. Closing of all banks in the state of Michigan gave warning of an impending **banking crisis.** Bank holidays spread from state to state until the climax was reached on the night of Mar. 3.

Mar. 4. **FRANKLIN D. ROOSEVELT, thirty-second president.** Banks closed and business virtually at a standstill.

Mar. 6. Banks closed for four days by proclamation of the president and an embargo placed on the export of gold in order to protect the gold reserve.

Mar. 9. Congress convened in special session, legalized the president's action with respect to banks and authorized the comptroller of the currency to take charge of insolvent banks. Within a week after the president's proclamation the sound banks began to reopen.

1933-1936. **NEW DEAL AGRICULTURAL LEGISLATION:** May 12, 1933, the Agricultural Adjustment Act became law. Its aim was the establishment of that parity for farm products which had existed in the period 1909–1914. This was to be achieved through removal of the agricultural surplus by means of compensated crop curtailment, financed through the licensing and taxing of the processors of farm products. Provision was also made for the refinancing of farm mortgages.

The Farm Credit Act (approved June 16, 1933) authorized the **Farm Credit Administration** to centralize *"all agricultural credit activities."*

The **Farm Mortgage Refinancing Act** (approved Jan. 31, 1934) created the **Federal Farm Mortgage Corporation** to aid further in the refinancing of farm debts and guaranteed both as to principal and interest federal bonds exchanged for consolidated farm loan bonds.

The **Farm Mortgage Foreclosure Act** (approved June 12, 1934) extended the lending authority of the land bank commissioner to permit him to make loans to farmers for the purpose of enabling them to redeem farm properties owned by them previous to foreclosure regardless of when foreclosure took place.

Frazier-Lemke Farm Bankruptcy Act (approved June 28, 1934) facilitated agreements between distressed farmers and their creditors and granted extension of time to farmers during which they might remain in possession of their farms.

The **Crop Loan Act** (approved Feb. 23, 1934) permitted the Farm Credit Administration to make loans to farmers in 1934 for crop production and harvesting.

The **Cotton Control Act** (approved April 21, 1934) placed the production of cotton on a compulsory rather than a voluntary basis.

Jones-Costigan Sugar Act (approved May 9, 1934) included among the basic crops of the original Agricultural Adjustment Act sugar beets and sugar cane.

Tobacco Control Act (approved June 28, 1934) placed the production of tobacco on a compulsory basis.

The Frazier-Lemke Farm Bankruptcy Act was subsequently declared unconstitutional, while Jan. 6, 1936, the Agricultural Adjustment Act met a similar fate. The objective of the latter act was then achieved by the **Soil Conservation Act** by which farmers were paid for planting soil-conserving crops in lieu of the ordinary staples.

1933-1934. **NEW DEAL BANKING LEGISLATION:** The **Emergency**

Banking Relief Act (approved Mar. 9, 1933) gave the president power to regulate transactions in credit, currency, gold and silver, and foreign exchange. It also authorized the secretary of the treasury to require the delivery of all gold and gold certificates; provided for the appointment of conservators of national banks in difficulties.

The **Banking Act of 1933** (approved June 16, 1933) extended federal reserve open-market activities; created the **Federal Bank Deposit Insurance Corporation** to insure deposits; regulated further the operations of member banks and separated security affiliates.

The **Bank Deposit Insurance Act** (approved June 19, 1934) amended deposit features of the Banking Act and raised the amount eligible for insurance of each depositor to $5000.

1933-1934. NEW DEAL HOME FINANCING: The **Home Owners' Refinancing Act** (approved June 13, 1933) created the **Home Owners' Loan Corporation** to refinance home mortgages.

The **Home Owners' Loan Act** (approved Apr. 27, 1934) guaranteed the principal of the HOLC's bond issues and permitted loans for repair of dwellings.

1933-1934. NEW DEAL MONETARY LEGISLATION: The **Gold Repeal Joint Resolution** (approved June 5, 1933) cancelled the gold clause in all federal and private obligations and made them payable in legal tender.

The **Gold Reserve Act of 1934** (approved Jan. 30, 1934) authorized the president to revalue the dollar at 50 to 60 cents in terms of its gold content; set up a $2,000,000,000 stabilization fund.

The **Silver Purchase Act** (approved June 19, 1934) authorized the president to nationalize silver.

1933-1935. NEW DEAL RELIEF LEGISLATION: The **Federal Emergency Relief Act** (approved May 12, 1933) authorized the RFC to make $500,000,000 available for emergency relief to be expended by the **Federal Emergency Relief Administration** created by the act.

The **Civil-Works Emergency Relief Act** (approved Feb. 15, 1934) appropriated an additional $950,000,000 available until June 30, 1935, for continuation of the civil-works program and for direct relief purposes under the FERA.

The **Emergency Relief Appropriation Act** of Apr. 8, 1935, was designed to provide relief and work relief and to increase employment by providing for useful projects; it appropriated $4,000,000,000 to be used nominally at the president's discretion. It further appropriated unexpended balances of several earlier appropriations aggregating about $880,000,000.

1933-1934. NEW DEAL SECURITIES LEGISLATION: The **Securities Act of 1933** (approved May 27, 1933) provided for filing with the federal trade commission and for transmission to prospective investors of the fullest possible information, accompanied by sworn statements, about new security issues sold in interstate commerce or through the mails.

The **Securities Exchange Act** (approved June 6, 1934) provided for the regulation of securities exchanges and established a securities and exchange commission.

1933-1935. NEW DEAL LABOR LEGISLATION: The **Labor Disputes Joint Resolution** (approved June 19, 1934) abolished the national labor board and created a federal agency for the investigation and mediation of labor disputes growing out of the **National Industrial Recovery Act** (NIRA).

The **Railway Pension Act** (approved June 27, 1934) provided a comprehensive retirement system for railway employees based on employer and employee contributions. This act was subsequently declared unconstitutional.

The **Crosser-Dill Railway Labor Act** (approved June 27, 1934) provided for the settlement of labor disputes on the railroads and outlawed company unions.

Wagner-Connery Labor Relations Act, of July 5, 1935, was designed to satisfy the complaints of labor organizations against provision of the Recovery Act of 1933 as it affected them, and also to remedy their disappointment at losing the advantage of these provisions by the invalidation of that act. It declared it the policy of the United States to encourage collective bargaining and to protect employees' freedom of self-organization, and their negotiating as to their employment through representatives of their own choosing. New **National Labor Relations Board** created.

1933-1936. FOREIGN POLICIES of the New Deal: Nov. 17, 1933, diplomatic relations with Russia were resumed, ending policy of non-recognition which had prevailed since the overthrow of the Kerensky government in 1917.

The **Johnson Debt Default Act** (approved April 13, 1934) prohibited financial transactions with foreign governments in default in the payment of obligations to the United States.

The **Cuban Treaty** (ratified May 31, 1934) abrogated the Platt amendment.

Pan-American Conference convened at Buenos Aires, Dec. 1, 1936, addressed by President Roosevelt in person, who outlined his program for an American peace program. Secretary Hull presented the plan for a neutrality pact for American nations.

1933-1935. OTHER NEW DEAL LEGIS-LATION: The Beer-Wine Revenue Act (approved Mar. 22, 1933) levied a tax of $5 on every barrel of beer and wine manufactured; re-enacted portions of the Webb-Kenyon Act as a protection to states whose laws prohibited liquors with alcoholic content in excess of 3.2%. The states were left in control of the sale and distribution of liquor.

May 18. The **Tennessee Valley Authority Act** created the Tennessee Valley authority to maintain and operate Muscle Shoals and to develop the water-power resources of the Tennessee Valley. Also to improve the economic and social status of the valley population.

June 16. The **Emergency Railroad Transportation Act** created a federal co-ordinator of transportation.

June 16. The **National Industrial Recovery Act** created a national recovery administration to supervise the preparation of codes of fair competition and to guarantee to labor the right to organize and bargain collectively; also made provision for a program of public works. The act was declared unconstitutional by the supreme court, May 27, 1935.

Dec. 5. Ratification of the **Twenty-First Amendment**, repealing the eighteenth or prohibition amendment.

1934, June 12. Reciprocal **Tariff Act**, authorizing the president, for a period of three years, to negotiate trade agreements with foreign countries without the advice and consent of the Senate; gave the president the power to raise and lower tariff rates by not more than 50%.

June 19. The **Communications Act** created a federal commission to regulate interstate and foreign communications by telegraph, telephone, cable, and radio. It abolished the federal radio commission and transferred its functions, and those of the interstate commerce commission, with respect to telephone and telegraph, to the new commission.

1935, Aug. 9. The **Motor Carrier Act** placed interstate bus and truck lines under control of the interstate commerce commission.

Aug. 14. Social Security Act. Its primary objects were: (1) To provide for establishing, in co-operation with each of the states, systems in the states for the payment of support to the needy aged;

(2) to pay sums to persons during limited periods after their loss of employment. Provision was also made for federal aid toward states' aid for needy, dependent children, for crippled children, for neglected children, for the vocational rehabilitation of the disabled, for health-service agencies, and for the blind. The purpose as to old-age pensions was to be effected in the first place by the government's matching states' allowance to needy persons over the age of 65 years, up to $15 a month for each case. A tax on employees and a tax at an equal rate on the payrolls of employers was to be levied, starting in 1937 at 1% and rising by steps to 3% in 1949, to provide a fund out of which, not before Jan. 1, 1942, qualified employees retiring at 65 would receive to the end of their life payments of from $10 to $15 per month.

To help states pay allowances to persons losing employment, the act created a separate tax of 1% the first year, 2 the second, and 3 the third, and thereafter on employers' payrolls, starting with the payrolls of 1936.

Aug. 26. Public Utility Holding Company Act. Purpose: (1) Doing away with holding companies among the public-utility enterprises serving communities with electricity except where such companies might be needful; (2) regulating the relations of remaining holding companies and their relations with the subsidiary companies that they controlled. The **Federal Power Commission** was made the administrative agency for these purposes. It was charged to proceed, after Jan. 1, 1938, to limit each holding company system to "a single, integrated public-utility system," save for minor and appropriate transgressions of the exact limit. It was to make exceptions in favor of a holding company's plural system or systems if these would suffer loss of economies by segregation, if systems were all in one state or in adjoining states, and where the combination of systems was not too great to admit of localized management, efficiency of operation, and effective regulation.

Aug. 30. Guffey-Snyder Bituminous Coal Stabilization Act. Provisions of the act followed in great measure those of the bituminous coal code under the NRA. A national bituminous coal commission created to administer the act, particularly to establish a code for the industry, embodying mandatory features detailed in the law. These included price-fixing features and a re-enactment of sec. 7-b of the Recovery Act, obliging employers to accept labor organizations and negotiate with representatives of the employees' own choosing. A tax of 15% on the selling price or market value of soft coal produced was imposed on producers, but nine-tenths of this was remitted to producers filing acceptance of the code. Thus producers were at liberty to stay out, but must pay heavily for non-conformity. Declared unconstitutional, May, 1936.

Aug. 30. Wealth-Tax Act. Use of federal power of taxation as a weapon against "unjust concentration of wealth and economic power." Increased surtaxes on individual yearly incomes of $50,000 and over.

1936, Nov. 3. Franklin D. Roosevelt re-elected president over Alfred M. Landon (Republican) by 524 electoral votes to 7. He carried every state except Maine and Vermont.

1937, Jan. 20. FRANKLIN D. ROOSE-VELT inaugurated for second term. He was the first president to be inaugurated on this day, set by the 20th amendment to the constitution.

Jan.-June. Widespread labor troubles resulting from efforts of the C.I.O. to organize the workers in the automobile and steel industries on the basis of industrial unionism. The **sit-down strike** made its appearance in the General Motors strike as a weapon of labor. The strike spread to Chrysler Corporation employees and to those of the Republic Steel Corporation, the Youngstown Sheet Steel and Tube Company, the Inland Steel Company, and the Bethlehem Steel Corporation. A strike among workers of the United States Steel Corporation was avoided when the company signed a contract with the C.I.O. Mar. 2. The strike of the employees of the Republic Steel Corporation resulted in bloodshed. Although the sit-down strikes and the aggressiveness of the C.I.O. in this period seriously divided public opinion, labor, through the application of the collective-bargaining provisions of the Wagner Labor Relations Act by the national labor relations board, made substantial progress in the unionization of the mass-production industries, where the principle of collective bargaining had never before been admitted by employers.

Feb. 5. President Roosevelt in a special message to Congress recommended the enactment of legislation empowering him to appoint "*additional judges in all federal courts without exception, where there are incumbent judges of retirement age who do not choose to resign.*" This proposal aroused widespread opposition in and out of Congress as an attempt on the part of the president to "pack" the **supreme court,** whose adverse decisions on various pieces of New Deal legislation had greatly displeased Mr. Roosevelt. After months of debate and controversy the bill failed of enactment, due largely to opposition of members of the president's party in the Senate.

Apr. 26. The President signed the Guffey-Vinson Act, successor to the Bituminous Coal Act of 1935, largely invalidated by the supreme court. The act created a **Bituminous Coal Commission,** to administer a code covering "unfair" practices, fixing minimum and, in some cases, maximum prices for coal, and dealing with arrangements for marketing.

May. Neutrality Act, reaffirming and somewhat enlarging statutes of Aug. 1935 and Feb. 1936. Whenever the president proclaimed a state of war outside of the Americas, the export of arms and munitions to the belligerents was to be prohibited. Certain materials designated by the president must be paid for before leaving the United States, and must be carried in foreign ships. All other trade with the combatants was subject to the cash, but not to the carry, restriction. In addition the act prohibited American citizens from traveling on belligerent ships and barred loans to warring powers.

Sept. 2. President Roosevelt signed the **Wagner-Steagall Act,** declaring a federal policy of employing government funds and credit to help states and their subdivisions to remedy the housing shortage.

Oct. A business recession, the gradual onset of which had been evident for several months, brought sharp declines in the stock market. By Nov. the recession had become general throughout the country.

Nov. 15. Congress assembled in special session, with earnest recommendation of the president that it carry forward his legislative program. A bill to regulate wages and hours passed the Senate, but was recommitted in the House by a combination of Republicans and southern Democrats. Congress adjourned Dec. 21, having accomplished little of a constructive nature.

1938, Oct. 24. Wages and Hours Law became operative. It provided for minimum wages and maximum weekly hours in industries affecting interstate commerce; it also prohibited child labor.

Nov. 8. State and congressional elections, showing substantial Republican gains for first time since 1928.

Dec. 24. The declaration of Lima adopted by 21 American states at the session of the Pan-American Conference expressed their determination to defend themselves against all foreign intervention and envisaged consultation in case peace, security or territorial integrity should be menaced (p. 1062). The United States government favored an even stronger statement and made every effort to close the ranks of the American nations in view of the activities of the totalitarian states of Europe.

1939, Jan. 12. President Roosevelt asked Congress for $552,000,000 for defense. Preparations were made for extensive fortifications in the Pacific and in the Caribbean (Puerto Rico and Virgin Islands). More and more openly the president indicated the sympathies of the United States for the European democracies. France was permitted to buy large numbers of military planes and the United States government itself embarked upon construction of 600 additional airplanes. After German annexation of Czechoslovakia the United States refused recognition of the change and imposed countervailing duties on imports from Germany. The danger of a German-Polish conflict led to

Apr. 15. Roosevelt's letter to Mussolini and Hitler asking for assurances that they would refrain from aggression on 31 named nations for 10 years and suggesting discussion of reduction of armaments and possibilities of restoring world trade. Hitler replied in a speech of Apr. 28 (p. 1005). Despite some senatorial opposition, American opinion appeared generally favorable to the president's initiative.

June. King George VI and Queen Elizabeth paid a four-day visit to the United States, the first reigning European sovereigns to set foot on American soil. Despite the obvious bid for American sympathy and support, the rulers were given a cordial reception.

Despite all efforts of the administration, Congress refused to modify the **Neutrality Act** which provided for an embargo on arms to belligerents. The president publicly stated that indirectly at least the Neutrality Act constituted an encouragement to a would-be aggressor. When, in August, the German-Polish conflict came to a head (p. 966), Roosevelt appealed to Victor Immanuel, Hitler and Moscicki, but without avail. The American government secured from the belligerents a promise not to bombard open cities, and

Sept. 5. The United States proclaimed neutrality in the European War.

2. THE DOMINION OF CANADA

1914, Aug. 4. Entrance of Great Britain into the World War. Message of Canada to the mother country: *"If unhappily war should ensue, the Canadian people will be united . . . to maintain the honor of the empire"* (Aug. 2). Special session of Parliament called (Aug. 18) and a war budget voted. 30,000 volunteers embarked for England by the end of Sept.

1914. Nationalization of the Canadian Northern Railway forced by fear of imminent failure and a collapse of national credit. The **Grand Trunk Railway** was nationalized in 1920. The government operated about 23,000 miles of railway representing a capital of $1,652,000,000, known as Canadian National Railways. Gradual co-ordination of lines. Sir Henry Thornton appointed in 1922 as the nonpolitical head of the system.

1915, Oct. 30. Death of Sir Charles Tupper, last of the "fathers of confederation."

Dec. 3. Internal war loan of $50,000,000 subscribed twice over; others for

$100,000,000 (1916) and $150,000,000 (1917) were also oversubscribed.

1916, Feb. 3-4. The Parliament buildings at Ottawa were destroyed by fire. New buildings were at once begun.

Nov. 11—1921. The DUKE OF DEVONSHIRE, governor-general.

1917, Sept. 26. Compulsory Military Service Act became law conscripting men between ages of 20 and 45.

Oct. 6. Parliament dissolved and a coalition cabinet formed. The Liberal Party was split, with Sir W. Laurier opposing conscription; French-Canadians were dissatisfied with conscription and with English language requirements in the schools and failed to enlist. The elections (Dec. 17) resulted in a sweeping victory for the coalition; Quebec unrepresented in the cabinet.

Dec. 6. Explosion in Halifax Harbor with heavy loss of life and destruction of property.

1918, Mar. Woman Franchise Bill passed

extending the federal vote to all women over 21 years of age.

Apr. Riots in Quebec city due to enforcement of conscription; several civilians killed.

Nov. 11. **Armistice declared** (see First World War). Canadian troops returned home in the next six months. Canada supplied 640,886 men for the war; cost to Canada, over $1,500,000,000.

1919, Feb. 17. **Death of Sir Wilfrid Laurier.**

May. Strike in Winnipeg among building trades which spread to general sympathetic strike lasting five weeks. One Big Union idea active.

1920, May 10. Official announcement that Canada would be represented at Washington by a Canadian resident minister; new international status; no appointment made until 1926, but treaties with the United States on North Pacific halibut fisheries (Mar. 1923), and for mutual assistance to prevent smuggling (June 6, 1924), both signed by a Canadian official (Mr. La Pointe).

July 10. Resignation of Sir Robert Borden. **Mr. Arthur Meighen** prime minister.

1921, Aug. 11. Arrival of **Lord Byng of Vimy** as governor-general (1921–1926).

Dec. 6. General elections resulting in Liberal (opposition) victory. **Mr. W. L. Mackenzie King** prime minister.

1923. Redistribution Bill increasing seats in House of Commons from 235 to 245, with the loss of 2 seats by the eastern provinces and the gain of 12 by the western.

1924, Mar. 21. A liquor treaty between Great Britain and the United States was ratified by the Dominion House of Commons and Apr. 4 by the Senate.

1925, Oct. 29. **National elections.** Liberal platform called for an adequate but moderate tariff, the reform of the Senate, a strong immigration policy, government steps to develop the foreign trade of the Dominion, the completion of the Hudson's Bay Railway and the reduction of grain rates. Conservatives advocated higher tariff. Liberals had 101 seats in the House of Commons, Conservatives, 118, Progressives, 23, Labor, 2, Independent, 1. The Progressives held the balance of power. Premier King decided to hold on until meeting of Parliament Jan. 7, 1926.

1926. **W. L. Mackenzie King** maintained a precarious hold on the government to June 28, when he resigned because

of customs scandal. **Arthur Meighen** then organized a cabinet which was defeated on the first government measure placed before Parliament.

Sept. 14. **National elections.** Liberals had 119 seats, but not a majority.

Sept. 25. Liberal cabinet, with **King** as prime minister.

Oct. 2. **Lord Willingdon,** new governor-general, came into office, superseding Lord Byng.

Nov. 10. **Vincent Massey** appointed first Canadian minister to Washington.

1927, Feb. **William Phillips** appointed American minister to Ottawa.

Nov. 15. **Election of Canada** to a seat in the council of the League of Nations.

1928. Appointment of **Canadian diplomatic representatives to Japan** and **France,** another evidence of Canadian nationhood. Proposal made that a British diplomatic representative to Ottawa be appointed since the governor-general is merely the personal representative of the king.

1929, Apr. 9. Canadian minister at Washington protested the sinking of the Canadian ship *I'm Alone* in the Gulf of Mexico by a United States coast guard prohibition patrol boat. Apr. 25 it was announced the case would be settled by arbitration.

Growing irritation in Canada at threat of hostile American tariff legislation against Canadian agricultural products.

Dec. 15. Agreement between Dominion government and the governments of **Alberta** and **Manitoba,** subject to ratification by Dominion Parliament and provincial legislatures, providing for return of natural resources to the two provinces and for continuation of the annual subsidies previously received by the provinces.

1930, May 2. **Dunning Tariff** became effective; most drastic tariff revision since 1907. Gave expression to uneasiness and resentment aroused in Canada by the high duties on Canadian articles contained in the Smoot-Hawley Tariff of the United States. Imports from Great Britain given preferential treatment.

July 28. **National election.** Basic issue the economic depression and the failure of the Liberal government to provide a policy for relief of unemployment. Conservatives asserted they would extend preferential tariff rates to Great Britain only in return for reciprocal concessions and that they would go much further than the Liberals in protecting Canadian products against American competition. Conservatives had 139 seats, a clear majority. **R. B.**

Bennett and Conservative cabinet took office on Aug. 7.

Sept. 8-22. Special session of Parliament to enact emergency unemployment and tariff legislation. Public works appropriation of $20,000,000 voted as an unemployment relief measure, supplemented by a similar amount from the provinces, substantial contributions by the municipalities and $21,000,000 by the railways, making a total of between 80 and 90 million available for expenditure within the next 12 to 18 months. Tariff duties increased on about 125 classes of goods, including textiles, shoes, paper, agricultural implements, cast-iron pipe, fertilizers, electrical apparatus, jewelry, and meats.

Oct. 1. Transfer of natural resources to Alberta and Manitoba.

1931. In accordance with the decision of the Federal-Provincial Conference held at Ottawa, Apr. 7 and 8, the **Statute of Westminster** stipulated that the British North America Act should remain unchanged. The Statute of Westminster, providing that laws of the United Kingdom do not apply to any dominion unless that dominion so requests, was adopted by Parliament without a division.

May 19. Parliamentary inquiry authorized into the **Beauharnois Company**, engaged in construction of a hydro-electric power project in the St. Lawrence River. Inquiry revealed that although the project was basically sound it had been ruthlessly exploited for the profit of company officials and three Liberal senators who were close friends of Mackenzie King, the former Liberal premier.

June 18. Tariff of 1930 revised upward. It was estimated that the new duties would cut off two-thirds of the goods previously imported from the United States.

1932, July 21-Aug. 21. IMPERIAL ECONOMIC CONFERENCE IN OTTAWA. Seven bilateral treaties signed by Great Britain, one of them being with Canada, gave raw material of the Dominion a preference of about 10% in the British market. The United Kingdom imposed new duties on wheat and other imports in order to give Dominions this preference. British preferential tariffs also imposed on foreign meat, butter, cheese, fruit, and eggs. For Canada's benefit Great Britain removed the restriction on Canadian live cattle, placed a tariff of 4 cents on copper and promised that the 10% *ad-valorem* tariff on foreign timber, fish, asbestos, zinc, and lead would not be reduced unless Canada agreed. In return, Great Britain

received concessions on manufactured goods entering Canada. Canada also signed new treaties with South Africa, Rhodesia, and the Irish Free State, and began the revision of existing treaties with Australia and New Zealand.

1933. Railway legislation embodying the recommendations of the royal commission in report of Sept. 1932. Three trustees for C.N.R. and co-operation between it and the Canadian Pacific.

May 12. Trade agreement with France signed, and went into effect June 10. It provided for reciprocal tariff preferences on 1148 items.

Aug. 25. Canada joined in **wheat agreement** with United States, Argentina, Australia, and Soviet Union. The countries agreed to export a maximum of 560,000,000 bushels for 1933-1934, and, except for the Soviet Union and Danubian states, promised to reduce either acreage or exports by 15%.

1934, July 3. The Natural Products Marketing Act assented to. It provided for the creation of a Dominion marketing board with powers to form local boards and to co-operate with marketing boards created by the provinces, and authorized the regulated marketing of any natural products, control by license of the export of any regulated products, and control of interprovincial marketing. The Dominion marketing board authorized to investigate and regulate price spreads in the handling of natural or regulated products.

Aug. 4. H. H. Stevens, minister of trade and commerce, in a privately printed pamphlet, made revelations which transformed widespread popular demand for governmental action to alleviate the depression into a demand for regulation of big business in Canada. Stevens resigned his cabinet position Oct. 27.

Oct. 1. The Dominion Companies Act went into force. Repealed the Companies Act of 1927 and established stringent regulations safeguarding the security of investors, shareholders, and creditors.

1935, Mar. 11. The Bank of Canada opened its doors, making effective the **Bank of Canada Act of 1934.** This privately owned but government-supervised institution served as a central bank.

Prime Minister Bennett early in the year proposed a sweeping **platform of social legislation** as the only means of escaping defeat in the face of growing popular dissatisfaction. Before adjourning July 5, Parliament enacted a comprehensive series of laws designed to cope with the economic situation. Among them were: The **Wheat Board Act**, establishing a board to buy wheat at a fixed minimum price, the government to absorb the loss if the board failed to sell the wheat at a profit over the fixed minimum. An act providing for a **Dominion trade and industry commission** to administer the **Combines Investigation Act**, prohibiting monopolies operating to the detriment of the public; a **Fair Wages and Hours of Labor Act**, guaranteeing fair wages on public works and a 44-hour week. An **Employment and Social Insurance Act**, providing for contributory unemployment insurance for workers receiving less than $2000 per year, with certain industries excepted; equal premiums to be paid by employers, employees, and federal government. The **Minimum Wage Act**, authorizing the establishment of a federal agency to fix minimum wages in manufacturing and commerce. The **Limitation of Hours of Work Act** providing for 8-hour day and 48-hour week for industrial workers.

Aug. 14. Dissolution of Parliament and call for general election.

Aug. 22. Victory of the Social Credit Party in Alberta, under leadership of William Aberhart, promising to every adult citizen of the province a regular income of $25 per month, funds for which were to be provided by a turnover tax of about 10% on domestic products. Death-blow to Alberta's credit.

Oct. 14. General election, a Liberal landslide gave Liberals 171 seats, with 8 seats held by independent Liberals who would ordinarily support the party.

Oct. 23. William Lyon Mackenzie King, prime minister for the third time.

Nov. 15. Prime Minister King signed at Washington the reciprocal trade agreement with the United States. The treaty granted Canada lower rates or other concessions on two-thirds of her exports by volume to the United States. The United States, in turn, received concessions on three-fourths of her dutiable exports to Canada.

Dec. 9-13. Conference of federal and provincial governments agreed unanimously that it was "imperative" to amend the constitution, and that Canada should have the power to amend its own constitution. A committee was appointed to study a procedure under which Canada could amend the British North America Act without recourse to the British Parliament.

1936, June 17. Supreme court of Canada invalidated most of "New Deal" legislation enacted by the Bennett government in 1935.

1937, Jan. 28. The judicial committee of the privy council in London, Eng., declared unconstitutional the bulk of the "New Deal" legislation of the Bennett government, thereby sustaining the decision of the supreme court of Canada of the previous year.

Apr. The demand of the C.I.O. for the recognition of the local branch of the N.A.W.A. (an affiliate of the C.I.O.) in the Oshawa, Ontario, plant of the General Motors Corporation led to a **sit-down strike**. Premier Hepburn of Ontario intervened, denounced the C.I.O., and brought about an agreement (Apr. 23) granting concessions to workers on wages and working conditions, but withholding recognition of the N.A.W.A.

The Dominion minister of justice announced (Mar. 24) that the sit-down strike was wholly illegal in Canada and that all the powers of the government would be used to prevent its use in the Dominion.

Aug. 15. Prime Minister Mackenzie King appointed a royal commission (Rowell commission) to study **amendment of the British North America Act**, which now seemed imperative in view of the court decisions on social and economic legislation. The commission was charged specifically to consider the economic and financial relations between the federal and provincial governments, but was given wide powers to investigate all phases of the confederation.

1939, May. Visit of King George VI and Queen Elizabeth to Canada. They were the first reigning sovereigns to visit the Dominion and were given an enthusiastic reception.

Sept. 3. England's declaration of war on Germany (p. 967) brought forth expressions of solidarity in Canada and the government at once took steps to aid the mother country in the great conflict.

3. NEWFOUNDLAND

1914, Aug. 4. Declaration of war by Great Britain. Newfoundland, like the other members of the empire, supported the mother country and sent troops.

1917. Resignation of Premier Morris, who was succeeded by Mr. (later Sir) W. F. Lloyd.

1919, May 23. The Hon. M. P. Cashin,

premier. Elections (Nov. 1) resulted in the overthrow of the Cashin ministry and Sir Richard A. Squires became premier.

1923. William R. Warren, premier.

Dec. 26. Grave charges of misappropriation of funds brought against Sir Richard Squires and others (later acquitted) by Premier Warren. The latter was defeated in the Assembly following the arrest of Squires (Apr. 22, 1924) and resigned. He was succeeded by **Mr. Walter Munroe.**

1933. NEWFOUNDLAND LOST ITS STATUS AS A DOMINION, and reverted to that of a crown colony, because of debt resulting from incompetence and corruption. A royal commission (appointed in Mar.) reported (Nov.) the following recommendations: (1) Replacement of the existing form of government by a special commission consisting of three British and three Newfoundlanders, with the governor as president. This commission was to have legal and executive authority subject to the supervisory control of the British government. (2) Readjustment and lowering of tariffs. (3) Assumption by the United Kingdom of responsibility for Newfoundland finances until the island should have become self-supporting. These recommendations were approved by the Newfoundland Parliament Nov. 29 and received the royal assent Dec. 21.

1934. Substantial progress toward economic and financial recovery.

Oct. 1. The commission announced that Jan. 1, 1935, import duties would be revised, generally downward.

1936-1937. The commission continued to devote itself to the problem of **economic rehabilitation,** giving particular attention to the development of alternative sources of employment, to the encouragement of subsistence farming, to the relief of poverty, and to the improvement of medical and educational facilities.

D. LATIN AMERICA

1. GENERAL

Though most of the Latin-American states, at the suggestion of the United States government, either declared war on Germany or broke off diplomatic relations, they played no part in the war from the military viewpoint. Nevertheless the war period was of utmost importance for the entire region, in view of the fact that the demand for raw materials made possible a **phenomenal expansion of trade.** Excepting for the slump of 1920–1921 this expansion was steady from 1916 to 1929. It was accompanied by **great capital investments,** especially by the United States, after the war, and by the emergence in the more advanced countries of a local industry. The **growth of the urban middle classes** enabled them to dispute with the great landholders the control of the government. At the same time the **agrarian proletariat** (on coffee, sugar, and other plantations) was reinforced by **workers in the oil-fields and mines,** as well as those in the factories. The result was increased **demand for social legislation** (carried out, however imperfectly, in several states), together with political organization of the lower classes (in many instances in alliance with the middle classes, at least for a time). These basic social changes created a ferment throughout the continent, the world depression adding its share to stimulate unrest.

Between the different Latin-American states and between Latin America and the United States co-operation along various lines became ever more common, despite periods of profound distrust between Latin America and the great neighbor in the north.

1915, May 24. The first Pan-American **Financial Conference** met at Washington.

May 25. Conclusion of an **arbitration treaty between Argentina, Brazil, and Chile** (the A.B.C. Powers).

1916, Apr. 3. A Pan-American **high commission,** meeting at Buenos Aires, worked out a scheme for improvement of telegraph and railway communication. A permanent high commission was created to elaborate uniform commercial laws.

1923, Mar.-May. The fourth Pan-American **Conference** at Santiago re-sulted in various conventions providing for fact-finding commissions in cases of disputes, for trademark regulations, publication of documents, etc., in addition to many resolutions touching health, education, etc.

May 3. Signature of the Pan-American treaty for the pacific settlement of disputes.

1928, Jan.-Feb. The sixth Pan-American **Conference** met at Havana. The Pan-American Union was placed on a treaty basis and various conferences arranged for matters of common interest. The United States, however, opposed a resolution directed against intervention in the internal affairs of other states.

Dec.—1929, Jan. The Pan-American **Conference on conciliation and arbitration** met at Washington, revised the treaty of May 3, 1924, declared for conciliation and arbitration of all disputes and set up commissions to deal with cases as they should arise.

1930, Sept. Meeting of the **first Pan-American Conference on agriculture** at Washington.

1933. President Roosevelt declared publicly against a policy of intervention in Latin America and did his utmost to demonstrate his policy of the "good neighbor." At the

1933. Seventh Pan-American Conference, at Montevideo, Secretary Hull did his utmost to remove distrust of the United States and impress upon the American states the need for confidence and collaboration.

1936, Dec. 1-23. Pan-American **Conference for the maintenance of peace,** in session at Buenos Aires. The American governments for the first time accepted the **principle of consultation** in case the peace of the continent should be threatened. A convention was drawn up to provide for a **common policy of neutrality** in the event of conflict between American states.

1938, Dec. 24. The Pan-American **Conference,** meeting at Lima (21 states represented) adopted the *Declaration of Lima,* which reaffirmed the absolute sovereignty of the various American states, but also expressed their determination to defend themselves against *"all foreign intervention*

CARIBBEAN SEA

PANAMA

Panama

Caracas

Orinoco R.

VENEZUELA

ATLANTIC

OCEAN

Bogota

COLOMBIA

Georgetown

BRITISH GUIANA

DUTCH GUIANA

FRENCH GUIANA

Paramaribo

Cayenne

Rio Negro

Quito

ECUADOR

Amazon

River

P E R U

Lima

B R A Z I L

Madeira R.

Araguaya

Sao Francisco R.

TACNA

ARICA

BOLIVIA

Sucre

CHACO

Pilcomayo R.

Paraguay R.

Paraná R.

PARAGUAY

Asuncion

Rio de Janeiro

PACIFIC

OCEAN

C H I L E

A R G E N T I N A

Santiago

Buenos Aires

Paraná R.

Uruguay R.

URUGUAY

Montevideo

ATLANTIC

OCEAN

SOUTH AMERICA
IN
1930

Shaded areas show territories
in dispute.

Scale of Miles

0   200   400   600   800   1000

or activities that may threaten them." It provided further for consultation in case *"peace, security, or territorial integrity"* of any state should be menaced. The declaration was a reflection of growing uneasiness, especially in the United States, with regard to possible designs of the fascist powers of Europe upon Latin-American territory, and, because of Argentine opposition, was less outspoken than the United States government would have desired.

2. ARGENTINA

1916-1922. HIPÓLITO IRIGOYEN, leader of the Argentine radicals, was **elected president** after an electoral reform (1912) had made possible the expression of popular (mass) sentiment. During his administration he carried through a **program of social reform** (factory acts, regulations of hours, pensions, etc.). Irigoyen refused to give up neutrality during the World War, although diplomatic relations with Germany were strained after the sinking of Argentine ships by German submarines (1917). Argentina supplied huge quantities of wheat and meat to the Allied Powers.

1920. Argentina became an original member of the League of Nations, but withdrew from the assembly in 1921 on rejection of an Argentine resolution that all sovereign states be admitted to the League.

1922-1928. MARCELO ALVEAR, president. In general he continued the policies of his predecessor in the sphere of social legislation.

1928. Irigoyen was again elected to the presidency, but

1930, Sept. 6. JOSÉ URIBURU forced him from office. Irigoyen's assumption of wide personal powers had aroused much criticism, while the distress created by the world depression had provoked a loud demand for further relief measures. With Uriburu the landowning and big business and other **conservative groups returned to power.** After a temporary dictatorship of Uriburu

1932-1937. AGUSTÍN JUSTO was regularly elected **president.** Political and social unrest continued and culminated in an unsuccessful **radical revolt** in the northeastern provinces (1933-1934).

1932, Nov. 17. Saavedra Lamas, the foreign minister, published a proposed South American **anti-war pact,** which had already been accepted by several states. Argentina also (1933) resumed full membership in the League of Nations, taking an active part in the negotiations concerning the war between Bolivia and Paraguay (p. 1066).

1933. The government launched a **program of national economic recovery,** which achieved marked success. A commercial treaty with Great Britain made possible the shipment of large quantities of beef and wheat.

1935. Conflict between the Conservative government of Justo and the opposition Radical and Socialist parties, which represented the majority of voters, reached serious proportions. **Fascist organizations** also opposed the government and formed a common front of the extreme Right (Oct.).

1936, Mar. In congressional elections, postponed from late in 1935, the Radical Party, under the leadership of former president Alvear, triumphed. A Leftist **Popular Front was organized** (May 1), but fascist groups continued to gain ground. The Rightist elements supporting the government formed a **National Front,** favoring a conservative dictatorship (May 31). The **Communist Party was declared illegal** (Nov. 10).

1937, Sept. 5. Presidential elections, bitterly contested. **Roberto M. Ortiz,** candidate of the government, was elected over the nominee of the Radical Party, Alvear. Efforts of the Leftist parties to prevent a quorum in a joint session of Congress to confirm the election failed when a majority was declared sufficient, and Ortiz was proclaimed elected. He was inaugurated Feb. 10, 1938.

3. CHILE

Chile remained neutral in the World War despite violation of her neutrality by both German and British warships. The export of nitrate in large quantities to the Allied Powers created a period of great prosperity.

1920, Jan. 10. Chile became a member of the League of Nations.

1920-1921. Chile suffered severely from the general world slump and the cessation of the demand for nitrate. The lower classes loudly demanded a more democratic régime and extensive social legislation.

1920-1924. ARTURO ALESSANDRI, elected president after a disputed election. He was the candidate of the **Liberal Alliance Party** and advocated wide political, religious, and social reforms. His election represented a **victory for the middle classes,** supported by labor elements. But during his term Alessandri was unable to achieve much, partly because of the stagnation of government under the parliamentary system. In 1924 he was forced from office. After control by a military junta under Gen. **Luis Altamirano,**

1925, Jan. 23. A *coup d'état* engineered by Maj. **Cárlos Ibañez** resulted in the recall of Alessandri and the promulgation of a

Sept. 18. New constitution, providing for responsibility of the cabinet to the president, broader suffrage, separation of Church and State, provincial autonomy, etc.

Oct. 1. Alessandri resigned, in view of the continued disorder and uncertainty. He was succeeded by

1925-1927. EMILIANO FIGUEROA, who was, in turn, forced out by

1927-1931. GEN. CÁRLOS IBAÑEZ, who made himself **dictator-president,** and then promulgated many of the social reforms which Alessandri had advocated.

1929, June 3. SETTLEMENT OF THE TACNA-ARICA QUESTION, which had embittered the relations of Chile and Peru for many years (diplomatic relations severed 1910). Efforts of the United States (1922-1926) to mediate and effect a settlement through a plebiscite led to no result, but served to bring about direct negotiations and the final agreement, by which **Chile received Arica** and **Peru was awarded Tacna,** Chile agreeing to accord Peru port and transportation facilities at Arica. Chile retained all territory taken from Bolivia (despite appeals of that country to the United States and Argentina), but accorded Bolivia a railway outlet to the Pacific. Thenceforth Chile and Bolivia drew closer. In 1936 they concluded a treaty providing for united diplomatic action. Closer economic and cultural relations followed (1937).

1931. Ibañez resigned because of the general discontent with his measures of economy (made necessary by the world depression).

1931. JUAN MONTERO, representative of the conservative elements, was elected in opposition to Alessandri. Political and social unrest continued, and

1932, June 4. Montero was overthrown. A junta headed by **Cárlos Dávila** assumed power and adopted a socialistic policy, but

Sept. 13. Dávila was overthrown by a military coup and Alessandri became president once more, after an election (Dec. 24).

1932-1938. THE GOVERNMENT OF ALESSANDRI, supported by a coalition of Conservative and Liberal parties, assumed ever greater control of economic activity, enacting far-reaching social reforms. Marked improvement of economic conditions after 1933 did not, however, relieve the political tension. The government was opposed on the one hand by **fascist groups,** on the other by **Communists.**

1937, Mar. 5. Alessandri and the Rightist bloc won a victory in the elections over the Popular Front parties.

1938, Sept. 5. A fascist (*Nacista*) uprising proved abortive, but in the ensuing elections the parties of the Left elected

1938- PEDRO AGUIRRE CEDRA, president. The Popular Front comprised Radicals, Socialists, and Communists, as against the combination of Conservative, Agrarian, and Liberal parties which supported **Gustavo Ross.** The new régime promptly embarked on a policy of helping the worker (low bread prices, housing, education), despite strong protests from the agrarian groups.

4. PARAGUAY

1912-1916. The presidency of **Edward Schaerer** was an era of progress and relative political stability. Trade, industry, grazing, and agriculture expanded, transportation and communications were improved, and foreign capital was invested. Paraguay remained neutral during the First World War, and in 1920 became an **original member of the League of Nations.**

1916-1919. Manuel Franco, president. On his death

1919-1920. José Montero, the vice-president, succeeded.

1920-1921. Manuel Gondra, president.

He was forced to resign by a revolutionary group. After the short presidencies of Eusebio Ayala (1921–1923), Eligio Ayala (1923–1924) and Luis Riart (1924),

1924-1928. ELIGIO AYALA was elected president. Representing the Liberal groups, he inaugurated a policy of social legislation.

1928-1931. JOSÉ GUGGIARI, president. During his administration

1928-1930. The dispute with Bolivia over the Chaco territory came to a head. Despite earlier agreements (1913, 1915) the respective claims were still unsettled. Dec. 6, 1928, the forces of the two states clashed and war seemed inevitable. Diplomatic relations were severed and Paraguay appealed to the League of Nations, but the Pan-American Conference at once offered to mediate. An arbitration convention was drafted (Aug. 31, 1929), but was rejected by both parties. Direct negotiations were agreed to, but skirmishes in the contested area continued until a temporary arrangement (return to *status quo ante*) was arrived at (Apr. 4, 1930).

1932-1935. THE CHACO WAR. The League of Nations and the Pan-American Union both called upon the two parties to desist from hostilities and accept neutral arbitration, but the numerous efforts to preserve peace resulted chiefly in added confusion. Neither side was ready to accept peace offers and the war continued. The Paraguayans, after a series of major campaigns, occupied the larger part of the Chaco, but failed in their attempts to invade Bolivian territory. During the war the relations between Paraguay and Chile became badly strained because of service of Chilean officers with the Bolivian army and employment of Chilean workmen by Bolivia.

1935. At the suggestion of the League of Nations, some 20 nations lifted the embargo on arms in favor of Bolivia, while retaining it against Paraguay. Thereupon Paraguay announced withdrawal from the League.

June 14. Paraguay and Bolivia concluded a truce, at the instance of the United States and five of the South-American governments. A peace conference at Buenos Aires was arranged for, and met in July. Definitive peace was not signed until July 21, 1938 (approved by plebiscite Aug. 10). The treaty provided for arbitration of boundaries between American states. The territorial award, made by six American presidents (Oct. 10), assigned the greater part of the Chaco to Paraguay, but provided Bolivia with an outlet to the sea by way of the Paraguay River.

1936, Feb. 17. A military revolt, provoked by opposition of the army to the supposed weakness of the government in the peace negotiations, led to the overthrow of President Ayala. Rafael Franco became provisional president. Supported by a junta of officers, and by radical and nationalist elements, he made himself a military dictator.

Mar. 11. Franco proclaimed a totalitarian state, and introduced economic, social, and financial reforms. These policies antagonized Paraguayan and foreign interests, which resented the heavy taxation.

1937, Aug. 15. Franco was forced to resign as a result of a bloodless *coup d'état*. Felix Pavia, of the Liberal Party, became provisional president and suppressed a number of counter-revolutionary movements.

Oct. 11. Pavia was elected constitutional president.

1939, Apr. 30. José Félix Estigarribia was elected president.

5. URUGUAY

Uruguay has, in the 20th century, enjoyed comparative stability and prosperity. During the administrations of

1907-1911. Claudio Williman,
1911-1915. José Batlle y Ordóñez,
1915-1919. Feliciano Viera,
1919-1923. Baltasar Brum, and their successors, many social and administrative reforms were initiated and the internal development of the country was rapid.

On the entry of the United States into the First World War, Uruguay expressed moral solidarity and later severed relations with Germany.

1919, Mar. 1. A NEW CONSTITUTION curtailed the powers of the president, created a national council of administration (9 members elected on proportional basis by popular vote and endowed with important functions), and disestablished the Roman Catholic Church.

1920. Uruguay joined the League of Nations.

1923-1927. José Serrato, president. He and his successor,

1927-1931. Juan Compisteguy, continued and accelerated the policy of social reform until Uruguay, like the rest of the world, began to feel the pinch of the depression.

1931-1938. GABRIEL TERRA, president. He represented the more advanced wing of the Liberal Party, and soon found himself in conflict with the national council of administration concerning the division of executive authority. In view of the political and social unrest and the consequent threat of civil war,

1933. Terra established a temporary dictatorship.

1934, Apr. 19. A new constitution provided for a strong executive, restricted the powers of Parliament, and established compulsory voting. Terra was re-elected president and

1935. A revolt against him was crushed.

1935-1938. The Terra government continued the work of social and economic reform, and Uruguay gradually experienced economic improvement.

1938- Alfredo Baldomir elected president to succeed Terra.

6. BOLIVIA

1917, Apr. 13. Bolivia severed relations with Germany, but did not declare war.

1917-1920. José Gutiérrez Guerra, president.

1920, Jan. 10. Bolivia became an original member of the League of Nations.

Mar. 16. In the Tacna-Arica dispute, the Bolivian government took the stand that neither Chile nor Peru was entitled to the provinces. The Bolivian government claimed access to the Pacific, preferably through the port of Arica. Nov. 1 Bolivia appealed in vain to the League of Nations to secure such an access.

July 11. A *coup d'état* led to the overthrow of Gutiérrez Guerra, and

1921-1925. BAUTISTA SAAVEDRA became president. His administration was marked by industrial development: public improvements, encouragement of agriculture and mining, flotation of large loans in the United States, etc. The exploitation of oil added greatly to the national resources.

1925, May 2. José Cabino Villanueva, president. His election was annulled (Sept. 1) by Congress, because of fraud. Villanueva fled the country and

1926-1930. HERNANDO SILES became president.

1928-1929. Dispute between Bolivia and Paraguay over the Chaco region; war temporarily averted through the League and mediation of the American powers (p. 1066).

1929. Settlement of the Tacna-Arica question (p. 1065). Bolivia definitely lost Atacama, but obtained the right

to use the Chilean-built railway between La Paz and Arica.

1930, May 28. Overthrow of President Siles, whose régime had become unpopular through economic depression, fall in the price of tin, closing of the mines, and resultant labor unrest. After a temporary government by a military junta, led by Gen. Carlos Blanco Galinda,

1931. DANIEL SALAMANCA was elected president.

1932-1935. THE CHACO WAR, between Bolivia and Paraguay (p. 1066).

1934, Dec. President Salamanca was overthrown by a military coup, following serious defeats of the Bolivian forces. The vice-president, Luis Tejada Sorzano, assumed the presidency.

1936, May 17. Another coup led to the fall of Tejada Sorzano, who was replaced by a joint civil and military junta under David Toro, who established a dictatorship. Measures to promote economic revival were adopted (virtual government monopoly over the petroleum industry; confiscation of Standard Oil Co. properties, Mar., 1937; efforts to control mining and banking). Toro's policies aroused much opposition and

1937, July 14. Toro was driven from office by fellow army officers.

1938- GERMÁN BUSCH succeeded as president.

1939, Apr. 24. Busch suddenly assumed dictatorial powers, dissolving congress and suspending the constitution. All connection with European totalitarianism was, however, denied.

7. PERU

1914, Feb. 4. A military revolt led to the overthrow of President Guillermo Billinghurst.

1914-1915. Col. Oscar Benavides served as provisional president.

1915-1919. José Pardo, president.

1917, Oct. 5. Peru severed relations with Germany, after attacks on Peruvian ships.

1919, July 4. A *coup d'état* led to the resignation and imprisonment of President Pardo, who was succeeded (Aug. 24) by

1919-1930. AUGUSTO LEGUÍA as president. Leguía's administration was noteworthy for great material progress. An extensive program of internal reform was undertaken, large loans were secured in the United States (1924, 1927, 1928), education was expanded, relations of Church and State revised, social and labor legislation enacted. For the rest Leguía's régime was notorious for corruption.

1919, Dec. 27. A new constitution (went into effect Jan. 18, 1920) introduced compulsory primary education, compulsory labor arbitration, income tax, etc.

1920, Jan. 10. Like most Latin-American states, Peru joined the League of Nations at the very outset.

1921-1929. The long-drawn dispute with Chile over Tacna and Arica (p. 1065), when finally settled, assigned Tacna to Peru.

1924, June 21. Signature of a protocol with Ecuador, envisaging negotiations concerning the old boundary dispute, and providing for arbitration in the event of failure of direct discussion.

1930, Aug. 25. RESIGNATION AND FLIGHT OF LEGUÍA, following a revolt led by Col. Luis Sánchez Cerro. Leguía was captured and tried, but was acquitted. Sánchez Cerro became provisional president, but

1931, Feb.-Mar. A series of revolts obliged Sánchez Cerro to give way to David Samanez Ocampo.

Oct. 11. Sánchez Cerro was elected president.

1932-1933. Threat of war with Colombia, over the disputed territory of Leticia. Peru took a strong line and prepared for war, though accepting proffered mediation of the League. The question was finally settled by agreement Nov. 2, 1934.

1933, Apr. 9. A new constitution was introduced.

Apr. 30. Assassination of Sánchez Cerro. He was succeeded at once by

1933-   OSCAR BENAVIDES, as president. Social and political unrest continued, despite the gradual recovery of the country from the depression. Benavides, supported by conservative and clerical elements, was opposed by the radical *Apra* (**Alianza Popular Revolucionaria Americana**), an organization in which the student element was strong. The Aprista opposition was held down with an iron hand.

1936, Oct. 11. The elections resulted in the defeat of Benavides' candidate by the Leftist groups, a Socialist being chosen president. Thereupon Benavides had the elections declared null and had his own term prolonged for three years.

Dec. 8. The constituent assembly was dissolved and **Benavides became virtually a dictator.** The radical opposition was suppressed (**Public Security Law of** Feb. 21, 1937) and efforts were made to counteract radicalism by the extension of social reform activities.

1938, June. The boundary dispute with Ecuador threatened to end in war when the troops of the two states clashed on the frontier. Oct. 12 Ecuador appealed to several American presidents to mediate, but Peru took an uncompromising attitude toward Ecuadorean demands for cession of territory.

8. ECUADOR

1916-1920. Alfredo Baquerizo Moreno, president.

1917, Dec. 7. Ecuador severed relations with Germany because of the submarine campaign, but did not, like most

other Latin-American states, join the League of Nations at the conclusion of the war. During the war and immediate postwar period much progress was made in education, social legislation, and above all sanitation (work of the American Col. Gorgas at Guayaquil, long a center of bubonic plague).

1920-1924. José Luis Tamayo, president. He was succeeded by

1924-1925. Gonzalo Córdova, who was driven from office by a military revolt led by Gen Francisco Gómez de la Torre (July 9, 1925).

1926-1931. ISIDRO AYORA, president. He introduced

1929, Mar. 28. A new constitution which ended the military régime set up in 1925, but paved the way for endless disputes between the executive and the legislature. Ayora had elaborate social and labor laws enacted and adopted many financial reforms.

1931, Aug. 25. Ayora resigned. Col. Luis Alba became provisional president, but was forced to flee after a *coup d'état* (Oct.). There followed a period of utter confusion, marked by conflict between the executive and legislature and between the conservative and liberal groups. After the suppression of a revolt (Aug. 1932), **Martínez Mera** became president, only to be replaced in Dec. 1933 by **J. M. Velasco Ibarra.**

1932-1934. The Leticia dispute between Peru and Colombia (p. 1068) gave Ecuador an opportunity to assert claims to portions of the Amazon Basin. In part motivated by these desires,

1934, Sept. 28. ECUADOR ENTERED THE LEAGUE OF NATIONS.

1935, Aug. 20. President Ibarra was overthrown by a military junta, after he had attempted to assume dictatorial powers. He was replaced by Antonio Pons, who, in turn, was forced to resign.

Sept. 26. A military dictatorship under Federico Páez was set up, to prevent the election of a conservative (the dominant Liberal Party was split by dissensions).

1935-1937. DICTATORSHIP OF PÁEZ. He suppressed a number of movements directed against his régime, but after a conflict with a constituent assembly, convened to promulgate a new constitution.

1937. Oct. 22. Páez was obliged to resign.

1937-1938. Gen. G. Alberto Enríquez became provisional president. With support of the army he adopted strong measures to maintain his authority. At the same time he liberated many political prisoners, abrogated objectionable repressive legislation, and embarked upon the work of financial and legal reform.

1938, June-Oct. Growing tension in relations with Peru, due to the long-standing dispute about the boundary (p. 1068).

Dec. 2. The Ecuador Congress elected Aurelio Mosquera Narváez president.

9. COLOMBIA

1914-1918. José V. Concha, president. He represented the conservative groups which had been in power since 1884 and which continued to rule the country until 1930. But even the conservative administrations of Colombia were obliged to initiate a measure of social legislation to meet growing pressure from the lower classes.

Colombia remained neutral during the First World War, but joined the League of Nations (Feb. 16, 1920).

1918-1921. Marco Fidel Suárez, president.

1919, Aug. 15. Signature of a contract with the Tropical Oil Company for exploitation of the Colombian oilfields, one of the most important sources of national wealth.

1921, Apr. 20. The United States Senate finally ratified the Thomson-Urrutia Treaty (concluded 1914) with certain modifications, thus ending the long dispute with regard to Panama. The Colombian Congress ratified it Dec. 22.

1922-1926. PEDRO NEL OSPINA, president.

1922, Mar. 24. An award by the Swiss Federal Council ended a long-standing boundary dispute with Venezuela in favor of Colombia. A boundary treaty with Peru settled the frontier on that side.

1926-1930. MIGUEL ABADIA MENDEZ, president. During his administration the growing social tension found an outlet in a number of major strikes, in the course of which many were killed by the police and government forces.

1930-1934. The election of ENRIQUE OLAYA HERRERA, a moderate liberal, brought to an end the long domination of the conservative groups. The world depression brought with it a rapid decline in coffee prices, and necessitated heavy borrowing.

1932-1934. THE LETICIA DISPUTE with Peru (p. 1068). Occupation of the town of Leticia by armed Peruvians brought the two countries to the verge of war. Under pressure from the Latin-American powers and the United States the disputants finally permitted supervision of the area by a League of Nations commission. By the final settlement (1934) Peru and Colombia proclaimed peace and amity and renounced armed action.

1934-1938. ALFONSO LÓPEZ became president, continuing the rule of the Liberal Party. The government now embarked upon far-reaching social reforms, aiming at government control of sub-soil riches, agrarian reforms, etc. Primary edu-

cation was made free and compulsory, and the Catholic Church was disestablished. All these policies called forth the opposition of the conservatives and clericals, who were further aided by the split in the Liberal ranks into moderate and progressive or even radical wings. Nevertheless, in the

1938. Election the Liberals were able to maintain a majority, and

1938- EDUARDO SANTOS, a moderate Liberal, became president. The Liberals won in the elections of Mar. 19, 1939.

10. VENEZUELA

1909-1935. Dictatorship of JUAN VICENTE GÓMEZ, who served during this period as either president or chief of the army. Gómez pursued a policy of nepotism and took care to have a congress entirely subservient to him. For the rest, the period of his rule was marked by striking material progress: administrative reforms were adopted, finances stabilized (national debt liquidated 1930), commerce and industry encouraged. After the opening of the Venezuela oil-fields (1918), the country soon became one of the leading oil producers, thus adding greatly to its wealth. On the other hand, the industrial development implied a growth of a proletarian class and a spread of radicalism which found much support among the students. The latter became active opponents of the dictatorship.

Venezuela maintained neutrality during the First World War, but

1920, Mar. 3. Joined the League of Nations.

1929, 1931. Revolts led by Gen. Arévalo Cedeño were put down, as were other opposition movements directed against the Gómez régime.

1935, Dec. 18. Death of President Gómez ended the dictatorship. Gen. Contreras became provisional president and succeeded in suppressing the disorders that broke out after the death of the strong man.

1936, Apr. 25. Gen. Eleazar López Contreras was elected president, and

July 16. A new constitution provided that the president's term should be limited to five years, with no eligibility for re-election.

1937, Jan. Elections were held for about one-third of the seats in Congress. These turned out to be a decisive victory for the Left parties, whereupon (Feb. 4) the government arrested many of the leaders of the Left (including newly elected congressmen) on the charge of communism. Most of these leaders were exiled, and most of the radical organizations (including the Federation of Students) were dissolved. The new president then did his utmost to suppress radicalism, but at the same time he embarked on a far-reaching program of social reform designed to meet the needs and demands of the lower classes and to check the spread of subversive tendencies.

11. BRAZIL

1914-1918. Wenceslau Braz Pereira Gomes, president.

1915, May 25. Agreement with Argentina and Chile (*A.B.C. Treaty*) providing for arbitration of disputes.

1917, Oct. 26. BRAZIL DECLARED WAR ON GERMANY. Relations had been severed Apr. 11 after sinking of Brazilian ships. During the war Brazilian warships co-operated with the Allies and Brazil furnished large stocks of food and raw materials.

1918. Rodriguez Alves, president. He died (1919) before assuming office, and was succeeded by

1919-1922. EPITACIO PESSOA as president.

1920, Jan. 10. Brazil joined the League of Nations as an original member.

1922-1926. ARTURO DA SILVA BERNARDES, president. Widespread discontent with the governmental system led to a

1924, July. Formidable revolt in São Paulo

and Rio Grande do Sul, led by Gen. Isidor Lopes. After suppression of the insurrection, the government undertook certain economic reforms.

1926, June 14. Brazil announced withdrawal from the League of Nations (effective 1928), after failure to secure a permanent seat on the council.

1926-1930. WASHINGTON LUIS PEREIRA DE SOUZA, president. He maintained order and tried, without much success, to improve the finances. Social unrest developed rapidly during this period and resulted in drastic measures against strikes and communism (strikes illegal, Aug. 13, 1927).

1930. The election of the Conservative Julio Prestes as president provoked

Oct. A GREAT REVOLT IN THE SOUTHERN PROVINCES, led by Getulio Vargas, governor of Rio Grande do Sul. Vargas accepted the presidency (Oct. 26) and forced Pereira de Souza to resign (Oct. 30).

1931. Establishment of the *National Coffee Department*, which year after year supervised the destruction of large quantities of coffee, in the hope of maintaining a good price in the world market. Coffee being Brazil's chief export article, the collapse of prices during the depression created much financial difficulty.

1932, July-Oct. A revolt broke out in São Paulo, which was successfully mastered by the government. The movement was the result of rivalry between São Paulo and Minas Gerães for control of the federal government.

1933. The government introduced a program of economic rehabilitation, with numerous social and political reforms, including

1934, July 16. A new constitution which involved greater centralization of control. The president was hence-

forth to be elected by Congress and was not to be eligible for re-election.

1934-1937. VARGAS was elected president under the new system. Economic conditions gradually improved, but social and political unrest increased. Among the industrial and plantation workers radical and communist propaganda made marked progress, while among the middle classes a strong fascist (*Integralista*) green shirt movement gained many adherents. The communist movement was said to be supported from Moscow, while the new Nazi government in Germany, whether connected with the *Integralista* group or not, unfolded an active and rather successful propaganda among the many Germans in the southern provinces. Barter arrangements with Germany resulted in a huge increase of trade between the two countries.

1935, Nov. A communist revolt broke out in Pernambuco and then in Rio de Janeiro. Though suppressed within a week, the revolt gave the government an excuse for the introduction of martial law. The president was granted almost dictatorial powers, a strict censorship was inaugurated and special tribunals were set up to try communist leaders.

1937, Nov. 10. VARGAS PROCLAIMED A NEW CONSTITUTION, after months of heated rivalry respecting the succession to the presidency. The new constitution gave the president full dictatorial powers and established a system of corporative nature (organization of a national economic council). The president announced that the new régime was not fascist, but the distinction was not very obvious.

1938, May 11. An Integralista rising was put down by the government without much difficulty.

1939, Mar. 9. Brazil concluded a series of agreements with the United States, thereby obtaining financial aid and support in the work of general economic development.

12. CENTRAL AMERICA

a. GENERAL

After the declaration of war on Germany by the United States, the states of Central America severed relations with Germany and ultimately declared war, mostly in 1918 (Panama, Apr. 7, 1917; Costa Rica, Mar. 23, 1918; Nicaragua, May 8, 1918; Honduras, July 19, 1918; Guatemala, Apr. 23, 1918). After the war almost all of them

became members of the League of Nations (Salvador joined in 1924, the others in 1920).

In the political sphere most of these states have continued in most unstable conditions, with numerous insurrections and overturns. Common to all of them has been the growing class consciousness of the laborers on banana, coffee, and sugar plantations, which came to constitute an ever more formidable challenge to the ruling groups. Despite representative machinery, the governments in many states are essentially dictatorships. During the 1920's the United States government intervened frequently in order to protect American lives and property. This policy, among other things, aroused much hostility toward the United States throughout Latin America, and has since been replaced by the "good neighbor policy," which eschews intervention.

1918, Mar. 10. The Central American court was dissolved after denunciation by Nicaragua and failure of the members to renew the arrangements.

1921-1922. THE PACT OF UNION between Costa Rica, Guatemala, Honduras, and Salvador, signed at San José (Jan. 19, 1921). The agreement set up an indissoluble and perpetual union, to be called the Federation of Central America. A provisional federal council was organized (June 17) and V. Martínez of Guatemala became president. Oct. 10 the federal constitution was completed, but once again the project of union was to be frustrated. Dec. 8 a revolution broke out in Guatemala, directed against the government's policy of federation. With its success the whole scheme fell through and the federation was dissolved (Jan. 29, 1922). Since that time there has been chronic trouble about frontiers between the different states, with occasional danger of war.

1922, Dec. 4—1923, Feb. 7. A Central American Conference met at Washington at the instance of the United States government, which hoped to terminate the dangerous friction between Nicaragua and Honduras. A general treaty of neutrality was drawn up, provision was made for the creation of a Central American court of justice, and measures to limit armaments and to further economic development were envisaged. The majority of the states ratified the treaties by 1926, but little was done to put them into effect.

b. PANAMA

1918. The constitution was amended to provide for the election of provincial governors.

1921. A boundary dispute with Costa Rica, inherited from the period of Colombian sovereignty, threatened to provoke war when Panamanian troops occupied disputed territory and armed clashes ensued (Feb.–Mar.). The United States government forced Panama to evacuate the area involved, which was then occupied by Costa Rica (Aug.).

Apr. 20. By the THOMSON-URRUTIA TREATY (p. 1050), Colombia recognized the independence of Panama. The boundaries, hitherto disputed, were adjusted, diplomatic relations were established, and various accords were signed (1924-1925).

1926, July 28. TREATY WITH THE UNITED STATES, designed to protect the canal in time of war. It provided that Panama consider herself at war when the United States was belligerent, and that Panama permit peacetime maneuvers by American forces on Panamanian territory. Opposition by the Panamanian Assembly because of infringement of sovereignty prevented ratification (Jan. 26, 1927). The question of sovereignty over the Canal Zone then arose, Panama denying that the United States possessed such sovereignty. Panama virtually appealed to the League of Nations to determine the question, but the League took no action and the president of Panama disavowed the appeal.

1931. President Florencio Harmodio Arosemena was forced to resign as a result of revolution (Jan. 2). A military government was set up and

1932-1936. HARMODIO ARÍAS became president.

1933, Oct. 17. President Arías conferred with President Roosevelt in Washington regarding the treaty relations between the two countries. The result was a declaration that Panama should be permitted all the commercial rights of a sovereign nation in the Canal Zone, and that there should be no American economic enterprise detrimental to Panama in the Canal Zone. The Panamanians having become more and more nationalistic,

1934-1935. Panama opened negotiations with the United States to secure modification of the Treaty of 1903, so as to eliminate the American guaranty of Panama's independence and the American right to intervene.

1936- JUAN AROSEMENA, president. The negotiations with the United States finally eventuated in

Mar. 2. A new treaty with the United States which met many of the objections raised by Panama to the earlier treaty.

c. COSTA RICA

1917, Jan. 27. President Alfredo Gonzales Flores was overthrown by a military coup led by Federico Tinoco. The United States refused recognition to the new régime and

1919, May 6. Tinoco was deposed by the Flores party. American marines were landed (June 4) to protect American interests. After the

Dec. 9. Election of Julio Acosta as president, the United States government granted recognition (1920).

1921. Conflict with Panama over the boundary (p. 1072).

1924-1928. Ricardo Jiménez, president.

1924, Dec. 24. Costa Rica withdrew from the League of Nations.

1928. Cleto Gonzáles Viquez, president.

1936- Léon Cortés Castro, president.

d. NICARAGUA

1914, Aug. 5. Conclusion of the Bryan-Chamorro Treaty with the United States, giving the latter the right to construct a canal across Nicaragua and lease sites for naval bases on both coasts. Costa Rica and Salvador at once protested against what they claimed was an infringement of their sovereignty.

1916, Apr. 13. The treaty was ratified by the United States, with the inclusion of a declaration that its provisions were not intended to affect the rights of other states.

1916-1921. EMILIANO CHAMORRO, president.

1917, Mar. 2. Salvador submitted the question of the Bryan-Chamorro Treaty to the Central American court of justice, which declared the treaty to be a violation of the treaties of 1907. Nicaragua ignored the decision and the efficacy of the court was thereby destroyed.

1917-1924. An American financial commission, in collaboration with the collector-general of customs, stabilized Nicaraguan finances.

1921-1923. Diego Chamorro, president.

1923-1925. Martínez Bartolo, president.

1925, Aug. 3. CÁRLOS SOLÓRZANO elected president. Like his predecessors he was a Conservative, but the new vice-president, Juan Sacasa, was a Liberal.

Oct. 25. A revolt, led by Emiliano Chamorro, forced Sacasa and other Liberals out of the government.

1926, Jan. 14. Solórzano resigned and Chamorro became president. The United States refused him recognition and when,

May 2. A Liberal insurrection was started by Gen. Agustino Sandino, the American government hastily landed forces. An armistice was effected by the United States (Sept. 23); Chamorro

resigned and the Nicaraguan Congress elected

Nov. 11. Adolfo Díaz (Conservative) president. But

Dec. 2. Sacasa returned from exile in Mexico and set up a Liberal government of his own, which was recognized by Mexico. During the civil war which ensued, the United States government supported Díaz.

1927, May 4. Henry L. Stimson, representing the United States, succeeded in bringing the two factions together. President Díaz was to complete his term of office, the opposition was to disarm, and the United States was to supervise the forthcoming elections.

1928, Nov. 4. José Moncada (Liberal) was elected, the United States government supervising the polling. Sandino, who had been continuing the fighting on his own account and who had gone so far as to attack the American troops, withdrew to Mexico, but in 1931 resumed the struggle.

1933. The Sandino insurrection was suppressed. Sandino himself was killed (1934), but sporadic outbreaks of his followers continued for some years.

1933-1936. JUAN SACASA, president.

1936, June 2. Sacasa was deposed by the National Guard, led by Gen. Anastasio Somoza.

1937- ANASTASIO SOMOZA, president. He made himself virtually dictator and proceeded with the utmost vigor against communists and other radicals. The introduction of rigid exchange control was designed to help the country economically, but met with indifferent success.

1939, Mar. 23. A constituent assembly approved a new constitution and re-elected Somoza to the presidency.

e. HONDURAS

1916, Mar. Francisco Bertrand became president following a successful revolution.

1919, Aug. Insurrection of Rafael López Gutiérrez, a Liberal. President Bertrand was obliged to flee, and American marines were landed (Sept. 11). Through American mediation a civil war was avoided and

1920-1923. Gutiérrez became president. When the elections of 1924 proved to be indecisive,

1924, Feb. 1. GUTIÉRREZ ESTAB-
LISHED A DICTATORSHIP.
The Conservatives, under Tiburcio Carías,
rose in revolt and marched on the capital.
The United States severed relations with
Gutiérrez and landed more troops. Gutiér-
rez was killed (Mar. 10), and

Mar. 31. The insurgents occupied the
capital. By the Pact of Amapala
(May 3), the civil war was ended. Vicente Tosta became provisional president
and suppressed an attempt at further
revolution by Gregorio Ferrara (Aug.–
Oct.). A new constitution was then framed
and

1925. MIGUEL PAZ BARAHONA became president, the United States
forces having prevented revolutionary leaders from becoming candidates. The United
States supported Barahona against further
attempts at revolt by Ferrara.

1928. Vicente Mejía Colindres, president.

1933. Gen. TIBURCIO CARIAS president.
He assumed practically dictatorial
powers.

1936, Apr. 15. The constitution was
amended to enable the president
to retain power until 1943. The
growing unrest in the country led
to numerous outbreaks and revolts.

1937, Jan.-Feb. A serious uprising, led by
Gen. Justo Umana, was crushed.
The government drove all opponents of the régime into flight
or else imprisoned them.

f. SALVADOR

The recent history of Salvador has been
much less spectacular than that of the neighboring states. The constitutional system
operated without much friction until

1931, Dec. 2. A *coup d'état* enabled Maximiliano H. Martínez to make
himself president.

1932. Martínez established a dictatorship.
Like near-by dictators, he devoted
himself to the suppression of communism and other radical movements.

1937, Aug. 10. Salvador withdrew from
the League of Nations.

1939, Jan. 20. A constitutional congress
abrogated the constitution of 1886
and adopted a new régime.

g. GUATEMALA

1920, Apr. 8. ESTRADA CABRERA,
president since 1898, was deposed
by the Assembly because of his opposition to the scheme of Central
American federation (p. 1072).

1920-1921. Cárlos Herrera, president. He
was overthrown by a revolution
(1921, Dec. 5) led by Gen. José
Orellana, who rejected the Central
American federation scheme.

1922-1926. Orellana, president.

1926-1930. Lázaro Chacón, president.

1930. Bautillo Palma, president. He was
overthrown (Dec. 16) by Gen.
Manuel Orellana, who was not
recognized by the United States
and who soon resigned.

1930-1931. J. M. Andrade, president, until

1931- GEN. JORGE UBICO made
himself President-Dictator. He
established close contact with the
dictators of Honduras and Salvador for the suppression of all
opposition.

1935. By "plebiscite" Ubico's term was
extended until 1943.

13. MEXICO

The revolution that convulsed Mexico
after the downfall of Díaz in 1911 (p. 822)
had reduced the country to a state of utter
confusion by 1914. Numerous leaders
(Huerta, Carranza, Obregón, Villa, Zapata,
etc.) held various parts of the territory,
installing their own presidents, fighting
each other, and creating difficulties with
Mexico's neighbors.

1914, Apr. 9. A group of American marines
was arrested at Tampico. The
United States government demanded satis-
faction (esp. a salute). On the refusal of
Huerta to meet American demands, United
States troops occupied Vera Cruz (Apr.

21). Huerta broke off relations with the
United States. The major South-American
states attempted to mediate, and Nov.
23 the American forces evacuated Vera
Cruz.

July 5. Victoriano Huerta was elected
president. He resigned almost at
once (July 15), admittedly because of the
refusal of the United States government
to recognize him, which made his position
impossible.

Aug. 15. Gen. Alvaro Obregón and
a constitutionalist army took
Mexico City and Venustiano Carranza became president. As yet the Constitutional-

ists controlled only part of the country. In the north **Francisco Villa** was practically dictator. He at once declared war on the Carranza régime, installing **Eulalio Gutiérrez** as president (deposed again Jan. 17, 1915). For a time Villa held Mexico City, but

1915, Jan. 27. Obregón recaptured the capital for the Constitutionalists.

Oct. 19. The United States government and a number of Latin-American states recognized **Carranza** as *de facto* president. Great Britain followed suit (Nov. 16).

1916, Mar. 9. Forces of **Villa's party** raided across the frontier into New Mexico. Thereupon American troops pursued him (Mar. 15). Carranza at once protested against the violation of Mexican territory and began to offer resistance. Clash of Americans and Mexicans at **Carrizal** (June 21). Ultimately conferences were arranged to arrive at some settlement. American troops departed Feb. 5, 1917.

1917, Jan. 31. THE NEW CONSTITUTION was adopted by the Mexican Congress (promulgated Feb. 5). This instrument had been worked out by a constitutional convention, in session since Nov. 21. Representing advanced nationalist and radical social views, the Constitution of 1917 at once became the **charter of the new Mexico.** It provided for universal suffrage, the curbing of foreign ownership of lands, mines, and oil-fields, restriction of the power and property of the Church and monastic orders, the 8-hour day, a minimum wage, arbitration of labor disputes, agrarian reform (breakup of large estates and distribution among the landless), housing reform, etc.

Mar. 11. CARRANZA was elected president, for a 4-year term. By the constitution he was ineligible for re-election, in 1921.

1918, Feb. 19. By decree, oil was declared an inalienable national resource and a tax was levied on oil lands and contracts made before May 1, 1917. Titles to oil lands were to be transformed into concessions. American and British companies, supported by their governments, at once protested. For the time being the matter was settled by compromise, but, as it turned out, the episode was only the first move in a long campaign to break the power and wealth of foreign companies.

1918. Formation of the Confederation of Labor (*Confederación Regional Obrera Mexicana*, popularly called the *CROM*). This became possible under the new constitution. The confederation was the counterpart of the American Federation of Labor, and before long was to be challenged by a more radical organization. For the time being, however, it was an important factor in the furtherance of the constitutional and social reform movement.

1920, Apr. 9. Three of the leading generals (Adolfo de la Huerta, Alvaro Obregón, and Plutarco Elias Calles) joined forces against Carranza, who was accused of attempting to dictate the presidential succession. The opposition proclaimed the Republic of Sonora and took the field. May 8 Obregón took Mexico City and thereafter many of the cities on the east coast. **Carranza was killed** (May 21) and **Villa surrendered** to the victorious insurgents (July 27; he was endowed with a handsome estate, which he enjoyed until his assassination in 1923).

Sept. 5. OBREGÓN was elected president. He was recognized by the United States (Aug. 31, 1923) upon agreement to respect titles to land acquired before 1917 and to accept an adjustment of American claims.

1923, Dec. 6. Adolfo de la Huerta led a revolt against the government of Obregón and the latter's candidate for the presidency, Calles. The United States government supported Obregón, who was able to crush the insurrection (1924).

1924-1928. PLUTARCO CALLES, president. After a long and serious controversy with the United States regarding the application of the constitution to foreign properties, an adjustment was finally arrived at (1927, Calles-Morrow Agreement), due to the more conciliatory attitude of the United States government and the mission of Dwight Morrow as ambassador.

Calles continued the work of **agrarian and educational reform** initiated in 1917, but soon came into **conflict with the Roman Catholic Church** over the application of constitutional provisions.

1927, Feb. The Church publicly repudiated the Constitution of 1917, but the government (Feb. 11) ordered **nationalization of Church property** and began to close Church schools. Foreign priests, monks, and nuns were deported. The struggle thus begun has continued with but little interruption and has frequently led to open conflicts.

1927, Oct. A great insurrection broke out and soon covered a dozen provinces. Calles proved himself the strong man of Mexico by proceeding at once and with great vigor against the rebels. Within a couple of months most of the leaders had been defeated, captured, and executed.

1928, July 1. Obregón was re-elected president, but was assassinated a few weeks later (July 17). Thereupon

1928-1930. EMILIO PORTES GIL served as provisional president. Calles remained the real power in the government and put down another

1929, Mar.-Apr. Insurrection, provoked by political and religious discontent and led by Gens. **Jesus María Aguirre and Gonzalo Escobar.**

June 21. A compromise agreement was reached with the Church, which relieved the tension for the time being.

Aug. 11. Promulgation of an extensive labor code, in accordance with the Constitution of 1917: 8-hour day, 6-day week, right to strike, minimum wage, compulsory insurance, etc.

1930-1932. PASCUAL ORTIZ RUBIO, president. Calles remained the dominant figure, and the new administration simply continued the policy of its predecessors.

1931, Sept. 9. Mexico joined the League of Nations.

1932, Sept. 3. President Ortiz Rubio resigned after a difference with Calles, who had (1931) assumed the ministry of war.

1932-1934. Gen. **Abelardo Rodríguez** served as provisional president.

1933. Adoption of a Six-Year Plan of social legislation and economic development, which really signified a move toward the Right on the part of Calles and the National Revolutionary Party, in so far as it deferred some of the more extreme measures earlier envisaged.

1934, July 2. GEN. LAZARO CÁRDENAS, the choice of Calles, was **elected president** after the constitution had been amended to extend the presidential term to six years. Conflict soon developed between Calles and the new president, who, though young, at once demonstrated a strong will-power. Representing the more advanced wing of the party, Cárdenas regarded Calles as too conservative. In 1935 he forced Calles into exile and, on the latter's return to Mexico (1936), had him arrested and sent off to the United States. Thereafter Cárdenas, undisputed master of the country, embarked upon an **accelerated program** of reform, in which he was supported by the new **Confederation of Mexican Workers** (Feb. 1936), led by **Vicente Lombardo Toledano,** next to the president

the most outstanding figure on the political scene. Within a couple of years as much land was expropriated as in the years 1917–1934. This was distributed to the peasants on the communal (*ejido*) basis. With regard to the Church, Cárdenas adopted a somewhat more conciliatory attitude, though he insisted on the elimination of the Church from politics and upheld the nationalization of Church property.

1936, Nov. 23. A new expropriation law empowered the government to seize private property when necessary for the "public or social welfare." Thereupon

1937, June 23. The National Railways of Mexico were taken over by the workers, and

Nov. 1. The sub-soil rights of the Standard Oil Company and other companies were **declared nationalized.** These steps inaugurated a new phase of the conflict with foreign interests. The federal labor board ordered American and British oil interests to increase the wages of workers by one-third, which the companies declared to be impossible.

1938, Jan. 19. A new tariff raised the rates from 100 to 200% on articles imported chiefly from the United States.

Mar. 1. The Mexican courts decided for the government and against 17 oil companies, in the wages dispute.

Mar. 18. THE GOVERNMENT TOOK OVER THE PROPERTIES OF THE AMERICAN AND BRITISH OIL COMPANIES, valued at $450,000,000. The governments at once protested against such action. The United States government, securing no encouragement to hope for settlement, discontinued silver purchases from Mexico, as a retaliatory measure. The British government suspended diplomatic relations. The issue raised tremendous excitement throughout Mexico, the people vigorously supporting the government.

May-June. Cárdenas proceeded against Gen. **Saturnino Cedillo,** former minister of agriculture and "boss" of the province of San Luis Potosí, who was reported on the verge of revolt in the interest of conservative groups. The movement was easily broken.

July 21. The United States government proposed arbitration of claims against Mexico for expropriation of lands held by Americans (valued at $10,000,000). The American government did not dispute the right of Mexico to expropriate, but insisted on full compensation. The Mexican government refused both arbitration and compensation (except in very general statements). On the contrary, it proceeded to conclude

Sept. 5. Oil barter agreements with Germany, Italy, and other nations, by which the oil should be exchanged for manufactured goods (previously imported chiefly from the United States and England). Nevertheless the United States government maintained a moderate attitude and showed great reluctance to abandon the "good neighbor" policy. Finally

Nov. 12. The United States and Mexico reached an agreement on the land question. Commissioners were to appraise the value of the properties and the Mexican government was to pay compensation at the rate of $1,000,000 per annum until the claims were liquidated. Repeated efforts to reach an agreement on the oil issue (spring, 1939) failed to produce results.

14. THE WEST INDIES

a. CUBA

1917, Apr. 7. Cuba declared war on Germany. The war period was one of great prosperity for the sugar industry, large quantities being shipped to the United States. But after the war the market collapsed with serious results for Cuba.

1920, Mar. 8. Cuba joined the League of Nations.

Nov. 1. Dr. Alfredo Zayas, candidate of the coalition National League, was elected by what his opponent, José Gómez (Liberal), declared to have been fraudulent methods. To prevent conflict the United States government sent Gen. Enoch Crowder, who arranged for new elections (1921, Mar. 15), which resulted in another victory for Zayas.

1921-1925. ALFREDO ZAYAS, president. Crowder was withdrawn (1923) and the Cuban government gradually adopted a policy of opposition to American influence.

1925-1933. GERARDO MACHADO (Liberal), **president.** He attempted to solve the problems of the sugar industry by restricting production, stimulated industrial development (higher tariffs), and promoted public improvements and health. The term of the president was extended to six years and **Machado was re-elected.** He made himself virtually dictator, but thereby aroused much opposition which was enhanced by economic difficulties arising from the world depression.

1930-1931. A revolt led by Marío Menocal was suppressed and various restrictive measures were introduced, but unrest and disorders continued (1931-1933). The United States had, at the outset, declared its intention not to intervene except in case of extreme anarchy. But it attempted to mediate, thereby arousing the resentment of Machado.

1933, Aug. 12. An army revolt forced Machado out of office. **Cárlos Manuel de Céspedes became president,** but disorder continued and the United States felt obliged to send warships to Cuba.

Sept. 5. **Céspedes was driven from office** by another army coup, led by **Fulgencio Batista,** who became practical dictator, though he eschewed political office.

Sept. 10. **Grau San Martín became president** and formed an extremely radical government, which was not recognized by the United States.

1934, Jan. 20. **Overthrow of Grau San Martín. Cárlos Mendieta became president** and succeeded in concluding with the United States

May 29. An agreement by which the **PLATT AMENDMENT** (p. 823) **WAS ABROGATED** and limitations on Cuban sovereignty were removed. Somewhat later (Aug. 24) the United States and Cuba signed a reciprocal trade agreement very favorable to the latter.

1935, Dec. 10. Mendieta resigned, and

1936, Jan. 10. Miguel Mariano Gómez was elected. Before the year was out,

Dec. 23. Gómez was forced from office by Batista, and

1936, Dec. 24-1940. FEDERICO LAREDO BRU became president. Batista remained the real dictator, and his régime, after 1933, embarked on a policy which apparently aimed at a corporative state along fascist lines. All political and social opposition was dealt with in drastic fashion. At the same time the government threw itself into radical social legislation and adopted (July 25, 1937) a **Three-Year Plan** which involved state control of the sugar and mining industries, the reorganization of agricultural schools, the distribution of land, etc. In

1940, Feb., a convention assembled to

draft a new constitution which came into force Oct. 10, with **General Fulgencio Batista** as head of the government.

b. HAITI

1914-1915. Haiti was wracked by revolutionary movements, one president following another in rapid succession and the country in chaos. American marines were landed to protect foreigners and foreign property, and finally to supervise an election in the hope of re-establishing some measure of ordered government.

1915-1922. PHILIPPE DARTIGUE-NAVE, president. He concluded

Sept. 16. A TREATY WITH THE UNITED STATES which gave the latter a practical protectorate. United States marines remained in occupation, and the United States government was given supervision of the customs offices and the power to organize a constabulary.

1918, June 19. A new constitution was introduced.

July 12. Haiti declared war on Germany.

1918-1919. A revolt directed against the American occupation and led by **Charlemagne Perlate**, caused much trouble, but was finally suppressed.

1920, June 30. Haiti joined the League of Nations.

1922-1930. LUIS BORNO, president. Opposition to his rule led to

1929, Dec. Serious disorders. Larger American forces were sent to the island, where they were attacked by the mobs. In view of the widespread anti-American feeling, the Washington government sent out

1930, Feb.-Mar. A commission of investigation, headed by **W. Cameron Forbes**. This commission recommended administrative reforms, the replacement of the military high commissioner by a civilian, and the continuation of the treaty relationship until 1936. It persuaded Borno to relinquish office, and

1930-1941 STENIO VINCENT became president. With American aid order was restored, finances and administration were reformed, public improvements introduced, and education was developed. At the same time a series of agreements were made providing for eventual termination of American control. These were blocked by the Haitian Assembly, which insisted on immediate withdrawal. After the advent of the Roosevelt administration in the United States arrangements were quickly made for complete termination of

American control and liquidation of the Haitian foreign debt.

1934, Aug. 6. The American forces were withdrawn. After a plebiscite and under executive pressure, the Haitian Assembly approved the agreements with the United States, and adopted

1935, June 17. A new constitution, which endowed the president with wide executive powers. Vincent's term was extended to 1941.

1937, Oct. An acute crisis developed in relations between Haiti and the Dominican Republic, because of maltreatment of Haitians (p. 1079). The Vincent government sought a peaceful solution and requested the good offices of the United States, Mexico, and Cuba. An agreement was finally reached Jan. 31, 1938.

c. THE DOMINICAN REPUBLIC

Chronic revolution and widespread disorder in Santo Domingo led to

1914, June 26. Intervention by the United States, which restored peace between the warring factions.

1916, May. Further outbreaks resulted in further intervention and

Nov. 29. PROCLAMATION OF AMERICAN MILITARY OCCUPATION. This step called forth opposition in the republic and in the United States also, with the result that from 1920 onward the American government sought to arrange for withdrawal.

1922, June 30. Agreement between the Dominican government and the United States. American rule ended Oct. 21 and the last marines were withdrawn Sept. 18, 1924. A provisional government was set up and

1924-1930. HORACIO VASQUEZ became president.

1924, Sept. 29. The Dominican Republic joined the League of Nations just as soon as the last American forces had left.

1929, Apr. An American commission, headed by **Charles G. Dawes,** at the request of the Dominican government investigated the finances and made recommendations.

1930, Feb. 23. President Vásquez was forced to resign as a result of a revolt.

1930-1938. RAFAEL LEONIDAS TRUJILLO, president. He adopted a policy of social reform and public works, developing communications, introducing sanitation, encouraging agriculture, and distributing lands. Opposition to his rule was dealt with harshly, so that members of opposition parties were obliged to flee abroad.

1937, Oct. The Dominican government drove a large number of immigrant Haitians back over the border, killing many in the process. This led to protests and demands for reparation from the Haitian government, which invoked American conciliation treaties for settlement of the dispute. By this method an agreement was arrived at (Jan. 31, 1938).

1938, May 17. Jacinto B. Peynardo was elected president after Trujillo had announced his forthcoming retirement.

d. PUERTO RICO

1917, Mar. 2. THE JONES ACT, making Puerto Rico a territory and granting American citizenship to its inhabitants. Voting was made compulsory. Proportional representation was established by means of a "limited vote" for certain senators and representatives. It was further provided that United States internal revenue collections on the island should be paid into the Puerto Rican treasury. (Subsequently permission was accorded the island, practically, to collect United States income taxes for the benefit of the local treasury.) With such assistance, the budget of the insular government increased from about $2,000,000 in 1901 to $11,000,000 in 1924. More than half of these funds were derived from what would normally be federal taxation.

May. The United States having declared war on Germany, the selective draft was extended to Puerto Rico by request of the insular government, after only two months of American citizenship. Some 18,000 men were inducted into service.

1918, June 2. The war, thus far rather distant, was suddenly brought home to the Puerto Ricans when a German submarine sank the *Carolina* near the end of her voyage from San Juan to New York.

Oct. 11, 24. A serious earthquake did much damage to towns on the west end of the island.

1924, Mar. A delegation, including Gov. Towner, came to the United States with the request that Puerto Rico be granted the rights of statehood without representation in Congress.

1928. The Puerto Rican legislature petitioned President Coolidge for the grant of autonomy without statehood. Autonomy was desired to provide homesteads for the peasantry, to free the island from American tariff restrictions, and to deal with the problem of absentee landlordism. President Coolidge replied, pointing out the advantages of American rule.

1930. Gov. Theodore Roosevelt was forced to appeal to Congress and to private philanthropy to aid the depressed population, of whom 60% were without employment.

1933. The Democratic administration in the United States took a much greater interest in the Puerto Rican situation and extended a large measure of relief, along lines followed in the United States itself. Nevertheless, there developed in the island an ever stronger demand for redefinition of status. Apart from a widespread sentiment in favor of statehood, there emerged a strong nationalist movement aiming at complete independence.

1936-1937. The Nationalists provoked demonstrations and riots, which in turn resulted in serious clashes with the police, arrest of many leaders, outbreaks of terrorism, etc.

1939, June 4. A committee of the legislature brought forth a demand for statehood and in the interval "demanded" an elective governor with power to appoint officials.

e. VIRGIN ISLANDS

1916, Aug. 4. AMERICAN-DANISH TREATY, by which Denmark agreed to cede the Danish West Indies (about 100 islands with a total area of 132 square miles) to the United States for $25,000,000. The treaty was ratified Jan. 17, 1917, and formal possession was taken Mar. 31 of the same year. Danish laws were allowed to remain in force.

The population (c. 26,000 in 1917) has suffered much from economic distress. The sugar industry of St. Croix had been in process of concentration and many small sugar mills had been abandoned. Ultimately all grinding was done in three large "centrals." Many laborers were thereby thrown out of employment. The loss of the free port status, which had existed under Danish rule, reduced the trade of the islands, especially of St. Thomas. The American prohibition law (1919) further destroyed the market for sugar products, though bay rum continued to be manufactured. The main achievement of the American administration has been in the development of education.

1924, Aug. 29-Sept. 1. Hurricanes damaged St. Thomas and St. John.

1931, Feb. After a succession of governors from the U.S. Navy, the United States established a civil government for the islands, making St. Thomas the capital. Paul M. Pearson became the first civil governor.

1931, Mar. The depression became so pronounced in the islands that President Hoover was able to refer to them as "an effective poorhouse" with 90% of the population dependent upon the bounty of the United States.

1933. The Roosevelt administration in the United States began to extend relief measures to the islands. Development of the tourist trade, expansion of the rum industry, etc., did much to ameliorate economic conditions.

1936, June 22. The Organic Act revised the political arrangements of government. The governor was to be assisted by a territorial legislative assembly, composed of the elected municipal councils of St. Thomas and St. Croix.

1938, Jan. 1. Universal suffrage went into effect under the new arrangements.

E. AFRICA

1. GENERAL

1915, Mar. Completion of a railroad and steamer route **from east to west** from Dar-es-Salaam to Lake Tanganyika and thence to the Congo River.

1918, May. The **Cape to Cairo Railroad** reached Bukama on the Lualaba River, making possible travel from the Cape to Cairo by rail and water with two short breaks (Tabora to Mwanza and Nimule to Rejaf).

1919, Sept. International agreement prohibiting the **manufacture and importation of liquor** into Africa and controlling the **arms and munitions** trade.

1920, Feb.-Mar. 20. Sir H. A. van Ryneveld and Sir C. J. Brand first flew from Cairo to the Cape.

Feb.-Mar. Maj. Vuillemin flew from Algiers to Gao on the Niger and thence to Dakar.

Dec. The Courtot expedition crossed the Sahara to Lake Chad by motor.

1921, Jan. 14. Rosita Forbes and Hassanein Bey visited the oasis of Kufra and traveled thence to Alexandria.

1922, Dec.-1923, Mar. The Haardt expedition crossed the **Sahara to the Niger** and back again with caterpillar motors.

1924, Feb.-Mar. Lieuts. Arrachard and Lemaitre flew across the desert to **Timbuktu and return.**

Nov.-1925, July. Capt. Delingette and his wife first crossed Africa by motor from **Oran to Capetown.**

1925, Nov.-1926, Feb. Alan Cobham flew from Cairo to the Cape in 94 flying hours.

1926, Sept. 25. An international slavery convention was signed by 20 states.

Nov.-1927, Mar. Cobham flew from London to Cairo and thence to Capetown.

1929, Jan.-Apr. Prince Sixtus of Bourbon opened a **motor route** from Algiers to Lake Chad.

Mar. Capt. Crofton and **Owen Tweedy** went by motor from Rejaf on the upper Nile to Lake Chad, the Niger River, and thence to Algiers.

1935, Jan. 14. The **first train crossed the Lower Zambezi bridge,** one of the longest in the world.

2. EGYPT AND THE SUDAN

1914, Dec. 18. Egypt proclaimed a British protectorate.

Dec. 19. Khedive Abbas Hilmi deposed.

1914-1917. SULTAN HUSSEIN KAMIL, uncle of Abbas.

1917, Oct. 9. Death of the sultan.

1917-1936. AHMED FUAD, brother of Hussein Kamil, became sultan, then king.

1919, Mar. 8. Saad Zaghlul Pasha and other Nationalist leaders, deported to Malta to prevent their going to the Paris peace conference. The Nationalist Party (*Wafd*) had grown tremendously during the war as a result of Egyptian resentment at British methods (forced labor conscription, requisition of materials, etc.). Its program was one of independence. The deportation of Zaghlul was followed by a serious national insurrection, which had to be put down by the British military under Field Marshal Allenby.

Oct. 17. Allenby appointed **high commissioner** for Egypt.

Dec. 7.-Mar. 6, 1920. Milner Commission to inquire into the disorders and suggest the future organization of Egypt.

1920, Mar. 10. A legislative assembly passed a **resolution in favor of independence.**

June 7-Nov. 9. Negotiations of Zaghlul and Milner, at London.

1921, Feb. 28. Publication of the **Milner** report, proposing independence with guaranties for British interests.

Apr. 5. Return of Zaghlul to Egypt. Attacks of the Nationalists on the government.

May. Numerous **outbreaks against foreigners,** in which many persons were killed.

Africa

July 12-Nov. 20. Further negotiations at London, conducted by the Egyptian premier, **Adli Pasha.** These broke down on the question of the retention of British troops in Egypt.

Dec. 22. Zaghlul and other Nationalists again deported.

1922, Jan. 23. The Wafd proclaimed a policy of passive resistance.

Feb. 28. TERMINATION OF THE PROTECTORATE by unilateral action on the part of Britain. Egypt declared independent, but the decision on security of communications, defense, protection of foreigners, and the future of the Sudan reserved for further negotiation.

Mar. 15. Fuad I assumed the title of *king.*

1923, Apr. 4. Zaghlul released by the British.

Apr. 19. PROMULGATION OF THE CONSTITUTION: it provided for a senate and a chamber, three-fifths of the former and the whole of the latter to be elected by universal suffrage; ministers to be responsible to the Chamber alone.

Sept. 27. Great victory of the Wafd in the elections.

1924, Jan. 28. Saad Zaghlul, premier.

June 24-25. Widespread anti-British riots.

Sept. 25-Oct. 3. Conferences between Zaghlul and Ramsay MacDonald failed to produce an agreement on the reserved questions.

Nov. 20. Death of Sir Lee Stack, sirdar of the Egyptian army and governor-general of the Sudan, assassinated by a fanatic. The Egyptian government at once expressed regret and promised punishment of those responsible.

Nov. 22. BRITISH ULTIMATUM, demanding punishment, apology, indemnity, suppression of political demonstrations, and withdrawal of Egyptian forces from the Sudan. Zaghlul agreed to these terms, excepting those relating to the Sudan. When the British insisted, he resigned in protest. His successor yielded (Nov. 24).

1925, Feb. 26. Sir George Lloyd, high commissioner.

Mar. 12. The Wafd again victorious in the elections; Zaghlul became president of the Chamber. The Nationalists blocked all measures of the government, which repeatedly dissolved the Parliament only to find a new Nationalist majority at the new elections.

1926, Jan. 21. Opening of the **Makwar** (Senaar) **Dam,** an important stage in the utilization of the Nile water. The Egyptians were much exercised by the development of cultivation in the Sudan, which might deprive Egypt of necessary water.

1927, Apr. 18. Sarwat Pasha, premier.

July 18. New draft treaty with Great Britain, envisaging British military occupation for 10 years.

Aug. 23. Death of Zaghlul Pasha; Mustafa Nahas Pasha became leader of the Wafd.

Oct. 30-Nov. 8. Further negotiations in London regarding the draft treaty.

1928, Mar. 4. The Egyptian Parliament rejected the British draft as incompatible with Egyptian independence.

Mar. 16. Nahas Pasha, premier.

Apr. 29. British ultimatum, forcing the Egyptian government to give up a bill providing for freedom of public assembly.

June 25. Dismissal of Nahas Pasha; Mohammed Mahmud (Liberal) became premier.

July 19. Parliament dissolved for three years; freedom of press and assembly suspended.

1929, Mar. 8-May 1. Resumption of discussions at London, the Egyptians hoping for concessions from the Labor government.

May 7. Agreement on Nile water: only Blue Nile water to be used for the Sudan, the water of the White Nile being reserved to Egypt.

Aug. 6. New draft treaty with England: British occupation to be replaced by a military alliance and British troops to be restricted to a few points on the Suez Canal; Egypt to join the League of Nations; the Sudan to be returned to an Anglo-Egyptian condominium.

Aug. 8. Sir Percy Loraine, high commissioner.

Oct. 31. Restoration of the constitution.

Dec. 21. The Wafd again swept to victory in the elections.

1930, Jan. 1. Nahas Pasha premier again.

Mar. 27-May 8. Negotiations in London regarding the British draft. These broke down chiefly on the issue of the Sudan.

June 21. ISMAIL SIDKY PASHA, premier. He was the appointee of the king, who chose him as an able administrator to deal with grave internal problems arising from the general world depression. The settlement with England was to be postponed, until the Wafd Party could be weakened.

June 26. The Wafd adopted a policy of

non-co-operation with the government and advocated non-payment of taxes. Nationalist outbreaks became common throughout the country.

Oct. 22. INTRODUCTION OF A NEW CONSTITUTION: the Senate to be three-fifths appointive; elections to the Chamber to be indirect. Loud Nationalist protests and riots. **Union of the Liberal Constitutional Party with the Wafd** in common opposition to the king and Sidky.

Dec. 8. Sidky Pasha organized a party of his own, **the People's Party.**

1931, Apr. 22. Treaty of friendship between Egypt and Iraq, the first link in the chain binding Egypt to the other Arab states in a community of attitude on subjects touching the Arab world.

May. Elections. Through prohibition of Wafd meetings and other repressive measures, the government party won a victory.

1933, June. Anti-missionary and anti-Christian outbreaks; formation of the *Committee for the Defense of Islam.*

Sept. 21. Sidky obliged to resign because of ill health. After the failure of a "palace" cabinet, the king accepted a

1934, Nov. Cabinet of Mohammed Tewfik Nessim, who attempted a policy of reconciliation and allowed Wafd activity. He insisted on the

Nov. 30. Suspension of the Constitution of 1930. Agitation of the Nationalists for restoration of the Constitution of 1923. This was not done, on British advice.

1935, Nov. Ethiopian crisis. This was made the occasion of a violent outbreak of Nationalist agitation (Nov. 13-Dec. 2) and a union of parties, designed to extract concessions from the British in their hour of need.

Dec. 12. RESTORATION OF THE CONSTITUTION OF 1923, long demanded by the Nationalists.

1936, Jan. 22. Cabinet of Ali Maher Pasha, a non-partisan government designed to put the revived constitution into effect.

Apr. 28. Death of King Fuad.

1936— FAROUK (b. 1920), king. His advent brought to an end the constant danger of usurpation of power by the king. The new ruler, simple and attractive, at once attained widespread popularity.

May 2. In the elections the Nationalists won a great victory. **A new Wafd**

cabinet was at once (May 10) formed under **Nahas Pasha.** This government negotiated the

Aug. 26. TREATY BETWEEN EGYPT AND ENGLAND. The British were to withdraw their forces, excepting for 10,000 men, to be restricted to the Suez Canal zone (in time of war the number might be increased); England to maintain a naval base at Alexandria for not more than 8 years; unrestricted immigration of Egyptians into the Sudan to be permitted; Egyptian troops to return to the Sudan; abolition of capitulations in Egypt envisaged; Egypt to become a member of the League of Nations; treaty of alliance between England and Egypt for 20 years, after which the agreement was to be re-examined.

Dec. 22. Ratification of the treaty by the Egyptian Parliament, despite criticism from several groups.

1937, Jan. 13. A British military mission arrived to advise the Egyptian government on the building-up of an army. In 1938 universal military training was introduced.

Apr. 12-May 8. Conference of Montreux between the powers enjoying capitulatory rights in Egypt. **Agreement to abolish the capitulations,** but to maintain the mixed courts for 12 years and extend their authority to criminal cases (hitherto handled by consular courts).

May 26. Egypt was admitted to the League of Nations at a special session.

Dec. 30. King Farouk dismissed the Nahas cabinet, after considerable friction, and appointed **Mohammed Mahmud Pasha,** leader of the Liberal Constitutional Party, as premier. The Wafd Party, which for years had lived on the Anglo-Egyptian antagonism, began to disintegrate as soon as a settlement had been reached. Opposition to Nahas within the party led to the withdrawal of a number of influential leaders and to the exclusion of others.

1938, Feb. 2. The king dissolved the Parliament, in which the Wafd Party still had a large majority.

Mar. 31-Apr. 2. In the elections the government party won a tremendous victory, Nahas not even winning a seat. Complete eclipse of the old Wafd Party. In June the premier reorganized his cabinet to admit a number of dissident Nationalists.

Nov. 19. In view of the international tension, the government embarked upon an **extensive program of armament** (air force, navy, munitions factories, etc.).

3. ETHIOPIA

1916-1930. ZAUDITU, empress. Her reign was marked by great instability and particularly by the growing antagonism between the Conservative, Church groups, led by the war minister, **Hapta Giorgis**, and the Liberal, westernizing party, led by the regent, **Ras Tafari**, who, as governor of Harrar, was building up a reliable force and introducing many improvements.

1919. Following the First World War, the Italian government proposed to the British a **scheme for co-operation in the exploitation of Ethiopia**; this was evaded by the British.

1921, Jan. Capture of Lij Yasu in Tigré. He was handed over to the custody of Ras Kassa, the powerful governor of the province.

1923, Sept. 28. ETHIOPIA WAS ADMITTED TO THE LEAGUE OF NATIONS. England had opposed the admission but it had been advocated by Italy and France, and Ethiopia was ready to accept the international arms traffic convention and to take steps against slavery.

1924. Slavery was officially abolished. Ras Tafari paid a prolonged visit to Europe, but evaded definite commitments, especially to England in the matter of building a dam at Lake Tsana.

1925, Dec. 14, 20. Exchange of notes between England and Italy, the British promising aid to Italy in the development of her sphere of influence in return for Italian support of British efforts to secure a dam at Lake Tsana.

1926, June 19. Protest of the Ethiopian government against the Anglo-Italian notes. Both sides gave assurances.

1928, Aug. 2. Conclusion of a **treaty of friendship with Italy** for 20 years: Ethiopia was to get a **free zone at Assab** and a road was to be jointly built and operated from Assab to Dessié.

Oct. 7. Ras Tafari became king (negus) following the death of Hapta Giorgis. Tafari thenceforth exercised the dominant influence and began to initiate his policy of modernization.

1929. A Belgian military commission was appointed to reorganize the army.

1930, Mar. 1. The negus granted a **concession for a dam at Lake Tsana** to the American J. G. White Corporation, which had the support of the British and Egyptian governments.

Mar. 31. A dangerous **revolt of Ras Gugsa**, the husband of Zauditu, was put down by Tafari, using the new methods.

Apr. 2. Death of the Empress Zauditu.

Nov. 2. Coronation of Ras Tafari as king of kings with the title of

1930-1936. HAILE SELASSIE I.

1931, July 16. Haile Selassie introduced a constitution providing for a parliament chosen by the provincial governments. This was part of his policy of governmental reorganization: appointment of younger men who had visited Europe to important governorships; establishment of schools; progressive measures to end slavery, etc.

1932. Rising of Ras Hailu of Gojjam. This was effectively suppressed.

1934, Dec. 5. Clash of Ethiopian and Italian forces at Ualual, in a disputed zone on the frontier of Italian Somaliland. The Italians demanded apology and reparation; the Ethiopian government insisted on an investigation of responsibilities.

1935, Jan. 7. Franco-Italian Agreement, including a cession of part of French Somaliland to Italy and the sale to Italy of shares in the Ethiopian railway.

Feb. Italy began to send troops to East Africa.

May. The council of the League of Nations arranged for an **arbitral tribunal** to deal with the Ualual dispute.

July. The tribunal having been unable to agree on procedure, the League arranged for a fifth arbitrator, but only to establish responsibility for the clash, not to determine the possession of Ualual.

Aug. 16. After a meeting of British, French, and Italian delegates at Paris, **Italy was offered wide opportunities for the development of Ethiopia,** subject to Ethiopian agreement. These offers were rejected, and it became more and more evident that Italy was bent on conquest.

Sept. 3. The arbitral board reported neither side to blame in the Ualual incident, since each side regarded the place as within its territory.

Oct. 3. BEGINNING OF THE ITALIAN INVASION OF ETHIOPIA.

Oct. 7. The League Council declared Italy the aggressor.

Oct. 11. The League Assembly voted to impose sanctions on Italy (for international aspects of the crisis, see p. 963).

Nov. 18. Sanctions were put into effect.

In the meanwhile the Italians advanced slowly in the north and south. The Ethiopians wisely avoided a pitched battle, but finally, in the spring of 1936, the Italians brought into full play their **air power** and began the use of **poison gas.** Unable to cope with these methods the valiant Ethiopian defense broke down.

1936, May 5. The Italians occupied Addis Ababa, the emperor having fled to the coast and thence to Palestine and England.

May 9. ETHIOPIA WAS FORMALLY ANNEXED TO ITALY, and, with Eritrea and Italian Somaliland, was organized as **Italian East Africa.** The King of Italy assumed the title *Emperor of Ethiopia.* The conquest was recognized by Italy's friends (Germany, Austria, and Hungary), but only after considerable delay by some of the other powers (England, France, 1938).

Pacification of Ethiopia. The Italians established posts and forts throughout the occupied territory, linking them up by roads. The great and immediate problem, however, was to defeat what native forces remained in the field and to disarm the Ethiopians. Isolated attacks on the Italians continued and

1937, Feb. 19. An attempt was made to assassinate the viceroy, Gen. Graziani, at Addis Ababa. He and a number of his staff were wounded. Wholesale arrests and executions in the capital, designed to intimidate the population.

Feb. 21. Ras Desta Demtu, the most formidable opponent of the Italians, was defeated outside the capital, and captured (executed Feb. 24).

4. NORTH AFRICA
(Morocco, Algeria, Tunisia, Libya)

1919, Feb. 4. In Algeria French citizenship was extended to all those who had served in the World War, to those who owned land, to literates, etc.

May 17. Civil government was re-established in Libya, which was divided into Tripolitania and Cyrenaica. Citizenship was granted to natives and a system of self-government with elected assemblies was established (July–Nov.).

July 11. Beginning of the attacks of Raisuli upon the Spanish possessions in Morocco.

Sept. 12. A Franco-Italian agreement led to the cession of several important oases in southeast Tunisia to Italy; Italian nationals were given the same status as Frenchmen in Tunisia.

1920, Oct. 25. The Italian government recognized Sheikh Sidi Idriss as head of the Senussi, with wide authority over Kufra and other oases.

1921, July 21. THE ANUAL DISASTER, in which a large Spanish force under Gen. Silvestre was destroyed by the Riff leader, **Abd el-Krim.** Fighting between the Spaniards and the Riffs became chronic, the Spaniards suffering heavy losses.

Nov. 8. A new nationality law decreed that children of foreign parents, if the latter were born in **Tunisia,** should be French subjects. Great Britain protested against this law and brought the matter before the permanent court, which found that the French legislation went beyond ordinary national powers. A **Franco-British agreement** (May 24, 1923) provided that the children in question might elect their nationality, but that the same should not hold for their own children.

1922, May 22. Gen. Badoglio began the offensive against the Arabs in Libya. The operations dragged on for years, though pressed more insistently after Mussolini's rise to power. By 1930 the conquest of the country by the Italians was at last completed.

July 13. Reorganization of the government of Tunisia, where the *Young Tunisians* (nationalists) had developed an extensive agitation for self-government. A complicated system of councils, composed of French and natives, was organized, but was given power only in economic matters.

Sept. 28. Submission of Raisuli; end of the war in the western part of the Spanish zone.

1923, Dec. 18. Tangier Convention signed by Spain, France, and Great Britain, after long conferences at London (July–Oct.) and at Paris. Tangier was to be governed for the sultan by a mixed com- mission, on which the French had the major influence.

1924, Dec. After repeated reverses, the **Spaniards were obliged to with- draw** from the interior and con- centrate on the coast.

1925, Jan. 27. Abd el-Krim captured Raisuli, who died soon afterward.

Apr. 13. Abd el-Krim began to attack the French, who were busy subduing the regions on the Riffian frontier.

July 26. A Franco-Spanish agreement provided for full co-operation against Abd el-Krim. The French gradually concentrated an army of 150,000 men against the Riffians.

Sept. 9. Under command of **Marshal Pétain,** the French and Spanish **began a major offensive,** driving back the Riffians.

Sept. 24. Resignation of **Lyautey** as French resident, after a long and brilliant career as pacifier of Mo- rocco.

Dec. 6. An Anglo-Italian agreement (the **Milner-Schialoja Agreement**) provided for the cession of the **Jarabub Oasis** and other parts of western Egypt to Italy.

1926, Apr. Conferences between the French and Abd el-Krim led to no result.

May 7. Opening of a **new Franco- Spanish offensive.**

May 26. ABD EL-KRIM SURREN- DERED. He was exiled to the island of Réunion and the Riffian war came to an end.

1927, Mar. 9. The system of **self-govern- ment in Libya was revoked.**

Nov. 17. Death of Mulai Yusuf, Sultan of Morocco. He was succeeded by his son, **Sidi Mohammed III.**

1928, Jan. 3. The Senussi leader in Cy- renaica surrendered, bringing to an end the war in eastern Libya.

July 25. The **Tangier Statute** was re- vised and Spain given somewhat larger measure of control. Italy became a signatory of the con- vention.

1929, Jan. 24. Tripoli and Cyrenaica were once more united under one gov- ernment.

1930. The **world economic crisis** made itself acutely felt in North Africa, Morocco in particular suffering from drought, locusts, and general falling-off of the demand for phosphate. Despite relief offered by the French government in vari- ous forms, the prevalent distress led to rapid spread of native unrest.

1931, Oct. Founding of a *League of Ulemas* at Constantine, Algeria. The pur- pose of this was to further the work of Moslem reform as outlined by the Moslem Congress at Jerusalem. It marked the extension of the new **Moslem-Arab renais- sance** (already widespread in Tunisia) to Algeria.

Dec. 29. Spanish Morocco was reorgan- ized under a high commissioner with civil and military authority. The establishment of the republic in Spain created much ferment in Spanish Morocco.

1932-1934. Completion of the **pacification of French Morocco.** Jan. 15, 1932, the French occupied the **oasis of Tafilet,** headquarters of the restless tribes- men. With the submission of the Atlas and Anti-Atlas regions, the conquest was completed.

1933, Nov. 28. Opening of the **Moroccan- Tunisian railway,** which united the French possessions and which, in time of war, would enable the government to send troops from Tunisia to Moroccan Atlantic ports and thus obviate the dangerous Mediterranean route.

1934, Jan. 1. Libya was divided into four provinces (Tripoli, Misurata, Ben- gasi, and Derna).

Aug. Violent **attacks upon the Jews** at Constantine and in other Algerian towns. Anti-Semitism was one of the main planks in the program of the Arab nationalists.

Nov. A group of young Moroccans, many of them educated in Europe, presented a *Plan of Moroccan Reforms* which may be taken as marking the **birth of Moroccan nationalism,** as distinct from the tribal opposition to foreign rule. The Moroccan nationalists drew much of their inspiration from Egypt and the Near East generally, and were deeply influenced by the developments in Iraq and by the Wafd struggle in Egypt.

1935, Nov. 13. An accord between France and Spain regarding Tangier pro- vided that the chief administrator and the bishop should be Spaniards. Owing to the outbreak of the Spanish civil war these arrangements had to be deferred.

1936. The electoral victory of the Left parties in Spain and France (Feb. and May) served as a great stimulus to radicalism and nationalism throughout North Africa. At the same time the French colonists, alarmed by concessions made by the home government to the lower classes, became extremely hostile to the Popular Front in France.

July 18. The Spanish civil war (p. 983)
broke out when the Spanish troops
in Morocco (under Gen. **Francisco Franco**)
rebelled and seized Melilla. Throughout
the war the Moroccan troops (Riffs, drafted
by Franco) played an important part in the
campaigns in Spain. In the meanwhile the
coastal towns were repeatedly bombarded
by Spanish Loyalist air forces.

1937, Jan. Acute tension resulted from
**rumors of the landing of German
forces** in Spanish Morocco. On demand,
the German government gave ample assurances, but there seemed no doubt that
German experts were busy fortifying the
region, exploiting the mines, etc.

**Mar. A Loyalist uprising in Spanish
Morocco** was put down with great
firmness.

**Mar. Spectacular visit of Mussolini to
Libya**, where he opened a great
new military road running the entire length
of the colony. Mussolini proclaimed **protector of Islam** and presented with a sword
of Islam. There remained no room for
doubt that the Italians were doing their
utmost to encourage the Arab and Moslem
movement throughout the Near East and
North Africa, as a convenient method of

embarrassing the British and French governments.

**Sept.-Oct. Nationalist uprising in Mo-
rocco.** The French government
rushed troops and airplanes and snuffed out
the movement as quickly as possible. Many
nationalist leaders were arrested. **Albert
Sarraut**, eminent French colonial administrator, was appointed to head a new *Commission of Co-ordination for North Africa*
with the objective of strengthening the
French position in all this region.

1938, Dec. Tunisia began to focus world
attention after vociferous demonstrations in the Italian Chamber and
throughout Italy calling for cession of Tunisia and Corsica to Italy. The French
government and nation were united in
uncompromising opposition to any such
concession, and

1939, Jan. The French premier, **M. Daladier, paid a visit to Corsica and
Tunis.** His enthusiastic reception in North
Africa appeared to demonstrate that the
Arabs, whatever their grievances against
France, had no desire to exchange French
rule for Italian. Tension between France
and Italy continued as the French government flatly declined to discuss any cession
of French territory.

5. WEST AFRICA AND THE SUDAN

The partition of Africa having been completed before the First World War, the
period after the war was devoted to the **consolidation of European rule** and the organization of the administration. In most of
the French and British colonies some form
of **representative government** (councils,
predominantly composed of officials, but
with representation of economic and native
groups) was established and the inhabitants were given some control over economic affairs. Consistent efforts were
made to put an end to slavery, to introduce primary and vocational education
for the natives, to organize justice and to
further economic development. Railroads
were built in most colonies and motor
roads were opened. In accordance with
international agreements, the import of
"trade spirits" (i.e. liquors not usually
consumed by Europeans) and of arms
and munitions was prohibited. Land legislation aimed at the prevention of a landless native proletariat.

1916, Mar. 4. An Anglo-French agreement
defined respective spheres in the
conquered **Cameroons** and **Togoland.** To
France was assigned by far the larger
part.

June 10. The laws of **Nigeria** were
applied to **British Cameroons.**

Aug. 21. The French part of **Togoland**
was **attached to French West
Africa.**

1917, July 8. French Cameroons was attached to French Equatorial Africa.

**Aug. 4. Liberia declared war on Ger-
many.**

1919, Mar. 1. The French organized a
separate colony of the **Upper Volta.**

May 6. The supreme council assigned
the German **Cameroons** and **Togoland** as **mandates to Great Britain
and France.** This was confirmed
by the League of Nations (July
20, 1922).

July 10. England and France made an
agreement defining the frontier of
their mandates in the Cameroons.

July 30. Conscription was introduced in
the French West Africa.

**1920, June 30. Liberia became a member
of the League of Nations.**

Dec. 4. The name of the French colony
Upper Senegal-Niger was changed
to the **French Sudan.** A superior council
(partly elective) was created for French
West Africa.

1921, Jan. 1. Mauretania was created a French colony.

Oct. 13. The French created a separate colony of the Niger.

Nov. 21. Establishment of the legislative council in Nigeria.

1923, Oct. 11. British Togoland was put under the government of the Gold Coast.

1924, Jan. 21. An Anglo-French agreement definitively fixed the frontier between the French Sudan and the Anglo-Egyptian Sudan.

June 19 (1925, Sept. 16). Agreement between the Liberian government and the Firestone Rubber Plantation Company provided for the lease to the company of one million acres of land for 99 years, and for a loan by the company of $5,000,000 (for 40 years at 7%).

Oct. 21. The city of **Dakar** (capital of French West Africa) was made an autonomous area, directly under the governor-general.

Nov. 25. Establishment of a legislative council in Sierra Leone.

1925, May 23. Establishment of a legislative council in the Gold Coast.

1927, Sept. 22. Slavery declared abolished in Sierra Leone.

1930, Mar. 8. A joint American-League of Nations investigation (Johnson-Christy Commission) to Liberia investigated the conditions of native labor and reported (Sept. 8) that slavery actually existed.

1932, Dec. 23. Liberia was forced to suspend payment of interest and amortization of the Firestone debt, which in 1931 had absorbed 55% of the revenue.

1935, June. The Liberian Legislature ratified an agreement with American interests, by which interest on the 1926 loan was reduced to 5% and all payments were made dependent on the state of revenue. The United States government resumed diplomatic relations with Liberia (broken off in 1930), and the British government followed suit (1936). Rapid development of the Firestone plantations secured the government greater revenue and enabled it to resume interest and amortization payments.

6. THE CONGO REGION

(French Equatorial Africa, Spanish Guinea, Belgian Congo, Angola)

1914-1918. Troops of the Belgian Congo assisted the British and French colonial forces in the **defense of Rhodesia** and the conquest of the **Cameroons.**

1916. Belgian forces occupied the districts of **Ruanda** and **Urundi,** part of German East Africa. Other German posts on the shores of Lake Tanganyika were taken, including **Tabora** (Sept. 19).

1919, May 30. An **Anglo-Belgian agreement** assigned Ruanda and Urundi to Belgium as a prospective mandate, but without the district of Kisaka. This was conceded to Belgium by agreement of Aug. 3, 1923, after which **Belgium accepted the mandate** (Oct. 20, 1924). The mandated territory was united administratively with the Belgian Congo (Aug. 21, 1925).

June 28. By the Treaty of Versailles, Germany retroceded to France that part of the **French Congo** (French Equatorial Africa), which had been ceded to Germany by the Agreement of Nov. 4, 1911.

1921-1924. Administration of Gen. **Norton de Mattos** in Angola. He at-tempted to open up the country by improved communications and other methods of encouragement, but met with great financial difficulties.

1921, Aug. 21. The Belgian government voted a credit of 300,000,000 francs for the **development of the Belgian Congo** through the construction of railways, etc.

1922, July 6. The Belgian Congo was given a wide **measure of autonomy,** with a system of administrative decentralization. Town government was introduced Jan. 12, 1923.

1924. An **Anglo-French agreement** defined the frontier between French Equatorial Africa and the Sudan (Wadai and Darfur).

1926, July 1. An **Anglo-Portuguese agreement** defined the frontier between Angola and Southwest Africa at the Kunene River.

1927, July 27. By an agreement between Portugal and Belgium, the latter ceded to the former 480 square miles on the southwest frontier of the Congo in return for 1 square mile of territory near **Matadi,**

required for the reconstruction of the Matadi-Stanleyville Railway.

1928, June. King Albert of Belgium visited the Congo and formally opened the new railway from the **Katanga Province** to the **Kassai River** (Bukama-Ilebo), providing direct communication by rail and water between Leopoldville and the rich Katanga copper mines.

1931, July 1. Opening of the **Benguella-Katanga Railway**, from Lobito Bay on the Angola coast to Katanga in the Belgian Congo, thus completing the first trans-African railway (Benguella-Beira, via Katanga and northern Rhodesia).

1934, May. Angola was reorganized, with division into five provinces.

June 18. Opening of the **air line from Algiers to Brazzaville**, by way of Fort Archambault.

July 10. Opening of the **railway from Brazzaville to the coast** at Pointe Noire.

1935, Apr. 16. Spanish Guinea (Rio Muni) **was divided**, Fernando Po being given separate administration.

7. EAST AFRICA
(Kenya, Uganda, Tanganyika, Nyasaland, Mozambique)

1919, May 7. The supreme council assigned German East Africa to Great Britain.

July 22. By ordinance the legislative council of British East Africa was enlarged to 11 elected members for the Europeans, 2 nominated members for the Asiatics (Anglo-Indians), and 1 for the Arabs. A majority to support the governor was assured by the appointment of sufficient official members.

Sept. 23. The supreme council assigned the **Kionga Triangle** (part of German East Africa) to Portugal.

1920, Jan. 10. THE BRITISH MANDATE OVER GERMAN EAST AFRICA went into effect. The name of the territory was changed to Tanganyika; the German settlers were sent home and their estates were sold.

July 23. British East Africa was renamed *Kenya* and was made into a crown colony. The coastal strip, leased from the Sultan of Zanzibar in 1887, became the **Kenya Protectorate**.

June 5. A nominated **legislative council** was established in Uganda.

1922, July 1. Opening of the **railway from Beira** to the south bank of the Zambezi, thus connecting Nyasaland with a good port.

1924, Jan. 4. In the Kenya the Indian element was given 5 seats in the legislative council (as against the previous 2) and the right to elect them by the communal system.

July 15. An Anglo-Italian agreement provided for the cession of Italy of a strip of territory from 50 to 100 miles wide on the British side of **the Juba River**, in fulfillment of the provisions of the Treaty of London of 1915 (p. 925). The cession was actually made June 29, 1925.

1925, Jan. 1. New immigration regulations for Tanganyika permitted the return of German settlers.

1926. A conference of **East African governors**, at Nairobi, discussed the possibility of an East African federation, much desired by the white settlers of Kenya. The idea has been frequently bruited since that time, but has met with staunch opposition from Zanzibar.

Mar. 19. A nominated **legislative council** was established **for Tanganyika**.

1928, Jan. 11. Opening of the **Nakuru-Mbulamuti-Jinja railway** line in Kenya, giving access to some of the most valuable territory for white settlement.

Feb. 13. Junction of the railway lines from the Katanga and from Beira, provided an outlet to the east for the rich mineral resources of Katanga.

Aug. 15. Opening of the **railway line from Tabora** (in Tanganyika) **to Mwanza** on the south shore of Lake Victoria.

Sept. 11. An important **convention between Portugal and the South African Union** regulated questions of transportation from the Transvaal to the coast, problems of labor recruitment, etc.

1929, Jan. 18. The Hilton-Young Commission recommended closer union of the East African and Central African colonies.

1934, Mar. The organization of the **legislative council for Kenya** was modified in the interest of broader representation.

1935, Jan. 14. Opening of the **Lower Zambezi bridge** (12,064 feet long and one of the longest bridges in the world), providing for uninterrupted rail connection between Beira and Nyasaland.

Sept. 10. A "parliament" of white settlers in Kenya met and denounced the government policy, especially on its financial side, and demanded closer union of Kenya, Uganda, and Tanganyika (rejected by a British parliamentary committee in 1931 as inopportune).

Oct. 7. The colonial office announced the appointment of **Sir Alan W. Pym** to inquire into the financial problems of the colony.

8. SOUTH AFRICA AND SOUTHWEST AFRICA

1919, Apr. Gen. Hertzog and a delegation of his Nationalist Party appeared at the Paris Peace Conference and asked for the recognition of complete independence for South Africa. During the war the party had become more and more pronounced in its secessionist and republican views. Since Hertzog represented a minority party in South Africa, nothing was done about the petition.

May 7. The supreme council of the Allied Powers assigned **German Southwest Africa as a mandate** to the South African Union. Botha had tried hard, but in vain, to have it ceded outright.

Aug. 28. Death of Gen. Botha. He was succeeded as prime minister and leader of the South African Party by Gen. Smuts.

1920, Mar. 10. In the elections the Nationalist Party won the largest number of seats (45, as against 40 for the South African Party, 25 for the Unionists, and 21 for the Labor Party). The Unionists now began to support the South African Party but the Laborites tended to join the Nationalists, thus creating a most delicate balance.

July 28. A native affairs commission was set up and the council system was extended to all native reservations. But the native question continued to be a burning one, partly because the reservations were wholly inadequate and partly because a very large part of the native population had become detribalized and settled as laborers on the farms of the whites, or as mine and industrial workers in the larger towns.

1921, Feb. 8. In new elections the South African Party (with which the Unionists had merged) secured 76 seats, as against 47 for the Nationalists and 10 for Labor.

1922, Jan.-Mar. A great strike movement on the Rand led to much radicalism and many serious outbreaks. Some 230 persons were killed in the disturbances.

Oct. 27. A popular referendum in Southern Rhodesia resulted in a heavy vote against joining the Union of South Africa, despite very attractive terms offered by Smuts. The English population of Rhodesia was evidently distrustful of the rising tide of Boer nationalism in the Union.

1923, July 25. The claims of the South Africa Company in Southern Rhodesia were finally settled along the lines laid down by the **Cave Commission report** (Jan. 1921). The British government agreed to a money payment, and the company thereupon resigned its administrative privileges.

Sept. 1. SOUTHERN RHODESIA BECAME A CROWN COLONY, with a system of responsible government.

1924, Apr. The South Africa Company abandoned its administrative powers in **Northern Rhodesia,** which also became a crown colony, but without responsible government.

June 17. ELECTIONS: victory of a coalition of the **Nationalists** and the **Labor Party** (resentful of the government's labor policy on the Rand and of the association of Botha's party with the Unionist mineowners) over the South African Party (53 seats as against 63 for the Nationalists and 18 for Labor).

June 30. Gen. Hertzog, leader of the Nationalists, **became prime minister.** In return for the support of the Labor Party he was, however, obliged to shelve the projects of secession and republicanism. The definition of Dominion status as laid down by the Imperial Conference of 1926 served further to meet the claims of the Nationalists.

1925, July 27. German Southwest Africa was given a constitution, providing for a legislative assembly. The German population became British citizens, but German was recognized as an official language.

1927, Feb. 21. A conference with representatives of the government of India finally led to arrangements for aid to those **Indians** who were willing to return home. Those that elected to stay were not to be subjected to further restrictions.

Nov. 11. The Nationality and Flag Act was passed after long and acrimonious discussion. The inclusion of the Union Jack in the South African flag was finally decided upon.

1929, June 12. In the elections the Nationalists renewed their victory of 1924.

1930, May 19. The franchise was extended to all white women.

1931, Aug. The reconstituted Labor Party repudiated its arrangements with the Nationalist Party and the coalition began to break down.

1932, Apr. In Southwest Africa the **Farmers' and Labor Party** was organized and began a drive for abolition of the mandate and establishment of the territory as a separate province with responsible government.

Dec. 27. The **Union government went off the gold standard,** last of the British Dominions to take this step, and then only after prolonged discussion and much disagreement.

1933, Jan. 24. Smuts called upon the government to resign in favor of a national government pledged to empire co-operation on non-racial lines.

Mar. 30. ESTABLISHMENT OF A NATIONAL GOVERNMENT. The two Labor members of the government dropped out, Hertzog remained prime minister, but Smuts and two other members of the South African Party joined the cabinet.

May 17. In the elections the national government won a great victory.

Aug. In Southwest Africa the victory of the National Socialists in Germany provoked an immediate response. The English settlers, by a narrow majority, put through a measure forbidding National Socialist "cells" and the wearing of uniforms. The English and Dutch settlers (a majority, owing to emigration of Germans and immigration from the Union after 1919) became more and more insistent on incorporation in the Union, which the Germans naturally opposed.

1934, June 5. Formal fusion of the South African Party (Smuts) **and the Nationalist Party** (Hertzog) under the new name of *United South African National*

Party (United Party). The non-fusion element in the Nationalist Party re-formed under the same name and became a group representing republican and anti-native policies (leader **D. F. Malan**).

June 12. Status of the Union Act, passed to define the position of the Union after the Westminster Statute. It established the Union as "a sovereign independent state" in every respect, though it left the field open for endless discussion regarding the "right of secession" from the British Commonwealth.

Nov. 29. The legislative assembly of **Southwest Africa petitioned** the Union Parliament **for admission to the Union** as a fifth province. A commission was sent out which reported (June, 1936) that the existing government was a failure and that there was no obstacle in the mandate to the incorporation of Southwest Africa. But in Dec. the government announced that it had no intention of changing the status of the territory, much less any intention of abandoning the mandate.

1936, Apr. 7. THE REPRESENTATION OF NATIVES ACT finally clarified the native policy of the government. The natives retained the right to register as voters in Cape Province, but they were to be put on a separate electoral roll and were to be permitted to elect three Europeans to represent them in the Union Parliament. A native representative council (22 members, 12 of whom elective) was to be established, but with purely advisory powers.

1937, Apr. 2. The Union government by decree prohibited **political activity by foreigners in Southwest Africa** (including non-naturalized German residents). Strong protests by the German government were of no avail. In Sept. a new German Party replaced the forbidden German *Bund.*

1937, Nov. A royal commission was appointed to visit Northern and Southern Rhodesia and Nyasaland, in order to investigate the possibility of closer union between them.

1938, May 18. The South African elections resulted in a victory for the United Party and Gen. Hertzog remained premier.

9. MADAGASCAR

1916. During the First World War a **secret anti-French society** was organized among native officials. This was discovered and suppressed with great severity.

1918. Opening of the railway from Tamatave to Tananarivo.

1923. Opening of the railway from Tananarivo to Antsirabe, first section of a line to the south.

1924, May 7. Reorganization of the administrative system, in the direction of decentralization and increase of the number of native officials. The governor-general was henceforth to be assisted by economic and financial councils, composed of an equal number of Europeans and natives, to advise him on public works and general budgetary matters.

F. ASIA

1. TURKEY

1918, July 4–1922, Nov. 1. MOHAM-MED VI, sultan.

Oct. 4. Collapse of Turkish armies; flight of Talaat and Enver.

Oct. 30. Armistice of Mudros (p. 948).

Dec. 8. Allied military administration of Constantinople.

1919, Mar. 7. Cabinet of Damad Ferid Pasha, with a policy of co-operation with the victorious powers.

Apr. 29. Landing of the Italians at Adalia, first step in the taking over of southwestern Anatolia.

May 14. Landing of the Greeks at Smyrna, with approval of the Allies.

May 19. MUSTAPHA KEMAL PASHA (b. 1880; hero of the battle at the Dardanelles and of the last battles in Syria; ardent Nationalist) arrived at Samsun as inspector of the 3d army. He at once began organization of resistance to the further dismemberment of Turkey and was officially dismissed by the sultan (July 8), and outlawed (July 11).

July 23–Aug. 6. Nationalist Congress at Erzerum, under Mustapha's lead.

Sept. 4. NATIONALIST CONGRESS AT SIVAS and **DECLARATION OF SIVAS** (Sept. 9): affirmed unity of Turkish territory and declared against Allied occupation and the formation of an Armenian state.

Sept. 13. The National Pact: enunciation of six principles, including self-determination, security of Constantinople, opening of the Straits, rights of minorities, abolition of capitulations.

Oct. Victory of the Nationalists in the elections to Parliament.

Oct. 5. Cabinet of Ali Riza, who attempted conciliation with the Nationalists.

1920, Jan. 28. The National Pact was adopted by the Parliament at Constantinople.

Mar. 16. To check the spread of the Nationalist agitation, Gen. Milne and an Allied force occupied Constantinople, while repudiating any idea of depriving the Turks of it. The announced object of the move was to keep open the Straits and to protect the Armenians. The Nationalists were denounced and many sent into exile. A new cabinet under Damad

Ferid was set up. Parliament was dissolved (Apr. 11).

Apr. 23. A provisional government was set up by the Nationalists at Angora (Ankara), with **Mustapha Kemal** as president.

Apr. The Nationalists concluded a military agreement with Soviet Russia, by which they secured necessary supplies.

June 10. THE TREATY OF SÈVRES presented to the Turkish government at Constantinople (terms, p. 954). Vigorous protests of the sultan and uncompromising opposition of the Nationalists, who received more and more popular support.

June 22. Beginning of the Greek advance against the Nationalists. The Greeks were strongly encouraged by Lloyd George, who meant to use them to force the peace terms on the Turks.

June 24. The Greeks defeated the Turks at Alashehr.

July 9. The Greeks took Brusa.

July 25. Adrianople surrendered to the Greeks.

Aug. 10. THE CONSTANTINOPLE GOVERNMENT SIGNED THE TREATY OF SÈVRES. Definitive break between the Nationalists and the sultan's government.

Oct. 21. In a campaign against the Armenian Republic, the **Turks took Kars.**

Dec. 3. Turco-Armenian peace treaty: Turkey got Kars and Ardahan, and Armenia (now a Soviet republic) was reduced to the province of Erivan.

1921, Jan. 20. The Fundamental Law adopted by the Angora Assembly: provided for sovereignty of the people; a parliament elected by manhood suffrage; responsible ministry; a president with extensive power.

Feb. London Conference of the Allied Powers, with both the Constantinople and the Angora governments represented, as well as the Greeks. Efforts to reach an adjustment broke down.

Mar. 13. Agreement of Mustapha Kemal and the Italians. The latter agreed to evacuate Anatolia in return for promises of extensive economic concessions. The last Italian forces left in June.

Mar. 16. TREATY OF MUSTAPHA KEMAL WITH SOVIET RUSSIA: Turkey was to retrocede Batum; in return Russia recognized the Turkish possession of Kars and Ardahan.

Mar. 23. Beginning of the new Greek offensive. The Greeks took **Afiun-Karahissar** and **Eskishehr** (Mar. 28–30), but were thrown back by the Turks (Apr. 2).

July 16-17. Battle of Kutahia. The Greeks took the town, as well as Afiun-Karahissar and Eskishehr.

Aug. 24-Sept. 16. BATTLE OF THE SAKKARIA. Desperate defense of the Turks. The Greeks failed to reach Angora. Though the Allied Powers proclaimed neutrality in the war and attempted to mediate, Lloyd George nevertheless encouraged the Greeks in their aggressive policy.

Oct. 13. Treaty of Kars: Turkey formally recognized the Armenian Soviet Republic.

Oct. 20. The Franklin-Bouillon Agreement between France and Mustapha Kemal. This followed months of hostility in Cilicia, which France now agreed to evacuate, in return for economic concessions.

1922, Mar. 26. The Allied Powers agreed to some revision of the Sèvres Treaty and attempted a settlement of the Greek-Turkish conflict. The Turks refused to grant an armistice until the Greeks had evacuated Anatolia. Further efforts at mediation (June) again failed.

July 29. The Allied Powers, in an ultimatum to Greece, forbade the occupation of Constantinople.

Aug. 18. Beginning of the Turkish counter-offensive against the Greeks. The Turks took **Afiun-Karahissar** (Aug. 30) and **Brusa** (Sept. 5). The Greek armies broke and fled in confusion to the coast.

Sept. 9-11. THE TURKS TOOK SMYRNA, which was to a large extent destroyed by fire (Sept. 13–14).

Sept. 15. Lloyd George appealed to the Allied Powers and the British Dominions to join in defense of the Straits against the Turks. The French took a negative stand, as did the Italians. Of the Dominions only Australia and New Zealand showed any great interest.

Sept. 16. A British force under Gen. Harington landed at Chanak.

Oct. 3-11. Conference and Convention of Mudania between the Allies and Ismet Pasha, representing the Turkish Nationalists. The Allies agreed to the return of Eastern Thrace and Adrianople to the Turks, and the Turks accepted the neutralization of the Straits under international control.

Nov. 1. Mustapha Kemal proclaimed the **ABOLITION OF THE SULTANATE.** Mohammed VI fled from Constantinople on a British ship.

Nov. 18. Abdul Mejid, cousin of Mohammed VI, proclaimed caliph.

Nov. 20. Lausanne Conference, to conclude peace between the Allies and the Turks. The conference broke up temporarily Feb. 4, 1923, after heated disputes about the abolition of capitulations and the status of Mosul. It resumed sittings Apr. 23 and concluded its work July 24.

1923, July 24. TREATY OF LAUSANNE: Turkey gave up all claims to the non-Turkish territories lost as a result of the World War, but recovered **Eastern Thrace** to the Maritza River, with **Karagach;** Turkey received **Imbros** and **Tenedos,** but the rest of the Aegean Islands went to Greece; Italy retained the **Dodecanese** and England **Cyprus;** the **capitulations** were abolished in return for a promise of judicial reforms; Turkey accepted **treaties to protect minorities;** Turkey paid no reparations, the **Straits** were demilitarized, with a zone on either bank; they were to be opened to ships of all nations in time of peace and in time of war if Turkey remained neutral; if Turkey was at war, enemy ships, but not neutrals, might be excluded. A separate **Turkish-Greek agreement** provided for **compulsory exchange of populations.**

Aug 23. Evacuation of Constantinople by the Allies. The Turks took possession Oct. 6.

Oct. 14. Angora was made the capital of the Turkish national state.

Oct. 29. FORMAL PROCLAMATION OF THE TURKISH REPUBLIC: Mustapha Kemal president, Ismet Pasha prime minister.

1924, Mar. 3. ABOLITION OF THE CALIPHATE; all members of the house of Osman banished.

Apr. 20. Adoption of the constitution, an elaboration of the Fundamental Law.

Aug. 6. The Anglo-Turkish dispute about the status of **Mosul** (left open by the Treaty of Lausanne) was submitted to the League of Nations.

Oct. 29. The League Council fixed a provisional line (*Brussels line*) assigning most of Mosul to Iraq.

1925, Feb.-Apr. Great insurrection in Kurdistan, directed against the religious policy of the government and aiming at autonomy. The suppression of the revolt cost much effort and blood. The leaders were executed. As a result of this rising and various attempts to assassinate Mustapha Kemal, his dictatorial powers were extended.

Aug. Polygamy was abolished and divorce introduced.

Sept. 2. Religious orders suppressed; a severe blow at the conservative opposition to the reforms of Mustapha Kemal.

Nov. Wearing of the fez forbidden. The use of the veil by women was made optional, but discouraged.

Dec. 16. Mosul award by the League Council; most of the territory, with rich oil-fields, was assigned to Iraq. Strong protests of the Turks.

Dec. 17. ALLIANCE WITH SOVIET RUSSIA, establishing close political and economic collaboration.

1926, Jan.-Feb. Introduction of the new civil, criminal, and commercial law codes, based respectively on Swiss, Italian, and German systems.

June 5. Treaty with England, disposing of the Mosul issue according to the League's decision.

Sept. 1. Civil marriage made compulsory.

1927, Sept. 2. Elections. Mustapha was empowered to name all candidates, so that his party (*The People's Party*) had a monopoly.

Oct. 15. Historic speech of Mustapha Kemal to the National Assembly, reviewing the whole course of the national revival and movement.

Nov. 1. Mustapha Kemal unanimously elected president for 4 years.

1928, Apr. 9. Abolition of the article of the constitution declaring Islam the state religion.

May 30. Conclusion of a non-aggression pact with Italy for 5 years.

June 13. Agreements with bondholders of the Ottoman public debt as to payments by Turkey.

June 15. Pact with Persia.

Nov. 3. Decree introducing the Latin alphabet, to be in universal use within 15 years. It was applied first to newspapers and then to books. All Turks under 40 years were obliged to attend schools to learn it. Arabic and Persian words were gradually rooted out.

1929, Mar. 6. Treaty with Bulgaria, settling many outstanding questions.

June. Introduction of a high protective tariff, in the effort to encourage Turkish industry. The government steadfastly rejected all foreign investment in Turkey and gradually bought up foreign concessions.

June. Suppression of communist propaganda making clear the limits placed by Mustapha Kemal on friendship with Russia.

Dec. 17. Treaty with Russia, extending and amplifying the Treaty of 1925.

1930, Mar. 28. The name of Constantinople was changed to *Istanbul*; Angora to *Ankara*; Smyrna to *Izmir*; Adrianople to *Edirne*, etc.

May. Formation of an opposition party (*Liberal Republican Party* under Ali Fethi Bey) permitted, in the effort to enliven political life. The new party favored a more moderate nationalism and greater co-operation with the west. After an extremely weak showing in the elections, Ali Fethi dissolved it, but an independent group of deputies continued to exist in the assembly.

June-July. Kurd revolt in the region about Mt. Ararat. Tension between Turkey and Persia, whence the insurgents operated.

Oct. 30. TREATY OF ANKARA between Turkey and Greece, following the settlement of property claims of repatriated populations and other outstanding questions. The two parties recognized the territorial *status quo* and agreed to naval equality in the eastern Mediterranean.

Oct. The Turks attended the first Balkan Conference, at Athens, and took an active part in the work of Greek-Bulgarian reconciliation and the formation of a Balkan pact.

Dec. 23. Dervish rising near Smyrna. This led to further measures to break the Moslem opposition, 28 leaders being executed.

1931, Mar. 8. Naval agreement with Russia: neither party was to add to its Black Sea fleet, excepting after six months' notice to the other.

May 4. Mustapha Kemal unanimously re-elected president for 4 years.

Oct. 30. Visit of Litvinov to Ankara: renewal of the Turco-Russian Alliance for 5 years.

Oct. 20-26. Meeting of the second Balkan Conference at Istanbul.

1932, Jan. 23. Settlement of the Turkish-Persian frontier dispute.

May 25. Visit of the Turkish foreign minister, **Tewfik Rushdi,** to Rome; extension of the agreement with Italy for five years and arrangements for development of trade between the two countries.

July 18. Turkey accepted the invitation to join the League of Nations.

1933, Apr. 22. New arrangement for payment **of the Ottoman debt.** The total was reduced from £T107,-000,000 to £T8,000,000.

Sept. 14. Conclusion of a non-aggression pact for 10 years between Turkey and Greece.

1934, Jan. Five-Year Plan for the development of industry, most of which was to be government-owned. The great depression necessitated a policy of rigid economy, but the encouragement of agriculture, opening of mines, construction of railroads and roads, etc., was continued.

Feb. 9. CONCLUSION OF THE BALKAN PACT, between Turkey, Greece, Rumania, and Yugoslavia (Bulgaria having refused to come in): the four powers mutually guaranteed security of their Balkan frontiers and promised to take no action with regard to any Balkan non-signatory without previous discussion.

May. Beginning of an active **policy of rearmament,** occasioned chiefly by distrust of Italian policy in the eastern Mediterranean.

Dec. 14. Women were given the vote and were permitted to sit in the Assembly (17 women elected in Mar. 1935).

1935, Jan. 1. Introduction of family names. Mustapha Kemal, at the suggestion of the Assembly, adopted the name *Kemal Atatürk* (father of the Turks).

Mar. 1. Kemal Atatürk re-elected president for 4 years.

1936, Apr. 11. The Turkish government appealed to the signatories of the Lausanne Treaty for permission to refortify the Straits (effect of the Ethiopian crisis, p. 963, and Turkish support of the League action).

July 20. The international conference at Montreux approved the Turkish request, Italy not voting. The Straits thereby were returned to Turkish control.

1937, May 29. The League of Nations Council, after acceptance by France and Turkey, adopted a **fundamental law for the Sanjak of Alexandretta,** which had been drawn up by neutral experts after an appeal by Turkey. 40% of the population of the sanjak is Turkish and a special régime for the district had been provided for in the **Franco-Turkish Agreement** of Oct. 20, 1921. The situation became acute after the conclusion of the **Franco-Syrian Treaty** (Sept. 1936) which envisaged Syrian independence. Despite acceptance of the new régime, which called for demilitarization, autonomy, and special rights for the Turkish population, disorders continued in connection with the forthcoming election.

July 9. SIGNATURE OF A NON-AGGRESSION PACT between Turkey, Iraq, Iran (Persia), **and Afghanistan,** securing the Turks on the Asiatic side as the Balkan Pact did on the European. Turkey generally recognized as a crucial force for peace in eastern Europe and hither Asia.

Oct. 25. Resignation of **Ismet Inönü,** close collaborator of Kemal Atatürk and since 1925 prime minister. He was succeeded by **Jelal Bey Bayar,** whose economic training made him especially suited for the management of the extensive industrial and agricultural program of the government.

Dec. 7. Beginning of the **Alexandretta crisis.** The Turkish government denounced the treaty of friendship with Syria (of May 30, 1926), whereupon the French government sent a military mission to Ankara. After bitter recriminations and threat of war

1938, July 3. The French and Turks came to an agreement: each to send 2500 troops into the sanjak to supervise the elections. The Turks entered the territory July 5. In the elections of Sept. the Turks secured 22 deputies out of a total of 40.

Sept. 2. THE REPUBLIC OF HATAY (i.e. Alexandretta), a new autonomous state, was voted by the new Assembly. The Turks were evidently in complete control and the republic existed only *pro forma.*

Nov. 10. DEATH OF KEMAL ATATÜRK, founder and president of the Turkish Republic. On the next day the National Assembly unanimously elected

1938- ISMET INÖNÜ, president.

1939, May 12. Conclusion of a **British-Turkish agreement of mutual assistance** in case of aggression or war in the "Mediterranean area." Despite close economic relations with Germany, the Turkish government identified itself with the British bloc designed to check German expansion into the Balkans. Negotiations for a similar pact between Turkey and

France gave promise of success since the French indicated readiness to abandon Hatay (Alexandretta) completely to the Turks.

June 23. France and Turkey concluded a **non-aggression pact**, and France agreed to the **incorporation of the Republic of Hatay** into Turkey. The Turkish Republic thereupon took its stand squarely by the western powers.

2. SYRIA

1918, Oct. 5. A French squadron took Beyrut, which was entered by British troops soon afterward. A Syrian state was proclaimed by Emir Faisal.

1919, July 2. A national congress at Damascus asked for **complete independence** for Syria, or, failing that, a mandate by the United States or Great Britain.

Sept. 15. The British gave over control to the French.

Oct. 9. Gen. Gouraud, high commissioner.

Dec. Fighting between the Arabs and the French.

1920, Mar. 8. A Syrian national congress again declared for complete independence.

Mar. 11. FAISAL PROCLAIMED KING. England and France refused to recognize him.

Apr. 25. The supreme council assigned the mandate for Syria to France (approved by the League, July 24, 1922).

July 25. The French took Damascus. Faisal was dethroned and forced to flee.

Sept. 1. Organization of the territory by the French: states of Aleppo, Damascus, Alaouite, loosely federated (1922) autonomous units, under one French commissioner; Great Lebanon (Christian) given a separate status.

Dec. 23. Anglo-French Agreement on frontiers with Palestine and Iraq.

1921, Mar. 4. A fifth state, Jebel Druse, recognized as autonomous.

Oct. 20. Agreement with Mustapha Kemal and the Turkish Nationalists, ending hostilities (p. 1095).

1923, Mar. 4. The Sanjak of Alexandretta was separated and given autonomy.

Apr. 20. Gen. Weygand, high commissioner.

1925, Jan. 1. Damascus and Aleppo united to form the state of *Syria*.

Jan. 2. Gen. Sarrail, high commissioner.

Feb. 9. Organization of the People's Party, a nationalist group demanding unity of the Syrian states and independence.

Apr. 2. Agreement with Turkey regarding the autonomy of Alexandretta.

July 11. Arrest of Druse notables who had been invited to a conference at Damascus. The Druses accused the French of favoritism toward the Christians.

1925, July 18—1927, June. GREAT INSURRECTION OF THE DRUSES, under Sultan Pasha. They soon controlled the countryside and attacked even the larger cities.

Oct. 14. Rising of Damascus, after the exposure of rebels' corpses by the French. The French withdrew from the city.

Oct. 18. Forty-eight-hour **bombardment of Damascus,** followed by tank and airplane attacks.

Nov. 6. Henri de Jouvenel, high commissioner.

1926, May 7. Second attack of the Druses on Damascus, followed by a **second bombardment** of the city by the French (May 8–19).

May 23. The Great Lebanon proclaimed a republic by the French.

Oct. 12. Henri Ponsot, high commissioner.

1927, June. End of the Druse insurrection, after a large-scale campaign. The leaders fled to Transjordania.

1928, June 9. A constituent assembly, summoned by the French, contained a large Nationalist majority. It drafted a constitution which gave no recognition to the French mandate and was therefore rejected by the high commissioner, who prorogued the assembly.

1929, Feb. 5. The constituent assembly was indefinitely adjourned.

1930, May 22. The high commissioner introduced a constitution of his own: Syria to be a republic, with a parliament elected for 4 years; this was to elect a president, with a 5-year term. Latakia was also established as a republic.

1932, Jan. Elections; through French pressure the majority turned out to be moderate.

June. The Parliament elected **Ahmed Ali Bey el-Abed** president, and he was approved by the French.

WESTERN ASIA

- - - Boundaries not yet definitely determined

Scale of Miles
0   50 100   200   300

1933, July. Damien de Martel, high commissioner.

Nov. 16. Treaty with France, following the lines of the Anglo-Iraqi Treaty: France to support Syria's admission to the League within 4 years; Syria to remain in alliance with France for 25 years, during which France would enjoy extensive control of foreign relations, army and finance. The treaty was not to apply to the other Syrian states.

1934, Nov. 3. Parliament was indefinitely prorogued because of opposition to the treaty (objection to separate treatment of the Syrian states and to continued French control), and widespread disorders.

1936, Jan. The Nationalist Party (founded 1935) was dissolved, after much Nationalist agitation and disorder. Violent street-fighting in most cities, followed by proclamation of martial law.

Feb. General strike in Syria. The French administration was obliged to permit the formation of a Nationalist cabinet (Feb. 23).

Sept. 9. SIGNATURE OF THE FRENCH-SYRIAN TREATY of friendship and alliance (ratified Dec. 26); mandate to end within 3 years and Syria to be admitted to the League of Nations;

Jebel Druse, Alouite, and Alexandretta to be included in the Syrian state, with special status; the Lebanon to retain its individuality. A treaty between France and the Lebanon was concluded Nov. 13.

Oct. 6. Outbreak of rioting in Alexandretta by way of protest of the Turkish population against the new arrangements. The problem, aggravated by Turkey's interference, was finally disposed of through League action and a separate Franco-Turkish agreement (p. 1097).

Nov. 30. The elections resulted in a huge Nationalist victory, whereupon (Dec. 21) a new president and premier took office.

1937, Jan. 4. The Lebanon Constitution, suspended some years previously, was restored.

July-Aug. Insurrection of the Kurds in northeastern Syria, who advanced claims to autonomy and separate status. The movement was put down by liberal use of the air forces.

Sept. 8. The Pan-Arab Congress at Bludan to deal with the Arab problem in Palestine. Syria became a center of Palestine insurgent activity during the Arab revolt of 1936–.

3. PALESTINE AND TRANSJORDANIA

1916, Apr. 26. Secret Anglo-French-Russian Agreement providing that Palestine should be placed under international administration.

1917, Nov. 2. BALFOUR DECLARATION, stating that the British government favored *"the establishment in Palestine of a national home for the Jewish people and will use their best endeavors to facilitate the achievement of that object, it being clearly understood that nothing shall be done which may prejudice the civil and religious rights of existing non-Jewish communities in Palestine."*

Dec. 9. The British armies took Jerusalem (p. 948).

1920, Apr. 25. The supreme council assigned the mandate for Palestine and Transjordania to Great Britain (approved by the League of Nations, July 24, 1922), on the terms set forth in the Balfour Declaration, excepting that provisions for a Jewish national home were not to apply to Transjordania.

July 1. Civil government instituted: Sir Herbert Samuel, high commissioner.

1921, Feb. An Arab congress demanded the establishment of a legislative assembly.

May 1-6. Serious anti-Jewish riots by the Arabs, who objected to the sudden influx of Jewish immigrants and to the acquisition of lands by Jewish interests.

Sept. 1. A constitution was promulgated by the high commissioner: there was to be an appointive executive council and a partly elective legislative council. The Arabs refused to vote for the council and therefore the constitution could not be put into effect. The territory was ruled by executive decree.

1923, May 26. Transjordania was organized as an autonomous state, ruled (since Apr. 1, 1921) by Emir Abdullah ibn Hussein, son of the Sherif of Mecca.

1925, Apr. 1. The Hebrew University at Jerusalem was opened by Lord Balfour.

July 1. Field Marshal Plumer, high commissioner.

1928, Feb. 20. Transjordania was recognized as independent, the British retaining military and some financial control.

July 6. Sir John Chancellor, high commissioner.

1929, Aug. FIRST LARGE-SCALE ATTACKS UPON THE JEWS, of whom many were killed. The conflict followed a dispute concerning Jewish use of the Wailing Wall in Jerusalem.

1930, Mar. 31. Report of an investigating commission under Sir Walter Shaw. It attributed the conflict to Arab hatred of the Jews and disappointment of the Arab hopes for independence.

May 17. A decree restricting Jewish immigration led to a Jewish strike of protest.

Aug. 25. Report of the League of Nations mandates commission on the clashes in Palestine, containing harsh condemnation of the British administration for having supplied inadequate police protection.

Oct. 20. THE PASSFIELD WHITE PAPER, following the report of Sir John Hope-Simpson. It stressed the plight of the growing Arab landless proletariat and the increasing land-hunger, and suggested that Jews be forbidden to acquire more land while Arabs were landless, and that Jewish immigration be stopped so long as Arabs were unemployed.

Nov. Acrimonious debate in the British Parliament on the Passfield Paper. The British government denied that any change of policy was envisaged. Nevertheless the confidence of the Jews was badly shaken.

1931, July 14. Sir Arthur Wauchope, high commissioner.

1932. Restrictions on Jewish immigration were somewhat relaxed, but this move simply led to more and more outspoken protests from the Arabs.

1933, Feb. 25. The high commissioner rejected an Arab demand that sale of Arab lands be forbidden and immigration restricted. Thereupon the Arab executive announced a policy of non-co-operation with the British and boycott of British goods.

Dec. Jewish protests and riots against restriction of immigration (this problem having become crucial in view of the persecution of Jews in Germany).

1935, Jan. 4. Opening of the great British oil pipeline from Mosul to Haifa.

1936, Apr. Formation of the Arab High Committee with the aim of uniting all Arabs in opposition to the Jewish claims. By this time the demonstrations and riots of the Arabs had reached the dimensions of open war against the Jews. Conciliatory efforts made by the four Arab rulers (Aug.) were of no effect. The Arabs called a general strike which continued until Oct. 12. To meet the situation the British government, somewhat belatedly, sent additional troops and appointed a commission of investigation and recommendation (Peel Commission), which took evidence in Palestine during the autumn. The Arabs boycotted it until just before its departure in Jan. 1937.

1937, July 8. Publication of the Peel Commission report. Convinced that Arabs and Jews could not get along together, the commission recommended a scheme for partitioning the mandate, making three states: (1) A Jewish state (about one-third of the whole) embracing the coastal territory from the northern boundary to just south of Jaffa. This state would contain about 300,000 Jews and about 290,000 Arabs; most of the land would be held by Arabs. (2) A British mandated territory comprising a strip from Jaffa along the railway to Jerusalem, both cities, as well as Bethlehem, to be included in it. (3) The rest was to be an Arab state, united with Transjordania.

Aug. 2. The Peel scheme was adopted by the World Zionist Congress, conditional on revisions in favor of the Jews. A minority voted against it and Jewish non-Zionist opinion throughout the world denounced the plan as a violation of the Balfour Declaration.

Aug. 23. The mandates commission of the League of Nations, and later the assembly, accepted the plan in principle.

Sept. 8. THE PAN-ARAB CONGRESS AT BLUDAN (Syria), composed of some 400 non-official representatives from all the Arab countries. The congress was called to deal with the Palestine situation and voted overwhelmingly against the Peel plan. Demands of the Arabs were: termination of the mandate and establishment of Palestine as an independent state in alliance with Great Britain; abandonment of the Jewish national home and cessation of Jewish immigration; the Jews to have merely the status of a guaranteed minority within the Arab state; partition unreservedly rejected. The congress arranged for a permanent executive, for economic support of the Palestine Arabs, and for extensive propaganda. Boycott of Jewish goods and enterprises, and eventually of the British, was provided for.

Sept. 26. Assassination of Yelland Andrews, British district commissioner for Galilee, brought on the most acute phase of the great Arab insurrection.

Oct. 1. The British administration arrested the members of the Arab High Committee and deported many of them to the Seychelles. The most influential Arab leader, the Grand Mufti of Jerusalem, **Haj Amin el Husseini,** took refuge in a mosque and later (Oct. 16) fled to Syria, which became the headquarters of the insurgents. The more radical elements (terrorist) secured ever greater control of the movement, and in Palestine outrages against the Jews multiplied to the point of pitched battles (Jerusalem, Nov. 14).

Nov. 11. The British commissioner set up **special military courts** to deal with terrorists: the mere carrying of firearms or bombs made an offense punishable by death.

1938, Jan. 4. The British government announced the **postponement of the partition scheme** and the appointment of a **new commission under Sir John Woodhead** to study the boundaries of the new states and to investigate economic and financial aspects. The commission took evidence in Palestine from Apr. until Aug., but was systematically boycotted by the Arabs.

Mar. 3. Sir Harold MacMichael arrived to replace Sir Arthur Wauchope **as high commissioner.** This was taken to presage more drastic repression of disorders. Before the end of the year the British had from 25,000 to 30,000 troops in Palestine.

June 29. Execution of Solomon ben Yosef, a young Jewish terrorist, representing the revisionist wing of Jewry which advocated retaliation on the Arabs. During July and Aug. Palestine was immersed in an undeclared war, with great **bombings in the Jerusalem, Haifa, and Jaffa Arab markets,** with considerable loss of life. By many it was claimed that these outrages were not the work of Jewish extremists, but of Arab terrorists who dominated the whole Arab population.

Oct. 2. Massacre of 20 Jews at Tiberias. The Arab extremists seized several towns, which were retaken by the British only with some difficulty (Bethlehem re-

taken, Oct. 10; the old city of Jerusalem, Oct. 18).

Nov. 9. Report of the Woodhead Commission. After analyzing various schemes of partition, the commission concluded that they were all impracticable. Thereupon the British government abandoned the plan and decided to convoke a **conference of Jews and Arabs,** the latter not only from Palestine but from the other Arab countries, all of which had demonstrated complete solidarity with the Palestinians.

1939, Feb.-Mar. The Palestine Conference in session at London. Neither Jews nor Palestine Arabs were ready to accept a British proposal, despite efforts of non-Palestine Arabs to effect a compromise. The conference closed (Mar. 17) without reaching a settlement. Thereupon,

May 17. The British Plan was published. It provided for an independent Palestine state in 10 years, in treaty relationship with Great Britain. Arabs and Jews were to share in the government "*in such a way as to ensure that the essential interests of each community are safeguarded.*" During a transition period Arabs and Jews were to serve as heads of departments (but with British advisers), and to take part in an advisory executive council according to population. After 5 years a representative body was to draft a constitution, which must provide for the different communities and for a Jewish home. In the matter of Jewish immigration the principle of absorptive capacity of the country was given up. Immigration was to stop after 5 years unless the Arabs agreed to its continuance. In that period 75,000 might be admitted, giving the Jews ⅓ of the population in 1944. The government was henceforth to prohibit or regulate transfer of land.

The British parliament approved this plan by a majority of only 89 as against the usual 200 or more (May 23), but it was violently denounced by the Jews throughout the world as making a "territorial ghetto" of the homeland. The Palestine Arabs also rejected it. Clashes and outrages again broke out in many parts of the mandate. The situation continued very unsatisfactory but was soon overshadowed by the crisis in Europe (p. 966). When England declared war on Germany (Sept. 3), the Zionist organizations at once proclaimed solidarity with Britain against persecuting Germany.

The (Wahabi) Dynasty of Ibn Saud

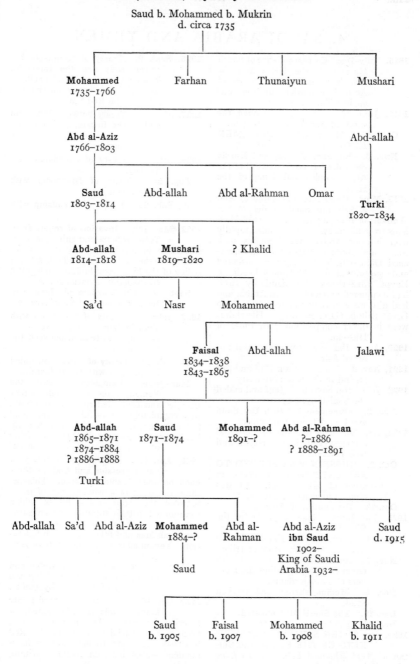

Saud b. Mohammed b. Mukrin
d. circa 1735

Mohammed
1735–1766 Farhan Thunaiyun Mushari

Abd al-Aziz
1766–1803 Abd-allah

Saud
1803–1814 Abd-allah Abd al-Rahman Omar **Turki**
1820–1834

Abd-allah
1814–1818 **Mushari**
1819–1820 ? Khalid

Sa'd Nasr Mohammed

Faisal
1834–1838
1843–1865 Abd-allah Jalawi

Abd-allah
1865–1871
1874–1884
? 1886–1888 **Saud**
1871–1874 **Mohammed**
1891–? **Abd al-Rahman**
?–1886
? 1888–1891

Turki

Abd-allah Sa'd Abd al-Aziz **Mohammed**
1884–? Abd al-
Rahman Abd al-Aziz
ibn Saud
1902–
King of Saudi
Arabia 1932– **Saud**
d. 1915

Saud

Saud
b. 1905 Faisal
b. 1907 Mohammed
b. 1908 Khalid
b. 1911

4. SAUDI ARABIA AND YEMEN

1915. July-Dec Correspondence of Sherif Hussein of the Hejaz and the British regarding the terms of Arab intervention in the war against Turkey (p. 937).

1916, June 27. Hussein proclaimed the establishment of the Arab state.

Oct. 29. HUSSEIN PROCLAIMED KING OF THE ARABS.

Nov. 6. England, France, and Russia recognized Hussein as head of the Arab peoples and King of the Hejaz.

1919, May. Hejaz forces defeated by Abd al-Aziz ibn Saud, leader of the Wahabis of Nejd, a puritanical sect of Moslems (rose about 1740 and extended rapidly over interior Arabia; the Wahabis took Mecca and Medina, 1803-1806, and threatened Damascus, 1808; they were defeated and suppressed by Mohammed Ali of Egypt, 1812-1820). Ibn Saud, by 1913, had conquered much of eastern Arabia and had also made a treaty of friendship with Great Britain (Dec. 26, 1915). His claims were in direct competition with those of Hussein.

1920, Aug. Ibn Saud conquered and annexed Asir.

1921, Nov. 2. Ibn Saud took **Hail** and put an end to the Rashid dynasty.

1922, July. Ibn Saud took **Jauf** and ended the Shalan dynasty.

Dec. 2. Agreement between Ibn Saud and Iraq defining the frontier.

1924, Aug. 24. The Wahabis of Ibn Saud attacked **Taif**, in the Hejaz, and took it (Sept. 5).

Oct. 3. HUSSEIN WAS FORCED TO ABDICATE by his subjects, in favor of his son **Ali.** Ali was obliged to evacuate Mecca.

Oct. 13. Ibn Saud took **Mecca.**

1925, Jan.-June. Siege of Jidda by the Wahabis.

Nov. 1. Agreement of Ibn Saud with Iraq regarding the frontier tribes.

Nov. 2. Agreement of Ibn Saud with Great Britain, regarding the frontiers of Transjordania.

Dec. 5. Medina surrendered to Ibn Saud.

Dec. 19. The Sherif Ali abdicated.

Dec. 23. Ibn Saud took Jidda.

1926, Jan. 8. IBN SAUD PROCLAIMED KING OF THE HEJAZ and Sultan of Nejd (changed Feb. 1927 to *King of the Hejaz and Nejd*).

1926, Sept. 2. Treaty of friendship between Italy and the Imam of Yemen; beginning of Italian efforts to establish influence on the east coast of the Red Sea.

1927, May 20. Treaty between Ibn Saud and Great Britain, which recognized the complete independence of the kingdom.

1929, Aug. 3. Treaty of friendship with Turkey.

Aug. 24. Treaty of friendship with Persia (Iran).

1930, Feb. 24. Treaty of friendship with Iraq.

1932, May-July. Invasion of rebels from Transjordania and subsequent insurrection in Nejd, evidently due to opposition to the westernizing and centralizing policy of the king (road-building, telegraph construction, aviation, etc.).

Sept. 22. The kingdom of Hejaz and Nejd was renamed *Saudi Arabia.*

1933, July 27. Treaty of friendship with Transjordania, ending years of hostility and tension between the two states.

1934, Feb. 11. Treaty of Sanaa concluded for 40 years with Great Britain.

Mar.-June. Campaign against the Yemen, after numerous border troubles and continued rivalry. Ibn Saud was completely successful, but the final peace (June 23), mediated by Great Britain, left Yemen independent, Ibd Saud acquiring only a rectification of the frontier.

1936, Apr. 2. Conclusion of a treaty of non-aggression and Arab brotherhood between Arabia and Iraq. This became the basis of a whole series of pacts between the Arab states, all of which were united in their stand on the Palestine question. General prevalence of the Pan-Arab idea and talk of an Arab federation. Yemen adhered to the treaty in Apr. 1937.

May 7. Agreement between Arabia and Egypt, the latter recognizing the annexation of the Hejaz by Arabia.

1937, Oct. 15. Renewal of the 1926 treaty between Italy and the Yemen, for a period of 25 years. The Imam of Yemen, occupying a crucial position on the Red Sea, has tried hard to maintain an independent status between Arabia, Britain, and Italy.

5. IRAQ

1919, Jan. 10. The British occupied Baghdad.

1920, Apr. 25. The supreme council assigned the **mandate for Iraq** to Great Britain, which accepted (May 5).

July-Dec. Great Arab insurrection against the British. Several British garrisons were besieged for weeks before the movement could be suppressed. It was simply the first indication of the determination of the Arabs to be independent.

Oct. 1. Sir Percy Cox named high commissioner.

1921, June 23. Emir Faisal, former King of Syria, arrived at Basra.

Aug. 23. Cox proclaimed **FAISAL KING OF IRAQ**, after a plebiscite had turned out 96% in favor.

1921-1933. FAISAL, king.

1922, Mar. 25. A military agreement was concluded with Great Britain, giving the latter a large measure of control.

June 18. Insurrection of the Kurds under Sheikh Mahmud. The movement aimed at independence or autonomy, and was not suppressed until July, 1924.

Oct. 10. An agreement with England transformed the mandate into an alliance relationship. Ratified by the Iraqi assembly June 11, 1924.

Dec. 2. Treaty with Nejd regarding frontiers. Nevertheless the following years were marked by constant border raids and clashes between tribes, some of which were divided by the agreement.

1923, Apr. 30. Protocol to the treaty of Oct. 10: Iraq was to become free when she joined the League of Nations and in no case later than four years after the conclusion of peace with Turkey.

July 24. Treaty of Lausanne. The decision regarding the **Mosul** area, rich in oil, was left to negotiation and led to a long-drawn dispute (p. 1095).

Sept. 25. Sir Henry Dobbs, high commissioner.

1924, Mar. 27. The Constituent Assembly met and ratified the agreement with Great Britain.

July 10. The Assembly adopted the **Organic Law** (constitution), introducing a liberal, parliamentary system of government.

July 19. End of the Kurd revolt.

1925, Nov. 1. Agreement with Nejd regarding the assignment and rights of the border tribes.

1926, Jan. 13. In accordance with the League recommendation that the relationship with England should be extended if Mosul was to be assigned to Iraq, a **new treaty** was signed extending the connection to 25 years, or until Iraq joined the League.

June 5. Settlement of the Mosul question, by agreement between England and Turkey. Most of the area went to Iraq.

1927, Nov. Visit of King Faisal to London, in an attempt to secure Iraq's admission to the League immediately.

Dec. 14. New treaty with Great Britain, which recognized the independence of Iraq and promised to support Iraq's admission to the League in 1932. In return Iraq granted Britain three new **air bases** and agreed that British officers should train the army.

1929, Mar. 2. Sir Gilbert Clayton, high commissioner.

Aug. 11. Treaty of friendship with Iran.

Oct. 3. Sir Francis Humphreys became high commissioner on the death of Clayton (Sept. 11, 1929).

1930, Feb. 24. Treaty of friendship with Nejd.

Sept. 11. New Kurd outbreak under Sheikh Mahmud. The sheikh surrendered in Apr. 1931.

Nov. 16. The Iraqi Parliament ratified the treaty with England, providing for admission to the League in 1932. The treaty confirmed Iraq's complete independence and sovereignty.

1931, Jan. 22. The Anglo-Iraqi Treaty was presented to the League.

1932, Apr.-June. Third rising of the Kurds. The rebels were driven over the Turkish frontier by Iraqi forces aided by the British air patrol.

Oct. 3. IRAQ WAS ADMITTED TO THE LEAGUE OF NATIONS after a favorable though somewhat dubious report of the mandates commission. Iraq was required to give **guaranties** for the protection of minorities, the rights of foreigners, freedom of conscience, recognition of debts, etc.

The Hashimite Dynasty

Hussein ibn Ali
King of the Hejaz
(abdicated 1924)

Ali	Faisal I	Abdullah
King of the Hejaz	King of Iraq	Emir and King
1924–1925	1921–1933	of Transjordan
		1921–1951
	Ghazi I	Tallal
	1934–1939	1951–
	Faisal II	
	b. 1935	
	King 1939–	

Nov. The frontier with Syria, long in dispute, was finally settled through the aid of the League of Nations.

1933, Aug. Massacre of the Christian Assyrians as they tried to recross the frontier from Syria, to which they had migrated earlier. The League took up the matter and tried to arrange for resettlement elsewhere, but with no success.

Sept. 8. Death of King Faisal at Berne.

1933–1939. KING GHAZI, son of Faisal.

1934, July 14. Opening of the great oil pipeline from Mosul to Tripoli in Syria. The line to Haifa was opened Jan. 14, 1935.

1935, Mar. Formation of a national government under Gen. Yasin Pasha el Hashimi. Incipient revolts were put down with vigor, and compulsory military training was introduced (June 19). The new government won a decisive victory in the elections of Aug. 6.

1936, Apr. 12. Conclusion of a treaty of non-aggression and Arab brotherliness with Saudi Arabia. This agreement became the basis for a general Arab alliance, the aim of the Pan-Arab movement. Other Arab states were invited to join.

Oct. 29. *Coup d'état* of Gen. Bakr Sidqi, a prominent Pan-Arab

leader. The king was a party to the movement, which was followed by the dissolution of Parliament and a practical dictatorship of Gen. Sidqi.

Nov. 26. Formation of a new party, the Society for National Reform, an organ of the governing group. Vigorous prosecution of road and railroad construction, irrigation, and other schemes of development.

1937, July 9. Conclusion of the Turkish-Iraqi-Iran-Afghan non-aggression pact, forming a loose Oriental entente of Moslem states able to offer effective resistance against imperialist designs of outside powers.

Aug. 11. Assassination of Gen. Sidqi by a Kurd. Formation of a new Pan-Arab cabinet. The Iraqi government took an active part in defense of the claims of the Palestine Arabs and became one of the prime movers in the cause of Arab solidarity.

1939, Apr. 4. Death of Ghazi in an automobile accident at Baghdad. In the ensuing disorders the British consul, supposed to have plotted the accident, was stoned to death. Ghazi was succeeded by his 3-year-old son,

1939-   FAISAL II, as king.

6. I R A N

The First World War may be said to have sealed the fate of the old régime in Iran (Persia until 1935). The government

1914, Nov. 1. Proclaimed neutrality, but was far too weak to enforce it.

The only troops available were the Cossack Brigade, under Russian officers, and the gendarmerie (since 1911) under Swedish officers who tended to sympathize with the Germans. Russian forces were still in oc-

The Pahlavi Dynasty of Iran

Abbas Ali Khan

Reza Shah Pahlavi
1925–1941

Mohammed Reza Pahlavi 1941–	Ali b. 1922	Gholam b. 1923	Abdor b. 1924	Ahmad b. 1925	Mahmud b. 1926	Hamid b. 1932

cupation of important towns in the north, while the British established themselves on the Gulf coast.

1915, Jan. 7. The Turks, campaigning against the Russians in the Caucasus, **took Tabriz,** which, however, was soon retaken by the Russians (Jan. 30). Persian territory was freely violated by both sides. At the same time the British, to strengthen their Russian allies, granted them a free hand in their zone under the 1907 Agreement, while the neutral zone was added to the British sphere.

Jan. Arrival in Persia of Herr Wassmuss, former German consul at Bushire. Wassmuss organized a number of tribes around Bushire and harassed the British, who were in occupation of the town. At the same time other German agents (**Niedermayer, Zugmayer**) established themselves in other towns of the interior, with the purpose of opening a route to Afghanistan and preparing a Turkish-German advance on India. One mission reached Afghanistan, but the amir evaded any commitment. For a time, however, the German influence was predominant.

Nov. The Russians invaded northern Persia in order to break the German influence at Tehran.

1916. The Turks, having defeated the British in Mesopotamia, **twice invaded Persia,** but were stopped by the Russians.

Mar. Sir Percy Sykes arrived at Bunder Abbas and began the organization of the **South Persia Rifles,** with which it was hoped that southern Persia could be protected from German influence and Turkish invasion. He marched to Kerman (May), Yezd (Aug.), Ispahan (where the Russians were already in occupation), and Shiraz (Nov.). His force ultimately numbered some 11,000 men, with which the British position was reinforced as against the Persian gendarmerie and the fractious tribesmen.

1917. Mar. The Turks, defeated at Baghdad, **fell back from Persia.**

Nov. The Russians, following the Bolshevik Revolution, also **began to withdraw** from the country. By this time the country was in a state of complete anarchy.

1918, Jan. Arrival of Gen. Dunsterville and a small British force, the object of which was to stiffen the Georgians and Armenians against the Turks and to establish a Caucasus front against possible German advance from the Ukraine. Dunsterville reached Enzeli from Baghdad, but, under threat from the Bolsheviks at Baku, was obliged to fall back on Hamadan. His force was gradually increased, and another, under **Gen. Sir. Wilfrid Malleson,** was sent to northeastern Persia to block a possible Bolshevik attempt on India from that direction.

Nov. A British flotilla, organized on the Caspian, **drove the Turks out of Baku.**

1919, May 21. Comm. D. T. Norris of the British flotilla, **defeated the Bolshevik naval force** at Alexandrovsk. In Aug. the British ships were handed over to the White Russians.

1919. The Persian government sent a **delegation to the Paris Peace Conference** and demanded abrogation of the 1907 Agreement, abolition of the capitulations and consular guards, restoration of Transcaspia, Merv, and Khiva, the Caucasus and Derbent, including Erivan and Baku, Kurdistan, and everything to the Euphrates River. This delegation, at the instigation of the British, was not officially recognized.

Aug. 9. THE ANGLO-PERSIAN AGREEMENT, negotiated by **Sir**

Percy Cox. Once again Britain reaffirmed the independence and integrity of Persia. Britain further engaged to furnish advisers and officers and to supply munitions for a force to preserve order. A loan was to be granted to Persia and aid to be given in railroad and road construction. The tariff was to be revised. This agreement was intended to seal the British ascendancy, and for that reason it brought forth at once widespread opposition in Persia. The Assembly (*Majlis*) refused to convene to ratify it.

1920, Jan. 10. Persia became one of the original members of the League of Nations.

May 18. The Bolshevik fleet, having defeated the counter-revolutionary forces, **took Enzeli and Resht,** and occupied most of Gilan (**Soviet Republic of Gilan,** to Oct. 1921). The British forces in northern Persia fell back on Kazvin.

Aug. 24. The Persian Cossack Brigade, commanded by Col. Storroselski, **took Resht** from the Bolsheviks, but was later defeated and driven back from Enzeli, after which the British helped to reorganize it.

1921, Jan. 18. The British began to withdraw from northern Persia.

Feb. 21. THE *COUP D'ÉTAT* OF REZA KHAN. The latter was born in Mazandaran in 1878 and was an officer of the Cossack Brigade. Highly intelligent, energetic and patriotic, he engineered the dismissal of the Russian officers after the defeat at Enzeli and then entered into negotiations with **Sayyid Zia ud-Din,** an eminent writer and reformer. With 3000 Cossacks Reza marched on Tehran and established a new government in which Zia ud-Din was prime minister and Reza himself minister of war and commander in chief.

Feb. 26. The first act of the new government was to drop the unratified British agreement and conclude a **treaty with the Bolsheviks.** The latter, in order to break down the British ascendancy, agreed to evacuate Persia, abrogate the capitulations, cancel all debts and concessions, and turn over, without indemnity, all Russian property in Persia.

Dec. 12. Persian-Turkish treaty of peace and friendship.

1922-1927. Financial mission of Dr. A. C. Millspaugh, an American expert. He was given wide powers and enjoyed the firm support of Reza Khan, though the finances of the army were kept beyond his control. With a new and enlarged army Reza suppressed a serious revolt in Gilan and (1922) subjected Azerbaijan.

1923, Oct. 28. Reza Khan took over the premiership. The shah, unable to approve the dictatorship, left for Europe, from which he never returned (died 1930).

1924, Mar. Rumors of the shah's return provoked a widespread **agitation for a republic.** Supposedly inspired by the Bolsheviks and by the events in Turkey, the movement was opposed by the religious leaders, who persuaded Reza of their view. Reza's threat of resignation brought the popular excitement to an end.

Oct. Campaign against Sheikh Khazal of Mohammerah and the Bakhtiari chiefs of southwestern Persia who, with the support of the Anglo-Persian Oil Company and the British government, had made themselves practically independent. They were all subdued and government control established throughout most of Persia.

1925, Feb. The Majlis invested Reza Khan with dictatorial powers.

Oct. 31. The Majlis declared the absent shah deposed.

Dec. 13. Reza Khan proclaimed shah by the Assembly. He was crowned Apr. 25, 1926, with the title

1925-1941. REZA SHAH PAHLAVI. The new shah consistently followed a policy like that of Mustapha Kemal in Turkey, excepting for the anti-religious aspect. He continued the work of restoring order, built up the army, developed roads, began the construction of a railway from the Caspian to the Persian Gulf, encouraged aviation, etc.

1926, Apr. 22. Persian-Turkish-Afghan Treaty of mutual security, concluded under Russian auspices. Nevertheless, friction between Persia, Turkey, and Iraq over the Kurdish populations in the boundary regions, continued to cause much unpleasantness.

1927, Feb. The Junkers Company (German) **opened regular air service** to Baku, Tehran, Ispahan, and Bushire. This continued until 1932.

Nov. 22. The Persian government advanced its **claims to the Bahrein Islands,** the Arab sheikh of which was under British protection. Discovery of oil gave the islands a new value. The conflicting claims have not yet been settled.

1928. Persia made an **agreement with Imperial Airways** (British), permitting regular flights along the Gulf coast to Karachi and India.

May 10. The Persian government, having introduced a **new judicial system** based on the French (1927), declared the capitulations abolished. New minimum tariff rates were offered to nations concluding treaties. Britain, followed by other powers, accepted the new system.

Sept. The National Bank of Persia was founded.

1929, Aug. 11. Persia recognized the Iraqi State and thus paved the way for better relations.

1930, Mar. 28. Introduction of the gold standard.

June-July. A great rising of the Kurds on the Persian-Turkish frontier strained relations between the two countries, but led to renewed efforts to establish a satisfactory frontier.

1931, Jan. Foreigners were forbidden to own agricultural land in Persia.

Feb. The government took over the Persian lines of the Indo-European Telegraph Company. At the same time the government established close control over all foreign trade, though private enterprise was permitted as before.

1932, Jan. 23. The Persian-Turkish boundary was revised in the vicinity of Mt. Ararat, thus obviating a constant source of trouble with Turkey.

Apr. 26. King Feisal of Iraq visited Tehran, paving the way for friendly relations.

Oct. Founding of the Persian fleet on the Gulf. The nucleus was a number of gunboats built in Italy for the Persian government.

Nov. 26. The Persian government cancelled the concession granted to **d'Arcy** in 1901 and taken over by the **Anglo-Persian Oil Company** in 1909. Long

negotiations to revise the concession had broken down. The British government, financially interested in the company since Aug. 14, 1914, and the largest single shareholder, brought the matter before the council of the League of Nations, which urged further efforts at direct negotiation. The result was the **new concession of May 29, 1933,** which extended the original contract from 1961 to 1993, but restricted the area from 500,000 square miles to 250,000 and after 1938 to 100,000. The company was to pay £225,000 annually in taxes for 15 years and £300,000 annually for a second period of 15 years. The minimum royalty was to be £750,000 annually.

1933, Apr. Swedish and Danish firms were awarded contracts to complete the Trans-Persian Railway.

1934, May. A concession granted to the Standard Oil Company of California to exploit for oil in the Bahrein Islands raised once again the Persian claim to ownership.

June 16-July 2. Visit of Reza Shah to Ankara and Constantinople. Persia and Turkey drew ever closer.

1935, Mar. 21. PERSIA BECAME OFFICIALLY *IRAN.*

1937, July 9. Conclusion of a **NON-AGGRESSION PACT** between **AFGHANISTAN, TURKEY, IRAQ, AND IRAN.** These four nations now formed an Oriental Entente comparable to the Balkan Entente.

1939, Jan. Opening of the **Trans-Iranian Railway** from the Caspian to the Persian Gulf. This important line, begun in 1927, was constructed entirely with Iranian capital.

7. AFGHANISTAN

Afghanistan remained neutral throughout the First World War, despite German and Turkish missions and despite widespread religious agitation for participation on the Turkish side. Heavy subsidies from the government of India no doubt played a considerable rôle in holding the amir to the policy of his father.

1919, Feb. 19. Assassination of Habibullah near Jelalbad, evidently because of his subservience to the British. His brother **Nasrullah was proclaimed amir** by the conservative, religious parties, but his son **Amanullah,** governor of Kabul, not only held the capital, but enjoyed the support of the army. Nasrullah therefore yielded.

1919-1929. AMANULLAH, amir. Borne

upon a wave of anti-British sentiment he took advantage of the war-weariness in India to proclaim a religious war and appeal to the Indian Moslems to rise against British rule. The Afghans began to invade India, but after a few initial successes were thrown back and threatened with invasion themselves. Neither side being prepared for a long struggle, they negotiated.

Aug. 8. The Treaty of Rawalpindi (supplemented by further agreements of Nov. 22, 1921), by which Britain recognized for the first time the complete independence of Afghanistan and the right to direct relations to other powers. The British subsidies were discontinued.

Rulers of Afghanistan since 1929

Mohammed Nadir
1929–1933

Mohammed Zahir
1933–

| Princess Bilkis | Mohammed Akbar b. 1933 | Ahmad Shah b. 1934 |

1921, Feb. 28. Conclusion of a treaty of friendship with Soviet Russia, similar to the Turkish-Russian treaty. There followed a period of several years during which Amanullah leaned rather heavily on the Bolsheviks as a protection against the British.

Mar. 1. Treaty of friendship and alliance with Turkey, laying the basis for a close relationship between the two powers.

June 22. Treaty with Persia (non-aggression), another link in the Oriental combination under the aegis of Russia.

1923, Apr. 9. PROMULGATION OF THE FUNDAMENTAL LAW, or constitution, modeled on the Turkish and representing Amanullah's desire to modernize his country. The amir retained extensive powers, but the new assembly (council of state), which was one-half appointed and one-half elected, had certain powers over legislation. The constitution was followed by a landslide of reform edicts, aiming at the establishment of an effective central administration, development of education, encouragement of trade and industry, opening of the country through roads, etc. Amanullah played the rôle of a Peter the Great, hastily overturning everything in his desire to modernize the country.

1926, June 10. Amanullah assumed the title of *king*.

Aug. 31. A neutrality and non-aggression pact was signed with Russia, supplementing the earlier agreement.

1927, Nov. 27. Conclusion of a second treaty of friendship and security with Persia.

1928, Jan.-July. Amanullah and his queen paid an extended visit to India, Egypt, and Europe, arranging for further contacts and for financial and advisory support.

May 25. Second treaty with Turkey.

Nov. Outbreak of a great revolt directed against the king and his revolutionary reforms. Opposition broke out on many sides, but drew its inspiration largely from the religious leaders and tribal chiefs.

1929, Jan. 14. Amanullah, unable to maintain himself, abdicated in favor of his older brother, **Inayatullah,** an easygoing and ineffectual person.

Jan. 17. Bacha-i-Saquao, a bandit leader with a small but determined following, captured Kabul and had himself proclaimed

1929. HABIBULLAH GHAZI. His position was challenged by many other claimants, among others by Amanullah, who collected an army at Kandahar, but was defeated in his advance on Kabul.

Mar. Arrival from Europe of **Gen. Mohammed Nadir Khan,** the most outstanding Afghan officer. He managed to collect an army and

Oct. 8. Took Kabul. Thereupon he was proclaimed (Oct. 16)

1929-1933. MOHAMMED NADIR SHAH. Habibullah Ghazi, having been captured, was executed, but the new ruler was faced by a large number of pretenders and followers of Amanullah, who were only gradually subdued. The general policy of Nadir was to continue the work of modernization, but in a less ostentatious and offensive way.

1932, Feb. A new constitution (*Fundamental Rules*) was issued. Its general tenor was much like that of the 1923 Constitution, but it provided for a two-chamber assembly, an appointed chamber of notables, and an elected council of state.

1933, Nov. 8. Assassination of Nadir Shah by a servant of one of his victims. The murder had no political significance, and the shah was succeeded without trouble by his son

1933- MOHAMMED ZAHIR SHAH, who, with the aid of his uncles, continued the wisely moderate but progressive policy of his father.

1936. The government granted to the Inland Exploration Company of New York a 75-year concession for the exploitation of oil.

1937, July 9. Afghanistan joined with Turkey, Iraq, and Iran in forming an Oriental Entente, apparently designed as a bulwark against pressure from any of the great European powers.

1938, June 20-24. Revolt of Shami Pir, a religious leader who operated from Waziristan. His movement was directed against the dynasty and its policy. After his defeat, Shami Pir fled to India, where he was arrested and transported to Syria.

8. INDIA

During the first two years of the First World War, the situation in India was comparatively quiet and the country co-operated loyally in the war. **Mahatma Gandhi,** saintly leader of the Indians in South Africa (p. 858), returned to India and threw his entire influence on the side of the government. India supplied about 1,200,000 troops (combatants and laborers), who took part in the campaigns in Europe, Mesopotamia, Palestine, Egypt, and East Africa. But during the second half of the war unrest became more and more prevalent. Rising prices and heavy taxation served as a stimulus to renewed agitation.

1916-1921. BARON CHELMSFORD, **Viceroy.** He was met at once with a demand for reform by the Indian members of the council, a demand which was vigorously supported (Dec. 29) by the **Indian National Congress** (chiefly Hindu) and the **All-India Moslem League,** which established common action by the **Lucknow Pact,** determining the electoral proportions of each group. The demand of these bodies was for an elected legislative assembly. At the same time revival of **radical nationalism** under **B. G. Tilak** and **Annie Besant.** To anticipate serious trouble, the British government, through the secretary for India, Mr. Montagu,

1917, Aug. 20. Announced a policy of developing **self-governing institutions** in India, with a view to introduction of responsible government. Mr. Montagu visited India in 1918 and together with Lord Chelmsford worked out a report (1918, Apr. 22) for limited self-government, which was presented to Parliament in July and which was at once denounced by the Indian National Congress as wholly inadequate.

1918-1919. Severe **crop failures** with acute distress and starvation, together with an **influenza epidemic** which caused 5,000,000 deaths, aggravated the situation still further and led to serious outbreaks.

1919, Mar. 21. THE ROWLATT ACTS, two anti-sedition measures which enabled the government to intern agitators without trial and entitled judges to try cases without juries, brought the discontent to a head, Hindus, Moslems, and Sikhs uniting in opposition to the government. Gandhi now proclaimed a campaign of passive resistance and non-co-operation. Stoppage of work, demonstrations and riots. The Punjab was in open rebellion, which culminated in

Apr. 13. THE AMRITSAR MASSACRE. Gen. Dyer, aiming to impress the populace with the strength of the government, ordered his troops to fire on an unarmed assembly; 379 persons were killed and 1200 wounded. Intense indignation throughout India. (An army council decided that Dyer's action was "an error of judgment," but a committee of the House of Commons condemned it.)

May 10-Aug. 8. The Afghan War, provoked by the Amir Amanullah in the hope that the Moslems would support his plans for conquering India. The amir entirely underestimated the strength of the British position and he was easily defeated.

Dec. 23. THE GOVERNMENT OF INDIA ACT introduced the Montagu-Chelmsford reforms and established the system known as *"dyarchy."* The Indian legislature was to consist of the viceroy, council of state (60 members, of whom 26 were to be officials), and legislative assembly (140 members, of whom 100 were to be elected). The Indian Parliament was opened at Delhi in Feb. 1921. The provincial governments were to have Indian as well as British ministers. Important matters were "reserved" for the governor and his executive council; the less important (sanitation, education, agriculture, etc.) were to be "transferred" to the Indian ministers. Provincial legislative councils were to be 70% elective, with a franchise rigidly limited by property qualifications.

The Indian National Congress rejected the new system out of hand, but the more moderate elements withdrew from the Congress and founded the **National Liberal Federation,** whose members co-operated with the government and in many places worked the new system with considerable success.

1920, Sept. 8. The National Congress, led by Gandhi, launched the **first non-co-operation campaign** (*satyagraha*) and boycott of British goods (*hartal*). Gandhi preached the wearing of homespun cloth and the revival of village industries (spinning-wheel). The whole movement aimed at "home rule" (*swaraj*) and supported the Moslem Khilafat movement, which was a protest against the treatment of the Turks by the victorious allies.

1921-1926. LORD READING, viceroy.

1921. Height of the revolutionary movement. Despite Gandhi's insistence on non-violent action, terrorist outbreaks were frequent, and in some parts of the country serious peasant risings against landlords and moneylenders took place: **rising of the Akalis** (Sikh peasant puritans) in the Punjab, Mar. 1921; **rising of the Moplahs** (Moslem peasants of Malabar) and widespread slayings of Hindu landlords. The latter episode resulted in a **rift between the Moslem League** (led by Mohammed and Shaukat Ali) **and the Indian Nationalists,** which in turn resulted in chronic clashes between Hindus and Moslems, with much bloodshed.

Nov. 2. The Ali brothers were convicted and sentenced to two years in prison for calling on the Moslem troops to desert.

Dec. 24. The Indian National Congress gave Gandhi sole executive authority. Gandhi denounced all violence and introduced **a campaign of civil disobedience** toward the law. Despite his great authority, violence continued to spread, culminating in

1922, Feb. 4. The Chauri Chaura affair. Insurgent peasants, led by Indian Nationalists, attacked the police station at Chauri Chaura (United Provinces) and killed 22 policemen. Gandhi at once ordered suspension of non-co-operation and civil disobedience, but the government took drastic measures.

Mar. 10. Gandhi was arrested and sentenced to six years' imprisonment. Therewith the first passive resistance campaign began to collapse.

1923, Sept. 25. Victory of the moderate element in the Indian National Congress. This group (the **Swaraj Party**), led by **C. R. Das,** favored participation in the elections with the aim of using its representatives in the legislature to obstruct government and so force the granting of home rule. In the elections the Nationalists did, in fact, win an impressive victory, but many of the elected deputies soon forgot about obstruction and began co-operation with the government. The leaders, Das and Motilal Nehru, began to advocate the grant of **dominion status** for India, leaving independence aside.

1924, Feb. 4. Gandhi was released from prison because of his precarious health. By this time the situation had quieted down considerably, and

Sept. 26. A United Conference at Delhi brought together representatives of the Hindus, Moslems, Parsees, Sikhs, and Christians, who agreed to set up local committees to prevent religious clashes.

1925, Sept. 7. The Nationalists in the Indian legislative assembly called for the establishment of round-table conferences to frame a scheme for responsible government.

1926-1931. BARON IRWIN, viceroy.

1926, Nov. 8. The British Parliament appointed the **Statutory** (*Simon*) **Commission,** with members from all British parties, to study the situation in India and the working of the Montagu-Chelmsford system. The Indians (both Hindu and Moslem) voted to boycott the commission because no Indians were included in it. The total effect of the move was to revive agitation and call forth further disorder.

1928. India was swept by a **great series of strikes** among the Bombay textile workers, railway employees, etc. These strikes marked the emergence of the industrial proletariat as an important factor. The movement had a pronouncedly revolutionary flavor.

Aug. 28. An All-Parties Conference at Lucknow voted for a scheme of Dominion status, worked out by a constitutional committee of the Indian National Congress (the **Nehru Report**). This decision aroused much dissatisfaction among the more radical elements and led to the

Aug. 30. Foundation of the Independence of India League by **Jawaharlal Nehru** (son of Motilal Nehru, author of the Dominion scheme). Similar independence organizations were founded by other groups.

Dec. 22. At the **All Parties Conference** in Calcutta Gandhi again assumed leadership and persuaded the conference to grant the government one year in which to introduce Dominion status, failing which another campaign of non-co-operation should be inaugurated.

1929, Apr. 12. The Trade Disputes Act and the Public Safety Act demonstrated the government's determination to deal firmly with radical labor leaders, communists, and terrorists, many of whom were arrested and imprisoned. Nevertheless, the situation in India became rapidly as bad as, if not worse than, in 1920–1921. The world depression made itself acutely felt and increased the misery of the lower classes.

Oct. 31. The government announced that round-table conferences would be opened with the objective of Dominion status. The viceroy thereupon opened discussions with Gandhi and other leaders (Dec.).

1930, Jan. 1. At the Indian National Congress at Lahore the extremists overruled the moderates, **voted for complete independence,** and decided to boycott the round-table conferences. Under Gandhi's guidance

Mar. 12. The second civil disobedience campaign was initiated. Amidst widespread rioting and innumerable arrests, Gandhi marched to the sea at Cambay and began to make salt illegally as a protest. The government replied by drastic censorship of the press and wholesale imprisonment of leaders.

May 5. Gandhi was again arrested. Height of the disorders: attacks on government salt works, risings of peasants and factory workers, terrorist attacks on officials, etc.

June 13, 24. Publication of the two volumes of the **Simon Commission's Report,** recommending administrative modifications, but denying full responsible government. Needless to say, these suggestions were condemned out of hand by the Indian Nationalists. The British government therefore left the report on one side and convoked

Nov. 12—1931, Jan. 19. The first Round-Table Conference, attended by representatives of the Indian princes and by Indian Liberals who were prepared to co-operate with the government. The conference decided in favor of the principle of federation and at least a measure of responsible government.

1931, Jan. 26. Gandhi was released from prison and, at Lord Irwin's request, entered upon discussions with the government. These resulted in

Mar. 4. The Delhi Pact (*Irwin-Gandhi Pact*); Gandhi agreed to discontinue civil disobedience and promised that the Congress would recognize the Round-Table Conferences; in return the government agreed to release political prisoners who had not been guilty of violence. End of the second passive resistance campaign.

Sept.-Dec. Second Round-Table Conference. Gandhi went to London to attend it, but the conference broke up without reaching agreement on the problem of representation of religious and other minorities.

1931-1936. THE EARL OF WILLINGDON, viceroy.

1932, Jan. 4. Gandhi and other Nationalist leaders were again arrested, and the Indian National Congress was declared illegal. These moves by the government had but little effect. In prison Gandhi embarked upon his "fasts unto death" in behalf of the untouchables, for whom he demanded the vote in the forthcoming constitutional revision. Outside his prison the struggle of the Nationalists and the masses was resumed. In the meanwhile

1933, Apr.—1934, Nov. 22. A parliamentary joint committee, reviewing the material of the Simon Commission and of the Round-Table Conferences, worked out a draft constitution.

1933, July 15. An All-India Congress at Poona, under Gandhi's lead, decided on resumption of civil disobedience Aug. 1.

Aug. 1. Gandhi was once more arrested and sentenced to 12 months' imprisonment, but he had to be released after a few days, in view of his health after a hunger strike.

1934, Oct. 24. Gandhi withdrew from the National Congress, without, however, renouncing all political activity.

1935, Apr. 1. The Reserve Bank of India, a central bank controlling the currency, was established to insure financial stability.

Aug. 2. THE GOVERNMENT OF INDIA ACT passed by the British Parliament. It embodied the results of the investigations and of the Round-Table Conferences, and completely transformed the governmental system of India. **Burma and Aden were separated from India** and became crown colonies. British India was divided into 11 provinces, each under an appointed governor and an appointed executive council. Each province was to have an elected legislature (bicameral in 6 provinces and unicameral in 5), representation to be based on a communal arrangement. The **provincial governments** were to enjoy wide autonomy, though the governors retained certain emergency powers. The ultimate objective was the establishment of an **All-India Federation,** to include the native states as well as the provinces of British India. Pending the adhesion of a number of provinces, this arrangement was postponed. But the 11 provinces together are under the governor-general and his executive council. A **central legislature** at Delhi consists of an upper house (*council of state*) composed of 34 elected members and 26 appointed members, and a lower house (*legislative assembly*) of 105 members elected by the provincial assemblies and 40 appointed members. The governor-general retained control of defense, foreign affairs, Christian Church affairs, etc. The act was to go into effect Apr. 1, 1937.

1936– **MARQUESS OF LINLITH-GOW,** viceroy and governor-general.

1937, Jan.–Feb. Elections for the provincial assemblies. The **All-India Congress** (chiefly Hindu and demanding complete independence) was the only well-organized party and so won absolute majorities in 6 provinces (and pluralities in 3 others). The objective of the party having been to force the abrogation of the new constitution and secure the convocation of an Indian constituent assembly, the leaders were now confronted with the problem whether or not to make use of such power as had been gained in the elections.

Mar. 18. In party congress at Delhi the moderate wing of the party (favoring co-operation with the government) won out over the extremists (led by **Pandit Jawaharlal Nehru,** who called for a thorough-going socialist as well as nationalist policy). But the moderates demanded assurances from the provincial governors that they would not use their emergency powers to frustrate the program of the party. The government having refused to bind itself to what amounted to a violation of the new constitution, the All-India Party abstained from forming administrations when

Apr. 1. The Government of India Act went into effect. In order to break the deadlock, the British government (Apr. 26) gave assurance that the provincial governors would not use their power "for detailed interference." This enabled the moderate wing to compromise and decide for co-operation. All-India governments were set up in 7 provinces. Once in power they liberated many political prisoners and restored the civil liberties. Attention began to turn more and more toward extensive social (especially agrarian) reform. The war in China and the revelation of Japanese imperial designs also contributed to greater cordiality and collaboration between the Nationalists and the British authorities.

1938. Further development of the split between moderates and radicals in the Congress Party. At the party congress at Haripura the left wing won out, and **Subhas Chandra Bose,** disciple of Nehru, was elected president over Gandhi's candidate. Gandhi declared the election fraudulent and threatened to leave the party.

1939, Mar. 2. Gandhi embarked upon another fast to force the ruler of the little native state of Rajkot to introduce reforms. The viceroy succeeded in effecting a compromise, but the episode apparently did much to revive the Mahatma's prestige.

Mar. 10–12. The party congress at Tripuri rejected a radical proposal to send the British government an ultimatum demanding independence, and

Apr. 29. Bose resigned as president of the Congress because of differences with Gandhi and the moderates. **Rajendra Prasad,** an adherent of the Mahatma, was elected to succeed. Gandhi began to advocate a policy of conciliation toward the native princes, but

June 12. Fifty native states rejected the British proposal for federation, while leaving the door open for other arrangements.

9. INDO-CHINA

a. SIAM

1917, July 22. Siam declared war on Germany and Austria-Hungary, and in the summer of 1918 sent a small expeditionary force to Europe. The war enabled the government to inaugurate the work of freeing the country of extra-territoriality and tariff restriction. By the peace treaties Germany, Austria, and Hungary were

obliged to abandon their claims in these matters.

1920, Jan. 10. Siam became an original member of the League of Nations.

Sept. 1. A TREATY WITH THE UNITED STATES did away with American extra-territorial rights and granted Siam tariff autonomy.

1924, Mar. 10. By treaty with Japan the latter power also gave up extra-territorial and tariff rights.

1925, Feb. 14. TREATY WITH FRANCE. France followed the example of the United States and Japan, gave up all special rights, arranged for arbitration of disputes, and finally agreed (Aug. 25, 1926) to the establishment of a demilitarized zone along the Indo-Chinese frontier. England concluded a similar treaty July 14, and the other European powers followed suit, so that by 1926 Siam had secured full jurisdiction and tariff autonomy.

1925-1935. RAMA VII (Prajadhipok), king, succeeding his brother. He appointed a council of state, composed of five royal princes, to aid him in government, and at once initiated a policy of economy, reduction in the number of officials, etc.

1927, Mar. 25. With the ratification of the last treaties with the powers, the consular courts came to an end and the Siamese government established a new tariff.

1931, Mar.-Oct. The king visited the United States in order to have his eyes operated on.

1932, June 24. A *COUP D'ÉTAT* PUT AN END TO ABSOLUTE GOVERNMENT in Siam and established constitutional government. The movement was organized by a group of young radicals, educated in Europe or imbued with European democratic theory, who formed a People's Party. The king, held captive for a short time, at once agreed to a constitution and the organization of a senate. The definitive constitution was adopted Dec. 10: provision for popular sovereignty; the council of state, though appointed by the king, to be responsible to a national assembly, half the members of which were to be appointed while the other half was to be elected by universal (male and female suffrage).

1933, Apr. 3. The king, convinced that the country would support him against the radicals, suspended the new constitution and set up a new council of state. This led to a new

June 20. *Coup d'état,* led by Col. Phya Bahol Sena and other army officers. While affirming their loyalty to the king, they forced the resignation of his council of state and recalled the National Assembly. Phya Bahol Sena became prime minister.

Oct. 11. Attempted counter-revolution by a number of princes and nobles, led by Prince Bovaradet. The movement failed miserably; several of the leaders were captured and most of the others fled the country.

1934, Jan. 12. The king left for a prolonged visit to Europe, from which he did not return.

1935, Mar. 2. Abdication of King Prajadhipok, who was dissatisfied with the new régime and found himself in conflict with the government over the execution of the counter-revolutionary leaders.

1935-1946 ANANDA MAHIDOL, the ten-year-old nephew of Prajadhipok, became king, and a council of regency, headed by Prince Aditya Dibabha, was set up in his behalf. The young ruler was being educated in Europe and did not even visit his kingdom until Nov. 1938. In the meanwhile the country was governed by a triumvirate consisting of the prime minister (Phya Bahol Sena), the minister of defense (Col. Luang Bipul Songgram) and the foreign minister (Luang Pradit), one of the chief figures of the popular movement and a man of decidedly advanced tendencies. The government has, in recent years, paid much attention to defense and the development of aviation, and has, thus far, succeeded in maintaining a position of neutrality as between England and France and, more recently, between China and Japan.

b. OTHER STATES

The situation after the First World War in Indo-China and Malaysia was a comparatively quiet one, marked by rapid expansion of administrative control, development of sanitation and education, and above all by increase of population and productivity. The extension of rubber plantation in particular had a profound effect on the economic setup in many of the states. Some progress was made toward the introduction of a popular element in government, and in all parts of the region (least in the Malay States) there was a growing demand for national recognition. The great depression after 1930 struck all states equally hard, led to the adoption of economic control measures by the governments, and called forth a considerable amount of labor agitation, with some communistic tinges. The great Far-Eastern crisis after 1931 revealed the exposed position of the whole area, and in all states measures were taken to strengthen defenses. The completion of the harbor works, dry-dock, air-field, and fortifications of Singapore (June, 1937) made that crucial port what was considered to be one of the strongest places in the world.

FRENCH INDO-CHINA. In 1922 a number of elected members were added to the colonial council which assisted the governor-general, and in 1927 a government council (60 members, of whom 35 are Frenchmen) was established and given advisory powers. The year 1930–1931 was marked by rather serious outbreaks in Tonkin, which were put down with considerable rigor. But agitation against French rule revived and, if anything, is constantly growing.

NETHERLANDS EAST INDIES. A legislative council (*Volksraad*) was created in 1916 and met in 1918. It was composed of 24 nominated and 24 elected members, the latter chosen by local councils. Racially there were 30 Dutchmen, 25 East Indians, and 5 members of other races (Chinese, e.g.). This body was given advisory powers in budgetary, military, and other matters. In 1922 the *Volksraad* became a genuinely legislative body when its assent was made obligatory for all government ordinances. In 1925 the entire administrative system was overhauled, and in 1929 it was decreed that in future the *Volksraad* should have 30 East Indian members (out of the 60). Despite the vigorous and efficient rule of the Dutch, there developed a movement for independence, represented by the **National Indonesian Party.** In 1937 the *Volksraad* unanimously petitioned the Dutch government to grant Dominion status within 10 years.

10. CHINA

1914, Aug. 23. The Japanese declaration of war against Germany was followed by **violation of China's neutrality** (Sept. 2) and capture of Tsingtao (Nov. 7).

1915, Jan. 18. JAPAN PRESENTED 21 DEMANDS in secrecy. An ultimatum extracted (May 8) modified acceptance of the first **four** groups: (1) Japanese succession to German rights in Shantung; (2) extension to 99 years of the leases in southern Manchuria with commercial freedom for Japanese there; (3) a half interest in the Han-yeh-p'ing Company which operated iron and steel mills at Han-yang, iron mines at Ta-yeh, and a colliery at P'ingshan; and (4) a declaration that no part of China's coast should be leased or ceded to any power. The **fifth** group, calling notably for Japanese advisers in political, financial, and military affairs, and railway concessions in the Long River Valley (Britain's sphere of interest), was set aside.

Dec. 9. Yüan Shih-k'ai, following the monarchist campaign by the **Ch'ou An Hui** (Aug. 14), and election and invitation by a hand-picked national convention, **accepted imperial office** for the ensuing Jan. 1, and adopted the reign title **Hung Hsien;** but in face of immediate successful **rebellion in Yünnan** led by Ts'ai Ao (Dec. 25),

1916, Mar. 22. Yüan cancelled his imperial plans and organized a republican cabinet under **Tuan Ch'i-jui,** senior general of the Pei Yang clique. Yüan died June 6 and was succeeded by **Li Yüan-hung,** who promptly restored the Constitution of 1912 and convoked the original Parliament of 1913.

1917, Jan. 23. Special rights were exacted by Japan in Manchuria and Inner Mongolia.

May 23. Dismissal of Tuan led to a rising of northern military governors. Chang Hsün, called to intervene, declared in Peking, with help of K'ang Yu-wei,

July 1. The restoration of the Manchu dynasty, which was again overthrown (July 12) by Tuan, who resumed the premiership. Resignation of Li left the presidency to the vice-president, **Feng Kuo-chang** (elected Oct. 1916). **Sun Wen** headed a secession government at Canton (Sept.).

Aug. 14. WAR WAS DECLARED AGAINST GERMANY AND AUSTRIA-HUNGARY, and labor battalions were sent to France, Mesopotamia, and Africa. China secured termination of German and Austrian extra-territoriality and Boxer indemnity payments, and return of their concessions at Tientsin and Hankow. The Allies postponed their Boxer payments five years.

1918, May 16. Japanese defensive alliance against any Communist Russian threat provided for action by Japanese-trained Chinese troops in Siberia under Japanese direction (notes Mar. 25, treaty May 16, clarified Sept. 6). Loans of perhaps 250,000,000 yen for Manchurian projects were contracted, about half through Premier Terauchi's agent, Nishihara, with Premier Tuan and his clique, now called the **An-Fu** (Anhui-Fukien) **Club**.

Aug. 12. A newly selected Parliament convened, and elected **Hsü Shih-ch'ang president** (Sept. 4–June 1922). Chinese politics continued, however, to be dominated by personal ambitions and the schism between the governments of Peking and Canton.

1919. Refusal of the Versailles Peace Conference to return the former German concessions in Shantung to China aroused violent resentment, refusal to sign the treaty (June 28), and (rather ineffective) boycott of Japanese goods.

Nov. 16. The Hutuktu of Urga placed **Mongolia again under Chinese suzerainty,** in recognition of a new Chinese garrison, but expulsion of the garrison by Mongols, led by White Russian Baron Ungern von Sternberg (Jan. 1921), and his expulsion by forces of the Far-Eastern Republic, resulted in formation of **the Mongolian People's Revolutionary Government** (July 6), under Soviet auspices.

1920-1926. CIVIL WAR between local military dictators left no real power to the national government, which struggled to maintain its envoys abroad. Revenues from customs and salt were already pledged and administered for service of foreign loans. Those from railways and land taxes were absorbed by local armies for which the civilian population felt no concern since they supported no local interests. Since the death of Yüan Shih-k'ai there was no personality, no concrete cause strong enough to direct or to claim the loyalty of all Chinese.

1922, Feb. 4. THE WASHINGTON CONFERENCE resulted in a **Nine-Power Treaty** to respect China's sovereignty, independence, territorial and administrative integrity, to maintain the "open door," and to afford China opportunity to develop stable government; a **Nine-Power Treaty** (Feb. 6) to grant immediate customs revenue increase to an effective 5%, and to call a conference to prepare for Chinese tariff autonomy; and a **Sino-Japanese Treaty** (Feb. 4), which was strictly observed, to evacuate Japanese troops from Shantung, and to restore to China all former German interests in Tsingtao and the railway to Tsinan, in return for their assessed value plus Japanese improvements. The mines were to be operated by a joint company. Britain announced (Feb. 1) **return of Wei-hai-wei** (actually effected Oct. 1, 1930). Joint resolution by 8 powers (Dec. 10, 1921)

called for re-examination of Chinese law and its administration in relation to extra-territoriality.

1924, Jan. 21. The first Kuo Min Tang national congress at Canton (Sun Yat-sen president) admitted Communists to the party, and accepted Russian advisers, notably **Michael Borodin** (arr. Sept. 1923) who reorganized the party for offense. **Chiang K'ai-shek** (Chieh-shih, b. 1887), himself trained in Japan, headed Russian and German instructors in a new **Whampoa Military Academy** (June). **Sun Wen** presented his platform in a series of lectures on the *San Min Chu I*, "Three Principles of the People" (Nationalism, Democracy, and Social Progress), which he had already defined in 1907. Upon death of Dr. Sun (March 12, 1925) he and his doctrine were promptly canonized as a focus for Chinese loyalty.

May 31. Soviet Russia, in fulfillment of repudiation (July 1919 and Sept. 27, 1920) of the tsar's ill-gotten gains, **gave up extra-territoriality, concessions** at Tientsin and Hankow, **and the rest of the Boxer indemnity,** to be used for education under Russian veto. The Chinese Eastern Railway was placed under joint management.

Despite Japanese objection to competition with the South Manchurian Railway, based on minutes of a Peking conference Dec. 4, 1905, the Chinese built two lines, Ta-hu-shan to Tung-liao and Kirin to Hailung.

Remission by the United States of the $6,000,000 Boxer indemnity balance (May 21) created the

Sept. 17. China Foundation for Promotion of Education and Culture which has since made annual grants for scientific education, and has housed and built up the National Library beyond any Chinese precedent.

1925. Sentiment against the "unequal treaties" and against the British, who used gunfire to disperse dangerous student demonstrations at Shanghai (May 30) and Canton (June 23), found effective expression in a strike and **boycott of British goods and shipping,** until Oct. 1926.

1926, July-Oct. Chiang K'ai-shek's northern campaign, with aid of Russian Gen. Blücher (then called Galens), followed the T'ai P'ing route from Canton through Hunan to Hankow (Sept. 6) and Wuch'ang (Oct. 10).

1927, Feb. 19-20. From the British, tired of boycott, and hopeful of wooing the Chinese from the Russians, the Nationalists extracted rendition of concessions at Hankow and Kiukiang.

Mar. 24. Seizure of **Nanking** gave the Communists a chance to foment trouble for Chiang by attacking foreigners (6 killed). An international force of 40,000 men protected Shanghai.

Apr. 18. Chiang and the conservative members of the Kuo Min Tang split with the radicals at Hankow and set up a **new government at Nanking.** Surface harmony was restored by a purge of Russians and Communists from Hankow in return for (temporary) retirement of Chiang from public life (Aug. 8). Advance to Peking was partly blocked by Japanese troops, sent to protect residents of Tsinan. Chiang married (Dec. 1) Soong (or Sung) Meiling, a sister of Sun Wen's widow, of T. V. Soong, minister of finance, and of the wife of H. H. K'ung, minister of industry, commerce, and labor.

1927-1934. A considerable body of the landless were organized on the Communist model of Soviet Russia in Kiangsi and adjacent Fukien, where they seized the land. Under **Mao Tse-tung** and **Chu Te** they defended themselves against all attacks from Nanking. When dislodged they effected an orderly long trek (1934–1935) through Kueichou and Szechüan into northern Shensi.

1928, Apr. 7. Chiang was recalled to lead a fresh northern campaign, in co-operation with **Yen Hsi-shan,** model governor of Shansi since 1912, **Feng Yü-hsiang,** a magnetic but erratic northern war lord since 1920, and two Kuangsi strategists, **Li Tsung-jen** and **Pai Ch'ung-hsi.** Despite conflict (May 3–11) with Japanese troops, again in Tsinan (withdrawn May 1929), **Peking was occupied** (June 8), renamed *Peip'ing,* and the capital transferred to Nanking. Chihli Province was renamed *Hopei.* The Chinese indicated their resentment at Japanese intrusion by a vigorous boycott (1928–1929). **Chang Tso-lin,** military governor in Manchuria since 1911 with Japanese approval, was forced to return there; and, since he now rejected Japanese advice, was assassinated (June 4). His son **Chang Hsüeh-liang** completed unification by recognizing the Nanking government (Nov.).

Sun Wen had indicated that, after military unification, a period of political tutelage must precede constitutional democracy. Accordingly

Oct. 10. The central executive committee of the Kuo Min Tang promulgated a **temporary organic law** which provided for a council of state headed by

the president (who is also the highest military authority), presiding over **five administrative divisions:** executive, legislative, judicial, civil service, and censorial. All appointments to these offices were to emanate from the central executive committee and the party congress.

A series of **treaties with 12 states** (July 25–Dec. 22) **recognized the Nanking government** and its right to **complete tariff autonomy** provided it practiced no national discrimination.

1929-1930. Japanese concern over the certainty of rapid loss of a large market for her cotton goods if the Chinese textile industry should receive protection dragged out treaty negotiations until May 6, 1930. Tariff autonomy, a substantial revenue source, was regained May 16. By 1930, 9 nationalities had lost **extra-territorial privilege** in China, and several more had by treaty agreed to its end when it should be universally abolished; but it was still (1939) retained by France, Great Britain, Japan, and the United States.

1930. A contract was given to a Dutch engineering company for a modern harbor at Hulutao near the head of the Gulf of Chihli, to serve as outlet for the railway system under Chinese ownership which would shortly enter competition with the South Manchurian Railway.

Oct. 1. **Wei-hai-wei restored to China** by Great Britain.

1931, May 5. A People's National Convention in Nanking adopted a **provisional constitution** which confirmed separation of five branches within the government, transferred power of executive appointment to the state council chairman, established autonomy of the (*hsien*) districts under provincial authority, and guaranteed personal freedom. The government pledged itself to free education and social insurance. A national congress to inaugurate full constitutional government should be called when autonomous district organization should be complete in a majority of provinces.

July 1. **Serious anti-Chinese riots in Korea,** stimulated by false report of a minor affair at Wanpaoshan in Manchuria, resulted in **renewal of the boycott against Japanese goods.** Report (Aug. 17) of murder by Chinese soldiers of a Japanese officer (Nakamura) in West Manchuria (June) inflamed Japanese opinion.

1931-1932. THE JAPANESE OCCUPATION OF MANCHURIA. The Kuantung army, engaged in night maneuvers at Mukden (Sept. 18), alleged an explosion on the railway as excuse for the preconcerted seizure before morning of the arsenal and of Ant'ung, Yingk'ou, and Ch'ang-ch'un, leaving to the Chinese troops no option save withdrawal. Amid foreign-office statements of intention to localize the incident, **Kirin was seized** (Sept. 21) and the whole of the **Three Eastern Provinces** was steadily occupied (Harbin, Feb. 5, 1932). Floods in the Long River Valley beyond recent precedent, added to Communist pressure, prevented any military effort to save Manchuria; but an immediate and more intense Chinese boycott cut Japanese exports (Nov.–Dec.) to one-sixth their usual figure. Subsequent vigorous flood-control measures averted new calamity and won popular esteem for the government.

1932, Jan. 7. United States Secretary of State Stimson notified all signatories of the Nine-Power Treaty of Feb. 4, **1922** that the United States would recognize no gains achieved through armed force contrary to the Pact of Paris of Aug. 27, 1928.

Jan. 28-Mar. 4. To compel the Chinese to abandon their economic war, 70,000 **Japanese troops landed at Shanghai** and drove the Chinese 19th Route Army from the vicinity of the International Settlement, destroying Chapei. An agreement (May 5) established a demilitarized zone about the settlement and termination of the boycott.

Feb. 18. INDEPENDENCE OF MANCHUKUO (Manchuria), to consist of the former Three Eastern Provinces with Jehol, was proclaimed at Hsin-ching (*New Capital*) the former Ch'ang-ch'un. **Henry P'u-i,** who abdicated the throne of China (1912), was installed as regent (Mar. 9), and promoted (Mar. 1, 1934) as **Emperor of the K'ang Te reign.** Japanese advisers and secretaries controlled from the first all important activities.

Sept. 15. A protocol established a close protectorate of Japan over Manchukuo.

Oct. 2. Report of a League of Nations commission of inquiry under the **Earl of Lytton** (signed Sept. 4) found that Japanese action Sept. 18–19, 1931, was not self-defense, and that creation of Manchukuo did not flow from a "genuine and spontaneous independence movement." It recommended establishment in Manchuria of an autonomous administration under Chinese sovereignty with international advisers and police, and recognition of Japanese economic interests.

1933, Feb. 24. Approving this report, the League Assembly adopted the **Stimson formula of non-recognition,** and

indicated that Japanese military pressure should cease.

Jan.-Mar. Japanese occupation of Jehol and advance south of the Wall (Apr.) forced

May 31. The T'ang-ku Truce, which required Chinese troops to evacuate the Tientsin area.

1934, Nov. China abandoned the silver standard for a managed paper currency compelled by an American policy of purchasing silver (June).

1935, Mar. 23. Russia sold to Manchukuo her interest in the Chinese Eastern Railway after negotiations begun in May 1933.

Apr. The government decreed one year of **military training for all male high-school and college students** to provide 100,000 reservists each year.

June 9. The Japanese army extracted the **Ho-Umezu Agreement** for withdrawal from Hopei of troops objectionable to the Japanese.

Continuing excessive cost of occupation of Manchukuo, in which bandits and irregular guerrillas prevented any durable pacification, led the Japanese army to attempt to force or buy, without actual invasion, formation of a local Chinese government willing to afford Japan opportunity for exploitation of resources and markets of North China. Efforts to secure secession of five provinces (Shantung, Hopei, Shansi, Chahar, and Suiyüan) having failed,

Nov. 24. An East Hopei autonomous régime was set up between T'ung-chou (outside Peking) and the sea. Japanese goods were openly smuggled wholesale into China through this area, and narcotics were poured from it upon the world market.

Dec. 18. A **Hopei-Chahar political council** was established at Peking under **Gen. Sung Che-yüan,** who rendered lip service to the Japanese but made no vital concessions.

1936, July 19. Chiang succeeded in gaining positive control of Kwangtung, in spite of Japanese aid to his adversaries, and of Kwangsi (Sept. 6), where the local leaders loudly demanded war against Japan, for which Chiang was still unprepared. The same demand was constantly voiced by the Chinese Communists, who had set up (Oct. 1935) orderly government in northern Shensi.

Sept. Japan presented seven secret demands (known Oct. 1) under threat of immediate invasion of both North and Central China. Most serious were: brigading of Japanese with Chinese troops against Communists everywhere (ground for action in any part of China), employment of Japanese advisers in all branches of government, autonomy for five northern provinces, and reduction of tariff to the level of 1928. Although Japan sent troops to Shanghai, Nanking stood firm.

Dec. 12-25. Gen. Chang Hsüeh-liang kidnaped Chiang K'ai-shek at Si-an to force him to declare war on Japan. Demonstration of loyalty to Chiang throughout China, even by the Reds whom he had pursued since 1929 and who now effected his release, testified to moral unity.

1937, Jan. 28. Negotiations terminated the long anti-Communist campaign, and brought the Shensi government into harmony with Nanking.

The Hankow-Canton Railway was completed with help from British Boxer indemnity funds, and a new Hangchow-Nanch'ang Railway was opened.

June 1. Szechüan was brought into the new national union, made effective by telegraph, long-distance telephone, and radio communication; Sino-American and Sino-German airlines; 75,000 miles of new motor roads; and a uniform stabilized paper currency. Achievement of political unity and stability (1927–1937) supplemented and accelerated fundamental changes which had been in progress since 1912 in many departments of life, often led by students returned from study abroad. Vital to China's clearly approaching struggle with Japan was introduction of modern finance and banking. Finance Minister T. V. Soong in 1932 announced a balanced budget, conversion of domestic debt, and abolition of *likin* transit dues which had been a vexation ever since the T'ai P'ing Rebellion. Substitution (Nov. 1934) of paper silver certificates for the new standard silver dollars (minted March 1, 1933) operated to concentrate in the treasury large deposits of silver bullion. These the United States treasury under the Pitman Act agreed (July 9, 1937) to exchange for gold, thus affording a large volume of credits abroad just when they were urgently required for purchase of arms.

Scholarship was immensely stimulated by close contact with western thought and literature. An official commission (1914–1928) drafted from the archives a *History of the Ch'ing Dynasty* to complete the standard series. **Wang Kuo-wei** (1877–1927) was a traditional scholar brilliant in decipherment of Shang oracular inscriptions as in textual and historical criticism. His elder friend **Lo Chen-yü** is noted for his archeological publications. Younger men have carried modern methodology into every domain of the humanities and sciences. **Hu Shih** (b. 1891) has led (since 1917) in developing a completely successful *pai hua* "plain speech" style of writing closely allied to colloquial speech and far easier to use and read than the terse classical style. It has won general acceptance for scholarly, literary, and practical purposes. Introduction of punctuation has facilitated understanding of both ancient and modern texts, and preparation of indexes makes their content accessible to a greater degree than ever before. A flood of periodicals, quarterly, monthly, and weekly (220 included in a current union index, 1934), afford a medium for scholarly publication and interchange of current views almost totally lacking in 1912. **Education** has been altered as much in content and method as in diffusion. Elementary pupils increased (1912–1935) from 2,793,633 to 11,667,888, and high-school students from 52,100 to c. 500,000. In place of 4 colleges in 1912 there were (in 1933) 40 universities, 40 colleges, and 29 technical schools, with 43,000 students, libraries totaling 4,500,000 volumes, and a budget of over $40,000,000 silver.

1937- THE JAPANESE CAMPAIGNS IN CHINA (no declaration of war, for technical reasons of international law). The conflict had been long in the offing, and the evidence would seem to indicate that Japan decided to act before the renaissance of China had gone too far.

July 7. The incident at Lukouchiao (near Peking): Japanese troops, on night maneuvers, clashed with Chinese. The fighting spread rapidly and led to the **seizure of Peking** (July 28) and **Tientsin** (July 29) by the Japanese. A large-scale campaign war begun in northern China. Without meeting much resistance, the **Japanese took Kalgan** (Sept. 3), **Paoting** (Sept. 24), **Shihchiachuang** (Oct. 10), **Kueisui** (Oct. 14), and **T'ai-yüan** (Nov. 9). By this time the Chinese had become better organized and were succeeding in slowing down the advance, though inferiority in equipment told heavily upon the Chinese throughout.

Aug. 8-Nov. 8. THE SHANGHAI CAMPAIGN. The killing of two Japanese marines at a Chinese military airdrome near Shanghai led to the landing of a Japanese naval force (Aug. 11) which soon found itself endangered by vastly superior Chinese forces. The Japanese were obliged to send an army which, after dogged resistance by the Chinese and very severe fighting, ultimately forced the Chinese back from the city (Nov. 8). The fall of Shanghai was followed immediately by the taking of Soochow (Nov. 20) and by an energetic drive up the Yangtze River. Merciless bombing of Chinese cities by the Japanese outraged world opinion.

Aug. 25. The Japanese naval blockade of South China was extended (Sept. 5) to the entire coast, but Tsingtao, Hongkong, Macao, and Kwangchou were excepted, out of consideration for foreign powers.

Aug. 29. Conclusion of a non-aggression treaty between China and Soviet Russia. This led to the sale of military aircraft to China and to shipment of large quantities of munitions after

Oct. 5-6. The League of Nations and the United States condemned the action of Japan. A conference of the powers at Brussels (Nov. 15) failed to effect mediation.

Nov. 20. The Chinese capital was moved from Nanking to Chungking (Ch'ung-ch'ing), though the executive power was, for the time being, established at Hankow.

Dec. 12. The *Panay* incident: attack of Japanese bombers upon American and British ships near Nanking produced acute tension between the powers. The United States government ultimately accepted Japanese explanations, but the Japanese government continued a high-handed policy toward foreign property and rights in China and evaded all protests from the United States, Great Britain, and France. The dangerous situation in Europe enabled the Japanese to pursue their aims without running serious risk of intervention.

Dec. 13. FALL OF NANKING, after heavy fighting. Horrible atrocities committed by the Japanese troops. The Chinese fell back, denying the Japanese a decision. The first six months of the war had demonstrated to an astonished world the moral unity of the Chinese people. All factions, including the Communists, acted on the orders of the central government. Chiang had the country behind him in the announced purpose of making no compromise at the expense of Chinese territory or independence.

Dec. 24. The Japanese took Hangchow and, advancing from the north, occupied Tsinan (Dec. 27).

1938, Jan. 10. Capture of Tsingtao by the Japanese, after the Chinese had destroyed the Japanese mills in that area. The Japanese then began the advance south along the Hankow Railway and through Shansi. They reached the Yellow River (Mar. 6), but mobile Chinese forces restricted the Japanese to the railway zone. More and more it became evident that the Japanese could capture the large cities and important communications, but that the countryside would remain in the hands of the Chinese guerrillas. During the spring of 1938 the Japanese forces suffered several reverses at the hands of the Chinese.

Mar. 28. The Japanese installed a Reformed Government of the Republic of China at Nanking, thus repeating the technique employed earlier in Manchukuo.

May. Resumption of the Japanese advance. They took Amoy (May 10), Suchow (May 20), Kaifeng (June 6), and Anking (June 12).

July 11-Aug. 10. Clash of Russian and Japanese forces at Changkufeng Hill, on the border between Siberian, Manchukuan, and Korean territory. After severe fighting a truce was finally arranged for, the Russians retaining their position.

Sept. 22. Creation of a United Council for China at Peking, under Japanese auspices. The Japanese made less and less of a secret of their intention to overthrow Chiang and his Nationalist régime and to transform China into a Japanese protectorate, as part of the projected "new order" in the Far East.

Oct. 12. The Japanese landed forces at Bias Bay, near Hongkong, evidently intending to realize on the acute crisis in Europe arising from the Czechoslovak affair (p. 965). They advanced inland and on

Oct. 21. THE JAPANESE TOOK CANTON, almost without a struggle. The city had been mercilessly bombed for months and a large part of the population had already fled. Capture of the city enabled the Japanese to cut the Canton-Hankow Railway, the most important line for transportation of supplies from abroad to the Chinese forces in the interior.

Oct. 25. FALL OF HANKOW to the Japanese. The Chinese government and army withdrew up the Yangtze to Chungking. Japanese control over the Yangtze below Hankow became ever more rigid, leading to repeated and insistent protests on the part of the western powers. The American secretary, Hull, reasserted the validity of the Nine-Power Treaty (Nov. 4) and was supported in his attitude by the British government. But protests made only the slightest impression in Tōkyō.

1939. The fighting continued in an inconclusive fashion over a large area. There was no indication of any slackening of Chinese determination, and the government of Chiang continued to receive supplies from Russia and other powers, even by the most devious routes. Both the United States and Britain made substantial loans to the nationalist government. The Japanese, unable to force a decision, developed an indirect attack on the position of foreign powers in China, demanding larger share in the Shanghai international concession and challenging foreign rights everywhere.

June 14. The Japanese established a blockade of the British concession at Tientsin (and incidentally also of the French), following refusal of the British authorities to surrender four Chinese accused of terrorism. Japanese spokesmen publicly announced that Britain must give up support of the Chinese nationalist régime and must co-operate with Japan in establishing the "new order" in the Far East.

11. JAPAN

1914-1918. THE FIRST WORLD WAR. During the war Japan manufactured and sent to Europe large quantities of munitions (especially to Russia). At the same time Japanese merchants took advantage of the conflict to supplant German commerce in eastern Asia.

1914, Nov. 7. Kiao-chow surrendered to the Japanese after a two months' siege (p. 918).

1915, Jan. 18. JAPAN SUBMITTED TO CHINA TWENTY-ONE DEMANDS (p. 1117), initiating the policy of subordinating China and establishing Japanese preponderance in the Far East.

Mar. 25. General election resulted in a victory for the government and the policy of vigorous imperialism.

July 30. Ōkuma ministry resigned because of bribery charges, but in Aug. Okuma formed a new ministry.

Oct. 19. Japan formally joined the Pact of London (Sept. 5, 1914) binding herself not to conclude a separate peace.

1916, July 3. Russo-Japanese Convention signed, by which Russia agreed to the extension of Japanese influence in China under agreements of 1915, and Japan recognized the Russian advance into Outer Mongolia.

Sept. 3. Fresh demands on China, increasing Japanese rights in South Manchuria and Inner Mongolia, followed a clash between Japanese and Chinese troops at Chêng-chia-tun (Aug.). Agreed to by China (Feb. 1917).

Oct. 9. Count Terauchi succeeded Ōkuma as premier, with a slight minority in the lower house.

1917, Apr. 20. The general election proved a victory for the government.

Nov. 2. Notes were exchanged with the United States (*Lansing-Ishii*

Agreement) by which the latter recognized the special interests of Japan in China and Japan gave pledges of good faith in the maintenance of Chinese integrity, independence, and the "open door."

1918, Apr. 5. British and Japanese marines landed at Vladivostok.

May 16. Sino-Japanese Treaty (p. 1118).

July 6. Allied commanders took command of Vladivostok. An announcement of intervention (Aug. 3) was issued.

Sept. 29. The Terauchi ministry resigned because of inability to cope with unrest caused largely by high prices resulting from war boom. Hara (first commoner premier) succeeded.

1919, Jan. 18. Peace Conference opened. Japan was favorable to the League of Nations, but her demand for a statement as to racial equality was refused.

Feb. 14. Acrimonious debate on universal suffrage in the Diet. The franchise then was limited to men over 25 paying a direct tax of 3 yen, thus excluding agricultural and industrial labor. Organized demonstrations in Tōkyō and dissolution of the Diet (Feb. 26) followed.

Apr. Rioting and open rebellion in Korea was mercilessly suppressed. There followed a revision of the Korean government substituting civil for military control and promising larger powers of self-government when the Koreans abandoned their independence movement.

Mar. 25. A reform act increased the electorate from 1,500,000 to 3,000,000.

May 10. A general election with the universal suffrage issue dominant resulted in 283 seats for the government party (*Seiyūkai*), which was opposed to it, 108 for the *Kenseikai*, and 68 for other parties.

Japanese Emperors since the Restoration

Kōmei
121st emperor
1846–1867

Meiji
Mutsuhito
1867–1912

Taishō
Yoshihito
1912–1926

Shōwa	Chichibu	Takamatsu	Mikasa
Hirohito	Yasuhito	Nobuhito	Takahito
1926–	b. 1902	b. 1905	b. 1915

Akihito
b. 1933

Masahito
b. 1935

1919. There was considerable industrial unrest and many strikes throughout the year.

1920, Jan. 10. Formal peace with Germany by exchange of ratifications. Japan, after initial satisfaction, became chagrined over the failure to secure recognition of Japan's special position in the Far East.

Dec. 17. Japan received as mandates from the League of Nations the former German islands of the Pacific north of the equator (Caroline, Marshall, and Marianas [Ladrone] archipelagoes).

Dec. 31. The First imperial census revealed population of 55,961,140 (including Sakhalin, Formosa, and Korea, 77,005,112).

1921, Mar.-Aug. The world tour of the crown prince, Hirohito, marked the first time a member of the imperial family had been abroad.

Nov. 4. Murder of Premier Hara by a political fanatic.

Nov. 12. Viscount Takahashi premier.

Nov. 12—1922, Feb. 6. Washington Conference (p. 957). Prince Tokugawa, Adm. Katō, and Baron Shidehara were the Japanese delegates.

Nov. 25. Crown Prince Hirohito constituted regent because of illness of the emperor.

1922, Feb. 11. Yap Treaty signed with the United States (p. 1050).

Feb. 23. Serious riots over universal suffrage.

June 2. Ratification of the Sino-Japanese Agreement on Shantung, resulting in more friendly relations with China and return of Kiaochow (Dec. 10).

June 11. Adm. Baron Katō succeeded Takahashi as premier.

July 6. Washington treaties ratified by Japan; naval budget reduced by 117,000,000 yen.

Sept. 6-24. The Ch'ang-ch'un Conference with Russia was a failure and Japan continued to occupy North Sakhalin.

Oct. The last of Japanese troops embarked from Siberia.

1923, Mar. 2. Universal Suffrage Bill defeated. Motion of opposition followed to impeach the government followed by wild scenes; Diet prorogued.

Aug. 28. Count Yamamoto succeeded Katō as premier.

Sept. 1. Great Tōkyō earthquake followed by great fires in Tōkyō, Yokohama, and neighboring cities, tidal waves and repeated shocks. 200,000 estimated killed; $1,000,000,000 estimated losses. Relief sent from abroad, particularly the United States. Program of modern reconstruction immediately commenced, financed by loans placed at home and abroad.

Dec. 29. Resignation of the ministry following an attack on the life of the prince regent; Viscount Kiyoura premier.

1924, Apr.-June. High feeling aroused by the American abrogation of the *gentlemen's agreement* and total exclusion of Japanese. Demonstrations and boycotts of American goods.

May 10. General election held; defeat for Kiyoura ministry; Katō premier and Baron Shidehara foreign minister (June 1924–Apr. 1927), with conciliatory policy toward China.

1925, Jan. 20. Russo-Japanese Convention (negotiated from Aug. 7, 1924, by Karakhan and Yoshizawa in Peking) re-established diplomatic relations: Russia recognized the Treaty of Portsmouth of 1905; the Fisheries Convention of 1907 was to be revised (new convention signed at Moscow Jan. 23, 1928); Japan received oil and coal concessions in North Sakhalin and agreed to evacuate her troops. This and subsidiary agreements formed a general settlement of issues between the two countries.

Mar. Bill passed granting universal male suffrage; voters increased from 3 to 14 million.

1926, Jan. 28. Premier Katō died and was succeeded by the new leader of the Kenseikai, Wakatsuki, the second commoner to become premier.

Dec. 25. The Taishō emperor died, and the prince regent succeeded. The year period was changed to Shōwa, marking the beginning of

1926- THE SHŌWA PERIOD.
After a few more years of the liberalism and internationalism of the Taishō period, a sudden strong militaristic and imperialistic reaction set in after the Mukden incident (1931). There was a partial repudiation of the intellectual and cultural aspects of Occidental civilization and a revival of older Japanese ideologies. Politicians lost their influence, and the army and, to a lesser extent, the navy became the dominant forces in the government, with the peasantry supporting the military against the city bourgeoisie and the capitalists. Under this leadership the nation embarked on a daring program of territorial expansion on the continent. Meanwhile, Japanese industry was growing rapidly, and Japanese manufactured goods began to flood the world market.

1927. Serious bank crisis, caused partly by huge loans for relief and reconstruction.

Apr. 17. Fall of Wakatsuki ministry; Gen. Baron Tanaka, leader of the Seiyūkai, became premier and foreign minister (until July 2, 1929), pursuing a "positive" policy toward China.

May-June. Japanese intervention in Shantung blocked the northward advance of Chinese Nationalist forces upon Peking.

1928. Apr. Japan again intervened in Shantung, leading to

May 3-11. Sino-Japanese clashes at Tsinan: Japan temporarily seized control of railways in Shantung; Chinese boycott movement against Japan lasted for over a year; incident settled Mar. 28, 1929; China to pay damages but not indemnity; Japanese troops withdrawn May 20, 1929.

1929. Growth of labor unions, begun particularly during 1915-1920, reached a total of 600 associations with a third of a million members; increase of labor disputes (576 in 1929).

July 2. Fall of the Tanaka ministry; cabinet formed under Hamaguchi of Minseitō; Shidehara returned as foreign minister.

1930. The population, which had been estimated at 26.5 million in 1726 and 34.8 million in 1872, doubled in following 63 years (69.2 million in 1935), the rate of increase accelerating steadily to a peak of 15.3 per thousand in 1930 before beginning to decline (14.4 in 1935). This rate of increase (c. 1 million a year by 1930) created a problem because of the high density of Japanese population already in the late Tokugawa period before the increase began. Public concern over the population question after 1922 and failure of emigration to provide a solution (total of all emigrants in modern period up to 1930 estimated to have been less than annual increase in 1930) led to emphasis on manufacturing and foreign trade as means to provide employment.

May 6. Sino-Japanese tariff agreement signed at Nanking by which Japan recognized China's tariff autonomy and received certain commercial safeguards and recognition of Japanese loans to former Chinese governments.

Oct. Japanese ratification of the London Naval Treaty (signed Apr. 22) following acrimonious debate in which the Seiyūkai attacked the policy of Hamaguchi and Shidehara.

Nov. 14. Premier Hamaguchi shot by an assassin in Tōkyō and succeeded by

1931, Apr. Wakatsuki, new leader of the Minseitō as premier.

Sept. 19. MUKDEN INCIDENT (p. 1119). Following Sino-Korean disorders at Wan-pao-shan (Kirin Province), the execution by Chinese of a Japanese major (Nakamura, June 27), and anti-Chinese riots in Korea, on the night of Sept. 18–19 Japanese troops in southern Manchuria seized Mukden and other strategic points and expelled the Chinese forces.

Dec. Fall of Wakatsuki ministry; cabinet formed by Inukai, leader of the Seiyūkai; Gen. Araki war minister.

1932, Jan. 28-Mar. 2. Sino-Japanese hostilities at Shanghai (p. 1120), precipitated by Japanese demonstration against the Chinese boycott (agreement signed May 5).

Feb. 18. Independence of Manchukuo (p. 1120).

May 15. Assassination of Premier Inukai by military reactionaries. A ministry chiefly of non-party members was formed under Adm. Viscount Saitō (later governor-general of Korea); Gen. Araki war minister, Takahashi finance minister. This marked the end of party government in Japan.

The abandonment of the gold standard (late 1931) led to depreciation of the yen in terms of foreign currencies and stimulated Japanese export trade. This led to the erection of tariff and quota barriers abroad.

1933, May 27. Following the report to the League of Nations of the Lytton Commission, Japan announced her withdrawal from the League (to take effect in two years).

May 31. Japanese invasion of Jehol (Jan.-Mar.) led to a truce signed at T'ang-ku which created a demilitarized zone in eastern Hopei under Japanese domination.

1934, Apr. 18. Foreign-office statement asserting virtual Japanese protectorate over Chinese relations with western powers.

July 7. Saitō ministry succeeded by that of Adm. Okada. Hirota continued as foreign minister (appointed Sept. 1933).

1935, June 9. Ho-Umezu Agreement (Japanese demands accepted in writing July 6 by Gen. Ho Ying-ch'in): China obliged to withdraw troops and cease anti-Japanese activities in Hopei.

Oct. 28. Enunciation of Foreign Minister Hirota's three points: establishment of a Japan-China-Manchukuo bloc, suppression of anti-Japanese activities in China, organization of a joint Sino-Japanese front against communism.

Nov. Failure of Japanese effort to create an autonomous North China. Instead, an "East Hopei Autonomous Council" was created (Nov. 25). This led to student demonstrations in Peking (Dec.).

1936, Feb. 20. In the election, the Liberal Mineseitō regained the leading position in the diet.

Feb. 26. Assassination of Viscount Saitō, Finance Minister Takahashi, and others in an uprising of young army officers at Tōkyō aiming at military dictatorship. Seventeen of the rebels were sentenced to death (July 7) by a military court.

Mar. 9. Hirota became premier, forming a cabinet dominated by the military (Gen. Terauchi); budget greatly increased; development of heavy industry pushed.

Nov. 25. German-Japanese anti-Communist Pact (p. 964).

1937, Jan. 23. Fall of the Hirota cabinet; Gen. Ugaki prevented by army leaders (Terauchi, Sugiyama) from forming a cabinet; Feb. 2 Gen. Hayashi formed a cabinet.

Apr. 30. General election went in opposition to the Hayashi ministry, which finally resigned May 31. Prince Konoye formed a "national union" cabinet with Hirota foreign minister, Sugiyama war minister (June 3).

July 7. SINO-JAPANESE HOSTILITIES (p. 1121).

Establishment of cabinet advisory council (Oct.) and imperial headquarters (Nov.) centralized the conduct of the war in the hands of the military and naval leaders, acting under direct authority of the emperor. Persons suspected of liberal or radical tendencies were arrested (371 on Dec. 14).

Nov. 3. Opening of the Brussels Conference, of powers connected with the Nine-Power Pact, except Japan; this failed to inaugurate negotiations to end the hostilities in China.

Nov. 6. Italy adhered to the German-Japanese anti-Communist Pact and recognized Manchukuo.

1938, Mar. 26. Passage of the National Mobilization Bill allowing state dictation of almost all phases of economic life (application of the law began May 5). Regular budget and war budget passed, totaling 8,365,000,000 yen.

May 26. Reorganization of the cabinet, military and naval officers taking six portfolios; Gen. Ugaki foreign minister.

Sept. 29. Resignation of Gen. Ugaki as foreign minister.

Oct. 29. Arita appointed Japanese foreign minister.

1939, Jan. 4. Resignation of Prince Konoye as premier; he was succeeded by Baron **Hiranuma**, who formed a cabinet including Konoye.

Apr. 2. A sharp dispute between Russia and Japan over fishing rights was settled by agreement for one year, Japan to participate on Soviet terms in auction of the fishing areas.

May. Outbreak of serious **fighting between Manchukuan and Mongolian forces** on the Mongolian frontier. The conflict, really one between Russia and Japan, assumed considerable dimensions in the course of the summer. At the same time Japanese relations with England were brought almost to the breaking point as a result of Japanese action at Tientsin (p. 1123). But

Aug. 23. Conclusion of the German-Russian Pact (p. 966) proved a tremendous shock to Japan, which at once scrapped the Anti-Communist Pact and resumed freedom of action.

Aug. 28. The Hiranuma cabinet resigned and a **new ministry under Gen. Abe** was formed to put the new policy into effect.

G. THE PACIFIC AREA

1. GENERAL

In the early months of the First World War, British ships with Australian and New Zealand forces, conquered the **German island colonies** south of the equator, while in Oct. 1914 the Japanese took possession of those north of the equator (the Mariannes, Carolines, and Marshalls). At the end of the war, Japanese, Australians, and New Zealanders all favored outright annexation of these territories, but because of American objections, they were finally classified as *C* mandates.

1919, May 7. The supreme council assigned **German New Guinea** and the neighboring German islands (Bismarck Archipelago) as a mandate to Australia; **German Samoa** (West Samoa) became a New Zealand mandate; the rich phosphate island of **Nauru** was mandated to the British Empire and by agreement the administration was divided between Great Britain, Australia, and New Zealand: Japan received the **German islands north of the equator** as a mandate. These arrangements were confirmed by the League of Nations Dec. 17, 1920.

1920-1922. The dispute about **Yap** between the United States and Japan. Yap was an important cable station and, according to the American view, had been excluded from the Japanese mandate and reserved for later arrangement. After much debate the matter was settled by agreement of Feb. 11, 1922, by which the island was recognized as part of the Japanese mandate, while the United States secured cable and radio rights.

1921, Dec. 13. THE PACIFIC TREATY, concluded by Great Britain, the United States, France, and Japan during the Washington Conference (p. 957) involved a reciprocal guaranty of possessions in the Pacific, while

1922, Feb. 6. The Naval Treaty between the five great powers included an engagement to maintain the *status quo* with regard to fortifications and naval bases in the Pacific (the American and Alaskan coasts not included).

1922, Apr. The Japanese government established civil government in the mandated islands (1400 islands with a total area of only 836 square miles, scattered over an immense area). The capital was set up at Korror Island (Palau group) and six branches of government were established in the major island groups. Much was done for sanitation, etc. For the rest the Japanese have ruled through appointed native headmen. Economically the development of the **sugar industry** has been most important. It has brought with it a considerable **influx of Japanese immigrants** (1933: native population 50,000; Japanese 32,000).

1933, May 27. Japan announced withdrawal from the League of Nations, to become effective in two years' time. At the same time the Japanese government made it clear that it had no intention of abandoning the mandate. Since the sovereignty in the mandates had never been very clear, the Japanese position was not seriously challenged.

1936, Jan. 1. With the **expiration of the international naval limitation treaties,** the provisions for the maintenance of the *status quo* of fortifications in the Pacific fell to the ground. Since 1932 there had been rumors of Japanese fortifications and submarine bases. After 1935 Australia and New Zealand were very active in coastal preparations and the United States government projected a great scheme of fortifications extending from the Alaskan coast and the Aleutian Islands to Midway Island, Guam, and Samoa.

2. AUSTRALIA

The outbreak of the First World War revealed all Australian parties united in loyalty to the mother country and in readiness to contribute in its defense. During the war Australia sent 329,000 men overseas, who took a prominent part in the Dardanelles campaign, the Palestine campaign, and the

fighting in France (after 1916). In May 1918 the five Australian divisions in France were organized as an **Australian army corps,** under the command of **Sir John Monash,** an Australian. The war was financed chiefly by borrowing and was accompanied, in Australia as elsewhere, by a great extension of government control, economic as well as political. Rising prices together with decline in real wages led to much **labor unrest** and a very extensive strike in Aug.-Sept. 1917. The failure of this strike resulted in stricter organization of the trade unions and greater concentration on economic rather than political aims. In the military field the Australian government took advantage of the opportunity to seize the German island colonies south of the equator.

1914, Sept. 5. The general elections resulted in a great **victory for the Labor Party** and in the formation (Sept. 17) of the **third Fisher cabinet.** In 1915 Mr. Fisher became high commissioner in London and his place was taken by

1915, Oct. 27. William M. Hughes as premier and leader of the Labor Party. Hughes, a very dynamic person, became the embodiment of Australian and British patriotism, and, after a visit to England in the summer of 1916, began to advocate **conscription** of men for service overseas. The suggestion roused much opposition among some of his colleagues, but

1916, Oct. 28. Conscription was defeated by a narrow margin in a popular referendum. The result was an open **rift in the Labor Party,** which ejected Hughes and several of his colleagues. The cabinet was reconstructed and ultimately

1917, Feb. 17. Hughes organized a National War Government, relying on the new **Nationalist Party** which was composed of Labor leaders who followed Hughes and by a large section of the Liberal opposition. The new party received a popular mandate in the elections of May.

Oct. 17. Completion of the **railroad from Port Augusta to Kalgoorlie,** thus first attaching West Australia by rail to the other states.

In order to meet the steady decline in voluntary enlistment, the prime minister, unwilling to enforce conscription by parliamentary action, decided once more to refer the matter to popular vote, but

1918, Jan. 10. Conscription was again defeated by referendum. Through the exertions of influential leaders voluntary enlistment was increased to some extent, but not enough to satisfy Hughes and his associates. In the summer of 1918 Hughes went to England and in the spring of 1919 took part in the Paris Peace Conference. There, with the support of the other Dominion statesmen, he succeeded in excluding from the covenant of the League of Nations any recognition of the principle of race equality. At the same time he intervened actively in the problem of the German colonies, so that on

1919, May 7. THE SUPREME COUNCIL ASSIGNED TO AUSTRALIA THE MANDATE FOR THE GERMAN COLONIES SOUTH OF THE EQUATOR, excepting Nauru Island and Samoa (which went to New Zealand). This arrangement was confirmed by the League Dec. 17, 1920. By agreement with England and New Zealand (July 2, 1919) Australia was given the administration of Nauru Island, which the three held together as mandatories.

Dec. 10. Sir Ross Smith arrived at Port Darwin by air, completing the flight from England in 27 days.

Dec. 23. The elections resulted in a victory for the Nationalist Party and the Hughes government continued in power.

1920, Jan. 10. Australia became an original member of the League of Nations with the full status of an independent nation.

1920. In a famous decision (**Engineers' case**) the Australian high court gave the commonwealth conciliation and arbitration court authority to regulate the conditions of labor of state employees. Thereby the commonwealth government secured preponderance over the state governments, a process already prepared by the expanded activity of the federal government during the war, the extension of its taxing power (income tax, inheritance tax), etc.

1921, Dec. 15. Adoption of a higher tariff, chiefly to protect the industries that had been born of the war. All parties were more or less united on the tariff issue. At the same time a **tariff board,** consisting of experts, was set up to advise the government. This board ultimately secured considerable power over the schedule of duties.

1922. By the **Empire Settlement Act,** the British government undertook to assist in the promotion of emigration to Australia and in the settlement of emigrants on the land.

Dec. 10. The elections resulted in 27 seats for the Nationalist Party, 29 for Labor and 14 for the **Country Party** (founded 1919), led by **Dr. Earle Page** and representing the farmer element. The Country Party held the balance of power and, being hostile to Hughes, finally forced the

1923, Feb. 3. Resignation of the Hughes government. The Nationalist Party began to disintegrate and

Feb. 9. Stanley Bruce, together with Page, formed a coalition cabinet composed of Nationalists and Country Party men.

1925, Sept. 23. A new immigration restriction act gave the governor-general authority to prohibit the entrance of aliens of any specified nationality, class, race, or occupation, either for economic or racial reasons. This act was never systematically applied, but it made possible restriction of Italian immigration, which had begun to arouse objections, especially among the labor groups.

1926. The Northern Territory was divided along 20° S.L. into Northern Australia and Central Australia, and a commission was set up to study possibilities of development.

1927, May 9. Parliament House was officially opened at Canberra. Thus far Parliament had sat at Melbourne while numerous schemes for the new capital were under debate. In a competition among architects, W. B. Griffin of Chicago received first prize and his plan became the basis for the new city.

June 8. Financial agreement between the commonwealth government and the state governments, following years of dispute concerning continued federal support to the states (the federal government having gradually absorbed most of the best springs of revenue). The federal government had already (Apr. 8) discontinued the *per capita* payments introduced in 1910. It now agreed to take over the state debts, which were to be liquidated within 58 years. In the interval the states were to pay part of the interest. A loan council was established to control future government borrowing, state as well as federal. In a short time this council established an effective control over much government expenditure, especially for development.

1928, June 9. Capt. Charles Kingsford-Smith arrived at Brisbane after his trans-Pacific flight from California.

1929, Oct. 12. The Labor Party won a resounding victory in the elections, whereupon

Oct. 22. James H. Scullin formed a Labor cabinet. For the most part Labor had remained extremely moderate in its policy, though in 1921 the party had adopted a program of socialization, and though in 1927 the Council of Trade Unions had been organized as a Left-Wing group associated with Moscow.

Nov. 1. Compulsory military service was given up and the voluntary system resumed, partly for reasons of economy, partly as an expression of Labor's pacifistic outlook.

1930- The great depression made itself acutely felt in Australia, where the government tried to combat it by drastic economy and other obvious devices. The rising price of gold and (after 1933) of wool, however, enabled Australia to recover more readily than many other countries.

1931. Foundation of the United Australia Party, composed of a number of dissident Laborites together with remnants of the Nationalist Party. The leader of the group was Joseph A. Lyons.

Dec. 19. The Labor Party was badly defeated in the elections, and a new Lyons cabinet was formed.

1932. The Financial Agreement Enforcement Act further strengthened the power of the federal government as against the states. The Labor premier of New South Wales, Lang, had refused (Apr. 1931) to pay his state's interest assessment to the federal government. The new enforcement act gave the federal treasurer power to take over certain revenues of a defaulting state. This was done in the case of New South Wales, thus precipitating the downfall of Lang's ministry.

1933, Apr. 8. West Australia voted 2–1 to secede from the commonwealth. Together with South Australia and Tasmania, the other agricultural states, West Australia had long protested against the "incidence of federation" and had demanded abatement of taxes or some form of federal relief. The government thereupon appointed a grants commission to investigate the claims of aggrieved states and to decide on compensation. Meanwhile (1934, Mar.) West Australia sent a petition to the king asking for legislation to effect secession. The British Parliament, however, refused to accept the petition without the previous approval of the Australian people as a whole.

May 26. The Australian government assumed authority over about one-third of the Antarctic continent (an area roughly the size of Australia itself).

1934, July 25. The government adopted a three-year defense program which involved the development of an air force, increase of naval power, mechanization of forces, etc. This program was later extended as international tension increased.

Nov. 7. The Lyons cabinet was replaced by a Lyons-Page combination, representing a coalition between the United Australia Party and the Country Party.

Dec. 8. Inauguration of a **weekly air-mail service** between England and Australia.

1936, May 23. A new and **higher tariff** was introduced, to replace the somewhat more modest tariff of 1932. The new schedule led to considerable **friction with Japan**, whose textiles were hard hit, but by an agreement of Dec. 27 the Australian government agreed to take as many Japanese textile products as in 1934, in return for Japanese purchase of a specified amount of Australian wool.

1937, Oct. 23. The Lyons-Page government won a sound victory in the elections (United Australia Party 28 seats; Country Party 17; Labor 29). The outstanding issue of the elections was the **defense problem**, the government advancing a program of naval construction, Labor calling for emphasis on air-armaments and less dependence on Great Britain. Australian expenditure for defense reached a record high in 1937.

1938, Oct. 25. The Duke of Kent was named as governor-general of Australia, the appointment reflecting the ever stronger attachment of the Dominion to the mother country as the international situation worsened.

1939, Apr. 7. Death of Premier Lyons, who was succeeded by Sir Earle Page.

Apr. 24. R. G. Menzies formed a new government which devoted itself wholeheartedly to the problem of defense. When (Sept. 3), England declared war on Germany, Australia unhesitatingly joined the mother country and arranged for assistance of all kinds.

3. NEW ZEALAND

New Zealand, like Australia, supported Great Britain enthusiastically throughout the First World War. Though conscription was introduced (Aug. 1, 1916), the great majority of men sent overseas (117,000) were volunteers. Together with the Australian forces they formed the Anzac divisions at Gallipoli and later took part in the French and Palestine campaigns. At home the war led to increased government control, both political and economic.

1914, Aug. 29. German Samoa surrendered to an expeditionary force from New Zealand, accompanied by the battle cruiser *Australia* and other British warships.

1915, Aug. 12. The cabinet of W. F. Massey (Reform Party) was reorganized as a **national war cabinet** through association of the Liberal Party (Joseph Ward, leader).

1919, May 7. The supreme war council assigned **Samoa as a mandate** to New Zealand, which shared with Great Britain and Australia the mandate for the rich phosphate island of **Nauru** as well. The New Zealanders would have preferred to have Great Britain assume the Samoan mandate, if only to avoid the problem of further colored populations.

Aug. 25. End of the coalition government. Massey and the Reform Party resumed the government, and in the elections of Dec. 17 secured a substantial majority in the legislature. The elections of 1922 and 1925 produced essentially the same results.

1920, Jan. 10. New Zealand became an original member of the League of Nations.

1925, May 10. Death of the prime minister. He was succeeded by Joseph G. Coates.

1927, July-Oct. Troubles in Samoa, where the native chiefs complained against the administration. An investigating commission vindicated the government and reported that the natives were instigated by Europeans. The government then proceeded to repatriate objectionable Europeans (Germans), whose properties were taken over.

1928, Nov. 14. In the elections the Reform Party was defeated by the United (i.e. Liberal) Party: Reform 28 seats; United 29; Labor 19.

Dec. 10. Sir Joseph G. Ward, leader of the United Party, formed a cabinet.

1930, May 28. George W. Forbes (United Party) became premier on the retirement of Ward for reasons of health.

New Zealand suffered very severely from the **world depression**, being essentially a producer of primary materials. The fall of prices and unemployment drove the government to a policy of drastic curtailment of expenditure (including salaries), restriction of imports, exchange control, conversion of the debt, etc. During the most critical years much of the famous social machinery was allowed to fall into disuse (notably wage and hour provisions, etc.). As a result the Labor Party withdrew its support from the government.

1931, May 19. Military training was returned to a voluntary basis, for reasons of economy.

Sept. 18. A coalition was effected between the United and Reform Parties, Mr. Coates entering the government. In the elections of Dec. 2 the government won a pronounced victory.

1935, Nov. 27. The Labor Party for the first time won a majority in the elections (Labor 53 seats; United and Reform Parties 20; Independents 7). Thereupon **Michael J. Savage formed the first Labor cabinet** (Dec. 5). The Labor Party came into power with an elaborate program of socialization and social reform. During the years 1935–1938 the major part of the program was translated into legislation. The chief measures were:

Nationalization of the Reserve Bank. All share capital was abolished and private shareholders paid off. The government thereby secured full control of the currency and of the country's credit.

By the **Primary Products Marketing Act** the government arranged to buy farm produce at a guaranteed price and dispose of it in London at the best available figure. Deficits were to be made up from reserve bank credit.

The **State Advances Corporation Act** remodeled the mortgage corporation as a state institution designed to liberalize government lending activities.

The **Industrial Conciliation and Arbitration Amendment Act** restored the compulsory arbitration system in disputes about wages and hours.

The **Government Railways Amendment Act** restored the railroads to complete government control and regulated road transport companies to prevent competition with railroads.

The arbitration court in 1936 fixed the **basic wage** for a man with wife and three children at £3 16s. per week.

1937, May 13. Formation of the **National Party**, a merger of the old Reform and United Parties, under leadership of **Adam Hamilton.** The new party was opposed primarily to the socializing policy of the government and presented a program of private enterprise and initiative.

1938, Oct. 15. In the elections the Labor government managed to retain its majority intact (Labor 54 seats; National Party 24).

1939, Sept. 3. British declaration of war on Germany. New Zealand, like Australia, at once decided on full support of the home country.

4. THE PHILIPPINES

1916, Feb. 4. National Bank of the Philippines chartered and made the depository of public funds. A **council of state** was created, composed of the governor-general, the presidents of both houses of the legislature, and the heads of executive departments.

Aug. 29. JONES ACT, abolishing the Philippine Commission and creating an **elective senate** of 24 members; greater powers vested in the Philippine government. Ultimate independence was promised as soon as stable government was established. As interpreted by Gov. Harrison, this act gave the islands practical autonomy.

1917, Apr. 25. A Filipino national guard was organized and its services offered to the United States.

1918, Nov. 20. A Filipino division was taken into federal service.

1919, Mar. 6. Use of the Spanish language in the courts was continued until 1930.

May. A delegation of forty prominent Filipinos, including **Manuel Quezon,** arrived in the United States and

asked for the fulfillment of promises of independence.

1920, Dec. 15. The legislature passed a bill providing 1,000,000 pesos annually to defray the expenses of the "independence commission."

1921, May 4, Sept. 12. The **Wood-Forbes Mission,** sent to investigate conditions in the islands. Its report declared that an immediate grant of independence would be *"a betrayal of the Philippine people"* and that *"under no circumstances should the American government permit to be established in the Philippines a situation which would leave the United States in a position of responsibility without authority."*

Oct. 5. Gen. Leonard Wood, governor-general.

1923, July 2. Manuel Quezon, president of the Senate, accused the governor of undue interference. July 17 the Filipino members of the council of state resigned for the same reason. The United States government, however, upheld the official acts of the governor.

1924, Feb. The insular auditor refused to honor vouchers for the funds of the independence commission, declaring it illegal.

Mar. 6. President Coolidge stated by letter: *"The Philippine people are by no means equipped, either in wealth or experience, to undertake the heavy burden which would be imposed upon them with political independence."*

May 6. A special mission, under Quezon, arrived in Washington and the Philippine legislature (Nov. 19) adopted a resolution demanding full and complete independence.

1925, Dec. 7. A petition from the legislature, **demanding independence**, presented to Congress.

1926, July 26. The legislature adopted a resolution calling for a plebiscite on independence. This was vetoed by the governor.

Dec. 7. Report of Carmi Thompson, sent to investigate conditions. He recommended that independence be postponed, but that the policy of home rule be extended and that the Philippine government should continue to liquidate its business enterprises.

1927, Aug. 7. Death of Gov. Wood. Henry L. Stimson appointed to succeed him (Dec. 13) and adopted a conciliatory policy.

1929, May 17. Dwight F. Davis, governor-general.

Earlier American opinion in favor of independence gradually became reinforced by **economic considerations:** (1) American economic conquest of the islands had not made great headway; (2) the American stake in the islands remained small; (3) the desire of the American sugar interests to be freed from competition of Philippine sugar. When the Smoot-Hawley Tariff was under consideration, Senator King of Utah and Senator Broussard of Louisiana introduced amendments calling for Philippine independence. These were defeated, however.

1931. Oct. President Hoover declared that *"economic independence of the Philippines must be attained before political independence can be successful."*

1933, Jan. 13. THE HOWES-CUTTING BILL passed over the president's veto. It provided for a **transitional commonwealth** for a period of 12 years, under a Filipino executive. The United States was to retain the right to military and naval bases and decisions of the Philippine courts were to be subject to review by the United States supreme court. During the probationary period tariffs were to be imposed on Philippine sugar, coconut oil and fibers

when introduced into the United States in excess of specific quotas. The Philippine legislature was to accept the independence measure within one.year.

Oct. The Philippine legislature rejected the proposed plan on the ground that it was not an independence bill, but a tariff against Philippine products and an immigration bill against Philippine labor.

1934, Mar. 2. President Roosevelt urged Congress to revive the Howes-Cutting Bill, with removal of the provision for American military reservations on the islands, and naval bases made subject to further negotiations.

Mar. 24. THE TYDINGS-McDUFFIE ACT adopted. It was essentially the Howes-Cutting Bill modified in accordance with the president's recommendations. The Philippine legislature, with misgivings, accepted the measure (May 1).

July 30. A constitutional convention convened to frame a constitution for the commonwealth. It completed its task Feb. 8, 1935, and President Roosevelt approved the document Mar. 23.

1935, May 14. The constitution was accepted by the voters of the islands.

Sept. 17. Elections to choose a president, vice-president, and national assembly. **Manuel Quezon, first president.**

Nov. 15. COMMONWEALTH GOVERNMENT FORMALLY ESTABLISHED. The president (elected for 6 years) enjoyed most of the powers of the governor-general. The legislature (National Assembly) was unicameral. The United States retained control of defense and foreign relations, exercised supervision over important phases of finance, and reserved the right to intervene to preserve the commonwealth government. Appeals from decisions of the Philippine courts might be carried to the United States Supreme Court.

Growth of opposition to President Quezon and his policy, linked with loud demands for immediate independence, in **1937, Feb.-Mar.** Brought President Quezon to the United States for conferences on the working of the independence act. He suggested independence in 1938 or 1939 in order to prevent the economic difficulties bound to arise from prolonged uncertainty. The United States government agreed to the establishment of a **joint preparatory committee**, composed of six Americans and six Filipinos. While this committee pursued its investigations, the outbreak of the Sino-Japanese conflict produced a reversion of feeling among the more conservative groups in the Philippines. Growing discussion of permanent Dominion status under American sovereignty as the only effective method of defense. President Quezon was rather favorable to this view, which was opposed by various opposition groups.

1938, May 20. **Report of the joint committee.** It recommended that the American tariff should be gradually extended to the Philippines, to become completely effective only in 1960 (instead of 1946).

Nov. 8. **In the elections** President Quezon's Nationalist Party won a decisive victory over the united opposition groups (**Popular Front**). The opposition, while bitterly criticizing Quezon for his dictatorial methods and infringements of civil rights, demanded independence in 1946, but no longer called for "immediate" independence, for which most Filipinos seemed to have lost the taste.

5. HAWAII

Hawaii has become more and more the key to the American strategic position in the Pacific. The naval base at **Pearl Harbor,** one of the finest deep water basins in the world, has been steadily developed since the channel was cleared and straightened in 1908–1910. Aug. 21, 1919, the great drydock was finally completed and there is now every facility for supplying and repairing warships.

Sugar and pineapple plantations comprise the main wealth of the islands, though the **tourist trade** has become of great economic importance. The population is extremely mixed, the figures for 1940 being: Hawaiian and part Hawaiian, 64,310; Caucasian, 103,791; Chinese, 28,774; Filipinos, 52,569; Japanese, 157,905; Korean, 6,851; Puerto Rican, 8,296.

1923, Apr. 26. "Bill of Rights" by which the territorial legislature defined and declared the claims of the territory concerning its status in the Union and provided for appointment of a commission to secure recognition of such claims by the federal government.

1927, June. **Maitland and Hegenberger** flew from California to Hawaii, a feat that was repeated by many other fliers in the ensuing years.

1937. **Samuel King,** the Hawaiian delegate in the United States Congress, introduced a bill to change the status of the islands from that of territory to that of state. A congressional committee, however, reported against the project, the mixed character of the population and the strategic position of the islands making it appear inadvisable.

1937. **Regular air connection** was established with California with the introduction of the trans-Pacific line to Manila.

1939. **The Hawaii Equal Rights Commission** created by Act of the territorial legislature to further claims for equal treatment and to oppose federal legislation discriminatory to the territory.

1940. The electorate of Hawaii, in an unprecedented plebiscite, voted more than two to one in favor of statehood for Hawaii.

H. THE SECOND WORLD WAR

(For events preceding Sept. 1, 1939, see above, p. 955, ff.)

1. POLITICAL AND INTERNATIONAL AFFAIRS
1939-1945

1939, Sept. 1. POLAND WAS INVADED by the German armed forces.

Sept. 2. Italy proclaimed its neutrality.

Sept. 3. GREAT BRITAIN AND FRANCE DECLARED WAR ON GERMANY.

Sept. 5. Gen. **Jan Christiaan Smuts** became prime minister of the Union of South Africa. A proposal that South Africa remain neutral was defeated in the legislature.

Sept. 21. Premier **Armand Calinescu** of Rumania was assassinated by members of the **Iron Guard**, a pro-Fascist group. Gen. **George Argeseanu** succeeded him, was replaced (Sept. 28) by **Constantine Argetoianu**, and the latter followed in turn by **Jorge Tatarescu** (Nov. 24).

Sept. 28. GERMANY AND RUSSIA ARRANGED TO DIVIDE POLAND BETWEEN THEM (p. 1145).

Oct. 2. The Pan-American Conference proclaimed a safety zone around the Western Hemisphere (p. 1154).

Nov. 3. The **United States Neutrality Act of May, 1937, was amended,** repealing the embargo on arms and placing exports to belligerents on a cash-and-carry basis.

Nov. 30. The Russian army invaded Finnish territory, opening the **Russo-Finnish War** which continued until Mar. 12, 1940 (p. 1145).

1940, Jan. 14. Admiral **Mitsumasa Yonai** formed a new Japanese cabinet.

Feb. 14-18. The cabinet and parliament of Paraguay resigned and the president, Gen. **José Félix Estigarribia,** took over the functions of government.

Feb. 15. A new cabinet was organized in Bulgaria under **Bogdan Philov.**

Mar. 20. **Edouard Daladier** resigned and **Paul Reynaud** formed a new French cabinet the following day.

Mar. 26. The Liberal Party won a decided victory in the **Canadian** elections.

Mar. 30. A puppet Chinese government under **Wang Ching-wei** was set up at Nanking with Japanese support.

Apr. 4. Winston Churchill was assigned general direction over the British defense program.

Apr. 9. GERMAN ARMED FORCES OCCUPIED DENMARK AND INVADED NORWAY (p. 1146).

May 10. THE GERMANS INVADED BELGIUM, THE NETHERLANDS AND LUXEMBURG (p. 1146).

NEVILLE CHAMBERLAIN RESIGNED as British prime minister and a coalition cabinet, including Conservatives and Laborites, took office under **WINSTON CHURCHILL.**

May 28. Leopold III of Belgium ordered his army to cease fighting. Leaders of the Belgian government on French territory declared Leopold deposed.

June 10. ITALY DECLARED WAR ON FRANCE AND GREAT BRITAIN.

June 13. THE GERMANS OCCUPIED PARIS. The French government moved to Tours and then to Bordeaux, Marshal **Henri-Philippe Pétain** replacing **Paul Reynaud** as head of the administration (June 16). Petain's first official act was to sue for peace (June 17).

June 22. FRANCE AND GERMANY CONCLUDED AN ARMISTICE. The United States Congress passed a **National Defense Tax Bill** to produce $994,300,000 a year, and raised the national debt limit from $45,000,000,000 to $49,000,000,000.

June 28. The Republican Convention at Philadelphia nominated **Wendell L. Willkie** and **Charles L. McNary** as candidates for the presidency and vice-presidency.

July 1. Rumania renounced the Anglo-French guarantee of territorial integrity and turned to Germany for support. **Ion Girgutu** formed a new cabinet (July 3).

July 5. The French government at Vichy severed relations with Great Britain following a **British attack upon French naval vessels at Oran** two days earlier.

July 7. Avila Camacho was elected president of Mexico amid considerable disturbance.

July 10. The French legislature voted to establish a **totalitarian form of government**, granting Marshal Pétain authoritarian powers.

July 14. Col. Fulgencio Batista was elected president of Cuba.

July 16. Prince Fumumaro Konoye was named prime minister of Japan to carry out a program of national consolidation and defense.

July 18. The Democratic National Convention at Chicago nominated **Franklin D. Roosevelt** as presidential candidate for a third term, and **Henry A. Wallace** as candidate for Vice-President.

July 20. President Roosevelt signed a bill providing for a **"two-ocean"** navy as part of a vast defense plan for the United States.

July 21. Lithuania, Latvia, and Estonia asked to be admitted to the Union of Soviet Socialist Republics.

July 27. The Pan-American Conference at Havana adopted plans for a joint trusteeship of European colonies in the Western Hemisphere.

Aug. 17. Germany declared the waters around Great Britain subject to a total blockade.

Sept. 6. Gen. Ion Antonescu assumed **dictatorial powers** in Rumania and opened negotiations with the Iron Guard. **King Carol** fled the country amid grave disturbances and was replaced by his son as **Michael V.**

Sept. 16. The **Selective Training and Service Act** was adopted in the United States. The act provided for the registration of all men between 21 and 36 years of age, and for the training, for one year, of 1,200,000 troops and 800,000 reserves. On Oct. 16, 16,400,000 men were registered, and the draft lottery commenced Oct. 29.

Sept. 22. Japanese armed forces commenced the **occupation of French Indo-China** after the French government had yielded consent for the use of three airfields and other concessions.

Sept. 26. President Roosevelt placed an **embargo on the export of scrap iron and steel** from the United States.

Sept. 27. GERMANY, ITALY, AND JAPAN CONCLUDED A THREE-POWER PACT at Berlin, pledging total aid of all to all members for a period of ten years. The avowed aim of the pact

was to "promote the prosperity of their peoples."

Oct. 11. German forces began to arrive in Rumania in considerable numbers, officially to train Rumanian soldiers and to protect the oil wells against British designs. **Rumania passed under German control.**

Oct. 28. Adolf Hitler and Benito Mussolini conferred in Florence while Italian forces launched an **attack upon Greece.**

Nov. 5. Franklin D. Roosevelt was re-elected President of the United States for a third term.

Nov. 20. The Hungarian government endorsed the **Rome-Berlin-Tokyo pact.**

Nov. 23. Rumania joined the **Rome-Berlin-Tokyo alliance.**

Nov. 27. The Iron Guard executed 64 former officials of King Carol's government while rioting spread throughout Rumania.

Dec. 6. Marshal Pietro Badoglio resigned as Italian chief of staff following reverses suffered by the Italian armies attacking Greece.

Dec. 14. Marshal Pétain expelled Pierre Laval from the French council of ministers.

Dec. 20. President Roosevelt named a **four-man defense board**, headed by **William A. Knudsen**, to prepare defense measures and to hasten aid to Great Britain. The German government denounced this action as "moral aggression" (Dec. 21).

Dec. 23. Anthony Eden became foreign secretary in the British cabinet, and Viscount Halifax was sent as British ambassador to the United States.

1941, Jan. 8. President Roosevelt appointed a four-man **Office of Production Management** to co-ordinate defense.

Feb. 28. The Churchill government was given a unanimous vote of confidence in the British Parliament.

Mar. 11. THE UNITED STATES CONGRESS PASSED THE LEND-LEASE ACT, empowering the President to provide goods and services to those nations whose defense he deemed vital to the defense of the United States.

Mar. 27. A military coup overthrew the government of the regent, **Prince Paul,** in Yugoslavia, and installed the young king, **Peter II.** This move was followed by a German invasion of Yugoslavia ten days later (Apr. 6). Belgrade was occupied by the Germans Apr. 10.

Apr. 13. RUSSIA AND JAPAN CON-CLUDED A NEUTRALITY TREATY.

May 2. In Iraq pro-Axis sympathizers attempted to control the government, but were defeated by British intervention.

May 17. The Icelandic Parliament announced that Iceland would separate from Denmark.

May 27. President Roosevelt proclaimed an unlimited state of national emergency.

May 31. The disturbances in Iraq were suppressed after the arrival of British reinforcements, and an armistice was concluded between the factions under British supervision.

June 16. The United States government ordered German consulates throughout the country closed. Three days later the German and Italian governments asked that United States consulates in Axis-controlled areas of Europe be closed.

June 22. GERMAN ARMIES IN-VADED RUSSIA along a two-thousand-mile front, opening a new stage in the war.

June 23. The French government at Vichy announced that it had granted the Japanese demand for military control of French Indo-China.

July 13. Great Britain and Russia concluded a mutual-aid treaty.

Aug. 14. THE ATLANTIC CHARTER. President Roosevelt and Prime Minister Churchill, representing the United States and Great Britain, issued a joint declaration of peace aims. They announced that their countries sought no aggrandizement, desired no territorial changes contrary to the wishes of the people concerned, respected the right of nations to choose their form of government, and wished to see sovereign rights and self-government restored to peoples who had been forcibly deprived of them. They likewise favored equality of economic opportunity with access to essential raw materials for all nations, they sought to promote friendly collaboration among the peoples of the world, fair labor standards, social security, freedom from fear and want, free traverse on the high seas, the abandonment of force, and the disarmament of aggressor nations.

Aug. 18. President Roosevelt signed a bill permitting the United States Army to keep men in service eighteen months longer.

The Reich commission in the Netherlands suppressed all representative bodies in the country in order to fortify the authoritarian principle in the administration.

Aug. 24. Prime Minister Churchill pledged British aid to the United States if the latter should become involved in war with Japan.

Aug. 25-29. British and Russian forces invaded Iran and established a régime that would co-operate with them. Riza Shah abdicated (Sept. 16) and was succeeded by his son, **Muhammed Riza Pahlevi.**

Sept. 20. A United States revenue measure, providing for defense expenditures of $3,553,400,000. became law.

Sept. 24. Fifteen governments (nine in exile) endorsed the Atlantic Charter. The list included Australia, Belgium, Canada, Czechoslovakia, the Free French, Great Britain, Greece, Luxemburg, the Netherlands, New Zealand, Norway, Poland, Russia, the Union of South Africa, and Yugoslavia.

Oct. 8. The Rumanian government by decree incorporated Odessa and an area beyond the Dniester (Transniestria) into Rumania.

Oct. 9. A political overturn in Panama deposed **Dr. Arnulfo Arias** and installed as president Señor **Ricardo Adolfo de la Guardia,** who was more friendly toward the United States than his predecessor.

Oct. 17. The cabinet of Prince Fumumaro Konoye was forced to resign and Gen **Hideki Tojo,** who was more pro-Axis in his attitude, became Japanese premier and minister of war.

Oct. 21. The assassination of a German officer at Nantes was punished by the execution of fifty French hostages.

Nov. 6. The United States extended $1,000,000,000 lend-lease credit to the Soviet Union.

Nov. 10. The National Defense Mediation Board of the United States government ruled against John L. Lewis and the United Mine Workers of America in the captive coal-mine dispute. Lewis accepted arbitration (Nov. 22).

Nov. 25. Bulgaria joined the Rome-Berlin-Tokyo alliance.

Nov. 26. The Lebanese government declared Lebanon an independent sovereign state.

Nov. 29. The Japanese prime minister, Gen. **Hideki Tojo,** declared that the influence of Great Britain and the United States must be eliminated from the Orient.

Dec. 2. President Roosevelt asked a definition of Japanese aims in Indo-China, and appealed (Dec. 6) to Emperor Hirohito to help in preserving peace.

Dec. 7. THE JAPANESE OPENED HOSTILITIES WITH A SURPRISE ATTACK ON HAWAII, THE PHILIPPINES, GUAM, MIDWAY ISLAND, HONGKONG AND MALAYA.

Dec. 8. THE UNITED STATES CONGRESS DECLARED A STATE OF WAR WITH JAPAN.

Dec. 11. GERMANY AND ITALY DECLARED WAR ON THE UNITED STATES.

Dec. 15. Congress passed an appropriation of $10,077,077,005 for the defense of the United States and for lend-lease aid. Four days later it extended the draft for military service to men from 20 to 44.

Dec. 21. A ten-year treaty of alliance was signed at Bangkok between Thailand and Japan. Thailand declared war on Great Britain and the United States a month later (Jan. 25, 1942).

Dec. 23. Free French forces took possession of St. Pierre and Miquelon, small islands off the coast of Newfoundland which had been administered by officials loyal to the Vichy government of France.

Dec. 25. Hongkong was captured by the Japanese, who continued to extend their hold on southeast Asia.

1942, Jan. 13. Donald M. Nelson became chief of the United States War Production Board, established to speed the armament program.

Jan. 15. An Inter-American Conference opened at Rio de Janeiro, summoned to unite the American republics against aggression (p. 1155).

Jan. 29. The Soviet Union and Great Britain agreed to respect the territorial integrity, sovereignty, and political independence of Iran.

Jan. 30. President Roosevelt signed the Price Control Act which was intended to limit inflation in the United States.

Jan. 31. Great Britain recognized the sovereign independence of Ethiopia, agreed to provide financial aid, to furnish technical and administrative advisers, and to re-establish diplomatic relations with the government of Haile Selassie.

Feb. 1. The German commissioner for Norway, Joseph Terboven, appointed Vidkun Quisling "minister-president" of a puppet régime. Quisling abolished the Norwegian Constitution (Feb. 7) and made himself virtual dictator.

Feb. 23. Gen. Alfredo Baldomir, President of Uruguay, dissolved both chambers of the legislature and created a State Council of members drawn from all parties except Communists and Herreristas.

Mar. 8. The Japanese occupied Rangoon in Burma. The United States and British governments approved the appointment of Gen. Joseph W. Stilwell to command the Chinese armies in Burma and act as chief of staff in the Chinese theater of war. To check the serious inflation in China, the Allied governments provided credits of £50,000,000 and $500,-000,000.

Apr. 4. The United States War Production Board halted all non-essential building, to conserve materials.

Apr. 11. The Indian Nationalist Leaders rejected an offer of autonomy for India after the war, with the right to secede, conveyed to them by Sir Stafford Cripps as emissary of the British government. Instead, they demanded immediate independence. Disturbances developed in India, and Mohandas K. Ghandi, Jawaharlal Nehru, and Abdul Kalam Azad, leaders of the independence movement, were arrested, but released later in the year.

Apr. 14. Marshal Henri-Philippe Pétain, who had removed Pierre Laval from the French governing council at Vichy (Dec. 14, 1940), was forced to reinstate him under German pressure.

Apr. 27. President Roosevelt proposed that the American people combat inflation by a seven-point program: (1) heavier taxes, (2) a ceiling on prices, (3) wage stabilization, (4) price control on agricultural products, (5) increased purchase of war bonds, (6) the rationing of essential commodities if scarce, (7) reduction of installment buying.

May 5. To forestall Japanese influence, British forces landed in Madagascar. The following Sept. 23 they entered the capital and an armistice was negotiated Nov. 5.

May 26. Prime Minister Winston Churchill and Foreign Minister Vyacheslav M. Molotov negotiated a twenty-year mutual aid treaty between Great Britain and the Union of Soviet Socialist Republics.

June 9. The United States and Great Britain agreed to pool all resources of food and production to assure victory.

June 17. A consultative board for the affairs of the **Netherlands East Indies** was set up in London to assist the Netherlands minister for the colonies.

June 18. Prime Minister Winston Churchill opened a series of **Anglo-American conferences** with President Roosevelt in Washington.

June 30. The United States Congress voted a record appropriation of $42,000,000,000 for military defense.

July. In Spain the Cortes, the national representative body, was re-established by Gen. **Francisco Franco,** but on Fascist lines. It was to form the supreme organ of the state and to be composed of 438 members, almost all selected by virtue of the fact that they had qualified for administrative or juristic posts.

July 6. President Castillo of Argentina announced that the republic would maintain its policy of neutrality.

July 16. The War Labor Board decreed that, in the interest of wage stabilization, wage increases would be granted equivalent to the rise in living costs between Jan. 1, 1941, and May, 1942. This was known as the Little Steel award.

Aug. 12. Prime Minister Churchill commenced a four-day visit to Moscow where he discussed the establishment of a **second front in Europe** with Joseph Stalin.

Aug. 30. The German Gauleiter announced the **annexation of Luxemburg to the German Reich** and the introduction of military conscription. Luxemburg workers responded with a general strike; a number were shot and others deported.

Sept. 14. The Vichy government of France established compulsory labor for men between 18 and 65 and for unmarried women between 20 and 35. This was regarded in France as an enforcement of German demands for labor collaboration.

Oct. 1. Germany formally annexed northern Slovenia and declared all the inhabitants German citizens.

Oct. 3. James F. Byrnes was appointed Director of Economic Stabilization for the United States.

Oct. 9. Great Britain and the United States announced their **relinquishment of extra-territorial rights** and special privileges **in China.**

Oct. 12. United States Attorney-General Biddle announced that 600,000 unnaturalized Italians in the country would no longer be classed as enemy aliens.

Nov. 8. **UNITED STATES FORCES LANDED IN FRENCH NORTH AFRICA** (p. 1160).

Nov. 11. In retaliation for the North African invasion, **German forces** moved into **Unoccupied France.** At Toulon, where most of the surviving ships of the French navy were stationed, the ships were sunk by their crews (Nov. 27) to prevent German efforts to seize them.

Nov. 17. Marshal Pétain appointed **Pierre Laval** his successor and gave him the power to make laws and issue decrees. This step reflected the increased German control over the Vichy régime.

Dec. 1. Admiral **Jean-François Darlan** assumed authority as **Chief of State in French North Africa,** with the approval of the British and United States governments. He was assassinated three weeks later (Dec. 24).

Dec. 16. The Seventy-Seventh United States Congress adjourned after the longest session in the nation's history.

1943, Jan. 14-24. CASABLANCA CONFERENCE. President Roosevelt for the United States and Prime Minister Churchill for Great Britain held a ten-day conference at the Moroccan seaport. They announced (Jan. 27) that the British and American chiefs of staff had worked out plans for an Allied offensive in 1943 designed to secure the "unconditional surrender" of the Axis powers. Churchill further intimated (Feb. 12) that there would be an invasion of Europe within nine months.

Feb. 6. Premier Benito Mussolini dismissed eleven members from the Italian cabinet, including his son-in-law, Count **Nobile Galeazzo Ciano,** and himself assumed the portfolio of foreign affairs.

Feb. 7. Lieutenant-General **Dwight D. Eisenhower** was appointed to command the separate Allied theater of operations in North Africa.

Feb. 10. President Roosevelt established as a wartime measure a **minimum 48-hour work week** for areas of the United States where there was a labor shortage.

Feb. 28. In Turkey the Popular Party elected all 455 deputies of the national parliament or *Kamutay*. Gen. Ismet Inonu was re-elected president of the Republic (Mar. 8).

Mar. 12. The United States Congress extended the lend-lease program for another year.

Mar. 15. Gen. **Henri Giraud**, successor to Admiral Jean François Darlan as head of the French government in North Africa, declared legislation passed there since 1940 was without effect, restored representative government, and promised that France would regain the right of self-determination after victory.

Mar. 22. Prime Minister Winston Churchill urged that plans be laid for a **new concert of nations** for Europe and Asia.

Apr. 9. In the United States an order of the President forbade wage increases above the level of the "Little Steel" formula, and restricted price rises for the future to the minimum prescribed in earlier proclamations.

Apr. 27. The **Soviet government severed relations with the Polish government-in-exile.** The following day Soviet spokesmen explained that relations were suspended rather than severed.

May 1. The United Mine Workers under John L. Lewis refused to return to work, whereupon President Roosevelt ordered the **seizure of the mines** (May 2) and Lewis proposed a 15-day truce (May 3).

May 5. The **Hungarian parliament was adjourned** *sine die.*

May 6. Marshal Stalin declared that Soviet Russia would hope to maintain friendly relations with a **strong, independent Poland** after the war.

May 12. Prime Minister **Churchill arrived in Washington** for a conference with President Roosevelt on the preparation of a second front in Europe and for discussion of general problems of the global war. He assured the United States Congress that Britain would fight side by side with the United States against Japan until the very end.

May 23. The **Third International** (Communist) **was dissolved.** It had been organized in Russia in 1919 to propagate communist ideals in other countries and direct communist organizations abroad. The Moscow dispatch announcing its dissolution asserted that communist parties in other countries would be autonomous henceforth.

May 29. President Roosevelt announced that the **Office of War Mobilization**, directed by James F. Byrnes, would be the supreme federal agency in the United States for the prosecution of the war effort on the home front.

June 4. A **French Committee of National Liberation** was formed, including both Gen. Charles de Gaulle and Gen. Henri Giraud. The committee pledged itself to support the Allied nations in their war against the Axis powers.

June 5. In Argentina the isolationist régime of President **Ramon S. Castillo** was overthrown by a military junta. The Congress was dissolved and a new government formed (June 8) by Gen. **Pedro P. Ramirez.**

June 26. The United States Congress passed the **Smith-Connally Anti-Strike Bill.** Anyone who instigated or aided in promoting strikes in government-operated plants or mines became subject to criminal penalties.

July 5. The Japanese government announced that it had approved the **cession to Thailand of six of the states of Malaya,** with a combined area of 74,770 square miles and a combined population of 2,870,000.

July 16. The **Office of Economic Warfare** was established by President Roosevelt, to supersede the Board of Economic Warfare and assume some functions of the Reconstruction Finance Corporation.

July 26. In Italy, **BENITO MUSSOLINI RESIGNED** with his cabinet and was placed under arrest. His place was taken by Marshal **Pietro Badoglio,** who announced (July 28) that the **Fascist Party was dissolved.** Mussolini, however, was rescued by German troops, and proclaimed (Sept. 15) the establishment of a **Republican Fascist Party** which achieved some authority in areas of Italy still under German domination (p. 1162).

Aug. 11-24. Quebec Conference. Prime Minister Churchill and President Roosevelt, with large staffs of advisers, conferred on the opening of a second front in Europe and other war projects of the United Nations. The **French Committee of National Liberation was recognized by** the United States, Britain, Russia and Canada as the administrative government of Algiers and of "French overseas territories which acknowledge its authority." The absence of a Russian representative at the conference, and the recall of the Russian ambassador from Washington during the sessions, caused speculation oʟ the possibility of a rift among the "Big Three."

Aug. 29. **King Boris III of Bulgaria** died suddenly and was succeeded by his six-year-old son as **Simeon II.** A council of regency, including the young king's uncle, **Prince Cyril,** the statesman **Bogdan Philov,** and Gen. **Nokola Michov,** was established and was approved by the Bulgarian parliament (Sept. 9).

Sept. 9. **THE BADOGLIO CABINET ACCEPTED TERMS OF SURRENDER FOR ITALY,** drawn up by the governments of Great Britain, the United States and Russia (p. 1162).

Iran declared war on Germany, and joined the United Nations (Sept. 14).

Sept. 11. German forces in Italy, learning that the Badoglio government had capitulated, seized control of leading cities including Rome, Milan, Trieste, Genoa, Bologna, Verona, and Cremona. Italian forces loyal to Badoglio occupied Sardinia and Free French troops secured Corsica (p. 1162).

Sept. 13. Gen. Chiang K'ai-shek was elected president of the Chinese Republic by the Central Executive Committee, which also permitted him to retain his post as commander-in-chief of the Chinese Army. The committee announced that democratic, responsible government would be established in China as soon as the war ended.

Sept. 25. The United States Office of Economic Warfare (created July 16) was further reorganized. A presidential decree consolidated the **Office of Economic Warfare** with **Lend-Lease Administration,** with the **Office of Foreign Relief and Rehabilitation,** the foreign procurement division of the **Commodity Credit Corporation,** and such sections of the **Office of Foreign Economic Co-ordination** of the State Department as it might be deemed advisable to transfer. The new organ was to be known as the **Foreign Economic Administration.**

Oct. 9. Yugoslav guerrilla forces commanded by **Marshal Tito** (Josip Broz) opened an offensive against Axis troops in the region of Trieste.

Nov. 9. The **United Nations Relief and Rehabilitation Administration** (UNRRA) was further defined and organized at Washington. Control was to be exercised by a director general, responsible to a central committee composed of representatives for the United States, Britain, Russia, and China. The central committee in turn was to report to a council to which each member state sent one delegate. There was to be an annual budget and all member states were to make contributions of a varying nature. UNRRA officials were to cooperate with the military commanders executing the plans of the United Nations in war areas, and the organization was to have legal authority to acquire, hold, and convey property, to enter contracts and undertake obligations.

Nov. 11. In Lebanon French authorities arrested the president, **Sheikh Beshara al-Khoury,** and his ministers, after the Lebanese Chamber of Deputies had proclaimed the independence of the republic. Strikes and rioting broke out and the prisoners were released (Nov. 22). On Nov. 27 the French yielded and the French Committee of National Liberation transferred all powers exercised by France under the terms of the mandate to the Lebanese and Syrian governments.

Nov. 28-Jan. 12, 1944. **TEHRAN CONFERENCE.** President Roosevelt, Prime Minister Churchill, and Marshal Stalin, after a series of talks, announced that they had concerted their war plans and reached complete agreement on the scope and timing of operations. They also issued a declaration (Dec. 1) pledging economic aid to Iran for the period of the war and after; in the interval Russian troops guarded the area north of Tehran, British forces occupied southern Iran, and some United States units patrolled supply routes. At the same time the United States, Britain, and China, represented by Roosevelt, Churchill, and Chiang K'ai-shek respectively, announced their joint determination to reduce Japan to surrender. **(Cairo Declaration, Dec. 1.)**

Dec. 21. In Bolivia the government of President **Enrique Peñaranda** was unseated by a group headed by **Major Gualberto Villarroel.** The new régime was not recognized diplomatically except by Argentina (Jan. 4, 1944). The United States refused recognition (Jan. 25, 1944).

Dec. 27-29. To forestall a strike of the railroad workers called for Dec. 30, the **United States Army took possession of the railroads,** without, however, actually operating them. The dispute was settled and army control lapsed after 22 days (Jan. 18, 1944).

1944, Jan. 27. The discovery of an espionage plot involving agents of the Axis powers led the **Argentine government to sever relations with Germany and Japan.**

Feb. 1. An amendment to the Constitution of the Union of Soviet Socialist Republics granted separate commissariats for defense and for foreign affairs to each of the constituent republics. Each could thus maintain its own army (which would form, however, a component element in the army of the U.S.S.R) and could conduct its own negotiations with foreign countries and conclude treaties with them.

Feb. 11. The civil administration of Sicily and Sardinia, and of the Italian mainland south of the northern boundaries of the provinces of Salerno and Potenza, was restored to the Italian government of liberated Italy (p. 1162).

Mar. 11. Eamon de Valera, prime minister of Eire, declined a request from the United States government that he close the German and Japanese ministries in Dublin to curb the possible transmission of military intelligence by Axis agents. Great Britain suspended all travel between the United Kingdom and Ireland (Mar. 13) and limited the privileges of foreign diplomats except those of Russia and the United States (Apr. 18).

Mar. 22. German troops occupied Hungary and a pro-German puppet government was set up the following day with Doeme Sztojay as prime minister and minister of foreign affairs.

Apr. 18. In Italy the cabinet of Marshal Pietro Badoglio resigned, but the king, Victor Emmanuel III, invited him to remain and form a new ministry.

May 3. The Spanish government agreed to restrict the shipment of minerals to Germany and to limit the activities of Axis agents in Spain. The United States thereupon cancelled its embargo on oil shipments for Spain.

June 4. THE UNITED STATES FIFTH ARMY ENTERED ROME, the first European capital to be liberated from Axis domination.

June 6. INVASION OF NORMANDY. The Supreme Headquarters of the Allied Expeditionary Forces (*S H A EF*) announced that Allied sea and air borne units had established beachheads on the Cherbourg Peninsula. This invasion, under the command of Gen. Dwight D. Eisenhower, marked the opening of a new, western front in the general attack on German-controlled territory (p. 1163 *f.*).

June 17. The Germans commenced a new type of bombing by sending pilotless planes, loaded with explosive and propelled by jet propulsion, against British cities.

Iceland, which had separated from Denmark (May 17, 1941), was established as an independent republic.

July 11. The United States recognized the French Committee of National Liberation, headed by Gen. Charles de Gaulle, as the *de facto* civil government of France in liberated areas of that country. Gen. Eisenhower warned the German government that French "Underground" forces were to be regarded as combatants.

July 18. Gen. Hideki Tojo, Japanese premier, resigned with his entire cabinet. Gen. Kuniaki Koiso became premier and Admiral Mitsumasa Yonai deputy premier.

July 21. Franklin Delano Roosevelt was nominated for a fourth term as President of the United States by the Democratic National Convention at Chicago. Harry S. Truman was named as candidate for Vice-President.

July 24. Russian forces drove the Germans from the last important Russian city by liberating Pskov, opening the way for an attack on German divisions holding Estonia.

July 27. The Soviet government recognized the Polish Committee of National Liberation established at Moscow and concluded a convention with it for the administration of liberated Polish territory.

Aug. 1. The president of Finland, Risto Ryti, resigned his office and the Finnish parliament voted that Marshal Karl Gustav Mannerheim should succeed him.

Aug. 23-24. King Michael of Rumania dismissed the cabinet of Gen. Ion Antonescu and accepted armistice terms from the United Nations. The Russians occupied Bucharest (Aug. 31).

German forces in Paris were compelled to capitulate as Allied armies approached and armed citizens liberated the city. The administration was turned over to Gen. de Gaulle with approval of the Allied commanders (Aug. 29).

Sept. 4. Brussels was liberated by the Second British Army.

Sept. 8. Bulgaria accepted armistice conditions laid down by the Russian government in accord with the Allied nations.

Oct. 2. The Polish forces of Gen. Bor (Tadeo Komorowski), which had risen against the German army of occupation in Warsaw, were driven to capitulate when Russian aid failed to arrive.

Oct. 13. Athens was occupied by Allied forces.

Oct. 20. Belgrade was occupied by Russian and Yugoslav forces.

Nov. 7. Franklin D. Roosevelt was elected for the fourth time as President of the United States, with Harry S. Truman as Vice-President.

The French Consultative National Assembly summoned by Gen. Charles de Gaulle held its first session. Municipal and departmental elections for the 89 *départements* were scheduled for February, with the franchise extended to all citizens, male and female, over twenty-one.

Nov. 10. In Finland Juho Paasikivi formed a new cabinet. The Communist Party, having secured recognition, prepared to contest the elections.

Nov. 26. Ivanoe Bonomi, Italian premier, **resigned**, but was persuaded to form a new cabinet (Dec. 9). The Allied governments, which had granted Italy full recognition (Oct. 23), approved the new ministry, after Great Britain had refused to accept Count **Carlo Sforza** as premier or foreign minister.

Nov. 27. Edward R. Stettinius succeeded Cordell Hull as United States Secretary of State when Mr. Hull resigned because of poor health.

Dec. 10. A Franco-Soviet treaty of alliance and mutual security, to run for twenty years, was negotiated at Moscow by Gen. Charles de Gaulle.

Dec. 25. The British prime minister, **Winston Churchill**, and his foreign secretary, Anthony Eden, **arrived in Athens** to arrange a settlement in the civil war between Greek factions. A regency government was proclaimed and Archbishop Damaskinos sworn in as regent after his appointment (Dec. 30) by the Greek King George II.

Dec. 31. Gen. Chiang K'ai-shek promised the Chinese people that a constitutional government would be established before the end of the war.

1945, Jan. 1. France joined the United Nations in full partnership three years after the Free French government in exile had offered its adherence.

Jan. 6. The Turkish government broke off diplomatic relations with Japan.

Jan. 11. The Greek civil war ended with a truce between the British and the leftist factions opposing British intervention. In Athens damage in the six weeks' strife was estimated at $200,-000,000, and the British casualties at over 2000.

Feb. 7-12. **CRIMEA CONFERENCE.** President Franklin D. Roosevelt for the United States, Prime Minister Winston Churchill for Great Britain, and Marshal J. V. Stalin, Chairman of the Council of Peoples Commissars of the U.S.S.R., conferred at **Yalta** in the Crimea, accompanied by members of their military and diplomatic staffs. An announcement issued Feb. 12 declared that they had concerted plans for the final defeat of Germany, and for the occupation, control, and collection of reparations from the vanquished nation. The three powers also pledged their joint efforts to assist liberated countries in Europe, and to support the formation of a general international organization to maintain peace and security. To this end, they endorsed the projected **United Nations Conference** scheduled to assemble Apr. 25 at San Francisco.

The **Polish government in exile** appealed for help against the arrest, deportation, and transfer of Polish population by the Soviet authorities.

Feb. 21. At the **Inter-American Conference in Mexico City** (Chapultepec) a proposal was introduced for the annual meeting of the foreign ministers of all American republics.

Feb. 26. Syria joined the **United Nations.** The Egyptian Parliament approved a declaration against the Axis.

Mar. 1. A new cabinet under Barbu Stirbey replaced that of Gen. Nicholas Radescu in Rumania.

Mar. 3. Finland declared war on Germany.

A constitution for an Arab League was drafted at Cairo and signed at a plenary session (Mar. 17).

Apr. 5. The Soviet Union denounced its 5-year non-aggression pact with Japan. Dated Apr. 13, 1941, this treaty had one year more to run, but might be denounced one year before its expiration by either party.

Apr. 12. President Franklin D. Roosevelt died suddenly at Warm Springs. Vice-President Harry S. Truman took the oath as President.

Apr. 21. Soviet Russia and the Polish Provisional Government signed a 20-year treaty of mutual assistance and co-operation. Russian efforts to obtain a seat for delegates of the Polish régime at the San Francisco Conference of the United Nations failed.

Apr. 28. BENITO MUSSOLINI WAS CAPTURED AND EXECUTED by Italian anti-Fascist forces when he attempted to escape to Switzerland.

A new **provisional Austrian government** was set up after the occupation of Austria by Allied armies.

May 1. ADOLF HITLER WAS REPORTED DEAD in Berlin as the Russians fought their way into the wrecked city. Admiral **Karl Doenitz** headed a provisional council which opened negotiations for surrender with the Allied governments (p. 1165).

May 6. Portugal severed diplomatic relations with the German government.

May 7. THE GERMAN PROVISIONAL GOVERNMENT UNDER ADMIRAL DOENITZ SURRENDERED UNCONDITIONALLY. Spain broke diplomatic relations with Germany.

May 9. Formal **ratification of the German surrender** was signed in Berlin.

May 12. Premier **Ivanoe Bonomi** of Italy requested the Allied governments to send troops to occupy **Trieste.** Marshal Tito was warned by Britain and the United States that Trieste must remain under Allied control.

May 18. President Truman informed the French ambassador that the United States would relinquish part of the American zone of occupation in Germany to the French.

May 20. United States troops were withdrawn from Trieste. Marshal Tito agreed to withdraw Yugoslav troops from Carinthia.

May 21. The governments of Syria and Lebanon broke relations with the French because the latter sent in troops without asking consent. The French forces were confined to barracks as rioting and resistance spread. In an attempt to assert control, the French army of occupation shelled Damascus (May 29).

May 30. The government of Iran requested the United States, Great Britain, and Russia to withdraw their forces from the country.

May 31. Prime Minister Churchill demanded that Gen. de Gaulle order the French forces in Syria and Lebanon to cease fire.

June 1. Fighting continued in Damascus. De Gaulle accused the British of meddlesome interference; the British declared the French were using lend-lease equipment against the Syrians and Lebanese; the French denied the charge (June 2).

June 9. The United States Department of State announced that Venezia Giulia, including Trieste, would be placed under a temporary military administration established by Great Britain, the United States, and Yugoslavia.

June 12. From London, Washington, and Moscow an announcement was endorsed to the effect that a tripartite commission would aid in the organization of a Polish government.

June 17. In Italy, **Ferruccio Parri** succeeded Ivanoe Bonomi as premier.

June 19. At San Francisco the representatives of the United States, Great Britain, Russia, France, and China decided that states which had sided with the Axis would not be admitted to the new security league until the Council invited them to become members.

June 23. A Polish national government was formed by adding five new members to the provisional (Russian inspired) régime at Lublin.

June 29. Czechoslovakia ceded Ruthenia to the Soviet Union.

The All-India Congress failed to agree on a common list of ministers for the new government and the deadlock between Moslem and Hindu leaders continued.

June 30. The French Communist Party voted for unity with the Socialist Party.

July 3. A three-way division of responsibility among the Russian, American, and British forces of **occupation in Berlin** replaced the single control which had been exercised by the Russians for two months.

July 10-19. The Japanese home islands were attacked with mounting intensity. Over 1000 carrier planes raided Tokyo (July 10); the United States fleet moved in to shell Honshu and Hokkaido (July 14-15); the British fleet joined in carrier raids against Japanese centers (July 17); and American and British fliers sank some of the last remnants of the Japanese Navy in Tokyo Bay (July 19). On July 26 the United States, Great Britain, and China demanded that Japan surrender unconditionally, but the demand was ignored.

July 20. Gen. **Francisco Franco** made changes in the Spanish cabinet, filled several government posts with men of reputedly royalist sympathies, and announced that the Spanish monarchy would be restored at a future date.

July 26. THE BRITISH LABOR PARTY WON 388 seats out of 640 in the national election of July 5; the ballots were counted three weeks later. A Labor Cabinet, with Clement R. Atlee as prime minister, replaced the coalition war cabinet of Winston Churchill which had held power since May 10, 1940.

Aug. 6-14. THE WAR IN THE PACIFIC ENDED in a week of disaster for Japan. An atomic bomb, the formula for which had been secretly perfected by United States and British scientists, and manufactured through an investment of $2,000,000,000, was dropped on the Japanese city of Hiroshima. It killed over 50,000 people, injured as many more, and leveled four square miles of homes and factories. Two days later, THE SOVIET UNION DECLARED WAR ON JAPAN and Russian armies swept into Manchuria (Aug. 8). On Aug. 9 a second atomic bomb shattered Nagasaki. The Japanese government offered to surrender if the Emperor Hirohito were permitted to retain his throne (Aug. 10), and on receiving this assurance THE JAPANESE ACCEPTED TERMS OF SURRENDER (AUG. 14).

Aug. 28-Sept. 2. UNITED STATES FORCES LANDED IN JAPAN to occupy strategic centers while the disarmament of Japanese military forces and the surrender of naval and air craft proceeded rapidly. FORMAL TERMS OF SURRENDER were signed by the Japanese envoys on board the U.S.S. *Missouri* in Tokyo Bay (Sept. 2) (p. 1170).

2. THE CAMPAIGNS IN POLAND AND FINLAND, 1939-1940

1939, Sept. 1. POLAND WAS INVADED by German forces estimated at 1,700,000 men. Headed by mechanized divisions and supported by overwhelming air power, the German thrusts disorganized and defeated the poorly equipped Polish armies. Though the latter had a numerical strength of 600,000 men, they were unable to mobilize effectively or to concert their resistance. The rapidity of the German convergence, from East Prussia, Silesia, and Slovakia, alarmed the Soviet government.

Sept. 17. Russian troops therefore invaded Poland from the east, meeting the advancing Germans near Brest-Litovsk two days later.

Sept. 27. After heroic resistance and destructive bombing, Warsaw surrendered and Polish organized opposition came to an end. The *Blitzkrieg* had lasted less than four weeks and the outcome had been determined in the first ten days.

Sept. 29. The German and Russian governments divided Poland. Germany annexed outright the Free City of Danzig (population 415,000) and 32,000 square miles between East Prussia and Silesia. In addition an area of 39,000 square miles, known as the *Gouvernement Général*, remained under German protection. The total German gains were estimated at 72,866 square miles with a population of 22,140,000. The Russians occupied 77,620 square miles of Eastern Poland, with a population of 13,199,000. Lithuania and Slovakia received small cessions of Polish territory.

Sept. 29. The Soviet government concluded a treaty with Estonia which gave Russia naval and air bases in Estonian territory.

Oct. 5. A similar pact with the Latvian government allowed the Russians to establish fortified bases in Latvia.

Oct. 10. Russia and Lithuania concluded a mutual assistance pact. The Russians acquired the right to occupy stations of military importance in Lithuania and ceded Vilna and surrounding territory to Lithuania in return. The assistance pact was to run for 15 years.

Nov. 26. The Finnish government rejected Russian demands similar to those accepted by the lesser Baltic states. The Soviet government demanded the withdrawal of Finnish troops mobilizing on the frontier.

Nov. 30, 1939-Mar. 12, 1940. RUSSO-FINNISH WAR. Russian armies attacked Finland on three fronts: (1) below Petsamo on the Arctic Sea, in central Finland, and on the Karelian Isthmus.

Dec. 14. Russia was expelled from the League of Nations for acts of aggression against Finland.

1940, Mar. 12. After three months of varying success but increasing pressure, the Russians breached the Mannerheim Line. Finland accepted peace, negotiated at Moscow, ceding to the Union of Soviet Socialist Republics the Karelian Isthmus, the city of Viipuri (Viborg), a naval base at Hangoe, and islands and territories totaling in all 16,173 square miles with a population of 450,000. Most of the Finns in the ceded areas were to be resettled in Finland.

3. THE INVASION OF DENMARK AND NORWAY, 1940

1940, Feb. 17. British naval forces entered Norwegian waters to rescue 299 prisoners of war from the German ship *Altmark*. The Norwegian government protested.

Apr. 8. The French and British governments announced that Norwegian waters had been mined to prevent the passage of German ships.

Apr. 9. German sea and air borne forces descended on Norway. Oslo, Bergen, Trondheim, Stavanger, and Narvik were rapidly invaded. At the same time German forces entered and occupied Denmark without formal resistance.

Apr. 11. Rallying from the surprise attack, Norwegian forces offered growing resistance. Three German cruisers and four troopships were lost in the invasion, and the German forces which had seized Trondheim and Bergen were driven out.

Apr. 13. British naval units attacked the Germans at Narvik, sinking all enemy warships in Narvik harbor and occupying the town until June 8.

Apr. 16-19. Anglo-French expeditionary forces landed in southern Norway, but were compelled to withdraw after two weeks (May 3).

Apr. 30. The Germans, reinforced steadily, captured Dombas, a key rail center, and Norwegian resistance was broken, though military operations were carried on until June 10. Haakon VII and his cabinet escaped to London to continue resistance.

Sept. 25. The German Reich-Commissar for Norway set aside the legal administration, dissolved all political parties except the *Nasjonal Samling*, and entrusted the government to thirteen commissars.

1942, Feb. 1. The German commissar, Joseph Terboven, appointed Vidkun Quisling "minister president" of the German-dominated régime. Disowned by the Norwegian government in London, Quisling abolished the constitution and made himself dictator (Feb. 7).

4. THE CONQUEST OF THE NETHERLANDS AND BELGIUM AND THE FALL OF FRANCE

1940, May 10. German armies, without warning, invaded the Netherlands, Belgium, and Luxemburg. Winston S. Churchill replaced Neville Chamberlain as British prime minister.

May 11. The French and British governments dispatched expeditionary forces into Belgium to co-operate with the Belgian army in its resistance. The Germans captured Fort Eben Emael, key Belgian defense position.

May 12. The Germans crossed the Meuse at Sedan.

May 13. Rotterdam surrendered to the Germans after part of the city had been blasted by an exterminating air attack. The Netherlands government, headed by Queen Wilhelmina, escaped to London. The Netherlands army capitulated May 14.

May 17-21. German mechanized divisions drove deep into northern France, racing down the Somme valley to the English Channel at Abbeville. The British and Belgian forces in Flanders were thus separated from the main French armies. Gen. **Maxime Weygand** replaced Gen. Gustave Gamelin as French commander-in-chief, but he was unable to arrest the French collapse. The **fall of Brussels** and Namur forced the British and Belgian armies back upon Ostend and Dunkerque.

May 26. Boulogne fell to the Germans. The Belgian armies, disorganized and short of supplies after eighteen days of fighting, could not sustain further attacks, and Leopold III ordered them to capitulate.

May 28. Exposed by the capitulation of the Belgians, the British expe-

BROWN, FRANCIS. *The War in Maps*. 3rd Edition. New York. Oxford Press. 1944

GERMAN ADVANCE IN EUROPE, WORLD WAR II

ditionary force of some 250,000 had to be withdrawn, chiefly from the beaches of **Dunkerque.**

June 4. By heroic efforts 215,000 British and 120,000 French troops were rescued, but were forced to abandon almost all equipment. British losses including prisoners totaled 30,000.

June 5. Having secured their right wing, the German invaders launched a wide attack against the French on an arc from Sedan to Abbeville.

June 10. ITALY DECLARED WAR AGAINST FRANCE AND GREAT BRITAIN. Italian forces invaded southern France.

June 13. Paris was evacuated before the continued German advance.

June 15. The French fortress of **Verdun was captured.** On the Baltic **Russian forces moved into Estonia, Latvia, and Lithuania** (June 15–17).

June 16. Marshal Henri-Philippe **Pétain** replaced Paul Reynaud as head of the French government.

June 17. Pétain asked the Germans for an armistice.

June 22. The requested **armistice was signed at Compiegne.** It provided that the French forces were to be disarmed, and that three-fifths of France be surrendered to German control.

June 23. Gen. **Charles de Gaulle,** at the head of a French National Committee in London, pledged continued French opposition against Germany. The British government supported De Gaulle

and severed relations with the régime of Marshal Pétain.

June 24. An armistice was concluded between France and Italy.

July 3. Battle of Oran. When the French crews refused to surrender, the British sank or captured a major section of the French fleet anchored at Oran, Algeria. The *Dunkerque* (26,000 tons), the *Provence* (22,000), the *Bretagne* (22,000), and an aircraft carrier (10,000) were destroyed.

July 4. All French ships in ports under British control were seized.

July 5. The French government at Vichy **severed relations with the British government.**

July 9. At Vichy, where the French government established its seat July 2, the parliament voted to give the Pétain régime the power to establish an **authoritarian government.** The vote was almost unanimous (395 to 3 in the Chamber of Deputies, 225 to 1 in the Senate). Pétain designated **Pierre Laval** as his vice-premier (July 12). On April 18, 1942, Laval became virtual dictator of France. On November 11, 1942, German forces entered Unoccupied France, following the Anglo-American invasion of North Africa. Pétain appointed Laval his successor and gave him authority to make laws and issue decrees. Laval thus became the puppet ruler of France under German direction. After the liberation of France a High Court of Justice declared Pétain guilty of plotting against the Republic and of intelligence with the enemy (Aug. 15, 1945). He was sentenced to death, but the sentence was commuted to life imprisonment. (For the Liberation of France see p. 1163 *f.*)

5. THE BATTLE OF BRITAIN

1940, June. The **Fall of France** and the loss of war material in the evacuation from Dunkerque led the British prime minister, Winston Churchill, to appeal to the United States government for military supplies. These were released by the War Department (June 3), and three weeks later a first shipment including 500,000 rifles, 80,000 machine guns, 900 75 mm. field guns, and 130,000,000 rounds of ammunition reached Britain.

July. On the fall of France the Germans occupied islands in the English Channel and intensified their air attacks on British cities, communications, and shipping.

Aug. 8. German bombing planes opened an ambitious **offensive** designed

to destroy British air strength by blasting the airfields and vital industries.

Aug. 15. One thousand German planes ranged as far north as Scotland. Croydon airfield was bombed. The British retaliated with heavy raids on Berlin, Duesseldorf, Essen, and other German cities.

Aug. 17. The German government proclaimed a **total blockade** of the waters around Great Britain.

Sept. 2. An important **defense agreement** was concluded **between Great Britain and the United States.** Fifty American destroyers were transferred to Britain to combat the air and submarine menace. In exchange the United States received a 99-year lease of naval and air bases in Newfoundland, Bermuda, the Bahamas, Jamaica, Antigua, St. Lucia, Trinidad, and British Guiana.

Sept. 7. Intensified bombing of London raised the casualties to 300–600 a day killed and 1000–3000 injured.

Sept. 11. The British bombed Continental ports, including Antwerp, Ostend, Calais, and Dunkerque, to frustrate German invasion preparations.

Sept. 16. Improved British defense measures inflicted heavy losses on German air raiders, 185 invading planes crashing in one day.

Sept. 27. A GERMAN-ITALIAN-JAPANESE PACT was concluded at Berlin providing for a ten-year military and economic alliance. The three contracting powers further promised each other mutual assistance in the event that any one of them became involved in war with a power not then a belligerent.

Oct. 10. Resuming the **air assault** with full intensity, the German *Luftwaffe* raided London heavily. Some Italian air squadrons joined in the attack. But shorter days, stormy weather, and improved defenses diminished the effectiveness of the air arm.

Nov. 10. In a supreme effort at crushing British industrial resources and demoralizing the population, the Germans blasted the industrial city of **Coventry** with destructive effect. Thereafter the air attacks became more sporadic. The British had survived the worst of the aerial *Blitzkrieg* and after November the winter weather made any attempt at invasion less likely. German losses in aircraft had been heavy: an official estimate placed them at 2375 German to 800 British planes destroyed in the period Aug. 8—Oct. 31. But many British cities had been severely shattered and burned, and 14,000 civilians had been killed in London alone. British losses at sea had also been heavy. On Nov. 5 Prime Minister Churchill declared that the **submarine boat** had become a greater menace than the bombing plane. (See *Naval Warfare and Blockade*, p. 1156 ff.)

Nov. 20. The **Stimson-Layton Agreement,** arranged between Sir Walter Layton, for the British Ministry of Supply, and Henry L. Stimson, United States Secretary of War, provided for a partial **standardization of military weapons and equipment** and initiated a general policy of pooling British and American technical knowledge, patents, and formulas in armament production.

1941. Great Britain became increasingly dependent upon arms, food, and raw material from the United States throughout 1941 as the German sea and air blockade was extended. President Roosevelt had proposed (Nov. 1940) an equal division of the American arms output between the United States and Britain. British credit in dollar exchange, which had amounted to $6,500,000,000, was exhausted by January, 1941, however, and British purchases had to be curtailed. This situation was eased by the signing (Mar. 11, 1941) of the **LEND-LEASE ACT.** The first shipments of food for Britain (Apr. 16) came just in time to avert a critical shortage there. Between April and December, 1941, one million tons of foodstuffs reached Britain from the United States.

May. Intensified German air attacks, facilitated by longer days and clearer skies, culminated in a shattering assault on London (May 10) which damaged the Houses of Parliament and the British Museum. Thereafter, however, secret German preparations for the invasion of Russia (June 22) reduced the number of bombers available for raids on Britain. Enormous damage had been endured by the British with remarkable courage. One home in every five was damaged or destroyed, factories shattered, and transport, gas, and water systems disrupted.

June 22. The **Battle of Britain subsided** with the opening of the Russian front in June, 1941. But the German submarine blockade remained a grave menace to British supply services throughout 1941 and 1942. It was gradually curbed by air and sea patrols, improved detection devices such as radar, and the extension of the convoy system. (See *Naval Warfare and Blockade*, p. 1156 ff.)

6. BALKAN CAMPAIGNS, 1940-1941

1940, June. The **fall of France** and the desperate position of Great Britain in the summer of 1940 caused a shift in the European balance. In the Balkans Rumania, which had won territory from all its neighbors in the twentieth century, was particularly menaced.

June 26. The **Union of Soviet Socialist Republics** demanded the return of **Bessarabia** and the cession of northern Bukovina. The disputed territory, 19,300 square miles with a population of 3,500,000, was occupied by Russian troops June 28.

Aug. 30. Under pressure from Berlin and Rome, the Rumanian government agreed to yield an area of 16,642 square miles with a population of 2,392,603 to Hungary (**Vienna Conference**).

Sept. 5. These reverses caused a political overturn in Rumania. Gen. **Ion Antonescu** became premier.

Sept. 6. King Carol fled from Rumania and was replaced by his son as **Michael V.**

Sept. 8. A further territorial cession of some 3000 square miles (**Southern Dobruja**) was demanded by, and yielded to, Bulgaria (**Treaty of Craiova**). These cessions cost Rumania in all about 40,000 square miles and 4,000,000 population.

Oct. 4. Hitler and Mussolini conferred at the Brenner Pass. The failure to break British resistance and increasing activity in the Balkan and Mediterranean areas forecast a shift in Axis strategy. Hitler also conferred with the French vice-premier, **Pierre Laval** (Oct. 22), with Gen. **Francisco Franco** of Spain (Oct. 23), with Marshal **Henri-Philippe Pétain,** head of the Vichy French Government (Oct. 24), and again with Mussolini, in Florence (Oct. 28).

Oct. 8. German troops entered Rumania to "protect" the oil fields.

Oct. 28. Greece rejected a demand of the Italian government for the use of Greek bases. Thereupon the Italians invaded Greece from Albania.

Oct. 30. British reinforcements were landed on Crete and other Greek islands. The Russian government delivered 134 fighter planes to Greece in accord with existing agreements.

Nov. 12. Vyacheslav Molotov, Soviet commissar for foreign affairs, **conferred with Hitler** in Berlin. Russian troops were massed on the Rumanian border.

Nov. 13. British bombing planes destroyed or damaged half of the Italian fleet anchored in the inner harbor at **Taranto.** At the same time Prime Minister Churchill announced the addition of five 35,000-ton battleships to the British navy.

Nov. 20. Hungary joined the Berlin-Rome-Tokyo Pact.

Nov. 23. Rumania joined the Berlin-Rome-Tokyo Pact.

Dec. 3. The Greeks broke through the Italian defenses in Albania, captured Porto Edda, and claimed a total of 28,000 prisoners. Agyrokastron was likewise captured five days later, and the Greeks overran one-fourth of Albania. The Germans dispatched 50,000 troops to reinforce the Italian armies. Combined with temporary successes of the British against the Italians in Africa, the Greek victories marked a blow to Axis prestige.

1941, Jan. 10. German air squadrons, transferred to Italy, attacked British naval forces off Sicily.

Feb. 10. The British government severed diplomatic relations with Rumania.

Mar. 1. Bulgaria joined the Rome-Berlin Axis and German troops occupied Sofia. The British delegation had left Feb. 24, and the Russian government warned the Bulgarians not to expect Soviet aid.

Mar. 25. Yugoslav envoys signed the Rome-Berlin-Tokyo Pact at Vienna.

Mar. 26-28. A political coup at Belgrade overthrew the regency of Prince Paul, and **Peter II** was proclaimed king. A new cabinet under Gen. **Simovich** announced that Yugoslavia would follow a policy of neutrality.

In naval engagements between Sicily and Tripoli the British sank an Italian warship, two cruisers and two destroyers.

Apr. 6. German troops, which had been massing on the German, Hungarian, Rumanian, and Bulgarian borders, **poured into Yugoslavia and Greece.** In Moscow official journals laid the responsibility for the spread of war upon the Germans.

Apr. 13. RUSSIAN AND JAPANESE DIPLOMATS SIGNED A MUTUAL NON-AGGRESSION PACT AT MOSCOW.

Apr. 17. The Yugoslav government capitulated after a campaign of 12 days. Resistance against the Germans and Italians was maintained by guerrilla forces.

Apr. 23. Greek resistance was broken and an **armistice signed.** King George II fled to Crete.

Apr. 27. The Germans entered Athens. Of the British expeditionary force in Greece 48,000 of the 60,000 men were evacuated, but much valuable equipment was abandoned.

May 2. In Iraq a pro-Axis régime under Premier **Rashid Ali** invited German aid, whereupon British forces entered the country.

May 20. German parachute troops invaded **Crete** and superior German air power inflicted serious losses and damage on the British cruisers and destroyers in Cretan waters.

May 31. Surviving British forces in Crete were evacuated to Cyprus and Egypt. The Axis position in the Eastern Mediterranean was greatly strengthened by the possession of Greece and Crete which made the Aegean Sea unsafe for British ships. Rebellion in Iraq ended when British troops entered Baghdad after Iraqi airfields had been bombed. Mosul was occupied June 4. An armistice was concluded and a government friendly to Great Britain installed. Iraq later declared war on Germany, Italy, and Japan (Jan. 16, 1943).

July 12. Confused fighting in **Syria** ended with an armistice after British and Free French forces moved on Beirut and Damascus. British naval units landed troops on the Lebanon coast. This occupation terminated the authority of the French Vichy government over Syria and Lebanon and cancelled the attempts of the Germans to obtain control of these territories. Possession of Syria and Iraq enabled the British to exert increased **pressure upon Iran**, the government of which was persuaded to co-operate (Aug. 28) after British and Russian forces entered the country. The danger that the German successes in the Balkans would bring Constantinople and the Straits under Axis control was fully realized in Moscow and the possibility that a Russian offensive might threaten the German flank explains in part why Hitler attacked Russia on June 22.

7. THE CAMPAIGNS IN RUSSIA, JUNE, 1941 — DECEMBER, 1944

1941, June 22. GERMAN ARMIES INVADED RUSSIA, opening hostilities on a front of 2000 miles, from the White to the Black Sea. The German invaders, with their allies, Italians, Rumanians, Hungarians, and Finns, were estimated at over 3,000,000 men. The Russians were credited with 2,000,000 men under arms, and an indefinite reserve. Prime Minister Churchill promised that Great Britain would extend all possible aid to the Russians.

June 29. The Germans reached Grodno, Brest-Litovsk, and Vilna.

July 1-2. **Riga,** capital of Latvia, was occupied by German troops, and the Russian retreat continued with heavy losses, especially around Bialystok.

July 13. A pact promising mutual aid was concluded between Great Britain and Russia.

July 16. The Germans captured Smolensk.

Aug. 1. Britain severed relations with Finland, which the Germans were using as a base for their invasion of Russia.

Aug. 19. The Germans claimed all Ukrainian territory west of the Dnieper except Odessa.

Aug. 25-29. British and Russian forces invaded Iran (Persia).

Sept. 4. The Germans commenced the beleaguerment of Leningrad, a state of partial siege which was not ended until Jan. 1943.

Sept. 19. Kiev and Poltava were stormed by the Axis forces, which continued their victorious advance to Orel (Oct. 8), Bryansk (Oct. 12), Vyasma (Oct. 13), Odessa (Oct. 16), Tanganrog (Oct. 19), and Kharkov (Oct. 24). By the end of October the Germans had entered the Crimea on the southern end of the vast front and had commenced the siege of Moscow in the north. The Soviet government transferred its headquarters to Kuibyshev.

Oct. 1. THE FIRST RUSSIAN PROTOCOL, signed at Moscow, provided that Great Britain and the United States would supply materials essential to the Russian war efforts for nine months. Purchase of American supplies was speeded by extending the Soviet government a credit of one billion dollars (Oct. 30). This was supplemented (June 11, 1942) by a Master Lend-Lease Agreement whereby the United States promised to supply the Soviet Union with such materials and services as the President might authorize. In return the Soviet government pledged that such articles or information would not be transferred to a third party without the consent of the President of the United

Axis, occupied areas & Finland—June 22,'41
Russian areas held by Axis—April 15,'43
Retaken by Russia since Nov. 19,'42
185,300 SQ. MILES

BATTLELINE AS OF
APRIL 15, 1943

RETAKEN
BY AXIS

BATTLELINE AS OF
NOV. 19, 1942

BROWN, FRANCIS. *The War in Maps.* New York. Oxford Press. 1944

RETREAT IN RUSSIA, WORLD WAR II

States. The arrangement was to continue until a date agreed upon by the two governments and materials unconsumed were to be returned to the United States at the end of the emergency.

Nov. 15. The siege of Sevastopol, an heroic epic of the war on the eastern front, commenced.

Nov. 16. The Germans captured Kerch. Rostov, entered by the invaders (Nov. 22), was retaken by the Russians a week later (Dec. 1). A counter-thrust temporarily relieved the pressure on Moscow (Dec. 6) and the Russians were also able to retake Kalinin (Dec. 16).

1942, Jan. 20. Continuing their winter offensive the Russians recaptured Mozhaisk. Dorogobuzh also fell to them (Feb. 23) and Rzhev (Mar. 20). In addition they scored advances toward Kursk (Apr. 29) and Kharkov (May 12).

May 26. The mutual aid pact between Great Britain and Russia was extended to a twenty-year treaty.

July 2. The Germans, who had opened a new summer offensive in southern Russia, captured Sevastopol which had sustained a siege of eight months. Driving powerfully toward the Caucasus, the Germans claimed Voronezh (July 7), Millerovo (July 15), and Rostov (July 24).

Aug. 9. Maikop fell to the invaders, who crossed the Don River (Aug. 20) and opened a vital offensive against Stalingrad (Aug. 22). This city was important as a communications center through which Volga River traffic, especially oil from the Caspian region, reached Russian distribution points. The Germans hoped not only to obtain needed supplies of petroleum for themselves, but to cripple the Russian war effort by cutting a major line of supply.

Sept. Russian agricultural supplies also were seriously reduced by the loss of the Ukraine and North Caucasus regions, for these areas had produced half the Soviet wheat and pork output. The grave deficiency was met in part after September, 1942, by increasing the shipments of canned meats, butter, fats, oils, dehydrated fruits and vegetables from the United States. By July, 1943, the Soviet Union had received 1,500,000 tons of foodstuffs under this arrangement.

Sept. 1. The Germans crossed the Kerch Straits and captured Novorossisk (Sept. 6). Farther north, a week later, they penetrated the city of Stalingrad (Sept. 14). Their summer offensive appeared on the point of succeeding, but they had overstretched their lines. Russian forces counter-attacked northeast of Stalin-

grad (Sept. 21) and ten days later (Oct. 1) opened a second thrust from southeast of the city.

Nov. 19. Without permitting the Germans time to entrench or to withdraw, the Russians intensified their pincer attack on the Stalingrad front while opening new drives toward Rzhev (Nov. 25) and Kharkov (Dec. 16).

1943, Jan. 1-18. The list of German defeats mounted to a débâcle. Russian forces recaptured Velikye-Luki (Jan. 1), entered Mozdok (Jan. 3), and relieved Leningrad from a 17-month siege. Twenty-two German divisions, cut off at Stalingrad, and reduced to 80,000 men, were forced to capitulate by Feb. 2. This second Russian winter offensive then rolled on, with the capture of Kursk (Feb. 8), Belgorod (Feb. 9), Rostov (Feb. 14), Kharkov (Feb. 16), Rzhev (Mar. 3), and Vyasma (Mar. 12). The losses of the Germans and their allies, in killed and captured, exceeded 500,000 for three months of winter fighting.

Mar. 15. Despite these casualties the Germans were able to open a spring drive, wresting Kharkov from the Russians once more (Mar. 15), and retaking Belgorod (Mar. 21). This checked the Russian tide of conquest temporarily and the lines were more or less stabilized. The Axis armies had been driven back halfway from the Don to the Dnieper. When they attempted to open a summer offensive in July, they found that the Russians had also been gathering men and material for a renewal of the struggle.

July. Military supplies from Great Britain and the United States helped materially to arm the Russian forces for the campaigns of 1943. The United States shipped 4100 planes, 138,000 motor vehicles, shiploads of steel, and industrial machinery for Soviet arms factories. Part of the equipment went by northern convoy routes to Archangel, part in Russian ships to Vladivostok, part via the Persian Gulf. Shipments through Iran increased to 100,-000 tons a month by July, 1943.

July. The Russian summer campaign of 1943. The Germans and their allies had 240-260 divisions, the Soviet armies had grown to 250-275, and the advantage in matériel had passed to the Russians. Anglo-American bombing was crippling German industry, greatly reducing the output of German planes, and this unhinged the plane-tank combination of mechanized warfare which had won earlier successes for the *Wehrmacht*. The output of Russian factories had increased greatly, and the United States shipments of planes to Russia, mounting to a total of 6500 by the autumn of 1943, deprived the Germans of their superiority in the air.

July 5. The Germans opened an offensive in the Orel-Belgorod sector, but were checked after a week's fighting.

July 11. A Russian counter-drive forced the Germans from Orel and Belgorod (Aug. 5).

Aug. 23. Broadening and gathering momentum the Russian drive swept on to **Kharkov.** In the south, Tanganrog fell (Aug. 30), in the center, Bryansk was recaptured (Sept. 17) and Smolensk (Sept. 25). By October the **Russians had reached the Dnieper** at several points, capturing Kiev (Nov. 6). The year closed with the reconquest of Zhitomir (Dec. 31).

1944. In January Novgorod in the north fell to the Russians (Jan. 20) and by February they had penetrated Estonia and were on the borders of prewar Poland.

Feb. 17. Ten German divisions, trapped in a pocket near Cherkassy, were largely destroyed, and the survivors made prisoner.

Mar. 26. The Ukrainian drives carried the Russians to the Rumanian border. Odessa fell to them on Apr. 10 and Tarnopol on Apr. 15. By May 9 they had taken Sevastopol, and the Crimea, like the Ukraine, was cleared of invading forces.

June 20. An offensive against the Finns delivered Viborg into Russian hands. Farther south Vitebsk fell to them (June 26) and Minsk (July 3). The opening of an Allied front in the west, following the **invasion of Normandy** (June 6), prevented the Germans strengthening the eastern front, and July and August brought an almost unbroken series of Russian triumphs. By the end of August they had reached the borders of East Prussia and were invading Poland and Rumania.

Aug. 24. THE RUMANIAN GOVERNMENT SURRENDERED when Russian troops reached the mouth of the Danube, and captured Jassy and Kishinev. The capitulation of Rumania trapped major units of the German Black Sea naval forces, although some of the smaller craft escaped up the Danube before the Russian advance closed that route of escape. Russian domination of the Black Sea opened a new and important supply route whereby cargoes could reach the Soviet Union.

Sept. 5. The Soviet Union declared war on **Bulgaria.** Three days later the Bulgarian government asked for an armistice (Sept. 8) and Russian columns moved into Sofia (Sept. 16).

Oct. 20. German forces of occupation in **Yugoslavia** were harassed increasingly by the *Partisans* and failed to halt the advance of the Russians who entered Belgrade (Oct. 20). Two weeks later they were at the gate of Budapest, but the Hungarian capital resisted savagely for over two months and was not conquered until Feb. 13, 1945.

Victorious in the Balkans, with their central armies pressing into Poland, and their northern (right) end of the line anchored on the Baltic after the **capture of Tallinn** (Sept. 22) **and Riga** (Oct. 13), the Russians opened their final drives into Germany (Jan., 1945). These maneuvers, synchronized with the Allied drives across the Rhine, merged into the **Battle of Germany** (p. 1164).

8. DEFENSE OF THE WESTERN HEMISPHERE

1939, Oct. 2. A Pan-American Conference at Panama declared that the waters surrounding the Western Hemisphere for a distance of 300 miles from shore and as far north as Canada constituted "sea safety zones" and must be kept free from hostile acts by non-American belligerent nations. The Conference also issued a **General Declaration of Neutrality** of the American Republics.

Nov. 4. President Roosevelt signed an amendment to the Neutrality Act which repealed the embargo on the sale of arms and placed exports to belligerent nations on a *cash-and-carry* basis.

Dec. 13. Three British cruisers attacked the German battleship *Graf Spee* and drove it into the harbor of Montevideo. When forced to leave harbor, it was scuttled by the German crew. In the name of the American republics the President of Panama protested to Great Britain, France, and Germany at this and other belligerent acts committed in American waters.

1940, May 16. President Roosevelt asked the Congress of the United States to appropriate $2,500,000,000 for **expansion of the army and navy** and proposed a productional goal of 50,000 airplanes a year. This program of expansion was to be supervised by a **Defense Advisory Commission.**

June 16. Congress authorized the sale of munitions to the government of any American republic. This measure, known as the **Pittman Act,** was extended by provisions authorizing the Export-Import-Bank to lend the American republics up to $500,000,000 (Sept. 26) and permitting them to procure munitions of a total value of $400,000,000 for their defense. These programs were taken over by the **Lend-Lease Administration** after its creation in March, 1941.

June 17. The United States Department of State notified European governments that it would not recognize the transfer of any geographic region of the Western Hemisphere from one non-American power to another non-American Power.

July 20. President Roosevelt signed a bill providing for a **two-ocean navy** as part of a vast defense plan for the United States in particular and the Western Hemisphere in general.

July 30. The republics of the Pan-American Union approved a convention setting up an **Inter-American Commission on Territorial Administration** to guard the sovereignty of the states of the Western Hemisphere. At this meeting at Havana, the delegates also approved an **Act of Havana** providing that the American republics, jointly or individually, should act as their own defense and that of the continent required.

Aug. 18. President Roosevelt and Premier **Mackenzie King** of Canada agreed to set up a **joint board of defense.**

Sept. 2. The United States obtained naval and air bases in Newfoundland, Bermuda, the Bahamas, Jamaica, St. Lucia, Trinidad, Antigua, and British Guiana on 99-year leases from Great Britain. In exchange Britain acquired 50 overage destroyers from the United States. The facilities at these bases were extended to the Latin American governments in conformity with understandings reached at the conferences of Lima, Panama, and Havana.

Sept. 16. The United States Congress passed the **Selective Service Act** providing for the registration of all men between 21 and 36 years of age, and for the training, for one year, of 1,200,000 troops and 800,000 reserves.

Dec. 20. The President of the United States named a defense board headed by **William A. Knudsen** to prepare defense measures and speed armament production.

1941, Feb. 1. The **United States Patrol Force** in the Caribbean area was raised to fleet status. Naval bases at Guantanamo Bay, Cuba; San Juan, Puerto Rico; and St. Thomas, Virgin Islands, were developed rapidly. A third set of locks was designed for the Panama Canal.

Mar. 11. The **Lend-Lease Act** was signed by President Roosevelt. It had passed the Senate by a vote of 60 to 31 and the House of Representatives by 317 to 71. Under this enactment "any country whose defense the President deems vital to the defense of the United States" became eligible to receive any defense article by sale, transfer, exchange, or lease.

Mar. The Republic of Panama granted the United States the right to extend its air defenses outside the limits of the Canal Zone. A **Pan-American highway,** to extend ultimately from Mexico City through Central America to Santiago, Chile, and thence across the Andes to Buenos Aires, and up the Atlantic coast to Rio de Janeiro, was two-thirds completed by December, 1941. A highway from Washington State to Alaska was also undertaken.

Apr. 9. The United States concluded an **agreement with Denmark,** undertaking to defend Greenland against invasion in return for the right to construct air and naval bases there.

July 7. **United States forces landed in Iceland** at the invitation of the Icelandic government, to relieve British troops in defending the island. Plans were completed (Sept. 25) for constructing air and naval base facilities in Iceland.

Nov. 24. The United States sent forces to **occupy Dutch Guiana,** to protect the resources and prevent possible activities by agents of the Axis powers.

Dec. 7. THE JAPANESE ATTACKED HAWAII AND THE PHILIPPINES.

Dec. 8. THE CONGRESS OF THE UNITED STATES DECLARED WAR ON JAPAN.

1942, Jan. 15. Representatives of the American republics met for an **Inter-American Conference at Rio de Janeiro.** It was summoned to concert measures for defending the Western Hemisphere against aggression.

Jan. 21. The representatives of 21 American republics, assembled at Rio de Janeiro, adopted unanimously a resolution calling for severance of relations with the Axis powers.

Mar. An Inter-American Defense Board was established to promote working co-operation among the American states in defense of the Western Hemisphere.

June 28. Eight German agents who had landed from a submarine on the shore of Long Island were captured by agents of the Federal Bureau of Investigation.

Sept. Ecuador granted the United States naval bases in the Galápagos Islands and the Santa Elena peninsula.

1943, Jan. 29. President Roosevelt visited President Getulio Vargas. They announced the joint determination of the governments of the United States and Brazil to safeguard the sea lanes of the Atlantic Ocean.

Mar. 11. The Lend-Lease Act was extended for one year by a vote of 82 to o in the Senate and 407 to 6 in the House of Representatives.

Apr. 21. President Roosevelt visited President Avila Camacho. They emphasized the good relations existing between the United States and Mexico as an example of the Good Neighbor policy.

Oct. 13. The government of Portugal conceded to Great Britain the right to use bases in the Azores Islands for air and naval patrol. This privilege was shared by United States ships and planes.

1944, Sept. 29. President Roosevelt called attention to the "growth of Nazi-Fascist influence" in **Argentina** and the failure of the Argentine government to fulfill its inter-American obligations. United States ships were forbidden to call at Argentine ports.

The **Mexican government** agreed to pay $24,000,000 with interest at 3 per cent for the property of United States oil companies expropriated in 1938.

1945, Feb. 21-Mar. 8. Inter-American Conference on Problems of War and Peace met in Mexico City. The United States offered an "economic charter for the Americas," to promote orderly reconversion and raise the standards of living. In addition, the United States government guaranteed for the duration of the war to aid any American state if its political independence or territorial integrity were attacked by a neighbor.

Mar. 3. The "Act of Chapultepec" was approved by the delegates of 19 American republics, providing for joint action to guarantee each American state against aggression. The states of the Western Hemisphere were to act collectively in their own defense unless and until the World Security Council should take effective measures to deal with an attack.

Mar. 27. The **Argentine Republic declared war on Germany and Japan.** One week later (Apr. 4) the Governing Board of the Pan-American Union admitted Argentina to membership and the Argentine régime was recognized (Apr. 9) by the United States, Great Britain, and France.

9. NAVAL WARFARE AND BLOCKADE

The gross tonnage of the merchant fleets of the leading nations in 1939 reflects the overwhelming advantage which Great Britain and her subsequent allies enjoyed on the sea. The ships of Norway, Holland, and Belgium, most of which escaped when these countries were overrun by the Germans in 1940, took service with the British and helped to build up the pool of **United Nations** shipping.

Merchant tonnage, 1939.

Great Britain	21,001,925	Japan	5,629,845
United States	11,470,177	Germany	4,482,662
Norway	4,833,813	Italy	3,424,804
Netherlands	2,969,578		
France	2,933,933		
Belgium	408,418		
Total	43,617,844		13,537,311

In 1939 the **world tonnage** for merchant ships of 100 tons or over was 68,509,432. More than half of this was destroyed, largely by submarine or air attack, in the course of the next five years. Yet so energetic was the shipbuilding program, carried out largely in American yards immune to air attack, that by May, 1945, Britain and the United States, through the **War Shipping Administration,** disposed of over 4000 ships with a deadweight tonnage of 43,000,-000. The Germans, Italians, and Japanese, on the other hand, found it increasingly difficult to make good their losses, and by 1945 their fleets, merchant and naval, had been almost completely eliminated.

1939, Sept. 3. The British government proclaimed a naval blockade of Germany.

Nov. 21. The British tightened the blockade on German imports and announced that German exports likewise would be halted.

Dec. 1. From this date neutral shippers were advised to obtain a "*navicert*"

BROWN, FRANCIS. *The War in Maps.* New York. Oxford Press. 1944

BATTLE OF THE ATLANTIC, WORLD WAR II

or certificate from British consular officials. These navicerts enabled a cargo to be passed through the patrols established by the British government in concert with its allies. Italy, the Netherlands, Belgium, and Japan protested against the British blockade measures.

Dec. 8. The United States Department of State questioned the British practice of seizing German goods on neutral vessels, and challenged (Dec. 14) the diversion of United States ships to British and French control bases. The State Department also protested (Dec. 27) against the British examination of neutral mail in the search for contraband.

Dec. 13. The German battleship *Graf Spee*, damaged by British cruisers in the South Atlantic, sought refuge at Montevideo. When forced to depart, it was blown up by order of the commander (Dec. 17).

1940, Feb. 16. A British destroyer invaded Norwegian coastal waters to attack the German ship *Altmark*, which was attempting to reach Germany with British prisoners of war aboard. The Norwegian government protested to London.

Apr. 8. The British and French governments announced that Norwegian waters had been mined to prevent the transit of German ships.

June 25. Japanese warships arrived at ports in French Indo-China.

July 3. BATTLE OF ORAN. British naval forces destroyed part of the French fleet stationed at Oran to make certain the ships would not be available for the Germans. The French officers had refused to surrender.

July 20. The United States Congress passed a bill calling for an unparalleled expansion of naval tonnage and the creation of a "two-ocean" navy.

Sept. 3. The United States acquired the use, on a 99-year lease, of naval and air bases in Newfoundland, Bermuda, the Bahamas, Jamaica, Antigua, St. Lucia, Trinidad, and British Guiana. In exchange, fifty overage destroyers were transferred to Great Britain.

Sept. 6. The United States Congress passed a defense measure appropriating $5,246,000,000 and providing for 201 ships of war, seven to be battleships of 55,000 tons each.

Sept. 22-25. British naval forces aided a "Free French" expedition, under Gen. Charles de Gaulle, in an attempt to take possession of Dakar in French West Africa. The forces holding Dakar for the Vichy government of France resisted and the attack was abandoned.

1941, Mar. 30. Battle of Cape Matapan. Three Italian cruisers and two destroyers were sunk by British naval forces in the waters between Crete and Greece.

Apr. 10. The United States declared Greenland under its protection and arranged with the Danish government to establish naval and air bases there.

May 24. The giant battleship *Bismarck* escaped into the Atlantic, where it sank the British dreadnought *Hood*, but was itself destroyed by combined British air and naval attack (May 27).

July 7. United States troops landed in Iceland to relieve British occupying forces, provide for the defense of the island, and develop air and naval bases.

July 31. Official London estimates of British, Allied, and neutral shipping losses for almost two years of war placed them at more than 7,000,000 tons.

Sept. 16. The United States navy assumed protection of all shipments as far as Iceland.

Oct. 17. The United States destroyer *Kearny* was torpedoed off Iceland, but reached port. The destroyer *Reuben James*, likewise torpedoed in the Atlantic, was lost (Oct. 31).

Dec. 7. THE JAPANESE OPENED A SURPRISE ATTACK ON HAWAII, THE PHILIPPINES, MALAYA, AND HONGKONG. (For developments in the Pacific area see p. 1167.)

1942, Apr. 18. Sixteen bombing planes from the United States carrier *Hornet*, led by Col. James Doolittle, bombed Tokyo.

Nov. 8. American and British Expeditionary Forces landed in French North Africa in the greatest amphibious invasion hitherto attempted. The British, American, and Allied warships, transports, and cargo vessels exceeded 850 ships (p. 1160).

Nov. 27. The greater part of the French navy, which had been rated the fourth largest in the world in 1939, was scuttled by the crews in Toulon harbor to prevent the Germans obtaining the ships.

1943, Mar. 17. The United States, Britain, and Canada issued official assurances that their governments were in agreement on the most effective methods for combating the **U-boat menace.**

July 10. American, British, and Canadian forces invaded Sicily in the second mass amphibious invasion of the war. Over 2500 vessels were involved. The conquest of all North African territory had given the Allied powers **control of the Mediterranean routes** and increased their advantages for transport and blockade.

July 16. President Roosevelt issued an order creating a new **Board of Economic Warfare.**

Aug. 24. At the **Quebec Conference** which ended on this date, Prime Minister Churchill and President Roosevelt announced important progress in curbing German submarine activity. "In the first six months of 1943 the number of ships sunk by U-boats was only half that of the last six months in 1942 and one-quarter that of the first six months of 1942." Figures subsequently released by the **Office of War Information** (Nov. 29, 1944) revealed that the tonnage of Allied and neutral merchant ships lost through enemy action between Sept., 1939, and Jan. 1, 1944, aggregated 22,161,000 gross tons. This was replaced by the output of United States shipyards alone, which launched 4308 ships with a deadweight tonnage of 44,082,000 in the same period.

Aug. 29. When the Germans attempted to seize the Danish naval vessels anchored in the navy yard at Copenhagen, the crews scuttled 29 of the 48 ships. Some of the smaller craft, 13 in all, escaped to Sweden, and 6 fell into German hands.

Sept. 3. With air and naval support **ALLIED FORCES CROSSED THE STRAITS OF MESSINA AND LANDED IN SOUTHERN ITALY.** This marked the first successful amphibious invasion of continental Europe in the course of the war.

Sept. 12. The major part of the **Italian fleet** escaped to the Allies after the Italian government of Marshal Pietro Badoglio surrendered.

Oct. 13. Portugal granted Great Britain the use of the **Azores Islands** as an Allied naval and air base.

1944. By 1944 the United Nations had achieved a position of **naval supremacy** which increased monthly and could no longer be seriously challenged. Despite improvements in submarine construction, 500 U-boats had been destroyed and merchant-ship losses from this cause sharply reduced. The Germans no longer had any capital ships in fighting condition and had all but ceased to build or repair shipping. What warships survived of the Italian and French navies were wrecked or in Allied control, part of the French fleet having been repaired at a cost of $200,-000,000. The Japanese still possessed a respectable navy, including 17 capital ships, but it was inadequate to protect the long route to the East Indies and Malaya, threatened increasingly by American and British aircraft and submarines. **Japanese air power** in particular was seriously reduced, and less than ten Japanese carriers survived, a fatal deficiency when the British carrier list had risen to 40 and the United States navy possessed over 100. Inability to maintain air protection for warships even in harbor was to doom the remnants of the Japanese navy in 1945.

1944, Jan. 23. The **Allies landed forces on the Italian coast south of Rome** in a second amphibious invasion of the Italian mainland (p. **1162).**

June 6. ALLIED FORCES LANDED AT SEVERAL POINTS ON THE CHERBOURG PENINSULA, with strong naval support, an armada of 4000 ships, and over 10,000 aircraft (p. 1163). For naval activities in the Pacific areas see *The War in the Pacific* (p. 1167 ff.).

10. CAMPAIGNS IN AFRICA, 1940-1943

1940, June 10. ITALY DECLARED WAR ON FRANCE AND GREAT BRITAIN.

Aug. 6. Italian forces invaded British Somaliland from Italian East Africa, completing their conquest by Aug. 19.

Sept. 13-15. An Italian army invaded Egypt from Libya.

Sept. 23. British naval forces and Free French troops under Gen. Charles de Gaulle attempted to occupy **Dakar** in French East Africa, but were repulsed. The attempt was abandoned Sept. 25.

Oct. 9. Free French forces under Gen. de Gaulle took possession of **Duala** on the Kamerun Coast, West Africa.

Dec. 8. The British opened a **surprise drive against the Italians** in North Africa. From Mersa Matruh in Egypt, to which they had retreated, Imperial troops outflanked the Italians, captured 1000 prisoners, and advanced so rapidly that they were in **Sidi Barrani** and had invaded Libya by Dec. 12.

1941, Jan. 5. The Italian garrison at Bardia surrendered to the Imperial forces, which took 25,000 prisoners and valuable war material.

Jan. 15. British forces from the Anglo-Egyptian Sudan and Kenya opened **drives into Italian East Africa** (Ethiopia) and also penetrated **Eritrea** (Jan. 19).

Jan. 22. Tobruk fell to the Imperial forces invading Libya. **Derna** surrendered (Jan. 24), **Benghasi**, capital of Cyrenaica, was entered (Feb. 7), and advance units reached **El Argheila** (Feb. 8). In a campaign of two months the Imperial divisions, commanded by General Sir **Archibald Wavell**, had captured over 114,000 prisoners at a cost of 3000 casualties.

Feb. 26. **Mogadiscio**, capital of Italian Somaliland, fell to the Imperial forces.

Mar. 22. **Neguelli** in southern Ethiopia was occupied by the British and Ethiopian forces, and the capital, **Addis Ababa**, capitulated (Apr. 6). Italian resistance in Eritrea collapsed by June, and before the end of 1941 all Italian East Africa was under British control.

Apr. 3. The Italians, reinforced by German divisions trained for desert fighting, and brilliantly commanded by Gen. **Erwin Rommel**, opened an attack against the Imperial outposts in Libya. Weakened by the dispatch of 60,000 troops to Greece, the British were forced to abandon their recent conquests in a costly retreat.

Apr. 14. The Germans reoccupied **Sollum** and **Bardia**.

Apr. 20. **Tobruk** was encircled, but the Imperial garrison held out with naval support. The drive of the Axis mechanized divisions stopped at the Egyptian frontier (May 29). Through the summer the British prepared for a counter-offensive.

Dec. 11. **Second British drive into Libya.** After relieving Tobruk, Imperial troops reached **Benghasi** for the second time (Dec. 25), but stopped short of El Argheila (Jan. 18, 1942). Gen. Rommel's reserves in Africa had been depleted because of the opening of the German drive on Russia (p. 1151).

1942, May 27. **Second Axis drive on Egypt.** Reinforced. Rommel

opened a powerful drive which captured **Tobruk** once more (June 21) and swept on to **Bardia** and **Bir-el-Gobi**. The victorious advance of the Axis troops was finally checked at **El Alamein**, only 70 miles from Alexandria. A four months' lull followed.

Oct. 23. **Third British offensive in North Africa.** The British Eighth Army under Gen. **Bernard L. Montgomery** drove east from **El Alamein** and expelled Rommel's divisions from Egypt by Nov. 12.

Nov. 8. **INVASION OF FRENCH NORTH AFRICA.** An Anglo-American invasion force, commanded by Gen. **Dwight D. Eisenhower**, disembarked in French Morocco and Algiers. This amphibious operation, on a scale hitherto unequaled in history, required 850 ships. The French garrisons at Casablanca, Oran, and Algiers were overcome after brief fighting, and an armistice arranged (Nov. 11) by Admiral **Jean-François Darlan**, who was in Algiers. Darlan, whose rôle as representative of the Vichy government was decidedly ambiguous, aided the Anglo-American forces to assume control of French North Africa and West Africa, but he was assassinated on Dec. 24.

Nov. 11. The Germans entered and took over control of Unoccupied France.

Nov. 27. The greater part of the **French fleet** which still survived was scuttled by the crews in **Toulon** harbor to frustrate the attempt of the Germans to obtain possession of the ships.

Dec. 1. Admiral **Darlan** retained his post as Chief of State in North Africa with Anglo-American approval. On his assassination (Dec. 24), Gen. **Henri Giraud** was designated to succeed him.

1943, Jan. 24. **Tripoli was occupied by the British Eighth Army** which pursued the retreating Axis forces into Tunisia.

Jan. 17-27. Conference at Casablanca, Morocco, with President Franklin D. Roosevelt, Prime Minister Winston Churchill, Gen. Henri Giraud, and Gen. Charles de Gaulle attending. The relationship between **Giraud** and the **De Gaulle** "Fighting French" party remained undefined, and Gen. Eisenhower took command of the unified North African operations. Plans for reducing the Axis powers to "unconditional surrender" were discussed at Casablanca but not disclosed.

Feb. 22. The Germans, who had rushed reinforcements to Tunisia, sought

BROWN, FRANCIS. *The War in Maps*. New York. Oxford Press. 1944

EUROPE AND AFRICA DURING GERMAN SEIZURE, WORLD WAR II

to hold this Protectorate, and seized **Kasserine Pass.** The Americans reoccupied it four days later.

Mar. 15. Gen. Giraud at Algiers restored representative government in French North Africa, declared legislation introduced there since 1940 void, and promised that after victory the French nation would decide its own form of government.

Mar. 19. American forces, striking east from Algeria, captured **El Guettar** in Tunisia.

Mar. 30. The British Eighth Army broke through the **Mareth Line** into southern Tunisia, meeting the advancing American Second Army Corps between Gabes and El Guettar on Apr. 8.

May 8-12. End of the Axis resistance in North Africa. British and United States forces captured the cities of **Tunis** and **Bizerte.** Possession of the whole North African coast opened the central Mediterranean to Allied shipping and exposed Italy to invasion. The threat to Egypt and the Suez Canal was ended and the Italian dream of a great African empire had proved a costly failure. Fighting in Africa was estimated to have drained the Axis powers of 950,000 men, killed or captured, 8000 airplanes, and 2,400,000 tons of shipping.

11. THE INVASION OF ITALY

1943, July 10. United States, British, and Canadian forces invaded Sicily under the command of Gen. Dwight D. Eisenhower. Over 2000 vessels were employed to convoy 160,000 men, and landings were effected along the southern coast. The Americans seized Gela; the British Eighth Army and Canadian troops, disembarking at Cape Passaro, drove along the east shore.

July 14. Port Augusta was captured.

July 19. Allied bombing planes wrecked **Naples,** and, after repeated warnings, attacked railway terminals and military objectives in Rome (July 20).

July 22. Half of Sicily was occupied, the Allied front stretching from Catania to Mazzara. Palermo fell July 24.

July 25. BENITO MUSSOLINI WAS FORCED TO RESIGN with his cabinet and his place was taken by Marshal **Pietro Badoglio.** This coup was virtually a revolution, breaking the 21-year period of Fascist rule. Badoglio declared the Fascist Party dissolved (July 28) and opened negotiations for an armistice.

Aug. 18. Resistance in Sicily collapsed with the fall of Messina. The campaign had cost the Allied armies an estimated 22,000 casualties, the Axis forces 167,000. At a loss of 274 planes the Allied airmen accounted for 1691 enemy aircraft.

Sept. 2. British and American forces crossed the Straits of Messina and landed in southern Italy.

Sept. 3. An armistice was signed at Algiers, ending hostilities between the Anglo-American forces and those of the Badoglio régime. It was announced (Sept. 8) that the Italian surrender was unconditional. The actual terms were not disclosed.

Sept. 15. Ex-Premier Mussolini, who had been held a prisoner near Rome, was rescued by German troops (Sept. 12) and proclaimed the establishment of a **Republican Fascist Party** (Sept. 15) in alliance with the German army of occupation. The Italian people were confused and divided, and the German divisions in the country seized the leading cities including Rome.

Oct. 1. After landing near Salerno (Sept. 9) American troops entered Naples. Thereafter, however, winter weather, the mountainous countryside, and stubborn German resistance stopped the Allied advance on a line south of Cassino.

1944, Jan. 22. Allied forces landed at Anzio in an attempt to outflank the German lines. The beachhead proved costly to hold and changed the situation little.

Feb. 11. Part of southern Italy, with Sicily and Sardinia, were returned to the jurisdiction of the Italian government. After occupation these areas had been administered with the aid of an **Allied Control Commission,** and **Allied Military Government** (A.M.G.), and an **Advisory Council** for Italy composed of representatives of the United States, Great Britain, the Soviet Union, and the French Committee of National Liberation.

Mar. 15. The Allied armies launched a heavy **assault against Cassino,** which fell May 18.

June 4. The Anglo-American troops entered Rome.

Aug. 12. Florence was captured after bitter fighting and Italy controlled by the Allies up to a line running from Livorno to Ancona. Thenceforth the Italian front remained a tense but unprogressive field of action until the final collapse of Germany in April and May, 1945.

The German divisions in Italy were forced to capitulate (Apr. 29–May 1), and the Fascist Republican Party dissolved. **Mussolini** was seized when he attempted to escape to Switzerland and was shot by his anti-Fascist captors without formal trial (Apr. 28).

12. THE LIBERATION OF FRANCE AND BELGIUM

1944, June 6. INVASION OF NORMANDY. For many months careful and elaborate plans had been matured by the Supreme Headquarters of the Allied Expeditionary Forces (SHAEF) for invading France. Command of this greatest amphibious operation in history was entrusted to Gen. **Dwight D. Eisenhower.** The British Isles provided the chief base for the concentration of men and war material, and the plan of campaign to follow the invasion date (D-Day) was rehearsed in exhaustive detail. Air control was to be maintained by the United States 8th and 9th Air Forces, and the British Royal Air Force, with a combined strength of over 10,000 planes. An American Naval Task Force and a British Naval Task Force were assembled to support the assault, and the invasion was planned to proceed under cover of an intense and accurately directed bombardment by 800 guns on 80 warships. To convey the troops and supplies across the Channel, 4000 other ships were utilized, and the lack of port facilities for disembarkation was overcome by a dramatic improvisation in engineering. Artificial harbors were to be constructed on an exposed coast by sinking lines of blockships and concrete caissons to form breakwaters, with floating pierheads and pontoon causeways to serve as wharves and docks.

June 6. United States and British forces succeeded in **landing on the Normandy coast** between St. Marcouf and the Orne River. Within a week a strip of beach 60 miles long had been occupied and the artificial harbors constructed.

June 18. An unusually severe gale with high waves delayed landing operations for three days and wrecked the major causeways in one artificial harbor. It was abandoned and traffic diverted to a British-built harbor which was less exposed and had suffered less severely.

June 27. The capture of Cherbourg placed a major port in Allied control. During the first hundred days following D-Day 2,200,000 men, 450,000 vehicles, and 4,000,000 tons of stores were landed.

This extraordinary achievement was rendered possible by perfecting the services of supply, on the basis of experience gained in the First World War, and in the amphibious landings in Africa and Italy. The enormous output of Allied factories and shipyards, which made it possible to duplicate all wrecked or damaged equipment, was also an important factor.

July 9. British and Canadian troops captured Caen. Allied tanks broke through German defenses near **St. Lo** and fanned out, disorganizing enemy resistance. Persistent bombing of all bridges and railways severely crippled the German attempts to bring up adequate forces to halt the Allied drives.

Aug. 15. In another amphibious operation the Allies effected successful **landings on the French Mediterranean coast** between Marseille and Nice.

Aug. 24. The citizens of **Paris** rioted against German forces of occupation as Allied armed divisions crossed the Seine and approached the capital. **French Forces of the Interior** (FFI), which had been organized for underground resistance and supplied with arms, rose against the retreating Germans.

Sept. 2. Allied forces, which had penetrated into Belgium, **liberated Brussels.**

Sept. 12. The American First Army crossed the German frontier near Eupen, and American armored forces entered Germany north of Trier. The Germans, however, manning the **Westwall** defenses, offered firm resistance and the Allied advance was halted. An Allied attempt to outflank the Westwall through the flat Dutch territory to the north (Sept. 17–26) failed, and survivors of an Allied airborne division which was dropped in Holland to **Arnhem** had to be withdrawn.

Sept. 15. The American Seventh and the French First Armies, sweeping up the Rhone Valley from beachheads won (Aug. 15) on the Riviera coast, joined the

American Third Army at Dijon. The American, British, and French forces were then reorganized in liberated France for a projected assault on Germany.

Dec. 16-25. BATTLE OF THE BULGE. The German supreme commander in the west, Gen. **Karl von Rundstedt,** under orders from Adolf Hitler, dislocated Allied preparations by a sudden drive against thinly held American lines in the Belgian and Luxemburg sector. Suffering heavy losses, the Allied forces were driven back to the Meuse, but they rallied to attack strongly on both sides of the "bulge" and the Germans were checked before the close of December.

With the opening of 1945, the American, British, and French drives into Germany from the west, co-ordinated with the rapid and powerful Russian thrusts from the Danube Valley, Poland, and East Prussia, fused into one vast combined operation.

13. THE BATTLE OF GERMANY, 1945

THE RÔLE OF AIR POWER. In twentieth-century warfare the assembly line has become as important as the battle line and consequently an equally vital target for attack. The strategy of blockade adopted by the Allied governments was designed primarily to starve, not the German population, but German industrial and military machines, chiefly by cutting off fuel and essential raw material. This aim could best be achieved by supplementing the naval blockade with a systematic **bombing of German factories, power plants, and transportation centers.**

At the commencement of the Second World War, in 1939, the Germans possessed the strongest air force in the world. By the close of 1943, however, their bombing squadrons were depleted, though they still had a peak force of 3000 first-line fighters. In 1944 the Allied air offensive was sharply intensified and German air strength declined decisively. Over 1000 *Luftwaffe* planes were destroyed in January and February and vital machine plants in **Essen** and **Schweinfurt** were crippled. Gen. **Henry H. Arnold,** commanding general of the United States Army Air Forces, later characterized the week of Feb. 20–26, 1944, as "probably the most decisive of the war" because of the shattering damage inflicted upon German installations in six days of favorable flying weather. By the end of hostilities the Germans had received 315 tons of explosive in retaliation for every ton of aerial bombs they had launched against Britain. Their loss in planes, by Jan. 1, 1945, had passed 50,000, in comparison with a total loss of 17,790 suffered by the United States Air Forces on all fronts. During the last four months of fighting, Allied air squadrons roamed Germany almost at will, destroying communications, obliterating plants and stores, and wrecking many of the remaining German aircraft on the ground, where they lay helpless for lack of fuel and repairs.

1945. The **military collapse of Germany** was consummated in four months by simultaneous drives launched by Russian armies in the east and south and American, French, and British Imperial forces in the west.

Jan. 12. Opening a powerful **drive into Poland,** the Russians took **Warsaw** (Jan. 17), swept into **Tarnow, Cracow,** and **Lodz** two days later (Jan. 19), and forced the Germans to abandon the whole **Vistula defense** line. By Feb. 20, Russian mechanized units, spearheads of an encroaching Soviet host that numbered 215 divisions, were within 30 miles of Berlin.

Feb. 7. Yalta Conference. While President Roosevelt, Prime Minister Churchill, and Marshal Stalin met at Yalta in the Crimea, to plan the final defeat and occupation of Germany (p. 1143), the United States Third Army crossed the German frontier at ten points. British and Canadian divisions opened an offensive southeast of **Nijmegen** (Feb. 8).

Feb. 22. The Third Army continued its progress, crossing the **Roer River.** American advance forces drove toward the **Ruhr Valley** (Feb. 23) and entered **Trier** (Mar. 2) and **Cologne** (Mar. 5). Supreme Headquarters of the Allied Expeditionary Forces announced that the total of German prisoners taken since D-Day (June 6, 1944) amounted to 954,377.

Mar. 7. The United States First Army **crossed the Rhine at Remagen,** and the German defense system on the east bank collapsed. By Apr. 11 the United States Ninth Army had reached the **Elbe River;** eight days later the Russians fought their way into **Berlin** (Apr. 20); and advance units of the **American and Russian armies met on the Elbe at Torgau** (Apr. 25).

Apr. 28. German resistance in northern Italy broke as American and British forces swept into the Po Valley. The **Fascist Republican régime disinte-**

grated, and Benito Mussolini, attempting to escape to Switzerland, was captured and shot by Italian Anti-Fascist partisans. The German divisions in Italy surrendered unconditionally.

May 1. BATTLE OF BERLIN. Russian forces continued to shell Berlin and fight their way into the capital. A German radio announcement from Hamburg declared that **Adolf Hitler had died** defending the Reichschancellery, and that **Admiral Doenitz** had succeeded him.

One million German and Italian soldiers in Italy and Austria laid down their arms.

May 4. The dissolution of the German National Socialist régime continued, with local military commanders making their own offers of capitulation. German divisions in northwestern Germany, the Netherlands, and Denmark surrendered.

May 7. A group of **German army leaders** sent envoys to Reims, where they **signed terms of surrender.**

May 8. President Truman for the United States and Prime Minister Churchill for Great Britain proclaimed the **end of the war in Europe (V-E Day).**

May 9. Marshal Stalin announced the end of the war to the Russian people. German army chiefs completed the formula of surrender in Berlin.

May 9-23. While German armed forces were being disarmed, the Allied governments transmitted orders through a **provisional German government** headed by Admiral Karl Doenitz. After two weeks this provisional régime was superseded. Doenitz, with several colleagues, and members of the German High Command and the General Staff, were taken into custody.

June 5. An **Allied Control Committee,** including Gen. **Dwight D. Eisenhower,** Field Marshal Sir **Bernard L. Montgomery,** and Marshal **Gregory K. Zhukov,** assumed full control throughout Germany. German territory, as of Dec. 31, 1937, was delimited in four **zones of occupation** under American, British, Russian, and French military administration.

14. THE WAR IN ASIA

1939. Economic penetration and military intervention enabled the Japanese to bring a widening area of China under their control after 1931, and especially after 1937. By the capture of Hankow in 1939, they forced the Chinese Nationalists to establish a new capital at **Chungking** (p. 1122). At the same time, the outbreak of war in Europe compelled the British, French, and Russian governments to concentrate their forces in that quarter, and left the United States the only Great Power in a position to oppose Japanese expansion.

Dec. 31. Russia and Japan reached an accord concerning the renewal of fishing rights and the settlement of debt claims between Russia and Manchukuo.

1940, Jan. 14. Admiral **Mitsumasa Yonai** formed a new Japanese cabinet.

Jan. 26. The **Trade Treaty between the United States and Japan,** first negotiated in 1911, expired. The State Department informed the Japanese government that commercial arrangements would continue on a day-to-day basis.

Mar. 30. The Japanese supported the establishment of a **puppet government under Wang Ching-wei** at Nanking to administer the areas of China under their control.

Apr. 17. Secretary of State **Cordell Hull** warned the Japanese that the United States would oppose any attempt to change the *status quo* of the **Netherlands East Indies** by other than peaceful means.

June 9. Russia and Japan reached an accord regarding the disputed frontier of Manchukuo.

June 25. With the **collapse of France** under the German invasion, the Japanese demanded the right to land forces in **French Indo-China.** Japanese warships arrived at several ports there.

July 16. Prince **Fumumaro Konoye** became Japanese premier with a mandate to organize the government on totalitarian lines.

July 18. The British government closed the **Burma Road.** This was the main route by which the Chinese Nationalist armies under Gen. **Chiang K'ai-shek** could obtain foreign war material. The Japanese agreed to discuss peace terms with the Chinese Nationalist government.

Aug. 9. British garrisons at Shanghai and in northern China were withdrawn.

Sept. 4. Secretary of State Hull warned the Japanese government that aggressive moves against Indo-China would have an unfortunate effect upon public opinion in the United States.

Sept. 26. After the French government at Vichy had conceded the use of three airfields and several ports in Indo-China, Japanese forces began the occupation of Indo-China and crossed into China 120 miles from Hanoi. The United States government placed an embargo on the export of iron and steel scrap after Oct. 15 to countries (except Great Britain) outside the Western Hemisphere. The Japanese ambassador at Washington described this (Oct. 8) as an "unfriendly act."

Sept. 27. JAPAN JOINED ITALY AND GERMANY in a ten-year tripartite pact "for the creation of conditions which would promote the prosperity of their peoples." The pact also contained mutual pledges of total aid in the event any of the partners became engaged in war with a country not yet a belligerent.

Oct. 18. Great Britain reopened the Burma Road.

1941, Jan. 31. Under Japanese auspices an armistice was arranged to end hostilities which had broken out between Thailand and French Indo-China. The Japanese obtained rice, rubber, coal and minerals from Indo-China, and confirmed their military occupation.

Mar. 11. France and Thailand concluded a convention, later signed at Tokyo (May 9) whereby Thailand acquired the section of Laos Province west of the Mekong River, three-fourths of the Campong-Thom Province, and territory in northern Cambodia.

Apr. 13. JAPAN AND RUSSIA CONCLUDED A NEUTRALITY PACT.

July 26. All Japanese credits in the United States were "frozen" by a presidential decree. Great Britain took similar action regarding Japanese assets in that country. All armed forces in the Philippine Islands were placed under the control of the United States, with Gen. Douglas MacArthur as Commander-in-Chief in the Far East.

Aug. 17. President Roosevelt warned the Japanese ambassador, Admiral Nomura, that any further policy of military domination in Asia by the Japanese would force the United States "to take immediately any and all steps necessary"

to safeguard legitimate American rights and interests. Prime Minister Winston Churchill declared a week later (Aug. 24) that Great Britain would support the United States if negotiations with Japan failed.

Oct. 17. Prince Fumumaro Konoye resigned as Japanese premier and was replaced by Gen. Hideki Tojo.

Nov. 17. Ambassador Joseph C. Grew at Tokyo cabled a warning to the United States that the Japanese might make a sudden attack.

Nov. 20. At Washington Admiral Nomura and a special Japanese envoy, Saburo Kurusu, proposed that the United States and Japan reopen trade relations and co-operate in securing the commodities of the Netherlands East Indies.

Nov. 26. Secretary Hull proposed as a basis of agreement that the Japanese withdraw their forces from China and Indo-China, recognize the territorial integrity of these countries and accept the Chinese Nationalist government. The United States and Japan could then negotiate a liberal trade treaty. Mr. Kurusu declared such proposals practically "put an end to the negotiations." Three days later (Nov. 29), Secretary Hull informed the British ambassador that diplomatic conversations between the United States and Japan had virtually broken down.

Dec. 6. President Roosevelt cabled a personal message to the Emperor of Japan urging him to use his influence to preserve peace.

Dec. 7. JAPANESE ATTACK ON PEARL HARBOR (p. 1167).

After December 7, when Japan was at war with the United States and Great Britain, the conflict in China was overshadowed by developments in the Pacific and the East Indies. Japanese conquest of Burma (1942) closed the Burma Road, the last practicable route by which military supplies could reach Chungking, for only a few tons a month could be flown in by air. Chinese armies remained in the field, and the Japanese kept an army of 1,000,000 men as an occupying force to protect towns and railway lines. The ultimate fate of these Japanese armies in Asia, and their communications with the Japanese home islands, depended upon the outcome of the war at sea.

15. THE WAR IN THE PACIFIC, 1941-1945

1941, Dec. 7. The JAPANESE SEA AND AIR FORCES LAUNCHED A SURPRISE ATTACK ON THE UNITED STATES BASE AT PEARL HARBOR, HAWAII, ON THE PHILIPPINES, and against British forces in **Hongkong** and **Malaya.** The United States forces were caught unprepared. At Hawaii five battleships and three cruisers were sunk or seriously damaged, three battleships less severely damaged, many smaller vessels sunk or crippled, and 177 aircraft destroyed. The casualties included 2343 dead, 876 missing, and 1272 injured.

Dec. 8. THE UNITED STATES DECLARED WAR ON JAPAN. Japanese air and naval forces attacked **Guam** and **Wake Island.** Resistance on Guam ended Dec. 13 and on Wake Island Dec. 20. **Great Britain declared war on Japan.**

Dec. 10. The British battleships *Prince of Wales* and *Repulse*, which had been dispatched to Singapore, were sunk by Japanese aircraft off the Malay coast.

Dec. 11. GERMANY AND ITALY DECLARED WAR ON THE UNITED STATES.

Dec. 21. A ten-year treaty of alliance was signed at Bangkok **between Japan and Thailand.** The Thai government agreed to aid Japan and declared war (Jan. 25, 1942) against Great Britain and the United States.

Dec. 25. British forces at **Hongkong** surrendered to the Japanese.

1942, Jan. 2. **Manila and Cavite were captured** by the Japanese. United States and Philippine forces fortified their position on **Bataan Peninsula** and held out until April 9. The island fort of **Corregidor** at the entrance to Manila Bay did not fall until May 6.

Jan. 11. Japanese forces commenced an **occupation of the Netherlands East Indies,** landing on Celebes, at Rabaul (Jan. 23), New Ireland (Jan. 25), the Solomon Islands (Jan. 26), and Amboina (Jan. 31).

Jan. 24-27. Allied forces sank five Japanese transports in a naval engagement in the **Macassar Straits.**

Feb. 15. Japanese forces, which had penetrated Malaya, captured **Singapore** from the north by land, taking 60,000 prisoners.

Feb. 27-Mar. 1. Battle of the Java Sea. Naval units of the United Nations were largely destroyed, opening the way for the Japanese conquest of the East Indies. Batavia fell on Mar. 6.

Mar. 7. The British evacuated **Rangoon** and the Japanese rapidly occupied Burma. **Lashio** was taken (Apr. 30), closing the Burma Road at that point, and **Mandalay** fell on May 2.

Mar. 9. The conquest of **Java** was virtually completed by the Japanese, who had won **Timor** (Feb. 20) also. The growing threat to Australia was checked in the jungles of New Guinea, and Gen. **Douglas MacArthur** assumed command of the combined Allied forces in the southwest Pacific (Mar. 17).

May 5. To avert possible Japanese penetration, British forces landed at **Diego Suarez,** naval base on the north end of Madagascar, and proceeded to occupy this French colony, entering the capital, Tananarive, on Sept. 23.

May 7. BATTLE OF THE CORAL SEA. Allied naval and air power frustrated a possible Japanese invasion of Australia or the New Hebrides by destroying 100,000 tons of Japanese shipping between New Guinea and the Solomon Islands.

June 4-7. A Japanese naval force attacked **Midway Island** and was dispersed with heavy losses by United States naval and air units.

June 12. Japanese invaders occupied **Attu** in the Aleutian Islands and later landed on **Kiska.** The Japanese tide of conquest was at its height, coinciding with the German drive for the Caucasian oil fields.

July 9. The Chinese Nationalist armies won a major success over the Japanese in Kiangsi Province.

Aug. 7. United States Marines landed in the Solomon Islands. **Tulagi** and Japanese airfields on **Guadalcanal** were captured.

Nov. 12. A three-day naval battle in the Solomon Islands ended in a victory for United States forces. One Japanese battleship and five cruisers were reported sunk, and twelve transports destroyed.

BROWN, FRANCIS. *The War in Maps.* New York. Oxford Press. 194'

1943, Mar. 4. Allied air squadrons destroyed a Japanese convoy approaching New Guinea.

July 1. Opening a concerted offensive in the South Pacific, Allied forces captured **Rendova Island** (July 2) while Australian troops linked up with American troops at **Salamaua** (July 3). The Japanese base and airfield at **Munda** on New Georgia Island fell Aug. 7. In September a Japanese force of 20,000 was encircled near **Lae** (Sept. 6–7), the airfield at Salamaua captured (Sept. 13), and **Finschhafen** occupied (Oct. 3). Allied forces disembarked on **Bougainville Island** (Oct. 31). Landing on the **Gilbert Islands** (Nov. 22), United States forces crushed Japanese resistance in three days' fighting, and Marines captured the important air base at **Cape Gloucester** on Dec. 31.

1944, Feb. 2. Invasion of the Marshall Islands. Roi was seized by the United States troops (Feb. 3), **Kwajalein** (Feb. 6), and an air base in **Einwetok** (Feb. 20). On March 1 American troops landed on the **Admiralty Islands**, and new landings were achieved in **New Guinea** (Apr. 24) at **Hollandia** and **Aitape**. The Schouten group was invaded (May 28) and the **Marianas** (June 16).

June 16. United States Superfortress bombing planes raided the Japanese home island of **Kyushu,** opening a campaign of destructive attacks on Japanese cities which ended only with the Japanese capitulation.

Aug. 11. The recapture of **Guam** was completed. On the Indian frontier the last Japanese invaders were driven back to Burma.

Sept. 14. American forces disembarked on **Morotai** in the Molucca Islands, and on the **Palau Islands** in the Carolinas (Sept. 15).

Oct. 19. United States invasion groups, commanded by Gen. Douglas MacArthur, **landed on the island of Leyte,** opening the campaign for the reconquest of the Philippines.

Oct. 21-22. **SECOND BATTLE OF THE PHILIPPINE SEA.** The Japanese fleet, having failed to halt the invasion, withdrew from Philippine waters (Oct. 25). It had suffered 40 ships sunk, 46 damaged, and 405 planes destroyed. More United States forces were promptly landed on the island of **Samos** (Oct. 26).

Nov. 26. A new phase of the Pacific War opened with the initiation of raids on Japan by United States land based B-29 bombers operating from **Saipan** in the Mariana Islands.

1945, Feb. 19-Mar. 17. The stubborn and protracted **battle for Iwo Jima** gave the United States air forces a base 750 miles from Yokohama, at a cost of 19,938 American casualties, including 4198 dead.

Mar. 21. United States carrier aircraft, penetrating Japanese inland waters, attacked principal units of the Japanese fleet, damaged 15 warships and destroyed 475 planes. No United States ship was lost.

Apr. 30. In Southeast Asia the 14th British Imperial Army (Admiral Lord **Louis Mountbatten**), with support from United States and Chinese forces, completed the destruction in fifteen months of the Japanese 15th, 28th, and 33d armies. Total Japanese casualties were set (May 5) at **347,000.**

Apr. 1. United States Marines and army troops invaded Okinawa. An attempt by the Japanese fleet to check this amphibious operation resulted in the sinking by American aircraft (Apr. 7) of the Japanese battleship *Yamato* (45,000 tons), 2 cruisers, and 3 destroyers. The last bitter resistance on Okinawa did not end until June 21, but the island provided an airbase 325 miles from Japanese cities.

May-Aug. In the greatest air offensive in history United States land-based and carrier-based aircraft destroyed or immobilized the remnants of the Japanese navy, shattered Japanese industry, and curtailed Japanese sea communications by submarine and air attack and extensive minefields. United States battleships moved in to shell densely populated cities with impunity and the **Twentieth Air Force** dropped 40,000 tons of bombs on Japanese industrial centers in one month.

After the collapse of Germany in May (p. 1165) the Japanese were left without allies, and the British and American resources in men and material were redirected toward the Pacific theater of war. Japanese strength was already half-broken and Japanese morale was beginning to disintegrate when two terrible strokes within one week hastened the conclusion of the war.

Aug. 6. AN ATOMIC BOMB, secretly prepared by British and American scientists, was dropped on the Japanese city of **Hiroshima** with obliterating effect. The city was more than half destroyed.

Aug. 8. SOVIET RUSSIA DECLARED WAR ON JAPAN and commenced a powerful invasion of **Manchuria.**

Aug. 10. The Japanese cabinet decided to make an **offer of surrender.** The Allied terms of capitulation were communicated to Tokyo and accepted four days later (Aug. 14). **United States** forces of occupation landed in Japan on Aug. 26.

Sept. 2. The **FORMAL TERMS OF SURRENDER WERE SIGNED**

by the Japanese officials and military leaders on board the U.S.S. *Missouri* in Tokyo Bay. Capitulation terms for Japanese forces in China, estimated at 1,000,000 men, were signed in **Nanking** (Sept. 9) by Japanese commanders and representatives of Generalissimo **Chiang** K'ai-shek.

16. THE ORGANIZATION OF PEACE

The **League of Nations,** formed at Versailles in 1919, failed to curb powerful aggressors or to protect its weaker members from attack. It was never a well-balanced, truly supra-national league, and proved itself unfitted to deal with economic problems or to enforce its decisions. When the Second World War opened in 1939, the League of Nations had lost almost all its prestige and influence.

The **international anarchy,** repudiation of treaties, acts of aggression, and final outbreak of a general war, which marked the 1930's, brought home to peaceful nations the need for an organization better adapted to adjust international tensions and disputes.

Three projects for international federation took form in the war years 1939–45. In Europe, Germany, Italy, and their satellite states forged an anti-Comintern, anti-democratic *bloc* which Adolf Hitler called his **"New Order."** In Asia and the East Indies the Japanese extended their power over a widening area, which they termed a **"Co-prosperity Sphere"** and in which they promulgated the doctrine of Asia for the Asiatics. Both the German and the Japanese hegemony had contracted and finally collapsed in defeat by the summer of 1945.

The **third international federation** formed in the war years came to be known as the **United Nations Organization.** It was based ideologically upon the foundations of the **Atlantic Charter** (p. 1137), structurally upon the wartime solidarity of the "Big Three," Britain, Russia, and the United States, and financially upon the credits (43 billion dollars) made available to nations which opposed the Axis by the Lend-Lease policy of the United States government. The victory of the United Nations, achieved in large measure through the effective mobilization of world resources, left their leaders in a position to write the peace treaties.

1943, Nov. 9. The **United Nations Relief and Rehabilitation Administration** held its first session at Atlantic City. This

international body, organized by the representatives of 44 nations, was created to aid countries which had been subjugated by the Axis powers. Its staff was intended to form in effect "an international civil service."

1944, Apr. A **United Nations Organization for Educational and Cultural Reconstruction** was proposed by the ministers of education from the Allied countries, meeting in London.

July 1-22. A **United Nations Monetary and Financial Conference** (*Bretton Woods Conference*) met for three weeks of discussion. To improve world economic conditions, the delegates of the United Nations proposed to create an **International Monetary Fund** and an **International Bank for Reconstruction and Development,** the first with a credit of $8,800,000,000, the second with a capital of $10,000,000,000. The major purpose was to avert currency disorders and stabilize exchange rates, and the plans, worked out by the financial experts of 44 nations, were referred to the governments concerned for approval.

Sept. 16-26. The Council of the **United Nations Relief and Rehabilitation Administration** held its second session, at Montreal. The allotment of $50,000,000 to Italy, partly for medical supplies, marked the first extension of aid by the United Nations to a former enemy country. Plans were laid to provide for a budget of $11,500,000 for 1945, by assessing member states. Whether UNRRA supplies and administrators would be admitted to countries liberated by the Russian armies remained undecided.

Oct. 9. Dumbarton Oaks Conference. Delegates representing the United States, the British Commonwealth, and the Soviet Union, after meeting from Aug. 21 to Sept. 27, published proposals for a permanent international organization to be known as the **United Nations.** The aim of the new society of nations was the preservation of world peace and security.

1945, Apr. 25-June 26. SAN FRANCISCO CONFERENCE. Delegates of 50 nations met at San Francisco to complete a **Charter for the United Nations Organization.** A preliminary draft was submitted to the Conference on June 22 by the United States Secretary of State **Edward R. Stettinius.** It provided for four organs in the new body: (1) a **General Assembly** as the major policy shaping forum; (2) a **Security Council** to supervise military and political problems; (3) an **Economic and Social Council** to deal with problems of economic and social conflict; and (4) an **International Court of Justice** for the adjustment of international disputes. The administrative work of the United Nations Organization was to be handled by a general **Secretariat** directed by a Secretary General.

July 17-Aug. 2. POTSDAM CONFERENCE. President **Harry S. Truman** for the United States, Prime Minister **Winston Churchill** for Great Britain, and Generalissimo **J. V. Stalin** for the Union of Soviet Socialist Republics met in Berlin to confer on plans for re-establishing peace. After July 28, Mr. **Clement R. Attlee,** head of the new British Labor Cabinet, replaced Mr. Churchill at the Conference. An agreement was reached that a **Council of Foreign Ministers,** representing the United States, Great Britain, Russia, France, and China, should be established to continue the task of drafting peace settlements. This Council held its first session in London (Sept. 11).

For Germany the decisions reached at the Potsdam Conference implied: (1) disarmament and demilitarization; (2) dissolution of National Socialist institutions; (3) trial of war criminals; (4) encouragement of democratic ideals; (5) restoration of local self-government and democratic political parties; (6) freedom of speech, press, and religion, subject to the requirements of military security.

Economic restrictions drafted by the Conference for Germany included: (1) prohibition of the manufacture of war materials and implements of war; (2) controlled production of metals, chemicals, and machinery essential to war; (3) decentralization of German cartels, syndicates, and trusts; (4) emphasis upon agriculture and peaceful domestic industries; (5) control of exports, imports, and scientific research. The methods whereby the victors would enforce these conditions were to be worked out in detail later.

The Conference further ordained "that Germany be compelled to compensate to the greatest possible extent for the loss and suffering that she has caused to the United Nations. . . ." The members of the Conference agreed in principle on the disposal of the German navy and merchant marine, but in this matter likewise the details were not worked out.

Peace treaties with Finland, Bulgaria, Hungary, Rumania, and Italy were to be drawn up as promptly as possible.

Sept. 2. FORMAL TERMS OF SURRENDER were signed by the Japanese civil and military envoys at Tokyo. The Japanese home islands were placed under the rule of a United States army of occupation, but the Emperor remained at the head of the state and the Japanese political and police officials continued to fulfill their functions. The high command and the military organizations were progressively disbanded. American forces also occupied island possessions regained or newly captured in the Pacific Ocean.

Korea was placed under Soviet and United States occupation, pending establishment of a Korean democratic government. The **Kurile Islands** and the southern part of **Sakhalin** were ceded to Russia, **Outer Mongolia** was recognized as part of the Soviet sphere of control, and Russia shared with China the facilities and supervision of **Port Arthur** and the Manchurian railroads. China regained sovereignty over **Inner Mongolia** and **Manchuria,** as well as the islands of **Formosa** and **Hainan. Hongkong** was reoccupied by the British, who likewise accepted the formal surrender at Singapore (Sept. 12) of all Japanese forces (585,000 men) in Southeast Asia and the East Indies.

VII. THE POST—WAR WORLD

A. THE UNITED NATIONS

1945, Oct. 24. The United Nations came into formal existence with the ratification of its Charter by 29 nations. The seat of the United Nations Organization was to be located in the United States.

1946, Jan. 10. The first session of the U.N. General Assembly opened in London, 51 nations attending. **Paul H. Spaak** of Belgium was elected its first president.

Jan. 12. The membership of the Security Council was completed with the election of the six non-permanent members (Brazil, Poland, Australia, Mexico, the Netherlands, and Egypt) to join the five permanent members (China, France, the United States, Great Britain, and Russia).

Feb. 1. **Trygve Lie** of Norway was elected **Secretary General** of the United Nations.

Apr. 18. The Assembly of the **League of Nations** dissolved itself after a last meeting at Geneva and transferred its assets to the United Nations.

Dec. 11. The General Assembly decided to bar **Franco Spain** from all U.N. activities and recommended that members break off diplomatic relations with Madrid.

Dec. 30. The **Atomic Energy Commission**, with Russia and Poland abstaining, approved the United States plan for far-reaching atomic control and inspection.

1947, Feb. 18. Soviet amendments to this plan opposed the degree of international control recommended in the first report of the **Atomic Energy Commission**. Subsequent efforts of the Security Council to find a plan for atomic control failed because of Soviet veto.

Apr. 2. The Security Council approved the appointment of the **United States** as **trustee for the Pacific Islands** formerly under Japanese mandate.

Aug. 1. The Security Council called for a cease-fire in **Indonesia** and formed a Committee of Good Offices to help settle the dispute between the Dutch and Indonesians.

Sept. 30. **Pakistan** and **Yemen** were admitted to membership.

Oct. 21. The General Assembly adopted a resolution calling on **Greece** and her northern neighbors (**Yugoslavia, Albania, Bulgaria**) to settle their disputes by peaceful means. A **Balkan Committee** was set up to observe the compliance of the four governments.

Nov. 14. The General Assembly recognized **Korea's** claim to **independence** and laid plans for the establishment of a national government and the withdrawal of occupation forces.

Nov. 29. Following the majority report of its **Special Committee on Palestine**, the General Assembly adopted a plan for the **partition of Palestine** into independent Arab and Jewish states. Jerusalem was to be placed under U.N. trusteeship.

1948, Jan. 20. The Security Council set up a Commission to settle the conflict between **India** and **Pakistan** over **Jammu** and **Kashmir**. Extended negotiations finally led to an arrangement for a plebiscite and a cease-fire (Dec. 23–25).

Apr. 19. **Burma** was admitted to membership.

May 20. **Count Folke Bernadotte**, President of the Swedish Red Cross, was appointed **United Nations Mediator in Palestine**. He was assassinated by Jewish terrorists on Sept. 17.

July 15. The Security Council ordered a truce in Palestine. While this did not entirely end hostilities, it helped prevent full-fledged and prolonged warfare.

Aug. 12. The **Commission for Conventional Armaments** decided that existing conditions prevented a program for the reduction and control of traditional armaments.

Oct. 25. The **Soviet Union** vetoed a proposal made by the non-permanent members of the Security Council for the settlement of the **Berlin blockade.**

Dec. 9-10. The General Assembly adopted the **Convention on the Prevention and Punishment of Genocide** and the **Universal Declaration of Human Rights.**

Dec. 12. The Assembly endorsed the government of **South Korea** as the only lawfully elected one and set up a Commission to aid in the unification of the country.

1949, Jan. 28. Continued warfare in **Indonesia** brought forth renewed attempts by the Security Council to halt hostilities and achieve a final settlement of the Indonesian question. Such a settlement was reached between the Netherlands and the Republic of Indonesia on Nov. 2.

Apr. 9. The **International Court of Justice,** in its first decision, held **Albania** responsible for the explosions in the **Corfu Channel** (p. 1189) and awarded damages to Great Britain.

May 11. **Israel** was admitted to membership in the United Nations.

May 14. The Assembly invited **India, Pakistan,** and the **Union of South Africa** to discuss the question of alleged discrimination against nationals of Indian origin in South Africa.

July 29. The **Atomic Energy Commission** voted to end its deliberations until a basis for agreement among the major powers could be found.

Dec. 5. The Assembly approved proposals by the **Commission for Conventional Armaments** that member states submit full information on their armaments and armed forces.

Dec. 8. The General Assembly, to promote **international stability in the Far East,** called upon all states to respect the political independence of **China** and the right of the Chinese people to choose their own political institutions.

Dec. 9. The General Assembly restated its proposal to place **Jerusalem** under a permanent United Nations régime.

1950, Jan. 3. The **Soviet Union,** after vainly trying to have Nationalist China excluded from the United Nations, **withdrew from all U.N. bodies in which Nationalist China was represented.**

June 25. Upon outbreak of the **KO-REAN WAR,** the Security Council called for immediate cessation of hostilities and withdrawal of North Korean forces. When the North Korean government failed to comply,

July 7. The Security Council set up a unified **United Nations Command** under the United States, to render aid to South Korea. This action was subsequently endorsed by 53 member nations, many of which contributed military or economic aid to the United Nations cause.

Sept. 28. **Indonesia** became the 60th member of the United Nations. Fourteen additional applicants (Austria, Ceylon, Finland, Ireland, Italy, Jordan, Republic of Korea, Portugal, Nepal, Albania, Bulgaria, Hungary, Mongolian People's Republic, Rumania) failed to gain the unanimous support of the Security Council, prerequisite for membership.

Oct. 7. The Assembly adopted a resolution calling for a unified, independent, and democratic **Korea,** and set up a **U.N. Commission for the Unification and Rehabilitation of Korea.**

Nov. 2. In a far-reaching resolution, the General Assembly provided for immediate emergency action, in case the Security Council, for lack of unanimity, should fail to function. In such a case the Assembly was to be summoned on 24 hours' notice, to decide on collective measures, including the use of armed force.

Nov. 4. The **U.N. Assembly rescinded its anti-Franco resolution** of Dec. 11, 1946, thus facilitating Spain's admission into the Western, anti-Communist camp.

B. EUROPE

1. INTERNATIONAL AFFAIRS

1946, July 29-Oct. 15. A PEACE CON-
FERENCE of the 21 nations which
waged war against the Axis in Europe
met at Paris to discuss the draft treaties for peace with Italy, Rumania, Hungary, Bulgaria, and Finland. These
treaties had been prepared by the Foreign
Ministers' Council of Great Britain,
France, the United States, and the Soviet
Union.

1947, Feb. 10. The Peace Treaties were
signed in Paris. Italy lost four
small border regions to France, her Adriatic
islands and most of Venezia Giulia to Yugoslavia, and the Dodecanese Islands to
Greece. She also renounced sovereignty
over her North African colonies and agreed
to the creation of the Free Territory of
Trieste. Her armed forces were reduced to
300,000 men and she agreed to pay $360
million in reparations. Rumania lost Bessarabia and northern Bukovina to the Soviet Union, but received back all of Transylvania. Hungary was left with her 1938
borders, except for a minor frontier rectification in favor of Czechoslovakia. Bulgaria retained the southern Dobruja. Finland ceded the port of Petsamo to the
Soviet Union and granted the Russians
a fifty-year lease of a naval base at Porkkala.

Mar. 4. France and Great Britain signed
a Treaty of Alliance at Dunkirk.

Mar. 10-Apr. 24. A meeting of the
Council of Foreign Ministers in
Moscow failed to make progress in
the drafting of peace treaties for
Austria and Germany.

July 12-15. Sixteen western European
nations met at Paris to discuss the
proposals for European recovery made by
U.S. Secretary of State Marshall (Marshall
Plan). A Committee of European Economic Co-operation was set up to direct the
drafting of a European Recovery Program
(ERP). The Soviet Union and her satellites earlier had refused to participate in
such a program, since it depended on American assistance.

Sept. A conference at Warsaw of the
Communist parties of Yugoslavia,
Bulgaria, Rumania, Hungary, Poland,
France, Czechoslovakia, Italy, and the
Soviet Union set up the Communist In-
formation Bureau (COMINFORM), to co-
ordinate the activities of European Com-
munism.

Oct. 29. Belgium, the Netherlands, and
Luxembourg ratified their agreement for a customs union.

Nov. 25-Dec. 16. A London Conference
of the Big Four foreign ministers
again failed to settle the German problem,
largely because of Soviet insistence on
$10 billion in reparations from Germany
and on four-power control of the Ruhr
region.

1948, Feb. 2. The United States and Italy
signed a ten-year treaty of friendship, commerce, and navigation.

Mar. 17. Great Britain, France, Belgium, the Netherlands, and Luxembourg signed the BRUSSELS TREATY,
a fifty-year alliance against armed attack in
Europe, providing for economic, social, and
military co-operation. A Consultative
Council was set up to co-ordinate the policies of the five signatories, and a Permanent
Military Committee was established
in London under the authority of the
Council.

Apr. 16. The nations behind the European Recovery Program met at
Paris and set up their permanent
machinery for economic co-operation, the Organization for European Economic Co-operation
(OEEC).

May 7. The International Committee of
the Movements for European
Unity convened the first Congress
of Europe in The Hague, under
the honorary chairmanship of
Winston Churchill, to discuss
plans for European Union.

June 28. The Cominform expelled Yugoslavia from membership for doctrinal errors and hostility to the
Soviet Union.

July 30-Aug. 18. A Danube Conference
of ten nations met at Belgrade to
discuss the future status of the Danube. A
new Convention, to replace that of 1921,
was introduced by the Soviet delegate. It
called for a Danube Commission confined
to the countries touching the river, and

hence was opposed by Great Britain, France, and the United States. The new Commission was set up on **Nov. 11, 1949,** over the protests of the three western powers.

Sept. 20. The **treaty of friendship and non-aggression** between **Spain** and **Portugal** was extended for ten years.

1949, Jan. A Council for Mutual Economic Assistance was formed in Moscow to further economic co-operation among the Soviet Union and her eastern European satellites. It was seen as a Communist reply to the European Recovery Program.

Mar. 13. Belgium, the **Netherlands,** and **Luxembourg** concluded an agreement providing for full **economic union** at an early date. **France** and **Italy** reached a similar agreement on Mar. 26.

Apr. 4. The **NORTH ATLANTIC TREATY** was signed in Washington by the foreign ministers of Great Britain, France, Belgium, the Netherlands, Luxembourg, Italy, Portugal, Denmark, Iceland, Norway, the United States, and Canada. It provided for mutual assistance against aggression within the North Atlantic area and for close collaboration in matters of military training, arms production, and strategic planning, under the direction of a **North Atlantic Council.**

May 5. The Statute of the **Council of Europe,** establishing an executive **Committee of Ministers** and a **Consultative Assembly** was signed in London by delegates from Belgium, Denmark, France, Great Britain, Ireland, Italy, Luxembourg, the Netherlands, Norway, and Sweden. It was subsequently signed by Greece, Iceland, and Turkey. **Strasbourg** was designated as the seat of the Council.

Sept. 27. The **Soviet Union denounced its treaty of friendship with Yugoslavia.** Her satellites subsequently followed the Russian example.

1950, Jan. 6. The **North Atlantic Council** approved the "master defense plan" prepared by the North Atlantic Defense Committee.

Jan. 29. In a series of bilateral agreements, the **United States agreed to provide arms and equipment** to its eleven associates under the **North Atlantic Treaty.**

Mar. 30-Apr. 1. The Committee of Ministers of the **Council of Europe decided to invite West Germany and the Saar** as associate members.

May 9. French foreign minister Robert Schuman proposed the **Schuman Plan** for the integration of the coal and steel industries of Western Europe.

Sept. 12-19. A conference in New York between the foreign ministers of the **United States, France, and Great Britain, agreed on a more liberal policy toward Western Germany** and the inclusion of a German contingent in a unified Western defense force.

Oct. 20-21. A **Conference at Prague,** attended by Soviet Premier Molotov and the foreign ministers of East Germany, Poland, Bulgaria, Hungary, and Rumania, **denounced the New York decisions of Sept. 19,** opposed the remilitarization of Germany, and called for German unification and a German peace treaty.

Dec. 18-19. General **Dwight D. Eisenhower** was appointed commander in chief of the North Atlantic Treaty forces, with headquarters in Paris.

Dec. 20. The **Consultative Council of the Brussels Treaty Powers decided to merge its military establishment with** that of the **North Atlantic Treaty Organization.**

2. THE BRITISH ISLES

a. GREAT BRITAIN

Post-war developments in Great Britain were shaped most decisively by the outcome of the national election of July 5, 1945, which brought a resounding victory to the Labor Party (p. 1145). The new government under Prime Minister **Clement R. Attlee** immediately embarked on an ambitious program of socialization, the ultimate aim of which was to make Britain a Socialist state. A brief period of post-war optimism was followed by an extended régime of economic austerity, due chiefly to the profound dislocation of Britain's economy as a result of the war. To facilitate reconversion to peace-time production, demobilization of manpower and industry was carried out only gradually. On

1945, Oct. 15. The House of Commons voted to extend the government's wartime emergency powers for five years. To make up for

the cessation of Lend-Lease, which
came as a deep shock to Britain's
economy,

Dec. 6. The **United States** granted a
loan of $3.75 billion to Great Brit-
ain. **Canada** subsequently provided a loan of $1.25 billion. Both
these loans became exhausted,
however, by the end of 1947, due
to high prices on the American
market.

1946, Feb. 13. Parliament repealed the
Trades Disputes Act of 1927,
which had made certain strikes
illegal and had hampered the political activities of labor unions.

Feb. 14. The **Bank of England** was
brought under public ownership.

May-July. In a burst of socialist legislation, Parliament passed a bill providing for the **nationalization of the coal
industry,** a **National Insurance Bill** (consolidating existing schemes of social insurance and extending them to a larger section
of the population), a **National Health Service Bill** (to make free medical services
available to everyone) and a **Cable and
Wireless Act,** nationalizing imperial communications.

July 21. Britain's export difficulties and
the world shortage of wheat com-
bined to necessitate the introduction of **bread rationing.** This was
followed by restrictions on most
other staple foods.

Oct. 30. Parliament approved the co-
ordination of the three armed
services under a **Defense Committee,**
headed by a Minister of Defense (**A. V.
Alexander**). In view of continued British
commitments abroad, the demobilization of
the armed forces was slowed down.

1947, Jan. 1. The **nationalization of the
coal mines** went into effect.

Jan.-Apr. A serious **coal shortage,** made
worse by severe weather condi-
tions, led to drastic fuel restrictions and
curtailment of industrial production. At
the same time, Parliament continued its
socialization program by adopting the
Transport Act, affecting railroads, road
transport, and inland waterways, the **Electricity Act,** nationalizing the electricity supply industry, and the **Town and Country
Planning Act,** which set up a new planning
system to regulate the growth of communities.

Mar. 4. An **Anglo-French Treaty of
Alliance** was signed at Dunkirk.

Nov. 1. **Municipal elections** to one-third
of the borough councils brought
heavy losses to Labor and simultaneous
gains to the Conservatives. Parliamentary

by-elections, on the other hand, testified
to the continued popularity of the Labor
government.

Nov. 20. **Princess Elizabeth** and **Philip
Mountbatten,** Duke of Edinburgh,
were married in Westminster Abbey.

1948, Jan. 1. The British railways passed
into public ownership.

Mar. 17. A 50-year **Treaty of Mutual
Assistance** between **Britain,
France, Belgium, the Netherlands,**
and **Luxembourg** was signed at
Brussels.

Apr. 1. The **British Electrical Authority**
took over the electricity industry.

July 30. The **British Nationality Act** received royal assent. It gave each
Dominion the right to determine
who were its citizens, while at the
same time conferring the status of
British subjects upon all citizens
of the Commonwealth.

Dec. The **National Service Act** con-
scripted all men between the ages
of eighteen and twenty-six.

1949, Feb. 1. Rationing of clothing was
discontinued, while meat, dairy
products, and sugar continued to
be on the list of restricted items.

June-July. A major **dock strike,** which,
according to the government, was
Communist-inspired, led to the
proclamation of a state of emergency before it was finally settled.

Sept. 18. To meet the rapid decline of
British exports and to remedy the
growing dollar deficit, the **British
government devalued the pound
sterling** from $4.03 to $2.80. This
set in motion a widespread devaluation of other European currencies.

Nov. 24. The **Iron and Steel Bill,** calling
for the nationalization of these key
industries, passed both Houses of
Parliament, after raising considerable opposition. It was not to go
into effect until 1951.

Dec. 16. Despite opposition from the
House of Lords, the **Parliament
Bill,** restricting the powers of the
Upper House to veto legislation,
was enacted into law.

**1950, Feb. 13. PARLIAMENTARY ELEC-
TIONS** reduced the Labor Party's
majority from 148 in 1945 to 7 in 1950. The
final count gave Labor 315 seats, the Conservatives and their allies 297, and the Liberals 9. The government of Prime Minister
Clement Attlee remained in office, although
its position was precarious, in view of its
slim majority. As a result, few controver-

Allied zones of occupation in Germany — American, British, Russian, French

CENTRAL EUROPE, 1950

sial measures were introduced into Parliament.

June 25. The outbreak of **war in Korea** found Great Britain on the side of the United States and the United Nations against the North Korean aggressors. She subsequently contributed naval and ground forces to the United Nations cause and embarked on increased defense production and expansion of her armed services.

b. IRELAND

1945, May 3. Prime Minister **De Valera** expressed official condolences to the German Minister in Dublin upon Hitler's death.

June 4. Elections in **Northern Ireland** favored continued Irish partition.

June 25. Dr. Douglas Hyde retired and **SEAN T. O'KELLY BECAME SECOND PRESIDENT OF EIRE.**

1948, Feb. 4. In a General Election for the Dail, **De Valera's Fianna Fail Party** lost its majority.

Feb. 18. James A. Costello of the Fine Gael Party was nominated Prime Minister.

Dec. 21. President O'Kelly signed the **Republic of Ireland Bill** calling for complete independence of Ireland at an early date.

1949, Feb. 8. Irish government declared that participation in the **North Atlantic Pact** was impossible so long as Ireland remained divided.

Feb. 10. Elections in **Northern Ireland** showed that at least two-thirds of the population favored continued union with Great Britain.

Apr. 18. The **REPUBLIC OF IRELAND** was officially proclaimed in Dublin on the anniversary of the Easter Rebellion of 1916. King George VI sent his good wishes.

May 17. The British House of Commons adopted the **Ireland Bill**, recognizing the independence of the Republic, but affirming the position of Northern Ireland within the United Kingdom. This provision met with protest from the Republic of Ireland.

1950, Jan. 26. Ireland concluded a **Treaty of Friendship, Commerce, and Navigation** with the United States.

3. THE LOW COUNTRIES

a. BELGIUM

Belgium, since her liberation, was governed by coalitions of her main political parties, with **Prince Charles** as Regent. Her major domestic issue was the return of **King Leopold**, which the Catholics favored and the Socialists opposed. Socialist Premier **Achille van Acker**, who had resigned when Leopold announced his intention to return, resumed office in July, 1945, thus causing the resignation of his Catholic colleagues. On July 17, 1945, Parliament passed a Bill making Leopold's return dependent upon parliamentary approval.

1946, Feb. 17. A General Election gave the Catholic **Christian Socialists** the largest number of votes; but continued disagreement over the future of the monarchy prevented the formation of a coalition cabinet. A number of predominantly Socialist cabinets, on the other hand, found themselves increasingly hampered by Catholic opposition and by growing dissent with their Communist members over economic issues.

1947, Mar. 19. Paul-Henri Spaak was able to form a coalition government of Catholics and Socialists, thus assuring greater stability in the handling of pressing economic problems.

Nov. 1. A **customs union** with Holland and Luxembourg (**Benelux**) became effective.

1949, June 26. In a General Election the Christian Socialists came within two seats of an absolute majority.

Aug. 10. Gaston Eyskens (Christian Socialist) formed a coalition cabinet with Liberal support. The Socialists refused to join.

1950, Mar. 12. A popular referendum voted 57.7 per cent in favor of King Leopold's return.

June 4. General Elections gave the Catholics an absolute majority, thus upholding the verdict of the referendum.

June 8. The first all-Catholic government in 30 years was formed by **Jean Duvieusart.**

July 22. King Leopold returned after six years of exile, greeted by violent protests from the Left, notably the Socialists. To avoid violence, Leopold decided to retire and abdicate when his son, Prince Baudouin, came of age in Sept. 1951.

Aug. 11. Prince Baudouin was invested with the royal powers as Prince Royal.

Aug. 18. Julien Lahaut, head of the Communist Party, was assassinated.

b. THE KINGDOM OF THE NETHERLANDS

The damage suffered by the Netherlands during the war was especially heavy, and large-scale famine was averted only by Allied aid.

1945, May 3. Queen Wilhelmina returned.

June 24. William Schermerhorn formed a coalition government.

1946, May 17-30. Parliamentary elections gave first place to the Catholic People's Party, with Socialist Labor running a close second. Dr. L. J. N. Beel formed a new coalition cabinet.

1948, Mar. 17. Signing of the Treaty of Brussels between Great Britain, France, and the Benelux countries.

July 7-8. General elections lost the government some support and a new coalition was formed under Labor's leader Drees.

Sept. 4. Queen Wilhelmina abdicated for reasons of health and was succeeded on Sept. 6 by QUEEN JULIANA.

1949, Aug. 3. Holland's Upper Chamber ratified the North Atlantic Treaty.

Dec. 27. Formal transfer of sovereignty to the United States of Indonesia.

4. FRANCE

The main tasks facing liberated France were the liquidation of her Vichy past and the establishment of the Fourth Republic.

1945, Aug. 15. Henri Philippe Pétain, head of the Vichy régime, was sentenced to death for treason, but his sentence was commuted to life imprisonment.

Oct. 9. Pierre Laval was sentenced to death for collaborating with the Germans. He was executed on Oct. 15.

Oct. 21. Elections for the Constituent Assembly showed a swing to the Left, the Communists receiving 152 seats, the Socialists 151, and the *Mouvement Républicain Populaire* 138.

Nov. 13. General Charles de Gaulle was unanimously elected President of the Provisional Government by the Assembly and on

Nov. 21, formed a cabinet of National Union.

1946, Jan. 20. President de Gaulle resigned abruptly because of continued Leftist opposition.

Jan. 22. Socialist Félix Gouin was elected President.

May 5. A Popular Referendum rejected the Draft Constitution which the Assembly had approved on Apr. 19.

June 2. Elections for a new Constituent Assembly resulted in a victory for the M.R.P., with the Communists in second and the Socialists in third place.

June 19. Georges Bidault was elected President of the Provisional Government.

Oct. 13. The revised Draft Constitution was adopted by 9,120,576 to 7,980,333 votes, with 7,938,884 abstentions. The new constitution closely resembled that of the Third Republic, except that the Senate was replaced by the Council of the Republic and France's relations to her overseas possessions were revised by creating the French Union.

Nov. 10. Elections for the National Assembly gave the Communists 186 seats, the M.R.P. 166, and the Socialists 103. The resulting deadlock between Communists and M.R.P. left a Socialist Premier as the only choice.

Dec. 16. After vainly trying to form a coalition, Léon Blum formed an all-Socialist cabinet.

1947, Jan. 16. PRESIDENCY OF VINCENT AURIOL. Blum resigned as Premier for reasons of health, and

Jan. 21. Ramadier formed a coalition cabinet.

Mar. 4. Anglo-French Treaty of Alliance was signed at Dunkirk.

Apr. 14. General de Gaulle assumed control of the nation-wide *Rassemblement du Peuple Français* to rally non-Communists to the cause of unity and reform.

May 9. The growing split between Communist and non-Communist members of the government, increased by economic difficulties and a wave of strikes, led to the exclusion of the five Communist ministers from the cabinet. An unbalanced budget, a poor harvest, and refusal of many peasants to deliver their grain further aggravated the situation in the summer and early fall.

Oct. 19-26. De Gaulle's R.P.F. emerged as the strongest group in the **Municipal Elections**, with the Communists in second place. In face of this growing extremism, the government and middle parties decided to co-operate and created a new *Third Force*.

Nov. A series of strikes, affecting nearly two million workers, was overcome by firm governmental action and a growing realization on the part of many workers that the leadership of their unions (C.G.T.) was Communist-dominated. The non-Communist members of the C.G.T.'s executive committee, on Dec. 19, seceded and formed the *Force Ouvrière*.

Nov. 19. At the height of the crisis, Premier Ramadier resigned.

1947, Nov. 23-1948, July 19. Cabinet of Robert Schuman, supported by a Third Force coalition of Socialists, M.R.P., and Radicals. After a brief period of economic stability, a renewed rise in prices and corresponding demands for higher wages temporarily deprived the government of Socialist support and thus led to its fall. André Marie and Schuman both tried unsuccessfully to form a lasting cabinet.

1948, Sept. 10. The Radical leader Henri Queuille formed a government with Schuman as Foreign Minister.

Oct.-Nov. To exploit the country's economic difficulties, the C.G.T. initiated another **wave of strikes**. Its cause was weakened, however, as the political, pro-Communist motivation of the strikes became obvious and the government took strong counter-measures.

Nov. 7. Elections to the Council of the Republic continued the swing to the Right, as de Gaulle's R.P.F. gained the largest number of seats.

1949, Feb. 22. Communist leader **Maurice Thorez** stated that French Communists would refuse to defend France against a Soviet army.

Oct. 5. Economic difficulties led to the **resignation of Henri Queuille.** After unsuccessful efforts of Jules Moch and René Mayer to form a cabinet,

Oct. 28. The Assembly approved a **coalition under Georges Bidault.**

Dec. 30. Transfer of sovereignty to Viet Nam (Indo-China).

1950, Mar. 8. The Chamber adopted a strict **anti-sabotage Bill,** primarily directed against Communist-inspired activities.

June 24. The **Bidault government** was defeated. After a short-lived cabinet under Henri Queuille,

July 11. René Pleven succeeded in forming a coalition based on economic compromise with the Socialists.

5. THE IBERIAN PENINSULA

a. SPAIN

Though not a participant in the war, Spain had been sufficiently partial to the Axis Powers to put herself in a position of almost complete post-war isolation. Her continued economic distress, on the other hand, made her reintegration into the world economy and the granting of foreign loans an imperative necessity. The first signs of such reintegration did not appear, however, until 1950, when the threat of Communism served to counteract the general aversion to the authoritarian régime of General Franco.

1945, Mar. 22. Don Juan, the Bourbon claimant to the Spanish throne, called for the resignation of General Franco and the restoration of the monarchy.

May 8. Spain broke off diplomatic relations with Germany.

May 12. Falangist officials attended a requiem mass for Adolf Hitler. Spain continued to give refuge to large numbers of Germans, despite Allied demands for their repatriation.

June 20. The **San Francisco Conference** excluded Spain from membership in the **United Nations.** A similar exclusion was contained in the report on the Potsdam Conference (Aug. 2).

Aug. 22. José Giral became Premier of a Republican government-in-exile at a meeting of the Cortes in Mexico City.

1946, Mar. 4. The **United States, Britain, and France appealed to the Spanish people to oust the Franco régime** and prepare the way for democratic elections.

Oct. 12. President Perón of Argentina presented General Franco with the highest Argentine decoration. This was followed on

Oct. 30, by a very advantageous Span-ish-Argentine commercial agree-ment. Señora Perón paid a state visit to Spain in 1947.

Dec. 11. The United Nations Assembly voted to bar Spain from all U.N. activities and urged its members to break off diplomatic relations with Spain.

1947, Feb. 9. Rodolfo Llopis formed a new coalition government-in-exile.

Mar. 31. General Franco announced a Bill of Succession (ratified, on July 6, by national referendum), according to which Spain again became a monarchy, the choice of the monarch being left to General Franco as Head of the State.

Apr. 2. Don Juan condemned the Bill of Succession and maintained his opposition to Franco.

Aug. 27. The Rodolfo Llopis government-in-exile resigned because of grow-ing collaboration between Repub-lican and Monarchist opposition groups. A new government was formed by Alvaro de Albornoz.

1948, Aug. 28. The exiled Monarchists and the anti-Franco Republicans (ex-cept the Communists) issued a "statement of accord."

Sept. 20. The Treaty of Friendship and Non-Aggression, concluded with Portugal in 1939, was extended for ten years.

1949, Sept. King Abdullah of Jordan was the first Head of State to visit Franco Spain.

Oct. 22-27. General Franco paid a visit to Lisbon, demonstrating the close relations between Spain and Portugal.

1950, Sept. 6. The United States Congress recommended, with certain re-strictions, a $62.5 million Mar-shall Plan loan for Spain.

Nov. 4. The United Nations adopted a resolution, sponsored by several Latin-American states, and supported by the United States, which rescinded the proposals of the earlier resolution of Dec. 11, 1946, thus opening the door to Spain's admission into the Western, anti-Commu-nist camp.

b. PORTUGAL

1945, May 3. The Government ordered official flags at half-mast because of Hitler's death. The defeat of the Axis, however, gave rise to demands for greater political free-dom, and on

Oct. 7, Premier Antonio de Oliveira Salazar permitted the formation of opposition parties. Censorship was re-moved on Oct. 12, and a political amnesty was granted. Yet on Oct. 14, because of immediate attacks against his government, Salazar reimposed the censorship of the press.

Nov. 18. The first general election in twenty years, because of a boycott by the opposition, brought victory for the National Union Party and the paternalist régime of Premier Salazar.

1946, June 2. The United States and Great Britain returned the bases they held in the Azores during the war.

Oct. 10. An attempted revolt of military officers was easily suppressed. Sporadic unrest continued into 1947.

1949, Feb. 13. President Antonio Carmona, 79, was re-elected after the single opposition candidate had with-drawn.

Apr. 4. Portugal signed the North At-lantic Treaty. She still was ex-cluded from the United Nations, however, by Soviet veto.

1950, Sept. 26-27. General Franco and Premier Salazar discussed ques-tions of Peninsular strategy and emphasized the solidarity of their two countries.

6. ITALY AND THE PAPACY

a. ITALY

1945, Nov. 24. The coalition cabinet of Ferrucio Parri resigned.

Nov. 30. The leader of the Christian Democrats, Alcide de Gasperi, formed a new government sup-ported by all major parties.

1946, Jan. 1. With the transfer of Bolzano province by the Allies, the whole country, except for Venezia Giulia (claimed by both Italy and Yugo-slavia), was under Italian sover-eignty.

May 9. King Victor Emmanuel III abdi-cated. His son proclaimed him-self King Umberto II.

June 2. Elections to the Constituent Assembly gave 207 seats (out of 556) to the Christian Democrats, 115 to the Socialists, and 104 to the Communists. At the same time a referendum rejected the Monarchy by 12,717,923 to 10,719,284 votes, thus making ITALY A REPUBLIC.

June 11. The Prime Minister, Alcide de Gasperi, was made temporary Head of State.

June 13. King Umberto, while refusing to accept the popular verdict against the Monarchy, left the country to prevent the outbreak of violence.

June 27. The Foreign Ministers of Great Britain, the United States, Soviet Russia, and France transferred the Dodecanese Islands from Italy to Greece and awarded the Briga and Tenda areas of northern Italy to France.

June 28. ENRICO DE NICOLA was elected PRESIDENT OF THE REPUBLIC by the Assembly.

July 12. Alcide de Gasperi formed a new coalition government.

1947, Jan. 20. Premier de Gasperi resigned, but resumed office on Feb. 1 at the head of a cabinet consisting of Christian Democrats, Communists, and Left-Wing Socialists.

Feb. 10. The PEACE TREATY with Italy was signed at Paris. Besides confirming earlier territorial changes, it made Trieste a Free Territory. A final decision on the future of Italy's colonies was postponed. Italian reparation payments, after the Western allies had waived their claims, were set at $360 million.

May 13. De Gasperi resigned again because of friction with the Left-Wing members of his coalition.

May 31. De Gasperi formed a new government of Christian Democrats and Independents.

Dec. 22. The Constituent Assembly adopted the new Constitution which called for far-reaching decentralization of government, a Chamber of Deputies and a popularly elected Senate. Relations between Church and State remained unchanged.

Dec. 28. Ex-King Victor Emmanuel died in exile.

1948, Mar. 26. A Franco-Italian Customs Union was concluded to become effective within one year.

Apr. 18. In the crucial first national elections under the new constitution, with Communist control as the main issue, the Christian Democrats won an absolute majority. The Popular Front of Socialists and Communists received 30.7 per cent of the votes cast.

May 11. Senator LUIGI EINAUDI was elected PRESIDENT OF THE REPUBLIC.

May 23. Prime Minister De Gasperi formed a new government, which was severely hampered by Communist-inspired unrest, such as the general strike proclaimed by the Communist-dominated Federation of Labor (C.G.I.L.) in protest against an attempt on the life of Communist leader Palmiro Togliatti (July 14), who was shot and seriously wounded by a student.

June 28. Italy was allocated $601 million under the Marshall Plan to aid her economic rehabilitation.

Oct. 18. The non-Communist elements in the C.G.I.L. seceded and formed a separate trade union.

1949, Apr. 4. Italy signed the North Atlantic Treaty despite strong opposition from the Left.

Nov. 21. The U.N. Assembly decided for eventual independence of Italy's former colonies. Until such time they were to remain under U.N. supervision.

1950, Jan. The government announced a ten-year economic plan, designed to wipe out Italy's large-scale unemployment. Some progress was made during 1950 with plans for much-needed agricultural reform, especially in the South.

Apr. 1. Italy assumed trusteeship under the United Nations over Somaliland, although she remained barred from U.N. membership by veto of the Soviet Union.

b. THE PAPACY

1946, Feb. 18. Pope Pius XII ordained thirty-two new cardinals.

May 3. Myron C. Taylor was appointed personal representative of President Truman at the Vatican. He resigned in 1950.

1949, June 20. The Vatican excommunicated all members of the government-sponsored Czech Catholic Action Committee.

July 13. A Vatican decree excommunicated all Catholics who followed and taught the Communist doctrine and denied the sacraments to those who "consciously and freely" supported Communist activities.

1950, June 30. A Papal decree excommunicated all plotters against legitimate ecclesiastical authorities.

Nov. 1. As climax of the twenty-fifth Holy Year, **Pope Pius XII pronounced the dogma of the bodily Assumption of the Virgin Mary.**

7. SWITZERLAND

1946, Mar. 19. Switzerland resumed diplomatic relations with the Soviet Union.

Mar. 25. An agreement between Switzerland and the Allied Powers provided for the disposal of German assets in Switzerland.

Apr. 2. Switzerland announced her decision to stay outside the United Nations, so as not to endanger her traditional neutrality.

1947, Oct. 28. General elections brought no important changes in the line-up of parties. The Progressive Democrats received 51, the Social Democrats 48, the Catholic Conservatives 44, and the Labor Party (Communist) 7 of the total 194 seats.

1950, Feb. Switzerland embarked on a **five-year plan of military preparedness** and announced that she would fight to defend her neutrality.

Sept. The **Federal Council expelled all Communists from government service.**

8. GERMANY

With the total defeat of the Hitler régime, no German government remained. Instead supreme authority was vested in an **Allied Control Council of Great Britain, France, the United States, and the Soviet Union.** Each of these powers administered its own occupation zone, with the Soviet Union holding the region east of the Elbe. The former capital, **Berlin,** was likewise divided into four sectors. The future policy toward Germany had been outlined at the **Potsdam Conference** (p. 1171), though its implementation varied in the different occupation zones. The most immediate measures of the victors were concerned with the liquidation of the Nazi system, the transformation of Germany's economy to peacetime production, and the transfer of administrative functions into German hands. On Nov. 20, the **trial of major Nazi leaders** opened at Nuremberg before an inter-Allied Tribunal. In addition, thousands of lesser Nazis were removed from office and held for trial. Germany's industrial power was drastically reduced by **dismantling of war plants** and the removal of equipment for reparations purposes. At the same time large stores of food were imported to maintain a minimum ration. In all occupation zones **political parties** were authorized by the end of 1945. In the Soviet zone administrative authority was vested in the provincial councils, which immediately initiated far-reaching land reforms. In the three western zones, **German self-govern-**ment was initiated on local and provincial levels. On Nov. 20, the Control Council approved the **transfer of 6.65 million Germans** from Austria, Hungary, Czechoslovakia, Poland, and the German region beyond the **Oder-Neisse line,** which had been handed to Poland at the Potsdam Conference, pending a final peace settlement.

1946, Jan. 27. **Local elections** in the **U.S. zone** resulted in victory for the **Christian Democrats,** with the **Social Democrats** in second place. Later elections in the **French and British zones** brought similar results.

Mar. 26. The **Allied Control Council** limited the future **level of German production** to half its 1938 volume, with German steel capacity set at 7.5 million tons. These limitations soon proved unworkable, since they seriously hampered German recovery.

Apr. 21. The **Social Democrats and Communists** in the **Soviet zone** merged into the Communist-directed **Socialist Unity Party (S.E.D.),** which received majorities in all subsequent elections. The Liberal Democrats and the Christian Democrats remained merely for purposes of democratic window-dressing.

June 30. Elections for Constituent Assemblies in the American zone brought victories for the **Christian Socialists** in Bavaria, the **Chris-**

tian Democrats in Wuerttemberg-Baden, and the **Social Democrats** in Greater Hesse.

July 2. The first of several political amnesties was declared by the Americans, to help overcome some of the difficulties of large-scale denazification.

Sept. 6. U.S. Secretary of State **James F. Byrnes**, in a speech at Stuttgart, announced a more lenient American policy toward Germany and called for a unified German economy.

Sept. 30. The International Tribunal at Nuremberg announced its decisions. The Nazi Leadership Corps, the S.S., the Security Police, and the Gestapo were found criminal organizations, while the S.A., the cabinet, and the General Staff were acquitted. Of the 22 defendants, Schacht, Fritzsche, and von Papen were acquitted, the rest received sentences ranging from ten years' imprisonment to death. Shortly before his scheduled execution, on Oct. 15, **Hermann Goering** committed suicide.

Dec. 2. James F. Byrnes and Ernest Bevin signed an agreement for the economic fusion of the U.S. and British zones (Bizonia) inviting France and Soviet Russia to join.

1947, Mar. 10-Apr. 24. The Moscow Conference of the **Big Four Foreign Ministers** revealed considerable disagreement on the German question between the Soviet Union and the West. Notably the Soviet demand for $10 billion in German reparations, to be paid from current production, ran counter to U.S.-British policy of making Western Germany economically self-supporting. The only agreement reached was on the formal **abolition of the state of Prussia.**

Apr. 20. "Landtag" elections in the British zone gave a majority to the Social Democrats in Lower Saxony and Schleswig-Holstein, and to the **Christian Democrats** in North Rhine-Westphalia.

May 18. "Landtag" elections in the French zone brought victory to the Christian Democrats and second place to the Socialists.

June 2. A German Economic Council was created to direct bizonal economic reconstruction.

Aug. 29. A revised plan for Western German industry set the 1936 production level as an ultimate goal and raised the yearly figure of steel production.

Oct. 5. Elections in the Saar brought victory to the **Christian People's Party** and the Socialists, which was seen as a popular endorsement of the new Saar Constitution adopted previously by these parties. Its first article proclaimed the Saar an autonomous territory, joined economically to France.

Nov. 25-Dec. 15. In another unsuccessful meeting of the Council of Foreign Ministers at London, the Soviet demand for German reparations from current production again proved the main obstacle to a general German settlement.

1948, Feb. 6. A new Bizonal Charter further perfected German administration of "Bizonia."

Feb. 13. As a counter-move, Soviet authorities conferred extensive powers on a **German Economic Commission** in the Soviet zone.

Mar. 20. The Soviet delegates walked out of the Allied Control Council, after charging the Western Powers with undermining the quadripartite administration of Germany.

Apr. 1. The Soviets began interfering with traffic between Berlin and Western Germany.

June 1. A Six-Power Agreement of the three Western Powers and the Benelux countries was reached, calling for international control of the Ruhr, German representation in the European Recovery Program, closer integration of the three western zones, the drafting of a federal constitution for Western Germany, and the creation of an **Allied Military Security Board.**

June 18. The Western Powers announced the introduction of currency reform in Western Germany, establishing the stable *Deutsche Mark*, and initiating a process of rapid economic recovery.

June 23. Soviet authorities introduced a currency reform for the Soviet zone.

July 24. Disagreement between the Soviet Union and the West over the latter's program of economic and currency reforms brought complete Soviet stoppage of rail and road traffic between Berlin and the West. To circumvent this blockade, the Western Powers began a large-scale air lift of vital supplies.

Sept. 1. A Parliamentary Council from the eleven Western German states began deliberations on a **Basic Law** for Western Germany.

Nov. 30. After ousting the democratic majority of the Berlin Municipal Assembly, the **Communists set up a new administration**, claiming authority **over the whole of Berlin**. In reply,

Dec. 5, elections in the western sectors of Berlin gave the Socialists 64.6 per cent of the vote, and Socialist Ernst Reuter became Lord Mayor.

Dec. 28. The United States, Great Britain, France, and the Benelux countries constituted themselves (and eventually Germany) as an **International Ruhr Authority** with far-reaching powers of control.

1949, Jan. 17. The **Western Allies** established a **Military Security Board** to supervise German disarmament and demilitarization.

Mar. 19. The Soviet-sponsored **People's Council** in Eastern Germany **approved a draft constitution** for a **Democratic Republic** of Germany and called for the election of a People's Congress.

Apr. 8. The three **Western Powers** agreed on an **Occupation Statute** for Western Germany, which assured the Germans of considerable self-government, while reserving far-reaching powers to the occupation authorities. Simultaneously dismantling provisions were eased and numerous industrial restrictions were removed, to meet German demand for greater economic freedom.

Apr. 23. Thirty-one minor **rectifications of the West German frontier** were carried out.

May 8. The Western Parliamentary Council adopted the **Basic Law** for the **FEDERAL REPUBLIC OF GERMANY**. While following in many respects the Weimar Constitution, the Basic Law tried to avoid the main shortcomings of its predecessor. It was subsequently ratified by all states except Bavaria. The **Federal Republic**, with Bonn as capital, **came into existence on May 23.**

May 12. The **Berlin blockade** was officially lifted.

May 16. Elections for a **People's Congress in Eastern Germany**, despite official pressure, gave only 66.1 per cent backing to the single list of Communist-approved candidates. On May 30, the Congress adopted the draft constitution of the **Democratic Republic**.

Aug. 14. Elections for the **Bundestag** (Lower House) in **Western Germany** gave the Christian Democrats a small lead over the Socialists, with the Free Democrats holding the balance. A **United States Court at Nuremberg** concluded the last of its **war crimes trials** with the sentencing of 19 German government officials and diplomats.

Sept. 12-15. **THEODOR HEUSS** (Free Democrat) was **ELECTED PRESIDENT** and **KONRAD ADENAUER** (Christian Democrat) **CHANCELLOR** of the **Western Republic**.

Sept. 21. The **Allied Occupation Statute** came into force. The functions of Military Government were transferred to the **Allied High Commission**.

Sept. 30. The **Berlin air lift** ended its operation after 277,264 flights.

Oct. 7. As a counter-move to developments in the West, the **GERMAN DEMOCRATIC REPUBLIC** was established in **Eastern Germany** without an election and with **WILHELM PIECK** as **PRESIDENT** and **OTTO GROTEWOHL** as **MINISTER PRESIDENT** of a predominantly Communist cabinet. The Soviet Military Government was replaced by a **Soviet Control Commission**. Politically and economically the new Eastern German state was merely another Soviet satellite.

Nov. 24. In the **Petersberg Agreement** the Allied High Commission made further economic concessions to Western Germany, in return for German membership in the International Ruhr Authority. Despite the fact that industrial production had reached 93 per cent of the 1936 level, the influx of more than 8 million Germans from the East had caused widespread unemployment. To speed economic recovery,

Dec. 15, Western Germany received the first allotment of E.C.A. funds, and thus **became a full participant in the Marshall Plan.**

1950, Jan. 16. The last rationing restrictions were ended in Western Germany.

Mar. 3. A **French agreement with the Saar**, confirming the region's autonomy and its economic union with France, created deep consternation in Western Germany.

May 9. The **Schuman Plan** calling for the integration of the coal and steel industries of Western Europe was welcomed by the Bonn government but received coolly by the Socialists and Trade Unions.

June 6. An agreement between **Eastern Germany** and **Poland** recognized the **Oder-Neisse line** as the final Ger man-Polish frontier and evoked protests in Western Germany.

June 15. The Bonn Parliament decided to accept an invitation to join the Council of Europe.

July 20. Appealing to the widespread hope for a reunited Germany, the **S.E.D.** convention in Eastern Germany called for the formation of a "national front," and for "national resistance" against the Western Powers.

Largely as a result of the Korean War, the status of **Western Germany during 1950 underwent a rapid change from that of a former enemy into that of a future ally.** This became clear when on

Sept. 19, the **Western Powers** announced that they would consider any attack against the Federal Republic or against Berlin as an attack upon themselves and that they would strengthen their military forces in Germany. At the same time they agreed to revise the Occupation Statute, to relax economic controls, to lift the limit on steel production, and to permit the Bonn government to establish diplomatic relations with foreign countries. A special security police was authorized to meet the threat of the much larger Soviet-sponsored "People's Police" of Eastern Germany. At the same time the Western Allies began considering possible **German participation** in a Western army under the **North Atlantic Treaty.** This growing collaboration in matters of military security between the Bonn government and the West, however, met with violent criticism from the **Socialist Opposition** and its leader, **Kurt Schumacher,** whose opposition to remilitarization found strong popular support, as was shown in the **Landtag elections** of the American zone (Nov. 19-26), which resulted in noticeable **Socialist gains.**

Oct. 15. Elections to the Eastern German Legislature brought the expected "victory" for the official list of candidates.

9. AUSTRIA

As a "liberated" rather than defeated country, Austria after the war was treated with leniency by the Western Allies, who did everything in their power to hasten her recovery. The Soviet Union, on the other hand, after initial requisitions of livestock and industrial equipment, made far-reaching demands for reparations from former German assets, thus seriously hampering Austria's economic reconstruction. Under these circumstances, the Austrian government was eagerly awaiting the conclusion of a final peace settlement and the withdrawal of the occupation forces.

1945, Apr. 25. A Provisional Government was set up with Socialist **Karl Renner** as **Chancellor.**

May 14. The **Democratic Republic of Austria** was re-established.

Aug. 8. The division of Austria and Vienna into **four occupation zones** was completed. The **Allied Council for Austria** assumed authority over matters affecting the whole of Austria.

Nov. 25. The first **general election** since 1930 gave the **People's Party** a majority over the Socialists and Communists.

Dec. 18. Leopold Figl (People's Party) formed a coalition cabinet with the Socialists.

Dec. 20. KARL RENNER was unanimously elected **PRESIDENT OF THE REPUBLIC** by the National Assembly.

1946, Jan. 7. The **occupying powers officially recognized the Austrian Republic** within its 1937 frontiers.

June 28. The Austrian government was given a large measure of authority by the Allied Council.

July 6. The **Soviets** claimed, as German assets, important **industrial establishments** in their zone.

Sept. 6. An **Austro-Italian agreement** gave considerable autonomy to the **South Tyrol.**

1948-50. Repeated **attempts to reach a peace settlement for Austria failed** because of Soviet and Yugoslav demands against Austria. To facilitate negotiations, the Western Allies renounced their own claims for German assets in Austria and made far-reaching concessions to Soviet claims for such assets, but the **deadlock continued through 1949 and 1950.**

1949, Oct. 9. **General Elections** brought losses to both the **People's Party** and the **Socialists,** as many former Nazis rallied behind the new **Union of Independents.** Communist strength remained negligible. The coalition government of People's Party and Socialists remained substantially unchanged, despite their basic disagreement on economic questions.

1950, Nov. 10-22. The Western Powers protested against Russia's indirect assistance to Communist-provoked strikes and riots.

Dec. 31. President Karl Renner died.

10. CZECHOSLOVAKIA

1945, Apr. 3. President Eduard Beneš appointed a National Front Government with **Zdenek Fierlinger** as Prime Minister.

May 10. The new government moved to Prague. In a sweeping political purge many collaborators were tried and executed. **Ex-President Hacha** died in prison, **Konrad Henlein** committed suicide.

June 29. Czechoslovakia ceded Ruthenia to the Soviet Union.

Aug. 3. All Germans and Hungarians in Czechoslovakia were deprived of their citizenship and subsequently expelled from the country.

Oct. 14. A Provisional National Assembly was elected by indirect suffrage.

Oct. 18. The government embarked on a far-reaching program of **industrial nationalization and agricultural reform.**

1946, May 26. Elections to the Constituent Assembly gave the **Communists** 2.7 million of the total 7.1 million votes and 114 out of 300 seats. As a result, Communist leader **Klement Gottwald** formed a new coalition cabinet.

June 19. The Assembly unanimously re-elected President Beneš.

1947, Apr. 16. Josef Tiso, former President of Slovakia, was condemned to death and **executed.**

July 7. Czechoslovakia first accepted, but later, under Russian pressure, **rejected an invitation** to participate in the **Marshall Plan Conference** in Paris.

1948, Feb. 25. COMMUNIST COUP. The Communists, having infiltrated most government services and trade unions, and enjoying Soviet support, threatened a *coup d'état* and thus secured President Beneš's signature to a **predominantly Communist government under Klement Gottwald.** In a drastic purge, lasting several months, democratic **Czechoslovakia was transformed into a Communist-run People's Democracy and a Soviet satellite.**

Mar. 10. Foreign Minister **Jan Masaryk** was killed in a fall from his office window, reported as suicide.

May 9. The **Constituent Assembly** adopted the new constitution.

May 30. The **National Elections** resulted in a victory for the single list of the Communist-dominated **National Front.**

June 7. President Beneš resigned on grounds of ill health. He died on Sept. 3.

June 14. KLEMENT GOTTWALD was elected **PRESIDENT.**

Oct. 25. Forced Labor Camps were set up to punish reactionaries and saboteurs.

1949, Jan. 1. A **Five-Year Plan** of industrial development was started to make Czechoslovakia economically independent of the West.

June. In an **attempt to destroy the influence of the Catholic Church,** the government founded its own **Catholic Action Committee** to take the direction of Church affairs away from **Archbishop Beran** and the Catholic hierarchy.

June 20. The Vatican, as a countermeasure, **excommunicated all active supporters of Communism in Czechoslovakia.**

Oct. 14. The **government assumed full control over Church affairs** and required all clergy to swear an oath of loyalty to the state. Most of the lower clergy complied.

1950. In an uninterrupted **series of political trials,** the government not only prosecuted its foes, but also some of its own members, who were accused of anti-Soviet, pro-Western leanings. In addition, several **Western diplomatic representatives were charged with espionage** and most Western correspondents were barred from Czechoslovakia.

April. The new **Minister of Defense,** Čepička, after dismissing several leading officers, announced a thoroughgoing **reorganization of the army along Soviet lines.**

11. HUNGARY

A provisional Hungarian government, established under **General Miklos** in 1944, concluded an **armistice** with the United Nations on **Jan. 20, 1945**, and henceforth co-operated in the war against Germany.

1945, Nov. 3. The first **General Election** gave an absolute majority to the anti-Communist **Smallholders' Party**, whose leader, **Zoltan Tildy**, formed a coalition cabinet.

The economic situation of the country was desperate as a result of the war, with serious food shortages and an unprecedented currency inflation. Large-scale Soviet requisitions further aggravated the situation.

1946, Feb. 1. A republic was proclaimed with Zoltan Tildy as President. **Ferenc Nagy** of the Smallholders' Party became **Premier** on Feb. 4.

1947, Feb. 10. The **HUNGARIAN PEACE TREATY** was signed at Paris. It called for the **return of Transylvania to Rumania**, a small frontier rectification in favor of Czechoslovakia, reparations, and the reduction of armed forces.

Feb. 25. The arrest of **Bela Kovács**, Secretary General of the Smallholders' Party, for alleged plotting against the occupation forces, ushered in the gradual purge of the party's anti-Communist wing.

May 31. Premier Nagy, accused of conspiracy by the Communists, resigned and was replaced by Smallholder **Lajos Dinnyes**.

Aug. 1. A **Three-Year Plan** went into effect, calling for a planned economy and nationalization of the banks.

Aug. 31. A General Election gave the **Communists the largest number** of seats. Premier Dinnyes continued in office at the head of a coalition cabinet of 15 members, including 5 Communists.

1948, Jan. 12. A fusion of Communists and Social Democrats into the **United Workers' Party** was engineered by the Communists.

July 30. President Tildy was forced to resign and was replaced by the chairman of the United Workers' Party, ex-Socialist **Arpád Szakasits**.

Dec. 9. After completing its purge of anti-Communist members, the Smallholders' Party called for **Premier Dinnyes'** resignation and put pro-Communist **István Dobi** in his place. The real power, however, was in the hands of the Communist Deputy Premier **Mátyás Rákosi**.

Dec. 27. The refusal of the Catholic Church to make concessions to the government led to the arrest of **Josef Cardinal Mindszenty** and other dignitaries on charges of conspiracy to overthrow the government. Cardinal Mindszenty was found guilty and sentenced to life imprisonment (Feb. 8, 1949).

1949, May 15. A General Election with open voting gave **complete victory** to the Communist-controlled **National Independence Front**.

June 16. The arrest of Communist Foreign Minister **Laszlo Rajk** on charges of conspiracy **set off a wholesale purge of Hungarian Communists** accused of deviating from the pro-Soviet line.

Aug. 7. A new constitution was proclaimed, following very closely that of the Soviet Union.

Dec. 28. The government decreed the nationalization of all major industries and announced the start of a Five-Year Plan.

1950, May-June. The remaining **ex-Socialists**, among them **Arpád Szakasits**, were dismissed from the government. Hungary, in its domestic and foreign affairs, had come completely under Communist and Soviet domination.

12. THE BALKAN STATES

a. YUGOSLAVIA

As the war ended, Yugoslavia was still theoretically a monarchy. The actual power, however, was wielded by **Marshal Tito** and his **National Liberation Movement**.

1945, Nov. 11. Elections for a Constituent Assembly gave a substantial majority to Tito's Communist-dominated National Front.

Nov. 29. The Assembly proclaimed a **FEDERAL PEOPLE'S REPUBLIC OF YUGOSLAVIA**, and on

1946, Jan. 31. A new constitution was adopted, closely resembling that of the Soviet Union. The new government was recognized by the Western Powers, though its leanings, from the start, were decidedly pro-Soviet.

Mar. 10. General Drazha Mihailovitch, wartime resistance leader, was captured, tried for collaboration with the enemy, and despite Western protests, was shot on July 17.

Sept. 18. Archbishop Stepinac, Catholic leader of Croatia, was arrested on similar charges and sentenced to sixteen years' hard labor.

1946-47. Yugoslavia concluded a series of political and economic agreements with Poland, Czechoslovakia, Albania, Bulgaria, and Hungary. She also became one of the founding members of the Cominform.

1947, Apr. 27. Marshal Tito announced a Five-Year Plan of industrial development.

Despite Yugoslavia's close outward association with the Soviet Union, Marshal Tito had repeatedly asserted Yugoslavia's own interests. As time went on, differences between the two countries became increasingly more frequent, so that finally, on

1948, Mar. 18. The Soviet Union recalled its military and technical advisers from Yugoslavia, and on

June 28. The COMINFORM EXPELLED YUGOSLAVIA from membership for doctrinal errors and hostility to the Soviet Union.

July 21-29. Marshal Tito denied the Cominform charges before a Congress of the Yugoslav Communist Party and received a vote of confidence. The party was later purged of Cominform supporters.

1949, June-July. The Soviet Union's Eastern satellites broke off all economic relations with Yugoslavia. As a counter-move, Marshal Tito concluded a series of economic agreements with the West, notably the United States.

Sept. 27. As a final gesture the Soviet Union denounced its treaty of friendship with Yugoslavia. Her satellites subsequently followed the Soviet example.

1950, Mar. 25. General Elections, in methods and results, differed little from those in other Communist-controlled countries and brought an overwhelming endorsement of the single list of People's Front candidates. Still, the *rapprochement*

between Yugoslavia and the West spread from the economic to the political sphere, as Yugoslavia opposed Chinese intervention in the Korean War, resumed diplomatic relations with Greece, and improved her relations with Italy, which had been disturbed by conflicting claims over Trieste. In the ideological field, Marshal Tito continued to adhere to his own brand of anti-Russian Communism or "Titoism."

b. ALBANIA

1945, Nov. 10. The Communist-dominated government of **Premier Enver Hoxha was recognized** by the Soviet Union and the Western Powers. It was upheld in

Dec. 2. General Elections, which returned the single list of official candidates.

1946, Jan. 11. The Constituent Assembly proclaimed the PEOPLE'S REPUBLIC OF ALBANIA. Its domestic and foreign policy followed closely the Communist, pro-Soviet line, taken by other Russian satellites. Relations with the West, and notably Great Britain, rapidly deteriorated.

May-Oct. Two naval incidents in the Corfu Channel, caused by Albanian coastal batteries and mines, and resulting in the loss of British lives, further increased British-Albanian tension.

1948-49. Relations between Albania and Yugoslavia, which had been particularly close, were broken as a result of the latter's exclusion from the Cominform.

1949, June 10. Koci Xoxe, former Communist Vice-Premier, and a number of other high officials, were convicted as Yugoslav agents. Xoxe was executed on June 11. As arrests for sabotage and espionage continued, large numbers of Albanians fled the country.

1950, May 28. A General Election confirmed the Hoxha régime. Albania fell completely under Soviet domination as she joined the Cominform and concluded a Treaty of Friendship with the USSR.

c. GREECE

The war left Greece a legacy of economic ruin, starvation, and domestic strife. The end of the civil war (p. 1143) did not bring political stability. The Regent, Archbishop Damaskinos, supported by British occupation authorities, appointed six different ministries during 1945, none of which was able to breach the gap between moderate and Left-Wing resistance groups.

1946, Mar. 31. The first General Election won an overwhelming majority for the Royalist Popular Party. The EAM and other leftist groups refused to participate in the voting.

1946, May-1949, Oct. Several thousand Communists, supported by Greece's Communist neighbors, engaged in extensive guerrilla activities, which soon developed into a regular CIVIL WAR.

Apr. 18. Populist leader Tsaldaris formed a cabinet.

Sept. 1. A plebiscite decided 69 per cent in favor of the monarchy, and

Sept. 28. King George II returned to Athens.

1947, Mar. 12. President Truman announced a far-reaching program of economic aid to Greece and Turkey (TRUMAN DOCTRINE).

Mar. 31. The Dodecanese Islands were returned to Greece.

Apr. 1. King George II died and was succeeded by his brother, Prince Paul.

Sept. 7. Themostokles Sophoulis formed a coalition government of Liberals and Populists.

Oct. 21. The U.N. General Assembly called on Yugoslavia, Albania, and Bulgaria to cease aiding the Greek guerrillas. A similar resolution was adopted in 1948. Both remained unheeded.

Dec. 24. "General Markos," leader of an estimated 20,000 guerrillas, proclaimed the establishment of the "First Provisional Democratic Government of Free Greece."

Dec. 27. The Greek government dissolved the Communist Party and EAM.

1949, June 30. Prime Minister Sophoulis died and was succeeded by Alexander Diomedes.

Oct. 16. After three years of fighting, the CIVIL WAR ENDED with the defeat of the rebel forces. This was made possible partly by American aid and because of the closing of the Yugoslav frontier as a result of Tito's quarrel with the Cominform.

1950, Mar. 5. A General Election gave the largest number of votes to the Populists, but the majority went to the Center and moderate Left. This distribution of forces, together with the aftermath of the civil war, greatly contributed to the instability of the government, as shown in a rapid succession of five cabinets during the remainder of 1950.

d. BULGARIA

Post-war developments in Bulgaria were decisively determined by the **Soviet invasion** of the country in 1944 (p. 1154). The Soviet-sponsored coalition government under Premier **Kimon Georgiev (Sept. 9, 1944)** contained only few Communists, though in key positions. Bulgaria formally capitulated on **Oct. 28, 1944,** and remained occupied by Soviet forces, which proved most advantageous to the Communists.

1945, Nov. 18. The first General Election gave overwhelming support to the single list of the Fatherland Front, a wartime coalition of major parties, by now under Communist control.

1946. In a sweeping purge, more than 1500 high-ranking and ten times as many minor figures of the old régime were killed.

Mar. 31. Premier Georgiev formed a Communist-dominated government.

Sept. 8. A referendum decided against the monarchy, and on

Sept. 15. Bulgaria was proclaimed a PEOPLE'S REPUBLIC. Young Tsar Simeon II went into exile.

Oct. 27. General Elections for a Constituent Assembly, carried on with considerable governmental interference, resulted in a Communist majority.

Nov. 21. Veteran Communist Georgi Dimitrov returned from Moscow to become Premier.

1947, Feb. 10. The BULGARIAN PEACE TREATY was signed in Paris. Bulgaria retained the Southern Dobruja, but had to pay reparations and reduce her armed forces.

Apr. 1. A Two-Year Plan was announced, followed by nationalization of banks and industries (Dec. 26).

June 6. Nikola Petkov, leader of the Agrarian Party, was arrested. He was convicted of treason and executed (Sept. 23).

Aug. 26. An extended campaign against the Opposition culminated in the dissolution of the Agrarian Party.

Nov. 27. Bulgaria and Yugoslavia signed a Treaty of Friendship and Mutual Aid.

Dec. 15. Soviet occupation forces left Bulgaria.

1948. The standard "Treaties of Friendship" were signed with the Soviet Union and her Eastern European satellites.

1949, Jan. 1. A Five-Year Plan was inaugurated.

June 25. Communist Deputy Premier **Traicho Kostov was arrested and charged** with ideological deviation and treason. Together with ten associates he was later found guilty and was **executed on Dec. 16.**

July 2. Premier Dimitrov, who earlier had gone to Russia for medical treatment, **died in Moscow.** He was succeeded by **Vassil Kolarov.**

Oct. 1. Bulgaria denounced her treaty of friendship with Yugoslavia.

Dec. 18. National Elections supported the official government list.

1950, Jan. 23. Premier Kolarov died and was succeeded by **Vulko Chervenkov,** head of the Communist Party. A large-scale purge of government officials, charged with complicity in the Kostov conspiracy, continued throughout the year.

Feb. 21. Similar charges of complicity against U.S. diplomatic representatives in Bulgaria led to a **break in U.S.-Bulgarian diplomatic relations.**

Apr. 1. The Communist Party revealed that **92,500 of its members had been expelled** during the previous 12 months.

e. RUMANIA

Although Rumania had surrendered in August 1944 (p. 1154), it took several months before a workable government could be established. Constant agitation of the Communist-controlled **National Democratic Front,** combined with direct Soviet pressure, finally brought results, when

1945, Mar. 2. **King Michael asked Petru Groza,** leader of the Left-wing Plowman's Front, **to form a government.** Based largely on the National Democratic Front, the new government from the start showed its Communist, pro-Russian leanings. It was only due to British and American pressure that

1946, Jan. 7. **Representatives of the Opposition parties were included in the government,** although the important posts continued to be in Communist hands.

May 17. General **Ion Antonescu,** wartime premier, was **condemned to death.**

Nov. 19. The **General Election,** preceded by a campaign of violence against the Opposition, resulted in a majority for the government.

1947, Feb. 10. The **RUMANIAN PEACE TREATY** was signed in Paris. It called for reparations, reduction of armaments, and the **return of Transylvania** to Rumania.

July 15. Julius Maniu, leader of the National Peasant Party, was **arrested,** together with some hundred members of the Opposition, on charges of espionage and treason. He was sentenced to solitary confinement for life.

July 28. The **National Peasant Party** was dissolved.

Nov. 5. Foreign Minister Tatarescu, non-Communist, resigned and was succeeded by veteran Communist **Ana Pauker.**

Dec. 19. Rumania and Yugoslavia signed a treaty of friendship and mutual aid.

Dec. 30. **KING MICHAEL ABDICATED** under Communist pressure.

1948, Mar. 28. In a General Election the official **People's Democratic Front** received 91 per cent of the votes. **Petru Groza** continued as Premier.

Apr. 13. A new constitution was adopted, modeled on that of Soviet Russia.

1949. The transformation of Rumania into a full-fledged Soviet satellite made further progress. An uninterrupted series of trials purged the country of all political opponents and the Communist Party of "deviationists." All **religious organizations** were **subjected to state control.** Catholic opposition led to the arrest of the remaining bishops and the **dissolution of all Roman Catholic congregations.** There was **collectivization of agriculture, nationalization of industry,** and the death penalty was imposed for even minor offenses against the state. **Relations with the Western Powers** further deteriorated as several Western diplomats were accused of espionage.

Oct. 21. **Rumania denounced its treaty of friendship with Yugoslavia.**

1950, July. The Rumanian Communist Party announced the expulsion of 192,000 members over the previous two years.

13. THE SOVIET UNION

The ability of Communist Russia to withstand the terrific shock of German invasion and her decisive contributions to Germany's defeat were generally recognized as signs of her great inherent strength. Yet with close to 25 million people rendered homeless by the war, and large areas in complete devastation, the Soviet government was faced with a tremendous task of reconstruction. Despite these domestic difficulties, the Soviet Union, in her foreign policy, was able with considerable skill and initial success, to use the inevitable international confusion of the post-war period for the advancement of Communist (and hence Soviet) influence.

1946, Feb. 10. The first **general elections** since 1937 for the **Supreme Soviet** returned the official list of approved candidates.

Mar. 15. The fourth **Five-Year Plan,** designed to increase pre-war industrial output by more than 50 per cent, was adopted by the Supreme Soviet. Much of the necessary industrial equipment was collected from regions under Soviet occupation.

Mar. 19. In a series of governmental changes, **President Michael Kalinin** resigned because of ill health and was **succeeded by** the former trade-union leader **Shvernik.** A **Council of Ministers** (with **Stalin** as Chairman and Foreign Minister **Molotov** as Deputy Chairman) **replaced** the former **Council of People's Commissars.**

June 28. The **Ministry of State Control** announced widespread dismissals in the industrial field for incompetence and dishonesty. This was followed in August by a similar purge of agricultural offenders.

Nov. 18. Marshal Koniev replaced **Marshal Zhukov** as **Commander-in-Chief** of Soviet armed forces.

1947, Mar. 3. **Stalin was succeeded as Minister of Defense by General Bulganin.**

Mar. 5. The **Soviet Union rejected** the report of the U.N. Atomic Energy Commission on **atomic control.**

July. The Soviet Union and her satellites refused to participate in European economic reconstruction under the **Marshall Plan.** Instead, the USSR further perfected the integration of Eastern Europe into a Soviet-dominated economic

bloc through a network of alliances and trade-agreements.

Oct. 5. The formation of a "Communist Information Bureau" (**COMINFORM**) was announced, to co-ordinate the activities of the Communist parties of Yugoslavia, Bulgaria, Rumania, Poland, France, Czechoslovakia, Italy, and the Soviet Union. Its headquarters was established at Belgrade.

According to official reports of the Soviet **State Planning Commission** (Gosplan), Russia's industrial output under the **Five-Year Plan,** while failing to reach its yearly goal in 1946, surpassed it in 1947. Shortage of manpower continued to be the main economic drawback. A severe food shortage, resulting from drought and crop failures in 1946, was relieved by an excellent harvest in 1947, and on

Dec. 15. The government was able to abolish food rationing. At the same time, on

Dec. 16. A drastic **currency devaluation,** at the rate of ten to one, brought renewed hardships to most people, but served to strengthen further the Soviet economy.

1948, Jan.-June. A number of high officials, including the Ministers of Justice and Finance, were replaced because of inefficiency.

Feb.-Mar. The USSR concluded treaties of friendship and mutual assistance with **Rumania, Hungary,** and **Bulgaria.**

Feb. 10. The **Central Committee of the Communist Party** accused Soviet composers, including **Shostakovich, Prokofief,** and **Khachaturian** of losing touch with the masses by showing bourgeois influences in their works. The accused confessed and repented.

Apr. 6. The USSR concluded a military assistance pact with **Finland.**

Aug. A further ideological shake-up occurred when the biologist, **T. D. Lysenko,** backed by the Central Committee, condemned the generally accepted "formal genetics," based on the findings of **Mendel** (p. 551), and substituted the outmoded teachings of **Michurin,** as in complete accordance with Marxian doctrine.

Aug. 31. A. A. **Zhdanov,** Deputy Premier and one of the party's leading ideologists, died.

1949, Jan. 25. The USSR and her Eastern satellites announced the formation of a **Council for Mutual Economic Assistance,** as a counterpart to the Western Economic Recovery Program.

Mar. 4. A series of governmental changes was initiated with the replacement of Foreign Minister **V. M. Molotov** by **A. Vyshinsky** and of Minister of Defense Marshal **N. I. Bulganin** by Marshal **A. M. Vassilievsky.** Both Molotov and Bulganin continued as members of the *Politburo.*

Sept. An atomic explosion was reported to have taken place inside the Soviet Union.

Sept. 28. The USSR repudiated her 1945 treaty of friendship with **Yugoslavia.**

Dec. 31. Stalin's seventieth birthday was the occasion for world-wide Communist celebrations. The announcement of several Stalin Peace Prizes was seen as a move in the Soviet **"peace offensive,"** which had become the main Communist propaganda weapon in the "cold war."

1950, Jan. 12. The **death penalty,** abolished after the war, was **reintroduced** for espionage, treason, and sabotage.

Feb. 14. The USSR and the Chinese People's Republic signed a 30-year treaty of alliance.

Mar. 12. Elections to the Supreme Soviet as usual supported the official list of government candidates.

14. POLAND

At the Yalta Conference (p. 1143), Poland's eastern territories were reduced approximately to the "Curzon Line" of 1919 (p. 1038), while her western border, pending a final peace settlement, was extended to the **Oder-Neisse** line in Eastern Germany. The leadership of post-war Poland was claimed by two rival groups, the Soviet-sponsored **Provisional Government at Lublin,** and the Polish **Government-in-exile** in London. After lengthy negotiations,

1945, June 28. A **Government of National Unity** was formed, under Socialist Premier **Osobka-Morawski** of the Lublin administration. It was recognized by the Western Powers, though its leanings turned out to be decidedly pro-Soviet. For this reason many Polish citizens, who, as displaced persons or members of Poland's armed forces, were still in Western Europe, refused to be repatriated.

1946, Jan. 6. The government announced the **nationalization of all industries** employing more than fifty workers.

June 30. A **popular referendum** approved the government's program of nationalization and land reform, and the establishment of a one-house parliament, as advocated by the Communists.

1947, Jan. 19. The first **General Election,** preceded by repressive measures against Deputy Prime Minister **Mikolajczyk's Peasant Party,** gave the government bloc 394 seats and the Peasant Party 28. Both Great Britain and the United States charged that the Yalta provisions for free and honest elections had been violated.

Feb. 4. **Boleslaw Bierut** was elected **President of the Republic** and **Joseph Cyrankiewicz** formed a new coalition cabinet.

Feb. 19. The Diet approved an **interim** constitution and proclaimed liberty and equality for all citizens.

Sept. 14. Poland denounced her Concordat and entered upon a series of conflicts with the Catholic Church.

Oct. 24. A campaign among pro-government members of the Peasant Party for his dismissal led to **Mikolajczyk's flight to London** and the purge of his followers from the ranks of the Peasant Party.

1948. The transformation of Poland into a Communist-dominated Soviet satellite made further headway as the Socialist Party was fused with the Communists, the Peasant Party joined the government bloc, a compulsory youth organization was set up, and the judiciary was changed along Communist lines.

June 26. A five-year **trade agreement** was signed with the Soviet Union to counterbalance the Marshall Plan, in which Poland had refused to participate.

Sept. 5. The Secretary General of the Communist Polish Workers' Party, **Wladyslaw Gomulka,** was forced to resign because of ideological deviation from the Soviet line.

1949, Jan. 25. Poland joined the **Council for Mutual Economic Assistance.**

Sept. 30. Poland again showed her adherence to Soviet and Cominform policy when she denounced her treaty of friendship with Yugoslavia.

Nov. 7. Soviet **Marshal Konstantin Rokossovsky** was appointed **Minister of Defense and Commander-in-Chief of the Polish army.** The latter was thoroughly reorganized along Soviet lines.

Nov. 11-13. The **Central Committee of the United Workers' Party** expelled a number of prominent members for "Titoist" leanings.

1950. **Poland's relations with the Western Powers,** which had deteriorated steadily since the war, **came close to the breaking point,** as several Western diplomats and correspondents were accused of hostile acts against the Polish government.

Mar. 20. Hostility between Church and State resulted in the **confiscation of Church lands** and other restrictions on Catholic activities.

June 6. The **Eastern German Democratic Republic recognized the Oder-Neisse line as final.** Most Germans east of this line had been expelled and the region had been thoroughly Polonized.

15. THE SCANDINAVIAN STATES

The chief concern of the Scandinavian countries during the post-war period was with military security. Negotiations between Denmark, Norway, and Sweden in 1948–49 for a joint defense pact broke down as Denmark and Norway (together with Iceland) decided to join the North Atlantic Pact, while Sweden was determined to do nothing that might impair her traditional neutrality. Finland likewise tried to maintain a middle course. But while she avoided carefully any association with the West, she could not very well refuse Soviet overtures for more cordial relations. She was careful, however, not to forego any of her independence.

a. DENMARK

1945, May 5. **Vilhelm Buhl,** Social Democrat, formed the first post-war cabinet.

Oct. 30. General Elections for the first time gave 18 of the 148 seats in the Lower House to the Communists. The Social Democrats lost an equal number, but still emerged as the strongest party. Since no coalition was possible, **Knud Kristensen** formed a Liberal minority government.

1947, Apr. 20. King Christian X died and was succeeded by his son, as **KING FREDERICK IX.**

Oct. 28. General Elections brought an increase of Socialist strength and a corresponding decline of the Communists.

Nov. 13. Hans Hedtoft formed a Social Democratic minority cabinet.

1949, Apr. 4. **Denmark signed the North Atlantic Treaty.**

1950, Sept. 5. In a **General Election** the Socialists showed further gains.

Oct. 28. The leader of the Liberal Agrarians, **Erik Eriksen,** formed a coalition cabinet of Liberals and Conservatives.

b. NORWAY

1945, June 26. The leader of the Labor Party, **Einar Gerhardsen,** formed the first post-war coalition government.

Sept. 10. **Vidkun Quisling** was sentenced to death and **executed** on Oct. 24.

Oct. 7. The first General Elections since 1936 gave a majority to the Labor Party, and **Einar Gerhardsen** formed a Labor government.

1947, Mar. 3. Parliament rejected a Soviet request for military bases on Spitzbergen.

1949, Apr. 4. **Norway signed the North Atlantic Treaty.**

Oct. 10. General Elections increased the majority of the Labor Party, while the Communists lost all their seats in the Lower House.

c. SWEDEN

1945, July 31. The coalition government of Per A. Hansson was replaced by a Social Democratic cabinet under Hansson.

1946, Oct. 5. Premier Hansson died and was succeeded by **Tage Erlander.**

1948, Sept. 19. General Elections maintained the Social Democrats as the strongest party, while the Communists lost seven of their fifteen seats.

1950, Oct. 29. King Gustav V died. He was succeeded by his son as **KING GUSTAV VI ADOLF.**

d. FINLAND

1945, Mar. 17-18. The General Election brought a swing to the Left.

Apr. 17. Juho Paasikivi formed a new coalition cabinet.

1946, Feb. 21. A number of wartime leaders, among them ex-President **Risto Ryti,** were sentenced to prison for involving Finland in the war or preventing the conclusion of peace. They were pardoned, over Soviet protests, in 1949.

Mar. 4. President Mannerheim resigned for reasons of health.

Mar. 9. JUHO PAASIKIVI was elected President.

Mar. 24. Mauno Pekkala formed a new coalition government.

1947, Feb. 10. The **FINNISH PEACE TREATY** was signed at Paris. The Soviet Union received the **Petsamo** area, a fifty-year lease of a naval base at **Porkkala,** and substantial reparations.

1948, Apr. 6. The USSR and Finland concluded a treaty of friendship and **mutual assistance,** directed primarily against Germany.

July 1-2. In the General Election the Communists lost one-fourth of their parliamentary seats.

July 29. K. A. Fagerholm formed a Social Democratic cabinet.

1949, Aug.-Sept. A wave of Communist-instigated strikes was defeated by firm government action and the loyalty of the non-Communist workers.

1950, Jan. 16-17. Parliamentary Elections gave a majority to the parties supporting **President Paasikivi,** who was re-elected on Feb. 15 for a term of six years.

C. NORTH AMERICA

1. THE UNITED STATES

1945, July 1. James F. Byrnes succeeded Edward R. Stettinius as Secretary of State.

Aug. 1. President Truman ordered the cessation of all Lend-Lease operations, which had cost the United States a total of $48.5 billion.

1945, Nov.-1946, Mar. Large-scale strikes in several leading industries, after seriously curtailing production, led to a first round of wage increases.

1945, Dec. 4. The Senate approved **United States participation in the United Nations.**

1946, Apr.-May. A second wave of strikes hit the soft-coal mines and the railroads. Before they were settled, the government had taken control of the railroads (May 17) and the coal mines (May 20).

June 25. The Senate passed a measure extending **Selective Service** until March 31, 1947. Prior to this, public pressure had brought about the **hasty demobilization** of close to 9 million men.

July 1-25. Experiments conducted at **Bikini** demonstrated the effect of an atomic explosion on warships and under water.

July 15. President Truman signed a bill extending a **credit of $3.75 billion** to Great Britain.

Sept. 20. Secretary of Commerce **Henry Wallace** was asked to resign following his criticism of the government's increasingly firm policy toward the Soviet Union.

Nov. 5. Congressional **Elections** gave the **Republicans substantial majorities** in both Houses.

Nov. 9. Following a futile battle with Congress to maintain price and wage controls, **President Truman virtually removed all controls** except those on rent and some foods.

1947, Jan. 7. James F. Byrnes resigned as Secretary of State and was succeeded by General **George C. Marshall.**

Feb. 2. The **United States and Canada** announced the continuation of their defense-co-operation under the **Permanent Joint Defense Board** of 1940.

Mar. 12. President Truman, in a message to Congress, outlined the **TRUMAN DOCTRINE** of economic and military aid to nations threatened by Communism. He specifically requested urgently needed aid for **Greece** and **Turkey**. The Greek-Turkish Aid Bill went into effect on May 22.

June 5. Secretary Marshall, in a speech at Harvard University, called for a **European Recovery Program**, initiated by the European Powers and supported by American aid (**MARSHALL PLAN**).

June 23. Congress, over the President's veto, passed the **TAFT-HARTLEY ACT**, which prohibited the use of union funds for political purposes, introduced a 60-day notice before a strike or lockout, outlawed the closed shop, and empowered the government to serve injunctions against strikes likely to cripple the nation's economy.

July 26. Congress approved the **unification of the armed services** under a Secretary of Defense (**James V. Forrestal**).

Sept. 2. The United States signed the **Treaty of Rio de Janeiro**, calling for mutual assistance between the American Republics.

1948, Mar. 14-31. Congress passed the Foreign Assistance Act (**Marshall Plan**) and authorized an initial $5.3 billion for European recovery. **Paul G. Hoffman** was appointed chief of the **Economic Co-operation Administration (E.C.A.)** on Apr. 6.

Apr.-July. Strikes in the coal, railway, and steel industries were stopped by government action and a third round of wage increases, to meet the constantly rising cost of living.

June 19. Congress passed a peace-time Selective Service Bill for men between 19 and 25.

Aug. 25. The Soviet Union broke off all consular relations with the United States when the latter refused to surrender a Soviet citizen against her will.

Nov. 2. Contrary to most predictions, Harry S. Truman was re-elected President over Thomas E. Dewey (Republican) by 303 electoral votes to 189. At the same time the Democrats gained a majority in both Houses.

1949. Growing fear of Communism. The spread of Communism in Eastern Europe and the Far East created a growing awareness among many Americans of a possible Communist danger at home. The trial and conviction for espionage of Judith Coplon, employee of the Justice Department, the revelations made in connection with the trial of Alger Hiss, formerly of the State Department, and the trial of the leaders of the American Communist Party, were only the more prominent among a large number of investigations and restrictive measures conducted by federal, state, and local authorities to uncover or prevent Communist infiltration, espionage, and sabotage.

Jan.-Oct. In one of its longest peace-time sessions, Congress, largely because of the opposition of the Southern Democrats, failed to give support to the major points of President Truman's "Fair Deal" program — the repeal of the Taft-Hartley Act and the enactment of federal civil-rights legislation. In the field of foreign affairs, on the other hand, Congress, on the whole, shared the administration's international orientation.

Jan. 7. Secretary of State Marshall resigned for reasons of health and was succeeded by Dean Acheson.

Jan. 20. HARRY S. TRUMAN was inaugurated for his second term. In his inaugural address, he presented a four-point plan for American foreign policy, Point Four of which called for "a bold new program" of assistance to economically underdeveloped areas.

Mar. 3. Secretary of Defense Forrestal resigned, worn out by his futile efforts to bring about the unification of the armed services. He was succeeded by Louis A. Johnson.

Apr. 4. The NORTH ATLANTIC TREATY was signed in Washington. It was ratified by the Senate on July 21 and signed by the President on July 25.

Apr. 19. The Foreign Assistance Act of 1949 authorized $5.43 billion for the European Recovery Program.

Aug. 10. President Truman signed a bill establishing a Department of Defense, with broader and more definite powers for the Secretary of Defense. General Omar N. Bradley was appointed chairman of the Joint Chiefs of Staff (Aug. 11).

Sept. 15. Congress extended the Reciprocal Trade Agreement Act for two years.

Oct. 6. President Truman signed the Mutual Defense Assistance Act appropriating more than one billion dollars for military aid primarily to members of the Atlantic Pact.

Oct. 14. The leaders of the American Communist Party were convicted of conspiracy to advocate the violent overthrow of the United States government and sentenced to fines and imprisonment.

1950, Jan. 25. Alger Hiss was found guilty of perjury for having denied his Communist affiliations and his role in the transfer of State Department secrets to the USSR prior to the war.

Jan. 31. President Truman instructed the Atomic Energy Commission to proceed with its work on the hydrogen bomb.

June 5. President Truman signed the third Foreign Aid Bill, appropriating close to $3 billion for the European Recovery and Point Four programs.

June 25. The invasion of South Korea by North Korean forces led to

June 27. UNITED STATES INTERVENTION IN THE KOREAN WAR, described as "police action" to support the United Nations, whose cease-fire orders had been disregarded by North Korea.

June-Sept. The administration's policy found immediate support in Congress. Selective service was extended, the military budget was almost doubled, and far-reaching military aid was appropriated under the Mutual Defense Assistance Program.

July 8. General Douglas MacArthur was appointed Commanding General of United Nations forces in Korea.

July 20. The charges made by **Senator Joseph McCarthy** of large-scale Communist infiltration into the State Department were found to be untrue by a Senate Committee. The senator's careless accusations brought great hardships to a number of people.

Sept. 12. Secretary of Defense **Louis A. Johnson** resigned and was replaced by General **George C. Marshall.**

Sept. 23. Congress, over the President's veto, adopted the **Internal Security Bill,** which called for the registration of Communists and Communist "front" organizations.

Oct. 15. A meeting at **Wake Island** between **President Truman** and **General MacArthur** tried to clarify differences between the administration and its Far Eastern commander over America's policy in Eastern Asia. MacArthur, on several occasions, and without authorization, had openly advocated a pro-National-

ist and anti-Communist policy in China. While such views were applauded by critics of the government's Far Eastern policy and of Secretary of State Acheson, the General's interference in matters outside his military sphere had caused considerable embarrassment to the administration's conduct of foreign policy.

Nov. 7. Congressional Elections reduced the Democratic majority in both Houses.

Dec. 16. Reversals suffered by United Nations troops in Korea, where the North Koreans had been joined by Chinese Communist troops, led to the **proclamation of a state of national emergency** by President Truman. **Charles E. Wilson** was made head of the newly created **Office of Defense Mobilization.**

Dec. 19. General **Dwight D. Eisenhower** was appointed **Supreme Commander of Western European Forces.**

2. THE DOMINION OF CANADA

1945, June 11. National elections held a majority for Prime Minister Mackenzie King's Liberal Party, thus endorsing the government's conduct of the war. The Progressive Conservatives came out second and the Co-operative Commonwealth Federation (Socialist) third.

1946, Apr. 12. Field Marshal Sir Harold Alexander succeeded the Earl of Athlone as Governor General.

July 1. Proclamation of the **Canadian Citizenship Act,** clarifying the definition of Canadian citizenship, but retaining the status of British subjects for Canadians. It went into effect on Jan. 1, 1947.

July 15. A Royal Commission, investigating the activities of a **Soviet spy ring** in Canada, reported on the disclosure of important secret information by Canadian officials and the existence of a Communist fifth column in Canada, directed by Soviet agents. Among the Canadians involved was the one Parliamentary delegate of the Labor-Progressive (Communist) Party.

Aug. 1. An **Anglo-Canadian wheat agreement** provided for British purchases of large amounts of Canadian wheat at prices considerably below the world market.

1947, Feb. 12. Prime Minister King announced continued **military cooperation between Canada and the United States.**

1948, July 22. A referendum in **Newfoundland** to decide between future self-government and confederation with Canada, by a narrow margin of 78,408 to 71,464 voted in favor of confederation. On March 31, 1949, Newfoundland joined Canada as a tenth province.

1949, Apr. 4. Canada signed the North Atlantic Treaty.

June 27. **National elections** gave the Liberal Party an overwhelming majority of 193 out of 262 seats in the House of Commons.

Nov. 22-Dec. 2. The British Parliament passed a **British North America Bill** granting the Parliament of Canada the right to amend Canada's constitution.

1950, June-Dec. Upon the outbreak of the Korean War, Canada immediately rallied to the support of the United Nations. The first Canadian troops arrived in Korea on Dec. 19. Earlier in the year the Canadian government had placed three destroyers at the disposal of the United Nations for action in Korean waters. Defense appropriations were more than doubled, and a 40 per cent increase of Canada's armed forces was authorized by Parliament. The **Essential Materials Act,** adopted in September, gave the government extensive control over defense industries.

D. LATIN AMERICA

1. GENERAL

1947, Sept. 2. The Inter-American Conference on the Maintenance of **Peace and Security** met at Rio de Janeiro and adopted the **INTER-AMERICAN MUTUAL ASSISTANCE TREATY** against aggression within a defense zone from Greenland to the Antarctic.

1948, Apr. 30. The ninth **Pan-American Conference** at Bogotá, Colombia, created the **Organization of American States** as a regional grouping under the United Nations, and set up an **Inter-American Defense Board.**

2. SOUTH AMERICA

a. ARGENTINA

1946, Feb. 24. Colonel **JUAN D. PERÓN** was elected President, and his supporters won a majority in both Houses. During the campaign the United States, on the basis of captured German documents, accused Argentina and Perón of collaboration with the Axis.

1947, Jan. 1. A Five-Year Plan of economic reform and industrialization went into effect.

1948, Mar. 4. Argentina and Chile agreed on the joint defense of their rights in the Antarctic and the **Falkland Islands** against British claims.

Aug. 13-14. The Chamber of Deputies gave **unlimited powers** to Perón in case of a national emergency and voted to reform the constitution. **Elections** for a constituent assembly (**Dec. 5**) gave the **Peronista Party** a substantial majority.

1949, Mar. 8. The **new constitution**, which was approved by the Assembly, largely confirmed Perón's policy of land reform, nationalization of industries, regulation of foreign trade, etc., and made the President eligible for re-election.

1950. Argentina had by now become a thinly disguised dictatorship under Perón, actively and ably seconded by his wife Eva. In domestic affairs, censorship of the press and far-reaching powers of arrest helped stamp out public criticism. In its foreign relations, the Perón régime claimed an intermediary position between Eastern Communism and Western capitalism.

b. CHILE

1946, Sept. 4. GABRIEL GONZÁLEZ VIDELA was elected President by a Left bloc to succeed **Don Juan A. Rios** (1942-46). He formed a coalition cabinet, including Communists, who later dropped out, as the régime moved to the right.

1947, Oct. Communist-led strikes brought the arrest of 200 Communists, the expulsion of two Yugoslav diplomats, and the **break of diplomatic relations with the Soviet Union and Czechoslovakia** (Oct. 21).

1948, Sept. 2. The Communist Party was outlawed, but Communist-inspired strikes and disorders continued.

1949, Mar. Parliamentary elections gave the government coalition a majority.

c. PARAGUAY

1946, July 26. General Higenio Morínigo, after revoking his 1940 ban on political activity, formed a two-party cabinet, thus ending his six-year dictatorship.

1947, Mar.-Aug. Civil War between the government and Left-wing forces under former President **Rafael Franco** ended with the latter's defeat.

1948-49. The retirement of President Morínigo ushered in a veritable procession of presidents: **Manuel Frutos** (June 6, 1948), **Natalicio González** (Aug. 5, 1948), **Raimundo Rolón** (Jan. 30, 1949),

Molás López (Feb. 27, 1949), and Federico
Chávez (Sept. 12, 1949).

d. URUGUAY

1946, Nov. 24. Tomás Barreta was elected
President. He died on Aug. 2,
1947, and was succeeded by Vice-
President Luiz B. Berres. Both
belonged to the Liberal Colorado
Party.

1950, Nov. 26. Andres Trueba was elected
President to succeed Berres.

e. BOLIVIA

1946, July 21. President Gualberto Villaroel was killed and his régime overthrown by rebellious workers, soldiers, and students. A provisional government promised a
liberal régime and was recognized
by Argentina and the United
States.

1947, Jan. 5. Enrique Hertzog, leader of
the Republican Socialist Union
Party was **elected President.**
Several subsequent attempts by
the **National Revolutionary Movement (M.N.R.)** to overthrow the
government were put down.

1949, May 1. Congressional elections gave
a continued majority to the government. A strike in the tin mines in May
and a rebellion by the outlawed M.N.R. in
September were put down by the army,
leaving the country on the verge of bankruptcy.

Oct. 19. President Hertzog resigned because of ill health and was succeeded by Vice-President **Mamerto Urriolagoita.** Disturbances
from the Right and Left continued, and on

1950, Apr. 10. The Communist Party was
outlawed.

f. PERU

1945, June 10. José Luis Bustamente was
elected President, supported by
Liberal and Aprista forces, to succeed **Pardo Ugarteche.**

1948, Oct. 29. President **Bustamente's**
government was overthrown and
replaced by a military junta under
General **Manuel Odría.** The
APRA and Communist Parties
were outlawed.

1950, July 2. General Odría was elected
President by a large majority and
transformed his junta into a cabinet.

g. ECUADOR

1946, Aug. 11. President Velasco Ibarra
was re-elected by the Assembly.

1947, Aug. 23. Colonel Mancheno, in a
successful revolt, ousted President
Ibarra, only to be overthrown himself on Sept. 3 by a Conservative
counter-revolution. Carlos Arosemena became Acting President.

1948, June 6. In the first popular elections
since 1940, Galo Plaza Lasso was
elected President.

1949, Aug. 5. An earthquake in central
Ecuador killed more than 4000
persons.

h. COLOMBIA

1946, May 4. Conservative leader **Mariano
Ospina Pérez** became President.
Because of a continued Liberal
majority in Congress, he formed a
coalition government.

1948, Apr. 9. The assassination of Left-
Wing Liberal **Jorge Gaitán** touched
off a major revolt which interrupted the
ninth **Pan-American Conference in Bogotá**
and caused 1400 deaths. Careful investigation failed to reveal the instigators of the
upheaval.

1949, June 5. Congressional elections gave
the Liberals a reduced majority.

Nov. 27. Following a violent campaign
costing over 1000 lives, the Conservative **Lauriano Gómez** was elected
President. The Liberals boycotted the
election.

i. VENEZUELA

1945, Oct. 18. President **Isaias Medina**
was overthrown by a revolt of
army officers and **Rómulo Betancourt** was made Provisional President on Oct. 22.

1946, Oct. 27. Elections for the constituent
assembly gave a majority to the
Democratic Action Party.

1947, Dec. 14. Rómulo Gallegos, well-
known literary figure, was elected
President, and his Democratic
Action Party maintained an overwhelming majority.

1948, Nov. 24. The government was overthrown and a military Junta under
Colonel **Carlos Delgado Chalbaud**
took control. Its program called
for close relations with the new
government of Peru and with
Franco Spain.

1950, May 13. The Communist Party was
outlawed.

Nov. 13. President **Delgado Chalbaud** was assassinated, and **Suarez Flammerich** became President of the Junta (Nov. 27).

j. BRAZIL

1945, Oct. 25. General demand for a more liberal government led to the forced resignation of **President Vargas** after almost fifteen years of dictatorship. He was succeeded by Chief Justice **José Linhares.**

Dec. 2. General **ENRICO DUTRA** was elected President. His Social Democratic Party won 40 per cent and the

National Democratic Union 33 per cent of the vote. The new government pledged co-operation with the United States abroad and the elimination of totalitarianism at home.

1946, Sept. 17. A new constitution authorized the government to outlaw any anti-democratic party.

1947, May 1. The Communist Party was outlawed.

Oct. 20. Brazil broke off diplomatic relations with the Soviet Union.

1950, Oct. 3. Economic difficulties and a rising inflation paved the way for the re-election of **GETULIO VARGAS** as President of Brazil.

3. MEXICO AND CENTRAL AMERICA

a. MEXICO

1946, July 7. **MIGUEL ALEMÁN** was elected President, the first civilian to hold that position. He named a cabinet of economic experts and embarked on an extensive program of internal reforms, including industrialization, electrification, irrigation, and transportation. Foreign capital was again welcomed, though under strict government control. **Relations with the United States** were extremely cordial, and for the first time an exchange of presidential visits took place in 1947.

1947, Sept. 30. A final settlement was made by the Mexican government for the 1938 expropriation of **United States oil properties.**

b. PANAMA

1948, Feb. 15. The **United States** announced the final **withdrawal of troops** from their wartime bases, thus settling a burning issue between the two countries.

May 9. **Presidential elections** brought a close and contested decision between former President Arnulfo **Arias** and the Liberal **Domingo Diáz Arosemena.** The latter finally won out, and on Oct. 1 succeeded **Enrique Jiménez** as President of Panama.

1949, Aug. 25-Nov. 24. The death of President **Arosemena** on Aug. 23 touched off a struggle for his succession, from which **Arnulfo Arias,** with the aid of the National Police, emerged victorious. He immediately began to suppress the Opposition.

c. COSTA RICA

1948, Feb. 8. Otilio Ulate of the National Union Party was elected President to succeed **Teodoro Picado.** When the government declared the election invalid, a civil war broke out, which was won by Ulate's followers under **José Figueras.**

May 8. **Figueras headed a military junta** which broke relations with the USSR, outlawed the Communist Party, and embarked on a program of political and economic reforms.

Dec. 10. **Costa Rica was invaded from Nicaragua** by Costa Rican exiles. Charges of Nicaraguan complicity were examined by a commission of the **Organization of American States** and dismissed as unfounded.

1949, Feb. 21. Costa Rica and Nicaragua signed a pact of friendship.

Nov. 8. Twenty-one months after his election, **OTILIO ULATE** was inaugurated as President, with full co-operation from **José Figueras.**

d. NICARAGUA

1947, Feb. 2. Leonardo Arguello was elected President to succeed Dictator **Anastasio Somoza.** The latter had supported Arguello as a possible figurehead, but when the new President showed signs of independence, he was immediately removed (May 27). In September, a puppet of Somoza's, **Victor Román Reyes,** was made President.

1950, Mar. 25. **General Somoza resumed the presidency** and in subsequent "elections" had his return endorsed by the people.

e. HONDURAS

1948, Oct. 10. President **Tiburcio Carías,** after 15 years of dictatorship, supported the election of Nationalist candidate **JUAN MANUEL GÁLVEZ** to become his successor. This did not keep the new President from adopting a program of moderate constitutional, social, and economic reform.

f. SALVADOR

1948, Dec. 14. President **Salvador Castaneda** (who had succeeded **Maximiliano Martínez** in 1944) was forced to resign. A provisional revolutionary government restored full constitutional liberties and called for

1950, Mar. 26-28. The first completely free elections since 1931. Major **OSCAR OSORIO** was elected President.

g. GUATEMALA

1944, Dec. 17-19. In Guatemala's first free elections, **JUAN JOSÉ ARÉVALO,** a university professor, was chosen President to succeed Dictator **Jorge Ubico,** who had been expelled. The new President followed a program of socialization and economic reform, which met with growing opposition from large landowners, foreign investors, and the military.

1950, Nov. 10-12. Colonel **JACOBO ARBENZ GUZMAN,** a consistent supporter of Arévalo's liberal program, was elected President.

4. THE WEST INDIES

a. CUBA

1948, June 1. **CARLOS PRÍO SOCARRAS** was elected President to succeed **Grau San Martín,** who finished his four-year term. Both were members of the Auténtico Party and anti-Communist.

b. HAITI

1946, Jan. 11. A military group under Colonel **Paul Magloire** ousted President **Elie Lescot,** took over the government, and installed **Dumarsais Estimé** as President.

1948, Feb. 11. The Communist Party was outlawed.

1950, May 10. President **Estimé** was overthrown by a military junta under Colonel **Paul Magloire,** who was subsequently elected President.

c. THE DOMINICAN REPUBLIC

1947, May 16. **RAFAEL LEONIDAS TRUJILLO,** who had controlled the country, directly or indirectly, since 1930, was re-elected President.

1947-50. The Dominican Republic repeatedly accused its neighbors, notably **Cuba** and **Guatemala,** of abetting subversive activities (such as the so-called "Caribbean League") directed against the Trujillo régime. The Council of the **Organization of American States** finally considered the matter and condemned the Dominican Republic as well as Cuba and Guatemala for engaging in conspiracies and attempted invasions.

d. PUERTO RICO

1948, Nov. 2. Popular Party candidate **LUIS MUÑOZ MARÍN** became the first elected governor of Puerto Rico.

1950, July 3. An act of the United States Congress permitted Puerto Rico to draft its own constitution.

Nov. 1. The attempt on President Truman's life by two Puerto Ricans led to the arrest of large numbers of Communists and Nationalists on the island. The latter were accused of plotting to overthrow the Puerto Rican government.

E. AFRICA

1. EGYPT AND THE SUDAN

1945, Jan. 8. A General Election (boycotted by the Wafd) secured a majority for the government of Prime Minister **Ahmed Pasha.** The Premier was assassinated on Feb. 24, after announcing Egypt's declaration of war against the Axis, and was succeeded by **Nokrashy Pasha.**

Sept. 23. The Egyptian government demanded that the **Anglo-Egyptian Treaty of 1936** (p. 1084) be revised, that British military occupation of Egypt be terminated, and that the **Sudan** be transferred to full Egyptian control.

1946, May 9. In face of growing anti-British agitation, the British government announced its readiness to withdraw its forces from Egypt.

1947, Jan. 25. Great Britain informed Egypt of her intention to prepare the **Sudan** for self-government.

Jan. 26. After breaking off negotiations with Great Britain for revision of the 1936 Treaty, the Egyptian government decided to refer the question to the **United Nations.** The matter came before the Security Council on Aug. 5, but no decision was reached.

1948, May 15. Egyptian forces moved into **Palestine** to intervene on the Arab side against the Jews.

July 15. A British ordinance introduced governmental reforms in the **Sudan,** over the protests of Egypt, and on

Nov. 15. Elections for a Legislative Assembly in the **Sudan** resulted in a majority for the anti-Egyptian Independence Front.

Dec. 28. Premier **Nokrashy Pasha** was assassinated and replaced first by **Abdul Hadi Pasha** and subsequently (July 26, 1949) by **Hussein Sirry Pasha.**

1950, Jan. 3. A General Election returned an overwhelming majority for the **Wafd** (Nationalist) Party, thus ending five years of government by minorities.

Jan. 12. Mustafa an-Nahas Pasha became Prime Minister and reopened negotiations with Great Britain for revision of the 1936 Treaty.

Nov. 20. The British government reiterated its intention to work toward a self-governing Sudan.

2. COLONIAL AFRICA

1945, May 8. Clashes between Nationalists and the French in **Algeria** caused the death of 88 French and over 1000 natives. A manifesto issued prior to the riots called for an autonomous Algeria, federated with France.

Oct. 11. The United States, Great Britain, France, and the Soviet Union set up a new international administration in **Tangier.**

Dec. 12. The British government announced formation of an **East African High Commission,** consisting of the governors of **Kenya, Uganda,** and **Tanganyika.** It went into effect on Jan. 1, 1948.

1947. A Central Bureau to co-ordinate the activities of the **North African independence movements** was created in Cairo. It worked in close collaboration with the Arab League.

Jan. 1. A new constitution in **Nigeria** provided for a certain degree of native self-government.

Mar. 29. A Nationalist revolt against French rule in **Madagascar** lasted until July and necessitated the sending of reinforcements from France.

Apr. 10. The first **Pan-African Trade Union Congress** met at Dakar and decided to organize the two million European and native workers in Africa.

Sept. 1. A new statute for **Algeria** granted French citizenship to all Algerians, created an Algerian Assembly, and gave financial autonomy to the region.

1948, Feb. 25. A Nationalist riot, involving some 50,000 persons, broke out in the **Gold Coast.**

Apr. 6-11. The new Central Legislative Assembly of **British East Africa** held its first session at Nairobi.

June-Oct. In a series of decrees, the absolute monarchy of Sultan Sidi Mohammed in **French Morocco** was liberalized through the creation of Consultative Chambers elected by Moslems and native Jews.

Aug. 3. The United Nations Trusteeship Council criticized Great Britain for the absence of democratic institutions and proper schools in **Tanganyika.**

Sept. 29. The first conference of representatives from the legislative councils of **Great Britain's African colonies** opened in London. Two-thirds of the participants were natives.

1949, Nov. 21. The General Assembly of the United Nations decided to grant **independence to Libya** on Jan. 1, 1952. **Italian Somaliland** was put under U.N. trusteeship, with Italy as trustee for ten years, after which the region was to gain independence.

1950. New constitutions for the **Gold Coast, Nigeria,** and **Sierra Leone** envisaged a large degree of native self-government with eventual independence for the Gold Coast.

Dec. 2. The United Nations Assembly adopted a plan for the **federation of Eritrea with Ethiopia,** under a federal government which would insure domestic autonomy for the former Italian colony.

3. THE UNION OF SOUTH AFRICA

1945, Oct. The end of the war also meant the end of the coalition government. The Labor Party and the Dominion Party withdrew, leaving Prime Minister **Jan C. Smuts** at the head of a cabinet composed entirely of members from the United Party.

1946, June 3. The **Asiatic Land Tenure and Indian Representation Bill** was enacted into law. It restricted land tenure for Asiatics and gave direct representation to Indians in the Natal provincial council. The Indian government, in protest, withdrew its High Commissioner and broke off trade relations with South Africa.

Dec. 14. The Assembly of the United Nations rejected the proposal of South Africa for the incorporation of **Southwest Africa** into the Union.

1947, Jan. 21. Prime Minister Smuts informed Parliament that his government would not place **Southwest Africa** under United Nations trusteeship. He later proposed to continue arrangements as they had been under the Mandate System.

1948, May 26. In the **GENERAL ELECTION** the coalition (United and Labor Parties) under Smuts was defeated by the Nationalist-Afrikaner bloc.

June 3. Daniel F. Malan, Nationalist leader, who had campaigned on a platform of racial segregation (*apartheid*), formed a new government with himself as Prime Minister and Minister for External Affairs.

1949, Jan. 13. Race riots between Zulus and Indians at Durban left more than 100 dead and 1000 injured.

June. The **South African Citizenship Act** discontinued the automatic granting of citizenship to British and Commonwealth immigrants, who now had to wait five years before receiving citizenship at the discretion of the government. At the same time the program of *apartheid* was put into effect as mixed marriages between Europeans and non-Europeans were forbidden and other measures of segregation were introduced.

1950, Apr. 27. The government announced a **Group Areas Bill** which assigned separate areas to the different races of South Africa. This and other segregation measures led to demonstrations and inter-racial riots and to protests from the Native Representative Council.

July 11. The International Court of Justice ruled that **Southwest Africa** was still a mandate, and that the Union of South Africa was obliged to sub-mit reports on its administration. This decision did not stop the South African government from further integrating Southwest Africa into the Union by giving representation to the territory in the Union Parliament.

Sept. 1. Jan Christiaan Smuts died

F. ASIA

1. THE MIDDLE EAST

a. TURKEY

1945, Mar. 19. The Soviet Union denounced the **Turco-Soviet Non-Aggression Pact of 1925.** Turkey subsequently rejected Soviet demands for territorial concessions and a revision of the Montreux Convention by the Black Sea powers.

1946, Jan. 8. Following repeated demands for an opposition party, the government admitted the **Democratic Party** under former Premier **Jelal Bayar.** The new party won 66 seats (against the official People's Party's 395) at the **General Election** on July 21.

Aug. 3. Recep Peker of the People's Party succeeded **Saracoglu** as Prime Minister.

Aug. 5. ISMET INÖNÜ was re-elected President.

1947, Mar. 12. President Truman announced a program of military and economic aid to Turkey (**Truman Doctrine**).

Sept. 10. Hassan Saka formed a new cabinet.

1948. As might be expected, Turkey's progress toward democracy was a slow one. Repeatedly President Inönü had to act as mediator between his own People's Party, reluctant to abandon its monopoly of power, and the Democratic Party, impatient to share that power. Gradually, however, the electoral system was re-formed, the power of the police was restricted, and civil rights were restored. In May, religious teaching, banned since 1923, was again permitted in primary schools. In foreign affairs, the non-aggression pacts with England and France were reaffirmed, while relations with the Soviet Union continued to be cool.

1950, Mar. 24. Turkey signed a **Treaty of Friendship and Conciliation** with Italy.

May 14. The General Elections testified to the democratization of Turkey, as the **Democratic Party** won an overwhelming majority, with 407 seats against 69 for the People's Party. Democratic leader **JELAL BAYAR** became President, and **Adnan Menderes** Prime Minister.

Sept. 20. Turkey sent a contingent of 4500 men to join the U.N. forces in Korea.

b. SYRIA

1945, Dec. 13. A Franco-British agreement pledged the **evacuation** of their troops from Syria. This was accomplished by Apr. 15, 1946.

1947, July 2. The first election under universal manhood suffrage gave only a minority of seats to the government. At the request of President **Shukri el-Quwatli,** Prime Minister **Jamil Mardam Bey** remained in office.

1948, Apr. 18. Shukri el-Quwatli was re-elected President.

1949, Mar. 30. In a bloodless *coup*, the government was overthrown by Chief of Staff **Husni Za'im,** who was elected President on June 23.

Aug.-Dec. In a second *coup* (Aug. 14), President Husni Za'im was arrested and executed. **Hashim al-Atasi** elected President on Dec. 14. In a third *coup* (Dec. 19) a number of government members, accused of plotting for a union with Iraq, were arrested.

1950, Sept. 4. A new constitution was adopted, limiting the powers of the President.

c. LEBANON

1946, Mar. 10. France and **Great Britain** agreed to evacuate Lebanon. The evacuation was completed by Aug. 31.

1947, May 25. Parliamentary elections gave the government 49 out of 55 seats in the Chamber of Deputies. The fairness of the election was questioned.

1948, May 27. President **Bishara el-Khoury** was re-elected for another six years.

1949, Mar. 23. Lebanon concluded an armistice with Israel, ending the invasion of Lebanon by Israeli forces.

d. PALESTINE (ISRAEL)

The immigration of Jews into Palestine had risen sharply during the war. In May, 1942, a conference of American Zionists had adopted the **Biltmore Program**, which repudiated the **British Plan of 1939** for an independent Palestine (p. 1102) and instead demanded a Jewish state and a Jewish army. As the war ended, both Jews and Arabs maintained military organizations in the Holy Land, in a state of uneasy truce.

1945, Aug. 13. The World Zionist Congress demanded that Palestine be opened to 1,000,000 Jews. President Truman (Aug. 31) requested the immediate admission of 100,-000 Jewish displaced persons from Europe.

Oct. 20. Egypt, Iraq, Syria, and Lebanon warned the United States that creation of a Jewish state in Palestine would lead to war.

1946, Apr. 29. An Anglo-American Committee of Inquiry advised against the partition of Palestine and instead recommended an independent state with local and provincial autonomy. This solution satisfied neither side.

July 22. Illegal Zionist activities reached a climax as British headquarters in the King David Hotel in Jerusalem were blown up, causing the death of 91 persons.

Sept.-Dec. At a London Conference on Palestine, boycotted by the Zionists, the Arab states proposed an Arab-dominated Palestinian state. The Zionist Congress at Basel, on the other hand, called for a Jewish state. Both Jews and Arabs favored the withdrawal of Britain from the Palestine mandate.

1947, Feb. 7. A final British proposal for the division of Palestine into Arab and Jewish zones and its administration as a trusteeship was rejected by Arabs and Jews.

Apr. 2. The British government referred the Palestine problem to the United Nations.

Nov. 29. Following the majority recommendation of its Committee on Palestine, the U.N. General Assembly voted the partition of the country into Jewish and Arab states. This was approved by the Jews, but rejected by the Arabs, and on

Dec. 17. The Arab League Council announced it would stop the proposed division of the Holy Land by use of force.

1948. Terrorist activities, especially by the Jewish Irgun, "Stern Gang," and (to a lesser extent) Haganah, took on warlike proportions and thousands of Arabs fled the country. The British government, unable to solve the Palestine problem, decided to withdraw its forces, and on

May 14. The British Mandate came to an end. The same day, a Jewish provisional government under David Ben Gurion proclaimed the STATE OF ISRAEL, with Chaim Weizmann as President. Within two days it was recognized by the United States and the Soviet Union.

1948, May-1949, July. WAR BETWEEN ISRAEL AND THE ARAB LEAGUE. Starting out on the defensive, Israeli forces soon gained the upper hand, due to superior equipment and fighting ability. United Nations efforts at mediation led to an uneasy truce (June-Oct.), during which the U.N. mediator, Count Folke Bernadotte, was assassinated by Zionist terrorists (Sept. 17). Continued U.N. efforts finally led to a series of armistices between Israel and the Arab League nations.

1948, Dec. 1. A Palestine Arab Congress at Jericho proclaimed King Abdullah of Transjordan as King of Palestine.

1949, Jan. 25. Israel's first elections brought victory to the Mapai Party of Premier Ben Gurion.

May 11. Israel joined the United Nations.

Dec. 14. Ignoring a resolution of the U.N. General Assembly for the internationalization of Jerusalem, the Israeli government moved to the city from Tel Aviv.

1950. As a result of the war and the continued immigration of unlimited numbers of Jews, Israel was faced with grave economic difficulties. These were increased by constant friction between the new state and its Arab neighbors. Efforts of the U.N. Palestine Conciliation Commission to reach a final peace settlement, remained unsuccessful.

e. TRANSJORDAN (JORDAN)

1946, Mar. 22. Great Britain recognized the independence of Transjordan and concluded a close alliance with the new state.

May 25. The **KINGDOM OF TRANS-JORDAN** was officially proclaimed, with Emir **Abdullah** as king. Its admission to the **United Nations** was vetoed by the Soviet Union.

1947, Jan. 11. Transjordan and Turkey signed a pact of friendship.

Apr. 14. Treaty of alliance concluded with Iraq.

Oct. 20. Elections to the National Assembly gave almost all seats to the official Revival Party.

1948, Mar. 15. A new treaty of alliance with Great Britain set up a Joint Defense Board.

May 15. The British-trained **Arab Legion** of Transjordan invaded Palestine and entered Jerusalem.

Dec. 1. A conference of Palestine Arabs proclaimed **Abdullah** sovereign of all Palestine, and on Dec. 13 the parliament of Transjordan approved a future union with Arab Palestine. This was criticized by the Arab League, since it acknowledged the partition of Palestine and presented a step toward Abdullah's scheme for a "Greater Syria" under his leadership.

1949, June 2. Transjordan was renamed "The Hashimite Kingdom of Jordan."

1950, Apr. 24. Final incorporation of Arab Palestine into Jordan over the protest of most of the Arab League.

f. IRAQ

1946, Mar. 29. Iraq concluded a treaty of friendship with **Turkey**, calling for joint control over the upper Tigris and Euphrates.

1947, Apr. 14. Treaty of alliance concluded with **Transjordan**.

Oct. 26. Great Britain announced the withdrawal of its army from Iraq, except for a military mission of two R.A.F. detachments.

1948, Jan. 15. The treaty of Portsmouth with Great Britain, which called for continued British participation in Iraq's defense, met with violent popular opposition and failed to be ratified. The treaty of 1930 thus remained in force.

g. IRAN

1945, Sept. 13. The Iranian government requested the **withdrawal of British, American, and Russian forces** and received assurances that evacuation would be completed by March 2, 1946.

Nov. 18. The **Tudeh Party** (Communist) organized a rebellion in the province of **Azerbaijan.** When government intervention against the rebels was prevented by the Soviet Union and Soviet troops failed to evacuate Iran,

1946, Mar. 19. The government protested to the **U.N. Security Council** against Soviet activities.

Apr. 5. Iran and the Soviet Union agreed on the **withdrawal of Russian troops** (completed by May 9), the introduction of reforms in Azerbaijan, and the creation of a Soviet-Iranian oil company for northern Iran.

June 13. Azerbaijan returned to Iranian control, maintaining some autonomy. Unrest in the province continued for some time.

Sept. 22. Rebellion in the province of **Fars** brought reforms and greater local autonomy to the southern tribesmen.

1947, Jan.-Feb. Parliamentary elections supported the government.

Oct. 6. An agreement with the United States arranged for an **American military mission** and the purchase of American military equipment.

Throughout the year, resentment had been growing against the oil concessions granted to the Soviet Union in April, 1946. Finally, on

Oct. 22. The Majlis (Parliament) nullified the **Soviet oil agreement.** Soviet protests against this action, as well as against American military assistance, were rejected.

1949, Feb. 5. The **Tudeh Party** was outlawed, following an attempt on **Shah Mohammed Reza Pahlavi's** life.

May 9. A revision of the constitution gave the Shah power to dissolve parliament.

May 10. Announcement of a **Seven-Year Plan** for the economic development of Iran, under the direction of American technicians.

July 18. A new agreement with the **Anglo-Iranian oil company,** calling for a larger share in the company's profits, was subsequently rejected by the Majlis.

h. AFGHANISTAN

1946, May. Prime Minister **Sirdar Mohammed Hashim Khan,** after 17 years in office, resigned and was succeeded by his brother Sirdar

Mahmud Shah Khan, who inaugurated a program of reform.

1949-50. In a border dispute with Pakistan, the government of Afghanistan demanded autonomy for the Pathan border tribes on the Pakistan side of the Durand line of 1893 (p. 868).

2. INDIA

a. BRITISH INDIA

1943-47. FIELD MARSHAL VISCOUNT WAVELL, Viceroy.

1945, Sept. 19. The new British Labor government proposed to discuss with Indian representatives the offer for Indian autonomy made by Sir **Stafford Cripps** in 1942 (p. 1138).

Sept. 20-23. The **All-India Congress** under Mohandas K. Gandhi and Pandit Jawarharlal Nehru, meeting in Bombay, declared this plan to be unsatisfactory, and called on Great Britain to "quit India."

Dec. 27. Elections to the Central Legislative Assembly gave the largest number of seats to the **Congress Party** and the **Moslem League.**

1946. Hindu-Moslem differences over the future of India, combined with a serious food shortage, led to frequent riots, causing thousands of deaths.

Mar. 14. The British government offered **full independence to India.**

Mar.-June. Negotiations between British and Indian leaders failed to draw up a plan which satisfied both the Congress Party and the Moslem League. The latter, under **Mohammed Ali Jinnah** insisted on a separate Moslem state of **Pakistan** and decided on "direct action" to achieve its goal.

Aug. 24. A new **Executive Council** (boycotted by the Moslem League) was formed as an interim government, including seven Congress members and five non-League Moslems. The Moslem League finally decided to join on Oct. 25.

Dec. 9. The **Constituent Assembly,** elected earlier, began its deliberations on the future of India. The Moslem League refused to participate.

1947, Feb. 20. To hasten developments, the British government declared its intention to transfer power into Indian hands not later than June 1948.

Feb. 20-Aug. 15. VISCOUNT MOUNTBATTEN, Viceroy.

May 29. The Constituent Assembly outlawed "untouchability."

June 3. Following negotiations with Hindu and Moslem leaders, the British government announced the new constitutional plan which called for **partition between India and Pakistan.** This plan was endorsed by the Moslem League on June 9 and the All-India Congress on June 16.

July 5. The **Indian Independence Bill** was introduced into Parliament. It called for two Dominions, **India** and **Pakistan,** and the termination of British authority over the remaining **Indian States.** The Bill became law on July 18.

Aug. 15. The **INDEPENDENCE OF INDIA** went into effect. The process of partition was accompanied by terrible acts of violence, notably in the Punjab region, between Moslems and Hindus. By the end of September, close to two million refugees had been exchanged between India and Pakistan. On

Sept. 21. The two new governments issued a joint statement stressing their readiness to remove all causes of conflict.

b. THE DOMINION OF INDIA

1947, Aug. 15. The **Dominion of India was inaugurated** in Delhi, with **Pandit Nehru** as Prime Minister and **Lord Mountbatten** as Governor General. Most of the **Princely States,** except Hyderabad, Kashmir, and Junagadh, joined the Indian Union. The Princes retained their titles, fortunes, and received a fixed civil list.

Oct. 26. The government of India admitted **Kashmir** into the Indian Union, thus precipitating a crisis with Pakistan, since Kashmir contained a majority of Moslems.

Nov. 9. The Indian government assumed control over the administration of the state of **Junagadh.**

Dominion of India

Dominion of Pakistan

Areas of uncertain status

INDIA–PARKISTAN, 1950

Dec. 30. After vain attempts to solve the conflict over **Kashmir**, the dispute was referred to the **United Nations.** Sporadic fighting continued in Kashmir between Indian and Moslem forces.

1948, Jan. 30. Mahatma Gandhi was assassinated by a Hindu for his part in the partition of India.

June 21. Chakravarti Rajagopalachari succeeded Earl Mountbatten as Governor General.

Sept. 7. The continued refusal of **Hyderabad** to join India or to grant parliamentary government provoked an ultimatum from Prime Minister Nehru, who threatened war unless Hyderabad joined the Dominion. In reply

Sept. 11. The Hyderabad government appealed to the United Nations.

Sept. 13. Indian forces invaded Hyderabad.

Sept. 17. Hyderabad surrendered and accepted India's demands.

1949, Jan. 1. Following the mediation attempts of a United Nations Commission, India and Pakistan agreed on a **cease-fire order for Kashmir.** A subsequent arbitration scheme, submitted by the United Nations, was rejected by India.

Nov. 26. The Indian Constituent Assembly adopted a new **Constitution** which made **India a Federal Republic.** The King continued to be recognized, however, as symbol of the free association of Commonwealth members.

1950, Jan. 26. Inauguration of the Republic and election of **Rajendra Prasad** as its first President.

Apr. 8. Mounting tension between India and Pakistan was eased by an agreement between Prime Ministers Pandit Nehru and Liaqat Ali Khan (**Delhi Pact**) promising fair treatment to each other's minorities. The continued deadlock over **Kashmir**, on the other hand, made any

really close relations between the two countries impossible.

June-Dec. India followed an independent course toward events in **Korea.** While condemning North Korean aggression, she was equally opposed to the crossing of the 38th parallel by U.N. forces. India also advocated the admission of **Communist China** to the United Nations.

c. PAKISTAN

1947, Aug. 15. The Dominion of Pakistan was inaugurated with **Liaqat Ali Khan** as Prime Minister and **Mohammed Ali Jinnah** as Governor General.

1948, Sept. 11. Mohammed Ali Jinnah died and was succeeded by **Kwaja Nazimuddin** as Governor General.

1950, Apr. 8. The **Delhi Pact** between India and Pakistan substantially reduced friction between the two Dominions.

June-Dec. Pakistan supported the United Nations cause in the **Korean War**, profiting economically from the sudden demand for her raw materials, brought on by the war.

d. CEYLON

1946, May 15. Ceylon was granted a **new constitution** which gave her almost complete self-government in domestic affairs.

1947, Sept. 26. The first cabinet under the new constitution took office, with Stephen Senanayaki as Prime Minister. The new parliament opened on Nov. 24. A series of agreements with the United Kingdom (Nov. 11) further reduced British influence in Ceylon, and finally, on

1948, Feb. 4. CEYLON BECAME A SELF-GOVERNING DOMINION in the British Commonwealth, the first non-European colony to achieve this status.

3. BURMA

1945, May 17. A British White Paper promised Burma **Dominion status** after the war.

1946, Dec. 20. The British government invited a Burmese delegation to meet in London and discuss the early achievement of **self-government** for Burma.

1947, Jan. 28. An agreement between British and Burmese leaders called for the

Apr. 9. Election of a Constituent Assembly. The **Anti-Fascist People's Freedom League** (A.F.P.F.L.), headed by **U Aung San**, received an overwhelming majority.

June 17. The Constituent Assembly unanimously adopted a resolution calling for an **"independent sovereign republic to be known as the Union of Burma."**

July 19. **U Aung San** and several members of his provisional government were **assassinated** by political opponents under the direction of former Premier **U Saw.** The assassins were tried and executed (May 8, 1948).

July 20. **Thakin Nu,** vice-president of the A.F.P.F.L., formed a new government.

Sept. 24-25. The **new constitution was adopted** by the **Constituent Assembly,** and **Sao Shwe Thaik,** the Sawbwa (ruler) of Yawnghwe (one of the largest of the Shan states), was elected provisional President.

1948, Jan. 4. The **UNION OF BURMA,** an independent republic free from any ties with the British Commonwealth, was officially proclaimed. **Sao Shwe Thaik** continued as President, and **Thakin Nu** as Prime Minister. The new state immediately embarked on a program of radical nationalization of resources and industries. Its program was not radical enough, however, to satisfy the two Communist parties of Burma, and in late

March. A **Communist rebellion broke out in Southern Burma.** The situation was further aggravated when in

August. The **Karens started a rebellion** to achieve an autonomous Karen state. Both Karens and Communists succeeded in occupying large parts of Southern and Central Burma. At the same time an element of the **"People's Volunteer Organization"** (part of the A.F.P.F.L.'s old army) ravaged Central Burma.

1949, June 14. The Karen rebels proclaimed a separate state, with headquarters at Toungoo.

1950, Mar. 19. Government forces captured **Toungoo.**

May 19. The main center of Communist resistance at **Prome** was taken by the army. The government was thus able to regain some control over the major towns and means of communication. **Rebel activity,** however, **continued,** and elections, already postponed several times, had to be postponed for another year. In the meantime the economic condition of the country, already seriously affected by the war, was steadily growing worse.

4. SIAM (THAILAND)

1946, Jan. 1. The state of war between **Great Britain** and **Siam** was officially ended. The **United States** resumed diplomatic relations with Siam on Jan. 4.

June 9. King **Ananda Mahidol** was found dead from a bullet wound. His brother, **Phumiphon Aduldet,** succeeded him.

Oct. 13. The Siamese government accepted the United Nations verdict to return to **Indo-China** the provinces acquired in 1941 (p. 1166).

1947, Nov. 8. In a bloodless *coup d'état*, an army group under Marshal **Luang Pibul Songgram** overthrew the government.

1948, Jan. 29. A general election resulted in a victory for the new government and on Apr. 8 **Luang Pibul Songgram** became Premier. There was considerable resistance, however, notably from the followers of **Nai Pridi Panomyang,** wartime resistance leader.

1949, May 11. Siam henceforth was to be known again as **Thailand.**

1950. The rise of **Communism** in Southeast Asia found Thailand on the anti-Communist side. On March 1 she recognized the **South Korean government,** and later on sent a contingent to participate in the **Korean war** on the U.N. side.

Mar. 24. King Phumiphon Aduldet returned from Switzerland, where he had been studying, and was crowned as

May 5. King **RAMA IX.**

5. INDO-CHINA

1945, Sept. 2. The **Viet Nam Republic** under its Nationalist President **Ho Chi-Minh** declared its independence, and on

1946, Mar. 6. **France recognized Viet Nam** as a free state within the Indo-Chinese Federation and the French Union. Yet

1946. Fighting continued between French and Vietnamese forces over the latter's desire for a greater measure of independence and the exten-

SOUTHEAST ASIA, 1950

sion of Viet Nam authority over the rest
of French Indo-China.

1949, Mar. 8. An agreement between the
French and the non-Communist
Viet Nam Nationalists under **Bao
Dai**, former Emperor of Annam,
recognized the **independence of
Viet Nam** (including Cochin China)
within the French Union.

June 14. The new state of Viet Nam was
officially established at Saigon,
with **Bao Dai** as Chief of State.

Yet armed conflict with the Communist
Viet Minh organization under **Ho Chi-Minh**
continued.

1950, Jan.-Feb. Communist China and the
Soviet Union recognized the **Viet
Minh** régime, while the **United States** and
Britain recognized **Viet Nam, Cambodia,**
and **Laos** as "Associated States within the
French Union." The Viet Minh forces now
received military aid from China, and Viet
Nam was given similar aid by the United
States.

6. THE REPUBLIC OF INDONESIA

1945, Aug. 17. Two days after the Japanese surrender, the Indonesian
leaders **Achmed Soekarno** and
Mohammed Hatta proclaimed the
independence of the Republic of
Indonesia. The Dutch refused to
recognize the new government.

Sept. 29-Oct. 3. British and Dutch
troops arrived in Batavia to disarm and repatriate the Japanese.
Before long, fighting was under
way between these troops and the
"**Indonesian People's Army.**"

Oct. 12. The Dutch government offered
to negotiate with those Indonesians, who were ready to agree to a
self-governing Indonesia within
the Netherlands Kingdom.

Nov. 13. **Soetan Sjahrir,** a young Socialist, became Premier of the new
republic while **Soekarno** became
President.

1946, Feb. 19. Negotiations began between
Dutch and Indonesian representatives, while Dutch and British
troops slowly pushed back the
Indonesian forces into central and
eastern Java.

Nov. 15. Following the conclusion of a
military truce, the Dutch and
Indonesians initialed the **CHERIBON
AGREEMENT** providing for **Dutch recognition of the Indonesian Republic** (Java,
Sumatra, and Madura), and the establishment of a **United States of Indonesia,** to
include, besides the Indonesian Republic,
the states of **Borneo** and the **Great East**
(Celebes, the Sunda Islands, and the Moluccas). The whole was to be joined with
the Netherlands in equal partnership under
the Dutch Crown. The agreement was
signed on March 25, 1947.

Nov. 29. The last **British** troops left
Indonesia.

1947, May-July. Attempts to carry out the
Cheribon Agreement revealed far-
reaching differences in its interpretation between Dutch and Indonesian authorities. On

June 26. Prime Minister **Sjahrir** resigned, but his successor, **Amir**
Sjarifoeddin, was no more successful in
solving the deadlock in the negotiations.
Both sides continued to violate the cease-
fire agreement, and when the Republic rejected a Dutch proposal for joint police
action against the disruptive Indonesian
forces,

July 20. The **Dutch launched a full-scale
offensive** in central and eastern
Java, making rapid advances.

Aug. 1. A resolution of the **U.N.** Security
Council, calling for a **cease-fire,**
was accepted by both sides but
was not strictly observed.

Dec. 8. Negotiations between Dutch
and Indonesian leaders were resumed under the auspices of a
U.N. Committee of Good Offices.

1948, Jan. 17. The Netherlands and the
Republic of Indonesia signed a
truce agreement on board the U.S.S. *Ren-
ville*, which laid down the principles to
serve as basis for future negotiations. Immediately, however, differences arose
as to the interpretation of these principles.

Jan. 31. A new Indonesian cabinet was
formed under **Mohammed Hatta.**

Sept. 18. Indonesian Communists, under the leadership of **Muso,** a
veteran Indonesian Communist recently
returned from Moscow, **set up a "soviet
government"** at Madioen (Java). The
government intervened successfully and
the Communists withdrew to the jun-
gle.

Dec. 18. After repeated breakdowns in their negotiations with Indonesia, the **Dutch resumed their offensive.** Within a few days they occupied the major Republican cities and **captured the Soekarno government.**

1949, Jan. 28. The **U.N. Security Council** called for an immediate end of hostilities, release of government leaders, and the transfer of sovereignty to the United States of Indonesia by July 1, 1950. Further United Nations efforts finally led to a **Round Table Conference at The Hague** between Dutch and Indonesian representatives.

Nov. 2. Complete agreement was reached on the transfer of sovereignty to the United States of Indonesia and on its relations with the Netherlands.

Dec. 16. Soekarno was elected first President and **Mohammed Hatta** became first Prime Minister of the United States of Indonesia.

Dec. 27. The **Netherlands** and the **Republic of Indonesia** formally **transferred sovereignty to the UNITED STATES OF INDONESIA,** a federal republic of 16 states, whose independence was proclaimed simultaneously at its capital of Jakarta (Batavia). The status of **Dutch New Guinea,** which remained outside the new federation, was to be determined in future negotiations.

1950. Local uprisings and guerrilla warfare continued in many parts of the new state, notably in East Indonesia.

May 19. A conference between the federal government and the states decided to substitute a **unitary state** for the United States of Indonesia. As a result,

Aug. 17. A provisional constitution was drawn up, establishing the **REPUBLIC OF INDONESIA.**

Sept. 6. **Mohammed Natsir** formed a new cabinet.

Sept. 28. The Republic of Indonesia was admitted to the United Nations.

7. CHINA

The end of the war found China still divided between the Nationalist forces of **Chiang Kai-shek** and the Red Army of **Mao Tse-tung.** The latter, having taken advantage of the sudden Japanese collapse, had overrun most of the northern provinces, and various efforts for a *rapprochement* between the two parties remained fruitless.

1945, Aug. 14. **T. V. Soong,** Premier of the Nationalist government, concluded a **treaty of friendship and alliance with the Soviet Union.** In return for Soviet recognition of the Nationalists as "the Central Government of China," the latter agreed to the independence of **Outer Mongolia,** gave the U.S.S.R. joint 30-year ownership of the **Manchurian Railway** and the port of **Dairen,** and agreed to the conversion of **Port Arthur** into an exclusively Chinese and Soviet naval base.

Aug. 26–Oct. 11. Negotiations between **Chiang Kai-shek** and **Mao Tse-tung** failed to settle their differences, and before the end of October heavy fighting was in progress between Nationalists and Communists in North China. Each side aimed at the control of Manchuria, which was being evacuated by the Soviet forces. At this point

Dec. 14. The United States intervened and sent **General Marshall** as mediator to effect a

1946, Jan. 10. Truce between **Nationalist and Communist forces,** followed by agreement to create a national army, form a coalition government, and draw up a new constitution. Yet, on

Feb. 17. The Communists demanded joint control with the Nationalists over **Manchuria.** When this was ignored,

Apr. 14. All-out civil war was resumed, interrupted by another uneasy truce (May 12–June 30) and intermittent peace overtures from both sides. During the initial campaigns, the Nationalist Government forces advanced all along the line.

May 1. The Nationalist Government returned from Chungking to Nanking.

Oct. 10. **Chiang Kai-shek was re-elected President** of China by the Kuomintang.

Nov. 4. **China** and the **United States** signed a treaty of friendship, commerce, and navigation.

Nov. 15. A National Assembly met (without Communist participation) and on Dec. 25 adopted a **new constitution,** which guaranteed political equality and civil rights to all citizens and vested supreme authority in the National Assembly. The government was to consist of a Legislative Yuan (Parliament) and an Executive Yuan (cabinet). The constitution went into effect on Dec. 25, 1946.

1947, Jan. 29. The United States officially abandoned its mediation efforts. General Marshall, in his final report, criticized both the reactionaries in the Kuomintang and the extremists in the Communist camp, who prevented a compromise.

Mar. 19. Nationalist successes against the Communists culminated in the capture of the Communist capital of Yenan. An almost immediate reversal resulted in Communist control over Manchuria by the end of 1947.

Nov. 21-23. Elections for the National Assembly aroused little popular interest. Most of the candidates belonged to the Kuomintang, since Communists and the Democratic League had been excluded.

1948. In the course of 1948, the decline of Chiang Kai-shek's forces, already evident in 1947, proceeded rapidly, and by the end of the year most of Northern China was in Communist hands. The Nationalists by now had lost most of their best troops, and corruption among their provincial leaders had led to the surrender or sale of vast amounts of American equipment to the Communists. The Nationalist economy, badly in need of reform and shaken by growing inflation, had long depended on American aid, which, since V–J Day, was estimated at more than $2 billion. In early 1948, an additional $400 million was allocated, but as time went on and the Nationalist government failed to liberalize and reform itself, American aid was drastically curtailed.

Mar. 29. The National Assembly convened at Nanking. After severely criticizing the government and its conduct of the war, it re-elected Chiang Kai-shek as President of China (Apr. 19) and gave him virtual dictatorial powers during the national emergency.

Sept. 1. The Communists announced the formation of a North China People's Government.

1949. The rapid decomposition of the Nationalist armies, the fall of Tientsin (Jan. 15) and Peiping (Jan. 21), and the Communist threat to the lower Yangtze Valley brought about a temporary change in the Nationalist government. On

Jan. 21. General Chiang Kai-shek resigned the presidency, leaving Vice-President Li Tsung-jen in charge of peace talks with the Communists. These broke down when

Apr. 20. Communist demands, including the formation of a coalition cabinet under Mao Tse-tung, and the punishment of "war criminals" (notably Chiang Kai-shek), proved unacceptable to the Nationalists. The Communists thereupon resumed their offensive, and in the course of the year drove the Nationalist armies off the Chinese mainland.

July 16. The Nationalists organized a Supreme Council under Chiang Kai-shek and began to prepare for withdrawal to the island of Formosa (Taiwan), which was completed by Dec. 8.

Aug. 5. The UNITED STATES issued a WHITE PAPER announcing the cessation of all aid to Nationalist China. The latter's collapse was attributed to the military, political, and economic incapacity of the Kuomintang leaders, who had come to rely on United States help to win the war and keep them in power.

Oct. 1. The Communist PEOPLE'S REPUBLIC OF CHINA was officially proclaimed at Peiping, with Mao Tse-tung as Chairman of the Central People's Administrative Council and Chou En-lai as Premier and Foreign Minister. The new régime was immediately recognized by the Soviet Union and her satellites, and later by Burma, India, and (Jan. 6, 1950) Great Britain.

1950. The unification of the country, together with a program of reconstruction and deflation, brought considerable economic improvement to the Chinese Republic. While some changes were introduced in agriculture, as land reform went into effect, there were no radical innovations, outside of over-all state planning, in industry. The "People's Liberation Army" carried on continued warfare against anti-Communist guerrillas.

At the same time, the Nationalist Government in Formosa at last introduced some of the reforms it had promised while still in control of the mainland.

Feb. 14. Mao Tse-tung signed a 30-year TREATY OF FRIENDSHIP, ALLIANCE, AND MUTUAL ASSISTANCE WITH SOVIET RUSSIA. It was followed by a series of economic agreements for the joint exploitation of Chinese resources.

Mar. 1. Chiang Kai-shek resumed the presidency of Nationalist China.

May 2. Communist forces completed occupation of Hainan.

Oct. Chinese Communist "volunteers" intervened in the Korean War on the North Korean side.

8. JAPAN

With the formal surrender of Japan (p. 1170), supreme authority passed into the hands of **General Douglas MacArthur,** as Supreme Commander for the Allied Powers (**SCAP**). Though aided by an Allied Control Council, and following the very general directions of an 11-nation Far Eastern Commission with headquarters in Washington, MacArthur pursued a quite independent policy. To facilitate his task, Japan's governmental structure was left intact and put under the direction of **Premier Shidehara** and a non-partisan cabinet. The most immediate task of the occupation authorities was to rid Japan of its imperialist past. In a series of decrees, General MacArthur restored civil liberties, liberated political prisoners, dissolved the secret police, liberalized the educational curriculum, granted the franchise to all adults, encouraged the formation of labor unions and the abolition of feudal land tenure, and ended the compulsory adherence to Shintoism. The climax of these moves to break with the past came on Jan. 1, 1946, when **Emperor Hirohito,** in a New Year's message, disclaimed the divinity that was accredited to him by the Japanese people.

1946, Apr. 10. The first **General Election** favored the moderate parties. Communist returns were negligible. A new government under **Shigeru Yoshida** took office on May 16.

A series of **purges,** initiated by SCAP, was directed against all "active exponents" of aggressive nationalism, including intellectuals and businessmen, and ultimately involved more than 1.5 million people. In addition, an **International Military Tribunal** in Tokyo began the trial of major war criminals, while separate British and Australian tribunals were set up in Southeast Asia and the South Pacific respectively.

Nov. 3. A **NEW CONSTITUTION** provided for an elected Upper House, transferred sovereignty from the Emperor to the people, safeguarded individual rights, and introduced a broad measure of local self-government. It became effective on May 3, 1947.

1947-48. The post-war **economic recovery** of Japan was extremely slow and heavily dependent on American aid. To improve matters, the initial Allied policy of dissolving the large industrial combines was abandoned in 1948, and **reparations** from capital equipment were drastically reduced. Japan's future **standard of living** was set at the 1930-34 level. Beginning in April, 1947, a limited resumption of private **foreign trade** was authorized, though by the end of 1948 Japan had only regained a small fraction of her former trade volume. To counteract the economic loss from numerous strikes, General MacArthur repeatedly imposed a ban on strikes. On Dec. 23, 1948, the **Diet prohibited all strikes** and collective bargaining **by government employees.** The initiative for Japan's economic revival came from the United States, seconded by Great Britain. It met with opposition from Australia and China, who feared a powerful Japan as a threat to their future security.

1947, April. Elections for both Houses of the Diet returned a Right-Wing majority for the **House of Councillors.** In the **House of Representatives** the Social Democrats received the largest number of seats. On May 23, the Diet elected Socialist **Tetsu Katayama** to head a coalition government.

1948, Feb. 7. The **Katayama government** resigned because of friction within the Socialist Party. A new coalition was formed by Democratic Party leader **Hitoshi Ashida** on March 9.

Mar. 15. A new Right-Wing Opposition party, the **Democratic Liberals,** was formed under the leadership of former Premier **Yoshida.** When

Oct. 7. Premier Ashida resigned, following a financial scandal involving members of his cabinet, **Shigeru Yoshida** formed a Democratic Liberal government on Oct. 14.

Nov. 12. The **International Military Tribunal** sentenced General **Hideki Tojo** and six others to death for major war crimes. Sixteen others were given life sentences.

1949, Jan. 23. National Elections showed a decided swing to the Right, with the Democratic Liberals gaining an absolute majority. Communist strength likewise increased. The Diet re-elected **Yoshida** as Premier.

May 12. The American representative on the Far Eastern Commission announced the **termination of reparation removals** to aid Japan's economic recovery. The inflationary tendencies of Japan's economy were gradually being overcome through a strict program of economic stabilization imposed by General MacArthur.

1950. Largely under the impact of the Korean War, severe restrictions were imposed on **Japan's Communists,** most of whose overt activities were suppressed. In the economic field, the war brought a much-needed increase in Japanese exports. The creation of a **National Police Reserve** of 75,000 men, to be used against domestic disturbances, was seen by some as the beginnings of a new Japanese army. In September, more than 10,000 prominent figures who had been dismissed at the beginning of the occupation were re-admitted to public life.

9. KOREA

According to decisions reached at the Crimea and Potsdam Conferences, the **United States** after the war occupied the southern half of Korea up to the **38th parallel,** while the **Soviet Union** took over the northern half. Each occupying power installed a group of Korean advisers, which was strongly conservative in the American and pro-Communist in the Russian zone.

1945, Dec. 27. The **Moscow Conference** between Great Britain, the United States, and the Soviet Union called for a **provisional Korean democratic government** under a five-year trusteeship of the three Powers and of China. Subsequent attempts of a **Joint Russo-American Commission** to put this agreement into force failed because of basic differences between the two parties over the definition of democracy. **Korea thus remained divided** into an agricultural south and an industrial north, with disastrous consequences to her economy.

1946, Dec. 12. A **Legislative Assembly,** half popularly elected, half nominated, was opened in the American zone. Its functions, at the start, were largely advisory.

1947, Sept. Following another futile attempt to settle the future of Korea by negotiations with the Soviet Union, **the United States referred the Korean problem to the United Nations.** The Soviet Union in turn proposed the simultaneous withdrawal of American and Soviet occupation forces.

1948, Jan. 8. A **United Nations Commission** arrived in Seoul (South Korea) to supervise elections for a **National Constituent Assembly.** It was refused admission to the Soviet zone. The Committee then recommended

May 10. Elections in South Korea for a new **National Assembly.** The parties of the Right gained a majority.

May 28. The **National Constituent Assembly,** meeting at Seoul, invited delegates from North Korea to attend. When this invitation was ignored,

Aug. 15. The **REPUBLIC OF KOREA** was proclaimed, with Dr. **Syngman Rhee** as President. United States Military Government was officially terminated and the new government entered into an agreement with the United States for the training of Korean forces.

Sept. 9. A Korean **PEOPLE'S DEMOCRATIC REPUBLIC,** claiming authority over the entire country, was inaugurated in northern Korea, under the presidency of veteran Communist **Kim Il sung.** Its institutions were modeled after those of the Soviet Union.

Dec. 25. The Soviet Union announced the complete withdrawal of its forces from North Korea.

1949, June 29. The United States completed the withdrawal of occupation forces from South Korea.

Sept. 2. The **United Nations Commission,** reporting on its failure to mediate between North and South Korea, **warned of a possible civil war.** There already was sporadic fighting along the 38th parallel, assuming the proportions of major battles.

Pusan perimeter
Greatest advance of North Korean forces
Greatest advance of UN forces

KOREA

1950, May 30. Elections for the **National Assembly of South Korea** gave the majority of seats to the moderate forces rather than to the extreme Right-Wing supporters of President Rhee.

June 5. North Korea proposed negotiations for an all-Korean assembly, but refused to deal with the government of Syngman Rhee.

June 25. Start of the **KOREAN WAR,** as North Korean troops crossed the 38th parallel at eleven points. The United Nations Security Council called for an immediate cessation of hostilities and withdrawal of North Korean forces.

June 27. The Security Council asked members of the United Nations to furnish assistance to the Republic of Korea. The United States intervened immediately, to help stem the North Korean advance.

July 8. Following a request of the Security Council, President Truman designated **General Douglas MacArthur** as commanding general of the U.N. forces in Korea.

Sept. 5. At its farthest advance, North Korea held most of the Korean peninsula except for a **U.N. beachhead around Pusan** in the southeast.

Sept. 13. American and South Korean forces launched a counter-offensive, co-ordinated with an amphibious landing at Inchon (Sept. 15). By the end of the month, **U.N. forces had reached the 38th parallel** and General MacArthur asked for the surrender of the North Korean forces. When his request was ignored,

Oct. 9. General MacArthur ordered the **crossing of the 38th parallel,** acting on implicit authority of the U.N. General Assembly. Within three weeks, **U.N. forces were approaching the Manchurian border,** reaching the Yalu River at several points.

Nov. 1. A North Korean counter-offensive halted, and in places **drove back U.N. forces.** The first Chinese prisoners were taken by MacArthur's forces. As the North Koreans failed to follow up their successes,

Nov. 24. General MacArthur launched a general assault in the west to end the Korean War.

Nov. 26. Substantial **CHINESE FORCES INTERVENED,** and by the end of the year had driven the U.N. forces back to the vicinity of the 38th parallel.

G. THE PACIFIC AREA

1. AUSTRALIA

1945, Jan. 29. The Duke of Gloucester succeeded Lord Gowrie as Governor General.

July 5. Prime Minister **John Curtin** died, after holding office since October, 1941. **Joseph B. Chifley** was elected leader of the Federal Labor Party and became **Prime Minister on July 12.**

Nov. 27-Dec. 15. A strike of coal workers in **New South Wales** seriously crippled Australian industry before it was settled by arbitration. To counteract absenteeism and strikes, and to improve coal production in general, Parliament, in August, 1946, adopted the **Coal Industry Bill,** setting up a Coal Board with wide powers of control over every aspect of the coal industry.

1946, Sept. 28. Parliamentary elections maintained the Labor government's majority in both Houses.

Oct. 31. A governmental ordinance called for radical improvements in the working conditions of natives in **Papua** and **New Guinea.**

1947, Jan. 27-Feb. 6. A meeting of representatives from Great Britain, France, the United States, the Netherlands, Australia, and New Zealand at **Canberra** established a **Regional Advisory Commission for the South Pacific** to deal with all common questions concerning the treatment and general improvement of the native peoples.

Mar. 11. **W. J. McKell,** an Australian citizen and member of the Labor Party, took office as **Governor General.**

July 22. To help alleviate the manpower shortage, Australia agreed to admit 12,000 Displaced Persons per year from Europe.

Nov. 27. The **Banking Bill,** calling for the nationalization of the banks, was passed after one of the most violent controversies in Australian history. Intended to aid in the prevention of depression and inflation, opponents of the bill branded its adoption as dictatorial and unconstitutional.

1949, June 27-Aug. 15. A Communist-inspired coal strike almost stopped all industrial activity. It was settled with the aid of emergency legislation and the use of troops in operating the mines.

Dec. 10. The **General Election** brought a decisive victory to the anti-Labor coalition of the Liberal and Country Parties. In pre-election campaigns they had opposed the government's socialist measures, especially the Banking Act, and had promised effective action against Communism. A new coalition government was formed by Liberal leader **R. G. Menzies** (Dec. 17). The Labor Party did maintain its majority in the Senate, where most of the new government's legislation was vetoed.

1950, Jan. A conference of Commonwealth countries at **Colombo** established the **Commonwealth Economic Consultative Committee** on economic aid **for Southeast Asia,** which in subsequent meetings drew up a six-year plan for that region.

June. Australia participated in United Nations action against **North Korea** and took measures to strengthen its armed forces.

Oct. 19. A bill dissolving the **Communist Party,** after passing both Houses, was appealed in the High Court.

2. NEW ZEALAND

1945, Aug. 21. The **war cabinet,** a coalition of the Labor and National Parties, in office since 1940, **was dissolved.**

Nov. As further steps in the **socialization program** of the Labor Party, the government, against strong opposition, provided for the nationalization of the Bank of New Zealand and adopted the New Zealand **National Airways Bill** to set up government-controlled airlines.

1946, June 17. General Sir Bernard Frey-
berg took office as Governor General.

Nov. 26. The Labor Party in the General Elections maintained a narrow majority with 42 seats against
the National Party's 38. **Peter
Fraser** continued as Labor Prime
Minister.

1948, Aug. 18. The British Nationality and
New Zealand Citizenship Bill
clarified the citizenship status of
New Zealanders, while maintaining their status as British subjects.

1949, Aug. 3. A referendum decided overwhelmingly in favor of peace-time
military service.

Nov. 30. Parliamentary elections
brought Labor its first defeat since
1935. The National Party won 46 and
Labor 34 seats. **Sidney G. Holland** formed
a new cabinet on Dec. 8, pledged to a program of private enterprise and initiative.
In fulfillment of this pledge,

1950. The government ended food rationing, removed wage and most price
controls, and reversed many of the
Labor government's nationalization measures, while maintaining
its social security program.

Aug. 19. Parliament voted to abolish the
appointed **Legislative Council**
(Upper House) as of Jan. 1, 1951, since it
served no real purpose. Plans for a new
Upper House were to be drawn up.

3. THE PHILIPPINE REPUBLIC

1946, Apr. 23. Manuel A. Roxas, head of
the Liberal Party, narrowly defeated Nationalist Party leader
Sergio Osmeña (who had been
President of the government-in-
exile) to become President of the
Philippine Commonwealth.

July 4. The **REPUBLIC OF THE
PHILIPPINES** was formally inaugurated at Manila. To aid the devastated economy of the new state, the United
States had earlier passed a **Rehabilitation
Act** for the payment of war damage claims,
and the **Bell Act,** which provided for eight
years of free trade between the two countries, after which time tariff restrictions
were to be gradually imposed by the United
States on Philippine imports. To prepare
their economy for these restrictions, the
Philippine government drew up a long-
range program of industrial expansion.

The economic problems of the new state
were intensified by continued conflicts between the government and the **Hukbalahaps**
("Huks"), a wartime, Communist-led,
peasant party concentrated in central
Luzon. The "Huks" already had appropriated much of the land from the landlords
and now demanded further land reform.
Government efforts to subdue these unruly elements were met by armed resistance.

1947, Mar. 11. A national referendum approved a **constitutional amend-
ment granting United States citizens equality with Filipinos** in the exploitation of national resources. The amendment had been
made a condition for American aid under
the Rehabilitation and Bell Acts.

Mar. 14. The United States was granted
a 99-year lease of Philippine military and

naval bases, and an American military
mission was to assist the formation of a
Philippine army.

Nov. 11. Elections for the Senate and
provincial offices showed a marked
gain for the Nationalists.

1948, Apr. 16. President Roxas died and
was succeeded by Vice-President
Elpidio Quirino.

July-Oct. To end the civil conflict between the government and the
Hukbalahap, a general amnesty
was granted on condition that the
latter surrender. Their failure to
comply brought on a full-scale
government offensive, which temporarily helped to check guerrilla
activities.

1949, Nov. 8. President Quirino was re-
elected over the Nationalist candidate (and puppet president under the
Japanese), José P. Laurel. Quirino's Liberal Party also won a majority in the Lower
House. One of the main issues of the extremely violent pre-election campaign had
been Laurel's opposition to Quirino's
close dependence upon the United
States.

1950, Oct. 28. A United States Economic
Survey Mission, appointed at the
request of the Philippine government,
painted a dark picture of inefficiency, corruption, economic backwardness and injustice, and recommended far-reaching economic, financial, and administrative reforms. Such reforms, it was felt, especially
in the agricultural field, might also help
to defeat the continued strong resistance
of "Huk" guerrillas, notably in central
Luzon.

LIST OF EVENTS FROM
JANUARY 1, 1951, TO APRIL 30, 1952

1951

Jan. 1. North Korean and Chinese Communist forces attacked and broke through **United Nations** lines along the 38th parallel. **Seoul** fell to the invaders on Jan. 4.

Jan. 2. The Eighty-first **United States** Congress adjourned.

Jan. 5. The **United States Senate** opened the "great debate" on American foreign policy with an attack on the administration by Senator **Robert A. Taft.**

Jan. 11. The **United Nations Truce Committee** proposed a five-point peace program for the **Far East.** After the government of **Communist China** rejected the proposal (Jan. 17), the **United States** entered a resolution that **China** be found guilty of aggression in **Korea.** The **United Nations General Assembly** so resolved on Feb. 1.

Jan. 17. A cabinet shuffle in **Great Britain** promoted **Aneurin Bevan** to Minister of Labor, demoted **George Isaacs** to Minister of Pensions.

Jan. 24. In the **Netherlands,** the coalition cabinet of **Willem Drees** fell. The crisis ended on March 13 when a similar four-party coalition government was formed.

Jan. 25. West German industrialists agreed to trade-union demands for a **"co-determination"** law giving labor a share in the management of the coal and steel industries.

United Nations forces in **Korea** opened a "limited offensive" in the western sector.

Jan. 31. **Getulio Darnelles Vargas** was sworn into office as President of **Brazil.**

Feb. 1. In the **United States** a strike of switchmen paralyzed rail communications. On Feb. 8, President **Truman** ordered the railroads to operate under Army control.

Feb. 8. The **French Government** announced an agreement with **Tunisia** giving that protectorate increased autonomy within the **French Union.**

Feb. 13. The **British Commonwealth Consultative Committee** met in Colombo, Ceylon, to discuss a development program for **South** and **Southeast Asia.**

Feb. 14. In Israel the government of **David Ben-Gurion** dissolved following a defeat in the **Knesset** on a question of religious education.

Feb. 21. General **Dwight D. Eisenhower** arrived in **Paris** to assume command of the **North Atlantic Treaty Powers'** European forces.

Feb. 22. The **Russian** press announced results of the recent elections for the **Supreme Soviet.** The Stalinist bloc won a popular majority of 99.76%.

Feb. 28. In **France** the center coalition government of **René Pleven** fell on the issue of electoral reform.

Mar. 1. The **Soviet Union** agreed to join the **United States, Great Britain,** and **France** in a meeting of deputy foreign ministers with a view to drawing up an agenda for a later foreign ministers' conference. The **deputy foreign ministers** met in **Paris** on Mar. 5 and quickly deadlocked on the question of disarmament measures.

Mar. 2. Reports from **Czechoslovakia** indicated that the **Czech Communist Party** was undergoing a purge of "Titoist" elements.

Mar. 7. Premier General **Ali Razmara** of **Iran** was assassinated by a member of a sect of religious and nationalist fanatics.

Mar. 9. **Ernest Bevin,** suffering from what proved to be a fatal illness, resigned as British Foreign Secretary to be replaced by **Herbert Morrison.**

Mar. 12. The **United States Senate committee** to investigate organized crime in interstate commerce (**Kefauver Committee**) held its first public hearings in **New York City.** Two weeks of sensational disclosures followed.

Mar. 13. The French National Assembly upheld the cabinet of Henri Queuille, thus ending two weeks of government crisis.

Mar. 15. Lt. Col. Jacobo Arbenz Guzman was sworn in as President of Guatemala.

Mar. 24. General Douglas MacArthur announced his readiness to meet in the field the commander of the North Korean and Chinese Communist forces for a discussion on means to end the bloodshed. He warned Communist China that she would face military disaster if the United States extended her operations to Chinese coastal and interior bases. The Peiping Government rejected his offer on Mar. 29. The governments of India (Mar. 31) and Great Britain (Apr. 2) urged that a truce be arranged.

Mar. 26. The foreign ministers of 21 American republics met in Washington, D.C., to discuss hemispheric problems.

Mar. 29. The United States completed the draft of a peace treaty with Japan and communicated it to the 14 co-belligerent powers including Russia.

Mar. 30. The United States Senate closed its debate on the sending of 4 additional infantry divisions to Europe.

Mar. 31. The International Trade Conference at Torquay, England, ended with the signing of a number of bi-lateral tariff agreements.

Apr. 2. French President Vincent Auriol finished an official visit to the United States with an address to a joint session of Congress.

Apr. 3. United Nations forces, having contained the Communists' first spring offensive, counter-attacked across the 38th parallel.

Apr. 5. The Israeli Air Force bombed Syrian military positions in retaliation for an alleged violation of the Israeli frontier. Border incidents continued until both sides heeded a United Nations Security Council cease-fire order on May 9.

Apr. 7. In Indo-China rebel chief, Ho Chi Minh, ordered his troops to abandon frontal assaults on French positions and resume guerrilla tactics.

Apr. 11. General Douglas MacArthur was relieved of all his commands in the Far East, to be succeeded by General Matthew Ridgway. In an address to a joint session of Congress on Apr. 19 MacArthur presented his arguments against the administration's policies.

Apr. 13. President Juan Domingo Perón of Argentina suppressed the newspaper La Prensa.

Apr. 18. In Paris delegates of France, West Germany, Italy, Belgium, the Netherlands, and Luxemburg signed a treaty embodying the Schuman Plan to set up a single market for coal and steel in the six nations. The treaty had then to be ratified by the several parliaments.

Apr. 22. Aneurin Bevan, British Minister of Labor, resigned from the cabinet in protest against a decision to give defense needs priority over the social services. The resignation signaled a revolt in Labor Party ranks.

Apr. 23. In Spain some 250,000 workers went on strike against rising living costs.

Apr. 29. The Iranian Senate and Majlis named the leader of the extremist National Front, Mohammed Mossadegh, as Premier to succeed Hussein Ala. The new government hastened legislation to nationalize the Iranian oil industry. The decree of nationalization took effect on May 2, retroactive to Mar. 20. Great Britain at once contested the legality of this unilateral abrogation of a 1933 concession treaty.

May 7. Secretary of Defense George C. Marshall appeared before the United States Senate Armed Services and Foreign Relations Committees to give testimony on the removal of General MacArthur. A succession of prominent witnesses went before the committee until the inquiry ended on June 25.

May 9. Rioting in Panama City followed the dissolution of the Panamanian National Assembly and the suspension of the constitution by President Arnulfo Arias. Next day the president was impeached and replaced by First Vice-President Arosemena.

May 15. Chinese Communist and North Korean armies launched their second spring offensive. After one week of heavy losses they were halted and forced into a general withdrawal.

May 16. The President of Bolivia resigned and delivered governmental power over to a military junta led by General Hugo Ballivan.

May 24. The French National Assembly ended its five years of existence. Israel charged that Jordanian National Guardsmen had invaded Israel twice within a week.

May 30. In **West Germany** Chancellor **Konrad Adenauer** demanded that the Western Powers allow the **Saar** to choose freely between Germany and France.

June 3. After months of **famine in India** the Indian Socialist Party staged a giant demonstration in **Delhi** to protest the government's failure to solve the food and housing problems.

June 13. Tabulation of votes cast in the **Italian local elections** which began on May 27 showed gains for the **pro-Soviet parties** and a decline of **Christian Democratic** strength.

Eamon de Valera again became Prime Minister of **Eire**. He was brought back to power by the defection of 5 members of **John Costello's** coalition.

June 17. Elections were held for the **French National Assembly.** On June 20 results showed that seats would be divided among 6 major groups: Popular Republicans (86), Radicals (95), Independents (99), Communists (101), Socialists (104), and De Gaullists (117).

June 19. President Truman signed a **military manpower bill** extending the draft until July 1, 1955, lowering the draft age to 18½ and authorizing universal military training to take effect at some unspecified date.

June 21. The four-power **deputy foreign ministers' conference** in **Paris** ended. The conference never succeeded in breaking the deadlock which set in at the beginning.

Defense Ministers of most of the British Commonwealth nations met in **London** to discuss stronger security measures for the **Mediterranean** and the **Near East.**

June 23. On a United Nations radio program **Soviet** representative **Jacob A. Malik** made a vaguely worded call for a cease-fire and armistice talks in **Korea.** Two days later President **Truman** replied that the United States was willing to engage in such talks. On June 29 General **Ridgway** broadcast to the **Commander-in-Chief** of **Communist Forces in Korea** an offer to negotiate an armistice.

June 28. A Hungarian court convicted Archbishop **Joseph Groesz** of conspiring to overturn the government.

June 30. In **Thailand** a naval revolt against the government of Premier **Pibul Songgram** was suppressed by loyal army and air force units.

July 3. Prime Minister **Nehru of India** lodged a formal complaint against **Pakistan** with the **United Nations Security Council.** He charged repeated violations of the cease-fire agreement in **Kashmir.**

July 4. The **Czechoslovak State Court** convicted an American correspondent, **William Oatis,** of espionage. After an official request for his release was refused on July 21, the United States prepared to take diplomatic reprisals.

July 5. **Ground action subsided in Korea** as arrangements for armistice talks went forward.

The **International Court of Justice** at **The Hague** ruled against Iran in her dispute with Great Britain over the nationalization of the **Iranian oil industry.** President Truman sent a personal message (July 9) and a special emissary, **W. Averell Harriman** (July 15), to urge a compromise settlement on **Iran.**

July 17. In **Belgium** King **Leopold III** abdicated in favor of his son **Baudouin.**

July 20. King **Abdullah of Jordan** was assassinated in **Jerusalem.** His heir, **Emir Talal,** was proclaimed King by the **National Assembly on Sept. 5.**

July 26. In **Italy** Premier **Alcide de Gasperi's** seventh **cabinet** was sworn in. The new cabinet was formed following a decision on July 3 that the government needed more liberal members.

Aug. 5. General **Ridgway** broke off **armistice talks in Korea.** He charged that **Communist** troops had violated the demilitarization regulations in **Kaesong.** Five days later talks resumed but deadlocked on the question of a truce demarcation line. On Aug. 23 the Communists suspended negotiations because of an alleged **bombing** of Kaesong by **United Nations** planes.

An **International Communist Youth Rally** in Berlin staged one of the largest Communist demonstrations in European history. More than a million youth took part.

Aug. 6. **Nikolai Shvernik,** President of the Presidium of the Supreme Soviet of **Russia** sent a message to President **Truman** proposing that their two nations agree to disarm and to ban atomic weapons. The message was a reply to a resolution of the **United States** Congress professing friendship for the Soviet people. On Aug. 7 the **United States** rejected the proposal and advised **Russia** first to honor existing obligations.

Aug. 11. The **French National Assembly** upheld the Center coalition cabinet of Premier **René Pleven**, ending the government crisis which had followed the June elections. On Sept. 3 the new government withstood its first serious test when the Assembly approved a bill to furnish indirect aid to **religious schools.**

Aug. 13. **Peru** asked the **United States, Argentina, Brazil,** and **Chile** to investigate border incidents with **Ecuador.** Fighting began on Aug. 11 over the old issue of access to certain **Amazon** tributaries.

Aug. 25. **United Nations** planes bombed the **North Korean** rail junction and port of **Rashin,** 20 miles below the **Siberian** border.

Aug. 30. The **United States** and the **Philippines** signed a **mutual defense pact.** This was to be the first of a series of such **security pacts** between anti-Communist Powers in the **Far East.**

Sept. 1. General elections in **New Zealand** confirmed Prime Minister **Sidney Holland's National Party** in power.

Sept. 4. The **Japanese Peace Treaty Conference** opened at San Francisco. Four days later the treaty was approved and signed by delegates of **Japan** and **48** other Powers. Defeated in their efforts at obstruction, the **Soviet** and other **Communist delegates** boycotted the final session.

Sept. 10. The foreign ministers of **Great Britain, France,** and the **United States** met in **Washington, D.C.,** for a two-day conference on measures to contain **Soviet** aggression. They agreed on plans for a **German** "peace contract" to replace the **Occupation Statute** and on the use of **West German** troops in a European army.

Sept. 13. The **United Nations Conciliation Commission** opened talks with **Israeli** and **Arab** delegates in **Paris** to effect a peaceful settlement in **Palestine.** The talks ended in failure on Nov. 21.

Sept. 15. Twelve member nations of the **North Atlantic Council** met in **Ottawa, Canada,** to discuss the defense of **Western Europe.** The conference ended on Sept. 20 with a recommendation that **Greece** and **Turkey** be admitted to the **North Atlantic** system.

Sept. 19. British Prime Minister **Clement Atlee** announced that he had asked the King to dissolve **Parliament.** General elections were scheduled for Oct. 25.

Sept. 23. **United Nations forces in Korea** capture "Heartbreak Ridge" after 37 days of hard fighting to secure strategic heights north of **Yanggu.**

Sept. 24. The results of **general elections** held in **Greece** on Sept. 9 gave the conservative **Greek Rally Party** of Field Marshal **Alexander Papagos** a clear plurality. But a parliamentary deadlock ensued because no party had an absolute majority.

Sept. 28. The **Argentine Government** easily put down a minor military uprising led by General **Benjamin Menéndez.**

Oct. 1. The **United Nations Security Council** voted to take up the **Anglo-Iranian** oil case. Two days later **Great Britain** finished evacuating technicians from **Iran.**

Oct. 5. The **United States House of Representatives** approved a $56.9 billion **armed forces appropriation** bill. **Senate** approval followed on **Oct. 12.**

Oct. 6. The **British High Commissioner** in **Malaya,** Sir **Henry Gurney,** was assassinated.

Oct. 8. **Princess Elizabeth** and **Prince Philip** arrived in **Canada** for a state visit.

The **high command** of the **Communist** forces in **Korea** agreed to resume armistice talks at a new site — **Panmunjom. United Nations** and **Communist** liaison officers held a series of meetings from Oct. 10 to Oct. 22 to resolve procedural issues. **Formal negotiations** were renewed on Oct. 25 for the first time since August.

Oct. 9. After 8 months of cabinet crisis in **Israel** Prime Minister **Ben-Gurion** formed a coalition government which commanded a firm majority.

Oct. 13. The government of **Venezuela** quelled a **revolt in Caracas** which was alleged to have been fomented by members of the illegal **Communist** and **Democratic Action** parties.

Oct. 16. Prime Minister **Liaquat Ali Khan** of **Pakistan** was assassinated while addressing a public meeting. Next day Governor General **Khwaja Nazimuddin** assumed leadership of the dominion.

Oct. 25. General elections in **Great Britain** gave the **Conservative Party** a parliamentary majority of 16 seats. Two days later **Winston Churchill** assumed the posts of Prime Minister and Minister of Defense. **Anthony Eden** was named Foreign Secretary. **Richard Austen Butler** became Chancellor of the Exchequer.

Oct. 27. Egypt formally abrogated her 1936 treaty of alliance with **Great Britain** and their 1899 condominium agreement covering the **Sudan.** The Sudanese Legislative Assembly rejected the Egyptian decision to restore the **Sudan** to Egyptian royal government.

Oct. 29. The French Commissioner in Cambodia, **Jean de Raymond,** was assassinated by a **Vietminh** rebel.

Nov. 2. Soviet Russia sent representatives to the **Japanese Diet** with attractive offers for a **trade treaty.**

Nov. 6. The **United Nations General Assembly** opened its 1951 session in **Paris.** Next day the Western Powers offered **Russia** broad **disarmament proposals.** These were formally presented to the **Assembly** on Nov. 8 by **United States** Secretary of State **Dean Acheson.** After several weeks of **Soviet counter-proposals** the disarmament talks reached a stalemate.

Nov. 10. France, Great Britain, the United States, and Turkey announced plans for a **security program** in the **Near East.**

Nov. 11. Argentine voters re-elected President **Perón** to another six-year term of office.

Nov. 12. In Nepal a century-long dynasty of royal prime ministers ended when the last of the **Ranas** resigned his post. Four days later King **Tribhubana** swore in a non-aristocratic government dominated by the pro-Indian **Nepali Congress Party.**

Nov. 14. The Eighth United States Army in **Korea** charged that **Chinese** and **North Korean** Communists had killed 2513 **American** prisoners of war. General **Ridgway** ordered an immediate and thorough investigation.

Nov. 16. Egypt offered to let the future status of the **Sudan** be decided by a plebiscite under **United Nations** supervision.

Nov. 21. United States Air Force Chief of Staff, General **Hoyt S. Vandenberg,** declared that the **Communists** in **Korea** were seriously challenging **United Nations** air superiority.

Nov. 29. A military *coup* in Syria led to the arrest of pro-Soviet Dr. **Maar-**

ouf Dawalibi, who had become Prime Minister the day before. The *coup* was executed by the Army Chief of Staff, Colonel **Adeeb** Shishekly, who on Dec. 2 took over all government authority.

Dec. 3. The **Russians** reported that the **Red Air Force** had forced down in **Hungary** a **United States Air Force** transport plane which had flown off its course. The four **crew members** were imprisoned until Dec. 28, when the **United States** paid **Hungary** a ransom of $120,000.

Dec. 6. Both the **East** and **West German Governments** agreed to send representatives to the **United Nations** to discuss the holding of free elections in Germany. On Dec. 19 a five-nation commission was approved to inquire into the possibility of such elections. **Soviet** opposition made the prospect unlikely.

Dec. 10. Iran agreed to submit the oil nationalization issue to the **International Court of Justice.**

Dec. 11. The **Union** of **South Africa** drew criticism from the **United Nations Trusteeship Committee** for refusing to place **Southwest Africa** under international authority.

Dec. 13. The **French National Assembly** ratified the **Schuman Plan** by a vote of 377 to 233.

Dec. 18. Communist negotiators in **Korea** gave the United Nations a list of 11,559 prisoners of war held in **North Korea.** There were serious discrepancies between the number of soldiers reported missing in action by **United Nations** commanders and the number of prisoners listed by the **Communists.**

Dec. 19. Russian Foreign Minister **Andrei Vishinsky** demanded that the **United Nations** call on the **United States** to revoke its **Mutual Security Act.**

Dec. 20. Greece was elected to the **United Nations Security Council** over the **Russian** candidate Byelorussia.

Dec. 24. The **Federation of Libya** began its official life as an independent state under King **Idris I.**

Dec. 27. The thirty-day armistice "trial period" lapsed in **Korea** with neither side proposing an extension. Armistice talks remained stalled on two issues: prisoner exchange and the building of airfields in **North Korea** during the prospective armistice.

Dec. 31. The **Marshall Plan** came to an end as the **Economic Cooperation Administration** was replaced by the **Mutual Security Agency.**

1952

Jan. 5. India and the United States signed a five-year "Point Four" agreement, whereby each nation would contribute an equal amount of money to develop the Indian economy.

Prime Minister **Winston Churchill** began talks with President **Truman** in **Washington, D.C.** Agreement was reported on 3 subjects: exchange of raw materials, support for the European Army plan, and measures to strengthen the North Atlantic Treaty Organization. On Jan. 17 **Churchill** addressed a joint session of **Congress.** He called for token **United States** forces in the **Suez Canal Zone** and promised better accord between British and American **Far Eastern** policies.

Jan. 7. French Premier **René Pleven's** government fell when the **Social-ists** voted against it on a question of reform for the nationalized railway and social security systems.

Jan. 9. In **Belgium** the government of **Joseph Pholien** resigned. Six days later **Jean Van Houtte** success-fully formed an exclusively **Social Christian** government with **Pho-lien** as Minister of Justice.

Jan. 11. The **West German Bundestag** ratified the **Schuman Plan** by a vote of 232 to 143. The **Commu-nists** and **Socialists** voted against it.

Jan. 14. The government of **Tunisia** appealed to the **United Nations Security Council** for a hearing on her demands for autonomy. The appeal was denied. **Anti-French** riots and disorders continued to shake the protectorate.

Jan. 18. The **British** cruiser *Liverpool* fired on **Port Said** as British troops clashed with **Egyptian** guerrillas there. Two days later British troops entered **Ismailia.** A climax of violence frightening to the **Egyptian Government** was reached on Jan. 26 when **riots** in **Cairo** brought death to over 20 people and wholesale destruction of foreign properties. Next day King **Farouk** named **Aly Maher Pasha** to succeed **Mus-tafa Nahas Pasha** as Premier.

Jan. 21. The **United States Congress** received President **Truman's** **budget message** calling for $84.9 billion in expenditure for 1953. Of this 76% was to be appropriated for national security programs.

Jan. 22. The French National Assembly approved the cabinet of **Edgar Faure.** The new cabinet represented the same parties which made up the **Pleven** ministry.

Jan. 24. **Vincent Massey** was appointed Governor-General of **Canada** to succeed Viscount **Alexander.** His was the first appointment of a Canadian to that post.

Jan. 25. The French Government de-cided to substitute a diplomatic mission for the **High Commissariat** of the **Saar.** This action created a furor in **West Germany** where on Feb. 4 Chancellor **Adenauer** demanded that the Western Powers consult **German wishes** on the **Saar** question.

Feb. 5. The 1951 session of the **United Nations General Assembly** ad-journed.

Feb. 6. King **George VI** of **England** died. Two days later Queen **Elizabeth II,** who had flown back from **East Africa,** took the oath of accession.

Feb. 19. The **French National Assembly** with some reservations approved the **European Army Plan** by a vote of 327 to 287.

Feb. 20. The **North Atlantic Treaty Or-ganization Council** met in **Lisbon, Portugal.** On Feb. 22 delegates approved the **European Defense Project** which had been previously drafted in Paris by **France, Italy, West Germany, Belgium, the Nether-lands,** and **Luxemburg.** Next day the Council agreed to raise **50 divisions** for the defense of western Europe by the end of 1952. The Council closed its session on Feb. 25 with the decision to bring **Morocco** and **Tunisia** into the North Atlantic sys-tem.

Feb. 26. Prime Minister **Winston Churchill** announced in the British **House of Commons** that **Britain** had produced its own **atmo bomb.**

Feb. 29. In **France** the government of Premier **Faure** resigned after its failure to secure the **National Assembly's** assent to a 15% tax increase. On Mar. 6 the Assembly endorsed **Antoine Pinay's** effort to form a moderately conservative "technicians'" government. The endorse-ment was carried with the support of 27 **De Gaullists** who thereby disobeyed party instructions.

Mar. 1. Final results of **India's** first na-tional elections gave Prime Minis-ter **Nehru's Congress Party** 364 of 489 seats in the National Assembly. **Pro-Soviet parties** won only 28 seats, but showed sur-prising strength in the **local assemblies.**

Egyptian Premier **Aly Maher Pasha** re-signed. He was replaced by **Naguib al Hilaili Pasha,** a former member of the **Wafd Party.** On Mar. 11 the **Wafd** took its parliamentary majority into oppo-sition.

Mar. 3. Puerto Rico by popular vote ratified its new constitution.

Mar. 4. The United States proposed an inquiry into **Chinese Communist** accusations that American forces were using germ warfare in **North Korea.** On Mar. 14 **Russia** repeated the charges but failed to acknowledge an offer by the **International Red Cross** to investigate them.

Mar. 8. The **Russian Supreme Soviet** approved the largest **budget** in its history. Some $28 billion was to be provided for defense in 1952.

Mar. 10. **Russia** delivered notes to the **United States, Great Britain,** and **France** calling for a four-power conference to discuss the **unification** and **rearmament** of **Germany.** On Mar. 23 the **Western Powers** replied in identical notes that they would consider the establishment of an **all-German government** only on the basis of **free elections,** that such a government should not be empowered to rearm, but could enter security agreements with other powers, that the German borders drawn at the 1945 **Potsdam Conference** were to be subject to revision.

In **Cuba** General **Fulgencio Batista** overthrew President **Carlos Prío Socarrás.** Batista assumed the titles of **Chief of State and Premier.** The presidency was left vacant pending elections.

Mar. 13. The United States Senate enacted into law an administration proposal to reorganize the **Internal Revenue Bureau.** This action followed public disclosures of widespread **corruption** among tax officials.

Mar. 20. The **Supreme Court** of the **Union of South Africa** invalidated the **race legislation** of Nationalist Prime Minister **Daniel Malan.** On Apr. 22 Malan introduced a bill to make **Parliament** a high court with power to pass on the constitutionality of its own acts.

The **United States Senate** ratified the **Japanese peace treaty.** It also approved several **Pacific security agreements** which had been contracted with **Japan,** the **Philippines, Australia,** and **New Zealand.**

Mar. 28. The **Bey of Tunis** yielded to French pressure and removed Premier **Mohammed Chenik,** who had supported the views of the **New Independence Party. Salah Eddine Ben Mohammed Baccouche** was appointed Premier.

Mar. 29. President **Truman** announced that he would **not** be a **candidate** for re-election in the 1952 presidential campaign.

Mar. 30. The **International Zone of Tangier** was torn by violently **anti-French** riots.

Apr. 3. **United States** Attorney General **J. Howard McGrath** dismissed his Special Assistant, **Newbold Morris,** who had been appointed to investigate government corruption. President **Truman** thereupon dismissed the **Attorney General** and appointed **James P. McGranery** to succeed him.

Apr. 4. The **Korean armistice talks** at staff-officer level recessed for 6 days as each side moved to break the deadlock on the question of **prisoner exchange.**

Apr. 5. At an **International Trade Conference** in Moscow, **Russia** offered to buy up to $10 billion worth of western goods in the next 2 years.

Apr. 8. In the **United States** the President ordered **government seizure** of the nation's **steel industry** to avert a **strike.** On Apr. 29 the **District Court of Washington, D.C.,** ruled that the seizure was unconstitutional. The administration then moved to carry the case before the **Supreme Court.**

Apr. 10. **Russia** continued the exchange of notes on **Germany** which began on Mar. 10. The new note proposed that **all-German elections** be held under a **four-power commission** rather than **United Nations** supervision. It rejected western views on the rectification of Germany's 1945 **frontiers.**

Apr. 11. A revolt in **Bolivia** overthrew the junta of General **Ballivan.** The leader of the **National Revolutionary Movement, Victor Paz Estenssoro,** was sworn in as President on Apr. 16. He promised to nationalize the **tin industry.**

Apr. 12. General **Dwight D. Eisenhower** announced that he had asked to be released from his duties as **"Supreme Allied Commander, Europe"** by approximately June 1. On Apr. 28 General **Ridgway** was appointed to succeed him. General **Mark W. Clark** was appointed to Ridgway's **Far Eastern** commands.

Apr. 15. A government **White Paper** declared that **Great Britain** was prepared to sign a **mutual defense treaty** with the **European Defense Community.**

Apr. 24. In **West Germany** Chancellor **Adenauer** proclaimed that the **unification** of Germany was his primary goal and that, once reunited, the nation could revise her **international commitments.**

APPENDIX I

ROMAN EMPERORS

27 B.C.– 14 A.D.	Augustus (Gaius Julius Caesar Octavianus)	222–235	Alexander Severus (Marcus Alexianus Bassianus Aurelius Severus Alexander)
14–37	Tiberius (Tiberius Claudius Nero Caesar)	235–238	Maximin (Gaius Julius Verus Maximinus "Thrax")
37–41	Caligula (Gaius Claudius Nero Caesar Germanicus)	237–238	Gordian I (Marcus Antonius Gordianus)
41–54	Claudius (Tiberius Claudius Nero Caesar Drusus)	238	Pupienus (Marcus Clodius Pupienus Maximus)
54–68	Nero (Lucius Domitius Ahenobarbus Claudius Drusus)	238	Balbinus (Decimus Caelius Balbinus)
68–69	Galba (Servius Sulpicius Galba)	238–244	Gordian III (Marcus Antonius Gordianus)
69	Otho (Marcus Salvius Otho)	244–249	Philipp "Arabs" (Marcus Julius Philippus "Arabs")
69	Vitellius (Aulus Vitellius Germanicus)	249–251	Decius (Gaius Messius Quintus Traianus Decius)
69–79	Vespasian (Titus Flavius Vespasianus)	251–253	Gallus (Gaius Vibius Trebonianus Gallus)
79–81	Titus (Titus Flavius Vespasianus)	252–253	Aemilian (Marcus Julius Aemilius Aemilianus)
81–96	Domitian (Titus Flavius Domitianus)	253–259	Valerian (Gaius Publius Licinius Valerianus)
96–98	Nerva (Marcus Cocceius Nerva)	259(255)–268	Gallien (Publius Licinius Egnatius Gallienus)
98–117	Trajan (Marcus Ulpius Nerva Traianus)	268–270	Claudius II (Marcus Aurelius Claudius Gothicus)
117–138	Hadrian (Publius Aelius Traianus Hadrianus)	270–275	Aurelian (Lucius Domitius Aurelianus)
138–161	Antoninus Pius (Titus Aurelius Fulvius Boionius Arrius Antoninus Pius)	275–276	Tacitus (Marcus Claudius Tacitus)
161(147)–180	Marcus Aurelius (Marcus Annius Aurelius Verus)	276–282	Probus (Marcus Aurelius Probus)
161–169	Lucius Aurelius Verus (Lucius Ceionius Commodus Verus)	281–283	Carus (Marcus Aurelius Carus)
180(172)–192	Commodus (Lucius Aelius Marcus Aurelius Antoninus Commodus)	284–305	Diocletian (Gaius Aurelius Valerius Diocles Jovius)
193	Pertinax (Publius Helvius Pertinax)	286–305	Maximian (Marcus Aurelius Valerius Maximianus Herculius)
193	Didius Julian (Marcus Didius Salvius Julianus Severus)	305(293)–306	Constantius I (Flavius Valerius Constantius Chlorus)
193–211	Septimius Severus (Lucius Septimius Severus)	305(293)–311	Galerius (Gaius Galerius Valerius Maximianus)
211(198)–217	Caracalla (Marcus Aurelius Antoninus Bassianus Caracallus)	306–307	Severus (Flavius Valerius Severus)
209–211	Geta (Publius Septimius Geta)	306–312	Maxentius (Marcus Aurelius Valerius Maxentius)
217–218	Macrinus (Marcus Opellius Severus Macrinus)	311(307)–324	Licinius (Gaius Flavius Valerius Licinianus Licinius)
218–222	Elagabulus (Marcus Varius Avitus Bassianus Aurelius Antoninus Heliogabalus)	311(306)–337	Constantine I, the Great (Flavius Valerius Constantinus)

337–340 Constantine II (Flavius Valerius Claudius Constantinus)

337–361 Constantius II (Flavius Valerius Julius Constantius)

337–350 Constans (Flavius Valerius Julius Constans)

361–363 Julian, the Apostate (Flavius Claudius Julianus)

363–364 Jovian (Flavius Jovianus)

364–375 Valentinian I (Flavius Valentinianus, in the West)

364–378 Valens (in the East)

375(367)–383 Gratian (Flavius Gratianus Augustus, in the West)

375–392 Valentinian II (Flavius Valentinianus, in the West)

379–395 Theodosius, the Great (Flavius Theodosius, in the East, and, after 392, in the West)

383–388 Maximus (Magnus Clemens Maximus)

392–394 Eugenius

395(383)–408 Arcadius (in the East)

395(393)–423 Honorius (Flavius Honorius, in the West)

408(402)–450 Theodosius II (in the East)

425–454 Valentinian III (Flavius Placidius Valentinianus, in the West)

450–457 Marcian (Marcianus, in the East)

455 Petronius (Flavius Ancius Petronius Maximus, in the West)

455–457 Avitus (Flavius Maecilius Eparchus Avitus, in the West)

457–461 Majorian (Julius Valerius Maioranus, in the West)

457–474 Leo I (Leo Thrax, Magnus, in the East)

461–465 Severus (Libius Severianus Severus, in the West)

467–472 Anthemius (Procopius Anthemius, in the West)

472 Olybrius (Anicius Olybrius, in the West)

473–474 Glycerius (in the West)

473–475 Julius Nepos (in the West)

473–474 Leo II (in the East)

474–491 Zeno (in the East)

475–476 Romulus Augustulus (Flavius Momyllus Romulus Augustus, in the West)

APPENDIX II

BYZANTINE EMPERORS

474–491 Zeno

491–518 Anastasius I

518–527 Justin I (Flavius Justinus)

527(518)–565 Justinian the Great (Flavius Justinianus)

565–578 Justin II (Flavius Justinus)

578(574)–582 Tiberius (Flavius Constantinus Tiberius)

582–602 Maurice (Mauritius)

602–610 Phocas I

610–641 Heraclius I

641 Constantine III (Constantinus)

641 Heracleon (Heracleonas)

641–668 Constans II

668–685 Constantine IV (Pogonatus)

685–695 and 705–711 Justinian II (Rhinotmetus)

695–698 Leontius II

698–705 Tiberius III (Apsimar)

711–713 Philippicus

713–715 Anastasius II

715–717 Theodosius III

717–741 Leo III (the Isaurian)

741–775 Constantine V (Kopronymus)

775–780 Leo IV

780–797 Constantine VI (Porphyrogenetus)

797–802 Irene (empress)

802–811 Nicephorus I

811 Stauracius (Staurakius)

811–813 Michael I (Rhangabé)

813–820 Leo V (the Armenian)

820–829 Michael II (Balbus)

829(820)–842 Theophilus I

842–867 Michael III

842–866 Bardas

867 Theophilus II

867(866)–886 Basil I (the Macedonian)

886–912 Leo VI (the Wise)

912–913 Alexander III

913–959 Constantine VII (Porphyrogenetus)

919–944	Romanus I (Lecapenus)	1204	Alexius V (Dukas)
959–963	Romanus II		*Latin Emperors*
963(976)	Basil II (Bulgaroctonus)	1204–1205	Baldwin I
–1025		1205–1216	Henry
963–969	Nicephorus II (Phocas)	1216–1217	Peter de Courtenay
969–976	John I (Tzimisces)	1218–1228	Robert de Courtenay
1025(976)	Constantine VIII	1228–1261	Baldwin II
–1028			
1028–1050	Zoë (empress)		*Nicaean Emperors*
1028–1034	Romanus III (Argyropolus)		
1034–1041	Michael IV (the Paphlagonian)	1206–1222	Theodore I (Lascaris)
1041–1042	Michael V (Kalaphates)	1222–1254	John Dukas Vatatzes
1042–1054	Constantine IX (Monomachus)	1254–1259	Theodore II (Lascaris)
		1258–1261	John IV (Lascaris)
1054–1056	Theodora (empress)	1259–1261	Michael VIII (Paleologus)
1056–1057	Michael VI (Stratioticus)	(1282)	
1057–1059	Isaac I (Comnenus)		
1059–1067	Constantine X (Dukas)		*The Paleologi*
1067	Andronicus	1261(1259)	Michael VIII
1067–1071	Romanus IV (Diogenes)	–1282	
1071–1078	Michael VII (Parapinakes)	1282–1328	Andronicus II (the Elder)
1078–1081	Nicephorus III (Botaniates)	1295–1320	Michael IX (co-emperor)
1081–1118	Alexius I (Comnenus)	1328–1341	Andronicus III (the Younger)
1118–1143	John II (Calus)	1341–1347	John V (Paleologus)
1143–1180	Manuel I	1347(1341)	John VI (Cantacuzene)
1180–1183	Alexius II	–1354	
1182–1185	Andronicus I	1355–1376	John V (restored)
1185–1195	Isaac II (Angelus-Comnenus)	1376–1379	Andronicus IV
1195–1203	Alexius III (Angelus)	1379–1391	John V (restored)
1203–1204	Isaac II (restored)	1390	John VII
1203–1204	Alexius IV	1391–1425	Manuel II
		1425–1448	John VII
		1448–1453	Constantine XI

APPENDIX III

THE CALIPHS, TO 1256

622(570)–632	MOHAMMED	720–724	Yazid II
		724–743	Hisham
	The Orthodox Caliphate	743–744	Walid II
632–634	Abu Bakr	744	Yazid III
634–644	Omar	744–750	Marwan II
644–656	Othman		
656–661	Ali		*The Abbasid Caliphate*
		750–754	Abu-l-Abbas al-Saffah
	The Omayyad Caliphate	754–775	Al-Mansur
661–680	Mo'awiya I	775–785	Al-Mahdi
680–682	Yazid I	785–786	Al-Hadi
683	Mo'awiya II	786–809	Harun Al-Rashid
684–685	Marwan I	809–813	Al-Amin
685–705	Abdalmalik	813–833	Al-Ma'mun (Mamun the Great)
705–715	Walid I		
715–717	Sulayman	833–842	Al-Mu'tasim
717–720	Omar ibn Abdul-Aziz	842–847	Al-Wathiq

847–861	Al-Mutawakkil	974–991	Al-Ta'i
861–862	Al-Muntasir	991–1031	Al-Qadir
862–866	Al-Musta'in	1031–1075	Al-Qa'im
866–869	Al-Mu'tazz	1075–1094	Al-Muqtadi
869–870	Al-Muqtadi	1094–1118	Al-Mustazhir
870–892	Al-Mu'tamid	1118–1135	Al-Mustarshid
892–902	Al-Mu'tadid	1135–1136	Al-Rashid
902–908	Al-Muqtafi	1136–1160	Al-Muqtafi
908–932	Al-Muqtadir	1160–1170	Al-Mustanjid
932–934	Al-Qahir	1170–1180	Al-Mustadi
934–940	Al-Radi	1180–1225	Al-Nasir
940–944	Al-Muttaqi	1225–1226	Al-Zahir
944–946	Al-Mustaqfi	1226–1242	Al-Mustansir
946–974	Al-Muti	1242–1256	Al-Musta'sim

APPENDIX IV

ROMAN POPES

(Names marked with an asterisk indicate popes sainted by the Church.
Names in italics are those of anti-popes.)

?42–?67	*Peter	311–314	*Melchiades	?538–555	Vigilius
67–?79	*Linus	314–335	*Sylvester I	556–561	Pelagius I
79–?90	*Anacletus I	336	*Marcus	561–574	John III
90–?99	*Clement I	337–352	*Julius I	575–579	Benedict I
99–?107	*Evaristus	352–366	*Liberius	579–590	Pelagius II
107–?116	*Alexander I	355–365	*Felix II*	590–604	*Gregory I
116–?125	*Sixtus I	366–384	Damasus I	604–606	Sabinianus
125–?136	*Telesphorus	366–367	*Ursinus*	607	Boniface III
136–?140	*Hyginus	384–398	*Siricius	608–615	*Boniface IV
140–?154	*Pius I	398–401	*Anastasius I	615–618	*Deusdedit
154–?165	*Anicetus	402–417	*Innocent I	619–625	Boniface V
165–174	*Soter	417–418	*Zosimus	625–638	Honorius I
174–189	*Eleutherius	418–422	*Boniface I	638–640	Severinus
189–198	*Victor I	418–419	*Eulalius*	640–642	John IV
198–217	*Zephrynus	422–432	*Celestine I	642–649	Theodore I
217–222	*Calixtus	432–440	*Sixtus III	649–655	*Martin I
222–230	*Urban I	440–461	*Leo I	655–657	*Eugene I
230–235	*Pontian	461–468	*Hilarius	657–672	*Vitalian
235–236	*Anterus	468–483	*Simplicius	672–676	Adeodatus
236–250	*Fabian	483–492	*Felix II (III)	676–678	Donus
251–253	*Cornelius	492–496	*Gelasius I	678–681	*Agatho
251–?258	*Novatian*	496–498	*Anastasius II	682–683	*Leo II
253–254	*Lucius I	498–514	*Symmachus	684–685	*Benedict II
254–257	*Stephen I	498–505	*Laurentius*	685–686	John V
257–258	*Sixtus II	514–523	*Hormisdas	686–687	Conon
259–268	*Dionysius	523–526	*John I	687	*Theodore II*
269–274	*Felix I	526–530	*Felix III (IV)	687–692	*Paschal I*
275–283	*Eutychian	530–532	Boniface II	687–701	*Sergius I
283–296	*Caius	530	*Dioscurus*	701–705	John VI
296–304	*Marcellinus	533–535	John II	705–707	John VII
308–309	*Marcellus I	535–536	*Agapetus I	708	Sisinnius
309(310)	*Eusebius	536–?538	*Silverius	708–715	Constantine

715–731	*Gregory II
731–741	*Gregory III
741–752	*Zacharias
752	Stephen (II)
752–757	Stephen II (III)
757–767	*Paul I
767–768	*Constantine*
768	*Philip*
768–772	Stephen III (IV)
772–795	Adrian I
795–816	*Leo III
816–817	Stephen IV (V)
817–824	*Paschal I
824–827	Eugene II
827	Valentine
827–844	Gregory IV
844	*John VIII*
844–847	Sergius II
847–855	*Leo IV
855–858	Benedict III
855	*Anastasius III*
855–857	*John IX*
858–867	*Nicholas I
867–872	Adrian II
872–882	John VIII
882–884	Martin II
884–885	Adrian III
885–891	Stephen V (VI)
891–896	Formosus
896	Boniface VI
896–897	Stephen VI (VII)
897	Romanus
897	Theodore II
898–900	John IX
900–903	Benedict IV
903	Leo V
903–904	Christopher
904–911	Sergius III
911–913	Anastasius III (IV)
913–914	Lando
914–928	John X
928	Leo VI
928–931	Stephen VII (VIII)
931–936	John XI
936–939	Leo VII
939–942	Stephen VIII (IX)
942–946	Martin III
946–955	Agapetus II
955–963	John XII
963–965	Leo VIII
965	Benedict V

965–972	John XIII
973–974	Benedict VI
974	*Boniface VII*
974–983	Benedict VII
983–984	John XIV
984–985	Boniface VII
985–996	John XV
996–999	Gregory V
997–998	*John XVI*
999–1003	Sylvester II
1003	John XVII
1003–1009	John XVIII
1009–1012	Sergius IV
1012–1024	Benedict VIII
1012	*Gregory VI*
1024–1032	John XIX
1032–1045	Benedict IX (a)
1045	*Sylvester III*
1045–1046	Gregory VI
1046–1047	Clement II
1047–1048	*Benedict IX (b)*
1048	Damasus II
1049–1054	*Leo IX
1055–1057	Victor II
1057–1058	Stephen IX (X)
1058–1059	Benedict X
1059–1061	Nicholas II
1061–1073	Alexander II
1061–1064	*Honorius II*
1073–1085	*Gregory VII
1084–1100	*Clement III*
1087	Victor III
1088–1099	Urban II
1099–1118	Paschal II
1105–1111	*Sylvester IV*
1100–1102	*Theodoric*
1102	*Albert*
1118–1119	Gelasius II
1118–1121	*Gregory VIII*
1119–1124	Calixtus II
1124–1130	Honorius II
1124	*Celestine II*
1130–1143	Innocent II
1130–1138	*Anacletus II*
1138	*Victor IV*
1143–1144	Celestine II
1144–1145	Lucius II
1145–1153	Eugene III
1153–1154	Anastasius IV
1154–1159	Adrian IV
1159–1181	Alexander III
1159–1164	*Victor IV*
1164–1168	*Paschal III*
1168–1178	*Calixtus III*
1179–1180	*Innocent III*
1181–1185	Lucius III

1185–1187	Urban III
1187	Gregory VIII
1187–1191	Clement III
1191–1198	Celestine III
1198–1216	Innocent III
1216–1227	Honorius III
1227–1241	Gregory IX
1241	Celestine IV
1243–1254	Innocent IV
1254–1261	Alexander IV
1261–1264	Urban IV
1265–1268	Clement IV
1271–1276	*Gregory X
1276	Innocent V
1276	Adrian V
1276–1277	John XXI
1277–1280	Nicholas III
1281–1285	Martin IV
1285–1287	Honorius IV
1288–1292	Nicholas IV
1294	*Celestine V
1294–1303	Boniface VIII
1303–1304	Benedict IX
1305–1314	Clement V
1316–1334	John XXII
1328–1330	*Nicholas V*
1334–1342	Benedict XII
1342–1352	Clement VI
1352–1362	Innocent VI
1362–1370	Urban V
1370–1378	Gregory XI
1378–1415	**The Great Schism**
1378–1389	Urban VI
1378–1394	*Clement VII*
1389–1404	Boniface IX
1394–1424	*Benedict XIII*
1404–1406	Innocent VII
1406–1415	Gregory XII
1409–1410	Alexander V
1410–1415	John XXIII
1417–1431	Martin V
1424–1429	*Clement VIII*
1424	*Benedict XIV*
1431–1447	Eugene IV
1439–1449	*Felix V*
1447–1455	Nicholas V
1455–1458	Calixtus III
1458–1464	Pius II
1464–1471	Paul II
1471–1484	Sixtus IV
1484–1492	Innocent VIII
1492–1503	Alexander VI
1503	Pius III
1503–1513	Julius II
1513–1521	Leo X

1522–1523	Adrian VI	1605–1621	Paul V	1740–1758	Benedict XIV
1523–1534	Clement VII	1621–1623	Gregory XV	1758–1769	Clement XIII
1534–1549	Paul III	1623–1644	Urban VIII	1769–1774	Clement XIV
1550–1555	Julius III	1644–1655	Innocent X	1775–1799	Pius VI
1555	Marcellus II	1655–1667	Alexander VII	1800–1823	Pius VII
1555–1559	Paul IV	1667–1669	Clement IX	1823–1829	Leo XII
1559–1565	Pius IV	1670–1676	Clement X	1829–1830	Pius VIII
1566–1572	*Pius V	1676–1689	Innocent XI	1831–1846	Gregory XVI
1572–1585	Gregory XIII	1689–1691	Alexander VIII	1846–1878	Pius IX
1585–1590	Sixtus V	1691–1700	Innocent XII	1878–1903	Leo XIII
1590	Urban VII	1700–1721	Clement XI	1903–1914	Pius X
1590–1591	Gregory XIV	1721–1724	Innocent XIII	1914–1922	Benedict XV
1591	Innocent IX	1724–1730	Benedict XIII	1922–1939	Pius XI
1592–1605	Clement VIII	1730–1740	Clement XII	1939–	Pius XII
1605	Leo IX				

APPENDIX V

HOLY ROMAN EMPERORS

800–814	Charlemagne	936(962)	Otto I, the Great; crowned 962
814–840	Louis I (the Pious); crowned 816	–973	
		973–983	Otto II
840–855	Lothar I	983–1002	Otto III; crowned 996
855–875	Louis II (in Italy)	1002–1024	Henry II, the Saint (Bavarian); crowned 1014
875–877	Charles II, the Bald (West Frankish)	1024–1039	Conrad II, the Salian (Franconian); crowned 1027
877–887	Charles III, the Fat (East Frankish); crowned 881	1039–1056	Henry III, the Black; crowned 1046
887–891	*Vacancy* during the war between the rivals, Guido of Spoleto and Berengar of Friuli	1056–1106	Henry IV; crowned 1084. *Rivals;*
		1077–1080	Rudolf of Swabia
		1081–1093	Hermann of Luxemburg
891–894	Guido (in Italy)	1093–1101	Conrad of Franconia
892–899	Lambert (co-regent-emperor with Guido)	1106–1125	Henry V; crowned 1111
		1125–1137	Lothar II (Saxon); crowned 1133
896–901	Arnulf (rival of Lambert; crowned by the pope)	1138–1152	Conrad III (Swabian); never crowned at Rome
901–905 (928)	Louis III, of Provence	1152–1190	Frederick I, Barbarossa; crowned 1155
905(915) –924	Berengar	1190–1197	Henry VI; crowned 1191
Italian Line		1198–1212	Otto IV (Brunswick); crowned 1209. *Rival:*
924–926	Rudolf of Burgundy	1198–1208	Philip II of Swabia; never crowned
926–945	Hugh of Provence		
945–950	Lothar III	1212–1250	Frederick II; crowned 1220. *Rivals:*
952–962	Berengar		
German Line		1246–1247	Henry Raspe; never crowned
911–918	Conrad I (Franconian); never crowned at Rome	1247–1256	William of Holland; never crowned
918–936	Henry I, the Fowler (Saxon); never crowned at Rome	1250–1254	Conrad IV; never crowned

1254–1273 *The Great Interregnum. Competitors:*
1257–1273 Richard of Cornwall; never crowned
1257–1272 Alfonso X of Castile; never crowned
1273–1291 Rudolf I (Hapsburg); never crowned, but recognized by the pope, 1274
1292–1298 Adolf I (Nassau); never crowned
1298–1308 Albert I (Hapsburg); never crowned
1308–1313 Henry VII (Luxemburg); crowned 1312
1314–1347 Louis IV (Bavaria); crowned 1328. *Rival:*
1325–1330 Frederick of Hapsburg, coregent
1347–1378 Charles IV (Luxemburg); crowned 1355. *Rival:*
1347–1349 Günther of Schwarzburg
1378–1400 Wenzel or Wenceslas (Luxemburg); crowned 1376
1400–1410 Rupert or Rupprecht (Palatinate); never crowned

1410–1437 Sigismund (Luxemburg); crowned 1433. *Rival:*
1410–1411 Jobst of Moravia
1438–1439 Albert II (Hapsburg); never crowned
1440–1493 Frederick III; last emperor crowned in Rome
1493–1519 Maximilian I; never crowned
1519–1556 Charles V; last emperor crowned by the pope (at Bologna)
1558–1564 Ferdinand I
1564–1576 Maximilian II
1576–1612 Rudolf II
1612–1619 Matthias
1619–1637 Ferdinand II
1637–1657 Ferdinand III
1658–1705 Leopold I
1705–1711 Joseph I
1711–1740 Charles VI
1742–1745 Charles VII (Bavaria)
1745–1765 Francis I (Lorraine)
1765–1790 Joseph II
1790–1792 Leopold II
1792–1806 Francis II

APPENDIX VI

BRITISH MINISTRIES SINCE WALPOLE

1721, Apr.—1742, Feb.
Sir Robert Walpole

1742, Feb.—1743, July
Lord John Carteret

1743, July—1754, Mar.
Henry Pelham

1754, Mar.—1756, Nov.
Duke of Newcastle (first ministry)

1756, Nov.—1757, July
Duke of Devonshire (William Pitt, secretary of state)

1757, July—1761, Nov.
Duke of Newcastle (second ministry)

1761, Nov.—1763, Apr.
Earl of Bute

1763, Apr.—1765, July
George Grenville

1765, July—1766, Aug.
Marquis of Rockingham (first ministry)

1766, Aug.—1770, Jan.
Duke of Grafton

1770, Jan.—1782, Mar.
Lord Frederick North

1782, Mar.—July
Marquis of Rockingham (2d ministry)

1782, July—1783, Feb.
Earl of Shelburne

1783, Apr.—Dec.
Duke of Portland (first ministry)

1783, Dec.—1801, Mar.
William Pitt (first ministry)

1801, Mar.—1804, May
Henry Addington

1804, May—1806, Jan.
William Pitt (second ministry)

1806, Jan.—1807, Mar.
Lord William Grenville

1807, Mar.—1809, Oct.
Duke of Portland (second ministry)

1809, Oct.—1812, May
Spencer Perceval

1812, June—1827, Apr.
Earl of Liverpool

1827, Apr.—Aug.
George Canning

1827, Aug.—1828, Jan.
Viscount Goderich

1828, Jan.—1830, Nov.
Duke of Wellington

1830, Nov.—1834, July
Earl Grey

1834, July—Nov.
Viscount Melbourne (first ministry)

1834, Dec.—1835, Apr.
Sir Robert Peel (first ministry)

1835, Apr.—1841, Aug.
Viscount Melbourne (second ministry)

1841, Sept.—1846, June
Sir Robert Peel (second ministry)

1846, July—1852, Feb.
Lord John Russell (first ministry)

1852, Feb.—Dec.
Earl of Derby (first ministry)

1852, Dec.—1855, Jan.
Earl of Aberdeen

1855, Feb.—1858, Feb.
Viscount Palmerston (first ministry)

1858, Feb.—1859, June
Earl of Derby (second ministry)

1859, June—1865, Oct.
Viscount Palmerston (second ministry)

1865, Nov.—1866, June
Lord John Russell (second ministry)

1866, July—1868, Feb.
Earl of Derby (third ministry)

1868, Feb.—Dec.
Benjamin Disraeli (first ministry)

1868, Dec.—1874, Feb.
William E. Gladstone (first ministry)

1874, Feb.—1880, Apr.
Benjamin Disraeli (second ministry)

1880, Apr.—1885, June
William E. Gladstone (second ministry)

1885, June—1886, Jan.
Marquis of Salisbury (first ministry)

1886, Feb.—July
William E. Gladstone (third ministry)

1886, July—1892, Aug.
Marquis of Salisbury (second ministry)

1892, Aug.—1894, Mar.
William E. Gladstone (fourth ministry)

1894, Mar.—1895, June
Earl of Rosebery

1895, June—1902, July
Marquis of Salisbury (third ministry)

1902, July—1905, Dec.
Arthur J. Balfour

1905, Dec.—1908, Apr.
Sir Henry Campbell-Bannerman

1908, Apr.—1916, Dec.
Herbert H. Asquith

1916, Dec.—1919, Jan.
David Lloyd George (first ministry)

1919, Jan.—1922, Oct.
David Lloyd George (second ministry)

1922, Oct.—1923, May
Bonar Law

1923, May—1924, Jan.
Stanley Baldwin (first ministry)

1924, Jan.—Nov.
J. Ramsay MacDonald (first ministry)

1924, Nov.—1929, June
Stanley Baldwin (second ministry)

1929, June—1931, Aug.
J. Ramsay MacDonald (second ministry)

1931, Aug.—1935, June
J. Ramsay MacDonald (third ministry)

1935, June—1937, May
Stanley Baldwin (third ministry)

1937, May—1940, May
Neville Chamberlain

1940, May—1945, July
Winston S. Churchill (first ministry)

1945, July—1950, Feb.
Clement R. Attlee (first ministry)

1950, Feb.—1951, Nov.
Clement R. Attlee (second ministry)

1951, Nov.—
Winston S. Churchill (second ministry)

APPENDIX VII

FRENCH MINISTRIES, 1815-1870

1815, July—Sept.
Charles-Maurice Talleyrand

1815, Sept.—1818, Dec.
Duke of Richelieu (first ministry)

1818, Dec.—1819, Nov.
Jean-Joseph Dessolles

1819, Nov.—1820, Feb.
Duke of Decazes

1820, Feb.—1821, Dec.
Duke of Richelieu (second ministry)

1821, Dec.—1828, Jan.
Jean-Baptiste de Villèle

1828, Jan.—1829, Aug.
Viscount of Martignac

1829, Aug.—1830, July
Prince of Polignac

1830, Aug.—Nov.
Duke of Broglie

1830, Nov.—1831, Mar.
Jacques Laffitte

1831, Mar.--1832, May
Casimir Perier
1832, May—1836, Feb.
Marshal Soult (first ministry)
1836, Feb.—Sept.
Adolphe Thiers (first ministry)
1836, Sept.—1837, Apr.
François Guizot (first ministry)
1837, Apr.—1839, May
Count Molé
1839, May—1840, Mar.
Marshal Soult (second ministry)
1840, Mar.—Oct.
Adolphe Thiers (second ministry)

1840, Oct.—1848, Feb.
François Guizot (second ministry)
1848, Feb.—June
Provisional government under Jacques-
Charles Dupont de l'Eure (Alphonse
de Lamartine, foreign minister)
1848, June—Dec.
General Louis Eugène Cavaignac (head
of the executive)
1848, Dec.—1849, Oct.
Odilon Barrot
1849, Oct.—1851, Jan.
Eugène Rouher
1870, Jan.—Aug.
Émile Ollivier

APPENDIX VIII

PRESIDENTS AND PRIME MINISTERS OF THE THIRD FRENCH REPUBLIC

1871, Feb.—1873, May PRESIDENCY OF ADOLPHE THIERS

1871, Feb.—1873, May
Jules Dufaure (first ministry)

1873, May
Jules Dufaure (second ministry)

1873, May—1879, Jan. PRESIDENCY OF MARSHAL MacMAHON

1873, May—Nov.
Duke of Broglie (first ministry)
1873, Nov.—1874, May
Duke of Broglie (second ministry)
1874, May—1875, Mar.
Courtot de Cissey
1875, Mar.—1876, Feb.
Louis Buffet
1876, Feb.—Mar.
Jules Dufaure (third ministry)

1876, Mar.—Dec.
Jules Dufaure (fourth ministry)
1876, Dec.—1877, May
Jules Simon
1877, May—Nov.
Duke of Broglie (third ministry)
1877, Nov.—Dec.
Grimaudet de Rochebouët
1877, Dec.—1879, Feb.
Jules Dufaure (fifth ministry)

1879, Jan.—1885, Dec. FIRST PRESIDENCY OF JULES GRÉVY

1879, Feb.—Dec.
William Waddington
1879, Dec.—1880, Sept.
Charles de Freycinet (first ministry)
1880, Sept.—1881, Nov.
Jules Ferry (first ministry)
1881, Nov.—1882, Jan.
Léon Gambetta
1882, Jan.—Aug.
Charles de Freycinet (second ministry)

1882, Aug.—1883, Jan.
Charles Duclerc
1883, Jan.—Feb.
Armand Fallières
1883, Feb.—1885, Aug.
Jules Ferry (second ministry)
1885, Aug.—1886, Jan.
Henri Brisson (first ministry)

1885, Dec.—1887, Dec. SECOND PRESIDENCY OF JULES GRÉVY

1886, Jan.—Dec.
Charles de Freycinet (third ministry)
1886, Dec.—1887, May
René Goblet

1887, May—Dec.
Maurice Rouvier (first ministry)

1887, Dec.—1894, June PRESIDENCY OF MARIE FRANÇOIS SADI-CARNOT

1887, Dec.—1888, Mar.
Pierre Tirard (first ministry)
1888, Apr.—1889, Feb.
Charles Floquet
1889, Feb.—1890, Mar.
Pierre Tirard (second ministry)
1890, Mar.—1892, Feb.
Charles de Freycinet (fourth ministry)
1892, Feb.—Dec.
Émile Loubet

1892, Dec.—1893, Jan.
Alexandre Ribot (first ministry)
1893, Jan.—Mar.
Alexandre Ribot (second ministry)
1893, Apr.—Nov.
Charles Dupuy (first ministry)
1893, Dec.—1894, May
Jean Casimir-Périer
1894, May—July
Charles Dupuy (second ministry)

1894, June—1895, Jan. PRESIDENCY OF JEAN CASIMIR-PÉRIER

1894, July—1895, Jan.
Charles Dupuy (third ministry)

1895, Jan.—1899, Feb. PRESIDENCY OF FÉLIX FAURE

1895, Jan.—Oct.
Alexandre Ribot (third ministry)
1895, Nov.—1896, Apr.
Léon Bourgeois
1896, Apr.—1898, June
Jules Méline

1898, June—Oct.
Henri Brisson (second ministry)
1898, Nov.—1899, Feb.
Charles Dupuy (fourth ministry)

1899, Feb.—1906, Feb. PRESIDENCY OF ÉMILE LOUBET

1899, Feb.—June
Charles Dupuy (fifth ministry)
1899, June—1902, June
René Waldeck-Rousseau

1902, June—1905, Jan.
Émile Combes
1905, Jan.—1906, Feb.
Maurice Rouvier (second ministry)

1906, Feb.—1913, Feb. PRESIDENCY OF ARMAND FALLIÈRES

1906, Feb.—Mar.
Maurice Rouvier (third ministry)
1906, Mar.—Oct.
Jean Sarrien
1906, Oct.—1909, July
Georges Clemenceau (first ministry)
1909, July—1910, Nov.
Aristide Briand (first ministry)
1910, Nov.—1911, Feb.
Aristide Briand (second ministry)

1911, Mar.—June
Ernest Monis
1911, June—1912, Jan.
Joseph Caillaux
1912, Jan.—1913, Jan.
Raymond Poincaré (first ministry)
1913, Jan.—Feb.
Aristide Briand (third ministry)

1913, Feb.—1920, Feb. PRESIDENCY OF RAYMOND POINCARÉ

1913, Feb.—Mar.
Aristide Briand (fourth ministry)
1913, Mar.—Dec.
Louis Barthou
1913, Dec.—1914, June
Gaston Doumergue (first ministry)
1914, June
Alexandre Ribot (fourth ministry)
1914, June—Aug.
René Viviani (first ministry)
1914, Aug.—1915, Oct.
René Viviani (second ministry)

1915, Oct.—1916, Dec.
Aristide Briand (fifth ministry)
1916, Dec.—1917, Mar.
Aristide Briand (sixth ministry)
1917, Mar.—Sept.
Alexandre Ribot (fifth ministry)
1917, Sept.—Nov.
Paul Painlevé (first ministry)
1917, Nov.—1920, Jan.
Georges Clemenceau (second ministry)
1920, Jan.—Feb.
Alexandre Millerand (first ministry)

1920, Feb.—Sept. **PRESIDENCY OF PAUL DESCHANEL**

1920, Feb.—Sept.
Alexandre Millerand (second ministry)

1920, Sept.—1924, June **PRESIDENCY OF ALEXANDRE MILLERAND**

1920, Sept.—1921, Jan.
Georges Leygues
1921, Jan.—1922, Jan.
Aristide Briand (seventh ministry)
1922, Jan.—1924, Mar.
Raymond Poincaré (second ministry)

1924, Mar.—June
Raymond Poincaré (third ministry)
1924, June
Frédéric François-Marsal

1924, June—1931, June **PRESIDENCY OF GASTON DOUMERGUE**

1924, June—1925, Apr.
Édouard Herriot (first ministry)
1925, Apr.—Oct.
Paul Painlevé (second ministry)
1925, Oct.—Nov.
Paul Painlevé (third ministry)
1925, Nov.—1926, Mar.
Aristide Briand (eighth ministry)
1926, Mar.—June
Aristide Briand (ninth ministry)
1926, June—July
Aristide Briand (tenth ministry)
1926, July
Édouard Herriot (second ministry)
1926, July—1928, Nov.
Raymond Poincaré (fourth ministry)

1928, Nov.—1929, July
Raymond Poincaré (fifth ministry)
1929, July—Oct.
Aristide Briand (eleventh ministry)
1929, Nov.—1930, Feb.
André Tardieu (first ministry)
1930, Feb.
Camille Chautemps (first ministry)
1930, Mar.—Dec.
André Tardieu (second ministry)
1930, Dec.—1931, Jan.
Theodore Steeg
1931, Jan.—June
Pierre Laval (first ministry)

1931, June—1932, May **PRESIDENCY OF PAUL DOUMER**

1931, June—1932, Jan.
Pierre Laval (second ministry)
1932, Jan.—Feb.
Pierre Laval (third ministry)

1932, Feb.—May
André Tardieu (third ministry)

1932, May—1939, May **FIRST PRESIDENCY OF ALBERT LEBRUN**

1932, June—Dec.
Édouard Herriot (third ministry)
1932, Dec.—1933, Jan.
Joseph Paul-Boncour
1933, Jan.—Oct.
Édouard Daladier (first ministry)
1933, Oct.—Nov.
Albert Sarraut (first ministry)
1933, Nov.—1934, Jan.
Camille Chautemps (second ministry)
1934, Jan.—Feb.
Édouard Daladier (second ministry)
1934, Feb.—Nov.
Gaston Doumergue (second ministry)
1934, Nov.—1935, May
Pierre Flandin (first ministry)

1935, June
Fernand Bouisson
1935, June—1936, Jan.
Pierre Laval (fourth ministry)
1936, Jan.—June
Albert Sarraut (second ministry)
1936, June—1937, June
Léon Blum (first ministry)
1937, June—1938, Jan.
Camille Chautemps (third ministry)
1938, Jan.—Mar.
Camille Chautemps (fourth ministry)
1938, Mar.—Apr.
Léon Blum (second ministry)
1938, Apr.—1940, Mar.
Édouard Daladier (third ministry)

1939, May—1940, July SECOND PRESIDENCY OF ALBERT LEBRUN

1940, Mar.—June | 1940, June—July
Paul Reynaud | Marshal Philippe Pétain

CHIEF OF STATE (VICHY RÉGIME)

1940, July—1944, August   Marshal Philippe Pétain

PRESIDENTS OF THE PROVISIONAL GOVERNMENT OF THE FRENCH REPUBLIC

1945, Nov.—1946, Jan. | 1946, Jan.—June
General Charles de Gaulle | Felix Gouin

1946, June—1947, Jan.   Georges Bidault

PRESIDENTS OF THE FOURTH FRENCH REPUBLIC

1947, Jan.—   Vincent Auriol

APPENDIX IX

ITALIAN MINISTRIES SINCE 1860

1860, Jan.—1861, June
Count Camillo Benso di Cavour

1861, June—1862, Mar.
Baron Bettino Ricasoli (first ministry)

1862, Mar.—Dec.
Urbano Ratazzi (first ministry)

1862, Dec.—1864, Sept.
Marco Minghetti (first ministry)

1864, Sept.—1866, June
General Alfonso La Marmora

1866, June—1867, Apr.
Baron Bettino Ricasoli (second ministry)

1867, Apr.—Oct.
Urbano Ratazzi (second ministry)

1867, Oct.—1869, Dec.
Federigo Menabrea

1869, Dec.—1873, June
Domenico Lanza

1873, July—1876, Mar.
Marco Minghetti (second ministry)

1876, Mar.—1878, Mar.
Agostino Depretis (first ministry)

1878, Mar.—Dec.
Benedetto Cairoli (first ministry)

1878, Dec.—1879, July
Agostino Depretis (second ministry)

1879, July—1881, May
Benedetto Cairoli (second ministry)

1881, May—1887, July
Agostino Depretis (third ministry)

1887, July—1891, Jan.
Francesco Crispi (first ministry)

1891, Jan.—1892, May
Marquis di Rudini (first ministry)

1892, May—1893, Nov.
Giovanni Giolitti (first ministry)

1893, Nov.—1896, Mar.
Francesco Crispi (second ministry)

1896, Mar.—1898, June
Marquis di Rudini (second ministry)

1898, June—1900, June
General Luigi Pelloux

1900, June—1901, Feb.
Giuseppe Saracco

1901, Feb.—1903, Oct.
Giuseppe Zanardelli

1903, Oct.—1906, Jan.
Giovanni Giolitti (second ministry)

1906, Jan.—May
Baron Sidney Sonnino (first ministry)

1906, May—1909, Dec.
Giovanni Giolitti (third ministry)

1909, Dec.—1910, Mar.
Baron Sidney Sonnino (second ministry)

1910, Mar.—1911, Mar.
Luigi Luzzatti

1911, Mar.—1914, Mar.
Giovanni Giolitti (fourth ministry)

1914, Mar.—1916, June
Antonio Salandra

1916, June—1917, Oct.
  Paolo Boselli
1917, Oct.—1919, June
  Vittorio Orlando
1919, June—1920, June
  Francesco Nitti
1920, June—1921, June
  Giovanni Giolitti (fifth ministry)
1921, June—1922, Feb.
  Ivanoe Bonomi
1922, Feb.—Oct.
  Luigi Facta
1922, Oct.—1943, July
  Benito Mussolini

1943, July—1944, June
  Marshal Pietro Badoglio
1944, June—1945, June
  Ivanoe Bonomi
1945, June—Dec.
  Ferruccio Parri
1945, Dec.—1947, Feb.
  Alcide de Gasperi

(Italy became a republic, June 10, 1946)

1947, Feb.—
  Alcide de Gasperi (reappointed)

APPENDIX X

LIST OF PRESIDENTS OF THE UNITED STATES

George Washington, 1789–1797
John Adams, 1797–1801
Thomas Jefferson, 1801–1809
James Madison, 1809–1817
James Monroe, 1817–1825
John Quincy Adams, 1825–1829
Andrew Jackson, 1829–1837
Martin Van Buren, 1837–1841
William Henry Harrison, 1841
John Tyler, 1841–1845
James Knox Polk 1845–1849
Zachary Taylor, 1849–1850
Millard Fillmore, 1850–1853
Franklin Pierce, 1853–1857
James Buchanan, 1857–1861
Abraham Lincoln, 1861–1865
Andrew Johnson, 1865–1869

Ulysses Simpson Grant, 1869–1877
Rutherford Birchard Hayes, 1877–1881
James Abram Garfield, 1881
Chester Alan Arthur, 1881–1885
Grover Cleveland, 1885–1889
Benjamin Harrison, 1889–1893
Grover Cleveland, 1893–1897
William McKinley, 1897–1901
Theodore Roosevelt, 1901–1909
William Howard Taft, 1909–1913
Woodrow Wilson, 1913–1921
Warren Gamaliel Harding, 1921–1923
Calvin Coolidge, 1923–1929
Herbert Clark Hoover, 1929–1933
Franklin Delano Roosevelt, 1933–1945
Harry S. Truman, 1945–1953

Index

Aachen, 162. *See also* Aix-la-Chapelle
Aaland Islands, occupied by Germans, 943; Convention of, 957; assigned to Finland, 1047; neutralized, **1048**
Aasen, Ivar, Norwegian grammarian, 699
Aba, Samuel, and the Hungarian throne, 245
Abacus, 131
Abbadids of Cordova, 233
d'Abbadie, Antoine Thomson, explorer, 826
Abbas, the Great, shah of Persia, 424; and the brothers Shirley, 424, 526
Abbas, uncle of the Prophet, 187
Abbas I, khedive of Egypt, 830
Abbas II, shah of Persia, 528
Abbas III, shah of Persia, 527, 529
Abbas Hilmi II, khedive of Egypt, 833; deposed, **834**
Abbasids, caliphs, 137, 187, 188
Abbeville, 1146, 1148
Abbey of Cluny, 216
Abbot, Sir John J. C., premier of Canada, **797**
A.B.C. powers, at Niagara conference, 791, **1062, 1070**
Abd-Ashirta, 33, 35
Abd-Ashtart, 33
Abd el-Kader, dey of Mascara, 837
Abd el-Krim, Riffian chief, 981, 1086, 1087
Abdera, 61
Abdiliti, king of Aewad, 33
Abdimilkat, 33
Abdul Aziz, sultan of Turkey, 728, 729
Abdul Aziz, sultan of Morocco, 838, defeated at Marakesh, 839; defeated by Mulay Hafid, 755
Abdul Hamid II, sultan of Turkey, 729; restores constitution, 731; deposed by parliament, 739, 757; died, 732
Abdul Mejid, sultan of Turkey, 725, 1095
Abdul-Mu'min, annihilates the Almoravid army, 233, 263
Abdul-Muttalib, grandfather of Mohammed the Prophet, 184
Abdullah, brother of Mundhir, 163
Abdullah, father of Mohammed the Prophet, 184
Abdullah, gov. of Syria, uncle of Al-Mansur, 188
Abdullah, grandson of Ja'far, leads Sh'ite insurrection, 188
Abdullah, ruler of Kandahar, 528
Abdullah II, leader of the Uzbeks, 526
Abdullah ben Yassin, Almoravid, conquers West Africa, 328
Abdullah el Taashi, khalifa, defeated at Omdurman, 832
Abdullah ibn Hussein, emir, ruler of Transjordania, 1100
Abdullah ibn Sa'd, gov. of Egypt, 186
Abdullah ibn Tashfin, founder of the Almoravid Berber dynasty, 233, 263
Abdullah ibn Zubayr, caliph in Arabia, Iraq, and Egypt, 186, 187
Abdulmalik, caliph, 187
Abdulmalik al-Muzaffar, defeated Christians in Spain, 164
Abdurrahman, founder of Moorish Spain, 163, 188
Abdurrahman, gov. of Spain, defeated by Charles Martel, 187
Abdurrahman, amir of Afghanistan, 868
Abdurrahman II, caliph, 163
Abdurrahman III, caliph and amir Al-Mu'minin, 163 *f*.
Abdurrahman Sanchol, succeeded his brother Abdulmalik, **164**
Abe, Gen. Nobuyuki, Japanese premier, 1127
Abe clan, in Japan, 353
Abel of Denmark, 203
Abélard, Peter, master at Paris, 229
Abensberg, battle of, 594
Abercromby, Gen. James, defeated at Ticonderoga, 516
Abercromby, Sir Ralph, attacked Puerto Rico, 824
Aberdeen, George Hamilton-Gordon, 4th Earl of, prime minister, 613; and the Spanish marriages, 645; and the near Eastern question, 726; gov.-gen. of Canada, 797
Abhayagiri Monastery, 132
Abhidharma, 129
Abhidharmakosa sastra, 131
Abhira tribe, 132
Abhorrers (court party, Tories), 428
Abibaal, 33
Abijah, 31
Abilene flints, 19
Abimelech, 30
Abimelek of Tyre, 33
Abö, Treaty of, 474
Aboukir, sunk by the German U-9, 917
Abraham, 29
Abrea, Antonio de, first sighted New Guinea, 894
Abruzzi, Luigi de Amedeo, Duke of the, expedition to Franz Joseph Land, 566
Absalom, 31
Abu Abdullah, Ismailian missionary, 262
Abu Bakr, first caliph, 184
Abu-l-Abbas al-Saffah, first Abbasid caliph, 188
Abu-l Ali ibn Marwan, established the Marwanids, **190**
Abu Muslim, leader of the Abbasids, 188
Abu Said, last of the Timurid dynasty, 330
Abu Simbel, 24
Abu Talid, uncle of Mohammed the Prophet, 184
Abu Yazid Makhlad, defeats Al-Qa'im, 266
Abydos, 21, 60

Abydus, 47
Abyssinian expedition, 614
Academic Legion, of Austria, 673
Académie Française, founded, 387; des Inscriptions et Belles-Lettres, des Sciences, des Beaux-Arts; des Sciences Morales et Politiques, 590
Academy in the Grove, founded by Plato, 67
Academy of Letters of China, 537
Academy of Naples, 293
Acadia, ceded by France to Britain, 433; name changed to Nova Scotia, 514
Acarnanians, 57, 58
Accident Insurance Law, in Germany, **690, 692**
Acco, 32
Achá, José de, pres. of Bolivia, 811
Achaea, 50, 56, 63, 65, 90
Achaean League, 79, 80, 90
Achaeans, 11, 47, 64, 90
Achaemenian kings, 40
Acheulean industry, 6, 8
Achilles, 47
Achilleus, raises revolt in Egypt, 118
Achinese, subdued by the Dutch, 877
Acosta, Julio, pres. of Costa Rica, 1073
Acquaviva, Rodolfo, Portuguese Jesuit, 533
Acragas, 47 *f.*, 53, 57, 62
Acre, captured, 725
Acropolis, at Athens, 62
Acropolis (city) capitulated to the Turks, 723
Acte, mistress of Nero, 106
Action Française, organ of French monarchists, 643
Act of Algeciras, 754
Act of Chapultepec, 1156
Act of Grace, 430
Act of Havana, 1155
Act of Mediation, for Switzerland, 590
Act of Settlement, of the English crown, **431, 432**
Act of Supremacy, 370, 372
Act of the Congress of Vienna, 602
Act of Uniformity, 372, 374; of the Clarendon Code, 426
Act of Union, established one parliament for England and Ireland, 437
Act of Unity and Security, in Sweden, 474
Act of 1651, a blow at Dutch shipping, 514
Act of 1673, imposing intercolonial duties, 514
Act of 1887, regulating railways, 784
Act of 1913, established Federal Reserve Bank districts, 791
Actium, battle of, 85, 99
Activists, German parties in Czechoslovak cabinet, **1011**
Acton, Sir John, an English adventurer, 458
Acts of Grace (*Tokusei*) in Japan, 357, 359
Adab, 25
Adad-nirari I, conquers Mitanni, 29; II, 35, 38; III, **27, 35**
Adalbert, archbishop of Hamburg-Bremen, 206
Adalbert of Treves, 208
Adalia, claimed by Italians, 986, 1094
Adam of Bremen, author of *Hamburg Church History*, 365
Adams, John (2d Pres. of U.S.); and the Boston Massacre Case, 519; leader of the Federalist Party, 764; elected pres.; defeated for re-election, 766
Adams, John Quincy (6th Pres. of U.S.), **771**
Adams, Samuel, Massachusetts, 519; leader of radicals at first Continental Congress, 520
Adams, Will, English pilot, 546
Adamson (William Charles) Act, 792
Addington, Henry, concluded peace with France, 437
Addis Ababa, occupied by the Italians, 991, 1086; Treaty of, 661, 835, 1160
Addled Parliament, 374
Adela, sister of Henry I of England, **193, 194**
Adelaide, Australia, founded, 900
Adelard of Bath, medieval scientist, 194
Adelheid, sister of King Conrad, **161, 162; imprisoned by Berengar II, 216
Adélie Land, in Antarctic, 577
Aden, occupied by the British, 725; separated from India and becomes a crown colony, 1113
Ader, Clement, 556
Adhemar of Puy, leader of the Provençals in First Crusade, **255**
Adil Shah, shah of Persia, 529
Aditya I, defeated and killed Aparajitavarman, 337
Aditya Dibabha, Prince, regent of Siam, 1116
Adkins (Jesse C.) case, 790
Adler, Alfred, on aspects of the subconscious, 552
Adlerkreuz, Gen. Carl Johann, arrests King Gustavus IV of Sweden, 595
Adli Pasha, premier of Egypt, 1083
Administration of Justice Act, 518–520
Admiralty Islands, 1169
Admonitions, 294
Adolf of Nassau, alliance with Edward I of England against Philip IV of France, 301; deposed, 301; confirms the status of Uri and Schwyz, 306
Adolph of Holstein, deprived of Lubeck, 210, 214

Adolphus Frederick, King of Sweden, 474
Adrenalin, 552
Adrian IV (Nicholas Breakspear), pope grants Henry II of England the lordship of Ireland, 169, 196; alliance with Frederick I against William of Sicily, 219, 223
Adrian VI (Adrian Dedel), last non-Italian pope, 395
Adrianople, battles of: Licinius defeated by Constantine, 119; Valens defeated by Visigoths, 120; Crusaders defeated by Greeks, 248; Crusaders defeated by Bulgarians, 259; Treaty of, 702, 712, 719, 724
Adua, battle of, 661, 745, 835; taken by the Italians, 991
Advance to the East, see *Drang nach Osten*
Advisory Council for Italy, 1162
Aedui, revolt of, 103
Aegates Islands, 86
Aegean migration of *Peoples of the Sea*, 34, 35, 36
Aegean Sea, 1151
Aegina, 50, 52, 55, 61
Aeginetans, 55, 56, 58
Aegospotami, 61
Aehrenthal, Alois Lexa, Count von, Austrian foreign minister, 755, 756
A.E.I.O.U., monogram of Frederick III, 304
Aemilianus, M. Aemilius, 115 *f.*
Aeneas, 69
Aeolians, 47, 48
Aequi, 71
Aeschines, negotiates peace between Philip and Athens, 64
Aeschylus, dramatist, 62
Aesop, of Lydia, 37
Aetheling, Edgar, brother of Margaret, wife of Malcolm Canmore, 201
Aëtios, general, supported the Empress Irene, 176
Aëtius, clears Gaul of barbarians, 121; defeats Huns at battle of Châlons, 121, 143; murdered by Valentinian, 121
Aetna, 57
Aetolia, 65
Aetolian League, 79, 89
Aetolians, declare war on Rome, 80, 87, 89
Affirmation Bill, legalizing affirmation in place of oath in the House of Commons, 616
Afghan Wars, 616, 866, 867, 871, 1111
Afghanistan, history of, 530, 866 *ff.*, 1109 *ff.*
Afghans at Kandahar, establish their independence, 530
Afiun-Karahissar, taken by the Greeks, retaken by the Turks, 1095
Afonso de Albuquerque, 364, 391
Afonso Henriques, founder of the Portuguese monarchy and of the Burgundian dynasty; arranges Treaty of Zamorra between Portugal and Castile; defeated at Badajos, 238 *f.*
Afonso II of Portugal, 239
Afonso III of Portugal; war with Castile, 239
Afonso V (the African), 287; leases the Guinea trade, 364
Afonso VI, of Portugal, 453
Africa, in the Palaeolithic period, 5 *f.*; in Post-Palaeolithic, 18; during the Middle Ages, 328, 363
African campaigns, 1159 *ff.*
African Lakes Trading Co., 847
African slave trade, prohibited in U.S., 768
Afridi clans, rebel, 871
Afrikander Bond, founded, 853; supports Rhodes, 855; merged in the South African Party, 858
Afshin, defeats Babek, 189
Aga Mohammed, founded the Kajar dynasty, 529; assassination, 862
Agamas, 129
Agathias, historian in the revival of Roman literature, 173
Agathocles, tyrant of Syracuse, 34; dies, 78
Agesilaus, 62
Aghlabid dynasty, in Tunis, 262, 263
Aghlabids of Egypt, 262
Agilulf, duke of Turin, founder of the Lombard state, 151
Agincourt, battle of, 268, 278
Agis I, restores Sparta's hegemony, 59
Agis III, defeated by Antipater, 65
Agis IV, executed, 79
Agnadello, battle of, 394
Agnes, mother of Henry IV of Germany, 206
Agnes of Poitou, wife of Henry III of Germany, 205
Agrarian League, amalgamated with the old Peasants' League, 691
Agrarian Society, in Piedmont, founded by Count Cavour, 655
Agricola, Cnaeus Julius, continues conquest of Britain, 108, 166
Agricultural Adjustment Act of U.S., declared unconstitutional, 1053
Agricultural depression in England, 616
Agriculture, in Post-Palaeolithic period, 10; traces in South Africa, 18
Agrigentum (Acragas), 62, 86
Agrippa I, 107
Agrippa II, 107
Agrippa, Marcus Vipsanius, defeats Pompey, 99; 102
Agrippa, Postumius, defeats Latins in battle of Lake Regillus, 71
Agrippina, wife of Germanicus, 103; exiled, dies, 105
Agrippina the Younger, niece of Claudius, 105, 106
Aguayo, Mar quis of, gov. of Coahuila, 492
Aguinaldo, Emilio, Philippine leader, 909; leads insurrection against the U.S., 787; proclaims independence, captured by Gen. Funston, 909
Aguirre, Anastasio, pres. of Uruguay, 811

Aguirre, Gen. Jesús María, a leader of insurrection in Mexico, 1076
Aguirre, José Antonio, pres. of the autonomous Basque provinces, 983
Agustín I, Emperor of Mexico, 821
Agyrokastron, 1150
Ahab of Israel, 27, 31
Ahalya Bai, ruled Indore, 535
Ahasuerus, see Xerxes I
Ahaz, 31
Ahaziah, 31
Ahenobarbus, Lucius Domitius, 105, 106. Hereafter referred to as Nero, *which see*.
Ahiram, 33
Ahlame, 34
Ahlmann, Prof. Hans, leads sledge tour to Northeast Land, 570
Ahmad, sultan as Al Musta'li; lost Jerusalem to the crusaders, 262
Ahmad Abu-l-Qasim, caliph under the title Mustansir l'Illah, 262
Ahmad ibn Tulun, founder of the Tulunid dynasty, 189
Ahmad Khan Durani, founded a powerful Afghan state, 529: expeditions to India, 530
Ahmad Shah, Indian ruler, 335
Ahmad Shah, 12-yr.-old sultan of Persia, 865
Ahmed, executed by his brother Sclim I, 421
Ahmed al Mansur, established the Sharifian dynasty, 524
Ahmed Ali Bey el-Abed, elected pres. of the Syrian Republic, 1098
Ahmed Bey, founded the Karamanli dynasty, 525
Ahmed Bey Zogu, premier of Albania; pres. of Albania; proclaimed king as Zog I, 1019
Ahmed Fenaketi, 345
Ahmed Fuad, sultan, then King of Egypt as Fuad I, 1081
Ahmed Gran, Moslem Somali Chief, 524
Ahmed Kiuprili, grand vizier of Turkey, 482 *f.*
Ahrenberg, Capt. Albin, airplane flight from Sweden to Angmagssalik, 568
Ahrensburg-Lavenstadt culture, 18
Aidan, Celtic Christian missionary, 166; founded Lindisfarne, 169
Aide-toi, le Ciel t'aidera, a Liberal electoral society, 627
Aigues Mortes, its walls built, 231
Aigun, Treaty of, 704, 879
Ain Jalut, battle of, 262
Ainus, Japanese race, 12, 138, 139
Air assault, by Germany, 1149
Airbrake, 556
Air mail (transcontinental) service between New York and San Francisco, 1150
Air power, the role of, 1164
Air raids, 946, 947
'Aisha, the Prophet's favorite wife, 185
Aisin Gioro, see Nurhachi
Aisne, battles of: first, 914; second, 939; third, 945
Aistulf, continues consolidation of Lombard kingdom, 152; besieges Rome, 153
Aitape, 1169
Aix-la-Chapelle, Treaty of, 435, 442, 451, 458, 466, 494, 515, 534
Ajanta, 43, 132
Ajatasatru, king 41
Ajayapala, ordered the massacre of Jains, 332
Ajnadayne, battle of, 184
Akalis, rise in the Punjab, 1112
Akbar, emperor of India, 530, 533, 534
Akbar, Prince, revolt of, 534
Akbar Khan, and massacre of the British, 866
Akhi, a semi-religious society among the Turks, 325
Akkad, 25
Akkadians, progress in sculpture, 25; raiders, 33; battled with Elamites, 39
Akra, battle of, 187
Akroinon, Byzantine victory over Arab invaders, 176; Peace of, 252
Alabama, admitted to statehood, 770
Alabama claims, for the depredations of the *Alabama* in the U.S. Civil War, 615, 781
Alai Darwaza, 333
Alalia, battle of, 53
Alamanni, defeated by Caracalla, 115; 116, 118, 120, 142
Al-Amin, Caliph, 188
Alans, defeated by Tacitus, 116; overrun Gaul, 121, 143
Alaouite in Syria, made a French state, 1098
Alarcón, Hernando de, reached the Zuñis; passed up the Colorado River, 492
Alarcón, Juan Ruz de, Spanish-American dramatist, 500
Alarcos, battle of, 234
Alaric I, leader of Visigoths, driven out of Greece, sacked Rome, 121; 142 *ff.*
Alaric II, 145
Alashehr, battle of, 1094
Alaska, sold by Russia to the U.S., 705, 781; settlement boundary dispute with Canada, 789, 797; given territorial status, 798
Alaska Highway, 1155
Ala-ud-din, consolidated the empire of the Khalji, 333
Alaungpaya, founder of the modern state of Burma, 529
Al-Aziz, conquered Syria and part of Mesopotamia, 262
Alba, duke of, defeated Pope Paul IV and his French allies, 396
Alba, Col. Luis, provisional pres. of Ecuador, 1069
Alba Fucens, 74

Albania, 761, 927, 1019 *ff.*, 1150
Albany, former Fort Orange, 512
Albany, in West Australia, established, 899
Albany Convention, 516
Albany Settlers, British colonists, 851
Albemarle, George Monk, 1st Duke of, defeated by De Ruyter and De Witt, 427
Alberic II, pope, 215
Alberoni, Giulio, Cardinal, 436; adviser of Elizabeth Farnese, 451, 463
Albert I, King of the Belgians, 623, 975
Albert I (Albrecht), supported Carobert in acquiring Hungary, 301
Albert II, King of Hungary and Bohemia, 304
Albert, Archduke of Austria, defeated the Italians in the second battle of Custozza, 659
Albert (town), in French hands, 914
Albert, Bishop of Livonia (Latvia), founded the Order of Swordbearers, 244
Albert of Austria, aids the Teutonic Order against the Poles, 310
Albert of Brandenburg (Hohenzollern), secularized East Prussia under the Polish crown, 310
Albert of Hapsburg, son of Emperor Sigismund, 318
Albert of Mecklenburg, deposed, 311
Albert of Saxe-Coburg-Gotha, consort of Queen Victoria of England, 609, 613
Albert the Bear, Margrave of Brandenburg, 208; war with Frederick I, 210; 214; helps drive back Poles, 242
Albert Nyanza, discovered, 826
Alberta, formed as a Canadian province, 797
Alberti, Leone Battista, Italian humanist, 290; 296
Albertus Magnus, Dominican teacher, 231
Alberuni of Khiva, scientist, 332
Albigensian (Catharist) Crusade, against heresy in southern France, 220 *f.*, 229, 257
Albinus D. Clodius Septimius, Roman emperor, 114
Albizzi, Maso degli, exiled the Alberti from Florence, 294
Albizzi, Rinaldo degli, exiled from Florence, 294
Alboin, Lombard king, 150
Albrecht of Wurttemberg, Prince, in command of 4th German army, 913
Albuera, battle of, 596
Albuquerque, Afonso de, conquered Ormuz, 364, 391; seized Malacca, 541
Alcaçovas, Treaty of, 363
Alcaeus, poet, 48
Alcantara, Pedro de, Emperor of Brazil, 817
Alchemy, practice of, 135
Alcibiades, commands expedition to Sicily, 59; annihilated Peloponnesian fleet, 60; recovered Byzantium, 61
Alcidas, admiral, 58
Alcmaeonids, 51, 52
Alcock, Capt. John, first to cross Atlantic in an airplane, 557
Alcolea, battle of, 646
Alcorta, José Figueroa, pres. of Argentina, 808
Alcuin, and the palace school of Charlemagne, 155, 166
Aldobrandini, Ippolito, Pope Clement VIII, 396
Aldrich, Nelson Wilmarth, co-author of the Payne-Aldrich Tariff, 790; and of the Aldrich-Vreeland Act, 791
Aldrich, Lt. Pelham, English explorer, 564
Aldrich-Vreeland Act, 791
Aldringer, Johann, defeated by Bernhard of Saxe-Weimar, 406
Aleppo, taken by the Greeks, 180; by the Moslems, 185; by British and Arabs, 948; made a French state, 1098
Alert (Br.) captured by the *Essex* (U.S.S.), 769
Alesia, 97
Alessandri, Arturo, pres. of Chile, 1065
Alessandria, siege by Frederick I, 209, 220
Aleutian Islands, 1167
Alexander I of Bulgaria, *see* Alexander of Battenberg
Alexander II of Epirus, assassinated, 66, 83
Alexander I of Greece, 1020
Alexander of Pherae, defeated by Epaminondas, 63
Alexander I of Poland, war with Ivan the Great; Constitution of Radom, 413
Alexander I of Russia, 482, 593; and the Treaty of Tilsit, 593, 595; at Congress of Erfurt, 594; at the Congress of Vienna, 601, 626, 702
Alexander II of Russia, his Emancipation Edict, 704; meeting of the three emperors, William, Francis Joseph, and Alexander, 733; 737; death, 705
Alexander III of Russia, 706
Alexander II of Scotland, 199
Alexander III of Scotland, 201
Alexander I of Serbia, 714, 715
Alexander, Serbian king, 715, 950, 1015, 1017, 1018, 1024
Alexander III the Great, 24, 25; rules Babylonia, 26; dominates the Jews, 32; takes Tyre, 33; conquers Syria, 35, 37, 38, 40; invades Sogdiana, 45; 55; defeats Memnon of Rhodes, marries Roxana, 65; defeats Porus in battle of the Hydaspes; son born, 66; rule of Parthia, 83; his death, 66, 67. 83
Alexander II, anti-pope, 168; blesses William's conquest of England, 191
Alexander II (Anselmo Baggio), pope, 218
Alexander III (Orlando Bandinelli), pope, excommunicates Frederick I, 220; 223; recognizes independence of Portugal, 234
Alexander IV, 66
Alexander V (Peter Philargès), pope, makes peace offers to Manfred of Sicily, 213
Alexander V, 78

Alexander VI (Rodrigo Borgia), pope, 290; the Naples succession, 293; grants lands to Catholic kings, 367; in the Holy League, 381; in the league against Charles VIII, 393; his bulls *Inter caetera* and *Eximiae devotionis*, 498; dies, 395
Alexander VII (Fabio Chigi), pope, friction with Louis XIV, 455
Alexander VIII (Pietro Ottoboni), pope, 455
Alexander, Bishop of Rome, 119
Alexander, Byzantine emperor, 179
Alexander, gov. of Peloponnese, 79
Alexander, Tiberius Julius, proclaims Vespasian emperor, 107, 113
Alexander of Battenberg, Prince of Bulgaria, 717; gov.-gen. of eastern Roumelia, 739
Alexander Severus, Marcus Aurelius, Roman emperor, 115
Alexandra, 32
Alexandra, Empress of Russia, 1028; murdered, 1032
Alexandretta, battle of, 724
Alexandretta, Sanjak of, 1097, 1098
Alexandria, 86; captured by Napoleon, 586; outbreak of riots, 831; bombarded by British fleet, 738, 832; 1160
Alexandrov, Todor, leads attempted rising of Macedonians, 1023
Alexeiev-Tseng Agreement, between Russia and the Chinese gov. of Manchuria, 750
Alexinatz, battle of, 734
Alexis, son of Peter the Great, 478
Alexis, Tsar of Russia, war with Poland; first contact with Turks in the Balkans, 478
Alexius II, Byzantine emperor, 320
Alexius III, Byzantine emperor, 253
Alexius IV, Byzantine emperor, and the Fourth Crusade, 254, 257
Alexius V (Dukas), Byzantine emperor, and sack of Constantinople, 254, 257
Alexius, Byzantine emperor, seizes Constantinople; defeated by Normans at Pharsalus; and by the Bogomils at Drystra, but annihilated the Patzinaks at Leburnion, 250; 255; founds the Empire of Trebizond, 259; defeated and captured by Theodore I, 259
Alfaro, Eloy, pres. of Ecuador, 814
Alfarrobeira, battle of, 287
Alfieri, Vittorio, Italian dramatist, 454
Alfonsine Tables, 235
Alfonso I, gives Church a share of lands conquered from Moslems, 164
Alfonso V (the Magnanimous), conquers Naples, 284; unites crowns of Naples and Sicily, 292; fled from Naples, 393
Alfonso VII, crowned "emperor," 233 *f.*; his death, 234
Alfonso VIII, victory at Las Navas de Tolosa, 234
Alfonso X (the Learned), 237, 282
Alfonso XI, defeated the Moslems at Salado, 280
Alfonso XII, son of Isabella, 644, 647
Alfonso XIII, King of Spain, 647, 981, 982
Alfonso I (the Warrior) of Aragon, captured Saragossa, 237
Alfonso III of Aragon, regrants privileges of Union, 283
Alfonso IV of Aragon, 284
Alfonso of Calabria, invades Tuscany, 296
Alfonso VI of Castile, resumes Christian reconquest of Spain, 333
Alfonso X of Castile, elected emperor in Germany, 213
Alfonso II of Leon, invades Aragon; his kingdom destroyed, 163
Alfonso of Poitiers, uncle of Philip III of France, 231
Alfonso IV (the Brave) of Portugal, 284
Alfonso, brother of Louis IX of France, 231
Alfonso the Wise, 199
Alfred the Great, of England, 167
Algarsson, Grettir, commands British Arctic expedition, 569
Algeciras Conference and Act on Morocco, 754, 789, 838
Algeria, under French rule, 837, 838, 1148
Algiers, taken by the French, 837; 1160, 1162
Al-Hadi, caliph, 188
Al-Hakim, the Mad Caliph, 262
Ali, cousin of the Prophet, caliph, 185, 187, 262
Ali, Rashid, Premier of Iraq, 1151
Ali, sherif of the Hejaz, 1048
Ali ben Khalifa, leads insurrection against the French in Tunisia, 838
Ali Bey, of Egypt, 524
Ali brothers, Indian nationalists, 1112
Ali Fethi Bey, heads opposition party in Turkey, 1096
Ali Kuli Khan, leader of the Bakhtiari tribe, 865
Ali Maher Pasha, premier of Egypt, 1084
Ali Murad, shah of Persia, 529
Ali of Gondar, Ras, of Ethiopia, 834
Ali of Janina, 722
Ali Pasha, Turkish statesman, 728, 729
Ali Riza, forms Turkish cabinet, 1094
Alid dynasty of Idrisids, in Morocco, 263
Alien Act of the U.S., 766
Alien Enemies Act of the U.S., 766
Aliens Expulsion Act passed in the Transvaal, 856
Aliens Immigration Restriction Act in the Transvaal, 856
Alishar Huyuk, 13
Aljubarrota, battle of, 284
Al Kase Al-Kabir (Three Kings), battle of, 392, 284
Al-Khoury, Sheikh Beshaka, 1141
Al-Khwarizmi, Arab scientist, 194
All-India Congress at Poona, 1113, 1114
All-India Federation established, 1114
All-India Moslem League, 1111
All-Parties Conference in India, 1112
All-Russian Congress of Soviets, 1028

Allah, as the One God, an article of Moslem faith, 184
Allen, Ethan, captured Ticonderoga, 520
Allenby, Gen. Edmund Henry Hyndman, British commander in Palestine, 257, 938, 939, 948; appointed high commissioner for Egypt, 1081
Allersheim, battle of, 407
Alles Erdreich ist Oesterreich unterthan, Frederick III's monogram, 304
Allia, 72
Alliance of Germany and Austria, 690, 694
Allied Control Commission, 1162
Allied Control Committee, 1165
Allied expedition to Japan, 889
Allied forces, landed on Cherbourg peninsula, 1159; at Anzio, 1162; on French Mediterranean coast, 1163
Allied Military Government, 1162
Allies in war against Napoleon, 600, 601, 602
Allison, William Boyd, co-author of the Bland-Allison Act, 783
Allouez, Claude Jean, Jesuit missionary, 507
Allthing, oldest parliamentary body in existence, 170
Alma River, battle of, 727
Almagro, Diego de, accompanied Pizarro on conquest of Peru, 489
Al-Mahdi, caliph, 188
Al-Mansur, real founder of the Abbasid dynasty, 188
Al-Mansur, son of Al-Qa'im, defeated Abu Yazid Makhlad, 262
Almanza, battle of, 453
Almazan, Peace of, 280
Almeida, Antonio José de, pres. of Portugal, 985
Almeida, Francisco de, first gov. of India, 364, 391; battle of Diu, 364, 530
Almenara, battle of, 450
Almeria, bombarded by four German warships, 984
Almerian culture, 17
Almohades, dynasty, 233, 263; Almoravid armies annihilated, 263; missionaries allowed to establish centers, 363
Almoravids, annihilated by Abdul-Mu'min, 233, 263; conquer West Africa, 328
Al-Mu'iz, son of Al-Mansur, recovers Morocco from the Omayyads, 262
Al-Mustanjid, Fatimid sultan, 262
Al-Mustansir, sultan, loses allegiance of Mecca and Medina, 262
Al-Mu'tasim, caliph; revolt of Jats or Gypsies; war with Byzantium, 189
Alp Arslan, conquered Georgia and Armenia, 254
Alphabet, invented by Phoenicians, 32, 33
Alpines, in the White group, 12, 16
Al-Qa'im, caliph, 262
Alsace-Lorraine, ceded to Germany, 636, 688, 693, 942; ceded to France by the Treaty of Versailles, 952
Altai, 136
Altamirano, Gen. Luis, rules Chile by a military junta, 1065
Altan Khan, Prince of the Ordos, 536
Altar of Peace dedicated, 102
Altar of Pergamum, 75
Altenstein, Karl, one of the founders of Berlin University, 594
Altgeld, John Peter, gov. of Illinois, 785
Althorp, Lord John Charles, 607
Altitude record in flying, 558
Altmark (against the Wends), 156; Treaty of, 415
Altmark, German ship, 1146, 1158
Altranstädt, Treaty of, 472, 475
Alva, Duke of, in the Netherlands, 380; victories at St. Quentin and Gravelines, 389
Alvarado, Pedro de, conquered Guatemala, 486; sought control of Quito, 489, 908; revolt of the Aztecs against the Spaniards, 491
Alvarez, Francisco, mission of Ethiopia, 524
Alvarez, Jorge, Portuguese explorer, 364
Alvear, Marcelo Torcuato de, pres. of Argentina, 1064
Alvensleben, Count Constantin von, convention for co-operation with Russia, 680, 705
Alverstone, Lord Richard Everard Webster, decides the Alaskan boundary question, 789
Alves, Rodriguez, pres. of Brazil, 818, 1070
Alyattes, King of Lydia, 37, 48
Al-Zahir, sultan, loses most of Syria, 262
Amadas, Philip, takes party of colonists to America, 508
Amadeo I, Duke of Aosta, accepts crown of Spain, 646
Amadeus of Savoy, *see* Felix V
Amalaric, grandson of Theodoric the Great, 146
Amalfi, a city republic, 217
Amalgamated Association of Iron and Steel Workers, 785
Amalgamated Society of Engineers, 611
Amals (Ostrogoths), 143
Amanullah, Amir of Afghanistan, 1109, 1110; provoked war with India, 1111
Amara, taken by Gen. Townshend, 927
Amaravati, 129, 131, 132
Amasis, 24; allied with Polycrates, 48
Amati, the Italian stringed instrument makers, 454
Amaziah, 31
Amba Alagi, battle of, 661, 835
Amberg, battle of, 585
Amboina, massacre of, 876; 1167
Amboise, conspiracy of, 384
Ambrose, Bishop of Milan, forces Theodosius to do penance, 120; 123, 142; supporter of monasticism, 142, 146
Amdrup, Lt. Georg Carl, surveyed the East Greenland coast, 566
Ameixal, battle of, 453

Amelia Island, taken by Federal navy, 776
Amenemhet I, II, III, 23
Amenophis I, 23
Amenophis III, 23, 28, 33
Amenophis IV (Ikhnaton), his religious reformation, 23, 29, 33, 35
America, in Post-Palaeolithic period, 19 f.; pre-Columbian period, 360 f., 371 f.; origin of the name, 368; its discovery, 387
American Anti-Slavery Society, 771
American Association for Old-Age Security, 791
American Colonization Society, 770
American Federation of Labor, 783
American Geographical Society, sponsor for Sir Hubert Wilkins' Antarctic flights, 576
American Peace Society, 771
American Red Cross Society, 783
American republics, neutrality of, 1154
American Revolution, *see* War of American Independence
American Tobacco Co., ordered dissolved by U.S. supreme ct., 790
American Trading Co. of Borneo, 877
American Woman's Suffrage Association, 781
Americans at Château-Thierry, 945; attack on the St. Mihiel salient, 950; reach Sedan, 950
Amherst, Gen. Jeffrey, with Gen. Wolfe took Louisburg, 516
Amherst, William Pitt, Earl of, British ambassador to China, 877
Amida, 127
Amiens, battle of, 950; Treaty of, 437, 452, 586, 590, 850, 875
Amini Commission, in India, 535
Amir al-Mu'minin (Prince of the Faithful), title assumed by Omar as caliph, 184
Amir al-Umara (Prince of the Princes), title granted to Mu'izz al-Dawla, 190
Amir Khusrav, Indian poet, 333
Amirids of Valencia, 233
Amitabha, Buddha of Boundless Light, 129 f., 136
Ammon, 29
Ammonites, 29, 30, 31
Amoghavarsha I, 336
Amorgos, Athenian fleet wiped out, 66
Amorites, 23; founded the Hammurabi dynasty, 25; 29, 33, 35
Amorium, captured, 189
Amos, 30, 31
Amosis, 23
Amoy, opened to trade, 879; taken by the Japanese, 1122
Amphibious mass invasions, 1139, 1158, 1159
Amphictyonic Council, 64; League, 64
Amphictyony of Anthela, 52
Amphipolis, 57, 59, 63, 64
Ampués, Juan de, founded Santa Ana de Coro, 488
Amratian culture, 18
Amr ibn al-'As, invades Egypt, 186
Amritsar Massacre, in India, 1111
Amsuvarman, King of Nepal, 331
Amundsen, Roald Engelbregt Gravning, flew across pole to Alaska; navigation of the northwest passage, 566; navigation of the northeast passage, 570; discovers South Pole, 575; lost in expedition to rescue Nobile, 566
Amursana, Prince of the Jungars, 540
An Lu-shan, Turkish adventurer, 341
Anabaptists, revolt of, in Thuringia, 400; in Münster, 401
Anacletus II, pope, 208, 219, 223
Anacreon, poet, 53
Anactorium, 58
Anadoli Hissar, 327
Analysis of the Phenomena of the Human Mind, by James Mill, 551
Ananda Mahidol, King of Siam, 1116
Anantavarman Codaganga, 337
Anarchism, 550
Anarchists, 640, 647
Anastasius I, emperor of the east; war with Persians, 122
Anastasius II, emperor; attempt to reorganize army, 175
Anatolia, history of, 252, 253, 256, 955, 1094 (*see also* Asia Minor)
Anau, 13
Anawrata, seized power in Burma, 347
Anaxagoras, philosopher, 62
Anaxandridas, king, helped form Peloponnesian League, 50
Anaximander, 48
Anaximenes, 48
Anchialus, battle of, 183
Anchieta, José de, Jesuit, established missions in Brazil, 501
Ancient School of pre-Sung Confucian commentators, 546
Ancón, Treaty of, 809, 813
Ancona, riots at, 663; 1163
Ancren Rewle, 201
Ancus Marcius, early King of Rome, 69
Ancylus Lake culture, 15
Andagoya, Pascual de, conquest of the Incas, 489
d'Andelot, François, 384
Anderson, Maj. Robert, defended Fort Sumter, 776
Anderson, Dr. Rudolph Martin, his study of Eskimos in Mackenzie Delta region, 567
Andes, 1155
Andhra Telugu (Dravidian) lands, 129, 132
Andhrabhrityas, the Satakani of the Puranas, 132
Andrade, Fernao Peres de, at Canton, 364
Andrade, José María Reina, pres. of Guatemala, 1074

d'Andrade, Simao, expelled from China, 536
Andrássy, Count Julius; Compromise of 1867 with Austria, 678; forms ministry, 695; agrees to *status quo* in Near East, 733; Andrássy note, 734; Congress at Berlin, 736, 737; favored the German-Austrian Alliance, 737
André, Maj. John, 522
Andrée, Salomon August, Swedish flyer, 565 *f.*
Andrew of Hungary, 214
Andrew I of Hungary, 245
Andrew II of Hungary, 245 *f.*
Andrew III of Hungary, 246
Andrews, Yelland, British district commissioner for Galilee, 1102
Andrianampoinimerina, King of the Hovas, 859
Andriscus, begins 4th Macedonian War. 80, 90
Androcles, 60
Andronicus II, Byzantine emperor, 321 *f.*; engages Roger de Flor to fight against the Italians, 322; in civil war with the emperor; obliged to accept grandson as co-emperor, 322
Andronicus III, grandson of Andronicus II, conquers Thessaly and part of Epirus, 322; defeated by the Turks at Maltepe, 325
Andronicus IV, son of John V, dethrones his father, 323
Andros, battle of, 79, 84
Andros, Sir Edmund, gov. of the Dominion of New England, assumes govt. of Connecticut, 512
Andrussovo, Treaty of, 475, 478
Anemia, 553
An-Fu (Anhui-Fukien) Club, 1118
Angara River, 7
Angelus, Isaac, Byzantine emperor, and the Bulgars, 247, 253; allies himself with Saladin; deposed, 253; restored to the throne, 254, 257
Angelus, John, Lord of Neopatras, 321
Angevin, the Plantagenet royal line in England, 194 *ff.*
Angevins, campaigns against them by Michael VIII, 321
Anghelu Ruju culture, 17
Anghiari, battle of, 295
Angles and Jutes, invade England, 166
Anglican Church (Church of England, Episcopal Church), established, 372
Anglo-American Conferences, 1139
Anglo-American Polar Expedition, 567
Anglo-American troops, entered Rome, 1162
Anglo-Austrian Agreement, 736
Anglo-Belgian Agreement on territory in the Belgian Congo, 1089
Anglo-Chinese commercial treaty, 883
Anglo-Chinese convention, recognizing British position in Burma, 872
Anglo-Dutch War, the first, 439; second war, 439
Anglo-Egyptian Convention, 833
Anglo-Egyptian Sudan, 1160
Anglo-French Agreement on boundary between Sierra Leone and French Guinea, 841; on Cameroons and Togoland, 1088; on French Sudan and the Anglo-Egyptian Sudan, 1089; on French Equatorial Africa and Wadai-Darfur, 1089
Anglo-French aid to Poles pledged; extended to Rumania and Greece, 966
Anglo-French conference at London on Germany's announcement of rearmament, 969
Anglo-French Convention settles question of bait-fishing in Newfoundland waters, 797
Anglo-French entente concluded, 752
Anglo-French forces, landed in Norway, 1146
Anglo-French rivalry begun with foundation of the French East India Co., 534
Anglo-French ultimatum to Russia demanding evacuation of the Danubian principalities, 727
Anglo-French-Austrian Treaty, 728
Anglo-French-Russian Agreement regarding Palestine, 1099
Anglo-German Colonial Agreement (Heligoland Treaty), 741–742, 848; future of Portuguese colonies, 748; Baghdad Railway problem, 761
Anglo-German loan to China, 882; second loan, 882
Anglo-German naval agreement, 969; estranges France, 963; 1003; denounced by Hitler, 971
Anglo-German Treaty, 911
Anglo-Irish trade pact, 973
Anglo-Italian agreement for cession of territory on the Juba River, 1090
Anglo-Italian Mediterranean Agreement signed, 970; ratified, 971
Anglo-Italian pact concluded, 965
Anglo-Japanese Alliance negotiations, 751, 892; reaffirmed, 888; renewed for ten years, 753, 892; ended, 958
Anglo-Norman culture, 194
Anglo-Persian Agreement, negotiated by Sir Percy Cox, 1107 *f.*
Anglo-Persian Oil Co., 865, 1108, 1109
Anglo-Portuguese Agreement, defined the frontier between Angola and Southwest Africa, 1089
Anglo-Portuguese Treaty, 843, 849
Anglo-Russian Entente concluded, 708, 754, 758, 865
Anglo-Russian-French agreement on the partition of Asiatic Turkey, 937
Anglo-Saxon kingdoms of Britain (Heptarchy), 166 *ff.*
Anglo-Saxon shires, 192
Anglo-Turkish agreement, secret, for the occupation of Cyprus, 736; mutual assistance pact announced, 966
Angora, battle of, 319, 323, 326, 330
Angora Assembly adopts a Fundamental Law, 1094; alliance

with Soviet Russia; treaty with England disposing of the Mosul issue, 1096
Angoulême, Count of, marries Claudia, dau. of Louis XII, 382
Anitta, King of Kushshar, 36
Anjou, Counts of, 226, 277
Anjou, Lt. Peter Feodor, surveyed Arctic coast of Siberia, 562
Ankara (Angora), new name of the capital of Turkey, 1096; visit of Litvinov, 1096; Treaty of, 1021, 1096
Ankarstrom, James Johan, assassin of Gustavus III of Sweden. 474
Anking, taken by Japanese, 1122
Anna, eldest daughter of Ferdinand I, 465
Anna, sister of Louis II of Bohemia and Hungary, 402
Anna of Austria, daughter of Philip III of Spain, 441
Anne, daughter of George II of England, 440
Anne, daughter of Ladislas II of Bohemia, 419
Anne, Empress of Russia, 481
Anne, Queen of England, 431 *ff.*
Anne of Austria, daughter of Maximillian II, wife of Philip II, 389
Anne of Bohemia, married Richard II of England, 267
Anne of Brittany, married to Charles VIII; then to Louis XII, 381
Anne of Cleves, 4th wife of Henry VIII, 369
Annexation Manifesto, in Canada, 795
Annibalianus, nephew of Constantine, 120
d'Annunzio, Gabriele, Italian poet, 662; expedition against Fiume, 955, 987
Anopheles mosquito, as malaria carrier, 552 ¶
Anschluss problem, between Austria and Germany, 1005, 1006
Anselm, Abbot of Bec, named Archbishop of Canterbury, 193; a religious reformer, 217; investiture battle in England, 219; 228 *f.*
Ansika, African kingdom, 843
Anson, Commodore George, trip around the world, 434
Antequera, José de, and the civil war in Paraguay, 799
Anthemios of Tralles, 173
Anthemius, 122
Anthony, King of Navarre, 384
Anthracite coal miners' strike, 788
Anthropoid apes, 1
Anthropoidea, 1
Anthropology, difficulty of classifying races, 12
Anti-Capetian Alliance of John of England, Otto IV of Germany, and the Counts of Boulogne and Flanders, 230
Anti-Catholic riots in Belfast, 973
Anti-clerical laws in the French Parliament, 638
Anti-Comintern Pact established by German, Italian, and Japanese agreements, 964; Spain joins, 966
Anti-Corn Law agitation, 611, 612
Anti-foreign movement in Japan, 888
Anti-Injunction Act (Norris), 1053
Anti-papal feeling in England, 266
Anti-papal laws in test by James II, 429
Anti-Saloon League.founded, 786
Anti-Semitic outbreaks in England under Richard I, 196
Anti-Socialist Law passed in Germany, 689
Anti-Trust Law (Sherman), 785
Antietam, battle of, 778
Antigonus (Cyclops), takes Syria from Ptolemy, 35; takes title of king, 77; killed at battle of Ipsus, 37, 78, 81, 84
Antigonus II (Gonatas), repels invasion by Pyrrhus, 79; in 2d Syrian War, 81, 84
Antigonus III (Doson), makes himself king, 79
Antigua, 1148 *f.*), 1155, 1158
Antioch, 96; taken by the Greeks, 180; captured by the Moslems, 185; Byzantine suzerainty recognized, 252; siege by the Emir of Mosul, 255
Antiochus I Soter, defeats Galatians, 81, 84
Antiochus II Theos, 37; in 2d Syrian War, 81, 84
Antiochus III the Great, divides Armenia, 38; 43, 80; in 4th Syrian War, 81, 83, 84, 89
Antiochus IV, Epiphanes, 82
Antiochus V Eupater, 82
Antiochus VI Epiphanes Dionysus, 82
Antiochus VII Euergetes Eusebes Soter Sidetes, 82, 83
Antiochus VIII Epiphanes Philomater Callinicus "Grypus," 82
Antiochus IX Philopater "Cyzicenus," 82
Antiochus X, XI, XII, XIII, 82, 83
Antiochus Hierax, 81
Antipas, tetrarch of Galilee and Peraea. 32
Antipater, 32, 65, 66: dies, 77, 83, 96, 102
Antitrinitarianism established in Poland, 414
Antivari, taken by the Italians, 947
Antoine, brother of John the Fearless of Burgundy, 379
Antoku, Japanese emperor, 354
Antonelli, Cardinal Giacomo, papal secretary of state, 659, 664
Antonescu, Ion, Rumanian dictator, 1136; 1142; premier, 1150
Antonines, 114, 116
Antoniniani, name given to his troops by Caracalla, 114
Antoninus Pius (Titus Aurelius Fulvus Boionius Arrius Antoninus), 109, 111
Antonio of Crato, prepares to reconquer the Portuguese throne, 393
Antonius, Lucius, Mark Antony's brother, 99
Antonius, Marcus, *see* Mark Anthony
Antony, St., his practice of monasticism, 123
Antwerp, bombarded by the Dutch, 622; 1149
Anual, battle of, 981
Anushirwan the Just (Chosroes), war with Rome, 126
Anushtigin, ancestor of the Khwarizm shahs, 255

An-yang, where first written Chinese documents were found, 14
Anyathian culture, 7
Anzacs, arrive in Egypt, 919
Anzan, 40
Anzio, 1162
Aoki, Shuzo, Viscount, and the Aoki-Kimberley Treaty, 891
Apamea, 127, 173
Aparajita, defeated by Vijayaditya III, 337
Aparajitavarman, crushed Varaguna II; killed by Aditya I, 337
Apennines, secured by Rome, 74
Apes, distinction from man, 1
Apia, in Samoa, acquired by U.S. in treaty with Germany, 911
Apion, son of Ptolemy VII, 84
Apocrypha, 30
Apolonius Rhodius, his *Argonautica*, 75
Apostles, 113
Apostolic succession, 141
Appeal to Rome, vindicated, 153
"Appeasement," policy of, 970
Appius Claudius (later Caecus) commits suicide, 72; 73, 91
Appomattox Court House, capitulation of Gen. Lee, 779
Apra (Alianza Popular Revoluncionaria Americana), a radical organization in Peru, 1068
Apraxin, Stephen, defeated the Prussians under Lehwald, 467
Apries, 24
Apuleius, Lucius, his *Metamorphoses*, 113
Apulia, 87; devastated by papal mercenaries, 211; under rule of Constantinople, 217
Apulians, 73
Aquae Sextae, 93
Aquileia, 120, 143
Aquillius, Moanius, 93
Aquinas, *see* Thomas Aquinas
Aquitani, 96
Arab High Committee, 1101; its members arrested, 1102
Arab League, 1143
Arabi, Ahmed, leader of the Egyptian nationalist movement, 738; war minister, 831
Arabia, in the Post-Palaeolithic period, 13; inhabited by tribes of Semitic race in the time of Mohammed, 184
Arabic, sunk, 923
Arabs, conquests of, 126, 163, 174 *ff.*, 329 *f.*
Arachosia, 39
Aradus, captured by Arabs, 185
Aragon, under Carolingian control; passes to Navarre; becomes independent, 237
Arakcheiev, Gen. Alexis Andreavich, adviser to Alexander I of Russia, 702
Araki, Gen. Sadao, Japanese war minister, 1126
Aram, puzzling inscription, 34
Aramaic kingdoms in 10th cent., 34
Arame, King of Urartu, 38
Arameans, 25, 29, 31; as "Semitic" Bedouins, 34
Aranda, Pedro Pablo Abarca de Bolea, Count of, Spanish reform minister, 452
Aratus of Sicyon, 79, 80
Araucanian Indians of Chile, 489; subjugated, 809
Arausio, 92
Araxes, 127
Arbela, 25, 26, 28, 40
Arbogast, Barbarian leader, 120
Arc lamp, invented, 553
Arc light, introduced by Brush, 783
Arcadia, 50, 54, 79; Academy of, in Italy, 454
Arcadian League, 63
Arcadians, 47, 50, 63
Arcadiopolis, battles of: Russians defeated by Greeks, 183; Greeks defeated by Bulgarians, 253
Arcadius, son of Theodosius, made Augustus in the east, 121, 143
Arce, Aniceto, pres. of Bolivia, 812
Arce, Manuel José, pres. of Central America, 819
Arch of Constantine, 122
Arch of Septimius, 116
Arch of Titus, 107, 113
Archaic culture, 20
Archangel, taken by Allied forces, 947; 1031, 1153
Archelaus, 32, 93
Archer, Scott, introduced wet collodion process, 553
Archidamus, King of Sparta, 58, 66
Archilochus, satirist, 48
Archimedes, 75, 87
Archinard, Col. Louis French conquests on the upper Niger, 841
Architecture in Spain, 237
Arcis-sur-Aube, battle of, 601
Arcola, battle of, 585
Arctic Air-Route Expedition (British), 569
Arctic culture, 18
Arctic Regions, Account of the, by William Scoresby, Jr., 562
Arctic Sea, 1145
Ardashir (Artahshatra, Artaxerxes), founds new Persian empire, 115; revolts against Artabanus, 124
Ardashir II, 125
Arda-Viraf, 124
Arden, Edward, plot against Queen Elizabeth, 373
Ardoin, revolt of, in Lombardy, 162
Ardvates, founded a dynasty in Armenia, 38
Ardys, of the Mermnadae, 37
Areopogus, 51
Aretino, Pietro, Italian Publicist, 393
Areus, King of Sparta, 79

Argentina, 806, 810, 1064, 1139, 1140, 1141; declared war on Germany and Japan, 1156
Argeseanu, George, Rumanian premier, 1135
Argesul, battle of, 935
Argetoianu, Constantine, Rumanian premier, 1135
Arginusae, battle of, 61
Argishtish I, II, 38
Argive League, 59
Argive School of sculpture, 62
Argolid, 47
Argonautica, of Apollonius Rhodius, 75
Argonne, battle of, 950
Argos, 46 *passim*
Argun, Il-khan of Persia, 346
Argyle, Archibald Campbell, 9th Earl of, 376, trial and condemnation, 429; executed, 429
Aria, 39
Arianism, causes Church strife, 119, 123; campaign against, 141, 144
Ariarathes I, II, 37
Arias, Arnulfo, President of Panama, 1137
Arias, Harmodio, pres. of Panama, 1072
Aribert, Archbiship of Milan, 217
Aricia, battle of, 71
Arikboga, brother of Kublai Khan, 345
Arima, a local lord of Japan, 543
Ariminum, 86 *ff.*
Arion, poet, 48
Ariosto, Ludovico, Italian poet, 393
Ariovistus, 96
Arista, Mariano, pres. of Mexico, 821
Aristagoras, revolt against Persians, 53
Aristarchus, 75
Aristides ("The Just"), 53, 55
Aristion, 93
Aristippus, Henry, translator of Plato and Aristotle, 223
Aristobulus I, 32
Aristobulus II, 32
Aristodemus of Cumae, 57, 71
Aristogeiton, 52
Aristomenes, in 2d Messenian War, 50
Ariston, king, and the Peloponnesian League, 50
Aristonicus, 82, 91
Aristophanes, Greek dramatist, 62
Aristophanes of Byzantium, 75
Aristophon, 64
Aristotle, Greek philosopher, 67; newly recovered during 12th century Renaissance, 231
Arita, Hachiro, Japanese foreign minister, 1127
Arius, 119
Arlington, Henry Bennet, Earl of, a member of the Cabal, 427
Armada of Spain, defeated by the English fleet, 373, 381, 390, 392
Armagnac, Count of, heads civil war against Burgundians, 278
Armat, Thomas, invented vitascope, 556
Armed neutrality at sea, advanced by Russia during the War of American Independence, 482
Armellini, Roman triumvir, 655
Armenia, in the Post-Palaeolithic period, 13; geography, population, civilization, and religion, 38 *f.*; history of, 110, 125, 744, 947, 1032, 1094
Armenian Massacres, 618, 732, 743, 744, 746, 919
"Armenoid," racial type, 36
Armentières, in the World War, 914, 945, 950
Arminius, annihilates Roman legions, 103
Armistice, between Austria and the Allied Powers, 950; final Armistice between Germany and Austria and the Allies signed and hostilities cease in World War, 951
Armistice, between France and Germany, 1135
Armitage, Lt. Albert, on the ice sheet of South Victoria Land, 574
Arms Traffic Convention; protocol signed prohibiting use of poison gas, 959
Armstrong, William George, rifling in artillery, 555
Army Law of 1868, providing for reorganization, 635
Army Regulation Bill, reorganized the British army, 615
Arndt, Ernst Moritz, German poet, 594; in the Frankfurt Parliament, 676
Arnhem, 1163
Arnim-Boytzenburg, Hans Georg von, captures Prague, 405; negotiates with Wallenstein, 406
Arnold, Benedict, American general, 520, 522
Arnold, Gen. Henry H., commander of U.S. Army Air Force, 1164
Arnold of Brescia, pupil of Abelard, leader of the Commune of Rome, 219
Arnon River, 29
Arnuandash I, II, 35
Arnulf, Archbishop of Reims, 216
Arnulf, Bishop, adviser to Dagobert, 147, 149
Arnulf, emperor, 152, 160
Arogee, battle of, 834
Aroostook County War, 773
Arosemena, Florencio Harmodio, pres. of Panama, 1072
Arosemena, Juan Demóstenes, pres. of Panama, 1072
Arpachiyah, 13
Arpad, 34, 35; led Magyars into Hungary, 244; dynasty extinguished, 317
Arques, battle of, 386
Arrachard, Lt. Paul, flew across the desert to Timbuktu, 1083
Arrapkha, Kingdom of, 28

Arras, battles of: first, 939; second, 950; Peace of, 279
Arretine ware, 113
Arretium, 87
d'Arriaga Brun da Silveira e Peyrelongue, Manoel José, first pres. of the Portuguese Republic, 650, 985
Arrondissements, in France, 587
Arrow (lorcha) incident at Canton, 879
Arsaces I, 81; founded Kingdom of Parthia, 83
Arsaces II (Tiridates I), founds Parthian Kingdom, 81, 83
Arsaces III (Priapatius), 81, 83
Arsaces IV (Priapatius), 83
Arsaces V (Phraates I), 83
Arsacid dynasty, 26; overthrown, 115, 124
Arses, succeeded Artaxerxes III, 40
Arsinoe II, 84
Art and architecture in Spanish America, 500
Artabanus I, 83, 124
Artabanus V, 115
Artabanus, King of Parthia, 105
Artabazus, 54
Artahshatr (Artaxerxes), 115, 124
Artanes, last King of Armenia, 38
Artaphernes, at battle of Marathon, 53
Artatama, 28, 29
Artavasdes, King of Armenia Major, 83
Artavasdos, revolt against Constantine V, 176
Artaxata, 106, 111
Artaxerxes I (Longimanus), 40
Artaxerxes II (Mnemon), 40, 62
Artaxerxes III (Ochus), 23, 33, 40, 55
Artaxias, ruler of Armenia Major, 38, 82
Arte della Lana (wool) of Florence, 294
Artemisium, Gulf of, 54
Arteveldt, James van, 264, 273
Arteveldt, Philip van, 277
Artha-sastra, 130
Arthur, brother of Henry VIII, 369
Arthur, nephew of John Lackland, 197
Arthur, Chester Alan, 21st pres. of U.S., 783
Arthur, Col. George, gov. of Tasmania, 899
Arthur of Brittany, in alliance with Philip II of France against his uncle John, 229
Articles of Baden, a program of religious reform in Switzerland, 666
Articles of Confederation establishing The United States of America, 521
Artificial harbors, 1163
Artigas, José, driven out of Montevideo by Portuguese, 502; led revolution in Banda Oriental, 801
Artisans' Dwelling Act, 615
Artois, battles of: first, 914; second and third, 921
d'Artois, Charles Philippe, Count, 579
Arundel, Earl of, executed for corresponding with Mary, Queen of Scots, 373
Arundel, Henry, 3d Baron Arundel of Wardour, accused in Popish Plot, 428
Arwad, 32, 33
Arya Sura, 131
Aryabhata, taught rotation of the earth, 131
Aryans, 39; at war among themselves, 41
Aryavarta, 130
Arzanene, 127
Arzashkun, 38
Asa, 31
Asad al-Kasri, gov. of Khorasan, 188
Asanga, founder of the Vijnanavadin or Yogachara school, 131
Ascalon, Kingdom, 30
Ascanians, great tenants-in-chief in Brandenburg, 213
Ascham, Roger, 372
Asding Vandals, crossed into Spain, 144
Asen, John and Peter, Bulgarian lords, 247
Asen, John II, ruler of the Second Bulgarian Empire, 251
Asen, Michael, son of John Asen II, 248, 260
Ashanti, Negro kingdom, British conquest and rule, 840 *ff.*
Ash'arites, orthodox school, 189
Ashbourne Act, 617
Ashburton, Alexander Baring, co-author of Webster-Ashburton Treaty, 611, 773, 795
Ashdod, Kingdom of, 30
Ashikaga (or Muramachi) Period in Japan, 359
Ashkalon, 27
Ashley, *see* Shaftesbury
Ashley, Lord Jacob, 378
Ashraf Shah, 528
Ashshur, 25 *ff.*
Ashurbanipal, 24; his library, 26; campaigns into Egypt, 27 *f.*; 33; helps Gyges defeat Cimmerians, 37; 39; destroyed Susa, 40
Ashurbelkala, 38
Ashur-nasir-pal II, 27, 33, 35, 38
Ashur-uballit, 28
Asia, in the Post-Palaeolithic period, 13 *f.*; Kingdom of Pergamum becomes Province of Asia, 91; the Second World War in, 1165 *f.*; for the Asiatics, 1170
Asia and Oceania in the Palaeolithic period, 6 *f.*
Asia Minor (Anatolia), in the Post-Paleolithic period, 13; geography and racial type, 36; invaded by Moslems, 188
Asiatic Registration Bill passed by Transvaal govt., 858
Asiatic Turkey, agreement on its future partition, 937
Asiento, 434, 450, 515
Aske, Robert, leader of Catholic rebellion in England, 370

Askia Mohammed, ruler of the Songhoy Empire, 329
Aslanduz, battle of, 862
Asoka, his Indian empire, 42, 132
Aspar, master of the troops for Leo I, 122
Aspern and Essling, battles of, 594 *f.*
Asperuch, *see* Isperikh
Aspromonte, battle of, 659
Asquith, Herbert, British prime minister, 620, 621, 929
Assab, bought by the Italian Rubbatino Co., 834; taken over by the Italian govt. and becomes Eritrea, 835
Assassins, an Ismailian fraternity, 254; suppressed and extinguished, 262
Assembly of Lenczyca, 242
Assertion of the Seven Sacraments, by Henry VIII, 370
Assignats, notes of the French govt., 580; their fall, 582; replaced by *mandats territoriaux*, 583
Assinarus, 57, 60
Assis Pacheco y Sampayo, Francis-Xavier, on Portuguese mission to China, 539
Assize of Arms, provides national militia in England, 195
Assize of Clarendon, civil legislation on heresy, 194, 196
Assizes of Jerusalem, a feudal code, 256, 257
Assizes of Romania, copied from the *Assizes of Jerusalem*, 261
Association of Merchant Adventurers, *see* Muscovy Co.
Associations Law in France, 642; applied to religious orders and schools in Japan, 982
Assumption Bill of U.S., 764
Assyria, civilization and religion, 26 *f.*; added to Rome, 110; invaded by Heraclius, 127
Assyrian Empire, first phase, 27
Astor, John Jacob, established the post of Astoria, 773
Astrology, 26
Asturian culture, 17
Astyages, deposed, 40; defeated by Cyrus, 48
Asvaghosha, his *Saundarananda*, 129
Aswan Dam, storage reservoir on the upper Nile, 833
Atabeg I-Azam, Persian minister, 865
Atabegs (regents) in the Seljuk Empire, 254, 256
Atahualpa, Inca monarch, 361, 489
Ataulf, begins conquest of Spain, 121, 144
Atbara River, battle of, 748, 833
Aterian industry, 5 *f.*
Athaliah, 31
Athanasian, attitude of the Church, 119
Athanasius, Christian theologian, 119; introduces eremitical monasticism in the west, 141, 142
Atharvaveda, 41
Athena of the Brazen House, temple of, 54
Athenian League, 56, 63
Athenion, 93
Athens, occupied by allied forces, 1142; 1143; entered by Germans, 1150
Atia, mother of Octavian, 98
Atkinson, Sir Harry Albert, New Zealand statesman, 907
Atlanta, battle of; evacuated by the Confederates, 779
Atlantic cable, brought to Newfoundland by Cyrus Field, 781
Atlantic Charter, issued, and endorsed by 15 states, 1137
Atlantic City, 1170
Atlantic Coast, 1155
Atlantic Ocean, 1156, 1158
Atomic bomb, energy, fission, 553
Atomic bombs, dropped on Hiroshima and Nagasaki, 1145, 1169
Atsiz, first independent Shah of Khwarism, 255
Atsutane, Hirata, in the Shinto movement, 887
Attalus, last pagan emperor, 121
Attalus I Soter, defeats Galatians, 37, 81
Attalus II Philadelphus, 82
Attalus III Philomater, bequeaths his kingdom to Rome, 82, 91
Attila, King of the Huns, 121, 143
Attlee, Clement R., British prime minister, 1145, 1171
Attu, occupied by Japanese, 1167
Aucassin et Nicolette, 231
Auckland, made capital of New Zealand, 905
Auckland, George Eden, Earl of, gov.-gen. of India, 870
Audacious (H.M.S.), sunk by German mine, 917
Audiencias in South America, 488 *passim*
Auersperg, Prince Adolf, Austrian minister, 694; second ministry, 694
Auerstädt, battle of, 592
Auffenberg-Komarow, Moritz von, Austrian commander, 914
Aughrim, battle of, 430
Augsburg, battle of, 244
Augsburg Edict, revoked, 401; Peace of, 402; Synod of, 216
August Convention between France and Russia, 742
Augustan, art, 113; Age (library), 112, 113, 434
Augustan Legion, 110
Augustenburg, Duke of, claimant to the duchies of Schleswig and Holstein, 676; son a claimant, 681
Augustine, Bishop of Hippo, 123; converted to Christianity, founder of western theology, 142; supported monasticism, 146; doctrines spread by Gregory the Great, 151; his death, 121, 145
Augustine of Canterbury, his mission to Britain, 151
Augustine the Monk, converts Kent to the Roman Church, 166
Augustinians, in Spanish America, 498
Augustovo, battle of, 921
Augustus, 32; his government, 101, 102; his death, 103; 107, 109, 110, 113, 116, 150
Augustus II, Elector of Saxony, King of Poland, 461, 471, 475
Augustus III, King of Poland, 463; claimant to the throne of Austria, 477

Auldcarn, battle of, 378
Aulic Council, 398
Aulick, John Henry, American commodore, 888
Aunjetitz culture, 17
Aurangzeb, Emperor of India, 533
Aurelian (Lucius Domitius Aurelianus), Roman emperor, 116
117, 124
Aurelius, Marcus, *see* Marcus Aurelius
Aureolus, pretender, 116
Aurignacian culture, 5, 6; industry, 6
Aurunci, 73
Ausculum, 86
Ausonius, Gallic poet, 123
Austerlitz, battle of, 437, 591
Austin, Capt. Horatio, in search of Sir John Franklin, 563
Australasian Federal Convention, 903
Australia, 896 *ff.*, 1128 *ff.*, 1167
Australia, British battle cruiser, helped in taking German
Samoa, 1131
Australia Agricultural Co., 898
Australopithecus, 1
Austria, 150 *ff.*, 299 *ff.*, 400 *ff.*, 465 *ff.*, 594 *ff.*, 670 *ff.*; republic,
1005 *ff.*, 1165
Austriae est imperare orbi universo, Latin version of Emperor
Frederick III's monogram, 304
Austrian annexation crisis, 970
Austrian Constitution of 1867, 694
Austrian Credit-Anstalt, failure of, 961
Austro-Asiatic Munda people, 41
Austro-German campaign in Serbia, 926
Austro-German crisis, annexation of Austria by Germany, 964,
965
Austro-Italian note to Greece demanding evacuation of Al-
bania, 761
Austro-Russian Agreement to maintain the *status quo* in the
Balkans, 695, 746; note to Balkan states, 759; conversations
resumed on Serbian situation, 762
Austro-Russian Treaty, 482, 485
Austro-Turkish Agreement recognizing the annexation of Bos-
nia and Herzegovina, 756
Authari, King of the Lombards, 150
Autogiro, 557
Automobiles, 556, 557
Avalokitesvara (*Lotus Sutra*), 130, 136
Avanti, King of, 41
Avanti, Mussolini's newspaper, 986
Avaris, 23
Avars, founded the first Mongol empire, 136; defeated by the
Franks, 150, 154; captured forts along the Danube; raided to
the gates of Constantinople, defeated at Viminacium by Pris-
cus, 173; emperor and Kuvrat, King of the Bulgars, in alli-
ance to break their power, 174; disrupted Great Bulgaria, 181
Avatamsaka-sutra, 130
d'Avaux, Count, French negotiator of Treaties of Westphalia,
408
Avellan, Feodor Karlevich, Russian admiral, 742
Avellaneda, Nicolás, Argentine statesman, 808
Aventine, 71, 72
Aventine Secession, 988
Averescu, Alexandre, Rumanian premier, 944
Averroës, ibn Rushd, Moslem scholar, 164
Avesta, divisions of its books, 39, 41
Avignon, papal court at, 223, 286
Avignonese Captivity, 268, 286, 302
Avignonese Line, of popes, 288
Ávila, Pedro Arias de, founded Panama; gov. of Nicaragua, 488,
489
Avilés, Pedro Menéndez de, founded St. Augustine, Fla., 493;
505
Avion, flying machine that did not fly, 556
Avis dynasty, established by John I of Portugal, 284
Avitus, deposed by Ricimer, 122
Axis, 1140 *passim*
Axum, Kingdom of, converted to Christianity by Frumentius,
328
Ayacucho, battle of, 802
Ayala, Eligio, pres. of Paraguay, 1066
Ayala, Eusebio, pres. of Paraguay, 1066
Ayllón, Lucas Vásquez de, established colony of San Miguel de
Gualdape in the Carolinas, 493
Ayn ud-Dola, Persian minister, 865
Ayodhya, 130
Ayora, Isidro, pres. of Ecuador, 1069
Ayuthia, destruction by the Burmese, 872
Ayyubid dynasty, founded by Saladin, 262
Azad, Abdul Kalam, 1138
Azaña, Manuel, prime minister of Spain, then president, 982,
983, 984
Azariah (Uzziah), 31, 35
Azarmidukht, daughter of Khusru Parviz, 127
Azcarate, Gumersindo, Spanish Republican leader, 648
d'Azeglio, Massimo Taparelli, Marquis, premier of Piedmont,
657
Azerbaijan, Atabeg house, founded by Ildigiz, 255; invaded by
Mongol armies, 262; declared independence, 947
Azes, an era, 128
Azes II, succeeds the Sakas in the Punjab, 128
Azilian culture, 17
Azilises, 128
Azione Cattolica, Catholic youth organization in Italy, 993
Aziru, 33, 35

Azores, discovered by Diogo de Seville, 363, 1156, 1159
Aztecs, civilization, govt., and culture, 20, 360; 491 *f.*
Azuchi-Momoyama Period, in Japan, 542 *f.*

Baal, worship of, 29
Baanes, defeated near Damascus, by Khalid, 184 *f.*
Baasha, 31
Babar, descendant of Timur, founded the Mogul Empire in In-
dia, 530
Babcock, Orville Elias, Grant's private secretary, implicated in
Whiskey Ring, 782
Babek, leader of Khurramites, terrorized North Africa, 189
Babenbergs, 240, 246
Babington, Anthony, plot against Queen Elizabeth, 373
Babism, founded by Sayyid Ali Mohammed, 864
Babylonia, of the Middle Kingdom, 22; early races, 24; civiliza
tion and religion, 25 *f.*; influence on civilization of Palestine, 28
Babylonian, or Avignonese, Captivity, residence of Pope Clem-
ent V in Avignon, 232; 399
Bacchiadae, rulers of Corinth, 50
Bacchylikes, distinguished in choral ode, 62
Bach, Alexander, Austrian minister of the interior, 678
Bacha-i-Saquao, bandit leader, captured Kabul and proclaimed
himself Habibullah Ghazi, 1110
Back, Sir George Arctic explorer, 563
Bacon, Sir Francis, British statesman and scientist, 374
Bacon, Nathaniel, leader of rebellion in Virginia, 513
Bacon, Sir Nicholas, lord privy seal under Queen Elizabeth, 372
Bacon, Robert, American envoy to Cuba, 823
Bacon, Roger, mediaeval scientist, 201
Bacon's rebellion, in Virginia, 513
Bactria, 39 *passim*
Badajoz, captured by rebels in Spanish civil war, 983
Badarayana, author of the *Brahma sutra*, 336
Badarian culture, 18
Baden-Powell, Robert Stephenson Smyth, defended Mafeking in
Boer War, 857
Badeni, Count Casimir, Austrian prime minister, 695
Badoglio, Marshal Pietro, Italian commander in Ethiopia, 991,
1086; chief of staff, 1136; premier, 1140; 1141, 1142, 1159,
1162
Baffin, William, English explorer, 561
Bagamoyo, German East Africa, bombarded; taken by the
British, 918
Bagehot, Walter, British political theorist, 552
Bagh, 131
Baghdad, founded, 188; made Moslem capital by Mamun, 188;
decline of the caliphate, 246; its capture and sack, 262; cali-
phate destroyed, 345; taken by the Turks, 528; occupied by
the British, 938, 1105; 1151
Baghdad Railway concession, secured by the Deutsche Bank,
692, 729, 749, 751, 757
Bagirmi, Negro kingdom, 840
Bagyidaw, King of Burma, 872
Bahadur, last of the active Indian sultans, 530
Bahaism, founded, 864
Bahamas, 1148 *f.*, 1155, 1158
Bahman Shah, 334
Bahmani dynasty founded, 334
Bahrain, 125
Bahram Gor, Sassanid king, 330
Bahrein Islands, claimed by Persia, 1108
Bahr-el-Ghazal region, 845
Baidukov, George Philip, North Pole flight, 558, 567
Baïhaut, Charles, in Panama Canal scandal, 640
Baikov, Feodor Isakovich, mission to China, 539
Bailly, Jean Sylvain, French revolutionary statesman, 579, 580,
583
Bairakdar, pasha of Rustchuk, 722
Bairam Khan, guardian of Akbar, 530
Bait Act, 797
Baker, Sir Samuel White, African explorer, 826, 830
Bakin, Kyokutei, Japanese author, 887
Bakr Sidqi, dictator in Iraq, 1106
Baku, Bolshevik govt. in, 947
Bakunin, Michael, Russian anarchist, 550, 640, 704, 705
Bal Gangadhar Tilak, *see* Tilak
Balaclava, battle of, 727
Balaic language, 36
Balaputradeva, King of Sumatra, 331
Balas, Alexander, slays Demetrius Soter, 82
Balathista, battle of, 180, 183
Balatoros, 33
Balban, founds a new Indian dynasty, 333, 334
Balbinus, D. Caelius Calvinus, Roman emperor, 115
Balbo, Count Cesare, Italian publicist, 651
Balbo, Italo, Fascist leader, 988
Balboa, Vasco Nuñez de, discoverer of the Pacific, 368, 486,
894; 488
Balchen, Bernt, in flight to the South Pole, 576
Baldomir, Alfredo, pres. of Uruguay, 1067, 1138
Baldwin I, Latin emperor of the East, 248, 255, 259
Baldwin II, Latin emperor of the East, 247, 248, 260, 320
Baldwin, Evelyn Briggs, explorer, 565
Baldwin Iron-Arm, son-in-law of Charles the Bald, 158
Baldwin, Stanley, British prime minister, 959, 968, 969
Balearic Islands, under Moslem domination, 158
Balfour, Arthur James, 1st Earl of, British prime minister, 617,
618, 619, 749, 929, 958, 1100 *f.*
Balfour, Sir William, leader of Covenanters, 428
Balfour Declaration, 1100, 1101

Bali, under Dutch control, 877
Balich, 28
Baliol, Edward, King of Scotland, 272
Baliol, John, claimant to the Scottish crown, 199, 201, 264
Balkan campaigns, 1149 ff.
Balkan Conference, first, at Athens, 961
Balkan Pact, 1026
Balkan wars, 695, 709, 712; first war, 759; second war, 760
Balkh, 124, 128
Ball, Albert, British aviator, 946
Ball, John, English preacher, 266, 267
Ballance, John, leader of the Liberal-Labor Party in New Zealand, 907
Ballard, John, plot against Queen Elizabeth, 373
Ballilla, a Fascist youth association, 989
Ballinger, Richard Achilles, controversy with Gifford Pinchot, 790
Balliol College, founded, 201
Ballivián, Adolfo, pres. of Bolivia, 811
Ballivián, José, pres. of Bolivia, 811
Balloon, invented, 553; first hydrogen built, 553; first dirigible, 555; stratosphere, 558
Balloon of Nassau, 554
Ballot Act, 615
Balmaceda, José Manuel, pres. of Chile, 809
Balodis, Gen. Francis Alexandrs, Latvian soldier, 1043
Balouba, African kingdom, 843
Balta, José, pres. of Peru, 813
Balta Liman convention, 719
Balthas (Visigoths), 143
Baltic Islands (Oesel, Moon, Dago), conquered by the Germans, 940
Baltic and North Sea Conventions, 755
Baltic region, in Post-Palaeolithic period, 18
Baltic states, 1041; treaties of the Entente and the Pact, 1042, 1043; 1145; Sea, 1154
Baltimore (U.S.S.), 809
Baltimore, George Calvert, Lord, in Maryland, 510
Baltimore & Ohio R.R. begun, 771
Balts (Letts), people, 142
Bambara kingdoms, replaced the Manding Empire, 525
Bambata Cave, 6
Bamboo Annals, 136
Bamiyan frescoes, 43
Bana, poet, 331
Banat of Temesvar, occupied by the Serbs, 949; divided between Yugoslavia and Rumania, 1016
Banavasi, 129
Banca Romana scandal, 661
Banda Oriental (Uruguay), 501, 502, 800, 801
Baner, Johan Gustafson, Swedish general, 406, 407
Bangkok, 1167
Bank Bill, vetoes by Pres. Jackson, 772
Bank Charter Act, 611
Bank Deposit Insurance Act, 1054
Bank failures in Canada, 798
Bank for International Settlements, 960
Bank of Canada, opened, 1059
Bank of England, 431, 961, 962
Bank of Japan, established, 890
Bank of the United States, 764; second bank, 770, 772
Banking Relief Act (Emergency), 1054
Banks, Sir Joseph, founder of the African Association, 525
Banks, Nathaniel Prentiss, Federal general, 778
Bannockburn, battle of, 264, 272
Banque d'Escompte de Perse, 864
Banque Imperiale Ottomane, established, 728
Bantam, in Java, British settlement; subdued by the Dutch, 876
Banting, Sir Frederick Grant, on insulin treatment, 553
Bantu, invasions, 18; history of, 328, 846, 851
Banu Asad tribe, 190
Banu Ka'b tribe of Arabs, 190
Banu Kilab tribe of Arabs, 190
Banzan, Kumazawa, his school of Confucian philosophy, 546
Bapaume, in the World War, 914, 938, 945, 950
Baptist Mission, at Ambas Bay, 840
Baptista, Mariano, pres. of Bolivia, 812
Baptista, Pedro, Portuguese explorer, 826
Barahona, Miguel Paz, pres. of Honduras, 1074
Barakzai dynasty, founded, 866
Baranov, Alexander, gov. of Alaska, 798
Baranovici, battle of, 932
Baratiere, Gen. Oreste, defeated at Adua, 661, 745
Barcelona, County of, 236 f., 981, 982, 983, 984
Bar Cocheba, Simon, Jewish leader, 32, 111
Bardas, Byzantine statesman, 177
Bardas Phocas, Byzantine general, 179, 180
Bardas Skleros, Byzantine general, 180
Bardi, Florentine bankers, 199, 293 f.
Bardia, 1160
Bardo, Treaty of, 638, 737, 838
Barebones, or Little, Parliament, set up by Cromwell in place of the Rump Parliament, 425
Barents, Willem, Dutch explorer, 559
Barghash Sayyid, Sultan of Zanzibar, 847
Bari, seized by Byzantine forces, 179; Synod of, 219
Baring, Sir Evelyn (Lord Cromer), resident and consul-gen. of Egypt, 832
Barkyaruk (Rukn al-Din), son of Malik Shah, 254
Barlaimont, Charles, Count of, 380

Barlow, Arthur, 508
Barmecides, rise to power and fall, 188
Barnato, Barney, South African financier, 854
Barnet, battle of, 271
Baronius, Caesar, Cardinal, historian of the Catholic Church, 397
Barqa, occupied by Arabs, 185
Barras, Paul François Nicolas, Count de, French revolutionary statesman, 584, 585
Barrekeb, 35
Barrère, Camille, French ambassador to Italy, 751
Barrère de Vieuzac, Bertrand, prosecutor of Louis XVI, 582, 584
Barrès, Maurice, French novelist and nationalist, 643
Barricades, Day of the, 386
Barrier Treaty of the Dutch with the empire, 439, 469
Barrios, Justo Rufino, pres. of Guatemala, 819
Barrot, Odilon, French statesman, 630, 631
Barrow, Sir William, British explorer, 562
Bar-Soma, establishes Nestorian Christological doctrine, 126
Barsur, 35
Bar-sur-Aube, battle of, 601
Bartering agreement, made by Germans, 1004
Barth, Heinrich, African explorer, 826
Barthélemy, François, Marquis de, member of French Directory, 585
Barthou, Jean Louis, French statesman, 643, 941, 958, 1018
Bartlett, Capt. Robert, Arctic explorer, 566, 567
Bartolo, Martínez, pres. of Nicaragua, 1073
Barton, Clara, pres. of Red Cross Society, 783
Barton, Sir Edmund, Australian statesman, 903
Barygaza, 129
Basava, created the Lingayat sect of fanatics, 339
Basel, Synod of, 218; Treaties of, 307, 452, 495, 584
Basel Mission (Swiss) on Gold Coast of Africa, 840
Bashō, Matsuo, Japanese poet, 547
Basil, favorite of Emperor Michael III, 177
Basil II (Bulgaroktonos), Byzantine emperor, 180 f., 183, 248
Basil I, founder of the Macedonian dynasty, 177
Basil I of Russia, 316
Basil II, Prince of Moscow, 316
Basil III, Russian tsar, 415
Basil of Caesarea, 123
Basil the Eunuch, illegitimate son of Romanus Lecapenus, 180
Basilica of Maxentius and Constantine, 122
Basilika, compiled under Leo VI, 179
Basiliscus, pretender, 122
Basra, occupied by a British force from India, 927
Bass, George, Australian explorer, 896
Bassano, battle of, 585
Bassein, Treaty of, 868
Bassermann, Friedrich Daniel, German politician, 676
Bast of Bubastis, 21
Bastarnae, 143
Bastidas, Rodrigo de, South American explorer, 368, 488
Bastille, storming of, 579
Basutoland, made a native state under British protection, 852, 853
Bataan Peninsula, 1167
Batanaea, 32
Batavia, founded by the Dutch, 538, 542; 1167
Batavian Republic, founded by France, 440, 584
Bates, John, tried for refusing to pay imposition on currants, 374
Bath, England, a center of Romano-British fashion, 166
Bathory, Sigismund, Prince of Transylvania, 420, 424
Bathory, Stephen, King of Poland, 415, 417
Baths of Caracalla, 114, 116
Baths of Diocletian, 122
Bathurst, Australia, founded, 898
Batista, Fulgencio, Cuban statesman, 1078, 1136
Batlle y Ordóñez, José, pres. of Uruguay, 1066
Batman, John, pioneer settler in Australia, 900
Battering-rams, 27
Battle-Axe People, 16; culture, 18
Batu, Mongol emperor, 244, 260, 344
Batum, in the World War, 1032
Bauer, Andreas, invented first cylinder printing press, 554
Bauer, Gustav, German statesman, 996, 997
Bauto, the Frank, 121
Bautzen, battle of, 599; Treaty of, 241
Bavaria, incorporated in Frankish Empire, 153; overrun by Magyars, 158; invasion by the French and Swedes, 407; Soviet Republic, 996
Baxter, Richard, dissenting clergyman, 428
Bayard, Pierre du Terrail, Seigneur de, 381
Bayazid, son of Suleiman the Magnificent, 423
Bayazid I, Turkish sultan, 319, 323, 325, 326
Bayazid II, Turkish sultan, 420
Baybars, Mameluke leader, 262
Bayeux Tapestry, 241
Bayin Naung, ruler of Burma, 541
Bayonne Conference, between Napoleon and Charles IV and Ferdinand of Spain, 452
Bazaine, Gen. Achille François, French commander, 636, 688
Beachy Head, battle of, 430
Beagle, on scientific voyage, 895
Beatrice, daughter of Ferdinand I of Portugal, 284
Beatrice, widow of Boniface, Marquis of Tuscany, 206, 217
Beatty, Adm. Sir David, British naval commander, 917
Beaufort, Henry, Bishop of Winchester, rivalry with Duke of Gloucester, 270

Beauharnais, Eugene, Napoleon's stepson, viceroy of Italy, 591
Beauharnais, Josephine, wife of Napoleon Bonaparte, 585; divorced by him, 595
Beauharnois Co., building hydroelectric power project in St. Lawrence River, 1059
Beaumarchais, Pierre Augustin Caron de, French playwright, 521
Beaumont, Lt. Lewis Anthony, English explorer, 564 *f*.
Beauregard, Pierre Gustave Toutant, Confederate general, 776
Bebek Seminary in Turkey, founded by Cyrus Hanlin, 728
Bebel, August, German socialist leader, 689
Beccaria, Cesare, Italian penologist, 455
Bechuanaland, a British protectorate, 854; attached to the Cape Colony, 856
Beck, Col. Joseph, foreign minister of Poland, 1039
Becket, Thomas, Archbishop of Canterbury, 194, 228
Becquerel, Antoine Henri, uranium rays, 552
Bedchamber Question, in Queen Victoria's reign, 609
Bede, father of English literature, 166, 167
Bedford, Duke of, *see* John, Duke of Bedford
Bedford, John Russell, Duke of, in the Pelham ministry, 434
Bedriacum, battle of, 107
Beecher, Rev. Henry Ward, American preacher, 781
Beechey, Capt. Frederick William, led Arctic expedition, 563
"Beer Hall Putsch" in Munich, 997
Beer-Wine Revenue Act, 1055
Beggars, party name in the Netherlands, 379 *f*.
Behring, Emil von, developed serum in diphtheria, 552
Beiruni, Persian poet, 190
Beirut, captured, 725; taken by British and Arabs and French naval forces, 948; Syrian state, 1098, 1151
Beisan, 13
Beit, Alfred, British capitalist, 854
Beke, Charles Tilstone, mapped Ethiopia, 826
Bela I, King of Hungary, 245
Bela II, King of Hungary, 245,252
Bela III, King of Hungary, 245, 253
Bela IV, King of Hungary, 246
Belalcázar, Sebastian de, gov. of Popáyan, 488, 489
Belcher, Sir Edward, Arctic explorer, 564
Belgium, 582, 623 *ff*., 974 *f*.; invaded by Germany, 1135, 1142; conquered, 1146; merchant tonnage, 1156; liberation, 1163 *f*.
Belgorod, 1153, 1154
Belgrade, captured by Turks, 422; Treaty of, 480, 484; taken by the Austrians, 916; retaken by the Serbs, 917; falls in Austro-German campaign, 926; again taken by the Serbs, 949; occupied by Germany, 1136; by Russia and Yugoslavia, 1143, 1154
Belgrano, Manuel, Latin American patriot leader, 800
Beliakov, Alexander Vasilievich, flew non-stop over North Pole, 558, 567
Belisarius, Byzantine general, 126, 144, 145, 172, 224
Belknap, William Worth, 782
Bell, Alexander Graham, invented the telephone, 555, 782
Bell, John, English representative in Ethiopia, 834
Bell, John, nominated for pres. by the Union Party, 775
Bell Beaker culture, 15 *ff*.
Bellarmine, Robert, Cardinal, defender of pope's temporal power, 396 *f*.
Bellasis, John Baron Bellassis, accused in Popish Plot, 428
Bellefonds, Linant de, African explorer, 826
Bellerophon, British warship, 603
Bellingshausen, Capt. Fabian Gottlieb von, Antarctic explorer, 571-573, 575
Bellini, Gentile, Venetian painter, 393
Bellini, Jacopo, Venetian painter, 299
Bellonte, Maurice, non-stop flight from Paris to New York, 558
Bellot, Capt. Joseph Rene, Arctic explorer, 564
Belshazzar, 26
Belskys, Russian noble family, 415
Belzu, Manuel, pres. of Bolivia, 811
Bemis Heights, battles of, first, second, 521
Benavides, Col. Oscar Raimundo, pres. of Peru, 1068
Beneckendorf and Hindenburg, *see* Hindenburg
Benedek, Ludwig, Ritter von, Austrian commander, 683
Benedetti, Count Vincent, French diplomat, 686, 687
Benedict V, Pope, deposed, 216
Benedict IX (Theophylactus), pope, 216, 217
Benedict XI (Niccolo Boccasini), pope, 222
Benedict XII (Jacques Fournier), pope, 286
Benedict XIII (Piero Francesco Orsini-Gravosa), pope, 288, 289, 457
Benedict XIV (Prospero Lorenzo Lambertini), pope, 457
Benedict XV (Giacomo della Chiesa), pope, 665, 942, 992
Benedict, St., founded monastery at Monte Cassino, his *Benedictine Rule*, 146, 151
Benedictine Rule, established by St. Benedict, 146, 151
Benefit of clergy, 194
Beneš, Eduard, President of Czechoslovakia, 959, 1009, 1010, 1023
Benevento, battle of, 213; conquered by Charlemagne, 152, 213; 217
Bengal, taken by the house of Balban, 334; captured from the Afghans, 533; partition, 871
Benghasi, 1160
Benguella-Katanga Railway, opened, 1090
Ben-Hadad I of Damascus, 35
Ben-Hadad II, 27, 31, 35
Ben-Hadad III, 35
Benin, 18
Benjamin, tribe of, 30

Benjamin of Tudela, rabbi, traveler, 362
Bennett, Floyd, American aviator and explorer, 566, 568
Bennett, James Gordon, financed the De Long expedition to Siberia, 565
Bennett, Richard Bedford, prime minister of Canada, 1059
Benningsen, Levin August, Count, Russian commander, 599
Bennington, battle of, 521
Bensley, James, invented first cylinder printing press, 554
Bentinck, Lord William, gov. gen. of India, 870
Bentinck, William, Earl of Portland, British statesman, 430
Benton, Thomas Hart, began the Webster-Hayne debate, 771, 773
Benyowski, Maritius Augustus, Polish adventurer, 859
Beran, Rudolf, prime minister of Czechoslovakia, 1013
Berar, 132
Berat, battle of, 321; taken by the Austrians, 927
Berbeo, Juan Francisco, leader of revolt in New Granada, 800
Berbers, in the White group, 12; revolts, 145; conquest of Spain, 163, 164; North Africa pacified, 187; revolt put down, 188; 333; tribesmen attack, 839
Berchtesgaden conference, between Chamberlain and Hitler, 1011
Berchtold, Leopold von, Austrian foreign minister, 759, 762, 923
Berengar I, grandson of Louis the Pious, 152, 215
Berengar of Ivrea, vassal of Otto the Great, 161
Berenguer, Gen. Damaso, Spanish soldier and statesman, 982
Berenice, sister of Agrippa II, 107
Berenice II, provokes 3d Syrian War, 81, 84
Beresina, crossing of the, by Napoleon's army on the retreat from Moscow, 598
Bergen, 1146
Bergerac or Poitiers, Peace of, 384
Berggren, Dr. Sven, Arctic explorer, 564
Berhoea, 127
Bering, Vitus Jonassen, Arctic explorer, 561, 798
Bering Sea seal fisheries in dispute between U.S. and Britain 785; arbitration, 798
Berkeley, Sir William, gov. of Virginia, 512, 513
Berlin, occupied by Napoleon, 592; Treaty of, 705, 714, 715, 717. 720, 729, 743; Sparticist revolt, 996; three-way occupation of, 1144; bombed, 1148, 1149, 1150, 1164; battle of, 1148
Berlin Conference on African Affairs, 739, 843
Berlin Congress, *see* Congress of Berlin
Berlin Decree, 768
Berlin-Rome Axis, established by German-Italian Pact, 964, 1003
Berlin-Rome-Tokyo Pact, signed by Hungary, Rumania, Yugoslavia, 1136, 1150
Berlin University, founded, 594
Bermuda, 1158 *f*., 1155, 1158
Bern, Dietrich von, 146
Bernabo, of the Visconti, 298
Bernadotte, Jean Baptiste Jules (Prince of Ponte Corvo), French general, 586; elected heir to the Swedish throne, 595; commands Swedish army with the Allies, 598, 599, 600; Sweden and Norway united under him as Charles XIV, 699
Bernard of Clairvaux, 208, 219, 228, 256
Bernardes, Arturo da Silva, pres. of Brazil, 1070
Bernhard of Lippe-Biesterfeld, Prince, marries Princess Juliana of Holland, 976
Bernhard of Saxe-Weimar, German general, 406
Bernier, Capt. Joseph Elzear, annexed Banks and Victoria Islands for Canada, 567
Bernini, Giovanni Lorenzo, Italian architect and sculptor, 454
Bernstein, Eduard, socialist writer, 693
Bernstorff, Count Andreas Peter, Danish statesman, 475
Bernstorff, Johann Heinrich, Count von, German ambassador at Washington, 923, 936
Berrhoe, battle of, 247, 253
Berri, Charles Ferdinand, Duke de, murdered, 626
Berry, Lt. Robert Mallory, Arctic explorer, 565
Berson, Prof. Arthur, altitude record, 557
Bertha, wife of Henry IV of Germany, 206
Berthelot, Gen. Henri Mathias, French general, 944
Berthier, Louis Alexandre, Prince of Neuchâtel, 592
Bertrand, Francisco, pres. of Honduras, 821, 1073
Berwick, James Fitzjames, Duke of, Spanish general, 450, 453
Berwick, Treaty of, 372
Besant, Annie (Wood), radical nationalist leader in India, 1111
Beseler, Gen. Hans von, German commander, 914
Besnagar, 43
Bessarabia, colonized by Bulgarians, 175, 183; acquired by Russia, 396, 701; 1149 *f*.
Bessarion, Johannes, Cardinal, Renaissance scholar, 289, 323
Bessemer, Henry, process of making steel, 554
Bessus, murdered Darius III, 65
Best, Charles Herbert, on insulin treatment, 553
Bethany Mission, German missionary station in South Africa, 853
Beth-Eden (Bit-Adini), Kingdom of, 35
Bethlehem Steel strike, 1056
Bethlen, Gabriel (Bethlen Gabor), Prince of Transylvania, 404, 420
Bethlen, Count Stephen, Hungarian prime minister, 1014, 1015
Bethmann-Hollweg, Theobald von, German chancellor, 692, 757, 762, 936, 942
Betsuzhev-Riumin, Alexis Petrovich, Count, Russian foreign minister, 481
Beyers, Christian Frederick, leads rebellion in South Africa, 859
Beynen, Koolemans, commands Dutch expedition for scientific observation in Spitsbergen area, 565

Beyrut, see Beirut
Bezabde, 125
Bezobrazov, Alexandre Mikhailovich, Russian adventurer, 752
Bhadrabuhu, high-priest, 42
Bhagavadgita ("Song of the Lord"), 43
Bhaja, 43
Bhanugupta, ruler in India, 331
Bharhut, 43, 129
Bhaskara, his *Siddhantasiromani*, 131
Bhavabhuti, Sanskrit dramatist, 331
Bhimadeva I, reconstructed the Saiva temple of Somanatha, 332
Bhoja (Paramara), Indian ruler, 332
Bhumaka, Saka satrap, 129
Bhutan, at war with British, 870
Bialystok, 1151
Bianchi, Michele, Fascist leader, 988
Bible, Gothic translation, 114; English translation, 372; translated by Luther, 400; translated into Bulgarian, 717
Bibliotheca Corvina, in Hungary, 318
Bibracte, 96
Bicocca, battle of, 394
Bicycle invented, 554; "safety," 555
Bidar, 335
Biddle, James, American commodore, 888
Bienville, Celoron de, takes possession of the Ohio Valley, 516
Big Bertha, German long-range gun, 557
Big Ten, at the Paris Peace Conference, 951
Bigge, John Thomas, Australian politician, 898
Bihar, 41
Bijnstis, King of Hatti, 36
Bilbao, falls to the insurgents in Spanish Civil War, 984
Bilhana of Kashmir, Indian writer, 337
Bill of Rights, 430; adopted by U.S. Congress, 764
Billaud-Varennes, Jacques Nicolas, French revolutionary statesman, 583, 584
Billinghurst, Guillermo Enrique, pres. of Peru, 1068
Bimbisara, king, 41
Binney, George, Arctic explorer, 569
Bir-el-Gobi, 1160
Birch, J. W. W., British resident at Pangkor, 875
Birger, King of Sweden, 204
Birger, Magnusson, statesman of mediaeval Sweden, 204, 244
Birney, James Gillespie, Liberty Party candidate for pres. of U.S., 773
Biron (properly Buhren), Ernst Johann, Duke of Courland, 478, 479
Biscoe, John, circumnavigated Antarctica, 573
Bishop, William Avery, British aviator, 946
Bishops, trial of the seven for seditious libel, 429
Bishops of Rome, in ecclesiastical quarrels, 113, 117, 118, 123; beginning of title *pope*, 141; under imperial control of the exarchate, 146
Bishops' Wars, 1st and 2d, 376
Bismarck, Otto Edward Leopold, Prince von, German statesman, appointed minister-president of Prussia, 680; the Polish insurrection, 680; the Danish War, 681; the alliance with Italy, 681; Seven Weeks' War, 682; relations with France, 681, 682; peace with France, 636; Kulturkampf, 688; alliance system, 733 f.; Tunis question, 838; resignation, 691, 741
Bismarck, giant German battleship, 1158
Bismarck Archipelago, discovered, 894; annexed by Germany, 895; Australian force landed, 918
Bissing, Gen. Moritz Ferdinand von, gov. of the occupied area of Belgium, 914
Bithynia, 37, 82, 93, 95, 110, 127
Bitlis, taken by the Russians, 929
Bittenfeld, Gen. Herwarth von, German commander, 683
Bittisfeva, 338
Bituminous Coal Stabilization Act, 1055, 1056
Biyushshilish, 35
Bizerte, 1162
Björkö, Treaty of, 753
Bjorn, King of Sweden, welcomes Carolingian mission, 170
Björnson, Björnstjerne, Norwegian writer, 699
Black Ball Line, initiated regular transatlantic service, 554
Black Death, reduction of population, 266; in Ireland, 275; in northern Europe, 276; in Florence, 294; in Bohemia, 302
Black Flags, guerrillas in Tonkin, 874
Black Hole, of Calcutta, 534
Black Hundreds, in Russia, 708
Black List, introduced, 929
Black Pagoda, at Konarak, 337 f.
Black Sea, Russian domination of, 1154
Black Stone, of Mecca, 190
Black Troop, standing army of Hungary, 318
Black War, carried on by Australian natives (the Black Line), 899
Blackheath, battle of, 369
Blacks (Neri), a Guelf faction of Florence, 293
Blaine, James Gillespie, American statesman, 783, 784, 785
Blake, Robert, English commander in war with the Dutch, 425, 437
Blanc, Louis, French socialist writer, 549, 550, 630, 636
Blanche of Castile, mother of Louis IX, 230
Blanco, Antonio Guzman, pres. of Venezuela, 816
Blancos, political party in Paraguay and Uruguay, 810, 811
Bland, Richard Parks, co-author of the Bland-Allison Act, 378
Bland-Allison Act, for free coinage of silver, 783
Bianqui, Louis Auguste, French revolutionary leader, 637

Blantyre, in East Africa, founded, 847
Blaxland, Gregory, English explorer in Australia, 893
"Bleeding Kansas," war for control, 775
Blenheim (Blindheim) and Hochstadt, battles of, 432, 446
Blériot, Louis, flew monoplane across English Channel, 557
Bligh, William, gov. of New South Wales, 898
Blignières, André (Le Barbier) de, minister of public works in the Nubar cabinet in Egypt, 831
Blind King Dom of Bohemia, slain at the battle of Crécy, 276.
    See also John of Luxemburg
Bliss, Gen. Tasker Howard, American soldier, 945
Blitzkrieg, 445, 449
Block, Adrian, Dutch explorer, 510
Blockade, defined by the League of Armed Neutrality, 482
Blockade of Germany, lifted by the Allies, 996
Blockade of Great Britain, proclaimed by Napoleon, 592; by Germany, 1149
Bloemfontein, 856, 857
Bloemfontein Convention, 856
Blois, Treaty of, 387
Blomberg, Werner von, German minister of war, 1004
Blommaert, Samuel, organized New Sweden Co., 511
Blood Purge (Hitler's), 1003
Blood River, battle of, 851
Bloody Assizes, 429
Bloody Assizes of Arad, 675
Bloody Sunday, in Russia, 707
Bloody Week, in Paris, 637
Blount, James Henderson, American envoy to Hawaii, 910
Blücher, German cruiser, 917
Blücher, Gebhard Leberecht von, Prussian general, 592, 598, 599, 600, 603
Blücher, Gen. Vasilie Knostantinovich, Russian general, 1118
Blue Shirts, in Ireland, 973
Blum, Léon, leader of the Socialist Party in France, 979
Blum, Robert, German Liberal in the Frankfurt Parliament, 674, 676
Boadicea, a misspelling of Boudicca, 106
Board of Commissioners for Trade and Plantations, 514
Board of Indian Commissioners, 790
Boards of Health, 780
Bobadilla, Francisco de, gov. of Española, 367, 496
Boccaccio, Giovanni, Italian humanist, 282, 294
Boccaro, Gaspar, Portuguese explorer, 524
Bockelsohn, Johann, Anabaptist, 401
Bocskay, Stephen, Prince of Transylvania, 420, 424
Bodawpaya, King of Burma, 872
Bodega y Quadra, Juan Francisco, Spanish explorer, 493
Bodenstein, Andrew (Carlstadt), Catholic theologian, 399
Bodh-Gaya, 42, 43
Bodhicharyavatara, 131
Bodhidharma, Persian, founder of the Ch'an Chinese sect, 341
Bodhisattva, 130, 131, 136
Bodmer, Johannes Jakob, 460
Body of Liberties, 511
Boelcke, Oswald, German aviator, 946
Boeotia, 47 *passim*
Boeotian League, 52, 56, 63
Boeotians, 47, 56, 59, 64
Boer War, 618, 749, 751, 857
Boers, revolt against the British, 856 f.
Boethius, Roman philosopher, 123, 146, 167, 267
Boettcher, Dr. Herbert, head of the Memel directorate, 1042
Bognaz Keui, 28, 36
Bogoliubski, Andrei, Prince of Suzdal, 244
Bogomils, heresy, 183, 318; driven into Bosnia, 246; their heresy spreads, 247; revolt in Thrace and Bulgaria, 250; 319
Bohemia, 207, 304 ff.; in the Thirty Years' War, 404; crown proclaimed hereditary in the house of Hapsburg, 418 f.; in the Seven Weeks' War, 683
Bohemia-Moravia, a German protectorate, 1004, 1013, 1016
Bohemian Brotherhood, 305, 418
Bohemian Crusade, led by John Ziska, 305
Bohemian Diet, 694
Bohemian Mark, 155
Bohemian nationalism, 302
Bohemund, Norman leader of the First Crusade, 250 f., 252, 255, 256
Boisdeffre, Gen. Le Mouton de, chief of French general staff, 641, 742
Boissy d'Anglas, François Antoine de, pres. of the National Convention in Paris, 584
Bokhara taken, 185, 187; intellectual center of Islam, 189; captured by Mongol armies, 260
Boleslav, Duke of Bohemia, 161
Boleslav I, of Bohemia, 239
Boleslav II, of Bohemia, 239
Boleslav I (Chrobry: the Brave), of Poland, 162, 209, 240, 241
Boleslav II (the Bold), of Poland, 241
Boleslav III (Wry-mouth), of Poland, 242
Boleslav IV, of Poland, 242
Boleslav V, of Poland, 242
Boleyn, Anne, second wife of Henry VIII, 369; executed, 370
Bolingbroke, Henry of, see Henry IV
Bolívar, Simon, South American liberator, 802, 803, 806, 811, 812, 814
Bolivia, 801 f., 806, 811 f., 936, 1067, 1141
Bolo Pasha, 929
Bologna, 220, 1141
Bolshevik *coup d'état* (Revolution) in Russia, 940, 1029

Bolsheviks, faction of the Social Democratic Party in Russia, 706
Bombay, acquired by the English, 534
Bombing of Britain, 1148 f.
Bona, bombarded by German cruisers, 919
Bonaparte, Jerome, King of Westphalia, 593, 599, 657
Bonaparte, Joseph, King of Spain, 452; King of Naples, 593, 596, 600, 799
Bonaparte, Louis, King of Holland, 593, 595
Bonaparte, Prince Louis Napoleon, pres. of French Republic, 631; coup d'état; becomes Napoleon III, 632 f.
Bonaparte, Lucien, 587
Bonaparte, Napoleon, see Napoleon
Bonar Law, Andrew, British prime minister, 958, 968
Bond, Sir Robert, premier of Canada, 798
Bond of Association, plot against Queen Elizabeth, 373
Bone carving, 5
Bonhomme Richard, defeated the Serapis, 521
Boniface, Marquis of Tuscany, 206
Boniface (Winfred), the Anglo-Saxon, his mission in Germany, 149, 150, 169
Boniface VIII (Benedetto Caetani), Pope, bull Clericis laicos, 199, 200, 222, 231 f.
Boniface IX (Piero Tomacelli), Pope, 288
Boniface of Montferrat, leader of the Fourth Crusade, 254; 257; King of Thessalonica, 258
Bonifatius, 121
Bonilla, Manuel, pres. of Honduras, 821
Bonner, Edmund, Bishop of London, 372
Bonnet, Georges, French foreign minister, 980, 1011
Bonnier, Ange Elisabeth Louis Antoine, French delegate to Congress of Rastadt, 587
Bonnivert, Guillaume Gouffier, Sieur de, French general, 400
Bono, Gen. Emillo di, Fascist leader, 988; in Ethiopia, 990
Bonomi, Ivanoe, Italian prime minister, 987, 1143, 1144
Bononia, 99
Book of Ceremonies of Constantine Porphyrogenitus, 181
Book of Common Prayer, 426
Book of Kells, 169
Book of Mormon, 771
Book of the Dead, 21
Books proscribed by Ch'in dynasty, 132, 133
Boomplats, battle of, 852
Boone, Daniel, clears wilderness road to Kentucky, 517
Booth, Sir George, 426
Bor (Tadeo Komorowski), Polish general, 1142
Borchgrevink, Carsten, Antarctic explorer, 573
Bordeaux, 1135
Borden, Sir Robert Laird, Canadian prime minister, 1058
Border Ruffians, in Kansas elections, 775
Bordereau, in the Dreyfus Affair, 641
Borgesius, Hendrik Goeyman, 626
Borghese, Camillo, becomes Pope Paul V, 397
Borgia, Caesar, son of Pope Alexander VI, 395
Boril, nephew of Bulgarian king Kaloyan, 248
Boris I, Tsar of Bulgaria, 177, 182
Boris II of Bulgaria, 183
Boris III, King of Bulgaria, 717, 745, 948, 989, 1018, 1022, 1024, 1141
Borno, Louis, pres. of Haiti, 1078
Bornu, see Kanem
Borobudur victory monument in Java, 348
Borodin, Michael, Russian diplomat, 1118
Borodino, battle of, 598
Boroughbridge, battle of, 264
Borromeo, Carlo, Archbishop of Milan, 396
Borsippa, 25
Bort, Balthasar, Dutch commander, 538
Bose, Subhas Chandra, pres. of the Congress Party in India, 1114
Boselli, Paolo, Italian prime minister, 930, 942
Boskop Man, 9
Bosnia and Herzegovina, occupied by Austria, 694, 714; annexed, 695, 708, 715, 731; insurrection, 694, 729, 755, 756
Boso of Provence, established Kingdom of Cisjuran Burgundy, 157, 159
Boston Massacre, 518
Boston Port Act, 518
Boston Tea Party, 518
Bosworth Field, battle of, 271
Botany Bay, English convict colony, 895
Botev, Christo, Bulgarian revolutionary, 717
Botha, Louis, South African statesman, 858; becomes prime minister of the Union, 858; takes Windhoek, 859; defeats Germans, 918; death, 1091
Bothwell Brigg, battle of, 428
Bothwell, James Hepburn, murdered Darnley, 373
Bottego, Vittorio, African explorer, 828
Botticelli, Sandro, painter, 290, 296
Bou Amama, leads uprising against the French in Algeria, 838
Boucicault, Jean, Marshal of France, 323
Boudicca, Queen of the Iceni, 106, 166
Bougainville, Louis Antoine de, French explorer, 894
Bougainville Island, 1169
Boulanger, Gen. Georges Ernest, French minister of war, 639, 740
Boulé, parliament of Greece, 710
Boulogne, fell to the Germans, 1146
Boundless Light Buddha, 130
Bounty, mutineers from, settled on Pitcairn Island, 895
Bounty, Queen Anne's, 432

Bourbon, House of, 386
Bourbon, Louis Henri, Duc de, 451
Bourbon family compact, 435
Bourbons in Naples, dethroned, 592
Bourgeois, Léon Victor Auguste, French statesman, 952
Bourges, Synod ot, 216
Bourgogne, Jean de, his Travels of Sir John Mandeville, 267
Bourke, Sir Richard, gov. of New South Wales, 899
Bouvet, Pierre, French naval officer, 571
Bouvines, battle of, 211, 230
Bovaradet, Prince of Siam, 1116
Boves, José Tomás, re-established Spanish control in Venezuela, 803
Bovianum, 74
Bowell, Sir Mackenzie, premier of Canada, 797
Boxer Rebellion, in China, 707, 750, 787, 882 f., 892, 1121
Boyaca River, battle of, 803
Boyars, Council of (Duma), 415
Boyars, Russia, 415, 417, 418
Boyen, Hermann von, Prussian general, 594
Boyer, Jean Pierre, pres. of Haiti, 824, 825
Boyle, Charles, 4th Earl of Orrery, enters cabinet of Queen Anne, 432
Boyne, battle of the, 430
Brabant, revocation of constitution, 469
Bracciolini, Poggio, Italian humanist, 271, 290
Braddock, Gen. Edward, English commander, 516
Bradford, William, gov. of the Pilgrims, 509
Bradlaugh, Charles, English politician, 616
Bradshaw, John, English judge, 379, 426
Bradstreet, Gen. John, English soldier, 516
Brady, Matthew, leader of Australian bushrangers, 899
Braga, Theophilo, Portuguese statesman, 649
Braganza, Constantine de, 530
Bragg, Braxton, Confederate general, 778
Brahma sutra, 131, 336
Brahmagupta, systematized mathematics, 131
Brahmanas, 41, 42
Brahmanism, 41
Brahmans, 129
Brahmo script, 42
Brahmo Samaj, reform association in India, 870
Braila, taken by Austro-German forces, 935
Bramante, Italian architect, 298
Branas, Alexius, Byzantine general, 253
Brand, Sir Christopher Joseph, British aviator, 1081
Brand, Jan, pres. of the Orange Free State, 853
Brandenburg, 208, 215
Brandywine, battle of, 521
Branibor (Brandenburg), created as a Mark, 160
Brankovich, George, Serbian prince, 319
Brankovich, Vuk, 319
Bransfield, Edward, 571
Branting, Hjalmar, Swedish premier, 699, 1047
Brasidas, killed at Amphipolis, 59
Bratianu, Dmitri, Rumanian statesman, 719
Bratianu, Ion, Rumanian premier, 926, 944, 1025, 1026
Bratianu, Vintila, leader of the Liberal Party in Rumania, 1026
Bratislav of Bohemia, 206
Brauchitsch, Gen. Heinrich Hermann Walther von, German chief of staff, 1004
Braun, Otto, German Socialist, 998
Bravo, Gonzalez, Spanish statesman, 646
Braz, Wenceslau, pres. of Brazil, 818
Brazil, Church and education in, 504; independence from Portugal, 648, 805, 817; United States of Brazil, 818; boundary controversies, 818; severs relations with German govt., 1070; war on Germany, 936; treaties with the U.S., 1071; 1156
Brazza, Count Pierre Paul François Camille Savorgnan de, African explorer, 828, 843, 844
Breadbasket Bill, 689
Breakspear, Nicholas, see Adrian IV
Breckinridge, John Cabell, nominated by southern Democrats for pres., 775
Breda, see Declaration of Breda
Breda, Treaty of, 427, 439, 514
Bréguet, Louis, helicopter, 557
Breitenfeld, battle of, see Leipzig
Bremen, Bishopric of, established, 153
Brenner Pass, Hitler and Mussolini, 1150
Brennus, barbarian leader, 37, 72
Brescia, in the League of Pavia, 220
Breslau, German cruiser, 919
Breslau, Treaty of, 466, 468
Brest-Litovsk, peace conference, 943; Treaty of, 946, 947, 951; 1043, 1044; 1145, 1151
Brewagne, French naval vessel, 1148
Brétigny, Peace of, 276
Bretislav I (the Restorer) of Poland, 240, 241
Bretislav II, 240
Bretton Woods Conference, 1170
Breuil, Henry Edouard Prosper, 5, 8
Breviarium Romanum, 396
Breviary of Alaric, 144, 163
Brian of Munster, defeated the Norse, 169
Briand, Aristide, French premier, 643, 930, 935, 936, 939, 941, 959, 960, 976, 977
Bridge, battle of the, 127, 186
Bridge of Calderón, battle of the, 804
Bridge of Dessau, battle of the, 404
Brienne, Loménie de, French minister of finance, 448

Brigandage, in Italy, 68
Brigantes, revolt suppressed, 111
Bright, John, English statesman, 611, 614
Brihaspati, a code, 130
Brihuega, battles of; Vendôme defeated by English, 446, 450; Loyalist victory in Spanish Civil War, 983
Brisbane, Sir Thomas Makdougall, gov. of New South Wales, 898
Brisbane, town founded, 899
Brissot de Warville, Jacques Pierre, leader of the Girondists, 580, 581
Bristol, John Digby, 1st Earl of, 575
Britain, invaded by Caesar, 97, 166; Caligula's campaign, 105; invaded by Aulus Plautius, 106; progress of Romanization, 108, 166; building operations of Hadrian, 110; evacuated by the Romans, 121, 166; prehistoric inhabitants, 164; battle of, 1148 f.
Britannicus, son of Emperor Claudius, 106
British attack on French naval vessels, 1135
British forces, invaded Iran, 1137; landed in Madagascar, 1138
British-Canadian Arctic Expedition, 567
British Central Africa, changed to Nyasaland Protectorate, 850
British Church Missionary Society, 840
British Columbia, 796; joins the Dominion of Canada, 796
British East Africa, renamed Kenya, 1090
British East Africa Co., 848; its dissolution, 849
British East India Co. chartered, 373; trading with Persia, 526; exemption from customs duties, 534; factories in Burma, 541; relations with Afghanistan, 866; charter renewed, 868, 870; govt. takes over its duties, 870; its rule ended, 875; stations in northern Borneo, 876
British Grand Fleet, under Adm. Sir John Jellicoe, 917
British Guiana, 1148 f., 1155, 1158
British India Steam Navigation Co., 847
British Isles, in Post-Palaeolithic period, 17; 164 ff.
British Labor Party, victory, 1145
British Museum, founded, 435; bombed, 1149
British North America, Report on the Affairs of, by Lord Durham, 795
British North America Act, 796
British Plan on Palestine, 1102
British Possessions Act, 795
British Somaliland, 1159
British South Africa Co., 855
British West African Settlements, 840
Britons, see Brythons and Cymri
Brittany, in union with the French crown, 383
Broca, Paul, physiologist, 551
Brocchi Plan, 1026
Brock, Gen. Isaac, 793
Brockdorff-Rantzau, Ulrich, Count von, chief of the German delegation at the Paris Peace Conference, 952, 996
Broglie, Achille Charles Leonce Victor, Duke de, French statesman, 628, 638
Broglie, Victor François, Duke de, French general, 467
Bronze Age of Greece, 46
Bronze culture, 2
Brooke, Sir James, Rajah of Sarawak, 877
Brooke, Gen. John Rutter, military gov. of Cuba, 823, 824
Broughton, Capt. William Robert, British explorer, 885, 887
Broussard, Senator Edwin Sidney, 1133
Brown, Lt. Arthur Whitten, first to cross the Atlantic in an airplane, 557
Brown, John, raid on Harper's Ferry, 775
Brown, M'Leavy, financial adviser to Korea, 886
Brown, Moses, applied machinery to cotton spinning, 764
Brownists, 372
Bruce, Edward, brother of Robert Bruce, 272
Bruce, James, explored Ethiopia, 525
Bruce, Margaret, daughter of Robert, 272
Bruce, Robert, claimant to the Scottish crown, 199
Bruce, Robert, King of Scotland, 199; 201; invades England, 264, 272
Bruce, Stanley Melbourne, Australian prime minister, 1129
Bruce, Dr. William Speirs, of the Scotch Spitsbergen Syndicate, 569, 574
Brue, André de, conquest of Senegal, 525
Bruges, taken by the Germans, 914; taken by the British, 950
Brühl, Heinrich, Count von, Austrian statesman, 466
Brum, Baltasar, pres. of Uruguay, 1066
Brundisium, 94, 96, 97, 99
Brune, Guillaume Marie Anne, French marshal, 460, 587, 588
Brunei, Sultan of Borneo, 877
Brunel, Olivier, 559
Brunelleschi, Filippo, Italian artist, 296
Brüning, Heinrich, German Chancellor, 999
Brünn, Treaty of, 302
Brunnow, Philipp Ivanovich, Count, Russian diplomat, 725
Bruno, Archbishop of Cologne, Pope Gregory V, 162, 216
Bruno, Giordano, Italian philosopher, 660
Bruno of Toul, see Leo IX
Brunswick, Charles William Ferdinand, Duke of, Prussian commander-in-chief, 581, 592, 595
Brunswick-Bevern, August Wilhelm, Duke of, Prussian General, 467
Brush, Charles Francis, introduced the arc light, 783
Brusilov, Alexei Alexeivich, Russian general, 914, 932, 940
Brussels, entered by von Kluck, 913; liberated, 1142
Brussels Act, for extirpation of the slave trade, 844
Brussels Conference of powers connected with the Nine-Power Pact, 1126

Bruttians, 85, 86
Bruttium, 88
Brutus, Decimus, assassin of Caesar, 98
Brutus, Junius Lucius, led revolt against Tarquin the Proud, 70
Brutus, Marcus Junius, led conspiracy in Caesar's assassination, 98, 99
Bryan, William Jennings, American statesman, 787, 789, 923
Bryan-Chamorro Treaty, 792
Bryansk, 1151, 1154
Brythons (Britons), a Celtic stock, 166
Brzezany, battle of, 940
Bubastis, 21, 24
Bubonic plague, 552
Buchanan, James (15th pres. of U.S.), 775
Bucharest, Treaties of, 596, 701, 719, 722, 739, 761, 944, 951
Buchlau Conference, 755
Buckingham, Edward Stafford, 3d Duke of, 370
Buckingham, Henry Stafford, 2d Duke of, leads rebellion against Richard III, 271
Buckingham, George Villiers, 1st Duke of, 374, 375, 427
Buczacz, Treaty of, 475
Budapest, 1154
Buddha, his death, 42, 136; symbols of presence, 43, 128, 129
Buddhacharita, 129
Buddhaghosha of Magadha, his Visuddhimagga, 132
Buddhism, founded, 41; 132, 134 ff.; adopted in Korea, 137; introduced into Japan, 139, 140; disappearance from India, 331; canon printed, 342; its problems of being and knowledge, 343 f.; most popular religion with the Mongols, 346; naturalized in China, 537; decline in Japan, 546
Budhagupta, last emperor of dynasty, 130
Buena Vista, battle of, 773
Buenos Aires, 808, 1155
Bugeaud de la Piconnerie, Thomas Robert, French marshal, 837
Bugis, from Celebes, 875
Buhlul Lodi, founded the Lodi dynasty, 335
Buhren, see Biron
Bukeshohatto, Japanese collection of maxims for warriors, 546
Bukharin, Nikolai Ivanovich, Bolshevik leader, 1034, 1036
Bukovina, taken by Austro-Germans, 922; 1149 f.
Bulgaria, modern independence declared, 731; first American mission, 717; Exarchate established, 717; abortive rising against Turkish rule, 717, 729; revolution at Philippopolis, 717; declaration of independence; conclusion of alliance with Serbia; treaty of alliance with Greece, 718, 759; Balkan wars, 719, 759, 760; Ferdinand of Saxe-Coburg-Kohary elected prince, 741; recognized by the powers, 745; World War, 926; alliance with Germany and Austria, 927; declares war on Serbia, 719, 927; Tsar Ferdinand abdicates, 948, 1023; post-war history, 1023 f.; 1135, 1137, 1141, 1142, 1150, 1171
Bulgarian Exarchate, 717
Bulgarian Horrors, 717, 734
Bulgaroktonos, slayer of the Bulgarians, see Basil II
Bulgars, converted to Greek communion, 158; defeated by the Byzantines, 176, 177; period of greatness under Tsar Symeon, 179; peace with Greeks, 180; Tsar Samuel builds up another great empire, 180; incorporated into the Byzantine Empire, 184; 2d Bulgarian Empire, 247 f.; revolt under Peter Deljan, 249; insurrection led by Peter and John Asen, 253; defeat Baldwin I and Doge Dandolo at Adrianople, 259
Bulge, battle of, 1164
Bull Run, battles of; first, 776; second, 778
Buller, Sir Redvers Henry, British general, 857
Bullock, William, invented the web printing press, 554
Bulnes, Manuel, pres. of Chile, 809
Bülow, Prince Bernhard Heinrich Karl Martin von, chancellor of Germany, 692, 747, 749, 750, 753, 757, 923
Bülow, Friedrich Wilhelm, Baron von, Prussian general, 599, 600
Bülow, Gen. Karl von, German general, 912, 914
Bulwer, Sir Henry, British ambassador at Madrid, 645
Bulwer, William Henry Lytton Earle, Baron Dalling and Bulwer, and the Clayton-Bulwer Treaty, 774, 788
Bunau-Varilla, Philippe Jean, and the Hay-Bunau-Varilla Treaty, 788
Bundelkand, 132
Bundesrat, the federal council of the North German Confederation, 686
Bundesrath, stopped on suspicion of carrying contraband, 749
Bunker Hill, battle of, 520
Buol-Schauenstein, Charles Ferdinand, Count von, Austrian foreign minister, 728
Buoncampagni, Ugo, becomes Pope Gregory XIII, 396
Buquoy, Charles Bonaventure, 404
Burckhardt, John Lewis, explored the Nile, 826
Bureau of Corporations, 791
Buresch, Karl, Austrian chancellor, 1006
Burgenland dispute, between Austria and Hungary, 955, 1006, 1014
Burgers, Thomas François, pres. of the South African Republic, 853
Burgoyne, Gen. John, British general, 521
Burgundians, overrun Gaul, 121, 143, 145; in civil war against the Armagnacs, 278
Burgundy, Duke of, see Philip, Duke of Burgundy
Burgundy, conquered, 147; Cisjuran kingdom, 157, 159; the duchy Kingdom of Burgundy passed to the empire, 225, 276
Burgwarde, 160
Burial of dead, in Post-Palaeolithic period, 13; under Pyramids, 21

Burian von Rajecz, Count Stephen, Austro-Hungarian foreign minister, 923, 942, 949
Burid dynasty of Damascus, 254
Burke (Charles Henry) Act, on Indians' property titles, 784
Burke, Edmund, British statesman and political theorist, 436
Burke, Robert O'Hara, Australian explorer, 901
Burke, Thomas, under-secretary for Ireland, 616
Burkersdorf, battle of, 468
Burlingame, Anson, American diplomat, 880
Burma, under Indian influence, 347; Dutch and English East India Co. opens factories, 541; modern state, 872; wars with the British, 872; British protectorate recognized, 881; separated from India, 1113; 1138, 1166, 1167, 1169
Burma Road, 1165, 1166, 1167
Burmese Wars, 1st, 868, 872; 2d, 870, 872; 3d, 871, 872
Burnes, Sir Alexander, British envoy to Afghanistan, 866
Burnet, William, gov. of Massachusetts, 512
Burni, revolt in Chahar suppressed, 539
Burnside, Ambrose Everett, Federal general, 778
Burr, Aaron, vice-pres. of U.S., 768; duel with Alexander Hamilton, 768
Burritt, Elihu, leader of American peace movement, 771
Burrough, Stephen, on Russian exploration, 559
Burrus, guard of Nero, 106, 107
Burschenschaften, German student organizations, 669
Bur-Sin, 26
Burton, Richard Francis, African explorer, 826
Busby, James, British resident in New Zealand, 905
Busch, Germán. pres. of Bolivia, 1067
Bushidō, a code of conduct in Japan, 546
Bushire, occupied by the British, 929
Bushmen in South Africa, 4, 850; Bushman-Hottentot, 12, 328
Bushranging Act, 899
Bushranging in Australia, 898; in Victoria, 902
Busiris, 21
Bussy-Castelnau, Charles Joseph Patissier, Marquis de, French administrator in India, 534
Bute, John Stuart, Earl of, British prime minister, 435
Butler, Gen. Benjamin Franklin, American soldier, 776
Butler, Walter, Count, 406
Butros Ghali, premier of Egypt, 834
Butt, Isaac, founder of Home Rule of Ireland Party, 616
Button, Sir Thomas, English explorer, 560
Buwayhids, 190
Byblos, 13, 33
Bye, a plot to imprison James I, 373
Bylot, Robert, English explorer, 560
Byng, George, Viscount Torrington, British naval commander, 432
Byng, Julian Hedworth George, 1st Viscount Byng of Vimy, gov-gen. of Canada, 1058
Byrd, Richard Evelyn, American Explorer; flight to North Pole, 566; flights over Ellesmere Land, 568; beginning of his polar flights, 569; expedition to the Antarctic; flies to South Pole, 576, 577
Byrnes, James F., Director of Economic Stabilization, 1139; Office of War Mobilization, 1140
Byzantine Crusade, 174
Byzantine history, 170 ff., 249 f., 320 ff.
Byzantium, 48 passim; reduced by Pausanias, 54; recovered by Alcibiades, 61

Cabal, its accession to power, 427
Caballero, Largo, Spanish statesman, 983, 984
Cabeçadas, Mendes, Portuguese insurgent, 985
Cabet, Etienne, French Utopian socialist, 549, 628
Cables, from Vancouver to Brisbane completed, 797; from Vladivostok to Shanghai, Hongkong, and Singapore, 880; to Australia, 907
Caboche, Simon, French insurgent, 278
Cabochian Ordinance, 278
Cabot, John, discoverer, 367, 507, 559
Cabot, Sebastian, discoverer; voyage to America, 367; reaches the Rio de la Plata, 490, 559
Cabral, Pedro Alvares, discoverer, 364; lands in Brazil, 368, 391
Cabrera, Estrada, pres. of Guatemala, 1074
Cabrillo, Juan Rodriguez de, explorer, 492
Cáceres, Andrés, pres. of Peru, 813
Cadamosto, Alvise da, Venetian explorer, 364
Cade, Jack, rebellion, 270
Cadillac, Antoine de la Mothe, sieur, founded Detroit, 507
Cadorna, Gen. Luigi, Italian commander, 925, 941, 945
Cadoudal, Georges, French conspirator, 590
Caecilius, 91
Caecina, Alienus, in battle of Bedriacum, 107
Caen, 1163
Caesar, Caius Julius, 74, 84, 92; conquest of Gaul, 96, 166; invasion of Britain, 97, 166; made dictator, 98; temple erected to him, 99; his Commentaries, 100, 142; 113
Caesar, Gaius, 102
Caesar, Lucius Julius, 93, 102
Caesarea, 32
Caesarea Mazaca, 124
Caesariensis, 106
Caesarion, son of Cleopatra, 97
Caetani, Cardinal, Pope Boniface VIII, 222
Cagni, Capt. Umberto, Arctic explorer, 566
Cagoulards (Hooded Ones), a terrorist group in France, 979
Caillaux, Joseph Marie Auguste, French premier, 643, 757, 941, 976
Caillé, René, African explorer, 826

Cairo Declaration, 1141
Caisse de la Dette, established in Egypt, 831
Calabria, taken by Byzantine forces, 179, 217; conquered by the Normans, 250
Calabrians, 86
Calah, 25, 27
Calais, taken by the English, 265, 267; 270; retaken by the Duke of Guise, 372, 383; restored to England, renounced, 372; 1149
Calatafimi, battle of, 658
Calcutta, founded, 534; captured; retaken by the English, 535
Calderón, Pedro, Spanish playwright, 389
Cale Acts, 57
Caledonians (Picts), 108, 110, 114, 121
Calendar, introduced, 21; reformed, 98; Gregorian, 396; French Revolution, 583
Calhoun, John Caldwell, American statesman, 771; treaty for annexation of Texas, 773; against Compromise of 1850, 774
Caligula, Roman emperor, 105
Calinescu, Armand, premier of Rumania, 1027
Calinescu, Armand, Rumanian premier, 1135
Caliphate, Orthodox, 184, 243, 485; abolished in Turkey, 1095
Calixtines of Bohemia, formulate the Four Articles of Prague, 305
Calixtus II (Guido), Pope, 207; arranged Concordat of Worms, 219
Calixtus III, an Aragonese imperialist antipope, 220, 290
Calleja, Felix, crushes revolution in Mexico, 804
Calles, Plutarco Elias, President of Mexico, 1052, 1075, 1076
Callias, Peace of, 56
Callicrates, 80
Callicratidas, 61
Calligraphy in China, 135; formal and cursive, 136
Callimachus, 75
Callinicum, battle of, 126, 172
Callistratus, 63
Calonne, Charles Alexandre de, French minister of finances, 448
Caltabelotta, Peace of, 290
Calthorpe, Adm. Sir Somerset Arthur Gough-, British naval commander, 948
Calvert, Cecilius, founder of Maryland, 510
Calvert, George (later Lord Baltimore), and Newfoundland, 510
Calvin, John, French reformer, 142, 401, 409
Calvinism, in the Netherlands, 379; dominant Protestant group, 401; established in Poland, 414; accepted in Transylvania, 420
Calvinist-Catholic coalition, in the Netherlands, 626
Camacho, Avila, President of Mexico, 1136, 1156
Cámara de Indias, 498
Camarina, 57
Cambacérès, Jean Jacques Régis de, appointed consul by Napoleon, 587
Cambodia, part secured by Siam, 873; French protectorate, 873; 1166
Cambon, Jules Martin, French ambassador at Berlin, 757
Cambrai, battle of, 940; Treaty of (Paix des Dames), 388, 394, 400; League of, 381, 393, 395, 397
Cambridge University, founded, 201; expeditions to Greenland, 569
Cambyses, 24; conquered Egypt, 40
Camden, battle of, 522
Camel, battle of the, 186
Camera, first image obtained, 554
Cameron, Charles Duncan, British consul in Ethiopia, 834
Cameron, Gen. Trevor, commander in New Zealand, 907
Cameron, Verney Lovett, African explorer, 828
Cameroons, invaded by British, 918
Camillus, Marcus Furius, 72
Camões, Luis Vaz de, Portuguese poet, 392
Camp of National Unity, a Polish party, 1040
Campagna, invaded by Frederick II, 212
Campania, 68, 69, 73, 98
Campbell, Andrew, and the rotary printing press, 555
Campbell, Archibald, and the Glencoe massacre, 431
Campbell, Sir Archibald, British commander in Burma, 872
Campbell, Sir Colin, and the relief of Lucknow, 870
Campbell-Bannerman, Sir Henry, British prime minister, 619, resigns, 620
Campeggio, Lorenzo, 400
Campero, Narciso, pres. of Bolivia, 812
Campero, Pedro Diaz, pres. of Peru, 813
Campi Raudii, 92
Campignian culture, 16, 17
Campo Formio, Treaty of, 585, 588, 591
Campomanes, Pedro Rodriguez, Count of Spanish reform minister, 451
Campong-Thom Province, 1166
Campos Salles, Manoel de, pres. of Brazil, 818
Camulodunum, 106
Canaan, 29, 30, 32
Canaanites, 30
Canada, campaign against, 520; takes possession of all islands north of continent, 567; settlement of loyalists, 792; republic rebellion in, 895; union of Upper and Lower Canada, 796; Red River Rebellion, 796; Canadian contingent sent to South Africa; entrance into World War, 797; Compulsory Military Service Act; Woman Franchise Bill, 1057; post-war history, 1058 ff.; 1140, 1158 f.
Canada Act, passed in British Parliament, 792
Canadian Arctic explorations, 567
Canadian elections, 1135
Canadian Northern Railway, 797, 1057

Canadian Pacific Railway Co., 797
Canadian troops, 1162, 1163
Canal Zone, boundaries defined, 819; 1154
Canalejas y Mendez, José, Spanish Liberal premier, 648
Canarese, 132; dynasty, 336
Canberra, New South Wales, 904
Cancer, Luis de, Dominican, 493
Candian War, between Venice and the Turks, 458, 483
Canet, Gustave, French soldier, 556
Canmore, Malcolm (Malcolm III), King of Scotland, 201
Cannae, battle of, 34, 87, 181
Canning, Charles John, Earl, gov.-gen. of India, 870
Canning, George, British prime minister, 604, 605, 606, 644, 723, 771
Cano, Alonso, Spanish sculptor, 389
Cano, Sebastian del, completed Magellan's voyage, 368
Canon of the Way and of Virtue, The, 44
Canonchet, chief of the Narragansetts, 511
Canossa, penance of Henry IV of Germany, 207, 219; Bismarck's defiant declaration, 689
Canova, Antonio, Italian sculptor, 454
Canovas del Castillo, Antonio, Spanish statesman, 647
Canrobert, François Certain, French commander in the Crimea, 727
Cantacuzene, John, Byzantine emperor, 322, 323, 325
Canterac, José, Peruvian statesman, 802
Canterbury (Christchurch), New Zealand, settled, 906
Canterbury, Stigand appointed Archbishop, 168; Lanfranc appointed, 191; Anselm succeeds, 193; Becket made Archbishop, 194; Stephen Langton named by the pope, 197; Winchelsey refuses grant to the crown, 200
Canton, opened to trade, 879; taken by the Japanese, 1122
Cantuar de mio Cid, 233
Canute, *see* Knut the Great
Canzaca, 127
Cão, Diogo, Portuguese explorer, 364
Cap de la Hogue, battle of, 431, 444
Cape Colony, first railway, 852; responsible govt. established, 853; customs union with Orange Free State, 854
Cape Gloucester air base, 1169
Cape Matapan, battle of, 1158
Cape Passaro, 1162
Cape St. Vincent, battle of, 452
Cape-to-Cairo telegraph and railway system, 743, 1081
Cape Town, founded by the Dutch, 524; in English possession, 850, 851, 857
Capelle, Adm. Eduard von, German minister of marine, 931
Capet, Hugh, King of France, 159, 225
Capital, by Karl Marx, 550
Capitol at Rome, burnt, 107; restoration, 108
Capitolinus, Marcus Manlius, 72
Capitulary of Kiersy, 158
Capitulary of Mersen, 158
Capitulations, abolished by Turkey, 919
Capo d'Istria, Agostino, Greek statesman, 724
Capo d'Istria, Giovanni Antonio, Count, Greek president, 722, 723, 724
Caporetto, battle of, 941
Cappadocia, 27 *passim*; Kingdom of, 37, 95, 96, 108, 188
Capper-Volstead Act on agricultural associations, 1051
Capponi, Niccolo, head of the Republic of Florence, 394
Capraca, 105
Caprivi de Caprara de Montecuculi, Georg Leo, Count von, chancellor of Germany, 691
Caps, Swedish party, 472
Capsian culture, 6, 17, 18
Captaincy-gen. of Guatemala, 804
Capua, 73, 74, 87 *f*.; 91, 94; supreme court established, 212; capital of a Lombard principality, 217
Capuchins, in Spanish America, 498; in Africa, 524
Carabobo, battle of, 803
Caracalla (Marcus Aurelius Antoninus Bassianus Caracalla), Roman emperor, 114, 115
Caractacus, British leader, 106
Caraffa, Gian Pietro, Pope Paul IV, 396
Caramania, 66
Caratheodory, Alexander, a Turkish diplomat, 736
Carausius, rebel, 118
Carbonari (Charcoal-Burners), Italian secret society, 650, 651, 663
Carbury Hill, battle of, 373
Carbutt, John, introduced celluloid film for photography, 556
Carcassonne, its walls built by Philip II, 231
Carchemish, 13 *passim*
Cárdenas, Gen. Lazaro, pres. of Mexico, 1076
Cardwell, Edward, British army reformer, 615
Carew, Sir Thomas, conspiracy of, against Queen Mary, 372
Carews, Normans, settle in Ireland, 169
Carey (Joseph Maull) Act, 786
Caria, 64, 65, 67, 84
Carians, as mercenaries, 37, 47
Carías, Gen. Tiburcio, pres. of Honduras, 1074
Carinthia, 1144
Carinus, Marcus Aurelius, Roman emperor, 116, 118
Carlist Party, in Spain, 647
Carlist War, 645, 646, 647
Carloman, brother of Charles the Fat, 152, 159
Carloman, son of Charles the Bald, 158
Carloman, son of Charles Martel, ruler of Austrasia, 150
Carloman. son of Louis the Stammerer, 150

Carloman, son of Pepin, receives northern Aquitaine, Burgundy, Provence, and Septimania, 153
Carlos I, King of Portugal, 649
Carlota Joaquina, sister of Ferdinand VII of Spain, 502
Carlsbad Decrees, 669
Carlsen, Capt. Elling, first circumnavigated Spitsbergen, 564
Carlstadt (Andrew Bodenstein), 399, 400
Carmathian revolt, at Mecca, 190
Carmer, Johann Heinrich Casimir von, Prussian jurist, 468
Carmona, Gen. Antonio de Fragoso, pres. of Portugal, 986
Carmona, Spain, captured by Arabs, 187
Carnarvon, George Edward Stanhope Molyneux Herbert, 5th Earl of, Egyptologist, 24
Carnarvon, Henry Howard Molyneux Herbert, 4th Earl of, and federation of the South African colonies, 853
Carnatic, 132
Carnegie Steel Co. strike, 785
Carnot, Lazare Nicolas Marguerite, member of the Committee of Public Safety in the French Revolution, 582, 584, 585, 639
Carnuntum, 119
Caro, Miguel, pres. of Colombia, 815
Carobert of Hungary, 222, 301
Carol I, King of Rumania, 720, 721, 925
Carol II, King of Rumania, 1025, 1026, 1027, 1136, 1150
Carolina, granted by king to eight proprietors, 513
Carolina Islands, 1169
Carolinas, reorganization of, 513
Caroline, American steamer, 772, 795
Caroline of Anspach, wife of George II of England, 434
Caroline of Brunswick, married to George IV, 605
Caroline Islands, discovered, 894; occupied by Japanese, 918
Carolingians, emergence in Austrasia, 149; protectorate over papacy, 152; disintegration of their empire, 157; Margraviate of Tuscany, 293
Carpatho-Ukraine, new name for Ruthenia, 1013; occupied by Hungary, 1016
Carpi, battle of, 445
Carr, Robert, Viscount Rochester, Duke of Somerset, 374
Carranza, Venustiano, pres. of Mexico, 791, 822, 823, 1074, 1075
Carrara family, defeated by the Venetians, 299
Carrera, José Miguel, defeated by Peruvians, 801
Carrera, Rafael, dictator of Guatemala, 819
Carrhae, 83, 97, 124
Carrier, Jean Baptiste, French revolutionary, 583
Carsidi, 74
Carson, Sir Edward, leads Ulster opposition to Home Rule, 621
Carta Mercatoria of Edward I of England, 309
Cartagena, Pact of, between Great Britain, France and Spain, 754
Cartel des Gauches, 977
Carter, Howard, Egyptologist, 24
Carteret, Sir George, receives grant of land in America, 512
Carteret, Philip, English explorer, 894
Carthage, 34, 52, 53, 86, 89; captured by the Arabs, 175, 187
Carthaginian wars, 34, 53, 66, 71, 86; killing of Scipi‹o›, 87, 88, 89
Cartier, Jacques, voyages, 505
Carus, Marcus Aurelius, Roman emperor, 116, 124
Carver, John, gov. of the Pilgrims, 508 *f*.
Carystus, 55
Casa de Contratación, 387, 496, 499, 500
Casablanca affair, 755, 839; bombarded by the French, 838; 1160; Conference, 1139, 1160
Casado, Gen. Segismundo, and Spanish civil war, 984
Casement, Sir Roger, and the insurrection in Ireland, 929
Caseros, battle of, 808
Cashel, Synod of, 169, 196
Cashin, Michael Patrick, premier of Newfoundland, 1060
Casimir I (the Restorer) of Poland, 241
Casimir II (the Just) of Poland, 242
Casimir III (the Great) of Poland, 314
Casimir IV, King of Bohemia, 310, 315, 316
Casimir-Périer, Auguste Casimir Victor Laurent, French statesman, 628
Casimir-Périer, Jean Paul Pierre, pres. of France, 641
Caspian region, 1153
Cass, Lewis, Democratic candidate for pres. of the U.S., 774
Cassander, 77 *f*.
Cassano, battle of, 587
Cassel, Sir Ernest, British financier, 757
Cassian of Marseilles, wrote *Institutes*, 123
Cassino, 1162
Cassiodorus, founded monastery at Beneventum, 123, 145
Cassius, Avidius, and the Sarmatian War, 111, 112
Cassius, Longinus Gaius, conspirator against Caesar, 98, 99
Cassius, Spurius, executed, 71
Cassivellaunus, king, defeated by Caesar, 97
Castagna, Giovanni Battista, Pope Urban VII, 396
Caste system, in India, 41, 42
Castelar y Ripoll, Emilio, Spanish statesman, 646, 647
Castelfidardo, battle of, 659
Castenedolo Man, 9
Castiglione, Baldassare di, Italian humanist, 393
Castiglione, battle of, 587
Castile, 164, 233 *ff*., 280 *ff*.
Castilla, Ramón, Peruvian statesman, 812 *f*.
Castillo, Ramon S., President of Argentina, 1139, 1140
Castle of Asia (*Anadoli Hissar*), 327
Castle of Europe (*Rumili Hissar*), 327
Castlereagh, Robert Stewart, Viscount, and Marquess of Londonderry, British foreign secretary, 600, 601, 604, 605
Castracani, Castruccio, 293

Castriota, George, *see* Scanderbeg
Castro, Cipriano, Venezuelan dictator, 788, 816, 817
Castro, León Cortés, pres. of Costa Rica, 1073
Castro, Gen. Pimenta de, dictatorship in Portugal, 985
Castro, Vaca de, gov. of Cuzco, 489
Catalan Co., band of mercenaries, 322
Catalonia, union with Aragon, 235, 237; Catalan republic, 390; invaded by Archduke Charles, 446; movement for autonomy, 980, 981, 982, 983
Catana, 48, 57, 59
Catania, 1162
Catargiu, Barbu, prime minister of Rumania, 720
Cateau-Cambrésis, Peace of, 383; Treaty of, 372, 388, 389, 395, 397
Catechismus Romanus, 396
Catesby, Robert, originator of the Gunpowder Plot, 374
Catharine I, Russian empress, 479
Catharine II (the Great), Empress of Russia, 468; favors Stanislas Poniatowski of Poland, 477; interference in Polish affairs, 481; armed neutrality at sea, 482; visit of Emperor Joseph II, 482, 485; Greek Scheme, 482, 485, 722; 2d war with the Turks, 482, 485; war with Sweden, 482; third partition of Poland, 482
Catharine of Aragon, first wife of Henry VIII, 369
Catharist, *see* Albigensian
Cathedral architecture, in England, 201
Cathelineau, Jacques, leader in the Vendée revolt, 582
Catherine, daughter of Charles VI of France, 270
Catherine of Braganza, married Charles II of England, 427
Catholic Emancipation Bill, 606, 663
Catholic League, led by Maximilian of Bavaria, 403
Catilina, Lucius Sergius, leader of discontented classes, 96, 100
Catinat, Nicholas, French general, 442; reduces Savoy, 444; defeated at Carpi, 445
Cato, Marcus Porcius (the elder), 89; his *Origines*, 91
Cato, Marcus Porcius (the younger), 96, 97, 98
Cato Street Conspiracy, 605
Catullus, Caius Valerius, lyric poet, 100
Catulus, Quintus Lutatius, 93, 95
Caudine Forks, 73
Caulaincourt, Armand Augustin Louis, Marquis de, French diplomat, 599, 600
Cavagnari, Sir Pierre Louis Napoleon, British agent in Afghanistan, 736, 868
Cavaignac, Louis Eugene, made dictator of France, 631
Cavalier Parliament, 426, 427, 428
Cavallotti, Felice Carlo Emanuele, radical Italian leader, 661
Cave, Stephen, report on the finances of Egypt, 831
Cave Commission, reports on claims of the South African Co., 1091
Cave-dwelling Man, in Italy, 68
Cave temples, 136
Cavendish, Lord Frederick, chief secretary for Ireland, 616
Cavendish, Henry, discovered hydrogen gas, 553
Cavendish, Thomas, English navigator, 494, 507
Cavendish, William Henry, Duke of Portland, second ministry, 437
Caves, of Palaeolithic Man, 4, 5
Caves of a Thousand Buddhas, 136
Cavite, 1167
Cavour, Count Camillo Benso di, Italian statesman, 655; becomes premier; enters Crimean War, at the Congress of Paris, 728; secret meeting with Napoleon III, war with Austria, 658; cession of Savoy and Nice; intervenes in the Papal States, 658 f.; dies, 659
Cawnpore massacre, 870
Caxton, William, English printer, 272
Cayley, Sir George, heavier-than-air machines, 556
Cecil, Edgar Algernon Robert, 1st Viscount Cecil of Chelwood, at the Paris Peace Conference, 952; treaty of mutual assistance, 959
Cecil, Sir William (Baron Burleigh), secretary of state under Queen Elizabeth, 372
Cecryphaleia, 55
Cedar Creek, battle of, 779
Cedar Mountain, battle of, 778
Cedeño, Gen. Arévalo, Venezuelan insurgent, 1070
Cedillo, Gen. Saturnino, revolt against Pres. Cárdenas of Mexico, 1076
Cedra, Pedro Aguirre, pres. of Chile, 1065
Celebes, island of, taken by the Dutch, 876; 1167
Celestine I, Pope, 141
Celestine II (Guido of Città di Castello), Pope, 219
Celestine V (St. Peter Clestine), Pope, 222
Celibacy of the clergy, decreed by local synods, 217
Cellini, Benvenuto, Italian sculptor, 393
Celman, Miguel Juárez, 808
Celtic invaders of Italy, 69; defeated Greeks at Thermopylae, 78
Celtic-speaking peoples, 16
Celts, invade Asia Minor, 37, 87, 142, 143; two stocks, 164, 166
Census of Japan, first imperial, 1124
Center Party of the Reichstag, 688
Central America, 1071; Pact of Union, 1072, 1154
Central Corporative Committee, established in Rome, 990
Central Executive Committee, China, 1141
Central Italy, Kingdom of, a proposed state in Federation, 657
Central Pacific R.R. chartered by Congress, 780
Ceos, 64
Ceramists, in China, 344
Cerezeda, Andrés de, acting gov. of Honduras, 491
Cerialis, Petillius, and Batavian revolt, 108

Cerignola, battle of, 393
Cerna, battle of, 934
Cernavoda, taken by Bulgar-German forces, 934
Cernius, Gen. Jonas, Lithuanian premier, 1043
Cernomen, battle of, 325
Cerro, Col. Luis M. Sanchez, pres. of Peru, 1068
Cerro Gordo, battle of, 773
Certosa, monastery, of Pavia, 298
Cervantes, Saavedra, Miguel de, his *Don Quijote*, 389
Cervini, Marcello, Pope Marcellus II, 396
Céspedes, Cárlos Manuel de, pres. of Cuba, 1077
Cettinje, taken by the Austrians, 927
Cetywayo, Zulu king, 853
Ceuta, taken by the Portuguese, 285
Ceylon, Tamil invasions, 339; a British crown colony, 536
Chabrias, crushed Spartan fleet, 63, 64
Chacabuco, battle of, 801
Chaco War, in South America, 1066, 1067
Chacón, Lázaro, pres. of Guatemala, 1074
Chaeronea, battle of, 65, 94
Chaga Bazar, 13
Chagar Beg, leader of the Seljuks, 254
Chagatai, son of Jenghiz Khan, 344
Chagatay Khan Suyurghatmish, Mongol ruler, 330
Chaillé-Long, Charles, African explorer, 828
Chaka, leader of the Zulus, 851
Chakri, a Siamese dynasty, 872
Chakste, Jan, pres. of Latvia, 1043
Chalcedon, 48, 63
Chalcidian League, 63
Chalcis, 52
Chalcocondylas, Laonicus, historian of the Byzantine Empire, 323
Chalcolithic (Stone and Copper) period, and culture, 2 f.
Chaldeans, 25, 27
Chaldiran, battle of, 421, 526
Chalgrove Field, battle of, 377
Challenger (H.M.S.), expedition of, 573, 895
Châlons, battles of; victory of Aurelian, 116; defeat of Huns, 121, 143, 144, 147
Chaltin, Col. Louis Napoleon (Belgian Congo), defeat of the Arab slave traders, 844
Chalukya-Chola dynasty, founded, 337
Chalukya or Solanki Rajput clan, India, 332; first dynasty, 335
Chalukyas of Kalyani, restored to power, 337
Chamber of Fasces and Corporations, in Italy, 992
Chamberlain, Joseph, British statesman, secedes from the Liberal Party, 617; colonial secretary, 618, 744; tariff reform, 619; advances to Japanese; discussions with German ambassador, 747; speech at Birmingham, 747; visit to South Africa, 857
Chamberlain, Neville, prime minister of England, 970; visit to Rome, 971, 980; resigned, 1135, 1146
Chambers of Reunions, established by Louis XIV, 443
Chambord, Henri Charles Ferdinand Marie Dieudonné, Count de, pretender to the throne of France, 637
Chambre des comptes, in Paris, 277
Chamorro, Diego, pres. of Nicaragua, 1073
Chamorro, Emiliano, pres. of Nicaragua, 792, 1073
Champa, 170
Champagne, battles of; first, 914; second, 921; third, 939
Champaubert, battle of, 600
Championnet, Jean Etienne, French general, 586
Champlain, Samuel de, explored the St. Lawrence River, 505
Champlitte, Guillaume de, 258
Champollion, Jean François, deciphered Egyptian hieroglyphics, 551
Chams, Malay people, 134; their capital sacked, 137
Ch'an, Chinese sect, 136, 341
Chancelade Man, 9
Chancellor, Sir John, high commissioner for Palestine, 1101
Chancellor, Richard, British merchant explorer, 417, 559
Chancellorsville, battle of, 778
Chandellas, Dravidian dynasty, 332
Chandragupta I (Sandracottus), founder of the Maurya dynasty, 42, 130
Chandragupta II Vikramaditya, ends Satrapy of Ujjain, 130, 132
Ch'ang-an, 133, 135, 136; western capital of the T'ang dynasty, 339
Chang Ch'ien, 133
Chang chih-tung, a leader in the Hundred Days of Reform, 882, 883, 884
Ch'ang-ch'un, occupied by Japanese, 962, 1124
Chang Hsüeh-liang, son of Chang Tso-lin, 1119; kidnaps Chiang Kai-shek, 1121
Chang Hsün, and restoration of the Manchu dynasty, 1117
Changkufeng Hill, clash of Russian and Japanese forces, 1122
Chang Ling, founder of Taoism, 135
Changsu, king of the Koguryo, 137
Chang Tso-lin, military gov. in Manchuria, 1119
Channel ports, taken by the British, 946
Chanson de Roland, 227
Chao Chung, 134
Chao dynasty, 44
Ch'ao Hsien, 133
Chao Ju-kua, traveler, 346
Chao K'uang-yin, or Tai Tsu, Chinese ruler, 342
Chao Meng-fu, Mongol painter, 346
Chao Ti, 134

Chao T'o, king of southern Yueh, 133
Chapas, a Gurjara clan, 331
Chappe, Claude, developed semaphore telegraph, 553
Chapultepec, battle of, 773; 1143
Charcot, Jean Baptiste, Etienne Auguste, Antarctic explorer, 574, 575
Chardin, Teilhard de, 8
Chares, 64
Charette de la Contrie, François Athanase, leader in the Vendee revolt, 582
Charge of the Light Brigade, battle of Balaclava, 727
Charlemagne, *see* Charles the Great
Charleroi, captured by the French revolutionary army, 583; battles of, 602, 912
Charles I, Emperor of Austria, 930; secret negotiations with French and British govts. to make peace, 936; reorganization of non-Hungarian part of monarchy, 949; abdicates, 950, 1005; returns to Hungary, 1014; march on Budapest, 957, 1014; exiled to Madeira, 957; Dethronement Act, 1014; dies, 957
Charles I of England, as Prince of Wales, 375; his first Parliament, 375; his 4th and 5th Parliament (Long Parliament), 376; royalist Parliament at Oxford, 377; in the Great Rebellion, 377 f.; sentenced to death and beheaded, 379
Charles I of Hungary, founder of the Anjou line, 317
Charles I, King of Naples and of Sicily, *see* Charles of Anjou
Charles I of Rumania, *see* Carol I
Charles II of England lands in Scotland; defeated at Worcester, 425; Declaration of Breda; proclaimed king by the Convention Parliament, 426; marries Catherine of Braganza, 427, 453; Treaty of Dover, 427; and parliament, 428
Charles II of Naples, 222, 292, 293, 318
Charles II of Rumania, *see* Carol II
Charles II, King of Spain, 445, 450
Charles III (the Simple), last Carolingian in France, 159, 160
Charles III of Naples, 292
Charles III of Spain, 452; in War of American Independence, 452, 494; reform measures, 497, 499; founded the San Carlos Academy of Fine Arts, 500, 799
Charles IV (the Fair), last Capetian of the direct line in France, 273, 276
Charles IV (Luxemburg), emperor, 288, 302; seeks to end Avignon captivity, 302; elected king of Bohemia as Charles 1, 304
Charles IV, King of Naples and Sicily, 458
Charles IV, of Spain, 452, 593
Charles V (the Wise), of France, 265; signs Peace of Bretigny, 276; reform and reconstruction, 277, 279; in Holy League against the Turks, 422; abortive expedition to Algiers, 524; his death, 277
Charles V, emperor (Charles IV of Spain), 372; wars with Francis I and with Henry II, 383; war with France, 388; expedition to Tunis, 388, 401; defeated at Algiers, 388, 401; Treaty of Cateau-Cambresis, 388; Treaty of Noyon: the Treaty of Madrid; League of Cognac; sack of Rome, 394, 400; Treaty of Crespy, 395; abdicates, 389, 402; at Diet of Worms, 400; wars with Francis, 400–401; war with Henry II of France, 402; grants land in Indies to the Welsers, 488, 496; sends an expedition to the Philippine Islands, 908
Charles VI of France, 268; attack of insanity, 277 f.; Treaty of Troyes, 270, 278; and the papal schism, 288; dies, 270
Charles VI, emperor; in War of Spanish Succession, 445 ff., 450; Pragmatic Sanction, 439 f., 463; death, 465
Charles VII, emperor, 465
Charles VII of France, crowned, 270, 278; renews war with English, 270, 279; favors Council of Basel, 279; separate Peace of Arras, 279; army reforms; treaty of alliance with Swiss cantons; retrial and rehabilitation of Jeanne Darc, 279, 293
Charles VIII of France alliance with Ludovico Sforza, 290; refused investiture by Pope Alexander VI, 293; invasion of Italy, 296, 298, 393, 409; Peace of Etaples, 369; married to Anne of Brittany; conquers Naples, 381; Treaty of Narbonne, 387; Sforza's appeal, 393
Charles VIII (Knut Knutsson) of Sweden, 313
Charles IX of France, 384
Charles IX of Sweden, 413
Charles X of France, Prince de Polignac, 627; Revolution of 1830, 628
Charles (X) (Cardinal of Bourbon) set up by the Catholic party in opposition to Henry IV, 386
Charles X, Gustavus of Sweden, 471
Charles XI of Sweden, 471
Charles XII of Sweden, 472; Northern War; battle of Poltava, 472, 479; return to Sweden, 472
Charles XIII of Sweden, 595
Charles XIV (Bernadotte) of Sweden; *see* Bernadotte
Charles XV of Sweden, 699
Charles, Cardinal of Lorraine, 383
Charles, Constable de Bourbon, battle of Pavia, 383, 394, 400; storms Rome, 400
Charles, Duke of Orléans, 278
Charles, Elector Palatine, 443
Charles, Prince of Denmark, ascends throne of Norway as Haakon VII, 701
Charles of Anjou, brother of Louis IX of France, accepts crown of Sicily, 213, 230; defeats Manfred, 213; quarrels with popes, 221; the Sicilian Vespers, 231, 247, 258, 290; Eighth Crusade, 258; defeated by Peter I of Sicily, 282; becomes Charles I, King of Naples and of Sicily, 290, 320; alliance with Baldwin II, 320; King of Albania, 321
Charles of Durazzo challenges the position of Emperor Sigismund, 317

Charles of Lorraine, Duke of Mayenne, *see* Mayenne
Charles of Lorraine, imperial general, captures Buda, 461; relieves siege of Vienna, 483
Charles of Nevers, claims Mantuan succession, 398
Charles of Valois, 222, 273, 293, 301
Charles, son of Lothair I, and the Kingdom of Provence, 157
Charles, son of Louis the German, receives Alamannia, 159
Charles, son of Pepin, 153
Charles the Bad of Navarre, 276
Charles the Bald, son of Louis the Pious, King of Italy, 152, 153, 158; King of the (West) Franks, emperor, 157, 158, 159
Charles the Bold, Duke of Burgundy, 271, 279; conference at Peronne; conquers Lorraine and makes war on Swiss cantons, 280; designs against Alsace, 306 f.; defeat and death, 271, 280
Charles the Fat, 152; king of the West Franks, 159; deposed, 160
Charles the Great (Charlemagne), Italian policy, 152; disintegration of his empire, 153; crowned emperor, 155; scholars at his court, 156, 157; invasion of Spain, 163; cited, 220; recognized Venice as Byzantine territory, 224; war of Christian reconquest of Spain, 162
Charles Albert, Elector of Bavaria, 465; emperor as Charles VII, 465
Charles Albert, King of Sardinia, 651, 654; abdicates, 655
Charles Anthony, Prince, father of Leopold of Hohenzollern-Sigmaringen, 687
Charles Augustus Christian, Duke of the Palatinate of Zweibrucken, 468, 469
Charles Edward, the Young Pretender, lands in Scotland, 435; defeated at Culloden, 435, 466
Charles Emanuel I of Savoy, 398
Charles Emanuel II of Savoy, 398, 457
Charles Emanuel III of Savoy, 458
Charles Felix of Sardinia, 651; 654
Charles Frederick, Duke of Holstein-Gottorp, his struggle with Denmark, 471; abandoned by Sweden, 472
Charles Ludwig, Archduke, brother of Emperor Francis II, 585; advances against Napoleon, 585; defeats Jourdan, 585; defeats Massena, 587; reorganizes Austrian army; begins invasion of Bavaria; defeated at Wagram, 595; agrees to Treaty of Schonbrunn, 595
Charles Robert of Hungary, 313, 315, 317
Charles Theodore, Elector Palatine, 468
Charleston surrenders to the British, 522
Charlotte Dundas, first practical steamboat, 553
Charte constitutionelle, Louis XVIII's constitution, 601
Charter Oak, 512
Charter of Franchises and Liberties for New York, 512
Charter of Lorris, 227
Charter of Worms, 206
Chartered companies, in Spanish America, 500
Charters, their sale by Henry I, 193
Chartist movement, 609
Charykov, Nikolai Valerianovich, Russian ambassador at Constantinople, 758
Chase, Salmon Portland, American statesman, 774
Chashtana, founds a dynasty of western satraps, 129
Chaslav, made first effort to unite Serbs, 246
Chastenoy, Peace of, 384
Château clique, in Lower Canada, 795
Château Gaillard, on the Seine, 229
Château-Thierry, battle of, 600
Chateaubriand, François René, Viscount de, French author and statesman, 663
Châtelperron, 5
Chatham, William Pitt, Earl of, British prime minister, 435, 436, 520
Chatillon brothers, leaders of the Huguenots, 384
Chattanooga, battle of, 779
Chaucer, Geoffrey, English poet, 267
Chauhan, King of Ajmer, 332
Chaumette, Pierre Gaspard, French revolutionist, 583
Chaumont, Treaties of, 600, 604
Chauny, in the World War, 938, 945
Chauri Chaura affair, in India, 1112
Chautemps, Camille, French premier, 979
Chauvin, Pierre, French colonizer, 505
Cheesman, Albert, Antarctic explorer, 576
Chefoo Convention, 880
Cheilon, King of Sparta, 50, 80
Chellean industry, 6
Chelmsford, Frederic John Napier Thesiger, Baron, viceroy of India, 1111
Chelyuskin, Lt. Simeon, Arctic explorer, 562
Chemin des Dames, taken by the French, 939
Cheng Ch'eng-kung, wrested Formosa from the Dutch, 537
Cheng Chih-lung, executed at Peking, 537
Cheng Chin, 539
Ch'eng Hao, initiated the Public Services Act, 343
Cheng Ho, chief eunuch of Yung Lo reign, 347; established tributary relations between Malay states and the Ming Empire, 348
Ch'eng I, discovered the *Ta Hsüeh*, 343
Cheng K'o-shuang, surrendered Formosa, 539
Ch'eng-tu, 135; *see also* I-chou
Cheng-tzu-yai, 14
Ch'en Jung, Chinese painter, 344
Chen-la, kingdom of, 137
Ch'en Leng, kills king of the Liu-Ch'iu Island, 137
Cheops, 23
Chepren, 23

Chera, 129
Cherasco, armistice of, 458; Treaty of, 387, 398
Cherbourg, captured by Allies, 1163
Cherbourg peninsula, 1159
Cherkassy, 1154
Chernaia, battle of, 657
Chernyshevsky, Nicholas Gavrilovich, Russian revolutionary, 705
Cherry Valley massacre, 521
Chersonese, 52, 63, 64
Chesapeake-Leopard affair, 768
Chesmé, battle of, 484
Chesney, Capt. Francis, Near Eastern explorer, 715
Che Tsung, Chinese reformer, 312
Chevalier, Michel, French political economist, 549
Cheyenne Indians, 780
Ch'i, 44
Chia Ching reign of Jen Tsung, 877
Chia Ching reign of Shih Tsung, 536, 543
Chiang Kai-shek, Chinese soldier and statesman, 1118; his northern campaign; new govt. at Nanking, 1118; gets control of Kwantung, 1118, 1120; kidnapped by Gen. Chang Hsüeh-liang, 1121; war with Japan, 1123, 1141, 1143, 1165, 1170
Chiang Sheng, Chinese scholar, 541
Ch'iang Tibetans, 134, 135
Chiao-chih, 134
Chiara, battle of, 445
Chibcha Indians, 20, 361, 488
Chichimec culture, 360
Chickamauga, battle of, 778
Ch'ien Hsuan, Mongol painter, 346
Chien-K'ang, 135
Chien, king, 128
Ch'ien Lung reign of Kao Tsung, 540
Ch'ien Ta-hsin, commentator on Chinese history, 541
Chigi, Flavio, nephew of Pope Alexander VII, 456
Chih-i, founder of the T'ien-t'ai school, 136
Chihli province renamed Hopei, 1119
Chi Ku Ko, 537
Child labor, legislation on, 790
Child marriage, 42
Childeric, Frankish king, 147
Children's Crusade, 257
Chile, 810; 808 ff., 1064 ff., 1155
Chilean Nitrate Co., 812
Chin, 44
Ch'in, 44, 45
Chin (or Kin) dynasty, 343
Ch'in dynasty, established, 132
Chin Hills, reduced by the British, 872
Chin Khan, see Nurhachi
Ch'in Kuei, Chinese ruler, 343
Ch'in Shih Huang Ti, 135
Ch'in Tsung, 343
China, in the Palaeolithic period, 6; language and civilization, 44; early history of, 44 ff.; 132 ff.; medieval, 345 ff.; modern, 541 ff.; 877 ff.; 1117 ff.; 1138, 1139, 1144, 1165 f., 1171
Chinese Eastern Railway, 882, 1035, 1120
Chinese Exclusion Act, passed by U.S. Congress, 783
Chinese Immigrants Act, in New Zealand, 907
Chinese labor, in the Transvaal, 619; in Australian colonies, 901
Chinese Republic, 1141
Chinese Revolution, breaks out, 884
Ch'ing dynasty, 537
Ching Ti, Chinese emperor, 347
Chinu culture, 20
Chios, 47 passim; battle of, 80
Chippewa, battle of, 769
Chippewa Plains, battle of, 793
Chir Tope, 128
Ch'i-shan, signs Ch'uanpi convention, 879
Chisholm v. Georgia, U.S. Supreme Ct. decision, 764
Chitral, disputed succession, 871
Chivington, Col. John Milton, and massacre of Indians at Sand Creek, 780
Ch'i-ying, signs Treaty of Whanghsia, 879
Chkalov, Valery Pavlovich, flew non-stop over North Pole, 558, 567
Chlodio, son of Merowech, 147
Chlorine gas, in World War, 921
Chloris, see Constantius
Chlothar, see Lothair
Cho-chun, 137
Ch'oe family, in Korea, 348
Ch'ŏei, Takano, favored opening Japan, 888
Chokier, Baron Surlet de, regent of Belgium, 622
Chola dynasty, of Tamil kings, 337
Ch'ŏlchong, King of Korea, 885
Cholera, 552
Chollet, battle of, 583
Cholm, taken by Austro-Germans, 922
Choral poetry, in Sparta, 50
Chorotegan culture, 20
Chōsen, Japanese name for Korea, 137, 887, 893
Chosen Council of Russia, 415
Chōshū, Satsuma fief of Japan, 889
Chosŏn (Jap.: Chosen), name of Korea, 137
Chosrew Pasha, Turkish grand vizier, 725
Chosroes, Parthian monarch, 110, 124
Chotusitz, battle of, 465
Ch'ou An Hui, Chinese monarchist society, 1117

Chou, change of name in a Chinese dynasty, 341
Chou dynasty, 44, 134
Chou-kou-tien, finding of skulls of Peking Man, 6, 8
Chou Ta-kuan, and the Mongol embassy, 345
Chou Tun-i, evolves a conception of causation, 343
Chouans, French insurgents, 584
Chou-li, Chinese ritual, 134
Chremonidean War, started by Ptolemy I, 79, 84
Chremonides, 79
Chrétien de Troyes, and the Arthurian romances, 231
Christ, controversy over substance, 119; the monophysite heresy, 123, 130, 134, 174; designation of Peter as founder of the Church, 141
Christian I (of Oldenburg), King of Denmark, Norway, and Sweden, 313
Christian II of Denmark, 410
Christian III of Denmark, 410
Christian IV of Denmark subsidy from Charles I, 375; defeated by Tilly, 405; Treaty of Lubeck, 405; war with Sweden, 407; in Thirty Years War; wars of Kalmar, 410
Christian VI of Denmark, 474
Christian VII of Denmark, 474
Christian VIII of Denmark, 697
Christian IX of Denmark, 681, 697
Christian X of Denmark, 699, 1045
Christian of Anhalt, defeated at battle of the White Mountain, 404
Christian of Brunswick, defeated by Tilly, 404
Christian Frederick, Danish Prince, 699
Christian, Prince of Holstein-Augustenburg, heir to Swedish throne, 595
Christian Era, 11, 13, 14, 18; its beginning, 102
Christian League, anti-Semitic organization in Rumania, 1026
Christian literature, proscribed in China, 877
Christian Socialists, in Austria, 1006
Christianity, 109; origin, 113; growth, 117, 118, 125; introduced into Saxony, 153; bureau for its care in China, 346; appearance in Japan, 544; introduced into Korea, 885; again permitted in Japan, 890
Christians, persecution in Rome, 106; in Trajan's administration, 110; 113; persecution by Decius, 115; Edict of Milan, 119; persecution spreads through Persia and Armenia, 125; exercise of religion guaranteed, 126; driven from Spain, 163; reconquer Spain, 164; persecution in Japan, 546; expelled from Annam, 874; persecution in Korea, 881, 885
Christianson, Hendrick, fur trader, 510
Christina, daughter of Henry IV of France, 398, 457
Christine, Queen of Sweden, 413, 471
Christophe, Henri, leader of the uprising in Haiti, 825
Christopher of Bavaria, ruler of Scandinavia, 313
Christopher, King of Denmark, 203
Christopher II of Denmark, 312
Chronicle (Anglo-Saxon), 167
Chrysler Corp. strike, 1056
Chrysoloras, Manuel, Greek scholar, 294
Chrysopolis, 119
Chrysostom, John, Patriarch of Constantinople, 123
Ch'u, 44
Chuang Chou, 45
Ch'uanpi Convention, 879
Chu-fu Yen, 133
Chu Hsi, Chinese philosopher, 343, 536, 537, 542, 546
Chu I-kuie, leads revolt in Formosa, 539
Chu I-tsun, author of Ching I K'ao, 540
Chu-ko Liang, chief minister of Shu dynasty, 135
Chulalonkorn, Phra Maha, founder of modern Siam, 873
Chün Chi Ch'u, Chinese military council, 540
Chungjong, Korean ruler, 542
Chungking, new capital of China, 1122, 1165, 1166
Church, Sir Richard, and Greek independence, 723
Church, William, designed first typesetting machine, 554
Church and state, their separation demanded by Roger Williams, 509 f.; attacks of French writers, 578, 637, 642; law in Portugal, 650; Spanish constitution proclaims separation, 982
Church of England, 372
Church of St. Sophia in Constantinople, 173
Church of the Holy Apostles (Ste. Geneviève), at Paris, 147
Church property, confiscated by the Soviet govt., 1030
Churchill, John (later Duke of Marlborough), British soldier, 429
Churchill, Winston Leonard Spencer, British statesman, 919, 920; prime minister, 1135 passim.
Churchill government, given vote of confidence, 1136
Churubusco, battle of, 773
Chūshingura ("Forty-Seven Rōnin") Incident, 548
Chu Te, a leader of landless Chinese, 1119
Chutu branch of the Satakani, 132
Chu Yuan-chang (Ming T'ai T'su), founder of the Ming dynasty, 346
Ciano, Count Nobile Galeazzo, Italian foreign minister, 992, 1012, 1139
Cibalae, 119
Cicero, Marcus Tullius, 69, 71, 89; prosecutes Verres, 95; his Orations Against Catiline, 96; executed, 99; influence on his age, 100; his De Officiis cited, 142
Ciceronian (language), Age, 112
Cid (Rodrigo Diaz) hero of Spain, 233
Cierva, Juan de la, designed the autogiro, 557
Cilicia, 65 passim; ravages of Arabs, 175; invaded, 187; ravaged by Byzantines, 189

Cilician Gates, in Asia Minor, 36, 114
Cimarosa, Domenico, Italian composer, 454
Cimbri, German or Celtic people, 93
Cimmerians, 27; invasion of Phrygia, 37; of Armenia, 38; destroyed Kingdom of Phrygia, 48
Cimon, defeated the Persians, 55; returns from exile, 56
Cincinnati, 778
Cincinnatus, Lucius Quinctius, 71, 72
Cinématographe, 556
Cinna, Lucius Cornelius, 93, 94, 96
Cinque Ports, 199
Cinvat bridge, 39
C.I.O. in strikes, 1056
Circassian officers' conspiracy against Egyptian govt., 831
Circus Maximus, 70
Cirrha, 52
Cirta, 92
Cisalpine Republic proclaimed, 585; renamed the Italian Republic, 590
Cisjuran Kingdom of Burgundy, established, 157, 159
Cisneros, Cardinal Jimenez de, Spanish statesman, 388
Cisplatine Province (Banda Oriental), 817
Cistercians, arrive in England, 193, 196, 228; influence on architecture in Spain, 235
Ciudad Real, military revolt, 981
Civil Code, enacted in Germany, 692
Civil Dominion, doctrines of John Wiclif, 266
Civil marriage, obligatory in the German Empire, 689; restored in Austria, 694; made compulsory in Turkey, 1096
Civil Rights Bill, passed, 780
Civil service, under Augustus, 101; reformed in England, 615
Civil Service Commission, in Canada, 797
Civil Service Law, in Nazi Germany, 1001
Civil War (U.S.), 776 *ff.*
Civil War, in Britain, 377; Second Civil War, 378
Civil War, in Spain, 983 *ff.*
Civil-Works Emergency Relief Act, 1054
Civilis, Julius, 108
Clactonian industry, 5, 6
Clam-Martinitz, Count Richard, Austrian prime minister, 931, 942
Clans, in Japan, 139
Clapperton, Hugh, African explorer, 826
Clarence, Duke of, 275
Clarendon (Sir Edward Hyde), Earl of, English statesman, 427, 428, 513
Clarendon, George William Frederick Villiers, 4th Earl of, British foreign minister, 726, 728
Clarendon Code, 426
Clark, George Rogers, American explorer and soldier, 521
Clark, Joshua Reuben, Memorandum of, on the Monroe Doctrine, 1052
Clark, William, member of the Lewis and Clark expedition, 768, 773
Clarke, James Freeman, American missionary, 717
Classical Comment of the Reigning Ch'ing Dynasty, 877
Classicus, Julius, 108
Clastidium, battle of, 87
Claudia, daughter of Louis XII, 382
Claudius (Tiberius Claudius Drusus), Roman emperor, 105; conquers Britain, 106, 166; marries Agrippina, 106, 113
Claudius II, Marcus Aurelius "Gothicus," first of Illyrian emperors, 116
Claudius, court poet, 123
Clausewitz, Karl von, Prussian general and military theorist, 594
Claverhouse, John Graham, 1st Viscount of Dundee, British royalist general, 428, 430
Clavering, Capt. Douglas Charles, Arctic explorer, 562
Clavière, Étienne, French statesman, 581
Clay, Henry, American statesman, 771, 772, 773, 774
Clayton, Sir Gilbert, high commissioner for Iraq, 1105
Clayton (Henry De Lamar) Anti-Trust Act, 791
Clayton, John Middleton, 788
Clayton-Bulwer Treaty, 774, 788, 818, 820
Clazomenae, 60
Cleander, 112
Clearidas, 59
Cleisthenes, 48, 52, 70
Cleitus, 65
Clemenceau, Georges Eugène Benjamin, French premier, 636, 639, 643; forms ministry. 941; at the Paris Peace Conference, 951; defeated for the presidency, 976
Clemens, Flavius, executed for atheism, 109
Clement II (Suidger), Pope, 206, 217
Clement IV (Gui Foulques), Pope, 213
Clement V (Bertrand de Gouth), Pope, and annates in England, 200; residence at Avignon, 222 *f.*, 232; suppression of the Order of Knights Templar, 232; 288; urges expedition to Italy, 301
Clement VI (Pierre Roger), Pope, and the revolution of Cola di Rienzi, 286
Clement VII (Giulio de' Medici), Pope, 278, 288
Clement VIII (Ippolito Aldobrandini), Pope, 396 *f.*
Clement IX (Giulio Rospigliosi), Pope, and mediation between Jansenists and Jesuits, 455
Clement X (Emilio Altieri), Pope, 455
Clement XI (Giovanni Francesco Albani), Pope, 455, 539
Clement XII (Lorenzo Corsini), Pope, 457
Clement XIII (Carlo della Torre de Rezzonico), Pope, 457
Clement XIV (Lorenzo Ganganelli), Pope, 457

Clément, Jacquet, murderer of Henry III, 386
Clement, neo-Platonist, 117
Clement, Prince of Bavaria, 443
Cleombrotus, defeated by Epaminondas, 63
Cleomenes I of Sparta, 50, 52
Cleomenes III, king, slain in Egypt, 79; 80
Cleon, leader of radicals in Athens, 58, 59
Cleonymus, 78, 79
Cleopatra I, regent for Ptolemy VI, 85
Cleopatra VII, 84, 90
Cleopatra Thea, 82
Cleophon, 60, 61
Cleph, succeeds Alboin, 150
Clericus laicos, bull of Boniface VIII, 200, 222, 232
Clermont, first successful steamboat, 553
Clermont, Synod of, 219, 255
Cleveland (city), established, 766
Cleveland, Stephen Grover (22d pres. of U.S.), defeats James G. Blaine, 783; defeated by Benjamin Harrison, 784; Pullman strike, 785; elected as 24th pres., 786; annexation of Hawaii, 910
Cleves-Julich succession, 386
Clifford, Lord George, attacked Puerto Rico, 824
Clifford, Thomas, 1st Baron Clifford of Chudleigh, a member of the Cabal, 427
Climate, evidence for dating, 2; changes, 3, 5; in Europe, 14; periods in Baltic region, 15
Climatic optimum, period of, 15
Clinton, George, vice-pres. of U.S., 768
Clinton, Sir Henry, British general, 521
Clive, Robert, British colonial soldier, seizure of Arcot, 534; battle of Plassey, 535
Cloaca Maxima, 70
Clodius, Publius, 96, 97
Cloelia, 71
Clonard monastery established, 169
Cloots, Jean Baptiste Du Val de Grace, Baron von, French revolutionary, 583
Clotilda, married to Clovis, 147
Clovis, 19
Clovis (Chlodovech), king of the Franks, 145, 147
Clubs, French Revolution, 580, 631
Cluny, France, 167, 191
Cnidus, 47, 62
Cnossus, 46, 47
Coal miners' strikes in England, 967, 968
Coalition, Third, against France, 437
Coanda, Gen. Constantine, Rumanian premier, 949
Coates, Joseph Gordon, prime minister of New Zealand, 1131, 1132
Cobbett, William, English journalist, 605
Cobden, Richard, British free trader, 611
Cobden-Chevalier Treaty, 613
Cobham, Alan, British aviator, 1081
Cobham, Henry Brooke, 8th Baron, plot to put Arabella Stuart on throne, 373
Cobham, Lord, *see* Oldcastle, Sir John
Coburg, Josias, Duke of, at Neerwinden, 582; at Fleurus, 583;
Cochrane, Lord Thomas, and Greek independence, 723; liberation of Peru, 801 805
Cocks, Richard, English industrialist, 546
Code Civil Ottoman, 728
Code of Hammurabi, 26, 27
Code of laws, Hittite, 36
Code of Lubeck, 307
Codex Justinianus, 173
Codos, Paul, world distance record in airplane, 558
Codreanu, Corneliu, leader of the Iron Guard in Rumania, 1026
Codrington, Sir Edward, British admiral, 723
Coele-Syria, 81, 84
Coercion Acts, 605
Coercion Bill in Ireland, 607
Coeur, Jacques, French financier, 279
Cohens *v.* Virginia, 770
Coinage, early, 37, 52, 56, 115
Coke, Sir Edward, English chief justice, 374
Colbert, Jean Baptiste, French controller-gen. of the finances, 442
Colchis, 93
Cold Harbor, battle of, 779
Coleman, Edward, confessor of the Duchess of York, 428
Colenso, John William, Bishop, translated Bible into Maori, 905
Colenso, battle of, 857
Colfax, Schuyler, accused in Credit Mobilier scandal, 782
Coligny, Adm. Gaspard de, 384, 505
Colijn, Dr. Hendryk, Dutch premier, 976
Colindres, Vicente Mejia, pres. of Honduras, 1074
Coliseum (or Colosseum) begun, 108, 113
College of Cardinals, established, 218
College of William and Mary, chartered, 513
Colley, Sir George Pomeroy, British general, 854
Colline Gate, battle of the, 94
Collins, Michael, Irish statesman, 972
Collinson, Capt. Richard, Arctic explorer, 564
Collip, James Bertram, on insulin treatment, 553
Colloredo, Rudolf, Imperial general, 406
Collot d'Herbois, Jean Marie, French revolutionary, 581, 582; conspiracy against Robespierre, 583; transported, 584
Cologne, 1164; Elector of, in the Grand Alliance War, 445
Coloman (Kalman) I of Hungary, 245

Colombia, United States of, 488, 799, 802 *f.*, 814 *ff.*, 1069 *ff.*
Colombo, Fernando, son of Columbus, 366
Colonia, founded, 501
Colonial Currency Act, 517 *f.*
Colonna, the, 293
Colonna, Sciarra, 222, 232
Colophon, 47
Color photography, first, 554
Colorado, as a territory, 780; admitted to statehood, 784, 790
Colorados, political party in Paraguay and Uruguay, 810, 811
Colored motion pictures, 557
Colt, Samuel, invented the revolver, 554, 772
Columba, Celtic missionary, 168, 169
Columban, St., of Leinster, Irish missionary, 146, 169
Columbus, Bartholomew, brother of Christopher, 367
Columbus, Christopher, 367 *f.*, 496, 824
Columbus, Diego, son of Christopher, 496
Column of Marcus, 113
Column of Trajan, 113
Combe-Capelle Man, 9
Combes, Émile, French premier, 642
Combination Acts in England, 606
Combines Investigation Act in Canada, 1060
Comitats, provincial govts. of Hungary, 317, 318
Comité d'Études du Haut-Congo, later the International Association of the Congo, 843
Commagene, 82, 103
Commercial Co. of Brazil, 502
Commines, Philippe de, French chronicler, 280, 296
Commission of the Luxembourg, 630
Commissioner of Indian Affairs, created, 771
Committee of General Security, 582
Committee of Imperial Defense, 619
Committee of Liberty, Turkish revolutionary group, 731
Committee of Public Safety, 582
Committee of Union and Progress, Young Turk organization, 731
Committees of Correspondence in Massachusetts, 518
Commodity Credit Corporation, 1141
Commodus, Lucius Aelius Aurelius, Roman emperor, 111, 112, 113
Commodus, Lucius Ceionius, 111
Common law in England, 195
Common Sense, Thomas Paine's pamphlet, 520
Commonwealth, 1649–1660 in England, 425
Commonwealth of Australia, *see* Australia
Commune of 1871, 637
Commune of Paris, 582, 583; 540
Commune of Rome, 219
Communications Act, 1055
Communism, 550; outlawed in Czechoslovakia, 1013; outlawed in Bulgaria, 1023; measures against it in Finland, 1048; illegal in Argentina, 1064; trial of leaders in Brazil, 1071; suppressed in Turkey, 1096; admitted to Kuo Min Tang in China, 1118
Communist Manifesto, by Karl Marx, 550
Communist Party, in Finland, 1143; in France, 1144
Comnenus, Andronicus, Byzantine emperor, 253
Comnenus, David, Emperor of Trebizond, 259
Comnenus, Isaac, Byzantine emperor, 249
Comnenus, John, Byzantine emperor, 252
Comnenus, Manuel, Byzantine emperor, wars with Hungarians, 252 *f.*; war with Venice, 253; war against the Seljuks, 253
Compactata of the Council of Basel, 302, 305
Compagnie du Canal Interocéanique, Panama Canal Co., 640
Compagnie des Indes Orientales, 534, 535
Compagnie d'Occident, which became *Compagnie des Indes*, 507
Company of the Hundred Associates, 505
Company of Isles of America, 505
Company of St. Christopher, 505
Companys, Luis, pres. of Catalonia, 983
Compass, mariner's, 343
Compiègne, 1148
Compisteguy, Juan, pres. of Uruguay, 1067
Compromise of Breda, 379
Compromise of 1107, in England, 193
Compromise of 1850, passed by U.S. Congress, 774
Compromise of 1867, in Austria, 678
Compon, Henry, Bishop of London, 429
Compulsory military service in France, 977; in Nazi Germany, 1002; in England, 929; in Canada, 1057
Comstock Lode, silver mine in Nevada, 783
Comte, Auguste, founder of Positivism, 550
Comuneros, uprising against Charles I, 388
Concentration camps, in Nazi Germany, 1001
Concha, José Vicente, pres. of Colombia, 816
Conciliar Movement, 288, 289, 302, 304
Concini, Concino, Italian statesman, 384
Concord, battle of, 520
Concordat between the papacy and Spain, 451, 645 *f.*
Concordat of Bologna, 382, 394
Concordat (1801) between France and the papacy, 588, 595, 642 *f.*
Concordat of 1482, 282
Concordat of 1741, 458
Concordat of Vienna, 304
Concordat of Worms, 208, 210, 219
Condé, Louis II de Bourbon, Prince of, French general, 407, 440, 442
Condé, Louis Henry Joseph, Prince of, French émigré leader, 579, 583
Conduriotis, Adm. Paul, *see* Kondouciottis, Adm. Paul

Confédéracion Regional Obrera Mexicana (Confederation of Labor), 1075
Confederate States of America, 776
Confédération Générale du Travail, in France, 641, 643
Confédération Générale des Bignerons, 643
Confederation of Bar, in Poland, 477
Confederation of Cologne, 309
Confederation of Europe, 603
Confederation of Milhaud, 384
Confederation of Radom, in Poland, 315
Confederation of Targowitz, in Poland, 477
Confederation of Vilna, 415
Confederation of the Equator, formed in Brazil, 817
Confederation of the Rhine, 592, 600
Conference of Calais, 270
Conference of Gela, 57
Confession of Augsburg, 401, 402, 413
Confession of Faith, adopted by the Scotch Estates, 372
Confessional Church, in Nazi Germany, 1001
Confessions of Augustine, 142
Confirmation of Charters, 200
Conflans, Treaty of, 279
Confucianism, in China, 133; in Japan, 546
Confucius (K'ung Ch'iu), his teachings, 45; Annals of, 133; Chinese rites to, 539; growth in Japan, 546
Congo, African Kingdom, 843
Congo Free State, 623, 739, 743, 844 *f.*; treaty with, 843, 847
Congregatio de propaganda fide, 397
Congregationalists, 372
Congress at Prague, 599
Congress at Utrecht, 446
Congress of Aix-la-Chapelle, 604
Congress of Angostura, proclaimed Great Colombia, 803
Congress of Berlin, 616, 710, 729, 736
Congress of Chatillon, 600
Congress of Erfurt, 594
Congress of Oppressed Austrian Nationalities, 949, 1016
Congress of Paris, 657, 719, 728
Congress of Rastadt, 586, 587
Congress of Troppau and Laibach, 604
Congress of Verona, 604
Congress of Vienna, 601, 666
Connaught, Arthur William Patrick Albert, Duke of, gov.-gen. of Canada, 619, 797
Connecticut, charter granted, 512
Connecticut Western Reserve, 766
Conon, Athenian commander, 61, 62, 63
Conquest of Constantinople, by Geoffroi de Villehardouin, 231
Conquistadores, 486
Conrad I, German emperor, 160
Conrad II (the Salian), German emperor, 158; campaign against Stephen of Hungary, 205, 245; recovers Lusatia, 205; his *constitutio de feudis*, 217, 223; divides Poland, 241
Conrad III, German emperor, on Second Crusade, 209, 256; renewal of expansion against Slavs and Scandinavians, 209
Conrad IV, German emperor, and King of Sicily, 213
Conrad, King of Arles, 161
Conrad, son of Frederick II, 213
Conrad, son of Henry IV of Germany, 207
Conrad of Masovia, Duke of Poland, 214 *f.*, 242
Conradi, Maurice, 994
Conradin, son of Conrad IV, 213
Consalvi, Ercole, Cardinal, papal diplomat, 601, 663
Conscription, introduced in England, 970; adopted for Ireland, 972; reintroduced in Austria, 1008; introduced in French West Africa, 1088
Consecration of bishops, in the Roman Church, 169
Consolidated Goldfields, 854
Conspiracy of Catiline, 96
Conspiracy of Minas, 502
Conspiracy of Pontiac, 516 *f.*
Constance, daughter of Manfred of Sicily, 213, 282, 290
Constance, daughter of Roger II, 210, 223
Constance, Peace of, 210; 306
Constans, son of Constantine, 120
Constans II (Constantinus), grandson of Heraclius, 151, 174
Constantia, 127
Constantine (Flavius Valerius Constantinus I the Great), 117, 119, 120, 121, 220
Constantine IV (Pogoratus), Byzantine emperor, 174
Constantine V (Kopronymos), Byzantine emperor, 176
Constantine VI, Byzantine emperor, 176, 177
Constantine VII (Porphyrogenitus), Byzantine emperor, 181, 183
Constantine VIII, Byzantine emperor, 248
Constantine IX (Monomachus), Byzantine emperor, 249
Constantine X (Dukas), Byzantine emperor, 249
Constantine XI, last Byzantine emperor, 323, 327
Constantine, King of Greece, 712, 920, 926, 932; abdicates, 940; restored; again abdicates, 1021
Constantine, Russian Grand Duke, 702
Constantinople, made Constantine's capital, 119, 120; conquered by the crusaders, 122; under siege, 127; indifferent to fate of Italy, 150; equality of Patriarchates of Constantinople and Rome, 151; Arabs, siege, 174, 175; schism with Rome, 178; blockaded by Byzantine fleet, 186; Moslem advance, 188; in Fourth Crusade, 254; 258; Greek army retakes city, 260; capture by the Turks, 290, 304, 322 *f.*; becomes the Turkish capital, 326 *f.*; occupied by a British force, 1094; evacuated by the Allies, 1095; name changed to Istanbul, 1096; Treaties of, 299, 719, 761, 833; 1151

Constantinople Conference, 734, 735
Constantinus II, Roman emperor, 120, 121
Constantius, Roman emperor, 121
Constantius II, Roman emperor, 120
Constantius, Flavius Valerius, Roman emperor, 118, 119, 125
Constantza taken by Bulgar-German forces, 934
Constituent Assembly in Spain, 982
Constitutio de feudis, 217
Constitution (U.S.S.) captures the *Guerrière*, 769
Constitution of Apatzingan, 804
Constitution of Radom, 413
Constitution of 1793, French, 582
Constitution of 1795, French, 584
Constitution of 1812, Spanish, 596, 643; of 1834 (Estatuto Real) of 1837, 645; of 1876, 647
Constitution of 1875, French, 637, 638
Constitution of U.S., 523
Constitutional Convention, at Philadelphia, 523
Constitutional Convention, in South Africa, 858
Constitutional Democratic Party (K.D. = *Cadet*), Russian progressives, 707
Constitutions of Clarendon, 194
Constitutions of Melfi, 212
Consulado, founded at Burgos, 387
Consulate, a French system of govt., 587
Consuls, of Milan, executive body, 297
Consuls of the Sea, established by Florence, 294
Consulship, law on re-election, 89
Conti, Nicolo di, traveler, 541
Continental Congress, first, 520; second, 520; calls a Constitutional Convention, 523
Continental System, inaugurated by Napoleon, 592
Continental Union Association, in Canada, 797
Contreras, Gen. Eleazar López, pres. of Venezuela, 1070
Convention Parliament, in England, 1660, 426, 429, 430
Conventions
    Alexandria, 725
    Alkmar, 597
    Cordoba, 804
    El Arish, 586
    Gastein, 681
    London (1861), 634; (1884), 854
    Marsa, 838
    Passau, 402
    Tauroggen, 598
    Uppsala, 413
    Vergara, 645
"Conversion of Nanda," 129
Convicts, at Botany Bay, 895; at Port Jackson (Sydney), 896; last to land in New South Wales, 900; last of them landed in West Australia, 902
Convocation, parliament of the clergy, 200
Convoy system, 1149
Conway, Henry Seymour, British statesman, 436
Conway, Sir Martin, Arctic explorer, 566
Conway Cabal, 521
Cook, Dr. Frederick Albert, Arctic explorer, 566
Cook, Capt. James, British explorer, 562, 571, 894 *f.*, 904; second voyage, 571; Sandwich Islands, 571, 895, 910; annexed South Georgia, 571; explorations on Alaskan coast, 798; discovered Christmas Island, 895; named east coast of Australia, 896
Cook, Sir Joseph, premier of Australia, 904
Cook Islands, under British protectorate, 896; annexed to New Zealand, 908
Coolidge, Calvin, 30th pres. of U.S., 1051, 1079, 1133
Cope, John Lachlan, Antarctic explorer, 576
Copenhagen, 1159
Copper Age, 11, 13
"Co-prosperity sphere," 1170
Coral Sea, battle of, 1167
Corbeil, Treaty of, 230, 237
Corbiesdale, battle of, 425
Corbulo, Gnaeus Domitius, 106
Corcud, a son of Bayazid II, 421
Corcyra, 46, 48, 58
Corday, Charlotte, assassinated Marat, 582
Corded Ware, 16
Cordeliers, French revolutionary club, 221; 580
Córdoba, Francisco Hernández de, Spanish conquistador, 488, 490, 491
Cordova, Spain, Omayyad dynasty, 164, 188; intellectual center of Europe, 163, 164
Córdova, Gonzalo, pres. of Ecuador, 1069
Cordova, Gonzalvo de, Spanish commander, 387, 393
Cordova, Jorge, pres. of Bolivia, 811
Corfinium, 93
Corfu, Pact of, 1016
Corfu incident, 988, 1021
Corinth, 46 *passim*
Corinth Canal, in Greece, 710
Corinthian War, 62
Corinthians, 55, 56, 58
Coriolanus, Gnaeus Marcius, 71
Corn Law in England, 604, 605, 606, 611, 612
Cornaro, Catharine, widow of James of Lusignan, 299
Cornu, Mme., 719
Cornwallis, Lord Charles, British commander, surrenders at Yorktown, 436, 522; battle of Camden, 522; gov.-gen. of India, 535; his Code of reforms, 536

Coronado, Francisco Vasquez de, gov. of New Galicia, 492
Coronation Durbar at Delhi, 871
Coronation stone of Scone, 199
Coronea, 56, 62
Coronel, battle of, 918
Corradini, Enrico, Italian nationalist writer, 662
Correggio, Antonio Allegri, Italian painter, 393
Corregidor, 1167
Corrupt and Illegal Practices Act, in England, 616 *f.*
Corsairs (French), 494
Corsica, under Moslem domination, 158; declared a papal fief, 218; subjugated by the French, 459; 141
Corte Real, Gaspar de, Portuguese explorer, 368
Corte Real, Michael de, brother of the foregoing, 368
Cortes, Hernando, Spanish conquistador, conquered Mexico, 486, 488, 490 *f.*; gov. and capt.-gen. of New Spain, 491, 492; expedition to the Philippine Islands, 908
Córtes of Spain, its origin, 280, 282; in the new Spanish constitution, 982, 983, 1139
Corti, Lodovico, Count, representative of Italy at the Congress of Berlin, 736
Corunna, battle of, 594
Corupedium, battle of, 78
Corvinus, Mathias (the Just), King of Hungary, 306; struggles against George Podiebrad, 318
Corvus, Marcus Valerius, 73
Cos, 47 *passim*; battle of, 79, 84
Cosa, Juan de la, commander of Columbus' vessels, 366
Cosgrave, William Thomas, pres. of the executive council of the Irish Free State, 972, 973
Cosimo III, grand Duke of Tuscany, 459
Cossack Brigade, established in Persia, 864, 865
Cossacks, Russian, and the conquest of Siberia, 415; conflict with boyars, 418; revolt in south and east, 418; under Stephen Razin, lead peasant revolt, 478
Cossus, Aulus Cornelius, 72
Costa, Gen. Gomes da, Portuguese revolutionary, 985
Costa Rica, 805, 819, 1071, 1072, 1073
Coste, Capt. Dieudonné, French aviator, 557
Cotta, Lucius Aurelius, 95
Cotton Control Act, 1053
Council for Mine plunder, 508
Council of Ancients (Elders), 584, 585
Council of Arles, 119
Council of Basel, 279, 289, 302, 305
Council of Blood, created in the Netherlands, 380
Council of Boyars, 415
Council of Chalcedon, 123, 142
Council of Constance, 268, 288, 289, 302, 305
Council of Constantinople, 151, 178
Council of Dad-Ishu, 125
Council of Ferrara-Florence, 289
Council of Five Hundred, 584, 585
Council of Florence, 316, 323
Council of Foreign Ministers, 1171
Council of Hieria, 176
Council of Lyon, 321
Council of Nicaea, 119, 125, 176
Council of People's Commissars, in Russia, 1029, 1032
Council of Pisa, 288
Council of St. Sophia, 177
Council of Sardika, 142
Council of Seleuccia, 125
Council of Ten, in Venice, 225
Council of Trent, 388, 396, 401, 414
Council of Valabhi, 42
Council of workers and soldiers, among Germans, 995
Council of Workers' and Soldiers' Deputies (Soviet), 1028
Council of the Indies (*Consejo de Indias*), 496, 497, 499, 503
Council of the League of Nations, 951
Counter-Reformation, 396, 397, 401, 415, 420
Countess of Scarborough (H.M.S.), defeated by John Paul Jones, 521
Country Party in Australia, 1129, 1130
Coups d'état: at Paris, 585; of Brumaire, 587; of Pres. Louis Napoleon, 632; at Constantinople, 760; in Prussia, 999
Coups de poing (hand-axes), in Palaeolithic period, 4
Cour de cassation, highest court of appeal in France, 642
Courbière, Guillaume René, Prussian general, 592
Courland, *see* Latvia
Court of Common Pleas, established, 200
Court of Exchequer, established, 200
Court of King's Bench, established, 200
Courtauld, Augustine, Arctic explorer, 569
Courten, Sir William, established the first colony on Barbados, 510
Courtenay, William, Archbishop, 268
Courtot expedition crossed the Sahara, 1081
Couthon, Georges, French revolutionary, 582
Coutras, battle of, 386
Covenant of the League of Nations, 952
Covenanters, *see* Solemn League and Covenant
Coventry, bombed, 1149
Coverdale, Miles, and the translation of the Bible, 370
Covilhã, Pedro de, and Alfonso de Paiva, Portuguese traveler, 364
Cowley, Henry Richard Charles Wellesley, 1st Earl, British diplomat, 728
Cowpens, battle of, 522
Cowper, Lord William, British statesman, 434
Cox, James Middleton, defeated for pres. of U.S., 1050

Cox, Sir Percy Zachariah, high commissioner for Iraq, 1105; 1108
Cracow, captured by Mongols, 211; conquered by Boleslav I, 239; reconquered by Boleslav the Brave, 240; made new capital of Poland, 313; battle of, 917; 1164
Cradock, Sir Christopher George Francis Maurice, British admiral, 918
Cradock, Sir John Hobart, 2d Lord Howden, mission to Mohammed Ali, 723
Craig, Sir James, Irish statesman, 972
Craiova, Treaty of, 1150
Crampel, Paul, French explorer, 844
Cranmer, Thomas, Archbishop of Canterbury, 370, 372
Crannon, 66
Crassus, Marcus Licinius, Roman general, 83, 95, 96, 97, 102
Crassus, Peter, 207
Craterus, regent for Philip III, 66, 77
Cravant, battle of, 278
Crawford, William Harris, American politician, 771
Crécy, battle of, 265, 276, 304
Credenza, of Milan, 297
Credit-Anstalt of Austria, 961, 999, 1006
Crédit foncier, 633
Crédit mobilier, 633
Crédit Mobilier scandal, in U.S., 782
Crefeld, battle of, 467
Cremera, battle of, 71
Cremona, 86, 87, 107; in the League of Pavia, 220; 1141
Crescentii, influential Roman family, 215
Crespo, Joaquin, pres. of Venezuela, 816
Crespy, Treaty of, 395, 401
Cressy, sunk by the German U-9, 917
Creswellian culture, 17
Cretan culture, 46, 47
Crete, of the Middle Kingdom, 23, 47; seized by Moslem free-booters, 177; reconquered from Saracens, 179, 180; taken from Byzantines, 189; revolt, 710, 745, 1022; union with Greece proclaimed, 710, 729; Organic Statute, 729; Pact of Halepa, 729; new reform scheme, 745; insurrection, 729, 746; union with Greece, 756; 1150; 1151, 1158
Crimea, annexed by Russia, 482; 1143; 1151, 1154, 1164
Crimea Conference, 1143
Crimean War, 613, 633, 678, 704, 727
Crimes Bill, in England, 617
Crimissus, 34, 66
Cripps, Sir Stafford, 1138
Crisa, 52
Crispi, Francesco, premier of Italy, 660, 661, 745
Crispus, Flavius Julius, son of Constantine, 119, 120
Cristea, Miron, Rumanian patriarch, 1027
Critias, at head of Thirty Tyrants, 61
Critolaus, 90
Crittenden Compromise Resolution, 775
Croatia, joined with Hungary, 246, 695
Croats, branch of southern Slavs, 239; conquered by the Franks, 246; seek separation from Hungary, 673; in opposition to the new kingdom, 1019
Croesus, of the Mermnadae, King of Lydia, 37, 38
Crofton, Capt. Richard, motored from Nile to Lake Chad, 1081
Croix de Feu, in France, 978
Cro-Magnon Man, 9, 68
Cromarty, a base for the British Grand Fleet, 917
Cromer, Lord, see Baring, Sir Evelyn
Cromwell, Oliver, Lord Protector of England; at Marston Moor, 377; at Preston Pans, 379; suppresses Irish rebellion; at, Worcester; made Lord Protector, 425; rejects title of king, 426; policy towards France, 439, 440; his body disinterred, 426
Cromwell, Richard, son of Oliver, 426
Cromwell, Thomas, minister of Henry VIII, 370
Cronje, Piet Arnoldus, Boer general, 857
Crop Loan Act, 1053
Cropready Bridge, battle of, 377
Croton, 53, 74
Crowder, Gen. Enoch Herbert, American envoy to Cuba, 1077
Crown Lands Ordinance (first), 850
Crown Point, taken from British, 520
Croydon airfield, 1148
Crozat, Antoine, Canadian trader, 507
Crusade of Nicopolis, 318
Crusades, of Richard I, Barbarossa, and Philip II, 196 f., 211; Edward with Louis IX, 198; failure of the Teutonic Knights, 214; First to Eighth Crusade, 219 ff.; against Turks, 318
Cruz, Sor Juana Ines de la, Spanish-American poetess, 507
Crysler's Farm, battle of, 793
Ctesiphon, 83 passim; battle of, 927
Cuauhtemoc, 491
Cuba, 823 f., 1077 f., 1136, 1155
Cuban Revolution, 647
Cuban Treaty, ratified by U.S., 1054
Cucuteni, 16
Culloden, battle of, 435
Cullom (Shelby Moore) Committee, 784
Cultures, methods of dating, 2, 3; climatic changes and modifications, 14; direction of movement, 15; in Greece and its areas, 11
Cum occasione impressionis libri, bull of Pope Innocent X, 455
Cumae, 48; battle of, 57
Cumans, in southern Russia, 243; in Theiss region, 246; support Stephen Nemanya, 247; invade Balkans, 250; revolt of Bogomils, 250

Cumberland, Federal warship, 776
Cumberland, William Augustus, Duke of, British general, 435; 467
Cuming, Sir Alexander, mission to the Cherokees, 513
Cunard, Samuel, founded Cunard Line, 554
Cunaxa, battle of, 40, 62
Cuneiform tablets, 23, 25, 27, 28, 32, 36
Cunimund, Gepid king, 150
Cunningham, Allan, Australian explorer, 899
Cuno, Wilhelm, German industrialist and statesman, 997
Curaçao, first all-steam vessel to cross the Atlantic, 554
Curia, reformed during Avignon period, 286
Curie, Pierre and Marie, radium, 552
Currency Act of U.S., 787
Currency deflation, in England, 604 f.
"Curse of the Alcmaeonids," 51
Curthose, Robert, son of William the Conqueror, 227
Curzola, battle of, 224
"Curzon Line," Poland's eastern frontier, 1038, 1042
Curzon of Kedleston, George Nathaniel, British statesman, 864, 871
Cushing, Caleb, American diplomat, 879
Custer, George Armstrong, massacred, 780
Custine, Adam Philippe, Count de, French general, 582
Customs Law, repealed in England, 612
Customs union of Germany and Austria, 999, 1006
Custozza, battles of, 654, 659, 674
Cuza, Prof. Alexander Constantin, leader of the Rumanian Christian League, 1026
Cuza, Alexander John, prince of Moldavia and Wallachia, 720
Cvetkovich, Dragesha, Yugoslav premier, 1019
Cyaxares, King of Media, 26, 29, 40, 48
Cyclades, 62, 79, 83, 84
Cylon of Megara, 51
Cyme, 47, 62
Cymri (Britons), a Celtic stock, 166
Cynoscephalae, battle of, 80; 89
Cynossema, 60
Cyprian, Bishop of Carthage, 117, 141
Cyprus, 32 passim; captured by Arabs, 186; acquired by Venice, 299; annexed by England, 919; offered to Greece, 927; 1151
Cyrenaica, 77, 1160
Cyrene, 24 passim
Cyril, Bulgaria, 1141
Cyril, missionary among the Slavs, 177, 239
Cyrus I, 40
Cyrus II, the Great, 26, 37, 40, 48
Cyrus, Patriarch of Alexandria, 186
Cyrus, son of Darius II, 61, 62
Cythera, 59
Cyzicus, battle of, 58, 60, 114
Czartoryski, Adam George, adviser to the Tsar of Russia, 601
Czartoryski, Frederick Michael, Prince, uncle of King Stanislas, 477
Czaslau, battle of, 465
Czech legions, in Siberia, 947, 1032
Czechs, branch of western Slavs, 239, 673
Czechoslovakia, declares its independence, 948, 1009; history of, 965 ff., 1004, 1009 ff., 1036, 1144
Czernin, Ottokar, Count, Austro-Hungarian foreign minister, 930, 936, 942; at Brest-Litovsk peace conference, 943
Czernowitz, taken by the Russians, 916, 932; retaken by the Austrians, 940

Dacian Wars, 110
Dacians, 109
Daendels, Herman Willem, Dutch marshal, 876
Da Gama, Vasco, Portuguese discoverer, 364, 571
Daghestan, ceded to Russia, 701
Dagobert, King of the Franks, 147, 239
Dagobert, Norman patriarch, 256
Dahlmann, Friedrich Christoph, German historian, 676
Dahomey, Negro kingdom, 840
Daibutsu, the Great Buddha, 350
Daigo II, Japanese emperor, 357
Dail Eireann (Irish Parliament), 972, 973
Daily Advertiser (London), 436
Daily Telegraph (London), 692, 756
Daimler, Gottlieb, invented internal combustion engine, 556
Daimyō (Japanese feudal chiefs), 888, 890
Dajōkan, great council of state in Japan, 350
Dakar, capital of French West Africa, 1089, 1158, 1159
Daladier, Édouard, premier of France, 967, 980, 1012, 1088, 1135
Dalai Lama, of Tibet, 536, 539, 540
Dale, Sir Thomas, in command of the Jamestown colony, 508
Dalhousie, James Andrew Broun Ramsay, 1st Marquess and 10th Earl of, gov.-gen. of India, 870
Dallmann, Capt. Eduard, German explorer, 573
Dalmatian pirates, reduced by the Venetians, 224
Dalmatius, Flavius Julius, nephew of Constantine, 120
Dalriada, in Scotland, 168
Dalrymple, Gen. Sir Hew Whitefoot, British commander, 593
Dalziel, Thomas, defeated the Scotch Covenanters, 427
Damad Ferid Pasha, Turkish statesman, 1094
Damaratus king, 50, 52
Damascene War, 80, 84
Damascus (city), taken by the British and Arabs, 948; 1144, 1151
Damascus, Kingdom of, founded, 35; captured, 127; seat of Moslem caliphate, 186; made a French state, 1098
Damaskinos, Greek archbishop, 1143

Damasus I, Pope, 173
Damasus II, Pope, 217
Damian, Peter, religious reformer, 217 f.
Damiens, Robert François, 447
Damietta, in Egypt, captured, 189; lost in Fifth and Sixth Crusades, 257
Dampier, William, explored coasts of Australia, 894
Dan no Ura, battle of, 354
"Dan to Beersheba," 29
Danaï, 24
Danby, Sir Thomas Osborne, 1st Earl of, British statesman, 428, 429, 430
Dandin, his romance *Dasakumaracharita*, 131
Dandolo, Enrico, doge of Venice, 254
Dandurand, Raoul, opposes Geneva Protocol, 959
Dane Mark, 155
Danegeld, 167
Danelaw, north of England, 167
Danes, move into northern islands (including British Isles), 158; incursion into Italy, 162; raid in England; invasion of Ireland, 166, 167; raids in British Isles, France, the Low Countries, 170; defeated at Bornhörde, 214
Danev, Sloian, prime minister of Bulgaria, 719, 760
Dangerfield, Thomas, discloses Meal-Tub Plot, 428
Daniel, 30
Daniel of Volynia, crusade against the Tatars, 244
Danilo I of Montenegro, 715
Danish East Greenland Co., founded, 568
Danish naval vessels, scuttled at Copenhagen, 1159
Danish West Indies, sold to U.S., 1045
Dante Alighieri, his influence on Castilian literature, 282; his *Vita Nuova*, the *Divine Comedy*, and *De Vulgare Eloquentia*, 294; his *De Monarchia*, 302
Dantidurga, overthrew the Chalukyas, 336
Danton, Georges Jacques, French revolutionary leader, 580, 581, 582, 583
Danube, 1154; Valley, 1164
Danube Statute, 958
Danubian culture, 16
Danubian Principalities, rise against Russian influence, 726, 727; under joint guaranty of the powers, 728. *See also* Rumania
Danzig, capitulation of, 477; free state, 953, 997, 1145
Danzig-Polish crisis, 971, 980
Darányi, Koloman, Hungarian premier, 1015
Daras, 126, 127; battle of, 126, 172
Darboy, Georges, Archbishop of Paris, 637
D'Arc, Jeanne, 270, 278 f.
D'Arcy, William Knox, British capitalist, 864, 865, 1109
Dardanelles, Treaty of, 596
Dar-es-Salaam, captured by Gen. Smuts, 918
Darfur, Sultan of, 929
Darimon, Louis Alfred, French Republican, 635
Darius I, 38; battle of Marathon, 40; exploration of the Indus, 42, 52
Darius II Nothus, 40, 62
Darius III Codomannus, 40, 53, 54, 65
Darlan, Jean-François, French admiral, chief of state in French North Africa, 1139, 1140; assassinated, 1139, 1160
Darling, Sir Ralph, gov. of New South Wales, 899
Darling Downs, discovered, 899
Darmsdenian industry, 4
Darnley, Henry Stuart, husband of Mary, Queen of Scots, 373
Dartiguenave, Philippe, pres. of Haiti, 825; treaty with U.S., 1078
Dartmouth College v. Woodward, decided by John Marshall, 770
Darwin, Charles, his *Origin of Species*, 551; 552; voyage of the *Beagle*, 895
Das, Chitta Ranjan, leader of the Swaraj Party in India, 1112
Dasakumaracharita, 131
Daszynski, Ignacy, head of provisional govt. at Cracow, 1038
Datames, gov. of Cappadocia, 40
Dating of Man, relative methods, 2; absolute methods, 3
Datis, at battle of Marathon, 53
Daudet, Léon, French royalist leader, 643
Daudi Chwa, King of Uganda, 849
Daumier, Honoré, French artist, 628
Daun, Leopold Joseph Maria, Count von, Austrian general, 467
Dauphin (Louis XVII), dies, 584
Davel, Jean Daniel Abraham, Swiss revolutionary, 460
Davenport, Rev. John, founds a theocratic colony at New Haven, 509
David I of Scotland, 201
David II of Scotland, 272
David, 30 f.
David, brother of Llewelyn, Prince of Wales, 199
David, Prof. Tannatt William Edgeworth, Antarctic explorer, 574, 576
Davids, Normans, settle in Ireland, 169
Dávila, Cárlos, President of Chile, 1065
Dávila, Gil González, Spanish explorer, 488, 491
Dávila, Miguel, pres. of Honduras, 821
da Vinci, Leonardo, Italiaa artist, 296, 298
Davis, Dwight Filley, gov.-gen. of the Philippines, 1133
Davis, Jefferson, pres. of the Confederacy, 775, 776, 779
Davis, John, Arctic explorer, 507, 559
Davis, John William, Democratic candidate for president, 1051
Davout, Louis Nicolas, French marshal, 591, 599
Davy, Sir Humphry, invented the arc lamp, 553

Dawes, Charles Gates, American banker and statesman, 959, 1051, 1078
Dawes (Henry Laurens) Act, to divide Indian lands, 784
Dawes Plan, 959, 998
Day of Dupes, 387
"Day of Indulgence," 206
Dayan, descendant of Jenghiz, 347
Daza, Hilarion, pres. of Bolivia, 812
D-Day, 1163
DDT, adopted by U.S. Army, 553
Déak, Francis, Hungarian statesman, 671, 673, 678, 695
Deakin, Alfred, Australian prime minister, 904
Dease, Peter Warren, of the Hudson's Bay Co., 563
De Beers Mining Corp, 854
Deborah, 30
Debs, Eugene Victor, American labor leader, 785
Debt Default Act (Johnson), 1054
Debts of the Allied Powers to U.S., 1051
de Burgh, Hubert, guardian of Henry III, 198
Decazes, Élie, Duke, French statesman, 626
Decazes, Duke of, French foreign minister, 638, 733
Deccan, dominated by Dravidian kings, 129
Decebalus, King of Dacia, 109
Decelea, 60
Decelean War, 58
Decembrist Rising, in Russia, 702
Dechanski, Stephen (Stephen Urosh III), Serbian prince, 319
Decius, Caius Messius Quintus Trainus, and persecution of Christians, 115
Decius Mus, Publius, 73
Decius Mus, Publius, son of the above, 74
Decken, Baron Karl von der, African explorer, 847
Declaration of Breda, 426
Declaration of Independence, American, 520
Declaration of Lima, 965, 1057, 1062
Declaration of London, 994
Declaration of Pillnitz, 581
Declaration of Rights, in England, 429 f.
Declaration of Rights and Grievances, 520
Declaration of Sivas, 1094
Declaratory Act, 518
Decree of Ravenna, 212
Deere, John, inventor of the steel plow, 554, 772
Deerfield, surprised by French and Indians, 511
Defender of the Faith, title conferred on Henry VIII, 378
Defenders of the Constitution, name of the Karageorgevich faction in Serbia, 714
Defenestration of Prague, 404, 419
Defense Acts, in Australia, 904
Defense Advisory Commission, 1154
de Forest, Lee, inventor, 557, 789
De Geer, Gerard Jakob, 3, 8
de Geer, Louis Gerhard, Norwegian prime minister, 699
de Got, Bertrand, Archbishop of Bordeaux, Pope Clement V, 222
Degrelle, Léon, leader of Rexists in Belgium, 975
Deiotarus, King of Galatia, 37, 96
Dejoces, 40
DeKalb, Johann, Baron, in the American Revolution, 521
De la Gardie, Magnus Gabriel, Swedish commander, 418
Delagoa Bay, 748, 749, 846, 852, 855
Delaware, Thomas West, Lord, gov. of the Virginia colony, 508
Delbos, Yvon, French foreign minister, 964, 979
Delcassé, Théophile, French foreign minister, 643, 748, 751, 752, 929
Delectissime nobis, encyclical of Pope Pius XI, 982
Delhi, Kingdom of, ruled by the Sayyids, 335, conquered, 330, 870; siege and capture, 870
Delhi Pact (Irwin-Gandhi), 1112
Delian League, 55, 56
Delingette, Capt. Alfred Charles, motored across Africa, 1081
Deljan, Peter, Bulgarian leader, 247, 249
Della Torre (Guelf), in Milan, 297
De Long, Lt. George Washington, Arctic explorer, 565
Delos, 62, 82, 95
Delphi, 52, 53, 56, 64
Delphic shrine, 52
Demak, Empire of, 876
Dembinski, Gen. Henry, Polish soldier, 674
Demetrius I (Poliorcetes) of Phalerum, 33, 35, 77, 78
Demetrius II, 79
Demetrius I Soter, 82
Demetrius II Nicator, 82, 84
Demetrius III, 82
Demetrius, King of Bactria, 43
Demosthenes, Athenian orator and statesman, 58, 59, 60, 64, 66, 67
Denain, battle of, 446
Denby, Edwin, American statesman, 1051
Dendrochronology, 3
Dengyō Daishi, *see* Saicho
Denham, Dixon, African explorer, 826
Denhardt, Gustav and Klemens, brothers, African explorers, 847
Denikin, Anton, white Russian leader, 952, 1031
Denmark, 170, 203, 315 ff.; 416, 474, 697 ff., 1045; occupied by Germany, 1135; 1142; invasion, 1146; 1155, 1165
Dennewitz, battle of, 599
Denshawi affair, 833
Department for spiritual affairs (Roman Catholic) in Germany, 689

Depretis, Agostino, Italian premier, 660
Der, 39
Derbend, 126
Derby, Edward George Geoffrey Smith Stanley, 14th Earl of, British prime minister, 613, 735
Dercyllidas, 62
Derebeys (lords of the valley), 484, 485
Derna, 1160
Dernburg, Dr. Bernhard, minister of German colonies, 692
De Robeck, John, British admiral, 920
Déroulède, Paul, French patriot leader, 740
De Ruyter, Michael, Dutch commander, 425, 427, 439, 442
Dervish rising, near Smyrna, 1096
Descent of Man, The, by Charles Darwin, 552
Deschanel, Paul Eugene Louis, pres. of France, 977
Desert Land Act, 782
Desèze, Count Raymond, counsel for Louis XVI, 582
Desiderius, Lombard King, 152, 153
Desmond, James Fitzgerald, Earl of, Irish insurgent, 373
Desmoulins, Camille, French revolutionary leader, 580, 583
De Soto, Hernando, discovers the Mississippi River, 493
Despensers, father and son, 264
Dessalines, Jean-Jacques, Haitian leader, 825
Dessolles, Jean Joseph Paul Augustin, French statesman, 626
Desta Demtu, Ras, Ethiopian chief, 1086
De Tham (Hoang-hoa-Tham), insurgent leader in Tonkin, 875
Dethronement Act, in Austria, 1014
Detroit, founded, 507; strengthened by the French, 516; surrendered, 769; taken by Gen. Brock, 793
Dettingen, battle of, 465
Deuteronomy, 30
Deutsche Kolonial Gesellschaft, 854
Deutschland, German commercial submarine, 932; German battleship, 984
Deva, 106
De Valera, Eamon, Sinn Fein leader, pres. of the Irish Republic, 971, 972, 973, 974; 1142
Devanampiya Tissa, founded the Mahavihara monastery, 132
Devapala, ruler of Bengal, 331
Devereux, Capt. Walter, assassinated Wallenstein, 426
Devil's Island, French penal prison, 641
Devonshire, Victor Christian Cavendish, Duke of, gov.-gen. of Canada, 1057
Devonshire, William Cavendish, Earl of, signs invitation to William of Orange, 429
De Wet, Christian Rudolf, Boer leader, 859
Dewey, George, American admiral, 787, 909
De Witt, Cornelius, Dutch commander, 427, 439, 442
De Witt, John, grand pensionary of Holland, 439, 442
Dezhnev, Simon, Cossack explorer, 561
Dhanga, Chandella, king, 332
Dhanis, Francis, Baron, Belgian commander, 844
Dharma Sastra of Manu, 130
Dharma Sutra of Vishnu, 130
Dharmalakshana school, 331
Dharmapala, ruler of Bengal, 331
Dhruva, defeated Nandivarman II, 336
Dhul-Nunids of Toledo, 233
Dhu-Qar, 127
Diaeus, 90
Dialogue of the Exchequer, The, 196
Dialogues of Gregory the Great, 151
Diamond Jubilee of 1897 (Queen Victoria), 619
Diamond necklace scandal, 448
Diana of Poitiers, Duchess of Valentinois, mistress of Henry II of France, 383
Dias, Bartolomeu, Portuguese discoverer, 364, 368
Dias, Dinis, Portuguese discoverer, 363
Diaz, Adolfo, pres. of Nicaragua, 821, 1073
Diaz, Armando, Italian general, 941, 949
Diaz de Solis, Juan, chief pilot of Spain, 368
Diaz, Diego, discovered Madagascar, 859
Diaz Porfirio, pres. of Mexico, 822, 1074
Diaz, Rodrigo (Ruy), of Bibar, the Cid, 233
Dibra, taken by the Bulgars, 927
Dido, legendary founder of Carthage, 34
Diebitsch, Hans Karl Friedrich Anton, Russian general, 598, 702, 724
Diego Suarez, Madagascar, taken by the French, 859, 860; 1167
Diesel, Rudolf, inventor of Diesel engine, 556
Diet of Augsburg, 401
Diet of Besançon, 210
Diet of Cologne, 398
Diet of 1435, 313
Diet of Frankfurt, 302
Diet of Mainz, 210, 289
Diet of Pressburg, 465
Diet of Princes at Leipzig, 405
Diet of Ratisbon, 209
Diet of Regensburg, 240 f., 461
Diet of Roncaglia, 220
Diet of Speier, first and second, 400 f.
Diet of Stans, 307
Diet of Tribur, 206
Diet of Worms, 398
Digambara sect, 42
Digenis Akritas, Byzantine epic, 181
Digges, Sir Dudley, 375
Dighton Rock, supposed Norse remains, 365
Dignaga, logician, 131
Dijon, 1164

Dilbat, 25
Dingaan, Zulu king, 851
Dingley (Nelson) Tariff Act, 787
Diniz (the Worker) of Portugal, 284
Dinwiddie, Robert, gov. of Virginia, 516
Diocles, reforms at Syracuse, 57
Diocletian (Caius Aurelius Valerius Diocletianus), Roman emperor, 114, 116, 117, 118, 119, 122, 141
Diodorus, 21
Diodotus I, King of Bactria, 81, 83
Diodotus II, 81, 82
Diogenes, Gen. Constantine, Byzantine soldier, 248, 250
Dioi, 44
Dion, regent for Dionysius II, 66
Dionysius I, Sicilian ruler, 34, 51, 66
Dionysius II, 66
Dipaea, 54
Diphtheria, 552
Diplomatic Revolution of 1756, 447, 481
Dipo Negora, leader of Javanese revolt, 877
Directory (Directoire), French form of government, 584, 585
Disability Pension Act, 785
Disarmament Conference, at Geneva, 962, 963, 1002
Disbanding Act, reducing the English army, 431
Disestablishment Act, 614
Dispersion (Diaspora) of the Jews, 111
Disraeli, Benjamin, British statesman; revolt against Peel's govt., 612; in third Derby ministry, 613; first ministry, 614; second ministry, 615; buys shares of the Suez Canal, 615, 733; elevated to the peerage, 616; in Russo-Turkish War, 734; at Congress of Berlin, 736; favorable to the German-Austrian Alliance, 737
Dissidents, adherents of the Protestant Reformation in Poland, 414, 477
Distraint of Knighthood, 200
Diu, battle of, 364
Divine Faith, a decree by Akbar, 533
Divisions of modern man, 12
Divyavadana, 131
Dixmude, in German possession, 914
Dixon, Jeremiah, English surveyor, 512
Dmitri, pretender to Russian throne, 418
Dmitri Donskoi (of the Don), conflict with the Tatars, 316
Dmowski, Roman, Polish party leader, 1037, 1038
Dnieper, 1151, 1153, 1154
Dniester, 1137
Dobbs, Sir Henry, high commissioner for Iraq, 1105
Dobropolje, battle of, 948
Dobruja, 1150
Dock strike, in London, 618
Doctors of the Five Classics, 133
Dodecanese Islands, 987, 1021
Doenitz, Karl, German admiral, head of provisional German government, 1144, 1165
Dogali, battle of, 660, 835
Dogen, introduced Soto branch of the Zen sect in Japan, 356
Dogger Bank, naval action, 917
Doheny, Edward Laurence, American capitalist, 1051
Doherty, John, labor leader, 608
Doiran, battle of, 934, 940
Dōkyō, Japanese monk, 351
Dolabella, Publius Cornelius, 99
Dole, Sanford Ballard, pres. of the Republic of Hawaii, 910
Dollfuss, Engelbert, Austrian premier, 990, 1007
Dolmens, 15, 17, 18
Domagk, Gerhard, sulfanilimide, 553
Dombas, 1146
Domesday Book, 193
Domesticated animals, in Post-Palaeolithic period, 10
Domingo, Marcellino, denounces Spanish monarchy, 981
Dominic, founder of the Dominicans, 221
Dominican Republic, established by revolt, 824; intervention by U.S. forces, 1078
Dominicans, in England, 198; in Spanish America, 499
Dominion Companies Act, in Canada, 1059
Dominion of Canada, formed, 796
Dominion of New England, formed, 512
Dominitian (Titus Flavius Domitianus), Roman emperor, 108, 109, 110, 112 f.
Dom Miguel, son of John VI of Portugal, 648
Domna, Julia, wife of Septimius, 115
Don, 1153
Don Carlos, brother of Ferdinand VII of Spain, 645, 647
Don Carlos, son of Philip II of Spain, 389, 463
Don Pacifico affair, 612, 613, 710
Don Quijote, 389
Donatello, Italian artist, 296
Donati, Corso, leader of the Blacks in Florence, 293
Donation of Constantine, 123, 290
Donation of Pepin, 152, 153, 176
Donatists, 117, 141
Donatus of Casae Nigrae, 117
Dongkur Hutuktu of the Ordos, 536
Doolittle, Col. James, bombed Tokyo, 1158
Doorn Kop, battle of, 856
Dor, 32
Dorchester Heights, occupied by Washington, 520
Dorchester laborers, sent to prison in England, 608
Dorcis, 54
Dorgun, regent of the Manchus, 537
Doria, Andrea, Genoese doge, 394, 397, 422

Doria, Gian Andrea, Genoese doge, 397
Doria, Gianettino, nephew of Andrea, 397
Doria, Luciano, Genoese admiral, 298
Doria, Pietro, Genoese admiral, 298
Doria, Tedisio, Genoese explorer, 363
Dorian phalanx, 50
Dorians, introduced the Iron Age, 47, 48, 52
Dorieus, 53
Doriscus, 55
Dorogobuzh, 1153
Dorpat, taken by the Germans, 943
Dorr Rebellion, in Rhode Island, 773
Dorylaeum, battle of, 252, 255
Dōshō, brought the Hossō sect to Japan, 351
Dost Mohammed, Amir of Afghanistan, 866
Douai, taken by the British, 950
Douglas, Stephen Arnold, American statesman, 774, 775
Douglass, Andrew Ellicott, 3
Doumer, Paul, pres. of France, 875, 978
Doumergue, Gaston, pres. of France, 977, 978
Dover, Treaty of, 427, 442
Dow, Neal, sponsored Maine prohibition law, 774
Downs, battle of the, 425
Dózsa, George, leads revolt of Hungarian peasants, 419
Draco, his laws published, 51
Dragina, battle of, 249
Dragonnades, in Languedoc, 443
Dragut, Turkish admiral, 423
Dragutin, Serbian prince, 318 f.
Drake, Edwin Laurentine, opens oil well, 555, 775
Drake, Sir Francis, British admiral, 373, 389 f., 490, 494, 507, 508, 571, 894
Drama, taken by Bulgar-German forces, 934
Drang nach Osten (Advance to the East) of Germany, 214
Drangiana, 39
Draper's Meadow, Virginia settlement, 515
Dravidian race, 12, 41; dynasty, 129, 132
Dreadnought, British warship, 557, 754
Dred Scott decision, 775
Drepana, 86
Dresden, battle of, 599, 600; Treaty of, 466, 468
Dresden, German cruiser, 918
Dreux, battle of, 384
Dreyfus Affair, 641, 642
Dreyfus, Capt. Alfred, 641, 642, 748
Dreyfus, Mathieu, brother of Alfred, 641
Dreyse, Johann Nicholas von, inventor of the Prussian needle-gun, 554
Drina, battle of, 916
Druids, 166
Drumclog, battle of, 428
Drummond, Sir James Eric, secretary-gen. of the League of Nations, 952
Drummond-Wolff, Sir Henry, British diplomat, 741, 833
Druses of Syria, their cult of Hakim, 263; rise against French rule, 977; insurrection under Sultan Pasha, 1098
Drusus, junior, known as Germanicus, which see
Drusus, Marcus Livius, 93
Drusus, senior, 102
Drusus, son of Germanicus, 105
Drygalski, Prof. Erich von, Antarctic explorer, 574
Dryopithicus, 1
Dryplate process, in photography, 555
Drystra, battle of, 250
Dual Control in Egypt, 736
Dual Shintō (Ryōbu Shintō), 350
Duala, taken by the British, 918; 1159
Du Barry, Jeanne Bécu, Countess (Jeanne Vaubernier), mistress of Louis XV, 447
Dubno, taken by the Austrians, 922
Dubois, Guillaume, cardinal and French statesman, 447
Dubois, Pierre, his De Recuperatione Sanctae Terrae, 232 f.
Duca, Ion G., Rumanian premier, 1026
Ducas, Byzantine historian, 323
Ducat, first coined, 224
Duces, in Italy, 146, 147
Ducetius, leader of the Sicels, 57
Duchesne, Gen. Jacques Charles René Achille, French colonial commander, 861
Duckworth, Sir John Thomas, British admiral, 592
Dudley, Edmund, 369
Due process clause, of the 14th amendment of the U.S. Constitution, 789 f.
Duesseldorf, 1148
Dufferin and Ava, Frederick Temple Hamilton Blackwood, 1st Marquess of, gov-gen. of Canada, 796, 832; viceroy of India, 871
Dufour, Gen. Guillaume Henri, Swiss commander, 666
Duguay-Truin, René, French naval officer, 501
Du Guesclin, Bertrand, Constable of France, 265, 277, 280
Duilius, Caius, 86
Duisberg, occupied by the French, 957, 959, 997
Dukhonin, Gen. Nicholas Nicholaievich, Russian commander, 1030
Dukhtar-i-Nushirwan frescoes, 43
Dulo family, Bulgarian, 182
Duma, Russian Parliament, 708
Dumbarton Oaks Conference, 1170
Dumouriez, Charles François, French revolutionary general, 581, 582

Dunbar, battles of; defeat of John Baliol, 199; victory of Cromwell, 425
Duncan I of Scotland, 201
Duncan, Scottish ruler, 168
Dundee, see Claverhouse
Dunes, battle of the, 390, 426
Dungi, 26
Dunkerque (city), 1146, 1148, 1149; French naval vessel, 1148
Dunkirk, surrendered to the English, 426; sold to France, 427; Treaty of Utrecht, 446
Dunlop, John Boyd, introduced pneumatic rubber tire, 556
Dunning Tariff, of Canada, 1058
Dunois, Jean, adviser of Charles VII of France, 278
Duns Scotus, medieval philosopher, 201
Dunstan, Archbishop, 167
Dunsterville, Gen. Lionel Charles, British commander, 947, 1107
Duperry, Louis Isidore, French explorer, 895
Dupleix, Joseph François, Marquis, French administrator, 534
Dupuis, Jean, Indo-Chinese explorer, 874
Dupuy de Lôme, Stanislas Charles Henri Laurent, naval architect, 555
Duquesne de Menneville, Marquis, French colonial commander, 516
Durand agreement, between England and Afghanistan, 868
Durando, Giacomo, Italian general of the papal forces, 654
Durazzo, 252; taken by Serbs and Italians, 925, 949
Durben, battle of, 215
Durham, John George Lambton, 1st Earl of, British statesman, 607, 795
Durham Cathedral as architecture, 193
Dürnkrutt, battle of, 246
Duroc, Géraud Christophe Michel, French general, 599
Dur-Sharrukin, 25, 27
Dushan, Stephen (Stephen Urosh IV), of Serbia, 319, 322, 325
Düsseldorf, occupied by the French, 957, 959, 997
Dutch, history of, 379, 437, 453, 509, 512, 524, 539, 600, 621 f., 875 f., 896, 957, 975
Dutch East India Co. founded, 437; factories in Burma, 541; in Cape Colony, 850; factory in Malaya, 875; end of the company, 876
Dutch Guiana, 1155
Dutch-Japanese dictionary, 548
Dutch West India Co. founded, 437; occupy Brazilian territory, 501; chartered, 510
Dvinsk, battle of, 922, 943
Dwelling Place culture, 18
"Dyarchy," system in India, 1111
Dybowski, Jan, African explorer, 844
Dyer, Gen. Reginald Edward Harry, British commander, 1111
Dynasties, 21–26

Eannatum, 25
Early, Jubal Anderson, Confederate general, 779
Early Bronze Age, 13, 29
Early Cycladic culture, 16
Early Dynastic (Sumerian) period, 13
Early Helladic culture, 16
Earthquakes: in Sparta, 55; in Japan, 138, 548; at Lisbon, 454; Regio and Messina, 662; Puerto Rico, 1079; in Tokyo, 1124
East Africa Protectorate (British), 849
East African Syndicate, 850
East Anglia, Anglo-Saxon kingdom, 166, 168
East India Co., see British East India Co.
East Indies, 1171
East Prussia, 1145, 1154, 1164
Easter, in the Roman Church, 169
Easter Island, discovered by Jacob Roggeveen, 894, 917
Easter Rebellion, in Ireland, 971, 972
Eastern Chin dynasty, 135
Eastern Empire, see Byzantine Empire
Eastern Roumelia, in revolution, 729, 739
Eastern Wei dynasty, 135, 136
Eastman, George, film manufacture, 556
Eaton, Theophilus, founds a theocratic colony at New Haven, 509
Eben Emael, Belgian fort, 1146
Eberth, Friedrich, pres. of Germany, 995, 998
Eberth, Karl, discovered typhoid germ, 552
Eboracum, 108, 114
Ebroin, Frankish leader, 149
Ecbatana, 39, 40, 66, 82
Ecclesia, 51, 55, 63
Ecclesiastical Titles Bill, 612
Ecclesiasticus, 30
Eck, John Maier von, Catholic theologian, 399
Eckardstein, Hermann, Baron von, German diplomat, 747
Eckardt, Tibor, leader of the Agrarian Party in Hungary, 1015
Eckener, Hugo, German aviator, 558
Eckmühl, battle of, 594
Eclectus, chamberlain of Commodus, 112
Ecloga, Byzantine law code, 175
Ecnomus, 86
Economic and Social Council, United Nations, 1171
Economic rehabilitation program, in Brazil, 1071
Economic restrictions, for Germany, 1171
Economic Warfare, Office of, 1140, 1141; Board of, 1159
Economics, 549
Ecthesis, of Emperor Heraclius, 151, 174
Ecuador, 489, 813 f., 1068, 1156
Eddas, Norwegian epics, 170

Eden, Anthony, British foreign secretary, 970, 990, 1136, 1143
Eden, Charles, gov. of North Carolina, 513
Edessa, 124, 127
Edfu, 21
Edgar, King of England, 167
Edgehill, battle of, 377
Edict of Boulogne, 384
Edict of Caracalla, 114
Edict of Milan, 119, 125
Edict of Nantes, 386, 443, 850
Edict of Restitution, 405
Edict of Tolerance, proclaimed by Joseph II, 469
Edict of Worms, 400
Edinburgh, Treaty of, 372
Edison, Thomas Alva, American inventor, 556, 782, 783
Edith, wife of Henry I, 193
Edmund, son of Henry III, 198
Edo, renamed Tokyo, 889
Edom, Kingdom of, 28, 29, 31, 32
Edom, son of Isaac, 29
Edrisi, Arab geographer, 223
Education, Palace School of Charlemagne, 155, 157; decrees of
 Fourth Lateran Council, 221; in Spanish America, 500; in
 China, 1121
Education Act in Belgium, 623
Education Act in England, 614, 619
Education Bill in France, the so-called Falloux Law, 631
Edward I (Longshanks) of England, 198 f., 200, 203, 272, 301,
 309, 374
Edward II, King of England, 199, 200, 264, 272
Edward III, King of England, 264 f., 272, 273, 276, 293, 370, 374
Edward IV, King of England, 271, 272, 273, 280, 369
Edward V, King of England, 271
Edward VI, King of England, 369, 370, 372
Edward VII, King of England, 619, 751, 754, 755
Edward VIII, King of England, 970
Edward (Duarte) I, King of Portugal, 285
Edward, the Black Prince, 265, 267, 276, 277, 280
Edward, King of England, 167, 168
Edward the Confessor, King of England, 168, 191, 200, 227
Edwin and Morca's uprising, 191
Edwin of Northumbria, defeated by the Mercians, 166
d'Effiat, Henri, Marquis of Cinq-Mars (Monsieur le Grand), 387
Egbert, Saxon ruler, 167
Egede, Hans, Norwegian priest, 561
Eglon, King of Moab, 30
Egmont, Lamoral, Count of, Belgian leader, 380
Egremont, Charles Wyndham, Earl of, British statesman, 435
Egypt, in the Palaeolithic period, 6; in Post-Palaeolithic, 18; an-
 cient history, 21 ff.; invaded by Arabs, 186, 187; modern his-
 tory, 729, 738, 828 f., 968, 1143, 1151, 1159, 1162
Ehud, 30
Eider Danes, 676
Eielson, Carl Ben, 576
Eight Articles, Protocol of the, 621
Eighth Crusade, 258
Einhard, biographer of Charlemagne, 155, 157
Einstein, Albert, relativity, 552; 553
Einwetok, 1169
Eion, 55
Eire, 1142
Eisai, branch of the Zen sect, 356
Eisenach Congress of workingmen's associations, 689
Eisenhower, Gen. Dwight D., commander of Allied Armies in
 Europe, 1139, 1160, 1162, 1165
Eisner, Kurt, German independent socialist, 995
Ekblaw, Walter Elmer, Arctic explorer, 567
Ekkehard of St. Gall, his Waltherius, 162
Ekman, Carl, premier of Sweden, 1047
Ekron, Kingdom of, 30
Ekumekus, sect in southern Nigeria, 842
El Alamein, 1160
El Argar culture, 17
El Argheila, 1160
El Arish, taken by the British, 938
El Caney, battle of, 787
El Cano, Juan Sebastian, discoverer of New Amsterdam Island,
 894
El Guettar, Tunisia, 1162
El Obeid, battle of, 738, 832
El Zanjón, Convention of, 823
Eladas, John, regent for Constantine VII, 179
Elagabalus (Heliogabalus), Roman emperor, 115
Elah, 31
Elam, 25 passim
Elam, Kingdom of, 40
Elamites, 39
Elamitic language, 28
Elandslaagte, battle of, 857
Elath, Gulf of, 29
Elbasan, taken by the Bulgarians, 927; taken by the Italians,
 949
Elbe River, 1164
Elbing, founded, 215
Elea, 53
Eleanor, daughter of Henry II, 194
Eleanor of Aquitaine, wife of Henry II of England, 196, 227, 228
Eleatic School, 53
Eleazar, priest of Jerusalem, 107, 111
Electoral Assembly at Regensburg, 405
Electoral Law, of France, 631

Electors of the Holy Roman Empire, 302
Electrical developments, 551, 554; telegraph, 554; incandescent
 light; locomotive, 554; long-distance transmission; street car,
 554
Elementary-school statute in Sweden-Norway, 699
Eleusinian Mysteries, 60, 87
Eleusis, 50, 61
Eleutheros, 33
Eleventh amendment to U.S. Constitution, 764
Elgin, James Bruce, 8th Earl of, gov. of Canada, 795, 870, 871,
 879
Eliada, 35
Eliot, Sir John, member of the Addled Parliament, 374, 375
Eliot, John, missionary to the Indians, 511
Elis, 54 passim
Elissa, legendary founder of Carthage, 34
Elizabeth, daughter of James I of England, 377
Elizabeth, Empress of Austria, 695
Elizabeth, Queen of England, 369, 370, 372, 373, 374
Elizabeth, Empress of Russia, 466, 481
Elizabeth of Luxemburg, 379
Elizabeth of Valois, wife of Philip II, 386, 389
Elizabeth of York, daughter of Edward IV, 271
Elizabeth City, captured by Federal navy, 776
Elizabethan Poor Law, 373
Elkins (Stephen Benton) Act, 789
Ellenborough, Edward Law, Earl of, gov.-gen. of India, 870
Elleporus, battle of, 66
Ellice Islands, discovered, 894; protectorate of Great Britain,
 896
Elliot, Capt. Charles, 879
Elliott, Sir George Augustus, British commander, 436
Ellsworth, Lincoln, American explorer, 566, 577
Elmenteitan culture, 18
Elphinstone, George Keith, British admiral, 850
Eltekeh, 27
Elulaios (Lule), 33
Elvas, battle of, 453
Elymians, 52
Emancipation Edict, liberating the serfs in Russia, 704
Emancipists, pardoned convicts in Australian colonies, 898
Embalming, 21
Embargo Act, American, 768
Embargo on scrap iron and steel, 1136
Emden, German cruiser, 918
Emergency Relief Appropriation Act, 1054
Emergency Tariff Act in U.S., 1050
Emeric I of Hungary, 245
Emesa, 115
Emessa, taken by Moslems, 186
Émigrés, French, 582, 584
Emin Pasha (Eduard Schnitzer), Egyptian gov. of Equatoria,
 832, 844, 848
Emma, wife of King Ethelred of England, 167, 168, 227
Emmanuel, Victor, III, King of Italy, 1142
Emmich, Gen. Otto von, German commander, 912
Empedocles, philosopher, 62
Emperor-worship, 115
Empire (first) of France, 578, 591
Employers' Liability Act, 616, 618
Employment and Social Insurance Act, in Canada, 1060
Emporiae, 87
Empress Frederick, of Germany, 742
Empress of Ireland, sunk in collision, 797
Empson, Sir Richard, 369
Ems telegram, 688
Ender, Otto, Austrian premier, 1006
Endicott, John, with colonists at Salem, 509
Engelbert of Cologne, 211
Engelbrechtson, Engelbrecht, Swedish leader, 313
Engels, Friedrich, Socialist writer, 550
d'Enghien, Louis Antoine Henri de Bourbon-Conde, Duke, 590
England, 164–168; 191 ff.; 264 ff.; 369 ff.; 425 ff.; 507 ff.; 517 ff.;
 604 ff.; 733 ff.; 912 ff.; 967 ff. See also Great Britain
English Channel, 1146, 1148
English culture, influence of the Conquest, 193 f.; progress of,
 201
English language, in courts of England, 266
Englishiki, supplement to the Japanese laws, 350
"Enlightened Despotism," 448
Ennius, 91
Enríquez, Gen. G. Alberto, pres. of Ecuador, 1069
Enryakuji, Japanese monastery, 352, 353, 359
Ensenada, Cenon de Somodevilla, Marquis de la, Spanish re-
 form minister, 451
Entente cordiale, between Britain and France, 619, 643, 838
Enver Bey, Turkish statesman, 731, 732, 760, 948, 1094
Enzeli, taken by the Bolshevik fleet, 1107
Enzio, son of Frederick II, 213
Eoanthropus dawsoni, 9
Epaminondas, Greek general, 63
Epanagoge, manual of Byzantine law, 178
Ephesus, 47 passim
Ephialtes, 54, 55
Ephthalites (Haytal), 125, 126
Epictetus, a Stoic, 114
Epicurus and Epicureanism, 77
Epidamnus, 58
Epidaurians, 58
Epidaurus, 50, 58
Epidemics, 780

Epîla, battle of, 284
Epipolae, 60
Episcopacy, restored in Scotland, 374; abolished, 376
Episcopal Church, 372
Episcopate, rise of, 141
Epoch of a Warring Country, century of warfare in Japan, 359
Eratosthenes, 75
Erech, 25, 26
Erectheum, 62
Eremitical monasticism, 141, 142, 146
Eretria, 52, 53
Erfurt Congress, socialist, 691
Erfurt Parliament, 677
Eric (V) Glipping of Denmark, 203
Eric (VI) Menved of Denmark, 203
Eric IX (the Saint) of Sweden, 204
Eric XIV of Sweden, 413
Eric Laespe of Sweden, 204
Eric of Pomerania, King of Denmark, Sweden, and Norway, 312, 313
Eric Plowpenny, King of Denmark, 203
Eric the Conqueror of Sweden, 203
Eric the Red of Iceland, 170, 558
Ericsson, John, inventor, 554
Ericsson, Leif, Norse leader, 365, 558
Erie Canal, completed, 771
Erie R.R., 774
Erik the Priest-Hater, of Norway, 204
Erik the Red, discovered Greenland, 365
Erik the Red's Land, 569
Eritrea, 1160
Ernest Augustus, Duke of Cumberland, King of Hanover, 669, 670
Erösd, 16
Errázuriz, Federico, pres. of Chile, 809
Errázuriz, Federico, son of the above, pres. of Chile, 810
Erskine, St. Vincent Whitshed, African explorer, 828
Ertebølle culture, 15, 18
Ertogrul, leader of a Turkish tribe, 325
Eryx, 86
Erzberger, Matthias, German statesman, 942, 951, 996, 997
Erzerum, captured by John Kurkuas, 179; taken by the Russians, 929; taken by the Turks, 947; Treaty of, 862
Erzingan, battle of, 260; taken by the Russians, 929
Escobar, Gen. Gonzalo, Mexican insurgent, 1076
Escolar, Pedro de, explorer, 364
Escorial, in Spain, 389
Eshmunazar I, II, 33
Eskimos, 20
Eskishehr, taken by the Greeks, retaken by the Turks, 1095
Espartero, Gen. Baldomero, "Duke of the Victory," Spanish statesman, 645, 646
Espionage Act, in the U.S., 1049
d'Espréménil, Jean-Jacques Duval, pres. of the *parlement* of Paris, 448
Essad Pasha, heads provisional govt. in Albania, 925, 1019
Essarhaddon (Ashur-ah-iddin), 24, 27, 33, 39
Essay on Population, by Malthus, 549
Essen, 1148, 1164
Essex, Anglo-Saxon kingdom, 166
Essex, Arthur Capel, 1st Earl of, British statesman, 428
Essex, Robert Devereux, 3d Earl of, English commander, 373, 377, 378
Essex (U.S.S.) captures the *Alert* (Br.), 769
Essling, battle of, *see* Aspern
d'Estaing, Charles Hector, Count, French admiral, 521
Estates-General, 232, 276 *f.*, 578, 579
d'Este, Maria, marries James, Duke of York, 427
Esterhazy, Major Marie Charles, and the Dreyfus case, 641
Esterhazy, Count Maurice, premier of Hungary, 941
Esther, Book of, 30
Estigarribia, José Felix, pres. of Paraguay, 1066, 1135
Estonia, 943, 966, 1028, 1031, 1044 *ff.*, 1136, 1142, 1145, 1148
Estonian Revolt, Teutonic Order takes Estonia from the Danes, 310
Estrup, Jacob, leader of the Conservative Party in Denmark, 697
Étaples, Treaty of, 381
Eteocretans, 47
Ethbaal, King of Tyre, 31
Ethelbert of Kent, 166
Ethelfreda of Mercia, 167
Ethelred the Redeless, Saxon king, 167, 168
Ethelstan, completes conquest of Danelaw, 167; crushes Scotch effort at revolt, 168
Ethiopia, 524, 660 *f.*, 754, 834 *ff.*, 963 *ff.*, 990, 1085 *ff.*, 1138, 1160
Ethiopian crisis, 963
Ethiopian dynasty, 24
Ethniké Hetairia, Greek organization, 746
Eton, founded, 271
Etruria, 68 *passim*
Etruscans, defeated Phocaean settlers, 53; defeated in naval battle, 57; first appeared in Italy, 68, 69; defeated at Lake Vadimo, 73; in the 3d Samnite War, 74, 93, 100
Etymologiae of Isidore of Seville, 163
d'Eu, Gaston d'Orléans, Comte, 817
Euboea, 46 *passim*
Eubulus, 64
Euclid, 75
Eucratides, 43
Eudes, *see* Odo

Eudes, Count of Chartres and Troyes, 225
Eudo, Duke, 187
Eudo, Prince of Oriel, 169
Eudocia, daughter of Valentinian, 145
Eudocia, widow of Valentinian, 145
Eudoxia, daughter of Bauto, 121
Eudoxia, daughter of Theodosius II, 121, 122
Eudoxia, widow of Constantine, 250
Eugene, Archduke, Austrian commander, 925
Eugene, Prince of Savoy, 444; imperial commander, 446, 457, 461, 463, 484
Eugenia of Battenberg, Queen of Spain, 647
Eugénie de Montijo, Empress of the French, 633
Eugenius, Roman emperor, 120
Eugenius, translator of Ptolemy's *Optics*, 223
Eugenius III (Bernardo Paganelli), Pope, 219, 256
Eugenius IV (Gabriel Condulmieri), Pope, 289, 292
Eumenes I, 37, 77, 81
Eumenes II, 37, 75, 80–84, 89
Eumenes III, 37
Eunomia, 50
Eunuchs, 37, 135
Eunus, captured, 90
Eupen, turned over to Belgium, 952, 974, 997; 1163
Euphrates, 24–25, 28, 29, 34
Euric, King of Toulouse, 144, 163
Euripides, Greek dramatist, 62
Eurymedon River, naval victory, 55
Eusebius, 23
Eusebius, Bishop of Caesarea, 123
Eusebius, Bishop of Nicomedia, 123
Eusebius, Bishop of Vercelli, 142
Eutaw, battle of, 522
Euthydemus, 43, 81, 83
Eutropius, 121
Euxine, 46, 47, 57, 62, 93
Evagoras of Cyprus, 63
Evangelical Church, in Nazi Germany, 1001
Evans, Sir George De Lacy, British soldier, 645
Evans, Oliver, invented high-pressure engine, 553
Evesham, battle of, 199
Exarchate of Bulgaria, established, 729
Exarchate of Ravenna, established, 146, 153; conquered by the Lombards, 176
Excavations in Africa, 5; in Asia, 6; in Mesopotamia, 13; in America, 19
Exhibition of 1851, in Hyde Park, London, 612 *f.*
Expression of the Emotions in Man and Animals, by Charles Darwin, 552
Expropriation Law, in Mexico, 1076
External Macedonian Revolutionary Organization, 718
Extinct animals, 6, 19
Extra-territorial rights in China, relinquished by Great Britain and the U.S., 1139
Eylau, battle of, 592
Eyre, Edward John, Australian explorer, 900
Ezekiel, 30, 31

"F's" (three) of the Tenant-Right League, 614, 616
Fabian Society, founded, 618
Fabius Pictor, Roman general, 90
Fachinetti, Giovanni Antonio, Pope Innocent IX, 396
Facta, Luigi, Italian prime minister, 987
Factory Act in England, 608
Factory inspection, in Germany, 691
Factory laws, in Sweden-Norway, 699
Fa-hsien, Buddhist pilgrim, 130, 136
Faidherbe, Louis Leon Cesar, French general, gov. of Senegal, 840
Fair Oaks, battle of, 778
Fair Wages and Hours of Labor Act, in Canada, 1060
Fairfax, Sir Thomas, general in English Civil War, 377, 378
Faisal, King of Syria, 1098; King of Iraq, 1105, 1106
Faisal II, King of Iraq, 1106
Falaba, sunk by submarine, 923
Falcón, Juan, pres. of Venezuela, 816
Falk, Adalbert, Prussian minister of public worship, 689, 690
Falk Laws, 689
Falkenhausen, Gen. Ludwig von, gov. of Belgium, 914
Falkenhayn, Gen. Erich von, German general, 917, 934, 958
Falkenstein, Gen. Vogel von, defeated the Hanoverians at Langensalza, 682 *f.*
Falkirk, battle of, 199
Falkirk Moor, battle of, 435
Falkland, Lucius Cary, Lord, Commons leader, 376
Falkland Dependency, 574
Falkland Islands, in dispute between Spain and England, 495; in controversy between U.S. and Britain, 806; battle of, 918
Fall, Albert Bacon, and the Teapot Dome oil scandal, 1051
Fallen Timbers, battle of, 522
Fallières, Clément Armand, pres. of France, 643
Fallmerayer, Philipp Jacob, in the Frankfurt Parliament, 676
Falloux, Frédéric Alfred Pierre, Count de, French statesman, 631, 633
Family Compact, between France and Spain, 451, 452, 495
Family Compact, in Upper Canada, 795
Famine, in Russia, 706, 742
Fan Noli, Bishop, Albanian leader, 1019
Fanning Island, discovered, 895; British cable station destroyed, 917
Fara, 13

Faraday, Michael, English inventor, 551, 5 54
Far Eastern Republic, in eastern Siberia, 1032, 1118
Far-Eastern Triplice, formed, 744
Farel, William, Swiss reformer, 409
Farewell, Francis George, declares Natal British, 851
Faria, Bento Pereyra de, on Portuguese mission to China, 539
Farías, Valentín Gómez, pres. of Mexico, 821
Farina, see La Farine
Farm Bankruptcy Act (Frazier-Lemke), declared unconstitutional, 1053
Farm Credit Act, 1053
Farm Mortgage Foreclosure Act, 1053
Farm Mortgage Refinancing Act, 1053
Farmers' and Labor Party in Southwest Africa, 1092
Farnese, Alessandro, Pope Paul III, 396
Farnese, Alexander, Duke of Parma, gov. of the Netherlands, 381
Farnese, Elizabeth, of Parma, marries Philip V of Spain, 452, 459
Farouk, King of Egypt, 1084
Farquhar, Sir Robert, seized French stations in Madagascar, 859
Farragut, David Glasgow, American admiral, 776, 778
Fars, 127, 128
Farther Spain (Hispania Ulterior), 88
Fascio di Combattimento, formed by Mussolini, 986
Fascist Congress at Naples, 988
Fascist Grand Council, made an official organ of Italy, 989
Fascist Republican régime, in Italy, disintegrated, 1164 f.
Fascisti Exposed, The, by Giacomo Matteotti, 988
Fashoda crisis, 641, 748, 833, 845
Fath Ali Khan, vizier of Afghanistan, 866
Fath Ali Shah, Shah of Persia, 862
Father Joseph, French diplomat, 387
Fatherland Front, in Austria, 1007, 1008
Fathpur Sikri, town near Agra, 533
Fatima, daughter of Mohammed, 187, 262
Fatimid dynasty, replaced by Omayyad dynasty, 164; in wars with the Mirdasids, 190; descent from Caliph Ali, 263
Fatio, Peter, leads an insurrection at Geneva, 460
"Fatti di Maggio," bread riots in Italy, 661
Fatyanovo culture, 16
Faulhaber, Cardinal Michel von, German churchman, 1002
Faure, Félix, pres. of France, 641, 642
Fauresmith culture, 6
Fausta, daughter of Maximian, 119, 120
Faustina, wife of Marcus Aurelius, 111
Faustrecht, 302
Favre, Jules Clause Gabriel, French Republican, 634, 636
Fawkes, Guy, and the Gunpowder Plot, 374
Fawkner, John Pascoe, pioneer settler in Australia, 900
Fayum, 21, 23; culture, 18
February Revolution, in Paris, 630, 673
Federal Bank Deposit Insurance Corporation, 1054
Federal Bureau of Investigation, 1156
Federal Council (Bundesrat) of the North German Confederation, 686
Federal Emergency Relief Act, 1054
Federal Farm Loan Bank Act, 792
Federal Farm Mortgage Corporation, 1053
Federal Power Commission, 1055
Federal Reserve Bank Act, 791
Federal tariff, in Australia, 904
Federal Trade Commission Act, 791
Federalist Party, U.S., 764
Fédération des Bourses du Travail, 641
Fédération des Syndicats, 641
Fédération du Parti des Travailleurs Socialistes de France, socialist political party, 639
Federation of Central America, formed, 1072
Federation of Labor, in New Zealand, 908
Federation of Organized Trades and Labor Unions, 784
Federation of Students in Venezuela, 1070
Federigo of Naples, deposed by the pope, 393
Federmann, Nicolaus, agent of the Welsers, 488
Fehrbellin, battle of, 442, 471
Fehrenbach, Konstantin, German premier, 997
Fejérváry, Baron Géza, Hungarian statesman, 696
Felix, beaten by Aëtius, 121
Felix, Antonius, procurator of Judea, 106
Felix V (Amadeus of Savoy), Pope, 289, 325
Felton, John, assassin of the Duke of Buckingham, 375
Feng Kuo-chang, pres. of China, 1117
Feng Tao, printed the nine Chinese classics, 341
Feng Yü-hsiang, Chinese war lord, 1119
Fengt'ai, attacked by Boxers, 883
Fenian Brotherhood, formed in New York, 614; raids in Canada, 796
Fenwick, Sir John, in plot to assassinate William III, 431
Ferdinand I, elected Prince of Bulgaria, 741; dismisses Stambulov, 718, 745; assumes title of tsar, 718, 755; abdicates, 948, 1022
Ferdinand I of Castile, 164, 284
Ferdinand II of Aragon, marries Isabella of Castile, 282; unites Aragon with Castile, 284; daughter Joanna married to Philip of Burgundy, 379; renews the Holy League, 381; Treaty of Narbonne; Treaty of Granada, 387; in coalition to despoil Venice, 393, 394; his death, 393 f.
Ferdinand III, takes Cordova and Seville from the Moors; helps Almohade emperor, 234 f.; African invasion, 235
Ferdinand I, Emperor of Austria, 671, 674

Ferdinand I, German emperor, 402; King of Bohemia, 419; war with John Zapolya; war against the Turks, 419 f., 422; succeeds to imperial throne, 423
Ferdinand II, German emperor; battle of the White Mountain, 404, 405; Treaty of Lubeck, 405; Treaty of Prague, 406 f.; his death, 407
Ferdinand III, German emperor, 407
Ferdinand I, King of Naples, 458; flees to Sicily, 586; dethroned by Napoleon, 592; restored to the throne, 602, 650
Ferdinand I (the Handsome) of Portugal, 283, 284
Ferdinand I, King of Rumania, 720, 721, 925, 1024, 1025
Ferdinand VI, King of Spain, 451, 452
Ferdinand VII of Spain, 502, 627, 643; 644; 645; South American colonies, 799, 800, 802
Ferdinand II (Bomba), King of the Two Sicilies, 654, 658
Ferdinand, Archduke of Austria, 591
Ferdinand of Austria, elected King of Rome and crowned, 400
Ferdinand of Braganza, heads revolt against John III, 286
Ferdinand of Brunswick, German general, 467
Ferdinand of Saxe-Coburg, declines throne of Spain, 646; marries Maria II, Queen of Portugal, 648
Ferdinand the Great, of Leon and Castile, 238
Ferdinand (the Constant Prince), youngest son of John I of Portugal, 285, 286
Ferghana, conquered by Li Kuang-li, 133; taken by Qutayba, 187
Ferguson, Major Patrick, defeated at the battle of King's Mountain, 522
Fermiers généraux (tax gatherers), in France, 578
Fernández, Gregorio, Spanish sculptor, 389
Fernández de Quiros, Pedro, discovered Tahiti and the New Hebrides, 894
Fernando Po, returned to Spanish rule, 840
Ferrante (Ferdinand I), of Naples, 284, 290, 292 f., 295, 393
Ferrara, Gregorio, Honduras leader, 1074
Ferrarese War, 290
Ferrer Guardia, Francisco, anti-clerical leader in Spain, 648
Ferry, Jules François Camille, French premier, 638, 639, 73/, 738, 739, 860, 874
Festival of the Supreme Being, 583
Feud of the Counts, civil war in Denmark, 410
Feudal holdings, in the Ottoman Empire, 728
Feudalism, 147, 149, 151, 153, 158; in Japan, 354 f.
Feuillants, moderate monarchists in French Revolution, 580
Fez, forbidden to be worn in Turkey, 1096
Fez, Kingdom of, 286; Treaty of, 839
Fichte, Johann Gottlieb, German philosopher, 594
Ficino, Marsilio, Italian humanist, 296
Fidenae, 71, 72
Fiefs in Japan, abolished, 890
Field, Cyrus West, brings Atlantic cable to Newfoundland, 78}
Field of the Cloth of Gold, 369, 383
Fieschi, Giuseppe Marco, Corsican radical, 628
"Fifteen, The," Jacobite rising in Scotland, 434
Fifteenth amendment to the U.S. Constitution, adopted, 781
Fifth Crusade, 257
Fifth Monarchy Men, 373, 426
Fiftieth Ordinance, allowing Hottentots to buy and hold land, 851
"Fighting French," 1160
Figueroa, Emiliano, pres. of Chile, 1065
Figure painting, in China, 135
Fiji, discovered, 894; annexed, 895
Filchner, Dr. Wilhelm, Antarctic explorer, 575
Filelfo, Francesco, humanist, 298
Filippo, Maria, of the Visconti, 298; war with Venice, 299
Filísola, Vicente, Mexican commander, 805
Fillmore, Millard, 13th pres. of the U.S., 774
Filonardi Co. leases Italian Somaliland for exploitation, 835, 836
Fimbria, Caius, 94
Finch, Sir Heneage (later Earl of Nottingham), in the ministry of Charles II, 427
Finiglacial stage, 15
Fink, Friedrich August von, Prussian general, 467
Finkenstein, Treaty of, 862
Finland, acquired by Russia, 699, 701; proclaims its independence, 943; German forces land; civil war, 943, 1047, 1048; post-war history, 966, 1047, 1048; 1028, 1029, 1031; invaded by Russia, 1135; 1142; declared war on Germany, 1143; campaign in, 1140 f.; 1151, 1154, 1171
Finno-Tatar race, 181
Finschafen, occupied, 1169
Firdausi (Abul Kasim Mansur), Persian poet, 190
Fire, use known to Palaeolithic period, 4
Firm, Joseph Lannison, invented straight-line printing press, 556
First Congress of U.S., 764
First Crusade, 219, 250 f., 255 f.
First International, 550, 635, 637, 689
First Principles, by Herbert Spencer, 550
First Treaty of Paris (1814), 601, 603, 851
Firuz (Perozes), makes peace with Ephthalites, 125
Firuz Tughluk, 334
Firuzan, Persian general, 128
Fisher, Andrew, Australian prime minister, 904, 1129
Fisher's Hill, battle of, 779
Fishing rights, on coasts of Newfoundland, 793, 798
Fitzmaurice, James, aviator, 558
Fitzmaurices, settled in Ireland, 169
Fitzroy, Capt. Robert, with Charles Darwin in the Beagle, 895, 906

Fiume, taken by the Italians, 949, 955, 959, **987**
Five Classics, in the Han dynasty, 133
Five Days in Milan, 673
Five Forks, battle of, 779
Five-Mile Act, of the Clarendon Code, 426 *f.*
Five-Year Plans, in Russia, 1034
Flaccus, Hordeonius, 107, 108
Flaccus, L. Valerius, succeeds Marius, 93, 94, 95
Flaccus, M. Fulvius, 91
Flagellants, 302
Flamininus, Titus Quinctius, Roman general, 80, 88
Flaminius, Caius, Roman general, 87
Flanders, granted by Charles the Bald to Baldwin Iron-Arm, 158; its influence in the Hanseatic League, 309
Flanders, Count of, in alliance with Edward I, 199; 231; refuses assistance to Edward III, 264
Flanders, Count of, son of Leopold II of Belgium, 720
Flandin, Pierre Étienne, French premier, 978
Flatters, Paul Francis Xavier, African explorer, 837
Flavius, Gnaeus, 73
Fleix, Treaty of, 384
Fletcher *v.* Peck, decided by John Marshall, 770
Fleurus, battle of, 583
Fleury, André Hercule de, cardinal and French statesman, 447
Flight of Mohammed (Hijrah, Hegira), 184
Flinders, Matthew, Australian explorer, 896
Flint, Mr., British interpreter at Tientsin, 540
Flint industry, 5
Flodden Field, battle of, 369
Flor, Roger de, with Catalan mercenaries, 322
Florence, early history, 293 *ff.*; center of the Italian Renaissance, 296; republic under Niccolo Capponi, 394; Alessandro de Medici hereditary ruler; Grand Duchy of Tuscany, 398; Treaty of, 588; captured by Allies, 1162
Flores, Alfredo Gonzales, pres. of Costa Rica, 1072
Flores, Juan, pres. of Ecuador, 813, 814
Flores, Venancio, pres. of Uruguay, 811
Florianus, M. Annius, 116
Florida, ceded to the U.S., 770
Floridablanca, Don José Moñino y Redondo, Count of, Spanish reform minister, 451, 452
Florin, first coined, 293
Florina, battle of, 934
Florus, Julius, leads revolt of the Treveri, 103
Foch, Gen. Ferdinand, 912, 941; on the Supreme War Council; commander-in-chief of the Allied armies in France, 945
Focsani, taken by Austro-German forces, 935; truce of, 944
Foix, Gaston de, Duke of Nemours, French general, 381
Foix, Germaine de, married Ferdinand of Aragon, 387
Fokker, Anthony Hermann Gerard, airplane designer, 557, 946
Follen, Karl, leader of the *Burschenschaft*, 669
Folsom point, 19
Fonck, René, French air fighter, 946
Fonseca, Hermes da, pres. of Brazil, 818
Fonseca, Juan Rodríguez de, Spanish minister of the Indies, 496, 499
Fonseca, Manoel Deodoro da, president of Brazil, 817, 818
Font, Robert, 5
Fontainebleau, Treaties of, 443, 452, 454, 468
Fontaney, Jean de, cured Chinese emperor, 539
Fontenay, battle of, 157
Fontenoy, battle of, 435, 466
Foochow, opened to trade, 879
Foods, of Palaeolithic period, 4; in Post-Palaeolithic, 10
Foot-binding, permitted to Chinese only, 537
Foraker (Joseph Benson) Act, establishing civil govt. in Puerto Rico, 824
Forbes, George William, premier of New Zealand, 1131
Forbes, Gen. John, took Fort Duquesne, 516
Forbes, Rosita, at the Kufra Oasis, 1081
Forbes, William Cameron, gov.-gen. of the Philippines, 910; heads commission to Haiti, 1078
Force Bill, enacted by U.S. Congress, 772, 784
Forced labor, Congo natives, 844
Ford, Henry, American industrialist, 557, 790
Fordney-McCumber Tariff Act, 1051
Foreign Economic Co-ordination Office of, 1141
Foreign Enlistment Act, of England, 645
Foreign Relief and Rehabilitation, Office of, 1141
Forest Cantons, of the Swiss Confederation, 301, 306
Forged Decretals, first papal citation, 153
Former (or Liu) Sung dynasty, 135
Formosa, 881, 890, 1171
Formosus, Pope, 152, 160
Forrest, Sir John, Australian explorer, 902
Forster, Albert, head of the Danzig Free State, 967, 1002
Forster, William Edward, English statesman, 615
Fort Dauphin, in Madagascar, founded, 859
Fort Donelson, surrenders to Grant, 778
Fort Douaumont, taken by the Germans, 930
Fort Duquesne, built by the French, 516
Fort Henry, surrenders to Gen. Grant, 778
Fort Le Boeuf, built by the French, 516
Fort Lee, surrendered to the British, 521
Fort Nassau, later Fort Orange, 510, 512
Fort Presqu' Isle, erected by the French, 516
Fort Rouillé, on site of present-day Toronto, 516
Fort Rüpel, occupied by a Bulgar-German force, 932
Fort Sumter, bombarded by Gen. Beauregard, 776
Fort Vaux, taken by the Germans, 930; retaken by the French, 931

Fort Washington, surrendered to the British, 521
Forts Clark and Hatteras, captured by Federal ships, 776
Fortescue, Sir John, chief justice of the King's Bench, ideas foreshadowed policies of Henry VII, 271 *f.*
Fortis, Alessandro, Italian premier, 662
"Forty-Seven *Rōnin*," 548
Forum Gallorum, battle of, 98
Forum of Trajan, in Rome, 69, 110
Fosna culture, 18
Fouché, Joseph, French revolutionary leader, 582, 583
Fouqué, Henry August, Prussian general, 467
Fouquier-Tinville, Antoine Quentin, public prosecutor at revolutionary tribunals, 583
Four Articles of Prague, 303, 305
Four-Power Pacific Treaty, 955
Four-Power Pact, 990
Four-Year Plan, of Nazi Germany, 1002
Four Years' War, 77 *f.*
Fourdrinier brothers, Henry and Sealy, invented paper-making machine, 553
Fourier, François Marie Charles, French sociological writer, 549, 628
Fourteen Points, of Pres. Wilson, 944, 1049; accepted by Germany and Austria, 950, 951
Fourteenth amendment to the U.S. Constitution, 780 *f.*
Fourth Crusade, 220 *f.*, 254, 256 *f.*
Fourth Lateran Council, 221, 257
Fox, Charles James, created Lord Holland, 435; 436; foreign secretary, 437; 768
Fox, Luke, English explorer, 560
Foxhall Man, 9
Franc, devalued, 978
France, 147 *ff.*, 225 *ff.*, 273 *ff.*, 440 *ff.*, 505 *ff.*, 578 *ff.*, 626 *ff.*, 912 *ff.*, 976 *ff.*; in Second World War, 1135, 1136, 1143, 1146 *f.*; 1148, 1156, 1163 *f.*
Franche-Comté, 395; occupied by Condé, 442; restored to Spain, 442; annexed to France, 459
Franchet-d'Esperey, Louis Félix Marie, French general, 920, 948
Franchise Bill, in England, 617
Francis I, of Austria, 581, 592, 601, 670 *f.*, 672
Francis I, of France, 369, 382 *f.*, 388, 394, 395, 400, 401, 505
Francis II, of France, 372, 384
Francis I, German emperor, 459, 464, 465, 467
Francis II, of Naples, 658
Francis II Rákóczi, 462 *f.*
Francis, Duke of Alençon, 384
Francis, Duke of Cadiz, 645
Francis IV, Duke of Modena, 650
Francis Charles, Austrian Archduke, 674
Francis Ferdinand, Austrian Archduke, 694; assassinated at Sarajevo, 695, 715, 761
Francis Joseph I, of Austria, 635, 674, 681, 693, 694, 695, 696, 733, 746, 755, 930
Francis of Assisi, 221
Francis, Sir Philip, 436, 535
Franciscans, in England, 198, 201; protest against luxury of popes at Avignon, 286; missions in Florida, 493; in Spanish America, 498 *f.*
Franco, Gen. Francisco, insurgent leader in Spanish Civil War, 983, 984, 1004, 1088; dictator, 1139, 1144, 1150
Franco, João, prime minister of Carlos I of Portugal, 649
Franco, Manuel, pres. of Paraguay, 1065
Franco, Rafael, pres. of Paraguay, 1066
Franco, Rafael, revolutionist, 814
Franco-Italian Agreement on Morocco and Tripoli, 661, 751; on Ethiopia, 1085
Franco-Prussian war, 688
Franco-Russian Alliance, 640, 742; extended, 748, 751, 963, 965
Franco-Russian loan to China, 882
Franco-Soviet Treaty, 1143
Franco-Spanish Campaign in Morocco, 981
Franco-Syrian Treaty, 1097
Franco-Turkish Agreement, on the Sanjak of Alexandretta, 1097
François, Hermann von, German general, 916
Frankfort, occupied by the French, 997; Treaty of, 636
Frankfurt Constitution, 677
Frankfurt National Assembly or Parliament, 675, 676, 677
Franklin, Benjamin, American statesman, 516, 517
Franklin, Lt. (later Sir) John, Arctic explorer, 562, 563 *f.*
Franklin, Lady, 564
Franklin relief expeditions, 563 *f.*
Franklin-Bouillon, Henry, French diplomat, 1095
Franks (Mervings), 116, 118, 120, 142, 144, 147
Franz Joseph Land, discovered, 564; claimed by Austria, annexed by Russia, 570
Fraser, Simon, English explorer, 793
Fraticelli, religious reformers, 288
Frederick I of Denmark, 412
Frederick III of Denmark, 474
Frederick IV of Denmark, took part in Northern War, 474; 561
Frederick V of Denmark, 474
Frederick VI of Denmark, 474
Frederick VII of Denmark, 676, 681, 697
Frederick VIII of Denmark, 697
Frederick IV Elector Palatine, leader of the Protestant Union, 402 *f.*
Frederick V (the Winter King), Elector Palatine, 404; elected King of Bohemia, 404, 419, 465
Frederick I (Barbarossa: Red Beard). king. 208; led Third Cru-

sade, 210, 247; executes Arnold of Brescia, 219; 220; excommunicated, 220, 223: 240; death, 256; 296
Frederick II (*Stupor Mundi*), German emperor, 199; 210 f.; abandons German Church to Innocent III, 211; 230; excommunicated; crowns himself King of Jerusalem, 211, 257; deposes and imprisons his son Henry, 212; excommunicated a second time, 212, 257; attempts at assassination, 213; 214 f.; became King of Jerusalem, 257; 293; 307; death, 213, 299, 592
Frederick III, German emperor, 289, 304, 305, 318
Frederick III, Emperor of Germany, 683, 688, 691
Frederick IV, German emperor, 306
Frederick I, King of Prussia, 461
Frederick II (the Great) of Prussia, 447, 465, 466, 467, 468, 469, 481, 484; his death, 469
Frederick I of Hesse-Cassel, King of Sweden, 473
Frederick III of Sicily, 284
Frederick, King of Sicily, 290
Frederick, Archduke, Austrian commander-in-chief, 914
Frederick of Antioch, 293
Frederick of Austria, last of the Babenbergs, 246, 306
Frederick of Brandenburg, 303
Frederick the Wise, of Saxony, 400
Frederick Charles, Prince of Hesse, elected King of Finland, 1047
Frederick Charles, Prussian prince, 683, 688
Frederick Henry of Holland, 438
Frederick William I, King of Prussia, 462, 465
Frederick William II of Prussia, 581
Frederick William III of Prussia, 586, 598, 601, 670
Frederick William IV of Prussia, 670, 676, 677; on the verge of war with Austria, 678, 680
Frederick William, Duke, imperial general, 467
Frederick William, the Great Elector of Brandenburg, 407, 442, 465 ff., 471
Fredericksburg, battle of, 778
Free City of Danzig, 1002
Free French, 1137; forces, led by Gen. de Gaulle, 1138, 1141, 1159
Freedmen's Bureau Bill, 780
Freedom of conscience, demanded by Cromwell's army, 378
Freeport heresy, avowed by Stephen A. Douglas, 775
Fregellae, 73, 91
Freiburg, battle of, 468
Freire, Ramón, pres. of Chile, 809
Frelinghuysen, Frederick Theodore, American secretary of state, 784
French, John Denton Pinkstone, 1st Earl of Ypres, British general, 857, 912, 920
French and Indian War, 516
French Cameroons, 1088
French Catholics, mission on Tahiti, 895
French Committee of National Liberation, 1140, 1141
French Communist Party, 1144
French Consultative National Assembly, 1143
French East India Co., 444
French Equatorial Africa, 846, 1088
French Forces of the Interior (FFI), French underground, 1163
French Guinea protectorate, 840
French hostages, executed by Germany, 1137
French in North America, 505 f.
French Indo-China, 874 f., 1117, 1136, 1158, 1165
French Mediterranean coast, 1163
French Morocco, 1160
French navy, scuttled, 1158
French North Africa, 1158, 1160 f., 1162
French Protestantism, its beginnings, 383
French Revolution, 578 ff.
French West Africa, 1158
Frequens, papal decree concerning general councils, 289
Frere, Sir Henry Bartle Edward, gov. of Cape Colony, 853
Frère-Orban, Walther, a leader of the Liberals in Belgium, 623
Fréron, Louis Stanislas, French revolutionist, 583
Freud, Sigmund, Austrian psychologist, 552
Freycinet, Charles de, French premier, 636, 639
Freycinet, Louis Claude, Desaulses de, French explorer, 895
"Friars' Lands," in the Philippines, 909
Friars Minor (Minorites, Grey Friars, Cordeliers), 221
Frías, Tomás, pres. of Bolivia, 812
Fribourg, Treaty of, 382
Frick, Wilhelm, minister of the interior under Hitler, 1000
Friedewalde, Treaty of, 402
Fritigern, Visigoth leader, 143
Fritsch, Werner von, German chief of staff, 1004
Friulian Mark, 155
Frobisher, Martin, British explorer, 507, 559
Froissart, Jean, French historian, 267
Frolic (Br.) captured by the *Wasp*, 769
Fronde, disturbances of the, 440
Frontenac, Louis de Buade, Count de, founded Fort Frontenac, 507
Frontiers, battle of, 913
Frost, John, English radical, 609
Froude, James Anthony, English historian, 853
Frumentius, converted the Kingdom of Axum to Christianity, 328
Fu, Chinese prince, 537
Fuad I, King of Egypt, 1083, 1084
Fuad Pasha, Turkish grand vizier, 728
Fuentes de Oñoro, battle of, 596
Fujiwara, Japanese clan, 140, 351, 352; period in Japanese history, 352; crushed by Yoritomo, 356

Fu-k'ang-an, invades Nepal, 540
Fukien, Chinese province, 882, 892
Full Bronze Age, 13
Fulton, Robert, American inventor, 553, 768
Fulvia, Antony's wife, 99
Fulvius, Marcus, defeats Rome in 2d Samnite War, 73
Fumumaro Konoye, Japanese prime minister, 1136, 1165, 1166
Fu-nan, suzerain of Chen-la, 137
Fundamental Constitutions, for Carolina, 513
Fundamental Laws, promulgated in Russia, 708
Fundamental Orders, establishing a general court in Connecticut, 509
Funding Bill of U.S., 764
Funk, Walther, minister of economics in Germany, 1004
Funston, Frederick, captures Aguinaldo, 909
Fürstenberg, Franz Egon von, Bishop of Strassburg, 443
Füssen, Treaty of, 466

Gabalas, Leo, Byzantine leader, 259
Gabbar, 35
Gabelle, salt tax, 276, 277, 578
Gabes, 1160
Gabinius, Aulus, 95
Gabinus, 84
Gablenz, Ludwig Karl Wilhelm, Austrian general, 682
Gabras of Trebizond, a feudal family, 253
Gad, tribe of, 29, 30
Gadsden Purchase, 774
Gaelic poetry, 169
Gaels, *see* Goidels
Gaeta, a city republic, 217; battle of, 393
Gaetulicus, conspiracy against Caligula, 105
Gag resolutions, against anti-slavery petitions, 773
Gagern, Heinrich von, pres. of the Frankfurt National Assembly, 675, 676
Gaines' Mill, battle of, 778
Gaiseric (Genseric) leads Vandals into Africa, 121; sacks Rome, 122, 142, 143, 144; takes Carthage, 145
Gaius, Roman jurist, 117
Gaius Caesar, *see* Caligula
Gaius Antonio, leader of revolt in New Granada, 800
Galapagos Islands, 1156
Galatia, Kingdom of, becomes a Roman province, 37; established by Celts, 78; invaded by Arabs, 187
Galatians, defeated by Attalus I, 37, 80, 81
Galba, Servius Sulpicius, Roman emperor, 107
Galdan, chief of the Olöt Jungars, 539
Galeazzo, of the Visconti, 298
Galerius (C. Galerius Valerius Maximianus), Roman emperor, 118, 119, 124
Galicia, taken by Austro-Germans, 922
Galilee, 29, 32
Galinda, Carlos Blanco, heads military junta govt. of Bolivia, 1067
Gallas, Matthias, imperial general, 406, 407
Galley Hill Man, 9
Gallieni, Joseph Simon, French general, 861, 914, 920
Gallienus, Publius Licinius Egnatius, Roman emperor, 116, 124
Gallipoli, campaign, 919 ff.
Galloway, Joseph, American statesman, 520
Gallus, half-brother of Julian, chosen as Caesar, 120
Gallus, C. Vibius Trebonianus, 115, 116
Gallwitz, Max von, German general, 922
Galton, Sir Francis, English scientist, 552
Galvani, Luigi, Italian physicist, 455
Gálvez, José de, occupies Upper California, 493
Gama, Christopher da, Portuguese conquistador, 524
Gama, Vasco da, Portuguese discoverer, 390, 524, 530
Gamarnik, Ian Borisovich, Bolshevik leader, 1036
Gamarra, Agustín, pres. of Peru, 811, 812
Gambetta, Leon, French statesman, 635, 636, 738, 831
Gambia, British settlement, 840
Gambier Island, protectorate established by the French, 895
Gamelin, Gustave, French commander-in-chief, 1146
Gandamak, Treaty of, 867, 868
Gandhara, 42, 43, 136; art, 129, 131
Gandhi, Mohandas Karamchand, Indian nationalist leader; in the Transvaal, 858, 859; returns to India; campaign of passive resistance and non-co-operation, 1111; withdraws from the National Congress, 1113; 1138
Gangas, wars with the Chalukyas, 336
Ganja, battle of, 862
Ganjin, Chinese monk, 351
Gapon, Father George, Russian labor leader, 707
Garashanin, Iliya, Serbian statesman, 714
Garay, Juan de, refounded Buenos Aires, 490, 492, 493
Garbai, Alexander, Hungarian Bolshevik leader, 953, 1013
García, King of Leon, 164
Gardanne, Gen. Claude Mathieu, reorganizes Persian army, 862
Gardiner, Stephen, Bishop of Winchester, 372
Gardoqui, Diego de, Spanish diplomat, 766
Garfield, James Abram, 20th pres. of U.S., 782, 783
Garibaldi, Giuseppe, Italian patriot, 655, 658, 659
Garigliano, battles of, 179, 387, 393
Garlande family, in France, 227
Garnier, Marie Joseph François, French colonial commander, 874, 880
Garrison, William Lloyd, established the *Liberator*, 771
Gas engine, 556
Gas lights, first introduced in London, 553
Gasca, Pedro de la, Spanish conquistador, 490

Gaspée affair, 518
Gaston, Jean Baptiste, Duke of Orléans, 387, 440
Gastone, Gian, ruler of Tuscany, 459
Gates, Gen. Horatio, American general, 522
Gath, Kingdom of, 30
Gathas, hymns in the Avesta, 39, 41
Gatling, Richard Jordan, invented the machine gun, 554
Gatty, Harold, circled globe alone by airplane, 558, 1052
Gaugamela, battle of, 40, 65
Gaul, conquest by Caesar, 96; revolt under Vercingetorix, 97; overrun by invaders, 121, 166
Gaulle, Charles de, French general, 1140, 1142, 1143, 1144; head of French National Committee, 1148; "Free French" leader, 1158, 1159; at Casablanca Conference, 1160
Gauls, sack Rome, 72, 74
Gautama, 41
Gaveston, Piers, favorite of Edward II of England, 264
Gaza, Kingdom of, 30; battles of, 35, 77, 938, 948
Gedrosia, 65
Gedymin of Lithuania, 313, 316
Geffrard, Fabre, pres. of Haiti, 825
Gela, 47, 57, 1162
Gelasius, Pope, 146
Gelasius II (Giovanni Coniulo), Pope, 219
Gelimer, Vandal usurper in North Africa, 172
Gelo, 34
Gelon of Gela, 57
Gempaku, Sugita, translator of a text on anatomy, 548
Genealogical charts, see table of contents
General Assembly, of the United Nations, 1171
General Confederation of Labor (C.G.T.), in France, 977, 980
General Court of Massachusetts Bay colony, 509, 511, 517, 518
General Motors strike, 1056
General Trades' Union, linking New York trade societies, 772
General warrants, declared illegal, 436
Genesis, 30
Genet, Edmond Charles Edouard, French minister to the U.S., 764
Geneva, adopts the Reformation, 409; annexed to France, 460; seat of the League of Nations, 994; Treaty of, 382
Geneva Protocol, 959
Genghis Khan. See Jenghiz (Chinjiz) Khan
Genji Monogatari, Japanese novel, 353
Genkū, founder of the Pure Land sect, 354, 356
Gennadios, Greek patriarch in Constantinople, 327
Genoa, Duke of, declines throne of Spain, 646
Genoa, 1141; Republic of, 397, 459; transformed into the Ligurian Republic, 585
Genoa Conference, on the Russian problem, 958
Genouilly, see Rigault de Genouilly
Genovesi, Antonio, Italian physiocrat, 455
Genroku year period, 547
Genshin, Japanese monk, 353
Gentil, Emile, united French possessions in Africa, 842, 845
Gentlemen's agreement between U.S. and Japan, 893; abrogated, 1051; between Italy and Great Britain, 991
Geochronology, 3
Geoffrey of Anjou, protector of Matilda as Queen of England 194, 227
Geoffrey of Monmouth, his History of the Kings of Britain, 194
Geology, method of dating, 2, 3
Geometric style in vase-painting, 47, 48
George I, King of England, 433 f.
George II, King of England, 465, 466
George III, King of England, 435, 436, 468, 517, 605, 669
George IV, King of England, 605, 606
George V, King of England, 620, 621, 969, 970
George VI, King of England, 965, 969, 970, 971, 979, 1057
George I, King of Greece, 710, 712
George II, King of Greece, 1021, 1022
George XII, last King of Georgia, 862
George, Prince, of Greece, high commissioner for Crete, 710, 746
George, Henry, American social critic, 618
George II Rákóczi of Hungary, 461, 482
George William, Elector of Brandenburg, 405, 407
Georgia, founded, 513
Georgia, Kingdom of, conquered by Arabs, 187; invaded by Mongols, 260; annexed by Russia, 701, 862; occupied by the British, 947; sets up Soviet govt., 1032
Gepids, 143; annihilated, 150
Gerard, Lord of Brogue, 217
Gerards, Normans, in Ireland, 169
Gerbert of Aurillac, 159; pope as Sylvester II, 162, 216. See also Sylvester II
Gerbillon, Jean-François, Jesuit, 539
Gergovia, 97
Gerhard, Count of Holstein, 312
Gerlache, Lt. Adrien de, Arctic explorer, 573
German African Society, 847
German East Africa, 847 ff., 1090
German East Africa Co., 847, 848
German-Austrian Agreement of 1936, 1003, 1008
German-Austrian Alliance of 1879, 741
German-Czech crisis of 1938, 965, 979, 980
German-Polish Agreement on Danzig, 1002
German Samoa, 1128, 1131
German Southwest Africa, 850 ff., 1091
Germanic Confederation, 602, 669, 670, 675, 676, 677, 681, 682 686, 687
Germanicus, Roman general, 103, 105

Germantown, battle of, 521
Germany, 153 ff., 205 ff.; 300 ff.; 398 ff., 460 ff. passim, 667 ff. 733 ff. passim, 912 ff. passim, 955 ff., 995 ff.; in Second World War, occupied Paris, 1135; invaded Poland, 1135, 1145; invaded Norway, occupied Denmark, 1135; armistice with France, 1135; pact with Italy and Japan, 1136; consulates closed in U.S., 1137; invaded Russia, 1137, 1151; declared war on U.S., 1138, 1167; annexed northern Slovenia, 1139; into unoccupied France, 1139, 1148, 1160; occupy Italian cities, 1141; jet planes against England, 1142; capitulated in Paris, 1142; occupied Hungary, 1142; driven from Pskov, 1142; surrendered unconditionally, 1144; divided Poland with Russia, 1145; Blitzkrieg, 1145; invaded Norway, 1146; mechanized divisions into France, 1146; bombed Great Britain, 1148; occupied Channel islands, 1148; submarine war, 1148 f.; sea and air blockade of Britain, 1149; invaded Rumania, Yugoslavia, Greece, 1150; penetrated Stalingrad, 1153; battle of, 1154, 1164 f.; merchant tonnage, 1156; North African resistance ended, 1162; capitulated in Italy, 1163; invaded by American First Army, 1163; invaded by Allied Armies, 1164; surrendered at Reims, 1165
Gero, Markgraf of Poland, 241
Gerry, Elbridge, American commissioner in France, 766
Gervais, Alfred Albert, French admiral, 742
Gervinus, Georg Gottfried, German historian and parliamentarian, 676
Gerzean culture, 18
Geta, Publius Septimius, brother of Emperor Caracalla, 114
Gettysburg, battle of, 778
Geza, Duke of the Magyars, 245
Geza I of Hungary, 245
Geza II of Hungary, 245
Ghana, Kingdom of, 328, 363
Ghazi, King of Iraq, 1106
Ghaznavids, dynasty, 190, 332
Ghent, taken by the Germans, 914; Treaty of, 769, 793
Ghiberti, Lorenzo, Italian artist, 296
Ghirlandaio, Domenico, Italian painter, 290
Ghislieri, Michaele, Pope Pius V, 396
Ghiyas-ud-Din Mohammed, ruler of Ghur, 332
Gia Long (Nguyen Anh), Emperor of Annam, 874, 880
Gian Galeazzo, of the Visconti, 298
Gian Maria, of the Visconti, 298
Giannone, Pietro, Italian historian, 455
Giants' Tombs, 17
Gibbons v. Ogden, decided by John Marshall, 770
Gibraltar, 163; taken by Sir George Rooke, 432, 446, 450; besieged by French and Spanish, 436
Gibson, Violet, attempts to assassinate Mussolini, 989
Gideon, 30
Giffard, Henry, and the first dirigible balloon, 555
Gijon, captured by Franco's troops, 984
Gilbert, Sir Humphrey, took possession of Newfoundland, 507
Gilbert Islands discovered, 895; under British protectorate, 896; 1169
Gilchrist, Percy, English inventor, 555
Gillan (Gillam), Zachariah, explorer, 561
Giluhepa, 26
Gimil-Sin, 26
Ginkel, Godart van, 1st Earl of Athlone, 430
Gioberti, Vincenzo, Italian statesman, 651
Giolitti, Giovanni, Italian prime minister, 661, 662, 925, 987
Giornico, battle of, 307
Giotto di Bondone, Italian architect, 222, 294
Giovanna, Princess, of Italy, 989, 1023
Giraud, Gen. Henri, French chief of state in North Africa, 1140, 1160, 1162
Girgutu, Ion, Rumania, 1135
Giron, Francisco, Peruvian insurgent, 490
Girondists, French revolutionary party, 580 f., 582, 583, 584
Gist, Christopher, founder of Cumberland, Md., 515
Gizeh, 23
Glabrio, M. Acilius, 89
Gladstone, William Ewart, British prime minister, 611, 614, 615, 616, 617, 618, 688, 734, 737, 742
Glagolithic (Slavic) alphabet, 177
Glanville, Ranulf de, English jurist, 195
Glasgow (H.M.S.), escapes destruction in battle, 918
Glaucia, Caius Servilius, 93
Glavatsky, Constantin Ivanovich, Lithuanian general, 1042
Glen, Alexander Richard, Arctic explorer, 570
Glen Gray Act, in the Cape Colony, 855
Glen Grey Falls, 6
Glencoe, Massacre of, 431
Glendower, Owen, revolts in Wales, 268
Glorious Revolution in England, 430
Gloucester, Duke of, 268
Glycerius, 122
Glynn, James, American commodore, 888
Gneisenau, German cruiser, 917, 918
Gneisenau, August Wilhelm Anton, Prussian general, 592, 594, 603
Gnosticism, 113
Gobineau, Count Joseph Arthur de, 551
Goblet, René, French premier, 639
Gobryas, takes Babylon, 26
God, Peace of, 217, 227
Godaveri, 129
Goderich, Frederick John Robinson, Viscount, British prime minister, 606
Godesberg conference, between Chamberlain and Hitler, 1012

Godfrey of Bouillon, King of Jerusalem, 255
Godfrey the Bearded, Duke of Upper Lorraine, 206, 217
Godolphin, Sidney, 1st Earl of, English statesman, 428, 432
Godoy, Manuel de, Spanish reform minister, 451, 452, 593
Gods and Goddesses: Adon, 32; Adonis, 32; Agni, 41; Ahriman, 39; Ahura Mazda, 39; Aleyan Baal, 32; Amon, 21, 24; Amon-Re, 21; Anat, 32; Angro-mainyu, 39; Anu, 25; Aphrodite (Astarte), 32; Aphrodite (Venus), 69; Apollo, 43; Ardini, 38; Arinna, 36; Ashera, 32; Ashur, 27; Astarte (Aphrodite), 29, 32; Athena, 46; Aton, 23; Attis, 36; Atum, 21; Atum-Re, 23; Baal Hammon, 32; Bacchus, 37; Bagbartu, 38; Baki, 37; Bast, 21; Bel, 26; Brahma, 43; Cybele (Ma), 36, 77; Dionysos, 37; Ea, 25; El, 32; Enlil, 25, 26; Eshmun, 32; Eunomia, 50; Friga, 170; Haldi, 38; Hari-Hara, 43; Hathor, 21; Hepa (Hepat), 28, 36; Hera, 46; Horus, 21; Huitzilopochtli, 360; Indra, 28, 41; Ishtar, 27; Isis, 21, 77; Jehovah, 29, 30; Krishna, 43, 331; Marduk, 26; Mars, 69; Melgarth, 31, 32; Minos, 46; Mithra, 28, 39, 77; Nasatya, 28,; Odin, 170; Ormuzd, 39; Osiris, 21; Ptah, 21; Rama, 43; Re, 21; Rurda 43; Sandon, 37; Santas, 37; Set, 21; Shepesh, 32; Sita, 43; Siva, 43; Soma, 41; Tammuz, 32; Tanit, 32; Tesheba, 38; Teshub, 28, 36; Thor, 170; Thoth, 21; Varuna, 28, 39, 41; Venus, 69; Vishnu, 43, 130, 332, 336, 338; Zeus, 46, 67
Godunov, Boris, Tsar of Russia, 417
Godwin, Earl of Wessex, 168
Godwin, Gen. Henry Thomas, in 2d Burmese War, 872
Godwin, William, English political theorist, 550
Goebbels, Dr. Joseph, German minister of propaganda, 1010
Goeben, German cruiser, 919
Goering, Gen. Hermann, National Socialist leader, 967, 990, 1000, 1004
Goethals, Lt. Col. George Washington, chief engineer of Panama Canal, 819
Goez, Benedict de, 537
Goga, Octavian, Rumanian premier, 1027
Goidels (Gaels), a Celtic stock, 164, 166
Goito, battle of, 654
Gokhale, a leader of the Nationalist movement in India, 871
Gold, discovered at Sutter's Fort, Calif., 774; on the Witwatersrand in southern Transvaal, 854
Gold Coast, made a separate British colony, 840, 1089
Gold mining, in Spanish America, 499, 501
Gold Repeal Resolution, 1054
Gold Reserve Act, 1054
Gold standard, introduced in Russia, 706
Golden (literary) Age, 112
Golden Bull, 303, 305; of Eger, 211; of Rimini, 214; of Frederick II, 240; 249
Golden Horde, 244, 262, 345
"Golden House" of Nero, 108
Golden Pavilion (Kinkaku), erected in Kyōto, 359
Goldie, Sir George Taubman, founder of the United African Co., 841
Goldoni, Carlo, Italian dramatist, 454
Goliath (H.M.S.) sunk, 920
Goltz, Gen. Colmar von der, gov. of Belgium, 914, 1007, 1043; drives the Bolsheviks out of Finland, 1048
Goluchowski, Agenor, Count, Austrian foreign minister, 744, 746
Gómara, Francisco, Spanish historian, 389
Gömbös, Julius, premier of Hungary, 990, 1014
Gomes, Fernão, leased the Guinea trade from Alfonso V, 364
Gomes, Manuel Teixeira, pres. of Portugal, 985
Gomes, Wenceslaus Braz Pereira, pres. of Brazil, 1070
Gómez, Esteban, explorer, 368
Gómez, José Miguel, pres. of Cuba, 823, 824, 1077
Gómez, Juan Vicente, pres. of Venezuela, 817, 1070
Gómez, Miguel Mariano, pres. of Cuba, 1077
Gompers, Samuel, American labor leader, 784
Gonatas, Gen. Stylianos, Greek leader, 1021
Gonçalves, Lopo, crosses the equator, 364
Gondopharnes, 128
Gondra, Manuel, pres. of Paraguay, 1065, 1066
Gongo Musa, ruler of the Mandingo Empire, 328 f.
Gonse, Gen. Charles, and the Dreyfus case, 641
González, Fernán, Count of Burgos, 164
Good Hope (H.M.S.) destroyed, 918
Good Neighbor policy, 1156
Good Parliament reforms under the Black Prince, 257
Goodwin, Sir Francis, 374
Goodyear, Charles, American inventor, 553, 772
Gorchakov, Alexander Mikhailovich, Prince, Russian chancellor, 733, 734, 736
Gordian I (Marcus Antonius Gordianus Africanus), Roman emperor, 115
Gordian II (Marcus Antonius Gordianus), Roman emperor, 115
Gordian III (Marcus Antonius Gordianus), Roman emperor, 115, 124
Gordillo, Francisco de, explorer, 368
Gordion, 37
Gordius, King of Phrygia, 48
Gordon, Gen. Charles George, in the Sudan, 617, 738 f., 830 f.; in China, 880
Gordon, George, Lord, riots in London against Catholic emancipation, 436
Goremykin, Ivan Longinovich, prime minister of Russia, 708, 930
Gorgas, William Crawford, 1069
Görgei, Gen. Arthur, Hungarian commander, 674
Gorges, Edward, receives grant of land in New England, 509

Gorges, Sir Ferdinando, member of the Plymouth Co., 508; receives grant of land in Maine, 509; restored to his heirs, 511
Gorgias, appeals to Athens for aid, 57; a Sophist, 62
Gorlice-Tarnow, battle of, 922
Gorman, Arthur Pue, co-author of the Wilson-Gorman Act, 786
Gorst, Sir John Eldon, British consul-gen. at Cairo, 833
Görz, Count Eustachius von, Prussian diplomat, 468
Goshen, made a Boer state, 854
Gōta Canal, opened, 699
Gotamiputa Siri Satakani, 129
Gothia, union with Svealand, 203
Gothic architecture, various influences, 239 f.; in Venice, 299
Goths, defeated by Caracalla, 115; 116, 143, 145
Götiglacial stage, 15
Gough, Gen. Sir Hubert de la Poer, British commander, 945
Gould, Jay, American capitalist, 784
Gounaris, Demetrios, prime minister of Greece, 926, 1021
Gouraud, Henri Joseph, French general, 1098
Gourgoulov, Dr. Paul, assassin of Pres. Doumer of France, 978
Gourgues, Dominque de, captured Fort Caroline, 505
Gourlay, Robert, leader in Canadian rebellion, 795
Government of India Act, 1111, 1113
Government of Ireland Act, 967, 972
Government of national defense, in France, 636
Government of the 5000, 60
Government Railways Amendment Act. in New Zealand, 1132
Govinda II, Indian ruler, 336
Govinda III, Indian ruler, 336
Gower, John, English author, 267; influence on Castilian literature, 282
Goyer, Pieter van, Dutch mission to China, 539
Gozan (Tell Halaf), Kingdom of, 35
Graah, Capt. Wilhelm August, Arctic explorer, 563
Grabski, Ladislav, premier of Poland. 1039
Gracchus, Gaius, 91, 92
Gracchus, Tiberius Sempronius, 91
Graf Spee, German pocket battleship, 1154, 1158
Graf Zeppelin, circumnavigation of globe, 558
Grafton, Augustus Henry Fitzroy, Duke of, British statesman, 429, 436
Graham Land Expedition (British), under John Rymill, 577
Grain Corporation in U.S., 1049
Gramont, Antoine Agenor Alfred, Duke de, French foreign minister, 628
Granada, its fall, 282, 387; Treaty of, 387, 393
Granada, Luis de, religious writer, 388
Granadan Confederation, designation of the New Granada Republic, 815
Grand Alliance, against France, 431, 444, 445, 446, 450
Grand Army of Napoleon, invasion of Russia, 596, 598
Grand Canal of China, 137; restored by Kublai Khan, 345
Grand Cañon of the Colorado, reached by the Spaniards, 492
Grand Catalan Co., 284
Grand College, created in China, 133
Grand Duchy of Moscow, 244
Grand Duchy of Tuscany, 398
Grand National Consolidated Trades Union, organized, 608
Grand Remonstrance in England, 376
Grand Trunk Pacific Railway, completed, 797
Grand Trunk Railway, nationalized, 1057
Grandi, Dino, Italian Fascist leader, 988
Grandidier, Alfred, explored Madagascar, 860
Grandson, battle of, 307
Granicus, battle of, 40, 65
Grant, James Augustus, explorer in Africa, 826
Grant, Ulysses Simpson (18th pres. of U.S.), 779, 781, 782
Granvella (Antoine Perrenot), Bishop, adviser of Margaret of Parma, 377
Granville, George Leveson-Gower, 2d Earl, British foreign secretary, 617, 832
Grasse, François Joseph Paul, Count de, French admiral, 436
Grassi, Giovanni, on the Anopheles mosquito, 552
Gratianus, Roman emperor, 120
Grau San Martin, Ramón, pres. of Cuba, 1077
Gravelines, battle of, 383, 389
Gravelotte, battle of, 688
Graves, passage, 15, 18; Red Ochre, 16; cut into rocks by Phrygians, 36
Gray, Capt. Robert, first to enter mouth of the Columbia River, 768, 773
Graziani, Gen. Rodolfo, Italian commander, 990, 1086
Grazing licenses, in Australia, 900; in New Zealand, 906
Great Bonanza, discovery of silver in Nevada, 782
Great Britain, name established by Union of England and Scotland, 432; in Second World War, declared war on Germany, 1135; blockaded by Germany, 1136; invaded Iran, 1137, 1151; treaty with Russia, 1137; pledged aid to the U.S. against Japan, 1137, 1140; Independence of demanded by India, 1138; twenty-year pact with Russia, 1138 f., 1153; at Casablanca Conference, 1139; at Quebec Conference, 1140 f., 1159; at Tehran Conference, 1141; at Crimea Conference, 1143; Italy declared war against, 1148; battle of, 1148 f.; German bombing of, 1148 f.; defense agreement with the U.S., 1148 f.; air defense of, 1149; lend-lease from the U.S., 1149; pacified Iraq, 1151; promised aid to Russia against Germany, 1151; severed relations with Finland, 1151; merchant tonnage, 1156; naval blockade of Germany, 1156 f.; exchanged air base leases for U.S. destroyers, 1155, 1158; evacuated Rangoon, 1167; at Potsdam Conference, 1171
Great Buddha (Daibutsu), dedicated in Japan, 350
Great Bulgaria, disrupted by Avars and Khazars, 181

Great Colombia (New Granada; Venezuela; and Ouito), 802 f., 814 f.
Great Commentary, see Mahabhashya
Great Cortract, affecting the income of James I, 374
Great Council of England, 191, 193, 194, 197, 198, 265
Great Council of Venice, instituted 224, 225
Great Diet of Mainz, 209
Great Diet of Verona, resolves on Holy war against Moslems. 216
Great Elector of Brandenburg, see Frederick William
Great (Ross) Ice Barrier. 573
Great Interregnum, in struggle of popes and emperors. 213
Great Jubilee, of Pope Boniface VII. 222
Great Khan of the Mongols, 246
"Great Learning," a work on knowledge 343
Great Lebanon, proclaimed a republic by France 1098
Great London fire. 427
Great migration, to Massachusetts Bay colony, 509
Great Mosque, at Ahmadabad, 335; at Champanir, 335; at Gulbarga, 334
Great Pagoda of Rajaraja I, 337
Great plague, in London, 427
Great Preslav, new capital of the Bulgars, 182, 183
Great Protestation, to James I, 375
Great Rebellion, in Britain, 377
Great Refusal, The, 222
Great Russians, branch of eastern Slavs, 239
Great Schism, in the Church, 277, 288, 302, 399
Great Seal of Britain, carried off by Charles I, 377
Great Trek, of the Boers, 851
Great Wall, of China, 132, 136
Greco, El, Renaissance painter, 389
Greco-Roman culture in Britain, 166
Greco-Turkish War, 618, 744, 746
Greece, history; ancient, 46 ff., 75 ff.; medieval, 170 ff., 248, 325 ff.; modern, 710 ff., 926, 932, 940, 1020 ff.; in Second World War, attacked by Italy, 1136; civil war, 1143; victories in Albania, invaded by Germany, signed an armistice, British forces evacuated, 1150; 1158
Greek culture, 67
Greek fire, 174, 176
Greek Orthodox Church, doctrinal controversy, 217
Greek Scheme, of Catharine the Great, 482, 722
Greek-speaking peoples, 16
Greeley, Horace, candidate for pres. of the U.S., 781, 782
Greely, Adolphus Washington, Arctic explorer, 565
Greene, Gen. Nathanael, American general, 521
Greenland, 568 f.; under U.S. protection, 1155, 1158
Greenville, Treaty of, 766
Gregorian calendar, adopted in England, 435; adopted in Japan, 890; introduced in Rumania, 1025; adopted by the Soviets, 1030
Gregorian Chant, 151
Gregory, Bishop of Tours, his History of the Franks, 147
Gregory of Nazianzus, Cappadocian, 123
Gregory of Nyssa, Cappadocian, 123
Gregory I (the Great), Pope, 150, 151, 152, 218
Gregory II, Pope, 151, 152, 176
Gregory III, Pope, 150
Gregory V (Bruno), Pope, 162, 216
Gregory VI (Johannes Gratianus), Pope, 216, 217, 218
Gregory VII (Hildebrand), Pope, 152, 168, 192; his Dictatus, 218; excommunicates Henry IV, 206 f., 218; deposed by the Synod of Worms, 218; sack of Rome, 207, 218; dies, 207, 220
Gregory IX (Ugolini Conti de Segni), Pope, excommunicates Frederick II, 211; canonization of Francis of Assisi and Dominic, 221, 230; his death, 212
Gregory X (Tebaldo Visconti), Pope, 213, 221, 258
Gregory XI (Pierre Roger de Beaufort), Pope, 288
Gregory XII (Angelo Coriaro), Pope, 288; resigns 289, 292
Gregory XIII (Ugo Buoncampagno), Pope, reformed the calendar, 396
Gregory XIV (Nicolò Sfondrato), Pope, 396
Gregory XV (Alessandro Ludovisi), Pope, 397
Gregory XVI (Mauro, or Bartolommeo Alberto Capellari), Pope, 651, 663
Grenville, George, British statesman, 435, 517
Grenville, Lord William, British prime minister, 437
Grévy, Jules, pres. of France, 638, 639
Grew, Joseph C., U.S. ambassador to Japan, 1166
Grey, Charles, 2d Earl, prime minister of England, 607, 608
Grey, Sir Edward, British foreign secretary, 619, 745, 754, 755, 758–762, 797, 845, 929, 935
Grey, Frances, granddaughter of Henry VIII, 372
Grey, Sir George, gov. of Cape Colony, 852; lt.-gov. of Adelaide, 900; gov. of New Zealand, 906, 907
Grey, Lady Jane, assigned the English crown by Edward VI, 372
Grey, Richard, executed by Richard, Duke of Gloucester, 271
Grey, Thomas, 2d Earl of Stamford, 428
Grey-Cambon correspondence, 760
Grey Friars, 221
Gribeauval, Jean Baptiste de, French general, 448
Griffin, Walter Burley, Chicago architect, 1130
Griffith, Arthur, Irish leader, 972
Grijalva, Juan de, Spanish discoverer, 368; 490 f
Grimaldi Dan, 9
Grimani, Girolamo, Italian admiral, 458
Grimke, Angelina and Sarah, in women's rights movement, 774
Grimm, Jakob, German philologist, 676
Grimoald, son of Pepin, 149
Grisons League, 409

Grito de Ypiranga (Cry of Ypiranga), Brazil. 805
Grodno, taken by the Germans, 922, 1151
Grolmann, Karl Wilhelm Georg von, Prussian general. 594
Gromov, Mikhail, Russian aviator, 558, 567
Gronau, Wolfgang von, German aviator. 568
Gröner, Gen. Wilhelm von, German quartermaster-gen.. 950
Grootfontein, surrendered by the Germans, 859
Grose, Francis, vice-gov. of New South Wales, 896
Groseillers, Médart Chouart. sieur de French explorer. 507
Grossbeeren, battle of, 599
Grosseteste, Robert. Bishop of Lincoln, 198: 201
Grossfriedrichsburg, Prussian fort in Africa. 525
Gross-Görschen, see Lützen, battle of
Grossjägerndorf, battle of, 467
Grote, George, South Australia colonization, 899
Grotefend, George Friedrich. deciphered cuneiform writing. 551
Grouchy, Emmanuel, Marquis de. French general, 603
Grove. Sir William Robert. invented incandescent electric light; 553
Grynetum, 42
Guadalajara, becomes capital of New Galicia. 492
Guadalcanal, 1167
Guadalete, battle of, 163
Guadalupe Hidalgo, Treaty ot. 774, 821
Guadet, Marguerite Élie, a leader of the Girondists. 580
Guam, 1138, 1167, 1169
Guano deposits of Peru, 813
Guantanamo Bay, 1154
Guaraní Indians of La Plata, 499
Guardia, Ricardo Adolfo de la President of Panama, 1137
Guatemala, 486 ff., 804 f., 819 f., 1074 ff.
Guchkov, Alexander, Russian statesman, 1028, 1029
Gudea, 26
Guébriant, Jean Baptiste, 407
Guelf and Ghibelline, in Florentine civil strife, 293. See also Welf and Waiblinger
Gueorguiev, Gen. Kimon, sets up dictatorship in Bulgaria, 1024
Guerra, José Gutiérrez, pres. of Bolivia, 1067
Guerrero, Manuel Amador, pres. of Panama Republic, 819
Guerrero, Vicente, pres. of Mexico, 804, 821
Guerrière (Br.) captured by the Constitution (U.S.S.), 769
Guesde, Jules Basile, French socialist, 639
Gueshov, Ivan Evstratiev, prime minister of Bulgaria, 718
Guggiari, José, pres. of Paraguay, 1066
Gugsa, Ras, husband of Zauditu, Empress of Ethiopia, 1085
Guibert, Jacques Antoine Hippolyte, Comte de, French military reformer, 448
Guibert of Ravenna, 207
Guicciardini, Francesco, Italian historian, 296, 392
Guido of Spoleto, consecrated emperor, 152; 215
Guienne, 231, 268
Guilds, formed under Henry III, 203; in Florence, 293
Guilford, battle of, 522
Guillaumat, Gen. Marie Louis Adophe, French commander, 948
Guillotine, reign of, 583
Guinegate, the Battle of the Spurs, 369, 382
Guiscard, Robert, Norman leader, 207, 217, 218, 250
Guise, Duke of, retakes Calais, 372
Guises, their influence, 384
Guizot, François Pierre Guillaume, premier of France, 628, 630; 645, 654, 666
Gujerat, 130; conquered, 533
Guldberg, Ove Høegh. Danish leader, 474 f.
Gulflight, 923
Gulistan, Treaty of, 862
Gulnabad, battle of, 528
Gumban culture, A and B, 18
Gumbinnen, battle of, 916
"Gun War," in Basutoland, 854
Gunda, architect of the temple of Virupaksha, 336
Gunderic, king of the Vandals and Alani, 144
Gundibald, King of Burgundy, 145
Gundicar, King of Burgundy, 145
Gunpowder, "formula" devised by Roger Bacon, 201
Gunpowder Plot, 374
Gupta dynasty, united Northern India, 130; 331
Gurdanaspa, 127
Gurdit Singh, 871
Gurgum, Kingdom, 35
Gurjara, central Asiatic nomads, 331
Gurjara-Prathihara dynasty, 331
Gurkhas, defeated, 540; invaded India from Nepal, 868
"Gushana Great King," inscription, 128
Gustavus I of Sweden, 412
Gustavus II Adolphus, of Sweden, 398, 405, 406, 413, 510
Gustavus III of Sweden, 474
Gustavus IV of Sweden, 595, 699
Gustavus V of Sweden, 701; 1047
Gustloff, Wilhelm, National Socialist leader, 995
Guthrun the Dane, divides England with Alfred, 167
Gutiérrez, Eulalio, pres. of Mexico, 1075
Gutiérrez, Leonidas Plaza, pres. of Ecuador, 814
Gutiérrez, Rafael López, pres. of Honduras, 1073, 1074
Gutium, 26, 39
Guy I of Athens, 258
Guynemer, Georges, French aviator, 946
Guyuk, Mongol khan, 344
Guzmán, Luisa María de, mother of Alfonso VI of Portugal, 453
Guzmán, Nuño de, pres. of first audiencia of New Spain, 492
Gwinner, Arthur von. German financier, 757

Gyges, King of Lydia, 24; 37, 48
Gylippus, 60
Gyllenborg, Count Karl de, prime minister of Sweden, 473 f.
Gyögi, Japanese monk, 350
Gypsies, on lower Tigris, 189
Gyroscope, invented, 556
Gytheum, 56
Gyulai, Gen. Franz, Austrian commander, 658

Haakon the Good, of Norway, 204
Haakon IV of Norway, conquered Iceland, 204
Haakon V of Norway, 204
Haakon VI of Norway and Sweden, 311
Haakon VII, of Norway, 701, 1046, 1146
Haardt expedition, crossed the Sahara, 1081
Haarfager (Fairhair), Harald, of Norway, 204; 558
Habeas Corpus Act, 428; suspended, 431, 437, 605; suspended for Ireland, 612
Habibullah Ghazi, see Bacha-i-Saquao
Habibullah Khan, Amir of Afghanistan, 868, 1109
Habicht, Theodor, Hitler's "Inspector for Austria," 1007
Habur, 28
Hacha, Emil, pres. of Czechoslovakia, 1013
Hadadezer (Hadad II), King of Zobah, 35
Hadippe, Kingdom of, 35
Hadrian (Publius Aelius Hadrianus), Roman emperor, 32, 34, 94, 109, 110; dies, 111; 113, 116, 166
Haeckel, Ernst Heinrich, German scientist, 551
Hafsid dynasty, 263
Hagenau, meeting of, 257
Hague Agreement, reduces Bulgarian reparations, 1023
Hague, first Peace Conference, 618, 748; Treaties of, 452, 583; Second Peace Conference, 754
Haian, 35
Haidar, son of Uzun Hasan, 526
Haidar Ali, usurped the throne of Mysore, 535
Haig, Sir Douglas, commander-in-chief of the British forces in the World War, 930, 941
Haile Selassie I of Ethiopia, 1085, 1138
Hailu, Ras, of Gojjam, Ethiopia, 1085
Hainan, 1171
Hainisch, Michael, first pres. of Austrian Republic, 1005
Haiti, 515, 825; American marines landed and martial law proclaimed, 791, 1078
Haj Amin el Husseini, Grand Mufti of Jerusalem, 1102
Hajj Omar, El, Tukulor chieftain in Senegal, 840
Hajjaj, Arab general, 187
Hakam, son of Hakam, 163
Hakam II, caliph, 164
Hakim, caliph, 255
Hakluyt, Richard, English explorer, 559
Hakuseki, Arai, Confucian scholar, 548
Haldane, Richard Burdon, 1st Viscount, British statesman, 693, 758
Halepa, see Pact of Halepa
Hales, Sir Edward, 429
Halicarnassus, 47
Halicyae, 56, 57
Halicz, retaken by the Austrians, 940
Halidon Hill, battle of, 265
Halieis, 55
Halifax, award in fishing dispute with U.S., 781
Halifax, Charles Lindley Wood, 2d Viscount, British foreign secretary, 964, 970, 971
Halifax, George Montagu Dunk, 2d Earl of, British statesman 434, 435, 515
Halifax, George Savile, 1st Marquis of, British statesman, 428, 430, 431
Halifax, Viscount, British ambassador to U.S., 1136
Hall, Charles Francis, American explorer, 564
Halle, battle of, 592
Halle, Albrecht von, 460
Halleck, Gen. Henry Wager, American commander, 778
Hallstatt, 11; culture, 16, 17
Hallushu, 38
Halycus, 66
Halys, 37, 48
Ham, taken by the Germans, 945
Hamadan, taken by the Russians, 927, 929, 938
Hamaguchi, Yūkō, premier of Japan, 1125, 1126
Hamath, 33, 34, 35
Hambach Festival, 669
Hamburg, 170; occupied by Russians; occupied by Davout, 599; Treaty of, 468
Hamburg Church History, by Adam of Bremen, 365
Hamdanids of Mosul and Aleppo, 190
Hamilcar, Carthaginian general, 34, 57, 78
Hamilcar Barcas, 86, 87
Hamilton, Adam, leader of the new National Party in New Zealand, 1132
Hamilton, Alexander, American statesman, 764, 768
Hamilton, Andrew, and freedom of the press, 513
Hamilton, Henry, British commander, 521
Hamilton, Gen. Sir Ian Standish Monteith, British commander, 920
Hamilton, James, Duke of, general of Charles I of England, 378
Hamlin, Cyrus, founder of Bebek Seminary in Turkey, 728
Hammidan, 40
Hammudids of Malaga, 232
Hammurabi, 26, 39; 35

Hampden, John, and opposition to Charles I, 376, 377 f.
Hampden, John (the younger), and the Restoration in England, 426
Han Lin Yüan, Academy of Letters in China, 537
Han Wu Ti, 135
Han Yü, Chinese poet, 341
Hanafite school of law, 188
Hanau, battle of, 599
Hancock, John, American patriot leader, 518
Han dynasty, 14, 44; Former or Western, 133; Later or Eastern, 134
Hand-Axe industry, 4–6
Han-Fei-tzu, 45
Hangchou, 137
Hangchow, taken by Japanese, 1122
Hangchow-Nanch'ang R.R., opened, 1121
Hangoe, 1146
Hanigalbat, 28
Hankel, Hermann, 131
Hankow, falls to the Japanese, 1122; 1165
Hankow-Canton Railway, completed, 1121
Hannibal, Carthaginian general takes Selinus and Himera, 34 80; crosses Apennines, 87; his army annihilated, 88
Hannington, Bishop James, murdered in Uganda, 847
Hanno, 34, 86
Hanoi, 1166
Hanover, Liberal constitution set aside, 669; Treaty of, 434, 451
Hanseatic League, its growth, 204, 205, 214, 302; definition of the term, 307; Peace of Stralsund, 309, 310, 559
Hansson, Per Albin, Swedish premier, 1047
Hansteen, Prof. Christopher, first magnetic chart drawn, 561
Hanzala, viceroy in North Africa, 188
Hapsburgs, in Germany, 213; origin, 299; 301; hereditary rulers of the Holy Roman Empire, 302; dynasty began with Frederick III, 304; 306 f.; Spanish branch, 399; their share of Hungary, 420. See also Germany, Austria
Hapta Giorgis, war minister of Ethiopia, 1085
Hara, Takashi, premier of Japan, 1123, 1124
Harald Bluetooth of Denmark, 203
Harappa, 13, 41
d'Harcourt, Henri, French ambassador to Spain, 445
Harcourt, Sir William George Granville Venables Vernon, leader of the House of Commons, 618
Hardenberg, Karl August von, Prussian reformer, 594; at Congress of Vienna, 601; 667
Hardie, James Keir, British labor leader, 618
Harding, Warren Gamaliel, 29th pres. of the U.S., 1050, 1051
Hardinge, Sir Charles, British viceroy of India, 655, 871
Hardinge, Sir Henry, gov.-gen. of India, 870
Hardrada, Harald, defeated at Stamford Bridge, 168, 204; defeated the Sicilian Saracens, 249
Hardy, Thomas, tried on charge of high treason, 437
Harem rule, in Persia, 533
Haremhab, 24, 30
Haria, 74
Harington, Gen. Sir Charles, British commander, 1095
Harisena, 132
Harivarman, 131
Harley, Robert (later Earl of Oxford), British statesman, 431, 432
Harmodius, 52
Harmsworth, Alfred Charles (Lord Northcliffe), 565
Harold, King of England, 168
Haroun, Ducos du, first to do color photography, 555
Harpagus, Gen., 48
Harpalus, 66
Harran, 28, 29, 127
Harrington, William Stanhope, Earl of, in the Pelham ministry, 434
Harris, Townsend, American consul-gen. in Japan, 888
Harrison, Benjamin (23rd pres. of the U.S.), 784, 786
Harrison, Francis Burton, gov.-gen. of the Philippines, 910, 1132
Harrison, William Henry (9th pres. of the U.S.), 769, 773, 793
Harrisonian industry, 4
Harsha, King of Thaneswar, 331, 335
Harshacharita, 331
Hart, Sir Robert, and the maritime customs service of China, 880, 881, 883
Hartford Convention, proposal for secession of the New England states, 769 f.
Hartington, Spencer Compton Cavendish, Marquess of, British statesman, 617, 518
Hartlepool, bombarded, 917
Hartog, Dirk, landed on the coast of West Australia, 894
Hartwig, Nicholas von, Russian minister at Belgrade, 759
Harun al-Rashid, caliph, 188
Harvard College, founded, 509
Harwich, British naval base, 917
Hasan, caliph, 186
Hasan-i-Dihlavi, Persian poet, 333
Hasdrubal, Carthaginian general, 34, 86, 88
Haselrig, Sir Arthur, impeachment ordered by Charles I, 377
Hassan ibn No'man, viceroy of Arabs, 187
Hassanein Bey, at the Kufra oasis, 1081
Hastenbeck, battle of, 467
Hastings, battle of, 168, 227
Hastings, John, claimant to the Scottish throne, 199
Hastings, Warren, gov.-gen. of Bengal, 535

Hastings, Lord William, executed by Richard, Duke of Glouces-
ter, 271
Hatay (Alexandretta), Republic of, 1097
Hathor of Dendera, 21
Hatra, 110, 124
Hats, party in Sweden, 474
Hatshepsut, 23
Hatt-i-Humayun, Turkish reform edict, 728
Hatt-i-sherif of Gulhané, Turkish reform decree, 725
Hattin, 35
Hattushash, 36
Hattushilish I, 36; III, 24, 36
Hau-Hau, a religious movement in New Zealand, 907
Hausen, Gen. Max von, German commander, 912
Haussa Confederation, in West Africa, 524
Haussmann, Georges Eugène, Baron, prefect of the Seine, 633
d'Hautpoul, Gen. Alphonse Henri, premier of France, 631
Havana, 1136, 1155
Havelock, Sir Henry, and the relief of Lucknow, 870
Hawaii (Sandwich Islands), discovered, 571, 895, 910; Republic
of Hawaii is proclaimed, 910; annexed by the U.S., 896, 910;
U.S. grants "Bill of Rights," Equal Rights Commission cre-
ated, plebiscite favoring statehood, 1134; attacked by Japan,
1138, 1155, 1158, 1167
Hawke sunk by submarine, 917
Hawke, Sir Edward, British admiral, 435
Hawke's Bay, New Zealand, established, 906
Hawkins, Sir John, defeat of the Spanish Armada, 373, 494, 507,
524
Hawkins, William, mission to India, 533
Haxey, Thomas, condemned for treason, 268, 271
Hay, John, American secretary of state, Open Door Note on
China, 749, 787; Hay-Pauncefote, Hay-Herran, and Hay-
Bunau-Varilla Treaties, 788, 815, 818; 882
Hayam Wuruk, Malaysian ruler, 348
Hayashi, Baron Tadasu, Japanese minister in London, 750, 892
Hayes, Dr. Isaac Israel, Arctic explorer, 564
Hayes, Rutherford Birchard (19th pres. of the U.S.), 782, 810
Haymarket Square (Chicago) Riot, 784
Haynau, Julius Jacob, Austrian general, 674
Hayne, Robert Young, debate with Webster, 771
Hayward, Henry O'Brien Frederic, Arctic explorer, 569
Hazael of Damascus, 27, 31
Hazaraspids, held Luristan, 255
Health and Morals of Apprentices Act, 437
Health Insurance Law, in Denmark, 697
Hearst, William Randolph, American publisher, 576
Hearth sites, 6
Heath, Sir Robert, 513
Heavenly Kingdom of Great Peace (background of the T'ai
P'ing Rebellion), 879
Heavenly Reason Society, in China, 877
"Heavy hydrogen," 553
Hébert, Jacques René, French revolutionary leader, 580, 583
Hebrew University of Jerusalem, 1100
Hebrews (Habiru), 23, 29
Hecatomnus, 64
Heceta, Bruno de, Spanish explorer, 493
Heckscher, Johann Gustav Mortiz, German statesman, 675
Heeringen, Gen. Josias von, German commander, 912
Hegenberger, Lt. Albert Francis, American aviator, 557, 1134
Hegira, Hijrah, see Flight of Mohammed
Heian period, in Japan, 352, 354
Heiji no Ran, second Japanese civil war, 354
Heimwehr, Austrian Christian Socialist private army, 1006, 1008
Heinsius, Anthony, grand pensionary of Holland, 439, 445
Heinz, Herr, pres. of the Palatinate govt., 998
Heipereides, organizes new Hellenic League, 66
Heisenberg, Werner, 553
Hejaz Railway, to the Holy Places in Arabia, 731
Helena, Byzantine Empress, 179
Helena, mother of Constantine the Great, 119, 255
Helena, wife of Constantius, 118
Helfferich, Karl, German statesman, 936
Heliaea (courts), 51
Helicopter, invented, 554
Heligoland, Treaty of, 741
Heligoland Bight, raided by the British, 917
Heliopolis, 21
Hellenic League, 65, 66, 78, 79
Hellenistic Age, 75–77
Helmholtz, Hermann Ludwig Ferdinand von, German scientist,
551
Helsingborg, battle of, 309
Helsingfors, taken by the Germans, 943
Helvetic Republic, decreed by French Republic, 460, 586
Helvetic Society, in Switzerland, 460
Helvetii, attempt to leave Switzerland, 96
Hemachandra, Jain monk, 332
Henderson, Arthur, British labor leader, 968
Henderson, Richard, organized Transylvania Co. for a settle-
ment in Kentucky, 517
Henlein, Konrad, leader of the Sudeten National Socialist Party,
1010, 1011
Henna, 90
Hennepin, Louis, Franciscan friar and explorer, 507
Hénon, Jacques Louis, French Republican, 634
Henrietta Maria, wife of Charles I of England, 375
Henriot, François, French revolutionary leader, 582
Henríquez y Carvajal, Francisco, provisional pres. of Santo
Domingo, 825

Henry, Cardinal, King of Portugal, 392
Henry, son of Emperor Frederick II, 211
Henry, Duke of Guise, 384
Henry, Duke of Brunswick-Wolfenbüttel, 401
Henry, Duke of Mecklenburg-Schwerin, marries Wilhelmina,
Queen of the Netherlands, 626
Henry, Duke of Saxony, successor of Conrad I, 160
Henry, Prince of Prussia, brother of Frederick the Great, 467
Henry of Burgundy, granted the County of Portugal, 238
Henry IV of Castile, 282
Henry of Langenstein, 288
Henry of Valois, King of Poland; see Henry III of France
Henry the Lion (Welf) of Saxony, 208, 209, 214, 242
Henry the Navigator, son of John I of Portugal, 285, 363, 364
Henry the Proud (Welf) of Saxony, 208
Henry the Wrangler, Duke of Bavaria, 161, 162
Henry I, King of England, 193, 196, 206, 207, 227
Henry II, King of England, 169, 170, 194 f., 229, 256
Henry III, King of England, 198, 199, 201, 203, 213, 230
Henry IV (Henry of Bolingbroke), King of England, 268
Henry V, King of England, 268, 270
Henry VI, King of England, 270, 271, 278
Henry VII, King of England, 194, 272, 369
Henry VIII, King of England, 369, 370, 372, 374, 382, 394, 401,
432
Henry I, King of France, 225
Henry II, King of France, 383, 395, 402
Henry III, King of France, 384, 386
Henry IV of France, 384, 386, 390, 501
Henry I (the Fowler), German emperor, 160, 208, 223
Henry II, German emperor, crowned Emperor of Rome, 162 f.,
169
Henry III (the Black), German emperor, 205 f., 217, 240, 245
Henry IV, German emperor, 206 f., 218 f., 240
Henry V, German emperor, 194, 207, 208, 219
Henry VI, German emperor, 196, 210 f., 223, 254, 256
Henry VII (Luxemburg), German emperor, 286, 293, 301, 306
Henry I, Latin emperor, 259
Henry II Trastamara, of Portugal, 265, 277, 280
Henry, Major (later Col.) Hubert, and the Dreyfus affair, 641
Henry, Patrick, American patriot, 517
Henry P'u-i, Chinese emperor, 1120
Henson, William Samuel, heavier-than-air machines, 556
Hentsch, Col. Richard, and the battle of the Marne, 914
Henty, Edward, settler in Australia, 900
Hephaestion, dies, 56
Hephthalites, see White Huns
Heptarchy of Britain, 166
Heraclea, 85
Heracleon, murders Antiochus VIII, 82
Heracleonas, Byzantine emperor, 174
Heracleopolis, 21
Heracles, 32
Heraclitus of Ephesus, 53
Heraclius I, Byzantine emperor, 127, 151, 173 f., 184, 186
Heraclius Constantinus, Byzantine emperor, 174
Herat, 42; taken by Persians, 864, 866
Hérault de Séchelles, Marie Jean, French revolutionist, 583
Herbert, Count of Vermandois, 159
Herculaneum, buried by eruption of Mt. Vesuvius, 108; excava-
tion of, 458
Heredia, Pedro de, founded Cartagena, 488
Heresy and heretics, campaigns against, 141, 221; suppression
promised by Frederick II, 212; of Constance, John Hus exe-
cuted by order of the Council, 288 f., 443
Hereward (the Wake), last stand, in Isle of Ely, 191
Heribert, Archbishop of Milan, 296
Hermae, mutilation charged to Alcibiades, 60
Hermannstadt, taken by Rumanians, 934
Hermocrates, 57, 58; defends Syracuse, 60
Hernández de Córdoba, Francisco, discovered Yucatan, 368
Hernici, 71, 73
Herod Agrippa II, 32, 107
Herod the Great, King of Judea, 32, 102, 105
Herodotus, 21, 24, 29, 34, 37, 62
Herostratus, 67
Herrán, Pedro Alcantára, pres. of New Granada, 788, 814
Herrenhausen, Alliance of, 463
Herrera, Cárlos, pres. of Guatemala, 1074
Herrera, Enrique Olaya, pres. of Colombia, 1069
Herrera, José Joaquin de, pres. of Mexico, 821
Herrera, Juan de, builder of the Escorial, 389
Herrero, insurrection in German Southwest Africa, 858
Herrin, riots in Illinois, 1050, 1051
Herriot, Edouard, French premier, 963, 976, 988
Hertford, Earl of, see Somerset, Duke of
Hertling, George, Count von, German chancellor, 942, 950
Hertz, Heinrich, verified existence of radio waves, 556
Hertzberg, Ewald Friedrich, Count von, Prussian minister, 477
Hertzog, James Barry Munnik, prime minister of South Africa,
858, 859, 1091, 1092
Heruls, 143
Herzen, Alexander, Russian Socialist, 704, 705
Hesiod, Greek poet, 47
Hesychast (Zealot), controversy in the Greek Church, 322, 323
Het Volk, Gen. Botha's organization in the Transvaal, 858
Heureaux, Ulises, pres. of Santo Domingo, 824 f.
Heyn, Piet, captured a Spanish plate fleet, 494
Hezekiah, 31
Hicetas, 66
Hicks, Gen. William, defeated by the Mahdi, 738, 832

Hidage, replaces Danegeld in England, 196
Hidalgo y Costilla, Miguel, initiates revolt in Mexico, 804
Hideki Tojo, Japanese premier, 1142, 1166
Hidetada, Japanese shōgun 546, 548
Hideyori, heir of Hideyoshi, 546
Hideyoshi, Toyotomi, Japanese ruler, 536, 544, 885
Hiero I, defeated Etruscans in naval battle, 57
Hiero II, king, 78, 86. 87, 90
Hieroglyphic writing 20, 46
Hieroglyphics, Hittite, 36
Hieronymus, 87
Hieropolis, 127
Higden, Ranulf, his *Polychronicon*, 267
High Seas Fleet, of the Germans, 917; surrenders at Rosyth, scuttled, 946
Hildebrand, *see* Gregory VII, Pope
Hill, Abigail, *see* Masham, Mrs.
Hill, Gen. Sir John, attempt to take Quebec fails, 514
Hill, Rowland, penny postage, 609
Hillsborough, Wills Hill Downshire, Lord, first British colonial secretary, 336, 517
Hilmi Pasha, grand vizier of Turkey, 731 *f.*
Hilton-Young Commission, recommend closer union of East and Central African colonies, 1090
Himera, 57; battle of, 34, 78
Himilko, defeated at Syracuse, 34
Hinayana, the Lesser Vehicle of Buddhism, 129, 347
Hincmar, Archbishop of Reims, 153
Hindenburg, Gen. Paul von, pres. of the German Republic, 916, 922, 938, 998, 999, 1000
Hindenburg burning, 558
Hindenburg Line, position on western front in World War, 938
Hindola Mahall, urban hall erected by Hushang Shah, 334
Hindu philosophy, schools, 130; culture, 132
Hinduism, 132; prohibited by Aurangzeb, 534
Hindus, refused entry to British Columbia, 797; 1144
Hipparchus, killed, 52; 53
Hipper, Franz von, German admiral, 917
Hippias, 52, 53, 62
Hippo Regius, siege, 121, 145
Hippocrates, defended by Thebans, 59
Hippocratic Oath, 131
Hira, ancient Lakhmid capital, 127, 184
Hiram I, King of Tyre, 31, 32; II, 33
Hiranuma, Baron Kilchiro, Japanese premier, 1127
Hirohito, Japanese emperor, 1124, 1138
Hiroshige, Andō, Japanese artist, 887
Hiroshima, 553, 1145, 1169
Hirota, Koki, Japanese premier, 1126
Hirtius, Roman consul, 98
Hisham, caliph, 163, 187
Hisham II, caliph, 164
Hisham III, last Omayyad caliph, 164
Hispania Citerior and, *Ulterior*, 88
Histoire du roi Saint Louis, 231
Historia Ottonis, 162
History of the Ch'ing Dynasty, 1121
History of the Franks, by Gregory of Tours, 147
History of the Lonbards, by Paul the Deacon, 151
Hither Spain (*Hispania Citerior*), 88, 95
Hitler, Adolf, German chancellor and president, 963–67, 997, 999, 1000, 1003–05, 1008, 1011, 1026, 1041, 1042, 1047, 1048, 1136, 1144, 1150, 1165, 1170
Hitotsubashi Yoshinobu, *see* Keiki
Hittin, battle of, 263
Hittite Kingdom, 24, 27, 35, 36, 68
Hittites, 23, 24, 29, 33
Ho Ch'üping, drives out the Hsiung-nu, 133
Ho Shen, corrupted civil service of the Ch'ien Lung Reign, 540
Ho-Umetzu Agreement, for withdrawal of troops from Hopei, 1120, 1126
Hoare, Sir Samuel John Gurney, British foreign secretary, 969, 991
Hobson, Capt. William, gov. of New Zealand, 905
Hoche, Lazare, French general, 437, 584
Hochkirch, battle of, 467
Höchst, battle of, 404
Höchstädt, *see* Blenheim, battle of
Hödel, Emil, attempts life of Emperor William I of Germany, 689
Hodža, Dr. Milan, Czechoslovak premier, 1010, 1011
Hoel, Prof. Adolf, surveying cruises for Norway, 569
Hofer, Andreas, leads revolt in Tyrol, 594, 595
Hoffmann, Gen. Max, German commander, 916
Hofmeyr, Jan, a founder of the Afrikander Bond, 853, 855
Hōgen no Ran, Japanese civil war, 354
Hogue, sunk by the German U–9, 917
Hohenfriedberg, battle of, 466
Hohenlinden, battle of, 588
Hohenlohe-Ingelfingen, Friederich Ludwig, Prince, 592
Hohenlohe-Schillingsfürst, Chlodwig Karl Viktor, Prince of, chancellor of Germany, 691, 692
Hohenstaufen, House of, 208
Hohenwart, Karl Siegmund, Count, prime minister of Austria, 694
Hohenzollern candidacy for Spanish throne, 646, 687
Hohenzollern property, claims settled by Prussian govt., 998
Hohenzollerns, in Germany, 213, 302, 310
Hojo, Japanese clan, 356 *f.*
Hokkaidō, Japanese island, 138, 1144
Hōkōji, monastery in Japan, 140

Hokusai, Katsushika, Japanese artist, 887
Holberg, Ludwig, Norwegian writer, 475
Holland, *see* Netherlands
Holland, John Philip, built first naval submarine, 556
Hollandia, 1169
Holles, Denzil, impeachment ordered by Charles I, 377, 378
Holstein, united with Schleswig under the crown of Denmark, 312
Holstein, Count of 203
Holstein, Friedrich von, German diplomat, 741, 744, 753
Holy Alliance, signed by Russia. Austria, and Prussia, 603, 604, 725, 771
Holy Cross, restored to Jerusalem. 173
Holy Lance, rivalry of Norman and Provençal, 256
Holy League, against Charles VIII of France, 381, 384; against France, 381 *f.*, 398, 400: against Turks, 422 *f.*, 423, 483
Holy Places, in Arabia, 422, 731
Holy Places, in Palestine, 726
Holy Roman Empire, established, 208, 213; history: *see* Germany
Holy War (*Jihad*), 184, 256, 919
Home Owners' Loan Corporation, 1054
Home Owners' Refinancing Act, 1054
Home Rule Bill, for Ireland, 617, 618, 620 *f.*
Home Rule for Ireland Party, founded by Isaac Butt, 616
Home School for Girls (later Constantinople Women's College), in Turkey, 728
Homer, his *Hades*, 25; 32, 47
Homeric war, end of Hittite Kingdom, 24; against Troy, 36
Homestead Act in U.S., 780
Homestead Law, for Alaska, 798
Hominidae, 1
Homo heidelbergensis, 9
Homo modjokertensis, found in Java, 7, 9
Homo Neanderthalensis, 9
Homs, taken by British and Arabs, 948
Hŏn-jong, King of Korea, 885
Hondō, largest Japanese island, 138
Honduras, 486 *ff.*, 804 *f.*, 821 *ff.*, 1073 *ff.*
Honganji, monastery of the New Pure Land sect, 359
Hongi, Maori chief of New Zealand, 905
Hongkong, ceded to Britain, 879; captured by Japanese, 1138; 1158, 1167, 1171
Honoria, sister of Valentinian III, 143
Honorius, Roman emperor, 120, 121, 123, 143, 144
Honorius III (Cencio Savelli), Pope, 211, 221, 258
Honorius IV (Jacopo Savelli), Pope, 221
Honshu, 1144
Hood, British dreadnaught, sunk, 1158
Hood, John Bell, Confederate general, 779
Hood, Robert, explored Canada, 562
Hood, Samuel, English admiral, 436
Hooker, Joseph, Federal general, 778, 779
Hooker, Rev. Thomas, led settlers to Hartford, 509
Hoorn, Philip de Montmorency, Count of, executed in the Netherlands, 380
Hoorn, Pieter van, Dutch mission to China, 539
Hoover, Herbert Clark (31st pres. of the U.S.), 961, 962, 1049, 1052, 1133
Hope-Simpson, Sir John, of the League mandate commission, 1101
Hopei, new name for Chihli Province, 1119
Hopei-Chahar, Chinese political council, 1120
l'Hôpital, Michel de, founder of the French Patriots, 386
Hopkins, Sir Frederick Gowland, discovery of vitamins in malnutrition, 552
Horace (Quintus Horatius Flaccus), Roman poet, 112
Horatius, Roman consul, 72
Horatius Cocles, 71
Horeb, 30
Horites, 28, 29
Hormisdas, 125
Hormisdas I, 124
Hormisdas IV (Hormazd), 127
Hormuz, 124
Hormuzd Rassam, British envoy to Ethiopia, 834
Horn, Count Arvid Bernhard, prime minister of Sweden, 472
Horn, Gustavus, commands Swedish troops, 406
Hornet, U.S. carrier, 1158
Hornsby-Akroyd oil engine, 556
Hornsrud, Christopher, Norwegian premier, 1046
Hortensius, Quintus, 74
Horthy de Nagybanya, Nicholas, regent of Hungary, 953, 1014, 1016
Hōryūji, monastery in Japan, 140
Hosea, 31
Hosokawa Katsumoto, war lord of western Japan, 359
Hospitalitas, revived, 150
Hospodars, rulers of Rumania, 719
Hossō sect, in Japan, 351
Hostilianus, put to death by Gallus, 115
Hostos, Eugenio Maria de, Puerto Rican leader, 824
Hôtel de Ville, of Paris, 628, 630, 636
Hotham, Beaumont, surrender of Napoleon after Waterloo, 603
Hottentots, 328, 850
Hötzendorff, Conrad von, Austrian chief of staff, 756, 914
Hou Han, 134
House, Col. Edward Mandell, adviser to Pres. Wilson, 935, 952
House of Burgesses, in Virginia, 518, 520
House of Douglas, in Scotland, 212

House of Lancaster, 268, 270; see England
House of Lies, 39
House of Lords, 266, 620
House of Valois, 273; see France
House of York, in Wars of the Roses, 270 f.; see England
Housecarls, in England, 168
Houses of Parliament, 1149
Hova (race), settlement in Madagascar, 524, 859; French conquest, 860, 861
Hovell, William Hilton, English explorer in Australia, 899
Howard, Catharine, wife of Henry VIII, 369
Howard, Charles, 1st Earl of Carlisle, in a confederation against Charles II, 428
Howard, William, Lord High Admiral, defeat of the Spanish Armada, 373
Howe, Elias, patented sewing machine, 554, 773
Howe, Joseph, Nova Scotian leader, 796
Howe, Richard, Lord, British admiral, 520
Howe, Gen. William, 520; occupies Philadelphia, 521
Howes-Cutting Bill, regarding the Philippine Islands, 1133
Howieson's Poort, 6
Hoyos, Alexander, Count, Austrian diplomat, 761
Hoysalas dynasty, 337
Hrihor, 24
Hrolf the Ganger, see Rollo
Hsi Hsia Kingdom, destroyed, 344
Hsi yü chi (Record of the Western Lands), 331
Hsia dynasty, 44
Hsia Kuei, Chinese painter, 344
Hsiang Yü, 133
Hsieh, viceroy, 128
Hsien, Chinese emperor, 135
Hsien Feng Reign, 879
Hsing-an, 132
Hsing Li Ta Ch'üan, a digest of Chinese moral philosophy, 536
Hsiu-ch'üan, founder of the Heavenly Kingdom of Great Peace, 879
Hsiung-nu, first Turkish Empire in Mongolia, 133, 135
Hsu Ch'ien-hsüeh, compiler of the T'ung Chih T'ang Ching Chieh, 540
Hsü Shih-ch'ang, pres. of Chinese Parliament, 1118
Hsüan Te dynasty, 347
Hsüan-tsang, Chinese pilgrim, 331, 340
Hsüan Tsung, Chinese emperor, known as Ming Huang, 340, 347
Hsüan Tsung, Chinese emperor, 877
Hsüan T'ung Reign, of the Emperor P'u-i, 884
Hsü Shen, completed first lexicon of archaic script, 135
Hsün K'uang or Hsün-tzu, his teachings, 45
Hu Jung, Chinese official, 135
Hua Hu Ching, aprocryphal Chinese text, 340
Huan, Chinese emperor, 135
Huang Tsung-hsi, Chinese philosopher, 540
Huáscar, son of Huayna Capac, ruler of the Inca Empire, 361, 489
Huayna Capac, conqueror of the Incas, 361
Hubertusburg, Treaty of, 468
Hübner, Joseph Alexander, Count, Austrian diplomat, 728
Hudaybiya, Treaty of, 184
Hudids of Saragossa, 233
Hudson, Henry, English explorer, 510, 560
Hudson's Bay, ceded by France to Great Britain, 432
Hudson's Bay Co., 514, 561, 773, 792, 793
Hué, Treaty of, 874 f., 880 f.
Huerta, Adolfo de la, leads revolt against Obregón govt. in Mexico, 1075
Huerta, Victoriano de la, pres. of Mexico, 791, 822, 1074
Hugenberg, Alfred, leader of the German Nationalists, 999, 1000
Hugh le Despenser, favorite of Edward II of England, 264
Hugh of Cluny, abbot, 207
Hugh of Lusignan, 197, 229
Hugh of Pajeus, founder of the Knights of the Temple, 258
Hugh of Provence, 161; King of Italy, 215
Hugh the Great, 159
Hughes, Howard, flight around the world, 558
Hughes, William Morris, premier of Australia, 904, 1129
Huguenots, 375, 384, 385, 386 f., 850
Hühnefeld, Baron Gunther von, German aviator, 558
Hui Tsung, Chinese ruler, 342 f., 344
Hulagu, destroyed the caliphate of Baghdad, 262, 345
Hull, Cordell, U.S. secretary of state, 1122, 1143, 1165 f.
Hull, Gen. William, surrenders Detroit, 769
Humayun, drove Bahadur Shah from Chitor, 530
Humbanigash of Elam, 39
Humbert I, King of Italy, 660, 661
Humble Petition and Advice of Cromwell's 3d Parliament, 426
Humboldt, Karl Wilhelm Baron von, Prussian statesman, 594, 599, 601
Hume, Hamilton, English explorer in Australia, 899
Hume, Joseph, radical member of Parliament, 606
"Humiliation of Olmutz," 678
Hummelauer, Baron, Austrian diplomat, 654
Humphrey, Duke of Gloucester, regent of England, 270, 271
Humphreys, Sir Francis, high commissioner for Iraq, 1105
Humphreys, Noel, discovers British Empire Mountains, 567
Hundred Days of Reform in China, 882
Hundred Years' War, 230, 264 f., 270, 273, 276–80, 309
Hundseid, Jen Valentinsen, premier of Norway, 1046
Hundsfeld, battle of, 242
Huneric, hetrothed to Valentinian's daughter Eudocia, 145
Hung Wu Reign potters, 537

Hungarian National Socialist Party, organized, 1015
Hungarian refugees, cause international crisis, 726
Hungary, 143, 206, 244 f., 317 f., 419 f., 671 ff., 930; 941 f., 953, 1013 ff., joined the Axis, 1136, 1150; occupied by Germany, 1142; resisted Germany, 1154; 1171
Hŭng-sŏn, regent of Korea, 885
Hung-wu, reigning title of Ming dynasty, 347
Huns, ravage Roman empire, 121, 143, 145; see Hungary
Hunter, John, gov. of New South Wales, 896
Hunters' Lodges, sympathizers with Canadian rebels, 795
Hunyadi, Janos, and wars against the Turks, 304, 318, 320, 326, 327
Hurr, successor of Musa ibn Nusayr, invades southern France, 187
Hurrian-Hittite culture, 35
Hurrians, 23, 25, 27–29, 36
Hus, John, Bohemian reformer, 288 f., 305
Husayn, caliph, 186, 189
Husbandman's Complaint, 201
Hushang Shah, erected the durbar hall of Hindola Mahall, 335
Husian, Shah of Persia, 528
Huskisson, William, English statesman, 605, 606
Hussein, Grand Sherif of Mecca, 937; King of the Arabs; King of the Hejaz, 937; abdicated, 1104
Hussein ibn Ali, founded the Husseinite dynasty, 525
Hussein Kamil, Sultan of Egypt, 1081
Hussein, son of Mohammed Ali, conquers Sudan, 830
Hussite wars, 302, 305
Hussites, begin break from the Roman Church, 302; background of the Reformation, 399
Hussy, Obed, invented reaping machine, 772
Hutchinson, Mrs. Anne, banished from Massachusetts Bay Colony, 510
Hutchinson, Thomas, lt.-gov. of Massachusetts, 518
Hutten, Ulrich von, German humanist, 400
Hutton, James, his Theory of the Earth, 551
Hutuktu of Urga, placed Mongolia under Chinese suzerainty, 1118
Huvishka, 129
Huxley, Thomas Henry, English scientist, 551
Hydaspes, battle of, 65
Hyde, Dr. Douglas, first pres. of Eire, 974
Hyde, Sir Edward (later Earl of Clarendon), British statesman, 426
Hydrogen gas, 553
Hydrophobia, 552
Hydroplane flight by Russians, 570
Hyksos (Rulers of Countries), 23, 28; expulsion from Egypt, 34, 35
Hyndman, Henry Mayers, English socialist leader, 618
Hyōgo (Kōbe), opened to foreign trade, 358, 889
Hyphasis, 65
Hypsilanti, Alexander, leader of the Greek insurrection, 722
Hyrcania, 81, 83
Hyrcanus, John, 32, 96
Hyrcanus II, 32
Hysiae, battle of, 50

I dynasty, in Korea, 349
I Wen Lei Chü, first Chinese literary encyclopedia, 340
Iamblichus, exponent of neo-Platonism, 117
Iapyges, of southern Italy, 68
Iaroslav (the Great) of Russia, 241, 243
Iazyges, of Sarmatia, 109
Ibáñez, Gen. Cárlos, pres. of Chile, 1065
Ibáñez, Vicente Blasco, Spanish writer, 981
Ibarra, Francisco de, gov. and capt.-gen., founded Durango, 492
Ibarra, José María Velasco, pres. of Ecuador, 1069
Iberia, 125, 126
d'Iberville, Pierre Moyne, sieur, started French colony in Louisiana, 507
Ibi-Sin, 26
Ibn al-Ash'ath, caliph, 187
Ibn Batuta, Arab traveler, 329, 334, 346, 363
Ibn Haukal, Arab, 328
Ibn Saud, Abd al-Aziz, King of the Hejaz and Nejd, 937, 1104
Ibrahim, leads Shi'ite revolt in Iraq, 188
Ibrahim, son of Mohammed Ali and Khedive of Egypt, 723, 724, 308
Ibrahim I, Ottoman sultan, 424
Ibrahim Pasha, Turkish vizier, 422
Ibrahim Shah, a patron of learning, 334
Ibsen, Henrik, Norwegian dramatist, 699
Ice Age, see Pleistocene period
Iceian industry, 4
Iceland, recognized as a sovereign state, 1045; 1137, 1142, 1155, 1158
Iceni, 106
I-ching, Chinese Pilgrim, 340
I-chou (renamed Ch'eng-tu), cultural center of China, 341
Iconoclasm, 152, 175, 177
Ida of Bernicia's realm, in Scottish history, 168
Idaho, organized as a territory, 780; admitted to statehood, 784
Ide, Henry Clay, gov. of the Philippines, 909
Idris ibn Abdullah, founder of the Alid dynasty, 263
Idris III, of the Empire of Kanem, 524
Idrisids of Egypt, 262
Idumaea, 96
Ieharu, Japanese shōgun, 548
Iemitsu, Japanese shōgun, 547

Iemochi, Japanese shōgun, 888, 889
Ienari, Japanese shōgun, 887
Ienobu, Japanese shōgun, 548
Iesada, Japanese shōgun, 888
Ieshige, Japanese shōgun, 548
Ietsugu, Japanese shōgun, 548
Ietsuna, Japanese shōgun, 547
Ieyasu, Tokugawa, Japanese shōgun, 543, 544, 546
Ieyoshi, Japanese shōgun, 887
Ifriqiya, North Africa, invaded, 186
Iglesias, Miguel, pres. of Peru, 813
Ignatiev, Nikolai Pavlovich, Count, Russian diplomat, 734, 735, 736, 879
Ignatius of Antioch, early martyr, 113
Ignatius, Patriarch of Constantinople, 152, 177
Ikhnaton, Pharaoh, 24, 29
Ikhshidids of Egypt, 190, 262
Iki, 138
Ikkō sect, 359
Ikshvaku dynasty, 132
Ile Dauphine, one of Madagascar's names, 859
Ilerda, 97
Ilg, Alfred, Swiss promoter, 835
Il-Ghazi, wars against Latin princes of Palestine, 254
Iliad, 46, 47
Ilium, 47, 98
Il-Khans of Persia, 262, 328, 345
Illinois, admitted to statehood, 770; 790
Illinois Central R.R., 774
Illyria, 89, 96
Illyrian Provinces, organized by Napoleon, 595
Illyrian Wars, 86
Illyrian-speaking peoples, 16, 47, 68
Ilow, Christian, imperial general, 406
Im (Lim J. Rin) family, in Korea, 349
Imad al-Dawla, gets part of Persia and Iraq, 190
Imad al-Din Zangi, founder of the Zangid dynasty, 254
Image-worship, disapproved by Emperor Leo III, 175 f., 177
Imamate, dogma developed by the Shi'ite sect, 187
Imbert, Paul, French traveler, 524
Imbros, 62
Immelmann, Max, German aviator, 946
Immigration Act, of the Union of South Africa, 859; in the U.S., 1050
Immigration Bill, limiting immigration to U.S., 1051
Immigration Restriction Act, of the Australian Commonwealth, 903
Imna, 140
Imperial Bank (Reichsbank), opened in Germany, 689
Imperial Bank of Persia, 864
Imperial Conference, of the British Empire, 968
Imperial Council, Russian upper chamber, 708
Imperial Economic Conference, in Ottawa, 1059
Imperial Federation League, in Canada, 797
Imperial (German) Insurance Code, 693
Implements arising from cultures, 2, 4–6; in Palaeolithic period, 7, 8; in Post-Palaeolithic, 10, 11; in South Africa, 18
Imredy, Bela, Hungarian minister, 1016
IMRO, Macedonian Revolutionary Organization, 1023
Imube clan, in Japan, 139
Inaros, 55
Inayatullah, King of Afghanistan, 1110
Inca Empire, conquered by Pizarro, 489
Incandescent lamp, perfected by Edison, 556, 783
Incas of Peru, civilization, religion, culture, and govt., 20, 360 f.
Income tax in U.S., 779; declared unconstitutional, 786
Indabigash, 40
Indemnifications, provided in Treaty of Lunéville, 590
Independence Club, in Korea, 886
Independence of India League, 1112
Independent Labor Party, 618
Independents, in England, 378
Index, of the Catholic Church, 663
India, early history, 6, 13 f., 41 ff., 64 f., 124 f., 128 ff., 330 ff.; modern history, 530 ff., 868 ff., 1111 ff.; demanded independence, 1138; 1144
India Act, Pitt's, 535
India Bill, ending political powers of the British East India Co., 613
Indian Councils Act, 871
Indian Mutiny, 613
Indian National Congress, 1111, 1112, 1113
Indian population of South America, 498; enslavement prohibited by New Laws, 498
Indian Territory, 780
Indiana, admitted to statehood, 770
Indians (American), 12, 19, 766, 780
Indo-China, 872 ff., 1114, 1115, 1138, 1160 f., 1166
Indo-European languages, 16, 36, 41, 47
Indo-European people, invading Italy, 68
Indo-Iranian, 23
Indonesia, 7, 12, 18
Indrapura, 136
Indus culture, 13
Indus Valley, 40
Industrial Conciliation and Arbitration Act, in New Zealand, 1132
Industrial courts, in Germany, 691
Industries of man in Palaeolithic period, 4–7
Inequality of Human Races, by Count Gobineau, 551

Inez de Castro, mistress of Peter, son of Alfonso IV of Portugal, murdered, 284
Infallibility, under Moslem law, 533; papal, 664, 694
Inflation, in U.S., 1138
Inflation of currency, by Germany, 959
Ingavi, battle of, 812
Ingeborg, wife of Philip II, of France, 221
Inglefield, Capt. Edward Augustus, Arctic explorer, 564
Injo, Korean ruler, 542
Inkerman, battle of, 727
Inland Exploration Co. of New York, 1111
Inland Steel Co. strike, 1056
Inner Mongolia, 1171
Innocent I, Pope, 142
Innocent II (Gregorio Paperescidei Guidoni), Pope, 208, 219
Innocent III (Lotario de' Conti di Segni), Pope, 197, 203, 211, 214, 219–24, 229, 231, 234, 257
Innocent IV (Sinibaldo Fiesco), Pope, 212 f., 316, 344
Innocent V (Pierre de Champagni, or Tarentaise), Pope, 293
Innocent VI (Étienne Aubert), Pope, 287
Innocent VII (Cosimo dei Migliorati), Pope, 288
Innocent VIII (Giovanni Battista Cibo), Pope, 290, 395
Innocent IX (Giovanni Antonio Fachinetti), Pope, 396
Innocent X (Giovanni Battista Pamfili), Pope, 455, 457
Innocent XI (Benedetto Odescalchi), Pope, 455, 504
Innocent XII (Antonio Pignatelli), Pope, 457
Innocent XIII (Michele Angelo Conti), Pope, 457
Inns of Court, established, 200 f.
Inönü, see Ismet Inönü
Inoue, Jonnosuke, Japanese foreign minister, 890
Inquisition, conducted by Franciscans and Dominicans, 221, 230, 232, 282, 379; in Portugal, 392; in Spanish America, 498; 504; re-established in Rome, 663
Institut National, reorganized, 588
Institute for Exploration of the North, 570
Institutes of Justinian, 116 f., 172
Instrument of Government, drawn up by Cromwell's army council, 379, 425
Insular Cases, decided by supreme ct., 788
Insulin, 553
Inter innumeras, encyclical of Leo XIII, 640
Inter-Allied Commission of Military Control, 960
Inter-American Arbitration Act, 960
Inter-American Commission on Territorial Administration, 1155
Inter-American Conference, Mexico City, 1143, 1156; Rio de Janeiro, 1138, 1155
Inter-American Defense Board, 1156
Intercursus magnus, commercial treaty between England and Netherlands, 365
Internal combustion engine invented, 555
Internal Macedonian Revolutionary Organization (IMRO), 718
Internal revenue taxes, 766
International African Association, 847
International Association for the Exploration and Civilization of Africa, 739, 828, 843
International Association of the Congo, 739, 843
International Chamber of Commerce, 1007
International Court of Justice, United Nations, 1171
International Economic Conference, at Geneva, 960; at London, 963
International Refugee Committee, 1001
International Workingmen's Association (First International), 550
Interstate Commerce Act, 784
Interstate Commerce Commission, 784
Inukai, Ki, premier of Japan, 1126
Invaders of the west, their origin and movements, 142, 143, 158
Inverlochy, battle of, 378
Invincible Armada, see Armada, Spanish
Ionia, 53, 81
Ionian Islands, retained by France, 585; Septinsular Republic, 587; ceded to Greece, 612
Ionian War, 58
Ionians, mercenaries, 37, 47, 54, 55, 62
Iorga, Prof. Nicholas, Rumanian historian and statesman, 1026
Ipek, taken by Austrians, 927; by Italians, 949
Ippolita, daughter of Francesco Sforza, 298
Ipsus, battle of, 35, 37, 78
Iraca, high priest of the Chibchas, 361
Irala, Domingo Martínez de, gov. of Buenos Aires, 490
Iran, 1106 ff.; invaded by British and Russian forces, 1137, 1151; 1138; declared war on Germany, 1141; joined United Nations, 1141; 1144; see also Persia
Iraq, 127, 128, 186, 190; mandated to Britain, 1105; independent, 1125 ff.; 1137, 1151
Ireland, racial origins, 168; given to Henry II, 196; 201, 203; Edward Bruce crowned king, 272 f.; Statute of Drogheda, 369; 370; Earl of Strafford's policy, 376; 607; recent history, 971 ff.
Irenaeus of Lyons, early martyr, 113
Irene, Byzantine empress, 176 f., 188
Irene, daughter of Emperor Isaac Angelus, 256
Ireton, Henry, completes Cromwell's work in Ireland, 425, 426
Irigoyen, Hipólito, pres. of Argentina, 1064
Irish Catholic insurgents, enlist with Charles I in English Civil War, 377
Irish Church, conforms to Rome, 169
Irish Free State, officially proclaimed, 972
Irish Home Rule Party, 615
Irish Land Act, 613

Irish monks, discover Faroe Islands, 365
Irish Nationalists, in British Parliament, 617, 620
Irish (Scoti) raids on Britain, 166
Irish Reform Bill, 614
Irkutsk, taken by Czech troops, 947
Iron Age, 2 *ff*., 11; cemeteries, 14; Hallstatt period, 15; spread of languages over Europe, 16; 17
Iron Cross, established, 598
Iron Guard, in Rumania, 1026, 1135, 1136
Ironclad frigate (*La Gloire*) built for Napoleon III, 555
Ironsides, army of Oliver Cromwell, 377, 378
Irredentist agitation, in Austria, 738
Irtish River, 14
Iruka, Kingmaker of Japan, 140
Irun, captured by rebels in Spanish Civil War, 983
Irwin, Edward Frederick Lindley Wood, 1st Baron, viceroy of India, 1112
Isaac, 29
"Is War in Sight?" article in Berlin *Post*, 733
Isabella of Angoulême, marries King John of England, 197
Isabella of Aragon, 230, 237
Isabella, daughter of Charles VI of France, 268
Isabella, daughter of Ferdinand and Isabella, 392
Isabella, daughter of King John of France, 298
Isabella, daughter of Philip IV of France, 264
Isabella, Princess, daughter of Dom Pedro II of Brazil, 817
Isabella, Queen of Castile, 282, 366, 387
Isabella, wife of Charles VI, 280 *ff*.
Isabella II, Queen of Spain, 644, 645, 646, 647
Isagoras, 52
Isaiah, 30, 31
Isandhlwana, battle of, 853
Isauria, 95
Isaurians, 122
Isca Silurum, 106
I-shan, signs Treaty of Aigun, 879
Ishbaal, 30
Ishmael, 29
Isidore of Kiev, Roman cardinal, 289
Isidore of Seville, his *Etymologiae*, 163
Isidorean Decretals, 217
Isidoros of Miletus, helped build Church of St. Sophia in Rome, 173
Isin dynasty, 26
Isis, religion, 113
Islam, its triumph, 136; organized by Mohammed, 184; Ottoman claims to leadership, 485; in China, 537; in Malayan archipelago, 876; in Egypt, 1084
Islamic conquest of West Africa, 328
Isly, battle of, 837
Ismail, Khedive of Egypt, 615, 736, 830, 831
Ismail, Shah of Persia, 526
Ismail II, Shah of Persia, 526
Ismail Sidky Pasha, premier of Egypt, 1083, 1084
Ismet Inönü, pres. of the Turkish Republic, 1095, 1097, 1140
Isonzo, II, successive engagements, 925, 932, 941
Isotopes, 552
Isperikh (Asperuch), Bulgarian ruler, 181
Ispuini, 38
Israel, 30
Israel, Kingdom of, 31
Israelites, led out of Egypt, 24; 30
Issus, battle of, 40, 65, 114
Istanbul, new name for Constantinople, 327, 1096
Isthmian Canal Commission, 819
Isthmian Canal diplomacy, 788
Isthmian Games, 80, 86, 88
Isvarakrishna, 131
Itagaki, Count Taisuke, head of Liberal Party in Japan, 890
Italia, Gen. Nobile's dirigible, in Arctic flights, 566
Italia Irredenta, agitation to acquire Trentino and Trieste, 660
Italia, Republic of, 93
Italian East Africa, 1159, 1160
Italian Lake Dwellers, 17
Italian Republic, Napoleon pres., 590
Italian Somaliland, 1160
Italian-French Entente, 751
Italian-German Agreement of 1936, 991
Italo-Yugoslav Agreement, 1015
Italy, early history, 17, 68 *ff*., 85 *ff*., 101 *ff*.; medieval history, 141 *ff*., 150 *ff*., 215 *ff*., 286, 288 *ff*.; modern history, 392 *ff*., 454 *ff*., 584 *ff*., 650 *ff*., 923 *ff*., 986 *ff*., 1086 *f*.; in Second World War, declared neutrality, 1135; declared war on France and Great Britain, 1135, 1148, 1159; on U.S., 1138, 1167; armistice with France, 1148; merchant tonnage, 1156; invaded Egypt, 1159; surrendered unconditionally, 1141, 1159; 1170, 1171
Itkhi-Teshub, 28
Itkhiya, 28
Ito, Prince Hirobumi, Japanese statesman, 751, 887, 891–893
Ittobaal, King of Byblos, 33
Ittobaal, priest of Astarte, 33
Iturbide, Agustin de, Emperor of Mexico, 804, 805
Iturrigaray, José de, viceroy of New Spain, 803
Ituzaingo, battle of, 806, 817
Ivan I Kalita, Grand Prince of Moscow, 316
Ivan II Krasnyi, Prince of Moscow, 316
Ivan III (the Great), Tsar of Russia, 317, 413
Ivan IV (the Terrible), Tsar of Russia, 415, 417, 418
Ivan V, co-tsar of Russia with Peter I, 478

Ivan VI of Russia, 479
Ivangorod, battle of, 916, 922
Ivory Coast, 840
Ivry, battle of, 386
Iwakura, Prince Tomomi, Japanese diplomat, 890
Iwo Jima, taken by U.S., 1169
Izmailov, Lev Vasilievich, Russian missionary, 539
Izumo clan, of Japan, 138
Izvolski, Alexander Petrovich, Russian foreign minister, 754, 755, 756
Izzet Pasha, grand vizier of Turkey, 948

Jabbock River, 29
Jabesh, 30
Jack Cade's Rebellion, 270
Jackman, Charles, on Russian exploration, 559
Jackson, Andrew (7th pres. of the U.S.), 769, 770, 771, 772
Jackson, Frederick George, arctic explorer, 565
Jackson, Frederick John, mission to Uganda, 848
Jackson, Gen. Thomas Jonathan ("Stonewall"), Confederate general, 776, 778
Jacksonville, occupied by Federal forces, 776
Jacobi, Moritz, rotary motor, 553
Jacobins, French Revolutionary club, 580, 584
Jacobites, second rebellion (The Forty-five), 435
Jacqueline, Countess of Holland, 379
Jacquerie, peasant uprising in France, 276, 310
Jadar, battle of, 916
Jadwiga (Hedwig) of Poland, 310, 314, 316
Ja'far, brother of Ali, 188
Jafar Shah of Persia, 529
Jaffa, evacuated by the Turks, 948
Jagellon dynasty, 414
Jagiello, Grand Duke of Lithuania, 310; King of Poland, 314, 316
Jagow, Gottlieb von, German foreign minister, 930
Jahan Shah, Indian ruler, 533
Jahangir, 533
Jahn, Friedrich Ludwig, developer of gymnastics, 594
Jahwarids of Cordova, 233
Jainism, 132, 337 *f*.
Jains, 41, 332, 335 *f*.
Jaipal, King of Bhatinda, 332
Jalandhara, 128
Jalayrs, succeed the Il-Khans in Iraq, 330
Jalula, defeat of the Persians, 128, 186
Jamaica, settled, 486; slaves emancipated, 609; 1148 *f*., 1155, 1158
Jamal Khan, minister of Ahmadnagar, 533
Jamal ud-Din el-Afghani, Moslem teacher, 738, 831, 864 *f*.
James of Aragon, exchanges Sicily for Sardinia and Corsica, 222, 290
James I (the Conqueror), of Aragon, 237, 258
James II, of Aragon (King of Sicily), 284
James of Lusignan, 299
James, Thomas, English explorer, 560
James Edward (the Old Pretender), 431, 432
James I, King of England, 373 *f*., 375
James II, King of England, 426 *ff*., 512
James I, King of Scotland, 272
James II, King of Scotland, 272
James III, King of Scotland, 272
James IV, King of Scotland, 369
James V, King of Scotland, 371
James VI, of Scotland, becomes James I of England, 373
Jameson, Dr. Leander Starr, South African statesman, 744, 855, 856, 858
Jamestown Colony, 508, 513
Janet, Pierre, on pathological psychology, 552
Janiculum, 74
Janissaries, in the Ottoman Empire, 420 *f*., 424, 482, 721, 722, 723
Jankau, battle of, 407
Jannaeus, Alexander, 31, 32
Jansenism, in conflict with Jesuitism, 455
Jansenius, Cornelius, Bishop of Ypres, founder of Jansenism, 455
Janson, Paul, Belgian premier, 975
Janszoon, Willem, Dutch explorer, 894
January Convention (Budapest), between Russia and Austria, 734
Japan, early history, 14, 138 *ff*., 349 *ff*.; modern history, 542 *ff*. 887 *ff*., 1123 *ff*.; in Second World War, attacked Hawaii, Philippines, Malaya, 1138, 1155, 1158, 1166, 1167; neutrality treaty with Russia, 1137, 1166; occupied Indo-China, 1136, 1138, 1158, 1167; navy, finished, 1144; merchant tonnage, 1156; U.S. credits frozen, 1166; 10-year pact with Germany and Italy, 1166; 10-year treaty of Alliance with Thailand, 1167; raided by U.S. superfortress planes, 1169; unconditional surrender, 1145, 1170, 1171
Japan current, 138
Jaqub, of the White Sheep, ruler of Persia, 330, 526
Jarmuk River, 29
Jarnac, battle of, 384
Jaroslav, taken by the Russians, 916; retaken by Austro-Germans, 922
Jarrès, Karl, Nationalist candidate for pres. in Germany, 998
Jask, battle of, 526, 528
Jason, succeeds his father, Lycophron, 63
Jassy, 1154; Treaty of, 482, 485
Jatakamala, 131

ats, or Gypsies, 189
Jaubert, Pierre, French mission to Persia, 862
Jaurès, Jean, French socialist leader, 643
Java, conquered by Hindu princes, 876, 1167
Java (Br.), captured by the *Constitution* (U.S.S.), 769
Java Sea, battle of, 1167
Javanese, revolt against Dutch, 876 *f.*
Jaxartes, 43; River, 39
Jay, John, American diplomat, 766, 793
Jay Cooke & Co., failure, 782
Jayadeva, his *Gitagovinda*, 504
Jayasimha Siddharaja, Indian ruler, 332
Jeanne, Queen of Navarre, 273
Jeannette, ship of De Long expedition to Siberia, 565
Jeb, 21
Jebdzun-damba Hutuktu of Urga, 536
Jebel Druse in Syria, autonomous French state, 1098
Jefferson, Thomas (3d pres. of the U.S.), 529, 764, 766, 767
Jeffreys, George, 1st Baron. English lord chancellor, 429
Jehan Shah, ruler of northwestern Persia, 330
Jehangir, of the Khoja family, 877
Jehoahaz, 31
Jehoash, 31
Jehoiachin, 31
Jehoiakim, 31
Jehoram, 30
Jehoshaphat, 31
Jehovah (Heb.: *Yahweh*), god of Israel, 30
Jehu, 31
Jekov, Gen. Nicolas, Bulgarian commander, 927
Jellachich, Baron Josef, gov. of Croatia, 674
Jellicoe, Sir John Rushworth, British admiral, 917
Jem (Djem), brother of Sultan Bayazid II, 420
Jemappes, battle of, 582
Jen Tsung, Emperor of China, 877
Jena, battle of, 592
Jenatsch, George, leads Protestant faction in the Valtelline, 410
Jenghiz (Chinjiz) Khan, ruler of All Mongols, 260, 325, 344, 362
Jenkins, Robert, English seaman, 515
Jenkinson, Anthony, English diplomat, 526
Jephtah, 30
Jeremiah, 31
Jericho, 13
Jeroboam I and II, 31
Jerome, church father, 123, 142, 146
Jerome, of Prague, 289
Jerusalem, 24, 31, 32, 107, 127, 186; Kingdom of, 255, 256, 256–258; recent history, 948, 1100, 1101; taken by Gen. Allenby, 948; Balfour Declaration, 1100; Hebrew University opened, 1100
Jesuits: in Europe, 392, 401, 409 *f.*, 413, 452, 454, 457, 493, 502, 638, 650, 663, 666, 982; in America, 493, 499, 504; in Africa, 524; in Asia, 539, 542, 982
Jesus of Nazareth, born, 32, 102; crucified, 105; religion of, 113. *See also* Christ
Jewish disabilities, in England, 613
Jewish immigration, in Palestine, 1101
Jews: early history, 29 *ff.*, 110 *f.*, 145; in England, 199; in France, 232; in Hungary, 246, 1013, 1015; in Spain and Portugal, 282, 392; in Russia, 706; in Rumania, 720, 1025; in Germany, 1001; in Czechoslovakia, 1013; in North Africa, 1087; in Palestine, 1100 *ff.*
Jezebel, 31
Jezreel, 29, 30
Jhangar culture, 13
Jhelum, battle of, 42
Jhukar culture, 13
Jibuti-Addis Ababa Railway, 745
Jiménez, Ricardo, pres. of Costa Rica, 1073
Jimmu, first Emperor of Japan, 139
Jingikan, department of religion in Japan, 350
Jingō, Japanese empress, 139
Jinsai Itō, Confucian commentator, 546
Jitō, Empress of Japan, 350
Jizya, tax on non-Moslems, in Persia, 533, 534
Joachim II of Brandenburg, 402, 465
Joan, daughter of Henry II, 194
Joan of Arc, *see* Darc, Jeanne
Joanna, daughter of Edward II of England, 272
Joanna, daughter of Ferdinand and Isabella, 379, 388
Joanna, daughter of John III, Duke of Brabant, 379
Joanna of Austria, mother of Sebastian I of Portugal. 392
Joanna of Naples, 290, 292
Joanna II, sister of Ladislas of Naples, 292
Joash, 31
Job, Book of, 30
Jōchō, Buddhist sculptor, 353
Jōdo Shin, see True Pure Land
Jōei-shikimoku, Japanese law code, 356
Joffre, Gen. Joseph Jacques Césaire, French commander, 913, 920, 921
Jofre de Loyasa, García, leads expedition to Philippine Islands, 908
Johannes, Byzantine usurper, 121
Johannes IV, Ethiopian emperor, 660, 834, 835
Johannesburg laid out, 854; captured in Boer War, 857
Johansen, Hjalmar, Arctic explorer, 565
John, Archduke of Austria, imperial general, 588, 594 *f.*
John, Despot of Thessaly and Emperor of the West, 250

John, Duke of Bedford, regent for Henry VI of England, 270, 279
John (the Fearless), Duke of Burgundy, 278, 379
John (Lackland), King of England, 197 *ff.*, 203, 221, 229, 230 *f.*, 257
John, King of Aragon and Sicily, 284, 292
John I, of Athens, 258
John II, King of Aragon, 284
John IV Lascaris, Byzantine emperor, 260
John V Palaeologos, Byzantine emperor, 298, 322 *f.*
John VII, Byzantine emperor, 323
John VIII, Byzantine emperor, 323, 326
John II, King of France, 265, 276, 298, 379
John III, King of Sweden, 413, 415
John I, Duke of Brabant, 379
John I, King of Portugal, 284, 285
John II, King of Portugal, 286, 364, 366, 367
John III (the Pious), King of Portugal, 392, 500
John IV, King of Portugal, 427, 453
John V, King of Portugal, 453
John VI, King of Portugal, 502, 648, 805
John VI Cantacuzene, *see* Cantacuzene
John II Casimir, King of Poland, 471, 475
John II Orsini, ruler of Thessaly and Epirus, 322
John II Zapolya (Sigismund), King of Hungary, 420, 422 *f.*
John III Sobieski, King of Poland, 462, 475, 483.
John Alexius III, Byzantine emperor, 320
John Asen II, Bulgarian Tsar, 247, 248, 260
John VIII, Pope, 159
John XI, Pope, 215
John XII, Pope, 161, 216
John XIII, Pope, 216
John XIV, Pope, 216
John XVI, Pope, 162
John XIX, 216
John XXII (Jacques Duèse), Pope, 290, 292
John XXIII (Baldassare Cossa), Pope, 289, 306
John of Austria, gov. of Netherlands, 381, 389, 424, 428, 675
John of Bohemia, aids Teutonic Order against Poles, 310
John of Braganza, King of Portugal, 392
John of Brienne, King of Jerusalem, 257, 260
John of Capistrano, preaches crusade against Turks, 318
John of Ephesus, historian, 173
John of Gaunt, Duke of Lancaster, 265, 266, 267, 271
John of Giscala, defeated at Jerusalem, 107
John of Luxemburg, King of Bohemia, 276, 304
John of Montecorvino, Roman missionary to China, 346, 362
John of Pian de Carpine, mission to the Great Khan, 362
John of Salisbury, 169, 194, 229
John of Werth, commands Bavarians at battle of Nördlingen, 406
John Albert, King of Poland, 413
John Frederick. Elector of Saxony, 402
John George, of Brandenburg-Jägerndorf, 404, 465
John George, Elector of Saxony, 405 *f.*
John Joseph, of Austria, 450
John Sigismund, Elector of Brandenburg, 403
John William, Duke of Cleve, 401, 403
Johns Hopkins University, opened, 782
Johnson, Andrew, 17th pres. of the U.S., 780, 781
Johnson, William, Indian guide, 515
Johnson-Christy Commission, to investigate conditions in Liberia, 1089
Johnston, Albert Sidney, Confederate general, 778
Johnston, Maj. George, commander at New South Wales, 898
Johnston, Sir Harry Hamilton, pacified Nyasaland, 849
Johnston, Joseph Eggleston, Confederate general, 776, 779
Johore, Sultan, 876
Joint-stock banks, in France, 633
Joinville, François Ferdinand Philippe Louis Marie, Prince de son of Louis Philippe, 837
Joinville, Jean de, *French chronicle*, 231
Jōjitsu sect, in Japan, 351
Jokichi Takamine, adrenalin, 552
Joliet, Louis, Jesuit missionary, 507
Jomonshiki culture, 14
Jonathan the Maccabee, 32
Joneid, Sheikh, head of dervish order, 526
Jones, Sir Harford, British emissary to Persia, 862
Jones, John Paul, American naval commander, 521
Jones (William Atkinson) Act, granting territorial status to the Philippines, 792, 1132
Jonnart, Charles, French envoy to Greece, 940
Joram, 31
Jordanes, his references to Scandinavia, 170
Jordanus of Severac, missionary to China, 362
José, Amaro, Portuguese explorer, 826
Joseph, Indian chief, 780
Joseph, Benjamin, of the Muscovy Co., 559
Joseph tribes, 30
Joseph I, German emperor, 419, 445, 446, 463
Joseph II, German emperor, 469, 482, 678
Joseph I, King of Portugal, 453, 502
Joseph Ferdinand, Archduke, Austrian commander, 922
Joseph Ferdinand, Electoral Prince of Bavaria, 445
Josephine Ford, Fokker monoplane, carried Byrd and Bennett to the pole, 566
Josephus, historian, 21, 23, 107
Joshua, 30
Josiah, 24, 31

Jotham, 31
Joubert, Barthélemy Catherine, French general, 586, 587
Joubert, Petrus Jacobus, proclaims Boer Republic, 853; 854, 857
Jourdan, Jean Baptiste, Count, French general, 584, 586, 600
Journey from St. Petersburg to Moscow, Radishchev's protest against serfdom, 482
Jouvenel, Henri de, French high commissioner for Syria, 1098
Jovellaños, Gaspar Melchor de, Spanish reform minister, 451
Jovianus, surrenders Mesopotamia to Persians, 120; concludes peace with Shapur, 125; dies, 120
Joyce, Cornet, carries Charles I as a prisoner to the army, 378
Juan-juan, *see* Avars
Juan Yüan, Chinese scholar, 877
Juárez, Benito, Mexican president, 634, 821; recognized by U.S., 822
Juba, king, 98
Juba River territory, 1090
Jubilee of 1450, 289
Jubilee of 1887 (Queen Victoria), 619
Juchên (Chin dynasty), 348
Juchi, son of Jenghis Khan, 344
Judah, tribe of, 29, 30, 31
Judaism, religion, 30, 31, 82
Judas Maccabeus, 32, 82
Judea, Kingdom of, 24, 26, 31, 32, 96, 102, 107
Judges, Book of, 30
Judicature Act, 615
Judiciary Act of 1789 of U.S., 764, 766
Jugurtha, 92
Jugurthine War, 92, 100
Julia, Caesar's daughter, 96, 97, 102
Julian "the Apostate" (Flavius Claudius Julianus), Roman emperor, 120, 125
Juliana, Princess, of Holland, 976
Julianus, M. Didius Severus, executed, 114
Jülich-Cleve quarrel, over succession, 403
Julio-Claudian house, 107
Julius II (Giuliano della Rovere), Pope, 290, 394, 395, 498
Julius III (Giovanni Maria del Monte), Pope, 396, 501
Julius Africanus, 23
Julius Agrippa I, wrongly called Herod Agrippa, 105, 106
July Revolution, in France, 606; repercussions in Germany, 669
June, Harold Irving, with Commander Byrd in flight to South Pole, 576
Jung, Carl, on aspects of the subconscious, 552
Jungars, Mongol tribe, 539, 540
Jung-lu, Chinese statesman, 882, 883
Junin, battle of, 802
Junius, *Letters of*, 436
Junker, Wilhelm, African explorer, 828
Junkers Co., German aviation line, 1108
Junnar, 129
Junot, Andoche, Duke of Abrantès, French general, 452, 593
Junta de Guerra y Armadas de Indias, 496
Junta of National Defense, 983
Juran Burgundy, Kingdom of, 157, 158
Jurchen Tungus tribes, 343
Justices in eyre, in England, 195, 196
Justices of the peace, 266
Justin Martyr, 113
Justin II, Byzantine emperor, 126, 170, 173
Justinian I, Byzantine emperor, 117, 122, 144–46, 150, 170, 173, 207
Justinian II, Byzantine emperor, 175, 182
Justinus I, Byzantine emperor, 122
Justo, Agustin Pedro, pres. of Argentina, 1064
Jutes and Angles, invade England, 166
Jutland (Skagerrak), naval battle, 931, 932
Juvenal (Decimus Iunius Iuvenalis), Roman satirist, 112

Ka'ab, at Mecca, 186
Kaas, Mgr. Ludwig, Centrist leader in Reichstag, 1000
Kabarega, in Uganda, 849
Kabul, 82, 128, 186, 187, 867, 868; captured by Dost Mohammed, 866
Kadamba dynasty, 132
Kadesh, 23, 30, 34, 36
Kadphises, 43. *See also* Kujula and Vima
Kaffirs, defeated by British, 852, 853
Kaffraria, set up as a native preserve, 852; joined to Cape Colony, 853; annexed by British, 853
Kafuan industry, 6
Kafur, a eunuch entitled Malik Naib, 333
Kagoshima, bombarded by British squadron, 889
Kahtaba, routed the Omayyad forces, 188
Kaifeng, taken by Japanese, 1122
Kaifuso, collection of poems in Chinese, 351
Kajar dynasty, founded, 529, 862
Kakatiyas, held an important kingdom under Ganapati, 338
Kakutsthavarman, 132
Kakwayhids of Kurdistan, 190
Kalamu, 35
Kaledin, Gen. Alexei Maximovich, White Russian leader, 1031
Kalgan, taken by Japanese, 1121
Kalhana, his *Rajatarangini*, 332
Kalidasa, playwright and poet of India, 131, 331
Kaliman I, Bulgarian ruler, 248
Kaliman II, Bulgarian ruler, 248
Kalinin, 1153
Kalisch, Treaty of, 598
Kalka River, battle of, 244, 260

Kallio, Kyosti, pres. of Finland, 1048
Kalmar wars, 410
Kálnóky, Gustav, Siegmund, Count, Austrian foreign minister, 740
Kaloyan (Joannitsa), Bulgarian ruler, 247 f., 254, 259
Kalpanamanditika, 129
Kamakura period, in Japan, 351, 354, 356, 357
Kama-sutra ("Laws of Love"), 130
Kamatari, Emperor of Japan, 350
Kamehameha I, conquered Sandwich Islands, 910
Kamenev (Rosenfeld), Leo, Bolshevik leader, 1034, 1035
Kamerun Coast, 1159
Kameyama II, abdicated, 358
Kamil, Hussein, Sultan of Egypt, 834
Kammu, Emperor of Japan, 351, 352
Kamutay, Turkish parliament, 1140
Kanagawa, Treaty of, 888
Kanaka (natives), traffic in Australia, 895, 901
Kan-ami, Japanese playwright, 359
Kanaris, Constantine, Greek admiral, 722
Kandahar, independent of Afghanistan, 530
Kane, Dr. Elisha Kent, Arctic explorer, 564
Kanem or Bornu, Empire of, 524
K'ang Hsi Reign of Sheng Tsu, 537, 539
K'ang T'ai, mission of Fu-nan, 135
K'ang Yu-wei, Chinese reformer, 882, 884, 1117
Kanishka, founds 2d Kushana dynasty, 128, 129
Kanishka II, 129
Kano, Japanese school of painting, 358
Kansas-Nebraska Act, 775
Kansu al-Gauri, Mameluke sultan of Egypt, 421
Kanvas, 43
Kao Hsien-chih, defeated by the Arabs at Talas, 341
Kao-li, in disastrous wars, 137
Kao Tsung of the Ch'ien Lung Reign, 540, 541
Kapolna, battle of, 674
Kapp Putsch, in Berlin, 997
Kappel, battle of, 409
Kara, 139
Kara Iskender, ruler of the Turkoman Black Sheep, 330
Kara Mustafa, Turkish grand vizier, 483
Kara Yusuf, head of the Turkoman Black Sheep, 330
Karageorge (George Petrovich), Prince of Serbia, 712, 722
Karageorgevich, Alexander, Prince of Serbia, 714
Karageorgevich, Peter, King of Serbia as Peter I, 715
Karamanli, dynasty, 525
Kardam, Bulgar ruler, 182
Kardis, Treaty of, 471
Karelian Isthmus, 1145
Karikalan, king, 335
Karim Khan of the Zand dynasty, 529
Karind, taken by Russians, 927, 938
Karli, 43
Karlowitz, Treaties of, 458, 461, 475, 479, 484
Karlsbad, program in Czechoslovakia, 1011
Karlsefni, Thorfinn, explorer, 558
Karluk, ship of the Canadian Arctic Expedition, 567
Károlyi, Count Julius, republican premier in Hungary, 953, 1013, 1014
Károlyi, Count Michael, pres. of Hungary, 1013
Kars, 529
Kartanagara, Malaysian ruler, 348
Karun River, in Persia, 864
Kashgar, 128
Kashgaria, conquered by Chao-hui, 540; defended against Jehangir and Mohammed Ali, 877; reconquered by Tso-Tsung-t'ang, 880
Kashmir, 129; center of Buddhist studies, 332, 866, 870
Kasim Barid, ruler of Bidar, 335
Kassapa, parricide king, 131
Kasserine Pass, 1162
Kassites, 25, 26, 39
Kasvin, taken by the Russians, 927
Katanga Co., in the Belgian Congo, 844
Kathiawar, 129
Katkov, Michael, Russian journalist, 704, 740
Katō, Takaaki, Japanese admiral and premier, 1124
Katsura, Viscount Taro, premier of Japan, 892, 893
Katyayana, 42
Katzbach, battle of the, 599
Kaulbars, Nicholas, Russian general, 718, 740
Kaunas (Kovno), capital of Lithuania, 1042
Kausambhi, 42, 130
Kaunitz, Wenzel Anton, Prince von, Austrian chancellor, 466
Kautsky, Karl, German Socialist, 693
Kavala, taken by Bulgar-German forces, 934
Kay, battle of, 467
Kazakistan, republic of the Soviet federation, 1034
Kazan, taken by Czech troops, 947
Kazan, Watanabe, favored opening Japan, 888
Kearney, U.S. destroyer, 1158
Kearny, Col. Stephen Watts, American commander, 773
Kegon sect, in Japan, 351
Keiki (Hitotsubashi Yoshinobu), Japanese shōgun, 888, 889
Keitel, Gen. William, German minister of war, 1004
Keith, Arthur Berriedale, 331
Kellermann, François Christopher de, French general, 581
Kellett, Capt. Henry, Arctic explorer, 564
Kellogg, Frank Billings, U.S. secretary of state, 960, 1052
Kellogg-Briand Pact (Pact of Paris), 960, 978

Kells, Synod of, 169
Kelvin, Lord, *see* Thomson, William
Kemal Ataturk, *see* Mustapha Kemal Pasha
Kemal Re'is, Turkish admiral, 420
Kemet, the black land, ancient Egypt, 21
Keng Ching-chung, grandson of Wu San-kuei, 539
Kennedy, Capt. William, Arctic explorer, 564
Kenneth I, King of Scotland, 168
Kenseikai, political party in Japan, 1123
Kenshin, Uesugi, rival of Nobunaga, 543
Kent, Anglo-Saxon kingdom, 166
Kent, Duke of, gov. of Australia, 1131
Kent, Edward, Duke of, 4th son of George III, 608
Kentucky Resolutions, written by Thomas Jefferson, 766
Kentucky, settled, 517; admitted to statehood, 766
Kenya, gets a legislative council, 1090; 1160
Kerala, 129
Kerbela, battle of, 186
Kerch, 1153; straits, 1153
Kerensky, Alexander Feodorovich, minister of war and prime
  minister of the Russian provisional govt., 940, 1028, 1029
Keresztes, battle of, 424
Kerguelen-Trémarec, Capt. Yves Joseph, discovered Kerguelen
  Island, 571, 895
Kermadec Islands, annexed to New Zealand, 907
Kerman, 126
Kerrl, Hans, German minister of Church affairs, 1001
Kerularios, Michael, Patriarch of Constantinople, 249
Kesseldorf, battle of, 466
Ketteler, Klemens, Baron von, German minister to China, 883
Keyes, Sir Roger, British admiral, 946
Keyser, Jacob van, Dutch mission to China, 539
Khabarov, Erofei, built fort at Albazin, 539
Khabarovsk, founded, 879; taken by Japanese, 947
Khadija, wife of Mohammed, 184
Khaidu, head of the house of Ogedei, 345
Khaireddin Pasha, Turkish admiral and corsair, 422, 423, 524
Khaki Election, in England, 967
Khalid ibn al-Walid, invaded Iraq, 127, 184
Khalji dynasty of Delhi, 333
Khanate of the Golden Horde, 244
Khandesh, in reconquest of the Deccan, 533
Khanikin, taken by Russians, 927, 929, 938
Khanua, battle of, 530
Kharijites (Azraqites), 186, 187, 188
Kharkov, occupied by Germans-Austrians, 943; 1151, 1153,
  1154
Kharoshti script, 42
Khartum, founded, 826, 830; captured by the Mahdi, 832; re-
  taken by the British, 833
Khazars, 126, 175, 181, 187, 242
Khevenhüller, Ludwig Andreas, Count, Austrian diplomat, 739
Khilafat movement, 1112
Khitan Mongols, conquer all Inner Mongolia, 341, 348
Khiva, 124
Khmelnitsky, Bogdan, hetman of Cossacks, 475, 478
Khoja dynasty, 540, 877
Khorasan, 125, 126, 188; devastated by Mongol armies, 260
Khorda Avesta, 39
Khorsabad, 25, 38
Khosroes II of Persia, 335
Khotan, 128
Khuen-Héderváry, Count Károly, premier of Hungary, 696
Khurramites, terrorize North Africa, 189
Khush-Newaz, Ephthalite Khan, 125
Khusru (Chosroes), satrap of Persian Armenia, 125, 172, 173
Khusru Parviz (Chosroes II), last king of Sassanian dynasty,
  127
Khuzistan, 127, 128
Khwarizm, 255 f.
Ki Tsurayuki, Japanese writer, 352
Kiakhta, Treaty of, 540
Kiamil Pasha, grand vizier of Turkey, 731, 760
Kiangsi Province, 1167
Kiao-chow, 893, 1123, 1124
Kibi-Teshub, 28
Kiderlen-Wächter, Alfred von, German foreign secretary, 757
Kieft, Willem, gov. of New Netherland, 510
Kiel, Treaty of, 600, 602
Kiel Canal, from the North Sea to the Baltic, 692, 754
Kielland, Alexander Lange, Norwegian writer, 699
Kiersy, Capitulary of, 158
Kiev, 244, 943, 1031, 1151, 1154
Kikkuli, treatise on horse-training, 28
Kilidj Arslan IV, Sultan of Rum, 253, 254, 260
Killiecrankie, battle of, 430
Kimberley, founded, 853; 857
Kimberley, John Wodehouse, 1st Earl of, British foreign secre-
  tary, 891
Kimbolton. Lord, impeachment ordered by Charles I, 376
Kinemacolor, a process of color photography, 557
Kinetoscope, first successful motion picture, 556
King, Mackenzie, Canadian premier, 1155
King, Philip Parker, gov. of New South Wales, 896, 898
King, Dr. Richard, explorer, 563
King, Samuel Wilder, delegate from Hawaii in U.S. Congress,
  1134
King, William Henry, U.S. senator, 1133
King, William Lyon Mackenzie, prime minister of Canada,
  1058, 1060
King George's War, 515

King Philip's War, 511
King William's War, 514
Kings, Book of, 30
King's Council (Small Council), 200, 266
King's Friends, 435, 436
King's Mountain, battle of, 522
King's peace, Greek settlement, 63
Kingsford-Smith, Capt. Charles, in trans-Pacific flight, 558,
  1130
Kinkaku, *see* Golden Pavilion
Kino, Eusebio, Jesuit, 499
Kinski, Wilhelm, imperial general, 406
Kioga, Lake, discovered, 828
Kionga Triangle, assigned to Portugal, 1090
Kiosseivanov, George, Bulgarian premier, 1024
Kirenzi, 28
Kirin, occupied by Japanese, 962
Kirk, Alexander Carnegie, introduced triple expansion engine,
  555
Kirk, Sir John, British consul-gen. at Zanzibar, 847
Kirk Kilissé, battle of, 759
Kirke, Col. Percy, relieves Londonderry, 430
Kirkuk, 28; battle of, 529
Kirmanshah, taken by Russians, 927, 929; taken by British, 947
Kirov, Serge, collaborator of Stalin, 1035
Kish, 13, 25
Kishiner, 1154
Kiska, 1167
Kisselev, Count Paul, gov. of the Danubian principalities, 719
Kistna, 129, 132
Kitabatake Chikafusa, Japanese warrior, 357, 358
Kitama, Egyptian tribe, 262
Kitasato, Shibasaburo, discovered germ of bubonic plague, 552
Kitchen Middens, 17
Kitchener, Horatio Herbert, 1st Earl, British general and war
  minister, 748, 833, 834, 845, 857, 904, 929, 937
Kitty Hawk, airplane flight of Wright brothers, 557
Kiyomasa, Katō, overran most of Korea, 544
Kiyomori, Taira, 354; Japanese premier, 354
Kiyoura, Keigo, Viscount, premier of Japan, 1125
Kizil-bashes, order of dervishes, 526
Klagenfurt, assigned to Austria, 1005, 1017
Klausener, Erich, German Catholic leader, 1003
Kléber, Jean Baptiste, French general, 586
Klebs, Edwin, discovered diphtheria germ, 552
Kleist von Nollendorf, Friedrich Heinrich Ferdinand Emil, with
  Bohemian army, 599
Klingsor, Gen. Wilhelm Mauritz, arrests Gustavus IV of
  Sweden, 595
Klokotnitsa, battle of, 248, 260
Klondike gold rush, 798
Kloster-Zeven, battle of, 467
Kluck, Alexander von, German general, 912, 913
Kmer people, of Siam, 347
Knights of Labor, in U.S., 783 f.
Knights of Malta, 258, 590
Knights of Rhodes, 258
Knights of St. John, or the Hospitalers, 258, 327, 420, 422
Knights of the Hospital of St. Mary of the Teutons, 214, 258
Knights Templar, *see* Order of the Knights Templar
Knights' War, 400
Knossos, 16
Knoviz culture, 17
Know Nothing Party, in U.S., 775
Knowles, Sir Charles, English admiral, 515
Knox, John, Scottish reformer, 372, 401
Knox, Philander Chase, U.S. secretary of state, 790
Knudsen, William A., head of U.S. defense board, 1136, 1155
Knut VI, 203
Knut the Great (Canute), King of Scandinavia and England,
  167, 203, 205, 241
Knutsson, Knut, *see* Charles VIII of Sweden
K'o Shao-min, prepared new *History of the Yüan Dynasty*, 88 f.
Kobad, 1st and 2d reigns, 126
Kobad II (Siroes), 127
Kōbō Daishi, *see* Kukai
Koc, Col. Adam, Polish leader, 1040
Koch, Lt. John Peter, Arctic explorer, 568
Koch, Lauge, Arctic explorer, 568
Koch, Robert, discovered germs of Bubonic plague, tubercu-
  losis, and cholera, 552
Kochubei, Victor Gavovich, Prince, Russian reformer, 701
Koehl, Capt. Hermann, German aviator, 558
Kogalniceanu, Enaki, prime minister of Rumania, 720
Koguryō, Korean state, 137
Koht, Halvdan, historian, foreign minister of Norway, 1046
Kojiki, record of Japanese history, 350
Kojong, King of Korea, 885, 886
Kok, Adam, Griqua chief, 852
Koken, Empress of Japan, 351
Kokinshū, anthology of Japanese poems, 352
Koko-nor, 127
Kokovtsev, Vladimir Nikolaievich, prime minister of Russia,
  708
Kolchak, Adm. Alexander Vasilyevich, Supreme Ruler of All
  Russia, 947, 952, 1032
Koldewey, Capt. Karl Christian, heads German Greenland ex-
  pedition, 564
Kolettis, Joannis, Greek leader, 724
Kolin, battle of, 467
Kolokotronis, Theodorus, Greek leader, 723

Kolowrat, Franz Anton, Count, finance minister of Austria, 671
Kolstad, Peter Ludvik, leader of Farmers' Party in Norway, 1046
Kolubara, battle of, 917
Komagatu Maru, Japanese ship, 797, 871
Komatsu II, Japanese emperor, 358
Komsa culture, 18
Kondane, 43
Kondouriottis, Lazaros, Greek leader, 723
Kondouriottis, Adm. Paul, pres. of the Greek Republic, 934, 1021
Kondylis, Gen. George, Greek statesman, 1022
Kongōbuji, Japanese monastery, 352
Koniah, battle of, 724
König, Friedrich, invented first cylinder printing press, 554
Königgrätz (Sadowa), battle of, 634, 686
Königsberg, founded, 215; Treaties of, 471, 593
Königsberg, German cruiser, 918
Königshofen, battle of, 400
Königsmark, Hans Christian, Swedish general, 407
Koniuchy, battle of, 940
Konoye, Fumumaro, Prince, premier of Japan, 1126, 1127
Kontors, 309, 310
Koppam, battle of, 337
Kopri :oi, taken by Russians, 929
Koran, 184, 186
Körber, Ernst von, Austrian prime minister, 695, 930
Korea, early history, 14, 137, 348 f.; modern history, 542, 743, 745, 747, 881, 885 ff., 890–893, 1119, 1123, 1171
Korfanty, Adalbert, Polish commissioner, 956, 997
Kormisosh, Bulgar ruler, 182
Kornilov, Gen. Lavr Georgievich, Russian counter-revolutionist, 940, 1029, 1031
Korsakov, Alexander Mikhailovich, Russian general, 587
Koryŏ period, in Korea, 348 f.
Kosala, 41
Kosambi, 41
Kosciuszko, Thaddeus, leads national uprising in Poland, 478
Kösedagh, battle of, 324
Kossovo, battles of, 319, 323, 324, 326
Kossuth, Francis, leader of the Independence Party in Hungary, 696
Kossuth, Louis, president of Hungary, 671, 673, 674, 796
Kotzebue, August von, German dramatist, 669
Kovel, battle of, 932
Kovno, taken by Germans, 922
Kowshing (Br.), sunk by Japanese, 881
Koxinga (Cheng Ch'eng-kung), 537
Koyata, Baron Iwasaki, purchases library of Lu Hsin-yüan, 884
Kraft durch Freude, German labor organization, 1002
Krasnov, Gen. Peter Nicolaievich, hetman of the Don Cossacks, 1031
Krassin, Russian ice-breaker, 567
Kray von Krajova, Paul, Austrian general, 586
Kremsier Constitution of 1849, 674
Kressenstein, Col. Kress von, German commander in Turkey, 929
Kreuzzeitung, German Conservative organ, 680
Krishnadeva, 338
Krishnaraja I, 336
Kristensen, Capt. Leonard, Antarctic explorer, 573
Krofta, Dr. Kamil, Czech foreign minister, 1010
Kronstadt, 934, 1033
Kropotkin, Prince Peter, Russian anarchist, 550, 640
Krüdener, Barbara Juliana, Baroness von, Russian mystic, 603
Kruger, Paul, pres. South African Republic, 744, 853, 854, 855, 856, 857
Kruger telegram episode, 692, 744, 856
Krugersdorp, battle of, 856
Krum, Bulgar ruler, 177, 182
Krumir tribes, from Tunisia, 838
Krylenko, Nicolai Vasilievich, Russian revolutionary leader, 1030
Kshitigarbha, 130
Ku I Ts'ung Shu, Chinese publication, 884
Ku k'ai-chih, refinement in figure-painting, 136
Ku Yen-wu, Chinese geographer, 540
Kuang Hsü Reign of Te Tsung, 880
Kuang Wu Ti, 134
Kuangchowwan, leased by China to France, 747
Kuan-yin, 136
Kublai Khan, Mongol Khan, 260, 262, 338, 345, 346, 357, 362; 366, 367
Kuchuk Kainarji, Treaty of, 481, 484 f.
Kudur-mabug of Elam, 39
Kudur-nahunte of Elam, 39
Kuei, Chinese prince, 537
Kueisui, taken by Japanese, 1121
Kufans, in Iraq, 186
Kühlmann, Richard von, German secretary for foreign affairs, 942, 943
Kujula Kadphises, unites tribes of Yue-chi, 128
Kūkai (kōbō Daishi), founder of the Shingon sect in Japan, 352
Kulevcha, battle of, 724
Kulikovo, battle of, 316
Kulin, ruler of Bosnia, 246 f.
Kulinism, 331
Kulm, founded, 211 f., 214; battle of (Nollendorf), 599
Kulturkampf, in Prussia, 664, 688, 690, 733
Kumanovo, battle of, 759
Kumaragupta I, his monastic community, 130

Kumarajiva, translator, 131, 136
Kumaralabdha, 131
Kumaralata, 129
Kumarapala, Jain ruler, 333
Kumarasambhava, 131
Kumaso, Japanese people, 139
Kume clan, in Japan, 139
Kun, Bela, Hungarian Bolshevik leader, 953, 1013, 1014
Kundersdorf, battle of, 467
K'ung An-kuo, his *Canon of History*, 136
Kung, Prince, regent for Te Tsung, 880
K'ung Ch'iu, *see* Confucius
K'ung Hsiang-hsi, Chinese minister of industry, 1119
Kung-sun family, in Korea, 137
Kuniaki Koiso, Japanese premier, 1142
Kuntala, 132
Kuo Hsi, Chinese painter, 343
Kuo Min Tang Party, in China, 884, 885, 1118, 1119
Kuo Shou-ching, maker of bronze instruments, 345
Kuo Tzu-i, suppresses rebellion in China, 341
Kural of Tiruvalluvar, 132
Kurbsky, Prince, leader of Russian boyars, 417
Kurdistan, religious policy of govt., 1096
Kurds, revolt in northeastern Syria, 1110; insurrection in Iraq, 1105
Kurile Islands, 1171
Kurkuas, John, Byzantine general, 179
Kuroda, Hideo, premier of Japan, 891
Kursk, 1153
Kurt, or Kubrat, 1st authenticated Bulgarian ruler, 181
Kurus, 43
Kurverein, formed at Rense, 302
Kusha sect, in Japan, 351
Kushan, "son of Heaven and King of Kings," 124, 130
Kushana Kingdom, in the Punjab, 134
Kushans, defeat Persians, 15
Kushshar, 36
Küstendil (Velbuzhde), battle of, 319
Kusunoki Masashige, Japanese warrior, 357
Kut, battle of, 938
Kutahia, Convention of, 724; battle of, 1095
Kutb Minar, a Delhi minaret, 333
Kutb-ud-din Aibak, 332
Kut-el-Amara, battle of, 927
Kuthah, 25
Kutusov, Mikhail Lairoinovich, Russian general, 591, 598
Kuya, Japanese monk, 353
Kuyper, Dr. Abraham, premier of the Netherlands, 626
Kviesis, Albert, pres. of Latvia, 1043
Kwajalein, 1169
Kwangsi, 44
Kwangtung, in control of Chiang K'ai-shek, 1120
Kyōto (formerly Edo), 354, 355, 358, 359, 889
Kyūshū, Japanese island, 14, 139, 1169
Kyūsō, Muro, Confucian scholar, 548

Labarnash (Tabarnash), founder of the old kingdom of the Hittites, 36
La Bassée, in German possession, 913, 921
Labor Disputes Resolution, 1054
Labor Party, in the Commonwealth of Australia, 903, 904, 1129, 1132
Labor Party, in England, 618, 968
Labor Party, in New Zealand, 908
Labor Relations Act (Wagner-Connery), 1054
Labor Representation Committee, in England, 618
Labor tax, abolished in Belgian Congo, 846
Labor troubles, in Switzerland, 994, 995; in U.S., 1056
Laborde, Jean, French consul in Madagascar, 860
Labyrinth, 23
Lacedaemon, 47
Lacerda, Francisco de, Portuguese explorer, 826
La Chaise, François d'Aix de, in Popish Plot, 428
Lachares, 78
La Cierva y Peñafiel, Juan, Spanish leader, 647
Lackland, John, *see* John (Lackland)
Laconia, 45, 48, 79, 80
Lactantius, 123
Ladd, William, founder of American Peace Society, 771
Lade Island, battle of, 53
Ladislas of Naples, 288, 292
Ladislas of Transylvania, 317
Ladislas II, King of Hungary, 418, 419
Ladislas III, King of Hungary, 245
Ladislas IV, King of Hungary, 246
Ladislas V, King of Hungary, 318
Lado enclave, 833, 834, 846
Ladulos, Magnus, King of Sweden, 204
Ladysmith, siege of, 857
Lae, 1169
Laelius, 91
Laenas, Caius Popilius, 89
Laënnec, René, invented the stethoscope, 551
Laetus, praetorian, 112
La Farina, Giuseppe, Italian statesman, 657
Lafayette, Marie Joseph Paul Yves Roch Gilbert Motier, Marquis, in American Revolution, 521; in French Revolution, 579, 581; in 1830 Revolution, 628
La Fère-Champenoise, battle of, 601
Laffitte, Jacques, French premier, 628
La Follette, Robert Marion, American statesman, 790, 1051

La France Orientale, one of Madagascar's names. 859
Lagash, 1st dynasty, 26
La Gloire, French ironclad frigate. 554
Lagos, battle of, 444
La Grandière, Pierre Paul Marie de. French admiral. 874
Lagrange, Joseph Louis, 131
La Harpe, Frédéric César de, Swiss revolutionary 460. 701
La Hire, Étienne, 278
La Hogue, Cap de, battle of, 431
Laidoner, Gen. John, in *coup d'état* in Estonia, 1044
Laing, Alexander Gordon, African explorer. 826
Laing's Nek, battle of. 854
Lakanal, Joseph, 583
Lake Champlain, battle of. 521
Lake Cochise, 19
Lake Erie, battle of. 769, 793
Lake George, battle of. 516
Lake Moëris, 21, 23
Lake Naroch, battle of, 932
Lake Presba, battle of, 940
Lake Regillus, battle of. 71
Lake Tatta, 35
Lake Trasimene, 87
Lake Urmia, battle of. 424
Lake Vadimo, 73, 74
Lakhta, battle of, 842
Lakshmanasena, author of *Gitagovinda.* 331
Lalitavistara, 129
Lallement, Pierre, developed two-wheeled velocipede, 555
Lally, Thomas Arthur, Count, besieged Madras, 535
Lamachus, expedition to Sicily, 59
Lamar, José de, pres. of Peru, 812
Lamarck, Jean Baptiste de, French scientist, 551
La Marmora, Alfonso Ferrero, Marchese di, Italian general and statesman, 727
Lamartine, Alphonse Marie Louis de, French poet and statesman, 630
Lambacsis, 110
Lambert, Gen. John; expels Rump Parliament; 426
Lambert of Spoleto, emperor, 152, 215
Lambros, Spyridion P., Greek prime minister, 934, 940
Lambruschini, Luigi, Cardinal, papal secretary of state, 663
Lamennais, Felicité Robert de, Catholic writer, 663
Lamia, 66
Lamoricière, Christophe Léon Louis Juchault de, French general, 837
Lamsdorff, Vladimir Nikolaievich, Count, Russian foreign minister, 750, 751
Lancaster, *see* Thomas, Duke of Lancaster
Land and Liberty, Russian secret society, 705
Land Law in U.S., 770
Land Occupation Act, in New South Wales, 901
Land of no return, 25
"Land of the Codfish," 366
Land Ordinance, in U.S., 522
Land Purchase Acts, in England, 617, 618
Landed Property Qualification Act, 432
Landfrieden, 212, 302
Lander, Richard, African explorer, 826
Landon, Alfred Moss, defeated for president of U.S., 1056
Landscape painting, in China, 343
Landshut, battle of, 467, 594
Landstad, Magnus, his *Norwegian Folksongs,* 699
Landsturm and Landwehr, established, 598
Lanfranc, Archbishop of Canterbury, 191, 193, 217
Lang, Capt. William, service in the Chinese navy, 881
Langensalza, battle of, 682
Langeron, Andrault de, 599
Langland, William, his *Piers Plowman,* 266
Langley, Samuel Pierpont, flew powered airplane, 556
Langlois, Capt., sent colonies to New Zealand, 905
Langside, battle of, 373
Langson, battle of, 874, 881
Langton, Stephen, Archbishop of Canterbury, 197, 221
Lannes, Jean, French general, 591
Lanrezac, Gen. Charles Louis, French general, 912
Lansdowne, Henry Charles Keith Petty Fitzmaurice, 5th Marquess of, British foreign secretary, 620, 751; gov.-gen. of Canada, 796; viceroy of India, 870
Lansing, Robert, U.S. secretary of state, 923, 949, 952
Lansing-Ishii Agreement, 1049, 1123
Lanston, Tolbert, invented monotype, 556
Lanza, Domenico Giovanni Giuseppe Maria, prime minister of Italy, 660
Laodice I, 81
Laodicea, 32
"Laodicean War," 81
Laomedon, 33
Laon, battle of, 600; taken by the Germans, 912
Laos, protectorate acquired by France, 875; Province, 1166
Laotians, 44
Lao-tzu, Chinese philosopher, 44; 135; 340
La Pérouse, Jean François Galoup de, French explorer, 895
La Plata, Viceroyalty of, 495, 497
La Pointe, Ernest, Canadian diplomat, 1058
Laptiev, Dmitri, Russian explorer, 562
Lapua, Finnish fascist organization, 1048
Laredo Bru, Federico, pres. of Cuba, 1077
La Révellière-Lépeaux, Louis Marie de, member of French Directory, 585

La Rochejaquelein, Henri du Vergier, Count de, a leader in Vendée revolt, 582
La Rochelle, battle of, 280
La Roque, Col. François, leader of the French *Croix de Feu,* 978
La Rothière, battle of, 600
Lars Porsena, attack on Rome. 71
Larsa, 25; dynasty, 26, 39
Larsen, Capt. Carl Anton, Norwegian explorer, 573, 574
La Salle, René Robert Cavelier, sieur de, French explorer, 507
Las Casas, Bartholomé de. Spanish missionary and historian, 389, 488, 493, 498
Las Palmas Island, awarded to the Netherlands, 975
Lascaris, Theodore. Byzantine emperor, 259
Lashio, 1167
Laskonogi, Vladislav, of Poland, 242
Lassalle, Ferdinand, German socialist, 550. 689
Lasso, Orlando di, Italian musician, 393
Latakia, a republic, 1098
La Tène culture, 15, 17
Late Bronze Age I, II, 29
Late Cycladic culture, 16
Late Helladic culture, 16
Late Neolithic culture, 13. 16
Later Han History, 128
Later Tsin dynasty, 341
Lateran Council, 395
Lateran Synod, 151, 218
Lateran Treaty of 1929, 660, 665, 989, 993
Lathyrus, son of Ptolemy VII, 84
Latimer, Hugh, English churchman, 372
Latimer, William, 4th Baron, impeached by Parliament, 267
Latin Alphabet, introduced in Turkey, 1096
Latin America, 366 *ff.,* 486 *ff.,* 799 *ff.,* 1062 *ff.*
Latin Church, of Constantinople, 220
Latin League, 70–73
Latin War, 73
Latins, 68, 70, 93, 252, 253
Latium, 68, 69, 71
Latour, Theodor Franz, Count Baillet von, Austrian minister of war, 674
Latvia (Courland), declares independence, 943, 966, 1031; history, 1043 *ff.,* 1136, 1145, 1148, 1151
Laud, William, Archbishop of Canterbury, 375, 376, 378
Lauderdale, John Maitland, Duke of, a member of the Cabal, 427, 428
Laudon, Gideon Ernst, Baron von, Austrian general, 467
Laudonnière, René de, established Fort Caroline, 505
Laufen oscillation, 4, 8, 9
Launay, Bernard René, Marquis de, gov. of the Bastille, 579
Laupen, battle of, 460
Laurier, Sir Wilfrid, premier of Canada, 797, 1057
Laurium, 53
Lausanne, Treaties of, 759, 839 (*see* Ouchy), 954, 1021, 1097, 1105 *f.*
Lausanne Conferences, 958, 959, 962
Lausitz culture, 17
Lautrec, Odet de Foix, Vicomte de, French general, 399, 400
Laval, Pierre, French premier, 969 *f.,* 979, 1136, 1138, 1139, 1148, 1150
Lavater, Johann Caspar, 460
Laveran, Charles, discovered malarial germs, 552
Lavigerie, Charles Martial Allemand, Cardinal, 640, 841
Lavrov, Peter, Russian populist leader, 705
Law, John, Scottish financier, 434, 447
Law of Guaranties, in Italy, 659 *f.*
Law of Indemnity, in France, 627
Law of Moses, 30
Law of Sacrilege, in France, 627
Law of the Double Vote, in France, 627
Law of the Septennate, in France, 637
Law of 1282, Florence, 293
Law of 22 Prairial, 583
Law on the Organization of the Public Powers (France), 637 *f.*
Lawrence, Sir John Laird Mair, viceroy of India, 870
Lawrence, Thomas Edward, British soldier and leader of the Arabs, 938, 948
Laws of Imitation, by Gabriel de Tarde, 552
"Laws of Love," 130
Lawson, Henry John, invented "safety" bicycle, 555
Lawson, William, Australian explorer, 898
Laxman, Lt. Adam, in Hakodate, 887
Lay, Horatio Nelson, inspector-gen. in China, 879
Lay investiture, struggle over, 206, 207, 216, 218
Layamon, his *Brut,* 201
Layton, Sir Walter Thomas, and the Layton-Wiggin report, 961; 1149
Lazar I, Prince of Serbia, 319, 324
Lazar III, Prince of Serbia, 320
Lazarevich, Stephen, Despot of Serbia, 319
Lazica, 126, 127
Le dynasty, in Annam, 347
League of Armed Neutrality, 482
League of Augsburg, against Louis XIV of France, 429, 439, 443, 461, 484, 514
League of Cambrai, to despoil Venice, 393 *f.,* 397, 398
League of Cognac, coalition against Charles V, 394, 400
League of Córdoba, in Argentina, 808
League of Heilbronn, 406
League of Liberators, in Estonia, 1044
League of Nations, 951, 956, 962, 963, 964, 1006, 1007, 1064, 1086, 1101, 1120, 1170

League of Nobles (Compromise of Breda), 379
League of Pavia, supports Frederick I on 2d expedition to Italy, 220
League of Sarnen, in Switzerland, 666
League of Sixteen, for the deposition of Henry III, 386
League of the Public Weal, a conspiracy against Louis XI, 279
League of the Russian Nobility, 708
League of the Three Forest Cantons, 306
League of Torgau, formed by Protestant princes, 400
League of Ulemas, founded at Constantine, 1087
Leakey, Louis Seymour Bazett, 6
Lebanon, 26, 29, 33, 1137, 1141, 1144, 1151
Le Bon, Gustave, his *Psychology of Crowds*, 552
Lebon, Joseph, French revolutionary, 582
Le Brix, Lt. Comdr. Joseph, French aviator, 557
Lebrun, Albert, pres. of France, 978
Lebrun, Charles François, Consul of the French Republic, 581, 587
Leburnion, battle of, 249
Lechfeld, battle of, 161
Lecompton Constitution, denounced by Douglas, 775
Lecomte, Gen. Claude Martin, in Paris Commune, 637
Ledru-Rollin, Alexandre Auguste, French radical, 631
Lee, Arthur Hamilton, first lord of British admiralty, 753
Lee, Richard Henry, resolution for "free and independent States," 520
Lee, Robert Edward, Confederate general, 778, 779
Lefèbvre d'Étaples (Jacques Faber), French reformer, 383
Leffingwell, Ernest de Koven, Arctic explorer, 567
Legal Tender Acts, in U.S., 779
Legatio Constantinopolitana, 162
Legations in Peking, under siege, 883
Legge Fascistissime, 989
Leghorn, purchased by Florence, 294
Legion of Honor, created, 590
Legislative Assembly, in the French Revolution, 578, 580 *f.*
Legislative Assembly (*Corps législatif*) under the French constitution, 632, 634, 635
Legislative Council, in New South Wales, 898, 900
Legnano, battle of, 210, 220
Leguía, Augusto Bernardino, pres. of Peru, 813, 1068
Lehwald, Gen. Hans von, Prussian general, 467
Leicester, Robert Sidney, 1st Earl of, commanded troops to aid Dutch Republic, 373
Leichhardt, Friedrich Wilhelm Ludwig, German scientist and explorer, 900
Leiningen, Count Karl August von, mission to Turkey, 715
Leipzig, or Breitenfeld, battles of; Gustavus Adolphus defeated Tilly, 405; Torstenson defeated Piccolomini, 407; Battle of the Nations, 599
Leipzig, German cruiser, 917; sunk, 918
Lelantine War, 52
Leleges, 47
Lemaire, Jacob, discovered Bismarck Archipelago, 894
Lemaitre, Lt. Henri, flew across Sahara, 1081
Lemanic Republic, organized by French, 460
Le Mans, battle of, 583
Lemberg, battles of, 475, 916, 922, 932
Lemnos, 62; battle of, 179; occupied by British, 920
Lenin, Nicolai (pseud. of Vladimir Ilyich Ulyanov), Russian Bolshevik leader, 706, 943, 1028, 1029, 1032, 1034
Leningrad, former Petrograd, 1030, 1151
Lens, in German possession, 913; taken by British, 950
Lenthall, William, speaker of Rump Parliament, 426
Leo of Tripoli, Saracen corsair, 179
Leo the Deacon, Byzantine historian, 181
Leo I, Byzantine emperor, 122
Leo II, Byzantine emperor, 122
Leo III (the Isaurian), Byzantine emperor, 151, 152, 175, 176
Leo IV, Byzantine emperor, 176
Leo V (the Armenian), Byzantine emperor, 177
Leo VI (the Wise), Byzantine emperor, 179
Leo I (the Great), Pope, 121, 123, 142
Leo IV, Pope, 152
Leo IX (Bruno of Toul), Pope, 206, 217, 249
Leo X (Giovanni de' Medici), Pope, 370, 395
Leo XI (Alessandro de' Medici), Pope, 397
Leo XII (Annibale della Genga), Pope, 663
Leo XIII (Gioacchino Pecci), Pope, 640, 660, 664, 665, 690, 993
Leoben, Peace of, 585
León, Luis de, theologian and poet, 388
Leon, Spanish ship, discovered South Georgia, 571
Leonard, Charles, in Johannesburg, 855
Leonardo da Vinci, Italian artist, 393
Leonidas, King of Sparta, 50, 54
Leonine Wall, built by Pope Leo IV, 152
Leonora, queen, *see* Telles
Leontini, 48, 57, 62, 66, 87
Leontius, Byzantine emperor, 175
Leontius of Preslav, Bulgarian patriarch, 183
Leopard, British ship, 768
Leopold, Duke of Austria, 196, 208, 306
Leopold of Anhalt-Dessau, Prince, 463
Leopold of Hohenzollern-Sigmaringen, Prince, 646, 687
Leopold I, King of the Belgians, 609, 622, 623, 645, 724
Leopold II of Belgium, **739, 743**, 828, 833, 834, 843, 844, 845, 846, 848
Leopold III of Belgium, 975, 1146
Leopold I, German emperor, 445, 461
Leopold II, German emperor, 470, 581

Leopold I; Grand Duke of Tuscany, 459, 654, 655
Leosthenes, 55, 66
Leotychidas, 54
Lepanto, battle of, 389, 396, 397, 424
Lepe, Diego de, explored Brazilian coast, 368
Lepidus, Marcus Aemilius, Roman triumvir, 95, 99
Lepreum, 59
Lerdo de Tejada, Sebastian, pres. of Mexico, 822
Lerma, Francisco, Duke of, favorite of Philip III of Spain, 390
Lerroux, Alejandro, premier of Spain, 983
Lesbians, 53
Lesbos, 47, 54, 56, 58, 60
Lesczinski, Stanislas, King of Poland, 447, 464, 472, 476 *f.*
Leslie, Gen. David, defeats royalists at Philiphaugh, 378
Lesseps, Ferdinand de, builder of Suez Canal, 555, 640, 655, 815, 830
Leszek I (the White) of Poland, 242
Leszek II (the Black) of Poland, 242
Leticia, dispute between Peru and Columbia, 1068, 1069, 1070
Letters of Junius, 436
Lettow-Vorbeck, Gen. Paul von, German commander in Africa, 918
Lettres de cachet (royal orders of arrest), in France, 578 *f.*
Letts, people, 124, 239
Leucimne, battle of, 58
Leucippus, philosopher, 62
Leuctra, 63
Leuenberg, Nicholas, heads peasant revolt in Switzerland, 459
Leukon Teichos, 56
Leuthen, battle of, 467
Levalloisean industry, 5, 6, 8
Levalloiseo-Mousterian industry, 6, 8
Levant, trade, 298, 424
Levelers, 373
Lever Act, in U.S., 1049
Levi, tribe of, 30
Lewis, John L., 1137, 1140
Lewis, Meriwether, heads Lewis and Clark Expedition, 768, 773
Lex Appuleia de maiestate imminuta, 93
Lex Aurelia, 95
Lex Caecilia Didia, 93
Lex Claudia, 85, 87
Lex de imperio Vespasiani, 108
Lex Gundobada, 145
Lex Hieronica, 90
Lex Iulia, 93
Lex Iulia de maritandis ordinibus, 102
Lex Iulia municipalis, 98
Lex Papia Poppaea, 102
Lex Plautia Papiria, 93
Lex Pompeia, 93
Lex Pompeia Licinia, 97
Lex Trebonia, 97
Lex Vatinia, 96
Lexington, battle of, 520
Leyte, 1169
Liakhov, Ivan, Russian merchant, discovers Siberian islands, 562
Liang, Empress, regent, 134
Liang Chi, killed by order of Emperor Huan, 135
Liang Ch'i-ch'oa, leader of the Harmony Party in China, 884
Liao, dynastic name, 341
Liaotung Peninsula, 881
Liao-Yang, battle of, 707, 892
Liapchev, Andrew, prime minister of Bulgaria, 1023
Libau, taken by Austro-Germans, 922
Libel of English Policie, pamphlet on sea-power, 271, 273
Liberal-Labor Party, in New Zealand, 907, 908
Liberal Party, in Hungary, 695, 696; in Denmark, 697; in Chile, 810
Liberal Republican Party, in U.S., 782; in Turkey, 1096
Liberal Union, in Turkey, 731
"Liberal Unionists," in England, 617
Liberator, established by William Lloyd Garrison, 771
Liberia, founded, 840; bankrupt, 842; recent history, 1088, 1089
Liberty, John Hancock's sloop, 518
Liberty of Conscience, Declaration of, issued by James II, 429
Libro de Montalvo, first codification of Spanish law, 282
Libya, Italian colony, 1086, 1087, 1088, 1159, 1160
Libyans, 24
Licensing Act, in England, 431
Lichchavi tribe, 130
Li-chi, early ritual text, 134
Lichnowsky, Felix von, Prince, in the Frankfurt Parliament, 676
Licinius, Caius, Roman reformer, 72
Licinius, Valerius Licinianus, defeated at Adrianople, 119
Licosa, battle of, 152
Lie, Jonas Lauritz Idemil, Norwegian writer, 699
Liebknecht, Karl, German Spartacist leader, 996
Liebknecht, Wilhelm Philipp Martin, German socialist, 689
Liége, in the War of the Spanish Succession, 431; in the World War, 916
Liegnitz, Moslems defeated the Poles and Germans, 262; Frederick the Great defeated the Austrians, 468
Light, Francis, at Penang, 875
Ligny, battle of, 603
Ligurian Republic, under French control, 585; incorporated with France, 591
Li dynasty, in Korea, 346

Li Hung Chang, Chinese statesman, 745, 880, 881, 882, 883, 885, 890, 891
Li Kuang-li, Chinese general, 133
Li Kuang-pi, suppresses rebellion in China, 340
Li Kung-lin, Chinese painter, 343
Li Po, Chinese poet, 340
Li Shih-min, founder of the T'ang dynasty, 338
Li Ssu, 45, 132, 133
Li Ssu-hsün, Chinese landscapist, 340
Li Tsung-jen, Chinese military strategist, 1119
Li Tzu-ch'eng, Chinese bandit, 536, 537
Li Yüan (T'ai Tsu), founder of the T'ang dynasty, 338
Li Yüan-Hung, pres. of the Chinese Republic, 884, 885, 1117
Li-Ito Convention, 881, 886, 891
Lij Yasu, Emperor of Ethiopia, 836, 1085
Liliuokalani, Lydia, Queen of Hawaii, 910
Lille, taken by Germans, 913; taken by British, 950
Lilybaeum, 86
Lima, 1155
Liman von Sanders, Otto, and German military mission to Turkey, 732, 761, 919
Limanova, battle of, 917
Limoges, sacked by the Black Prince, 265
Lin Tse-hsü, forces surrender of opium, 878
Linares, José Maria, pres. of Bolivia, 811
Lincoln, Abraham (16th pres. of the U.S.), 775, 776, 779, 780
Lincoln-Douglas debates, 775
Lindbergh, Charles Augustus, American aviator, 557, 1052
Linden, Cort van der, Dutch premier, 626
Lindenmeier site, 19
Lindi, captured by Gen. Smuts, 918
Lindman, Arvid, premier of Sweden, 1047
Lindsay, Martin, leads British Trans-Greenland Expedition, 569
Lindum, 106
Line of Demarcation, in South America, 495, 502
Linear script, replaces hieroglyphics, 46
Linga-worship, 132
Lingayat sect, in India, 338
Lingones, 108
Liniers, Jacques de, forced British out of Buenos Aires, 800
Linlithgow, Victor Alexander John Hope, Marquess of, viceroy of India, 1114
Linotype, invented, 556, 783
Linsingen, Alexander von, German general, 922
Lionel, Duke of Clarence, viceroy of Ireland, 273
Lionel, son of Edward III of England, 298
Liotard, Victor, French commissioner, of the upper Ubangi, 845
Lipara, 57, 86
Liquor trade, forbidden in Belgian Congo, 846
Lira, devalued in Italy, 991
Lisbon, taken by the Portuguese, 239; destroyed by an earthquake, 454
Lisht, 23
List, Friedrich, German economist, 549
Lister, Joseph, initiated antiseptic surgery, 551
"Literature of the Five Monasteries," Zen school in Kyōto, 358
Lithuania, 215, 239, 316 f., 317, 413 f., 999, 1031, 1042 ff., 1136, 1145, 1148
Little Big Horn, battle of, 780
"Little Clay Cart," 131
Little Entente, 956, 960, 963, 965, 990, 1009, 1010, 1015, 1018
Little Parliament, see Barebones
Little Steel Award, 1139
Litvinov, Maxim, Russian commissar for foreign affairs, 960, 1036 f.
Liu An, Prince of Huai-nan, 133
Liu Fang, suppressed rebellion in Annam, 136
Liu Hsiang, on contents of the Chinese imperial library, 134
Liu Hsin, his inventory of Chinese literature, 134
Liu K'un-i, adviser of the empress dowager of China, 883
Liu Pang, founder of the Han dynasty, 133
Liu Pei, founder of the Shu dynasty, 135
Liu Teh, Prince of Ho-chien, 133
Liu-ch'iu Islands, 137
Liudolf, Duke of Swabia, 161
Liutprand, Lombard ruler, 150, 152
Liutprand of Cremona, his Historia Ottonis and Legatio Constantinopolitana, 162
Livadia, Treaty of, 880
Liverpool, Earl of, 437
Liverpool-Manchester Railroad, 554
Livia, 3d wife of Octavian, 99, 103, 105
Livingston, Robert R., American minister to France, 553, 768
Livingstone, David, African explorer, 826, 828, 847
Livius Andronicus, 90
Livonian Brothers of the Sword, unite with Teutonic Knights, 211, 214, 215
Livonian War, 413, 414, 417
Livorno, 1163
Livy (Titus Livius), Roman historian, 71, 112
Llewelyn, Prince of Wales, 199
Lloyd, Sir George, high commissioner for Egypt, 1083
Lloyd, Sir William Frederick, prime minister of Newfoundland, 1060
Lloyd George, David, British prime minister, 620, 758, 929, 935, 936, 939, 941, 944, 951, 967, 968, 1095
Lobanov, Alexis Borisovich, Russian foreign minister, 746, 886, 891
Lobengula, king of the Matabele, 855
Lobositz, battle of, 467

Locarno, Conference and Treaties, 959, 960, 977, 998, 1003
Location Commission, in Natal, 852
Locke, John, English philosopher, 513
Lockwood, Lt. James, Arctic explorer, 565
Locomotive, 553
Locrians, 54
Locris, 56, 74
Lodi, battle of, 585
Lodz, 1164; battle of, 917
Loewenhaupt, Count, Swedish general, 472
Löffler, Friedrich, isolated diphtheria germ, 552
Lohan (saints), 136
Lollardy, 266, 398
Lollius, Marcus, Roman general, 102
Lolo, 44
Lombard, Peter, Bishop of Paris, 229
Lombard League, 210, 220. See Second Lombard League
Lombard Republic, set up by Napoleon, 585
Lombards, 149, 150, 152, 153, 158, 173, 206, 210
Lombard-Venetian Kingdom, given to Austria, 602
Lombroso, Cesare, Italian scientist, 552
Lomonosov, Michael Vasilyevich, Russian scientist, 481
Londinium, 106
London, forfeits charter, 428; treaties of, 687, 723, 760, 936; 1144, 1146; bombed, 1149, 1158, 1170
London Co., 508
London Conference, to save the Danes, 681; on Greek independence, 724; on reparations, 956, 958
London Missionary Society, 860
London Naval Conference, 756, 961, 970, 1052
London Naval Treaty, 1052, 1126
London Peace Conference of 1912–1913, 760
London Resolutions, 796
Long Barrows culture, 17
Long Island, battle of, 520; 1156
Long Parliament of Charles I, 376 ff., 426
Longjumeau, truce in French religious wars, 384
Longwy, taken by Germans, 912
Lookout Mountain, see Chattanooga
Loos, battle of, 921
Lope de Vega, Felix, Spanish playwright and poet, 389
Lopes, Gen. Isidor, leads revolts in Brazil, 1070, 1071
López, Afonso, pres. of Colombia, 1070
López, Cárlos, pres. of Paraguay, 808, 810
López, Francisco Solano, pres. of Paraguay, 810, 811
López, José Hilario, pres. of New Granada, 815
López de Legazpi, Miguel, founded Manila, 908
Loraine, Sir Percy, high commissioner for Egypt, 1083
Lord Dunmore's War, 517
Lord of Milan, title established, 296
Lords Appellant, in England, 268
Lords of Articles, control Scottish Parliament, 272
Lords of Trade, in England, 512
Lords Ordainers, in England, 264
Lordship of Athens, 258
Loredano, made Doge of Venice, 299, 326
Lorentz, Hendrik Antoon, electron theory, 552
Loris-Melikov, Gen. Michael Tarielovich, Russian minister of interior, 705
Lorne, John George Douglas Sutherland Campbell, 9th Duke of Argyll and Marquess of, gov.-gen. of Canada, 796
Lorraine, overrun by Magyars, 158; restored to Germans, 160. See also Alsace-Lorraine
Losada, Diego de, founded Caracas, 488
Lothair I, Emperor, 157
Lothair II, Emperor, 208, 219
Lothair, King of France, 159, 162
Lothair I (Clothar), King of the Franks, 147
Lothair II, King of the Franks, 147
Lothair II, King of Italy, 215
Lothair, King of Lorraine, 153, 157
Lotharingia, the modern Lorraine, 157, 379
"Lotus of the Good Law," 129
Lotus School of Buddhism, 340
Lotus Sutra, 130
Loubet, Emile, pres. of France, 642, 752
Loucheur, Louis, French financier and statesman, 956
Loudoun, John Campbell, Earl, commander of the British forces in America, 516
Louis I, Duke of Anjou, 292
Louis II, King of Bohemia and Hungary, 402, 419, 422
Louis I, the Child, King of Germany, 160
Louis II, German emperor, 152, 153, 157
Louis IV, German emperor, 301, 306
Louis II, King of France, 159
Louis III, King of France, 159
Louis IV, King of France, 159
Louis V, King of France, 159
Louis VI, the Fat, King of France, 227 f.
Louis VII, the Young, King of France, 196, 228, 229
Louis VIII, King of France, 197, 198, 229, 230
Louis IX (St. Louis), King of France, 199, 212, 213, 229–31, 257 f., 345, 384
Louis X, King of France, 273
Louis XI, King of France, 271, 280, 295, 307
Louis XII, King of France, 298, 381 f., 393 f., 398
Louis XIII, King of France, 375, 386
Louis XIV, King of France, 390, 427, 429, 431, 441 f., 443, 445 ff., 455, 458, 460, 461, 483, 525
Louis XV, King of France, 447, 448, 477
Louis XVI, King of France, 448, 450, 579, 580, 582

Louis XVIII, King of France, 601, 602, 603, 626
Louis, King of Holland, 440
Louis the Great, King of Hungary, 310, 314, 317, 324
Louis I, King of Portugal, 648
Louis, King of Saxony, 159
Louis I, King of Spain, 451
Louis of Baden, imperial general, 461
Louis of Bavaria, 444
Louis of Brandenburg, 310
Louis the Cardinal, 384
Louis of Condé, 384
Louis of Nevers, Count of Flanders, 273
Louis of Orange, 380
Louis of Provence, "emperor of Italy," 215
Louis the German, King of the East Franks, 157, 158, 159
Louis the Pious, emperor, 155, 157, 215
Louis Philippe, King of the French, 582, 622, 628, 630, 860
Louisbourg, capture of, 515
Louise Elizabeth, of Orléans, 451
Louisiana, ceded by France to Spain, 452; returned to France, 452; sold to the U.S., 495, 766, 768; admitted to statehood, 770
Lounda, African kingdom, 843
Louval, Louis Pierre, assassin of the Duke de Berry, 626
L'Ouverture, Toussaint, leader of the uprising in Haiti, 825
Louvois, François Michel Le Tellier, Marquis de, French minister of war, 442, 444
Lovett, William, English radical, 609
Low, Frederick Ferdinand, U.S. minister to Peking, 885
Lowell, Francis Cabot, combined processes of cotton manufacture, 764
Lowestoft, battle of, 427, 931
Lowicz, battle of, 917
Loyalists, in Spanish Civil War, 983
Loyalty Islands, annexed by the French, 895
Loyang, 44, 134–36; eastern capital of the T'ang dynasty, 338
Loyola, Ignatius de (Inigo Lopez de Recalde), founder of the Society of Jesus, 388 f., 401
Lu, 44, 45
Lu Chiu-yüan, a disciple of Mencius, 344
Lu Hsin-yuan, editor of the Shih Wan Chuan Lou Ts'ung shu, 884
Lü Pu-wei, his Pythagorean musical scale, 45
Lu Wen Ch'ao, Chinese scholar, 541
Luang Bipul Songgram, Siamese minister of defense, 1116
Luang Pradit, Siamese foreign minister, 1116
Lübeck, 208, 210, 214, 307; Treaty of, 405; Congress, 693
Lublin, Union of, 414; taken by Austro-Germans, 922; 1144
Luca, 97
Lucan (Marcus Annaeus Lucanus), in conspiracy against Nero, 107, 112
Lucanians, 73, 74, 78, 85–87
Lucca, Ramon Barros, pres. of Chile, 810
Luccheni, Luigi, Italian anarchist, 695
Lucilius, 90
Lucius II, Pope, 219
Lucknow, relief of, 870
Lucknow Pact, in India, 1111
Lucretia, raped by Sextus Tarquinius, 70
Lucretius Carus, Titus, his De rerum natura, 100
Lucullus, Lucius Licinius, Roman general, 39, 83, 93, 94, 95
Ludendorff, Erich von, German general, 916, 922, 938, 941, 945, 950, 997
Lüderitz, Franz Adolph Eduard, establishes German colony in Southwest Africa, 738, 854
Lüderitz Bay, taken by British, 918
Ludi Saeculares, religious ceremonies, 102
Ludovisi, Alessandro, Pope Gregory XV, 397
Ludovisi, Ludoviso, nephew of Gregory XV, 397
Luftwaffe, 1149
Lugalzaggisi, King of Erech, 25
Lugard, Sir Frederick John Dealtry, British commander in Uganda, 848, 849
Lugdunensis, 107
Lugdunum, 114, 120
Luisa Fernanda, Spanish princess, 645
Lukuchiao, clash of Japanese troops with Chinese, 1121
Lulé Burgas, battle of, 759
Lull, Ramon, Catalonian writer, 237
Lullubu, 28
Lumière, Auguste and Louis, cinematographe, 556
Lumley, Lord Richard, signs invitation to William of Orange, 429
Luna, Tristán de, to colonize the Carolinas, 493
Lunacharski, Anatoly Vasilievich, Russian Bolshevik leader, 1028
Lund, Treaty of, 443
Lundy's Lane, battle of, 769, 793
Lunéville, Treaty of, 588, 590
Lung-men, 136
Lupescu, Magda, mistress of King Carol of Rumania, 1025, 1026
Lupton (Frank) Bey, surrenders to the Mahdi, 832
Luque, Hernando de, accompanied Pizarro on conquest of Peru, 489
Lusatia, created as a Mark, 160; recovery by Germans, 205
Lusignan, Guy de, buys Cyprus from Richard I, 256
Lusitania, war in, 90
Lusitania, sunk by German submarine, 791, 923
Lusitanians, 88, 95
Luste, Eugene, invented sound production on film, 557

Lutf Ali Khan, last of the Zand dynasty in Persia, 529
Luther, Hans, German prime minister, 998
Luther, Martin, German reformer, 142, 304, 370, 395, 399, 400
Luther am Barenberge, battle of, 405
Lutipri, 38
Lutsk, taken by Austrians, 922; retaken by Russians, 932
Luttrell, Col. Henry Lawes, elected to House of Commons in place of Wilkes, 436
Lützen, Gustavus Adolphus defeated Wallenstein, 406
Lützen, or Gross-Görschen, battle of, 598
Luvian, Hittite dialect, 36
Luxembourg, François Henri de Montmorency-Bouteville, Duke of, French general, 442, 444
Luxemburg, 440; Napoleon's efforts to acquire the duchy, 686; annexed by Germany, 1139; 1146
Luxemburg, Rosa, German Spartacist leader, 693, 996
Luxemburgs, in Germany, 213
Luynes, Charles d'Albert, Duc de, favorite of Louis XIII, 386 f.
Luzzara, battle of, 445
Luzzatti, Luigi, prime minister of Italy, 662
Lvov, Prince George, heads provisional govt. in Russia, 1028, 1029
Lyautey, Louis Hubert Gonzalve, marshal of France, resident-gen. in Morocco, 839, 1087
Lycaonia, 36
Lycée of Galata Serai, in Constantinople, 728
Lycia, 37, 84, 96
Lycians, 24
Lycophron, 63
Lycurgus, Athenian lawgiver, 50, 51, 66
Lydenburg, joins South African Republic, 852
Lydia, Kingdom of, 37, 40, 48, 77
Lydians, 37
Lyell, Sir Charles, his Principles of Geology, 551
Lygdamis of Naxos, 31
Lynch Bros., of London, open Karun River to navigation, 864
Lyons, falls after two months' siege, 583, 628; Synod, 212, 221
Lyons, Joseph Aloysius, prime minister of Australia, 1130, 1131
Lyons, Richard, impeached by the Good Parliament, 267
Lyons-Page govt. in Australia, 1131
Lyric poetry, in Greece, 48; in Rome, 100
Lys, battle of, 945
Lysander, defeats squadron off Notium, 61
Lysias, one of the ten Attic orators, 67, 82
Lysimachus, 37; takes title of king, 77; slain, 81
Lysippus, 67
Lytton, Edward Robert Bulwer, 1st Earl of, viceroy of India, 870
Lytton Report on Manchuria, 962

Ma Jung, invents double-column commentary, 135
Ma Yüan, Chinese painter, 344
Ma Yüan, conquered Tonkin and Annam, 134
Mabuchi, Kamo, in Shinto movement, 887
Macao, Portuguese settlement in China, 536, 538
MacArthur, Gen. Douglas, commander-in-chief in the Far East, 1166, 1167, 1169
Macarthur, John, soldier of fortune in New South Wales, 896, 898
Macartney, George, Earl of, British representative at Peking, 540
Macassar Straits, 1167
Macbeth, King of Scotland, 201
Maccabeus, Judas, led Jewish insurrection, 81
MacDonald, Jacques Étienne Joseph Alexandre, French general, 587, 588, 599, 600
MacDonald, Maj. James, suppressed mutiny in Uganda, 849
MacDonald, James Ramsay, British prime minister, 618, 959, 963, 968, 969
Macdonald, Sir John Alexander, premier of Canada, 796, 797
Macdonough, Thomas, lieutenant (later captain), won naval battle of Plattsburg, 769, 793
MacDowell, Irvin, Federal general, 776
Macedonia, under Spartan and Theban hegemony, 62 f.; under Philip and Alexander the Great, 64 ff.; insurrection, 731; 752, 1017, 1022, 1023
Macedonian Revolutionary Organization (IMRO), 1023
Macedonian Wars, 79, 80, 87–90
Machado, Bernardino, pres. of Portugal, 985
Machado, Gerardo, pres. of Cuba, 1077
Machanidas, regent for King Pelops, 80
Machek, Dr. Vladko, leader of the Croats, 1017, 1018, 1019
Machiavelli, Niccolo, Italian historian, 280, 393, 395
Machine gun, invented, 555
MacIan of the MacDonalds, in massacre of Glencoe, 431
Mack von Leiberich, Karl, Baron, Austrian general, 586, 591
Mackay, Dr. Alistair Forbes, Arctic explorer, 574
Mackay, Gen. Andrew, defeated at Killiecrankie, 430
Mackensen, August von, German general, 916, 926, 934
Mackenzie, Alexander, premier of Canada, 792, 796, 798
Mackenzie, William Lyon, Canadian rebel leader, 795
Mackinder, Halford John, first ascent of Mt. Kenya, 849
MacKinnon, Sir William, British promoter, 743, 844, 847, 848
Mackintosh, Capt. Aeneas Lionel Acton, Antarctic explorer, 575 f.
MacLeod, James Walter, on insulin treatment, 553
MacMahon, Marie Edmé de, pres. of French Republic, 637, 638, 688, 847, 853
MacMichael, Sir Harold, high commissioner for Palestine, 1102
MacMillan, Donald Baxter, Arctic explorer, 567
MacMillan, Kirkpatrick, invented first real bicycle, 554

MacMurdo, Edward, American promoter, 847
MacMurrough, Dermond, 169
Macnaghten, Sir William Hay, British envoy to Afghanistan, 866
Macon's Bill No. 2, 769
MacPherson, John, interim gov.-gen. of India, 535
Macquarie, Col. Lachlan, gov. of New South Wales, 898
Macrinus (Marcus Opellius Severus Macrinus), Roman emperor, 115
"Mad Mullah" (Mohammed ben Abdullah), in Somaliland, 836
Madagascar, 525, 859 ff., 1093, 1138, 1167
Maddox, Robert Leach, introduced dry plate process in photography, 555
Madeira Islands, explored, 363
"Mademoiselle," Anne Marie Louise d'Orléans, Duchesse de Montpensier, in the Fronde, 440
Madero, Francisco, pres. of Mexico, 822
Madhava. wrote the Sarva darsana samgraha, 339
Madhyamika school, 130
Madhyamika Sutra, 130
Madison, James (4th pres. of the U.S.), 768
Madras, site of, granted to an Englishman, 533
Madrid, established as capital, 389; under siege by the Insurgents, 983, 984, 985; Peace of, 400; Treaty of, 388, 394, 454, 495, 501
Madrid Convention, regarding Morocco, 838
Madsen-Mygdal, Thomas, premier of Denmark, 1046
Maecenas, patron of literature, 112
Maelius, Spurus, 72
Maesa, Julia, ruled empire of Elagabalus, 115
Maesolia, 129
Mafeking, invested by Boers, 857
Mafia, Italian secret organization, 989
Mafra palace, in Lisbon, 453
Magadha, 41, 43, 132
Magadha kings, follow Gupta dynasty, 130
Magas, 84
Magdeburg law, 240, 242
Magdelian culture, 5
Magdhaba, taken by the British, 938
Magellan, Ferdinand (Fernão de Magalhães), circumnavigated globe, 368, 390, 571, 894, 908
Magenta, battle of, 658
Magersfontein, battle of, 857
Magi, privileges restored under Ardashir I, 124, 125
Magic, belief in, 4; practices, 26; cult of, 135
Maglemosean culture, 15, 17, 18
Magna Carta (Great Charter), signed by King John, 197 f.
Magna Graecia, 52 f.
Magnano, battle of, 586 f.
Magnentius, Magnus, pretender, defeated by Constantius, 120
Magnesia, 38, 47, 82; battle of, 89
Magnetic polarity, known to the Chinese, 343
Magnus VII (Smek) of Sweden, acquired Norwegian crown, 312
Mago, defeated at Syracuse, 34
Magoon, Charles Edward, gov. of Cuba, 823
Magyar, substituted for Latin as the official language in Hungary, 671
Magyars (Hungarians), cross Carpathian Mountains, 158; 160, 179, 211, 215, 244 f. See also Hungary
Mahabharata, 43
Mahabhashya (Great Commentary) of Patanjali, 43
Mahadaji Sindia, Maratha leader in India, 536
Mahanaman, 132
Mahaniddesa, 132
Maharashtra, 132
Mahasanghikas, 42
Mahavihara, or Great Monastery, 132
Mahayana, the Great Vehicle of Buddhism, 129, 131
Mahdavi heresy, 533
Mahdi (Mohammed Ahmed ibn Seyyid Abdullah), religious leader in the Sudan, 533, 738, 832
Mahendravarman I (Pallava), converted to Sivaism, 335
Mahmud I (Begarha), Indian ruler, 335
Mahmud II, Ottoman ruler, 722, 725
Mahmud (the Idol-Breaker), master of Khorasan, 190
Mahmud, ruler of Kandahar, 528
Mahmud of Ghazni, 332
Mahmud Gavan, minister of Mohammed III, 335
Mahmud Shah, ruler of Afghanistan, 866
Mahmud Shevket Pasha, Turkish general and statesman, 732
Maidalchini, Olympia, sister-in-law of Pope Innocent X, 455
Maiestas Carolina, code of laws for Bohemia, 305
Maigrot, Mgr. Charles, condemns Chinese rites, 539
Maikop, 1153
Maillotins, in revolt in Paris, 277
Main, a plot to dethrone James I, 373
Maine, restored to the heirs of Sir Fernando Gorges, 511; admitted to statehood, 770
Maine (U.S.S.), blown up in Havana Harbor, 787, 823
Maine prohibition law, 774
Maintenon, Françoise d'Aubigné, Marquise de, mistress of Louis XIV, 443
Mainz, recovered by the Prussians, 582 f.
Maipú, battle of, 801
Maison Carrée, at Nîmes, 113
Maisonneuve, Paul de Chomedy, sieur de, founded Montreal, 507
Maistre, Casimir, African explorer, 844
Maistre, Joseph de, Catholic writer, 663
Maitland, Lt. Lester James, American aviator, 557, 1134

Maitrakas dynasty, in western India, 331
Maitreya, a divine incarnation in the Jebdzun-damba of Urga, 130, 136, 536
Majestic (H.M.S.), sunk, 920
Majid, Sultan of Zanzibar, 846
Majlis (national assembly of Persia), 865, 1108
Majorianus, 122
Majuba Hill, battle of, 854
Majunga, bombarded by a French squadron, 860
Makallé, fortress in Ethiopia, 991
Makarov, Stephen Osipovich, Russian admiral, 566
Makino, Shinken, Baron, Japanese diplomat, 952
Makran, king, submits to Ardashir, 124
Makura no Sōshi (Pillow Book), by Sei Shōnagon, 353
Makwar Dam, on the Nile, 1083
Malabranca, Cardinal, 222
Malacca, taken from the Dutch by Portuguese, 536; retaken by the Dutch, 539; 541 f., 875
Malaga, captured by rebels in Spanish Civil War, 983
Malamir, Bulgar ruler, 182
Malan, Daniel François, leader of a South African republican group, 1092
Malatesta, Enrico, leader of a general strike in Italy, 663
Malay states, in treaty of federation, 875 ff., 1116
Malaya, British, its settlement, 875; its organized states, 876; 1138, 1140, 1158, 1167
Malaysia, 348; trade with Europe, 541 f., 1116 f.
Malchus, 34, 53
Malcolm II, King of Scotland, 168
Malcolm, Sir John, mission to Persia, 862
Male, Louis de, last Count of Flanders, 277
Malesherbes, Chrétien Guillaume de Lamoignon de, counsel for Louis XVI, 582
Malfante, Antonio, African explorer, 363
Malietoa Laupepa, King of Samoa, 911
Malietoa Talavou, King of Samoa, 911
Malietoa Tana, in civil war in Samoa, 911
Malik-al-Kamil, Sultan of Egypt, 221, 257
Malik Shah, Seljuk sultan, 250, 255
Malinov, Alexander, Bulgarian prime minister, 948, 1023
Mallarino, Manuel, pres. of New Granada, 815
Malleson, Gen. Sir Wilfrid, British commander in Persia, 1107
Malmaison, battle of, 939
Malmédy, turned over to Belgium by Versailles Treaty, 952, 974, 997
Malmö Armistice, between Denmark and Frederick William IV, 676
Malocello, Lanciloto, Portuguese explorer, 363
Malolos Constitution, proclaimed, 909
Malory, Sir Thomas, his Morte Arthure, 272
Malplaquet, battle of, 432, 446
Malta, besieged by Turks, 423; taken by Napoleon, 586; restored to Knights of Malta, 590
Maitepe, battle of, 324
Malthus, Thomas Robert, Essay on Population, 549; 551
Malvern Hill, battle of, 778
Malvy, Louis Jean, French politician, 941
Malwa, 42, 43, 129, 130
Malypetr, Jan, Czechoslovak prime minister, 1010
Mamaea, Julia, 115
Mambanos, see Nahapana
Mamelukes, in Egypt, 262; 363, 364, 828
Mamercus, Aemilius, 72
Mamertines, 78, 86
Mamun the Great, caliph, 188 f.
Man, his place among the animals, 1, 2; as a toolmaker, 8; modern races, 12
Manasseh, tribe of, 29, 31
Manavalla, enthroned in Ceylon, 335
Mancaphas, Theodore, Byzantine leader, 259
Manchester Anti-Corn Law Association, 611
Manchester School of Politics, 611
Manchu dynasty, in China, 536, 541, 542, 1117
Manchukuo, 1165
Manchuria, early history, 14; Russian-Japanese War, Boxer insurrection, 707; returned to China by Treaty of Portsmouth, 803; protectorate established by Japan, 1120; 1169, 1171
Mandalay, taken in 3d Burmese War, 872; 1167
Mandats territoriaux, financial notes, in France, 584
Manding Empire, in Africa, 328 f., 525, 840
Mandokoro, an administrative board in Kyōto, 355
Manegold of Lautenbach, medieval controversialist, 207
Manetho, his history of Egypt, 23
Manfred, father of Constance, wife of Peter III of Aragon, 282
Manfred, King of Sicily, 213, 293
Mangasha, Ras, Ethiopian chieftain, 835
Mangin, Charles Emmanuel, French general, 931
Manhattan Island, purchased from the Indians, 510
Mani, founder of Manichaeism, 124
Maniakes, Georgios, Byzantine general, 249
Manichaeans, under caliphate of Al-Mahdi, 188; in China, 341
Manichaeism, 124, 142; condemned, 340; state religion of the Uighur Turks, 341
Manikka Vasagar, a Tamil saint, 336
Manila, founded, 909; captured by American forces, 909; 1167
Manila Bay, battle of, 787, 909
Manilius, Caius, 95
Manin, Daniele, Italian statesman, 657
Maniu, Julius, premier of Rumania, 1025, 1026
Manjusri (Avatamsakasutra), 130, 536
Manly, Charles Matthews, gasoline engine, 556

Mann, James Robert, co-author of the Mann-Elkins Act, 789
Mannerheim, Baron Karl Gustav, Finnish general, 1047; President of Finland, 1142
Mannerheim Line, 1145
Manning, Thomas Henry, in charge of the British-Canadian Expedition, 567 f.
Mannock, Edward, British aviator, 946
Manorialism, 158
Mansfeld, Ernst, Graf von, German general, 375, 404 f.
Mansfield, William Murray, Lord, attacked in Letters of Junius, 436
Mansion House speech, of Lloyd George, 758
Mantegna, Andrea, Italian painter, 393
Manteuffel, Otto von, prime minister of Prussia, 678
Mantinea, 54, 63, 80; battle of, 59
Mantua, 398, 585
Mantua, Ferdinand Charles, Duke of, 445
Manu, the Dharma Sastra, 130
Manuel I (Comnenus), Byzantine emperor, 246
Manuel II, Byzantine emperor, 323
Manuel, Greek emperor, 245
Manuel I (the Great, the Fortunate), of Portugal, 390, 392, 500
Manuel II, of Portugal, 649
Manuel, brother of Theodore of Epirus, 248, 260
Manuel, despot of the Morea, 322
Manuel Alexius II, Byzantine emperor, 253
Manyema, African kingdom, 843
Man'yōshū, a collection of poems in Japanese, 351
Manzikert, battle of, 250, 254, 255
Mao Chin, Chinese scholar, 537
Mao Tse-tung, a leader of landless Chinese, 1119
Maoris, of New Zealand, 904, 906 f.
Map, Walter, his story of the Grail, 194
Mar, John Erskine, Earl of, leads Jacobite rising in Scotland, 434
Mar Yabalaha, patriarch, 346
Maranhão, founded by French, 501
Maranhão Co. of Brazil, 503
Mar'ash, 35
Marat, Jean Paul, French revolutionary leader, 580, 582
Maratha govt., in the Deccan, 534
Maratha leaders, in India, 868
Marathon, battle of, 40, 53
Marbaal, 33
Marbury v. Madison, decision by John Marshall, 766
Marcel, Etienne, Parisian leader, 276
Marcellae, battle of, 182
Marcellus, Marcus Claudius, Roman general, 86, 87, 88
Marcellus II (Marcello Cervini), Pope, 396
March Days of 1848 in Berlin, 675
March Laws in Hungary, 673
March (1918) offensive, 945
"March on Rome," by the Fascists, 988
Marchand, Jean Baptiste, French mission to the Nile region, 745, 748, 833, 836, 845
Marches of Italy, vote for union with north, 659
Marchfeld, battle of, 241, 299
Marcia, concubine of Commodus, 112
Marcian, Emperor of the East, 121
Marcomanni, 109, 111, 112
Marconi, Guglielmo, Italian inventor, 556
Marcus Aurelius (Marcus Aelius Aurelius Antoninus), Roman emperor, 109, 111, 112, 113, 117
Mardonius, killed at Plataea, 54
Marengo, battle of, 588
Mareth Line, 1162
Marfori, Carlos, favorite of Isabella II of Spain, 646
Margaret, Countess of Salisbury, 370
Margaret, Maid of Norway, heir of Alexander II of Scotland, 199, 201
Margaret, wife of Charles the Bold, Duke of Burgundy, 271, 280, 369
Margaret, wife of Charles of Valois, 293
Margaret, wife of Emanuel Philibert of Saxony, 395
Margaret, wife of James IV, King of Scotland, 369
Margaret, wife of Malcolm Canmore of Scotland, 201
Margaret, wife of Philip the Bold, 276, 379
Margaret of Anjou, wife of Henry VI of England, 270, 271
Margaret of Denmark, wife of Haakon VI of Norway, 311 f.
Margaret of Parma, ruler of the Netherlands, 379 f.
Margaret of Provence, wife of Louis IX of France, 230, 237
Margary, Augustus Raymond, Chinese interpreter, 880
Marghiloman, Alexandre, Rumanian prime minister, 948
Margravate of Azilia, in Carolina, 513 f.
Margraviate of Tuscany, 293
Margus, 116
Mari (Ben-Hadad III), 35
Maria I, Queen of Portugal, 454, 502
Maria II, Queen of Portugal, 648
Maria, wife of Emperor Honorius, 121
Maria, wife of Emperor Sigismund, 314; queen of Hungary, 317
Maria of Antioch, wife of Emperor Manuel Comnenus, 252, 253
Maria Anna, wife of Joseph I of Portugal, 454
Maria Antoinette, daughter of Emperor Leopold I, 445
Maria Carolina, wife of Ferdinand I, King of Naples and Sicily, 458
Maria Cristina, Regent of Spain for Alfonso XIII, 647
Maria Cristina, Regent of Spain for Isabella II, 644, 645, 646
Maria da Gloria, see Maria II
Maria Louisa of Bourbon-Parma, 650
Maria Theresa, Empress, 447, 459, 463, 465, 468

Maria Theresa, wife of Louis XIV of France, 390, 440, 442, 443, 447
Mariana, Juan de, Spanish historian, 389
Marianas, 1169
Marianne Islands, occupied by Japanese, 918
Marie Antoinette, wife of Louis XVI, 448, 583
Marie Louise, Archduchess, wife of Napoleon, 595, 601
Marie Louise of Savoy, first wife of Philip V of Spain, 451
Marie de France, at the court of Henry II, 194
Marie of Edinburgh, Princess, marries Prince Ferdinand of Rumania, 720
Marienwerder, in Germany, founded, 212, 215
Marignano, battle of, 382, 394, 409
Marignolli, John, papal legate to Peking, 362
Marinids of Morocco, 263, 363
Marion, Francis, his defense of South Carolina, 522
Maritza River, battle of, 319
Marius, Gaius, Roman dictator, 92, 93 f., 96
Marj-Dabik, battle of, 422
Mark, collapse in Germany, 997
Mark Antony (Marcus Antonius), Roman general, 83, 84, 85, 98, 99, 102, 105, 109
Marketing Act, in U.S., 1051
Markham, Albert Hastings, Arctic explorer, 564
Marks, German, their establishment, 155
Marlborough, N.Z., established, 906
Marlborough, John Churchill, Duke of, British general, 431, 432, 434, 446
Marmont, Auguste Frédéric Louis Viesse de, Duke of Ragusa, French general, 595, 596, 599, 601
Marmousets, 277
Marne, 1st battle of the, 914; 2d, 945
Maroboduus, King of Bohemia, 103
Marozia, mistress of Pope Sergius III, 215
Marqash, 35
Marquesas Islands, discovered, 894; taken by French, 895
Marquette, Jacques, Jesuit missionary, 507
Marquez, José de, pres. of New Granada, 814
Marradas, Don Balthasar de, imperial general, 406
Marranos, converted Jews, 282
Marroquin, José, pres. of Colombia, 815
Marsaglia, battle of, 444
Marsden, Samuel, mission in New Zealand, 905
Marseille, 1163
Marshal, William, Earl of Pembroke, guardian of Henry III, 199, 203
Marshall, John, American jurist, 766, 770
Marshall Islands, discovered, 894; annexed by Germany, 895; occupied by Japanese, 918; 1169
Marsiglio of Padua, medieval controversialist, 288, 301
Mars-la-Tour, battle of, 688
Marston Moor, battle of, 377
Martel, Charles (i.e., the Hammer), 150, 152, 163, 188
Martel, Damien, high commissioner for Syria, 1099
Martens, Frederick, German surgeon, 561
Martial (Marcus Valerius Martialis), epigrammatist, 112
Martignac, Jean Baptiste Silvère Gay, Viscount de, prime minister of France, 627
Martin, king of Aragon and Sicily, 284
Martin I, pope, 151, 174
Martin IV (Simon Mompitié de Brion), Pope, 221, 231
Martin V (Otto Colonna), Pope, 289
Martin, Pierre, open hearth method of steelmaking, 555
Martin of Tours, advocate of monasticism, 123, 142
Martínez, Maximiliano Hernández, pres. of Salvador, 1074
Martínez, Vicente, of Guatemala, pres. of the Federation of Central America, 1072
Martinitz, Jaroslav, and the Defenestration of Prague, 404
Martino (Della Torre), established the catasta, a tax, 297
Martinuzzi, George, Cardinal, organizes Transylvania, 420
Martyr, Maj. Cyril Godfrey, reconquest of the Sudan, 849
Martyropolis, 127
Marwan II, caliph, 188
Marwan ibn al-Hakam, caliph, 186 f., 188
Marwanids of Diyar-Bakr, 190
Marx, Karl, Socialist writer, 549, 550, 689
Marx, Wilhelm, German prime minister, 998
Mary, Duchess of Suffolk, sister of Henry VIII, 370, 382
Mary, Queen of Scots, 370, 372 f., 374, 384, 390
Mary, wife of Charles VII of France, 293
Mary, wife of Charles I of Hungary, 317
Mary, wife of Emperor Maximilian, 280, 304, 379
Mary, wife of Louis II of Hungary, 419
Mary, wife of William of Orange, 427, 431
Mary of Portugal, wife of Philip II of Spain, 389
Mary the Catholic, Queen of England, 369, 372, 389
Masako, mother of Yoriie, head of the Japanese Minamoto, 356
Masamoto, drove the shōgun Yoshitane out of Kyōto, 355
Masamune, Date, a lord of northern Japan, 546
Masaniello (Tommaso Aniello), leads revolt of Naples, 390, 398
Masaryk, Thomas Garrigue, pres. of Czechoslovakia, 1009, 1010
Masatochi, Hotta, brother of Shōgun Ietsuna, 547
Masham, Mrs. Abigail Hill, Queen Anne's favorite, 432
Mashin, Draga, marries Alexander I of Serbia, 715
Maslama, brother of Caliph Sulayman, 187
Mason, Charles, English surveyor, 512
Mason, James Murray, Confederate commissioner to Great Britain, 776

Mason, John, receives grant of New Hampshire and northern Massachusetts, 509, 511
Masonic lodges, at Saloniki, 731
Maspero, Gaston Camille Charles, 134
Massachusetts, 508 *f.*, 511 *f.*, 790
Massachusetts Government Act, 519
Massacre of the Boulevards, in Paris, 632
Massacre, of Hindus, 335; of Protestants in Ulster, 376
Massacre of St. Bartholomew, 390
Massalia, 47
Massari, Alfonso Maria, African explorer, 828
Massasoit, Indian chief, 511
Masséna, André, French general, 586, 587, 588, 591, 596
Massey, Sir Edward, defended Gloucester in English Civil War, 377
Massey, Vincent, Canadian minister at Washington, 1058
Massey, William Fergusson, prime minister of New Zealand, 908, 1131
Massilia, 53
Massinissa, King of Eastern Numidia, 88, 90, 92
Masson-Ourself, 88, 89, 92
Master of Stair, *see* Stair
Masudi, Arab, 328
Masurian Lakes, battle of, 916
Mataafa, king of Samoa, 911
Matabele Wars, 855, 856
Matanbaal, 33
Mataram, Empire of, conquered by Moslems, 876
Mathias of Csak, "little king" of Hungary, 317
Mathias of Hungary, King of Bohemia, 306
Mathura, 42, 43, 129
Matilda, Countess of Tuscany, 207, 218, 219, 293
Matilda, wife of Henry the Lion, 194
Matilda, wife of Henry V of Germany, 194, 207, 227
Matildine lands, 207, 208, 217, 219, 220, 223
Matin de Bruges, massacre of French, 232
Matsukata, Count Masayoshi, Japanese premier, 891
Matteo, of the Visconti, *imperial vicar*, 297 *f.*
Matteotti, Giacomo, Italian Socialist Deputy, 988
Matteucci, Pellegrino, African explorer, 828
Matthew, assertion of the Petrine theory, 141
Matthias, Count of Thurn, heads revolt in Prague, 404
Matthias, German emperor, 402, 403
Mattiwaza, 29
Mattos, Gen. Norton de, administrator of Angola, 1089
Matz, battle of, 945
Maubeuge, taken by Germans, 913
Mauchamp, Dr. Emile, murdered in Morocco, 838
Maud, *see* Edith
Maude, Sir Frederick Stanley, British general, 938
Maues, 128
Maunoury, Michel Joseph, French general, 913, 914
Maupéou, René Nicolas Charles Augustin, chancellor of France, 448
Maurepas, Jean Frédéric Phélippeaux, Count de, French prime minister, 448
Mauretania, 98, 105; created a French colony, 1089
Maurice, Byzantine emperor, 127, 146, 173
Maurice, Duke of Saxony, 402
Maurice of Nassau-Siegen, Prince gov. of Brazilian territory for Dutch West India Co., 501
Maurozomes, Manuel, Byzantine leader, 259
Maurras, Charles, French royalist leader, 643
Maurya, dynasty, 42, 43
Mausolus, in "War of the Allies," 64, 67
Mawson, Douglas, Antarctic explorer, 574, 575, 576, 577
Max, Prince of Baden, chancellor of Germany, 950, 995
Maxen, battle of, 467
Maxentius, Aurelius Valerius, Roman emperor, 119; 123
Maxim, Sir Hiram, English inventor, 556
Maximian (Marcus Aurelius Valerius Maximianus), Roman emperor, 118, 119
Maximilian, Duke of Bavaria, heads Catholic League, 403, 404, 407, 423
Maximilian I, German emperor, 280, 304, 369, 379, 382, 393, 394, 398 *f.*
Maximilian II, German emperor, 402
Maximilian of Austria, Archduke, Emperor of Mexico, 616, 634, 822
Maximilian, Joseph, 466, 468
Maximin, Caius Julius Verus Maximinus ("Thrax"), Roman emperor, 115
Maximum Freight Rate Case, 784
Maximus, M. Clodius Pupienus, Roman emperor, 115
Maximus, Magnus, executed by Theodosius, 120
Maximus, Quintus Fabius (Cunctator), dictator, 87, 88
Maxwell, James Clerk, on radio waves, 556
May Laws, or Falk Laws, in Germany, 689
Maya revolt, 492
Mayas, of Yucatan, civilization, culture, religion, govt., 20, 360 *f.*
Mayenne, Duke of, heads Catholic revolt against Henry III, 386
Mayflower, brought Pilgrims to America, 509
Mayflower Compact, 509
Mayo, Richard Southwell Bourke, Earl of, viceroy of India, 870
Mayr, Michael, Austrian prime minister, 1005
Maysville Road Bill, in U.S., 771
Mazarin, Jules, Cardinal, and French statesman, 387, 407, 440
Mazarin Bible, printed at Mainz, 304
Mazdak, high priest of Zoroastrianism, 126
Mazeppa, Cossack hetman, 472, 480

Mazyadids of Hilla, tribe of the Banu Asad, 190
Mazzaro, 1162
Mazzini, Guiseppe, Italian revolutionist, 651, 655
McAdoo, William Gibbs, U.S. secretary of treasury, 1049
McCarthy, Justin, leader of Irish Nationalists, 617
McClellan, George Brinton, Federal general, 776, 778
McClintock, Capt. Leopold, Arctic explorer, 564
McClure, Capt. Robert, Arctic explorer, 564
McCormick, Cyrus Hall, American inventor, 554, 772
McCrary (George Washington) Bill, in U.S., 784
McCudden, James Thomas Byford, British aviator, 946
McCulloch *v.* Maryland, decided by John Marshall, 770
McCulloch, John Ramsay, Scottish economist, 549
McKinley, Capt. Ashley Chadbourne, Antarctic explorer, 576
McKinley, William (25th pres. of the U.S.), 786, 787, 788
McKinley Tariff Act, 785, 786, 797
McLemore (Atkins Jefferson) Resolution warning Americans from traveling on armed ships, 791
McLeod, Alexander, Canadian, acquitted for murder in N.Y. courts, 772 *f.*
McNary-Haugen Bill, in U.S., 1051
Meade, George Gordon, Federal general, 778
Meal-tub plot, in England, 428
Meares, Capt. John, established fur post at Nootka, 792
Mecca, 184, 187, 262
Mechanicsville, battle of, 778
Mecklenburg, colonized, 210
Mecklenburg, Dukes of, withdraw from Confederation of Rhine, 598
Media, 40, 83
Median Empire, founded by Cyaxares, 40
Medicean Portolano, 363
Medici, the, papal bankers, 290; dominance in Florence, 294; patrons of Italian Renaissance, 296; driven out of Florence, 394
Medici, Alessandro de', Pope Leo XI, 397
Medici, Alessandro de', hereditary ruler of Florence, 398
Medici, Catherine de', queen of France, 384
Medici, Cosimo de', 289 *f.*, 293, 294, 295, 296, 298, 398
Medici, Giovanni Angelo, Pope Pius IV, 398
Medici, Giovanni de', 294
Medici, Giovanni de', Pope Leo X, 395
Medici, Giuliano de', in the Pazzi conspiracy, 290; 295
Medici, Giulio de', Pope Clement VII, 396
Medici, Lorenzo de' (the Magnificent), 289, 290, 293, 295
Medici, Marie de', queen of France, 386, 387
Medici, Piero de', driven out of Florence, 393
Medici, Salvestro de', Gonfalonier, 294
Medina, 184, 187, 262
Medina Sidonia, captured by Moslems, 163, 187
Mediolanum, 116, 118
Mediterranean Agreements, 647, 740, 741
Mediterranean Coalition, 691
Medum, 13
Meerut, sepoy mutiny, 870
Megabyzus, defeated Athenians, 56
Megacles, 51, 53
Megalithic culture, 15
Megalopolis, 63
Megara, 47 *passim*
Megara Hyblaea, 48
Megarians, 58
Megarid, 55, 56, 58
Megasthenes, his account of India, 42
Meghaduta, 131
Megiddo, 13, 23, 24, 31; battle of, 948
Mehmed Jemal, representative of Turkey at Congress of Paris, 728
Mei Wen-ting, Chinese mathematician, 540
Meighen, Arthur, prime minister of Canada, 1058
Meiji Period, in Japan, 889
Mein Kampf, by Adolf Hitler, 997
Meissen, created as a Mark, 160
Mekong River, in Cochin-China, 874, 1166
Mela, references to Scandinavia, 170
Melanchthon, Philipp, German reformer, 401
Melanesians, 12
Melas, Michael, Austrian general, 587, 588
Melbourne, founded, 900
Melbourne, William Lamb, 2d Viscount, British prime minister, 608, 609, 611
Melesias, 56
Melfi, Synod of, 218
Melgarejo, Mariano, pres. of Bolivia, 811
Méline, Félix Jules, French premier, 640, 641
Melitene, 108; captured by John Kurklas, 179, 188
Mello, Custodio José de, Brazilian admiral, 818
Melos, 59
Melville Island, post established by British, 899
Memel, founded, 215; taken by Germans, 921; annexed, 966, 1004, 1042, 1043
Memnon of Rhodes, defeated by Alexander, 65
Memphis, 21, 23, 55, 56
Menahem, 31
Menander, Greek dramatist, 43, 67
Mencius (Meng K'o), Chinese philosopher, 45, 344
Mendaña de Neyra, Alvaro de, Spanish discoverer, 894
Mendel, Gregor, Austrian scientist, 551
Mendez, Miguel Abadia, pres. of Colombia, 1069
Mendicant Orders, 221
Mendieta, Cárlos, pres. of Cuba, 1077

Mendoza, Andrés Hurtado de, viceroy of Peru, 490
Mendoza, Antonio de, viceroy of Peru, 490, 492, 497, 500, 908
Mendoza, García Hurtado de, founded the town of Mendoza, 489 f.
Menelek, Emperor of Ethiopia, 660, 661, 745, 835, 836
Menes, 21, 23
Meng T'ien, 133
Mengli Girai, Khan of the Crimea, 317
Menocal, Mario García, pres. of Cuba, 823, 824, 1077
Menou, Baron Jacques François de, French general, 586
Mensheviks (moderates), faction of Social Democratic Party in Russia, 706
Menshikov, Alexander Danilovich, Prince, Russian statesman, 480
Menshikov, Alexander Sergeievich, Prince, Russian emissary to Turkey, 726
Mentana, battle of, 659
Menua, 38
Menved, Eric of Denmark, 310 f.
Menzies, Robert Gordon, Australian premier, 1131
Mera, Martínez, pres. of Ecuador, 1069
Mercator, Isidorus, supposed author of forged decretals, 217
Merchant Marine Acts, in U.S., 1050
Merchant Shipping Act, in U.S., 615
Merchant tonnage, 9 countries, 1156
Merchants' Handbook, by Francesco Pegolotti, 362
Mercia, Anglo-Saxon kingdom, 166, 168
Merciless Parliament, 268
Mercy, Franz, Austrian general, 407
Mergenthaler, Ottmar, invented linotype, 556, 783
Mergentheim, battle of, 407
Merida, captured by Moslems, 163, 187
Merimdean culture, 18
Mermnad, Dynasty of, 37, 48
Merneptah, 24, 30
Merodach-baladan, 27, 39
Merovingians, 147, 149
Merrimac, Confederate frigate, 776
Mersa Matruh, Egypt, 1159 f.
Mersen, Treaty of, 157, 159, 379; Capitulary of, 158
Merton College, founded, 201
Merv, 124, 128
Mervings (Franks), 143
Mesembria, battle of, 177
Mesha, King of Moab, 31
Meshachev, Ivan Illarionovich, Arctic explorer, 570
Mesilim, King of Kish, 25
Mesolithic (Intermediate Stone), period and culture, 2 ff.
Mesopotamia, early history, 2, 13, 25, 110, 125, 127, 186
Mesopotamian culture, 41
Messalina, 105, 106
Messana, 57, 78, 86
Messapians, 68
Messene, 63, 80
Messenia, 48, 54, 55, 63
Messenian War, 1st and 2d, 50; 3d, 54 f.
Messina, destroyed by earthquake, 662; 1162
Messines Ridge, battles of, 939, 945
Mestizos, 503
Metaurus River, battle of the, 88
Metaxas, Gen. John, premier of Greece, 1022
Metcalfe, Charles Theophilus, Baron, gov.-gen. of India, 870
Metellus, Quintus Caecilius, 90, 92
Metemma, battle of, 835
Methodius of Thessalonica, missionary to the Slavs, 177, 239
Methuen, Paul, 3d Baron, British general, 857
Methuen, Treaty of, 432, 453
Methymna, 58
Metinna (Mattan), 33
Metropolitans, precedence recognized, 141; heads of independent Russian Church, 316
Metternich, Clemens Wenzel Nepomuk Lothar, Prince von, Austrian chancellor, 599, 601, 604, 650 f., 667, 669, 671, 673, 722
Metz, established as a capital, 147
Meun, Jean de, completed William of Lorris' *Roman de la Rose*, 231
Meuse, 1146, 1164
Meuse-Argonne, battle of, 1049
Mexico, conquest of, 490 f.; history of, 791, 803 f., 821 ff., 1074–1077; 1136, 1155, 1156
Meyer, Edward, German historian, 21
Mezzabarba, Carlo Ambrogio, conflict over Chinese rites, 539
Mi Fei, Chinese painter, 343
Miaja, Gen. José, heads National Defense Council in Madrid, 984
Miao Ch'üan-sun, Chinese bibliographer, 884
Miao tribes, lose central South China, 132; revolt suppressed, 540, 879
Miao-tzu, 44
Michael, Prince of Serbia, 714, 717
Michael I, Byzantine emperor, 155, 177
Michael II, Byzantine emperor, 177
Michael III, Byzantine emperor, 177
Michael IV, Byzantine emperor, 249
Michael V, Byzantine emperor, 249
Michael VI (Stratioticus), Byzantine emperor, 249
Michael VII (Parapinakes), Byzantine emperor, 250
Michael VIII (Paleologus), Byzantine emperor, 257, 260, 320, 321
Michael IX, Byzantine emperor, 322
Michael I, King of Rumania, 1025

Michael V, King of Rumania, 1136, 1142, 1150
Michael the Brave, of Moldavia, 424
Michael, Despot of Epirus, 248
Michael II, Despot of Epirus, 260, 320
Michael Angelus, Despot of Epirus, 258, 259
Michaelis, George, chancellor of Germany, 942
Michelangelo, Buonarroti, Italian artist, 296, 393, 396
Michinaga, 353
Michmash, 30
Michor, Nokola, Bulgarian general, 1141
Micipsa, king, 92
Microliths, 5
Micronesia, 18, 19
M.I.C.U.M. (*Mission interalliée de controle des usines et des mines*), 959
Midas, ruler of Phrygia, 37, 48
Middle Bronze Age, of Palestine, 29
Middle Cycladic culture, 16
Middle Helladic culture, 16
Middle Kingdoms, 44
Middle Stone Age, 6
Middleton, Christopher, explorer, 561
Middlesex election, 436
Midhat Pasha, Turkish grand visier, 729, 734
Midlothian, constituency of Gladstone, 616
Midway Island, 1137, 1138, 1167
Mieszko I, first historical ruler of Poland, 241
Mieszko II, King of Poland, 241
Mieszko III, King of Poland, 242
Migrations, of the Germanic race, 143
Mihailov, Ivan, Macedonian revolutionary, 1023
Mihira, or Bhoja, Indian ruler, 332
Mihran, Persian commander, 186
Mikhail of Serbia, crowned by papal legate, 246
Miki, Maekawa, founder of Tenri Sect in Japan, 887
Mikiracula, ruler in India, 331
Mikkelsen, Einar, Arctic explorer, 567, 568
Miklas, Wilhelm, pres. of Austrian Republic, 1006, 1007, 1008
Milan, 141, 142, 151, 220, 295 ff.; 397, 458 f., 654, 1141
Milan, Decree of, on blockade against British trade, 593, 768
Milan, King of Serbia, 714, f., 737
Milan, Prince of Serbia, 714
Milazzo, battle of, 658
Mildenhall, John, of the British East India Co., 533
Milescu, Spatar, mission to China, 539
Miletus, 37 *passim*; Treaty of, 60; 81; 84
Military Collapse of Germany, 1164
Military League, in Bulgaria, 1024
Military supplies, from Great Britain and U.S. to Russia, 1153
Miliukov, Prof. Paul Nikolaievich, Russian historian and statesman, 707, 940, 1028, 1029
Milkiasaph, 33
Mill, James, English philosopher, 549, 551
Mill, John Stuart, English philosopher, 550
Millerand, Alexandre, pres. of France, 977
Millerovo, 1153
Millesimo, battle of, 585
Millspaugh, Dr. Arthur Chester, heads financial mission to Persia, 1108
Milne, Sir Berkeley, British admiral, 919
Milne, Gen. Sir George Frederick, British commander, 1094
Milner, Sir Alfred, British statesman, 856, 967, 1081
Milner-Schialoja Agreement, 1087
Milo, 85
Milo, Titus Annius, 96, 97
Mi-lo-fo (Maitreya), 136
Miltiades, 52, 53
Miltitz, Charles von, papal chamberlain, 399
Milvian Bridge, battle of the, and device of *in hoc signo vinces*, 119
Milyutin (Stephen Urosh II), King of Serbia, 319
Mimana, 139
Min, Queen of Korea, 885 f., 891
Mina, Francis Xavier, Mexican revolutionist, 804
Minaean Kingdom, 13
Minamoto, Japanese clan, 352, 355
Minas Geráes, discovery of gold, 501
Minden, battle of, 467
Mindon Min, King of Burma, 872
Mindovg, Lithuanian chieftain, 316
Miners' Federation, of Great Britain, 618
Ming dynasty, founded, 346, 348, 362, 363
Ming, emperor, 134, 536, 537
Minghetti, Marco, prime minister of Italy, 660
Minh-Mang, Emperor of Annam, 874
Minimum 48-hour work week in U.S., 1139
Minimum Wage Act, in Canada, 1060
Minimum wage schedules, in U.S., 790
Ministry of Blockade, in England, 929
Ministry of Education, in Japan, 890
Minorites, 217
Minseito, Japanese party, 1126
Minsk, 1154
Minto, Gilbert John Elliot-Murray-Kynynmond, 4th Earl of; gov.-gen. of Canada, 797; gov.-gen. of India, 868, 871
Minturnae, 74
Minuit, Peter, purchased Manhattan Island from Indians, 510; 511
Minusinsk region, 7, 14
Miocene Indian and France, 1
Miquelon, 1138

Mirabeau, Honoré Gabriel Riquetti, French revolutionary leader, 579, 580
Miranda, Francisco de, Latin American patriot, 800, 802
Mirbach, Count Wilhelm von, German ambassador to Russia, 1032
Mirdasids, of Aleppo, Arab tribe of Banu Kilab, 190
Mirdite Republic, established at Prizrend, 1019
Mironescu, George, premier of Rumania, 1025
Mirza Shah, Moslem dynasty in Kashmir, 334
Mirza Taki Khan, Persian prime minister, 864
Mise of Amiens, Louis IX's agreement favoring Henry III against barons, 198 f.
Mise of Lewes, exacted from Henry III by Simon de Montfort, 198
Misenum, Pact of, 99
Mishna, 30
Misitheus, *see* Timesitheus
Missale Romanum, 396
Missing Link, 1
Missionaries, in Africa, 840, 847, 851, 853; Portuguese, in Madagascar, 859, 860; French in Korea, 885; British and French, on Tahiti, 895; American, in Hawaii, 910
Missionary Ridge, *see* Chattanooga
Mississippi, admitted to statehood, 770
Mississippi Bubble, in France, 434, 447
Missolonghi, Greek fortress, 722, 723
Missouri, admitted as a slave state, 770
Missouri, U.S. Battleship, 1145
Missouri Compromise, 770, 775
Mistra, capital of Morean province, 320, 323
Mitanni, 23; Kingdom of, 28, 29, 36
Mitau, taken by Austro-Germans, 922
Mitchell, Sir Francis, 374
Mithras, religion of, 113, 117
Mithridates I, 37, 81, 83
Mithridates II (the Great), 81, 83, 97, 128
Mithridates VI Eupator, 37, 85, 94, 95
Mithridatic Wars, 93–95
Mitre, Bartolomé, gov. of Buenos Aires, 808
Mitsuhide, Akechi, 543
Mitsukuni, Tokugawa, compilation of a *History of Japan*, 547
Mitsumasa Yonai, Japanese admiral, 1135, 1142, 1165
Mittelholzer, Lt. Walter, Swiss aviator, 569
Miura, Viscount, Japanese resident in Korea, 886
Mo Ti, 45
Moab, and Moabites, 29, 31
Mo'awiya, founder of Omayyad dynasty, 186
Mo'awiya II, caliph, 186
Mobile, founded, 507
Mobile & Ohio R.R., gets land grant, 774
Mocenigo, Pietro, Venetian admiral, 458
Mochitoyo (sōzen), Yamana, war lord of western Japan, 359
Moctezuma, ruler of the Aztecs, 490 f.
Model Parliament, 200
Modena, uprising in, 651
Modon, battle of, 420
Moesia, 103, 109, 115, 122
Moewe, German cruiser, 932
Moffat, John Smith, South African promoter, 855
Moga "Great King," an era, 128
Mogadiscio, 1160
Mogul Empire, in India, founded, 530; 533 f.; its end, 870
Mohacs, battles of, 419, 422; 2d battle, 461, 483 f.
Mohallib, 186, 187
Mohammed, brother of the sultan Barkyaruk, 254
Mohammed, the Prophet, 184
Mohammed, leads Shi'ite revolt in Iraq and Medina, 188
Mohammed, ruler of Seljuk kingdom of Iraq, 255
Mohammed I, Emir of Cordova, 163
Mohammed I (Bahmani), Indian ruler, 334
Mohammed I (the Restorer), Turkish sultan, 326
Mohammed II (the Conqueror), Turkish sultan, 323, 326 f.
Mohammed III, Ruler of Delhi, 335
Mohammed IV, Turkish sultan, 424, 483 f.
Mohammed V, Turkish sultan, 732, 948
Mohammed VI, Turkish sultan, 948, 1094, 1095
Mohammed of Ghur, Mu'izz-ud-Din, 332
Mohammed Ahmed, *see* Mahdi
Mohammed (Mehemet) Ali, of Egypt, 723, 724, 725, 828, 830
Mohammed Ali, of Khokand, 877
Mohammed Ali, leader of the Moslem League, 1112
Mohammed Ali Shah, Persian ruler, 865
Mohammed Ali ben Abdullah, *see* "Mad Mullah"
Mohammed Bey, ruler of Egypt, 525
Mohammed ibn Abi 'Amir, *Hajib Al-Mansur*, 164
Mohammed ibn Qasim, conquers Sind, 187
Mohammed ibn Tumart, founder of the Almohades dynasty, 233, 263
Mohammed Khudabanda, Persian prince, 526
Mohammed Kiuprili, Turkish grand vizier, 424, 482
Mohammed Mahmud Pasha, premier of Egypt, 1084
Mohammed Nadir Shah, King of Afghanistan, 1110, 1111
Mohammed Said, Egyptian Khedive, 830
Mohammed Shah, Persian ruler, 862
Mohammed Sökölli, Turkish grand vizier, 423
Mohammed Tewfik Nessim, premier of Egypt, 1084
Mohammed Tughluk, Mongol ruler, 333, 334, 338
Mohammed Zahir Shah, King of Afghanistan, 1111
Mohammedan Union, in Constantinople, 731 f.
Mohammedans (Panthays) in Yünnan revolt, 879, 880
Mohenjo-daro, 13, 41

Moir, James Reid, 4, 8
Moira, Lord (Francis Rawdon-Hastings, 1st Marquess of Hastings), gov.-gen. of India, 868
Mokanna, veiled prophet, revolts in Khorasan, 188
Mola, Gen. Emilio, insurgent leader in Spanish Civil War, 983
Molasses Act, 515, 517
Moldavia, held by Bulgarians, 181; principality of Rumania, 719, 720; Hypsilanti in revolt, 722; declared an independent govt., 1031
Moldavian (Bessarabian) Republic, 943; union with Rumania, 944
Molé, Louis Mathieu, Count, French prime minister, 628, 630
Mollien, Gaspard, African explorer, 826
Mollwitz, battle of, 465
Molon, 81
Molossus, 64
Molotov, Vyacheslav M., Russian commissar for foreign affairs, 1037, 1138 f., 1150
Molteno, John, South African statesman, 853
Moltke, Helmuth Carl Bernhard, Count von, German general, 636, 680, 683, 733, 762
Moltke, Helmuth von, German general, 913
Molucca Islands, 1169
Mommu, Emperor of Japan, 350
Mompesson, Sir Giles, 375
Mona, 106
Monagas, José Gregorio, pres. of Venezuela, 816
Monagas, José Tadeo, pres. of Venezuela, 816
Monash, Sir John, in command of Australian army in World War, 1128, 1129
Monasticism, 123, 142, 146, 167, 169, 175
Monastir, battles of, 760, 934, 940
Monastir-Doiran, battle of, 948
Moncada, José, pres. of Nicaragua, 1073
Monchijo, a court of appeal in Kyōto, 355
Monck, Charles Stanley, 4th Viscount, gov.-gen. of Canada, 796
Moncontour, battle of, 384
Mondovi, battle of, 585
Monge, Gaspard, in provisional govt. of French Revolution, 581
Mongka, Mongol khan, 344 f.
Mongol Empire, reunited, 345
Mongolia, under Chinese suzerainty, 1118; Inner, 1171; Outer, 1171
Mongolia People's Revolutionary Govt., under Soviet auspices, 1118
Mongoloid group of Man, 12, 19
Mongols, first appearance in Europe, 211; invade Poland, 242; 244, 246, 262; in Anatolia, 320, 324; Central Asian Empire, 344, 346; invade Japan, 357; overthrown in China, 362
Monitor, Federal ironclad, 776
Monk, George (later 1st Duke of Albemarle), English general, 425, 426, 439
Monks of Studion, banished, 77
Monmouth, battle of, 521
Monmouth, Duke of, natural son of Charles II, 428, 429
Monmouth (H.M.S.), destroyed, 918
Monomakh, Vladimir, Prince of Kiev, 244
Monophysite heresy, 123, 171, 249
Monoplane, flown across English Channel, 557
Monopoli, battle of, 249
Monothelete controversy, 151
Monotype, invented, 556
Monroe, James (5th pres. of the U.S.), 644, 768, 770
Monroe Doctrine, 644, 770 f., 816, 1052
Mons, battle of, 913
Monserrate, Antonio, Portuguese Jesuit, 533
Montagu, Edwin Samuel, secretary for India, 1111
Montagu-Chelmsford reforms, in India, 1111
Montague, Charles, chancellor of the exchequer under William III, 431
Montague, Richard, 375
Montalembert, Charles Forbes René de Tryon, Count de, French Liberal Catholic, 633
Montana, organized as a territory, 780; admitted to statehood, 784
Montañés, Martínez, Spanish sculptor, 389
Montanism, 113, 117
Montano, Arias, at Council of Trent, 388
Montaperti, battle of, 293
Montcalm de Saint Véran, Louis Joseph, Marquis, French general, 435, 516
Montdidier, in French hands, 914; taken by Germans, 945
Monte, Giovanni Maria del, Pope Julius III, 396
Monte Cassino, held by Moslems, 158
Montecuccoli, Raimondo, Count of, imperial general, 442, 483
Monteil, Col. Parfair-Louis, French colonial commander, 743, 745, 841, 845
Montenegro, independence recognized in Treaty of Berlin, 715, 729, 734, 737, 756, 759, 760, 1016
Montereau, battle of, 600
Monterey, founded, 493
Montero, José, pres. of Paraguay, 1065
Montero, Juan Esteban, pres. of Chile, 1065
Montes, Ismael, pres. of Bolivia, 812
Montespan, Françoise Athénaïs, Marquise de, mistress of Louis XIV, 443
Montesquieu, Charles Louis de Secondat, French political theorist, 457, 728

Monteverde, Juan Domingo, Spanish commander in Venezuela, 802
Monteverdi, Claudio, Italian composer, 454
Montevideo, founded by Spaniards, 501; besieged, 811; 1154, 1158
Montfort, Simon de (the elder), 221; leads Albigensian-Waldensian crusade, 229
Montfort, Simon de, 198 f.
Montgolfier, Joseph and Stephen, invented the balloon, 553
Montgomery, Sir Bernard L., British Field Marshal, commander of British Eighth Army, 1160, 1165
Montgomery, Richard, British commander in Canada, 520
Montgomery, Sir Robert, and the Margravate of Azilia, 513 f.
Montijo, see Eugenie de Montijo
Montijo, battle of, 453
Montmédy, taken by Germans, 913
Montmirail, battle of, 600
Montmorency, Anne, Duc de, constable of France, 387
Montpensier, Antoine Marie Philippe Louis, Duke of, husband of Luisa Fernanda of Spain, 645, 646
Montreal, 1170
Montrose, James Graham, Marquis of, 376; defeats Covenanters in English Civil War, 378; flees to continent, 378
Monts, Pierre de Guast, sieur de, French colonizer, 506
Montt, Jorge, pres. of Chile, 809
Montt, Manuel, pres. of Chile, 809
Montt, Pedro, pres. of Chile, 810
Monzaemon, Chikamatsu, Japanese playwright, 547
Mookerheide, battle of, 380
Moore, Sir John, British general, 594
Moore, William, explorer, 560
Moors, expelled from Spain, 282
Moplahs in India, uprising of, 1112
Mopsuestia, fortified against Byzantine raids, 188
Moraes Barros, Prudente de, pres. of Brazil, 818
Morales, Agustín, pres. of Bolivia, 811
Morat, battle of, 280, 307
Moratorium on inter-Allied debts and reparations, 961, 1052
Moravia, Kingdom of, 239, 241
Moravians, branch of western Slavs, 239
Morazán, Francisco, pres. of Central American provinces, 819
More, Sir Thomas, English humanist, 370
Morea, conquest of the, 458, 722
Moreau, Jean Victor, French general, 584, 586, 588, 590
Morel, Edward Dene, British publicist, 845
Morelos, José María, revolt in Mexico, 804
Moreno, Alfredo Baquerizo, pres. of Ecuador, 814, 1068
Moreno, Gabriel García, pres. of Ecuador, 814
Moreno, Mariano, sought control of Banda Oriental and Paraguay, 800
Moresby, Capt. John, explorer, 902
Moresnet, assigned to Belgium, 952, 974
Moret, Sigismond, Spanish statesman, 647
Moreton Bay, convict settlement, 899
Morgan, Henry, English freebooter, 494
Morgarten, battle of, 306
Mōri family, in western Japan, 543
Morillo, Pablo, defeated revolutionists in New Granada, 803
Morinaga, Japanese shōgun, 357
Moriscos, expelled from Spain, 389, 390
Morley, John, British statesman, 618
Mormon Church, organized, 771
Mornington, Richard Colley, 1st Baron (later Marquess Wellesley), gov.-gen. of India, 868
Morny, Charles Auguste Louis Joseph, Duke de, half-brother of Napoleon III, 632
Moro, Ludovico, ruler of Milan, 381
Moroccan crisis (1905), 619, 692, 753, 838; second crisis (1911), 693, 757, 758, 839
Moroccan Reforms, Plan of, offered by Young Moroccans, 1087
Moroccan-Tunisian Railway, opened, 1087
Moronobu, Hishakawa, Japanese artist, 547
Morosini, Francisco, Venetian commander, 458
Morosini, Pier, Latin patriarch of Constantinople, 257, 258
Morotai, 1169
Morrill Act, in U.S., 780
Morrill Tariff, in U.S., 779
Morris, Sir Edward, premier of Newfoundland, 1060
Morris, Sir Edward Patrick, premier of Canada, 798
Morrison, American ship, 887
Morrison, Robert, missionary to China, 877
Morrow, Dwight Whitney, U.S. ambassador to Mexico, 1052, 1075
Morse, Samuel Finley Breese, developed electric telegraph, 554, 773
Morte Arthure, by Sir Thomas Malory, 276
Mortier, Edouard Adolphe Casimir Joseph, Duke of Treviso, French marshal, 601
Mortimer, Roger, paramour of Isabella, queen of Edward II, 264
Mortimer's Cross, battle of, 270
Morton, John, Bishop of Ely, 271
Morton, Dr. William Thomas Green, first used ether as an anaesthetic, 551, 773
"Morton's Fork," method of raising money, 369
Moscicki, Ignace, pres. of Poland, 1039
Moscoso, Louis de, Spanish explorer, 493
Moscow, 244, 316, 598; Treaty of, 1042; 1140, 1144, 1151, 1153
Moscow Gazette, 740
Moscow Scientific Maritime Institute, 570
Moses, 24, 30

Moshesh, leader of Basutos, 852, 853
Moslem faith, 184
Moslem League, in India, 1112
Moslem Spain, 232, 234, 255
Moslems, 150, 152, 184 ff., 215, 232 ff., 255 ff., 1144; see also names of individual states
Mosquera, Tomás Cipriano de, pres. of New Granada, 814, 815
Mosquito Indians, protectorate of Great Britain, 820
Mossel-bay, 6
Mosso, 44
Mosul, occupied by British, 947; awarded to Iraq, 1096, 1105
Mota, Antonio da, 364
Motor Carrier Act, 1055
Mototsune, dictator of Japan, 352
Mott, Lucretia, in women's rights movement, 774
Mott, Peter, Arctic explorer, 569
Motya, 52
Mound Builder area, 20
Mount Asama, in Japan, 548
Mount Graupius, 108
Mount Hermon, 29
Mount Ithome, 55
Mount Lovchen, guarding Montenegro, 927
Mount Lycaeum, 50
Mount Vesuvius, 95; eruption, 108
Mountain, French Revolutionary party, 580, 581, 582
Mountbatten, Lord Louis, British admiral, commander of 14th British Imperial Army, 1169
Mountjoy, William Stewart, Lord, subjugated Ireland, 373
Mousterian industry, 5
Moving pictures, 556
Mowinckel, John Ludwig, premier of Norway, 1046
Mozambique, allotted to Germany, 748
Mozambique Co., chartered by Portugal, 849
Mozdok, 1153
Mozhaisk, 1153
Mrichchakatika ("Little Clay Cart"), 131
Msidi, King of Katanga, 844
Mtesa, King of Uganda, 847
Mu Tsung, Emperor of China, 880
Mucianus, Licinius, 107
Mueller, Ludwig, national bishop of Germany, 1001
Müffling, Friedrich Karl Ferdinand von, Prussian general, 724
Mugwumps, reform wing of Republican Party, 783
Mühlberg, battle of, 402
Mu'izz al-Dawla, gets part of Persia and Iraq, 190
Mukden, battle of, 707, 892; occupied by Japanese, 962; Chinese forces expelled, 1126
Mulai Hafid, Sultan of Morocco, 755, 839
Mulai Hassan, Bey of Tunis, 422
Mulai Yusuf, Sultan of Morocco, 839, 1087
Mularaja, leader of the Chalukya clan, 332
Mulcy, al-Tawa'if, dynasties of Moslem Spain, 232
Mulligan (James), letters, 782
Muluk, al-Tawa'if, dynasties of Moslem Spain, 232
Mummies, 21
Mummius, Lucius, crushes Achaean League, 80, 90
Mumtaz Mahal, wife of Shah Jahan, 533
Munch, Peter Andreas, Norwegian historian; 699
Münchengratz Agreement, 724 f.
Munda, 97 ff., 1169
Munda kings, 129
Mundhir, 163
Munetada, Kurozumi, founded the Kurozumi sect, 887
Munich Agreements, 971, 1012, 1040
Municipal Corporations Bill, 608
Munja (Paramara), Indian ruler, 333
Münnich, Burkhard Christoph, Count, Russian general, 480, 484
Muñoz, Augustin Fernandez, Duke of Riansares, secret marriage to Maria Cristina of Spain, 645
Munro, Sir Charles, British general, 921
Munroe, Walter, premier of Newfoundland, 1061
Münste, Georg Herbert, Count, German ambassador to Great Britain, 737
Münster, Treaty of, 438
Muntasir, caliph, 189
Münzer, Thomas, leader of the Anabaptists, 400
Muqtadi, caliph, 189
Muqtadir, caliph, 190
Muqtafi, caliph of Egypt, 189 f.
Murad I, Ottoman sultan, 319, 324
Murad II, Ottoman sultan, 323, 326
Murad III, Ottoman sultan, 424
Murad IV, Ottoman sultan, 424, 528, 529
Murad V, Ottoman sultan, 729
Murakami, emperor of Japan, 353
Muraic Shikibu, Japanese woman novelist, 353
Murat, Joachim, French general and King of Naples, 452, 586, 592, 594, 602, 603
Muraviev, Michael, Count, Russian foreign minister, 746, 749
Muraviev, Nicholas, Count, gov.-gen. of Siberia, 703, 879
Muret, battle of, 229, 235, 237
Murfreesboro, or Stone River, battle of, 778
Murillo, Bartolomé, Spanish painter, 389
Muromachi, see Ashikaga
Murray, Sir Archibald, British commander in Egypt, 937 f.
Murray, James Stuart, revolted against Mary, Queen of Scots, 373

Mursa, 120
Murshilish I, King of the Hittites, 35, 36; II, 36
Mürzsteg program, of reforms for Macedonia, 731, 752
Musa, Moslem conqueror, 163
Musa, brother of Sultan Mohammed I, 326
Musa ibn Nusayr, pacifies North Africa, 187
Mus'ab, gov. of Iraq, 187
Musair, 38
Musaylima, false prophet, 184
Muscovy Co., 507, 559 f.
Muses, temple of, 75
Mush, taken by Russians, 929
Mushanov, Nicholas, Bulgarian premier, 1023
Musical scale (Pythagorean), 45
Muslim ibn Quraysh, 190
Mussolini, Benito, Italian prime minister, 663, 925, 963, 965,
    986, 988, 989, 991, 992, 1003, 1008, 1012, 1088, 1136, 1139,
    1140, 1144, 1150, 1162, 1163, 1164 f.
Mustafa, son of Sultan Suleiman, 423
Mustafa Kiuprili, Turkish grand vizier, 484 f.
Musta'in, caliph, 189
Mustansir l'Illah, caliph, 262
Mustapha, pretender to Turkish throne, 323, 327
Mustapha IV, Ottoman sultan, 722
Mustapha Kamel, leader of Nationalist Party in Egypt, 834
Mustapha Kemal Pasha, President of the Turkish Republic,
    920, 954, 1094, 1095, 1096, 1098
Mustaqfi, caliph, 190
Musta'sim, caliph, 262
Mu'tadid, caliph, 189 f.
Mu'tamid, caliph, 189
Mutannabi, Arab poet, 190
Mutawakkil, brother of the caliph Wathiq, 189
Mutawakkil, 422
Mu'tazilites, in the caliphate of Mamun, 189
Mu'tazz, caliph, 189
Muthanna, defeats Persians under Mihran, 186
Mutina, 87; battle of, 98
Mutineers from the Bounty, 895
Mutiny, sailors at Spithead and the Nore, 437; in the German
    fleet at Kiel, 951, 995; in the British navy at Invergordon,
    969; on Dutch training ship Zeven Provincien, 976
Mutiny Act, in England, 430
Mutsuhito, Emperor of Japan, 889, 893
Mutual aid pact, Great Britain and Russia, 1138 f., 1151
Muwatallish, defeats Ramses II, 36
Muybridge, Edward, first to apply moving picture principle,
    555
Muzaffar ud-Din, Persian ruler, 864, 865
Muzaffarids, succeed the Il-khans in Fars, Kirman, and Kurdi-
    stan, 330
Muziris, 129
Muzzarelli, Mgr. Carlo, papal statesman, 655
Mwanga, King of Uganda, 847, 848, 849
Mycale, 40, 47, 54
Mycenae, 46, 47, 50, 54
Mycenaean culture, 16, 29, 33
Mycerinus, 23
Mylae, 78, 86
Mylius-Erichsen, Ludvig, Danish expedition to Greenland, 568
Myonnesus, 82
Myron, sculptor, 62
Myronides, 55
Mysians, 36
Mysore, 132; War, 868
Mysticism, cult of, 135
Mytilene, 47, 51, 58, 63; battle of, 61

Nabis, King of Sparta, 80, 88
Nabonidus, 26
Nabopolassar, King of Babylonia, 26, 28, 40
Nachtigal, Gustav, African explorer, 826, 841
Nadab, 31
Nadir Duli, shah of Persia, 528–530, 534
Nadir Shah, drove Turks out of Persia, 484
Naevius, 91
Näfels, battle of, 306
Nagabhata I, ruler of western India, 331
Nagabhata II, 331
Naganori, Asano, Lord of Akō, 548
Nagarjuna, founder of the Madhyamika school, 130
Nagarjunikonda, 132
Nagasaki, opened to foreign trade, 543; 1145
Nagpur, 132
Nagyvarad, Peace of, 419
Nahapana, named Mambanos, 129
Nahas (Mustafa) Pasha, Egyptian nationalist leader, 1083
Nahor, 29
Nairi, 38
Naissus, 116
Nakamaro, Japanese monk, 351
Nakamura, Maj., Japanese officer, 1119, 1126
Nakatomi clan, in Japan, 140
Nakatomi Kamatari, founds Fujiwara clan, 140
Naklo, battle of, 241, 242
Nalanda, 130
Namik Kemal, Turkish dramatic and political writer, 728
Namur, taken by Germans, 913; 1146
Nancy, battle of, 280, 307
Nandivarman II, III, Pallava rulers, 336
Nangis, battle of, 600

Nanking, seized by Communists, 1119; taken by Japanese, 1122;
    Treaty of, 879; 1135, 1165, 1170
Nansen, Dr. Fridtjof, Arctic explorer, 565
Nanto-Bordelaise Co., French colonizers, 905
Nantwich, battle of, 377
Naosuke, Japanese statesman, 888
Napata, 24
Napier, Sir Charles James, British general, 725
Napier, Sir Robert Cornelis, British commander in Ethiopia,
    834
Napier, Lord William John, superintendent of British trade in
    China, 878
Naples, 217, 290, 292 f., 390, 397, 458, 650 ff., 654; Kingdom of,
    657, 658, 659; bombed, 1162; entered by American troops, 1162
Napoleon I, Emperor, 440, 452, 458, 460, 502, 578, 583 ff., 626,
    721, 766, 768, 769, 799–802, 859, 862
Napoleon III, Emperor, 437, 555, 616, 623, 632 ff., 646, 655 ff.,
    667, 680, 681, 686, 688, 720, 727, 822
Nara period, in Japan, 138; 350
Narada, a code, 130
Naram-Sin, 25, 35
Narasimha, 337
Narasimhavarman (Pallava), 335
Narbonne, captured by Samh, 187; Treaty of, 387
Narcissus, freedman, 105
Narcissus, wrestler, 112
Nares, King of Persia, 118, 124, 125, 146, 172
Nares, Sir George Strong, Arctic and Antarctic explorer, 564;
    572, 895
Nariakira, Tokugawa, 888, 889
Narnia, 74
Narodna Odbrana, Serbian propagandist society, 715
Narutowicz, Gabriel, pres. of the Polish Republic, 1039
Narva, battle of, 472, 479; taken by Germans, 943
Narváez, Aurelio Mosquera, pres. of Ecuador, 1069
Narváez, Pánfilo de, expedition to punish Cortes, 491, 493
Narváez, Gen. Ramon María, Spanish soldier and statesman,
    645, 646
Narvik, 1146
Nasca culture, 20
Naseby, battle of, 377, 378
Nashville, abandoned by Confederates, 778
Nashville Convention, 774
Nasik, 129, 132
Nasir ud-Din, Persian ruler, 863, 864, 865
Nasir ul-Mulk, Persian prime minister, 865
Nasiriya, taken by British, 927
Nasjonal Samling, Norwegian parliament, 1146
Nasr, defeated by Kahtaba, 188
Nasrids, of Granada, 233
Nasrullah, Amir of Afghanistan, 1109
Nasi, Joseph, 423
Natal, 851, 852, 855
Nathalia, wife of Milan, King of Serbia, 714
Nathorst, Dr. Alfred Gabriel, Arctic explorer, 566
National Assembly, in the French Revolution, 579, 580, 630,
    631; of the Third Republic, 636, 637, 638
National Association for the Protection of Labor, 608
National Association of the United Trades for the Protection
    of Labor, 611
National Bank of the Philippines, chartered, 1132
National Banking Act of the U.S., 779
National Christian Party, anti-Semitic organization in Ru-
    mania, 1026
National Coffee Department in Brazil, 1071
National College of China, 137
National Congress of India, 871
National Constituent Assembly, at Weimar, 996
National Convention of Chartists, 609, 611
National Convention of France, 578, 582, 584
National Council at Zagreb, 1016
National Council of Corporations, in Italy, 989
National debt, its beginning, 431
National Defense Council, organized at Madrid, 984
National Defense Mediation Board, 1137
National Defense Tax Bill, 1135
National Guard (Blue Shirts), in Ireland, 973
National Guard of France, 579, 627, 637
National Indonesian Party, of Netherlands East Indies, 1117
National Industrial Recovery Act, in U.S., 1054, 1055
National Insurance Act, in England, 620
National Labor Relations Board, in U.S., 1054
National Labor Union, 783
National Liberal Party, in Prussia, 686
National Pact, adopted by Constantinople Parliament, 1094
National Party, in New Zealand, 1132
National Party of Work, in Hungary, 696
National Peasants' Party, in Rumania, 1025
National Progressive Republican League, in U.S., 790
National Prohibition Act, in U.S., 1050
National Prohibition Party, in U.S., 1061
National Railways of Mexico, 1076
"National register" for war service, in England, 971
National Socialist German Workers' Party, 1000
National Socialists (Nazi) in Germany, 974, 999,
National Society for the Unification of Italy, 657, 658
National System of Political Economy, by Friedrich List, 549
National Union, in Johannesburg, 855
National Union, in Portugal, 986
National Woman's Suffrage Convention, in U.S., 781
National workshops, in Paris, 630

Nationalist Congress, in Egypt, 834
Nationalist movement, in India, 871, 1112
Nationalist Party, in Australia, 1129
Nationalist Party, in Syria, 1099
Nationalist Union, of Lithuania, 1042
Nationalists, in Turkey, 1094, 1095, 1097
Nationality and Flag Act, for South Africa, 1092
Nationality Statute, in Czechoslovakia, 1011
Natives Land Act, of the Union of South Africa, 859
Natufian culture, 6, 13; industry, 6
Naturalization Act, of U.S., 766
Naucratis, 24, 47
Naupactus, 55, 58; Treaty of, 80, 87
Nauru, German island colony, 1128
Naus, M., administrator of Persian customs, 864
Naval Defense Act, of Britain, 618, 741
Naval limitation treaties, 1128
Naval warfare and blockade, 1156 ff.
Navarino, battle of, 723
Navarre, 237
Navarrete, battle of, 265, 277, 280
Navarro, Pedro, 386
Navas de Tolosa, battle of, 233, 234, 237
Navetas, 17
Navicert, 1156 f.
Navigation Acts, in England, 267, 427, 437, 439, 514
Navy Department, created in U.S., 766
Navy Law, first in Germany, 692, 747
Naxis, 52
Naxos, 50 passim
Nay, Cornelis, Dutch explorer, 559
Nayanmars, Tamil saints, 336
Nazarbek, Avetis, Armenian revolutionary leader, 743
Nazi Labor Front, 1002
Nazi Revolution, in Germany 1000 f.
Nazi Storm Troops, 999
Nazi-Fascist influence, in Argentina, 1156
Nazis, abortive coup in Vienna, 990, 1003, 1006, 1007
Neanderthal Man (Homo neanderthalensis), 5, 9
Neanthropic Man, 9
Near-Eastern Triplice, 743
Nearchus, Macedonian general, 42, 65
Nebraska, admitted to statehood, 784
Nebuchadrezzar, 24, 25, 26, 31, 33, 39
Necho, 24, 26, 31
Necker, Jacques, Swiss banker, 448, 579, 580
Nedao, 145
Neerwinden, battle of, 431, 582
Negri Sembilan, Malay federation, 876
Negrillos, 328
Negrin, Juan, premier of Spain, 984
Negroid group of Man, 12, 19, 68
Negroponte, battle of, 290, 299
Neguelli, 1160
Nehawand, battles of, Persians defeated, 186; Omayyad forces
    routed, 188
Nehemiah, 31
Nehru, Motilal, leader of the Swaraj Party in India, 1112
Nehru, Pandit Jawaharlal, founded Independence of India
    League, 1112; 1114, 1138
Nei Ko, Chinese grand secretariat, 540
Nelidov, Alexander Ivanovich, Russian diplomat, 744
Nelson, Donald M., chief of War Production Board, 1138
Nelson, Horatio, British admiral, 586, 591
Nemea, 62
Nemours, Jeanne de, mother of Victor Amadeus II, 457
Nemours, Louis Charles Philippe Raphael, Duke of, 622
Neolithic (New Stone) period and culture, 2 ff.; earliest remains,
    11; in Greece, 47; Neolithic Man in Italy, 68
Neon, 64
Neo-pagan movements, in Nazi Germany, 1001
Neo-Persian Empire, 124–32
Neophytos, Bulgarian monk, 716
Neo-Platonic Academy, at Athens, 172
Neo-Platonism, 117, 142
Neo-Pythagoreanism, 113, 117
Nepal, 868
Nepos, Cornelius, Roman writer, 100
Nepos, Julius, Roman emperor, 122, 147
Nerchinsk, Treaty of, 478, 539
Nero, son of Germanicus, 105
Nero (Claudius Nero Caesar), Roman emperor, 106, 107, 112
Nero, Caius Claudius, 88
Nero, Tiberius Claudius, 99
Nerva, Marcus Cocceius, Roman emperor, 103, 109, 110
Nervii, 96
Nesib, battle of, 725
Nesselrode, Karl Robert, Count, Russian chancellor, 601
Nestorian Christians, in China, 346, 537
Nestorian Christological doctrine, established by Bar-Soma, 126
Netherlands, 379 f., 437 ff., 602, 621 ff., 975 ff.; in Second World
    War, 1137; overrun by Germany, 1146 f.; merchant tonnage,
    1156; 1163, 1165
Netherlands East Indies, 1117, 1139, 1165, 1167
Nettelbeck, Joachim Christian, Prussian general, 592
Neufchâtel, problem of, 666 f.
Neuhof, Theodore Stephen, Baron von, German adventurer,
    459
Neuilly, Treaty of, 953, 1023
Neurath, Constantin von, German foreign minister, 999, 1013
Neustria, 147

Neutrality Act (1794) passed in U.S., 764; (1937), 1056, 1057,
    1135, 1154
Neutrality, General Declaration of, 1154
Neutrality Pact, Japan and Russia, 1137, 1166
Nevada, organized as a territory, 780; admitted to statehood,
    784
Neville's Cross, battle of, 265, 272
Nevski, Alexander, Prince of Novgorod and then of Vladimir,
    244
New Albion, named, 507
New Amsterdam, settled, 510; seized by the English, 439; name
    changed to New York, 512
New Amsterdam Island, discovered, 894
New Berne, N.C., captured by Federal forces, 776
New Caledonia, annexed by the French, 895
New Christianity, The, by Count Claude Henri de Saint-Simon,
    549
New Deal legislation, in U.S., 1053–56
New Economic Policy (NEP), in Soviet Russia, 1033
New England Anti-Slavery Society, 771
New England Confederation, 511
New England Emigrant Aid Society, 775
New Georgia Island, 1169
New Granada, 488, 497, 802 f., 814 ff. See also Colombia
New Guinea, 894, 896, 902; renamed Papua, 904, 918, 1167,
    1169
New Hampshire, separated from Massachusetts, 511; 523
New Hebrides, discovered, 894; England and France establish a
    condominium, 895, 1167
New Holland, part of Australia, 896
New Ireland, 1167
New Jersey, territory granted to Lord Berkeley and Sir George
    Carteret, 511
New Laws, of Peru, 490, 497, 498
New Mexico, admitted to statehood, 784
New Netherland Co., 510
"New Order," Hitler bloc, 1170
New Orleans, founded, 507; battle of, 769
New Panama Canal Co., 788
New Plymouth, settled, 906
New South Wales, 896, 899–904
New South Wales Corps, 896
New Spain (Mexico), 490 ff.; Viceroyalty created, 497; 803 f.
New Sweden Co., 510 f.
New York, occupied by the British, 521
New Zealand, 904 ff., 1131 ff.
New Zealand Association founded, 905
New Zealand Co., 905, 906
Newbold, Charles, patented the iron plow, 553, 764
Newburn on the Tyne, battle at, 407
Newbury, battle of, 377
Newcastle, Thomas Pelham-Holles, Duke of, British statesman,
    434, 435
Newcastle Program, 618
Newcastle proposals, submitted to Charles I, 378
Newfoundland, 432, 793, 797 f., 1060, 1061, 1148 f., 1155, 1158
Newfoundland fisheries, 790
Newlands, Francis Griffiths, resolution ratifying annexation of
    Hawaii, 910
Newlands Act, in U.S., 788
Newman, John Henry, Cardinal, 612
Newport, Treaty of, 379
Newport, Capt. Christopher, English colonizer, 508
Newton, Sir Isaac, English scientist, 431
Ney, Michel, French Marshal, 591, 598, 599
Nez Percé Indians, 780
Niagara Conference, of A.B.C. powers, 791
Niazi Bey, Turkish revolutionary, 731
Nicaea, 114, 119, 250, 252, 255, 257
Nicaean Empire, founded by Theodore I (Lascaris), 259
Nicaragua, 790, 820 f.; finances stabilized by American commis-
    sion, 1073
Nice, Treaty of, 388, 395; 1163
Nicene creed, 119
Nicephorus, Byzantine emperor, 188, 224, 321; 176 f.
Nicephorus III (Botaniates), Byzantine emperor, 250
Nicephorus Briennius, revolts in Albania, 250
Nicephorus Gregoras, Byzantine historian, 323
Nicephorus Phocas, Byzantine emperor, 179 f.
Nichiren, founded the Lotus sect, 356
Nicholas, Nicolaievich, Grand Duke, Russian commander-in-
    chief, 914, 922
Nicholas of Cologne, and the Children's Crusade, 257
Nicholas of Hereford, coadjutor of John Wiclif, 266
Nicholas of Rumania, Prince regent for Michael I, 1025
Nicholas I, king of Montenegro, 715, 950, 1016
Nicholas I, Pope, 152, 153
Nicholas II (Gerard), Pope, 206, 218
Nicholas III (Giovanni Gaetano Orsini), Pope, 221
Nicholas IV (Girolamo Masci), Pope, 221, 346
Nicholas V (Tomaso da Sarzana), Pope, 289 f.
Nicholas I, Tsar of Russia, 674, 680, 726, 727
Nicholas II, Tsar of Russia, 706, 707, 731, 745, 754, 755, 757,
    761, 762, 882, 1028, 1032
Nicholson, Francis, British general, 514
Nicholson's Nek, battle of, 857
Nicias, Conservative leader in Athens, 58, 59, 60
Nicias, Peace of, 59
Nicolaiev, occupied by Germans-Austrians, 943
Nicolet, Jean, French explorer, 506 f.
Nicolle, Charles, control of typhus, 553

Nicolle, Leon, Swiss Socialist Deputy, 995
Nicomedes I, 37
Nicomedes III, 37, 93, 95
Nicomedia, 118, 120
Nicopolis, battle of, 319, 323, 326
Nicuesa, Diego de, founded Nombre de Dios, 486
Niebuhr, Barthold Georg, German historian, 551, 594
Niedermayer, Oskar von, German agent in Persia, 1107
Niemoeller, Martin, German churchman, 1001 f.
Nien Fei, captured Shanghai, 879
Niepce, Joseph Nicéphore, made the celeripede, 554
Nieuport, held by British, 914
Nigel, Bishop of Ely, 196
Niger, French colony, 1089
Niger, Justus Caius Fescennius, Emperor of Syria, 114
Nigeria, 6; north and south, British colonies, 842, 1088
Nightingale, Florence, nursing services in Crimean War, 727
Nihonshoki (or Nihongi), history of Japan written in Chinese, 350
Nijmwegen, Treaty of, 443, 450
Nika Insurrection, in Constantinople, 172
Nikayas, 42, 129
Nikolas, Patriarch, 179
Nikolsburg, Peace of, 686
Nikon, Patriarch, reforms Russian Orthodox Church, 478
Nile, battle of, 586
Nîmes, 113
Nine-Power Treaty, 1118
Nine Years' War, of Japan, 353
Nineteenth amendment, of U.S. Constitution, 1050
Ninety-Day Embargo, by U.S., 769
Nineveh, 13, 25, 27, 28, 40, 127, 174
Ningpo, opened to trade, 879
Niño, Alonso, Spanish explorer, 488
Nioroan culture, 18
Nippur, 25
Nirvana, 42
Nisaea, 59, 60
Nish, taken by Bulgars, 927; taken by Serbs, 949
Nishi, Kwanjiro, Viscount, Japanese general, 749, 886, 892
Nishihara, Japanese agent in Manchuria, 1118
Nisibis, 28, 124 ff.
Nitard, Everard, Jesuit adviser of Marie Anne of Austria, 450
Nitti, Francesco Saverio, Italian premier, 987
Nivelle, Gen. Robert Georges, French general, 930, 938
Nixon, Sir John Eccles, British general, 927
Niza, Fray Marcos de, Spanish missionary, 491
Nizam al-Mulk, vizier, 254
Nizar, 262
Nō, Japanese lyric drama, 358, 546
Noae, 57
Noailles, Louis Marie Antoine, Viscount de, in the French Revolution, 579
Nobile, Gen. Umberto, Arctic explorer, 566, 569 f.
Nobiling, Dr. Karl, attempt on Emperor William I of Germany, 689
Nobilior, Marcus Fulvius, subdues Aetolians, 80
Nobrega, Manuel de, Jesuit missionary in Brazil, 501
Nobunaga, Oda, sets up puppet shōgun in Kyōto, 542, 543
Nobuyori, 354
Nogaret, Guillaume de, threatens Pope Boniface VIII, 222, 232
Nogi, Count Maresuke, Japanese commander, 892
Noir, Victor, French Republican journalist, 636
Nola, 87
Nomura, Admiral, Japanese envoy to U.S., 1166
Non-Aggression Pact, Russia and Japan, 1150
Nonconformists, and Common Prayer Book, 426
Non-Intercourse Law, in U.S., 769
Non-intervention agreements on Spain, 970, 983
Non-jurors, in England, 430
Norbanus, Caius, 94
Nordenfeldt, Thorsten, built first naval submarine, 556
Nordenskiöld, Prof. Nils Adolf Erik, Arctic explorer, 564, 565
Nordenskiöld, Dr. Otto, Arctic explorer, 574
Nordics, 12, 16
Nördlingen, battle of, 407
Norfolk Island, 896, 898, 899, 901
Norge, Gen. Nobile's dirigible, 566
Noricum, 102, 150
Norinaga, Motoori, a Shinto scholar, 887
Noriyori, brother of Yoritomo, 354
Norman Conquest, 167
Normandy, 158, 159, 225, 227, 268, 270, 278; invaded by Allied Expeditionary Forces, 1142, 1154
Normandy, Duke of, 225
Normans, on coast of Spain, 163; colony in Ireland, 169; in Italy, 249 f., 252; in Balkans, 253
Norodom, King of Cambodia, 874
Norris, David Thomas, British naval commander, 1107
Norse, in Scotland, 168; in Ireland, 169
Norsemen, on American continent, 365; early Arctic exploration, 558
North, Frederick, Earl of Guilford, British prime minister, 436, 520, 521
North Africa, 1140, 1159 f.
North America, 505 ff.
North American Act, British, 1060
North Borneo Co., chartered by Britain, 877
North Briton, No. 45, 435
North Carolina, established as a royal govt., 513
North Caucasus, 1153

North Dakota, admitted to statehood, 784
North Foreland, Van Tromp defeated by the English, 425; Albemarle defeated by De Ruyter and De Witt, 427
North German Confederation, 635, 686
North Pole, conquest of, 566
Northampton, battle of, 270; Treaty of, 272
Northbrook, Thomas George Baring, Earl of, viceroy of India, 870
Northeastern Confederacy, planned by American Federalists, 768
Northern Ch'i dynasty, overthrown by Northern Chou, 136
Northern Pacific Panic, 789
Northern Pacific R.R., completed, 783
Northern Rhodesia, under administration of South Africa Co., 858
Northern Securities Co., 789
Northern Society, secret organization at St. Petersburg, 702
Northern Territory of Australia, 901; becomes federal possession, 904
Northern War, 471, 474, 480
Northern Wei dynasty, in China, 43, 135
Northumberland, Anglo-Saxon kingdom, 166, 168
Northumberland, John Dudley, Duke of, lord protector, 373
Northwest Co. of Canada, 792
Northwest Ordinance, for govt. of the Northwest, 522 f.
Northwest Rebellion in Canada, 797
Northwest Territories, purchased from the Hudson Bay Co., 796
Northwestern Alliance, in U.S., 785
Norway, 170, 204, 312, 410, 474 f., 569 f., 577, 602, 699 ff., 966, 1045, 1046 ff.; in Second World War, invaded by Germany, 1135, 1146; 1138, 1146; merchant tonnage, 1156; 1158
Norwegian Society, of Copenhagen, 475
Norwegian-Swedish expedition, by sledge to Northeast Land, 570
Noske, Gustav, German statesman, 996
Notium, 61
Nottingham, Daniel Finch, Earl of, English statesman, 430, 434
Novaesium, 108
Novara, Austrian scientific expedition, 895
Novara, Swiss defeated French, 382, 388, 394, 409; Piedmontese defeated by the Austrians, 655
Nova Scotia, formerly Acadia, 514
Novatians, 117
Novellae of Justinian, 173
Novgorod (St. Peter's Yard), 307, 318, 1154
Novi, battle of, 587
Novi Bazar, taken by the Italians, 949
Novo-Georgievsk, stormed by Germans, 922
Novorossisk, 1153
Novosiltsov, Nikolai Nikolaevich, Russian reformer, 701
Noyon, in Germans' possession, 914, 938, 945; taken by British and French, 950; Treaty of, 394
Nripatungavarman, 337
Nubar Pasha, Egyptian prime minister, 831
Nubia, 23, 24
Nullification doctrine, in U.S., 771
Numa Pompilius, early King of Rome, 69, 86, 99
Numantia, 90
Numerianus, Marcus Aurelius Numerius, co-Augustus, 116
Numidia, 98
Nuñez, Rafael, pres. of Colombia, 815
Nuño Tristam, explorer, 363
Nur al-Din, opponent of the crusaders, 254, 262
Nur Jahan, wife of Jahangir, 533
Nuraghis, 17
Nurhachi, Manchu leader, 536
Nürnberg, German cruiser, 917, 918
Nürnberg, Peace of, 401
Nürnberg Laws, in Nazi Germany, 1001
Nushirwan, last of the Il-Khans of Persia, 262, 330
Nuzi, 28
Nyasa, Lake, discovered, 826
Nyaya, 131
Nygaardsvold, Johan, premier of Norway, 1046
Nymphaion, Treaty of, 260
Nymphenburg, alliance against Austria, 465
Nyon Conference and Agreement, 984
Nystadt, Treaty of, 474, 480

Oates, Titus, Popish Plot, 428
Oath of abjuration, in England, 431
Oath of Salisbury, 191
Oaths of allegiance and supremacy, 430
Oaths of Strassburg, 157
Ob River, 7, 14
Obando, José María, pres. of New Granada, 815
Obaydullah al-Mahdi, of the Fatimids, caliph, 190, 262
Obelisks, as symbols, 21; 23
Oberlin College, 771
Obolla, taken by Moslems, 127, 184
Obradović, Dositey, Serbian scholar, 721
Obregón, Gen. Alvaro, president of Mexico, 1074, 1075
Obrenovich, Milosh, Prince of Serbia, 712, 714, 722
O'Brians of Munster, 169
O'Brien, William Smith, heads Young Ireland Party, 612
Obruchev, Prof. Sergei Vladimirovich, Russian explorer, 570
Obry, Ludwig, invented the gyroscope, 556
Ocampo, David Samanez, pres. of Peru, 1068
Ocampo, Sebastian de, Spanish explorer, 368
Ocaña, battle of, 394
Occasional Conformity Bill, in England, 432, 434

Occultism, cult of, 135
Oceania, 7, 18
Ochrid, patriarchate of, 183, 184
Ochs, Peter, Swiss radical, 460
O'Connell, Daniel, Irish leader, 606, 607, 612
O'Connor, Feargus Edward, chartist leader, 609
O'Connors, of Connaught, 169
Octavia, Octavian's sister, 99, 106
Octavian (Gaius Julius Caesar Octavianus), Roman emperor, 85, 98, 99, 101. *See also* Augustus
Octavius, Cnaius, 93
Octavius, Marcus, 91
October Manifesto, in Russia, 709
Octobrist Party, in Russia, 707
Oda, Dane, Archbishop of Canterbury, 167
Odenathus, Septimius, ruler of Palmyra, 116, 124
Oderic of Pordenone, medieval traveler, 346, 362
Odessa, bombarded, 919; occupied by Germans-Austrians, 943; taken by the Bolsheviks, 1031; 1137, 1151, 1154
Odo (Eudes), Count, King of the West Franks, 158–60
O'Donnell, Leopold, Duke of Tetuan, Spanish statesman, 646
O'Donojú, Juan, viceroy of Mexico, 804
Odovacar (Odoacer), 122, 144
O'Duffy, Gen. Owen, leader of the United Ireland Party, 973
Odysseus (Ulysses), 47
Odyssey, 46, 47
Ōe Hiromoto, Japanese scholar, 355
Oecumenical councils of the Church, 119, 141, 175, 178
Oenophyta, 56
Offa II, King of Mercia, 166
Offnet, 16
Ogdensburg, French mission, 515
Ogedei, Mongol khan, 344, 345
Oglethorpe, James, English colonizer, 514, 515
O'Higgins, Bernardo, supreme director, in Chile, 801, 808
O'Higgins, Kevin, Irish statesman, 972, 973
Ohio, admitted to the Union, 766
Ohio Co., 515, 766
Oil, Drake's well, 555; fields in Persia, 865
Oil pipe-line, from Iraq to Haifa, 1106
Oirat, chief of a Mongol confederation, 347
Ojeda, Alonso de, Spanish conquistador, 367 *f.*, 486
Ōjōyōshū, religious movement in Japan, 353
Ōkada, Adm. Keisuke, premier of Japan, 1126
Okhrid, taken by Bulgars, 927
Okinawa, 1169
Okitsugu, Tanuma (Mototsugu), 548
Oklahoma, admitted to statehood, 784
Ōkubo, Toshmichi, of the Satsuma, 899, 890
Ōkuma, Marquis Shigenobu, Japanese premier, 890, 891, 1123
Olaf, ruler of Denmark, 311
Olaf (I) Trygvesson of Norway, 204
Olaf II (St. Olaf), of Norway, 204
Old-Age and Invalidity Insurance Law, in Germany, 690 *f.*, 692
Old-Age Pension Law, in England, 620; in Denmark, 697; in Australia, 904
Old Believers, Church of, in Russia, 478
Old Stone culture, 2
Old Stone Mill (Newport), supposed Norse remains, 365
Old Testament, Sheol, 25; 29, 30, 32
Oldcastle, Sir John (Lord Cobham), leading Lollard, 268
Older Stone Age, 6
Oldowan industry, 6
Oleg, Russian prince, 243
Olga, Princess of Russia, 179, 243
Olgerd, Lithuanian prince, 316
Olid, Cristobal de, Spanish conquistador, 488, 491
Oliva, Treaty of, 475
Olivares, Gaspar de Guzman, Count, Duke of Santander, administrator for Philip IV of Spain, 390
Oliveira Salazar, Antonio de, Portuguese premier, 986
Oliver, James, invented plow with chilled steel moldboard, 781
Ollivier, Émile, French statesman, 634, 635
Olmo Man, 9
Olney, Richard, American statesman, 785, 786
Oltenitza, battle of, 727
Olybrius, 122
Olympias, 77
Olympic Games, revived in Greece, 709
Olynthus, 63, 64
Omalian culture, 17
Omar, viceregent of Mohammed, assumed title of Amir al-Mu'minin (Prince of the Faithful), 184, 186
Omar ibn Abdul-Aziz, caliph, 187
Omar Khayyám, Persian poet, 254
Omar Pasha, Turkish general, 715, 727
Omar Zarhuni, pretender to Moroccan throne, 838
Omayyad Caliphate, 186
Omayyad dynasty of Cordova, 163, 164, 188; fall of caliphate, 176; fall of the kingdom, 187, 188, 262
Omdurman, battle of, 748, 833
Omens, interpretation of, 26
Omortag, Bulgar ruler, 182
Omri, 31
Omsk, taken by Czech troops, 947
Ōmura, opened Nagasaki to foreign trade, 543
On, 21
Oñate, Juan de, secured submission of New Mexico, 492
O'Neill, Hugh, Earl of Tyrone, leads Irish rebellion, 373

O'Neills of Ulster, 169
Onin War, over succession in great Japanese families, 359
Ono Imoko, first official envoy of Japan, 140
Onomarchus, defeated by Philip II, 64
Open Door Note, on China, 749
Opera, its development, 454
Opis, 25
Opium, trade in, 871, 877, 878, 879, 883, 959
Opium War, 609
Oporto, revolution, 648
Oppert, Ernst, expedition to rifle royal tombs of Korea, 885
Optants' dispute with Hungary, settled, 1026
Oqba ibn Nafi, conquers North Africa, 186, 187
Oran, 1135; battle of, 1148, 1158; 1160
Orange Free State, 852, 853, 855, 857, 858
Orange-Nassau, Prince of (Later William IV), 440, 850
Orange River Sovereignty, 852
Orangia Unie, organization in the Orange River Colony, 858
Oranian culture, 6, 8
Orations, Olynthiac, Philippic, 64; Mark Antony over Caesar, 98
Orations against Catiline, 96
Orbegosa, Luis, pres. of Peru, 811, 812
Orchomenos, 46, 52, 64, 94
Orchon inscriptions, 324
Ordaz, Diego de, South American explorer, 488
Ordenaçoes Affonsinas, law code of Portugal, 286
Ordinance of Secession, in U.S., 775
Ordinance of 1293, in Florence, 293
Ordonnances, first issued by Louis IX, 231
Ordono III of Leon, 164
Örebro, Synod of, 410 *f.*
Oregon, adopts principle of recall of all elective officials, 789
Oregon Boundary Treaty with U.S., 612, 795
Orel, 1151, 1154
Orellana, Francisco de, sought to conquer Amazonian territory, 489
Orellana, Gen. José, pres. of Guatemala, 1074
Orellana, Gen. Manuel, pres. of Guatemala, 1074
Orestes, defeated in battle, 122
Organic Act of Alaska, 798
Organic Statute, in Rumania, 719
Organization of Labor, by Louis Blanc, 549
Oribe, Manuel, headed *Blancos* in Uruguay, 811
Oriental religions, 113
Origen, neo-Platonist, 117
Origin of man, 1, 2
Origin of Species, The, by Charles Darwin, 551
Orissa, 43
Orkhan I, Ottoman sultan, 322, 330
Orlando, Vittorio Emanuele, Italian premier, 942, 987
Orlando Furioso, poem by Ariosto, 392
Orléans, city of, 147, 270, 278
Orléans, Duke of, attacked Guienne, 268
Orléans, Duke of, proposed marriage to daughter of Charles V, 395
Orléans, Duke of (Philippe Egalite), in the French Revolution, 581, 583
Orléans, Louis Philippe Robert, Duke of, Arctic explorer, 568
Orlov, Alexis Fedorovich, Prince, Russian diplomat, 728
Orlov, brothers, Alexei Grigoryevich, Count, and Grigori Grigoryevich, and palace revolution in Russia, 481
Orm, his *Ormulum*, 201
Ormond, James Butler, 2d Duke of, British commander-in-chief, 432, 434
Orne River, 1163
Orodes I, defeated Crassus, 83
Orontes, 23
Orosius, Paulus, his *History* translated by Alfred the Great, 167
Orsini, the, 293
Orsini, Clarice, wife of Lorenzo de' Medici, 295
Orsini, Felice, attempts to assassinate Napoleon III, 613, 633, 657
Ortiz, Roberto Marcelino, pres. of Argentina, 1064
Ortiz Rubio, Pascual, pres. of Mexico, 1076
Ortuqid dynasty of Diyar-Bakr (Diarbekr), 254 *f.*
Ōsaka, allied naval demonstration, 889
Ōsaka Castle, destroyed, 546
Osborn, Sherard, Arctic explorer, 564
Osborne, visit of Napoleon III to, 720
Osborne, Sir Thomas (later Earl of Danby), English statesman, 43
Oscans, 68
Oscar I, King of Sweden-Norway, 699
Oscar II, King of Sweden, 699, 701
O'Shea, Capt. William Henry, and the Parnell divorce suit, 617
Oslo, 1146; Convention, 1045
Osman (Orthman) I, founder of the Ottoman dynasty, 324
Osman Beg Kara Iluk, founder of the White Sheep dynasty, 330
Osman Digna, lieutenant of the Mahdi, 832
Ospina, Mariano, pres. of New Granada, 815
Ospina, Pedro Nel, pres. of Colombia, 1069
Ostend, in German possession, 914; taken by British, 946, 950; 1146, 1149
Ostend East India Co., 434, 439 *f.*
Ostend Manifesto, on the acquisition of Cuba by U.S., 775
Ostermann, Andrei Ivanovich, foreign minister of Russia, 479
Ostermann-Tolstoi, Alexander Ivanovich, Count, Russian general, 599
Ostmark (against the Avars), 155

Ostracism, 53–57
Ostrogoths (Amals), 121, 122, 143, 144, 145–47
Oswald of Northumbria, 166
Oswego, established, 513
Otago, in New Zealand, settled, 906, 907
Otawi, taken by Gen. Botha, 918
Othman, member of the Omayyad family of Mecca, 186
Otho, Marcus Salvius, husband of Poppaea Sabina, 106, 107
Otis, Gen. Elwell Stephen, head of Philippine govt., 909
Otis, James, American revolutionary, 517
Ōtomo clan, in Japan, 139
Ottar (Othere), Norse explorer, 558
Ottawa, parliament buildings destroyed, 1057
Ottawa Imperial Economic Conference, 969
Otto I (the Great), German emperor, 160, 161 f., 216, 220
Otto II, German emperor, 162, 216
Otto III, German emperor, 159, 162, 216
Otto I, King of Greece, 709, 724
Otto, claimant to throne of Austria-Hungary, 956, 1014
Otto of Bavaria, King of Hungary, 317
Otto of Brandenburg, regent for Wenceslas II, 241
Otto of Brunswick (Welf), against Philip of Swabia (Waiblinger), 211
Otto, Nikolaus, his silent gas engine, 555
Ottokar I, Bohemian king, 240
Ottokar II (the Great), Bohemian king, 213, 215, 240 f., 246, 299
Ottoman Bank, attacked by Armenian revolutionaries, 746
Ottoman National Debt Administration, 729
Ottoman Turks (see also Turks), history, 299, 324 ff., 420 ff., 482 ff., 596, 721 ff., 734 ff., 759 ff., 919 ff., 963, 1103 ff.
Ottonian Renaissance, 162
Otumba, battle of, 491
Ouchy, Convention, 974, 976; Treaty of, 662
Dudenarde, battle of, 432, 446
Oudh, 130; annexed by Britain, 870
Oudinot, Nicolas Charles, Duke of Reggio, French general, 598, 599, 600
Oudinot, Gen. Nicolas Charles Victor 2d, Duke of Reggio, French general, 631, 655
Oudney, Walter, African explorer, 826
Ourcq, battle of, 914
Ourique, battle of, 238
Outer Mongolia, 1171
Ou-yang Hsiu, his New History of the T'ang, 343
Ovando, Nicolás de, gov. of Española, 496
Overweg, Adolf, African explorer, 826
Ovid (Publius Ovidius Naso), Roman poet, 112
Oviedo, Gonzalo de, Spanish historian, 389
Owen, Maj. Douglas Charles, at Wadelai, 849
Owen, Robert, English Socialist, 549, 608, 771
Owen, Adm. William FitzWilliam, at Delagoa Bay, 846
Oxenham, John, English mariner, 494
Oxenstierna, Axel Gustafsson, chancellor of Sweden, 406, 413
Oxenstierna, Count Johan Axelsson, son of the preceding, 908
Oxford, Robert Harley, Earl of, English statesman, 433, 434
Oxford Movement, 612
Oxford University, 194, 567, 569, 570
Oxley, John, explores interior of Australia, 898
Oyama, Prince Iwao, Japanese general, 892

Paardeberg, battle of, 857
Paasikivi, Juho, Finnish statesman, 1143
Pacheco Pereira, Duarte, Portuguese discoverer, 367, 368
Paches, fleet commander, 58
Pacific, Second World War in the, 1167 ff.
Pacification of Dunse, 376
Pacification of Ghent, 381
Pacification of Limerick, 430
Pacifico, David, claim against Greek govt., 612
Pacifist agitators, in France, 939
Pacores, 128
Pact of Amapala, 1074
Pact of Biac-na-bato, 909
Pact of Bordeaux, 637
Pact of Halepa, 729, 731, 745
Pact of Paris, 960, 1052
Pacte de famille (Family Pact), between France and Spain, 451
Pacte de famine, an attempt to corner the grain trade, 448
Pacuvius, 91
Paderborn, 103
Paderewski, Ignace Jan, premier of Poland, 1038
Padilla, Juan de, leads uprising against Charles I in Spain, 388
Padlock Law, in Spain, 648
Padma-sambhava, modifies the Buddhism of Tibet, 340
Padua, given to the Carrara family, 299
Paekche, Korean state, 137, 140
Pães, Gen. Sidonio, president of Portugal, 985
Paestum, discovery of the temples, 458
Paets, Konstantin, president of Estonia, 1044
Paetus, L. Caesennius, defeated by Armenians, 106
Paetus, Thrasea, Stoic, 107, 108
Páez, Federico, pres. of Ecuador, 1069
Páez, José Antonio, pres. of Venezuela, 803, 816
Páez, Pedro, missionary to Ethiopia, 524
Pagan, Bulgar ruler, 182
Pagan Min, King of Burma, 872
Paganism, campaign against, 141, 151; in Ireland, 169
Page, Charles, electric locomotive, 554

Page, Dr. Earle Christmas Grafton, leader of the Australian Country Party, 1129
Page, Walter Hines, American diplomat, 935
Pago Pago, in Samoa, acquired by U.S., 911
Pahlavas, in eastern Iran, 128
Pahleri, Mohammed Riza, Iran leader, 1137
Pai Ch'ung-hsi, Chinese military strategist, 1119
Paine, Thomas, his Common Sense, 520
Painlevé, Paul, French premier, 939, 941
Painted Porch, 77
Paintings, in caves, 5
Paisi, monk, his History of the Bulgarian People, 717
Paisiello, Giovanni, Italian dramatic composer, 454
Paithan, 129
Paiva, Alfonso de, expedition to Ethiopia and India, 364
Paix des Dames, Treaty of Cambrai, 400
Paixhans, Henri Joseph, introduced the shell gun, 554
Palace School, of Charlemagne, 155, 157
Palacio, Raimundo Anduza, pres. of Venezuela, 816
Palácky, Francis, Czech historian, 673
Palaeobotany, method of dating, 2
Palaeolithic period, 1–9; culture, 2, 4, 5, 17, 44; in Greece, 47; cave-dwelling Man in Italy, 68
Palaeologi, Byzantine dynasty, 319, 320
Palaeologus, Constantine, conquers Frankish Morea, 323
Palaeologus, Thomas, 323
Palaeontology, method of dating, 2
Palafox y Melzi, José de, Spanish patriot leader, 594
Palamas, Gregory, disciple of the Hesychasts, 323
Palau Islands, discovered, 894; bought by Germany, 896; occupied by Japanese, 918; 1169
Palembang, factory set up by the Dutch, 876
Palembang, Prince of, 347
Palermo, taken by the Arabs, 23; 1162
Palermo stone, 23
Palestine, early history, 29, 32; conflicts between Arabs and Jews, 1101
Palestine, Conference of Jews and Arabs, in London, 1102
Palestine mandate, 970
Palestine-Syria, in Post-Palaeolithic period, 13; of the Middle Kingdom, 23
Palestrina, Giovanni di, Italian musician, 392
Pali Theravadins, see Sthaviravadins
Palice, 57
Palladius, Bishop, mission in Ireland, 169
Pallas, freedman, 105, 106
Pallava, warrior dynasty, 130, 335
Pallavicini, Giorgio, Italian leader, 657
Palm, Johann Philipp, bookseller of Nürnberg, 592
Palma, Bautillo, pres. of Guatemala, 1074
Palma, Tomás Estrada, pres. of the Cuban Republic, 822
Palmer, Nathaniel Brown, explored Palmer Archipelago, 573
Palmerston, Henry John Temple, 3d Viscount, British statesman, 612, 613, 622, 645, 654, 666, 676, 725, 726, 830
Palmyra, 34
Palo Alto, battle of, 773
Pamir boundary, with Afghanistan, 868
Pamphylia, 84, 96
Pan Ch'ao, Ruler of Turkestan, 128, 134, 135
Pan Ku, compiled History of the Former Han, 135
Panactum, 59
Panaetius, 91
Panama, 791, 815, 818, 819, 1072, 1137, 1154, 1155; Republic of, 1155
Panama Congress, planned by Simón Bolívar, 771
Panama Tolls Bill, 791
Pan American Airways, Transoceanic service, 558
Pan-American Conferences, 784; at Buenos Aires, 1054 f.; Declaration of Lima, 1057, 1062; 1135; at Havana, 1136; at Panama, 1154
Pan-American Highway, 1155
Pan-American Union, 784, 1156
Panammu I and II, 35
Pan-Arab Congress, at Bludan, 1100, 1101, 1104, 1106
Panay (U.S.S.), attacked by Japanese bombers, 1122
Panchakrama, 331
Panchan Lama, at Tashalumpo, 540
Panchasiddhantika, 131
Panchatantra, 131
Pandects, of Justinian, 173
"Pandion," a king, 129
Pando, José, pres. of La Paz, 812
Pandulph, papal legate in England, 198
Pandus, 43
Pandya, 129
Pangalos, Gen. Theodore, Dictator of Greece, 1021
Pangkov, Treaty of, 875
Panhard and Levassor, develop automobiles, 556
Panic of 1857, 775; of 1893, 786
Panini, gives earliest Sanskrit grammar, 42
Panipat, battles of; Babar defeated Ibrahim Shah Lodi, 530; Ahmad Shah defeated the Marathas, 530, 535
Panis, Étienne Jean, and the September massacres in Paris, 581
Panium, battle of, 81
Pannonia, 103, 150
Pannonian legions, revolt suppressed, 103
Panormus, 52, 86
Pansa, Roman consul, 98
Pan-Slav Congress, 673
Pan-Slav movement, 705

Pantheon, 113
Panther, gunboat, on a mission to Agadir, 693, 757, 839
Panticapaeum, 57
Pantjar, 128
Pao T'ing-po, Chinese author, 541
Paoli, Pasquale, Corsican leader, 459
Paoting, taken by Japanese, 1121
Papacy, early years, 141, 142, 206, 215 *ff.*, 286 *ff.*, 395 *ff.*, 454 *ff.*, 663 *ff.*, 992 *ff.*
Papak, vassal-king of Parthia, 124
Papal coronation, 155
Papal infallibility, 664, 688
Papal Legations, in insurrections, 658
Papal States, *see* Papacy
Papeete, bombarded, 917
Papen, Col. Franz von, German chancellor, 990, 999
Paper, manufacture of, 135
Paper currency, in China, 1121
Paper-making machine, 553
Paphlagonia, 37, 93
Papineau, Louis Joseph, Canadian rebel leader, 795
Papinian, Aemilius, murdered by Emperor Caracalla, 114; 116
Papists' Disabling Act, 428
Pappenheim, Gottfried Heinrich, Count of, imperial general, 406
Papua, new name for New Guinea, 904
Papuans, in the Negroid group, 12, 18
Parachute troops, German, 1151
Paraetacene, battle at, 77
Paraguay, 799, 801, 808, 810, 1065 *f.*, 1135
Paraguayan War, 808, 811, 817
Parakramabahu I and II of Ceylon, 338
Paramaras of Dhara, Munja, and Bhoja, 332
Pardo, Manuel, pres. of Peru, 813
Pardo y Barreda, José, pres. of Peru, 1068
Pareto, Vilfredo, his *Treatise of General Sociology*, 551
Parinirvana-sutra, 136
Paris, established as a capital, 147; 158–60, 231, 270, 279, 601, 623, 628, 636, 637
Paris, Treaties of, 230, 435, 436, 451, 494, 495, 502, 516, 535, 703, 728, 787, 823, 859, 864, 866, 909
Paris Commune, *see* Commune
Pâris, François de, archdeacon, 447
Paris, International Exposition of, 1855, 633
Paris, Louis Philippe Albert d'Orléans, Count of, 630, 637
Paris, Matthew, monk of St. Albans, 201
Park, Mungo, African explorer, 826
Parker, Alton Brooks, defeated for presidency of U.S., 789
Parkes, Sir Harry Smith, British envoy to China, 879
Parkes, Sir Henry, pres. of first Australasian Federal Convention, 902, 903
Parlamento of Milan, 296
Parlements of France, 448
Parliament, its origin, 198; development, 200
Parliament Bill, 620
Parliament House, in Australia, 1130
Parliament of England, 265 *ff.*; 425, 426, 432 *ff.*, 966
Parliament of Ravennika, 259
Parliament of Westminster, 264
Parliament of York, 264
Parliamentary reform, in England, 605
Parma, 220
Parmenides of Elea, 53
Parmenio, 65
Parnell, Charles Stewart, Irish leader, 616, 617
"Parnellism and Crime," articles in London *Times*, 617
Paros, 53
Parr, Catharine, 6th wife of Henry VIII, 369
Parry, Lt. Edward, Arctic explorer, 562, 563
Parry, William, plot against Queen Elizabeth, 373
Parsashatar, 28
Parsis, refugees in Kathiawar, 337
Parsons, Sir Charles, compound steam turbine, 556
Parsons' Cause, 517
Parsya, 41
Parthenon, temple of Athens, 62
Parthenopean Republic, 586
Parthia, 81–83
Parthian War, 99, 110, 114
Parthians, 26, 39, 97, 102
Parti Ouvrier Français, 639
Parti Ouvrier Socialiste Revolutionnaire Français, 639
Partisans, in Yugoslavia, 1154
Partito Popolare, Catholic party in Italy, 986
Paschal II, Pope, 207, 219
Paschal III, anti-pope, 220
Pashich, Nicholas, Serbian statesman, 714, 715, 1017
Paskievich, Ivan Feodorovich, Russian general, 674, 702, 724, 862
Pass of Thermopylae, 54
Passage graves, 15, 18
Passarowitz, Treaty of, 458, 484
Passchendaele, in German possession, 914
Passfield White Paper, on landless Arabs, 1101
Pasteur, Louis, French scientist, 552
Paston Letters, 271
Pastoral, of Gregory the Great, 151
Pataliputra, 42, 130
Pataria, a movement for clerical celibacy, 217 *f.*
Paterson, William, vice-gov. of New South Wales, 896
Patiño, José, Spanish reform minister, 451
Patriarch of Constantinople, 142, 151, 175

Patriarchate, set up at Preslay, 180, 183, 184
Patriarchs, position in Church, 141, 175
Patricians, of Rome, 69, 71, 73
Patrick (St.), missionary to Ireland, 168 *f.*
Patrimonium Petri, 215, 216
Patriot Party, of Holland, 440
Patriotic National Movement, dissolved by Finland, 1048
Patrons of Husbandry, in U.S., 782
Patroons, in New Amsterdam, 510
Patterson, Robert, Federal general, 776
Patzinaks (Pechenegs), 183, 243, 245, 248, 250, 252
Paul I, Tsar of Russia, 482, 586
Paul II (Pietro Barbo), Pope, 290
Paul III (Alessandro Farnese), Pope, 396
Paul IV (Gian Pietro Caraffa), Pope, 396
Paul V (Camillo Borghese), Pope, 397
Paul, apostle, 141
Paul, jurist, 116
Paul, Prince, regent of Yugoslavia, 1018, 1136, 1150
Paul the Deacon, his *History of the Lombards*, 151
Paulinus, Gaius Suetonius, Roman general, 106
Paulicians, campaign against them, 178, 183
Paullus, Lucius Aemilius, Roman general, 80, 87, 89
Pauncefote, Julian, 1st Baron, British diplomat, 788
Pausanias, King of Sparta, 54, 61
Pavia, 122; Lombard capital, 150, 152, 162; battle of, 370, 388, 394, 400
Pavia, Félix, pres. of Paraguay, 1066
Pavón, battle of, 808
Payer, Julius, Arctic explorer, 564
Payne-Aldrich Tariff, 790, 909 *f.*
Payne, Sereno Elisha, co-author of Payne-Aldrich Tariff, 790
Pazmany, Peter, Cardinal, promotes Counter-Reformation in Transylvania, 420
Pazzi, the, Italian bankers, 290
Pazzi Conspiracy, 290, 295 *f.*, 298
Peace, of Aix-la-Chapelle, 435, 442; of Akroinon, 252; of Almazan, 280; of Arras, 279; of Augsburg, 402; of Bergerac or Poitiers, 384; of Bretigny, 265, 276; of Callias, 56; of Caltabelotta, 290; of Cateau-Cambrésis, 383 *f.*; of Chastenoy, 384; of Constance, 210, 306; of Étaples, 369; of God, 217, 227; of Leoben, 585; of Madrid, 400; of Nagyvárad, 419; of Nicias, 59; of Nikolsburg, 686; of Nürnberg, 401; of Phoenice, 80, 87; of Pyrenees, 426, 449; of San Germano, 211; of Stralsund; 309; of Thorn, 302, 310, 314; of Troyes, 373; of Vossem, 442; of Wedmore, 167; of Westphalia, 390; of Wordingborg, 309; of 562, 172; of 955, 164; of 1126, 252; of 1176, 253; of 1295, 222; of 1302, 222; organization of, after Second World War, 1170 *f.*
Peace Conference at Paris, 951, 952, 1118, 1123
Peace Congress, at Paris, 633
Peace Convention, at Washington, 775
Peace Preservation Act, in Ireland, 614, 616
Pearl, The, mystical poem, 267
Pearl Harbor, in Hawaii, 910, 1166
Pearse, Patrick Henry, leads Easter Rebellion in Ireland, 971
Pearson, Paul Martin, gov. of the Virgin Islands, 1080
Peary, Lt. Robert Edwin, Arctic explorer, 565, 566
Peasant Party, in Bulgaria, 1022, 1023
Peasant uprising, in France, 579
Peasants' League, in Germany, 691
Peasants' Revolt, in England, 267
Peasants' War, in Germany, 400
Peč, Patriarchate, 319
Peçanha, Nilo, pres. of Brazil, 818
Pedius, Roman consul, 98
Pedro I, Emperor of Brazil, 648, 817
Pedro II, Emperor of Brazil, 817
Pedro the Cruel, *see* Peter (Pedro the Cruel)
Peel, Robert, British prime minister, 605, 606, 608, 609, 611, 612
Peel, Thomas, 899
Peel, William Robert Wellesley, report on Palestine mandate, 970, 1101
Pegolotti, Francesco, Florentine trader, 362
Pehrsson, Axel, premier of Sweden, 1047
P'ei Chü, appointed to command in the west, 137
Peip'ing, new name for Peking, 1119
Peisander, 60
Peisistratids, 48
Peisistratus, 51, 52
Peixoto, Floriano, pres. of Brazil, 818
Pekah, 31
Pekahiah, 31
Peking, 879, 1119, 1121; Treaty of, 703
Peking-Hankow Railway, 882
Peking Man (*Sinanthropus pekinensis*), 6, 9, 43
Pelagius, papal legate, 257, 302
Pelagonia, battle of, 260
Pelayo, creates Kingdom of the Asturias, 164
Pelham, Henry, prime minister, 434
Pellegrini, Cárlos, pres. of Argentina, 808
Pelliot, Paul, French orientalist, 884
Pelloux, Gen. Luigi, prime minister of Italy, 661
Pelopidas, 63
Peloponnese, 46 *passim*
Peloponnesian League, 50, 56, 58
Peloponnesian Wars, 55–62
Peloponnesus, cultures in, 16
Pelops, King of Sparta, 80
Pelusium, 24, 127
Pembroke, Richard de Clare, 2d Earl of, 169

Peña, Luis Sáenz, pres. of Argentina, 808
Peña, Roque Sáenz, pres. of Argentina, 808
Peñaranda, Enrique, President of Bolivia, 1141
Pendleton, George Hunt, author of the Pendleton Act, 783
Penicillin, 553
Peninsula Campaign, in American Civil War, 778
Peninsular & Oriental Line (P. & O.), 554
Peninsular War, 593
Penitentiary pilgrimages, to Jerusalem, 255
Penn, William, given a charter for Pennsylvania, 512
Penna, Affonso Augusto Moreira, pres. of Brazil, 818
Pennsylvania, charter granted, 512
Penny postage instituted, 609
Penrith, battle of, 435
Penruddock, John, uprising suppressed, 425
Pentapolis, occupied by Arabs, 186
Pentathlus, beaten by Elymians, 53
Pentland Hills, battle of, 427
Pentonville system, in transportation of convicts, 900
Peoples of the Sea, 24, 29, 34, 36
People's Court, in Germany, 1001
People's National Convention, in Nanking, 1119
People's or Populist Party, in U.S., 785
People's Party, in Turkey, 1096
Pepe, Gen. Guglielmo, leads revolt of the Carbonari, 650
Pepin I, of Landen, founder of the Carolingians, 147, 149, 150
Pepin II, of Heristal, 149, 150
Pepin III (the Short), of Neustria and Burgundy, 150, 152, 153
Pepin, King of Italy, 155; 163
Pepin, son of Louis the Pious, 157
Pepperell, William, colonial commander, 515
Peraea, 32
Peralta Barnuevo Rocha y Benavides, Pedro de, Spanish-American scientist, 500
Perceval, Spencer, British prime minister, 437
Percies, revolt in Wales, 268
Perdicaris, Ion, kidnaped in Morocco, 838
Perdiccas, 37, 66, 77, 83
Pereire, Isaac and Emile, founders of the *Crédit Mobilier*, 633
Perennis, praetorian, 112
Perestrello, Bartholomew, 366
Peretti, Felice, Pope Sixtus V, 396
Pérez, José Joaquin, pres. of Chile, 809
Pérez, Juan, Spanish explorer, 493
"Perfect Wisdom," 130
Pergamene school of art, 75
Pergamum, 75 *passim*; Kingdom of, 37, 81; Roman province, 91
Pergolesi, Giovanni Battista, Italian composer, 454
Periander of Corinth, 48, 50
Pericles, 55–58, 62
Periods: Abbevillian, 4, 5; Acheulian, 5, 6; Al Ubaid, 13; Amarna, 29, 30, 33; "Annals" (China), 44, 45; Atlantic, 15, 18; Aurignacian, 9; Boreal, 15, 18; Chellean, 5, 6; Demotic, 21; Early Bacsonian, 14; Early Minoan, 16; First Pluvial, 6; Gambian Pluvial, 6; Geometric, 16; Glacial, 4; Günz glacial, 4, 8; Hallstatt, 15, 17; Hieratic, 21; Hieroglyphic, 21; Hoabinhian, 14; Hyksos, 29; Kamasian Pluvial, 6; Keo-Phay, 14; Late Bacsonian, 14; Late Minoan, 16; La Tène, 15, 17; Lower Oligocene, 1; Lower Palaeolithic, 4; Lower Pleistocene, 6; Magdalenian, 9; Mesolithic, 10; Middle Minoan, 16; Mindel glacial, 4, 8; Minoan, 16; Mousterian, 5, 6; Neolithic, 2, 10; Pleistocene, 1, 2, 4, 5, 10; Pliocene, 1, 2; Pre-Boreal, 15, 17; Pre-Chellean, 4, 5; Prehistoric, 1–3; Pre-Palaeolithic, 40; Riss glacial, 4–8; Second Pluvial, 6; Solutrean, 9; Sub-Arctic, 15; Sub-Atlantic, 15; Sub-Boreal, 15, 18; Third Pluvial, 6; Upper Palaeolithic, 5, 6; Upper Pleistocene, 6; Urak, 13; Würm glacial I, II, 4, 8
Peripatetics, 77
Periplus, 129
Perlate, Charlemagne, revolt in Haiti, 1078
Permanent Court of International Justice, 958, 994
Permanent Settlement, in Cornwallis's Code, 536
Péronne, in the World War, 914, 938, 945, 950
Peroz, Sassanid king, 330
Perpendicular Gothic, 266, 267
Perperna, Marcus, 95
Perpetual Peace of 532, 172
Perrers, Alice, dominates Edward, the Black Prince, 266
Perry, Commodore Matthew Calbraith, negotiated treaty with Japan, 725, 888
Perry, Oliver Hazard, American naval commander, 769, 793
Perryville, Ky., Battle of, 778
Persecution of Christians, 115, 117, 119; of Persian Christians, 125; of monks, over iconoclasm, 177; of Protestants in England, 372; of Christians in Japan, 546; of religious dissenters in Russia, 706; Christians in Korea, 881; Jews in Nazi Germany, 1001; and in Czechoslovakia, 1013
Persepolis, 13, 39, 40, 65
Perseus, King of Macedon, 80, 90
Pershing, John Joseph, American general, 791, 822
Persia, early history, 13, 40, 48, 124, 172, 190, 260, 330, 484, 526, 701, 754, 862 *ff*., 1107
Persian Cossack Brigade, 1108
Persian Gulf, 1153
Persian Wars, 53, 54, 124 *ff*., 172–74, 421 *f*., 424, 484, 701, 702
Persius (Aulus Persius Flaccus), satirical poet, 112
Personal property taxes, in England, 196
Perth, founded in West Australia, 899
Pertinax, Publius Helvius, 114
Peru and the west coast, 489, 497, 799, 801 *f*., 812 *f*., 813, 1065, 1067, 1068, 1155

Perugino, Italian painter, 290
Perusia, 99
Peruvian area, 20
Peruvian-Bolivian Confederation, 809
Peruvian Corp., 813
Peruzzi, the, Florentine bankers, 199, 293 *f*.
Peruzzi, Rodolfo, exiled from Florence, 294
Pescara, Fernando, Marquis of, 388
Peshawar, 128; conquered by Ranjit Singh, 866; Treaty of, 866
Pessoa, Epitacio, pres. of Brazil, 1070
Pestel Paul, Russian revolutionary, 702
Pesti Hirlap (*Pest Journal*), organ of the Hungarian radicals, 673
Pet, Arthur, on Russian exploration, 559
Pétain, Gen. Henri-Philippe Benoni Omer Joseph, French general, 921, 930, 939, 1087; head of French government, 1135, 1136, 1138, 1139, 1148, 1150
Petar, last ruler of Croatia, 246
Peter I (Vladika, or prince-bishop) of Montenegro, 715
Peter II, King of Montenegro, 715
Peter I (the Severe) of Portugal, 284
Peter II of Portugal, 453
Peter V of Portugal, 648
Peter I (the Great) of Russia, 472, 478, 479, 528, 529, 561
Peter II of Russia, 479
Peter III of Russia, 468, 481
Peter I of Serbia, 715, 950, 1017
Peter III, King of Sicily, 213; crowned as Peter I of Sicily, 282; 284, 290
Peter IV of Sicily, 284
Peter II, King of Yugoslavia, 1018, 1136, 1150
Peter of Bracheuil, attempt to conquer Bithynia, 259
Peter, Bulgar ruler, 183
Peter, St., 141
Peter (Pedro the Cruel) of Castile, 265, 277, 280
Peter of Chelchich, 305 *f*.
Peter of Courtenay, Latin emperor, 259 *f*.
Peter the Hermit, in the First Crusade, 255
Peterborough, Charles Mordaunt, Earl of, captures Barcelona, 432
Peterloo Massacre, 605
Petermann, Dr. August Heinrich, Arctic explorer, 564
Peters, Karl, German colonialist, 847, 848
Peterwardein, battle of, 484
Petherick, John, African explorer, 826
Pétion, Alexandre, control in South Haiti, 825
Pétion de Villeneuve, Jérôme, mayor of Paris, 581, 582
Petition of Right, in England, 375
Petitioners (country party, Whigs), 428
Petliura, Gen. Simon, Russian counter-revolutionary, 1031
Petra, 126
Petrarch, Italian humanist, 267, 282, 294
Petre, William, 4th Baron Petre, accused in Popish Plot, 428
Petri, Olaus, Swedish reformer, 410
Petrine theory, 141
Petrograd, formerly St. Petersburg, 1028
Petroleum, discovery of, in Pennsylvania, 555. *See also* Oil
Petroleum Law, of Mexico, 1052
Petronilla, daughter of the monk Ramiro, 237
Petronius, legate of Syria, 105
Petronius (Gaius Petronius Arbiter), Roman writer, 107, 112
Petronius Maximus, 122
Petropolis, Treaty of, 812
Petrovich, *see* Karageorge
Petsamo, 1145
Peucker, Gen. Eduard von, Austrian minister of war, 675
Peynardo, Jacinto Bienvenido, pres. of the Dominican Republic, 1079
Pezet, Juan Antonio, pres. of Peru, 813
Pfrimer, Walter, proclaimed "dictator" in Austria, 1006
Phaestus, 46, 47
Phags-pa, Tibetan lama, 346
Phalaris, 53
Pharaoh, as deity, 21; the kings, 23
Pharisees, 32, 106
Pharnabazus, 60, 61
Pharnaces I, 82, 97
Pharsalus, 97, 98; battle of, 250
Phasael, 31
Pheidias the Athenian, 62
Pheidon, King of Argos, 48, 50
Pherae, 63
Philadelphia, Pa., 512, 521
Philae, 21
Philaret (Theodore Nikitich Romanov), father of Tsar Michael Romanov, 418
Philetaerus, 37, 80
Philhellenism, 723
Philibert, Emanuel, of Savoy, 395, 398
Philip I, King of France, 207, 219, 227
Philip II (Augustus), King of France, 197, 198, 211, 229, 256 *f*.
Philip III (the Rash), King of France, 231, 232
Philip IV (the Fair), King of France, 199, 223, 231 *f*., 264, 301
Philip V (the Tall), King of France, 273
Philip VI, King of France, 264, 265. 273
Philip III (Arrhidaeus) of Macedon, 66, 77 *f*.
Philip IV of Macedon, 78
Philip V of Macedon, 79, 80, 81, 87, 89
Philip II, King of Spain, 372, 379, 381, 389, 392, 493, 908
Philip III, King of Spain, 390, 445, 503
Philip IV, King of Spain, 390, 440, 445

Philip V, King of Spain, 445, 447, 450, 451, 458, 463
Philip I, King of Portugal, *see* Philip II of Spain
Philip, New England Indian chief, 511
Philip, tetrarch of Batanea, 32
Philip, Capt. Arthur, governor of New South Wales, 896
Philip, Dr. John, English missionary to South Africa, 851
Philip of Anjou, *see* Philip V of Spain
Philip of Hesse, 402 *f.*
Philip of Macedon, 63, 64, 65, 82, 83
Philip of Orléans, French regent, 447, 450, 451
Philip of Swabia, German emperor, 211, 221, 256
Philip the Arabian, *see* Philippus
Philip the Bold, Duke of Burgundy, 265, 270, 276 *ff.*, 379
Philip the Good, Duke of Burgundy, 279 *f.*, 377
Philip the Handsome, Duke of Burgundy, 379, 388
Philip Louis, Prince of Neuburg, 402
Philiphaugh, battle of, 378
Philippa of Hainault, wife of Edward III of England, 264, 265
Philippi, 99
Philippicus, Byzantine emperor, 175
Philippine Bill, passed by U.S. Congress, 909
Philippine Commissions, 909, 1132, 1133
Philippine insurrection, 787
Philippine Islands, discovered, 368, 408; 492; Aguinaldo's insur-
  rection, 909; civil govt. established, 909; Wood-Forbes Mis-
  sion, 1132; commonwealth govt., established, 1133, 1134; at-
  tacked by Japan, 1138, 1155, 1158, 1166; 1167
Philippine Sea, second battle of, 1169
Philippopolis, battle of, 248
Philippus (Marcus Julius Philippus "Arabus"), Roman em-
  peror, 114, 115
Philistia, 29
Philistines, 24, 29, 30
Phillips, William, American minister to Canada, 1058
Phillips, W. H., invented first helicopter, 554
Philo, Q. Publilius, 73
Philo, Judaeus, 73
Philocrates, negotiates peace between Philip and Athens, 64
Philomelon, battle of, 252
Philopoemen, 80
Philotas, murdered, 65
Philov, Bogdan, Bulgarian statesman, 1135, 1141
Phipps, Capt. Constantine John, Arctic explorer, 562
Phips, Sir William, gov. of Massachusetts, 512, 514
Phocaea, 47
Phocas, Byzantine emperor, 127, 173
Phocians, 47, 54, 64
Phocis, 56, 64, 79
Phoenice, 80; Peace of, 80, 87
Phoenicia, 23, 32–34, 84
Phoenicians, invention of the alphabet, 47, 48
Phoenix Park murders, 616
Phonograph invented, 556; patented, 782
Phormio, 57, 83
Photius, attempts to depose Pope Nicholas I, 153, 177 *f.*, 179
Photography, 554, 555, 569
Phraates I, *see* Arsaces V
Phraates II, 82, 83
Phraates III, 83
Phraates IV, 83
Phrantzes, Georgios, Byzantine historian, 323
Phraortes, 40
Phrygia, 36–37, 48, 60, 77, 127
Phrygians, civilization and religion, 36
Phya Bahol Sena, prime minister of Siam, 1116
Phyle, 61
Physics and Politics, by Walter Bagehot, 552
Physiocrats, school of economics, 448
Pi Yüan, his supplement to the history of Ssu-ma Kuang, 541
Piacenza, 206, 220; Synod of, 219, 255
Piast, semi-mythical family of Poland, 241
Piatakov, Georgei Leonidovich, Bolshevik leader, 1036
Piave, battle of, 949
Picard, Auguste, Belgian scientist, 558
Picard, Louis Joseph Ernest, French Republican, 634
Picardy, battle of, 914
Piccolomini, Aeneas Sylvius, Pope Pius II, 289, 290
Piccolomini, Francesco, Pope Pius III, 395
Piccolomini, Octavio, imperial general, 406, 407
Picentes, 68, 73
Pichegru, Charles, French general, 440, 583, 584, 585, 590
Pichincha, battle of, 803 |
Pichon, Stéphen Jean Marie, French foreign minister, 941, 952
Picot, Georges, French diplomat, 937
Picquart, Col. Georges, and the Dreyfus Case, 641
Pictographs, invade of cuneiform writing, 25, 40
Picts, raids on Britain, 166; converted, 168
Piedmont, *see* Savoy
Piedmont Valley, settlement, 512
Pierce, Franklin (14th pres. of the U.S.), 774
Pierlot, Hubert, Belgian premier, 975
Piero della Vigne, in plot to assassinate Frederick II, 213
Piero the Gouty, son of Cosimo de' Medici, 295, 296
Piérola, Nicolás de, pres. of Peru, 813
Piers Plowman, 266
Pietermaritzburg, founded, 851
"Pig War" of Serbia with Austria, 715
Piggott, Richard, Irish journalist, 617
Pigneau de Béhaine, Pierre, French missionary in Annam, 874, 880
Pilgrim of Passau, German missionary to Hungary, 245
Pilgrimage to Mecca, 184

Pilgrims, arrival at Cape Cod, 508, 509
Pillar of Asoka, 42
Pillsbury, John Sargent, flour-milling process, 782
Pilotless jet planes, first used, by Germans, 1142
Pilsudski, Josef, Polish soldier and statesman, 955, 1037, 1039, 1040
Piltdown Man (Eoanthropus dawsoni), 9
Pinchot, Gifford, and Ballinger-Pinchot controversy, 790
Pinckney, Charles Cotesworth, American commissioner to France, 766
Pinckney, Thomas, negotiates American treaty with Spain, 766
Pindar, Greek poet, 53, 62
Pindari tribes, in India, 868
Pineda, Alvárez, Spanish explorer, 368
Ping-yang, battle of, 881
Pining, Didrick, gov. of Iceland, 365
Pinto, Anibal, pres. of Chile, 809
Pinto, Francisco Antonio, pres. of Chile, 809
Pinto, Serpa, Portuguese explorer, 828
Pinturicchio, Italian painter, 290
Pinzón, Martin, commanded one of Columbus' vessels, 366
Pinzón, Vicente Yañez, voyages, 368
"Piracy" in the Mediterranean, 984
Pirates, in early Corsica, 68; of Queen Teuta, 86; defeated in Mediterranean, 95; Moslem, 179; Dalmatian, 224; Saracen, 249; Victual Brothers, 309; Japanese, 349; deys of Algiers, 525
Pires, Thomé, Portuguese emissary to Peking, 536
Pirna, battle of, 467
Pirot, taken by the Bulgars, 927
Pisa, bought by Florence, 252, 294
Pisano, Vittorio, Italian admiral, 298
Piso, Gaius, Calpurnius, 106
Piso, Licinianus, murdered, 107
Piso, Lucius Calpurnius, accused of poisoning Germanicus, 103
Pitalkhora, 43
Pitcairn Island, settled by mutineers, 895
Pithecanthropus erectus, 7, 9
Pithom, 24
Pitt, William (later Earl of Chatham), in the Pelham ministry, 435; in ministry of Newcastle, 435; chancellor of the exchequer, 436
Pitt, William the Younger, 436; first ministry, India Bill, 437; proposes concessions to Catholics, resigns, dies, 437
Pitti, Luca, 295
Pittman Act, 1155
Pius II (Aeneas Silvius), Pope, 290, 304, 327
Pius III (Francesco Piccolomini), Pope, 395
Pius IV (Giovanni Angelo Medici), Pope, 396
Pius V, Saint (Michele Ghislieri), Pope, 396, 423
Pius VI (Giovanni Angelo Braschi), Pope, 588, 595, 650, 663
Pius VII (Baranaba Chiaramonti), Pope, 588, 595, 650, 663
Pius VIII (Francesco Castiglioni), Pope, 663
Pius IX (Giovanni Maria Mastai-Ferretti), Pope, 631, 634, 651, 660, 664, 690
Pius X (Giuseppe Sarto), Pope, 662, 665, 992
Pius XI (Achile Ratti), Pope, 993
Pius XII (Eugenio Pacelli), Pope, 993
Pizarro, Francisco, Spanish conquistador, 486, 488, 489
Pizarro, Gonsalo, brother of the preceding, 489
Pizarro, Hernando, brother of Francisco, 489
Place, Francis, English radical, 606
Place Bill, in England, 431
Placentia, 86–88
Placidia, Galla, half-sister of Honorius, 121, 144, 145
Plague, in Athens, 56, 58; brought to Rome, 111, 116; in Attila's army, 143; in Portugal, 285
Plain, a party in the National Convention of France, 580, 581
Plains Indians, 780
Plains of Abraham, battle of, 516
Plan of Iguala, Mexico's independence of Spain, 804
Planck, Max, quantum theory, 552
Plano, Carpini, envoy of Pope Innocent IV in China, 344
Planta, Rudolf, seized the Valtelline Pass, 409
Plantagenet, House of, 194
Planudes, Maximus, Byzantine scholar, 323
Plassey, battle of, 535
Plastiras, Gen. Nicholas, Greek insurgent, 1021, 1022
Plataea, 40, 52, 54, 58, 59
Plato, Greek philosopher, 66, 67
Platonic Academy, founded by Cosimo de' Medici, 296
Platonism, 123
Platt Amendment, affecting Cuba, 788, 823; abrogated, 1077
Plattsburg, battle of, 769, 793
Plautianus, praefect, 114
Plautius Aulus, invades Britain, 106
Plautus, 91
Plebeians, of Rome, 69, 71–73
Plehve, Viacheslav Constaninovich, Russian minister of the interior, 707
Pleistarchus, 78
Pleistocene Age, 5
Plekhanov, George Valentinovich, Russian socialist, 706
Plethon, Georgius, Byzantine scholar, 323
Plevlje, taken by the Austrians, 927
Plimsoll, Samuel, shipping reforms, 615
Pliny the Elder (Gaius Plinius Secundus), his *Natural History*, 112; 115, 129, 170
Pliny the Younger (Gaius Plinius Caecilius Secundus), reorgan-
  izes Bithynia, 110; his *Letters*, 112
Plotinus, exponent of neo-Platonism, 117
Plowden, Walter, English emissary in Ethiopia, 834

Plows, of iron, of steel, 554
Plumer, Gen. Herbert Charles Onslow, British general, 939, 1100
Plural marriage, 42
Pluto, ninth planet, 553
Plymouth, settlement by Pilgrims, 509
Plymouth Co., granted charter, 508
Pneumatic rubber tire, introduced, 556
Po, Fernando, Portuguese discoverer, 364
Po Chü-i, Chinese poet, 341
Po Valley, 1164
Pobiedonostsev, Constantine Petrovich, adviser to Alexander III of Russia, 706
Podiebrad, George, King of Bohemia, 304, 305, 318
Poetilius, his law on debtors, 73
Pogroms, in the Ukraine, 706
Pohl, Hugo von, German admiral, 931
Poiarkov, Vasili, Russian explorer, 539
Poimanenon, battle of, 259
Poincaré, Raymond, French premier and president, 643, 759, 762, 936, 958, 976, 978
Poitiers (Tours), Charles Martel defeated Abdurrahman, 188; Edward, the Black Prince, defeated the French, 265, 276; Synod of, 216
Pola, battle of, 298
Poland, 207, 241 ff., 310, 312, 413, 477, 478, 602, 702, 943, 953, 955, 958, 965, 966, 971, 1028, 1037, 1038, 1039, 1040, 1041; in Second World War, invaded by Germany, 1135, 1140, 1145 f., 1154; 20-year treaty with Russia, 1143; divided between Germany and Russia, 1145; 1164
Polar stations, international, 565
Pole, Reginald, Cardinal, archbishop of Canterbury, 370, 372
Polianov, Treaty of, 415, 418
Polignac, Jules Auguste Armande, Prince de, French prime minister, 579, 627, 724
Polish constitution, abrogated, 702
"Polish Corridor" demanded by Hitler, 966
Polish Committee of National Liberation, 1142
Polish government-in-exile, 1140, 1143
Polish-Lithuanian crisis, 965
Polish national government, formed, 1144
Polish Revolution, 702, 703, 704
Polish-Russian War, 955, 1038
Polish War, 310
Polished stone tools, in Post-Palaeolithic period, 10
Political economy, 549, 550
Politis, Nicolas Socrate, Greek statesman, 959
Polk, James Knox (11th pres. of the U.S.), 773
Pollentia, battle of, 121, 143, 144
Pollock, Gen. Sir George, British commander in Afghanistan, 866
Pollock v. Farmers Loan and Trust Co., income tax decision, 786
Polo, Marco, son of Nicolo, 337, 346, 368, 537
Polo brothers, Nicolo and Maffeo, Venetian Travellers, 362
Poltava, battle of, 472, 479, 1151
Polybius, 90, 91
Polycarp of Smyrna, early martyr, 113
Polychronicon, by Ranulf Higden, 267
Polycleitus, sculptor, 62
Polycrates, allied with Amasis of Egypt, 48, 50
Polygamy, abolished in Turkey, 1096
Polygnotus, painter, 62
Polyperchon, 77
Polytheism, 39
Pombal (Sebastião José de Carvalho e Mello), Marquis de, Portuguese reformer, 453, 495, 502, 503
Pomerania, converted, 208
Pompadour, Jeanne Antoinette Poisson Le Normant d'Étioles, Marquise de, mistress of Louis XV, 447, 466
Pompeians, 97
Pompeii, 108, 113
Pompey (Gnaeus Pompeius), Roman soldier and statesman, organized Syria, 33, 37, 39, 83, 94–96, 97
Pompey, Sextus, brother of the above, 95, 96, 97, 99
Pomponius, his reference to Scandinavia, 170
Ponce de Leon, Juan, Spanish explorer, 368, 493
Poncet, Charles Jacques, emissary of Louis XIV, 525
Pondoland, annexed by British, 855
Poniatowski, Stanislas, King of Poland, 477, 481
Pons, Antonio, pres. of Ecuador, 1069
Ponsot, Henri, French high commissioner for Syria, 1098
Pontgravé, François Gravé, sieur de, attempts to colonize Tadoussac, 505
Pontius Pilate, and crucifixion of Christ, 105
Pontus, 82, 93–95
Poole, Gen. Frederick Cuthbert, British general at Murmansk, 947
Poole, Jonas, whale-fishing, 561
Poor Law, in England, 608, 609
Pope, John, Federal general, 778
Popham, Sir Home Riggs, capitulates at Buenos Aires, 800
Popish Plot, in England, 428
Poplicola, Lucius Valerius, 71, 72
Poppaea Sabina, mistress of Nero, 106, 107
Populist movement, in Russia, 705
Populonia, 74
Porcelain, 340
Porphyrius, exponent of neo-Platonism, 111
Port Arthur, 707, 881, 891, 892, 1171
Port Augusta, 1162
Port Hamilton, in Korea, 886

Port Hudson, surrenders, 778
Port Nicholson, landing of first British colonists, 905
Port Philip Association, 900
Port Royal, captured by Sir William Phips, 514
Portal, Sir Gerald Herbert, British agent in Uganda, 849
Portáles, Diego José Victor, pres. of Chile, 809
Portes Gil, Emilio, pres. of Mexico, 1076
Portland, see Cavendish
Portland, battle of, 425
Porto, Silva, Portuguese explorer, 826
Porto Eddo, Albania, 1150
Porto Novo, battle of, 535
Portocarrero, Louis Manuel Fernandez de, Cardinal, 445
Portsmouth, Treaty of, 707, 753, 883, 887
Portugal, 234, 238 f., 284 ff., 329, 390 f., 446, 450, 452, 524, 525, 530, 536, 542, 593, 648 ff., 748, 843, 844, 875, 876, 881, 985; broke with Germany, 1144; 1156, 1159
Portuguese America, 500 ff.
Positivism, 550
Possevino, Antonio, Catholic churchman, 417
Post, Wiley, American aviator, 558, 1052
Post of Berlin, publishes "Is War in Sight?" 733
Postal Congress (International), 667
Postal reform, promoted by Rowland Hill, 609
Postal service, established in Japan, 890
Postal workers, in Paris strike, 643
Posthumus, Ladislas, King of Hungary and Bohemia, 304, 305
Post-Palaeolithic culture, 10
Postumius, Sp., 73
Postumius, L., defeats Samnites, 73
Postumus, emperor in Gaul, 116
Potemkin, Gregory Alexandrovich, Prince, 485
Potemkin episode, 707
Potenza, 1142
Potgieter, Andries Hendrik, Boer leader, 851
Pothorst, Hans, voyage to Iceland, 365
Potidaea, 58, 64
Potocki family, of Poland, 477
Potsdam Agreement, 693
Potsdam Conference, 1171
Pottery, 4, 7; in Post-Palaeolithic period, 10
Pottinger, Eldred, defended Herat, 862
Pottinger, Sir Henry, English diplomat, 879
Poulsen, Valdemar, invented the arc transmitter, 557
Poulter, Dr. Thomas Charles, Antarctic explorer, 577
Poussin, Louis de la Vallée, on the Pahlava era, 128
Poutrincourt, Jean de Biencourt de, re-established Port Royal, 505
Powell, George, British surveyor, 573
Powys, William Herbert, Duke of, in Popish Plot, 428
Poynings' Law, see Statute of Drogheda
Pozharsky, Dimitri, Russian patriot leader, 418
Prado, Mariano Ignacio, pres. of Peru, 813
Praetor's Edict, codified, 110, 116
Pragmatic Sanction of Bourges, 279, 289
Pragmatic Sanction of Charles VI, 440 f., 451, 463
Pragmatic Sanction of Justinian, 146
Pragmatic Sanction of Mainz, 289, 304
Pragmatic Sanction of 1439, 289
Pragmatic Sanction of 1720, incorporating Bohemia in Hapsburg empire, 419
Prague, battle of, 467; bombarded, 673; Treaties of, 406, 686
Praguerie, a series of coalitions, 279
Prajadhipok, see Rama VII
Prajnaparamita ("Perfect Wisdom"), 130
Prakrit inscriptions, 129
Prasad, Rajendra, Indian nationalist, 1114
Prasenajit, king, 41
Pratimoksa, 42
Pratishthana, 129, 132
Pratt, Gen. Thomas Simson, British commander in New Zealand, 907
Praxiteles, Greek sculptor, 67
Prayer-Book, of Edward VI, 372
Pre-emption-Distribution Act, 773
Prefectures, established in France, 587
Prehistory, 1
Pre-Mousterian industry, 5
Premysl, House of, 239, 240, 241, 301, 304
Prendergast, Sir Harry North Dalrymple, British commander in Burma, 872
Prenzlau, battle of, 592
Presbyterian mission (British), in Nigeria, 840
Presbyterianism, in England, 378
Presbyterians, 372
"Presidency in charity," enjoyed by Rome, 141
Presidential Succession Law, in U.S., 783
Presidios, system established, 497 passim
Press law, in Japan, 890; in Spain, 646
Pressburg, Treaty of, 591
Prester John, legendary Christian king, 363
Prestes, Julio, pres. of Brazil, 1071
Preston, battles of, 379, 434
Preston, Capt. Thomas, commanded troops in Boston Massacre, 518
Prestonpans, battle of, 435
Pretender (Old), 434, 446
Pretoria, 852, 855, 857, 858; Treaty of, 854
Pretorius, Andreas. Boer leader, 851

Pretorius. Marthinius, pres. of the South African Republic, 852, 853
Preussisches Wochenblatt, organ of the German Moderates, 680
Prevention of Crimes Bill, in England, 616
Prevesa, battle of, 422
Priapatius, see Arsaces IV
Price control, in French Revolution, 581, 584
Price Control Act, 1138
Pride, Col. Thomas, purges parliament, 379
Pride's Purge, 378, 426
Prie, Jeanne Agnes Berthelot de Pléneuf, mistress of Louis Henri de Bourbon, 447
Priene, 75
Priestman, William Dent and Samuel, oil engine, 556
Prieto, Indalecio, defense minister of Spain, 984
Prilip, taken by the Bulgars, 927
Prim, Juan, Marqués de los Castillejos, prime minister of Spain, 646, 687
"Prima Porta," statue of Augustus, 113
Primary Education Law, in France, 628, 639
Primary Products Marketing Act, in New Zealand, 1132
Primates, 1
Primogeniture, in England, 196
Primus, Antonius, in 2d battle of Bedriacum, 107
Prince Edward Island, joins Dominion of Canada, 796
Prince of Wales, institution of the title, 199
Prince of Wales, British battleship, 1167
Princeton, battle of, 521
Princip, Gavrilo, assassin of Francis Ferdinand. 761
Principalities of Moldavia and Wallachia, 719, 728; see also Rumania
Principality of Achaia, 258
Principles of Geology, by Sir Charles Lyell, 551
Principles of Physiological Psychology, by Wilhelm Wundt, 552
Principles of Political Economy, by John Stuart Mill, 550
Principles of Political Economy and Taxation, by David Ricardo, 549
Printing, 312, 340, 500, 554, 555, 556
Priscus, defeats Avars, 173
Priscus, Helvidius, 108, 109
Pristina, taken by the Bulgars, 927
Prithivipati I, Indian ruler, 337
Prittwitz, Friedrich Wilhelm von, German general, 916
Prizrend, taken by Bulgars, 927
Probus, Henry, brief reign in Poland, 242
Probus, Marcus Aurelius, Roman emperor, 116
Procheiros Nomos, parts of the Justinian Code, 178
Proclamation of 1763, by George III, 517
Procop the Great, Bohemian Hussite leader, 305
Procopius, Byzantine writer, 170, 173
Proculians, jurisprudence schools, 116
Prodicus, Sophist, 62
Production Management, Office of, 1136
Professio Fidei Tridentina, see Pius IV
Program of Belleville, 635
Progress and Poverty, by Henry George, 618
Progressist insurrection, in Spain, 645
Propagandist societies, in Serbia, 715
Propertius, Sextus, 112
Property tax, first levied, 58; 61, 62
Propliopithecus, 1
Propylaea, entrance gate, 62
"Proscription" of the optimates, 93
Prosopitis, 56
Protagoras, Sophist, 62
Protection, in New South Wales, 901; in New Zealand, 907
Protectionist system, 605 f.
Protective Tariff Acts in England, 969
Protestant Church, in Germany, 1001
Protestant doctrines, in England, 370, 372
Protestant missions, in Uganda, 847; in China, 880
Protestant succession, in England, 496
Protestant Union, 402, 404
Protestants, 399 ff.; in Ulster, 376
Protocol of London (1830), gave Greece independence, 724; (1852), succession to the duchies of Schleswig-Holstein, 676, 681
Protoguerov, Alexander Nicholoff, Macedonian revolutionary, 1023
Proto-Hattic language, 36
Proto-Mousterian industry, 5
Proudhon, Pierre Joseph, French socialist, 549, 637
Provence, French naval vessel, 1148
Provence, Kingdom of, 157
Proverbs, 30
Provisions of Oxford, 198, 264
Prusias I, 82
Prussia, origins, 211, 214 f.; see also Germany
Pruth, Treaty of the, 472, 479, 484
Przasnysz, battle of, 922
Przemysl, invested by Russians, 916; taken by Austro-Germans, 922
Przemyslav II, King of Poland, 242
Psalms, 30
Psamtik (Psammetichus), Saïtic revival in Egypt, 24, 27; 37, 47
Psamtik II, 24
Psamtik III, 24, 56
Psellus, Michael, Byzantine scholar, 181, 250
Pskov, taken by Germans, 943, 1142
Psychoanalysis, 552
Psychology, 552

Psychology of Crowds, by Gustave Le Bon, 552
Ptolemies, 24; rule the Jews, 32; rule Phoenicia, 33, 37; administration of Egypt, 75; 84; 89
Ptolemy, Greek geographer, 571
Ptolemy I Soter, 33, 35, 77, 79, 80, 84
Ptolemy II Philadelphus, 81, 83
Ptolemy III Euergetes, 81, 84
Ptolemy IV Philopater, 84
Ptolemy V Epiphanes, 84, 129
Ptolemy VI Philomator, 82, 84
Ptolemy VII Euergetes II, 84
Ptolemy VIII Soter II, 84
Ptolemy IX Alexander I, 84
Ptolemy X Alexander II, 84
Ptolemy XI Auletes, 84
Ptolemy XII, 84, 97
Ptolemy XIII, 85, 97
Ptolemy Ceranunus, 78
Public domain, created in U.S., 522
Public Health Act, in England, 615
Public Safety Act, in India, 1113
Public Schools Act, in New South Wales, 902
Public Services Act, in China, 343
Public Utility Holding Company Act, in U.S., 1055
Pueblo area, 20
Puerto Rico, discovered, 824; San Juan founded, 486; ceded to U.S., 824, 1079; 1155
Pueyrredon, Juan Martin de, director in Rio de la Plata, 801
Pugachev, Yemelyan Ivanovich, Russian insurgent, 481
P'u-i, emperor of China, 884
Pulakesin II (Chalukya), 335
Pulcher, Appius Claudius, 86
Pulcheria, sister of Theodosius II, 121
Pulci, Luigi, 296
Pullman, George, built first sleeping-car, 555
Punctation of Olmütz, 678
Punic, language of Carthage, 34
Punic Wars, 34, 78, 86, 87, 89
Punjab, 6, 42, 43, 81, 124, 187, 866, 870, 1111
Puranas, 43, 129, 132
Purandukht, daughter of Khasru Parviz, 127
Purchas, Samuel, English explorer, 561
Pure Food and Drug Act, in U.S., 789
Pure Land, of the Buddha, 353; sect founded, 354
Puritans, nonconformists of Anglican Church, 372, 426
Purvey, John, coadjutor of John Wiclif, 266
Pushyamitra, 43
Putna, battle of, 944
Putnam, Gen. Israel, American soldier, 520
Pydna, 63, 64, 80, 89
Pygmalion, ruler of Carthage, 34
Pygmy, in the Negroid group, 12, 18, 33
Pylos, 58, 59, 60
Pym, Sir Alan William, and Kenya Colony, 1091
Pym, John, leader of parliamentary party in England, 375, 377; 426
P'yŏngyang, battle of, 138; 891
Pyramids, 21, 23; battle of the, 586
Pyrenees, Peace of the, 426, 448; Treaty of the, 390, 440
"Pyrrhic victory," 86
Pyrrhus, King of Epirus, 34, 78, 79, 83, 85, 86
Pythagoras, philosopher, 53, 113
Pytheas, references to Scandinavia, 170
Pythian games, 64

Qadarites, of the Omayyad period, 189
Qadisiya, battle of, 182, 186
Qais tribe, in Syria, 186, 187
Qarqar, 27, 31, 35
Quadi, 109, 120
Quadrilateral, fortresses in northern Italy, 654
Quadruple Alliances, 59, 435, 451, 463, 603, 604, 608, 645, 647
Quakers, in West New Jersey, 512
Quang-nam, 134
Quantum theory, 552
Quartering Act, in American colonies, 518, 520
Quatre Bras, battle of, 603
Quebec Act, 520
Quebec, battle of, 435
Quebec Conference, 1140 f., 1159
Quebec Convention, Resolution, 796
Queen Anne's War, 514
Queensland, established as a separate colony, 901; 913
Queenston Heights, battle of, 793
Querétaro, founded, 492
Quervain, Dr. Alfred de, Swiss scientist, 568
Quesada, Gonsalo Jiménez de, Spanish conquistador, 486, 488; 489
Quetta, in India, occupied by British, 870
Quexos, Pedro de, explorer, 368
Quezon, Manuel, President of the Philippines, 1132, 1133, 1134
Quiberon Bay, battle of, 435
Quincy, Josiah, 518
Quinine, 553
Quintana, Manuel, pres. of Argentina, 808
Quintilian (Marcus Fabius Quintilianus), Roman author, 112
Quintuple Alliance, 604
Quisling, Vidkun, puppet president of Norway, 1138, 1146
Qurna, taken by Anglo-Indian forces, 927
Qutayba, Arab conqueror, 187

Rabah, Zobeir, African ruler, 842
Rabaul, 1167
Rabban Sauma, negotiates with Pope Nicholas IV, 346
Racconigi Agreement, between Russia and Italy, 757, 839
Races of Man, 12
Radagaisus, barbarian leader, 121, 143
Radama I, King of the Hovas, 860
Radama II, King of the Hovas, 860
Radar, 1149
Radek, Karl, a Bolshevik leader, 1028, 1036
Radescu, Nicholas, Rumanian general, 1143
Radetzky, Joseph, Austrian general, 654, 655, 674
Radich, Stephen, leader of the Croats, 1017
Radicalism and "utopian" socialism, in France, 628, 635
Radio broadcasting, first commercial station, 557
Radioactive minerals, 3
Radishchev, Alexander Nicolaievich, Russian writer, 481
Radisson, Pierre Esprit, French explorer, 507
Radium, 552
Radomir (or Romanus), Gabriel, Bulgarian tsar, 183, 184, 247
Radoslavov, Vasil, Bulgarian prime minister, 719, 948
Radowitz, Joseph Maria von, Prussian statesman, 670, 676, 677
Radzin, Treaty of, 478, 483
Rae, Dr. John, Arctic explorer, 563
Raffael Santi, Italian painter, 392
Raffles, Sir Thomas Stamford, occupies Singapore, 868, 875; 876
Raghid Pasha, Turkish grand vizier, 484
Raghuvamsa, 131
Raglan, Fitzroy James Henry Somerset, 1st Baron, British commander in the Crimea, 727
Raiders of the Sea, 932
Railroad Transportation (Emergency) Act in U.S., 1055
Railway Act, in France, 628
Railway Labor Act, in U.S., 1054
Railway legislation in Canada, 1059
Railway Pension Act, in U.S., 1054
Railway scandal, in Canada, 796
Railway workers, in France, 643
Railways, American, 553, 774, 793; foreign, 554, 633, 683, 755, 812, 815, 836, 850, 852, 854, 855, 883 *f.*; 890, 901, 902, 907, 1121, 1129
Rain, battle of, 406
Rainfall, fluctuations in the Pleistocene period, 5
Rainilaiarivony, Hova prince, 860
Raisuli, Ahmed ben Mohammed, Moroccan bandit, 838, 1086, 1087
Rajadhiraja I, 337
Rajagriha, 42
Rajaraja I, hegemony over the Deccan, 337, 338
Rajatarangini of Kalhana, 332
Rajendra Choladeva, king, 337, 338
Rajich, Vuk Stefanovich, Serbian writer, 721
Rajputs, defeated by Subaktagin, 190
Rákóczi (George I), Prince of Transylvania, 407, 420
Rakovski, George, Bulgarian revolutionary, 717
Raleigh, Sir Walter, 373, 374, 508, 513
Ram Hormuz, 128
Ram Mohun Roy, organized *Brahmo Samaj*, 870
Rama I (Phra Buddha Yod Fa Chulalok), King of Siam, 873
Rama II (Phra Buddha Loes Fa Nobhalai), King of Siam, 873
Rama III (Phra Nang Klao), King of Siam, 873
Rama IV (Phra Chom Klao Mongkut), King of Siam, 873
Rama V (Phra Maha Chulalonkorn), King of Siam, 873
Rama VI (Vajiravudh), King of Siam, 873
Rama VII (Prajadhipok), King of Siam, 1116
Rama Kamhing, Mongol ruler, 345
Rama Tiboti, founder of the Tai Kingdom in Siam, 347
Ramadi, captured by British, 938
Ramanuja, interpreted the *Vedanta*, 336, 337
Ramaraja, 338
Ramayana, 43
Ramdas, Hindu poet, 534
Ramek, Rudolf, prime minister of Austria, 1006
Rametta, battle of, 249
Ramillies, battle of, 432, 446
Ramirez, Gen. Pedro P., President of Argentina, 1140
Ramiro, Spanish monk, 237
Ramses II, 24, 30, 35, 36
Ramses III–XII, 24
Ranavalona I, Queen of the Hovas, 860
Ranavalona II, Queen of the Hovas, 860, 861
Rand strike movement, 1091
Randolph, Edward, collector of customs in Boston, 511
Rangaku, "Dutch Learning," 888
Rangoon, taken by the British, 872; 1138; 1167
Ranjit Singh, Sikh chieftain, 866, 868, 870
Ranke, Leopold von, German historian, 551
Rantzau, Josias, German general, 407
Rapallo, Treaties, 955, 958, 987, 997, 1017, 1033
Raphia, battle of, 84
Rapson, Edward James, on sequence of Indian rulers, 128
Ras Makonen, Ethiopian chieftain, 661
Ras Shamra, 13, 28, 32
Rashtrakuta dynasty, 336
Rasmussen, Knud, Arctic explorer, 568
Rasoherina, Queen of the Hovas, 860
Raspe, Henry, Duke of Thuringia, 212
Rasputin, Gregory Yefimovich, a Russian mystic, 708, 1028
Rastadt and Baden, Treaty of, 447, 450
Rathenau, Walter, German statesman, 956, 997
Ratkau, battle of, 592

Raucoux, battle of, 466
Ravachol (Koenigstein), François Auguste, anarchist, 640
Ravaillac, François, assassin of Henry IV, 386
Ravenna, 122; capital of the West, 146, 655; seat of the exarch, 153; conquered by the Lombards, 176
Ravenna, battle of, 381, 394
Rawalpindi, Treaty of, 1109
Raymond Berenguer IV, union of Catalonia and Aragon, 235, 237
Raymond of Antioch, 252 *f.*
Raymond of Toulouse, 230, 255, 256
Rayy, 13
Razin, Stephen, heads peasant revolt in Russia, 478
Razumovsky, Prince Andreas, adviser of Tsar Alexander I, 601
Reading, Rufus Daniel Isaacs, Lord, viceroy of India, 1112
Reagan (John Henninger) Bill, in U.S., 784
Reason culture, in French Revolution, 583
Reate, 107 *f.*
Rebellion Losses Bill, of Canada, 795
Reccared, King, 163
Reciprocal Tariff Act, in U.S., 1055
Reciprocity agreement between U.S. and Canada, 790, 797
Recoinage Act, in England. 431
Recollet friars, arrive at Quebec, 505
Reconstruction, Joint Committee of Fifteen on, in U.S., 780, 781
Reconstruction Finance Corp. in U.S., 1053, 1140
Recopilación de Leyes de las Indias, 496
Recuperatione Sanctae Terrae, De, 232
Red Ochre Graves, 16
Red River, in Indo-China, explored, 874; 880
Red River Rebellion, in Canada, 796
Reding, Aloys von, leads revolt in Switzerland, 460
Redistribution Bill, in England, 617; in Canada, 1058
Redmond, John, leader of the Irish Nationalists, 617, 971
Reed, Walter, yellow fever, 552
Reeves, William Pember, head of Labor Dept. of New Zealand, 908
Reflections on Violence, by Georges Sorel, 550, 641
Reform Bills, in England (1831), 607; (1867), 613
Reform era, in England (1830–1846), 606 *ff.*
Reform of finances, in France, 442
Reform (Conservative) Party, in New Zealand, 908, 1131
Reformation, beginnings, 213; 289, 399 *f.*; in England, 370; 395; in Denmark and Sweden, 410; in Hungary, 419
Reformed religion (Calvinist), 402
Refrigeration, in railway transportation, 555, 781
Regensburg, battle of, 394
Reggio, destroyed by an earthquake, 662
Régis, Jean Baptiste, prepared first maps of China, 539
Regulating Act, applied to British India, 535
Regulus, Marcus Atilius, Roman general, 86
Rehoboam, 31
Reichsbank, opened in Germany, 689
Reichsrat, of Denmark, 309; of Austria, 996
Reichstadt Agreement, between Austria and Russia, 734, 735
Reichstädte, imperial cities of Germany, 213
Reichstag, in Germany, 214, 686, 996, 1000
Reid, George Houstoun, Australian premier, 903, 904
Reid, Robert Gillespie, railroad builder in Canada, 797
Reid Moir industry, 4
Reign of Terror in French Revolution, 578, 582, 584; in Russia, 1033
Reims, German surrender, 1165
Reims, Synod of, 219
Reinach, Jacques, Baron, in Panama scandal, 640
Reinsurance Treaty, between Germany and Russia, 741
Relander, Lauri, pres. of Finland, 1048
Relativity, 552
Religion, in the early empires, 21, 23; in Japan, 350 *f.*, 355; debates instituted for Moslems, 533
Religious wars, of France, 384 *ff.*, 390
Remagen, 1164
Remedello culture, 17
Remigius, Bishop, 147
Remouchamps culture, 18
Renaissance, 146, 298, 299
Rendova Island, 1169
René, Angevin claimant to throne of Naples, 292, 293
Rennenkampf, Gen. Pavel Karlovich, Russian general, 916
Renner, Karl, chancellor of Austria, 1005
Rennyo, head of the New Pure Land sect, 359
Rense, formation of an electoral union (*Kurverein*), 302
Rentenbank, in Germany, 998
Reparations, 956, 997
Repeating rifle, 555
Report on Manufactures, 764
Republic of the Don, 1031
Republic Steel strike, 1056
Republican army, in Ireland, 973
Republican Fascist Party, Italy, 1140, 1162
Republican Party, formed, in U.S., 775
Republicanism, in France, 635
Repulse, British battleship, 1167
Requesens y Zúñiga, Luis de, Spanish commander in Netherlands, 380
Requin, Col. Édouard, treaty proposal to League of Nations, 959
Rerum novarum, encyclical of Leo XIII, 993
Res Gestae Saxonicae, 162
Resaca de la Palma, battle of, 773
Resaina, 124

Reserve Bank, in New Zealand, 1132
Reserve Bank, of India, 1113
Reshid Pasha, Turkish commander, 723
Reshid Pasha, Turkish reformer, 725, 728
Resht, taken by Bolshevik fleet, 1108; retaken by Persian Cossack Brigade, 1108; Treaty of, 529
Restoration monarchy, in France, 626 *ff.*
Restrepo, Carlos, pres. of Colombia, 816
Resumption Act, for specie payment, in U.S., 782, 783
Retes, Ortiz de, named New Guinea, 894
Retief, Piet, slain by Zulus, 851
Retz, Jean François, Cardinal de, in the Fronde, 440
Reuben, tribe of, 29, 30
Reuben James, U.S. destroyer, 1158
Reuter, Ludwig von, German admiral, 946
Reuter, Paul Julius de, concession for Imperial Bank of Persia, 864
Reval, founded, 204; taken by Germans, 943
Revocation of the Edict of Nantes, 443
Revolt of the *ciompi*, in Florence, 294
Revolutionary tribunals, 583
Revolver, invented, 554
Rewbel, Jean François, member of the French Directory, 585
Reyes, Rafael, pres. of Colombia, 815, 816
Reynaud, Paul, France, 1135, 1148
Reynier, Jean Louis, French general, 599
Reza Khan (Reza Shah Pahlavi), Shah of Persia, 1108, 1109
Rezanov, Nicolai Petrovich de, Russian ambassador to Japan, 887
Rezin, King of Damascus, 31, 35
Rezon, founded, Kingdom of Damascus, 35
Rhaetia, 102, 109
Rhagae, 39
Rhandeia, 106
Rhea Silvia, traditional mother of Romulus, 69
Rhegium, 48, 57
Rheims, in the World War, 913, 914; *see also* Reims
Rhine, 1154, 1164
Rhine League, 302
Rhineland, evacuation, 961, 978; Republic, 996, 997
Rhode Island and Providence Plantations, chartered, 511
Rhodes, 47 *passim*; siege of, 327; captured by the Turks, 422
Rhodes, Cecil John, South African capitalist and statesman, 854, 855, 856
Rhodesia, 855, 856, 918, 1089
Rhodesian Man, 9
Rhone Valley, 1163
Riade, battle of, 160
Riarios of Naples, in Pazzi conspiracy, 290, 295
Riart, Luis, pres. of Paraguay, 1066
Ribaddi, 33
Ribaut, Jean, Huguenot settlement in South Carolina, 493, 505
Ribbentrop, Joachim von, German foreign minister, 1004, 1012
Ribeiro, João, leads Portuguese revolt against Spanish rule, 392
Ribera, José (Spagnoletto), Spanish painter, 389
Ribot, Alexandre Félix Joseph, French prime minister, 936, 939, 941
Ricardo, David, English economist, 549
Ricasoli, Bettino, Baron, prime minister of Italy, 659
Ricci, Matteo, with Jesuits in China, 537
Richard I (*Coeur de Lion*), King of England, 196 *f.*, 229, 260
Richard II, King of England, 267, 268, 273, 309
Richard III, King of England, 271
Richard, Count of Autun, 158
Richard, Duke of York, claims throne of France, 270
Richard of Clare (Strongbow), expedition to Ireland, 169, 196, 203
Richard of Cornwall, elected emperor in Germany, 198, 213, 257
Richardson, murdered near Yokohama, 889
Richardson, Dr. John, Arctic explorer, 563
Richardson, William Adams, U.S. secretary of the treasury, 782
Richelieu, Armand Emmanuel du Plessis, Duke de, French premier, 626
Richelieu, Armand Jean du Plessis, Cardinal-Duke of, French statesman, 387, 405, 407; 505
Richemont, Arthur, adviser of Charles VII of France, 278
Richet, Charles, helicopter, 557
Richthofen, Manfred von, German aviator, 946
Ricimer, deposes Avitus, 122
Ridley, Nicholas, English churchman, 372
Riebeeck, Jan van, founded Capetown, 524
Ried, Treaty of, 599
Rienzi, Cola di, Italian revolutionist, 286
Riel, Louis, Canadian rebel, 796, 797
Riesco, Germán, pres. of Chile. 810
Rif tribes, in Morocco, 838, 839, 981, 1086
Riga, founded, 214, 244; battle of, 940; Treaty of, 1033, 1038, 1043; 1151, 1154
Rigault de Genouilly, Charles, French admiral, 874
Riggs, Elias, American missionary, 717
Rights of Man, Declaration of the, in French National Assembly, 579
Rigveda, book of hymns, 41
Riiser-Larsen, Capt. Hjalmar, Antarctic explorer, 576, 577, 1046
Riksdag, parliament of Sweden, 311
Rim-Sin, defeated by Hammurabi, 26, 39
Rio Branco Law, of Brazil, 817
Rio de Janeiro, sacked, 501; 1155
Rio de la Plata, 800 *f.*; blockaded by French and English, 808
Ripon, Treaty of, 376

Ripon, George Frederick Samuel Robinson, Marquess of, viceroy of India, 870
Ripperdá, John William, Baron de, adventurer, 451
Ripurian Franks, 143
Risorgimento, Il, Italian newspaper, 657
Ristich, Jovan, prime minister of Serbia, 714
Ritsu sect, of Japanese Buddhists, 351
Ritterschaft, in Germany, 214
Rivera, Fructuoso, leader of *Colorados* in Uruguay, 811
Rivera, Luis Muñoz, Puerto Rican leader, 824
Rivera, Gen. Miguel Primo de, Spanish dictator, 909, 981
Rivers, Earl (Richard Woodville), executed, 271
Riviera coast, 1163
Rivière, Henri, French administrator, 874, 880
Rivoli, battle of, 585
Rizal, Dr. José, Philippine leader, 909
Rizzio, David, favorite of Mary, Queen of Scots, 373
Rjurik, founder of a Russian dynasty, 243
Roanoke Island, captured by Federal navy, 776
Robber Council, of Ephesus, 142
Roberjot, Claude, French diplomat, 587
Robert II (the Pious), King of France, 225, 238
Robert II, King of Scotland, 272
Robert III, King of Scotland, 272
Robert, brother of Henry I of France, 226, 227
Robert, Count of Paris, 159
Robert of Chester, 194
Robert of Courtenay, Latin emperor, 259
Robert (Angevin) of Naples, 292
Robert, son of Charles II of Naples, 222
Robert, son of William the Conqueror, 193
Robert the Strong, 158, 159
Robert brothers, built first hydrogen balloon, 553
Robert College, in Turkey, 728
Robertians, 159
Roberts, Frederick Sleigh Roberts, Earl, British general, 857
Robertson, James, 517
Roberval, François de la Roch, seigneur de, viceroy of Canada, 505
Robespierre, Augustin, brother of the following, 582
Robespierre, Maximilien Isidore, French revolutionary leader, 580–83
Robin Hood, 267
Robinson, George, in Tasmania, 899
Robles, Gil, Spanish Catholic leader, 983
Roca, Julio, pres. of Argentina, 808
Rocafuerte, Vicente, Ecuadorian leader, 813, 814
Rochambeau, Jean Baptiste Donatien de Vimeur, Count, French admiral, 522
Roche, Marquis Alexandre de la, French colonizer, 505
Roche, Otto de la, of Athens, 258
Rochefort, Jannequin, sieur de, French explorer, 524
Rochelle, under siege, 387
Roches, Peter des, tutor of Henry III, 198
Rochester, *see* Carr, Robert
Rochester, Laurence Hyde, Earl of, British statesman, 428
Rock, carvings, in caves, 5
Rockingham, Charles Watson-Wentworth, Marquis of, British prime minister, 436
Rocroi, battle of, 390, 440
Rodbertus, Johann Karl, German socialist, 549, 550
Roderick, Visigothic king of Spain, 163, 164, 187
Rodjestvensky, Zinovy Petrovich, Russian admiral, 752
Rodney, George Brydges, English admiral, 436, 516
Rodríguez, Gen. Abelardo, pres. of Mexico, 1076
Rodríguez de Francia, José, Dictator of Paraguay, 801, 810
Rodríguez, Simón, Spanish republican, 802
Roe, Sir Thomas, British diplomat, 533
Roehm, Ernst, German Nazi leader, 1003
Roentgen, Wilhelm Konrad, X-rays, 552
Roger of Salisbury, organized English exchequer, 196
Roger of Sicily, 252, 256
Roger I, lord of southern Italy, 218, 219
Roger II, of Sicily, 208, 210, 212, 219, 223
Roger-Ducos, Pierre, French revolutionary leader, 587
Rogers Bill, in U.S., 1051
Roggeveen, Jacob, Dutch discoverer, 894, 911
Rogier, Charles, Belgian statesman, 622, 623
Rohan, Benjamin de, defended Rochelle, 387
Rohan, Henri, Duc de, gov. of the Valtelline, 410
Rohlfs, Gustav, African explorer, 826
Roi, 1169
Rokuhara Tandai, Kyōto governors, 356
Roland, Cardinal, 210
Roland de la Platière, Jean Marie, Girondist leader, 581
Roland, Mme., 581
Roll silk, as writing material, 133, 135
Rolle, John, Englishman, refused to pay tonnage and poundage, 375
Rollo (Hrolf the Ganger), baptized as Robert, Norman leader. 159, 170; 204
Roma, Italian airship, 557
Roman, Prince of Galicia, 244
Roman Catholics, people German lands, 144; under Theodoric the Great, 145; persecuted, in Russia under Alexander III 706; *see* Papacy
Roman de la Rose, 231, 267
Roman Empire, in the west, 155, 162, 216
Roman Line, of Popes, 288
Romaña, Eduardo de, pres. of Peru, 813
Romanos, creator of religious poetry, 173

Romanov, Michael, Tsar of Russia; see Michael I
Romanov, Nikita, Russian boyar, 417
Romansch, language, 995
Romanus II, Byzantine emperor, 179
Romanus III (Argyropolus), Byzantine emperor, 249
Romanus Diogenes, 250
Romanus Lecapenus, Byzantine co-emperor with Constantine VII, 179, 183
Rome, 68 ff., 85 ff., 141, 150; Synod of, 217, 218; for later history see Papacy, Italy; 1141, 1150, 1159, 1162
Rome-Berlin Axis, 964, 991, 995, 1015
Rome-Berlin-Tokyo Pact, signed by Hungary, Rumania, Yugoslavia, 1136, 1150
Rome Protocols, 990, 992, 1007, 1015
Römer, Friedrich, German politician, 676
Rommel, Gen. Erwin, commander of German forces in North Africa, 1160
Romulus, traditional founder of Rome, 69
Romulus Augustus (nicknamed Augustulus), Roman emperor, 122
Roncesvalles, defeat of Franks, 155; Charlemagne's rear-guard annihilated, 163
Rooke, Sir George, British admiral, 431, 432
Roon, Albrecht Theodor Emil, Count von, Prussian minister of war, 680, 687
Roosebeke, battle of, 277
Roosevelt, Franklin Delano (32d pres. of the U.S.), 963, 966, 1053–56, 1057, 1133, 1136 passim; elected for fourth term, 1143; died, 1143
Roosevelt, Theodore (26th pres. of the U.S.), 753, 754, 788, 789, 790, 791, 892, 1079
Root and Branch Bill, in England, 376
Root-Takahira Agreement, 789, 893, 1049
Rosamund, daughter of Cunimund, 150
Rosas, Juan Manuel de, gov. of Buenos Aires, 806, 808, 810, 811
Roscellinus, champion of nominalism, 228
Rosebery, Archibald Philip Primrose, 5th Earl of, British prime minister, 618, 742, 743, 849
Rosecrans, William Starke, Federal general, 778
Rosen, Roman Romanovich, Baron, Russian diplomat, 747, 886
Ross, Gustavo, Liberal leader in Chile, 1065
Ross, James Clark, Arctic explorer, 563, 573
Ross, Capt. John, Arctic explorer, 562, 563
Ross, Sir Ronald, on transmission of malaria, 552
Ross Dependency, in Antarctica, 576
Rossa, O'Donovan, Irish agitator, 614
Rossbach, battle of, 467
Rossetti, Constantine, Rumanian leader, 719
Rossi, Maurice, world distance record in airplane, 558
Rossi, Count Pelegrino Luigi Edoardo, Papal statesman, 549, 654 f.
Rostopchin, Feodor Vasilyevich, Russian general, 598
Rostor, 1153
Roswitha, nun of Gandersheim, 162
Rosyth, British naval base, 917, 946
Rothari, becomes Roman Catholic, 150, 151
Rotterdam, blasted by Luftwaffe, 1146
Roubaix, taken by British, 950
Rouher, Eugène, French statesman, 631
Round Barrows culture, 17
Roundhead, parliamentarian Puritan, 377
Round-table conferences, in India, 1113
Rous, Sir John, motion censuring Lord North, 436
Rousseau, Jean-Jacques, French political theorist, 460, 728
Rouvier, Maurice, premier of France, 740, 753
Roux, Sylvain, in Madagascar, 859
Rovere, Francesco della, Pope Sixtus IV, 290
Rovere, Giuliano della, Cardinal, Pope Julius II, 395
Roveredo, battle of, 585
Rowanduz, taken by Russians, 927
Rowlatt Acts, in India, 1111
Roxana, wife of Alexander the Great, 65, 66, 77
Roxelana, wife of Sultan Suleiman, 423
Royal African Co., 433, 525
Royal Titles Bill, in England, 616
Royalist plot, in France, 979
Roye, abandoned by Germans, 938; taken by British and French, 950
Roze, Pierre Gustave, French admiral, 885
Rubattino Co., of Italy, 834
Rubicon, crossed by Caesar, 97, 99, 100
Rubber, vulcanizing process, 554
Rudini, Antonio Starabba, Marquis de, prime minister of Italy, 660 f.
Rudolf I, German emperor, 158, 240 f., 246, 299
Rudolf II, German emperor, 402
Rudolf III, of Burgundy, his death, 205
Rudolf I, King of Juran Burgundy, 157
Rudolf III, of Swabia, 306
Rudolf, Austrian Archduke, 694
Rudolf, Duke of Burgundy, 159; elected King of Italy, 215
Rudolf of Swabia, anti-king against Henry IV, 207
Rudolf, Lake, discovered, 828
Rudradaman, 129
Ruel, Treaty of, 440
Rufinus, 121
Rufus, Faenius, in conspiracy against Nero, 107
Rufus, Lucius Verginius, Roman general, 107
Rufus, Publius Rutifius, reforms Roman military system, 92
Rufus, Publius Sulpicius, 93
Ruge, Arnold, German politician, 676

Rugians, 143
Ruhr, invaded by French and Belgians, 958, 974, 977, 997
Ruhr Valley, 1164
Ruhrort, occupied by French, 956, 959, 997
Ruiz de Apodaca, Juan, viceroy of Mexico, 804
Rukh, Shah, son of Timur, 330
Ruhk, Shah of Persia, 529
Rukn al-Dawla, gets part of Persia and Iraq, 190
Rukn-i-Alam, a Persian saint, 333
Rule-of-reason, doctrine, 790
"Rule of the 'colonels,'" in Poland, 1039
Rum Rebellion, 896, 898
Rumania, 719 ff., 738, 760, 925, 934, 935, 944, 948, 949, 956, 977, 1009, 1024 ff.; 1135, 1136, 1137; occupied by Russia, 1142; 1143, 1149, 1150; surrendered to Russia, 1154; 1171
Rumili Hissar, see Castle of Europe
Rump Parliament, in England, 379, 425, 426
Runciman, Lord Walter, British statesman, 971, 1011
Runes, in Viking period, 170
Runnymede, signing of Magna Carta, 197
Rupert III, Elector, 298
Rupert, Prince, Stuart general, 377, 427
Rüppell, Edouard, African explorer, 826
Rupprecht of Bavaria, Prince, 913
Rusas I, II, III, 38
Rush, Richard, American minister to England, 644
Rush-Bagot Agreement, 770
Russell, Edward (later Earl of Orford), British admiral, 428, 431
Russell, Lord John, British prime minister, 606, 607, 612, 613, 795, 906
Russell, Lord Odo, British diplomat, 733
Russell, Lord William, in confederation against Charles II, 428, 431
Russia, history, 16, 242 ff., 316 ff., 415 ff., 471 ff., 596 ff., 701 ff., 741 ff., 913 ff., 1027 ff.; in Second World War, invaded Finland, 1135; invaded Iran, neutrality treaty with Japan, mutual aid treaty with Great Britain, invaded by Germany, 1137; 20-year treaty with Poland, 1143; invaded Poland, 1145; expelled from League of Nations, 1145 f.; non-aggression pact with Japan, 1150; invaded by Germany, 1151; campaigns, 1151 ff.; first Russian protocol, 1151; 1153; declared war on Bulgaria, 1154; declared war on Japan, invaded Manchuria, 1169, 1171
Russian-American Fur Co., 798
Russian Arctic development, 570
Russian armada, defeated by the Greeks, 179
Russian-Austrian Agreement, of 1897, 695, 746, 751, 757
Russian-Bulgarian Agreement, of 1909, 757
Russian-Chinese Agreement, of 1902, 751
Russian-Chinese Treaty, 882
Russian Church, independent of Constantinople, 417
Russian-German Treaty, of 1887, 741–743
Russian-Japanese War, 886 f.
Russian Law, earliest law code, 243
Russian Revolution, 938, 940, 941
Russian Turkestan, in Post-Palaeolithic period, 13
Russians (Varangians), first appearance, 177; 179, 215, 247, 316
Russo-Finnish War, 1135, 1145 f.
Russo-Turkish War, 616, 705
Rustam, Persian commander, 128, 186
Rustam Shah, of Persia, 330, 526
Rustenburg, at Capetown, 850
Rusticus, Junius Arulenus, executed, 109
Ruthenia, renamed Carpatho-Ukraine, 1013; 1144
Rutherford, Ernest, radio-activity, 552; 553
Rye House Plot, in England, 428
Ryerson, Egerton, Canadian rebel leader, 795
Rykov, Alexei Ivanovich, Russian Bolshevik, 1036
Rymill, John, Antarctic explorer, 577
Ryō no Gige, commentary on Japanese laws, 350
Ryō no Shūge, on Japanese laws, 350
Ryōbu Shintō, Japanese religious belief, 350
Ryswick, Treaty of, 431, 439, 444, 445, 447, 494, 514
Ryti, Risto, President of Finland, 1142
Rzher, 1153

Sá Mem de, founded São Paulo, 501; and Rio de Janeiro, 501
Saalfeld, battle of, 592
Saar, plebiscite in, 1003
Saar River, 1164
Saavedra, Bautista, pres. of Bolivia, 1067
Saavedra Cedron, Alvaro, expedition to Philippine Islands, 908
Sabaean Kingdom, 13
Sabin, Bulgar ruler, 182
Sabine, Capt. Edward, magnetic observatory on Pendulum Island, 562, 563
Sabines, 68, 70, 74
Sabinians, jurisprudence schools, 116
Sabinus, Julius, 108
Sabinus, Nymphidius, praefect, 107
Saburai-dokoro, 355
Saburo Kurusu, Japanese envoy to U.S., 1166
Saburov, Pierre Alexandrovich, Russian diplomat, 737
Sacasa, Juan, pres. of Nicaragua, 1073
Sacheverell, Henry, preached ultra-Tory sermons, 432
Sacken, Gen. Dmitri, Russian general, 599
Sacraments, decreed by Fourth Lateran Council, 221
Sacred Mount, 71, 72
Sacred Wars, 52, 56, 64, 65
Sacrosancta, superiority of council over pope, 289

Sacrovir, Julius, leads revolt of the Aedui, 103
Sa'd ibn-Abi-Waqqās, leads Arabs against Persians, 128, 185
Sadanobu, Matsudaira, Japanese regent, 548
Sadaqa, The, of the Mazyadid dynasty, 190
Saddharma-pundarika-sutra, 129, 136
Sadducees, 32
Sadi-Carnot, Marie François, pres. of France, 639, 640
Sadowa, see Königgrätz, battle of
Sadyattes, of the Mermnadae, 37
Safavid dynasty, in Persia, 330
Saffarid dynasty, 189
Safi, Aurelio, Roman leader, 655
Safi, Shah of Persia, 528
Safi al-Din of Ardabil, 526
Sagas, Norwegian, 205, 365
Sagasta, Práxedes Mateo, Spanish statesman, 647, 823
Saguntum, 87
Saichō (Dengyō Daishi), founder of the Tendai sect in Japan, 352
Saigo of Satsuma, leader in the Satsuma Rebellion, 889, 890
Saigon, Treaty of, 874, 880
Saikaku, Ibara, Japanese author, 547
Sailendra dynasty, in Malaysia, 348
St. Adalbert, of Prague, 244
St. Albans, battle of, 270
Saint-Arnaud, Armand Jacques Leroy de, French general, 632, 727
St. Augustine, Church father, 142
St. Augustine, in Florida, 514
St. Bernard, of Clairvaux, 228
St. Christopher, settled, 510; ceded to England, 514
St. Clair, Gen. Arthur, 766
St. Germain, truce of, 384; Treaty of, 953, 1005
St. Germain, Comte de, war minister of Louis XVI, 448
St. Germain-en-Laye, Treaty of, 443, 471
St. Giles' riot, in Edinburgh, 376
St. Gothard Railway, in Switzerland, 667
St. Gotthard, battle of, 483
St. Helena, island, 603
St. Jean de la Croix, reformed monasteries, 389
St. Jean de Maurienne conference, 937
St. John, Henry, Viscount Bolingbroke, English statesman, 432, 433, 434
St. John, Oliver, resists imposition of a benevolence, 374
St. John, of Rila, 183
St. John the Greater, 164
St. John's Chapel, in Tower of London, 193
Saint-Just, Louis de, French revolutionary leader, 582
St. Kunigunde, wife of Henry II of Germany, 162
St. Lo, 1163
St. Ladislas, of Hungary, 245
St. Leger, Gen. Barry, 521
St. Lucia, 1148 f., 1155, 1158
St. Lucia Bay, annexed by Britain, 854
St. Marcouf, 1163
St. Mark's Church, Venice, 224
St. Michael, Shrine of, 217
St. Mihiel, in the First World War, 914, 921, 950, 1049
St. Paul (Saul of Tarsus), 106; 113
St. Paul's Cathedral, London, 427
St. Peter's Yard, Russia, 307
St. Petersburg, founded, 479; renamed Petrograd, 1028; Treaties of, 468, 596, 880
St. Petersburg Protocol, 723
St. Pierre and Miquelon, 1138
St. Quentin, battles of, 372, 383, 389, 395, 950
Saint-Ruth, French general, 430
St. Sava, Archbishop of Serbia, 247
Saint-Simon, Count Claude Henri de, Utopian socialist, 549, 628
St. Stephen (I) of Hungary, 241, 245
Ste. Theresa de Jesus, Carmelite nun, 389
St. Thomas, 1154
St. Wenceslas, murdered, 239
Saionji, Marquis Kimmochi, premier of Japan, 892, 893, 952
Saipan, 1169
Sais, 21, 24
Saitic revival, 24
Saito, Makoto, Viscount, premier of Japan, 1126
Saiyid-i-Edjil Chams al-Din Omar, Mohammedan financier, 345
Saka rulers, of India, 128, 129
Sakanoue Tamuramaro, 351
Sakas subdued, 43, 124
Saker, Edward, Baptist mission at Ambas Bay, 840
Sakhalin, 1171
Sakje-Geuzi, 13
Sakkara, 23
Sakkara, battle of, 1021; 1095
Sakuntala, 131
Sakya, 42
Sakyamitra, 331
Sakyamuni, 129
Saladin (Salah al-Din), 254, 256, 257, 262 f.
Salado, battle of, 280, 284
Salamana, 1169
Salamanca, Daniel, pres. of Bolivia, 1067
Salamis, battle of, 40, 54, 56
Salandra, Antonio, prime minister of Italy, 662, 925, 930, 988
Salankayana of Vengi, 132
Salasco, Carlo Canera di, Italian general, 654
Salazar mission, 687
Salbai, Treaty of, 535

Saldanha, Manuel de, Portuguese ambassador to China, 539
Salerno, capital of a Lombard principality, 217; 1142, 1162
Salgharids, hold Fars, 255
Salian Franks, 143, 147
Salian House, of German emperors, 205, 208
Salic Law, in France, 273, 442; in Spain, 450, 644; in Hanover, 669
Salim, Prince, see Jahangir
Salinator, Marcus Livius, 88
Salisbury, in Mashonaland, 855
Salisbury, Robert Arthur Talbot Gascoyne-Cecil, 3d Marquess of, British prime minister, 617, 618, 619, 734, 735, 744, 747, 750, 786
Salisbury, Robert Cecil, Earl of, 374
Sallust (Caius Sallustius Crispus), Roman historian, 100
Salvador, El, 1071, 1074
Salvaterra, Juan Maria, Jesuit missionary, 499
Salvius, John Adler, Swedish diplomat, 408
Salvius, Julianus, 110, 116
Salza, Hermann von, leader of Teutonic Knights, 211, 214, 257
Salzburg, votes for union with Germany, 1006
Sam'al, Kingdom of, 34, 35
Samanids, dynasty, 189, 190, 332
Samantabhadra, 130
Samara, taken by Czech troops, 947
Samarcand, taken by Moslems, 186
Samaria, 27, 31, 32
Samarra, reached by British, 938
Samaveda, 41
Sambhaji, Raja of the Marathas, 534
Samh, captures Narbonne, 187
Sami, Mahmud, premier of Egypt, 831
Samians, 53, 54
Samkara of Malabar, 336
Samkhya-karika, 131
Samnite Wars, 73, 74
Samnites, 68, 73, 74, 78, 86, 87, 94
Samo, Frankish tradesman, 239
Samoa, 784, 894, 896, 911, 918
Samoan Islands, divided, 749, 911
Samoilovich, Prof. Rudolph Lazarevich, Russian scientist, 570
Samori, Mandingo ruler, 841, 842
Samos, 47 passim
Samos, Philippine island, 1169
Samosata, 108
Samothrace, 63
Sampson, William Thomas, American admiral, 824
Samson, 30
Samsonov, Alexander Vasilyevich, Russian general, 916
Samudragupta, 130
Samuel, 30
Samuel, Bulgarian tsar, 180, 181, 183, 249
Samuel, Sir Herbert, high commissioner for Palestine, 969, 1100
San, battle of, 922
San Diego, founded, 493
San Francisco Conference, 1144, 1171
San Germano, peace of, 211
San Giovanni di Medua, 925, 927, 949
San Giuliano, Antonio Paterno-Castelli, Marquis di, Italian foreign minister, 923
San Ildefonso, Treaties of, 452, 495, 502
San Jacinto, battle of, 772
San Jacinto, American steamship, 776
San Juan, 1154
San Juan Hill, battle of, 787
San Lorenzo, Treaty of, 766
San Marco library, 296
San Martin, Grau, pres. of Cuba, 1077
San Martin, José de, commander in Rio de la Plata, 800, 801, 802, 803, 806
San Mateo, Treaty of, 802
San Remo Conference, 987
San Salvador, in the Bahamas, 367, 805
San Sebastian, taken by the Insurgents in Spanish Civil War, 983
San Stefano, Treaty of, 705, 717, 735
Sanaa, Treaty of, 1104
Sanchi, 42, 43, 129, 131
Sancho II, of Castile, 233, 239
Sancho I, of Portugal, 239
Sancho, of Leon, 164
Sancho, son of Alfonso X of Castile, 235
Sancho the Fat, of Leon, 164
Sancho the Great, of Navarre, 164, 237
Sanclemente, Miguel, pres. of Colombia, 815
Sancroft, William, Archbishop of Canterbury, 429
Sand, Karl, German revolutionary, 669
Sand River Convention, 852
Sanderson, William, English explorer, 559
Sandino, Gen. Agustino, Nicaraguan rebel, 1073
Sandler, Rickard, premier of Sweden, 1047
Sandracottus, 81
Sandwich Islands, see Hawaii
Sandys, Sir Edwin, in Virginia colony, 508
Sanetomo, Japanese shōgun, 356
Sanfuentes, Juan Luis, pres. of Chile, 810
Sang Hyang-yang, 134
Sanga, 345
Sanhedrin, 105, 107
Sanjō II, Emperor of Japan, 353
Sanjurjo, Gen. José, Spanish insurgent, 982, 983

Sankey, John, 1st Viscount, 967
Sanron sect, in Japan, 351
Sanskrit, 42, 131, 132
Santa Anna, Antonio López de, pres. of Mexico, 821
Santa Cruz, Andrés, pres. of Bolivia, 802, 809, 811
Santa Cruz Islands, discovered, 894
Santa Elena peninsula, 1156
Santa Fé, founded, 492
Santa Hermandad, union of Castilian towns, 282
Santa Margherita, Treaty of, 988
Santa Maria, Domingo, pres. of Chile, 809
Santa Sophia, in Constantinople, 327
Santander, Francisco de Paula, pres. of New Granada, 803, 814
Santarem, João de, explorer, 364
Santiago, battle of, 787
Santiago, Chile, 1155
Santiago de Campostella, 164
Santideva, his poem *Bodhicharyavatara*, 131
Santo Domingo, 486, 789, 824, 825
Santos, Eduardo, pres. of Colombia, 1070
Santos-Dumont, Alberto, Brazilian aeronaut, 557
São Paulo de Loanda, settled, 524
Sapieanza, battle of, 298
Sappho, Greek poetess, 48
Saracens, defeat Otto II, 162; 212; raid into Lombardy, 215; defeat Adriatic pirates, 249. *See also* Moslems
Sarafov, Boris, Macedonian revolutionary, 718
Saragossa, captured by Moslems, 163, 187; battle of, 450; Treaty of, 908
Sarah, Duchess of Marlborough, 431
Sarajevo, assassination of Francis Ferdinand, 761
Saratoga, *see* Bemis Heights, battle of
Sarawak, ceded to Sir James Brooke, 877
Sarbadarids, in Khorasan, 330
Sardinia, 34, 86, 99, 158, 218; *see* Savoy, Piedmont; 1141, 1142, 1162
Sardinians, 24
Sardis, 37, 48, 53, 60
Sardur I, II, III, IV, of Armenia, 38
Sargon I, 25, 35; II, 27, 33, 38, 39
Sari Bair, battle of, 920
Sarikamish, battle of, 919
Sarmatians, attack on Danube frontier, 111, 120
Sarmiento, Domingo, pres. of Argentina, 808
Sarnath, 43, 131
Sarrail, Maurice Paul Emmanuel, French general, 927, 934, 948, 1098
Sarraut, Albert, premier of France, 979, 1088
Sarsfield, Patrick, defeated at Aughrim, 430
Sarva darsana samgraha, 338
Sarvastivadin, a sect, 128
Sarwat Pasha, premier of Egypt, 1083
Sasbach, battle of, 442
Saskatchewan, Canadian province, 797
Sassanian dynasty, 26, 124–32, 136
Satakani, 129
Satakani Empire, 132
Satala, 108
Satavahana, 129
Satsuma Chōshū, Tosa, and Hizen, offer to abolish feudalism, 899
Sattasai, poems, 129
"Saturnians," 90
Saturninus, Lucius Appuleius, 93, 109
Saudi Arabia, new name of Kingdom of Hejaz and Nejd, 1104, 1106
Saul, 30
Saundarananda, 129
Saushshattar, 28
Sautrantika school, 131
Savage, John, plot against Queen Elizabeth, 373
Savage, Michael Joseph, premier of New Zealand, 1132
Savage Island, 896; annexed to New Zealand, 908
Savannah, founded, 514; captured by British, 522
Savannah, steamship, 770
Saviors of the Nation, with Albanians in insurrection against Turks, 732
Savonarola, Girolamo, Dominican friar, 290, 296
Savov, Michael, Bulgar general, 719, 760
Savoy, 397, 458, 463
Saxa Rubra, 119
Saxe, Maurice, Count de, French marshal, 434, 466
Saxo Grammaticus, his *Historia Danica*, 399
Saxons, 121, 142; in England, 166; 245, 246
Saxony, conquered by Charlemagne, 153; overrun by Magyars, 158; 160, 465, 466, 468, 599
Say, Jean Baptiste, French political economist, 549
Saye and Sele, William Fiennes, Lord, rights to Connecticut River Valley, 509
Sayf al-Dawla, captured Aleppo, 190
Sayyid Ali Mohammed, founder of B'abism, 864
Sayyid Khalifa, Sultan of Zanzibar, 848
Sayyid Said, representative of Sultan of Muscat, 847
Sayyid Zia ud-Din, Persian writer, 1108
Sazonov, Sergei Dmitrievich, Russian statesman, 721, 757, 758, 920, 925, 930
Scaevola, Quintus Mucius, 71, 100
Scaligers, of Verona, 299
Scanderbeg (George Castriota), Albanian hero, 327
Scandinavia, 170, 203 *ff*., 311 *ff*., 410 *ff*., 471 *ff*., 697 *ff*., 1045 *ff*.
Scapa Flow, British naval base, 917, 946, 996

Scarborough, bombarded, 917
Scerdilaidas, 87
Schacht, Hjalmar, German financier and statesman, 998; 1004
Schall von Bell, Johan Adam, reformed dynastic calendar, 537, 539
Scharnhorst, German cruiser, 917
Scharnhorst, Gerhard Johann David von, Prussian general, 594, 599
Schärtlin, Sebastian, in the Schmalkaldic League, 402
Schauenberg, Alexis Henry Antoine Balthasar, Baron de, 460
Scheer, Reinhard, German admiral, 951
Scheidemann, Philipp, German Socialist leader, 951, 995
Schérer, Barthélemy Louis Joseph, French general, 586
Schill, Ferdinand Baptista von, Prussian general, 592, 595
Schism Act, 433, 434
Schleicher, Gen. Kurt von, German chancellor, 999, 1003
Schleicher, Matthias Jakob, cell theory in physiology, 551
Schleiermacher, Friedrich Daniel Ernst, German philosopher, 594
Schleswig, 160, 203, 312
Schleswig-Holstein question, 676, 681, 697, 953, 996
Schlieffen Plan, in World War, 913
Schmalkaldic League, 401
Schmalkaldic War, 402
Schmerling, Anton, Austrian minister for foreign affairs, 675
Schmidt, Prof. Otto, Russian explorer, 567, 570
Schnaebelé, Guillaume, French customs official, 639, 691, 740
Schnitzer, Eduard, *see* Emin Pasha
Schober, Johann, Austrian premier, 1006
Scholarius, George, Byzantine theologian, 323
Schomberg, Friedrich Hermann, English general, 443
Schomberg, Meinhart, Duke of Leinster, 430
Schön, Wilhelm Eduard von, German foreign minister, 755
Schönbrunn, Convention, 733; Treaty of, 595, 596
Schouten, Willem Cornelisz van, Dutch explorer, 894
Schouten Group, 1169
Schroeder-Stranz, Lt. Hans G. Leo, Arctic explorer, 569
Schumacher, Peter (afterward Count Griffenfeld), treatise on absolutism, 474
Schurman, Jacob Gould, on Philippine Commission, 909
Schuschnigg, Kurt, Austrian chancellor, 1004, 1007, 1008
Schutzbund, Socialist private army, 1006
Schwarzenberg, Prince Félix, Austrian statesman, 654, 674, 677
Schwarzenberg, Karl Philipp, Austrian general, 596, 599, 600
Schweinfurt, 110
Schweinfurth, Georg August, African explorer, 828
Schwerin, Kurt Christoph, Count von, Prussian general, 466
Scientific thought and progress, 551 *ff*.
Scipio, Aemilianus, destroyed Carthage, 90; 91, 92
Scipio, Cnaius Cornelius, 86, 87
Scipio, L. Cornelius (*Asiaticus*), 89
Scipio, Lucius, 94
Scipio Nasica, P. Cornelius, 91
Scipio, Publius Cornelius (Africanus), 87, 88, 89
Scipio, Publius Cornelius, defeated by Hannibal, 88
Scipio, Quintus Caecilius Metellus Pius, 95, 97
"Scipionic circle," 91
Sciri, 143
Sclaveni, early name of the Slavs, 239
Scolvus, Johannes, explorer, 365
Scopas, 67
Scoresby, William, Arctic explorer, 562
Scoresby, William, Jr., Arctic explorer, 562
Scoresby Sound Committee (Danish), 569
Scotch Reform Bill, 613 *f*.
Scotch Spitsbergen Syndicate, 569
Scotland, 167, 199, 201, 272, 607, 1148
Scott, Sir Francis Clayton, British general, 842
Scott, Capt. Robert Falcon, Antarctic explorer, 574, 575, 576
Scott, Thomas, executed in Red River Rebellion, 796
Scott, Walter, designed first color press, 556
Scott, Winfield, American general, 773, 776
Scottish Free Church Association, settled Otago, 906
Scottish invasion, stopped by the Percies, 268
Scottish Kirk, established, 376
Scottish National Expedition, led by Dr. W. S. Bruce, 574
Scottish War, 264
Scrap iron and steel, embargo on, 1136
Screw propeller, 770
Scribonia, second wife of Octavian, 99
Scrope, Richard Le, rebellion against Henry IV, 268
Scullin, James Henry, premier of Australia, 1130
Sculpture, among the Assyrians, 26; among the Greeks, 53, 67
Scutage, levied in England, 196
Scutari, taken by the Austrians, 927; taken by the Italians, 949
Scyrus, 62
Scythians, 83
Sealers, in exploration, 571
Seamen's Security Law, in Norway, 1046
Se-ami, Japanese playwright, 359
Sebaste, 32
Sebastian I, King of Portugal, 392, 524
Sébastiani, Horace François Bastien, Count, French general and diplomat, 592
Sebastopol, in the Crimea, 727, 728, 919, 943, 1153, 1154
Sebastopolis, battle of, 175
Sebilian, industry, &c; culture, 18
Secession states, 776
Second Crusade, 219, 228, 252 *f*., 256
Second International, 550
Second Lateran Council, 219

Second Lombard League, 211, 212
Second Peace of Paris, 603
Secretariat, United Nations, 1171
Secretariat of the Indies, 496
Secret societies, in France, 627; in Italy, 650
Sects, in Japanese Buddhism, 351 *f.*
Securities and Securities Exchange Acts, in U.S., 1054
Security Council, United Nations, 1171
Sedan, battle of, 636, 688; 1146, 1148
Seddon, Richard John, prime minister of New Zealand, 907, 908
Sedeño, Antonio de, Spanish colonizer, 488
Sedgemoor, battle of, 429
Sedgwick, Adam, English geologist, 551
Sedition Act, of U.S., 766, 1049
Sedow, Lt. Georgii Yakovlevich, Russian explorer, 570
Seeadler, German cruiser, 932
Segesta, 56, 57, 59, 66
Sei Shōnagon, Japanese woman writer, 353
Seidler, Dr. Ernst von, Austrian prime minister, 942
Seine, 1163
Seipel, Ignaz, premier of Austria, 1006
Seisachtheia (laws), 51
Seiyūkai, party in Japan, 1123
Seize Mai, crisis of, in France, 638
Sejanus, Lucius Aelius, 101; 103; 105
Sejm, Polish parliament, 1038, 1040
Sejong, King of Korea, 349
Sekigahara, battle of, 544
Selborne, William Waldegrave Palmer, 2d Earl of, high commissioner in South Africa, 858
Selden, John, imprisoned for signing the Great Protestation, 375
Seldte, Franz, in Hitler cabinet, 1000
Selective Training and Service Act, 1049, 1136
Seleucia, 83, 111
Seleucids, dynasty of, 25; 32, 33, 37, 38, 43, 75, 80–83
Seleucus I Nicator, 33, 35, 37, 42, 77, 78, 81, 83
Seleucus II Callinicus, 81, 83
Seleucus III Soter, 81
Seleucus IV Philopater, 81, 82
Seleucus V and VI, 82
Self-Denying Ordinance, in England, 378
Seligenstadt, Synod of, 216
Selim I (the Grim), Ottoman sultan, 420 *f.*, 422, 423, 524, 526
Selim II (the Sot), Ottoman sultan, 402, 423
Selim III, Ottoman sultan, 485, 715, 721, 722
Selinus, 34, 57, 59, 66, 110
Seljuk Empire of the East, 254 *f.*
Seljuk Turks, 181, 190, 248 *ff.*, 254 *f.*, 320, 324
Selkirk, Thomas Douglas, 5th Earl of, his settlement on Red River, 793
Sella, Quintino, Italian minister of finance, 660
Sellasia, battle of, 79
Selves, Justin Germain Casimir de, French foreign minister, 758
Selwyn, George Augustus, Bishop of New Zealand, 905
Semainian culture, 18
Semaphore telegraph, 553
Semendria, Serbia, falls, 526
Semenov, Gen. Nicolai, Russian counter-revolutionary, 1032
Seminole War, in Florida, 770
Semiramis (*Shammu-ramat*), 27
Semites, 23; language, 25
Sempach, battle of, 306
Senate (France), 632, 635, 636, 638
Senate of Napoleon I, 587, 588, 591
Senatus consultum (decree of a senate), 632, 633, 636
Seneca, adviser of Nero, 106, 107, 112
Seneca, Lucius Annaeus, philosopher, 112, 113
Senecio, Herennius, executed, 109
Senef, battle of, 448
Senior, Nassau William, English economist, 549
Senjirli, 28, 35
Senlis, Treaty of, 381
Sennacherib (*Sin-ahê-erba*), 27, 31, 33, 39
Senones, annihilated by the Romans, 74
Sentinum, 74
Senussi Arabs, 839, 840, 929, 1086, 1087
Separate Graves culture, 18
Separatist movement in Rhineland, 998
Separatists, in England, 372
Sepeia, battle of, 50
Sepoy mutiny, 870
September Laws, in France, 628, 630
September massacres, in Paris, 581
Septennial Act, in England, 434
Septimius Severus, Lucius, Roman emperor, 114, 166
Septinsular Republic, 587
Septuagint, Hebrew Bible, 75
Sequeira, Ruy de, explorer, 364
Serai (New and Old), palaces in Constantinople, 327
Serapis, defeated, 521
Serbia, 183, 246 *ff.*, 318 *ff.*, 712 *ff.*, 926, 932, 941, 1016
Serbian-Austrian tariff war, 755
Serbs, branch of southern Slavs, 239
Serbs, Croats, and Slovenes, Kingdom of, 1016; name officially changed to Yugoslavia, 1017
Seres, taken by Bulgar-German army, 934
Serfdom, established in Russia, 478; abolished, 703
Sergent, Antoine François, French revolutionary, 581
Sergius, Duke, defeats the Moslems, 152
Sergius, Patriarch, 173, 174
Sergius III. Pope. 215

Serna, José de la, viceroy of Peru, 802
Serrano y Dominguez, Francisco, Spanish regent, 646, 687
Serrato, José, pres. of Uruguay, 1066
Sertorius, Quintus, 95
Servan de Gerbey, Joseph, in French Revolution, 581
Servetus, Michael, executed, 409
Servien, Abel, French diplomat, 407
Servile Wars, 90, 92, 93, 95
Servius Ahala, 72
Servius Tullius, 69, 70
Servus Servorum Dei, papal style, 151
Sesostris I, II, 23; III, 23, 29
Sesshū, Japanese painter, 358
Sestos, 54
Seti I (Sethos), 24, 30
Sevar, Bulgarian ruler, 182
Sevastopol, *see* Sebastopol
"Seven Centuries" poems, 129
Seven Cities of Cibola, legend of, 492
Seven Days, battle of, 778
Seven Weeks' War, 682 *ff.*
Seven Years' War, 435, 447, 452, 454, 466 *ff.*, 481, 484, 517, 521
Seventeen Article Constitution, of Japan, 140
Seventeen Standard Histories, Chinese, 537
Seventh Crusade, 257 *f.*
Severi, 116
Severus, 22
Severus, Flavius Valerius, Roman Caesar, 119
Sèves, Col. Joseph (Soliman Pasha), organized Egyptian army, 828
Sevier, John, 517
Seville, captured by Moslems, 163, 187; Treaty of, 434, 451
Seville, Diogo de, discovered the Azores, 363
Sèvres, Treaty of, 954, 1020, 1094
Sewing machine, 554
Seward, William Henry, U.S. secretary of state, 774, 776
Sextius, Lucius, 72
Seymour, Frederick Beauchamp Paget, British admiral, 832
Seymour, Sir George Hamilton, British diplomat, 726
Seymour, Jane, 3d wife of Henry VIII, 369
Seymour, Thomas, brother of the Duke of Somerset, 370
Seyss-Inquart, Arthur, Austrian Nazi leader, 1008
Sfondato, Nicoló, Pope Gregory XIV, 396
Sforza, Count Carlo, Italian foreign minister, 987, 1143
Sforza, Francesco, 292 *f.*, 295, 298, 397, 400, 401, 409
Sforza, Francesco Maria, 395
Sforza, Galeazzo Maria, 298
Sforza, Gian Galeazzo, 298
Sforza, Ludovico (il Moro), 290, 296, 298, 393
Sforza, Maximilian, 394
Sforza, the, rulers of Milan, 298
Sguros of Greece, a feudal family, 253
Shabaka, King of Napata, 24
Shackleton, Edward, Arctic explorer, 567
Shackleton, Lt. Ernest Henry, Antarctic explorer, 574; 575 *f.*
SHAEF, 1142
Shaftesbury, Anthony Ashley Cooper, 1st Earl of, British statesman, 427, 428
Shah, Riza, ruler of Iran, 1137
Shah Shuja, Amir of Afghanistan, 866
Sha-ho, battle of, 707
Shahr-Baraz, subjugates Egypt, 127
Shallum, 31
Shalmaneser I, 29, 38; III, 27, 31, 33, 35, 38, 40; IV, 38; V, 26, 27
Shamash-Shum-ukin, 27, 40
Shami Pir, religious leader, 1111
Shamiramalti, 13
Shamshi-Adad V, 27, 38
Shams-ud-din Iltutmish, slave ruler, 333
Shan, 44
Shan States, 872
Shang Chih-hsin, 539
Shang dynasty, in China, 14, 44
Shanghai, 879, 962, 1121, 1165
Shang Yang, 45
Shanhaikwan, occupied by Japanese, 962
Shansabani Persian Princes, of Ghur, 332
Shansi, 44
Shantung, Treaty of, 958, 1124
Shapley, Harlow, star distances, 553
Shapur (*Sapor, Shahpuhri*), 115, 116, 124
Shapur II and III, 125
Share-croppers, 51
Sharifian dynasty, 524
Sharki dynasty, 334
Sharon, 29
Sharpe, Archbishop James, 428
Shattuara, King of Hanigalbat, 29
Shaukat Ali, leader of the Moslem League, 1112
Sha'ul (Saul), 35
Shaw, George Bernard, Irish dramatist, 618
Shaw, Sir Walter, report on Palestine, 1101
Sheba, 13
Shechem, 31
Sheep-raising, in New Zealand, 906
Sheikh Khazal, of Mohammerah, 1108
Sheikh Mahmud, Kurd leader, 1105
Shelburne, William Petty Fitzmaurice, Earl of, British prime minister, 436
Shemakha, ceded to Russia, 701

Shemyaka, in civil war in Russia, 316
Shen Chia-pen, Chinese jurist, 883
Shen Tsung, Chinese ruler, 342, 536
Sheng Hsüan-huai, Chinese railway administrator, 884
Sheng Tsu, of the K'ang Hsi Reign, 537, 540
Shepstone, Sir Theophilus, annexation of South African Republic, 853
Sher Ali, Amir of Afghanistan, 736
Sher-Shah, the Afghan, 530
Sheridan, Philip Henry, Federal general, 779
Sheridan, Richard Brinsley, under-secretary of state, 437
Sheriffmuir, battle of, 434
Sheriffs, in England, 191
Sherman, William Tecumseh, Federal general, 779
Sherman Anti-Trust Law, in U.S., 785, 787
Sherman Silver Purchase Act, in U.S., 785, 786
Shi'a, Moslem teaching, 526
Shibasaburo Kitasato, bubonic plague germ, 552
Shidehara, Baron Kijuro, Japanese diplomat, 1124, 1125
Shigemori, son of Kiyomori, 354
Shih Chi, general history of China, 134
Shih Huang Ti, 132
Shih Tsu, dynastic name of Kublai Khan, 345
Shih Tsu, of the Shun Chih Reign, 537
Shih Tsung, of the Chia Ching Reign, 536, 543
Shihchiachuang, taken by Japanese, 1121
Shi'ites, 186, 187, 188, 526
Shikibu, Takenouchi, Japanese scholar, 548
Shikoku, island, 138
Shiloh, battle of, 778
Shimabara, uprising of peasants, 547
Shimonoseki, Treaty of, 743 f., 881, 886, 891
Shingen, Takeda, 543
Shingon, Japanese sect, 352
Shinran Shōnin, founded New Pure Land sect, 356
Shintō, religion in Japan, 138
Shipbuilding, the use of iron, 554
Ship-money, tax in England, 376
Shipping Board of U.S., 792
Shipping Control Commission in England, 929
Ship subsidy policy of U.S., 775
Shir Ali, Amir of Afghanistan, 867
Shirase, Lt. Choku, Japanese explorer, 575
Shirawaka, Emperor of Japan, 354
Shirawaka II, Emperor of Japan, 354
Shire system, in England, 167
Shirkuh, vizier of Egypt, 262
Shirley, Sir Anthony and Sir Robert, English adventurers, 424, 526
Shirley, William, captured Louisburg, 515
Shishman, Tsar of Bulgaria, 322, 324
Shitennōji, monastery in Japan, 140
Shōgun, Japanese title, 356, 544
Shōin, Yoshida, anti-foreign Japanese, 888
Sholes, Christopher Latham, use of typewriter, 555, 781
Shōmu, Emperor of Japan, 350
Shore, Sir John, gov.-gen. of India, 536
Short-Cut School, 340
Shoshenk (later Sheshonk), 24
Shōtoku, Emperor of Japan, 140, 351
Showa Period, in Japan, 1125
Shrewsbury, Charles Talbot, Earl of, English statesman, 429, 430, 431, 434
Shu or Shu-Han dynasty, 135
Shubbiluliu, King of the Hittites, 29, 35, 36
Shubun, Japanese painter, 358
Shufeldt, Capt. Robert Wilson, American emissary to Korea, 885, 890
Shuh Chih Reign of Shih Tsu, 537
Shuisky, Basil, Russian tsar, 418
Shuiskys, Russian noble family, 415
Shurur, battle of, 526
Shuster, 124
Shuster, William Morgan, treasurer-gen. of Persia, 758, 865
Shutarna, 29
Shutruk-nahunte, raided Babylonia, 39; II, 39
Shuvalov, Peter Andreievich, Russian diplomat, 736
Siam, 347, 541, 872 f., 1114
Siamese, 44
Siberia, in Palaeolithic period, 7; in Post-Palaeolithic, 14; coast surveyed, 562
Sibittibaal, 33
Sibiu, battle of, 934
Sibley, Henry Hastings, American general, 780
Siccardi, Giuseppe, Italian statesman, 657
Sicels, displace Sicans, 52; 57
Sicilian Vespers, War of, 222, 231, 258, 290, 321
Sicilians, 24; originally Sicans, 53
Sicily, ancient, 52, 53, 57, 66, 78, 86; conquered by Moslems, 158, 177, 215, 217; medieval, 210 f., 212, 213, 218, 290, 292, 447; revolution, 651; 659; modern, 1142; invaded by American, British, and Canadian forces, 1159, 1162
Sickingen, Franz, von, German knight, 400
Sickness Insurance Law, in Germany, 690, 692
Siculan cultures I, II, III, 17
Sicyon, 43, 50, 52, 79, 90
Siddhanta, 42
Siddhartha, founder of Buddhism, 41
Sidi Barrani, 1160
Sidi Idriss, Sheikh, head of the Senussi, 1087
Sidi Mohammed, Sultan of Morocco, 525

Sidi Mohammed III, Sultan of Morocco, 1088
Sidney, Algernon, in a confederation against Charles II, 428
Sidney, Henry, signs invitation to William of Orange, 429
Sidney, Sir Philip, English poet, 373
Sidon, 27, 32, 33, 53
Sidonians, 32
Siebener Concordat, in Switzerland, 666
Siege engines, 27
Siegebert, Ripuarian Frank, 147
Siemens, Werner von, introduced the electric street car, 556
Siemens, Sir William, open hearth method of steel-making, 555
Sien-pi, Mongols, 134, 135
Sierra Leone, British colony, 840, 1090
Sievershausen, battle of, 402
Siéyès, Emmanuel Joseph, Abbé, French revolutionary leader, 579, 587
Sigeric, 144
Sigeum, 51, 52
Sigismund I, King of Poland, 415
Sigismund II (August), King of Poland, 413, 414
Sigismund III, King of Poland, 415-418
Sigismund, German emperor, 288, 289, 302, 305, 306, 307, 314, 318, 324
Sigismund, King of Sweden, 413
Sigüenza y Góngora, Carlos, Spanish-American scientist, 500
Sikhs, a religious order, 534, 868, 870
Sikorsky, Igor, developed twin-motored planes, 557
Silaharas, a dynasty, 337
Siles, Hernando, pres. of Bolivia, 1067
Silesia, 239, 240, 1145
Silesian Wars, 1st and 2d, 465, 466; 3d or Seven Years', 466
Silesians, defeated by Mongols, 211
Siling Vandals, in Spain, 144
Silistria, taken by Bulgar-German forces, 934
Silius, Gaius, revolt in Gaul, 103
Silk floss paper, 135
Silla, Korean state, 137 f., 140, 348
Silva, Antonio Maria da, Portuguese prime minister, 985
Silva Xavier, Joaquim José da, revolution in Minas Geráes, 502
Silvela, Augustino Francisco, Spanish statesman, 647
Silver (literary) Age, 112
Silver mines, of Potosi, 489, 492; of Mexico and Peru, 489
Silver Pavilion (Ginkaku), in Kyōto, 359
Silver Purchase Act in U.S., 785, 786, 1054
Silver standard, abandoned by China, 1120
Silvestre, Fernandez, Spanish general, 981, 1087
Simbirsk, taken by Czech troops, 947
Simeon, tribe of, 20
Simeon I, Prince of Moscow, 316
Simeon II, King of Bulgaria, 1141
Simhavishnu (Pallava), 335
Simiidae, 1
Simnel, Lambert, English pretender, 369
Simon, Sir John, British statesman, 969
Simon, Jules (Jules François Simon Suisse), French premier, 638
Simon, the Maccabee, 32
Simonides, poet, 53, 62
Simony, 205, 206, 208, 216, 217
Simorich, Gen., Yugoslavian premier, 1150
Simpson, Thomas, of the Hudson's Bay Co., 563
Simpson, Mrs. Wallis Warfield, marries Duke of Windsor, 970
Simuka, 129
Sinai, 23, 30
Sinanthropus pekinensis, 6, 9
Sinclair, Harry Ford, American promoter, 1051
Sind, 43; conquered, 186; 187; treaty with England, 868; annexed, 870
Singapore, occupied by British, 868, 875; 1167, 1171
Singara, 125
Sinn Fein, in Ireland, 971
Sinobaldo Fiesco, see Innocent IV
Sino-Japanese tariff agreement, 1126
Sino-Japanese War, 707, 881, 886, 891
Sinuessa, 74
Sinuhet, story of, 23, 29
Sioux Indians, defeated, 780
Sippar, 25, 39
Siricius, author of the earliest decretal, 142
Sirovy, Gen. Jan, Czechoslovak prime minister, 1011
Sismondi, Jean Simonde de, French political economist, 549
Sistan, 124
Sistine Chapel, in Rome, 290
Sistova, Treaty of, 485
Sit-down strikes, in France, 979; in U.S., 1056
Sitka, Alaska, founded, 798
Sitting Bull, Sioux Indian chief, 780
Siut, 21
Siva, 132
Sivaism, 331
Sivaji, wins title of raja, 534
Sivamara II, King of Mysore, 336
Sivapithecus, 1
Six Acts, of British Parliament, 605
Six Edicts, of Turgot in France, 448
Six National Histories, of Japan, 350
Six Nations, American Indians, 513
Six-Year Plan, in Mexico, 1076
Sixth Crusade, 257
Sixtus, Prince, of Bourbon, in the First World War, 936, 942
Sixtus IV (Francesco della Rovere), Pope, 290, 295
Sixtus V (Felice Peretti), Pope, 396

Skagerrak, *see* Jutland
Skalds, of Iceland, 205
Skandagupta, repulsed White Huns, 130
Skobelev, Michael Dmitreievich, Russian general, 738
Skopin-Shuisky, Michael, Russian leader, 418
Skoropadski (Skoropadsky), Pavel, hetman of the Ukraine, 943, 1031
Skottowe, Capt., English representative at Canton, 540
Skouloudis, Sophocles, premier of Greece, 927
Skull, as a drinking-cup, 150
Skupshtina, parliament of Serbia, 713, 714
Skutkonung, Olaf, ruler of Sweden, 203
Skwarazynski, Gen. Stanislas, Polish nationalist leader, 1040
Skylax, Greek admiral, 42
Slater, Samuel, applied machinery to cotton-spinning, 764
Slatin (Sir Rudolf Carl von) Bey, surrenders to the Mahdi, 832
Slaughter House Cases, in U.S., 781
Slave-raiding parties, in Brazil, 501; in East Africa, 847
Slave Trade Commissioners, take over Fernando Po, 840
Slavery and the slave trade, in Greece, 48; in Rome, 100; in Spain, 237; 282; forbidden by Henry the Navigator, 363; in America, 486, 496; 604, 770, 780; in British colonies, 607; 739, 768; in New Granada, 815; in Brazil, 817; 824, 830, 840, 844, 847; abolished throughout British Empire, 437, 851; 860, 873, 895
Slavic-speaking peoples, 16
Slavonic Welfare Society, in Moscow, 705
Slavs, 161, 208, 210, 239
Slawata, William, imperial emissary, 404
Sleeping-car, 554
Slidell, John, Confederate diplomat, 773, 776
Slivnitza, battle of, 714, 718, 739
Sloane, Sir Hans, and the British Museum, 435
Sloka metre, used by Brahman legal writers, 130
Slovakia, 239, 1012, 1013, 1145
Slovaks, branch of western Slavs, 239
Slovenes, branch of southern Slavs, 239; 1018
Slovenia, northern, annexed by Germany, 1139
Sluys, battle of, 265, 276
Smendes, 24
Smetana, Antanas, pres. of Lithuania, 1042
Smigly-Rydz, Gen. Edward, head of Polish army, 1040
Smith, Adam, his *Wealth of Nations*, 549
Smith, Alfred Emanuel, defeated for pres. of U.S., 1052
Smith, Edmund Kirby, Confederate general, 779
Smith, Sir Francis, application of the screw propeller, 554
Smith, George Albert, first process of colored motion pictures, 557
Smith, Sir Harry George Wakelyn, gov. of Capetown, 852
Smith, James Francis, gov. of Philippines, 909
Smith, Capt. John, with Jamestown colony, 508
Smith, Joseph, organizes Mormon Church, 771
Smith, Leigh, English traveler, 565
Smith, Sir Ross, British aviator, 1129
Smith, Sir Thomas, gov. of East India Co., 559
Smith, William, geologist, 551
Smith, Capt. William, takes possession of South Shetland Islands, 571
Smith-Connally Anti-strike Bill, 1140
Smith-Dorrien, Horace Lockwood, British general, 913
Smithfield culture, 18
Smokeless powder, introduced by the French, 556
Smolensk, destroyed by the French, 598; 1151, 1154
Smoot-Hawley Tariff Act, in U.S., 1052, 1133
Smuts, Jan Christian, South African statesman, 859, 918, 952, 1092; prime minister, Union of South Africa, 1135
Smyrna, 1020, 1094, 1095
Smyth v. Ames, decision by U.S. supreme ct., 782
Snefru, 23
Snorri Sturleson, his *Younger Edda*, 205
Snowden, Philip, British chancellor of the exchequer, 968, 969
Soan industry, 6
Sobeslav I, 240
Sobieski, John, *see* John III Sobieski
Social Credit Party, in Alberta, 1060
Social Democratic Federation, in England, 618
Social Democratic Party, in Denmark, 697; in New Zealand, 908; in Russia, 706; in Sweden, 699
Social Democratic Workingmen's Party, German, 689
Social experiments, in Greece, 75
Social Revolutionary Party, in Russia, 706
Social Security Act, in U.S., 1055
Social War, 64, 80, 85, 93, 95
Socialism, in the 19th cent., 549, 550; 618, 640, 647, 941, 942, 978, 1007
Socialist Congress, at Gotha, 689; at Bologna, 987; at Livorno, 987; at Stockholm, 942
Socialist Party, at Tours Congress, 977; in France, 1144
Socialist and Republican Union, in France, 978
Socialist Workingmen's Party, in Germany, 689
Société des Indes Orientales, 859
Society for the Cultivation of Heaths, in Denmark, 697
Society for the Emancipation of Italy, 659
Society for National Reform, in Iraq, 1106
Society for Propagating the Gospel, in New England, 511
Society Islands, under French protectorate, 895
Society of Jesus (Jesuits), 389
Socrates, Greek philosopher, 67
Soddy, Frederick, radio-activity, 552
Sofia, 1150
Sofia Cathedral, bombed, 1023

Soga clan, in Japan, 139, 140
Sogdiana, 39, 45, 83, 128, 133
Sogdianus, 40
Soil Conservation Act, in U.S., 1053
Soissons, 147; in World War, 913, 914, 921, 945
Soissons vase, 147
Sokoto, Kingdom of, 525
Solaro della Margarita, Clemente, Count, Italian statesman, 654
Soldiers' Bonus Bill, in U.S., 1051
Soldiers of the keys, papal mercenaries, 211
Solemn League and Covenant (Covenanters), 376, 377, 426, 427, 428
Solferino, battle of, 658
Soliman Pasha, *see* Sèves
Sollum, 1160
Solo Man, 7
Solomon, builds temple, 31
Solomon, defeated for Hungarian throne, 245
Solomon ben Yosef, Jewish terrorist, 1102
Solomon Islands, discovered, 894; annexed by Germany, 895; 1167
Solon, Greek reformer, 51, 61, 70, 72
Solórzano, Cárlos, pres. of Nicaragua, 1073
Solus, 52
Solutre, 9
Solutrean culture, 5
Solway, 110
Solway Moss, battle of, 370
Somers, Sir George, 510
Somers, John, British lord keeper of the seal, 431
Somers Islands Co., to colonize Bermuda, 510
Somerset, Edmund Beaufort, Duke of, 270
Somerset, Edward Seymour, Duke of, and Earl of Hertford, lord protector of England, 370, 372
Somerville, William, English missionary in Bechuanaland, 826
Somesvara I, 337
Somesvara IV, 338
Somme, battle of, 931, 946, 950
Somme valley, 1146
Somoza, Gen. Anastasio, pres. of Nicaragua, 1073
Somrong-Sen culture, 14
So-nam gya-tso, called the Dalai Lama, 536
Sonderbund, league of the Catholic cantons of Switzerland, 666
Song of Deborah, 30
Song of Roland, 163
Song of the Battle of Lewes, 201
"Song of the Lord," 43
Sŏnggye, of the I dynasty in Korea, 349
Songhoy Empire, in Africa, 328, 329, 524
Sonnino, Sidney, Baron, Italian statesman, 661, 662, 923, 936, 952
Sonora, Republic of, 1075
Sontoku, Ninomiya, Japanese peasant-philosopher, 887
Soochow, taken by Japanese, 1122
Soong, T. V., Chinese minister of finance, 1119, 1121
Soong, Mei-ling, marries Chiang Kai-shek, 1119
Soor, battle of, 466
Sophagasenus, 81
Sophia, Princess of Hanover, 431, 432
Sophia, regent for Ivan V and Peter I, 478
Sophia, wife of Ivan the Great, 415
Sophia-Augusta of Anhalt-Zerbst, *see* Catharine II
Sophists, teachers of Greece, 62
Sophocles, Greek dramatist, 62
Sora, 74
Soranus, Barea, Stoic, 107
Sorbon, Robert de, endowed University of Paris, 231
Sorel, Georges, his *Reflections on Violence*, 550, 641
Sorzano, Luis Tejada, pres. of Bolivia, 1067
Sosibius, 84
Soubise, Benjamin de Rohan, Duke of, French general, 387, 467
Souchon, Wilhelm, German admiral, 919
Soulouque, Faustin, pres. of Haiti, 825
Soult, Nicolas Jean de Dieu, French general, 588, 591, 594, 596, 600, 628
Sound moving picture, 557
Sound on film, invented, 557
South Africa Act, approved by British Parliament, 858
South Africa Co., 848, 855, 856, 858
South African Party, 858
South African Republic, 852, 853, 855
South African Union, 1091, 1092
South Atlantic, 1158
South Australia, 899, 903
South Australia Association, chartered, 899
South Carolina, established, 513
South Carolina Exposition, 771
South Dakota, admitted to statehood, 784
South magnetic pole, 574, 576
South Pole, discovered, 575, 576
South Sea Bubble, financial panic, 434, 447
South Sea Co., 432
Southampton, Henry Wriothesley, 3d Earl of, 375
Southern Alliance, part of the Populist Party, 785
Southern Ch'en dynasty, 135, 136
Southern Ch'i dynasty, 135
Southern Liang dynasty, 135
Southern Pacific R.R., completed, 783
Southern Rhodesia, becomes crown colony, 1091
Southern Society, Russian revolutionary organization, 702

Southland, in New Zealand, 906
Southwold Bay, battle of, 427
Souza, Martin Affonso de, founded São Vicente, in Brazil, 500
Souza, Thomé de, gov.-gen. of Brazil, 500
Souza, Washington Luis Pereira de, pres. of Brazil, 1071
Souza y Menezas, Affonso Martimho de, Portuguese mission to China, 539
Soviet government, *see* Russia
Soviet Union, *see* Russia
Spa Conference, 997
Spaak, Paul, premier of Belgium, 975
Spagnoletto, *see* Ribera
Spain, 17, 88, 144, 163 *ff*., 218, 234 *ff*., 280, 282, 284, 366 *ff*., 393 *ff*., 450 *ff*., 643 *ff*., 991 *ff*.; 1139, 1142; broke with Germany, 1144
Spalato, 123
Spalirises, one of the King of Kings, 128
Spallanzani, Lazaro, Italian naturalist, 455
Spanish-American War, 647, 787, 823, 909
Spanish Guinea, divided, 1090
Spanish Inquisition, *see* Inquisition
Spanish March (or Mark), 155, 236
Spanish Morocco, reorganized, 1087; uprising, 1088
Spanish Netherlands, 443, 446
Spanish Republic, First, 646; Second, 981, 982
Spanish Revolution of 1820, 803
Sparta, 46 *passim*
Spartacist revolt, in Berlin, 996; in Ruhr, 997
Spartacus, Roman gladiator, 95
Spartans, 50, 52, 56, 58, 60, 62, 64
Spearheads, 5
Speculum Maius, 231
Spee, Maximilian von, German admiral, 917, 918
Spencer, Herbert, English philosopher, 550
Spencer, John Poyntz, 5th Earl, British statesman, 742
Speransky, Michael Michaelovich, Count, Russian reformer, 701, 702
Sphacteria, 59
Sphrodias, 63
Spinola, Ambrose, 404
Spirit of St. Louis, Lindbergh's monoplane, 557, 1052
Spitamenes, beaten by Alexander, 65
Spitsbergen, discovered, 558
Spoils system, in U.S., 77
Spoleto, conquered by Charlemagne, 152
Spoletum, 87
Spoliation claims, paid by France, 772
Spooner, John Coit, amendment for civil govt. in Philippines, 909
Spotsylvania Court House, battle of, 779
Spottswood, Alexander, gov. of Virginia, 513
Spurs, battle of the, 232, 369
Spytihnev, King of Bohemia, 240
Squires, Sir Richard Anderson, premier of Newfoundland, 1061
Sravana Belgola, 132
Srimaravarman, King, 336
Srong-tsan-sgam-po, King of Tibet, 331
Ssu-ma Ch'ien, compiled history of China, 134
Ssu-ma Kuang, his history of China, 134
Stack, Sir Lee, British gov.-gen. of the Sudan, 1083
Stadion, Johann Philipp Karl Joseph, Austrian statesman, 594
Staffarda, battle of, 444
Stafford, William Howard, Viscount, in Polish Plot, 428
Stahlberg, Karl Juho, pres. of Finland, 1047
Stahremberg, Prince Ernest Ruediger von, Austrian politician, 1008
Stahremberg, Rüdiger von, defended Vienna, 483
Stair, James Dalrymple, 1st Viscount, and the massacre of Glencoe, 431
Stalin, Joseph, Russian Marshal, 1029, 1034, 1139, 1140, 1164, 1165, 1171
Stalingrad, 1153
Stamboliski, Alexander, Bulgarian premier, 1022
Stambulov, Stephen, Bulgarian statesman, 718, 745
Stamford, battle of, 271
Stamford Bridge, battle of, 168, 204
Stamp Act, put through Parliament, 518
Stamp Act Congress, 518
Standard Oil Co., 1067, 1109
Standard Oil Trust, 785, 790
Stanford, Leland, California senator, 555
Stanhope, Charles, Earl, first printing press with iron frame, 553
Stanislav, taken by Austro-Germans, 922, 940
Stanley, Edward Geoffrey Smith, 14th Earl of Derby, British colonial secretary, 607
Stanley, Frederick Arthur, 16th Earl of Derby, gov.-gen. of Canada, 797
Stanley, Sir Henry Morton, African explorer, 739, 828, 843, 844, 847
Stanton, Elizabeth Cady, in women's rights movement, 774
Staple Act of 1663, 514
Star Chamber, in England, 369, 376
Star of the West, fired on at Charleston, 776
Stargard, Truce of, 418
State Advances Corporation Act, in New Zealand, 1132
States-General, of France, 386
States-General, of Holland, 438, 439, 440
Statute *de Heretico Comburendo*, 268
Statute of Drogheda (Poynings' Law), 369
Statute of Gloucester, 200
Statute of Kilkenny, in Ireland, 273

Statute of Laborers, 266
Statute of Mortmain, 200, 268
Statute of Niessawa, 315
Statute of Piotrkow (Magna Carta of Poland), 413
Statute of Praemunire, 266, 268
Statute of Provisors, 266, 268
Statute of the Six Articles, 370
Statute of Wales, 199
Statute of Westminster, 969; 1059
Statute of Westminster (*Second*), 200
Statute of Westminster (*Third*), 200
Statute of 1327, 266
Statutory Commission (Sir John Simon), to study situation in India, 1112, 1113
Stauning, Theodor, premier of Denmark, 1046
Staurakios, Byzantine general, 176, 177
Stavanger, 1146
Stavisky, Alexandre Sacha, Russian promoter, 978
Stcherbatsky, 131
Steam engine, 554, 628
Steamboat, 553
Steamship service, between England and India, 870
Steamships, first to cross Atlantic, 554
Steel-making, 555
Steel strike, in U.S., 1049, 1050
Stefano, of the Visconti, 298
Stefansson, Vilhjalmur, Arctic explorer, 567, 570
Stein, Aurel, orientalist, 884
Stein, Heinrich Friedrich Karl, Baron vom und zum, Prussian reformer, 594, 600, 601
Steinkirk, battle of, 431, 444
Steinmetz, Karl Friedrich von, Prussian general, 688
Stela, of the Vultures, 25; of Hammurabi 39
Stellaland, a Boer state, 854
Stellenbosch culture, 6
Stem (Stamm) duchies, 160
Stephanie, Lake, discovered, 828
Stephen I (St. Stephen) of Hungary, 205, 241, 245
Stephen II of Hungary, 245
Stephen III of Hungary, 245
Stephen V of Hungary, 246, 317
Stephen II, Pope, 152, 153
Stephen V, Pope, 160
Stephen IX, Pope, 217
Stephen, Bishop of Rome, 117
Stephen, son of Henry I of England, 194
Stephen of Blois, 194
Stephen of Vendôme, and the Children's Crusade, 257
Stephen Nemanya, founder of the Nemanyid dynasty in Serbia, 246 f.
Stephen Nemanya II, son of the preceding, 247
Stephen Urosh II, *see* Milyutin
Stephen Urosh III, *see* Dechanski, Stephen
Stephen Urosh V of Serbia, 319
Stephens, Alexander Hamilton, vice-pres. of Confederate States, 776
Stephens, James, Irish agitator, 614
Stephens, Uriah Smith, American labor leader, 783
Stephenson, George, adapted steam engine to the railroad, 554
Sternberg, Baron Ungern von, White Russian leader, 1118
Stesichorus, poet, 48
Stettinius, Edward R., U.S. secretary of state, 1143
Stevens, Capt. Albert William, American aeronaut, 558
Stevens, Henry Herbert, Canadian minister of trade, 1059
Stevens, John, developed screw propeller, 554
Steyn, Martinus Theunis, pres. of the Orange Free State, 856
Sthaviravadins (Pali Theravadins), 42, 128
Sthenelaïdas, 58
Stibbs, Bartholomew, 525
Stigand, Archbishop of Canterbury, 168, 191
Stilicho, Flavius, 121, 123, 143, 144
Stillbay industry, 6
Stilwell, Gen. Joseph W., U.S. and British Chief of Staff in Chinese theater of war, 1138
Stimson, Henry Lewis, U.S. secretary of state, 1052, 1073, 1120
1133, 1149
Stimson-Layton Agreement, 1149
Stirbey, Barbu, Rumania, 1143
Stirling, Capt. James, British colonialist, 899
Stockach, battle of, 586
Stockholm, Treaty of, 434, 474
Stockmar, Christian Friedrich, Baron von, adviser to Queen Victoria, 609
Stockton & Darlington R.R., 554
Stofflet, Jean Nicolas, a leader in Vendée revolt, 582
Stoicism, 77, 111, 113
Stoke, battle of, 369
Stokes, Maj. Claude Bayfield, in Persia, 865
Stolbovo, Treaty of, 413, 418
Stolietov, Gen. Nikolai Gregorievich, Russian emissary to Afghanistan, 867
Stolypin, Peter Arkadevich, Russian prime minister, 708
Stone tools, 4, 5, 6
Stony Desert, in Australia, 900
Stopford, Sir Robert, British admiral, 725
Storroselski, Col. Peter Makarovich, with Persian Cossack Brigade, 1108
Storting, of Norway, 701
Story of Wen Amon, 24
Stowe-on-the-Wold, battle of, 378
Stoyadinovich, Milan, premier of Yugoslavia, 964, 1019

Strabo, geographer, 34, 129
Strabo, Gnaius Pompeius, 93
Stradivarius, Antonio, Italian stringed instrument builder, 454
Strafford, Thomas Wentworth, 1st Earl of, English statesman, 376
Stragna, battle of, 249
Straits Convention, 726, 755, 1097
Straits Settlements, British crown colony, 875
Stralsund, Peace of, 309
Strasser, Gregor, German Nazi leader, 1003
Strategopulos, Alexius, Byzantine general, 260
Stratford de Redcliffe, Stratford Canning, British diplomat, 726
Stratigraphy, method of dating, 2; 5
Straw, Jack, a leader in the Peasants' Revolt, 267
Streeruwitz, Ernst, chancellor of Austria, 1006
Strength Through Joy, German labor front, 1002
Stresa Conference, 963, 990, 1003
Stresemann, Gustav, German statesman, 998, 999
Strikes, in England, 620; in Italy, 661 f.; in Russia, 707; in Winnipeg, 1058
Stringfellow, John, heavier-than-air machines, 556
Strode, William, impeachment of, 377
Stroganov, Paul Alexandrovich, Russian reformer, 701
Stroganov family, of Russia, 415
Struensee, John Frederick, prime minister of Denmark, 474
Strypa, battle of, 932
Stuart, Arabella, 373
Stuart, House of, 373
Stuart, James, English explorer, 793
Stuart, John M'Douall, crossed Australia, 901
Stuart line, on Scottish throne, 272
Stulgenskis, Antanas, pres. of Lithuania, 1042
Stumm, Ferdinand, Baron von, German diplomat, 757
Stupor Mundi, see Gerbert of Aurillac and Frederick II
Sturdee, Sir Frederick Charles Doveton, British admiral, 918
Sturdza, Michael, Prince, ruler of Moldavia, 719
Stures, of Sweden, 312
Stürgkh, Count Carl, Austrian prime minister, 930
Stürmer, Boris Vladimirovich, Russian minister-pres., 930
Sturt, Charles, Australian explorer, 899, 900
Sturzo, Don Luigi, Italian Catholic leader, 988
Stuyvesant, Peter, Dutch settler, 511
Su Ch'in, 44
Suárez, Francisco, Jesuit, 388
Suárez, Marco Fidel, pres. of Colombia, 1069
Subaktagin, founder of the Ghaznavid dynasty, 190, 332
Submarine Blockade, 1149
Submarine campaign, 931, 936, 939
Subutai, Mongol leader, 244, 261 f.
Suchet, Marshal Louis Gabriel, French general, 600
Suchow, taken by the Japanese, 1122
Sucre, Antonio José de, Latin-American leader, 802, 803, 811, 812
Sudan, 745, 828 ff.
Sudbury, Archbishop Simon of, 267
Sudeten Germans, 1010, 1012
Sudraka, his drama Mrichchakatika, 131
Suetonius (Gaius Suetonius Tranquillus), Roman writer, 112
Suevi, overrun Gaul, 121, 144
Suez Canal, 555, 615, 729, 733, 738, 752, 830, 833, 919, 929, 1162
Suffolk, Henry Grey, Duke of, in conspiracy against Queen Mary, 372
Suffolk, William de la Pole, Duke of, favorite of Henry VI, 270
Suffolk Resolves, 520
Sugar Act, 517; Jones-Costigan Act, 1053
Sugawara Michizane, Japanese envoy to China, 352
Suger, tutor of Louis VI of France, 227, 228
Sugiyama, Lt-Gen. Gen. Japanese war minister, 1126
Sui court, in China, 140
Sui dynasty, 136, 348
Suidgar, Pope Clement II, 217
Suiko, Empress of Japan, 137, 140
Sujin, 10th Emperor of Japan, 139
Sukchong, brings Confucianists to Korea, 542
Sukhavati, see Western Happy Heaven
Sukhavativyuha, 129
Sukhomlinov, Gen. Vladimir, Russian war minister, 930
Sukman, Turkish prince, 254
Sukman Qutbi, Shah of Armenia, 254
Sulayman, caliph, 164
Sulayman, caliph, 187
Suleiman, Shah of Persia, 528
Suleiman I (the Magnificent), Ottoman sultan, 365, 402, 422–423
Suleiman, Sultan of Turkey, 326, 401
Suleiman III, Ottoman sultan, 484
Sulla, Lucius Cornelius, Roman statesman, 89, 92–95
Sullivan, Gen. John, gives up siege of Newport, 521
Sully, Maximilien de Bethune, Duc de, French statesman, 373, 386
Sumangaru, ruler of Soso, 328
Sumer, 25
Sumerians, in Babylonia, 25, 33, 39. See also Early Dynastic
Sumitomo, Japanese pirate, 353
Summa Theologiae, of St. Thomas Aquinas, 231
Sumter, Thomas, defeated, 522
Sun Ch'üan, founder of Wu dynasty, 135
Sunderland, Robert Spencer, 2d Earl of, British statesman, 428, 429, 431, 434
Sun Diata, King of the Mandigos, 328
Sung, 44

Sung dynasty, in China, 341 f.; southern Sung, 343
Sunga dynasty, 43
Sunga-Kanva, 129
Sung-Che-yüan, Chinese general, 1120
Sung-yün, Chinese pilgrim, 136
Sun Hsing-yen, Chinese scholar, 877
Sunium, 53
Sunjo, King of Korea, 885
Sunnites, 528, 529, 533
Sun Wen, heads secession govt. at Canton, 1117–28
Sun Yat-sen, pres. of the United Provinces of China, 881, 883, 884, 1118
Supreme Council, at Paris Peace Council, 952
Supreme Court of Canada, 1060
Supreme War Council, 945
Sur dynasty, 530
Suraja Dowla, Nawab of Bengal, 534
Surashtra, 129, 130
Surendranath, Banerji, Indian Nationalist, 871
Suring, Dr. Reinhard Joachim, German aeronaut, 557
Surrey, Henry Howard, Earl of, 370
Suru, 35
Susa, 13 passim
Su Shih (Su Tung-p'o), Chinese statesman and poet, 343 f.
Sushun, Japanese emperor, 140
Susiana, 128
Sussex, Anglo-Saxon kingdom, 166
Sussex, sinking of, 791; 931
Suti, 34
Sutoku, Japanese emperor, 354
Sutralamkara, 129
Sutras, 46
Sutri and Rome, Synods in, 217
Suttee, in India, 130; 870
Sutters' Fort, discovery of gold, 774
Suvla, landing of British troops, 920
Suvorov, Alexander Vasilyevich, Russian general, 485, 587
Suvorov Island, annexed to New Zealand, 908
Svatopluk, Moravian prince, 239
Svealand, origin of Swedish Kingdom, 203
Sven I (Forked Beard), King of Denmark, 167, 203
Sverdrup, Johan, in Norwegian storting, 701
Sverdrup, Otto Neuman, Arctic explorer, 565, 570
Sverker, King of Sweden, 204
Sverre, King of Norway, 204, 205
Svetambara sect, 42
Sviatopolk-Mirsky, Pierre Dimitrievich, Prince, Russian minister of the interior, 707
Sviatoslav, Russian prince, 180, 183, 243
Svinhufvud, Pehr Evind, pres. of Finland, 1048
Swabian League, 307
Swakopmund, taken by Gen. Botha, 918
Swaraj Party, in India, 1112
Swaziland, 855
Sweden, 170, 203 f., 310 f., 471, 595, 602, 699 f., 966, 1046, 1047, 1159
Swedes, penetrate into Russia, 158–170, 564
Swedish-French period, of Thirty Years' War, 407
Swiderian culture, 18
Swiss Confederacy, history, 301, 306 f., 408 f., 459, 590, 602, 666 f., 994, 995
Swiss guards, of the Tuileries, 581
Swiss Lake Dwellings, 16
Swiss mercenaries, 459
Switzerland, 1165
Swynford, Catherine, mistress of John of Gaunt, 271
Syagrius, Gallo-Roman general, 147
Sybaris, 48, 53
Sybota, 58
Sydney, Australia, 901, 902
Sydney-Melbourne railway, 902
Sykes, Sir Mark, British diplomat, 937
Sykes, Sir Percy Molesworth, 1107
Syllaeum, battle of, 174
Sylvester I, Pope, 123
Sylvester II (Gerbert of Aurillac), Pope, 216
Sylvester III, a rival pope, 217
Sylvis, William H., American labor leader, 783
Syme, David, Melbourne editor, 901
Symeon, Tsar of Bulgaria, 179, 182 f.
Symington, William, built Charlotte Dundas, first practical steamboat, 553
Symira, 32
Symmachus, pagan, 122
Symmes Co., in southwestern Ohio, 766
Syndicalism, 550, 551
Synod of Augsburg, 216; of Bari, 219; of Basel, 218; of Bourges, 216; of Cashel, 169, 196; of Clermont, 219, 255; of Kells, 169; of Lateran, 218; of Lyons, 212, 221; of Melfi, 218; of Orebro, 410; of Piacenza, 219, 255; of Poitiers, 216; of Reims, 219; of Rome, 217, 218; of Seligenstadt, 216; of Toledo, 163; of Troyes, 268; of Vienne, 222, 232, 258; of Whitby, 166, 168; of Worms, 206, 207, 218, 219
Synods in Aquitaine and Burgundy, 217; of Sutri and Rome, 206, 217
Syphax, King of Numidia, 87
Syphilis, 552
Syracuse, 48 passim
Syria, 13 passim, 34, 35, 184, 186, 728, 1098, 1100, 1143, 1144, 1151
Syrian Wars, 80, 81, 83, 84, 88 f.

Szálasi, Ferenc, Nazi leader in Hungary, 1015
Széchenyi, Count Stephen, Hungarian reformer, 671
Szechůan, 44, 135, 1121
Szegedin, Treaty of, 320; Truce of, 326
Szeklers, in Hungary, 245; 420
Sztojay, Doeme, Hungarian prime minister, 1142

Ta Ch'in, 134
Ta Tai Li-chi, early ritual text, 134
Taaffe, Eduard Franz Joseph, Count von, prime minister in Austria, 694
Taanach, 28
Tabaristan, conquered, 187, 188
Tabarnash, see Labarnash
Tabeel, 35
Tabin Shwehti, King of Burma, 541
Table of Deputies, lower house of Hungarian Diet, 671
Table of Magnates, upper house of Hungarian Diet, 671
Tabnit, 33
Taboos, in theory of caste defilement, 42
Tabor, captured, 305
Tabora, captured, 918
Taborites, of Bohemia, 305
Tabrimmon, 35
Tabriz, taken by Turks, retaken by Russians, 919
Tacitus, Marcus Claudius, 116
Tacitus, Publius Cornelius, Roman historian, 107, 112, 142, 170
Tacna and Arica, 809, 813, 1065, 1067, 1068
Tadahira, Japanese regent, 353
Tadakiyo, Sakai, Japanese prime minister, 547
Tadakuni, Mizuno, Japanese reformer, 888
Tafari, Ras, of Ethiopia, emperor as Haile Selassie I, 836, 1085
Taff Vale case, in England, 619
Tafna, Treaty of, 837
Taft, William Howard (27th pres. of the U.S.), 789, 790, 820, 823, 909
Tagina, battle of, 172
Tagliacozzo, battle of, 213
Taharka, 24
Tahir, siege of Baghdad, 188
Tahirids, of Khorasan, 189
Tahiti, discovered, 894; made a French colony, 895
Tahmasp I, Shah of Persia, 526
Tahmasp II, Shah of Persia, 528, 529
Tahunian culture, 13
T'ai (Thai) peoples, 44, 132; in Siam, 348
T'ai P'ing Rebellion, 879
T'ai P'ing Yü Lan, Chinese encyclopedia, 343
Tai Sheng, compiled early ritual texts, 134
Tai Teh, compiled early ritual texts, 134
T'ai tribe, in Central South China, 132
T'ai Tsu, see Chao K'uang-yin
T'ai Tsung (Li Shihmin), Chinese emperor, 340, 341, 342
T'ai-tsung, invaded Korea, 542
Tai Wen Kun, see Hŭng-sŏn
T'ai-yüan, taken by Japanese, 1121
Taihō Laws, in Japan, 350
Taika Reform (Japanese), 349
Taila III of India, 338
Taillandier, Saint-René, French diplomat, 753, 838
Taira, Japanese clan, 352, 355
Taishō Period, in Japan, 893, 1125
Taj Mahal, 533
Takahashi, Korekiyo, Viscount, premier of Japan, 1124, 1126
Takakuni, Japanese shōgun, 359
Takauji, general, 357, 358
Takht-i-Bahi inscriptions, 128
Takshasila, 42
Talaat Pasha, Turkish minister, 732, 948, 1094
Talavera, battle of, 594
Talayots, 17
Talgai, Man, 9
Talha, companion of the Prophet, 186
Talikota, battle of, 533
Talking pictures, successfully introduced, 557
Tallage, in England, 186
Talleyrand-Perigord, Charles Maurice de, French statesman, 594
Tallien, Jean Lambert, French revolutionary leader, 582, 583
Tallinn, 1154
Talmud, 30, 32
Tamasese, King of Samoa, 911
Tamatave, occupied by French, 859; 860
Tamayo, José Louis, pres. of Ecuador, 1069
Tamil, 132; saints, 355, 356
Tammany Hall, in New York, 784
Tammaritu, ruler of the Elamites, 40
Tammaritu II, ruler of the Elamites, 40
Tamworth Manifesto, of Robert Peel, 608
Tanagra, 56
Tanaka, Baron Giichi, Japanese premier, 1125
Tananarive, 1167
Tancred of Hauteville, 217, 255
T'ang, Chinese prince, 537
T'ang dynasty, in China, 137, 338
T'ang T'ai-tsung, Emperor of China, 331
T'ang Ying, at the imperial Chinese kilns, 541
Tanga, battle of, 918
Tanganrog, 1151, 1154
Tanganyika, British mandate, 1090
Tanged-point culture, 18

Tangier, battle of, 286; Treaty of, 837; ceded to England, 525; 1086
Tangier Convention, 981, 1086
Tangier statute, 1087
T'ang-ku, Truce of, 1120, 1126
Tanis, 21, 24
Tanks, first use by British, 931
Tanlongo, Bernardo, Italian financier, 661
Tannenberg, battle of, 302, 310, 314, 916
Tantrism, 331, 340
Tanucci, Bernardo, prime minister of Naples, 458
Taoism, cult, 135, 136, 440
Tara, Kingdom of, 168
Taranaki, formerly New Plymouth, 906
Taranto, 1150
Taraori, battle of, 332
Taras, 48, 57
Tarde, Gabriel de, his Laws of Imitation, 552
Tardenoisian culture, 15
Tardieu, André Pierre Gabriel Amédée, premier of France, 955, 1007, 1009
Tarentines, 78
Tarentum, 48, 85, 87, 90, 91; 2d pact at, 99; taken by Byzantines, 179
Tariff issue, in Canadian elections, 796
Tariff Law, in Germany, 690, 692
Tariff of Abominations, in U.S., 771, 772
Tariff of 1816 in U.S., 770; of 1832, 772; of 1857, 775; 783
Tariff Reform League in England, 619
Tariff war, between Britain and Ireland, 973
Tarim Basin, conquered, 133
Tariq, Berber, invader of Spain, 163, 187
Tarleton, Sir Banastre, English general, 522
Tarnopol, battle of, 922, 940; 1154
Tarnow, 1164
Tarpeian Rock, 72
Tarqui, battle of, 812
Tarquinius Collatinus, Lucius, 70
Tarquinius Priscus, 69, 70
Tarquinius Sextus, 70
Tarquinius Superbus (the Proud), 69, 70
Tarra conensis, 107
Tarshish, 32
Tarsius, 1
Tarsus, 99, 106, 119
Tartarescu, George, premier of Rumania, 1026
Tartu, Treaty of, 1044, 1047
Tasian culture, 18
Tasman, Abel Janszoon, Dutch navigator, 571, 894, 904
Tasmania, 894, 898, 899, 901
Tassilo, Duke of Bavaria, 153
Tatarescu, Jorge, Premier of Rumania, 1135
Tatars, 314, 316, 317, 417, 483, 485; see also Mongols
Tatatonga, chancellor of Jenghis Khan, 344
Ta-t'ung, 135, 136
Tauenzien, Bogislaw Friedrich Emanuel, Prussian general, 599
"Taungs skull," 1
Tauromenium, 90
Tauromomon, battle of, 250
Tavoras, conspiracy of the, 454
Tawney, Richard Henry, British historian, 399
Taxila, 43, 128
Taxiles, invite Alexander into India, 65
Tayacian industry, 6
Taylor, Zachary (12th pres. of the U.S.), 774
Te Rauparaha (Satan), Maori chief, 905
Te Tsung, Emperor of China, 880, 882
Tea, first mentioned, 343
Teapot Dome scandal, in U.S., 1051
Tecumseh, Indian chief, 769, 793
Tegea, 48, 54, 63
Tegetthoff, Wilhelm von, Baron, Austrian admiral, 659
Tehran Conference, 1141
Teispes, king, 40
Tejpala, 332
Telamon, 87
Telegraph, in Seven Weeks' War, 683; 688; in Persia, 864; India to England, 870; Shanghai to Tientsin, 880; across Australia, 902
Telegraphy, 554, 556, 773
Teleki, Count Paul, Hungarian premier, 1016
Teleki, Count Samuel, Hungarian Scientist, 828
Tel-el-Kebir, battle of, 738, 832
Telephone, 555, 782
Telepinuš, 36
Telerig, Bulgar ruler, 182
Telets, Bulgar ruler, 182
Television, 557
Telipinuš, 35
Tell Ahmar, 28
Tell-el-Amarna letters, 24, 26, 29, 32
Tell Halaf, 13, 28
Tell Judeideh, 13
Telles, Leonora, Queen of Portugal, 284
Tellini, Gen. Enrico, Italian general, 988, 1021
Tello, 13
Telugu, 130, 132
Temesvar, battle of, 674
Tempe, pass of, 54
Templars and Hospitalers in the Holy Land, 214, 222, 232, 258. See also Knights Templar

Temple, Sir William, British statesman, 426, 427
Temporal power, of the papacy, see Papacy
Temujin, see Jenghis Khan
Temur Oljaitu, of the Yüan dynasty, 345
Ten Points, or March Laws, in Hungary, 673
"Ten Thousand," the, Greek, 40; 63
Ten Years' War, 823
Tenant-Right League, in Ireland, 614
Tenants-in-chief, 213
Tenchi, Japanese emperor, 140
Tencteri, 96
Tendai, Japanese sect, 352
Teng, Chinese Empress, 134
Tennes, 33
Tennessee, admitted to statehood, 766
Tennessee Valley Authority Act, in U.S., 1055
Tennis court meeting, of the National Assembly in France, 579
Tenos, 63
Tenri sect, of faith healers in Japan, 887
Tenure-of-Office Act, in U.S., 781
Tepe Giyan, 13
Tepe Hissar, 13
Tepe Mussian, 13
Teplitz, Treaty of, 599
Terauchi, Count Seiki, Japanese premier, 893, 1118, 1123, 1126
Terboven, Joseph, German commissioner for Norway, 1138
Terchan, battle of, 330
Terence, 90, 91
Terillus, 57
Terra, Gabriel, pres. of Uruguay, 1067
Terra, Hellmut de, archaeologist, 6, 8
Terramare culture, 17; peoples, 68
"Terrible Day" at Anagni, 222, 232
Terrorism, in Ireland, 616
Tertiary Pleistocene epoch, 44
Tertry, battle of, 149
Tertullian, 117
Teruel, battle of, 984
Tervel, Bulgar ruler, 182
Teschen, Duchy of, 955, 1009, 1012, 1040; Treaty of, 468
Tesla, Nikola, method of long-distance transmission, 555
Test Act, in England, 427, 428, 432, 606
Tetricus, at battle of Châlons, 116
Tettenborn, Friedrich Karl, Baron, 598
Teumman, defeated by Ashurbanipal, 39
Teusina, Treaty of, 413
Teuta, Queen, 86 f.
Teutoberg Forest, battle of, 103
Teutones, 92
Teutonic conquest of Britain, 166
Teutonic Knights, 211, 214 f., 242, 244, 258, 302, 310, 312, 316, 413, 415
Teutonic-speaking peoples, 16
Tewfik Pasha, Khedive of Egypt, 736, 831
Tewfik Rushdi, Turkish foreign minister, 1097
Texas, declares independence, 772, 821; 773
Texel, battle of, 425
Thailand (Siam), 1138, 1140, 1166, 1167
Thales, predicted eclipse, 48
Thälmann, Ernst, German Communist, 998
Thames River, battle of, 793
Thapsus, 97, 98
Tharawaddi Min, King of Burma, 872
Thasos, 55, 61, 63
Theagenes, 48
Thebans, at Plataea, 58; defeat Hippocrates, 59
Thebes, 21 passim
Thegnhood, in England, 167
Thelwall, John, 437
Themes, as a system of govt., 174; 179
Themistocles, 52, 53, 54, 55
Theobald, Archbishop, 194
Theobald of Navarre, 257
Theocritus, 75
Theodolinda, married Duke Agilulf of Turin, 150
Theodora, Byzantine empress, 249
Theodora, Byzantine regent, 177
Theodora, daughter of Maximian, 118
Theodora, wife of Justinian, 170, 172
Theodora, wife of Theophylact, 215
Theodore I (Lascaris), Emperor of Nicaea, 259
Theodore II (Lascaris), Emperor of Nicaea, 248, 260
Theodore I, Tsar of Russia, 417 f.
Theodore III, Tsar of Russia, 478
Theodore, brother of Heraclius, 184
Theodore, Emperor of Ethiopia, 834
Theodore of Epirus, 248, 259
Theodore of Tarsus, Archbishop of Canterbury, 166
Theodore Dukas Angelus, Despot of Epirus, 259
Theodoric, son of Strabo, 122, 123
Theodoric the Great, 122, 143, 145, 146
Theodoros of Studion, 177
Theodosia, bombarded, 919
Theodosian Code, 121
Theodosiopolis, 126
Theodosius I (Flavius Theodosius "the Great"), 119, 120, 142, 143
Theodosius II, Emperor of the East, 121
Theodosius III, 175
Theogony, 47
Theophano, wife of Otto II, 162, 180

Theophilus, Byzantine Emperor, 177
Theophylact, Roman senator, 215
Theopompus, King of Sparta, 50
Theory of the Earth, The, by James Hutton, 551
Thera, 48
Theramenes, 60, 61
Theravadin, 42 f., 132
Theresa, wife of Henry of Burgundy, 238
Thermidoreans, in the French Revolution, 584
Thermopylae, 54, 64, 78, 99; campaign of, 54, 78, 80
Thermum, 80
Theron of Acrages, 57
Theseus, King of Athens, 50
Thespians, 54
Thespis, originated tragedy, 53
Thessalian cultures, I, II, III, IV, 16
Thessalian League, 52
Thessalonica, 179, 258, 259, 260, 323
Thessaly, 46 passim
Theutberga, wife of Emperor Lothair, 153
Thiaumont, battles of, 930
Thibaud, G., ascended the Nile, 826
Thibaw, King of Burma, 872
Thibron, 62
Thierry, Baron Charles de, French adventurer, 905
Thiers, Louis Adolphe, French president, 628, 630, 634, 636, 637, 725
Thieu-Tri, Emperor of Annam, 874
Third Crusade, 220, 253 f., 256
Third Estate (tiers état), in France, 579
Third International, founded, 1033; 1035; dissolved, 1140
Third Lateran Council, 220
Third Party, in French Chamber, 634, 635
Third Republic, in France, 636
Thirteen Classics with Commentaries, Chinese, 537, 877
Thirteenth amendment to U.S. Constitution, 780
"Thirty Tyrants," in Athens, 61; in the reign of Gallienus, 116
Thirty Years' Peace, 56, 58
Thirty Years' War, 387, 390, 403 f., 410, 419, 420
Thirty-nine articles of religion, 372
Thiudareiks, corrupted into Theodoric, 145
Thomas, Byzantine general in Anatolia, 177
Thomas, Duke of Lancaster, 264
Thomas, George Henry, Federal general, 779
Thomas, Jacques Léonard Clément, French general, 637
Thomas, St., 128
Thomas, James Henry, British labor leader, 969
Thomas, Sidney Gilchrist, process for removing phosphorus from iron ore, 555
Thomas Aquinas, his Summa Theologiae, 231; 664
Thomist rationalists, 201
Thompson, Carmi Alderman, American administrator, 1133
Thompson, David, explorer, 792, 793
Thompson, George, explorer, 524
Thompson, Sir John Sparrow David, premier of Canada, 797
Thompson, William, English socialist, 608
Thomson, Charles Edward Poulett, Baron Sydenham, gov. of Canada, 795
Thomson, Joseph, African explorer, 828
Thomson, Thaddeus Austin, and the Thomson-Urrutia Treaty, 816, 1069, 1072
Thomson, William (Lord Kelvin), British scientist, 555
Thorbecke, Johan, and Netherlands constitution, 625
Thorfinn Karlsefni, Viking leader, 365
Thorn, founded, 211 f., 215; Peace of, 302, 310, 314
Thrace, 51 passim
Thracians, 47, 52
Thracybulus, tyrant, 48, 57, 60, 61, 63
Thrasydaeus, 57
Thrasyllus, 60
Three Emperors' League, 690, 694, 706, 733, 737
Three Hundred Champions, battle of, 50
Three Kingdoms period, in Korea, 137, 340
Three Kings, see Kasr el-Kabir, battle of
Three-power naval conference, 960
Three-Power Pact, Germany, Italy, Japan, 1136
Three Years' War, of Japan, 354
Thrice-crowned Chola, 337 f.
Throgmorton, Sir Nicholas, Spanish plot, 373
Thucydides, Greek historian, 56, 58, 59, 62, 67
Thugs of India, 333
Thurii, 56, 74, 78, 85
Thuringia, overrun by Magyars, 158; 997
Thuringian Mark, 155
Thuringians, 142
Thurlow, Edward, English lord chancellor, 436
Thutmosis I (Thothmes), II, 23; III, 23, 27–29, 33, 35, 36
Ti, people, 135
Tiahuanacan culture, 20
Tiastanes, 127
Tiberias, 32
Tiberius, Byzantine emperor, 174
Tiberius II, Byzantine emperor, 126, 173
Tiberius III, Byzantine emperor, 175
Tiberius (Claudius Nero Caesar), Roman emperor, 101, 102, 103, 105, 116
Tiberius Gemellus, 105
Tibesti, occupied by French, 843
Tibet, 341, 540, 752, 754, 871
Tibetan Buddhism, reformed, 536
Tibetans, 44

Tibeto-Burman peoples, 44
Tibni, 31
Tibullus, Albius, 112
Ticinus, 87
Ticonderoga, 516, 520
T'ien-tai school, 136
Tientsin, 880, 1121; Treaties of, 874, 879, 881, 890
Tiepolo, Bajamonte, rebellion of, 225
Tiepolo, Giambattista, Italian painter, 454
Tierra de Vera Cruz, name given to Brazil, 368
Tiglath-pileser I, King of Babylon, 27, 38
Tiglath-pileser III (Pul), King of Babylon, 26, 27, 31, 33, 35
Tigranes I, King of Armenia, 33, 38 83, 95
Tigranocerta, 95, 106
Tigris, 28; eastern boundary of Roman Empire, 110
Tikhomir of Durazzo, 247
Tikrit, captured by British, 938
Til Barsip, 35
Tilak, Bal Gangadhar, Indian Nationalist, 871, 1111
Tilden, Samuel Jones, candidate for pres. of U.S., 782
Tilly, Jan Tserklaes, Baron of, imperial general, 404 f.
Tilsit, Treaty of, 593, 595, 701, 862
Timbuktu, founded, 329, 524
Time of Troubles, in Russia, 413, 415, 418
Times (London), 554, 555, 617
Timesitheus, C. Furius, 115
Timocrates, attack on Sparta, 62
Timoleon, defeated the Carthaginians, 34, 66
Timor, divided between Dutch and Portuguese, 877; 1167
Timotheus, 63
Timur (Tamerlane), Mongol leader, 326, 330, 334, 363, 530
Timur shah, King of Afghanistan, 535
Timurids, 330
Tin Darwaza (Triple Gateway) of Ahmadabad, 335
Tinchebray, battle of, 193
Tindale, William, his translation of the Bible, 370
Tingitana, 105
Tinoco, Federico, Costa Rican insurgent, 1073
Tintoretto (Jacopo Robusti), Venetian painter, 393
Tippamuir, battle of, 378
Tippecanoe, battle of, 769
Tipperary insurrection, 612
Tippoo Sahib, 2d Mysore War, 535; 3d Mysore War, 536
Tirana, Treaty of, 1020
Tiridates, King of Armenia, 83, 106, 124
Tiridates I, see Arsaces II
Tirlemont, battle of, 913
Tirpitz, Alfred von, German admiral, 692, 747, 758, 917, 931
Tirujnana Sambandhar, a Tamil saint, 336
Tiruvalluvar, 132
Tiryns, 46, 55
Tirzah, 31
Tiso, Mgr. Joseph, premier of Slovakia, 1013
Tissaphernes, 60–62
Tisza, Kálman, premier of Hungary, 695, 762
Tisza, Count Stephen, premier of Hungary, 696, 941
Tithe War, in Ireland, 607, 609
Tithes, in Ireland, 169
Titian (Tiziano Vecelli), Italian painter, 393
Tito (Josip Broz), marshal of Yugoslavia, 1141, 1144
Tittoni, Tommaso, Italian foreign minister, 987
Titulescu, Nicholas, Rumanian foreign minister, 1026
Titus (Titus Flavius Vespasianus), Roman emperor, 108
Toba, Emperor of Japan, 354
Toba II, Japanese emperor, 356
Toba Tatars, 135
Tobacco Control Act, in U.S., 1053
Tobacco cultivation, in Virginia, 508
Tobiesen, Capt. Sivert Kristian, Arctic explorer, 564
Tobruk, 1160
Tochari (Scythians), 83
Tochev, Andrew, premier of Bulgaria, 1024
Todleben, Franz Eduard Ivanovich, Russian military engineer, 727
Tōgō, Count Heihachiro, Japanese admiral, 892
Togoland, British, 1088
Togoland, German, 918, 1088
Tojibids of Saragossa, 233
Tokihira, Japanese dictator, 352
Tokimasa, head of the Minamoto, 356 f.
Tökölli, Imre, insurrection in Hungary, 461
Tokt, Bulgar ruler, 182
Tokugawa, Yoshinobu, Prince, 1124
Tokugawa Period, in Japan, 544
Tokumine, beats off Mongol invasion, 351
Tokusei, see Act of Grace
Tokyo, bombed by U.S. planes, 1144, 1158; 1170; Bay, 1170
Tokyo-Berlin-Rome Pact, signed by Hungary, Rumania, Yugo-slavia, 1136, 1150
Toledano, Vicente Lombardo, Mexican labor leader, 1076
Toledo, Synod of, 163
Toledo, Francisco Alvarez de, Viceroy of Peru, 489
Tolentino, battle of, 602
Toleration Act, in England, 430
Tolkappiyam, Tamil grammar, 132
Tolly, Barclay de, Russian general, 595, 598
Tolmides, 56
Toltec culture, 20
Tomashevich, Stephen, heir to Bosnian throne, 320
Tombs, Egyptian, 23, 69
Tomislav, King of Croatia, 246

Tonga (Friendly Island), discovered, 894; British protectorate, 896
Tonghak Society, in Korea, 881, 891
Tongoland, annexed by British, 855
Tonkin, insurrection in, 874; 875
Tonnage and poundage in England, 374, 375
Tonty, Henri de, French explorer, 507
Tooke, John Horne, Irish leader, 437
Tools, of Palaeolithic period, 4 ff.
Topete, Juan Baptista, Spanish admiral, 646
Toqtamish, Khan of the Golden Horde, 330
Tordesillas, Treaty of, 367, 502
Torgau, battle of, 467, 1164
Torgud, 540
Tories, English party, 427
Tornikios, Leo, 249
Toro, battle of, 282, 286
Toro, David, pres. of Bolivia, 1067
Torpedo, 553, 555
Torquatus, Titus Manlius, 73
Torre, Gen. Francisco Gómez de la, revolt in Equador, 1069
Torre, Miguel de la, in command in Venezuela, 803
Torrington, Arthur Herbert, Earl of, British admiral, 430
Torstenson, Leonard, Swedish general, 407
Tosa, Japanese school of painting, 358
Tosa, Satsuma fief of Japan, 889
Toscanelli, Paolo, Florentine geographer, 366
Tosta, Vicente, pres. of Honduras, 1074
Tostig, made Earl of Northumberland, 168
Totila, Ostrogoth leader, 172
Totonac, a Mexican people, 491
Tottleben, Gottlob Heinrich, Russian general, 467
Tou, Chinese Empress, 134
Tou Hsien, Chinese general, 134
Toulon, siege by British, 583; 1158
Toulouse, Kingdom of, 144, 163; battle of, 601
Tourane, 134, 136
Tournay, ceded to England, 369
Tournon, Charles Thomas Maillard de, 539
Tours, battle of, 150, 163; 1135
Tourville, Anne-Hilarion de Cotentin, Comte de, French admiral, 431, 444
Tower of London, 267
Towner, Horace Mann, gov. of Puerto Rico, 1079
Townshend, Charles, British statesman, 436
Townshend, Charles Vere Ferrers, British general, 927, 948
Townshend Acts, 518
Towton, battle of, 270
Tractarians, advocates of Oxford Movement, 612
Trade Disputes Act, in India, 1113
Trade Disputes Bill, in England, 620
Trade guilds, in France, 448
Trade treaty between U.S. and Japan, 1165
Trade Union Act, in France, 639
Trade-union congress, in Australia, 902; in France, 641
Trade-unionism, 606, 608, 635, 639, 640
Trade-Union Law, in England, 968
Trade unions, in Russia, 1030
Trading-with-the-Enemy Act, in U.S., 1049
Trafalgar, battle of, 452, 591
Tragedy, Greek, 53
Traikutaka dynasty, 132
Traitorous Correspondence Bill, 437
Trajan (Marcus Ulpius Traianus), Roman emperor, 32, 109, 110; 112 f.
Transatlantic cable, 775
Transatlantic telephone, 558
Transcaucasia, in the Post-Palaeolithic period, 13
Transcaucasian Republic, 947, 1031
Transcaucasian Socialist Soviet Republic, 1032
Trans-Greenland Expedition, 569
Trans-Iranian Railway, 1109
Transjordania, 1100, 1101
Transmarine Council, of Brazil, 503
Trans-Missouri Freight Association case, 785
Transniestria, 1137
Transoxania, 187, 189, 260
Transportation Act, in U.S., 1050
Trans-Siberian Railway, 707, 744, 745, 1032
Transubstantiation dogma, at Fourth Lateran Council, 221
Transylvania, 420, 934
Transylvania Co., in Kentucky, 517
Trautmannsdorf, Count Maximilian von, imperial diplomat, 408
Travels of Sir John Mandeville, by Jean de Bourgogne, 267
Travendal, Treaty of, 472
Treason Act, in England, 431
Treason law, Roman, 109
Treatise of General Sociology, by Vilfredo Pareto, 551
Treaty of Craiova, 1150
Treaty of Pacification, with Scotland, 376
Treaty of Partition, 445
Treaty of 1221, 257
Treaty of 1537, 410
Treaty of 1618, 424
Treaty of 1783, 764
Treaty of 1800, 766
Treaty of 1839, 974
Treaty of 1888, 752, 833
Treaty of 1889, 784
Treaty on seal fisheries, 785

Trebia (Trebbia), battle of the, 87, 587
Trebizond, Empire of, 259; 929, 947
Trent, British steamer, 613, 776
Trenton, battle of, 521
Trepani, battle of, 224
Trepov, Alesander, Russian minister, 930, 1028
Treveri, revolt of the, 103, 108
Trevithick, Richard, invented high-pressure engine, 553
Trianon, Treaty of, 1014
Tribonian, Roman jurist, 172
Tribunal of Constitutional Guaranties, in Spain, 982
Tribunate of 100, in France, 587, 591
Tricoupis, Charilaos, Greek statesman, 718
Tridentine Decrees, 401
Triennial Act, in England, 376, 379
Triennial Bill, in England, 431
Trier, 1163, 1164
Trieste, taken by Italians, 949; 1141, 1144
Trifanum, battle of, 73
Trimurti, 43
Trinidad, 1148 *f*., 1155, 1158
Trionfans, Augustino, 302
Triparadeisus, 77
Tripartite Pact, Great Britain, France, Italy, 836; Germany, Italy, Japan, 1166
Tripartite treaty, to restore Shuja to Persian throne, 866
Tripartitum, Hungarian constitution, 419
Tripitaka ("Three Baskets"), 42, 132
Triple Alliance, 427, 434, 439 *f*., 442, 660, 690, 694, 737 *f*., 740; 742, 748, 751, 754, 760, 923
Triple expansion engine, 555
Tripoli, 1160
Tripolitan Wars, 662, 758, 759, 768
Tripolye cultures A, B, 16
Trireme, 53
Triumph (H.M.S.), sunk, 920
Triumvirates, Roman, 96, 97, 98, 99
Trocadero, battle of, 644
Trochu, Gen. Louis Jules, pres. of the French govt. of national defense, 636
Troezen, 56
Trojan War, 47, 69
Tronchet, François Denis, counsel for Louis XVI, 582
Trondheim, 1146
Troppau Protocol, 604, 651
Trotsky, Lev (Leon Bronstein) Davidovich, Bolshevik leader, 943, 1029, 1034
Troubridge, Ernest Charles Thomas, British admiral, 919
Troy (Ilium), 47, 106
Troy I and II, 13, 24
Troyes, Peace of, 372; Synod of, 258; Treaty of, 270, 278
Trozene constitution, for Greece, 723
Truce of God, 217, 227
True Cross, captured in sack of Jerusalem, 127, 174
True Pure Land (*Jodo Shin*) sect, 356, 359, 543
Trujillo, Rafael Leonidas, pres. of the Dominican Republic, 1079
Truman, Harry S., President of U.S., 1144, 1165, 1171
Truter, Sir John, English missionary in Bechuanaland, 826
Tryphon, 92, 94
Trzka, Adam Erdmann, imperial general, 406
Ts'ai Ching, 342
Ts'ai Lun, eunuch, 135
Ts'ai Yung, 135
Tsaldaris, Panyoti, premier of Greece, 1021
Ts'ang Ying-hsüan, supervisor of Chinese imperial kilns, 540
Ts'ao P'ei, founder of Wei dynasty, 135
Ts'ao Ts'ao, son of preceding, 135
Tsar, title first assumed, 415
Ts'e Fu Yüan Kuie, Chinese encyclopedia, 343
Tseng Kuo-ch'üan, T'ai P'ing Rebellion, 880
Tseng Kuo-fan, T'ai P'ing Rebellion, 880; 884
Tser, battle of, 916
Tsewang Rabdan, seizure of Lhasa, 539, 540
Tsingtao, 918, 1122
Tso-chuan, archaic Chinese text, 134
Tso Commentary, 45
Tso Tsung-t'ang, T'ai P'ing Rebellion, 880; 881
Tsong-kha-pa, 536
Ts'ui Shu, Chinese scholar, 884
Tsunayoshi, Japanese shōgun, 547
Tsungli Yamen, foreign office of China, 880, 892
Tsushima, occupied by Russians, 889
Tsushima Straits, battle of, 707, 892
Tu Duc, Emperor of Annam, 874
Tu fu, Chinese poet, 340
Tu Hawaiki, Maori Chief of New Zealand, 905
Tu Yu, compiled the first Chinese encyclopedia, 341
Tuan Ch'i-jui, Chinese premier, 1117
Tuan Fang, gov.-gen. of Nanking, 884
Tuan Yü-ts'ai, Chinese scholar, 541
Tuaregs, sack Timbuktu, 329; defeated by French, 841
Tuberculosis, 552
Tubertus, A. Postumius, 72
Tuchins, revolt in Languedoc, 277
T'u-chüeh (western Turks), 136, 340
Tucker, Stephen Davis, inventor of the rotary press, 555
Tudkhaliash II, III, IV, 36
Tudor, House of, 271, 369
Tugendbund, German patriotic organization, 594
Tughril Beg, leader of the Seljuks, 254

Tughtugin, founder of the Burid dynasty, 254
Tuileries, stormed by mob, 581
Tuka, Voitech, Slovak deputy, 1009
Tukaram, Hindu poet, 534
Tukhachevski, Michael, Soviet marshal, 1036
Tukulors, 840
Tukulti-Ninurta I, 38
Tulagi, 1167
Tulayha, false prophet, 184
T'u-li-ch'en, ruler of Ili, 540
Tullius Hostilius, early King of Rome, 69
Tului, son of Jenghis Khan, 344
Tulunids, an Egyptian dynasty, 262
Tuman Bey, Sultan of Egypt, 422
Tumbian culture, 18
Tumuli, Phrygian, 37
Tumulus culture, 17
T'ung Chih Reign of Mu Tsung, 880
Tung Chung-shu, Confucian training, 133
T'ung Meng Hui, union of Chinese societies, 883
T'ung Tien, first Chinese historical encyclopedia, 341
Tung Yüan, Chinese painter, 343
Tungus, 135
Tun-huang, 136
Tunis, occupied by French, 638, 729, 837
Tunisia, govt. reorganized, 1086, 1160 *f*., 1162
Tupac Amarú, revolt of, 800
Tupper, Sir Charles, premier of Canada, 797, 1057
Turakina, widow of Ogedei, 344
Turan, 124
Turco-Armenian peace treaty, 1094
Turco-Greek War of 1897, 731
Turco-Russian Alliance, 1096
Turcoing, battle of, 583
Turenne, Henri de la Tour d'Auvergne, Vicomte de, French general, 407, 440, 442
Turgot, Anne Robert Jacques, Baron de l'Aulne, French reform minister, 448
Turin, Treaty of, 658
Turin papyrus, 23
Turkestan, lost to China, 341
Turkey, 1140, 1143, 1151
Turkhan Pasha, pres. of Albania, 1019
Turkish-Greek exchange of populations, 1095
Turkish Republic, 1095
Turkmanchai, Treaty of, 702, 862
Turkmenistan, Soviet republic, 1034
Turkomans, Black Sheep and White Sheep, 330
Turks (*see also* Ottoman Turks), 126, 127, 136, 304, 317–20, 423 *f*., 424, 461, 463, 475, 484, 485, 526, 592, 662, 701, 714, 719, 758, 937, 947, 948, 966, 978, 1094–98, 1107, 1109, 1110
Turpin, Eugène, developed smokeless powder, 556
Tuscany, 212, 220, 398, 459, 463, 586
Tuscarora War, in North Carolina, 513
Tusculum, Counts of, 216
Tushita heaven, 130
Tushpa, 38
Tushratta, King of Mitanni, 28 *f*.
Tutankhamen, tomb of, 24
Tutor, Julius, 108
Tuttlingen, battle of, 407
Tutuila, American island of Samoa, 911
T'u-yü-hun, Mongol, 137
Tvrtko I, Lord of Bosnia, 319
Tweedy, Owen, African explorer, 1081
Twelfth amendment to the U.S. Constitution, 767
Twelve Apostles of Ireland, 169
Twelve Articles, in German Peasant War, 400
Twelve Tables, laws of the, 71, 72, 94
Twelve Years' Truce, 381
Twenty-first amendment to U.S. Constitution, 1055
Twenty-one Demands on China, 1123
Tydings-McDuffie Act, on Philippines, 1133
Tyler, John (10th pres. of the U.S.), 773
Tyler, Wat, leader in Peasants' Revolt, 267
Tyndaridas (Tyndarion), tyrant, 57
Tyne, 110
Typesetting machinery, 554, 556
Typewriter, 555
Typhus, 553
Typology, method of dating, 2
Typos of Emperor Constans II, 151
Tyrants in Greece, 48
Tyrconnel, Richard Talbot, Earl of, joins James II, 430
Tyre, 26, 27, 32, 53
Tyrol (Austrian) plebiscite, 1006
Tzirallum, 119
Tzu Hsi, dowager empress of China, 880, 881, 882, 883

U 235 (isotope of Uranium), 553
Ualual, battle of, 990, 1085
Ubico, Gen. Jorge, pres. of Guatemala, 1074
Ucciali, Treaty of, 660, 661, 745, 835
Uda, Emperor of Japan, 352
Udayana Buddha, 129
Udena, king, 42
Udyana, 136
Ueno, battle of, 889
Ugaki, Gen. Kazushige, Japanese foreign minister, 1127
Uganda, 847, 848
Ugarit, 32, 33

Uighur Turks, 341
Uitlander agitation, in Transvaal, 855, 856
Ujjain, 41, 128–30, 132
Ukraine, becomes a Soviet republic, 1030; 1153, **1154**
Ukrainian territory, claimed by Germany, 1151
Ukrainians, or Little Russians, 239; treaty with Central Powers, 943
Ulfilas, 123, 144
Ulfsson, Günnbjorn, explorer, 558
Ulloa, Francisco de, 492
Ulm, Treaty of, 404, 407; battle of, 591
Ulmanis, Karlis, pres. of Latvia, 1033
Ulpian (Domitius Ulpianus), Roman jurist, 116
Ulrika Eleonora, Queen of Sweden, 472
Ulster, 621
Ulster Plantation, 374
Ulundi, battle of, 853
Umako, Soga chieftain, 140
Umana, Gen. Justo, crushes Honduras uprising, 1074
Umbrians, 68, 73, 93
Umma, 25
Umman-haldash I, II, 39; III, 40; III, imprisoned, **40**
Ummanigash, 39, 40
Umman-menanu, fought against Sennacherib, 39
Umor, Bulgar ruler, 182
Umpanda, Zulu king, 851
Unam sanctam, bull of Boniface VIII, 222, 232
Unamuno, Miguel de, Spanish author, 981
Underground Railroad, 773
Underwood Tariff Act, in U.S., 791, 910
Uniate Church, 415
Unigenitus, papal bull, 447, 457
Unión Cívica, party in Argentina, 808
Union for Liberty, rights and duties of Aragon nobility, **284**
Union Indo-Chinoise, 875
Union Jack, national flag of Great Britain, 432
Union of Liberation, in Russia, 706
Union of Kalmar, 311 *f.*
Union of Socialist Soviet Republics, 1029, 1033; *see also* Russia
Union of South Africa, 858, 1091, 1092
Union of True Russian Men, 708
Union of Unions, in Russia, 707
Union or Death, Serbian propagandist society, 715, 761
Union Pacific R.R., 780
Unionist Party, in South Africa, 858
Unis, 23
Unitarians, 372
United African Co., 841
United Australia Party, 1130
United Council for China, 1122
United East India Co., 510
United Federation of Labor, in New Zealand, **908**
United Irishmen, 437
United Kingdom, union of Great Britain and Ireland, **437**
United Kingdom of Portugal, Brazil, and Algarves, 502
United Kingdom of the Serbs, Croats, and Slovenes, 950
United Landtag of Prussia, 670, 675, 680
United Mine Workers of America, 1137, 1140
United Nations, 1156 *passim*
United Nations Monetary and Financial Conference, 1170
United Nations Organization, 1170
United Nations Organization for Educational and Cultural Reconstruction, 1170
United Nations Relief and Rehabilitation Administration (UNRRA), 1141, 1170
United Principalities of Moldavia and Wallachia, 720
United Provinces of Central America, 805, 819
United Serbian Youth (*Omladina*), 714
United States of America, 521, 764 *ff.*, 935 *ff.*; 1049 *ff.*; in Second World War, 1135 *passim;* Lend-Lease, 1136, 1137, 1140, 1149; mines seized, 1140; declared war on Japan, 1138, 1167; Department of State, 1144, 1158; naval and air bases from Great Britain, 1155, 1158; merchant tonnage, 1156; Greenland, under protection of, 1158; embargo on scrap iron and steel, 1166
United States, armed forces of, 1142; *passim*, landed in North Africa, 1139, 1158; entered Rome, 1142; destroyed Hiroshima and Nagasaki with atomic bombs, 1145, 1169; landed in Japan, 1145, 1170; planned a "two-ocean" navy, 1155, 1158; landed in Iceland, 1155, 1158; bombed Tokyo by plane, 1158; entered Naples, 1162; captured El Guettar, 1162; crossed German frontier, 1163; crossed the Rhine at Remagen, 1164; landed on the Solomons, 1167; air offensive immobilized Japanese communications, industry, navy, 1169; carrier aircraft penetrated Japanese inland waters, 1169; landed on Leyte, 1169; invaded Okinawa, 1169
United States captures *Macedonian*, 769
United States of Brazil, *see* Brazil
United States of Colombia, *see* Colombia
United States Steel Corp., 787, 1056
Universal German Workingmen's Association, 689
Universal suffrage, in Spain, 647; in Hungary, 796; in Japan, 1123, 1124
University College, 201
University School of Explorers, 569
University of Alcala, 238
University of Constantinople, 181, 728
University of Lisbon, 284
University of Naples, 212
University of Paris, 228, 231, 278
University of Peking, 882

University of Prague, 302, 305 *f.*
University of Salamanca, 238
University of Sydney, 901
University of Uppsala, 312
University Tests Act, at Cambridge and Oxford, **615**
Unkiar Skelessi, Treaty of, 704, 724
Unstrut, battle of the, 599
Untouchables, of India, 1113
Upanishads, 41, 131, 336
Upper Acheulean industry, 6
Upper Italian Kingdom, 657
Upper Mesopotamia (Mitanni), 28
Upper Silesia, League of Nations award, **997**
Upper Volta, French colony, 1088
Upper Yenisei, 7, 14
'Uqaylids of Mosul, 190
Ur, 13, 24–27, 35
Uranium rays, 552
Urartu, *see* Van
Urban, Hungarian renegade, 327
Urban II (Eudes de Lagary), Pope, 218 *f.*
Urban IV (Jacques Pantaléon), Pope, 213
Urban V (Guillaume Grimoard), Pope, 288
Urban VI (Bartolommeo Prignano), Pope, 288
Urban VII (Giovanni Battista Castagna), Pope, **396**
Urban VIII (Maffeo Barberini), Pope, 397
Urban, Charles, first process of colored motion pictures, 557
Urbicus, Quintus Lollius, legate of Britain, 111
Urdaneta, Andrés de, Spanish navigator, 894
Urdiñola, Francisco de, conquers San Luis de Potosí, 492
Urey, Harold Clayton, "heavy hydrogen," 553
Uriburu, José, pres. of Argentina, 808, 1064
Urkhiteshub, 30
Ur-Nammu, 26
Urnfield culture, 17
Urosh I of Serbia, 245, 318
Urquhart, David, English publicist, 725
Urquiza, Justo José de, pres. of Argentina, 808, 811
Urrutia, Francisco José, Spanish diplomat, 816
Ureolo, Peter, King of Hungary, 245
Uruguay (Banda Oriental), 801, 806, 810 *f.*, 817, 1066, 1067, 1138
Urukagina, social reforms, 25
Urumilki, King of Byblos, 33
d'Urville, Dumont, French explorer, 895, 899
d'Urville, Capt. Jules Sébastien César Dumont, Antarctic explorer, 573
Usipetes, 96
Üsküb (Skoplje), taken by Bulgarians, 927
Usman dan Fodio, Tukulor chief, 525
Usselinex, William, 510
Utah, admitted to statehood, 784
Utensils, of Palaeolithic period, 4
Utica, 32, 33, 98
Utraquism and Utraquists, 305, 404
Utrecht, Treaty of, 432, 446, 450, 457, 458, 463, 494, 500, 514, 645; Union of, 381
Utu-hegal, King of Erech, 26
Uxbridge, Treaty of, 377
Uzbekistan, Soviet republic, 1034
Uzbeks, driven out of Khorasan, 526
Uzun Hasan, ruler of the White Sheep, 330, 526

Vaca, Alvar Nuñez Cabeza de, gov. of Buenos Aires, 490, 492, 493
Vadier, Marc Guillaume Albert, French revolutionist, 584
Vadimo, Lake, battle of, 73
Vaez de Torres, Luis, explorer, 894
Vahan, leader of revolt, 125
Vaibhashika school, 131
Vaida-Voevod, Alexander, premier of Rumania, 1026
Vaillant, Auguste, French anarchist, 640
Vairochana, Indian cult, 331
Vais, Ghilzai chieftain, 528
Vaisali, 42
Vaiseshika-sutras, 131
Vakatakas, its domain, 132
Vakpatiraja, Prakrit poet, 331
Valabhi, 131
Valdivia, Pedro de, founded Santiago in Chile, 489
Valenciennes, taken by the British, 950
Valens, Fabius, Roman emperor, 107, 120, 143
Valentina, wife of Louis of Orléans, 298
Valentinian I (Flavius Valentinianus), Roman emperor, dies on an expedition, 120
Valentinian II, Roman emperor, 120, 122
Valentinian III, Roman emperor, 122, 142, 143, 145
Valerian (Publius Licinius Valerianus), 115 *f.*, 124
Valerius, Roman consul, 72
Valla, Lorenzo, humanist, 290
Valley Forge, 521
Vallière, Louise de la, mistress of Louis XIV, 443
Valmiki, 43
Valmy, battle of, 581
Valois kings, claims to Naples, 293
Valona, occupied by the Italians, 1019
Valparaiso, bombarded, 809; Treaty of, 809, 812
Valteline Pass, 409
Van (city), taken by the Turks, 947
Van (Urartu), Kingdom of, 38, 40
Van Buren, Martin (8th pres. of the U.S.), 772

Van Diemen's Land, changed to Tasmania, 901
Van Diemen's Land Co., 898
Van Eyck, Hubert and Jan, Flemish painters, 280, 282
Van Kerckhoven, Capt. Guillaume François, Belgian commander, 844
Van Keulens, father and son, cartographers, 561
Van Ryneveld, Sir Helperus Andrias, Dutch aviator, 1081
Van Tromp, Maarten, Dutch admiral, 425, 439
Van Zeeland, Paul, premier of Belgium, 975
Vancouver, Capt. George, explorer, 791
Vandal Kingdom, in Africa, 121, 144, 145
Vandalia Co., 517
Vandalic Wars, of Justinian, 145
Vandals, overrun Gaul, 121; in southern Spain, 144; treaty with Constantinople, 145
Vandamme, Dominique René, defeated by Bohemian army, 599
Vanderbilt, Cornelius, 819
Vannic language, 28
Varaguna I, suzerain over Pallavas, 336
Varaguna II, 336, 337
Varahamihira, his *Pañchasiddhantika*, 131
Varahran I, 116, 124; II, 124; III, 124; IV, 125; V, 125
Varahran (Bahram), Persian general, reigns as Bahram VI, 127
Varangians, *see* Russians
Vardhamana Mahavira, 41
Vargas, Getulio Dornelles, pres. of Brazil, 1071, 1156
Varna, battle of, 314, 318, 323, 326
Varro, antiquarian, 69, 71, 100
Varro, Caius Terentius, Roman general, 87
Varttikas, 42
Varus, Publius Quinctilius, Roman general, 103
Vasa, Gustavus Eriksson, Gustavus I of Sweden, 410
Vasishka, 129
Vasquez, Horacio, pres. of Dominican Republic, 1078
Vasubandhu, philosopher, 131
Vasudeva, 129
Vasushka, 129
Vatatzes, John Dukas, Nicaean emperor, 248, 253, 259, 260
Vatican City, temporal domain of the pope, 993
Vatican Council of 1870, 664, 688
Vatsaraja, ruler of western India, 331, 336
Vatsyayana Mallanaga, 130
Vattagamani, founded the Abhayagiri Monastery, 132
Vauban, Sébastien le Prestre, Marquis de, French general, 442
Vaubernier, Jeanne, *see* du Barry
Vaucelles, Truce of, 402
Vauchamps, battle of, 600
Vaughan, Sir William, sells part of Newfoundland, 510
Vaugoin Karl, chancellor of Austria, 1006
V-E Day (Second World War), 1165
Vedanta, 131, 336
Vedas, 41, 130
Veientines, 71
Veii, 71, 72
Vela, Blasco Nuñez, viceroy of Peru, 490
Velasco, Luis de, expedition to Philippines, 908
Velásquez, Diego de, conquered Cuba, 369, 486, 490, 491
Velásquez, Diego, Spanish painter, 389
Velikye-Luki, 1153
Velocipede, 555
Vendée, revolt in the, 582–84
Vendidad, book of the Avesta, 39
Vendôme, Louis Joseph, Duke de, French general, 442, 446, 457
Veneti, 68, 96
Venetia, overrun by Magyars, 158; ceded to Italy, 659; *see also* Venice
Venetians, trading privileges with Constantinople, 252, 253; 258, 328, 420, 423; Treaty of the, 299
Venezia Giulia, 1144
Venezuela, 488, 618, 786, 802, 816 f., 1070
Venice, 223, 224 f., 252, 253, 298 f., 319, 397, 424, 458, 655
Venizelos, Eleutherios, Greek prime minister, 709, 710, 759, 920, 926, 940, 1020, 1021
Venizelos-Tittoni Agreement, 1020
Venloo, in War of the Spanish Succession, 431
Venusia, 74
Vera Cruz, 791, 821
Verbiest, Ferdinand, his perpetual calendar, 539
Verbőczy, Stephen, constitution for Hungary, 419
Vercellae, 92
Vercingetorix, leads revolt of Gaul, 97
Verdun, 914: 1st battle of, 930; 2d, 939, 946; Treaty of, 157, 158; fortress, captured by French, 1148
Vereeniging, Treaty of, 751, 857
Vergennes, Charles Gravier, Count de, French minister, 448, 521, 522
Vergniaud, Pierre Victurnien, French revolutionary leader, 580, 582
Vermont, admitted to statehood, 766
Verneuil, battle of, 270, 278
Vernon, Edward, English admiral, 434
Verocchio, Andrea del, Italian artist, 296
Verona, 100, 119, 1141
Verrazzano, Giovanni, Italian explorer, 505
Verres, prosecuted by Cicero, 95
Verri, Pietro, Italian economist, 455
Versailles, Treaties of, 452, 469, 495, 951, 952, 960, 1003, 1038, 1170
Verulamium, 97

Verus, Lucius Aurelius, shares powers with Marcus Aurelius, 111, 117
Verus, Marcus, Annius, made Caesar, 111, 112
Vervins, Treaty of, 386, 390
Vesontio, 96
Vespasian (Titus Flavius Vespasianus), Roman emperor, 32, 107, 108
Vespucci, Amerigo, Spanish discoverer, 368
Veturius, T., 73
Via Aemilia, 88
Via Appia, 73
Via Flaminia, 74, 87, 88
Via Valeria, 74
Vibhasha, 129, 131
Viborg, taken by Germans, 943; battle of, 1047; Manifesto, 708; 1154
Vicente, Gil, Portuguese playwright, 392
Vichy government, 1135, 1138, 1139, 1148, 1158, 1166
Vicksburg, surrender of, 778
Vico, Giambattista, Italian philosopher, 455
Victor, Bishop of Rome, 141
Victor II, Pope, 217
Victor III, Pope, 218
Victor IV, Anti-Pope, 220
Victor Amadeus, Duke of Savoy, 387; 398, 444, 450
Victor Amadeus II of Savoy, 457
Victor Amadeus III of Savoy, 458, 585
Victor Emmanuel I of Piedmont, 650
Victor Emmanuel II, King of Piedmont, 655, 658, 659, 660, 733
Victor Emmanuel III, King of Italy, 661
Victoria, Queen of England, 609, 611, 613, 619
Victoria, settled, 900; 901, 902
Victoria, Guadalupe, pres. of Mexico, 821
Victoria Falls, discovered, 826
Victoria Nyanza, discovered, 826
Victual Brothers, Swedish pirates, 309
Vieille, Paul, developed smokeless powder, 556
Vienna, besieged by Turks, 422, 483; taken by French, 591; Treaties of, 434, 451, 458, 463, 468, 651, 659, 697; 1150
Vienna Four Points, 727
Vienne, Synod of, 222, 232, 258
Viera, Feliciano, pres. of Uruguay, 1066
Viipuri (Viborg), 1145 f.
Vijayabahu, ruler of Ceylon, 338
Vijayaditya III, 337
Vijayanagar, center of Brahman studies, 338
Vijñanavidin (Idealist) school, 131
Vijnaptimatratasiddhi, 331
Vikings, 167, 170
Vikrama, an era, 128
Vikramaditya II (Chalukya), 336
Vikramaditya VI, 337
Vikramankacharita, 337
Vikramortasi, 131
Vilayet Law, in Turkey, 729
Vilkitski, Capt. Boris Alexandre, Russian explorer, 570
Villa Francisco (Pancho), Mexican revolutionist, 791, 822, 1075
Villafañe, Angel de, gov. of the Carolinas, 493
Villafavila, Treaty of, 388
Villafranca, Treaty of, 658
Villalar, battle of, 388
Villalobos, Ruy Lopez de, 894, 908
Villani, Giovanni, Italian chronicler, 294
Villanova culture, 17
Villanovans, 68, 69
Villanueva, José Cabino, pres. of Bolivia, 1067
Villarroel, Maj. Gualberto, Bolivia, 1141
Villars, Claude Louis Hector, Duke de, French general, 440, 447
Villaviciosa, battle of, 446, 450
Villazón, Eleodoro, pres. of Bolivia, 812
Villegagnon, Nicholas Durand de, French colonizer, 501
Villehardouin, Geoffroy de, French chronicler, 231, 258
Villehardouin, family, 258
Villèle, Jean Baptiste Séraphin Joseph, Count de, prime minister of France, 627
Villeroy, François de Neufville, Duc de, marshal of France, 444, 446
Villiers, George, Duke of Buckingham, 374
Villius, 89
Villmergen Wars, in Switzerland, 448
Villon, François, French poet, 280
Vilna, 922, 925, 1038, 1042, 1145, 1151
Vima Kadphises, conquers northwestern India, 128
Vimala Saha, builder of a Jain temple, 332
Vimeiro, battle of, 593
Viminacium, battle of, 173
Vimy Ridge, taken by Canadian troops, 939
Vinaroz, in Spanish Civil War, 984
Vincent, Stenio, pres. of Haiti, 1078
Vincent of Beauvais, his *Speculum Maius*, 231
Vincenzo II (Gonzaga) of Mantua, 398
Vincke, Ernst Friedrich Georg, German politician, 676, 680
Vindelicia, 102
Vindex, Caius Julius, his revolt, 107
Vindhyas, 129, 131, 132
Vindobona, 112
Vinegar Hill, battle of, 437
Vinekh, Bulgar ruler, 182
Vio, Thomas de, Cardinal of Gaëta, summoned Luther, 399
Viquez, Clito Gonzáles, pres. of Costa Rica, 1073

Viraballala III, ruler of southern India, 338
Virarajendra, 337
Virchow, Rudolf, German parliamentarian, 688
Virgil (Publius Virgilius Maro), Roman poet, 112
Virgin Islands, 792, 1079, 1080, 1155
Virginia, daughter of Virginius, 72
Virginia, its charter revoked, 508
Virginia convention, 520
Virginian Resolutions, 766
Virginius, stabs his daughter, 72
Viriathus, assassinated, 90
Visconti, Filippo Maria, 292, 295
Visconti, Giovanni, 294
Visconti, Matteo, 224
Visconti, Otto, 297
Visconti, Valentina, 381
Vishnu, the *Dharma Sutra*, 130, 132
Vishnukundins, a dynasty, 132
Vishtasp (Hystaspes), King of Bactria, 39
Visigothic Kingdom, of Spain, 144, 163
Visigoths (Balthas), 120, 143, 144, 145, 147, 163, 173
Vispered, book of the Avesta, 39
Vistula, line, 1164
Visuddhimagga, 132
Vitalian, pretender, 122
Vitamins, 552; D, 553; A, 553
Vitascope, 556
Vitebsk, 1154
Vitellius, Aulus, Roman Emperor, 107
Viten, Lithuanian prince, 316
Vitergo, Treaty of, 320
Vitoria, Francisco de, pioneer in international law, 388
Vitoria, Tomas Luis de, Spanish musician, 389
Vitovt, *see* Witold
Vittoria, battle of, 600
Vittorio Veneto, battle of, 949
Vivaldo, Ugolino, Genoese explorer, 363
Vives, Luis, professor at Oxford, 388
Viviani, René, French premier, 762, 929, 930
Vizcaino, Sebastian, explorer, 492
Vladimir, Bulgarian ruler, 182
Vladimir, Prince, of Russia, 180
Vladimir the Saint, 243
Vladislav I, King of Bohemia, 240
Vladislav II, King of Bohemia, 240
Vladislav I (Ladislas) Hermann, King of Poland, 241
Vladislav II (Ladislas), King of Poland, 242
Vladislav IV (Lokietek), King of Poland, 312
Vladislav V (Jagiello), King of Poland, 314
Vladislav VI, King of Poland and Hungary, 314, 318
Vladislav VII, King of Poland, Bohemia, and Hungary, 314, 415, 418
Vladislav, King of Serbia, 247
Vladislav, John, Bulgar ruler, 184
Vladislavitch, Sava, 540
Vladivostok, 704, 879, 947, 1123, 1153
Vlamingh, Willem de, 561
Voeslau, Treaty of, 714
Vogel, Sir Julius, railroad builder, 907
Vogt, Karl, German politician, 676
Voitech, George, uprising in Bulgaria, 247
Voldemaras, Augustine, premier of Lithuania, 1041, 1042
Volga River, 1153
Volksraad, legislative council of Netherlands East Indies, 1117
Volmar, Dr., negotiated Treaties of Westphalia, 408
Vologesus (Balas), 125, 126
Vologesus I, Parthian ruler, 83
Vologesus III, of Parthia, 111
Vologesus V, of Parthia, 115
Volosin, Augustin, leader in Carpatho-Ukraine, 1016
Volsci, 71, 73
Volstead Act, in U.S., 1050
Volta, Alessandro, Italian physicist, 455, 551
Voltaire, François Marie Arouet de, French writer, 457, 460
Voltri, battle of, 588
Vonones, one of the Kings of Kings, 128
Vorarlberg, votes for union with Switzerland, 994
Voronezh, 1153
Vorovsky, Vaslav Vaslovovich, Russian diplomat, 994
Vossem, Peace of, 442
Vouillé, battle of, 147, 163
Voyage to Icaria, by Etienne Cabet, 549
Vranje, taken by the Serbs, 949
Vratislav II, King of Bohemia, 240
Vreeland, Edward Butterfield, American politician, 791
Vuillemin, Maj. Joseph, French aviator, 1081
Vukan, ruler of Montenegro, 247
Vulcan, introduction of iron in shipbuilding, 554
Vulcan Pass, 934
Vulgate, 123, 396
Vulso, Lucius Manlius, 86
Vyasma, 1151

Wabash, St. Louis & Pacific R.R. *v.* Illinois, decision by U.S. supreme ct., 782
Wace, his *Roman de Brut* and *Roman de Rou*, 194
Wadai, Negro kingdom, 840
Waddington, William Henry, French statesman, 736
Wadjak Man, 9
Wadsworth, Capt. William, hid charter of Connecticut, 512
Wady-el-Mughara, caves, 6

Wafd, Egyptian party, 1083, 1084
Wages and Hours Law, in U.S., 1056
Wagner-Stegall Act, in U.S., 1056
Wagram, battle of, 595
Wahabis, revolt of, 540, 828, 1104
Wahehe War, in German East Africa, 849
Wailing Wall, in Jerusalem, 1101
Waitangi, Treaty of, 905
Wakatsuki, Reejiro, premier of Japan, 1125, 1126
Wake Island, 1167
Wakefield, Edward Gibbon, English colonialist, 899, 905
Walcher of Malvern, 194
Waldeck, George Frederick, Prince of, in battle of Fleurus, 444
Waldeck-Rousseau, Pierre Marie René, French premier, 642
Waldemar II (the Conqueror), King of Denmark, 203, 210, 242, 244
Waldemar IV, King of Denmark, 309, 311
Waldemar, King of Sweden, 204
Waldemar of Denmark, Prince, 718, 740
Waldemar the Great, King of Denmark, 203
Waldensian Crusade, *see* Albigensian
Waldmann, Hans, *bürgermeister* of Zürich, 307
Waldo, Peter, leader of the Waldensians, 229
Waldsemüller, Martin, geographer, 368
Wales, conquered, 166; Norman penetration, 196, 199
Walewski, Alexandre Florian Joseph Colonna, Count, French foreign minister, 728
Walfish Bay, 853, 859
Walid I, caliph, 187
Walid II, caliph, 188
Walker, Sir Hovenden, British general, 514
Walker, William, American adventurer, 819
Wall of Antonius, 111, 114
Wall of Hadrian, 110, 114, 166
Wall painting, 113
Wallace, Alfred Russel, British scientist, 551
Wallace, Henry A., U.S. vice-president, 1136
Wallace, William, Scottish leader, 199
Wallachia, 181, 719, 720, 722. *See also* Rumania
Wallenius, Gen. Kurt, Finnish Fascist leader, 1048
Wallenstein, Albrecht Wenzel Eusebius von, Duke of Friedland, imperial general, 404, 405, 406
Waller, Sir William, in English Civil War, 377
Wallia, Visigoth, 121, 144
Wallis, Samuel, English explorer, 894
Wallon, Henri Alexandre, French politician, 638
Walls of Aurelian, 116
Walo, papal legate, 242
Walpole, Sir Robert, prime minister of England, 432, 434
Walsh, Thomas James, American senator, 1057
Walsingham, Sir Francis, British statesman, 373
Walsingham, Thomas, his *Chronicle*, 267
Walter, Hubert, Archbishop of Canterbury, 196
Walter, John, British publisher, 555
Walter of Brienne, Duke of Athens, 294
Walter the Penniless, in First Crusade, 255
Walters, Lucy, mistress of Charles II, 428
Waltherius, 162
Wan Li Reign of Shen Tsung, 536, 537
Wang An-shih, Chinese reformer, 342, 343
Wang Ching-wei, head of Chinese puppet government, 1135, 1165
Wang dynasty, 346
Wang Hsi-chih, 136
Wang Hsien-ch'ien, Chinese historian, 884
Wang Hsüan-tse, Chinese emissary, 331
Wang Mang, Chinese emperor, 134
Wang Ming-sheng, commentator on Chinese history, 541
Wang Shou-jen (pen-name of Wang Yang-ming), 536, 537
Wang Wei, Chinese landscapist, 340
Wang Yang-ming, school of Confucian philosophy, 546
Wanghsia, Treaty of, 879
War chariot, introduced into Egypt, 28
War Finance Commission, in U.S., 1049
War Hawks, for war with England, 769
War Industries Board, in U.S., 1049
War Information, Office of, 1159
War Labor Board, 1139
War Mobilization, Office of, 1140
War Production Board, 1138
War Shipping Administration, 1156
War of American Independence, 436, 448, 449, 452, 495, 520–23
War "of Berenice," 81
War of Chioggia, 298
War of Devolution, 442, 450, 461
War of Jenkins' Ear, 434, 451, 494, 515
War of 1812, 769, 770
"War of the Allies," 64, 80, 93
War of the Austrian Succession, 434, 447, 451, 459, 465, 479, 484, 494, 517, 534
War of the Axe, 852
War of the Bavarian Succession, 468
War of the Emboabas, 501
War of the Mantuan Succession, 398
War of the Mascates, 502
War of the Oranges, 454
War of the Pacific, 809, 812, 813
War of the Polish Succession, 447, 451, 458, 459, 463, 477, 479
War of the Reform, 821

War of the Second Coalition, 482, 586
War of the Seven Reductions, 495
War of the Spanish Succession, 431, 439, 445, 450, 457, 459, 461, 494, 501, 514
War of the Third Coalition, 452, 591, 699, 701
War of the Three Henrys, 384
Warad-Sin, ruler of Larsa, 39
Warbeck, Perkin, English pretender, 369
Ward, Frederick Townsend, helped suppress T'ai P'ing Rebellion, 880
Ward, Joseph, New Zealand leader, 1131
Ward, Sir Joseph George, premier of New Zealand, 908, 1131
Warner, Seth, American commander, 520
Warren, William Robertson, premier of Newfoundland, 1061
Warrior class, in Japan, 890
Wars of Independence and Liberation, in Latin America, 799 ff.
Wars of the Roses, 270 ff.
Warsaw (city), battles of, 471, 916, 922; surrendered, 1145; 1164
Warsaw, Grand Duchy of, 702
Wartburg Festival, 669
Wartenburg, battle of, 599
Warwick, Lord, see Northumberland, Duke of
Warwick, Edward Plantagenet, Earl of, executed by Henry VII, 369
Warwick, Richard Neville, Earl of, regent in France, 270, 271
Warwick, Sir Robert Rich, Earl of, granted much of Connecticut River Valley, 509
Washburn, Cadwallader Colden, flour-milling process, 782
Washington, capital of U.S., 766, 769; Treaty of, 781; 1141, 1144, 1166
Washington (state), admitted to statehood, 784; 1155
Washington, George (1st pres. of U.S.), 516, 520, 521, 764, 766
Washington Conference, 956, 958, 1050, 1118, 1124
Washshukanni, 29
Wasp (U.S.S.) captures the Frolic (Br.), 769
Wasserman, August von, syphilis, 552
Wassmuss, Herr, German consul at Bushire, 1107
"Water Beggars," capture Brill, 380
Waterboer, Nikolaas, Griqua chief, 853
Waterloo, battle of, 603
Water-Power Act, in U.S., 1050
Wathiq, caliph, 189
Watkins, Henry George, Arctic explorer, 569
Watson, John Christian, premier of Australia, 903, 904
Watt, James, invention of modern steam engine, 553
Wauchope, Sir Arthur, British high commissioner for Palestine, 1101
Wavell, Sir Archibald, victorious commander of British forces in North Africa, 1160
"Way of Purity," 132
"We don't want to fight," music hall song, 735
Wealth of Nations, by Adam Smith, 549
Wealth-Tax Act, 1056
Weaver, James Baird, candidate for pres. of U.S., 785
Webb, Sidney and Beatrice, members of Fabian Society, 618
Webb-Pomerene Act, in U.S., 1049
Weber, Max, German sociologist, 399
Webster, Daniel, American statesman, 611, 771, 772, 773, 774, 795
Weddell, Capt. James, Antarctic explorer, 573
Wedel, Count Botho von, mission to Vienna, 923
Wedell, Richard Georg von, German general, 467
Wedmore, Peace of, 167
Wegener, Dr. Alfred, Arctic explorer, 568, 569
Wehrmacht, 1153
Wei dynasty, 44, 135, 137
Wei-hai-wei, 881, 891, 1118, 1119
Wei Pao, his version of the Chinese Canon of History, 341
Weimar, Constitution, in Germany, 996
Weiser, Conrad, 515
Weissenberg, battle of, 688
Wekerle, Alexander, prime minister of Hungary, 696, 941
Welf and Waiblinger in Germany (Guelf and Ghibelline in Italy), 208, 212
Welfs, in Brunswick, 213
Welle River, in Africa, 828
Wellesley Province, given to British, 875
Wellington, capital of New Zealand, 907
Wellington (Sir Arthur Wellesley), Duke of, British general 593–595, 596, 600, 601, 602, 603, 606, 607, 609, 723, 899
Wellman, Walter, Arctic explorer, 565
Wells, Dr. Horace, nitrous oxide as an anaesthetic, 551, 773
Welsers, bankers of Augsburg, 488
Welsh Disestablishment Bill, 621
"Welsh" refugees, political group in Scotland, 168
Wen Tsung, 880
Wenceslas (Vaclav) I, King of Bohemia, 240
Wenceslas IV, King of Bohemia, 302, 305
Wenceslas I, King of Poland, 242, 317
Wenceslas II, King of Poland, 241
Wenceslas III, King of Poland, 241, 304
Wenceslas, German Emperor, 298
Wenden, battle of, 417
Wends, 160, 208
Wentworth, Thomas, member of the Addled Parliament, 374; 376
Wentworth, Thomas, attack on Cartagena, 434
Wentworth, William Charles, Australian explorer, 898, 900, 902

Wergeland, Henrik, Young Norway Party, 699
Werth, Johann, 407
Wesley, John and Charles, English religious reformers, 434
Wesleyan mission, in New Zealand, 905
Wessex, Anglo-Saxon kingdom, 166, 168
West Africa, 1159, 1160
West Australia, govt. established, 903
West Indies, 486 f.
West Virginia, admitted to statehood, 780
Western Chin dynasty, 135
Western Empire, resurrected by Charlemagne, 177
Western Happy Heaven (Sukhavati), of O-mi-t'o (Amitabha), 136
Western Hemisphere, defense of, 1154 ff.
Western Wei, 136
Westernport, British post, 899
Westinghouse, George, patented the airbrake, 555, 781
Westinghouse Electrical Co., 1050
Westland, in New Zealand, 906, 907
Westminster, Treaty of, 427, 439, 466
Westminster Assembly, 377
Westphalia, Peace of, 390; Treaty of, 381, 408, 440, 455; Kingdom of, 593, 600
Westwall, German, 1163
Wettins, in Saxony, 213, 302
Wettstein, John Rudolf, 410
Weu, Prince of Wei, 44
Weygand, Gen. Maxime, French commander-in-chief, 1033, 1098, 1146
Weymouth, George, colonization in America, 508
Weyprecht, Carl, Arctic explorer, 565
Whalers, off coasts of Japan, 887
Whaling industry, 562
Whampoa, Treaty of, 879
Whampoa Military Academy, in China, 1118
Wharton, Thomas, British secretary of state, 431
Wheatstone, Sir Charles, electrical developments, 554
Whig Party in U.S., 772
Whig Tariff, 773
Whiskey insurrection, in western Pennsylvania, 764
Whiskey Ring, 782
Whitby, Synod of, 166, 168
White, Sir George Stuart, British general, 857
White, John, English colonizer, 508
White, Rev. John, settlement at Salem, Mass., 509
White Cloud, secret fraternity in China, 537
White Fathers, Mission of the, in Africa, 841
Whitefield, George, collaborator of the Wesleys, 434
White group, of man, 12, 19
White Huns, of Hephthalites, 330
White Lotus Society, secret fraternity in China, 537; 540, 877
White Mountain, battle of the, 404, 429
White Oak Swamp, battle of, 778
White Plains, battle of, 527
White Russians, branch of eastern Slavs, 239
White Terror, in France, 626
Whitehead, Robert, invented locomotive torpedo, 555
Whitelocke, Gen. John, occupied Montevideo, 800
Whites (Bianchi), Guelf faction in Florence, 293
Whitney, Eli, introduced the cotton gin, 764, 770
Whitworth, Sir Joseph, rifling in artillery, 555
Wiclif, John, English reformer, 266, 267, 288, 305, 398
Widukind of Corvey, his Res Gestae Saxonicae, 162
Wielopolski, Alexander, Marquis, Polish leader, 704
Wiesloch, battle of, 404
Wiesner, Friedrich, Baron von, Austrian jurist, 762
Wiggin, Albert Henry, the Layton-Wiggin Report, 961
Wilberforce, William, English abolitionist, 608
Wilderness, battle of the, 779
Wilhelm, German Crown Prince, 913, 930
Wilhelmina, Queen of the Netherlands, 626, 996, 1146
Wilkes, Capt. Charles, at Antarctica, 573
Wilkes, John, publisher of the North Briton, 435 f.
Wilkins, Sir George Hubert, Antarctic flights, 576
Will of the People, Russian radical society, 705
William X, of Aquitaine, 227
William I (the Conqueror), King of England, 168, 193, 201, 218, 225, 227
William II (Rufus), of England, 193, 201
William III, see William of Orange
William IV, of England, 606, 607, 609, 669
William I, German emperor, 667, 680, 681, 686–688, 689, 691, 736
William II, German Emperor, 691, 733, 741, 742, 744, 746, 749, 753, 754, 756, 757, 762, 838, 942, 951, 995
William I, King of the Netherlands, 621, 622, 625
William II, King of Holland, 438, 439, 625, 888
William IV, of Orange-Nassau, 440
William V, of Holland, 440
William I, King of Sicily, 219, 223
William II, of Sicily, 223
William, Duke of Urach, King of Lithuania, 1041
William, Duke of Württemberg, King of Lithuania, 944
William of Holland, King of Germany, 212 f.
William of Lorris, his Roman de la Rose, 231
William of Nassau, Prince of Orange (William the Silent), 380
William of Occam, opponent of Thomism, 201; 301
William of Orange (later William III), 380, 381, 427, 429, 430, 439, 442, 444, 512, 513
William of Rubruck, envoy of China, 345, 362

William of Villehardouin, Prince of Achaia, 321
William of Wied, Prince, King of Albania, 925, 1019
William of Wykeham, founder of Winchester School, 267
William the Lion, King of Scotland, 199, 201
William the Pious, Duke of Aquitaine, 216
Williams, Henry, first Anglican clergyman in New Zealand, 905
Williams, Roger, 509
Willibord, Christian missionary to Scandinavia, 170
Willigis, Archbishop of Mainz, 162
Williman, Claudio, pres. of Uruguay, 1066
Willingdon, Freeman Freeman-Thomas, 1st Earl of, gov.-gen. of Canada, 1058; viceroy of India, 1113
Willkie, Wendell L., 1135
Willoughby, Sir Hugh, expedition to Russia, 559
Wills, William John, Australian explorer, 901
Wilmington, Spencer Compton, Earl of, British statesman, 434
Wilmot Proviso, in the House of Representatives, 774
Wilson, Sir Charles Rivers, in Nubar cabinet in Egypt, 831
Wilson, Daniel, son-in-law of Pres. Grévy of France, 639
Wilson, Dr. Edwin Adrian, Antarctic explorer, 574
Wilson, Sir Henry Hughes, British general, 945
Wilson, (Thomas) Woodrow (28th pres. of the U.S.), 791, 792, 923, 935, 944, 948, 949, 951–55, 986, 987
Wilson, William Lyne, co-author of the Wilson-Gorman Tariff Act, 786
Wilson-Gorman Tariff Act, 786
Wilton cultures A, B, C, 18
Wimbledon, Edward Cecil, Viscount, expedition against Cadiz, 375
Wimpfen, battle of, 404
Winchelsey, Robert, Archbishop of Canterbury, 200
Winchester, battle of, 779
Winchester, Oliver Fisher, introduced the repeating rifle, 555
Winchester School (St. Mary's College), 267
Winckelmann, Johann Joachim, German scholar, 458
Windhoek, capital of Southwest Africa, 859, 918
Windischgrätz, Prince Alfred, Austrian general, 673, 674, 676
Windischgrätz, Princess, 673
Windmill Hill culture, 17
Windsor, Duke of, see Edward VIII of England
Windsor, Treaty of, 285, 749
Windthorst, Ludwig, German political leader, 688
Wine industry, in France, 643
Wineau, taken by Austro-Germans, 922
Wingate, Sir Francis Reginald, British general, 833
Winrich of Kniprode, grand master of the Teutonic Knights, 215
Winter, Sir James Spearman, premier of Canada, 798
Winterkönig, Philip, on Russian exploration, 559
Winthrop, John, emigrates to Massachusetts Bay, 509
Winthrop, John, Jr., 509
Winzingerode, Ferdinand von, 599
Wireless telegraphy, invented, 556
Wirth, Julius, prime minister of Germany, 997
Wisconsin, first direct primary law, 789
Wisiniowiecki, Michael, King of Poland, 475
Wissmann, Hermann von, African explorer, 828, 848
Witan, Anglo-Saxon council, 167, 168, 191
Witchcraft, in Salem, 512
Witiges, Ostrogoth king, 172
Witold (Vitovt), Grand Duke of Lithuania, 314, 316
Witos, Vincent, leader of Peasant Party in Poland, 1039
Witte, Sergei Yulievich, Count, Russian statesman, 706, 707, 708, 746, 747, 750, 751, 752
Wittelsbachs, in Upper Bavaria, 213
Wittgenstein, Ludwig Adolf Peter, Russian general, 598, 599
Wittstock, battle of, 406, 407
Witu, protectorates, 847, 848
Witu Co. formed, 847
Woermann & Co., German traders in Africa, 840
Wojciechowski, Stanislas, pres. of the Polish Republic, 1039
Wolfe, James, British general, 435, 516
Wolff, German cruiser, 932
Wolseley, Sir Garnet Joseph, 1st Viscount, British general, 738, 796, 832, 841, 853
Wolsey, Thomas, British statesman, 369, 770
Woman suffrage, in Australia, 904; in England, 968
Women's Rights Convention, in U.S., 774
Wood, Leonard, American general, 823, 1132, 1133
Wood blocks for printing, 340, 342
Wood-Forbes mission, to the Philippines, 1132
Wood Lake, battle of, 780
Woodhead, Sir John, and commission on Palestine, 1102
Woodlands area, 20
Woodville, Elizabeth, wife of Edward IV, 271
Woolens Act, 514
Worcester, battle of, 425
Wordie, James Mann, Arctic explorer, 567, 568
Wordingborg, Peace of, 309
Workers' insurrection, in Moscow, 707 f.
Workers' Security Law, in Norway, 1046
Working hours in factory, restricted, 692
Workingmen's Association, in England, 609
Workingmen's Compensation Act, in England, 620; in France, 977; Maryland first state to adopt law, 788
Workingmen's Party, in New York, 771
Works and Days, of Hesiod, 47
World Court, 960, 999, 1006

World Economic Conference, at London, 969
World Security Council, 1156
World War, First, 434, 763; western front, 913–16, 921, 938; eastern front, 914, 916–17, 923, 932; at sea, 917, 918; colonies, 918: Ottoman front, 919–21; submarine warfare, 922, 939; Italian intervention, 923–25; Balkan front, 925–27; Mesopotamian, 927–29, 930 ff.; armistice, losses, peace settlements, 951, 952, 953
World War, Second, 1135 ff.
World War Foreign Debt Commission, in U.S., 962
World Zionist Congress, 1101
Worms, Concordat and Synod, 206, 207 f., 210, 212, 218, 219
Worship of God, abolished, 583
Worsley, Frank Arthur, Arctic explorer, 569
Wörth, battle of, 688
Wrangel, Ferdinand Petrovich, Baron, Russian explorer, 562
Wrangel, Gustavus, Swedish admiral, 407
Wrangel, Gen. Peter Nicolaievich, Russian counter-revolutionary, 1031
Wren, Sir Christopher, English architect, 427
Wright, Sir Almroth Edward, introduced anti-typhoid inoculation, 552
Wright, Frances, women's rights movement in America, 774
Wright, Gen. Luke Edward, gov. of the Philippines, 909
Wright brothers, Wilbur and Orville, pioneers of aviation, 557, 789
Writing, 21
Writs of assistance, 517
Wu, Chinese empress, 340
Wu dynasty, founded, 135
Wu-k'ung, pilgrimage to India, 341
Wu Liang, 135
Wu-ling, Prince, 44
Wu San-kuei, Ming general, 537, 539
Wu Tao-hsüan, Chinese figure-painter, 340
Wu Ti, The Martial Emperor, 133, 137
Wu Tsung, Chinese ruler, 341
Wu Ying Tien, books printed from movable wooden type, 541
Wundt, Wilhelm, German psychologist, 552
Wurschen, battle of, 599
Württemberg, Prince of, 592
Würzburg, battle of, 585
Wusterhausen, Treaty of, 463
Wyatt, Sir Francis, gov. of the Virginia colony, 508
Wyatt, Sir Thomas, conspiracy against Queen Mary, 372
Wyoming, made a territory, 780; admitted to statehood, 784
Wyoming massacre, in Pennsylvania, 521

X-rays, 552
X.Y.Z. affair, 765
Xanthippus, 53, 86
Xaquixaguana, battle of, 489
Xavier, St. Francis, Jesuit missionary, 542
Xenophon, his Anabasis, 40, 62, 67
Xerxes, King of Persia, 38, 54, 89
Xerxes I (Ahasuerus), 40
Xerxes II, 40
Xois, 23

Yadavas, possessions of the Chaluykas, 336
Yagoda, Genrikh Grigorevich, Bolshevik leader, 1036
Yajnavalkya, a code, 130
Yajurveda, 41
Yakinlu, 33
Yakub, Amir of Afghanistan, 867, 868
Yakub Beg, ruler of Kashgaria, 880
Yakub Khan, Amir of Afghanistan, 736
Yale College, founded, 512
Yalta, Crimea, 1143, 1164
Yalu River, battles of the, 138, 881, 891, 892
Yamagata, Aritomo, Japanese premier, 746, 886, 891, 892
Yamamoto, Tatsuo, premier of Japan, 893, 1124
Yamashiro no Oe, heir of Prince Shōtoku, 140
Yamassees, Indian tribe in Carolina, 513
Yamato, Japanese battleship, 1169
Yamato culture, 14, 139
Yamatodake, Prince, victories over Japanese clans, 139
Yamini, see Ghaznavid
Yang Chien (Wen Ti), founded Sui dynasty, 136
Yang Chu, 44, 45
Yang Hsiu-ch'ing, in the T'ai P'ing Rebellion, 879
Yang-shao culture, 14
Yang Shou-ching, Chinese envoy to Japan, 884
Yang-ti, Emperor of Korea, 348
Yangtze Agreement, between England and Germany, 750
Yap, Island of, dispute between U.S. and Japan, 1128
Ya'qub ibn Layth, Persian ruler, 189
Yaqut, Arab geographer, 362
Yarmouth, 917, 931
Yarmuk, battle of, 174, 186
Yasht, hymns of the Avesta, 39
Yasin Pasha el Hashimi, premier of Iraq, 1106
Yasna, hymns of the Avesta, 39
Yasodharman of Mandasor, 331
Yasovarman, King of Kanauj, 331
Ya'udi (Senjirli), Kingdom of, 35
Yavanas, 43
Yayoishiki culture, 14

Yazid I, caliph, 186
Yazid II, caliph, 187
Yazid III, caliph, 188
Yazid ibn Muhallib, revolt against caliph, 187
Ye, 135
Year Books, in England, 200
"Year of Pacification," in Germany, 208
Yeardley, Sir Thomas, gov. of the Virginia colony, 508
Yehawmelek, 33
"Yellow-Dog" contracts, in U.S., 1053
Yellow fever, 552
Yellow Turbans, in rebellion, 135
Ye-lü A-pao-chi, founder of the Khitan (Mongol) dynasty, 341
Ye-lü Ch'ü-ts'ai, chancellor of Jenghis Khan, 344, 345
Ye-lü Ta-shih, founded Kara-Khitai, 343
Ye-lü Te-kuang, son of A-pao-chi, 341
Yemen, Treaty of, 1104
Yen, 44
Yen, Chinese empress, 134
Yen Hsi-shan, gov. of Shansi, 1119
Yen K'o-chün, Chinese scholar, 877
Yeni-Shehr, battle of, 420
Yen-men, 137
Yermak, Cossack chief, 416
Yersin, Alexander, discovered germ of bubonic plague, 552
Yezdigird the Wicked of Persia, 125
Yezdigird II of Persia, 125
Yezdigird III of Persia, 127, 128
Yin dynasty, 44
Ying Tsung, Emperor of China, 347
Yogachara (Mystic) school, 131, 331
Yoga-sutras, 131
Yodogimi, widow of Hideyoshi, 546
Yokohama, 888, 890, 1169
Yolanda, wife of Peter of Courtenay, 259
Yoldia Sea, 15
Yōmei, Emperor of Japan, 140
Yonsangun, Korean ruler, 542
Yoriie, head of the Minamoto, 356
Yorimasa, in uprising against Taira clan, 354
Yorimichi, Japanese regent and dictator, 353
Yoritomo, uprising against Taira clan, 354, 355
Yoriyoshi, destroyed the Abe clan in Japan, 353
York (Toronto), captured, 793
York, Duchess of, 428
York, Frederick Augustus, Duke of, in War of the Second Coalition, 586
York School, 166
York von Wartenburg, Hans David Ludwig, Count, Prussian general, 596, 598, 599
Yorktown, surrender of Lord Cornwallis, 437, 522
Yōrō Laws, in Japan, 350
Yosheiie, destroyed the Kiyowara family, 354
Yoshifusa, regent of Japan, 352
Yoshihito, Emperor of Japan, 893
Yoshimasa, Japanese shōgun, 359
Yoshimitsu, Japanese shōgun, 359
Yoshimune, Japanese shōgun, 548
Yoshinaka, drives Taira clan out of Kyōto, 354, 356
Yoshinaka, Kira, 548
Yoshino period, in Japan, 358
Yoshisada, vassal of the Hōjō family in Japan, 357
Yoshishige (Sārin), Ōtomo, convert to Christianity, 543
Yoshitane, Japanese shōgun, 359
Yoshitoki, regent of the shōgun, 356
Yoshitomo, in second civil war, 354
Yoshitsune, Japanese general, 355
Young, Sir John (Lord Lisgar), gov.-gen. of Canada, 796
Young, Owen D., American industrialist, 1052
Young Czechs, radical group in Bohemia, 694
Young Europe movement, organized by Mazzini, 651
Young Ireland Party, 612
Young Italy, Italian revolutionary society, 651
Young Norway Party, 699
Young Plan, 960, 999, 1052
Young Poland, Union of, 1040
Young Tunisians, 1086
Young Turk movement, 731, 732, 755
Younghusband, Col. Francis Edward, expedition to Tibet, 752, 871
Youngstown Sheet Steel & Tube Co., strike, 1056
Youth Movement, in Nazi Germany, 1002
Ypres, 1st battle, 914; 2d. 921; 3d, 939; 4th, 950
Yser, battle of, 914
Yu, Chinese king, 44
Yu Yün-wen, used explosives in defeating the Chin, 343
Yüan dynasty, 345
Yüan Shao, orders massacre of eunuchs, 135
Yüan Shih-k'ai, president of China, 881, 883, 884, 885, 1117
Yudenitch, Gen. Nicolai Nicolaievich, Russian counter-revolutionary, 1031
Yue-chi, Indo-European people, 43, 83, 128, 133, 134
Yüeh, 133
Yüeh Fei, Chinese general, 343
Yugoslavia, 949, 953, 956, 977, 987, 988, 992, 1009, 1016, 1017, 1018; invaded by Germany, 1136; 1141, 1144; capitulated, 1150
Yü-hsien, Manchu gov. of Shantung, 883
Yukiie, uncle of Yoritomo, 356
Yukinaga, Konishi, overran most of Korea, 544
Yuma point, 19

Yung Cheng Reign of Shih Tsung, 540
Yung Lo Reign of Ch'eng Tsu, 346, 537
Yung Lo Ta Tien, Chinese encyclopedia, 537
Yung Wing, 880
Yungay, battle of, 809, 811, 812
Yün-kang, 136
Yünnan, conquered, 346
Yuri, in civil war with Basil II of Russia, 316
Yussupov, Prince Felix, assassin of Rasputin, 1028
Yusuf Adil Shah of Bijapur, 530
Yusuf ibn Tashfin, led Berbers in Spain, 233

Zab, battle of, 188
Zabern affair, in Alsace, 693
Zabinas, Alexander, slays Demetrius II, 82
Zadriades, ruler of Armenia Minor, 38
Zaghlul (Saad) Pasha, Egyptian premier, 1081, 1083
Zaimis, Alexander, Greek premier, 710, 926, 940, 1021
Zain-ul-Abidin, 335
Zaionczek, Gen. Joseph, viceroy of Poland, 702
Zakir, King of Hamath, 35
Zakonnik, Serbian law code, 319
Zaldúa, Dr. Francisco Javier, pres. of Colombia, 815
Zallaka, battle of, 233
Zama, battle of, 34, 88
Zaman Shah, ruler of Afghanistan, 866
Zamasp, Persian ruler, 126
Zamora, Treaty of, 238
Zamora, Alcalá, pres. of provisional govt. in Spain, 982
Zamosc-Komarov, battle of, 914
Zand dynasty, 529
Zangid dynasty, of Mesopotamia and Syria, 254 f.
Zankov, Alexander, premier of Bulgaria, 1023
Zanzibar, 847, 848, 849
Zápolya, John II, King of Hungary, 402, 419 f., 423
Zapolya, Stephen, Prince of Transylvania, 419
Zaque, ruler of the Chibchas, 361
Zara, taken in Fourth Crusade, 257
Zarathustra (Zoroaster), 39
Zauditu, Empress of Ethiopia, 836, 1085
Zayas, Dr. Alfredo, pres. of Cuba, 824, 1077
Zayas, Fernando Mompó de, in civil war in Paraguay, 800
Zayd, in Shi'ite revolt in Iraq, 188
Zayd ibn Thabit, official redaction of the Koran, 186
Zayrids of Granada, 233
Zbigniew, brother of Boleslav III of Poland, 242
Zealots, 32; see Hesychast
Zechariah, 31
Zedé, Gustave, built first naval submarines, 556
Zedekiah, 31
Zeebrugge, German submarine base, 946, 950
Zelaya, José Santos, pres. of Nicaragua, 820
Zeligowski, Lucien, leads Polish freebooters, 955, 1038, 1042
Zemgalis, Gustav, pres. of Latvia, 1043
Zemlin, taken by the Serbs, 916
Zemski Sobor, national assembly in Russia, 415
Zemstvo Law, in Russia, 705, 706 f.
Zen sect, in Japan, 355, 358
Zeno, 122, 126, 147
Zeno, founder of Stoicism, 77
Zenobia, Queen of Palmyra, 116, 124
Zenodotus, 75
Zenta, battle of, 461, 484
Zeppelin, Count Ferdinand von, his rigid airship, 557, 569
Zeppelin raids, 429
Zeus Ammon, claimed by Alexander as his father, 66
Zhitomir, 1154
Zhivkovich, Gen. Peter, premier of Yugoslavia, 1017
Zhu-Zhu Empire in Asia, 143
Zhukor, Gregory K., Russian marshal, 1165
Ziboetes, King of Bithynia, 37
Ziegler, William, Arctic explorer, 565
Ziethen, Hans Ernst Karl von, Prussian general, 603
Zimbabwe, stone ruins of Rhodesia, 328
Zimisces, John, Byzantine general, 180, 183, 244
Zimmerman, Arthur, German diplomat, 792, 930, 936, 942
Zimri, 31
Zimrida, 31
Zindiqs, communistic sect in Khorasan, 188
Zinoviev, Grigori Evseyevich, Russian diplomat, 968, 1028, 1034, 1035
Zipa, political ruler of the Chibchas, 361
Ziska, John, Hussite leader, 305, 314
Zita, Empress, widow of Charles I of Austria-Hungary, 956
Ziyad ibn Abihi, vicegerent of Mo'awiya, 186
Ziyadatullah, driven from Egypt, 190
Ziyanids, successors of the Almohades, 263
Ziyarids, as independent sovereigns, 190
Zlatev, Gen. Petko, premier of Bulgaria, 1024
Zloczow, battle of, 940
Zobayr, companion of the Prophet, 186
Zobeir Rahama, slave-trader, 830, 842
Zoë, Byzantine empress, 248 f.
Zoë, mother of Constantine VII, 179, 183
Zoë (Sophia), wife of Ivan III of Russia, 317
Zog I, King of Albania, 1020
Zographos, Georgios Christaki, proclaims independence of northern Epirus, 1019

Zola, Émile, French writer, 641
Zollverein (customs union), in Germany, 669; 680, 687
Zorndoff, battle of, 467
Zoroastrianism, 39, 115, 124–26
Zoser, 23
Zoutpansberg, joins South African Republic, 852
Zrinyi, Nicholas, Hungarian soldier, 402
Zsitva-Torok, Treaty of, 424
Zubow, Prof. Nicolai Nicolaievich, Arctic explorer, 571
Zugmayer, Erich Johann Georg, German agent in Persia, 1107

Zulu War, against British, 616, 854
Zululand, 852, 854, 856
Zur Kritik neuerer Geschichtschreiber, by Leopold von Ranke, 551
Zuravna, Treaty of, 475, 483
Zurbarán, Francisco, Spanish painter, 389
Zuravno, taken by Austro-Germans, 922
Zürich, 409; battle of, 587; Treaty of, 658
Zutphen, battle of, 373
Zwentibold, illegitimate son of Arnulf, 152, 160
Zwingli, Ulrich, Swiss reformer, 399, 409

Supplementary Index

Covering events from January 1, 1946, to April 30, 1952.]

Abdul Hadi Pasha, Egyptian Premier, 1203
Abdullah, King of Jordan, visit of, to Franco, 1181; assassinated, 1225
Acheson, Dean, U.S. Secretary of State, 1197
Acker, Achille van, Belgian Premier, 1178
Adenauer, Konrad, Chancellor of the Federal Republic of Germany, 1185
Afghanistan, resignation of Prime Minister Sirdar Mohammed Hashim Khan, 1208; reforms by successor, Sirdar Mahmud Shah Khan, 1209; border dispute with Pakistan, 1209
Ahmed Pasha, Egyptian Premier, assassination of, 1203
Albania, Communist government, Premier Enver Hoxha, 1189; People's Republic, 1189; Corfu Channel incidents, 1189; breaks relations with Yugoslavia, 1189; general election (1950), 1189
Albornoz, Alvaro de, Premier of Spanish Republic-in-exile, 1181
Alemán, Miguel, President of Mexico, 1201
Alexander, A. V., British Minister of Defense, 1176
Alexander, Field Marshal Sir Harold, Governor General of Canada, 1198
Algeria, fighting between Nationalists and French troops, 1203; French citizenship for Algerians, 1203; national assembly and financial autonomy, 1203
Allied Control Council (Germany), 1183; Soviet delegates "walkout" of, 1184
Allied Council for Austria, 1186
Allied Military Security Board, 1184, 1185
All-India Congress Party, 1209
Aly Maher Pasha, Egyptian Premier, 1228
Ananda Mahidol, King of Siam, death of, 1212
Anti-Egyptian Independence Front (Sudan), 1203
Anti-Fascist People's Freedom League (Burma), 1211, 1212
Antonescu, Rumanian wartime Premier, condemned to death, 1191
Arab Conference at Jericho proclaims Abdullah King of Palestine, 1207
Arab League Council, 1207
Arab Legion of Transjordan, British-trained Arab troops, invade Palestine, 1208
Arévalo, Juan José, President of Guatemala, 1202
Argentina, Juan D. Perón elected President (1946), 1199; Five-Year Plan, 1199; agreement with Chile on Falkland Islands, 1199; new constitution (1949), 1199
Arguello, Leonardo, Nicaraguan President, 1201
Arias, Arnulfo, President of Panama, 1201; impeachment of, 1224
Arosemena, Alcibiades, First Vice-President of Panama, 1224; replaces Arías as President, 1224
Arosemena, Carlos, 1200
Arosemena, Domingo Díaz, President of Panama, death of, 1201
Ashida, Hitoshi, Japanese Premier, 1217
Athlone, Earl, Governor General of Canada, retirement of, 1198
Atomic Energy Commission (U.N.), approves U.S. control plan, 1172; U.S.S.R. opposes U.S. plan, 1172; the hydrogen bomb, 1197
Attlee, Clement R., British Prime Minister, 1175, 1176, 1226
Auriol, Vincent, President of France, 1179; visit of, to U.S., 1224
Australia, strike of coal workers, 1221; elections (1946), 1221; displaced persons from Europe, admitted, 1221; nationalization of banks 1221; Communist strikes, 1221; election (1949), 1221; joins U.N. forces in Korea, 1221; Communist Party dissolved, 1221
Austria, Western Allied Powers, lenient treatment of, 1186; harsh demands by U.S.S.R., 1186; provisional government, Karl Renner, Chancellor, 1186; Republic re-established, 1186; four occupation zones, 1186; Leopold Figl's coalition with Socialists, 1186; Karl Renner elected President, 1186; autonomy for the South Tyrol, 1186; deadlock on peace settlement, 1186; death of President Renner, 1186
Auténtico Party (Cuba), 1202

Baccouche, Salah Eddine Ben Mohammed, pro-French Tunisian Premier, 1229

Ballivan, Gen. Hugo, head of military junta, Bolivia, 1224; government overthrown, 1229
Bao Dai, Chief of State of Viet Nam Republic, 1214
Barreta, Tomás, Uruguayan President, 1200; died in office, 1200
Batista, Gen. Fulgencio, 1229
Bayar, Jelal, Premier of Turkey, 1206; elected President (1950), 1206
Beel, Dr. L. J. N., Netherlands Premier, 1179]
Belgium, post-war coalitions, with Prince Charles as Regent, 1178; Socialist opposition to King Leopold's return, 1178; referendum favors King's return, 1178; coalition governments, 1178; all-Catholic government, Jean Duvieusart, Prime Minister, 1178; customs union with Holland and Luxembourg, 1178; King Leopold III abdicates, 1225; Prince Baudoin succeeds father, Leopold III, 1225
Benes, President of Czechoslovakia, 1187; resignation and death, 1187
Ben-Gurion, David, Premier of Israel, 1207
Bernadotte, Count Folke appointed U.N. mediator in Palestine, 1172; assassinated by Jewish terrorists, 1172
Berres, Luiz B., Vice-President and President of Uruguay, 1200
Betancourt, Rómulo, 1200
Bevan, Aneurin, British Minister of Labor, 1223; resignation of, 1224
Bevin, Ernest, British Foreign Minister, 1184; resignation and death, 1223
Bidault, Georges, French Premier, 1179, 1180
Bierut, Boleslaw, first President of the Republic of Poland, 1193
Bikini, demonstration of atomic bombs exploded under water, 1196
Bishara el-Khoury, President of Lebanon, 1206
Bizonia, economic fusion of British and American zones in occupied Germany, 1184
Blum, Léon, Socialist Premier of France 1179
Bolivia rebellion in (1946), 1200; Enrique Hertzog, elected President, 1200; strikes in tin mines, 1200; resignation of Hertzog, 1200; succeeded by Vice-President Mamerto Urriolagoitia, 1200; Communist Party outlawed, 1200; military junta usurps government, 1224; junta overthrown, 1229
Bonn, Germany, capital of Federal Republic of Germany, 1185
Bradley, Gen. Omar N., chairman of U.S. Joint Chiefs of Staff, 1197
Brazil, Dictator Vargas resigns, 1201; Chief Justice José Linhares, head of government, 1201; Enrico Dutra elected President (1945), 1201; new constitution adopted, 1201; Communist Party outlawed, 1201; relations with U.S.S.R. broken, 1201; Vargas chosen President (1950), 1201
Briga awarded by Allies to France, 1182
British East Africa, Central Legislative Assembly, first session of, 1204
British India, Cripps autonomy plan rejected, 1209; elections in (1945), 1209; Hindu-Moslem riots, 1209; British offer of full independence (1946), 1209; Moslems demand separate state, 1209; meeting of Constituent Assembly, 1209; Indian Independence Act, 1209; violent disturbances, 1209
Brussels Treaty, 1175; signatory powers merge military forces authorised with North Atlantic Treaty Organization, 1175
Buhl, Vilhelm, Social Democrat, head of post-war government of Denmark, 1194
Bulganin, Gen., succeeds Stalin as U.S.S.R. Minister of Defense, 1192
Bulgaria, Soviet-sponsored coalition under Premier Kimon Georgiev, 1190; discussed by Soviet army, 1190; Fatherland Front, 1190; People's Republic, 1190; peace treaty signed, 1190; Two-Year Plan, 1190; Agrarian Party dissolved, 1190; treaty with Yugoslavia, 1190; treaties with U.S.S.R. and satellites, 1191; Five-Year Plan, 1191; treaty with Yugoslavia denounced, 1191; national elections, 1191; purge of government officials, 1191; diplomatic relations with U.S., broken, 1191; members of Communist Party expelled, 1191
Burma, Union of, independent republic (1948), 1212; constitution adopted, 1211; Communist rebellion in, 1212
Bustamente, José Luis, Peruvian President (1945–48), 1200
Butler, Richard Austen, British Chancellor of the Exchequer, 1227

Byrnes, James F., U.S. Secretary of State, 1184, 1196

Cairo, Egypt, violent riots in, 1228
Canada, Dominion of, election (1945), 1198; Canadian Citizenship Act, 1198; Soviet spy ring, 1198; Anglo-Canadian wheat agreement, 1198; military co-operation with U.S., 1198; Newfoundland tenth provinces (1948), 1198; North Atlantic Treaty signed, 1198; election (1949), 1198; joins U.N. forces in Korean War, 1198
Carías, Tiburcio, Dictator-President of Honduras, 1202
Caribbean League, 1202
Castaneda, Salvador, President of Salvador, forced resignation of, 1202
Catholic Christian Socialist Party (Belgium), 1178
Catholic People's Party (Netherlands), 1179
Ceylon, new constitution, 1211; Dominion in British Commonwealth (1948), 1211
Chalbaud, Col.¡Carlos Delgado, leader of military junta in Venᵇ ezuela, 1200; assassinated, 1201
Chávez, Federico, Paraguayan President (Sept. 12, 1949), 1200
Cheribon Agreement, 1214
Cherzenkov, Fulko, head of Bulgarian Communist Party, Premier, 1191
Chiang Kai-shek, President of Nationalist China, 1215, 1216, 1217
Chifley, Joseph B., Australian Premier, 1221
Chile, Communist strikes, 1199; relations with U.S.S.R. broken, 1199; Communist Party outlawed, 1199; election (1949), 1199
China, Nationalists (Chiang Kai-shek) and Communists (Mao Tse-tung), 1215; treaty with U.S.S.R., 1215; civil war, 1215; treaty with U.S., 1215; new constitution, 1215–16; mediation by U.S., 1215; elections for National Assembly (1947), 1216; decline of Nationalists (1948), 1216; Communist successes (1949), 1216; Nationalist forces withdraw to Formosa, 1216; Communist People's Republic of China, 1216; anti-Communist guerrillas, 1216; reforms by Nationalists in Formosa, 1216; Communist treaty with U.S.S.R., 1216; Communist forces capture Hainan, 1217; intervene in Korean War, 1217
Christian X, King of Denmark, death of, 1194
Christian Democratic Party (Italy), 1181, 1182
Christian Democrats (German political party), 1183, 1184
Christian People's Party (Saar), 1184
Churchill, Winston S., chairman of first session of Congress of Europe, 1174; British Prime Minister, 1227; visit to U.S. and address to Congress, 1228
Colombia, coalition government (1946), Mariano Ospina Pérez, President, 1200; revolt in (1948), 1200; congressional elections (1949), 1200; presidential election (1949), 1200
Cominform (Communist Information Bureau), 1174; expels Yugoslavia, 1174
Commission for Conventional Armaments (U.N.), 1172
Committee of European Economic Co-operation (Marshall Plan), 1174; U.S.S.R. refuses to participate, 1174
Conference of British African colonies, meeting of, London, 1204
Congress of Europe, first meeting of, at The Hague, 1174
Coplon, Judith, 1197
Costa Rica, election (1948) declared invalid, 1201; civil war, 1201; military junta government, relations with U.S.S.R. broken, 1201; Communist Party outlawed, 1201; invasion from Nicaragua by exiled Costa Ricans, 1201; pact with Nicaragua (1949), 1201; Otilio Ulate inaugurated as President (1949), 1201
Costello, James A., Eire Prime Minister, 1178
Council of Europe, Statute of, 1175; offer of membership to Western Germany, 1175
Council of Ministers (U.S.S.R.), 1192
Council of Foreign Ministers (France, Great Britain, U.S.S.R., U.S. — "Big Four"), Moscow and London meetings, 1174; meeting of deputy ministers in Paris, 1225
Council of Mutual Economic Assistance (U.S.S.R.), 1193
Cuba, Carlos Prío Socarras elected President (1948), 1202; government overthrown (1952) by Gen. Fulgencio Batista, 1229
Curtin, John, Australian Premier, death of, 1221
Customs union of Belgium, the Netherlands, and Luxembourg (Benelux), 1175
Cyrankiewicz, Joseph, Premier of Poland, 1193
Czech Catholic Action Committee, 1182, 1187
Czechoslovakia, National Front Government, Zdenek Fierlinger, Premier, 1187; Ruthenia ceded to U.S.S.R., 1187; all Germans and Hungarians banished, 1187; provisional National Assembly, 1187; industrial nationalization and agricultural reform, 1187; Constituent Assembly elections, 1187; coalition cabinet, ᵇKlement Gottwald, Communist leader, Premier, 1187; Marshall Plan rejected, 1187; Communist coup, 1187; new constitution, 1187; Communist victory in elections (1948), 1187; forced labor camps, 1187; five-year industrial plan, 1187; Catholic Action Committee, 1187; control by state of Catholic Church, 1187; political trials, 1187; Western diplomatic representatives charged as spies, 1187; army reorganized, 1187

Danube Conference, Belgrade, 1174
Democratic Action Party (Venezuela), 1200
Democratic Liberal Party (Japan), 1217, 1218
Democratic Party (Turkey), 1206
Denmark, post-war Social Democratic government, 1194, general election results, 1194; death of King Christian X, 1194; Frederick IX succeeds as King, 1194; North Atlantic Treaty

signed, 1194; coalition government of Liberals and Conservatives (1950), 1194
Department of Defense (U.S.), 1197
De Valera, Eamon, 1178
Dewey, Gov. Thomas E., Republican candidate for President, 1197
Dimitrov, Georgi, Bulgarian Communist Premier, death of, 1191
Dinnyes, Lajos, Hungarian Premier, 1188
Dodecanese Islands, awarded by Allies to Greece, 1182
Dominican Republic, the, President Trujillo re-elected(1947), 1202; troubles with conspiracies, 1202
Dominion Party (South Africa), 1204
Drees, William, Socialist Labor Premier of the Netherlands, 1179
Dutra, Enrico, Brazilian President, 1201
Duvieusart, Jean, Belgian Premier, 1178

EAM, Greek leftist party, 1190
East African High Commission, 1203
Ecuador, Velasco Ibarra, re-elected President (1946), 1200; revolts against, 1200; counter-revolution, 1200; popular elections (1948), 1200; severe earthquake (1949), 1200; border incidents and fighting with Peru, 1226
Eden, Anthony, British Foreign Minister, 1227
Egypt, election (1945) boycotted by Wafd Party, 1203; Premier Ahmed Pasha assassinated, 1203; demand for revision of Anglo-Egyptian Treaty of 1936, 1203; anti-British feeling, 1203; reference to United Nations, 1203; intervention in Palestine (1948), 1203; protests British moves in Sudan, 1203; anti-Egyptian party in the Sudan, 1203; Premier Nokrashy Pasha assassinated, 1203; election (1950), 1203; negotiations reopened with Great Britain, 1203; Treaty of 1936 abrogated (1951) by Egypt, 1227; violent fighting and riots, 1227; King Farouk dismisses Nahas Pasha, Wafd (Nationalist) Premier, 1227; unsettled conditions continue (1952), 1228
Einaudi, Luigi, elected (1948) President of Italy, 1182
Eisenhower, Gen. Dwight D., appointed Commander-in-Chief of North Atlantic army, 1175, 1198; released from command in Europe, 1229
Elizabeth, Princess, eldest daughter of King George VI, marriage to Philip Mountbatten, Duke of Edinburgh, 1176; state visit to Canada, 1226; accedes to throne as Queen Elizabeth II, 1228
Eriksen, Erik, head of coalition of Liberal and Conservative government of Denmark, 1194
Eritrea, federation with Ethiopia, 1204
Erlander, Tage, Premier of Sweden, 1194
Estimé, Dumarsais, President of Haiti, 1202
European Recovery Program, 1174, 1196
Eyskens, Gaston, Belgian Premier, 1178

Fagerholm, K. A., Social Democratic Premier of Finland, 1195
Farouk I, King of Egypt, 1228; assumes control of government (1952), 1228
Faure, Edgar, French Premier, 1228
Federal Labor Party (Australia), 1221
Federal People's Republic of Yugoslavia, 1188
Fianna Fail Party (Eire), 1178
Figueras, José, head of Costa Rican military junta, 1201
Fine Gael Party (Eire), 1178
Finland, election (1945), 1195; resignation of President Mannerheim, 1195; peace treaty signed, 1195; treaty with U.S.S.R., 1195; election (1948), 1195; Communist strikes, 1195; election (1950), 1195
Flamerich, Suarez, head of military junta government (Venezuela), 1201
Foreign Assistance Act (Marshall Plan), 1196
Forrestal, James V., U.S. Secretary of Defense, 1196; resignation of, 1197
Four-Point Plan of President Truman, 1197
France, Fourth Republic, 1179; Henri Philippe Pétain, convicted of treason, 1179; Pierre Laval, conviction and execution of, 1179; elections for Constituent Assembly, 1179; Gen. Charles de Gaulle, President of Provisional Government, but resigns, 1179; Félix Gouin, Socialist President, 1179; constitution rejected, 1179; new Assembly, 1179; Georges Bidault President, 1179; revised constitution, 1179; Communists predominate in National Assembly, 1179; Léon Blum forms all-Socialist cabinet, 1179; Vincent Auriol elected President, 1179; Ramadier's coalition cabinet, 1179; Communist strikes, 1179; Anglo-French alliance, 1179; municipal election results, 1180; strikes of Communists, 1180; new non-Communist workers' union (Force Ouvrière), 1180; Ramadier resigns, 1180; Schuman's short-lived cabinet, 1180; Henri Queuille's coalition cabinet, 1180; wave of C.G.T. strikes, 1180; Council of Republic elections, 1180; Communist Maurice Thorez and Soviet army, 1180; economic troubles, Queuille cabinet resigns, 1180; Georges Bidault coalition cabinet 1180; Viet Nam government (Indo-China) established, 1180; successive governments fail to solve economic troubles, 1185–1228; agreement with Tunisia, 1223; Schuman Plan ratified, 1227
Franco, Gen. Francisco, visit of, to Salazar of Portugal, 1188
Franco, Rafael, Paraguayan rebel leader, 1199
Frederick IX, King of Denmark, 1194
French Union, 1179
Frutos, Manual, Paraguayan President (June 6 to August 5, 1948), 1199

Gaitán, Jorge, Colombian Left-Wing leader, assassination of, 1200
Gallegos, Rómulo, Venezuelan President, 1200
Gálvez, Juan Manuel, President of Honduras, 1202
Gandhi, Mohandas K., Hindu leader, 1209; assassination of, 1211
Gasperi, Alcide de, Italian Premier, 1181
Gaulle, Gen. Charles de, 1179, 1180
General Assembly (U.N.), Franco Spain barred from U.N., 1172; appoints Balkan Committee, 1172; on Korean independence, 1172; partition of Palestine favored, 1172; convention on genocide, 1173; endorses South Korean government, 1173; favors internationalization of Jerusalem, 1173
Georgiev, Kimon, Bulgarian Premier, 1190
Gerhardsen, Einar, head of Labor government (Norway), 1194
Germany, Allied Control Council in control, 1183; Berlin divided into four sectors, 1183; Nazi leaders on trial at Nuremberg, 1183; war plants dismantled, 1183; diverse administrative authority in four zones, 1183; transfer of more than 6,000,000 Germans, 1183; local elections, results of, 1183; German production limited, 1183; merger of Social Democrats and Communists, Soviet zone, 1183; elections, American zone, 1183–84; political amnesty, 1184; American policy announced, 1184; decision in Nazi trials, 1184; economic fusion of British and U.S. zones, 1184; abolition of State of Prussia, 1184; Landtag elections in British and French zones, 1184; economic council, 1184; elections in the Saar, 1184; new Bizonal charter, 1184; Economic Commission in Soviet zone, 1184; Soviet blockade of traffic in Berlin, 1184; air-lift by Western Powers, 1184; international control of the Ruhr, 1184; currency reform in Western Germany, 1184; currency reform in Soviet zone, 1184; Basic law for Western Germany, 1184; Communists claim authority in all Berlin, 1185; elections in western sectors of Berlin, 1185; Federal Republic of Germany, 1185; Berlin blockade lifted, 1185; elections for the Bundestag, 1185; Allied High Commission, 1185; Theodor Heuss elected President, Konrad Adenauer, Chancellor, of Western Republic, 1185; Berlin air-lift, end of, 1185; German Democratic Republic (Communist), Wilhelm Pieck, President, and Otto Grotewohl, Minister President, 1185; E.C.A. funds allotted Western Germany, 1185; French agreement with the Saar, 1185; Schuman Plan favored by the Bonn government, 1185; Oder-Neisse line, agreement to, by Eastern Germany and Poland, over protests by Western Germany, 1185; Bonn government joins Council of Europe, 1186; S.E.D. Party (Communist) convention, 1186; Western Germany Occupation Statute, revision of, agreed, 1186; remilitarization opposed by Socialists, 1186; Landtag election results, 1186; Communist elections, Eastern Germany, 1186
George VI, King of England, death of, 1228
Giral, José, Premier of Spanish Republic-in-exile, 1180
Goering, Hermann, suicide of, 1184
Gold Coast, Africa, nationalist riot, 1203; new constitution for, 1204
Gómez, Lauriano, Colombian President, 1200
Gomulka, Wladyslaw, Secretary of the Polish United Workers' Party, 1193
González, Natalicio, Paraguayan President (Aug. 5, 1948, to Jan. 30, 1949), 1199
Gottwald, Klement, Communist President of Czechoslovakia, 1187
Gouin, Félix, French Socialist, 1179
Gowrie, Lord, Governor General of Australia, 1221
Great Britain, program of socialism, 1175–76; Trades Disputes Act repealed, 1175; marriage of Princess Elizabeth and Philip Mountbatten (created Duke of Edinburgh), 1176; dock workers' strike, 1176; pound sterling devalued, 1176; veto power of House of Lords restricted, 1176; general election of 1950, Labor majority reduced, 1176; Anglo-French alliance, 1176; treaty of mutual assistance with the Benelux states, 1176; conscription act passed, 1176; joins U.N. Powers in Korean War, 1178; protests Iran seizure of oil properties, 1224; general election (1951), Conservative Party victory, 1226–27; atom bomb produced, 1228; ready to sign mutual defense treaty with European Defense Community, 1229
Greece, chaotic post-war conditions, 1190; plebiscite favors monarchy, 1190; guerrilla activities and civil war, 1190; return of King George II, 1190; the Truman Doctrine of economic aid, 1190; Dodecanese Islands, 1190; coalition government, 1190; "First Provisional Government of Free Greece" (rebel guerrilla), 1190; Communist Party outlawed, 1190; defeat of rebel forces, 1190; general election (1950), 1190; general elections (1951), 1226
Greek Rally Party, 1226
Groess, Joseph, Hungarian Archbishop, 1225
Grotewohl, Otto, Minister President of the German Democratic Republic (Communist), 1185
Groza, Petru, Communist Premier of Rumania, 1191
Guatemala, free elections (1944), 1202; socialist program, 1202; election of 1950, 1202
Gurney, Sir Henry, British High Commissioner to Malaya, assassinated, 1226
Gustav V, King of Sweden, death of, 1195
Gustav VI Adolf, King of Sweden, 1195
Guzman, Col. Jacobo Arbenz, President of Guatemala, 1202

Hacha, ex-President of Czechoslovakia, death of, in prison, 1187

Haganah, Jewish terrorist band, 1207
Haiti, military revolt in (1946), 1202; Communist Party outlawed, 1202; military junta in control (1950), 1202
Hansson, Per A., death of, 1194
Hashim al-Atasi, President of Syria, 1206
Hashimite Kingdom of Jordan, the, 1208
Hatta, Mohammed, Indonesian Premier, 1214, 1215
Hedtoft Hans, head of Social Democratic government of Denmark, 1194
Henlein, Konrad, suicide, 1187
Hertzog, Enrique, President of Bolivia, 1200; resignation of, 1200
Heuss, Theodor, President of Federal Republic of Germany, 1185
Hilaili Pasha, Naguib al, Egyptian Premier, 1228
Hirohito, 'apanese Emperor, 1217
Hiss, Alger, convicted of perjury, 1197
Ho Chi-Minh, Communist leader in Indo-China, 1212, 1214
Hoffman, Paul G., chief of Economic Co-operative Administration, 1196
Holland, Sidney G., New Zealand Premier, 1222
Honduras, election of 1948, 1202; reforms, social and economic, 1201
Houtte, Jean Van, Belgian Premier, 1228
Hoxha, Enver, Albanian Premier, 1189
Hungary, armistice concluded with Allied forces, 1188; republic established, 1188; peace treaty signed 1188; three-year plan, 1188; Communists predominate, 1188; fusion of Communists with Social Democrats, 1188; new constitution proclaimed, 1188; five-year plan, 1188; arrest and conviction of Cardinal Mindszenty, 1188; Communist government established, 1188; purge of Communist party, 1188; all former Socialists dismissed, 1188
Hussein Sirry Pasha, Egyptian Premier, 1203
Hyde, Dr. Douglas, retires as President of Eire, 1178

Ibarra, Velasco, President of Ecuador, 1200
India, Dominion of, 1209–11; disputes with Pakistan, 1209; fighting in Kashmir, 1211; Hyderabad province, 1211; mediation in Hindu-Pakistan by U.N., 1211; new constitution (1949), 1211; Federal Republic of India, 1211; Delhi Pact, 1211; attitude of, in Korean War, 1211; favors admission of Communist China to U.N., 1211; "Point Four" agreement with U.S.
Indo-China, Viet Nam Republic, 1212, 1214; Communist rebellion, 1212, 1214; Communist China and Soviet Union and the Communist rebels, 1214; U.S. and Great Britain aid Viet Nam Republic, 1214
Indonesia, independence disputed by the Netherlands, 1214; negotiations result in Cheribon Agreement, 1214; Communists set up rival government, 1214; final agreement with Netherlands, 1215; guerrilla disturbances, 1215; Republic of Indonesia joins United Nations, 1215
Inönü. Ismet, President of Turkey, 1206
Inter-American Conference, Rio de Janeiro, 1199
Inter-American Mutual Assistance Treaty, 1199
Inter-American Defense Board, 1199
International Committee of the Movement for European Unity, 1174
International Communist Youth, rally of, in Berlin, 1225
International Court of Justice, Albania held responsible for Corfu Channel explosions, 1173; ruling by, on status of Southwest Africa, 1205; ruling on oil dispute in Iran, 1224
International Military Tribunal (Japan), 1217
International Red Cross, offer by to investigate Communist charges of germ warfare, 1229
International Ruhr Authority, 1185
International Trade Conference, Torquay, England, 1224; Moscow, Soviet Russia, 1229
Iran, Communist rebellion in province of Azerbaijan, 1208; Soviet activities, 1208; Soviet-Iranian oil company, 1208; Azerbaijan autonomy, unrest continues, 1208; province of Fars, 1208; parliamentary elections (1947), 1208; American military mission, 1208; Soviet oil agreement repudiated, 1208; Tudeh Party outlawed, 1208; constitution revised, 1208; Seven-Year Plan, 1208; American technicians, 1208; Anglo-Iranian Oil Company, new agreement (1949), 1208; oil industry nationalized, 1224
Iraq, treaty with Turkey, 1208; alliance with Transjordan, 1208; Treaty of Portsmouth with Great Britain, 1208
Ireland (Eire), elections in North Ireland, 1178; Sean T. O'Kelly elected President, on retirement of Dr. Hyde, 1178; general election, results of, 1178; independent Republic proclaimed, 1178; declines North Atlantic Treaty, 1178; treaty with United States, 1178
Irgun, Jewish terrorist band, 1207
Isaacs, George, British Minister of Pensions, 1223
Ismailia, Egypt, occupied by British troops, 1228
Israel. See Palestine
Italy, coalition cabinet of Parri resigns, 1181; Alcide de Gasperi, Premier, 1181; Bolzano province, 1181; abdication of King Emmanuel III, 1181; King Umberto II proclaims himself, 1181; Italy a republic, 1181; Umberto leaves country, 1182; Dodecanese Islands transferred to Greece, 1182; Briga and Tenda awarded to France, 1182; Enrico de Nicola elected President, 1182; peace treaty signed, 1182; new constitution adopted, 1182; Franco-Italian customs union, 1182; death of Victor Emmanuel III in exile, 1182; national election (1948), 1182; Luigi Einaudi President, 1182; De Gasperi forms new Christian Democrats cabinet, 1182; Communist

strikes, 1182; Palmiro Togliatti, Communist leader, attempted assassination of, 1182; allocated $601,000,000 under Marshall Plan, 1182; non-Communist union formed, 1182; North Atlantic Pact signed, 1182; ten-year economic plan, 1182; assumes trusteeship of Somaliland, 1182; barred from U.N. by U.S.S.R. veto, 1182

Japan, post-war conditions in, 1217; election (1946), 1217; new constitution, 1217; elections (1949), 1218; end of reparations, 1218; Communist restrictions imposed, 1218; National Police Reserve, 1218
Jiménez, Enrique, President of Panama, 1201
Jinnah, Mohammed Ali, Governor General of Pakistan, 1211; death of, 1211
Johnson, Louis A., U.S. Secretary of Defense, 1197; resignation of, 1198
Juan, Don, Spanish claimant to throne, 1180

Kalinin, Michael, U.S.S.R. President, resignation of, 1192
Karen, Burma, rebellion in, 1212
Katayama, Tetsu, Japanese Premier, 1217
Kefauver Committee, 1223
King George II, King of Greece, return of, from exile, 1190; death of, 1190
Khachaturian, Soviet composer, 1192
King Michael of Rumania abdicates, 1191
King, William Mackenzie, Canadian Prime Minister, 1198
Kolarov, Vassil, Bulgarian Premier, death of, 1191
Koniev, Marshal, Commander-in-Chief of U.S.S.R. army, 1192
Korea, division of, into North and South, 1218; futile negotiations, 1218; problem referred to U.N., 1218; U.N. Commission, 1218; elections in South Korea, 1218; Republic of Korea for South, People's Democratic Republic for North, 1218; U.S.S.R. and U.S. withdraw occupation troops, 1218; elections (1950) in South Korea, 1220; start of war by invasion from North Korea, 1220; Chinese forces all North Koreans, 1220
Korean War, outbreak of, 1173; continued fighting (1951–52), 1223–29; armistice talks, 1225–29; bombing of rail junctions and supply stations by U.N., 1226; "Heartbreak Ridge" captured by U.N. forces, 1226; American prisoners of war, charges by U.N. commander, 1227; Communists charge U.N. using germ warfare, 1229
Kostov, Traicho, Communist Deputy Premier of Bulgaria, executed, 1191
Kovacs, Bela, Secretary of Smallholders' Party, Hungary, 1188
Kristensen, Knud, head of Liberal government of Denmark, 1194

Labor Party (New Zealand), 1221, 1222
Labor Party (South Africa), 1222
Lahaut, Julien, Belgian Communist Party leader, assassinated, 1179
La Prensa, leading Argentine newspaper, suppressed, 1224
Lasso, Galo Plaza, President of Ecuador, 1200
Laurel, José P., 1222
League of Nations dissolves, 1172
Lebanon, parliamentary election (1947), 1206; armistice with Israel, 1206
Leopold, King of Belgium, abdicates in favor of son, Prince Baudouin, 1178
Lescaot, Elie, President of Haiti, 1202
Liaqat Ali Khan, Prime Minister of Pakistan, 1211; assassinated, 1226
Liberal Colorado Party (Uruguay), 1200
Liberal Party (Philippines), 1222
Libya, independence of, granted, 1204
Lie, Trygve, Secretary General of United Nations, 1172
Linhares, José, Brazilian Chief Justice, 1201
Llopis, Rodolfo, Premier of Spanish Republic-in-exile, 1181
López, Atilio, Paraguayan President (Feb. 27 to Sept. 12, 1949), 1200
Lysenko, T. D., Soviet biologist, 1192

MacArthur, Gen. Douglas, Commander-in-Chief of U.N. forces in Korean War, 1197; meeting with President Truman at Wake Island, 1198; Supreme Commander for the Allied Powers (SCAP) in Japan, 1217; appointed Commander-in-Chief of U.N. forces in Korea, 1220; offer to enemy commander, 1224; warns Communist China, 1224; relieved of all commands in Far East, 1224; address to joint session of Congress, 1224; U.S. Senate committee of inquiry on removal, 1224
McCarthy, Senator Joseph, 1198
McGranery, James P., U.S. Attorney General, 1229
McGrath, J. Howard, U.S. Attorney General, 1229
McKell, W. J., Australian Governor General, 1221
Madagascar, nationalist revolt in, 1203
Magloire, Col. Paul, head of military junta, Haiti, elected President (1950), 1202
Malan, Daniel F., South African Prime Minister, 1204; ignores ruling by International Court of Justice, 1205; introduces bill to make Parliament supreme, 1229
Malik, Jacob A., Soviet delegate to United Nations, 1225
Mancheno, Col., leader of revolt in Ecuador, 1200
Maniu, Julius, leader of Rumanian Peasant Party, sentenced to life imprisonment, 1191
Mannerheim, Carl, President of Finland, resignation of, 1195
Mao, Tse-tung, Communist leader in China, 1215, 1216
Mapai Party (Israel), 1207

Mardam, Jamil Bey, Syrian Prime Minister, 1206
Marín, Luis Muñoz, first elected governor of Puerto Rico, 1202
Markos, Gen., Greek rebel leader, 1190
Marshall, Gen. George C., U.S. Secretary of State, 1174, 1196; suggests European Recovery Program, 1196; resignation of, 1197
Marshall Plan for European Recovery, 1174, 1196; U.S.S.R. refuses to participate, 1174
Martínez, Maximiliano, 1202
Masaryk, Jan, Czechoslovakian Foreign Minister, death of, 1187
Massey, Vincent, Governor General of Canada, 1228
Medina, Isaias, Venezuelan President, 1200
Menderes, Adnan, Turkish Premier, 1206
Menendez, Gen. Benjamin, 1226
Mexico, election (1946), Miguel Alemán President, 1201; industrial program, 1201; cordial relations with U.S., 1201
Mihailovitch, Gen. Drazha, trial and execution of, 1189
Miklos, Gen., 1188
Mikolajczyk, head of Polish Peasant Party, 1193
Mindszenty, Cardinal Josef, sentenced to life imprisonment, 1188
Ministry of State Control (U.S.S.R.), 1192
Mohammed Chenik, anti-French Tunisian Premier, 1229
Molotov, Vyacheslav, Deputy Chairman of U.S.S.R. Council of Ministers, 1192
Morínigo, Higenio, Dictator and President of Paraguay, 1199
Morocco, French, elective Consultative Chambers of, 1204
Morrison, Herbert, British Foreign Minister, 1223
Morris, Newbold, 1229
Moscow Conference of Big Four Foreign Ministers (1947), 1184; Big Four meeting, London, 1184
Moslem League (India), 1209
Mossadegh, Mohammed, Premier of Iran, 1224
Mountbatten, Lord Louis, Viceroy of British India (1947) and Governor General of Dominion of India, 1209
Mountbatten, Philip, 1176, 1226, 1228; marriage of, as Duke of Edinburgh to Princess Elizabeth, 1176
Mouvement Républicain Populaire, French Catholic Party, 1179
Muso, Communist leader, Indonesia, 1214
Mustafa an-Nahhas Pasha, Egyptian Premier, 1203

Nagy, Ferenc, Hungarian Premier, 1188
National Democratic Front (Rumania), 1191
National Democratic Union Party (Brazil) 1201
National Front Party (Iran), 1224
National Front, Yugoslavia, 1188
National Front Government (Czechoslovakia), 1187
National Independence Front (Hungary), 1188
Nationalist Party (Philippines), 1222
National Liberation Movement in Yugoslavia, 1188
National Peasant Party (Rumania), dissolved, 1191
National Revolutionary Movement (Bolivia), 1200, 1229
National Union Party (Costa Rica), 1201
Nazimuddin, Khwaja, Pakistan Governor General, 1211, 1226
Nehru, Pandit Jawarharlal, Prime Minister of India, 1209, 1211
Netherlands, Kingdom of the, return from exile of Queen Wilhelmina, 1179; abdication of, 1179; coalition government, 1179; general election (1946), 1179; Treaty of Brussels, 1179; Dr. L. J. N. Beel, Premier, 1179; elections (1948), William Drees (Socialist Labor Party), Premier, 1179; Queen Juliana, 1179; North Atlantic Treaty ratified, 1179; transfer of sovereignty of East Indies to United States of Indonesia, 1179
New Independence Party (Tunisia), 1204
New Zealand, socialist program of Labor government (1946), 1221; British Nationality and New Zealand Citizenship Act, 1222; peace-time military service voted, 1222; parliamentary elections (1949), 1222; Legislative Council abolished, 1222
Nicaragua, election (1947), Leonardo Arguello, President, displaced by Dictator Anastasio Somoza's puppet President Victor Román Reyes, 1201; Somoza President again (1950), 1201
Nicola, Enrico de, elected by Assembly (1946) President of Italian Republic, 1182
Nigeria, native self-government for, 1203
Nokrashy Pasha, Egyptian Premier, negotiations by, with British government, 1203; assassinated, 1203
North African Independence Movement, Central Bureau, 1203
North Atlantic Treaty, 1175
North Atlantic Treaty Organization Council, meeting of, in Ottawa, Canada, 1218; in Lisbon, Portugal, 1228
North China People's Government (Communist), 1216
Norway, Labor Party coalition government, 1194; Soviet bases on Spitzbergen refused, 1194; North Atlantic Treaty signed, 1194

Oatis, William, convicted of espionage by Czechoslovakia Court, 1225
Occupation Statute for Western Germany, 1185
Oder-Neisse line, 1183
Odría, Gen. Manuel, head of military junta, President of Peru, 1200
Office of Defense Mobilization (U.S.), 1198
O'Kelly, Sean T., President of Eire, 1178
Organization of American States, 1199
Organization for European Economic Co-operation, 1174
Osmeña, Sergio, Nationalist Party leader (Philippines), 1222
Osobka-Morawski, Socialist Premier of Polish Lublin government, 1193

Osorio, Oscar, President of Salvador, 1202

Paasikivi, Juho, President of Finland, 1195
Pakistan, Dominion of, 1211; Delhi Pact, 1211; supports U.N. in Korean War, 1211
Pakkala, Mauno, Finnish Premier, 1195
Palestine, increased immigration, 1207; Biltmore Program, 1207; Anglo-American Committee of Inquiry, 1207; serious riots in Jerusalem, 1207; London Conference, 1207; Palestine problem referred to U.N., 1206; partition voted by U.N., 1206; terrorist activities, 1207; State of Israel, 1207; war with the Arab League, 1207; mediation efforts by U.N., 1207; uneasy truce, 1207; election (1949), 1207; Israel joins U.N., 1207; government moved to Jerusalem, 1207; economic trials and friction with Arabs, 1207
Pan-African Trade Union Congress, meeting of, at Dakar, 1203–04
Panama, U.S. troops withdrawn, from wartime bases, 1201; presidential elections (1948), 1201; death of President Arosemena, 1201; Arías election (1949), 1201; rioting and impeachment of Arías (1951), 1224
Pan-American Conference (ninth), Bogotá, Colombia, 1199
Papacy, the, Pope Pius XII ordains 32 new cardinals, 1182; President Truman appoints (1948) Myron C. Taylor personal representative, 1182; Taylor resigns in 1950; Czech Catholic Action Committee members excommunicated, 1182; all Catholics following Communist doctrine excommunicated, 1182; Pope Pius XII announces the dogma of bodily assumption of the Virgin Mary, 1183
Papagos, Field Marshal Alexander, 1226
Paraguay, dictatorship ended, 1199; two-party government, 1199; civil war, 1199; President Morínigo retires, 1199; procession of Presidents, 1199, 1200
Parri, Ferrucio, Italian Premier, 1181
Pauker, Ana, Communist Foreign Minister of Rumania, 1191
Peace Conference at Paris, treaties with Axis Powers, except Germany, 1174
Peasant Party (Poland), 1193
People's Congress (Eastern Germany), elections for, 1185; constitution for the Democratic Republic (Communist) adopted, 1185
People's Council (Eastern Germany) approve draft constitution for German Democratic Republic, 1185
People's Democratic Front (Rumania), 1191
People's Party (Austria), 1186
People's Party (Turkey), 1206
People's Republic of Bulgaria, 1190
People's Republic of China, 1216
Permanent Joint Defense Board (U.S. and Canada), 1196
Perón, Col. Juan D., President of Argentina, 1199; unlimited powers granted, 1199
Peru, José Luís Bustamante, elected (1945) Presidente, 1200; government overthrown by military junta (1948), 1200; Gen. Odría President, 1200; Communist Party outlawed, 1200; border incidents with Ecuador, 1226
Petersburg Agreement, 1185
Petkov, Nikola, Bulgarian Agrarian Party leader, executed, 1190
Philippine Republic, the, inaugurated (1946), 1222; Hukbalahap rebellion, 1222; lease to U.S. of military and naval bases, 1222; U.S. Economic Survey Mission (1950), 1222
Pholien, Joseph, Belgian Premier, 1228
Picado, Teodoro, President of Costa Rica, 1201
Pieck, Wilhelm, President of German Democratic Republic (Communist), 1185
Pius XII, Pope, ordains new cardinals, 1182
Pleven, René, French Premier, 1180, 1226
Progressive Democratic Party (Swiss), 1183
Popular Front (Socialists and Communists parties, Italy, 1182
Poland, Lublin provisional government, 1193; Polish London government-in-exile, 1193; Oder-Neisse tentative boundary line, 1193; National Unity government, 1193; nationalization of industries, 1193; Republic of Poland proclaimed, 1193; Vatican concordat denounced, 1193; fusion of Communists and Socialists, 1193; trade agreement with U.S.S.R., 1193; Yugoslavia treaty denounced, 1194; Western diplomats accused of hostile acts against the government, 1194; Church lands confiscated, 1194; Oder-Neisse line declared final by government, 1194
Port Said, Egypt, clashes in, British troops and Egyptian guerrillas, 1228
Portugal, half-mast flags flown at death of Adolf Hitler, 1181; opposition parties in, 1181; general election (1945), Salazar régime endorsed, 1181; Allied bases in Azores returned, 1181; revolt of army officers suppressed, 1181; President Antonio Carmona re-elected, 1181; North Atlantic Pact signed, 1181; visit of Franco, 1181
Prasad, Rajendra, President of Republic of India, 1211
Prince Charles, Belgian Regent, 1178
Prince Paul succeeds his brother, King George II, as King of Greece, 1190
Prokofiev, Soviet composer, 1192
Puerto Rico, election (1948), 1202; new constitution for, authorized, 1202; plots by Communists, 1202

Queuille, Henri, French Premier, 1180
Quirino, Elpidio, Vice-President and President of Philippine Republic, 1222

Quisling, Vidkun, trial and execution of, 1194

Rajagopalashari, Chakravarti, Governor General of India, 1211
Rajk, Laszlo, Hungarian Foreign Minister, 1188
Ramadier, M., French Premier, 1179
Rassemblement du Peuple Français, French anti-Communist party, 1179
Raymond, Jean de, French Commissioner to Cambodia, assassinated, 1227
Razmara, Ali, Premier of Iran, assassinated, 1223
Regional Advisory Commission for South Pacific, 1221
Renner, Karl, Austrian President, death of, 1186
Republican Socialist Union Party (Bolivia), 1200
Revival Party (Transjordan), 1208
Reyes, Víctor Román, 1201
Ríos, Juan A., defeated for President of Chile (1946), 1199
Rokossovsky, Konstantin, Polish Minister of Defense and Commander-in-Chief of army, 1194
Rolón, Raimundo, Paraguayan President (Jan. 30 to Feb. 27, 1949), 1199
Roxas, Manuel A., President of the Philippine Republic, 1222; death of, 1222
Rumania, Left-Wing government established (1945), 1191; peace treaty signed, 1191; treaty with Yugoslavia, 1191; abdication of King Michael, 1191; Communist constitution adopted, 1191; Yugoslavia treaty denounced, 1191; purge of members of Communist Party, 1191
Ryti, Risto, ex-President of Finland, 1195

Saar, the, recognized by French government as independent within French Union, 1228; furor in Germany follows, 1228
Saka, Hassan, Turkish Premier, 1206
Salvador, revolution in (1948), 1202; election (1950), 1202
San Martín, Grau, Cuban President, 1202
Schermerhorn, William, head of coalition government in Netherlands, 1179
Schumacher, Kurt, German Socialist leader, 1186
Schuman, Robert, French Foreign Minister, 1175
Schuman Plan, 1175; initialed by French Assembly, 1227, and by West German Bundestag, 1228
Security Council (U.N.), membership completed, 1172; approves U.S. as trustee for Pacific islands, mandated to Japan, 1172; appoints committee to aid Dutch and Indonesian settlement, 1172; commission appointed in Pakistan and Indian Kashmir dispute, 1172; orders truce in Palestine, 1172; proposal by non-permanent members to end Berlin blockade vetoed by U.S.S.R., 1173; votes to set up U.N. command in Korea, 1173; and the Anglo-Iranian oil dispute, 1226; Greece elected to membership, 1227; appeal of Tunisia to, 1228
Senanayaki, Stephen, Ceylon Prime Minister, 1211
Shostakovich, Soviet composer, 1192
Shidehara, Japanese Premier, 1217
Shukrai-Quwatli, Syrian President, 1206
Shvernik, Nicolai, President of the Presidium of the Supreme Soviet, 1192, 1225
Siam (Thailand), return of Indo-China provinces, 1212; army coup d'état, 1212; election (1948), 1212; name changed to Thailand, 1212; joins U.N. in Korean War, 1212; naval revolt, 1225
Sídí Mohammed, Sultan of Morocco, 1204
Sierra Leone, native self-government for, 1204
Simeon II, Tsar of Bulgaria, exiled, 1190
Six-Power Agreement, 1184
Sjahrir, Soetan, Premier of Indonesia, 1214
Smallholders' Party (Hungary), 1188
Smuts, Jan Christiaan, Prime Minister of South Africa, 1204; death of, 1205
Socarras, Carlos Prío, President of Cuba, 1202
Social Democratic Party (Brazil), 1201
Social Democrats (German political party) 1183, 1184
Socialist Labor Party (Netherlands), 1179
Socialist Party (Japan), 1217
Socialist Unity Party (Eastern Germany), 1183
Soekarno, Achmed, Indonesian leader, 1214; elected President of Indonesia, 1215
Somaliland, Italian, U.N. trusteeship, with Italy as trustee, 1204
Somoza, Gen. Anastasio, Dictator-President of Nicaragua, 1201
Songgram, Pibul, Thailand Premier, 1225
Sophocles, Themistocles, Greek head of coalition government of Liberals and Populists, 1190
Soviet Control Commission (Eastern Germany), 1185
Spaak, Paul H., first President of United Nations, 1172; Premier of Belgium, 1178
Spain, Don Juan, seeks restoration of the monarchy, 1180; economic distress in, 1180; breaks diplomatic relations with Germany, 1180; requiem mass for Hitler, 1180; excluded from membership in U.N., 1180; José Gíral, Premier of government-in-exile, 1180; Franco receives Argentine order, 1181; treaty with Argentina, 1181; visit of Señora Perón, 1181; Franco's Bill for succession of the monarchy opposed by Don Juan, 1181; accord between exiled monarchists and anti-Franco Republicans, 1181; non-aggression treaty with Portugal, 1181; treaty with King Abdullah of Jordan, 1181; U.S. Congress recommends loan, 1181; U.N. rescinds resolution of 1946, 1181; workers' strikes, 1224
Stalin, Josef, Chairman of U.S.S.R. Council of Ministers, 1192
State Planning Commission (Gosplan, U.S.S.R.), 1192

Stepinac, Catholic Croatian leader, sentences to prison, 1189
Stettinius, Edward R., U.S. Secretary of State, 1196
"Stern Gang," Jewish terrorists, 1207
Strasbourg, seat of Council of Europe, 1175
Sudan, the, demands by Egypt for full control, 1203; self-government planned by the British, 1203; elections for legislative assembly (1948), 1203; assembly rejects Egyptian demands, 1227; Egypt proposes plebiscite, 1227
Supreme Court of South Africa, ruling by, on race legislation, 1229
Switzerland, diplomatic relations with U.S.S.R. resumed, 1183; agreement with Allies for disposal of German assets, 1183; decides not to join U.N., 1183; general election (1947), results of, 1183; five-year plan of military preparedness, 1183; expels all Communists from government service, 1183
Sweden, Social Democratic government, 1194; general election of 1948, 1195; King Gustav dies, 1195; King Gustav VI Adolf succeeds as King, 1195
Syria, election (1947), 1206; government overthrown (1949) by successive coups, 1206; new constitution adopted, 1206
Szakasitz, Arpad, 1188

Talal, Emir, King of Jordan, 1225
Tangier, new international administration, 1203; anti-French riots, 1229
Tatarescu, Rumanian Foreign Minister, 1191
Taylor, Myron C., 1182
Tenda, awarded by Allies to France, 1182
Thaik, San Shwe, President of Burma, 1212
Thailand. See Siam
Thakin Nu, Burmese Prime Minister, 1212
Thorez, Maurice, French Communist leader, 1180
Tildy, Zoltan, leader of Hungarian Smallholders' Party, 1188; President of Hungary, 1188
Tiso, Josef, former President of Slovakia, execution of, 1187
Tito, Marshal, dominant figure in Yugoslavia, 1188, 1189
Togliatti, Palmiro, Italian Communist leader, attempted assassination of, 1182
Tojo, Hideki, execution of, as war criminal, 1217
Transjordan, independent state, 1207–08; admission to U.N. vetoed by U.S.S.R., 1208; treaty with Turkey, 1208; alliance with Iraq, 1208; election (1947), 1208; alliance with Great Britain, 1208; Palestine invaded by troops of, 1208; renamed "The Hashimite Kingdom of Jordan," 1208; Arab Palestine incorporated into Jordan, 1208,
Treaty of Rio Janeiro, 1196
Trieste, made Free Territory by Allies, 1182
Trueba, Andreas, Uruguayan President, 1200
Trujillo, Rafael Leonidas, President of Dominican Republic, 1202
Truman, President Harry S., 1190, 1196, "Fair Deal" program, 1197; "Four-Point" Plan, 1197; meeting of, with Gen. MacArthur at Wake Island, 1198; proclamation by, of national emergency, 1198; attempted assassination of, 1202; announces he will not be candidate for President, 1229
Truman Doctrine, the, aid to nations against spread of communism, 1196
Tsaldaris, Greek Populist leader, Premier of Greece, 1190
Tunisia, French protectorate, demands for autonomy, 1228; anti-French riots, 1228; changes in government by the Bey, 1229
Turkey, U.S.S.R. denounces Treaty of 1925 (non-aggression), 1206; Soviet demands for revision of Montreux Convention rejected, 1206; general election (1946), 1206; aid to, by U.S., 1206; disturbed conditions in, 1206; treaty with Italy, 1206; election of 1950, 1206; joins U.N. forces in Korean War, 1206

U Aung San, 1211; assassinated, 1212
Ubico, Jorge, Dictator-President of Guatemala, 1202
Ulate, Otilio, President of Costa Rica, 1201
Union of Socialist and Soviet Republics, withdrawal of, from U.N. bodies in which Nationalist China is represented, 1173; council of mutual economic assistance for Eastern Europe, 1175; denounces treaty with Yugoslavia, 1175; opposes militarization of Western Germany, 1175; post-war reconstruction tasks, 1192; elections to Supreme Soviet, 1192; fourth Five-Year Plan, 1192; rejects U.N. plan for atomic control, 1192; refuses participation in the Marshall Plan, 1192; Eastern European economic bloc, 1192; Communist Information Bureau (Comminform), 1192; currency devalued, 1192; treaties with satellite countries, 1192; pact with Finland, 1192; atomic explosion reported, 1193; denounces treaty with Tito's Yugoslavia, 1193; alliance with Communist China, 1193; "peace offensive" (Stalin Peace Prizes), 1193; elections to the supreme Soviet, 1193; series of notes to Britain, France, and U.S. on Germany, 1229
Union of South Africa, Prime Minister Jan Christiaan Smuts' government, 1204; Asiatic Land Tenure and Indian Representative Act, protested by Indian government, 1204; Southwest Africa, 1204; general election (1948), 1204; racial segregation, 1204; race riots, 1204; South African Citizenship Act, 1204; Malan ignores ruling of International Court of Justice and incorporates Southwest Africa into the Union, 1205; Group Areas Bill, 1204–05; race legislation invalidated by Supreme Court, 1229
United Nations, the, charter of, ratified, 1172; seat of, U.S.,

1172; first session of General Assembly, London, proceedings, 1172; Paul H. Spaak of Belgium, President, 1172; Trygve Lie of Norway, Secretary General, 1172; Pakistan and Yemen chosen as members, 1172; Burma made member, 1172; Israel made member, 1173; Indonesia made member, 1173; favors a United Korea, 1173; provides for emergency action by General Assembly, 1173; rescinds anti-Franco resolution, 1173; Commission on Korea reports, 1218; intervention U.N. forces in Korean War, 1220; proposal of. for peace rejected, 1223
United Party (South Africa), 1204
United States, lend-lease operations cease (1945), 1196; large-scale strikes, (1945–46), 1196; participation in U.N. approved by Senate (1945), 1196; strikes (1946) in coal mines and railroads, government control, 1196; Selective Service Act extended, 1196–97; atomic explosion under water at Bikini, 1196; Congressional elections (1946), 1196; forced resignation of Secretary of Commerce Wallace, 1196; controls of prices removed, 1196; the Truman Doctrine, 1196; the Taft-Hartley Act, 1196; unification of the armed services, 1196; Treaty of Rio Janeiro, 1196; Foreign Assistance Act (Marshall Plan), 1196; nation-wide strikes (1948), stopped by government, 1196; U.S.S.R. breaks consular relations, 1197; re-election of President Truman (1948), 1197; Communist trials, 1197; "Fair Deal" program, 1197; North Atlantic Treaty, 1197; Department of Defense established, 1197; Reciprocal Trade Act extended, 1197; Mutual Defense Assistance Act, 1197; allotment of funds to E.R.R., 1197; intervenes in Korean War, 1197; charges of Communist infiltration in State Department, 1198; Internal Security Act, 1198; congressional elections (1950), 1198; White Paper on China, 1198; withdraws occupation troops from Korea, 1218; U.S. forces aid to South Korea, 1220; aid to Philippine Republic, 1222; debate in Senate on foreign policy, 1223; switchmen strike, railroads under army control, 1223; Kefauver Committee, 1223; peace treaty with Japan, 1224, 1226; changes in Far East command, 1224; visit of President Auriol of France, 1224; Manpower Act, 1225; meeting of British, French, and U.S. foreign ministers, Washington, 1226; ransom paid Hungary for release of air crew, 1227; visit of Prime Minister Churchill, 1228; congress has 1952 budget message, 1228; inquiry proposed into Communist charges of germ warfare rejected, 1229; inquiry as to charge of corruption in Department of Justice, 1229; government seizure of steel plants, 1229
United Workers' Party (Hungary), 1188
United Workers' Party (Poland), 1194
Urriolagoita, Mamerto, Vice-President and President of Bolivia, 1200
Uruguay, Tomás Barreta, President (1946), 1200; death of, 1200; Vice-President Luis B. Berres succeeds, 1200; Andreas Trueba elected President (1950), 1200
U Saw, Burmese Premier, executed for treason, 1212

Vandenberg, Gen. Hoyt S., U.S. Chief of Staff of Air Force, 1227
Vargas, Getulio, Dictator of Brazil for 15 years, resigns (1945), 1201; chosen as President (1950), 1201
Vassilievsky, A. M., U.S.S.R. Minister of Defense, 1193
Venezuela, revolt in (1945), 1200; election in, for constituent assembly, 1200; Rómulo Gallegos. President, 1200; government overthrown (1948), 1200; Communist Party outlawed, 1200; revolt (1951) by Communists suppressed, 1226
Videla, Gabriel González, President of Chile, 1199
Viet Minh, Communist organization in rebellion against Viet Nam Republic, 1212, 1214
Viet Nam (Indo-China), 1180
Viet Nam Republic, 1214
Villaroel, Gualberto, Bolivian President, rebellion against in which he is killed, 1200
Vishinsky, A., U.S.S.R. Foreign Minister, 1193, 1227

Wafd Party (Egyptian Nationalist), 1203
Wavell, Field Marshall Viscount, Viceroy of British India, 1209
Weizmann, Chaim, President of Israel, 1207
Wilson, Charles E., head of U.S. Office of Defense Mobilization, 1198
World Zionist Congress, 1207

Xoxe, Koci, former Vice Premier of Albania, execution of, 1189

Yoshida, Shigeru, Premier of Japan, 1217, 1218
Yugoslavia, elections for Constituent Assembly, 1189; Federal People's Republic, 1188; new constitution, 1189; economic agreement with Poland, Czechoslavia, Albania, Bulgaria, and Hungary, 1189; five-year plan, 1189; disagreements with U.S.S.R., 1189; expelled by Cominform, 1189; purge by, of Cominform followers, 1189; break with Soviet satellites, 1189, agreements concluded with Western Powers, 1189; U.S.S.R. denounces treaty with, 1189; general elections (1950), 1189

Za'im, Husni, Chief of Staff, Syria, overthrows government (1949) and elected President of Syria, 1206; arrested and shot, 1206
Zhdanov, A. A., Deputy Soviet Premier, death of, 1192